# SELECT CONSTITUTIONS

**[UK, USA, FRANCE, CANADA, SWITZERLAND, JAPAN, CHINA AND INDIA]**

**SIXTEENTH EDITION**

**ANUP CHAND KAPUR**

**K.K. MISRA**

**S Chand And Company Limited**

**(ISO 9001 Certified Company)**

**S Chand And Company Limited**
**(ISO 9001 Certified Company)**
***Head Office:*** Block B-1, House No. D-1, Ground Floor, Mohan Co-operative Industrial Estate, New Delhi – 110 044 | Phone: 011-66672000
***Registered Office:*** A-27, 2nd Floor, Mohan Co-operative Industrial Estate, New Delhi – 110 044 Phone: 011-49731800
www.**schandpublishing.com**; e-mail: **info@schandpublishing.com**

**Branches**

| | | |
|---|---|---|
| Chennai | : | Ph: 23632120; chennai@schandpublishing.com |
| Guwahati | : | Ph: 2738811, 2735640; guwahati@schandpublishing.com |
| Hyderabad | : | Ph: 40186018; hyderabad@schandpublishing.com |
| Jalandhar | : | Ph: 4645630; jalandhar@schandpublishing.com |
| Kolkata | : | Ph: 23357458, 23353914; kolkata@schandpublishing.com |
| Lucknow | : | Ph: 4003633; lucknow@schandpublishing.com |
| Mumbai | : | Ph: 25000297; mumbai@schandpublishing.com |
| Patna | : | Ph: 2260011; patna@schandpublishing.com |



*First Edition 1956*
*Subsequent Editions and Reprints 1983, 89, 93 (Twice), 94, 95, 97, 99, 2001, 2002*
*Sixteenth Edition 2006*
*Reprints 2008, 2010, 2012, 2013, 2014 (Twice), 2015, 2016, 2017 (Twice), 2018 (Thrice), 2019, 2020, 2021*

***LPSPE 2022***

**ISBN:** 978-93-550-1093-3 **Product Code:** H5CNS41PLSC10ENAA21L

PRINTED IN INDIA

By Vikas Publishing House Private Limited, Plot 20/4, Site-IV, Industrial Area Sahibabad, Ghaziabad – 201 010 and Published by S Chand And Company Limited, A-27, 2nd Floor, Mohan Co-operative Industrial Estate, New Delhi – 110 044.

# Preface to the Sixteenth Edition

Dr. A.C. Kapur's classic text has been edited and enlarged by me in order to make the book more useful to students and other readers interested in the subject. A general critique of the various political systems and a discussion of their respective political traditions have been added to enrich the institutional approach of the original author of the book.

*80, Kadambari Apts.*
*Rohini, Sector IX*
*Delhi - 1100 85*

**K.K. MISRA**

# Preface to the Fifteenth Edition

For compelling reasons the fourteenth edition of this book is made available in the market after a lapse of near about two years. The unpredictable rise in the cost of production compelled the Publishers to advise reduction in the volume of the book if its price was to be kept at the old level. There was no option but to agree and it was an arduous and time consuming process to prune the subject-matter without detriment to the text itself and, at the same time, to incorporate the recent changes and development and their constitutional impact on the working of the government concerned.

Perestroika and glasnost, the twin reforms, which Mikhail Gorbachev initiated in the 1980s to restructure the Soviet Society by combining economic reforms with political changes resulted into the disintegration of the Soviet Union and the demise of Communism for all practical purposes in the land of the Soviets. The Constitution of the erstwhile USSR has, consequently, been omitted.

Efforts have been made all through to keep the text up-to-date.

*''Gokal Niwas''*
***Turner Road***
*Clement Town*
*Dehra Dun-248 002*

**ANUP CHAND KAPUR**

# Preface to the First Edition

This book is an attempt to explain the working of the governmental systems as obtainable in England, United States of America, Switzerland, USSR and India, and has been designed to meet the needs of students appearing for University and various competitive examinations. Efforts have been made to keep the text as nearly abreast of the times as the rapid changes in events in every country have permitted. Endeavour has, also, been made to make comparative study of the forms, structure and organisation of modern constitutional governments. Wherever possible case-law has been cited. In fact, no book on Constitutions can serve a useful purpose, whether it is meant for the legal profession or statesmen and parliamentarians or students of Political Science and Comparative Governments unless it is adequately supplemented by judicial decisions. A Constitution is what the judges make it. Chief Justice Hughes of the Supreme Court of the United States observed, "The Constitution is what the Supreme Court says of it".

I have tried to consult the best available sources of information in respect of the various subjects dealt within the book and I take this opportunity of acknowledging my indebtedness to the renowned authorities from whom I have borrowed so profusely and drawn the inspiration for preparing this book.

With a view to encouraging students to read as widely as possible, I have placed at the end of each Chapter a selected bibliography dealing with the subject treated in the chapter, and have cited many additional authorities in the footnotes.

My cordial thanks are due to Shri R.L. Niroda, Secretary, Pepsu Vidhan Sabha, for permission to make use of his Secretariat Library, and Shri Thakar Das Jand, Librarian, Mahendra College and his assistants for their unfailing courtesy in making available library books at all odd hours. My wife helped me, as usual, in pushing the book through the press.

**ANUP CHAND KAPUR**

*Civil Lines*

*Patiala*

*June 15, 1956*

# Contents

## THE GOVERNMENT OF CANADA (CONSTITUTION OF 1982) 415—462



## THE GOVERNMENT OF SWITZERLAND 463—529



## THE GOVERNMENT OF JAPAN 530—596



## THE GOVERNMENT OF THE PEOPLE'S REPUBLIC OF CHINA ( CONSTITUTION OF 1982) 597—652

*Chapters* *Pages*

## PART – II

**THE GOVERNMENT OF THE INDIAN REPUBLIC** **1—416**

# PART I

## Governments of The United Kingdom, The United States of America, France, Canada, Switzerland, Japan and China

# CHAPTER I

# Nature and Content of the Constitution

## Nature of the British Constitution

In almost every country in the world, except the United Kingdom the term 'Constitution', means a selection of the legal rules which delineate the government of that country which have been embodied in one or several documents. Such a document may have been drawn up either by a Constituent Assembly, or it may be the handiwork of a legislature, or it may have been granted by a King binding himself and his successors to govern according to the provisions of the Proclamation. The Constitution thus understood means a written, precise and systematic document containing the general principles under which government functions. It is distinct in character, the supreme law of the land, which is held in special sanctity. The 'Constitution' is amended and altered by a procedure different from that required in amending a statutory or ordinary law. The statutory law must be consistent with the letter and the spirit of the Constitution otherwise it is held unconstitutional or *ultra vires,* as soon as a court has an opportunity to review it.

But the British Constitution has never been devised and reduced to writing.[1] It remains undefined, unsystematized and uncodified. It lacks precision and coherence. The Englishmen never drew out their political system in the shape of a formal document and, consequently, there is no single place in which 'The Constitution' as a whole is clearly and definitely written down. Many books may be found which describe the British Constitution, but no one of them can be said to contain it. There are, no doubt, some enactments of Parliament which make the British Constitution, but these enactments do not bear the same date. They are scattered as they were made as and when they were needed and the circumstances demanded. But the most important part of the British Constitution is just what is kept out of the written law and given over to the sole guardianship of custom. Nor is there any law in the United Kingdom of which we can say that since it is a part of the Constitution, it can be altered by a procedure different from the one required for altering the statutory law. Here the Constitutional Law and Statutory or Ordinary Law stand at par with one another. Both emanate from the same source and undergo the same procedure in passing and amending them. Obviously then, no court or any other authority can legally refuse to enforce and set aside any enactment of Parliament.

The British Constitution is, therefore, to a large extent an unwritten and flexible Constitution. It is the product of history and the result of evolution. It has grown with the growth of the English nation, changed with its wants, and adapted itself to the needs of various times. Jennings has aptly remarked, "If the Constitution consists of institutions and not of the paper that describes them, the British Constitution has not been made but has grown—and there is no paper."[2] The institutions necessary for carrying out the functions of the State were established from time to time as the need arose. "Formed to meet immediate requirements they (institutions) were then adapted to exercise more extensive and sometimes different functions. From time to time, political and economic circumstances have called for reforms. There has been a constant process of invention, reform and amended distribution of powers. The building has been constantly added to, patched, and partly recon-

1. Except for the Instrument of Government of 1653. The Instrument of Government which made Cromwell Lord Protector and established a new legislature was, however, the British Constitution for a few years only. Restoration put an end to it and England returned to the old form of government.

2. Jennings, W. Ivor, *The Law and the Constitution,* p. 8.

structed, so that it has been renewed from century to century, but it has never been razed and rebuilt on new foundation."[3] In other words, the British Constitution is "the child of wisdom and chance,"[4] it is the result of a process in which many elements, like charters, statutes, judicial decisions, precedents, usages and traditions, have entered piling themselves one upon the other from age to age and shaping the political institutions of the country according to the exigencies of time. The British Constitution is ever growing and always undergoing modifications. It is a dynamic Constitution with its roots in the past and branches in the future. Lord Morrison cogently said, "But as a whole, ours has been a peaceful development, learning as we moved on, establishing the foundation of further progress."[5] No man in 1688 could have foretold, with any measure of accuracy, what the Constitution of present day Britain would be, and no man of our times can predict how the Constitution will evolve a few decades hence.

Briefly, the British Constitution is a body of basic rules indicating the structure and functions of political institutions and the principles governing their operation. It is just the same in nature as the constitution of any other country, the only difference being that the British Constitution has never been systematized, codified and put in an orderly form. Probably, no attempt will be made in future, too, to bring all these rules and principles together to make the Constitution a consistent and coherent whole. In fact, it is an impossible task, for not only do the usages and traditions cover a wide range, but many of them are not sufficiently definite to be reduced to writing. Moreover, the Englishman, as a political entity, has never favoured a system of government based upon fixed principles involving the application of exact rules. He is practical, matter of fact, and zealous for business. Expediency is the guiding principle of his life and he seizes opportunity by the forelock. He knows no logic and the British Constitution lacks all logic. The result, as Ogg says, " is a constitutional structure which lacks symmetry, governmental system which abounds in the illogical." But it does not mean that it is a mere hotchpotch of heterogeneous elements. The rules and principles which govern the governmental machinery have been deduced from British experience and consciously adhered to and applied.

Thomas Paine and Alexis de Tocqueville were the two prominent among many writers who were of the opinion that the British Constitution did not exist. Thomas Paine, a great champion of written constitutions, categorically declared that where a Constitution "cannot be produced in a visible form, there is none." In a spirited reply to Burke, who eminently defended the British Constitution in his *Reflections on the French Revolution,* Paine asked, "Can Mr. Burke produce the English Constitution ?" If he cannot, we may fairly conclude that though it has been so much talked about, no such thing as a Constitution exists or ever did exist." De Tocqueville, the celebrated French writer on Foreign Governments, a generation later said that in "England the Constitution may go on changing continually or rather it does not exist."[6] Whatever be their reasons for making these assertions, Paine and de Tocqueville were both wrong. There can be no State without a constitution. It is true that there is no single document intended to comprise the fundamental rules of constitutional practices to which a student of the British Constitution may turn for reference, as one does in the United States or in India, but there is no constitution which is either wholly written or entirely unwritten. Written and unwritten elements are present in every constitution. All written constitutions grow and expand with the passage of time either as a result of customs or judicial interpretations. Written constitutions, remarked Bryce, become "developed by interpretation, fringed with decisions, and enlarged by customs so that after a time the letter of their texts no longer conveys their full effect." Nor can the makers of a written constitution foresee the future and shape the constitution to fulfil the needs of the people to come. Man is dynamic and so are his political institutions. The conventional element in any system of government is inevitable. Finally, a written constitution does not contain all the rules relating to all

3. *Ibid.*
4. As Strachey has called it in his *Queen Victoria* and quoted by F. A. Ogg in his *English Government and Politics,* p. 68.
5. Lord Morrison, *British Parliamentary Democracy,* 2.
6. "En Angleterre la constitution pent changer sans cease : Ou plutot ellen'existe point." It will be observed that de Tocqueville's emphasis is more on the flexible character of the British Constitution. He could not reconcile himself to the fact that the constitutional law and the statutory law should emanate from the same source and both be amended by ordinary legislative process. He, accordingly, concluded that the British Constitution did not exist.

the institutions of government. A selection is made of both. For instance, the Constitution of the United States of America contains only seven Articles and occupies about ten pages. The Constitution of India, on the other hand, is the lengthiest Constitution in the world containing 395 Articles and twelve Schedules. The difference between the two Constitutions is suggestive, for it shows that within limits a written constitution may contain as much or as little as is thought desirable by the father framers. And yet no constitution is complete by itself. "It is a framework, a skeleton which had to be filled out with detailed rules and practices. It is concerned with the principal institutions and their main functions, and with the rights and duties of citizens which are, for the time being, regarded as important. It may contain more or less, according to the circumstances of the moment and the special problems being faced by the State while it is being drafted." All written constitutions provide for amendments in order to cater to the future needs of the people. Customs and judicial decisions, too, supplement the constitutional provisions. The difference between a written and unwritten constitution is, therefore, one of degree rather than of kind. Wherever there are rules determining the creating and operation of governmental institutions, there exists a constitution. Britain has such institutions and such rules; "and certainly long before the times of Paine and de Tocqueville England had such a body of rules, with Englishmen equally conscious of its existence and proud of its history."[7]

## COMPONENT PARTS OF THE CONSTITUTION

### Sources of the Constitution

The sources from which the British Constitution is drawn are many and diverse and these may be divided into seven main categories.[8] In the first place there are certain great Charters, Petitions, Statutes and other landmarks such as Magna Carta (1215), the Petition of Rights (1628), the Act of Settlement (1701), as modified by the Abdication Act of (1936), the Act of Union with Scotland (1707), the Great Reform Act (1832), the Parliament Act of 1911, as amended in 1949, the Government of Ireland Act of 1920, the Public Order Act of 1936, the Ministers of the Crown Act of 1937, Representation of the People Act, 1949, the Life Peerage Act, 1958, the Peerage Act, 1963, the Statute of Westminster 1931, the Indian Independence Act, 1947, etc. Most of these are Acts passed by Parliament. But a document like Magna Carta is considered to be a part of the Constitution as it makes a great landmark in national history, and various Acts of Parliament "may, without undue violence to the facts be regarded as in direct line of descent from Magna Carta."[9] Elder William Pitt called Magna Carta, the Petition of Rights and the Bill of Rights as the Bible of the British Constitution. One thing, however, very significant about these Charters and Statutes is that they were the product of political stress and crisis and they contain the terms of settlement of that crisis. They are a part of the Constitution because of what they deal with. It is the context of the constitutional struggle within which they originated that they bear the impress of the constitutional law.

Secondly, there are a good number of Statutes, which Parliament has passed from time to time, dealing with suffrage, the methods of election, the powers and duties of public officials, etc. These Statutes, unlike the constitutional landmarks enumerated in group one, are not the outcome of a constitutional struggle. They were passed as and when the exigencies of time demanded them under the ordinary process of things. For example, none of the laws extending the right to vote, which were passed between 1867 and 1948, aroused popular excitement as the Reform Act of 1832. Nonetheless, all these Statutes are vitally important for the development of political democracy and any attempt to repeal them would now be regarded against the "constitutional sense" of the nation. In fact, the system of Government obtainable in Britain, would become unworkable if ever an attempt is made to repeal any one of such Statutes, though Parlia-

7. Ogg, F. A., and Zink, H., *Modern Foreign Governments,* p. 26.
8. Sir Maurice Amos divides the rules of the Constitution into three kinds: (i) Rules of Law; these include Rules of the Common Law, Rules of Statute Law, and the law or so-called "privileges" of Parliament; (ii) the conventions of the constitution; and (iii) principles which relate to the liberty of the subjects, *The English Constitution,* p. 24.
9. Gooch, F. K., *The Government of England* p. 64. Magna Carta, writes Gooch "is technically an enactment of the King, with the advice of his great council; parliament grew out of the great council; and even at present, an Act of Parliament is technically enacted by the King with the advice and consent of Parliament." Similarly, Gooch tries to prove that the Petition of Rights does not differ in principle from an Act of Parliament: "the Bill of Rights is, in the most literal sense, itself an Act of Parliament." *Ibid.,* pp. 64-65.

ment is a sovereign body and it has "the right to make or unmake any law whatever."[10]

The third source of constitutional rules is to be found in the decisions of judges on cases heard by them in the law courts. When judges decide cases, they interpret, define and develop the provisions of the great Charters and Statutes. While doing so, their judgments create precedents which succeeding judges respect. Since many of these judgments related directly to constitutional matters, the legal principles and judicial precedents of these judgments are an important element in the British Constitution; they resemble and correspond to the decisions of the Supreme Court of the United States which have helped to clarify and expand the provisions of the American Constitution. The decision in the case of the Sheriff of Middlesex in 1840 established the principle that Parliament has the right to punish its own members for a breach of privilege, no other legal authority being necessary. The judgment in *Bradlaugh v. Gossett* in 1884 established the supremacy of Parliament over the courts in all matters concerning the internal affairs of Parliament.

In the fourth place, are the principles of the Common Law and several matters of major constitutional importance covered by them. It is from the Common Law, for example, that the King derives his prerogative,[11] and that Parliament derives its supremacy. The civil liberties of the people, which in America are embodied in the Bill of Rights, are ensured in Britain by the rules of the Common Law. Freedom of speech, of press and of assembly, the sanctity of a citizen's home, and the right of jury trial are Common Law rights which today have their effective meaning in the long line of decisions judges have made. The laws of Parliament may redefine or modify the manner of exercising these rights, but such laws are in their turn subject to judicial interpretation made in the light of the many precedents of the past.

The principles of the Common Law are not established by any law passed by Parliament or ordained by the king. They grew up entirely on the basis of usage. Common Law, according to Blackstone, consists of customs "not set down in any written statute or ordinance, but depending on immemorial usages for their support." The judges recognised "the customs of the realm", applied them in individual cases, and set precedents for decisions in later cases. As these decisions were "broadened down from precedent to precedent there grew up a body of principles of general application which stand as a bulwark of British freedom and an essential part of the British Constitution."[12] The Common Law, like statutory law, is, thus, "continually in the process of development by judicial decisions."[13]

Another source of constitutional rules is to be found in usages or conventions. The conventions of the constitution, as they are called, are the centre and soul of the constitutional law in Britain. The fundamental convention, from which practically all others flow, is the convention of the Cabinet Government. Although the validity of the conventions of the constitution cannot be the subject of proceedings in courts of law, yet they cover some of the most important parts of the British political system and are observed with due respect. Conventions are, says Herman Finer, "rules of political behaviour not established in statutes, judicial decisions or Parliamentary customs but created outside these, supplementing them, in order to achieve objects they have not yet embodied. These objects, in the British Constitution, can be summed up thus : to make the executive and the legislature responsible to the will of the people. To add concreteness we could use the terms *Crown, Government, or Cabinet* in place of *Executive* and *Parliament,* meaning the House of Commons (especially) and the House of Lords, in place of *Legislature.*"[14]

Next but less reliable are the commentaries by eminent writers whose works have come to be regarded as authoritative expression on the British Constitutional Law. These commentators have systematised the diverse conventional rules, established a definite relation of one to another, and, then, linked them into some degrees of unity by reference to central principles. In certain cases such writers have provided compendious and

10. Dicey, A. V., *Introduction to the Study of the Law of the Constitution* p.10.
11. The term prerogative was in origin used to denote the sum of the rights ascribed to the King as a feudal overlord. But the expression is used today to refer to the Crown's discretionary authority, that is, to what the King or his servants can do without the authority of an Act of Parliament.
12. Carter, M. G., and Others, *The Government of Great Britain,* p. 43.
13. Common Law may be regarded as that part of the Law of the land which is traditional and judge-made. "The explanation of the adjective "common" is that in medieval times the law administered by the King's superior courts was the "common custom of the realm", as against the "particular customs with which local jurisdictions were concerned." Harrison, W., *The Government of Britain,* Appendix 'B, pp. 161-62.
14. Finer, Herman, *Governments of Greater European Powers,* p.46.

detailed accounts of the operation of particular categories of rules and their works have acquired the status of constitutional documents, probably, the most authoritative of such works is Erskine May's *Treatise on the Law, Privileges, Proceedings and Usages of Parliament.* It is the classic guide to the procedure and privileges of Parliament and is constantly referred to by the Speakers of the House of Commons on the formulation of their rulings on question of privilege and procedure. Also (although to a much lesser extent) A.V. Dicey's *Law of the Constitution* has acquired over the years an authority that makes it more than merely a commentary on constitutional practice.

Finally, the exercise of the Royal prerogative forms another aspect of constitutional practice. The power to declare war, make treaties, pardon criminals and dissolve Parliament are important functions performed by Royal Prerogative. They are executed through *Orders* in Council or through proclamations and writs under the great seal. Today, these functions are performed by Ministers on behalf of the Monarch, and, as such, the authority for the decision comes from the Crown rather than from Parliament.

The nature of the British Constitution may be summed up in the words of Anson. It is, he wrote, "a somewhat rambling structure, and like a house which many successive owners have altered just so far as suited their immediate wants or fashion of the time, it bears the marks of many hands, and is convenient rather than symmetrical. Forms and phrases survive which have long since lost their meaning, and the adaptation of practice to convenience by a process of unconscious change has brought about in many cases a divergence of law and custom, of theory and practice."[15] Walter Bagehot in his classic work : *The English Constitution* [16] asserted that such a system of Government as obtainable in Britain was possible because there existed certain prerequisites : mutual confidence among electors, a calm national mind, and the gift of rationality. All these qualities add up to an adult and practical nation. The obvious result is that the "British for the most part think that the nature of their Constitution is most sensible and that a codified constitution like the American is more trouble than it is worth....."[17]

## CONVENTIONS OF THE CONSTITUTION

### Sanction behind Conventions

The Conventions of Constitution,[18] the name given by Dicey to the indefinite number of customs, traditions and precedents, form an integral part of the British Constitution.[19] So deep-rooted have these conventions been found in the habits of the Englishmen, and so firmly the mechanism of government is erected on their foundation that without them the Constitution becomes maimed if not absolutely unworkable. And yet they are not the law of the Constitution; they are nowhere written down in any formal or official document.

A distinction is very often made between laws of the Constitution and conventions of the Constitution. But conventions are not really very different from laws and it is frequently difficult to place a set of rules in one class or the other. Jennings has rightly said that the Conventions, like most fundamental rules of any Constitution, rest essentially upon general acquiescence. "A written constitution is not law because somebody has made it, but it has been accepted." Conventions are based on usage and acquiescence and their binding force, like laws, is derived from the willingness of the people to be so bound. If obedience to law is deemed a fundamental duty, obedience to conventions is among the political obligations, because they help the wheels of political machine going in accordance with the will of the people. Both, law and conventions, are inevitably similar as they serve the common purpose of regulating the structure and functions of government aiming at the good of the people and are the result of common consent. "What is law and what is convention," Jennings maintains, "are primarily technical questions. The answers are known only to those whose business it is to

15. Anson, W. R., *Law and Custom of the Constitution,* Vol. I., p. 1.
16. The book was first published in London in 1867.
17. Brogan, D. W., and Verney, D. V., *Political Patterns in Today's World,* p. 87.
18. John Stuart Mill referred to them as " the unwritten maxims of the constitution", while Anson, referred to them as "the customs of the constitution." None of the phrases, according to Jennings, exactly expresses what is meant. Dicey's phrase has, however, now been sanctioned by common use. *The Law of the Constitution,* op. cit.,p. 80.
19. "Though in 1837 the terms 'conventions of the constitution' had not attained regular currency, the thing meant thereby was in effective operation and had been so in essence since the revolution." Keith. A. B., *The Constitution of England from Queen Victoria to George VI,* Vol. I, p. 12.

know them. For the mass of the people it does not matter whether a rule is recognised by the judicial authorities or not. The technicians of Government are primarily concerned.''

Technically, the difference between laws and conventions spreads to three aspects. In the first place, laws emanate from a legally constituted body and carry with them greater sanctity. Conventions are extra-legal and they grow out of practice. Their existence is determined by usage. In the second place, law is usually expressed in more precise terms and it has the added dignity of extracting unquestioning obedience from everybody. Conventions are never formulated. They grow out of practice, they are modified by practice, and at any given time it may be difficult to say whether or not a practice has become a convention. Finally, law is enforced by the courts and it is the duty of judges to consider whether Acts are legally valid and to take such steps that they are obeyed. Conventions are not enforced by the courts and judges cannot force their obedience as they have no legal sanction.

But even from the technical point of view no definite boundary line can be drawn between legislation, on the one hand, and conventions, on the other hand. If a given provision is a part of the British Constitution, it is either law or convention and the fundamental conventions have well-nigh been recognised by many Acts of Parliament. The Preamble to the British North America Act, 1867, (now Canada Act), an enactment of British Parliament, read : ''the Provinces of.......have expressed their desire to be federally united into one Dominion under the Crown of the United Kingdom.......with a constitution similar in principle to that of the United Kingdom.''[20] The Constitution of the United Kingdom is a body of rules determining the structure and functions of political institutions and the principles governing their operation. These rules and principles of political governance are primarily unwritten and lie scattered in the various Charters, Statutes judicial decisions and conventions and mark a steady transference of power from the King as a person to a complicated impersonal organisation called the Crown. The King has become the Crown and that is the core of the constitutional system in the United Kingdom and around it revolves the entire machinery of government. Recognition to constitutional conventions was, again, accorded by Article 2 of the Agreement for a Treaty between Great Britain and Ireland in 1921, when the law, practice, and constitutional usage governing the relationship of the Crown or of its representatives, or of the Imperial Parliament to the Dominion of Canada, were made applicable to the Irish free State. In Section 4 of the Status of the Union Act,1934, of the Union Parliament, specific reference is made to the constitutional conventions regulating the use by the Governor-General of his legal power of summoning and dissolving Parliament, and of appointing ministers.[21] Some of the conventions regulating relationship between the Dominions and the United Kingdom have been inserted in the Preamble to the Statute of Westminster, particularly those relating to alterations in the law touching the Succession to the Throne, or the Royal Style and Titles,[22] and the legislative authority of the British Parliament.[23] The importance of the first of these conventions was demonstrated in the abdication of Edward VIII. The change in the Royal Style and Titles after the Indian Independence Act,1947, was brought about by the full assent of the Dominion Parliaments.

The Cabinet system of Government presupposes the pre-eminence and leadership of one single person and he is the Prime Minister. Abolish the institution of Prime Minister or diminish any part of his powers, the entire political struc-

20. Mackenzie King, the Prime Minsiter of Canada, said, '''This British Constitution we love. It is partly unwritten, it is partly written; it finds its beginning in the core of th past, it comes into being in the form of customs and traditions, it is found on the common law; it is made up of precedents, of Magna Carta, of Petition and Bill of rights; it is to be found partly in the statutes and partly in the usages and practices of Parliament itself. It represents the highest achievement of the British genius at its best. No one has ever seen it; no one has ever adequately described it; yet its presence is felt whenever liberty or right is endangered, for it is the creation of the struggle of centuries against oppression and wrong, and embodies the very soul of freedom.''

21. Refer to H. V. Evatt, *The King and his Dominion Governor,* Appendix, pp. 229-306.

22. ''Inasmuch as the Crown is th symbol of the free association of the members of the British Commonwealth of Nations, and as they are united by a common allegiance of the Crown , it will be in accord with the *established constitutional* position (emphasis mine) of all members of the Commonwealth in relation to one another that any alteration in the law touching the succession to the Throne or the Royal Style and Titles shall hereafter require the assent as well as of the Parliaments of all the Dominions as of the Parliament of th United Kingdom.''

23. ''It is in accord with the *established constitutional* position (emphasis mine) that no law hereafter made by Parliament of the United Kingdom shall extend to any of the said Dominions as that of the law of that Dominion otherwise than at the request and with the consent of that Dominion.''

ture would be destroyed. And yet neither the institution of Cabinet nor the office of the Prime Minister[24] were known to law before 1937. The Ministers of the Crown Act, 1937, provided for the payment of a salary of £ 10,000 a year "to the person who is the Prime Minister and the First Lord of the Treasury."

The same Act provided for the salaries of the Ministers who "are members of the Cabinet". It also recognised "Party", "Opposition" and "the Leader of the Opposition." It may, however, be noted that the provisions of the Ministers of the Crown Act do not validate or legalise these conventions. What it does is to recognise them that they exist. But once their existence is recognised by legislation, conventions do not really remain very different from laws. Jennings asserts that the "conventional system of the British Constitution is in fact much like the system of the common law."[25]

Conventions are essentially of three kinds. First, those which ensure harmony between Parliament and the Executive in the light of Parliamentary Sovereignty. The Glorious Revolution of 1688 settled once for all that Parliament had supreme power and it could control every aspect of national life. The powers of the King were limited and the constitutional development was the emergence of the Cabinet. Convention, therefore, alone provides for the essential rules of the Cabinet Government. It demands that the Ministers of the King must be the members of Parliament, they should belong to the majority party in the House of Commons, and function under the party leader designated as the Prime Minister. It further demands that the Cabinet is responsible to Parliament for its actions and it remains in office so long as it retains the confidence of the House of Commons. If the majority is reduced to minority and the Commons withdraw their support, the Cabinet either resigns or appeals to the electorate for mandate. The Ministry must resign if the verdict of the electorate is against it, allowing the Party in Opposition to form the government. If there are more opposing parties than one, and the result of the general election does not give clear majority to one single party, it may meet Parliament and allow a vote of the House of Commons to decide its fate as the Conservative Ministry did in 1924. "But it cannot ask another dissolution, nor should the Crown concede it if it were asked."[26] Conventions insists on the collective responsibility of Cabinet to Parliament for all its public acts, and that its duty is to initiate legislation. Convention, again, determines that the Ministry should combat domestic crisis with all the authority at its disposal, but it must summon Parliament immediately to consult with it. Similarly, the Ministry shall have full regard to the will of the Commons in the conduct of foreign affairs and "shall not declare war, or neutrality or make peace, or enter into important treaties without securing as soon as possible endorsement by the Commons, which so far as possible should be taken into counsel before the Crown is committed to any definite course of action."[27]

Secondly, there are conventions which relate to legislative procedure and the relations between the two Houses of Parliament. That Parliament meets annually and that it consists of two Houses rest on custom. The essential principle of the initiative of the House of Commons in matters of finance, under the authority of the Cabinet, and the subordination of the Lords rested solely on convention until the Parliament Act of 1911. The Act of 1911, as amended in 1949, put definite limitations on the legislative powers of the House of Lords which had hitherto been regulated by convention only. The principle that no peer other than a Law Lord sits when the House of Lords is acting as a Court of Appeal is also customary. Then, there are many conventions regulating parliamentary procedure. It is a matter of convention that every Bill must have three readings before finally voted upon. It is, again, a convention which determines that a speech from the Government benches is to be followed by a speech from the Opposition. Indeed, the whole idea of His or Her Majesty's Opposition is a product of convention. Convention, too, demands that the Speaker of the House of Commons should become a no-party man and he must resign from the membership of the party to which he belonged on his election as Speaker. It was another convention till very recently that the retiring Speaker must be returned unopposed

24. In fact, the office of the Prime Minister came to be recognized by legislation in 1917 when the Chequers Estate Act enabled the official "popularly known as the Prime Minister" to occupy the Chequers Estate as a furnished country residence.
25. Jennings, W. I., *Cabinet Government,* p.5.
26. Keith, A. B., *The British Cabinet System* (Second Edition by N. H. Gibbs), p. 2.
27. *Ibid*, p. 3.

and he should be elected Speaker as many times as he pleases.

Finally, there are conventions which aim at securing harmony between government and legislative action, on the one hand, and the verdict of the electorate, on the other. One convention of this character is that government should not initiate legislation of a controversial nature unless they have a mandate from the electorate. The "mandate convention", as it has now come to be known, is vindication of the principle of popular sovereignty.[28] It makes necessary that any item of policy which involves radical changes must have been a part of the programme on which government fought the previous election, or, "if it was not, that the Opposition should show by its action or inaction that this is not a matter of keen controversy." The Conservative majority in the House of Lords in the years immediately following Labour victory in 1945, approved bills embracing such measures as nationalization on the ground that Labour had received a mandate from the electorate.[29] This convention does not apply only to legislation, but also to foreign policy. Another example of this nature is that when an appeal to the electors goes against the Ministry they are bound to retire from office and have no right to dissolve Parliament a second time. "Behind these conventions", according to Greaves "there is something of a political sanction."[30]

Another type of conventions are those which determine the relations between the Dominions and the United Kingdom. As said before, the Statute of Westminster, 1931, embodies in a legal form the conventions which at one time regulated inter-Imperial relations thereby giving a constitutional sanction to the legislative independence of the Dominions. But the methods of inter-Commonwealth co-operation are still essentially conventional. For example, in matters relating to the Dominions the King acts on the advice of the Ministers of the Dominion concerned and not on that of his Ministers constituting the Government in Britain. Then, the British Parliament does not pass any law for a Dominion unless it has been expressly authorised by the Dominion concerned to do so. The rules for making of treaties by any part of the Dominions are still be found in the Reports of the Imperial Conferences in 1923, 1926 and 1930. Similarly, the position of the Dominion Governor-General was determined by agreements at the Conferences of 1926 and 1930. The co-operative link between the Commonwealth countries and their functioning as a single organism are matter of common understanding and mutual agreements.

It is generally asked why conventions are so scrupulously observed in Britain ? This has been partly explained by Dicey.[31] His conclusion was that violation of conventions ultimately means breach of law. He takes the example of convening a session of Parliament every year and argues if no session of Parliament is summoned annually, it is only a breach of convention and not a violation of law. But if no session of Parliament is called annually, it is not possible to raise revenues and pass the Army and Air Force (Annual) Act. In that case it becomes illegal to maintain army and air force on money raised from unauthorised taxes. Any one doing so can be brought before a court for breach of law and punished accordingly. It, therefore, becomes essential rather imperative that Parliament should be summoned at least once a year. If it is not, it means indirect collision with the laws of the land. Similarly, the Ministry may come to grief, if it does not resign after it has lost the confidence of the House of Commons.[32]

---

28. In 1945 Labour Party's manifesto read, ".......we give clear notice that we will not tolerate obstruction of the people's will by the House of Lords."
29. Viscount Cranborne, the leader of the Conservative Party in the House of Lords, said, "Whatever our personal views, we should frankly recognise that these proposals were put before the country at the recent General Election and that the people of this country, with full knowledge of these proposals, returned the Labour Party to power. The Government may therefore, I think, fairly claim that they have a mandate to introduce these proposals. I think it would be constitutionally wrong, when the country has so recently expressed its views, for this House to oppose proposals which have been definitely put before the electorate." The idea of the electoral mandate is by no means new, although the concept of the mandate had been much more vague with the Liberals and the Conservatives. But the Labour had always believed since 1918, that a party should go to the electorate with a set of concrete proposals which, if successful, it is thereby mandated to put it into practice. Refer to A. H. Birch's *Representative and Responsible Government, An Essay on the British Constitution,* pp. 116-22.
30. Greaves, H. R. G., *The British Constitution,* p. 18.
31. Dicey, A. V., *The Law of the Constitution,* Ch.XV.
32. But a Ministry can continue to remain in office for a sufficiently long time even if it has lost the confidence of the House of Commons. When Parliament has passed the annual budget, and it is usually done by the beginning of July, the House of Commons does not exercise any control over the Ministry. For, no session of Parliament may be summoned until April next and the Ministry may continue to remain in office without breaking the law, though it no longer enjoy, the confidence of the House of Commons. There are other means,too, by which the Ministry can retain office. Cf. H. J. Laski, *Democracy in Crisis,* Ch. II.

But this does not cover the whole case. Lowell has correctly pointed out that Britain is not obliged for ever to hold annual sessions of Parliament. Being a sovereign body, Parliament can pass a permanent Army and Air Force Act and grant the existing annual taxes for a number of years. Moreover, there are some conventions the violation of which does not necessarily lead to breach of law. For example, no breach of law would follow if the Speaker does not resign from the membership of his party after his election to that office, or if the Government does not recognise His or Her Majesty's Opposition, or if all the conventions relating to the conduct of business in the House of Commons are not observed. Similarly, there is no breach of law if the Prime Minister is taken from the House of Lords. At the same time, precedents may be broken if the altered political conditions of the country demand that. The Labour Government violated convention of ministerial collective responsibility when members of the Cabinet in 1931 "agreed to differ". It was justified by Baldwin and he maintained that conventions were altered by circumstances. One of the merits of the conventions is the flexibility they impart in the governance of the country. Disraeli, in 1868, disregarded the well-established usage by resigning without meeting Parliament on defeat at the general election. In 1929, Baldwin reverted to the old convention and considered it wholly constitutional for him to meet Parliament and receive its verdict. The conventions, as Jennings points out, "do not exist for their own sake; they exist because there are good reasons for them."[33] And the good reason is that conventions are related to the idea of a constitutional government and democracy with which almost all Britishers find themselves in agreement. Neumann succinctly remarks: "This remarkable island race simply prefers to retain proven procedures when there is no particularly strong reason to adopt innovations, and has thereby produced a system of time-honoured customs and conventions which are observed because they are based not only on precedent but also on reasons."[34] The conclusions of Dicey, therefore, do not command unqualified support.

Lowell believes that conventions are supported by something more than the realization that their violation might mean the violation of some law. Unlike the laws of the Constitution, conventions go to constitute a moral code for the guidance of public men in the field of practical politics. "In the main," he says, "the conventions are observed because they are a code of honour. They are, as it were, the rules of the game, and the single class in the community which has hitherto had the conduct of English public life almost entirely in its own hands is the very class that is peculiarly sensitive to obligation of this kind. Moreover, the very fact that one class rules, by the sufferance of the whole nation, as trustees for the public, makes that class exceedingly careful not to violate the understandings on which the trust is held."[35] The additional sanction for conventions comes from public opinion. The power of government rests in the last resort on the consent of the electorate and the powers of different departments of government must be exercised in accordance with that principle. Any deviation therefrom will go to make the action of government 'unconstitutional'[36] though not illegal. Legally, there is nothing wrong if conventions are violated. But a legal truth in Britain may become a political untruth. Even a popular and dynamic personality like Edward VIII could not go against the wishes and advice of his Ministers in marrying the woman of his choice. The conventions are really obeyed because of the political difficulties which follow if they are violated. To raise the question of their violation is, therefore, in large measure, fruitless, for conventions are not violated. If one is at all violated, as it was done by the House of Lords in 1909, by rejecting the famous Lloyd George budget, there is an immediate demand to have this convention enacted into law. The electorate gave to the Liberal Party their unequivocal consent in defining the financial and legislative powers of the House of Lords and the result was the Parliament Act, 1911, which made it impossible for the Lords to delay Money Bills for more than one month. The same Act limited its legislative powers too.

33. Jennings, W. I., *Cabinet Government*, P. 7.
34. Neumann, R. G., *European Comparative Governments*, pp. 25-26.
35. Lowell, A. L., *Government of England*, Vol. I., pp. 12-13.
36. Robert G. Neumann writes : "But since there is no constitution in any formal sense, 'unconstitutional' means, in effect, only one thing namely, that it is not proper. This brings us to the core of the British system of government which is not a constitutional document, nor an elaborate system of checks and balances, but rather the generally held and clearly understood belief that certain things simply are not done by gentlemen." *European and Comparative Government*, pp. 4-5.

"Government," according to Jennings, "is a co-operative function, and rules of law alone cannot provide for common action."[37] It implies integration of the activities of many individuals. Each individual must follow certain rules if he is to play his part well, and rules are generally obeyed because of the habit to obey them, no matter whether they are laws or conventions.[38] Conventions are, therefore, rules of political behaviour, first established to solve some specific problems and subsequently they were followed as they seemed just and reasonable to follow. They established intelligent practices and continue their authority as such. Dicey's view is that the Crown shall be converted into the privileges of the people. "Our modern code of constitutional morality," he observed. "secures through in a roundabout way what is called abroad the 'sovereignty of the people,"[39] It is in this context that Jennings wrote that "conventions are obeyed because of the political difficulties which follow if they are not." Marshall and Moodie give a more matter of fact explanation. They say, "conventions describe the way in which certain legal powers must be exercised if the powers are to be tolerated by those affected."[40] This fact has been clearly expressed by the Judicial Committee of the Privy Council in *British Coal Corporation* v. *Rex* (1935) when it interpreted the Statute of Westminster, 1931. The Committee declared : "The Imperial Parliament could as a matter of abstract law, repeal or disregard Section 4 of the Statute. But that is theory and has no relation of realities."[41] The Conventions have democratised the Executive by making Parliament the centre of gravity enabling thereby the democratic system operate in a unitary government. Parliamentary practices emerging out of this process of democratization enable the Government and the Opposition to sit together, discuss and work together for the development of national welfare. Conventions have also revolutionised the Judiciary by making the Law Lords to constitute the highest Court of Civil Appeal in Britain. They have also enabled inter-Commonwealth relations and the collaboration of the member nations to the common advantage.

Conventions are not static like laws. They, "provide the flesh which clothes the dry bones of law" and, consequently, conventions have enabled a rigid legal framework of government to keep an organic pace with the changing political ideas and needs of the people. New needs demand a new emphasis and a new orientation even when the law remains fixed. Men have to work the old law in order to satisfy the new needs and conventions are the motive power of the British Constitution. They lubricate the machinery of government and keep the machine going more smoothly. In their absence the structure of government is sure to collapse and the nature of the British Constitution might well be very different from what it is now. The British system is the best example of democracy and especially of parliamentary democracy.

Something more is served by conventions. "No written constitution," remarks Herman Finer, "any more than the ordinary law, can express the fulness of life's meanings and demands, because the human imagination, even at its most talented, falls far short of reality." The real constitution is a living body of general prescriptions carried into effect by living persons. Conventions are flexible and growing and they can be easily adjusted to the future requirements without creating a political stir which an amendment of the constitution creates. They harmonise relations where a purely legal solution of practical problems is impossible. "In converting a monarchical into a democratic constitution, and in passing from the seventeenth to the twentieth century, the British eschewed writing the new articles : they preferred to rely on the growth and inheritance of customs—that is, conventions."[42]

## SALIENT FEATURES OF THE CONSTITUTION

From the nature of the Constitution flow

37. Jennings, I., *The Law and the Constitution,* pp. 12- 13.
38. "A usage in constitutional matters, it will be found on investigation, is normally based on some definite convenience or utility in relation to the constitutional system of the day, and with the passing of the years it is followed under the influence of the normal psychological principle of limitation and willingness to follow precedent." Keith, A. B., *The British Cabinet System,* p.5.
39. Dicey, A. V., *The Law of the Constitution,* p. 431.
40. Marshall, Geoffery, and Moodie, G. C, *Some Problems of Constitution,* pp. 16-18.
41. Section 4 of the Statute of Westminster stipulates that no law enacted by the United Kingdom Parliament shall extend to the Dominions without the consent of the latter.
42. Finer, H., *Governments of Greater European Powers,* pp. 49-50.

the following important features :

1. *It is Mostly Unwritten.* The British Constitution to a large extent is of an unwritten nature. It is not a pre-arranged pattern according to which government must be carried on. Nor is it the result of conscious creation. Its sources are several and the course of its development has been sometimes guided by accident and sometimes by high design. Being a "child of wisdom and of a chance," its growth has been piecemeal and gradual expressing itself in different Charters and Statutes, precedents, usages and traditions whatever the exigencies of time demanded. There is, accordingly, no single document which can be said to contain the general principles of political governance. In fact, no attempt has ever been made to embody these principles in a documentary form. They remain scattered. Some of these rules and principles have been reduced to writing and are embodied in the Acts of Parliament, but a greater part still remains unwritten and is "simply carried in men's minds as precedents, decisions, habits, and practices." The written elements taken by themselves do not comprise the Constitution, though they have considerably affected it.

2. *A Specimen of Development and Continuity.* The British Constitution has grown like an organism and developed from age to age. It fulfils Sir James McIntosh's dictum that constitutions grow instead of being made. It is the product of evolution and the result of slow and steady development and successive accretions spreading over a thousand years. And all through this period, Britain has never witnessed political upheavals of a revoultionay character. In fact, all political revolutions, if they may be described as revolutions, have been of conservative nature. Britain has all through moved along an essentially continuous constitutional pathway readjusting her institutions slowly and cautiously to the changing conditions and needs of the country and its people. The political changes, as Ogg says, "have as a rule been so gradual, deference to traditions so habitual, and the disposition to cling to accustomed names and forms even when the spirit has changed, so deep-seated, that the constitutional history of Britain displays a continuity hardly paralleled in any other land."[43] Lord Morrison is of the opinion that such a peaceful evolution of the British Constitution is "more permanent, more satisfactory and less painful, than if it were the result of the violent bloody revolution," and he thinks that his "country has been lucky in that respect."[44]

3. *Difference between Theory and Practice.* The gradualness of the constitutional evolution and the English habits of retaining traditional forms, despite radical changes in the position of power, have produced a marked difference in theory and practice. The government in the United Kingdom in ultimate theory is an absolute Monarchy, in form, a limited constitutional Monarchy, and in actual character, democratic republic. In theory, or, to be accurate, legally, the government of the United Kingdom is vested in the Monarch. All officers of the State, civil and military, are appointed and dismissed in Her Majesty's name. The Ministers are Her Majesty's Ministers and they remain in office during the Royal pleasure. The Monarch is the source of law and fountain of justice. Her Majesty summons, dissolves and prorogues Parliament. No parliamentary election can be held without the Royal writ. Laws made by Parliament are not valid and cannot be enforced without the Royal assent and if the Monarch so wishes may veto any law passed by Parliament.

The Monarch is also the Commander-in-chief of all the British forces during peace and war. War is declared in Her Majesty's name, peace and treaties are negotiated and concluded in the name and on behalf of the Monarch. Government documents are published by Her Majesty's Stationary Office. All people in the United Kingdom are the loyal subjects of the Monarch and their national Anthem is : "God save the Queen." In short, there is no act of government which is not attributed to the Monarch's name and person. Her Majesty's powers, in terms of law, are uncontrolled, unrestricted and absolute.

But all this is in theory. In practice, the Monarch does nothing by doing everything. The Revolution of 1688 finally settled that in the last resort the King must give way to Parliament. Since then, the whole development of the British Constistution has been marked by a steady transfer of powers and prerogatives from the Monarch as a person to the Crown as an institution. The King has now long ceased to be a directing factor in government and he virtually performs no offi

43. Ogg, F. A., *English Government and Politics,* p.68. Even the war and revolution of the seventeenth century have not been deemed a catastrophic change from the past. On the other hand, "closer examination reveals that what was really happening was only the winning of full and lasting triumph for principles and usages that had long been growing up." *Ibid.*

44. Morrison, Herbert, *British Parliamentary Democracy, pp. 1-2.*

cial act on his own initiative. If the King were to exercise any of the powers which he exercised in the past, and this he can legally do even now, he will be signing the warrant of his own abdication. The real power rests with the King's duly constitued Ministers and His Majesty remains only a symbol of authority, or to put it in the language of the British Constitution : "The King can do no wrong."

The Ministers of the Monarch are members of Parliament and they remain in office as long as Parliament wishes it. But the real power of Parliament rests with the House of Commons, a representative House of the People. The responsibility of the Ministers is to the House of Commons. The Prime Minister and other principal Ministers belong to it. All this means the supremacy of the House of Commons and ultimately that of the people, for the people decide the complexion of the House at a general election. It is the verdict of the people which determines the government. No government can remain oblivious of public opinion, if it is to continue in office, control and direct administration, and to maintain support for the future too. Such a government is a government by consent. "Government with us," says Jennings, "is government by opinion, and that is the only kind of 'self- government' that is possible." [45] Practice, thus outruns theory in Britain and she presents one of the most democratic systems of government in the world. The Webbs[46] used for the system of government as obtainable in the United Kingdom the phrase a "crowned republic". While defending British Monarchy, Lord Morrison succinctly observed, "But it takes good countries to run monarchies and it takes good monarchs to be the heads of States. And may I add that it takes a good Republic to appreciate a good monarch."[47]

4. *Sovereignty of Parliament.* The British Constitution establishes the supremacy of Parliament. It means that Parliament is supreme. It can make and unmake any kind of law and no court in the realm can question its validity. The authority of Parliament is transcendental and absolute, and it embraces both the enactments of ordinary laws and the most profound changes in the government itself. There is no judicial review and no authority can declare that the laws made by Parliament are *ultra vires.* Even the veto power has become obsolete and the Monarch must signify his assent to all measures passed by Parliament. Whether Parliament is really sovereign or not, it is a separate question. So far as law, pure and simple, is concerned, it is.

5. *A Flexible Constitution.* As already pointed out, there is no codified and basic constitutional law having superior sanctity to statutory law. The power to make and amend the constitutional law is vested in Parliament and no special procedure is required than that attends the enactment of an ordinary bill. Furthermore, the popular ratification of constitutional amendments, required in countries like Switzerland and Australia in the nature of referendum, is unkown in Britain.[48] The Constitution of United Kingdom is flexible and responsive. It carries with it the advantage of centring public opinion according to the needs of the time. There is in it a facility of reform, an adaptability superior to written and more rigid constitutions. James Callaghan, the former Labour Prime Minister, expressed the opinion that constitutions "should not be lightly tampered with, but neither should they be rigid and inflexible. They must adjust to meet the real aspirations of a nation."

The supremacy of Parliament and the ordinary easy method of changing constitutional law have been the subject of some legal controversy. Supremacy of Parliament, it has been asserted, is a legal fiction, for it is exercised in the spirit of responsibility and responsibility in actual practice means the maintenance of majority in Parliament. As long as a Party can maintain its majority in Parliament, it can get anything done. But this is really not so. How easy it is to make constitutional changes depends on the general nature of the political system prevailing in a country and the attitude of the people towards constitutional amendments. Democratic principles and responsible institutions are the heritage of Englishmen and Parliament has never changed the law lightly

45. Jennings, I., *Cabinet Government,* p. 19. The Joint Select Committee on Indian Constitutional Reform (1934) observed that there "arise two familiar British conceptions, that good government is not acceptable substitute for self-government and that the only form of self-government worthy of the name is government through ministers responsible to an elected legislature." Vol. I, Part I, p. 5.
46. Sidney and Beatrice Webb.
47. Morrison, Herbert, *British Parliamentary Democracy,* p. 5.
48. Referenda had been recently sought on two occasions, but in no way connected with laws, constitutional or statutory. The first referendum was on the question of British joining the European Economic community and second over proposals to set up separate Assemblies in Scotland and Wales.

and casually. There are profound psychological checks and voluntary restraints on the exercise of its legal authority, whatever be the extent of majority the Party in power may command. "Parliament, after all," remarks Ogg, "is composed of men who with few exceptions, are respected members of a well-ordered society, endowed with sense, and alive to their responsibility for safeguarding the country's political heritage. They live and work under the restraint of powerful traditions and will no more run riot with the Constitution if it were weighed down with guarantees designed to put it beyond their control."[49] The "mandate convention" is indicative of the political temperament of the poeple. It enjoins that no far-reaching changes in the governmental system should be made until the voters have had a chance to express their opinion upon the proposals at a general election. Asquith's Liberal Government went to the country with the scheme of Second Chamber reform. In 1923, Stanley Baldwin appealed to the electorate on the issue of tariff. In 1931, general election was held to elicit support of the people for the National Government under Ramsay MacDonald. The Labour Party in 1945 fought general election on the issues of nationalization and granting self-government to India and other subject countries. Similarly, in the election of 1964 the Labour Party put before the electorate its programme of re-nationalization. Although the Party secured a precarious majority, yet Harold Wilson told the people immediately after forming the government : "Having been charged with the duties of Government we intend to carry out those duties. Over the whole field of Government there will be many changes which we have been given a mandate by you to carry out. We intend to fulfil that mandate."[50] Legally, therefore, the constitution of Britain is undeniably the most flexible in the world, but actually it is considerably less fluid than might be inferred from what the writers say. The flexibility of the Constitution does not depend wholly, or even largely, upon the simplicity of its amending process.

6. *A Unitary Constitution.* The British Constitution is unitary and not like that of the United States of America or India, federal. There is, of course, devolution, but all authority flows from the Central Government centred at London. The local areas, as they exist in Britain, derive their powers from the Acts of Parliament which may be enlarged or restricted at its will. Parliament is constitutionally supreme, and the local government machine is merely an agent of the Central Government. The essence of a federation, on the other hand, is union and not unity and the powers and jurisdiction exercised by the units, which compose a federation, are original, clearly demarcated, and are derived from the constitution. Neither the Central Government nor governments of the federating units can encroach upon each other's sphere. If any change is desired to be brought about, it must be done by amending the constitution and the process of amendment is prescribed therein. This establishes the supremacy of the constitution. It means that the distribution of powers is maintained by a constitution-amending authority which is superior to both central and local governments. In Britain Parliament is supreme and the local areas are subordinate units with such powers as it chooses to bestow. It can, if it so wished, abolish the whole complex structure of local government by a simple enactment. The existence of a unitary form of government is one of the reasons why Britain is able to manage without a written constitution. A written and a rigid constitution are the pre-requisities of a federal polity. If the devolution referendum in Scotland and Wales had been accepted it would have moved the United Kingdom away from the highly centralized State that has characterised the British system over the past 250 years. The proposal envisaged to set up separate Assemblies in those areas with specified powers.

7. *A Parliamentary Government.* The British Constitution provides for a Parliamentary form of government as distinct from the Presidential type of government. The King, who is a legal sovereign, has been deprived of all his powers and authority. The real functionaries are the Ministers who belong to the majority party in Parliament and they remain in office so long as they can retain its confidence. The Ministers are both the executive heads and members of Parliament and they co-ordinate the Legislative and Executive departments of government. The Cabinet in Britain, as Bagehot defines it, is a

49. Ogg. F. A., *English Government and Politics,* p. 72. Munro in this connection maintains : "Legislators come from the people; they think and feel as the people do; they are saturated with the same hopes and fears; they are creatures of the same habits and when habits solidify into traditions or usages they are stronger than laws, stronger than the provisions of a written constitution." Munro, W. B., *The Governments of Europe,* p. 23.

50. The *Statesman,* New Delhi, October 19, 1964.

"hyphen that joins, the buckle that binds the executive and legislative departments together." There can be no disagreement between the Executive and Legislature. They work in agreement and the dangers involved in deadlock between the law-making, tax-granting authority and the Executive are absent. If ever the House of Commons votes against the Executive and defeats its policy or if ever it should pass a legislation which has not the favour of the Cabinet, one of the two things would happen. The Cabinet must either resign and enable the Opposition to form government, or it should advise the King to dissolve Parliament and order new elections and thereby give an opportunity to the electorate to approve or disapprove the action of the Cabinet. There can be no continued conflict of policy between the Executive and the Legislature as it may happen in the United States, where there is separation between the Executive and Legislative departments. The right to govern in Britain, observes Greaves, "flows through the legislature to the Cabinet; is not separately conferred on a popularly elected Chief Executive and in a popularly elected Parliament; the right is not capable therefore of conflicting interpretation by two bodies having an equal moral claim to speak for the public. The risks of conflict or of inanition which result from such a separation of power are attested by a wide experience, whether it be the Weimar Constitution of Germany, the federal Constitution of America, or the 1848 Constitution of France."

8. *Two-Party System.* Parliamentary government means party government as it provides the machinery to secure a stable government under a unified command of the politically homogeneous and disciplined leaders. The members of the government rise and fall in unison and they are individually and collectively responsible for the policy which the Cabinet initiates and they carry out. Since Parliamentary government is a party government, without political parties Parliamentary government is impossible. Such a system of government, which combines responsibility with representation, functions best when there are two parties, one forming the Government and the other forming the Opposition. Two-party system enables the views of the electors to have coherent expression and Britain provides the classical example of two party system. It originated in the seventeenth century and for two hundred years thereafter only two parties functioned. With the emergence of the Labour Party as a major political force in 1921 brought three parties in the political field. With the collapse of the Liberal Party there were again two parties and the government alternated between the Conservatives and the Labour. There was a split in the Labour Party in 1981 and a Social Democratic Party came into existence. The Social Democrats in alliance with the Liberals gave an impressive performance in the early stages of their emergence. But they were not able to make a significant dent on the two major parties. The alliance was short-lived and the Liberals are at present unrepresented in the House of Commons. Many prominent Social Democrats, too, have shifted their loyalty to their parent Labour Party. In fact, the British Constitution has grown and evolved under the two party system and its working tends to maintain and perpetuate it.

9. *The Rule of Law and Civil Liberties.* One of the fundamental principles of the British Constitution is the Rule of Law. It is based on the Common Law of the land and is the product of centuries of struggle of the people for the recognition of their inherent rights and privileges. In Britain, unlike the United States of America, or the Republic of India, the Constitution does not confer specific rights on citizens. Nor is there any Parliamentary Act which lays down the Fundamental Rights of the people. Yet there is maximum liberty in Britain and according to Dicey, it is due to the existence of the Rule of Law.

The Rule of Law has never been enacted as a Statute. It is implicit in the various Acts of Parliament, judicial decisions and in the Common Law. According to Lord Hewart, the Rule of Law means "supremacy or dominance of law, as distinguished from mere arbitrari-ness, or from some alternative mode, which is not law, of determining or disposing of the rights of individuals".[51] It is sufficient for the present to say, that when powers of government are exercised according to settled and binding rules and not arbitrarily, then, the subjects of that government are living under the Rule of Law. Such conditions of life can be possible only when there is equality of all before the law, its supremacy, uniformity, and universality. The citizens, the courts, the administrative officials, are all subject to it. In other words, under the Rule of Law, obligations may not be imposed by the State, nor property

51. Hewart, Lord, *The New Despotism,* p. 19.

interfered with, nor personal liberty curtailed except in accordance with the accepted principles of law and through the action of legally competent authorities. These principles are recognised by the courts and as a result judiciary is the unfailing guardian of the liberties of the people in Britain, though there is no Charter of rights to guarantee them.

Sovereignty of Parliament and the Rule of Law are closely connected. By its sovereign power, Parliament can curtail or suspend the liberties of the people and set aside the Rule of Law itself. Parliament has very often done it, but it always did it at times of national emergency. Drastic restrictions were imposed upon commonly recognised rights of the people during World War I. In 1934 and 1936, Incitement to Disaffection Act and Public Order Act were passed which imposed stringent restrictions on the rights to speech, assembly and press. Throughout World War II, drastic restraints were imposed under Emergency Powers (Defence) Act, 1939. But traditions of the country and political temperament of the people do not tolerate such infringement of their liberties when conditions of national emergency or danger are not prevailing. There is a sense in which Parliament itself is subject to the Rule of Law. It cannot, and in fact it does not, make laws which unnecessarily encroach upon the liberties of the people. Laws in Britain are passed to promote liberty and not to restrict liberty. "Freedom of speech is as truly a part of the British way of life as the responsibility of ministers. Neither rests upon written law; neither would be observed more consistently if it did so."

10. *Hereditary Character.* Another specially distinctive feature of the British Constitution is the recognition given to the hereditary principle, which has been, for so long, discarded by the great majority of other countries. Monarchy rests on the hereditary principle and the House of Lords is primarily composed of hereditary peers. It is true that neither the King nor the House of Lords play any effective role in the political set-up of the country, yet their continuance appears hardly reconcilable with the democratic ideals which Englishmen cherish so fondly. And still Englishmen had never been in a mood to abolish these historic institutions. Attlee observed, "I would claim that, despite the maintenance of monarchical and oligarchical elements, the British system is the best example of democracy and especially of parliamentary democracy."

**Development of the Constitution**

We note from the above description one leading characteristic of the British Constitution that it is the result of continuous development. Freeman emphasised this feature with unquestionable accuracy. He said, "The continual national life of the people, notwithstanding foreign conquests and internal revolutions, has remained unbroken for fourteen hundred years. At no moment has the tie between the present and the past been wholly rent asunder, at no moment have Englishmen sat down to put together a wholly new constitution in obedience to some dazzling theory. Each step in our growth has been the natural consequence of some earlier step; each change in our law and constitution has been, not the beginning in anything wholly new, but the development and improvement of something that was already old. Our progress has in some ages been faster, in others slower; at some moments we have seemed to stand still, or even to go back but the great mark of political development has never wholly stopped; it has never been permanently checked since the days when the coming in of the Teutonic conquerors first began to change Britain into England."[52] The starting point of the British Constitution and the principles which govern their working lie scattered into the past and the present mechanism of government can only be understood if we analyse the process of this growth; how the British Constitution came into being and how it assumed its present form and stature.

It is customary to divide this process of growth into six distinct periods, but we divide them into three as a matter of practical utility. The first period extends from the time of the Angles and Saxons through the Norman and Angevin dynasties to 1485. This period may be called the period in which were laid the foundations of the Constitution. The second period extends from 1485 to 1689 and covers the establishment of the Tudor dynasty through the early and later Stuart periods and embraces the Puritan Revolution and Commonwealth. This period is called the period of reconstruction of the Constitution. By the end of the fifteenth century Parliament had begun to show marks of its strength and the King's power had definitely eclipsed. The

52 Freeman, F. A., *Growth of the English Constitution*, p.19.

great institutional foundation of the modern English Constitution had been firmly laid. The years to come were in the nature of further growth and adjustment of these institutions leading to altered balances of power and mechanisms of control.

The third period extends from 1689 to the present and it is of more direct interest to the students of British Government today. In this period came the rounding out, or fructification of the Constitution. The Glorious Revolution of 1689 drew to a close, the great constitutional struggle of the seventeenth century. Kings in future held the throne by the grace of Parliament. Kings could be made and unmade by Parliament. Parliament was, therefore, Supreme. The Bill of Rights embodied the constitutional rules and principles which should guide the transactions of the King in his dealings with Parliament. It stated clearly and definitely the limitations on the powers of the king, and in one specific clause decreed that no future ruler of England could be a Roman Catholic or could marry a Roman Catholic.

The Bill of Rights marked the culminating point in the evolution of the fundamentals. The centre of gravity had shifted from the King to Parliament. But it was many years before the change became clearly understood. It took time for seeds which had been sown in earlier periods to germinate to this and to grow into fully matured institutions of popular government. Following are the main lines of growth and development which complete our account in making the British Constitution what it stands for today: diminished powers of the King, emergence of the cabinet and consequently responsible Ministry; rise of political parties; leadership of the Prime Minister; shifting of power within Parliament; democratisation of the House of Commons as a result of enactment of a series of Reform Bills beginning from 1832; and the great constitutional changes which altered the character of the British Empire. The latest change was made by the Labour Government recently when it reduced the absolute number as well as the hereditary element in the composition of the House of Lords.

## SUGGESTED READINGS


Amery, L.S. : *Thoughts on the Constitution.*

Amos, M. : *The English Constitution*, Chaps. I, II.

Anson, W.R. : *Law and Custom of the Constitution*, Vol I. pp. 1-13.

Bagehot, Walter : *The English Constitution.*

Birch, A.H. : *Representative and Responsible Government, An Essay on British Constitution*, Chap. I , pp. 116-122.

Dicey, A.V. : *Law of the Constitution*, Chaps. I, II, XIV, XV.

Gooch, R.K. : *The Government of England,* Chaps. VI, VII.

Greaves, H.R.G. : *The British Constitution*, Chap. I.

Finer, H. : *Governments of Greater European Powers,* Chap. 2.

Jennings, W.I. : *Cabinet Government,* pp. 1 - 19.

Jennings, W.I. : *The Law and the Constitution*, Chaps. II, III.

Keith, A.B. : *The Constitution of England from Queen Victoria to George* VI, Vol. I. pp. 12 -19.

Keith, A.B., and Gibbs, N.M. : *The British Cabinet System,* pp. 1-21.

Laski, H.J. : *Parliamentary Government in England*, Chaps. I & II.

Laski, H.J. : *Reflections on the Constitution.*

Low, S. : *The Governance of England*, pp. 1-14.

Lowell, A. L. : *Government of England,* Vol. I, pp. 1-15.

Morrison , Herbert : *British Parliamentary Democracy.*

Muir, Ramsay : *How Britain is Governed.*

Munro, W.B. : *The Governments of Europe,* Chap. II.

Ogg. F.A. : *English Government and Politics,* Chap. III.

Philips, O. Hood : *Constitutional and Administrative Law.*

Wheare, K.C. : *Modern Constitutions.*

Yardley, D.C. : *Introduction to British Constitutional Law.*

# CHAPTER II

# The British Political Tradition

### Liberal Political Tradition

The most important contribution to the growth of the liberal political tradition in the west has come from the people of England. The English political system is a product of a slow and gradual evolution. Unlike France, Russia and China, no successful violent revolution ever interrupted the steady development of a unique political system in Britain. Though we should not minimise the significance of the Republican revolution of 1649 under the leadership of Cromwell, yet the constitutional development of England is more intimately connected with the events of 1688. After this, the growth of the British political tradition was interrupted neither by any internal catastrophic armed uprising nor by a successful external invasion. The Industrial Revolution and colonial exploitation by building a worldwide empire enabled her to become the richest country in the world during the nineteenth century. As a result, economic contradictions of the British society never exploded into revolutionary political conflicts. By exploiting the wealth of the colonies, the capitalist ruling class of Britain was able to transfer a share of this wealth to the people as well. The British people, therefore, did not attempt to change the political structure of their country through a violent struggle directed against their ruling class.

Some writers on the British constitution have attributed the success of the British constitutional experiment to some special traits of the British national character. Laski, however, presents a dissenting note: "It is tempting to attribute it, as eulogists are wont to do, to some special British genius for the difficult art of self-government. That explanation, however, is an unsatisfactory one, since obviously, it is a deduction from the history rather than a principle informing it. A passion for simplicity usually works havoc with political philosophers; and it is rare indeed for a phenomenon so complex as the success of the British government to be capable of explanation in terms of a single principle. Explanations which base themselves upon some supposed virtue in a national character rarely deceive any save those who are responsible for their making. Anyone who compares the impression produced by Englishmen upon Frenchmen in the seventeenth and eighteenth centuries respectively will recognize at once that judgments of national behaviour are always a dangerous enterprise. There is a presumption in them both of unity and objectivity which rarely coincide with the facts themselves.'[1]

### Socio-Economic Conditions and Political Change

The social structure and economic system of a country largely determine its form of government and political institutions. The British political system and its parliamentary government are no exceptions to this general rule. They were the products of the middle class social revolution in Europe, which destroyed the power of the feudal class. A new social class, the urban bourgeoisie, emerged on the historical stage to claim a share in political power.

In medieval Europe, including Britain, political power was widely dispersed among the feudal barons. In a technical sense, the feudal chiefs were regarded as the king's vassals but actually the position of the monarch was no better than that of any his most powerful barons. The king asked for military assistance from his vassals at the time of foreign invasion or internal revolt. Thus, the very survival of a king depended on the support of his feudal chiefs. The peasants, who tilled their land, were their serfs and the other people who lived on their territory were their subjects. The traders, the craftsmen and the peasants were, in different ways, the victims of feudal exploitation. However, leadership in the anti-feudal revolts, came from the rising commercial and industrial classes in the cities.

1. Laski H.J., *Parliamentary Government in England*, p. 1

Some far-sighted monarchs recognised the emerging trends of political change, and laid the foundations of a new absolute monarchy by destroying the power of the feudal lords with the cooperation of the rising bourgeois class. In England, the Tudor dynasty represented an absolute monarchy of the new type where the king, though autocratic, sought the cooperation of Parliament in governing the country. To some extent, the emerging social strata of the bourgeoisi found representation in Parliament. When the Stuart monarchs challenged these class interests, the social classes adversely affected by this challenge put an end to their rule and instituted a Republic under Cromwell's leadership, with a written constitution to incorporate the new changes.

The Republican political system did not prove stable in England. After a short interval, the Stuart dynasty was restored to power. The Stuart monarchs made another attempt to regain their autocratic powers. But the Bloodless Revolution of 1688 abolished the system of absolute monarchy in Britain for ever. The Parliamentary leaders established a limited monarchy and put Mary and William jointly on the English throne. in place of James II who was ousted from power. Thus the first middle class political revolution was successfully accomplished in the history of the world. The revolution abolished the state power of British aristocracy along with the system based on monarchical absolutism.

However, this revolution did not undermine the economic and administrative privileges of the landowning aristocracy. Unlike the French Revolution, their estates were not confiscated and distributed among the peasants. The members of aristocracy participated in large number both in parliament and the government. But the British society and economy was increasingly dominated by the rising commercial and industrial classes of England during the eighteenth century. After the accomplishment of the Industrial Revolution, the industrial magnates and the big financiers of the City emerged as the new rulers of England. Parliament and the cabinet, though mainly aristocratic in composition, took orders from them. The aristocratic class had no independent role to play now. After the mechanisation of their farms and diversion of a part of their surplus capital to industry, the British aristocracy was assimilated in the capitalist class. According to Laski, it is this class which still exercises a preponderant power in the working of the British political system precisely because it still owns the main instruments of production like land and capital.

**Stages in Political Development**

(a) Tribal-Communal Society—In order to understand the political development of England in modern times, it is necessary to have some knowledge of its historical antecedents. The Iberian and the Alpine tribes were the first settlers of the British Islands, who owned their land and cattle in common and normally led a peaceful life. Celtic tribes invaded Britain in the 7th century B.C. and assimilated the original inhabitants into their own tribal structures, while reducing some of them to slavery. They also introduced agriculture and carried on some trade with the Gauls in France.

(b) Roman Colonial Rule—Julius Ceasar, Roman Emperor, invaded England in 52 B.C. and converted the country into a colony of the Roman Empire. The English people suffered from colonial rule for about four centuries. The Romans developed commerce and transport and granted the municipal status to five English cities. The Imperial rulers also introduced the system of agricultural estates owned by landlords. The British upper classes became completely Romanised and were transformed from Celtic tribal chiefs into Roman landowners and officials, Thus the land which was formerly under collective ownerships of the tribal clans was converted into private property of a few British and Roman aristocrats. As the Roman economy depended on a large class of slaves, the tribal democracy and equality gave way to class rule and racial inequality and exploitation. The British slaves were recruited in the army, worked on the farms and carried to Italy and other parts of the empire to be sold in the open market. When the Celtic incursions put an end to Roman rule in 450, tribal-communal social structures partially reappeared and destroyed the Roman social and political innovations to a great extent. This implied revival of tribal democracy, coltectivism and equality to a limited extent.

(c) The Anglo-Saxon Political System—The invasions of the Anglo-Saxon tribes began in the later half of the fifth century and continued till the end of the sixth century. Their social structure was partly tribal and partly feudal. After destroying the tribal communal democracy of the Celts, the Anglo-Saxon conquerors laid of the Celts, the Anglo-Saxon conquerors laid the foundations of territorial kingdoms in Britain which were half-feudal and half tribal, a cross between tribalism and feudalism. These Teutonic tribes—Angles, Saxons, Jutes and Danes had come from Germany and Denmark. The present English language has evolved from the Anglo-Saxon dialects. The dialects of the defeated Celts are still represented in the spoken tongues of the Irish, Welsh and Scottish peoples, but have left no imprints on modern English.

As the Anglo-Saxon tribes, like the Celts, lived on agriculture, the urban and commercial civilization of the Romans vanished from Britain. Unlike the colonising Romans, the Anglo-Saxons did not create large agricultural estates to be worked with the help of a slave army. Britain again became a land of small villages and nomadic tribes. Slowly the social organisation of the Anglo-Saxon tribes was feudalized. The entry and propagation of Roman Catholicism in the 7th century expedited the process of feudalization in England.

The first important social division arose in England between the warriors and peasants. The bonds of kinship loosened and successful warriors put forward claims for territorial sovereignty. As a result of continuous warfare, the victorious tribal leaders emerged as territorial feudal rulers. In this way, seven kingdoms of Kent, Sussex, Wessex, Essex, Mercia, East Anglia and Northumbria were established. Land originally allotted to clans and families on a collective basis was seized as private property by the ambitious clan leaders. Big farmers were named thanes and small peasants were called the ceorls. Gradually, the social class of barons arose from the thanes and all other peasant cultivators were reduced to serfdom. However, feudal political rule in the real sense began in England with the Norman conquest in the 11th century.

Wales and Ireland had accepted Christianity earlier than England but this did not affect their tribal mode of living. The life of the Celtic Christian monks was simple and ascetic and the Celtic Church did not own any land or property. The Anglo-Saxon conquerers were polytheistic and regarded Celtic Christianity with contempt as a religion of their defeated subjects.

Therefore, the Roman Church, whose messenger Augustine entered England in 597, represented the rising social forces of European feudalism. The Queen of Kent had already embraced Christianity and the King was converted to the new faith on the insistence of Augustine and his queen. Gradually all other royal households and Anglo-Saxon ruling chiefs were converted from paganism to the Roman religion. This was the second victory of Rome over England and thus a new social elite of the priests played a significant role in the feudalization of the British society and polity. The priests soon rose to the position of civil servants and ministers of their royal superiors. They explained to the king the value of Roman laws and written charters.

The king granted land to the Church by these charters and also used them to confirm the propriotory rights of the thanes over the land under their possessions. Thus the land collectively owned by the peasants became the private property of the bishops and feudal landlords. Free peasants living under a tribal democracy were converted into slaves, serfs or workers attached to the land of their masters. The feudalizing process, which had reached an advanced stage in Europe, was slowly maturing in England too. Scandinavians attacked Britain in the ninth century and later settled in the north-eastern parts of the country. They founded new towns and developed commerce with other European peoples. But they also collected huge tributes, which further impoverished the peasants.

In 1018, King Canute of Denmark, proclaimed himself as the Emperor of Norway and England. After his death, England became a free country again. But in 1066, William, who was the Duke of Normandy owing allegiance to the French King, invaded and conquered England. The Witan proclaimed William as the new king of England. According to Frederick Ogg, the Witan was an assembly of the most important men of the kingdom, lay and ecclesiastical. It had no fixed membership, but consisted of such persons as the king chose to summon to three or four meetings commonly held each year. According to some writers, the Witan could be regarded as the forerunner of the English Parliament.

**Feudal Political System**

George B. Adams says that the history of the English constitution upon English soil began with the Norman conquest. William, the founder of the Norman dynasty, had consolidated his sovereign power upon the whole of England by 1069. He confiscated the property of the Saxon

the members of the royal family and Norman nobles. He adopted the same pattern of feudal organisation as had already existed in France. A new aristocratic class was created in England based on the French descent, language and culture whose descendents still own large landed estates on the dawn of the 21st century and are proud of their noble origin.

The British constitution during the Norman rule operated on the basis of a balance of power between the king and his barons. The king governed in consultation with his barons. All power was based upon ownership of the land in this feudal polity and the essential political feature of feudalism was the downward delegation of power. The king was the sole and ultimate owner of all the land in his kingdom and granted it to his feudal vassals in return for military and political services and payment of customary dues and tribute.

The feudal lords administered the regions under their control and adjudicated the disputes of their subjects in their private courts. They also collected taxes and received services from their tenants. The main obligation of the barons was to support their king in war. Some of the prominent barons advised the king in running the administration. In England the conquerers had imposed feudalism on a defeated people from above. Therefore, the feudal system reached a higher regularity and completeness than in most other countries. In Europe, the king's ownership of all the land was a legal fiction and the feudal lords obtained rights over their land by force. William himself was technically the feudal vassal of the French king in Normandy but Paris had no control over the actions of the Duke of Normany. In England, he owned the land effectively and allocated it to barons on very harsh terms. No baron was allotted such amount of land as to make him a contender for the king's power.

The king retained a very large estate for himself so that he could successfully compete against the combined power of all the barons. Therefore, the British monarch, through dependent on the barons in certain ways, could exercise autocratic powers from the beginning of Norman rule. But despite the absolutist character of the king's authority, the Saxon peasantry regarded the Norman King as their protector from the oppression of their barons and sided with their king in his conflict with a baron. The king recruited the Saxon soldiers in his army and could rely on their perfect loyalty. England, therefore, had a constitutional development that was unique in European history. From the start the power of the state was greater and the power of the feudal aristocracy was less.

The supremacy of the king was evident from the fact that William could hold a national census of the families and evaluate their property just twenty years after coming to power. The commissioners were sent to each town and village to measure the land. This was not possible in Saxon England and equally impossible in any other feudal country of Europe. The survey revealed that 91% of the English people were agriculturist who could be divided into the following social classes : slaves : 9%; serfs –70%; freemen –12%; and others, living in towns, about 9% only. This showed that about 80% of England's total population of two million consisted of slaves or serfs at the close of the eleventh century.[2]

The Normans introduced in England a body of written and rigid rules, which tended to force all cultivators into a uniform class of serfs with no legal rights against the lord of the manor. The Pope Innocent III, a contemporary of King John, narrated the miserable condition of the serfs as follows : "The serf serves; he is terrified with threats, wearied by corvees (forced services), afflicted with blows, despoiled of his possessions; for if he possesses naught he is compelled to earn; and if he possesses anything he is compelled to have it not; the lord's fault is the serf's punishment; the serf's fault is the lord's excuse for preying on him.....O extreme condition of bondage! Nature brought freemen to birth but fortune hath made bondmen. The serf must needs suffer, and no man is suffered to feel for him, he is compelled to mourn, and no man is permitted to mourn with him. He is not his own man, but no man is his."[3]

Such was the law of feudalism. It was very harsh for the peasants and some lords enforced it strictly. But the serf could retain a certain amount of personal freedom basing it

---

2. Morton, A.L., *A People's History of England,* p. 64.
3. *Ibid.* p. 67

certain amount of personal freedom basing it on custom and ancient tradition. After doing the lord's work, he could claim a little time for himself. The lord could not sell his serf or a member of his family. He could even appeal against his lord in the king's court . The lord could not take his life without proving him guilty for an offence which required a death sentence. The serf of medieval England was different from the slave of the Roman empire. He was a person and human being who could claim for himself certain customary rights. The English serf enjoyed a better social status than his counterpart in contemporary feudalised Europe. The absolute monarchy placed certain limits on the tyrannical power of the English barons.

**Revolt of the Barons and Magna Carta**

When Queen Matilda ascended the English throne after the death of Henry I, a section of the English barons raised their banner of revolt. The civil war of the barons continued for two decades. They built their fortresses and followed the example of the European feudal lords in exploiting and oppressing the peasants. But Matilda's son, Henry II, succeeded in suppressing this rebellion, destroyed their fortresses and prohibited the barons from fortifying their manors. He dismissed a large number of the sheriffs and prohibited all illegal exactions from the peasants.

The fiefs of the English Crown never became rival sovereignties to be absorbed one by one in the process of national unification as in France, until all were gone and only royal absolutism was left. The English barons were administrative subordinates of the Crown, dangerous to weak kings through casual combinations, but never able to act in opposition to the Crown save by joining their forces and appealing for general support, a process which involved terms and conditions, the setting forth of which produced constitutional documents.

The power of the Church increased during the Norman rule. Competition began between the King's Courts and the tribunals set up by the Church. The bishops claimed exclusive jurisdiction over the cases involving the priests and awarded them lighter punishments as compared to those awarded to other citizens in the king's courts. The laws enforced by the Church were based on the Roman system of jurisprudence. The royal courts enforced the Common Law based on usages and customs followed by the Saxon people of England. The Pope not only intervened in the appointment of the bishops but also claimed a share of the revenues and income of the Church.

Henry succeeded in claiming jusisdiction over the civil cases involving the priests who could now be tried in the King's Courts. He also started the convention of the Circuit Courts trying cases in different manors as mobile representatives of the King's authority.

This practice brought down the influence of the courts set up by the barons. The trial by jury began but members of the jury were not as yet impartial adjudicators. Their object was to assist the court in punishing the accused and presumed from the start that he was guilty and acted as the King's witnesses.

French continued as the language of the royal court and Norman aristocracy till the end of the thirteenth century. The Norman lords also participated in the feudal wars of France on the continent. Thus London emerged as a great centre of trade for the English and French merchants, Foreign traders arrived to settle in London from all parts of Europe. When the third Crusade began, England was trading with commercial centres as far as Italy.

When King Richard demanded money from the rich bankers and merchants to raise an army to fight in the third crusade, they asked for the charters granting them civic autonomy in return for the financial contribution. The merchants in small towns demanded similar charters of civic autonomy from the local barons. Traders' Guilds came into existence in several English cities and towns. Free cities thus emerged in a feudal environment. The brief reign of Richard has acquired great constitutional significance due to the adoption of those charters for civic freedom. Richard's departure to Europe further proved that the King's administration could be successfully carried on by other persons in his absence exploding the myth of the monarch's indispensability.

Magna Carta or the great charter is regarded as the greatest event of the Norman era. Some writers like Keith regard it as one of the basic documents of the British Constitution. But the contemporary significance of the great charter was very limited. It does not mention the democratic rights of the people at all but merely reiterates the customary privileges of the barons or feudal lords. King John, who was an efficient and strict ruler, violated thereby some customary privileges of the English barons. He raised a few new taxes, deprived some barons of the ownership of their manors and compelled others to pay higher rents for the land they possessed. The merchants, who had grown accustomed to civic autonomy were asked to pay higher taxes on their increasing profits. John refused to recognise the appointment of Archbishop Langton by the Pope. France deprived John of his dukedom in Normandy and confiscated the land of the Norman barons settled in England.

King John, thus, antagonised the barons and bishops of England, the Pope and the French monarch simultaneously. Even the merchants of London and the Saxon militia refused to cooperate with the king. John, therefore, had to accept the terms of the Magna Carta reluctantly, presented to him by the barons on 15 June, 1215. The historical value of the Magna Carta is that the feudal lords of England united with the merchants of London to place certain limits on the autocratic powers of the Norman monarchy. But reduction in the authority and jurisdiction of the King's courts was a reactionary step. A committee of 25 barons was formed to safeguard the terms of the great charter. The Magna Carta, thus, was a mutual contract confirming the rival claims and privileges of various sectors in the feudal establishment such as the monarch, the barons and the church hierarchy. How could it safeguard the liberty of the English people? The majority of the British nation still consisted of the serfs oppressed by this feudal establishment.

### Growth of Parliamentary Power

When the powers of Parliament increased in England during the succeeding centuries, the importance of the Magna Carta was also enhanced. The process of the decline of feudalism started during the thirteenth century. New social classes emerged in the British society. They saw new meanings in the words used in the Magna Carta and pleaded for the recognition of their new rights disguised as ancient customs. The evolution of Parliament began, which was used first by the British aristocracy and later by the bourgeisie to achieve its own political supremacy in the state. Nobody remembered the Magna Carta during the Tudor rule. Shakespeare did not even allude to the great Charter in his play entitled **King John**. The long forgotten document however, was dug out of the government archives and Parliament, then, used it in support of certain new rights claimed by it. In course of time, the Magna Carta was converted by bourgeois liberal mythology into a symbol of the struggle between Royal Absolutism and Democratic Freedom.

Professor Adams claims that there were two fundamental doctrines proclaimed by the Magna Carta. The first doctrine asserted that there are certain essential laws forming the basis of every political system which ought to be adhered to by a king or his government. The second doctrine stipulated that if these basic laws are violated, the nation will either compel the government to recognise them or overthrow it and set up a new regime in its place.

The evolution of Parliament began in the thirteenth century. The Norman kings abolished the Saxon Witan, which was a council of their tribal chiefs and created in its place two new councils of the Norman barons. They were known as Great and Small Councils. Parliament arose from the great Council and the Privy Council and Cabinet emerged from the small Council at a much later stage in British constitutional history. To begin with, the Great council was an assembly of the barons, who owned large estates. Small landlords, merchants and priests were added to it during the thirteenth century. Originally, the barons, knights, burgesses and clergymen sat together in the same assembly. Later the king asked them to deliberate separately asking them to divide into two or three separate groups on the basis of their status and wealth.

The king summoned the Council according to his own needs. Its most important act was to approve the taxes proposed by the monarch. Parliament normally obeyed the king's orders. Its power, therefore, was very limited. But the fact that the merchants and small landowners were represented in Parliament was in itself a revolutionary change. It signified the declining prestige and power of the English feudal class.

Gradually Parliament was divided into two chambers on a definite basis. The representatives of nobility constituted the House of Lords. The traders and small landowners formed the House of Commons. Some priests were also included in the House of Lords but the majority of them lost contact with Parliament. If we compare these changes with the development of the medieval councils in Europe, we note two significant differences between them. In Europe, the medical council was divided into three segments i.e., (1) the big and small landowners, (2) the clergymen, and (3) the merchants or burgesses.

In England, on the other hand, Parliament had only two segments from which the priestly class was almost excluded and the small landlords, escaping the tutelage of their aristocratic superiors, rubbed their shoulders with their socially inferior burgesses or traders. In Europe, the monarchy, the aristocracy and the Church hierarchy remained closely united and created a common reactionary front against the rising bourgeois. In England the city bourgeois and small landlords combined together under the leadership of their monarch to destroy the political sovereignty of the feudal aristocracy and the allied Church hierarchy.

**Decline of Feudal Government**

The feudal political system declined and disintegrated in England owing to the following reasons :

(1) In England a section of the landlords realized that the productive capacity of a free agricultural worker was greater than the enslaved serf. Thus arose a new social class of enterprising landowners and a class of liberated peasants working together to enhance agricultural productivity.

(2) Some serfs migrated to towns and became industrial workers. Commercial agriculture and growing trade created a prosperous middle class of merchants manufacturers and bankers exerting greater influence on politics.

(3) The Hundred years' War in France weakened the feudal system, awakened a sense of English nationhood, and anglicised the French-speaking Norman nobility and monarchy. Joan of Arc became the symbol of French resistance to English invasion of France.

(4) Peasant uprisings grew in number and intensity during the fourteenth and fifteenth centuries in England. They developed political consciousness and inspired the struggle for basic human rights. The feudal class became frightened of the potentialities of a peasant revolution.

(5) Instead of looking after their estates, the English nobles became more interested in the politics of London, participating in palace intrigues and provoking internal factional struggles. In 1455 the Wars of Roses began in which the nobles fought on both sides either supporting the cause of the House of York or that of the House of Lancaster. The victory for the House of York signified the strengthening of the monarchy and further weakening of the baronial power.

(6) Although leadership of both the warring factions was provided by the aristocrats only, the sympathy of merchants and landowning agriculturists lay with the House of York exclusively. The supporters of the House of Lancaster came from the nobles of frontier regions who wanted to restore rigid feudalism on English territory. Therefore, the victory of the House of York represented the first political success of the new rising social classes of England. Edward IV ascended the throne who followed policies which were later carried forward by the Tudor rulers. He confiscated the land of hostile nobles and concluded new agreements with the merchants of London, thus increasing the income of the kings' treasury.

(7) The monarch thus secured financial independence as he was no longer dependent exclusively on Parliamentary grants. His rule, therefore, may be regarded as a preamble to the new chapter of Tudor rule in British constitutional history. The Tudor administration, though still autocratic in substance, sought legitimacy by seeking and obtaining the support of the middle class, especially the commercial bourgeoisie.

**Middle Class Revolution in England**

The modern age began in England with the foundation of the Tudor dynasty and the beginning of a middle class social revolution. To fix a definite date for the closure of the middle ages may arouse controversy for any other country, but is now universally agreed that the inauguration of the reign of Henry VII marked the end of the medieval period in England. The military and political power of the nobles was destroyed. The king confiscated the lands of the old aristocracy, expanded the royal estates and created a new social class of landowners drawn from the upper middle classes. The Tudor monarchs used Parliament for ratifying the policies which were in essence formulated by them. According to A.L. Morton, the Tudor monarchy "rested on the fact that the bourgeoisie were strong enough in the sixteenth century to keep in power any government that promised them elbow room to grow rich, but not yet strong enough to desire direct political power as they did in the seventeenth."[4]

Henry VII married a princess of the House of York and persuaded Parliament to approve the Tudor dynastic succession. Henry VIII laid the foundations of the National Church of England and liberated England from the international control of the Roman Catholic Church. When the king wanted separation from his Spanish queen Catherine, the Pope disallowed it. As a result, Henry VIII himself led the Protestant movement in England. He confiscated the estates of the Church and resold them to small landowners. Thus a new social class of the landowning squires was created. The squires worked as Justices of the Peace and constituted honorary officials of the new regime. Parliament approved Henry's reforms about the Church supporting them enthusiastically. All those, who got a share in the confiscated lands of the monasteries, became ardent admirers of the Tudor monarchy and loyal followers of the Auglican Church.

The King was recognised not only as the Chief of the English State but also as the Head of the Anglican Church. When Queen Mary ascended the throne, she tried to revive Catholicism in England but failed to restore the confiscated estates of the monasteries. During the long reign of Queen Elizabeth I, England became a Protestant nation irreversibly. Like her predecessors, Elizabeth was an absolute ruler but she was very efficient and talented as a Queen. With minor exceptions, she too received, like other Tudors, the support of Parliament for her policies.

The sixteenth century is regarded as a period of transition in European history. In England also important changes took place in agriculture, industry and commerce. The landlords enclosed the public lands and claimed them as their private property. Some landlords took possession of the lands belonging to free peasants. The medieval trade guilds were replaced by a new type of capitalist traders. The craftsmen's guilds also came to an end. The owners of small workshops reorganised production by employing wage workers. A large number of peasants, craftsmen and unemployed retainers of the old nobility became beggars, thieves and vagabonds belonging to the lumpen-proletariat. While capital was accumulating in the hands of the favoured few, the majority was facing starvation and unemployment. The law provided that a citizen could arrest a vagabond, force him to work as his slave and could even whip him.

**Absolute Monarchy of the Tudor Period**

During the reign of Elizabeth, absolute monarchy was modified partially and socio-economic conditions also improved to some extent. However, the rapid increase in the circulation of bullion and the Tudor policy of debasing the coinage brought about a galloping inflation in the country which enabled the landlords, farmers and traders to earn huge profits. Elizabeth and her merchant subjects showed great interest in building ships and establishing chartered companies for trade and piracy. The Queen had regular shares in the booty looted by the English pirates who regularly attacked Spanish ships on the high seas.

It was the age of commercialism. Spain was the chief rival of England. The victory of the English sailors over the Spanish armada during Elizabeth's reign signified the beginning of a new era. It was the triumph of a bourgeois mercantile England over the reactionary pro-feudal elements in Europe. The Spanish monarchy was the patron of Roman Catholicism and feudal forces of the European society. After destroying the Maya and Aztek civilizations of Central and South America, a corrupt, oppressive and luxury-loving Spanish aristocracy, in alliance with the church hierarchy, was ruling over Spain and her trans-Atlantic colonies, reducing the Spanish and colonial peasantry to a position of near serfdom. As compared to Spain, Elizabeth's England was a progressive, national monarchy where commerce and industry flourished and the peasantry had been liberated from its medieval bondage.

Queen Elizabeth was a popular ruler. She neither needed a standing army for her security nor a salaried bureaucracy to carry on her administration unlike contemporary European monarchs and the future Stuart kings of England. She neither claimed divine sanction for her rule nor showed any disrespect to Parliament. She followed the Tudor tradition in supporting the progressive elements of the state and also in using state power in accordance with laws as

4. Morton, A.L. *A People's History of England,* p. 169.

well as in seeking and obtaining Parliament's approval for her policies and actions. For this reason, the rising social classes as represented in Parliament also gave their consistent support to all Tudor monarchs. Like her foresighted predecessors, she knew that the unruly horse, she was riding, could not be controlled by the crack of a whip but only by loving persuasion. This alone unravels the mystery of Parliament's obedience to the sovereign and success of absolute monarchy during the Tudor period.

**Parliament's Struggle Against Monarchy**

With the start of the Stuart reign in England, the conflict between the king and Parliament began for a division of state power between them. Such tendencies had manifested even during the last stage of Elizabethian reign. It was obvious that the rising English middle class was not prepared to suffer indefinitely the monopoly of political powers in the hands of an autocratic monarch governing in the interest of nobility. The Queen often granted exclusive rights in trade or production of a particular commodity to her own favourites. When Parliament opposed this in 1601, the Government adopted a policy of accommodation.

James I ascended the throne in 1603. He did not possess Elizabeth's cleverness or tolerance. Earlier he had ruled Scotland where Parliament did not exist. He claimed a divive basis for his autocratic rule. He displeased the merchants of London by his financial policies. Elizabeth's annual budget amounted to £ 400,000 only. James thought this amount was too small for his needs. Parliament always opposed the raising of new taxes and invariably reduced the demands made by the king. It was also dissatisfied with the king's foreign policy and opposed the alliance proposed by him with Catholic Spain or equally Catholic France.

When Charles I became the king of England in 1625, Parliament's conflict with monarchy grew more intense. When it decided to impeach the king's favourite minister, the Duke of Birmingham, Charles dissolved the House of Commons. He imposed new taxes without the approval of Parliament. The merchants and landlords, who loved their property, did not want to pay these taxes raised by the king without the consent of their representatives.

Liberty for the bourgeoisie meant safeguards for their private property. In 1628 the Commons presented the Petition of Rights to the king protecting against he tyranny of the martial law, illegal detention of citizens and forcible collection of new taxes and loans. Forcibly keeping the Speaker in his chair, the House of Commons also adopted three resolutions. It was resolved that anyone trying to restore property in England, or advising the king to impose taxes without the consent of Parliament, or paying these illegal taxes to the Government will be deemed an enemy of the state, nation and England's freedom. Charles dissolved Parliament and refused to summon it for eleven years.

In the absence of Parliament, Charles sold monopoly rights in trade and production, increased duties on imports and exports and imposed a new tax on ships. Though these policies were opposed by a few courageous individuals, yet no political crisis or popular discontent developed for another decade. However, the policies of Charles and Laud as leader of the Anglican Church displeased the Presbyterians of Scotland, who characterized one Anglican Church under Laud as a disguised form of the Catholic Church.

The Presbyterians felt that the king, bishops and ritual ceremonies had no place in true religion. Their religion was based on austerity, pious life, private prayer and thrift. They called themselves as Puritans and condemned music, drinking and luxuries. Such ideas were gradually affecting the English middle class as well. When Charles wanted to bring Scotland under the Anglican Church, the people of Scotland revolted against him.

Charles asked the London merchants for a loan to conduct war against the rebels. This was refused. Seeing no other way out, he summoned a meeting of the Commons in 1640. The Commons led by Pym sent a petition opposing the war against Scotland. Charles had no further hope of his demands being approved by the Commons. Parliament was dissolved again giving rise to direct confrontation between the king and the Commons.

When it was summoned again, an organised opposition party had come into existence in Parliament. Pym and Hampden toured the country to organise a powerful Presbyterian party and London emerged as their stronghold. The Commons impeached the king's favourite minister Strafford for treason but the Lords did not agree. The next step on the part of the

Commons was to demand his death sentence through a bill of attainder. Frightened by the revolutionary atmosphere in London, Charles acceeded to this demand. About two hundred thousand residents of London watched the hanging with obvious glee.

## Republican Interlude and Monarchical Restoration

This led to new political developments in England culminating in the downfall of monarchy and establishment of a Republic. But this Republic was short-lived and lasted just for twelve years. Republican rule in a way broke the chain of constitutional growth in England for some years.

When Charles asked for monetary grants for crushing the Irish revolt, a group of members defected to the monarch's camp. Differences arose in Parliament on the issue of reforming the Anglican Church. The civil war alone could now resolve the disputes between the Royalists and the Republicans. The king was supported by a reactionary coalition of big landowners, Anglican bishops and Catholic nobles. He was opposed by the bankers and merchants of London, the urban middle class, small landowners and free peasants of East Anglia. The English sailors were on the side of Parliament. The workers and poor peasants were not involved on either side. For them it was a war of two ruling classes. On the whole, the cause of Parliament was progressive, in a relative sense, and its victory proved beneficial to the English people on a long-term view.

Gradually, Cromwell seized the leadership of the revolution. As a leader of the Independents, he represented the interests of the peasants and the lower middle class. The Levellers constituted a branch of the Independents who advocated a radical version of Republicanism. The Diggers formed the extreme left-wing of the Independent Party demanding equal distribution of land among the peasants. Cromwell disapproved the programme of the Levellers as well as the Diggers as impractical. Charles was defeated in the civil war and sentenced to death. England was proclaimed a Republic in 1649. This happened one hundred forty years before the French Revolution of 1789 when France was declared a Republic for the first time.

The House of Lords, the citadel of British feudalism, was abolished by a new revolutionary constitution. The House of Commons was to be re-elected on the basis of a revised, and broader- based franchise. Cromwell and the revolutionary leaders failed to secure the necessary support from the Commons for their progressive policies as the House was still entrenched with feudalist elements. Cromwell, therefore, was obliged to transform his government into a military dictatorship. He squandered public funds in the repression of the Irish people and in a war with Holland. As a result, even the forces which had supported him earlier turned against his dictatorial rule. Cromwell's death jeopardized the survival of the Republic. Although this experiment in Republican government proved short-lived but the flames of revolution succeeded in destroying the evil of monarchical absolutism in England for ever. Frederick Ogg says, "Like revolutionists everywhere, seventeenth century Englishmen found it easier to destroy than to build."[5]

If this revolution had failed in 1649 leading to the victory of counter-revolutionary monarchist forces in the civil war, England would have been saddled with an absolute monarchy, on the pattern of continental states like Spain or France, based on military power and governed by a centralized bureaucracy drawn from an aristocratic class. It would have changed the direction constitutional growth in England. The Bloodless Revolution of 1688 would have been impossible without the violent overthrow of absolute monarchy in a Republican Revolution in 1649.

In 1661 the heir of the Stuart line was restored to the English throne. The loyalists won the election to the next Parliament. The squires and merchants, who had supported the Republic earlier, switched their allegiance towards the new monarchy and formed the backbone of the Tory Party in future. After some time, the Whig Party was organised to function as an opposition faction in the Commons. The Tory Party consisted mainly of the rural landowners and the Anglican priests who were both devout royalists now. Catholic nobles were not allowed to participate in politics but in a crisis their sympathies lay with the monarch. The Whig Party was led by the aristocrats and supported by the city merchants and intellectuals

5. Misra, K.K., Quoted in Contemporary Political Theory, p. 343

belonging to the dissenting sects. Charles II ruled with the support of a loyal Tory Parliament. However, James II had to confront the opposition from a powerful Whig Party.

James put an end to the disabilities imposed upon them earlier and gave them equal political rights. This displeased the Tory supporters of the king. James tried to become independent of Parliament by obtaining financial aid from France. He raised an army led by Catholic officers. The majority of the Tory statesmen then realized that the king was determined to revive his autocratic rule.

**Establishment of Constitutional Monarchy**

The Tory and Whig statesmen of England jointly invited King William of Holland to invade England in order to put an end to the autocratic rule of James and establish a constitutional monarchy in its place. The supporters of James deserted him and so he fled from England to save his life. Parliament offerred the British Crown jointly to Mary and William and proclaimed a Bill of Rights depriving the monarch of his/her control over the armed forces and the courts.

The monarch, after the Revolution of 1688, could neither veto any particular law passed by Parliament nor delay its enforcement. He could not raise any tax without the approval of Parliament. It was made obligatory to summon at least one session of Parliament in three years. The term of the Commons was three years. On these conditions, the Whigs also turned royalists like the Tories. The Revolution brought the Central Government and the Local Administration of London and other cities under the control of the Whigs for about a century.

However, the Tory squires and landlords continued to rule over the rural counties and districts. Karl Marx observes : "The Glorious Revolution brought into power, along with William of Orange, the landlord and capitalist appropriators of surplus value. They inaugurated the new era by practising on a colossal scale thefts of state lands that had hitherto been managed estates, were given away, sold at a ridiculous figure or even more modestly. These annexed to private estates by direct seizure. All this happened without the slightest observation of legal etiquette. The Crown Lands thus fraudulently appropriated, together with the Church estates, so far as these had not been lost again during the republican revolution, form the basis of the todays' princely domains of the English oligarchy. The bourgeois capitalists favoured the operation with the view, among others, to promoting free trade in land, to extending the domain of modern agriculture on the large farm system, and to increasing their supply of agricultural proletarians ready to hand. Besides, new landed aristocracy was the natural ally of the bankocracy, the new-hatched *haute finance* and of the large manufacture, then depending on protective duties."[6]

The Glorious Revolution of 1688 demonstrated the supremacy of Parliament over the king but the actual responsibility of government still remained with the monarch. A big assembly like Parliament was not suitable to function as a governing agency. During the succeeding centuries, the responsibilities of governance were gradually transferred from the king to the cabinet which was in its origin and status a Committee of Parliament.

Another significant change took place in the position of the House of Lords. Its powers gradually declined in relation to those of the House of Commons. The change took place on the basis of conventions, which were later ratified by an act of Parliament. Another change, which ought to be mentioned, related to franchise which was gradually broadened to give representation to new social classes of the British society. Lastly, an important change occurred in the character and role of British political parties in the working of the parliamentary system of government in England.

During the reign of Mary and William, the Whig Ministers formed the government. However, Queen Anne appointed Tory or coalition ministries which were not responsible to Parliament. William also could appoint his ministers in his discretion and was not bound by their advice but he treated them with some consideration as they had the support of the majority faction in Parliament. Queen Anne regarded the ministers as her servants and claimed the right to hire and fire them at her sweet will. She was not prepared to change her ministers merely because a certain party lost or won a particular Parliamentary election. The ministers were mere subodinate administrators

6. Morton, A.L. *A People's History of England*, pp, 277-278.

of their particular departments under the Queen's leadership and control. She presided over the meetings of her Council of Ministers and took a lead in decision-making.

In 1714 George I of the Hanover dynasty was crowned as the king of England. He was the ruler of a small German principality and was ignorant of political conditions prevailing in England. He could not speak English. He, therefore, took no interest in the affairs of the state. The ministers were consequently deprived of monarchical leadership in government. They developed the convention of appointing the most senior minister as their chairman to preside over the meetings of the Council of Ministers. This Chairman was later known as the Prime Minister of England.

During the eighteenth century, the Whigs were able to maintain their majority in Parliament. Robert Walpole, who was an efficient administrator and a senior leader of the Whig Party for a long time, may be regarded as the first working Prime Minister of England without any formal recognition of his status. Actually, his contemporaries did not visualize him in this role. Walpole's colleagues did not function as a collective body and did not regard themselves as responsible to Parliament. This implied that the cabinet system had not developed as yet in the true sense.

**Oligarchical Nature of Government**

The form of government in the eighteenth century England was oligarchical, Not wen 10% of the adult population could vote. The constituencies were irrational and contained grossly unequal number of voters. The ruling party employed corrupt methods to secure its majority in Parliament. The Whigs retained power by practising corruption from 1714 to 1761. This was the age of great advances in commerce and agriculture. The military technology was undergoing rapid change and to satisfy the growing demands of the armed forces became a profitable business. A new social group of contractors flourished. London emerged as the centre of international trade and finance. The Tory squires had no share in running the central government but they continued to administer counties and districts and lived affluently on the incomes derived from their farms.

The foreign policy of England was also meeting with success. England won the Seven Years'. War (1756-1763) against France and acquired French Canada (Quebec) as war booty. The defeat of the French in this war paved the way for the British conquest of India. Scotland was now part of Britain and the colonial hold over Ireland was being consolidated.

The necessary conditions for the coming Industrial Revolution were maturing in England. The British emigrants were colonising North America. The Whig leaders of the British government and the Directors of the East India Company were mutual friends. Accumulation of capital from trade and colonial tribute was laying the foundation of England's rapid industrialisation. All social classes, which were politically conscious and possessed economic power, were quite happy with the policies pursued by the Whig Party. It was inevitable under these circumstances that the dictatorship of the Whig oligarchy continued without interruption for half a century.

When George III was crowned, he tried to overthrow the Whig rule. He was an ambitious monarch. The cabinet system had not yet fully developed. Factionalism brought dissensions in the Whig ranks. The character of the Tory Party was also changing. A section of the city merchants entered the Tory Party. With the help of the Tories and by using his personal influence, the monarch succeeded in winning the support of a majority in the Commons. Thus he formed a new cabinet entirely consisting of his friends and supporters, who allowed him to intervene directly in the affairs of government.

However, the positions taken by George III and the former Stuart monarchs were not identical. While the Stuart kings believed in autocratic government, George III played the same political game to which the Whig aristocrats had grown accustomed during the last fifty years, The method was to give jobs, licenses and contracts to the voters and ensure the election of the favourite candidates to Parliament through these acts of patronage. The members of Parliament could also be suitably bribed and benefitted so that they voted in support of ministerial policies out of a sense of personal gratitude. George III learnt this art from the Whig leaders and succeeded in appointing his cabinets drawn from his loyal servants.

To begin with, he appointed Lord Bute, his former teacher, as a minister. He obeyed the king as his loyal servant and formed a pro-monarchical faction in Parliament. This enabled Georged III to instal cabinets of his choice for a decade. On an adverse vote of the House of Lords, he dismissed all ministers who had been opposing him. He appointed the younger Pitt, a young man of twentyfive, as the new Prime Minister. The House of Commons expressed lack of confidence in the new Council of Ministers on several occasions. The king, in a mood of indignation, dissolved the House of Commons and ordered a general election. He used his patronage and influence openly. The new House of Commons endorsed the king's choice of the younger Pitt as the Prime Minister.

The Torty Party was strengthened by the king's patronage. The merchants, manufacturers and landowners, who had supported the Whigs in the past, turned their allegiance towards the Tory Party. The independence of the American colonies and the success of the French Revolution made England a more conservative and reactionary state. By establishing colonial rule in Ireland, Canada and India, Great Britain became an Impenial Power, *par excellence,* The Industrial Revolution created a new net-work of industrial workshops and factories in England. In them arose a new social class of factory workers destined to play a new role in world history.

In capitalist Britain at this time, the members of this growing labour force were not granted any political rights. How could the Whig and Tory elites agree to grant them suffrage? They viewed the working class as a slave army which should toil in the coal-mines, steel mills, textile factories or agricultural farms so that their affluent Whig and Tory masters could maintain their monopoly rights over the nation's wealth, politics and culture. In fact, Tories and Whigs did not constitute two different political parties in terms of their basic ideology and fundamental policies. They were just two different designations adopted by an identical, dominant class clique ruling the United Kingdom of Great Britain in the eighteenth century.

**Burke and the British Condition**

A section of the British ruling class supported the cause of American independence. Burke said that the Americans were fighting for the achievement of these aims which are recognised as the basic principles of the English Constitution. It was commonly agreed that no tax should be imposed without the consent of the tax payers or their elected representatives. The British Parliament, therefore, could not justifiably impose any tax on the American taxpayers without first giving them representation in Parliament. As this representation was denied them, the American people were justified in waging their struggle for independence.

However, the British dominant classes with one voice opposed the French Revolution. Only a small liberal group among the remnant Whigs expressed sympathy towards this democratic revolution. Burke condemned it outright in the his *Reflections on the French Revolution* — a treatise that proved popular among the Tory rulers of England. The French Revolution was led by the bourgeoise in France and so the bourgeois classes of the European Continent were sympathetic towards it. Consequently, the bourgeois parties and the people in general in South Germany as well as in Italy welcomed the revolutionary armies of France as instruments of their liberation from feudal oppression.

Why did, then, the English bourgeois rulers oppose this Revolution? The reason was obvious. The European bourgeois class was still denied a share in political power, Its class interests, therefore, coincided with those of the peasants and the common people. The European bourgeoisie wanted to put an end to the oppressive rule of the monarch and the nobility, allied to him, by leading a democratic revolutionary upsurge against them. The English bourgeoisie, on the other hand, had already become a ruling class and had formed on alliance both with the aristocracy and monarchy. Any democratic revolution could endanger their rested interests and therefore, the oligarchical constitution of England satisfied them fully. In Parliament franchise was limited to the members of the bourgeoise and the aristocracy. This led Burke to sing panegyrics of the British constitution.

The slogan of the French Revolution was *Liberty, Equality and Fraternity.* How could Tory England accept equality and fraternity between the capitalist and the worker or the landlord and his tenant? The French revolutionaries confiscated the estates of the nobles and distributed them among the peasants. How could the Tory landowners approve this act of sacrilege? The Constituent Assembly of France proclaimed manhood suffrage with no property restrictions. The English ruling class was puzzled. Even revolutionary Cromwell did not commit this outrage. This was, according to the dominant class perception, no liberty but a license to anarchy and chaos.

**Violation of Human Rights**

In order to crush the Revolution ary France, the Tory England imposed repressive practices on the progressive popular movement, which was demanding human rights for the English people, and simultaneously entered into a military alliance with reactionary monarchist powers like Austria, Prussia and Spain. The revolution in France was not only a political menace to British social structure, a bourgeois France ruled by the capitalists could develop into a serious colonial and commercial rival of an imperialistic England. The war against the French Republic and later against Napoleon continued till 1815 and ended in the restoration of the reactionary Bourbon regime in Paris. This inaugurated a period of political repression and large scale violation of civil liberties in England.

In 1794 Pitt began the persecution of persons professing radical republican views by suspending the *Habeus Corpus* rule. Thomas Paine's popular treatise *Rights of Man* was banned. The author sought political asylum in France and lived there or in the United States of America for the rest of his life. Democratic associations were also banned. The strikes, bread-riots and sabotage occurred in factories on a large scale. When soldiers expressed sympathy for the agitators, a mounted police corps was organised which was recruited from members of the upper class. The police and the army were instructed to guard the factories. Every radical citizen was regarded as a Jacobin or a French agent.

Even after the end of the war in 1815, the civil liberties remained suspended. When six thousand citizens of Manchester started on hunger-march to London, the police resorted to violence and dispersed the marchers. In August 1819, eighty thousand people assembled in Manchester at Peterloo to listen to the speech of a Radical leader Hunt. As soon as Hunt stood up to begin his speech, the mounted police arrested him and attacked the peaceful assembly with pointed spears killing eleven people on the spot and injuring four hundred people including one hundred women. It was probably a rehearsal of the Amritsar massacre perpetrated on British territory itself by the forefathers of Brigadier-general Dyer. The British working-class still commemorates the grim tragedy of the Peterloo massacre even today. This was the naked dance of capitalist dictatorship prevailing at that time in England. In Tory England then the rule of law had given way to the rule of the sword.

Parliament passed laws to suppress civil liberties. The magistrates were empowered to prohibit any assembly of fifty people and could order the search of any house on the suspicion that the arms were concealed there. Flags and bands could not be used in a procession. Mass physical exercise and drills were declared unlawful. Additional tax was imposed on political newspapers and publications to make them costlier for the common people. Several publishers of radical literature were arrested and prosecuted for spreading disaffection. Some of them were exiled. Popular movement was thus crushed by the British ruling class.

**Extension of Representative Government**

The Industrial Revolution in England created a new social class of industrial capitalists, who demanded that all social classes should be represented in Parliament, which ought to instal a government of people's representatives. The Tory Party was under the influence of big landowners, big bankers and big merchants. The industrial class was discontented with the Tory administration and, therefore, the members of that class started a reformist liberal movement under the leadership of a small group of liberal Whig leaders. The new Liberal Party was very critical of the electoral system for the House of Commons. Industrialisation brought about significant changes in the distribution of population. The population of cities like London, Manchester, Birmingham, Sheffield, Leeds etc. multiplied rapidly.

However, there was no corresponding increase in the representation of cities in Parliament. Several cities did not send, even one member to Parliament. Many constituencies known as the pocket boroughs, controlled by the Tory landlords, consisted of depopulated rural areas. The emerging class of industrial capitalists scarcely had any representation in Parliament. As the industrial workshops were small, the employers maintained personal contact with the workers under their employment. The Trade Unions were still unlawful. The workers at that moment looked upon their employers as their well- wisheres and leaders.

Thus the united front of the British industrialists and the workers challenged the oligarchical rule of the Tory reactionaries. In 1831 the Liberal Party, supported by a powerful mass movement, succeeded in reforming the electoral system for the House of Commons despite the obstruction of the Tory Party aided by the House of Lords. The pocket boroughs were abolished, forty two new constituencies were created for London and other cities and sixty five counties with new urban settlements.

The franchise was extended from 220,000 voters before the reform to 670,000 citizens entitled to vote after the reform. Even this number was quite small in view of the fact that England's' population at that time was estimated as 14,000,000. However, the political significance of the change should not be underestimated. The industrial bourgeoisie of England, riding on the shoulders of a loyal working. Class, had by this measure successfully challenged the aristocratic Tory patrons of finance capital. This was the secret of the rise and success of the Liberal Party in the later half of the nineteenth century. The franchise was not extended to the English working-class by the Reform Act of 1832. However, by actively participating in a mass movement led by the Liberal Party, the working-class established itself as a force to be reckoned with in the subsequent political history of the United Kingdom.

**Constitutional and Political Reforms**

The nineteenth century was an era of reforms in England. These included central administration, local government, the electoral system, civil liberties, free trade, rapid industrialisation, reduction in the monarch's powers, growth of cabinet system, decline in the privileges of the House of Lords etc. The century also witnessed the Liberal-Tory political dialogue and competition, failure of the Chartist Movement, progressive development of the labour movement and organisation of the trade unions.

In 1867, the Tories passed a new Reform Bill about elections to the House of Commons. The Radical Associations led by Bright and Cobden and the British workers now organised in trade unions struggled for voting rights and held large suffrage rallies. Though both parties opposed their demands in the beginning, Disreli finally agreed to enfranchise the workers and petty-bourgeois sections as he wanted to project a new image for his Tory Party of which he was the leader. The agricultural workers and industrial labourers living outside municipal limits got the right to vote by the Act of 1885.

The Dissenters, Catholics and Jews were also granted civil and political rights on an equal basis. Thus the privileges of the Anglican church were discontinued. The capitalist oligarchy that existed in the eighteenth century was gradually transformed into a bourgeois democracy, Although workers voted in elections to the House of Commons, yet no member of the working class or any trade union activist had a chance of being elected to Parliament at that historical juncture. The Labour Party was not yet in existence. Politically the working class was still a subject class.

Imperialism and British Democracy

Laski has rightly pointed out that there was a symbiotic relationship between the growth of imperialism abroad and British democracy at home. Along with constitutional reforms in England, the nineteenth century also witnessed complete colonisation of India the cruel opium wars in China, brutal colonial wars all over the globe, violent suppression of freedom struggle in Ireland etc. France, Germany and Russia emerged as commercial and colonial rivals of great Britain in different parts of the world.

In 1880 a new era commenced in world history. This was the age of global imperialist expansion and domination of finance capital. Great Britain and other capitalist powers joined hands in the colonial partition of Africa, in dividing China into spheres of influence, in consolidating the chain of Colonial exploitation in western and southern Asia, in the construction of the Suez Canal and in extending economic imperialism to Latin America in conjunction with the United States. Imperialist rivalry led the British and German capitalists to fight the first world war. British democracy like the Athenian democracy of ancient Greece was founded on a restrictive concept of democracy which denied freedom and equal rights to the slaves in one case and colonial subjects in the other. Race and or class fixed the boundaries of democratic rights in both the cases.

**Party System and Responsible Government**

During the phase of the rise of Imperialism, the two-party system in England was consolidated. The British ruling class, first divided between the Whigs and Tories, later adopted the Liberal and Conservative designations. The existence of two major parties facilitated the growth of parliamentary government in England. To begin with, Parliament did not represent the British people. While the upper house was constituted on a hereditary basis, the lower house was elected on severely restricted franchise and under a thoroughly corrupt electoral system. The British political system was oligarchical in its essence. With the extension of suffrage, new social classes found representation in the House of Commons but the government remained under the effective control of the two bourgeois parties.

The Conservative and Liberal Parties could later be regarded as two wings of the same ideological party, in fact just two factions of the quarrelling bourgeoisie. Industrial capital eventually joined hands with the finance capital. Consequently, the industrialists supporting the Liberal Party turned Conservative. Radical intellectuals and manual workers thought in terms of creating a separate political association. Thus the organised Trade Unions and radical petty-bourgeois individuals jointly laid the foundation of the British Labour Party at the beginning of the twentieth century. With the rise of large-scale mechanized production, the size of factories and trade unions went on growing bigger and thus giant trade union organisations came into existence.

When the working-class got vote, the Labour Party based on the organised power of trade unions was bound to emerge sooner or later as a third political grouping. Manhood suffrage was first demanded by the Chartists but the ruling class delayed its grant for another fifty years. Capitalism not only denied franchise to the workers, it also refused to grant it to women for a century. Adult franchise was ultimately won in the United Kingdom as a result of the working class agitation and the suffragist movement of the British women.

The Liberal Party was gradually absorbed by the new Conservative Party. The Labour Party finally emerged as the main rival of the Conservatives in the British parliamentary politics. Between the two world wars, the state power mostly remained with the Conservative Party. The minority Labour Governments of 1924 and 1929 were short-lived, which could not implement their programme. Thus the Conservatives were able to maintain their status as the chief ruling party of the United Kingdom as well as the British Empire for a long time.

After the second world war, the Labour Party got an opportunity to form its government by securing a majority in the House of Commons for the first time. This time the Party did get a chance to carry out its programme. However, the Conservatives were voted to power again in 1952, continued to rule till 1964 and undid some of the measures of the previous Labour administration. The Labour Party got another chance to govern in 1964 but was replaced by the Conservatives in 1970, who ruled till 1974. Between 1974 and 1979, Labour Party exercised power again. Then Thatcher and Major ruled England on behalf of the Conservatives for eighteen uninterrupted years. In 1998, Labour has been reelected to power under Tony Blair. It turns out that while the Tory or Tory-led governments ruled Britain for 66 years after the first world war, Labour Party was in power for about eighteen years only. That shows that the British two-party system is heavily loaded in favour of the Conservatives and against the Labourites.

**Theory and Practice of British Democracy**

In theory, it can be claimed that despite the presence of the monarchy and a predominantly hereditary House of Lords, Britain has established political democracy. The people elect the House of Commons directly and the leader of the majority party there is automatically chosen as the Prime Minister by the monarch . The elected popular leader forms his own cabinet, which is collectively responsible to the House of Commons.

In practice, the class which owns the means of production in the United Kingdom governs the country through its direct agents in the Conservative Party or its indirect spokesmen in the rightwing leadership of the Labour Party. However, Great Britain, unlike a fascist regime, cannot be described as a naked and vulgar dictatorship of the bourgeoisie. The existence of the Labour Party, recognition of civil liberties in normal times, highly organised trade unions, the right to criticise the government in Parliament, relatively independent judiciary, Labour control over some municipal governments, the formation of Labour ministries occasionally at the Centre etc. demonstrate the fact that Great

Britain has developed a political system which ought to be described as essentially bourgeois-democratic.

The twentieth century, like the sixteenth is an age of transition in world history. During the sixteenth century, the bourgeois revolution commenced in feudalist Europe. During the last five centuries, the capitalist Powers of Europe, the U.S.A. and Japan brought the whole world under capitalist influence and domination.

Political systems based on Socialism and led by Communist and Workers' Parties emerged in the Soviet Union, Eastern Europe, China, North Korea, Viet Nam and Cuba during the twentieth century. It is true that counter-revolutionary regimes have now replaced the formerly socialist governments in Europe, that does not mean that the agenda for socialism has disappeared from the world for ever. The working- class continues its allegiance to Labour, Socialist or even Communist Parties in many countries. Socialist and Labour Parties are ruling at present in eleven West European countries including the United Kingdom. In Russia also, the Communists and their allies have obtained a majority in the Duma i.e. Russian Parliament and their candidate lost narrowly in the Presidential election against Yeltsin.

The national liberation movements in Asia, Africa and Latin America were increasingly attracted by socialist ideals. Decolonization of the British Empire had put socialist-inclined regimes in power in several of the new nation-states, emerging in the former British colonies. Britain is also passing through this transitional phase in her history, while the Conservative and Right-wing Labour leaders have joined in an unholy alliance to defend capitalism, the organised power of the working class is challenging the *status quo* in various ways.

**Laski's Interpretation of British Democracy**

According to Laski, the real rulers of Britain are those who own the movable and immovable wealth of the country. The British constitution, from a political point of view, is an expression of a democratic form of government but it does not reflect an egalitarian or democratic social order. The reasons for this contradiction between the political philosophy of the construction and the character of the socio-economic system of the United kingdom are: recognition of the right of private property, capitalistic economic system, unequal distribution of wealth in society, the aristocratic tradition, class orientation in education, racial chauvinism of the ruling class based on its colonial heritage, colour prejudices of the elites and masses, feudal pomp of the royal household eulogies by the mass media and films of the affluent style of living practised by the upper classes, support that the Church gives to the sentiments of class hierarchy and propaganda by the media and other fora controlled by the upper strata of society that all radical and socialist associations are either atheistic or anti-national etc. In spite of these limits, the democratic form of government in Britain has proved relatively more successful than in some other countries.

Not only Harold Laski but H.R.G. Greaves, James Harvey and Katherine Hood have argued that an economic oligarchy is still entrenched in the Conservative Party, which mostly occupies the seats of government, and operates as an agent of this oligarchy. Democracy, according to laski, has been married to capitalism in the United Kingdom and its state institutions, therefore, have to function within a narrow capitalistic framework. The industrial workers have constituted a majority of the British electorate and the nation for more than a century and the Labour Party has also been active in British politics for about a hundred years. Yet this party secured absolute majority only in four general elections and its rightwing leaders occupied the seats of authority for less than twenty years. Leaving aside a few exceptions the Tory establishment has been continuously ruling Great Britain after World War I. Laski has rightly observed that political power is the handmaiden of economic power. Those who own the wealth and capital of the country, also thereby govern the British people through the instrumentality of the Conservative Party. Those, who direct and manage its banks and industries, create public opinion by controlling the mass media and finance the propagandist and organisational activities of the Conservative Party.

**Conservative and Colonial Heritage**

The majority of the British people belongs to the Anglican Church, which invariably supports the Conservative Party. Educational institutions are managed by the members of the upper class and special schools are maintained for the students belonging to higher social strata.

of the armed forces,. the majority of the judges, the highly placed bureaucrats, the bishops and archbishops, the citizens of aristocratic origin, big industrialists and bankers, the editors of the large national newspapers, the university professors, the eminent doctors and lawyers, retired civil servants etc. remain stable supporters of the Conservative Party.

It is not very easy for any political party to confront these vested interests. It has been estimated that about ten per cent people of Britain, who constitute the upper strata of the British social hierarchy, consistently vote for the Conservative Party in all general elections. This explains the relatively weaker position of the Labour Party in the British political system. When the British people use their votes to defeat the party of the vested interests and enable the Labour Party to form its Ministry, the Labour Government soon discovers that it cannot govern without entering into a humiliating compromise with these powerful forces of the British social-economic system. The right wing leadership of the Labour Party then tries to bring some reforms in the living conditions of the working class within the bounds of the capitalistic system. In order to attract the labour votes, the Party has occasionally raised socialist slogans and some ordinary members and intellectuals of this Party have genuinely believed in socialist ideals, but the policy of its mainstream leadership has always been that of a compromise and 'constructive' criticism of the vested interests. Actually the Labour Party is the twentieth century version of a Liberal Party.

During the hey-day of the British Empire, there was no place for political equality between the British people, who formed the ruling nationality, and the people of the colonies, who were treated as subject, therefore inferior, nationalities. The right of national self-determination was denied to Asian and African nations for a long time. England's Parliament, whose sovereignty extended to millions of subjects living in several continents, did not include a single representative of the colonised areas, and therefore, they could not regard it as a democratic assembly. It was rather an Imperialist Parliament used by the British capitalists for exploiting the people of India, Africa and other colonies. As pointed out earlier, democracy in the United Kingdom had a narrow social base just like its predecessor in classical Greek cities like Athens because the majority was denied equal rights of citizenship in both political systems.

After the loss of colonies, Great Britain has become worried about her political and economic prospects as a small nation. It has finally decided to join the European Community and is represented in the European Parliament, though it has opted out, for the time being, of the common European currency called euro, preserving the pound as its national currency. Britain is also a member of the U.S- led military alliance, N.A.T.O and unlike France, continues as a staunch American ally. Margaret Thatcher demonstrated her imperial concerns in the Falklands' war gains Argentina. Tony Blair shows his solidarity with Bill Clinton by participating in aerial bombardments of Iraqi people. Colonial heritage has been lost but colonial temperament survives in post-Imperialist British democracy.

### Tony Blair's Reform Projects

The present Labour Prime Minister of Great Britain has introduced some significant constitutional changes in the first half of his term in office. Tony Blair's plan of granting devolution to Scotland and Wales and the planned abolition of the rights of hereditary peers have probably produced the greatest shake up in the British political system in centuries. A change in the voting system for the House of Commons, which seeks to introduce proportional representation, is also under active consideration. Great Britain has so far followed the relative majority rule in single-member constituencies. If Tony Blair's plan of changing the electoral system bears fruit, it would alter the nature of British politics beyond recognition. At the heart of all these reforms, There has been a desire to bring the government in close conformity with public opinion and achieve modernisation and democratisation of the political process.

In fact, Tony Blair intends to severe the trend of the centralisation of power that had occurred during the years of Margaret Thatcher, The Labour Party has a majority of over 400 members in Parliament and most party MPs are loyal to their leader. William Hague, Conservative Party leader at present, has failed to make much of an impact so far and so the Tories are languishing in the opinion polls. Tony Blair has successfully co-opted the Libral Democrats, Britain's third Party, on his side. In fact, he is trying to build up a grand left-centre coalition that may present the Conservatives from coming to power for several generations. For this purpose, he is attempting to create an informal alliance with the Liberal Democrats.

As the initial step, Tony Blair has asked Paddy Ashdown, leader of the Liberal Democrats, and his senior colleagues to join a Cabinet committee dealing with constitutional reforms. This is the first instance in recent history when opposition members have been invited to join a Cabinet committee. The Blair governmental has a challenging task ahead. Apart from formulating and implementing constitutional changes, there are a series of elections to be fought to the European Parliament, to the Scottish and Welsh Assemblies and to various municipal bodies. His electoral success will determine the fate of his reforms.

## SUGGESTED READINGS

Adams, W.B. : *Constitutional History of England.*
Greaves, H.R.G. : *The British Constitution*
Harvey, J. & Hood, K. : *The British State*
Laski, H.J. : *Democracy in Crisis.*
Laski, H.J. : *Parliamentary Government in England*
Moore Jr., B. : *Social Origins of Dictatorship and Democracy*, Chapter I
Morton, A.L. : *A People's History of England*
Ogg, F.A. : *English Government and Politics*

# CHAPTER III

# The King and the Crown

## The King and the Crown

In early days all powers of the government were centred in the man who wore the crown—the state cap of royalty. In the course of history those powers have been almost entirely transferred from the King[1] as a person to a complicated impersonal organisation called the "Crown." It does not mean the exit of the monarch from the body politic of the country. The King is still there as head of the State and he wears, as before, the diadem or the crown. Now, as then, the King is the Chief Executive and the supreme legislative power rests with the King-in-Parliament. His Majesty is, as ever, the 'fountain of honour.' He is the commander of the military forces of the realm by land, sea and air. Even postmen deliver His/Her Majesty's mails. The King, in short, is still the source of all authority, the 'Great Leviathan' embodying in his own person the sovereignty, the dignity and the unity of the State.

Such are the legal powers of the monarch. But a legal truth is very often a political untruth in Britain. Down to 1688, the King was an efficient factor in the Constitution. He ruled as well as reigned. Thenceforward it became otherwise. The King/Queen still reigns, but he/she has gradually ceased to rule. And the fact of the Constitution today is that the King/Queen personally has nothing to do with any affairs of Government. The actual exercise of powers and rights connected with the office of the King/Queen belong to the Crown.

The Crown is not a living tangible person. It is an artificial contrivance; an abstract concept. Sir Sidney Low calls it "a convenient working hypothesis."[2] Sir Maurice Amos says, "The crown is a bundle of sovereign powers, prerogatives and rights—a legal idea."[3] Historically the rights and powers of the Crown are the rights and powers of the King/Queen. Legally this is still in general the case. But Parliament has now enchained the King/Queen and the Constitution requires these powers and rights to be exercised, in substance, not by the King/Queen personally. They are exercised in the King's/Queen's name, as the personal bearer of the powers and rights comprised in the Crown, by Ministers who derive their authority from Parliament and are solely responsible to Parliament. This somewhat intangible synthesis of authority is what we call the Crown. The Crown is, thus, a "subtle association" of King or Queen, Ministers and Parliament and all three combined make an abstract concept of supreme authority. The King/Queen is its physical embodiment whereas Ministry, a creature of Parliament, is its most concrete visible embodiment.

There are two main stages which stand conspicuous in the transfer of powers from the King/Queen as a person to the Crown as an institution. The first is what we may call the "institutionalising" of the King. Kingship in Anglo-Saxon days was elective. Succession to the throne was not determined by hereditary principle. Every monarch reigned personally and independently of his predecessors and, consequently, when a King died there was an "interregnum" or break in government till another was established as a new King. After William, the Duke of Normandy came to the English throne in 1066, but essentially in the twelfth and thirteenth centuries title to the throne became hereditary and the next in line succeeded to the rights and privileges connected with royalty.[4] The result was the emergence of the institution of the kingship or the monarchy; a continuous political system which remained uninterrupted by the coming and going of individual monarchs.

---

1. The word "King" is here used as a term common to either sex. The Head of the State is now a Queen, Queen Elizabeth II.
2. Sidney Low, *Government of England*, p. 255.
3. Maurice Amos, *The English Constitution*, p. 88.
4. King John was the English King, who styled himself *Rex Angliae* (King of England) and not, *Rex Anglorum* (King of the English) and it so happened that he was the first English King to be succeeded by his eldest son when that son was still a boy.

A vital distinction was, in this way, made between the person and the office of the monarch. The distinction is now reflected in the maxim of the British Constitution: "The King is dead; long live the King." This announcement, made at the time of the Royal demise, means in the words of Blackstone, "Henry, Edward or George may die, but the King survives them all", that is, the King as a natural person may die, but long live the office (the Crown) which one monarch passes on to another. The Crown, as an institution, never dies; it is permanent. There is no interregnum between the death of one Sovereign and the accession of another. Immediately on the death of his or her predecessor the new Sovereign is proclaimed at an Accession Council.

The distinction between the monarch as an individual and the King/Queen as an institution paved the way for the transfer of political functions from a personality to an institution and as the chance would have it, it began with King John. The pace was slow and the process was not fully complete till the middle of the nineteenth century. But the constitutional struggles of the seventeenth century transferred final authority from the King to Parliament and thereafter led by logical evolution to government by Ministers responsible to Parliament. The whole of this process has been beautifully explained in a fairy tale and it runs : "once upon a time there was a king who was very important and who did very big and very important things. He owned a nice shiny Crown, which he would wear on specially grand occasion, but most of the time he kept it on a red velvet cushion. Then somebody made a Magic. The Crown was carefully stored in the Tower; the King moved over to the cushion and was transformed into a special kind of Crown with a capital letter....The name given to the Magic is the Constitutional Development." And the course of the Constitutional development, during the past nine centuries, had been that most of the functions which were at one time performed by the monarch are now exercised on the advice of Ministers, though still in the King's name. George Ponsonby, speaking in the House of Commons (June 11, 1812), said that it is an essential principle of the Constitution "that the servants of the Crown shall be alone responsible." When a King speaks on political questions, he always speaks as the mouthpiece of his Ministry. The Duke of Windsor, the former King Edward VIII, began the radio address on the day after his abdication with these words : "At long last I am able to say a few words of my own. I have never wanted to withhold anything, but until now it has not constitutionally been possible for me to speak."[5]

To sum up, the King is a natural person and he wears the crown, the state-cap of royalty. But when we use a capital letter in writing the word Crown, it stands for the Kingship as an institution. The distinction between the King and the Crown, thus, becomes obvious. Broadly speaking, it is two-fold. First, the King is a person, the Crown is an institution. The King as a person dies or may abdicate or may even be dethroned whereas the Crown as an institution is permanent ; it is neither subject to death nor abdication nor dethronement. This has been succinctly explained by Kerr. He says, "Nobody toasts the Crown or prays God to save it,"[6] people pray to God to save the King. Secondly, the King does not exercise the powers which belong to the Crown on his own initiative and authority. They are exercised by the King at the behest of those who exercise the will of the people, that is, Ministers and Parliament make a synthesis of supreme authority and it is called the Crown. The Crown is the key-stone of the country's constitutional structure.

*Title and Succession.* The events of 1688-89 finally established the supremacy of Parliament and determined that the Sovereign's right to rule rested upon the consent of the governed as expressed through Parliament. The basic Act in the matter of title to the Crown is the Act of Settlement passed by Parliament in 1701. It provided that the Crown shall be hereditary in the line of the Princess Sophia of Hanover,[7] so long as it remained Protestant[8]. The succession is now

5. The Duke of Windsor, *A King's Story* (1951), p. 411.
6. Kerr. W.G. *European Governments and their Backgrounds.*
7. Sophia, the gand-daughter of James I, was the widow of the ruler of one of the smaller German States, the Electorate of Hanover.
8. The Act was passed in the reign of William III after the death of his wife, Queen Mary. It anticipated that neither William nor his cousin and sister-in-law, who became Queen Anne, might have children. The Act, accordingly, provided that in the event of such default of isue, "the Crown and regal government ....., with the royal state and dignity ...... and all honours, styles, royalties, prerogatives, powers, jurisdiction and authorities to the same belonging and appertaining, shall be, remain and continue to the .... most excellent princess Sophia and the heirs of her body, being Protestants ..." On the death of Queen Anne in 1714, Sophia's son, the King of Hanover, become King of Great Britain with the name of George I.

vested in the House in Windsor, a name adopted during World War I to relieve the House of Hanover of any suggestion of German connections. The principle of hereditary is determined by the rule of primogeniture at Common Law. The basic rules are that an elder line is preferred to a younger and that, in the same line, a male is preferred to a female. If there are no sons, the daughters in order of their seniority succeed to the Throne. In any event the heirs must be Protestants. If all Protestant heirs are extinct or if there be no heir within the prescribed degrees of relationship to succeed, Parliament is competent to bestow the Crown on another family and thereby start a new dynasty. But succession cannot now be altered, under a provision of the Statute of Westminster, 1931, except by common consent of the member nations of the Commonwealth which owe allegiance to the Crown.[9]

The Royal Marriages Act of 1872 provides that until the age of twenty-five, the consent of the King is necessary to a marriage that might affect the succession to the Throne. After twenty-five no consent is required, except a year's notice of Privy Council. But Parliament may disapprove such a marriage. The issue arose with respect to the possibility of a marriage between Princess Margaret, sister of Queen Elizabeth, and a commoner, Peter Townsend, who had divorced his wife. The Princess finally gave up the idea of marriage. When the heir to the throne is a minor (under 18 years of age) or whenever the reigning sovereign becomes physically or mentally incapacitated a regency is set up in conformity with the terms of Regency Acts passed by Parliament. The latest of these Acts, the Regency Act, 1953, laid down that the first potential regent should be the Prince Philip, the Duke of Edinburgh and thereafter the Princess Margaret and then those in succession to the Throne who are of age. In the event of the Sovereign's partial incapacity or absence abroad, provision is made for the appointment of Counsellors of State (generally speaking, the wife or husband of the Sovereign, and the four adult persons next in succession to the Sovereign)[10] to whom the Sovereign may delegate by Letters Patent certain royal function. But Counsellors of State may not, for instance, dissolve Parliament, except on the express instructions of the Sovereign, nor create peers.

The title of Her Majesty Queen Elizabeth II depends on the Abdication Act, 1936. King Edward VIII abdicated in 1936 on the issue of His Majesty's marriage with Mrs. Simpson.[11] The Duke of York, then, next in succession to the throne, succeeded thereto as George VI[12]. George VI had no son and his elder daughter, Princess Elizabeth, became Queen in 1952 upon the death of her father.

*Royal privileges and immunities.* The sovereign enjoys numerous personal privileges and immunities. He may acquire, hold and dispose of property of all kind[13] precisely in the same manner as any private citizen. But the King is above law. He cannot be called to account for his private conduct in any court of law or by any legal process, not even, as Dicey humorously observed, if he were to shoot his own Prime-Minister. He is exempt from arrest. He cannot be made a defendant in a law-suit, his goods cannot be seized by officers of law in default of any kind of payment, and no judicial processes can be served against him so long as a palace remains a royal residence.

The monarch receives a large annual grant from the State treasury. This grant is made available by Parliament in the form of an appropriation for the Civil List. The Civil List is granted by an Act of Parliament to the Sovereign for the duration of his or her reign and for a period of six months afterwards. On March 9, 1982 the Chancellor of the Exchequer announced an increase

9. The Preamble to the Statute of Westminster, 1931, provides that "it would be in accord with the established constitutional position of all the members of the Commonwealth in relation to one another that any alteration in the law touching the succession to the throne of the Royal Style and Titles shall hereafter require the assent as well of the Parliaments of all the Dominions as of Parliament of the United Kingdom."

10. The Regency Act, 1953, provided that Queen Elizabeth, the Queen Mother, should be added to the persons to whom royal functions may be delegated as Counsellors of State.

11. Mrs. Simpson, a lady of United States origin, became a British subject by a second marriage after she had obtained a divorce from her Amercian husband, Edward VIII, who was a bachelor till then, desired to marry Mrs. Simpson and the lady lodged a petition for divorce from her second husband. The Cabinet took exception to this marriage and eventually on December 10, 1936 the King executed an instrument of abdication renouncing the throne for himself and his descendants.

12. The Abdication Act was duly assented to by Parliaments of the Commonwealth countries, thus, fulfilling the requirements of the Statute of Westminster 1931.

13. Queen Victoria handed down more than £ 2,000,000 and the personal fortune of the Royal Family is not diminished by death duties. In addition there are valuable Royal collections of jewellery, stamps and pictures. Estimates as to the total value of the Royal Family's personal wealth vary from £ 10,000,000 to £ 600,000,000. Anthony Simpson, *The Anatomy of Britain Today,* p. 22. Also refer to Martin, K. *The Crown and the Establishment* p. 134.

of 8.1 per cent pay rise of the Royal family. Queen Elizabeth's income from public funds to cover her expenses as monarch, thus, rose from £ 3.26 million to £ 5.54 million. The first rise of £ 3.26 million was made by the Conservative Government in 1980. On both the occasions the rise angered some members of the Opposition Labour Party in the House of Commons.

In 1971 the Queen asked Parliament for an increase in her annual grant. It evoked public criticism and Richard Crossman, an influential Minister in the last Labour Government, described the Queen's request for more money as impertinent. He voiced his opinion, as Editor of *The New Statesman* weekly in an article, denouncing the Queen as a "tax dodger." Crossman's principal target of attack were the Queen's private wealth and tax exemptions. He observed that the Queen inherited assets conservatively valued at more than £ 50 million. "But on the top of all this and unlike any other multi-millionairess, the expansion of her private fortune has been accelerated by public tax-privileges granted to her precisely because she is not a private person, yet she still asks for more."[14] The *Daily Mirror* reported in its issue of June 1, 1971 that its readers had voted overwhelmingly against giving Queen Elizabeth a pay increase.

## POWERS OF THE CROWN

The powers of the Crown are those which belong to the office of the King or to the Kingship as an impersonal institution. These powers are never exercised by the Monarch himself. They are exercised in the King's name by Ministers who derive their authority from Parliament and are responsible to Parliament for the use they make of these powers. As the Crown powers are not the King's personal powers, they may be described as nominal powers of the King as distinct from his actual powers. So extensive is the authority of the Crown that it embraces all fields and functions of Government and yet it is still growing. The province of the State, during recent years, has increased considerably and keeping pace with these political developments, the activities and functions of Government, too, have enormously expanded. This means fresh duties of direction and control by the Government and consequently augmentation of powers of the Crown. Lowell, writing in the first decade of the present century, observed, "All told the executive authority of the Crown is in the eye of law, very wide, far wider than that of a Chief Magistrate in many countries, and well-nigh as extensive as that now possessed by the monarch in any government, not an absolute despotism; and although the Crown has no inherent legislative power except in conjunction with Parliament, it has been given by statute, very large powers of subordinate legislation."[15] The powers of the Executive, under any system of government, cannot be rigidly divided into watertight compartments. Under the Parliamentary system of government Ministers of the Crown are the real functionaries. There is no divorce between the Executive and the Legislature. The Crown has as much to do with legislation as with the executive and administrative matters. It has, also, to do something with justice. The Crown, thus, forms a part of the Executive, Legislative and Judicial mechanism. It is the keystone of the country's constitutional structure. It mayapparentlyseem paradoxical, although it is logical to the nature of the British Constitution "that the powers of the Crown have expanded as democracy has grown."[16]

The powers possessed by the Crown are derived from two sources : prerogative and statutes. Statutory powers of the Crown refer to those duties which have been assigned to the Executive authorities by Acts of Parliament. They include not only the greater part of powers under which the different departments of the Government function, but also the powers by which Whitehall exercises control over the local government authorities and other bodies distinct from the Crown. The powers of the Crown under this category are various, wide, and growing. Acts of Parliament have, really, become a prolific source of Crown power, particularly with the development of the practice of delegating legislative powers to the Executive.

The powers and privileges which the Crown derives from the Common Law constitute the prerogative. Dicey defines it as "the residue of discretionary or arbitrary authority which at any time, is legally left in the hands of the Crown."[17] The prerogative was, in origin, the sum of the rights ascribed to the King as a feudal

14. As reported in *The Times of India, Bombay*, 29, 1971.
15. Lowell, A.L., *The Government of England*, Vol. I., p. 26.
16. Ogg and Zink, *Modern Foreign Governments*, p. 51.
17. Dicey, A.V., *Law of the Constitution*, p. 424.

overlord and it continued to be the basis of authority till parliamentary control of public affairs became an established fact. The seventeenth century was one continuous struggle between the use of prerogative power by the person of the King and the determined attempt of Parliament to control such powers either by statute or by Ministers responsible to Parliament. Parliament emerged victorious out of this struggle and the King, to the most part, was deprived of the prerogative powers which inhered in his person. Some were abrogated by statutes,[18] some have been lost by disuse, and the residue which remain have been inherited by the Crown. It is impossible to draw a list of the prerogatives of the Crown. The existence and limits of some raise difficulties of constitutional law. But the undoubted prerogatives include the summoning of Parliament, declaration of war or neutrality, ratification of treaties, appointment to offices, to dismiss the servants of the Crown, and to regulate the conditions of their service, and the power to pardon offenders.

The expression prerogative is, then, used to refer to Crown's discretionary authority, that is, what the King or his servants can do without the authority of an Act of Parliament. It provides a convenient mechanism of various important activities of Government. Although the prerogative has no statutory authority yet it is ac knowledged by courts. Most of the prerogative powers derive authority from the Common Law and the rules of Common Law form part of the law of the Constitution in Britain. It may, also, be added that some prerogative powers have been conferred upon the Crown by statute[19] and it is within the competence of the courts to determine whether an Act of Parliament is within the prerogative or to what extent royal power has been abridged or abolished by Statute.[20] In brief, the Crown possesses the prerogative powers that still inhere in the Monarch, and those powers conferred by parliamentary legislation in total constitute a vast reservoir of authority.

**Executive Powers**

The Executive powers of the Crown are so numerous that only some of the most important can be mentioned here. They have increased in the past, are increasing in our own time and must continue to increase so long as the functions of the modern governments continue to expand. The Crown is the supreme Executive head and it must, as such, see that all national laws are duly observed and enforced. It directs the work of the administrative branch and national service; collects and expends, according to law, national revenues; appoints all higher executive and administrative officers, judges, bishops and the officers of the army, navy and air force, regulates the conditions of services; and suspends and removes these officers, except judges[21] and other employes of government from service. The Crown holds the supreme command over the armed establishments The Crown supervises, and in some instances directs, the work of local government, especially that of boroughs and counties. The officers of local government and other bodies, like the British Broadcasting Corporation, are not the officers of the Crown. No doubt, these bodies are created by the Acts of Parliament, but they do not represent the Crown. The Crown simply exercises supervisory functions over them. Its right to control and direction is limited to certain specified matters.

The modern tendency is to assign powers to Ministers, or to civil servants, "without any necessity of royal intervention."[22] The exercise of the prerogative of mercy, for example, is now primarily a matter for the Home Secretary, and the Royal share is mainly formal. In the same way, the practice of delegated legislation vests powers in the Ministers, rather than in the King-in-Council as originally the practice was, to make rules, regulations, and orders.

**Conduct of Foreign Relations**

The Crown conducts the foreign relations of Britain with other countries; sends and receives ambassadors or other diplomatic agents, and all foreign negotiations are carried on in the name of the Crown. The declaration of war and making of peace are prerogative of the Crown. The Crown is also the treaty- making authority and all international agreements are made in its

18. Refer to the clauses of the Bill of Rights forbidding, suspending or dispensing with laws; the Act of Settlement and various other Acts of Parliament of the like nature.
19. For example, in 1876, the Appellate Jurisdiction Act gave the Crown the power to create four judicial life peerages, the number has since been increased.
20. Refer, for example, to the case of *Wilts United Dairies* (1921).
21. Judges can be removed only on joint address by the two Houses of Parliament. See *Infra.*
22. Keith, A.B., *The Constitution of England from Queen Victoria to George VI,* Vol. I, pp. 49-50.

name. Treaties concluded by the Crown are not subject to ratification by Parliament unless it is specifically conditioned upon parliamentary approval, or anything else is involved in it, like the cession of territory, payment of money, changes in the laws of the land, that require the assent of Parliament in order to make it valid. But "any treaty of high moral import," as the Locarno Treaty of 1925, is essentially laid before the two Houses of Parliament.

When the Treaty of Versailles was submitted to Parliament in 1919, for its approval, a section of the people, who were strongly wedded to the principle of democratic control over foreign relations, had hoped that in future no treaty would be made without parliamentary assent. Labour leaders, too, had long pleaded for it. But the Labour Governments of Ramsay MacDonald and C.R. Attlee never attempted it. Perhaps, they did not find such a policy feasible and treaties continued to be negotiated and ratified by action of the Crown alone.

It is true that no government can venture to declare a war unless there is assurance that Parliament will supply the funds to carry it to a successful end. But Parliament itself has no authority to declare a war. This power belongs exclusively to the Crown. Both in 1914 and 1939, the Ministers made the decisions and in the name of the Crown they led the country to war. And both the times the declaration of war took the form of a Royal Proclamation authorised by Order-in-Council. The question of Parliament's expressing disapprovalof the Government's policy, or its refusal to grant supplies does not at all arise. So long as the Ministry can command a stable majority in Parliament, its support is *ipso facto* there.

**Legislative Powers**

The powers of the Crown are mainly, though not exclusively, Executive. In the United States of America, the Executive, Legislative and Judicial functions are clearly defined among three separate departments, although the framers of the Constitution could not maintain the purity of the doctrine of the Separation of Powers when they came to details. In the United Kingdom little or no distinction is given to this doctrine of Separation of Powers. The law-making function is vested in the King-in- Parliament. Every Statute declares itself to have been enacted "by the King's Most Excellent Majesty, by and with the advice and consent of Lords Spiritual and Temporal and Commons in Parliament assembled and by the authority of the same," and here, as everywhere else, the King has yielded his power to the Crown. The Crown is, therefore, an integral part of the national Legislature and its assent is essential to the enactment of laws.

The Ministers of the Crown, who constitute the country's real Executive, are members of Parliament. They control and guide the work of Parliament and determine how conveniently it can be transacted. The Crown, accordingly, summons, prorogues, and dissolves Parliament. When a new Parliament meets it is usually greeted by the Monarch in a Speech from the Throne, which is usually delivered by the King or Queen in person from the Throne in the House of Lords with the Commons present. The Speech from the Throne outlines the legislative programme of the Crown and expresses the views and opinions of Government on various matters of national and international importance. But the Speech from the Throne is not the King's or Queen's speech. It is the Government's speech. It is put in the hand of the Monarch to be read. "The Monarch can, however, talk to the Prime Minister about it and sometimes minor amendments are sggested because it may be felt that the revised language suits the Monarch better than the official language which is set out. But alterations about policy are not made. That is for the Government responsible to Parliament, and everybody knows it."[23]

As has just been said, the Royal assent is essential to the validity of laws passed by Parliament. It means that the King may refuse assent to, or veto, any law passed by Parliament. But the veto power has never been exercised since 1707. It has become obsolete. Disraeli in 1852, however, considered that the King's right to refuse assent to legislation still existed and was not an "empty form." But no Monarch exercised this power. The passing of the Parliament Act, 1911, revived the issue and suggestions were made in 1913 that the King could refuse his assent to the Irish Home Rule Bill. Bonar Law asserted that the King's veto was "dead" only so long as the House of Lords was not liable to be overridden by the House of Commons, and as the Home Rule Bill was being put through Parliament under the Parliament Act of 1911, the King could exercise his "right of refusing assent to matters not suffi-

23. Lord Morrison, *British Parliamentary Democracy*, pp. 60-61.

ciently considered by the people which the Lords had been supposed to exercise."[24]

George V, as Jennings points out, was "himself inclined to accept the same idea," and insisted upon an appeal to the country.[25] Lord Esher, who was advising the King, did not agree with this viewpoint and insisted that it would be dangerous for the Monarch to refuse to accept the advice of Ministers. Sir William Harcourt, too, was of the same opinion and in a personal interview with the King insisted that if there were to be general election, an appeal to the electorate would not be made on the issue of Home Rule. The sole question would be—"Is the country governed by the King or by the people? and that would mean an attack on the person of the King."[26]

If some headstrong King refuses assent to a Bill passed by Parliament ignoring the advice tendered by his Ministers, then, what would happen? There is no reason to believe that such a situation is ever likely to arise, but if it does, the Ministry would forthwith resign. In that case, there would be two alternatives before the King. One, to summon the Leader of the Opposition and commission him to form the Ministry. The House of Commons would refuse to support such a Ministry, because it would be tantamount to approving the action of the King as the Government ousted formed the majority in the House. So there would be no other option for the King, but to dissolve Parliament and order new elections. "That would be a dangerous step," as Munro says, "for any King to take, because an "adverse decision at the polls would inevitably suggest his abdication."[27] This is the verdict of British history. As long as the Ministry has a majority in Parliament, and so long as Parliament remains representative of the people, it carries with it the verdict of the people. There is, under the circumstances, no need for the exercise of the veto. This is exactly what Asquith submitted to George V in a Memorandum on the contro- versy of 1913. The Prime Minister asserted, "We have now a well established tradition of 200 years, that, in the last resort, the occupant of the Throne accepts and acts upon the advice of his ministers ....."[28] This point was abundantly clarified by the Duke of Windsor, the former King Edward VIII. He said, "whenever the Prime Minister 'advises' the King he is using a respectful form of words to express the will and decision of the Government. The King is virtually bound to accept such 'advice.' Furthermore, he cannot seek 'advice' elsewhere. However, if, in the exercise of his undoubted powers, he chooses not to accept the 'advice' thus formally tendered, then his Ministers resign, and he must try to form a new Government from the Opposition."[29] Asquith also pointed out to the King in 1913 that "the veto could be exercised only by the dismissal of the Ministry, for no Government would accept a refusal to assent to a Bill without resigning."[30]

The King has now ceased to give assent to Bills personally. The assent is given by a Royal Commission appointed by the Crown under the Royal Sign Manual. The Lord Chancellor or Senior Commissioner simply says that His Majesty not having seen fit to be personally present upon this occasion, has appointed a Royal Commission and that they shall indicate the Royal Assent has been given to the Bills as good and proper Acts of Parliament. The assent to Bills, is, therefore, only a picturesque formality.

The Crown, acting alone, has the power to issue measures authorising certain executive actions. The Orders-in-Council,as they are known, are issued by the King and Privy Council. There are two varieties of Orders-in-Council. First, those which are merely administrative rules and govern the various branches of government in their routine business. Others are promulgated only by virtue of authority expressly granted by Parliament and are frequently called statutory orders. Such orders have actually the force of law, because they are based upon the authority of Parliament. This kind of "subordinate legislation" is now of steadily increasing importance and the subject is dealt with more fully at its appropriate place.[31]

**Judicial Powers**

The King is still described as the 'fountain

24. Keith, A.B., *The Government of England from Queen Victoria to George VI*, Vol. 1, p. 358.
25. Jennings, W.I., *Cabinet Government*, p. 369.
26. Esher Papers III, p. 132. As quoted in Jenning's *Cabinet Government*, p. 370.
27. Munro, W.B., *The Governments of Europe*, p. 63.
28. Spender, J.A., *Life of Lord Oxford and Asquith*, Vol.-II, pp. 29-31
29. A King's Story, *op. cit.*, p. 343
30. Spender, J.A., *Life of Lord Oxford and Asquith*, Vol. II, pp. 29-31. Asquith's memorandum.
31. See Chap. VII *infra*.

of justice' and this historic expression reflects that the King's conscience spoke the last word in the administration of justice. This is not the case now. The principle of the independence of Judiciary has freed for all practical purposes, the judges and courts from control at the hands of the Executive. And yet the courts are not entirely outside the Crown's widesweeping orbit. Judges, including the Justices of Peace in the counties and boroughs, are appointed by the Crown. The Lord Chancellor, a member of the Cabinet, exercises general judicial supervision. All issues which come before the Judicial Committee of the Privy Council are decided by the Crown. Finally, the Crown exercises the prerogative of mercy and may grant pardon to persons convicted of criminal offences. This is done by the Home Secretary.

**'King Can Do No Wrong'**

Such, in brief, are the powers of the Crown. The Crown, no doubt, is closely associated with the person of the King, but the King in person is for the most part the principal formal element of the State and its Executive. The actual or potential element is the Crown. The position of the King has been cogently summed up by Lowell. He says: "According to the early theory of the Constitution the ministers were the counsellors of the King. It was for them to advise and for him to decide. Now the parts are almost reversed. The King is consulted, but the ministers decide." In many cases the Monarch may personally know little what they decide or even if he knows, he may have little liking for them, although the Crown powers are exercised in his name. His Majesty's servants have become His Majesty's masters.

There are two important principles on which the constitutional structure rests in Britain. First, the Monarch may not perform any public act involving the exercise of discretionary powers, except on advice of the Ministers. Second, for every act performed in the name of the Monarch the Ministers are responsible to Parliament, and hence the meaning of the phrase: "The King can do no wrong." That is to say, the King can do nothing right or wrong, of a discretionary nature and having legal effect. Whatever may be the personal views of the Monarch, he must, as a constitutional Monarch, give way to his Ministers, feeling that they have behind them a majority of the people's representatives and they can be called upon to account for their acts, singly or collectively, by Parliament.[32] This is now a well established tradition of nearly three hundred years. Conventions are an integral part of the Constitution and every King of Britain at the time of coronation swears to maintain the Constitution and uphold constitutional Monarchy.

Nor can any Minister plead the orders of the King in defence of the wrongful act or for an error of omission and commission. Thomas Osborne, Earl of Danby,[33] was impeached in 1679 of "high treason, and diverse high crimes and misdemeanours." Danby's plea was that whatever he had done was by order of the King, and the King could do no wrong. He even produced, at the time of his impeachment, the Royal pardon. Parliament held Danby's plea illegal and void.[34] It was definitely laid down that the Ministers can not plead the command of the King to justify an illegal and unconstitutional act, and thereby shield themselves behind the legal immunities of the occupant of the Throne.

## JUSTIFICATION OF MONARCHY

**Can Royalty Survive?**

The almost wholly formal position of the Monarch in the British system of government and the fact that conventions prevent him from exercising the powers that he legally possessed, raises the question why kingship in Britain should not be abolished ? To some people Monarchy does not appear to be worth it costs the nation. To a few more it appears a political anachronism. But the real fact is that the great mass of the British people are not willing to see Kingship disappear. The seventies of the last century witnessed a

32. Back in the days of Charles II one of the courtiers wrote on the door of the Royal bedchamber :
"Here lies a Great and Mighty King,
Whose Promise none relies on:;
He never says a foolish thing,
Nor ever does a wise one".
"Very true," retorted the King, "because while my words are my own, my acts are my minister's".
33. Danby succeeded Clifford as Lord High Treasurer and consequently he had become virtually the first minister of the Crown.
34. Resolution concerning the Royal Pardon in Bar of Danby's Impeachment. Admas, G.B., and Stephens, H.M., *Select Documents of English Constitutional History,* p. 439.

strong republican movement.[35] It even caused sensation, when persons like Sir Charles Dilke joined its ranks,[36] and Chamberlain could predict that the "Republic must come and at the rate at which we are now moving it will come in our generation."[37] Yet a few years later the movement collapsed, "and Queen Victoria was able to impose a public recantation upon Dilke before accepting him as a Cabinet minister."

Since then, Monarchy in Britain had been more popularly acclaimed and it was generally accepted by all political views without discussion.[38] "Monarchy, to put it bluntly," wrote Laski, "has been sold to democracy as the symbol of itself, and so nearly universal has been the chorus of eulogy which has accompanied the process of the sale that the rare voices of dissent have hardly been heard. It is not without significance that the official daily newspaper of the Trade Union Congress devotes more space, of news and pictures, to the royal family than does any of its rivals."[39] Although the cost of the Crown in Britain and elsewhere reveals a glaring disparity,[40] yet a little suggestion is made that the people fail to get "their money's worth." Ceremony, pomp, and ritual connected with royalty involve, no doubt, a certain amount of lavishness and many people contrast this display with the poverty and distress of a great mass of the people. But to raise such a question, says Gooch, is not necessarily to resolve it against Kingship.[41] "Democratic Government", according to Jennings, "is not merely a matter of cold reason and prosaic policies. There must be some display of colour, and there is nothing more vivid than royal purple and imperial scarlet."[42] Ernest Barker says that to think of politics in terms of pure reason and cold utility is to think wrongly. "There is a world of unbought and uncalculated sentiments which matters vitally in politics. Emotions, loyalties, feelings, chivalries—these are things that count, and count profoundly. The man who releases, the man who attracts, the man who expresses, this world of unbought and uncalculated sentiments is doing an incalculable service to the community. Reason has her sphere and victories. Sentiment has also her triumphs; and they are not the least notable of triumphs."[43] The Monarch is the symbol of unity, a magnet of loyalty, and an apparatus of ceremony and the King or Queen serves to attract every Britisher's feelings and sentiments into the service of the community. The Kingship, in the words of Winston Churchill, "is most deeply founded and dearly cherished by the whole association of our people."[44] Clement Attlee, who had been active in the socialist movement in Britain for more than half a century, claimed that during the period he had taken part in bringing about a number of changes in British society by helping to abolish some old things, such as Poor Laws, "there is one feature of it which I have never felt any urge to abolish and that is the monarchy. I have never been a republican even in theory, and certainly not in practice."[45]

This patriotic admiration of the mass of the Sovereign's subjects for Monarchy is due to somewhat complex considerations of history, of human motives and sentiments, and of utility. Event Lord Altrincham, the Conservative Peer who criticised the Queen and the Court in an article published in *The National and English Review,* the magazine he edited, said on television on August 6, 1957, that he regretted any

35. A Republican demonstration was held in Trafalgar Square in September 1870 and early in 1871 and a Republican Club was formed in London with Charles Bradlaugh as its first President. While speaking at its inauguration, Bradlaugh said that "the heir-apparent to the throne has neither the intelligence, nor the virtue, nor the sobriety, nor the high sense of honour, which might entitle him to take a front rank in this Great Nation."
36. At a crowded meeting at Newcastle, Dilke attacked on the excessive cost of the Crown. He asserted, "If you can show me a fair chance that a republic here will be free from the political corruption that hangs about the monarchy, I say, for my part, and I believe that the middle classes in general will say—let it come."
37. Among other sympathisers of the movement the notable were Bright, Odger the Trade Unionist, Mundella, M.P. for Sheffield, and John Morely.
38. There are even now some people who would prefer in principle that Britain were a republic. A few members of Parliament desired its substitution after the abdication of Edward VIII. "Had Edward VIII not abdicated in 1936," writes R.M. Punnett, "there might have been an evolution of Monarchy into a form akin to the Scandinavian model but George VI and Elizabeth II have sought to preserve much of the Monarchy's remoteness and mystique." *British Government and Politics*, p. 254. A recent prediction is that Monarchy at the most can survive during the life-time of Elizabeth II.
39. Laski, H.J., Parliamentary Government in England, p. 392.
40. Refer to Greaves, H.R.G., *The British Constitution*, pp. 83-84, See also Punnett, R.M., *British Government and Politics*, pp. 256-57.
41. *The Government of England*, p. 10.
42. Jennings, W.I., *The British Constitution*, p. 116.
43. Barker, E., *Essays on Government*, p. 5.
44. Broadcast Speech at the death of George VI in early 1952.
45. *Observer,* Clement Attlee on Monarchy.

impression that he "was hostile to the Queen or trying to attack her in a personal way or be beastly about it." Lord Altrincham's criticism of Queen Elizabeth aroused nation-wide controversy. He had described the Queen's speaking as a "pain in the neck" and her utterances as those of "priggish schoolgirl," and called for a "truly classless Commonwealth Court" to replace her present entourage of "people of the tweedy sort." *The Reynold News,* a Left-wing Sunday newspaper, supported the criticism of the young Peer because he "has said aloud what many people are thinking: Buckingham Palace is not in tune with the Britain of 1957." [46] The general mass of the people were angry with Lord Altrincham and many suggested that he should be shot. Lord Altrincham was actually slapped as he left the television studio. The man, who struck him, said, "That's for insulting the Queen."[47] Herbert Morrison said, "You get funny people breaking out now and again like Lord Altrincham, but nobody would know him if he was not a Lord; he is a Lord only because he is the son of his father. But he says funny things. They got him headlines in newspapers and even get him on television, which no doubt pleases him no end. But don't worry about these jokers."[48] The general body of the British people support the British Monarchy and Morrison cited an instance which he said he could never forget. "I shall never forget," wrote Morrison, "seeing, at the time of the Coronation of King George VI, a banner going right across the street of an East End slum in London which said : 'Lousy but loyal.' And I think that was one of the greatest compliments that has ever been paid to the British Royal Family."[49] As long as the Monarch "behaves constitutionally," concludes Morrison, the Labour Peer, "as I have every expectation, I think it will remain a popular institution in my country."[50]

It is more than true. The British Monarchs for the last more than three hundred years—ever since the Revolution of 1688—have been wise enough to forget past pretensions, to learn new lessons, to change their position with the changing time, and to join with their subjects in bringing about changes in other institutions. They acted in obedience to the unwritten rule of the British national life which prescribes that the power of the King shall be used in accordance with the will of the people. "They stood above party; they watched the nation; and they joined with their subjects in bringing about change when the will of the nation was set for change—and only when it was so set "[51] They changed their position with the growth of a cabinet system and the rise of the office of Prime Minister. In the nineteenth and twentieth centuries they helped in the passage of the Reform Bill of 1882 and the Parliament Act of 1911; the former made the House of Commons more democratic and the latter made the House of Lords less able to thwart or check the purposes of the House of Commons. The Parliament Act of 1911 was amended in 1949 to reduce the delaying action of the Lords on ordinary Bills to one year only. Attlee's Labour Government carried through substantial nationalisation of industry in its period of office, 1945 to 1951, and fiscal reforms of an equalitarian nature. The Life Peerage Act, 1958 and the Peerage Act, 1963, aimed to change the complexion of the House of Lords and both these Acts came from the Conservative Governments. The Monarchs joined with their subjects in effecting all these changes.

1977 Britain saw the year long celebrations of Queen Elizabeth's Silver Jubilee of her accession to the throne in 1952. It was a year of crowded pageantry and of cultural, sporting, dramatic and musical events. The Queen and her husband Prince Philip visited every region of Britain, including the terrorist-ridden Ulster and the Commonwealth countries in the Pacific, including Australia and New Zealand. The Government spared no expenditure, in a year of severe economy cuts, and it became a festival of nostalgia and an emotional hinge for things past for the British people. But there were many politicians, who looked at the Jubilee as a sort of Royal farewell since they claimed to see portents of the end of monarchical system in Britain. One of the British astrologers actually put the disappearance of British royalty within just fifteen years.

What is the necessary background of this political or astrological speculation? Queen Elizabeth was crowned as an Empress on June 2,

46. As reported in *The Tribune*, Ambala Cantt., August 6, 1957.
47. As reported in the *Hindustan Times*, New Delhi, August 9, 1957.
48. Herbert Morrison, *British Parliamentary Democracy*, p. 5.
49. *Ibid.*
50. *Ibid.*
51. Barker, E., *Essays on Government*, p. 2.

1953 when the British Empire, even after the freedom of Indian sub-continent, still straddled much of the world and was a world power economically and politically. In her nearly five decades long reign Britain has lost her world status and is economically near the bottom of European Economic Community table. The British Sovereign was an essential props and focus of loyalty in the Imperial era and a symbolic tie of Commonwealth. With the Empire gone and the Commonwealth fading, the international need or justification of Britain to have a sovereign has eroded, it is claimed.

The portents are even more evident in Britain itself. There is no doubt, however, that Queen Elizabeth is held in high esteem if not affection by a majority of the British people today. She has during her long reign performed her duties conscientiously and with grace. Talking about the popularity of the monarchy Sir Harold Wilson suggested that it is partly because of the remarkable character of the Queen and her close interest in ordinary people. "I think the monarchy and she herself personally and her family are much more popular now than 25 years ago." In a survey conducted by the *Mirror*, London, it was reported that 89 per cent, of those questioned expressed support for monarchy. Those queried were asked to rank members of the royal family according to "best impression." The Queen led by 78 per cent, followed by 83 year— old Queen Mother Elizabeth, with 73 per cent, and Prince Charles , 66 per cent. Princesses Anne and Margaret were at the bottom of the list. Strangely enough the two sections of the population that regard the Royal family most warmly are the aristocracy and the less privileged class, the former whose future is inevitably tied with the royalty and the latter "to whom the glamour and romance of royalty is a form of escapism." In between the middle classes, skilled workers and trade unionists, are either indifferent or they seriously question the need of maintaining the royal house and the pageantry surrounding it at such high national expense.

Perhaps, the biggest cloud in the royal horizon was the Home Rule Plan for Scotland and Wales. In December, 1976 the Labour Government published its proposals to give Home Rule to Scotland and Wales. Earlier, the Queen in her traditional address to Parliament had announced that a Bill would be introduced immediately "for the establishment of Assemblies to give the Scottish and Welsh people direct and wide ranging responsibilities for the domestic affairs within the economic and political framework of the United Kingdom." The Bill introduced in Parliament was so complex that it tied down Wales a Scotland with thousands of threads and hundreds of straps that the Welsh and Scottish nationalists, especially the latter, gave it a hostile reception. The Bill was certainly provocative.

The Bill provided for referenda, both in Wales and Scotland, to seek the approval of both nationalities to set up separate assemblies in their areas. In Wales, the proposal was rejected by a majority of four to one and possibly the main cause was fear of Welsh linguistic nationalism comparable to the French linguistic nationalism in Quebec. In Wales there are fairly well-defined English and Welsh-speaking areas, with a tendency among local authorities of the latter to impose their language on the former. In a subsequent referendum the people of Wales have accepted the creation of an Assembly for their region. The Scottish Nationalist Party and their allies supporting devolution gained a majority of little more than 2 per cent over their opponents. But as the total turnout at the referendum was 64 per cent of voters eligible, this was short of 40 per cent electorate required under the Bill to endorse the devolution. The Scottish National Party resented the fact that a bare majority was not permitted to prevail and they avenged their defeat by withdrawing their support to the Callaghan's minority Government resulting into the exit from office of the Labour on a vote of no confidence. In a subsequent referendum, Scotland won the people's approval for a Scottish Parliament and regional autonomy.

The Scottish Nationalist Party is committed to winning eventual independence, including control of the rich North Sea oil field lying off the east coast of Scotland. It supported devolution only as stepping stone to complete separation from the "auld (old) enemy England." One of the Scottish Members of Parliament provoked by the devolution Bill declared, "very soon we shall have our own independence day in Edinburgh." Earlier, Queen Elizabeth's personal anxiety about the danger of the break up of the United Kingdom through separatist movements had upset leaders of the Scottish Party and they called her comments "ill advised" and "unfortunate." In an address on May 4 to Parliament on the start of the Jubilee celebrations, Queen Elizabeth said: "I number Kings and Queens of England and

Scotland, and Princes of Wales among my ancestors and so I can readily understand these aspirations.'' But, ''I cannot forget'', the Queen added with some emotion, ''that I was crowned Queen of the United Kingdom of Great Britain and Northern Ireland. Perhaps this Jubilee is a time to remind ourselves of the benefits which union has conferred at home and in our international dealings, on the habitants of all parts of the United Kingdom.'' Donald Stewart, leader of the 11 Scottish Nationalist Party MPs, declared the same day the Queen addressed Parliament, ''if it comes to a choice between independence and the monarchy, we would choose independence.''

This potential danger to the British union and the Sovereign at its head was demonstrated by the most royalist of British parties, the Conservatives opposing the Home Rule Bill. Even if the plan for independence is eschewed, the devolution plan, which is in line with the policy of the Labour Party, is sure to ultimately change the geographical and political structure of the United Kingdom and to have an impact on royalty too. The emotions and loyalties engendered by the Queen's Silver Jubilee in 1977 and Prince Charles' wedding celebrated in July, 1981, in full blaze of pomp and publicity, may stop the trend against royalty and towards breaking the union of Britain for sometime, probably during the life of Queen Elizabeth, but the Throne cannot be said to be secure for her successors. The economic cost to the nation for the upkeep of royalty would have been justifiable in an era of Empire and world status, but now these expenditures palpably intrude on a weaker and poorer Britain with more than two million unemployed, falling standards of living and a stupendous expenditure, averaging 5 million pounds a day, incurred for regaining Falkland islands and that, too, when the country was battling its way out of recession.[52] The March 1982, pay rise of the Queen by more than 8 per cent was widely resented and the people questioned the need to continue with royalty. Not less importantly, there is an exemplary moral rectitude that the British people traditionally expect from the Royal family and that expectation has been fulfilled in the case of the Queen. But prevailing social commotion cannot be kept out of palaces and the recent affairs of Princess Margaret with a youngman and her separation from her husband as also the much publicised goings on of Prince Charles before his marriage and Prince Andrew's mysterious ''affair'' for a week with an American actress have tarnished this tradition, just as they have made royalty look more human and common.

## FUNCTIONS OF THE MONARCHY

According to Jennings the functions of the Monarchy may be said to be four. First, appearing in an impersonal fashion as the Crown, the Monarch's name is the cement that binds the Constitution. Secondly, the Monarch similarly binds the units of Commonwealth. Thirdly, there are political functions of the highest importance which the Monarch performs personally. Fourthly, the Monarch is a social figure exercising important functions outside the political sphere. We begin the elaboration of these functions first taking the personal functions of the Monarch, though it upsets the order in which Jennings enumerates them.

### Personal Authority of the King

In the actual conduct of the work of government the Monarch still personally performs certain specific acts and the most important of these is that the King must make certain that he/she has a Government in the United Kingdom. The Government is headed by the Prime Minister and the Prime Minister selects his own team to make a Government. The King, thus, chooses a Prime Minister and the latter then prepares a list of Ministers and submits it to the King for his approval. But when choosing the Prime Minister, the King must remember that a Ministry must have the support of a majority of the House of Commons otherwise it will be unable to govern.

Now-a-days, the choice of such a person who is to be the Prime Minister and can lead the majority in the House of Commons is obvious. The leader of the majority party in the House of Commons is summoned and commissioned to form government. ''The essential point'', writes Herbert Morrison, ''is that the new Prime Minister should be able to command a majority in the House of Commons, and not merely be able to form a government, for the government cannot live without a parliamentary majority.'' If the Government is defeated on a hostile vote in the House of Commons, the Sovereign summons the Leader of the Opposition and commissions him to form a new government. Even if the Prime Minister dies in office the choice of his successor

52. Bhatte, V.R., ''*Can Royalty Survive in U.K.? The Hindustan Times*, New Delhi January 18, 1977.

can be reasonably obvious, though careful consideration would be given to the likelihood of the person appointed being acceptable to a majority in the House of Commons. Since Churchill's War Government has emerged the office of the Deputy Prime Minister, though it has not been constitutionally recognized. "When the Prime Minister dies in office" says Morrison, "the Deputy Prime Minister might be specially considered by the Sovereign, though there would be no obligation to do so especially as I gather, that the Sovereign does not recognise such an office."[53] In 1951, when Winston Churchill again returned to office, he submitted to George VI the name of Anthony Eden as Secretary of State for Foreign Affairs and Deputy Prime Minister. The King "pointed out that the latter office was unknown to the Constitution, and on his instructions it was deleted from the new Foreign Secretary's appointment."[54]

But if no party commands a real majority, or when a Prime Minister retires and when the majority party has not yet designated its leader, the choice of the Prime Minister is not easy. The Sovereign makes, in such a case, a personal decision to whom to send for, although he is always careful to follow that course which is least likely to arouse criticism. "The Sovereign's choice in these conditions," writes Morrison, "has much constitutional significance. The choice may be a very delicate one and involve embarrassing complications. The Sovereign would, of course, take all relevant considerations into account, and be at great pains not only to be constitutionally correct, but make every effort to see that the correctness is likely to be generally recognised."[55] It is the Sovereign's undoubted right to seek or not to seek the advice of the outgoing Prime Minister and is also free to receive counsel and advice from such Privy Councillors whom the Monarch may wish to consult. When the Conservative Prime Minister, Bonar Law, resigned because of ill-health on May 20, 1923 King George V passed over the claims to succession of Sir Austen Chamberlain and Lord Curzon and sent for Stanley Baldwin to form the government.[56] In 1924, no party had a clear majority in the House of Commons. George V sent for Ramsay MacDonald, and not Asquith, to form the Government, although the Labour Party had behind it only about one-third of the members of the House. A minority Labour Government under MacDonald, dependent on Liberal votes, took office again in 1929. The events of 1931 or "the crisis of 1931" as Herbert Morrison described, "were more complicated" and the act of George V in commissioning Ramsay MacDonald to head the National Government was characterised by Professor Laski "as much the personal choice of George V as Lord Bute was the personal choice of George III."[57] King George V "was, I feel sure," wrote Herbert Morrison, "actuated by sincere motives. And certainly the financial and economic situation of the country was serious. Nevertheless I think his judgment was at fault."[58] The King would "have been wise", he adds, "to have ascertained what was likely to happen by inquiry of one or more Labour Privy councillors likely to know. He might have asked the Prime Minister to ascertain the view of the Labour Cabinet; but no action was taken to ascertain the general Labour view."[59] Morrison even questioned the need of the National Government and was of the opinion "that a Conservative-Liberal coalition could have done all that the so-called National Government did."[60]

Whenever the Labour Party secured a majority it insisted on the right of the Labour members of Parliament to choose their own leader and the Sovereign's choice of the Prime Minister was, accordingly, obvious. But the Conservative Party did not follow this practice and the Sovereign had, thus, a choice when the Conservative Party had a majority but no leader. Baldwin became leader in 1923 and Chamberlain in 1937, because they were Prime Ministers. This practice of the

---

53. A major reconstruction by Harold Macmillan was announced on 13th, 16th and 18th July 1962. The new post of first Secretary of State was specially created for Mr. R.A. Butler, who would, according to the announcement, "act as Deputy Prime Miniter.". But Butler did not step into office of the Prime Minister when Macmillan resigned.
54. Petrie, C., *The Modern British Monarchy,* p. 193.
55. Herbert Morrison, *Government and Parliament*, p. 77
56. Lord Curzon's peerage was advanced as a disqualification in his case. But according to L.S. Amery, a Minister of the time, "the final decision was, to the best of my belief, made mainly on the issue of ....... personal acceptability ......... If a constitutional precedent was created, it was largely as the ex-post facto cover for a decision taken on other grounds." L.S. Amery, Thought on the Constitution, p. 22.
57. Laski, H., Parliamentary Government in England, p. 403,
58. Herbert Morrison, *Government and Parliament,* p. 79.
59. *Ibid.*
60. Ibid., p. 78. Also refer to H.J. Laski, *Parliamentary Government in England*, pp. 402-408.

Conservative Party evoked a severe criticism from the Labour Party when Sir Anthony Eden resigned on January 9, 1957 and the Queen appointed Harold Macmillan as the new Prime Minister.Until the moment Macmillan went to the Palace the nation was left guessing whether he or R.A. Butler, the Lord Privy Seal, would become Sir Anthony Eden's successor. The Queen sought the advice of Sir Winston Churchill and the Marquess of Salisbury and it was believed that the advice of Churchill was a powerful factor in deciding the issue. The *Times* in an editorial said that ultimate responsibility for the choice of Harold Macmillan was the Queen's alone and that time and events would show how wisely she had judged. Labour Party chiefs at a specially called meeting of their 'shadow cabinet' Parliamentary committee, expressed the fear that the Crown had been brought into party politics in a most undesirable way. James Griffiths, Labour Deputy Leader, in the absence of the leader Hugh Gaitskell, said in a radio interview, on January 11, 1957 : "We do not question that the Crown acted with due constitutional propriety," but, he added, "we do believe it is important that parties themselves should decide on their leaders and that the Crown should not be put in the embarrassing position of having to make a choice between rival claimants for the Premiership from the same party." Griffiths further asserted that if this position was to recur often there would be a full case for examining the procedure, because "this is bringing the Crown into internecine party warfare which is very bad for the Constitution."

The historical method of choosing a leader by the Conservative Party underwent a considerable strain when Sir Alec Douglas-Home was asked to take over from Harold Macmillan in 1963 and eventually led to the retirement from politics of R.A. Butler. In 1965, the party changed its method of selecting a leader. Today, a ballot is held of all Conservative MPs, and to be elected a leader on the first ballot a candidate has to receive an overall majority of votes, and also he has to receive 15 per cent more votes than his nearest rival. If he/she does not achieve this, as Mrs Margaret Thatcher could not, a second ballot is held two or three days later, for which the contestants have to be renominated and for which new candidates can also be nominated. To be successful in the second ballot a candidate merely has to secure an overall majority of votes. If this is not still achieved, a third ballot is held. The third ballot is restricted to the three leading candidates of the second ballot and the voters indicate their first and second preferences on the ballot paper. After the votes have been counted, the third candidate is eliminated, and the votes secured by him are redistributed, according to the second preferences, between the two remaining candidates. The successful candidate is then presented to a party meeting consisting of Conservative MPs, Peers, prospective candidates, and members of the National Union Executive Committee.[61] This process was first used in July 1965, when Sir Alec Douglas-Home resigned as party leader. The new democratic method, thus, ended the hoary tradition of evolving a sort of consensus after private soundings of Conservative members of Parliament, prospective MPs., Peers and the party executive. In past when the Conservatives would be in power the retiring Prime Minister had always a big say about his successor. All this led to intrigue and wire-pulling in the party. Thus ended the monarch's conventional privilege of selecting a conservative Prime Minister through informal consultations.

The new method of selecting the Conservative party leader was in line with the method followed by the Labour Party till 1980, and it mitigated the possibility of the monarch's intervention in active politics. Till 1980, for the selection of a Labour Party leader, a ballot of the Parliamentary party was held in which a candidate for the post was required to receive an absolute majority. If no candidate received the requisite majority, a second ballot was held, dropping out the candidates at the bottom in the first ballot, a week later and this process was repeated until a candidate secured a majority[62]. Since 1980, the party leader elected by the Parliamentary party is to be approved by an electoral college

61. When Sir Alec Douglas-Home resigned in July 1965, as party leader, Edward Heath, Reginald Maudling, and Enoch Powell were nominated to contest to succeed him. In the first ballot Heath got 150 votes. Maudling 133 votes and Powell 15 votes Heath, thus, did not have the required 15 per cent more votes than Maudling. Before the second ballot was held Maudling and Powell withdrew from the contest and Heath was left the only choice to be duly approved by the party meeting.

62. In February 1963, in the election to choose a successor to Hugh Gait skell, in the first ballot Harold Wilson received 115 votes, George Brown 888 votes, and James Callaghan 41 votes. As Wilson could not secure an absolute majority. Callaghan dropped out, and in the second ballot, a week later, Wilson was elected with 104 votes to George Brown's 103.

consisting of members of Parliament, constituency delegates and trade union representatives.

When the monarch exercises a choice in selecting the Prime Minister he or she is no mere figurehead. The monarch, as Jennings says, "does not steer the ship, but she (Queen) has to make certain that there is a man at the wheel. Nor is it always easy to know when the problem will arise. Neville Chamberlain in 1937 had a large majority, but by 1940 George VI was looking forward for a Conservative Prime Minister who could secure Labour as well as Conservative support and found him in Mr. Churchill."[63] It is, however true, Jennings, admits, that these cases are exceptional. Normally the machine runs efficiently, because the Government has a majority and if it loses at an election, the Opposition steps in to form the Govrnment. The existence today, of the Labour and Conservative Parties' procedures for electing their leaders does not in itself effect the constitutional prerogative of the Monarch, in that the Monarch remains free to choose whoever may be regarded as suitable. Nevertheless, in practice it seems inconceivable that the Monarch would choose as Prime Minister anyone who had not first been elected party leader, provided that in a crisis time was allowed for the election to take place. It is possible, however, that the Monarch could still play an effective role in selecting a Prime Minister if it was not clear which party could form a government.

It is sometimes asserted that the dismissal of Ministers and the dissolution of Parliament may be undertaken by the King without the consent of Government. No Government has been dismissed by the Sovereign since 1783, although it is still maintained by many constitutional experts that the King has the right to dismiss Ministers, if he has reason to believe that their policy though approved by the House of Commons has not the approval of the people.[64] But, as Jennings correctly points out, such an argument "is an argument for dissolution and not a dismissal of Ministers."[65] Ministerial dismissal by the Head of the State is not the essence of the Parliamentary system of Government and no King would venture it, whatever be the legal opinion, unless he is determined to gamble in the most dangerous manner.

The duration of Parliament in ordinary circumstances is for five years, but conditions may arise in which a dissolution of Parliament may be desired before the expiry of its full term of life. There might, for example, be an important difference of opinion within the Cabinet which would make it impossible for the Government to carry on, or a Government may desire to take the verdict of the electorate on an important matter of policy on which it had no mandate, or there might be revolt within the ranks of the Government Party which caused the Government to be defeated in the House of Commons on some matter of importance. In circumstances such as these the Prime Minister might request the Sovereign to exercise his Royal prerogative of dissolving Parliament and direct new elections to be held.

The Sovereign's right to dissolve Parliament has been a subject of deep controversy. It has been maintained that the Sovereign is not bound to accept ministerial advice on this matter. This, indeed, seems to have been the view of Queen Victoria and some of her contemporaries. Even Keith held similar opinion. "The prerogative of the Crown to dissolve Parliament," he wrote ,"is undoubted. The manner of dissolution does not, as often said, strictly speaking, involve the aid of ministers, for the King could still present himself in the House of Lords, and by word of mouth, dissolve the Parliament."[66] But in practice dissolution takes place by a proclamation under the Great Seal, which is based on the advice of the Privy Council for whose summons the Lord President accepts responsibility. Consequently, the King cannot secure a dissolution without advice. If the Ministers refuse to give such advice, he can do no more than dismiss them and we know how hazardous it is for the Sover-

63. Jennings, Ivor, *The Queen's Government,* p. 43.
Also refer to N.H. Brasher's *Studies in British Government*, p. 12

64. Gladstone appears to have thought in 1878 that the right to dismiss still existed. Disraeli also held the same view. In 1886, Queen Victoria had made efforts to overthrow the Liberal Government because to her mind the Government was not governing with integrity for the welfare of the country. Decey, too, was of the opinion that the King could dismiss Ministers in order to ascertain the will of the nation. Asquith, on the other hand, rebutted Dicey's arguments and maintained that "a practice so long established, and so well justified by experience should remain unimpaired."

65. Jennings, W.I. *Cabinet Government*, p. 380.
Also refer to N.H. Brasher's Studies in british Government, p. 12.

66. "There was no doubt of the power and prerogative of the Sovereign to refuse a Dissolution—It was one of the very few acts which the Queen of England could do without responsible advice." *Letters of Queen Victoria,* Edited by Bensor and Esher Vol. VIII, pp. 314-465.

eign to dismiss Ministers who command the confidence of the House of Commons. A forced dissolution, therefore, is impossible, "though one induced by royal pressure is perfectly in order."[67] There have been two definite occasions during the last eighty years when dissolution took place at the express desire of the King. The first was over the budget in 1910 at the desire of Edward VII and, the second. over the power of the Lords in the same year, at the desire of George V. In each case, maintained Laski, "the ministers, however, reluctantly, acquiesced in the King's desire and the dissolution was, accordingly amply surrounded by the cloak of ministerial responsibility; though the King took the initiative in pressing a dissolution upon the government. In each case, also, the government accepted the advice."[68] But there are many instances as well, for example, in 1866,1873, 1885, 1895, and 1905 when the Cabinet did not wish to dissolve, in spite of the royal sanction.[69]

The right of the King to dissolve Parliament without advice became a matter of practical discussion in 1913 over the Home Rule Bill. The Home Rule Bill had been passed by the House of Commons in two successive sessions but rejected by the House of Lords in each of these sessions. The Unionists claimed that the Government had received no mandate from the electorate at General Election for such a measure in 1910, and; thus, demanded a dissolution before the Bill was submitted to the House of Commons the third time and passed under the Parliament Act, 1911. The Unionists realised that Asquith was unlikely to advise dissolution and they discussed the power of the King to dissolve without advice. George Cave argued that the King had an undoubted right to dissolve Parliament and that he should exercise the right on this occasion to satisfy himself that the House "does indeed represent the democracy of today." Sir William Anson admitted that the advice of the Ministers was constitutionally necessary, and that if the Government was not willing to give such an advice, the King would have to ascertain, presumably from the Opposition, whether the alternative Ministry could take office and to accept the responsibility for a dissolution. Dicey agreed with Anson, but Professor Morgan insisted that such independent action on the part of the King " would almost inevitably be equivalent to dismissal of his ministers," and that if once a dissolution was effected by the King's choice, "no dissolution would be free from ambiguity, and speculation as to the degree of responsibility of the Sovereign would be a feature of every election." Commenting on this issue Jennings comes to the conclusion that "there cannot be the least doubt that Professor Morgan was wholly in the right. Either the King 'persuades' the ministers to 'advise' a dissolution or ministers resign." In other words, the King cannot exercise his prerogative of dissolution without advice.

During the last more than a hundred years there is no instance of a refusal of a dissolution when advised. Nevertheless, opinion has always prevailed, and there exists a persistent tradition that it could be refused, if the necessary circumstances arose. Summing up the discussion of the right of the King to refuse dissolution, Keith says, "It appears that there is some divergence of view among the authorities on the question whether the King can refuse a dissolution to a Prime Minister who asks for it, the better opinion is that the power still exists, but that it could be properly exercised only in exceptional circumstances."[70] What those exceptional circumstances can be Stannard gives one specific instance. The contingency for refusal was there, he says, if Neville Chamberlain had advised a dissolution in May, 1940 when the Germans were crossing the Albert Canal. At such critical moments, he says, "the limits of the convention that keeps the Crown out of politics are reached, and the reigning Sovereign must himself decide, in the last resort, where his duty lies."[71] Similarly, the right to a dissolution, as Keith says, "is not a right to a series of dissolution." The King would not give the Ministry, which had obtained dissolution and lost an election, another dissolutions". The circumstances are which should enforce the retirement of the Ministry, although it is also true that a defeated Ministry would not ask for a second dissolution.

The conclusion is that dissolution is normally ordered by the Sovereign on the advice of the Prime Minister, but it is quite wrong to infer that the personal opinion of the Monarch is never

67. Keith, A.B., *The British Cabinet System*, p. 297.
68. Laski, H.J., *Parliamentary Government in England*, p. 412.
69. Keith, A.B., *The British Cabinet System*, p. 297
70. Keith, A.B., *The British Cabinet System*, p. 302
71. Stannard, H., *The Two Constitutions*, p. 17.

of any account in matters affecting the dissolution of Parliament. In his biography of George VI, Sir John Wheeler Bennett has vividly described the attitude of the King during the 1950-51 Labour Government when the stability of the Government was severely hampered by the precarious majority of eight votes it held in the House of Commons.[72] The Opposition, failing to bring down the administration by a series of adverse motions, adopted a system of guerrilla warfare. "It was not pleasant", wrote the Prime Minister, "to have Members coming from hospital at the risk of their lives to prevent a defeat in the House."[73] This instable equilibrium was a source of anxiety to the King and on June 24, 1951, he raised question of dissolution with the Prime Minister, who replied that he would ask for one in autumn. Parliament was dissolved on October 24. Attlee denied that he was pushed into asking for a dissolution by some pressure from the King. "There is no substance in this, but, the position of the King was one which I personally had to take into account."[74] Attlee, speaking on B.B.C. television in February 1963, stated that the strain on the health of Labour Members of the House of Commons to maintain the Government's slender majority was his predominant motive in seeking a dissolution. He was no doubt also influenced by the desire to secure the most politically opportune moment for the election. Commenting upon this issue Brasher says, "Yet if royal wishes were not decisive in 1951 neither were they negligible. Implicit in Lord Attlee's attitude is an acceptance of the fact that the monarch still retains a measure of responsibility for the maintenance of political stability."[75] It cannot be merely accidental that the King's pressures to dissolve Parliament in 1924, 1931 and 1951 have come only to dislodge Labour governments.

The King summons and prorogues Parliament. On the opening of Parliament, the King reads the Speech from the Throne.[76] But the Speech which the Sovereign reads is not his own work and may be read for the King by the Lord Chancellor. The King assents to the election of the Speaker of the House of Commons and here too, he may act by proxy. Orders-in-Council cannot be passed except for the presence of the King. Similarly, the appointment of the Lord Chancellor and the Secretaries of State are the personal acts of the King, consisting in actual handing of the seals of office to the designated ministers. The Monarch receives ambassadors in person, though this too is a sheer formality.[77] The King may convoke a conference of party leaders, as did George V in 1914, with a view to avoid a constitutional crisis, though such a step the King can take only upon advice received from his ministers.[78]

The Sovereign is the 'fountain of honours'. "It is the essence of honours of any kind" says Keith, "that they should appear to be the personal gift of the Sovereign, and for this reason all honours are submitted to and formally approved by the Sovereign,and whenever possible the investiture with the insignia or other act in connection with its bestowal is performed by King in person or at least the royal signature is attached to the instrument conferring it'." But the principle in the great majority of cases of the conferment of honours is that the recommendation to the Sovereign goes from a Minister, and normally the Prime Minister. The grant, however, is not entirely on advice. The Sovereign is able to resist the grant of honours of which he does not approve. In 1859, Queen Victoria refused to consent to a Privy Councillorship for John Bright. In 1869, she refused to sanction a peerage for Sir L.de Rothschild; and in 1881, she firmly resisted Gladstone's advice to make Sir Garnet-Wolseley a Peer. In 1906, Edward VII objected to several peerages and Privy Councillorships, although on

72. Wheeler Bennet, J. W., *King George VI : His Life and Reign*, pp. 791-96.
73. Attlee, C., *As It Happened*, p. 206.
74. *Observer*, August 23, 1959.
75. Brasher, N.H., *Studies in British Government*, p. 13.
76. It has been accepted since 1841, that the Speech from the Throne is a statement of ministerial policy for which the Sovereign accepts no responsibility. In 1881, Queen Victoria objected to a paragraph in the Queen's Speech on the proposal of withdrawal of troops from Kandhar. Lord Spencer and Sir William Harcourt, who were Ministers-in-Attendance, "impressed upon Sir H. Ponson by that Speech from the Throne was in no sense an expression of Her Majesty's individual sentiments but a declaration of policy made on the responsibility of her Ministers". As cited in Jennings, W.I. *Cabinet Government*, p. 373. Also refer to Herbert Morrison's *Government and Parliament*, p.75
77. In 1929, George V raised objections to receiving an ambassador from the Soviet Union. The Foreign Secretary, politely but firmly, told the King that there was a Cabinet decision to that effect. The King then received the ambassadar.
78. The King summoned the Home Rule Conference of July 1914, on the advice of Asquith, the Prime Minister. The speech which George V delivered to the Conference was sent to and approved by the Prime Minister, Jennings, W.I., *Cabinet Government, pp. 361-62.*

pressure he ultimately gave way. A few honours, that is, the Order of Merit, the Order of Companions of Honour, the Royal Victorian Order, the Most Noble Order of the Garter, and the Most Noble and Most Ancient Order of the Thistle, are in the Sovereign's personal gift.

**The King as Adviser**

Far more important is the Monarch's role as a critic, adviser and friend of the Ministers. In the oft-quoted phrase of Bagehot,[79] the Sovereign has "three rights—the right to be consulted, the right to encourage, the right to warn." And "a King of great sense and sagacity," he further added, "would want no others. He would find that his having no others would enable him to use these with singular effect." Or, as stated by Winston Churchill, "under the British constitutional system the Sovereign has a right to be made acquainted with everything for which his Ministers are responsible, and has an unlimited right of giving counsel to his government."[80] Since the time of George I, the Sovereign has not attended a Cabinet meeting, but the King is better informed than the average Cabinet Minister on all matters which are brought before the Cabinet. He sees all Cabinet papers, whether they are circulated by the Cabinet office or by the Departments. He receives the Cabinet agenda in advance and can discuss memoranda with the Ministers responsible for them. If he requires information from a Department he can ask for it. He also receives a copy of the Cabinet minutes, reports of Cabinet Committees, including the Defence Committee and the Chiefs of Staff Committee and the "daily print" of dispatches circulated by the Foreign Office.[81] He follows debates in Parliament by means of the "Official Report". If other information would be helpful, he can ask his Private Secretary to obtain it. Moreover, he has a staff to keep him informed of the development of political events. In short, the Prime Minister must keep the King abreast of what happens within and without the country, always tell him of Cabinet decision and he must be ready to explain the reasons for any policy. "In some respects," says Jennings, "notably on foreign affairs and on matters dealing with the Commonwealth, he may be better informed than the Prime Minister."

The King would, thus, acquire some knowledge and experience which no other statesman in control of governmental machine can claim. Bagehot rightly showed that the King has two advantages over the Prime Minister. One, while Prime Ministers and Ministers change, the King, goes on until he dies. Cabinet business, therefore, is continuous for him and a change of government "is merely a change of personnel." All this makes the King a mentor whom a wise Minister is not only obliged, but positively desires, to consult. "In a word, the King knows the mistakes made by a Premier's predecessors, and probably why they made them." Writing about the advantages of Monarchy, just after the death of George VI, Clement Attlee said, "Yet another advantage is that the Monarchy continuously in touch with public affairs, acquires great experience," whereas the Prime Minister might have been out of office for some years. "He (Prime Minister) has no doubt kept himself as fully informed as possible and, on coming into office, can avail himself of the experience of the civil service, but this is not the same thing as having access, year after year, to all the secret papers...... King George VI was a very hard worker and read with great care all the state papers that came before him.......A Prime Minister discussing affairs of state with him was talking to one who had a wider and more continuous knowledge than any one else."[82] Since the Prime Minister must discuss his policies with the Monarch, speak of new developments, and listen to what he has to say; and what the Monarch says is the result of his perennial knowledge and experience, he is in an excellent position to influence the man who has the power to decide on policy. "To express a doubt," as Jennings says, "is often more helpful than to formulate a criticism; to throw in a casual remark is often more helpful than to write a memorandum. The easy personal relationship that George VI maintained with his Ministers

79. Bagehot, W., *The British Constitution* (The World Classics ed.), p. 69.

80. Churchill, Winston, S., *The Finest Hour,* p. 379.

81. Herry Hopkins wrote after lunching with Their Majesties on 30th January 1941 : "The King discussed the Navy and the Fleet at some length and showed an intimate knowledge of all the high-ranking officers of the Navy, and for that matter, of the army and the air force. It was perfectly clear from his remarks that he reads very carefully all the important dispatches and among other things, was quite familiar with a dispatch which I had sent Sunday night throug the Foreign Office." Sherwood, Robert E., *Roosevelt and Hopkins*, p. 251.

82. *Life*, February 18, 1952.

probably had more influence than the letters which Queen Victoria wrote in profusion.[83] John Wheeler-Bennet, in his biography of George VI points out that the King believed, as did his father, that the Crown "must of necessity represent all that was most straightforward in the national character, that the Sovereign must set an example to his people of devotion to duty and service to the State, and that, in relation to his Ministers, he must closely adhere to—and never abandon—the three inalienable rights of the King in a constitutional monarchy; the right to be consulted, the right to encourage, and the right to warn."[84]

The views of the King are particularly valuable, because they are not clouded by political controversy. He has no party objective at all, nor is he concerned with intra-party intrigues. He is in the words of Lord Attlee, "the general representative of all the people and stands aloof from the party political battle."[85] The former Conservative Prime Minister Sir Alec Douglas-Home was of the opinion that the "Queen has a constitutional role of great importance, because after all everything is done in the name of the Queen and Parliament so they are one...........So I think her power lies in her influence, and the authority which she naturally carries after 25 years of the most intimate experience of national and international affairs. I think she is influential. Nor that she would take a political part, not at all but obviously the Prime Minister discusses with her political issues of the first importance both to our country and overseas. And on all of those the Queen will have a point of view which is her own, born of very considerable experience. Her influence is important and accepted. I think, because people realise, in this country, that she puts public service above everything, and far above, of course politics in which she does not herself intervene." On the same point Sir Harold Wilson, another former Prime Minister, said, "Her role is important, not in terms of power but in terms of, for example, the weekly audience the Prime Minister has with her. These are very useful for the Prime Minister, because, for instance, he is talking in absolute confidence to some one with lot of experience and a lot of understanding, sometimes a lot of sympathy. He has to collect in his mind all the things he wants to talk about which have happened over the past week, and she will put a lot of questions, always friendly and helpful. It is a very pleasant oasis in a Prime Minister's life and constructive one." Then, there is the traditional reverence for the Monarch's office which must add weight to his opinions. Asquith, wrote in his Memorandum on the Rights and Obligations of the King, that "He is entitled and bound to give his ministers all relevant information which comes to him; to point out objections which seem to him valid against the course which they advise; to suggest (if he thinks fit) an alternative policy. Such intimations are always received with the utmost respect and considered with more respect and deference than if, they proceeded from any other quarter."[86]

Jennings gives a matter of fact summing up. He says, "Thus, the King may be said to be almost a member of the Cabinet, and the only non-party member. He is, too, the best informed member and the only one who cannot be forced to keep silent. His status gives him power to press his view upon the Minister making a proposal and (what is sometimes even more important) to press them on the minister who is not making proposals. He can do more, he can press those views on the Prime Minister the weight of whose authority may in the end produce the Cabinet decision. He can, if he likes to press his point, insist that his views be laid before the Cabinet and considered by them. In other words, he can be as helpful or as obstreperous as he pleases......in the end, of course, he is bound by a Cabinet decision, but he may play a considerable part in the process by which it is reached."[87]

The King's function is advisory only. He can press his opinions as forcefully as he likes. He may resist the advice given to him by his Ministers, but he must not persist and in the last resort give way if Ministers refuse to accept his opinion. He cannot carry his point so far as to threaten the stability of his Government. There are two reasons for it. In the first place, the King cannot act unconstitutionally so long as he acts on the advice of a Minister supported by a majority in the House of Commons. Ministerial responsibility is the safeguard of the Monarchy. The saying that the 'King can do no wrong'

---

83. Jennings, I., *The Queen's Government*, p. 46.
84. Wheeler-Bennet J.W., *King George VI : His Life and Reign*, p. 132.
85. Attlee on Monarchy, Observer, *op. cit.*
86. Spencer, J. A., *Life of Lord Oxford and Asquith*, Vol. II, pp. 29-31.
87. Jennings, I., Cabinet Government, pp. 327-28.

precisely illustrates that the Monarch cannot make decisions of a political or controversial character. The price of his popularity and position is in the abstention from politics. In the second place, if the King forces his opinion which the Ministers are not willing to accept the Cabinet must resign. The King's action, then, immediately enters into political controversy. But the real power of the King depends upon "his willingness to keep respectable and to keep off politics." The Throne cannot stand for long amid the gusts of political conflict and the storm of political opinion. "The road of least criticism is the road for the King." Lord Esher, who was advising George V on the dispute over the Home Rule Bill controversy, most correctly summed up the position of the King. He wrote in a memorandum : "Every constitutional monarch possesses a dual personality. He may hold and express opinions upon the conduct of his ministers and their measures. He may endeavour to influence their actions. He may delay decisions in order to give more time for reflection. He may refuse assent to their advice up to the point where he is obliged to choose between accepting it and losing their services."[88]

**The King as Mediator**

The King very often acts as a mediator and uses his prestige to settle political conflict or "diminish the virulence of Opposition." As he wields no political power and makes no political enemies his advice is deemed valuable and is generally accepted. In 1872, Queen Victoria wrote to Lord Russel, without Gladstone's knowledge, and urged upon him not to move for papers on the Alabama question so that the Government should not be embarrassed. In 1881, the Queen asked General Ponsonby to see Sir Stafford Northcote and Lord Beaconsfield to secure agreement about the Government's proposals to meet Irish obstruction. The Queen's mediation was again very useful in resolving differences between the two Houses of Parliament. In 1913 and 1914 George V made efforts to secure agreement on the Home Rule Bill. The leaders of the Parties did not reach agreement, but he did bring them together. In his address at the Buckingham Palace Conference on July 21, 1914, the King said , "My intervention at this moment may be regarded as a new departure, but the exceptional cir- cumstances under which you are brought together justify my action." There is also some evidence available that in 1916, Lord Stamfordham, as the King's Private Secretary, endeavoured to settle the dispute between Asquith and Lloyd George which led to the resignation of Asquith. George V had much conspicuous part to play in 1921 over the Irish Home Rule tangle. "A King is," as Attlee says, "a kind of referee, although the occasions when he has to blow the whistle are now-a-days very few." But even then, they do happen. *The Financial Times* reported that Queen Elizabeth II, as Head of the Commonwealth, intervened to end the Commonwealth crisis over the question of imposing sanctions against South Africa, to ward off a clash between Prime Minister Margaret Thatcher and other heads of the Commonwealth. The occasion was necessitated by Mrs. Thatcher's reiteration of outright opposition to sanctions in the House of Commons. The Queen's anxiety was to prevent a break-up of the Commonwealth and her mediation had a little cooling effect on the rigid attitude adopted by the Prime Minister.

**A Symbol of Unity**

The King of Britain is at once the King of Canada and other Dominions. In his welcome speech on the visit of George VI to Canada in 1939, Prime Minister Mackenzie King said : "Here you will be in the heart of the family that is your own. We would have your Majesties feel that in coming from the old land to the new, you left one home for another." The constitutional developments of 1911 to 1931, ending with the Statute of Westminster, have given the Dominions complete independence both in matters of legislation and in matters of policy. But the King is still, in the language of the Preamble to Statute of Westminster, a symbol of the free association of the members of the British Commonwealth of Nations. Subordination to the Government at Westminster is inconsistent with Dominion Status, but common "allegiance to the King" is not. The King, therefore, provides an indispensable symbol of unity of the far-flung Commonwealth countries.[89] It is "the last link of the Empire that is left," as Baldwin reminded Edward VIII. Break this link which is furnished by Royalty and nothing remains in common among the autonomous partners in the Commonwealth. With a view to stabilize the bonds of unity the Statute of Westminster provides that any change

88. *Ibid.*, p. 329.
89. Attlee on Monarchy, *Observer, op. cit.*

made in the order of succession to the throne must have the consent of the members of the Commonwealth. "Queen Elizabeth is the Queen of all territories that admit allegiance to her. She is one Queen and not a score of Queens. The Queen is a person and not an institution, and so she is one Queen." The essential factor in this scheme of governance was, and still is, the Monarchy. The person of the King moves as a single animating force through the whole of that Commonwealth.

Then, the Sovereign is the symbol of the free association of the members of the Commonwealth including the Republic of India and some fifty other Sovereign and independent States. The position of the Sovereign as head of the Commonwealth countries, who do not owe allegiance to the King, was best explained by Prime Minister Jawaharlal Nehru. In a broadcast speech on May 10, 1949, Nehru said, "It must be remembered that the Commonwealth is not super-state in any sense of the term. We have agreed to consider the King as a symbolic head of the free association. But the King has no function attached to that status in the Commonwealth. So far as the Constitution of India is concerned the King has no place and we shall owe no allegiance to him." This is the correct position, yet the King provides the link which brings about the free association of sovereign nations which meet and think over problems of common interests and derive means of mutual amity. The King is, in the words of Winston Churchill[90] "a mysterious link, indeed, I may say, the magic link, which united our loosely bound but strongly inter-woven Commonwealth of nations, states and races." The King may be a symbol for India and other countries like her, but he is also in that capacity "the Head—the one and single Head—the Head of the body which is all the more united because it now has, and henceforth acknowledges, a Head.[91]

**The King as Chief of the Nation**

British Kingship, wrote Earl of Balfour, "like most other parts of our Constitution, has a very modern side to it. Our King, in virtue of his descent and of his office, is the living representative of our national history. So far from concealing the popular character of our institutions .......he brings it into prominence. He is not the leader of a party nor the representative of a class; he is the chief of the nation......He is everybody's King."[92] He is really everybody's King and that is precisely the feeling of all British people. The accession of the King, his coronation, his jubilee, are the occasions for unparalleled demonstration of popular and patriotic devotion. Enthusiastic and loyal subjects throng the route to watch and cheer the King when he drives in State to open a new session of Parliament. In fact, every item of royal activity is newsworthy and it is flashed through by every device that modern publicity can utilize. "Some of the tributes," said Laski, "devoted to the person of the Monarch since the war would certainly have been more suited to the description of a demi-god than to the actual occupants of the throne in the last sixty years."[93]

Monarchy, therefore, provides a useful focus for patriotism particularly where it has a long and glorious history. "We can damn the Government," says Jennings, "and cheer the King."[94] A person can be loyal to his King and yet oppose the Government. The Conservatives "served the King" in 1914, although they opposed some aspects of the Liberal Government's policy. The patriotic fervour of the people is more easily stimulated when the "King" declares war and asks for recruits for the "royal forces." The national appeal: "Your King and country need you" is sufficient to remind them that they are one nation. The King is the most concrete symbol of this oneness and unity. According to Llyod George, "the King in 1917 enormously assisted in allaying industrial unrest by his visits to munition works and other places when suspicion of war motives was being aroused."[95] The visit of George VI to various theatres of War and the bombed areas in England imbued the soldiers and the civilian population alike with a new spirit of patriotism. They made a heroic bid to win the war and the loyal subjects of the King ultimately won it. "God save the Queen" is their National Anthem, and they do and die for the Sovereign who for them personifies the State. Or to put it in the words of Amery, "Human nature not only

90. Broadcast Speech on the death of George VI.
91. Barker, E.., *Essays on Government*, p. 19.
92. Introducation to Bagehot's *English Constitution* p. XXV.
93. Laski, H., *Parliamentary Government in England*, p. 389
94. Jennings, W.I., *The English Constitution*, p. 111.
95. As cited in Jennings, W.I., *Cabinet Government*, p. 364.

craves for symbols but prefers them to be personal and human."[96] The Monarch is, thus, a more personalised and attractive symbol of national unity "than a vague concept of the state, the flag, or even a President, and the hereditary system at least solves the problem of succession."[97]

Queen Elizabeth's plea for unity in an address to Parliament, on May 4, 1977 at the start of Jubilee celebrations, stirred up unprecedented political controversy as it was a departure from the tradition that the Monarch did not intervene in political affairs. But it did indicate her personal anxiety about the danger of break up of the United Kingdom through separatist movements in Scotland and Wales. It was reported that the speech was written in Buckingham Palace and that the Queen wanted to speak her mind about separation. Prime Minister James Callaghan had seen a copy of the speech earlier but had not offered advice and had not been asked about this passage.

**King as a Social Figure**

The King is not merely a part of the political machine, he is also an important part of the social structure and wields a great social influence. He is the leader of society by general precedence dating back from the fourteenth century and sustained until the present day by Royal Ordinances, ancient usage, established custom and the public will. The Royal family sets morality, fashion[98] and aptitude even in art and literature. The Royal patronage is an enormous asset to any cause and ensures for it popular support. Such a national appeal no other person, however eminent, could give. His presence at ceremonies such as the laying of the foundation stones, the launching of ships, and the opening of new works, enables people of opposing views to associate without suppressing their mutual opposition. Government is a collective concern and it requires the willing co-operation of all sections of people. The presence of the King adds personal touch to the individuals feeling a personal responsibility for the collective action. No government is averse to use the personal popularity and social influence of the Sovereign to strengthen its own popular appeal. The Jubilee and Diamond Jubilee celebrations of 1887 and 1897 strengthened popular support for the imperialistic ideas of the Conservative Governments then in office. It is certain, too, that the Silver Jubilee of 1935 strengthened the "National Government, whose popular support had until then been rapidly diminishing." The Silver Jubilee celebrations of Queen Elizabeth II in 1977 were intended to regenerate emotions and loyalties of the nation to stop the trend gainst Royalty which several forces combined to demonstrate recently.

Thus, these "dignified" functions, as Bagehot called them, are far more important than the King's Government functions. If democracy means the government by the people as well as for the people, the presence of the King helps to make it so. When the people cheer the Queen and sing her praises, " wrote Herbert Morrison, "they are also cheering our free democracy.[99] The proper part of the Monarch, as Laski emphasised, "has been that of a dignified emollient rather than of an active umpire between conflicting interests."[100]

**The King and Parliamentary System**

The Cabinet system of government has nowhere proved a workable plan without the presence of some titular Head of the State, whether he be a King, as in Britain, or a President, as in India. But from the political point of view a person who is free of party ties and stands above party considerations is the most desirable adjunct of the Parliamentary system of government. An elected Head of the State is a promoted politician and howsoever sincerely he may endeavour to forget his past party associations, he cannot do it. Even if he can, others cannot. But the Sovereign, unlike an elected President, has no party associations or partisan leanings. His august position, as the occupant of the throne, puts him in an altogether different atmosphere. He is everybody's King and he does not form party loyalties. As a result, not only is he in a position to act more impartially, but also, what is of more importance, he is believed by others to be impartial. If Parliamentary government in

96. Amery, L.S., *Thoughts on the Constitution*, p. 139.
97. Punnet, R.M., *British Government and Politics*, p. 257.
98. Princess Rose, now Queen Elizabeth II, and her sister Princess Margaret, began going out for their evening walks, in the spring of 1939, without hats, and this set a fashion for children in London causing a considerable diminished sale in children hats. A deputation of children-hat dealers waited upon the Queen and explained to Her Majesty how hard they had been hit. The Queen asked her daughters to use hats for their evening walks and it set a fashion for children to follow.
99. Morrison Herbert, *Government and Parliament*, p. 92.
100. Laski, H. J., *Parliamentary Government in England*, p. 395.

Britain is to be retained in the classic form in which it has been developed, then, the best representation of such a "dignified and detached" figure is the King. "Thus far, beyond doubt, the system of limited Monarchy has been an unquestionable success in Great Britain. It has, so far, trodden its way with remarkable skill amid the changing habits of the time. Its success has been the outcome of the fact that it has exchanged power for influence; the blame for errors in policy has been laid at the door of ministers who have paid penalty by loss of the office." Monarchy has been no bar to the progressive democratization of the Government otherwise it would have been thrown overboard long ere this. "The security and popularity of the British Monarchy today," wrote Herbert Morrison, "are largely the result of the fact that it does not govern and that government is the task of ministers responsible to a House of Commons elected by the people. The Monarchy as it exists now facilitates the process of parliamentary democracy and functions as an upholder of freedom and representative government."[101]

The popularity of the British King and the role which he plays in the British politics is now an undisputed fact. In Britain, there had been moves to end or mend the House of Lords; even to reform the House of Commons and the Cabinet, but Monarchy has withstood the test of time. People realise and appreciate its "unifying, and stabilising influence." If it were to be abolished the substitute would be either like the type of Indian Presidency or the American Presidency. The former is not a good substitute, because the President of India neither rules nor reigns; and if he rules it is the negation of Parliamentary government. The limited period of office of a President has disadvantages as compared with the continuing reign of a hereditary Monarch. The type of American Presidency would entail revolutionary changes in the existing political set-up of the country. An Englishman will never agree to it. The institution of Monarchy is something with which all Britons have grown up; it is a part of their heritage and their political culture. They have shaped it so that it does not interfere with their social and political development and they see no reason to substitute some other institution for this venerable institution. Lowell has aptly said, "If the King is no longer the motive power of the state, it is the spar on which the sail is bent, and as such it is not only a useful but an essential part of thevessel." So despite its anachronism in a democracy, the Kingship is impregnably entrenched in the British constitutional system. Ernest Barker has aptly said, "When a nation has preserved continuity with its past, and continues to feel some piety towards its past, it will naturally fly the flag of monarchy which it has inherited from its past. But the monarchy which it preserves will be a changing and moving monarchy—changing and moving with the times and actively helping the times to change and move. That, for the last 300 years, has been nature of the British monarchy. That is the secret of its survival, and that is the source of its strength." Even the present strains on Monarchy, with the liquidation of the Empire, the economic cost to the nation on the upkeep of royalty, and Scotland's determination to win independence, are not likely to liquidate this venerable institution. It will continue to command respect, loyalty and affection for no other reason than that it works. And for a nation with a long history, it gives a sense of continuity, of stability. So the crowds hoping for a view of the Queen, will continue to stand outside the Buckingham Palace, where the guards will also continue their time-honoured ritual. And the Monarch perhaps typified by Elizabeth II and her son Prince Charles, will survive.

**The Ruling Elite**

The ruling class of the United Kingdom today uses the monarchy in three ways : firstly, as an ideological weapon for maintaining the equilibrium of the political system; secondly, as a direct or indirect means of intervention in political events at critical junctures; and thirdly, because of its constitutional rights, the monarchy is potentially a reserve weapon to be used in crisis. That is why Bagehot had felt that "without the queen in England, the present English government would fail and pass away." Baldwin regarded it as "The guarantee in this country...against many evils that have affected and afflicted other countries." The great value of the monarchy to the ruling class has been, as we have seen, its facade of neutrality, its pretence of representing the nation as a whole. Once the monarch showed partisanship openly on a controversial question, the pretences of impartiality would be undermined and the great merit of a

101. Morrison, Herbert, *Government and Parliament*, P. 92.

troversial question, the pretences of impartiality would be undermined and the great merit of a monarchy would vanish from the point of view of the ruling elites. The crown would then become "the football of contending factions."

Recently, the institution of monarchy has been subjected to adverse criticision due to scandalous conduct of some members of the royal household, including Prince Charles. Some critics have argued that monarchy has outlined its utility and should be abolished after the reign of the present reigning Queen. However, this still remains a minority opinion.

## SUGGESTED READINGS


Amery, L : *Thoughts on Constitution.*

Anthony Sampson : *The Anatomy of Britain Today.*

Bagehot, E. : *English Constitution.*

Barker, E. : *Essays on Government*, Chap. I.

Benemy, F. W. G. : *The Queen Reigns: She does not Rule.*

Blake, R. : *The Unknown Prime Minister.*

Brasher, N. H. : *Studies in British Government*, Chap. I.

Campion, Lord and others : *British Government Since 1918*

Cathcart, Helen : *Her Majesty.*

Dorothy Laird : *How the Queen Reigns.*

Finer, H. : *Governments of Greater European Powers*, Chap. 9.

Greaves, H. R. G. : *The British Constitution* , Chap. IV.

Grigg, John : *Is the Monarchy Perfect ?*

Hardie, F. : *The Political Influence of British Monarchy.*

Jennings, W. I. : *The British Constitution*, Chap. V.

Jennings, W. I. : *The Queen's Government*, Chap.2.

Keith, A. B. : *The Constitution of England from Queen Victoria to George VI*, Vol. I, Chaps. II, III.

Keith, A. B. : *The King and the Imperial Crown.*.

Laski, H. J. : *Parliamentary Government in England*, Chap. VIII.

Lowell, A. L. : *The Government of England* (1908), Vol. I, Chap. I.

Marriot, J. A. R. : *Mechanism of the Modern State* (1927), Vol. II, Chaps. XXIII, XXIV.

Martin, Kingsley : *The Magic of Monarchy.*

Martin, Kingsley : *The Crown and the Estabilishment.*

Morrison, Herbert : *Government and Parliament*, Chap. V.

Morrah, Dermot : *The Work of the Queen.*

Munro, W. B. : *The Governments of Europe*, Chap. IV.

Nicolson, Sir H. : *George V.*

Ogg, F. A. : *English Government and Politics* (1936), Chaps. IV, V.

Ogg, and Zink, H. : *Modern Foreign Governments*, Chap. III,

Pterie, Sir Charles : *The Modern British Monarchy.*

Stannard, H. : *The Two Constitutions*, Chap I.

Wheeler Bennett, Sir J. W. : *George VI : His Life and Reign.*

William, E. N. : *The 18th Century Constitution*, 1688-1815.

Windsor, Duke of : *Crown and Public*, 1920-53.

# CHAPTER IV

# Privy Council, Ministry and Cabinet

The powers of the Crown are exercised through different agencies. Some are exercised by Ministers acting singly in the Departments over which they preside, some are performed by the Privy Council and its various Committees, some by the Cabinet and some are carried on with the help of the permanent Civil Servants. It will, therefore, be meaningful to know the nature and organisa- tion of these institutions and how do they actually function.

## THE PRIVY COUNCIL

### Origin and Development

From early times there had been a Council, a group of men attendant on the King, fulfilling certain duties and acting as the King's advisers. The Privy Council is an official name given in law to the body of persons who are the advisers of the Sovereign. In its origin, the Privy Council is the descendant of the King's Council, the *Curia Regis,* which dates from Norman days, and has had, under various names, a continuous history. An attempt was made under the Lancastrian Kings to make it directly subordinate to Parliament, but it could not succeed. In the sixteenth century the King's Privy Council became the powerful instrument of Tudor despotism. In the next century its powers were considerably eclipsed by an inner circle of the King's advisers which eventually came to be known as Cabinet.

As the Privy Council had become an unwieldy body for purposes of effective consultations, the later Stuart King started the practice of consulting with a few members of the Council who met the King in his closet or "Cabinet". It became a regular practice and by 1679, the old Privy Council may be said to have been virtually abolished, except for formal business and as a Court of Law. This change can be observed from the farewell speech of Charles II, in the same year to his Privy Councillors. The King said : "His Majesty thanks you for all the good advice which you have given him which might have been more frequent if the great numbers of the Council had not made it unfit for the secrecy and dispatch of business. This forced him to use a smaller number of you in a foreign committee, and sometimes the advice of some few among them upon such occasions for many years past."

### Composition and Organisation

The Privy Council was, therefore, the chief source of executive power in the State. As the system of Cabinet Government developed, the Privy Council became less prominent. Many of its powers were transferred to the Cabinet as an inner committee of the Privy Council, and much of its work was handed over to newly created government Departments, some of which were originally the committees of the Privy Council. The present day Privy Council is the body on whose advice and through which the Sovereign exercises his statutory and a number of prerogative powers. It, also, has its own statutory duties, independent of the power of the King in Council.

The Privy Council includes all Cabinet Ministers, past and present,[1] the Prince of Wales and the Royal Dukes, the Archbishops and the Bishop of London, and a large number of other people of distinction in the field of politics, arts, literature, science or law who are elevated as Privy Councillors. Ambassadors are now usually made Privy Councillors and since the precedent of 1897 Dominion Premiers are regularly offered its membership.[2] The Speaker of the House of Commons, too, is normally offered Privy Councillorship. The title of "Right Honourable" is borne by all members of the Privy Councillors and the membership of the Privy Council is re-

1. Once appointed to the Privy Council, a person ordinarily retains his membership for life.
2. General Hertzog and De Valera, however, refused Privy Councillorship.

tained for life .

The Privy Council is convened by the Clerk of the Privy Council and is presided over by the Sovereign or, when the Sovereign is abroad or ill, by Councillors of State. Three Privy Councillors from a quorum, but, as a rule, not fewer than four are summoned to attend. Rarely is anyone invited to attend a Council meeting who is not a Cabinet member. The whole Privy Council is called together only on the death of the Sovereign or when the Sovereign announces his or her intention to marry.

The Privy Council is responsible for advising the Sovereign to approve Orders in Council, of which there are two kinds, differing fundamentally in constitutional principle. Those made by virtue of the Royal Prerogative, for example, Orders approving the grant of Royal Charters of Incorporation, and, secondly, those made under Statutory powers, which are the highest form of delegated legislation. It is an accepted principle that members of the Privy Council attending meetings at which Orders in Council are made do not thereby become responsible for the policy upon which the Orders are based; this rests with the Ministers whose Departments are responsible for the subjects of the Orders in question whether or not they are present at the meeting. Certain Orders in Council must be published in the *London Gazette*, which is an official periodical published by the authority of the Government. The Privy Council also advises the Crown on the issue of Royal Proclamations, some of the most important of which relate to the prerogative acts (such as summoning or dissolving Parliament) of the same validity as Acts of Parliament.

The Privy Council serves, as in ancient times, as a panel for the composition of the committees. The meetings of the committees differ from those of the Privy Council itself in that the Sovereign cannot constitutionally be present. These committees have only advisory functions. The committee relating to Jersy and Guernsey is of long historical lineage. Similarly, there are committees for the Universities of Oxford and Cambridge and the Scottish Universities. Early in the reign of Queen Victoria it was found convenient to entrust the Privy Council, acting through a committee, various functions, which later on were handed over to Departments. The connection of the Council with education, however, remained considerably longer and it was only in 1899, that a Board of Education with an independent President was substituted for the committee. The administrative work of the Privy Council committees is carried out in the Privy Council office under the control of the Lord President of the Council.

The most noteworthy of such committees is the Judicial Committee of the Privy Council created in 1833. This Committee is generally selected from Lord Chancellor, ex-Lord Chancellors, and Lords of Appeal in Ordinary, although other members of the Privy Council who have held high judicial office (including Chief Justices and certain other judges from other Commonwealth countries who have been sworn members of the Privy Council) may also be asked to sit when business of the Judicial Committee is heavy. The Judicial Committee does not deliver judgment. It advises the Sovereign who acts on its report and approves an Order in Council to give effect thereto. Its decisions, though not binding on the English courts, are treated with great respect by them.

The Judicial Committee of the Privy Council is the final court of appeal from the courts of United Kingdom dependencies and certain States of the Commonwealth, including certain countries of which Her Majesty is no longer the Queen, but have not elected to discontinue to appeal. It derives its appellate jurisdiction in respect of such appeals from the principle of English Common Law which recognises, "the right of all the King's subjects to appeal for redress to the Sovereign in Council", if they believed that the Courts of Law had failed to do them justice. The Judicial Committee is also the final court of appeal from the ecclesiastical courts of England, from the Channel Islands and the Isle of Man, and from Prize Courts[3] in the United Kingdom and dependencies. It hears appeals from members of the medical, dental and certain kindred professions against decisions of their respective disciplinary bodies.

Lord Samuels describes the Judicial Committee of the Privy Council as "one of the most august tribunals in the world." Members of the Judicial Committee hold or have held certain high judicial offices in the United Kingdom or the Commonwealth and the Privy Councillors. Appeals are admitted only by leave given by the courts overseas according to local law or , failing that, by the Judicial Committee itself.

3. Prize courts deal with matters concerning property captured in time of war which, by the grace of the Crown, falls to the forces which assist in the capture.

## THE MINISTRY

### Ministry and Cabinet

The term Ministry is used in two senses. Sometimes it is used to mean Cabinet as if the two terms are synonymous. Sometimes it is used to mean both the Cabinet and other Ministers who are not members of the Cabinet. The second meaning is preferable. When a new Prime Minister is appointed, he has to fill hundred or so posts, major and minor, which together make up the Ministry. For example, the Cabinet formed by Winston Churchill in 1951 contained sixteen members. In addition to these Ministers in the Cabinet, there were twenty-two Ministers who were not in the Cabinet. Then, there were over fifty junior Ministers and this total of about ninety constituted Churchill's Ministry. The Labour Government formed by Harold Wilson in October 1964 con tained a total 101 Ministers and Parliamentary Secretaries. The Cabinet contained 23 members, like its Conservative predecessor Government, under Sir Alec Douglas Home. The Ministry is, thus, a convenient concept that embraces all categories of Ministers collectively with varying shades and degrees, who go to make up the political side of the Executive. That is her Majesty's Gov ernment.

The Ministers vary in nomenclature and in importance. About twenty or more of the most important out of the Ministry are the members of the Cabinet.[4] They meet collectively, decide upon policy, and in general "head up" the government. It does not, however, mean that every Cabinet Minister must necessarily preside over an administrative Department. There are a few sinecure offices which involve no substantial departmental duties. Men of great political importance whose capacity for departmental work has been lessened by the passage of time, or those who have no taste for administration, but whose counsel is always of immense value,[5] are assigned offices with a few or no duties attached. For example, the duties of the Lord Privy Seal were abolished in 1884 and yet he is always a member of the Cabinet. The Lord President of the Council, too, has only nominal duties. Sometimes these offices are usefully occupied by Ministers who are entrusted with major responsibilities of a general rather than of a departmental kind. This was true of Lord President from 1940-43, and Herbert Morrison who became Lord President in the Labour Government of 1945. In Macmillan's Government (1961) the Lord President of the Council was entrusted with the general duty of promoting scientific and technological development as Minister of Science. The Lord Privy Seal handled foreign office business in the House of Commons. The Earl of Home (later Sir Douglas-Home), the Foreign Secretary, was in the Lords.

Another expedient is the appointment of Ministers without Portfolio. From 1915 to 1921 ten cases occurred of Ministers in the Cabinet without Portfolio.[6] But this system ended in 1921 after a scathing criticism in the House of Commons. It was revived in Baldwin's Ministry of 1935 when Lord Eustace Percy and Anthony Eden received Ministries.[7] Arthur Greenwood held the office of Minister without Portfolio during his membership of the War Cabinet and also for a short while in 1947. W.F. Deedes was appointed Minister without Portfolio by Harold Macmillan in a major reconstruction of Cabinet in July 1962 and October 1963 Douglas Home appointed two Ministers without Portfolio. But it is not usual for such a Minister to be created.

In the second place, there are certain Ministers who are designated as of "Cabinet rank". Attlee's Labour Government, formed in January 1949, had fifteen such ministers. The ministers of "Cabinet rank" are the heads of the administrative departments, and although they are formally of Cabinet status and are paid the same salary as Cabinet Ministers, but they are not members of the Cabinet itself. They attend the Cabinet meetings only when specifically invited by the Prime Minister to deal with matters concerning their Departments. This division of Ministers was observed by Churchill in 1951 and he had eighteen Ministers under this category. The Ministers of "Cabinet rank" vary in numbers from government to government; it is a matter

4. Anthony Eden, who succeeded Winston Churchill after the latter retired from active politics, had eighteen Cabinet Ministers. Harold Macmillan continued with more or less the same number. Harold Wilson's Cabinet formed in 1964 had twenty-three members, though Wilson advocated 15 to 20 members, to make an ideal Cabinet, BBC Publications, *Whitehall and Beyond,* p. 26.
5. John Bright proved poor administrator at the Board of Trade in 1868, but was later valuable as Chancellor of the Duchy.
6. Keith, A. B., *The British Cabinet System,* p. 45.
7. Lord Eustace Percy found his position anomalous and resigned office, later leaving parliamentary life. Anthony Eden was given the duty of dealing with League of Nations' affairs, but on Sir Samuel Hoare's retirement in 1935, he was appointed in his place.

for the Prime Minister's discretion. In Heath's Government (1972) there were seven Ministers of this kind.

Then, come the "Ministers of State", who are "deputy minister" in Government Departments where the work is particularly heavy and complex, or when it involves frequent travelling overseas. A Minister of State may,if circumstances demand, hold independent charge of a Department, though there is no precedent so far. Compared with ten Ministers of State in Douglas-Home's Government there were sixteen in Harold Wilson's Government and eleven in Heath's Government. The Ministers of State usually have a status intermediate between that of a full Minister and of a Parliamentary Secretary. The first Minister of State ever created was Lord Beaverbrook in May 1941 and since then the practice has come to stay. "In practice the general idea of the Minister of State", says Herbert Morrison, "is to create minister of higher status than that of a Parliamentary Secretary who could relieve heavily burdened departmental ministers of material parts of their work to an extent which might not be considered appropriate in the case of Parliamentary Secretaries." It would appear that any action taken by a Minister of State who is subordinate to the Minister in charge of a Department, would be on behalf of the Minister under delegated powers. The Minister-in-charge of the Department is answerable to Parliament for all intents and purposes.

Finally, there are the Parliamentary secretaries, or 'junior ministers'. Each departmental Minister has usually a Parliamentary Secretary, but in some of the larger Departments there may be two. A Parliamentary Secretary may not be confused with the Permanent Secretary who is a senior member of the Civil Service in the Department. Parliamentary Secretaries are mostly members of the House of Commons, or if not, then, of the House of Lords. They belong to the majority party and are selected by the Prime Minister in consultation with the Minister concerned. They remain in office as long as the Ministry is there or the Prime Minister wishes them to be there. But they are not Ministers of the Crown and constitutionally have no 'power'. The primary function of the Parliamentary Secretary is to relieve their senior Ministers of some of their burden by taking part in parliamentary debates, and answering parliamentary questions, and by assisting in departmental duties. There are also five "political" officials of the Royal Household, including the Treasurer, the Comptroller, and Vice-Chamberlain. These offices carry a political complexion and their incumbents are ranked as Ministers.

All these categories of Ministers, who make the Ministry, are members of Parliament[8] and belong to the majority party in the House of Commons. They are individually and collectively responsible to the House of Commons and continue to remain in office as long as they can retain its confidence. The Ministry may, thus, consist of the whole number of Crown officials having seats in Parliament, sustaining direct responsibility to the House of Commons and holding office subject to a continued support of a working majority in the latter body. But the Ministry has no collective functions. It is the function of the Cabinet. The Cabinet is a committee of the Ministry, chosen by the Prime Minister who meet together for four or five hours each week to deliberate, formulate policy, supervise and co-ordinate the work of the whole Government machine. The Ministry as a whole never meets and it never deliberates on matters of policy. The duties of a Minister, unless he is Cabinet Minister, are individual uties relalting to the administrative Department or Departments to which he is attached. In sum, the Cabinet officer deliberates and advises; the Privy Councillor decrees; and the Minister executes. The three activities are easily capable of being distinguished, even though it frequently happens that Cabinet officer, Privy Councillor, and Minister are one and the same person.

**Size of the Ministry**

The overall size of the Ministry (excluding Parliamentary Secretaries) has more than doubled from early this century; rising from about forty five in the Governments of Balfour, Campbell Bannerman, and Asquith before 1914, to

8. It is a well settled convention that Ministers should be either Peers or members of the House of Commons. There have been however, occasional and temporary exceptions. Gladstone held the office of Colonial Secretary in 1845 for nine months without a seat in Parliament. Sir A. G. Boseawen, Minister of Agriculture, was a similar case in 1922-23. General Smuts was a Minister without Portfolio and a member of the War Cabinet from 1916 until the end of War without a seat in Parliament. Ramsay MacDonald and his son Malcolm MacDonald were members of the Cabinet though not in Parliament from November 1935 until early in 1936. MacDonalds were defeated at the General Election held in November 1935 Patrick Gordon-Walker was appointed Foreign Secretary by Harold Wilson despite his failure to get elected in October, 1964. Gordon-Walker had to quit on his defeat in the by-election too.

more than one hundred in the Wilson Government formed in 1964. This increase has created the danger of excessive executive domination of the Legislature. Although members of the House of Commons appointed to Ministerial office no longer have to secure re-election to the Commons, there do exist statutory limits on the number of Ministers allowed to serve in the Commons at any one time.

The Ministers of the Crown Act, 1937, provided that only eighteen out of twenty-one senior Ministers could serve in the House of Commons at any one time. This meant that if all the twenty-one posts were filled, at least three had to be held by members of the Lords. In addition, the Act of 1937 provided that no more than twenty Junior Ministers could sit in the Commons at any one time. During World War II, under the provisions of the emergency legislation, these figures were exceeded, while many of the ministerial posts created after the War were specifically excluded from the limitations imposed by the Act of 1937. In 1941, the Select Committee on Offices and Places of Profit under the Crown recommended that only sixty Ministers in all should serve in the House of Commons.[9] In pursuance of this recommendation the House of Commons Disqualification Act, 1957, specified that not more than seventy Minister of all categories could serve in the House of Commons at one time. This limit was not exceeded by Macmillian or Home. When the Labour Government came in power in 1964 it created the new Ministerial posts which correspondingly increased the size of the Ministry and, accordingly, the necessity of new legislation arose. The Ministers of the Crown Act, 1964, increased from seventy to ninety-one the total number of Ministers who could serve in the Commons at any one time, and abolished the limit on the number of senior Ministers that could be drawn from the Commons. Since the figure of ninety-one fixed by the 1964 Act, as the maximum number of Ministers that could be drawn from the House of Commons, was below the total number of Ministerial posts in the Wilson Government, the Act recognised the principle that some posts should be filled by the Lords. It means that Ministers over and above the number of ninety-one would come from the Lords thereby increasing the strength of the Peers in the Ministry.

## THE CABINET

### Not Known to Law

The Cabinet is the core of the British constitutional system. It is the supreme directing authority; "the magnet of policy," as Barker calls it,[10] which co-ordinates and controls the whole of the executive government, and integrates and guides the work of the Legislature. According to Bagehot, the Cabinet is a "hyphen that joins, the buckle that binds the executive and legislative de- partments together." Lowell calls it "the keystone of the political arch." Sir John Marriot describe it as "the pivot round which the whole political machinery revolves." Ramsay Muir speaks of it as "the steering-wheel of the ship of State." Sir Ivor Jennings succinctly says that the Cabinet "provides unity to the British system of government." With whatever colourful phrase it may be described and from whatever angle it is approached, the Cabinet is the motive power of all political action in Britain. And yet it is not known to law.

Like various other political institutions of the country, the Cabinet, too, is the child of chance. Until 1937, it was not even mentioned in any Act of Parliament, and in the Ministers of the Crown Act there is just an occasional reference to it.[11] As the Cabinet has no legal existence, its actions have not the force of law. The judicial acts of the Cabinet are formally made the actions of the Privy Council which body has existence in law. The machinery of the Cabinet system is, thus, based upon conventions, unwritten but always recognised and stated with almost as much precision as the rules of law. This, indeed, is the most remarkable outcome of the British Constitution.

### Development of the Cabinet

The name Cabinet referred originally to a small body of ministers whom the later Stuart Kings commenced consulting in preference to the Privy Council of their predecessors.[12] Then, came the Revolution of 1688, and the consequent increase in the powers of Parliament. Wil-

9. The Herbert Committee Report, H. C. 120 of 1941.
10. Barker, E., *Britain and the British People* (1943), p. 54.
11. The Ministers of the Crown Act, 1937, referred to it while providing higher salaries for those Ministers who were members of the Cabinet.
12. The smaller inner group of persons to whom the King came to give his special confidence was variously known as the '*Junto*'(a term first used during the reign of Charles I), the 'Cable' (after the initial letters of the inner group of 1671—Clifford, Arlington, Buckingham, Ashley and Lauderdale), the 'Cabinet Council' or the 'Cabinet' (the cabinet being the private room or closet of the King's palace in which the group met).

liam III on ascending the throne formed a Ministry drawn both from the Whigs and the Tories. But he soon realized that the Tories were very critical of his policy and their opposing views made it impossible for him to carry out smooth administration. He, therefore, gradually dismissed all the Tories from his Ministry and got, for the first time, a body of Ministers chosen from one political party. The Whig Junto of 1696 is regarded as the real beginning of the Cabinet system. Queen Anne carried the development a stage further by letting the inner circle *decide policy* while her precedecessors *tolerated only advice*. But she still continued to dismiss her Ministers when they forfeited her favour. At the same time, both William and Anne presided in person at the meetings of the cabinet

The system of Cabinet Government can be said to have really emerged when the King was excluded from the meetings of the Cabinet. This happened, by chance in 1714, when George I ceased to attend the meetings of the Council because he did not understand English. The King designated Sir Robert Walpole to preside in his place. The Cabinet thereupon ceased to meet at the palace with the Sovereign presiding, and met instead at the House of the First Lord of the Treasury. The First Lord became a kind of Chairman to the Cabinet and Walpole furnished the required leadership in the absence of the King and the colleagues looked to him for direction. As Chairman of the Cabinet, he presided at its meetings, guided and directed its deliberations, reported the decisions arrived at the Cabinet meetings to the King, and reported to the Cabinet the opinion of the King. Moreover, as a member of Parliament he served as a link between the Cabinet and Parliament. This new position and duties of Walpole in effect involved the origin of the office of the Prime Minister, although he resented and repudiated the suggestion that his position was of that kind. Necessity, thus, grafted the Premiership as well as the Cabinet constitution.

Another outcome of the absence of the King from meetings of the Cabinet was that Ministers, instead of tendering individual advice, began seeking for unanimity. Walpole could hardly go to the King with a dozen or fifteen different opinions. Differences amongst themselves the Ministers began to resolve inside the Cabinet, and thereby agreed advice was conveyed to the King. Out of this emerged another development. The Cabinet, if it were to tender unanimous advice, had to be a homogeneous body. When distinct political parties had begun to emerge, it became convenient to draw all Cabinet Ministers from a single majority party to be sure of parliamentary approval.

For twenty years Walpole headed the Government and during that period a system that was in its infancy gathered strength and a certain measure of stability. In fact, in Walpole's administration are found the essential characteristics of present-day Cabinet government. "It was Walpole who first administered the Government in accordance with his own views of our political requirements. It was Walpole who first conducted the business of the country in the House of Commons. It was Walpole who in the conduct of that business first insisted upon the support for his measures of all servants of the Crown who had seats in Parliament. It was under Walpole that the House of Commons became the dominant power in the State, and rose in ability and influence as well as in actual power above the House of Lords. And it was Walpole who set the example of quitting his office while he still retained the undiminished affection of his King for the avowed reason that he had ceased to possess the confidence of the House of Commons." It was, again, Walpole who used No. 10 Downing Street while he was in office, which subsequently became the official residence of the Prime Minister.

At the same time, there had developed the principle of ministerial responsibility; the principle that a Minister was responsible to Parliament for all his public acts, and that he could be brought to book by Parliament if ever it considered his acts prejudicial to the interests of the country. The principle of ministerial responsibility evolved slowly. For the first time Strafford in the reign of Charles I was made to answer to Parliament for what was considered the bad advice he had given to the King. The King did his best to shield him, but, and in spite of the best efforts of Charles himself, Strafford was made to pay the penalty imposed by Parliament.[13] Exactly the same happened in Danby's case during the reign of Charles

13. Strafford was impeached of high treason by the House of Commons "for endeavouring to subvert the ancient and fundamental laws and government of His Majesty's realms of England and Ireland and to introduce an arbitrary and tyrannical government against law in the said kingdom." Adams, C. B., and Stephens, H. M., *Select Documents of English Constitutional History*, p. 361.

II.[14] Since then the principle of ministerial responsibility has been recognised as the *sine quo non* of the parliamentary system of government.

It does not, however, mean that the Cabinet system of government had become an accomplished fact in the eighteenth century, and the King was a mere cipher in his relations to the Cabinet. Even Sir Robert Walpole felt himself very much the King's servant and dismissable by him. George III demanded the inclusion of some members in the Cabinet, though they belonged to the opposing party. George IV made efforts to create among the Ministers division by getting their individual opinions on Canning's foreign policy. William IV, once or perhaps, twice, contemplated the dismissal of a Cabinet which enjoyed the confidence of the House of Commons and the electorate.

Thus, the complete theory and practice of the Cabinet system, as it emerged out of the eighteenth century, did not take its present form before the reign of Queen Victoria. "Under Peel, Disraeli, and Gladstone the system reached a kind of climax : indeed the classic exposition of its working is still a chapter in the *Life of Walpole,* written by one of Gladstone's colleagues (Morley) with his master's assistance."[15]

It is early to analyse the development of the Cabinet during the twentieth century. But two significant observations may be made here. The first is, that the membership of the Cabinet has increased from twelve or less to eighteen or more. Sir Robert Peel was content with thirteen members; Disraeli in 1874 tried as few as twelve. Since then the Cabinet has tended to grow steadily until recent times. With the expansion of the functions of government, it became a practice to include in the Cabinet the heads of all important Departments as well as number of Ministers without departmental duties, like the Lord President of the Council and the Lord Privy Seal, and sometimes even the Chancellor of the Duchy of Lancaster. Between the two world Wars the number was seldom less than twenty. In 1935, it was twenty-two. But there were constant complaints against the swelling size of the Cabinet. It was contended that a Cabinet of twenty-one or twenty-two members was too large for an effective deliberative body. A Cabinet, say of twelve persons, like Disraeli's in 1874, can amicably and conveniently settle questions by intimate discussion around a table. A Cabinet of more than a score, on the other hand, verges upon "a public meeting: it must have a formal procedure, a considerable committee organisation, a substantial secretariat, and so on. A small Cabinet can usually take decisions by a consensus of opinion, a large Cabinet may find it easier to take vote."[16]

Experienced statesmen prefer a small cabinet. Attlee reduced the number of his Cabinet Ministers to seventeen in 1949, Winston Churchill still further reduced it to sixteen in 1951, with a separate provision of 'ministers not in the Cabinet.' In 1962, there were twenty Cabinet Ministers and the number increased to 23 in 1964. In January 1967, it stood at twenty. In 1974, it again went upto 21 whereas Callaghan came down to 20. Mrs. Margaret Thatcher had 22 whereas John Major, who succeeded her in November 1990, had 21. The nomenclature of Ministers was adhered to in the succeeding Cabinets, except that holders of the most of the newly created posts by Wilson Government had the formal title of Ministers whereas those who held older posts had special titles for instance, the Chancellor of the Exchequer and the President of the Board of Trade. The holders of nine offices (some ancient and other of recent creation) were known as 'Secretaries of State.' The 'Ministers not in the Cabinet' carried the same status as the Cabinet Ministers, received all the Cabinet conclusions, except those of the utmost secrecy, and took their full share in the Cabinet Committees. But they participated in the deliberations of the Cabinet only when summoned, and matters concerning their Departments were under discussion.

Closely connected with it are two other phases. First, to cope with the increased work of the Cabinet, the system of standing Cabinet Committees, which discuss and settle all contentious matters, has been introduced on the extended scale. Secondly, the Labour Government began to meet twice a week whereas before the War one meeting a week was generally sufficient. The War Cabinet of 1940-45, also, met twice a week in the ordinary way, but naturally there were many more special meetings than in peace time, some of them late at night. Now it meets for a few hours once or twice a week during Parliamentary sitting, and rather less frequently

14. See ante, Chap. III.
15. Derry, K., *British Institution of Today* (1948), p. 41.
16. Jennings, W. I., *The Queen's Government,* p. 116.

when Parliament is not sitting. Additional meetings may be called by the Prime Minister at any time.

The second significant development of the twentieth century is that the Cabinet has sacrificed much of its party character at periods of national emergencies in the efforts to achieve national solidarity. Britain, it had always been argued and the same conviction holds good even now, hates a coalition, because it is deemed distortion of the parliamentary system of government. And yet in the inter-War period of about twenty-one years, four years were occupied by Lloyd George's Coalition Ministry surviving from the previous War, and eight years by the National Government headed by MacDonald, Baldwin and Chamberlain which carried on into succeeding War of 1939. There were also two periods of minority government—again a distortion of the parliamentary system—the Labour Governments of 1924 and 1929-31. Taking, thus, the whole period between 1918 and 1945, less than six years were occupied by governments of the normal type when there was one single-party government with a working majority.[17] In October 1974 the Labour Party won 319 seats out of a total of 635 membership of the Commons. But this precarious majority was soon eroded for one reason or another and Callaghan's minority Government remained in office with the support of the Liberal and Scottish Nationalist parties till it was defeated on a vote of no confidence when both these parties withdrew their support. In the General Election held in May 1979, the Conservative Party was given a clear mandate by the electorate winning 339 seats. Mrs. Margaret Thatcher, the first woman Prime Minister Britain had, formed the Government and she remained in office for 11 years and six months and after her resignation in November 1990 was succeeded by John Major, the Chancellor of Exchequer in her Cabinet. He was really her choice.

Whatever be the demerits of coalition government, this twentieth century development is characteristic of the adaptability of the British people. Jennings, while referring to the War coalition, points out that "the coalition which saved civilization between 1940 and 1945 seems to have been at least as united as the ordinary party government.[18] The National Government in 1932 maintained its unity by strange device of an "agreement to differ,"[19] an exception to collective responsibility.[20]

## PRINCIPLES OF CABINET SYSTEM

The Cabinet is, thus, a wheel within a wheel. Its outside ring consists of a party that has a majority in the House of Commons; the next ring being the Ministry, which contains men who are most active within that party; and the smallest of all being the Cabinet, containing the real leaders or chiefs. By this means is secured that "unity of party action which depends upon placing the directing power in the hands of a body small enough to agree and influential enough to control." The Cabinet is, in brief, the driving and the steering force. But despite its importance, it has no legal status as an organ of government. Its existence and working hinge s upon some well established customs, traditions and precedents. There is, however, one supreme virtue in it. The conventional character of the Cabinet makes it a highly flexible institution easily adjustable to meet emergencies or any other special circumstances. In fact, the stupendous success of the Cabinet system in Britain, for the past two and a half centuries, may be properly attributed to the Cabinet's high degree of adaptability. The whole system is based upon the fact that the government is carried on in the name of the King, by Ministers who are members of the majority party in Parliament, and are responsible to Parliament for all their public acts both individually and collectively. These important features of the Cabinet system which have now become classical need analysis.

### A Constitutional Executive Head

Cabinet government means that the King is no longer the directing and deciding factor responsible before the nation for the measures taken. The whole of the political and executive power of the Crown is exercised in the King's

17. These were Bonar Law and Baldwin Governments from October 1922 to January 1924 and the second Baldwin Government from November 1924 to June 1929. Normal single party Government was again restored in 1945 and it continued. The October 1959 elections with a very comfortable majority for the Conservatives ensured its continuance. The Labour Party in the election of October 1964 could secure a precarious majority of five only, but in the following General Election it was able to muster a comfortable majority.
18. Jennings, W. I., *Cabinet Government*, p. 247.
19. Refer to Laski's admirable thesis, *Crisis and the Constitution* (1932).
20. The "Samuel Liberals" disagreed with the tariff policy of their colleagues. For a time an "agreement to differ" was observed. Before long, however, they withdrew from the Government.

name by political men who belong normally to the majority party in Parliament. These political men can be criticised, attacked and compelled to answer questions, and they are liable to be turned out of office, if their policy is not approved by Parliament. As the King takes no part in politics, he does not participate in the confidential discussions in which his ministers decide the advice they will give him. In other words, the King does not preside over Cabinet meetings. The abstention of the King from Cabinet meetings was originally a matter of sheer accident, but it was a step of great constitutional importance in the development of the responsible Ministry. It does not, however, mean that the King has nothing to do with the Cabinet and what it does. As Jennings has said, the Monarch "may be said to be almost a member of the Cabinet, and the only non-party member."[21] Though, he keeps off the politics, yet he commands a position to influence the decisions of the political leaders constituting the government of the day. But it must be repeated that influence is not power and in the end the Monarch is bound by the Cabinet decision.

**Chosen from Parliamentary Majority**

Ministers are members of Parliament and, generally, in modern times, of the House of Commons, and they are chosen from that party which has a majority in that House. These two facts, taken together are of fundamental importance. The membership of Parliament gives to Ministers a representative and responsible character. It also binds together the Executive and Legislative authorities and there can be no working at cross purposes between these two organs of Government. The harmonious collaboration thus brought about ensures a stable and efficient government. Such a government is always responsive to the needs of the people. Moreover, Cabinet Ministers are leaders of the majority party in the House of Commons and, consequently, they must assume direction of principal activities of Parliament. This offers an effective opportunity to the Executive to present, to advocate, and to defend its views and proposals.

It is now a well-settled convention that Ministers should be either Peers or members of the House of Commons, though there had been exceptional occasions when Ministers held office out of Parliament. General Smuts was a Minister without Portfolio and a member of War Cabinet from 1916 and until the end of the War without his being a member of Parliament. Sir A.G. Boscawen, as Minister of Agriculture, is another identical case in 1922-23. Ramsay MacDonald and Malcolm MacDonald were both members of the Cabinet though not in Parliament from November 1935 until early in 1936. Patrick Gordon Walker was the Foreign Secretary in Wilson's Government till he was defeated in the by-election. "The House of Commons is, however extremely critical of such exceptions ....... In truth, the conduct of government business in the House of Commons is such a onerous task that the absence of an important minister places a considerable burden on the rest.[22] Even in the House of Lords the representation of many Departments, the piloting of their legislation, and the explanation of their policy demand the presence of a good number of Ministers and the Ministers of the Crown Act, 1965, recognises the principle that some Ministerial posts must be filled by members of the Lords. Practical convenience as well as constitutional convention, therefore, compels the Prime Minister to confer office only upon members of Commons or peers."[23] Ministers remain out of Parliament only while they are trying to find seats. If they cannot get in, and are unwilling to be created Peers,they resign from their offices.

Cabinet government means party government. This was explained by Professor Trevelyan in his Romanes Lecture. He said, "The secret of British Constitution as it was developed in the course of the eighteenth century was the steady confidence reposed by the parliamentary majority in the Cabinet of the day. If that confidence is withdrawn every few months government becomes unstable, and men cry out for a despotism, old or new. In eighteenth-century England the requisite confidence of Parliament in the Cabinet could have been obtained in no other manner than through the bond of a party loyalty held in common by the Cabinet and by the majority of the House of Commons."[24] Party provides the machinery which secures a stable government under a unified command of the politically homogeneous and disciplined leaders.

It was an easy task to form a Ministry from one single political party, which commanded the majority in Parliament, so long as there were only

21. Jennings, I., *Cabinet Government*, pp. 327-28.
22. *Ibid.*, p. 53.
23. *Ibid.*
24. As quoted in *The English Constitution* by Sir Maurice Amos, p. 70.

two political parties. With the emergence of the Labour Party in the beginning of the twentieth century,the position became a little uncertain because sometimes it might happen, as it did in 1924 and 1929, that no single party could command a majority with it in the House of Commons. Ramsay Mac Donald on both these times formed Govern- ment on the distinct support of the Liberal party. In times of national emergencies, as the two world wars, and grave crisis, like the Economic Depression of 1931, there were coalition Ministries. But it is a rare feature as a coalition government is essentially anomalous in Britain, because "it contradicts the fundamental principle that a Cabinet represents a party united in principle."[25] Coalition Government is a combination of strange bed-fellows who pursue rival policies and rival ambitions. The truth of the matter is that coalitions do not love each other and except in times of unusually abnormal political circumstances, the Government in Britain has always been a unified whole representing one single political party. The coalition formed in May, 1940, was a true National Government as it represented all parties. But its sole aim was the successful prosecution of the War and it failed to survive the defeat of Germany by more than a few weeks. At that point, disagreements about post-War reconstruction proved more fundamental than the common wish to go on to defeat Japan. The future of the two-party system, however, appeared bleak with the split in the Labour Party and formation of the Social Democratic Party in alliance with the Liberal Party. It was widely predicted that the three—party system had come to stay in Britain and coalition government might become the future norm. But the alliance was just short-lived and the Social Democratic Party itself could hardly make any headway. The old pattern of two-party system prevails with its past vigour.

**Leadership of the Prime Minister**

The Cabinet is a team which plays the game of politics under the captaincy of the Prime Minister. The Prime Minister, according to Morley "is the keystone of the arch." Although in the Cabinet all its members stand on an equal footing, speak with equal voice and act in unison, yet the Chairman of the Cabinet is the first among equals and occupies a position of exceptional and peculiar authority. He is the leader of the Parliamentary majority and all Ministers work under his accepted leadership. It is true that the Prime Minister is technically appointed by the King, but in practice the choice of the King is pretty strictly confined to a man who is designated as a leader of the party.

It is from the time of Walpole we have the convention that the Prime Minister selects his own Ministers. The Ministers, no doubt, are appointed by the King, but in actual practice they are the nominees of the Prime Minister. The King simply receives and endorses the list prepared and presented to him by the Premier.[26] If the Prime Minister has the power to make his Ministers, it is also his constitutional right to unmake them. The identity of the Ministers is not known without the Prime Minister. In 1931, Ramsay MacDonald tendered the resignation of his Cabinet without the knowledge of his colleagues and, in the words of Laski, "with the announcement of the national government the ministers learnt of their own demise." A party lives on party spirit and as an instrument of government it preserves its continuous corporate identity under the leadership of the Prime Minister. All this accounts for unity and close association between Ministers on the one side and the Cabinet and the parliamentary majority on the other. Or, as Barker says, "The unity and the corporate character is sustained and maintained by the dominance of the Prime Minister. This is the essence of Ministerial Responsibility."

**Ministerial Responsibility**

Ministerial responsibility is the first and foremost principle of the Cabinet system of government and collective responsibility is Britain's principal contribution to modern political practice. According to Birch the term " responsible Government " may be applied to the British political system in three main respects.[27] In the first place, it may be regarded as a characteristic of the British system that governments do not act irresponsibly. That is to say, they do not abuse wide legal powers which they possess. "In this sense, responsible government means 'trustworthy government', and is a general description of the British political culture."[28] Secondly, re-

25. Jennings, W. I., *Cabinet Government,* p. 246.
26. In 1945, King George VI "disagreed" with Clement Attlee on the appointment of Sir Hugh Dalton as Foreign Secretary and asked him to appoint Ernest Bevin in his place, which he did. *King's Diary,* quoted by Wheeler-Bennett in *George VI: His life and Reign,* p. 635.
27. Birch, A. H., *Representative and Responsible Government,* p. 131.
28. Punnett, R.M., *British Government and Politics, p. 178.*

sponsible government is responsive to public opinion, and it acts in accordance with the wishes of the majority of the people. The third and the most specific meaning of responsible government is that the government is answerable to Parliament for all its acts. This meaning is based on the principle that Ministers are members of Parliament and secondly, they must be drawn from the majority party and they remain in office so long as they can command the support of the majority of the members of the House of Commons. From this flow the doctrines of collective responsibility of the government and individual Ministerial responsibility to Parliament.

Ministerial responsibility to Parliament has two aspects : the collective responsibility of Ministers for the policies and actions of the Government, and their individual responsibility for the work of their Departments over which they preside, that is, a Minister incharge of a Department is answerable for all its acts and omissions and must bear consequences of any defect of administration. Both forms of responsibility are embodied in conventions. According to Birch, "Both conventions developed during the nineteenth century, and in both cases the practice was established before the doctrine was announced."[29] Woodward, too, states that in 1815, "the responsibility of the cabinet as a whole was difficult to establish", and that "no ministry between 1783 and 1830 resigned as a result of defeat in the House of Commons; no ministry before 1830 ever resigned on a question of legislation or taxation."[30]

Implicit in the doctrine of collective responsibility is the unity of the Government. Cabinet is a unit— "a unit as regards the Sovereign and a unit as regards the legislature." Cabinet Government is a Party Government and its members (Ministers) come into office as a unit under the leadership of a person whom the party acclaims. All Ministers stand for the political programme of the party and represent the uniformity of political opinion. They must, therefore, swim and sink together because the fall of the Ministry is the fall of the party and, consequently, its political programme.

The essence of the Cabinet is its solidarity; a 'Common front' and collective responsibility had its origin in the need for Ministers in the eighteenth century to represent a united front to the Monarch on the one hand, and to Parliament on the other. "Today, collective responsibility", writes Punnett, "enables the Government to present a common face to its party supporters inside Parliament, to the party outside Parliament, and to the electorate generally—the maintenance of a united Government front being an essential prerequisite of preservation of party discipline in the House, and to the answering of Opposition and public criticism of Government policy."[31]

Collective responsibility applies to all Ministers alike, from senior Cabinet Ministers to Junior Ministers and one who is not prepared to defend the Cabinet decision must resign.[32] General Peel and three other Ministers resigned because they did not agree with and support Disraeli's Reform Bill. Lord Morley and Burns resigned in 1914 as they could not approve of the decision to go to War. Sir Herbert Samuel and other Liberals, and Viscount Snowden resigned in 1932 because they could not support the Ottawa Agreement. Anthony Eden resigned in 1938 because he was unable to agree with the foreign policy adopted by Neville Chamberlain and the Cabinet. In 1950, when a Junior Minister not in the Cabinet criticised the Government's agricultural policy and resigned immediately afterwards, the *Economist* commented that he would "have been in a stronger position if he had resigned first and made his criticisms afterwards, rather than transgress an accepted rule of the Constitution."[33] In 1958, when the Chancellor of the Exchequer resigned because of the disagreement with other Ministers on the question of economic policy, the public could know the disagreement only when the resignation was announced. The practice, as established now, is that

29. Birch, A. H., *Representative and Responsible Government*, p. 131.
30. Woodward, E. L., *The Age of Reform*, p. 23.
31. Punnett, R. M., *British Government and Politics*, p. 178.
32. Lord Salisbury expressed this rule clearly in 1878 : "For all that passes in Cabinet, each member of it who does not resign is absolutely and irretrievably responsible, and has no right afterwards to say that he agreed in one to a compromise, while in another he was persuaded by the colleagues...........
........It is only on this principle that absolute responsibility is undertaken by every member of the cabinet who, after a decision is arrived at, remains a member of it, that the joint responsibility of Ministers to Parliament, can be upheld, and one of the most essential principles of parliamentary responsibility established." Cecil, Gwendolyn, *Life of Lord Salisbury*, Vol. II, pp. 219-220.
33. *The Economist*, April 22, 1950.

the doctrine of collective responsibility applies even to the unpaid Parliamentary Private Secretaries. In 1965, Frank Allaun, Parliamentary Private Secretary to the Colonial Secretary, resigned his post because he could not accept Government policy towards the crisis in Vietnam. In 1967, the Prime Minister forced a group of Parliamentary Private Secretaries to resign when they declined to support specific aspects of Government economic policy.[34] But this aspect of the convention was broken in the 1970's, when Prime Minister Wilson allowed ministers to remain in office, although they openly disagreed over the continuation of Britain's membership of the European Economic Community. The breach of the convention was logically acceptable, because the final decision was left to the nation in a referendum so that neither the ministers nor Parliament had responsibility for the decision. Mrs. Margaret Thatcher, however, dismissed the Navy Minister, Keith Speed, because he had not only opposed the proposed cuts in the department but had publicly criticised the Government policy. Hal Miller,Parliamentary private secretary to the Leader of the House, Francis Pym, resigned because he did not agree with the Government policy on the steel industry.

But if a Minister does not resign, then, the decision of the Cabinet is as much his decision as that of his colleagues even if he protested against it in the Cabinet. This means that the Minister must vote for the decision in Parliament and, if necessary, defend it either in Parliament or in public. He cannot rebut the criticism of his opponents on the plea that he did not agree in the decision when the matter was being discussed in the Cabinet. Lord Melbourne emphasised this aspect upon his colleagues after his Cabinet had come to a conclusion on the Corn Laws. He said, ''Bye the bye, there is one thing we have not agreed upon, which, is, what we are say. Is it to make our corn dearer or cheaper, or to make the price steady ? I do not care which : but we had better all be in the same story.'' That is to say, all Ministers should vote for the government and tell the same story wherever it was to be told. Gladstone would even insist that a Minister absenting at the time of division in Parliament should be censured.

The duty of the Minister is not merely to support the Government, but to refrain from making any speech which is contrary to the Cabinet policy or make a declaration of policy in a speech upon which there is no Cabinet decision.[35] In 1922, Edwin Montagu., the Secretary of State for India, was virtually dismissed, as he had permitted the Government of India to publish a telegram involving major policy without Cabinet sanction. In 1935, the Foreign secretary, Sir Samuel Hoare, was at least ''allowed'' by the Baldwin Government to resign, because his secret proposals with the French Premier, Laval, on the Italo-Ethiopian question had met with nationwide disapproval.[36]

The Cabinet is, thus, by its nature a unity and collective responsibility is the method by which this unity is secured. There is no other condition upon which that team work, which is the *sine qua non* of the Cabinet system,can become possible. All Ministers whether members of the Cabinet or not, share collective responsibility, including that for Cabinet or Cabinet Committee decisions in the reaching of which they have taken no part whatever. ''This may sound rather rough,'' wrote Morrison, and ''indeed from time to time it is. But the government must stand together as a whole and Ministers must not contradict each other, otherwise cracks will appear in the government fabric. That is liable to be embarrassing or possibly fatal,and indeed injurious to good government. All this is part of the contract of service. It has to be endured as condition of acceptance of office.'' Moreover, collective responsibility begets mutual confidence, and it makes possible that give-and-take in the shaping of policy without which any effective mutual confidence is rarely attained. There is still

34. In 1838, Lord Fitz Roy, the Vice-Chamberlain, was dismissed from his post for voting against the Government. In 1856, Queen Victoria asked Lord Palmerstone ''to make it clear to the subordinate members of the Government that they cannot be allowed to vote against the government proposal about the National Gallery tomorrow, as she hears that several fancy themselves at liberty to do so.''

35. The duty of the minister in respect of speeches was stated by Lord Palmerstone in a letter to Gladstone in 1864 : ''A member of the government when he takes office necessarily divests himself of that perfect freedom of action which belongs to a private and independent member of Parliament, and the reason is this, that what a Member of the Government does and says upon public matters must to a certain degree commit his colleagues, and the body to which he belongs if they by their silence appear to acquiesce; and if any of them follow his example and express publicly opposite opinions, which in particular cases they might feel obliged to do, differences of opinion between members of the same government are necessarily brought out into prominence and the strength of the government is thereby impaired.''

36. ''Subsequently action by the Cabinet showed that it really shared the Foreign Secretary's views, and in few months he was back as First Lord of the Admiralty. For the time being however, he was encouraged to make himself a scapegoat.''

another reason. If it were regarded as possible for a Cabinet Minister to free himself from the decision of his colleagues, after the course decided upon had proved unsuccessful or unpopular, both the trust and the secrecy which are so essential to the working of the Cabinet would be destroyed. This would further mean that the most private transactions in the Cabinet would of necessity be divulged to the public. "Such a position is really frightful, because it might lead to the emergence of another body to replace the Cabinet, as the Cabinet once upon a time replaced the Privy Council, as organ for the discussion of policy."

Collective responsibility means, then, that an attack on a Minister is attack on Government. It also means that members of the Cabinet express a common opinion, prudent and mutually consistent. To repeat the phrase of Lord Melbourne "they must all be in the same story." The theory of the Cabinet is that it must not disagree. Of course, it sometimes does, but not in public. To put it in the poignant words of Herbert Morrison, "It must not seem to disagree."[37] Ministers must aim at preserving not only the spirit "but the appearance of Cabinet solidarity."[38] Collective responsibility is associated with cognate principle of Cabinet secrecy. Disclosures of Cabinet discussions plague the Government and bring into open a Cabinet split. "A Cabinet split" as Jennings says, "may become a party split and a party split may lose the next election."[39]

The idea of collective responsibility, first developed in the eighteenth century as a protection for Ministers against the King, and then it grew as a device for maintaining the strength and unity of the party. In 1782, there occurred the first instance of the collective resignation of a Ministry, when Lord North resigned in anticipation of a certain parliamentary defeat. All his Ministers, with the one exception of the Lord Chancellor, resigned with him. Following this, Pitt did a great deal to develop conventions relating to collective responsibility[40] and by 1832, it was well-recognised. But the concept of "responsible government," that the Government should resign if it lost the confidence of Parliament, appears not to have been introduced "into British political debates until as late as 1829, and then in relation to Canada rather than Britain."[41] After the Reform Act, 1882, it came to be regarded as axiomatic that the Government must respond to a Parliamentary defeat on a major issue. Peel resigned in 1835 saying that he considered "that the Government ought not to persist in carrying on public affairs ........ in opposition to the decided opinion of a majority of the House of Commons."[42] Since then, collective responsibility of the Cabinet to Parliament has become a cardinal feature of British politics. The last instances where a single Minister resigned on an adverse vote of the House of Commons were those of Lowe in 1864, and Lord Chancellor Westbury in 1866. It does not, however, mean that no Minister does resign individually if ever he incurs the wrath of Parliament or his public transactions prove highly unpopular with the public. At an emergency session of Parliament on April 3, 1982 Mrs. Margaret Thatcher's Government was subjected to fierce attack on Argentina's occupation of Falkland islands and the criticism was mainly directed against the Foreign Secretary, Lord Corrington, and Defence Secretary John Nott. The Labour Opposition leader. Michael Foot, described the Government's conduct as "the great betrayal of the trust" reposed by the people of Falkland islands in Britain. The Foreign Secretary, along with his two colleagues at the Foreign Office, Humphery Atkins and Richard Luce, as also the Defence Secretary, John Nott, owned the responsibility for the crisis and resigned. The resignation of Lord Corrington and his two colleagues at the Foreign Office was accepted whereas the Prime Minister declined to accept Nott's resignation. Mrs. Margerat Thatcher felt that the debacle over Falkland islands was not so much the fault of Nott as he was relying on the information supplied to him.

If the causes of complaint were an official discretion or misconduct on the part of a Minister, he would be asked to resign voluntarily before his conduct comes under fire and is forced out of office by a hostile vote in the House. J.H. Thomas was asked to resign in 1936 because of the leakage in the budget.[43] Sir Hugh Dalton, the Chancellor of the Exchequor, had to resign because of

37. Herbert Morrison, *British Parliamentary Democracy,* p. 13.
38. *Ibid.*
39. Jennings, W. I., *The Queen's Government,* p. 119.
40. But in the first two years of his office, Pitt refused to resign despite numerous defeats in Parliament.
41. Birch, A. H., *Representative and Responsible Government, An Essay on the British Constitution,* p. 131.
42. As quoted in above, p. 135.
43. J. H. Thomas was the Colonial Secretary. He betrayed budget secrets to two friends. The information so conveyed enabled them to save themselves from some taxes.

similar indiscretion.[44] Sir Samuel Hoare resigned in 1935 before the House could condemn his Italo-Ethiopian proposals.[45] John Profumo, the War Secretary in the Macmillan Government, resigned because he had lied to the House of Commons in denying improper relations with the model, Christine Keeler. In a letter to the Prime Minister, Profumo wrote, "I have come to realize that by this deception, I have been guilty of a grave misdemeanour."

It is not possible, says Herman Finer, "to operate collective responsibility without a safety valve: individual scapegoats", and he assigns two reasons for it. First, there are more departmental policies and it becomes unreal to impute responsibility to all of them jointly. Secondly, if a Cabinet could be overthrown every time on trivial matters or it involved some error on the part of an individual Minister and Parliament was not prepared to condone it, it may mean too many reorganisations of the Cabinet. "It could not be tolerated, " concludes Finer, "in the British economic and social system, where a high degree of stability and continuity to policy is essential to the standard of living and the peace of mind of the population."[46]

If the question were on policy, then, the Government would, save in very exceptional cases, assume the responsibility of that policy, treating a hostile vote as a vote of no confidence in itself. Ogg and Zink graphically sum up this aspect of ministerial responsibility : "When a Minister either because of this own action or because of actions of a subordinate for which he is responsible falls into such predicament, he is not left by his colleagues merely to sink or swim while they look on from the distant shore. Either they jump in and push him under, or they haul him into their boat and accept his fate as their own; in other words, they repudiate him and throw him out before his trouble drags him down or they rally to his support and make common cause with him. The latter course is pursued far more frequently than the former—so much so that Cabinet solidarity, and, therefore, collective responsibility may normally be taken for granted."[47] L.S. Amery, a Cabinet Minister at various times between 1922 and 1945, puts it rather more succinctly. "The essence of our Cabinet system", he says, "is the collective responsibility of its members." All major decisions of policy are, or are supposed to be, those of the Cabinet as a whole. They are supported by speech and vote by all its members, and, indeed, by all the members of the Government in the wider sense of the world. The rejection or condemnation by Parliament of the action taken upon them affects the Cabinet as a whole, and is followed, if the issue is one of sufficient importance, by its resigna- tion. The secrecy of Cabinet proceedings, originally based on the Privy Councillor's oath and antecedent to collective responsibility, is in any case the natural correlative of that collective responsibility. It would obviously be impossible for ministers to make an effective defence in public of decisions with which it was known that they had disagreed in the course of Cabinet discussion."[48]

Birch, however, is of the opinion that while the doctrine of collective responsibility remains unchanged, its practical importance has been greatly reduced with the diminution of Parliamentary power as a result of the growth of party discipline."[49] "The idea underlying the doctrine of collective responsibility," he maintains, "is that the government should be held continuously accountable for its actions, so that it always faces the possibility that a major mistake may result in a withdrawal of Parliamentary support. In the modern British political system it does not happen."[50] A major blunder in the policy of the Government may lead to an immediate and sharp swing in the public opinion, but the Government thrives upon its Parliamentary majority and firmly holds on to office. The Government, thus, gets an "ample opportunity to recapture public support before the next general election is held." The Labour Government of 1945-50 survived through the fuel crisis of 1947, the collapse of its Palestine Policy in 1948, and the fiasco of the ground-nuts scheme in 1949. In 1950 it was returned to power, though with a reduced major-

44. Sir Hugh Dalton gave a reporter some advance information in the budget and this appeared in the reporter's newspaper fifteen minutes before the Chancellor of the Exchequer rose in his place in the House of Commons to deliver his budget speech.
45. Sir Samuel Hoare concluded a secret pact with Premier Laval of France that about half of Ethiopia be given to Italy with a view to ending the war then going on between Italy and Ethiopia.
46. Finer, H., *Government of Greater European Powers*, p. 151.
47. Ogg. F., and Zink, H., *Modern Foreign Governments*, p. 103.
48. Amery, L. S., *Thoughts on the Constitution*, p. 70.
49. Birch A. H., *Representative and Responsible Government*, p. 136.
50. *Ibid.*, p. 137.

ity. The Conservative Government of 1955-59 succeeded not only in surviving after the debacle of Suez, but winning an increased majority at the next election.

Birch, therefore, concludes "that the doctrine of collective responsibility does not occupy the place in the present political system that is commonly claimed for it." A crisis that would have brought down a Government "a hundred years ago now acts as an opportunity for its Parliamentary supporters to give an impressive display of party loyalty, and stimulates its leaders to hold on to the reins of power until public attention is diverted to a sphere of policy which puts the Government in a more favourable light." It, no doubt, ensures common front, but in the zeal to maintain it, the traditional sanctity which collective responsibility carried with it does not exist any more. According to the new usage of responsibility, "a government is acting responsibly, not when it submits to Parliamentary control but when it takes effective measures to dominate it."[51] If ever it permits members, as it did in 1936, on the question of capital punishment and in 1959, on the Street Offences Bill, a free vote, the Government is accused of "evading responsibility."[52]

**Secrecy and Party Solidarity**

The Cabinet is a secret body collectively responsible for its decisions. It deliberates in secret and its proceedings are highly confidential. The secrecy of Cabinet proceedings is safeguarded by law and convention. The Privy Councillors' Oath[53] imposes an obligation not to disclose Cabinet secrets. The Official Secrets Act of 1920, forbids communication to unauthorised persons of official documents and information and provides legal penalties for disclosures made as such.[54] But the effective sanction is neither of these two. The rule is primarily one of practice. Its theoretical basis is that a Cabinet decision is advice to the King and the monarch's sanction is necessary before its publication. Its practical foundation is "The necessity of securing free discussion by which a compromise can be reached, without the risk of publicity for every statement made and every point given away."[55] There must be, as Lord Salisbury said, "irresponsible licence in discussion,"[56] if mature, rational independent contribution to the process of policy making is desired from men who are engaged in a common cause and who come together for the purpose of reaching an agreement. It is, therefore, essential that Ministers deliberating in a Cabinet meeting should speak freely and frankly, "toss their thoughts across the table, make tentative propositions and withdraw them when the difficulties are pointed out, express their doubts without reserve, discuss personalities as well as principles.[57] This kind of discussion cannot be conducted in the public. Nor can anybody express his opinions without reserve if he knows that it is likely to be quoted in Parliament or in the press. Publicity reduces the independence of mind of Ministers in relation to each other and harmony of views becomes impossible if there is a chance that whatever they speak will be broadcast. Moreover, a knowledge of divergence of opinion offers vulnerable points to the attacks of the Opposition which is always on its toes to plague the party in power. Secrecy is of special urgency in these days of high nationalism and warlike friction between impassioned nations "so that the Cabinet's state of mind may not be made the

51. *Ibid.*, p. 138.

52 "On some issues where there is no clear party line, the members of government are sometimes allowed to join in the 'luxury' of a free vote, uninhibited by the Party Whips or by the doctrine of collective responsibility. Even on some occasion when back benchers are allowed a free vote, however, the government's collective view is often made clear. The government is expected to give lead on practically all issues, and for the government not to do so can be seen as an abdication of duty." Punnett, R. M., *British Government and Politics*, p. 180.

53. The main terms in the oath of the Privy Councillor deserve notice:
"You shall swear to be a true faithful servant unto the Queen's Majesty, as one of Her Majesty's Privy Council.......You shall, in all things to be moved, treated and debated in Council, faithfully and truly declare your Mind and Opinion according to your heart and conscience, and shall keep secret all matters committed and revealed unto you or that shall be treated of secretly in Council. And if any of the said Treaties or Councils shall touch any of the Councillors, you shall not reveal it unto him, but shall keep the same until such times as, by consent of Her Majesty, or the Council, Publication shall be made thereof."

54. Edgar Lansbury, son of the former Cabinet Minister George Lansbury, was fined in 1934 for publishing a memorandum submitted to the Labour Cabinet of 1929-31 by his father.

55. Jennings, W. I., *Cabinet System*, p. 248.

56. Lord Salisbury declared that privacy of discussion "could only be made completely effective if the flow of suggestions which accompanied it attained the freedom and fulness which belonged to private conversations—members must feel themselves untrammelled by any consideration of consistency with the past or self-justification in the future." Cecil, Gwendolen, *Life of Lord Salisbury,* Vol. II, p.223.

57. Jennings, W. I., *The Queen's Government*, p. 121.

subject of distracted and inflammatory debate until it has arrived at a considered policy". Secrecy is, thus, an essential part of the Parliamentary system. Secrecy helps to produce political unanimity and political unanimity is a very important condition of party solidarity, which in its turn assists secrecy. Both "help to concentrate responsibility on a single unit, the Cabinet, and since no exact discrimination appears before the real and supposed authors of a policy until long after the event, the more care has to be taken about the inclusion of people in the Cabinet, for no one may be included who is so incapable as to cause its better members to fall."

A difficulty obviously arises when a Minister or Ministers feel bound to resign as a result of serious Cabinet division. A Minister who resigns from the Cabinet usually desires to make an explanation in Parliament. Since this involves an explanation of Cabinet discussion, the Minister concerned must secure the permission of the King through the Prime Minister,[58] and it is always given. But the Minister's right is limited to the explanation of the circumstances which led to his resignation. It "gives no licence to make further disclosure."[59] He must not disclose other occasions on which he differed from the rest of the Cabinet. This is an important precaution. "Usually the issue on which a Cabinet Minister resigns is not an isolated incident. It is the culmination of a series of disagreements, the straw which broke the camel's back. If he gives a long history of disagreements the other members must disclose why they disagreed with him, and much of the procedure of the Cabinet will inevitably come into public discussion. Such discussion is not merely unfortunate for the party in power; it is undesirable in the public interest; for if there is a risk that his remarks will be discussed, no Minister will be able to speak freely and frankly.[60]

Some other means also exist by which more or less reliable information respecting views expressed or decisions taken often get out. "There are few Cabinet meetings," observes Laski, "in which the modern Press is not a semi-participant."[61] During the War of 1914-18, the representatives of the press were able to secure information from the Prime Minister's Secretariat in the "Garden suburb." Since then the Prime Minister or some other Minister, on his behalf, gives to the press a guarded statement, in order to promote opinion about the policy they intended to pursue. Professor Laski makes a bold statement when he says, "and there have been fewer Cabinets still in which some member has not been in fairly confidential relations with one eminent journalist or another."[62] Revelations also occasionally appear in writings of former Cabinet Ministers, especially when in a Cabinet crisis like that of 1931, Ministers are keen to have their position and the stand they took clarified.

Down to the time of the First World War no record was kept of matters discussed or actions taken in the Cabinet meetings. The taking of notes other than by the Prime Minister was long forbidden. The Ministers would simply indicate to their Departments what the decisions were if they could remember what exactly concerned their Departments.[63] This system of Cabinet proceedings, however, completely broke down under the stress of War and one of the first acts of Lloyd George was to institute a Cabinet Secretariat to organise the business of the War Cabinet. The Machinery of Government Committee in 1918 recommended that the Secretariat should be permanently maintained "for a purpose of collecting and putting into shape agenda, or providing the information and the material necessary for its deliberations, and of drawing up the result for communication to the departments concerned."[64] In 1922, Bonar Law desired to abolish it, but its utility by then had been clearly established and it was decided to continue with it

58. Lord Melbourne objected in 1834 to the King's giving consent without consultation with the Prime Minister. He maintained that for the King to act direct would be "subversive.....of all the principles upon which the government of their country has hitherto been conducted."

59. Lord Derby in 1878 received the Queen's permission to make an explanation to Parliament after his resignation. In reply to Lord Derby's explanation, General Ponsonby wrote : "Her Majesty expects that, whenever a Privy Councillor makes any statement in Parliament respecting proceedings in Her Majesty's Council, the Queen's permission to do so should first be solicited, and the object of the statement made clear; and that the permission thus given should only serve for the particular instance, and not be considered as an open licence."

60. Jennings, W. I., *The Queen's Government,* p. 121.

61. Laski, H. J., *Parliamentary Government in England,* p. 255.

62. *Ibid.*

63. During Asquith's Government it was quite common for a minister's private secretary to telephone to the Prime Minister's private secretary to ask what the decision had been.

64. As quoted in W. I., Jennings' *Cabinet Government,* p. 226.

though its functions were narrowly defined.[65]

Cabinet records are strictly confidential and no formal reports of proceedings are published.[66] Great care is taken to ensure the secrecy of the Cabinet minutes. The Secretary to the Cabinet has instructions that while drafting minutes he should avoid reference to opinions expressed by any individual member and to limit the minutes "as narrowly as possible to the actual decision agreed to." The minimum staff is employed in the reproduction of the minutes and all notes are destroyed as they are transcribed. Then, the copies are sealed immediately in special envelopes addressed to the Ministers, and law officers entitled to receive them. Theses envelopes are locked in the Cabinet boxes and delivered by special messengers. A record copy is kept in the Cabinet office under the immediate control of the Secretary.[67]

**Relationship with the Monarch**

One of the important powers of the Queen is to give her advice to the Cabinet and Prime Minister. She can correspond with and summon for consultation the prime minister as well as other ministers and even opposition leaders. The ministers patiently listen to her views and are influenced by them. MacDonald was influenced by the suggestions of the monarch to such an extent that he betrayed his own Party losing its sympathy and leadership. The Queen remains in constant touch with the Foreign Affairs Ministry and her influence on British foreign policy is not negligible. She not only meets members of the cabinet but can hold consultation with the opposition leaders. George V participated in this type of 'conspiracy' against the ruling Labour Party in 1931..

The monarch maintains close relationship with Defence Ministries and exercises influence in the appointments of senior military officers. When some military officers were threatening a civil war in 1914 on the question of freedom for Ireland, the king was considered a patron of these conspirators who were ready to resist the grant of home rule to the Irish people even by violence. That is why Dr. Jennings thought that the monarch is one of the most forceful members of the Cabinet, the weight of whose authority may ultimately impose a decision on the British government.

The Cabinet's relationship with the monarch remains shrouded in mystery. The public cannot know it during the reign of a particular monarch. Publication of records after the death of Queen Victoria, or Edward VII, or even George V have shown how they were constantly pressing their cabinets to accept their views on such significant issues as division of Ireland, the Bolshevik Revolution in Russia, Labour Cabinet's policies towards Egypt and India, formation of the National government in 1931 etc. Roger Fulford suggests that George VI opposed the appointment of Dalton to head the Foreign Affairs Ministry and prevailed upon Attlee to give the job to Conservative Bevin in 1945.

When the official biography of George VI is published, it may confirm the guess that he exerted the same pressure for the partition of India in 1947 with Churchill's support and Lord Mountbatten's complicity, who was related to him as his father, George V, did for the division of Ireland with Tory connivance. Those documents, which may enable us to evaluate the role of George VI in giving a reactionary orientation to the foreign policy of the Labour Government of 1945-51 are still not available for research. Similarly the actual nature of Elizabeth II's relationship with her cabinets cannot be fully known in her life-time.

The monarchy, as Laski says, is greatly eulogised by conservative writers on the British constitution. This is because he or she, due to his or her social upbringing, has natural preference for the conservative values and ideals. For a conservative cabinet, the Queen's weight in politics today amounts to a fragrant flower, but a Labour cabinet should be ready to receive her affectionate scoldings and pinpricks. If a really progressive Socialist government ever came to power in England determined to push an anticapitalist programme into a action, it will probably encounter stiff resistance from the queen.

---

65. The functions of the Cabinet Secretariat are :
    (a) to circulate the memoranda and other documents required for the business of the Cabinet and its Committees;
    (b) to compile under direction of the Prime Minister the agenda of the Cabinet and under the direction of the Chairman, the agenda of a Cabinet Committee;
    (c) to issue summons of meetings of the Cabinet and its Committees;
    (d) to take down and circulate the conclusions of the Cabinet and its Committees and to prepare the reports of Cabinet committees; and
    (e) to keep, subject to the instructions of the Cabinet, the Cabinet papers and conclusions.
    During World War II an Economic Section and a Central Statistical Office were added to the Cabinet Secretariat.
66. Two partial Reports were, however, published in 1917 and 1918.
67. Jennings, W. I., *Cabinet Government*, p. 254.

## CHAPTER V

# The Cabinet at Work

### Meetings of the Cabinet

The Cabinet now meets usually twice a week during sessions of Parliament and once a week out of it or possibly not at all during the autumn recess. Additional meetings may be called by the Prime Minister at any time, if a matter urgently requiring discussion should arise. It is not tied to any one place but ordinarily meets at 10 Downing Street, the official residence of the Prime Minister. Sometimes it meets in the Prime Minister's room at the House of Commons. The agenda for the meetings is prepared by the Cabinet Secretariat which is circulated among the members before they meet. A Minister who wishes to place an item on the agenda, after setting it with his officials that the matter is worth the Cabinet's consideration, writes a paper on it for the use of his colleagues. The Secretariat will print it and circulate it among all the members of the Cabinet, if possible a week before the meeting. The other Ministers look into it, partly for the general principles involved and partly for its probable effects on the Departments under their charge. They may discuss its implications with the Minister initiating the proposal for the policy or his officers in the Department and if they feel necessary print papers of their own on it for the Cabinet. It is from these communications that the Secretariat prepares the agenda in consultation with the Prime Minister.

The Prime Minister opens the meetings informally and he may bring any matter not on the agend, if he deems it necessary. The members discuss issues and reach decisions, avoiding details. As a rule, it concentrates on principles only. The Ministers discuss until agreement is reached. Votes are not taken. The Prime Minister interprets the consensus. ''That would be shocking !'' says Herbert Morrison, ''That would give the whole thing away. That would exhibit a disunity in the Cabinet''[1]

### Cabinet Committees

The burden of the Cabinet, as Finer says, is titanic. It cannot adequately meet its huge tasks. In its traditional form, it is a general controlling body and it usually meets twice a week and that too for a few, generally two, hours at a time. Then it, has too many members for effective discussion and many of them are departmental Ministers and they are too pre-occupied in their departmental duties. The Cabinet, therefore, neither desires nor is able to tackle all the numerous details of Government. The result is the emergence of the Cabinet Committees.

The origin of the system of standing Cabinet Committees can be traced back to the committee of the Imperial Defence, which was formed in 1902 as a permanent committee to supplement the Cabinet's general responsibility for defence. Cabinet Committees had been formed earlier too to deal with particular questions, but the Imperial Defence Committee was the first Standing Committee of the CAbinet. A Home Affairs Committee was created in 1919 and more Standing Committees emerged in the inter-War period. With the Second World War an extensive Cabinet Committee system was adopted as the basis of the means of co-ordinating the expanding governmental machine. Attlee retained this committee system in 1945, and he had some fifteen committees composed of Cabinet and non-Cabinet Ministers, each presided over by a senior member of the Cabinet.

Some of the Cabinet Committees are continuous and , thus, permanent bodies; other are ad hoc, i.e. created for single time-limited matter; dealing with a special problem or a critical situation and composed of the Ministers primarily concerned. They deliberate, report and disband. Some important Standing Committees of the

1. Morrison, Herbert, *British Parliamentary Democracy,* p. 14. If there is a narrow division of opinion and the Prime Minister does not know which side of the argument is in the minority, the problem is solved by the stratagem of ''collecting the voices.'' The Prime Minister ''goes right round the table saying to each Minister : 'Are you for or against'? This is collecting the voices. Somebody under the counter, so to speak, probably the Secretary of the Cabinet, is making a little slip and counting up those for and against. Certainly he adds up the figure on each side. Now that's not taking a vote. The British will not wish to admit doing naughty things even if we have to remedy matters 'under the counter'. So that is collecting the voice''. *Ibid.*

Cabinet are : (1) The Legislation Committee formerly known as the Home Affairs Committee. The functions of the Legislation Committee are to review legislation proposed by individual Ministers, make recommendations to the Cabinet on legislative priorities, set their time-table and to consider the Parliamentary procedure to be followed to help the passage of the Bill; (2) The Defence Committee is one of the largest and most important. It was first set up in World War II with the Prime Minister as Chairman. Its membership includes the Minister of Defence, the Lord President of the Council, the Foreign Secretary, the Chancellor of the Exchequer, the Minister of Labour, the Minister of Supply, the First Lord of the Admiralty, and the Secretaries of State for War, Air, Commonwealth Relations, and Colonies. It is advised by the Chiefs of Staff Committees consisting of the professional heads of the three military services. The Defence Committee concerns itself with the present and future defence problems, the preparation of plans over the whole field of government activity, both civil and military, for mobilising the entire resources of the nation in case of war and then the problems of reconstruction in the post-war period; (3) The Lord Presi dent's Committee, presided over by the Lord President; (4) The Economic Policy Committee, with the Prime Minister as Chairman; and (5) The Production Committee.

The number and composition of the Cabinet Committees are largely determined by the Prime Minister, and he is guided by his own working methods, the nature of the problems which his Cabinet faces, and the talents and temperaments of his ministerial associates. Names of the committee members and their chairmen are kept private. The chairmen of the committees are responsible to the Cabinet, and not to Parliament, for their role as committee chairmen. "Despite the anonymity," writes Punnett, "the chairmanship of a Cabinet Committee involves a lot of work, and the need to include in the Cabinet sufficient men capable of filling the role is one of the factors that a Prime Minister has to bear in mind when forming his government."[2]

"The Cabinet Committees," says Herman Finer "are deliberative or action-integrative, sometimes both,"[3] They provide a means whereby certain problems and issues can be studied and discussed by Ministers most concerned and some kind of compromise reached before they are brought before the whole Cabinet. It obviously assists consideration of a subject in Cabinet meetings if the principal issues involved have been identified and thrashed out by a small ministerial group and agreed recommendations submitted. Cabinet Committees are also useful to co-ordinate policy and administration. The political, economic, social and administrative implications of the most vexed and the complex problems can be investigated and ways and means devised to mobilize efforts for their fulfilment and, at the same time, help to eliminate conflicts or duplication of programmes. Moreover, committees can be employed to keep a critical problem under continuous review. It is neither possible nor desirable for the whole Cabinet to concentrate its attention on any aspect of national policy for an indefinite period of time. Finally, by including non- Cabinet Ministers the Committee system can extend the Cabinet's co-ordinating activity to wider areas of governmental affairs. It is not also uncommon for senior members of the permanent services to attend as advisers to their Ministers. There are certain Cabinet Committees which have no political importance and civil servants are made fullfledged members of these committees with the right to speak when they are asked for advice maintaining, of course, the responsibility of the Ministers for policy.

The Cabinet Committees, thus, combine two functions: co-ordinating the Departments, and decentralizing the policy. They customarily report to the whole Cabinet and seek to submit agreed reports and recommendations. But a Minister who is not satisfied with the recommendations of a committee can appeal to the Cabinet, where, under the chairmanship of the Prime Minister, differences are tried to be resolved. If the dissenting Minister still does not reconcile himself to the Cabinet decision, the only course left for him is to resign.

**Cabinet Secretariat**

We traced in the last Chapter the origin of the Cabinet Secretariat. Today, the Secretariat has become an indispensable part of the machinery of government. It prepares an agenda of business, under the guidance of the Prime Minister, to come before the Cabinet and circulates to Cabinet Ministers any memoranda or Cabinet

2. Punnett, R. M., *British Government and Politics*, p. 209.
3. Finer, H., *Governments of Greater European Powers*, p. 164.

Committees' reports that they must study before undertaking the discussion of items on the agenda of the Cabinet meeting. It keeps a record of the minutes and advises members of the decision reached in the meetings. It also serves the various Cabinet Committees and inte- grates their progress.

During the Second World War the Cabinet offices were expanded to include besides the Secretariat proper an Economic Section and a Central Statistical Office. The Economic Section maintains a constant watch on the economic trends and developments and advises the Cabinet as they affect the country and its people. It prepares the annual *Economic Surveys* of the nation's targets and the planning for production and capital investment. The Central Statistical Office was established "to produce a developing statistical series, general and comprehensive in nature, to be an index to economic, and social trends." It publishes the *Monthly Digest of Statistics.* In addition, a Central Policy Review staff has been appointed to work under the supervision of the Prime Minister, with and through Departments to assist Cabi- net Ministers collectively by providing them with an assessment of Government policies and programmes as a whole.

## FUNCTIONS OF THE CABINET

"Thus, the Cabinet is surrounded by expert help channelled to it or its committees or to individual Ministers, marshalled as and when the Cabinet needs it to be used as its wisdom requires. Going up to the Cabinet are sifted facts and sifted evaluations and ideas. From, it, outward and downward to the departmental officials flow will policies, and desires asking guidance, counsel, facts."[4] This is how the Cabinet is enabled to perform its arduous and complex functions of governance. The Report of the Machinery of Government Committee officially defined the functions of the Committee as :[5]

(i) The final determination of policy to be submitted to Parliament;

(ii) The supreme control of the national executive in accordance with the policy prescribed by Parliament; and

(iii) The continuous co-ordination and delimitation of the activities of the several Departments of the State.

### Policy-Determining Functions

The Cabinet is a deliberative and policy formulating body. It discusses and decides all sorts of national and international problems and attempts to reach unanimous agreements among members regarding the Government's policy concerning each. However much the members may disagree among themselves, they must present to Parliament and to the world a united front. If an individual member finds it impossible to agree with the conclusions of the Cabinet, the only course left for him is to resign.[6]

When the Cabinet has determined on a policy, the appropriate Department carries it out either by administrative action, with in the framework of the existing law, or by submitting a new Bill to Parliament so as to change the law in conformity to the policy. Legislation is, thus, the handmaid of administration and Cabinet is instrument, which, according to Bagehot, links the Executive branch of government to the Legislative. The Cabinet directs Parliament for action in a certain way and so long as it can command a majority in the House of Commons, it gets the approval of the sovereign organ of the State Parliament. This is how the Cabinet asks Parliament to take necessary steps with a view to carrying of the policy determined into effect.

These are essentially the legislative functions of the Cabinet. But we cannot make a vivid and precise distinction between legislation and administration. "In the modern state," writes Jennings, "most legislation is directed towards the creation or modification of ad- ministrative powers." The Cabinet, accordingly, plans the legislative programme at the beginning of each session of Parliament. Public Bills are introduced and piloted in Parliament usually by a Cabinet Minister or by some other Minister acting on Cabinet's approval. In legislation, the control of the Cabinet over the Ministry is complete for no Bill can be promoted except with its sanction, and the Legislation Committee of the Cabinet discusses at the beginning of each session what Bills shall be promoted in a session. In short, it is no exaggeration to say that the Cabinet legislates with the advice and consent of Parliament. Ogg has aptly said that Cabinet Ministers formulate policies, make decisions and draft Bills

4. Finer, H., *Governmentsof the Greater European Powers,* pp. 167-68.
5. The Committee was set up in 1918 to review the machinery of Government in Britain. It was presided over by Lord Haldane and is popularly known as the Haldane Committee.
6. No action was taken against Erie Heffer, Minister of State for Industry in Harold Wilson's minority government, when he publicly criticised sale of four warships to Chile.

on all significant matters which in their judgment require legislative attention, asking of Parliament only that it give effect to such decisions and policies by considering them and taking the necessary votes. As long as the Government has a majority in Parliament, it is rare to challenge Cabinet policy. The Cabinet takes office if it thinks it enjoys the confidence of Parliament, and once in office Cabinets tend to act as masters rather than servants of Parliament.

**Supreme Control of the Executive**

The Cabinet is not an executive instrument in the sense that it possesses any legal powers because it is entirely a product of non-legal conventions. Legally, the Executive power still vests in the King, though practically the Crown is the Executive. But the Crown is rather a concept than a tangible authority. The real authority that acts for the Crown and in its name are Ministers. These Ministers, except for the holders of three or four sinecure offices,[7] preside over the major Departments of government and carry out the policy determined by the Cabinet and approved, by Parliament. In carrying out the work of their Departments, Ministers, whether in the Cabinet or not, scrupulously follow the directions of the Cabinet and enforce its decisions and policies. Any deviation thereform is against the rigid discipline of the party government and may consequently lead to the removal of Minister.

As heads of the Departments, the Ministers are responsible for the policies pursued by their Departments and for their administrative efficiency. They decide policy issues that arise in their Departments, give instructions to their principal subordinates and supervise the Departmental activities to such an extent as to enable them to know that their Departments work in the desired direction. The Ministers are also answerable to Parliament for all acts of omission and commission and, accordingly, they must look for the efficient management of departmental business and see that it is responsive to the needs of the people. John Staurt Mill appropriately said that the Minister must receive "the whole praise of what is well done, the whole blame of what is ill"[8] in the work of his Department, and that in consequence he must resign if serious blunders are exposed.

The Cabinet may adopt the device of Orders-in-Council, instead of going to Parliament for approval, to give effect to some more general line of policy including even a declaration of war. Both the World Wars were declared by Orders-in-Council. The supreme national executive is, therefore, the Cabinet. The power of delegated legislation has still more enhanced Cabinet's Executive authority. Parliament may give to the King-in-Council, to individual Ministers of the Crown or to other persons or bodies the right to make rules and regulations. Legislation, during recent times, has become more voluminous and more technical. Parliament frequently passes laws in skeleton form, leaving it to the Cabinet or Ministers to fill the gaps and make rules and regulations in order to give effect to those laws as and when need arises.

**Cabinet as Co-ordinator**

The essential function of the Cabinet is to co-ordinate and guide the functions of the several Departments of Government. Administration cannot be rigidly divided into twenty or more Departments. The action of one Department may affect the work of another Department and, indeed, every important problem cuts across departmental boundaries. A foreign policy decision must often be made in relation to defence and trade policy. An educational policy decision may affect health, labour or taxation policy. Even if no other Department is affected, it certainly concerns the Treasury Department. The Cabinet does the vital task of co-ordinating policy and its implementation. "This means not only the linking of specific administrative decisions by reference to a general policy, but the expression of the same general policy in legislation." On purely inter-departmental matters the Departments endeavour to resolve their differences and try to reach agreement. If they cannot agree, the Prime Minister might act as an arbitrator and co-ordinator. In the last resort, there is appeal to the Cabinet.[9]

The emergence of the Cabinet Committees and the increased problem of co-ordination has

7. Non-Departmental Ministers are : The Lord President of the Council, the Chancellor of the Duchy of Lancaster, the Lord Privy Seal, the Paymaster-General and Ministers without Portfolio.
8. Mill, J. S., *Consideration on Representative Government,* p. 246.
9. The Cabinet instructions are that proposals affecting other Departments must not be submitted to the Cabinet until they have been thoroughly discussed with those Departments at the official level and if necessary with the Ministers. Wherever there is a conflict of interests between Departments, it should not be submitted to the Cabinet unless all possibilities of agreement at lower level have been explored and exhausted, Jennings, W. I., *Cabinet Government,* p. 228.

brought about a significant expansion in the work of the Cabinet office. The Prime Minister and the Chairmen of the Cabinet Committees now primarily rely upon the corps of expert assistants in the Cabinet Secretariat to supply them with the requisite information and advice in integrating the work of the different departments. The functions of the Cabinet Secretariat, *inter alia,* are: to take down and circulate the conclusions of the Cabinet and its Committees and to prepare the reports of Cabinet Committees. "The Cabinet Secretariat," writes Herbert Morrison, "has now become an important element in the organisation of Government. It serves not only the Cabinet but also its Committees and at times, *ad hoc* meetings of selected Ministers to settle a particular matter which may be a subject of inter-departmental disagreement."

Apart from the Cabinet Committees, the most ambitious post-1945 experiment in the co-ordination of government Departments was the system of "Overlords" introduced by Sir Winston Churchill in his 1951-55 Government. In the 1951 Cabinet of sixteen members, formed by Churchill, there were six Peers three of whom were "Overlords" entrusted with the task of co-ordinating various Departments. Lord Leathers was Minister for the Co-ordination of Transport, Fuel and Power; Lord Cherwell was Pymaster-General and he was to Co-ordinate scientific research and development; and Lord Woolton, Lord President of the Council, was to co-ordinate the work of the Ministry of Agriculture and Fisheries and the Ministry of Food. Lord Alexander was made Minister of Defence in 1952 thereby increasing the number of "Overlords' to four. The object of Churchill's scheme was to group and co-ordinate the Departments by means other than the Cabinet Committee system and to reorganise the nature and structure of Cabinet composition.

But there were a number of weaknesses in the system, especially the confusion that it caused as to who was the responsible Minister, the Departmental Minister or the "Overlord". Since the "Overlordis" were Peers and not accountable to the House of Commons, the Opposition attacked the system as it threatened the authority of the House of Commons. After the 1952 Transport crisis, the experiment of "Overlords" was gradually abandoned.

**Cabinet and the Budgets**

Two more functions may be added to those enumerated above :

The Cabinet is responsible for the whole expenditure of the State and for raising necessary revenues to meet it. The annual Budget Statement is excluded from the scope of the Cabinet decisions, but being a matter of political importance, it is always brought before the Cabinet and the Chancellor of the Exchequer makes an oral statement about it a few days[10] before his Budget speech in the House of Commons. The reason for this peculiar procedure is the fundamental importance of secrecy. But it is within the discretion of the Cabinet to ask for longer notice and effective discussion.[11] On the estimates, the control of the Cabinet is complete.[12] With regard to new proposals for taxation, if they involve any major change of taxation policy, they must be considered at length before the Budget is produced. Winston Churchill said in 1937, that "although the general layout of financial policy should emanate from the Chancellor of the Exchequer personally, and should be submitted to the Cabinet only in its final form, there ought to be, and there nearly always has been a special procedure in respect of new and novel imposts......... It would be in my opinion, a departure from custom, for any Chancellor of the Exchequer to present to a Cabinet, only a few days before the opening of the Budget, some great schemes of new taxation, which had not been examined." Moreover, the Cabinet can always insist on modifications after the Budget has been presented to Parliament. The Cabinet can also overthrow a Budget altogether, at the risk of the resignation of the Chancellor of the Exchequer, in deference to parliamentary or public opinion.

But Mrs. Margaret Thatcher, fearing opposition to her £ 33 billion deflationary budget, which had raised taxes all around, avoided holding any pre-budget Cabinet meeting to discuss the Government's overall economic strategy. By thus springing a surprise on her colleagues she grievously undermined the principle of collective cabinet responsibility, demanding their loyalty without respecting their views. Lord Carrington,

10. The usual time is four or five days.
11. In 1860 the Cabinet asked for details of Gladstone's Budget a month before it was announced. As the financial year had not then closed, Gladstone was unable to agree, but he gave a week's notice.
12. It was a result of Cabinet disagreement on the estimates that Lord Randolph Churchill resigned in 1866 and Gladstone in 1894.

Lord Soames, Sir Francis Pym, Ian Gilmour, Jim Prior and Walker, all senior Cabinet Ministers, were extremely unhappy with the Prime Minister's methods and her monetarist policies. The budget provoked open rebellion in the Conservative Party. At the end of the four-day budget debate in the House of Commons, the Government's proposal to impose a 15 per cent increase in petrol taxes was passed by 295 votes to 281, a margin of only 14 when her Government had a majority of 44. Eight Conservative MPs voted against the Government while 25 others abstained. Brocklebank-Fowler caused a sensation by crossing the floor to join the ranks of the Labour dissidents who soon formed the Social Democratic Party.

**Cabinet and Appointments**

Appointments do not normally come before the Cabinet. But all major appointments to great offices of the State, at home and abroad, are the responsibility of the Cabinet. The employment of a member of the Royal Family as Governor-General must always be dealt with by the Cabinet. Similarly, certain key positions like the Secretaryship to the Treasury, and the Chief Planning Officer might be made with the approval of the Cabinet. In the case of the Viceroy of India, the Cabinet had on several occasions intervened because this post had always been considered of special importance. In the case of Sinha's appointment to the Governor-General's Council the Cabinet was consulted. "The King objected to the principle of appointing to that Council any Indian and only agreed to the appointment when the Cabinet unanimously advised that the appointment should be made as part of the reform scheme in India."

**Dictatorship of the Cabinet**

"A body which wields such powers," observes Ramsay Muir, "as these may fairly be described as 'omnipotent' in theory, however, incapable it may be of using its omnipotence. Its position, whenever it commands a majority, is a dictatorship only qualified by publicity. This dictatorship is far more absolute than it was two generations ago."[13] A Government which has a real majority can be reasonably certain of maintaining itself in power as long as Parliament lasts. This almost mechanical source of power makes Cabinet a powerful institution. It determines how most of the time available in the House of Commons shall be used. It decides which proposals to change the law it will submit to Parliament. Then, it possesses the means to see that all measures so submitted become the Acts of Parliament. The rigidity of the party discipline enjoins upon all members to attend Parliament at the crucial moment of voting and the "energy of whip's organisation" assures blind support to the party. Woe betide a member who has no satisfactory explanation for ignoring a three line whip. But the most effective weapon to keep the House under control is the Prime Minister's power of dissolution. The dissolution, as Jennings says "can hold the member's head like a big stick." No individual member likes to take the risk of an election contest. It demands both time and money and at the end of it he may not be returned. There is, therefore, unflinching obedience to the Whip and so long as the rank and file of the Government supporters obey the Whip, the Cabinet will remain supreme. Amery had maintained that Parliamentary Government was already dead and had been replaced by Cabinet government. Summing up the whole process of development Brogan and Verney maintain : "The struggle of the seventeenth century was between the House of Commons and the King. More recently the Commons have fought the Lords, and in both battles the Commons was triumphant. Or at least it appeared to be. It is apparent today, as it was not to Bagehot a hundred years ago, that much of the power has in fact been transferred not to the Commons but to the Cabinet."[14]

Flushed with the majority and intoxicated with power, a Government, can press unplatable measures on the House of Commons. It might even violate the solemn pledges which it made at the time of the General Election, as it happened in 1938. The Conservative Party, in 1935, won a heavy majority in the House of Commons on its professions of fidelity to the League of Nations and its unequivocal condemnation of the rape of Abyssinia by Italy. The Party's election manifesto, *inter alia*, stated, "The League of Nations will remain, as heretofore, the keystone of British foreign policy.......We shall, therefore, continue to do all in our power to uphold the Covenant and to maintain and increase the efficiency of the League. In the present unhappy dispute between Italy and Abyssinia, there will be no wavering in the policy we have hitherto pursued." In later years, the Government followed a policy which

13. Ramsay, Muir, *How Britain is Governed*, p. 89.
14. Brogan, D. W., and Verncey, D. V., *Political Patterns in Today's World, p. 75.*

was a grave departure from the principles of the League and a complete violation of the promises given by the Conservatives at the time of the General Election. Britain was negotiating under an ultimatum with Italy, although the latter had violated the League Covenant in Abyssinia and was making frantic efforts to make Spain its protectorate in pursuance of its policy of establishing Italian hegemony in the Mediterranean, and replacing Britain in control of Egypt and the Suez Canal. "If this is to be taken as a precedent," observed Keith, "then, any Government can feel fully entitled boldly to ignore, if in power, any limitation imposed upon it by the terms of its election promises."[15]

Then, once in power the Government is subject to no Parliamentary limitation, except the Standing Orders under which the House of Commons functions. These Standing Orders are not Statutes. They are passed by the House of Commons alone by means of majority resolutions. A Government can, so long as it continues to command its majority, alter these Orders when it wishes in order to facilitate the passage of its measures. This danger was much in evidence during the tenure of office of the Labour Government of 1945-50. The Government wedded to a programme of nationalisation pushed it too fast in Parliament. It applied guillotine to the proceedings on the Transport Bill and the Town and County Planning Bill both in the Standing Committee and in the subsequent stages in the House of Commons. It was for the first time in the history of the House of Commons that such a drastic procedure had been applied to proceedings on a Bill in the Standing Committee. "As a result, 37 Clauses and 7 Schedules of the Transport Bill were not discussed at all in the Standing Committee, and the discussion on several more was cut short by the guillotine. In the case of the Town and County Planning Bill, about 50 Clauses and 6 Schedules were not discussed at all in the Committee. On the Report stage the guillotine was applied again."[16] While summing up these episodes Professor Keith remarked, "What is clear, however, is that a Government, with a large majority is limited in its legislative programme only by its own good sense and its respect for those rules of debate which generations of men in all parties have agreed upon."[17] It is further argued that debates are mere formalities, tolerated by the Government only because they do not affect the result in the lobby division.

There are bitter criticisms of the growth of delegated legislation and of the consequential growth of Administrative Law and it is maintained that the Rule of Law and freedom of the citizens are gravely menaced by these developments. "When the legislature confers," says Barker, "a measure of legislative powers on the executive it takes something away from itself; but when it confers upon the executive a measure of judicial power, it is diminishing not itself, but an organ other than itself." Delegated legislation and administrative justice have, therefore, immensely added to the powers and supremacy of the Cabinet.

It does not, however, follow, and "it is not true," as Jennings observes, "that a government in possession of majority forms a temporary dictatorship."[18] The House of Commons is not a place in which a victorious party exhibits its unchecked authority and dictates to the defeated and politically important minority. Nor can it remain oblivious of outside influences. The process of Parliamentary government involves parliamentary forbearance. The minority agrees that the majority should govern, and the majority agrees that the minority must criticize. The Standing Orders are, no doubt, constructed to ensure that the will of the majority shall prevail. But the Orders do not present the complete picture of the Government's position. They are supplemented by the customs of the House. The customs of the House demand a scrupulous observance and respect by the majority for those rules of debate "which generations of men in all parties have agreed upon." Originally, these customs arose for the protection of the individual member of the House and today they continue for the "Private Member," as he is still called, and, as such, for His Majesty's Opposition. The Speaker is the impartial custodian of the rights of the members of the House. His conduct really reflects the spirit which, according to Brier, is ultimately more important than the forms of government.

The customs of the House very considerably modify the rigours of the majority rule. Take, for example, the Standing Order relating

15. Keith, A. B., *The British Cabinet System*, p. 248.
16. *Ibid.*
17. *Ibid.*, p. 249.
18. Jennings, I., *Cabinet Government*, p. 442.

to a Private Member's right to put questions to Government in order to elicit information on any matter of public importance or with regard to administration. So important is this right that the Select Committee on Parliamentary Procedure maintained in its Report that the exercise of the right of asking questions "is perhaps the readiest and most effective method of parliamentary control over the action of the executive. But custom goes much further." Parliamentary time is allowed to the Opposition so that it may criticise the Government's work. The various stages through which a Bill passes in its career in the House-the First and Second Readings, Committee Report, and Third Readings-are arranged with this end in view. In the Committee of Supply the choice of subjects for discussion rests with the Opposition. The actual time to be spent on various stages of business is, as far as possible, arranged "behind the Speaker's Chair" or through the usual channels; that is to say, the Government and Opposition Whips, in consultation with their respective leaders, settle the time to be allowed by informal discussion. They even settle the subjects to be debated, the information to be provided and the line of attack.

His Majesty's Opposition is second in importance to His Majesty's Government. The public duty of the Opposition is to oppose. It must attack upon the Government and upon individual Ministers. Diligent performance of this duty by the Opposition is the major check which the Parliamentary system provides upon corruption and defective administration. It is also the means by which individual injustice can be prevented. The Government, too, recognizes its duty that it must govern openly and honestly, and that it should meet criticism not by suppressing Opposition, but by rational arguments which should have the approbation of the electorate. A Government which does not respect the traditions of the House and neglects the Opposition does so at its own peril. His Majesty's Opposition is the prospective Government. The lapses of the Government are its opportunities and it uses them to appeal to the public opinion. "The House is its platform, the newspapers are its microphones, and the people is its audience." The Government which loses the popular support will ultimately lose its majority and when majority disappears, the government, too, will disappear. The Cabinet, no doubt, is normally the master of the House of Commons, but, as Laski, says "there are always limits to its mastery of which it must take account."[19]

Nor is the Government insensitive to the reaction of its own followers. It is true that a member of Parliament is returned on the party support and his political career depends upon the support he gives to his party. But it does not mean that he is entirely docile and immune to influences other than of his party leaders. He is in constant touch with his constituency and keeps himself abreast with the flow of public opinion therein. If he feels that the popularity of the Government is receding, he becomes clamorous because it means a fall in his electoral support. Then, there are interest-groups within the party. These groups maintain a constant watch on the activities of Government and they are vocal on issues that concern them. Thus, the government works against a background of constant outside appraisal which also finds its echo in the lobbies of the House and it is a function of the Whips to keep informed on trends of opinion both in the country and in the House. Signs of unrest in the constituencies, amongst interested groups, or on the part of sufficient number of backbenchers, may lead to changes in a Government's plans and proposals. A Government which is not susceptible to those influences and does not alter its direction is not a government of the people and by the people. It ignores the maxim of parliamentary democracy that tomorrow is the day of election.

The Cabinet is, therefore, the supreme interpreter of majority opinion and it rules both majority and minority. It dare not ride roughshod over public opinion. The ultimate appeal rests with the people, and it must remember those to whom it will have to account in the future as well as those who entrusted it with power. In 1934, there was a great outcry against the provisions of the Incitement of Disaffection Bill. The National Government had an unprecedented majority and, no doubt, the Bill was passed, but the Bill as passed was very different from the Bill as presented; and public opinion had amended it. So, spontaneous was the outburst against the Anglo-French proposal for a settlement of the Italo-Ethiopian dispute in December 1935, that the Cabinet was forced to reverse its decision. It "felt that there could not be that volume of public opinion which it is necessary to have in a democ-

19 Laski, H. J., *Reflections on the Constitution,* p. 96.

racy behind the Government in a matter so important as this.'' Sir Samuel Hoare, the Foreign Secretary, resigned because, as he put it, he had not ''got the confidence of the great body of opinion in the country, and I feel that it is essential for the Foreign Secretary, more than any other Minister in the country to have behind him the general approval of his fellow- countrymen. I have not got that general approval behind me today, and as soon as I realized that fact, without any prompting without any suggestion from anyone, I asked the Prime Minister to accept my resignation.'' In 1940, public opinion compelled the Government under Neville Chamberlain to resign. Again, in 1946 the Government had to concede considerable alterations over the powers and functions of the Steel Board. In the Suez crisis of 1956, the Government had ultimately to bow before the public opinion. Members of Parliament, too, have not completely surrendered themselves to the Party and they protest, though it is quite rare, against the policy of the Government. In February 1962, for instance, three conservative M.Ps voted against the scheme for reorganisation of Greater London. In May 1963, fifteen Conservative M.Ps either abstained or voted against the Government decision to deport Chief Enaharo to Nigeria. In 1988, Prime Minister Margaret Thatcher suffered her most embarrassing rebuff when 38 members of her own Conservative Party joined Opposition members in voting against the controversial tax legislation that sought to impose a flat rate local tax on all adults. Another 12 abstained inspite of heavy pressure from Government Whips. The Bill could pass with a majority of 25 votes only 320-295. ''Defections of this kind,'' says Brasher, ''are not followed by the immediate retribution of the withdrawal of the whip. For the Conservative Party particularly, if any penalty at all is incurred it is more likely to be the penalty of not being readopted for the next election than expulsion from the Parliamentary party......Even when the Chief Whip interviews M.Ps hostile to some aspect of Government policy his primary purpose is persuation rather than coercion.''[20] Laski, has, therefore, said that ''the public feeling is always a fact in determining the breaking-point of members' loyalty to the Cabinet they normally support.''[21]

The fate of the Government today, as before, is normally determined by a General Election and not by a vote in Parliament. The real function of Parliament is not to govern but to see that it governs according to the wishes of the people. The Cabinet leads Parliament and the country on the clear understanding that the Government is not the master but the servant of the people. It was cogently said by Bagehot that the real function of Parliament was to ''express the mind of the people'', to ''teach the nation what it does not know'' and to make the people ''hear what we otherwise should not.'' This Parliament does admirably well.

Yet, it cannot be denied that changing political, social and economic circumstances in modern Britain demand a strong Executive. It requires additional powers to meet additional demands, but such powers are used, in general, with discretion, and with the full realisation that the Cabinet is answerable to Parliament, and ultimately, to the electorate itself. Moreover, as Brasher says, '' there are restraints on the Cabinet less tangible than so far described, but more effective. These are the restraints which spring from the habitual attitudes of governors and governed, from conventions, from tacit assumptions on what constitutes a reasonable degree of Government control over the activities of the people it rules. These are the real limitations on Cabinet authority. Their effectiveness will last as long as public opinion is sufficiently educated to recognise them.''[22]

## THE PRIME MINISTER

### Informal Basis

''The Prime Minister '', said John Morley, ''is the keystone of the Cabinet arch.'' It would, however, be more accurate, says Jennings ''to describe the Prime Minister as the key-stone of the Constitution.'' The phrase is as precise as it is picturesque, for, as Jennings, again says,''All roads in the Constitution lead to the Prime Minister. From the Prime Minister lead the roads to the Queen, Parliament, the Ministers, the other members of the Commonwealth, even the Church of England and the Courts of law.''[23] The Prime Minister is by far the most powerful man in the country. He has been the principal benefi-

20. Brasher, N. H., *Studies in British Government,* p. 25.
21. Laski, H. J., *Reflections on the Constitution,* p. 96.
22. Brasher, N.H, *Studies in British Government,* pp. 34-35.
23. Jennings, W. I., *The Queen's Government,* p. 40.

ciary of the Cabinet's growth in power. The prerogatives lost by the King have fallen for the most part into the Prime Minister's hands. Those which have not been acquired by him have gone to the Cabinet. But the Prime Minister "is central to its formation, central to its life, and central to its death."[24] He forms it; he can alter it or destroy it. "The Government", as Greaves puts it, "is the master of the country and he is the master of the Government."[25]

And yet the office of the Prime Minister remained unknown to the law until recently. Like the various other institutions of the country, it is the result of mere accident, the child of chance. No statute settled the status of the Prime Minister and his salary is still drawn in part as First Lord of the Treasury, an office bound up with Premiership since 1721.[26] Not until 1878 did the term make its appearance in any public document when Lord Beaconfield who signed the Treaty of Berlin was referred to in the opening clause as "First Lord of Her Majesty's Treasury, Prime Minister of England". This designation, in the opinion of Sir Sidney Low, was just "a concession to the ignorance of foreigners, who might not have understood the real position of the British plenipotentiary if he had been merely given his official title.[27] It was only in 1906 that the formal position in the order of precedence in State ceremonials was accorded to the office. The Prime Minister was made the fourth subject of the realm, just after the Archbishop of York. The Chequers Estate Act, 1917 referred to "the person holding the office popularly known as Prime Minister" and provided for the use of Chequers by the incumbent of the office.[28] The Ministers of the Crown Act, 1937, recognised for the first time, the office of the Prime Minister by giving him the salary of £10,000 a year as Prime Minister and First Lord of the Treasury.[29] The Ministerial Salaries and Members' Pensions Act, 1965, and the Ministerial and Other Salaries Act, 1972, reiterated it. But these provisions do not confer any powers on the Prime Minister. "These are casual recognitions of a constitutional situation, not the legislation of that situation." The Prime Minister has no legal powers as such. His powers are derived from and are limited by constitutional conventions. Basically it is as true today as when Gladstone said it that "nowhere in the wide world does so great a substance cast so small a shadow; nowhere is there a man who has so much power, with so little to show for it in the way of formal title or prerogative."[30]

**Choice of the Prime Minister**

The formation of a Cabinet depends essentially on the Royal choice of a Prime Minister. During the eighteenth century, it frequently happened that there was no proper cohesion within the Cabinet and the royal favour was as necessary as the popular support for the Chief Minister of the Crown. In the early part of the reign of George III an attempt was made to reassert the power of the King, the object being to choose such Ministers as were acceptable to himself. This attempt failed and by 1832 the position of the Prime Minister as the leader of the predominant party in the House of Commons had become recognised.[31]

It is a well-settled rule now that the Prime Minister must be either a Peer or a member of the House of Commons. Every Prime Minister since Sir Robert Walpole has been in one of the Houses. No Peer had been Prime Minister since the resignation of Lord Salisbury in 1902. In 1923, the question, whether a Peer should be a Prime Minister, was definitely raised. The resignation of Bonar Law left the King with a choice between Lord Curzon and Stanley Baldwin. Long before this it had been felt that the Prime Minister must belong to the House which made and unmade a government. It had also been asserted that the House of Commons had a right to expect that " its chief representative should be within its influence and personally accountable to it."[32] Curzon, no doubt, was a Peer, but it was not the only issue.

24. Laski, H.J., *Parliamentary Government in England,* p. 228.
25. Greaves, H. R. G., *The British Constitution,* pp. 108-09.
26. "The Prime Minister", declared Balfour, "has no salary as Prime Minister, his name occurs in no Acts of Parliament, and though holding the most important place in the constitutional hierarchy, he has no place which is recognised by the laws of his country. This is a strange paradox." As quoted in Marriot's *English Political Institutions,* p. 85.
27. Sidney Low, *The Government of England,* p. 156.
28. Chequers is now the official country house of the Prime Minister.
29. ....There shall be paid to the person who is Prime Minister and First Lord of the Treasury an annual salary of ten thousand pounds."
30. Quoted in Marriot's *English Political Institutions,* p. 86.
31. For the choice of the Prime Minister see Chapter III, *ante.*
32. Hercourt quoted in Jennings *Cabinet Government,* p. 22.

The scales were heavily weighted against him because of his personality.[33] Both these factors put together resulted in the selection of Stanley Baldwin, whose Cabinet experience was limited to eight months of Bonar Law Government, as Prime Minister. It is claimed that the decision of the King was finally determined by the advice given by Earl Balfour,[34] although George V had also consulted other prominent Conservatives including Lord Long, Lord Salisbury and L.S. Amery. Lord Stamfordham, on behalf of the King, explained to Lord Curzon that "since the Labour Party constituted the official Opposition in the House of Commons and were unrepresented in the House of Lords, the objections to a Prime Minister in the Upper Chamber were insuperable."[35]

A single precedent, however, does not create a rule that a Prime Minister must necessarily be from the House of Commons. But "the Election of a peer," as Keith rightly remarks, "for that office would be abnormal."[36] If the Government owns responsibility to the House of Commons alone, a vote in that House only can compel the Government either to resign or to advise a dissolution. Moreover, the Prime Minister is also responsible for the party organization. Party organization matters only in the House of Commons and not in the House of Lords. If, in brief, the Prime Minister is to correctly feel the pulse of Parliament and in the ultimate analysis that of the electorate, he can do so in the House of Commons. "The precedent that the Prime Minister should belong to the House of Commons must, therefore, be regarded as decisive. Baldwin did not show the slightest desire to continue his Premiership on his transfer to the House of Lords. Professor Keith is of the opinion that had Baldwin decided to continue, such a decision would certainly have been popular enouggh in the country after he had established his reputation by his brilliant handling of the abdication of Edward VIII. He holds that "it remains possible that a Prime Minister might retain that office after transfer to the Upper House.[37] But it is doubtful if any Prime Minister will ever venture it now. Earl Home disclaimed his peerage, under the peerage Act, 1963, and became Sir Alec Douglas-Home and succeeded Harold Macmillan as the Prime Minister. The new methods of choosing a prime minister adopted by both Labour and Conservative parties preclude the possibility of a Peer being elevated to this august office now

**Functions of the Prime Minister**

The Prime Minister is the corner-stone of the Constitution. In his hand is the key of Government. His duties are onerous and his authority enormous. Gladstone described these thus: "The Head of the British Government is not a Grand Vizier. He has no powers, properly so called, over his colleagues: on the rare occasions when a Cabinet determines its course by the votes of its members, his vote counts only as one of theirs. But they are appointed and dismissed by the Sovereign on his advice. In a perfectly organised administration as that of Sir Robert Peel in 1841-46, nothing of great importance is matured, or would even be projected, in any department without his personal cognizance and any weighty business would commonly go to him before being submitted to the Cabinet. He reports to the Sovereign its proceedings, and he also has many audiences of the august occupant of the throne."[38] There is much truth in what Gladstone had said. But nearly all recent developments have tended to increase the authority of the Prime Minister. "Indeed, the tendency of the British politics has been to steadily transfer power, not only from the House of Commons to the Cabinet but within the Cabinet to a small group and from the small group to one man, the Prime Minister."[39] There are and were very many good reasons for this change. The extension of the franchise, the prestige which Gladstone and Disraeli conferred upon the office give to the Prime Minister position and authority almost comparable with the President of the United States. He is even likened to a dictator, not perhaps the 'ideological dictator' of our times, but the 'benevolent despot' of the eighteenth century history with his all perva-

33. The defects of Lord Curzon's character are immortalised in the lines :
"George Nathaniel, Viscount Curzon,
Is really a very popular person."
34. Keith, A. B., *Cabinet System of Government,* p. 29.
35. Jennings, W. I., *Cabinet Government,* p. 23.
36. Keith, A. B., *Cabinet System of Government,* p. 29.
37. *Ibid.*
38. Quoted in Keith's *British Cabinet System,* p. 65.
39. Brogan, D. W., and Verney, D. V., *Political Patterns in Today's World,* p. 75.

sive influence in society. This is, indeed, an exaggeration, although the powers of the Prime Minister are very wide, and his status and prestige enviable.

The Prime Minister makes the government. With the selection of the Prime Minister the essential work of the King is completed, for it rests with the former to make up his list of Ministers and present it for the Royal assent. Technically, the last word rests with the King, because it is he who appoints them, But in practices, the decision belongs to the Prime Minister and the Royal assent is more or less a formality. Even Queen Vectoria never carried her objections on political grounds.

The Prime Minister in constituting his Government has to consider the claims and views of leading members of his party in both Houses. But, as Amery puts it, "subject to Parliament putting up with his selection of his colleagues and his arrangement of offices, he has a very free hand in shaping his government according to his own view of what is likely to work best and according to his personal preference."[40] It is for him to decide on the size of the Cabinet and the Ministers to be included in it. In fact, the British Prime Minister has never been under any sort of direct dictation either from Parliament or from a Party Executive in making his government. He may even select colleagues outside the ranks of his Party, or even outside Parliament, if in his judgment a particular person is specially fitted for particular job. For example, in 1903 Balfour offered the Colonial Office to Lord Milner, when he was still the High Commissioner in South Africa and had no parliamentary experience to his credit. MacDonald in 1924, made Lord Chelmsford, a non-party ex-Viceory of India, First Lord of the Admiralty. The most remarkable example is that of Baldwin's appointment in 1924 of Winston Churchill as Chancellor of the Exchequer. The Conservative Party was vehemently opposed to this appointment. But "the appointment was made and the Conservative Party in Parliament, though never quite reconciled to it, grumbled and submitted.[41] Harold Wilson appointed Patrick Gordon-Walker to such an exalted office as the Foreign Secretary, though defeated in the General Election. L.S. Amery while summing up this power of the Prime Minister says, "Few dictators, indeed, enjoy such a measure of automatic power as is enjoyed by a British Prime Minister while in process of making up his Cabinet."[42]

Many of the choices of the Prime Minister, however, are obvious. He must include among his Ministers men of standing with the Party. The history of how Arthur Henderson became Foreign Secretary in 1929, shows that in a party's government a vital member of the party can always set limits to the discretion a Prime Minister can exercise; he must include "essential men" This is perhaps particularly important in fact of the diverse elements within the British parties. In 1964 and 1974, Harold Wilson included in his Cabinet Ministers drawn from various sections of the Labour Party, including 'militants' like Frank Cousins and Barbara Castle. Harold Macmillan included in his Cabinet in 1957 both the left and right wingers like R.A. Butler and Lord Salisbury. The Prime Minister, while composing his Cabinet has often to decide whether a particular extremist in the party would be a threat to party in or out of the Cabinet. He may decide to 'buy silence' from a potential rebel by entrusting him with Ministerial office. This perhaps influenced Attlee's inclusion of Aneurin Bevin in his Cabinet, and Wilson's inclusion of Cousins and Barbara. Nevertheless, Prime Minister's discretion, as Laski puts it "is both wide and mysterious." Herman Finer expresses the same view in his own characteristic way. He says, "The Prime Minister has to make the Cabinet work; it is his; he must give it cohesion; he must arbitrate differences of view and personality; he must fit all the necessary talents together into a reputable team."[43]

In the allocation of offices, as well, the Prime Minister offers posts in his discretion, although politicians of standing can safely decline what is given, if they command so much support in the party as to make it unwise to dispense with their services. But rarely the Prime Minister's final allocation is rejected, because refusal may mean exclusion from office not merely for the term of that Parliament, but, perhaps, for ever. Sir Robert Horne, who had been a successful President of the Board of Trade and Chancellor of the Exchequer, refused in 1924 the Ministry of Labour that Baldwin offered him and

40. Campion and Others, *Parliament : A Survey,* p. 63.
41. *Ibid.*
42. Campion and others, *Parliament: A Survey,* p. 63.
43. Finer H. *Governments of the Greater European Powers,* p. 144.

he was never considered again for any future office. "It is only exceptionally forceful or fortunate political rogue elephant;" says Amery, "that once extruded from the governing herd, can find their way back into it, as both Mr. Churchill and the present writer (Amery himself) discovered for a decade after 1929."[44]

If the machinery of the government is to work efficiently and effectively, then, it is the undoubted right of the Prime Minister to appoint, reshuffle, or dismiss his colleagues. He is free, in the exercise of his impartial judgment, to make what appointments may seem good to him. He must also, from time to time, review the allocation of offices among his various colleagues and consider whether that allocation still remains the best that can be effected. Both as captain of the team and at the helm of administration, it is his duty to request any of his colleagues, whose presence in the Ministry is, in his opinion or judgment, prejudicial to the efficiency, integrity or policy of the government, to resign.

The Prime Minister can also advise the Sovereign to dismiss a Minister. According to law a Minister holds office at the pleasure of the King and he can be dismissed whenever it pleases His Majesty. It is now a well-established custom that the prerogative of dismissal is exercised solely on the advice of the Prime Minister. It is, however, doubtful if ever a Prime Minister would advise dimissal except in very extreme cases. All the same, the right of the Prime Minister is there. Sir Robert Peel maintained that, "under all ordinary circumstances if there were a serious difference of opinion between the Prime Minister and one of his colleagues, and that difference could not be reconciled by an amicable understanding, the result would be retirement of the colleague, not of the Prime Minister.[45] But such a crisis would never come. In Britain "there is a tradition—a kind of public school fiction—that no minister desires office, but that he is prepared to carry on for the public good.[46] This tradition implies a duty to resign when a hint is given. There are many instances of such resignations, Lowe and Aryton resigned in 1873, Seeley in 1914, and Austin Chamberlain in 1917. Montagu in 1924; and Sir Samuel Hoare in 1935. But Mrs. Margaret Thatcher dismissed the Navy Minister, Keith Speed, when he was asked to resign and made "excuses", and forced another, Hal Miller, Parliamentary Private Secretary, to resign.

To sum up, it is a purely personal authority of the Prime Minister to ask a colleague to resign or to accept another office. Removal from office is always a stronger step and it may have its repercussions in the House of Commons and in the constituencies.[47] It may even lead to the breaking up of the Cabinet. Moreover, it is a declaration of weakness and defective judgment in placing the Minister in office, or suggests error of policy on the part of the Prime Minister. No Prime Minister will, therefore, go to the extreme of dismissing a colleague. There are other polite methods of doing things. The Prime Minister can rid himself of an undesired colleague by a general reshuffle of the Ministry and it is the best way of avoiding a slight on a person who may have considerable parliamentary and popular support.[48] The recent tendency, begun by Churchill, continued by Attlee and invariably followed by his successors, has been to make changes more frequently to weed out unwanted incumbents. In a major reshuffle of her Cabinet on 14 September 1981, Mrs Thatcher dropped three so-called "wets"—persons who had openly questioned her economic policies and shifted Keith Joseph from the Industry Ministry to the comparatively innocuous department of education. Among those dropped were Mark Carlisle, Lord Soams and Peter Thorneycraft. In fact no British Prime Minister has sacked more Ministers than Mrs. Thatcher and at the time of her resignation from the office of Prime Ministership in November 1990, only three of her original Cabinet Ministers remained in office. To remain more dignified some Prime Ministers "elevated" the offending Ministers in order to get rid of them. This is one of the chief, though least used arguments for the retention of the House of Lords.

Then, the Prime Minister is the leader of

44. Amery, L. S., *Thoughts on the Constitution,* p. 64.
45. As cited in Keith's *British Cabinet System,* pp. 82-83.
46. Jennings, W. I., *Cabinet Government* , p. 197.
47. Lord Salisbury dared not dismiss his Home Secretary, Mathews, in 1890. He wrote to the Queen : "At present Lord Salisbury does not think that a bare dismissal would be admissible. It would be looked upon as very harsh and beget numberless intrigues.....There is no instance of dismissal, and it would require some open and palpable error to justify it."
48. In September 1947, on rearranging the government, Attlee asked Greenwood, one of his senior colleagues, to retire on grounds of age. Some quarters hold the opinion that Attlee exercised a clear power of dismissal.

his Party. The general election is in reality the election of a Prime Minister. The wavering voters who decide elections support neither a party nor a policy. They support a leader. The Prime Minister has, therefore, to give effective leadership. He must feel the pulse of the people and try to know true and genuine public opinion on matters which confront the nation. He must also guide public opinion by receiving deputations, and discuss issues by public speech at party conferences, and on other important occasions which demand proper attention. He should also give the Opposition a feeling that the Government will not ride rough-shod over the wishes of the minorities. For all this, he needs strength of character, the gift of leadership, patience, tact and a devotion to principles. He must also guide and inspire those he has chosen as Ministers and should enjoy the confidence of a majority in the House of Commons. In short, the Prime Minister must be a capable evaluator of public opinion and at the same time an expert in propaganda. He must know what to say, when to say, and when not to say anything.

Jennings gives a graphic picture of the qualities which a Prime Minister should possess. He says: ''Since his personality and prestige play a considerable part in moulding public opinion, he ought to have something of the popular appeal of a film actor and he must take some care over his make-up—like Mr. Gladstone with his collars, Mr. Lloyd George with his hair, Mr. Baldwin with his pipes and Mr. Churchill with his cigars. Unlike a film actor, however, he ought to be a good inventor of speeches as well as a good orator. Even more important, perhaps, is his microphone manner, for few attend meetings but millions look to broadcasts. Finally, it is essential that he should be able to retain the loyalties of his political friends; and it helps considerably if he remembers their names, asks the right questions about their families, realizes when sympathy or congratulation is required, and generally is good mixer with exactly the right measure of condescension.[49]. To this, we should add now his television appeal and mannerism, including debating skills.

A party which has not a leader cannot function. Its condition, in fact, becomes hopelessly chaotic. In the same way, a party with a weak leader is in a weak position. It is not possible for it to attract popular support and be in a position to form government. It has been claimed that in 1964 and 1966 the Labour Party won and the Conservatives lost the elections largely because of the impression, made by their leaders. During the winter of 1965-66 the Rhodesian crisis had raised Wilson's stature as a Prime Minister, whereas by March 1966 Heath had been leader of the Conservative Party for only seven months, ''and was still very much the 'new boy'. In the Conservative Party the leader is the Party. He controls the Party organisation and its funds. He also carries with him disciplinary authority and uses this weapon of decisive power against anyone who dare challenge his authority. The Chairman and Leader of the Labour Parliamentary party is recognised as the Leader of the Labour Party not only in Parliament but also in the country; he is *ex officio* a member of the National Executive Committee of the Labour Party and he is free to attend any of the Sub-Committees of the Executive as an *ex officio* member if and when he wishes to do so. In fact, the prestige of the Prime Minister and the party are closely intertwined. It is the party which makes the leader, but once the leader had been elected the party support is concentrated in the leader. The majority which the party receives at the polls is a party majority, but it owes its allegiance to the leader and it is spoken of as his party. Party prestige with the electorate demands it and this is the real strength of the Prime Minister. A Prime Minister must, therefore, strive for the unity of his party and his personality should be capable of inspiring loyalty in his colleagues and trust in the country.

The Prime Minister is the Chairman of the Cabinet. He must pick a team and keep it as a team, and, accordingly, his task as Chairman of Cabinet meetings, in which Government policy is hammered into shape and decisions taken, is of crucial importance. The Prime Minister is the leader of the Party and his colleagues in the Cabinet owe him a personal as well as a party allegiance. He controls agenda and it is for him to accept or reject proposals for discussion submitted by Ministers. The Ministers always consult him before important proposals are put forward and his support solicited. It is also well recognized that in Britain and the Anglo-Saxon countries generally the ''Chairman of any committee attracts a special kind of loyalty engendered by the vague feeling that business is expe-

49. Jennings, W. I., *Cabinet Government*, p. 163.

dited and improved by order and that one must be prepared to suffer the Chairman's ruling for the sake of the collective enterprise.[50] A casting vote, too, is inherent in the Chairman.[51] All this gives pre-eminent authority to the Prime Minister as Chairman of the Cabinet. But Cabinet in Britain does not take decisions by votes now.[52] Since votes are not taken, the Prime Minister's power to sum up in Cabinet discussions is very important. Jennings says, "A team of politicians is probably the most difficult to handle because, though each of them knows that his political future depends on the success of the team, there will usually be a few who are anxious to become captain.[53] The management of the Cabinet is, thus, certainly the Prime Minister's most difficult function "because it compels him to take difficult decisions not only on the substance but also on the tactics.[54] The Prime Minister may seek to persuade a minority or convince a majority. He may feel it necessary sometimes to give way to the majority even when he does not agree or try to force his own opinion on the Cabinet as Gladstone almost always did. But in the latter case the Prime Minister must run the risk of splitting the party. He must reconcile the differences of opinion between Ministers. If he fails, he may shatter the Government and the Party and "leave his leadership self-condemned, as Balfour's was by 1905.[55]

Some Prime Ministers had really been good Chairmen. They had always striven to see the main issues and the questions of principle. By dint of their commonsense and good judgment they guided the discussions towards a definite conclusion ensuring harmonious and efficient teamwork. Lord Samuel has given an excellent description of Ramsay MacDonald as Chairman of the Cabinet. He says, MacDonald "was a good Chairman of Cabinet, carefully preparing his material beforehand, conciliatory in manner and resourceful. In the conduct of a Cabinet when a knot or a tangle begins to appear, the important thing is for the Prime Minister not to let it be drawn tight; so long as it is kept loose it may still be unravelled. MacDonald was skilful in such a situation—and there were many.[56]

As the guide to the Cabinet the Prime Minister is the chief co-ordinator of the policies of the several Ministers and Ministries. He, more than anyone else, must endeavour to see the work of the Government as a whole and bring the variety of Government activities into reasonable relationship with one another. He is, in fact, the Manager-in-Chief of the Government's business. Sir Robert Peel is universally acclaimed the model Prime Minister. He supervised and was genuinely familiar with the business of each Department. Though he had an able Chancellor of the Exchequer, in whom he had full confidence, he himself introduced the budgets in 1842 and 1845. The War Office, the Admiralty, the Foreign Office, the administration of India and Ireland felt his personal influence as much as the Treasury and Board of Trade.

Such close attention is no longer possible now. The functions of Government have expanded so widely and its activities have become so complex that even if a Prime Minister is to regard Sir Robert Peel as a model and intervene when he considers it necessary, the result will be equally disastrous to him and to the country. But the Prime Minister must keep an eye on what goes on in the Departments and must know enough to be ready to intervene if he apprehends that something is going wrong. Usually, he exercises supervision through the eagerness of the Ministers to consult him, but he must have the ability to give sound advice almost on the spur of the moment. "If he is intellectually lazy like Baldwin or difficult of approach like MacDonald, he cannot exercise these functions properly."[57]

The work of co-ordination is done by the various Committees of the Cabinet, but the Prime Minister is, as Herbert Morrison said, "eminently a co-ordinating Minister." He decides what Cabinet Committees there will be, appoints the Chairmen and presides over some Commit-

50. Finer, H., *The Theory and Practice of Modern Government*, p. 592.
51. The decision to arrest Dillon in 1881 was carried by Gladstone's casting vote.
52. The practice of taking votes and deciding by a majority did not originate until 1880. The question of the removal of the Duke of Wellington's statue from Hyde Park in 1883 was decided by a show of hands. But votes are not taken now. "Now this is not done by voting for the holding up of hands or the calling of 'Aye' and 'No'," "would not only be regarded as a breach of Cabinet decorum but would also be felt to symbolize and demonstrate, nakedly and unashamedly, a lack of Cabinet unity and solidarity which is always deprecated." Morrison, H., *Government and Parliament*, p. 5.
53. Jennings, W. I., *The Queen's Government*, p. 137.
54. *Ibid.*, p. 138.
55. Brasher, N. H., *Studies in British Constitution*, p. 39.
56. As cited in Jennings, W.I., *Cabinet Government*, pp. 176-77.
57. Jennings, W. I., *The Queen's Government*, p. 139.

tees himself Attlee was Chairman of the Committee for Commonwealth Affairs, Far Eastern Affairs, Economic Policy, Housing, National Health Service, Food and Fuel, and Indian Affairs, during the two Ministries, 1945-51. The Prime Minister must also keep in touch with the work of the other Cabinet Committees. And with a wide ministerial experience to his credit before stepping into 10 Downing Street the Prime Minister can perform this function efficiently and effectively, as did Winston Churchill, Clement Attlee, Harold Macmillan and Harold Wilson, to take just a few examples from a long list of modern Prime Ministers.

The Prime Minister must be in the closest contact with the Foreign Secretary and the Chancellor of the Exchequer. For the rest, his door must ever be open, "his mind clear and his judgment rapid and efficient." Foreign affairs are always on the agenda and decisions of great importance demand speedy determination. There may be no time to summon a meeting of the Cabinet. In such cases the Prime Minister and the Foreign Secretary consult each other and a decision is reached. The Prime Minister may even man the entire policy. Neville Chamberlain adopted a foreign policy of his own, forced it on the Foreign Office and compelled the Foreign Secretary, Anthony Eden, to resign. But foreign policy cannot be divorced from the defence and trade policy. Chamberlain used the Principal Economic Adviser to the Government as his principal assistant in the conduct of his foreign policy. Churchill's task was fundamentally different. In war-time there is one supreme function of the Government and it is to win the war, and it must inevitably be the Prime Minister's personal concern. All else is subordinated to it. In the main, the nature of international relations today, with 'summit meetings' of Heads of States and the need for speedy military decisions in the nuclear age, forces the direct and personal involvement of the Prime Minister in foreign affairs. The effect of two Wars on the machinery of Cabinet government was to concentrate power in the hands of the Prime Minister and his close advisers. This increased authority has been retained to some extent in peacetimes too.

The Prime Minister's responsibilities for the co-ordination of the administration are further indicated by the fact that he leads the Civil Service Department established in 1968, in pursuance of the recommendation of the Fulton Committee. The Civil Service Department is under the control of the Prime Minister as Minister for Civil Service, with responsibility for the day-to-day work of the Department delegated to a senior Minister assisted by a Parliamentary Secretary. The Department's Permanent Secretary is also the official head of the Home Civil Service.

The Prime Minister is the real leader of the House of Commons. Now the tendency is that he designates another colleague as Leader of the House and delegates to him the specific function of arranging the business of the House,[58] but this delegation cannot deprive the Prime Minister of his function as leader of the Government. "The problem is not," as Jennings says, "that the Government runs the risk of defeat—for unless the party breaks up, or has no majority, or has a very small majority,[59] the Government cannot be defeated—but that it runs the risk of being worsted in the argument." The House is 'the finest platform in Europe', "the only debating society in Britain whose debates are read, or at least glanced at, by millions. If the Government is to keep its majority in the country, it must consistently make a good case."[60] All principal announcements of policy and business are made by the Prime Minister and all questions on non-departmental affairs and upon critical issues are addressed to him. He initiates or intervenes in debates of general importance, such as those on defence, foreign affairs, and domestic issues of primary character. In fact, the House always looks to him as the fountain of policy. He is also recognised to have an immediate authority to correct what he may consider the errors of omission and commission of the colleagues.

The party Whips in the House are under the Prime Minister's direct supervision and through them he issues orders to the rank and file of the party. He assists the Speaker and the Chairman in maintaining order and decorum in the House.

58. Asquith separated the offices of Prime Minister and leader of the House of Commons in 1915. Since 1945 no Prime Minister has attempted to combine the two roles.

59. Harold Wilson's minority Government, which assumed office in March1974, was defeated quite a number of times on major issues of economic policy. But the Conservative Party did not demand its resignation. Similar had been the lot of James Callaghan who headed a minority government throughout his tenure, except for a brief spell to begin with. But Callaghan's Government was defeated on a vote of no confidence when the Liberals and the Scottish Nationalists withdrew their support in early 1979.

60. Jennings, W. I., *The Queen's Government*, p. 139.

In brief, the House comes to a large extent under the control of the Prime Minister. The management of the Government's majority and the maintenance of smooth relations with the Opposition depend upon his inspiring lead and parliamentary skill. The Prime Minister ought to be what is called 'good House of Commons man', a man who observes its traditions and knows to handle it, a man like Baldwin or Churchill.

The Prime Minister wields the supreme power of dissolution and, thus, "holds the security of Members on both sides of the gangway in the House in his hands." It means that the members of the House of Commons hold their seats at the mercy of the Prime Minister's use of this "terrifying power," for it means new elections without certainty that they will be elected. "Men do not like to run the risks," observes Byrum Carter, "which are involved in this process, if little is to be gained from incurring the danger."[61] The threat of dissolution, thus, hangs over their heads, "restraining them, restricting their independence, leading them into the government's body."[62]

There is some divergence of opinion among the authorities on the question whether the King can refuse a dissolution to a Prime Minister who asks for it. Winston Churchill stated during the course of the debate on the Education Bill in March, 1944, that although advice to dissolve comes from the Prime Minister, it is only advice and may, in exceptional circumstances, be disregarded.[63] What those exceptional circumstances can be have been explained by Sir David Keith in his *Constitutional Histroy of Modern Britain.* He writes : "The King's prerogative, however circumscribed by convention, must always retain its historic character as a residue of discretionary authority to be employed for the public good. It is the last resource provided by the Constitution to guarantees its own working."[64] It is, however, difficult to imagine circumstances in which the King could refuse dissolution to a Prime Minister. Laski clearly stated that this part of the royal prerogative is as obsolete as the royal veto power.[65] If the King refused a dissolution to a Prime Minister, he would be substituting his judgment about the need for and timing of a General Election for that of his Chief Minister. The Prime Minister, under such circumstances, will presumably resign, though he had with him a clear majority in the House of Commons. When the Prime Minister resigns, the King will naturally send for the Leader of the Opposition and commission him to form the Government. Such a Government cannot continue in office unless it is supported by the House of Commons. As there is no majority for the new Government, the King will be compelled to dissolve Parliament and General Election held. But the King could hardly grant a dissolution to the second Prime Minister after refusing to the first. If he does and he must do it, his neutral position will be fatally compromised. Jennings concludes that "thus, while the King's personal prerogative is maintained in theory, it can hardly be exercised in practice.[66] During the last more than hundred years there has been no instance of a refusal of a dissolution by the King when advised.

The right to advise a dissolution was long assumed to belong to the Cabinet. The decision to dissolve now rests with the Prime Minister and this has been done since 1918. In fact, since that time no decision to dissolve "has been brought before the Cabinet, and Prime Ministers now assume a right to tender advice to dissolve on their own account.[67] This aspect was further explained by Sir John Simon in 1935. He wrote that "the decision whether there shall be an immediate general election, and, if so, on what date the country should go to the polls, rests with the Prime Minister, and until the Prime Minister has decided, all anticipations are without authority.[68] Keith is of the opinion that the Cabinet should be consulted and decide the issue of dissolution and if the older practice has been departed from, to some degree, it is no ground that

61. Carter, Byrum, E., *The Office of the Prime Minister,* p. 274.
62. *Ibid.,* p. 275.
63. Keith, A. B., *British Cabinet System,* p. 30. Also refer to Asquith's affirmation in 1924. But Asquith had a design to put Ramsay MacDonald into difficulty while in office, so that the King would turn to him to form the Ministry.
64. Keir, D; *Constitutional History of Modern Britain,* p. 491.
65. Laski, H. J., *Reflections on the Constitution,* p. 72.
66. Jennings , W. I., *Cabinet Government,* p.395.
67. Keith, A. B., *The British Cabinet System,* p. 304.
68. As cited in above, *Ibid.* Harold Wilson did not succumb to the demands of his colleagues in the Cabinet, especially the Chancellor of the Exchequer, Mr. Healy and the Employment Secretary, Mr. Michael Foot, to dissolve Parliament and hold new elections.

further departure should take place. "It is derogatory," he says," to the dignity of other Cabinet Ministers, and tends to make them appear in the public eye the servants, rather than equals, of the Prime Minister. It runs counter to the best aspects of the Constitution, the doctrine of collective responsibility and deliberation, and it presumes that for some reason or other, in this vital issue, the Prime Minister has pre-eminence in other issues denied to him."[69] Morrison said that the presence of members of the Secretariat at Cabinet meetings precludes the discussion of such matters as the political factors involved in a dissolution.[70] But in 1966 and on other past occasions, informal discussions took place between the Prime Minister and some of his colleagues.

The Prime Minister is the only channel of communication with the Crown on matters of public concern, although there are many examples of the Crown's connection with individual Ministers "behind the back of the Prime Minister."[71]Apart from the Cabinet conclusions, which are drawn by the Cabinet Secretariat and a copy sent to him, the King has no official means of knowing of the Cabinet discussions, except what the Prime Minister may choose to tell him. This account "is not revised by his colleagues." He is also the chief adviser of the Sovereign and in emergencies the Monarch will first consult the Prime Minister. The Prime Minister advises the King on royal activities of an official character such as a visit to a foreign country, or tour of a part of the kingdom or empire or Commonwealth countries. The consultations between Queen Elizabeth II and Macmillan, which preceded the royal visit to Ghana in 1961, when there seemed to be an element of personal danger involved for the Monarch, is a recent example. Stanley Baldwin regarded it both a duty and right to offer counsel to Edward VIII on his contemplated marriage with Mrs. Simpson. He consulted the Cabinet only at that stage when differences of an irreconcilabe nature had developed between him and the King. The Prime Minister, then, became" as usual the link between the King and Cabinet interpreting the opinions and decisions of one to the other."[72]

The Prime Minister has wide powers of patronage including the appointment and dimissal of Ministers. In 1962, Harold Macmillan virtually dismissed a third of his Cabinet. Margaret Thatcher repeated it in 1981 and again in 1986. Sir Geoffery Howe, Deputy Prime Minister in Thatcher's Government resigned on November,1990 over differences with the Prime Minister on her approach to European Economic and Monetary Union. In an age when professional politicians predominate, the Prime Minister's ability to affect the career of ambitious Members of Parliament, inevitably gives him or her considerable power and authority. In a BBC programme early in 1988, Margaret Thatcher's former Defence Minister Sir John Nott accused her of "going over the top" in her dealings with cabinet colleagues,promoting a cult of personality. "The Cabinet was never more than a rubber stamp", he said.

The distribution of general patronage through the Honour list gives the Prime Minister an influence in many sectors of national life. Though Lloyd George's abuse of patronage discredited the whole system, and since 1922, a Committee of the Privy Council has vetted all proposed awards, but no grant is made without the Prime Minister's recommendation. The patronage, therefore, remains a valuable political weapon in the hands of the Prime Minister.

The Prime Minister's power of appointment is not as extensive as that of the President of the United States, but it is considerable nevertheless. All Ministerial positions are his gifts. So is the allocation of Ministerial offices. He will either himself select new occupants or be consulted by the Minister concerned when there are vacancies in the chief diplomatic, military, judicial and ecclesitical offices. Though Departmental Ministers have particular responsibility for their departmental officials, the Civil Service as a whole is controlled by the Treasury under the direction of the Prime Minister as First Lord. The Permanent Secretary of the Treasury advises the Prime Minister and he himself makes appointments of the Permanent Secretary or the permanent UnderSecretary, Deputy Secretary or the Deputy Under- Secretary and the principal establishment officers in each of the Government Departments. Thus, as with the Ministerial hierarchy, the Prime Minister can be seen as head of the permanent administrative structure. Then, there are a good many special appointments in

69. *Ibid.*, p. 305.
70. Morrison, Herbert, *Government and Parliament*, p. 24.
71. Finer, H., *The Theory and Practice of Modern Government*, p. 592.
72. Greaves, H. R. G., *The British Constitution*, p. 110.

which the Prime Minister is interested—Governors-Generals in the Dominions, High Commissioners in the Commonwealth countries, British representatives to important international organizations, and Board members of nationalised industries. He will certainly be consulted about many of these, and frequently the choice is his.

The Prime Minister also recommends to the Sovereign for the appointment of Church of England Archbishops, bishops and certain other senior clergy, as well as for appointments to high judicial offices, such as Lords of Appeal in Ordinary, Lord Chief Justice and Lord Justices of Appeal. He also advises the Crown on appointment of Privy councillors, Lord Lieutenants of counties[73] and certain civil appointments, such as, Lord High Commissioner of the General Assembly of the Church of Scotland, Poet Laureate, Constable of the Tower and some University appointments which are in the gift of the Crown.

The Prime Minister may occasionally attend and participate in international conferences or meetings. Lord Beaconsfield attended the Congress of Berlin, Lloyd George participated in the Peace Conference at Paris, and Neville Chamberlain led the meetings in Germany preceding the Munich Agreement. Churchill attained new heights during the Second World War in his six meetings with President Roosevelt and two with Stalin. Ramsay MacDonald personally discussed with Dr. Dawes in 1929 on the most important phase of Anglo-American relations. He also went to the United Staes to confer with President Hoover on the limitation of armaments. The recent practice of holding Summit Conferences has further enhanced the powers and prestige of the Prime Minister.

He conducts relations in matters of Cabinet rank with the Commonwealth countries. A classical example was afforded by the negotiations over the mode in which effect was to given to the abdication of King Edward VIII.

The Prime Minister acts, though infrequently, either without authorization by the Cabinet or even against previously determined Cabinet policy. Lloyd George decided upon his own initiative to call a session of the Imperial War Conference and announced it in Parliament without receiving the proper authorization of the Cabinet. Stanley Baldwin raised in 1923 the issue of protection without previously consulting his Cabinet. Baldwin also took the initial steps in the action which led to abdication of Edward VIII without previously consulting his Cabinet. In the Second World War, Winston Churchill made a speech on 22nd June 1941, offering all possible assistance to the Soviet Union without consulting the Cabinet and he added, "nor was it necessary."[74]

Whenever the prime Minister acts as such, the Cabinet is rather in a difficult position, for it must either accept the policy enunciated by the Prime Minister or run the risk of losing its leader "unless it is possible to find a compromise which will save the prestige of both." But such a course of action is unusual as it endangers Cabinet unity and at the same time the security of the Prime Minister.

**Prime Minister's position**

Such is the magnitude of the powers of the Prime Minister. But what is his position as compared with his colleagues ? Lord Morley described him as *primus inter pares.* He said, "Although in Cabinet all its members stand on an equal footing, speak with equal voice, and, on the rare occasions when a division is taken, are counted on the fraternal principle of one man and one vote, yet the head of the Cabinet is *primus inter pares,* and occupies a position which so long as it lasts, is one of exceptional and peculiar authority." Herbert Morrison also held the same estimation of the position of the Prime Minister. He says, "As the head of the Government he (Prime Minister) is *primus inter pares* . But it is today far too modest an appreciation of the Prime Minister's position."[75] Ramsay Muir considers such a description as "non-sense" when "applied to a potentate who appoints and can dismiss his colleagues. He is, in fact, though not in law, the working head of the State, endowed with such a plenitude of power as no other constitutional ruler in the world possesses, not even the President of the United States."[76] Another writer says, "if one must have a Latin phrase, a better one, no doubt, is Sir William Vernor Harcourt's *luna inter stella minores*—a moon among lesser stars—although even this may not really be strong enough."[77] Jennings says that the Prime

73. The office of the Lord Lieutenant of the county was first created in the sixteenth century. Its holder was chief among the county justices and commander of the county milita.
74. Churchill, W., *The Grand Alliance,* p. 370.
75. Morrison, H., *Government and Parliament,* p. 97.
76. Ramsay Muir, *How Britain is Governed,* p. 83.
77. As quoted in Ogg and Zink, *Modern Foreign Governments,* p. 90.

Minister is not merely *primus inter pares.* He is not even *luna inter stellas minores.* "He is, rather, a sun around which planets revolve."[78]

The earlier conception of the Prime Minister as first among equals, *primus inter pares,* does not reflect real difference in status and responsibility between the person who holds the first position, and is the Prime Minister, and even his senior colleagues. Sir Winston Churchill clearly expressed this distinction and it bespeaks of the Prime Minister *vis-a-vis* his Cabinet colleagues. He says, "In any sphere of action there can be no comparison between the positions of number one and number two, three, or four. The duties and problems of all persons other than the number one are quite different and in many ways more difficult. It is always a misfortune when number two or three has to initiate a dominant plan or policy. He has to consider not only the merits of the policy, but the mind of his chief; not only what to advise, but what it is proper for him in his station to advise; not only what to do, but how to get it agreed, and how to get it done. Moreover, number two or three will have to reckon with numbers four, five, and six, or may be some bright outsider, number twenty.......

"At the top there are great simplifications. An accepted leader has only to be sure of what it is best to do, or at least to have made up his mind about it. The loyalties which centre upon number one are enormous. If he trips, he must be sustained. If he makes mistakes they must be covered. If he sleeps, he must not be wantonly disturbed..."[79] Among his colleagues the Prime Minister has never been the first among equals at any time since Gladstone became Prime Minister in 1868. If he is described first among equals even now, it is simply to stress the democratic nature of his position. The Prime Minister is really a sun around which planets revolve and in the blaze of the sun the planets even lose their identity. The actual power of the Prime Minister, however, varies according to his personality and the extent to which he is supported by his party. "But within the limits of prudence and commonsense", as Byrum Carter observes "he may exercise a directing authority which is the envy of political leaders of other states."[80]

At the root of the primacy of the Prime MInister is the fact that since the Reform Act of 1867, the elections have become the issues of personality. Many members of the electorate equate the party with its leader. The party leader has become the hub of the party's appeal and the centre of the party loyalty. A General Election is now a plebiscite between alternative Prime Ministers, Gladstone, while referring to the election of 1857, rightly said, "it is not an election like that of 1784, when Pitt appealed on the question whether the Crown should be slave of an oligarchic faction, nor like that of 1831, when Grey sought a judgment on reform, nor like that of 1852, when the issue was the expiring controversy of protection. The country was to decide not upon the Canton river, but whether it would or would not have Palmerston for Prime Minister." Again, in the election of 1880, Gladstone, in his famous Midlothian campaign, carried a relentless criticism of Beaconsfield Government. The only question which electors asked themselves was whether they wished to be governed by Lord Beaconsfield or Gladstone, though the latter was no longer the leader of his party. It was the personal triumph of Gladstone and he became Prime Minister by the choice of the people. The General Election of 1945 was a personal appeal to the electors by Churchill to re-elect him. The Conservative Party hoped to "cash in on his personal popularity." Every hoarding had a picture of the Prime Minister headed by slogan : "Help him finish the job" and underneath in comparatively small letters was the almost irrelevant injunction to "vote for the Bloggs."

The Conservative Party did not even issue its manifesto. But Churchill issued one of his own and it began appropriately with the word "I". Candidates, too, ignored their party labels and called themselves "Churchill candidates." The newspapers played their own part by emphasising that the issue lay between "Churchill or Chaos" or "Churchill and Laski, Harold Laski being the current bogyman."[81] The electorate was, in other words, asked to choose for or against Churchill and they chose against.

The object of this sort of electioneering , "necessarily, is to give the Prime Minister a national standing which no colleague can rival so long as he remains the Prime Minister."[82] It

78. Jennings, W. I., *Cabinet Government, p. 183.*
79. Churchill, W., *Their Finest Hour,* p. 15.
80. Carter, B. E., *The Office of the Prime Minister,* p. 334.
81. *Ibid.,* p. 186.
82. Laski, H. J., *Parliamentary Government in England,* p. 241.

strengthens his hands against his colleagues in the Government and Parliament. And, then, he appoints and dismisses his colleagues. He can shuffle his pack as and when he pleases. He alone determines whether and when Parliament shall be dissolved. In the inter departmental disputes he is the arbitrator and if these disputes become a Cabinet question, his voice carries weight. To defy authority of the Prime Minister and to challenge his position is suicidal to the political ambitions of a Minister unless the Prime Minister "has handled his job so badly that there is a widespread feeling" of his unfitness for it.

But the Prime Minister's position is bound up with the party system. His prestige, no doubt, is one of the elements that make for the success of the party. He is also responsible for party cohesion. But, without his party, he is nothing. He goes to the electorate not as an individual, but as a leader of the party. Whatever he is and whatever he can claim to be is due to what the party has made him. So long as he retains the hold of his party, "he is able, within limits, to dictate his policy." Once the party disowns him, he meets the fate of Ramsay MacDonald. Sir Robert Peel lost his party in 1845 and it ended his career. Gladstone returned to power in 1892, because he had never left his position in the party. The Prime Minister's power in office, thus, depends in part on his personality, in part on his own prestige, and in part upon his party support. Defined powers legally conferred do not determine the position of the incumbent. "The office is", as Jennings says, "necessarily what the holder chooses to make it and what other ministers allow him to make of it". His authority is great, but his authority is a matter of influence in the context of the party structure. If he is a popular and dynamic figure, it is difficult for his colleagues to oppose him. Even the resignation of a leading Minister as that of Lord Salisbury in 1957 and of Thorneyeraft, Powell and Birch in 1958, may not unhinge the Prime Minister from his position. But he can be forced from office when faced with a substantial discontent in his Cabinet or his party. The resignations of Asquith in 1916, Lloyd George in 1922, MacDonald in 1935, and Chamberlain in 1940 came primarily as a result of discontent within the Government. Anthony Eden in 1957 and Harold Macmillan in 1963 were widely criticised within the party before 'illness' brought their resignations. Within the first two years of her tenure as Prime Minister there was a silent but sizable revolt against Mrs. Margaret Thatcher in the Conservative Party. The Party Chairman Thornycraft and the leader of the House of Commons, Francis Pym, publicly criticised her economic policy. There was again difference of opinion between Mrs. Thatcher and her Foreign Secretary Francis Pym on the Falkland Islands issue and it became evident in the House of Commons on May 13, 1982 when certain supporters of the Prime Minister seemed to back up Enoch Powell's call for Pym to resign. Sir Harold Wilson, the former Labour Prime Minister, had earlier predicted that she would be ditched by her own colleagues. It came out true. Mrs. Thatcher's position within the party and the Ministry had always been frail and ultimately she was compelled by her Party colleagues to resign on November 23, 1990, after she failed to get the requisite votes in the first round of balloting to the post of the Party leader. Ideally, the Prime Minister should have a personality which earns him or her not only the loyalty of her own Party but also a measure of ungruding respect from the Opposition. Mrs. Thatcher lacked both.

**Comparison with American President**

The office of the British Prime Minister is often compared with that of the American President. The comparison is significant for both resemble in many respects. But it would be too much, as Laski says, "to say that the position of a modern Prime Minister has approximated to that of an American President."[83] Even Churchill who attained new heights of power and authorty had not the personal powers of the President of the United States. Harry Hopkins, in a report to President Roosevelt, wrote, "Your former 'naval person' (Winston Churchill) is not only the Prime Minister, he is the directing force behind the strategy and the conduct of war in all its essentials. He has an amazing hold on the British people of all classes and groups. He has particular strength both with the military establishments and the working people."[84] Churchill, too, admitted that "never did a British Prime Minister receive from Cabinet colleagues the loyal and true aid which I enjoyed during the five years from these men of all parties in the State. Parliament, while maintaining free and active criticism,

83. *Ibid.*
84. As cited in Jennings, W. I., *Cabinet Government,* p. 181.

gave continuous, overwhelming support to all measures proposed by the Government, and the nation was united and ardent as never before.''[85] But Churchill accomplished all this because he had a united Cabinet, a united Parliament, and a united people behind him. Both the Cabinet and Parliament supported his policy. He could not act without his Cabinet as President Roosevelt could do. To illustrate the difference in the position and powers of the President of the United States and the British Prime Minister, Jennings says that ''the President pledged the United States in the realization of the objectives of the Atlantic Charter while the War Cabinet, not the Prime Minister, pledged the United Kingdom.''[86]

This is the essence of the difference between the authority of a Prime Minister and a President of the United States. Churchill had to observe the constitutional norms by seeking the approval of the Cabinet and the Cabinet was dependent upon the unswerving support of the House of Commons. The Prime Minister is not the master in his Cabinet as the American President is in his. The Cabinet of the President is essentially a group of advisers appointed by and responsible to him. They are bound to give advice to the President should he ask for it, but have no authority to it. They do meet regularly and consider what the President likes to put before them, but they have no corporate rights which are recognised by custom. The difference between the British Cabinet and the American becomes clear by these two anecdotes. Melbourne ending the discussion on Corn Laws said, ''It does not matter what we say, but we must all say the same story.'' Lincoln, on the other hand, could say on putting the question in his Cabinet. ''Noes seven, ayes one, the ayes have it.''

The Prime Minister can less easily brush aside the opinions of his colleagues. His powers are large, but he has to secure the collaboration of his colleagues. His Cabinet consists of the party's most important leaders. They all share publicity with him to a greater extent. Sometimes one of them may even attract greater public interest and popular enthusiasm. Then, the Prime Minister is still officially the first among equals in his Cabinet. His status must not, therefore, be thought of involving his superiority to and independence of his Cabinet, though in time of crisis or when he happens to be a man of outstanding personality, he may become the complete master of the situation. All the same, the Prime Minister ''is solid with his colleagues; the party has cemented them together as a multiple but a corporate executive.''[87] Churchill had such effective power that no British Prime Minister had had before. But the War Cabinet or Parliament could have ejected him if he would have lost the confidence of either of the two. The thought, therefore, that the Prime Minister stands high above and aloof from his colleagues and that he orders and decides ''top policy'', like the President of the United States is, according to Herman Finer, ''ridiculous : it is wishful thinking; it is misleading for Britain and for the United States.'' Even Harry Hopkins, who had reported in 1941, to President Roosevelt that ''Churchill is the government in the every sense of the word,''[88] could find the differences between the authority of the Prime Minister and the President of the United States when he observed during three days of the Conference in the Atlantic that Churchill was constantly reporting and consulting the War Cabinet.[89] Whereas Roosevelt took all the decisions by himself, subject only to the advice of his immediate and self-selected entourage, which advice he could accept or reject, Churchill could do so only by inspiring those whom he had chosen as Ministers, and carrying them with him.

In his book, *The Office of Prime Minister,* Byrum E. Carter observes, ''Comparisons between unlike systems are always inherently misleading, but it does seem safe to say that the power of the Prime Minister and his senior colleagues is substantially greater than that of the American President."[90] Carter assigns two reasons for his conclusion. First, the American President has no power to dissolve Congress and it sits for its specified period of time in the Constitution. The Congress may and it very often does drastically amend proposals which emanate from the administration. The President has, no doubt, certain means by which he can attempt legislation, ''but they are not comparable in effectiveness to those wielded by the Prime Minister."[91] Secondly, the

85. Churchill, W. *The Second World War, Vol. II.*, p. 24.
86. Jennings, W. I., *Cabinet Government,* p. 181.
87. Finer, H., *The Theory and Practice of Modern Government, op. cit.*, p. 593.
88. Sherwood, Robert E., *Roosevelt and Hopkins.*, p. 243.
89. More than thirty communications passed between Churchill and Clement Attlee, the Lord Privy Seal.
90. Carter, B. E., *The Office of the Prime Minister,* p. 336.
91. *Ibid.*

President is the head of the party, "but it is party in which the central organisation has little control."[92] The real basis of a party organisation in the United States has historically rested in the States and it is difficult for the central party to exercise discipline. The Prime Minister, on the other hand, heads a disciplined party and since a General Election is now fought on personalities this "inevitably enables the party leader to extend his power against that of the rank and file members of the Party, and even as against those individuals who exercise substantial intra-party influences themselves."[93] Summing up the differences in the powers and position of the British Prime Minister and the American President, Punnett says, "Certainly, the Prime Minister's power is greater than the authority of the President within the United States system, where the federal nature of the Constitution and the separation of powers raise barriers to the President's authority which do not exist for Prime Minister in Britain."[94] In Britain, the unitary nature of the Constitution, and the unification rather than separation of powers make the authority of the Prime Minister, no matter how much he may be limited by the Cabinet, necessarily greater than that of the American President. But the President, wrote Woodrow Wilson, just before his first inauguration, "is expected by the Nation to be leader of his party as well as the Chief Executive officer of the Government, and the country will take no excuses from him. He must play the part and play it successfully or lose the country's confidence. He must be Prime Minister as much concerned with the guidance of legislation as with the just and orderly execution of law, and he is the spokesman of the Nation in everything, even in the most momentous and most delicate dealings of the Government with foreign nations." Laski puts it in a matter of fact way when he says that "The President of the United States is both more and less than a King; he is also both more and less than a Prime Minister. The more carefully his office is studied, the more does its unique character appear."[95]

**Prime Ministerial Government**

The confussion in not clearly demarcating the powers and position of the Prime Minister and the American President is closely linked with the popular belief that Britons no longer have Cabinet Government, but instead live under Prime Ministerial Government. Crossman argues that ".......The post-war epoch has been the final transformation of Cabinet Government into Prime Ministerial government........"[96] Mackintosh also said : "Now the country is governed by a Prime Minister, his colleagues, Junior Ministers and civil servants with the Cabinet acting as a clearing house and court of appeal."[97]

Is it true, then, that the Prime Minister, for all practical purposes, is the Executive in Britain? Are the members of the Cabinet little more than his dependants, selected at his will and hold office so long the Prime Minister wishes them to ? What real influence other Ministers exercise in the formulation of Cabinet policy in the context of the individual responsibility for the Departments under their charge as well as collective responsibility for Cabinet decisions ?

It is now generally agreed that the Prime Minister's powers are today great, and in many respects are growing. The post-war period has many instances to provide the primacy of Prime Minister's power. For example, the decision to make the atom bomb by the first Labour Government was not taken in the Cabinet but in the Defence Committee of the Cabinet. The Suez adventure of 1956 was largely the personal policy of the Prime Minister, Anthony Eden. The decision to try to take Britain into the Common Market in 1961 was essentially that of the Prime Minister, Harold Macmillan. The decision of the Labour Government in 1965 to attempt a new approach to Europe also rested ultimately on the Prime Minister, Harold Wilson. The first seventeen months of Labour Government's regime after the 1964 General Election disclose how greatly the Prime Minister was personally responsible for the tone and decisions of the Government as a whole. The decision to dispatch the Royal Navy Armada on April 5, 1982 to recapture the Falkland Islands seized by Argentina, was Mrs. Thatcher's alone. Similarly, the British Government's policy against the racist regime of South Africa was essentially the determination of Prime Minister Margaret Thatcher, though

92. *Ibid.*
93. *Ibid.*
94. Punnett, R. M., *British Government and Politics,* p. 307.
95. Laski, H. J., *The American Presidency,* p. II.
96. Crossman, R. H., *Introduction to English Constitution,* p. 51.
97. Mackintosh, J.P., *The British Cabinet,* p. 524.

compelling reasons obliged her to soften and to bring in a streak of flexibility. Tony Blair joined Bill Clinton on his own in synchronizing British bombing attacks on Iraq in 1999.

Even then it does not mean that the Prime Minister is assuming the role of 'Presidential authority' and that the increase in the authority of the Prime Minister has produced a basic change in the system of the Cabinet Government in Britain. Herbert Morrison rejected the thesis of Prime Ministerial Government and said that the Prime Minister, ".....is not the master of the Cabinet", and he ".......ought not to, and usually does not, presume to give directions or decisions which are proper to the Cabinet or one of its Committees."[98] Morrison is supported by many other writers and statesmen. They all accept that the Prime Minister is powerful, yet assert that he is not overwhelmingly supreme as the Cabinet remains a collective executive body. A Prime Minister cannot ride roughshod over the will of the Cabinet. And as stated earlier, "he is both a captain and a man at the helm."[99] But he can remain at he helm only if he plays the game of politics like a captain. A captain must carry the team with him. Without a team there can be no captain just as without a captain there can be no team. The reality of collective responsibility, therefore, is not disproved by the great power of the Prime Minister in modern political conditions. Prime Ministerial power must be understood as varying with political circumstances and with the personal fortunes of the man who wields it. "The fundamental fact about the position of the Prime Minister is that he must operate flexibly within parliamentary and cabinet system in which power is distributed and which gives the Prime Minister as much command of the political situation as he can earn."[100] If his influence is as great as that of the American President, even then he is very far from having the powers of the President who is accountable to nobody except the electorate and that too after a specified period of four years. The Prime Minister, in varying degrees, is, on the other hand, accountable to his Cabinet colleagues, his party and even, in some degree, to the Opposition, as he considers it his duty to consult with the Leader of the Opposition at moments of national crisis, as for example, in the case of Falkland Islands.

98. Morrison, Herbert, *Government and Parliament*, p. 52.
99. Amery, L. S., *Thoughts on the Constitution*, p. 72.
100 Ronald Butt, *The Power of Parliament*, p.427.

**Prime Minister and Monarchy**

When no single party emerges as the majority party in Parliament, the monarch has to exercise his discretion in appointing the Prime Minister. In 1924 and 1929, the king appointed Ramsay Mac Donald as Prime Minister who formed minority Labour Governments with the outside support of the Liberal Party. In both cases, George V exercised his discretion correctly. However, in 1931 the political developments that followed the resignation of Mac Donald have aroused considerable controversy. The king, according to Laski and Greaves, played an activist role in the formation of the Coalition Government with MacDonald, traitor to his own Labour Party, presiding over a predominantly Conservative Cabinet in which few defectors from the Labour and Liberal parties were also included. The new government passed the National Economy Act, dissolved Parliament, fought a general election with the king's blessings under conditions of mass hysteria and received a massive electoral victory."

Both Laski and Greaves severely criticise the monarch's activist role in influencing his Labour Prime Minister so that he conspired secretly to bring the downfall of his own party's cabinet without its knowledge and without consulting his own Parliamentary Labour Party. In the name of 'Nationalism', the nominal rulers of Italy and Germany put dictators like Mussolini and Hitler in power so that they could safeguard capitalism. The British monarch used his political influence to overthrow the Labour Government and assemble the so-called National Coalition under MacDonald, the defecting Labour Prime Minister, so that he could resolve the economic crisis in England on the terms acceptable to the British capitalist class. The new Prime Minister, in fact, implemented the actual Tory policies in a 'national' disguise.

It is an established historical fact that monarchy, despite its cloak of neutrality, is emotionally and practically an essential part of the Conservative establishment. Some Liberal and Labour Prime Ministers have often felt that there is a certain degree of apathy and aloofness, even antipathy and aversion occasionally, in their relations with the monarch. Asquith in 1910 and Attlee in 1951 faced pressure from George V and

George VI respectively to dissolve the House of Commons, as demanded by the Conservatives at those occasions. Despite this, no Prime Minister has ever felt the need for abolishing monarchy as an institution. Even Lord Attlee believed "that it is right to have a certain amount of pageantry, because it pleases people and it also counteracts a tendency to other forms of excitement." (*The Times, July* 9, 1952). The present Prime Minister of the Labour Government, Tony Blair, is trying to abolish the institution of hereditary peers in the House of Lords and may succeed in doing so but he has no quarrel with hereditary monarchy. The reason is that no Prime Minister ever feels threatened or thwarted by the existence of a ceremonial monarchy. The monarch cannot influence him in changing any of his policies unless he is himself willing to be influenced in that direction.

The present initiative of the Labour Prime Minister, Tony Blair, is playing an activist and supportive role to the American President, George Bush, in the Afghan War against the Taliban and Osama bin Laden's *Al Quaeda*, without obtaining the concurrence of his cabinet, shows that the British Prime Minister is supreme in determining the foreign policy of his country. The cabinet lacks real control over his authority.

## SUGGESTED READINGS


Amery, L.S. : *Thoughts on the Constitution.*

Amos, A.: *The English Constitution*, pp. 130-149

Anderson, Sir J. (Ed.): *British Government Since* 1918.

Bagehot, W. : *The English Constitution.*

Birch, A.H.: *Representative and Responsible Government, An Essay on the British Constitution*, Chaps. 10-13.

Brogan, D. W. : *The American Political System*, Chap. II.

Compion and Others : *British Government Since* 1918, Chapt. II.

Campion and Others : *Parliament : A Survey*, Chaps. II,III.

Carter, Byrum, E. : *The Office of Prime Minister*

Crossman, R. H. : *Introduction to English Constitution.*

Daalder, Hans :*Cabinet Reform in Britain*, 1914-1963.

Derry, K. : *British Institutions of Today*, Chap. IV

Ehrmann, J.: *Cabinet Government and War*, 1890-1940

Finer, H. : *Government of Greater European Powers*, Chap. VII.

Finer. H. : *The Theory and Practice of Modern Government*, Chap. XXIII.

Greaves, H.R.G. : *The British Constitution*, Chap. V.

Howard, A. and West, R. : *The Making of a Prime Minister.*

Jennings, W.I. : *The British Constitution*,Chaps. VII, VIII

Jennings, W.I : *Cabinet Government*, Chaps. II, III, VIII, IX, XIII.

Jennings, W.I. : *The Queen's Government*, Chaps. 6, 7.

Keith, A. B. : *The British Cabinet System* (1952 revised by Gibbs), Chaps. II-V.

Laski, H. J. : *The Crisis and the Constitution.*

Laski, H, J. : *Parliamentary Government in England*, Chap. V.

Laski, H.J. : *Reflections on the Constitution*, Chaps. VIII-X.

Lowewenstein, K. : *British Cabinet Government.*

Powell, A.L. : *The Government of England*, Vol.I, Chaps. II,III.

Mackintosh, John P. : *The British Cabinet.*

Marshall, G. and Moodie, G. C. : *Some Problems of the Con- stitution.*

Mathiot, Andre : *The British Political System*, pp. 135-136.

Morrison, Herbert : *Government and Parliament*, Chaps. I—IV.

Morrison, Herbert: *Parliamentary Government.*

Muir, R. : *How Britain is Governed*, Chap. III.

Ogg, F.: *English Government and Politics*, Chaps. VI, VII.

Ogg, F. and Zink, H. : *Modern Foreign Governments*, Chaps. IV,V.

Stannard, H. ; *The Two Constitutions*, Chap. II.

Wisemen, H.V. : *Parliament and the Executive.*

# CHAPTER VI

# The Machinery of Government

## THE DEPARTMENTS AT WORK

### Working of the Departments

The preceding Chapter analyses how the Cabinet does its work. But the Cabinet is only policy formulating body. All details with the working out of policies so formulated, and all routine business connected thereto are left to the various Ministries or Departments of the State located in the Whitehall, just in the vicinity of Parliament These Departments are presided over by Ministers—usually, but not without exception, Cabinet Ministers—no matter what they are called, First Lord, Chancellor of the Exchequer. Foreign Secretary, President of the Board, or by any other designation. The Minister, who is a political chief, is responsible for all activities of organisations within the Department with a view to successful implementation of policy of the Government. As the Minister cannot himself know about all the activities and operations of a large Government Department, he must rely upon subordinates in whom he has confidence. A successful Minister is one who can develop a competent team of principal assistants and who can infuse the entire staff in the Department with his personality so that the organisation functions in a desirable and creditable manner. Harold Nicholson has written : "A Minister of strong personality immediately alters the whole atmosphere of his department and in the shaping of events, atmosphere is a far more important element than written word."

Below the Minister in a typical Department are one or two Junior Ministers designated as Parliamentary Under-Secretary of State or Parliamentary Secretary, who is also a member of the Ministry.[1] It is a frequent practice for one of those two Ministers to be chosen from the Lords and the other from the Commons in order that there may be some person in each House competent to represent the Department and answer queries with regard to its work.[2] They all go in and out of office with the change in the party control of Government. Hence their tenure of office is temporary and is dependent on the life of the Ministry. The function of the Junior Ministers is to relieve their senior Ministers of their burden by taking part in Parliamentary debates and answering Parliamentary questions, and by assisting in their departmental duties. Writing about the duties of a Parliamentary Under-Secretary, Winston Churchill said that he was often changed, "but his responsibilities are always limited. He has to serve his chief in carrying out the policy settled in the Cabinet, of which he is not a member and to which he had no access." He cannot dictate or determine policy that is the function of the Minister alone. This point came into prominence during the investigations of the Lynskey Tribunal in 1949. The Tribunal brought out that one Parliamentary Under-Secretary had on occasions overruled the advice of the permanent officials in his Department without consulting the Minister. When this was revealed, Prime Minster Attlee laid down the definite ruling that a Junior Minister should not override the advice of the permanent officials in his Department without reference to his political chief, who alone is responsible to Parliament for the policy and efficient functioning of his Department.

Below in the departmental chain is the Permanent Secretary[3] who occupies a position of the very highest responsibility and importance. Then, there are a Deputy Secretary, Under-Secretary, Assistant Secretaries, Principals, Assistant Principals, and many others who do merely Secretarial work of a purely routine character.

---

1. Where a Senior Minister is a Secretary of State, the Junior Minister has the title of Parliamentary Under-Secretary.
2. The Ministers of the Crown Act, 1937, specified that only eighteen out of twenty-one Ministers listed in the Act could serve in the House of Commons at one time. The House of Commons Disqualification Act, 1957, declared that not more than twenty- nine senior Ministers listed in the Act, and not more than seventy Ministers in all, could serve in the House of Commons at one time. The Ministers of the Crown Act, 1964, increased from seventy to ninety-one the total number of Ministers to serve in the House of Commons and abolished the limit on the number of senior Ministers.
3. Known as the Permanent Under-Secretary of State in those Departments where the Minister is a Secretary of State.

Highest and lowest, these non-political agents of administration make up, in general, the Civil Service Civil Servants are those servants of the Crown, other than holders of political or judicial offices, who are employed in a civil capacity, and whose remuneration is paid wholly and directly out of moneys voted by Parliament.[4] Their tenure of office is permanent and they continue to function regardless of all political changes in the country. They are outside the domain of politics and this is one of the most characteristic features of the Civil Service in Britain The permanent heads have in most cases been so long attached to their respective Departments that they acquire a complete grasp of affairs within their own spherers. With their expert knowledge, they help the Ministers to see that the Department works efficiently and in a particular direction determined by the policy of the Government. Lord Balfour has given a true picture of the position which Civil Servants occupy in Britain. "They do not control policy; they are not responsible for it. Belonging to no party, they are for that very reason an invaluable element in Party Government. It is through them, especially through their higher branches, that the transference of responsibility from one party or one minister to another involves no destructive shock to the administrative machine. There may be change of direction, but the curve is smooth."[5] Indeed, to a large extent they direct the actual working of the Department, and the Minister who controls the Department relies mainly upon the Civil Service for any new course of action which he desires to take.

The Permanent Secretary of a Department is the chief civil servant of the Department and he occupies a pivotal position. In the first place, he is the general manager in charge of the administrative work of the Department. At the head of the entire administrative hierarchy he is responsible to the Minister for the proper functioning of the Department. Secondly, he serves as chief adviser to the Minister on all matters of departmental policy and administration. But between the Minister and the Permanent Secretary these must exist mutual trust and confidence.

Below the Permanent Secretary the organisation of the Department fans out. Usually he has below him one or two Deputy Secretaries who supervise various branches of Ministry. They in turn have under them one or two Under-Secretaries each controlling several Assistant Secretaries and below the Assistant Secretaries come the Principals and Assistant Principals. All lines of responsibility within the Department converge inward and upward to the permanent Secretary and through him to the Minister.

The functions of the Departments may be said to be four. First, a Department must answer for its administration to the public. To put it more accurately, the officials of the Department must provide to their political chief all relevant information so that he may defend the actions of his Department in Parliament and on the public platform. That is to say, the policy of the Department is so framed that it must be capable of "articulate rational defence." The second function of the Department is the drawing up of its policy. It performs this both from its own administrative experience and from the direction given to it by its political chief. The Department prepares the draft of the scheme, works out its details in accordance with the general policy of the Ministry and consults the interests likely to be affected by it. If the scheme of policy cannot be carried out within the existing framework of the law, then, it passes into the stage of proposals for the Bill. After its approval by the Cabinet Committee, it is sent to the Parliamentary Counsel to the Treasury to be drafted as a Bill to be laid before Parliament. The Bill is sponsored and piloted by the Minister and it is his responsibility to see it through. But permanent officials of the Department will have to be in attendance in the "box" of the House and Committees to assist him with information and advice. It will, thus, be clear that even if the inspiration for the Bill may have come from the Minister, the preparatory work is the task of the Departments and in great part the result of the influence exerted by the Civil Servants.

Finally, it is the implementation of the policy. When the policy has been determined, presented, and sanctioned, it becomes the duty of the permanent officials of the Department to see that it is faithfully carried out, even if it is not exactly what they might have advised. There is little evidence in Britain on civil servants sabotaging the policy of the responsible political head of their Department.

Most modern statutes are "skeleton legislation." Parliament legislates in general terms only, empowering the Department concerned to work out the detailed regulations necessary to

4. Based on a definition given by the Royal Commission on the Civil Service 1929-31 (The Tomlin Commission).
5. Introduction to Bagehot's *English Constitution*, p. XXIV.

give effect to the Statute. It may also merely empower a Department to make rules with regard to a specific matter. The regulations made by the Department have the force of law. The "statutory in- struments" are so numerous that ever since 1890, Parliament has provided for the publication of an annual volume of "statutory rules and orders." Thus the Department will, probably, concurrently with its preparation of the Bill, have been working out regulations and other acts of subordinate legislation, and shortly after the Bill becomes law will issue them in a form drafted by its own lawyers. This process of delegated legislation had been the subject of severe criticism and Lord Hewart, in his book,*The New Despotism,* characterised this practice, cou pled with administrative adjudication—as "the new despotism" of the civil service.

Some administrative policy-making takes a quasi-judicial form. For example, the Minister of Town and Country Planning is empowered to decide what "development charge" shall be levied on land developers and where a new town shall be located. Similarly, it is for the President of the Board of Trade to determine what regions of the country shall be declared "development areas" in which industry will be financially encouraged to locate. Decisions of these kinds are not truly judicial as they do not determine legal rights. "They are, however, an extremely important means by which administrators make policy and shape the nation's future, within the framework of powers agreed to by Parliament."[6]

**Departments of Government**

It is not possible within the compass of this book to give a thorough description of work done by each Department. But it is worthwhile to look into the working of Departments arranged in groups by reference to similarity of work undertaken. The main Departments may be grouped thus:

(1) *General Departments.*
- The Treasury.
- The Home Office.
- The Scottish Office.

(2) *Economic Departments:*
- Ministry of Agriculture, Fisheries, and Food.
- Board of Trade.
- The Board of Customs and Excise.
- Ministry of Fuel and Power.
- Ministry of Labour and National Service.
- Ministry of Supply.
- The Post Office.
- The Ministry of Works.
- Ministry of Housing and Local Government.
- Ministry of Transport and Civil Aviation.

(3) *Social Welfare Departments:*
- Ministry of Education.
- Ministry of Health.
- The Department of Technical Co-peration.
- Ministry of Pensions and National Insurance.
- The Department of Scientific and Industrial Resarch.

(4) *Imperial and Foreign Departments :*
- The Foreign Office.
- The Colonial Office
- The Commonwealth Relations Office.

(5) *Defence Departments:*
- The Admiralty.
- The War Office.
- The Air Ministry.
- The Ministry of Aviation.
- The Ministry of Defence.

This is not a comprehensive list. A full list is published at intervals by the Stationery Officer under the title : "His/Her Majesty's Ministers and Heads of Public Departments." The Ministry formed by Sir Winston Churchill in 1951 contained the holders of thirty-eight offices. In October 1961 there were thirty-five in the Government of Harold Macmillan. The Labour Government of Harold Wilson created five new Departments and also made certain major adjustments in the jurisdiction and functioning of the already existing Departments. The newly created Departments were : The Department of Economic Affairs, The Ministry of Technology, The Ministry of Overseas Development, The Ministry of Land and Natural Resources, and the Welsh Office.

The "Senior" Department is the Treasury. Nominally, the heads of the Treasury are the Lords Commissioners : The First Lord of the Treasury (now always the Prime Minister), the Chancellor of the Exchequer and five junior Lords. In practice, the Lords Commissioners never meet as a Board and their responsibilities are carried by the Chancellor of the Exchequer assisted by the Chief Secretary to the Treasury, the Financial Secretary and the Minister of State. There is also a Parliamentary Secretary to the Treasury, who is the Chief Government Whip in

6. Marx, *Foreign Governments (1952)*, p. 87.

the House of Commons.

The functions of the Treasury fall under four main headings : finance, control of expenditure, general civil service establishment matters, and co-ordination of economic policy. Since the Treasury has "the power of the purse", it has won for itself a position of supremacy and from the very early stage it is the most powerful Department of the Government. "The power of the purse of the Treasury," Sir Robert Chalmers, the Permanent Secretary to the Treasury, told the MacDonald Commission, "means that all acts of administration requiring money (and practically all do in one form or another) come before the Treasury, and as a sort of shadow of that, there necessarily follow, and there are, intimately connected with, all the staff questions as to how to carry out the administrative problems that come before the Treasury."[7] One of the Permanent Secretaries of the Treasury is the Head of the Civil Service.

*Parliamentary Council to the Treasury.* The office of the Parliamentary Council is responsible for the drafting of all Government Bills, except those Bills or provisions of Bills extending exclusively to Scotland, which are handled by the Lord Advocate's Department. The office drafts all financial and other parliamentary motions and amendments moved by the Government during the passage of the Bills. It advises Departments on questions of parliamentary procedure, and attends committees and sittings in both Houses. It also drafts subordinate legislation when specially instructed, and advises the Government on legal, parliamentary and constitutional questions falling within its special experience.

**Advisory Bodies**

There are several hundred Committees and Councils attached to Government Departments for the purpose of consultation or expert advice, of which about 500 are permanent bodies attached to the main Departments. The advisory bodies are appointed by the Minister concerned and their membership includes civil servants, industrialists, trade unionists, university and industrial scientists, local government officials and experts from many other walks of life. There are three main types of such bodies, in which representatives of the Government meet representatives of groups outside Government; expert bodies, which formulate recommendations for action in a particular field; and bodies which have advisory status but which in practice decide matters themselves, e.g. the Central Training council in child care, the Air Transport Advisory Council, the Safety Board, etc.

In addition to these advisory committees there are *ad hoc* committees which the Government frequently sets up to examine and make recommendations on specific matters. For certain important inquiries a Royal Commission, whose members are selected on the grounds of their wide experience and diverse knowledge of the subject under study, may be appointed by Royal warrant. A Royal Commission examines written and oral evidence from Government Departments and other interested organisations and individuals. The Commission makes recommendation which the Government may accept in whole or in part or may take no action thereon. Public inquiries are also undertaken by departmental committees appointed by the head of the appropriate Department.

## CIVIL SERVICE

### Growth of the Civil Service

The Civil Service, as Graham Wallace said, "is the one great political invention in nineteenth century England."[8] Originally, the work of Government was done by persons of the Royal Household. With the development of the Cabinet system of government they came to be recruited by patronage, though it did not assume the form of Spoils System as it had prevailed in the United States. Once appointed, an official could expect to be retained so long as he was in good health and reasonably efficient. But in the late eighteenth and early nineteenth centuries such a system of recruitment was severely condemned by persons like Burke, Bentham and Carlyle. The Hailebury experiment, which aimed to give a rigorous training for youngmen destined to go to India in the service of the East India Company, provided an impetus for immediate reform of the British Civil Service. By the middle of the nineteenth century competitive examinations were introduced, first for the Indian Civil Service, and then, in 1870, for the British Civil Service. A Civil Service Commission was established through the initiative of Gladstone, which was alone empowered to admit persons to the service. Since that time several careful studies and a number of Orders-in-Council have furnished the basis of increased efficiency in matters of re-

7. See Finer., H., *The British Civil Service* (1937), p. 51.
8 *Ibid.*

quirement, division of the services into different grades, admission of women, determination of pay scales, etc. The result has been a large degree of unification.

In 1966, the Government appointed a Committee under the chairmanship of Lord Fulton, then Vice-Chancellor of the University of Sussex, to examine the structure, recruitment and management, including management training, of the Civil Service. The Fulton Committee submitted its report on the Civil Service in June 1968 and as a result of which an important programme of reconstruction and reform was undertaken.

The programme launched by the Civil Service is designed to make it more effective in carrying out its changing and expanding tasks, and will take several years to complete both because of its complexity and because of the resources in money and manpower that its full implementation requires. Nevertheless, since the Government's acceptance of the main Fulton proposals, action has been taken on quite a number of points. The Civil Service Department, under the control of the Prime Minister, has been in operation since November 1968; the Civil Service College has been opened since June 1970, with two centers in England and one in Scotland, and a greatly extended training programme has been introduced throughout the service; and a merger into a new administration group of the former administrative, executive and clerical classes, up to assistant secretary level, was effected in January 1971. In addition, a plan to absorb all posts from permanent secretary down to and including Under-Secretary and equivalent grades into a single, separate unit is now complete.

The number of civil servants is more than 500,000[9] and out of these 200,000 are industrial civil employees (primarily post office Engineers and employees in naval dockyards and Royal Ordinance Factories). But the term civil servants is generally used to cover non-industrial members of the staffs of the various Government Departments in the United Kingdom or working overseas. The total number of industrial and non-industrial civil servants employed in all Departments ( at home and overseas), is about 855,000 nearly one-third are women. The great expansion in State planning is essentially responsible for this huge number of civil servants. It has also led to further reorganisation.

**Organisation of the Service**

The guiding principles of Civil Service organisation are simple and obvious. They are three: a unified service; recruitment by open competition; and classification of posts into intellectual for policy and clerical for mechanical work, to be filled separately by separate examinations. In 1920, as a result of the recommendations of the Reorganization Committee—a Committee of the National Council—Civil Service was reorganized and an executive grade was interposed between the administrative and clerical. The report set out a simple two-fold division. "The administrative and clerical work of the civil service may be said, broadly, to fall into two main categories. In one category may be placed all such work as either is of a simple mechanical kind or consists in the application of well-defined regulations, decisions and practice to particular cases; in the other category, the work which is concerned with the formulation of policy, with the revision of existing practice or current regulations and decisions, and with the organization and direction of the business of Government." Each of these two main categories contains two of the four existing general classes.

The top administrative group is the pivotal and directing class of the whole Civil Service. They "are responsible for transmitting the impulse from their political chief, from the statutes and declarations of policy through the rest of the service and out of the public."[10] On this group rest the responsibilities for advising Ministers on questions of policy, and for controlling and directing Departments. It is a body of advisers, "a permanent brains trust," who find solutions for various administrative problems that arise outside the normal routine of departmental work, supply suggestions which may form the ingredients of supreme policy, and interpret regulations applying them to difficult cases. Sir Warren Fisher cogently explained the principles on which civil servants act : "Determination of policy is the function of Ministers, and once a policy is determined it is the unquestioned and unquestionable business of the civil servant to strive to carry out that policy with precisely the same goodwill whether he agrees with it or not. That is axiomatic and will never be in dispute. At the same time, it is the traditional duty of civil

9. Including part-time Staff—two part-time officers being reckoned to one whole time officer.
10. Finer, H., *The Theory and Practice of Modern Government*, p. 767.

servants, while decisions are being formulated, to make available to their political chiefs all the information and experience at their disposal, and to do this without fear or favour, irrespective of whether the advice thus tendered may accord or not with the minister's initial view. The presentation to the minister of relevant facts, the ascertainment and marshalling of which may often call into play the whole organization of the department, demands of the civil servant greatest care. The presentation of inferences from the facts equally demands from him all the wisdom and all the detachment he can command.''[11]

The Administrative class itself formulated its duties in a statement submitted to the Tomlin Commission.[12] These duties have been succinctly summed up by Jennings. He writes that the civil servant's function is ''to advise, to warn, to draft memoranda and speeches in which the Government's policy is expressed and explained, to take the consequential decisions which flow from a decision on policy, to draw attention to difficulties which are arising or are likely to arise through the execution of policy, and generally to see that the process of government is carried on in conformity with the policy laid down.''[13] Sir Horace Wilson, then Permanent Secretary in the Ministry of Labour, defined the duties of the Administrative class to the Tomlin Commission. He said : ''Broadly speaking, the main quality that is required seems to me to be a capacity to take the facts about a particular subject, to put them into shape, to suggest the deductions that might be drawn from them, to propose the lines of policy that might be adopted in relation to them, and generally to apply a constructive analytical mind to what I would call the policy of the Ministry.

For the efficient performance of these arduous duties the Administrative Officers must necessarily possess a trained mental equipment of a high order capable of the ready mastery of complex and intricate problems. The qualities exactly wanted in an Administrative Officer are judgment, *savior faire,* insight and fairmindedness. For, the men who enter this class are not, as Finer says, ''merely secretarial; they are the young shoots who may twenty years hence be permanent heads of the departments or very closely associated with it.''[14] Its members are, in majority of cases, university graduates who attained front rank eminence at the universities. After having entered service, through competitive examination, they get a general training, in more or less every branch of administration up to a comparatively late age. This is, according to the argument of Macaulay and Jowett, a better qualification for intellectual work than a special training, and that success in that training is likely to indicate desirable qualities of character. It also accounts for the liberal outlook of the civil servants in England.

The members of administrative class are recruited by a severe competitive examination. Recruitment to this class is by no means confined to ordinary competition entrants and to candidates of University standard who entered by special competition in the two post-war periods. About 40 per cent of the total are recruited from other classes, within the service, by promotion, limited competition, or transfer. This is partly due to the pressure from staff associations representing the other classes, anxious to secure opportunities of promotion for their members and partly due to the greater needs of government than could be met from the regular planned intake into the class.

The specialist classes (General and Departmental), which number about 130, 000 include Scientific, Professional and Technical classes and other classes which carry out the wide range of specialised activities now undertaken by the Government. The categories include Accountants, Architects, Doctors, Economists, Engineers, Lawyers, Librarians, Statisticians, Surveyors and Scientists in all branches of science. The recruitment to such jobs is not subject to competitive examination. Specialists who possess duly recognised qualifications and a particular standard of training and experience are appointed for individual jobs. Vacancies are advertised and the selection is made through the method of interview.

In addition, there are many other departmental classes where employment is peculiar to one Department, for example, Post Office, Factory Inspectorate of the Department of Employment and Productivity, School Inspectorate of the Ministry of Education and Science, the Inspectorate of Children's Department of the Home

11. As cited in Jennings' *Cabinet Government,* pp. 114-115.
12. It is reproduced in full in Herman Finer, *The Theory and Practice of Modern Government,* pp. 769-770.13.
13. Jennings, W. I., *Cabinet Government,* p. 116.
14. Finer, H., *The Theory and Practice of Modern Government,* p. 770.

Office, and the Mines Inspectorate of the Ministry of Power.

The Diplomatic Service is a separate self-contained service of the Crown, which provides the staff (comprising some 6,200 civil servants) for services in the Foreign Office and Commonwealth Office and at United Kingdom diplomatic missions and consular posts in foreign and in independent Commonwealth countries. Its functions include advising on policy, negotiating with overseas governments and conducting business in international organization, promoting British exports and the advancement of British trade; presenting British ideas; and protecting British interests abroad.

The service has its own grade structure, corresponding by salary with the grades of the Administrative, Executive and Clerical classes of the Home Civil Service. It also has Secretarial, Communications and Security Guard branches. Various specialists and advisers from Home Departments or the armed forces may serve at overseas posts on secondment or attachment to the Diplomatic Service.

## CIVIL SERVICE EVALUATED

### Role of the Civil Service

The growth of the Civil Service in Britain is a comparatively modern phenomenon. During this period the British Civil Service has assumed a great constitutional prominence. Three factors are of particular importance in this respect. The first is the change from the negative State to the positive State. As the functions of the State increased, the services of a professional staff were increasingly recognised necessary and the complexity of the work involved compelled the Minister's to leave to their officials all but the largest decisions on major policy. But when the issue is one which must be submitted for the Minister's personal decision, it has even then to be fully and fairly presented to him so that all the material facts and considerations are before him. Civil Servants matter in the determination and presentation of the relevant material.

This is, indeed, a rough classification, but the fact remains that a very large number of decisions is taken by senior Civil Servants. Even if the decision is taken by the Minister or the Cabinet, the case must be prepared. Information is collected by an Executive and he gives his suggestions, if he is asked to do. His memorandum goes to the Administrative Secretary who gives his own comments and if he does not approve the work of the Executive he may prepare it anew. Then, the file may travel to others in the same Department or in other Departments, if it concerns any other, for their remarks, and all concerned may add their comments of agreement or disagreement. At the end, when the file goes to the Minister, it contains a definite statement of the practicable alternatives, with the arguments for and against each of them. He can see the file if he wishes, but generally there is no need, because the combined wisdom of the Department has brought the question down to an issue where commonsense and political *savoir faire* are the qualities required. If he says that he must consult the Cabinet, he makes up his own mind and gets an Executive to state the case in a Cabinet Memorandum.

The second is the method of recruitment by open competition conducted by an independent body, the Civil Service Commission. The open competitive examination is not an examination in special and professional subjects deemed necessary as a preparation for a career of professional administration. Such a system of examina tion has, no doubt, certain tangible defects. But the British system of competitive examination aims at testing the general ability of candidates. Coupled with the written test is the *viva voce* test. The object of the interview is to fathom their intelligence and alertness, vigour and strength of their character, and potential qualities of leadership so that the administrators of tomorrow may not only think, argue, and write but also devise, act and lead.

It does not, however, mean that there is in Britain no political or purely personal influence on appointments or promotions. But the grossest forms of patronage are certainly absent. This is one of the very important reasons of the high standard of efficiency maintained by the Civil Service. The civil servant in Britain is not so ruthlessly subjected to the disappointment and irritation caused, as for instance in Canada, and for many reasons in India, by the imposition over their heads of ministerial proteges of minor capacity. The British public service traditions encourage honest opinion and fearless criticism. But so long as politicians can influence in any vulgar sense appointments, promotions and the distribution of honours there is, as Jennings aptly says, "a risk of toadying, flattery and self-seeking."

The third important reason is the ethics of the British Civil Service or the code of conduct which every civil servant is required to observe. This is a code laid down partly in Acts of Parliament and partly in orders, regulations, and instructions issued by the Government and by Departments of the Government. "It is a stringent code," as Barker put it, "designed to pre vent any chance of economic corruption and any opportunity of political influence." The principles it enjoins and the standards it sets work as effectively as the professional codes of the doctor and the lawyer in that country and like them the British administrative code of ethics, too, rapidly became a moral for the whole world.

The British civil servant is rigidly neutral and rigorously impartial in economic and party political issues. He "may not make political speech, print a partisan article or tract, edit or publish a party newspaper, canvass for a party candidate or serve on a party committee." He probably by nature, but most certainly by training, stands somewhat aloof from political parties. He has neither any personal motive nor any design. By virtue of his security of tenure he represents the principle of continuity in government. He is a link between successive Ministries, and the repository of principles and practices which endure while governments come and go. He serves with equal fidelity whatever be the complexion of Government. In 1932, when Britain became protectionist the officials of the Treasury and the Board of Trade did their best to produce the most efficient protective system that their ingenuity could devise. When MacDonald succeed- ed Lord Curzon, in 1924, at the Foreign Office, the official who had served Lord Curzon continued as MacDonald's Private Secretary. The Labour Party had really no occasion in 1924, in 1929 or in 1945, as also in 1964, in 1966 and in 1974 to change the occupants of some of the key positions in public service. "To prevent any possible difficulty in foreign policy," writes Jennings, "Mr. Arthur Henderson, who became Foreign Secretary in 1929, circulated in the Foreign Office copies of the official Labour Party programme, *Labour and the Nation.* By 1945, however, the views of Labour politicians were sufficiently well understood to make such a precaution unnecessary." The fact is, that the civil servants are servants of Her Majesty, the Government—whatever the political colour of that Government may be—and of the nation as a whole.

There is no evidence to show any kind of intrigue between Civil Servants and the Opposition. All civil servants feel a temporary allegiance to the party in power and its programme, no matter what their bias or personal conviction. All do their jobs with honesty. The men at the top give their advice frankly until their chief has reached his decision. But once the decision is there they deem it their duty to carry that out loyally. The British Civil Service is loyal to the Government of the day. Herbert Morrison relates an important incident to illustrate it. "Some American officials", he writes, "in attendance on the United States Government representatives at the Potsdam Conference in 1945 had an experience which to them was surprising. During the first part of the Potsdam discussions between representatives of the Governments of the United States, the Soviet Union and the United Kingdom, the British General Election was proceeding. some of the Americans said to some of the British: 'If there is a change of Government as a result of the election in your country there will be, we suppose, changes in your important civil servants. So may be we shan't see these British civil servants any more.' They were assured though they were not wholly convinced, that this would not happen; they were genuinely surprised and could not follow it when Mr. Attlee turned up as Prime Minister and head of the British delegation in the second part of the Conference, instead of Mr. Churchill, accompanied by the same civil servants as served Mr. Churchill."[15]

Confidential communications—and they are numberless — the Civil Servants treat as secret even from their next parliamentary chief. If one Minister prepares a scheme which never materialises, the permanent Secretary of the Department may refuse to show the relevant documents to the succeeding Minister and the beauty is that the latter would recognise the propriety of such a course. Here is an anecdote given by Herbert Morrison. He writes, " In talking in my younger days to a high civil servant who had formerly worked under me I was vigorously—perhaps in the circumstances too vigorously—denouncing the policy of his new master, my successor in office. At a moment when it became clear that I was somewhat embarrassing him, he said, "Well, Mr. Morrison, I can only say that different Ministers have different ways, which illustrated the meritorious loyalty which the civil

15. Morrison, H., *Government and Parliament,* pp. 319-20.

service quite properly owes and practises towards Ministers.''[16] Nor must the civil servant use any information gained through his work to improve his personal position or to gain pecuniary benefits. Examples are very rare when a Permanent Secretary, as it happened in 1936 when Secretary of the Air was dismissed for using his knowledge of public negotiation for his own private advantage, may be removed from office for violation of the principles of the civil service code. Morrison says, ''We are proud of the British Civil Service. As a whole, they are efficient, public spirited, incorruptible; very,very rarely does a British Civil Servant get convicted of bribery, corruption, nepotism, treachery or favouri- tism.''[17]

**Should Ministers be Experts ?**

It is very often complained that ministers are amateurs in the art of government and the administration is actually carried on by the civil service. It is, no doubt, true that Ministers are laymen[18] with no knowledge of the Department they have to preside.[19] Then, their appointment and allotment of portfolios is a matter of political consideration and expediency rather then their liking or aptitude for the work they are expected to perform. Even if a Minister is able to get a Department of his own choice, it is impossible for him to qualify as an expert. The work of a Department is a vast mass of administrative details. It is not possible for the Ministers to follow all the details and go into the heaps of files to master the case, particularly when their attention is largely engrossed in the more active field of politics; the Cabinet, Parliament, the press and the platform. They have, therefore, no decisions of their own to make and simply endorse what their subordinates tell them to do. It is, accordingly, suggested that only those persons should be appointed Ministers and Departments assigned to them who have adequate professional experience related to the work they will be expected to supervise. It is further asserted that if in France and other Continental countries it is not uncommon to put military and naval men in charge of War and Marine Ministries, why cannot a similar practice be followed in Britain ? Another example cited is that of the United States where there is now a growing tendency to place at the head of at least a few of the Executive Departments, like agriculture and labour, experts in the work with which they are concerned.

But this is not the problem of the Parliamentary system of government. The essence of Cabinet Government is ministerial responsibility; responsibility for which the electorate had given its verdict at the time of the General Election and responsibility which the Government must conscientiously own and discharge during the tenure of its office. The government is wedded to a particular policy and its first concern is to see it through to the satisfaction of those who have returned them to authority. Perhaps, the best simple statement of the basic principle involved is that of Sir George Cornewell. It is quoted by Bagehot and has been times out of number repeated : ''It is not the business of a Cabinet Minister to work his department. His business is to see that it is properly worked.'' Ramsay MacDonald put it still more graphically ''The Cabinet,'' he said, ''is the bridge linking up the people with the expert, joining principle to practice. Its function is to transform the message sent along sensory nerves into command set through motor nerves. It does not keep the departments going; it keeps them going in certain directions.'' The work of a Minister is, thus, to helps framing general policies and to see that they are carried out by the staff employed for the purpose. The authority of the Civil service and for that matter of the experts is one of influence, not of power. ''it indicates,'' as Laski says, ''consequences; it does not impose commands. The decision which results is the Minister's decision; its business is the provision of the material within which, in its judgement, the best decision can be made.''

There are many advantages if the head of a Department is a layman. A layman sees the De-

16. *Ibid.*, pp.38-39.
17. Morrison H., *British Parliamentary Democracy*, p. 17.
18. Sir Winston Churchill was successively Under-Secretary of State for Colonies, President of the Board of Trade, Home Secretary, First Lord of the Admiralty, Chancellor of the Duchy of Lancaster, Minister of Munitions, Secretary of State for War and Air, Secretary of State for the Colonies, Chancellor of the Exchequer, First Lord of the Admiralty, and the Prime Minister.
19. ''We require,'' wrote Sidney Low, ''some acquaintance with technicalities of their work from the subordinate officials, but none from the responsible chiefs. A youth must pass an examination in arithmetic before he can hold a second-class clerkship in the Treasury, but a Chancellor of Exchequer may be a middle-aged man of the world who has forgotten what little he ever learnt about figures at Eton or Oxford'', *The Government of Britain*, p. 201. Disraeli, while forming a Ministry, offered the Board of Trade to a man who wanted instead the Local Government Board. '' It does not matter'' said Disraeli, ''I suppose you know as much about trade as the First Lord of the Admiralty knows about ships.''

partment as a whole. His vision is broad and his attitude compromising and progressive. The mental attitude of an expert is narrow and he is apt to exaggerate the importance of technical questions. When an expert supervises the work of an expert, there is likely to be friction and disagreement, for it is the habit of experts to disagree and are rigid in holding their point of view. In order to produce really good results and avoid the dangers of friction, and, consequently. inefficiency and bureaucracy, it is necessary "to have in administration a proper combination of experts and men of the world."[20] An amateur Minister may again serve as an intermediary between one Department and the other and his own Department and the House of Commons, to which body he is responsible for carrying out a certain policy. Government is one single whole and there is and must be an organic unity in the various aspects of administration. A layman who takes a general view of a Department considers himself and his Department a part of the bigger whole and endeavours to shape his policy in accordance with the general policy, and will see that its various parts keep in line, and in particular watch that experts remember that they are to work as members of a team as servants of the Crown, that is to say, of the Queen's Ministers, and that they provide a store of knowledge and experience.

It is true that the political head of a Department should be well informed of the work to be carried on under his direction. But it does not mean that he is expected to qualify as an expert. In every Department there is division of labour and scores of problems come which demand high order of practical and technical proficiency, and even departmental experts with permanent tenure cannot claim specialisation in all those problems. How can, then, it be possible for a Minister, whose tenure of office is short and precarious, to master everything which concerns his Department ? The permanent heads of Departments cannot be experts in the sense that a great physicist, a great surgeon, or a great artist is an expert. But, "They do not live in a realm", says Laski, "into which the ordinary cannot enter." Any one who remembers the intellect and power of grasping details of Sir John Simon or Sir Stafford Cripps will agree that these are the qualities which a Minister requires in his relation with his Department. "We send men into the Treasury," concludes Laski, because "they have good general minds, not because they are trained economists; so also in the Ministry of Agriculture or the Board of Education. They are valuable as administrators less because they have expert knowledge of a technical subject-matter but because we believe, on the evidence rightly, that their training will endow them with qualities of judgment and initiative without which no Government can be successfully run. But these are exactly the qualities a politician must have if he is to be successful, normally, in the struggle for place."[21]

**Tendency towards Bureaucracy**

An important criticism against Whitehall is the danger of bureaucracy. Ramsay Muir maintains that "bureaucracy" in Britain "thrives under the cloak of ministerial responsibility." He asserts that the continuous and persistent influence of the permanent civil service in the three functions of administration, legislation and finance is the dominating fact of British governance today and, as such, the element of bureaucracy is of vital importance, "though its strength is masked by the doctrine of ministerial responsibility."[22] This criticism implies that permanent officials control the life of the nation. Various, and not without much truth, arguments are advanced in this connection. First, it is contended that in the carrying out of established policy, many acts are done every day which involve a policy. The Minister simply conveys the general direction of a policy approved by Parliament and directs the Department to carry it through. He has no time to look to the daily working directions. The permanent civil servant is an expert fully conversant with the details and their implications and he, accordingly, tends to shape the day-to-day policy of the administration.

Secondly, in devising new policy, which may take the form of Bills to be put before Parliament, the influence exercised by the civil servants is supreme. Ministers simply receive vague indications of policy from their party or Cabinet. But the material to serve the basis for a draft Bill has to be provided by officials of the Department concerned. Then, the actual drafting of a Bill is a complicated and a difficult task. A layman will make the worst of a job if he attempts

20. Lowell, A. L., *The Government of England,* Vol. I., p. 173.
21. Laski, H.J., *Parliamentary Government in England,* p. 293.
22. Ramsay Muir, *How Britain is Governed,* Chap. 11.

it. It is done by the officials of the Parliamentary Counsel under the Treasury. "Only an expert can fit the new policy into the old administration; and the permanent official may often have to suggest to the political Ministers what can and what cannot be done, as well as how to do what can be done. Thus, new policy is very often the actual product, and still more often the result of corrections and suggestions of the permanent civil servants."[23] It is not the civil servants at the top who exert the influence alone and shape policy. There are many less important decisions and even some elements of policy which are influenced by the lower ranks of the civil service. In every Government Department responsibility must be delegated. This involves giving some control over policy of civil servants lower on the ladder.

Thirdly, the method of asking questions in Parliament is deemed to be method by which the governed can exercise some control over the acts of the administrative departments and getting redress of wrong done. But the critics point out that this method "is crude and largely ineffectual." The questions are, undoubtedly, answered by the political heads of Departments, yet the answers are formulated by the permanent officials. It is very difficult for a Private Member to get information if the answers prepared by experts tend to obscure the issue. More than this, even if the officials be willing and keen to tell the whole truth, the questioner is often at a disadvantage, because he does not know enough to frame an effective question. And even if the question is effective, it is put after the administration has acted and there is no effective method yet devised to control the day-to-day policy of a Department before it is formed.

Then, there is actually a clear and rigid hierarchy of authority from the Minister down to the most junior official and all this inevitably creates what is popularly known, "red tape." It means that many official decisions "are taken by rather wooden, rule-of-thumb methods." The citizens feel aggrieved, because of the stereotyped method of disposal of the cases and rigid application of the rules without taking cognisance of the peculiarities involved therein. The system also takes pretty long time to dispose of finally. All this is nothing short of bureaucracy which defeats the purposes of a democratic government, more so parliamentary democracy. "The faults most commonly enumerated are over-devotion to precedent; remoteness to the rest of the community, inaccessibility, and faulty handling of the general public; lack of initiative and imagination; ineffective organization and misuse of man-power; procrastination and unwillingness."[24] The officials regard the routines more important than the results and value the means employed more than the needs aimed at. "The trained official," as Bagehot said, "hates the rude, untrained public. He thinks that they are stupid, ignorant, reckless."[25]

But the real danger of bureaucracy it is pointed out, is the process by which the Departments have been made a source of legislation in the shape of orders and regulations issued in supplement of the legislation passed by Parliament and source of jurisdiction, in the sense of issuing decisions on a number of contentious issues which arise in the course of their work. In other words, the exercise of what is described as delegated legislation and administrative adjudication are really a great enhancement in the powers of the Executive. It is true that, in form, such powers of legislation are exercised in the name of the political chief of the Department, but, in fact, they are actually exercised by administrative officials. Then, the Executive goes a step further by establishing departmental tribunals or quasi-tribunals, which decide disputes arising under these orders and regulations. As long as the decision is within the scope of broad grant of powers given by Parliament, it is legal and the justice or wisdom of the Minister's decision cannot be questioned in a court of law; it is final. But at the back of this final decision of the Minister is some anonymous civil servant. Moreover, the Minister, or rather the civil servant, is not governed by the rules of judicial procedure, which are incumbent upon the courts, and may, therefore, make decisions without giving an opportunity to the affected party to submit evidence or to plead and argue his case. It would, accordingly, seem that both these powers of legislation and jurisdiction have made the authority of the administrative departments arbitrary and unduly free from restraint. For, both the methods oust Parliament and the courts of law from the exer-

23. Burns, C.D., *Whitehall*, p. 69.
24. Report of the Committee on the Training of Civil Servants (1944).
25. Bagehot, W., *The English Constitution*, p. 172.

cise of their respective authority and the natural outcome is omni-competent bureaucracy.[26]

But this is, again, not a correct appraisal. Lowell suggested in his now classical book, *The Government of England,* that in England the danger of bureaucracy had disappeared through the particular type of relationship between amateur and professional involved in the clear distinction of political from non-political agents.[27] Bureaucracy, according to Laski, ''is the term usually applied to a system of government, the control of which is so completely in the hands of the officials that their power jeopardizes the liberties of ordinary citizens.'' The permanent officials in Britain are not the masters of the situation. The Civil Service is, no doubt, the reservoir of experience and knowledge. They furnish the Cabinet and Parliament with much of the information and material which is required in shaping and enacting policies on a multitude of subjects. But they do not dominate the administration and fix the tone and character of the Government. At the head of every Department is a responsible political chief who really rules. It is he who is responsible to Parliament and the people for carrying out the policy, and the civil servants must adjust themselves to carry out that policy. If a member of Parliament, who represents the people, feels that an injustice has been done to an individual or a wrong principle is being applied, he may ask the Minister privately for an explanation. And all Ministers do it readily. If the explanation offered does not satisfy him, he can ask the question in the House. If the answer, again, does not meet his criticism, he may raise like subject in a debate. But a responsible Minister will like to avoid such an eventuaity, because, as Jennings remarks, ''even more important than the fact that questions are asked is the fact that questions may be asked.''[28] This fact makes the Minister alert. He must not make mistakes because he is responsible. He will exercise a greater degree of care and caution because he can be questioned in Parliament about the mistakes of the most junior official. The Civil Servants, also, know the precarious position of their political chief, and, therefore, they, too, must not make mistakes. This they have to remember all the time and at every step.

A bureaucracy controlled by Parliament, and subject to Parliamentary chiefs is not a bureaucracy. The Civil Service in Britain is part of a democratic and responsible form of government in which abuse of power would lead to a quick and drastic public reaction which would cause some ''heads to roll''. The responsible Minister, who is at the head of the civil servants, would continue reminding them the inner meaning of Sir William Hercourt's remark ''what the public won't stand.''[29] This is the primary function of a Minister and this is the real meaning of Cabinet Government. The whole development is, accordingly, permissive development proceeding from Parliament, subject to Parliament, and terminable by Parliament. The difficulties created by 'red tape' are perhaps a small price to pay for compensating advantages.

**Bureaucratic Influence**

A contrary view of the British bureaucracy was expressed by Professor Graham Wallas in his *Human Nature in Politics* (p. 249) as follows: " The real 'Second chamber', the real 'constitutional check' in England, is provided not by the House of Lords or the Monarchy, but by the existence of permanent Civil Service appointed on a system independent of the opinion or desires of any politician, and holding office during good behaviour''.

Senior bureaucrats exercise great influence on Cabinet ministers and even the Prime Minister unobtrusively. James Harvey and Katherine point out in *The British State* (p-196-197): ''Since Mr. Attlee was from the beginning surrounded by Mr. Churchill's advisers on foreign affairs, it is not at all surprising that the foreign policy of the Labour governments received the general approval of the Conservative Opposition throughout their period of office. The immense influences which the highest officials in the Foreign Office can exercise over the Foreign secretary... is very great indeed because the Foreign secretary is almost completely dependent on his officials and ambassadors for all his information about foreign countries.''

The power of the leading civil servants is still further enhanced by the fact that some matters are so secret that even the Cabinet and most of the Ministers are kept in ignorance about them. This applies chiefly to military affairs and to the

26. Hewart, Lord, *The New Despotism.*
27. Vol. I, Chap. VIII.
28. Jennings, W. I., *The British Constitution, op. cit.*, p. 134.
29. As quoted in H. J. Laski's *Parliamentary Government in England,* p. 288.

secret police. For example, the war-time atomic energy agreement between Churchill and Roosevelt, though known to certain bureaucrats, was not revealed to Attlee who was at that time deputy Prime Minister of the War Cabinet.''

Professor Chester rightly observes. ''The Characteristics (of the Whiteball Machine) which struck me most forcibly were : the great weight and vastness of the machine which on occasion almost amounted to an immovable object, if you were against it, but was an irresistible force if you were on its side; and the tremendous power which lay in the hands of Ministers and in the hands of their nearest personal advisors.'' (*Lessons of British War Economy, p. 19*) It is not difficult to imagine the degree of immorality which this bureaucratic machine would present to a government desirous of making radical socio-economic changes.

While political leaders in England wear specific party labels, administrative elites are not expected to be partymen. On the contrary, the claim is made that they are politically 'neutral' and their exclusive concern is to advance the business of the state 'under the direction of their political masters.' However, the top civil servants are not mere executants of their policies, as they themselves play a significant role in their determination. Regarding the manner in which this power is exercised, the notion of 'neutrality' is surely misleading, because the bureaucrats undoubtedly are not likely to be free of certain definite ideological inclinations, which must affect the orientation and character of their advice and action. Ideological inclinations of top civil servants, in England are bound to be generally conservative due to their social upbringing and elitist education and so they may be neutral, more less, as between different conservative groupings and parties which succeed each other in office. As Ralph Milihand rightly points out, '' Nor even need there be any departure from such 'neutrality' when that spectrum is somewhat widened, as when social-democratic governments accede to office.'' (*The State in Capitalist Society,* p. 108).

Any government bent on 'radical' changes is most likely to find many of these bureaucrats quite possibly hostile. This is because the civil servant's ''profession requires him to care more for the continuity of the realm than for the success of party.'' (C.H. Sission, *The Spirit of Administrati*on, p, 124.) This conservatism of British civil servants should be seen in specific terms, related to their national hierarchies and class configurations. Their objective is simply the defence of the particular social order prevailing in England. Bureaucrats are, therefore, conscious and unconscious allies of existing social and economic elites in contemporary capitalist order of Britain.

Ralph Miliband says : ''The state bureaucracy, in all its parts, is not an impersonal, un-ideological, apolitical element in society, above the conflicts in which classes, interests and groups engage. By virtue of its ideological dispersions, reinforced by its own interests, that bureaucracy, on the contrary, is a crucially important and committed element in the maintenance and defence of the structure of power and privilege inherent in advanced capitalism. The point applies at least as much to economic 'technocrats'... contemporary capitalism has no more devoted and more useful servants than the men who help administer the state's intervention in economic life.'' (*The State in Capitalist Society, pp. 115-116).*

Perhaps even more than the members of the administrative elites, top military men are portrayed as altogether free from the political and ideological biases and partisanship, who are dedicated to a 'national interest' and to 'martial virtues' like honour, discipline, courage etc. Here too, as in the case of the bureaucracy, the notion of the military elite as ideologically uncommitted and politically unbiased is manifestly false. The weight of the high ranking military officers in influencing state decision is considerable, and not only in matters pertaining to the armed forces but also foreign policy, internal security and even economic policies.

Like civil servants, their beliefs and convictions are essentially conservative not only in general sense but also in the specific sense of preserving the social and economic status quo and opposing any meaningful alternative to that system. In this perspective, the important point is not so much that the military elite does weild a great deal of influence in the British state system. More important is the fact that the military hierarchy is very likely to use this influence to reinforce the conservative bias of their governments and do their best to limit the impact of any radical proposal put forward by a liberal or social democratic regime. ''Given their whole ideological orientation, military and police elites may always be expected to support with particular zeal the determination of the civil power to combat 'internal subversion'. at least from the Left '' zeal the determination of the civil power to combat 'internal subversion', at least from the Left.'' (*Ibid.*, p. 123).

In periods of strife and class conflict, these managers of the state's coercive function reliably and loyally serve any conservative regime in suppressing the striking workmen, agitating left wing political activists, and other such enemies of peace and challengers of the status quo. On the other hand, this could not quite so readily be taken for granted in the case of political dissenters and activists at the other end of the political spectrum such as neo-fascists and fascists of all hues.

Political sociology is concerned with the changes brought about by bureaucracy in a modern state. Max Weber suggested that the process of bureaucratization and democratization have acompanied each other. This may be true of political developments in Britain or france. Weber thought that bureaucracy represents rational legal authority based on recruitment of administrators from broad sections of society. They possess the technical means to operate the engines of a modern state but the administrative processes serve the community through the programmes of the party in power and not the private interests of an administrative elite.

## SUGGESTED READINGS


Benemy, F.W.G. : *The Elected Monarch : The Development of the Power of the Prime Minister.*

Bridges, Sir Edward : *Portrait of a Profession.*

Burns,C.D. : *Whitehall.*

Campbell, G.A. : *The Civil Service in Britain.*

Campion and others : *Parliament : A Survey,* Chap. VI.

Clarke, J.J. : *Outlines of Central Government.*

Critchley,T.A. : *The Civil Service Today.*

Dunnil, Frank : *The Civil Service.*

Finer, H. : *The British Civil Service.*

Finer, H. : *Governments of Greater European Powers,* Chap. 8

Finer, H. : *The Theory and Practice of Modern Government,* Chap. XXX.

Hewart, Lord : *The New Despotism.*

Jennings,W.I. : *British Constitution,* Chapt VI.

Jennings, W.I. : *Cabinet Government,* PP. 110-133.

Keith, A.B. :*The British Cabinet System.*

Laski, H.J. : *Parliamentary Government in England,* PP. 263-308 and Chapt VI.

Laski, H.J. : *Reflections on the Constitution,* Chaps. XI-XIII.

Low, S. : *The Governance of England,* Chapt. VI.

Lowell, A.L. : *The Government of England,* Vol. I, Chaps. VII,VIII.

Mackintosh, J.P. : *The British Cabinet.*

Mackenzie, W.J.M. and Grove, J.W. : *Central Administration in Britain.*

Muir, R. : *How Britain is Governed* , Chap. II.

Ogg, F.A. and Zink, H. : *Modern Foreign Governments,* Chapt. VI, VII.

Ogilvy Webb, M. : *The Government Explains.*

Robson, W.A. : *The British Civil Servants.*

*Royal Commission on the Civil Service.*

Wheare, K.C. : *The Civil Service in the Constitution.*

Wilson, F.M.G., And Chester, D. N. : *The Organization of British Central Government.*

# CHAPTER VII

# Parliament

## Origin and Growth of Parliament

Parliament is described by its critics as a mere 'talking shop'. This description is used opprobriously and yet that is what the word parliament means and to a great extent it describes the actual institution. It is a place where people talk about the affairs of the nation.

The earlier document in which the word 'parliament' is found is the eleventh-century *Chanson de Roland,* where it is used simply to refer to a conversation between two persons. But the word early acquired a derivative meaning, that of an assembly of persons in which discussion took place. A contemporary referred to the meeting Runnymede as the parliament in which King John "gave his charter to the barons."[1] Anyway, by 1258 parliament had evidently begun to acquire a special meaning. In June, of the same year, one of the reforms demanded by the barons at Oxford was three parliaments a year "to treat the business of the King and Kingdom." Clearly, therefore, the essence of parliament is discussion and when the word was first applied to the great councils of the English Kings it was with the view to emphasise their deliberative function.

The origin of parliament may be traced to two ideas and both these ideas are of great antiquity. The one is that the King, though himself the supreme law-giver, always sought the advice and counsel of the wisest and most experienced of his subjects. In Saxon times, Kings governed with the advice and counsel of the "Witanagemot," or meeting of wisemen. The other idea is that of representation. The Norman Kings held their courts in different parts of the country, and summoned therein for discussion of national affairs prominent members of the Church, big landlords, and Knights. They were really not representatives of the people in the sense in which we understand them today, but it does indicate the idea of selecting some prominent individuals, even by the Norman Kings whose power was unlimited, for purposes of consultations. This kind of consultation took a significant shape in 1213 when King John, who was hard pressed for money, ordered the Sheriff of every Shire to send up four 'Knights' from his Shire to discuss the affairs of the realm with the King. Here are the seeds of a modern idea of Parliament; a representative assembly of the people, where their affairs are discussed and laws made for them.

The growth of Parliament was more or less spontaneous, slow, and sometimes haphazard.[2] But its form was very different from what it is today. And so were its powers. It took eight centuries to transform Parliament into a governing body resting on the suffrage of all adult persons in the country and the process has only been completed in our own times. All these eight centuries had been a period of struggle which had been more intense during the reign of evil Kings. It began with King John. All of us know how the barons, in desperation, took the King prisoner and made him sign at Runnymede, on June 15,1215 *Magna Carta* or the *Great Charter.*

This was not a victory of the people over the King, but a victory of the rich and powerful men of Britain over the King. The *Magna Carta,* all the same, gave them, *inter alia,* assurances against arbitrary arrest and it provided that the King could not impose taxes on his chiefmen without the common counsel for the realm. For the next eighty years the struggle was between the Kings who were anxious to get money, and the other great men of the land who claimed the right to meet, and consider whether the King's demands were reasonable or not, and get their grievances redressed. Out of this struggle emerged the present political dogma of no taxation without representation, and the conversion of these assemblies into legislative bodies.

The original idea of calling 'Parliament' was, thus, associated with the pressure of the money demands of the Kings. It was called when the King wanted it and its primary business was

1. Mackenzie. K. R., *The English Parliament,* p. 12
2. *See ante Chap. II*

to hear from the King why money was needed, how it was going to be spent, and to consult those who had been summoned as to the best means of raising it. This is still the most important business of Parliament.

The 'Parliament' summoned by Simon de Montfort, in 1265, is generally described as the first parliament in anything like the modern meaning of the word. For, he called two knights from each county and also representatives from certain towns, although much of the credit for its being representative is lessened by the fact that he summoned only his own supporters. In 1295, Edward I, who needed money for wars, called together, what has been named, the 'Model Parliament.' To this were summoned archbishops, bishops, abbots, earls and barons; all of whom attended as landholders on personal writs. General writs were also issued to the Sheriffs for the election of two knights from each county, two citizens from each city, and two burgesses from each borough. Representatives of the lesser clergy were also summoned through the bishops, Thus, a large representative element was added to the feudal council.

Two important things emerged out of this kind of transacting of business. The persons summoned to the King's Parliament only discussed the best way of raising money by taxes. They grumbled, no doubt, but they could hardly afford to come into conflict with the King and question the propriety of his demands. But whenever they came to attend the meetings of 'parliament', they brought with them their local grievances and presented petitions to the King detailing the wrongs and injustices done in their part of the country and prayed for their redress. If the King refused to redress the grievances, the apprehension was that the representatives of the tax-payers might create difficulties about meeting the financial needs of the King. Gradually, therefore, was established the principle that the redress of grievances should precede the grant of supply. With the lapse of time another development took place. The grievances were at first personal and particular. But it was soon discovered that many people and many localities had common grievances. They, accordingly, began talking about it in 'Parliament' and if other members supported them in their requests, then, they would send a petition from 'Parliament' to the King. If the King agreed to grant what they asked, he would send back the petition with the words *Le roy le veult* (the King wills it) written on it. If he did not accept it, he would send the petition back with the words *Le roy s' avisera* (the King will think about it). Even today public Bills are assented to with the words *Le roy le veult. Le roy s' avisera* has not now been used to a measure since 1708 as it amounts to vetoing a Bill.

Even more important was the second development. There began a custom that the King could not tax his people unless Parliament voted him the money and devised ways of raising it. This finally became a mighty law, and the struggle between Cromwell and Charles is the culminating point in this connection. Another important result of this struggle was the decision of the issue: who was to govern in Britain—King or Parliament. The struggle ended in the execution of King Charles by Parliament and subsequently the supression of Parliament for some years by Cromwell. But the Glorious Revolution of 1688 finally decided the supremacy of Parliament. With abdication of the last Stuart King, Parliament turned to the Hanoverian dynasty. It had two definite results of constitutional importance. First, Monarchy became the gift of Parliament, and secondly, any future Monarch of Britain would be a constitutional Monarch acting on the advice of his Ministers responsible to Parliament. This ended four centuries old conflict between the Kings and Parliament, and, then, followed the process of democratization of Parliament.

The *Magna Carta* had curtailed the King's powers over his barons. The struggle between Cromwell and Charles had represented the claim to a share in power of the new rising class. The Revolution of 1688 had established the sovereignty of Parliament by reducing Monarchy to dependence upon it. But Parliament was still very far from being a democratic Parliament. Before 1832 there were only a few thousands of voters spread all over the country, and parliamentary seats—"pocket boroughs" or "rotten boroughs" as they were called- were in the gift of rich men, and were bought and sold like shares on the Stock Exchange. The First Reform Act of 1832 was a cautious measure which left the working class completely unrepresented. After all it added only 1,00,000 persons to the voters lists and it represented just the partial acceptance of the claim of the middle class. Parliament was, therefore, still a long way from being a people's Parliament.

At intervals after 1832 extending to 1928 there has been successive electoral reforms. First to the more substantial middle class, then to the lower middle class and the workmen in the towns, then to the mass householders, then to adult males over twenty-one years of age and most women over thirty and afterwards to almost every person over twenty-one of either sex. The age of voting has now been reduced from January 1, 1970 to 18; adding another two million to the voting population of the country.

The essential changes which these eight centuries have brought about may, thus, be summarised :—

1. Eight centuries ago Parliament was called when the King wanted it. When it met, it could not make laws. All that it had to do was to grant the King the money he asked for, and to discuss the best way of raising the money by taxes. Today, the King must call a Parliament. It has become a regular thing and its meetings, except for intervals of recess, go all the year round.

2. From being a selected thing it is now an elected thing. The King does not select whom he will call to a Parliament. Members are elected by the people at regular intervals.

3. The right to take part in the election of members of Parliament, instead of restricted to a small section of the people, is enjoyed by all adults, men or women in the country who had attained the age of eighteen. This right they express through a system of secret ballot.

4. Power has passed from King to Parliament. The King is only a constitutional head of the State who acts on the advice of his Ministers and they in turn are responsible to Parliament.

5. That within Parliament, power has passed from Upper to Lower Chamber-from the Lords to the Commons.

**Sovereignty of Parliament**

The development of Parliament discloses how it conducted a struggle with the Kings to determine the residence of authority and to vindicate sovereignty for itself. This issue was practically determined in the seventeeth century and cosolidated in the eighteenth. Three landmarks illustrate the result. It was Parliament mutilated and under the control of the army but nevertheless Parliament that resolved in December 1648 to bring Charles I to trial[3] and his subsequent execution in 1649."[4] It was, again, the same Parliament that abolished[5] Monarchy by an Act and declared Britain to be a Commonwealth.[6] In 1660, it was, again, Parliament which restored Charles II to the throne, and on the condition of his co-operation with Parliament.

The second landmark was the Revolution of 1688 when James II, failing to co-operate with Parliament was made to abdicate, and it was again Parliament which supported the invitation to William of Orange to come over to defend Britain's rights against James II.[7] Parliament also determined, by the Bill of Rights of 1689. not only who should reign next, but also on what express conditions he should reign.[8] In 1701, Parliament made the Act of Settlement, an Act, which, *inter alia,* actually determined the suecession to the throne.[9]

The third landmark is 1783 when, with the accession of Younger Pitt to office, the Cabinet system in all its essentials was finally fixed, and the King ceased to choose and dismiss his Ministers. Henceforth, in reality if not in form, Ministers came to be chosen and dismissed by parliament.

The power of Parliament is supreme and unlimited. It embraces a vast field including the making of laws, levying of taxes, the sanction for declaring of war and making of peace. It controls and supervises all governmental machinery. It can dethrone Kings; it can elect Kings; it can abolish Kingship. The power and jurisdiction of Parliament, said Sir Edward Coke, "is so transcendent and absolute, as it cannot be confined either for persons or causes within any bounds." Blackstone held the same view and used language to the same effect. Erskine May said, "The constitution has assigned no limits to the authority of Parliament over matters and persons within its jurisdiction. A law may be unjust and contrary

3. Act Erecting a High Court of Justice for the Trial of Charles I, Adam and Stephens, *Select Documents of English Constitutional History,* p. 389.
4. Sentence of the High Court of Justice upon Charles I, *Ibid.,* pp. 391-393.
5. Act abolishing the office of the King, *Ibid.,* pp. 397-399.
6. Act declaring England to be Commonwealth, *Ibid.,* p. 400.
7. It was called the *Convention Parliament,* the assembly resembled Parliament in every way, except that it was not convened by the King's writ, a state of affairs rendered inevitable by the flight of James II, and by the fact that William had not yet been crowned as King. The proceedings were, however, validated by the Confirmation Parliament Act passed on February 20, 1689, *Ibid.,* pp. 454-456.
8. *Ibid.,* pp. 462-69.
9. *Ibid.,* pp. 475-79.

to sound principles of government; but parliament is not controlled in its discretion, and when it errs, its errors can only be corrected by itself." De Lolme declared that "Parliament can do everything but to make a woman a man, and a man a woman." But like various other remarks made by De Lolme this statement also involves confusion. If the power of Parliament be envisaged wholly from the legal point of view, the proposition that Parliament cannot make a man a woman is inaccurate. Should Parliament enact a law causing a confusion in the sexes, legally speaking, a man would be a woman and no other body can set the law aside on the grounds that it is unconstitutioal or undesirable. Parliament is not legally subject to any physical limitation.

"The Sovereignty of Parliament," said Dicey, "is from a legal point of view the dominant characteristic of our political institutions," and the principle of Parliamentary Sovereignty, he added, "means neither more nor less than this, namely, that Parliament thus defined has, under the British Constitution, the right to make and unmake any law whatever; and further no person or body is recognised by the law of England as having a right to override and set aside the legislation of parliament"[10] Dicey, thus set the following propositions:—

(1) That there is no law which Parliament cannot make; and

(2) That there is no law which Parliament cannot unmake.

From the above two follows the third :

(3) That there is under the British Constitution no marked or clear distinction between laws which are fundamental or constitutional and laws which are not; and

(4) That there is no authority recognised by the law of Britain which can set aside and make void such legislation.

Finally, Dicey added:

(5) That Parliamentary Sovereignty extends to every part of the King's Dominions.

To sum up, Parliament can legislate what it pleases, as it pleases, and that what Parliament enacts is law. What Parliament has enacted, the courts interpret and apply unless Parliament has otherwise provided. Parliament is both a legislative body and a Constituent Assembly. No formal distinction is made in Britain between constitutional and other laws, and the same body, Parliament, can change or abrogate any law whatsoever and by the same procedure. An Act of Parliament cannot be called into question in any court of law. Nor can it be declared invalid, for no law exists in Britain higher than that made by Parliament. Although Equity and Common Law are the oldest and most fundamental to the British Constitution, yet neither Equity nor Common Law can overrule the laws enacted by Parliament. If two Acts of Parliament are in conflict with each other, a more recent Act of Parliament takes precedence over a less recent and supersedes any earlier statutory provisions inconsistent with it.

The principle of the legal supremacy of Parliament also helps to explain the status of certain "fundamental and historical documents," like Magna Carta, the Petition of Rights, the Bill of Rights, the Habeas Corpus Act, the several Acts dealing with suffrage, etc., which are accepted as a distinct element or source of the British Constitution. In reality such "documents" possess the general character of statutes, and as they are connected with the structure or functions of government, they carry with them greater sanctity than an average statute. But any recent statute, though it is unlikely to be in conflict with the provisions of these legal landmarks, would nonetheless in law take precedence over them.

Finally, the right to this legislative supremacy resides in Parliament and in Parliament alone. Executive in Britain has not the power of issuing decrees which have the force of law save in so far as that power is conferred on it by Parliament itself and so can be taken away by Parliament.[11] Neither through the Royal Prerogative nor by any other means can any legal limitation be placed on Parliament. As a corollary, the right to impose taxes resides with Parliament alone. Again, Parliament alone has the right to legalise the past illegalities. Legally, therefore, Parliament can make or unmake any law, destroy by statute the most firmly established convention or turn a convention into a binding law, and legalise past illegalities reversing the decisions of courts. It even has power to prolong its own life by legislative means beyond the normal period of five years as determined by the Parliament Act, 1911.

Sovereignty of Parliament, however, is re-

---

10. Dicey, A., *Introduction to the Law of the Constitution,* pp. 39-40.
11. The famous exception, the Statute of Proclamations which only remained in force for a few years, is in one sense an illustration itself of this principle, since it was considered necessary to confer the decree-power on Henry VIII by an Act of Parliament.

ally nothing but a legal fiction and a legal fiction may assume anything. Dicey, and many others like him, dealt with only legal aspects of sovereignty divorcing it from the realities of actual life. And the reality of actual political life in Britain is that a legal truth very often turns out to be a political untruth. Parliament cannot do any and everything, and make or unmake any kind of law. There are many moral and political checks which limit its powers, and Parliament would find many other things as difficult to accomplish as to make a man a woman. Blackstone correctly said that, "It (Parliament) can, in short, do everything that is not naturally impossible." All proposals for law are considered on the touchstone of practical utility and moral considerations. In a law-abiding community, such as the British community, the very fact that Parliament has enacted a law is strong presumption that it will be obeyed. The ordinary citizen does not readily set up his own private judgment against that of Parliament. But there are limits to obedience too. "If a legislature decided," as Leslie Stephen suggests, "that all blue-eyed babies should be murdered, the preservation of blue-eyed babies would be illegal; but legislators must go mad before they could pass such a law and subjects be idiotic before they could submit to it." In fact, no legislature can even think of such a legislation, particularly in a country like Britain where public opinion is strong and has the ready means of expression. Democracy is a government by consent and laws in a democratic government must necessarily be the manifestation of the will of the people. If they are not, the political sovereign takes his revenge. The supreme legislature, therefore, always takes care to keep itself within the practical restraints, though legally there may be none.

It is true, as Dicey said, that law is a law whether it is moral or not and legislation passed by Parliament may not have any reference to the moral aspect. But Parliament cannot pass a law which is against the facts of nature or is against the established codes of public or private morality. Similarly, it dare not pass legislation against the established customs of the country unless the people want it. Even the supremacy of Parliament is itself nowhere laid down as a fundamental and unalterable law. It is the expression of custom, the result of a long and ultimately successful struggle against the ordinance-power of the King. The will of the people triumphed in making Parliament supreme and sovereign and in this way sovereignty of Parliament became an organic principle of the British Constitution. And so are the conventions which carry with them the acquiescence of the people; the supreme and sovereign will. The conventions of the Constitution are, thus, an organic principle of the British Constitution as the Sovereignty of Parliament itself is and, accordingly, they are beyond the practical possibility of the competence of Parliament. This is a significant restraint against the Sovereignty of Parliament.

Another important feature of the British Constitution is the Rule of law. The conception of the Rule of Law was given classical exposition by Dicey as he had given to the Sovereignty of Parliament. The Rule of Law means that the ordinary law of the land is of universal application, that there is no exercise of arbitrary authority, and that there is no division into separate systems of law, one for officials and another for the ordinary citizens. It also carries with it the rule that the remedies of the ordinary law will be sufficient for the protection of the rights and liberties of the citizens, and, there is nothing in Britain as the Fundamental Rights. The Rule of Law is closely interwoven with the supremacy of Parliament. To put it in another way, Parliamentary supremacy is, in part, only tolerable, because the Rule of Law is recognised. If Parliament passes a legislation which is contrary to the principles of the Rule of law, it imperils its own supremacy, Sovereignty of Parliament and the Rule of Law remarks Barker, "are not only parallel; they are also interconnected, and mutually interdependent. On the one hand, the judges uphold and sustain the sovereignty of Parliament, which is the only maker of law that they recognise (except in so far law is made, in the form of 'case law', by their own decisions) ; on the other hand Parliament upholds and sustains the rule of law and the authority of the judges, who are the only interpreters of the law of the land."[12] Rule of Law is, therefore, an effective limitation on the legal Sovereignty of Parliament.

The most decisive proof of the legislative sovereignty of Parliament are those Acts which fix the limits of its own duration. The Triennal Act provided that no Parliament should last

12. Barker, Ernest, *Britian and the British People,* pp. 24-25. It should, however, be noted that the Executive has now acquired a power of administrative jurisdiction.

longer than three years, and the Septennial Act of 1716 enacted that it should last for seven years unless previously dissolved by the King. The Parliament Act of 1911 reduced its life to five years, and the same Parliament that introduced the change extended its own life by successive statutes until it had sat for almost eight years. All these extensions were made in times of war with the express approval of all the political parties and the tacit consent of the nation. What is more important to note is that in 1945, after the precedent of the First World War had been followed for almost five years, it was universally recognised that the Conservative majority in Parliament must not get another extension without the consent of the Labour minority. Accordingly, when Churchill asked his Labour colleagues to remain in the National Government without a General Election until the end of the Japanese War, he coupled his request with a suggestion that the electorate should be asked to signify its approval of the postponement of General Election by a referendum. The Labour Party did not agree and though Britain was still in the midst of hostilties. General Election was held and the electorate returned the Labour in majority to form the Government. No Parliament, therefore, dare extend its duration, permanent or temporary, until it has with it the tacit consent of the nation. While discussing the question of Sovereignty of Parliament, Heman Finer says, "All is true except that, in fact, there are limitations in practice to the authority of Parliament, limitations that are embodied in the authority of the electorate, mediated or not through the political parties. The sovereignty of Parliament, is limited by the power of the people—but by no other instrument."[13]

Yet, what is Parliament ? Jennings says, indeed, we talk in "fictions on concepts even when we mention 'Parliament'. Parliament is not an institution."[14] Parliament consists of the King, the House of Lords, and the House of Commons. All the three functionaries join together to complete the actions of Parliament. We need say nothing about the King, for his part in legislation has become little more than formal. The House of Lords and the House of Commons are two different institutions having different characteristics and different functions. The authority of the House of Lords with the passage of the Act of 1911, as amended in 1949, has become rigorously limited and if today the House of Commons were to pass a law abolishing the House of Lords, it can do it and the Queen must give her assent thereto. There is nothing to obstruct it. The conception of the Sovereign Parliament, therefore, now stands fundamentally changed. Under the present circumstances Parliament really is the House of Commons, and in the broader sense it means the majority party in the House which in its turn is the Cabinet. Parliament endorses what Cabinet proposes. And yet it is normally the joint action of the Queen, the Lords, and the Commons which law requires to make legislation possible. This is evident from the words with which an Act of Parliament opens : "Be it enacted by the Queen's most excellent Majesty, by and with the advice and consent of the Lords Spiritual and Temporal, and Commons, in this present Parliament assembled, and by the authority of the same...."

Though, Parliament may legally legislate for the Dominions, yet its powers are rigidly limited by constitutional limitations. As a result of these constitutional limitations it is in accord with the constitutional position of all the Dominions, "in relation to one another that any alteration in the law touching the succession to the Throne, on the Royal Style and Titles shall hereafter require the assent as well of the Parliaments of all the Dominions as of Parliament of the United Kingdom." Moreover, no Act of British Parliament passed after 1931 is to extend to a Dominion unless the Act expressly affirms that the Dominion concerned has requested and assented to it. Legally, North America Act of 1967, till April 1982, when Canada "patriated" its Constitution, could be amended by the British Parliament. But the convention which then governed the constitutional amendment was that it proceeded from the Canadian Parliament and the British Parliament quickly passed the required amendment. This process nullified Dicey's assertion that the right or power of Parliament extended to every part of the King's dominion. The Canadian Constitution Act, 1982, put an end to this anachronistic practice by which Canada, a full sovereign nation, had still to ask a foreign (British) Parliament to make changes in their own Constitution. The British North America Act, 1867, with all its amendments remains in existence but sans its previous nomenclature. It has now become the Canadian Constitution Act,

13. Finer, H., *Governments of Greater European Powers*, p. 47.
14. Jennings, W. I., *Parliament*, p. 2.

1867, together with its various amendments.

But the great inroad made on the sovereignty of Parliament is by the delegated legislation. Dicey, perhaps, did not visualise this modern development when he maintained that legislative supremacy lies in Parliament and in Parliament alone. Parliament cannot find time for all the work it has to do, and so lightens its task by permitting other bodies to take share in law-making. In some cases the Crown acting on its prerogative powers, is left to issue Orders, usually Orders-in-Council, and in other and numerous cases an Act of Parliament gives some Minister, Department, or other authority, the power to make Orders and Regulations. It is true that it is the Act of Parliament which authorises the issuing of Rules and Regulations, but a great mass of these Rules and Regulations practically remain unknown except to those who administer them. Cecil Carr divides the "Statutory Instrumentts", as these Rules and Regulations are now called under the Statutory Instruments Act of 1946, into separate classes, 'general and local' and estimates that their average exceeds 1,200 a year.[15] In 1946 the total just topped 2,287. Their number has since then still more increased. Parliament does not and cannot keep a check on this tremendous increase in the delegated legislation and they have the force of law and the courts can intervene only when the rules and regulations so made are against the delegation of power or when proper procedures have not been used.

The jurisdiction of Parliament is also limited by practices of International Law. It is now a recognised principle of the British Constitution that International Law is a part of the Municipal Law of the land. It was decided in *West Rand Gold Mining Co.* vs. *The King* "that whatever has received the common consent of civilised nations must have received the assent of our country." Any legislation which is repugnant to the principle of International Law Parliament cannot enact.

Dicey himself recognised the formal and purely legal aspect of the doctrine of the Sovereignty of Parliament and proceeded to point out that this formal concept operated within two limits, external and internal. Ultimately, the legal sovereign derives its authority from the political sovereign. Political sovereignty is tersely but fully stated in Labour Party pamphlet circulated in the elections of 1945:

"It really does rest with you. You may complain about statesmen and politicians. You may criticise Parliament. But you give statesmen power. You elect politicians to Parliament. You determine the membership and thereby the policy of the House of Commons.[16]

You meant the voters, and the House of Commons is really Parliament; it is the principal pillar on which national democratic government rests. Legally, Parliament can make and unmake any kind of law, but in actual practice it must bow to the will of those who determine the membership and policy of the House of Commons. It cannot ignore the wishes and interests of those who are likely to be affected by its legislation.

Finally, with the accession of Britain to the European Community on January 1, 1973, the provisions of the European Communities Act (passed by Parliament) applying the Treaty of Rome became operative, and Parliament subjected itself to various types of Community legislation, including regulations made thereunder and directives issued from time to time by the Council of the Community. These directives are binding upon each member-State of the Community to which they are directed. The British Parliament can make no deviation therefrom. The only option allowed to Parliament is to choose the form and method of implementation. Under the Treaty of Rome the Parliaments of all member-States delegated a number of their members to sit in the European Community Parliament, to deliberate and decide matters coming before it. European Parliament is now elected directly by the people of the member-states. Parliament in Britain has adopted special parliamentary procedures to keep its members informed about Community developments, and enable them to scrutinise and debate matters which are to be decided by the Community's institutions. But Britain's accession to the Community, as a result of the nation-wide referendum—which itself negates the sovereignty of Parliament—completely erodes the concept of Parliament's sovereignty. The British Parliament cannot legislate on or take decisions on matters that conflict with the decisions of the Community's institutions. The decisions and directives the British Government receives are binding and take direct effect. Lord Dunning ruled in April, 1980 in the case of

15. Campion and Others, *Parliament : A Survey,* p. 241.
16. Finer, H., *Government of Greater European Powers,* p. 59.

stockroom manageress Wendy Smith that the European Common Market Law took priority over the English statute law. He held that the Common Market Law, by virtue of Britain's accession to the Treaty of Rome, was binding and, consequently, overriding. This, perhaps, is the first instance in which an Act of British Parliament has been overruled in deference to a non-British Law, thus, reducing the Sovereignty of Parliament to less than a legal fiction.

The Sovereignty of Parliament, therefore, operates within the limits imposed by conventions, public opinion, morals of the community, expediency, International Law, and International Agreements.

## THE HOUSE OF LORDS

Parliament now consists, apart from the King himself, of two Houses—the House of Lords or the Upper Chamber, and the House of Commons or the Lower Chamber. It was not always so, and on the most formal occasions it is not so even today. When the King opens Parliament, or prorogues it, or when his assent to the Bills is announced, all members of Parliament—Lords Spiritual and Temporal and Commons—assemble in one Chamber, and there listen to the King in his person or his message. Ordinarily, however, the Peers do their business in one Chamber and the Commons in another.

In Britain nothing is arranged. It just grows and the House of Lords is the child of this growth. When Edward I called his Model Parliament in 1295, all the different classes of people summoned to attend met in one single assembly. But afterwards they broke into three groups or "estates"—Nobles, Clergy and Commons—to hear separately the King's plea for money and "to make such response as they individually chose". Gradually, however, practical interests led to a different arrangement. The greater barons and the greater clergy[17]had many interests in common and they, accordingly, associated together in one body. The lesser clergy found attendance at Parliament very irksome. Moreover, they were jealous of their clerical privileges and preferred to make their money grants to the King in their "Convocation." They soon ceased to attend Parliament altogether. Similarly, the Knights, after a good deal of wavering, found their interests identical with the burgesses and finally united with them for all purposes. The result was the division of Parliament into two Houses. In one House sat the Peers—Temporal and Spiritual—in the other, the representative Knights of the Shires and the representative Townsmen. The first, which became the House of Lords, was a non-representative House, as it was composed of men who attended in response to personal summons. The second was a completely representative House, called the House of Commons, as it consisted of the representatives of the Shires and the Boroughs.

How and when exactly this arrangement came about, nobody knows. It was accidental and the result of social and economic circumstances. By the close of the reign of Edward III, this bicameral organisation seems to have been fully established.[18] Thenceforward the distinction between the two Houses became political.

The hereditary principle came into being similarly. The term "peer" means *equal* and originally it referred to the feudal tenants-in-chief of the King all of whom were legally peers of one another. After the division of Parliament into two Houses in the fourteenth century, it was being used for those members of the baronage who were "accustomed" to receive a personal writ of summons when a Parliament was to be held. There is no evidence to show that the Kings had ever a mind to create a peerage of a hereditary character. It was, however, a custom that a King, whenever he summoned a Parliament, would send for the same peers who had sat in an earlier one, or if in the meantime they had died, for their eldest sons. In course of time, custom became a right and a seat in the House of Lords descended from father to eldest son, just as did the family estate under the rule of primogeniture.

### Composition of the Lords

Potential membership of the House of Lords is over 1,000, but this number is reduced to about 760 by a scheme which allows Peers who do not wish to attend to apply for leave of absence, either for the duration of a particular Parliament or for a single session.[19] Average daily attendance is upwards of 250 but more may attend when some matter in which they have a special interest is under discussion. Its composition may be divided into the following seven categories :

17. The greater clergy were not simply clergies, but they were feudal landholders too.
18. Adams, G. H., *Constitutional History of England,* pp. 194-95.
19. Provision is made for a Peer to terminate his leave of absence on giving a month's notice.

1. The Princes of the royal blood, who now-a-days take no part in the proceedings of the House.[20]

2. *The Lords Spiritual,* 26 in number and include the two Archbishops of Canterbury and York, the Bishops of London, Durham and Winchester, and 21 most senior Bishops of the Church of England. When a sitting Bishop dies or resigns, the next senior on the list becomes entitled to a writ.

3. The *Lords Temporal* subdivided into:

(i) all hereditary Peers and Peeresses, now 700 in number who have not disclaimed their Peerages under the Peerage Act, 1963. Hereditary Peers carry with them a right to a seat in the House of Lords, provided the holder is 21 years of age or over. Under the Peerage Act, 1963, however, anyone succeeding to Peerage may, within twelve months of succession, disclaim that Peerage for his or her life time. Those who disclaim their Peerages lose their right to sit in the House of Lords, but are eligible for election to the House of Commons;

(ii) until 1963 the Scottish Peers elected for each Parliament sixteen representative Peers to sit in the Lords. The Peerage Act, 1963, opened membership of the Lords to all Scottish Peers;[21]

(iii) nine Lords of Appeal in Ordinary (commonly called the Law Lords), appointed under the provisions of the Appellate Jurisdiction Act, 1876, to assist the House of Lords in the performance of its judicial functions. They hold their seats for life; and

(iv) life Peers and Peeresses created under the provisions of the Life Peerage Act, 1958.[22] There are at present more than 200 life Peers.

By far the most important and the most numerous are the hereditary Peers and they account for more than seventy per cent of the total membership of the House. A great bulk of them hold their seats simply as a result of chance as they happen to be the eldest son of an eldest son back to an ancestor who was first created a peer. They are the "accidents of an accident", as Bagehot has called them. Nearly one half of the total of the hereditary Peers are the creation of the twentieth century. Another 300 go to the nineteenth century, and the rest go up to the thirteenth century. The bulk of the Peerage is, therefore, of recent origin. No hereditary peerage has, however, been conferred since 1965.

The power of the Crown to create hereditary peers, until 1965, was unlimited and till then it had been used with great freedom. Normally, it was usual to create anything from two to half a dozen new Peers a year and the object was to honour men of distinction in law, letters, science, politics, diplomacy, war, or for any other meritorious services, But it had also been an important constitutional weapon in the hands of the Crown to change the complexion of the House of Lords in order to overcome its resistance to the avowed policy of the party in power. It was actually used by the creation of twelve Tory Peers in 1711 in order to secure approval of the Treaty of Utrecht. In 1832 the continued resistance of the House of Lords to the Reform Bill incurred the threat to create as many new Peers as Earl Grey's Ministry deemed necessary to get the measure passed. A similar situation arose over the Parliament Bill of 1909. Once again, the reluctant House of Lords succumbed to the threat. In view of the provision of the Parliament Act of 1911 and scrupulous adherence to the "mandate convention" there had been no more occasion to resort to this method of securing the assent of the House of Lords over an issue on which electorate had given its verdict.

Sometimes the Government of the day needs spokesmen in the Lords or must fill Royal Household appointments. Peerage is, accordingly, conferred on men of talent and loyalty. Lord Passifield, formerly Sidney Webb, was raised to peerage in the first Labour Government and scores of others were elevated from 1945 to 1965.

*Privileges and disabilities.* Members of the House of Lords have certain privileges and are under certain disabilities. They enjoy freedom of speech and are exempt from arrest while the House is in session. The Lords can individually approach the King to discuss public affairs. They have also right of recording a protest against any decisions of the majority in the House in its

20. There are now three peers of royal blood; Prince Charles, the Prince of Wales, Dukes of Gloucester and Kent.
21. By the Act for the Union of Great Britain and Ireland, the Irish Peers were entitled to elect 28 representatives, but no elections have been held since the creation of the Irish Free State (now the Irish Republic) in 1922, and no Irish Peers now remain.
22. Some of the appointments under the 1958 Act, are recommended by the Prime Minister after consultation with the Leader of the Opposition or with the Leader of the Liberal Party and its alliance.

Journals. They have the right to commit for contempt of their privileges and that right extends beyond a session. A Peer when charged with treason or felony had the right to demand trial by his fellow Peers but the privilege with regard to felony was withdrawn in 1936. The Peers have, also, the right to act as a court of final appeal for the realm, but this right is now exercised by the Law Lords only.

The members of the House of Lords had no right to vote at Parliamentary elections, and they were disqualified for election to the House of Commons. They could not divest themselves of their titles or refuse inherit them when their elders died. Consequently, it was a matter of much tribulation "when their heir who has made a career for himself in the Commons and Ministry must leave the excitement of these centers of government with the prospects of high office, even the Prime Ministership, to go to the House of Lords". Three recent examples are good to illustrate the point. One is Quintin Hogg, son of Lord Hailsham, an eminent lawyer and once a Commoner who bitterly suffered his "promotion". The other was the Marquess of Salisbury. Lord Stansgate's son and heir, Anthony Wedgwood Benn, in vain fought hard to avoid eventually inheriting his father's title Winston Churchill was willing to be kinghted, but he firmly refused the peerage, for he rejoiced in remaining a "House of Commons man".

With the passage of the Peerage Act, 1963, the old position is changed. It now enables any hereditary Peer with political ambitions to disclaim peerage, and seek election to the House of Commons. Wedgwood Been, Viscount Stansgate, was the first to renounce his title and won back his seat as Labour M.P. The enactment of Peerages Act was the result of nearly ten years' struggle of this "reluctant peer." Persons who disclaim their peerages lose their right to sit in the House of Lords, but they are able to vote at parliamentary elections and are eligible for election to the House of Commons. Lord Home disclaimed his peerage and became Sir Alec Douglas-Home. He became Prime Minister after the resignation of Harold Macmillan.

The membership of the House of Lords was hitherto entirely male. Although there were some twenty-six peeresses in their own right, holding titles by virtue of decent from male ancestors, but they were not admitted. Even now those who are allowed to sit and vote in the House of Lords are the life Peeresses. The male Peers, who have not renounced their titles cannot seek elections to the House of Commons, but the wives of Peers may sit, as did Lady Astor for many years. Similarly, the husbands of new life Peeresses retain their right to seek election to the House of Commons, as they will get no title.

The Peers receive no salary for their parliamentary work, but they are entitled to travelling expenses from their homes to the Palace of Westminster, provided they attend at least one-third of the number of sittings. They may also claim, with the exception of the Lord Chancellor, the Lord Chairman of Committees, the Law Lords and any member in receipt of a salary as the holder of a ministerial office, payment for expenses incurred for the purpose of attendance at the House (except for judicial sittings). The Leader of Opposition in the Lords receives an annual salary.

**Procedure and Organisation**

The two Houses of Parliament must invariably be summoned simultaneously and both are prorogued[23] together, but adjourned[24] separately. The House of Lords meets only for four days in a week—Monday to Thursday—and normally for two hours or thereabout. Friday sittings are arranged when pressure of business demands. The precedent is that except under direct pressure, discussion must be concluded in time to enable the noble Lords to dress for eight o'clock dinner. The House is sparsely attended. The usual attendance used to be from 70 to 80 members and that, too, on occasions when a matter of first rate importance was being discussed. Now the average daily attendance at a sitting is over 250. It is one of the results of the Reform Act of 1957. Three members constitute a quorum, but at least thirty must be present in order to pass any Bill. According to Standing Orders promulgated by the House in 1958 holders of peerage are asked, at the beginning of each Parliament, whether they will attend the sittings of the House as reasonably as they can or whether they desire to be relieved of the obligation to attend. If they so desire, they

---

23. At the end of a session of Parliament the King dismisses it and tells to reassemble on a certain date to begin a new session's work. This dismissal is called proroguing. Parliament prorogation both ends a session and terminates all pending business.
24. To adjourn means merely to interrupt the course of business temporarily. At the end of each day's work, and whenever it takes a holiday, Parliament adjourns.

are requested to apply for leave of absence, either for the duration of Parliament or for a shorter period, during which they are on their honour not to attend, and not to vote without notice. Failure to send a reply to the Lord Chancellor is tantamount to the wish not to attend. This is a useful step to wards rationalising the composition of the House of Lords.

The debate is more leisurely than in the House of Commons. Freedom of speech is virtually unrestricted and the presiding officer, the Lord Chancellor, has far more limited power over debate than enjoyed by the Speaker in the House of Commons. The Lord Chancellor is a Chairman, not a Speaker as in the Commons. The level of debate is high and on certain occasions higher than that of the House of Commons.

The organisation of the House of Lords closely parallels that of the House of Commons. The Lord Chancellor is the presiding officer. The Crown, by commission under the Great Seal, appoints several Peers to take their place on the "Woolsack" in order of precedence in the absence of the Lord Chancellor. The first of the deputy speakers to act for him is the Lord Chairman of Committees, who is appointed each session and takes the chair in all Committees, unless the House otherwise directs. He also has important duties in connection with Private Bills Legislation in which he is assisted by his Counsel, who is a permanent salaried officer of the House. The House also appoints a number of Deputy Lord Chairmen of Committees. The permanent officers of the House include the Clerk of the Parliament, who is charged with keeping the records of proceedings and judgments and who pronounces the words of assent to Bills, the Gentleman Usher of the Black Rod, who enforces the order of the House, and the Sergeant-at-Arms, who attends the Lord Chancellor. The appointment of the Sergeant-at-Arms and that of the Gentleman Usher of the Black Rod are now held by the same person.

The Committee system of the House of Lords is more simple than that of the House of Commons. The Lords conduct some of their business in the Committee of the Whole House and it consists of the members present. It is presided over by the Lord Chairman of Committees and it operates under less formal Rules of Procedure than when the House is in regular session. The House has no Standing Committees except one for textual revision to which Bills are referred after passing the Committee of the Whole House. Sessional and Select Committees are utilised for the consideration of special kinds of legislation or for gathering of additional information on pending Bills. Sessional Committees may consist of all members present during the session or of small number as determind by the House. There are a number of Select Committees on Private Bills, consisting of five Peers, appointed in each session.

### The Lord Chancellor

The presiding officer of the House of Lords is the Lord Chancellor, a member of the Cabinet. He presides while sitting on the traditional "Woolsack", a large and rather shapeless divan. The Lord Chancellor is usually a Peer and if he is not, he is created one immediately after his appointment. It does not, however, mean that a Commoner cannot be chosen to that office. The "Woolsack" is technically placed outside the precincts of the House of Lords to enable those who are Commoners to perform their official duties as presiding officers of the House.

The powers and functions of the Lord Chancellor are many and varied. Here we are only concerned with those connected with the occupant of the Woolsack.[25] His powers as presiding officer are absolutely insignificant as compared with the Speaker of the House of Commons. They even fall far short of those commonly assigned to a moderator. The questions regarding procedure are decided by votes of the House. For example, if two or more members simultaneously attempt to address the House, the House itself, and not the Chair, decides who shall have the floor. The proceedings of the House of Lords are extremely orderly, but if order in debate is to be enforced, it is done by the House and not by the presiding officer. When the members speak, they do not address the Chair, but the House and begin with "My Lords." If the Lord Chancellor is a Peer, he may join in the debates of the House. When he does so, he steps away from the Woolsack. He may even vote, on party lines, like any other member, but in no case does he have a casting vote.

## POWERS AND FUNCTIONS OF THE LORDS

### Powers before 1911

As said earlier, Parliament began its career as an advisory body of the monarch without any

25. For other functions of the Lord Chancellor see Chap. IX, *infra*.

legislative power. But gradually Parliament established the principle that the King should not levy taxes without the consent of Parliament, and how Parliament granted supplies to the King on the redress of grievances. But while this struggle between the King and Parliament was continuing, there developed a struggle within Parliament as to which House should speak for Parliament on financial matters. The Commons in the reign of Richard II, demanded the right to be consulted on money matters, and in the reign of Charles I they claimed that the grants of money given to the King were exclusively their right. Later in 1671, they maintained that though grants of money required the consent of the House of Lords, but it was not within the power of that House to offer amendments to any financial proposals from the Commons.

In 1678, the Commons passed another resolution of a still more comprehensive character. It asserted "that all aids and supplies, and aids to His Majesty in Parliament, are the sole gift of the Commons, and all Bills for the granting of such aids and supplies ought to begin with the Commons; and that it is the undoubted and the sole right of the Commons to direct, limit and appoint in such Bills, the ends, purposes, considerations, conditions, limitations and qualifications of such grants which ought not to be changed or altered by the House of Lords." The House of Lords never admitted this claim to sovereignty by Commons on financial matters, although by usage gradually the Lords acquiesced to the claims of the representatives of the people. In 1860, however, the House of Lords made a bold attempt to reject a Bill for the repeal of duties on paper. But the Commons made a defence and got it through. Control over financial matters, they reiterated, was the exclusive business of the House of Commons and any attempt on the part of the Lords to tamper with or in any way modify the financial powers of the Commons would be regarded by them as an infringement of their privileges.

The beginning of the present century witnessed another bid on the part of the House of Lords to revive its powers. Having become bold by rejecting some legislative measure in 1832, 1889, and 1893 they rejected the proposals of Lloyd George which aimed to levy certain new taxes on landed property and claimed it to be their political right to do so. This became a regular issue of first rate constitutional importance with the Liberal Government which was placed in power early in 1906 by the most sweeping electoral victory. The outcome of this struggle was the passage of the Parliament Act of 1911. This Act not only confirmed the sovereignty of the House of Commons in money matters, but made it "omnipotent in matters of ordinary legislation too." The Act virtually abolished the power of the Lords either to amend or reject a Money Bill.

With regard to ordinary legislation the House of Lords possessed co-equal powers with the House of Commons. All Bills, except Money Bills, could, and still may, originate with the Lords, although by usage nine-tenths of them start their career in the Commons.[26] The House of Lords could, and it did, amend or reject a Bill passed by the House of Commons. It might continue to reject a Bill passed continually by the House of Commons and it did this on various occasions. When after a bitter struggle, Gladstone could see his second Home Rule Bill through the Commons only to have it rejected in the Lords he felt that "the cup of grievances was full." In his last speech in Parliament, the retiring Prime Minister referred to the struggle that had begun between the two Houses and predicted that it would have to go forward to an issue. The prediction came out true and the issue was brought to a head in 1909 which ultimately ended into the Act of 1911 thereby curtailing its powers over ordinary legislation too.

Before the Parliament Act, 1911, the House of Commons had no means to assert its will. The only alternative with the Prime Minister was to ask the King to create enough Peers to swamp the House of Lords. But it was a drastic measure and no Prime Minister would ask for it without being sure that he had the support of the electorate. The only recourse for him, under the circumstances, was to ask for dissolution of the House of Commons and put the issue before the public at a general election. If it was ratified by the electorate, the Lords were expected to give way and this they usually did. But when the verdict of the people was sought in 1910, they did not care for the precedent. On November 16, the King agreed that if the Liberals were returned after a second General Election and the House of Lords rejected the Government's Bill to limit the power of the House of Lords to reject Bills, he would create sufficient new Peers sympathetic to the Govern-

26. Most of the Bills which originate in the House of Lords are Private Bills and other non-controversial Bills, like a Judicial Bill.

ment to ensure the Bill's passage.[27] The General Election held later in the year showed little change, and the Parliament Bill was, accordingly, introduced again. Eventually the news of the King's pledge to create sufficient new Peers was made public; and when it came to a vote on the Bill in the House of Lords, a number of opponents of the measure abstained, and it became a law of Parliament.

**The Parliament Act, 1911**

The Parliament Act, 1911, is of fundamental constitutional importance. It sealed the victory of the House of Commons statutorily. Under this Act the House of Commons attained a recognition of three principles, and thereby of its own final and conclusive sovereignty. The first principle was that the Commons alone had control of all Money Bills. The House of Lords could only delay and its delaying power was limited to one month only. Out of this emerges the second that the House of Commons alone had control over the Cabinet, and, finally it could pass by itself alone and without the concurrence of the Lords, any legislative measure which was affirmed by its vote in three successive sessions (whether of the same Parliament or not); the Lords exercised only delaying power for two years. The Act also declared that a Second Chamber constituted on a popular rather than a hereditary basis would be set up. The relevant clauses specified:—

1. "If a Money Bill, having been passed by the House of Commons, and sent up to the House of Lords at least one month before the end of the session, is not passed by the House of Lords without amendment within one month after it is sent up to that House, the Bill shall, unless the House of Commons directs to the contrary, be presented to His Majesty and become an Act of Parliament on the Royal assent being signified, notwithstanding that the House of Lords have not assented to the Bill."

It means that should the House of Lords withold its assent to a Money bill for more than one month the Bill would be presented to the King and become law on receiving the Royal assent, nothwistanding that the House of Lords have not assented to the Bill.

2. The term Money Bill was so defined as to include measures relating not only to taxation, but also to appropriations and audits. The Speaker was empowered to certify whether a given measure was or was not a Money Bill.

3. "If any Public Bill (other than a Money Bill or a Bill to extend the maximum duration of Parliament) is passed by the House of Commons in three successive sessions (whether of the same Parliament, or not), and having been sent up to the House of Lords at least one month before the end of the session, is rejected by the House of Lords in each of those sessions, the Bill shall on its rejection for the third time by the House of Lords, unless the House of Commons direct to the contrary, be presented to His Majesty and become an Act of Parliament on the Royal assent being signified thereto, notwithstanding that the House of Lords have not consented to the Bill : Provided that this provision shall not take effect unless two years have elapsed between the date of the second reading in the first of those sessions of the Bill in the House of Commons and the date on which it passes in the House of Commons in the third of those sessions."

This clause provided that a Bill passed three times by the Commons in successive sessions, and each time rejected by the Lords might be presented to the King for his assent provided two years had elapsed between the initial proceedings of the Bill in the House of Commons and its final passing in that House in the third session.

**The Amending Act, 1949**

In addition to the specific provisions of the Parliament Act, 1911, there was an understanding that the House of Lords would not reject a measure for which there was a mandate from the electorate at the preceding General Election. But the Labour Party was not satisfied with the statutory limitations which the Act of 1911 imposed, particularly relating to ordinary legislation in forcing a delay of two years before a Bill could be finally enacted. The 1945 manifesto of the Labour Party affirmed : " .....We give clear notice that we will not tolerate obstruction of the people's will by the House of Lords." When the Labour Party came into power something dramatic was expected. But nothing actually happened till October 1947, when the Speech from the Throne disclosed the Government's intention

27. "After a long talk (with Asquith)", wrote the King in his diary, "I agreed most reluctantly to give the Cabinet a secret understanding that in the event of the Government being returned with a majority at the General Election, I should use my prerogative to make the Peers if asked for. I disliked having to do this very much, but agreed that this was the only alternative to the Cabinet resigning, which at this moment would be disastrous." Nicolson, H., *King George the Fifth,* p. 138.

to introduce immediately a Bill to amend the Parliament Act, 1911, by reducing from three sessions to two and from two years to one the maximum period during which measures passed by the House of Commons could be held up. This sudden announcement was necessitated by the Government's determination to nationalise the iron and steel industry. The Government could rightly anticipate the opposition of the House of Lords and it was, accordingly thought necessary to clear the way for the passage of the measure in the fourth year of its term of office. The Amending Bill was introduced in November 1947 and at all stages it met a stout opposition from the Lords.[28] It, however, passed over the Lords' veto two years later modifying thereby the procedure of the Parliament Act, 1911, relating to ordinary legislation.

According to the Amending Act of 1949, a Bill may now become law despite its having been rejected by the House of Lords if it has been passed by the House of Commons in two successive sessions (instead of three as provided in the Act of 1911), and, if one year (instead of two) has elapsed between the date of the second reading in the first session in the House of Commons and the final date on which the Bill is passed by the House of Commons for the second time. The 1949 Act, thus, reduced from two years to one the period during which the Lords may delay Bills which had passed the Commons.

**Present Powers and Functions**

The powers and functions of the House of Lords are fixed by the Parliament Act, 1911, as amended in 1949. They may be reduced into four main groups :—

(1) The power of amending or delaying legislation other than financial legislation;

(2) The power of influencing Government and people by debate;

(3) Executive powers; and

(4) Certain judicial powers.

On the Money Bill the power of the House of Commons is absolute. If the House of Lords withhold their assent to a Money Bill and what is a Money Bill is determined by the certification of the Speaker of the House of Commons, for more than a month, the Bill would be presented to the King and become a law on receiving the Royal assent. What is meant by a Money Bill was defined in the Act, but each such Bill has to bear a certificate by the Speaker that the Bill is a Money Bill within the meaning of the Act.

A non-money Bill passed by the House of Commons in two successive sessions with an interval of at least one year between its first and second readings and final passage in the House of Commons will become a law after having received the Royal assent irrespective of its having been rejected by the House of Lords.

The second function of the House of Lords is the influencing of Government and the people by its debates. Among the Peers, who make a habit of participating in the debates and votes, are generally elder statesmen and others who have spent their lives in public service and whose talents place them high in the world's esteem. No Government which is obliged to submit to criticism and to the need for explaining its actions and views can ignore the opinion expressed by such elder, seasoned and veteran statesmen and politicians. The debates are free, outspoken and sometimes reach a much higher dialectical level than in the House of Commons. This is obviously due to many reasons. The Lords are not subject to so many restrictions on debates as the Commoners are. Their discussion is all the more free because of the impossibility of overthrowing a Government by an adverse vote in the House of Lords. The furthest that the Lords can do is to delay the passage of legislation for one year. Secondly, their positions are secure. Not being subject to dissolution, and not being liable to seek re-election every five years, the Lords do not have to speak with one eye on the reactions of their voters to their speeches. They are responsible to no one but then no one is responsible to them. They need not follow the Party Whip and are free from that form of parliamentary pressure known as "lobbying." Moreover, the House of Lords is an august Chamber, a reservoir of expertise knowledge. It contains amongst the galaxy of its members past Prime Ministers, may be three or four at a time,[29] and Ministers, who had made their mark on the political life of the nation.

As it is, the result is that debates in the House of Lords, which are based upon experience and ability, set a very high standard of discussion and a thorough thrashing of the issues. Lords'

28. In the House of Commons the vote on third reading was 323 to 195, with Liberals supporting the Government whereas in the Lords it was 204 to 34 for rejection with the Liberals opposing the Government. It was a vote of very unusual size for the House of Lords.

29. There was in November 1986 only one, Harold Macmillan. On his death there is none now.

debates can and do exercise a very definite influence on Government, and through the press, on the public opinion generally. "It is sometimes a truer sounding board than the House of Commons itself."[30] Herman Finer gives a beautiful summing up of the influence which Lords exercise. He says, "The House of Lords had and still has important legislative authority, but this is distinctly inferior to that of the Commons. Yet still retains some, far from negligible. Beyond this, it remains one of the most distinguished forums of public debate in the world, for it has the right to discuss any phase of legislation, policy, and administration,....a substantial part of its membership is of exceptional distinction in intellect and political, social and business experience. These constitute a body of public-spirited experts, able to talk with great intelligence and knowledge, and really to do so with an aloofness from immediate partisan politics because they are not dependent for their status on appeals for popular election, and with abundant time to deliberate, as the Lords are far less pressed with decisive business than the Commons. This candid expertise has influence with the public, the government, and the civil service."

**Executive Powers**

The Lords had and still they have the power to ask questions, to elicit information from the Government on any aspect of administration and a full right to debate its policies. They exercised and still exercise equal power with the Commons to approve or disapprove the Statutory Instruments and jointly participate with the Commons on the removal of the Judges. In the course of the sixteenth century the Lords lost actual power to control the Executive. But they still enjoy a share in the Cabinet membership, partly because the House of Commons Disqualification Act, 1957, as amended by the Ministers of the Crown Act, 1964, limits the number of Ministers who may sit in the House of Commons, and partly because every Government must be assured of spokesmen of standing to expound its intentions and actions to the House of Lords. In recent years, it has been usual for the House of Lords to include about 20 office-holders, among whom are the Government Whips, who are members of the Royal Household, and act as spokesmen for the Government in debate. The number of Cabinet Ministers in the House of Lords varies; there are usually between two and four out of a total number of about 20. In the Government of June 1955, Lord Chancellor, Lord President, the Minister for Colonies, the Minister for Air, Paymaster-General, Minister without Portfolio, Minister of State for Foreign Affairs belonged to the Lords. Only the first four were in the Cabinet. In the Labour Government of 1950 three Cabinet Ministers, two outside the Cabinet, and five Under-Secretaries were in the Lords. Prime Minister Harold Macmillan appointed a Peer, the Earl of Home, as the Foreign Secretary. The appointment produced a storm of opposition from the House of Commons. Mrs. Margaret Thatcher, once again, appointed a peer, Lord Carrington, as Foreign Secretary. Two other Foreign Secretaries, to sit in the House of Lords in this century, were Lord Curzon in 1923 and Earl of Halifax before the outbreak of World War II in 1939.

The House of Lords performs two judicial functions. The first is the trial of unpeachment cases on charges preferred by the House of Commons. With the acceptance of the principle of ministerial responsibility this power of the Lords has become obsolete. The last impreachment occurred in 1805. The second judicial function is that the House of Lords is the Supreme Court of Appeal in civil cases for Great Britain and Northern Ireland. But the whole House now never meets as a Court of Appeal. It is only the Lords of Appeal or the nine Law Lords, with the Lord Chancellor presiding, who do the judicial work of the House. The Law Lords are, so to speak, a small specialised committee of the House of Lords to whom the function of hearing appeals has been delegated.

## REFORMING THE LORDS

No other political institution in Britain has been criticised to such an extent as the House of Lords. The slogan of the Labour Party since 1907 is to end the House of Lords as a hereditary Chamber is a political anachronism in a democratic age. The Liberal Party, on the other hand, had its political creed for reforming it and a comprehensive reform of both the composition and the powers of the House of Lords was envisaged in the Preamble to the Parliament Act of 1911, but the former was not enacted. Abolition of the Lords has not been attempted by any Labour Government, "partly it would seem because the Second Chamber is recognised as being capable of performing useful legislative and deliberate functions, especially for Labour Govern-

30. Brown, W. J., *Everybody's Guide to Parliament* (1952), p. 52.

ments which tend to have heavier legislative programmes than Conservative Governments."[31] Since 1911 two measures affecting the composition, but not the powers, of the Lords have been passed : The Life Peerage Act, 1958, and the Peerage Act, 1963. Both these Acts came from the Conservative Governments. The general attitude of the Conservative Governments towards the House of Lords in this century has been to defend its obstructive powers and advocate minor reforms of its composition "in order to make it more respectable and thus more justifiable in the use of its existing powers."[32] Proposals to eliminate the present hereditary basis of the House of Lords and to reduce its powers were published in a White Paper and legislation to give effect to these proposals was promised within a year's time, but nothing came out of it.

The drastic amendments of the "Socialist Bills"—nationalisation of aircraft and shipping industries—by the House of Lords in November, 1976, once again, brought into sharp focus the role of the House of Lords as a second chamber of legislature. Eric Varley, Minister of Industries in the Callaghan Government, gave a warning to the House of Lords to desist from wrecking and mutilating the Bill coming from the House of Commons. He called on the Lords to realise that if they forced a confrontation with the House of Commons, "there can only by one outcome—the abolition of the House." The Conservative Lords, supported by some Liberal Peers, rejected Varley's warning and said that they would continue to obstruct these "Socialist Bills." The anger in Labour ranks against the House of Lords was indicated by a Labour Member of Parliament calling on the Prime Minister to create 400 new peers to redress the balance between the Lords and Commons. By an overwhelming majority of $6\frac{1}{2}$ million to 91,000 the annual conference of the Labour Party, in October 1977, voted to abolish the House of Lords. The Party prepared a 2-policy document which proposed to abolish the rights of hereditary Peers, and to revise the system of life Peerage, which was a compromise that the Labour Party had accepted earlier. The membership of the reformed House was to be drawn from both sides of the industry, employers and unions, from the public and private sectors and from Local Government elected or nominated by their respective organisations. The House so constituted would be named Lords of Parliament or Parliamentary Aldermen. The House would have no veto or delaying power over the House of Commons.

But the Labour Government, headed by James Callaghan, had a precarious majority of one which was ultimately reduced to a minority Government depending upon the support of the Liberals and Scottish Nationalists could not dare to abolish an institution that rightly boasted of some of the greatest minds that Britain had ever produced. When the Liberals and the Scottish Nationalists withdrew their support in March 1979, Callaghan was defeated on a vote of no confidence. The Conservative Party received the electoral mandate in May 1979 General Election and formed the Government with a comfortable majority in the House of Commons. The issue of abolishing the House of Lords had no meaning during the Conservative regime. Nor is there any possibility that the House of Lords would be abolished in the very near future even if the Labour Party, which itself has split, comes into office. Tony Blair has declared that he would institute drastic reforms in the composition and functions of the House of Lords during the current tenure of the Labour Government.

**Arguments against the Lords**

The arguments which are generally advanced against the House of Lords are :

The House of Lords as at present constituted is a political anachronism in a country with thoroughly democratic institutions. The composition of the House still remains what it has been for centuries and more than seventy per cent of the Peers sit in their places because their forefathers sat before them. There may be hereditary genius on a large and sweeping scale. Even if it may be conceded that all the Peers have the making of capable legislators, no test of their aptitude has been applied. And even if ability of all the Peers were positively proved "the modern world," as Finer points out, "has rejected the application of ability to government unless it is representative of the interests of those expected to obey the Law."[33] No elective principle, popular or occupational, characterises the composition of the House of Lords. The Peers are responsible to nobody save themselves. They take their seats by their own right. They need no party labels, and no jealous constituency watches their

31. Punnett, R. M., *British Government and Politics*, p. 275.
32. *Ibid.*
33. Finer, H., *The Theory and Practice of Modern Government*, p. 407.

votes or takes a note how diligently and regularly they attend to their duties. In other words, as Jennings points out: "They have not to trim their sails to the breeze of public opinion."[34] And yet they claim that they are representatives of the people enjoying their full confidence. Webbs, Sidney and Beatrice, had aptly remarked, "Its (House of Lords) decisions are vitiated by its compositon; it is the worst representative assembly ever created...[35] Patrick Gordon Walker, speaking for the Labour Party in the House of Commons on the Peerage Bill maintained (June 19, 1963) that it should be considered only a first step towards complete abolition of hereditary peerage. The Life Peerage Act, 1958, was designed as means of infusing new life into the House of Lords. But the Labour Party criticised the measure as an attempt by the Conservative Government to give no authority to the Lords, while avoiding the basic problem of the hereditary element. The Peerage Act, 1963, has not at all helped to change the complexion of the House. The hereditary principle remains intact as the Act specified that the title could pass, on the Peer's death, to his heir and that too if the heir also chose to disclaim. In the first twelve months of the operation of the Act, only eight Peers chose to disclaim and among the eight were Lord Home and Lord Hailsham, who were able to disclaim at the time of the Conservative Party leadership crisis in 1963. During the total span of more than two decades the Act did not lead to any attractive figure of exodus. The general effects of both the Acts of 1958 and 1963, were, therefore, that the original basic problem of composition of the House of Lords was left untouched. On November 21, 1968, the House of Lords approved by 251 to 56 votes planned abolition of its 600-year old aristocratic, privilege in law-making. the Labour Government promised detailed legislation within a year, but nothing came out.

The latest proposal for reforming the House of Lords came from the Conservatives themselves. Apprehending that the Labour Party would make it an election issue and if they gained electoral majority at the next General Election a serious attempt would be made to abolish the House of Lords. The reform proposal sponsored by the Conservatives aimed to make the House a body in some respects resembling the United States' Senate elected by the method of proportional representation. The proposal received an active support from some Cabinet Ministers of Mrs. Margaret Thatcher's Government. But the proposal was extremely vague. It did not, for example, discuss what would possibly happen to the Law Lords, let alone the Bishops. Equally vague was what power the new body would possess, particularly in relation to the House of Commons. The net result is that for the umpteenth time there is talk in Britain for reforming the House of Lords and for the umpteenth time little if anything seems likely to come of it.

The meagre attendance which the House attracts, and lack of interest which the Lords evince in their legislative duties is an argument by itself for either ending or mending it. Normally sixty or seventy members had participated in its deliberations.[36] Now the daily attendance on the average is rather less than two hundred, while one–hundred and fifty are regularly engaged in the work of the House. Many Peers so seldom show their faces in this gilded Chamber that the attendants even do not recognise them.[37] One half of its membership has perhaps never spoken at all in the Lords. The number who have spoken several times is something like one in eight of the entire membership, and those who speak are largely Ministers or ex-Ministers. It is only on rare occasions that they "bring up the big battalions when the defeat of a progressive measure is desired."[38] And the quorum is only three. The smallness of the number of Peers who participate frequently in the work of the House is a grave defect, as Bagehot pointed out: "The real indifference to their duties of most Peers is a great defect, and the apparent indifference is a dangerous defect....An assembly–a revising assembly especially–which does not assemble, which looks as if it does not care how it revises, is

34. Jennings, W. I., *The British Constitution,* p. 90.
35. Sidney and Beatrice Webb, *A Constitution for Socialist Commonwealth of Great Britain,* p. 63.
36. "In 1932 and 1933, 287 Peers never attended the House. Beween 1919 and 1931, 111 Peers never voted, and more than half never spoke; there were only 13 divisions out of over 440 in which more than 200 voted. In the whole period only 98 Peers spoke on an average more than once a year, and those were largely ministers and ex-ministers." Greaves, H.R.G., *The British Constitution,* p. 53.
37. In 1893 when the Lords made a great rally in order to defeat Gladstone's Second Home Rule Bill, one Peer was stopped by the door-keeper who asked him if he were really a Peer. He replied, "Do you think if I weren't I would come to this blankety, black hole".
38. At the second reading of the Bill to amend Parliament Act, 1911, in 1947, the voting in the House of Lords was 204 to 34 for rejection. This was a vote of very unusual size for the House of Lords.

defective in a main political ingredient. It may be of use, but it will hardly convince mankind it is so.''[39] Lord Samuel's remark on the composition of the House of Lords that the efficiency of that House was secured by the almost permanent absenteeism of most of its members was a telling blow aimed at the Lords.

Then, the large and predominant majority of these hereditary members belong to one political party, the Conservative, which appears to be permanently entrenched in the House of Lords. Of those whose party membership is known, it is computed that two-thirds of the members, belong to the Conservative Party, and one- third are Liberal and Labour. The result is that whatever be the direction of the popular vote, and no matter which party controls the House of Commons, the Conservative Party, and even worst of it, its more reactionary members, remain in unchallenged mastery of the House of Lords. Some members of the House openly admit the claim of Lord Balfour that it was the duty of the Lords to see that the Conservative Party ''should still control whether in power or whether in Opposition the destinies of this great Empire '' And the Lords have proved true to their professions. A Conservative Government is always certain of its majority. No Bill promoted by a Conservative Government has been rejected by the House of Lords since 1832, ''and, for the last fifty years at least no Conservative Bill has been amended against firm Government opposition.''[40] When any other Party is in power, the position is quite different. The Conservative majority in the Lords determines its strategy in consultation with the Conservative leaders in the House of Commons. Nothing passes the House of Lords except what the Conservative Party permits, no matter whether that Party is in office or in Opposition.

The House of Lords has become also, what Ram- say Muir has termed, the ''common fortress of wealth.'' There is now no great national industry, says Harold Laski, whose leadership, so far as its capitalist side is concerned, does not find its appropriate representation in the House of Lords.[41] In fact property has always been the basis of the Upper Chamber, and is still adequately represented there. ''Over one-third of them are Directors (some multiple) of the staple industries of the nation. One-third of them also own very large estates. Many of them are related by marriage, birth and business connections with the Conservative members of the House of Commons.''[42] The Peers are, therefore, predominantly an economic interest. It also provides a sufficient data to establish that the division between parties in Britain is in essence a class division and Peers are drawn from one class only. How can it be possible, then, that this capitalist class with vested interests can look to proposals for radical social and economic reforms with any desirable sympathy ? The answer to this question can be found from what Lord Acton wrote to Gladstone's daughter in 1881, when the Lords opposed the Irish Land Bill. He said, ''But a corporation, according to a profound saying, has neither body to kick nor soul to save. The principle of self-interest is sure to tell upon it. The House of Lords feels a stronger duty towards its eldest sons than towards the masses of ignorant, vulgar, and greedy people. Therefore, except under very perceptible pressure, it always resists measures aimed at doing good to the poor. It has almost always been in the wrong—sometimes from the prejudice and fear and miscalculation, still oftener from instinct and self-preservation.''[43]

When the House of Lords is invariably wedded to the principles and policy of a single party and it has avowedly retarded the forces of progress, then, the existence of the House of Lords, as Herman Finer puts it, is a gross anomaly, ''without justification in this era.'' The views of Abbe Sieyes, that if the Second Chamber agrees with the first it is superfluous, while if it disagrees, it is obnoxious, seems to many in Britain, according to Prof. Laski, ''common sense.''[44] The formal policy of the Labour Party, though it has not contributed anything towards its realization, is still in favour of a single Chamber. Laski, while arguing his case for abolishing the House of Lords has maintained that an undemocratic institution like the House of Lords cannot survive in a democratic society unless it

39. Begehot, W., *The English Constitution,* pp. 101-102.
40. Jennings, W. I., *The British Constitution,* p. 90.
41. Laski, H. J., *Parliamentary Government in England,* p. 112.
42. Finer, H., *The Theory and Practice of Modern Government,* pp. 407-408. ''There were 246 landowners in the House in 1931, while directors of banks numbered 67, railways 64, engineering works 49, and Insurance Companies 112, to name only a few.'' Greaves, H.R.G., *The British Constitution,* p. 54.
43. As cited in Herman Finer's *Theory and Practice of Modern Government,* p. 48.
44. Laski, H. J., *Parliamentary Government in England,* p. 123.

is always able to adjust its behaviour to the demands of democracy. And the demands of democracy are the *speedy responsiveness* to the public opinion and the social needs. The House of Lords cannot fulfil these demands, because, "where it is tempted to be active in defence is just where democracy is tempted to be active in offence." [45] The House of Lords, in simple words, is wealth and privilege personified and the real conflict is between wealth and the masses. Democracy stands for the masses and in democracy nothing should exist which comes in conflict with their interests. The need is to end the House of Lords or to radically mend its composition.

**Arguments in Favour**

In spite of the determined policy of the Labour Party to abolish the House of Lords and the vigorous efforts of the Liberals to substitute for it a Chamber constituted on a popular instead of hereditary basis, the House of Lords still remains what it has been for centuries in the past. It is essentially a hereditary Chamber of Peers. The Liberals could not adopt a workable plan to democratize it. Even the Labour Party made no attempt in its five regimes either to end or mend it. The only change which the Labour was able to bring on the Statute book was an amendment to the Parliament Act of 1911 in 1949.

The first and really the conservative argument advanced for its preservation is that the British people will not tolerate this historic institution to be obliterated. In Britain nothing is created anew. Everything evolves gradually, over a long period of time and so it is that every British institution preserves into the present elements of the past. If the British had ever sat down to refashion the whole of their political machinery, it is possible that the hereditary House of Lords would have disappeared. If they had ever set out to reduce their Constitution into writing, the Lords might also have disappeared. But that is not their instinct and their method of doing things. They take everything as it is and put up with it as long as it works tolerably well. When its shortcomings are experienced, they are tried to be remedied as a matter of course. And when the inadequacies become unendurable, it is amended to the extent it is necessary to meet the revealed inadequacy or difficulty. It is not obliterated, because the British people intuitively know that life is more than logic. And having admitted that a hereditary House of Lords in a democracy is illogical, the practical way of life tells them that on the whole it works well, and in some ways "surprisingly" well. "The very irrationality of the composition of the House of Lords and its quaintness," said Herbert Morrison, "are safeguards for our modern British democracy."[46] Because changes intended to make the House of Lords democratic and representative would have undemocratic results. It would tend to make the Lords equal to the Commons, thus creating rivalry, conflicts and deadlock between the two.

And democracy needs a second chamber. The United States of America expressly provided for a second chamber—the Senate—which exercises vastly wider powers than does the House of Lords. The French, who are a very logical people, have included a second chamber in all their Constitutions. So have the Scandinavian democracies. Even those countries which experimented with a single chamber ultimately reverted to the double chamber system because of the demands of democracy. Unless it is acceptably proved that democracy does not need a second chamber, it is not democratic to abolish one in Britain when the Parliament Act has destroyed the power of the Lords to interfere with Money Bills, and limited its power on other Bills to "delaying action" and, that, too, just for a year. Life Peerages Act, 1958, and the Peerage Act, 1963, tend to democratize it, accepting the democratic utility of bicameralism. Even the Labour Party, except for some members, do not favour its abolition. Lord Morrison portrayed the attitude of the Labour Party when he said, "So the powers of the Lords have been much diminished over the years. I think rightly so. But it remains an assembly of considerable importance where good debates are held. There are men of great experience in the Lords' Chamber. The debates are of pretty good quality as a rule and in legislative revision, improving and polishing up parliamentary Bills, the House of Lords is useful and effective. Although its powers are more limited, its standing is still pretty high."[47]

An argument that the House of Lords ought not to have a permanent Conservative majority is not necessarily an argument that there ought

45. *Ibid*, p. 136.
46. Morrison, H., *Government and Parliament*, p. 194.
47. Morrison, H., *British Parliamentary Democracy*, pp. 7-8.

not to be a House of Lords. Conservatism is needed to check the radicalism of the Lower House. It is just like the appeal from Philip drunk to Philip sober. A second chamber in a unitary State is a means of checking what a nineteenth century Lord Chancellor called "the inconsiderate, rash, hasty, and undigested legislation of the other House." The House of Lords is a brake of considerable advantage on the decisions of a popularly elected House, sometimes reached under stress of great national emotion. When radicalism is injected with conservatism it is reason without passion and this is precisely what laws ought to be. Then, the real question which needs a straight answer is whether the House of Lords should be hereditary or elective.

There are certain advantages about having a non-elective second chamber. If the second chamber is to be the replica of the Lower Chamber, then, there is no point, or little point, in having the second chamber. The essence of the second chamber is that it should not be subject to the same impulses and the same pressures as the Lower Chamber. No member of the House of Commons can afford wholly to disregard the wishes of his constituents. "Some indeed, are little more than the echoes of the popular emotions of their constituents, and trim their political sails to every wind of popular feeling. Even the most courageous and honest must keep a 'weather eye' on popular feeling." But a member of the House of Lords rarely speaks for the sake of speaking. He has no advantage to keep the debate going. He can speak freely, express unpopular views, and advocate unconventional remedies. Nor has he any constituents to please. A Peer's constituency, it is claimed, is under his hat. At the end of the debate when all kinds of views have been expressed and opinions given, there is usually no division. Even if there is one, it is of no political consequence, for an adverse vote does not involve the fate of the Government. The Lords also know that the Parliament Act, 1911, as amended in 1949, sets a limit to their capacity of defying the will of the Commons. They, accordingly, resist but do not persist.

The result is that the House of Lords can afford to have full and free debates on legislative and non-legislative issues which the Commons "are too busy to discuss or which party leaders may consider too explosive to touch," because a Lords' vote does not of itself imperil the government. The proceedings of the House of Lords receive wide publicity and the people at large find cue to their opinions in the utterances of these reverential statesmen. This is how the Lords prepare the public for the consideration of the important issues, educate public opinion, and make the Government susceptible to such reactions. The House of Lords, thus, performs a very useful function of influencing the people and the Government. Debates and votes on Motions in the Lords "can and at times do", writes Morrison, "stir public opinion, or they may ventilate true public grievances or have repercussions in the House of Commons so they make the Government conscious of some failure or shortcoming. No Government, therefore, whatever its political complexion, studiously and systematically ignores the opinion of the House of Lords. Indeed, it is the duty of the Leader of the House of Lords in the Cabinet to indicate to his colleagues the feelings of his House on subjects under considerations."[48]

Then, the House of Lords acts as a legislative chamber. Bills can be introduced there instead of in the House of Commons. The Bryce Committee stated that partially non-controversial Bills, when they originate in the House of Lords, may find an easier passage in the House of Commons if they have been fully discussed and put into a well considered shape before being submitted to it. Moreover, a finished Act of Parliament must be word-perfect. For, if mistakes are made, the Government may be involved in administrative embarrassment or confusion or it may place the community in grave difficulties as a result of legally correct but unexpected and disturbing decisions of the courts. The House of Lords is a specially valuable institution in this matter of spotting lack of clarity or doubtful matters of drafting, because it includes not only distinguished lawyers but a number of members who have functioned on the bench of a High Court of Justice, and also include the Law Lords.

The House of Lords usefully does the examination and revision of Bills, after they have passed through all the stages in the House of Commons. This is now more needed since the House of Commons almost on all Bills is obliged to act under special rules limiting debates, thereby, curtailing the possibilities of free and fuller discussion. The House of Lords functions under no such limitations. Moreover, the Lords

48. Morrison, H., *Government and Parliament*, p. 176.

is properly said to be a ventilating chamber consisting of men who have distinguished themselves in the field of public activity, and possessing varied and diverse experiences. Glancing down the list of those who have been created Peers during recent years, one notices that in addition to persons who may be described as "politicians" there are to be found former Diplomats, Admirals, Generals, Labour Union Officials, Businessmen,Newspapers proprietors, University Professors, Doctors, and civil servants. Such a galaxy of men with expertise knowledge in the various fields of public life can with confidence engage themselves in practical and highly intelligent discussion and criticism. Nearly a century ago Walter Bagehot wrote, "The House of Lords has the greatest merit which such a chamber can have; it is possible. It is incredibly difficult to get a revising assembly, because it is difficult to find a class respected revisers....The Lords are in several respects more independent than the Commons....The House of Lords, besides independence to revise judicially and position to revise effectually, has leisure to revise intellectually. These are great merits, and, considering how difficult it is to get a good second chamber, and how much with our present First Chamber we need a second, we may well be thankful for them."[49]

The House of Lords is still a forum of debate on the administrative activities of the Government. The Lords had and still have the power to ask questions and a full right to debate its policies. The House of Commons has not the time to discuss all issues and problems, national and international, whereas the House of Lords has sufficient time and opportunity to do so. This is a useful national service rendered by the distinguished men whose views matter with the people and government. Even the apathy of the Peers to attend the meetings of the House has been characterised as a virtue in disguise. It would be impossible to get through the business of the House under present conditions if all who were entitled to attend and participate did so; a staggering number of more than 1,000. "The working of the House is made possible only," maintained Viscount Samuel, "by the absenteeism of a large number of members, and we should be grateful to those who grace the meetings of this House by their absence."

The Lords also relieve the Commons of the work of considering Private Bills. Most of these Bills are examined in the first instance by committees of the House of Lords. Such Bills undergo a "quasi-judicial" process which may take much time when they are opposed. A Bill opposed in one House is usually not opposed in the other; and the result is that the Peers diminish by one third the heavy and uninteresting labours which would have to be undertaken by members of the Commons if there were no House of Lords. Provisional Order Bills and Special Orders are much in the same position.

Interposition of delay is needed to crystallise public opinion on all Bills before they become Acts. In fact, it is of considerable advantage that the decisions of a popularly elected Chamber should be given a second thought and that, too, under conditions of calmer atmosphere in a Chamber which is less susceptible to immediate popular pressure. The problem of second thought is much needed in Bills which affect the fundamentals of the Constitution, or introduce new principles of legislation, or raise issues upon which opinion of the people may appear to be almost equally divided. George Washington illustrated the need for interpostion of delay by pouring a cup of hot liquid into a saucer and allowing it to cool. "We pour legislation into the senatorial saucer to cool it," he said.

But the real point is how long the House of Lords should be allowed to interpose delay in the enactment of legislation ? Churchill was of the opinion that all controversial legislation should be passed in the first two years of a Government's term of office, and thereafter the Lords should apply the brake to radical change until such time as "the engine of the popular will is refuelled by popular election." To this Attlee replied that it would mean that "the engine had to go to be repaired every five years for a Conservative Government and every two years when a Labour Government was in power." In the three party conference, convened to consider the composition and powers of the House of Lords, when in 1947 the amending Bill to Parliament Act had passed in the Commons, the Conservatives suggested a delay of eighteen months after the second reading of the Bill. But the Labour's proposal was for nine months from the third reading. No agreed compromise could be arrived at and the result was interposition of one year's delay after the second reading was determined by the Act of

49. Bagehot, W., *The English Constitution*, pp. 99-100.

1949.

Perhaps, the greatest merit of the House of Lords, as Bryce emphatically maintained, is its moral authority. "A Second Chamber," he said, "ought to possess, if possible, the largest measure of moral authority. By moral authority I mean.... the influence exerted on the mind of the nation which comes from the intellectual authority of the persons who compose the chamber, from their experience, from their record in public life and from the respect which their characters and their experience inspire... This House has a moral authority as well as the prestige, the unequalled prestige, of its long antiquity. There is no assembly in the world which can look back over so long and glorious a career as the great Council of the Nation, the *Magnum Concillum* of early Norman times, the form of which remains in this House as its oldest member...I cannot help hoping that, whatever new Chamber is constructed, every effort will be made to preserve for it both the prestige of antiquity and the moral authority which this House inherits."[50] The House contains Peers who are members of ancient families in whom a sense of public service is ingrained by long traditions. Then, there are ex-Cabinet Ministers who have earned their titles through their political work.[51]

Finally, it is argued that the House of Lords is also useful as a seat for Ministers, in that any figure who is called upon to serve in the Government, but who does not wish to enter the party political fray of the House of Commons can be raised to Peerage and thereby made eligible for Ministerial office. In 1957 Sir Percy Mill was created a Peer and he took up the post of Minister of Power in Macmillan's Government. Lords Bowden, Cadogan, Chalfont, and Gardiner were given Life Peerage in 1963 and 1964 and were, thus, made eligible for Ministerial office. But this argument does not cancel the case for abolition of hereditary Peerage. The most important aspect of the debate is that conservative writers favour its retention, while the radicals distrust it as a group.

## REFORM PROPOSALS

### Proposals for Reform : 1869-1918

With the enactment of Parliament Amending Act, 1949, the issue of the powers of the House of Lords had been decided and the Labour Party did no longer argue for its abolition till 1977 when the demand was renewed. But the Labour Party is now split and its stage back to power in the near future is not probable. The next question then is reforming its composition. This question is as old as several generations. Lord Russel introduced in 1869, a Bill in Parliament providing for the gradual infiltration of Life Peers. But it was rejected. In the same year a project of Earl Grey came to a naught and the same fate awaited the proposal of Lord Rosebury in 1874 and Lord Salisbury in 1888. No more was heard of the House of Lord reform until 1907. In 1907, the House set up a Select Committee to consider the suggestions made from time to time to increase the efficiency of the House in legislation. The report of the Committee suggested new constitution of the House consisting of Peers of the royal blood; the Lords of Appeal ordinary; 200 representatives elected by the hereditary Peers; hereditary peers possessing special qualifications; Spiritual Lords of Parliament, and Life Peers.

But it was too late. In the meantime the struggle between the Lords and the Commons had commenced and that, too, with great momentum. The result of the struggle was the Parliament Act of 1911. The 1911 Act was declared to be only a stage towards a more fundamental reform and its *Preamble* was indicative of it. The *Preamble* said that it was "intended to substitute for the House of Lords as it at present exists a Second Chamber constituted on a popular instead of hereditary basis." But the overwhelming occupation of the Asquith Ministry left the subject unpressed. Then, came the First World War and the issue remained untouched till 1917 when a Committee, consisting of 30 members equally chosen from both the Houses and representing all shades of opinion, presided over by Viscount Bryce, was appointed.

The Bryce Committee submitted its Report in the spring of 1918. It expressed the opinion that "in so far as possible, continuity ought to be preserved between the historic House of Lords and future Second Chamber, which obviously would mean that a certain portion of the existing peerage should be included in the new body." At the same time, the Committee agreed that its membership should be open to all the people so that it might represent adequately their thoughts and sentiments and no one set of political opinion should exercise therein a marked permanent dominance.

The Committee proposed that the reconstituted House of Lords should have 327 members,

50. Speech in the House of Commons, March 21, 1921. As cited in Sidney Bailey, *British Parliamentary Democracy.*
51. Brasher, N.H., *Studies in British Government,* p. 108.

three-fourths (246) to be elected by an electoral college composed of the members of the House of Commons grouped into 13 regional divisions. The Commoners from each region would elect the quota to which their area on the basis of population was entitled to. The remaining 81 members were to be chosen from the whole body of Peers by a Standing Joint Committee of both the Houses. The tenure of office was fixed at 12 years, one-third members in each group retiring after four years.

With regard to the functions of the House of Lords, the Committee agreed that the reconstituted Chamber ought not to have equal powers with the House of Commons. Nor should it aim at becoming a rival of the Commons, particularly in making and overturning Ministers or of voting Money Bills. The Committee considered the following functions appropriate to a Second Chamber in Britain:—

(1) The examination and revision of Bills brought from the House of Commons.
(2) The initiation of Bills dealing with subject of a comparatively non-controversial character.
(3) The interposition of so much delay (and no more) in the passing of a Bill into law as may be needed to enable the opinion of the nation to be adequately expressed upon it.
(4) Full and free discussion of large and important question.[52]

**Reform Plans : 1918-1934**

The Bryce Committee Report and the plan it recommended was too much of a compromise and it pleased neither the Conservatives nor the progressives. The Government of Lloyd George, however, in 1922 moved in Parliament a resolution embodying the essentials of the Bryce plan. The plan was coldly received and three months after when the Coalition Government resigned it was left without official sponsorship. The short-lived Conservative Government marked its own time, and the first Labour Government under Ramsay MacDonald dared not touch the problem because of its own precarious position.

When the Conservative party came to power, it showed a genuine desire to do something in the matter so that Labour Government if it again came to office might not take some drastic measures. In fact, the Conservative werre pledged to the reform of the House of Lords in the elections of 1924, but the Prime Minister was not keenly interested in it and the matter hanged on. In 1925, Lord Birkenhead brought to the House of Lords a plan with no tangible results. In 1927, the Lords adopted a resolution declaring that they would welcome "a reasonable measure limiting and defining the membership and dealing with defects inherent in the Parliament Act." Nothing came out of it as well. In 1928, Lord Clarendon suggested a plan according to which 150 members should be elected by the peers and 150 nominated by the Crown in proportion to the strength of the various parties in the House of Commons, and a few Life Peers. The Labour when in office in 1929 did not consider the matter important to take it up and the National Government was pre-occupied in other things.

In 1932, a Conservative Party Committee made a fresh study of the subject and published the results of its deliberations in the document entitled Report of a Joint Committee of Peers and Members of the House of Commons. The Committee presented a plan for a Second Chamber with 320 members. Then, came the Salisbury plan in December 1933. It suggested that the House should consist of 300 members. The definition of the Money Bill was to be more restricted and interpreted by a Joint Select Committee of both the Houses with the Speaker as Chairman. No Bill, other than the Money Bill, was to be passed under the Parliament Act until after a dissolution. The Bill was passed by the House of Lords by 83 to 34 votes on the first reading and by 171 to 82 on the second reading. Baldwin, however,brought about the discontinuance of the discussion.

**Reform by Labour Government**

In 1934, the Labour Party passed a resolution that: "A Labour Government meeting with sabotage from the House of Lords would take immediate steps to overcome it; and it will in any event take steps during its term of office to pass legislation abolishing the House of Lords as a legislative chamber." The Labour Manifesto in 1945, read : "...We give clear notice that we will not tolerate obstruction of the People's will by the House of Lords". This, of course, implied curtailing its powers rather than reforming its composition and the 1947 Amending Bill to Parliament Act, 1911, was a clear testimony of the intentions of the Labour. The Bill aimed to reduce the delaying action of the Lords on ordinary Bills

52. Committee on the Reform of the Second Chamber, 1918 (Report) p. 4.

to one year only and it became an Act in 1949 despite its rejection by the House of Lords.

When the Bill of 1947 was passed in the House of Commons an intra-party conference, under the Chairmanship of the Prime Minister, was convened early in 1948, the issue for discussion being the relationship of the composition to the powers of a second chamber. There appeared to be a "substantial agreement" on the following general principles with regard to the composition of the Lords :

(1) The Second Chamber should be complementary to and not a rival to the Lower House, and, with this end in view, the reform of the House of Lords should be based on a modification of its existing constitution as opposed to the establishment of a Second Chamber of a completely new type based on one system of election.

(2) The revised constitution of the House of Lords should be such as to secure as far as practicable that a permanent majority is not assured for any political party.

(3) The present right to attend and vote based solely on heredity should not by itself constitute a qualification for admission.

(4) Members of the Second Chamber should be styled "Lords of Parliament", appointed on grounds of personal distinction or public service. They might be drawn either from Hereditary Peers, or from Commoners who would be created Life Peers.

(5) Women would be capable of being appointed Lords of Parliament in like manner as men.

(6) Provision should be made for the inclusion in the Second Chamber of certain descendants of the Sovereign, certain Lords Spiritual and the Law Lords.

(7) In order that persons without private means should not be excluded, some remuneration would be payable to members of the Second Chamber.

(8) Peers who were not Lords of Parliament should be entitled to stand for election to the House of Commons, and also to vote at elections in the same manner as other citizens.

(9) Some provision should be made for the disqualification of a member of the Second Chamber who neglected, or became no longer able or fit, to perform his duties as such.

**Life Peerage Act and Peerage Act**

Life Peerage Act, 1958, empowers the Queen without prejudice to Her Majesty's Powers as to the appointment of Lords of Appeal in Ordinary, to confer on any person a peerage for life. The Act also made women eligible for the conferment of life peerage. For the first time the Act of 1958 gave women the right to sit and vote in the House of Lords. In 1963 further changes in the composition of the House of Lords were affected by the Peerage Act, which gave a Peer the right to disclaim his peerage for his life time and to renounce for himself, but not for his successors, the rights and privileges of a peerage and at the same time remove his disqualifications to sit in the House of Commons and to vote in parliamentary elections. The Act also equated the position of Peeresses in their own right with that of hereditary Peers for parliamentary purposes, and gave full rights of admission to all Peers and Peeresses of Scotland thus bringing to an end the system of representative Peers.

**Future of the House of Lords**

In spite of the general recognition of the fact that a hereditary legislative chamber is an anachronism in a modern democratic State, there had been no progress in reconstituting the House of Lords. The Peerage Act, 1958, and the Peerage Act, 1963, made no material difference in its composition. In 1967, the Labour Government announced its proposals for a major reform of composition together with proposals for further reduction in the powers of the House of Lords. It was planned to abolish the 600–year old privilege of law-making. It was, indeed, a sweeping reform that would have virtually, if enacted, made the hereditary peers extinct as a political force. The House would have, of course, retained its ancient right to function as a brake on legislative measures sent to it from the House of Commons. The Labour Government promised a detailed legislation incorporating its proposals within a year, but nothing came out. Nor would there have been any certainty of Callaghan's minority Government to succeed in its plan of reforming the Lords if it had been attempted. Still, change appeared to be on the way. Some observers saw Britain moving eventually from a unitary to a federal system in view of developments in the European Community and the devolution referenda in Scotland and Wales, although the proposal did not envisage federalism. The Scottish Nationalists have now declared as their goal the independence of Scotland and the possibility of a federation, if at all there was any, is completely out of the question. The renewed Labour Party's threat to abolish the

House of Lords and to include the issue in the Party's next General Election manifesto induced the Conservatives to anticipate the impending danger and with the support of some members of Mrs. Margaret Thatcher's Government set afoot a proposal for reforming the Lords and making the new body resemble the United States' Senate in some respects. The proposal is vague in many respects and it is doubtful if the Conservatives themselves will own the proposal and initiate reform proposal. A divided Labour Party has indefinitely eclipsed its chances of securing an electoral majority and pursuing its plan of abolishing the House of Lords. The splinter group of the Labour Party—Social Democratic Party–in alliance with the Liberal Party had not any such proposal on its cards.

Two issues, however, are definitely clear. In future, the House of Lords will not be composed of aristocrats whose seats are guaranteed by hereditary birth-right alone. Abolition of the House of Lords is not the scheme of reform. What it is intended is that privilege should no longer remain the basis of entrance ticket to the House of Lords. And, secondly, it will be left with an obstructive power that amounts to a nominal delay. The Labour Party recognises the utility of the Lords as a revising and deliberative chamber. Herbert Morrison cor- rectly expressed the point of view of the Labour Party. He said, "whilst willing to respect the House of Lords for the value and standard of its debates, and for its capacity as chamber of legislative revision, we should not tolerate, from such an institution, any undue interference with the will of the House of Commons or of the people."[53] It should exist as a second chamber strong enough for revision and weak enough to be no rival to the Commons. It is really ironical that so much learned controversy should continue over the merits of an essentially undemocratic institution three-hundred-fifty years after it was abolished by the first democratic revolution of the world as early as 1649 in the English Civil War.

**Abolition of the House of Lords?**

As we know, the Republican Revolution of 1649 had abolished the House of Lords along with the monarchy as the Republicans regarded both these institutions as feudalist and anti-democratic in character. They were reactivated twelve years later as an act of counter-revolution. The present Labour government led by Tony Blair is not committed to its abolition as such but, nevertheless, it is determined to put an end to the institution of hereditary peerage. The Labour majority, with cooperation of the Liberal-Democrats, has not yet decided about the future shape of the second chamber but both these parties are unanimous to give a representative character to this 'archaic' relic of the past.

The conservatives have not yet reconciled themselves to the prospects of a radical change in the character of the House of Lords which according to them, has a 'democratic' legitimacy! T.E. Utley once told a conservative audience, "We as a party are always having to think up enlightened reasons for doing things which we believe in on other grounds. When, in the late nineteenth century, Lord Salisbury was struggling in the House of Lords to prevent the process, which has gone up, of diminishing the power of the Upper House, he thought up an argument of the highest possible importance in our constitutional history; that the House of Lords must be allowed a veto on legislation – not in the interests of stability or security or anything glum like that, which a democratic electorate would not like – but in order to protect the electorate against the danger that a government, having been returned to power, might neglect its mandate. He presented the House of Lords as the assembly which protects the community against the abuse of its mandate by a popularly elected government." (James Harvery and Katherine Hood, *The British State*,. pp. 82-83

The grandson of Lord Salisbury repeated the same thesis : "We on this side of the House ask no more than that issues affecting the welfare of the electorate, where their judgment is unknown or doubtful, should be referred for their consideration, or at least deferred for a short time to enable their view to be found out. That is the whole reason for our stand for an effective Second Chamber." Lord Balfour pointed out : The doctrine that the majority in the House of Commons has a right to do what it likes in the fourth and even in the fifth year of Parliament.... seems to me a negation of democracy." The Earl of Glasgow, opposing the reform bill of 1949, declared, "If this Bill passes, no longer will the people of this country, when their liberty and way of life are threatened, be able to say, 'Thank God we have a House of Lords." (*Ibid*... p. 83).

Lord Teviot, asserting that the House of

53. Morrison, H., *Government and Parliament.*

Lords was a defender of true democracy, asked a ridiculous question, "Is not this bill another attempt to override still further government by traditional constitutional methods in this country, and to continue the drive to totalitarianism which would wreck democracy by the removal of the last barrier between government and total power?" (Ivor Jennings, *Cabinet Government*, p 360). There is no doubt that so long as the House of Lords survives even in its existing form, it will be used by the vested interests for safeguarding their special privileges. In future too it will continue to resist progressive and radical legislation. The left-wing supporters of the Labour Party consider its existence dangerous for ary attempt to bring about social transformation in the direction of socialism. A genuinely socialist government, in the opinion of Laski and Greaves. which wants to bring about far-reaching socio-economic changes in Britain, cannot succeed in realizing its aims without abolishing the House of Lords. The capitalist forces, says Laski, will certainly support the continued existence of the second chamber by every means at their disposal. Even Tony Blair, at the close of the twentieth century, is not proposing the *abolition*, of this 'fortress of wealth'. As Labour Prime Minister, with a huge majority in the House of Commons, he can easily abolish this permanent citadel of Conservatism, but he does not possess the political will for doing so.

The House of Lords in England has a social basis in the large class of English landowners who still possess huge landed property and pursue an aristoeratic coiratic style of living. They are now an adjunct of the British capitalist class. As Laski pointed out, capitalist democracy in England does not regard an aristocratic chamber as incongruous with its parliamentary system of governance.

## SUGGESTED READINGS

Bailey, Sidney D. (Ed.) : *The Future of the House of Lords.*
Boardman, Harry : *The Glory of Parliament.*
Bromhead, P. A. : *The House of Lords and Contemporary Politics.*
Brown, W. J. : *Everybody's Guide to Parliament,* Chaps. II VII, XVIII.
Campion and Others : *Parliament: A Survey,* Chaps. IV, IX.
Carter, G. M., and others : *The Government of Great Britain,* (The World Press Ltd., Calcutta), pp. 148-55.
Chorley, Lord, Crick, B., and Chapman, B. : *Reform of the Lords.*
Finer, H. : *The Theory and Practice of Modern Government,* pp. 406-42.
Gordon, Strathearn: *Our Parliament.*
Greaves, H. R. C. : *The British Constitution,* Chap. III.
Hansard Society : *The Future of the House of Lords.*
Jennings, W. I. : *The British Constitution,* Chap. IV.
Jennings, W. I. : *Parliament,* Chaps. I, XI.
Laski, H. J. : *Parliamentary Government in England,* Chap. III.
Lindsay, Martin : *Shall We Reform the Lords ?*
Lowell, A. L. : *The Government of England,* Vol. I, Chaps. XXI, XXII.
Mackenzie, K. R. : *The English Parliament,* Chaps. I, II, XII.
Marriot, J. A. R, : *English Political Institutions,* Chaps. VI, VII.
Morrison, H. *British Parliamentary Democracy.*
Morrison, Herbert : *Government and Parliament,* Chap. IX.
Muir, R. : *How Britain is Governed,* Chap. VII.
Ogg, F. A. and Zink, H. : *Modern Foreign Governments,* pp. 40-42, Chap. X.
Stout, H. M.: *British Government,* Chap. VII.
Wade, E. C. S. and Philips, G. G. : *Constitutional Law,* pp. 35-44.
Weston C. C. : *English Constitutional Theory and the House of Lords.*

# CHAPTER VIII

# Parliament (Continued)

## THE HOUSE OF COMMONS

### Composition and Organisation

The House of Commons has always been a purely elective body, but both the electorate and constituencies varied greatly in the course of centuries. There are 635 seats in the House of Commons: 516 for England, 36 for Wales, 71 for Scotland and 12 for Northern Ireland.

The age of voting has been reduced from January 1, 1970 to 18. But adults getting the right to vote are not eligible to become members of the House or serve in the Jury before attaining the age of 21. Members are elected from single member constituencies and the law relating to parliamentary elections is contained principally in the Representation of the People Act, 1949, as amended by the Act of 1969.

All British subjects, of either sex, provided they are 21 years old or over, and from whatever part of Her Majesty's dominions they come, are eligible for election, provided they are not lunatics, bankrupts, persons convicted of certain crimes including corrupt practices, clergymen of the established Churches of England and Scotland and the priests of the Roman Catholic Church, and Peers of England and Scotland and the United Kingdom, and the holders of certain offices under the Crown, as also those expressly precluded under the House of Commons Disqualification Act, 1957 (for instance, holders of judicial offices, civil servants, members of the regular armed forces and police forces, members of the legislature of any country or territory outside the Commonwealth, and holders of other public offices listed in the Act).

The life of the House of Commons is for five years unless previously dissolved. But normal Parliament is dissolved by the Sovereign, acting on the advice of the Prime Minister, before the expiry of the full legal term and General Election held. Where a particular vacancy occurs in the period between General Election, for example, on the death or resignation of a member, a by-election is held to fill the vacant seat. According to the ancient theory, service in the House of Commons is like a jury service, not a right but duty. Technically, a member may not resign his office. But resignation is possible through a fiction. There is a sinecure office "the Steward of the Chiltern Hundreds" and the "Steward of the Manor of the Northstead" and a member intending to resign applies to the Chancellor of the Exchequer for appointment to one or other of these offices. Such a request is granted as a matter of course. The appointment automatically results in the vacating of a seat in the House of Commons, because it is a paid post under the Crown. Then, the office of the stewardship is promptly resigned.

The House of Commons, according to the usual practice, must meet at least once a year because certain essential legislation, including taxation and expenditure of public funds, is passed only for a year at a time and must be renewed annually. The session normally begins in October or November and continues for twelve months, except for brief adjournments. The session is brought to an end by prorogation and all business unfinished at the end of the session is terminated (with certain minor exceptions) until Parliament is again assembled. This means that a Bill not completed in one session must be reintroduced in the next, unless it is to be abandoned. The dispersal of the House through adjournment does not affect uncompleted business.

Since 1947 the normal times of meetings of the Commons have been the first five days of each week, except when Parliament is in recess. The hours of sitting for normal business are : Mondays to Thursdays from 2.30 p.m. to 10.00 p.m. and Fridays 11.00 a.m. to 4.30 p.m. Certain business is exempt from normal closing time and other business may be exempted if the House so chooses, so that the Commons often sits later than 10.00 p.m. on the first four days of the week, and all night sittings are not uncommon. On all these occasions time has to be rationed. From 2.30 till not later than 2.45 on Mondays to Thursdays private business is taken, questions following until 3.30. Immediately after questions is the time at which members may seek leave to move a motion of adjournment in order to discuss a matter of urgent public importance. If leave for the motion has been granted it stands over till 7 o'clock. It is only after such like preliminaries that comes the order for the day for the transaction of public business. This continues until 7 p.m., when adjournment motion or opposed private business may be taken. After that the interrupted business is resumed and continues until 10 p.m.

Members of the House of Commons were paid an annual salary of £4,500 under the Ministerial and other Salaries Act, 1972, subject to income tax. Members were also entitled to a number of special facilities and allowances, including the stationery, postage and telephone calls from within the House of Commons; travel or car mileage allowances; a tax-free subsistence allowance of £1,050 a year for provincial members and a secretarial allowance of £1,750 a year. Members' pensions, first introduced in 1965, are now regulated by the Parliamentary and other Pensions Act, 1972. This provided for a compulsory contributory scheme to pay pensions to members after four years' service on retirement from the House if they had reached the age of 65. Provisions had also been made for widows' and orphans' benefits.

**Closure of Debate**

As the time of the House of Commons is carefully rationed in order to provide for an orderly conduct of business, some measure for an enforced closure of debate is necessary. Ordinarily, an agreement is made "behind the Speaker's Chair" between the Chief Whips of the Government and the Opposition with regard to allocation of time to debate on different measures and the Speaker will see to it that the agreement is carried out. If such an arrangement fails, then, there are several expedients to cut short debates. This system of shortening the debates is known as the closure.

"A time must come," remarks Herman Finer, "when debate ceases and action is taken. This is, alas, a law of life itself."[1] Before 1880, the procedure in the House of Commons was designed to obstruct and prolong discussion rather than produce laws or oversee administration. In 1881, the Irish Nationalists adopted tactics by obstructing the business of the House. They would speak for hours on any subject, relevant or irrelevant, and yet the Speaker had no authority to stop that confusion and end such obstruction. The sitting of the House, which began at 4 o'clock on Monday, January 24, 1881 ended only at 9.30 a.m. on the following Wednesday. Speaker Brand declared, "The dignity, the credit and the authority of this House are seriously threatened, and it is necessary that they should be vindicated. Under the operation of the accustomed rules and methods of procedure the legislative powers of the House are paralysed. A new exceptional course is operatively demanded."[2] He declined to call any more members to speak, put the question, asked the House to change its rules or give the Speaker more authority.

The House did both. It altered the rules of debate so that time wasting and obstruction could be checked, and increased the authority of the Speaker in controlling the debate. Deliberate obstruction is rare now, and to some extent the members can be relied upon to recognise an obligation to be reasonably brief in what they have to say. But occasion may arise when cutting short the debate may become expedient. Closure may, then, take one of the following forms:

(1) After a debate has been going on for some time, a member may move that the "the question be now put" –that is, that the subject on which discussion is taking place may be put to the vote. It is the discretion of the Speaker to accept or refuse the motion. He will refuse it, if he thinks that such a motion is an abuse of the rules of the House, or an infringement of the rights of the minority. If the Speaker permits it, and the motion is carried by not fewer than a hundred votes, the debate is closed and the matter under discussion is voted upon. If it is negatived, the debate is resumed.

The procedure of closing the debate in this way makes the Government, if it is despotically minded, the master of the debate. With a comfortable majority at its back, it can get the motion to put the question moved, get 100 members to support it, and carry the issue. It is only the impartiality of the Speaker which can stem such designs of the Government and see that the right of the Opposition to have sufficient say is not choked.

(2) In addition to the simple closure device, which may be used on any kind of motion, there are other devices whose use in general practice, is confined to legislation. This kind of closure

1. Finer, H., *Governments of Greater European Powers,* p. 113.
2. As cited in above. *Ibid.*

involves allotting a certain amount of time to various parts of a measure or to its several stages, and at the appointed time taking a vote no matter any part of the measure or even its important aspects had been discussed or not.

The closure by compartment or the "guillotine" is introduced in a resolution before the House, planning the various stages, and provides that at the end of each, at a time fixed, the Speaker shall "put the question" without further debate. This kind of closure has been developed in order to deal with long and obstinate Opposition, and in order to give the Opposition some measure of choice as to how the time allotted for discussing the various parts of the Bills is to be used. Since 1946 Standing Committees use the "guillotine" also.

(3) Another form of closure provided for in the Standing Orders is known as the 'Kangaroo.' It was first used in 1909, by which the Speaker is empowered to select those clauses and amendments to be proposed which he thinks most appropriate for discussion. That is to say, the Speaker at the Report Stage is invested with power to decide which amendments may be debated when several have been submitted to the same clause. The practice of missing some amendments is called the Kangaroo since the Speaker "leaps over" some amendments either because they are not in order or had been talked about before, or are merely time wasting. Kangaroo may be used either in conjunction with Guillotine or separately. The Chairmen of Committees, too, possess a similar power. The device of Kangaroo invests the Speaker with grave responsibility, but there is virtually no evidence of real abuse. The principle which the Speaker follows in the application of the Kangaroo is to select those amendments that raise the most important points of principles and concern the most important sections of opinion, and the most effectively worded in this sense.

**Parliamentary Privileges**

Each House of Parliament enjoys certain privileges and immunities designed to protect the House from unnecessary obstruction in carrying out its duties. These privileges apply collectively to each House and individually to each member.

In the House of Commons the Speaker formally claims from the Crown for the Commons "their ancient and undoubted rights and privileges" at the beginning of each Parliament. These include freedom from arrest in civil proceedings for a period from forty days before to forty days after a session of Parliament; freedom of speech, so that Members of Parliament cannot be prosecuted for sedition or sued for libel or slander anything said in the House or reported in Parliamentary publications and the right of access to the Crown, which is a collective privilege of the House. Further privileges include the right of the House to control its own proceedings ; the right to pronounce upon legal disqualifications for membership and to declare a seat vacant on such grounds; and the right to penalise those who commit a breach of its privileges.

Parliament claims the right to punish not only for breaches of its privileges, but contempt, which is an offence or libel against its dignity or authority. An offender may be detained within the precincts of the House, though such a punishment has not been given since 1880. Nowadays the House would probably direct offenders to be reprimanded. An offender who is not a member of the House is brought to the Bar by the Serjeant-at-Arms, and is there reprimanded by the Speaker in the name, and by the authority of the House. If the offender is a member he receives the Speaker's admonition or reprimand standing in his place. An offending member may also be suspended or, in extreme cases, expelled[3] from the House. Offenders other than members, may be ordered to attend at the Bar of the House; all may be heard in extenaution of their offences, or in mitigation of their punishment, before the House decides what action to take.

## OFFICERS OF THE HOUSE

The chief officer of the House of Commons is the Speaker who is elected by the Members to preside over the House immediately after a new Parliament is formed. Other officers of the House are : the Chairman of the Ways and Means, and one or two Deputy Chairmen, all of whom may act as Deputy Speaker. The Speaker had a salary of £13,000 a year plus £3,000 parliamentary allowance and residence within the Palace of Westminster. On retirement he is offered peerage and is provided with a pension. The Chairman of the Ways and Means and the Deputy Chairman were paid salaries of £6,750 and £5,500 respectively, in addition to their parliamentary allow-

3. In 1947 Garry Alligham was expelled from the House on account of critical articles he had written about Parliament.

ance of £3,000. They neither speak nor vote in the House other than in their official capacity. Permanent officers of the House, that is, those who are not members of Parliament, include the Clerk of the House of Commons, who is charged with such matters as keeping the records, endorsing bills and signing orders, and the Serjeant-at-Arms, who attends the Speaker in the House.

**The Speaker and His Role**

At the appointed hour for the House of Commons to meet, the Speaker enters the chamber with time-honoured ceremonial. The *Oxford English Dictionary* defines the Speaker as "the member of the House of the Commons who is chosen by the House itself to act as its representative and to preside over its debates." This is a fairly correct definition and it brings out three important points : that the Speaker is himself a member of the House of Commons and elected like all the others; that the House itself elects its own Speaker; and that he is the House's accredited deputy and the chairman of its deliberations. The dictionary definition, however, gives no idea of the Speaker's indispensability. Without the Speaker the House cannot meet. On the death of Speaker FitzRoy,[4] for instance, the House rose at once and could not function until the election of his successor, although the country was in midst of the Second World War.

The Speaker is an office the origin of which is obscure, but it is an office of much dignity, honour and authority. The first Speaker officially recorded in the Rolls of Parliament was Sir Peter de la Mare in 1376. In old days the Speaker was the spokesman for the Commons when they wished to lay their petitions before the King and in a sense he is that still. Today, in all his work, both in and out of the Chair, the Speaker interprets the will of the House and speaks for it as well as to it. For more than six hundred years the office has developed, but not essentially changed.

In the earlier days the King appointed the Speaker, but long after when the office became elective the usage was, as Coke testified in 1648, that the Sovereign would "name a discreet and learned man" whom the Commoners would then proceed to "elect". It was not till the reign of George III that the Royal influence wholly ceased to be exercised in the choice of a Speaker. Even now the election of the Speaker is subject to the approval of the Crown. But the real choice is that of the House of Commons, and normally the practice is to have unanimous election of the Speaker[5]. He is chosen by the Party in power from its own benches when there is a vacancy. The Opposition is always consulted before his name is proposed and if the Opposition objects, his name is withdrawn. As the Speaker is expected to be as impartial as any human being can be, the candidate proposed for the Speakership is one who has not been a violent partisan, or a member of the Government, and has ordinarily served a long apprenticeship as Chairman or Deputy Chairman of the Ways and Means or of some other Committee. The purpose is to secure general respect, and "no violent animosity." In 1945 when Labour had a majority of over 200, it did not oppose the re-election of Colonel Clifton Brown, who had been the Conservative nominee in1943. In 1959 the Conservatives thought that they might elect a Speaker from the Labour Party. It could not materialise as the Conservatives insisted that the choice of the candidate should be theirs. Sir Frank Soskice refused the appointment and the Conservatives refused to consider any other.

The Speaker, thus, elected continues in office for the whole life of Parliament[6]. But once elected he continues in office for so long as he wishes no matter whether or not the party which first proposed him for the Speakership is returned in majority[7]. The practice had been that once elected, the Speaker retains office until death or voluntary retirement. It is a tribute to the impartiality of the presiding officer of the House. Onslow, who was Speaker for thirty-four years

4. Fitz Roy died in 1943.
5. A contest for the Speakership is possible. Shaw Lefevre was elected for the first time (in1839) in a contest and so was Speaker Gully in 1895. Another contest over the election of a new Speaker took place in 1951 when the Conservatives were returned to Office. The Labour Party, in Opposition, did not object to the Conservative candidate for the office, but at the same time proposed that the former Deputy Speaker was most suitable a candidate because of his greater experience. Votes were taken and the Conservative candidate ex-Minister W.S. Morrison was elected defeating Major Milner of the Labour Party. The contest is not rare now.
6. The Speaker remains in office after dissolution until the next Speaker has been elected. He does not, however, after the dissolution execute duties such as issuing writs, etc., as he does during Parliamentary recess.
7. During the nineteenth century, for instance, only three Speakers were elected from the Conservative Party. The Party came to office in 1841, 1874, and 1895, but in each case the Speaker already in office was reappointed although he was elected to Parliament as a Liberal and to the Chair under a Liberal Government. In 1945, when Labour had a clear majority, Clifton- Brown, a Conservative, was retained as Speaker.

at the beginning of the eighteenth century, set a good example of impartiality by resigning his office as Treasurer of the Navy in order to show that he was independent of the government. But his successors for the next hundred years did not adhere to his conception of office. Not until the nineteenth century, it became the generally accepted principle, never questioned since 1870, that a Speaker, once elected takes no further part in party politics.

Since the time of Shaw Lefevre it has come to be understood that the Speakership is a strictly judicial office, wholly divorced from politics. As the Speaker abstains from any kind of political activity, its natural corollary is that a Speaker should not have to fight an election. Accordingly, for a long time there was a tradition to re-elect him unopposed. Since 1832 this had been the general rule. But in 1935 and again in 1945 the Labour Party contested the re-election of Conservative Speakers, FitzRoy and Clifton-Brown, though without any success. In 1951, no official Labour candidate opposed the Speaker. But an independent Labour candidate who ran against him was overwhelmingly defeated. In 1955 General Election the Speaker was opposed but re-elected by a large majority. It appears that the electorate feels alive to its duty of re-electing the Speaker unopposed and are determined to continue with a tradition which is now more than a century old, although since the end of the Second World War the Speaker has, almost always, been opposed. But when a candidate at the polls, the Speaker remains aloof from party issues, standing as 'the Speaker seeking re-election'. The endeavour has been, as Herman Finer remarks, "to make the Speaker the objective embodiment of the rules and laws of the Commons, purgating from him the last milligram of partisanship"[8].

An impartial arbiter in the proceedings of the House, the duties of the Speaker are many and arduous. Some of these duties depend on age old practice, some on statutory authority, and some on the Standing Orders of the House. We divide them into three main categories.

On occasions he acts as spokesman of the House, *e.g.*, when he claims the Commons' privileges, and executes its orders and decisions. Sometimes he bears their loyal address to the Throne. The Commons have access to the King only through the Speaker, or, in a body, with the Speaker at the head. In the name of the Commons the Speaker conveys thanks and censures. He presents Money Bills at the Bar of the House of Lords.

In certain ways, the Speaker acts as the House's representative and executive. He is its active and the only constitutionally recognised deputy. He issues a number of warrants in the name of the House for various purposes. For example, when a seat falls vacant during a session, the House directs Mr. Speaker to cause a writ to be issued for new election. Similarly, he issues warrants for the commitment of offenders and for the attendance of witnesses in custody.

The Speaker is also in charge of the administrative department, specifically called the Speaker's Department of the House of Commons. To it belong the Clerk of the House, a Librarian and staff, an Examiner of Petitions for Private Bills, officers of the vote office, and various others.

Occasionally, the Speaker is required to preside over a constitutional conference like the Buckingham Palace Conference in 1914 and the Speakers' Conference in 1920.

Gladstone once said that the Speaker's chief function was to defend the House against itself. He does this when he presides in the Chair of the House during the debate. In the Chair, his functions are threefold. First to keep order in the House, second; to keep members in order; and third, to select the speakers in the debate.

The Speaker presides over the sittings of the House of Commons, except when it sits as a Committee of the Whole, and decides who shall have the floor. All speeches and remarks are addressed to the Chair. In any political assembly feelings are apt, from time to time, to run high. When they do, there is always the possibility of disorder. It is the business of the Speaker to see that the proceedings of the House are conducted with decorum and, if possible, with effect. He has, accordingly, wide powers to check disorder, irrelevance, tedious repetition and unparliamentary language or behaviour. It is a rule that when the Speaker stands, no member must remain on his feet. When he finds signs of disorder, the Speaker will stand and with a few well-chosen words of admonition or appeal will try to cool down the passion of Members, and thus, avoid disorder. Usually this is effective, but if any Member persists in disorder, the Speaker may ask him to resume his seat. If he still continues to be

8. Finer, H., *Governments of Greater European Powers*, p. 107.

disorderly, the Speaker may order him to withdraw from the House.[9] If he does not go, the Speaker will 'name' the Member. This means expulsion of the Member from the House. If the Member refuses to leave the House he will be escorted out (by force if necessary) through the Serjeant-at-Arms.[10]He adjourns the House, if the disorder becomes serious. A Standing Order to this effect was brought in after certain Irish Members had forced Speaker Gully into a very difficult position and it was applied in May 1905[11].

On November 13, 1980 the House witnessed rowdy scenes when Labour M.Ps blocked the prorogation ceremony denying the Queen's messenger, Black Rod, bearing summons from the Lords, access to the Commons Chamber. The Speaker was forced to suspend the stormy sitting twice, first for ten minutes and then for 15 minutes, before the Government bowed to the Opposition's demand for the withdrawal of the Conservative document on the proposed increase of council house rents, the issue which had sparked off the uproar. Michael Hasaltine, Secretary of State for Environment, emphasised that he was withdrawing the consultative document because the authority of the Speaker was at stake. But such occasions are very rare in the parliamentary life of Britain.

Here is a lengthy quotation from Herbert Morrison to illustrate the high traditions of the office and the great reverence with which the Members hold the incumbent. "The Speaker, "says Morrison, "has no bell with which to restore order not even a gravel. When he rises in his place and says, 'Order,' it is rare for the House not to come to order at once. And if some Members should be noisy a large proportion of the House will aid the Speaker by crying 'Order, Order' until the noisy and disorderly ones are quietened, or a Member standing at the same time as the Speaker rises resumes his seat. One evening between the wars I was impressed by a comparison with the French Chamber of Deputies. The occasion was exciting and the Deputies were thoroughly enjoying themselves in one of their occasional outbursts of noisy and persistent disorder. The President sat in his place ringing the bell vigorously and at length, it almost seemed that the louder he rang the bell, and the longer he rang it, the worse the disorder became. I could not help thinking, with some British Parliamentary pride of Mr. Speaker in the House of Commons."[12]

His second function is to keep members in order and this relates to the judicious conduct of debates. The Speaker is "Lord of Debate." He must see that the debate centres on the main issues before the House and Members do not wander, accidentally or deliberately, in the realm of irrelevance. Any Member can point out to Mr. Speaker that the Member who is speaking is out of order. But generally, the Speaker himself calls such a Member to order. Then, there are constant direct appeals to him for his rulings on points of procedure. Here the Speaker acts as a judge interpreting the law of Parliament. His ruling is final which need not be contested.[13] Each decision of the Speaker ranks as a precedent, to be heeded like the judgment of a court on the next occasion. Similarly he advises the Members and the House on points not covered by Law. He puts questions and announces the results of votes.

The Speaker's third duty in presiding over Commons debates is to "call" the Members to participate. He decides who is to speak, for so little time is available now-a-days that only those who are fortunate enough "to catch the Speaker's eye" can hope to speak. The Speaker is guided in his choice by many considerations. He will usually give a Member a chance of making his first, or maiden speech, but generally he will choose those Members who, in his opinion, are likely to be in a position to make the best contribution to the debate; the Government and Opposition leaders share a conventional priority. And since his object is to give opportunities for the

---

9. On the first occasion when the member is named he must stay away for five days. On the second, for twenty-one days. On the third, until the end of that sitting of Parliament.
10. The Serjeant-At-Arms attends the Speaker with the Mace (the symbol of Speaker's authority) and arranges the policing of the House. The Speaker can also order the arrest of a member and confinement to the Tower of Big Ben. In 1930, one member in a fit of anger seized the Mace and lifted it from the Table.There was talk of Mr. Speaker using this power for the offence, which by Parliamentary standards, was very grave, but he did not use it and the offending member was merely expelled for a period.
11. For one whole hour the House refused a hearing to the Colonial Secretary. The Deputy Speaker was in the Chair and he adjourned the House.
12. Morrison, H., *Government and Parliament,* pp. 204-205.
13. During the 1958-59 session, a number of Labour Members grumbled about Speaker Morrison's actions. It has been mentioned that some Members were discourteous to the Speaker in raising pointless points of order, and they disputed his decisions.

expression of all the main shades of opinion, he exercises his judgment most discreetfully. In fact, Members apply to the Speaker beforehand through their Whips, so that his choice is by no means haphazard, and, of course, the Leaders of the House and Opposition decide who shall be their principal speakers. But he preserves his freedom to depart from this list.

Another less obvious function of the Speaker is to protect the House against the encroachments of the Government. When Ministers tend to encroach upon the freedom of Members, or refuse to answer questions, or do not give sufficient information, it is to Mr. Speaker that the Member appeals to safeguard and enforce the rights of Members against the executive.

There are some other functions of the Speaker and they are of crucial importance. He can prevent the putting of the question to a vote, when moved by a Member of the majority and usually a Government Whip, until he is personally satisfied that the minority has been given due opportunity to debate its views. After all Closure is an infringement of the rights of the minority and it is the duty of the Speaker to protect the liberties and rights of debate of the minority. He, also, decides whether to admit or rule out amendments. Then, he has the power of decision on the admissibility of questions. He may, on his own judgment, decide whether a matter is of definite public and urgent importance and so put it on the immediate agenda for debate. The Act of 1911 empowers the Speaker to certify that a Bill is a Money Bill and thereby eliminates the obstruction of the House of Lords. He decides how Bills are to be allocated between the various Standing Committees, and in this respect has a comparatively free hand. The Speaker also appoints the Chairmen of Standing Committees, whom he chooses from the Chairmen's panel, a list of not less than ten Members drawn up by the Committee of Selection. It is for the Speaker to decide who is the leader of the Opposition should this ever be in any doubt.

The umpire-like quality of the Speaker is characteristic of the trust which the Commons repose in him. He does not vote, except in a case of a tie. But the Speaker usually endeavours to give his casting vote in such a way that it maintains the *status quo,* upholds established precedents and previous decisions of the House, and avoids making himself personally responsible for bringing about any change. What he really does is to put a temporary stop to the debate on an issue that will probably be revived at a later date.

What precisely the office of the Speaker is and his functions have been succinctly described by Douglas Clifton-Brown, who was Speaker from 1943 to 1954. On the occasion of his re-elction in 1945, he said, "I have to try to see that the machine runs smoothly. The Speaker can help here, in the Chair and behind the Chair. I have to see that the Government business, while I am not responsible for it, is not unduly hampered by wilful obstruction. I have to see that minority views have a fair hearing .......Of course, there will be various shades of opinion on all sides of the House and all these have to be considered when one is calling speakers. Free speech and fair play for all must be my main duty....As Speaker, I am not the Government's man, nor the Opposition's man. I am the House of Commons man and I believe, above all, the back-benchers' man .....As Speaker, I cherish the dignity of the office very much. I wish to uphold it, and I shall." Sir Harry Hylton-Foster, on his election to Speakership in October 1959, pledged his service to the cause of Parliament. It would be his whole ambition in life, he said, to serve the House faithfully "to maintain in full vigour those traditions that have made this House at once the origin and the example of parliamentary institutions throughout the world.[14]

The Speaker is, in brief, the impartial custodian of the rights of the members of the House. For him, the humblest back-bencher is no less than a Member, and the greatest Minister is no more than a Member. The essence of his impartiality lies in the way he maintains an atmosphere of fair play by ensuring that the Opposition have an opportunity to express their views and criticisms, yet at the same time seeing that there is no parliamentary obstruction to hinder the Government in its task of governing the country. "It is Mr. Speaker's function to safeguard the privileges and rights of the Members of the Commons not only against the Crown and Lords but as between each other, to the end that the whole basis of Parliament, as a forum in which the elected representatives of the people speak their minds and say what they think—popular or unpopular should be reserved."[15] The Speaker's conduct reflects the spirit, as Briers says, which is ultimately more important than the forms of

14. As cited by Ronald Young, *The British Parliament,* p. 125.
15. Brown, W. J., *Guide to Parliament,* p. 61.

Government. "In some measures he is responsible for the continued existence of the House of Commons, for it will survive only so long as its procedure and facilities are adequate for the functions it has to perform; and the adjustment of established procedure to novel conditions is the Speaker's task."[16] The Speaker must, accordingly, possess high and varied qualities of character and intellect. He should be able, vigilant, imperturbable, tactful, enthusiastic for and interested in the institution of Parliament. Sir William Harcourt said of the Office: "We expect dignity and authority, tampered by urbanity and kindness; firmness to control and persuasiveness to counsel: promptitude of decision and justness of judgment; tact, patience, and firmness; a natural superiority combined with an inbred courtesy, so as to give by his own bearing an example and a model to those over whom he presides; an impartial mind, a tolerant temper, and a reconciling disposition; accessible to all in public and private as a kind and prudent counsellor." The Speaker seldom speaks, but when he does "he speaks for the House, not to it."[17]

The varied qualities needed in an ideal Speaker are not commonly found. But the ideal is recognisably there and for all these burdens the Speakership carries compensation in social status and material well-being. In the official precedence he ranks before the Prime Minister and just after the Archbishop of Canterbury. He is the only subject of the Queen who holds levees at which court dress must be worn, and to which invitations are in the nature of commands . On retirement, he gets a handsome pension and is created a Peer. Speaker Whitley (1921-28) was the first to refuse peerage. On his retirement Labour Members opposed the grant of his pension. They thought that the Speaker's pension was too much whereas his salary too little.

## FUNCTIONS OF THE HOUSE

The House of Commons has, broadly speaking, three functions: legislation, financial business, and deliberation and criticism or controlling the Government. The Clerk of the House of Commons once defined the functions of the House as follows : "(1) Representation of popular opinion, (2) the control of finance, (3) the formulation and control of policy, (4) legislation." The Clerk of the House, as well as Walter Bagehot, listed legislation last, and that, too, for cogent reasons. Legislation developed from the practice of petitioning the King. Financial functions were the original and the procedure involved therein originated in the practice of granting "aids". The critical and deliberative functions are the earliest, rudimentary in the beginning but the most essential feature of the governmental system in Britain. It is, perhaps not always realised that the prime task of the House of Commons is not to govern or legislate, but to criticise and control the executive government and it is the essence of parliamentary democracy. John Stuart Mill illustrated this point in his own characteristic way. "The meaning of representative government is, that the whole people, or some numerous portion of them, exercise through deputies periodically elected by themselves the ultimate controlling power, which, in every constitu- tion, must reside somewhere....The proper duty of a Representative Assembly in regard to matters of administration is not to decide them by its own vote, but to take care that the persons who have to decide are subject to its constant control." We, however, for obvious reasons take legislation first.

## LEGISLATION

### Process of Legislation

The process of making laws is the business of Parliament as a whole; King, Lords and Commons. The House of Commons can by itself do nothing. But, in practical terms, the role of the Monarch in Parliament is just formal, and in a number of respects the legal power and political authority of the House of Lords is subservient to that of the Commons. Today, the Commons composed of the 635 elected representatives of the people, is the dominant element in Parliament, so that in almost all practical (though not legal) respects Parliament and the House of Commons are interchangeable terms. The House of Commons can initiate any measure, ordinary and financial, and most of the great contentious and important laws originate there and the verdict of the House of Commons finally determines their fate.

Every law begins as a Bill[18] which is read three times in each House of Parliament and after receiving the King's assent becomes an Act. Why the Bill is read three times, it is difficult to say.

---

16. Briers, P. M., *Papers on Parliament: A Symposium* p.27.
17. Speaker Lenthall said to Charles I in 1842 that he had "neither eye to see nor tongue to speak in this place, but as the House is pleased to direct me, whose servant I am."
18. A Bill is a draft Act of Parliament.

It may only be assumed that if the House has given its assent to a measure three times there can be no question of unpremeditated acquiescence to it. The practice of reading a Bill three times dates from medieval times, "when the number three was regarded with especial reverence; and by the end of the sixteenth century it appears to have become invariable."[19] It is, indeed, a sensible practice, but it is only a practice and not a legal necessity.

Bills, in Britain are classified in accordance with two important distinctions. In the first place, Bills are divided on the basis of a difference of *substace,* into *Public Bills* and *Private Bills*. Public Bills are of general application and contain subject-matter applicable uniformly to the public as a whole or to large parts of it. On the other hand, Private Bills affect particular local or private interest and are concerned with establishing legal arrangements that will apply to specific person, corporation, group, community or the like. They are not generally of public concern and are passed by a special procedure distinct from Public Bills. Most Private Bills come from local government authorities.

Public Bills are subdivided, according to a formal distinction, into Government Bills and Private Members' Bills. Both Government and Private Member's bill are, as far as subject-matter is concerned, Public Bills but their origin is different. A Government Bill, as its name implies, is a Public Bill introduced by a Minister on behalf of the Government.[20] A Private Member's Bill is a Public Bill promoted by a Member of Parliament, who is not a member of the Government. Public Bills run between 90 to 150 per year as finally enacted laws, of which a very small numbers originate from Private Members. Public Bills may originate in the Commons or in the Lords, but usually they find their origin in the Commons.

A Public Bill, in becoming law passes through three readings but five stages in the House of Commons. The five stages are: (1) First Reading; (2) Second reading; (3) Committee stage;(4) Report stage; and (5) Third Reading. If there are financial clauses in a Bill, and most Bills have succh clauses, there will be two extra stages, either before or after the Second Reading. A financial resolution is moved and debated in the Committee of the Whole House (the House without the Speaker ) and report to the House itself; the Speaker presiding.

Before a Public Bill begins its career in the House of Commons, the Cabinet discusses the proposal to introduce a Bill at the initiation of the Minister concerned. If the Cabinet accepts the proposal, a memorandum is sent to the Office of the Parliamentary Counsel, a subordinate department attached to the Treasury set up in 1869 and staffed by non-practising lawyers, containing a general description of the scope of the Bill. The Parliamentary Counsels are the skilled lawyers who draw up the Bill on the lines suggested by the memorandum. Then , the draft Bill is laid before the Cabinet for approval, printed and discussed with the representatives of the various interests affected. No Government can afford to ignore or trample upon the various groupings of opinion. There is the next general election to be always remembered. It means that there are endless negotiations, deputations and interviews before even a final draft of the Bill is settled. The Bill may have to be redrafted many times and this process may occupy a considerably long time. At the end of such consultations the Bill may have to receive Cabinet approval once again.

When the Bill has been finally approved by the Cabinet, it stands its turn for introduction. There are two ways of introducing a Bill. It may be introduced on a motion, or it can be introduced on written notice. The former procedure has now fallen into disuse as far as Government Bills are concerned. The normal method of introducing a Bill is on written notice and is prescribed in Standing Order No. 35 of the House of Commons. On the day appointed, of which notice had been given, the introducer merely comes forward and hands to the Clerk of the House a "Dummy Bill" . The Clerk reads out the title of the Bill. The "Dummy" does not contain the text of the Bill. It is just a special form of stationery officially furnished on which the title of the Bill is written down. There is no debate and discussion and that finishes the first reading of the Bill. The Bill is printed as soon as it is ready and Members get its copies to study. The measure then waits its turn for the Second Reading. The First Reading is this a formal stage.

The crucial stage in the life of a Bill is the

19. Taylor, E., *The House of Commons at Work*, p. 131.
20. Proposals for legislative changes are set out by the Government in White Papers which are debated in Parliament prior to introduction of a Bill. Since the late 1960's the Government has also adopted the practice of publishing 'Green Papers' from time to time setting out for public discussion major ministerial proposals which are still at the formative stage.

Second reading and, *ipso facto,* the second stage in its career. On a day fixed in advance, which varies between one day and several weeks depending on the nature of the Bill by an order of the House, the Minister-in-charge of the Bill will rise and move that "the Bill be now read a Second time." He will explain, elaborate and elucidate what the proposed measure will do, and how the necessity of such a measure is important and urgent. Some leading Members of the Opposition will follow the minister. He might move to amend the Minister's motion and say that "the Bill be read a second time this day six months hence." Or he might propose a substantive amedment to the policy embodied in the Bill. Then would ensue a general debate in which many Members on both sides of the House would participate, and it would end with the Minister winding up for the Government. Upon the conclusion of the debate there would be a division. If the Government were defeated it would have to resign. But it would never be defeated so long as it commands a majority. In the Commons non-controversial Bills may be referred to a Second Reading Committee to recommend whether it should be taken as read a second time. Likewise, a Public Bill relating exclusively to Scotland, may, in certain circumstances, be referred by the House of Commons to the Scottish Grand Committee at the second reading stage. When this happens, the Committee must consider the Bill in relation to its principles and report that it has done so. The Bill thus returned to the House has not been read a second time, but when it comes up for the second reading again a motion may be made to commit it to a Scottish Standing Committee. If this motion is carried the Bill is deemed to have been read a second time.

The second reading is not the time for detailed discussion or amendments and vote upon the clauses. It is the Bill as a whole, its merits and principal policy issues involved, which are discussed and amendments are proposed not to the Bill, but to the motion that "the Bill be now read a second time." The object is to approve the Bill or throw it out entirely. The second reading in Britain, corresponds more exactly to the Continental practice of "discussion generale," which usually precedes passage to the specific articles. Erskine May, the former Clerk of Parliament, said that "The second reading is the most important stage through which the Bill is required to pass: for its whole principle is then at issue, and affirmed or denied by a vote of the House"[21]. But the truth is that one stage in the course of the Bill is as important as the other. In fact, decisions are made in the Committees and not in the second reading. The organs of opinion and interested groups, as Herman Finer maintains, are "extremely vocal from now onward and seek to exert influence upon the Minister-in-charge of the Bill. They obtain their opportunity for concrete amendments in the states of cogitation which immediately precede, and operate during consideration in committee."[22]

Upon being read a second time, ordinary Public Bills[23] go automaticaly to one of the Standing Committees unless some member rises immediatelly after the second reading and moves that the Bill be committed to a Committee of the Whole House or to a Select Committee or to a Joint Committee of Lords and Commons. Public Bills to which Cabinet attaches great importance are often sent to the Committeee of the Whole House. In the House of Lords, unless otherwise ordered a Bill is committed to a Committee of the Whole House.

The Committee stage provides the occasion for a detailed discussion of the Bill. Every clause must be put separately to the Committee and accepted, amended or rejected, with or without debate. Discussion is generally of a very restrained, persuasive character. "The Minister is generally terse and quiet and the speeches of the critics have something of the same dry, business like flavour." The government maintains with persistence its guiding hand throughout the Committee stage. It does not relinquish its leadership to a Reporter, as in France or to a "member-in-charge" as in the United States. A Minister, in Britain, sponsors the Bill in Parliament and pilots it through all stages. The fate of the Bill depends almost exclusively upon him. He must guide the Bill through the Committee with tactful, and if necessary forthright firmness in respect of principles, and with the appearance of amiable resignation and broad-mindedness in connection with unimportant detail.

A member of Committee may speak any number of times to the same question without

21. As cited in Herman Finer, *The Theory and Practice of Modern Government,* p. 485.
22. *Ibid.*
23. The exceptions are Bills for imposing taxes, Consolidated Fund Bills and Provisional Orders Bills.

being exactly repetitive or demonstrably irrelevant. To avoid such obstructionists, the Government may be forced to apply a 'guillotine' motion, or by moving the Closure on every amendment. This is a salutary if not a drastic remedy and yet it cannot prevent obstruction. If the Opposition feels inclined they will force a division on every clasue.[24]

But once a Bill is passed through the second reading, its fundamental principles are supposed to have been accepted. It is out of order to propose an amendment in a Committee intended to negative the effect of the Bill. Similarly, amendments which are not strictly relevant to the subject-matter of the Bill, and amendments which are not in conformity with the general intention of the Bill are out of order. Then, the amendments must not be inconsistent with whatever has already been agreed to in the Committee on the Bill, and "they must not be trifling, vague or jesting."

The Committee stage has existed for centuries. The Commons had in the past, when the Spekaer was the servant of the King and "an office-seeking spy" always wanted to discuss affairs without the presence of the Speaker. Now the Committees derive their importance and utility from the increased legislation and inability of the House to spend time on its detailed discussion. The modern Committee system was established in 1882. "It was ," as Finer says, "one answer (the other was Closure) to the congestion of the House with business, aggravated at that time by the ingenious obstructive tactics of the members from Ireland, who had made up their minds that if Ireland was not to be freed to govern herself, they would not let England govern herself." The main purpose of the Committee system was decongestion to save the time to the House of Commons by devolving its business to other bodies of the House which functioned at other times.

There are five types of Committees : (1) Committee of the Whole House ;(2) Standing Committees; (3) Select Committees; (4) Joint Committees; and (5) Private Bills Committees. The Private Bills Committees are for the discussion of private and local legislation and have nothing to do with the Public Bills. The Joint Committees are Select Committees of the House of Commons and the House of Lords and consist of an equal number of members from each House to consider Bills or other matters in which both Houses are interested.

The Committee of the Whole House is the first in importance. It consists of all the members of the House of Commons. But it is distinguished from the House itself that it is presided over not by the Speaker, but by a Chairman of the Committee or in his absence by the Deputy Chairman.The Mace which is the symbol of authority of the Speaker is placed, so long as the Committee is in session under the Table. Then, the Rules of Procedure in the Committee are relaxed. The motion need not be seconded and the members are allowed to speak any number of times on the same question. There is no restriction on speech in the Committee of the Whole House and all devices which aim at cutting off debate cannot be moved.

Committee of the Whole House meets for four distinct purposes. There is the Ordinary Committee of the Whole House on a Bill; the Committee of the Whole House on a Money Resolution; the Committee of Supply and the Committee of Ways and Means. The first comes into being whenever the House resolves that an ordinary Bill shall go to the Committee of the Whole House rather than to a Standing or Select Committee. When the work of the Committee is done, it rises. The House of Commons again comes into session, and the Speaker occupies the Chair and the Mace is placed on the Table. The Chairman of the Committee, then, approaches the Chair and says, " I beg to report that the Committee have made progress in matters referred to them, and ask leave to sit again." The Speaker asks when the Committee is to sit again and one of the Government Whips answers him. The appointed day is announced from the Chair and it becomes an order of the House. If a Committee has completed its assigned task, its Chairman says,"The Committee have come to a certain resolution." The Committee of the Whole House is not set up permanently. It is a temporary body appointed from day to day.

The Committee of the Whole House on a Bill is rare. If it is desired to send the Bill to a Committee of the Whole House, a motion to that effect must be moved immediately after the Bill is read a second time. Other- wise the Bill will go

24. "In Standing Committee on the Cinematograph Films Bill 1927, a minority of six Members divided the Committee no fewer than three hundred times, and prolonged the Committee stage from April to July: twenty-five sitting days. In 1948, the Opposition prolonged the debate on the Gas Bill for months in Committee and even forced several all-night sittings on the Bill—the only case where a Standing Committee had sat all night." Taylor, E., *The House of Commons at Work*, p. 139.

automatically to a Standing Committee. The Committees of Supply and of Ways and Means are Committees of the Whole House of Commons which discharge the financial duties of the House concerning the grant of public money and the levying of taxation.

After the Second Reading automatically a Bill, other than a Money Bill, goes to one of the Standing Committees, unless the House resolves that the Bill would go either to the Committee of the Whole House or to a Select Committee. "Constitutionally important Bills" are referred to the Committee of the Whole House, because the House has always preferred to deal with them directly rather than in smaller Committees. A Bill is referred to a Select Committee when examination of expert evidence is necessary to carry the legislation with technical efficiency involved therein.

Most Bills, therefore, go to the Standing Committees. Originally, there were two Standing Committees. In 1907, their number was raised to four; in 1919; to six; and in 1947 to "as many as shall be necessary." Currently, there are seven such Committees appointed, though the number can be increased at need. The Committees are not named as in other Legislatures by subject-matter, for example, Education, Health, Armed Services, etc. In the House of Commons they are distinguished only by a letter of the Alphabet: A, B, C, D. Only four Committees—the Second Reading Committee, Scottish Standing Committee, the Scottish Grand Committee and the Welsh Committee—are distinctly named. The Standing Committees are appointed by the Selection Committee, a body normally consisting of eleven members drawn from the main parties in the Commons at the beginning of each session. The members of a Standing Committee are constantly changing, from session to session. Each Committee consists from sixteen to fifty members, who are specialists and experts in the subject which is the substance of the Bill. The parties are represented in proportion to their numbers in the House. Chairmen of Standing Committees are appointed by the Speaker from a Chairmen's Panel consisting of not less than ten persons nominated by the Selection Committee. The Committees meet in the mornings from 10.30 a.m. to 3.30 p.m., with the recess, and may continue even afterwards. The House has now admitted that a Committee might sit while it is in session. The "guillotine" form of closure has more recently become applicable to Standing Committees. The Government may also use its power to move the Closure on each amendment. The procedure of a Standing Committee is generally similar to that of a Committee of the Whole House.

Bills come to the Standing Committees quite arbitrarily, according to their order on a calendar and according to which Committee finishes its work first. There is no specialisation on different topics. The Standing Committees are composed of members of Parliament and have no vestige of executive power. They cannot summon persons and papers before them. They cannot debate or discuss matters irrelevant to the actual text of the Bill before them. They are legislative Committees and not investigative Committees. All information that is needed is supplied by the Minister-in-charge of the Bill. The Opposition supplies the contrary information. The public are admitted to meetings of a Standing Committee, unless the Committee decides to exclude them.

In addition to the normal Standing Committee, there are three others, the Scottish Standing Committee, the Scottish Grand Committee and the Welsh Grand Committee. The Scottish Standing Committee consists of thirty members nominated from Scottish consituencies with up to twenty other nominated members; in its plenary form, as the Scottish Grand Committee, it comprises all the members for the Scottish constituencies and not less than ten or more than fifteen others. These Committees have three functions: to discuss for two days of each session matters of exclusively Scottish concern; to consider for six days such estimates as refer exclusively to Scotland; and also to consider the principles of any Bill which the Speaker certifies as relating exclusively to Scotland. Such a Bill can then, on the motion of a Minister, be referred to its Committee stage to a Scottish Standing Committee. The Welsh Grand Committee consists of 36 members for constituencies in Wales and Monmouthshire, with up to 5 other nominated members. The Committee considers the Annual Report for Wales and certain selected subjects for debate.

Select Committees are appointed to inquire into and report to the House on special matters of great importance or to give special consideration to Bills that are controversial and propose radical changes. They are employed on specialised tasks which the House itself is unsuited to perfom. They chiefly carry out inquiries rather than discuss legislative details. Since Select Com- mittees are specialised Committees they seldom have more than fifteen members who are more or less technical experts adequately familiar with matters referred to them for investigation. They hold hearings, collect evidence examine witnesses, sift evidence, and draw up reasoned conclusions to report to the Commons. As soon as the investigation conducted by a Select Committees is completed and its report submitted to the House, the Committee passes out of existence. The findings of a Select Committee are not binding . It simply makes recommendations to the House.

Apart from temporary Select Committees of this kind, a number of perennial Select Commitees on various topics are appointed every year and they remain in existence throughout the session of Parliament. Hence, these are called Sessional Select Committees. Examples of Sessional Select Committees are : the Selection Committee, the Committee of Privileges, the Committee on Public Petitions and Committees on Public Accounts, on Estimates, on Statutory Instruments, on Nationalised Industries and European Legislation. In addition, a number of 'specialist' committees have been set up: The Committee on Agriculture, the Committee on Science and Technology, the Committee on Education and Science, the Standing Orders Committee and the Committee on Race Relations and Immigration which considers matters affecting immigrants and race relations in Britain.

But in 1980 Mrs. Margaret Thatcher's Government, backed by the Opposition Labour Party, brought about a radical change, despite the stiff opposition from some members of Parliament, in the Committee system, by establishing twelve Select Committees and phasing out the existing Select Committees, except the Public Accounts and European Legislation Committees. These Select Committees, consisting of nine to eleven members selected by an all-Party group of nine Members of Parliament, are of the nature of special ''watchdog'' committees endowed with investigative powers and keeping constant control on the working of the Department to which a Committee is attached. But, unlike the Congressional Committees in the United States they have not the power to amend Bills. Nor can they compel Ministers to attend their meetings. The Government is publicly pledged to co-operate with the Committees and it is, accordingly, presumed that Ministers will not refuse to appear once invited to do so. The Government is also committed to give more powers to these Committees if deemed expedient and necessary.

Joint Committees are committees composed, usually of an equal number of Members of each House appointed to consider either a particular subject or a particular Bill or Bills, or to consider all Bills of a particular description, for instance, Bills dealing with statute law revision and consolidating Bills. A Joint Committee to consider a particular subject may be appointed at the instance of either House, but the proposal that a particular Bill should be committed to a Joint Committee must come from the House in which the Bill originated.

The members of a Joint Committee are usually chosen in equal numbers by the respective Houses. The Committee has only such authority as both Houses agree to give it. The time and place of its meetings are also fixed by agreeement between the two Houses. The Chairman is elected by the Committee itself from among its members. Decisions are taken by vote and the Chairman votes like any other member of the Committee.

The Report of a Joint Committee is presented to both Houses—by the Chairman to the House of which he is a Member, and by a member selected by the Committee for the purpose to the other House.

Finally, are the Private Bill Committees. The constitution, functions and procedure of the Committees on Private Bills depend on whether a Bill is opposed or unopposed. An opposed Bill, in this sense, is not a Bill which has been opposed in Parliament, but a Bill against which a petition has been deposited, or a Bill which the Chairman of the Ways and Means or the Lord Chairman of the Committees report should be treated as unopposed Bill, athough no petition has been presented against it. The Committee on an opposed Bill before the House of Commons consists of four members of the House (appointed by the Committee of selection) who must have no personal or local interest in theBill. For an unopposed Bill, the Committee consists of the Chairman of the Ways and Means and a deputy Chairman and three other members chosen by the Chairman from a panel appointed by Committee of Selection at the beginning of each session. In the House of Lords, Committees on opposed Bills consist of five members, unopposed Bills are referred to the Lord Chairman of Committees.

**The Committee System**

In Britain as early as the r eign of Queen

Elizabeth I it was not unusual to refer a Bill after the second reading to a committee which can be compared to a Select Committee of our times. The Committee system, in its present form was established to relieve the congestion of business in the House of Commons, caused partly by the obstructive tactics of the Irish Nationalists, as mentioned earlier. They have, consequently, no resemblance whatever between the Committees of the American or Continental type. The Committees in the United States and European countries are bodies of relatively stable membership specialising in particular aspects of public policy. In the United States there are Committees of Congress which formulate policy, and intervens in the actions of the Government. In the Third Republic of France a system of elven Commissions, chosen by lot from the Chamber of Deputies, performed the same functions to an even greater extent. The Fourth Republic constitutionalised Commissions. Article 15 of the Constitution provided that "the National Assembly should study in its Committees the Bills laid before it.........." They were nineteen in number and were powerful enough to find themselves often in conflict with the Government.

But such a conception of Committee system is entirely foreign to the spirit of the British Constitution. The Committees of the House of Commons are not small expert bodies undertaking special studies of the merits of the Bills and possessing the power of life and death over them. They are rather miniature editions of the House headed by a Chairman whose powers and functions are very much like those of the Speaker including the Closure rules. They have no permanence or individuality. Their members are constantly changing. The Standing Committees of the House are distinguished only by a letter of the alphabet, and they have no special subjects to deal with.[25] The Speaker assigns Bills to them more or less at will. The purpose of the Committees is to put the Bill into final shape for adoption after its general character has already been approved at the second reading and before it has to be reported out. Public hearings are not conducted by Standing Committees and they take no evidence.[26] The House of Commons still jealously guards its responsibility of making laws and criticising policy in full session. Its Committees are only auxiliaries, "the mere accessories of the legislative and critical machine".

The Committee system, as it obtained in Britain, had engaged the attention of parliamentarians and public men and they had been advocating since long for the creation of specialized committees of the House of Commons, each concentrating on the affairs of a department or group of Departments. The advocates of specialized committees included Lloyd George, L.S. Amery, Sir Stafford Cripps, Sir Ivor Jennings, Harold Laski, D.W. Brogan and two recent Clerks to the House of Commons, Lord Campion and Sir Edward Fellowes.The many reforms that have been suggested along these lines vary in details. But all are agreed that specialised committees would enable Members to acquire the detailed information about the work and problems concerning the Department if they are to conduct diligent and useful debates on administrative matters and on legislation necessary to meet administrative needs of the Department. Secondly, specialised committees would enable Members to acquire information about and criticise those aspects of defence policy whch "are now shrouded in secrecy." Members are generally ignorant of the defence policy of the country during peace time and, accordingly, it is free from parliamentary control, although it involves the expenditure of 20 per cent of Government's annual revenue. Thirdly, specialised committee would discuss administrative matters in a non-partisan way and, finally, membership of the committees would help Members of the Opposition not only to criticise the Government "in an informal way, but also to prepare themselves to take over responsibility for the departments if they should win an election."

The suggestions for reform of the committee system have been widely discussed in the press, platform, books, in debates in the House of Commons, and before the Select Committees on Procedure of 1930-31, 1945-46, 1958-59, and 1964-65. But "they have met unyielding opposition from the spokesmen of whatever government to be in power." [27] The Government point

---

25. The Public Accounts Committee and the Estimates Committee have special functions in connection with the expenditure of public funds.
26. The Public Accounts and Estimates Committees have the power to send for persons and papers. In some ways they have functions like Congressional investigating committees, though they act in a non-partisan manner and within the policy limits laid down by the House.
27. Birch, A. H., *Representative and Responsible Government*, p. 161.

of view had been that Britain should not try to copy the institutions of foreign countries and if American or French pattern was adopted, "we would be doing something absolutely opposite to British constitutional development."[28] Herbert Morrison, in his evidence to the Select Committee of Procedure, 1945-46, maintained that Parliament "is not a body which is organised for current administratio–not in this country. They have had a go at it in France and the United States, and I do not think too much of it." It had further been maintained that specialised committees would constitute a radical constitutional innovation, which would be a challenge to the responsibility of the Minister that he is individually accountable to the House as a whole for the work of his Department.

But Birch remarks that it is no answer to say that reform would constitute a breach of traditional practice. "because this is what the reform is intended to." He is of the opinion that most of the arguments by the opponents of the proposed reform are irrelevant. He even suggests that it will be appropriate to consider the nature of responsible government in Britain, if ministerial responsibility blurs by the creation of specialised committees.[29] Whatever be the merits or otherwise of specilised Committees it cannot be denied that the British Committee system was defective and Parliament could not control administration because M.Ps lacked knowledge about administrative affairs, and the House lacked time for detailed discussion. To remedy the position partially three specialized Committees were set up : the Committee on Agriculture, the Committee on Science and Technology, and the Committee on Education and Science. They were in addition to Public Accounts Committee, the Select Committee on Estimates and the Select Committee on Statutory Instruments. All these Committees are set up at the beginning of each session of Parliament, but are in effect a permanent feature of the House of Commons Commiittee system. R.H.S. Crossman, Leader of the House of Commons, while pleading for reform in the Parliamentary procedure gave a note of warning. He said, "....we must take care to see them up in the right way. We cannot make the American-style Committees. They must be in our tradition. We must take trouble and care on this. We are on the edge of getting it right, but do not let us set up too many committees."[30]

The M.Ps Committee charged to look into the procedure of the House of Commons submitted its report in December, 1979 and suggested radical reforms. When the Conservative Government came into office in May,1980 the Government accepted the Committees' recommendations and backed by the Labour Opposition brought forward the most important changes in Parliament during the present century. The Government believed that the proposed reforms would assert the historic role of the Commons in checking and controlling the Executive and bringing members of Parliament into the heart of Government's decision-making process. It refuted the argument of the critics of reform that the creation of special "watchdog" committees to oversee the work of each Government department would mean usurpation of the role of the Government itself, and asserted that the administration would, in fact, benefit from the constant scrutiny of the work of Ministers and Civil Servants.

In pursuance of the recommendations of the MPs Committee twelve Select Committees, each comprising between nine and eleven members of the House, selected by an all Party group of nine members of the Commons, were established. They cover : agriculture, defence, education, employment, energy, envioronment, foreign affairs, home affairs, industry and trade, social services, transport, and all Treasury and Civil Service matters. Another Committee supervises the work of the independent Ombudsman who investigates complaints of maladministration brought up by MPs on behalf of individuals. There could also be up to four sub-committees looking into such matters as overseas aid, immigration, and State-owned industries. The hitherto, existing Select Committees are to be phased out except for the vital Public Accounts and European Legislation Committees.

The new investigative committees meet in public or on occasion in private if members agree that that is expedient. They have the power to send for persons, papers, records and any other material relevant to the matter at issue. But they do not possess the authority to compel Ministers to attend their meetings, though it is certain that

28. R. A. Butler in a debate in the House of Commons in 1958 and as cited in Birch's *Representative and Responsible Government,* p. 162.
29. Birch, A. H. *Representative and Responsible Government,* p. 164.
30. Extract from Parliamentary Speeches on Reform given in Bernard Crick's *The Reform of Parliament.,* Appendix D, p. 308.

once invited they shall not refuse to appear. The Government is publicly pledged to co-operate with these committees and, if need be, to ask Parliament to make them stronger. Yet they do not have, unlike the United States Congressional Committees, the power to amend or pigeonhole the Bills.

To enable each Committee to function smoothly and efficiently provision has been made to appoint special staff to weigh and assess evidence and deal with other routine work. Previous committees lacked such support, with the result that MPs themselves had to perform time-consuming administrative chores instead of concentrating on their main investigating role.

Opinion, however, still exists that the "watchdog" committee might weaken the central constitutional primacy of the full House of Commons and some MPs have still not reconciled to the change, though it has full support of the Government as well as the Labour Opposition. There are others who feel that the "watchdog" powers to the new Select Committees are too circumscribed. The majority, however, regard the new system as a major step towards greater democratic control. When the MPs were given the freedom to vote on the procedure reform Bill according to their conscience they did so by a vast, 200 plus majority in support of the change.

The next stage in the career of a Bill is called the Report Stage, when the bill is reported back to the House by the Committee. If the Bill has been dealt within the Committee of the Whole House, the report stage is formal. Where it has been dealt with "in Committee upstairs,"[31] debate may arise and amendments may be moved on the Report. The Government sometimes avails itself of the opportunity to make amendments which were promised at an earlier stage, but could not be drafted or could not be moved or amendments which it is felt are so important that they ought not to be in a Committee. There is always a tendency for the Report stage to lengthen out "the tendency of a parent body", as Finer puts it, "to re- consider the discretion it gave its offspring." To save the time of the House , the government resorts to motions for Closure and " the Speaker assists by keeping the debate to the clauses rather than generalities."

The third stage in the House is that of the Third Reading of the Bill. The rules governing Third Reading are substantially those which apply to Second Reading. There is a debate again on the principles of the Bill as a whole. The idea of the debate at this stage is that the Bill "having been approved in principle on the Second Reading, having been licked into shape in detail on the Committee stage, the House should take one more look at the Bill as amended before it finally gives its approval." Only amendments involving verbal alterations are accepted. When the motion that the Bill be read for the third time is carried, its career in the House of Commons comes to an end. "The Third Reading", remarks Herman Finer, "is a political mustering : the Government expresses its thankfulness that it has been able to do the country some good in spite of the Opposition; and the Opposition replies by claiming that it has made a bad bill better than the Government first presented it, and that, even so, it has doubts for the future of the country's prosperity."[32]

The Bill passes through much the same stages in the House of Lords. If the House of Lords has no amendments to offer, then it becomes an Act of Parliament after receiving the formal assent of the King. The House of Lords may amend the Bill or even throw it out altogether. But overthrowing a Bill by the Lords makes operative the Parliament Act of 1911, as amended in 1949. In case of amendments, they have to be approved by the Commons. On the day appointed for the consideration of amendments, the Speaker puts the question : "That the Lords' amendments be now considered." As such amendment is read by the Clerk, the Minister-in-charge of the Bill rises and moves : "That the House doth not agree with the Lords in the said amendment" or "That this House doth agree with the Lords in the said amendment." In case of disagreement, a Committee is appointed to "draw-up reasons" for not agreeing to amendment. Then, an exchange of messages takes place between the two Houses. If there is no agreement and both the Houses insist on their own plea, the Bill is lost unless the Commons invoke the Parliament Act of 1911, as amended in 1949. That shows that the House of Lords an delay the passage of Bills and even kill them occasionally.

The ceremony by which Bills receive the Royal assent represents one of the many exam-

31. 'Upstairs' signifies that the Standing Committee meets in a Committee Room on the floor above the Chamber, so the phrase commonly used.
32. Finer, Herman, *Governments of the Greater European Powers*, p. 119.

ples of ancient parliamentary pageantry. It is sometimes given by the King in person, but more often by a Royal Commission. It takes place in the House of Lords. The King is represented by Lords' Commissioners, who sit in front of the Throne. At the bar of the House stands the Speaker of the House of Commons who has been summoned from that House. The Clerk of the Crown reads out the title of each Bill and the Clerk of Parliament pronounces the Royal assent—*Le Roy le veult*, the King (or Queen) wills it. With the Royal assent the Bill has become a law.

The procedure for the Public Bills introduced by Private Members is slightly different. What actually happens is that before the beginning of session the Private Members send their Bills to be introduced in Parliament. Then, ballots for precedence are drawn. Private Members' Bills must be introduced on a Friday, for the Government monopolises the time of the House on the earlier days of the week. The Members who are successful in the ballot for precedence on Friday present their bills upon written notice. There is another method to introduce the Bills under the "Ten Minutes Rule." This method gives to the sponsor of the Bill an opportunity to make a short speech, for ten minutes, in favour of the Bill. This will usually be followed by an equally brief speech from a Member or Members who oppose the Bill. After that the Speaker will put the question that leave be given to bring in the Bill. If the motion is carried the Bill is presented and has its first reading. However, Private Members' Bills are not always debated owing to pressure on parliamentary time. Many of those which are debated proceed no further than second reading; but a few succeed in becoming law.

Private Members' Bill may be introduced by Peers in the House of Lords at any time during the session, without notice. The time that can be given to the Commons is, however, strictly limited, and few become Act of Parliament.

The Private Members's Bill suffers from certain important disabilities. In the first place, the time allotted is absolutely insufficient. The time allotted for all stages of all Private Members' Bill is ten days in the session. Secondly, the Private Members, in comparison with Members of Government, lie under a heavy disadvantage in the drafting of the Bill. Finally, even if it is well drafted, its passsage depends on a combination of various circumstances. If the Government is opposed to the Bill, it will have no chance. If the Government is indifferent, various procedural difficulties stand in the way. If the Government definitely approves it, as to make its own, the Bill would, of course, become a Government Bill. "However, it would appear that if the Private Member is popular or at least not unpopular; if the Bill is popular or at least not unpopular, and if the member possesses some skill in respect of parliamentary procedure the Bill will have a fair chance of being passed into law."

Apart from these rather restricting circumstances, Private Members' Bills follow exactly the same course of Public Bills promoted by the Government.

**Private Bills**

Private Bills are quite different from Private Members' Bills. A Private Bill is a measure only which affects specific private interests as opposed to the general classes of the community which are affected by most Public Bills. They deal with a special situation or a limited locality, and the great majority of such Bills concern the rights and powers of local authorities. Private Bills resemble Public Bills in that most of the work is done before the Bill reaches Parliament. There are lengthy negotiations, conference on disputes between the interested parties and every effort is made to 'settle' opposition before the Bill is presented in order to reduce the expenses to which parties are liable and in case of contested Bills they are enormous.

A Private Bill is presented in the form of a petition by the promoters and it is deposited in the Private Bill Office of the House of Commons. The promoters are not the members of Parliament, but outside persons or bodies acting through a firm of parliamentary agents. Thereafter the agents must appear before the Examiners[33] of Petitions for Private Bills and prove that they have observed the provisions of all the Standing Orders relative to giving notice to interested persons and the general public. The Examiners report to both the Houses simultaneously and if their report is favourable the Bills are presented in one or the other House within the dates prescribed by Standing Order, and read a first time.

The presentation and first reading of Private Bills are mere 'book entries' and the Members of Parliament normally have nothing to do with them until they come up for Second Read-

33. The Examiners are permanent officials appointed jointly by the two Houses.

ing.The Second Reading is also likely to be entirely a formality, except in the rare case where an important new principle is contained in the measure. The real hearing takes place at the Committee stages. Opposed Private Bills go to an ordinary Private Bill Committee—a Committtee known as a "Private Bill" group, *i.e.,* a Committee on a group of Private Bills. It consists of four members, chosen in the Lords by the House and in the House of Commons by the Committee of Selection. Members selected on the Committee must sign a declaration that they are not personally interested in the Bill before the Committee, and that their constituents are not locally affected by it.

In Committee the semi-judicial nature of private legislation is seen at its plainest. A Committee on a Private Bill is to decide whether the Bill is justified at all; whether the promoters really need it; whether it is the only way of furthering their ends. The Committee must decide whether it is to the public advantage that the Bill should pass into law. Above all, it must also assess the claims of the opponents of the Bill who appear before them. Persons who are interested in the passage of a Private Bill support it before the Committee. Those who oppose it, marshal their objections. Both sides are presented by expensive legal lawyers, expert in this kind of work.

The Committee, then, makes a report which for practical purposes is its decision. This is normally accepted as a matter of course by the House. The Report and Third Reading Stages are, therefore, with few exceptions, formalities. After Third Reading the Bill passes to the other House, and in due course, if no mishap occurs, becomes an Act.

Private Bills which are unopposed go to an unopposed Bill Committee consisting of five members. The proceedings of this Committee are brief and usually formal. The senior partner of the firm of parliamentary agents appears before the Committee, explains the general purpose of the Bill, produces the formal evidence, and accounts for any clauses of an unusual nature. In fact, most of the work is done in private conferences between the Speaker's Counsel and the parliamentary agents.

**Provisional Order Bills**

Instead of promoting of Private Bill, the company or Local authority may in some cases obtain an order from a Government Department allowing them to proceed. In all such cases the Department concerned holds a local inquiry, and if it is satisfied that the application is justified, issues the order and presents a Bill in Parliament to confirm the Provisional Order. Most ofthe work has, thus, been done before the bill, which is called a Provisional Order Bill, reaches Parliament. Almost all Provisional Order Bills are unopposed as the Department is not likely to make an order to which Parliament would object. If there is opposition, the Bill goes to a Select Committee, but the chances of its being defeated are negligible.

**Delegated Legislation**

Delegated legislation is a term used to describe the Statutory instruments–Rules, Orders, and Regulations–issued by Government Departments to supplement, amplify and apply statutes passed by Parliament. We have seen how slow and complicated is the process of law-making. This is in order that every detail of the Bill may be carefully examined by the representatives of the people, and British legislation is always lengthy and detailed. Although the draftsmen of a Bill try to provide for all contingencies, but there is a limit to the details which a Bill can contain. And, then the conditions vary and circumstances change. To meet those varying conditions and circumstances Parliament delegates through its statutes power to Ministers and their administrative assist ants to make Orders and Regulations in their discretion, that is, to apply the provisions of the statutes to the situations they are intended to regulate. "Much of our social and economic legislation", L.S. Amery said, "covers so vast and detailed a field that no statute, however, cumbrous and many of them are already cumbrous and unintelligible enough–could possibly provide for all contingencies. Some power of ministerial variations or interpretations is obviously necessary, subject to the attention of Parliament being drawn to what is being done."[34]

The main purpose for which powers are delegated by Parliament to the Executive are : to allow the amendment of existing legislation in order to bring it up to date; to create machinery to administer the Act; or, most generally, to allow the Departments to decide details within the framework of legislation that consists only of broad principles. This often also involves, subdelegation, whereby the Minister is empowered by the Act to delegate these powers to his De-

34. Amery, L. S, *Thoughts on the Constitution,* p. 50.

partmental officials, subject to his confirmation. In this way, two or three tiers of delegation can be involved in the granting of delegated power.

Delegated legislation, accordingly, means the function of sub-legislation by the Executive. It is legislation not by direct functioning of Parliament, but by powers conferred on the Executive by an Act of Parliament (or, more rarely, by Royal Prerogative). The Committee on Ministers' Power defined it "as the exercise of minor legislative power by subordinate authorities and bodies in pursuance of statutory authority given by Parliament itself." It is not an original power of the Executive itself, but delegation of authority by Parliament and strictly subordinate to the terms of the Statute authorising delegation. It is, as such, termed delegated legislation and sometimes subordinate legislation. If it is inconsistent to the parent law, or is in excess of the power granted, it is void. Otherwise, it has the force of law and the law courts cannot interfere therein. What a supreme body delegates no other agency of Government can abrogate. Parliament, being sovereign may delegate powers to whomever it wills and may similarly withdraw the powers that it has delegated. This is unlike the powers of the American Congress. Congress there is itself a delegated agency and the Constitution forbids a delegated agency to delegate any further on.

The power to legislate when delegated, is normally confined to matters of detail bordering upon administration, but in case of sudden emergency power may be delegated to legislate on major matters. In 1931 the Gold Standard (Amendment) Act empowered the Treasury to legislate for the control of the Exchange. The National Economy Act empowered the King-in-Council to effect reductions, including cuts in salaries, in certain public services.The Foodstuff (Prevention of Exploitation) Act authorised the Board of Trade, subject to annual resolution by either House of Parliament, to control supply price of certain foodstuffs.

Prof. Laski points out that " the habit of delegated legislation is not new."[35] The Report of the *Committee on Ministers' Powers*[36] gives examples of delegation of legislative powers in the sixteenth, seventeenth and eighteenth centuries. It existed even in the fourteenth century; a Statute ordered that "no wool should be exported until the King and his Council do otherwise provide." It delegated to the King-in-Council the specified power of deciding when to end the ban on exporting wool. But it is only during the last century and half that the bulk of delegated legislation has enormously increased to meet the ever increasing needs of a modern State. For example, in 1800, 168 of such Instruments (till 1946 called Rules and Orders) were issued ; in 1913, 444; in 1937, 1,500; and never less until in 1945 it rose to 1,706; it then fell from 1,166 in 1951 to 706 in 1952 and now again they run into four figures. The factors which are responsible for this over accelerated pace are:

So long as the functions of the State were limited and it existed mainly for maintaining internal order and external security, Parliament had few laws to make and, accordingly, it could provide conveniently the necessary legislation. Nowadays the province of the State has increased considerably and so have the activities of govern- ment. Schemes of social welfare and economic problems of a national and international character form the primary functions of the State. The provision of social services, like national health insurance, unemployment insurance, town and county planning, involve the making of detailed regulations to provide for industrial benefits. The exercise of economic control involves the imposition of a variety of restrictions and positive duties. It is obvious that when we are using duties, quotas, bounties, licences and various other expedients as instruments of policy, some accurate, flexible and speedy means must be found to give effect to the policy of Parliament. And whenever it seemed clear to the House of Commons that it was a convenient way of operating a statute, it has never hesitated to grant such a power through the means of delegated legislation. Jennings rightly points out, "The power to make delegated legislation must grow in number as the scope of Government power increases through the development of collectivism. Although such a system was not unknown in the 18th century and not uncommon in the early 19th century, it has grown in number and importance with the development of the period of collectivism which is usually said to begin from 1870. Formerly, the legislation used to deal with local government and public utility services but since 1906, the Central Government has been given many direct administra-

35. Laski, H., *Reflections on the Constitution,* p. 43.
36. The Committee was appointed in 1929 under the Chairmanship of Lord Donoughmore.The Committee submitted its Report in 1932.

tive functions, and there has consequently been an increase in the Rules and Regulations issued by the Departments to supplement the legislation applying to their own Centrally administered services.''

Moreover, Parliament no longer has the time, nor, indeed, the necessary data to enable it to produce the mass of detailed regulations which the present functions of government required. Delegated legislation relieves the pressure on Parliamentary time by removing details of administration to settle broad principles without entering into highly technical details. The Committee on Ministers' Powers noted : ''The National Insurance Act, 1946, contained 79 clauses and schedules, ''but if it had not provided for ninetynine sets of regulations, it would have contained at least three hundred clauses.''[37] Delegated legislation has, thus, the merit of shortening Bills and consequently the time of considering them. ''The province of Parliament'', wrote Lord Thring, Parliamentary Counsel to the Treasury, in 1877, ''is to decide material questions affecting the public interest, and the more procedural and subordinate matters can be withdrawn from their cognisance, the greater will be the time afforded for the consideration of more serious questions involved in legislation.'' This is probably ''the only mode in which Parliamentary government can with respect to its legislative functions be satisfactorily carried on.''

Delegated legislation enables the Executive to provide for all unforeseen contingencies without having to return to Parliament for amending Acts or additional powers. The details can be regulated after a Bill passes into an Act with greater care and minuteness, and to better adaptation to local or the special circumstances. Besides, Statutory Instruments mitigate the inelasticity which would often otherwise make an Act unworkable. Even the smallest and most uncontroversial amendment of an Act requires the passage of another Act going through all the parliamentary stages in both the chambers. It may also happen that no parliamentary time may be available to push the amending Bill through. This would frustrate the object of the original legislation. Delegated legislation, on the other hand, can rapidly be revised by the issue of another Statutory Instrument. Parliament has the same rights over such a changed Instrument as over the original.

Delegated legislation is ideal in an emergency. It is the means by which the Executive can be armed with power to take immediate action and without public discussion.The Economy Act of 1931, enabled the Government to effect economies they deemed necessary by Orders-in-Council. The Defence of the Realm Act, 1914, and the Emergency Powers (Defence) Act, 1939, and 1940, empowered the Government to do whatever it deemed necessary to meet the wartime emergencies. The Committee of Ministers' Powers, while dealing with this aspect, reported : ''In a modern State there are many occasions when there is a sudden need for legislative action. For many such needs delegated legislation is the only convenient or even possible remedy.''

Sir William Graham Harrison, First Parliamentary Counsel to the Treasury, assigned another reasons in favour of delegated legislation. He says, ''I should like also to emphasise a side of the question which appeals to me particularly as one who has drafted, not only a large number of statutes, but also a very large number of Statutory Rules and Orders, *viz.*, the superiority in form which, as a result of the different circumstances and conditions under which they are respectively prepared and completed, delegated legislation has over statutes. In most cases the time available for drafting Bills is inadequate, and their final form when they have passed both Houses is generally unsatisfactory. On the other hand, Statutory Rules can be prepared in comparative leisure and their subject-matter can be arranged in a logical and intelligible shape uncontrolled by the exigencies of Parliamentary procedure and the necessity for that compresion which every Minister (however much in debate he may use the draftsman as a whipping boy) invariably requires in the case of a Bill.''[38] Delegated legislation, thus, provides a speedy, convenient and accurate means of giving effect to the policy of Parliament and also to meet the ever-increasing need to speed in the governmental process.

Delegated legislation is quite inescapble. But delegated legislation, its critics point out; is a clear threat to Parliamentary system of government as it offends the principle that legislation should be made in Parliament. If Parliament uses its unlimited legislative powers to delegate that

37. Molson, Hugh, *Papers on Parliament, A Symposium,* p. 97.
38. As cited in W.I. Jennings in Parliament, pp. 457-58.

power to another body, parliamentary government itself is suspended. In Germany, this was, in fact, the method used by Hitler. Long before the collapse of France in 1940, the Government had been authorised to issue decrees by French Parliament which thereafter scarcely ever met. It means that Parliament abdicates its own proper functions to the Executive. Then, the ever-expanding scope of Government action has resulted into an inconceivable regulation of the citizens' life. "Bureaucrats tend to exalt administrative convenience and the national advantage at the expense of the individual and his freedom. The official in his zeal to achieve a desirable result may impose an unreasonable burden upon the subject. The power under a statute to make rules gives him just the opportunity that he wants." The Committee on the Ministers' Powers pointed out that delegated powers might be so wide as to deprive the citizens of protection by courts against action by the executive which is harsh or unreasonable. The courts can declare delegated legislation *ultra vires* only when the rule is against the delegation of power or when proper procedures have not been used. They cannot ensure that powers are exercised reasonably in the wide sense.

Some public anxiety at the practice of delegating legislative power was occasioned on the publication in 1928 of a vigorously written book, the *New Despotism,* by Lord Chief Justice Hewart. Lord Hewart claimed that the Old Despotism of Royal domination had been replaced by the New Despotism of Executive domination of Parliament, which was proving to be just as big a threat to Parliament's authority and to public liberties, with Parliament being used as a cloak for Executive Despotism. Similarly, W.A. Robson in his book, *Justice and Administrative Law,* emphasised the constitutional problems involved in these developments. Much of the concern of the critics was not over the delegation of powers to Ministers, but was over the sub-delegation of powers to civil servants. The disquiet that was thus aroused led to the Government in 1929 to set up a committee under the Chairmanship of the Earl of Donoughmore to consider the powers exercised by or under the direction of (or by persons or bodies appointed by) Ministers of the Crown, and to report what safeguards were considered necessary. It was a distinguished Committee and its recommendations were of great importance. The Committee on the Ministers' Powers reported in 1932 and came to the conclusion that whether good or bad the development of the practice of the delegated legislation was inevitable. The system of delegated legislation, the Committee concluded, was "legitimate......for certain purposes, within certain limits, and under certain safeguards." Nothing was done to implement the recommendations of the Donoughnmore Committee until the War, when the Select Committee on Statutory Instruments was set up in 1944.

In 1946, the Select Committee on Procedure criticised the existing machinery for Parliamentary scrutiny and in 1952 the Select Committee on Delegated Legislation made a more detailed analysis of the problem. The main criticisms that emerged from these post- war enquiries were that the Executive was assuming the legislative role of Parliament to an extent that endangered liberty, and that many of the powers that were delegated to Ministers were too loosely defined. It was pointed out that prior consultation with those affected by delegated legislation was not always possible, and that the protection of the courts was denied by many of the regulations.

The post-war period also witnessed a further spate of literature, for example, Christopher Hollis's : *Can Parliament Survive? and G.W. Keeton's : The Passing of Parliament,* which criticised the effect of delegated legislation in increasing Parliament's subservience to the Executive. In recent years, however, concern over the question of delegated legislation has been less marked.

Dangers of delegated legislation are not inherent in it. With proper safeguard they can be avoided. The validity of the Statutory Instruments can be questioned on the ground that they conflict with the parent laws and are *ultra vires.* This is a most important safeguard. The fact that there are special draftsmen for these instruments is another important technical safeguard. Moreover, acutest care is taken to consult representative interests who are likely to be effected by rules and orders and this procedure of prior consultation before the Bill is introduced is deemed considerable protection against arbitrariness. But the real safeguard against the abuse of power to legislate must be sought in Parliamentary control. Herbert Morrison said, "The principle of delegated legislation is, I think right, but I must emphasise that it is well for Parliament to keep a watchful and even jealous eye on it at all stages."[39]

Thus, Parliamentary scrutiny of the actual granting of delegated powers remains the most important safeguard. The existing methods of scrutiny are based primarily on the Statutory Instrument Act, 1946. The Act clarified and modified the existing method of control. The term 'Statutory Instrument' was used to describe the documents that grant delegated powers (replacing the multiplicity of Rules and Orders that had existed before), and the Select Committee that had been set up in 1944 to scrutinize the process of delegated legislation, was put on a permanent basis as the Statutory Instruments Committee. Now the methods of Parliamentary control rest partly on the activities of the Statutory Instrument Committee and partly on the initiative of individual Members of Parliament.

All Statutory Instruments are published by Her Majesty's Stationery Office and are placed on general sale for the information and use of the public. They are formally presented to Parliament, with copies being sent to the Speaker and the Lord Chancellor, and to all Members of Parliament who asked for them. A Member of Parliament can take action according to the prescribed procedure. There are three distinct procedures which can be used for the presentation of Statutory Instruments, the parent Act defining the procedure to be adopted. The first is, simply to present the Statutory Instruments to both Houses of Parliament. They become operative immediately after presentation to Parliament. Neither of the Houses has the power to annul them. Nor any positive acceptance of the Instrument is necessary. It is only a method of publicity and generally it is used for minor matters. This method, accordingly, affords little chance of Parliament control.[40]

The second procedure is for the Statutory Instruments to be laid before both Houses of Parliament for a period of forty days. Under this procedure no Statutory Instrument can come into operation until it has been approved by the affirmative resolution of both the Houses. The third and the most used procedure is for the Statutory Instrument to be laid before both Houses for a period of forty days and the Instrument is operative until, or unless, it is annulled by a prayer for annulment in either House in this period. It may, however, be noted that an Instrument can be annulled, but it cannot be amended. The difference between the second and third procedure is obvious. According to the second procedure the Instrument does not become operative unless the Government takes the initiative and secures by a resolution of both Houses its positive approval. According to the third procedure, the Instrument becomes automatically operative unless there is successful move to stop it.

Another safeguard is the process of scrutiny. The Committee on Ministers' Powers recommended "the appointment of a small Standing Committee of each House to consider the report on Bills conferring lawmaking powers and on regulations and rules made in pursuance of such powers and laid before Parliament." In 1944 a Select Committee on Statutory Instruments–known as the Scrutiny Committee–was established and its existence is renewed each session. The Committee consists of eleven members based on party composition in the Commons, with the Chairman coming from the Opposition. The function of the Scrutiny Committee is to consider every Statutory Instrument or draft instrument laid before the House and draw the attention of the House to provisions that impose a charge on the public revenues; that are made under an enactment which excludes challenge in the law courts; that appear to make some unusual or unexpected use of the powers conferred by Statute; that have been withheld from publication by unjustifiable delay : that call for elucidation of their form or substance.

In the House of Lords the Special Orders Committee examines and reports on all statutory Instruments which require on affirmative resolution of the House. The Committee does not report the expediency of an order but reports its opinion as to whether the order raises important questions of policy or principle and how far the order is founded on precedent; it also advises the House whether the order can be passed without special attention, or whether there ought to be a further enquiry before the House proceeds to a decision.

The Select Committee on Statutory Instruments is reputed to spend much and useful time on shifting those instruments which ought to be brought to the attention of the House of Commons. The Speaker and his Counsel assist the Committee with advice. It may summon civil servants for explanation what it cannot under-

39. Morrison, Herbert, *Government and Parliament,* p. 151.
40. Punnett, R. M., *British Government and Politics,* p. 322.

stand, and finally reports to the House within the time limit for action. From 1944 to the end of 1954, 19,400 Instruments were made and out of these 10,250 had to come before Parliament. The Select Committee scrutinized 7,000 and drew the attention of the House to 93 of them. In other words, as Finer says, "over eight years about1,000 public[41] instruments per year were made; about 900 a year were scruitinised; and on an average of 11 per year were brought to the attention of the House."[42]

It follows from the supremacy of Parliament that no Court of Law can question the validity of a Statute. But the same does not apply to Statutory Instruments. They are only valid if they comply in substance and in form with the provisions of the parent Acts. It must, however, be emphasised that the courts cannot consider the wisdom or otherwise of a Statutory Instrument, "If it is bureaucratic, vexatious, embarrassing and harassing to the subject, it is for Parliament to take a decision and object in whatever way is appropriate."[43]

Moreover, powers are delegated to the Queen in Council or to authorities directly responsible to Parliament, *i.e.,* to Ministers of the Crown, to Government Departments for which Ministers are responsible, or to organisations whose legislation is subject to confirmation or approval by Ministers who thereby become responsible to Parliament for it. Certain Acts also require direct consultation with organisations which will be effected by delegated legislation before such legislation is made.

Laski maintained that "the protest against the growth of delegated legislation collapses as soon as it is submitted to serious scrutiny."[44] The existing safeguards offer Parliament, the court, and the public the chance to keep delegated legislation in its proper place. No administration, much like the one in Britain, can remain oblivious of the reactions of Parliament and pressure groups when it is formulating regulations. In fact, there is always some form of prior consultation between a Department exercising legislative powers and the interests most likely to be affected, although it is not a formal obligation. Nonetheless, here, too, as it is in so many other activities of Government, the price of liberty is eternal vigilance. It is wise to delegate power of legislation but Parliament must ensure that the powers given to Ministers are not abused and the law courts must retain their power to see that they are not abused and the law courts must retain their power to that they are not exceeded. There is, however, one missing element in the whole scheme of parliamentary control. When a proposed instrument is debated in the House it has no power to amend it. It can only pass or reject it as a whole. The House, accordingly, has to accept the part, that is objected to, in order that the rest, which it approves, may be passed.

## FINANCIAL FUNCTIONS

### Money Bills

"Who holds the purse holds the power", wrote Madison in the *Federalist.* It was through the control of the nation's purse that the House of Commons rose to supremacy. Hence, it is no matter of surprise that Money Bills should occupy a large portion of time that the House devotes to its work. The Parliament Act, 1911, defines Money Bill as a public bill, which in the judgment of the Speaker of the House of Commons, contains provisions dealing with all or any of the following subjects, namely, the imposition, repeal, remission, alteration or regulation of taxation; the imposition, for the payment of debt or other financial purposes of charges on the Consolidated Fund, or on money provided by Parliament, or the variation or repeal of any such changes; supply; the appropriation, receipt, custody, issue or audit of accounts of public money; the raising or guarantee of loan or the repayment thereof; or subordinate matters incidental to those subjects or any of them.

The enactment of Money Bills is somewhat different from that of others. In the first place, they must originate in the House of Commons and in the Committee of the Whole. The House of Commons cannot vote money for any purpose nor impose a tax except at the demand and responsibility of the Crown, which in effect means the Cabinet. The Government, thus, has complete and undivided power of initiative in financial matters. Likewise the power of the House of Commons is complete and decisive. The Parliament Act of 1911 prescribes that Money Bill passed by the House of Commons and sent to the House of Lords one month before the ending of

41. Public Instruments are those which had to come before Parliament.
42. Finer, Herman, *Governments of Greater European Powers,* p. 134.
43. *Hansard Society, Papers on Parliament : A Symposium,* p.107.
44. Laski, H. J., *Parliamentary Government in England,* p. 350.

session, may be submitted to the Royal assent and become law after one month whether passed by the House of Lords or not. The role of the House of Lords in matters of Money Bills is, accordingly, formal.

The principal financial function performed year to year is the preparation, consideration, and authorization of the Budget. ''Budget'' is an old word meaning a bag containing pages or accounts. The use of the word in public finance originated in the expression ''The Chancellor of the Exchequer opened his Budget,'' which was applied in Parliament to the annual speech of the Chancellor of the Exchequer explaining his proposals for balancing revenue and expenditure.

The Budget speech is the main occasion of the year for reviewing the Exchequer finances and the economic state of the nation, and its formal basis is the Chancellor's proposals for raising money by taxation. Viewed in simple outline, it involves, on the one hand, estimates of annual financial expenditure and, on the other, a calculation of anticipated revenue. The formal action by Parliament that renders legal the expenditure of public money takes the form of an act of Parliament. Such an Act authorises the payment of money out of the Consolidated Fund. Consolidated Fund is a great reservoir into which all the revenues of the Kingdom are poured and out of which all the money required for public expenditure is drawn. Consolidated Fund has no physical existence. It is just an account lodged with the Bank of England and money is paid out from it when authorised by Acts of Parliament. The principal Act of this kind is the Annual Appropriation Act.

The Consolidated Fund is replenished through money paid into it by the authority of an Act of Parliament which gives legal validity to the raising of revenues. The principal Act in this respect is the Annual Finance Act. Annual Budget prepares a way for the passage of Appropriation Act and Finance Act.

The financial year begins on April first. The estimates for the coming financial year are presented to the House of Commons somewhat in the second or third week of February. A little later the Chancellor of the Exchequer makes his Budget speech reviewing the finances of the past year and detailing the financial programme of the current year, particularly as regards new taxes, or increased taxes, or reduced taxes. The estimates are discussed in the Committee of the Whole on Supply. This Committee, like Committee of Ways and Means, meets under the Chairman of Ways and Means, or his Deputy, in place of the Speaker. The precedure is more informal than in a sitting of the House. Motions do not have to be seconded, debate cannot be cut off by Closure rules and members may speak any number of times.

The estimates are presented in sections and each section is taken up in ''votes'' or groups of items. The number of days allotted to consideration of the annual estimates are fixed at twenty-nine, all of which must be taken before August 5. The debates in Supply on the Estimates are very seldom devoted to properly financial matters. They are almost invariably general debates on the policy of the Government to the services provided for. This gives an opportunity to the Ministers to explain and defend their proposals and to the Opposition an opportunity to air their grievances or to criticise the general policy of the Government. The Members may propose to strike out or reduce any item of expenditure, but they have no right to add or increase any amount. The debates must be concluded within the allotted time. When the estimates have all been debated, the whole is then embodied in an Appropriation Bill and put through the usual stages and passed by the House.

But the Appropriation Bill is not passed until July or August. It follows that money must be provided for the Government between April 1, and the passing of the annual Appropriation Act. So the Departments draw up provisional estimates of the money they are likely to require during those four months. These estimates are presented to Parliament as a *Vote on Account* and considered as expeditiously as possible. In the case of Service Departments—Army, Navy and Air force—no Vote on Account is usually necessary. The item 'Pay, etc., of Officers and Men' is brought up, and debated which is invariably passed before the beginning of the financial year. Unlike the Civil Departments, Service Departments may use for one purpose money voted for another. It must, however, be noted that the Committee of Supply sanctions all expenditure of public money which is not (a) otherwise sanctioned by an Act of the same session, or (b) paid directly out of the Consolidated Fund.''[45]

The Committee of Ways and Means has

45. Certain high officials are paid out of the Consolidated Fund, *e.g.*, Judges, the Speaker, the Comptroller and Auditor-General. This means that their salary has not to be voted annually. They are supposed to be above political considerations. Interest on the National Debt is also paid directly out of the Consolidated Fund, and it is by far the largest of the amounts so paid.

two functions to perform. In the first place, before any money voted in the Committee of Supply can be withdrawn from the Consolidated Fund, it must be authorised by a resolution of the Committee of Ways and Means. But the second and more important function of the Committee of Ways and Means is the raising of revenues. Revenue, like expenditure, is partly raised under statutes that continue until repealed, partly under the authority of annual statutes. The bulk of the revenue is raised by the former method. Proposals are taken up in groups or sections and approved by the Committee in the form of resolutions. The rules prevent private members from moving any increase in the taxes or imposition of any new tax. Their action is only restricted to approving, striking out, or lowering the taxes proposed by the Government. After the Committee of Ways and Means have voted all the revenue proposals, its resolutions are embodied in annual Finance Bill, just as the resolutions of the Committee of Supply are emobodied in the Appropriation Bill. The Finance Bill is, then, introduced and put through the different stages prescribed for an ordinary public Bill. After passing through the Commons the Finance Bill goes to the House of Lords. The Lords debate the Finance Bill in general terms. They do not examine it in detail, nor do they suggest any amendments. The Parliament Act, 1911, requires that it must be returned to the House of Commons before the expiry of a period of one month.[46]

## CONTROLLING THE EXECUTIVE

A third great function of the House of Commons is that of controlling the Executive. The responsibility of the Ministry to the House of Commons involves a constant control of the House over the Government. Control and responsibility go naturally hand in hand. Since responsibility of Government means its resignation from office whenever the policy of Government proves fundamentally unacceptable to the House of Commons, "an obligation rests upon the House of Commons to exercise a day-to-day control over the Ministry in such a way that fundamental disagreement between the executive and the representatives of the people will be clear and manifest." If the actual and possible mistakes of government were not apparent, the Government might become irresponsible. Control by the House of Commons prevents this. It tends to keep the Ministers constantly conscious of the fact that they will be called upon to give an account of what they do. "A Government," says Laski, "that is compelled to explain itself under cross-examination will do its best to avoid the grounds of complaint. Nothing makes responsible government so sure."[47]

The House of Commons maintains its control in two ways. The first is the constant demand in the House for *information* about the actions of Government; the second is the *criticism* that is constantly aimed at the government in the House. These two methods are closely related to each other and take various froms.

### Question Time

The most effective instrument by which the House of Commons seeks information from the Executive is the oral or written question. "Parliamentary Government," asserts Laski, "lives and dies by the publicity it can secure not only on governmental operations, but on all the knowledge it can obtain on the working of social processes."[48] Any member of the House of Commons may, by following prescribed regulations, direct questions at Ministers and for four days in a week–Monday, Tuesday, Wednesday and Thursday–at the beginning of the sitting of the House, Ministers devote almost an hour to answering questions which have been put to them. An average of 15,000 questions are asked every year. Except for "Private Notice" questions, which are questions of an urgent character of which the normal advance notice is not given, two days' notice of a question is normally required. Questions may be answered orally or in writing. A member cannot put down more than two questions for oral answer on any one day. Supplementary questions arising out of the original answer may be allowed at the discretion of the Speaker. Questions either seek for information or press for action. The person to whom they are addressed, must be officially responsible for the sub- ject-matter of the question. They may deal with the grievances of individual citizens or with great issues of public policy. The former relate to specific Departments of the Government and are answered by their Ministry. Questions relating to public policy are answered by the Prime Minister or his deputy who leads the House of Commons.

---

46. *See ante.*
47. Laski, H. J., *Parliamentary Government in England,* p. 149.
48. *Ibid.,*p. 159.

The device of asking questions has important results. In the first place, it brings the work of the various Departments of Government under the public scrutiny. This fact makes all concerned with the working of the machinery of Government realise that their efficiency and honesty are being regularly tested. Secondly, it mitigates the danger of bureaucratic habits, because "men who have to answer day by day for their decisions will tend so to act that they can give account of themselves."[49] Finally, it is the most effective check on the day-to-day administration. Questions, in brief, bring to light the activities of Government and subject Government to the public scrutiny, and this is, according to Herman Finer,"the fundamentally characteristic British way of keeping the Cabinet painfully sensitive to public opinion."[50]

**Debates and Discussion**

The House of Commons is also a debating assembly. "A society that is able to discuss," writes Laski. "does not need to fight ; and the greater the capacity to maintain interest in discussion, the less danger there is of an inability to effect the compromises that maintain social peace." [51] If the original meaning of the word Parliament is not used opprobriously, it is really a place where people talk about the affairs of the nation. This is done when laws are made and policy of the government is under review. The most important function of His Majesty's Opposition is to criticise matters of administration and policy-making and make the Government to defend its intentions and practices. The best opportunity for the Opposition to criticise governmental policy as a whole is when it debates the reply to the King's "Gracious Speech". At the beginning of each Session of Parliament, the Government's legislative programme is announced in the King's or Queen's Speech—known as Speech from the Throne. An address in reply to the Speech from the Throne is moved and seconded and followed by a debate, usually lasting six days, on the policy of the Government as outlined in the Speech and on amendments from the Opposition regretting that the Speech contained no reference to some matter, or was in some other way unsatisfactory. Then, discussion of public finance, more especially of proposals for expenditure, offers a very real opportunity for discussion and criticism. If the Opposition disapproves the Government's foreign policy, it uses the debate on appropriations for the Foreign Office as an occasion for criticism. Indeed, the House of Commons devotes to criticism of the Government the whole time allotted to the examination of the estimates.

**Adjournment Debates**

The normal occasion for criticism of the Executive is a debate on a motion for adjournment. A Member may, during a sitting, between the time when all questions have been answered and the time for the beginning of the public business, move adjournment of the House for discussing a definite matter of urgent public importance. If the motion is supported by forty members and the Speaker has agreed that the matter is definite and urgent, the sitting is suspended until evening when a full debate on the issue is held. What is important to note is that even a Government which commands an overwhelming majority in the House of Commons cannot prevent the ventilation of an important grievance. Even the weakest Opposition can conveniently command the support of at least forty votes and once the Speaker, who is an impartial and non-party man, recognises the urgency of the matter, the debate is assured. "Such motions", says Herman finer, "are roughly only twice a year. Yet the possibility of instantaneous arrangements keeps the Government alive to opinion in the House of Commons and efficient and lawful relationships with the millions who are under its democratic power."[52] What has been called the "Half-Hour" adjournment debate takes place at the end of each day's regular business—between 10 P.M. and 10.30 P.M. A Member may raise a matter of which he has given informal notice, but which does not involve new legislation. A short reply from the Government follows. This enables a grievance to be ventilated without a formal motion and without a vote. Immediately before Parliament adjourns for recess there are a series of general debates similar in character to the regular "Half-Hour adjournment debates." In addition to these, the most extreme form of Opposition attack on government policy is the vote of censure which is tantamount of expressing lack of confidence in the Ministry. Such a motion is really a crucial occasion in the life of a Govern-

49. Laski, H. J., *Parliamentary Government in England,* p. 151.
50. Finer, H., *Parliaments of Greater European Powers,* p. 162.
51. Laski, H. J., *Parliamentary Government in England,* p. 155.
52. Finer, H., *Governments of the Greater European Powers,* p. 162.

ment, because it decides its fate. So long as a Government can command a comfortable majority, it is not possible for such a motion to get through. But still it creates embarrassments in the ranks of the Ministry and shakes its prestige.

The Commons, therefore, spearheaded by the Opposition, possess adequate and effective opportunities for controlling the Government. And such a control is more urgent today than before, for the functions of the Government are so extensive now that they touch the very bones of individual lives. "The government departments", remarks Finer, "are virtually forty great monopolies; they need a strong force outside them to shake them up,"[53] and this the Opposition does on so many counts. It is Her Majesty's Opposition, now statutorily recognised. It has its own leader, who is "the obverse of the leader of the House,"[54] with its own 'shadow Cabinet'. Her Majesty's Opposition is prospective government. According to Tierney, the duty of Her Majesty's Opposition is "to propose nothing, to oppose everything and to turn out the Government.

**Investigation Committees**

Then, there is the technique of investigation committees. "Investigation by committees," says Laski, has been one of the most vital techniques contributed by the parliamentary system to the methodology of representative government: and it has been possible only by the fact that the parliamentary system exists." The answers given to questions and the information supplied therein often disclose a sorry state of affairs and a general resentment is expressed. The Minister in a bid to placate a special or general public opinion, which insists for more information, may appoint a Select Committee of the House, a departmental committee or a Royal Commission to report upon the problem. He may also appoint such a committee on his own initiative when he thinks that some question ought to come into the public view, on which there is inadequate knowledge, or confused or irritated public sentiment. A Committee will investigate, find out the facts and make recommendations upon which, at a later stage, Government may take necessary action. This process of investigation has been in operation for a sufficiently long time now and quite a few reports issued by these bodies have created landmarks in the history of their subjects. "In education, in the improvement of factory conditions, on poor-law reform, on the machinery of government, on the reorganisation of the army, on the limits of ministers' powers, on the principles of local administration, we have reports that have profoundly affected the contours of our policy."[55]

The twelve newly established perennial Select Committees of Parliament have added new dimension to the process of overseeing the working of Whitehall departments. Over the past one hundred years the constitutional balance had tilted diametrically from the House of Commons to an increasingly powerful Civil Service and Government. These special "watchdog" committees meet in public and are empowered to send for persons, papers and records. Armed with specialist staff to weigh and assess evidence, they re-assert the historic role of the House of Commons in checking and controlling the executive.

**Scrutiny of Expenditure**

The House of Commons is assisted in discharging the responsibilities for the national finance by the Comptroller and Auditor General and by the Public Accounts and Expenditure Committees. The Comptroller and Auditor General, who holds a permanent appointment, as an officer of the House of Commons, is charged with controlling the entries and issues of public money to and from the Exchequer account and the National Loans Fund, with auditing departmental accounts, and with the submitting reports on the appropriation of parliamentary grants, as required by Statute, to Parliament. He has also been encouraged by successive Committees of Public Accounts to examine departmental expenditure with a view to drawing attention to any cases of extravagance or waste.

The Public Accounts Committee was first set up in 1861 to ensure that expenditure was properly incurred for the purpose for which it had been voted and in conformity with any relevant Act of Parliament. These terms of reference have been widely interpreted by successive committees which have investigated whether full value has been obtained for the sums spent by the departments, and examines cases in which the administration appears to have been faulty or negligent. The Committee has therefore, become an instrument for the exposure of waste and inefficiency. It embodies its findings in reports

53. *Ibid.*, p. 132.
54. Jennings, W. I., *Parliament*, p. 162.
55. Laski, H. J., *Parliamentary Government in England*, p. 152.

which are regularly debated each session in the House of Commons. Its recommendations are considered by the Treasury in consultation with Departments, and put into effect, so far they are accepted, according to Treasury instructions. If the recommendations are not acceptable, a reasoned reply has to be submitted to the Public Accounts Committee which may either accept the objections or return to the charge in subsequent reports.

The Expenditure Committee was established in 1971 to replace the former Estimates Committee, following a recommendation of the Select Committee on Procedure in the session in 1968-69. The work of the Committee is designed to effect an improvement in the control by the House of Commons over the pattern of public expenditure, and involves the examination of any public expenditure, and papers on public expenditure represented to the House by the Government, and such of the estimates as seem fit to it. In particular it is charged with considering : (a) how the policies implied in the figures of projected expenditure and in the estimates could be carried out more economically, and (b) the form of the papers and estimates presented.

The Committee has established a Steering Sub-Committee and six functional Sub-Committees on Public Expenditure (General ), Defence and External Affairs, Trade and Industry, Education and the Arts, Employment and Social Services, and Environment and Home Office. Its most important reports, like those of the Public Account Committee, are debated in the House.

**Parliamentary Commissioner (Ombudsman)**

There is the Parliamentary Commissioner (Ombudsman), an officer of the House of Commons independent of the Executive. His function is to investigate complaints of maladministration brought to his notice by members of Parliament on behalf of members of the public. His powers of investigation extend to actions taken by Central Government Departments in the exercise of their administrative functions, but not to policy decisions. Certain administrative actions are also outside his jurisdiction. These include matters affecting relations with other countries and the activities of British officials outside the United Kingdom. In the performance of the functions, the Parliamentary Commissioner has access to all departmental papers, and reports his findings to the member of Parliament who presented the case. The Commissioner reports annually to Parliament and may submit such other reports as he thinks fit. A permanent Select Committee now exists to supervise the work of the Parliamentary Commissioner.

**Parliament and the Nationalised Industries**

Public corporations operating the nationalised industries are appointed by an appropriate Minister and are responsible to him, and through him to Parliament. Such Ministers can give the corporations general directions, can call for information, and have extensive powers over the use of capital funds, but they do not normally use these powers to interfere in the day-to-day operations of the industries, and have refused on grounds of public policy to answer questions on day-to-day administration.

In general, therefore, Ministers may be questioned in Parliament on the general policies of the Government towards the nationalised industries but not on routine administrative matters. Debates on the nationalised industries may take place on the presentation to Parliament of the annual reports and accounts of the various public corporations, on the reports of the Select Committee on Nationalised Industries, on questions by Private Members, on adjournment motions or on Bills affecting one or more industries.

**Parliament and the European Community**

Following British accession to the European Community at the beginning of 1973 arrangements have been made in both the Houses of Parliament to keep members informed about Community developments and to enable them to scrutinise and debate matters which are to be decided in Community institutions. Members of the House of Commons can obtain copies of, and information about, European Community documents. In addition, to the information of the House, explanatory memoranda are provided by the Government on each legislative proposal made to the Council of Ministers by the Commission of the European Community. A monthly list of subjects likely to be dealt with at the next meeting of the Council is also prepared by the Government, and is accompanied by an oral ministerial statement. When community business of a substantial nature has been transacted a Government Minister makes a statement to the House of Commons and answers Members' questions.

Government reports on Community matters generally are to be made twice a year to Parliament, and are debated on two allotted dates. Four further days are allotted to general Community matters, and a place for parliamentary questions related to Community affairs has been specifically allocated in the question rules. The normal opportunities for debates are also available for discussion of European Community business, and, if necessary, special adjournment motions can be moved under the rule providing for such motions on specific and important matters that should have urgent consideration. So that Parliament may be involved in the consideration of proposals for European Community legislation before decisions are taken by the Council of Ministers, a Committee on European Secondary Legislation (set up in May, 1974) helps members of the House of Commons to identify important proposals which affect matters of principles or policy or involve changes in United Kingdom law. Ministers are available to give evidence to the Committee about particular proposals, and a senior official of the House has been appointed to help the Committee to deal with the legal implications of proposals.

The Government has assured the House that debate of any proposal which the scrutiny recommends for debate should take place before a final decision is taken in the Council of Ministers. Procedures are broadly similar in the House of Lords, and there is a special Select Committee for the scrutiny of European Community instruments.

## DECLINE OF PARLIAMENT

### Parliament an Instrument of Government

According to Ramsay Muir the growth of Cabinet dictatorship "has, to a remarkable extent, diminished the power and prestige of Parliament, robbed its proceedings of significance, made it appear that Parliament exists mainly for the purpose of maintining or somewhat ineffectually criticising an all good but omnipotent Cabinet and transferred the main discussion of political issues from Parliament to platform and the members." In 1934 Sir Ivor Jennings published a book on Parliamentary Reform in which he observed that "during the past fifty years Parliament has become progressively less effecient,"[56] and noted that the back bench member " is almost impatient in the House."[57] In 1935 Sir Bryan Fell regretted that the spirit of independence among MPs was "nearly dead" and that the Executive was becoming more and more impatient of criticism. He thought that the Government's control over the time of the House "was not without dangers which might even threaten the very existence of our Parliamentary institutions."[58]

In 1949 Christopher Hollis pointed, in his book, *Can Parliament Survive?*, that Members of Parliament had become servants of the party machines, and observed that it would be "simpler and more economical if a flock of tame sheep, kept conveniently at hand, were driven through the division lobbies in the appropriate numbers at agreed times."[59] Lord Cecil of Chelwood moved, in 1950, a resolution in the House of Lords that the growing power of the Cabinet was "danger to the democratic constitution of the country."[60] Sir Arthur Salter remarked in a public lecture that the British Parliament "has a past glory, a present of frustration, a future of uncertainty. Our destiny turns largely I think upon our ability to restore the traditions and the authority of Parliament so that it can be once more the effective guardian of our liberties."[61] But the most sweeping of all attacks came from Professor G.W. Keeton. In his book, *The Passing of Parliament*, he criticises the growth of party discipline, the decline in the independence of Parliament, the extension of delegated legislation, the erosion of the Rule of Law and the general lack of effective checks on the powers of administration. He observed that the nineteenth century assumption that Parliament, strengthened by successive extensions of franchise, could effectively control the Executive had "proved completely fallacious"[62]; and described the twentieth century developments as involving "the relentless advance of administrative tyranny."[63]

The pith of all this criticism is that Parliament has merely become an instrumnent in the hands of the Government and it simply endorses its decisions so long as the Government can command majority. A Private Member has neither any will of his own nor initiative of any kind.

56. Jennings, W. I., *Parliamentary Reform*, p. 7.
57. *Ibid.*, p. 9.
58. Refer to A. H. Birch, *Representative and Responsible Government*, p. 79.
59. Christopher Hollis, *Can Parliament Survive ?*, pp. 64-65.
60. Quoted in Hansard Society, *Parliamentary Reform*, 1933-1958, p. 158.
61. Reprinted in Campion's *Parliament : A Survey, p. 199.*
62. Keeton, G. W., *The Passing of Parliament*, p.199.
63. *Ibid.*, p. 201.

There had been an inconceivable growth of the power of the Party Whips and the Party machines over the individual Members of Parliament. The result is that there is neither freedom nor spontaneity in speech and vote to the back-benchers who belong to a party. Take, for example, the Labour Party. The Parliamentary Labour Party works under a set of rules which regulate the conduct of its members. A Labour Party candidate is required to pledge in writing that he would scrupulously observe the rules of the Party and one of which lays down that a Labour Member of Parliament may not vote in a sense different from that determined by the Party. This is not objectionable, if the whole party were to meet to determine the course of voting. But the Party meets only once a week for an hour or so, ''and plainly cannot deal with more than a fraction of the business which will come before Parliament in the following week.''[64] In practice, it means that a Labour Member of Parliament must vote according to the behest of the Party Leaders who decide the issues and whose orders the Party Whips obey. There is all the difference in the world between voluntary general cooperation in pursuit of agreed political ends and a dull mechanical discipline which reduces Members of Parliament to the level of robots. This is, in fact, ''robotizing'' of politics, M. Ostrogorski, in his monumental study of *Democracy and the Organisation of Political Parties,* has painted an alarming picture of the consequences of the growth of caucuses. He says that they dominate Parliament, destroy the independence of the backbenchers, convert Parliamentary leaders into party dictators, and act as an arbiter ''between Parliament and outside opinion.''[65]

A hundred years or so ago, the number of electors in any constituency was very small. It did not require a highly organised policical machine to establish contact between the candidate and his electors. The candidate could keep and, in fact, he did keep personal contacts. But a typical constituency today possesses sixty or seventy thousand electors, and it is, for all practical purposes, impossible for a candidate to keep the old bonds of personal contact. He must, accordinlgy, if he is to fight with any prospect of success, need the support of a powerful local and national political machine. And the machine gives its support on its own terms. The terms are that the member should, if elected, do as he is told and he is told to religiously follow the Party Whip. Almost every vote taken in both the Houses of Parliament is governed by a strict system of Party discipline. Any one recalcitrant in duty towards the Party to which he belongs is to pay a heavy price of expulsion and if it is not felt politically convenient, then to refuse his adoption at the next election and both the eventualities entail the end of his political career. This is not the way of democracy and more so of Parliamentary democracy.

The Party discipline has certain obvious ad- vantages. But its results are too obvious. It helps to determine the Party policy in the ''back room of the party caucuses, imposed by this disciplinary set-up on the House of Commons, and by the House on the country. In principle, policy should spring from popular need, be freely ventilated in Parliament, and then express itself in Government action.'' Secondly, it makes for irresponsibility in Government. If ''a government knows that sane or silly, right or wrong, drunk or sober, it can force its proposal through the House by virtue of this disciplinary set-up, it is under a lessened necessity to exercise its powers with the maximum of care and responsibility. This makes for slack, careless and bad government.'' Finally, rigid Party discipline makes Members of Parliament cow- ards and subservients, as they lose honesty, courage and independence. It is practically unheard for a Member to vote against his Party. On a small number of questions of no political significance when government ''takes off the whips'' that the Members vote according to their personal convictions. All this had diminished the independence of Parliament both as a legislature and a body that made and unmade ministers.

The reforms in the procedure of the House of Commons, too, have considerably diminished the importance of a Private Member and the authority of the Government has correspondingly increased. The timetable for Bills, the guillotine, the selection of amendments and other devices which aim to cut short debate are, undoubtedly, a requirement of an efficient legislative procedure. But they reduce to the minimum the influence of Members. The legislative initiative has gone from the Private Member and it now belongs to the Departments under the direction of the Cabinet '' which together have become in practice the first chamber in our law-making mecha-

64. Brown, W.J., *Guide to Parliament,* p. 162.
65. Ostrogorski, M., *Democracy and the Organization of Political Parties,* Vol. I, pp. 215-216.

nism."[66] This is partly due to the technicality of modern legislation which ordinary Members of Parliament are quite incompetent to understand. It is reported that only two Members understood the Local Government Bill of 1928, and one of them was the Minister who presented the Bill and who had been very minutely instructed by the civil servants who drew it up.[67] The result is that the Parliamentary process becomes a dull, meaningless and routine affair. The actual work is done by the permanent civil servants and legislation becomes their concern.

Another result of the technicality of modern legislation is that legislative powers are freely delegated by Parliament without the Members of the two Houses fully realizing what is being done. Orders made in pursuance of these powers have, it is true, generally to be submitted to Parliamentary scrutiny, but their quantity and complexity are such that it is no longer possible to rely for such scrutiny on the vigilance of Private Members acting as individuals. It was argued before the Donoughmore Committee,[68] and the critics of delegated legislation still argue , that the real danger lies in the volume and character of delegated legislation : that the delegation of legislative power has passed all reasonable limits and assumed the character of a serious invasion on the sphere of Parliament by the Executive; and that no standardization of practice or use of procedural device can alter the fact that delegated legislation essentially threatens the sovereignty of Parliament and the Rule of Law. Lord Hewart, in his frontal attack on the increasing pace of delegated legislation and as a consequence the growth of Executive powers, observed : "The citizens of a State may indeed believe or boast that.......they enjoy.........a system of repre sentative institutions ......But their belief will stand in need of revision if, in truth and fact, an organized and diligent minority equipped with convenient drafts, and employing after a fashion part of the machinery of representative institutions, is steadily increasing the range and power of departmental authority."[69]

The control of public finance is the prerogative of the House of Commons. But of all the functions of the House of Commons this is the least efficiently performed. "When it deals with legislation, if it does not initiate, it does at least substantially alter the Bill submitted to it, and often makes a mess of them. When it deals with the general policy of the Cabinet......its debates even if not leading upto any definite resolution or decision, exercise a very important influence. But when it deals with the all-important subject, its own special subject or finance it seems to be almost impotent."[70] The initiative in finacial matters, as in other fields of policy, is taken by the Cabinet, and Parliament may only criticise and attempt to alter what is proposed by the Government. The Ministerial majority in the House of Commons ensures to sustain the Cabinet's financial programme and to vote down threat of any kind from the Opposition. Then, Parliament has little time to delve deep into the Government's financial proposals. The twenty-nine days of debate allotted to the estimates allow only a superficial examination of most of them. The result is that the debate is centred on policy issues rather than on financial aspect involved in the Budget.

The Expenditure Committee, the successor of Estimates Committee, was set up in order to have a more searching examination of the estimates, and to suggest, if any, economies consistent with the policy implied in those estimates. But the Committee has so far only had a limited success. Although the Committee is even working through sub-committees, yet it cannot consider all the Departmental estimates every year. It chooses for examination those estimates which, for one reason or another, have aroused some special interest or concern. The work of the Public Accounts Committee is restricted. All that the nation can be sure of is that money which had been voted for a particular item was spent on that item. But it cannot be sure that it has been spent properly on that item. There is another direction in which the finance of the country has escaped almost entirely from the con- trol of Parliament and that is with regard to the National Debt. A very large part of the revenue of the State goes to pay interest on the National Debt and it is paid directly out of the Consolidated Fund under permanent legislation and needs no annual sanction

66. Greaves, H. R. G., *The British Constitution*, p. 31.
67. One was Neville Chamberlain, the Minister of Health, and the other was Sidney Webb, who had made a detailed academic study of grants-in-aid. Refer to W. I. Jennings, *Parliament Must be Reformed*, p. 43.
68. The Committee on the Ministers' Powers. (1929).
69. Hewart, Lord, *The New Despotism*, p. 12.
70. Muir, R., *How Britain is Governed*, p. 221.

from Parliament. It is true that since it is paid under legislation, and Parliament being the legislature, it must have determined that it should be so. "But it must be remembered that huge loans raised in time of national emergency and coming eventually to swell the National Debt to fantastic figures are rushed through Parliament on the strength of that national emergency which results in a general mitigation of scrutiny; and also that the cumulative effect of several Acts of Parliament, and of many transactions performed under Acts of Parliament, may be very different from what a Parliament would be justified in sanctioning if it had to vote the money annually."[71] Inevitably, as expenditure increases and borrowing too increases, the opportunities for real financial scrutiny diminish and the control of the House of Commons becomes less effective.

**Criticism Answered**

But the "years during which procedure was being worked out." said Lord Kennet, "were the years of struggle between the legislature on one hand and the Crown on the other . The chief care of the Commons was at first to prevent the Crown from getting money except through Parliament, and in later years to prevent it from spending money on purposes other than those for which Parliament had provided it. Their procedure was planned to act as a check on the Crown in the interests of themselves, the economizers. But times have changed. The rule of Parliament is established, and the power of the Crown is gone. A check upon the Executive's power over the purse is still needed by the Commons as much as ever, but the Executive upon whose power the check has to be exercised is now not the Crown but its Ministers responsible to Parliament. Procedure planned to check the Crown is out of date."[72] For that purpose it is certainly out of date. And yet it is essentially desirable if the financial procedure could be made an effective control of national finance. The procedure, as it stands, is still extremely useful. "It provides the cue on the soundest constitutional basis that redress of grievances should precede supply of money—for debates which must take place, and which need a motion of sufficient gravity to register the feeling of the House, without tying the hands of Executive."[73] Instead of trying to pit its judgement against the experts responsible for working out the details of estimates and expenditure, the House of Commons very wisely concentrates on the political aspects of the Government proposals, which are singled out by the Opposition. The functions of the Commons are, in fact, one aspect of their control over the general policy of the Government. The Government cannot behave in a completely arbitrary fashion. It must take account of the political situation and public opinion.

There are various devices which help Parliament to keep proper scrutiny of expenditure. There is the Treasury to control expenditure and it derives its power from the responsibility to Parliament of the Chancellor of the Exchequer for the financial policy of the Government. Control over issues of money to Departments and the audit of accounts is exercised by the Comptroller and Auditor-General, who holds a permanent appointment with the status of an officer of the House of Commons. As Comptroller of the Exchequer, he controls receipts and issues of public money to and from the Exchequer Account, and as Auditor-General he audits Departmental Accounts and submits his report on the Appropriation Accounts and other accounts, as required by law to Parliament. His statutory function is to ensure that all expenditure is properly incurred. In addition, he has been encouraged by successive Committees of Public Accounts to examine Departmental expenditure with a view to drawing attention to any cases of apparent waste or extravangance.

The accounts of each Department and the reports on the accounts made by the Comptroller and Auditor-General are considered by a Select Committee called the Public Accounts Committee. The business of the Committee is to ensure that expenditure is properly incurred in accordance with the purpose for which it was voted and within relevant Act of Parliament. It is a powerful instrument for the exposure of waste and inefficiency. The Expenditure Committee is another Select Committee and its functions are to examine the Estimates, to report, how if at all, the policy applied in the Estimates can be carried out more economically and to consider the principal variations between the Estimates of the current year and those of the previous year and the form in which estimates should be presented.

It is true that the Public Accounts Commit-

71. Taylor, E., *The House of Commons at Work*, pp. 222-23
72. Young, E. H., *The Finance of Government*, p. 42.
73. Taylor, E., *The House of Commons at Work*, p. 225.

tee and the Expenditure Committee can only partially remedy the present incomplete supervision of national finance, but it must be conceded that the Government Departments are really nervous of these Committees. Herbert Morrison illustrated it from a personal experience. He had an argument with his Permanent Secretary of the Home Office, Sir Alexander Maxwell, when he was keen on spending a little money for a public purpose. Sir Alexander Maxwell told Morrison that it would be *ultra vires* of law as he had no power to spend money "out of our estimates on that particular subject." Morrison argued that he had the power and did not agree with his Permanent Secretary. Sir Alexander Maxwell replied, "Secretary of State, the matter could become serious. I may be called before the Public Accounts Committee, and the Committee might ask me why did I allow it when it was *ultra vires?* Am I then to say that I advised the Secretary of State that he could not, but he insisted on spending it. Whereupon, Home Secretary you will be in an awful trouble in the House." Morrison had to yield. Summing up, Morrison says, "This is one of those devices whereby a Minister who is trying to do something that in strict law he is not entitled to, even the civil service can pull him up, which is a good thing."[74]

"It is fashionable now-a-days." wrote Prof. Laski, "for critics of the present position to lament almost with tears over the decline of his (Private Member) status." But, "the lament," he said ,"is wholly misconceived. It mistakes the functions the modern House of Commons has to perform; it mistakes the purpose of parties in the modern State; it is an anachronistic legacy of a dead period in our history when politics was a gentleman's amusement; and the sphere of governmental activity was so small that an atomistic House of Commons was possible. The only way to restore to the Private Member the kind of position he occupied eighty or even fifty years ago, is to go back to the historic conditions which made that position possible. History does not permit us to indulge in such luxuries."[75] The old days of *laissez- faire* do not exist any longer. Every Government introduces proposals for legislation which Gladstone and Disraeli alike would have described as "socialisitc" and which "would have shocked Cobden or Peel."[76] The immensely greater area of functions with which the modern Government is to deal, and the growing concentration of economic power necessitate that legislation, if it can be real, co-ordinated and intergrated legislation, must become Government legislation. It cannot be left to the uncoordinated action and vagaries of Private Members. This is not all. The problem of modern Government is a problem of time and this is, according to Laski, the basic reason why the initiative in legislation has passed from the Private member.

Saving of time, as it is generally demanded, to consider the increased volume of legislation is much more difficult to effect. The frequent attempts made by the Select Committee on Procedure, consisting of experienced Parliamentarians, to find a solution suggest that there is likelihood now of anything except slight changes. The Select Committee on Procedure of 1958 approved in general only those suggestions which involved fuller use of Committees, reduction in the volume of oral questions, and greater opportunities for back-benchers to speak in debates. These suggestions were debated in the House of Commons in July 1959, and February 1960 but for variety of reasons few changes were made. The House of Commons generally shows a determination to keep most stages of its business in the hands of the House as a whole. This may be due to the innate conservatism of the parties over Parliamentary procedure. But on its own side " the Government has to consider the possibility of its work being hampered by procedural changes which might lessen its authority."[77] And the Government alternates in Britain.

But the Private Member in spite of his loss in the legislative function, has still many important functions to perform. The ventilation of grievances, the extraction of information, the criticism of administration, and initiation of debate still remain with him and he can make a great contribution in representing the direction of public opinion. He can also serve on Committees of enquiry. If Parliament needs to be reformed[78] and Private Member to get a due place then, as Laski suggests, let it be done "without treading upon the essential right of Government to initiate legisalation." The function of legislation is not the only function of Parliament. Its real function is to watch the process of administration and to

74. Morrison, Herbert, *British Parliamentary Democracy,* pp. 88-89.
75. Laski, H.J., *Parliamentary Government in England,* pp. 165-66.
76. Jennings, W. I., *Parliament Must be Reformed,* p. 40.
77. Brasher, N. H., *Studies in British Government,* pp. 81-82.
78. Refer to Jennings, *Parliament Must be Reformed,* p.40.

safeguard the liberties of private citizens. "In the proper scrutiny of delegated legislation, in the improvement by analysis, by criticism, by suggestion, of departmental work in the enlargement of the place of the Select Committee of enquiry, in our system, there is a wide range of service awaiting the private member of which we do not, in the present organisation over the House, take anything like full advantatge."[79]

It does not, however, mean that such an enlargement of Private Member's functions should in any way interfere with the Cabinet's control of the mainstream of parliamentary activity. If it is to amount to an interference of the Cabinet's control "coherence of policy would at once be lost and with it the ability to place responsibility where it truly should lie." The real success of the British system of Government, in the opinion of Prof. Laski, "lies precisely in the exact allocation of responsibility that it makes possible."[80]

Nor does it amount to the dictatorship of the Cabinet or domination by the permanent Civil Servants. The chief task of the House of Commons is to maintain a Government. For this there must be a coherent majority in agreement wilth the general policy of the Cabinet, "willing to entrust it with vital decisions, looking to it for leadership, and broadly having confidence in the persons who compose it."[81] It is now admitted on all sides that administration is at the centre of the modern State. A vast sphere of the activities of Government is beyond the control of Parliament. Administrative discretion must, accordingly, exist and decisions rest with the Minister. At the same time, the Cabinet is a Government by consent. It has to conduct its operations in full publicity. It is subject to constant criticism, both within and without Parliament and sometimes the criticism is devastating. Its main problem, therefore, is to maintain the loyalty of its supporters despite the impact of this criticism upon them. It means that the Cabinet must diligently follow the drift of public opinion and always remember the next General Election.

The Government is at all times alive to the fact that in the making of every policy there are limits beyond which it must not go. A serious lapse or blunder may easily disturb the foundation of its majority. A clear drift of electoral opinion away from its support may sow a spirit of rebellion in the House before which even a Government with vast majority is impotent. "Maintaining a majority, "remarked Laski, "is never a simple and straightforward matter; the discipline of followers is not the obedience of private soldiers to their commanders. There enter into its making a host of subtle psychological considerations the accurate measurement of which is vital to the Cabinet's life."[82] Ramsay MacDonald had to give way on the Unemployment Assistance Regulations in 1934. Baldwin had a thumping majority, but he had to sacrifice Sir Samuel Hoare in the Abyssinian crisis of 1935. Similarly, Chamberlain had to yield on his National Defence Contribution of 1937. An unpopular policy always creates the fear that it may lead to defeat at the next General Election, and Members are unwilling to serve under a Government which does not recognise that it is leading them to a defeat. Had Baldwin refused to withdraw the Cabinet's proposals on Abyssinia, it was evident that a large majority of his followers in Parliament would have voted against him with the obvious result that either he would have resigned or would have asked the King for dissolution. Laski had convincingly said that "it is dangerous to run the House on too tight a rein. Excessive secrecy, grave discourtesy, continuous threat of resignation or dissolution, inability to quell an angry public opinion outside, always breed revolt. A Cabinet maintains control in the degree that it is successful in not going too far beyond what the House approves. It must know when to yield: and it is important to yield gracefully. A Cabinet that tries to carry off its policy with too high a hand is almost always riding for a fall."[83]

There is, as Herbert Morrison says, "balance of power" between the Government and the House and that is the essence of British parliamentary democracy. The Government in introducing its legislation or administering its policy always tries to be reasonable, rational, polite, and considerate. If it conducts itself as if it is the master of the House, which really it is so long as it has a majority, it is asking for trouble. "Ministers must take into account the forces that are against them, the possible critics–public opin-

79. Laski, H. J., *Parliamentary Government in England.* p. 167.
80. *Ibid.*
81. Greaves, H. R. G., *The British Constitution,* p. 44.
82. Laski, H. J., *Parliamentary Government in England,* p. 172.
83. *Ibid.*

ion, the Press, and above all, the House of Commons; at times the House of Lords. Therefore, the Cabinet tries not to ride for a fall. It tries to develop a sense of what it can get the House to accept and what it cannot get the House to accept.''[84] If the Government is defeated, it means some of its own sup- porters have gone against it. It also leads to a General Election and the party in power goes to the country divided and the people know all about it. It damages the prestige of the party and injures the prospects of the Government at the election. ''So the Cabinet has to be careful. Ministers have to look ahead.......They may get to know that the House won't stand for it,'' and will make a concession.[85]

Parliament, thus, stands unique and by no means deprived of its political significance. Parliament now works harder than it did before, and there has been no formal decree depriving it of its ancient rights. If the governmental control has widened, Parliamentary controll too has also been widened with the introduction of new established Select Committees which assume the role of ''watchdog'' Committees over the Departments and wherever there are loopholes efforts are made to plug them to save administration from the vigilant scrutiny of these Committees which are vested with investigatory powers. But one thing is certain that in parliamentary democracy as in Britain, there is no question of Cabinet dictatorship. Jennings has very aptly said that dictators who have to appeal to the country at frequent intervals are the servants of the people and not their masters. There is the periodic and daily assessment of their actions. The House of Commons compels the Government to be responsive to the public opinion at all times. The Opposition is there to remind it of the vulnerability of its position and the weakness of its policies. There are, therefore, very strong and exceedingly democratic forces within Parliament to restrain the Government from acting arbitrarily. That is, its responsiveness and responsibility as the constitutional system, according to L.S. Amery '' is one of democracy by consent and not by delegation.''[86] There is, therefore, not much justification[87] in Richard Crossman's statement that Parliament ''has declined, is declining, and should not decline any further.''[88] In a Welfare State leadership of the Executive is its sine qua non, but constitutionalism is its most vital and effective restraint.

**Subordination of Parliament**

The House of Commons has gradually become more and more subservient to various external influences exerted by the organised interest groups. Several members of Parliament represent personally or socially the industrial, banking, landowning or trade union interests and plead the cases of organised social classes in the House and its various committees with natural eagerness. Big business corporations engage salaried barristers to advocate their interests before the Ministers and influential members of the House to affect the course of legislation in their favour. There is an element of truth in Lenin's critique : " The whole history of bourgeois democracy, particularly in the advanced countries, has transformed the parliamentary tribune into the principal, or one of the principal, arenas of unprecedented fraud, of the financial and political deception of the people, of careerism, hypocricy, and the oppression of the toilers". (Quoted in *The British State*, James Harvey and Katherine Hood, p. 56).

Nevertheless, the House of Commons does retain a certain degree of influence. While major interests tend to consider Parliament as an auxiliary instrument in the advancement of their purposes, they still find it worth- while to exert their pressures through elected representatives. In this instance too, however, corporate interests are much better placed than their competitors. For one thing, it is conservative parties of one denomination or another which have continued, throughout the outgoing century, to dominate the House of Commons and other legislatures in the major capitalist countries. These conservative majorities in parliament have for the most part consisted of men drawn from the upper and middle classes, who have taken a favourable view of capitalist activity and correspondingly an unfavourable view of policies detrimental to it.

While the extreme case in this respect is the U.S. Congress, even in the British House of Commons "it is normally interests associated with business and property which have had the

84. Morrison, H., *British Parliamentary Democracy,* pp. 70-72.
85. *Ibid.*, p. 74.
86. Amery, L.I., *Thoughts on the Constitution,* p. 12.
87. Refer to Ronald Butt, *The Power of Parliament,* p. 412.
88. Extract from Parliamentary Speeches on Reform as given in Bernard Crick's *The Reform of Parliament,* Appendix D, p. 307.

big parliamentary battalions on their side."

Moreover, the Parliamentary Labour Party and its trade union leaders and officials have often acted, at the behest of their rightwing leaders, " on a view of 'national interest' which required them, not to advance working class interests but to help subdue them." Most of the Labour Party members have easily succumbed to the disease of parliamentary 'cretinism', causing them to see the world through parliamentary haze which blurred their class perspective on relevant issues. "Of all the forces which have contained socialist parliamentarians in social-democratic parties, none has been more effective than their own leaders and fellow parliamentarians". (Ralph Miliband, *The State in Capitalist Society*, p. 149). In fact, "The Parliamentary Labour Party is a classic example of this phenomenon". (*Ibid.*, footnote). Notwithstanding universal suffrage and competitive politics, the House of Commons has remained much more the instrument of the dominant classes than of the subordinate classes. It may help to attenuate the pattern of class domination, but it also remains one of its means.

Today, the House of Commons has become synonymous with British Parliament as the role of the House of Lords has continuously declined and is further declining in the British parliamentary system of governance. Morover, the House of Commons has acquired a universal dimension as it has evolved conventions which have become globally applicable in various countries opting for parliamentary institutions.

## SUGGESTED READINGS


Bernard Crick : *The Reform of Parliament.*

Birch, A. H. : *Representative and Responsible Government, An Essay on British Constitution.*

Broadman,H. : *The Glory of Parliament.*

Brown, W. J. : *Everybody's Guide to Parliament.*

Campbell, George: *Parliament.*

Campion and others :*Parliament, A Survey,* Chaps. I, IV, VI, XI, XIII.

Campion, Lord: *Introduction to the Procedure of the House of Commons.*

Chester, D.N. and Bowring, Nona: *Questions in Parliament.*

Coombes David : *The Members of Parliament and Administration.*

Finer, H. : *Governments of Greater European Powers,* Chaps. V, VIII.

Finer,H. : *The Theory and Practice of Modern Government,* Chaps. XX, XXI.

Foot, M. : *Parliament in Danger.*

Greaves, H.R. G. : *The British Constitution,* Chap. II.

Gordon, S. :*Our Parliament.*

Hanson,A. H. and Wiseman. H.V. : *Parliament at Work*

Hill, A. and Whichelow, A. : *What is Wrong with Parliament?*

Ilbert, Sir C. : *Parliament.*

Jennings W.I. : *Parliament,* Chaps. VI-X,XIII.

Jennings, W.I. : *Parliament Must be Reformed.*

Laski, H.J. : *Parliamentary Government in Enland* . Chap. IV.

Laski, H.J. : *Reflections on the Constitution* Chaps I-VII.

Laundy, Philip: *The Office of Speaker.*

Mackenzie, K.R. : *The English Parliament,* Chaps. V.VIII_XI.

Morrison, H. : *Government and Parliament,* Chaps. VI. IX-XI.

Morrison, H. : *British Parliamentary Democracy.*

Muir, R. : *How Britain is Governed,* Chaps. V, VI.

Munro, W.B. and Ayearst, M. : *Government of Europe,* Chaps. IX-XIV.

Ogg, F.A. and Zink, H. : *Modern foreign Governments,* Chaps. XII-XIII.

*Papers on Parliament, A Symposium.* The Hansard Society Publication, pp. 1, 73, 96-109.

Pollard, A. F. : *The Evolution of Parliament.*

Richards, Peer: *Honourable Members.*

Ronald Butt: *The Power of Parliament.*

Tylor, E. : *The House of Commons at Work,* Chaps, IV-VII.

Wade, E. C. S. and Philip , G. G. : *Constitutional Law* pp. 71-121, 325-355.

Wheare. K.C. : *Government by Committe.*

Young, Roland: *The British Parliament.*

# CHAPTER IX

# Law and the Courts

The previous part ended with the process of democratization of the British system of government and the working of the political institutions which emerged therefrom. But the maintenance of democracy must depend in a large measure on the just and efficient working of the courts of law. Judiciary, indeed, is the never-failing custodian of the liberties of the people in Britain and British justice—honest, impartial, intelligent, and available alike to rich and poor—has been the pride of Englishmen for centuries together.

## KINDS OF LAW

### Common Law

There are in Britain three kinds of law: Common Law, Equity and Statute Law. Common Law, arising from ancient customs, finds its origin to about eight hundred years back, Before the Norman conquest there was no uniform legal system. The courts were local bodies and the laws had varied a great deal in different places. The Norman and the Angevin Kings were determined to unite the nation and ''to make the strength of Monarchy felt, or, in the legal phrase, to make the King's writ run,'' throughout the length and breadth of the land. They found that their judicial power was the most effective instrument for this purpose, and their practice was to send their judges to tour the country and to see that it was being properly governed. In the beginning, the travalling judges listened to cases in the local courts and applied the customs which they found in different places. Gradually, they began to iron out the differences and applied the same principles everywhere without much regard for particular local customs. By the process of unification the judges built a system of rules which was the same or ''common'' for the whole of the realm. This was the origin of what we still call the Common Law. It was the origin, too, of the ''Assizes,'' the courts which the judges still hold under the King's commission when they tour the country ''on circuit.''

This early unification of the law in Britain has been an event of abiding importance. It gave the country a strong law, and perhaps it is partly the strength of law that has made Englishmen one of the most law-abiding nations in the world. Another result of the unification of the law or at least the method by which it came about was to give to the office of the judge a prestige and influence far above that which it holds in any other system. The Common Law was in origin a judge-made law. The decision of one judge was followed by others, because that was the easiest thing to do. In this way precedents and the doctrine of *stare decisis* (''let the rule stand'') were evolved. The doctrine embraces even the Statute Law and it is an invariable rule of British jurisprudence that a decision given by a judge as to what the Common Law is or what the Statutes mean, shall be accepted as a rule to be applied in all similar cases, until it is set aside by a judge of a higher court or until a new Act of Parliament settles the matter beyond doubt.

The Common Law is therefore, a body of rules which had never been ordained by any Monarch, or enacted by any legislative body. It grew by decision and record. It is still the most fundamental element in the British system. In particular, it covers the general principles of the law of contracts and the civil wrongs. The criminal law, too, was the Common Law, though most of it has now been put into statutory form.

### Equity

With the lapse of time, however, the Common Law became sufficiently inflexible as to give rise to serious complaints. Judges ceased to adapt it to the changing needs of British society. There were many cases in which the Common Law provided no remedy and sometimes there were manifest injustices because of rigid adherence to precedence. Feudalism was disappearing and money was taking its place about the fifteenth century. The country at that time was passing through a period of social, economic and political instability in which justice often required a procedure less technical and dilatory and method of enforcement more summary, than those that the Common Law was providing. The development of Equity, the second strand in English Law, provided remedies for deficiencies in the Common Law and saved the situation.

The law had always regarded the Kings as the fountain of justice, and the courts were his courts. If his courts failed to give justice an aggrieved subject was entitled to appeal to the King and to pray him to grant a remedy out of his grace. In the beginning, the King tried to deal with each petition on merit, giving the matter his personal attention and sometimes discussing it with his Council. But he soon found that if he kept on dealing with all the petitions himself, he would have time for nothing else. The King, therefore, passed on such petitions for consideration by his Chancellor, who was not then a judge as he is today. The Chancellor was the legal member of the King's Council and "Keeper", as it was said, of the King's conscience. Thus, arose the Court of Chancery, which at first was not so much of a court as an administrative department of the State charged with reconciling law and justice. In effect, an aggrieved subject who could not get justice from the law in a civil suit, appealed to the Chancellor for the redress of his grievance in accordance with the accepted ideas and common sense.

Equity was rooted not in custom but in conscience. "It was based on the belief that law should correspond to the moral standard of the community." Since Equity provided remedies where the Common Law could only impose penalties, and as it recognised the existence of new problems to which the law had not been adapted, much business came to the Chancery. From the decisions of the successive Lord Chancellors was framed a body of rules known as Equity, not in opposition to the law, but as an addition to it. Equity included such principles as the following:

"Equity will not suffer a wrong to be without a remedy.
He who seeks equity must do equity
Delay defeats equity.
Equality is equity.
Equity looks to the intent, rather than to the form."

It was not until the beginning of the eighteenth century that the principles of Equity became well settled and the method of their development from case to case had been the same. It meant that the Chancellor had become a judge and his Chancery had become a court of justice. It also meant that there emerged two independent systems of courts applying two separate kinds of law. This extraordinary state of things actually lasted until 1873. The Judicature Act established for the first time a single system of courts and the rules of both Law and Equity were administered both in the King's Bench and Chancery. It must, however, be noted that the Judicature Acts of 1873 did not amalgamate Common Law and Equity, but it settled the relation between them by enacting that where they conflicted, Equity was to prevail.

To sum up, Equity consists of a miscellaneous collection of principles, "not systematically related to one another, but each tending to make this or that rule of the Common Law more equitable than would otherwise be."[1] It has many things in common with the Common Law. Both the Common Law and Equity were shaped by judges to fit the needs of the period in which they were formed, though the needs were different in each case. Common Law provided a basic system of law based upon ancient customs, but moulding them in conformity to the centralized royal authority. Equity simplly added to the rules of the Common Law in order to make it more equitable and thereby to remove the rigidity or inadequacy of law. Equity was thus, complementary to the Common Law. But gradually, like the Common law, it too, became a system bound by precedents and in the eighteenth century, a Chancellor declared that the doctrines of Equity "ought to be as well settled and made as uniform almost as those of the Common law."

**Statute Law**

The Statute Law is composed of Acts passed by Parliament and this is by far the largest source of law in modern times. Until the nineteenth century almost all civil and criminal law was Common Law or Equity. Even when the civil and criminal law had been embodied in the Acts of Parliament their basis still remained Common Law. It must, however, be noted that Statute Law overrides the Common Law. This is unlike Equity, because it does not contradict Common Law. It simply mitigates Common Law or meets its deficiencies. In case of a conflict between Statute and Common Law, the former is always upheld. For the Statute Law has final voice; whatever the Common Law, or past Statutes, or decisions based on them may have prescribed, that can be altered by a new Statute. In fact, the

1. Brier, J.L., *Law and Government*, p. 130.

need for Statutory Law was felt to remove the anomalies by the precedents which did not fulfil changing needs of society and were in conflict with the new standards.

When we turn from the sources to the contents of law, the most important distinction is the one between civil and criminal law. The object of civil proceedings, which is called "action", is to give redress, usually, in the form of pecuniary damages, to some private party whose rights another has infringed, On the other hand, in criminal proceedings or "prosecutions" the law does not regard the wrong act as directed to a particular person only. It considers that there is a public interest at stake and its aim is to protect society against such acts by punishing the offender.

## THE COURTS

### Civil Courts

The Courts that apply the law in the United Kingdom are broadly speaking divided into civil and criminal courts although no rigid line can be drawn since the distinction is a comparatively modern one. Quite a number of civil cases are, in fact, heard in criminal courts while occasionally a criminal case may be heard in what is primarily a civil court. For civil cases the lowest courts are the county courts, which decide cases in which the amount involved does not exceed £750, or where, in actions for the recovery of land, the ratable value of the land is not more than £400 a year. The growth of social and economic legislation has added to the jurisdiction of the County Courts. Workmen who consider they have not received due compensation for injury suffered in their employment and tenants and landlords disputing about their rights under the Rent Restriction Act, bring their cases to the County Courts.

County Courts (of which there are nearly 400) are so located that no part of a county is more than a reasonable distance from one of them. They are presided over by a paid judge who almost always sits alone, although he may sit with a jury consisting of eight persons if either party wishes it and the court makes an order to that effect. There are 106 County Court Judges now in office, each having a circuit, which is either one court, or a group of courts depending upon the work to be done.

In addition to the County Courts there are still a few local courts with somewhat similar jurisdiction. Most of these are survivals from the medieval borough courts and have little or no work to do at the present time, but the Liverpool Court of Passage, the Salford Hundred Court and the Mayor's and City of London Court are still well used.

Above the County Courts, there is one Supreme Court of Judicature consisting of two parts: the Court of Appeal, in which sit the Master of Rolls and Eight Lord Justices of Appeal, and the High Court of Justice, in which the judges are the Lord Chief Justice and about 68 Justices.

The High Court is organised into three divisions: the Chancery to which most of the cases which formerly belonged to Courts of Equity are assigned; the Queen's Bench for the Common Law cases; and Probate, Divorce and Admiralty.[2] The Court of the Appeal and the High Court sit in London, but the Judges of the Queen's Bench Division also hear criminal cases in the county at the Assizes. Petitions for divorce are also now heard at the Assizes. Appeals from the Country Courts rest with the High Court. On its original side it has jurisdiction in cases in which the amount involved is sufficiently large. Then, there is the Court of Appeal which receives appeals both from the County Courts and the High Courts of Justice. The Court of Appeal sits on two or three divisions or occasionally all Lord Justices sit together in cases of great importance. Above the Court of Appeal stands the House of Lords, the highest Court of Appeal in the realm both in civil and criminal cases. The whole House of Lords never sits as a court. In 1876 seven Peers for life were created to hear appeals and they are known as Lords of Appeal in Ordinary or more popularly as Law Lords. The Appellate Jurisdiction Act 1947, changed the number to nine. All appeals are now heard by ten Law Lords, namely, the Lord Chancellor and nine Lords of Appeal in Ordinary. The Lord Chancellor is the presiding officer and is a member of the Cabinet. The nine Law Lords are invariably men of high judicial distinction, eminent judges or lawyers who are made life Peers.

The Judicial Committee of the Privy Council is an exalted appeal body which, strictly speaking, does not belong to British judicial hierarchy. Technically, it is not a court which renders decisions, but a body which gives advice to the King or Queen on cases referred to it although its recommendations are always accepted.

2. Under the provisions of the Administration of Justice Act, 1970, the Division has been renamed the Family Division.

When the Long Parliament abolished the Star Chamber in 1641, it took way the right of the Privy Council to hear appeals from the English courts, but it did not touch the right of appealing to the Council from the overseas possession of the Crown. The Privy Council is, therefore, still the highest Court of Appeal from courts overseas, except in so far as its jurisdiction has been curtailed by legislation, as it has been in some of the Dominions.[3] It acts now by virtue of an Act of 1933 through the Judicial Committee, the members of which are Privy Councillors aided by their overseas colleagues on matters affecting their particular territories. The members of the Judicial Committee number about twenty jurists, but most of the work is done by the same judges as sit in the House of Lords, acting here, however, not as Peers, but Privy Councillors. The Law Lords are salaried life Peers, and when this category of Peers was created, it was decided that they could carry the bulk of work both in the House of Lords and in the Judicial Committee.

The Judicial Committee of the Privy Council has one special jurisdiction which associates it with the British court. In time of war it is the highest court of the whole of the Empire in naval prize cases.

**Criminal Courts**

In Britain when a person stands charged with a crime he is brought before one or more Justices of the Peace (J.P.) or, in the larger towns, before a Stipendiary Magistrate. The former serves without pay, whereas the latter receives regular salaries or stipends from their respective boroughs or urban districts, hence their title. The Stipendiary Magistrates are appointed by the Secretary of State for Home Affairs and are barristers of seven years' standing. Justices of the Peace are appointed by the Lord Chancellor[4] on the recommendations of the Lord-Lieutenants of the counties. The Magistrates have jurisdiction over the same classes of cases as Justices of the Peace and also some additional powers.

Acting singly, Justices of Peace and Magistrates have jurisdiction over petty cases which are punishable by a fine of not more than twenty shillings or by imprisonment for not more than fourteen days. More serious cases are tried by a Bench of two or more Justices or a Magistrate. When two Justices sit as a Bench, it is called a Court of Petty Session. The courts have summary jurisdiction and may impose maximum fines ranging from £50 to £100 or even £500 in certain specified cases, or they may impose a sentence of imprisonment up to six months or in a very few cases, a year. If the offence is punishable by imprisonment for more than three months, the accused may be tried by a Jury.

Then, there is the Court of Quarter Sessions, composed of two or more of the Justices from the whole of county. In the larger towns it is presided over by a single paid Magistrate, the Recorder, appointed by the Home Secretary. All indictable offences, save the most serious, can be tried here, and appeals from the Courts of Summary Jurisdiction are heard. In fact, it is the court in which majority of grave crimes are tried.

Courts of Assizes are branches of the High Court of Justice. They are held in the county towns and in certain big cities three times a year. A Queen's Bench judge is the presiding officer of the court assisted by a jury. The Assizes Judges work on circuits covering England and Wales, and travel from one country to another in the course of their duties. They can try any indictable offence committed in the county. The judge at a criminal trial, according to English practice, is much in the position of an umpire. In English law it is not the function of a judge to discover the truth. He is there to see that the rules are observed and both sides to the case have fair play. The truth will be known when the jury give their verdict. If the jury returns the verdict of not guilty, the accused is forthwith discharged. If on the other hand, it finds him guilty, the judge pronounces judgment. If the jury cannot agree, there may be a new trial with a different set of jurors.

From Quarter Sessions or the Assizes the accused may appeal to the Court of Criminal Appeal. The prosecu-tion cannot appeal if once the accused is found not guilty as no one can be again tried on the same accusation. The Court of Criminal Appeal consists of Lord Chief Justice and not fewer than three Judges of the Queen's Bench. The Court sits in London and without a jury. Under the Administration of Justice Act, 1960, a further appeal from the Court of Criminal Appeal to the House of Lords can be brought if the Court certifies that a point of law of general public importance is involved and it appears to the Court or the House of Lords that the point is

3. All the Dominions except New Zealand have restricted the right to appeal to the Judicial Committee of the Privy Council.
4. Or by the Chancellor of the Duchy of Lancaster.

one that ought to be considered by the House. The House of Lords is the highest Court, as stated previously, both in civil and criminal cases. But its criminal business is quite exceptional. Since 1948 the House of Lords has voted away the historic rights of its members to be tried for treason or felony by a jury of Peers of their own or higher rank. The House no longer exercises any original jurisdiction.

## FEATURES OF THE JUDICIAL SYSTEM

There is no single form of judicial organization that prevails throughout the country. The system of courts described in the preceding pages is one obtainable in England and Wales. The law of Scotland differs both in principle and procedure and the organization of Courts there is different. Northern Ireland has still another system, although it is more like the English.

There is now integration of the courts in England and Wales. Two generations before the country was "cluttered up with unrelated overlapping and sometimes useless tribunals." Cases multiplied and it was difficult to determine which court had the jurisdiction and each type of court had its own peculiar forms of practices and procedure. As a result of the reforms brought about by the Judicature Acts extending between 1873-76 the judicial system has been thoroughly reorganised. Practically all the courts[5] have been brought together in a single centralised system removing the old anomalies and conflicts of jurisdiction.

There are no separate administrative courts in Britain just as there are in France and other Continental countries. In these countries, there are two distinct types of law, ordinary and administrative, and two separate courts, ordinary and administrative. The officers of the Government are amenable to the administrative courts for certain acts done in their official capacity and the law applicable therein is the administrative law. The Common Law in Britain recognises no distinction between the acts of Government official and ordinary citizens. All are amenable to the same ordinary courts and to the same law, though the system of administrative adjudication is inevitably developing.

But the great virtue of the British judicial system is the independence, promptness and impartiality with which justice is administered. The judges are not influenced by any consideration except that of justice and fair play. This is primarily due to their absolute position of independence. They are appointed by the Crown and hold office during good behaviour. They can be removed only by joint address of both Houses of Parliament to the Crown and their salaries are fixed so that no pressure can be brought to bear upon them. When in 1931, a special law was passed to enable the salaries of all government servants, from the Prime Minister downwards, to be reduced as an economy measure, the judges protested against their inclusion as involving an encroachment upon their absolute independence.

There is no system of judicial review in Britain. Parliament is supreme and it is beyond the competence of courts to declare a law *ultra vires.* The courts have to accept the law as it emerges out of Parliament no matter even if it is repugnant to the provisions of *Manga Carta,* the Petition of Rights, or any previous Act of Parliament itself such as the Habeas Corpus Act, the Parliament Act, 1911, the Statute of Westminster, or "any other so-termed consitutional landmark." Nor do the courts concern themselves with what Parliament meant to say: they simply look at the words of any statute.

But an important issue arose in January, 1977. Can judicial pronouncements change or modify a duly enacted law? While granting an injunction against the postal workers' decision to boycott, for a week, the services to South Africa, the Court of Appeal asked the Attorney-General to explain why he had declined to authorise judicial action against the Union. In the Judges' view, the boycott was a criminal offience since it violated the 1953 law. Instead of complying with the Court's directive, the Attorney-General Samuel Silken, questioned the Court's authority to demand an explanation from him for the refusal. He also contended that the court could not grant such an injunction. His contention was that as a parliamentary officer he was answerable to Parliament alone and that his action could not be challenged by the courts. The Attorney-General relied on the principle that it was for the Government to decide whether or not to prosecute a person or group.

The Judges and courts in Britain are custodians of the liberties of the citiziens. The Englishmen have no constitutional rights in the sense we have them in India. There is liberty in Britian because there is Rule of Law. Plainly put, it

5. Except those of the Justice of the Peace.

means that it is the law of Britain that rules the country and not the arbitrary will of an individual. The judges are jealous guardians of the Rule of Law. MacIlwain said that Britain needs no written constitutional guarantees because her traditions of government are so old and so firm, and these are traditions of the Rule of Law; the common heritage of the British uniform impression.

Judicial procedure, especially in Criminal Courts, is accusatorial rather than inquisitorial. The complainant must prove his case. Before trial and at trial, an accused person is stringently protected against any kind of inquisitorial procedure. It is not for the judge to probe into the matter. He acts with complete impartiality as an umpire between the contestants and decides according to the evidence as presented to him. And the evidence itself is strictly limited. Only the sworn testimony of witnesses, subject to cross-examination, can be heard. There must be no hearsay, no evidence on previous offences or bad character. The trial must take place in open court, in the full limelight of press publicity.

The jury system in Britain is the first expression of the Rule of Law. The verdict of a jury in favour of the accused cannot be reviewed at the instance of the prosecution. It means that juries are able to tamper justice with mercy and to refuse to convict wherever the law is seriously out of touch with public opinion. The power of adjusting the law of the land to difficult cases, which is indispensable to every human and enlightened system of justice, is vested not in the officers appointed and under the control of government, but in ''chance groups of citizens,'' who are selected at random on each occasion from the general mass of the people and retire after doing their duty into the obscurity from which they came. On several occasions the juries ''have struck vigorous and effectual blows for the liberty of the subject when the law has, for the time at least, been illiberal.''

The independence of judges came rather later than that of juries. Besides the statutory security of judges in their office, the method by which they are appointed has provided another safeguard for their independence. In most other countries judges start their judicial career at an early age in subordinate positions and gradually work their way up the ladder by promotion. Naturally, therefore, they must look to government or possibly to popular election, and a weak man may sacrifice his judicial independence in a temptation to win over the favour of those who can help him to improve his prospects. In Britain, on the other hand, a judgeship is the crown and not the starting point of a career. Judges are appointed generally in later middle life from among the leading members of the Bar. Once appointed, a judge has no favours to look for either from government or from anyone else. A County Judge has no chance of promotion to the High Court. A promotion from the High Court to the Court of Appeal or the House of Lords does not add much, although it does add something to the dignity or the income of a judge. The obvious result is that ''judges on the whole, so far from being subservient to government, tend to be critical of it, and regard themselves as the watchdogs of the ordinary man against anything savouring of bureaucratic tyranny.''

Finally, there is the acceleration of judicial business, and the cases move rapidly. This is due to two reasons. In the first place, judges in Britain possess greater discretion in dealing with legal technicalities. Secondly, the judicial Rules of Procedure are made by a special ''rule committee'' consisting of the Lord Chancellor and ten other persons who are eminently familiar with law. They know the technicalities and frame rules so as to ensure speedy justice. This is not possible when Rules of Procedure are made by legislature, as in the United States, composed of laymen. Courts in Britain, therefore, ''do not tolerate the pettifogging, dilatory, hair-splitting tactics which lawyers are so freely permitted to use in American halls of justice. The Judge rules his courtroom, pushes the business along, and declines to permit appeals from his rulings unless he sees good reason for doing so.''[6] Moreover, the higher courts do not upset in appeal the judgments of lower courts for merely technical errors.

## RULE OF LAW

### Meaning of the Rule of Law

One of the very important features of the British constitution is the recognition of the Rule of Law. It is based on the Common Law of the land and is the product of centuries of struggles of the people for the recognition of their inherent rights and privileges. It means three things. First, that what is supreme in Britain is law. There is no such thing as arbitrary power and every rule by which the government governs must be au-

6. Munro and Ayearst, *The Governments of Europe,* p. 260.

thorised by law, either Statute Law, passed by Parliament, or by the ancient principles of Common Law, which have been recognised for many hundreds of years now. In other words, the Latin tag *populi supreme lax*–the welfare of the people is the supreme law—cannot be used by the government as an excuse for pursuing its own idea of the public interest without regard for legality. Second, that everyone is subject to the law and no one can plead that he acted under orders. His business like everyone else is to obey the law. The government and its officials derive such power as they possess from the ordinary law. Third, the Rule of Law makes the government subject to Parliament, and through Parliament to the people. To put it another way, Parliamentary supremacy is, in part, only tolerable because the Rule of Law is recognised.

The meaning of the term Rule of Law can best be understood by considering what government can be like without it. In France before the Revolution the nobility enjoyed special privileges and immunities and they could disregard the ordinary law. They could imprison and punish their inferiors without putting them through any form of trial. In Britain the law gives no such privileges and everyone is subject to the same law. The Crown and Government, the Executive and its officials, are subject to exactly the same laws administered exactly in the same courts as the most humble citizen. This is the meaning of the phrase ''equality before law.'' In Germany, Hitler's expressed wishes were law and his government had power to imprison people without trial, or even people who had been tried and acquitted by a duly constituted court by law. Where the Rule of Law prevails no one can suffer any penalty or loss of liberty unless he has been tried and sentenced by a court. At one time it was the practice in periods of emergency in Britain to pass Acts of Parliament suspending the issue of the writ of Habeas Corpus. In the two World Wars, it was thought desirable not to take this course. The Government was, however, empowered to intern suspected persons without trial, though special committees were appointed by the Home Secretary to consider cases of persons so detained and advised him whether or not he ought to release them. But these emergency provisions were among the first to be abolished as soon as the emergency had ceased.

The other side to the Rule of Law is the possibility which it affords the ordinary citizen of reacting against interferences with his rights by any other person even though he is a government servant. The law in this respect was formerly imperfect. It has now been considerably improved by the Crown Proceedings Act, 1947, which makes the Crown liable to action like any other ordinary person, and reduces to a minimum its privileges in litigation.

**Dicey's Exposition of the Rule of Law**

The conception of the Rule of Law was given classical formulation by A.V. Dicey. Dicey gave to the Rule of law three meanings.[7] It means in the first place, ''that no man is punishable or can be lawfully made to suffer in body or goods except for a distinct breach of law established in the ordinary courts of the land. In this sense the rule of law is contrasted with every system of government based on the exercise by persons in authority, of wider arbitrary or discretionary powers of constraint.'' This principle implies that no person may be arbitrarily deprived of life, liberty or property, no one may be arrested and detained except for a definite breach of law which must be proved in a duly constituted court by law. Cases are not tried behind closed doors but in open courts to which public has free access. The accused has the right of being represented and defended by a counsel and in all serious criminal cases he must be tried by a jury. Judgment is rendered in open court and the accused has the right to appeal to higher courts. All this reduces to the minimum the possibility of executive arbitrariness and consequently oppression. It establishes absolute supremacy of law.

The Rule of Law, in the second place, means: ''Not only with us is no man above the law, but (what is a different thing) here every man, whatever be his rank or condition, is subject to the ordinary law of the realm and amenable to the jurisdiction of the ordinary tribunals.'' It implies, in the first place, the equality of every citizen, irrespective of his official or social status, before the law. Secondly, there is only one kind of law in Britain to which all Englishmen are amenable. All public officials, high or low, are under the same responsibility for every act done by them. If public officials do any wrong to an individual or exceed the power vested in them by law, they can be sued in the ordinary courts and tried in the ordinary manner subject to the provisions of the ordinary law. The equality of all in

7. *Law of the Constitution,* 8th edition, p. 179. Also refer to Jennings, *The Law and the Constitution,* 3rd ed. ,Chap. II.

the eyes of law minimises tyranny and irresponsibility of the Executive. Dicey in elaborating the principle of equality before law says: "With us every official, from the Prime Minister to constable or a collector of taxes, is under the same responsibility for every act done without legal justification as any other citizen."

Finally, the Rule of Law means that with the British "the general principles of the Constitution are..., the result of judicial decisions determining the rights of private persons in particular cases brought before the Courts." In Britain rights of the citizens do not flow from the Constitution, but from judicial decision in particular cases, as in the famous Wilkes' case, and not from statements of general constitutional principles.

Dicey was a great admirer of the Rule of Law. He maintained that there was liberty in Britain becuse there was the Rule of Law. But in reality there are some significant departures from the meanings given by Dicey to the concept of the Rule of Law. Dicey himself admitted these exceptions, although his admission "did little to modify the widespread influence of the mistaken views he had propagated so effectively."[8]

In considering Dicey's first meaning of the Rule of Law, a distinction must be made between arbitrary power and discretionary authority. It is still an essential principle of the constitutional government in Britain that there should be no exercise of arbitrary authority. When Dicey referred to "ordinary law", he had in his mind the Common Law or the Statute Law. Today, criminal law includes innumerable offences which are created by statutory regulation.[9] The power to create offences by regulations made by Government Departments or subordiate bodies has become an inevitable task of the modern State. The growth of delegated legislation touches upon the principle of the Rule of Law.

Wherever there is delegated legislation there is discretionary authority. If discretionary authority is contrary to the Rule of Law, then, the Rule of Law is inapplicable to any modern Constitution. When Dicey in 1885 wrote the first edition of the *Law of the Constitution,* the primary functions of the State were preservation of law and order, defence and foreign relations. Today, the functions of the State are more positive and they regulate the national life in multifarious ways. Discretionary authority in every sphere is, thus, inevitable and administrative authorities have to be left a reasonable amount of discretion to meet the exigencies of time and peculiarities of a situation or a problem. Discretion does not mean absolute or arbitrary power and it must not be exercised unreasonaly, wantonly and maliciously. It is "a science of understanding to discern between falsity and truth, between right and wrong...(and) not to do according to will and private affections." According to Lord Halsbury discretion should be exercised according to "the rules of reason and justice, not according to private opinion, according to law, and not humour." Robson has aptly said that "Discretion in public affairs is seldom absolute; it is usually qualified. It must be used judiciously..."[10] Arbitrary power, on the other hand, is the power exercised by an agent responsible to none and subject to no control.

Dicey's second meaning of the Rule of Law is also subject to certain qualifications. In the first place, there remain, even after the operation of the Crown Proceedings Act, 1947, certain privileges and immunities which are open to public authorities and their officers. The Public Authorities Protection Act, 1893, as amended by Section 21 of the Limitation Act, 1939, makes it necessary that all proceedings against public officials for the excess, neglect, or default of the public authority must be started within six months of the act. If it is not done, the proceedings lapse. Heavy penalty by way of costs is to be paid, if a citizen's law suit against a public authority fails. Judges are not liable for anything done or said in the exercise of their judicial functions, even if they exceed their jurisdiction,[11] unless the judge ought to have known the facts ousting his jurisdiction.

Secondly, common with all civilised States, Britain too affords immunities, to the persons and property of other States, their rulers and diplomatic agents, in the forms of process in courts, though not from legal liability as such.[12] The significance of these immunities has been widely applied in favour of recognised international agencies and their officers, particularly

8. Campion and Others, *British Government since 1918; Administrative Law in England* by W.A. Robson, p. 86.
9. See ante Chap. VIII.
10. Robson, W.A., *Justice and Administrative Law,* p. 401.
11. Immunity does not attach to a ministerial, as opposed to a judicial, act. Thus an action lies for a wrongful refusal to hear a case, but not for a wrongful decision. Refer to Wade and Philips, *Constitutional Law, p. 236.*
12. *Dickinson* v. *Delsolar* (1930), I. K. B. 376.

after 1944. In the third place, there are one or two instances where internal political expediency has required the conferment of special immunities. The Trade Disputes Act,1906, prohibits the bringing of any action against a trade union in respect of a tort. Similarly, it is impossible to bring an action against an unincorporated body, *e.g.,* social clubs and many other charitable institutions, though individual members or officers are liable for wrongful acts in which they take part.

It is true that the officials are amenable to the jurisdiction of ordinary courts, and the law of England knows nothing of exceptional offences punished by extraordinary tribunals. But during the last sixty years Government Departments, which are not courts in Dicey's sense, have been made final courts of judgment in regard to many matters which fall within the scope of their work. For example, the Home Secretary has the discretion to grant or refuse the certificates of naturalisation of aliens. He has also full power of deporting an alien and his actions cannot be challenged in any court of law. The Crown alone has the power to issue or refuse passports and the exercise of this power cannot be questioned in a court of law. Similarly, the Minister of Health, the National Health Insurance Commissioner, the Ministry of Education, the Board of Trade, the Minister of Transport, the Railway Rates Tribunal, and other authorities, not being ordinary courts of the country or constituted as such, finally decide questions affecting the person and property of the citizens. There is, thus, a considerable distribution of administrative power and, therefore, Dicey's Rule of Law is, in practice, considerably modified.

A citizen is not only subject to the ordinary law of the land, he is also amenable to the special law affecting his particular profession and that special law may be enforced by a special tribunal relevant to the profession or occupation. The armed forces of the country are subject to military law or naval law in addition to the ordinary law of the land and offences against that law are triable by a court-martial. Likewise, the clergy are liable to ecclesiastical law enforced by ecclesiastical courts. The members of the medical profession are subject to the jurisdiction of the General Medical Council which is competent to try them for professional misconduct. The General Dental Council exercises similar jurisdiction over the members of the Dental profession. All this is not in conformity with and in accordance to the meaning given to the Rule of Law by Dicey. But it is now believed that group law is not inconsistent with the Rule of Law provided proper judicial methods are applied and arbitrariness of any kind is avoided.

Finally, in his third meaning to the Rule of Law, Dicey only refers to the fundamental political rights and maintains that the citizen whose fundamental rights are infringed may seek remedy in the courts and he will rely, not upon a constitutional guarantee, but on the ordinary law of the land. He does not refer to the mass of rights derived from Statutes, e.g., pensions, insurance or free education. Even the rights at Common Law, like the right to personal freedom, the right of self-defence, the right to bring an action for wrongful arrest, assault or false imprisonment, the right to speech, etc., really find their effectiveness from various Statutes. The writ of Habeas Corpus existed at the Common Law, but was made effective by the Habeas Corpus Acts of 1679 and 1816. The right to arrest is governed partly by Common Law and partly by Statutes, *e.g.,* the Criminal Justice Act 1925. The Law of Libel is primarily Common Law, but various Statutes, as the Law of Libel (Amendment) Act, 1888, give special privileges to the Press. The Public Order Act of 1936 is an important part of the Law on public meetings.

The conception of the Rule of Law as explained by Dicey, therefore, needs modifications in the context of the modern conditions. The Rule of Law still remains a principle of the British Constitution, but it needs restating in the light of present conditions. According to a recent statement, the Rule of Law "involves the absence of arbitrary power; effective control of and proper publicity for delegated legislation, particularly when it imposes penalties: that when discretionary power is granted the manner in which it is to be exercised should as far as practicable be defined; that every man should be responsible to the ordinary law whether he be private citizen or public officer; that private rights should be determined by impartial and independent tribunals; and that fundamental private rights are safeguarded by the ordinary law of the land."[13] Such a statement takes account of developments with respect to administrative law and justice which have important bearings on the rights of citizens. Since the principle of the Rule of Law is connected with the supremacy of Parliament, in ul-

13. Wade and Philips, *Constitutional Law,* p. 58.

timate resort the principle must guide the conduct of a political party which is in majority in Parliament and is in a position to influence the course of legislation.

**Administrative Law and Justice**

A feature of the Continental jurisprudence is the existence and use of a body of law known as administrative law. It regulates the conduct of official business and pertains to the relations of private citizens and the governmental authorities. In France and other countries, which have modelled their judicial system upon those of Continental Europe, Administrative Law is dispensed in a separate system of courts called Administrative Courts. A French citizen, for example, who is involved in a dispute with a Department of the Government, would seek redress, in an administrative rather than ordinary Court of Law, and if some injury or loss is sustained by a citizen by the action of an officer of the government and the court holds it to be an abuse or excess or wrongful exercise of authority, he would collect damages or compensation from the Government.

Anglo-Saxon jurisprudence has never favoured the establishment of a separate body of law and separate courts for this kind of justice. Dicey had held that there was no system of administrative law in Britain,[14] and it was antithetic to the Rule of Law as it conferred a privileged status on officials and, thus, protected them from acting arbitrarily and irresponsibly.[15] He, accordingly, argued to keep officials, in both their private and public capacities, answerable to the same law as the private citizens and to maintain the ordinary courts as the usual places for hearing and deciding cases arising out of the performance of administrative functions. Administrative Law, according to Dicey, is nothing more than the generalisation from the judgment rendered in the special courts, the *tribunaux administrativs* for officials in their relations with the public.

But Dicey's is not a correct appreciation of the Administrative Law. Nor are his conclusions acceptable. Herman Finer states the truth that "wherever there is administration and law, there is administrative law."[16] In Britain, there is such a body of law and its sources, as Prof. Robson writes, include not only the law controlling public administration, (*i.e.*, Statutes, Common Law and Equity), but also the law emanating from the executive organs in the exercise of their duly authorised powers. "Thus, Statutory Instruments, administrative orders, and the determination of administrative tribunals can be as authentic sources of administrative law as legislation and decisions of courts. Moreover, just as the usages and conventions of the Constitution form an important part of constitutional law, so the uses and conventions form an essential part of administrative law."[17]

Moreover, there are many administrative 'Courts' functioning in Britain. They have developed on an *ad hoc* basis, though they form no system of judicial organisation as in France and other Continental countries. The modern tendency towards conferring judicial functions on Departments of the Government or on tribunals controlled, directly or indirectly, and appointed by the Ministers of the Crown, began more than a hundred years ago, and that too during the lifetime of Prof. Dicey. It originated mainly in social legislation such as the Public Health Act of 1875, but "one powerful stream of tendency." Robson writes, "flowed through the successive Railway and Canal Commissions which were set up to regulate the railways in 1873 and 1888."[18] With the beginning of the present century the activities of the Government widely expanded embracing various places of the social and economic life of the people. Parliament could not legislate for everything in a detailed manner. The result was a vast volume of delegated legislation that was passed and that continued to be passed by Parliament. And the factors that made it desirable to delegate legislative authority from Parliament (the need for speed, and the technical nature of the issue) also made it necessary to create administrative adjudication machinery to consider aspects of the maladministration of the matter concerned. By 1920, judicial functions had been conferred on a wide variety of administrative tribunals, such as, the Minister of Health, the Board of Trade, the Ministry (then the Board) of Education, the District Auditor, the Home Secretary, the Electricity Commission, the London Building Tribunal, the pension appeal bodies

14. Refer to W. A. Robson, *Administrative Law in England, 1919-1948; and Campion's British Government Since 1918,* p. 86.
15. Dicey, A. V. *Law of the Constitution,* p. 329.
16. Finer, H., *Theory and Practice of Modern Government,* p. 924.
17. Robson, W. A., *Administrative Law in England 1919-1948, p. 86.*
18. *Ibid.,* p. 125.

and several others. Their jurisdiction covered an extensive range of subjects, including public health, housing, education, unemployment insurance, health insurance, pensions of all kinds, trade unions, public utilities and other matters. The most conspicuous development of the following years is the adoption of the three-man tribunal as the typical type. This type was adopted for the discharge of judicial functions in connection with the new national insurance scheme, the postponement of call up for military service, reinstatement of ex-servicemen in civil employment, unemployment assistance, the control of rents for furnished buildings, the regulation of road and rail transport. But, at the same time, there is still a tendency of conferring judicial powers specifically on a Minister and this has occurred in town and county planning, education, the national medical service, police appeals and the superannuation of local government officers.

The continuing expansion of governmental activity and responsibility for the general well-being of the community has, thus, greatly multiplied the occasions on which the individual may find himself at issue with the administrator or with another body of persons or an individual. Consequently, there has been a substantial growth in the number of tribunals—there are over 2,000 in existence now—and in the range of their activities during the past thirty years. Their constitution follows a fairly general pattern; all consist of an uneven number of persons so that a majority decision can be reached.

Administrative tribunals may be broadly classified as follows:

(i) those which have permanent members appointed for their special knowledge and a Chairman who may be a lawyer of experience as the Transport Tribunal, and the Lands Tribunal;

(ii) those which are purely administrative, for instance, the special Commissioners of Income Tax, who hear appeals on matters relating to Income Tax from the ruling of the Inland Revenue official;

(iii) those which deal exclusively with matters of interest to one Government Department or public authority, for instance, the Pensions Appeal Tribunals, which hear appeals against the rejection by the Secretary of State for Social Services of war services pension claims; and

(iv) those which consist of ordinary people appointed by a Minister to arbitrate between individuals, for instance, the Rent Tribunals, which have jurisdiction in the determination of rents of certain properties.

Although there is no general provision respecting appeals from statutory tribunals, the Tribunals and Inquiries Act, 1958, and other Acts provide for an appeal, at least on a point of law from all the more important tribunals to the High Court or, in Scotland, to the Court of Session. An appeal may also lie to a specially constituted appeal tribunal, to a Minister of the Crown or to an independent referee. An Advisory body known as the Council on Tribunals exercises general supervision over the tribunals and reports on particular matters, those peculiar to Scotland being dealt with by the Scottish Committee of the Council.

Britain has, therefore, a large body ofAdministrative Law and most of this law originates in Statutes and Statutory Instruments. The great majority of Acts of Parliament passed and Ministerial regulations made in recent years relate to matters of public administration. And wherever there is administration and law, ther is administrative law. There are also many administrative 'Courts'—Ministers, other administrative officials and special tribunals hearing and deciding cases.

**Reform of Administrative Justice**

It is now generally believed in Britain that it is unrealistic under modern conditions to give to the Rule of Law the strict interpretation placed upon it in the nineteenth century. Delegated legislation and administrative jurisdiction are both inescapable. One justification of administrative tribunals is that in their absence the Law Courts would be extremely overworked. But it may be added that tribunals have advantages over the courts for citizens and the State alike. Tribunals are cheap, speedy, less legal formalities to be observed, easily accessible to the public, and are composed of experts in the matter to be dealt with. There is, therefore, greater possibility of a right judgment and expert decision. The objections in principle to the system of administrative tribunals, however, are based partly on opposition to the increase in the executive authority and the extent of executive influence, and partly on the argument that justice cannot be expected in administrative tribunals because the administration is both the offender and the judge of the offence. It offends against the principle that no party should judge a case in which it is itself involved.

Whatever be the reasons and merits of

administrative adjudication there is need in the reform of administrative justice. In hearing and deciding cases administrative officers and administrative tribunals do not follow a judicial-like procedure; the Rules of Procedure followed by regular courts. The decision rendered are not published and the authorities deciding cases are not required to give the reasons—or at least the grounds—for their decisions. And then the right of appeal from the decisions of administrative tribunals is often limited or even non-existent. This may mean miscarriage of justice. These are some of the defects which require to be eliminated.

Lord Hewart's[19] *The New Despotism,* published in 1929 reflected the attitude of considerable body of alarmed jurists and he called to the attention of the public the dangers that he believed to be attendant on this new development, delegated legislation and administrative adjudication. Two other books, F.J. Port's *Administrative Law* and Dr. C. K. Allen's *Bureaucracy Triumphant* pertinently brought the issue before the public eye. This was followed by the appointment of the Committee on Ministers' Powers in 1929 to deal with these two hotly debated questions. Its terms of reference were to consider the powers exercised by or under the direction of Ministers of the Crown by way of (a) delegated legislation, and (b) judicial or quasi-judicial decision, and to report what safeguards were desirable or necessary to secure the constitutional principles of the sovereignty of Parliament and the supremacy of the law.

The Committee's findings about administrative adjudication were the same as with regard to delegated legislation that both are essential and desirable under the modern conditions but subject to certain safeguards. Purely judicial functions, the Committee recommended, should not be entrusted, as a rule, to the Ministers, but quasi-judicial functions may and even must. The safeguards suggested were: that the High Court should have a right to prevent a Minister or Ministerial tribunal from exceeding their statutory power; that the aggrieved party should have a right to appeal to the High Court on a question of law; that the adjudicatory procedure should conform to the principles of natural justice which require that a man may not be a judge in his own case; that no party should be condemned, that the parties affected must know in good time the case they have to meet; that the parties are entitled to know the reasons of the decision; and that inspector's enquiry report should be published along with the decision given on its basis. The Committee rejected Professor Robson's proposal, who was also a member of the Committee, for establishing Administrative Courts. It made no recommendation about the reform of the constitution of the exising tribunals or for co-ordinating them to a system pattern.

Since the Committee submitted its report in 1932 there has been a substantial further development of administrative justice and the three-man tribunal as the typical body for dispensing it. In 1955 a Committee under the Chairmanship of Sir Oliver Franks was appointed to report on the functioning of the administrative tribunals and it submitted its report early in August 1957.

The Report of the Franks Committee is a document of great importance. It rejected the Treasury view put before the Committee that the administrative tribunals were part and parcel of the machinery of Government and consequently were not judicial institutions. The conclusion of the Committee was that administrative tribunals were independent organisations of adjudication for the impartial assessment of the individual's claim. The three points on which the report was based were: (1) all decisions of administrative tribunal should be subject to review by the ordinary courts in points of law; (2) the decision should be entrusted to a court rather to a tribunal in the absence of special considerations that make a tribunal more suitable and if possible to a tribunal rather than to a Minister; (3) the determination that the citizen should not suffer in the protection of his legal rights from the substitution of a tribunal or a Ministerial inquiry or hearing for a court of law. "We regard both tribunals and administrative procedures," the Report noted "as essential powers to society. But the administration should not use these methods of adjudication as convenient alternatives to the courts of law." The emphasis of the Report is that whosoever be the arbiter of the rights of the individual, he must be an independent arbiter and the scope for decision must be confined to points of law; neither to policy, nor to administrative expediency or efficiency. The procedure that has been recommended by the Committee is: openness in inquiry or hearings, fairness and impartiality. "The intention of Parliament," adds the Report

19. Lord Hewart was the Lord justice.

"to provide for independence is clear and unmistakable."

As regards the composition of the administrative tribunals, the Committee recommended that the Chairman should be appointed by the Lord Chancellor and not by the Minister. The proceedings of the tribunal should be open and the citizen who is a party has a right to be told in good time the case he is to meet. The reason for the proposals and the background of Minister's policy must also be stated. There must be a full statement of the cases together with relevant evidence and the parties concerned should know the reasons for the decision. The Minister's final orders must contain his reasons in full.

It seems unlikely that Britain will ever acquire a separate and unified system of administrative courts as it exists in France. The British are more apt to proceed by the way of gradual change and adaptation. What it is necessary to emphasize is the improvement in the quality of administrative justice. This can be brought about if "throughout the executive establishment there can be developed procedures for hearing cases that are fair and that accord the citizen his elementary rights, and if judicial-mindedness can be instilled into officials exercising judicial duties, then the dangers in the present situation will be removed to a large extent." The recommendations of the Franks Committee, acceptable to the government, were embodied in the Tribunals and Inquiries. Act of 1958, and the Town and County Planning Act of 1959. By the former Act, a Councial for Tribunals in England, Wales and Scotland was set up, Chairman appointed jointly by the Lord Chancellor and by the Secretary of State for Scotland and other members by the Department concerned. Its purpose is to exercise general oversight over the composition and procedure of tribunals. The detailed application of openness, fairness and impartiality could obviously not be defined by Statute alone. But Ministers have brought these principles specifically to the notice of officials concerned in tribunal work. The Act also effected an improvement in that members of public concerned now receive much fuller information than before.

**The Parliamentary Commissioner**

But the dissatisfaction with the system of administrative tribunals continued. It was argued that the existing tribunal system was an inadequate means of dealing with public grievances and there were many complaints that were not covered by the Tribunal system. Since redress through Parliament was becoming increasingly difficult as Government activities continued to expand, it was suggested that there was a need for some supplementary means of dealing with grievances and a similar official as the Ombudsman, which had worked satisfactorily in Scandinavia, New Zealand and other countries, could usefully be introduced in Britain. Accordingly a Parliamentary Commissioner was created in 1967 to examine complaints of maladministration.

The Parliamentary Commissioner is an officer of the House of Commons, independent of the Executive. His function, under the Parliamentary Commissioner Act, 1967, is to investigate complaints of maladministration brought to his notice by Members of Parliament on behalf of their constituents. His powers of investigation extend to any action by a Government Department in the exercise of its administrative functions, but not to policy decisions (which are the concern of the Government), nor to matters affecting relations with other countries or the activities of British official outside the United Kingdom. Certain other matters are also excluded from the scope of his investigations, but may be brought within the scope by Order-in-Council. The Commissioner does not normally intervene in cases where a complaint has an alternative remedy, whether to an administrative tribunal or a Court of Law, but he has discretion in such cases whether or not to investigate. Decisions taken by a Government Department or other authority in the exercise of a discretion vested in the Department or authority are not reviewed by the Commissioner by way of appeal

In the performance of his duties the Parliamentary Commissioner has access to all departmental papers and, generally speaking, reports his findings to the Member or Members of Parliament who presented the case. A select Committee has been appointed to which the Commissioner submits his annual report and any other report raising important general principles.

The creation of the post of the Parliamentary Commissioner was hailed, no doubt, but the limitations imposed on his powers by the 1967 Act caused disappointment to many. The Parliamentary Commissioner is an officer of Parliament and he acts only on complaints he receives through a Member of Parliament. He has no executive authority of his own, and can only enquire into and report to Parliament, on any complaint referred to him, while Ministers retain the right to veto the disclosure of any official document. Then, the investigations of the Commissioner are confined to the Departments of the Government alone and do not extend to Local Government or the nationalized industries. The innovation of an Ombudsman, therefore, left untouched many of the general criticisms of the existing machinery dealing with questions of alleged maladministration.

**Class Bias of Judiciary**

The English jundiciary system, according to Laski, is the product of Parliaments and judges who have the same political, economic and moral outlook as that of the ruling class which they represent. It is not the expression of principles of 'natural justice' derived from the minds of judges and legislators but actually reflects the property relations which have been established in British society. Thus the English law of property protects the right of the capitalists to the private ownership of the mean of production, and the right of the great landowners to the private ownership of their estates. The law of contract provides the necessary conditions for the carrying on of capitalist trading relations, the law of master and servant protects the right of the capitalist employer to hire workers for wages and then fire them at his will when he no longer needs them, and company law regulates the complex relations between companies and their share-holders."

There are, of course, some branches of the law, which are not directly related to property relations e.g. the law of marriage and divorce and criminal law ; but even these laws broadly reflect the outlook of a ruling class which owes its dominant position to the private ownership of capital. In fact, the British legal system and its judicial apparatus safeguard capitalist relations of production and the political and ideological structures which are based on them"

However, it would be a grave over-simplification to argue that the English law is a direct, unmitigated manifestation of capitalist interests. But unlike French law which was restructured as the Napoleonic Code as a result of the French Revolution, English law is a product of gradual evolution from feudal conditions to its present bourgeois and liberal forms. The working class has also been able to exert an increasing influence on law-making and judicial system. The judges have striven to create a logically consistent system of law in the context of all these historical forces. Even then, human rights remain subordinate to the property rights of the dominant class.

## SUGGESTED READINGS


Allen, C.K. : *Bureaucracy Triumphant.*

Allen, C.K. : *Administrative Jurisdiction.*

Archer, Peter : *The Queen's Courts.*

Campion and Others : *British Government since* 1918, chap IV.

Campion and Others : *Parliament, A Survey,* Chap. X.

Carter, G.M. and Others : *The Government of Great Britain,* Chap. VIII.

Devlin, Lord : *Trial by Jury.*

Dicey, A.V. : *Law of the Constitution,* Chaps. IV, VIII, Introduction pp. lxvii to xciv ; Appendix Section I.

Finer, H.: *Theory and Practice of Modern Government,* Chap. XXXVI.

Gibbs, F.T.: *The Magistrates' Courts.*

Griffith, J.A.G. and Street, H.: *Principles of Administrative Law.*

Hewart, Lord: *The New Despotism.*

Jackson, R.M.: *The Machinery of Justice in England.*

James Philips: *Introduction to English Law.*

Jennings, W.I.: *Law of the Constitution,* Chap. II.

Laski , H.J. : *Parliamentary Government in England,* Chap. VII.

Munro, W.B., and Ayearst, M.: *The Governments of Europe,* Chap. XVII.

Rhodes, G. : *Administrators in Action.*

Robson, W.A. : *Justice and Administrative Law.*

Robson, W.A. : *The Government and the Governed.*

Wade, H.W.R. : *Towards Administrative Justice.*

Wade, R.C.S., and Philips, G.G. : *Constitutional Law,* pp. 48-58, 215-37, 267-79.

Whyatt, John : *The Citizen and the Administration.*

Yardley, D.C.M. : *Introduction to British Constitutional Law.*

# CHAPTER X

# Political Parties

**Indispensability of Parties**

Political parties are recognised as a natural and inevitable piece of machinery of democracy. Democracy needs them for two reasons. First, political parties are the means by which the citizens get an opportunity to choose their rulers and, secondly, they explain to them and educate them in the merits and dangers of alternative policies. MacIver defines a political party, "as an association organised in support of some principle or policy which by constitutional means it endeavours to make the determinant of government."[1] A party is, thus, a voluntary association, which in a system of parliamentary government, as obtainable in Britain, formulates a programme, presents to the electorate the candidates who represent that programme, and return to Parliament a majority of members who will carry the programme into effect through the agency of their leaders organised in a Cabinet. A party is, accordingly, a link, a bridge, between society and the State; it affects the electorate, Parliament, and the Cabinet.

Yet political parties in Britain are not organs or institutions of the State specifically regulated by its laws, as is the case in some countries. The law does not even mention them. Their only nearer approach to official recognition is in the rules for the formation of Committees of the House of Commons.[2] But without political parties the whole nature of the British constitution would be changed, and many of its conventions would become unworkable. Her Majesty's Government is a party Government and the Prime Minister is the leader of the majority party in the House of Commons. The party in opposition is Her Majesty's Opposition and it is recognised as a necessary and vital element in the working of the British Constitution. The functions of the Opposition are to criticise and vote against the policy of the Government, the party in office, with a view to overthrowing it and taking its place. Ivor Jennings has, therefore, aptly said that "a realistic survey of the British Constitution today must begin and end with parties and discuss them at length in the middle."[3]

**The Two-Party System**

In 1882, W.S. Gilbert wrote :

"How nature always does contrive
That every boy and every gal
That's born into this world alive
Is either a little liberal
Or else a little conservative"

Gilbert, of course, ignored the Irish Nationalist Party at that time and many other smaller parties and groups. During the last hundred years, Governments without a party majority have been in office for thirty years and Coalition Governments for twenty-nine years. Yet in substance Gilbert was right and there is a 'national' tendency for Britain to follow the two-party system. Taking recent examples, in the General Election of 1950 there were 1,868 candidates who contested the 625 seats and stood under as many as thirty-three different labels.[4] It is true that every label did not indicate a separate organised party, but even then, by grouping together parties which supported each other's candidates and omitting those whose organisation was too rudimentary, there were eleven organised parties or groups of parties. In the General Election held in October 1959 there were again eleven organised parties or groups of parties. In all there were 1,536 candidates standing for elections for 630 seats. "The list of eleven parties," observes Ivon Thomas, "...looks like the analysis of a cricket eleven's innings with a long string of 'ducks' following a big stand by the opening pair and a slight contribution by the first wicket down; one player has retired hurt and there is a little wag in the tail."[5] Two main features of the General Election of 1950 were that there was a complete

1. MacIver R. M., *The Modern State,* p. 396.
2. Stewart, M., *The British Approach to Politics,* p. 158.
3. Jennings, W. I., *The British Constitution,* p. 31.
4. Thomas, I., *The Organisation of Different Parties. Parliament, A Survey,* p. 169.
5. *Ibid.*

rout of all Independents and all the candidates of minor parties. Even the Liberal party was not able to get more than nine seats, though it put 475 candidates and two of them were elected with Conservative support. The Communists put 100 candidates and got none elected. Labour secured 315 seats and the Conservatives 298. In 1951 General Election, a closely fought General Election, the Conservatives won 322 seats, Labour 294, Liberals and others 9. In 1955 General Election the Conservatives won 345, Labour 277, Liberals 6 and Sein Finn 2. In the General Election held in October 1959, the representation was: Conservatives and supporters 365, Labour and Co-operatives 258, Liberals 6 and Independent one.[6] In 1964 General Election the Labour won 317, Conservatives 303, Liberals 9. Others, which included Communists, Scotch and Welsh, Republicans, Independents, and members of Individual parties, 0. In the 1966 General Election Labour secured 363 seats, Conservative and Associates 258, Liberals 12, Republican Labour 1, and The Speaker 1. Communists, Scottish and Welsh Nationalist Independents and members of individual parties could secure no seat. In the 1970 Elections the party-wise strength was: Conservatives and Associates 330; Labour 287; Liberals 6; Scottish Nationalists 1; Unity (Northern Ireland) 1; Protestant Unionists (Northern Ireland) 1; Independents 2; The Speaker 1. February 1974 General Election failed to give any clear-cut verdict and Harold Wilson formed a minority government, Labour securing the larger number of seats, though it secured 37.2 percentage of votes cast. The Conservatives secured 294 seats as against Labour's 301 with 33.2 per cent of the votes cast. Eight months later another election was held and this time the Labour Party could secure 319 seats, a majority of just three votes. In the elections held in May 1979, after the defeat of the Labour Government on a vote of no confidence in March 1979, the Conservatives secured 339 seats as against 296 for all the other parties put together.

General Election in Britain till 1981 has been between two gigantic machines and two-party system was the essence of governance in Britain. The British political parties started in the seventeenth century had two important and conflicting views on the constitutional questions, and consequently two parties.[7] For many years to follow there continued to be two parties. There is, indeed, a certain logic in the system. The policies which a Government can adopt are necessarily conditioned by the circumstances of the time and for the most part in Britain the real question has not been "what policy shall be followed, but the speed at which the nation shall move towards predestined end. Some wish to move rapidly and others more slowly."[8] The cautious conservative found his place in the Conservative Party and the more adventurous in the Liberal or the Labour Party.

Since 1846, the two main parties have tended to represent different class interests. If there has not been further split of an ostensible character, it is because of the striking homogeneity of the British economic life. And none of the class divisions have been so distinct as to entail sub-divisions. "As land decreased in importance, the 'Country Party' claimed the support of other kinds of capital. As the workers gained the franchise the employer and the salaried employee moved over with the *rentiers*. We have no peasants' party because we have no peasants. We have no agrarian party because the owners of land are also shareholders and company Directors. We have no farmers' party because, in the main, the interests of land owners and farmers have been the same and, indeed, it would be impossible to distinguish the two classes."[9]

Again, it is assumed that British Ministries must be homogeneous. "England does not love coalitions" is an old but still a widely accepted maxim, although in national emergencies Britain had always formed National Governments. In fact, party leaders had always striven for the two-party system whenever the possibility of the

6. The relative strength of parties as on July 31, 1962, was : Conservatives 365; Labour 249; Liberals 7; Independents 8, excluding Speaker, Chairman and Deputy Chairman, Ways and Means; Vacant 3.
7. The formation of two parties in Parliament dates back to the struggle over the Exclusion Bill in 1679. To check the passage of the Exclusion Bill, which was desinged to prevent the succession of James II, Charles II dissolved Parliament. The supporters of the Bill began immediately to petition for a new Parliament, and came to be known as "Petitioners" while their opponents expressed their abhorrence of the attempt to force the King to summon Parliament and were consequently nicknamed "Abhorrers." Soon afterwards the Petitioners became known as "Whigs" and the Abhorrers as "Tories." The two parties remained opposed in principle, though their views underwent a good deal of change in the course of time. The Whigs aimed at the restriction of the power of the Crown in favour of that of Parliament. The Tories, on the other hand, upheld Royal Power and opposed Dissent.
8. Jennings, W. I., *The British Constitution*, p. 57.
9. *Ibid.*, p. 58.

split had been in evidence. Disraeli, more than anyone, recognised that, "he must build his party and keep it under one roof." Lord Salisbury went to the extent of compromising with Randolph Churchill until he could be sure that if he went he would go alone. "Campbell Bennerman perfomed Herculean feats to keep the two wings of the Liberal party together during the Boer War; and Balfour wrote strange economics and played even stranger politics to prevent Chamberlain from splitting another party."[10] Even the Constitution itself was developed under the two- party system and "does its best to compel it." The single member system of election does not contemplate the existence of more than two parties. The electors, too, have become so accustomed to the two-party system that an election is really a choice of a government. The great majority of the people are not interested "in political principles, but they are concerned with what party obtains a majority," the party in power or the one in Opposition.

In the House of Commons arrangements rest on an assumption that there shall be two parties and two only. There most of the benches are divided into two ranks, facing each other across an intervening space. On the front Government or Treasury bench, sit Ministers and on the front bench opposite, sit the Leader of the Opposition and his associates. The procedure of the House of Commons provides for a definite part to be played by the Opposition and the Opposition is assumed to be united. The Opposition has its own "Shadow Cabinet" and its Leader is paid a salary from public funds. The Government proposes and the Opposition opposes with a view to defeat the party in power as Opposition is the alternative government. "The third party", as Jennings remarks, "is thus constantly butting into what appears to be a private fight."[11] It should either support the government or vote with the Opposition, or keep aloof and abstain from voting. If it constantly supports one party and opposes the other, it loses its separate identity. If it supports sometimes the one and sometimes the other, the electors regard it inconsistent and without any conviction for a programme. The decline of the Liberal Party is primarily due to its support to the Labour government in 1924. In the General Election of 1950, the Liberal Party contested 475 seats and secured only 9 seats, polling 9.11 per cent of the total votes. In 1955 General Election they secured 6 seats polling 2.08 per cent of the total votes. In 1959 the six seats were retained polling 16,40,761 votes. But in 1964 they polled 3,093,316 or 11.2 per cent of the votes and won 9 seats. In 1966 they polled 2,327,533 or 8.6 per cent of the votes and secured 12 seats. In 1970, their strength was only 6 and in February 1974, 14 with 19.3 per cent votes.

These are some of the reasons which have helped the emergence and maintenance of the two-party system in Britain. It has, no doubt, some tangible defects. But it does not mean overthrowing it. "The British Constitution", says Jennings, "is a nicely balanced instrument, and a change anywhere produces a change everywhere."[12] Its greatest merit is that two-party system ensures permanent and stable government. The political homogeneity of the Government produces a well organised and a responsible team of workers who play the game of politics with singleness of purpose under the captaincy of their accredited leader, the Prime Minister. They rise and fall in unison and are individually and collectively responsible for the policy which the Cabinet initiates. Minority Governments are weak because they cannot govern.[13] Coalition Government is uncertain of its existence from day to day, because it is the result of compromise. They continue to work together so long as they can be made to agree. "In a world where strong and rapid government is necessary" concludes Jennings, "only the two-party system works well."[14]

## THE PARTIES

### Origin of Parties

In the beginning when Parliament was an advisory body of the King the question of parties did not arise. Parliament was asked for advice and it gave it. When given, the Crown might, or might not, take any notice of it. Two conditions were necessary for the emergence of the party system. The first that Parliament should become

10. *Ibid.*, p. 61.
11. *Ibid.*, p.63.
12. *Ibid.*, p. 64.
13. Harold Wilson's minority government in 1974 and Callaghan's Government too were dependent for support of the Liberals and Scottish Nationalists. When the Liberals and the Scottish Nationalists withdrew their support, the Government fell in March 1979.
14. Jennings, I., *The British Constitution*, p. 65.

a legislative body in all its essentials and its rights fully established. This stage was not reached until the late seventeenth century. And the second was that there should be political issues of a broad and deep-character about which and on which men could combine in parties. This stage was also reached in the latter part of the seventeenth century. If any date as such can be chosen for the origin of political parties, it is 1679.

The original line of cleavage was between the Tories and the Whigs. The Tories represented the country interests, those interests surviving from feudalism and which were in danger of being eaten into by the rising mercantile interests of the towns. The Whigs represented the new interests which later transformed the economic and social structure of Britain. By the same token, the Tories were associated with the Church of England, while the Whigs were associated with the Dissenters. The aristocracy, for the most part, sided with the Tories, but elements of it favoured the Whigs. By the nineteenth century these two parties had become the Conservative[15] and the Liberal and in spite of many changes and contradictions something of the old differences between them survived. They competed with each other for power throughout the latter part of the nineteenth century and well into the twentieth century till Labour Party replaced the Liberal Party in the political arena.

Barker cites an old story which once upon a time was widely current in Britain. The story went that when Liberty, Equality and Fraternity had to be distributed between France, England, and the United States, the English came first and took away Liberty, the French came next and took Equality, and the Americans coming last, took the residuary gift of Fraternity.[16] If these gifts, continues Barker, were to be distributed among the three political parties in Britain, it would be just to say that the Liberals took Liberty, the Conservatives took the gift of Fraternity and the Labour Party adopted the residuary gift of Equality. The Liberals were the party of progress, reform, improvement and liberty. The Conservatives were the party of authority, tradition, conservatism and fraternity. The Labour Party views man as a man on an equal basis and stands for removing the hindrances and obstacles which divided men into conflicting classes because of the uneven distribution of wealth.

**The Conservative Party**

The Conservative Party, as said earlier, has passed through many names. The name Conservative which has now been for more than a century its general name, hardly denotes its essential nature. It values, according to Herbert Morrison, traditions and precedents.[17] "The essence of conservatism," says Finer, "is to be discovered in the social institutions of which it approves and its attitude to the idea of progress. The social institutions favoured by Conservatives are Crown and national unity, church, a powerful governing class, and the freedom of private property from State interference."[18] It would, thus, appear that Conservatives steadfastly adhere to old traditional forms and solemn ceremonies. They dislike criticism to old institutions, such as Monarchy, and emphasise the duty of loyalty to the King and the State which he personifies. The Conservative sense of nationality is intense "and its most frequent judgment is that such and such a foreign country or sect is untrustworthy."[19] It has faith in the superiority of the race to all other races. It believes in the mission of the race, popularly called the white man's burden to civilise other peoples, even against their will, and "even with violence to the point of brutality." Its attitude, as revealed in Britain's history for a century or more, was neither conservative nor cautious. It has been rather a fanatical clinging to the notion of fraternity or unity. Empire is its very breath and Churchill's famous remark, that he had not become His Majesty's first Minister to preside over the dissolution of the British empire, was no accident. The Conservative Party clung down to 1922 to the unity of the United Kingdom in face of the pressing demand, which eventually took a revolutionary form, for Irish Home Rule. It again clung, under the inspiration of Disraeli and later of Joseph Chamberlain, to the unity of the British Empire by economic ties. Today, it clings, in the face of the idea of the class division, to the idea of social unity and homogeneity of the nation.

Since one of the chief things to be con-

15. The Conservative Party is sometimes referred to as the Tory Party and the Labour Party as the Socialist Party. But the official titles are Conservative Party and Labour Party.
16. Barker, E., *Britain and the British People*, p. 43.
17. Morrison, H., *Government and Parliament*, p. 131.
18. Finer, H., *Theory and Practice of Modern Government*, p. 312.
19. *Ibid.*, p. 313.

served today is the structure of capitalism, the Conservative Party is allied to the cause of private property and private enterprise. The great industrialists are, thus, joined to the old aristocracy in the conservative ranks. This union, encouraged by Peel in the second quarter of the nineteenth century, was indeed, the making of the Conservative Party as distinct from the old Tory Party of the landed classes. The Tory element still remains, forming the Right wing of the party; a few of these called "Diehards" are inclined to regard all changes with disfavour. Majority of the Conservatives however, urge that capitalism must be justified not only to the rich but to all classes; democracy should be preserved and social services extended. Nor, in their view, must support of capitalism mean complete abandonment of industry to private enterprise; the Government should keep watch and where necessary, give assistance in such forms, as tariffs, subsidies and marketing organisations. Nationalist feelings and the interests of industrialists combine to make the party favour the protection of home industries as a remedy against unemployment. In the twentieth century it took the form of Imperial preference and extension of inter-Imperial trade.

Among the younger members of the party a sharp swing towards a vigorous and progressive programme competing with the Labour Party has recently been in prominent evidence. The publication in 1947 of the *Industrial Charter* which accepted the need for central planning, and the emphatic endorsement of this Charter by the Conservative Conference of 1947 is not only indicative of the victory of this group, but also a vital change in the attitudes of the Conservatives. *The Right Road of Britain,* the Conservative statement of policy in 1949, pledged the "maintenance of full employment" and endorsed the importance and utility of social services. The Conservative Party manifesto of 1951 emphasised the need for housing and pledged to it a priority second only to national defence. In 1955 the Conservatives pledged to "prosperity through free enterprises." In October, 1959 the election manifesto read, "the main issues at this election are simple: (1) Do you want to go ahead on the lines which have brought prosperity at home? (2) Do you want your present leaders to represent you abroad?" In a personal preface Harold Macmillan observed, "I do not remember any period in my lifetime when the economy has been so sound and the prosperity of our people at home so widely spread." In 1964 General Election the Conservative slogan was "Prosperity with a Purpose." Labour appealed on "New Britain" programme. The only difference between the two programmes was on emphasis, otherwise distinction between the two was none.

But May 1979 General Election brought a sharp change in the attitude of the Conservative Party. Mrs. Margaret Thatcher, the leader of the Parliamentary wing of the Party, believed that successive Conservative Governments since World War II had been bullied into bowing before intellectual premises postulated by the Socialists. She asserted that a return to Conservative ethos of self-help, near monopoly capitalism, with a heavy emphasis on *laissez faire* economics, strict fiscal and monetary control was the only way to get the nation back to its feet. She insisted that the philosophy that made Britain "great" in the nineteenth century must work equally well in the later half of the twentieth. The Conservative Party, accordingly, put before the electorate in May 1979 General Election the choice of the Socialist Welfare State as envisaged by the Labour Party and individualism. By voting for the Conservative Party the electorate endorsed its policy of cutting direct taxes, trimming of public bureaucracy by halting the further growth of State-owned enterprises, curbing the power of the trade unions and stringently tightening the Immigration Law. The Speech from the Throne delivered on the opening of the new Parliament on May 15, 1979 hinted at steps to prune the public sector. It was widely believed in Britain that the Conservative Government, at no distant date, would enact legislation to offer parts of the ship building and aerospace industries for sale to private enterprise. The dispatch of the Royal Navy Armada in April 1982 to regain Falkland islands from Argentina was in pursuance of the Conservative concept of an Empire. There is no change in the Party's programme and policy since 1980 and Mrs. Thatcher has stood by it steadfastly in spite of vehement criticism by a section of the Party and even within the Government. The Prime Minister managed to get rid of the inconvenient Ministers.

The Party derives its support from the possessing and patriotic and traditional governing class, of the wealthy, the aristocratic and the subaristocratic, the gentry, the upper and middle class, as well as working-class patriots, disgruntled workers, and high-skilled workers whose pride aligns them with the party that preaches the rewards and opportunities of free enterprise.

Till recently the Conservative Party was built around the Party leader. He was not elected on a sessional basis; once elected he remained the leader until he either died or resigned from the post as Churchill did. A Conservative Prime Minister was always a party leader even if he was not very palatable to other important luminaries of the party. When Churchill was appointed Prime Minister in succession to Nevile Chamberlain, his leadership of the party came as a matter of course despite his unpopularity with the die-hards.

The Conservative Party has now broken with its hoary tradition regarding the election of its leader. The members of the House of Commons and the Lords elect their leader by free ballot from among themselves.

The leader of the Conservative Party possesses powers beyond those of the leader of the Labour Party. He appoints the Chairman of the party organisation at the Central office and is responsible for the elaboration of party policy and statements issued thereunder. While in Opposition he selects from the party members of the House of Commons and Lords those who act with him in the 'shadow cabinet'.

**The Liberal Party**

The Liberal Party is not a major party now, though for many generations it had been one of the two large parties and even today the Liberals are not a minor party in their intellectual capacity or the quality of their leadership. But it has become an army of generals without any adequate body of troops. In 1945 it secured about two and a quarter million votes and of 306 candidates it put, only twelve were elected, and seven of this total represented districts in Wales. In 1950 the number of votes cast in favour of the Liberal Party was over two and a half million, but only 9 candidates were elected, and 319 lost their deposits. In 1951 there was a sharp decrease in the number of votes and it could get in only six Liberal members. In 1955 and again in 1959 General Elections they retained the old number, though as a result of by-elections the number increased to 7 by July 31, 1962. In the 1964 General Election the number of votes cast in favour of Liberals was 3,093,316 and they won 9 seats. In 1966, their number rose to 12, although the percentage of votes cast fell from 11.2 to 8.6. In March 1974 they secured 14 seats despite a respectable 19.3 per cent of the votes cast. In the 1979 General Election the previous number was retained. But at present there is none.

The Party has stood, at all times, for liberty in all its aspects. It has championed the cause of religious liberty and particularly the right of the Nonconformists to worship freely and to gain emancipation from the civic disabilities under which they suffered. It has championed the cause of political liberty, the right of every citizen to an equal share of the suffrage, and the right of the House of Commons, elected popularly, to a final and sovereign voice. The Parliament Act of 1911, was the triumph of the Liberals and a vindication of their creed of liberty.

The Liberals were opponents of Government restraint and championed *Laissez-faire.* In the mid-nineteenth century they represented the trading and manufacturing classes as against the landed class. The popular element in Liberalism, however, caused the Party to advocate social reforms which conflicted with the individualism of the nineteenth century. Today, the Liberals have recognised that there is a liberty of the worker which has also to be secured. The Capitalist- Socialist issue for them is not as important as it is often supposed. The Conservatives' fondness for aristocracy and for tariff and Labour's plan for collectivist control all appear to Liberals as dangerous to the liberty of the individual. While rejecting Socialism, they advocate considerable reforms in Capitalism. They are prepared to socialise some industries if it can be proved that this would increase efficiency, but do not regard nationalisation is essential for the proper arrangement of society. They go still further and advocate the diffusion of property, *i.e.,* the workers in each enterprise are gradually to become partners by receiving a share of its profits in the form of share in its capital. They also advocate the democratization of enterprise and would have each industry governed by an industrial council representing both workers and employers. In the same way they would have each work or factory provided with a works council representing both sides. The Liberal Party, in brief, proposes a kind of partnership of management of labour in industrial affairs. Private ownership and management would remain, but through representative councils and profit-sharing schemes the workers would achieve a stake in the business.

The Liberals are not Socialists but they approach Socialism in two directions. **First,** by advocating the socialisation of all enterprises which can be best conducted by the State, and secondly, by seeking to introduce the principle of social co-operation in the manner just described. "They believe neither in a regime of private enterprise, nor in one of pure socialism, but in a mixed regime which combines features and elements of both, according to the needs of the nation, and progressively changes the proportion of the elements with the movement of national needs." The aim of the Liberal Party is to build a liberal Commonwealth, in which every citizen will possess liberty, property and security, and none shall be enslaved by poverty, ignorance or unemployment. The Liberals, accordingly, claim that they represent not a single class but the whole nation and are not tied to a theory; they consider every proposal on its merits. They oppose the tariff policy of the Conservatives and on immediate problems in the Imperial and foreign field and take a view very similar to that of Labour.

The Party is supported by those of moderate incomes and by a lesser proportion of both the rich and the poor. In some districts there is a strong liberal tradition, often associated with Non-conformity. But many of the Liberals feel that they can now make them of more effect by supporting the Conservative and Labour parties and thereby bringing a liberalising influence on their policies. In fact, in a country with a political system which groups citizens into two sides—the side of the Government and the side of the Opposition—the position of the third party with numbers inferior to the other two is inevitably shaken. Moreover, today it is an almost irresistible temptation to "make one's vote to count" by supporting a party which has a chance to win and the party to win is either the Conservative or the Labour. "The result has been a downward spiral Liberal power." It will be interesting to note that whereas in 1950 the Liberals "bitterly rejected the overtures of the Conservatives, in 1951 seven Liberal candidates received Conservative support."[20] Yet, it is claimed in many Liberal circles that Proportional Representation would allow the strength of Liberal feelings in the country to be fairly expressed. The possibility of such a reform is, indeed, remote in Britain. The Liberals though on the upsurge, since March 1974 election, are not likely to make any spectacular mark in the body politic. The Party was till very recently in alliance with the Social Democratic party, a splinter group of the Labour Party, but they have since separated, Liberals have not a single member in the House of Commons at present.

**The Labour Party**

The Labour party which is a political expression of a working class movement, belongs to the present century, though traces of the movement can be found from the Industrial Revolution which created large masses of urban workers divorced from the occupation of land or ownership of the means of production. This movement manifested itself in Trade Unions, and in co-operative societies and in the Chartist agitation which demanded universal male suffrage. But it was not until the franchise was extended in the late nineteenth century that an effective political party could arise. The Labour Party was formed in 1906 and from that date it has grown rapidly and emerged from the General Election of 1922 as the second largest party.

Labour presents itself as the party of democratic socialism and the socialist objectives of the party embrace the public ownership of the key industries and those economic enterprises that are natural monopolies. In all, the Labour Party considers that roughly 20 per cent of the economic life of the country should be owned and managed by the State and the remaining 80 per cent should continue under private ownership, but strictly regulated by Government in conformity with the economic planning of the State.

According to Labour Party policy, economic planning and control should be directed by a democratically chosen Government. The Party believes that through persuasion a majority of the population can be won to the Labour Programme. The regulation and control which a socialist economy require should not, according to the Labour Party, impinge upon the basic civil liberties of the citizen. Freedom of discussion and criticism, they believe, should be adequately safeguarded, and the socialist way must win its victory in free competition with the programmes of other political parties. Here, the Labour Party is sharply opposed to the Communist philosophy, however much their economic and social objectives may be alike.

The driving force of the Labour Party is less a passion for socialism than a passion for social equality. It strives to achieve political, social and economic emancipation of all the people, and more particularly of those who directly

20. Carter, G. M., and Others, *The Government of Great Britain,* p. 81.

depend upon their own exertions by hand or brain for the means of life. It is, as has been suggested, a "party of levellers" in a country which needs levelling, and protect the wage-earning class from the various disabilities which retard their progress and amelioration. In brief, the Labour Party aims to safeguard the individual citizen from the cradle to the grave by providing remedial measures against all social ills and devising means to constantly improving standard of living for all citizens of the country. This programme is the content of a Welfare State. The Labour Party, thus, "seeks to light Britain for- ward into a new era of equality with less of a zest, perhaps, for the technique of social change, and less of concern for the question whether or not that technique involves a policy of socialism and more, far more of a passion for the reality of social change and the actual coming of equality."[21] It carried through substantial nationalisation of industry in its period of office, 1945 to 1951, and fiscal reforms of an equalitarian nature. The Party is sincerely, genuinely, and deeply liberal and democratic and is "inspired by the Bible," as Finer says, "rather than *Das Kapital.*"[22]

Labour's view of the Empire is that self-government should as soon as possible be extended to those territories which do not yet enjoy it. For the realization of that end, they would encourage the development of colonial resources, the extension of social services and the encouragement of native trade union and co-operative activity. In international affairs, while its ultimate aim is a world Socialist Commonwealth, but its immediate aim is to strive and strengthen the bonds between the United Nations and the establishment of that collective security which the League of Nations failed to secure. The student of party programmes will, however, observe that the avowed differences between different parties in Britain are mostly with regard to the ownership and control of means of production. In "social, imperial and international affairs the professed immediate policies of all parties are very similar : the elector has to judge whether Capitalism or Socialism is more likely to produce the desired results, and, perhaps which party is by its nature, personnel and record the more capable of progress."[23]

Labour Party finds its support among wage-earners in the town, and to much less degree, in the country-side. A number of middle class people, who are hostile to capitalistic structure of society and consider it a meance for the future, also support Labour. And, in fact, from all walks of life come persons who have adopted the socialist view of life.

In organisation, the Labour Party presents a Federation embracing Trade Unions, socialist societies like the Fabian Society, and individual members. Its structure is more elaborate than that of other parties and the resolutions passed at its annual conference determine its policy. There is no "leader" in the same sense as the Conservatives had till 1980. The leader was elected by the Parliamentary Labour Party, composed of all members of the Party who had seats in the House of Commons. Now the election of the leader has to be approved by an electoral college consisting of Members of Parliament, Constituency delegates and trade union representatives. As long as the party is in Opposition, its day-to-day policy is decided upon in caucus, but when the Party is in power, direction rests in the hands of the leaders who are of course, in the Cabinet. Even then constant liaison exists between leaders and back-benchers and periodic conferences are held in which the Government's policy is discussed. These conferences become quite stormy when a "rebellion" brews, but discipline usually prevails in the end and the party leaders have their way. Such rebellion usually comes from the left wing of the Party and the most recent example is that of Aneurin Bevin, who was disowned by the parliamentary Labour Party and recommended that the whip be withdrawn, though Bevin was given another opportunity by the Party Executive to "mend" himself.

The basic organisation of the party is the Annual Party conference. It is composed of delegates from all member organisations. One vote is cast for each 1,000 members of affiliated organisations. The trade unions with their million members have by far the majority. The Party conference elects the National Executive Committee. It manages Party affairs and directs the central office. In theory, the National Executive Committee is subordinate to the conference, but in actuality it is its leader. The leader of the Parliamentary Party is its ex-officio member. The

21. Barker, E., *Britain and the British People,* p. 48.
22. Finer, H., *Governments of Greater European Powers, op. cit.,* p. 61.
23. Steward, M., *The British Approaches to Politics,* p. 164.

Executive Committee is usually the author of the Party programme and directs, through the central office, all the vast activities of the Party. What makes the Executive Committee really powerful is the rule that no one may carry the Party label in an election without its approval. Moreover, it has the power to expel individual members or to disaffiliate organisations from the Party, though such actions are subject to review before the Party conference.

The Labour Party secured a precarious majority of five votes to form the government in the elections of 1964. The total number of votes cast in favour of the Party were 2,205,507 (44.1 per cent) and won 317 seats as compared with Conservatives' votes of 12,002,407 (43.4 per cent) and 303 seats. In 1966 elections it won 363 seats, thus ensuring a majority of 97 votes and polled 47.9 per cent votes. In March 1974, no Party could secure a clear-cut majority but Wilson formed the minority Government as leader of the largest Party. Whereas the Labour Party with 301 seats, polled 37.2 per cent of votes cast, the Conservative secured 296 seats polling 38.2 per cent of the votes cast. Eight months later another election was held and this time the Labour Party was able to secure 319 seats, a majority of just three votes which soon dwindled to a minority Government headed by James Callaghan. Callaghan's Government remained in office till March 1980 when it was defeated on the withdrawal of support by the Liberals and Scottish Nationalists on a vote of no- confidence. In the election held in May 1980 Conservatives secured 339 seats against 296 for all other parties put together.

Internal strife had ever plagued the Labour Party and it reached a new and higher stage in 1979 when it was embroiled in a demoralising ideological struggle between the leftist faction led by the former Energy Minister Anthony Wedgwood Benn and the moderate group led by James Callaghan. Wedwood Benn dominated the executive of the Party and openly spoke out against Callaghan's views on many issues. It was at this stage that the fierce struggle between the Left and the Right was feared to cause a split in the Labour Party, eventually leading to the emergence of a viable Centre party.

James Callaghan resigned from the leadership of the Party on October 15, 1980 and Michael Foot was elected the new leader. The split was averted for the time being, although the extreme Right was highly dissatisfied with the result of the leader's election. But the split became inevitable after the massive victory of the Leftists. The delegates at a one-day conference decided that the Party's next leader should be chosen by an electoral college and not by the elected Members of Parliament as the practice hitherto was. In this electoral college the Parliamentary Labour Party and the Constituency Labour parties each were allocated 30 per cent of the votes and the remaining 40 per cent were given to the trade unions. This was something of a "last straw" for the Right wing Members of Parliament led by David Owen, Mrs. Shirley Williams, William Rodgers and Roy Jenkins. They formed the Council of Social Democracy—possibly a prelude to the formation of a new Party. It proved true despite the desperate efforts of Michael Foot, the leader of the party, and the Deputy leader, Healey to keep the Party united and fight the leftward drift from within. The split, thus, changed the historic role of the Labour Party to be an electoral alternative, at least for the present, to the Conservative Party.

A fierce row has erupted between Labour and its political backbone, the Unions, over a remark by a junior Labour leader, Stephen Byers, to four lobby journalists during a dinner with them at a restaurant in Blackpool, where the annual conference of trade unions was being held in September 1996, that a Blair Government could sever links with the unions.

Byers told the political correspondents from *The Times*, the *Daily Telegraph, the Daily Mirror* and the *Daily Express*, that the Party leadership was planning to ballot members on whether they preferred unions retaining voting rights at Party Conferences and seats on the national executive. "But what has stoked the row and made union leaders jive with anger is the assertion by Mr. Byers that Mr. Blair would put all this to ballot if he, on becoming Prime Minister, was to face a summer of discontent through disruptive strikes." But Unions "refuse to play the second fiddle to Labour Party". The result is that a sort of war of words has erupted between the Labour leadership and the Unions with just 15 days to go for all important Party annual conference, the last before the elections. The sharp divisions could lead to a final show down between the modernisers and the Unionists. The outcome of the "battle would not only" decide the fate of the Labour Party but could radically affect the British polity." Mr Blair however, is not expected to bow down to the hard-core Union conservatives. "He knows that the middle-class voter has to be convinced about the modern approach of his new Labour and its fears of disruptive strikes *et al* driven out, if he is to win the next polls". [24]

**Social Democratic Party**

In April, the Social Democratic Party was formed as a result of the split in the Labour Party, which had then twelve seats in the House of Commons. Roy Jenkins, who ended his term as President of the European Community Commission in February 1981 had made clear in 1980 that he believed Labour had moved too far to the left and that he planned to launch by December (1980) a rival political party. The left-wing drive led by Anthony Wedgwood Benn and the dismal record of Mrs. Margaret Thatcher's Government both contributed to the emergence of the Social Democratic Party which entered the country's political arena by contesting the Warrington by-election with Roy Jenkins contesting the seat. Warrington had been a traditional rock solid Labour stronghold. Roy Jenkins received 42 per cent of the votes cast, while Labour candidate Douglas Hoyle just won by obtaining 48 per cent—down from 61 per cent in 1979. The Conservative candidate lost his deposit. The result, which was described variously as "startling", "magnificent" and "sensational", was considered to be a barometer of the prevailing political climate in Britain showing deep discontent with Mrs. Thatcher's policies and disappointment with the Labour Party, torn by its internal wrangles and dissensions.

The Warrington result gave a greater confidence to the Social Democratic Party. It ended its annual convention in London in October 1981 expressing confidence that it could win the country's next general election in alliance with the Liberal party. The new Party set for itself the middle course between what it viewed as a dangerous leftward drift in the Labour Party and the extreme conservatism of the Government of Mrs. Thatcher. The Party chose the slogan "A Fresh start for Britain" to characterise what it hoped would be a departure from the traditional mould of British Party politics. The Liberal-Social Democratic Party alliance defeated in a special election in Croydon North-West the ruling Conservative Party candidate. In November Mrs. Shirley Williams won the traditional conservative seat in Crosby. What made the Liberal-SDP alliance more bright was that both the Parties were 'Centrist' and the fact that important sections of capital and labour supported the alliance. At one time there were 22 Social Democrat Members of the House of Commons and 34 Peers who supported the Centrists and they were almost entirely former Labour Party members. The Duke of Devonshire, a former Conservative Government Minister and a nephew of former Premier Harold Macmillian, left the ruling Conservative Party, on 13 March 1982 to join the Social Democratic Party. Roy Jenkins, one of co-founders of the SDP declared, "it was a characteristically courageous decision. We are delighted to have him." Roy Jenkins also found his berth in the House of Commons by defeating both the Conservative and Labour Candidates. But the future of the Party seems to be bleak with its disintegration with the Liberal Party. Quite a number of Social Democrats have gone back to their parent Labour Party. Britain has, thus, reverted to its time-honoured two-party system.

**The Myth of Bipolarity**

The central feature of the two-party system has been that the leadership of both the principal political formations has unanimously accepted the rationality of the socio-economic foundations of British society. Rousseau and Marx pointed out that the British people were only free to decide periodically which members of the ruling class were to misrepresent them in Parliament. Despite the gradual growth of franchise and the emergence of strong labour movement, Parliamentary democracy in England continues to fulfil the wishes of Balbour: "our alternating cabinets, though belonging to different parties, have never differed about the foundations of society. And it is evident that our whole political machinery presupposes a people so fundamentally at one that they can safely afford to bicker ; and so sure of their own moderation that they are not dangerously disturbed by the never-ending din of political conflict. May it always be so". (Bagehot, *The English Constitution*, p. xxiv).

It is a historical truth that the two major parties of England, alternating in government, have always been in agreement on basic questions of home and foreign policy. As Harold Laski put it correctly :"Since 1689 we have had for all effective purposes, a single party in control

24. "Unions Refuse to Play Second fiddle to Labour Party", Vijay Dutt, as reported in the *Statesman,* New Delhi, September 18, 1996.

of the state. It has been divided no doubt, into two wings [but] its quarrels have always been family quarrels in which there has always been room for compromise." (*Parliamentary Government in England*, p. 94). In this passage, Laski was referring only to the Conservative and Labour parties. But the leaders of the Labour Party have been just as loyal to the basic institutions of capitalism as have been the leaders of the other traditional parties. Tony Blair has now given up all pretentions that the Labour Party can have any connection with any 'socialistic' programme. But the history of Labour leadership from MacDonald to Attlee to Wilson clearly shows that its socalled commitment to any kind of 'socialism' was pure illusion. Bipolarity of British parliamentary democracy, therefore, remains a convenient fiction.

Behind the facade of bipolarity the dominant classes of England have been fortunate enough to rely on the Conservative Party as the major 'party of government' which is rarely a 'party in opposition'. One of the most remarkable thing about the conservative party is that it has very successfully adapted itself to the necessities of populist politics. Thus old, aristocratic, pre-industrial Tory party first adopted itself to the new industrial environment and accommodated in its leadership the representatives of the industrial bourgeoisie; and then consciously set out, after the second Reform Act of 1867 to develop a kind of popular base with mass membership in the country. The erstwhile Tories became new Conservatives, who have never ceased to retain their broad electoral base since then. The Whigs were transformed into the Liberal Party, which after a century was overtaken by the Labour Party that claims to represent organised labour.

The Conservative Party, despite its multi-class electoral appeal and rhetoric of piecemeal social reform, remains chiefly the defence organisation, in the political sphere of property and business. The party aggregates and articulates the different interests of the dominant classes. It reconciles, coordinates and fuses the divergent interest of the socio-economic blocs supporting it into a workable policy and programme. It also provides an ideological disguise to this policy appropriate for political competition in the age of 'Mass politics.' Major Conservative leaders are familiar figures in the boardrooms of large corporations. They are united with the business world by ties of kinship, friendship, mutual interest and common outlook. They can always depend upon the capitalists to finance generously their election campaigns and other needs. By contrast, the Labour Party is associated with subordinate and intermediary classes and its leaders cannot be found in the councils of the great corporations. They depend on Trade Union funding and small subscriptions. They may occasionally win elections but they have neither the will nor the capacity to make any dent in the consolidated structures of capitalism. The two-party system in England is, therefore, characterised by a situation of imperfect competition.

## SUGGESTED READINGS


Bailey, S: *Political Parties and the Party System of Britain.*

Barker, E.: *Britain and the British People* (1943) Chap. II.

Birch, N.: *The Conservative Party.*

Blondel, J.: *Parties and Leaders.*

Briers, P. M. and Others: *Papers on Parliament, A Symposium* (1949), "The Party System and National Interests."

Bulmer-Thomas, Ivor : *The Party System in Great Britain.*

Campion and Others: *Parliament: A Survey,* Chap. VIII.

Cruikshank, R., *The Liberal Party.*

Finer, H.: *The Theory and Practice of Modern Government,* Chap. XVI.

Gollan, J.: *The British Political System.*

Gooch. R. K.: *The Government of England,* Chap. V.

Greaves, H.R.G.: *The British Constitution.* Chap. VI.

Hall, G.: *The Labour Party.*

Jennings, W.I.: *The British Constitution.*, Chap. I.

Laski, H.J.: *Parliamentary Government in England,* Chap. II.

Lowell, A.L.: *The Government of England.*

Vol. I, Chaps. XXIV-XXX.

Vol. II, Chaps. XXI-XXXVII.

Mckenzie, R. T.: *British Political Parties.*

Morrison, H.: *Government and Parliament.* pp. 78-8, 114-15 and Chap. VII.

Neumann, R.G.: *European and Comparative Governments,* Chap. VIII.

Rose, R. (Ed.): *Studies in British Politics.*

Stewart, M.: *The British Approach to Politics,* Chap. XIII.

William, F.: *Fifty Years' March: The Rise of the Labour Party.*

# CHAPTER XI

# Local Government

### School for Democracy

"The local assemblies of citizens," wrote Alexie de Tocqueville more than a century ago, "constitute the strength of free nations. Town meetings are to liberty what primary schools are to science; they bring it within the people's reach, they teach men how to use and how to enjoy it. A nation may establish system of free government, but without the spirit of municipal institutions it cannot have the spirit of liberty." The educative value of representative government largely depends on the development of local institutions. Local government is a school for democracy. It cultivates a sense of civic duties and inculcates among citizens a corporate spirit of common administration of common interests. All problems of administration are not certain problems. It should, accordingly, be the responsibility of the inhabitants of the area concerned to solve their local problems which are peculiar to that area. Neighbourhood makes us automatically aware of interests which impinge upon us more directly than upon others. And what is done by common counsel in the solution of the common problems gives us a degree of satisfaction which is unobtainable when it is done for us by others from outside. Local government may, accordingly, be defined as government by popular elected bodies charged with administrative and executive duties in matters concerning the inhabitants of a particular district or place and vested with powers to make bylaws[1] for their guidance.

### Fundamental Aspects

The history of local government in Britain is one of gradual development. Blackstone had correctly maintained that "the liberties of England may be ascribed above all things to her free local institutions. Since the days of their Saxon ancestors, her sons have learned at their own gates the duties and responsibilities." The marked genius of the British for self-government may, thus, be traced to the root of local self-government. Parliament became strong, and a system of Parliamentary democracy was eventually established, because the countries and boroughs from which the members of Parliament were drawn "had a sap of native vigour and an instinct for self-government." The old methods of local government have, indeed, been greatly altered by the legislation during the past century or so, but "the whole of the change," as Barker puts it, "has only strengthened an old and vigorous system of national liberty – so old that it is anterior to the system of national liberty; so vigorous that it has supplied the sap and the stimulus to that system." The general main-spring and the fountain of initiative is locally elected bodies. These elected bodies determine local policies and are organs of Local Government. As organs of government, they make their own local rules or by-laws, raise and spend their own local rates, and appoint and control their own administrative staffs for carrying out their functions of local services. But as organs of government in local areas, they are parts of the general system of government in the country and, as such, subject to the control of Parliament and the Central Government. Parliament determines and can always modify their activities and their powers. The Central Government and its administrative staff audits, inspects and supervises their activities and such a supervision and direction becomes all the more necessary because Parliament subsidizes the local rates by 'grant-in-aid' from the central taxes. In spite of this control Local Government in Britain is infinitely more self-reliant than is customary on the Continent of Europe. There is no all-powerful Minister of the Interior. as in France, whose hand weighs heavily on the shoulders of local authorities. "under such circumstances, free men may assemble in their councils, pretty much as of yore, and impress the mark of their personalities on their environment." Many leading statesmen of the country, in the past and during our own times, began their careers in the councils of Local Government. Taking recent Examples, Joseph and

1. Laws of local application which must be approved by the appropriate Minister.

Neville Chambelain were both Lords Mayors of Birmingham. Herbert Morrison first became prominent as President of the London County Council.

**Development**

Until modern times the machinery of local government was not organised in accordance with any particular plan, but grew up haphazard to satisfy particular needs. Since there was no coordination, the overlapping of functions, disorder, and a loss of efficiency were inevitable. The present counties and parishes find their origin in the shires and hundreds, vills or townships of pre-Norman days. The Central Government was largely superimposed upon existing local organization. In the Middle Ages each county or shire had its court or governmental assembly, presided over by the Sheriff as the royal representative and composed of the freemen of the county. The county court performed general governmental as well as judicial functions. Within the county were hundred courts similarly composed and under the supervision of the Sheriffs. The manorial courts of the feudal system were the courts of the smaller units, the vill and the township. Boroughs which obtained Charters from the Crown, possessed varying degree of automony. From the time of Henry II royal justice began to cover the whole country through the circuits of justices. The local and manorial courts were superseded and with them the office of the Sheriff lost much of its former importance. In the fourteenth century the newly created justices of the peace acquired judicial, administrative and police powers. The parish which was hitherto an ecclesiastical unit also became the unit of local administration. I was the parish which was responsible for the repair of roads and later for the administration of Elizabethan poor low.

No attempt was made after the Revolution Settlement in 1689 to reimpose central administrative control. Apart from the boroughs, which were largely autonomous acting under their Charter powers, general local administration was in the hands of the county justices sitting in the Quarter Sessions. This was all altered by the century of reform between 1835 and 1935. The results were mainly three. One was the reform and democratization of the organs of local government. The second was a reform and clarification of the powers aud functions of local government. The third was a reform and elucidation of the connection between local and Central Government. The reform of the organs of local government was a long and complicated process, because from 1835 to 1888 Britain pursued the curious policy of creating a new ad hoc authority to deal with each new local need that emerged. Not only that, each new authority was given a different area of operation from that of the old authorities. The Local Government Act of 1888 drastically altered all this. It instituted democratic county councils, with a general competence, in place of the old system of Justices of the Peace, mixed with the ad hoc bodies which had recently been added to it. The light has progressively grown. The existing system of Local Government is based mainly on six distinct types of authority—the Administrative County, the County Borough, the NonCounty Borough, the Urban District, the Rural District, and the Parish. Of the authorities responsible for the government of these six, the first and the second date from 1888; the third from 1835, subject to modifications made in 1882; the fourth and fifth and sixth from 1894. The London County Council was set up in 1889, as successor to the indirectly elected Metropolitan Board of Works.

With regard to the power and functions of Local Government, and their progressive reform and clarification since 1835, there now exists a system of what may be called *integral Local Government*, under which each major authority generally conducts the whole of local government in its area. The system of integral local government gives local authority a large initiative in such matters as roads and transport, police, public health, public education, public assistance and the supply to public services such as housing, gas, water, and electricity. Here is a large field for the determination and conduct of local policy. It will thus be obvious that a progressive authority can take action which will vitally affect the health, the growth of mind, and the general well-being of all its area. It may, however, be noted that since 1945, local authorities have lost their responsibility for hospitals, and for gas and electricity services, and at present there is much pressure for the nationalisation of other services, especially education, police and water distribution.

**Local and Central Governments**

It is here that the connection of local government with the central government begins to show its importance. It becomes, accordingly, necessary to know the development and the present method of that connection. The Central Government has obviously a duty of stimulating local initiative where it is backward and checking it where it abuses its authority or does things beyond its powers. This necessitates a system of contact, or co-operation, and of interaction between local elected bodies, with their local administrative staffs, and the Departments of the Central Government with their administrative officers. The system of "grants-in-aid" paid from the public funds in subvention of local finances is a significant step directed to control and supervise the activities of local bodies. In fact, grants-in-aid are paid only on condition that Central Government and its officials inspect and supervise their spending and the operation of the services on which such grants are spent. The power of the purse of the Central Government may, therefore, be said to have *bought* a measure of control over Local Government and it has cost heavily to the autonomy of the local bodies. Another way of financing by the Central Government is the system of block grants.

Like all other institutions, Local Government, too, is subject to the supreme authority of Parliament and such laws as it may enact. Beyond that the various Government Departments supervise the work of local government and see that the statutory authority is fulfilled. The Home Office inspects and to a certain extent supervises the police forces, except in the Metropolitan District of London, where the police is directly administered by the Home Office. The latter is also in charge of local civil defence work, especially the Home Guard. In addition, Ministerial consent is required for certain actions by local authorities, including the making of by-laws, and the appointment of some officials. Building plans require Ministerial approval, and the administration of some services, particularly the police, fire brigade, and education is subject to examination by Ministry Inspectors. Some legislation that gives powers to local authorities, particularly with regard to planning and land development, allows for appeals to the appropriate Minister. The Treasury must give its consent to borrowing local government. Generally speaking, the appropriate Central Government Departments supervise work of local authorities, keep them in line, and establish rules with regard to procedure, organisation qualifications of officials, equipment, and general objectives. The Department of the Environments, recently set up, under a Secretary of State, to assume responsibility in England for the range of functions affecting the physical environment in which people live and work, which was formerly divided between the Ministry of Housing and Local Government, the Ministry of Public Building and Works, and the Ministry of Transport, is the main link between the local authorities and the Central Government in England. In Scotland, the Scottish Development Department is responsible for general policy in regard to Local Government, in Wales, the Welsh office and in Northern Ireland the Ministry of Development.

Since local powers and duties originate from Acts of Parliament and are enforced by courts, the Central Government may obtain from the High Court a writ requiring any neglect of legal duty to be repaired. Any private person who has suffered loss as a result of negligence of local authority can bring a civil action. In like manner, the courts are used to check action which is *ultra vires*. Central Government may also invalidate local ordinances which may go beyond powers granted to the local authorities. In health, housing or other services where neglect can have the gravest results, a Justice of Peace, or simply four rate-payers in the area, can invoke the aid of the Ministry of Health to enquire into local inefficiency and, perhaps, take over the duties itself.

Changing social conditions and broadening conceptions of the functions of government have broken new ground for Central Government control, and the end is not in sight. New central agencies, notably of the kind we call public corporations, are established to undertake new services or to replace the agencies of Local Government. Considerable transfer of functions takes place from smaller or larger geographical units in the existing Local Government structure and even the word "local" takes a new significance.[2] The policy of coordination and standardization, which is so prominent a feature of our times, has deeply penetrated the realm of Local Government. The statutory provisions concerning meetings, committees and the form of audit of accounts ensure that in each area there shall be similar machinery whatever the extent to which it is used. Meanwhile the Central Government brings a constant influence to bear through its inspectors. Not only are satisfactory reports from them the condition of grants-in-aid, but the re-

2. Campion and Others, *British Government Since 1918*, p. 198

sulting accumulation of knowledge shows to the Central Government what changes in the law have become necessary. Circulars acquaint local authorities with the policy which the Central Government wishes them to pursue and if the latter finds its legal powers insufficient, it can always propose new laws and bring them on the statute. Occasionally, if the local authority uses its power in a way of which the government strongly disapproves, a special Act will be passed handing over the powers to Commissioners appointed by the Minister of Health.

It will, thus, be seen that the methods of central control are numerous. Local Government though still admired and ardently cherished in Britain, has now become a hazy spheres of local action distinct from Central Government. Certain services once accepted as purely local have assumed national significance. The local school is part of a national educational system; public assistance is no longer a community task but a national responsibility, even gas and electricity, once characteristically municipal service, have now been nationalised. Much premium has, during recent years been placed on administrative considerations in demarcating the sphere of central and local government. J.H. Warren, while reviewing the changes which have taken place in the scope and system of Local Government in Britain, writes: "The particular sphere to be assigned to local government is not a question which is, or wholly can be determined by consideration of democratic freedom and responsibility, viewed as capable of development by ties of neighbourhood and the activity of local communities; or even by the consideration that local self-government is an educative process and invaluable to democracy on that account. The assignment of local government functions must have some regard to administrative consideration."[3] The assignment of local government functions, particularly after the First World War, is significant of this fact.

Nonetheless local administration and to a limited extent the framing of policy remain functions of local authorities. The Central Government secures the cooperation of local authorities and the relationship is one of friendly partnership. Local authorities are not branches of Departments in Whitehall, though they operate some of the central services on an agency basis. Their members are elected by the districts they serve. Their services are administered by their own officers. The overall record of the councils and their committees is splendid. In any system of political governance, the Central Government must control the local, however, autonomous the Local Government may be. But there is.one important difference between the control of Local Government in Britain and in other countries, such as France. In France the control of the Central Government over the local is a control of an executive character, which goes so far that it practically eliminates local government, in any exact sense of the word, and remits the control of local policy to local administrative officials acting for the central executive. The British system of Local Government, on the other hand, is a halfway House which combines both legislative and executive control. "The value of this system," according to Barker, "is that it is kinder to local government than pure executive control and more elastic in its application to the differences of local governing bodies than purely legislative control. Parliament offers grants to local authorities as an equal might offer to equals: the executive, watching the actual operation of spending of these grants, can use an elastic discretion to suit each particular case-seeking indeed to standardise, but seeking to do so by stimulating the laggard and holding back the impatient, according to the needs and demands of each particular case." The preoccupation of the local councils and committees with administrative matters guarantees that democratic procedures are maintained on all levels. Government's control over local authorities is kept to the minimum.

## PRINCIPAL TYPES OF LOCAL AUTHORITY

For purposes of Local Government, England and Wales and Northern Ireland are divided into county boroughs and administrative counties. Administrative counties (outside London) are further divided into three types of county district: non-county borough; urban districts; and rural districts. Rural districts are themselves subdivided into parishes (except in Northern Ireland). Scotland is divided into counties (including four counties of cities) which are independently administered; large and small boroughs; and districts. Each local authority division

3. *Ibid, p.* 195

is administered a different council. The London Government Act, 1963, which came into force on April 1, 1965, has reduced the number of county, borough and urban district councils in England.

**The Parish**

Although England is divided into Parishes for church purposes, the Parish, as a local authority, exists only in the countryside. Where the population is less than three hundred there is usually no council and the affairs of the Parish are managed by a parish meeting which all ratepayers may attend. In the larger Parishes a council of from five to fifteen members is elected at a Parish meeting and they hold office for three years. The duties of the Parish Council or Meeting are slight. It acts as a minor education authority and may provide public works, recreation grounds, and protect local rights of way. Sometimes an Act may enable them to see to the lighting of the village, and higher authorities may hand over to them the care of the water supply and the repairing of footpaths. A Parish may have paid clerk, but there is no other paid official.

**The District**

A group of Parishes forms a Rural District and if the development of industry turns a Parish into a small town, it may request the County Council to make it into an Urban District. The Councils of both types of Districts are elected for a period of three years, one-third retiring after every one year. The Chairman may be one of the Councillors, or chosen from outside, but in either case he has the powers of a Justice of Peace during his term of office.

The Districts enjoy greater dignity and power than the Parish. They are used by Central Government as housing authorities, and, thus, have the power to acquire land and to build, and the duty of dealing with slums and overcrowding. As sanitary authorities, District Councils may provide for water supply and other sanitary measures. Trunk roads are maintained directly by the Ministry of Transport and other major roads by counties, whereas the unclassified roads for which no grant is made by the Ministry, must be maintained by the Urban District Councils. In the countryside, although the county is the responsible authority, it frequently delegates the work to the Rural Districts.

District Councils have often owned or shared in the management of public utilities. With the nationalisation of gas and electricity, however, this field of activity has been greatly reduced. District Councils keep a number of paid officials, e.g., Clerk, Treasurer, Medical Officer of Health, Sanitary Inspector, and Surveyor of Highways. An Urban District Council has some additional powers, such as that to provide allotments, libraries and public baths. Where the population exceeds 25,000 a Stipendiary Magistrate can be appointed. There is, in fact, little to choose between the large Urban District and the small Borough.

**The County**

England still clings to the county system of the past that has come down through the centuries. The fifty-two historical counties are relics of former times and are shorn of all important functions. They have no elected councils and have only three principal officials, the Local Lieutenant, the Sheriffs and the Justice of the Peace. The office of the Local Lieutenant has great dignity and is usually held by a wealthy county gentleman. He has charge of the county records and recommends suitable persons to be Justice of the Peace. The Sheriff is responsible for making all the preparations necessary for the holding of assizes.

There are now sixtytwo Administrative Counties superimposed over the historical councils. Every Administrative County is divided into Electoral Divisions, each returning one Councillor at the elections, which are held once every three years. The Councillors, when elected, choose a number of Aldermen equal to a third of their own number. Frequently Councillors themselves are Aldermen, and this necessitates a by-election to provide a new Councillor. The term Aldermen goes back to the times of the Saxons when it meant men chosen for their maturity of age and experience to assist in government. Today, it has no reference to age. They are elected for six years, one-half retiring at the time of each Council election. Greater length of office, no doubt, equips them with experience of the Council work. It also enables talented persons, who do not wish to face the mud and mire of election campaigns, of get elected. The Chairman of the County Council is elected in the same manner as the Chairman of District Council, and has the same right of acting as a Justice of the Peace. The Council can pay a salary to the Chairman and the travelling expenses incurred by members when doing Council work.

The County Councils are responsible for

the policy and the administration of the county and supervise the work of subordinate bodies. The Councils also act as agents for the Central Government, cooperating with it to administer Public Assistance and the Pensions. They maintain the ordinary local services, building and asylums. They also administer the licensing laws except for liquor, and appoint the regular administrative personnel of the county.

New and very considerable powers and duties have been imposed on the Councils as a result of two important Statutes; the Education Act of 1944, and the Town and County Planning Acts of 1944 and 1947. The Education Act of 1944 has made counties responsible for the education service at all stages. This task was previously shared between Counties, Boroughs and Urban Districts. Legislation passed after the war of 1939-45 has made the County the responsible authority for the Health Service and for Town and County Planning, the latter had become necessary for the reconstruction of war devastated areas in line with a general plan. In addition to this general work, the County Council must give attention to agriculture, and its duties in this respect have been considerably increased.

The old and new forms of county government are brought together by the Standing Joint Committee, half of whose members are Justices, and half County Councillors. This Committee appoints the Chief Constable of the County, and organises a police force in accordance with the law and the Home Office regulations. The police are inspected annually by the Home Office, and if the result is satisfactory, half the expenses will be met by the Central Government. Subject to this control, the County police are responsible for all police duties within their area.

**The Borough**

A unit of local government of a special type is the Borough, which is simply a Town with a Charter. An Urban or Rural District which desires to become a Borough petitions to Her Majesty in Council for a Charter. If as few as five per cent of the local ratepayers object an Act of Parliament will be necessary.

The Borough is governed by a Borough Council constituted similar to a County and District Council. The Borough is divided for election purposes into wards, each returning three, or a multiple of three, Councillors. One-third of the Councillors retire each year. The Councillor choose Aldermen to one-third of their number, as for County Councils. The Borough Council selects its own Mayor either from among the Councillors or from outside; and he holds office for a year and may be reelected. Besides being the Chairman of the Council, he presides over the local bench of the Justices of Peace during his year of office, and continues to act as Justice of Peace for the following year. Generally, his functions are ceremonial.

The Borough status gives a town a much greater degree of dignity and civic pride. It also means larger expenses for pomp and ceremonial occasions. All Boroughs possess, as a minimum. the powers of a large Urban District Council, and those additional powers which the Charter confers. Any Borough may by ancient custom or Royal Order be called a city, but this is only a dignity and involves no legal powers. The Mayors of some of the most famous cities are called Lord Mayors. Just like the County Council, the Borough Council operates chiefly through Committees. The Council manages the corporate estate and the borough fund. It establishes the borough rates. It has its own budget and appropriates money. Subject to approval by the Central Government, it may borrow money. It also administers the municipal services which are often quite extensive.

**The Government of London**

London is the largest capital city and with the exception of New York, the greatest metropolitan area in the world. Today, there is still the old city keeping its boundaries, street names and forms of local administration which as they were centuries ago. Round this city have grown the dwellings of millions, rich and poor. Systematic government for this huge district dates back on to the last century.

The City of London properly speaking is an area of about one square mile located in the heart of London, primarily the business and financial centre, in which over a million people are active during the day but in which few people live at night. It is divided into twenty-six wards each of which returns, according to its size, number of Councillors to the Court of Common council elected by those with residence or business qualification in the city. In addition to the 206 councillors elected annually, the Court of Common Council contains 26 Aldermen, elected directly by citizens and holding their office for life. These together with the Lord Mayor, form a separate Court of Aldermen. Another, and the third body is called the Court of Common Hall and it consists of the Court of Aldermen and the Liverymen of the city companies. These companies are the survivors of the ancient guilds. Today they have none of their old duties and in reality these are now private societies of wealthy men. The Court of Common Hall annually selects two Aldermen, one of whom will be elected Lord Mayor by the Court of Aldermen.

The Court of Common Council is the real governing body of the city. It relies on the county for its municipal services, although it has a small police force and courts. It also controls certain areas outside the city limits. The city of London is the scene of magnificent ceremonies especially on the annual Lord Mayor's Day held at the Guild Hall.

**The London County Council**

The Act of 1888 set up a County Council for London. Its structure and that of Metropolitan Boroughs are now consolidated in the London Government Act, of 1939. The London County Council, bears only a general resemblance to other County Councils, there being three important differences. It is organised differently, for the electoral divisions are those used in the return of members of Parliament for the Metropolis, the County Councillors being twice as numerous; the Aldermen are in the proportion of one to six, instead of one to three Councillors; and Chairman of L.C.C. is a very dignified president with no control of policy. Secondly, an ordinary County Council receives authority once for all over the ancient county areas, minus its County Boroughs. The L.C.C. received authority over the Administrative County of London. The third difference is that the L.C.C. inherited the functions of the old Board of Works as well as acquiring those of the County Council.

The hundred and twentynine Councillors choose twenty Aldermen who hold office for six years, half on them retiring at the end of a three-year period. The Chairman of the Council may be chosen from outside as was Lord Snell in 1934. The powers of the L.C.C. are extensive indeed. It is the sole authority with respect to main sewers and sewage disposal, fire protection tunnels and ferries and bridges. It is responsible for street improvements which are metropolitan. Its power also extends to the construction and operation of tramways, and it has undertaken several rehousing schemes, involving the demolition of slum areas and the erection of workmen dwellings. It is, also, responsible for maintenance of the larger London parks and provision for public recreation. It has comprehensive functions in the matters of education, elementary, secondary, and technical.

**The Metropolitan Borough**

The County area, apart from the city, is divided into 28 Metropolitan Boroughs. The Councillors are elected for a threeyear period and they choose Aldermen to one-sixth of their number for a period of six years, one-half retiring every three years. The Mayor is chosen as in a Municipal Borough and enjoys the same power and dignity except that he is an ex-officio J. P. for his year of office only, not the subsequent year as well. In their functions the metropolitan Boroughs resemble closely the small Municipal Boroughs which have no separate police force, and are not education authorities. Health services are shared between L.C.C. and Boroughs, Some Boroughs have their own housing schemes.

From April 1, 1965, under the provision of the London Government Act, 1963, the London County Council and the Middlesex County Council have been abolished and the area hitherto administered by them, together with adjacent areas of Essex, Hertfordshire, Kent and Surrey, form the Greater London area. This area is administered by the Councils of 32 London boroughs and the City of London, which retains the independent status, and the Greater London Council

**Proposals for Restructuring Local Government**

Since the nineteenth century, when conception of a comprehensive system of locally elected councils to manage various services provided for the benefit of the community was first incorporated in statute law, there has been increase in the population, and a massive transformation in the range, complexity and scale of local authority functions. As a result of this, Local Government in Greater London was reorganised in the 1960's. Government proposals for a major restructuring of Local Government throughout the remainder of Great Britain were announced in 1971 and were intended to come into effect by 1975. The existing 1,800 authorities are replaced by 51 county and some 375 district authorities in England and Wales, and 8 regional and 49 district authorities in Scotland (outside the Orkney and Shetland Islands, which have separate, virtually all purpose authorities). The new county and regional authorities normally provide those services most suitably administered on a large scale, including major planning, roads, education and social services, while the independently elected district authorities provide the more local services such as housing, refuse collection, and the provision of amenities. The main exceptions are the provisionally styled 'metropolitan' counties, where the districts are responsible for education and the social services.

The Northern Ireland Government is committed to a reorganisation programme which it intended to implement by April 1973. According to this programme it was proposed that the Local Government functions which were of a regional character should be transferred to Northern Ireland Government. Planning, roads and water and sewerage services would be administered by the Ministry of Development, while education, personal health and personal social services would be the responsibility of area boards acting as agents of the ministries concerned. It has been decided that the remaining Local Government functions will be provided by 26 new district authorities. Housing has already become the responsibility of the new Northern Ireland Housing Executive.

### A Critique of Local Government

The British system of local government is often held up as a model for other counties representing the principle of democratic decentralisation at its best. *The Labour Party Speakers' Handbook* even claims that the functions of local authorities have now developed 'to the positive ones of giving to every citizen the best possible opportunities for a full and happy life," This attitude completely ignores two tendencies which are a marked feature of the existing system of local governance in England — "firstly, the progressive tightening up of administrative, legal and financial control over all local authority activities by the central government; secondly, the increasing tendency to take away the powers of local authorities altogether." (James Harvey and Katherine Hood, *The British State*, p. 241).

The principal weapon of central control is finance. But a progressive county or borough council is obstructed also in ways not connected with finance. Denial of financial aid is a big hindrance for any local authority that is planning social services for the deprived section of the population. However, the most important restriction on its powers is derived from the doctrine of *ultra vires.* While an ordinary citizen can do anything which is not forbidden by law, local authorities are allowed to do only those things for which there is express statutory sanction. As a result, the various units of local government constitute today, to a greater or lesser degree, "an extension of central government and administration, the latter's antennae or tentacles. "In an advanced capitalist country like Britain, sub-central government is rather more than an administrative device.".

Ralph Miliband concludes : "In addition to being agents of the state these units of government have also traditionally performed another function. They have not only been the channels of communication and administration from the centre to the periphery but also the voice of the periphery or of particular interests at the periphery ; they have been a means of overcoming local particularities, but also platforms for their expression, instruments of central control and obstacles to it." (*The State in Capitalist Society,* p. 49). While centralisation of power has grown in the British political system, local organs of government in the United Kingdom have continued as power structures in their own right. Therefore, they have been capable of influencing the lives of the people they have governed to a great extent.

## SUGGESTED READINGS

Campion and Others : *British Government Since 1918, Chap. VI*

Clarke, J.J. : *Outlines of the Local Government of the United Kingdom.*

Cole, G.D. H.: *Local and Regional Government.*

Drain, G. : *The Organization and Practice of Local Government.*

Finer, H. : *English Local Government.*

Griffith, J.A.G. : *Central Departments and Local Authorities.*

Golding, L. : *Local Government.*

Maud, J.P.R. : *Local Government in Modern England.*

Hart, William O. : *Introduction to the Law of Local Government.*

Jackson, R.M. : *The Machinery of Local Government.*

Jackson, W.E. : *Local Government in England and Wales.*

Jackson, W. E. : *The Machinery of Local Government.*

Jackson, W. E. : *The Structure of Local Government.*

Jennings, Sir Ivor : *Principles of Local Government.*

Jwell, R.E.C. : *Central and Local Government.*

Lofts, D. (Ed.) : *Local Government Today and Tomorrow.*

Robson, W. A. : *The Development of Local Government*

Warren. J.H. : *The English Local Government System.*

Warren, J.H. : *Municipal Administration*

# THE GOVERNMENT OF THE UNITED STATES OF AMERICA

## CHAPTER I

## The American Political Tradition

### A Nation of Immigrants

Within the span of a hundred years in the seventeenth and early eighteenth centuries, a tide of emigration set from Europe to America. The most impelling single force which induced emigrants to leave their European Homelands was the desire for economic opportunity and England was the first to seize it. Between 1620 and 1635 economic difficulties of an unprecedented character had swept England and there was no work for a multitude of people. Even the best artisans could earn just a bare living. Bad crops added to the distress. In addition, England's expanding woollen industry demanded an increasing supply of wool to keep the looms working and the sheep, raised in their anxiety to make best of the opportunity, began to encroach upon soil hitherto given over to tillage.

Simultaneously, religious upheavals played their part. A radical sect of Puritans, known as the Separatists had migrated to Holland during the reign of James I in order to practise their religion as they wished. Some years later a part of this group decided to emigrate to the New World where in 1620 they founded the "Pilgrim" colony of New Plymouth. In Britain, too, immediately after the accession of Charles I to the throne, Puritans, who had been subjected to increasing persecutions, followed the Pilgrims to America and established Massachusetts Bay Colony. But Puritans were not the only colonists driven by religious motives. Dissatisfaction with the lot of Quakers led William Penn to undertake the founding of Pennsylvania. British Catholics, also, under Cecil Calvert's inspiration founded Maryland. The pace of emigration accelerated during the arbitrary and despotic rule of Charles I. After the triumph of Cromwell many Cavaliers—"King's men" left Britain in sheer horror and colonized in Virginia.

In Germany the oppressive policies of various petty princes helped to mount high the number of the emigrants. On the whole, the settlers who came to America in the first three-quarters of the seventeenth century, the overwhelming majority was the British. There was sprinkling of Dutch, Swedes, and Germans in the middle region, a few French Huguenots in South Carolina and elsewhere, and a scattering of Spaniards, Italians, and the Portuguese. But they were hardly ten per cent of the total population. After 1680, however, Britain did not provide any appreciable number of immigrants. A majority of them had come from Germany, Ireland, Scotland, Switzerland, and France for varied reasons. For a considerably long time immigration remained a steady stream and the population which numbered to about a quarter of a million in 1760 amounted to more than two and a half million in 1775.

### Towards Independence

The immigrants from Britain not only brought with them English language, but also Anglo-Saxon traditions of civil liberty and self-government reinforced as they were by *Magna Carta,* the Bill of Rights and the *Habeas Corpus* Act. They transplanted all these traditions, in fact, the whole fabric of the Common Law in their new homelands. For the most part, the non-English Colonies adapted themselves to the traditions of the original settlers as they adopted the English language, law, customs and habits. The process of amalgamation had the obvious result of intermingling the different cultures and thereby producing a new culture—a blend of English and Continental characteristics conditioned by the environments of the New World.

Before Colonies could be established in

America, it was necessary to have legal authorisation to do so. This was granted by the King of Britain in Charters, granted in some instances to trading companies, in others to individuals and in still others to the colonists. The basis of government in each colony was the supremacy of the Crown, although there was the lack of controlling influence on the part of the Government in Britain. The colonies were , during the formative period, free to a large degree to develop as their inclinations or force of circumstances dictated. This large degree of self-government exercised by the colonists resulted ''in their growing away with Britain'' whenever in the years to come the Government attempted to regulate their conduct. The colonists had indeed, become with the lapse of time, increasingly''Americans'' rather than ''English'' and this tendency was strongly reinforced by the blending of other national groups and cultures which was simultaneously taking place. How it operated and the manner in which it laid the birth of a new nation was vividly described in 1782 by St. John Crevecouer: ''What then is the American, this new man? He is either an European, or the descendant of an European, hence that strange mixture of blood, which you find in no other country.........I could point out to you to a family whose grandfather was an Englishman, whose wife was Dutch, whose son married a French woman, and whose present four sons have now four wives of different nations. He is an American, who leaving behind him all his ancient prejudices and manners, receives new ones from the new mode of life he has embraced, the new government he obeys and the new ranks he holds.........''

In 1763 at the end of the Seven Years' War the French were driven from the North American Continent. New territories came under British control, and money was needed to administer them. The British Government had incurred huge debt fighting the French and it was decided that the Colonies should bear a part of the expenses of administration and defence of the Colonies. At the same time, attempts were made to enforce the trade laws more rigorously, and to tighten the control over Colonial affairs. It spread a wave of deep resentment amongst the Colonies. ''Businessmen wanting to develop their own industries; merchants and shippers wishing to trade with nations other than England; planters believing they could get better prices from the Dutch and French than from the English; speculators wishing to buy western land—all these and others found reason to chafe under the heavier taxes and harsher restrictions.''[1]

But those who resented and protested had hardly thought of independence. What they exactly wanted was the repeal of the onerous laws and to leave the Colonists as much alone as possible. Their protests, however, stirred up popular feelings and radical men like Sam and John Adams in Massachusetts and Patrick Henry and Thomas Jefferson in Virginia seized the opportunity and appealed to the emotions of the colonists in the name of natural rights of men, and of government resting on the consent of the governed. They quoted Locke on individual liberty and human rights.

The result was a deliberate disobedience of the ''obnoxious'' laws and orders. The Colonial Legislatures frequently withheld appropriation of salaries for officials and soldiers until their demands were conceded to or their grievances redressed. After the accession of George III to the throne in 1760, the British Government decided to deal firmly with the recalcitrant subjects. This caused resentment fanned to revolutionary fervour. All attempts at conciliation failed and by 1776 the Colonists were faced with the alternatives of submission or rebellion and they chose the latter.

**The Declaration of Independence**

The Declaration of Independence adopted on July 4, 1776 announced the birth of a new nation. It declared the Colonies States, each independent of the Crown and politically independent of others. At the same time, it set forth a democratic philosophy of man's natural rights, popular consent as the only just basis for political obligations, a limited government, and the right of the people to revolt against tyrannical government.

The Revolutionary War dragged on for about six years with fighting in every Colony. With Cornwallis's surrender on October 19, 1781 the military effort to halt the Revolution was, however, over. When the news of Americann victory reached Britain, the House of Commons voted to end the war. Soon after Lord North's Government resigned and the new Government assumed office to conclude peace on the basis of the Declaration of Independence. The Treaty was finally signed in 1783. It acknowledged the inde-

1. Burns and Peltason, *Government by the People,* p. 92.

pendence, freedom and sovereignty to the thirteen Colonies which became the States.

The Continental Congress which managed the common affairs of the Colonies during the early stages of the Revolution met and functioned without any constitution or fundamental law. It was created to meet an emergency and was looked upon merely as a temporary expedient. But when war appeared imminent and the advantages of union became more manifest, it was resolved to place the common government on a firm and permanent basis with larger powers and definite authority. On June 12, 1776, the day after a committee was appointed to prepare a declaration of independence, Congress appointed another committee consisting of one member from each Colony " to prepare and digest the form of a Confederation to be entered into between these Colonies." In November 1777 an instrument called the *Articles of Confederation* was finally adopted by Congress, which was to go into effect when ratified by all the States. All States except Maryland ratified the Articles during the year 1778 and 1779. Maryland, too, ratified them on March 1, 1781 and on the same date the Articles went into effect. They constituted the first Constitution of the United States of America.

The Confederation, thus, formed was styled a "firm league of friendship," under the name of the United States, and its declared purpose was to provide for the common defence of the States, the securities for their liberties, and their natural and general welfare. For "the more convenient management of the general interests of the United States" an annual Congress of delegates, to be chosen by the States, was established. No State was to send less than two and more than seven delegates, and each State was entitled to only one vote regardless of its size or other considerations. Unlike the Continental Congress, the Congress of the Confederation had definite and express powers to deal with certain subjects of common concern to declare war and make peace, to send and receive diplomatic representatives; to enter into treaties to coin money; to regulate trade with the Indians; to borrow money; to build a navy; to establish a postal system; to appoint senior officers of the United States Army (composed of state militants); and a few other powers of a like character. Approvals of nine of the thirteen States was required to make important decisions.

The Articles of Confederation, however, did not give two most important functions to Congress, *i.e.*, those of taxation and regulation of commerce. All that the Congress could do was to ask the States for funds. The Central government, therefore, existed on the doles of the State Governments. Nor had the Articles made any provision for an executive department or for a national judiciary, with the single exception of a court of appeal in cases involving captures on the high seas in time of war.

During the revolutionary period it did not matter much. But the post-war complications created insoluble problems. The war had inflated the currency and it circulated at about one-thousandth of its face value. The sky- high prices had dislocated the economy of the country and everybody groaned under the crushing burden of the excessive prices. In the absence of a uniform rate of exchange the international trade had come to a standstill. The Central treasury was nearly empty and the States had become defaulters in their payments. Creditors were reluctant to lend and public securities were sold at a fraction of their face value. The Congress was helpless and it had no means to remedy the chaos. The conditions were yet more demoralising in the dealings of the States with each other and the Central Government. The latter had, according to the Articles of Confederation, sole control of the international relations, but a number of States had begun their own negotiations with foreign nations. Nine States had organised their independent armies and several had little navies of their own. There was a curious diversity of coins minted by a dozen foreign nations, and a bewildering variety of State and national paper bills. Each State regulated its commerce and some States even discriminated against their neighbours. The result was continuous jealousies, dissensions, and sometimes reprisals and retaliation between themselves. For purposes of foreign and inter-State commerce each State was, in sum, a nation by itself, and the Confederation was simply a non-entity.

**Movement for Revision**

The climax was reached when all attempts to improve the Articles of Confederation had failed and the States were on the verge of Civil War. Washington, Hamilton and many other political leaders, who had laboured to bring together the States in bonds of Union, were convinced that the Government of the Confederation must either be revised or superseded entirely by a new system. The Congress of the Confederation was a government of the States and not of the people. It was weak because it lacked four things which every strong national government must possess: the power to tax, to borrow, to regulate commerce, and to maintain an army for the common defence. And to have a strong government possessing all these four powers, the Central Government must really be a government of the people belonging to one single nation. Washington wrote: "I do not conceive that we can exist long as a nation without our having lodged somewhere a power which will pervade the whole Union in as energetic a manner as the authority of the State governments extends over the several States."

Disputes between Maryland and Virginia over navigation in the Potomac River led to a conference of representatives of five at Annapolis in September 1786. Alexander Hamilton, one of the delegates, convinced his colleagues at the conference that the subject of trade regulation was bound up with other essential questions and it was, accordingly, necessary to call upon all the States to appoint representatives in order to "devise such further provisions as shall appear to them necessary to render the constitution of the Federal Government adequate to exigencies of the Union." The Annapolis convention adopted a resolution for a general convention of delegates from all the States to meet in Philadelphia in May 1787. The Continental Congress was at first indignant over this bold step, but finally it reluctantly endorsed the idea in February of that year. All the States except Rhode Island appointed delegates to participate in the convention.

**The Philadelphia Convention**

The Philadelphia Convention was in reality a constitutional convention as it was charged with the purpose of revising the Articles of Confederation. It assembled on the second Monday in May, 1778 and was composed of fifty-five members. It was, in the words of Jefferson, "an assembly of demi-gods." A French *Charge,* writing to his government said : "If all the delegates named for this Philadelphia Convention are present, one will never have seen, even in Europe, an assembly more respectable for talents, knowledge, disinterestedness and patriotism than those who will compose it." The men who actually guided the destinies of the emerging nation were George Washington, James Madison, Alexander Hamilton, Benjamin, Franklin, Edmund Randolph, Gouverneur Morris, James Wilson, and many other distinguished gentlemen.

The Convention actually met on May 15, 1787, in the Independence Hall and unanimously selected George Washington as the Chairman of the Convention. It was then decided that voting should be by States, each State having one vote; that the deliberations of the Convention should be behind closed doors and kept secret; that a quorum should be seven States and that a majority vote would be competent to ratify all decisions.

Within five days of its meeting the Convention made a momentous decision when it adopted Edmund Randolph's resolution : "that a national government ought to be established consisting of a supreme legislative, executive and judiciary." Thus, as Madison later wrote, the delegates "with a manly confidence in their country" simply threw the Articles aside and proceeded ahead with the consideration of a wholly new form of government. The delegates recognised that the predominant need was to reconcile two different powers—the power of the autonomous States and the power of the central government. They adopted the principle that the functions and powers of the national government, being new, general, and inclusive had to be carefully defined and stated, while all other functions and powers were to be understood as belonging to the States." They recognised, however, the necessity of giving the national government real power and, accordingly, accepted the fact that it be empowered among other things, to coin money, to regulate commerce, to declare war, and make peace.

At the end of sixteen weeks of deliberations and after ironing out many vexing problems, on September 17, 1787, a brief document incorporating the organisation of the new government of the United States was signed "by unanimous consent of the States present." But a crucial part of the struggle for a more perfect union was still ahead. The Convention had decided that the constitution would become operative when it had been approved by Conventions in nine out of the thirteen States. By the end of 1787 only three had ratified it. There was a widespread controversy. Many were alarmed at the powers which the constitution envisaged to give to the Centre. These questions brought into existence two parties, the *Federalists* and the *Anti-federalists;* those favouring a strong central government and those who preferred a loose association of separate States. The controversy raged in the press, legislatures, and the State conventions. Impassioned arguments poured forth on both sides. Patriots like Patrick Henry, Richard Henry Lee, and others opposed the proposed constitution on the plea that it contained no Bill of Rights and, consequently, it would prove dangerous to the liberties of the people.

The *Federalists* conceded to the demand of the inclusion of a Bill of Rights as soon as the new government was organised. This promise, which was carried out soon after the new government came into being by the adoption of the first ten amendments, enabled the wavering States to support the constitution. The Constitution was finally adopted on June 21, 1788.[2] The Congress of the Confederation enacted that the new government should go into effect on March 4, 1789. In the meantime Senators and Representatives were elected as the first members of the new Congress, and George Washington was chosen first President of the Union. Thus the old Confederation passed away and the new Republic entered upon its career.

Today, the United States of America consists of fifty States including the States of Alaska and Hawaii. The country covers an area of more than nine million square kilometers. Hawaii lying in the Pacific 3,200 kilometers from the mainland, and Alaska 3,170 kilometers (by the Alaskan Highway through Canada) to the north-west. It is a varied land of mountains, plains and plateaus. About two-thirds of the people live in towns and cities, one-third in rural areas. A publication of the United States Information Service, thus, describes the land and the people: "The United States is a country of great diversity—vast cities and small villages; roaring factories and quiet fields, busy streets and small churches for meditation. Geographically, there is a variety too—lakes and deserts; prairies and mountain ranges; rocky sea coasts and sunbaked plains. And at the core of this varied land are the people—the most varied of all, for they stem from countries and social levels throughout the world. But in spite of many differences, certain traditions—freedom, equality, individual rights are common to all and are taught in the home, in the church, and in the schools."[3]

**The Native Americans — A Tragic Story**

A tragic chapter of the American political tradition is the genocidal violence directed against the native American people who numbered about a million when the white emigrants set foot on the territory which is today known as the U.S.A. As distinguished with other native American cultures and nations such as the Mayas and Azteks of Mexico and the Incas of Peru, who had developed advanced civilizations, the North American Indians had remained sociologically at a less developed level. These forest dwelling communities lived partly by the cultivation of corn and partly by hunting and fishing. As Parkes points out, "Most of them were relatively peaceful, though a few, like the Iroquois in what is now upstate New York, became highly militant. Their political organisation was simple and fairly democratic. The chieftain of an Indian tribe had limited powers, and important decisions were made by the tribal council"[4].

Fields and hunting areas were held by these Indian communities in common and were not divided into private properties. Agriculture was often managed by the women while the men engaged in hunting and fighting. The European settlers learned from them how to grow maize crops, a number of vegetables, medicinal and narcotic plants, particularly tobacco. The Europeans began to occupy their common lands, clearing forests and claiming all such land as their private properties. This brought them into conflict with the Indians. There was continuous fighting between the two races. The average European "usually came quickly to the conclusion that the only good Indian was a dead Indian." That is how the genocidal war against the Indian people commenced.

Henry Parkes concludes: "For nearly three hundred years the record of white-Indian relations in the United States was a tragic story of misunderstandings, broken agreement, treacheries and massacres, Eventually the white peoples took possession of almost the whole country, and the surviving Indians, reduced to one - fifth of their original number as a result not only of warfare but also of the liquor and diseases brought by the white men, were herded on to reservations."[5]

By 1875 the United States army had broken the back of Indian resistance and their struggle

2. North Carolina ratified the Constitution in November 1789, and Rhode Island in May 1790, after Congress had threatened to deprive her of the privilege of trading with the Union, and secession had been threatened by several countries in which Federalist sentiment was strong.
3. *Facts about the United States* (1956), p. 4.
4. Parkes, Henry Bamford : *The United Stctes of America : A History*, p.23.
5. Ibid; p. 24.

for freedom and democratic rights. Most of the Indian communities were forced to settle on desert and semi-desert lands assigned to them. ''But no sooner had the program been completed than gold was discovered in the Black Hills country in the South Dakota reservation, and a flood of white adventures invaded the lands of the Indians. This led to the most serious Indian conflict, the serious war of 1876. In addition to being driven out of their land, ''the Plains Indians had also lost the economic base of their society. For countless centuries they had acquired food, clothing, and shelter from the meat and skins of the buffaloes who had roamed across the Plains in immense herds totalling perhaps 13,000,000 animals. But the white men almost exterminated them within a quarter of a century.''[6]

There is an important lesson for us to learn from this ongoing genocide of the heroic Indian race, lasting for three centuries, that the American political tradition is rooted in violence and there is a link between this genocidal violence and dropping of atomic bombs on two Asian cities of Hiroshima and Nagasaki as well as America's desire to retain nuclear weapons, capable of destroying the whole human race, for eternity.

But there is a silver lining to this tragic saga. Citizenship was ultimately granted to all Indians by the American Government in 1924. Some of the Indians became educated and to a large degree assimilated into white civilization. Their population, which was reduced to 200,000, by now, has started increasing slowly. They are now researching their ethnic cultural roots and may ultimately enrich the multi-ethnic character of America's political democracy by their free and equal participation. After all, it is their country which was usurped by the European emigrants and aggressors and the indigenous inhabitants fully deserve a share in the fruits of modern American development and enjoyment of democratic rights.

**The Institution of Slavery**

Another negative feature of the American political tradition has been the institutionalised oppression and exploitation of the Afro-American people who were brought from Africa by the British and other European slave traders and sold into slavery to the planter aristocracy of the southern United States. First, they had employed poor whites as servants on contract basis to till their fields but soon found out that a permanent labour force in the form of Negro slaves imported from West Africa was much more profitable. The first cargo of Negro slaves reached Virginia from Africa in 1619 and in the early years of the 18th century the black slaves almost completely replaced the white servants. According to Henry Parkes, "English slave-traders and American planters were led by economic interest to fasten upon American society an institution which was to cause irreparable harm for many generations to come ... a plantation-owning aristocracy was slowly emerging .. In accordance with the English feudal tradition, it was generally assumed .. that wealthy landowners were entitled to exercise leadership and become a ruling class ... the average small farmer accepted upper-class rule as being in accord with the laws of God and nature.''[7]

Thus it is not true to argue that America had no feudalist tradition. Slavery, as an institution, was even more oppressive and exploitative than medieval serfdom. The total slave population increased from nearly 800,000 to 4, 000, 000 in 1860. Most of them worked as farm labourers on the cotton plantations of rich landowners who sold their produce to British traders. Modern slavery, in its origin and usage was, therefore, an instrument of rising capitalism. In this respect, it can be distinguished both from Greco-Roman slavery and medieval European feudalism. Despite its profitability for the plantation landlord, the rising Northern bourgeoisie was opposed to it as these capitalists wanted the emancipated slaves of the South to come to the North and work in their factories as wage-workers.

Abraham Lincoln proclaimed the liberation of the slaves from January, 1863. But the social and political implications of this supposed emancipation were negligible. Direct disfranchisement of the Negroes was prohibited by the Fifteenth Amendment. But the same result could be obtained through indirect methods such as poll tax or literary tests which were fraudulently used even to disfranchise Negro graduates. Intimidation was another device to keep the blacks away from politics and voting. The black people gradually migrated to the Northern cities and practically almost to all other states in search of jobs and were concentrated in the urban ghettos and slums. They were continuous victims of discriminatory racial laws and economic exploitation.

6. *Ibid*; p. 424
7. *Ibid*; p. 32.

By long-established traditions, the Negro people were considered inferior to the whites, in sharp contradiction to proclaimed American ideals of liberty and equality. In the middle decades of the twentieth century these traditions were increasingly under attack. In the 1950's and 1960's there was a sharp increase in Negro militancy. The Supreme Court and Federal Administration had propounded new definitions of Negro rights but so far they had little concrete effect in improving social and economic conditions of the Negro masses. In the earlier phases of the movement, it was led by a moderate Negro priest, the Reverend Martin Luther King who believed in non-violent resistance to discrimination. The white racists resorted to violence killing many activists of the movement and thus wanted to intimidate all other agitators into submission. A civil rights march of 200,000 participants persuaded Congress to pass its most effective and comprehensive measure for Negro rights in July 1964.

This legislation, however, did not change the basic grievance of the Negro people which was simply economic misery. By mid-sixties a new group of young militants had largely taken control of all Negro organisations. Their favourite slogan was "Black Power." Starting in the summer of 1965, the mass poverty of the slum population produced a frightening series of violent explosions in several American cities. Rioting became widespread killing and injuring thousands and destroying properties on a huge scale. The police retaliated with brutal violence and shootings, thereby demonstrating to the Negroes the government's hostility to the cause of Black liberation. In April, 1968, Martin Luther King, the apostle of non-violence, was martyred and his assassination sparked renewed ghetto riots. The Negro freedom-fighters were crushed by greater state violence but the outcome of the struggle was the recognition by the ruling elites that greater participation will have to be allowed to the Black people in running the American political system in future and their living conditions will have to show a marked improvement both in social and economic spheres.

**Growth of Pluralist Democracy**

American society, according to S.E. Finer, "is highly pluralistic, where a myriad freely-formed associations co-exist, of all types and traditions." U.S. society "contains a large number of sub-cultures" based on ethnic origin, religion or region while government is founded upon, dependent upon and accountable to the organised public opinion in society, the social structure is relatively much more fragmented, unstable and inherent. It would be wrong to say that American society is open-ended. Yet there may be some truth in arguing that, unlike Europe, it does not have a traditional aristocracy, a sort of ruling elite, that dominates high positions of the state. At the other end of the scale, the American working class does not have a party of its own, on the European pattern, which can fight its class battles against the dominant class in American society.

There was indeed a landlord class before the war of Independence in 1776, which sided with the British Crown, so it was as much a civil war in thirteen colonies as a war of liberation against British rule. After the defeat of the British, the estates of the Loyalist landowners were confiscated. This was the first great blow at the landed aristocracy. The second occurred when the planters' aristocracy was destroyed in 1865 as a result of the defeat of the Southern confederacy in the Civil War. In the absence of a hereditary ruling class based on landed property, America has lacked any kind of permanent ruling elite in the European sense. However, the growth of capitalist industry gradually created a new upper class in American society based on the possession of wealth.

However, it is difficult to agree with S.E. Finer when he says: "Whereas the one great cleavage that still persists in Britain is the horizontal one between capital and labour, this is not only greatly attenuated in the United States, but is simply one amongst a great number of other cleavages, which are very different in kind"[8] While the social structures of all advanced capitalist countries in Europe and North America may not be exactly identical, the cleavage between capital and labour is their most characteristic feature everywhere. So pluralist democracy there functions within the constraints of a system that recognises the ascendency, even supremacy, of a power elite, to use a phrase popularized by C. Wright Mills in the context of the American society after the second world war.

In the United states, citizens enjoy universal franchise, free and regular elections, repre-

8. S.E. Finer, *Comparative Government,* p. 196

sentative institutions and fundamental rights. Both individuals and groups take full advantage of these rights, under effective protection of laws, and independent judiciary and a free political culture. As a result, no U.S. government can fail to respond to the desires and demands of competing interests, whether related to labour or capital, which are both treated supposedly on an equal footing. A leading theorist of this democratic-pluralist view argues that in this political system'' all the active and legitimate groups in the population can make themselves heard at some crucial stage in the process of decision.''[9] Other pluralist writers "suggest that there are a number of loci for arriving at political decisions, that business men, trade unions, politicians, consumers, farmers, voters and many other aggregates all have an impact on policy outcomes, that none of these aggregates is homogeneous for all purposes; that each of them is highly influential over some scopes but weak over many others; and that the power to reject undesired alternatives is more common than the power to dominate over outcomes directly.''[10]

Another writer, who himself disagrees with the plurist interpretation of the American polity, summarises it as follows in relation to the United States : ''Congress is seen as the focal point for the pressures which are exerted by interest groups throughout the nation, either by way of the two great parties or directly through lobbies. The laws issuing from the government are shaped by the manifold forces brought to bear upon the legislature. Ideally, Congress merely reflects these forces, combining them... into a single social decision. As the strength and direction of private interests alters, there is a corresponding alteration in the composition and activity of the great interest groups — labour, big business, agriculture. Slowly, the great weatherman of government swings about to meet the shifting winds of opinion.''[11]

There are elites in different social, economic, political, administrative, professional and other spheres. But they lack cohesion to constitute what C. Wright Mills called a 'power elite'. Elite pluralism is a guarantee that power in society will be diffused and not concentrated in a dominant class.

Harold J. Laski contested the Pluralist 'democracy' thesis in his monumental work entitled *The American Democracy*. Ralph Miliband criticised its assumptions in *The State in Capitalist Society*. Both have argued that in the ultimate analysis, capital dominates labour in the American political system. Business groups, rather than trade unions, finance and control political parties as well as state institutions.

## SUGGESTED READINGS

*An Outline of the American History,* Distributed by the United States Information Service.

Burns, J.M., and Peltason, J.W.: *Government by the People,* Chaps. III, IV.

Ferguson, J.H., and McHenry, D.E. : *The American System of Government,* Chaps. II, III.

Garner, J.W. : *Government of the United States,* Chap. IX.

Munro, W.B. : *Government of the United States,* Chaps. II, III.

Swisher, C.B. : *American Constitutional Development.*

9. R.A. Dahl, *A Preface to Democratic Theory,* pp. 137-138
10. R.A. Dahl, *et. al. Social Science Research of Business : Product and Potential*, p. 36.
11. R.P. Woolf, *A Critique of Tolerance*, p. 11.

# CHAPTER II

# Essentials of the American Constitution

### Constitution as a Document

The Constitution that emerged from the Philadelphia Convention was a model of draftsmanship, of linguistic elegance, of brevity, and of apparent clarity. It could not be otherwise, for it was designed to bring unity into the diversity of the new nation. Its provisions were built around several fundamental principles enshrined in the Declaration of Independence and upon these principles the American governmental system has since operated. So enduring and inspiring are these principles that the Constitution has, for more than two centuries now withstood the onslaughts of time and has served the country in war and peace, in calm and crisis, without fundamental change; 73 of the original 84 clauses of the Constitution stand exactly as they came from the fluent pen of Gouverneur Morris. The people of the United States have so much abiding faith in the sagacity, moderation, and "sense of the possible" shown by the makers of the Constitution that the original document is virtually worshipped. Until 1952, it was kept, along with the Declaration of Independence, in an illuminated shrine in the Library of Congress. Both these documents are now housed in the National Archives building in "a stronghold believed adequate to protect not only against the moth, the rust, the thieves but the atom bomb."[1] The words of Max Lerner are typical of the feelings of every American for their Constitution and its makers. He writes: "Here was the document into which the Founding Fathers had poured their wisdom as into a vessel; the Fathers themselves grew ever larger in stature as they receded from view; the era in which they lived and fought became a Golden Age. In that Age there had been a fresh dawn of the world, and its men were giants against the sky; what they had fought for was abstracted from its living context and became a set of 'principles' eternally true and universally applicable."[2]

The Constitution of the United States is the oldest written Constitution in existence and the shortest of the Constitution of any other nation, except the Chinese. It contains only 4,000 words, occupying ten or twelve pages in print which can be read in half an hour. Never was it in the minds of the Fathers of the Constitution to work out in all details a complete and final scheme of government for the generations to come. They sought merely a starting point and provided a skeleton to be clothed with flesh by customs, exigencies, national emergencies, economic development, and various other factors affecting the welfare of the nation. The Constitution is, thus, a living document; growing, developing and expanding, and it will continue to grow while the nation endures.

Gladstone called the Constitution of the United States, "the most wonderful work ever struck off at a given time by the brain and purpose of man." But actually its roots go deep, into the past. Some of its provisions are traceable to the *Magna Carta* and for other its authors drew ideas from the writings of John Locke, Montesquieu and Blackstone. Some basic concepts had an even more ancient origin, as the doctrine of consent. Following are the fundamental principles and distinctive features of the Constitution.

## ESSENTIAL FEATURES

### Popular Sovereignty

A prime feature of the Constitution is that it gives recognition to the principle of popular sovereignty. The right of the people to ordain, abolish and alter their own institutions of government was asserted in the Declaration of Independence. This inalienable right of the people received constitutional sanctity and the Preamble declares that "we the people of the United States......do ordain and establish this Constitution for the United States of America." The Constitution also provides the methods by which it may be altered or abolished and to institute new form and organs of government which are most

1. Brogan, D. W., *An Introduction to American Politics*, p. 2 f. n.
2. *Ideas for the Ice Age*, pp. 241-42.

likely to guarantee the safety and welfare of the people. It means that the voice of the people is supreme in all matters of political determination in the United States and they reign, said de Tocqueville, "as Deity does in the Universe."

The doctrine of popular sovereignty attributes ultimate sovereignty to the people and consequently substitutes constitutional system of government for arbitrary and despotic authority of any kind. When it is recognised that the people are the safest depository of supreme power and that the will of the people is a better guarantee of wise, efficient, and moderate government, it really means respect for human rights, and in the language of Abraham Lincoln, a government of the people, by the people and for the people. "The American system," James Madison said, "is based on that honourable determination which animates every votary of freedom to rest our political experiments on the capacity of mankind for self-government." Since the incorporation of the doctrine of popular sovereignty in the American Constitution, "it has," as Bryce said, "become the basis and watchword of democracy."

On the concept of popular sovereignty is erected another pillar of democracy. The Preamble states the great objects which the Constitution and the Government established by it are expected to promote: national unity, justice, peace at home and abroad, liberty and the general welfare. The early State loyalties were strong and loyalties to the States are still strong, but there is the triumph of the nation and unmatching prosperity of the people built on the bastions of democratic ideals which disdain privileges of all kind. The Preamble, in fact, echoes the immortal saying of Thomas Jefferson :

> The God who gave us life gave us liberty at the same time.
> Error of opinion may be tolerated where reason is left to combat it.
> The earth belongs always to the living generation.
> Nothing is unchangeable but the inherent and alienable rights of man.

**Limited Government**

A natural corollary of the doctrine of popular sovereignty is the concept of a limited government, possessing only such powers as have been conferred upon it. The Constitution-makers had, indeed, a horror of unlimited power. While assuming that the people were sovereign, the organisation and powers of their governments were set forth in written documents. After carefully stating what powers they wished the Federal Government to exercise, they left all residual powers to the States composing the Union. Next, they separated the three branches of government, Executive, Legislative and Judiciary, and made them to operate with elaborate checks and balances. The Constitution also imposed certain positive restraints on all public authorities in the country, high and low, by setting limits and bounds to the actions they might take and the manner in which they exercise their powers. These limitations are designed to protect the person, property and civil liberties of the individual against arbitrary encroachment by government officials. In some matters the individual is protected against the Central Government, in others against State and Local governments, and in still others against all governments, Central, State and Local. The Fifth and Fourteenth Amendments together forbid Congress and State Legislatures to deprive any person of life, liberty, or property without due process of law. In a strict sense every line in the Constitution is a vindication of the sovereign rights of the people and a limitation on Government. "In framing a government which is to be administered by men over men," wrote Madison, "the great difficulty lies in this: You must first enable the government to control the governed; and in the next place oblige it to control itself." In this sense the Constitution serves a dual function. It is a positive instrument of government enabling the Governors to control the governed. It is also a restraint on the Government, a device by which the governed check the Governors.[3]

**Federal System**

The delegates at the Philadelphia Convention met to find means for establishing an effective national government. At the same time, there was no serious discussion in the Convention of proposals which might have lowered the dignity of the individual States. It is true that Hamilton pleaded for subjecting the State Governments to rather complete Central control but, "while many applauded his eloquence and admired his youthful brilliance, none followed his suggestion."[4] They knew that the overwhelming majority of the people were too much deeply

3. Burns and Peltason, *Government by the People,* p. 92.
4. Gosnell, C. B., and Others, *Fundamentals of American National Government,* pp. 67-68.

attached to their State Governments and they would not permit a scheme of government aiming at their complete subordination to a Central Government. The framers of the Constitution were, therefore, confronted with a difficult task : how to make the Central Government strong enough for its duties without impairing rights of States; how to preserve the integrity of the States without weakening the Central Government. By heroic efforts they devised a plan of government which now carries the nomenclature of a federation.

The Fathers of the Constitution, thus, established a dual system of government within the States of the United States of America. There is the National Government with a complete set of its own governmental agencies—Legislative, Executive, and Judicial—exercising powers delegated to it by the Constitution which are of common national interest. Paralleling this system in each State is another complete set of Legislative, Executive and Judicial organs acting upon the persons within that State and exercising the residuary powers, that is, the powers not delegated to the National Government or denied to the States by the Constitution. Under the Constitution, therefore, the National Government is one of enumerated powers only. Residuary powers rest with the State Governments. Each of these two sets of Government within its own sphere is autonomous and independent; neither encroaching on the other. If any change is desired to be made in the division of powers it can be done only by amending the Constitution and the method of amendment is provided in the Constitution.

Fears and doubts in the minds of the people existed at the time of the adoption of the Constitution about the practicability of the federal union. Before 1861, lively arguments were waged over whether a State composing the Union had a constitutional right to secede. But the Civil War settled once for all this controversial issue. As the Supreme Court declared in *Texas* v. *White* (1869): ''The Constitution in all its provisions looks to an indestructible union, composed of indestructible states.'' No State, therefore, can break its constitutional bonds, for the Union is perpetual and indissoluble.

The United States of America is today the oldest federal union in existence. In fact, this type of polity originated therefrom. So successful it has been that many other countries have followed the American model. Quite a sizeable number of people spread all the world over even visualize a world organised on federal basis.

**Federal Supremacy**

Though the powers of the federal government are enumerated, yet federal law within its sphere is supreme over all state laws. This was the imperative necessity which the Fathers of the Constitution had fully realised. A federal union establishes two sets of government, each independent within its own sphere of jurisdiction. With demarcated powers and authority, conflicts between the National and State Governments are bound to arise and that, too, frequently. Such disputes might threaten the union if the Constitution does not provide for their settlement. The Constitution of the United States provides that disputes arising between the National Government and the State Governments must be settled in the Federal Courts. To guide judges in their decisions, the Constitution says: ''The Constitution, and the laws of the United States......and all treaties...........shall be the supreme law of the land.........'' It means that the Federal Constitution is paramount over all forms of law, State or National. Federal law, therefore, if validly enacted under the Constitution, ranks above the State Law. State Laws which conflict with the National laws or treaties may be declared unconstitutional ; and the Supreme Court at Washington is the tribunal of last resort for deciding all cases of conflict of jurisdiction between the Federal and State authorities. But treaties and Acts of Congress must be in accordance with and in conformity to the Constitution if they are to out-rank State Constitutions and laws. Compared with one another, Acts of Congress and treaties are on a plane of equality. If one conflicts with another, the measure passed most recently prevails.

A good example of the operation of the Federal supremacy occurred in 1956, when by a 6 to 3 vote the Supreme Court declared the Pennsylvania Sedition Act null and void on the ground that by passing numerous Federal sedition laws Congress ''had occupied the field to the exclusion of parallel state legislation.'' The Court also held that ''dominant interest'' of the Federal Government in protecting the nation against subversion, and the possibility that the administration of State sedition laws would conflict with the operation of the federal plan were further reasons for declaring the Pennsylvania Sedition Act inoperative.

## Separation of Powers

That the three functions of Government—Legislative, Executive and Judicial—must each be vested in a separate organ or department seemed to most Americans as undebatable as the laws of nature. James Madison wrote, in the *Federalist* : "No political truth is certainly of greater intrinsic value or is stamped with the authority of more enlightened patrons of liberty, than that..........the accumulation of all powers—legislative, executive and judiciary—in the same hands.....may justly be pronounced the very definition of tyranny." The theory of limited government, which formed the basis of political thought of that time, presupposed separating the three branches of government in order to prevent tyranny and absolutism. The Framers of the Constitution had, accordingly, no hesitancy about invoking the principle that political direction of authority should not concentrate in any one of the branches of government. They had rebelled against the tyranny of the British Government and wished to prevent such rulers from coming to power in the United States.

There is in the Constitution itself no direct statement of the doctrine of Separation of Powers. It is inferred from the opening sentence of each of the Constitution's three Articles. Article One begins by saying: "All legislative powers herein granted shall be vested in a Congress of the United States,.........."Article Two begins with the statement that : "The Executive power shall be vested in a President of the United States of America......." Article Three states: "The judicial power of the United States shall be vested in one Supreme Court, and in such inferior courts as the Congress may from time to time ordain and establish....." The Constitution-makers, thus, provided that the operation of each of the three processes of government should be entrusted to a separate agency. The Legislative process be operated by an independent Congress, the Executive process by an independent President and the Judicial process by an independent Supreme Court and subordinate courts.

On the basis of this arrangement the doctrine of Separation of Powers has from the first been early established as a principle of governmental organisation in the United States and it has been enforced by the courts exactly as any other legal rule. One of the many statements of it is found in the judgment of the Supreme Court in *Kalbourn* v. *Thompson.* The Court declared: "It is believed to be one of the chief merits of the American system of written constitutional law that all powers entrusted to government, whether state or national, are divided into three grand departments—the Executive, the Legislative and the Judicial; that the functions appropriate to each of these branches of government shall be vested in a separate body of public servants; and that the perfection of the system requires that the lines which separate and divide these departments shall be broadly and clearly defined. It is also essential to the successful working of this system that the persons entrusted with power in any one of these branches shall not be permitted to encroach upon the powers confided to others but that each shall by the law of its creation be limited to its own department and no other."

## Checks and Balances

But even the most convinced believers in the doctrine of the Separation of Powers acknowledged that an absolute separation of the three departments of government would make government itself impossible. Madison, the ardent advocate of the doctrine of Separation of Powers, wrote in the *Federalist,* that the principle "does not require that the legislative, executive and judiciary departments should be wholly unconnected with each other." He proceeded to prove that "unless these three departments be so far connected and blended as to give each constitutional control over the others, the degree of separation which the maxim requires as essential to a free government can never in practice be duly maintained." Unlimited power, it was argued, was always dangerous and the very definition of tyranny unless power was made a check to power. It could also be possible that different officials exercising different kinds of powers might pool their authority together and act in a tyrannical way.

The Framers of the Constitution, accordingly, introduced modification to the doctrine of Separation of powers when they came to details by setting up what are called 'checks and balances'. Having divided government into a threefold process and having assigned to each process a supposedly independent branch, the Philadelphia Convention authorised a very considerable amount of participation in, or 'checking' of the affairs of each branch by the other two. Expressed in simple words, instead of complete separation of the three branches of government, each was given enough authority in other functional areas to give it a check on its companion branches. The object was to make exercise of power limited, controlled and diffused. The final constitutional arrangement, thus, gives to each Department of government exclusive powers appropriate to that Department, but at the same time, these powers are shared by other Departments lest it should corrupt those who wield power. The Legislative branch is checked by President through his veto power but Congress, if it can muster a two-thirds vote, may enforce its view by overriding his veto. The Constitution also armed the President with another kind of veto, described as "pocket veto." This veto kills a Bill presented to the President for his signature if he does not assent thereto within a period of ten days and in the meantime Congress adjourns. The President is, thus, able to check Congress. The Legislative Department, in its turn, checks the Executive through its powers to appropriate money and to impeach. The Senate confirms the appointments made by the President and approves treaties made by him. The President can declare war on the authority and approval of Congress. The Supreme Court depends upon Congress in several respects, for instance, appropriations and appellate jurisdiction as also for the number of justices who serve on that tribunal. Congress may impeach and remove federal judges from office. The President is empowered to appoint Judges of the Supreme Court, and grant pardons, reprieves, commutations and amnesties. And the Supreme Court, shortly after the Constitution became operative, developed the practice of ruling on the validity of Acts passed by Congress and approved by the President. Such a system of checks and balances has been described by Bryce : "The ultimate fountain of power, popular sovereignty, always flows full and strong welling up from its deep source, but it is thereafter diverted into many channels, each of which is so confined by skilfully constructed embankments that it cannot overflow, the watchful hand of the judiciary being ready to mend the bank at any point where the stream threatens to break through."

No feature of American Government, national, state and often local, writes Frederic Ogg, "is more characteristic than the separation of powers, combined with precautionary checks and balances."[5] He further adds, "Nothing quite like it can be found in any other leading country of the world."[6] It was not the intention of Montesquieu, the author of the concept of Separation of Powers, to neatly divide the powers of government into three separate and distinct departments. What precisely he desired to establish was that power should be a check to power, *Le pouvior arrete le pouvior,* and in accordance with this dictum the Framers of the American Constitution divided government into three distinct departments and wove an intricate system of 'checks and balances' in order to avoid tyranny emanating from any source. They were thinking not alone of the tyranny of a monarch, as Montesquieu had thought, but the possible tyranny of the people or even of majority under a system of majority rule. "They knew, as we do, that no drug and no beverage is more intoxicating than power over men and that intoxicated men are not to be trusted as unrestrained rulers."[7] The Framers had, thus, a deep horror of the tyranny of the majority rule and they were not disposed to make any exception for a government conducted in the name of the people themselves. If the proper checks and balances are maintained no group is permitted to dominate and the programme of government is refined by the consideration from varied points of view.

The arrangement of government as established by the Constitution was designed to promote co-operation among the three branches of government as well as checking and balancing them. Without it the machinery of government, the Constitution Framers thought, would break down. But in actual practice, the system of checks and balances has prevented unity, frustrated leadership, divided responsibility and slowed up action. "Not all the objects which the Fathers had in view," says Herman Finer, "have been realized, but their main intention, effectively to separate the powers, has been achieved; for they destroyed the concept of leadership in government which is now so important in the present age of ministrant politics."[8] By establishing the Presidential system of government, the Fathers of the Constitution, adds Finer, "separated the executive sources of knowledge from the legislative centre of their application; severed the connection between those who ask for supplies

5. Ogg, F., *Essentials of American Government,* p. 38.
6. *Ibid.*
7. Swisher, Carl Brent, *The Theory and Practice of American National Government,* p. 62.
8. Finer, H., *The Theory and Practice of Modern Government,* p. 101.

and those who have the power to grant them; introduced the continuous possibility of contest between two legislative branches; created in each the necessity for separate leadership in their separate business; and made this leadership independent of the existence and functions of the executive." With powers divided between the Executive and Legislative Departments without any means of proper co-ordination, there is always inordinate delay to arrive at an agreement even on pressing matters which demand expeditious disposal. One branch of government may be operating on one policy whereas the other two may follow quite a different one, particularly when the Executive belongs to one party and the Congressional majority to another. Some Presidents have succeeded to bridge the gap separating them from the Legislature, but "while an emergency may bring temporary co-ordination, and the use of patronage can usually be counted upon to pave the way to some action, the national government is still torn into parts by the provision which the framers made for separation of powers."[9]

From the very beginning of the establishment of the Union, Congress has always emphasised its independent existence and its independent will. Whenever there had been unity of purpose and unity of will, as in an emergency like that of 1933, or during the two World Wars, Congress reasserted itself either by rejecting or by altering or modifying Presidential measures. And very often it does so "to draw attention to itself that he (the President) is not the unqualified master of the nation."[10] When in 1940 the United States became more and more involved in the Second World War, Congress conferred immense powers on the President. Protests soon followed both in Congress and outside that the President was gathering legislative power into his own hands violating the doctrine that the powers of government are sepa- rated by the Constitution. It was partly in response to this criticism that the new Congress, which commenced its life in January 1943 exhibited a revolt against the leadership of Roosevelt by rejecting many proposals which the President had recommended and accepting many Bills to which the President had objected including the two fundamental Acts which he had vetoed. The result is, as Finer remarks, "Legislative procedure had come to differ essentially from that in Britain and France, financial procedure is worlds apart; there is no co-ordination of political energy or responsibility; but each branch has its own derivation and its morsel of responsibility. All is designed to check the majority, and the end is achieved."[11] But, "At what cost?" Finer puts it. The cost, he replies, cannot be calculated unfortunately in dollars. And yet the principle of the Separation of Powers, as Professor Beard observes, " is indeed a primary feature of American government and is constantly made manifest in the practices of government and politics."[12] Somewhat ironically, even checks and balances "designed to promote over all equilibrium, often operate rather to aggravate than to ameliorate the ill efforts of separation, as for example, in the case of Presidential veto and senatorial assent to treaties."[13]

Corwin remarks that "lately the importance of this doctrine (the Separation of Powers) as a working principle of government under the Constitution has been much diminished by the growth of Presidential leadership in legislation, by the increasing resort by Congress to the practice of delegating what amounts to legislative powers to the President and other ad-ministrative agencies, and by the emergence in the latter of all the three powers of government, according to earlier definitions thereof."[14] The rise of political parties, a fact which was unforeseen by the Framers of the Constitution, and their functions have tended to redistribute the authority divided by the Constitution and have established the leadership of the Executive to a considerable extent indeed. Congress, too, has, not stood in the way of prompt and forceful action in times of emergencies. It has also on its own initiation delegated to the Executive the power of making rules and regulations in the pursuit of positive governmental programmes, and all such rules and regulations have the effect of statute law. Still there are limits beyond which the breaking down of the division cannot be permitted to go. Congress can delegate to the President a great

9. Zink, Harold, *Government and Politics in the United States,* p. 12.
10. Tourtellot, A. B., *An Anatomy of American Politics,* p. 83.
11. Finer, Herman, *The Theory and Practice of Modern Government,* p. 101.
12. Beard, C. A., *American Government and Politics,* p. 16.
13. Ogg, F. A., and F. O. Fay, *Essentials of American Government,* p. 39.
14. Corwin, S. E., *The Constitution and What It Means Today,* p. 2.

deal of power, but it cannot abdicate its functions and delegate its legislative authority to him. Even if it does, as Congress did in 1933, the Supreme Court intervenes declaring such delegation of authority void. The Supreme Court held in *Field* v. *Clark* (1892), that "the Congress cannot delegate legislative power to the President is a principle universally recognised as vital to the integrity and maintenance of the system of government ordained by the Const itution." The Court in 1935, unanimously invalidated the National Industrial Recovery Act partly on the ground that Congress had by that law delegated to the President its power to make what amounted to laws and, consequently, such a delegation of authority violated the principle of the Separation of Powers. However, the Court's subsequent policy has been to permit administrative rule-making provided the terms of the law are reasonably specific. And what is reasonably specific is, again, determined by the Court.

Both the principles of American government—Sepration of Powers and checks and balances—have frequently been a cause of confusion and conflict. They have resulted in great variations in the relationship bet- ween the President and Congress, variations in terms of personalities as well as external events. It is also impossible to deny, as Woodrow Wilson remarked, that "this division of authority and concealment of responsibility are calculated to subject the government to a very distressing paralysis in moments of emergency." Certainly, the Separation of Powers had been used, at various periods of American History to check and balance government so effectively that nothing could be accomplished even when the need for governmental action was most apparent. The more power is divided the more irresponsible it becomes. Power and accountability are the essential constituents of a good government. And today, when the area of governmental activity has broadened so enormously, can the system of Separation of Powers and checks and balances be reconciled with the need for strong, effective and responsible government ? This issue was brought into the forum of serious discussion by Woodrow Wilson's *Congressional Government,* and since then many proposals designed to bring about greater harmony in the Executive and Legislative Departments have been suggested. Woodrow Wilson had urged the superiority of a reasonable Cabinet system of government and his doctrine has been championed by effective writers. A few have, on the contrary, wielded the cudgels in defence of the American system. Some suggest a compromise by establishing a joint executive legislative Cabinet, that is, the Representatives and Senators should be included in the President's Cabinet. Still others suggest that Secretaries of the Government ('Cabinet' members) may be permitted to appear in the two Houses of Congress to explain Government's programme and policy, and answer questions. A few advocate changing the Constitution to prevent the Supreme Court from declaring law unconstitutional. Nothing tangible has come out so far although under the existing conditions the Separation of Powers on the whole is working better than the Framers could have foreseen. The system of checks and balances has been greatly modified by the political parties. Political parties join what the Founding Fathers had separated. The increasing important function of the President as legislative leader and other aspects of American political process owe their existence to adjustments necessitated by the Separation of Powers. Summing up the system of Separation of Powers and checks and balances, William Havard remarks, "The system as a whole is a going one despite a certain cumbersomeness in its general operation; to attempt to shift to some of parliamentary government, as a great many critics have urged, would seem to be as uncertain in practical effect as it is unlikely in terms of political feasibility."[15]

**Presidential Type of Government**

The system of government emerging from the principles of Separation of Powers and limited government is quite different from parliamentary democracy. Americans separated their institutions of government whereas there was fusion of governmental institutions in Britain. There was another important factor which influenced the deliberations of the Philadelphia Convention, Parliamentary democracy is unworkable without distinct political parties, each with its own programme and platform. The Framers of the Constitution forthwith rejected such a system of government which weakened national solidarity and created sharp cleavages and narrow loyalties. They strove to establish an energetic yet dignified Executive capable of enforcing laws firmly and one that should lend a note of stability.

15. Havard, William C., *The Government and Politics of the United States,* p. 33.

That is the Presidential Government.

It is a single Executive. The President is alone; one combining the functions of the Head of the State and Head of the Government. He is responsible to the people who elected him and to the Constitution to which he swore allegiance when he took office. He has no seat in the Legislature and is not accountable to that body. Nor does he depend upon it for the retention of his office; it goes by calendar.The Secretaries he appoints and make his 'Cabinet' and over which he presides, is not what Bagehot called a "Committee of the House of Commons." They are the President's nominees, appointed by him and responsible to him; it is his family. If any one is a member of the legislature at the time of his appointment, he must resign his seat therefrom before accepting such an appointment. The Executive department is, therefore, independent of and co-ordinate with the Legislative department and, as such, this system of government is the negation of Parliamentary system which joins the two, the Executive and the Legislative departments.

## A Rigid Constitution

A Constitution that is written and establishes two sets of government with defined powers and both are equal in status, must be rigid. The procedure for amending it is prescribed in the Constitution and is distinct from the procedure adopted in making a statutory law. The amendment of the Constitution also necessitates participation of both sets of government. It is, consequently, unlike that of Britain. The Constitution provides two definite methods for amending it and we discuss these methods in the later part of this Chapter. The methods are extremely elaborate and rigid and account for only twenty-six amendments during the last 204 years.[16] Yet, in spite of its rigidity, it is the remarkable adaptability of the Constitution that has enabled it to survive the rigours of democratic and industrial revolutions, the turmoils of the Civil War, the tension of a major depression, and the dislocation of the two global Wars.

## Judicial Review

As a corollary of the twin doctrines of a limited government and Separation of the Powers, there has developed the doctrine of judicial review by which courts exercise the power of annulling any Legislative measure or Executive action which in their opinion goes beyond the Constitution. The federal judiciary acts as a guardian of the Constitution. It interprets the constitution and decides the competency of Congress or State legislatures. If in the opinion of the courts a particular act is beyond the authority given to Congress or State legislatures or that it encroaches upon the domain of either of the two legislatures or seeks to deny or abridge the civil liberties of the people, then, such an act is declared unconstitutional or *ultra vires* and hence inoperative. Similarly, any act of the Executive , which is deemed in excess of or beyond its constitutional authority, may be held unconstitutional. When in 1933, Congress in a desperate effort armed the President with large discretionary powers to deal with the economic crisis, the Supreme Court intervened and in the *Panama Refining Company* v. *Ryan* held that this was an invalid delegation of legislative power to the Executive. Another part of the National Industrial Recovery Act authorised the representatives of each industry to make codes of fair practices applicable to all members of the industry under the supervision of the President and empowered him to promulgate the codes as law. This provision the Supreme Court also declared void.[17] "We think", the court rule "that the code making authority thus conferred is an unconstitutional delegation of legislative authority."

The doctrine of judicial review has been subjected to severe criticism during recent times. Its supporters defend it as necessary to preserve a free and limited government, and that it also helps to establish a stable government by guarding against legislative precipitancy and executive arbitrariness. The critics, on the other hand, assert that the courts infringe upon the Legislative and Executive functions and retard the working of representative government. It is further maintained that the process of judicial review delays pressing social and economic policies so necessary to meet changing conditions. We shall revert to the details of this controversy at its appropriate place.[18]

## The Bill of Rights

The Constitution as it emerged out of the Philadelphia Convention did not contain the Bill

16. The Twenty-fifth Amendment setting out the way the office of President is filled in the event of his incapacity became law on February 10, 1967.
17. *Schechter* v. *United States*, 295 U.S., 495 (1935).
18. See Chap. VII infra.

of Rights embodying the rights and liberties of the people. Repeated efforts were made towards the end of the deliberations of the Philadelphia Convention to secure a Bill of Rights to the draft constitution, but all failed. Omission, however, became such a burning issue that it nearly defeated ratification of the constitution by the States. The Federalists ultimately conceded to the demand of the inclusion of Bill of Rights as soon as the new government was organised and the First Ten Amendments were added to the Constitution in 1791 to constitute the Bill of Rights. In these provisions are enshrined the rights and liberties of the people of the United States. A zone of freedom is, thus, established wherein no government may legally operate. Although the boundaries so set by Articles incorporating the Bill of Rights are by no means self-defining, yet they do whatever can formally be done to safeguard those individual rights which history has found to be the hallmark of a just and free society—freedom of speech, of worship, the right of *habeas corpus,* from arbitrary deprivations except by due process of law, and no unreasonable searches and seizures.

A few peculiarities may be noted. Some rights are mentioned in the body of the Constitution, but most of them are contained in the first Ten Amendments, popularly known as the Bill of Rights. Additional guarantees are made in other amendments, especially the Thirteenth, Fourteenth, Fifteenth, Nineteenth and Twenty-fourth. In addition to the basic rights, the Constitution refers to privileges or immunities but does not define them Section 1 of the Fourteenth Amendment says, "No State shall make or enforce any law which shall abridge the privileges or immunities of citizens of the United States...." Without going into the legal complexities involved, civil rights are guaranteed to all persons whereas privileges and immunities extend only to citizens of the United States of America. "Although privileges or immunities," write Ferguson and McHenry, "have never been completely listed, experience suggests that they entitle citizens to have governmental protection while on the high seas or in foreign countries; expatriate, except when the nation is at war; have access of ports of United States, navigable waters, and agencies of the Federal Government, including courts of law; run for Federal office and vote for Federal officers; enjoy all rights and advantages secured by treaties; assemble peaceably and petition for redress of grievances; petition for writ of *habeas corpus;* enter the country and prove citizenship if questioned, and inform the Federal government of violation of its laws."[19] Privileges or immunities such as these, it is stated, are inherent in national citizenship and cannot be infringed either by the Federal or any State government. Aliens may be permitted to these privileges or immunities "as a matter of grace," but they cannot demand them as citizens can.

Rights in the United States are relative and not absolute. The Declaration of Independence refers to "natural" and "inalienable" rights and the Constitution too uses words that suggest the same ideas. For example, the first Amendment says, "Congress shall make no law respecting the establishment of religion, or prohibiting the free exercise thereof; or abridging the freedom of speech, or of the press; or the right of the people peaceably to assemble, and to petition the government for a redress of grievance". Amendment IX prescribes, "The enumeration in the Constitution of certain rights shall not be construed to deny or disparage others retained by the people." Some Judges of the Supreme Court maintained that the rights conferred by the First Amendment are either absolute or "preferred," but the majority view is that rights are relative.

Both the Federal and State governments are forbidden to deprive anyone of life, liberty, or property, without the due process of law. The due process of law means that anyone suspected of violating the law must be dealt with according to established rules and not arbitrarily. It also means that the government must be the product of law and "powers must be applied not erratically to some people or to others as governors see fit, but uniformly to all people similarly situated." Finally, due process of law means that acts of Legislatures and Executives, both at the Centre and the States, must be reasonable. There has been a good deal of controversy over what is reasonable and what is not. Before 1880, the courts had held that what was reasonable was a political decision and, therefore, reserved to Legislatures and Executives to determine it. Since that time, however, courts have said that the "due process of law" clauses require the courts to make the final determination as to whether actions or laws are reasonable or not. This has led

19. Ferguson, John H., and McHenry, Dean, E., *The American System of Government,* p. 118.

judges to disagree sharply among themselves and has provoked widespread criticism. Nevertheless, the courts insist that "due process of law" guarantees both proper procedure and the reasonableness of the law themselves.

## GROWTH OF THE CONSTITUTION

The Constitution as it emerged out of the Philadelphia Convention was a brief document consisting of a Preamble and seven Articles condensed into 89 sentences. Since then the Constitution has been steadily changing, developing, expanding and adapting itself to the new conditions. The Framers knew that if the Constitution was to endure, it must he a living Constitution capable of flexibility and adaptability to cater to the expanding needs of the people and the country. They did not try to reduce all details into writing but rather left room for the system to grow. Chief Justice Marshall observed in *McCulloch* v. *Maryland:* "A constitution is intended to endure for ages to come, and, consequently, to be adapted to the various crises of human affairs. To have prescribed the means by which government should, in all future time, execute its powers, would have been to change, entirely, the character of the instrument,and give it the properties of a legal code.It would have been an unwise attempt to provide, by immutable rules, for exigencies which, if foreseen at all, must have been seen dimly, and which can best be provided for as they occur." The American Constitution, as Bryce says, "has necessarily changed as the nation has changed, has changed in the spirit with which men regard it, and therefore, in its own spirit." A written Constitution does not mean a set of clear-cut rules which inexorably control political authorities in the discharge of their public duties. "It is," according to Charles Beard, "a printed document explained by judicial decisions, precedents and practices and illuminated by understanding and aspiration. In short, the real Constitution is a living body of general prescriptions carried into effect by living persons."[20]

The American Constitution is, thus, not the written fundamental instrument of the Federal Government framed at Philadelphia together with its amendments. It also includes statutes enacted by Congress, particularly those dealing with the organisation of the government and the powers assigned to the agencies Congress has created; executive orders and actions which enable the government to function efficiently; the monumental decisions of the Supreme Court interpreting the Constitution and thereby affecting the powers and operations of the government; and the innumerable political habits and governmental usages which chisel the Constitution to achieve the dynamic political purposes of the flourishing nation of fifty States. Considered in that manner, the difference between the Constitution of the United States and of Britain remains only of a degree. Judge Cooley defined a Constitution as "the body of rules and maxims in accordance with which the powers of sovereignty are habitually exercised." And Woodrow Wilson described the Constitution as a "vigorours taproot" from which have evolved "a vast constitutional system—a system branching and expanding in statutes and judicial decisions as well as in unwritten precedent."[21]

### Development by Statutes

As said earlier, the Constitution is concise and brief and its makers left many matters to be determined by the Acts of Congress in order to complete the framework of government. The Judiciary Article (Article III), for example, states only that there shall be "one Supreme Court," and "such inferior Courts as Congress may from time to time ordain and establish." The Judiciary Act 1789 laid the foundation of the American judicial system, fixed the number of Judges of the Supreme Court and their salaries, provided for the Court's organisation, and set forth its jurisdiction. This Act has been amended from time to time. Several times Congress has passed laws changing the number of Judges of the Supreme Court. Similarly, Article II of the Constitution assumes administrative departments, but it says almost nothing about them. The elaborate organisation of the federal administration has been established by statutes, with federal departments or independent agencies created, reorganised, or given new functions by Congress. Still more, nowhere does the Constitution prescribe the precise way in which minor officers of the Government are to be selected. Congress enacted a civil service law providing for their appointment by competitive examinations.

Some of the manifold laws of Congress are so basic that they are more a part of the total Constitution than many of the written sentences.

20. Beard, C. A., *American Government and Politics* (1932), p. 15.
Wilson, Woodrow, *Congressional Government*, p. 9.

The Presidential Succession Act, 1947 determines succession to the Presidency, and in the event of the death of Vice-President the officers who will follow him. It is the Act of Congress that specifies that members of the House of Representatives shall be chosen from single-member districts. The Act of 1887 fixes in detail the method of counting electoral votes. The Rules of Procedure and internal organisation and practices of Congress itself are the result of statutory authority.

After enumerating the various powers of Congress, the Constitution concludes with a sort of general grant empowering Congress to make all laws which it may deem necessary and proper for carrying into execution the jurisdiction assigned to it. This is sometimes called "the elastic clause" and many matters that Congress might not otherwise feel authorised to deal with have been covered under this provision. In the same way, by broadly interpreting the Constitution, Congress has established a huge defence establishment, created scores of administrative boards and bureaus, entered into the business of education, banking, insurance, construction, transporting, generating electric power, and found authority to regulate the economic and social life of a highly industrialised nation. The policy of liberal interpretation was first adopted by Chief Justice Marshall and his associates, and with rare exceptions has been followed by the Court throughout its entire history. The Supreme Court has declared as a fixed principle that it will show great respect for the interpretations of Congress and will overrule them only when they are clearly and palpably wrong. In *Ogden* v. *Saunders* the Supreme Court ruled : "It is but a decent respect due to the wisdom, the integrity, and the patriotism of the legislative body in which any law is passed to presume in favour of its validity, unless its violation of the Constitution is proved beyond all reasonable doubt."Charles Beard is of the opinion that this axiom is often disobeyed "and there would seem to be reasonable doubt when four Supreme Court Justices dissent from the views of the majority, it is a canon of interpretation which, if generally followed would eliminate many disputes over the meaning of the Constitution."[22]

**Development by Executive**

Likewise, the nation's Chief Executives have greatly helped to develop the Constitution by their decrees, orders and actions. It is no exaggeration that Presidents Jackson, Lincoln, and both Roosevelts have had an impact on the Constitution at least equal to that of any of the original framers. By their vigorous use of the Presidential powers they made the Presidency an office of Legislative as well as Executive leadership. In fact, a considerable number of political techniques in the United States rest on precedents set by one or another President. The Constitution is silent about the existence of the 'Cabinet' and the President's obligation to consult it. But Washington created one and began consulting it. This practice has been followed since then making the 'Cabinet' an established organ of the government that meets ordinarily once a week. The Constitution states that only Congress can declare war, but the Presidents have used their authority to send troops into action in such a way as virtually to assure the creation of a state of war. Woodrow Wilson did it and so did Franklin D. Roosevelt. Constitutionally, all treaties must be approved by a two- third majority of the Senate, but recent Presidents have often substituted 'executive agreements' or 'gentlemen agreements' for treaties made and concluded by themselves not requiring Senate approval and yet considered by the Supreme Court as binding. Such power, the Court held, is inherent in the nature of the executive function. President Franklin D. Roosevelt assumed uprecedented powers manning the entire life of the nation during World War II, under his authority as Commander-in-Chief of the armed forces.

Various Presidents have asserted that they acted within their powers in sending armed forces anywhere in the world in order to protect the lives and property of the Americans without obtaining the approval of Congress. Franklin D. Roosevelt maintained that the Constitution was broad enough to justify a far reaching programme of recovery and reform.

Then, by statutes passed under the authority of the constitutional provisions, and regulations made thereunder it is determined how commerce is carried on, the process of the naturalization, the procedure and the methods of taking census, obtaining of patents and copyrights. Congress has also delegated to various executive official and administrative boards the power to supplement statutes by regulations and orders. These regulations are not laws but they have the force of law. "They are, as it were, the twigs on

22. Beard, C. A., *American Government and Politics* (Tenth edition), p. 28.

the branches which have sprung from the main trunk, which is the Constitution.''[23]

**Development by Interpretation**

In the oft quoted observation made by Chief Justice Hughes lies the truth how the American constitutional system has developed through the process of judicial interpretation. He said, ''We are under the Constitution but the Constitution is what the judges say it is.'' The judges have to interpret the Constitution and the Constitution, like that of United States, written in concise, general words and phrases often admits of varying interpretations. And to give a phrase a new interpretation is to give it a new meaning; and to give it a new meaning is to change it. Almost every clause of the Constitution has been before courts and interpretations of the judges have virtually remade parts of the Constitution. The doctrines of implied powers, of inherent powers, of the sanctity of contracts and many other decisions of the Supreme Court stand unique in determining the course of government. The Supreme Court vested the power of dismissal in the President excluding the Senate altogether, although in terms of the Constitution it shares with the President the power of appointment. The Constitution entrusts the Federal Government with power to control the means of communication and transport. The Supreme Court ruled that the means of communication embraced telegraphic, telephonic and air media communication. In the means of transport were included rail-road and airways. A similar liberal interpretation was given to the ''armed'' forces broadening thereby the jurisdiction of the federal authority. The Constitution declares that ''Congress shall have power ...to regulate commerce.'' What is meant by the word commerce and what does it include, the Supreme Court has given it varied meanings to suit new situations and make it responsive to new problems. ''It has been the work of the Supreme Court, through its power of judicial interpretation,'' says Munro, ''to twist and torture the term'Commerce' so that it will keep step with the procession.''[24]

Edwards S. Corwin stated in 1938 that, ''the Supreme Court has handed down not far from 30,000 opinions...and of this total probably one-fourth at least comprises cases involving constitutional points.''[25] It means that by 1938 some7,500 decisions rendered by the Supreme Court involved interpretation of some part of the Constitution or appealed some fundamental doctrine of the American constitutional system. The court has the last word; its declaration of meaning is final, unless and until some subsequent decision gives yet a different interpretation.

Thus, judicial interpretation has been the most important method of determining the meaning of the Constitution. ''Whatever is enacted by Congress and approved by the Supreme Court,'' declared Howard Lee McBain, '' is valid even though to the rest of us it is plain violation of an unmistakable fiat of the fundamental laws. There is no limitation imposed upon the national government which Congress, the President, and the Supreme Court, ''acting in consecutive agreement, may not legally override. In this sense the government as a whole is clearly a government of unlimited powers; for by interpretation it stakes out its own boundaries.''[26] It means that the Supreme Court is the final arbiter on questions of constitutional interpretation and it determines what the Constitution realy means in the context of the new developments which emerge in the country. Woodrow Wilson maintained that the Supreme Court is ''a kind of constitutional convention in continuous session,'' constantly adjusting constitutional provisions to new circumstances. It adapts the document of 1789 to a changed nation of 1991 and 2000. The Supreme Court has, thus made the Constitution a living growing thing; has modernized it in each successive decade. And the Court's power to do so has not been brought about by any formal provision or amendment, but by interpretation of the Court itself in the case of *Marbury* v. *Madison* in 1803.

**Development by Usage**

The Constitution has, also, considerably developed, expanded and modified by usages and customs. What habit is to the individual, usage is to the State. Nations, like men, get into the habit of doing things in a given way. Habit then hardens into usage, which becomes difficult to change. These political customs and usages, which have their basis neither in laws nor in judicial decisions, are essential parts of the basic framework of the fundamental rules of the government. In

23. Munro, W. B., *The Government of the United States,* p. 69.
24. *Ibid.*, p. 70. The Supreme Court has rendered more than a hundred decisions in answer to what includes the term 'Commerce.'
25. Corwin, E. S., *The Living Constitution,* p. 78.
26. Corwin, E. S., *Supreme Court over Constitution,* pp. 93-4.

fact, the Constitution has been greatly modernized, amended and democratised through the development of the unwritten rules. They make flexible the otherwise rigid Constitution.

The most notable example is the extra-constitutional development of the political parties. It is scarcely possible to conceive of the Federal or State government in the absence of political organisations. Yet the Constitution makes no provision of the political parties. It is, again, the political parties which bring about co-ordination between the Legislative and Executive branches, and the Presidential office has been made more responsible to the people.

Another example is that of the 'Cabinet' which advises the President. There is no basis for this in the Constitution. The Congressional statutes have simply set up the departments from which the 'Cabinet' members are drawn up. President Washington found it useful to have a small group of advisers to whom he could look for counsel and other Presidents have continued with it and today, it is impossible to dispense with such a body. Senatorial courtesy, presidential nominating conventions, and other party activities, the residence requirements in the case of the Representatives all these rest, not upon the Constitution, but upon usage. Legislative Committees are not authorised in the Constitution, but custom and usage have made them as permanent as if they were.

A familiar example how a custom changes or supplements constitutional provisions is found in the procedure of electing the President. The Constitution makes a simple provision that he shall be elected by electors, chosen in their respective States. The Constitution-makers assumed that these electoral groups in the States would be actually deliberative bodies and that they would weigh the relative merits of each candidate before exercising their choice. But custom has rendered the Presidential election direct and nullified the intention of the Constitution-makers, if not the spirit of the document itself. To cite another equally important example, the Constitution provides that Money Bills must originate in the House of Representatives, but Senate's consideration of revenue measures by tradition is as much recognised as that of the House of Representatives.

President George Washington set precedent that the President should not seek election for more than two terms. This became a custom and was scrupulously followed till 1940 when Franklin D. Roosevelt sought election for the third time and was elected. He was elected for the fourth term as well. Under the stress of national emergencies and influenced by the dynamic personality of Roosevelt, the people succumbed to violation of the custom. But the popular opinion in the United States was so much in favour of the two-term election that eventually a constitutional amendment was made in 1951, limiting the tenure of office of the President to two terms. The custom became a constitutional law and that shows the sanctity of customs. The growth of the American Constitution has, therefore, heavily depended upon customs and usages. Professor Beard makes a bold statement when he says that customs and usages in the American system of government form as large an element as it does in the British Constitution.[27] This is, however, not exactly correct although customs have in some respect changed the basic characteristics of the American Constitution.

**Growth by Amendment**

The Constitution-makers prudently realised that future context of things and experience would need a change to foster the growth of the nation and, accordingly, they provided the process of the formal amendment of the Constitution. Article V provides—

"The Congress, whenever two-thirds of both Houses shall deem it necessary, shall propose amendments to this Constitution, or on the application of the Legislature of two-thirds of the several states, shall call a convention for proposing amendments, which, in either case, shall be valid to all intents and purposes, as part of this Constitution, when ratified by the Legislatures of the three-fourths of the several states, or by conventions in three-fourths thereof, as the one or the other mode of ratification may be proposed by the Congress...."

The process by which the Constitution is amended may be divided into two parts: proposing an amendment (initiation or proposal of the amendment), and ratifying an amendment. There are two ways in which an amendment may be proposed:

(1) by a two-thirds vote of both Houses of Congress, or
(2) by a national constitutional convention called by Congress upon request of the

27. Beard, Charles A., *American Government and Politics*, p. 60.

Legislatures of two-thirds of the States.

It may be ratified:

(i) by the Legislatures of three-fourths of the States, or

(ii) by special conventions in three-fourths of the States.

An amendment may be proposed by Congress, in which case it may be introduced in either House as a joint resolution, and must pass in both the Houses separately by a majority of two-thirds vote. Or an amendment may be proposed by a national convention convened by Congress upon request of the Legislatures of two-thirds of the States. Such a request might indicate a general nature of the amendment that is desired or it might simply ask that a convention be called for the purpose of revising the Constitution. Congress would then prescribe the number of delegates, mode of their election and the time and place of their meeting. But the difficulties inherent in this procedure have ruled it out as mode of initiating amendments to the Constitution.Therefore,all the amendments hitherto proposed have originated with Congress, that is, in accordance with the first method.

In whatever manner the proposal for amendments is initiated, Congress prescribes which of the two ratification procedures is to be followed : State Legislatures or state Conventions. State Legislatures have been used in all instances, except in the case of the Twenty-first amendment when Congress provided that State Conventions were to be used. When State Conventions are used, the Legislatures of each State decides on the size of the convention, how the delegates are to be elected, and the time and place of meeting. Two limitations were written into the amendment clause (Article V) and both these limitations were considered essential to safeguard the political compromises of the Constitution. These provided : (1) that no amendment prior to 1808 should affect the constitutional provisions barring federal interference with the slave trade or forbidding direct taxes not apportioned among the States according to population, and (2) that no amendment should deprive a State of its equal representation in the Senate without the consent of the State concerned.

A few important observations with regard to the process of amendment may be noted. The relevant Article in the Constitution does not say anything on the following points:—

(i) What does "two-thirds of both Houses" means; two-thirds of the total membership of each House or two-thirds of those present and voting? The Supreme Court has ruled that a two-thirds of those present and voting fulfils the constitutional provision. This interpretation has prevailed and it now means two-thirds of the members present.

(ii) It does not, also, say whether or not the action of Congress in voting to propose a constitutional amendment requires the assent of the President and Governors. The Supreme Court has held that amendment is solely a legislative function and the President need not sign proposed amendments before they are sent to the States.[28] Nor do the State Governors need to sign instruments of ratification.

(iii) Can a State Legislature, which has ratified the constitutional amendment, later before the necessary three-fourths has been obtained, rescind its previous decision? Congress by its resolution has declared that it cannot. But a State Legislature may, however, first refuse to ratify it and, then, at a later date may ratify it.

(iv) The Constitution does not fix any time limit within which the ratification must be completed. But Congress may do it on its own initiative as it was done in the case of the Eighteenth, Twentieth, and Twenty-first amendments and fixed seven years as the maximum time for ratification in each case. The Supreme Court has held that it is within the competency of Congress.

(v) Can a State Legislature, when a proposed amendment comes before it for ratification, refer it to the people for their approval? It has been held that it may be done provided the State Legislature itself takes formal action after the people have given their verdict. But a State Legislature, may not submit an amendment to the people for final decision, thereby abdicating its own powers. The Supreme Court has held that it was neither within the constitutional power of National or that of the State governments to alter the methods of ratification which the Constitution itself prescribes.

(vi) Are there any limitations, express or implied, on the subject-matters of amendment? The Constitution provides for only one limitation, that no State shall be deprived of its equal representation in the Senate without its consent. This limitation is designed to protect individual States or a small group of them from a discrimi-

28. *Hollingsworth et al* v.*Virginia.*

natory action by a dominant three-fourths of the States. Legally, therefore, any provision of the Constitution, except for a State's equality of representation, can be altered by amending the Constitution.

The process of amending the Constitution is difficult and circuitous and, consequently, there had been only twenty-six amendments during a span of two centuries since the Constitution became operative in 1789. The first ten amendments were "the price of ratification" and were embodied in 1791. The Constitution of 1789 was accepted by the States of Massachusetts, Virginia and New York on the definite assurance that a series of amendments guaranteeing individual rights would be speedily added to the original document. These amendments are called the Bill of Rights. The next sixteen amendments, the twenty-sixth ratified on July 5, 1971, brought about various alterations, deleting many provisions and adding new ones to fit in the needs of time and consistent with the political aspirations of the people.

Following are some of the important points of criticism of the amendment procedure:—

1. The inconsistency of majority rule requiring two-thirds votes of both Houses of Congress and ratification by three-fourths States is really inconceivable. Even two-thirds votes of Congress are difficult to secure. So far, out of thousands of resolutions introduced in Congress only twenty-nine had mustered the necessary two-thirds votes of both Houses. Out of these twenty-six have been ratified by the necessary number of States and have become effective. It has been suggested that only a majority vote in both Houses of Congress and ratification by two-thirds of States should be made necessary to effect constitutional amendments. But the proposal has not evoked sufficient enthusiasm.

2. For ratification, States rather population are required. It is asserted that this is too conservative a system, for thirteen small States may pool together and hold up the aspirations of an overwhelming majority of population. This is tantamount to a veto of an absolute nature. In other words, about one-tenth of the people of the nation, distributed in the thirteen geographical districts, can prevent nine-tenths of the people from effecting innovations in their system of government.

3. The submission of amendments to Legislatures instead of to ratifying conventions has been criticised as undemocratic. It means that the ratification is to be effected by a relatively small number of persons who happen to be in the Legislatures. And these legislatures had been elected for other purposes than the issue involved in the constitutional amendment. This objection can be removed by providing for ratification through State conventions. When the Twenty-first amendment was submitted to the ratification of State conventions it was hoped that a new precedent had been set and that in future this democratic method would continue to be followed. But when Congress in 1947 proposed the Twenty-second amendment, to limit the Presidential tenure, it reverted to the previous practice and submitted the amendment to state Legislatures for ratification.

4. Finally, there is no prescribed time limit for ratification unless specifically determined by a resolution of Congress as in the case of Eighteenth, Twentieth and Twenty-first amendments.[29] Absence of such a prescription makes the issue a plaything of the States and indefinite delay takes away the purpose underlying the amendment. For example, the child labour amendment was proposed by Congress in 1924 without specifying the time limit for ratification. So far only twenty-eight States have ratified it, the last one being Kansas in 1937.[30] On one occasion Ohio ratified an amendment submitted 80 years earlier.[31] Connecticut, Georgia and Mas sachusetts voted in 1939 to ratify the first Ten Amendments— 150 years after they had been submitted to them for their ratification, although these constituting the Bill of Rights, have been operative in those as in other States since 1791. On the whole the time required for ratification "has been rather short, varying from three years and eleven months for the Twenty-second Amendment to seven months for the Twelfth. The Twenty-third was ratified in nearly record-breaking time : slightly over nine months."[32]

Amendment is an integral part of the Constitution and the twenty-six amendments made to

29. The Supreme Court in *Dillon* v. *Miller* (1921) held that proposed amendments "died of old age" unless a time limit was stated. But in 1939 the Court ruled differently in *Coleman* v. *Miller* and held that the child labour amendment was still "alive" after fifteen years and that the question of a time limit was political.
30. Burns and Peltason, *Government by the People,* p. 108. But the prohibition of child labour under the Fair Labour Standards Act, 1938 has substantially eliminated interest in the pending amendment.
31. Ferguson, J. H. and McHenry, D. E., *The American System of Government,* p. 70.
32. *Ibid.,* p. 73.

date have an equal influence on the American political life as any other factor that has contributed to the development of the Constitution. All the amendments, except the Twenty-Second, seem to have had direct or indirect democratising tendency. The expansion of suffrage and lowering the voting age, the direct election of Senators, the protection of individual rights, the social and economic implications of the graduated income-tax and even the adjustments in Presidential elections and the dates of assuming office "have all made some contribution to the conception of a government resting on as broad a basis of popular sovereignty as possible."[33]

## FEDERAL CENTRALIZATION

### Growing Needs of the State

Centralization is the shifting of governing authority from lower or member units to higher units, with a tendency for power to grow at the top. Federal centralization is, accordingly, the tendency for the natio- nal government to assume influence or control over functions which formerly were considered under State jurisdiction. The Constitution limited the authority of the Central Government by prescribing that Congress might exercise only those powers expressly enumerated while the residuary powers were given to the States. This was specifically stated in the Tenth Amendment. But it was inevitable in the state of things in which United States began its career as a federation that the process of centralization should grow rapidly and the development in the expansion in the power and authority of Federal Government had been continuous. There were three principal factors which significantly contributed in increasing federal authority. The first is the part played by Federal Judiciary. Secondly, the express powers of Congress have considerably expanded and in effect added to by legislative, judicial and administrative interpretation. Finally, certain express powers of Congress, particularly the commerce clause, have been chiefly responsible for centralizing tendencies.

"A chief actor in the entrenchment of a strong federal government was John Marshall of Virginia, staunch Federalist and Chief Justice of the United States from 1801 to 1835."[34] His decision in the famous case of *Marbury* v. *Madison* gave the power to the courts to interpret the Constitution and declare Acts of Congress unconstitutional, although the Constitution itself contained no express provision to this effect. In 1819 Marshall, again, in the case of *McCulloch* v. *Maryland* established the doctrine of federal supremacy over the States, and enunciated the principle of implied powers[35] of Congress. Both these doctrines are landmarks which made federal centralization inevitable. But Marshall went even beyond the doctrine of implied powers by invoking the theory of resultant power. A resultant power is a power that is deducible from two or more express powers. "Thus where the doctrine of implied powers has a broadening effect, the concept of resultant powers has no limits at all except the judiciary itself exercises restraint."[36]

Marshall also declared in *McCulloch* v. *Maryland* that the United States was a union of the people and that the Central Government was both in theory and in fact a national government resting directly on the people. He aimed to emphasise that the federal government was held to have its powers direct from the people and not by way of the States. The Constitution only established a framework in which a national government could and should develop. This point was further stressed by Justice Holmes in *Missouri* v. *Holland.* The words of the Constitution, he observed, "called into life a being, the development of which could not have been foreseen completely by the most gifted of its begetters. It was enough for them to realize or to hope that they had created an organism; it has taken a century and has cost their successors much sweat and blood to prove that they created a nation." The nation has grown and expanded and so have its needs. Since 1787 United States has grown from a poor, sparsely populated, agricultural country to a rich and densely populated and highly integrated industrial nation. Until recently the United States had no positive foreign policy. Her isolated geographic position, a favourable balance of power in Europe, and no embroilment in Asia, enabled her to keep aloof and repose in her security. Today, it has all changed and the United States takes on herself the burden of maintaining world peace and assumes the role of super-power. The obvious result is that all these

33. Havard, William C., *The Government and Politics of the United States,* p. 41.
34. Dimock, Marshall Edward and Dimock Gladys Ogden, *American Government in Action,* p. 70.
35. An implied power is a power that is deducible from an express power, *See ante.*
36. Dimock, M. E., and Others, *American Government in Action,* p. 134.

changes involve a powerful impact on government. The altered social, economic, political and international conditions require re-allocation of responsibilities and the overall general tendency has been strengthening the national government at the expense of the States. With all these changes there has been simultaneous change in people's attitude towards the national government, irrespective of the party in power. Determined to make America great and strong, the platforms of both the major parties reflect the wishes of the people and their programmes call for greater activity by the Central Government helping its domain to grow.

In fact, from the beginning the logic of events has helped the national government's sphere to expand. But the real swing in the Federal-State relations begins from 1860 when the Federal Government began to exercise what had hitherto been regarded as exclusively the reserved powers of the States. Many factors and various devices have contributed to that end and the National Government is today doing more things, spending more money and coming much closer to the people than was contemplated by the framers of the Constitution. It engages in such activities as public health, agriculture, poor relief, highway construction, labour relations and many others and yet the formal constitutional powers of the national government remain the same today as they were in 1789.

An important way to bring about the present Federal-State inter-relations is the system of grants-in-aid, that is, the amount of funds flowing from the national to State treasuries. The Committee of the Council of State Governments defines federal grants-in-aid as "payment made by the national government to state and local governments, subject to certain conditions for the support of activities administered by the states and their sub-division."This aid is given under the power granted in the taxation clause[37] which authorises the use of Federal funds to provide for the "general welfare." The practice is based on the assumption that some activities conducted by the States and local governments, like housing, agriculture, education and health, are matters of "general welfare" and, consequently, justify support by the Federal Government. Then, the revenue resources of the Federal Government are enormous as compared with those of the States. Grants-in-aid are the means by which the Federal government provides aid in financing State functions which otherwise would have been either insufficiently performed or tardily performed. Finally, the modern idea of the functions of the State does not compartmentalise its role within geographic jurisdictions of administration. All functions are national in scope and though there is virtue in their local administration, yet, they must be standardised at a high level. The Central Government, therefore, gives to the States financial aid up to a certain proportion of the total amount of expenditures on the beneficent departments, on the condition that the States and their local units administer the programme in accordance with rules laid down by Central Government.

The earliest grants made to States were in land or money without the imposition of conditions on their use. Today, the grants given are almost wholly conditional. This means that grants are made for specified purposes and subject to conditions stipulated by Congress or the administrative agency. It is a matter of common experience that one who gives money has a loud voice in calling the tune. Grants-in-aid are a prolific source of centralisation. They offer "a middle ground between direct Federal assumption of certain state and local functions and their continuation under exclusive state and local financing, with haphazard coverage and diverse standards. It makes possible the achievement of national minimum standards, yet retains most of the benefits of administration close to the people."[38] Thus, by the grants-in-aid the Federal Government is able to promote programmes in schemes of social services which it could not do otherwise without amending the Constitution.

Federal grants have increased stupendously, in 1911-12 their total was near about $ 5 million, but during the mid 1950's, the total was about $ 3 billion annually. In the late 1960's, all forms of Federal grants, including grants-in-aid, shared revenues, emergency grants, and payments to individuals within States exceeded $ 15 billion per year.[39] This figure enormously swelled in the decades to follow.

One of the vexatious problems of the Confederation period was the trade barriers which the States had been erecting against one another. The Annapolis Conference of 1786, which led di-

37. Article 1, Sec. 8, Clause 11.
38. Ferguson, J. H., and McHenry, D. E., *The American System of Government,* p. 174.
39. *Ibid.*

rectly to the Constitutional Convention of the following year, was really summoned to relieve the embarrassing commercial situation so created. The Constitution, therefore, contains a clause conferring upon Congress the "power to regulate commerce with foreign nations and among the several States....."[40]. In defending this power of Congress, Hamilton wrote in the *Federalist*[41] that "a unity of commercial as well as political interests, can only result from a unity of government." What Hamilton meant was that the political power "must be commensurate in its range with the matter which it is permitted to regulate."[42] Today, the problem of inter-State and foreign commerce is not the same as it existed in 1787. It is now a gigantic problem and includes all commercial activities covering production, buying, selling, and transporting of goods. The power of Congress to regulate commerce should, accordingly, grow at equal pace with the growth of that commerce. The Supreme Court has consistently accepted this argument. Laws have, therefore, been enacted, upheld by the Supreme Court and subsequently administered in such fashion as to indicate that apparently no appreciable area of economic life lies outside the sphere of federal intervention.

The power to regulate is the power to prescribe rules by which commerce is governed, that is, the right to foster, promote, protect and defend all commerce that affects more states than one. Since today there are few aspects of the United States economy that do not affect commerce in States more than one, and as the term commerce now includes the whole complex mass of transactions covered by the word 'business,' most business transactions are subject to national regulation. As such, significant aspects of employment as collective bargaining, hours of work, wages, working conditions, and the conduct of strikes in large sectors of American industry have been largely withdrawn from the jurisdiction of the States. Summing up the astounding expansion of Federal Government's power under this heading, Ferguson and McHenry remark," in the decade of 1930 to 1940 alone, Congress has validly employed the commerce power to regulate labour relations, control radio broadcasting, provide retirement system for railroad employees, fix minimum wages and maximum hours, regulate inter-State bus and truck lines, control small streams even of doubtful navigability, regulate stock exchanges, forbid transportation of strike breakers, punish extorters, kidnappers and vehicle thieves."[43] All these are federal encroachments on the constitutional powers of the States.

The Central Government is constitutionally responsible for protecting the country from external aggression and, when necessary, for waging war. The problem of common defence today is entirely different from what it was in 1787. No country can afford to wait for defence until war is declared. It must always be prepared to ward off the probabilities of war and to win, if it actually comes. It means the ability to man the industrial resources of the country and to apply nation's scientific knowledge to the task of defence. Everything from the physics course taught in schools to the conservation of national resources and the maintenance of economy affects the war-making potential. When the country is in the midst of hostilities it must gear up the entire life of the nation in a bid to win war. It means to conscript men, control all the channels of production, transportation, distribution, and in fact every aspect of economic and social life in the country.

And when the war ceases the government must tackle problems of demobilization and post-war reconstruction. The change-over from wartime conditions to peace-time conditions must be smooth and it needs proper planning and co-ordination. It must also give aid to war veterans and to remove the maladjustments in the economy caused or aggravated by war. "In brief, the national government has the power to wage war and wage it successfully. In total war this means total power. As long as we live in a world where war is an ever-present possibility, the defence activities of the government will be many and varied, and they will impinge on all aspects of our lives."[44]

The people of the country at all stages of its development had always looked to the national government for solving their problems. Their desire to make the country big and prosperous necessitated "big business, big agriculture, big labour", and, "all add up to 'thirties big govern-

40. Article I, Section VIII, Clause 3.
41. No. 11.
42. Gensell, C.B. and Others, *Fundamentals of American System of Government,* p. 73.
43. Ferguson, J. H. and McHenry, D.E., *The American System of Government,* p. 122.
44. Burns and Peltason, *Government by the People,* p. 142.

ment.'' The World Economic Depression of 'thirties of the present century considerably enhanced the prestige of the Central Government. There were over twelve million unemployed out of a total labour force of fifty million, and many more million were destitute. The resources of the states were absolutely inadequate to give relief on such a mass scale and simultaneously devise means to steer the country out of economic and financial difficulties. The Federal Government came to the rescue of the people and the bold policy of Roosevelt led the country to the path of recovery.

Simultaneously to the increased confidence of the people in the national government, there has been decreasing tendency to holding on to the traditional ties of loyalty to States. This is due partly to the development in the means of communication and transport and, consequently, greater mobility of the population. Secondly, most of the States had no independent existence prior to their becoming members of the Union. There developed, accordingly, no strong feelings of local pride and the original settlers long looked to the Central Government for their betterment. The States themselves, too, are in a way responsible for it. Even within the limits of their jurisdictions and their resources most States have not kept abreast and, thus, failed to instil local loyalty. Washington D.C. is ''almost a model of perfection when compared to some state capitals which are graft-ridden, inefficient, and unable to provide the services that the people expect.''

**Co-operative Federalism**

All this process of centralization raises a question as to whether the United States is any longer properly classified as a federation. ''Constitutionally speaking,'' observes Griffith, ''it would appear as though the Supreme Court would no longer impose any substantial barriers to national legislation in the economic sphere as constituting an invasion of the states' rights. As for all other areas of constitutionlly permissive governmental action, it would appear to be open to the National Government to dictate or at least to dominate policy through the use of conditional subsidies.''[45] He concludes that exclusive jurisdiction, even in the most traditional State and local functions, the smaller units may no longer have. But autonomy they still have in large measure. ''Their vitality is still very great. The same social conscience that was among the factors causing the Supreme Court to let down the barriers to increased governmental activity nationally has had its counterpart in its wide extension of the sphere of permissible state activity.''[46] Congress too, in practice has shown very considerable restraint in curtailing State discretion through conditional grants-in-aid. Internal-level co-operation has considerably increased and regional administrative units, often federal in nature, are created with problems (chiefly river basin conservation and development) on wider than State lines. Loyalties to the States are still strong among all the fifty States. ''The traditional advantages of federalism—experiment, differentiation, political education, diffusion of power—still have great opportunities for expression in the United States to a degree very largely lost in Britain.''[47] But in term of governmental functions, it cannot be denied that federal government has assumed inconceivable powers and federalism, as practised in the United States, is today no obstacle in assuming functions which in the interest of national strength it is important to handle at the national level.

But as Carl Friedrich says, ''It would be a mistake........., to declare federalism in the United States dead; in some areas the states have recaptured some of their power through more vigorous insistence on their participation in the federal administration.''[48] A new con ception of federal interrelations has developed lately. Co-operative federalism, as it is described, emphasises mutual administrative assistance among the different levels of government instead of administrative competition and conflict. ''Co-operative federalism,'' observes Potter, ''may be, as some charge, often less efficient, surreptitious centralization. It may be, as others charge, often less efficient than full centralization. But in view of the fiscal supremacy of the national government on the one hand, and the strength of local political sentiments on the other , it is almost certain to remain one of the most important aspects of the administrative element of American federalism.''[49] According to Richard M. Leach, a United States expert on federalism, ''In operation, feder-

45. Griffith, Ernest, S., *The American System of Government*, p. 24.
46. *Ibid.*
47. *Ibid.*, p. 25.
48. Friedrich, C. J., *Constitutional Government and Democracy*, p. 218.
49. Potter , A. M., *American Government and Politics*, p. 66.

alism requires a willingness, both to cooperate across governmental lines, and to exercise restraint and forbearance in the interests of the entire nation.''

The traditional theory of federalism stands modified to fit into the needs and demands of the present conditions. No society can afford the luxury of a rigid division of powers which was possible in the social and economic conditions of the eighteenth century.

There is, accordingly, not much of substance in President Reagan's assertion that he made on January 20, 1981 in his inaugural address. The new President emphasised that it was his intention ''to curb the size and influence of the Federal establishment and to demand recognition of the distinction between the powers granted to the Federal Government and those reserved to the states or the people.'' He reminded the nation that the Federal Government ''did not create the states; the states created the Federal Government.'' This is true, but the course of United States' constitutional development now extending to more than two centuries cannot be so summarily changed. It is an unavoidable conclusion that older patterns of decentralization—whether in the form of local autonomy under a unitary system or of States' rights in a federal union ''were doomed to dissolve in the corrosive acids of twentieth century politics, economics and technology: virtually all the great driving forces in modern society combine in centrist direction.''[50] The traditional theory of federalism is a political anachronism now. Vile expresses the opinion that co-ordinate status of the federal and regional governments is as difficult to sustain as their independence in the spheres assigned to them. Their status of equality ''may be defensible in legal terms, but it is very difficult to interpret in terms of power and influence.''[51] The leadership of the federal government is unchangeable and all federal unions have moved alike in the same direction.

Of late, a new concept of ''creative federalism'' has emerged in the United States and is widely advocated. It puts emphasis on getting the job done without regard to who is in the pivotal role, the centre or the units of a federal polity. This is in sharp contrast to President Reagan's commitment to ''revitalised federalism'' which he made in his inaugural address. It is defined as a return of authority and revenues to State and local governments; the essence of the federal polity with which United States started her career.

## SUGGESTED READINGS


Beard, C.A. : *American Government and Politics,* Chaps. II, III.

Beard, C.A. : *The Supreme Court and the Constitution.*

Benjamin Barker and Stanley H. Friedelbaum: *Government in the United States,* Chaps. 1 to 3.

Birch, A. H. : *Federalism, Finance and Social Legislation in Canada, Australia and The United States.*

Bowie, R.R. and Friedrich, C.J., (Eds.) : *Studies in Federalizm.*

Benson, George, C. S. : *The New Centralization.*

Brogan, D.W. : *The American Political System,* Chaps. I, II.

Brogan, D.W. : *An Introduction to American Politics* , Chap. I

Burns and Peltason: *Government By the People,* Chaps. IV, V.

Carr, R.K. : *The Supreme Court and Judicial Review.*

Clark, J.P. : *The Rise of a New Federalism.*

Corwin, E.S. : *The Constitution and What it Means Today.*

Corwin, E.S. : *Understanding the Constitution.*

Dimock, M.E., and Dimock, G.O .: *American Government in Action,* Chaps. II, III.

Elazar,. Daniel, J. : *The American Partnership.*

Ferguson, J.H., and McHenry, D.E.: *The American System of Government,* Chaps. IV, VI.

Finer, H. : *The Theory and Practice of Modern Government.*

Griffith Ernest : *The American System of Government.*

Irish, Marian D. and Prothro,James W. : *The Politics of American Democracy,* Chap. IV.

Lees, John D. : *The Political System of the United States,* Chaps. 1-3.

McBain, H.L.: *The Living Constitution.*

Munro, W.B.: *The Government of United States,* Chaps. IV, V.

Nicoll, Donald E. (Ed.) : *Creative Federalism.*

Swisher, Carl, B: *American Constitutional Development.*

Swisher, Carl, B: *The Theory and Practice of American National Government,* Chaps. 1,2,4.

Thursby, Vincent V.: *Inter-State Co-operation.*

Vile, M.J.C.: *The Structure of American Federalism.*

Zink, H. : *A Survey of American Government,* Chaps. III, V.

Wilson, Woodrow : *Congressional Government.*


50. Lipson, L., *The Great Issues of Politics,* pp. 315-16.
51. Vile, M. J. C., *The Structure of American Federation,* p. 199.

# CHAPTER III

# The Presidency

## ORGANISATION, MODE OF ELECTION, AND POWERS

### A Single Executive

One of the grave weaknesses in the organisation of government under the Articles of Confederation was the absence of executive authority to carry into effect the determinations of Congress and the treaties of the United States. The imminent need with the framers of the Constitution at the Philadelphia Convention was to provide an executive department co-ordinate with the legislative department. It was, accordingly, declared that the executive power should be vested in an officer called the President of the United States.

The basic considerations dominated the discussions relating to the Presidency. The first was the need to have an "energetic yet dignified" executive capable of enforcing national laws firmly, and one which should lend a note of stability to the new government. The other was, a fear that the people would be critical if the executive was made too strong. Many alternatives were suggested and discussed. Men, like James Wilson, wanted a strong executive independent of the legislature. It was argued, and Locke and Montesquieu were freely quoted in support of their advocacy, that if, the Separation of Powers was desirable, it was logical to have three co-ordinate branches of government with no one predominant over the others. There were others who wished to have the "executive magistracy" appointed by Congress and subject to its mandate. Some delegates favoured one-man executive; others advocated a plural executive composed of two or three men possessing equal power.

The final decision on the Presidency was a compromise. The President was to be single and independent of the legislature. Even after the single executive was agreed upon, many argued to associate with the President an executive council which would share with him the exercise of executive power in certain important fields. The proposition was rejected and in its place the Senate was charged with acting as an executive council to the President in negotiating treaties and the making of appointments. The Philadelphia Convention, in brief, finally decided to vest in the President considerable executive power, but he was hemmed in by the system of checks and balances. In this way, the framers of the Constitution accomplished both their objectives. By making him independent of the legislature and eligible for re-election, stability and continuity were assured. By sufficiently checking his powers the fears of the people at that time who had a horror of unlimited power, were avoided. Sections 2 and 3 of Article II of the Constitution are devoted to enumeration of Presidential powers. But much of the President's authority has accrued to him by virtue of factors beyond the powers conferred upon him by the Constitution. "No important institution," as Harold Laski says, "is ever that the law makes it merely. It accumulates about itself traditions, conventions, ways of behaviour, which, without ever attaining the status of formal law, are not less formidable in their influence than law itself could require."[1] And the growth in power and prestige of the Presidency of the United States is a prominent example of the unforeseen possibilities of a written Constitution. If with the Founding Fathers the problem was, how strong should the executive be, the same problem confronts the Americans even today. The people also ask : Why has the President become so powerful? Is this a dangerous tendency ? We will deal with this aspect later in the Chapter. But one thing is clear. No longer could a James Bryce write on the subject, "Why Great Men are not chosen Presidents."

### Qualifications and Compensation

The Constitution requires that the President shall be a natural born citizen, that he must have attained the age of thirty-five years, and must have been for fourteen years a resident of the United States. The question of residence was

1. Laski, H. J., *The American Presidency*, pp. 13-14.

raised by the opponents of Herbert Hoover who had not been a resident for fourteen consecutive years immediately prior to his election in 1828, although he had resided in the United States considerably more than fourteen years altogether. According to Ferguson and McHenry the interpretation of Article II requiring residence for fourteen years "continuously and immediately preceding election appears unwarranted."[2] These constitutional requirements apart, Congress has in effect added to them by providing that persons convicted of various federal crimes will, in addition to other penalties, "be incapable of holding office under the United States."[3]

The salary and other emoluments of the President are fixed by Congress. They cannot, however, be increased or diminished during his term of office. From 1909 to 1940, the salary of the President was $ 75,000 a year. In 1949 it was raised to $100,000 plus $50,000 tax-free expense allowance. In 1953, the tax-free features of the latter sum were eliminated and the salary became $150,000 for all practical purposes. According to the Presidential Increase Act, 1969, the salary was increased to $200,000 and a general expense fund of $50,000. Both are subject to income-tax. The legislation was assented to by President Johnson on January 18, 1969, two days before he relinquished his office. President Richard Nixon was the first recipient of the new increase in salary. Separate budgetary provisions are made for his travel, official entertaining, and White House, the official residence of the President. After relinquishing office, Ex-Presidents, under a Presidential Retirement Law of 1958, get an annual pension of $60,000, free office space and up to $ 96,000 a year for office staff. The President is immune from arrest for any offence and is not subject to the control of courts. No process can be issued against him or compel him to perform any act. He can be removed from office only by Impeachment but after removal he is liable to arrest and punishment according to law.

### Presidential Term

There was a vexing discussion in the Philadelphia Convention regarding the term of office of the President. It was first agreed that the term should be seven years with provision against re-election. On reconsideration, however, it was ultimately fixed at four years and nothing was said with regard to re-eligibility. When the Constitution simply stipulates that "he shall hold his Office during the term of four years,"[4] the framers, no doubt, allowed the indefinite re-eligibility of the President. The first President, Washington, set a two-term custom and it was followed for a century and a half, although two unsuccessful bids were made for a third term by Grant and Theodore Roosevelt. Grant failed to secure the party nomination whereas Theodore Roosevelt was defeated at the polls. When the question of possible third term for Calvin Coolidge first arose, the Senate passed a resolution declaring that any departure from the two-term tradition "would be unwise, unpatriotic, and fraught with peril to our free institutions."

Thus, the tradition seemed to have been fairly well established when in 1940 President Franklin D. Roosevelt decided to accept the Democratic nomination for the third successive term and his victory at the polls repealed the tradition. He was elected even for the fourth term in 1944, although he died soon after the inauguration.[5] But the breaking of the tradition by Franklin Roosevelt was not to become a precedent for indefinite re-election. The Twenty-Second Amendment, adopted in 1951 bars any person from being elected more than twice[6]. Nor can a President be elected more than once if he has served more than half the term to which another President was elected. For example, Gerald Ford assumed office in the second year of Richard Nixon's four-year term, he could serve as President only for one more term.

### Mode of Election

Perhaps no other question consumed so much time of the Philadelphia Convention as that relating to the method of choosing the President. Various schemes were proposed. Some proposed a direct election by the people, while others urged election by the Congress. The direct method of election by the people was ruled out for various reasons. The framers of the Constitution intended to establish a method which would, as Hamilton

2. Ferguson and McHenry, *The American System of Government*, p. 301.
3. Pritchett. C. Herman, *The American Constitution*, p. 285.
4. Article II, Section 1. President Jimmy Carter said, in an interview on April 30, 1979, that he had come to believe that the President should serve only one six-year term.
5. Franklin Roosevelt died in April, 1945.
6. This was not applicable in the case of Harry Truman who was President when the Amendment was proposed. Truman, however, did not seek election for the third term.

put it, "afford as little opportunity as possible to tumult and disorder," and would not "convulse the community with any extraordinary or violent movements." Against the method of election by Congress, it was argued that such a method was the negation of the unanimously accepted principle of the Separation of Powers and that it would make the President a mere creature or tool of that as- sembly.

The finally adopted plan was the expedient of indirect election. The Constitution provided that the President will be chosen by electors appointed in each State in such manner as the legislature of that State may direct, and each State to have as many electors as it has Senators and Representatives in Congress.[7] The method, thus, adopted, enabled the electors to meet in due course, each group in its own State, and give their votes in writing for two persons, of whom at least one must not be an inhabitant of the same State as elector. The ballots were then sealed and transmitted to the presiding officer of the Senate who counted them in the presence of both the Houses and announced the result. The person receiving the highest number of votes was to be the President and the one obtaining next to him was to be the Vice-President, provided, both had obtained a clear majority of the electoral votes. In case, no one obtained a majority of the electoral votes, the House of Representatives was to choose, voting by States and each State having one vote, from among the five highest. In the event of a tie in the electoral vote, it was provided that the issue would be settled in the same way.

The Founding Fathers had expected that the electors of the different States would be talented and leading citizens presumably well acquainted with the qualifications and merits of the candidates for Presidency. They had also hoped that the electors would meet at their respective State capitals, discuss among themselves the qualifications and merits of each candidate, and, then, exercising their best judgment, cast their votes for the fittest. In the first two elections the quiet and dignified procedure contemplated by the framers, functioned exactly as they had expected. At the third election (1796), however, a new shape of things began to emerge and long before the electors met, it was well known that most of the Presidential electors would vote for either John Adams or Thomas Jefferson, although in no case were any pledges exacted.

By this time two national parties, the Republicans and the Federalists, had come into existence and when the Presidential election took place in 1800, the electors were party functionaries pledged to vote for the candidates of their own parties. The Republicans, who elected a majority of their electors, had their candidates, Jefferson for President and Aaron Burr for Vice-President. It so happened that Jefferson and Burr had polled exactly seventy-three votes each. In accordance with the constitutional provision the election was thrown to the House of Representatives which was still controlled by the Federalists. It was with the greatest difficulty that Jefferson was elected, because some of the Federalists had toyed with the idea of making Burr the President. However, this incident revealed that the mode of election was defective and must be amended. Immediately there- after the Twelfth Amendment was adopted [8] to avoid the repetition of such an incident. Each voter now separately votes for the President and Vice-President and one who secures the majority of votes in each case stands elected. If no candidate for Presidency secures a majority of electoral votes, the House of Representatives chooses from among the three men with the highest electoral votes. The House votes by State delegation, with each delegation casting one vote. A majority of the members of each delegation determine how the State's single vote will be cast. If members of a delegation are evenly divided, then that State's vote is not counted. A majority of all the States is needed for election.

If no man receives a majority of the votes cast for Vice-President, the Senate chooses between the two men with the highest votes. Each Senator casts one vote, and election requires a majority of full members of the Senate. A law of 1887 declares that each State will determine the authority of its selection of electors.

Thus, the constitutional indirect method of Presidential election has been upset by the growth of political parties and political practices. Although the language of the Constitution relating to Presidential election remains unchanged, but the business of nominating candidates for Presidency, carrying on campaigns, and casting ballots has become a popular operation of national importance. The real choice of the President, graphically remarks Charles Beard, "has been transferred to the national convention of the

7. Article II, Section I.
8. It was adopted in 1804.

winning party, and the mass of voters supporting the party at the polls. In this way, the deliberative, dignified procedure contemplated by the framers of the Constitution has been replaced by a popular operation of the first magnitude. It fills the land with discussions and agitations for six months or more every four years. It puts at stake the ambitions of individuals in quest of power, the interests of classes, and the fortunes of the country. Nearly everybody takes part in it, from the President, busy re-electing himself or helping to select his successor,[9] down to ordinary citizens who discourse on the merits of candidates with as much assurance as on the outcome of the latest prize fight. The performance involves endless discussions, public and private, oratory, uproar, surveys, the election of thousands of delegates to elaborate national conventions, the concentration of opinion on a few ambitious leaders, a nation-wide propaganda as the sponsors for various aspirants exhibit the qualifications of their favourites to the multitude, and the expenditure of millions of dollars on publications, meetings, 'rounding up delegates' and 'seeing that goods are delivered.''[10]

Until recently candidates could raise funds from any source available and were totally free to spend as much money as they wanted. Successful fund raisers or independently wealthy candidates were often accused by their opponents of "trying to buy the electors." Sustained efforts were made to reform the process of campaign financing and ultimately Congress, in 1971, 1974 and 1976, passed election laws that impose strict limits on both contributors and candidates. The new laws also provide for public funds to be made available to candidates who have successfully raised some funds within the prescribed limits and who agree to limitations on their campaign spending, both in primaries and general elections. The funds for candidates come directly from tax-payers, instead of from regular Treasury appropriations. Taxpayers "voluntarily may check a box on their income-tax forms to express their support for the matching-fund system. Each taxpayer who checks the box, funnels $ 1 of taxes into a special fund, which is later distributed to qualified candidates." To qualify for federal aid in the primaries, candidates must raises at least $5,000 in individual contributions of $ 250 or less in each of the 20 States. The Federal Government matches these contributions dollar to dollar. Presidential candidates must also stay within an overall spending ceiling determined by an inflation-based formula and expected to be about 15.9 million for 1980. For the general election, the Democratic and Republican nominees may neither receive nor spend private funds if they want to qualify for public funds. In 1980 they were eligible for grants of approximately $2.5 million. In 1976, public funds were the only source of revenue for Jimmy Carter and Gerald R. Ford, either of whom received about $21.8 million.

What happens now is that within the constitutional framework described above, a standardized State procedure has developed under which electors are elected on a general ticket basis. The list of electors is made up by the official party organisation in each State and this honour goes to distinguished citizens or to partisans willing to make liberal contribution to campaign funds. On the election day the voter does not directly vote for President and Vice-President, but for all the Presidential electors put up by his party in his State. Normally, the party which secures a plurality of the popular votes in any State is entitled to all the electoral ballots of the State for President and Vice-President. Not too many hours after the polls close, it is usually known who will be the next President of the United States. However, the voters' verdict in the election of the electors is the last act in the Presidential drama. Technically, the voters have only elected the electors and it is the job of the latter to elect the President.

Each of the States possesses as many Presidential electors as it has Senators and Representatives in Congress. The total number of electors constituting the electoral collage is 538 including the District of Columbia, although it is

9. Dwight Eisenhower not only picked up Richard M. Nixon as his successor but helped in his campaign for the Presidency.
10. Beard, Charles A., *American Government and Politics,* pp. 179-80.
The costs of Presidential electioneering are impossible to estimate exactly. But they are growing at an alarming rate. For what the figures are worth, the President's 1962 Commission estimated joint expenditure on Presidential and Vice-Presidential candidates by the National Committees of the two major parties as follows:
1952 $ 11.6 million
1956 $ 12.6 million
1960 $ 20.0 million
The Commission estimated the total expenditure on all candidates in 1960 at $ 165–$ 175 million.

not entitled to have any member in the Senate or the House of Representatives. A simple majority of 538 electoral vote total (270) is needed to win the Presidency. The electors automatically vote for their party's nominee since no elector dare break faith with the party which nominated him, and the work of the electoral college is a final formality before the successful candidate becomes the constitutionally elected President. In this way, the deliberative, judicial, non-partisan system designed by the framers of the Constitution has been overthrown by political custom.[11]

If no candidate for the Presidency receives the necessary electoral majority on election day, the issue is thrown for decision into the House of Representatives. There, each State, irrespective of its population and size, casts vote for one of the three men who earlier had received the maximum electoral votes in the elections. There have been only three occasions in the American history in 1800, 1824, and 1876 elections, when the Statewise voting in the House of Representatives has decided the Presidential election.

The precise practice as it prevails today, may, thus, be summed up: the first stage to the Presidency is the selection of delegates to the national convention of the political parties. In most States, delegates are selected by the parties at their State conventions. But in 15 States they are chosen by the voters at primary elections—usually in March, April and May of the year preceding the Presidential election. The second stage comprises holding the convention when the party selects its candidates for President and Vice-President, and adopts a programme of objectives. In the first week of September starts the election campaign and the candidates for Presidency and Vice-Presidency selected by their parties crisscross the nation, explaining their positions on key issues, domestic and international. By train, plane, bus and car they travel to nearly every State. They make hundreds of public appearances, and scores of speeches from platforms, over radio stations, and before television cameras. As many as 20 speeches may be given in a day. Then, comes the polling day for the election of the electors early in November (on Tuesday following the first Monday in November). It is a legal holiday in most States. In other states, employees are given time off so that they may vote conveniently. The polling stations open as early as 6 in the morning for 12 hours or more. The ballot is direct and secret. Individual votes are counted State by State and by custom the presidential candidate receiving the most votes within a State is declared the winner of the State's electoral votes. The result is known in a few hours after the election is over. Once the outcome is clear, it is customary for the defeated candidate to make a concession speech thanking his supporters for their efforts and congratulating his opponent on the victory.

The formal balloting for President takes place long after polling day through the machinery of the Electoral College. The practice now is for the Electors to vote for the candidate who carried their State in the November Presidential election. The Electoral College does not actually meet. The various state groups of electors assemble at their respective State capitals, as required by the national law of 1934, on the Monday following the second Wednesday in December after their November election to vote for President and Vice-President. The votes of the State electoral groups are sent to the President of the Senate, opened and counted before a joint session of Congress on January 6, and formal announcement of the result of the election made. The new President is inaugurated at noon on January 20 to run a four-year term of office.

Since 1797, when Representative William L. Smith introduced the first proposed Constitutional Amendment for reform of the Electoral College, hardly a session of Congress has passed without the introduction of one or more resolutions on the subject. Presidents from Jefferson to Jimmy Carter have suggested changes. But only one—the 12th Amendment ratified in 1804—has been approved. The 23rd Amendment, ratified in 1961, gave three electoral votes to the District of Columbia, but that does not basically change the system.

Modern critics, for example, the American Bar Association, have described the Electoral College "as archaic, complex, indirect and dangerous." Public interest in change has been spurred by the close elections of 1960, 1968 and 1976. In the most recent of these, a shift of fewer than 10,000 votes in Ohio and Hawaii from Carter to Ford would have elected Ford despite his 107 million deficit in the popular vote. The direct vote plan, whose principal sponsor was Democratic Senator Birch Bayh, attracted the most attention, but was defeated in the Senate in July, 1979.

11. Beard, Charles A., *American Government and Politics*, p. 160.

Under his plan, the President was to be elected by a direct popular vote on a nationwide basis. If no candidate received at least 40 per cent of the votes, "there would have been a runoff between the top two candidates."

In the final analysis, no one is really certain of the impact of abolition of the Electoral College of the American political system. For this reason, passage of any future amendments and their ultimate ratification by the States are dubious. Both Congress and the States will be wary of change. A witness, Eddie N. Williams, in his testimony in 1977, stated the matter succinctly: "There is no conclusive evidence of the effect such proposals would, or would not have."

**Removal from Office**

Removal from office of a President is by impeachment and only for treason, bribery, or other high crimes and misdemeanours. No President has ever been so removed. President Andrew Johnson's impeachment failed by one vote. The House of Representatives has the power to initiate Impeachment proceedings by a majority vote. The case is tried by the Senate with the Chief Justice of the Supreme Court presiding. It requires two-thirds vote for conviction, which makes the President liable to removal from office and disqualification. He is also liable to trial under ordinary judicial procedure.

## THE VICE-PRESIDENCY

The Vice-President must meet all the qualifications of President since he may succeed to the Presidency in the event of the President's death, resignation or removal. The framers of the Constitution might have omitted the Vice-Presidency but when the method of electing the President through the medium of Electoral College was decided upon, it became necessary to provide for an office the incumbent of which should succeed to the Presidency without delay. It would have been politically undesirable to leave the office of the President vacant until new electors could be chosen and they had chosen the President. But even when the office of the Vice-President had been created, the framers were not too enthusiastic about it. Benjamin Franklin took the position so slightly that he proposed to have its holder addressed as "His Superfluous Highness." This is, in fact, an apt description. John Adams, the first to hold the office of Vice-President, lamented to his wife : "My country has, in its wisdom, contrived for me the most insignificant office that ever the invention of man contrived or his imagination conceived." Thomas Jefferson, his successor, said something more apparent and meaningful than he realized when he described the "second office of government" as "honourable and easy," "the first" as "but a splendid misery." The rise of the political parties and the Jefferson-Burr episode and the consequent adoption of the Twelfth Amendment further contributed to the decline of the office of the Vice-President. It is an office of obscurity and not glory and it is rarely occupied by a man for whom the majority of the people would have voted as a candidate for the Presidency. Even the potential importance of the Vice-President as 'heir-apparent to the President', and ten had succeeded it in 185 years, had not been sufficient to attract leading political figures to seek it as a matter of course. "Most men of ability and ambition," observes Clinton Rossiter, "would still rather be a leading Senator or Secretary of State than Vice President, even after all the good and exciting times that Richard Nixon has had."[12] The Vice-Presidency is, therefore, "an office unique in its functions or rather lack in its functions."[13] Woodrow Wilson described the position of the Vice-President as "one of anomalous insignificance and curious uncertainty." Franklin Roosevelt said that he would rather be a Professor of History than Vice-President. John Nance Garner, who was Roosevelt's running-mate in 1932 and 1936, described the post as "not worth a pitcher of warm spit." Thomas R. Marshall, who was Vice-President under Woodrow Wilson, described himself as "a man in a cataleptic fit," who "is conscious of all that goes on but has no part in it." Such are the dimensions of importance of the Vice-Presidency "and impotence is the mark of a second-class office."[14]

**Mode of Election**

The Vice-President is elected in the same way as the President and according to the original provisions of the Constitution (Article 2, Section 1, Ch. 2) the man getting the highest number of votes next to the President-elect was declared the Vice-President of the United States. The Twelfth Amendment changed the method of election. The

12. Rossiter, Clinton, *The American Presidency,* p. 102.
13. Corwin, E. S., *The President: Office and Powers,* p. 73.
14. Rossiter, Clinton, *The American Presidency*, p. 102.

electors have now to vote separately for the President and the Vice-President. There are two considerations which govern the choice of a candidate for this office. First, he would not be from the same geographical district as the Presidential candidate.[15] If the President is from the Middle West, the Vice-President will be from the East, and *vice versa.* Wilson was from New Jersey; Marshall from Indiana. Harding came from Ohio; Coolidge from Massachusetts, Franklin D. Roosevelt came from New York; Garner from Texas. Second, by no means so strictly applied, that the candidates for the office of President and Vice-President shall represent different wings of the party. In 1940 Henry Wallace of Iowa was united with Franklin Rosevelt, and Charles McNary of Oregon with Wendel Wilkie of New York and Indiana. For the election of 1944 Roosevelt designated Harry Truman of Missourie as his "running- mate."

**Functions and Duties**

The Constitution-makers thought it desirable to give the Vice-President something to do besides the death, resignation, incapacity, or removal of his chief. The Constitution, accordingly, ordains that he should preside over the sessions of the Senate. Even as a presiding officer of the Senate his responsibilities of office are not great. The Senate is a body with customs and traditions that the presiding officer must respect and accept. He votes only in case of a tie and in all other matters plays an impartial role. The Senate refused to accept, in fact it refused to listen patiently, to the proposal of Vice-President Dawes who tried to modernize the House. The result is that a "vigorous man gets restive under such conditions; his frustration is noticed and the prestige of office degenerates accordingly."

During recent years, however, the potentialities of the office have been demonstrated. President Harding associated Vice-President Coolidge with Cabinet work. Franklin Roosevelt entrusted many responsibilities to Henry Wallace. Although less close to Roosevelt in outlook, Truman was able to help the President with Congressional problems. The Vice-President, as Rossiter says, "has experienced something of a renaissance" under Truman and Eisenhower. Alben Barkley was probably the most distinguished man nominated for the office since John C. Calboun and he proved extremely useful to Truman as a link to Congress. In 1949, the Vice President was made by law a member of the National Security Council. Richard Nixon was the busiest and most useful Vice-President in memory. Eisenhower believed that no President in the future could relegate the Vice-President to its former stand by status in the government. He showed the path that the Vice-President must be a working member of the administration, fully informed of every detail. He deputed Nixon on an itinerary of Latin America, the Middle East countries, India and Pakistan, and the extent of the economic and military aid given by the United States to Pakistan was largely based upon his report. Nixon sat by invitation in the Cabinet and even presided over some Cabinet meetings in the absence of President Eisenhower. Vice-President Johnson in the Kennedy administration continued in the Nixon pattern, with assignments overseas and chairmanship of several inter-departmental Committees. Johnson was also Kennedy's counsellor as a member in the "Ex Com" of the National Security Council, an *ad hoc* group of a dozen top administration officials who aided the President in working out his responses to the 1962 Cuban crisis. Hubert H. Humphery was used for numerous political and diplomatic assignments. President-elect Jimmy Carter deeply involved Walter Mondale during the transition period in setting up the administration, joining in the interviewing and selection of Cabinet members and frequently advising on foreign policy. He received the same Central Intelligence briefings as Jimmy Carter. The President told his cabinet that Mondale was "his chief staff person" and added that all White House staff had been instructed that "he is their boss." The Vice-President had an office in the White House, close to the President, with special areas of responsibility, such as crime and to represent the President abroad as well as working with the Senate and House of Representatives. Mondale had become a partner in administration. But George Bush, under Reagan, did not enjoy that enviable position and authority.

The 'New look' which Eisenhower gave to the office was intended to give to the Vice-President training at least with the major national and international policies so that if he is compelled to take over the White House he may be able to steer through domestic problems and international complexities. Truman said, "It is a terrible

15. Amendment XIII provides : "The Electors will meet in their respective states and vote by ballot for President and Vice-President, one of whom, at least, shall not be an inhabitant of the same state with themselves...."

handicap for a new President to step into office and be confronted with a whole series of critical decisions without adequate briefing." But the powers of the Vice-President are only potential; authority comes to him only with the demise or other incapacity of the President. So far as the office of the Vice-President itself is concerned, it is up to the each future President to make whatever can be made "of this disappointing office." In all, the Vice-President has been chiefly useful to the President by relieving him of ceremonial duties and making goodwill journeys abroad.

**Succession to Presidency**

Ten Vice-Presidents have so far succeeded to the Presidency and nine in the event of death during their terms. The tenth Gerald Ford succeeded on Nixon's resignation. The Constitution provides: "In case of the removal of the President from office, or of his death, resignation, or inability to discharge the powers and duties of his said office the same shall devolve on the Vice-President...."[16] This provision does not give the Vice-President any constitutional right to assume the title of the President. It simply provides that the duties and powers of the Presidential office shall devolve upon the Vice-President. But John Tyler, the Vice-President to fill a vacancy, took the title of the President for all practical purposes and did not differentiate himself in position and powers from the regularly elected holders of office. His example has since been followed. According to the Twenty- second Amendment a man succeeding to the Presidency and serving more than two years may be elected President in his own right only once."[17]

No case of Impeachment has made a vacancy for a Vice-President.[18] Nor had there been an occasion on which "the inability to discharge the powers and duties" on the part of the President may have resulted into the moving up of the Vice-President. President Garfield was physically unable for more than two months in 1881 to perform any important official work. President Woodrow Wilson was similarly incapacitated for a considerably long time during the latter part of his second term. Even absence from the United States for months together, as it happened during the terms of office of Woodrow Wilson, Franklin Roosevelt and Harry Truman, did not constitute "inability to discharge the duties" of Presidency. This is for two reasons. In the first place, neither the Constitution, till the Twenty-fifth Amendment became law on February 10, 1967, nor the laws provided who was competent to determine and under what circumstances a President might be considered unable to discharge his duties. Secondly, there had been extreme reluctance on the part of even ailing Presidents and their families to surrender authority. The result was that the question of succession to Presidency, except in case of death, remained obscure.

The Twenty-fifth Amendment provides that the Vice-President would take over the duties and responsibilities of the Presidency: (1) if the President states in writing to the President *pro tempore* of the Senate and the Speaker of the House that he is unable to carry out his duties, and (2) if the Vice-President and a majority of the Heads of Executive Departments believe that there is Presidential disability and send to Congress a declaration to that effect. But, in such an eventuality, it is only in his acting capacity that the Vice-President takes over the office of the President. When the President resumes office after the incapacity does not exist, he reverts to his original office of Vice-President. If, however, the Vice-President and a majority of the principal officers of the Executive Departments inform in writing to the President *pro tempore* of the Senate and the Speaker of the House of Representatives that the President was unable to discharge the duties of his office, Congress then decides whether the President was unable or not to discharge his duties. If it decided that incapacity still existed the Vice-President countinues to remain the Acting President otherwise the President shall resume the duties of his office. President Reagan after he was shot and operated upon for a major chest surgery with a cracked seventh rib and who needed two tubes to drain liquid from his lungs, still remained the effective President and conducted business from a hospital suite. How well did he fulfil his many Presidential functions, some of which could be very arduous, calling for long hours of continuing activity and that too at

16. Article II, Section 1, Clause 5.
17. "No person shall be elected to the office of the President more than twice and no person who has held the office of President, or acted as President, for more than two years of a term to which some other person was elected President shall be elected to the office of President more than once...."
18. Richard Nixon resigned in order to avoid the possibility of impeachment. But Exertt CarlLadd Jr. says that Richard Nixon ended his Presidency by "de facto impeachment and conviction." *Fortune*, December 3, 1979.

the age of 70 is a big question mark.

Succession to the Presidency in the event of both the offices of the President and the Vice -President having fallen vacant is covered by the Presidential Succession Act of 1947. In such an unhappy event, the law provides that the Speaker of the House of Representatives shall, upon his resignation as Speaker and as Representative in Congress, act as President. If there is no Speaker, or if the Speaker fails to qualify as Acting President, then President *pro tempore* of the Senate shall, upon his resignation as President *pro tempore* and as Senator, act as President. If there is no Speaker or no President *pro tempore,* or if neither is qualified, as for example, neither is a natural born citizen, the line of succession then runs down through the cabinet to the first of its members not under disability to discharge the powers and duties of the office of the President. Such a man would be an acting President until a Speaker or President *pro tempore* had qualified to take over. There is no provision for a special election.

The Presidential Succession Act, 1947, has been a subject of criticism. It has been contended that the Speaker and the President *pro tempore* may not be of the Presidential stature and may even belong to the Party in opposition to the late President. But the most weighty criticism is that both the Speaker and President *pro tempore* are likely, since seniority has much to do with their selection to be too old to carry the burden of the White House. Following the assassination of John Kennedy, when Lyndon Johnson was sworn in as President on November 22, 1963. John W. McCormack, the Speaker of the House, was nearly seventy-two, and Senator Carl Hayden, the President *pro tempore,* was eighty-six. It has, therefore, been suggested that the Succession Act of 1947 needs a revision. Alternatives recently discussed include holding a special election, reassembling of the members of the Electoral College to choose a Vice-President, returning to the old form of having the cabinet officers—beginning with the Secretary of State—succeed, and having the former Vice-President designate a successor, with the consent of the Senate or of the whole Congress. One of these, or some variant, it has been pointed out, is likely before long to replace the present order of succession.

## POWERS AND DUTIES OF THE PRESIDENT

### Sources of Presidential Authority

The powers and duties of the President are partly determined by the Constitution, partly by Acts of Congress and treaties, partly as a result of usages and precedents, and partly by judicial interpretations. Article II of the Constitution, which deals with the office of the President, is primarily devoted to the methods of election, his term, qualifications, compensation, and oath of office. The clauses relative to his powers and duties are few and brief. Some of them are specific, but many of them are general in terms and hence open to interpretation. But a great deal of responsibility which now rests on the shoulders of the President may be traced to laws which Congress has, from time to time, enacted. Congressional statutes authorise the President to determine policies which may have far-reaching effects, make important appointments, and to issue orders which for all practical purposes have the force of law. Congress may also bestow upon him the exercise of wide discretionary powers within the framework of the laws passed by it. In 1933, for example, Congress vested the President with the discretionary power to reduce the gold contents of the dollar, to issue additional paper money, and to purchase silver as a partial currency. In 1941 the Lend-Lease Act gave to the President enormous discretionary powers in the matter of furnishing ships, munitions and supplies to the countries fighting against the Axis powers. Similarly, the programmes of economic and military aids in different parts of the world give to the President a wide range of discretion in the allocation of money and direction of aid.

The Supreme Court, too, has defined Presidential powers; for example, it has held that the President's power to remove from office can be exercised without consulting the Senate.[19] Where the Constitution is silent, the judiciary has been called upon to articulate. The Constitution gives the President the power to pardon offenders, but it does not say whether he may pardon a man before he is convicted. The Supreme Court held that the President possesses such a power and may pardon the offender even before he is convicted.[20] In some cases the Supreme Court has refused to take jurisdiction on the ground that the

19. *Myers* v.*United States* (1926).
20. *Ex-parte Garland* (1886).

matter involved political questions belonging to the sphere of the President or Congress as it was held in *Luther* v. *Borden* (1949). The Court affirmed that the constitutional guarantee to every State of a "republican form of government" presents a 'political question.' But more recently Justices "have appeared willing, even eager, to jump into what Mr. Justice Frankfurter aptly called 'the political thicket.'[21]

Finally, some Presidential powers and duties have been acquired through custom and usage. For example, the President is accepted as the leader of his party and is conceded the right to be consulted on all matters affecting the interest of his party both inside and outside Congress. The custom of Senatorial courtesy has now developed into a well-recognised policy for purposes of political patronage. Washington assumed he was master of his own family (the Cabinet) and Congress eventually concurred. He also established himself as the sole vehicle of communication with foreign governments and in the "Whisky Rebellion" he established the responsibility of his office for suppression of domestic disorder. President Jackson is responsible for the exercise of veto power over legislation on policy grounds; previously it had been more or less assumed that the use of the veto was to be confined to questions of unconstitutionality.

**Extent of Presidential powers**

But the real extent of the powers of the President depends upon his own personality, the influence the wields, and the state of affairs under which the office is administered. In times of national emergencies the powers of the President may be so expanded as to be limited in effect only by the necessities of the national existence. The powers wielded by President Lincoln during the Civil War were so enormous that he was frequently referred to as a dictator.[22] Both Wilson and Franklin Roosevelt assumed vast and unprecedented powers and so did George Bush during the Gulf War in January 1991.

Since many provisions of the Constitution relating to the powers of the President are general in terms, it all depends upon how the President takes a view of his responsibilities and duties as the Chief Executive. He may take a narrow view and may be satisfied with the bare duties of enforcing the Constitution and the law and conduct of routine administration. One may, like President Coolidge, not strive to be "a great President." Some may take a broad view of his powers and responsibilities, as did Theodore Roosevelt, who asserted that it was the President's right "to do anything that the needs of the nation demand unless such action is forbidden by the Constitution or the laws." The famous Monroe Doctrine laid down in 1823 the essentials of United States foreign policy and it still continues to hold good.[23] In the early stages of the First World War President Woodrow Wilson so defined the American rights of commerce and travel that it dragged the country eventually into war. Immediately after his inauguration in 1933 President Franklin Roosevelt assumed leadership to steer the country out of the economic crisis through his policy of New Deal. Later, he so formulated his foreign policy towards the Axis powers that it involved the United States in actual hostilities. It was Harry Truman who ordered atomic bombs dropped on Hiroshima and Nagasaki in 1945 and then refused to use them against any other foe. It was the Truman Doctrine (March 1947) that shattered the long United States tradition of peacetime isolation by supporting Greece and Turkey against Communist threats. It was Truman's Marshall Plan that committed United States resources to the rebuilding of Europe. Later Truman defied the Soviet blockade of Berlin and risked war by authorising the airlift. Still later, he met the Communist invasion of South Korea by ordering United States forces in the field. The role of the President is, therefore, affected by the personality and the time. Winston Churchill, at dinner on the Presidential yacht Williamsburg in 1952, spoke to Truman with blunt generosity: "The last time you and I sat across a conference table was at Potsdam. I must confess, Sir, I held you in very low regard. I loathed you taking the place of Franklin Roosevelt. I misjudged you badly. Since that time, you, more than any other man, have saved western civilisation."[24] The people and the times,

21. Irish, Marian D., and Prothro, James W., *The Politics of American Democracy,* p. 136.
22. Justifying the use of his executive prerogative in the absence of expressly granted authority, Lincoln declared, "No organic law can ever be framed with a provision specifically applicable to every question which may arise. The whole of the laws are being resisted and all will be destroyed if not protected....I am to sacrifice one law in order to save the rest......The Constitution is silent on the emergency."
23. President James Monroe in a message to Congress in 1832 laid down his foreign policy commonly known as the Monroe Doctrine.
24. *Newsweek,* January 8, 1973, p. 28.

the complicated and fast-moving stream of events of the twentieth century, need strong and decisive leaders to occupy the White House. But there may be a unscrupulous President, like Richard Nixon, who impaired the traditional character of the Presidency by his crowding usurpation of powers and violation of the historic concept of Presidency or one like Jimmy Crater who was castigated for ineffectual weakness; a man of confused ideas and lack of direction.

The powers of the President may be divided broadly into: (1) those chiefly or exclusively executive in character; (2) those arising out of the legislative process; and (3) those which flow to him as a national leader. The executive powers of the President may further be divided under the following headings : (i) supervision over the administrative agencies of the federal government; (ii) enforcement of the laws; (iii) to make appointments and removals; (iv) granting of pardons; (v) to conduct diplomatic relations and negotiate treaties; (vi) to act as Commander-in-Chief of the armed forces of the United States and (vii) to act in emergencies.

## EXECUTIVE POWERS

### President as Chief Administrator

The President assumes high technical responsibilities as head of the national administration. It is the duty of the President, as Chief Executive, to see that the Constitution, laws and treaties of the United States, and decisions rendered by the federal courts are duly enforced throughout the country. He may, accordingly, direct the heads of the Departments and their subordinates in the discharge of the functions vested in them by the Acts of Congress. It is true that Congress has assumed the power of deciding the structure and extent of authority of administrative Departments, but it does not detract the right of the President to control administration. There are some Departments which are placed by law under his direct control. Moreover, the Constitution entrusts him with the duty of the faithful execution of the laws. The Constitution also permits him to "require the opinion, in writing, of the principal officer in each of the executive departments, upon any subject relating to the duties of their respective offices." This provision when supplemented by the decision of the Supreme Court that the President is bound to see that an officer faithfully carries out the duties assigned to him by law makes the legal position of the President supreme. Finally, the President has the power to remove the head of the Department who refuses to obey his orders. His authority to determine and direct, within the framework of law, the steps to be taken by that officer is clear and definite. "He is not likely, of course," observes Charles Beard, "to quarrel with a Cabinet officer over details but when there is a serious conflict over important public policies, the President, if firm in his views, will prevail, and the officer will yield, resign, or be dismissed."[25] Such a conflict occurred in the administration of President Coolidge in 1924, between the President and the Attorney-General Harry M. Daugherty; and the Attorney-General was forced to resign under protest. In 1946, President Truman ousted Henry A. Wallace from the Department of Commerce after a clash of opinions over foreign policy. Secretary of State Cyrus Vance resigned in April 1980 because he disagreed with President Carter's decision to attempt a military rescue of the American hostages in Iran. So did General Haig, Reagan's Secretary of State and a few more resigned on the issue of mandatory sanctions against South Africa and secret supply of arms to Iran.

Thus, upon the President rests the overwhelming responsibility for the administration of the national government. The simple provision of the Constitution which vests in him the duty of seeing that all the laws of the United States are properly executed carries "the awesome significance of this responsibility." The Report of the Hoover Commission on Organisation of the Executive Branch of the Government stated: "The critical state of world affairs requires the government of the United States to speak and act with unity of purpose, firmness, and restraint in dealing with other nations. It must act decisively to preserve its human and material resources. It must develop strong machinery for the national defence, while seeking to construct an enduring world peace. It cannot perform these tasks if its organisation for development and execution of policy is confused and disorderly, or if the Chief Executive is handicapped in providing firm direction to the departments and agencies."[26]

When Jefferson became President, the federal government employed 2,120 persons. Today by latest count, the President heads a colossal

25. Beard, Charles A., *American Government and Politics*, p. 170.
26. *General Management of the Executive Branch*, p. 2 (1949).

establishment of over $2\frac{1}{2}$ million Federal civilian employees, These employees work in 2,117 component units of federal administration—in 2,117 departments, services, bureaus, commissions, boards, governmental corporations and other types of agencies. They are spread throughout the world and their wages alone amount to over 18 billion dollars a year. It is impossible for any President, whatever be the extent of his drive and however dynamic personality he may possess, to keep proper supervision over all the administrative agencies. And despite the immensity of the job, the President is only a part-time administrator. His other tasks demand most of his time, attention and energy. It, therefore, necessitates some integrated system of organization which should facilitate the President for leadership and control.

This is provided, in the first place, by the Presidential Secretariat consisting of the President's Secretaries and the staff that functions under them. They make a total of over 250 employees in the White House Office. The Secretaries are an able core of attaches to aid him in keeping abreast of administrative work. A recent development is the authorisation of administrative assistants to the President in addition to the executive Secretaries. The President's Committee on Administrative Management urged that the lack of staff assistants to the President be remedied by the appointment of six administrative assistants who "should be possessed of high competence, great physical labour, and passion for anonymity." The Administrative Reorganisation Act of 1939 provided for six Administrative Assistants for the President. Their duties are not precisely described by law but they include: collecting information for the President on all matters of interest to him as Chief administrator and head of his party, smoothing out troubles in politics and administration; scrutinizing and reporting on appointments to offices and work done by the civil servants, keeping the President in touch with Congress and a liaisoning between the President and Congress, and keeping the President informed about the fluctuations in the public opinion, grievances and needs of the citizens and of States and local government with respect to the work of the federal agencies.

In addition to the three Secretaries and six administrative assistants, the President has his personal staff consisting of an assistant to the President, a special counsel to the President, an executive clerk, and Army, Navy and Air Force aides. Outside this inner circle are the heads of a number of staff agencies who advise the President on policy and "help him run the administrative leviathan." The most important of these is the Director of the Bureau of the Budget. Several other Presidential agencies have also vital function especially in the making of economic and military policies. They are: the Council of Economic Advisers, Office of Emergency Planning and the National Security Council, the Office of the Defence Mobilization, Board of Impartial Analysis, and Office of the Personnel, etc.[27] The Executive Office of the President has since been expanded to a personnel of some 1, 200 Executive Secretaries, officials, assistants, clerks and other employees. Within this large group is the White House Secretariat.

**Power of Law Enforcement**

The Constitution commands the President to "take care that the laws be faithfully executed."[28] It also prescribes that the President, before he enters on the execution of his office, shall take an oath or affirmation that "he will to the best of his ability, preserve, protect and defend the Constitution of the United States."[29]As law enforcement official for the nation, the President's responsibility is not limited to the execution of the specific provisions of Congressional statutes. It includes, as well the duty of protecting the whole constitutional system of government, guarding it against attack from any source, and ensuring to all citizens protection against rebellion or other danger to the rights, the Constitution guarantees to them. The President's power, to take care that the laws be faithfully executed embraces all phases of the Constitution as interpreted by courts. If the enforcement of laws encounters a resistance, the President "shall commission all the officers of the United States," including the armed forces, to see that the laws are faithfully executed. President Eisenhower dispatched federal troops to Little Rock, Arkansas on September 24, 1957 to enforce Federal Court's ruling on desegregation.

27. The new President, on assumption of office, may create a variety of new organisations reflecting his some pet projects and may even jettison an existing one as Kennedy did to the National Security Council machinery of Eisenhower administration.
28. Article II, Section 3.
29. *Ibid.*, Section I, Clause 7.

Addressing the American nation on the situation in the Little Rock and justifying the presence of federal troops there, the President said : "When large gathering of obstructionists made it impossible for the decrees of the court to be carried out, both the law and national interest demanded that President take action." Five years later (September, 1962) there occurred the greatest clash since the Civil War, between the Federal Government and the State of Mississippi, where Governor Bamett defied a Federal Court injunction to admit a negro, James Meredith, to the hitherto all white University of Mississippi. Seven hundred Federal Marshals were sent to enforce the law against the State National Guards who surrounded the University on the Governor's orders and even threatened to resist by force if the Federal Marshals brought Meredith to the University. President Kennedy ordered the mobilization of the Mississippi National Guards, thus, placing it under the command of the Federal Government. Troops and military police were also sent and James Meredith was finally enrolled. In 1894 President Cleveland, despite the protests of the Governor of Illinois, sent soldiers to Chicago where a great railway strike, affecting the movement of commerce and mail, had taken place. President Wilson, too, resorted to the same action on the occasion of the labour dispute among the steel workers at Gary, Indiana. Even if the President apprehends that laws are not likely to be obeyed, or there is the possibility of their being obstructed, he may order out the troops. President Harding ordered the troops to stand by in 1922 when a strike threatened to tie up the railways. Troops were sent to take over the plant of the North American Airplane Corporation in 1944 when strikers refused to heed the repeated appeals of the President.

The extent of the President's authority as chief law-enforcement officer of the nation is nowhere better illustrated than in the Supreme Court's decision in *re Neagle,* one of the most dramatic cases in American Constitutional History. In 1890 the Attorney-General of the United States, under direction of the President but without any specific statutory authority detailed United States Marshal Neagle to act as bodyguard of Justice Stephen J. Field of the Supreme Court whose life had been threatened by a citizen of California. The Justice was attacked in a railroad restaurant when Neagle shot to death the assassin. Neagle was arrested and indicted for murder by the Californian authorities. Neagle sought a writ of *habeas corpus* to secure his release from Californian authorities, an action eventually appealed to the Supreme Court. His defence hinged upon finding legal authority for his special assignment, that is, the authority of the President's appointment of an agent without statutory authorization. The Supreme Court held that inasmuch as it is the duty of the President "to take care that the laws be faithfully executed" there was vested in the President authority for Neagle's assignment, although there was no specific statute of Congress allowing the President and the Attorney-General to direct the Marshal to protect Supreme Court Judges. The Court further declared that the President's duty was not confined "to the enforcement of the Acts of Congress or of treaties of the United States according to their express terms," but included "the rights and obligations growing out of the Constitution itself, our international relations and all the protection implied by the nature of the government under the Constitution."

Presidents before and after Neagle's time have not hesitated to use the immense power which the Constitution vests in them as such. But it does not mean that the President's power is not without limit. It is true, that the Chief Executive may sometimes act, as President Washington did in sending troops (15,000 of them) in crushing the Whisky Rebellion of 1794; Lincoln took immediate action, with Congress not even in session, to move against, 'treasonable individuals' who defied the power of the Union in southern States, or as is in Neagle's case, without specific authorization from Congress, but he has no *carte blanche* to do so in all cases. The Supreme Court recently acted as a brake to slow down unlimited expansion in the powers of the President. In 1952 President Truman seized the nation's steel mills justifying his action on the grounds of the grave national emergency facing the nation if the strike should take place. The President was not supported in his action by authorization of Congress. The Supreme Court, in *Youngstown Sheet and Tube Co.* v. *Sewyer,* found the President's action invalid. The majority of the Court held that the President had transcended his authority, for no support of the seizure order could be found in the Acts of Congress in the President's power as Commander-in Chief of the Armed Forces, or in the general constitutional grants of executive power to the President. The President, in this instance, was making basic law rather than executing it and the exercise of such a power he did not have under the doctrine of the Separation of Powers. The minority opinion, on the other hand, stressed the paramount responsibility of the President faithfully to execute the laws.

**Power of Appointment**

The power to appoint is one of the most important and effective in the list of Presidential powers. It gives the President the means to command the allegiance of a huge number of federal officers and enables him to secure the active support of the members of Congress for his programme. The Constitution gives the President the power to nominate, and by and with the advice and consent of the Senate to appoint "ambassadors, other public ministers and consuls, judges of the Supreme Court and all other officers of the United States, whose appointments are not herein otherwise provided for, and which shall be established by law; but the Congress may by law vest the appointment of such inferior officers, as they think proper, in the President alone, in the courts of law, or in the heads of departments."[30] Thus, appointments to the federal services fall under two groups: officers whose appointment is entrusted by the Constitution or by an Act of Congress to the President and Senate, and "inferior officers" whose appointment is vested by Congress in the President alone, the courts of law, or the heads of departments.[31] There has never been made a logical line of division and distinction between the "superior" and "inferior" officers. In the first category, however, are included heads of departments, judges, diplomats, regulatory Commissioners, Marshals, and Collectors of Customs. Some bureau chiefs and virtually subordinate employees fall under the second category.

Taken together, the officers belonging to superior category may number several thousand. In filling these posts the President and the Senate are subject to no restrictions, except in some cases when Congress by law may fix some qualifications as citizenship, professional qualifications, technical training, etc. The Tenure of Office Act of 1820 fixed the tenure of great bulk of offices at four years, and even where the term is not prescribed by Statute, the custom is to replace most of them at the expiration of four years. So in practice the four years' tenure is universal, except for federal judges, and each President during his term has at his disposal an enormous extent of patronage, subject to the approval of the Senate. During 1954 Eisenhower sent in 45,916 appointments to the Senate for confirmation. Not one of these was rejected. Of the total, 42,057 were military appointments, which are customarily automatically confirmed. Of the 3,859 civilian appointments, just half were postmasters.

There are some appointments which are the personal choices of the President and the usual practice for the Senate is to ratify them promptly and without objections even if the Senate is in the hands of the party in opposition to the President. It rarely interferes with the President's selection of his own 'Cabinet,' that is, heads of Departments, ambassadors and Supreme Court Justices. The only two exceptions during the last forty years or so were Charles B. Warren nominated by President Coolidge as Attorney-General and rejected by the Senate, and its refusal to confirm Eisenhower's nominee for Secretary of Commerce, Lewis, L. Strauss, for political reasons.[32] The choice of the diplomatic representatives is also left largely to President's discretion, although Senate's rejection of Martin Van Buren as Minister to Britain will be remembered from the Jackson administration. On occasions, the President may be obliged to withdraw the diplomatic nomination on grounds of political expediency. In 1943, President Franklin Roosevelt nominated Edward J. Flynn to the post of ambassador to Austria. A storm in the Senate broke out and Flynn was attacked as a politician with a "clouded past and a man utterly unqualified for the position in question." President Roosevelt withdrew his name. Military and naval appointments, especially in times of crisis, are principally subject to Presidential determination. Finally Supreme Court Justiceships are filled by the President and nearly always approved. The Senate, however, refused to approve President Hoover's appointment of Circuit Judge John J. Parke in 1930 largely because of labour and negro opposition. It also refused to confirm President Johnson's nominations of Abe Fortas for Chief Justice and William H. Thornberry for associate Justice. Similarly, in November 1969 Clement Haynsworth's nomination was rejected. The Senate on April 8, 1970 rejected President Nixon's

30. Article II, Section 2.
31. The only appointments made by courts of law are : clerks, reporters, and other ministerial officers. There are, however, a large number of inferior officers in the various Departments who are appointed by the Heads of Departments.
32. Altogether there had been eight such rejections.

nomination of Harold Carswell to the Supreme Court.

In all other instances Senate freely uses its power to ratify or reject the appointments as it sees fit. As a rule, the Senate usually gives its consent unless there are substantial reasons to reject. Much, however, depends upon its political complexion. If the majority of the Senators belong to the President's party, then all Presidential appointments are usually confirmed, for it requires just a bare majority of the Senators present. Confirmation of appointments need not require a two-thirds vote as in the case of ratification of treaties. Paul C. Warnke's appointment the Senate ratified on personal appeal of President Carter, despite Democratic majority. But it forced withdrawal of Theodore C. Sorensen, Carter's first nominee for Director of the Central Intelligence Agency.

A good many of the federal offices, specially those of a local nature, are subject to a custom called *senatorial courtesy.* This is an unwritten rule which requires that the President would confer with and secure the consent of the Senator or Senators of his party from the State to which appointment is to be made. If the President does not do so and insists on his own personal choice, the other Senators, acting under the rule of senatorial courtesy, will probably reject the nomination. One of the best examples of the operation of senatorial courtesy was the Floyd H. Robert case of 1938-39. President Roosevelt appointed Robert as judge of the Federal District Court for Western Virginia. This appointment was objected to by both the Senators belonging to the State of Virginia, and the President's party. The President without heeding to their objection sent the name to the Senate for confirmation and the Senate rejected it. A similar conflict occurred in 1951 between President Truman and Senator Paul H. Douglas (Democrat) over two federal judgeships. When the President refused to accept the Senator's candidates, Douglas opposed the President's nominees[33] and the Senate unanimously refused to confirm the Presidential appointments. In case the federal vacancies to be filled are located in the State which has no Senators of the President's party, the President has some discretion, but even there he is bound to consult party leaders in the regions concerned.

The above statement of senatorial courtesy is not the actual practice. Ordinarily, the Senators do not wait to be consulted. They keep their eyes on the possible vacancies and send messages, through the President's liaison representative for Congressional affairs, requesting that certain of their followers be nominated to the positions. The President may attempt to inquire into the qualifications of the nominees of the Senators, but in many instances he simply endorses their desires. In fact, he has no time for all that.

Another class of officer subject to Presidential nomination are minor authorities like revenue officials, marshals and Federal Attorneys within Congressional districts. The custom is that the Representative, if he belongs to the President's party, names the person to be appointed for his district and the recommendation is always accepted unless for special reasons the President desires to make a ''personal'' appointment. If the Representative does not belong to the President's party, the patronage may go to the Senator if there is one of the President's political party. Extension of such a kind of patronage to the Representatives is of considerable utility for maintaining their political organisation.

Finally, are the great variety of federal appointments to minor offices which do not require confirmation of Senate at all. The power of all such appointments is vested by the Act of Congress in President alone or in the heads of various Departments and more than 95 per cent of federal appointments come under this category. By far the greater portion of them are now regarded as ''classified services'' and the appointment is made under civil service rules. Still, from 20 to 30 per cent are treated as patronage. When Congress carries the majority of the party to which the President belongs, and the relations between the two are harmonious, then, it is inclined to increase the proportion of officials whose appointment is vested in the President alone or in heads of Departments. But in times of conflict Congress exhibits its hostility. For example, in 1943, Congress was in ''revolt'' against President Roosevelt's domestic policy and it severely criticised some of the appointments made by him. The Senate went to such an extent as to actually pass a Bill providing that the selection of all officials, with certain exceptions, carrying

33. When Truman's nominations reached the floor of the Senate with adverse recommendation of the Senate Judiciary Committee, Senator Douglas stated, '''I do not want to label the nominees themselves as being personally obnoxious to me. I regard them as estimable men and fine citizens. But I should like to point out that they were nominated without consultation with me, without any indication of the reasons for their selection, and contrary to the recommendations of the much more highly qualified men whose names I had forwarded and who were supported by the heavy preponderance of informed opinion in Illinois.''

a salary of $4,100 a year or more, should be subject to the approval of the Senate. Such a threat is always 'a gun behind the door' which Congress may employ in controlling the exercise of the President's appointing power.

While the Constitution expressly authorises the President to appoint officers with the consent of the Senate, it is completely silent on the question whether he may remove an officer, either with or without the consent of the Senate. The only provision in the Constitution in regard to removal is that by impeachment. But this process of removal is cumbersome and unwieldy. Moreover, the resort to impeachment to remove a person from a petty inferior office "would be," as Garner puts it, "very much like shooting birds with artillery intended for destroying battleships."[34]

The issue of dismissal assumed an important topic in the first session of Congress. There was difference of opinion as to whether that power lay with the President alone or he could do so with the consent of the Senate only, or whether the power lay with Congress to prescribe how removals might be made. It was finally decided that the President may remove alone and there was no necessity of securing the consent of the Senate. This interpretation was accepted by the Supreme Court. In 1866, Congress passed the Tenure of Office Act forbidding the President to make removals except with the consent of the Senate. The Act of 1866, thus, reversed the custom which had been in practice for seventy-eight years and recognised the right of the President to remove officers only on securing the assent of the Senate. President Andrew Johnson violated this Act regarding it as unconstitutional and it was one of the causes of his Impeachment in 1868. The Act was, however, repealed in 1887.

In 1876 an Act of Congress was passed providing that certain classes of postmasters could not be removed from office except with the advice and consent of the Senate. The constitutionality of this Act was contested in the Supreme Court and it was decided in *Myers* v. *United States* that the statute was unconstitutional and that the power to remove was implied not only from the power to appoint, but also from the general authority of the Executive to see that the laws are executed faithfully.[35] But this decision was modified in 1935. The Supreme Court held in Humphery's case that a regulatory commission's powers are quasi-legislative and quasi-judicial in nature and that the President's removal authority could be limited in respect to officers exercising such powers."[36]

To conclude, as to purely administrative offices, for which the President bears constitutional responsibility for the faithful performance of the duties thereof, complete and independent removal power rests in the President to be exercised on any ground. But three classes of officers cannot be removed by the President. First, the judges of the Federal Courts who can be removed by impeachment only. Second, members of the various Boards and Commissions with part legislative and part judicial powers who are protected by statutory limitations on the removal power. Third, all officers and employees who are appointed under Civil Service rules and may not be removed "except for such causes as will promote the efficiency of the service."

**Power of Pardon**

The President's power to grant pardons and reprieves is judicial in nature, and it is exclusive. The Constitution authorises the President "to grant reprieves and pardons for offences against the United States except in case of Impeachment." The President cannot, of course, pardon offences against State laws. Nor can he do it in regard to impeachment offences. Otherwise, his authority of granting pardons is very wide and if he chooses he may grant pardon before as well as after conviction. President Ford granted general pardon to his predecessor Richard Nixon against all offences during his tenure as President. A reprieve postpones the execution of the penalty. A general pardon, granted to a large number of offenders, is called an amnesty and is granted by proclamation. A good example of amnesty is Jefferson's freeing all persons convicted under the Sedition Act of 1798. In 1865 Andrew Johnson issued a proclamation offering amnesty to all those who had borne arms against the United States, with certain exceptions and subject to certain conditions. President Roosevelt issued a last minute pardon to Dr. Francis E. Townsend, who was held in contempt of a House of Repre-

34. Garner, J. W., *Government in the United States*, p. 303.
35. Justice McReynalds, Brandies and Holmes did not agree with the majority opinion. The majority opinion declaring the Act of 1876 unconstitutional and giving full power of removal to President was written by the former President, Chief Justice Taft.
36. *Humphery's Executor (Rahbun)* v.*United States (1935).*

sentatives investigating committee.

In actual practice, the President does not himself exercise his discretion in granting pardons. He has delegated his responsibility to a large extent to the Department of Justice and acts upon its recommendations, though he may take, as President Harding personally took, steps to arrange pardon for Deles.

**Military Powers**

The Constitution declares that the President shall be the Commander-in-Chief of the army and navy and the State militia when called into the service of the United States.[37] Provisions of law empower the President to appoint military and naval officers with the advice and consent of the Senate and in time of war to dismiss them at will. The power to declare war belongs to Congress, though the President may through the conduct of the foreign affairs of the country bring about the situation when declaration of war may become a virtual necessity. President McKinley despatched a battleship to Havana, where it was blown up, and it helped precipitate war with Spain. In 1918 President Wilson sent American forces to Siberia to help Allied troops, when no state of war existed between the United States and Russia, fighting the Bolsheviks. Under Harding and Coolidge armed forces were employed to suppress ''disorders'' in certain Caribbean countries. The United States declared war against Germany in 1941, but the navy had begun to fire on submarines threatening the convoys to Britain long before that. In fact, ''a shooting war' had started in 1940. President Truman had no authorization from Congress in 1950 when he ordered American forces to resist aggression in Korea. President Nixon arrogated to himself ''the power to initiate a war, to invade a foreign country without a declaration of war, to keep secret for three years a massive air attack upon a neutral country....''[38]

When war actually comes, there is tremendous enhancement in President's power both as Executive head and as Commander-in-Chief. As Commander-in- Chief, he decides where the troops are to be located and where the ships are to be stationed. It is upon his orders that troops are mobilised, the fleets assembled, and the militia of the State called out. He may direct the campaign and might, if he wished, take command of military operations, though in practice he never does so. But all major decisions of strategy, and many of tactics as well, are his alone to make or to approve. Congress may still more add to his powers by enacting blanket legislation, giving him discretionary authority in matters of vital importance, in domestic and foreign affairs. In World War I, President Wilson was given power to control production, purchase and sale of various kinds of material for war purposes and food supplies for troops. He had power to take over factories, mines, pipelines, etc. In fact, he had a vast reservoir of power in planning broad strategy, raising military and industrial manpower, and mobilizing the nation's economy for war. In World War II, Congress again delegated vast authority to the President and Roosevelt became a sort of constitutional dictator. Roosevelt used ''Lincolnian as well as Wilsonian'' precedents. In 1942, he demanded that Congress must repeal within a month a provision in the Price Control Act that protected the farmer and which it had refused to repeal earlier. This threat of Roosevelt was characterised as ''a claim of power on the part of the President to suspend the Constitution in a situation deemed by him to make such a step necessary,''[39] Roosevelt's threat succeeded and Congress ''meekly'' repealed the provision. The Supreme Court has expressed its unwillingness to pass judgment on war policies. In the West Coast—Japanese curfew regulations case in 1943—the Court declared : ''The Constitution commits to the Executive and to Congress the exercise of the war power....It has necessarily given them wide scope for the exercise of judgment and discretion....It is not for any court to sit in review of the wisdom of their action or substitute its judgment for theirs.''[40] In the nuclear age of absolute weapons in which we live the next wartime President will have the right of which Lincoln spoke, to take ''any measure which may best subdue the enemy.'' This is fully illustrated by the directions issued by George Bush to the Commander of the Allied Forces engaged in the conduct of the Gulf war.

Some forms of the Constitution, no doubt, are suspended during actual hostilities. But two basic constitutional rights do remain or have so far remained during all wars of the United States.

---

37. Article 2, Section 2, Clause 1.
38 Henry Steele Commager, ''Nixon's Impact on U.S. Presidency.'' *The Tribune,* Chandigarh, August 19, 1974.
39. Corwin, E.S., *Total War and the Constitution,* p. 64.
40. *Hirabayashi* v. *United States (1943).*

One is the ultimate control of the President by the people, that is, Presidential elections must be held during peace and war. In the midst of Civil War, Lincoln had to campaign for re-election and seek the verdict of the people, Roosevelt had twice to do the same in World War II. Similarly, despite certain restrictions, the basic liberties of free speech and free press "have survived the hard test of war."

The President may establish military government in conquered territory and in territory acquired through cession, subject to the Acts of Congress. After World War II, military governments were set up by the United States in Italy, Japan, and in certain sections of Korea, Germany and Austria. These military governments functioned until the signing of the peace treaty and were administered by a combination of American and local personnel.

At home the President may use troops in executing federal laws against resistance that cannot be overcome by ordinary civil process. It is also his constitutional duty to guarantee to each State of the Union a republican form of government, protect it against invasion, and to order out troops to suppress domestic violence upon the application of the State Legislature or Executive.

**Conduct of Foreign Affairs**

The Constitution does nowhere expressly declare that the President is the chief foreign policy maker and the accredited official spokesman of the country in international affairs. But constitutional interpretations and practices accept him so and ascribe such functions to him. In 1799, John Marshall spoke of the President as "the sole organ of the nation in its external relations, and its sole representative with foreign nations." In the Curtiss-Wright case,[41] the Supreme Court referred to the "exclusive power of the President as the sole organ of the Federal Government in the field of international relations—a power which does not require as a basis for its exercise an act of Congress, but, which like every other governmental power, must be exercised in subordination to the applicable provisions of the Constitution." According to the Constitution, the President appoints ambassadors, and other public ministers, by and with the advice and consent of the Senate, he negotiates and concludes treaties with foreign governments, subject to the ratification of two-thirds majority of the Senate, and he receives ambassadors and other public ministers from foreign countries.

The power to appoint ambassadors and to receive them is important, because it involves the vital power of recognition. The President has complete discretion to recognise or not, new governments or States. In 1902, Theodore Roosevelt recognised the new State of Panama a few hours after a revolt had been staged with the help of United States forces. President Wilson withheld recognition from Mexican Governments which he disapproved. President Hoover tried to restrain Japan from an aggressive policy by refusing to recognise its puppet Manchukuo. Roosevelt recognised the government of Soviet Russia in 1939.[42] President Carter recognised China and terminated United States' link with Taiwan in January 1979. Withdrawal of diplomatic agents or alterations in their assignments or instructions amounts to disapproval with the policy of the country concerned. For example, after the conquest of Ethiopia by Italy in 1936, the American legation in Addis Ababa was reduced to a consulate. A more extreme form of indicating displeasure with a country involves closing its consulates as in the case of Germany in 1940.

The President shares his treaty-making power with the Senate. But there are many other methods by which the President may bypass the Senate. The first of this kind are the Executive agreements. Executive agreements are pledges of certain action by Executives of two countries. A famous example is the "gentleman's agreement" between President Theodore Roosevelt and the Emperor of Japan under which Roosevelt agreed to exert his influence and persuade Congress to kill exclusion legislation and the Emperor of Japan agreed to prohibit the emigration of coolies (labourers). Some Executive agreements have marked famous events : The Boxer Protocol of 1901, the Atlantic Charter, and the "destroyer bases" agreement. The Supreme Court has held that Executive agreements within range of the President's power are to be the law of the land. "Such precedents," says E. S. Corwin, "make it difficult to state any limit to the power of the President and Congress, acting jointly, implement effectively any foreign policy, upon which they agree, no matter how the recalcitrant third plus one man of the Senate may feel about the matter."[43]

41. *United States* v. *Curtiss-Wright Export Corp.* See also *University of Illinois* v. *United States.*
42. Wilson, Harding, Coolidge and Hoover had refused to recognise the Russian Soviet Government from 1917 to 1933.
43. Corwin, E. S., *The Constitution and What It Means Today*, p. 102.

In addition to the Executive agreements, Congress may confer authority on the President to make agreements with other nations. The most notable example of such Congressional authority is the Reciprocal Trade Act of 1934 which authorised the President, for a period of three years, to enter into trade agreements with foreign countries, and lower tariff rates by proclamation to the extent of fifty per cent without securing the ratification by the Senate. This Act was extended once in 1937 and again in 1940. In 1943 the term was extended for two years only. These reciprocal trade agreements, although not submitted to the Senate for confirmation, are fully enforceable in the courts.

The President may resort to secret diplomacy and consequently enter into secret agreements with foreign powers and commit himself to the pursuit of a specific policy. This he does by appointing personal emissaries of ambassadorial rank, without submitting their names to the Senate for confirmation as required in the case of more permanent appointees. President Theodore Roosevelt sent a high emissary to Tokyo in 1905 and came to terms with Japan on certain important matters in the Far East. On her part Japan undertook to respect American dominion in the Philippines. Roosevelt, on his part, committed his government to accept the establishment of Japanese sovereignty on Korea. He also impressed upon the Japanese Premier that the people of the United States were determined to see that peace is maintained in the Far East and that "whatever occasion arose, appropriate action of the government of the United States....for such a purpose could be counted upon by them quite as confidently as if the United States was under the treaty obligation." The whole negotiations were so quietly arranged that nothing was known about it in America until after the death of Theodore Roosevelt. Before and after United States entered into World War II, Franklin Roosevelt held top secret conferences with the British Prime Minister and heads of other governments. Some of the agreements reached at these conferences were made public, others were kept secret. From Washington's Proclamation of neutrality in 1793 to Eisenhower's decision to go to the Summit in 1955, Presidents have repeatedly committed the nation to decisive attitudes and actions abroad, more than once, to war itself. President Truman was not exaggerating much when he told an informal gathering of the Jewish war veterans in 1948, "I make American policy." Reagan in his inaugural address on January 20, 1981 enunciated his Government's foreign policy which he truly translated into action immediately after assuming office. He declared, "To those neighbours and allies who share our freedom, we will strengthen our historic ties and assure them of our support and firm commitment. We will match loyalty with loyalty." In an obvious reference to the USSR, the new President affirmed that as "for the enemies of freedom, those who are potential adversaries, they will be reminded that peace is the highest aspiration of the American people. We will negotiate for it, we will not surrender for now or ever. Above all we must realize that no weapon in the arsenal of the world is so formidable as the will and moral courage of free men and women. It is a weapon our adversaries in today's world do not have. Let that be understood by those who practise terrorism and prey upon their neighbours" (as in Afghanistan).

If properly evaluated the powers of the President as chief foreign policy maker and as Commander-in-Chief are, indeed, real, matter of fact, and colossal. And it is not surprising that the President's figure looms large in world politics. In an age of international complexities and mounting tensions in which we live, every word uttered by the President of the United States is searched for meaning in foreign offices throughout the world. Whenever people talk in the capitals of their respective countries "what is the United States going to do?" they actually mean therefrom "what is the President going to do." As Commander-in-Chief, he deploys America's armed forces abroad and occasionally supports policies with what is known as "Presidential war making." It must, however, be noted that in spite of the immensity of his powers in the field of foreign relations much depends upon the personality of the President, the state of conditions prevailing in the country and his ability to persuade Congress to approve or at least finance his programme. The President has, no doubt, the authority and capacity to act even independently of Congress, but he cannot act beyond Congress. Congress provides money and unless it provides what the President asks for no President can succeed in his efforts. Checks and balances operate in foreign policy-making and these cannot be ignored.

**Emergencies**

Emergencies arise in the life of every nation and it is the fundamental right of every State to meet them and preserve its existence. Emergencies in the past concerned with the security of the State and martial law had long been justified as an emergency power to be exercised at the time of great stress to restore law and order and ensure the security of the State. But during the last six decades emergencies have been used as a reason for the exercise of other governmental powers as well, chiefly in order to combat economic emergencies that seemed to threaten the life of the nation. "In recent years," writes Gosnell, "crisis has followed crisis; emergencies have appeared to create new emergencies. One wonders if the United States will ever return to what was formally considered normal times."[44] An associated cause of the growth of Presidency, according to Griffiths, is the shattering series of emergencies, both foreign and domestic, that has been America's lot during the past century. Rossiter makes us to accept an axiom of Political Science that great emergencies in the life of a constitutional State "bring an increase in executive power and prestige, always at least temporarily, more often than not permanently."[45] He cites the examples of Lincoln, Wilson and Franklin Roosevelt. "Each of these men left the Presidency a stronger instrument, an office with more customary and statutory powers, than it had been before the crisis."

The Constitution of the United States does not specially provide for any kind of emergency. The Supreme Court, too, has held that "emergency does not create power" nor does it increase power already given in the Constitution.[46] The exercise of emergency power of the President is based either on his military power, his responsibility to see that the laws are faithfully executed or an emergency power delegated to him by Congress. In times of military emergency the President has always resorted to extraordinary means. But, it was not until 1933 that the President first made use of emergency powers to meet an economic crisis and since then Presidents have issued proclamations declaring both "limited" and "unlimited" national emergencies.

The laws passed by Congress are not uniform concerning actions which may be taken in case of emergencies. Under a few such laws the President may act only after Congress itself has declared that an emergency exists. But ordinarily Congress authorises the President himself to determine whether there is an emergency. The use of emergency powers is both salutary and dangerous. Properly used they are restorative; improperly used, they may become a prelude to dictatorship.

But such a contingency cannot happen in the United States. The system of checks and balances limits the emergency powers of the President. The Supreme Court, in *Youngstown Sheet and Tube Co.* v. *Sawyer* (1952), refused to uphold President Truman when he issued an order directing the Secretary of Commerce to take possession of and operate most of the nation's steel mills. The President's justification for his action was that in order to avert national catastrophe it was necessary. The Supreme Court declared that there was no source of authority for the President's action either in the Constitution or in any Act of Congress. It was not even a valid exercise of the military power of President, for, according to Justice Black, the Commander-in-Chief does not have the power "to take possession of private property in order to keep labour disputes from stopping production. This is a job for the nation's law-making, not for its military authorities....The Constitution does not subject this law- making power of Congress to Presidential or military supervision or control."

From the decision in the *Youngstown Sheet and Tube Co.* v. *Sawyer* following inferences may be drawn when the President may act without the authorization of law : (1) There must be a real emergency; (2) it must be of a type for which Congress has not already legislated; (3) and it must be one which has arisen suddenly not affording sufficient time for action by Congress. These are valid limitations to the exercise of emergency powers of the President, yet the President may still act in time of emergency. There may be times when these limits are obscure. Justice Clark agreeing with the majority decision in the case cited above, declared, "In may view....the Constitution does grant to the President exclusive authority in times of grave and imperative emergency. In fact, to my thinking, such a grant may well be necessary to the very existence of the Constitution itself." This is "but a substantiation of the doctrine," says Gosnell, "that when emergency power is used properly, it is restorative in nature."

So long as America held relatively aloof

44. *Fundamentals of American National Government*, p. 185.
45. Rossiter, Clinton, *American Presidency*, p. 65.
46. Refer to *Home Building and Loan Association* v. *Blaisdell* (1934).

from the world, cognisance of national emergencies could be taken alone. Now America has assumed for itself the status of the only super power and it has upset the old balance of the nineteenth century completely and finally. Woodrow Wilson wrote, in Theodore Roosevelt's last year in office: "The President can never again be the mere domestic figure he has been throughout so large a part in our history. The nation has risen to the first rank in power and resources. The other nations of the world look askance upon her, half in envy, half in fear, and wonder with a deep anxiety what she will do with her vast strength....our President must always henceforth, be one of the great powers of the world, whether he acts greatly or wisely or not....We can never hide our present President again as a mere domestic officer....He must stand always at the front of our affairs, and the office will be as big and influential as the man who occupies it." Rossiter maintains that it may be taken as an axiom of Political Science that the more deeply a nation becomes involved in the affairs of other nations, the more powerful becomes its executive branch. "The authority of the President", he says, "has been permanently inflated by our entrance into world politics and our decision to be armed against threats of aggression, and as the world grows smaller, he will grow bigger."[47]

## LEGISLATIVE POWERS

The Presidential system of government, spearates the Executive and Legislative branches, as signing to each a major role in the government. No machinery is provided for integrating the two. But while the chief duty of the President is to execute the laws, he is at the same time given a share in their making. Rossiter characterises the President as the Chief Legislator, though it appears to be an extravagant title. He says, "Congress still has its strongmen, but the complexity of the problems it is asked to solve by a people who assume that all problems are solvable has made external leadership requisite of effective operation. The President alone is in a political, constitutional, and practical position to provide such leadership, and he is therefore expected, within the limits of constitutional and political propriety, to guide Congress in much of its lawmaking activity."[48] President's share in law-making is both positive and negative.

### Presidential Messages

The Constitution ordains that the President "shall from time to time give to the Congress information of the State of the Union, and recommend to their consideration such measures as he shall judge necessary and expedient; he may, on extraordinary occasions, convene both Houses, or either of them, and in case of disagreement between them, with respect to the time of adjournment, he may adjourn them to such time as he shall think proper...." The Constitution in the presence of this specific provision contemplates Presidential leadership in matters of legislation and, indeed, as Charles Beard says, "it is not too much to say that the fame of most Presidents rests upon their success in writing policies into law rather than upon their achievements as mere administrators."[49] Presidents who successfully directed Congress in policy-making are Jackson, Lincoln, Theodore Roosevelt, Wilson, and Franklin Roosevelt. The nation had rated them "great" Presidents.

The information required to be furnished is contained in an annual message (State of the Union message) conmmunicated at the beginning of each session, and in special messages communicated from time to time during the session. The Presidential message may be delivered orally in the presence of both Houses, or sent to them in a document. The annual message is major in significance and may roughly be compared to the Speech from the Throne in England. Washington and Adams came in person to Congress to deliver information and make recommendations. Jefferson adopted the practice of communicating what he had to say in the form of a written message. This was the rule for 113 years, when in 1913, President Wilson returned to Washington's custom and began delivering his messages to Congress personally. While reviving the earlier precedent Woodrow Wilson said, "the President of the United States is a person, not a mere department of the government hailing Congress from some isolated island of jealous power, sending messages, not speaking naturally and with his own voice; he is a human being trying to co-operate with other human beings in a common service."

For a time Wilson's successors followed in his footsteps. President Hoover read his first

47. Rossiter, Clinton, *The American Presidency,* p. 64.
48. *Ibid,* p. 19.
49. Beard, C. A., *American Government and Politics,* p. 203.

message to the general public over the radio as well to Congress, but subsequently he resumed the old practice of sending written messages. Franklin D. Roosevelt restored the practice of reading personally the messages as a means of drawing the attention of the whole nation to his programme with the invaluable help of radio and camera. This was followed at short intervals by a succession of special messages, each dealing with a particular problem and outlining in some detail the administration's proposed measures for dealing with it.

The annual message contains a review of the activities of government during the preceding year, a declaration of party policies, and recommendations for such legislation as the President deems the interests of the country require. Sometimes the message may contain an important announcement, warning some other country against pursuing a certain course of action. It may also contain a momentous statement of principles as the Monroe Doctrine incorporated in President Monroe message of December 1823 or Roosevelt's four freedoms which summarised objectives of American foreign policy in 1941. In March 1947, Truman appealed to Congress for aid to Greece and Turkey in their resistance to Russian aggression in the name of communism. In 1954 session of Congress, President Eisenhower presented some sixty-five proposals for new legislation in his opening address and even supplementary in later messages plus the budget message and the annual economic report.

Less obvious, but equally important, are the frequent written messages sent from the White House to Congress on a vast scale of public problems. These messages are read by a clerk, often indistinctly, and printed in the Congressional Record. They indicate the needs of the government and the necessity for an appropriate legislation and, thus, is a gesture to friendly legislators to the President to initiate the required measures, Often, these messages are accompanied by detailed drafts of legislation and the friendly legislators take them up as they are.

The consideration which the Presidential messages receive at the hands of Congress depends upon the influence which the President wields with the two Houses. If he belongs to a different political party from that which is in control of Congress, or if for other reasons Congress is out of sympathy with his policies, his recommendations receive very little consideration. Franklin Roosevelt assumed unprecedented leadership in legislation and every important measure enacted by Congress between 1933 and 1943 either emanated from the Executive Departments or was sponsored by the President. But the Congressional election of 1942 made a sharp change in the attitude of Congress with a reduced Democratic majority and a general disapproval of his domestic policy. The new Congress struck down one after another measures sponsored or favoured by President Roosevelt. A similar position happened in 1973, when a political crisis developed between Republican President Nixon and Congress controlled by the opposition Democratic Party. The most immediate issues were the ending of United States involvement in Vietnam and what many members of the Senate and the House of Representatives looked upon as the usurpation of Congressional power by the President. Democratic leaders of the 93rd Congress pledged to take strong counter-measures to reassert the authority of Congress as a co-equal branch of the Government with the Executive.

President Jimmy Carter could sense the tough and aggressive attitude of the Congressmen whose minds were moulded by the decade in which Presidents acted like monarch in determining foreign policy, making wars and subverting the executive structure of the Federal machine. He demonstrated that he needed more Congress expertise for his domestic measures and in the making of America's foreign policy. It was an established White House ritual that Jimmy Carter met from two to a couple of dozen members of Congress and informally discussed matters with them. The two-to-one Congressional majority of Democrats over Republicans, no doubt, worked to Carter's advantage on routine issues, but, with impressive insistence, the 95th Congress declared its intention to share in the making of foreign policy,"unlike any we have seen in history." The House of Representatives voted to trim foreign aid in general than to deny United States Funds in international lending agencies to certain countries. Some of these restrictions were endorsed by the Senate, despite the appeal of the White House that such action would deny administration needed flexibility to conduct foreign policy. So familiar did the White House become with the issue of Congressional intrusion into foreign policy that President Carter declared, "I have some good days on Capital Hill, but I have some bad days." The House of Representatives rejected Carter's recommendation to send nuclear fuel to India whereas the Senate decided in favour of the Presidential recommendation. Reagan began courting Congress extraordinarily when he organised a political action committee, called Citizens for the Republic, to finance Republican candidates for national and State offices. During the 1980 campaign, Reagan supporters in Congress created a network of Congressional advisory committees to develop policy positions for him and advise him "on key concerns of constituents." The courtship of Congress intensified during the transition—the period in between his election and inauguration when the opinion of Doles and Senator John Tower, Storm Thurmond, and other Republicans heavily influenced Cabinet choices. Reagan aides promised regular bipartisan leadership meetings with the President. Reagan himself "met with a number of Senators....Democrats and Republicans......touching all the right keys," Doles said. still Reagan had some very uneasy time with Congress and he had to give way or compromise on a number of crucial issues.

All the same, legislative leadership of the President cannot be discounted. The impact of the President's personality aside, the delivery of the oral messages, heard by tens of millions over the radio and heard and seen by additional millions, through television and newsreel, give greater emphasis to executive recommendations. The attendant publicity is frequently a factor in mobilizing public opinion in support of Presidential proposals. If, in addition, they receive popular approval, the Presidential prestige is enhanced considerably. In summing up the legislative powers of the President, Rossiter says, "The President who will not give his best thoughts to guiding Congress, more so the President who is temperamentally or politically unfitted 'to get along with Congress' is now rightly considered a national liability." John F. Kennedy in his "A Candidate's view of the Presidency" declared that the President "cannot afford 'for the sake of the office as well as the nation—to be another Warren G. Hardinge' described by one backer as a man who 'would, when elected, sign whatever bills the Senate sent him and not send bills for the Senate to pass'. Rather he must know when to lead the Congress, when to consult it and when he should act alone."[50]

**Power to Call Extraordinary Sessions**

The President is empowered to call extraordinary sessions of Congress for consideration of special matters of an urgent character. The President cannot of course, compel Congress to adopt his recommendations at a special session any more than at a regular session but "he can some time hasten action and if he is backed by a strong public opinion he may be able to accomplish even more." In earlier days when the second regular session of every Congress ended on March 4, with the next regular session not commencing until after the following December, special sessions were fairly numerous to deal with extraordinary situations specially in years like 1909, 1913, 1921, 1929 and 1933. Under the new calendar introduced by the Twentieth Amendment the need for special sessions is less, because the intervals between regular sessions are shorter, and the new President after his inauguration finds a new Congress already in session.[51] In 1939, a special session was necessitated by the outbreak of War. Since 1939, there had been only one occasion when President Truman called "a Congress back to Washington after it had gone home without expectation of returning."

The President is also given the power to adjourn Congress when there is disagreement between the House of Representatives and the Senate as to time of adjournment. But this power has never been exercised, for Congress has always been able to agree on this subject.

**Budget**

A sound, complete, effective and practical Budget system was inaugurated in 1921 under the Budget and Accounting Act. Before there was an Executive office to enable the President to discharge the responsibilities of a Manager with regard to the expenditure of the administrative agencies. Each Department of Government submitted and defended its budget directly to Congress and the President did not review the financial demands of Departments and independent agencies. The Budget and Accounting Act, 1921 vests in the President the sole responsibility for requesting the grant of funds by Congress and empowers him to assemble, correlate, revive, reduce or increase the estimates of the several Departments and Establishments. He is required

50. Cornwell Elmere, *The American Presidency : Vital Center,* p. 20.
51. The Amendment was adopted on February 6, 1933. Section 1 reads, "The terms of the President and Vice-President shall end at noon on the 20th day of January, and the term of Senators and Representatives at noon on the 3rd day of January........"Section 2 provides, "The Congress shall assemble, at least, once in every year and such meeting shall begin at noon on the 3rd day of January, unless they shall by law appoint a different day."

to submit to Congress a complete statement—Budget—of estimated revenues and expenditure and activities of the government as recommended programme. Budget is, thus, a detailed statement of policy objectives with means of achieving them for the guidance of Congress.

The Act of 1921 created the Budget Bureau as the organ for performing the work required of the President. It is empowered to supervise the spending activities of the various agencies and to advise the President on steps to be taken to introduce greater economy and efficiency in the administrative services. The Director of the Budget, who is head of the Bureau, is appointed by the President and acts directly and solely under the President. Since 1939, the Bureau has been located in the Executive Office of the President and has become the President's largest and most valuable staff agency. The Act also created the independent General Accounting Office, headed by the Comptroller General. "In taking the initiative for transferring the Bureau of Budget to the Executive office of the President, providing high level advisers within the White House Office and creating an executive planning organization, Roosevelt made it possible for a President to come closer to fulfilling the charges of the office than would have been conceivable before these steps were taken."[52]

**Power to Issue Ordinances**

Under the legislative functions of the President may be included what is known as the ordinance power, that is, the power to issue certain orders and regulations having the force of law. The issuing of ordinances or "executive orders" as it is sometimes called, has now become such an important phase of the President's legislative powers that in 1935 Congress passed a law,[53] requiring that all executive orders, decrees or proclamations having general applicability and legal effect must be published in the *Federal Register,* which is issued daily.

Some of these regulations are issued by the President and other administrators under express authority conferred upon them by Acts of Congress; others are issued as a result of the necessity of prescribing means for carrying into effect the laws of Congress and the treaties; while still others are issued in pursuance of the constitutional powers of the President, and this he does as Commander-in-Chief of the armed forces. It has now become a normal practice with Congress to pass laws in general terms leaving discretionary authority with the President or the executive Departments to fill in the gaps and this is tantamount to legislating in fact. The National Emergency Act, 1933, authorised "the President to organise and regulate the industries of the United States to create new agencies, to make regulations for them, to delegate functions for subordinates, and to do other things deemed necessary to bring about economic prosperity." The Trade Agreement of 1934 empowered the President to make the trade agreements with foreign nations and lower the existing tariff rates by 50 per cent. And even more radical kind of delegation was contained in the Reorganisation Act of 1939. Franklin Roosevelt, in fact, broke all records. Within a short time after his inauguration he prevailed upon Congress to delegate large powers to him and, thus, started an era of executive orders. Senator Herink Shipstead compiled the statistics and figured that President Roosevelt had issued 3,073 executive orders prior to 1944. During the same period 4,553 laws were passed by Congress.

The Congressional delegation of discretionary authority to the Executive has been a subject of deep controversy and described by many as a violation of the theory of Separation of Powers and an inroad on the legislative competence of Congress. The Supreme Court has established the general rule which requires that Congress should set standards and enunciate the policy under which the ordinance power is to be exercised by the President or his subordinates. In the National Industrial Recovery Act, 1933, for example, the Court found that the Congress had given the President power without required constitutional standard or policy to guide the Executive. The second case arose over the general National Recovery Act (NRA) code-making authority which the Court found delegated lawmaking to an even greater extent and was therefore unconstitutional.[54]

**Veto Powers**

Finally, the President is given an important share in legislation through his veto power. The

52. Harvard, William C., *The Government and Politics of the United States,* pp. 96-97.
53. The Federal Register Act.
54. *Schechter Poultry Corp.* v. *United States* (1935).

Constitution requires that all Bills and resolutions, except proposed constitutional amendments, must be submitted to the President before becoming law. If he approves, he appends his signatures thereto and it is promulgated as law. If he disapproves, he returns it to the House in which it originated with his objection, within ten days. Congress, by a two-third vote in each Chamber, may then pass it over his veto. If the President fails to sign or veto the Bill within ten days, excluding Sundays, it becomes law without his signatures. If Congress adjourns within ten days after the President receives the Bill and he takes no action, the Bill is automatically killed. This is known as the *pocket veto* and it is absolute. Towards the end of a session numerous Bills and resolutions are passed by Congress in order to clear up its accumulated business. A considerable number of the last-minute Bills, to which the President may be opposed or for which he does not want to take responsibility, thus, fail to become law and the Presidents have rather generously used this device. President Jimmy Carter killed in a single day (November 11, 1978) three Bills he considered inflationary.

The veto power has been used more vigorously during recent times than formerly. Eight Presidents, John Adams, Jefferson, J.Q. Adams, Van Buren, W. H. Harrison, Taylor, Filmore and Garfield, did not veto any Bills. The first six Presidents vetoed only three Bills. But in contrast to this Franklin D. Roosevelt alone vetoed 63 Bills (9 were overridden). Truman vetoed 251 Bills (12 overridden) and Eisenhower 86. The share of Jimmy Carter and Ronald Reagan is no less. Both Franklin D. Roosevelt (1944) and Harry Truman (1948) ventured into new territory when they vetoed Tax Bills, though both were overridden by Congress.

Washington and other early Presidents vetoed only those Bills which they regarded unconstitutional. Jackson was the first President to use this power to safeguard the Executive branches of government against the encroachments of the Legislature. Now Presidents veto Bills which they regard "as inexpedient, contrary to public policy, or for any other reason that is considered compelling." Eisenhower vetoed the first Farm Bill to come to him in 1956 on the ground that it was "bad legislation."

But Congress too has often reasserted its authority by overriding the Presidential veto. The Democratic majority in the Congress overrode President Ford's veto for 11 times during his tenure of office. Only President Andrew Johnson (15 times) and President Harry Truman (12 times) had their veto quashed by Congress more often than Gerald Ford, who had served only half as Andrew Johnson and less than one- third as long as Harry Truman.

## THE PRESIDENT AS A LEADER

### A Party Leader

The President combines in his person the two offices of King and Prime Minister, or as Theodore Roosevelt said, "A President has a great chance; his position is almost that of a King and Prime Minister rolled into one." On the one hand he is a party leader, the spokesman and representative of popular majority "more or less organised in the party that he heads." Originally, the Chief Executive was not a party man and Washington thought himself identified with no party. But when political parties had become definitely established, we have it from Jefferson's time that Presidents began to be elected as party men and party leadership became as truly a function of the President as of the British Prime Minister. And today his position as a political leader of the party is as much a source of his power as the authority which the Constitution confers upon him. Chosen as a party man to head a government operated under a party system, the President surrounds himself with advisers of his own faith, consults usually with men belonging to his party in Congress for appointments, confers with his own men in the party in framing policy, and he uses his power as chief legislator to push through the party's programme to a crowning victory. Sometimes it troubles good Americans to watch their dignified chief of the State deeply submerged in party politics, which torment Washington's spirit. "Yet if he is to persuade Congress, if he is to achieve a loyal and cohesive administration, if he is to be elected in the first place (and re-elected in the second) he must put his hand firmly to the ploy (plough) of politics." John F. Kennedy, commenting upon President Eisenhower's preference to "stay above politics," maintained that no President "can escape politics. He has not only been chosen by the nation—he has been chosen by his party. And if he insists that he is 'President of all the people' and should, therefore, offend none of them—if he blurs the issues and differences between the parties—if he neglects the party machinery and avoids his party's leadership—then he has not only weakened the political party as an instrument of the democratic process he has dealt a blow to the democratic process itself. I prefer the example of Abe Lincoln, who loved politics with the passion of a born practitioner.''[55]

**Voice of the People**

At the same time, the President is the voice of the people; the leading formulator and expounder of public opinion in the United States. While he acts as a political leader of some, he serves as a moral spokesman for all. Woodrow Wilson, well before he could become the President, explained the essence of this role: ''He (President) is the only national voice in affairs. Let him once win the administration and confidence of the country, and no other single force can withstand him, no combination of forces will easily overpower him. His position takes the imagination of the country. He is the representative of no constituency, but of the whole people. When he speaks in his true character, he speaks for no special interest. If he rightly interprets the national thought and boldly insists upon it, he is irresistible; and the country never feels the zest for action so much as when its President is of such insight and calibre. Its instinct is for unified action and it craves for a single leader.'' The President is the head of the State and the personal spokesman of the people, even of those who voted against him and who still oppose him, Former President Truman in a TV-radio interview with Edward R. Munrow in 1958, graphically described the President as ''lobbyist for all the people.'' In his address to Democratic National Convention, which nominated him to be the Party's presidential candidate for the second term, Jimmy Carter described the President as ''the steward of the nation's destiny. He must protect our children—and the children they will have—and the children of generations to follow. He must speak and act for them. This is his burden—and his glory.''[56]

As an administrator the President must faithfully administer the laws, no matter whether these laws were passed by Democratic or Republican majorities in Congress. As Commander-in-Chief he represents the whole nation. He does not direct war for the benefit of any single party or any class of people. He, indeed, acts for all the people. The rank and file of the people identify the President with the federal government, and even with the American way of life. The White House is one of the few national sacred buildings. The President embodies the nation and as well leads it. The people naturally look to him for guidance in all sort of matters. It is he who labours to make the United States a better and prosperous place to live in. Even in democracy the people need a leader. ''They need some one who will personalise government and authority, who will simplify politics, who will symbolise the protective role of the State, who will seem to be concerned with them.'' The eyes of the whole nation are, in fact, riveted towards its first citizen. There is a corps of astute journalists in Washington who shadow the President wherever he goes. They are always after to catch even the most trivial phrase that falls from his lips at press conferences, at fireside chats, or off-hand and spread it broadcast throughout the length and breadth of the country. His message to Congress (State of the Union) stirs the country and it is the one great public document which is most widely read and discussed. The President, wrote Woodrow Wilson just before his first inauguration, ''is expected by the Nation to be leader of his party as well as the Chief Executive Officer of the Government, and the country will take no excuses from him. He must play the part and play it successfully or lose the country's confidence. He must be Prime Minister, as much concerned with the guidance of legislation as with the just and orderly execution of law, and he is the spokesman of the Nation in everything, even in the most momentous and most delicate dealings of the Government with foreign nations.'' John F. Kennedy said, that the White House is not the centre of political leadership. It must be the centre of moral leadership—a 'bully pulpit,' as Theodore Roosevelt described it. ''For only the President represents the national interest. And upon him alone converge all the needs and aspirations of all parts of the country, all departments of the government, all nations of the world.''[57] In his farewell address to the nation on January 14, 1981, President Jimmy Carter observed, ''The President is the only elected official charged with representing all the people. In the moments of decision, after the different and conflicting views have been aired, it is the President who then must speak to the nation and

55. ''A Candidate's View of the Presidency'', reproduced in Elmer E., Cornwell's *The American Presidency, Vital Center,* p. 21.
56. Reproduced in *Span,* New Delhi (The International Communication Agency, American Center), October, 1980.
57. ''A Candidate's View of Presidency'', reproduced in E. Cornwell's *The American Presidency, A Vital Center,* p. 21.

for the nation."[58]

**Head of the State**

In an essay on British Government Ernest Barker described the monarch as a symbol of unity, a magnet of loyalty, and a centre of ceremony.[59] The President as head of the State serves the American people in the same capacity. Apart from the Chief Executive, the Constitution makers had expected him to perform, like the Monarch, what Bagehot called, the "dignified functions." Today, the "dignified" functions of the President surpass the expectations of the Founding Fathers. "Throwing out the ball at the first base ball game, lighting the White House Christmas tree, sponsoring Easter egg rolling on the White House lawns, receiving monarchs and delegations of almost reverential school children, the President is a dignified embodiment of the nation in a nation where official dignity is scarce and the supply normally exceeds the demand."[60] The American people need such a symbol and it has been useful "as a cement of national feeling." This symbolic character of the office of the President has strengthened its practical powers.

Speaking of the President's powers in general, Justice William O. Douglas of the Supreme Court said in a recent opinion, "the great office of President is not a weak and powerless one. The President represents the people and is their spokesman in domestic and foreign affairs. The office is respected more than any other in the land. It gives a position of leadership that is unique. The power to formulate policies and mould opinion inheres in the Presidency and conditions our national life." Harold Laski simply epitomises the whole truth when he said, "The President of the United States is both more or less than a King; he is also both more or less than a Prime Minister. The more carefully his office is studied, the more does its unique character appear." His military role, his ceremonial functions, and his national responsibilities combine to make him a powerful chief of the State representing the whole nation.

**Presidential Power: Peril or Promise**

The issue of the powers of the President has echoed and re-echoed throughout the history of American nation. Writing about President Andrew Jackson, Henry Clay said, "we are in the midst of a revolution, hitherto bloodless, but rapidly leading towards a change of the pure republican character of the government and to the concentration of all power in the hands of one man." The problem has become more critical in the present century. Amaury de Riencourt, writing under the caption *"The Coming Caesars,"* says, "In truth, no mental effort is required to understand that the President of the United States is the most powerful single human being in the world today. Further crisis will inevitably transform him into a full fledged Caesar, if we do not beware. Today, he wears ten hats—as Head of State, Chief Executive, Minister of Foreign Affairs, Chief Legislator, Head of Party, Tribune of the people, Ultimate arbitrator of Social Justice, Guardian of Economic Prosperity, and World Leader of Western Civilization. Slowly and unobtrusively, these hats are becoming crowns and this pyramid of hats is slowly metamorphosing itself into a tiara, the tiara of one man's imperium."[61] John F. Keneddy, in his address, *A Candidate's View of Presidency,* said, "whatever the political affiliation of our next President, whatever his views may be on all the issues and problems that rush in upon us, he must above all be the Chief Executive in every sense of the word. He must be prepared to exercise the fullest powers of the office—all that are specified and some that are not. He must master complex problems as well as receive one-page memorannda. He must originate action as well as study groups. He must re-open the channels of communication between the world of thought and the seal of power."[62] Kennedy's comments on the Presidential office were a kind of counter-attack against the reaction President Eisenhower had represented against the Roosevelt-Truman era. "Roosevelt fulfilled," he said, "the role of moral leadership. So did Wilson and Lincoln, Truman and Jackson and Teddy Roosevelt. They led the people as well as the Government—they fought for great ideals as well as bills. And the time has come to demand that kind of leadership again. And so, as this vital campaign begins, let us discuss the issues the next President will face—but let us also discuss the powers and tools with which he must face them. For he must endow the office with extraordinary strength and vision."[63]

---

58. Reproduced in *Span,* New Delhi (The International Communication Agency, American Center), March 1981.
59. Barker, E., *Essays on Government,* p. 6.
60. Brogan, D. W., *An Introduction to American Politics,* p. 273.
61. Cornwell, Elmer E., *The American Presidency : Vital Center,* p. 44.
62. *Ibid.,* p. 19.
63. *Ibid.,* p. 21.

Wars and emergencies, political and economic, are the main harbingers of Caesarism. In grave emergencies, leadership can never be collective and the people of United States are now living in an age of permanent emergency. The Government has to fight "hot wars" and wage "cold wars", solve critical and explosive issues involving abuse of diplomatic immunities as in the case of American hostages in Iran, prevent periodic trade and financial crises and create conditions of security in all avenues of the nation's life. The Government must also mitigate labour-management conflict, check monopolistic trends, vitalise the economy by removing roadblocks that slowed the economy and reduced productivity, provide decent housing, educational and health facilities and secure civil rights. President Carter maintained, "Today, we are asking our political system to do things of which the founding fathers never dreamed. The government they designed for a few hundred people now serves a nation of almost 230 million people. Their small coastal republic now spans beyond a continent, and we now have the responsibility to help lead much of the world through difficult times to a secure and prosperous future."[64] Such an immense increase in the efforts of the Government to achieve desirable results has literally forced a modern President to be what Woodrow Wilson called "a big man." Amaury Reincourt succinctly said, "Presidential power in America has grown as American power and expansion has grown, one developing within the other."

The "big man" as a symbol of power for good and evils has evoked varying responses. There are those who share the view that the Presidential power has increased, is increasing and ought to be diminished. They warmly supported the Twenty-Second Amendment to the Constitution which limited the President's tenure to two terms in office. By this limitation they hoped that the vast expansion of executive power will not lead to dictatorship and the destruction of representative democracy. Corwin, on the other end, suggests that such fears of Presidential dictatorship or domination are exaggerated. He notes the restraints on Presidential power that still exist. He reminds us that public opinion in the United States has strongly demanded vigorous Presidential leadership. Corwin, however, emphatically urges improved relationship between the President and Congress as a possible solution of the still inadequate status of the Presidency today.[65]

Laski finds many hindrances to the exercise of effective Presidential leadership. Instead of fearing power, he maintains, that power, "equal to the function the President has to perform, and suitably criticised and controlled, should be given to the Chief Executive."[66] Laski endorsed the views of the President's (1937) Committee on Administrative Management which were, in general, shared by the Hoover Commission, supporting administrative reorganisation in the interest of a strong, energetic, unified, efficient and responsible executive. Both the President's Committee and the Hoover Commission agreed that the President must be given administrative authority commensurate with his constitutional responsibility."[67]

The Presidency of the United States is, indeed, an office of great power. A number of factors, some historical and some institutional, have converged in modern times and have changed radically the character of the office as it was conceived by the framers of the Constitution. At the same time, the limits upon the Presidency are many and they have a way of exerting themselves even in the midst of grave crisis. No significant policy can be made effective without the approval of Congress, the law making and money appropriating body, and always jealous to assert its authority and independence. Congress also investigates, through its committees, the activities of the Executive Departments and their agencies. No unconstitutional action can escape the probity of the Supreme Court. "The opposing party, the free and active press, the permanent civil service, the governments of the fifty States and the giant corporations and labour unions, and

64. President Jimmy Carter's farewell address to the nation, January 14, 1981, *Span,* New Delhi, March, 1981.
65. Corwin, E.S., *The President : Office and Powers,* pp. 356-358.The peculiarities of the American electoral system make it possible for one Party to gain the White House while the other wins a majority of Seats in the House and the Senate. Such divided victories have occurred only five times since 1848—in 1956, 1968, 1986, 1988 and 1990. In 1980 and 1982 the Republicans gained majority in the Senate while they remained in minority in he House of Representatives. The majority of the Democrats increased by 25 more members in 1982. It is in the "Off-year" (mid-term non-Presidential) elections that the Party not in control of the White House is more likely to obtain control of Congress. Such a division has occurred in 13 of the 26 "off-year" elections since 1884.
66. Laski, H. J., *American Presidency,* p. 97.
67. *Report,* pp. 1-3, 53.

universities, all these independent centres of power can frustrate any President who attempts to overstep the boundaries of his rightful authority''[68] Jimmy Carter maintained in his farewell address to the nation (January 14, 1981): ''This is at once the most powerful office in the world—and among the most severely constrained by law and custom. The President is given a broad responsibility to lead—but cannot do so without the support and consent of the people, expressed formally through the Congress and informally through a whole range of public and private institutions.'' Every President's conscience, training and sense of history, remarks Clinton Rossiter ''have joined to halt him short of the kind of deed that would destroy his fame and his standing with the people.''[69] If he becomes so desperate to cross the boundary, he may meet the fate of Richard Nixon and make himself liable for impeachment, though Nixon was saved by President Ford by giving him general pardon against all offences during his tenure of office.

American Presidency, therefore, has a promise that it is an instrument of constitutional government. ''And it is one of the two prides of the American people that no one of their Presidents has been a scoundrel or a tyrant.'' The second is the tradition of American democracy, personal liberty and moral behaviour. This is the real strength of Presidency: Ronald Reagan had not met the fate of Richard Nixon, but the 'Irangate' scandal (arms for hostages deal) had a much more serious impact on America's status as a major economic and political power than Water-Gate did. And what shocked most the Americans was that their President (Reagan) lied to the American public, that he played foul with some of its premier institutions, (for example Congress,) that he failed to meet those uniquely American standards of decency, morality and democracy. In short, Regan betrayed that ''mythic self-image of American exceptionalism.''

Concluding his discussion on *The Coming Caesars,* Amaury de Riencourt says that the rise of Caesarism in America is considerably eased by a number of American features. The first is, '''democratic equality, with its concomitant conformism and psychological socialization, which is more fully developed in the United States than it has ever been anywhere, at any time.'' The second important feature is that Caesarism can come to America constitutionally, without having to alter or break down any existing institution. ''The White House is already the seat of the most powerful tribunician authoritty ever known to history. All it needs is amplification and extension.. Caesarism in America does not have to challenge the Constitution as in Rome or engage in civil warfare and cross any fateful Rubicon. It can slip in quite naturally, discreetly, through constitutional channels.''[70] Carl J. Friedrich says, ''indeed, two modern developments have brought with them a curb to presidential power as contrasted with Jackson's days : one is the professional expert and administrator, and the other is the techinques of mass communication and of polls which has brought the citizen's view into limelight.''[71] The Water-gate revelations blurred President Nixon's public image. There had also been revelations of wholesale falsehoods in regard to the bombing of Cambodia. By a vote of 71 to 18, the Senate approved a Bill on July 20, 1973 limiting the power of the President to commit the United States armed forces to future hostilities without firm Congressional approval. Speaking on the Bill, Senator Jacob Javits, a Republican, angrily asked, ''What gives him (the President) the pre-eminence and patriotism that is denied to us ? I do not understand it. He is human and mortal, as we are. If you had any doubt about it yesterday, you should not have it today. What is the basis for the assumption that he is infallible and cannot make a mistake and that only we are capable of mistakes ? Nixon was on record saying that the American people were like children and his opinion of their elected representative was not mere flattering. It had also been reported that Nixon based his actions on the theory that the President knew all the facts and he had the right to order burglary of the files of Dr. Daniel Ellsbergs, the psychiatrist. But what ultimately was Nixon's fate? A self-condemned person who brought Presidency to shame. No less was the contribution of his Vice-President, Spiro Agnew, to loss of faith by the people in the institution of the President.'' Agnew resigned in 1973, because of the ''kick charges.'' At that time he did not contest charges of evading $29,000 in income taxes. in April 1981 he was fined

68. Clinton Rossiter, ''The Presidency of the U.S.A.'' *The Indian Express,* New Delhi, November 6, 1964.
69. *Ibid.*
70. Cornwell, Elmer E., *The American Presidency : Vital Center,* p. 45.
71. Friedrich, C.J., *Constitutional Government and Democracy,* pp. 380-81.

$250,000 to pay Maryland for accepting ''kick-backs'' while Governor of the State from 1967 to 1969.

The country's reaction against Lyndon Johnson, Richard Nixon and Ronald Reagan demostrates that Americans do not want a President to become too powerful, to take too much authority to himself, to cut too many corners, to abuse the office, to ride roughshod over Congress. Yet the country certainly wants him to have ample power to cope with all emergencies, to be firmly in command of the sprawling bureaucracy, ''really to run things.'' In fact, Congress and the public push at the President new authority to handle new problems. Election results and opinion polls indicate that the voters also respond to a just, humane, decent person—but one who can also be tough and ruthless when necessary. Time and again, an Alladi Stevension (1952 Democratic candidate) or a George McGovern (1972 Democratic candidate) or even Jimmy Carter for the second term in 1980, is dismissed as ''too nice'' or ''too decent'' for the White House. ''The public seems to want a soft-hearted but hard-nosed President, and that is a hard role to cast.'' They want someone they can look up to and respect. Despite Ronald Reagan's landslide victory in the 1980 Presidential election and even the Democrats voting with his economic policies, especially to cut government spending, the public opinion poll (published by the *New York Times* in March 1982) showed the steady erosion of popular support for his domestic and foreign policy. It was found that only 45 per cent of those asked approved Reagan's ''handling the job'' as President. The Hollywood style of conducting the state affairs the nation did not accept from the occupant of the White House and that too, at the age of 70. The John-Tower Edmund, Muskie-Bent Scowropt-review Board exonerated Reagan of any personal wrong-doing in the so-called Iran-gate scandal, in which arms were sought to be sold to Tehran in exchange for American hostages held in Iran and the funds from the arms sale got diverted to Contra rebels in Nicaragua. In a broadcast speech to the nation, President Ronald Reagan acknowledged that his once-secret Iranian initiative ''deteriorated,'' into an ''arms for hostages'' deal and said, ''it was a mistake'' and ''as President, I cannot escape responsibility.'' The Iran-Contra affair has been the biggest crisis of the Reagan Presidency. But the political damage done to the Presidency cannot be repaired at any cost, though he had owned full responsibility for his own actions and for those of his administration and acknowledged : ''I've paid a price for my silence in terms of your (nation's) trust and confidence.''

## SUGGESTED READINGS


Agar, Herbert : *The United States, The President, The Parties and the Constitution.*

Beard, C.A. : *American Government and Politics,* Chap. VII.

Brinkley, W.E. : *President and Congress.*

Brogan, D.W. : *The American Political System,* Part Four, Chap. 1.

Brogan, D.W. : *An Introduction to American Politics,* Chap. VIII.

Brown, S. : *American Presidency.*

Brownlow, L. : *The President and the Presidency.*

Cornwell, Elmer E. : *The American Presidency, Vital Center.*

Corwin, E.S. : *The Constitution and What it Means Today.*

Corwin E.S. : *The President: Office and Powers.*

Haight, D.E., and Larry D. Johnson: *The President: Roles and Powers.*

Hayman, S. : *The American President.*

Herring, E.P.: *Presidential Leadership: The Political Relations of Congress and the Chief Executive.*

Irish, M.D. and Prothro, J.W : *The Politics of American Democracy,* Chap. 10.

Koeing, Louis W. : *The Chief Executive.*

Laski, H.J. : *The American Presidency.*

Marcus Cunliffei : *American Presidents and Presidency.*

Milton, G.F. : *The Use of Presidential Power.*

Munro, W.B. : *Government of the United States,* Chaps. X, XII.

Neustadt, Richard E. : *Presidential Power: The Politics of Leadership.*

Ogg, F.A. and Ray, P.O.: *Essentials of American Government,* Chap. XX.

Polsby, Nelson W. : *Congress and the Presidency.*

Rossiter, Clinton : *The American Presidency.*

Smith, J. Malcolm, and Cornelius P. Cotter : *Powers of the President during Crises.*

Sorenson, Theodore C. : *Decision-making in the White House.*

Swisher, Carl B. : *American Constitutional Development.*

Warren, Sidney: *The President as World Leader.*

Wilson, W. : *The President of the United States* (1916).

Zink, Harold : *Government and Politics in the United States,* Chaps. XIV, XV.

# CHAPTER IV

# The 'Cabinet' and the Executive Departments

### Origin and Nature of 'Cabinet'

The Executive Departments of the Government of the United States are: State; Treasury; Defence; Interior; Justice; Agriculture; Commerce; Labour; Health, Education and Welfare; Housing and Urban Development; and Transportation. Each Executive Department is headed by a Secretary appointed by the President with the consent of the Senate. The ten Secretaries and the Attorney- General are recognised as the top political figures in the national administration and they were in the line of succession to the Presidency. They sit in the 'President's Cabinet.'[1] The Constitution has nothing to say about a 'Presidential Cabinet.' It simply mentions that the President "may require the opinion, in writing, of the principal officer in each of the executive Departments, upon any subject relating to the duties of their respective offices."[2] But the framers of the Constitution had in their minds the importance of counsel in determining policies, though they "apparently deemed it unnecessary to insert any formal provision, taking it for granted that the President would have sufficient sense to avail himself of advice upon important occasions."[3] They did, of course, give to the Senate a measure of such authority in connection with appointments and treaty making.

Washington had in the beginning expected that the Senate would serve the same purpose that the Upper Chambers in the Colonial Legislatures had fulfilled, that is, it would be an advisory council with as much executive as legislative responsibility. The Constitution more or less implied this function of the Senate when it provided that the President shall have the power "by and with the advice and consent of the Senate" to make treaties and appointments. Washington sought the advice of the Senate in connection with America's Indian affairs but was "snubbed." Relying on the precedent of English and Colonial courts, the President sought the assistance of the Supreme Court, to render opinions of an advisory nature, but here again he was "rebuffed." Washington, therefore, began talking over certain questions with the principal officers of government and by 1791, he called regular conferences of key officials for consultation not only on matters pertaining to their particular Departments but in regard to questions of general executive policy. Since 1793, the name "Cabinet" came to be applied to these joint meetings of the Chief Executive with his heads of the Departments. Unknown to the Constitution, Cabinet is an extra-legal institution and is a child of custom and tradition. But it is simply an advisory body, though its growth is an example of the manner in which usage has shaped the Constitution to meet the pressure of necessity.

Early in his administration, Andrew Jackson dispensed with Cabinet meetings altogether and acted on the advice of several of his intimate friends. This "Kitchen Cabinet," as it popularly came to be known, served the purpose of the President's advisers. His successors, however, followed the custom of calling the heads of the principal Departments into an informal conference for the discussion of complicated problems, and thus, began a series of Presidents who depended rather heavily on their Cabinets. With the coming in of Woodrow Wilson the reverse phase began.[4] He preferred his own sources of advice or depended upon the council of a very few personal agents such as Colone l Edward M. House. Wilson's successor, President Harding, however, was excessively reliant on his Cabinet, invited the Vice-President to attend its meetings and included in its membership "men who knew a great deal more about public affairs than did he himself." President Roosevelt did not lean heav-

---

1. Others may be invited to Cabinet meetings at the discretion of the President.
2. Article II, Section 2, Clause 1.
3. Zink, H., *A Survey of American Government,* p. 254.
4. Woodrow Wilson did not even bother to discuss the sinking of the *Lusitania* or the declaration of war with it. "For some weeks," wrote his Secretary of Interior, Franklin Lane," we have spent our time at cabinet meetings largely telling stories."

ily on his Cabinet, although he did not dispense with its regular meetings.[5] In the beginning, particularly in fashioning his New Deal, he looked for advice to a little group of younger people known as the ''brain trust.'' For a time, he tried a ''super cabinet,'' the National Emergency Council, which included in its membership more than thirty persons drawn from the Cabinet and independent establishments. But eventually he returned to the old system, although Roosevelt and Truman leaned heavily on personal friends such as Harry Hopkins and George Allen. President Eisenhower did his best to restore the Cabinet to full duty. He invited such key officials as the Director of the Budget and the Chairman of the Civil Service Commission to attend regularly. He even established a formal Cabinet Secretariat to organise its work and to keep the necessary records. Eisenhower, accordingly, used an expanded and augmented Cabinet quite extensively as a sounding-board and policy-making group. President Kennedy, on the other hand, preferred to deal directly with those Cabinet members involved in a particular problem and he avoided large-scale formal meetings. Eisenhower, Kennedy, Johnson, Nixon, Ford, Carter and Reagan included the Vice-Presidents in their Cabinets. Carter described his Cabinet officers—10 Secretaries and the Attorney-General—as ''almost perfect'' and directed them to ''honor (honour) my commitments to the American people.''

Though unknown to law yet it has become an integral part of the institutional framework of the United States of America.[6] But it is really not a cabinet in the sense in which we understand it under a system of parliamentary government. The members of the American Cabinet are not members of Congress and neither they take part in its debates nor do they go there to initiate and pilot legislation or to defend the policy of Government or stand in need of seeking its confidence. They are essentially the advisers of the President. The President can, and often he does, override the opinions of his 'ministers' or he may not seek it or even if he does seek, it is for him to decide whether to consult them individually or collectively. The use of the Cabinet depends on the President's desire. Harold Ickes, who was at times enraged at what transpired in the Cabinet, wrote in his Diary after a meeting in 1935: ''Only the barest routine matters were discussed. All of which leads me to set down what has been running in my mind for a long time, and that is just what use the Cabinet is under this administration. The cold fact is that in important matters we are seldom called upon for advice. We never discuss exhaustively any policy of government or question of political strategy. The President makes all of his own decisions.'' Henry Morgenthan, another member of Roosevelt Cabinet wrote: ''The important things were never discussed at Cabinet.'' Lincoln too ignored his Cabinet and at one time seemed on the verge of doing away with the meetings altogether. Gideon Welles, Lioncoln's Secretary of the Navy, complained, ''There is really very little of a hearing at this time so far as most of the cabinet are concerned, certainly but little consultation in this important period.'' Again, he said, ''But little was before the cabinet, which of late can hardly be called a council. Each Department conducts and manages its own affairs, informing the President to the extent it pleases.''

The Cabinet meets ordinarily once a week and it is for the President to decide what matters come before it.[7] Proceedings are decidedly informal and there are no rules of transaction of business.[8] Only rarely is there a vote and that too, when the President asks for one. No minutes or official records were kept of its proceedings. President Eisenhower established a Cabinet Secretariat to organise its work, keep its records and follow through on decisions. In addition to setting up a sub-Cabinet to support the Cabinet itself, he continued the practice of authorising Cabinet level committees to deal with special problems. Eisenhower appointed, in November, 1954, Maxwell M. Rable as the Secretary of the Cabinet of the United States. But Cabinet members have no

5. ''The President ordinarily began with a recital of pleasantries, telling stories which ticked with him or joshing cabinet members about their latest appearances in the newspapers. Then he might throw out a problem for a generally rambling and inconclusive decision. Or, turning to the Secretary of State, he might say without ceremony, ''Well, Cardell, what's on your mind today? Then he would continue around the table in order of precedence.'' Cornwell, Elmer E., *The American Presidency: Vital Center, pp, 67-68.*
6. The term Cabinet is referred to by name in Chief Justice Marshall's decision *Marbury* v. *Madison* (1803).
7. President Taft observed : ''As it is, the custom is for the President to submit to its members questions upon which he thinks he needs their advice, and for the members to bring such matters in their respective departments as they deem appropriate for Cabinet conference and general discussion.''
8. It is reported that Franklin Roosevelt sometimes related a story or an amusing incident. Lincoln, too, was fond of stories.

corporate rights which are uniformly recognised by custom. This is well illustrated by two anecdotes, one relating to America and other to Britain. "Ayes one, noes seven. The ayes have it," announced Lincoln following a Cabinet consultation in which he found every member against him. The only vote that counts is the President's own. This is so often contrasted with Lord Melborne putting a question on Corn Laws to the vote in his Cabinet and saying, "it does not matter what we will say, as long as we all say the same thing." Unanimity of decisions is the basic principle of Cabinet government and essence of collective responsibility. The Cabinet members in America may make speeches in support of the general policy of the administration. They may even initiate a line of policy which, having been approved by the President, may be described as their own special contribution, as the agricultural policy of Wallace and the reciprocal low tariff agreements of Hull, in Roosevelt's administration. "But, in general, the American Cabinet minister lives and moves and has his being in the context of Presidential thought. However able and distinguished, he is bound to be eclipsed by the major significance of his chief."[9]

The Cabinet in the United States is, in fact, the "President's family." President Monroe thought himself as merely a *primus inter pares.* But as Brogan puts it, "even Monroe was primus and he had chosen his peers."[10] A British Prime Minister may have a choice in selecting his colleagues upon whom he can rely, yet the party expects certain men to be in the Cabinet and the country, too, expects them to be there. In America, the President, unlike the Prime Minister in Britain, does not make a team. The considerations which influence his choice are different from those of a Prime Minister belonging to a country with a Parliamentary system. Some of his colleagues may hardly be known to him when he chooses them. President Wilson had never met Lindley Garrison, his Secretary of the Interior. He may, again, appoint persons not belonging to his own party, though since 1975 the principle of party solidarity has been adhered to rather closely.[11] Cleveland appointed Walter G. Gresham as Secretary of State and he had been thought of as a Republican candidate for the Presidency. Theodore Roosevelt and Taft each appointed a Democrat Secretary of War and Hoover made a Democrat Attorney- General. Roosevelt appointed Henry L. Stimon as Secretary of War, and Frank Knox as Secretary of Navy in 1940, although both were prominent Republicans and the latter had only four years previously been his party's candidate for Vice-President. Eisenhower thought it good politics to recognize the "Democrats for Eisenhower" by naming Texas Democrat, Mrs. Oveta Culp Hobby, as his first Secretary of Health, Education and Welfare. President Kennedy's Cabinet included two Republicans, the Secretary of Treasury, Douglas Dillon, and Secretary of Defence Robert McNamara. Lyndon Johnson continued with the members of Kennedy's Cabinet, after his assassination.

If the President makes his Cabinet, he can also unmake it at his will. It is true that the choice of the President is not so unrestricted as it is generally imagined. He is limited by party necessities, geographical considerations and it is politics also to recognise the major religious groups. President Kennedy appointed his brother Robert Kennedy as Attorney-General and it was obviously a personal matter. Wilson was compelled to make Bryan as Secretary of State and for the same reasons that compelled Gladstone to take in Chamberlain in 1880 and Lord Palmerstone to offer a place in his cabinet to Cobdon. But once Wilson had become settled, he was able to drop Bryan with no trouble at all. It happens only in the United States, because there cannot be a Cabinet crisis in the British sense. Leaving aside Lincolns and Wilsons even weaker Presidents can get rid of any member of the Cabinet as

9. Laski, H. J., *The American Presidency*, pp. 79-80. President Roosevelt did not refer to his Cabinet the proposal to reforming the Supreme Court as contained in his message to Congress in 1937. This is narrated by the late Harold Ickes and it illustrates how the President may commit the administration to a bold or even a rash course of action without consulting his Cabinet. Harold Ickes said, "I have always deprecated the fact that President Roosevelt did not consult his Cabinet in advance and that nobody knew about the particular plan, except the President himself and the Attorney-General. The Cabinet was called together hastily at eleven o'clock one morning. The message was already on the way to the Hill (*i.e.,* Congress). Even if our advice had been sought, it would have been ineffective. We were confronted with a choice of supporting the President—or of resigning from the Cabinet and opposing it." As quoted by D. W. Brogan in *An Introduction to American Politics,* pp. 176- 277 f.n.
10. Brogan, D. W., *An Introduction to American Politics* p. 275.
11. Washington made Jefferson Secretary of State and Hamilton Secretary of the Treasury. But friction soon arose and it proved desirable '"to bring the chief offices into the hands of men who saw eye to eye in political matters."

president Arthur got rid of Blaine, the most popular Republican and the greatest force in the party. The conclusion is obvious. In the United States the Cabinet is only what the President wants it to be. "It is his tool" and as for its members, "a breath unmakes them as a breath has made." Its compositon is unpredictable. Many of its members, after their terms of office, retire into the obscurity from which their elevation had brought them.[12] "Cabinet office," in the words of Professor Laski, "is an interlude in a career; it is not itself a career. There is no technique of direct preparation for it; there is no certainty that it will continue because it has begun; there is no assurance that the successful performance of his functions will lead to a renewal of office in a subsequent administration."[13] A President can get rid of all his Cabinet as Jackson did; he can get rid of his prodecessor's Cabinet as Taft and Truman did. He can dismiss a member of the Cabinet as Truman dismissed Wallace. In July, 1979, Carter dismissed Joseph Califano, Secretary of Health, Education and Welfare, and Secretary of the Treasury. He allowed Attorney-General Griffin Bell and the Secretary of Energy, James Schlesinger, to resign. The Secretary of Transport, Brock Adams resigned before he was dismissed. The Secretary of State, Cyrus Vance resigned in April, 1980, because he disagreed with Carter on the rescue of hostages in Iran.

**Utility of the Cabinet**

Nevertheless the Cabinet has a character and importance of its own. Membership in it continues to be the ambition of many politicians.[14] And although there is considerable variation in its prestige and influence from administration to administration, yet it must meet once a week and transact two types of business. In the first place, the broad policies of the government are examined and discussed. The President may frequently consult the Cabinet on matters of top policy. He may accept their opinion or not, but the discussions bring out useful information and opinion, clarify views and promote morale in administration. Cabinet discussions help to sustain the President and render him more responsible to the people.

The second type of work it does is rather more routine. The President co-ordinates the activities of different Departments and resolves interdepartmental conflicts which are bound to arise in a complicated and gigantic administration, as one finds in the United States. What the President does is that he frequently meets the individual departmental heads and agency chiefs, listens to their complaints and limitations and, then, asks the Cabinet to attempt co-ordination. Cabinet meetings and discussions help to iron out departmental differences and misunderstandings. The Cabinet meeting may also serve to produce a sense of administrative responsibility and coherence in an administrative structure that is fragmented, specialised, and diffused.

While evaluating the role of the American Cabinet, it may be noted that it is a body of advisers to the President and not a council of his colleagues with whom he has to work and upon whose approval he depends. Cabinet discussion, as Professor Laski says, "is the collection of opinions by the President with a view to clarifying his own mind, rather than a search for a collective decision." The Cabinet members cannot publicly oppose the direction of the President. Roosevelt made it significantly clear. He said, "when a Cabinet member speaks publicly, he usually speaks on the authorization of the President, in which case he speaks for the President. If he takes it upon himself to announce a policy that is contrary to the policy the President wants carried out, he can cause a great deal of trouble."[15]

A few significant suggestions have been made for making the Cabinet a more potent factor in administration. One suggestion is that the Cabinet could be transformed into a vigorous institution simply by making the proper appointments. "A good Cabinet," commented Professor Laski, "ought to be a place where the large outlines of policy can be hammered out in common, where the essential strategy is decided upon, where the President knows that he will hear, both in affirmation and in doubt, even in negation,

12. Laski, H. J., *American Presidency*, p. 80.
13. *Ibid.*, p. 95.
14. Prof. Brogan cites a case in which he was an eye witness. He writes, "I was present towards the end of 1948, at a discussion of the new Cabinet, Mr. Truman was expected to announce. It was suggested that Mr. Dean Acheson would be made Secretary of State and it was objected that he had resigned as Under-Secretary of State on the ground that he couldn't afford the job. A friend of Mr. Acheson's remarked, "He couldn't afford Under-Secretary, but anybody can afford to be Secretary of State." Brogan, D. W., *An Introduction to American Politics*, p. 277 f.n.
15. Truman, Harry S., *Memoirs*, Vol. I. p. 329.

most of what can be said about the direction he proposes to follow." A Cabinet functioning in this spirit could, indeed, stimulate administrative leadership, but thus far the Cabinet has fallen short of such an ideal. Alexander Haig, Secretary of State in Reagan Cabinet suggested: "if a government as large and complex as ours is to function," the President "must delegate a measure of authority. How well, consistently and effectively the executive branch functions will depend to a great extent on how wisely its President chooses, and uses, his Cabinet."[16] The basic criteria of selection, he says, should be excellence and competence, "preferably demonstrated by successful experience in fields at least related to those for which any particular Cabinet officer is to be made responsible."

Haig also proposed that a President "cannot squander time on minutiae; Cabinet members must be responsible for managing their respective departments for which they need a delegation of requisite authority or the right kind of presidential support and backing." On policy matters affecting the responsibilities or interests of more than one cabinet department the President "should compel every cabinet officer to make policy recommendations to the President in front of, and open to challenge by, other Cabinet officers—especially those whose responsibilities or interests are affected by the issue in question." Every Cabinet officer must have periodic private access to the President, "otherwise the officer's morale, prestige and hence effectiveness will be gravely undermined."[17]

Suggestions have also been made to establish closer relations between the members of the Cabinet and Congress by giving them seats in the Senate and the House of Representatives and the right to participate in debate without the right to vote. The Secretaries (Cabinet members) are now limited to appearing before the Congressional Committees. The proposed arrangement could conceivably be a mutual advantage. It has been contended that there is no constitutional obstacle if this arrangement is brought about. But there seems slight prospect in fact of the adoption of this plan. Congress itself is hesitant. Alexander Haig noted that Cabinet members can be invaluable in expounding, defending and lobbying for the President's own programme in Congress, without making any institutional changes, with the media, and through each Cabinet officer's personal range of contacts. "Cabinet officers will want to be as responsive as possible to congressional needs and desires—in fact they have to be, since Congress controls their department's budgets."

## ADMINISTRATIVE ORGANISATION

The Constitution is silent regarding the administrative structure. The framers of the Constitution were not concerned with the organisation of the executive branch other than the office of the President. But having provided for the three Departments: Foreign Relations, the Military Forces, and Fiscal Affairs, it was evidently assumed that Congress would provide for additional Departments as the needs arose. This conclusion is supported by the constitutional provision that the President can require an opinion in writing from the principal officers in each of the Executive Departments. The Constitution further provides that Congress may vest by law the appointment of inferior officers in the President alone, in the Courts, or in the heads of the Departments. It is on this basis that Congress creates departments, commissions and other federal authorities.

Today, the Executive branch of government is made up of the following types of administrative organisations: (1) Executive Departments, ten in number, each headed, except the Department of Justice which is headed by the Attorney-General, by an officer with the title of Secretary; (2) executive agencies outside the ten regular Departments headed by single administrators; (3) boards and commissions, which may be further divided into regulatory, nonregulatory and advisory; and finally, (4) the government corporations. Agencies outside the ten Departments are usually termed "independent," in the sense that they are not responsible to the head of any Department. Some of these enjoy a large degree of independence of the President while others do not, but all are subject to legislative control by Congress.

The bureaux or the agencies directly associated with the President in an overall planning and control play a vital role in the administrative set-up of the country. There are between 200 and 400 bureaux in the Federal Government of which about 65 report directly to the President. Important out of these are the President's personal staff

16. Reproduced in *The American Review*, New Delhi, Autumn 1980, Winter 1981, p. 51.
17. *Ibid.*, pp. 51-52.

of Secretariat, personal advisers, and administrative assistants; and Bureau of the Budget; the Council of Economic Advisers; Science Adviser; the National Security Council; Civil and Defence Mobilization and the Central Intelligence Agency.

The Independent Commissions are another type of agency and these arose along with the growth of government regulation. Typically they are given regulatory powers over some sector of economy—rail and truck transport, trade practices, power, communications, aviation, tariffs. The Commission membership ranges from three to eleven. Commissions are appointed by the President with the approval of the Senate for a stated number of years. The power of the President to remove a commissioner during his tenure is usually limited.

Then, there are the 'government corporations.' Corporations, in America, as in other countries, enjoy a degree of freedom and flexibility in the performance of their functions which is not open to the more orthodox type of agency. Usually, but not always, the corporation is created to undertake some specific project or to conduct some business undertaking. The Tennessee Valley Authority is the best known of the examples of the Corporation.

**Organisation of a Department**

At the head of each Department, except the Justice and the Post Office, is the Secretary. Secretaries are the political appointees who express the policy of the party in office. They are also members of the President's Cabinet and are responsible to him for all intents and purposes. If any Secretary is selected by the President from the opposition party, he selects only those who are friendly to his cause. In most of the Departments the second ranking official is the Under-Secretary who is the deputy of the departmental head and like his superior is a political appointee. There are no permanent Under-Secretaries comparable to those serving in the British Ministries. Each Department has Assistant Secretaries, in some one, in others to the maximum four, who again are usually political appointees. Many of them may be career men.

Customarily, the Departments are divided and sub-divided into subordinate units, such as "bureaus," "divisions," "offices" and "services." The basis of division may differ from one Department to the other, but the most common basis is functions and actually speaking there is often much less difference among them than the titles would imply. A bureau in one Department is very similar in form and functions to a division in another Department. An office, however, may differ only in minor details from a service.

**Powers and Duties of the Secretaries**

While commenting upon the powers and duties of a head of the Department, John Sherman, a former head of the Treasury Department, declared: "the President is entrusted by the Constitution and laws with important powers, and so by law are the heads of Departments. The President has no more right to control or exercise the powers conferred by law upon them than they have to control him in the discharge of his duties....If he (a departmental head) violates or neglects his duty he is subject to the removal by the President or impeachment....but the President cannot exercise or control the discretion reposed by law in...any head or subordinate of a department of the government."[18] But this is not the real position. The President, as said earlier, is the Director of Administration. He is invested with the power of removal and by virtue of vast discretionary powers conferred upon him by laws has a wide choice of ways and means to get his will dominate. Whatever be the theory, the practice is otherwise. Being a political appointee, the Secretary is expected to inject the policies of the President in the conduct of the affairs of the Department he heads, especially when a strong-willed President is determined to carry out a fixed policy. When he does not belong to the Presidential party, he must be friendly to the President's policy.

The head of a Department is a legislator too, for he enjoys to a certain extent freedom in issuing orders pertaining to matters over which he presides. By a general Act of Congress, he may prescribe regulations, not inconsistent with law, for the government of his Department, the conduct of its officers and clerks, the distribution and performance of its business, and the custody, use and preservation of the records, papers, and property pertaining to it. This broad provision is very often supplemented by legislation giving him power to issue ordinances over particular matters.

The Secretary of a Department, also brings circuitous influence on actual legislation. He must submit to Congress annually certain specified reports bearing on the activities of his De-

18. As cited by Charles A. Beard, in *American Government and Politics*, p. 276.

partment. He must also appear before various Committees of Congress in order to explain, give information and answer to inquiries on legislation pending before Congress.[19] Secretaries write letters to Senators and Representatives, having political affinities with them, urging or opposing measures for discussion. "Indeed they sometimes submit to Congress, on their own motion, elaborate draft of Bills which they wish to have enacted into law."[20]

Finally, several heads of Departments exercise powers which are judicial in character. With the multiplication in the functions of government and growth of subordinate legislation and power of making Rules and Regulations, it has been thought expedient to give the heads of certain departments the authority to hear cases carried up from the lower administrative divisions under their control.

## FEDERAL PERSONNEL AND THE MERIT SYSTEM

Those entrusted with the administrative duties are divided into two groups: political appointees and those who belong to the executive civil service. The Secretaries, Under-Secretaries and Assistant Secretaries, bureau chiefs, division heads, members of the boards and commissions form only a minor fraction of all over $2\frac{1}{2}$ million men and women who carry on the civilian activities of the national government. Such a staggering number of Federal government employees present a difficult problem, for the greatness of any government and the quality of its administration depend in large measure on the ability, loyalty and devotion of the men and women who constitute its staff and carry on its activities. Selection and retention of capable employees, therefore, is a prime requirement of public administration.

### The Spoils System

For a generation or more the selection and appointment of administrative officers and other employees were based on competency, "fitness for office," a tradition set by President Washington. With the emergence of political parties more weight began to be given to political considerations when filling posts as they fell vacant or when new ones were created. John Adams, who succeeded Washington, was a party man, but he maintained to a considerable extent the principles established by Washington. The advent of Jefferson marked the first change in American public personnel practice. Though he agreed in principle with Washington's concept of "fitness for office" and there were only limited removals during the first two years of his first administration, he found the Departments of government and other administrative agencies peopled with those who were his political and personal enemies. Being a shrewd politician he was also aware of the political significance of the power of appointment. He was, accordingly, moved to remark: "How are vacancies obtained ? Those by the death are few, by resignation none." He found it necessary to remove some officials who had been appointed by his Federalist predecessors. Here is the start of the system known as "spoils," the requirement of party loyalty rather than fitness for office became the prime criterion for public employment.

The real fillip to the spoils system was given by a Congressional Act of 1810. It provided that terms of District Attorneys, Collectors, Surveyors of Customs, Navy Agents, Paymasters, and certain other office-holders should henceforth be limited to four years. It paved the way for rotation in office with the change in administration. For twenty-eight years Jefferson's party remained in power but Madison, Monroe, and John Quincy Adams did not follow the path of their great leader and made only a few removals. When Andrew Jackson occupied the White House, the concept of a public office as "spoils" had attained complete dominance in the governments of the States and vigorous pressure was being exerted for the extension of the principle to the operations of the Federal Government. Jackson welcomed the change as he believed that political parties need something besides "intellectual cement" to hold them together."

Andrew Jackson explained and defended his appointment programme which may be reduced to four propositions. First, since the administration of government is a simple process any person of normal intelligence and industry is capable of performing administrative duties; second, democratic principles support the idea of rotation in office; third, office-holders who remain over a great number of years are corrupted by a sense of power dangerous to the existence of democracy—more is lost by the long continuance of men than is generally to be gained by their

19. A recent Secretary made more than 400 appearances on Capitol Hill.
20. Beard, C. A., *American Government and Politics*, p. 277.

experience; and fourth, democracy is "prompted by party appointment by newly elected officials." The new President did not make a clean sweep of "anti-Jacksonian office-holders," nevertheless he removed in the first year of office nearabout 700 employees in the Executive Departments and filled all the new vacancies with his own party men.

The spoils system, therefore, is the practice, resorted to by political parties as well as factions, of filling appointed offices with their supporters when they come into power. "To the victor belong the spoils of the enemy," said Senator William L. Mercy in a debate in the Senate in 1832, and since then the phrase gained wide currency. While Andrew Jackson did not inaugurate the spoils system, he religiously initiated it and all appointments for party reasons became part of the accepted order of things in the national, State and municipal administrations. It flourished unchecked between 1820 to the close of the Civil War.

To job spoils were added other types of spoils—contracts, grafts, and the like. In the following years of the Civil War public opinion began to question some of the extreme practices associated with the spoils and the assassination of President Garfield at the hand of a disappointed office seeker served to arouse public opinion, as perhaps never before, on the evils inherent in the spoils system. While the spoils system has not been wholly eliminated even today,[21] important reforms were proposed and adopted in the two decades after the Civil War.

**Movement for Civil Service Reform**

The price of the spoils system had been too high indeed. The spoils system and political patronage had always produced incompetent and inexperienced public servants, and sometimes grafting and corrupt ones. By the sixties of the last century the standard of the Federal Service was at such a low ebb that civil service reform had become the aim of a popular political crusade. The goal of the civil service reformers was to establish a merit system under which appointments to the public service would be based on ability, experience, knowledge and training rather than on party loyalty. In 1868, Democratic Party urged in its platform that corrupt men be expelled from office and the useless offices be abolished. In 1872, both major political parties advocated civil service reform. The death of President Garfield in 1881 by a disappointed office-seeker aroused the nation's demand for a change in the system by which Federal offices were filled. In 1883, Congress passed the Federal Act, better known as the Pendleton Act.

The Pendleton Act set the basic pattern of national civil service and it is still the fundamental law governing recruitment. It created a Civil Service Commission consisting of three members, no more than two of the same party, appointed by the President and the Senate. The Act divided the administrative employees of the national government into two categories: (1) those in the unclassified; and (2) those in the classified service. Power to determine under which service most administrative agencies of government were to operate were granted to the President. Admission to the classified service was made dependent upon merit as manifested through the process of competitive examination conducted by the Civil Service Commission. Although appointments were still to be made by the President or the heads of the Departments, but the choice was limited to those who ranked at the top on the eligible list prepared by the Civil Service Commission on the results of the examination conducted by it. Also, all classified employees were required to abstain from active participation in politics, and they were to be protected in their jobs against political activity.

At the outset, the reform did not extend far and the number of positions affected did not exceed 14,000. After the turn of the century, the number was greatly increased and in 1937 over 60 per cent of the total positions were subject to the Civil Service Commission. By the Ramspeck Act, which came into force on January 1, 1942, many New Deal positions that had been outside the merit system were brought within its scope—a number estimated at well over 100,000."[22] At the time the Chairman of the Civil Service Commission declared that more than eighty per cent of the regular employees of the national government belonged to the competitive class.

The Civil Service Reform League bluntly declared in 1937 that Congress was always the chief obstacle to progress. It had repeatedly failed, when enacting legislation calling for ad-

21. Some positions are actually under a merit plan, but still they do not seem to receive adequately qualified incumbents. Others are exempted by Law from the competitive system.
22. Ogg, F. A., and Ray, P. O, *Essentials of American Government,* p. 325.

ditional appointments, to name them as classified services. Such instances were glaring when party long out of power suddenly found itself in control of Congress, *e.g.*, when the Democrats took over in 1886, 1913, and 1933, and Republicans in 1807 and 1921. Roosevelt's accession to Presidency in 1933, followed by his policy of New Deal, gave a rude shock to the merit system. The Democrats were back to power after 12 years, and the rank and file were hungry for offices. Creation of new agencies connected with the recovery plan multiplied the number of new jobs and in great majority of cases Congress exempted from competitive system the new entrants, thus, leaving the way open for spoils. The President by his first executive order on record withdrew from the classified service positions in the Bureau of Foreign and Domestic Commerce, which his predecessors had placed therein. "As a result of wholesale exemption by statute and of spoil raids in a good many of the older establishments as well, the service as a whole so far slipped back" and the proportion on a merit basis sank to hardly 60 per cent in the middle of 1936.

There was renewed agitation for reforms. In 1937, the President's Committee on Administrative Management recommended an extension of the merit system not only "upward and outward," but also "downward" so as to embrace skilled workers and labourers. President Roosevelt, too, urged, on Congress that all except policy making positions be placed on a merit basis. In 1938, the President ordered into classified service all New Deal non-policy determining positions. The Ramspeck Act did the rest. It authorised the President to include in the service, at Presidential discretion, all positions except those subject to Presidential appointments and subject to the confirmation of the Senate, and a few other limited groups of technical nature. In 1951, the proportion of the service operated under the merit plan was approximately 92 per cent. When President Eisenhower assumed office in 1953, he found only 17,382 jobs open for his patronage. The remaining, approximately 2,500,000 persons employed by the Federal Government at that date, were protected by the merit system. Of the 17,382 jobs not protected by civil service, practically all were either at very high or very low levels. Thus, the reform so modestly begun, today embraces a very large part of the federal civil personnel, over 85 per cent.

A significant feature of the American Political System in the ease with which ministers and civil servants in American Government interchange their positions with similar positions in corporate management. In fact, thene is a contact flow of senior managers from business to government and of senior bereaucates to industry and private banks.

## SUGGESTED READINGS


Beard, C.A.: *American Government and Politics*, Chap. X.

Blau, Peter M: *The Dynamics of Bureaucracy.*

Brogan, D.W.: *The American Political System,* Chap. II.

Corwin, E.S.: *The President's Office and Powers,* Chaps. III, IV.

Fenno, Richard F.: *The President's Cabinet.*

Ferguson, J.H., and McHenry, D.E.: *The American System of Government,* Chaps. XXI, XXII.

Greaves, W.B.: *Public Administration in Democratic Society,* Chaps. VIII-XIV.

Harris, Joseph P.: *Congressional Control of Administration.*

Hermans, Somers: *Presidential Agency.*

Hyneman, S.: *The American President,* Chap. XIII.

Hyneman, Charles: *Bureaucracy in a Democracy.*

Koeing, Louis W.: *The Chief Executive.*

Laski, H.J.: *The American President,* Chaps. I, IV.

Marx, F.M. (Ed.) : *"Federal Executive Reorganisation—A symposium,* Amer, Pol. Sc. Review, XI, pp. 1124-1168 (Dec. 1946), XLI, pp. 48-56 (Feb., 1947).

Ogg, F.A., and Ray, P.O.: *Essentials of American Government* XIX, XXI, XXII.

Riper, Paul P.: *History of the United States Civil Service.*

Swarthout, John M., and Bartley, Earnest R.: *Principles and Problems of American National Government,* Chaps. VI, XVII.

White, L.D.: *Introduction of the Study of Public Administration,* Chaps. XXII-XXXI.

# CHAPTER V

# Congress : Structure and Composition

### Role of Congress

The first Article of the Constitution provides for the legislative branch of government : "The Congress of the United States" and vests all legislative power in it. The Acts of Congress are the supreme laws of the land. But the framers of the Constitution had no intention of making it all-powerful. The demands of the doctrines of limited government and federalism are such as to deny unlimited powers to any governmental agency. Yet, the importance of Congress in the final analysis cannot be discounted. In fact, Congress today exercises an almost incomprehensibly great authority to set the course of the public policy. For, Congress has not only the power given by the actual words of the Constitution, but also powers that may be reasonably implied from those delegated powers. So vast is the extent of the implied powers as also resultant powers that it embraces more or less the entire life of the nation. Unless Congress grants money, the Executive and Judicial Departments of government cannot operate, new policies cannot be enforced and the entire machinery of the government comes to a dead stop. It was, accordingly, not out of reason that the framers would have devoted the first Article in the Constitution to the organisation and powers of Congress.

### Congress is Bicameral

Regarding the desirability of creating a national legislature consisting of two chambers there was little difference of opinion among the members of the Philadelphia Convention.[1] The Congress which operated under the Articles of Confederation was a single Chamber assembly, but the framers of the Constitution did not consider it worthy of emulation. They were familiar with the successful functioning of bicameral State legislatures. They also knew that in Britain, too, bicameral Parliament existed. The reasons, however, which prompted bicameralism were the result of a "great compromise" without which perhaps the Union would not have come into being. Under the Articles of Confederation, all States stood on a footing of equality. They would not agree to the new administrative set-up unless their old status was preserved in one branch of the legislature and where they could be represented as constituent political units. On the other hand, the larger States, which had sponsored the movement to federate, would not agree to a plan unless they were given adequate representation in proportion to their superior numerical strength. There were economic reasons too. The North, the more populous part of the country, was commercial in interest whereas the South, the sparsely populated part, was agricultural. The division of the legislature into two Houses based on two different principles of representation was in part influenced by these considerations in order to balance and harmonise the two distinct economic interests in the national government. At the same time, the Fathers of the Constitution entertained a fear of the majority rule and they desired to set up the Senate as a conservative check on the "turbulence of democracy." And if it was to be an effective check on the radicalism of the popular House, then it ought not to be a mere duplication of the latter both in its composition and powers. Accordingly, Congress was based on States as political entities and on population, the Senate representing the former and the House of Representatives the latter. The Senate was to be smaller in size, its members chosen for a long term of office and by a different method, higher age and residence qualifications were required. It was given certain specific powers, such as share in the appointing, treaty making and judicial powers, which were not conferred on the House of Representatives.

---

1. The story is told that when Thomas Jefferson returned from France after the Philadelphia Convention had completed its labour, he objected to the bicameral feature of the national legislature and asked Washington why the Convention had taken such a step. The conversation took place at breakfast, and Washington is said to have asked Jefferson, "'Why did you pour your coffee?" "To cool it," replied Jefferson. "Even so,'" answered Washington, "We pour legislation into the senatorial saucer to cool it." Max Farrand, *The Framing of the Constitution,* p. 74.

## THE HOUSE OF REPRESENTATIVES

### Composition and Organisation

The Constitution does not specify the size of the House beyond stipulating that "representatives shall be apportioned among the several states according to their respective numbers," and that there shall not be more than one member for every thirty thousand people and that every state is entitled to, at least, one representative irrespective of its population.[2] The actual enumeration was to be made within three years after the first meeting of the Congress and within every subsequent period of ten years in such manner as determined by law. Elections are to be held every second year by the people of the several States.[3] The times, places and manner of holding elections shall be prescribed in each State by the legislature thereof; but the Congress may at any time by law make or alter such regulations.[4]

Apportionment of seats has caused periodic controversies. The original 65 members of the House were allocated in the Constitution. Thereafter allocations were made by Congress after each census, ranging from the basis of one representative for each 30,000 in 1792 to one for 4,12,000 in 1961. After 1920 census Congress failed to carry out the constitutional mandate to reapportion seats after every ten years. The Reapportionment Act of 1929 set the "permanent" number of the House at 435. The admission of Alaska in 1958 and of Hawaii in 1959 brought the total membership to 437, but it dropped back to 435 in 1962 and remained there.

The formal qualifications which a member of the House of Representatives should possess are: that he must not be less than twenty-five years old, should be a citizen of the United States of, at least, seven years standing, and an inhabitant of the State from which he is elected. Custom has laid an important qualification regarding residence. The Constitution requires only legal residence in the State. It has since been modified to mean residence of the Congressional district. Custom has been so insistent on the locality rule that no choice of the candidate is likely to be made unless he is resident of the locality from which he seeks election. In fact, no candidate offers himself for election from a district in which he does not reside. Franklin D. Roosevelt, Jr., after deciding to run for the New York Congressional seat vacated by the death of Sol Bloom, rented an apartment in the district and announced that address as his legal residence. Helen Gahagan Douglas rented a hotel room in the industrial commercial district in Los Angeles which she represented, though she continued to live in fashionable Beverly Hills. In case of death or resignation of a member during his term, the Governor of his State may call a special election for the unexpired portion of the term.

The Constitution provides certain disqualifications. It provides that no person holding any office under the United States shall be a member of either House of Congress during his continuance in office.[5] This provision was adopted for the purposes of keeping separate, as far as practicable, the Executive and Legislative Departments. Secondly, no Senator or Representative may, during the time for which he or she is elected, be appointed to any civil office which shall have been created or the emoluments of which shall have been increased during such time.[6] The purpose of this provision is to prevent Congress from creating new offices or increasing the salaries of existing offices for the benefits of members who might desire to be appointed to them.

The Constitution provides that Congressmen will be paid salary and other perquisites of office as determined by law. The law fixed the salary subject to the national income tax. In addition to it, travelling allowance is paid for one trip in each session from the Member's home to Washington. Every member has a "franking privilege" too—of free postage on official correspondence and all other official mail matter, such as pamphlets and reprints of speeches sent free to the constituents. Stationery and office supplies, telephone and telegraph service are provided. Free medical service is made available to all members. Allowances for clerks and secretarial service are also made : \$12,500 per year for a Representative and \$25,000 to \$60,000 per year for a Senator, depending upon the population of his home State. Retirement annuities have been

2. Article I, Section 2, Clause 3.
3. Article I, Section 2, Clause 1.
4. Article I, Section 4.
5. Article I, Section 6, Clause 2.
6. *Ibid.*

provided since 1946.[7]

Congressmen are exempt from legal process in all civil actions while attending the sessions of Congress and when going to or returning thereto. This immunity, however, does not cover indictable criminal offences. They are also legally immune from prosecution or suit, as for libel and slander, for anything they may say on the floor of the House.

The House of Representatives has a term of two years only. In 1966 President Johnson proposed that the term of Representatives be increased to four years. This would, it was argued, relieve members of the House of fresh elections after every two years. It was also argued that synchronisation of the term of the House with that of the office of the President would reduce considerably the possibility of deadlock with a President of one party and the House majority of another. But the four-year term of the House is likely to create problems in connection with the term of the Senate, as the present constitutional arrangement requires election of one-third of the Senators every two years. If the term of the Senate is increased to eight years, one-half of the Senators retiring after every four years, this scheme too, might lead to deadlock between a President and the Senate majority if both belong to two different parties. The other alternative is to reduce its term to four years. But the Senate is not likely to agree to it, two-thirds of which must vote affirmatively to submit the necessary constitutional amendment.

Before the adoption of the Twentieth Amendment in 1933, the term of the Representatives began on March 4, following election, although they did not assemble till next December unless called in a special session.[8] The old Congress, therefore, remained in office and continued functioning for about four months after a new Congress had been elected. The members defeated at elections would continue to make laws for their constituents who had not approved their re-election. These defeated members were popularly known as ''lame-ducks'' and the session of the House so convened as ''lame-duck'' session. The Twentieth Amendment sought to remove the evils inherent therein by providing that Congress must assemble at noon on January 3, unless another date is provided by law. It means that a new Congress fresh from elections of November, must begin legislative work early in January. Under the Legislative Reorganization Act, 1946, the regular session adjourns on July 31 unless otherwise provided by Congress.

The President may call either House or both in a special session. The Senate in particular is called to confirm appointments or ratify a treaty. As a rule, the President only summons the legislature in special session to deal with a matter of national urgency and usually announces his purpose well in advance so as to focus the attention of Congress and the country sharply to the business in hand.

The Constitution permits both the Houses to adjourn simultaneously. But what is to be done, if crisis happens during the adjournment and the members desire to assemble in a session ? The need for a decision on this issue happened in 1939 after the outbreak of the Second World War. The opponents of Roosevelt feared that, by taking drastic actions during an adjournment, he might involve the country in the War and consequently Congress remained almost in continuous session in 1939, 1940 and 1941. In 1941, it was in session for 365 days; in 1942, for 346 days, with a brief recess in December. In 1943, between January and July, it was in session for 184 days, and the need for a vacation was generally recognised. But many members were unwilling to adjourn even for a brief recess without making some specific provision for meeting earlier than the stipulated date in a resolution of adjournment. The resolution, accordingly, provided for adjournment on July 8 and reassembling on September 14, 1943, or until three days after they were notified to reassemble whichever event occurred first. The President of the Senate and the Speaker of the House were authorised to call the Houses ''whenever in their opinion legislative expediency might warrant it.'' The resolution further provided that Congress was to be recalled ''whenever the majority leader of the Senate and the majority leader of the House, acting jointly, or the minority leader of the Senate and the minority leader of the House, acting jointly, file a written request with the Secretary of the Senate and the Clerk of the House that Congress reassemble for the consid-

7. Members who choose to join the retirement provisions are required to pay into the fund 7.5 per cent of their salaries. This entitles them to receive a retirement allowance, after the age of sixty-two and a minimum of six years service, of 2.5 per cent of their average salary multiplied by their years of service. Retirement pay may not exceed 75 per cent of final congressional salary.
8. Article I, Section 4. Clause 2.

eration of legislation." According to this precedent, Congress can now reassemble on the call of the majority or minority leaders and it has been freed from the pleasure of the President to call a special session.

The Rules of the House of Representatives provide for securing the attendance of members if the required quorum for the transaction of official business is not present. Fifteen members of the House may compel the attendance of absentees by instructing the Sergeant-at- Arms to arrest them and bring them in the House.

**The Speaker**

With regard to the internal organisation of the House of Representatives, the Constitution simply says that members "shall choose their Speaker and other officers."[9] It does not say anything about his powers and functions. Nor does the Constitution require that the Speaker must be a member of the House, although every Speaker has been at the time of his selection a member of the House.

The election of the Speaker takes place at the beginning of each new Congress and the nominee of the majority party is invariably elected by the House. Here it differs from the office of the Speaker of the British House of Commons. Unlike Britain, the election of the Speaker of the House of Representatives is not unanimous. Nor the Speaker of the preceding House need always be elected, although the tradition is now well established that Speakers are re-elected in subsequent Congress if their party maintains a majority; Sam Rayburn remained in office for 16 years. With the coming in of the other party in majority, the Speaker must change. Seniority is, no doubt, an important consideration in choosing a Speaker, but personal popularity and political backing are the most important prerequisites.

Unlike the impartial and judicious Speaker of the British House of Commons, the Speaker of the House of Representatives acts as a leader of his Party and uses the powers of his office to promote his Party's programme. There are two important reasons for such a development. The Constitution did not provide the House with an official leadership. Apparently the statesmen of 1787 took it for granted that the House would lead itself. As the House grew in numbers and its legislative business expanded, the need for guidance and leadership developed and this devolved upon the Speaker as a leader of the majority Party. "Beginning with Henry Clay, the Speaker gradually became the recognised leader of the majority party, and hence of the House as a whole. He became the man on whom the majority depended for getting its measures safely through the maze of rules. More and more authority was absorbed into his hands until he became a vital dictator of legislation."[10] During the decade around the turn of the present century Speaker Thomas B. Reed was frequently referred to as "Czar" Reed. Jeseph G. Cannon, popularly known as "Uncle Joe," held the same position. "A simple Chairmanship," as Ogg and Ray put it, "grew into a vital dictatorship carrying the power over life and death over almost everything that the House undertook to do." [11]

Before the "revolution of 1910-11" which was directed against the Speaker of the House, he appointed all Standing as well as Select Committees and the Committee appointments went to those who could be depended upon to follow his wishes. And as legislation in the United States is really the work of the Committees, he had the virtual power in the shaping of legislation. As a Chairman of the Rules Committee, he would give place on the order of the business only those measures which he desired to be enacted. Moreover, until 1910, his power of "recognition," that is, the power to grant or withhold the right of discussion, enabled the Speaker to a large degree to prevent consideration of measures to which he was opposed and to cut off debate by members of the minority Party.

The Speaker's denial of the right of debate in many cases, together with the necessity of going to his room in advance in order to secure a promise to recognition, led in 1910 to revolt against "Cannonsism"[12] by a wing of the Republican party, the "insurgents." They were joined by the Democrats. The coalition of Democratic minority leaders and progressive Republican "insurgents" brought about several amendments to the rules. The Speaker was removed from the Rules Committee and the power of selection of all Standing Committees was restored to the House itself. His power of recognition, the chief source of complaint, was also taken away. All

9. Article I, Section 2.
10. Munro, W. B., *The Government of the United States*, pp. 324-25.
11. Ogg, F. A., and Ray, P.O., *Essentials of American Government*, p. 212.
12. Joseph G. Cannon was Speaker from 1903 to 1910.

told, the blow to the powers of the Speaker was so severe that the office has never been since then quite the same.

Nevertheless, the Speaker is still the "Commanding" figure in the House and many important duties belong to the office. He presides over the sittings of the House, arranges for the orderly conduct of the business of the House, preserves order and decorum. In case of disturbance or disorderly conduct he may either suspend business or instruct the Sergeant-at-Arms to quiet any disorder in the House. But the Speaker cannot censure or punish a member; only the House itself can do that. Then, he "recognises" members desiring the floor; the only power left out of the Speaker's three potentially great powers. The rules of the House provide that if two or more members rise, "the Speaker shall name the member who is first to speak." This in effect gives the Speaker wide discretion.

The Speaker has the right to interpret the rules of the House. Though he must follow the established precedent, but it is within his power to disregard them and to create new ones, provided that the House agrees. A majority of the House of Representatives may overrule the interpretation placed on a rule by the Speaker, but they rarely exercise this prerogative. All the same, the ruling of the Speaker is not final as it is with the Speaker of the House of Commons in Britain. He puts questions to a vote, signs all acts, addresses joint resolutions, writs, warrants and subpoenas ordered by the House. The Speaker appoints Select and Conference Committees and has the right to refer bills to Committees, though the Bills now are automatically sent to Committees by the Clerk of the House on the basis of their subject-matter. Occasionally, when the competency of a Committee which is to receive the Bill is disputed, the Speaker decides.

As a member of the House, the Speaker has the same right to speak and vote as other members, although he does not vote, except when the House is voting by ballot or when there is a tie. But the Speaker of the British House of Commons never participates in its deliberations and he votes only when there is a tie and that, too, he does according to the established customs of the House.

The Speaker of the British House of Commons becomes a non-party man immediately after his election to that office. But unlike his British counterpart, the Speaker of the House of Representatives is actively and openly identified with his party's organisation in the House. As a leader of the majority party in the House, the Speaker is frequently called to the White House to go over legislative matters with the President.

Today, the Speaker is relatively weak, yet he still has many "weapons" which he can use to influence the course of legislation. He is by tradition and practice the active member of the majority party in the House, the "elect of the elect"[13] and is second in succession to the Presidency. He, therefore, occupies an office of great prestige and importance in the Federal Government.

**House Floor Leaders**

Each of the parties, majority and minority in the House, has a Floor Leader, chosen or approved by the party caucus, to take charge of the party interests during legislative sessions. As his title indicates, the floor leader is normally the chief strategist and tactician on the floor for his party. The majority leader, when of the same party as the President, often is the administrative spokesman. Each floor leader is manager of his party's programme on the floor of the House and has effective control, through co-operation with the Speaker, over important aspects of procedure. He takes the initiative in planning the course of debate on the floor, determines the order in which members of his party may speak, and maintains party regularity. If the floor leader is the party general in the Chamber, the party whips are its colonels.

Dimock analyses the qualities of a floor leader and says, "The successful leader must be a born politician in the best sense of the word. He must be personally popular, be a good judge of men, have his ear to the ground, and know what not to believe. He must be able to cooperate with party leadership and the chief executive and yet have a mind of his own. He must possess that keen sense of timing and the judgment and finesse which characterises the successful executive."[14] When the Republican Party assumed majority in 1947, it designated as floor leader Charles A. Helleck of Indiana, who had been a member of the House since 1935, and the Democrats designated as minority leader Sam Rayburn of Texas, who had long served as Speaker of the House.

13. Polsby, Nelson W., *Congress and Presidency,* p. 51.
14. Dimock, M.E., *American Government in Action,* pp. 377-78.

## THE SENATE

### Composition and Election

The Senate is a small body of only one hundred members, two from each State irrespective of population or area, elected for a term of six years, one-third retiring every two years. It is so arranged that the terms of both Senators from a particular State do not terminate at the same time. It is a continuous body as only one-third of the Senators face re-election for any Congress. A long term of office, with frequent possibilities of re-election, puts Senators in more comfortable and advantageous position than Representatives. Unlike the latter with a two-year term. they have time even in a single term to acquire experience, master legislative procedure and to attain a certain degree of leadership. It is not uncommon for a Senator to run 18 to 24 years of service. The continuous existence of the Senate is also highly beneficial. The Senate never finds itself in a position in which the House of Representatives is found every two years. The latter is entirely a new body with greatly altered membership, "obliged to organise from the ground up." The Senate is continuous and always organised. Two-third of its members are already in office. Precedents and traditions of the House are therefore, "carried along on the current of a never-ending stream."

All States have an equal representation in the Senate and the Constitution recognises the sacredness of this political dogma when it prescribes that "no state, without its consent, shall be deprived of its equal suffrage in the Senate."[15] The concept of equality of representation was a great compromise which resulted in the establishment of the United States Union and proved a great balancing factor in the North and the South. George Hamilton asserted that, once the new government was in operation, there never would be a conflict of interests between large and small states. This prediction has proved true and throughout the course of American history, whether the State is large or small, it has made little or no difference in its political attitudes and alignment. The Senators, too, do not now consider themselves as ambassadors of their States. They deem themselves as representatives of the nation and their interests are national rather than regional. It has been suggested, during recent times, that the anomalies of equal representation should be removed, because, it is a gross violation of the democratic theory that geographical units should be the basis of representation. Moreover, geographical representation gives to the States with only one-fifth of the population more than one-half of the Senators and if these States with few people are "gauged up" against the thickly settled ones, there might be perpetual and intolerable conflict and hostility and inconceivable repercussions. For instance, California has more than seventy times the population of Alaska, yet both are entitled to the same number of Senators.

These complaints of "Senatorial tenderness towards farm and allied interests" are frequently heard in industrial areas. To remedy the situation it has been suggested that a State be allowed an additional Senator for every million inhabitants in excess of some fixed number. "The proposal, however" as Ogg and Ray say, "is little short of fantastic, because to carry it out would require not only a constitutional amendment, but the express consent of every State whose representation would become less than that of some other States—a prerequisite which could not possibly be met."[16] Even if the proposal would have been practicable, the increased strength of the Senate, it is suggested, would reduce its efficiency as a deliberative body. And, the Senate and House of Representatives would become both representative of the same people in the same proportions. It means duplication and the need for a second Chamber disappears. The whole question of change, therefore, remains an academic one.

The qualifications prescribed for eligibility to the Senate are the same in principle as those required of Representatives, though there is a little difference in degree. The Senator must be not less than thirty years old, an inhabitant of the State for which he is elected, and a citizen of the United States for nine years. The framers of the Constitution thought that the longer term and higher qualifications would tend to give greater strength and dignity to the Senate than would be found in the House of Representatives and, at the same time, a higher average ability.

There is no constitutional provision that a Senator should be a resident of a particular part of the State. In some States, however, custom came to be established that the two Senators shall be taken from two different parts. Sometimes

15. Article V.
16. Ogg. F. A, and Ray, P. O, *Essentials of American Government,* p. 201.

when there is a large city in the State, the custom is to take one of the Senators from the city and the other from the country. For a long time Maryland had a statutory provision that one of the Senators should be an inhabitant of the eastern shore and the other of the western shore.

In regard to the mode of election of the Senators there was a sharp difference of opinion among the members of the Philadelphia Convention. The method finally agreed to was that the Legislatures of the States should elect them. There were two main reasons for adopting this method. In the first place, the Founding Fathers thought that the choice by Legislatures would be the best means of forming a connecting link between the State governments and the national government thereby cementing the bonds of union. The jealousy of the State governments towards the National Government was so manifest at that stage that all possible efforts were made by the Constitution-makers to bring about cohesion through the mechanism of the newly established government. Secondly, it was believed that choice by Legislatures would enable the selection of Senators of greater ability as the legislators would be in a better position to evaluate the qualifications and merits of the candidates than the mass of the people.

But the working of this indirect method of elections belied the expectations of the Fathers of the Constitution. With the development of the party machinery, the actual choice of the Senator was made in the State party convention or in the legislative caucus, and both were controlled by bosses. It frequently led to long and stubborn contests which very often ended in deadlock. Not infrequently the Legislatures failed to elect a Senator and the State with vacancy in the Senate would go unrepresented. From 1890 to 1912 not less than eleven States at one time or another were represented in the Senate by one member only. In 1901 Delware had no Senator at all at Washington to speak for the State. And, then, the breaking of deadlock was sometime accomplished by bribery and other corrupt influences. Indeed, charges of bribery and corruption came to be very common, "and there is little doubt that between 1895 to 1910 a number of wealthy men found their support."[17] Finally, prolonged senatorial contests gravely interfered with the regular business of the State Legislatures. The obvious result was a spirited movement to secure the amendment of the Constitution and after a tiring effort the Seventh Amendment was adopted in 1913. It provides that the two Senators from each State shall be "elected by the people thereof for six years...." They are elected by vote of such persons as are entitled to vote for members of the Lower House of the State Legislature. It further provides that in case there occurs a vacancy in the Senate, the Governor of the State in which the vacancy occurs may fill vacancy by temporary appointment until the next General Election at which time a successor is elected for the balance of the former Senator's term.

**The Presiding Officer**

The Presiding officer of the Senate is the Vice-President of the United States and despite his much exalted position, he is little more than a moderator. He is not a member of the Senate, and, indeed, may belong to a different political party that controls the Chamber. He does not appoint the Committees of the Senate and so has no power of predetermining the character of legislation, and he votes only in case of a tie. Moreover, he cannot control debate through the power of recognition, as the Speaker of the House of Representatives does. The President of the Senate must recognise the members seeking the floor in the order in which they rise. The tradition requires that he shall treat the members of both parties impartially in according recognition for purposes of debate. The Senate does not expect leadership, as is the case with the Speaker of the House, from its Presiding Officer and would resent it most bitterly as Vice-President Dawes learnt to his sorrow in 1925, when he attempted to change the Senate rules.

The Senate also elects from among its own members a *President pro tempore,* who presides in the absence of the Vice-President. The *President pro tempore,* though nominally elected by the Senate itself, is really chosen by the majority of the caucus and is, like the Speaker of the House, the ranking member of the party. Though the President *pro tempore* is a position provided for in the Constitution, he follows the Speaker in the line of the succession to the Presidency, and his election carries with it such perquisites as an official automobile, but the occupant is not equivalent of the Speaker of the House. Since he presides in the absence of the Vice-President, whose position is of no consequence in the Senate's power structure, he gains no significant

17. Garner, J. W., *Government of the United States,* p. 183.

powers from this role. As a member from a State, he can vote on all issues. He presides permanently if the Vice-President succeeds to the Presidency.

The Senate has its own majority and minority floor leaders. They are elected in the same manner as the Party floor leaders of the House of Representatives and their position and influence are also identical. In 1947, when Republicans assumed majority in the Senate they chose as floor leader Wallace H. White, who had served for years first in the House of Representatives and then in the Senate. The Democrats, on their part, designated as minority floor leader Senator Alben Barkley, who had been their ''masterful'' majority floor leader since 1937. Necessarily the majority floor leader is potentially the more influential, especially if the President is also of the same party, but his opposite number on the minority side may be of only slightly less consequence.

**The Filibuster**

The principal point of difference between the Senate and the House procedure lies in the rules respecting debate. Limitation on debate in the House is a relatively simple matter and closure rules are rigid and strict. Senate is extremely jealous of its freedom of debate and a member can speak as long as his physical capacity enables him to hold the floor. The advantage of this privilege is occasionally taken by the Senators near the close of the session for purposes of ''filibustering'' a measure to which they are opposed. Sometimes the Senators opposing a Bill ''talk it to death'' by refusing to yield the floor until the supporters of the measure agreed to drop it from discussion. Many important measures had actually been abandoned on a mere threat of the use of filibustering. Individual filibusters of note include those staged by Huey Long and Robert Lafollette, Sr., who held the floor continuously for 18 hours in 1908. The all-time record for continuously holding the floor was achieved in 1953 by Senator Wayne Morse of Oregon; he talked for 22 hours and 26 minutes. A filibuster against an atomic energy Bill produced a Senate impasse for twelve days in July 1954, including a four-day around the clock session. The longest filibuster speech so far recorded is that of Strom Thurmond, who spoke for more than twenty-four hours against the civil rights legislation of 1957.

More commonly filibuster is conducted by a group of Senators talking in relays, each yielding the floor to a colleague known to be friendly and bound to continue the delaying action. Southern Senators have used the filibuster relay to great advantage in preventing the consideration of civil rights legislation. Very often, they had gained their ends merely by threatening to take and hold the floor. In 1917, a small group of Senators filibustered to prevent the Senate from taking a vote on a Bill to give to President authority to arm American merchant vessels notwithstanding the fact that nearly all the other Senators desired to pass the Bill. President Woodrow Wilson expressed the general public resentment over the obstructionist tactics by declaring: ''The Senate of the United States is the only legislative body in the world which cannot act when its majority is ready for action. A little group of wilful men, representing no opinion but their own, have rendered the great government of the United States helpless and contemptible.''

The Senate had long recognised the serious repercussions of filibustering, but the incident of 1917 resulted in a movement to limit the filibuster and adoption of a new rule by the Senate which made it possible, by a two-thirds vote, to limit the debate on any measure to one hour for each Senator. This rule was applied for the first time in 1919, to bring to an end the discussion on the Treaty of Versailles. Since then it had been successfully used for three times more. The closure (cloture) rule of 1917 was amended in 1949, after a filibuster on civil rights legislation. A revised closure was made applicable on any matter under Senate proceedings, except change of rules. According to Rule XXII as amended in 1949, a vote of two-thirds members of the total membership of the Senate was required to carry closure. The old rule of 1917 required two-thirds votes of the members present and voting. The amendment of 1949 had, thus, made closure more difficult to use. A ceaseless effort was made to change the closure rules, but it was always opposed by Southern Senators who were out to filibuster the Civil Rights Bill. In 1959, on the proposal of the majority leader Johnson, the pre-1949 formula permitting two-thirds of members present and voting to impose closure was adopted. But the controversy has not ended. Current proposals centre around a closure by a majority vote or, alternatively, by a three-fifths vote of those present and voting.

Filibuster is, thus, a device by which an insistent minority can, if it feels strongly, usually block action on a proposed Bill and frustrate the business of the Senate. But ''fortunately resort to filibuster,'' remark Professors Swarthout and Bartley, ''is infrequent. It is the ultimate weapon of the intransigent few.'' The fact is that even on most controversial matters the Senators are usually able to reach a unanimous agreement that the debate must end at stipulated time on a given day. ''This self-imposed curb on unlimited debate,'' add Swarthout and Bartley, ''is the rule; the filibuster is the rare exception,''

## SPECIAL FUNCTIONS OF THE SENATE

The Senate was intended to be more than an Upper Chamber of Congress. The Founding Fathers designed it to be, in a way, the counterpart of the Privy Council in Britain and it was for this reason that they provided in the Constitution that the ''advice and consent'' of the Senate would be required in certain executive actions, for example appointments and treaties. President Washington, during his first term of office, sought the advice of the Senate in person. But the Senators refused to sit with the President in executive session and declined the proposal. Washington, accordingly, gave up his plan of personal conferences with the Senate and substituted the practice of sending business to it in written communications. In this way, the Senate ceased to be anything like a Privy Council and its ''prerogative became one of consent rather than advice.''[18]

Even then, its power of consenting to certain actions of the executive together with coequal legislative powers with the House of Representatives, and judicial powers relating to impeachment cases, gives to the Senate a unique position and it has eclipsed in prestige and authority the popular Chamber, the House of Representatives.

### Share in Appointments

The President shares with the Senate the power of appointing federal officers. The President nominates and the Senate confirms officers of the United States by simple majority. The underlying idea was to restrain the unlimited powers of the President by a system of checks and balances and thereby ensure the appointment of honest and capable men to office. The Constitution-makers never intended to give the Senate anything more than the negative power of rejecting the nominations of the President.[19] But the practice of *senatorial courtesy* gives to the Senators of the State concerned, where an appointment is to be made, both a positive as well as a negative function.[20] According to law the President sends the nomination to the Senate, where it is referred to the appropriate Standing Committee. An appointment to the federal Judiciary, for instance, is referred to the Senate Judiciary Committee; an appointment to the military establishment to the Armed Services Committee. If the nomination is contested, hearing may be held at which those actively favouring or opposing the nomination are heard. If a Committee majority is favourable, a report to that effect is made to the Senate itself. On rare occasions, the Committee reports unfavourably. The Senate, then, votes and if it refuses to confirm a nominee, his appointment is not possible.

But the actual process of appointment has greatly altered the provisions of the Constitution. For a proper understanding of the procedure in vogue the principal officers of the United States may be divided into two groups: (I) those who serve the nation as a whole, as do Supreme Court Judges, 'Cabinet' members, officers of the military establishments, ambassadors, etc., and (2) those who serve as federal officers, within a particular state, as do federal district judges, certain classes of post-masters, distinct attorneys, marshals, etc. Presidential appointments of principal officers are rarely rejected by the Senate, though there have been a few outright rejections in recent years.

Appointees whose federal duties are confined within the boundaries of a single State, and referred to under category 2 above, come under the custom of senatorial courtesy. The custom demands that the President should consult the senior Senator of the State in which the appointment is to be made. If the senior Senator does not belong to the President's party, he must do so with the junior Senator. If neither Senator is of the President's party, the President is not bound to consult with either Senator, but he will often do so. Even if he does not consult, the President will rarely appoint a personal enemy of the Senators concerned. The Senate is jealous of its traditional prerogative and will rarely approve an appointment which is personally obnoxious to the Senator most concerned. In 1938, President Roosevelt tried to break this iron-clad tradition

18. Munro, W. B., *The Government of the United States*, p. 287.
19. See *ante*, Chap. III. Also refer to J. W. Garner's *Government in the United States*, p. 191.
20. The role of the Senate in making appointments has already been discussed in connection with the powers of the President, Chap. III, *ante*.

and nominated a federal Judge in Virginia, without first clearing his choice with the senior Senator from Virginia, Carter Glass. The latter, though himself a Democrat, asked his colleagues to reject the nomination as he had been bypassed. The Senate refused the nomination by 72 to 6 votes. In 1951, President Truman was unable to secure confirmation of two nominations of federal district judges in Illinois, because of the opposition of Senator Paul Dougals, senior Senator from the State. The nomination of Justice Fortas by President Johnson in 1968 for appointment as Chief Justice of the Supreme Court raised a storm and was rejected. Within five months, November 1969-April 1970, the Senate rebuffed for the second time President Nixon in his attempt to appoint a Conservative Southerner as Supreme Court Judge.

**Share in Treaty-making**

The Senate also shares with the President the power of making treaties. All treaties negotiated by and on behalf of the President are laid before the Senate and a two-thirds vote of the Senators present is necessary to the validity of the treaty.[21] The Fathers of the Constitution probably wanted the President and Senators to sit down together and jointly work out a treaty. It is evident from the use of the words "advice and consent" of the Senate used in the Constitution. Washington, who thoroughly knew the mind and intentions of the Philadelphia Convention, visited the Senate to discuss a treaty which he desired to be concluded with the Southern Indians. Having received the rebuff from the Senate, Washington "started up in a violent fret," and said that "this defeats every purpose of my coming here."[22] And since then no President has conferred directly with the Senate. Nonetheless the Senate plays a significant role in making treaties and ratifying treaties. If the President entertains doubts on the repudiation of a treaty by the Senate, he consults members of the Foreign Relations Committee in advance and solicits their views. In fact, the Secretary of State usually works closely with the Foreign Relations Committee of the Senate.

How important is the treaty-ratifying power of the Senate is given by John Hay, once the Secretary of State. He said, "A treaty entering the Senate is like a bull going into the arena; no one can say just how or when the final blow will fall. But one thing is certain—it will never leave the arena alive." This is rather too sweeping a statement and particularly when it comes from a former Secretary of State. It is true that the extraordinary two-thirds majority required for the approval of a treaty has frequently proved a great handicap and led to the defeat of a number of treaties. It is also true that a small majority can sometimes threaten to defeat a treaty and to reap political advantage thereby. Some of the rejected treaties such as Taft Knox arbitration treaties of 1911-12, the Treaty of Versailles, and the protocol for participating in the World Court, were of supreme importance. But the Senate, too, has unconditionally approved about 900 of the approximately 1,100 or more submitted to it; many of the remainder were passed with amendment or reservation. There is, however, strong agitation to modify the Senate's treaty-ratifying power. It is demanded that this power should be given to a simple majority either of the Senate or of the two Houses. There is evidently no marked sentiment for change and the Senate is not likely to surrender the power given to it by the two-thirds majority requirement so long as the proposing of an amendment to mark the change requires a two-thirds vote of both Houses of Congress.

**A Court of Impeachment**

Another special function of the Senate is that of acting as a court for the trial of impeachment cases. The Constitution prescribes that the President, Vice-President, and all Civil officers[23] shall be removed from office on impeachment for and conviction of treason, bribery, or other crimes and misdemeanours. The House of Representatives initiates the charge and the Senate sits as a court of trial. On such an occasion the Senate is on a judicial mien and issues writs, sub-poenas to witnesses, and administers oaths. When a President is on trial, the Chief Justice of the Supreme Court presides. A Committee of Representatives appointed by the House appears at the bar of the Senate and prosecutes the impeached official.

21. On June 13, 1952 three treaties were ratified when the Senator acting as Presiding officer voted 'aye' and the only other Senator in the Chamber remained silent.
22. As cited in Burns and Peltason, *Government by the People,* p. 422.
23. Military and Naval officers are tried by court martial. The members of Congress are not liable to impeachment. In the case of William Blount, a Senator from Tennessee in 1907, the Senate decided that it had no jurisdiction of the case.

A two-thirds vote of the Senate is required for conviction and the penalty which it can impose is removal from office and disqualification from holding office in the future. It cannot inflict punishment ranging to imprisonment or fine. But the person convicted and removed may be indicted and tried by courts under the ordinary procedure of law as any other criminal may.

The procedure of removing an officer by impeachment is so cumbersome and unwieldy that it is very seldom resorted to. The Senate has sat as a Court of Impeachment on twelve occasions so far, and it has given the verdict of guilty only four times. The most notable trial was that of President Andrew Johnson, who in 1868 escaped conviction by only one vote after a three-month sitting of the Senate as a Court of Impeachment.

## SENATE : CAUSES OF ITS STRENGTH

### Not a Subordinate Branch

In addition to the three general functions which the Fathers of the Constitution assigned to the Senate, it is also a legislative body. But it is a co-ordinate body and not a subordinate branch of Congress and exercises co-equal powers with the House of Representatives in making the national laws. There is no law in the the United States, as it is in Britain,[24] which empowers the House of Representatives to veto the Senate. The only eminence which the House enjoys over the Senate is the one relating to raising of the revenues and the Constitution simply provides that such measures must "originate" in the House of Representatives. But it, also, prescribes that the Senate "may propose or concur with amendments as on other Bills." It means that the Senate can agree to, amend, modify or reject any measure relating to revenues and sometimes it so drastically mutilates it that it becomes beyond any possible recognition, as it did a few years back with the Tariff Bill. The Senate can, thus, virtually initiate new revenue proposals under the guise of amendments. The Tariff Bill was so completely amended that it struck out everything in the Bill except the enacting clause. Then, it inserted a new tariff of its own and transmitted the measure back to the House of Representatives "as amended." The House unnecessarily grumbled over this invasion of its special privilege and in the end accepted the tariff as amended by the Senate. On another occasion, a tariff measure came back from the Senate to the House of Representatives with no less than 847 amendments. And every Bill, money or nonmoney, carries with it the introductory clause stipulating: "Be it enacted by the Senate and the House of Representatives of the United States, in the Congress assembled." According to the letter of the law the revenue Bills must originate in the House of Representatives, but in practice the Senate can also do that[25] and as Munro says, "it has found a way of doing what the Constitution did not intend it to do."[26]

With regard to the appropriation Bills, the Constitution is silent and the only logical inference is that in the absence of any constitutional prohibition, the Senate may originate appropriation Bills, including the national budget, if it wishes to do so. The custom, however, is and the House has guarded it "with great jealousy" that it has the exclusive right to originate appropriation Bills. Yet it cannot be denied that the Senate's fiscal role rivals that of the House of Representatives.

### Investigative Powers

The Senate has very often undertaken special investigations embracing varied matters. Among the constitutional powers of Congress to which the investigating function is ancillary are those of legislation, impeachment, determining the qualifications and elections of its members, the consideration of treaties and agreements requiring Senate action, and the confirmation of Presidential nominees for public posts. Apart from this, as a result of the implied powers, which the Supreme Court has held as the valid jurisdiction of Congress, the investigation committees may exercise the power to delve deep from time to time into many aspects of the activities of the Executive. The Legislative Reorganisation Act, 1946, charges the Standing Committees of Congress with "watchfulness" over the corresponding agencies on the administrative side. In this "watchdog" capacity, the Committees may be concerned with the handling of appropriation, the personal or official probity of Executive appointees or with matters touching the national security.

The investigation committees may sit in Washington or they may go about the country to find facts, ideas, opinion and information, and seek advice that may be of utility in coming to a

24. Refer to the Parliament Act of 1911 as amended in 1949.
25. Lodge, Henry Cabot, *The Senate of the United States*, p. 9.
26. Munro, W. B., *The Government of the United States*, p. 302.

conclusion. It may summon witnesses, official and non-official, require them to produce papers and documents considered necessary for purposes of the investigation. In 1857 provision was made by law for one year imprisonment on conviction for refusal to testify. The Supreme Court has held the Act of 1857 constitutional. In *McGrain* v. *Daugherty* (1937) the Supreme Court while upholding the Senate's authority to probe into the official conduct of a former Attorney-General, did not indicate that a witness might refuse to answer if the bounds of power were exceeded by a committee or if the questions were not 'pertinent' to the matter under inquiry. In 1953, the Supreme Court held in *United States* v. *Rumely* that if the subject under examination lies outside the authority of the investigating committee, a witness is under no legal obligation to answer its questions. In 1957, in the case of *Watkins* v. *United States* the Supreme Court set aside the conviction of a witness for contempt of Congress because the questions he had refused to answer had not been demonstrated to be pertinent to the subject under investigation.

Bryce credits committees of the Senate with having more than once "unearthed dark doing" which needed to be brought to light. There is now increasing emphasis in the United States on the "watchdog" function of the investigation committees. The only way Congress can check the administration is through the questioning of official witnesses in the committees when appropriation Bills are under consideration, or through interim investigations of its own into the way Executive agencies are being run. The Committee can summon any official of the United States, from a member of the Cabinet to the routine clerk to testify in public and private hearings. It is, indeed, an effective method of checking administration. But to say, as Munro observes, that "they are merely seeking data as a basis for legislation is to use the words with Pickwickian versatility. What they often are seeking is ammunition that can be used in the next election campaign."[27] The inquiries are, therefore, largely political in nature. The Senators dominate the politics of the country and Congress, and its investigation committees are always politically vigorous. Many famous investigations have since taken place and the most recent was the Truman Committee during World War I which probed into waste and inefficiency, made many constructive suggestions, and helped put its chairman (Harry Truman) in the White House. Another important investigation committee was the Kefauver Committee inquiry into organised crime. The Water-gate Committee and the Tower Commission remain unsurpassed in making public sensational disclosures. Special Investigation Committees have all the powers of Standing Committees, except that they normally may not introduce legislation.

There is a mortal terror of these senatorial investigations and many official "dread the loaded questions of hostile Congressmen." Errors are likely to arise here and there in the conduct of administration which when discovered are widely publicized for political gains, and investigations thrive on publicity. Senatorial investigations operate "directly in spotlight" and often the "proceedings are covered by newsreel and television cameras and reported by the host of newsmen." Recently, some investigators have so fanatically sought publicity that "they have indulged in defamation of character, bullying and mistreatment of witnesses, and outright partisanship."[28] Such a situation is viewed with alarm even by the members of Congress. Senator Scott W. Lucas has warned that "unless Congress reforms its methods of conducting investigations, unless it puts some limits of responsibility both upon the interrogation of witnesses and upon the type of testimony which witnesses are allowed to give—unless, indeed, it adopts a wholly new and more judicious attitude—one of the great and important instruments of legislative process will be destroyed."

But the intrinsic utility of investigation committees cannot be denied if they conduct their investigations keeping in view the objects they are charged with. Brogan has correctly said that the investigation committees are "one of the most important modifications of the separation of powers and, consequently, one of the indispensable driving belts of the American system."[29] To put in the words of Galloway, they are "the buckle that binds, the hyphen that joins the legislature to the executive."[30] The investigatory power is an essential adjunct of the law-making authority, for investigatory function is used to

27. *Ibid.*, p. 303.
28. Burns and Peltason, *Government by the People*, p. 41.
29. Brogan, D. W., *The American Political System*, p. 328.
30. Galloway, G. B., "Investigation Functions of Congress." *The Political Science Review*, Vol. XXI, No. 3.

seek information in matters in which legislation is contemplated to ascertain the effectiveness with which laws are being executed, to uncover the wrongs and excesses of the government and thereby to put before the public problems essential to the country's welfare. It is only by such investigations that Congress can discover what has been going on, as it has not the day-to-day contact with the executive Departments the question time gives to the House of Commons in Britain. Some of the investigations conducted by the Senate Committees, especially by the Foreign Relations Committees, have been marvellously revealing and advantageous in keeping administration on its toes.

**Conference Committees**

In case of disagreement between the Senate and the House of Representatives the differences are resolved through a Conference Committee. The members of this Committee called "managers" are equally drawn, generally three and in exceptional cases five, from each Chamber and they confer together. Each Chamber votes as a unit and the conferees may be given instructions by their respective Houses. It is natural that the Senators, who are seasoned statesmen and stalwart politicians with longer and maturer parliamentary experience, should have better of the gain. And considering the degree of solidarity often exhibited by the Senators the conferees are usually supported by the Senate. The Senate, in fact, usually gives a free hand to its representatives on Conference Committees whereas the House binds its conferees more than often to instructions. That is done as the House feels that its managers are too easily out-talked by the Senators.

**Political Role of the Senators**

"Senators are somewhat a different breed of political animal from the average representatives."[31] The Senators represent, as compared with Representatives, more people and greater areas and thus, are not subject to the fluctuating public opinion and personal idiosyncrasies of the electors of a particular locality. A Representative must cater to local needs and remain susceptible to the influence of a few interest groups and handful of local party bosses. The Senators, and a majority of them, enjoy nationwide reputation for their political sagacity. Their opinions are reckoned with and even Presidents at times have to defer to the wishes of some eminent Senators, especially those who are the prospective candidates for the Presidency. Senators also very often command important positions and dominating influences in the organization and policies of their party in the state which they represent.[32] Their party position is essentially linked with their control of federal patronage. The power of the Senate to confirm Presidential appointments is important constitutionally as well as politically. The former is indicative as a part of the system of checks and balances whereas the latter emphasises that the individual Senator has virtually a veto power over major appointments in his State.

**Senatorial Solidarity**

Closely allied with it is solidarity exhibited by the Senators. "In a sense the Senate is a mutual protection society." Each Senator jealously guards the rights and privileges of others irrespective of party ties and whenever an onslaught had been made to break its solidarity, as Roosevelt did to bypass the traditional method of senatorial courtesy in 1938, it has always stood together. Washington correspondents have frequently reported that two Senators may attack each other in vehement language on the floor, only to be seen a short time later strolling arm in arm in the corridors outside. They thrive on the principle of live and let live and their code of behaviour is to speak well of the Senate as an institution. Such a sense of solidarity enables them to ward off all encroachments from outside. "The Senate," remark Swarthout and Bartley, "is alert against any possible threat of pressure by either of these two (the President or the House of Representatives) sources, and it is quick to resent any action it considers to be a danger to its prerogative or its tradition." In its solidarity lies the independence and assertiveness and these qualities make the Senate one of the most powerful legislative assemblies in the world.

**Independent Spirit**

One of the most important factors which accounts for the authority and independence of the Senators is the continuity, stability and traditions of the Chamber which the House of Representatives has not been able to develop. The entire membership of the House of Representatives must stand for re-election every two years and every time it is faced with the laborious task of

31. Burn and Peltason, *Government by the People*, p. 420.
32. As in the case of Huey Long of Louisiana, Joseph Guffey of Pennsylvania, Nelson Aldrich of Rhode Island, or, more recently, Robert A, Taft of Ohio, and Harry of Virginia.

reorganising itself. The Senate, on the other hand, has been continuously organised since 1789, for only one- third of its members stand for re-election in each two-year period. Coupled with this fact is the six-year Senate term. There are many members who gain election for three terms and some even see six Presidential terms come and go. The continued long service gives to the Senators a standing and prestige and they carry with them the sense of senatorial pride. They regard themselves as senior lawmakers of the country and custodians of the balance of powers between the Legislative and Executive departments. Each Senator strives to become a specialist, working hard "at unglamorous legislative work."

Membership in the Senate is, in fact, greatly coveted. A high proportion of its members are former Representatives or former State Governors. The tendency of many of the most able House members to seek Senate seats has constituted a drain on the talent of the House of Representatives. The loss of the House is the advantage of the Senate. Similarly, the presence of around twenty-five former State Governors not only adds to the prestige and stature of the Senate, but also imparts an active quality to Senate behaviour less evident among the House membership, where talent is depleted by the locality rule and some other factors.

**Conservative Character**

The Constitution-makers had thought that the Senate would prove the bulwark of conservatism. They had, accordingly, designed it and given it special powers so that it might serve as a check on the more radical House of Representatives. The Senate has fulfilled the expectations of its designers and acted as a conservative obstacle to hotheaded action as was illustrated some years ago when it opposed President Truman's proposal to draft rail-road strikes into the army. "It is from Senators," writes Charles Beard, "rather than Representatives that public may expect staunch defence of constitutional methods and powerful opposition to violent, high-handed and bigoted opinions and actions." But the Senate no longer remains a 'rich man's club', as it appeared before 1913. The Seventeenth Amendment to the Constitution made the Senate popularly elected and it has almost lost its "plutocratic" element. In recent years it has usually been more liberal than the House of Representatives, but it has never been swayed by violent gusts of passion. The Senate has justifiably fulfilled the expectation of the framers of the Constitution and to put it in the words of Washington "we pour legislation into the senatorial saucer to cool it."

**Influence on Foreign Policy**

The Senate has been the Congressional spokesman on foreign policy, and the House its junior partner. This is due to the Senate's treaty-ratifying authority and its veto power over Presidential appointments of ambassadors, ministers and other important officials. The Senate can, also, influence the foreign policy through investigations. The investigations of the Nye Committee paved the way for neutrality legislation in 1930. In 1951, the Senate Investigation on the question of dismissal of General Douglas MacArthur brought Truman's foreign policy in the Far East under fire and the administration was obliged to clarify its position.

But the present trend is to undertake international obligations by legislation rather than by treaty. The notable examples of such a joint action by the Senate and the House are the Greek-Turkish Air Programme, the European Recovery Programme, Point Four, the Indian Grain Programme, etc. Some Senators have vehemently protested against such an encroachment as well as the President's frequent use of executive agreements. They stress that no obligations be incurred except by formal treaty procedure.

The obvious result is that all through these times the Senate has kept its supremacy. The longer term and greater dignity of a Senator attract political leaders to the Senate than the House of Representatives and their appearance in the Senate enhances the prestige of being a Senator still more. The Senate is the smaller body and generally speaking its fellowhip includes citizens older in years and wider in political experience. They are usually better acquainted not only with the problems of law-making, but also with the inner working of the federal administration. It is through the Senate that most national patronage is siphoned to the State party machines. The Senate has more influence than the House over the conduct of foreign affairs. James Bryce remarked that the Senate "has succeeded in effecting the chief object of the Fathers of the Constitution, *viz.*, the creation of a centre of gravity in the government, an authority able to correct and check on the one hand the democratic recklessness of the House, on the other, the monarchical ambitions of the President. Placed between the two, the Senate is necessarily the rival and often the opponent of both. The House can accomplish nothing without its concurrence. The President can be checkmated by its resistance. There is, so to speak, the negative success on its positive side, it has succeeded itself eminent and respected.'' There has been a good deal of overlapping of actions of the Senate and the House during recent times, but if either body has increased its powers relative to the other, it is the Senate. While Upper Chambers in other parts of the world have been declining in power and importance, the Senate has added to its strength and prestige. It is not only the most powerful Second Chamber in the world, but also one of the most powerful legislative assemblies in the world.

According to C. Wright Mills, the American Congress operates at the middle level of state power. It generally registers dicisions made elsewhere by the American ''Power Elite'' which consists of theree inter-related, dominant elites : (1) heads of a few largest corporations; (2) top military generals, admirals and air force officers; and (3) a few hundred top leaders of the two main American Parties. Both Senators and Congressmen belongingto the lower house obey the dictates of what he calls the economic, military and politcal elites fused into an interconnected ''power elite''.

## SUGGESTED READINGS

Bailey, S. K.: *The New Congress.*

Beard, C.: *American Government and Politics,* Chaps. IV, V.

Brogan, D. W.: *The American Political System,* Part Five, Chaps. III, IV.

Bryce, James: *The American Commonwealth,* Vol. I, Chaps. X- XIII.

Dimock, Marshall E.: *Congressional Investigating Committees.*

Finletter, T. K.: *Can Representative Government Do the Job?*

Galloway, George, B.: *Congress at the Crossroads.*

Galloway, George, B.: *History of the House of Representatives.*

Griffith, E. M.: *Congress, Its Contemporary Role.*

Haynes, G. H.: *The Senate of the United States: Its History and Practice,* Vol. I, Chaps III-VII.

Kaufauver, E., and Laven, J.: *A Twentieth Century Congress.*

Matthews, Donald R.: *Senators and their World.*

Munro, W. B.: *The Government of the United States,* Chaps. XVII-XX.

Ogg, F. A., and Ray, P. O. : *Essentials of American Government,* Chaps. XIII-XIV.

Polsby, Nelson, W.: *Congress and the Presidency.*

Riddick F.M. : *The United States Congress.*

Rogers, L. : *The American Senate.*

Vinyard, Dale: *Congress.*

White, William S. : Citadel : *The Story of the U.S. Senate.*

Wilson, W. : *Congressional Government.*

Young, R. : *This is Congress,* Chap. III.

Zink, H. : *A Survey of American Government,* Chaps. XVI-XVII.

# CHAPTER VI

# Congress : Functions and Powers

## FUNCTIONS AND POWERS OF CONGRESS

The Senate and the House of Representatives make the national Legislature of Congress of the United States. Article 1 of the Constitution vests all legislative power in Congress and then enumerates the functions it shall have to perform and the powers it is authorised to exercise. If the Founding Fathers had strictly adhered to the application of the doctrine of Separation of Powers, Congress would have been only a law-making body. But the system of checks and balances gives it non-legislative functions as well, and these functions are in no way less important than its Legislative functions. Broadly regarded, Congress is the instrument by which the people frame, declare, and supervise the policies of the nation. Under the non-legislative functions, we may include: (1) constituent, (2) electoral, (3) executive, (4) judicial, (5) directive and supervisory, and (6) investigative. With regard to legislative functions, it must be observecd that Congress is not the only law-making authority notwithstanding what Article I of the Constitution says.

## NON-LEGISLATIVE FUNCTIONS

### Constituent Functions

The proposal to amend the constitution should either be made by a two-third vote of Congress or by a national Convention which Congress calls at the request of the legislatures of two-thirds of states.[1] Whatever method is adopted, and only the Congressional method has ever been invoked, not a syllable of that document can be changed without the intervention of Congress. In addition to the initiation of proposals for the alteration of the Constitution, Congress determines the manner to be used for ratification by either the legislatures of three-fourths of the States or by conventions in three-fourths of the States, and may specify time limit for ratification. Moreover, Congress has important duties in expanding and interpreting the original Constitution and this, as we have discussed,[2] is one of the most important factors to make the Constitution dynamic.

### Electoral Functions

Congress and each of its Houses have electoral functions to perform. As a matter of routine, it meets in joint session every fourth year to count the electoral votes cast for the President and Vice-President. If no candidate receives a majority of the electoral votes for President, then, the House of Representatives selects, each State voting as a unit, the President from among the candidates with three highest votes. When no candidate secures a majority of the electoral votes cast for the Vice-President, the Senate makes the choice from among the two candidates with the highest number of votes. Only one Vice-President had been so far elected in this manner and that, too, in 1837, when the party system was not fully developed. Such a contingency cannot happen now. Congress by law determines who shall be the President in the event of the death or disability of the President and Vice-President. Congress, also, has authority to legislate on the times, places, and manner of holding elections for Senators and Representatives, and that it judges the qualifications of its own members, including the validity of their elections.[3] It may disqualify persons whose conduct a majority of the members disapprove.[4] In 1926, for example, the Senate "refused to seat" William S. Vare because of his excessive campaign expenditure.

### Executive Functions

Executive functions extend to appointments and treaty making. Administrative functions we take under the heading directive and supervisory. This bifurcation has been made for purposes of clarity. In relation to more than sixteen thousand officials who are nominated by

1. See *ante*, Chapter II.
2. Chap. V, *ante*.
3. Article I, Sections, 4, 5.
4. The constitutionality of this practice has been questioned, although there are many precedents to support it.

the President and confirmed by the Senate, the Congressional role is specially outstanding. The Senators and the Representatives, but especially Senators, actually determine the vast majority of these appointments. Senators who belong to the President's party do not wait to be asked which candidate they would like to favour. They immediately proceed on their own initiative to suggest names of the candidates whom they desire and, except in rare cases, they get their recommendations accepted. If no Senator from a State belongs to the President's party, Representatives claim their privileges to recommend such names. Sometimes, even when there are party Senators, an agreement may be worked out under which the Senators share the patronage with the Representatives.

The Senate has the important functions of ratifying treaties.[5] In the negotiations of treaties, the President has the exclusive authority, but discreet and far-sighted Chief Executives consult the leading Senators and take their opinion in anticipation in order to facilitate its ratification.

Congress, as a whole, has intimate interest in the international relations of the United States. The President reviews the international situation in his messages and Congress permits the expenditure to be incurred on international obligations. The present tendency to incur international obligations through legislation rather than treaty emphasises the need of a joint action by the Senate and the House.

**Judicial Functions**

Impeachment proceedings of the President, Vice-President, Judges and other federal officials can be brought about by the Senate as a Court of Trial (the Chief Justice of the United States presiding when the impeachment of the President is being tried).

Each Chamber exercises disciplinary powers over both its own members and to a limited extent over private persons. Members of Congress are not subject to impeachment as they are not, according to the decision of the Supreme Court, civil officers of the United States. Both the Chambers, therefore, determine how to discipline their members, and a two-thirds vote of his own House is sufficient to expel a Congressman, though it is a most uncommon proceeding.

Each House has also the inherent power to punish private persons whose conduct directly interferes with the due transaction of Congressional business. If, for example, a witness before a Congressional Committee refuses to answer a question, the Chamber concerned to which the Committee belongs can sit as a court and convict him of contempt. It may order the Sergeant-at-Arms to hold him in custody. But he cannot be held longer than the time Congress remains in session. Such a power, however,Congress normally does not exercise. The matter is referred to the United States Attorney-General for punishment under the law whenever there is case of contempt of the House or the Senate.

**Directive and Supervisory Functions**

The President and his principal subordinates, no doubt, actually direct and supervise administration, but it is Congress which creates all the administrative Departments and agencies. The. Constitution does not say anything about their organisation. Nor does it define their powers and functions. The form, the organisation and the powers to be exercised, by the administrative Departments are all defined by Acts of Congress. And, then, Congress provides money for carrying on their activities. All this ''opens a way for watchfulness over the work performed, for requests for information and reports for assignments of tasks and duties, and, of course, for curtailment of activities, or even termination of them altogether (perchance of the agency itself), by denial of funds.'' The Legislative Reorganisation Act of 1946, stressed the importance of continuous vigilance over the execution of all laws by the Standing Committees of both the Houses. Then, Congress may from time to time see fit to pass laws directing the administrative Departments to report to it. Thus, the Controller-General has been made responsible to Congress rather than to the President. Congress may sometimes pass a resolution directing the administration to follow a certain course of action in the event of a particular situation.

Direction and review are a continuous process and both are complementary. Almost all agencies are required to make annual reports to Congress. Members of Congress may call for information and explanation. Congressional Committees may undertake a review of a particular agency or problem. Confirmation by the Senate of an appointment or confirmation of a treaty may necessitate widespread resentment or criticism and may, thus, lead to a Congressional inquiry. But the most appropriate occasion of a

5. See *ante* under the heading Special Functions of the Senate.

thorough review is when representatives of the various agencies appear before Committees to defend budgetary demands.

**Investigative**

While discussing the role of the investigative committees, it was pointed out how these "watchdog" Committees help to keep administration within its bounds.[6] But appointment of such committees is not the peculiar function of the Senate alone. In fact, investigations by committees of Congress are as old as Congress itself, "Legislative oversight of administration is familiar and well-grounded assumption of responsible Government," writes Arthur Macmalon, and Congress can look into any subject whenever it deems necessary in order to carry out its law making, amending, electoral, directive and supervisory, or other duties. Alexander Hamilton and the Treasury Department were investigated into by the Second Congress; Presidential and Cabinet officers have been frequently investigated ever since.

Congressional investigations help to make administration accountable. A proper function of the Legislature, a body representative of the people, is to keep constant watch and control over the activities of the Government which they support and to make public its policies and acts. Under a parliamentary system there are many devices available to do so. In the presidential system there are no such means available and responsibility cannot be adequately enforced. Legislative investigations are, therefore, a major technique, even though it is sometimes cumbersome and has fearful implications for holding the Executive and administrative agencies accountable. Still, the need for throwing adequate light of publicity on what the administration does has become really imminent during recent times. As Congress has been required to extend the area of governmental functions, it has also been compelled to delegate regulatory powers, to authorise wide increase in the number of administrative bureaus, and to support by "appropriation and sustain by law a great and complex government machine involving an expenditure of over $ 42,000,000,000 (which has exceeded by more than a million by now) annually and the activities of over two million (which now touches the figure by a little more than half a million) government employees."[7]

Many Americans have held investigatory powers of Congress as un-American and have pleaded that they should be outlawed. Actually the Constitution does not provide for such investigations, but, at the same time, they are deeply rooted in American legislative procedure.[8] It is true that there has been extravagant abuse of the investigatory powers by the politically inspired members of these Committees, but "corruption and bribery have often been revealed only through Congressional investigations. The inadequacy of old laws and the necessity for new ones have been determined only by investigations. The abuse of offices, inefficiency, misapplication of powers have all been curtailed not only by investigation but by the constant possibility of an investigation."[9]

## LEGISLATIVE FUNCTIONS

**Extent of Legislative Functions**

In spite of the importance and immensity of its non-legislative functions, after all Congress is primarily a legislature and to it the Constitution assigns "all legislative power herein granted." The words "herein granted" have two important meanings. In the first place, it means that consistent with the principle of limited government, the powers of Congress, too, are limited and they are enumerated in two lengthy Sections of the Constitution.[10] There are some eighteen different categories on which it has been made competent to enact laws. Secondly, the subjects not enumerated are beyond the authority of Congress but at the same time, the Constitution expressly details what Congress cannot do.[11] The general conclusion is that Congress may exercise those powers which are expressly granted and not definitely prohibited by the Constitution, and the rest remain within the jurisdiction of the States.

After expressly enumerating in succession the various powers of Congress, the Constitution concludes with a sort of general grant, empowering Congress to make all laws which shall be necessary and proper for carrying into execution

6. *See ante,* Chap. V.
7. Tourtellot, A. B., *The Anatomy of American Politics,* p. 98.
8. The colonial assemblies of America were authorized to conduct specific investigations. The Constitutions of some of the original thirteen States contained general authorization of this kind.
9. Tourtellot, A. B., *The Anatomy of American Politics,* p. 99.
10. Article I, Sections 7 and 8.
11. Article I, Section 9.

"the foregoing powers, and all other powers vested by this Constitution in the Government of the United States, or in any Department or officer thereof."[12] Within a few years after the founding of the Constitution, Congress desired to pass laws relating to matters that the Constitution did not mention particularly in connection with the proposal of Hamilton to establish a United States bank. Hamilton contended that the authority to establish such an institution was clearly implied in the power to borrow money and pay the debts of the United States. A federal bank, he asserted, was a proper, if not necessary, means for carrying into effect these important powers of Congress, just as the establishment of mint was necessary to carry out the power relating to the coinage of money. Jefferson and his associates maintained that Congress had no right to exercise any power which was not expressly conferred. As a result of the liberal attitude which ultimately prevailed and the policy of liberal interpretation, which Chief Justice Marshall of the Supreme Court and his associates adopted, Congress has profusely relied upon the doctrine of implied powers for its authority to legislate on many important questions. "Let the end be legitimate," said Marshall speaking for the Court, "let it be within the scope of the Constitution, and all means which are appropriate, which are plainly adapted to that end, which are not prohibited, but consistent with the spirit and letter of the Constitution, are constitutional."[13] Implied powers are, therefore, those that may reasonably be deduced from delegated or enumerated powers or, to use the language of the Constitution, those that are "necessary and proper" for carrying delegated or enumerated powers into execution. Implied powers do not give the Federal Government a *carte blanche* to do anything it wishes. Implications can be made from some delegated or enumerated powers in the Constitution and the end should be, as Chief Justice Marshall remarked, "legitimate" and all means adopted to achieve that end are "appropriate."

But Chief Justice Marshall In *McCulloch* v. *Maryland* went even beyond the doctrine of implied powers when he invoked the theory of the resultant power. The result has been to strengthen the National Government in order to enable it fulfilling the great purpose for which it was created.

The doctrine of implied powers has been further cemented by the express provisions in some of the Amendments that Congress shall have the power to enforce them by "appropriate legislation."[14] The "General Welfare Clause" has further helped the authority of Congress to expand. The Constitution provides that "Congress shall have the power....to provide for the common defence and general welfare of the United States." It means that Federal Government possesses powers which are neither specifically enumerated nor implied, under the constitutional provision of the common defence and general welfare of the United States. For example, when States cannot adequately handle particular problems, which fall within their jurisdiction of residual authority, then, it devolves upon the National Government, under the General Welfare Clause, to assume the power in an attempt to relieve the situation. This opinion was supported by Justice Stone[15] in his dissenting opinion to support the Agricultural Adjustment Act. A similar opinion was expressed in *Steward Machine Company* v. *Davis* and *Helvaring* v. Davis in 1937. Justice Cardozo, delivering the majority judgment, used the "General Welfare Clause" to justify the Social Security Act. Since then, Congress has legislated on many matters embracing diversified problems covered by this mystic constitutional provision.

Reliance has also been placed on the so-called "emergency powers." During the economic depression of the thirties and the World War II, Congress passed emergency legislation on subjects beyond its normal jurisdiction. Congress has no emergency powers and the Constitution does not prescribe any. Nevertheless Congress has enacted laws, when the country was in the midst of economic or international crisis, which it never would have passed under ordinary circumstances. The Supreme Court, however, held that the "emergency does not create power," nor does it increase power already given in the Constitution. The powers which Congress wields at such time are not special powers. It relies on powers which it already has, but for which there is little or no need to use ordinarily.[16]

12. Article I, Section 8, Clause 18.
13. *McCulloch* v. *Maryland.*
14. Refer to Amendments XIII, XIV, XV, XIX and XXIV.
15. *United States* v. *Butler (1936).*
16. *Home Building and Loan Association* v. Blaisdell (1934).

Thus, the powers expressly given to Congress do not convey the extent of the powers actually exercised today. Two of the eighteen express powers relate to levying taxes, spending public money, and borrowing on federal credit. The third brings in foreign and inter-state commerce. These three items alone have been expanded so amazingly that despite the six lines of type which they require in an ordinary printed copy of the Constitution, they now constitute the basis for hundreds and even thousands of far-reaching statutes which Congress has from time to time enacted. The Commerce clause has been invoked during the past three decades, to justify the regulation of business practices, the protection of organised labour, the regimentation of the coal-mining industry, and the stabilization of the stock and grain markets. The remaining gap was filled by the general welfare clause and the crowning event was made under common defence. When the economic depression began there was some feeling that Congress lacked adequate powers to tide over the difficulties in which the country was placed at that time. Today, no such fear can be entertained even remotely. Indeed, the chief apprehension in many minds at present seems to be that too much responsibility has been loaded on Congress, especially in those fields which were long left to private and state control.

## THE MAKING OF LAWS

### Legislative Procedure

The British and Americans, says Griffiths, are alike in their ideals as to how to legislate. "Both strive to provide thorough discussion and consideration. Both are determined that the minority shall have a fair opportunity to be heard, to criticize, to offer alternatives. Both offer opportunity to criticize the administration and call it to account."[17] And he concludes that such differences as there are in two countries are chiefly differences in procedural methods rather than in objectives. Griffiths makes two important observations here. American procedure, he says, provides much greater legislative specialization in substance and in detail and this suits well the enormity of legislation which Congress has before it. Much of it, which in part concerns details, in Britain is left to departmental orders or private Bills. Secondly, in comparison to the simple standing orders of the House of Commons and the precedents thereunder, Rules of Procedure and precedents in both the House and the Senate "present a maze, a mystery which even those of long standing membership often find it difficult to master completely."[18]

Each Congress in its two years of existence faces over 10,000 Bills and resolutions, of which less than 2,000 are private Bills, which follow a simplified procedure. The remaining Bills are public. A Bill introduced in the first session of a two-year Congress does not have to be re-introduced in the second session of the same Congress. With the election of the new Congress all previously introduced Bills, which have not been enacted into laws, lapse and these must be re-introduced, if need is felt to do so, with the coming in of the new Congress. The principal reason for this huge number of Bills is the doctrine of equality among the membership. A backbencher and a Chairman of a Committee rank equally. No distinction is also made between a minor Bill and an important measure, both are of equal importance. There is no such distinction, as it is in Britain, between a Government and a Private Member's Bill.

The greater part of the work of the Senate and the House of Representatives is transacted through the medium of Bills or joint resolutions. There is practically no difference between the two, except that the latter are narrower in scope and more temporary in purpose. Otherwise, they are similar to Bills, undergo the same procedure and after having been passed by both the Chambers are sent to the President, and if assented to by him, have the full force of law. But joint resolutions differ from *concurrent resolutions* and *unicameral* or *simple* House or Senate resolutions. Concurrent resolutions are employed to express an attitude, opinion and objective of both the Chambers. They are not submitted to the President for his approval and consequently have no legal effect unless prior enactment has been made dependent upon them. Unicameral or simple House or Senate resolutions express the opinion, purpose, or intention of the Chamber concerned and are not to be endorsed by the other. That is to say, unicameral resolutions concern the operations of either Chamber alone and may be covered by a simple resolution, acted upon in only the Chamber concerned. Unicameral resolutions, like the concurrent resolutions, are not submitted to the President and have no legal

17. Griffiths, *The American System of Government*, p. 39.
18. *Ibid.*

effect.

There is a good deal of variation among Bills themselves. Some of the Bills are of fundamental importance and embody major programmes of government policy and cover important details spreading to fifty, seventy-five or even more printed pages. Other Bills pertain to private affairs, for example, to provide pensions for widows of former Presidents, or appropriate money to pay for damages caused by post office or army trucks. The former are known as *Public Bills* and the latter as *Private Bills* that is, they do not concern public matters. *A* private Bill is primarily of interest to some individual or group of individuals and aims at their benefit. But here, too, as in the case of Bills and joint resolutions, the distinction is not always followed in practice.

There are six major stages that a public bill usually passes through before it becomes law after receiving the assent of the President: (1) drafting and introduction of the bill; (2) consideration and approval by committee in the Chamber in which the bill is introduced; (3) consideration and approval by that Chamber itself; (4) consideration and approval by committee in the second Chamber; (5) consideration and approval by the second Chamber; and (6) ironing out differences between the two Chambers in conference.

Unlike Britain, where bills are introduced, sponsored and piloted by the government, there are no government bills in the United States. The government has no place in Congress and all bills, public or private, are introduced and defended by members of Congress. It does not, however mean that all proposals to enact legislation originate among the Senators or the Representatives. Some bills have their origins primarily within Congress. They may reflect the wishes and labours of Congressmen who introduced them. Or a bill may have its birth in the deliberations of a standing committee which has given much time and consideration to the need for new legislation in a particular field. Most new tax bills are so prepared by the House Ways and Means Committee. Some Bills originate with, or at least are inspired by pressure groups, or persons outside of Congress.[19] But a majority of the bills come from the administration, that is, from the President or from one of the Executive Departments or independent agencies. Whatever be the source of origin, a bill must become a member's child and he may appear in one of the Chambers as its sponsor.[20] The Senators and the Representatives generally act as intermediaries rather than originators in the making of laws.

With very few exceptions, any member of either Chamber may introduce a bill or resolution dealing with any subject over which Congress has jurisdiction. But the Constitution requires that revenue bills be introduced in the House of Representatives, and by custom appropriation bills are so considered first by the House. Under the Constitution, resolutions proposing the impeachment of federal officers may also be introduced in the House. The ratification of treaties, confirmation of appointments, and trial of impeachment cases are all restricted by the Constitution to the Senate, and accordingly, any motion or resolution bearing on these matters can be presented only by a Senator.

The member introducing a bill endorses the copy with his name and drops it in the "hopper," a box on the Clerk's desk in the House and the Secretary's in the Senate. The bill is immediately numbered and sent to the Government Printing Office and made available to members next morning at the document room. With this procedure the first stage in the career of a bill is over. The introduction of a bill by a member does not necessarily mean that he endorses it. Many bills bear the notation, "By request," which means that the member has introduced the bill as a matter of courtesy.

Reference to a Committee is the next step in the legislative procedure. In the great majority of cases the bill goes to an appropriate Standing Committee of the House, into which it is introduced, automatically. The title of the bill indicates what particular Standing Committee should receive it. Before 1910-11, the Speaker in the House of Representatives determined the Committee to which a Bill was to go. But now the Speaker has been deprived of this power. Sometimes, however, a Bill is of such a nature that it might be referred with almost equal propriety to any one or two or more appropriate Committees. In all such exceptional cases, the Speaker decides

19. It was widely reported that certain Sections of the 1954 Act revising the federal income tax were originally written by business groups and reflected the desires of business for more favourable tax treatment.

20. An Act of Congress is frequently known by the name of the Representative or Senator who introduced the Bill out of which the Act emerged, *e.g.*, the Sherman Act. If a Bill originates from a Committee an Act is sometimes known by the Chairman of the Committee that handled it, *e.g.*, the Taft-Hartley Act.

to which Committee a Bill shall be referred. But it is the accepted practice for Speakers to exercise the discretion freely and without party prejudices. In the Senate the reference to a Committee is even more automatic than in the House, because the Presiding Officer there has never had the discretionary authority to assign Bills to Committees.

In Committees, Bills are first given a preliminary examination and a decision is taken whether the proposal has merit or not. The Bills which are deemed worthy of consideration are sorted and the rest are entrusted to the Committee files. It means, Bills meriting no consideration are ''pigeon-holed.'' It is estimated that from 50 to 75 per cent of the Bills introduced in Congress come to final rest in Committee files and are never heard of again. The more important Bills which merit consideration are studied in details, and relevant information is gathered both from official and public sources. The Committee may seek to obtain all the light on the subject. Specified portions of the measure or even the whole of it may be assigned to a sub-committee. The sub-committees are very much like regular Committees, ''sorting the wheat from the chaff,'' deciding what changes should be recommended in a certain Bill, and otherwise preparing to dispose of the business entrusted to them. In 1946 Congress decided to provide a research staff for each Committee.

Committees charged with the consideration of important Bills frequently hold public meetings at which interested parties may appear and present arguments for and against the measures under consideration. In addition to the prepared statements of witnesses, numerous questions are often put by members of the Committees for the purpose of elucidating certain points or eliciting further information. Apart from the testimony received in connection with public hearings, Standing Committees are very often subjected to outside influences. The President may himself talk personally or even write letters to top-ranking members of the Committee for their due consideration of important measures. Officials of administrative agencies may ask the Committees to be heard in person or they may submit detailed statements with their reasons for a favourable action by the Committee on a certain Bill. Representatives of pressure groups also manage to make their influences felt whether public hearings are held or not. Sometimes they manage to get themselves invited to the private hearings of Committees.

On the basis of its own investigations, the information gathered at public hearings, the opinion elicited from high Government officers and the influence exercised by pressure groups, the Committee meets in executive (closed) session to arrive at its verdict. Before the final meeting is held the sentiments of various members are canvassed. It may take by majority vote one of the following courses:

(1) it may recommend the Bill back to the Chamber concerned with recommendation that it be passed;

(2) it may amend the Bill and recommend that it be passed as amended;

(3) it may entirely change the original Bill except its title and report a new one in its place;

(4) it may report the Bill unfavourably and recommend that it need not be passed;

(5) it may ''pigeon-hole'' the Bill, that is, to take no action on the Bill at all, or report it so late in the session that it may not find an opportunity for consideration.

The Report to the House is usually made by the Chairman of the Committee or someone designated by him. On important matters Committee Report may be extensive and exhaustive; on minor matters it may convey a little more than a simple affirmative note. Hearings of the major Committees on important legislation are published, some in the 'documents' series of Congress. Minority reports may also be filed.

**The Caucus System**

Before describing the next stage in the legislative procedure, it is necessary to briefly refer to the caucus system. We have already referred to the absence of leadership in Congress and consequently the need for devising some other means to see the Bills through or to oppose them. The mechanism which has been developed to meet the situation is known as the ''caucus'' or ''conference.''

There are numerous Bills which are non-controversial and do not demand much political interest. Such Bills are left to find their own way in Congress and the individual members are permitted by their parties to take stands as they please. But the most important legislative proposals cannot be left to themselves and it is here that the caucus system intervenes. A caucus is a meeting of the members of a political party both belonging to the Senate and the House and all members are expected to attend unless they have a valid reason for absence. The caucus at its first meeting of the session elects its party leader, steering committee, floor leader, whips and party assignments on Congressional Committees. The caucus of the majority party plans a positive programme for the particular session of Congress. The minority caucus has less an active role to play, although it may decide to oppose certain controversial Bills which, "are regarded especially dear to the majority party." In the caucus meetings members are free to express their opinions and persuade the caucus to accept their view. But once the decision has been taken and a particular stand determined, all members of the caucus are expected to abide by its decision no matter what their personal views on the measure may be.

The caucus system is used more in the House of Representatives rather in the Senate. The caucus of the Senate used to be as strong as that of the House of Representatives, but during the last two decades the caucus in the Senate "have limited themselves to setting up party machinery and arranging committee assignments, leaving Senators free to divide themselves as they like on pending Bills."[21] It does not, however, mean that the party Whip is not issued to the members to pass a Bill which is deemed in the best interests of the party, but no official caucus is taken which would bind the party Senators in voting.

**Procedure on the Floor**

Each Bill reported out of a Committee to the floor of the House is placed on one of the three principal calendars. A Legislative Calendar is a docket or list of measures reported from Committees and ready for consideration. The House of Representatives maintains three of these for different types of measures: (1) A Calendar of the Committee of the Whole House on the State of the Union, to which are referred all public Bills raising revenues or involving a charge against the government. It is also called the Union Calendar. (2) A House Calendar for all public bills not raising revenues nor appropriating money or property. (3) A Calendar of the Committee of the Whole House for all private bills; also called the Private Calendar. Bills are listed on these Calendars in the order in which they are received from the committees and remain there until the final adjournment of Congress, unless they are removed for consideration. All Bills are not invariably called up from the calendars in the order in which they are listed. Most important bills are lifted out of their sequence on the lists and put in a preferred position. If this is not done, there may not be any chance of their being taken up for consideration and hundreds of bills "die on the calendars" in every Congress.

Both Houses guard jealously the right of the minority to be heard. In the House of Representatives it usually takes the form of apportioning an equal amount of time on a given measure to its opponents and proponents. In the Senate it appears in the facilities extended for almost unlimited debate.

When the time fixed for bringing a Bill to the floor of the House of Representatives has arrived, the House ordinarily meets as a Committee of the Whole. The Senate before 1930 used Committee of the Whole more frequently than the House, but it has now abandoned this practice for the consideration of ordinary Bills, except in debating treaties. The Committees of the Whole are of two kinds: a Committee of the Whole House for consideration of private Bills, and a Committee of the Whole House on the State of the Union of considering public Bills. When the House goes into the Committee of the Whole, the Speaker leaves the chair and calls someone else to preside in his place. The presence of 100 members constitutes a quorum. Debate in the Committee of the Whole is conducted rather informally, and greater freedom of discussion is allowed. Divisions are taken only *viva voce,* by rising vote or by tellers and no record is kept how members vote. Motions to refer or to postpone are not permitted and when discussion is completed the Committee votes to rise, the Speaker resumes the chair and the mace is again placed on a marble pedestal on the right of the chair.

The device of the Committee of the Whole is really important, because it enables all Finance Bills and most other important Bills to be considered in such a way that ordinarily every member who desires to speak and offer amendments can do so. He is, in fact, given an opportunity for that. It also, affords large number of amendments to be presented, explained and disposed of speedily. "It facilitates rapid fire, critical debate which commonly shows the House at its best. And, for better or worse, the absence of recorded ayes and nays enables members to register their sentiments without check or restraint such as published votes

21. Zink, H, *A Survey of American Government,* p. 353.

sometimes impose.''

Three readings of each Bill are required by House rules. The first requirement is satisfied by printing the title of a Bill in the *Congressional Record and the Journal.* Then, the measure goes to the Committee and if reported back, is placed upon its Calendar for a second reading. The second reading occurs at the time the Bill is taken up for consideration in the House or in the Committee of the Whole. This is the actual reading in full with opportunity for debate and for amendments to be offered. Some amendments are general, ''considered'' amendments are seriously intended as alterations in the Bill. Others are *pro forma*, involving the striking out of the last word or two of a section. In the conduct of the Bill the top-ranking members of the Committee who had supported the Bill pilot it through in the House. The minority members of the Committee oppose it. Time for debate is generally predetermined and is equally divided between the supporters and opponents of the Bill.

At the conclusion of the consideration, the Speaker states: ''The question is on the engrossment and third reading of the Bill.'' If adopted, the Bill is ordered engrossed and read a third time. After this ''the question is on the final passage of the Bill.'' If it is passed, then, it is sent, duly signed by the Speaker, to the Senate.

**Action by the Senate**

The engrossed Bill is sent to the Senate through a messenger where it is received with due dignity. The President of the Senate refers it to the appropriate Standing Committee in conformity with the rules. The Senate Committee gives the same kind of detailed consideration as it received in the House of Representatives, and may report it with or without amendment. Then, it is placed on the Calendar.

The Rules of Procedure in the Senate differ from those in the House of Representatives. The Senator making the report may ask consent of the Chamber for the immediate consideration of the Bill. If there is no objection and the Bill is of non-controversial nature, the Senate may pass the Bill even without a debate after a brief explanation of its purposes and effect. Any Senator may also move an amendment thereto. If there is any objection to its immediate consideration, the report, must lie over one day and the Bill is placed on the Calendar. Unlike the House of Representatives, there is only one Calendar of Bills in the Senate.

At the conclusion of the morning business for each legislative day the Senate proceeds to the consideration of the Calendar of Bills. Bills that are not objected to are taken up in their serial order permitting each Senator to speak for five minutes only on any question. Objections my be raised at any stage. When the Bill has been objected and passed over on the call of the Calendar, it is not necessarily lost. The majority party of the Senate determines the time at which the debate takes place and a motion is made to consider the Bill. The motion may lead to filibuster. Closure may be applied if 16 Senators sign a motion to that effect and the motion is carried by two-thirds of the members voting. Amendments may be moved even at this stage, and these, including those proposed by the Committee that reported the Bill, are considered separately.

After final action on the amendments, the Bill is ready for engrossment and the third reading . The Presiding officer then puts the question upon the passage and the vote is taken *viva voce*. A simple majority is necessary to pass the Bill. The original engrossed House Bill, together with the engrossed amendments, if any, is returned to the House with a message stating the action taken by the Senate.

On return to the House, it is placed, with all the relevant papers, on the table of the Speaker to await further action. If the amendments are minor these are accepted by the House, and the Bill is ready for enrolment for presentation to the President. If the amendments are substantial or controversial and the House does not agree thereto, a member may request for a conference. At the conference only matters in disagreement are considered. In many instances the result of the conference is a compromise. If no agreement is reached the matter is reported by the conferees to their respective Chambers.

**Bill Becomes Law**

A Bill cannot become a law until it has been approved in identical terms by both Houses of Congress. When the Bill has finally been approved by both Houses it is sent to the President for his assent. If he approves the Bill he signs it and usually writes ''approved'' and it becomes law. If the President decides to veto it, he returns it with a message stating the objections to the Chamber in which the Bill originated. If the measure is repassed by both the Houses, with two-thirds votes in each, it becomes law without the signatures of the President. If two-thirds vote is not forthcoming the veto stands. If the President keeps a Bill for ten days without signing it while Congress is in session, it becomes law without his signatures. But if Congress adjourns within ten days and the President does not sign the Bill, the Bill is killed. This has been called the "pocket veto."

**Committee System Analyzed**

Law-making in the United States is a labyrinth, complicated and tortuous process wherein Committees play the key role. It is here that the Bills languish and die and the Chairmen of the Committees play a strategic role in the process of selecting the Bills that the Committees will take up, in shaping the size and jurisdictions of the sub-committees, and in selecting members who may sponsor legislation. In countries with parliamentary system the part which the Committees play is secondary. Their purpose is to give the Bill a final shape and it comes to them when the Chamber itself has already approved its general character. The Minister sponsoring the Bill holds its charge throughout : it is his child. It is just the other way in the United States. Woodrow Wilson appropriately characterised American Government as "Government by the Standing Committees of Congress."

The Committees are of two types in the United States: Standing or "Legislative " Committees and Special Committees. The House of Representatives has twen-ty-two Standing Committees and the Senate sixteen. They are permanent Committees, each of which watches over a particular segment of legislative business. The number of Committees though slightly different, the division of responsibility among Committees is very similar in both Houses. Each of the Senator is assigned two of the Committees, though three even four Committee assignments are sometimes made, whereas one Representative, with some exceptions, however, gets only one. Many Committees constitute their Sub-Committees, some of which are permanent and are subject to little control by the parent Committee.

A House Committee, a phrase commonly referred for a Standing Committee of the House of Representatives, consists of nine to fifty-one members, and a Senate Committee usually has eight to twenty-six members. All the Standing Committees in both the Chambers are bipartisan in character and the proportion is fixed by the Party in majority for the time being. There is a tendency to appoint members to Committees in the work of which they are interested. It is a forum of specialised interests, for example, ex-soldiers seek places on the Committee dealing with veterans, members from the farm States go to the Committee on Agriculture and the industrial states of the North and East are represented on the Finance Committee. Special or Select Committees may be created at times to perform specific tasks. Their members are appointed by the Speaker and are created by a simple resolution. The best known Select Committees are investigating committees. When the function has been carried out the Select Committee automatically expires. In recent years, however, such Committees are seldom appointed and investigations are assigned instead to the relevant Standing Committees.

Special Investigating Committees are sometimes set up to gather information on some subjects as an aid to law-making, to check on the administration of laws, or to investigate into alleged undesirable practices or conditions. The House of Representatives frequently votes itself into the Committee of the Whole for the purpose of expediting business and reaching agreements on detailed provisions of Bills. When the House meets as a Committee of the Whole, all its members sit as a committee with an appointed chairman.

Joint Committees consisting of an equal number of Representatives and Senators have been created by law in a few well-demarcated fields, such as, the Joint Committees on Atomic Energy, on the Economic Report, on the Library of Congress, on Internal Revenue Taxation. Conference Committees are a special form of Joint Committee used to iron out differences on Bills as passed by the two Houses. The Speaker appoints House conferees, and the Vice-President those of the Senate. Normally the House appoints three or five conferees, but the Senate tends to appoint more.[22] If the conferees agree on a compromise they report the result to their respective Chambers. Should the House and Senate both agree to accept the recommendations of the Conference Committee, the Bill is deemed to have passed in the form the Conference Committee proposed it. If one or both Chambers refuse to accept the recommendations of the Conference

22. In a recent Congress, Senators outnumbered Representatives on one Conference Committee by fourteen to five and on another by thirteen to five.

Committee, the Bill dies or another Conference Committee meeting may be arranged to resolve the differences in the light of the deliberations and sentiments expressed by the House and the Senate.

The real work of legislation, which averages 5,000 to 7,000 Bills in a session, is done through the Standing Committees. These Committees call out those Bills which they regard important and recommend to Congress for enactment. In fact, most Bills are enacted in the form given them in the Committees. Some Bills are redrafted *de novo* in Committee rooms. The Standing Committees, therefore, play a vital role in the Congressional legislative process. The reduced number of Standing Committees, 61 prior to 1927, 47 from 1927 to 1946 and since then 22, has resulted in the greater use of sub-committees as the work-load of Committee work remained the same after 1946.[23]

In theory Chairmen of the Committees in each House are designated by the Committee on Committees of the majority party. But in practice each assignment goes to that Member of the majority party who has the longest unbroken service on the Committee. This seniority rule in the appointment of Chairman is a subject of deep controversy as it ignores ability and puts premium on continuous service on the Committee itself. The American Political Science Association appointed, in 1945, a Committee on Congress and it recommended the abandonment of the seniority rule. The Committee suggested two alternatives to the prevailing system. First, the Chairmen of Standing Committees should be selected at the beginning of each Congress by a Committee on Committees of the majority party on the basis of merit, or, if seniority remains the dominant consideration, then an automatic limit of six years be placed on the term of all Chairmen, thereby forcing a reasonably regular rotation of office.

The role of the Chairman of a Committee in the legislative process is extremely important. He has the power to arrange the meetings of the committee; to select its professional staff; to appoint the members of the sub-committee; to determine the order in which it considers Bills; to decide if public hearings on a Bill are desirable; to arrange to have a Bill, favourably reported by the committee, brought to the floor of the House; and serve as a manager on the Conference Committee on a particular Bill, should one be necessary. "In theory the manner in which a Chairman exercises these powers is subject to review and even control by the committee as a whole, but it is a rare committee that even undertakes to check or rebuke its Chairman." It also goes to the credit of a Chairman that he does not seek to ride roughshod over a majority of his Committee members.[24]

A significant merit of the Committee system in the United States is that the Committees are well equipped to consider measures referred to them. The members of the Committees are sufficiently experienced, many members having first-hand information on the subject covered by a bill. In addition to the clerical staff, each committee is authorized to appoint not more than four professional staff members on a permanent basis.[25] The Legislative Council and the Legislative Reference Service of the Library of Congress render assistance to the Committees for the successful and efficient performance of their duties. But the vital source of information is the testimony given by Government officials, representatives of organized groups, and private citizens at public hearings.

In addition to making recommendations on legislation, the Standing Committees scrutinize administration of laws by the Executive branch of Government. The Legislative Reorganization Act, 1946, directs each Committee of Congress to "exercise continuous watchfulness of the execution by the administrative agencies concerned of any law, the subject-matter of which is within the jurisdiction of such Committee."[26]

## FINANCIAL FUNCTIONS

The Constitution establishes the financial supremacy of Congress by specifying that "no money shall be drawn from the Treasury but in consequence of appropriation made by law." The Constitution also provides that all Bills for raising revenue shall originate in the House of Representatives. The usage adds to it that the appropriation Bills are also initiated there. The Senate possesses co-equal powers with the

23. The Legislative Reorganization Act, 1946, reduced the number of Senate Standing Committees from 33 to 15. But now there are 16 whereas in the House there are 22.
24. Galloway, G. B., *The Legislative Process in Congress*, p. 280.
25. The Appropriation Committee in each House is authorized to appoint such staff as it determines to be necessary.
26. Section 136 of the Legislative Reorganization Act, 1946.

House of Representatives in accepting or rejecting Financial Bills, but in practice it "functions as a Court of Appeals in financial legislation often mending defects of such measures sent over from the House."

The budgetary powers of Congress are, indeed, great as both Congress and the President shape national policy-making. It is "a system of separated institutions sharing powers."[27] How Congress shares powers with the President is succinctly explained by David E. Bell, President Kennedy's first Director of the Bureau of the Budget. The Budget, he said, is "............a major means for unifying and setting forth an overall executive programme....." It "reflects (the President's) judgment of the relative priority of different federal activities. Thus, the President's budget necessarily reflects his policy judgments and the Congress in acting on the President's budget necessarily reviews these policy judgments as to the relative importance of alternative uses of national resources.

......The essential idea of the budget process is to permit a systematic consideration of our Government's programme requirements in the light of available resources; to identify marginal choices and the judgment factors that bear on them; to balance competing requirements against each other; and finally, to enable the President to decide upon priorities and present them to the Congress in the form of a coherent work programme and financial plan."[28]

## GENERAL APPRAISAL OF CONGRESS

The Founding Fathers, who drafted the Constitution of 1787, had great hopes for Congress. Congress was conceived as the dominant and most powerful of all three branches of government. It was given a place of precedence and it is the first and the longest Article of the Constitution—longer than all other original Articles combined. The Constitution gives to Congress control of the laws of the nation, the finances of the nation, the strength of the armed forces of the country. By implication it possesses unlimited investigatory powers. It has the right to impeach the President, the Vice-President and other officers of the United States, exercises complete supervisory powers over administrative agencies and has the choice to select the President and Vice-President if no candidate receives an electoral majority. In brief, because of its supervisory and appropriation power, Congress has stronger ultimate administrative powers than the Presidency, and because of its impeachment powers, including the impeachment of the judges themselves, it is a higher Court of justice than any other, including the Supreme Court, in the land. The powers of Congress, except for certain exceptions, are clearly constitutional and detailed carefully to cover eighteen different phases of national life and emerging therefrom are the Implied powers and Resultant powers. Members of Congress are the only officials who are exempt from arrest while attending sessions, except for treason, felony or breach of peace and from libel law.

Its working and achievements disclose that Congress stands out as one of the successful Legislatures of the democratic world. It has endured for more than two hundred years and has never failed to serve the country loyally. Nevertheless, Congress has from the beginning not fulfilled the expectations of the framers of the Constitution. It has suffered declining prestige, weakened influence, and a more or less chronic inability to get its work done, as the Presidency has in general grown and as the Supreme Court has on the whole held its own.

### Not a Really National Representative Body

Primary among the reasons of its declining prestige and authority is the fact that Congress is not, in very real sense, a national representative body. It is an assemblage of State delegations. "Its historic development, unlike the Presidency, has been along generally regional lines; its major pre-occupation has been the resolution, usually by compromise, of conflicting regional interests; its ordinary approach to national legislation has been through the avenue of the effect of such legislation, not on the welfare or the opinion of the nation as a whole, but on the interests and the reaction of the area from which the Senators and Representatives come and to which they must return."[29] Congress, is, as Professor Laski pointed out, the legislature of a continent and a member of Congress is expected to think in terms of sectional interests. He must think about the effect of a measure upon the particular area for

27. Neustadt, Richard E., *Presidential Powers,* p. 33.
28. Statement of David E. Bell, Hearings Before the *Sub- committee on National Policy Machinery,* as quoted in Polsby's *Congress and the Presidency,* p. 83.
29. Tourtellot, A. B., *An Anatomy of American Politics,* p. 79.

which he sits rather than its effects on the country as a whole. This regional attitude of Congress has given it a position of backwardness, but to the advantage of Presidency which Americans regard as the pivot of national solidarity.

At the position of Congress and its members is the working of the "locality rule." The Constitution demands that the Senators and Representatives shall be residents of the States they represent and convention insists that Representatives shall, in addition, be residents of the congressional district that they wish to represent. A member of the House of Representatives is constantly aware that every two years he will be judged by his constituents and this awareness makes him far more responsive to his judgment of what will please them. The obvious result is that every Congressman keeps his ear to the ground and sacrifices national for local and sectional interests. Locality rule accounts in part of the comparative local-mindedness of the American Congress.

A memmber of Parliament in Britain cannot afford to disregard the party whip and go against the behest of the party even if the decision of the party may be antagonistic to the wishes of his constituents. In America, neither the Senator nor the Representative can afford to obey the party call against the wishe of the State or a district he represents. He knows that if he is defeated it will mean the end of his Congressional career. The President or the party can do nothing for him, "cannot procure for him a seat outside his own bailiwick, can only solace him with a job—and cannot always do that." The result is that the whims of the local party boss, if his fate depends upon his judgment, or that of an important section of his "home-folks" are more near and dearer to him than the national leaders of his party. Voters, too, feel that if they elect a man he should be the local champion. All these factors combined together do not make Congress really a national representative body and, consequently, its authority and prestige are grievously impaired.

**Separation between Executive and Legislature**

The Presidential system of government envisages a distinct mechanism of government. Parliament, in Britain, is only formally a legislative body. Its real business is to endorse the decisions of the Cabinet and make them effective. Parliament may bring about minor amendments here and there in the measures before it, but fundamentally legislation is shaped in the Whitehall and not in Westminster. With Congress, it is just the reverse. Legislation is the main business of both the Chambers in the United States. The Senate and the House do not act under the instructions of the President. They, no doubt, co-operate with him, particularly during times of national emergencies but Congress is a co-ordinate branch of government with the Executive. To put it still more explicitly, the Executive and the Legislature are co-equal partners in working the governmental machinery. There is, however, no cohesiveness and the party ties which bind the Executive and Legislative departments of government are too flimsy for an integrated policy as obtainable in Britain and other countries with a parliamentary system of government. To put it in the words of Laski, the party ties which bind the two wings of government "never bind them into a unity." The interests of Congress are separable from those of the President.

From the very beginning of the establishment of the Union, Congress has always emphasized its independent existence and its independent will, except only during war, or an emergency like that of March 1933, where there had been unity of purpose and unity of will. This is for two reasons. First, the realisation of the fact that administration does not depend for its existence on Congress if it acts on its own way; and, secondly, every individual Congressman endeavours to assert himself and his rights that Congress cannot be overshadowed by the President. To put alterations and modifications to the measures of the President "is to draw attention to itself that he is not unqualified master of the nation." Sometimes the "very political survival of the Congressman, who is, after all, subject to renomination and re-election on the local level, demands that he break on one or more issues with the President of his own party."[30]

The provisions of the Constitution with respect to foreign policy are "an invitation to struggle" between the President and Congress, in the opinion of Professor Edward S. Corwin. The invitation lies in the intricate system of checks and balances by which the framers of the Constitution sought to ensure that neither the President nor Congress would totally dominate the other. Congress has not always accepted the

30. Polsby, Nelson E., *Congress and the Presidency,* p. 114.

Constitution's invitation to struggle with the President over foreign policy. There had been periods when Congress was content to leave the matter to the President—because of the strong personality of a particular President, because of Congessional indifference, or, most importantly, because Congress generally agreed with what the President was doing. The most recent such period of relative Executive-Congress peace lasted approximately 20 years, from World War II till about the middle of 1960's. This broad consensus between Congress and a succession of Presidents, in American public opinion generally was cracked by President Lyndon Johnson's intervention in the Dominican Republic in 1965 and then shattered by the deepening U.S. involvement in Vietnam beginning the same year. Since that watershed Congress has become increasingly assertive of its constitutional rights and prerogatives. Through a variety of legislative devices, it has sought and secured a much greater measure of detailed control over Executive branch agencies. The technique of consensus which Roosevelt, Truman, Eisenhower, John Kennedy and Lyndon Johnson could hammer out and enlist the aid of key congressional leaders and Committee Chairmen has become a casualty of 1970s. "Neo-Congressional government," observes Alexander Haig, "would not be harmful if we had a parliamentary system. But our Congress is neither temperamentally nor structurally adapted to discharge executive branch responsibilities, nor is its constitution mandated to do so." He, therefore, concludes that the eighteenth century concept of balance is "as essential to our constitution as is its emphasis on checks. The machinery of government becomes harmonious not in paralysis but in balanced action."

**Short-sighted Policy of Congress**

The net result is incoherency and irresponsibility. The Executive has no place in Congress to coordinate its activities and establish a hyphen between the Executive and Legislative departments of government. Legislation is every Congressman's concern, but it is no one's child. To impress upon his constituents his worth as a legislator and in order to cater to the local sentiments and to justify the trust reposed in him by his electors, every Congressman has a mania to rush in all kinds of measures. Congress is, accordingly, charged of wilful parochialism and neglect of national needs. It has, consequently, seldom succeeded in formulating and enacting long range and lasting policies unless they were imposed upon it by a strong President.

Polsby maintains that even the "efficient minority" of Congressmen, who stand eminent in the legislative sphere, determine the consequences of their behaviour from the point of their careers. "The questions he must continually pose to himself are: How will my behaviour today affect my standing in the House tomorrow, the next day, and in years to come? How may I act so to enhance my esteem in the eyes of my colleagues ? How may I lay up the treasures of my obligation and friendship against my day of need? Or, if he is oriented to public policy: How may I enhance the future chances of policies I favour."[31] Such a state of mind has made Congress "the butt of jokes among all the people, the subject of despair among the enlightened and the instrument of hope among the ruthless."[32] It has, therefore, been correctly observed : "If the law is regarded—as properly it should be—as a codification of the moral judgment of the community as a whole, which in this case is the nation, then, Congress has been strangely and unbelievably obtruse in determining that judgment."

The Congress, thus, speaks in a confusion of tongues and the long decline of Congress has contributed greatly to the rise of Presidency. It cannot operate successfully without leadership, which none but the President can offer. When Congress finally gave up its primary responsibility for preparing the national Budget in 1921, it had no choice but to call on the President to come to its rescue. By abdicating this ancient and primary function, it exercised the most short-sighted policy since it gave a tremendous boost to the power of the President, not only to control his administration, but to influence the legislative process too.

**Inefficient Working of Congress**

Even a cursory observer of the working of Congress would regret the amount of legislative time wasted on relatively minor issues, and the haste, especially in the House in which matters of great importance are dealt with. The rules of filibuster and the two-thirds votes required for ratifying treaties in the Senate are a great hindrance in the way of the majority and Congress carrying out its purpose. The Rules of Procedure

31. *Ibid.*, p. 102.
32. Tourtellot, A. B., *The Anatomy of American Politics*, p. 88.

followed in both the Houses encourage minorities to obstruct its business by making frequent points of order and time consuming motions, introducing irrelevant business, and repeatedly demanding quorum calls.

The Congressman is not only a legislator, but he is also expected to serve his constituents as an "errand-boy" in varied fields divorced from legislation. An active Congressman once said, "Nevertheless at least half of my time is taken up with matters that has nothing to do with my legislative duties. Answering letters from my constituents, trotting around to the Departments doing their errands, trying to represent them in one way or another as a broker, a factor, an attorney, an agent, an emissary, and whatever you will takes up about half the time of the average Congressman. And I don't have to do it if I don't want to. All I have to do is to neglect it; then I get licked at the next election.......[33]Such kind of work seriously interferes with Congressman's real usefulness as a national law-maker. The theory of representation as prevailing in the United States demands that the representative gives his attention, first to his constituents and secondly, to national affairs. Local sentiment and pressure are, thus, intensified. Though neither residence in the district nor the elements of short term of office are present in the Senate, " the attitude fostered by the relationship of constituents to their representative,"write Professors Swarthout and Bartley, "is transferred over to the Senator in similar, though diminished, fashion."

The criticism of many members of Congress themselves, together with those of other officers of government and outside commentators, about the adequacy of Congress to meet the challenges of the twentieth century, are compiled on the Hearings of the Joint Committee on the Organization of Congress,, which were held from March to June 1945, and which culminated in an enactment of the Legislative Reorganization Act of 1946. The Director of the Bureau of the Budget, Harold E. Smith, in his testimony urged the Joint Committee to "consider broadly what the role of Congress should be in the government of the United States." He developed his point as follows: "we are familiar with the observation that this is a different sort of world from that which existed when the Constitutional Convention devised the framework of our government. Yet we still lack a penetrating and practical restatement of the role of representative assemblies in the light of the changed problems with which they deal and the altered conditions under which they operate. We are up against the fact that legislative bodies have not changed very much but the kinds of problems with which they must cope have changed radically. Your own talents and the keenest minds you can command could very well be devoted to rethinking the functions of the Congress under present conditions. A sound formulation of the role of the representative body is basic to all the work of your committee. Only on such a basis can one develop standards by which to judge and develop proposals for changes in organization, procedure, staffing, and other matters."[34]

**Influence of Lobby**

A Congressman is further bedevilled by the presence in the national capital of numerous individuals who press him at every turn to support or reject given legislation. There is no open bribery or graft, but the methods employed by the 'lobbyist' are frequently so subtle that the "unsuspecting legislator is under lobby influence before he is quite aware of what has happened." The 'lobbyists'[35] are the representatives of the special groups economically or otherwise interested in the legislation before Congress. They are called 'lobbyists' because they buttonhole individual members of Congress in the lobbies and elsewhere too. The members succumb to the special interest groups. The existence of lobbies is a serious problem to Congress, because they place on the legislator a burden "from which he cannot always disassociate himself. The pleadings—and threats—of special interest groups are constantly in his ears. Even many of the church groups of the nation now mantain paid lobbyists in the nation's capital." Lobbying, no doubt, is good and it frequently performs necessary services, "but it has outgrown its evil associations and more sordid ways" with shocking results on the reputation and integrity of Congress as a national legislative body. The Federal Regulation of Lobbying Act is an important section of

33. Also refer to Ferguson and McHenry, *The American System of Government,* pp. 281-82.
34. Organization of Congress, Hearings before the Joint Committee on the Organization of Congress (1945), pp. 670-71.
35. The term lobby arose from the use of lobbies, or corridors, in legislative halls as places to meet with and persuade legislators to vote a certain way. Thirty years ago there were 2,000 lobbies, and now there are more than 15,000 of them registered at Washington, D. C. spending some two million dollars, to push their real projects.

the Legislative Reorganization Act of 1946, which aimed to remedy some of the glaring defects in the "lobby." The Lobbying Act requires persons, corporations, and organized groups of all kinds seeking to influence the passage or defeat of legislation by Congress "to register, list contributions, and file quarterly statements of expenditures with the Clerk of the House of Representatives." But it is no remedy and does not help to elevate the stature of Congress.

**Rigours of the Committee System**

The Committee System is also subjected to severe criticism and it centres to a considerable degree on the methods used in Committees of Investigation. The seniority rule in choosing Committee Chairmen, sometimes almost dictatorial power of Committees Chairmen, and broad authority of the Committees to "pigeonhole" legislation are matters which are disturbing and they have since long troubled some students of Congress. "Yet curtailing these powers, without generally overhauling the entire congressional machine and drastically altering philosophy of the members would result in an impossible volume of work for Congress." As regards purposes of Congressional investigations, other reasons aside, investigations are often motivated by the desire of a political party to advance its own interests or to embarrass its adversary. In 1920 and 1930, the Democratic Party did its best to discredit the Republican Party through investigations into the scandals of Harding Administration and the evils of bankers and businessmen. The Republican Party took its revenge in 1947-48 and 1953-54 to expose the shortcomings of Roosevelt and Truman administrations. Thus instead of giving fair, impartial information to Congress and to the public for constructive use, an investigating committee usually starts out to prove something and hunts the evidence which will support this proof and this vicious circle continues without any qualms of conscience. The public can hardly expect Congress to function with wisdom under the circumstances.

**Judicial Review**

The process of judicial review also depresses the enthusiasm of the legislators. While the last word rests with the Supreme Court, the legislators while initiating any legislative measure have not only to think that what their constituents want, or will stand, but also whether what Congress does decide will be acceptable to the Supreme Court in case its validity is challenged. No one can predict what the Supreme Court will do, but the apprehension is there. "When all legislation," observes Professor Brogan, "has to run this kind of gauntlet, the results are apt to depress the legislator and his supporters, to blunt the edge of zeal and hope to turn the minds of both parties to more practicable and tangible achievements, favours and jobs."[36]

**Unification of Socio-economic Interests**

In the context of the present state of affairs in the country there has been the growing unification of the nation's economic and social interests. The sectional economic issues are fast disappearing and all sections of the people now stand together for their common interests. The rejection of Jimmy Carter for the second Presidential term and even his own South repudiating him, except his own State of Georgia and there, too, his own huge margin of 1976 whittled down by almost 20 per cent, clearly indicates that national politics have now few sectional aspects and it is not easy to split the country geographically on economic issues. The nation accepted Reagan's economic policy and even the Democratic Congressmen had supported some aspects of that policy. Socially, too "the Midwest farmer, the Farwest rancher and the Eastern plant manager are becoming unified in their tastes and values; their children no longer go solely to their own sectional colleges and universities; their travel and vacations are no longer within sectional limits." But there is no change in the attitude of Senators and the Representatives. "The senior Senator from Tennessee is no more concerned with or closer to the residents of Oregon that he was two or three generations ago. In the halls of Congress sectional values, sectional attitude and sectional roots remain."

The result is that the people with their new national standards do not look favourably towards Congress. They are, indeed, unwilling to place great faith in a legislature which, while still protecting what local interests remain, frequently "by procrastination, indecision or opportunistic compromise endangers the nation's interests." They look to the President as the embodiment of national unity and national solidarity. This really is dangerous to the prestige of Congress and a grave cause of its weakness.

36. Brogan, D. W., *The American Political System,* p. 138.

## STRENGTHENING THE CONGRESS

### Executive-Legislative Coordination

It should, thus, be obvious that the problem of coordinating the Executive and Legislative branches has been aggravated by the fact that usage has intensified a separation that the Constitution only implied. This happened immediately after the inauguration of the Constitution when the first Congress required the Secretary of the Treasury, Alexander Hamilton, to make his reports in writing instead of orally, which he was ready and eager to do. Since then this practice has been rigidly followed with the consequence that the Executive is entirely divorced from the legislature and as Judge Story described a century ago: ''The Executive is compelled to resort to secret and unseen influences, to private interviews and private arrangements to accomplish his own appropriate purpose instead of proposing and sustaining his own duties and measures by a bold and manly appeal to the nation in the face of the representatives.'' The nation cannot stand at ease when the President and Congress wrangle and deadlock over important issues. The President, being the representative of the nation, the generalissimo of administration, and the people's choice, is the leader of the nation. His leadership can only be established and stabilized, if there is proper co-ordination and cooperation between the Executive and the Legislative departments. The co-ordination really means strengthening Congress itself and thereby aiming to remove the instinctive and inherent tendency of Congress to be anti-Presidential. Three-quarters of a century ago, James A. Garfield, after a long service in the House of Representatives, declared : ''It would be far better for both departments if members of the Cabinet were permitted to sit in Congress and participate in the debates or measures relating to their several departments but, of course without a vote. This would tend to secure the ablest men for the chief executive offices; it would bring the policy of the administration into the fullest publicity by giving both parties ample opportunity for criticism and defence.''

There are some students of Congress who have gone so far as to advocate the abolition of the entire concept of presidential government and the substitution in its stead of the cabinet system of government. If America is to remake her constitution, it will most surely be a parliamentary system. But this will not happen. Some discussion on the merits of the British cabinet system took place before the Joint Committee on the Organisation of Congress when that Committee was making plans for the Legislative Organization Act of 1946. Walton H. Hamilton of the Yale Law School, expressed his alarm on the pace at which adoption of the British system was being advocated and observed that the situation in which Americans were placed and their needs had not been correctly analysed. He remarked: ''The clash of executive and the Congress is greatly overdone; it presents no more than a minor problem. The character of the English system is missed; the distinctive conditions of American society, which it would never fit, are overlooked; the activities which make up our pattern of government are not adequately taken into account. The life of any political system is function; imitation, especially where situations are unlike, can never spell functions.[37] The conviction that the British cabinet system would not meet American needs is widely held and it is believed that the presidential system ''with all its operational groanings and creakings has afforded a different, but equally practical and probably better adopted solution to the problem of governmental power in the United States.

Even proposals to introduce Executive initiative in legislation and to make administration responsive and responsible within the existing framework of government have not been well received. Two years after Garfield's recommendation, referred to above, young Woodrow Wilson proposed giving ''the members of the Cabinet seats in Congress with the privilege of the initiative in legislation.'' In 1883, he urged that President Cleveland ''now assume the role of Prime Minister with the Cabinet as the agency of co-ordination to accomplish the popular will.'' And when he became President, he wanted in very truth to be a Prime Minister. He stressed his function as the leader of his party, addressed Congress in person, and promoted and carried out a programme of notable legislation. When he faced possible defeat on the proposed repeal of the exemption of American vessels from payment of Panama Canal tolls he declared: ''In case of failure of this matter I shall go to the country after my resignation is tendered.'' In 1918, he appealed to the country for the returning of a Democratic majority to both the Senate and the House of Representatives. ''I am your servant.''

37. Organization of Congress, Hearings before the Joint Committee on the Organization of Congress (1945), pp. 702-03.

he said in his appeal to the electorate "and accept your judgment without cavil, but my power to administer the great trust assigned to me by the Constitution would be seriously impaired should your judgment be adverse, and must frankly tell you so because so many critical issues depend upon your verdict.," The American electorate appeared to resent the appeal and a Republican Congress was elected although many other factors doubtlessly contributed to that event. "President Wilson learned eventually," remark Professors Binkley and Moos, "that such a system does not conform to American traditions and apparently cannot be institutionalised in the American setting."[38] Don K. Price, an authority in the field of Public Administration, has remarked, "Perhaps only a psycho-analyst could explain America's peculiar nostalgia for the obsolescent institutions of the mother country."[39]

Another proposal of Congressional—Executive relations has been suggested on somewhat different and less radical lines. It is suggested that ex-Presidents be given lifetime seat in the Senate. But such an arrangement is not likely to cement the relations between the occupant of the White House and Congress, though it would provide to the Senate additional knowledge of the problems surrounding it which that body might not otherwise gain.

M. La Follettee Jr. advocated for the creation of a permanent group consisting of important Congressional leaders—Vice-President, Speaker, majority floor leaders of the two Houses, chairmen of major Committees—and key Cabinet members who should regularly meet and plan in outlines the broad basis of national policy. Regular meetings between the Congress leaders and the executive chiefs would enable them to know one another well and, thus build a team spirit. "The penalties for excluding Congress from the national council are high," says Roland Young. "Their exclusion means a continuance of the localism which are so often a predominant characteristic of Congressional behaviour. When Congress feels ignored it often retaliates irrationally, by sulking, by refusing to pass needed legislation, and by passing ill-advised legislation. When Congress is nettled, it is well to treat her like a desperate woman and walk the other way."[40]

There are cumbersome and awkward methods of obtaining information on administration by Congress. For example, Congress may pass resolutions of inquiry directed to heads of Departments. Hearings may be conducted by Congressional Committees and too often these investigations are not held jointly by both Houses. Departmental information may be obtained by personal interviews or by correspondence of Congressmen with administrative officials. Recent Presidents have held weekly press conferences at the White House with leaders of the Senate and the House. The substitution of the question hour, modelled after the British practice, taking the place of the prevailing American practices, has been proposed by Representative Kefauver and Senator Fullbright. According to this plan, it is suggested that during the question hour in both Houses, "Cabinet" members and other key administrators should be present to answer to questions put by members. The reform, it has been maintained, would bring administrators and Congressmen together thereby removing the element of indifference that now exists. But introduction of the question hour has been considered by many thoughtful men in the United States as a sheer waste of time of the already overburdened Congress. Walton Hamilton observed, in his testimony before the Joint Committee on the Organization of Congress that "we have a device here which is vastly superior to that (question hour), and that is the appearance of the administrative officer before the Congressional Committee where the matter is a great deal more searching than it could ever be before the House."[41]

The outcome is not clear, though the need for co-ordination and harmony between the Executive and Legislative departments is keenly felt on all sides, but within the existing system of government. "Congress and the Presidency," observes Polsby, "are like two gears, each whirling at its own rate of speed. It is not surprising that, on coming together, they often clash. Remarkably however, this is not always the case. Devices which harmonize their differences are present within the system, the effects of party loyalty and party leadership within Congress, presidential practices of consultation, the careful restriction of partisan opposition by both Con-

38. Binkley, W. E., and Moos, *President and Congress,* p. 382.
39. Price, Don, K., "The Parliamentary and Presidential Systems," *Public Administration Review,* Vol. II, p. 317.
40. Roland Young, *This is Congress,* p. 257.
41. Organization of Congress, Hearings before the Joint Committee on the Organization of Congress (1945), p. 705.

gressional parties, and the readily evoked overriding patriotism of all participants within the system in periods—which now-a-days, regrettably, come with some frequency—universally defined as crises.''[42]

But this is not sufficient. Congress need be strengthened and the legislative-executive relationship urgently requires to be improved. An often repeated suggestion is that candidates for membership in Congress be permitted to run for election in any constituency which they might choose, or in which they might be chosen, without regard to residence. If candidates are thus freed from the grips of local politics, the persons elected would have a national stature and a national outlook towards problems confronting the country. The Report of the Joint Committee to study the Organization of Congress (1945) called for the creation of majority and minority policy committees in each Chamber of Congress, a joint legislative-executive council, restructured committees of the House and the Senate, an increase in services and aids to Congress, reduction of ''petty duties'' that take time of Congress, and more adequate compensation of members. Many of the recommendations of this Joint Committee were enacted into law with the passage of the Congress Reoganization Act of 1946.

Another identical Joint Committee was again appointed in 1966. The Report of this Committee advocated few major reforms, but it did also recommend safeguards for majority rule and fair procedure in committees, to strengthen fiscal control of Congress,to provide added services by the Library of Congress, to lighten regulation of lobbying and some realignment of committees. A modest reform Bill was introduced in the Senate and it passed therefrom in 1947, but the House of Representatives did not concur.

Neither the 1946 nor 1966 Joint Committee proposed any bold solution or challenged the sacrosanct seniority rule. ''If Congress does establish'', observe Ferguson and McHenry, ''the joint committee on congressional operations recommended in the 1966 report, it will have a device for self-criticism and self-improvement.''[43]

During the last four decades, American Presidents have acquired increasing supremacy not only due to their national leadership but also due to their international leadership making Congress more and more subordinate and subzervient to the wishes of the President, who is now the leader of the only super power left in the world.

## SUGGESTED READINGS


Bailey,Stephen : *Congress Makes A Law*

Bingley, W.E. : *President and Congress.*

Brogan, D.W. :*The American Political System.* Part Five, Chaps. I-IV

Brown, G.R. : *The Leadership of Congress.*

Burns, J.M., and Peltason, J.W.: *Government By the People,* Chaps. XV-XVII

Corwin, E.S.: *The President's Office and Powers,* Chap. VII.

Kefauver, E. and Levin, J.A. : *Twentieth Century Congress.*

Galloway, G.B.: *Congress at the Crossroads.*

Gross, Betram: *The Legislative Struggle.*

Haynes, G.M.: *The Senate of the United States.*

Herring, E. Pendleton : *Presidential Leadership*

Laski, H.J.: *The American Presidency,* Chap. III.

Lawrence, H.C. :*The President, Congress and Legislation.*

Ogg, F.A, and Ray, P.O. : *Essentials of American Government,* Chap, XVI-XVII.

Polsby, Nelson, W. : *Congress and the Presidency.*

Tourtellot, A.B.: *The Anatomy of American Politics,* Chap. III.

William Y. Elliot: *The Need for Constitutional Reform.*

Wilson, W. : *Congressional Government,* Chap. V.

Young, R. : *This is Congress,* Chaps. II, V-VI, VII.

Zink, H.: *A Survey of American Government,* Chaps. XV, XVIII, XIX.

Zinn, Charles J. *: How American Laws are Made.*


---

42. Polsby, N. E., *Congress and the Presidency,* p.115.
43. Ferguson, J. H., and McHenry, D. E., *The American Federal Government,* p. 297.

# CHAPTER VII

# Federal Judiciary

## Need for a Federal Judiciary

The Articles of Confederation made no provision for a national judiciary. Hamilton declared this to be the crowning defect of the old Goverrnment, for laws, he asserted, were dead letter without courts to expound their true meaning and define their operations. During the period of Confederation all judicial controversies were left to the State Courts, and each State having its own legal system presented a variety of conflicting decisions which created conditions of uncertainty and innumerable complexities. The major task of the Founding Fathers was to evolve out a judicial system which should preserve the integrity of the new government to be established and remove the chaotic conditions which were existing then.They also realised that under the system of govenment they were establishing, disputes between the States would become more frequent in the future and an impartial umpire, standing outside them all, would be needed to settle their controversies. Similarly, there would be questions bearing on the relations of the United States with foreign nations on matters covered by treaties which could not, even for reasons of political expediency, be left to the State courts. To do them so, meant placing the peace and well-being of the country at the mercy of thirteen conflicting authorities. Then, disputes were certain to arise as to the meanings of various provisions of the new constitution and with regard to the interpretation of laws passed by Congress. To leave such disputes to the courts of the different States would have meant invitation to chaos, for each State court would give different decisions, one opposed to the other.

Finally, the framers of the Constitution were planning for a "more perfect union" and to "estabilsh justice." If the new constitution and the laws and treaties made under it could achieve the objects set, it was imperative, they concluded, that there should be a distinctive federal court, supreme, and independent of the States.

Guided by these reasons, the Constitution-makers made a provision (Article III) in the Constitution for the federal judiciary, and while doing so they made the judicial power co-ordinate with Executive and Legislative powers. It is a brief reference and the Constitution does not say much about its structure and organisation. Article III merely states that judicial power will be vested in one Supreme Court and such inferior courts as Congress may from time to time ordain and establish. Thus, Congress is given authority for the proper functioning of the Supreme Court, and to create additional courts as and when it deemed necessary and expedient. But in order to maintain the independence and integrity of the judges of all such courts, the Constitution provides for permanence of tenure during good behaviour and a compensation for their services which cannot be diminished during their continuance in office.

In spite of these constitutional provisions, Congress has still the means to control the federal judiciary. True, Congress cannot abolish the Supreme Court, or diminish the salaries of the Justices, or remove any one of them from office, except by due process of impeachment, but it can make significant changes in so many other ways. Congress can by law reduce the number of Justices by prescribing that on death, or resignation of any of them them the vacant post shall be abolished, or accept a plan, as one proposed by President Franklin Roosevelt, to appoint new Justices up to six to the Supreme Court when Justices after reaching the age of seventy fail to resign within six months, and thus to increase the number of Justices and secure the right kind of "appointments." With regard to the inferior courts, control by Congress has been real and more comprehensive. In 1802 during Jefferson's Presidency, it repealed the law of the preceding year creating sixteen posts of Circuit Judges which President Adams had filled, with men strong in federalist conviction at the close of his term of office. Congress can, also by law, prevent certain classes of cases from coming before the Supreme Court by refusing to provide a system of appeals. But on the whole, it can be safely said that except in times of crisis the Federal Judiciary enjoys a high degree of independence from legislative interference.

**Appointment and Tenure of Judges**

The Constitution merely stipulates that the President and Senate are to appoint Justices of the Supreme Court and authorises Congress to vest the appointment of such "inferior officers" as it thinks proper in the President alone, in the court of law, or in the heads of Departments. All Justices of the Supreme Court are, thus, nominated by the President and appointed by and with advice and consent of the Senate. With regard to the inferior courts, it has been settled by uniform practice that judges of all lower federal tribunals are not "inferior officers" and their appointment should not, therefore, vest in any other authority than the President and the Senate.

The Constitution does not state what qualifications are demanded of Justices of the Supreme Court, either as to age, citizenship, and legal competence, or as to political views and background. From the time when President Washington submitted to the Senate his first list of Supreme Court appointments, the attempt has been made almost invariably to select men of high prestige and outstanding ability. Appointments have been made from time to time, it is true, "to pay political debts, to show deference to a particular section of the country, or even to provide representation for a political party, which would not otherwise be represented." But even then the calibre of the men selected has been exceptionally high. It is also true that Democratic Presidents have appointed Republicans to the Bench and Republican Presidents have selected Democrats. The men appointed to the Supreme Court are, usually, well advanced in age at the time of their appointment.[1] Since Justices do not readily give up office even with the approach of senility, the membership of the Court has often included men past the age when they could carry the share of their work.

One reason for the reluctance of aged Justices to resign from the Court is that they hold office during good behaviour and they can be removed only by impeachment. There has been much criticism of life appointments. By the Act of 1937, Justices of the Supreme Court may retire, without resigning, after 10 continuous years of service and upon reaching the age of 70. The membership of the Supreme Court has been fixed at nine.[2] No Justice of the Supreme Court has been removed by impeachment. Samuel Chase is the only Supreme Court Justice to have been impeached, but he was not convicted.[3]

## FEDERAL JURISDICTION

**Jurisdiction of the Federal Judiciary**

The powers of the Federal Government being delegated they are limited. The jurisdiction of the federal judiciary, accordingly, extends over only those classes of cases as enumerated or implied in the Constitution. The State Courts have jurisdiction over all others.

**1. Cases under Constitution : Laws and Treaties**

Article Three section Two of the Constitution provides :"The judicial power of the United State shall extend to all cases, in law and equity arising under this Constitution, the laws of the United States, and treaties made, or which shall be made under their authority." It means that only cases of a justiciable character can come before the Federal Courts. It cannot decide questions executive or legislative in character unless such a question involves the interpretation of the Federal Constitution, or a federal law, or a treaty in which the United States is a party. Anyone who claims that an executive action or legislative Act encroaches upon his rights guaranteed to him by the Constitution, laws or treaties of the United States, he can bring an action against the appropriate authority for the restoration of his rights. The situation is well summed up in this statement of the Supreme Court: "The jurisdiction of the courts of the United States is properly commensurate with every right and duty created, declared, or necessarily inspired by and under the Constitution and laws of the United States. But the right must be a substantial and not merely an incidental one in order to warrant its assertion in the Federal Courts. It must appear on the record.............that the suit is one which does really and substantially involve a dispute or controversy as to a right

1. Joseph Story became a member of the Supreme Court at the age of thirty-two and served from 1811 to 1845. Justices James Iredell, Bushrod, Washington and William Johnson were appointed before they were forty years old.
2. President Reagan appointed Mrs. Sandra Day O' Connor to serve on the United States Supreme Court and, thus broke almost two centuries of male exclusivity in the high ranks of the American Judiciary. Another has been added by George Bush.
3. Chase was impeached in 1804 on charge of partisanship. The charges were not supported by the Senate and he was acquitted. He remained on the Bench until his death.

which depends on the construction of the Constitution or some law or treaty of the United States, before jurisdiction can be maintained."

Congress and the President cannot, therefore, ask the Justices of the Supreme Court to express themselves on the constitutionality of a proposed legislation. The Court is not an advisory body and will not give advisory opinions. It will render its decision only as and when a real dispute is presented to it for decision. Consequently, there must be a party of interest to challenge the constitutionality of law in toto or in part. Nor has Congress powers to assign the Judiciary any duties other than judicial. This was definitely established in the *Hayburn* case. Congress in this instance had instructed Circuit Judges to function as pension Commissioners. The Judges individually refused and the Supreme Court upheld their action.

**2. Cases Affecting Ambassadors and Others**

In the second place federal jurisdiction extends to all cases affecting diplomats accredited to the United States. But according to the well accepted principle of International Law diplomatic agents of foreign States are immune from prosecution in the court of the country to which they are accredited. The provision in the Constitution extending federal jurisdiction to all cases affecting diplomats is intended to check the State Courts from the infringement of International Law. If a diplomatic agent commits an offence, his recall may be requested or he may be even expelled, but so long as he remains a duly accredited diplomat his immunity from legal process is guaranteed.

**3. Admiralty Cases**

Admiralty and maritime cases relate to American vessels on the high seas or in the navigable waters of the United States and they embrace all cases arising from disputes on freight charges, wages of the seamen, damages due to collison and marine insurance. In time of war, it covers cases relating to prize vessels captured at sea. The reason for giving admiralty jurisdiction to Federal Courts was twofold. In the first place, admiralty is a distinct branch of jurisprudence and it differs in substance and procedure from the common law and equity appiied in ordinary courts of law. Secondly, foreign commerce is a federal subject and the framers of the Constitution thought it best to vest admiralty and maritime jurisdiction in the Federal Courts.

**4. Cases Relating to U.S. or States**

The jurisdiction of the Federal Courts extends to all disputes to which United States in one of the parties, or when the dispute is between a State and a citizen of another State. As originally provided in Article Three, Section Two of the Constitution, suits could be brought before Federal Courts against a State by citizens of other States, or by citizens of foreign countries. Soon after the Constitution went into effect a citizen of South Carolina named Chisholm, sued the State of Georgia (1793) for the recovery of a debt. The Supreme Court entertained the suit and ruled that such suits could be maintained.

This decision caused a widespread popular indignation as it had been openly asserted, when the Constitution was before the States for their ratification, that no State could be sued by an individual without its own consent. The Government of Georgia felt that it was derogatory to the dignity of a sovereign State. A demand was, accordingly, made that the Constitution be suitably amended so as to prevent such "suits" in future. As a result of this demand the Eleventh Amendment was adopted in 1795, which expressly forbids Federal courts to take cognisance of any suit brought against a State by a citizen of another State, or by citizens or subjects of any foreign State. Such suits can only be brought in the courts of the State concerned aspermitted by law. If there is no legal authorisation courts cannot entertain such suits. But a State can be sued in Federal Courts when the other party is the United States, or another State of the Union or a foreign State.

**5. Cases between Citizens of Different States**

Finally, the judicial power of the Federal Courts extends to all cases between citizens of different States, between citizens of the same State claiming lands under grants of different States and between a State, or the citizens thereof, and foreign States, citizens or subjects. It means that disputes between foreigners and citizens of the foreign States and between citizens of different States can be brought before the Federal Courts. For purposes of this provisión corporation or Company is a citizen of the State in which it was incorporated.

**Exclusive Concurrent Jurisdiction**

Although the cases mentioned above may come before Federal Courts, the Constitution does not insist that Federal Courts must assume exclusive jurisdiction in all such cases. The Constitution gives the Federal Courts no exclusive jurisdiction whatsoever. Congress is free to distribute jurisdiction over them as it pleases and, indeed, it may completely divest Federal Courts of jurisdiction in some instances. As matters stand, Federal Courts have exclusive jurisdiction over: (1) all cases involving crimes against laws of the United States; (2) all suits for penalties brought under laws of the United States, all suits under admiralty and maritime jurisdiction, or under patent and copyright laws; (3) all bankruptcy proceedings; (4) all civil actions in which the United States or a State is a party, except between a State and its own citizen; and (5) all suits and proceedings brought against ambassadors, others possessing diplomatic immunity, and foreign consuls.

Over practically all other kinds of cases to which the federal judicial power extends, Federal and State Courts have concurrent jurisdiction. That is to say, in all such cases, which of necessity are always civil, and involve amounts of $ 3,000 or more, the plaintiff has the choice to commence it in a Federal court or, in the Courts of a State to which he belongs, or in the Courts of a State where the defendant resides. The defendant is, however, given the privilege of having the case removed to a Federal Court if it has been instituted in a state Court provided the request is made before the latter has reached a decision.

Federal Courts are denied jurisdiction over cases involving parties with diverse citizenship and are for amounts less than $ 3,000. These cases must be tried in State Courts, if at all.

**Federal Court Writs**

In the exercise of national judicial power granted by the Constitution, the Federal Courts have the authority to use the writs of *habeas corpus, mandamus, injunction* and *certiorari.*

## TYPES OF FEDERAL COURTS

There are two general types of courts: Constitutional and Legislative.

**Constitutional Courts**

Constitutional Courts are established under the authority of Article III to exercise the Judicial power of the United States. They consist of the Supreme Court, Federal Courts of Appeal, and District Courts. The Constitution provides only for the Supreme Court and empowers Congress to ordain and establish the ''inferior courts.'' The establishment of inferior courts is, therefore, not mandatory. They have been created and their jurisdiction is defined by the statutes of Congress starting with the Judiciary Act of 1789. The Congress can, thus, at will abolish the ''inferior courts,'' but not the Supreme Court.

**Legislative Courts**

Legislative courts are created by Congress and their authority is outside of Article III. They do not exercise the judicial powers of the United States, but are special courts created to aid the administration of laws enacted by Congress in pursuance of powers delegated to it or implied in such powers. For example, Article I, Section 8 grants to Congress the power to impose and collect ''taxes, duties, imposts and excises.'' In order to decide disputes about the valuation of goods and subject to import duties, Congress established the United States Customs Court, composed of nine Judges. Similarly, Congress is given power to govern territories and has created territorial court systems under that authority. Congress can set rules in regard to patents and has created the United States Court of Customs and Patent Appeals which handles appeals from the decisions of the United States Patent Office, the Customs Court and Tariff Commission. There is also a civilian court of Military Appeals to hear appeals from military courts martial.

All these are courts and they follow a judicial procedure. But they have been created under the Congressional power and not under the Judicial Article of the Constitution. The difference between the Constitutional and Legislative Courts, thus, lies in the source of their respective authority and the nature of the cases over which they have jurisdiction. Article II mentions the types of cases and controversies to which the federal judicial power extends and these must all come before constitutional Courts. Legislative Courts, on the other hand, carry into execution such powers as those of regulating inter-state commerce, spending public finds, laying and collecting import duties and governing territories.

Yet another difference may be marked between the two. All Judges in the Constitutional Courts are appointed by the President with the advice and consent of the Senate and they hold office during good behaviour. They can be removed from office only by impeachment. Judges in Legislative Courts are similarly appointed, but almost always they serve for fixed terms and can be removed by methods other than impeachment.

In spite of these differences, the Legislative Courts are tied into the regular Federal judicial machinery. Appeals may be taken from their decisions to specified courts of the regular system, usually to Federal Court of Appeals.

In the District of Columbia, Congress has set up a complete system of local courts including a Municipal Court. The District has also a U.S. District Court and a U.S. Court of Appeals. These are based partly on Article III and partly on Articles 1 s.s cl. 17, which authorises Congress to exercise exclusive jurisdiction over the seat of Government of the United States.

## CONSTITUTIONAL COURTS

### Supreme Court

At the apex is the Supreme Court and it is the creation of the Constitution and specifically mentioned in Article Three, Section one. It was first organised under the Judiciary Act of 1789 with the Chief Justice and five associate Justices. Its membership has, however, varied and the present strength of a Chief Justice and eight associated Justices was fixed in 1869 where it has remained ever since.[4] The Court held its first two terms in Wall Street in New York City. Its next two terms were held at Philadelphia and thereafter it met at Washington.

Justices of the Supreme Court are appointed by the President with the advice and consent of the Senate. The Constitution does not prescribe any qualifications hence the President may appoint anyone for whom Senatorial confirmation can be obtained. Terms of Federal Judges are for life or during good behaviour and they are removable by impeachment only. After reaching the age of seventy they may retire or resign and receive full salary, provided they have served for ten years or more. Or they may retire at sixty-five with fifteen years of service, at full pay. If they retire, and not resign, they are still Federal Judges and can be given an assignment.[5] Their salaries are fixed by an Act of Congress, and while they can be raised at any time no dimunition can be made during the tenure of office of any judge.

The jurisdiction of the Supreme Court is both original and appellate. The original jurisdiction, however, is extremely limited and an average of only four or five cases come before the court each year for original trial. The Constitution opens the court to such trials when (1) a foreign ambassador, minister or consul, or (2) one of the States is a party. This jurisdiction of the Supreme Court is the grant of the Constitution itself and the Supreme Court has decided, in the famous *Marbury* v. *Madison* that Congress can neither increase nor reduce the jurisdiction of the court in this respect. Legislative action, however, has granted concurrent trial power to the District Courts in some of these cases. Under the present Judicial Code the following original cases must be brought to the Supreme Court: (1) cases against foreign ambassadors and ministers and (2) cases between one of the States and the United States, a foreign State or another one of the States.

In all other cases the Supreme Court has appellate jurisdiction both as to law and facts "with such exceptions and under such regulations as Congress shall make." In accordance with this provision, Congress has defined in detail the appellate jurisdiction of the Supreme Court. At present, cases come to it from State Courts, Federal Courts of Appeal and in a few instances, Federal District Courts. The expectation is that the Supreme Court should not devote its time "upon mere settlement of law suits in the manner of an ordinary law court, but rather upon constitutional interpretation and policy, especially in economic and social fields, appeals lacking in this higher interest are likely to encounter no very warm reception."[6]

There are, thus, two general sources from which cases may reach the Supreme Court on appeal:

(a) Cases from the highest State Courts where a federal question is presented, namely, when the State Court has held that a federal law, treaty, or executive action violates the Constitution of the United States or has held that the law enacted by the State or the State action is valid under the Constitution and when that finding of the State Court is challenged. The power of the Supreme Court to review laws is based upon the constitutional provision that the laws made by Congress and treaties concluded by the Federal Government are supreme law of the land and, consequently, supersede the Constitutions and laws enacted by the State Legislatures. Some of the Court's greatest decisions have been rendered in such cases, where an appeal has been taken to

4. President Roosevelt made an attempt in 1937 to have the membership of the court vary between nine and fifteen depending upon Justices who did not resign at the age of seventy. The plan did not succeed.
5. There has been only one instance of a Supreme Court Justice to have been reappointed after an interim of private life. Justice Charles Evans Hughes was appointed on May 2, 1910, by President Taft. He resigned in 1916 to be Republican candidate for Presidency. On February 13, 1930, he was appointed Chief Justice by President Hoover.
6. Ogg and Ray, *Essentials of American Government,* p. 351.

it when a State Court has denied a claim based upon an alleged federal right.

(b) Cases from the lower Federal Courts, chiefly from the Courts of Appeal. But the cases coming to the Supreme Court on this count are insignificant, only one in thirty cases, since final determination had been vested by law in these courts in many types of cases between private individuals. But when a litigant claims that a constitutional right has been denied to him, it is a case for the Supreme Court.

Two special proceedings may, also, be noted. The Supreme Court may require a Court of Appeal to transmit a case to it, either before or after decision, when, on a petition of a party to the suit, the Court concludes that the case is of such significance as to make decision by the highest court desirable. A Court of Appeal may also take the initiative of certifying to the Supreme Court questions or propositions of law involved in a case that it requires instructions from a superior court to enable it to make a proper decision. The Supreme Court may, on such a reference, merely answer the question or it may require that the whole case be submitted to it for final decision.

Cases in a few instances may go directly from a District Court to the Supreme Court. If a District Court holds a Federal law to be unconstitutional in a case in which the United States is a party or in a case between two private parties in which the United States has been made a ''party by intervention'' direct appeal goes to the Supreme Court. The Judiciary Act of 1937 permits such direct appeals to the Supreme Court. An occasional case also goes up from one of the special courts.

The Supreme Court meets on the second Monday in October for a session which generally extends through to June. Special session may be called by the Chief Justice when the Court is adjourned, but the occasion must be of unusual urgency and importance.[7] Six Justices constitute a quorum no matter whether the Chief Justice is present or not. When a case has been argued, the court holds a conference where the Justices discuss their views and, then, vote. The Chief Justice usually states his opinion first and other Justices follow him in order of their seniority. The meeting culminates with a vote conducted by the Chief Justice who calls upon his associates in reverse order according to the dates of their commission and himself voting last. If the Chief Justice belongs to the majority opinion, he may request one of his associates to prepare the opinion of the Court, or he may prepare it himself, after which it is scrutinised by the Court at a second conference and approved. Any member of the Court who disagrees with the majority may file a dissenting opinion, a right frequently taken advantage of. The concurrence of at least five of the nine Judges is necessary to the validity of a decision[8] and, as a matter of fact, many important decisions have been rendered by a bare majority of the Court, that is 5 to 4.

**Federal Courts of Appeal**

Next below the Supreme Court are Federal Courts of Appeal, known before 1948 as the Circuit Courts of Appeal, 12 in all, one for each of the eleven judicial circuits in which the United States is divided and an additional one for the District of Columbia created in 1948. These Courts were created in 1891 to relieve the overburdened Supreme Court of a great deal of its appellate jurisdiction by making many decrees and judgments of the Circuit Courts final. The Chief Justice is assigned by law to the Federal Court of Appeal of the District of Columbia. The eight associate Justices are distributed by assignment among the other circuits. Six of them are assigned to one district and each of the remaining two are assigned to other districts. The requirement of the original Judiciary Act that Justices of the Supreme Court travel on circuit has been repealed and they now only rarely if ever choose to do so. A Court of Appeal must have at least three Judges, two of whom are necessary for a quorum. The number of Judges in each circuit varies from three to nine. Appeal Judges are appointed by President with the advice and consent of the Senate for terms of good behaviour.

The Federal Courts of Appeal have essentially appellate jurisdiction, that is, they hear and determine only cases appealed from the lower courts, and their decisions are final in most cases except where the law provides for a direct review by the Supreme Court. This relieves the Supreme Court of all but the most important cases and

7. In 1942 the Court was called to a special session on July 29 to consider a petition for writ of *habeas corpus* of seven German ''saboteurs.''

8. There is a difference between opinion and decision. An opinion is the statement of the reasoning by which the Court fortifies a decision in a particular case. The decision is reached by secret vote of the Justices, and the Chief Justice then assigns a Justice the task of writing the opinion.

enables it to dispatch its business more promptly. Federal Courts of Appeal also review and enforce orders of the Legislative Court, and quasi-judicial boards and commissions. The Supreme Court may call up from a Federal Court any case on a writ of *certiorari* involving an important constitutional or legal point.

**District Courts**

The lowest grade of Federal Courts is the District Court, ninety-four in number. In some cases a State constitutes one district in other cases a State is divided into two or three districts. Districts have from one to twenty-four judges; in a few instances one judge serves two or more districts. The judges are appointed by the President with the approval of the Senate for terms of good behaviour.

Excepting the few cases which originate in the Supreme Court, and those of special character that commence in the Legislative Courts, most other cases, civil and criminal, under the laws of the United States, start in District Courts. Their jurisdiction is original and no case comes to them on appeal, although cases begun in State Courts are occasionally transferred to them. Ordinarily, cases are tried with one judge presiding. Since 1937, three judges must sit in most cases involving the constitutionality of federal statutes. Appeals in such cases may be taken directly to the Supreme Court and it was a part of President Roosevelt's proposal to reorganise the Federal Courts. Otherwise, appeals as a rule, go first to the appropriate Court of Appeal.

The jurisdiction of the Federal Judiciary may thus, be summed up:

**SUPREME COURT**

**Original Jurisdiction:**

1. Action by the United States against a State.
2. Action by a State against a state.
3. Cases involving ambassadors and other public ministers.
4. Action by a State agains citizen of another State or aliens (jurisdiction is not exclusive).

**Appellate Jurisdiction:**

1. From lower Federal Courts.
2. From state Courts when a 'federal question' is involved.

**11 COURTS OF APPEAL**

**Appellate Jurisdiction only:**

1. From certain District Courts.
2. From certain Legislative Courts.
3. From certain great commissions, such as, Securities and Exchange Commission.

**89 DISTRICT COURTS:**

**Original Jurisdiction:**

1. Over cases of crimes against the United States.
2. Over civil actions by the United States against an individual.
3. Over cases involving citizens of different States.
4. Over actions by a State against an alien or citizen of another State.
5. Over cases of admiralty and maritime jurisdiction.
6. Over such other cases as Congress may validly prescribe.

## JUDICIAL REVIEW

**Power of Judicial Review**

The Supreme Court is the most powerful judicial agency in the world. Alexis de Tocqueville, writing in 1848, observed: "If I were asked where I placed the American aristocracy, I should reply without hesitation.........that it occupies the judicial bench and bar......scarcely any political question arises in the United States that is not resolved sooner or later into a judicial question." Exactly a century later Professor Harold Laski wrote: "The respect in which the Federal Courts, and above all, the Supreme Court are held is hardly surpassed by the influence they exert on the life of the United States."[9] What accounts for this great influence and prestige of the Supreme Court is its power to interpret the Constitution. Justice Frankfurter put it rather bluntly that "the Supreme Court is the constitution." When Justices interpret the Constitution, they make policy decisions and thereby have the final say over the determination of the social and economic issues that confront the country. They uphold or declare null and void and, consequently, of no effect the acts of Congress or State Legislature or Executive orders which are in conflict with the Constitution. By doing so the Supreme Court becomes the guardian of the constitutional system of the United States.

9. Laski, H. J., *American Democracy,* p.110.

Professor Henry J. Abraham defines the term "Judicial review" to mean "the power of any court to hold unconstitutional and hence unenforceable any law, any official action based upon it, and any illegal action by a public official that it deems.......to be in conflict with the Basic Law, in the United States and its Constitution."[10] Theoretically, any court in the United States can declare a law or an executive action unconstitutional, but the Supreme Court is the final arbiter. Actually, however, the Supreme Court will not review every case in which questions of constitutionality are raised. It has established maxims or criteria and cases coming before the Court must fulfil the set criteria, numbering sixteen.[11] This has been done to eliminate the very large number of appeals which otherwise would have come before the Court.

There is no direct authority in the Constitution which empowers the Supreme Court to declare the constitutionality or otherwise of State or Federal Acts. Some writers, however, hold that the framers of the Constitution did not intend to confer such a power, at least over Federal Acts, upon the courts of the United States and the exercise of authority of holding Federal Acts, or orders unconstitutional is the usurpations of power. President Jefferson had unequivocally declared that the "design of the Fathers" was to establish three independent departments of Government and to give the Judiciary the right to review the acts of Congress and the President was not only the violation of the doctrines of the Separation of Powers and limited government, but it was also in violation of the intentions of the makers of the Constitution.

There are others who consider that judicial review is inherent in the nature of a written Constitution. There are two important provisions of the Constitution, it is maintained, which are indicative of the intentions of its framers. One is Article VI, Section 2, which reads, *inter alia*: "This Constitution, and the laws of the United States which shall be made in pursuance thereof; and all treaties made, or which shall be made, under the authority of the United States, shall be the supreme law of the land; and the Judges in every state shall be bound thereby, anything in the Constitution or laws of any state to the contrary notwithstanding." The second provision is found in Article III, Section 2, which says: 'The judicial power shall extend to all cases, in Law and Equity, arising under this Constitution, the laws of the United States, and treaties made, or which shall be made, under this authority...."Both these provisions are sufficient to fill in the gap which the Constitution failed to expressly provide for. The thread of the intention of the framers of the Constitution can be connected with what Hamilton wrote in the *Federalist* "The interpretation of the laws is the proper and peculiar province of the courts. A Constitution is, in fact, and must be, regarded by the judges as a fundamental law. It must, therefore, belong to them to ascertain its meaning, as well as the meaning of any particular act proceeding from the legislative body. If there should happen to be irreconcilable variance between the two, that which has the superior obligation and validity ought, of course, to be preferred; in other words, the Constitution ought to be preferred to the statute, the intention of the people to the intention of their agents."[12] Professor Beard remarks that there is good reason for thinking that a majority of the prominent members of the Philadelphia Convention "took a similar view of the federal judicial powers."[13] In fact, judicial review was already in existence in the American States after their break with Britain in 1766. If it was not expressly provided in the Constitution, it was because the framers believed the power to be clearly enough implied in the language used in Articles III and VI.

---

10. Abraham, Henry, J., *The Judicial Process,* p. 251.
11. Some of these maxims are :

"(1) Before the Court will glance at particular issue or dispute, a definite 'case' or 'controversy' at law or in equity between bona fide adversaries under the Constitution must exist, involving the protection or enforcement of valuable legal rights, or the punishment, prevention, or redress of wrongs directly concerning the party or parties bringing the justiciable suit.

(2) The party or parties bringing suit must have standing.

(4) Not only must the complainant in federal court expressly declare that he is invoking the Constitution of the United States, but a specific live rather than dead constitutional issue citing the particular provision on which he relies in that document must be raised by him; the Court will not entertain generalities.

(6) The federal question at issue must be substantial rather than trivial; it must be the pivotal point of the case; and it must be part of the plaintiff's case rather than a part of his adversary's defence."

12. No. LXXVIII.
13. Beard, C. A., *American Government and Politics,* p. 233.

Chief Justice Marshall made the issue clear. Whatever may have been the intention of the framers of the Constitution, the issue was finally decided by Chief Justice Marshall in 1803 in the famous case of *Marbury* v. *Madison* and since then judicial review has become a part of the constitutional law, in fact, its very cornerstone. The facts of the case, briefly stated, were that Congress had provided in the Judiciary Act of 1789, that requests for *writs of mandamus'*[14] could be made to and granted by the Supreme Court. On the night of March 3, 1801, Marbury was appointed Justice of Peace for the District of Columbia by President Adams, whose term of office expired before the commission of his appointment could be delivered to Marbury. The new President Jefferson and his Secretary of State, Madison, refused to deliver the commission to Marbury who petitioned to the Supreme Court for a *writ of mandamus* ordering Madison to deliver the commission. Marshall, in writing the opinion of the Court, held that Marbury was entitled to his commission and that *mandamus* was a proper remedy in the situation, but the Supreme Court had no authority to issue the writ. The issuance of such a writ, declared Marshall, was in violation of the constitutional provision of Article III as it clearly does not include such writs. The Judiciary Act of 1789, which empowered the Supreme Court to issue writs enlarged the original jurisdiction of the Supreme Court and Congress was devoid of authority to enlarge its original jurisdiction. Marshall argued that Justices were bound by oath to support the Constitution, and when they found that one of its provisions was in conflict with the law they must hold the latter repugnant and void.

The argument of Chief Justice Marshall, in brief, was that the Constitution is the supreme law of the land and the Justices are bound to give effect to it. When the Court is called upon to give effect to a statute passed by Congress which is clearly in conflict with supreme law of the Constitution, it must give preference to the latter, otherwise the declaration of the supremacy of the Constitution would have no meaning. The implications in Chief Justice Marshall's decision may be summarised as under :—

(1) that the Constitution is a written document that clearly defines and limits the powers of government;

(2) that the Constitution is a fundamental law and is superior to the ordinary law passed by Congress;

(3) that the Act of Congress which is contrary to and in violation of the fundamental law is void and cannot bind the courts; and

(4) that the judicial power conferred by the Constitution together with the oath to uphold Constitution,[15] which the Justices take on the assumption of office, require that the courts should declare, when they believe, that the Acts of Congress are in violation of the Constitution.

Since Marshall's decision in 1803, the power of the Supreme Court to declare Acts of Congress invalid has been resented, evaded, and attacked but never overthrown. The principle of judicial review is now firmly embedded in the American System of government and *Marbury* case forms the basis of the important authority exercised by the Supreme Court. During the first eighty years only in the key case of *Marbury* v. *Madison* and subsequently in the *Dred Scot* v. *Sonford*[16] a federal law was disallowed. Since then more than eighty Acts of Congress, in whole or part, have been invalidated. In the four years between 1933 and 1937, thirteen federal and fifty-three state Acts were declared null and void. Since 1937, no economic measure enacted by Congress has been held unconstitutional and the Supreme Court "has displayed a tolerant attitude toward economic regulations enacted by the States. In this area the judicial neutralism advocated by Justice Holmes has become dominant."[17] Statistically the incidence of judicial review on Congressional legislation has been extremely slight. State laws have been more frequently the subject of Supreme Court disallowance.

Since Marshall's time, the Supreme Court has emphasised repeatedly that it is not concerned with the policy, wisdom or expediency of legislation but only with its constitutionality. In its own words, it "neither approves nor con-

14. Judicial orders commanding government officials to perform duties required by law.
15. Without prescribing any specific form, the Constitution requires (Art. VI), all judicial as well as executive officers to take oath to support the Constitution. The wordings of this oath were fixed by the Act of 1868.
16. In this case the Supreme Court held that negroes were not citizens of the United States. Chief Justice Taney ruled, such persons were considered as "subordinate and inferior class of beings." The Fourteenth Amendment reversed this decision.
17. Saye, Albert B., and others, *Principles of American Government,* p. 403.

demns any legislative policy. Its delicate and difficult office is to ascertain and declare whether the legislation is in accordance with, or in contravention of, the provisions of the Constitution; and having done that, its duty ends.'' In another case the Court ruled, ''Even should we consider the act unwise and unprejudicial to both public and private interests, if it be fairly within delegated power, our obligation is to sustain it.''

Although the final judgment in cases of this kind is made by the Supreme Court of the United States, judicial review is a prerogative of all courts from the highest to the lowest. Even a Justice of the Peace may exercise this authority in proper cases, although his decision would certainly be appealed. When a court declares a legislative Act unconstitutional, it means that it cannot be enforced as its inconsistency with the Constitution deprives it of the character of law. But the courts have no power at their disposal to carry out their decrees. It is for the Executive to enforce them and it may be possible for an executive officer to ignore them and this has actually happened in a few cases as, for example, in a famous case in connection with which President Andrew Jackson wrathfully remarked that ''John Marshall has made his decision, now let him enforce it.'' Generally, however, ''the prestige of the doctrine is so great that a pronouncement of the Court is accepted as final even when the act declared unconstitutional is a popular one.'' As Bryce expressed it, the Supreme Court is ''the living voice of the Constitution,'' and, as such, the country obeys, both by inclination and habit.

**Process of Judicial Review Examined**

Those who have critically studied the power of judicial review contend that as a result of it the Supreme Court has expanded its authority to such an extent that it has become a non-elective super-legislature. The judges while giving their decisions, and in whatever legal dress such decisions are clothed, are political decisions. The judges do not confine themselves to such legal questions as the limits of Federal or State jurisdiction, or the carrying out of legal regulations which are essential to make due process of law, but they discuss the advisability of legislation, its essential justice, and its conformity to the law of reason. The law of reason and essential justice, are what the temperments, characteristic attitudes, and views of the Justices are. The Justices have their own political, economic and social predilections and to which they very often owe their appointments. The appointments of the Judges are customarily, but not exclusively, partisan. And in interpreting and applying phrases, like ''regulate,'' ''commerce,'' and ''due process of law,'' they hardly can fail to be swayed consciously or unconsciously by their social philosophies and general outlook on affairs. Between the Civil War and the New Deal, Republicans were in White House for all but sixteen years. Regardless of party affiliations, most of the Presidents and Senators believed in the policy of complete *laissez faire* and looked with suspicion any proposal which restricted the right to economic freedom regarding it ''dangerous, socialistic, populistic and anarchic.'' And these were the men who appointed most of the Justices of the Supreme Court. With the appointment of Melville Fuller as Chief Justice in 1888, a new period began in the history of the Supreme Court. Between 1888 and 1937, it became ''an aristocracy of the robe and twisted the due process clause into a moat around all forms of private property.'' It censured and invalidated all kinds of legislation which, in the opinion of the Justices, unreasonably interfered with the use of private property. The Court gave a narrow meaning to the inter-State commerce and, thus, in many ways clipped the powers of Congress. It did not even hesitate to veto all attempts by Congress to forbid child labour.

In 1895 the Supreme Court reversed an old and well-accepted and hitherto practised precedent and made it impossible for the Federal Government to levy income-tax. It was a decision of five to four Justices and Justice Field made manifest the feelings of the majority opinion about such experiments. He regarded income-tax as a sheer assault on capital and contended that ''it will be but the stepping stone to others, large and more sweeping, till our political contests will become a war of the poor against the rich, a war constantly growing in intensity and bitterness.''[18] When the Supreme Court retarded the manifestation of public opinion by imposing upon the nation its own construction what the social and economic order ought to be, it really assumed the power of super- legislature but not in its representative capacity. The popular opinion took a political revenge by adopting the Sixteenth Amendment in order to reverse this decision. In

18. *Pollock* v. *Farmers Loan and Trust Co.*

the "notorious" *Atkins* case Justice Sutherland, speaking for the majority, "defined the role of the court," as Brogan says, "in a way that a radical critic could hardly have bettered."[19] And referring to this case Boudin remarked : "the announcement that the court has constituted itself in a super-legislature is perhaps plainer than in any other case."[20] Justice Sutherland had unequivocally asserted that "there are limits to power and when these have been passed, it becomes the plain duty of the Courts in the proper exercise of their authority to so declare." Such decisions are, indeed, political in nature, and are not impressive, impartial and worthy of any special respect as the decision of a court should generally command.

It may also be noted that all such decisions had come forth with five to four majority and if Justice Sutherland is to be relied upon that it was the plain duty of the courts, in proper exercise of their authority, to declare invalid any exercise of authority which passed beyond the limit, it follows that the four dissenting Justices had always been oblivious of their plain duty. In the Atkins case particularly the minority included the very conservative Chief Justice Taft.

The Supreme Court's assumption of power as a super-legislature has always been contested by a minority of the Justices. Justice Oliver Wendell Holmes (1902-32), who spent well over thirty years on the Court, consistently and ceaselessly protested "against his colleagues' habit of writing their own economic predilections into the Constitution." Holmes was a conservative with a little faith in social reform in legislation, but he never allowed his personal views to become the measure of the constitutionality of legislation and he was, accordingly, in dissent. Louis D. Brandies too, appointed in 1914, by President Wilson, joined with Holmes in protesting against "the major direction of the Supreme Court's opinions and exposing the reasons behind the Court's majority." With the coming in of Harlan Fiskstone, in 1923, "Holmes, Brandies, and Stone dissenting" became a familiar phrase in the law review.

There is yet another aspect of the problem. While interpreting and applying the spirit and language of the Constitution the Justicess also decide questions of public policy. When an Act of Congress comes before the Supreme Court, the Justice are either accepting or rejecting a policy embodied therein. The policy once rejected by them has no chance of enforcement until a differently constituted court at some later time takes a different attitude. The Supreme Court is the least responsive to public opinion. If the Constitution is supreme because it is an expression of the people's ideas then those agents who most directly represent those ideas have the best right to interpret the Constitution. It is, therefore, pertinently asked why should five men, who constitute a majority of the Court, holding office for life and brought to their posts for their strong political, social and economic predilections, have power to tell Congress and the President, elected by the people, what they may not do ? The undue partiality and excessive dependence on legal formula shown by the Supreme Court has seriously retarded progress in the United States.

The claim of Chief Justice Hughes that "we are under a Constitution but the Constitution is what the judges say it is" or to express the same what Justice Frankfurter tersely said, "The Supreme Court is the Constitution" is difficult to accept so long as some, at least, of the Justices are keen politicians by training and are keen enough "to yearn for the Presidency even after they have becomes Justices of the Supreme Court."[21] It is not, indeed, an exaggeration to say that, at any given time, one or two of the Justices are potential candidates for Presidency. It would not also be out of place and unimportant to mention here that Chief Justice Taft did not "think it compatible with his high office to act as a personal adviser to Mr. Coolidge throughout his Presidential terms."[22] Chief Justice Hughes and some of his associates, it is alleged, played a considerable part in the defeat of President Roosevelt's Court plan in Congress. When Judges are politicians and become active politicians, the prestige of judiciary does not carry with it the esteem which it should carry as an impartial custodian of the Constitution.

Judicial review assumed a new aspect after

---

19. Brogan, *The American Political System,* p. 22.
20. As *cited.* in above.
21. Laski, H. J., *The American Presidency,* p. 68. Justice Charles Evans Hughes was appointed on May 2, 1910 by President Taft. He resigned in 1916 to be a Republican candidate for Presidency. On February 13, 1930, he was appointed Chief Justice by President Hoover.
22. *Ibid.*

the appointment of Earl Warren as Chief Justice in 1954. It is known as "judicial activism." Prior to Warren's appointment judicial review had only been used to invalidate legislation on the ground that it was in conflict with the Constitution; a negative concept indeed. During the tenure of Chief Justice Earl Warren's office, judicial review had been used positively to create legislation. The Court accepted a modern liberal style of judicial review—the discussion of economics, the references to political history, the use of the sociological treaties, "the absence of appeals to precedents as wholly controlling." The rules of the Constitution were applied in a "reflective and broad-gauged manner consistent with the intention of the Framers and the needs of public policy."[23] It was claimed that the judicial process during the two decades following Warren's appointment "was being brought to bear in favour of a progressive, democratic, libertarian society."[24] Apart from its "leadership in the black revolution, the most significant piece of egalitarian reformist activitism in which the Warren Court engaged was its imposition of the 'one man one vote' principle upon representation" in State Legislatures and Congress. The Court threw precedents and the "political questions" doctrine overboard and held by a six to two majority in *Baker* v. *Car* ( 1962) that State legislative apportionment properly was subjected to judicial scrutiny under the equal protection clause.

There was an avalanche of criticism directed at the Court. The gist of the criticism was that the Court had unwisely fashioned itself "into a kind of permanent libertarian constitutional convention, which sat from day to day intent on solving all of the political and social ills of the country through a continuous process of judicial intervention." The Justices, it was argued, disregarded precedents and long-standing rules of law and on occasion even resorted to spurious "law office history" in order to endow their decisions with a superficial constitutional plausibility. All this seriously violated the democratic process in that it "imposed" reform without regard to majority will or the normal legislative organs for effecting social change.

Dissatisfaction with such experiments in "venturesome constitutionalism,"[25] as one of the critics described the Supreme Court decisions, was widespread in the entire country and by the end of 1969, the legislatures of thirty-three States petitioned Congress to call a constitutional convention.[26] Earlier in 1958 the conference of the Chief Justices (of the Supreme Courts of the 50 States) had adopted a resolution calling on the United States Supreme Court to "depart from politics and return to the law."[27]

Warren Burger who succeeded Earl Warren, had never been accused of being a flaming liberal. But the appointment of William H. Rehnquist, in succession to Chief Justice Burger, evoked widespread criticism. He was criticised, at a gruelling Senate hearing to confirm his nomination by President Ronald Reagan, for his extreme views on race, the poor, rights for women and freedom of speech. Senator Edward Kennedy described Rehnquist as "too extreme to be Chief Justice." When Richard Nixon nominated him on the Supreme Court in 1971, the minority report, filed by members of the Senate Judicial Committee, declared that Rehnquist had "failed to show a demonstrated commitment to fundamental human rights", that "he was outside the mainstream of American thought" and, therefore, should not be confirmed.

Political historians generally agree that the most permanent legacy that a United States President leaves to the nation is the appointments he makes to the Supreme Court. This is because the nine Supreme Court Justices enjoy life-time tenure and their interpretation of the Constitution is the final word in the United States. There is no final appeal. Reagan's appointment of Chief Justice William Rehnquist was the President's phenomenal success in changing the ideological face of America's judiciary. The ideological tilt was expected to be advanced by Justice Rehnquist's accession. He was fully conservative as President Reagan's most conservative instincts. The President's ultimate aim was to pull the nine-member Supreme Court away from its

23. Emette S. Redford, and others, *Politics and Government of the United States*, p. 519.
24. Kelly, Alfred H., and Harbison, Winfred A., *The American Constitution: Its Origins and Development*, p. 1017.
25. Dissenting in the Reapportionment cases of 1964, Justice Stewart observed : "I am convinced that these decisions mark a long step into that unhappy era when a majority of the members of this Court thought by many to have convinced themselves and each other that the demands of the Constitution were to be measured not by what it says, but by their own notions of wise political theory...What the Court has done is to convert a particular philosophy into a constitutional rule, binding upon each of the 50 States......*Lucas* v. *Colorado* (1964).
26. *Congressiosnal Quarterly*, August 1, 1969, p. 1572.
27. *Report of the Committee on Federal-State Relationships.* The Conference of the Chief Justices, August 1958, p. 14.

slight liberal inclination. Only a conservative could expect to reach the Supreme Court Bench. It was a calculated move of President Reagan that by the end of his term of office in 1988, at least half of the Justices should be his nominees.[28]

**Suggestions for Reform**

The system of judicial review has, from time to time, been violently assailed and many remedies have been suggested. One reform suggested is not to permit invalidation of statutes by mere majorities of the Court or even by the votes.[29] The spectacle of important Congressional legislation being overthrown by votes of five to four does not add to the prestige of the Supreme Court. In fact, it adds to the scepticism of "judicial infallibility." It has, therefore, been proposed that an exercise of the power of judicial review should require the concurrence of seven of the nine Justices of the Supreme Court. Such a kind of reform, it is contended, can be accomplished by an Act of Congress. But it is doubtful if the Supreme Court would declare this kind of Act valid. Two other proposals have been suggested. One is to abolish the power of judicial review by constitutional amendment. But this is an impossible task. There has actually been little or no demand for abolishing judicial review; its continuance being assumed even by various schemes for altering the personnel and jurisdiction of the Courts. The second is that Congress may repass a law set aside by the Court as it may override a Presidential veto. But this, too, would require a constitutional amendment.

The remedies which require a constitutional amendment are not deemed sufficiently efficacious, because of the difficulties of uncertain results and circuitous methods involved therein. It took nearly twenty years for the Sixteenth Amendment to come into effect and, thus to undo the work of the Supreme Court. One of the most drastic proposals suggests that the Constitution be amended to establish a "Court of the Union" composed of the Chief Justices of the Supreme Courts of 50 States, with power to review and reverse decisions of the United States Supreme Court when States' rights are involved. But critics of this proposal rightly ask: would this not lower the prestige of the Supreme Court and impair its effectiveness? Is it practicable to have a court composed of fifty members? Would the Chief Justices of the Supreme Courts of the States most of whom are popularly elected, be of high quality and capable of taking a detached view?

During more recent times there have been serious proposals afoot to curb the powers of the Supreme Court. When the Court struck down State anti-subversion laws in the 1950s or, in the *Miranda* case of 1966, defining the rights of prisoners undergoing interrogation, dozens of Bills came before Congress to restrain it. Most of them were intended to keep the so-called "moral" or "social" issues—principally abortion, school prayer, and school desegregation—outside the scope of unifying federal decision, such as, the Supreme Court would provide. The conservatives, who dominated the Senate argued that the role of the federal judiciary had been unjustifiably enlarged and that the Supreme Court was not the sole interpreter of the Constitution. The legislative authority towards curbing the Supreme Court was chosen because it is relatively quick and easy. None was passed. But will the Supreme Court Stand it if Congress passed any of such measures? It still has the power to review legislation passed by Congress. The Court may not, therefore, be so much vunerable to attack by a legislative measure as conservatives propose and suppose.

None of the proposals, referred to above, has evoked popular enthusiasm, and most Americans continue to hold the system of judicial review a desirable feature of the governmental system as obtainable in the United States. "Generally speaking," as Burns and Peltason put it, "Americans have never been willing to put full trust in the majority. An independent judiciary with the power to judicial review has been the major institutional sign of this fear of unchecked legislative and popular majorities."[30] But how far independent are judges? Enough has been said about it, but one more illustration will be relevant in this connection. Chief Justice Taft feared to

28. President Reagan appointed one another Supreme Court Justice, Mrs. Sanda Day O' Cornor who was also a conservative. The Court's two leading liberals, Justices William Brennan and Thurgood Marshall (the Court's only black) were 80 and 77. Two moderates, Justices Lewis Powell and Harry Blackmun, were 78 and 77. Therefore, the chances of additional vacancies through death or voluntary retirement caused by illness or age during the remaining period of Reagan's presidency were weighted in his being able to leave behind a Supreme Court with at least a solid five-conservative majority.
29. In the event of tie, the decision of the inferior Court is affirmed.
30. Burns and Peltason, *Government By the People, op. cit.*, p. 582.

resign lest the "radical" Hoover be allowed to appoint someone in his place. In 1929 he wrote, "I am older and slower and less acute and more confused. However, as long as things continue as they are, and I am able to answer in my place, I must stay on the Court in order to prevent the Bulsheviki from getting control."[31]

But a serious problem that faces the Supreme Court is the number of cases before the Court which have increased manifold during recent years. Chief Justice Warren E. Burger, in 1983 gave the quantum of the case-load that already was. In 1953, Chief Justice Earl Warren's first year, there were 1,463 filings and in 1981, there were 5,311 cases on the docket and if the increase continued at the current rate, the Chief Justice said, that during his tenure on the Court there would be 7,000 to 9,000 cases a year on the docket. "No nine people in the world can handle that many cases and handle them properly." To maintain the quality of justice, he suggested, fundamental changes in the United States Judicial System, such as creating a Second Court of last resort. In his annual report to the American Bar Association, the Chief Justice called on Congress to create a commission to look into the whole problem. So far Congress has done nothing in this respect, though the Chief Justice had viewed the problem of massive and mounting case-load as "very serious."[32]

**Roosevelt Proposals**

President Franklin Roosevelt's battle with the Supreme Court is a more recent and "more dramatic attempt by a political leader to influence the course of judicial decisions." President Hoover left office in March 1933, in the midst of the great economic depression. On the same date, President Roosevelt entered upon his duties promising a "New Deal" and steer the country out of the economic chaos. Under his leadership Congress passed in quick succession laws of far reaching importance in record breaking time. Haste was justified by the emergency.

By 1935, these measures began to come before the Supreme Court. The Supreme Court declared five of the New Deal Statutes unconstitutional during the Court term beginning in October 1935. In all it invalidated, within three years of its battle with the President, twelve New Deal statutes or its provisions thereof. It is instructive to note something about the composition of the Supreme Court at that stage. Between 1933 to 1937, the Supreme Court consisted of nine judges, all of whom had been appointed before 1933, and except two, McReynolds and Brandies, the rest were appointed by Republican Presidents. Their average age was seventy-two (in 1937), the highest in the Supreme Court history, and it so happened that four (McReynolds Sutherland, Butler and Van Devanter) of the six, who were over seventy, were "conservatives" while the fifth (Hughes) was a "middle of the roader" and only the sixth (Brandies) a "liberal". On most of the measures which came before the Supreme Court the Justices were divided into two definite blocs: "conservative" and "liberal."

Early in 1937, when the conflict between the President and the Supreme Court was moving towards its climax, Roosevelt presented to Congress his own programme to reorganise the federal judiciary. The President and the Democratic Party had given no indication of such a reorganisation during the Presidential election campaign. His message to Congress on February 4, 1937, embodying his reorganisation proposals had, therefore, a dramatic effect. The most significant proposal was to give the President the power to appoint an additional Justice for each member of the Court who had served for ten years and who remained on the Bench after reaching the age of seventy, provided the maximum number should never exceed fifteen. The object of the proposal was to "rejuvenate" the Supreme Court and to make it more efficient so that it could keep up with its work.

The proposal was defeated in its entirety. The only redeeming feature which emerged out of it was that Congress permitted Supreme Court Justices with ten years of service to retire at seventy with full pay. Although it was a political defeat for Roosevelt, yet, as it has been observed the President "lost his battle but won his war." In 1938, Justice Roberts wrote another majority opinion, this time holding that the Agricultural Adjustment Act of 1938, which also aimed to regulate agriculture, was constitutional. It is true that by the fall of 1937, the "liberals" were clearly in majority in the Supreme Court and by September 1942, only Justices Roberts and Stone remained out of the old lot. But even before any changes could be made in the personnel of the

31. *Ibid.*, pp. 583-84.
32. *News and World Report,* February 14, 1983, published at Washington, D. C.

Supreme Court, the Court manifested a change of mind by reversing its previous attitude towards State Minimum Wage Law for women, by redefining the Commerce clause as to include 'manufacturing,' by upholding the Social Security Act and the Labour Railway Act.

The Switching on of Chief Justice Hughes and Justice Roberts, who had up to that time voted with 'conservative' Justices, indicated the truthfulness of the newly coined political terminology: "A switch in time saved the Nine." Within four years most of that which President Roosevelt had sought to achieve by his proposal to liberalise the court had been achieved without changing its structure. Since 1936, only two minor sections of two Federal Laws had been declared unconstitutional. The Court now interprets the Constitutions in the light of the social and economic condition prevailing in the country. It treats the Constitution as a body of living principles and consequently has validated a large expansion in the authority of the Centre under the commerce clause and in a new interpretation of the welfare clause. The result is the emerging legislation in the context of a Welfare State.

Another significant feature of the Supreme Court's 'modernization' is a substantial change in its regard to precedents. Justices of the old school had adhered to precedents to the point of religious devotion which robbed the Constitution of its adaptability to changing conditions. The new Court attitude freed constitutional interpretation from the restrictions of *stare decisis*. In 1941 and 1957 the Court reversed its previous decisions in child labour and women's minimum wages respectively. The new Court attitude was best expressed by Justice Reed. He declared in *Eire Railroad Company* v. *Tompkins* (1938), "In this court *stare decisis,* in statutory construction, is a useful rule, not an inexorable command."

But all this was feared to be reversed by the Rehnquist Court. Central to Rehnquist's view was his obligation to the political activism encompassed by the phrase "The living Constitution." Fidelity to the "original intent" of the framers is the cornerstone of Rehnquist's constitutional interpretation. The constitutional language, for him, is not infinitely elastic, to be shaped to perceived needs of succeeding generations. His belief in the centrality of original intent as a search for "what the words they (the framers) used meant to them" runs consistently in his public pronouncements, particularly in his judicial decisions already on record.

## SUGGESTED READINGS


Backer, T. H.(Ed.): *The Impact of Supreme Court Decisions.*

Beard, C. A.: *The Supreme Court and the Constitution.*

Beth, Loren P. : *Politics, the Constitution, and the Supreme Court.*

Brogan, D. W. : *The American Political System,* Part one, Chap. II.

Carr, R.K. : *The Supreme Court and the Judicial Review.*

Corwin, E. S. : *Twilight of the Supreme Court.*

Corwin, E.S. : *Court Over Constitution : A Study of the Judicial Review as an Instrument of Popular Government.*

Cushman, R.E. : *Ten Years of Supreme Court* (1937-47), "American Political Science Review,"Vol. XLII (Feb. 1948), pp. 42-67.

Curtis, Charles, P. : *Lions under the Throne.*

Ferguson. J.H., and McHenry, D.F. : *The American System of Government,* pp. 63-67, Chap. XV

Frend, P.A. : *On Understanding the Supreme Court.*

Haines, C.G. : *The Role of the Supreme Court in American Government and Politics.*

Harris, R.J. : *The Judicial Power of the United States.*

Beard, C. A. : *American Government and Politics,* pp. 46,58 Chap. VIII.

Hynemann,C.S. : *The Supreme Court on Trial.*

Laski, H. J. : *The American Democracy,* pp. 73-78, 110-16, 671-73.

Lytle, C.M. : *The Warren Court and Its Critics.*

Mason, A.T. : *The Supreme Court from Taft to Warren.*

Mendelson, Wallace: *Capitalism, Democracy and the Supreme Court.*

Miller A.S. : *The Supreme Court and American Capitalism.*

Ogg, F.A. and Ray, P.O. : *Essentials of American Government*, pp. 42-46, Chap. XXII.

Pound, Roscoe: *Organization of the Court.*

Roberts, O.J. : *The Court and the Constitution.*

Rodell, F. : *Nine Men; A Political History of the Supreme Court from 1790 to 1955.*

Schlesinger, T. M. : *The Supreme Court.*

Shapiro, M. : *Law and Politics in the Supreme Court.*

Swisher, C.B. : *The Growth of Constitutional Power in the United States,* Chap. IX.

Warren,Charles : *Congress, the Constitution and the Supreme Court.*

# CHAPTER VIII

# Political Parties

## Origin of the Party System

Political parties are indispensable for the working of a democratic government. Without them, says MacIver, "there can be no unified statement of principle, no orderly evolution of policy, no regular resort to the constitutional device of parliamentary elections nor of course any of the recognized institutions by means of which a party seeks to gain or to maintain power." If there are no parties, politics would be a sheer babel of tongues and the power of the people, termed as popular sovereignty, would dissipate itself into numberless channels and become quite ineffective and futile. A disorganised mass of people can neither formulate principles nor can they agree on policy and the obvious result is complete chaos. Political parties provide necessary leadership and direct reservoir of popular sovereignty. They bring order out of chaos by putting before the people for what they stand and educate them with their programmes. The people approve the programme of a party which they deem best and return it to power. The party returned in majority forms the Government and pursues its programme vigorously. The primary business of a political party is, in brief, to educate the electorate and mould the public opinion, to win elections and to form the government.

But the men who framed the American Constitution shared the common opinion that political parties were highly detrimental to national solidarity as they encouraged strife, division, chicanery, and personal manipulation. Planning as the Fathers were for the United States as a whole, they sought to provide a mechanism of government which would be free from all "violence of the faction," as Madison called it. They apprehended that their young republic, too, might meet the fate of the republics of the ancient world and of medieval Italy, if the system of government they were establishing permitted the growth of factitious spirit. The Philadelphia Convention had, therefore, to transcend party and the device of division of powers and the system of checks and balances were designed, among other objects, to prevent party domination, no matter how noble its purpose be.

Yet, within a few years of the career of the Union, party divisions and party spirit were sufficiently evident. In fact, hardly had Washington taken the oath of office that he noticed the signs of an emerging party split. To give "the fledgling government" a sense of unity and to rise above faction and party, Washington included both Alexander Hamilton, the leading federalist, and Thomas Jefferson, the most influential anti-federalist, in his Cabinet. But Jefferson resigned as Secretary of State in Washington's second administration to devote full time to the job of welding together a great party following. Washington deplored the emerging state of affairs and in his Farewell Address he warned his countrymen against "the common and continuous mischief of the spirit of party are sufficient to make it the interest and duty of a wise people to discourage and restrain it. It serves always to distract the public councils and enfeeble the public administration. It agitates the community with ill-founded jealousies and false alarms, kindles the animosity of one part against another....." But Washington was no political philosopher and he did not see the inevitability of partisanship. In the Presidential election of 1796, the third under the Union and the first in which Washington was not a candidate, there were two national parties, one supporting John Adams and the other supporting Thomas Jefferson. By 1800 the party system had settled itself quite firmly in the government, even to the extent of necessitating the addition of the Twelfth Amendment so as to make the Electoral College method workable.

It scarcely need be added that since that time political parties have played a very vigorous role in the United States. Sometimes they have been more vigorous than others. National emergency may cause their temporary eclipse or an independent President may be able to transcend them for a time, but the party system has never received a setback. It has grown from generation to generation, and today this extra-constitutional growth forms the hub of the political life of the nation. "But for the appearance of a national party system," as Professor Brogan realistically points out, "the election of a President really enough of a national figure to carry out his duties, might have been impossible. And it is certain that the greatest breakdown of the American constitutional system, the Civil War, came only when the party system collapsed."[1]

**Basis of American Party System**

The basis of the American party system is not the same with which political parties are traditionally associated. "American parties have never been bodies of men united on some general principles of government and united to put these principles into concrete form by legislation and administration." The line of division in the Philadelphia Convention was between large and small States with slavery issue looming large in the background. It was in interests and reactions of an economic and sectional nature that the parties started on their career in early years of the republic. The Federalist party relied upon the commercial, financial and industrial elements of the New England and the Middle States, whereas the backbone of Jefferson's Party were agrarian interests, planters and farmers, of the South and rural North.

Both Hamilton and Jefferson were genuinely prompted by their keen desire to build a strong, vigorous and free nation and they concentrated their best energies in achieving that virtuous purpose. But "each had a distinctive road to strength, vigour and freedom." Hamilton believed in a strong Federal Government and he attempted to build it, enjoying an advantageous position as Washington's Secretary of the Treasury, on real and sound financial basis. He caused the national bank to be founded, passed excise taxes and extended in general the authority of the national government within the framework of the Constitution in order to make the people of the United States feel that they really made a nation and the national government represented the nation; it was no confederation of States.

Thomas Jefferson took a serious objection to Hamilton's methods and there was a rift in the Cabinet. Jefferson resigned and devoted his political talents to building a party to combat "Hamiltonians," as Hamilton and his followers came to be nicknamed. Jefferson's irritation was that all the measures of the government are directed to strengthen the mercantile class without any consideration of the interest of the yeomanry. Devoted as he was to the ideal of an agrarian democracy, he concluded that whole Federalist programme would result into the creation of an oligarchy, the rule of the propertied few in the interests of a propertied few. He could think of no other means to remedy it, except to plead for State rights and a narrow construction of the constitutional powers of the Central Government.

It may appear rather confusing that Jackson, Polk, Cleveland, Wilson and Franklin Roosevelt differed from the founder of their party and depended on the extension of the authority of the national government and a broad interpretation of the Constitution. But Jefferson's attitude of mind cannot be divorced from the context of the "extra-political conditions of the early days". The lack of communication and transport, the provincial values, the absence of a national spirit and of an identity of the people with the new nation, all these factors retarded the growth of national sentiments and the Central Government being regarded as the custodian of the interests of the nation. Jefferson, consequently, felt that only by reserving a great body of rights solely to the States could mean protection of the interests of the people. "There was, therefore, no essential contradiction in his historic position as the founder of the Democratic Party and his overt defence of state rights against national encroachment."[2]

The two great American parties were and are combination of interests and their strength is local. Roughly speaking, United States may today be divided into four groups. The manufacturing North-Eastern group is in the main Republican; the agricultural south is overwhelmingly Democratic. The support of the central farming States is sought by both the parties. Another development of the present century is the political importance of the still mainly agricultural and grazing but rapidly industrialising West. It is the constant endeavour of both the parties to go beyond their citadels of strength and secure the support of either of the two uncertain groups, or preferably both. These two groups are, in fact, the determining factors of Presidential and Congressional majorities and to enable the Republican and the Democrats to bank upon their support

1. Brogan, D. W., *An Introduction to American Politics*, p. 45.
2. Tourtellot, A. B., *An Anatomy of American Politics*, p. 168.

means a high degree of political organization. But so long as North remains Republican and South Democratic, locality will continue to embrace the party politics of the country.

### The Two-Party System

Throughout its history the United States had, barring a few minor parties, two major political parties. Various explanations for such a development have been offered. First, the people belonging to the English-speaking countries are less doctrinaire and more inclined to compromise. Second, the problems of race, nationality and religion are not so prominent to divide them into different factions as compared with Continental countries of Europe. Third, the two-party system is a legacy of the Colonial regime and it has since then perpetuated. Fourth, the two-party system is the consequence of the American voting system, especially the Electoral College and the single member district plan of electing legislative representatives. It is true that the electoral method of electing the President would be very undemocratic if a strong third party should emerge. If no majority wins in the Electoral College, the House of Representatives elects the Chief Executive head of the State from the highest three, each State casting one vote. The single member district scheme of electing representa- tive also discourages the development of minor parties.

Two-party system has certain important results. Under the parliamentary system, one party which carries the mandate of the electorate forms the government and with its legislative majority has the power to carry out that mandate. But under the presidential system, the separation of powers, upon which hinges the framework of government may, occasionally create conditions of deadlock between the Executive and Legislative departments, though normally it results in a situation where the President has a Congressional majority of his own party. In the event of joint Congressional majority being of one party and the President of another, the nation suffers because of the friction and critical role which both play. During the last two years of Truman's first administration, the Republican Congress enacted legislation not liked by the President and President Truman spent a good deal of time criticising it. At the same time, the President was conducting the government through the execution of his constitutional and statutory functions and Congress spent a good deal of time criticising him. A more piquant situation arises when the Senate is of one party and the House of Representatives of another and the President necessarily divided in his attitude towards Congress.

Under the two-party system the parties become moderate and compromising bodies highly sensitive of their responsibility. Each party endeavours to rally round as many interests as it possibly can to win power. And as each party is at all times either the government or the opposition it remains in touch with realities and can ill-afford to make wild and irresponsible statements of policy. Finally, multiple party system would make continued functioning of the electoral college virtually impossible.

It does not, however, mean that minor parties have never existed in the United States. From early times, dissatisfied elements have launched "third" parties; totalling at least a score. But the one redeeming feature is that third parties have come and gone and during the last 150 years none except the Republican Party has ever gained sufficient strength to displace an existing major party. Several times minor party candidates for the Presi- dency have polled sufficient votes to hold the balance of power between the two majors, but they have been unable to keep their separate identity or strength for long. On six different occasions since Civil War, third parties have played respectable roles and the most recent one was that of Robert M. La Follette, the progressive candidate for Presidency in 1924, who polled $4\frac{1}{2}$ million votes.

The role of the minor parties in the American politics cannot be discounted.[3] They are generally the innovators of policy, if not holders of office. "The old parties have not hesitated to take plank after plank from Populists, Greenbackers, Socialists, and Progressives and install them in their own platforms." Minor parties are almost invariably radical than the old line organisations and much of what these left-wing parties advocated two or three decades ago may be found in the Democratic and Republican platforms of today. There may not be a future for the third parties in the United States, but those who promote them have the satisfaction to see their programmes, for which they worked, become the law of the land under the auspices of old parties.

## HISTORY OF AMERICAN PARTIES

### The Democratic Party

The Democratic Party is nearabout two

3. For the influence of third parties, see John D. Hicks, *The Third Party Tradition in American Politics.*

century old and was established under the leadership of Thomas Jefferson during Washington's administration. Known under various names, including Anti-federalists, Republicans, Democratic Republicans, and Democratic, the party has survived under the most difficult circumstances. Early in history it took a stand against protected tariffs, ship subsidies, imperialism, and the extension of the powers of the national government through "constructions" of the Constitution. Its historic centre of gravity was long in the agricultural interests of the country, although a large proportion of importing merchants and urban mechanics were soon brought into its fold. After the extinction of the Federalist Party around 1816, the Democratic Party enjoyed a period of virtual political supremacy. During the Jacksonian era, however, considerable split appeared and the party now known as Democratic soon faced a formidable Whig opponent. It receded to opposition after the Civil War and continued a minority for decades together, but at intervals spirited up with vigour in Congress and captured the Presidency twice with Grover Cleveland, twice with Woodrow Wilson, and four times with Franklin D. Roosevelt. John F. Kennedy occupied the White House with a comfortable Congressional majority of his Party and Lyndon Johnson in the 1964 election secured the biggest, popular majority in the United States history. Jimmy Carter unseated in 1976 Gerald Ford, a personally popular President, but in 1980 he lost to Ronald Reagan. Republican Reagan again winning in 1984. A noticeable trend is that a greater proportion of young and new voters support Republican candidates. It is also apparent that the more education a person has the more likely he is to support Republican candidates. Jimmy Carter, who became the 48th President, had a solid backing of Southern States but Virginia. The rest of America's States were divided between the two candidates. Carter defeated President Gerald Ford. Ford was the first incumbent President to be turned out of office since President Herbert Hoover's bid for re-election during the 1932 economic depression. Jimmy Carter was also defeated in 1980. He was the first President from the more rural and more impoverished South since President Zachary Taylor's election in 1848.

**The Republican Party**

The Republican party of today is in essence successor of two earlier major parties. The Federalist Party led by Hamilton, which had championed strong national government and a liberal construction of the Constitution, had expired after making tactical errors during the War of 1812. It appeared first as National Republican and then Whig during Jackson's time. The Republican Party was founded in 1854 and nominated John C. Fremont as Presidential candidate in 1856. It took a strong stand on slavery. Fremont lost to a Democratic coalition still strong enough to win. Four years later Lincoln gained victory on a Republican platform that proposed abolition of slavery and favoured internal improvements including a "satisfactory homestead measure for farmers," and "liberal wages for working men and mechanics." From 1860 down to 1913, it controlled the Executive department of government continuously with exception of eight years when Grover Cleveland was President (1885-1889; 1893-1897). It was, however, not a smooth sailing for the party. It suffered from the exposure of the corruption during Grant's administration. It was also shaken by internal divisions "between East and West, between conservative businessmen and not-so-conservative farmers and workers, between reform-minded Liberal Republicans and stand-patters, between party regulars (Stalwarts) and not-so-conservative farmers and workers, between many different combinations of these." In spite of these divisions and shakings, the party could stand abreast and succeed, "because by design or by chance" its leaders "could assuage the different elements." William Mckinley saved the party from collapse when important labour and rural elements were on the verge of deserting the party towards the end of the century. When in the following years reformists against the conservatism of the party policy, Theodore Roosevelt, a progressive Republican, reoriented the party's appeal.

The Republican party capitalised upon the popularity of a military hero, Dwight D. Eisenhower to win the Presidency in 1952, and to retain it in the election of 1956, despite a Democratic victory both in the Senate and the House of Representatives. The Democratic Party lost the Presidency in the election of 1960. The Party itself was badly divided over the policy towards the war in Vietnam. "Waste, overlapping programmes, and rank inefficiency had caused the public to be disillusioned with President Johnson's Great Society and alleged war on poverty." Richard M. Nixon won the Presidency in 1968 and retained it in 1972. But his ouster as a result of Water- gate Scandal brought the party to disrepute. The Party came back to White House with Ronald Reagan in the 1980 election. He was re-elected in 1984 to be followed by George Bush in 1988, his Vice-President.

The party has stood for a liberal interpretation of the Constitution, especially those parts relating to the powers of the national government, and has shown less sympathy than the Democratic Party for the rights of the States. It is the champion of the protective tariffs, of internal improvements under federal auspices, of colonial expansion, liberal pensions for veterans, subventions for the merchant marine, Negro suffrage, and gold monetary standard.

**Features of the Party System**

One of the most significant features of the American political parties is their decentralization. Although the Republican and the Democratic parties are two national parties, much of the power in the party system is concentrated in the State capitals and rooted organizationally in the county and municipal levels. Apart from the selection of Presidential and Vice-Presidential nominees and the preparation of national platforms, the Party's central agencies are virtually powerless. Control remains with State and local leadership in conducting the campaign and in deciding upon candidates for office. "A sense of discipline to higher authority is almost unknown, and, if pressed, doubtless would be met by indignation and resistance on the part of the local units concerned."[4] Professor Key says that the national party is little more than "gathering of sovereigns (or their emissaries) to negotiate and treat with each other."[5]

There is , however, evidence of a countertrend in the direction of a greater concentration of power and this is essentially due to the centripetal tendencies of a modern government. This is a universal phenomenon and American party system cannot escape therefrom. For example, the Presidential party increasingly has come to be identified as national in outlook no matter whether the occupant of the White House is a Republicon or a Democrat.On the other hand, localism still remains strong in the Congressional party. The result is a wide gap between the President and Congress in the formulation of policy. But the reality is otherwise. The two wings of the party are not so sharply divided due to the "nationalisation" of politics and if this process continues the sectionalism is sure to disappear from the American party system.

Another important characteristic of the American parties is their reluctance to become tied to any rigid ideological doctrine. The party division is rather blurred and no distinct line of demarcation can be drawn to separate their programmes. Agriculture is not now the predominant occupation of the Americans, and the greater part of the annual wealth does not come from the soil. Large sections of the Middle West and the South, once the strongholds of agrarian democracy, have become industrialised and there is a corresponding change in the attitude of the people. Their needs have also changed and so they look towards government with changed spectacles. Then, the interests of industry, trade and agriculture overlap and dovetail in many ways. There can be no divorce between them. Within industry itself there is a sharp difference and different points of views are put forward to remedy their disabilities. For example, automobile and allied industries are not inclined to protective tariffs; investors of capital abroad and bankers favour low tariffs.

These complexities in the economic life of the country have made the Democrats to shift to new grounds. They have abandoned their old slogan to "tariff for revenue only" and stand for protection, if somewhat modified by reciprocal trade agreements. The Republicans, too, extend considerable support to this programme. The result is, as Professor Beard says, "that the cleavage between the right and left wings of each is greater than the gulf between the parties themselves, especially in the Senate where agrarian states have a disproportionate weight."[6]

James Bryce, after a deep study of the American system, observed that these two great parties were like two bottles. Each bore a label denoting the kind of liquor it contained, but both were empty. It is not true, according to Beard, "that the two parties are exactly identical except as to their labels."[7] There are two important facts to be observed in this connection. The first is, loyalty to tradition which makes the strongholds of both the parties to continue in their support to the parties concerned. Secondly, the old senti-

4. Barker, Benjamin and Fiedelbaum, Stanley, H., *Government in the United States*, p. 147.
5. Key, V.O., *Politics, Parties and Pressure Groups*, p. 363.
6. Beard, C. A., *American Government and Politics*, p. 67.
7. *Ibid.*, p. 68.

ments and opinions still determine the attitude of different interests and characterise the divisions among the voters. This can be illustrated by a sample poll taken by the American Institute of Public Opinion and cited by Professor Charles Beard. According to this sample poll the Democratic candidate, President Roosevelt, ''received 28 per cent of the votes in the upper income group of citizens, 53 per cent in the middle income group, and 69 per cent in the lower income group, while his Republican opponent, Wendell Wilkie, received 72 per cent of the votes in the upper group, 47 per cent in the middle group, and 31 per cent in the lower group.'' A similar poll was again taken in 1943 and identical results were obtained, except for some minor changes in the percentages.

To sum up, the major parties in the United States are deep-rooted in capitalism. The only difference between the two is that the Republicans think that the more government leaves capitalism alone the more it flourishes. The Democrats maintain that unless capitalism is constantly adjusted to social, technological and economic changes, it may perish of its own inflexibility. In international politics the Democrats play the ''strange role of the party of nationalism, strong armies and navies, international intervention and war leaving to the Republicans—at any rate for the time being—the less glamorous and rather unfamiliar role of advocating caution, restraint and even isolationism.'' But Reagan and George Bush disproved it.

An important feature of the American party system is its non-ideological character. In Europe, parties are organised on ideological basis where conservative parties support capitalism and labour, socialist and communist parties criticise capitalism and propose various degrees of reform in the social system. In America, there has been no labour, socialist or communist party of any national relevance. Both the leading national parties in America are firm supporters of the capitalist system and consider socialism of any variety as un-American and antinational.

## SUGGESTED READINGS


Beard, C.A. : *American Government and Politics,* Chap. III.

Bone, H. A. : *American Politics and the Party System,* Chaps. I—X.

Brogan, D.W. : *An Introduction to American Politics,* Chaps. II—V.

Brogan, D.W. : *The American Political System. Part Two,* Chaps. I—IV.

Bruce, H.R. : *American Parties and Politics.*

Duverger, M. : *Political Parties.*

Key, V.O. : *Political Parties and Pressure Groups.*

Mackenzie, C. W. : *Party Government in the United States.*

Merriam, S.E. and Gosnell, H.F. : *The American Party System.*

Milnor, A. (ed.) : *Comparative Political Parties*

Penniman, H.R. : *American Parties and Elections.*

Rohlfing, C.C. and Charlesworth, J.C. : *Parties and Politics.*

Sindler, A.P. : *Political Parties in the United States.*

Stannard, T. : *The Two Constitutions,* Chap. VI.

Tourtellot, A.B. : *The Anatomy of American Politics,* Chap. VIII

Zink, H. : *A Survey of American Government,* Chaps. VIII—XI.

# CHAPTER IX

# The American Political System

### Concentration of Economic Power

In the United States, Professor C. Kaysen notes, "there are currently some 4.5 million business enterprises ... Corporations formed only 13 per cent of the total number."[1] The political history of the United States would have been different if the concentration of economic power had been as rapid as Marx throught it must become. In fact as Professor E.S. Mason says about the United States, "the largest corporations have grown mightily, but so has the economy."[2] Ralph Miliband dissents and regards advanced capitalism "all but synonymous with giant enterprise"which dominates key sectors of its industry, commerce and finance. In regard to the United States, Carl Kaysen admits,"A few large corporations are of overwhelmingly disproportionate importance in our economy, and especially in certain key sectors of it. Whatever aspects of their economic activity we measure — employment, investment, research and development, military supply — we see the same situation."[3]

Professor Galbraith says: "In 1962 the five largest industrial corporations in the United States, with combined assets of $ 36 billion, possessed over 12 per cent of all assets used in manufacturing. The fifty largest corporations had over a third of all manufacturing assets. The five hundred largest had well over two thirds corporations with assets in excess of $10,000,000, some two hundred in all accounted for about 80 per cent of all resources used in manufacturing in the United States ... In the first half of the decade (June 1950 - June 1956), a hundred firms received two thirds by value of all defence contracts, ten firms received one-third."[4] According to Galbraith twentyeight corporations provided about 10 per cent of all employment in manufacturing, mining and trade. Four corporations accounted for about 22 per cent of all industrial research and development. Three hundred and eightyfour big corporations accounted for 55 per cent of these expenditures, but 260,000 small fims accounted for only 7 per cent.

There is every reason to believe that this domination of America's economy by giant corporations has become even more marked in recent years. State intervention itself tends to expedite this process despite its professed desire to curb monopolies and safeguard the interests of small business. The enormous political signification of this concentration of private economic power on the American polity is a major concern of this chapter. Moreover, it should be noted that this growth of the giant enterprise is not merely a national phenomenon. A growing number of the largest American firms are assuming more pronounced transnational character, both in terms of ownership and management. Much of this has been brought about as a consequence "of the equation by American corporations of a rapidly expanding stake in the economic life of other advanced capitalist countries, often to the point of actual control of the latter's major enterprises and industries". But American capitalism is international also in another, more traditional, sense as "large-scale capitalist enterprise is deeply implanted in the under-industrialised areas of the world ... in Latin America, the Middle East, Africa and Asia."[5]

What is the political significance of these corporations from the point of view of power structures? C. Wright Mills explains : "Not

---

1. *The Corporation in Modern Society,* p. 86
2. *Ibid.,* p. 10
3. Kaysen, Ibid, p. 86
4. J.K. Galbraith, *The New Industrial State,* pp. 74-75.
5. Ralph Miliband, "*The State in Capitalist Society,* pp. 14-15

great fortunes, but great corporations are the important units of wealth, to which individuals of property are variously attached. The corporation is the source of, and the basis of, the continued power and privilege of wealth. All the men and the families of great wealth are now identified with large corporations in which their property is seated.''[6] It should be emphasized that the location of power inside rather than outside the typical giant corporation renders anachronistic the theory of the 'interest group' as a fundamental unit in the structure of capitalist society. A whole series of developments have loosened or broken the ties that formerly bound the great interest groups together.

**Nature of American Democracy**

Except in times of crisis, the normal political system of capitalism, whether competitive or monopolistic, is liberal democracy, which Marxists may call bourgeois democracy. Votes are the nominal source of political power, but money is the real source. The political system, in other words, is democratic in form, but plutocratic in content. This was even recognized by Lord Bryce who talked about the enormous power that money wielded in American elections. All the political activities and functions, which characterize this system such as indoctrinating and propagandizing the voting public, organising and maintaining political parties, running electoral campaign "are managed only by means of money, in fact, lots of money."And since in monopoly capitalism the big corporations are the source of big money, they are also the main sources of political power.''[7]

It is true that there is an inherent contradiction in this system. The voters, who do not own much property but constitute an overwhelming majority of the population, may form their own mass organisations, such as trade unions, political parties etc., raise funds through subscriptions and thereby become an effective political force. If they win formal political power and then threaten the economic power and privileges of the wealthy oligarchy, the system will face a crisis unless the oligarchy gives up peacefully. Since no privileged class has behaved this way in history, we can discount this possibility. It is more likely that it will abandon democracy and adopt coercive ways of some kind of fascism. Such a breakdown of liberal democracy may occur for other reasons such as war, economic crisis or political instability. Laski has argued in the *American Democracy* that a fascist solution is not unthinkable in the American political system in a period of intense economic or political crisis.

In general, the moneyed oligarchy of the United States prefers democratic rule to any type of authoritarian government. The stability of the system is enhanced by periodical elections which give legitimacy to plutocratic rule. Popular ratifications of capitalist, oligarchic rule enables it to avoid certain very real dangers of personal or military dictatorship which plague the presidential political regimes of many Latin American countries. Hence in the United States and other advanced capitalist democracies, wealthy oligarchies as a rule do not resort to authoritarian method in dealing with opposition movements. They devise more indirect and subtle means for achieving their ends.

The capitalists make concessions to weaken and soften trade-union militancy and political radicalism of the working-class. They buy off their leaders with money, flattery and honours. When such leaders acquire power, they remain within the limits of the system and try to win a few more concessions to keep their electoral supporters content. They never challenge the real bastions of oligarchic power in the economy and in the coercive branches of the state apparatus. The oligarchy also shapes and alters the machinery of government in order to check the deadlocks and stalemates which might lead to breakdown of democratic procedures. For example, the number of political parties is deliberately limited to prevent the emergence of government by unstable coalitions.

By these methods, democracy is made to serve the interests of the capitalist oligarchy far more effectively and durably than authoritarianism. However, the possibility of a shift to authoritarian rule remains embedded in the constitutional system. Indeed, the American constitutional system, like other democratic constitutions, makes provision for such autocratic rule in times of emergency. However, this is not the favoured form of government for

6. C. Wright Mills, ''*The Power Elite,* p. 116

7. Paul A. Baran and Paul M. Sweezy : *Monopoly Capital,* p. 157

normally functioning capitalist societies. The United States also preferably maintains a system of liberal democracy. "In constitutional theory, the people exercise sovereign power; in actual practice, a relatively small moneyed cligarchy rules supreme. But democratic institutions are not merely a smoke- screen behind which sit a handful of industrialists and bankers making policies and issuing orders. Reality is more complicated than that." In fact, the nation's founding Fathers were conscious of this "latent contradiction in the democratic form of government , as indeed were most political thinkers in the late eighteenth and early nineteenth centuries"[8]

Many writers such as Charles Beard, Harold Laski and D.W. Brogen recognised the possibility that the propertyless majority might use its power to vote to turn its nominal sovereignty into real authority and thereby the security of property, which the capitalists considered as the basis of civilised society. The framers of the constitution therefore devised the well-known system of checks and balances. Its purpose was to make it as difficult as possible to subvert the existing system of property relations.

America's capitalist democracy later developed in a context of several conflicts among various groups and segments of the wealthy classes, which unlike Europe, had never united by a common struggle against feudal power because the United States had no feudal class to contend with for the reasons, the state institutions in the United States have been terribly anxious to protect the privileges of the property-owning minorities against the people. We know "how the separation of powers was written into the Constitution, how states' rights and local autonomy became fortresses for vested interests, how political parties evolved into vote gathering and patronage-discussing machines without programme or discipline. The United States became a sort of utopia for the private sovereignties of property and business."[9]

The very structure of the polity prevented effective action in many areas of the economy and social life. City planning is the worst casualty of the chaotic number of authorities that rule American cities. Robest C. Wood in his *1400 Governments* refers in its title to the number of separate governmental authorities that are operating within the New York metropolitan area. Each of these authorities is the repository and representative of vested interests. There is no over all authority to co-ordinate and control their policies. It is ridiculous to talk of 'planning' in such circumstances.

The system of political representation and the absence of responsible political parties has given an effective veto power to short-term and long-term coalitions of vested interests. Moneyed classes in America are united only on one programme i.e. extension of territorial sovereignty (that is how thirteen original colonies expanded into fifty contemporary states through war, purchase and conquest and protection of the interests of American investors and traders abroad (U.S. economic imperialism). In fact these two activities have been the first concern of the federal government throughout the nation's history. R.W. Van Alstyne, in *The Rising American Empire,* highlights this aspect of America's developing capitalist democracy.

## Social Structure and Class Distribution

The common economic features of developed capitalist systems such as the U S A, Britain, France, Canada, Japan etc. provide these countries with a broadly similar 'economic base'. But this commonality of their economic base is also responsible for creating many significant similarities in their social structure and class distribution. We find therefore in all these countries, including the United States a relatively small number of people who own a markedly disproportionate share of personal wealth and whose income is predominantly derived from ownership of private properties.

Many of these rich persons also control the uses to which their assets are put. But some wealthy individuals may own a small part of those large assets which they control and manage in reality. It is these owners and controllers, taken together, who institute the ruling class of the United States and other capitalist countries. Whether this usage is correct for a democracy will be examined in this chapter later. At this stage, we may just note the existence of economic elites which through ownership or control do command the most important sectors of all

8. Baran and Sweezy : *Monopoly Capital,* p. 159
9. *Ibid,* p. 160

developed capitalist economies.

At the other end of the social scale, we find in all these countries, a working class mostly composed of industrial workers with agricultural wage-earners a steadily diminishing element in the work force.

This implies that the main form assumed by the 'relations of production' in the United States is that between capitalist employers and industrial wage-earners. Like other social classes, the working class of the United States is highly diversified, it is a distinct and specific social formation due to its characteristics as distinguished from those of other classes. Ralph Miliband says "The most obvious of these characteristics is that here are the people who, generally, 'get least of what there is to get', and who have to work hardest for it. And it is also from their ranks that are recruited the unemployed, the aged poor, the chronically destitute and the sub-proletariat of capitalist society"[10]

While apologists of capitalism talk of its "classlessness", the proletarian condition remains still harsh in the work process, in levels of income, in lack of opportunities and in the social definition of existence. The economic and political life of all capitalist societies including the United States is chiefly shaped by the relationship, determined by the capitalist mode of production, between these two classes– the owners of property on the one hand and the workers on the other. The confrontation of these two opposite social forces powerfully determines the political systems of developed capitalism and the United States is no exception to this general rule. The political process is virtually concerned with this antagonism. It is, in fact, intended to legitimate the terms of their unequal relationship.

However, it would be wrong to assign a merely nominal role to other social classes and strata in capitalist America. In fact, their existence and activity greatly helps to prevent the political polarisation of a capitalist society. In the United States, a large and growing class of professional people — lawyers, doctors, scientists, administrators, technocrats etc. plays a significant economic and political role in the system — then we have a middle class associated with small and medium-sized enterprises, which cannot be assimilated into the upper class of the corporate rich. Finally, a capitalist society includes a large number of 'cultural workmen— writers, poets, critics, journalists, priests and intellectuals.

The brief enumeration of classes and strata given here is not exhaustive. We have disregarded the lumpen and criminal elements and also excluded those who actually run the state as politicians, civil servants, judges and military men. Their role will be taken up separately a little later, one point may be noted that classes may exist and yet they may not be conscious of their class positions and actual relations between classes. As C. Wright Mills says, "The fact that men are not 'class conscious, at all times and in all places does not mean that 'there are no classes' or that 'in America everybody is middle class'. The economic and social facts are one thing. Psychological feelings may or may not be associated with them in rationally expected ways. Both are important, and if psychological feelings and political outlooks do not correspond to economic or occupational class, we must try to find out why, rather than throw out the economic baby with the psychological bath, and so fail to understand how either fits into the national tub."[11]

In his Introduction to *Democracy in America,* Alexis de Tocqueville says that this book was written "under the impression of a kind of religions dread produced in the author's mind by the contemplation of this irresistible revolution which had advanced for so many centuries in spite of all obstacles."[12] He was here speaking of the progress in the direction of democratic egalitarianism. Since then many writers have echoed de Tocquville's sentiments. J. 4. Meisel spoke about the 'myth of the most potent socio-political solvent of modern times. Theories have been advanced about the 'mass society, the 'end of ideology', the 'end of history' and 'classlessness'.

However, Professor Kolko maintains that there was "no significant trend towards income equality" in the United States between 1910 and 1959[13]. H.P. Miller also notes that "in the

10. *Miliband, R. The State in Capitalist Society,* p. 161
11. I. L. Horowitz (ed) *Power. Politics and People,* p-317.
12. A. de Tocqueville, *Democracy in America,* Vol 1-7 p.4
13. G. Kolko, *Wealth and Power in America* p. 13

absence of remedial action, this nation may soon face with an increase in the disparity of incomes''[14]

Professor Meade has drawn our attention to 'a really fantastic inequality in the ownership of property' and equalisation is a myth in the context of significant economic inequalities that exist in all developed capitalist countries including the United States. For the United States, R.J. Lampman notes that the share of wealth accruing to the top 2 per cent of American families in 1953 amounted to 29 per cent (instead of 33 per cent in 1922):[15] and that one per cent of adults owned 76 per cent of corporate stock, as compared with 61.5 per cent in 1922.[16] This hardly justifies the belief in 'People's Capitalism;

This shows that despite tall claims about the levelling process, there continues to exist a relatively small class of people who own large amounts of property and also receive very large incomes derived from that ownership. On the other end, there is a very large class of people who own very little or no property, whose income depends on the sale of their labour power and who live a life of actual poverty.

The findings of an official conference on Economic Progress in the United States which reported in 1962 are ; ''thirtyfour million people in families and four million unattached individuals lived in poverty; thirty-seven million people in families and two million unattached individuals lived in deprivation. The total of seventy-seven million comprised two-fifths of the U.S population in 1960.''[17]

The phenomenon of managerialism does not significantly alter the class and social polarisation of the American society. ''In practice'', Adolf Berle writes about the United States, "institutional corporations are guided by tiny, self-perpetuating oligarchies. These in turn are drawn from and judged by the group opinions of a small fragment of America—its business and financial community.''[18] But this view is not true because the corporate managers are seldom free from the direct pressures of the owners and also because they themselves are usually part of the owning fraternity. In the United States, according to Kolko, "the managerial class is the largest single group in the stockholding population, and a greater proportion of this class owns stock than any other.''[19] Thus modern managerial class is an indivisible component of the ruling capitalist class and the work process under both remains one of domination and subjection.

Professor Kolko concludes: ''The signal fact of American business history is the consensus among businessmen ... that the capitalist system is worth maintaining.'' It may tolerate ''decisive innovation in the economic sphere'', but is opposed to radical economic programmes that might, in the process of altering the concentration of economic power, also undermine the sterility, if not the very existence of the status quo.[20] The question now is whether this economically dominant business elite is also a ruling class in the sense that it exercises a decisive degree of political power; whether its control and ownership of the industrial-commercial complex enables it to dominate the state in the political environment of developed capitalism.

**The State System and the State Elite**

According to Paul Baran, Paul Sweezy and Ralph Miliband, the ruling class of a capitalist society is that class which owns and controls the means of production and which "is able by virtue of the economic power thus conferred upon it, to use the state as its instrument for the domination of society." The theorists of liberal democracy and often of social democracy, on the other hand, "have denied that it was possible to speak in a really meaningful way of a capitalist class at all, and that such economic power as could be located in capitalist society was so diffuse, fragmented , competitive, and so much subject to a multitude

---

14. H.P. Miller, *Rich Man, Poor Man,* p. 54
15. R.J. Lampman, *The Share of Top Wealth Holders in National Wealth*, p. 26
16. *Ibid*., p. 209.
17. H. Magdoff, ''Problems of United States Capitalism'' in *The Socialist Register,* 1965, p.
18. A. A. Berle, *The XXth Century Capitalist Revolution,* p. 180
19. G. Kolko, *Wealth and Power in America,* p. 67
20. G. Kolko, *The Triumph of Conservatism,* p. 12

of countervailing checks as to render impossible its hegemonic assertion *vis-a-vis* the state or society. "[21] You may find, therefore, in a capitalist country like the United States, a plurality of competing economic, political and other elites, which are, by the very fact of their pluralistic competition, their lack of common purpose and absence of cohesion is capable of forming a dominant class that can weild effective state power.

It may easily be conceded that there does exist a plurality of economic and other elites in a developed capitalist society like the United States. Despite the integrating trends of its capitalism, these elites do from distinct interests and groupings, whose completion greatly influences the political process. However this elite pluralism cannot obstruct the various elites of the U S A's capitalist society from integrating into a dominant economic class, showing great solidarity and cohesion because their common interests and shared objectives transcend their specific disagreements and differences..

But the most important question in this context is whether this dominant class in the economic sense also constitutes the ruling class in the political sense. Of course, no one can deny that this economically dominant class does wield substantial political power and influence. The question is a different one altogether, namely whether this dominant class also exercises a much greater degree of power and influence than any other class, whether it exercises a decisive degree of political power; whether its ownership and control of crucially important areas of economic life also ensures the control of political decision-making in the particular environment of advanced capitalism[22]

The first element of the state system is its government. It is surprising that government and state should often appear synonymous. The assumption of governmental power is not equivalent to the acquisition of state power. When the Republicans or the Democrats win an election in the United States, they form a government which in Weber's words, can ''successfully plan the monopoly of the legitimate use of physical force'' within U.S. territory. A second element of the state system is the administrative one, which now extends far beyond the traditional bureaucracy of the state. It includes a wide variety ministerial departments, public corporations, regulatory commissions, central banks, etc., which are concerned with the management of economic, social cultural and other activities.

Formally, bureaucracy is at the service of the political executive, its tool and instrument. Actually it is a part of the political process. Karl Mannheim noted that ''the fundamental tendency of all bureaucratic thought is to turn all problems of politics into problems of administration.''[23] Administrators cannot divest themselves of their ideological convictions when they tender their advice to ministers or when they are in a position to take independent decisions. Professor Meynaud correctly points out, ''The establishment of an absdute separation between political and administrative sectors had never represented much more than a simple juridical fiction of which the ideological consequences are not negligible.''[24]

These considerations apply to all other elements of the system. They equally apply to a third such element, namely, the armed forces, to which may be added the para-military, security and police forces of the state. They together constitute that branch of the state system which is concerned with the 'management of violence'. In the United States, this coercive apparatus has developed, since the second world war, into a vast, resourceful and expanding establishment. Its professional leaders, a new race of *warlords,*[25] are persons of high status and extra-ordinary influence, inside state system and in society, similar increase had occurred in the forces of internal security. In no other capitalist state, except in Nazi Germany, police repression and militarization ever reached a grander scale than in the post-war United States.

The fourth element of the state system is the judiciary, which is also non-elective as the administrative and coercive apparatuses are. But unlike them, it is not the constitutional obligation of the judges to serve the government of the day. They are constitutionally independent of

21. Ralph Miliband, *The State in Capitalist Society,* p. 21
22. *Ibid.*, p. 45
23. Karl Mannheim, *Ideology and Utopia,* p. 105
24. Meynaud, *La Technocratie,* p. 68
25. See C. Wright Mills, *The Power Elite,* Chapter 8.

the political executive and protected from it by security of their tenure and other guarantees. In addition, they are expected to defend citizens' rights and freedom against any encroachment by the political executive. Even then, the judiciary is an integral part of the state system which profoundly affects the exercise of state power.

Various units of sub-central or local government constitute the fifth element of the state system. For all the centralisation of power, which is a major development in all capitalist countries,'' sub-central organs of government, notably in federal systems such as that of the United States have continued as power-structures in their own right, and therefore able to affect very markedly the lives of the population they have governed"[26]

Representative assemblies of developed capitalist counters constitute the sixth element of their state and, as an elective element, can be viewed as the most democratic segment. Their life revolves around the government. In the United States, they are formally independent institutions of political power. Their relationship with the executive is one of conflict and co-operation. Opposition parties cannot be wholly uncooperative. By taking part in the work of the legislature, they help the government's business. Government parties are seldom single minded in their support of the political executive. Dissenters "must be persuaded, cajoled, threatened or bought off." Both sides, thus, reflect this duality. Ralph Miliband says: "It is in the constitutionally-sanctioned performance of this cooperative and critical function that legislative assemblies have a share in the exercise of state power. That share is rather less extensive and exalted than is often claimed for these bodies"[27]

It is through these six components of the state system that presidents, prime ministers and their ministerial colleagues, high civil servants and other state bureaucrats, top military men, judges of superior courts, some eminent parliamentary leaders, political and administrative leaders of sub-central government exercise their political power. These are the people who together constitute the state elite. But the state system is only a part of the political system which is broader and includes many institutions such as political parties and pressure groups. They influence the political process and vitally affect the functioning of the state system. It further includes such non-political institutions as giant corporations, churches, the mass media etc. Obviously the men who lead and govern them wield political power but they should be distinguished from the state elite which exercises state power as a distinct and separate entity.

In the case of the United States, it is necessary to analyse the relationship of the state to the economically dominant class. It may well be discovered that this ''relationship is very close indeed and that the holders of state power are, for many different reasons, the agents of private economic power, that those who wield that power are also, therefore, and without unduly stretching the meaning of words, an authentic 'ruling class;.''[28]

From this point of view, ''the phrase 'what is good for General Motors is good for America' is only defective in that it tends to identify the interests of one particular enterprise with the national interest. But if General Motors is taken to stand for the world of capitalist enterprises as a whole, the slogan is one to which governments in capitalist countries do subscribe, often explicitly''[29] The American government like capitalist governments elsewhere, does so because it accepts the view that the economic rationality of capitalism provides the best possible set of social arrangements for human welfare and progress. Representing the view of the state elite in America, President Eisenhower said: ''I believe in our dynamic system of privately owned businesses and industries. They have proven that they can supply not only the mightiest sinews of war, but the highest standard of living in the world for the greatest number of people .... But it requires someone to take these things and to produce the extraordinary statistics that the United States with 7 per cent of the world's population produces 50 percent of the world's manufactured goods. If that someone is to be given a name I believe that his name is the American businessman.''[30]

**Bureaucratic, Military and Judicial Elites**

Top civil servants in the United States,

---

26. Ralph Miliband, *The State in Capitalist Society,* p. 49
27. *Ibid.,* p. 50
28. *Ibid.,* p. 51
29. *Ibid.,* p. 69
30. S.E. Harris, *''The Economics of Political Parties,* p. 5

specialists at upper levels of established career services, "have almost unlimited reserves of the enormous power which consists of sitting still" in defence of the *status quo*. Bureaucracy works as the conscious ally of the business class in all capitalist countries with the United States in the lead, candidates to and members of the civil service are subjected to screening procedures in order to eliminate men and women suspected of any radical orientation. But the most important factor that reinforces the conservative outlook of higher civil servants that turns them into firm supporters of the interests of corporate capitalism is their closeness to its environment.

Furthermore, bureaucracy and large enterprises are now increasingly related in terms of an interchanging personnel. This is particularly true of the new breed of 'technocrats' who man both national and superannuation institutions. The same is also true of independent regulatory agencies in the United States. They may be independent of the political executive, but ideologically and politically, they are integrated into the world of corporate capitalism, Labour, on the other hand, does not possess any links or advantages in the bureaucratic world. American civil servants are not neutral in class conflicts but, in fact, the allies of capital against labour.

Miliband, therefore, concludes, "The state bureaucracy in all its parts, is not an impersonal un-ideological, a-political element in society, above the conflicts in which classes, interests and groups engage. By virtue of its ideological dispositions, reinforced by its own interests, that bureaucracy, on the contrary , is a crucially important and committed element in the maintenance and defence of the structure of power and privilege inherent in advanced capitalism. The point applies at least as much to economic technocrats ...In this light, contemporary capitalism has no more devoted and more useful servants than the men who help administer the state's intervention in economic life."[31]

Similarly, the notion that the military elites in America are ideologically neutral is manifestly false. As in the case of civil servants, military conservatism is also specific in the sense that it is finaly committed to protect and maintain capitalist values and purposes. Professor Huntingtion says: "Few developments more dramatically symbolised the new status of the military in the post-war decade than the close association which they developed with the business elite of American society .... Professional officers and business men revealed a new mutual respect. Retired generals and admirals in unprecedented numbers went into the executive staffs of American corporations; new organisations arose bridging the gap between corporate management and military leadership. For the military officers, the business represented the epitome of the American way of life"[32]

F.J. Cook has given a well-documented analysis of this process in his book *The Warfare State.* C. Wright Mills has forcefully argued that in the United States, the steady militarisation of life and the abnormal growth of the 'military domain' has produced a situation in which the military must be regarded as a power group coequal with the corporate elite and the 'political directorate'. The military elite is their trusted ally "against striking workmen, left-wing political activists, and other such disturbers of the *status quo*" [33]

Judicial elites are mainly drawn from the upper and middle layers of society. In the United States, they are men of a conservative disposition, in regard to all the major economic, political and social arrangements of their society. The Supreme Court, by assuming the role of a third chamber, has used its judicial discretion to determine social policies though one judge enunciated the view in 1824 that "public policy is an unruly horse and dangerous to ride." [34] But many judges of the Supreme Court have nevertheless been compelled to ride that horse, for good or bad reasons. Judges have taken a rather poor view of radical dissent and even connived in the erosion of civil liberties in the conditions of a long-tern 'Cold War'. They have consistently displayed a bias in favour of privilege, property and capital. The history of trade unionism in America is also a history of continuous struggle against the courts' attempts to curl the rights of the working-class.

31. Ralph Miliband : "*The State in Capitalist Society,* pp. 115-116
32. S. Huntington, *The Soldier and the State* pp. 361-362.
33. R. Miliband, *The State in Capitalist Society,* p. 123
34. Quoted in Miliband's *The State in Capitalist Society,* p. 125

**Legitimation and Imperfect Competition**

The claims of democratic diversity and free political competition which are made on behalf of capitalist democracies like the United States appear valid in the field of communications — the press, radio, television, education etc. The value of this freedom and opportunity of expression cannot and should not be underestimated. ''Yet the notion of pluralist diversity and competitive equilibrium" Milliband points out,'' is here as in every other field rather superficial and misleading for the agencies of communication and notably the mass media are, in reality, and the expression of dissident view notwith-standing, a crucial element in the legitimation of capitalist society'[35] In the context of the United States, the freedom of expression mainly means the free expression of ideas which assist the established system of power and privilege.

Even P.F. Lazarsfeld and R.K. Merton, two mainstream sociologists, have admitted this regarding the United States, ''Increasingly the chief power groups, among which organised business occupies the most spectacular place, have come to adopt techniques for manipulating mass public through propaganda in place of more direct means of control Economic power seems to have reduced direct exploitation and turned to a subtler type of psychological exploitation, achieved largely by disseminating propaganda through the mass media of communication ... These media have taken on the job of rendering mass publics conformative to the social and economic status quo.''[36]

The ideological function of the media is obscured in the United States by the absence of state dictation, the existence of debate and controversy and the looseness of the conservative doctrine allowing variations within its framework. Yet the fact remains that the mass media in capitalist democracies are mainly intended to perform a highly 'functional' and legitimising role, both as the expression of a system of domination and a means of reinforcing it. The press radio and television may preserve fair degree of impartiality between the Republican and Democratic parties, but this does not preclude adverse criticism of all views opposed to this bi-party consensus. Radical views are specially marked for hostile condemnation. Socialism for them has always been a devil incarnate. Similarly, the press and other media in the United States remain a deeply committed anti-trade union force. Since 1945 the U.S. media was virulently hostile not only towards international communism but also national liberation struggles and revolutionary movements everywhere.

Conservative, pro-capitalist attitudes of the mainstream media are derived from the ownership and control of the 'means of mental production.' The mass media in the United States are overwhelmingly in the private domain which is dominated by large-scale capitalist enterprises. "The Hearst empire," for instance, ''includes twelve newspapers, fourteen magazines, three television stations, six radio stations, a news service, a photo service, a feature syndicate, and Avon paperbacks''; and similarly ''in addition to magazines, *Time, Inc.,* also owns radio and television stations, a book club, paper mills, timber land, oil wells, and real estate''.[37]

The ideological dispositions of the owners of the capitalist mass media oscillate between soundly conservative to utterly reactionary. Newspaper proprietors closely control the editorial policies of their newspapers as well. James Wechsler, the editor of the *New York Post* said, ''The American press is overwhelmingly owned and operated by Republicans who fix the rules of U.S. political debate. And I use the words 'fix' advisedly ...It is a press that is generally more concerned with tax previleges of any fat cat than with the care and feeding of any underdog ... It is a press that is far more forthright and resolute in combating Communist tyranny in Hungary than in waging the fight for freedom in the United States''[38]

In capitalist democracies, there are certain political parties which are the chosen instruments of the business classes and of the dominant classes generally. In most countries, one major party perform that role, though a second or third party may also enjoy a similar patronage. Thus the Republican Party in the United States is

35. R. Miliband, *The State in Capitalist society,* p. 197
36. B. Rosenberg and D.M. White (eds.), *Mass Culture — The Popular Arts in America,* p. 457.
37. G.W. Domhoff, *Who Rules America,* p. 81.
38. Quoted in J.E. Gerald, *The Social Responsibility of the Press,* p. 108

pre-eminently the "party of business" and of businessmen, but the Democratic Party, for that reason, is not denied necessary business support or corporate funding of its electoral compassion. H.E. Alexander had made this point clear in his book, *Financing the 1964 Election.* As a pressure group *vis a vis* the state, business enjoys a vast degree of superiority ideological, political and cultural hegemony on society. This hegemony includes influence on the Republican and Democratic party machines, the mass media, other agencies of political socialisation, and various organs of government.

America may be suitably described as a 'business civilization' permeated by a business culture and a business ethos. Business has set up and financed 'promotional groups' to disseminate free enterprise propaganda in defence and calibration of the capitalist economic system. A concerted effort for ideological indoctrination has gone furthest in the United States:..."The attitudes, opinions arguments, values and slogans of the American business community are a familiar part of the landscape of most Americans. In recent years, the business point of view has found abundant expression in every kind of medium: placards in buses on the economics of the 'miracle of America'; the newspaper and magazine advertisements on the perils of excessive taxation, speeches of business executives on the responsibilities and rights of management; editorials deploring the size of the national debt; textbooks sponsored by business associations, explaining the working of free enterprise economy; pamphlets exposing the dangers of unwise political intervention in business affairs; testimony by business spokesmen before Congressional committees on a host of specific issues of public policy."[39]

Political competition between labour and capital is imperfect and most unequal in the United States. One obvious reason for this is absence of an authentic working-class party which could have become the vehicle of a rival ideology and politics. In these circumstances, as an American writer, Professor Heilbsoner points out," The striking characteristic of our contemporary ideological climate is that the 'dissident' groups, labour, government, or academics, *all seek to accommodate their proposals for social change to the limits of adaptability of the prevailing business order.* There is no attempt to press for goals that might exceed the powers of adjustment of that order. Indeed, all these groups recoil from such a test. ...thus, it falls to the lot of the business ideology, as the only socio-economic doctrine of consequence, to provide for non-business groups and in particular, for the intellectual community the sense of mission and destiny that is the part usually emanated from rival ideologies."[40]

The presidency of John F. Kennedy provides an illuminating example of the power wielded by big corporations on the American government. President Kennedy found himself engaged in a "spectacular power struggle" with the Business Advisory Council, "an exclusive and self-perpetuating club of top corporate executives that had enjoyed a private and special relationship with the government since 1933" and which "from Administration to Administration ...had continuous privilege to participate in government decisions with no public record or review"[41] When the Commerce Secretary, Luther H. Hodges, wanted to include a broad cross-section of American business—big, medium and small-sized in the BAC, it severed its official connections and renamed itself the Business Council. In fact, Hodges had even thought of broadening the Council to include representatives of labour, agriculture and education.

The confrontation resulted in the withdrawal of all plans for reform. A rapprochement was made and small committees of the Business Council were assigned to each of various government departments and agencies, and to White House itself. On the other hand, "labour leaders complained about the Kennedy campaign against 'inflationary wage increases', itself part of Kennedy's assurance to business that he was playing no favourites. But the President wanted to restore a good working relationship with Business Council regardless of labour's concerns."[42]

In the light of the strategic position which

39. Sutton, et al, The *American Business* Creed, p. 11-12
40. R.L. Heilbroner, "The View from the Top-Reflections on a Changing Business Ideology", in Cheit, *The Business Establishment*, p. 2 (italics in text)
41. Rowen, *The Free Enterprise. Kennedy, Johnson and the Business Establishment,* pp. 61-62
42. *Ibid,* p. 73

as a 'veto group' on par with labour. For labour has nothing of the power of capital in the day-to-day decision-making of capitalist enterprise. A firm's policies regarding production, export, investment etc. are determined by the capitalist owner. In this sense, labour lacks a firm basis of economic power, and consequently has much less pressure potential *vis-avis* the state. In the international sphere, there is no labour equivalent of the World Bank, the International Monetary Fund, or the O. E. C. D. and the G-7, to ensure that governments do not take anti-labour measures in order to please the business elites .While international solidarity of the working-class is a hallowed rhetoric, the unity of world capitalism has become a concrete and permanent reality. The outstanding characteristic of trade union movements in the United States has been division, not unity. Labour, as a pressure group, is extremely vulnerable to internal and external influences that erode its will and strength. American governments have generally felt it unnecessary to treat labour with that respect which they have invariably accorded to capital.

The most important political fact about the United States as an advanced capitalist society is the continued existence of ever more concentrated economic power. The assumption that the United States has long achieved political equality, whatever may be the case in regard to economic and social equality, constitutes one of the great myths of the epoch. Political equality, save in formal terms, is impossible in the conditions of advanced capitalism. Economic life cannot be separated from political life. Unequal economic power...... inherently *produces* political inequality .... whatever the constitution may say.''[43]

## SUGGESTED READINGS


Charles A. Beard. *American Government and Politics.*

Paul Baran, *The Political Economy of Growth.*

Paul Baran and Paul Sweezy, *Monopoly Capital.*

A.A. Berle, *The XXth Century Capitalist Revolution.*

D.C. Blaisdell, *American Democracy under Pressure.*

A.R. Brady, *Business as a System of Power.*

F.J. Cook, *The Warfare State.*

R.A. Dahl, *Who Governs? Democracy and Power in an American City.*

Eckstein H., and Apter, D. (eds) *Comparative Politics.*

Finer, S.F. *The Man on Horseback.*

Huntington, S.P. *The Soldier and the State.*

Kolko, G. *Wealth and Power in America.*

Laski, H.J., *The American Democracy.*

Mason, E.S. *The Corporation in Modern Society.*

Mills, C. Wright, *Power Elite.*

Miliband, R. The *State in Capitalist Society.*

Tocqueville, Alexie de, *Democracy in America.*


43. Ralph Miliband, *The State in Capitalist Society*, p. 237

# THE GOVERNMENT OF FRANCE

## CHAPTER I

# The French Political Tradition

### Democratic and Authoritarian Tendencies

French citizens created the Fourth Republic in 1946. They built it out of the ruins of the War and the ravages of four years of the German occupation of the Second World War. The fact that it is a Fifth Republic suggests that there had existed other governmental systems than that which prevails at present. During the century and a half following the French Revolution, France experienced three further revolutions,[1] two *coups d' etat* [2], and three wars.[3] She adopted and rejected, during this period, more than a dozen constitutions,[4] three of them monarchic, two dictatorial, three imperial and four republicans. Besides these constitutional experiments, for a number of years she was governed by provisional systems, not based on any written text as the *Comite de salut public,* the provisional government of 1848, and the government of National Defence of 1870. "Each time a constitu- tion was made," remarks Herman Finer, "large elements of the nation were resolved never to make it work, or to work within it, but to destroy and replace it by another that must equally outrage rival millions of the population."[5]

Several times, thus, in between the history of the four republics France has passed through many phases and tried many experiments. Among the countries in which popular government has prevailed France, according to James Bryce, is in two respects unique. "She adopted democracy by a swift and sudden stroke, without the long and gradual preparation through which the United States and Switzerland and England passed, springing almost at one bound out of absolute monarchy into the complete equality of all citizens." And France did this not merely because "the rule of the people was deemed the completest remedy for pressing evils, not because other kinds of government had been tried and wanting, but also in defence of general and abstract principles which were taken for self-evident truths."[6] The democratic and authoritarian tendencies in France, therefore, form an indispensable background for the proper appreciation of the present political system there. No country can rid itself of its past, but past in France most conspicuously runs in the present and may go deep in the future as well.

### Heritage of the Revolution

The "old Regime from which France extricated herself during the last decade of the eighteenth century was marked by the Declaration of the Rights of Man. Men, it was affirmed, were born free and remained free and equal in rights; the aim of all political associations was the preservation of the natural and impersceptible rights of man, namely, liberty, property, security and resistance to oppression. The Declaration of the Rights of Man was founded on the ideas of Voltaire, Montesquieu and Rousseau and the same declaration was made a part of the preambles of the Constitutions of Fourth and Fifth Republics.

During the next decade France experimented with four Constitutions. The Constitution of 1791 was the result of the labours of the National Assembly and it attempted to carry out the ideas which brought about the French

---

1. In 1830, 1848 and 1870.
2. In 1799 and 1851.
3. In 1793, 1870 and 1914.
4. One of them, the *acte additionel*, lasted only for twenty-one days.
5. Finer, Herman, *Government of Greater European Powers*, p. 272.
6. Bryce, J., *Modern Democracies*, Vol. II, p. 232.

Revolution. The Revolution which had started in 1789 as an attempt to reform ended in 1792 and 1793 by abolishing of the monarchy and executing the King.

The Convention was summoned by the extreme radicals and it prepared another Constitution to replace the Constitution of 1791. It established a collegiate executive composed of 24 men and established a legislative assembly on a broader popular basis. The draft Constitution could never be put into effect as a result of political circumstances and remained a dead letter. The Convention, then, set up another Constitution in 1795, the system of Directory.

The Constitution of 1795 established a plural executive or Directory, as it was called, composed of five members chosen by the legislature. It provided a bicameral legislature chosen by voters with property qualifications. The Directory failed to distinguish itself. Its members were men of mediocre ability and were divided amongst themselves and they failed to control the situation. Anarchy again threatened the country and the Directory was replaced in 1799 by a Consulate, a system which derived its name from the fact that the executive authority was vested in the three consuls. Napoleon Bonaparte was the first consul.

The Constitution of 1799 was strictly authoritarian and its machinery was placed under the exacting control of the First Consul, Napoleon Bonaparte. He did not believe in the popular constitutions. To all intents and purposes, France had again become a monarchy and in 1804 Napoleon proclaimed himself Emperor of France and made the office hereditary in his family.

Napoleon abdicated in 1814 and in terms of the agreement with the victorious allied powers the Bouborns were restored to the throne in the person of Louis XVII. Louis was pledged to advance a limited monarchy patterned somewhat close to that of England. But the Frenchmen soon discovered that it was far easier to transplant the form than the spirit of the government. The monarchs, too, had never caught the spirit of the Constitution which they had sworn to uphold. Charles X violated certain provisions of the Constitution and, thus, the "July Revolution" of 1830. Charles X had to abdicate and France, once again, was faced with the problem of providing herself with a new government.

Most Frenchmen believed that the monarch was at fault and not the monarchy and, therefore, changed the line of Kings. Louis Philippe, of the House of Orleans, was put on the throne on a clear understanding that he would be a strict constitutional ruler. But the royal ineptness and partisan squabbles, owing to the multiplicity of political parties, made the parliamentary system unworkable. Gradually, the system of government lost all support and the sentiment in favour of a republic grew apace. Paris was once more flamed into revolution and on February 24, 1848 Louis Philippe abdicated and quitted the country. A provisional government was set up on May 4, 1848 and France was proclaimed a republic, known in history as the Second Republic.

The Constitution of the Second Republic was based on the American type of Presidency. But the people were in no mood to accept the new type of government. When the first National Assembly was elected, two-thirds of its members turned out to be avowed monarchists. On December 2, 1848 the French people went to the polls and, by overwhelming majority elected Louis Napoleon, nephew of Napoleon I, the first President of the Republic. Louis Napoleon was himself certainly no republican. He began manoeuvring and after three years in office, staged a *coup d' etat* and gave the country a new Constitution. On November 7, 1852 the Senate decreed the re-establishment of the Empire. It was submitted to the people for their approval and they gave an affirmative vote. The imperial power became as fully centralised under Napoleon III as it had been in the days preceding Waterloo, though some important changes were made in the plan of government.

For a decade things went reasonably well. In time, however, the original popularity of the Emperor was on the wane. Anticipating bad times, he initiated a number of reforms and a new Constitution of the Second Empire was drafted on May 21, 1870. But on July 19, the Emperor plunged the country in a hasty and ill-conceived war against Prussia. At the disastrous battle of Sedan Napoleon surrendered. He was subsequently released by his German captors and went to England where he died in 1875.

The period of 1870 to 1875, says Neumann, "not only gave rise to the Third Republic but also created the foundations of the Fourth, its nearly identical successor." The Government created in 1875, after experimenting with various make-shift arrangements, was a Parliamentary Republic. It was nominally headed by the President of the Republic elected by majority of both Houses of the legislature for a term of seven years with eligibility for re-election. The President was seemingly equipped with vast powers, but the actual leadership of the government was in the hands of the Prime Minister, officially known as the President of the Council of Ministers. The role of the two "presidents" was the same under the Third Republic as it was under the Fourth, but not under the Fifth.

The legislature was bicameral. The Upper Chamber, the Senate, had 300 members indirectly elected by electoral colleges formed in each department. A tenure of nine years, one-third retiring every three years, and a minimum age of forty years were prescribed for Senators. The Chamber of Deputies, the Lower Chamber, was directly elected by universal suffrage, although women did not possess the right to vote, for a period of four years. In theory, it could be dissolved by the President of the Republic with the consent of the Senate, but since 1877 no attempt was made to dissolve it. The lack of dissolution proved a distressing feature of French politics; the short life of French Cabinet. There was no provision for resolving a deadlock between the two chambers and it placed the Senate in an advantageous position.

**Vichy Interlude**

The Third Republic did not live through World War II. It collapsed after eight weeks of fighting in 1940. The war time Premier, Paul Renaud, resigned and he was succeeded by Marshall Petain, a hero of World War I. Negotiations were promptly opened for an armistice. According to the terms of the armistice France was divided into an occupied and unoccupied zone. The French Government in Vichy, though in unoccupied zone, was in no way free from German influence.

The National Assembly in a joint session of the two chambers, which met to ratify the armistice, "voted all power to the Government of the Republic under the authority and signature of Marshal Petain," who was also authorised to frame a new constitution. Petian never promulgated a new constitution, but on the day after the National Assembly had given him full powers, he promulgated two Constitutional Acts. The first made him the chief of the State to serve indefinitely. The second Act essentially set up a dictatorship; making laws and to control the budget. He was also vested with emergency powers. As to the existence of emergency, Petain was the sole judge. It was, thus, at Vichy, under the guidance of Marshal Petain, that the Third Republic was finally killed.

**The Provisional Government, 1944-45**

The Vichy Government and the simultaneous occupation, first of part and then of all the country met with vigorous opposition, which came to be known as Resistance, from several groups at various points in the country. In 1943, a National Council of Resistance was formed together with "the government in exile" which General De Gaulle had formed in London. With the liberation of France by the Allied troops, De Gaulle entered Paris on August 20, 1944 and shortly after as President of the provisional government formed his ministry known as Commissioners.

The first act of De Gaulle when he entered Paris was to issue a decree declaring the Vichy legislation null and void. In pursuance of this declaration the first national elections came on 21 October 1945, when the French people were called to elect a representative Constituent Assembly. In part, the election took the form of a referendum, in part, it was to designate the members of the Assembly. The first part included two questions : "(1) Do you wish that the Assembly to be elected at this time should be a Constituent Assembly?; (2) Do you approve of the public powers being organised, until the establishment of the new constitu- tion, in conformity with the bill, the text of which was given on the other side of the ballot ?" If the electorate answered "yes" to the first question, it meant the election of the Constituent Assembly empowered to draw up a new constitution replacing one of the Third Republic. In case of a negative decision the members elected would constitute a Chamber of Deputies under the Third Republic and performed its functions accordingly.

The Voters repudiated by an overwhelming majority the Constitution of the Third Republic and indicated their desire for an entirely new constitution. The Drafting Committee of the Assembly set to work without delay on the constitution. The Drafting Committee submitted the new constitution to the Assembly on April 19, 1946. Its main features were a single legislative Chamber; the Chamber was to elect the President of the Republic for a term of six years and he was not to serve for more than two terms; the powers and functions of the President in general, were less extensive than that of the President under the Third Republic; the Prime Minister was to be elected by the Assembly and he would form his own Council of Ministers responsible to the Assembly. The draft also contained a formidable array of rights-civil, economic and social.

The Assembly approved the Draft Constitution by a Communist–Socialist majority in spite of the determined opposition of the other moderate parties. When the Draft Constitution was submitted to a referendum for approval , it was rejected. The defeat of the Draft reflected the fear that the Communists would seize power through the all powerful unicameral legislature on which they had particularly insisted in the Constituent Assembly.

The Second Constituent Assembly was elected on June 2, 1946. The Assembly was able to produce a final draft within four months of its composition. On October 13, 1946, the people adopted the new constitution.

**The Fourth Republic**

The Constitution of the Fourth Republic came into effect on Christmas eve 1946. Commenting upon the nature of the new Constitution, Munro remarked: ''What ultimately emerged from the Constituent Assembly in October 1946, was a considerably diluted form of parliamentary government, with some hitherto untried features-a rather curious political mosaic with some provisions which are by no means certain to prove workable. In its essential features, notably the provision of a cabinet responsible to the Assembly but normally without the power to procure a dissolution, it is astonishingly similar to that of the repudiated Third Republic.''

The Fourth Republic inherited all those problems which the Third Republic was powerless to solve. Ministries in France had risen and fallen almost as rapidly since 1946 as before. Prime Ministers came and went with disturbing frequency as the majorities shifted back and forth in the Assembly. The twelve years of the Fourth Republic saw 20 cabinets, an average of one every seven months.

**The French Political Tradition**

France is a classic land of revolutions and a continued revolutionary tradition is the major contribution of the French people to politics, from the bourgeois-democratic revolution of 1789, the second popular, liberal-democratic revolution of 1848, to the Paris Commune of 1871 and the New Left uprising of 1968. The central message of the French Revolution of 1789 that one may discern in the origins, evolution and effects of the violent annihiliation of the *ancien regime* was a crucial step of France on the long road toward democracy. Marx says: "The centralized State power with its ubiquitous organs of standing army, police, bureaucracy, clergy and judicature—organs wrought after the plan of a systematic and hierarchic divisions of labour-originates from the days of absolute monarchy..... Still, its development remained clogged by all manners—medieval rubbish, seignorial rights, local privileges, municipal and guild monopolies and provincial constitutions. The gigantic broom of the French Revolution..... swept away all of these relics of bygone times, thus clearing simultaneously the social soil of its last hindrances to the superstructure of the modern state edifice raised under the First Empire, itself the offspring of the coalition wars of old semi-feudal Europe against modern France."[7]

It is necessary to emphasize that the revolutionary violence was crucial for France's advance, where the obstacles democracy faced were different from those in England. French society did not "generate a parliament of landlords with bourgeois overtones, in the English manner. Previous trends in France had made the upper classes into an enemy of liberal democracy, not part of democracy's entering wedge. Hence, if democracy were to triumph in France, certain institutions would have to be gotten out of the way.... for this very reason, the Revolution was all the more decisive."[8]

Under absolute monarchy, the French landowners adapted to the generally gradual intrusion of capitalism by putting greater pressure on the peasants but left them in a condition of *de facto* ownership. Till the mid-eighteenth century the crown was the main agency of modernisation in France. This process brought about a fusion between nobility and bourgeoisie

7. Quoted in Theda Skocpol, *States and Social Revolutions*, (Cambridge University Press, 1984), p. 174.
8. Barrington Moore Jr., *Social Origins of Dictatorship and Democracy,* (Penguin University Books, 1973).

quite different from that in England. This resulted in the "feudalisation" of a large section of the French bourgeoisie while sections of the English feudalists, through the law of primogeniture, were forced to adopt bourgeois ways of living. Without the Revolution, the ongoing feudalisation of the French middle class would have forced the French monarchy to carry out a form of conservative modernisation from above, similar in its main outlines to what happened in Germany and Japan.

But the Revolution did prevent this conservative, antidemocratic outcome for France. When the French bourgeoisie consummated its political revolution in 1789, it had not yet seized the commanding heights of economic power. In fact, the bourgeois class rose to state power by climbing on the backs of radical movements within the urban artisans and workers. These radical forces prevented the revolution from turning backward. The rich and middle peasants took advantage of the situation to force the dismantling of the seigneurial system, which was the main achievement of the Revolution.

The radical revolution was an integral part of the revolution on behalf of private property and the rights of man. The anticapitalist elements in the *sans-culottes* revolution and the protest of poor peasants were a reaction to hardship resulting from capitalist features of the prevailing economy. The radicals, however, cannot be regarded as an excrescene on the liberal and bourgeois revolution. The one was impossible without the other. The democratic revolution would not have gone as far as it did without pressure from the radicals. In short, Barrington Moore points out, "it is very difficult to deny that if France were to enter the modern world through the democratic door she had to pass through the fires of the Revolution, including its violent and radical aspects."[9]

Political scientists point to the gashes left by the French Revolution as a major cause of the instability of French political institutions. Nevertheless, it is true that social transformation brought by the Revolution was ultimately favourable to the development of parliamentary democracy in France. By destroying monarchy, landed aristocracy and feudal rights, it sanctified the right of bourgeois property and equality before the law. "To deny that the predominant thrust and chief consequences of the Revolution were bourgeois and capitalist is to engage in a trivial quibble.... Put this way, the thesis [of bourgeois revolution] overemphasises the independent influence of such interests."[10]

During the restoration, a Bourbon King reigned from 1815 to 1830. The failure to share regal power with *haute-bourgeoise* proved its undoing and the main cause of the revolution of 1830. At this point the old aristocracy vanished from the political arena as an effective social force. The Revolution of 1848, the establishment of the seond republic and later the rule of Nepoleon III paved the way for unquestionable ascendancy of the industrial and financial bourgeoisie in France. The war with Bismarck's Germany resulted in the defeat of Louis Bonaparte, the rise of the Paris Commune, signifying the formationn of first Workers' Republic in 1871, and finally the establishment of the Third Republic in 1875. Despite the succession of several constitutions in France, two empires and five republics, the steady depelopment of parliamentary democracy was never halted by any counter-revolution.

France has been consistently, for the most part of its post-Revolutinary history from 1789 to the present day, an authentic capitalist democracy. But France also has been a land where different schools of socialism, from utopiamism of Fourierists and Saint-Simonians to revolutionary syndicalism and Marxism have flourished. The Communist and Socialist Parties have been two major political formations of the working class, the peasantry and the radical intelligentsia during the twentieth century. The workers and other oppressed strata have played a significant role in democratic revolutions of 1789, 1830 and 1848. The Paris Commune of 1871, antifascist struggles from 1936 to 1945, trade union struggles in general, and May-June mass movement of 1968 in particular against Charles de Gaulle.

It is this working class radicalism both in thought and action, which distinguishes the French political tradition from American and British conservatism. The explosion of May-June,1968, was largely the expression of the accumulated discontent of the French people after ten years of de Gaulle's rule. Half a million

9. Ibid.,p.105.
10. Ibid,. pp.105-106.

workers had lost jobs; their wages were frozen by the government and the big corporations while prices and profits were soaring. Even the students in university campuses were rebellious. Police brutality against them on 10th May sparked off "the wave of protests that swept over France, culminating in the great strike of nine million workers and the massive factory occupations which tied up the whole country for several weeks."[11]

Waldeck Rochet, the general secretary of the French Communist Party, declared that the people "are fed up with being subjects. They want to be citizens."[12] For ten years the French working-class had struggled against de Gaulle's procapitalist policies through strikes and mass campaigns through the General Confederation of Labour led by the Communist Party. When de Gaulle came to power in 1958, he secured 80% of the votes in the referendum for his Bonapartist Constitution. The Communist Party was the only party calling for its rejection and 20% voted against it. It was the Communist Party which had fought againt de Gaulle's regime of personal dictatorship single-handed for the last ten years.

The increased support for Communist Party, especially among the workers, many towns and regions, enabled it to elect some 30,000 Communist councillors and bring about a larger political unity of all left wing parties. The Left Bloc obtained 45% votes against de Gualle's 55% in 1965 presidential election and 47% votes against 53% for the Gaullists in the 1968 parliamentary election. That is why when the Communist Party and the CGT, along with other trade unions called for mass demonstrations and general strike on 13th May, in solidarity with the students, 800,000 marched in Paris, 60,000 in Lyons, 50,000 in Toulouse, Marseilles and Bordeaux, and 30,000 in Mans, and nine million joined the general strike throughout France. Contrary to hopes aroused by the nation-wide masss movement, "the balance of class forces made it impossible to put on the order of the day the instant establishment of socialist power. On the other hand, it was possible to oust the Gaullist power.... opening the path to socialism. What was lacking for putting this very real possibility into practice was unity of the workers and the democratic forces."[13]

After the disintegration of the Soviet Union and fall of the Communist system, the French Communist Party not only lost its electoral influence but also changed its ideology embrassing the programme of democratic socialism. The French political system today is based on co-existence of a right-wing conservative party and a reform-oriented socialist party who share power between themselves as President and Prime Minister or function as formal rivals as a party of government and that of opposition.

## SUGGESTED READINGS

Alfred Coblan : *The Social Interpretation of the French Revolution.*

Barrington Moore Jr : *Social Origins of Dictatorship.*

Georges Lefebre : *The French Revolution*, 2 Vols.

Theda Sakocpol : *States and Social Revolutions.*

P. Abril : *Politics in France.*

D.W. Brogan : *The Development of Modern France.*

---

11. Jack Woddis, *New Theories of Revolution,* International Publishers, New York, 1974), p.348.
12. Quoted in *Ibid,* p. 349.
13. Ibid.,p.105.

# CHAPTER II

# The Fifth Republic

## THE NATURE OF THE CONSTITUTION

### Fall of the Fourth Republic

A story has often been told how a French book-seller when asked on one occasion for a copy of the French Constitution, replied that he did not deal in periodical literature. ''This anecdote,'' remarks Gooch, 'embodies a reference to an important formal fact in French political history and, at the same time, indicates a prevalent attitude toward that fact.'' On June 1, 1958, the Fourth Republic came to an end. The change came about somewhat abruptly with a marked element of melodrama at the final stage. The Government was unable to meet the challenges of the time especially the Algerian crisis. In May 1958 President Rene Coty unequivocally and firmly told the National Assembly that he would resign if a government led by General De Gaulle was not formed. The National Assembly submitted reluctantly, but the Assembly signed its own death warrant when it adjourned and handed over its law-making power to General De Gaulle's Government for six months. When the Deputies had agreed without argument to disperse until October, M. Andre Marlaux, the General's Minister for Information, remarked, ''now one may be able to govern.'' With no party and no programme, General De Gaulle had obtained dictatorial powers previously accorded by the French Parliament only to Marshal Petain under the menace of German tanks. De Gaulle promised that at the end of six months ''order will have been re-established in the State,hope refound in Algeria and union re-made in the nation, thus permitting the public powers to resume their normal functioning.''

Among the powers that French Parliament had delegated to De Gaulle's Government was constitu- tion-making. The General had categorically told the National Assembly that if he was not provided with the mandate and the means of reforming the Constitution, he would resign at once and retire again into private life. ''My Government has been formed,'' he told the Assembly, ''for the explicit purpose of making these changes I have the impression that in voting for my investiture you indicated that you wanted these changes....If you cannot agree on the Bill submitted to you I imagine it will be up to some other government than my own to try, after so many other governments have tried in vain.

There was no other alternative but to submit to De Gaulle's challenge and accept his terms. The Reform Bill, proposed by the General, was approved by the National Assembly by 350 votes to 163. It sought to take away the existing power from the Assembly to change the Constitution and invest in the government the power to submit proposed constitutional changes directly to the electorate by referendum without going through Parliament. It also provided for a consultative committee of parliamentarians whose advice would be sought in drawing up the terms of the proposed reform, but without binding the government to accept their advice. The Universal Suffrage Commission had proposed to eliminate the consultative committee and to make it compulsory for the government to submit its reform proposals to the vote of Parliament, while nevertheless allowing the government subsequently to put its constitutional reform proposals to the people in any form it liked, even if the parliamentary vote was unfavourable. But General De Gaulle wasted no time in telling the Assembly that this would not do and unless the Deputies adopted the Bill as submitted to them, he would resign. ''The attitude of this Assembly's Universal Suffrage Commission, '' he said, '' is in plain contradiction with the objects for which the Government was formed.'' He said that it was obvious that if the government were to submit the constitutional reform to the National Assembly before it was submitted to the nation by referendum, it would start a new constitutional debate and all precedents in France had shown that these debates could not get anywhere. ''It was impossible to foresee the atmosphere three months hence in which such a debate would take place,'' he added.

### The Proposed Constitutional Reform

What constitutional reforms General De

Gaulle proposed to bring about could be predicated to a great extent. As President of the Provisional Government after the War, De Gaulle believed that France would never be an effective force in the world unless its political structure was overhauled. He called for a regime in which political power should not depend on the vagaries of party politics.'' He pleaded for a constitution which provided for a strong central government with a president elected by the nation and invested with authority to act much on the lines of the United States system. Parliament should pass the legislation and supervise the government, but the president should appoint ministers, promulgate laws, issue decrees and preside at cabinet meetings. The instability and weakness of successive governments in post-war France–26 of them—had hardened the General's belief to give France a stable government, which multiple parties had hitherto denied it. On the eve of the recess of the National Assembly, the General told the Deputies that he dearly loved the republican institutions and that the Assembly elected by universal suffrage ''would remain the principal Assembly in tomorrow's Parliament.'' This statement gave immense relief to those who had believed that De Gaulle would repudiate the French democratic tradition and set up an authoritarian regime. But the General's statement also emphasised that the dependence of the executive upon the legislature would be reduced through various means and to the minimum. If the new system of government was to be parliamentary, it would just be a semblance of it. Anyway, the new constitutional reforms were intended to end the Fourth Republic.

De Gaulle had opposed the Constitution of the Fourth Republic from the very start. He resigned the Premiership and retired from politics before the Constitution came into force. It was only natural that on his return to power 12 years latter he should have refused to accept institutions that he had already considered deplorable. ''Besides by that time, many other Frenchmen, too, had come to treat the Constitution as the scapegoat for the failings of the Fourth Republic.[1]

The Constitution of the Fifth Republic emerged out of the Enabling Act of June 3, 1958, in which the National Assembly provided, by the requisite majority of the three-fifths, that the Constitution ''will be revised by the government formed on June 1, 1958,''[2] that is, General De Gaulle's Government. The draft was first drawn up by a small Cabinet Committee, headed by the Minister of Justice and later Prime Minister, Michel Debre. General De Gaulle himself was not a member of this Committee. But there is little doubt that the Committee had always kept in view the General's constitutional theories, particularly his emphasis on the need of a strong President. The most important landmark was the speech made by General De Gaulle at Bayeux on June 16, 1946, wherein he outlined the ideas that were to serve as the foundations of the new constitution. ''The rivalry of parties,'' he said, 'in our country, is a fundamental character, which leaves everything in doubt and which very often wrecks its superior interest. This is an obvious fact that ...our institutions must take into consideration in order preserve our respect for laws, the cohesion of governments, the efficiency of the administration and the prestige and authority of the State. The difficulties of the State result in the inevitable inalienation of the citizen from his institutions........All that is needed then is an occasion for the appearance of the menace of dictatorship.'' To avoid this menace, De Gaulle outlined that following institutional changes:

''1. The legislature, executive and judiciary must be clearly separated and balanced.
2.. Over and above political contingencies there must be a national 'mediation' (arbitrage).
3. The voting of the laws and the budget belonged to the Assembly elected by direct and universal suffrage.
4. A second Assembly elected in a different manner, was needed to examine carefully the decisions taken by the first, to suggest amendments and proposed bills.
5. The Executive power should not emanate from Parliament. Otherwise the cohesion and authority of the government would suffer, the balance between the two powers vitiated, and the members of the executive would be merely agents of the political parties.
6. A President of the Republic (chief d'

---

1. Dorothy Pickles, *The Fifth French Republic,* p. 14.
2. For a detailed study refer to Macridis, Ray, and Brown Bernard, *The De Gaulle's Republic : Quest for Unity,* Chap. X.

Etat), embodying the executive power above political parties, should be elected by a college, which included the Parliament, but is much broader than Parliament........to direct and work the policy of the government, promulgate the laws and issue decrees, preside over the meetings of the Council of Ministers; serve as mediator above the political contingencies; invite the country to express its sovereign decisions in an election, be the custodian of national independence and treaties made by France and appoint a Prime Minister in accord with the political orientation of Parliament and the national interest."[3]

The Cabinet Committee prepared the Draft of the constitution in two months. The Draft was considered by the Constitutional Consultative Committee consisting of 39 members; 26 representatives of the National Assembly and the Council of the Republic, and 13 members of the Government. The Consultative Committee endorsed the new text of the constitution after suggesting minor modifications which the Government accepted. It was submitted to the people at a referendum held on September 28, 1958. France gave a triumphal vote of confidence to General De Gaulle and the constitution was ratified by a majority of 79.25 per cent votes.

## SALIENT FEATURES OF THE CONSTITUTION

### Reconstruction of Power

The Constitution of the Fifth Republic, though framed within a short period of time under the stress and strains of the Algerian war, introduced prominently the revisionist ideas that General De Gaulle had uttered and sternly advocated. Two major themes constitute the hub of the entire framework of the Constitution: first, the reconstitution of the authority of the State under the leadership of a strong executive, and, second. the establishment of a 'rationalized'' Parliament, that is, Parlia- ment with limited political and legislative powers. The new Constitution established a parliamentary system, in accordance with the undertaking given by General De Gaulle's government on taking office to preserve Republican traditions, but in which Parliament was no longer in a position to dominate the Executive as it did in the period of the preceding Republics. Michael Debre, the Chairman of the Cabinet Committee, which drafted the Constitution, and later became the Prime Minister, himself pointed out that the ''objects of constitutional reform was to reconstruct State power.' Thus, the crucial task of the constitution makers was to create a strong and stable government to succeed a Parliamentary system that could not produce stable majorities. The perennial dilemma of the French body politic had been multipartism, always shifting loyalties and manoeuvring for power.

### Republican Traditions

The new Constitution respects the French Republican traditions. The Preamble solemnly affirms the attachment of the French people to the Declarations of the Rights of Man and the principles of national sovereignty as defined by the Declaration of 1789, confirmed and completed by the Preamble of the Constitu- tion of 1946. Article 2 of the Constitution proclaims that ''France is a Republic, indivisible, secular, democratic, and social.'' It ensures the rights of all citizens and respect for all beliefs. The national emblem remains the blue, white and red tricolour flag and the national anthem is the *Marseillaise.*[4] The motto of the Republic is liberty, equality and fraternity. The government is that of the people, by the people and for the people, Article 3 affirms all sovereignty stems from the people. But this sovereignty is not to be exercised solely through the representatives of the people but also through referendum. The suffrage may be direct or indirect, but always ''universal, equal and secret.'' Respect for political parties is reiterated in Article 4, where, however, it is stated that the parties ''must respect the principles of national sovereignty and democracy.'' Many thought that this provision was aimed at the Communist Party, which had become powerful.

### Constitution the Result of Compromise

The Constitution of the Fifth Republic is a compromise, an expression of two very different and probably conflicting principles. The first is the modified version of the traditional Parliamentary system and the second is the introduction of a strong President who would em-

3. As cited in Roy C. Macridis and Robert E. Ward (Eds.), *Modern Political systems : Europe*, p. 52.
4. The French Revolutionary hymn composed by Rought de Lisle in 1792, sung by volunteers of Marseilles as they entered Paris, 30th July.

body the legitimacy of the nation, and could, in an emergency, prevent the disruption of the political system. There are the familiar organs of Parliamentary system, a politically irresponsible head of the State as distinct from the head of government; the Prime Minister appoints and dismisses his colleagues and he directs the policies of the government and is responsible to the lower Chamber of Parliament, the National assembly; the National Assembly has the right to censure and overthrow the Cabinet and the Prime Minister; the two Houses of Parliament are democratically elected; and the Judiciary is independent.

At the same time, the Constitution delegates broad powers to the Chief of the State, the President, and places serious limitations on Parliament. There is a new principle, the rule of incompatibility which makes partiamentary seat and a ministerial post incompatible to each other. This rule requires that a member of Parliament who becomes a Minister must quit his parliamentary seat and is replaced by the "substitute" who runs at the same ticket at the legislative election. The legislative and the executive powers are thus separated and this is clearly the negation of the Parliamentary system where the Cabinet is a hyphen that joins, a buckle that fastens the Executive and Legislative departments.

Thus, the Constitution of 1958 was the result of a compromise between the "republicans" belonging to the political parties of the Fourth Republic, generally in agreement about the case for some measure of change which would increase the stability and effectiveness of the executive, and De Gaulle and his followers, who wanted essentially to enhance the role of the President. In delegating its constituent powers to De Gaulle's Government on June 3, 1958, the National Assembly refused to let the new head of the government establish a Presidency on the American model. Perhaps, somewhat surprisingly, De Gaulle accepted this limitation to his freedom to shape the Constitution. The 1958 Constitution, accordingly, deems the President an "arbiter" not a "leader" or "guide." Article 5 of the Constitution reads, 'The President of the Republic shall see that the Constitution is respected. He shall ensure, by his arbitration, the regular functioning of the governmental authorities, as well as the continuance of the State. He shall be the guarantor of national independence, of the integrity of the territory, and treaties." Admittedly, arbitration, remark Jean Blondel and Drexel Godfrey, "is an ambiguous concept; one could vary the interpretation from the idea of a more positive role (clearly De Gaulle's view) to that of a neutral function (clearly the "correct" interpretation of the law of the Constitution)."[5]

With so many compromises in principles, it is not surprising that the Constitution should have been ambiguous in part and that efforts should have been made to modify both the letter and the spirit of the law. De Gaulle was the holder of the power and occupant of the Presidential office for near about two terms and from the inception of the Constitution,[6] he had constantly made efforts to mould and remould "the original text in the direction he thought best, and he has been helped by circumstances." The Algerian war and the strain on the morale of the army led to various covert and overt attempts at overthrowing the Government were sufficient to endow the President with emergency powers and Article 16 of the Constitution provides for such powers. The President established the weight of his stewardship of the State at the time of the Algerian crisis. De Gaulle also benefited from the hitherto unprecedented fact of having the support of a majority of Deputies in the National Assembly belonging to his own Party which was disciplined and solidly behind him.[7] He, therefore, intervened in a number of matters which were not clearly within the province of the President according to the Constitution. With Michel Debre as his first Prime Minister, the President did not find any difficulty in over-stepping the bounds set by the Constitution in the exercise of constitutional powers. His move for a change in the election of the President, from indirect to direct, and the first election of the President by universal suffrage, in December 1965, vindi-

5. Jean Blondel and E. Drexel Godfrey, *The Government of France*, p. 33.
6. 1958 to 1965 and 1965 to 1969. He resigned as a result of unfavourable verdict at the referendum in April 1969 on the reorganisation of the Senate and regional reforms.
7. The Gaullist Party, the U.N.R., was the largest party at the First General election of the Fifth Republic in 1958 and it obtained almost an overall majority at the subsequent election in 1962 after De Gaulle had dissolved the National Assembly when it overthrew the Government by a vote of censure. It is significant to note that censure dissolution and return of a majority had not taken place in France for over half a century.

cated De Gaulle's assertion that the popular election of the President would by itself increase the authority of the incumbent of that office.

"The popular election of the President." observe Jean Blondel and Godfrey, "may thus come to be a springboard in future moves towards presidential rule; it may equally be De Gaulle's last effort to bring the country round to his view of the political system. Only time will tell, but it is clear that the changes which have taken place between 1958 and 1965 have been at least as important (if not more important) for the shaping of the new regime as the test of the Constitution itself."[8]

**Limited powers of Parliament**

The new constitution establisheda "rationalized" Parliament—a Parliament with limited powers. Only two sessions of the National Assembly and the Senate take place in a year.The first session, the Constitution prescribes, begins on October 2 and lasts for eighty days, and the second on April 2, and it cannot last for more than 90 days, a maximum of five months and twenty days in all.[9] Extraordinary sessions may take place at the request of the Prime Minister or of a majority of the members of the National Assembly "on a specific agenda." They are convened and closed by a decree of the President of the Republic.[10] But De Gaulle was of the opinion that the President had the last word on whether to convene an extraordinary session or not, despite the terms of the Constitution.

Parliament can legislate only on matters defined in the Constitution. The Government can make laws on all other matter by simple decree. Articles 37 of the Constitution provides: "Matters other than those which are in the domain of law shall be subject to rule-making power." Laws to be voted by Parliament are enumerated in Article 34. The distinction between the law- making and rule-making authorities may not be incompatible with parliamentary government, but it certainly reverses the traditional relationship between the legislative and rule-making authorities in France and is in conflict with the Republican traditions of the country. Hitherto Parliament was supreme and it could delegate legislative powers to the government. But there had, also been "special" powers granted and withdrawn at the will of Parliament. The supremacy of Parliament had, therefore,remained intact.. Henceforth, power to legislate is definitely limited by the Constitution, and, outside these limits, powers belong to the rule-making authority, the Government.

The Constitution also allows Parliament to delegate law-making power to the executive. Article 38 says : "The government may for the execution of its programme ask Parliament to authorize it to take by ordinances, within a limited period of time, measures which are normally reserved to the domain of law. " Such ordinances come into force as soon as they are promulgated, but they are null and void if a bill for their approval is not submitted by the government to Parliament within the prescribed period of time or if the approval of the bill is rejected.

It is not Parliament, but Government which fixes the order of business.[11] The President of the National Assembly is now elected for the whole legislative term whereas the President of the Senate is elected for three years.[12] Hitherto the President of the National Assembly was elected every year and this placed him at the merey of the various parliamentary groups. He could, under the circumstances, neither be independent nor impartial. Nor could he command the same dignity and prestige as his counterpart does enjoy in Britain.

Parliament is no longer free to establish its own Standing Orders. Such orders must be found to be in accord with the Constitution by the Constitutional Council, before they become operative..[13] The number of the Parliamentary Committees–Standing Committees—has been fixed and their functions are strictly circumscribed.[14] Now only the Government Bills and not the amendments made by the Committees and counter- proposals suggested by them come before Parliament for consideration. A Minister alone introduces, pilots and defends the Bill.

8. Blondel, J., and Godfrey, E.D., *The Government of France*, pp. *34-35.*
9. Article 29.
10. Article 30.
11. Article 48.
12. Article 32.
13. Article 61.
14. Article 43.

Though not a member of Parliament, a minister is constitutionally empowered to appear in both the Chambers, introduce Bills and take part in debates. The Government has the right to reject all amendments and to demand a single vote on its own text with only those amendments that it accepts—the procedure as the 'blocked'' vote.[15]

All these provisions are directed against government by Assembly and eliminate the practices which had hitherto plagued governments. Many of the Procedural Rules ''reflect a genuine desire to check some of the more flagrant abuses of the past and are consistent with the strengthening of executives in modern democracies. Others, however, are designed to weaken Parliament.''[16]

**Parliament is Bicameral**

Parliament is bicameral, composed of the Nation-al Assembly and the Senate. The Deputies are elected directly whereas the members of the Senate by indirect suffrage. The Senate assures representation of the territorial entities of the Republic and Frenchmen residing outside France are duly represented in the Senate. Depu ties are elected for a nine years term and one-third of its membership is renewed every three years.The Constitution increases somewhat the powers of the Senate. In the fourth Republic, the Council of the Republic, the upper chamber named then, had no overriding power to veto legislation. It could in practice only force the National Assembly to discuss for the second time the bills that it had passed. Though a reform had taken place in 1954, which had slightly increased the powers of the Council of the Republic, but the main limitation was not substantially removed. The makers of the Constitution of 1958 attempted to increase the authority of the Senate and magnify its position. The Senate was given an ironclad veto over legislation if the Prime Minister and the Government desired it. Article 35 ordains that all laws shall be voted by Parliament. Articles 45 empowers the Prime Minister to convene a joint conference of members equally drawn from both Chambers to iron out the differencess, if any . It is, therefore, up to the Prime Minister to call a meeting of the joint conference, and if he does not do so, the Bill *ipso-facto* dies.

**Ministerial Responsibility**

The Government continues to be responsible, as in the previous Republics, to the National Assembly.[17] An Assembly can overthrow the Government by half of the total of its membership plus one, that is, by an absolute majority. It means that Deputies who abstain from voting are counted as having voted for the Government.[18] But signatories to the motion of censure or no confidence, if the motion is lost cannot move another one in the course of the same legislative session. There is, however, no such bar if the motion of censure is moved by the same signatories when the Prime Minister himself seeks a vote of confidence from the National Assembly on any general issue of policy or on any given legislative bill.

The power to dissolve Parliament, which is the prerogative of the Prime Minister in countries with Parliamentary system, belongs to the President of the Republic in France under the Constitution of 1958. The President can dissolve the National Assembly at any time and for any reason solely at his discretion.[19] There is only one limitation. He cannot dissolve it twice within the same year. The Constitution also enjoins another formality. The President is required to consult the Prime Minister and the Presidents of the two Chambers while announcing dissolution.

**The Referendum**

Another innovation of the 1958 Constitution is that the President of the Republic can bring certain issues before the people at a referendum. Article II provides that the President of the Republic ''on the proposal of the government....or on joint resolution by the two legislative assemblies........may submit to a referendum any bill dealing with the organisation of public powers, the approval of an agreement of the Community, or the authorization to ratify a treaty, that without being contrary to the Constitution would effect the functioning of existing institutions.'' Article 89 also provides for a referendum on amendment of the Constitu-

15. Article 44.
16. Macridis, R. C., and Ward, R. E. (Eds.), *Modern Political Systems : Europe*, p. 261.
17. Article 17.
18. Article 49.
19. Article 12.

tion. The President has, thus, the power to submit to a referendum the approval of a projected bill concerning the organisation of public institutions and an amendment of the Constitution. But the calling of a referendum is the personal act of the President. He may elicit or refuse it depending on the circumstances.

In the case of a constitutional amendment, the President may decide that constitutional amendment proposed by the Government to Parliament need not be submitted to a referendum after it has been adopted by Parliament. In this event the pròposal is sent to a joint meeting of the two Chambers instead of going through the two Chambers separately and the proposed amendment becomes effective when approved by a three-fifths majority of votes. This provision was, perhaps, intended to accelerate the procedure in cases of rather technical amendments and was used in 1960, in order to make it possible for the Community to be transformed into a loose confederation of independent states, and in 1963, to change the timing of the sessions of Parliament.

The use of referendum under Article 11 is limited to three types of measures : those concerning the organization of the public authorities; approving an agreement with the Community; or authorizing ratification of a treaty which would effect the functioning of institutions. 'This Article,' observe Jean Blondel and Godfrey, "has led to the clearest cases of unconstitutional action on the part of the President, both in spirit and letter."[20] The constitutional provision is that the President may, on the proposal of the government during parliamentary sessions or on the joint proposals of the two assemblies, submit to a referendum any bill dealing with any of the measures referred to above. This Article had been applied on three occasions, twice over Algeria, and on the last occasion over the method of election of the President, "the initiative clearly came from De Gaulle himself; the form of a 'proposal' by the Government was respected, admittedly, but no one doubted who the real originator of the proposal was."[21] The second implication of Article 11 is, though it does not expressly state so, that the Bill be discussed and adopted by Parliament and, then, submitted to the people at a referendum for their approval. This is the only logical interpretation in view of the practice hitherto followed in France. Nor had there been any suggestion that a Bill might be adopted either by Parliament or by the people. In the absence of a specific provision to this effect, the only inference is that the President may refer a Bill to a referendum of the people only when it had, in the first instance, been adopted by Parliament. But the President in all these three cases—twice over Algeria, and, then, on the method of Presidential election–bypassed Parliament and submitted the projected Bills to a referendum.

Article 11 does nowhere specify that the procedure prescribed therein covers an amendment of the Constitution. The procedure for amending the Constitution has been clearly and definitely stated in Article 89, and provides for a referendum too. But De Gaulle utilised Article 11 to introduce the proposal that the President of the Republic be elected by universal suffrage. Any change or modification in the method of election of the President requires amendment of Article 6 of the Constitution. It was clearly an unconstitutional act of the President. But its validity was not questioned in the Constitutional Council.

**The Constitutional Council**

The Constitution establishes a Constitutional Council and it replaces the Constitutional Committee of the Fourth Republic. France had never in the past any judicial organisation to review legislation and determine its constitutionality or otherwise. The Constitution of the Fourth Republic provided for the Constitutional Committee to ensure that the proposed laws were in conformity with the Constitution and that any law of doubtful constitutionality could be put into effect only by amending the Constitution according to the prescribed procedure. The Constitutional Committee was a non-judicial body consisting of Presidents of the two Chambers, seven members chosen by the National Assembly from the beginning of each session from outside its own membership, and three members similarly chosen by the Council of the Republic (Senate of the Fifth Republic), a total of 12, sitting under the chairmanship of the President of the Republic. The function of the Committee was to examine any law passed by the National Assembly, prior to promulgation, whenever so requested by the President of the Republic and the Presiding officer of the

20. Blondel J., and Godfrey. E. D., *The Government of France*, pp. 44.45.
21. Ibid.

Council of the Republic. Whenever the Council of the Republic had doubts about constitutionality of a measure passed by the Assembly, it passed a resolution requesting its own presiding officer and the President of the Republic to refer the matter to the Constitutional Committee. The Committee would examine the disputed measure and endeavoured to iron out the differences between the two Chambers. If it could not succeed to bring about an agreement the Constitutional Committee would give its decision. If it decided that the objection raised by the Council of the Republic was not valid and the measure in dispute did not conflict with the Constitution, it was promulgated forthwith. If it decided that the measure was in conflict with the Constitution, it would be sent back to the National Assembly with a direction that the proposed legislation should be passed in conformity with the Constitution or the Constitution be duly amended. It was for the National Assembly to determine whether to abandon the measure or to proceed to amend the Constitution.

The Constitutional Council of the Fifth Republic is composed of nine members who serve for a period of nine years. Three are nominated by the President of the Republic, three by the President of the National Assembly and three by the President of the Senate. They are renewed by a third every three years. In addition to these nine members, all former Presidents of the Republic are members ex-officio; General Charles De Gaulle refused the Council seat when he resigned as President in 1969. The President of the Council is appointed by the President of the Republic and he exercises a casting vote in case of a tie.

The Constitutional Council has four distinct functions. First, it supervises the regularity of the election of the President of the Republic, and the referendums and announces the result. The Council is responsible for declaring the office of the President vacant, if for any reason or cause the President of the Republic cannot carry out his duties. It decides cases in which the regularity of parliamentary elections is contested. Before 1958, contests arising out of parliamentary elections were decided by each House. The Constitutional Council has taken speedy decisions thus avoiding bitter and long controversies in the legislative assemblies in the past.

Second, the Constitutional Council must be consulted on the conformity with the Constitution of Organic laws and the Standing Orders of both the Houses of Parliament. The Council merely pronounces on the constitutionality, leaving the government or Parliament, as the case may be, to take the appropriate step to regularize the situation. Its decision is final. There had been a sharp conflict between Parliament and the Council with regard to the constitutionality of the Standing Orders. Parliament re-introduced various clauses in the Standing Orders along lines of pre-1958 arrangements, which the Constitutional Council felt were in conflict with the new Constitution and, accordingly, held them unconstitutional. One of these had allowed for the possibility of vote following debate on questions. This would have indirectly brought back, though in a limited way, the practice of interpellation if the Constitutional Council had not pronounced against it. Interpellations had been the bane of French politics during the preceding Republics.

Third, the Council acts as an advisory body to the President of the Republic if he is contemplating the assumption of emergency powers. Article 16 of the Constitution requires that the Constitutional Council must be consulted by the President, both with ragard to the existence of the emergency (on which its opinion, with reasons, must be published), and the measures that he proposes to deal with it. But the President is not constitutionally bound to accept its advice. It is just a consultation and it is for the President to accept the opinion of the Constitutional Council or not. It may be noted that whereas consultation with regard to threat to the integrity of the country, independence of the nation, or danger to the execution of international commitments, and interruption to regular functioning of the constitutional organs of government is mandatory with the Prime Minister, the Presidents of the Chambers and the Constitutional Council, consultation with the latter alone is necessary with regard to the measures which the President may deem necessary to meet the threat or to deal with it.

Finally, all bills (other than organic), including treaties, may be referred to the Constitutional Council, before their promulgation, by the President of the Republic, the Prime Minister, or one of the Presidents of the two Chambers to seek its ruling. A declaration of unconstitutionality suspends the promulgation of the bill or the application of the treaty. It is also the guardian of legislative-executive relations. It decides all claims made by the government whether Parliament has exceeded its legislative competence or not. The decisions of the Council are binding on the Executive and Parliament and on all judicial and administrative authorities.

"It is as yet too soon," observed Jean Blondle and Godfrey, "to state whether the Constitutional Council will remain a part of 'living' Constitution."[22] But the process of constitutional review provided by the Constitution of the Fifth Republic essentially differs from the process of Judicial review obtainable in the United State of America. The Constitution of 1958 does not provide for anything that could be described as judicial review. It simply creates a body which, within certain specific and narrowly defined limits has the function of deciding on the constitutionality of governmental or Parliamentary acts. The Council has no general responsibility for ensuring respect for the Constitution. It can express its opinion only if consulted on matters enumerated above and on the initiative of the persons mentioned. it has no power to enforce its decisions. If the President of the Republic, the Prime Minister and Presidents of both Houses of Parliament were to agree among themselves to refrain from consulting the Constitutional Council on a matter where consultation is optional, there is no means by which the Council can make its views known. A citizen cannot appeal to it nor can any Court of Law. It is not competent to judge matters where individual rights are violated. The Constitutional Council is not, therefore, in any sense comparable to the United States Supreme Court.

Nevertheless, on matters on which the Constitutional Council must be consulted, it has served so far as a watchdog over Parliament. There was a sharp conflict of opinion between Parliament and Government on the question of taking votes on resolutions as provided in the original Standing Orders. The Constitutional Council, whose approval of Parliamentary Orders must be obtained according to the Constitution of 1958, decided that votes on resolutions were unconstitutional. In January 1982 the Council threw out the original nationalisation Bill (involving five major industrial groups, 39 banks and two financial holding companies) ruling that certain clauses—notably those dealing with compensation to stockholders—were unconstitutional. The Government subsequently improved compensation terms, revised other clauses and streamlined the revamped Bill through the Socialist controlled National Assembly. The Bill was promulgated after the Constitutional Council rejected objections by Opposition parties to parts of a revised version of the Government Bill. The Council has, on the whole, widely received approbation for its admirable work and all parties, except the Communists, appear anxious to expand its jurisdiction. The programme of all the major non-Communist organizations for the 1967 General Election included a section aiming at creating a "real" Supreme Court .

**Emergency**

When the institutions of the Republic,the independence of the nation, the integrity of its territory, or the execution of international engagements are menaced in a grave and immediate manner and the regular functioning of the public powers is interrupted, the President of the Republic may take whatever measures are required by the circumstances. This is a personal and discretionary act of the President. The President needs only to inform the nation by a message, and to consult the Constitutional Council. The National Assembly, however, convenes automatically and cannot be dissolved during the period of emergency. We shall revert to this aspect of Presidential powers in the following Chapter.

**Revision of the Constitution**

Like the Constitution of the Fourth Republic, the Constitution of 1958 includes a special procedure for revision. It is relatively simple. There are two methods to amend. The right of initiative for the revision of the Constitution can come either from the President of the Republic on the proposal of the Prime Minister, or from private members of Parliament. A proposal for amendment must, to be effective, be voted first in indentical terms by both Houses of Parliament and then ratified at a referendum. A proposal stemming from the President of the Republic and approved by the two Chambers by a simple majority in each House may go, at the President's discretion, either before the two Chambers meeting jointly in a congress and passed by a three-fifths majority, or

22. Blondel J., and Godfrey, E. D., *The Government of France*, p. 37

to the people at a referendum. Thus, an amendment emanating from the Government, may either go before the congress of two Houses or direct to the people at a referendum. A proposal stemming from a private member of either House must always be submitted to the people at a referendum. President De Gaulle, however, claimed, by invoking Article 11, that an amendment can also be submitted directly by the President to the people at a referendum, thus, bypassing Parliament.

There are two limitations on the right to amend the Constitution. The Republican form of government is not subject to revision, and the amendment procedure may not be initiated or pursued when the integrity of the country is at jeopardy.

The procedure for amending the Constitution gives to the Senate an effective veto as the first stage of revision is required, under Article 89, to be voted in identical terms, in both the Houses of Parliament. If the Senate does not agree to the amendment, it fails. Under the Fourth Republic the Council of the Republic had no power to initiate a resolution for amending the Constitution. It originated from the National Assembly and after having passed therefrom it was referred to the Council of the Republic. If it disagreed with the National Assembly, its consent was not necessary if the National Assembly could gather a two-thirds majority on the second reading of the Bill. If the requisite two-thirds majority could not be secured a referendum was held.

There are certain other ambiguities as well in the amending procedure. Article 89 does not say anything regarding the voting of a proposal for revision. Article 126 of the Standing Orders, however, makes it legal that the ordinary legislative procedure is to be used, that is, a simple majority is required for an amendment to pass in both the Houses of Parliament.

**Appraisal of the Constitution**

The Constitution which established the Fifth Republic, adopted by the people at a referendum by an unprecedented overwhelming majority, was a personal triumph of General De Gaulle. The Communists and others, including a section of the Socialists, Radicals and the Radical Socialists, who opposed the Constitution, failed to rally the people to their side partly because they were in a mood to accept any reasonably alternative to a discredited Constitution of the Fourth Republic and partly because the voters knew that a negative vote would mean the dictatorship of the army. General De Gaulle came to power as it was thoughtt that he alone was acceptable to the army which was threatening to seize power and subvert democratic institution.

The 1958 Constitution was designed to give France a stable and strong government by eliminating the pitfalls of the earlier Constitutions. The Fifth Republic retained the parliamentary system of government, but, at the same time, rendered the President of the Republic exceptionally strong and endowed him with emergency powers and others more extensive than even those possessed by the American President. But a powerful Head of the State is the negation of the theory and practice of a Parliamentary system that the 1958 Constitution established. The Cabinet still remains there, but its has been deprived of even its basic and essential functions and responsibility. The President of the Republic nominates the Prime Minister and other ministers are appointed on the recommendation of the Prime Minister. In the presence of the multiplicity of parties and in the absence of a constitutional provision or a convention that the President shall appoint a Prime Minister-designate after fullest consultation with the various party leaders, his choice significantly matters. Then, the rule of incompatibility, which makes it obligatory for a minister to relinquish on appointment his seat in Parliament, and the provision that even outsiders who had not contested election for a parliamentary seat can be appointed ministers, destroys the team spirit and cohesiveness of the Cabinet which is the *sine qua non* of ministerial responsibility that the Constitution specifically enjoins. The Head of the State in a Parliamentary system keeps aloof from politics and he does not preside over the Cabinet meetings where policy is formulated and decided. The 1958 Constitution provides that the President of the Republicc presides over the Cabinet meetings. It is the prerogative of the Prime Minister, in Parliamentary system, to advise the Head of the State to dissolve Parliament and such an advice is generally accepted. But in France, the President dissolves Parliament in consultation with the Prime Minister and the presiding officers of the Senate and the National Assembly. It is a mere consultation and the decision is that of the President alone. The President makes treaties and takes steps during emergency to combat it in order to safeguard the independence of the nation, territorial integrity of France and ensure execution of international agreements. What is an emergency and what measures are necessary to combat it is the sole determination and decision of the President. The President simply consults the Prime Minister and the presiding officers of the Senate and the National assembly, and the Constitutional Council without necessarily having their approval on the measures taken to meet emergency.

The Constitution of the Fifth Republic is neither Presidential nor Parliamentary. The responsibility of the government to Parliament is in conflict with the basic principles of the Presidential system which hinges upon the Separation of Powers and checks and balances. The powerful and independent position of the President of the Republic runs counter to the Parliamentary system. In the opinion of some, the French Constitution of 1958 is essentially a monarchical constitution in a republican disguise and its parallel existed in France during the reign of Louis Phillips from 1830 to 1848. Under that system the monarch guaranteed the stability and continuity of government. He ruled rather than governed and left the day-to-day administration of the government to cabinet. But when a crisis arose he stepped in and decided with finality the measures to meet the crisis and resolve the problems arising therefrom.

The 1958 Constitution had a special mission which General De Gaulle was committed to fulfil and he designed the Constitution in that direction. France was in dire need of a stable and strong government and the General, under compulsion of circumstances to retain republican institutions, combined democracy with authority concentrated at a single point avoiding the vagaries of the elected representatives by cutting short the power and functions of Parliament. But the price of orderly, responsible and stable government is too high in terms of a Parliamentary system.

Parliamentary procedure, has been modified in order to rationalise Parliament to enable the Government to exercise effective control over legislative business. The downfall of the Ministry has been rendered much more difficult than before. The President has been vested with the power to refer back a Bill duly passed by Parliament within fifteen days of its approval by the latter to debate it all over again or in part and Parliament has no right to refuse re-consideration. The President can also submit to a referendum of the people a projected Bill concerning the public power. He can bypass Parliament, as De Gaulle did on three occasions, and directly submit to a referendum Bills amending the Constitution under the cover of Article 11. There is another significant provision in the 1958 Constitution which essentially curtails the legislative powers of Parliament. Parliament votes only essential and fundamental laws. On less important matters it has no vote. These will be decided by Government and enforced by decrees.

The Constitution, therefore, seeks to make the President and the Government very strong *vis-a-vis* Parliament . And in a bid to do so, it is ambiguous and confusing at very many places. It is the living specimen of compromise, and the Constitution of the Fifth Republic has been described as an ''untidy constitu- tion.'' This curious amalgam of irreconcilable principles must sooner or later lead to conflict between the President and the Cabinet or between the Executive and Parliament. Fortunately, nothing untoward happened during the life-time of De Gaulle and his continued occupation of the office of the President from 1958 to 1969, but portents are there. De Gaulle is dead and the habits of a nation seldom die as they do not with the individual. The conflict may end in the Presidency virtually becoming what it used to be under the Fourth Republic unless the voters back the President by giving him a Parliament which is amendable to his control, or decide to follow the pattern of Presidency as obtain- able in the United States of America. French democracy had not functioned smoothly and efficiently in the past and the same possibilities are in store for the future because of sharp divisions among the people which are reflected in her party system as also because of so much bitterness and violent antagonism among political elements. The nation has neither forgotten old conflicts nor taken steps to resolve new conflicts. French politics is more ideological rather than practical.

# CHAPTER III

# The Presidency

### Mode of Election

The framers of the 1958 Constitution endeavoured to make the President of the Republic the repository of prestige and prerogatives so that the office may provide for the continuity of the State, cement the bonds between France and her former colonies, and vigilantly supervise the decorous functioning of the Constitution. The President, in their opinion, was the "Keystone of the arch" of the Constitution to be established; both the symbol and the instrument of reinforced executive authority. In order to accomplish it, they modified the manner in which the President of the Republic was to be elected. Under the Fourth Republic he was elected at a joint session of both the Houses of Parliament for a term of seven years and was eligible for re-election for one term more. Originally, the Constitution of the Fifth Republic provided for an indirect election by an electoral college consisting of some 80,000 "grand electors" that included members of Parliament, of the General Councils and of the Assemblies of overseas Territories and elected municipal Councillors and supplementary delegates from the larger municipal councils. Representation in the electoral college was roughly proportionate to population, but the smaller rural communes were over-re-presented.

This system of Presidential election was widely criticised by many political leaders and constitutional lawyers "who saw in it the perpetuation of the old political forces of the Fourth Republic."[1] In the middle of September 1962, General De Gaulle proposed to modify the mode of Presidential election and suggested that after the end of his own term of office early in 1966, or in the event of his death in office, the President should be elected by direct popular vote. In a message to Parliament in October 1962, he put the issue succinctly and said : "when my seven-year term is completed or something happens that makes it impossible for me to continue my functions,[2] I am convinced, that a popular vote will be necessary in order to give.... to those who will succeed me the possibility and the duty to assume the supreme task...." In a broadcast message to the nation he announced that Articles 6 and 7 of the Constitution would be revised by a Bill to be voted on at a Referendum and by a procedure as laid down in Article 11, that is, the proposed amendment would be submitted directly to the people for their approval or rejection without being debated by the two Houses of Parliament as provided in Article 89 relating to amendment of the Constitution.

The Constitution amending Bill met with stout opposition. The President's decision to invoke the provisions of Article 11 was characterised as unconstitutional and for the first time the political parties joined hands to oppose it tooth and nail. They tabled a vote of censure against the Government and the motion was carried by 280 votes. General De Gaulle thereupon dissolved the National Assembly and proceeded with his plans to hold the referendum on the proposed amendment. The legislative election was postpond till then.[3] On October 28, 1962 the people endorsed De Gaulle's proposal[4] and Articles 6 and 7 of the Constitution, thus, stood amended.

The President is now elected by universal direct suffrage, and by two ballots unless a candidate obtains an absolute majority of the votes cast at the first. If the requisite majority is not obtained at the first ballot, the second is held on the second Sunday after the first. At the second ballot only two candidates may stand—the two at the top of the poll or who had been left in

1. Macridis J., and Ward, A. E., *Modern Political Systems : Europe,* p. 255.
2. The President missed assassination the previous month at L Petit Clamart.
3. According to Article 12 a General Election takes place not less than twenty days nor more than forty days after the dissolution.
4. 12,808,600 voted "Yes", 8 million "No", and 6 million abstained from voting.

that position by the withdrawal after the first ballot of candidates who polled more votes.

The President is elected for a term of seven years, as in the previous Republic. The Constitution is silent on the question of re-election. It is presumed that the President can offer himself and be elected for as many terms as he may like. There is no limit to his re-eligibility. The Constitution simply provides that the President shall be elected for seven years by universal suffrage[5]. No qualifications for the office are mentioned either. The sole disqualification mentioned in the Constitution of the Fourth Republic that the members of the families who had reigned over France could not be eligible for the post of Presidency has been dropped. Nor does the Constitution prescribe any minimum age limit for the Presidential office.

**Succession to the Presidency**

The supervision of the Presidential election, including the investigation of alleged irregularities at the election and the promulgation of result, the Constitution entrusts to the Constitutional Council.[6] The election of the new President takes place not less than twenty and not more than thirty-five days before the expiry of the term of office of the retiring President. In case the Presidency falls vacant, for any reason, the President of the Senate replaces the President until the President resumes his functions. If the Constitutional Council declares, on petition of the Government, by an absolute majority of its members, the President to be permanently incapacitated the President of the Senate temporarily performs the functions of the President until the new incumbent is elected. The new President must be elected within not less than twenty and not more than thirty-five days from the date of the Constitutional Council's declaration of the vacancy or incapacity.[7] In his capacity as Acting President of the Republic, the President of the Senate, is specifically prohibited by the Constitution[8] from using Articles 11 and 12 (governing respectively the use of the referendum relating to any Government Bill dealing with organization of the political branches of government or ratification of a treaty, and dissolution of the National Assembly), and Articles 49, 50 and 89 (governing, respectively conditions in which a government may be defeated, its obligations in this eventuality, and the revision of the Constitution.

## POWERS OF THE PRESIDENT

**Traditional Functions**

The Constitution of the Fifth Republic maintains the political irresponsibility of the President and as Head of the State he continues to enjoy the prerogatives or the traditional functions that were vested in the office in the past. The President appoints the Prime Minister and accepts his resignation.[9] On the proposal of the Prime Minister, the President appoints and dismisses the other members of the government.[10] He presides over the meetings of the Council of Ministers,[11] of Councils and Committees of National Defence[12] and of the Superior Council of the Judiciary.[13] The President is the Commander-in-Chief of the Armed Forces of the country.[14] He negotiates and ratifies treaties,[15] accredits ambassadors and Envoys Extraordinary to foreign powers and receives ambassadors and Envoys Extraordinary accredited to him[16] and makes appointments to some civil and military posts of the State.[17] He signs the Ordinances and decrees that have been considered in the Council of Ministers,[18] sends messages to parliament,[19] promulgates laws,[20] and may ask for the re-examination of a Bill or some of its articles, which cannot be refused.[21]

5. Article 58.
6. Article 7.
7. Article 7.
8. *Ibid.*
9. Article 8.
10. *Ibid.*
11. Article 9.
12. Article 15.
13. Article 65.
14. Article 15.
15. Article 52.
16. Article 14.
17. Article 13.
18. *Ibid.*
19. Article 18.
20. Article 10.
21. *Ibid.*

He is kept informed of all negotiations leading to the conclusion of international agreements.[22] The President has the right of pardon.[23]

In exercising these formal functions, the President, like his predecessors, acts with the concurrence of the Prime Minister, whose countersignature, together with that of any other responsible minister, is necessary.[24] The most important exception to the countersignature of the Prime Minister is the appointment of the Prime Minister under Article 8 and it is understandable because the resigning government cannot take responsibility. But De Gaulle claimed, in his Press conference on January 31, 1964, that the President has the right to dismiss the Prime Minister. M. Pompidou implicitly accepted this view when he said (April 24, 1964) that it was inconceivable that a Prime Minister should remain in office if he had lost the President's confidence.[25] When differences developed between General De Gaulle and Prime Minister Debre, he resigned. George Pompidou resigned in July, 1968, because of differences of opinion on the President's plan to institute a system of participation of workers and employees in the management and profits of enterprises.

The Constitution vests in the President the power of pardon and consults the Higher Council of the Judiciary under conditions determined by an organic law. The Higher Council of Judiciary also assists the President in the appointment of High Court Judges.

**Personal or Discretionary Powers**

Besides the traditional functions, the Constitution vests the President with personal or discretionary powers and in the exercise of which the countersignatures of the Prime inister are not required. They are truly and substantially Presidential acts and he exercises them solely in his discretion. The Constitution specifically mentions four of them. In the first place, the President can dissolve the National Assembly at any time, on any issue and for any reason. The Constitution imposes only one limitation on the President's power of dissolution. He cannot dissolve it twice within the same year.[26] The other limitation that the President, before announcing dissolution of the National Assembly, should consult the Prime Minister and the Presiding officers of the two Houses of Parliament is a sheer formality. In Britain and other countries having parliamentary system, powerr of dissolution is the sole right of the Prime Minister and it is never refused by the Head of the State whenever it is asked. The Head of the State has no right to dissolve Parliament on his own initiative. In France, the initiative rests with the President of the Republic and he only consults the Prime Minister and the Presiding officers of the two Chambers. Consultation is not consent and, accordingly, it has no binding force. The ultimate decision is that of the President.

The President may refuse dissolution when asked by the Prime Minister. It was reported that Michel Debre had wanted a dissolution after the Algerian cease-fire agreement had been ratified by the people at a referendum, but President De Gaulle decided against dissolution. On the other hand, when the combined Opposition parties defeated the Government on a vote of censure in 1962, the President promptly dissolved the National Assembly although the Prime Minister had submitted the resignation of his Government. But General De Gaulle decided not to accept the resignation of the Government and to dissolve the National Assembly instead.

The second personal power of the President relates to the submission of Bills to the people at a referendum. Calling of referendum is a personal act of the President and the Constitution specifically provides that it does not require the countersignature of the Prime Minister.[27] It is his decision to elicit or refuse submission of a Bill of specified nature or a treaty to a referendum. The President may decide that a constitutional amendment proposed by the Government need not be approved at a referendum after it had been adopted by Parliament. In such an event, the proposal is sent to a joint meeting of the two Houses of Parliament and if adopted by a three-fifth majority of the votes cast, it becomes an amendment of the Constitution. Whatever be the exigencies of designing this procedure, it is a Presidential act no doubt and the President determines it in his discretion.

22. Article 52.
23. Article 17.
24. Article 19.
25. Dorothy Pickles, *The Fifth French Republic*, p. 133 f.n.
26. Article 12.
27. Article 19.

On the other hand, the President is required to submit certain Government Bills to the referendum of the people. Such Bills relate to the organization of public authorities, carrying approval of a Community agreement, or proposing to authorize the ratification of a treaty which, without being contrary to the Constitution, would effect the functioning of institutions.[28] Article 11 which contains these provisions categorically enjoins that the President on the proposal of the Government during (Parliamentary) sessions or on a joint motion of the National Assembly and the Senate may submit to referendum all measures enumerated above. But on all three occasions when the provison of this Article were invoked the initiative invariably came from the President and not from the Government of Parliament. In the second place, the President invoked this Article in 1962 and claimed that this Article empowered him to submit directly to the people amendments to the Constitution ignoring the procedure prescribed in Article 89. It means that the President did not give any opportunity to the representatives of the people, by bypassing Parliament to discuss or move amendments to the proposals emanating from government.

When the institutions of the Republic, the independence of the nation, the integrity of the territory of France, the execution of international engagements are menaced in a grave and immediate manner and the regular functioning of the public powers is interrupted, the President may take whatever measures he deems necessary to combat the menace.[29] This is, again, a personal act of the President exercised in his discretion. The President needs only to inform the nation by a message and to consult the Constitutional Council on the measures taken or contemplated to be taken. The National Assembly however, convenes automatically and it cannot be dissolved during the tenure of the emergency. Thus, the President alone is entitled to decide when an emergency, as defined by the Constitution, exists, and what measures should be taken. His obligations are merely to consult the Presidents of the two Houses and the Constitutional Council and to inform the nation. The provision that Parliament meets as of right and it cannot be dissolved during the period of emergency as also that the opinion of the Constitutional Council with regard to the measures taken or intended to be taken must be published, does not provide any real safeguard against the Presidential exercise of emergency powers. The President has the right to assume full powers even if he acts unconstitutionally.

The Constitution also vests explicity in the President certain other powers that he can exercise in his discretion. He has the power to nominate persons to civil and military posts unless it is otherwise provided by an organic law (a law passed by an absolute majority of the Senate and the National Assembly separately).[30] He signs all decrees and ordinances prepared by the Council of Ministers.[31] He promulgates the laws passed by Parliament. The Constitution enjoins upon him to do so within a period of fifteen days following the transmission to the Government the laws so passed. But he may send back, before the expiration of the specified period, to Parliament and ask for reconsideration of the law or of certain of its articles (clauses). Parliament has no power to refuse such a reconsideration. The President can raise question of unconstitutionality on a bill or on a law before the Constitutional Council.[32] He may send messages to Parliament and if not in session, it may be convened specially for that purpose.

**The President as Mediator (Arbiter)**

Article 5, which is the first in Title II of the Constitution and relates to the President of the Republic, explicity charges the President to guarantee the functioning of the institutions of government. It reads: ''The President of the Republic shall take care to see that the Constitution is respected. He shall ensure, by his arbitration, the regular functioning of the governmental authorities, as well as the continuity of the State. He shall be protector of the national independence of the nation, of its territorial integrity, and of respect for treaties and Community agreements.'' This is an all-embracing responsibility which the Constitution bestows upon the President. Mediation is a personal act involving the exercise of judgment. As a result, it gives to the President unlimited

28. Article 11.
29. Article 16.
30. Article 13.
31. *Ibid.*
32. Article 61.

field of action. His mediation spreads over almost every conceivable aspect of policy, domestic or foreign. He must see that the Constitution is duly respected and its commands unflinchingly obeyed. He devises means to ensure that by his arbitration the proper functioning of the institutions of the government is guaranteed and the continuity of the State is uninterruptedly preserved. He is the protector and, thus, the guardian of the national independence, of the integrity of the territory of the country, and of respect for Community agreements and teaties. The range of the President's responsibilities, in brief, extends to matters of war, foreign policy, the preservation of internal peace, and the functioning of governmental institutions. And above, all, the powers of the President are overriding, final and decisive. Speaking one week after his election to the Presidency in 1958, General de Gaulle reaffirmed his conception of the office and his own personal role. He said: ''The national task that I have assumed, for the past 18 years is confirmed. Guide of France and chief of the republican State, I exercise supreme power to the full extent allowed and in accord with the new spirit to which I owe it.''

The President rules as well as reigns. He is the custodian of the national unity. He may delegate his powers for the realization of national objectives to other organs of government, the Prime Minister, the Cabinet and Parliament, and they may take appropriate decisions thereon, but subject, in the case of conflict among Ministers or between the Cabinet and Parliament to the President's arbitration. This was at least De Gaulle's ideal and he ceaselessly strove for it. On three important occasions, he interpreted the Constitution in a manner which limited the powers of Parliament and on all three occasions President De Gaulle's decision was accepted. In the first instance, an absolute majority of the Deputies, which is the constitutional requirement under Article 29, demanded that Parliament should be convened in an extraordinary session, but the President asserted his right to decide whether it would be justifiable or not to convene an extraordinary session. He did not consider that the demand of the Deputies was cogent enough and refused to convene an extraordinary session.

On the second occasion in 1961, the emergency had been proclaimed and consequently Parliament was in session as required under Article 16. But when it adjourned for the summer vacation there had taken place farmers demonstrations in a number of Departments and parliamentarians decided to hold a special session of Parliament in order to introduce a bill dealing with the causes of agricultural discontentment and the remedial measures. Since Parliament was in session and it had only adjourned for a brief recess it was up to the Presiding officers to convene a special session. But De Gaulle intervened and opposed the convening of a special session on the ground that agricultural problems were totally unrelated to the exercise of his powers under Article 16, and for which purpose Parliament had been convened. He maintained that the special session, though constitutionally in order, was politically unnecessary, since the proposed legislation could be introduced a few weeks later during the regular autumn session.

The third was the familiar and now oft-repeated instance when De Gaulle decided to submit directly to the people on October 28, 1962, a bill modifying the constitutional provision relating to the election of the President of the Republic. This act of General De Gaulle has been held by an overwhelming majority of the French jurists as unconstitutional. A constitutional amendment is governed by the provisions of Article 89, and before its submission to the people at a referendum it must pass through both the Houses of Parliament. But De Gaulle bypassed Parliament and this act of the President was a clear contravention of the Constitution, though the President had defended his action under Article 11 of the Constitution. This Article, as pointed out earlier, does not relate to constitutional amendments.

**Extent of the Powers of the President**

The President of the Republic under the Constitution of 1958 is meant to be the Head of the State and, according to the letter and spirit of the Constituttion, he should in normal crircumstances be no more than that. Though the reality of the Constitution had become more presidential during the tenure in office of General De Gaulle, the basis of the government is parliamentary. Michel Debre, the chief architect of the Constitution, had unequivocally maintained that the ''parliamentary regime was the only one suitable for France. The system of government the constitution of 1958 establishes in France, has two basic features, which characterise all the parliamentary systems of government in Great Britain, Canada, Australia, India and many others. First, the executive is divided in two organs, the Head of the State,[33] and the government,[34] which led by the Prime Minister, is responsible for policy-making and policy-implementation.[35] Second the Government is collectively responsible to the National Assembly,[36] the representative Chamber, which can, by censure, force its resignation.[37]

Like his predecessors, under the Third and Fourth Republics, the President is politically irresponsible, except in the case of high treason, for which he can be tried before the High Court of Justice.[38] In few respects the Constitution of 1958 gives to the President, even where his traditional functions are concerned, a little more freedom and scope for action than his predecessors have had. For instance, the President negotiates treaties.[39] Under the Constitution of 1946, the President was simply "kept informed" of the negotiations. Then, the list of offices to which the President has now the right to make appointments[40] is far larger than that contained in the 1946 Constitution. The President of the Fifth Republic appoints the Prime Minister and Ministers proposed by him[41] without going through the process of designation as provided in the Constitution of the Fourth Republic. But in one respect he has less opportunity to act independently than his predecessors. In the exercise of his right to pardon the President now requires a countersignature of the Prime Minister and a responsible Minister. The previous Constitution made no provision as such. The first President of the Fourth Republic, M. Auriol, no doubt, sought advice on matters of pardon, but he did not submit his orders for countersignature.

All the same, it does not mean that the 1958 Constitution, vesting the President with such powers, eliminates the basic elements of parliamentary democracy. They are there, yet the President is vested with some special powers, which the previous Constitution did not contain. These are: the power of dissolution,[42] submission of Bills to the people at a referendum,[43] reference of certain Government Bills to the people for their approval or rejection,[44] and assumption of full powers in certain emergencies.[45] These powers, by their very nature and the restrictions that the Constitution imposes were intended to be exercised at rare intervals or in emergencies alone. But President De Gaulle made full use of these powers. His sole object in doing so was to strengthen and exalt his position. Accordingly, the Constitution of the Fifth Republic has been variously described. Some suggest that it was "tailor-made" for General De Gaulle, who was to become the first President of the Republic in December, 1958. But Jean Blondell and Drexel Godfrey remark, "This is, in fact, only partly true; it would be truer to say that the Constitution is becoming more and more tailor-made for De Gaulle, partly as a result of the constitutional amendment, partly as a result of customary change."[46]

General De Gaulle put the new conception of the office of the President under the Constitution tersely when he said in 1964 that the President "elected by the nation is the source and holder of the power of the State," the only man to "hold and to delegate the authority of the State." This assertion of the President meant, in the ultimate analysis, that the President can concentrate the powers of the State in his own hands, provided he holds his office as a result of the mandate of the people and as long as specific reforms, irrespective of the nature

33. Article 5 clearly establishes it, although it does not say so in clear and specific terms.
34. Article 20.
35. Article 21.
36. Article 20.
37. Article 49 and 50. In 1958, motion of censure against the government was carried in the National Assembly by 280 votes. The government resigned, though the President did not accept the resignation but dissolved the National Assembly.
38. Article 68.
39. Article 52.
40. Article 13.
41. Article 8.
42. Article 43.
43. Article 45 and 89.
44. Article 11.
45. Article 46.
46. Blondell, J., and Godfrey, E. D., *The Government of France*, p. 29.

and scope, are approved by the people by their own votes at a referendum.

The Constitution of the Fifth Republic as said earlier, is the result of compromise between two irreconcilable principles—principles which govern the parliamentary system in sharp contrast of a presidential system. The Algiers rebellion and the inability of the government of the Fourth Republic to deal with it effectively had abundantly proved that the strengthening of the Executive was an imperative need of the country. In fact, many political leaders had been suggesting, since more than a decade, various methods by which this could be achieved. General De Gaulle wanted that type of Executive wherein the President should have a much ''higher'' role and he should be concerned with the ''permanent'' interests of the nation. He had opposed the Constitution of the Fourth Republic from the start, resigned from the Premiership and retired from politics before it came into force. It was only natural that on his return to power twelve years later he should have refused to accept the institutions that he had already considered deplorable.

The compromise between the two diametrically opposed points of view was difficult to arrive at, because French ''Republican'' tradition was opposed to and suspicious of the presidential system of government. This suspicion goes back to the miiddle of the nineteenth century when the second Bonaparte overthrew the regime and established an Empire. At the same time, French people had not forgotten the failures of the Third Republic. The experiences of the Vichy regime, under the German occupation, were also living memories with them. The Algiers rebellion hardened their conviction that a parliamentary regime must be coupled with a strong and energetic Executive. The 1958 Constitution combined both, a strong Executive and a ''rationalized'' Parliament within the framework of a Parliamentary system.

Though General De Gaulle had agreed to the system of government with parliamentary institutions, but he saw potentialities in the various provisions of the Constitution, more especially in Articles 5 and 16 to nullify their impact. Gradually, from the conception of an arbiter, he assumed the role of the ''Guide'' of the nation and vested the office of the President with broad leadership functions. Presidency became the centre of policy-making not only in foreign affairs but also in domestic issues. He established specialised bureaus and offices where policy alternatives were thrashed. The Prime Minister and his government knew nothing what was happening at the Elysee, the Presidential palace. The President, thus, emerged as the key policy-making organ bypassing the Prime Minister and his Cabinet, who, in terms of the Constitution, are charged with the duty of determining and directing the national policy and are collectively responsible for that to Parliament. The President adopted the device of directly appealing to the nation to vote for his policies and programmes. In the second term of his office, which began in January 1966, he decided, without any consultation with Parliament and most probably without the full knowledge of the Prime Minister and his Cabinet, to ask for the withdrawal of the United States forces from France, and, in effect, withdrew from NATO. In his various trips abroad, De Gaulle advocated his own foreign policy which often took the Ministers at home by surprise. When he advocated the ''liberation'' and ''independence'' of Quebec in the summer of 1967, even his own foreign Minister was taken by surprise.

Besides the impressive powers that the Constitution conferred on the President, General De Gaulle added new dimensions to the Presidency by considering himself to be the ''Saviour'' of the nation who was destined to usher in an era of stability and prosperity not only for the generation of his own times but for the coming generations too. Before his second term election in December 1965, he reminded his countrymen the role he had played in the past and what the country expected him to do in the years ahead. He said: ''seven years ago I believe it was my duty to return to her head in order to save her (France) from civil war, to spare her from financial and monetry bankruptcy and to build her institutions to meet the requirements of the modern times and world. Since that time I have believed it was my duty to exercise the powers of Head of State so that France might on behalf of all her children, make an unprecedented stride forward in her internal development, restore complete peace and acquire throughout the world a political and moral position worthy of her. Today, I believe it is my duty to hold myself ready to continue my task weighing, with full knowledge of the facts, the effort involved, but convinced that at this time it is best in order to serve France.''[47]

De Gaulle ruled supreme for more than a decade and throughout his tenure he regarded both government and Parliament ''as being, in their different ways, mere agents of the President.'' Public interest was focussed in him and not in the Prime Minister. There were protests in Parliament and the President paid no heed to them. In Oral Questions addressed to the Prime Minister on April 24, 1964, two Deputies, M. M. Mitterand and Coste-Floret, criticised the President in general for taking decision without consulting his Ministers and for ignoring both the Cabinet and Parliament ''and also specifically for transferring to the President which should constitutionally be the Prime Minister's functions in the field of nuclear policy.''[48]

On January 31, 1964, M. Coste-Floret addressing the Prime Minister observed, 'We were told that you did not exist. Why did you not resign immediately?'' Prime Minister M. Pomipidou defended the President and his interpretation of the Constitution He admitted that there was a profound modification of Presidential functions, but explained that in the referendum of 1962, the people had clearly and definitely confirmed their approval of General De Gaulle's conception of his functions and the manner in which he carried them out. The Prime Minister expressed the view that the importance of both the Prime Minister and the Government was enhanced ''by their responsibility—on the one hand to the President and on the other to the National Assembly. Immediately after his death in 1970, Pompidou paid handsome tribute to his mentor. He said, ''General De Gaulle is dead, France is a widow.''[49] He appealed to his countrymen to follow the path he carved for the country and emulate the lesson he taught. ''Let us gauge,'' he maintained, ''the duties which gratitude imposes upon us. Let us promise to France not be unworthy of the lessons which have been dispensed to us and let De Gaulle live eternally in the national soul.''[50]

De Gaulle relinquished Presidency in April 1969, when his proposals relating to the organization of the Senate, and regional reforms were rejected at a referendum. His successor M. Pompidou was not even a fragment of his mentor, although he tried to maintain glory of the Presidency that he had inherited. But the process of the ''Presidentialisation'' of the regime was reinforced by Valery Giscard d' Estaing, Pompidou's successor. Giscard won the 1974 Presidential election as an apostle of unity—a reformer who promised change without convulsion, a healer who sought to melt the ''icy antagonism between Right and Left into a vigorous convivial center.'' But he could not fulfil his promise because France's historic division not only persisted but had become sharp. His handling of the foreign policy was impressive and abroad he powerfully consolidated the President's influence and prestige. He took the initiative of supporting Zaire, Chad and Mauritania and enunciated a clear African policy for France. He put forward a plan for European monetary union and boldly came out in favour of the entry of Spain and Portugal into the European Economic Community despite the political and economic problems to rise in his own country.

Giscard established himself the real leader of the nation and he emulated the lesson De Gaulle had taught, whose Finance Minister he was from 1962 to 1966, about the role of the Presidency. He regarded all affairs of the State as his ''reserved domain'' as foreign policy and defence were called under General De Gaulle. Giscard even interfered in the small details of policy execution, like the nomination of officials that his predecessor had left to the jurisdiction of the Prime Minister. He used the powers at his disposal in a far more thoroughgoing manner than even De Gaulle did. He issued instructions direct to Ministers and interested himself in the tiniest details of administration. He had formed around him a team of about 40 able, mostly young officials, many of them the product, like Giscard himself, of the Ecole Nationale d' Administration. Many people believed that it was this team at the Elysee, not the elected representatives of the people, who really governed France.

---

47. French Affairs, 183 (New York : Embassy of France, Press and Information Service (November 4, 1965), pp. 1-2.
48. The decrees of July 10, 1962 and January 14, 1964, were held to constitute a transference to the President the responsibility for the general direction of defence and of the right to decide on the use of the nuclear deterrent, Dorothy Pickles, *The Fifth French Republic*, p. 156 f.n.
49. *The Tribune*, Chandigarh, November 11, 1970.
50. *Ibid.*

"The trouble with Giscard," General De Gaulle is supposed to have said, *"c'est le peuple."* He had no common touch with the people. The system of governning the country, he ventured, caused resentment and hostility among the intellectuals and political strata. "For the first time, France is being governed by technocrats", snapped Madame Marie-France Garraud, the only woman candidate for 1981 Presidential election; "there is now a gap between the governed and the governors." And a distinguished ex-official, who worked closely with De Gaulle at the Elysee, was in no doubt that "Giscard has deformed the Constitution."

The victory of the Socialist leader, Francois Mitterand, over Valery Giscard d' Estaing in the 1981 Presidential election was essentially an expression of the people's desire of a change of 23 years' conservative rule rather than their willingness to take the country to the Left. The other factors that led to Mitterand's victory included Giscard's failure to cure the nation's ailing economy (rate of inflation running at 12.5 per cent and over a million and a half without jobs) and the unpopularity that he had gathered over the diamonds he had received from the deposed Emperor Bokassa.[51] By and large, however, Mitterand's success was the backing he got from the youth who needed jobs and security and the Communists who wanted to oust Giscard at any cost.[52]

The Socialist Party's main priority was decentralisation—to take from Paris the control of the regions and give them to local councils by proportional representation. Other equally important pledges made by the President related to the nationalisation of banks, 11 big industries and a few insurance companies. The President started his job fairly well to the admiration of the masses. The measures he had taken made Mitterand popular with even his opponents. Mitterand's victory heralded a qualitative change in the Elysee and in the government. He was known to the French as the "quiet force" the serene father-figure who never talked too much. He carried this image with him in the Elysee. There had been no rush to the media to explain himself. He controlled his Ministers discreetly, with little of the direct meddling, badly suffered from president Giscard. Mitterand's socialism is moral and patriotic. "Morality and national pride now combine in Mitterand's overiding determination that France should make up the ground it lost in the opportunistic, materialistic years of Gaulist and Giscardian economic progress." His foreign policy was distinguished for its leaning towards the third world countries rather than heavily tilted towards the advanced and capitalist countries. Nor had the President forgotten his relations with USSR despite the Communists unconditionally supported him in his election and were till 1983 participants in the government too.

In the March 1986 elections to the National Assembly the Socialist Party emerged as the single largest party and the right-wing headed alliance between the Gaullist Rally for the Republic (PRP) and the former President Giscard De Estaing's Union For French Democracy (UDF) won 291 seats in a 577-member House. It was the first time in the 28 years of the Fifth Republic that the Presidency and the Assembly were controlled by different parties. Prior to the poll, President Mitterrand had warned that he would order an early Presidential election (due in 1988) rather than be "a cut-rate" President. But immediatly after the poll he announced his decision to appoint a Prime Minister from the victorious right-wing coalition and, thus, put to rest that he would utilise his Presidential power to appoint a Prime Minister and thereby to foist an unrepresentative government on France. He appointed Jacques Chirac the Prime Minister.

The right-wing alliance was committed to the policy of 'privatization' of over-sweeping of nationalisation of banks and a dozen of France's powerful industrial groups. And Chirac wanted to do most of it by Presidential decrees meaning that President Mitterrand would have to undo under his own singnatures what his socialist government had done five years before. On July 14, 1986 in an interview on French Television, the President cast his political decision in decorous moral terms. To sign the 'privatizatin' decree, he indicated, would be to sell off France's national interests to "foreign interests." It meant that the only option with the Prime Minister was to go slow with his

51. "If I was a cannibal," complained Bokassa, "he was a cannibal. For 10 years, I was with Giscard. If I stole diamonds, he should be punished, too, because he got his diamonds." *The Sunday Standard,* New Delhi, May 24,1981.
52. Georges Marchais, who himself was candidate for the Presidency and eliminated at the first round of election, pledged unconditional support for Mitterand at the second round.

programme and refer all such changes, he intended to make, to Parliament and get its verdict thereon. If the President did not bend to his conservative Cabinet plan and the Prime Minister was not inclined to follow the parliamentary process, the resultant confrontation could prove fatal to, what had been widely described, ''cohabitation'' between strange bed-fellows.

The year 1987 opened with the French government of the Prime Minister, Jacques Chirac, under fire from at least three different counts: a disruptive rail strike; domestic-based terrorism; and Libyan aggression in Chad. A series of strikes called by the pro-Communist General Confederation of Labour in support of the railwaymen, bus, metro and electrical workers disrupted their respective services in a show of labour opposition to the general economic policies of the conservative Prime Minister. The Chad problem and the persistent threat of hit-and-run terrorists strikes by Action Direct inevitably aggravated the ''cohabitation'' tensions between President Francois Mitterrand and Prime Minister Chirac. In their messages of New Year greetings to the nation, the two leaders exchanged thinly shielded barbs in an effort to pin the blame for the prevailing turmoil. One French commentator on television characterised the situation as ''a guerrilla struggle at the summit.'' The conservative government also stepped up its charges that the railway strike had become primarily ''political'', with the aim of undermining it. All this did not augur well for France with its historical background.

France has demonstrated that a combination of American-style Presidency and British-style cabinet is practically a working proposition. The socialist Milterand-led Presidential government could successfully cobalit with a conservative Ministry. Today Jacques Chirac has reversed these roles. He is a conservative President and at present (2002) successfully cobalits with a socialist cabinet led by Jaspers as Prime Minister.

# CHAPTER IV

# The Government

### The Cabinet

In the language of the Constitution, the Cabinet, composed of the Prime Minister and other Ministers, constitutes the Government which determines the policy of the nation and is responsible to Parliament.[1] While the role of the President is to ensure a ''guardianship'' of the Nation,[2] the role of the Government is to govern. The President of the Republic, no doubt, chairs the Council of Ministers,[3] but it is the Government as a whole, and in particular its leader, the Prime Minister, who is responsible for the policy of the Nation.[4] The Constitution accords special recognition to the office of the Prime Minister by custom known as the Premier.

The office of the Premier, before the 1946 Constitution, had always been precarious in authority and in tenure because of Ministries necessarily being formed from heterogeneous parliamentary groups. The framers of the Constitution of 1946 were fully alive to the defects inherent in the French political system and they attempted to stabilise the position of Premier, as much as they could. In fact, the position of the Premier, as Phillip William pointed out, ''was the keystone of the constitutional settlement of October 1946.''[5] The Reporter of the Constitution to the Second Constituent Assembly in 1946, could boast that the President of the Council of Ministers ''has become a Prime Minister in the English sense.'' Actually, wrote F. Ogg, he had be- come ''more than that—a head of the government, with powers at some points considerably transcending those of the British ministerial chief.'' But it was clearly not so. The Constitution prescribed that he exercised some of his powers with the countersignatures of one of the relevant Ministers. The most important limitation in the exercise of his powers was political. In the absence of a coherent Ministry, the Premier could not become an effective leader and was never in a position to form a stable, strong and effective government.

The Constitution of the Fifth Republic creates the office of the Prime Minister and retains in essence some of the provisions of the 1946 Constitution which establish his supremacy and leadership as much as is compatible with the position of the President of the Republic and the collective character of the Government. He '''directs'' the operation of the Government and is ''responsible'' for national defence. He ''ensures'' the execution of the laws and exercises the rule-making power subject to the condition that all decress and ordinances are signed by the President of the Republic.

The Prime Minister determines the composition of the Cabinet,[6] presides over its meetings, and directs the administrative services. He defends his policy before Parliament, answers questions addressed to him by members of Parliament, states the overall programme of the Government in special declarations and puts the question of confidence before the National Assembly.[7] He makes appointments to the posts which the President of the Republic is not specifically designated to appoint.[8] He presides over the councils and committees of the defence establishment in place of the President of the Republic when the occasion arises.[9] The Prime Minister may, in exceptional circumstances, take his place as chairman of a meeting of the Council of Ministers by virue of an express delegation of authority and for specific agenda.[10]

The Prime Minister exercises legislative

1. Article 20.
2. Article 5.
3. Article 9.
4. Article 21.
5. Phillip Wiliam, *Modern Foreign Governments,* p.540.
6. Article 8.
7. Article 49.
8. Article 21 as read with Article 13.
9. Article 21 as read with Article 15,
10. Article 21 as read with Article 9.

initiative concurrently with the other members of Parliament.[11] Parliament assembles in an extraordinary session at the request of the Prime Minister or of the majority of the members composing the National Assembly, for a specific agenda. Only the Prime Minister may ask for a new session before the end of the month following the decree of closure of Parliament after the completion of the agenda for which it had been convened in extraordinary session.[12] Moreover, throughout the Consittution the Prime Minister is called for advice as specifically in cases of dissolution of the National Assembly[13] and in the use of emergency powers by the President of the Republic under Article 16.

**The Cabinet and Collective Responsibility**

The Government in France, like other parliamentary democracies, remains legally a collective organ and the decisions of the Government are the decision of all its members. Collective decision-making is implicit in Articles 13 and 20 of the Constitution. Article 13 provides that the President of the Republic shall sign the Ordinances and decrees that have been considered by the Council of Ministers. This nature of collective decision making is supported by Article 38 which provides : "The Government may, in order to implement its programme, request of Parliament authorization to take by ordinance, during a limited period of time, measures which are normally in the domain of law. Ordinances shall be enacted in the Council of Ministers after consultation with the Council of State." But Article 20 makes it abundantly explicit when it says that Government shall determine and direct national policy.

Article 20 associates collective decision-making with the collective responsibility of the Government After stating that the Government determines and directs the policy of the nation, it also provides that the Government shall be responsible to Parliament. The Constitution prescribes three methods of enforcing Government's responsibility to Parliament. The first method is found in Article 49. It states: "The Prime Minister after discussion by the Council of Ministers shall commit the Government before the National Assembly to responsibility for its programme or possibly, for a general policy declaration." The National Assembly can defeat the Government either on its programme or on a declaration of general policy and in such an eventuality the Government as a whole resigns and quits office.

Second, the National Assembly can defeat the Government by passing a vote of censure. The Constitution prescribes a definite procedure for moving a vote of censure and its consequential effects.[14] A motion of censure is required to be signed by at least one-tenth of the members of the National Assembly and the vote thereupon takes place not less than forty-eight hours after the motion had been introduced. Only those votes are counted that are favourable to the motion and the motion is considered adopted only if it is supported by a majority of all the membership of the Assembly. If the motion is defeated the signatories to the motion of censure which had been defeated cannot propose another motion censuring the Government for the rest of the session. But others, who had not been signatories to the defeated motion may propose such a motion of censure.

Third, the Prime Minister may, after discussion in the Council of Ministers, make an issue a matter of confidence. If he does so, confidence is presumed to heave been accorded, and the proposal in question is presumed to have been carried without a vote being taken, if a motion of censure has not been moved within twentyfour hours. Such a motion of censure is subject to the same conditons as a motion of censure on the Government's policy. If the motion is lost, the proposal is carried. There is no limit to the number of censure motions that may be presented by the same members of the National Assembly on matters on which the Government has made questions of confidence.

There is one important difference between the two kinds of vote of confidence. If the Government seeks a vote of confidence, a simple majority of the members present and voting is sufficient to bring down the Government. If a vote of cencusre is moved against the Government an absolute majority of the total membership of the National Assembly is necessary to carry a vote of censure. The absolute majority

11. Article 39.
12. Article 29.
13. Article 12.
14. Article 49.

of the total membership of the Assembly renders the adoption of the vote of censure extremely difficult followed by a deterrent action that the signatories to the lost motion cannot move another vote of censure for the rest of the Assembly session.

When the National Assembly passes a motion of censure or rejects the programme or a general policy of the Government, the Prime Minister must submit to the President of the Republic the resignation of the Government.[15]

**Functions of the Cabinet**

Whatever be the provisions of the Constitution with regard to collective decision-making and the responsibility of the Government as a whole to the National Assembly, the functions of the Cabinet became drastically modified under General De Gaulle as well as Giscard. Three reasons can be assignel for it. The first is the rule of incompatibility as provided in Article 23 of the Constitution. It states, "Membership in the Government shall be incompatible with the exercise of any parliamentary mandate, with the performance of any national function in a trade or professional organization, with public employment, or with any professional activity. An organic law shall determine the conditions in which the holders of such mandates, functions, or employment shall be replaced. Members of Parliament shall be replaced in a manner conforming to the provisions of Article 25." This Article was introduced in the Constitution at specific request of De Gaulle in his bid "to reduce the temperature of politics."[16] It forbids ministers to remain members of Parliament after they had been appointed to the Government. Whatever be the merits of this provision, it is, indeed, incongruous in the context of a parliamentary democracy. Government, in a parliamentary system, emanates from the majority Party in the representative Chamber and it remains in office so long as it can retain its confidence. It defends its policies and programmes on that basis of majority. It is true that members of the French Government do attend the meetings of both Houses of Parliament and participate in, their deliberations without the right to vote,[17] but their simple participation is not enough for a parliamentary democracy if the representative Chamber is really to be the barometer of public opinion. The representatives carry with them the mandate of the electorate expressed at the time of the General Election and they pursue their programme in accordance with that mandate. But the Constitution of the Fifth Republic prohibits it. De Gaulle had hoped that the rule of incompatibility would force Ministers to abandon their "politician's outlook and take a ministerial," presumably "statesmanlike", attitude on becoming members of the Government. This hope of De Gaulle, however, has not been realized. The procedure does not appear to have led to considerable variations in the attitude of the Ministers. For, though a Minister ceases to be a member of the Assembly or the Senate after his appointment, he does not eschew his membership of the Party to which he belonged. He has to fight election again after the expiry of his term of office as a Minister and for that he has to depend upon the Party if his reelection is to be ensured. He contests election on the ticket of a party, supports its programme and participates in party campaigns.

Then the Government is no longer composed of parliamentarians who simply resign their electoral mandate. Since 1958, more than one third of the Cabinet members have been civil servants, technicians, professors and intellectuals who had never been in Parliament and who had never desired to do so. De Gaulle attempted it to effect a "depoliticization" of the Government in order to bring about a change partly on the ground that the Government should in some sense be "above the daily turmoil of political life," and partly because the General conceived of politics "as an activity which somehow can be divorced from state policy-making." On coming back to power, in May 1958, and before the new Constitution was drafted, De Gaulle appointed to his Cabinet members of the civil, foreign and colonial services, a practice which had been abandoned, except in time of war, for over half a century, and placed these men in key positions. It had two effects. First, it vitiated the basic principle of a parliamentary system and, secondly, it was against the traditional, but universally recognized, maxim that the representative Chamber is the authentic expression of popular sovereignty. Cabinet cohesion and collective responsibility have no political utility in this context.

15. Article 50.
16. Blondell, Jean and Godfrey, E.D., *The Government of France*, p. 51.
17. Article 31.

In fact, both the non- parliamentarians and parliamentarians, as Macridis and Ward maintain, "who renounce their parliamentary mandate are therefore presumed to be independent of immediate political and electoral consideration, only, however, to become increasingly dependent upon the President, from whom they hold their ministerial position."[18]

The Cabinet is a deliberative and policy-making body. It discusses and decides all sorts of national and international problems confronting the country and thereby an attempt is made to reach unanimous agreements embodying Government's policy. It must present to Parliament and to the world unified policy of action if collective responsibility is to be fully realized. Meetings of the Council of Ministers under President De Gaulle were frequent and prolonged. Reports prepared by the Ministers or their aides were debated, but generally the discussion revolved "around the suggestions and directives of the President."[19] In contrast, the Cabinet meetings under the Prime Minister, wherein national policy would have been determined and for which the Constitution holds it responsible to Parliament,[20] had become rare. Instead, several inter-ministerial committees were set up "to implement the decisions reached in the Council of Ministers by President De Gaulle or at the Elysee."[21] The Cabinet had, thus, become a mere instrument for the execution of policy and in some matters, especially defence and foreign policy, it was "simply bypassed." Giscared followed his mentor, whose finace Minister he was. Mitterand, who inherited the Gaullist presidential system, tailor-made for his opponents, which he himself opposed because it gave the President too much power, has controlled his Ministers discreetly, with little of the direct meddling.

The only redeeming feature of the constitutional provisions is that ministerial instability that had plagued France throughout its parliamentary career has sharply decreased. The rule of incompatibility was designed to remove any temptation to overthrow the government and manipulate another. In the earlier Republics every Deputy was a prospective minister and every minister aspired to become a Prime Minister without any qualm of conscience. Under the rule of incompatibility there is no possibility of a former minister, who had been ousted from office, again resuming his old seat in Parliament because that had been occupied by a substitute who had to be designated under the 1958 electoral law. It can, therefore, be said that the threat of losing a parliamentary position as a price of membership of government is real and effective. Moreover, the incompatibility of ministerial position with function of professional representation on a national level yields to the result that office–bearers of the labour unions or employers' federations or chambers of commerce or agricultural associations cannot become ministers. They have to resign their positions before joining the government in order to assume the role of statesmen.

In the first seven years of the Fifth Republic, France had only two Prime Ministers, Michel Debre (1959-62) and Georges Pompidou (1962—1968). Maurice Couve de Murville came in July 1968. In contrast, only two Premiers of the fourth Republic lasted for over a year and no Prime Minister since 1875 lasted continuously in office as long as Pompidou. The cabinet has shown also a corresponding stability. Only on three occasions there have been important reorganizations. Maurice Couve de Murville remained in charge of Foreign Affairs for about ten years to become Prime Minister in 1968. The Ministry of the Interior and Army were each headed by the same one Minister, respectively, for over six years. This is a "remarkable stability," observe Macridis and Ward, "that compares favourably, if not better, with the stability of the British or the American cabinet."[22]

**Parliamentary Control**

Parliament supervises the work of the Government in three main ways. During sessions of Parliament, opportunity is provided for exchanges of opinions during debates. It is here that the Government comes under close scrutiny and its lapses or achievements come into limelight. Parliament is a place where matters are debated and society, writes Harold Laski, "that is able to discuss does not need to fight; and the greater the capacity to maintain interest

18. Macridis, Roy C., and Ward, Robert E., *Modern Political System : Europe,* p. 260.
19. *Ibid.*
20. Article 19.
21. Elysee is the official residence of the President of the Republic.
22. Macridis, Roy C., and Ward, Robert E., *Modern Political Systems : Europe, p. 260.*

in discussion, the less degree there is of an inability to effect the compromises that maintain social peace.''[23] The most important function of the Opposition is to discuss and criticize matters of administration and policy–making and thereby to make the Government obliged to defend its intentions and practices. It must, however, be said that there must be a well-organised and strong Opposition to create an effective stir in the Government by its criticism.

But the main method of supervision in France is during the first stage of legislative procedure, by the examination of Bills in Commissions. All members of recognised parliamentary groups are members of a Commission, though not of more than one. The Commissions are parliamentary committees empowered to examine, discuss and report Bills before they can be debated in the Assembly and they have even been powerful engines of supervision and control very often leading the Government to wilderness. The Commissions can summon both the Ministers and the Civil Servants, examine them on matter being discussed before it and ask them to provide explanation and justification thereto.

In addition to the permanent Commissions, there are special Commissions too. A special Commission consists of thirty members, of whom not more than fifteen may be drawn from the same permanent Commission and a Bill may be sent to it for examination and report instead of one of the permanent Commissions. The Chamber may itself ask for this procedure to be adopted, and this has become the rule rather than the exception. There are also Commissions of Inquiry, similar to the Select Committees of the House of Commons, and Supervisory Commissions, which supervise the management and finances of the nationalised industries and public services.

Information about the transaction and affairs of the Government may be obtained by the members of Parliament through the medium of either written or oral questions to the relevant Minister. Questions on general policy of the Government are addressed to the Prime Minister. Written questions are printed in the *Journal Officiel.* Ministers are required to reply to the questions addressed to them within a period of one month and their replies are printed in the *Journal Officiel.* They may, however, delay their replies for one month, and sometimes two, and may even refuse to reply on the ground that it would not be in the public interest to divulge the required information. If the reply to a written question is unduly delayed the Presiding officer of the Chamber may ask the member concerned whether he would prefer to put his question orally.

Oral questions are replied once a week at a sitting reserved for this purpose, and in the National Assembly it is on Fridays, Oral questions may be with or without debate. Questions without debate are called by the President of the Chamber and the member who is the author of the question is allowed to speak for five minutes and it is followed by the Minister's reply. No other speeches are allowed. Questions with debate are put by their authors in the course of a speech the duration of which may last up to half an hour. After the Minister concerned has given its reply, the President of the Chamber may allow other members to speak for a period not exceeding fifteen minutes in each case. The minister may give a final reply, if he so desired.

Finally, the motion of censure is really a potential device of controlling the Government. It the motion is accepted the Government resigns. But the framers of the Constitution of 1958 invented the technique of censuring the Government, as contained in Article 49, which is not only drastic but clumsy too, as pointed out earlier. Control of the Assembly and even discussion of policy is very limited indeed.

## SUGGESTED READINGS


1. Blondel and Godfrey, *The Government of France*
2. Finer, S.E. *Comparative Government*, Chap. 7.
3. Macridis and Ward, *Modern Political Systems in Europe.*
4. Pickles, Dorothy, *The Fifth French Republic*


23. Laski, H. J.,, *Parliamentary Government in England,* p. 149.

# CHAPTER V

# Parliament

## Parliament in Retrospect

The Parliament of Fifth Republic is, as in the past, bicameral, consisting of the National Assembly and the Senate. The Upper House, the Senate, has regained its title, which it had lost in the 1946 Constitution, but not all the powers, which it had under the Third Republic. The Lower House, the National Assembly, has kept its name which the Constitution of 1946 had given it. Bicameralism has a chequered history in France. During the three-quarters of century after the Revolution, France had a series of Constitutions, some of which provided for a single chamber legislature and some for two chambers. "There was no fixed tradition", as Munro observed, "but, in general, the monarchists preferred the bicameral system while the republicans felt that one chamber was enough."[1] Hence the Third Republic began its career with a single chamber legislature, called the National Assembly.

But the National Assembly was not merely a legislative body, it was also a Constituent Assembly. The National Assembly was sharply divided whether the new constitution should provide for one legislative chamber or for two. The anti-republicans, the monarchists, the imperialists and other conservatives, who formed an influential majority in the Assembly, were by no means reconciled to the republican form of government. They entertained a fear that a single elective chamber "might too easily be stampeded" and in order to check the turbulence of democracy they desired to set up a conservative Senate with effective powers, the same motives which, *inter alia,* swayed the framers of the American Constitution. They ultimately triumphed and the National Assembly agreed to provide for a bicameral legislature in the Constitution of the Third Republic. Because of the lengthy term of office (elected for nine years, one-third retiring every three years), the tradition of reelecting outgoing members, and the higher average age of the Senators, the Senate proved to be a sober and dignified body and as it was natural influence went with seniority. It attracted the ablest politicians and seasoned statesmen which increased its authority and attractiveness at the cost of the representative chamber, the Chamber of Deputies.

The Senate possessed co-equal powers with the Chamber of Deputies. But it rarely rejected Bills outright. Those it disliked were simply buried in committees from which they never emerged. In the beginning, the Senate did not challenge Governments. The provisions of the Constitution were vague regarding the responsibility of the Government. Custom rather than the law, however, became the decisive factor and the Senate was responsible for dismissing two Ministries before 1914 and a third in 1925. In the last ten years of the Third Republic it dismissed four.

When the collapse of 1940 occurred, the two chambers sitting together as a National Assembly voted themselves out of authority and abdicated their powers in the hands of Marshal Petain thereby signing the death warrant of the Third Republic. After the liberation, provisional government was set up in Paris with General De Gaulle at its head, aided by a ministry and a consultative assembly. The first constitution, which was submitted to a referendum of the people in May 1946, and rejected, contained no second chamber at all. The Socialists and the Communists combined together and refused to compromise in this matter. While no considerable group desired a restoration of the old Senate, as it had functioned under the Third Republic, there was nevertheless a widespread feeling that some kind of upper chamber was desirable.

In the Second Constituent Assembly the battle was fought out between the Radicals and their supporters who fovoured a virtual return of the old Senate. M. R. P., like De Gaulle, wanted a broadly corporate chamber, representing colonial and professional interests as well as local authorities. The Communists and the Socialists preferred no second chamber at all, but recognizing that there must be one if the constitution was to be accepted at the poll, it

1. Munro, W. B., *The Government of Europe,* p. 397.

must be feeble and submissive. The Constitution of 1946, therefore, provided for two chambers, the national Assembly and the Council of the Republic, a shadowy bicameralism indeed. The framers of the constitution had intended the Council of the Republic to act simply as "a council of reflection", and not a "council of action" M. Paul Coste-Floret, General Reportter on the Constitution, while summing up the legislative structure established for the Fourth Republic, maintained that it was one of "incomplete bicameralism" or of "tampered mono cameralism."

The Senate under the 1958 Constitution is indirectly elected for a term of nine years, one-third retiring after every three years. Except for age, which is 35 years for the Senators, other qualifications are the same for candidates seeking election to this Chamber as those required for election to the National Assembly, including the obligation to name a substitute. The National Assembly is a representative chamber elected for a term of five years by universal suffrage. General De Gaulle conceived the Senate as the Chamber whose detachment and wisdom would provide for a balance against the National Assembly. While deprived of the right to overthrow the Cabinet, the Senators were given an ironclad vote over legislation if the Prime Minister and the Government desired it.[2] The two Chambers have equal powers, except that the budget originates in the National Assembly. The Senate cannot introduce a vote of censure, the cabinet is responsible only to the National Assembly. In case of persistent disagreement between the two Chambers, which had not been resolved even at their joint conference, the Prime Minister may ask the National Assembly to rule "definitivly.

Unlike the British monarch and the President of India, the French President under the Fifth Republic is not a component part of Parliament. Article 24 of the Constitution states that Parliament "shall comprise the National Assembly and the Senate." This provision is comparable to the Constitution of the United States. Article I provides, "All legislative powers, herein granted, shall be vested in a Congress of the United States which shall consist of a Senate and House of Representatives." But unlike the American President, the Constitution of France vests in its President significant legislative powers.

**A "Rationalised" Parliament**

In order to bring about a change in the behaviour of parliamentarians, the framers of the 1958 Constitution created a "rationalised" Parliament in an effort to enhance the position of the Government and remove the defects of "Assembly Government" as experienced during the previous two Republics. Their object was to limit Parliament to the performance of its proper functions of deliberation and supervision and not of blocking executive action, that is, to protect the executive from "legislative encroachments."[3] The Constitution, accordingly, deals with legislative procedure in much more details than previous Constitutions had done. "A number of matters traditionally left for Parliament to decide are now constitutionalized."[4] Parliamentary Standing Orders, for example, must be found in accord with the Constitution by the Constitutional Council before they become effective. Only two sessions of each Parliament are to be held on dates specified in the Constitution and their duration has also been determined by the Fundamental law.[5] Extraordinary sessions may take place on the request of the Prime Minister or of the majority of the members of the National Assembly "on a specific agenda."[6] They are convened and closed by a decree of the President of the Republic,[7] who, it appears now, seems to have the last word on whether to convene an extraordinary session or not, despite the terms of the Constitution. The number of Parliamentary Commissions has been reduced and their functions are carefully curtailed.[8] The Government now determines the order of business in a Chamber,[9] and Parliament can legislate on matters defined in the Constitution.[10] Matters

2. Chap. III *ante*.
3. Macridis, Roy C. and Ward, Robert E., *Modern Political Systems : Europe*, p. 261.
4. Pickles, Dorothy, *The Fifth French Republic*, p. 89.
5. Article 28.
6. Article 29.
7. Article 30.
8. Article 43.
9. Article 48.
10. Article 34.

other than those defined in the Constitution are subject to the rule-making power of the Government.[11] Annual election of the President of the National Assembly has been changed into the whole legislative term and the Senate elects its President every three years. Both the Presidents, therefore, no longer depend upon the mercy of the Chambers every year. This provision has enhanced the prestige and authority of the presiding officers and ensures their independence and impartiality. The Government is empowered to reject all amendments and to demand a single vote on its own text with only those amendments that it accepts.[12]

By constitutionalizing the procedural rules, the framers of the Constitution made a genuine effort to correct some of the more flagrant abuses of the past, to diminish the opportunities of conflict in the general organization of Parliament, and to reduce possibilities of "guerrilla and open warfare" during the debates over general legislation. The process and operation of censure motions have been severely restricted[13] and the classic procedure of the "interpellation" abolished. The extended power of dissolution[14] given to the President of the Republic makes the members of the National Assembly less disposed to show vindictiveness against the Government "if they know that they might rock their own boat trying to sink the executive ship."[15] Finally an overall control of parliamentary activity is provided by the possible intervention of the Constitutional Council.[16]

Thus, the constitutional provisions and Parliamentary Standing Orders are designed to weaken the Parliament and to strengthen and enhance the influence and prestige of the Executive. The powers of the National Assembly have, in the last analysis, diminished in relation to the Government and its prestige has suffered in relation to the Senate. In the Fourth Republic, the Senate, renamed the Council of the Republic, had no overriding power to legislation. The framers of the 1958 Constitution increased the powers of the Senate and magnified its position especially by giving the authority to veto all Bills if the Government so desired.

**Restrictions on Parliament**

The Constitution of 1958, like its predecessor Republican Constitution, establishes a secular, democratic and social Republic"[17] and proclaims that sovereignty belongs to the people "who shall exercise it through their representatives and by way of referendum."[18] The authentic expression of popular channels are, therefore, the institutions of Parliament and the referendum. The Parliament is not the only institution to express it and its will can be negatived by the people themselves at a referendum. Referendum, accordingly, cancels the proposition that the Parliament is the manifestation of the will of the people and mirror of their sovereign power. But the most important innovation of the Constitution of the Fifth Republic is the restrictions imposed on the jurisdiction and scope of activity of the Parliament. Through the device of a "rationalised" parliament, a deliberate attempt was made by the framers of the Constitution to diminish the powers of the National Assembly in relation to the Government and undermine its prestige in relation to the Senate, not a popularly elected Chamber.

**Functions of Parliament**

The Constitution describes and defines the functions of Parliament and they are distinctly three in number. Its legislative functions are defined in Article 34 and extend to:

"the rules concerning civil rights and the fundamental guarantees accorded to citizens for the exercise of civil liberties; the obligations imposed for national defence on the persons and property of citizens; nationality, status and legal capacity of persons; marriage agreements; inheritance and gifts: determination of crimes and misdemeanours as well as the penalties applicable to them: criminal procedure; amnesty; the creation of new types of jurisdiction and the status of the judiciary;

the basis, rate and method of collecting taxes of all kinds; the currency system:

the electoral systems for the Houses of Parliament and the local assemblies:

11. Article 37.
12. Article 44.
13. Article 49, Chap. IV *ante.*
14. Article 12.
15. Blondell, Jean, and Godfrey, E. D., *The Government of France,* p. 60.
16. Article 61. Chap. II *ante.*
17. Article 2.
18. Article 3.

the creation of categories of public corporations;

the fundamental guarantees accorded to the civil and military personnel of the State:

the nationalization of enterprises and the transfer of the property of enterprises from the public to the private sector;

(and the) fundamental principles of:

the general organization of national defence: the free administration of local entities, the extent of their jurisdiction and of their resources;

education;

property rights, civil and commercial obligations;

legislation pertaining to employment, unions and social security.''

After enumerating the legislative scope of Parliament Article 34 provides: ''The provisions of the present article may be elaborated and completed by an organic law.'' It means that this enumeration of legislative power cannot be enlarged except by an organic law, that is, a law passed by an absolute majority of members of both Houses of Parliament. Organic laws are promulgated only when the Constitutional Council has declared that they are in conformity with the Constitution. Article 37 makes this point clear. It states. ''Matters other than those which are in the domain of law shall be subject to the rule-making power.'' It goes even further and adds, ''Documents in the form of laws, but dealing with matters falling within the rule-making field, may be modified by decrees issued after consultation with the Council of State.'' Thus, laws enacted under the Fourth Republic dealing with matters that are declared by the Constitution of 1958 to be beyond the competence of Parliament can be modified by a decree. They are, therefore, ''delegalized.''

Apart from the rule-making power of the executive, the Government may also with the permission of Parliament, take over, for a limited period, responsibility for dealing with matters defined by the Constitution in Article 34 as properly belonging to Parliament. Article 38 prescribes: ''The Government may, in order to impelement its programme, request of Parliament authorization to take by ordinance, during a limited period of time, measures which are normally within the domain of law.''

There is nothing exceptional or extraordinary in authorizing the executive to make rules and regulations in pursuance of authority delegated to it, or to issue decrees or promulgate ordinances. Such had been the practice in the Third and Fourth Republics. But all such decrees or ordinances were temporary measures devised for exceptional circumstances or to meet exceptional conditions. All the same, supremacy of Parliament was kept intact. Parliament remained the final judge of the extent and duration of special powers accorded to Governments to legislate by decrees. And to crown this, such decrees were subject to ratification by Parliament. But under the Constitution of the Fifth Republic the legislative scope is neatly defined and beyond that the Government deals by executive action and may even take over, for a limited period, with the permission of Parliament responsibility for dealing with matters defined by the Constitution as properly belonging to the domain of law and, accordingly, within the competence of Parliament itself. This is, really, uprcedented. Moreover, to define a 'legislative sphere' is really the first serious attempt in French Republican history. ''The legislative domain,'' as Dorothy Pickles remarks, ''was, up to 1958, anything claimed by Parliament as such.''[19] There may be a reasonable justification in the arguments that by curtailing the legislative sphere the intention was to remove the disabilities of the Third and Fourth Republics when the Government had to fight inch by an inch to survive, but this is no answer to the question. By strictly limiting its legislative sphere Parliament has lost its incentive to efficiency and reduced its capacity to adequately control and supervise the executive.

With regard to budget and financial bills the 1958 Constitution ''consecrates the 'executive budget','' as Macridis and Ward remark.[20] The procedure for voting finance bills is designed to prevent the National Assembly from using delaying tactics as it did under the Fourth Republic. The finance bill is submitted by Government to Parliament. Proposals emanating from members of Parliament are out of order if their adoption entails either a reduction in public revenues or an increase in public expenditure.[21] Article 47 prescribes the procedure for enacting the finance bill. If the National As-

19. Dorothy Pickles, *The Fifth French Republic*, p. 101.
20. Macridis, Roy C., and Ward, Robert E., *Modern Political Systems : Europe*, p. 263.
21. Article 40.

sembly does not complete the first reading of the Finance Bill within forty days, the Government sends the Bill to the Senate to be read within two weeks. If the Senate does not vote it within seventy days the Government may promulgate and put into effect its provisions by ordinance. If the Government has failed to introduce the Finance Bill in time to be promulgated before the beginning of the financial year, it may ask Parliament to authorize taxation by decree and to authorize expenditure in respect of any estimates previously accepted by the National Assembly.

Whatever be the merits of procedure prescribed for voting Finance Bills, it is really unimaginable to think of "executive budget" in a Republican Government and by-passing Parliament in case its two Houses fail to reach an agreement.[22] And agreement between two Houses on fiscal matters is as undemocratic as an "executive budget.' A representative Chamber in all democratic countries is the embodiment of popular sovereignty and an arbiter of financial matters. The origin of Parliament can, indeed, be found in the old but ever resplendent democratic axiom: no taxation without representation and that had been the course of history in every democratic country.

The Constitutional Council limits the authority of Parliament in three ways. Firstly, the Constitutional Council "regulates the regularity" of election of the Deputies and the Senators and ensures the regularity of referendum procedure and declares results thereof[23]. Both these cases fall within the traditional domain of the Parliament and, as such, diminish the authority of that body. Secondly, Parliamentary Standing Orders, which determine the legislative procedure and are the legitimate right of legislative assemblies, are required to be submitted to the Constitutional Council, before they become operative, and decision obtained there from about their conformity to the Constitution.[24] Finally, my Deputies and Senators have questioned the impartiality of the Constitutional Council, particularly on matters relating to specific disputes arising between Government and Parliament with a view to ensure that each organ of Government keeps within the sphere of its own jurisdiction. All this in effect have further added to the restrictions imposed by the Constitution on the powers and jurisdiction of Parliament. The decisions of the Constitutional Council, remarks Dorothy Pickles, "during the first years of the regime were, in fact, always restrictive of what parliament held to be its rights. The Constitutional Council played a not unimportant part in bringing about the worsening of relations between Government and Parliament which became one of the most characteristic features of the regime."[25]

### Privileges of Members

Members of Parliament enjoy certain privileges. No member of Parliament can be prosecuted, sought out, arrested, retained or tried on account of opinions expressed or votes cast by him in the performance of his functions. No member of Parliament may be prosecuted or arrested on criminal or misdemeanour charges during sessions of Parliament without authorization of the House of which he is a member, except in case of *flagrante delicto* (in the very act).[26] In the latter cases (when caught *flagrante delicto)* he may be arrested, though the House is still free to stop proceedings. When Parliament is not in session, a member can be arrested only with the authorization of the bureau of the House to which he belongs, except in cases where the arrest is *flagrante delicto,* or where a court has made a final finding, or where arrest had been authorized in a previous session.

### Obligations of the Members

The Constitution also prescribes certain obligations of the members of Parliament. Certain occupations are incompatible with membership of Parliament. Most of such incompatibilities were also present in the Third and Fourth Republics. The Constitution of the Fifth Republic has added to this list and, among others, include directorship of nationalised and State subsidised concerns, or of concerns carrying out public-works contracts, legal representation of concerns involved in actions against the State. In all these cases the member's resignation is followed by a by-election.

Article 27 prohibits mandatory instructions to membess of Parliament. The same Arti-

22. Article 59.
23. Article 60.
24. Article 61.
25. Dorothy Pickles, *The Fifth French Republic,* p. 107.
26. Article 26.

cle also prohibits members from voting by proxy. The voting right of members of Parliament, it says, is personal. Under the Fourth Republic absenteeism was a regular feature and proxy voting used to be general. Either one member of the group cast the votes for whole group, or members of a group handed over their signed voting papers to one or more proxies, who voted on their behalf. "One result of this system was that debates which were in actual fact conducted before almost empty benches could be followed by votes including upwards of 75 per cent of the membership of the House."[27] The Constitution of the Fifth Republic has attempted to change all this. A member of Parliament may now delegate his vote for five reasons, duly notified in writing in advance.[28] They are: absence from a sitting on grounds of illness, accident or family circumstances; absence on a Government mission or on military service; absence from France on the occasion of a special session of Parliament; or due to representation of the Senate or Assembly at a meeting of an international Assembly. No single member can cast more than one proxy vote at a time.

The Constitution also requires that members must vote regularly. The salary of the members is now divided into two parts: the basic salary, and an 'attendance bonus'. The exact nature of determining the 'attendance bonus' and the manner by which members are to be penalized for non-attendance is decided by each House itself. The Standing Orders of the National Assembly provide that absence from three consecutive Commission sittings without valid reasons entails the resignation of the member concerned from the Commission and a loss of a third of the attendance bonus, until the opening of the following session of the Assembly in October. Absence without valid reasons from more than a third of the votes by ballot in any month entails the loss of one-third of the monthly attendance bonus. If a member absents himself from exercising votes personally, he forfeits two thirds of his attendance bonus.

## GENERAL ORGANIZATION OF PARLIAMENTARY BUSINESS

### Sessions of Parliament

Parliament now meets on fixed dates and for a fixed duration. Article 28, as amended in December 1963, provides for two regular sessions, the first beginning from October 2 and it lasts for 80 days. The second session opens on April 2 and its duration is not to exceed ninety days. Parliament, therefore, now sits for a maximum of less than six months in a year whereas under the Fourth Republic it sat for a minimum of seven months. The first session beginning in October deals mainly with the budget and the second with the legislative programme. Extraordinary session is held at the request by the President of the Republic, or the Prime Minister or of a majority of the members of the National Assembly, for a specific agenda. If the extraordinary session is held at the request of a majority of members of the Assembly, the session must be closed as soon as the specific agenda has been completed and, in any case after a period not exceeding twelve days.[29] In addition, Parliament meets on two occasions, after an election, for a special session of up to a fortnight, and during a period of application of Article 16, when it is entitled to sit for the duration of the emergency.

### Presiding Officer

Each House elects its bureau, at the beginning of the October session, consisting of its President, Vice-Presidents (six for the Assembly, and four for the Senate), Secretaries (twelve for the Assembly and eight for the Senate) and the *Questeurs* (three for each House). The Secretaries supervise the production of the official records and check the votes. The *Questeurs* are responsible for administrative and financial arrangements. The functions of the *bureau* as a collective body are to organize and supervise the different services in the House, and if required to assist the Presiding officer on a number of points, particularly on disciplinary matters and the admissibility of Bills or resolutions.

The Presiding officer (President) of each House is elected at the first meeting of the session, Formerly elected annually, the President of the National Assembly is now elected for the duration of the House. The President of the Senate is, however, elected after each partial re-election of the House; after every three years. The President of the Senate now performs the

27. Dorothy Pickles, *The Fifth French Republic*, p. 91.
28. Article 27 provides, "Organic law may, in exceptional circumstances, authorize proxy voting. In that case no one may exercise more than one proxy."
29. Article 29.

functions of the President of the Republic if incapacitated, and not the President of the National Assembly as heretofore.

In the main, functions of the two Presidents are similar. But neither of the two approximates the Speaker of the House of Commons. They resemble the Speaker of the House of Representatives more or less. Though of necessity impartial in the actual conduct of debate, ''they do attempt to influence, by informally talking to members, the conduct of business.''[30] Before 1958, these offices were stepping stones to the Presidency. Vincent Auriol was the President of the National Assembly when he was elected President of the Republic.

The 1958 Constitution vests in both the Presidents certain specific powers. The Presidents of the National Assembly and the Senate must be consulted by the President of the Republic as to the existence of an emergency as defined in Article 16. A private member's Bill, resolution or amendment which the President of the House holds to be constitutional, but the Government challenges it as unconstitutional, must be either submitted by him to the Constitutional Council or ruled out of order.''[31] Under the Standing Orders of the Assembly and the Senate the Presidents of both the Houses enjoy somewhat more discretion than their predecessors under the Third and Fourth Republics, particularly in calling members to order, and in calling for the closure of the debates.

The Parliamentary timetable is drawn up every week by *la Conference des Presidents, a* meeting of the President and Vice-Presidents of the Assembly, and of heads of Parliamentary groups, Presidents of Commissions, and the *rapporteur general* (Reporter General) of the Finance Commission. Voting in this body is weighed in proportion to party strength. Previously, the prestige of the Government and the extent of its persuasiveness influenced its decisions. The Constitution of 1958 now gives the Government effective control over the timetable by giving priority to Government Bills and to those Private Members' Bills acceptable to the Government.[32]

In France there exist quite a number of Parliamentary groups not always classified as belonging definitely to Government or to Opposition side. French Parliamentary procedure has been taking into account the existence of such Parliamentary groups. But only organized groups, that is, groups with membership of 30 or more are now represented at the *Conference des Presidents* and on the Parliamentary Commissions into which each House is divided for purposes of legislation. The traditional method of evading the regulations of minimum membership, by tacking on a number of isolated members or small groups for administrative purposes, is now prohibited. Groups are now represented on Commissions in proportion to their strength in the House, including affiliates (apparentes-affiliated members or groups). If there remain any more vacancies after seats have been allotted to groups, isolated members can become members of Commissions provided they are elected by the whole House.

## LEGISLATIVE PROCEDURE

### How a Bill Becomes Law

Bills may be introduced in either of the two Houses of Parliament and have their first reading in the House where they originate, except for finance Bills which must be submitted and read first in the National Assembly.[33] The legislative initiative is exercised concurrently by the Prime Minister and by the members of Parliament.[34] Private members' Bills are not in order if they involve a decrease in public revenues or the creation or increase of public expenditure.[35] If it appears in the course of legislative process that a Private member's Bill, or amendment thereto is not constitutional, the Government may request the President of the House to rule it out. In case of disagreement between the Government and the President of the House concerned, the Constitutional Council, at the request of either the Government or President of the House, gives a ruling thereupon within one week from the date of its reference.

Immediately after the introduction of the bill. it is sent to one of the six Commissions (committees) of the House, or, on the request of

30. Blondell, J., and Godfrey, E. D., *The Government of France*, p. 63.
31. Article 41.
32. Article 48.
33. Article 39.
34. *Ibid.*
35. Article 40.

either Government or the House itself, to an ad hoc Commission. The Commission discusses the bill, may adopt it, dismiss or amend it. Each Bill has a *Rapporteur* from the Commission who reports it to the House, which discusses the Bill first in general, then article by article and votes on each article. There is then a final vote on the Bill as a whole, as amended. This completes what is called the first reading. It then goes to the other House, which follows the same procedure. If both Houses agree on the same text, the Bill is sent to the President of the Republic within fifteen days of its transmission to the Government. The President has no veto power, but he possesses a sort of suspensive veto. Article 10 provides, ''He may, before the expiration of this limit (fifteen days), ask Parliament for a reconsideration of the law or of certain of its articles. This reconsideration may not be refused.'' It is, however, very rare that the President asks for reconsideration of the Bill by Parliament, but if asked for it is normally on the ground of technical errors which had been overlooked by Parliament.

In case of disagreement between the two Houses of Parliament, the Bill is read for the second time in each House. If the disagreement still continues, a joint committee of the two Houses, comprising an equal number of members of each House, is set up with a view to proposing a common text for the provisions on which disagreement remains. The text prepared by the joint committee may be submitted by the Government for approval of the two Houses. No amendments are in order unless the Government agrees thereto.

If the joint committee does not adopt a joint version, the Government may, after a new reading by the National Assembly and the Senate, ask the National Assembly to rule definitely. In that case, the National Assembly may take either the version prepared by the joint committee, or the last version passed by the Assembly, modified as appropriate by one or more of the amendments adopted by the Senate.[36] If the Government does not intervene and ask the Assembly to rule definitely, the Bill dies. The Senate, thus, possesses a veto power over the National Assembly, if the Government so desires.

**Financial Procedure**

The voting of finance is subject to special procedure laid down in the Constitution. The procedure is designed to prevent the Assem bly from using delaying tactics. Before 1958, French Parliaments were notorious for their delaying action in respect to the budget. As Jean Blondell and Godfrey point out, ''....; indeed, the budget was customarily one of the hurdles which few Governments passed safely, and this in turn increased delays, as a new Government had to be formed and rethink the budget before the finance bill could be approved,''[37] In order to redress this situation, the Constitution of 1958 consecrates the ''executive budget.'' The budget is submitted by the Government first to the National Assembly. Proposals stemming from members of Parliament ''are not receivable if their adoption would result in a reduction in public revenues or the creation or increase of public expenditures.''[38]

The Constitution of 1958 prescribes a limit of forty days within which the National Assembly must complete the first reading of the Finance Bill. If it does not vote within the specified period, the Government sends the Bill to the Senate to be read within two weeks. If the Bill has not been voted after seventy days, the Government becomes entitled to promulgate the Finance Bill by Ordinance.[39] If the Government has not submitted the Finance Bill in time to be promulgated before the beginning of the fiscal year,[40] it may ask Parliament to authorize taxation by decree and to authorize expenditure in respect of any estimates previously accepted by the National Assembly.[41]

It may be noted that the Finance Bill is voted by both the Houses of Parliament. The Constitution only requires that it should be voted first by the National Assembly.[42] There is no law in France, fundamental or organic, which empowers the National Assembly to override the Senate, as the House of Commons can do in Britain. If the National Assembly and

36. Article 45.
37. Blondell, J., and Godfrey, E. D., *The Government of France,* p. 71.
38. Article 40.
39. Article 47.
40. Financial year ends on 31st December in France.
41. Article 47.
42. Article 39.

the Senate disagree, the procedure for resolving the difference between the two Houses is the same as governing disagreement on an ordinary Bill.[43]

**The Committee system**

Until the Constitution of the Fifth Republic became operative in 1958 the legislative committees in France were engines of power and control and were often in conflict with the Government. They decided the fate of virtually any Bill by amending it, pigeonholing it, or failing to report it. Only the amended text of a Bill could come from the Committee to the floor of the Assembly. And when it reached there, the *Rapporteur* (reporter) of the Commission piloted the Bill and took the lead in the debate and was usually the first on the tribune. He intervened at any time in debate and would make his chief contribution at a point favourable to the success of the debate and the work of the Committee. It would very often even mean vigorous criticism of the Government, for Committee Chairmen and Rapporteurs were potential candidates for ministerial office. ''The leaders of the committees,'' observed Philips Williams. ''had an evident interest in opposing the Government: and the greater the prestige and solidarity of their committee, the liklier they were to succeed.''[45]

This situation has drastically been altered by the Constitution of 1958. Article 43 limits to six the number of permanent Committees in each House.[46] They formerly numbered 19, each having 44 members. The purpose sought in reducing the number of Committees is twofold. First, to reduce the authority of the Committees, whose Presidents when the field of activity of the Committees coincided with that of a Ministry, tended to become shadow Ministers. Secondly, in pre 1958 Parliaments a Bill, whose scope was such as to interest more than one Ministry, was submitted to many Committees and it was a time consuming process. For instance, the bill to ratify the E.D.C. Treaty in 1954 was submitted to the Foreign Affairs Committee to report, and also to four other Committees for their opinion. The reduction in the number of the Committees now aims to prevent the time-wasting process, although the Standing Orders also provide for the practice of submitting Bills to more than one Committee.

The composition of the six regular Committees varies from 60 to 120 members, nominated to represent proportionately the political parties. Only organized groups, with thirty members or more, are now represented on the Committees. Isolated members can become members of Committees only if elected by the whole House to any vacancies remaining after the seats have been allotted to group members. The composition of the Committees has, thus, become more compact and responsible. They no longer remain subject to the vagaries of the unaffiliated groups and isolated members.

The Committees receive the Bills, examine them, hear the Minister, and suggest changes. But the Government has the last word on bringing the Bills on the floor of the House and on accepting or rejecting the amendments made. Article 42 states that the discussion on the floor of the House has to take place on the Government's text. The procedure followed is that debate on a Government Bill begins with a ministerial declaration and, then Committee's report is presented. Formerly, the debate took place on the basis of the Committee's amended text and not on the Government's Bill, and the *Rapporteur,* not the Minister, was responsible for piloting the Bill through the House. The 1958 Constitution has changed all that and the result is that the legislative work has been expedited and improved in many respects, while the Government no longer remains at the mercy of Committees that were often inspired by parochial considerations.

**Relations between the two Houses**

Both the Houses possess identical powers, except that the Finance Bill has its first reading in the National Assembly. The 1958 Constitution does not permit the Assembly to override the Senate, as it could under the Constitution of the Fourth Republic, unless the Government decides to intervene on the side of the Assembly. In other words, the Senate has been given veto over legislation if Government so desires. If the Government does not intervene, a Bill on which both the Houses disagree can shuttle between the national Assembly and the Senate indefinitely. Moreover, Article 45 does not provide for putting an end to persistent dis-

---

43. Article 45.
44. Philip Williams, *Politics in Post-War France,* p. 238.
45. They are : Foreign Affairs; Finance, National Defence; Constitutional Laws, Legislation, and General Administration; Production and Trade; and Cultural, Social, and Family Affairs.

agreement between the two Houses. The Joint Committee of the two Houses set up at the request of the Prime Minister in case of disagreement deals only with articles on which agreement has still not been reached, that is, provisions on which disagreement remains.

If the Government intervenes, "it may do either passively or actively." In the former case, the Prime Minister may, after the Bill has been read twice in each House, ask for setting up a joint committee composed of equal number of members from each House. If the joint committee reaches an agreement the version prepared by it is then submitted by the Government for approval by the two Houses. No amendment is in order without the Government's agreement. If the Joint Committee does not agree, or if the version of the Committee is rejected by either House, the two Houses may make further efforts to agree or drop the Bill, or shelve it. But if the government intervenes actively, the Government may ask the National Assembly to rule definitely thereon; if the disagreement still persists. In order to override the Senate the Assembly requires only an ordinary majority vote on the Bill, unless it is organic.

All this means that in case the Government is not interested in the enactment of a legislative measure, the Senate can effectively block legislation. The relationship between the two Houses, then, assumes the same form as it existed between the two Houses under the Constitution of 1875, that is, both Houses of Parliament possessing co-ordinate powers, independent and equal to each other.

The Senate does not control the executive and the Government is responsible to the National Assembly alone. Obviously a subordinate chamber, it really possesses co-equal legislative powers with the National Assembly and exercises an effective right of veto over any change in its status. In fact, the Senate's position has considerably been improved and its authority increased by the 1958 Constitution. The President of the Senate replaces the President of the Republic; if incapacitated, until the new President is elected. It is the constitutional duty of the President of the Republic to consult the President of the Senate before the application of emergency measures under Article 16, and on the desirability of dissolution. The President has the right to submit certain Bills in certain circumstances to the Constitutional Council, and, like the President of the National Assembly, to nominate three members to the Constitutional Council. The Senate has the right to equal representation with the Assembly in the High Court of Justice. The National Assembly needs the concurrence of the Senate before requesting a referendum. Finally, the Senate has the right to receive Presidential messages from the President. Article 18 provides: "The President of the Republic shall communicate with the two Assemblies of Parliament by means of messages, which he shall cause to be read and which shall not be an occasion for any debate."

## SUGGESTED READINGS

Ambler, J.S., *The French Army in Politics.*

Ardagh, J., *The New French Revolution.*

Aron, Raymond, *France, Steadfast and Changing.*

Avril, P. *Politics in France.*

Campbell, P. *French Electoral Systems.*

Crawley, A. *De Gaulle.*

Ehrmann, H.W. *Politics in France.*

MacRae, D., *Parliament, Parties and Society in France.*

Pickles, Dorothy, *The Fifth French Republic.*

Thombon. D., *Democracy in France.*

Williams, P.M. *The French Parliament.*

# CHAPTER VI

# French Law and Law Courts

## Sources and Nature of French Law

In the main French law is built solidly upon Roman Law. The Romans held Gaul for a longer time than they occupied Britain and left upon it permanent impress of their culture and their laws. The law of Rome, once planted, was never uprooted and has persisted as a basic influence throughout all later times. And when the country ''arrived at a single, uniform legal system, the Roman heritage supplied much of the foundation, framework and ornamentation of the structure.''[1]

During the Middle Ages the field was largely taken by the customary law. France became the classic land of feudalism. But there the feudal kings had never been able to extend their actual jurisdiction beyond their own dominions. The dukes and counts were too powerful in their own dominions to be controlled by their king. Hence there grew up in every local area its own system of customary law, its own *Coutume,* as it was called. These in due course of time were put into written form and administered by the local courts. No attempt was ever made to weld these customary laws into a single nation-wide system comparable to the English common law. As late as the middle of the eighteenth century Voltaire remarked that a traveller in his country had to change laws almost as often as he changed horses. Added to this complexity and confusion were an increasing number of royal decrees, ordinances or edicts applying sometimes to the entire country, sometimes to specified sections only. Before such edicts could take effect, they were required to be registered by the various regional courts, known as *parliaments.* Some parliaments, one like that of Paris, even refused to register certain edicts. But this did not create any serious impediment, because the king could force such *parliament* to register the edict.

The leaders of the French Revolution were fully seized of the weakness of such a confused and overlapping legal system. They knew that the legal decentralisation as it prevailed in France constituted a barrier to the creation of national unity and impeded the growth of fraternity *(fraternite)* which the Revolution was seeking to establish. They also felt that the *coutumes* were mediaeval in spirit and, accordingly, incompatible with the new political and social order. The revolutionists, therefore, set to the task of abolishing customary law and overhauling or rescinding the ordinances. New and uniform laws, in the form of statutes, were enacted, and old and new laws were consolidated and codified. In 1791 and 1795, the first Penal Code and Code of Criminal Procedure were enacted.

But it was not until Napoleon Bonaparte came into power, as first Consul, that the work of codifying the whole jurisprudence of France was speeded up and finished. The Corsican went at the project with characteristic energy, and completed it within a few years. The Civil Code which was published in 1804 was the first of a series followed in 1807 by a Code of Civil Procedure. Other Codes were enacted subsequently. In all of them, the predominant influence of Roman Law was paramount. These Codes have been revised and amended, but the fundamentals remain unchanged and are the living law of France as also that of numerous other countries which have since adopted them.

## Characteristics of French Law

The law of France today consists primarily of the Napoleonic Code as amended, revised and extended at intervals to meet the new conditions and needs of the country, especially those flowing from increasing industrialization and other economic changes. This brings in four outstanding characteristics of French law. France has, in the first place, a uniform system of law throughout the country. There is unity and symmetry in it and the law, as embodied in the codes, is clear and easily available. In the second place, it is a written law and, as such, essentially differs from the law of English-speaking countries. There is no doubt, much of the written law in England and America, but in

1. Ogg, F., and Zink, H., *Major Foreign Governments*, p. 563.

both countries, that great mass of jurisprudence as the common law is largely unwritten and uncodified. In France, there is virtually no law that is not codified and cannot be read in the books.

In the third place, French law is enacted or statutory, although at many points it may be rooted in customs. In England and in the United States the law is being constantly developed, expanded and even altered by judicial decisions and both these countries have built up great bodies of judge-made law. It is true that according to the theory of Anglo-American Jurisprudence the judges cannot make law. They only interpret and apply it, but they do in fact make changes and often far-reaching changes. A judicial decision rendered sets a precedent and there is a traditional respect with the courts to a doctrine of *stare decisis,* that is, a court will always be guided by a previous decision unless there is a compelling reason for reversal. The result is that "one judicial decision advances little upon another, and so on year after year, until there exists a wide gulf between the law as it is and the law as it was. Simple words and phrases receive new shades of meaning, and ultimately acquire new meaning altogether." In this way, the doctrine of *stare decisis* gives a definite drift and direction. In France there is no such doctrine. The judges decide every case independently on its merits in conformity with the statutory law aiming at justice in the particular case and not in conformity with the precedent. No court is under any obligation to be guided by its own previous decisions or even by the decisions of a higher court. Precedents are cited in French courts, but no great reliance is placed upon them and the judges "are free to disregard even the weightiest precedents if they feel so inclined."

Finally, distinction is made in France between the ordinary law and administrative law and, consequently, there are two separate systems of courts, ordinary tribunals and administrative tribunals. In case of conflict on the jurisdiction of courts, there is a Tribunal of conflicts which decides whether a case falls within the competence of one set of courts or the other.

## JUDGES AND JUDICIAL PROCEDURE

With regard to organisation of Ordinary courts there are certain important general features :

1. The first is the unity of civil and criminal justice. That is, unlike England and the United States where there are separate civil and criminal courts, civil and criminal actions in France are for the most part handled by the same court. The same judges sit in both courts. The practice is some judges sit in the civil courts and they are drawn for the trial, when necessary, of criminal cases. Similarly, the public prosecutors, known as the *parquet,* are occupied with civil as well as criminal cases, though attached to the civil courts. There is, however, a separation between the two in the higher courts and they are divided into civil and criminal sections.

2. There is in France no system of circuit courts except in the case of Assize Courts. The courts are stationary and litigants go to the judges rather than judges going to the litigants. The English and American system of circuit judges has never been adopted in France.

3. French courts are collegial. No French court is allowed to give judgment, as in England, with only one judge making the court, and no judgment is valid unless concurred in by at least three of the judges constituting the bench. The principle of collegiality is insisted by the French to rule out prejudice and, thus, as a condition of justice.

4. Trial by jury is not ubiquitous in France and one of the reasons for it is that courts are manned by a collegial arrangement. The tendency of the juries to be swayed by passionate pleadings does not commend their spread beyond the courts in which they are employed. One well-known French jurist declared that in many cases the courts might as well "allow justice to depend upon a throw of the dice as upon the verdict of the jury." Others have stigmatised the French jury, "as a sacrifice of common sense to an Anglo-Saxon superstition, and one that merely works havoc with the orderly administration of justice."

In the courts where jury continues to be employed, it consists of twelve persons chosen by lot from a panel of citizens. The decisions are reached by majority vote. When votes stand six to six, or seven to five, for conviction, the three judges, if they are unanimous, may render a verdict of acquittal.

### Appointment of Judges

During the Third Republic judges were appointed by the Minister of Justice. This method of appointment was severely criticised as it interfered with the independence of judges and very often politically unpopular judges could be denied promotion. The Constitution of the Fourth Republic attempted to remedy this by creating the Higher Council of the Magistracy. This Council consisting of 14 members including the President of the Republic as chairman and the Minister of Justice, evaluated the qualifications and merits of the judge-candidates and recommended a panel of names to the President of the Republic and selection was made therefrom. The Constitution of the Fifth Republic retains the Higher Council of Judiciary but with restricted functions and somewhat different methods of appointment. It consists of the President of the Republic (chairman), the Minister of Justice *(ex-officio* chairman), and nine members appointed by the President of the Republic. The Council nominates judges to the higher judicial posts and rules on matters involving the judicary.[2] The *magistrature*, the magistracy, in which there are clearly defined ranks and schedules of promotions, and which is entered through a specialised school, the *Centre National d' Etudes Judiciaries,* is open to law graduates successful in a competitive examination. The judiciary at the lower level is a career service.

**Independence of the Judiciary**

"By and large," say Ogg and Zink, "French courts and Judges compare favourably in capacity, integrity, independence and impartiality, with those of any other country." Article 64 of the 1958 Constitution specifies that judges shall be irremovable. The Constitution of the Fourth Republic had made a similar provision. The Constitution of 1948 declared irremovability incompatible with the responsibility of officials in the Republican system of government and the judiciary in France had always been considered as a public service. The Third Republic's constitutional law did not even mention judiciary. According to the Constitution of 1958 judges can be removed from office on charges of gross misconduct only and that too on the recommendation of the Higher Council of Judiciary, which has been entrusted with the constitutional duty of acting as disciplinary council of the judges. The President consults the Higher Council of Judiciary on questions of pardon under conditions determined by an organic law.

**Procedure is Judge-animated**

In the law courts in the United States and Britain criminal cases are initiated by an attorney who prosecutes on behalf of the public. It is his business to make a case. The prisoner is defended by an attorney paid by himself, or, provided he is too poor, by the public funds. The judge is an impartial arbiter between the two rival parties, prosecution and defence. He may ask questions to counsels and witnesses and the accused is tried in an open court. But he is not an interrogator. Nor is there any previous inquisition, except in cases where a grand jury is required for an indictment. The position is different in France. Before the case comes before the judges in court, there is preliminary investigation and this is done by the *juges d' instruction. Juges d' instruction* has the power to order arrest of the suspects and hold them until his investigation is complete. He interrogates them and seizes all documents material to the case. *Juges d' instruction* are attached only to courts of first instance and do not form part of the higher judiciary. They are under the *supervision* of the *parquet.* "Such a man's ambitions," remarks Finer, "are extremely pointed toward promotion. It is a sensitive point in the course of justice, especially since it is connected with the problem of arrest and detention."[3] Finer further adds, "the judge is more than the English judge, a kind of party to the issue : he seeks the facts, whether there is jury or not."

A famous feature of the French courts is the institution of the *parquet,* otherwise known as *the ministere public* or men who act for the public weal. To each court is attached a *parquet* headed by a *procureur,* or state attorney, and composed of a number of assistants to him. In the courts of first instance they are called *substiuts;* in the courts of appeal they are called *arocats-generaux* or *substiuts generaux.* The *parquet* represents the State in courts and conducts prosecutions. For the due performance of his duties the services of the detective are loaned to him. "It embodies the dual interest of securing a conviction, yet also ensuring justice or fairplay for the prisoner." The members of the *parquet* are irremovable and move upward in their own hierarchy. Their main business is in criminal cases, but they may also act in civil cases which are of interest to the State. They

2. Artiole 65.
3. Finer, H., *Governments of Greater European Powers,* p. 516.

see that the judgments and petty decrees are executed.

**Absence of Habeas Corpus**

Nothing resembling *habeas corpus* exists in France. It was tried to be remedied in the Constitution of 1946 which was rejected at the polls. It provided that ''No one may be detained unless within forty-eight hours he has appeared before a judge called to rule upon the legality of his arrest and unless this judge confirms the detention each month by motivated decision.'' The Constitution of the Fourth Republic did not contain any such provision. Article 65 of the 1958 Constitution briefly provided that no person may be detained arbitrarily. It is further provided that judicial authority, ''guardian of the liberty, shall assure respect for this principle in conditions to be determined by law.'' This may be described as a provision for a writ of *habeas corpus,* but there is no express mention thereof.

## THE ORDINARY COURT SYSTEM

**Justice of Peace**

France was covered with a network of numerous courts in order that justice might be easily accessible to all. The organisation of the courts was simple enough. At the bottom was the justice of the peace *(juge de paix),* who was a salaried official with some judicial experience though not ordinarily a law degree. There was one such court at each canton. In some cases, however, the jurisdiction of a justice would extend to two or more cantons. There were in all more than 3,000 such courts. They had a limited and summary jurisdiction over minor offence and civil disputes. A major reform in the number of courts, both civil and criminal, took place in 1958, and as a result of that the 3,000 or so Justice of the Peace courts were abolished. The lowest court is now the *tribunal d' instance* and there are some 454 such courts in France. For most important cases litigants go to the *tribunal de grande instance.* There are 172 such tribunals, less than two on an average per *departement.* These tribunals hear appeals especialy from the judgments of some of the specialized courts, such as *tribunaux de commerce* which deals with commercial cases. Another important set of courts of this kind are the *conseils de prud' hommes,* which deal with disputes between employers and employees over the implementation of labour contracts. *Tribunal de' instance* consists of only one judge, who in addition of his more formal powers also acts much as the Justice of the Peace did in the past. The *tribunal de' grande instance* have three or more judges.

Simple criminal cases are dealt in the Police courts, which function in almost all localities of any importance. More serious cases are brought before the *tribunaux correctionnels* where judges (the same as those of the *tribunaux de' grande instance)* decide cases without juries. Finally, the more serious cases are decided by *cours de assises* (one per *department)* which consists of three judges and nine jurors.

Appeals on matters of facts are generally allowed in civil cases, unless they are not trivial, but not in criminal cases. Appeals on interpretation of laws are always allowed. Both on these counts appeals go to courts of Appeal; twentythree in number.

**Court of Cassation**

The highest court in France is the Court of Cassation. It is called *Cassation* because it may ''break'' the law of the lower court, not the judgment. Cases are brought from any court of last resort for the proper interpretation of law. It accepts the facts determined by previous courts and interprets law remanding the case to another court having the same jurisdiction as that from which the case was brought.

## ADMINISTRATIVE COURTS

**Administrative Courts**

The French courts, fall into a dual hierarchy : the Ordinary Courts dealing with the statutory law, and the Administrative Courts, from the *Conseil de prefecture* (renamed *tribunaux administratif in 1952)* up to the *Conseil d' Etat.* The Ordinary Courts are concerned with the litigation among citizens themselves, and the application of law to citizens. The Administrative Courts are concerned with the acts of the administrative authorities in conflict among themselves, local or central, and the grievances that citizens may have against these authorities.

The reason for this distinction is to be found in the determination of the Revolutionary leaders that the judiciary should have no interference in administration. In their law reforms of August 1790, they declared, ''Judicial functions are distinct and shall always remain separated from administrative functions.'' With the lapse of time it was found that administration could abuse its powers and needed a corrective. Yet the rigid adherence to the theory of separation of powers did not permit the corrective to be administered by the ordinary courts. The Constitution of 1799 established administrative courts and since then administrative courts have become the most lasting institution of France.

**Jurisdiction of Administrative Courts**

State officials and the municipalities as corporate bodies are responsible for their actions and consequently can be sued in the administrative courts and pay damages for any prejudice to life and property caused by defective action. Defective action means the action of the official which is the result of bad judgment or is arbitrary, that is, the result of the violation of the prescribed forms, violation of a law, misuse of power. Maurice Houriou, the eminent authority on administrative jurisprudence, defines defective action as "the negligences, the omissions, the errors among the habits of administration when those habits are bad." The rules which are applied in deciding such cases are called the administrative law. Dicey defines administrative law as that "body of rules which regulate the relations of administration of the administrative authority towards private citizens." The administrative law is not embodied in a code, like the civil law. Some of the rules have been established by the issue of executive decrees, but in large part they have been accumulated by the decisions of the administrative courts, especially by the decisions of the Council of State, *Counsel d' Etat.* Administrative law, thus, somewhat resembles the common law in England which has been slowly built up in the regular courts by one decision after another.

Such a nature of the French system of administrative law covers a wide range. It deals not only with the liability of the State and the municipal bodies for the wrong done to private individuals or their property, but with the rule relating to the validity of the administrative decrees, the methods of granting redress when public officials exceed the authority vested in them by law, the awarding of damages to private individuals for injuries which result from faults of the public service, the distinction between official and personal acts on the part of public officers, and many other allied matters. In sum, if "gives redress in many cases, where none would be available in the United States" and in England where there are no duly constituted administrative courts.

The French system of administrative courts essentially differs from the system of justice obtainable in Britain. In Britain all men and women, officials or not, are amenable to one set of courts—the ordinary courts and the same judges—and are under one system of law. This is the essence of the classic doctrine of the Rule of Law as enunciated by Dicey. Suits against the State and its officials do not form an extensive and separate branch of jurisprudence, though there may exist special courts and commissions for the purpose of adjudicating claims brought by private individuals against the government. The ordinary courts can quash the orders of administration and issue writs commanding action or cessation of action, its correction, or the payment of damages. But in France the ordinary courts can do nothing of the kind. Recourse in such cases must be had to the administrative law courts.

The immunity of public officials from the jurisdiction of the ordinary courts does not extend to anything done by them in a personal or non-official capacity. It does not even extend to acts performed in an official capacity, if the injury results from the personal fault or personal negligence of the officer concerned. The State is suable and will pay where the official acts in good faith for the public. If he does something in office which is not truly in pursuance of its purpose, the official himself is responsible and not the State. He will be sued personally before the ordinary courts for damages and it is the *Tribunal des conflicts* (The Court of Conflicts) which decides whether it is a personal fault or not. For example, an official posts an electoral list, but may make some error in this. This may lead to an administrative case suable in the administrative court. But if the official concerned makes public the view that one of the electors has been excluded because of bankruptcy, this becomes a personal fault, not done in good faith for the public, and the officer is suable by the bankrupt for damages in ordinary courts, not Administrative Courts.

## ORGANISATION OF THE ADMINISTRATIVE COURTS

**Tribunaux Administratifs**

The principal administrative courts in France are the Tribunaux Administratifs and the Counseil d' Etat, the Council of State. At the lower level, the ninety-odd *Counsels de Prefecture* of Napoleon were reduced to twenty-three in 1926 and were renamed *tribunaux administratifs* in 1952. All these twenty-three tribunals are full-fledged courts of first instance in administrative cases. In general, these tribunals hear complaints made by the individuals against the actions of administrative officials. The most prolific source of such complaints is the tax assessments. Other matters over which they have jurisdiction are those relating to public works, especially highways and the conduct of local elections. Each Administrative Tribunal consists of a President and four members appointed by the Minister of the Interior from among persons who hold, or had held, public administrative positions.

**Conseil d' Etat**

At the upper level an appeal court in many cases, but directly competent for the more important problems, is the *Conseil d' Etat.* It is composed of 150 members who are almost entirely recruited through the School of Administration. The Council is divided into several sections, the main distinction being between four advisory sections and a judicial section. The judicial section, in its turn, is divided into a number of chambers in which normally five councillors (conseillers) decide cases on the report of more junior members. More important cases may be decided by as many as ten or fifteen councillors. The Council of State has, thus not only a wide original jurisdiction, but it has also the power of cassation in some cases and appellate authority in others. It has attempted to curb the actions that are inherent in a centralized administrative system and to protect the individual in all the cases where he has no redress before the civil courts.

The Council of the State is an impressive body enjoying the public esteem and confidence. Its litigation section devotes the whole of its time hearing appeals that come before it from the regional courts, hearing also the large number of cases that come to it as a court of first instance, annulling decrees, even of the Council of Ministers as being *ultra vires,* irregular in form, or flowing from the misuse of power, and generally safeguarding the rights and interests of the people. Access to the court is easy, convenient and cheap. Appeals may be lodged in the Council through mail and need include only an official form, on which the complaint is described, and the necessary supporting documents. Even the small fee that the appellant pays is refunded to him if a decision is given in his favour.

French system of administrative law and administrative courts have been the subject of severe criticism in countries which base their legal system on Anglo Saxon law. The critics maintain that justice cannot be expected from and obtained in the administrative courts when administrative branch of the government is made the sole judge of its own actions. When administration is both the offender and the judge of the offence, there can be neither impartiality in the decisions nor the authorities rendering the decisions can act independently. This is a pure and simple encroachment on the essential liberties and fundamental rights of the people. It is further contended that the distinction between *contentions administratives* and *contentions civiles,* the former within the sphere of the administrative courts and the latter within the sphere of the civil courts, is only a subtlety and no harm would come from sending administrative cases to ordinary courts on the Anglo-American plan as this system provides a strict adherence to law. The fact that the ordinary courts deal with cases effecting the administration side by side with other cases makes the officers of the government more responsible and they are kept aware of the necessity of adhering to the regular laws of the land. Finally, advocates of the Anglo-Saxon system point out that the Anglo-Saxon notion of personal liability for abuse of power, regardless of the fact whether the act is committed under orders or not, ''places the weight of personal responsibility, directly on every official and prevents him from 'passing the buck' to his superior.''

But in the light of French experience, it is not true to say that administrative law and the administrative courts jeopardise the rights and liberties of the people. On the contrary, Frenchmen consider it the corner-stone of their liberties. Duguit, the eminent French jurist, affirmed that the great body of case law worked out by the Council of the State affords the individual. ''almost perfect protection against administrative action'' Professor Garner, in his famous article on ''French Administrative Law'' asserted that ''without fear of contradiction in no other country of the world are the rights of individuals so well protected against administrative abuses and the people so sure of receiving reparation for injuries sustained from such abuses.''

There is no justification for suspecting the administrative courts for partiality in favour of the officials. The Council of the State, as the highest administrative tribunal, has established admirable traditions of impartiality. ''Personal acquaintance with a number of *counseillers,* younger and older,'' observes Finer, ''and an insight into the preparation at the *Ecole Nationale d' Administration* (the National School of Administration), warrants the judgment that they have a superb grasp of the law, the doctrine, the nature of the society served by their administration, and an assurance of their probity. They are not bureaucratic tyrants, but men of just and comprehending mind.''

In the context of the Welfare State and consequently the ever-expanding State activity embracing the entire life of the nation involves complicated and technical issues which the lawyer-judges cannot properly appreciate and render judicious decisions. Administrative courts consist of experts on the administrative side who understand the technicalities involved and are in a position to thrash all issues theadbare in order to arrive at the truth and dispense justice. There is always greater possibility of a right judgment when decision is rendered by experts. Moreover, citizens get better and real redress for the injuries sustained, for litigation in the administrative courts is cheap and it is executed repidly. The procedure is simple and there exists decentralized administrative jurisdiction in the twenty-six regional courts, which are courts of first instance, and it cannot be said the justice delayed is justice denied.

Finally, the French system of administrative courts protects public officials against ''vexatious and absurd obstacle such as are often interposed by English and American courts on grounds of mere technicality; in particular by substituting State for personal liability it gives them greater assurance for independence in making decisions and enforcing laws.'' Berthelemy's opinion about the nature of administrative justice is important to cite here. He says, ''Let one be guarded against considering administrative justice as 'exceptional' justice....Administrative justice is not a dismemberment of the justice of the law courts. It is the judicial organ by which the executive power imposes on the active administration the respect for law. The administrative courts have not taken their role from the judicial authority; they are one of the forms by which the administrative authority is exercised. To put the mater even more precisely, it may be said that the administrative tribunals are, towards the acts and decisions of administration, what the courts of appeal are to decisions of inferior courts.''

To sum up, the administrative law and the administrative courts do not invade liberties of private citizens. On the other hand, they provide positive and effective restraint, more particularly the Council of the State ''to which all Frenchmen look with high approval as the Argus-eyed defender against official arbitrariness and oppression.'' The critics of administrative jurisprudence, notably in England and America, have in the recent years grown more sympathetic towards the French system. They have felt that the operations of the State in the sphere of business necessitate the building of an administrative edifice in which law and administrative courts must have their due place. Wherever there is administration there is administrative law and both England and America have themselves developed agencies having all the essential characteristics of administrative courts.

# CHAPTER VII

# French Political Parties

### Main Tendencies of Party Divisions

Political parties as definite organisations based on a precise political programme, there were none in France until the end of the nineteenth century. It took a hundred years of political activity, and fifty of universal suffrage for the conflict of ideas inseparable from politics to find channels of expression. And yet the French political parties have not even now attained what may be regarded as the essentials of a true party system: internal discipline and cohesion and an exact correspondence between divisions outside Parliament and the grouping of the members within. At the root of all this is the traditional multiplicity of parties. In the Fourth, as in the Third, Republic, "French government," remarks Finer, "is bedevilled by the existence and passionateness of many parties."[1] Their number usually exceeds a dozen.

Various reasons can be ascribed to the multiplicity of parties and, consequently, a source of political confusion in France.

The first is the lack of political continuity. "In French political life," says M. Goguel, "the past has as great an influence, if not more influence, than the present."[2] France has seen many political upheavals and experimented with different forms of government each time beginning anew. Beginning from 1775, she had been republic on three different occasions, an absolute monarchy, a constitutional monarchy and twice an empire. "And every form of government," rightly says Lowell, "that has existed in France has its partisans, who are irreconcilable under every other; while the great mass of the middle classes and the peasants have no strong political convictions, and are ready to support any government that maintains order." Political parties cannot exist and develop unless there is something approaching a consensus on the general nature of the political structure of the State. It is only with the beginning of the present century that the French, as a nation, have reconciled themselves to the republican form of government as a permanent institution. Even in the years immediately preceding the Second World War there were groups of Royalist and Fascist extremists who would have liked the republic to do away. The same attitude continued to prevail under the Fourth Republic and there were many who merely paid lip ser-vice to republicanism. The Communists now constitute a powerful and well organised party in France and they, too, avow their adherence to a republican form of government. But their methods are not what a republican system demands and their programme envisages a dictatorship. The differences between the Communists and the Socialists are vital and they do not make the forces of the Left, though the former helped the victory of the Socialist Mitterand in the 1981 Presidential election and were, till 1983 participants in the Government. The result is, as Ogg and Zink observe, on many broad and fundamental issues, "individuals and groups assume the most varied and irreconcilable positions. Political disagreement is no more a matter of Right and Left, otherwise we might look for a gradual shaking down of two opposing sets of political elements into two great parties. Clash of attitudes on all of the issues....releases cross-currents of opinion that keep the scene perpetually agitated and frustrate nearly every tendency toward compromise and coagulation."[3]

In the second place, multiplicity of political parties and parliamentary groups is due in part to certain traits in the general temperament of the French people. "French politics," remarks Siegfried, "are often both unrealistic and passionately ideological."[4] A Frenchman is by temperament more a philosopher with idealistic conceptions of life. He thinks of politics in intellectual rather than in practical terms and holds steadfast to his views no matter what

1. *Governments of Greater European Powers*, p. 336.
2. *France under the Fourth Republic*, p. 140.
3. *Modern Foreign Governments*, p. 548.
4. *Modern France : Problems of the Third and Fourth Republics*, p. 13.

those views are and their practical repercussion. Such an attitude of mind creates political fanatics and it is difficult for such fanatics to reconcile in practical politics where compromise is needed for realizing the common end. Lowell remarked that a Frenchman "is inclined to pursue an ideal, striving to realize his conception of a perfect form of society and is reluctant to give up any part of it for the sake of attaining so much as lies within his reach. Such a tendency naturally gives rise to a number of groups, each with a separate ideal, and each unwilling to make the sacrifice that is necessary for a fusion into a great party."

There is in France what Lord Bryce calls a legacy of revolutionary habits and this anarchical tendency leads to resentment of authority; to reluctance to work as one of a team and to sink one's personality into an anonymous unit, the party, An average voter does not allow others to think for himself. He does not relish the idea of being yoked to the programme and policy of any party. He disdains party discipline in order to maintain his personality. Any attempt to control and to regulate his political conduct is deemed as an invasion on his liberties. He accordingly, makes at elections his own choice of personalities who appeal to his own way of thinking. Politicians, too, are emotionally enthusiastic. They are subject to strong personal likes and dislikes and are easily swayed to extremes in one direction or the other. For the Frenchman "politics," as Ogg puts it, "is a battle rather than a game." The minority does not trust the majority for fair treatment and each party sees in its tenure of power an opportunity for revenge for previous persecution.

A Frenchman, at the same time, is deeply religious. Religion is a part of the individual's life in France and it has influenced her social political and economic structure. The French political life is, accordingly, divided both vertically and horizontally. Prolonged and bitter relations between the Church and the State produced different parties espousing one cause or the other and adherents to the State cause pursuing different means for realizing it and they still continue with the same old track.

No less important a factor to help to perpetuate their political attitudes is French economic stability, or as some would say, economic stagnation. The traditional economy of France is one of small enterprise in both agriculture and industry. It is a country of small towns and villages, of scattered farms and small one-man or family business. Small town economics have encouraged small-town politics and the ordinary Frenchman's way of life is less visibly affected by the activities of governments and parliaments. They think of politics in terms of symbols and doctrine rather than of concrete policies. The result is as Phillip Williams sums up: "strictly, France is not, as is sometimes claimed, a peasant country—the peasants are not a majority of the population though they are a large and very influential segment of it. But her atomised, small-scale structure promotes political individualism, strong local loyalties, and a political psychology more adapted to resistance than to positive construction. It reinforces the old tendency to *incivisme,* the lack of civic consciousness which makes so many Frenchmen regard the state as an enemy personified in the tax collector and the recruiting sergeant."[5]

The nature of the French parliamentary system itself had helped the growth of political groups. The success of parliamentary system of government in France inevitably depended upon the consolidation of existing party organizations and groups in such a way as to afford the ministry a reasonable assurance of stable support. But the system of second election, the method of organizing committees in parliament, the device of interpellation, the practice of putting government measures in charge of reporters, and the lack of dissolution had considerably contributed in the Third Republic and before to the political confusion. The Constitution of the Fourth Republic in a way sought to remedy these defects, but without any change in the situation. The second election encouraged small party groups to enter their candidates in the first election with the hope that they could lend their support to some one else in the second for a suitable consideration. The interpellation procedure had also helped to keep the groups in flux. Dissolution did not hang on the head of a deputy in France like a big stick as it does in England. He had nothing to lose by deserting his party. He might, indeed, profit, by changeover necessitating reshuffling of offices.

**Parties under the Fifth Republic**

Since the beginning of the Fifth Republic

5. *Politics in Post-War France,* p. 3.

party system in France has undergone a transformation. Some parties almost disappeared, others became just skeletons of their former selves, others were in the process of combining under a single name and on the verge of amalgamating their organizations into one. The result is that in the General Election of 1967, there were only four major parties which confronted each other. A number of factors account for this trend.

In the first place the Gaullists Party "has managed to swallow (but not digest) many of the Conservative and Centre groups. The overwhelming majority which General De Gaulle's party commanded forced the Left both to unite and cooperate. Two of the oldest parties-the Socialists and the Radicals-formed a federation, the Federation of the Socialist and Democratic Left. The Democratic Centre was a combination of some four of five different political parties or groups.

Apart from electoral considerations, there were institutional reasons, too, to support this trend. The direct election of the President of the Republic by universal suffrage, and the requirement that only two candidates confront each other on the second ballot was another important factor to encourage combining and co-operating process. Presidential elections also brought into the field of contest new leadership and disciplined parties to challenge De Gaulle's unprecedented majority.

The Constitution of 1958 empowers the President to dissolve Parliament. De Gaulle during his tenure of office threatened many a time the National Assembly to use the big stick the Constitution had given him and thereby attempted to curb opposition. It gave an impetus to the opposition parties and groups to combine and co-operate. New Rules in the National Assembly also helped to develop unity. A party now needs 30 Deputies to form a Parliamentary group and it helped the splinter groups to affiliate and cooperate. Only a Parliamentary group can secure representation on the legislative committees. The new electoral law stipulates that a candidate who fails to receive ten per cent of the registered votes in his constituency has to withdraw from the second balloting or lose his deposit unless he receives five per cent of the votes.

Another important factor is the modernization of France and diminution of peasantry in size, thus, the base of undisciplined parties or of the undisciplined factions tends to shrink. Localism has disappeared to a great extent and a new national consciousness has appeared in the French politics. The invasion of the Gaullist Party, first in 1958, but more so in 1962, in places where the traditional Right used to be strong demolished the traditional beliefs and behaviours. "For the first time, national feelings replaced sectional behaviour; men voted for candidates whom they did not know, simply because they were Gaullists; and the 'notables' of the countryside suffered astounding defeats where they had been assumed to be, up to then, almost unchallengeable."[6]

The process of simplification of the party system in France, thus, started. Whether the trend of combination and co-operation, is a permanent trend it is yet to be seen. It was apprehended that with the exit of De Gaulle from the political scene the Gaullist party itself might disintegrate into a number of formations, making the unity for the Centre and for the Left less compelling. But nothing tangible has happened so far and one may hope that multipartism may finally lead to a three or four-party system with party leadership and discipline.

**The Communist Party**

The French Communist Party dates from 1920 and it came into being when a split in the Socialist Party occurred. At the Tours Congress the majority of the delegates voted for affiliation to the Third International whereupon the minority seceded. The majority established its separate entity and adopted the name of the Communist Party. It accepted Marx-Lenin programme and the Communists aimed at overthrowing capitalism, and socialisation of the means of production, distribution and exchange.

But the initial success of the movement was not followed up. The internal feuds within the Party and the resentment of revolutionary Frenchmen at receiving instructions from Moscow contributed to a sharp decline in its membership. Between 1924 and 1928 Communist membership fell from 88,000 to 52,000 and its electoral support came mainly from the traditional voters from the Left. Bitter personal and political rivalries plagued the Party for some years, but expulsions, reorganisations and

6. Blondell, J., and Godfrey, E. D., *The Government of France*, pp. 84-85.

changes in line gradually built the Party into a compact and thoroughly disciplined movement. When the Party joined with Leon and the Radicals in the Popular Front, it assumed the role of a national party and its membership rose to 350,000. There was again a decline in its membership with the Hitler and Stalin pact and at the outbreak of the Second World War the Party was legally banned and went underground. All the 72 Deputies of the Communist Party in the Chamber and two Senators were excluded from Parliament. Similar, exclusion of the Communists was made from local governments. On the invasion of France by Hitler, the Communists remerged and they became stout members of the Resistance. When the War was over the party grew in numbers and capitalizing on its services to the country during Vichy regime and the German occupation, it was able to capture 159 and 150 seats in the First and Second Constituent Assemblies respectively. Its record was still more impressive in local elections. In combination with minor affiliated groups, the Party held in 1946 a total of 182 seats in the National Assembly and constituted the largest bloc. In 1951, its strength was reduced to 103 seats though its popular vote fell only about 10 per cent. Under the Fifth Republic, despite electoral setbacks, the Communists found themselves in a good tactical position. They had led the opposition to General De Gaulle's return and together with some splinter groups and individual leaders had taken a firm stand against the 1958 Constitution. Speaking against the Gaullist system of Government, Waldeck Rochet, the Party leader, said that it was a personal Bonapartist system that should be reformed and it represented the interests of the monopolists and the capitalists that should be done away with.

The Communist Party is the best organised political party in France. The basic unit of the Party is the cell, composed of from three to thirty members who work in the same establishment. The cell meets at least weekly, but when the unit is based on the place of work there is infact continuous contact between them. Other members, not working in large establishments, are organised in local cells based on the street, ward or cmmune. Each cell elects a secretary or *Bureau* or the executive committee. The higher level above the cell is a territorial unit called the *section,* manned by delegates from the cell secretaries and bureau. Above the *sections* are *departmentale federations* (departmental federations), again consisting of delegates from the sections, meeting every six months. The federation secretaries are chosen by the regular bureau selected by the sectional delegates in consulation with national leadership.

The highest authority in the Communist Party is the National Congress, composed of delegates by the conference in each department. Once in two years, or more often if necessary, a national Congress is convoked. But this is in theory only and "the Congress misses beats" as Finer remarks. The National Congress elects a Central Committee of sixty to eighty members, meeting at least every two months and acting as a consultative assembly of the Party. This Committee chooses at the Congress,several other bodies, like the political bureau, the Secretariat, a Central Committee. The Political Bureau, like the Presidium of the Central Committee (Politbureau before the organisation of the party) in the estwhile Soviet Russia there is the iron hand of the party organisation and the principle of democratic centralism is rigidly applied. In the Assembly the Deputies elected on the Communist Party ticket vote unitedly as a solid *bloc* and according to the Party executive whip. "The *discipline de vote* operates absolutely only in this party of all the parties in this French system."

The clientele of the party is nationwide. Its main strength is in the Northern Industrial area, the rural departments on the northern and western edge of the *massif central,* and the predominantly agricultural Mediterranean Coast, together with part of hinterland. In the south and centre almost all the Departments where communism is strongest have been on the Left since the beginning of the Third Republic and in the northern industrial areas the Party owes its position primarily to a working class appeal. The influence of Communism on the peasantry is a "remarkable phenomenon, not confined to the poor metayers of the centre but extending to prosperous southern farmers and vine growers, owning their own land and voting to express a political rather than a social choice."

It is, thus, essentially a working-class party, though many middle class intellectuals have gained positions of power as cadres. Of all the Communist voters, only half are industrial workers, some 8 per cent are agricultural workers, another 18 per cent are salaried employees,

5 per cent are civil servants, 5 per cent farmers, and the rest are members of the middle class, and of the professions, and intellectuals, teachers, artisans, merchants, etc.

As a Marxist workers' party, the Communists stand for the State control of the means of production and handing over of the land to the peasants. In day-to-day politics, the Communists have consistently supported claims for increase in wages. In matters of foreign policy the Party used to take its cue from the former Soviet Union.

The Birth of Euro-Communism in the mid Seventies as a revolt against Soviet hegemony inflicted a real danger to Marxism. The French, the Italians and the Spanish emerged as the three key partners in Euro-Communism. In 1975 Enrico Berlinguer and Georges Marchais, leaders of the Italian and French Communist parties signed a joint statement in Rome committing the two parties ''for the plurality of political parties, for the right of existence and activity of the opposition parties, and for democratic alternative between the majority and the minority.'' The eventual building of a Socialist Society in Italy and France, the statement added, would be characterised by a ''continued democratization of economic, social and political life'' and the existing ''bourgeois'' liberties would ''be guaranteed and developed.'' Realising that there was a remote possibility of revolution, as envisaged by Marx, in Western Europe, the Euro-Communists placed added emphasis on electoralism, on seeking popular support through calls for gradual reforms, on winning the co-operation of other left-wing parties even at the cost of doctrinal and political concessions and on the building of party's image as a progressive and responsible organisation within the existing political system whose creed was not to everthrow the prevailing social and political structure but to preserve and transform it.

The French Communist Party formed an alliance with the French Socialists in a bid for left unity, but it ended in a fiasco amidst mutual bickerings. As a consequence in the 1978 General Election the Communists lost heavily as compared with the Socialists; 86 seats as compared with 104 seats won by the Socialists, in the National Assembly with a total membership of 491. The French Communists afterwards drifted back to Moscow for guidance and initiative.

But the Party suffered a further setback in the 1981 Presidential election and elections to the National Assembly. M. George Marchais, the Communist Party leader got only 15.3 per cent of the total vote in the Presidential election and the Communist candidates could secure 44 seats, just half of 1978, in June 1981 General Election. Several leading spokesmen of the Party disappeared from the New Assembly. In the Presidential election after his elimination in the first round Marchais pledged unconditionally his support to Mitterand the Socialist candidate, and this support helped Mitterand to enter Elysee. After the General Election the Socialist President gave four cabinet posts to the Communists after a series of negotiations at which Communists modified their declared stand on Afghanistan and Poland as the price for a share in the Socialist Government. But this cooperation ended in 1983, and the four ministers withdrew from the Government.

In the March 1986 General Election the Communist Party won 34 seats securing 9.8 per cent of the votes, as compared with 22 per cent in 1981. Since then there had been a growing pressure on Georges Marchais to step down and the Party should shed its doctrinaire approach which had become an electoral liability. With the anuoncement of Marchais that he would not be the Party's candidate in the next Presidential election, due in 1988, and even with relative liberalisation and greater acceptance of social democracy, the Communist Party was unlikely to be able to retain its lost ground. With the resignation of the top functionaries Charles Popreu and Marcel Rigout, January 1987, who were dubbed by Marchias as ''renovators'' and ''liquidators'' of the Party, the French Communist Party faced a grave crisis worsened by the reforms, peresstroika and galsnost, initiated by Mikhail Grobachev in the USSR. With the liquidation of Communism in East European countries and the collapse of Soviet Russia and the disbandment of the Communist Party the future of Communism is bleak in France as also in other countries of the world. Even Marx and Lenin have been degraded and denounced.

**The Socialist Party**

The Socialist Party was originally formed in 1879, but it took real inspiration from Jean Jaures and was firmly established in 1905, It is referred to officially by the initials of S. F. I. O., meaning *section francaise de l' internation-*

*ale ouvriere,* the French section of the Second International. The Socialist Party pursued the programme of evolutionary socialism till 1915, when extremist elements reasserted the traditional pacific and international tenets of the party. The extremist movement gradually gained strength being especially influenced by the Russian Revolution which found eventual expression in the split at Tours when the Communist Party came into being.

The old socialist Party had not by 1924 retrieved its electoral position, but had the advantage of an alliance with the Radicals and formed the left wing of M. Herriot's parliamentary majority. But Socialists and Radicals differed too deeply over economic policy and the alliance could not prove enduring. The Radicals joined hands with the Conservatives. In 1928, the electoral alliance with the Radicals was restored. In 1936, the Socialist Party was the largest group in the new Assembly and for the first time it took over the leadership of the government. This short-lived victory, however, did not put an end to the dissensions within the party. The deterioration international situation caused a serious division, which grew more acute as Nazi power increased. With the outbreak of hostilities, followed by the debacle of June 1940, and the establishment of the Vichy regime; the socialists were badly split up. Some of its leaders, like Leon Blum and Vincent Auriol, never swerved in their loyalty to France and the Republic and they took an active and creditable part in the Resistance. Others opposed the war against the Nazis and in many cases, accepted or collaborated with the Vichy regime. Its policy of social services, welfare, nationalisation, a reformed constitution, democratic freedom and civil rights, and true internationalism brought the Socialists the promise of a bright political future at the Liberation, "but the evolution of political parties," remarks Finer, "worked grindingly against Socialist. strength." The elections of 1945 showed that the Socialists were only the third largest party.

In post-war as in pre-war France, the Socialist Party has been handicapped by the incongruity of its position and following. Though it stands for Socialism, yet it has never been representative of the working class. Few of the active members of the Party are industrial workers and except in northern regions, the industrial and mining departments of Nord and Pasde-Calais, the S. F. I. O. has never satisfied the deeply felt class consciousness of the French workers on which the Communists have capitalized so successfully. French workers mistrust the bourgeoisie and those who are actively associated with the Party are teachers, professional and other white-collar workers and lower grade civil servants. At the same time, the rank and file of the Party is slowly becoming less proletarian. Then, the Socialist appeal to youth, and in general to new elements outside its traditional ranks, has proved decidely ineffective. The Socialist Party constitution requires five years membership as a qualification for becoming a delegate to the Party Congress or National Council, for election to the executive committee, for editorship of the party newspaper, or for adoption as a parliamentary candidate. This does not make it easier to recruit new leaders or to maintain rapid promotion.

S. F. I. O. is the drfender of the democratic Republic and is, accordingly, anti-revolutionary. It is the party of the Welfare State, planned economic investment, public housing, industrialization, educational opportunity, a more equal tax structure service. The Socialists follow the western foreign policy leading to the Brussel Treaty, NATO, the Schuman Plan, the Western Union Pact, the Council of Europe. The Party, as a whole, is the foe of old type of authoritarian French colonialism and an advocate of extended self-government of the colonies.

The Socialists opposed De Gaulle and objected to his economic and political policies at home. They opposed his personal government and disputed on a number of points the interpretation he gave to the Constitution of the Fifth Republic. They vehemently criticised and opposed the device of referendum which undermined Parliament and reinforced personal government. Together with all other parties, the Socialists voted against the reform of the Constitution allowing for the direct election of the President of the Republic.

The Presidential election by direct vote again caught the party in internal rivalries and contradiction. Mitterrand, who assumed the leadership of the non-Communist Left, gradually brought the Socialists into a co-operative frame-work of the Federation of the Democratic and Socialist Left. The Socialists contested the 1967 election as candidates of the Federation and for the first time in the present century they did not form a Parliamentary group. But the Socialists still jealously guarded their independence within the Federation, and resisted all effort to allow it to become a genuine party with its own independent organization and leadership.'

Mitterrand made his third try for the Presidency and defeated President Giscard d' Estaing in May 1981 election by 35 per cent of the vote, thus, avenging the socalist's loss in the 1974 election. Eleven days after assuming office Mitterrand dissolved the 491 member National Assembly and called for new elections. The Socialists and the Communists agreed to a mutual support for the Assembly elections. In the 1978 elections the Socialists had won 104 Assembly seats but in June 1981 it was a landslide victory for them capturing 284 seats, with a comfortable majority in the National Assembly and the first scialist occupant of the Elysee, the Socialist Party moved ahead with their wide-ranging plans to establish what Mitterrand said in his election campaign a more just social order.

Early measures—raising the minimum wage, family allowances, pensions and rate rebates–taken by the Socialist Government were only palliatives to reduce increasing inequalities. The linchpins of the new policy were reflation combined with social and institutional reform. Twelve financial holding companies were nationalised. Small business, on the other hand, were helped by cheap credit and rebates of social security payments for new employees. The death penalty, the special Security Court and the army's special courts were abolished and the Napoleonic highly centralised administration was decentralised. Prefects were abolished, while electoral bodies were taken over by executive power in the regions, departments and town and villages. The country returned to the system of proportional representation.

These were the salient achievements of the Socialist Government. It was an impressive start to entrench the Socialist in the mass support. But the course of politics has never run smooth, more so in France. After the Parliamentary elections the Socialists were eclipsed by the Chirac Gaullists to make a strong base in the country side. As a consequence in the General Election in March 1986, the Socialist Party secured 32 per cent of vote. The alliance of Centre-Right parties, the Rally for Republic (RPR) led by a former Prime Minister, Jacques Chirac, and the Union for French Democracy (UDF) led by the former President of the Republic, Varley Giscard d' Eastaing, and their supporters won 291 seats in the 577-member Assembly—a majority of just seven. The Socialists remained the largest single Party with 216 seats which was more than President Mitterrand had expected. The latent divisions and dissensions within the Party gave a set back to the Socialists. Mitterrand was re-elected in 1988 for the second term by a reduced margin. Disputes that were largely silenced for the sake of national unity during the Gulf War reappeared as the Party prepared to discuss its concept of a new World Order. The cease-fire in the Gulf tiggered a resumption of feuding between the leaders, Mitterrand and his Prime Minister Michel Rocarrd, who ultimately had to quit.

**The Radicals**

The Radical Party, whose full title is the *Parti republican radical et radical socialiste* (the Radical Republican and Socialist Radical Party) is the oldest of all French parties, having been founded in 1901. As the most important party of the Third Republic, "the governmental *par excellence,* the radical party was associated in French minds at the end of the War with all that they disliked in pre-war French politics."

The Party had been compared to a radish, red outside and white inside—with "its heart on the Left and its pocket book on the Right." It throve on the single-member constituencies and was the leading party of the Third and Fourth Republics. It promised all things to all men, nothing to anyone in particular, and steadily against any substantial welfare for the industrial workers. Its clientele were small farmers, rural doctors, shopkeepers, school-teachers and the lawyers. The party's contribution to the Resistance movement was not impressive.

The Radical Party was not only itself more loosely organised but, since 1946, had been allied with a number of smaller groupings to form the R. G. R., "a coalition whose character and organization nobody has found it easy to define with any degree of precision." The R. G. R. had been described as a body of men of the Right, seated in the centre. Radical Party membership has never exceeded 2,000,000. Today it is doubtful it there are more than 10,000 members.

The Party is more or less extinct now. Severe conflicts within it have ended in its disintegration. With the waning of the significance of anti-clericalism and the general acceptance of economic planning and State social and economic controls, the Radicals found themselves not only without men, but also without ideas. Some moved to the Gaullist Party, others to the Left, while a third group went to the centre. A group of its leaders joined the Federation of the Democratic and Socialist Left as one of its constituent units. It is in the name of the Federation that they are represented in Parliament, not more than 25. Those who remained in the centre became part of the Democratic Centre. The Radical Party is, thus, virtually dead.

**The Convention of Republican Institutions**

A notable development of the Fifth Republic is the flowering of "political clubs" consisting of students, intellectuals and leaders of student and professional organizations for the purpose of debating the future of the country. These clubs discuss and examine critically the policies of the Government and institutions of the country, and take a stand against the Gaullists. Six such clubs, located in different cities, took steps to bring them all together in a common meeting.

*The Convention des Institutions Republicaines* was, thus, established in 1964, in an effort to bring the non-Communist-Left together against General De Gaulle. The Convention was explicitly dedicated to economic and social planning, a democratic government clearly opposed to the personal rule of De gaulle, and to European unity. The Convention held its Congress and it decided to exercise influence on the political parties of the Left. These youngmen, who commanded sufficient influence, offered "to act as a catalyst in the constant dialogue among the Radicals, the Socialists, the P.S.U., and even the Liberal Catholics and the Communists, in order to set the foundations from which a coherent opposition to De Gaulle would emerge and a coherent democratic force would develop." They played an important role in setting up one common candidate of the Left for the Presidential election, and simultaneously worked hard to create a Federation. In this way they became a part of the Federation of the Democratic and Socialist Left. The Convention has negligible political strength.

**The Democratic Centre**

Many political parties in Frnace claim to be Centrist, but no political party has deliberately called itself a Centrist party. The Centre has, all through, consisted of splinter groups: Moderates, unaffiliated Independents, Peasants, Republicans, etc. Only in the years following Liberation one political party, *M.R.P. (The Movement Republicain Populaire),* managed to form a political formation, formulated a programme and attracted more than 25 per cent votes. All others changed their names very often and shifted their alliance in an unpredictable manner—sometimes to the Left and sometimes to the Right. From 1945 to 1962, for example, the Centre consisted of the M.R.P., the Left Republicans, some of the Moderates and Peasants, dissident Radicals, and Left-Centre groups. Since 1962 none of these parties has been able to elect an adequate number of Deputies so as to form a group in the National Assembly.

But the direct election of the President in 1965 forced the Centre groups to unite behind a single candidate and the formation contrived as such was given the name of Democratic Centre. The support this combination received in the legislative elections of 1967 gave little hope of its continuity. As long as the Left is represented by a co-operative arrangement between the Communists and the Federation, there is very little hope for the Democratic Centre to survive.

**Parties of the Right**

The Right is composed in the post-war, as it was in the pre-war France, of a number of small groups, whose membership and names changed frequently. But in the post-war period two groups emerged which distinctly advocated the outright overthrow of the Republic and its substitution with an authoritarian regime. Those two formations may be described as anti Republican Right: The Poujadist movement and the Activists. The former emerged in 1954 from groups that had been traditionally most loyal to the Republic and to Parliamentary government. Shopkeepers, artisans, small farmers, and many small political leaders, who supported this movement, were called Poujadists, after the name of the movement's leader, Pierre Poujade. Beginning as a strong pressure block called the Uniion for the Defence of Merchants and Artisans, whose aim was to lighten the tax burdens on small businessmen, the movement later became a party, the Union and French Fraternity. It demanded the complete overhaul of the political institutions, Parliament to be replaced by the Estates General and the leaders of the Fourth Republic tried before a "High Court."

By 1955, Poujade, the leader of the movement, organized local and departmental federation throughout France. His slogan was: "throw out the rascals" the Deputies of the National Assembly. Poujade nominated candidates in many Departments, refused to ally himself with any other political party or group, and appealed for a big support. He was able to capture 25 seats in the National Assembly. With the return of De Gaulle in 1958, the Poujadist movement collapsed.

The second anti-republican formation was the "Activists." Some Army officers attempted in the course of the war in Algeria to rise against the Fifth Republic and General De Gaulle. They were supported in Algeria by the French settled there, and in France proper by small secret groups—a few of the remaining disciples of authoritarian ideology, and some outright Fascists and Extremists. They formed a formation called O.A.S., the *Organization de L' Armee Secrete* and indulged in indiscriminate acts of terrorism and assassination. It also conspired to assassinate De Gualle, and proclaimed its determination to keep Algeria French. It was in 1961 that the leaders of O.A.S., including two Generals were arrested and the organization was smashed.

**The Republican Right**

In this group of political division are included the independents and the Gaullists. The first, like the Radicals and the M.R.P., appeared to be on the way out while the Gaullist constituted a well-knit organisation and was the well-organized political party of France.

The Independents have had virtually no organization and membership, except for an alliance among departmental and political leaders. They supported the Fifth Republic and by extending their support to the Gaullists did well in the 1958 elections securing 20 seats. They became the conservative party in the Assembly in matters of economic and social reform, and in regard to Algeria. This resulted into De Gaulle's displeasure and divided them sharply amongst themselves. The election of the President by direct vote and later the legislative election of 1962 sharply divided them and a group called the Independent Republicans joined hands with the Gaullists. The residue joined hands with other Centrist groups.

**The Gaullists**

General De Gaulle returned to France in 1944 at the head of the Provisional Government. He advocated the establishment of a strong Presidential government, the overhauling of the stagnant economy of the country and broad social welfare measures. But within eighteen months of his regime he resigned. He re-entered politics as the head of a large political movement, the Rally of the French People, with the avowed object of establishing a new Constitution by replacing the Constitution of the Fourth Republic which suffered from the same defects as the Constitution of the Third Republic. By the end of 1947 the R.P.F. had a membership of 800,000 and it won a sweeping victory in the municipal elections of 1947. It subsequently gained more than one-third of the seats in the upper chamber of Parliament. The Gaullists, then, pressed for dissolution of Parliament and new elections.

But in the elections of 1951, the Centre parties with the support of Socialists to the Left and Independents to the Right checkmated their intentions. They could secure only, 117 seats in the National Assembly. the Parliamentary group of the P.R.F. showed signs of disintegration soon. De Gaulle freed his followers from the pledge to follow him and himself withdrew from politics. In the elections of 1956, the Gaullists were reduced to just a handful of Deputies—the Social Republicans. Yet the devout and select group of De Gaulle remained active and awaited for the opportunity enabling their leader to return.

It did not take long. The deterioration of the war in Algeria and the inability of the Government of the Fourth Republic to keep an effective control over the Army provided the requisite opportunity for De Gaulle to return first as the Prime Minister and then after the Constitution of 1958 became operative as the first President of the Fifth Republic. A strenuous effort was made to revive the Gaullist Party. In the election of 1958, the Gaullist contested elections under the label of U.N.R—the Union of the New Republic. They captured 189 seats and with the help of their Deputies who joined them the Gaullists mustered a strength of 210 and became the largest Parliamentary group. In the elections of 1962, they won 275 seats out of a total of 482.

The Gaullists drew their strength from the Right and the Centre, especially the Catholic votes. It is a party which is supported by more women than men and it is a party that failed to appeal to the young. Thirteen per cent of the voters for the party are farmers and about twenty-seven per cent are workers. Employed and managerial groups. Executives, industialists and merchants vote for the Gaullists.

The future of the Gaullists eclipsed after General Charles De Gaulle's resignation in 1969 from the Presidency. There was no dynamic leader to keep them together and make them a force to count. With the Gaullist era ending began the Giscardian era. In 1978, the Centre-Right coalition won the genral election but Chiracs' Gaullist prodominance in the coalition was reduced by 20 seats. Chirac had by then acquired a kind of charisma among the Gaullists. Although he had been Giscard's Prime Minister for two years (1974-76) but he never acted subserviently.

Jacques Chirac waged his own campaign for 1981 Presidency and seriously splitted right forces. He, however, earned the enmity of many conservative leaders when, after finishing third in the first ballot of Presidential election, he withheld his wholehearte support from his voters for Giscard in the second round. He declared that he would give his vote in favour of Giscard, but left it to his followers to vote as they pleased. It went in favour of the Socialist leader Mitterrand and he was elected. The Socialists also secured an absolute majority in June 1981 elections to the National Assembly. In March 1986 elections Chirac-Giscard alliance secured 291 seats in the National Assembly, a water-thin majority, no doubt, but France, once again, went to the Right. Chirac considered it a good stepping for the next Presidential election in 1988. But the Socialists succeeded in taking over the Presidency. After the two-term of Presidency of Socialist Mitterand, Jacque Chirac won the French Presidency for the Conservative political forces. The 1958 Constitution has polarised the French political system between the right-wing conservative parties led by the Gaullists on one side and the leftwing political parties led by the Socialists on the other.

# CHAPTER VIII

# The French Political System

**Revolutionary Legacy**

Every great revolution, says Franz Borkenau, "has destroyed the State apparatus which it found. After much vacillation and experimentation, every revolution has set another apparatus in its place, in most cases of quite a different character from the one destroyed; for the changes in the state order which a revolution produces are no less important than the changes in the social order."[1] Social revolutionary crises in France in 1789, 1793, 1830 and 1848 set in motion political and economic conflicts that culminated in fundamental structural transformations. Bourgeois, peasant and working class revolts transformed social and economic relations. Autocratic and 'feudalistic' monarchies were overthrown and constitutional, bureaucratic and bourgeois, democratic national-states came into existence after each of these successive revolutions in France.[2]

The prerevolutionary landowning classes lost their exclusive privileges in social and political spheres and were largely deprived of their shares of the agrarian surpluses through regional and local quasi-political institutions. The emergent political elites were, however, obstructed, by counter-revolutionary attempts at home and military interventions from abroad in building new state organisation to consolidate the Revolutions. The new State structures, nevertheless, were more centralized and rationalised than those of the *ancien regime.* The outcomes of the various French Revolutions favoured the bourgeoisie. The French revolutionary upheavals created and consolidated "a professional-bureaucratic state that coexisted sysmbiotically with, and indeed guaranteed the full emergence of, national markets and capitalist private property..... And despite the massive presence in society of the French state as a uniform and centralized administrative framework, further, national economic development and social differentiation remained primarily market-guided and outside the direct control of the government." One reason for a focus on state building as a legacy of the French Revolution is in the words of Samuel P. Huntington: "A complete revolution involves..... the creation and institutionalisation of a new political order."

The course of the ongoing French revolutions and counter-revolutions was shaped by social and political crises in which liberal stabilization proved very difficult, and by the emergence of centralized state bureaucracy that paved the way for Bonapartist regimes, As a prelude to this analysis, let us first consider the social character of the revolutionary break in France. Of course, Alexis de Tocqueville placed the state at the centre of his analysis in *The Old Regime and the French Revolution.* In this book, he made a penetrating analysis of the French Revolution, emphasizing the elements of continuity between the monarchy which it overthrew and the Republic which it established: "The despot fell; but the most substantial portion of his work remained; his administrative system survived his government."[4]

Unlike Marx, de Tocqueville believed that the democratic revolution was not entirely the achievement of the bourgeoisie but the crowning result of multiclass effort, not excluding a section of the nobles. It was ideological revolution in which the principle of social equality and spirit of Christianity prevailed. He thus implicitly refutes some of the propositions of both liberal and Marxist historiography. He did not think that "*discrepancy between political equality and economic inequality,* would be indefinitely accepted by a democratic people. He saw that the first phase of the democratic world revolu-

1. Quoted in Theda Skocpol, *States and Social Revolutions,* p. 161.
2. Theda Skocpol, "*States and Social Revolutions,*" p. 162.
3. Samuel P. Huntington, *Political Order in Changing Societies,*. p.266.
4. Quoted in W. Ebenstein: *Great Political Thinkers*, p.523.

tion, political in nature would inevitably lead to a second phase, which would be primarily social and economic..... The July Revolution of 1830 was the last purely political revolution in France.... and he foresaw that the next upheaval would result from economic grievances."[5]

The February Revolution of 1848 was the first in which the French working class played a crucial role. Even before the revolutin began, de Tocqueville predicted, "Before long, the political struggle will be restricted to those who have and those who have not; property will form the great field of battle." After the Revolution, he told the Chamber of Deputies that the passions of the working class have turned from political to social questions and that they were forming ideas aiming "not only to upset this", or that law, ministry or even form of government, but society itself, until it totters upon the foundations on which it rests today."[6] De Tocqueville, however, hated this revolutionary spirit of the workers not merely because he opposed socialism but also because it might provoke the property-owning classes to opt for an absolute government, that Marx later called Bonapartism. De Tocqueville said, "The insane fear of socialism throws the bourgeois headlong into the arms of despotism. As in Prussia, Hungary, Austria and Italy, so in France the democrats have served the cause of the absolutists. But now that the weakness of the Red party has been proved, people will regret the price at which their enemy has been put down."[7]

But this was not the end of the social revolution process which, de Tocqueville believed, would continue to refashion social and political institutions in future.

In *'Recollections'*, he explained the legacy of the French Revolutions in the following words, "will socialism remain buried in the contempt that so justly covers the socialists of 1848?..... I am sure that in the long run the constituent laws of our modern society will be drasticlly modified; many of the main parts of them have already been substantially modified."[8] An abortive socialist revolution occurred in France in 1871 known in history as the Paris Commune. Marx lent his public support to this revolutionary event despite the fact that it took place in a not yet fully industrialized society, with a poorly organised working class and a leadership consisting of largely petty-bourgeois groups.

Marx even predicted that the Commune could never succeed. In his essay entitled 'The Civil War in France' he explained the accidental circumstances which enabled the workers of Paris to liberate themselves from the capitalist government of France. Explaining the role of accidents in a revolution, Marx said, "World history would indeed be very easy to make, if the sruggle were taken only on condition of infallible favourable chances. It would, on the other hand, be of a mystical nature, if 'accidents' played no part."[9] For Marx, the Revolutions of 1789 and 1848, were partial, political revolutions of the bourgeoisie lacking a social content. The proletariat alone could represent the interests of society as a whole through a social revolution. Thus for Marx, the Paris Commune was the the "political form of social emancipation".

**Bonapartist Heritage**

From Nepoleon Bonaparte to Louis Bonaparte to General de Gaulle, Bonapartism has been a recurrent feature of the French political system. The reason for this is to be located in the fact that the French dominant class, from the begining, had less capacity than the English to make an effective liberal political revolution against the monarchy. The English Parliament was a functioning national institution for a century, at least, before the English Revolution and it brought together prosperous landlords and the rising bourgeoise class in the English system of government. In France things were quite different. The dominant class was divided internally from the very beginning as to what kind of representative institutions it wanted *vis-a-vis* monarchy. In the early phases of the Revolution there was great distrust of any centralized executive power and so no workable system could be created to replace the monarchical one. As testified by Alfred Cobban, the fundamental reality was "that before

5. Quoted in *Ibid,*. pp522-523.
6. Quoted in *Ibid.*, p.529.
7. Alexie de Tocquerville, *The European Revolution and Correspondence with Gobineau,* p. 22.
8. Alexie de Tocqueville, *Recollections,*. pp; xiv-xv
9. Karl Marx, *The Civil War in France,* p. 86.

1789....there ws not a single truly elected assembly in the country, but only government officials, in 1790 there was no longer a single official, but only elected bodies."[10]

This kind of pervasive anarchy first led to revolutionary dictatorship of the Jacobins. After the fall of Robespierre, the Thermidorean Convention dismantled the judicial apparatus of the Terror and the centralized controls of the revolutionary government. Once again an attempt was made to consolidate the Revolution in a conservative liberal form. But the liberal republican Directory was no more successful than the pre-1792 constitutional monarchy, as it faced similar problems and chaotic conditions. However, it retained most civil servants and expanded central administrative structures. "The central bureaucracy was thus given a renewed stability which paved the way for the vital role it was to play in the new state moulded by Napoleon and bequeathed by him to later generations,"[11]

In these circumstances, Napoleon Bonaparte seized power in a *coup d'etat,* who established himself, step by step, first as *de facto* dictator, then as First Consul for life, and finally as full-fledged crowned emperor, significant institutional developments took place under Napoleon. He legalised the social and economic accomplishments of the Revolution and reintroduced administrative centralisation. "The Directory owed its fall partly to the narrowness of its political foundations. Bonaparte, well aware of that fact, looked for allies on the Right as well as on the Left, and his most successful method of winning sympathy was to appoint men from all sections of the political world to the new posts which were opening.... Some had been terrorists, others belonged to the nobility."[12]

He dispensed with mass mobilisations and expressions of ideological commitment and weilded the symbols, rituals, and propaganda of a highly generalized French patriotism. He embellished his essentially authoritarian regime with symbolic concessions to the inherited factions: plebiscitary and patriotic rituals for the radicals: "consultative councils with restricted franchise for the liberals, and a Concordat with the Catholic Church for conservatives."[13] The destruction of the old regime and the gaining of fundamental rights by all citizens made possible the creation of truly national army. France had many political regimes since Napoleon's dictatorship, which lasted only until 1814. It was followed by a restored Bourbon monarchy, then a 'bourgeois' monarcly, a Second Republic followed by a Second Empire of Louis Bonaparte, then an ephemeral, socialist Paris Commune, drowned in blood by the Theirs dictatorship, followed by a Third Republic, destroyed by the Nazi conquest and the creation of a fascistic Vichy regime. It was replaced by a Fourth Republic, set up after liberation, only to be overthrown by a Bonapartist regime of Charles de Gaulle in 1958.

Thus three Bonapartist regimes have ruled over France from 1804 to 1814 by Nepoleon, from 1852 to 1870 by Louis, and from 1858 to 1969 by Gaulle. All of them became necessary because of some inherent weaknesses of the civilian, liberal Republican governments which they had to replace. Yet as Herbert Leuthy correctly points out, an observer who concentrates only on the periodically changing constitutional forms cannot comprehend the real basis and enduring power of French government. He says: "If one looks at a constitutional handbook one will find no mention of.... any of the great institutions on which the permanence of the state depends..... No mention is made of the Ministries which remain after the Minister of the day has departed. No mention is made of the Council of State which, because of its jurisdiction over the administrative machine, rules supreme over the instruments of state power, is indispensable to an executive incapable of carrying out its will without it, interprets according to its own code the true content of laws passed by Parliament or quietly buries them, and as the universal advisor of, Government usually gets its own way even in the formulation of government policy, because it has authority and permanence, and the Government has not."[14]

Herbert Leuthy goes on to describe the

10. Afred Cobban, "Local Government during the French Revolution," in *Aspects of the French Revolution*, p.118.
11. Theda Skocpol, States and *Social Revolution* p. 193.
12. Quoted in *Ibid*, p. 195.
13. Ibid,. p. 195, See Leo Gorshoy, *The French Revolution and Napoleon pp.* 375-381, 451-467.
14. Herbert Leuthy, *France Against Herself*, trans. Eric Mosbacher, p.p. 18.

Bonapartist contribution to the French political system with the same passion: "No mention is made of the general staff of the financial administration, which is able to modify and interpret the budget passed by Parliament as autocratically as the Council of State is able to modify and interpret its laws, and by its control over state revenue and expenditure is able to exercise a decisive influence over the life and death of governments.... Not one of these instituions is derived 'from the people'. They represent the state apparatus of the absolute monarchy, perfected and brought to its logical conclusion under the First Empire. When the crowned heads fell, the real sovereignty was transferred to this apparatus. But it works in the background, unobtrusively, anonymously, remote from all publicity and almost in secret.... It is not so much a state within a state as the real state behind the facade of the democratic state." Crystallization of this Bonapartist state in the womb of revolutionary democracy, which began with Napoleon and was consolidated by Louis, was later given a modernized appearance by Charles de Galulle in the twentieth century. Thus Bonapartism and now Gaullism are as much authentic elements of the French state structures as liberal parliamentarism. In fact, Bonapartist heritage is integrated with the functioning of democracy in France.

**Advanced Capitalist Democracy**

Despite travelling different trajectories, in their ascent towards modern constitutionalism, Great Britain, France and the United States today are equally developed members of the international league of advanced capilatist democracies. They may have different histories, traditions, cultures and political institutions, but they aiso have in common two crucial characteristics: the first is that they are all very highly industrialised societies; and the seond is that their means of production, trade and finance are under capitalist ownership and management. As A. Schonfield says, "There are big differences between the key institutions and economic methods of one country and another. The differences are often the subject of sharp ideological cleavages. Yet when the total picture is examined, there is a certain uniformity in the texture of their societies. In terms of what they do, rather than of what they say about it, and even more markedly in terms of their behaviour over the period of years, the similarities are striking."[16]

Notwithstanding all levelling proclamations, there continue to exist in France wealthy economic elites who own large amounts of property in one form or another, and who also receive large incomes, derived wholly or partially from their ownership or control of that property. On the other hand, France also contains a very large class of people who own very little property and whose income is derived from the sale of their labour. Poverty is a fluid concept but the 'affluent society' of France has failed to eradicate it. There is enough evidence to show that it is not a marginal or residual phenomenon but an endemic condition affecting a substantial part of its population.

Managerialism represents an important phenomenon in the development of French capitalism too. Along with the owners, these managers who also are part-owners constitute self-perpetuating oligarchies in the French corporations. As Baran and Sweezy explain, "profits, even though not the ultimate goal, are the necessary means to all ultimate goals. As such, they become the immediate, unique, unifying, quantitative aim of corporate policies, the touchstone of corporate rationality, the measure of corporate sucess."[17] In fact, the modern manager can pusue profit more vigorously than the old-style entrepreneur, with the aid of market analysts, economic consultants, and other specialists. In both, the work-process remains one of domination and subjection.

In a sense, the spread of managerialism reinforces the advantage of what Harold Laski used to call the 'careful selection of parents'. Access to the upper layers of capitalist enterprise requires high university qualifications available only to the sons of the rich. Two French authors have pointed out., "An approximate calculation of chances of access to university according to the father's profession shows that these are of the order of less than one per cent for the sons of agricultural wage earners to nearly 70 per cent for the sons of businessmen and to more than 80 per cent for members of the liberal professions. These statistics clearly demonstrate

16. A Schonfield, *Modern Capitalism*, p.65.
17. Baran and Sweezy : *Monopoly Capital*, p. 40.

that the educational system operates, objectively, a process of elimination which is more thorough as one reaches the most unprivileged classes."[18] Those who fear a 'meritocratic' society in which every one will be judged on 'merit' alone, need not be unduly alarmed, as the race is still rigged, against the working-class.

Raymond Aron laments the fact that he found the capitalists of France, those acursed 'monopolists', without any 'hegemonic virtue' as they did not have "a definite and unanimous opinion, either on the policy to be followed in Indo-China or on the policy to be followed in Algeria." They had in fact "most often no political conceptions."[19] This is a superficial view because differences "among the French economic elites about Indo-China or Algeria occurred inside a field of *Conservative* options, and severely excluded any other. There may have been some among the members of these elites who wished for rapid decolonisation but history, somehow, does not record a massive degree of pressure on the part of any segment of the French bourgeoise on behalf of the Vietnamese and Algerian liberation struggles-or for the nationalisation of private enterprise, or for a major redistribution of wealth, or for a radical extension of social benefits, or for an extension of trade union rights; and so forth."[20] This elite pluralism does not prevent the separate economic elites in France's capitalist society from constituting a dominant, political class with a high degree of cohesion and solidarity.

The administrative class in France also contributes directly and substantially to the exercise of state power. If the regime is weak and plagued with cabinet instability as happened under the third and fourth Republics, bureaucrats would step into the vacuum to play a dominant role in decision-making. But even when political executive is strong, as is the case in the Fifth Republic from 1958 onwards, top civil servants have succeeded in influencing the policies of successive Presidents from Charles de Gaulle to Jacques Chirac. State intervention has assumed more elaborate institutional forms in France than anywhere else in the capitalist world. As Schonfield points out, "in some ways, the development of French planning....can be viewed as an act of collusion between senior civil servants and the senior managers of big business. The politicians and the representatives of organised labour were both passed by."[21]

In France, the main channel of entry to top administrative positions is the *Ecole Nationale d' Administration.* The same is also true of the high military and judicial parts in the French State. Two French authors point out that social origin is important not only for selection but also for promotion, "If a student of modest origin has successfully negotiated his university course, the entrance examination of the E.N.A. and.... the final examination where the cultural sifting is perhaps more severe than on entry, he will not, nevertheless, be on the same level as the offspring of great bourgeois families or of high officials: the spirit of caste and personal family relations will constantly work against him when promotions are made."[22]

The state elite in France does not view its commitment to capitalism as involving any element of class partiality. It subscribes to Hegel's exalted view of the state as an embodiment of reason and national unity, particularly reflected in the statement of its charismatic leader, General de Gaulle, when he said, "I belong to everyone and I belong to no one." He thus visualised himself, far above the interests of the lesser men, whether they were capitalists or workers, farmers or businessmen, the young or the old. De Gaulle's perception of his political role is similar to the historical role attributed to the two Bonapartes in the French politics of their own times. Yet his conduct of affairs showed that he protected economic and political arrangements in which large-scale capitalist enterprise played a crucial role. But that is, more or less true of other Presidents of the fifth Republic, including the Socialist Mitterand, from 1969 to the present day.

The evidence conclusively suggests that in terms of social origin, education and class situation, the persons who have occupied command positions in the French state system have been mostly drawn from the world of business property or from the professional middle classes.

---

18. P.Bourdieu and J.C. Passeon, *Las Heritiers, pp. 13-14.*
19. R. Aron, *Sociologic des Societes Industrielles, Esquis\se d' une Theorie d'es Regimes Politiques*, p. 81.
20. R. Miliband, *The State in Capitalist Society*, p. 43.
21. A Schonfield, *Modern Capitalism*, p. 128
22. Bon and Burnier, *Les Noveaux Intellectuals*, p. 165.

But the men and women born into the subordinate classes, which form the vast majority of the French population have fared badly not only in administration, the judiciary and the military, the non-elected segments of the state system but also in the legislatures and the cabinets which are exposed to competitive party politics on the basis of universal adult franchise, "In an epoch when so much is made of democracy, equality, social mobility, classnessness and the rest, it has remained a basic fact of life in advanced capitalist countries that the vast majority of men and women in these countries has been governed, represented, administered, judged and commanded in war by people drawn from other, economically and socially superior and relatively distant classes."[23] This applies equally to advanced capitalist democracy as practised in France.

**Left Wing Governments in France**

The first such government to require consideration is the Popular Front government of Leon Blum, brought to power in 1936 which had won 376 seats with 147 seats for the Socialist Party, 106 to the bourgeois Radical-Socialist Party, and 72 to the Communist Party, the rest being shared by smaller parties of the Left. The opposition had 222 seats dispersed over a number of Rightwing parties. This victory of the Left was quite clear and decisive, thus constituting its biggest electoral success in the inter-war years. It signalled a grand show of radical, left wing and democratic strength against the internal and external threat of fascism. The victory of the Popular Front was immediately given a new dimension by the massive wave of strikes, with the occupation of factories by the workers. These strikes swept the whole country. This revolution of 1936 was a dramatic working-class uprising, although mainly peaceful, against capilatist oppression along with forceful demands for improvement in living conditions.

The Popular Front government was formed on 4 June, one month after the elections, with Leon Blum becoming its Prime Minister. It was composed of Socialists and Radicals, with Communists giving issue-based support from outside. In this potentially dangerous conflict between labour and capital, relief came to the besieged fortress of capital from the new left wing government itself. Roger Salengro, the new socialist minister of the interior, had promised on the eve of his appointment, "Let those whose task is to lead the trade union movement do their duty. Let them hasten to put an end to this unjustified agitation. For myself, my choice is made between order and anarchy. Against whosoever it may be, I shall maintain order."[24]

The Popular Front government did not try to establish industrial peace by using coercive power of the state. It brought the representatives of capital and labour on a negotiating table and made them sign the famous Matignon agreement. It endorsed the 40 "hour week, a general increase in wages and enlarged trade union rights. J. Bannier remarks, "the economic and social measures of the Popular Front, which were thought at the time to be quite revolutionary, seem now extraordinarily timid when compard to what has been achieved since then in France and abroad, not only by governments of the left, but also by governments making no profession whatever of radicalism."[25]

This assessment underestimates the difficulties and the opposition which the Blum government faced. The point is also relevant to the foreign policy of the government, especially its attitude to the Spanish Civil War. It adopted a policy of neutrality and non-intervention towards it. This failed to appease the Right, but helped to divide and demoralise the Left. Once relieved of its immediate fears, the opposition regained into confidence and began, with ever greater strength, to challenge the lift-wing regime, which then began a process of retreat. It resulted in the resignation of the Blum cabinet in June 1937. Leon Blum had made absolutely clear, after the elections, that he wanted merely to "administer the bourgeois state and, therefore, to "put into effect the Popular Front programme, not to transform the social system,"[26] So the fact is that the short-lived Blum regime did even try to overcome the political, financial and international obstacles in its path. Blum had no wish to transform the *exercise* of power into *its conquest*.[27] Thus the impact of the Popular Front 'experiment' upon the French social sys-

24. Quoted in *Ibid.*, p. 94.
25. J. Bannier, *Les Grandes Affaires Francaieses*, p. 35
26. Dorothy M. Pickles, *The French Political Scene*, p. 130.
27. G. Lefranc, *Histoire du Front Populaire*, p. 141. For a perspective discussion of this distinction in Leon Blum's thought, see C. Audry, *Leon Blum on la Politique du Juste*.

tem was very limited because it did not fundamentally influence the distribution of political and economic power in French society.

Another case of a left-wing regime in France occurred at the time of its liberation in 1944, when traditional elites were massively discredited by their wartime record of collaboration with the Nazis. They were bereft of political influence when a resurgent and armed Left appeared on the verge of capturing state power in post-liberation France. But here also the reality was much less dramatic. There were two main reasons why appearance belied reality. The first was the status of General de Gaulle as the recognised leader of all Resistance movements in France including the Communists and consequently the potential leader of the post-liberation French government. But the general was determinded to deprive the left, especially the Communists, from an important role in the post-liberation settlement. In this de Gaulle was eminently successful.

But that achievement was facilitated "by a second factor in the political situation of France at the time of the Liberation, namely that the French Communist Party, though bent upon major economic and social reforms, was in no sense committed to anything resembling a revolutionary bid for power."[28] The Communist Party, therefore, was satisfied with a marginal role in the reconstructed Provisional Government which de Gaulle formed on 9 September, 1944. It included two Communists, with minor ministries of public health and air, and four right wing socialists and the rest of his Cabinet consisted of conservatives. Some acts of nationalisation followed but they did not intend to transform the French economic and social order, whose continued capitalist character was taken for granted both by de Gaulle and socialist ministers of his Cabinet. As the Social ist Minister of Production put it at the time, "a wide free sector remains the fundamental condition of French activity and economic recovery."[29]

A year after the Liberation, on 21 October, 1945, general elections gave the Communist and Socialist Parties an absolute majority in the new Constituent Assembly, and also in the country. The 'classical Right' had been utterly defeated at the polls. But the Mouvemente Republican Populaire (M.R.P.) regrouped the Right, gaining 141 seats, against 148 for the Communists and 134 for the Socialists. The M.R.P., as a crucially important instrument of conservatism, could play a role in governance because the Socialist Party insisted on its participation in a tripartite government that included the Communists. The M.R.P. and the Socialists also desired de Gaulle to continue as President, who insisted on the exclusion of the Communists from strategic ministries, such as defence, interior or foreign affairs. Instead, the Communists got four 'economic' ministries and their leader was given a portfolio signifying more rank than power.

In accepting so many insults and compromises, the Communists were trying to project their 'nationalist' image. Probably they believed that their participation in a clearly non-socialist and even anti-socialist government led by de-Gaulle, may ultimately lead to a socialist conquest of power, with their own party at the head of affairs. This proved to be a miscalculation. Communist participation actually 'deradicalised' the government by subduing the militant elements of the working class movement. This was what de Gaulle had hoped for when he took Communists into his government. He said later, "At least for a certain time, their participation under my leadership would help to assure social peace, of which the country had such great need."[30]

The situation did not undergo much change when de Gaulle suddnelly tendered his resignation on 20 January 1946. Maurice Thorez became vice-premier with the Socialist Felix Gouin as Prime Minister. Inspired by the spirit of Yalta the French Communist Party proudly described itself as 'the Party of Reconstruction'. "But the 'reconstruction' in which it played so notable a part was that of a predominantly capitalist economy, and the renovation which occurred was was that of a regime whose main beneficiaries were not the working classes but those capitalist and other traditional elites whose situation had at the time of liberation seemed so perilous.... it can at any rate hardly be doubted that the Communist presence in the government between 1944 and1947, when the Communist

28. R. Miliband, *The State in Capitalist Society*, p. 103.
29. Quoted in B.D. Graham, *The French Socialists and Tripartisme* - 1944-47, p. 48.
30. Charles de Gaulle, *Memoires de Guerre*, p. 276.

ministers were forced out, entailed no threat to the French dominant class, and was in fact of quite considerable advantage to it."[31]

### The Gaullist Republic

The French politics during the Fourth Republic from 1946 to 1958 was characterized by dissensus and deadlocks. In 1947, once the Communists had gone into opposition, there were 183 opposition deputies out of 635. In 1951 there were 221, made up of the Communists on the left and the Gaullist R.P.F. on the right. In 1956 there were still 201 although most of the Gaullists had left the Assembly and their place was taken by a neo-fascist group led by Poujade. Thus the fraction from which the government majority had to be structured was 452 in 1947 and 414 in 1951, needing 318 votes out of a possible 635. Besides, the ruling bloc itself was sundered by France's historic cleavages. For these reasons, cabinets were unstable and their average life was less than seven months.

The Assembly of 1956 contained few Gaullists. Under instructions from de Gaulle, the R.P.F had dissolved itself. But his friends in the Assembly, the Senate, the army and the bureaucracy did not give up their efforts to recall the General at a suitable opportunity. It came in 1958 over the war in Algeria. This polarised French public opinion. The Communists supported the cause of Algerian independence, the far right demanded total repression and the ruling parties all split down the middle. The defection of the army proved the final straw. A cabinet crisis followed. The military officers in Algiers started an insurrection. France feared a civil war. On 15 May, the General declared his readiness "to assume the powers of the Republic."

The officers of the armed forces publicy demanded the return of de Gaulle and the members of Parliament echoed their call. Faced by an army threat to invade France from Algerian soil, the French government resigned. On 1 June 1958 the Assembly expressed confidence, by 329 votes to 224, in de Gaulle as new Prime Minister, with full powers of governance for the next six months, authority to revise the constitution, and an immediate adjournment of the Assembly. It was really a Bonapartist *coup d'etat*. In the words of S. F. Finer, "The General was back in the saddle again. This time he would ride." It was a "swing from parliamentary institutions to some kind of Bonapartism."[32]

The Gaullist constitution was drawn up rapidly and submitted to the French people on 28 September 1958 for their approval in a referendum. Only the Communist Party opposed it but 80% of the voters approved it. De Gaulle was chosen President by an electoral college consisting of regional and local councilors. "Superficially the Constitution looks much the same as before.....But there are four vital differences. The parliamentary representation of the public has been deliberately distorted. The legislature has been muzzled. The executive has been given a much greater weight in decision-making; and, notably, the presidency has been exalted at the expense of the prime minister and the Cabinet."

But this exaltation is due "more to practice than to the letter of the Constitution. On paper the prevalent notion is of a 'two headed executive' with a division and balance between the president..... and the prime minister." But in terms of "the other constitutional innovations....the presidential usurpation of power is clearly displayed."[33] To begin with, the Prime Minister is *appointed* by the President in his discretion. Next, the president has the right to dissolve the Assembly whenever he thinks fit. Thirdly, he has a qualified right to bypass the legislature by ordering a referendum. Fourthly, the President possesses an emergency power of great dimension under Article 16. Finally, he is the 'arbitrator' under Article 5. "In practice this clause has thrown the cloak of constitutionality around flagrant breaches of the Constitution and enabled Charles de Gaulle to make it mean what it suited him to mean."[34]

Through the connivance of his Prime Ministers the President used his referendum power both as a personal plebiscite and, in one flagrant case in 1962, to amend the constitution in flat contradiction of Article 89. From 1958 to 1969, De Gaulle could remove a recalcitrant Prime Minister and choose his successor; he could override unruly opposition in the Assembly by

31. Relph Mcliband, *The State in Capitalist Society*, pp. 105-106.
32. S.E. Finer, *Comparative Government*, p. 300.
33. *Ibid,* p. 302.
34. *Ibid.* p. 304.

using procedural rules; he could ignore the constitutional rules by invoking his power of arbitration.

How did this happen? First, a new electoral law favoured the united Gaullists over a divided opposition, and discriminated particularly against the Communists. In the 1958 election, the Gaullists and their conservative allies got 320 seats with 49% votes. The opposition parties secured 51% votes but received only 144 seats. The Communists with 21% votes cast in their favour could get only 10 seats while the Gaullists with 28% could claim 188 seats. Though his party was in a minority, de Gaulle nominated Michel Debre from his own party as his first Prime Minister. Paradoxically, the minority status of the Gaullist party enabled de Gulle to expand the role of the presidency. As he proceeded to conciliate the Aligerian rebels, he came into clash with the inflamed, chauvinists among the 'Moderates' on his right but in the process received the support of the left-wing parties. They even overlooked his usurpations of the constitutional authority.

The General climaxed these unconstitutional usurpations of his authority in September 1962 by putting his constitutional amendment, to provide for a direct election of the President, directly for a popular referendum, in violation of the procedures clearly laid down in Article 89. The entire non-Gaullist majority of the Assembly passed a vote of no- confidence in the Gaullist cabinet. The President then dissolved the Assembly and called for a general election. The outcome stupefied all the opposition parties, both left and right. For the Gaullists, the election was a landside.

S. E. Finer says, "In vain did the General's opponents claim that the moral victory was theirs since the parties which had opposed de Gaulle's unconstitutional referendum had won sixty per cent of the total popular vote. For the hard political fact was that, with his minority vote of forty per cent, de Gaulled had picked up 229 metropolitan seats—only thirteen short of an absolute majority in the Assembly's and since in this election the Independent Republicans of M. Giscard d'Estaing had fought as allies of the Gaullist party, and had won twenty seats, this ensured the General and his prime minister something no government had possessed since the beginning of the Third Republic, and something that Debre, who was the chief architect of the 1958 Constitution, had never envisaged when he pioneered its drafting: namely, an absolute governmental majority in the assembly."[35]

The opposition parties of centre and left began to take the lesson of the electoral system with its second ballot to heart. The new mode of election for the president, adopted in 1962, requiring an absolute majority of the electorate either at first ballot or the second between two leading candidates of the first ballot, facilitated polarisation of the parties into two opposing blocs. The Gaullist party formed the nucleus of one of these blocs and the Socialist Party gradually developed into the nucleus of a rival bloc after a decade of trial and error. The Communists on the left and the neo-fascist groups on the right were electorally and politically isolated and marginalised and were compelled to align with what they believed was the lesser evil. Consequently, in the 1965 presidential election De Gaulle and Mitterrand received 44.6% and 31.7% votes respectively in the first ballot, and 55.2% and 44.8% votes respectively in the second ballot. By this time the Fifth Republic began to institutionalise itself.

In the words of de Gaulle, "The keystone of our regime in the new institution of a president of the Republic, designated by the reason and feelings of the French people to be the head of state and the guide of France." Then follows an extra-ordinary catalogue of the president's powers, real and fanciful, related to administration, defence, foreign policy, public safety and "the outstanding responsibility for the destiny of France and of the Republic.' (Broadcast, 20 December, 1962.) The General established this exalted conception of his office through four avenues. The first was the docility of his cabinet, which became almost a rubber stamp for his decisions. The General ruled his cabinet and through it the Assembly. The second avenue was an over-use of the government's decrce powers. When the Gaullists lost their majority in 1967 in the Assembly, the President relied on decrees to enact laws under Article 38. In constrast to this, the president invoked the emergency powers under Article 16 only once at the time of the Four Generals' Revolt in Algeria

35. S.E. Finer, *Comparative Government*, p. 308.

in April 1961. Finer argnes that the proclamaion of emergency was unconstitutional as there was no interruption in "the regular functioning of the constitutional organs of government" as required by Article 16.

The third avenue was de Gaulle's usurpation of the right to interpret the Constituition under cover of article 5. Despite the provision of a Constitutional Council and the *Counseil d'Etat* to deal with such matters, the President preferred to impose his personal interpretations. In 1960 he disallowed the convening of a special session of Parliamant under Article 29 requested by a majority of deputies to discuss the farmers' grievances. A somewhat similar case arose in 1961, once again provoked by argicultural unrest. Again , unable to prevent the Parliament's meeting, the President simply refused to let it debate agricultural bills because his view was that it must confine its deliberation to issues related to emergency alone. This unexpacted interpretation provoked widespread anger. The opposition immediately tabled a motion of censure but the President of the Assembly ruled the censure motion out of order on the strange grounds that in his view the General did have the right of interpreting the constitution under Article 5. As Finer says correctly, this bizarre logic defies analysis.

However, the classic utilization of the 'arbitration power' to violate the Constitution was the use of referendum to amend the Constitution in 1962; when the mode of Presidential election was changed from indirect to direct without the required approval of Parliament under Article 89. So the final avenue to presidential supremacy has been the abuse of referendum and debilitation of Parliament. His charismatic leadership transformed the Gaullist Republic into a plebiscitary dictatorship. The General told the voters in his broadcasts, "Iam the country's guide. To succeed I must have the support of the nation. That is why I appeal to you over the heads of inter mediaries."[36]

**Legitimation of the Fifth Republic**

From a capitalistic point of view, Gaullism had given France political stability, public order, a booming economy, a vast gold hoard, peace in Algeria and a nationalist and seemingly anti-American but pro-European foreign policy. At this moment, the tranquillity of the French social and political life was rudely disrupted and the entire fabric toppled and seemed to distintegrate. The very legitimacy of the Fifth Republic was in question. The government was paralysed by a month-long general strike of ten million workers. Finer says,"The way was clear for a ***coup d' etat.*** It did not not happen, because of a covert...complicity between the socalled revolutionary party, the Commuists, and the Gaullist government, Brought to the jump, the Communist race-horse 'refused', the government regained the initiative and in new general elections scored a momentous victory over all its opponents of the centre and the left."[37]

The immediate conclusions from this Gaullist crisis of legitimacy can be drawn as follows:(1)the tradition, nay the cult of insurrection and Revolution, was still alive in France; (2) the Communist Party of France at this occasion did not prove to be an extra-constitutional and insurrectionary force; (3) the concept of a unified 'opposition of all the lefts', symbolized in the 1968 common programme was credible so long as the combined left, led by the Communists, was kept away from state power; and (4) General de Gaulle took advantage of this fundamental cleavage within the ranks of the French Left to resurrect his authouity and legitimise the Fifth Republic.

The revolutionary crisis of 1968 proved to be a five-act play. The first act began with the activities of the ultra-left student agitators leading to a general strike of the French workers on 13 May, the tenth anniversary of the Fifth Republic. The second act included occupation of factories by the workers and M. Pompidou's decision to negotiate a settlement with the trade unions on economic issues. The third act involved a harassed Charles de Gaulle offering a popular referendum on a concept called 'participation' but the effort failed. Then began the riots in capital leading to failure of all talks between the government and the workers and the number of strikers reaching *ten million.*

Finer describes the scenario, "This was the revolutionary climax. The government clearly had no control over the situation and widespread demands were voiced for the resignation of the prime minister and for the re-

36. Quoted in Finer, *Comparative Government* pp.324-325.
37. S.E. Finer, *Comparative Government*, p. 326.

tirement of de Gaulle. The political parties staked their calims to the succession: Mitterrand, leader of the Federation of the Left. declared he would be a presidential candidate in the event of an election, the Communists stated that they would naturally expect to share in any government, and Mendes-France, the leader of the doctrinaire P.S.U., himself announced his willingness to head a new government of 'all the lefts.' But nobody *did* anything to bring all this about. They sat, apparently expecting the government would quit."[38]

The fourth act in the drama was the General's broadcast. He told the nation that he was not resigning; that he had cancelled referendum on 'participation;' and that he was dissolving Parliament and calling for immediate elections. The moment for taking a revolutionary action had passed. The negotiations with the trade unions began to bear fruits. The Gaullists started counter-demonstrations against what they described as the Communist-totalitarian threat to the Republic. France slowly returned to work in mid-June. The police moved to eject students from the premises which they had occupied and met no resistance. Social peace had been re-established. That is how the fifth act of the drama came —the denouement. The result of the election was a land-slide victory of the Gaullists and their allies. It was a giant step in the direction of legitimisation of the Fifth Republic.

At this stage, we can make five hypotheses. (1) The most important element in the development of the Fifth Republic during its first decade was the personal charisma of General de Gaulle. (2) Leaving out the charismatic personality of the leader, the constitution provided no solution for the situation where a non-charismatic President faced an Assembly in which his party was in a minority, and was compelled to work with a Prime Minister of a different political complexion. (3) The French dissensus had perished and the desined polarisation had not occurred. (4) the General could not be defeated in an election by a fractured opposition but could lose a referendum, as he did in 1969, leading to his resignation. (5) Except the Communists, all other parties had given their acceptance to the Gaullist Constitution.

The General's plan to reform the Senate, to reshape it in the Gaullist image, and to acquire new powers through a constitutional amendment, were rejected in a referendum held on 27 April,1969 with 47.58 per cent votes in favour and 52.41 per cent votes against the proposal. The General's ambition to alter, delete or replace no less than 23 of the 89 articles of the current Constitution was thwarted by the people. As Finer put it, "Having by the illegal use of Article 11, whipped the French electorate on its bare arse, the General was now inviting it to kiss the rod as well."[39] This meant that one General's attempt to delegitimise his own constitution of the Fifth Republic by suggesting comprehensive amendments had failed and his resignation after this event was a correct step in the direction of its further legitimisation.

This next election brought M. Pompidou to Presidential office with 44 per cent votes in the first and 57.6 per cent votes in the second ballot. The election closed the de Gaulle chapter. It opened another. This had been a free, fair and open election. All parties had taken part in it, including the far left, and the Gaullist candidate had won. Now Mitterrand's complaint that the Gaullist clique was retaining power through force or fraud was no longer valid. For the first time, the credentials of the President were not suspicious. In 1974, the French people elected Valery Giscard d'Estaing, a non-Gaullist conservative, as their President. Both in 1981 and 1988, the electorate chose Socialist Mitterrand as their President. Jacques Chirac was elected to Presidency in 1995 as a Gaullist leader. The succession of these leaders belonging to different parties in the Presidential office demonstrated conclusively that the Fifth Republic had finally achieved full legitimacy.

In a sense, the strategy and tactics of the French Communist Party during the revolutionary crisis of 1968 also helped in the ultimate legitimisation of the Fifth Republic. Jack Woddis believes that by abstaining from any adventurist call for an insurrection: "It avoided another Indonesian catastrophe, in which at least half a million Communists and others were massacred in 1965 after abortive *coup* against the military leaders; it secured material and democratic gains for the workers; it increased the

38. *Ibid*. p. 328.
39. *bid*, p. 338

cred in 1965 after abortive *coup* against the military leaders; it secured material and democratic gains for the workers; it increased the people's desire to have done with de Gaulle, who was compelled to resign within a year of the general strike."[40]

The most important test of the Fifth Republic came when the Socialist President had to appoint a Gaullist Prime Minister in 1986 but despite their different political complexions, the experiment in cohabitation proved successful. The same Gaullist Prime Minister Chirac, who coexisted with the Socialist President Mitterand at that time is now at the Elysee as President and he has to coexist with the Socialist Prime Minister, Jospin. The Communists are occasionally represented in Socialist cabinets without causing any constitutional or political embarrassment. Capitalist democracy is not weakened by their presence in some governments led by the Socialist Party; this in fact strengthens it.

The French system of a combined Presidential Parliamentary government was adopted in Sri Lanka by Jayawardhene in 1976. In 2002, Sri Lankan democracy faces now a similar dilemma, which France has faced during the last fifteen years i.e. how to cohalit successfully Chandrika Kumartung-led Presidency with a cabinet led by the United National Party that is opposed to the President ideologically as well as programmatically.

## SUGGESTED READINGS

Barrington Moore, *The Social Origins of Dictatorship and Democracy*
Blondel and Godfrey, *The Government of France*
Dorothy Pickles, *The Fifth French Republic*
Finer, S.E., *Comparative Government*, Chap.7.
Jack Woddis, *New Theories of Revolution*
Macridis, J. and Ward, A.E., *Modern Political Systems —Europe.*
Ralph Miliband, *The State in Capitalist Society.*
Theda Skocpol, *States and Social Revolutions.*

40. Jack Woddis, *New Theories of Revolution*, p. 365

# THE GOVERNMENT OF CANADA
## (CONSTITUTION OF 1982)

## CHAPTER I

# Political Tradition and the Constitution

**Historical Background**

Canada, which today has an area of almost 10 million square kilometers and a population of 23,500,000, out of which 6,000,000 are French, was originally founded in 1608 by the French colonists. The Seven Years' war between the French and the English had its repercussions in Canada too. General Wolfe, Commander of the British forces in North America, conquered Quebec in September, 1759 and Montreal a year later. As a result of the Treaty of Paris, 1763, France recognized the cessation of Canada to Britain. The Treaty, however, provided that "His Britannic Majesty, on his part, agrees to grant liberty of the Catholic religion to the inhabitants of Canada."

The King of Britain thereafter appointed a Governor to rule Canada on his behalf. He was assisted by a Council and an Assembly. But complications soon arose because of the heavy influx of British immigrants. Parliament passed an Act in 1774 which aimed to remove the grievances and disabilities of the Roman Catholics. But the situation again worsened when a large number of Loyalists from America, immediately after the Declaration of Independence by the thirteen Colonies, entered and settled in Canada. Parliament thereupon passed the Constitution Act, 1791, which divided Canada into two Provinces, the Upper Canada with a British majority and the Lower Canada with a French majority. Each Province had its own Council and Assembly, the former nominated and hereditary and the latter was elective. The Governor was independent of the legislature and he received instructions from the Colonial Office in London. But even this system of administration did not remedy the situation. In Lower Canada the British dominated in the Council whereas the French were in majority in the Assembly. This resulted into unceasing deadlocks between the two Chambers and the irresponsive Executive and representative Assembly. The ethnic and religious controversy, French versus English, became unmanageable. Louis-Joseph Papineau, the leader of the French, declared an open revolt against the King of Britain. The rebellion was suppressed and Papineau fled, but the smouldering embers of discontent were not finally extinguished. In Upper Canada, too, things were not running smooth. The British majority there could not reconcile itself with an irresponsive popular control over the administration.

The British Government suspended the Constitution Act and sent Lord Durham to Canada with full administrative authority. Lord Durham went deep into the problems of Canada and after two years of his stay submitted to the British Government his report which is eminently known as the Durham Report. The Durham Report constituted a landmark in British constitutional history as it set a political way for Canada. Lord Durham recommended, *inter alia,* that establishment of responsible government should alone bring the English and the French to an enduring national integration. Parliament passed an Act in July 1840 uniting the Upper and Lower Canada. For two decades the system of government thus established functioned no doubt, but new problems emerged which finally necessitated the union of all the Canadian areas in a Federal polity.

**Birth of a Dominion**

The four Provinces in 1867 that became the federal Provinces of Ontario, Quebec, Nova Scotia and New Brunswick were little more than scanty pockets of settlement, subsisting on forests, farms, fisheries, industries and localised manufacture. They possessed only three cities—Quebec, Montreal and Toronto—with more than 300,000 inhabitants, and a little more than 12 per cent of the people lived in towns with a population of over 5,000. There were a variety of conditions which favoured the union of these struggling Colonies and the potentially hostile political bodies. At the Montreal Inter-Provincial banquet of 1861, Joseph Howe maintained, in the after-dinner speech, that if public men of the ''various Colonies could only get together as were then doing, they would discover what excellent fellows they all were and the barriers between them would soon go down.'' Here were the germs of the second political miracle occurring on the North American Continent; the first having occurred when thirteen States united to form the United States of America.

The idea of a union of the Colonies in the British North America dates back to the time of the American Colonies winning their independence. But the cooperating circumstances which would have resulted into the materialization of such ideas never took place. Lord Durham, while favouring a union, wrote in his famous Report: ''I found two nations warring in the bosom of a single state; I found a struggle, not of principles, but of races; and I perceived that it would be idle to attempt any amelioration of laws or institutions until we could first succeed in terminating the deadly animosity that now separates Lower Canada into the hostile divisions of French and English.'' The situation was no better in other Provinces and to the situation in Lower Canada were added all the problems and difficulties that were found in the other Colonies as well.

The two major recommendations of the Durham Report were the re-union of Upper and Lower Canada and the immediate grant of responsible government. Lord Durham had considered that only union between the two Canadas could eliminate the racial conflict in Lower Canada and, thus, make it possible for responsible government to function effectively. But the separate cultures of the two peoples complicated the working of responsible government and created endless frictions which resulted in political deadlock, sudden ministerial changes, and general instability. The demand in Upper Canada for representation according to the numbers threatened to upset the political balance. The French, in Lower Canada, which was less populous, feared it as an attempt to destroy their separate culture and concluded that they could survive only as distinct community within the framework of a true federation. Federation, they considered, was the best possible solution for harmonising the diverse cultural groups in a larger political unit. Professor Alexander Brady sums up the circumstances that helped the birth of a federation. He says, ''it was a means of preserving their identity; for other colonists it was an escape for colonial inferiority to self-government in a generous national *plane*, with an ever widening horizon of expansion.''

Economic problems also plagued a divided Canada. The repeal of the Navigation Laws and the abandonment of the preferential tariffs in the forties and fifties gave a new and convincing impetus to the proposal for union. Economic embarrassments were apprehended by all to become more acute with the expiration of the Reciprocity Treaty with the United States as it would result into serious loss of markets for the Canadian producers. The only solution of these and other difficulties following in their wake was enlargement of political and economic boundaries where all Canadians in union with each other ''strengthen their position as best as they might in a highly dangerous and competitive world.'' Defence was no less important. The many-sided menace from the United States ''cast a shadow over all the colonies; the bellicose statements of many American politicians, the exceptional military power of the country engaged in a prolonged civil war; the danger frequently apparent of becoming embroiled in war through British-American quarrels; and the threat to the colony of Canada, although this in a sense was a common threat also, of having the United States isolate the whole north-eastern corner of North America from the remainder of the continent by taking possession of all empty western territory.''

Finally, the pre-federation period was a time of great economic upheaval which disturbed the economies of all the Colonies. With their limited resources and undeveloped means of communication and transport the Colonies could not adjust themselves to the new technological and industrial needs. ''The shift from wood to iron,'' says Prof. Creighton, ''from water-power to steam boats became virtually an accomplished fact. All these changes fell with jarring force upon provincial economies which were unprepared to sustain the tremendous and expensive adjustments involved.''

The cumulative effect of all these circumstances was that the Canadian federation became a matter of practical politics in the spring of 1864, when Dr. Charles Tupper, the Prime Minister of Nova Scotia, introduced a resolution in its provincial legislature for the appointment of delegates ''to confer with delegates who may be appointed by the governments of New Brunswick and Prince Edward Island for the purpose of considering the subject of the union of the three provinces under one Government and Legislature.'' The Nova Scotia Legislature unanimously endorsed Trupper's resolution, and similar resolutions were passed by the Legislatures of the two Maritime Colonies, New Brunswick and Prince Edward Island. A conference was called to meet at Charlottetown on September 1, 1864. On June 30, a new coalition government was formed in the Province of Canada which pledged to use its best efforts to bring about federation in the British North American Colonies. The proposed Charlotte- town conference was considered propitious by Canadian Government and at the request of his Cabinet, Lord Monck entered into communication with the Lieutenant-Governors of the Maritime Colonies and asked if a Canadian delegation might join the conference and participate in its deliberations. The request was granted and eight Canadian Ministers, including MacDonbald, Brown Carter and Galt, joined the conference. Nova Scotia, New Brunswick and Prince Edward Island sent five delegates each, making a total of twenty-three delegates in all.

The conference met as scheduled. The Canadian representatives put forward their proposals for a comprehensive union of all the Colonies. The delegates from the Maritime Colonies, proceeded to the separate considerration of the proposals to which their respective Legislatures had agreed and authorised them to confer. But it became soon apparent that the union among themselves could not hope for success. Federation was the only feasible plan and the delegates reached a decision that a formal conference of all the delegations, including New Foundland should re-assemble at Quebec in October.

On October 10, 1864 there assembled at Quebec one of the most epoch-making conferences in the Canadian history. Canada had its twelve delegates, New Brunswick and Prince Edward Island seven each, Nova Scotia five,and New Foundland two, in all thirty-three. The fundamental principle accepted at Charlotte- town was endorsed unreservedly at Quebec that is, that the new government should be a federation. In less than eighteen days seventy-two resolutions were agreed on, which practically became the subsequent North America Act of 1867. These resolutions were approved by Parliament of Canada, but met with considerable opposition in the Maritime Provinces. This led to the convening of a conference by the British Government in London consisting of the representatives of Nova Scotia, New Brunswick and Canada. The outcome was the passage of the British North America Act of 1867, which received royal assent on March 29, and was proclaimed on May 22, and came into effect on July 1.

Thus, on July 1, 1867, came into being the Dominion of Canada consisting of four Provinces—Ontrario, Quebec (United Canada redivided), New Brunswick and Nova Scotia. The Queen was given power, on the advice of the Privy Council and on the address from Parliament of Canada and the legislatures of New Foundland, Prince Edward Island and British Columbia, to admit the remaining Colonies or any of them into the Dominion, and with the same advice she was given power to admit Ruppert's Land and North- Western territory on address from Parliament of Canada. Ruppert's Land and North-Western territory were, accordingly, adminted in 1870. The Province of Manitoba was admitted at the same time, and in the following year came in British Columbia. Prince Edward Island was admitted two years later in 1873. In 1905 two Dominion statutes transferred a large block of the western territory into the Province of Alberta and Saskatchewan. Finally, in 1949, New Foundland became the tenth province of the Dominion of Canada.

**The Canadian Constitution Act, 1982**

Canada is now made up of ten constituent units, called the Provinces. Canada achieved political independence between the years 1919 and 1931. The Statute of Westminster, 1931, gave legal expression to what was already a fact. The Balfour Declaration of 1926 had reconginsed the equality of the Dominions and the United Kingdom. It was reinforced by the Imperial Conference of 1930. The Statute of Westminster statutorily established that the dominions enjoyed complete autonomy in their internal and external affairs and the ties which bound them together and with the United Kingdom were of equality and not subordination. The allegiance of the Dominions to the reigning monarch of the United Kingdom did not assign to them a place of inferiority so far as their relations with the British Government were concerned. He was as much their King as of the United Kingdom; several monarchs wrapped up in one person, completely distinct from one another. The King acted on the advice of Dominion Ministers in all matters relating to the administration of the Dominion. The Dominion was free to make any law and there was no limit on its legislative power. No Dominion statute could be declared void because it was repugnant to the law of the United Kingdom, and no act of the Parliament in the United Kingdom was to extend to the Dominion unless the act specifically declared that the Dominion had requested and consented to its enactment.

But Canada could not amend its Constitution, the British North America Act, 1867. The British North America Act, unlike the Commonwealth of Australia Constitution Act, contained no amending clause whatever. The framers of the 1867 Constitution felt that if any amendments to the basic Act of 1867 were necessary, Canada would address the authorities in London to amend the British North America Act and the British would do accordingly. The British Parliament had always acted a little more than an automaton and quietly and quickly passed the required amendment. The Statute of 1867 was amended 23 times till 1982. The British Parliament was, thus, simply an agent in the realization of the wishes of the Canadian Parliament.

But this procedure of amending the British North America Act by an Act of British Parliament placed Canada, in the opinion of the vast majority of Canadians, in a humiliating position. Canada would have acquired an amending formula and had "patriated"[1] its Constitution in 1931, but the Provinces and the Federal Government could not agree on the content of the amending formula. Thus, it was agreed that the power to amend the British North America Act, 1867, would be left with the Westminster Parliament. But the efforts to find an agreed formula were not abandoned and negotiations between the federal and Provincial Governments were held in 1935, 1949, 1960, 1964, 1978, 1979 and 1980, all ending in disagreement. An agreement between the federal and nine Provincial Governments in November 1981 on the contents of the Constitution Act, 1982, which included an amending formula, ended the 55 years' impasse. Quebec did not give its assent to the Agreement of Ten (Federal and nine Provincial) Governments.

On December 2, 1981, by a 246 to 24 vote, the Canadian House of Commons adopted the text of the address as it stood amended by an Agreement of the Ten. The Senate passed it on December 8, by a vote of 59 to 23, and the same evening the Address left for London. This address was a solemn request to the British authorities to amend the basic Statute of 1867. The text of the Address read:

"THAT, WHEREAS in the past certain amendments to the Constitution of Canada have been made by the Parliament of the United Kingdom at the request and with the consent of Canada;

AND WHEREAS it is in accord with the statutes of Canada as an independent state that Canadians be able to amend their Constitution in Canada in all respects:

AND WHEREAS it is also desirable to provide in the Constitution of Canada for the recognition of certain fundamental rights and freedoms and to make other amendments to the Constitution;

A respectful address be presented to Her Majesty the Queen in the following words;

To the Queen's Most
Excellent Majesty:
Most gracious Sovereign:

We, your Majesty's loyal subjects, the House of Commons of Canada in Parliament assembled, respectfully approach your Majesty, requesting that you may graciously be pleased to cause to be laid before the Parliament of the United Kingdom a measure containing the recital and clauses hereinafter set forth...."

Two Acts were proposed for adoption by the British Parliament. The first was the Canada Act, the instrument of "patriation". Appended

1. "Patriation" means that Canada "would obtain or recover from the British Parliament the power to amend the Constitution of Canada, in the sectors common to both orders of government and, for the British Parliament, it would mean letting go of a power that it retained in spite of itself in 1931, as a favour to Canada". Gerald A. Beaudoin, *The Patriation of the Canadian Constitution,* issued by the Canadian High Commission, New Delhi.

to this Act was the Constitution Act, 1982, which included, *inter alia,* the Chapter of Rights and Freedoms, the amending formula, etc.

In December 1981, the Government of Quebec approached the Court of Appeal at Montreal with the following question: was there a constitutional convention giving Quebec the right to veto amendments to the Constitution which would have the effect of making the Agreement of the Ten unsconstitutional from the viewpoint of convention? Meantime, in London, in January 1982, the Native Peoples were held "nonsuited" by the Biritsh Court of Appeal on the question of the jurisdiction of the Crown over their rights. All legislative power over them the court ruled, belonged to Canada and the Crown no longer had any authority whatsoever in that area.

Legally, nothing stood in the way of the British Parliament to amend the British North America Act, 1867. The British Government felt that the Agreement of the Ten met a "substantial measure of provincial consent"[2] criterion decreed by the Supreme Court of Canada on September 28, 1982. In his letter of December 19, 1981, Premier Levesque of Quebec asked Prime Minister Mrs. Margaret Thatcher to suspend proceedings on the resolution of the Canadian Parliament in the Parliament of U.K. until Quebec gave its consent to the resolution or until the court had decided on the Quebec right of veto question. Mrs Thatcher in her reply to Premier Levesque on January 14, 1982 wrote that she intended to proceed with the resolution and that the question of the Quebec veto was a purely Canadian one in view of the decision of the Supreme Court.

The British Parliament passed the Twenty-Third amendment to the British North America Act, 1867, enacting the Constitution Act, 1981, "which shall have the force of law in Canada and shall come into force as provided in that Act." It also provided that no act of Parliament of the United Kingdom "passed after the Constitution Act,1981, comes into force shall extend to Canada as part of its law." With this enactment which was cited as the Canada Act the process of "patriation" was complete and Canada acquired the right to amend or repeal the Canada Constitution.

The Proclamation bringing Canada's new Constitution Act into law was signed by Queen Elizabeth II in a historic ceremony in Parliament Hill in Ottawa, on April 17, 1982. Prime Minister Pierre Trudeau said at ceremony proclaiming the Act: "After 50 years of discussion we have finally decided to retrace what is properly ours. It is with happy hearts, and with gratitude for the patience displayed by Great Britain, that we are preparing to acquire today our complete national sovereignty." Quebec decided not to participate in the ceremony. In addressing the Quebec's decision the Prime Minister said: "I know many Quebecers find themselves pulled in two directions by that decision. But one need not look only at the results of the referendum in May 1980 (some 60 per cent of Quebecers refused to give mandate to the Provincial Government to negotiate a new political relationship with the rest of Canada, an arrangement described as "sovereignty-association") to realize how strong is the attachment to Canada among the people of Quebec. By definition, the silent majority does not make a lot of noise. It is content to make history."[3] The Queen later addressed about 32,000 people attending the outdoor ceremonies on Parliament Hill. She lauded Quebec's cultural contribution despite her sorrow that the Province had refused to participate in the Proclamation of the country's new Constitu-

2. The Prime Minister and the Provincial Premiers met in Ottawa (September 8-13, 1980) to consider patriation, a charter to rights, distribution of powers, federal institutions etc. No unanimous agreement was reached. Prime Minister, Trudeau announced a plan of action which included patriation, an amending formula, a Charter of Rights, etc. Six Provincial Premiers announced their opposition to the Federal Patriation resolution and their intention of challenging the proposal in Courts. Manitoba asked its Court of Appeal for a ruling, *inter alia,* on the constitutionality of the patriation resolution. The New Foundland and Quebec Governments also sought rulings from their respective Provincial Courts of Appeal. The Manitoba Court of Appeal ruled (three to two) that the Federal Government could ask the United Kingdom Parliament to amend the Canadian Constitution of the Provinces. The New Foundland Court of Appeal ruled unanimously that consent of the Provinces was necessary before the Constitution could be amended by the U.K. Parliament. The Quebec Court of Appeal ruled (four-to-one) that the resolution was within the constitutional authority of the Senate and the House of Commons. The Supreme Court of Canada heard appeals from the decisions of all the three Provincial Courts of Appeal. On September 28, 1981 the Supreme Court declared that the Federal government's constitutional resolution was valid but that by convention, it required a substantial measure of provincial consent." The Court stated, however that it was up to the political actors to define what was meant by "substantial provincial consent".

3. *Canada Weekly,* April 28, 1982.

tion. "Although we regret the absence of the premier of Quebec, it is right to associate the people of Quebec with this celebration because without them, Canada would not be what it is today," she said in French.[4]

**Basis of the Constitution (1982)**

The Constitution Act, 1982, is not a new Canadian Constitution. The Biritsh North America Act, 1867, together with all its amendments (23 in number, the last being the passage of legislation allowing the Constitution Act, 1982, to come into force) as well as other important laws that touch on constitutional matters remain in existence and are incorporated in the Constitution Act, 1982. For example, the British North America Act now becomes the Constitution Act 1867, and so do other Acts that from time to time amended the original Act.

The Constitution Act 1867, is, thus, the pivot on which hinges the constitutional framework of Canada. It is the instrument that created the Dominion of Canada by uniting the four original Provinces and binds together in perpetual common ties the Provinces that today make the federation of Canada. As the Constitution Act, 1867, was designed to bring unity not the diversity of the new nation, it contains the scheme of distribution of powers between the Centre and the Provinces, and organisation of governments at both levels.

Apart from the written part of the Canadian Constitution there are innumerable conventions and judicial practices that have moulded and shaped the Constitution during the 115 years of its career. The Preamble to the Act had been the main innovator of the constitutional conventions when it declared in 1867 that it was the desire of the original Provinces to be united "with a constitution similar in Principle to that of the United Kingdom." It means that all those principles which are basic to the cabinet system of government in the United Kingdom and find their origin and continuance in the conventions of the constitution would be observed in Canada too. The Constitution Act, 1867, did not incorporate any of these conventions. The Preamble is not a part of the Act, but the direction it contains for the fulfilment of the objective makes a vital difference in theory and practice.

**Amending Procedure**

At the time of writing of the Act of 1867, the founding fathers of Canada took the attitude that if future changes to the Act were needed, Canadians could simply ask the British Parliament to amend it, and it had always been done without demur. The Constitution Act, 1982, puts an end to this anachronistic practice by which Canada, a fully sovereign nation, still had to ask a foreign Parliament, to legislate changes in its Constitution.

Part V of the 1982 Constitution, covering Sections 38 to 49 contains a procedure for amending the Constitution of Canada. The amending procedure spells out how Canadians, through their National and Provincial Governments, can make changes in their Constitution. This procedure contains essentially five amending powers.

An amendment of the Constitution may be made by a resolution of the House of Commons and the Senate and by resolutions of the Provincial Legislative Assemblies of at least two-thirds of the Provinces that have in the aggregate, according to the then latest general census, at least fifty per cent of the population of all the Provinces.[5] An amendment may be initiated either by the House of Commons or the Senate or by the Legislative Assembly of a Province. This general amending formula has two important aspects: the amending procedure spells out, for the first time, a role for the Provinces in making constitutional changes, and, secondly, no single Province, big or small, can veto a constitutional amendment. That requires the consent of both the Houses of Parliament and seven Provincial Legislatures representing at least 50 per cent of the population of all the Provinces. Article 39 (I), as a measure of abundant caution, provides that no proclamation shall be issued by the Governor-General declaring that the Constitution stands amended before the expiry of one year from the adoption of the resolution by the Parliament unless the Legislative Assembly of each Province has previously adopted a resolution of assent or dissent. After the expiry of one year the proclamation can be issued by the Governor-General even if all the Provincial Assemblies had not signified their

4. *Ibid.*
5. Section 38 (1)

assent or dissent, provided Assemblies of seven Provinces representing 50 per cent of the population of all the Provinces had assented to the amendment as passed by Parliament. But no proclamation shall be issued after the expiration of three years from the date of the adoption of the resolution initiating the amendment. It lapses.[6]

If the amendment affects the rights, prerogatives or proprietary rights of Provinces or privileges of the legislature for government of a Province, it requires the support of a majority of the total membership of each House of Parliament and the Legislative Assemblies of at least two-thirds of the Provinces representing at least 50 per cent of the population. Such an amendment shall not have effect in a Province the Legislative Assembly of which has expressed its dissent supported by a majority of its total membership prior to the issue of the proclamation unless that Legislative Assembly, subsequently, by resolution supported by a majority of its total membership revokes its dissent and authorizes the amendment. The resolution of dissent may be revoked at any time before or after the issue of the proclamation.

Where an amendment is made, transferring Provincial legislative powers relating to education or other cultural matters from the jurisdiction of the Provincial Legislatures to Parliament, the Federal Government shall provide reasonable compensation to province which had ''opted out'' of the change (that is, has refused to accept the transfer for itself). Of course, there is a limit of three Provinces that can choose to opt out because if more than three Provinces opposed an amendment, it would not be adopted as the consent of at least seven Provinces is required to render the amendment valid.

For the following five subjects an amendment requires the consent of Parliament and the Legislative Assembly of each Province, that is, the Parliament and ten Legislative Assemblies must agree thereto; even a single dissent may defeat the amendment:

(a) the office of the Queen, the Governor-General and the Lieutenant-Governor of a Province;

(b) the right of a Province to a number of members in the House of Commons not less than the number of Senators by which the Province is entitled to be represented at the time the Procedure for amending the Constitution (Part V) comes into force;

(c) subject to Section 43 (amendment of provisions relating to some but not all Provinces) the use of the English or the French language;

(d) the composition of the Supreme Court of Canada;

(e) an amendment to Part V relating to the Procedure for Amending of the Constitution.

When an amendment concerns some or more Provinces, but not all including any alteration to boundaries between Provinces, and any amendment to any provision that relates to the use of English and French, the amendment must be the result of consent of the two Houses of Parliament and of Provincial Assemblies involved.

Finally, Parliament may exclusively make laws amending the Constitution of Canada in relation to the executive and legislative authority of Canada. But the amendment to the Constitution of Canada in relation to the following matters can be made only in accordance with the general procedure for amending the Constitution, that is, the consent of the Canadian Parliament and seven Provincial Legislative Assemblies representing at least 50 per cent of the population of all Provinces:

(a) the principle of proportional representation of the Provinces in the House of Commons prescribed by the Constitution of Canada;

(b) the powers of the Senate and the method of selecting Senators;

(c) the number of members by which a Province is entitled to be represented in the Senate and the residence qualifications of the Senators;

(d) the Supreme Court of Canada subject to Section 41(d) which provides that any amendment relating to the Supreme Court requires the consent of the Parliament and the Assemblies of all the ten Provinces;

(e) the extension of the existing provinces into the territories; and

(f) notwithstanding any other law or practice, the establishment of Provinces.

6. Section 46 (1)

The Legislatures of the Provinces, as had been the case before the proclamation of the Constitution Act, 1982, can exclusively make laws amending their Constitutions.

Article 49 provides for the setting up of a Constitutional Conference composed of the Prime Minister of Canada and the first ministers of the Provinces within fifteen years after the Procedure for Amending Constitution of Canada, as contained in Part V, comes into force to review the provisions of this Part.

**Federalism**

Canada is a federal State, established in 1867. In that year, at the request of three separate colonies (Canada, Nova Scotia and New Brunswick), the British Parliament passed the British America Act (now the Constitution Act, 1867) which federally united the three "to form.... one dominion under the name of Canada." The Act merely embodied, with one modification (providing for the appointment of extra Senators to break a deadlock between the two Houses of Parliament), the decisions that delegates from the Colonies—the "Fathers of Federation" -had themselves arrived at.

The Act divided the Dominion into four Provinces. The pre-Confederation "province of Canada" became the Province of Ontario and Quebec, while Nova Scotia and New Brunswick retained their former limits. In 1870, the Parliament of Canada created Manitoba; British Columbia entered the Union in 1871 and Prince Island in 1873. In 1905 the Parliament of Canada created Saskatchewan and Alberta and in 1949 New Foundland joined.

But the Fathers of the Canadian Constitution were not wedded to the narrow ideas of federalism and they did not follow the path carved out by the framers of the American Constitution. The United States had been engaged from the days of Jefferson in the long and bitter controversy over rights and powers of the States which culminated in the tragic Civil War. Canadian leaders had the opportunity to become wiser from the experience of their neighbours. The majority of the delegates assembled at the Quebec Conference had the abiding conviction that the outstanding lesson to be learned from the menacing circumstances of the American Republic was the necessity of strengthening the centripetal forces in a federation, which they proposed to set up. The best way, they decided, was to give a few enumerated subjects of jurisdiction to the constituent units and leave the residue for the Central Government. "The true principle of confederation," asserted Sir John MacDonald, "lay in giving to the Central Government all the principles and powers of sovereignty, and that the subordinate or individual states should have no powers but those expressly bestowed on them. We should, thus, have a powerful Central Government, a powerful Central Legislature, and a decentralized system of minor legislatures for local purposes." At another occasion MacDonald confidently claimed: that "Here we have adopted a different system. We have strengthened the Central Government. We have given the Central Legislature all the great subjects to legislation. We have thus avoided that great source of weakness which has been the cause of disruption of the United States."

The distribution of powers in the Canadian Constitution was, thus, in vast contrast to that of the Constitution of the United States and it was directly the result of the events that followed the inauguration of the American federation culminating into the Civil War. Unlike the United States, the Provinces in Canada were assigned exclusive jurisdiction on subjects enumerated in Section 92 of the Act and the Dominion had jurisdiction over the rest and for "greater certainty" Section 91 of the Act enumerated 29 subjects which were assigned to the Dominion (Federal) Parliament. The enumerated subjects assigned to the Provinces were just 16 in number and they were essentially of a local nature. Some subjects, which in the United States had been left with the States, such as marriage and divorce and criminal law (Entries 26 and 27 Section 91) were given in Canada to the Dominion (Federal) Parliament. But that was not enough. Section 91 also empowered the Federal Parliament "to make laws for the peace, order and good government of Canada in relation to all matters not coming within the classes of subjects by this Act assigned exclusively to the legislatures of the Provinces." This is an all-embracing provision which enables the Federal Parliament to make laws on subjects which are within the exclusive jurisdiction of the Provinces on the plea that they affected the peace, order and good government of Canada. At top of this, the Federal Government was given the power to disallow any law passed by a Provincial Legislature within a year of its enactment.

The Federal Government possessed the power of appointing and removing the Lieutenant-Governor in each Province. It could also instruct the Lieutenant-Governor to withhold his assent to Bills or reserve them for the consideration of the Governor-General. All important judicial appointments in the Provinces were vested in the Federal Government. The members of the Senate were nominated by the Federal Government and the representation of the Provinces in the Senate, unlike the United States, was not based on equality. The Canadian Senate, thus, significantly differed from its namesake in the United States.

The Canadian federation was designed by its architects to depart radically from the federal principle which divides and distributes powers between a central government and governments of the constituent units, and accepts both sets of government within their respective spheres of jurisdiction as coordinate and independent. The most essential characteristic of the federal government is that neither the central government nor the regional governments can render the one helplessly dependent upon the other for its existence or proper functioning. But the Canadian Provinces were desired to be inferior bodies "possessing little more prestige and authority," as Dawson says, "than inflated municipalities." In the discussions at the Quebec Conference, Provincial Legislatures were repeatedly described as "subordinate," "minor," and "inferior" bodies. Speaking on the Quebec Resolution in Parliament of Canada on February 6, 1865, John MacDonald said, "We... strengthen the Central Parliament and make the confederation one people and one government, instead of five peoples and five governments, with merely a point of authority connecting us to a limited and insufficient extent...this is to be one United Province with the local governments and legislatures subordinate to the general government and legislature." The amplification of this point by Charles Tupper is yet more blunt. He said, "we propose to preserve the Local Governments in the Lower Provinces because we have no municipal institutions." But he was also careful to state that "while we should diminish the powers of Local Governments we must not stock too largely the prejudices of the people in that respect." Thus, it was the definite intention of the Constitution-makers to make the Provincial Governments in Canada subordinate to the Central Government and not coordinate with it. Their purpose was not to repeat the events that had happened in the United States of America. Whatever the intentions of the Founding Fathers, it must be admitted that they defeated the purpose of a federal polity.

The powers of disallowance and veto further rendered the Provinces helplessly dependent upon the Central Government. The British North America Act empowered the Dominion Government to prevent the Provincial Legislature from making laws upon its own allotted subjects, if the Dominion Government happened to disapprove the policy involved in such laws. In *Re-Disallowance* and *Reservation* (1938) the Supreme Court of Canada held that the Dominion Government's powers of disallowance and veto were unrestricted in law and extended to all kinds of legislation, financial and ordinary. This is tantamount to placing the Provincial Governments entirely at the mercy of the Dominion Government.

All these are unitary elements and Professor K.C. Where, a renowned authority on federalism, tersely put it, "Could there be a more powerful weapon for centralising and unifying the government than this?"[7] Wheare, then, examines the controversial question whether Canada has a unitary or federal type of government. His conclusion is that in spite of these unitary elements, '"the federal principle is not completely ousted" from the Canadian Constitution; it does find a place there and an important place. "Yet if we confine ourselves to the strict law of the constitution," he adds, "it is hard to know whether we should call it a federal constitution with considerable unitary modifications, or a unitary constitution, with considerable federal modifications. It would be straining the federal principle too far, I think, to describe it as a federal constitution, without adding any qualifying phrase For this reason I prefer to say that Canada has a quasi-federal constitution."[8]

But Professor Kennedy, another renowned scholar, categorically says that "Canada is a federation in essence." His conclusions are based upon a series of legal decisions, and that reduces them into four:

(1) The Federal Parliament is not a delegation from the British Parliament or from the

7. Where, K. C., *Federal Government,* p. 20.
8. *Ibid.*

Provinces. It has full and complete powers over its sphere of jurisdiction.

(2) The Provincial Legislatures are not delegation from the British Parliament. Their authority is plenary within the limits prescribed by the Constitution and, as held in *Hodge* v. *The Queen* within the sphere so prescribed "the local legislature is supreme and has the same authority as the Imperial Parliament or the Parliament of the Dominion."

(3) The Provincial Legislatures are not delegations from the Federal Parliament and their status is in no way analogous to municipal bodies. In the liquidators of the *Maritime Bank of Canada* v. *The Receiver- General of New Brunswick,* Lord Watson declared: "That Act of 1867.... nowhere professes to curtail in any respect the rights and privileges of the Crown or to disturb the relations then subsisting between the sovereign and the provinces. The object of the Act was neither to weld the provinces into one, nor to subordinate provincial governments to a central authority, but to create a Federal Government in which they should all be represented, entrusted with the exclusive administration of affairs in which they had a common interest, each province retaining its independence and autonomy...As regards those matters which by Section 92 are specially reserved for provincial legislation of each province continues....as supreme as it was before the passing of the Act."

(4) The Provinces remain independent and autonomous. Professor Kennedy summing up the position and status of the Federal Government and Provinces says that both governments "exercise co-ordinate authority and are severally Sovereign within the sphere specifically or generically or by implication constitutionally granted to them."[9] This construction, he holds, agrees with the Preamble of the British North America (Canada) Act which reads "whereas the Provinces of Canada, Nova Scotia, and New Brunswick have expressed their desire to be federally united."

A federal constitution is really what the Judges declare it to be. Interpreting the Constitution of the United States the Supreme Court adopted a definite theory of federalism. It had been assumed that the States retained their 'sovereignty' in all matters which were not expressly taken away from them and as such no legislation of Congress must interfere with powers which remained with the States, and no legislation of the States must be allowed to interfere with the exercise of powers specially assigned to the Federal Government. The Supreme Court has the power to declare unconstitutional Federal or State legislation which, in its opinion, offended against the limitations imposed by the Constitution. Moreover, in interpreting the Constitution, the Supreme Court has always remembered that a Constitution is not an ordinary law. It is a fundamental law providing the machinery of government and it has to be interpreted according to the conditions which it has to meet and solve. Mere reliance on the letter of the law and the intentions of its framers would make the Constitution static thereby preventing the organs of government adapting themselves to changing social and economic conditions.

But the Supreme Court of Canada and the Judicial Committee of the Privy Council (till 1949) had not followed the practice of the American Supreme Court. They regarded the British North America (Canada) Act as a statute to be interpreted like other statutes. And faithful to the traditional rules of statutory interpretation, the Judges had been concerned with the literal meaning of the words in the Act of 1867 without reference to historical facts, or the intentions of the framers of the Constitution, or the changing social and economic conditions of the country to which the machinery of the government must fit in. The result is that there has not been a straight line interpreting the British North America (Canada) Act. Lord Haldane, in the *Attorney-General of Australia* v. *Colonial Sugar Refining Co.,* held that the Constitution of Canada could not be described as federal except in a loose sense. In spite of the conflicting interpreations of the British North America (Canada) Act, history has proved otherwise. The American federation began its career with a theory of State rights. Today, we find there the ever-increasing growth of central power and the process of centralization is in full swing, that is, the national government assuming influence or control over functions which formerly were considered under State jurisdiction. Canada began its political existence with the scales highly tilted in favour of the central authority. Today, the Canadian Provinces enjoy powers almost greater than those in the States in the American federation.

9. *The Constitution of Canada,* p. 408.

Many factors are responsible for this development, but it has been essentially determined by the attitudes of mind prevalent among those vested with political authority. Sir John MacDonald, the most outstanding statesman of the early period and, in fact, the architect of the Canadian federation, had convincingly, viewed the Provincial Legislatures subordinate bodies and regarded the Lieutenant-Governors as nominees of the Federal Government whose interests he expected them to safeguard as dutiful servants. MacDonbald also set the precedent of disallowing Provincial legislation and twenty-nine Acts were victims in the first decade of the career of the federation. But the Liberal Party, partycularly as represented in the person of Oliver Mowat, Prime Minister of Ontario (1872-1896), strongly protested and fought against MacDonald's wide use of Dominion authority and essentially its powers of disallowance. The Liberals urged the view that within their sphere of jurisdiction, the Provinces were as supreme as the Federal Government within its own. By 1887, the dissatisfaction against the centralist policies of the Federal Government had reached a pitch. In a conference held at Quebec the representatives of the five Provinces met to vindicate the plenary nature of Provincial authority, and agreed to agitate for: (1) curtailment of the federal jurisdiction; (2) abolition of the power of disallowance; (3) recognition of the Lieutenant-Governor as the representative of the King rather than servant of the Federal Government; and (4) each Province should nominate some members to the Senate.

When the Liberal Party assumed office at the Centre in 1896, it adopted a responsive attitude and tried to lessen a fear of centralisation prevalent in the new growing nation. It did not repudiate any of the powers which the British North America (Canada) Act conferred upon the Federal Government. Nor did it set to make those powers become obsolete. But since then the power of disallowance had been more cautiously used, an exceptional rather than a normal expedient or as Brady says, "an extreme medicine of the Constitution." The present position is well explained by Dawson. He says, "Sporadic revivals of disallowance have occurred during the past thirty-five years, but it is a far from being the active agent in assuring to the Dominion that oversight which was contemplated by the Canadians that the true judge of the mistakes and injustices of the provincial legislature is the electorate and not the Dominion Government. Since the Dominion Government has now definitely assumed a federal aspect, it balances divergent interests, thus, subordinating the legal powers to the federal principle in practice."

The conventions of the parliamentary system of government go still further. The 1867 Act empowered the Federal Government, to appoint a Lieutenant-Goverrnor, and by law the Lieutenant-Governor appoints his Ministers who hold office at his pleasure.But the parliamentary system of government demands that the Lieutenant-Governor must appoint his Ministers only those persons who belong to the majority party in the Provincial legislature and command its confidence. The real functionaries are, thus, the choice of the people who returned them in majority at elections and the Federal Government must accept their choice and endorse their policies for which they hold a mandate. In fact, the Federal Government cannot afford to do otherwise as it is itself the choice of the people and it has to appeal to the people at periodic intervals for return to power. This custom of the Constitution renders almost nugatory the intention of the Quebec Conference that the Dominion influence over the Provinces would be effectively exercised through the agency of the Lieutenant-Governors. Similarly, although the Federal Government has the power to make all the important provincial judicial appointments, yet it exercises this authority with due discretion and has not attempted to pack the courts with partisans opposed to Provincial powers. Professor Wheare, accordingly comes to the conclusion that "Canada is politically federal and that no state Government which attempted to stress the unitary elements in the Canadian Constitution at the expense of the federal elements would survive."[10]

Professor Wheare does not entirely rely upon the law of the Constitution for determining whether it is federal or not. The practice of the Constitution, he says, "is more important almost than the law of the Constitution", for a country "may have a federal Constitution, but in practice it may work that Constitution in such a way that its government is not federal. Or a country with non-federal Constitution may

10. Wheare, K. C., *Federal Government*, p. 21.

work in such a way that it provides the example of a federal government.'' Professor Wheare's conclusion is obviously clear. ''It seems justifiable to conclude,'' he says, ''that although the Canadian Constitution is quasi-federal in law it is predominantly federal in practice. Or to put it in another way, although Canada has not a federal Constitution, it has a federal government.''[11]

Canada has really a federal government. The unitary elements are being so worked that they do not conflict with the federal principle. The Provinces now enjoy wide political and legislative authority. Within the sphere of powers granted to them, they are practically autonomous. The power of disallowing Provincial legislation is sparingly used and is confined only to acts which infringe the principle of legislative power and contravene the interests of the Commonwealth. A Lieutenant-Governor is no longer an instrument of the Central Government. His appointment by the Federal Government is, in fact, an evidence of the federal link and does not mean subordination once he is legally appointed.

Although the Constitution Act, 1982, is not primarily concerned with the allocation of powers in the Canadian federal system, there are two constitutional provisions that will benefit directly the Provinces and their ability to exercise their constitutional responsibilities. The well-accepted practice of using federal revenues to help the less wealthy Provinces, the principle of equalization, is now enshrined in the Constitution. Section 36 in Part III of the Act provides: ''without altering the legislative authority of Parliament or of the provincial legislatures, or the rights of any of them with respect to the exercise of their legislative authority, Parliament and the legislatures together with the Government of Canada and the provincial governments, are committed to (a) promotion of equal opportunities for the well-being of Canadians; (b) furthering economic development to reduce disparity in opportunities; and (c) providing essential public services of reasonable quality to all Canadians.'' The Federal Government is constitutionally committed to making equalization payments for this purpose to further the commitment.[12]

The other provision constitutionally confirms the exclusive Provincial authority over natural resources and gives the Provinces new powers respecting the inter-Provincial sale of resources and the indirect taxation of non-renewable resources.[13]

## CHARTER OF RIGHTS AND FREEDOMS

### Entrenchment of Rights

Canadians have traditionally enjoyed extensive human rights and they are the foundation of the Canadian way of life. But few of them had been set down in the form of laws. They had grown steadily and were handed down from generation to generation. In times of danger when the security of the nation was threatened, some of those rights could be temporarily withdrawn. Even under such circumstances the consent of the people was given through their representatives in the Parliament. By incorporating basic human rights and freedoms in the Constitution, the 1982 Act has given them constitutional sanctity. They are guaranteed and in case of any infringement or denial redress can be sought in a court of law. The Charter of Rights and Freedoms enables the courts to determine whether a Federal or Provincial law is commensurate with it and to declare any legislative measures that contravene it. The criterion is that which ''can be demonstrably justified in a free and democratic society.'' The entrenched rights and freedoms can be limited only by rule of law, within limits that are reasonable and can be justified in the context of a free and limited society. It applies to all legislation, past, present or future. This innovation brings the Canadian Constitution closer to the American Constitution on the question of fundamental rights.

However—and this is an innovation—the Canadian Charter of Rights and Freedoms, or the ''Carta Canadiana'', has what is known as a ''notwithstanding'' clause applied to a few of its parts. These parts refer to fundamental rights, legal guarantees and equality rights, except for women, where the ''notwithstanding'' clause does not apply. Parliament and the Provincial Assemblies each acting in their jurisdictions, can derogate from this Charter, provided that they expressly state

11. *Ibid.*
12. Section 36 (2)
13. Section 92 A added immediately after Section 92 of the Constitution Act, 1867 (formerly named the British North America Act, 1867).

in their laws that they are doing so. Such derogation is valid only for five years. To extend its duration, it is necessary to repeat the express declaration required by Section 33. There can be no complications with the democratic rights. They are an integral part of the Constitution, and the legislators can in no manner use the ''notwithstanding'' clause.

## SPECIFIC RIGHTS

The Charter is divided into specific heads and each head enumerates the Rights and Freedoms relevant to it:

**Fundamental Freedoms**

Many of the liberties spelt out in the Charter are those associated with a free society. These include fundamental freedoms—freedom of conscience, religion, thought, and expression, freedom of the press and other media of communication, freedom to assemble and associate freely. All these fundamental freedoms are guaranteed, but they are subject to the ''notwithstanding'' clause under which it is possible to derogate from them.

**Democratic Rights**

Every citizen has the right to vote in an election of members of the House of Commons or of a Legislative Assembly and to be elected as its member. The duration of the House of Commons and a Provincial Assembly is fixed at five years from the date for the return of the writs at a General Election of its members. But in time of real or apprehended war, invasion or insurrection, the life of the House of Commons may be extended by the concerned legislature beyond the specified period of five years, provided such an extension is not opposed by the votes of more than one-third of the members of the House of Commons or the Legislative Assembly as the case may be. The Constitution does not fix the period for which the life of a legislature can be extended. It all depends upon the circumstances then prevailing and the judgment of the concerned Government. But the Constitution does not give a *carte-blanche* to the legislature to extend its life because it imposes a limitation by providing that such a continuation should not be opposed by the votes of more than one-third of the total membership of the House of Commons or the Provincial Legislative Assembly, as the case may be. If more than one-third of the members of the Legislature concerned opposed the extension in its life, the proposal is defeated and its duration does not go beyond the specified term of five years.

The Constitution also provides that there shall be a sitting of Parliament and of each Provincial Assembly at least once every twelve months. Both these provisions are a unique feature of the 1982 Constitution. Duration of the term of the Legislature and summoning of its sessions are the relevant parts of the provisions relating to the Legislature and all the constitutions of the world have followed the same pattern. But the Canadian Constitution enshrines them in the Chapter relating to Fundamental Rights and Freedoms. Section 20 of the British North America (Canada) Act 1867 which has been repealed by the Constitution Act, 1982, ordained: ''There shall be a Session of the Parliament of Canada once at least in every year, so that twelve months shall intervene between the last sitting of the Parliament in one Session and its first sitting in the next Session.''

**Mobility Rights**

Freedom of mobility and settlement, prior to the proclamation of 1982 Constitution, was protected in large by the courts, but imperfectly. Mobility Rights are now enshrined in the Constitution and their guarantee is explicit. Every Canadian citizen and every person who has the status of a permanent resident of Canada has the right to move freely from one Province to another, to live and seek a job anywhere in Canada as well as to enter, remain in or leave the country. However, a Province, in which the employment rate is below the national average possesses the right to undertake ''affirmative action programmes'' for socially and economically disadvantaged individuals. Section 6 (4) provides that the right to move and gain livelihood ''do not preclude any law, program (programme) or activity that has its object the amelioration in a province of conditions of individuals in that province who are socially and economically disadvantaged if the rate of employment in that province is below the rate of employment in Canada.'' It means that a Provincial Legislative Assembly has the constitutional right to prohibit entry and settlement of individuals seeking jobs in a Province in which the rate of unemployment is above the national average till that time when the national average is reached.

**Legal Rights**

The Constitution guarantees to ''everyone'' citizen or an alien, the right to life, liberty and security of person and the right not to be deprived of any such right except in accordance with the principles of fundamental justice. It means that there must be a valid cause prescribed by law that ''can be demonstrably justified in a free and democratic society.'' In case of its capricious application either by executive action under the law or the provisions of law that violate the rule of law and cannot be demonstrably justified the Courts have the right to intervene when approached by the aggrieved party and nullify such action and hold the law itself *ultra vires* of the Constitution. Enforcement of rights is a right by itself and any person whose rights have been infringed or denied can apply to a court of competent jurisdiction to obtain such remedy as the court considers appropriate and just.

The Constitution protects ''everyone'' against unreasonable search or seizure or arbitrary detention or imprisonment. A person who has been arrested or detained has the right to be informed without unreasonable delay of the charge against him and has also the right to engage a legal counsel and to retain and instruct him. It is the obligation of the arresting or detaining authority to inform the arrested person or the detenu of his right to legal aid. He has also the right to have the validity of his detention determined by way of *habeas corpus* and be released forthwith if the detention is held unlawful.

Any person charged with an offence has the right to be informed without unreasonable delay of the specific offence and to be tried in a court of law within a reasonable time. No one should be compelled to give evidence against himself in a criminal case and he should be presumed innocent until he is proved guilty according to law in a fair and public hearing by an independent and impartial court. The accused person is not to be denied reasonable bail without just cause. Except in the case of an offence under military law tried by a military tribunal, the accused person has a right to be tried by jury where the maximum punishment for the offence is imprisonment for five years or more severe punishment. No person can be found guilty on account of any act or omission, unless, at the time of the act or omision, it constituted an offence under Canadian or international law or was criminal according to the general principles of law recognised by the community of nations. If finally acquitted of the offence, the accused person cannot be tried for the same offence again and, if finally found guilty and punished for the offence, he cannot be tried or punished for it again. If found guilty of the offence and if the punishment for the offence has been varied between the time of the commission of the offence and the time of sentencing, the accused has the right to the benefit of the lesser punishment.

Every person has the right not to be subjected to any cruel and unusual treatment or punishment. A witness who testifies in any proceedings has the right not to have any incriminating evidence given by him used to incriminate him in any other proceedings, except in a prosecution for perjury or for the giving of contradictory evidence. A party or witness in any proceedings who does not understand or speak the language in which the proceedings are conducted or who is deaf has the right to the assistance of an interpreter.

As in the case of Fundamental freedoms, Legal rights, too, can be derogated, though both are guaranteed.

**Equality Rights**

Every individual is equal before and under the law and has the right to the equal protection and equal benefit of the law without discrimination and, ''in particular, without discrimination based on race, national or ethnic origin, colour, religion, sex, age or mental or physical disability.'' For the first time in the Canadian history, the Constitution recognizes the equality of women. As such women's groups can now challenge laws that discriminate against women. This provision, however, does not rule out ''affirmative action'' programmes or activities aimed at improving the situation of the disadvantaged individuals or groups. Section 15(2) provides that equality before law and under law and equal protection of law and benefit of law against discrimination ''does not preclude any law, program (programme) or activity that has its object the amelioration of conditions of disadvantaged individual because of race, national or ethnic origin, colour, religion, sex, age or mental or physical disability.'' Because the scope of equality rights is so extensive and affected so many laws, they came into effect three years after patriation (return) of the Constitution to Canada to enable the federal and Provincial Governments to make any necessary adjustments to their laws.

**Official Language Rights**

Official Language Rights provide every person with the right to use English or French in dealing with institutions of the Canadian Parliament and Federal Government. French and English are the official languages of Canada and have equal status in the institutions of Parliament and the Government of Canada. New Brunswick joins Quebec and Manitoba in providing constitutional protection to the use of French or English in its Legislative, Courts and Parliamentary documents. In New Brunswick citizens have the right to communicate in French or English with any office of the Provincial Government, and the two languages are made official in that Province.

The Constitution also preserves the rights and privileges acquired or enjoyed either before or after the commencement of the Charter of Rights and Freedoms with respect to any language that is not English or French.

The Constitution also preserves any legal or customary right or privilege acquired or enjoyed either before or after the coming into force of the Charter with respect to any language that is not English or French.

**Minority Language Education Rights**

A Canadian citizen educated in Canada in English may send his or her children to a school in English in Quebec. In addition, a Canadian citizen who has a child being educated in English in Canada may continue to send any of his or her children to a school in English if she or he moves to Quebec.

The above provisions apply to the French minority in the other nine Provinces. In addition, the other nine Provinces have agreed that any Canadian citizen whose mother tongue is French will be entitled to send his or her children to a school in French. This right has specially been provided to enable Canadians who have to move around the country, or English or French-speaking minorities living in a Province of another language group to have their children educated in their own language.

**Enforcement of Rights**

Any person whose rights or freedoms, as guaranteed by the Charter in Part V of the Constitution, have been infringed or denied may apply to a court of competent jurisdiction to obtain such remedy as the court considers appropriate and just in the circumstances. Where in such proceedings a court concludes that evidence was obtained in a manner that infringed or denied any rights or freedoms guaranteed by the Charter, the evidence shall be excluded if it it established that, having regard to all the circumstances, the admission of it in the proceedings would bring the administration of justice into disrepute...

**General**

The Charter includes certain rights and freedoms under the caption General:

(1) Aboriginal rights and freedoms are not affected by the provisions of the Charter. Section 25 states that the guarantees of certain rights and freedoms incorporated in the Charter of Rights and Freedoms ''shall not be construed so as to abrogate or derogate from any aboriginal, treaty or other rights or freedoms that pertain to the aboriginal peoples of Canada including—

(a) any rights or freedoms that have been recognised by the Royal Proclamation of October 7, 1963; and

(b) any rights or freedoms that may be acquired by the aboriginal peoples of Canada by way of land claims settlement.''

In addition, Section 35 of Part II dealing with Rights of the Aboriginal Peoples of Canada provides that the existing aboriginal and treaty rights of the aboriginal peoples of Canada are recognised and affirmed. The aboriginal peoples include the Indian, Inuit and Metis of Canada.

(2) The guarantees of this Charter of certain rights and freedoms are not to be construed as denying the existence of any other rights or freedoms that exist in Canada. It means that in addition to the rights and freedoms contained in the Charter of Rights and Freedoms there exist other rights as well which have that much sanctity as the rights forming part of the Charter. The only difference between the two is that the latter are not guaranteed rights and, consequently, they cannot be enforced as provided in Section 24.

(3) Canada is a multicultural State and while interpreting any provision of the Charter this aspect would essentially be kept in view. Section 27 provides that the Charter ''shall be interpreted in a manner consistent with the preservation and enhancement of the multicultural heritage of the Canadians.''

(4) The right to equality extends to all Canadian citizens without discrimination based on

race, colour, religion, sex, age or mental or physical disability. But at the same time Section 15 dealing with equality rights places a bar of ''affirmative action'' and as the scope of equality clauses is extensive affecting so many laws, these rights were to go into effect three years after the return of the Constitution to Canada. But this bar did not apply to the equality of women with men. It immediately went into effect. Section 28 provides, ''Notwithstanding anything in this Chapter, the rights and freedoms referred in it are guaranteed equally to male and female persons.''

(5) No provision of the Charter on Rights and Freedoms abrogates or derogates from any rights or privileges guaranteed by or under the 1982 Constitution of Canada in respect of denominational, separate or dissentient schools.

(6) Finally, as a measure of abundant caution and to avoid any kind of doubt Section 31 provides: ''Nothing in this Charter extends the legislative powers of any body or authority.''

Canada demonstrated successfully how federal system of governance can be combined with the theory and practice of parliamentary government. Earlier in the United States, federalism co-existed with a Presidential system of government. The Indian constitution makers benefitted much from Canadian experience and Joined the concept of federation to a parliamentary type of regime both at the centre and the constituent units.

## SUGGESTED READINGS

Cheffins, R.I., *The Constitutional Process in Canada.*

Clokie, H. McD., *Canadian Government and Politics*

Dawson, R.M., *Democratic Government in Canada.*

Laskin, B. *Canadian Constitution Laws.*

Stanley, F.G., *A Short History of the Canadian Constitution.*

# CHAPTER II

# The Executive

### The Crown

The Government in Canada proceeds from the Crown with a capital letter; and this new Crown be of the British North America Act 1867, (now the Constitution Act, 1867) stated: that "the Provinces of....have expressed their desire to be federally united into one Dominion under the Crown of the United Kingdom.... with a Constitution similar in principle to that of the United Kingdom." The Constitution of the United Kingdom is a body of rules indicating the structure and functions of political institutions and the principles governing their operation. These rules and principles of political governance lie scattered in the various Charters, Statutes, Judicial decisions, usages and traditions, and all mark a steady transference of power from the King as a person to a complicated impersonal organisation called the Crown. The King is still there and legally all government radiates from the person of the Monarch but in actual practice the King has become the Crown. The King does not exercise the powers which belong to the Crown on his own initiative and authority. He does so at the behest of those who exercise the will of the people, that is, Ministers responsible to Parliament. The King, Ministers and Parliament make a synthesis of supreme authority and it is called the Crown. The principles governing the operation of all the three political institutions essentially embody the British Constitution. The nature of the British Constitution has been beautifully summed up in a fairy tale and it runs: "once upon a time there was a King who was very important and who did very big and very important things. He owned a nice shiny crown, which he would wear on especially grand occasion, but most of the time he kept it on a red velvet cushion. Then somebody made a Magic. The Crown was carefully stored in the Tower; the King moved over to the cushion and was transformed into a special kind of crown with a capital letter; and this new Crown became in the process something else; no one knows exactly what, for it is one thing today, another thing tomorrow, and two or three things the day after that. The name given to the Magic is the Constitutional Development."

Her Majesty Elizabeth the Second, is the Queen of Canada, Australia and other Dominion countries, and the reigning Monarch of Britain. In fact, she is several monarchs wrapped up in one person, but each is completely separate from all the rest. She is the Queen of Canada not because she is the Queen of the United Kingdom, but because she is the Queen of Canada separately. At each step of the evolutionary process of constitutional development in Canada, the relationship of the Crown to Canada was altered to meet the aspirations of the growing nations until the present association emerged in which Elizabeth the Second is the Queen of Canada as distinct from her status as Monarch of the United Kingdom. Her Majesty is simply a symbol, the symbol of Canada's free association with British and the other Commonwealth nations, and a symbol of the history and traditions which a majority of the Canadian people revere.

In December 1952, it was decided by the Prime Ministers of the Commonwealth countries, meeting in London, to establish new forms of title for each country. The title for Canada was approved by Parliament and established by a Royal Proclamation on May 29, 1953. The title of the Queen, so far as Canada is concerned, now is:

> "Elizabeth the Second, by the Grace of God of the United Kindgom, Canada and Her other Realms and Territories Queen, Head of the Commonwealth, Defenders of the Faith;"

In fact, Britain had herself consistently encouraged this gradual advance to partnership, "possibly because she had learned her lesson the hard way in the days of the Third George, and that this attitude, more than any other factor, is responsible for Canada's retention of the symbol of the Crown as the tie which binds the partnership." When the Canadians desired a Constitution similar in principle to that of the United Kingdom what they had in mind were the Monarchy, a Cabinet to advise it, a Parliament consisting of two Houses and the Cabinet responsible to its representative Chamber, the law courts and the common law.

The functions of the Canadian Crown, which are substantially the same as those of the Queen in relation to the Government of Britain, are generally discharged by her representative the Governor-General. A few Canadian prerogative powers, such as the granting of honours and awards and the appointment of ambassadors and ministers plenipotentiary, are dealt with by the Queen personally; most are, however, performed on her behalf by the Governor-General, and in either case the prerogative is exercised on the advice of the Government of Canada.

## GOVERNOR-GENERAL

### Appointment and Term

The Monarch of Canada occupies the Canadian throne, but the permanent home of the occupant is not Canada but Britain. As the Monarch cannot reign herself from a distant land which is her permanent home, she appoints a personal representative to act on her behalf and he is the Governor-General of Canada. Formerly, the Governor-General was appointed by the Sovereign on the advice of the Colonial Secretary, a British Minister of the Crown. In 1890, the old practice was altered. The Dominion Government was consulted before making the appointment, though this procedure had not invariably been followed, as in 1916 when the Duke of Devonshire was appointed without any preliminary consultation. The Imperial Conference of 1926 made a revolutionary change. It was decided at the Conference that if the Governor-General ''is not the representative or agent of His Majesty's Government in Britain or of any Department of that Government,'' the British Government must not have to do with anything in making the selection. Since then the appointment of the Governor-General had been made by the Dominion Government. The Prime Minister of Canada recommended the appointment to the King or the Queen and the advice so tendered was invariably accepted. Britain simply checked up the availability of the person so advised to be appointed if he happened to be her national in Britain. In 1936, Prime Minister Bennet devised another method. When Lord Tweedsmuir's name was being considered, Bennet first discussed the matter with the Leader of the Opposition, Mackenzie King. His object was to make the appointment non-partisan in character by carrying the approval of the leaders of both major political parties. The procedure was hoped to become a practice, but the appointment in 1952 of Vincent Massey, the first Canadian to be appointed to that office, was widely criticised. Massey was prominently identified with the Liberal Party and he was once a Cabinet member when that Party was in office. Many people in Canada did not view it a healthy practice of appointing a Governor-General from among the Canadians themselves. They feared, remarked Leslie Robert, ''that once the appointment of one of their own has became accepted practice, little time will elapse before the Governor-Generalship becomes a political plum—the ripest in the gift of government.''[1] But with the appointment of Roland Michener, it appeared that this objection did not carry much significance. Michener succeeded General George P. Vainer who died on March 5, 1967 and was the third Canadian to become his country's Governor-General. Since then the Governor-General has invariably been a Canadian.

The term of office of the Governor-General. writes Dawson, ''may be simply, if somewhat ambiguously, stated as being officially recognised as six years, customarily treated as five years, while on occasion it has been seven years.''[2] Therefore, the Governor-General traditionally serves for a term of five years.[3] He may be removed from office by the Queen acting on the advice tendered by the Canadian Cabinet.

In the event of the death or incapacity or, generally, the absence from Canada of the Governor-General, the powers and authorities granted to him are vested in the Chief Justice of Canada as ''Administrator.'' In the event of the latter's death, incapacity, removal or absence, the powers are vested in the Senior Judge for the time being of the Supreme Court of Canada.

### Powers of the Governor-General

The powers of the Governor-General are extensive and he exercises his authority under the Letters Patent constituting the office of the Governor-General, and the provisions of the Constitution Act, 1867, (formerly British North

1. Leslie Robert, *Canada, the Golden Hinge*, p. 58.
2. Dawson, R. M., *The Government of Canada*, p. 176.
3. *Reference Papers No. 70.* Information Division, Department of External Affairs, Ottawa, Canada.

America Act). But, like his master, the Monarch, the Governor-General has ceased to rule now and he has personally nothing to do with the affairs of government. The actual exercise of powers and rights associated with the office of the representative of the Monarch belong to Her Majesty's responsible Ministers in Canada. "The Governor-General," writes Dawson: "has tended to follow the same path which had been marked out a few generations earlier by his august principal and he now shares substantially the same disabilities. He is a legal survivor who has contrived to remain a political necessity—the once supreme chief whose powers have largely passed into other hands, yet who has nevertheless retained a substantial residue of his former ascendancy and importance."[4]

The British North America Act, 1867, vested the Executive government and authority in the Crown[5] to be exercised by the Governor-General with the aid and advice of a Council chosen and summoned by him and liable to be removed by him at his pleasure.[6] But law is not practice and the Executive power is actually exercised in the Queen's name by Ministers who derive their authority from the Federal Parliament and are responsible to it for the use they make of their powers. As a constitutional head the way is carved out for the Governor-General by the established practices of the parliamentary system of government, which the British North America Act, 1867 established in Canada similar in principle to that of the United Kingdom. He follows the usual course of summoning the leader of the majority party in the House of Commons and entrusts him with the duty of forming the Council of Ministers and the Ministers remain in office so long as they command the confidence of the House of Commons. The constitutional position of the Governor-General was explained in a formal statement by the Imperial Conference in 1926. The statement affirmed that the Governor-General of a Dominion was the "representative of the Crown and not of any department of the British Government, and that his position in relation to the administration of public affairs in the Dominion was essentially the same as that of His Majesty the King in Great Britain." The Governor-General has nothing to do with the determination and execution of the policy, and he does not take part in the deliberations of the Ministers, that is, Cabinet meetings. The Duke of Argyll (1878-83) discontinued attending meetings of the Cabinet and since then this practice has been invariably followed.

The Governor-General is the Commander-in Chief of the land, naval and air forces of the Federation. He appoints representatives of Canada to the United Nations and signs treaties of minor importance which are not signed by the Crown directly. He also appoints and receives those ordinary agents and ministers who are not appointed and received by the Government directly. Till 1926 the Governor-General performed certain ambassadorial functions on behalf of the British Government and was charged with the duty of guarding the wider interests of the Empire. But the Imperial Conference of 1926 not only clarified the position of the Governor-General with relation to the government of a Dominion, but it also declared his complete separation from the British government. Accordingly, in 1928, all such functions of the Governor-General were transferred to the High Commissioner stationed in Canada as representative of the Government in London.

The Governor-General appoints, according to law, the Lieutenant-Governors of the Provinces and can remove them from office as well. In practice, all such appointments and dismissals are made by the Federal Ministry. The Governor-General also appoints the Speaker of the Senate, the Judges of the Supreme Court, Provincial Courts, Commissioners, justices of the peace and officers of various other categories. And like his various other acts, these appointing functions are really those of his duly constituted Ministers responsible to the House of Commons.

The Governor-General summons, prorogues and dissolves Parliament. But like the various other powers of the Governor-General, these are also his nominal powers. The Bying episode of 1926, finally decided that the right to ask for dissolution belongs to the Prime Minister and the Governor-General cannot refuse it.The power of the Governorr-General to veto a Bill or to reserve it for the assent of Her Majesty is an obsolete practice now. The Imperial Conference of 1926, and the Conference on the

4. Dawson, R. M., *The Government of Canada*, p.165.
5. Article 9, North America Act, 1867.
6. Article 11.

Operation of Dominion Legislation, and Merchant Shipping Legislation (1929) definitely decided that the disallowance of Dominion legislation by British authorities and reservation by the Governor-General did not conform to the equal status of the autonomous communities within the British Empire. The explicit obligation placed by the British North America Act, 1867, to keep the British Government informed of the Acts passed by the Canadian Parliament was faithfully observed until 1942, when it was quietly discontinued. This was followed in 1947 by the passage of an Act amending the Canadian Statute which had provided for transmission of copies of current Acts to the Governor-General and to the British Government. The Constitution Act, 1982 repeals this part of the Act.

Such are, then, the powers of the Governor- General. According to law there is no sphere of administration where the authority of the Governor-General does not intervene. But in practical politics Lord Bying's episode finished once for all the controversy and conflict of opinion as to the exercise of powers by the Governor-General, and the Imperial Conference of 1926 vindicated his constitutional position. There are, however, certain functions which the Governor-General does not exercise on ministerial advice. The most important of them is the appointment of a Prime Minister. No one else except the Governor-General can commission a new Premier in the form required by the established custom of the parliamentary system of government. The task of the Governor-General is simple, if the party commanding parliamentary majority has an accredited leader. But if the office becomes vacant, because of a sudden death or resignation of the incumbent or when party dissension may make the office of the Prime Minister to fall vacant and there is no obvious leader, the Governor-General has, then, the discretion to select a person who may command the confidence of a stable majority in the House of Commons and be in a position to form government. He may even seek the advice of those whom the Governor-General feels can give some advice, as Lord Aberdeen did in 1897, in his search for a successor to Sir John Thompson. The Governor-General may adopt another procedure by tapping the potential Prime Minister and discover for himself who can form a Cabinet. In 1896, Lord Aberdeen, after first sounding out Sir Donald Smith, eventually commissioned Sir Charles Tupper to succeed Sir Mackenzie Bowell. Aside these two occasions, the Governor-General had not the opportunity to exercise his judgment in selecting the Prime Minister, but the contigency is still there and it may happen as it did in 1916 and 1923 in Britain or as it occured in Australia in July, 1945. Then, he has the prerogative to refuse to grant a dissolution of the House of Commons and the right to dismiss a government. The Governor-General's discretion is, however, closely regulated by previous usage and "the counsel of constitutional doctrine, and rarely involves more than the formal recognition of an existing situation."

The second function of the Governor-General is that he acts as a mediator and uses his influence to settle political disputes between political leaders whenever occasion may demand it. As the Governor-General wields no political power his advice is deemed valuable and generally accepted. The Duke of Devonshire in 1917, summoned Sir Robert Borden, Sir Wilfrid Laurier, and four others to a meeting at Government House to discuss and amicably decide the conflicting issues regarding conscription, postponement of elections during War, and the possibilities of forming a coalition government. This is how the King intervened in Britain in 1914 in his efforts to secure agreement on the Home Rule Bill. The Governors-General have sometimes intervened to settle quarrels between the Dominion and a Province, as Lord Dufferin endeavoured to remove the bitterness between British Columbia and the Dominion immediately after the latter's membership of the federation. Twenty years later Lord Aberdeen held a series of interviews with the Premier and Attorney-General of Manitoba.

Governors-General have also been expected at times to act as quasi-diplomatic agents of their country. In early days, Governors-General paid official visits to the United States with a definite diplomatic purpose and under instructions from the Government in London. Today, their visits are neither diplomatic nor are undertaken on the instructions of the British Government. They are goodwill visits to strengthen the ties of friendliness between the two neighboring countries undertaken with the approval of the Canadian Government. All the same, as Dawson points out, "It is, indeed, probable that these social calls are still occasionally used to review unofficially and tentatively matters which are of common interest to the two nations, although their usefulness for purposes of diplomatic intercourse is obviously restricted.''

The Governor-General, like the King of Britain, is also an important part of the social structure and he wields a great social influence. His patronage is an enormous asset to any cause and ensures for popular support. His name is always associated with multifarious activities and various fields of art, music, literature, theatre, social service, youth movement, etc., which are organised under his patronage. These ''dignified'' functions, as Bagehot described these are more important than the government functions.

Closely connected with the social activities are the Governor- General's ceremonial duties as the representative Chief Executive Head of the State. He opens Parliament, receives foreign diplomatic agents, and he is Canada's busiest host. He is also Canada's most travelled VIP and goes on tours throughout the country once or twice a year. The ceremonial functions of the Governor-General have been graphically described by Leslie Roberts. He writes: ''the Governor-General receives, dines and wines foreign and domestic celebrities at Government House, his official residence at Ottawa. He pins medals on heroes and welcomes visiting celebrities. He travels the country from end to end unveiling monuments, opening hospitals, launching charity drives, and taking his ease with the war veterans in their sanctuaries. He is primarily a goodwill ambassador, but it is not goodwill for Britain that the Governor-General works to create, but goodwill between Canadians and goodwill toward Canada on the part of the nation's distinguished and official guests,''

The Cabinet government, in short, presupposes the presence of some titular head of the State, some central and impartial figure, and the Governor-General fulfils that purpose as the representative of the Queen. His position is very often compared and made analogous to that of the King in Britain. The influence of the Governor-General is not negotiable. But there is a subtle distinction between the role of the King and his representative. The Governor-General is the nominee of the Canadian Government, and since he comes and goes within a relatively short period of time, he cannot enjoy the national prestige of the Monarch himself. The King is the chief of the nation, he is everybody's King and provides a useful focus for patriotism. People live and die for the Monarch. He personifies the State. ''We condemn the government,'' says Jennings, ''and cheer the king.'' The Governor-General is, as Sir Robert Borden not inaptly described him, ''a nominated President'' who can seldom appeal to popular sentiment in the same magnetic way as the Monarch. ''However much he may graciously act as the King himself would act, he is still a substitute. Consequently, he loses much as a potent symbol and mirror of the nation. For such a symbol Canadians must look beyond him to the king in person.'' The Governor-General may offer informal counsel to his Ministers and like the Monarch he has the right to be consulted, the right to encourage and the right to warn,but he has not the same continued and ripe experience of life-time as that of the King. The King acquires political knowledge and experience, which makes him a mentor and a wise Minister is not only obliged but positively desires to consult him. After a short span of office, the Governor-General goes into oblivion.

## THE CABINET

### The Privy Council and the Cabinet

In a parliamentary system of government cabinet is the motive power of all political action. It is the magnet of policy and the supreme directing authority which co-ordinates and controls the whole of executive government, and integrates and guides the work of the Legislature. Yet, as in Britain, it has no legal status in Canada. It is an extra-constitutional body, a committee of Queen's Privy Council, whose acts are formally made the actions of the Privy Council which body has existence in law.[7] The whole machinery of the cabinet system is based upon conventions, unwritten but always recognised and stated with almost precision as the rules of law. It is by convention, that the members of the Cabinet are members of either House of Parliament and the Cabinet resigns office when it no longer holds the confidence of the House of Commons.

The British North America Act, 1867, now the Constitution Act, 1867, provides for the Privy Council. Section II states that ''there shall be a council to aid and advise in the government of Canada, to be styled the Queen's

7. Articles 11 and 12, North America (Constitution) Act, 1867.

Privy Council for Canada; and the persons who are to be Members of that Council shall be from time to time chosen and summoned by the Governor- General and sworn in as Privy Councillors, and members thereof may from time to time be removed by the Governor-General.'' The legal body, therefore, to be constituted for aid and advice in the Government of Canada is the Privy Council. It is chosen and summoned by the Governor-General and is subject to removal by him. But in practice, the Privy Council as a whole does not aid and advise the Governor-General. Nor is it removed by him as a whole. The real advisers of the Governor-General are the members of the Cabinet, the active part of the Privy Council, and they aid and advise him in the Government of Canada only by custom. All members of the Cabinet are, no doubt, members of the Privy Council, but all members of the Privy Council are not members of the Cabinet. The Privy Council consists chiefly of present and former ministers of the Crown and they generally retain their membership for life. In 1953 the Chief Justice of Canada, the Speaker of the House of Commons and the Senate, and the Leader of the Opposition were all made members of the Privy Council before they left for coronation of Queen Elizabeth to form a part of Canada's official delegation.

The Privy Council as a whole holds no meeting and this practice has been followed ever since 1867, except only for two occasions. It met for the first time in 1947, to receive the formal announcement by the King of his consent to the marriage of princess (now Queen) Elizabeth, and for the second time in 1952, to hear the proclamation of the accession of Queen Elizabeth on the death of her father, George VI. The Privy Council does not meet as a functioning body, and its constitutional responsibilities as adviser to the Crown are exclusively performed by Ministers who constitute the Cabinet of the day. In this way, Privy Council and Cabinet are two aspects of the same constitutional organism. In practice most of the executive powers exercised by the Governor-General-in-Council, such as, the making of Orders-in-Council, are performed by Cabinet resolving itself into a sub-committee of the Privy Council. The resulting Orders-in-Council are then signed by the Governor-General.

**The Ministry and the Cabinet**

The Cabinet and the Ministry in Canada are usually treated as if they are synonymous, and the fact is that during the large part of the Canadian history there had been no difference between the two. But there does exist a difference between them as it is in Britain, because not all the members of the Government formed by a Prime Minister make the Cabinet. A Cabinet consists of a select circle of colleagues of the Prime Minister who meet together from time to time to decide matters of high policy. The number of Ministers not in the Cabinet had remained till recently absolutely insignificant and it is only since the Second World War that this ''penumbral group'' has become fairly large. Before the War there used to be one or more members. In 1943, out of a total of twenty-seven members of the Government, twenty were in the Cabinet and seven not in the Cabinet, and in 1954 the number of the members not in the Cabinet increased to eleven. Since then this level has been maintained.

It means that Ministers in Canada, too, are not alike in status and they differ in importance. The first group comprised the great bulk of the personnel of the Cabinet, usually fourteen or fifteen in number, who ''head up the government'' and are also the immediate associates of the Prime Minister. Then, come the Ministers without portfolio, three or four, who are surely the members of the Cabinet, but are not the political heads of the Departments of administration. Britain, on the other hand, has not liked such a category of Ministers, though from 1915 to 1921 ten cases occurred of Ministers in the Cabinet without Portfolio. It ended in 1921 after ruthless criticism in the House of Commons. Baldwin revived it in 1935, but just for a brief period. In Canada it is a usual practice to have ministers without portfolio and there are one or two others who ''may for a wide variety of reasons be similarly honoured.''

Finally, is ''the penumbral group'' which has recently become fairly large. The most numerous of this quasi-ministerial group are the recently created parliamentary assistants, who are members of the House of Commons appointed to relieve the Cabinet Ministers of some of their less important duties. They are members of Parliament and they come and go out of office as the Cabinet Ministers do, but they have no place in the meetings of the Cabinet and have nothing to do with the determination of policy. Nor do they head up the Departments of administration. They may be considered analogous to ''Junior Ministers'' in Britain.

A Canadian Cabinet differs from the British in its composition, but it is strikingly like the British in the thorough manner in which it accepts the pre-eminence of the Prime Minister along with the rules of homogeneity, collective responsibility and secrecy. The Cabinet government means party government and solidarity of the government demands its political homogeneity so that as a team all should play the game of politics under the captaincy of the Prime Minister. Like Britain, Canada hates coalition government and since 1867 there had been only one instance of a coalition Government when a Union Government was formed during the First World War to enforce the terms of the Conscription Act of 1917. The principle of homogeneity in government had such an impress on the mind of the Canadians that they have carried it through with unfaltering conviction. ''There is something more required to make a strong administration,'' wrote Joseph How over a hundred years ago, ''than nine men treating each other courteously at a round table. There is the assurance of good faith—towards each other—of common sentiments, and kindly feelings propagated through the friends of each, in society, in the Legislature and the Press, until a great party is formed....which secures a steady working majority to sustain their policy and carry their measures.''

But in the selection of his colleagues, the Canadian Prime Minister does not exercise an unrestricted choice as the British Prime Minister does. The Canadian Cabinet is always designed to represent the principal races, religions and regions of the country. The representativeness of a member is sometimes much more evident than his ability. ''The inevitable consequence is,'' as Dawson remarks, ''that the choice of the Prime Minister is seriously restricted and he is often compelled to push merit to one side in making some of his selections.'' The first requisite of Cabinet composition is that every Province must have, if at all possible, at least one representative in the Cabinet. It makes the Cabinet federalised. This practice was begun while constituting the first Dominion Cabinet and since then it has hardened into a rigid convention.

The convention that each Province, if at all possible, must have at least one representative in the Cabinet makes another convention almost mandatory, namely, that the two large Provinces must each be given more than one representative. An effort is usually made to obtain at least one Protestant English-Speaking representative from Quebec and three and even four French. This gives to Quebec the minimum of four members. Ontario must also have four, and possibly five members and one of them should be a Roman Catholic of Irish extraction. ''Provincial representation,'' remarks Dawson, ''has frequently been further elaborated in that a few portfolios have been commonly recognised as the special preserve of certain areas.'' This kind of conscious and planned representativeness is deemed imperative in order to strengthen the Executive in a country having diverse religious, linguistic and economic interests. It helps to ensure that in reaching decisions the Cabinet will hear and discuss all the major interests and harmonise them in such a way as to satisfy all without jeopardising the national interests. ''I feel,'' remarked Mackenzie King in 1922, ''that the whole purpose of confederation itself would be menaced if any great body of opinion, any considerable section of this Dominion of Canada, should have reason to think that it was without due representation in the shaping of national policies.''

**Ministerial Responsibility**

The Cabinet must speak as one on all questions of Government policy. A Minister who cannot support that policy must resign. Each Minister of a department is answerable to the House of Commons for that Department and the whole cabinet is answerable to the House of Commons for Government policy and administration generally. If the Cabinet is defeated in the House of Commons on a motion of want of confidence, it must either resign office or seek dissolution of Parliament.[8] Defeat of a major Government Bill is ordinarily considered as a vote of want of confidence, and leads to the same consequence—when the Governor-General will summon the leader of the Opposition and commands him to form a Cabinet or the outgoing Prime Minister may seek dissolution of the House of Commons. But

8. Joe Clark's Government resigned in December 1979 and the House of Commons was dissolved.

Cabinet can choose to consider any such defeat not decisive. It is open to the House of Commons to vote straight want of confidence.

The Cabinet forms a link between the Governor-General and Parliament. It is, for virtually all purposes, the real executive. The Cabinet's primary responsibility in the Canadian political system is to determine priorities among the demands expressed by the people (or discerned by the Government) and to define policies to meet those demands. The Cabinet is responsible for the administration of all Government Departments, prepares by far the greater part of the legislative programme of Parliament and exercises substantial control over all matters of finance—subject to Parliamentary approval of the expenditure of public funds.

## THE PRIME MINISTER

Jennings describes the Prime Minister of Britain "as the keystone of the Constitution." The position of the Canadian Prime Minister is exactly the same, for like his prototype in Britain, he is the most powerful man in the country. He forms the Cabinet; he can alter it or destroy it. "The Government," to put it in the words of Greaves, "is the master of the country and he is the master of the government." And yet the office of the Prime Minister, like various other institutions in Canada, is not known to law. The Cabinet system of government pre-supposes the per-eminence and leadership of one single person and he is the Prime Minister. There are no legal powers which may determine the extent of his powers, but constitutional conventions, upon which is firmly erected the mechanism of government, give him the whole weight of government. Abolish the institution of the Prime Minister or diminish any part of his powers, the entire political structure would be destroyed.

The choice of the Prime Minister, as stated before; is obvious. The Governor-General summons a recognised leader of a political party having a clear majority in the House of Commons and that leader becomes the Prime Minister. But on occasions when the choice is neither obvious nor simple, as in the event of a sudden death or resignation of the Prime Minister or party dissensions, the Governor-General has some discretion in the selection of a Prime Minister. But such occasions do not occur frequently and since 1896, the Governor-General has not been called upon to use his own judgment in selecting a Prime Minister. It does not, however, mean that the power of the Governor-General has become obsolete. Dawson points out that "the conscription crisis in Canada in 1944 might easily have resulted in the Governor-General being compelled to choose a successor to Mr. Mackenzie King."

### Powers of the Prime Minister

The powers of the Prime Minister, said Arthur Meighen, "are very great. The functions and duties of a Prime Minister in Parliament are not only important, they are supreme in their importance." Talking about the powers of the British Prime Minister Lord Oxford and Asquith, himself the occupant of that office in the first decade and a half of the present century, said, "the office is what its holder chooses to make it," and only a few holders exhibit any marked desire to lightly view their responsibilities and duties as heads of government.

The Prime Minister is the corner-stone of the Constitution and in his hand is the key of government. The Prime Minister makes the government, allocates offices, and has unabridged power of reshuffling or dismissing his colleagues. In the selection of his colleagues, the choice of the Prime Minister, as said before, is seriously limited, but once the Ministry has been formed the control of the Prime Minister over its members is unchallengeable. It is purely the personal authority of the Prime Minister to ask a colleague to resign or to accept another office. While referring to the question of ministerial responsibility, Professor Dawson writes, "The members of the Canadian Cabinet acknowledge three separate and distinct responsibilities: responsibility to the Governor-General, which is now rarely invoked in any aggressive sense; a responsibility to the Prime Minister and to one another, which produces what is called the 'solidarity' of the Cabinet; and a responsibility, both individual and collective, to the House of Commons."[9]

It is from Lord Argyll's time that the Prime Minister presides over the meetings of the Cabinet and as the Chairman of the Cabinet he attracts, like the British Prime Minister, a special kind of loyalty. He exercises a casting vote and it is inherent in the Chairman. If there arises difference of opinion in Cabinet discussions, the Prime Minister is the major influence in helping to arrive at decisions. Then, he determines the Cabinet agenda and thereby accepts or rejects proposals for discussion put forward by Cabinet Ministers. In this way, the Prime Minister leads the Cabinet. As the leader and guide of the Cabinet, the Prime Minister is al-

9. Dawson, R. M., *The Government of Canada*, p. 205.

ways consulted by every Minister before an important proposal is put forward. In fact, he is the chief co-ordinator of the policies of the several Ministers and Ministries.

The Prime Minister, as the leader of the parliamentary majority, guides the deliberations of Parliament. He leads the House of Commons, makes all principal announcements of policy and business, answers all questions on departmental affairs and upon critical issues, initiates or intervenes in debates of general importance, and corrects the errors of omission and commission of his colleagues. He apportions the time of the House of Commons and submits the measures of his Government for its approval.

The source of the authority of the Prime Minister lies in his ''prerogative'' to recommend the dissolution of Parliament. This prerogative, which in most circumstances permits him to precipitate an election, is a source of considerable power both in his dealings with his colleagues and with the other parties in the House of Commons.

Another source of the Prime Minister's authority derives from the appointments he recommends, including Privy Councillors, Cabinet Ministers, Lieutenant Governors of Provinces, Speaker of the Senate, Chief Justices of all federally-appointed Courts, Senators and certain senior executives of the Public Service. The Prime Minister also recommends the appointment of a new Governor-General to the Monarch, although this normally follows consultation with his Cabinet.

The Prime Minister is the leader of the parliamentary majority party, and, like the British Prime Minister, he may on special occasions man the entire policy. He is the link between the Governor-General and the Cabinet on matters of public concern and is in a special sense the chief adviser of the former. He also has the primary responsibility for the Council of Ministers advising the Governor-General when Parliament should be convened and when it should be dissolved. The Prime Minister may, also, attend and participate in international conferences or meetings and conduct relations of Cabinet rank with the Common wealth countries.

**Position of the Prime Minister**

The most apt description of the position of the British Prime Minister is the one given by Jennings, though Lord Morley's description that he is *primus inter pares* has now become classical. Dawson says that the Canadian Prime Minister ''cannot be first among equals for the very excellent reason that he has no equals.''[10] The actual authority of the Prime Minister is, indeced, great and his powers potentially enormous. One who appoints and can dismiss his colleagues and is, in fact, though not in law, the working head of the State, he can have no peers. The Prime Minister, therefore, ''is, rather, a sun around which planets revolve.''

But the Prime Minister's position is bound up with the party. So long as he retains the hold on his party, he is able, within limits, to dictate his policy. But a hold on the party has also an important reference to the relationship of the Prime Minister with his colleagues in the Cabinet. Dawson remarks that the quotation *primus inter pares* ''contains, however, some truth: it calls attention to one very important aspect of this relationship, namely, that the other ministers are the colleagues of their chief and not his obedient and unquestioning servants.''[11] A Prime Minister who treats his colleagues as his subordinates and issues orders to his Ministers or interferes persistently in their departmental work heads towards his downfall. Prime Minister Bowell attempted such an attitude and unnecessarily began interfering in the departmental work of their ministries with the result that seven members of his Ministry chose to rebel and he was compelled to agree to the terms dictated by them. Commenting on this outstanding Cabinet rebellion in Canadian history, Dawson remarks, ''All members of the Cabinet are responsible to the House; and while they gladly acknowledge the leadership of the Prime Minister and will, in fact, usually bow to his decisions, they can never completely surrender their individual judgment or responsibility.''[12] The office of the Prime Minister is, as Jennings says, necessarily what the holder chooses to make it and what other ministers allow him to make of it. His power and prestige essentially depends upon his personality and his personality significantly counts in leading the Cabinet, the Parliament and the nation.

## SUGGESTED READINGS

1. Dawson, R-M (ed.) *The Government of Canada.*
2. Hutchinson, B. *Mr. Prime Minister, 1867-1966.*
3. Ricker, J.C., *How Are We Government* ?
4. Saywell, J.T., *The office of Lieutenant-Governor.*

# CHAPTER III

# Parliament

### The Parliament

The federal legislative authority is vested in Parliament of Canada, consisting of the Queen, an Upper House styled the Senate and Lower House known as the House of Commons. The Queen is represented by the Governor-General. The part of the Governor- General in the process of legislation has become little more than formal, for he must follow the advice of his Cabinet. This is the way of the parliamentary system of government. The Senate and the House of Commons are two different institutions having different functions and different characteristics. The Senate is in theory an independent legislative body and the British North America (Constitution) Act, 1867, endowed it with co-equal powers, but in practice it usually surrenders before a potent and consistent pressure of public opinion reflected in the votes of the Commons. Democracy demands that the Upper Chamber must not persist, though it should resist, and in strict obedience to this democratic principle the Canadian Senate has cautiously avoided a clash with the popular Chamber. It has, in fact, always submitted to the wishes of the House of Commons. It is really a recording Chamber and Parliament is surely the House of Commons. Yet it is the joint action of the Governor-General, the Senate, and the House of Commons, which law requires, to make legislation possible.

Under section 91 of the Constitution Act, 1867 (formerly the British North America Act, 1867), as amended, the legislative authority of the Parliament of Canada extends to the making of laws for the peace, order and good government of Canada. It includes authority to legislate[1] in respect of: the public debt and property; the regulation of trade and commerce; unemployment; insurance; the raising of money by any mode or taxation; the borrowing of money on the public credit; postal service; the census and naval service, and defence; the fixing and providing for the salaries and allowances of civil and other officers of the Government of Canada; beacons, buoys, lighthouses, and Sable Island; navigation and shipping; quarantine and the establishment and maintenance of marine hospitals; sea coast and inland fisheries; ferries between a Province and any British or foreign country or between two Provinces; currency and coinage; banking, incorporation of banks and the issue of paper money; savings banks; weights and measures; bills of exchange and promissory notes; interests; legal tenders; bankruptcy and insolvency; patents of invention and discovery; copyright; Indians and lands reserved for the Indians; naturalization and aliens; marriage and divorce; the criminal law except the constitution of courts of criminal jurisdiction, but including the procedure in criminal matters; the establishment, maintenance and management of penitentiaries. The Dominion Government also exercises all powers which are not specifically granted to the Provinces that is, residuary powers.

In addition, under Section 95 Parliament of Canada may make laws in relation to agriculture and immigration concurrently with Provincial Legislatures, although in the event of conflict, federal legislation is paramount.

## THE SENATE

### Bicameralism a Necessity

The democratic demand for bicameralism and more so in a federal polity was fully recognised and the British North America (Constitution) Act, 1867, recognizably provided for one. But the Senate in Canada, unlike its counterpart in the United States, was not planned to perform a strict federal function. Curiously enough, there was only one suggestion from the delegates of Prince Edward Island, at the Quebec Conference, that representation in the Up-

1. Clause 1 of Section 91 of the North America Act, 1867 in respect of amendment of the Constitution was repealed by the Constitution Act, 1982.

per Chamber should be on the strictly federal basis of equal representation of all the constituent units, big or small. Even this proposal was substantially modified by its proposer almost as soon as it was put forward and today Provinces, large and small, are much less concerned with representation into the Senate than representation into the Cabinet. "The most likely explanation of this lack of assertiveness on the part of the small provinces," observes Dawson, "is that the Conference (Quebec) regarded this feature of the American Constitution as one of the grave dangers implicit in the doctrine of State rights."

Another departure from the federal principle was the mode of appointment of the members of the Senate. The American experience with an elected Upper Chamber had not impressed the delegates of the Quebec Conference. They were convinced that inasmuch as responsible government was identified with the Lower Chamber, it was not desirable to create a possible rival by making the Upper Chamber as an elected body. The Conference, therefore, decided to have the members of the Senate appointed for life by the Governor-General.

And, then, the Senate was intended to be "the minor legislative partner"; a revising and restraining body. Sir John MacDonald affirmed at the Quebec Conference that the Senate "must be an independent House, having a free action of its own, for it is only valuable as being a regulating body, calmly considering the legislation initiated by the popular branch, and preventing any hasty or ill-considered legislation which may come from that body, but it will never set itself in opposition against the deliberate and understood wishes of the people." The Senate was, also, intended to represent property and conservatism. In the sixties of the last century when the constitution for the union was being discussed, there existed much distrust of "pure democracy." MacDonald and his associates were anxious to preserve minority rights and to erect bulwarks against the unheeded democratic tide. They desired to establish a constitutional system wherein "marked popular majorities" would not solely dominate, and "the sudden gusts of popular passion" would be controlled. "The right of minority," remarked Sir John, "must be protected, and the rich are always fewer in number than the less rich."[2]

The authors of the Canadian Constitution, therefore, sought to establish a Second Chamber which should reflect the will, not of more numbers, but of those with special position. Sir John MacDonald claimed that all colonial leaders at the Quebec Conference believed that the basic principles of the British Constitution should be conserved, "namely, that classes and property should be represented as well as numbers." And in accepting an appointed Chamber with distinct property qualification, the Senate was brought closer to the House of Lords and ensured, as Brady remarks, "the nineteenth century Whig ideal of a balanced representation of social interests."[3]

**Composition and Term**

From an original membership of 72, the Senate now has 104 members. The break up is 24 members from each of the four regions and six from New Foundland. The division into four regions is: (1) Ontario; (2) Quebec; (3) the Maritime provinces (10 Senators are allotted to Nova Scotia, 10 to New Brunswick and 4 to Prince Edward Island); and 24 the Western Provinces (6 Senators being allotted to each of the four Provinces of Mantioba. British Columbia, Alberta and Saskatchewan). Two Senators represent the Yokon and the North-West Territories. If at any time on the recommendation of the Governor-General the Queen thinks fit that four or eight members be added to the Senate, the Governor-General may appoint them, but the number of Senators must not at any time exceed 118. That is the legal maximum limit of membership of the Senate.

Section 23 of the North America (Constitution) Act, 1867, provided that a Senator must be at least thirty years of age, a natural-born or naturalised subject of the Queen, resident within the Province in which he is appointed and possesses property real or personal, to the value of four thousand dollars. In the case of Quebec, he must be a resident of the electoral district for which he is appointed. A Senator loses his seat for any of the following reasons: (i) if for two consecutive sessions of Parliament, he fails to attend the Senate; (ii) if he takes an oath of allegiance or makes a declaration of allegiance to a foreign power or does an

2. Refer to Alexander Brady's *Democracy in the Dominions*, p. 71.
3. *Ibid.*, p. 72.

act whereby he becomes a subject or a citizen of a foreign power; (iii) if he becomes bankrupt or insolvent or a public defaulter; (iv) if he is attained of treason or convicted of felony or of any infamous crime; (v) if he ceases to be a resident of the Province by shifting to some other; and (vi) if he resigns his seat in the Senate.

Senators are appointed by the Governor-General, who acts on the recommendation of the Prime Minister. Originally, they were appointed for life, but in 1965, a mandatory retirement age of 75 was set. ''Senatorship has been invariably regarded'', writes Dawson, ''as the choicest plums in the patronage basket, and they have been used without compunction as rewards of faithful party service.'' Appointments are made, as a rule purely on party lines, although every Prime Minister admits that the system is unsatisfactory as it promotes narrow party interests. And yet every Prime Minister continues with it. There is only one solitary example when Sir John A. MacDonald appointed an opponent, John MacDonald, a Liberal. Party appointments undermine the efficiency of the Senate. Summing up the system of appointments, Dawson says: ''There is no doubt that many of those appointed are a credit to the Senate; there is no doubt that the system is most useful as an instrument of party discipline and service; but there is equally no doubt that the chief purpose underlying these appointments is not the public good, but party patronage and advantage, and that this is reflected in the general low regard in which the Senate is popularly held.''

**Powers of the Senate**

The British North America Act, 1867, (now the Constitution Act, 1867) does not define or limit the powers of the Senate excepting that the House of Commons has the sole power to originate all Bills for the raising or spending of money. The absence of any specific provision gives to the Senate co-equal legislative power with the Commons. But taking into consideration the intentions of the framers of the Constitution that the Senate was to act as a revising and restraining body to deal with possible errors or impulses of the Commons, and the fact that the Ministry is responsible to the Lower House as the prime guardian of expenditure, and survives only as long as it commands support from that House, the Ministry introduces all important legislation and defends its policies in the House of Commons. There is another important reason for the exclusion of the Senate. Since the twenties of the present century and as a result of the precedent set by Mackenzie King, only one Minister and that too without Portfolio sits in the Senate. This fact reduces the significance of the Senate in the enactment of laws and in the control of policy. Ministers introduce all important legislation in the Commons where they sit as members and are able to defend such legislation.

The tendency of Ministers to introduce all their measures in the House of Commons has, thus, deprived the Senate of any major part in the initiation of legislation. During recent years there has been an extraordinary change and between 1946-53, 138 Bills were introduced in the Senate as compared with 36 between 1924-45. The explanation of this increase lies in the fact that between 1946- 53, ''Parliament has been overhauling and consolidating the bulk of the Canadian Statutes, and the Cabinet has generously allowed the Senate to participate in this very arduous labour.'' But this practice, Prof. Dawson observes, ''cannot be extended indefinitely, if for no other reason than that the really able, energetic, and willing Senators are relatively few.''[4] Private Bills usually originate in the Senate.

But once Bills reach the Senate, after they have passed the Commons, its effective participation ensures by proposing amendments or rejecting the entire Bill, if the Senators so desire. The Senate has never taken the position that its powers of rejection and amendment are absolute and independent of public opinion, ''but it has ventured to oppose the Commons on the ground that the measure was not only inadvisable but that the Lower House had no popular mandate for this particular proposal.'' It rejected the Old Age Pension Bill in 1926, but accepted it next year because the Bill had received the mandate of the electorate at the new General Election and the government initiating it had been returned to office. There has, thus, established a sort of 'mandatory convention', as in Britain. Both the Senate and the Lords do not reject a Bill on which the mandate of the electorate has been obtained.

In revising Bills the Senate does really

4. Dawson, R. M., *The Government of Canada,* p. 343.

useful work. Bills are often sent from the Commons badly drafted, hastily assembled, and, in some instances, almost unworkable. Senators have more leisure and fewer distratctions than the members of the House of Commons. The talent and wider experience of some Senators make it possible for them to improve the Bills in a logical shape and draftsmanship. Then, they have no specific electorate to placate and they speak less to the gallery, for in truth there is seldom a gallery in the Senate. The investigatory work of the Senate's Standing Committees and Special Committees is also often distinguished. Detailed examination of the measures before the Senate is done in the Standing Committees at which the public may be invited to present their views and even members of the Cabinet may appear to give information and explain a particular proposal.

With regard to financial measures the British North America (Constitution) Act, 1867 definitely states that Money Bills originate in the House of Commons.[5] The Senate's power to amend them is a matter of dispute between the two Chambers. The Act itself is silent on this point. The House of Commons, taking precedent from its counterpart in Britain, asserts that the Senate has no power to amend Money Bills. "All aids and supplies granted to His Majesty by Parliament of Canada, are the sole gift of the House of Commons, and all Bills for granting such aids and supplies ought to begin with the House, as it is the undoubted Right of the House, to direct, limit, and appoint in all such Bills, the ends, purposes, considerations, limitations and qualifications of such grants which are not alterable by the Senate."[6] The Senate has "indignantly rejected" this right of the House of Commons. It has been maintained that such a power to be exclusively exercised by the Commons is an addition to the Constitution. The Senate argues that when the British North America (Constitution) Act, 1867, explicitly refers to the origin of Money Bills in the House of Commons, the omission in the Act with regard to amendment or rejection of Money Bills by the Senate is conclusive evidence that the framers of the law had no intention to place any restriction on the power of the Senate. The Senate has also urged that if it is to act as the guardian of the Provincial rights, it must possess the power to interfere in financial legislations that is detrimental to Provincial interests.

But these are only theoretical arguments. In practice the Senate has repeatedly amended Money Bills. "At such times," writes Professor Dawson, "it has not been at all uncommon for the Lower House to acquiesce in the Senate's amendments while adding the quite futile clause that the incident was not to be considered as precedent."[7] The Senate does not openly reject a pure Money Bill. It amends it, but when it puts amendments which are not acceptable to the Commons, it is tantamount to its power of rejection. And here the power of the Senate is superior to that of the House of Lords, which functions under constitutional limitations, as provided in the Act of 1911 amended in 1949.

Apart from its legislative and financial functions, the Senate has successfully conducted investigations at different times into current political and social problems. A Special Committee of the Senate held an inquiry in 1946, into the operation of the War Income-Tax Act and Excess Profits Tax Act and it did the job admirably well. Such inquiries can most fruitfully be conducted by the Senate, and every year there are innumerable inquiries which demand some scrutiny and drastic overhauling, and the Senate has the leisure, ability and freedom to investigate them.

The Senate was intended to be the "minor legislative partner" and this intention of the Constitution-makers finds expression in the two constitutional provisions. One relates to the composition of the House of Commons which provides that it will be an elected Chamber. Whatever be the reasons for an appointive Senate, this single provision gives to the Commons unquestioned position of eminence and authority as a representative Chamber. An elected Chamber is the mirror of public opinion and it must translate into practice the policy which has been endorsed by the people at the General Election. This is the first principle of a democratic government. Secondly, representation and taxation go together. Section 53 of the British North America (Constitution) Act, 1867,

5. Section 53.
6. House of Commons Standing Orders and Rules, No. 61.
7. Dawson, R. M. *Government of Canada,* p. 349.

gives powers to the House of Commons by providing that all Bills for the raising or spending of money shall originate in the House of Commons.

Apart from these two constitutional provisions, the eminence and authority of the House of Commons, and, consequently, weakness of the Senate, depends upon the practices of the parliamentary system of government. The essential feature of such a system of government is the responsibility of the Cabinet to the representative Chamber and the Constitution ordains that the Representative Chamber is the House of Commons. Once these three fundamental propositions are put in their proper context the position of the Senate becomes permanently settled, although there may be still room for development and adjustment of the functions which fall within the areas of the two Chambers.

There are certain functional weaknesses of the Senate too. Critics regard it as a sleeping beauty which neither acts as an effective brake to the hasty and ill-considered legislation passed by the Commons nor does it properly serve the purpose of revision. Sir George E. Foster in the course of a debate remarked: "Who on the street asks to know what is the opinion of the Senate upon this or that question ? Who in the press really takes any trouble to know whether the Senate has any ideas, and if so, what they are upon any branch of legislative concern or upon conditions which require the best and most united work of all in order to arrive at a successful conclusion." There are others who regard the Senate merely as a House of echoes. Sir J. A. Marriot writes, "It will be observed that the Canadian Senate attempts to combine several principles, which if not absolutely contradictory, are clearly distinct. Consequently, it has never possessed either the glamour of an aristocratic and hereditary Chamber, or the strength of an elected assembly or the utility of a Senate representing the federal as opposed to the national idea. Devised with the notion of giving some sort of representation to provincial interests it has, from the first, been manipulated by party leaders to subserve the interests of central executive."

But Professor Dawson is of the opinion that despite the severe handicaps from which the Senate suffers, it has been able to do some genuinely useful work. "It revises and checks legislation sent up from the Commons and it takes by far the greater part of the load of private Bill legislation from overworked Commons. It has, however, not been a conspicuous success in guarding the rights of provincial or other minorities, although this was one of the chief reasons for its creation. Its attitude on social legislation has often been criticised as reactionary, but the evidence on this point is conflicting. The Senate, in short, has its merits, although they fall far short of justifying its continuance in its present form."[8] Professor Alexander Brady says that the relative success or failure of the Senate is a matter of opinion. "Its virtues," he further adds, "have usually been unhonoured or even unrecognised; its defects well publicized. It has failed to rivet on itself wide popular attention and esteem. It is commonly neglected by newspapers and seldom does it influence profoundly policies and legislation."[9] The Senate, as it is, is a weak Chamber and stands no comparison to the eminence, authority and importance of the House of Commons.

The first great handicap placed on the Senate was the system of appointment of its members. "The founders of the Dominion," says Professor Dawson, "accepted as inevitable the fact that if the Cabinet appointed the Senators, it would be for party reasons: but even they could scarcely have expected party gratitude to become so dominant a motive."[10] Except for the original appointments made in 1867, which represented all political groups, the Senatorship has always been a party spoils and it had gone to the orthodox members of the party in office who had served it long and with a meritorious credit. Former members of the House of Commons who had been defeated at the General Election or are "too old to battle further for office," moneyed persons who had liberally contributed to party campaigns, and others who had aided their party receive their reward and they constitute a considerable number of the appointees.

The result is, as Professor Brady remarks, "Whatever the zeal and ability of appointees or the depth of their experience—often they are men of distinguished achievement—they can

8. Dawson, R. M., *Democratic Government in Canada*, pp. 412-13.
9. Brady, A., *Democracy in the Dominions*, p. 72.
10. Dawson, R. M., *Government of Canada*, p. 432.

seldom escape in the public mind from the stigma of receiving a reward rather than a call to service.'' Leftist parties have been highly critical of such party appointments and have never failed to emphasise the high percentage of Senators who sit on the boards of powerful commercial corporations. Here the Canadian Senate loosely resembles the House of Lords. It has become, like the Lords, a fortress of wealth and, consequently, the Senators are predominantly an economic interest who cannot and do not look to proposals for radical, social and economic reforms with any desirable sympathy. The composition of the Senate, therefore, is fundamentally responsible for the general low regard in which the Chamber is popularly held.

Another result of the composition of the Senate is the ''air of superannuated indolence'' which Lord Bryce discerned in the House of Lords. Life term of office, which has now been changed into mandatory retirement at 75, inevitably led to a larger number of Senators remaining in the Chamber long after they had passed the age of genuine usefulness. The great bulk of these superannuated members could not perform their duties with the same energy, zeal and effectiveness as youngmen, and the youngmen had no reason to go to the Senate as it gave them no hope to future career. The old men went there with the sense of opening up the last chapter of their career. Sir George E. Foster, after his appointment as a Senator, commented in his diary: ''How colourless the Senate—the entering gate coming to extinction.''

The Senatorship is, thus, a refuge for those whose active life is almost over,[11] and who are primarily concerned with a pleasant, secure and not very strenuous old age. Gratten O' Leary succinctly put the issue when he said, ''the Senatorship isn't a job. It's a title. Also it's a blessing, stroke of good fate; something like drawing a royal straight flush in the biggest pot of the evening, or winning the Calcutta sweep. That's why we think it wrong to think of a Senatorship as a job; and wrong to think of the Senate as a place where people are supposed to work. Pensions aren't given for work.''

Here is an obituary, quoted verbatim, of Senator Dessaulles who died in 1930, in his 103rd year, and it bears eloquent testimony on the usefulness or uselessness of the Senate:—

> ''Senator Dessaulles, dead at St. Hyacinthe, who held a seat in the Senate of Canada since 1907, had a remarkable record. So far is recalled by those around the Senate since he was there, he never once participated in any debate or gave expression to an opinion; but he followed the discussions closely and was there when the division bells rang. He was a kindly old man, held by all parties in venerable respect because of his great age.''

The result is clear. The Senate may supply the opportunities to do useful work, but it does not supply at all adequate incentive for work. Political ambition is there dead. But there is the assurance of a secure existence and the salary is ample. There is, thus, ''a general sense of futility in the red Chamber; few people listen to the speeches, the usual drama and excitement of politics are lacking, no vital issues hang on the Senate's votes, there are no reputations to be made, there are no fresh, aggressive, stimulating young minds to satisfy.''

More fundamental than the above factors is the fact that despite the formal equality of powers of the two Chambers, the Ministry is responsible to the House of Commons and it survives only as long as it commands support from that House. Before the twenties usually one and occasionally two and even three Senators were included in the Cabinet and they were assigned definite portfolios. But Mackenzie King set a precedent and since then there is only one single Minister from the Senate and that, too, without a Portfolio. This reduces the importance of the Senate in the enactment of laws and in the control of policy. Ministers introduce legislation in the House to which they belong and where they can explain and defend their policies and it is in the House of Commons that explanation and defence really matters. The Minister without Portfolio has no portfolio to look after, no policy to defend and no work to account for. It is a sinecure assignment. The Senate and the House of Commons enjoy equal legislative powers, but Money Bills must originate in the House of Commons and its voice is decisive. In case of a deadlock between the two, the Governor-General may appoint four to eight Senators to resolve the deadlock. Since Senate appointments are party appointments, the party

11. In the 1945 Senate thirty-three out of the ninety-five had been over sixty years of age at the time of their appointment and this proportion more or less still continues.

in power will naturally make appointments to facilitate its triumph. The opposition of the Senate to the House of Commons matters nothing in the final analysis.

When all legislation originates in the House of Commons in the early part of a session of Parliament, the Senate has no business to transact. It must either wait or adjourn until the legislation of the session comes before it. "Year after year," complained Senator Arthur Meighen, "the services of this House are allowed to slumber for a good portion of the session." It is not uncommon for the Senate to adjourn for long periods immediately after the passage of the Address in reply to the Speech from the Throne. And when it meets, it functions leisurely and the debates are short. In 1938, for example, the Senate sat for 61 days and in 1939 for only 47 days. The debates generally cover less than 10 pages per day of the Hansard.[12] "While the value of the contributions made by the members of the Canadian Parliament," remarks Professor Dawson, "can scarcely be measured by the convenient method of totalling pages of debate, it is difficult to believe that the Senators have achieved so remarkable a brevity without losing much of the content in the prodigious effects of concentration. A perusal, of their remarks amply confirms the accuracy of this observation."

The Senate has also not succeeded in protecting property, Provincial, and minority rights although these were the original aims for creaing the Upper Chamber in Canada. Professor Mackay has specially gone into this aspect and his conclusions are that the Senate "has no consistent record as an upholder of the rights of the provinces, and the party lines have usually proved stronger than those of the section and province affected." Quebec is the only Province which reposes confidence in the Senate as the protector of its position and culture against encroachment or abuse. Other provinces are much less concerned with representation in the Senate. They are really concerned with representation in the Cabinet, which in Canada is a truly federalised institution. In the maintenance of rights of other minorities, "the Senate has proved," says Prof. Dawson, "to be of moderate but no exceptional service; although its alertness in Private Bill legislation has been of considerable help in protecting private property rights and public interests against the attacks of predatory corporations."

**Reforming the Senate**

The Senate, thus, suffers from its own handicaps and disabilities. It has been regarded as the weakest second Chamber in the world. All the same, it has been by no means a useless body and the Senators have performed a creditable service in revising and amending legislation. The Senators are frequently charged with partisanship, especially when a majority is hostile to the party then in office. "Yet ordinarily," says Professor Brady, "they are less motivated by party loyalty and less regimented by party discipline than members of the Commons. They are not without partisan spirit, and divide into the Government group and the Opposition, seated to right and left of the Speaker. But they are more impartial in discussing Bills, and in committees pursue their task with impressive care." With no specific electorate to placate, they are less inclined to oppose merely for the sake of partisan end, and speak less to the gallery, for in reality there is seldom a gallery. Being secure in their positions and not being subject to dissolution, like the Lords in Britain the Senators do not speak with one eye on the reactions of their voters to their speeches. They are responsible to no one, but, then, no one is responsible to them. The result is that although the debates in the Senate are usually brief, yet they are based upon ability and experience and often set a high standard of discussion. The Commons take due cognizance of what the Senators say. Even in financial legislation their voice counts. The question of its abolition, accordingly, does not arise. And democracy needs a second Chamber. Unless it is acceptably proved that democracy does not need a second Chamber, it is not democratic to abolish one in Canada.

But there has been from early times a demand for reforming the Senate, as no one has desired to maintain it in its present unsatisfactory condition. The difficulty of devising a second Chamber is no less acute in Canada than in other countries with parliamentary system of governments. In fact, there are certain special difficulties inherent in the Canadian structure of government. The population of the Maritime Provinces is more generously represented in the Senate than any other main section of Canada and they would be unfriendly to any scheme of reform which would tend to reduce the number

12. The official compilation of the proceedings of Parliament.

of its representatives. Quebec will be no less hostile to any consideration of senatorial reform and it has always been suspicious "of every constitutional innovation, traditionally on the defensive, guarding its culture and institutions against inter- ference from English-speaking Canada."

The Inter-Provincial Conference held in 1927, to discuss senatorial reform decisively rejected the proposal for an elective Chamber and accordingly, it continues to be nominated. "Thus, the Senate" Brady remarks, "remains as it is because no strong interests seek, and many would oppose, its reform and the indifference of the multitude gives it security." As a matter of fact, the question of Senate abolition or reform tends to become an issue with the Opposition or Government when the party balance in the Chamber swings the other way. Senate appointments are frequently used to give not only Provincial representation, but also representation to economic, racial and religious groups in the Provinces and Prime Ministers have very often placated the temporary irritations of minorities.

Some measures of reform, however, may not be impossible within the given framework. The Senate could be utilised to better advantage by initiating more bills in it. At the same time, the powers of the Senate should be limited, like the House of Lords, so that it could exercise only suspensive veto over ordinary legislation and exercise no control over Money Bills. Ministers should be permitted to introduce bills and speak in either Chamber, although they would vote only in the Chamber to which they belong, or the practice, as in Britain, may be utilised by placing a number of junior ministers in the Senate, or if more ministers were re-admitted in the Senate their junior ministers may be placed in the Commons.

## THE HOUSE OF COMMONS

"The Canadian House of Commons, although it is not the oldest among the legislative Chambers patterned upon Westminster, is the first wherein representatives from federal colonies convened the inheritor of parliamentary traditions from the colonial legislatures which attained responsible government in the nineteenth century, and the forum for some eighty years where men of French and British descent have discussed their common affairs and achieved that delicate balance of interest on which the Canadian national state rests." The House of Commons is the great democratic organ of State government where public will finds expression and exercises its ultimate political power. It is the "grand inquest of the nation" where policies are discussed and legislative measures are hammered and to which body the Executive must turn to justify its public acts and get approval.

### Composition and Organisation

The fundamental importance of the House of Commons is derived from its representative character. Canada has today full adult suffrage and, generally speaking, every man and every woman enjoys the right to vote if he or she is eighteen years of age, is a Canadian citizen, has been ordinarily resident in Canada for twelve months preceding the election and has been ordinarily resident in the electoral district at the date of issuing the writ authorising the election. Qualifications for representatives are not given in the North America (Constitution) Act, 1867 but are determined by statute. The present statutory qualifications are simple: The members of the House of Commons must be Canadian citizens and at least twenty-one years of age. Property qualifications disappeared in 1874. All but four of the members are elected from single member constituencies. Two constituencies—Halifax and Queens—elect two members each. The maximum term of the members is five years and the actual duration of membership depends upon the dissolution of Parliament. According to the Constitution Act, 1982, the maximum term may be extended "in time of real or apprehended war, invasion or insurrection....by the Parliament of Canada if such continuation is not opposed by the votes of more than one-third of the members of the House of Commons." The usual term is four years. It has, indeed, become a tradition of Canadian political life that no Prime Minister will allow a term to run for the full five years if it can possibly be avoided. This is based on experience as well as on other practical considerations.

Section 37 of the British North America (Constitution) Act, 1867, had provided that the House of Commons shall consist of 181 members. Further, under Section 51, it was enacted that, after the completion of the census of 1871 and each of subsequent decennial census, the representation of the four Provinces should be readjusted. Membership of the House of Commons was accordingly increased from time to time until it reached 255. In 1949, as a result of the Union of New Foundland, provision was made for its representation by seven members. This increased the membership of the House to 262. By Chapter 15 of the Statute of 1952, Parliament of Canada amended Section 51 of the British North America (Constitution) Act, providing for a new method of re-adjustment of representation of the House of Commons. Pursuant to this amendment a new Representation Act was passed, providing for a total of 265 members of the House of Commons. A further change in representation was assented to on March 13, 1975 when the North-West Territories Representation Act was approved. Provision was, accordingly, made for representation of the Yukon Territory by one member and the North-West Territories by two members. The membership of the House of Commons is now 282.

A member of the Canadian House of Commons, unlike his fellow member in Britain, is allowed to resign his seat. Absence from the sitting of the House is penalized. A member is allowed 21 days unexcused absence and for every day missed over that number, $60 is deducted from the total payment of his salary.

**The Opposition**

The Opposition occupies an essential place in Constitutions based on the British parliamentarry system. Like many other institutions in Canada, such as the Prime Minister and Cabinet, the Opposition, too, is founded on unwritten customs.

The choice of the Canadian electorate not only determines who shall govern Canada, but by deciding which Party receives the second largest number of seats in the House of Commons, it designates which of the major parties becomes the official Opposition. The function of the leader of the Opposition is to offer intelligent and constructive criticism of the Government and its policies. If it succeeds in overthrowing the Government, the leader of the Opposition might form the Government. If Parliament is dissolved on the advice of the Prime Minister and electorate approves the policy of the Opposition by returning it in majority at election its leader becomes the Prime Minister.

Although the position of the leader of the Opposition was not recognized in the British North America Act, 1867, it received statutory acknowledgment in Canada in 1927. The Senate and the House of Commons Act of the year provided for an annual salary to be paid to the leader of the Opposition in addition to the indemnity as a Member of the House. In 1963, the Senate and the House of Commons Act was further amended to provide for an annual allowance to each Member of the House of Commons (other than the Prime Minister or the leader of the Opposition in the House of Commons) who is the leader of a party that has a recognised membership of 12 or more persons in the House.

The function of the Parliamentary Opposition is to offer constructive criticism of the Government of the day, to ensure that Government proposals are carefully reviewed before they pass into law, to ensure the accountability of the Cabinet for the executive policies and activities, and to suggest alternative policies for the governing of Canadians. The final objective of the Opposition is to secure majority in the House; and while this can rarely be obtained by the direct alienation of Government supporters, it could occur as the result of a following General Election.

**Parliamentary Procedure**

In structure, Rules and Procedure the Canadian House of Commons inherits the British parliamentary customs and usages. The general principle is that whenever a matter of legislative practice or procedure is not modified or replaced by the Canadian House, the usages and the customs of the British House of Commons will be followed.

Immediately after the General Election the Governor-General-in-Council summons the House of Commons and after taking the oath the members proceed to elect their Speaker. The name of the candidate for Speakership is conventionally proposed by the Prime Minister and seconded by a member of the Cabinet and almost invariably the Opposition parties express their approval. In Britain, the Speaker of the last Parliament is normally re-elected irrespective of party changes or his own party affiliation. In Canada, on the other hand, a new Speaker is usually chosen for each Parliament, and he must belong to the Government Party. This practice enables the House to alternate more frequently the Speakers from English and French Canada; the convention being that if the Seaker of one Parliament is of British origin, the Speaker of the next Parliament must be a French Canadian, and both the Speaker and the Deputy Speaker must not come from the same race.

The duties of the Speaker are as onerous as that of his prototype in Britain. He presides over the deliberations of the House, maintains decorum, puts questions to the House, reads any motion or resolution and protects the person of the Members from insult. He maintains the conduct of debate in accordance with the rules and practices of the House and is the guardian of the powers, the dignities, the liberties and the privileges of the House. The Speaker votes only in case of a tie.

After the election of the Speaker the House breaks, but it reassembles shortly before the time appointed by the Governor-General when the Usher of the Black Rod announces that the Governor-General desires the attendance of the House in the Senate. The Governor-General then reads Speech from the Throne outlining the policy of the Government and the legislation which it intends to bring in Parliament in the coming session. After the Speech had been delivered, the Commons return to their Chamber. The Speech comes before the House for discussion on a Motion of Thanks from the Treasury Benches. It gives an opportunity to the Opposition to offer criticism against the policy of the Government and the Leader of the House—the Prime Minister—gives his explanation for pursuing such a policy. When the House adopts the Motion of thanks, it expresses the confidence in the Government.

The basic procedure in the passage of public Bills is the same, and here, again, Canada follows Britain in making distinction between Government Bills, Private Members' Bills, and Private Bills. The procedure is that Bills receive three readings in the House, three in the Senate, and then go to the Governor-General for his assent, if approved by both the Houses. In case of differences between the two Houses, a conference is held between representatives of each House to discuss and if possible to reconcile the differences. If agreement is not reached, the Governor-General may nominate four to eight Senators to resolve the deadlock; the position similar to one available in Britain to create more peers to resolve the deadlock between the Lords and Commons prior to 1911. The Canadian Committee system also resembles the British Committee system; the Committee of the Whole, the Select Committees, and the Standing Committees. The procedure followed herein is also similar.

**Functions of the House**

Theoretically, the Commons and the Senate possess co-equal legislative powers. But with the stabilization of the parliamentary government and because of two specific provisions in the British North America (Constitution) Act, 1867, —the Senate is appointive whereas the House is popularly elected, and that all Money Bills must originate in the House of Commons—the Commons has become the pivot of all legislation and the Senate is lost in oblivition. Bills may be introduced in either House, but Bills imposing any charge on the people or making any grant for the services must originate in the House of Commons. The Rules of Procedure lay down that ''all aids and supplies granted to His Majecty by the Parliament of Canada are the sole gift of the House of Commons, and all Bills for granting such aid and supplies ought to begin with the House, as it is the undoubted right of the House to direct, limit and appoint in all such Bills the ends, purposes, considerations, conditions, limitations and qualifications of such grants, which are not alterable by the Senate.'' Money Bills must be introduced by the Ministers.

The House of Commons must invariably ratify all measures which the Cabinet submits, but in the process of making laws it provides an opportunity to discuss and criticise. In fact, the deliberative function is a part of the legislative function of Parliament wherever the parliamentary system of government exists. The most important function of the Opposition is to criticise matters of administration and policy-making and, thereby, to make the Government to defend its intentions and practices. Even the opinion expressed by members of the majority party may carry enough weight to bring about substantial modifications in the Cabinet's proposals. The Opposition may also be able to secure a few modest concessions. No government, whatever be its majority, can remain oblivious of the criticism of the Opposition. A government which neglects the Opposition does so at its own peril, because the lapses of the Government are the opportunities of the Opposition and it uses them to appeal to the public opinion. Nor is the government insensitive to the reactions of its own followers. Signs of unrest against its policy in the constituencies, amongst interest groups or on the part of a sufficient number of back-benches, may lead to changes in the government's plans and proposals.

The Rules of the House allot most of the time to the Government business and the Government has the sole power to move closure. But the Rules are careful also to provide abundant opportunity for the Opposition to question, criticise and attack. Twenty-five days of each session are specifically allotted to the Opposition to debate any subject it pleases, and on six of these days it can move a motion for want of confidence.

A vital aspect of the critical function of the House of Commons is its power of controlling the Executive, or its powers of general supervision. The responsibility of the Ministry to the House of Commons involves a constant control of the House over the Government. Indeed, control and responsibility go hand in hand. The House of Commons exercises its control in two ways. The first is the constant demand in the House for information about the actions of the Government and this is done through the medium of oral or written questions. The members of the House are given opportunity normally on three days in a week to address questions to Cabinet Ministers concerning various phases of public affairs. Supplementary oral questions are sometimes allowed, but they are not very common, and are definitely not encouraged. The House may conduct investigations into the administration of Departments and, thus, bring out the activities of the Government into the light of publicity.

The second is the criticism that is regularly aimed at the Government. This is done when laws are made and the policy of the Government is under review. The best opportunity for the Opposition to criticise the policy of the Government as a whole is when it debates the Speech from the Throne which incorporates the policy of the Government which it intends to pursue and the legislation it proposes to enact. Discussion of public finance, more especially of proposals for expenditure, offer a very real opportunity for discussion and criticism. If the Opposition, for example, disapproves the Government's foreign policy, it uses the debate on appropriations for the Foreign Office as an occasion for criticism.

In addition to these regularly scheduled debates; the normal occasion for criticism of the Executive is the debate on a motion of adjournment. A member may ask leave to move the adjournment of the House "for purposes of discussing a matter of urgent pubic importance." If the Speaker decides that the matter is urgent and at least twenty members support it, the motion is allowed. If less than twenty but more than five support it, the question of leave is at once referred to the House for a decision. The most direct method of launching an attack on the Cabinet is the motion of no confidence. Motion for a vote of no confidence is really a crucial occasion in the life of the Cabinet, because it decides its fate. As long as a Government can command a comfortable majority, it is not possible for such a motion to get through, still it creates embarrassments in the ranks of the Ministry. Amendment to a Government's motion or an immediate attack on a Government measure inferentially becomes an issue of "no confidence." There are times when a Cabinet may itself take the initiative and demand a vote of confidence from the House as it was done in January, 1926.

The House of Commons is a selective body. It is here that the national talent is exhibited and the members make their mark. The House does not actually pick the Cabinet, but the fact that the Cabinet must always be able to retain the support of a majority of the House gives the Chamber a negative power of choice. The House selects ministers indirectly in yet another way. It provides the rigorous environment in which ministerial talent must prove its worth and establish its right of office. The prospective ministers usually serve an arduous apprenticeship in the House; and while many cease to be serious contenders long before their party comes to power or vacancies occur in the Cabinet, the few able survivors have had ample opportunity to develop their capacity before they are called upon to assume office. And as Professor Laski observes, there is "no alternative method that in any degree approaches it."[13]

The House of Commons educates and leads public opinion on many questions. All that comes before the House of Commons had not been before the people at the time of the General Election and their mandate could not

13. Laski, H. J., *A Grammar of Politics*, p. 300.

be obtained thereupon. Many matters are new and many problems emerge out of the national and international movement of events which could not be anticipated. The House talks, argues, investigates, opposes, decides, and very often postpones action on various matters, and while doing so it arouses interest and helps to create a more enlightened opinion throughout the county. Referring to this process in Britain, and it is equally applicable in Canada, Professor Ivor Jennings says, ''So the discussion radiates from Westminster in waves of ever-decreasing elasticity. Arguments are transmitted, prevented, simplified, perhaps distorted. A 'Common opinion' develops, and creates new waves which find their way back to Westminster. They set going new arguments in the smokeroom and more formally in the House. In their turn these arguments produce new rays which go back to the ordinary people. In this way there is a constant interchange between Parliament and people which does produce a constant assimilation of opinion....The purpose of Parliament is to keep them (the Cabinet) in touch with the public opinion, and to keep public opinion in touch with the problems of government.''[14]

Finally, the House of Commons is a unique institution of national importance ''which presents in condensed form the different interests, races, religions, classes and occupations, whose ideas and wishes it embodies with approximate exactness.'' In the land of diversity, as Canada is, it brings unity. The representatives of the people of all shades and opinions, languages and religions, territories and occupations meet together, talk and discuss their viewpoints, hammer the issues and reconcile the differences in order to present the people one single united policy. The House is, thus, to use Mill's phrase, ''the nation's committee of grievances and its Congress of opinions,'' the members of which with their varied experiences and diverse samplings, are genuinely and actively concerned with the promotion of the national welfare. This gives strength to the government of the time and enables the Cabinet to proceed with far more assurance and certainty to work which lies before it. Mackezie King declared in the gloomy days of 1940: ''I can say frankly to honourable members that it is a source of comfort rather than the opposite to have Parliament in session at a time such as this. I say that quite sincerely. There is comfort in the sense of knowing that where the situation is as serious as it is, the body of the people's representatives are here and can express freely their views, as can the Government its views and what it is doing, in a manner which it is not possible to do through the press....I would not wish a long period to elapse, with the country and the World in the state in which it now is, without having an opportunity of consulting with the members of Parliament and having them fully informed with respect to what the Government is doing.''

## SUGGESTED READINGS

Bissonnelte, B., *Essai sur Constitution du Canada.*

Dawson, R.M., *Democratic Government in Canada.*

Kennedy, W.F.M., *Statutes, Treaties and Documents of the Canadian Constitution.*

Kung, F.A. *The Modern Senate of Canada.*

Varcoe, F.P. *The Distribution of Legislative Power in Canada*.

14. Jennings, I., *Parliamentary Reforms,* pp. 18-19.

# CHAPTER IV

# The Federal Judiciary

### System of Courts

The system of courts obtainable in Canada possesses certain characteristics which are due to the federal nature of the government. But it has not followed the American idea of what a system of courts should be under a federation. In the United States there are two sets of courts, Federal and State, distinctly constituted and with well demarcated jurisdiction. Within their own field of jurisdiction the Supreme Court of the United States and the Supreme Courts of Appeal in the States are the final Courts of Appeal. In certain circumstances a dispute may be transferred from one to the other. For example, if a case involves the interpretation of the Constitution or a federal statute, it may be transferred from the jurisdiction of a State Court to that of a Federal Court. Such transfers, however, do not make the rule and a case will normally finish in the system in which it originated.

The British North America Act, 1867, (now the Constitution Act, 1867) established two systems of courts, Federal and Provincial, but the dividing line between them is horizontal rather than vertical. Parliament is empowered to create a general court of appeal and may establish any additional courts for the better administration of the laws of Canada.''[1] The Provinces exercise jurisdiction over the administration of justice, including the constitution, maintenance and organisation of Provincial Courts, both of civil and criminal jurisdiction, and including procedure in civil matters in those courts.''[2] Procedure in criminal matters is within the competence of the federation. The Federal Government also controls the appointments, the remunerations and the removal of Judges at the Centre and in the Provinces (with a few minor exceptions).[3] The great majority of cases originate in one of the Provincial courts and can go up to the Supreme Court of Canada on appeal, and until 1949 from there to the Judicial Committee of the Privy Council in Britain. The Exchequer Court of Canada, which is a Federal Court, has been given a specialised jurisdiction, and is, accordingly, not like a Federal Court on the American model.

Under Section 99 of the British North America Act, 1867, (Constitution Act, 1867) the Judges of the superior courts hold office during good behaviour but are removable by the Governor-General on an address of the Senate and the House of Commons. By virtue of the British North America Act, 1960, (the Constitution Act, 1960), Judges of superior courts now cease to hold office upon attaining 75 years of age. The tenure of office of county court judges is fixed by the Judges Act as being during good behaviour, and their residence is required to be within the county or union of counties for which the court is generally established.

### Federal Judiciary

The Parliament is empowered by Section 101 of the Constitution Act, 1867 (formerly the British North America Act, 1867), to provide, from time to time, for the constitution and organization of a general Court of Appeal for Canada and for the establishment of any additional courts for the better administration of the laws of Canada. Under this provision, Parliament has established the Supreme Court of Canada, Federal Court of Canada, and certain miscellaneous courts.

### Supreme Court of Canada

At the apex of the Canadian system of courts is the Supreme Court of Canada, established in 1875 and is now governed by the Supreme Court Act, 1962. The court consists of a Chief Justice, eight puisne judges. Originally, the court consisted of a Chief Justice and five

1. Section 101, The North America Act, 1867 (now the Constituttion Act, 1867).
2. Section 92, sub-section 14, *Ibid.*
3. Sections 96-100, *Ibid.*

judges. The number of Judges was raised to six in 1927 and then to eight in 1949. The Chief Justice and the puisne judges are appointed by the Governor-General-in-Council, and they hold office during good behaviour and are only removable by the Governor-General on address of both the Senate and the House of Commons. They cease to hold office upon attaining the age of 75. The Court sits at Ottawa and exercises general appellate jurisdiction throughout Canada in civil and criminal cases. The Court is also required to consider and advise upon questions, referred to it by the Governor-General-in-Council and it may also advise the Senate and the House of Commons on Private Bills referred to the Court under any rules or orders of the Senate or the House of Commons. It should be noted that the Supreme Court of Canada and the Provincial Courts apply both Federal and Provincial laws and that their division of authority is not coincident with the division of legislative authority between the Federal and provincial Governments.

Generally speaking, in civil cases appeals may be brought from any judgment of the highest court of final resort in a Province only when leave to appeal has been sought and secured either from the highest court of final resort in that Province or from the Supreme Court of Canada itself. In the latter case leave may be granted even when such leave has been refused by any other court, when, with respect to the particular case sought to be appealed, the Supreme Court is of the opinion that any question involved therein is, by reason of its public importance or the importance of any issue of law involved in such question, one that ought to be decided by the Supreme Court. The former automatic right of appeal to the Supreme Court in civil cases where the sum claimed was in excess of $ 10,000 was repealed in January, 1975.

In criminal cases the appellate jurisdiction of the Supreme Court is conferred by Sections 613-624 of the Criminal Code. Aside from cases in which a person stands sentenced to death or in jeopardy of such a sentence, persons convicted of indictable offences may appeal to the Supreme Court only on question of law on which a Judge of the Provincial Court of appeal dissents or on a question of law with leave of the Supreme Court.

Appeals from the Federal Court, primarily the Federal Court of Canada, are regulated by the statutes establishing them. Such appeals may essentially be made only with leave of the Court.

The Supreme Court is also a final Court of Appeal and its judgment is conclusive in matters of constitutional interpretation, and in cases, where validity of Federal and Provincial statutes is in dispute.

The Judicial Committee of the Privy Council was until recently the final court of appeal for Canada for all but criminal cases. This had eclipsed the position of the Canadian Supreme Court. For a very long time, therefore, it had been a growing feeling in Canada that to send appeals to the Judicial Committee of the Privy Council in London was below the dignity of a nation marching towards statehood. Attempts were made on various occasions to abolish it, but this could not be accomplished. When the Statute of Westminster, 1931, removed the limitations on the competency of the Canadian Parliament, criminal appeals were abolished in 1933. An amendment to the British North America Act, passed in 1949 provided an authority for the Parliament of Canada to legislate in respect of constitutional matters and in the same year a Canadian Statute abolished all appeals to the Privy Council and made the Supreme Court a court of final appeal in all cases. Its judgments in all matters are conclusive.

**Federal Court of Canada**

As a result of a sweeping revision in 1970, the Exchequer Court of Canada, established in 1875, has been replaced by the Federal Court. This Court consists of two divisions, Trial and Appeal, with a total of 12 judges. Both divisions sit throughout Canada. There is a now retirement age of 70 for these judges. They hold office during good behaviour and are only removable by the Governor-General on address of the Senate and House of Commons. The Federal Court of Appeal has as part of its jurisdiction the competence to review all decisions and orders of a judicial or quasi-judicial nature rendered by federal boards or other tribunals, on questions of error in law, excess of jurisdiction, or failure to apply the principles of natural justice. The intent of this reform is to speed up proceedings and to encourage the development of a coherent body of administrative law. The Trial Division's jurisdiction included jurisdiction in respect of such matters as admiralty, patents, customs and excise, and income tax. It also has jurisdiction in claims involving industrial property and in suits involving the Crown in right of Canada. In effect, the Crown in right of Canada is now in the same position before the court as an ordinary litigant.

An appeal lies to the Supreme Court of Canada from any judgment of the Federal Court of Appeal with leave of that court when in the opinion of the Court of Appeal, the question involved in the appeal is one that ought to be submitted to the Supreme Court for decision. Further, an appeal to the Supreme Court lies from a final or other judgment or determination of the Federal Court of Appeal, whether or not leave to make such appeal has been refused by the latter Court, when, in the opinion of the Supreme Court, the question involves a matter of public or legal importance. As with civil appeals to the Supreme Court of Canada, the former automatic right to appeal from a judgment of the Federal Court of Appeal in cases in which the amount in controversy exceeded $10,000 was repealed as of January 27, 1975. An appeal to the Supreme Court continues to be from any decisions of the Federal Court of Appeal in the case of a controversy between Canada and a Province or between two or more Provinces.

## SUGGESTED READINGS

Ohmsted, R.A., *Decisions of the Judicial Committee of the Privy Council Relating to the Canadian Constitution - 1867-1954.*

Trudeau, P.E. *Federalism and the French Canadians.*

# CHAPTER V

# Political Parties

## Party System in Canada

The democratic government as it is understood and practised in Canada simply cannot function without well organised political parties. Like various other institutions inherited from the mother country, the Canadian statesmen in the early days of federation adopted the same pattern of political parties and even gave them the same names—the Conservatives and the Liberals. It does not, however, mean that there had been no other political party beyond the two. Third parties have frequently arisen, but none of them has yet been in a position to challenge effectively the predominance of the Liberals and Conservatives. But the main items in the party programmes were included by a ''sheer chance of the cards.'' Thus, the Conservatives became protectionists and the Liberals opposed such a policy. It is really surprising that in a country inhabited by two races of different languages and religions these differences have not accounted for the division of the parties, although they have occasionally been assisted in the climb to power by skilfully exploiting sectarian and racial jealousies, especially on the issues of bilingualism and denominational schools.

The most important characteristics of the political party system in Canada are, therefore : (1) there is no clear-cut line of division of affinities among the people. Each party commands allegiance from the people in different walks of life. The rich and the less rich, for one can hardly talk of the poor in Canada, the farmers, merchants, manufacturers, shopkeepers, professional men have been found in both the major parties. The Canadian party system is, accordingly, not based upon any distinct ideology. Party membership is the result of chance. (2) The party feelings in Canada do not introduce bitterness in society. No party in Canada can go very far unless it derives support from two or more regional areas in the country and as a consequence of this a national party must take as its primary purpose the reconciliation of the widely scattered aims and interests of a number of these areas and bring together people possessing divergent interests and beliefs. The differences with the parties are, thus, frequently more acute than between the parties themselves. (3) Canada has consistently followed the two-party system and it is only within the past forty years or so that the third parties have emerged. The political parties in Canada have acquired a prominence hitherto unknown. The emergence of the Labour Party and the organisation of the famers into a separate party with definite objects are threatening to the two-party system, as they challenge claims of the other associations to represent adequately the diverse interests within the nation.

Canada has now four political Parties: (1) The Progressive Conservative Party; (2) The Liberal Party; (3) The New Democratic Party: and (4) The Social Credit Party of Canada.

## The Progressive Conservative Party

The origin of the Progressive Party, till 1942, known as the Conservative Party, may be traced back in 1857, when a number of separate groups in the Province of Canada brought together a temporary coalition, which proved afterwards to be permanent, under the name of Liberal-Conservative. It was composed of extreme Tories, moderate Liberals from Upper Canada, together with French moderates, and some English-speaking members from Lower Canada. The coalition soon fell under the leadership of John A. MacDonald who by dint of his domineering personality and afterwards by a dogged desire to see confederation established in Canada, was able to weld the members together. He drew members from other groups and Provinces and, thus, formed a genuine political party. So strong a hold it afterwards exercised on the people that the party was able to retain office, with but one five-year interval, until 1896.

The role and outlook of John A. MacDonald and the Conservative Party have been compared to those of Hamilton and the Federalists in the United States. This is correct, and MacDonald and his successors in the leadership of the Conservative Party often paid genuine tributes to Hamiltonian doctrines. Like the Federalists, the Conservatives stood for centralisation, identified themselves with the propertied, commercial and industrial interests, and above all with these interests succeeded in solving the practical task of nation-making. The centralising influence and the policy of unifying the people of diverse interests, origins and beliefs into one single whole found expression in the national policy of a protective tariff, in the construction of the trans-continental railway, and in many other policies which were directed towards that end. Economic nationalism was, therefore, considered the best means of welding the people in a community of different interests and aspirations. And this continues to be the policy of the party even now and its programme includes schemes of social insurance, abolition of child labour, fixing of minimum wages and maximum hours of work.

In May 1979 General Election the Progressive Conservative Party won 136 seats in a 282-member House of Commons and formed the minority government, ending 16 years of Liberal Party's rule. But the minority Government was defeated after nine months in office and new elections were held in February 1980. The Progressive Conservatives could secure only 101 seats and, consequently, made way for the Liberal Party to form the government.

**The Liberal Party**

The origin of the Liberal Party remains hazy, but it, undoubtedly, goes back to the early reformers who fought for responsible government. After the establishment of the Confederation, however, the separate elements in the Provinces did not put any energetic effort to combine themselves and constitute a genuine political party. Many of the Liberals had opposed the confederation and when it came into being, they became lukewarm. But the centralizing policy of the Conservative Government forced them to defend the rights of the provinces. The Liberals, or the Clear Grits, as they were called in Upper Canada, were inspired by Jeffersonian ideas and his Anti-Federalist party. There was another close resemblance between the Liberals and the Anti-Federalists. Both were based on frontier agrarian democracy with distinct radical tendencies. ''The Clear Grits were indeed,'' writes Prof. Dawson, ''definitely influenced by the successors to the Jeffersonians, the Jacksonian Democrats. They were opposed to wealth and privilege in any form, and they favoured soft money, universal suffrage, frequent elections, and various other 'republican' measures well known south of the border.'' Another group which was affiliated with the Liberals was the Rouge party from Quebec. It was anti-clerical and had aroused the opposition of the Roman Catholic Church and after Confederation it had definitely declined in size and importance. To these two elements were joined some reformers, secessionists and independents from New Brunswick and Nova Scotia.

The first Liberal Government came into power in 1973, after the Pacific Scandal, when all the three groups, the Clear Grits, Quebec Rouge, and the Progressive Liberals, combined together under the leadership of Alexander Mackenzie, although the groups acknowledged also a separate allegiance to their own leaders. Various factors were responsible for the defeat of the disunited Liberals and their remaining in the wilderness for about almost two decades. When Laurier became the Liberal leader in 1887, he welded the different groups and made a genuine national party. Laurier had realized the urgent need for national unity. ''Brilliant in speech, masterly in tactics, Laurier warned his countrymen from the Conservative loyalty, attached them to his own Gladstonian Liberalism, and sought no less skilfully than MacDonald to win support through the whole country by emphasizing the policies of material expansion. He exalted the spirit of compromise whereby alone a national leader in Canada could survive. Above all, he purged the Liberal creed of anti-clericalism of the Rouge Group, and, thus securely anchored his party in the French Province.'' Laurier's successor was Mackenzie King and he followed the high ideals and traditions set by his leader with strict fidelity with the result that Mackenzie King could command in Quebec even more unqualified support. And from 1887 to 1948, for full sixty-one years, the Liberal Party had two leaders to shape its destiny whereas the Conservative Party had ten during this period. ''From this unbroken continuity of political strategy it derived great prestige and formidable weight.'' It continues to retain its strength in Quebec and obtains enough support in other regions and is the most truly national party in Canada. It was ousted from office by the Conservatives in the elections of 1957. The Liberals returned to power in the next General Election and remained in office till May 1979 when the Progressive Conservative Party formed the minority government with 136 seats. But the Liberals were again returned to power in February 1980 General Election with a comfortable majority of 146 seats.

The Liberal Party stands for low tariff and does not advocate the interference of the State in the economic life of the country. It still champions the right of the Provinces and the Sovereign status of Canada within the British Empire. It stands for making trade agreements not only with the members of the British Empire, but also with the foreign countries on the basis of reciprocity. The analysis of the programmes of the Conservative Party and the Liberal Party will reveal that the former stands for economic nationalism whereas the latter for political nationalism and the truth is that political and economic nationalism are merely twin sisters with little difference.

Early in 1978, Prime Minister Pierre Trudeau made public his proposal for a new Constitution which was to be a Canadian-based statute. But the publication of the draft constitutional proposal immediately provoked widespread criticism. After prolonged discussion an agreement was reached between the government of Canada and nine Provincial Governments, in November 1981, to patriate the Canadian Constitution and entrench a Charter of Rights and Freedoms and an amending formula. The resolution on the Constitution was adopted by Parliament in December 1981 and the British Parliament enacted it forthwith. The Proclamation bringing Canada's new Constition Act of 1982 into law was signed by Queen Elizabeth in Ottawa on April 17, 1982. It was Trudeau's personal achievement and a triumph of the Liberal Party as it ended the anachronistic practice of British Parliament amending the Constitution of a sovereign State.

**The New Democratic Party**

The New Democratic Pary dates from 1961, when the major trade union federations (the Canadian Labour Congress) and the Cooperative Commonwealth Federation party joined forces to launch a new Party. The Cooperative Commonwealth Federation had been founded in 1932 by a group of farmer and labour parties in the Western Provinces. Prior to 1939 the labour movement was industrially and politically weak, and produced no party with sufficient electoral strength to achieve more than a meagre representation in some Provincial legislatures. This was due to the socio-economic causes. In 1932, however, the Cooperative Commonwealth Federation was formed in order to pool together their political interests. The C.C.F. was able to make some general appeal to members of all occupations. It had a socialist programme and contemplated a new social order based upon sweeping economic changes. It advocated socialisation of all financial agencies, transportation, communication, and public utilities, social insurance---covering old age, illness, accident and unemployment—freedom of association, socialistic health services, crop insurance, encouragement of co- operatives, abolition of the Senate, etc. It urged repeal of the Immigration laws and stands for equal rights of citizenship for all irrespective of sex, class, origin, or religion; restoration of civil liberties; and the right of labour to organize itself. The party advocated repeal of taxes on the necessaries of life, taxation on land values, exemption of small income from forms of militarism. The programme of the new party substantially remains the same. In May 1979 General election the New Democratic Pary won 26 seats whereas in February 1980 Elections it increased its strength to 33.

## SUGGESTED READINGS


Baurinot, John : *Canada.*

Borden, R. L. : *Canadian Constitutional Studies.*

Bradley, A. C. : *Canada.*

Brady, Alexander : *Democracy in the Dominions.*

Bryce, J. : *Modern Demcracies,* Vol. I, Chaps. XXIII—XXVII.

Clement, W. H. P. : *The Law of the Canadian Constitution.*

Clokie, E. M. : *Canadian Government and Politics.*

*The Constitution Act, 1982.*

Dawson, R. M. : *Constitutional Issues in Canada.*

Dawson, R. M. : *The Government of Canada.*

Durham, Lord : *Report on the Affairs of British North America.*

Evatt, H. V. : *The King and His Dominion Governors.*

Jennings, I., and Young, C. M. : *Constitutional Law of the Commonwealth.*

Keith, A. B. : *The Constitution, Administration and Laws of the Empire.*

Keith, A. B. : *Dominion Autonomy in Practice.*

Keith, A. B. : *The Dominions As Sovereign States.*

Kennedy, W. P. M. : *The Constitution of Canada.*

Lajole, Paul Gerin : *Constitutional Amendment in Canada.*

Lefroy, A. H. F. : *Canada's Federal System.*

Mansergh, Nicholas : *Documents and Speeches of British Commonwealth Affair,* Vol. I.

Newton, A. P. : *Federal and Unified Constitutions.*

Porritt, E. : *The Evolution of the Dominion of Canada.*

Riddle, W. R. : *The Canadian Constitution in Form and Facts.*

Roberts, Leslie : *Canada, The Golden Hinge.*

Ross, G. : *The Senate of Canada.*

Trotter, R. C. : *Canadian Federation.*

Wheare, K.C. : *Federal Government*

Wheare, K. C. : *Statute of Westminster.*

# CHAPTER VI

# The Canadian Political System

## A Nation in Making

Canada's political tradition represents a fragmented past both structurally and in terms of development. The territories which now constitute Canada were originally the homelands of the native Indian tribes in the eastern, central, southern and western parts of the country as well as of the Eskimos in the cold northern areas which have an arctic climate. The Indian population now numbers 245,000 and the Eskimo population is estimated at 17,000. A tragic element of Canada's colonial history was the systematic genocidal violence directed against the tribal people who were forcibly displaced from their settled areas and compelled to migrate further west and north under threat of mass extermination. Most of these tribes were relatively peaceful and their political organisation was fairly democratic. The tribal chief possessed specified powers and important matters were decided by the tribal council.

The Indian and Eskimo tribes had no notion of private property in land. Land and forests were considered collective possessions of the entire tribe. Agriculture was often managed by women while men generally engaged in hunting and fighting. The Europeans began to occupy their common lands, clearing forests and claiming all such land as their private property. This brought the whites and Indian communities into conflict and defeat and dispersal of the latter who were thus ejected from their age-old, rightful habitat. Most of the Indians and Eskimos, who have survived the white onslaughts, are now confined to the Northwest Territories or Reservations in other Canadian Provinces. Today a Cabinet Ministr in charge of Indian Affairs and Northern Development looks after their welfare and development.

After three centuries of oppression and exploitation, they are gradually being brought into the national mainstream. A vast new autonomous territory of Nunavut has been created from part of Canada's North-west Territories on April 1, 1999 where mostly Eskimo tribes live. About 27,000 residents of this area recently elected a 19-member assembly, which is almost entirely Intuit in character. The assembly has been invested with a wide range of powers over a territory equal in size to Western Europe. Voter turn out in Nunavut topped 80% in temparature of –30°C. This is a big step in the integration of indigeneous communities within the multinational Canadian nation.

Like the United States, Canada is also a nation of immigrants. The territories, constituting Canada now, came under British colonial rule at various times by conquest, cession or settlement. Nova Sctotia was occupied in 1628 by settlement at Port Royal, was ceded back to France in 1632 and was finally returned by the French in 1713, by the Treaty of Utrecht. The Hudson's Bay Company's charter was granted in 1670, which conferred rights over all the territory draining into Hudson Bay. Canada, with all its dependencies, including New Brunswick and Prince Edward Island, was formally ceded to the United Kingdom by France in 1763, Vancouver Island was acquired by the Oregon Boundary Treaty of 1846 and British Colombia was created as a separate British colony in 1858. The British North America Act of 1867 granted the right of self-government for the people of Canada. Adjoining provinces and territories were ceded to the Canadian Confederation in 1869,1871,1873,1905 and 1949. In 1931 Norway formally recognised the Canadian title to Sverdrup group of Arctic islands. Canada now holds sovereign rights over the whole Arctic sector north of the Canadian mainland.

The Canadian nation has been formed by uniting and integrating two major immigrant nationalities—The French and the English. In 1961, 5,540,346 people were of the French origin and 4,195,175 were of the English descent. The total of the people of the British origin, however, was 7,996,669 which included the Scottish and the Irish as well. The rest of the Canadian nation includes people of German,

Scandinavian, Italian, Russian, Ukrainian, Jewish, other European, Chinese, Japanese, other Asian and Negro origin as well. Canada, like the United Sates, can be regarded as a melting-pot of several nationalities. At present, both English and French are recognised as official languages and right to education is available to school-going children through the medium of French as well as English. The Province of Quebec, which has a French-speaking majority, exhibits separatist tendencies. In a referendum held a few years ealier, almost 49% voters wanted independence for Quebec, and are at present being ruled by a Party that stands for Quebec's separation from Canada.

Canada is also divided into a large number of religious sects and denominations. Roman Catholics constitute the largest single denomination (9 million), followed by United Church of Canada (4 million) and Anglican Church (3 million) respectively. Other lesser sects are Presbytarian, Baptist, Lutherani, a Ukranin, Greek Catholic, Greek Orthodox, Jewish etc. Each provincial government is responsible for its education system but the general plan is similar for all provinces. separate elementary and secondary schools for minority groups, mainly Roman Catholic are found everywhere. In general, education is free upto the end of the secondary level. The principal sources of revenue are provincial government grants and direct taxation for school purposes. Except in Quebec the number of private schools is small, their enrolment being just 3% of the total in elementary and secondary grades. The federal government operates schools for Indians and Eskimos with an enrolment of 35,000. An additional 40,000 attend non-federal schools. Canada has many institutions of higher learning, teaching courses in liberal arts, sciences, engineering, medicine etc. Education has been a great instrument of cultural amalgamation and national integration in Canada. At the same time, a system of private elitist education also co-exists with the qualitatively inferior schooling provided by government-aided institutions.

**Developed Capitalist Dependency**

Some years ago *The National Geographic* wrote about a quiz for school-children of the United States belonging to higher grades in which a majority answered that Canada was a northern state of the USA. They were geographically wrong but not so incorrect in terms of political and economic relationship between these two neighbouring North American nations. Canada, for all practical purposes, can be treated as a developed, industrialisd dependency of its southern, neighbouring capitalist super-power. American multinationals have very substantial investments in various sectors of the Canadian economy. They have played a leading role in the industrial development of Canada. The United States and Canada along with Mexico are the Members of the North American Free Trade Area (NAFTA). This facilitates intimate commercial ties between the two countries. American businessmen, therefore, have a feeling that though Canada is technically a sovereign, independent state, it is fully integrated economically with the United States. Canada is also a military ally of the USA as a founding member of the North Atlantic Treaty Organisation (NATO) led by the United States.

There is probably no better way to make the sovereign-satellite relationship between the United States and Canada intelligible "than by summarising the world-wide scope and character of what is unquestionably the leading United States 'multinational corporation'—Standard O.C of New Jersey.... In terms of dollar assets, Jersey Standard is the largest industrial corporation in the United States.... Jersey's foreign investments were half as large as its domestic investments but its foreign profits were twice as large as its domestic profits.[1] The number of subsidiaries of Standard Oil in the United States was 77 and 37 in Canada. It also had 54 subsidiaries in Europe, 43 in Latin America, 14 in Asia and 9 in Africa. This showed the crucial importance of Canada as an area for the expansion of the foreign assets of Standard Oil, the largest American corporation.

The tremendous scope and diversity of Jersey's foreign operations might give the impression that over the years the company has been a large and consistant exporter of capital. It is not true. Apart from a small initial export of capital several years ago, the expansion of Jersey's foreign asset has been financed from the profits of its foreign operations. These foreign profits have been so large that huge sums have been remitted to the parent company in the United States. Baran and Sweezy have, therefore, concluded: "In a word: Standard Oil

1. Baran and Sweezy, Monopoly Capital, pp. 192-93

of New Jersey is a very large and consistant *importer* of capital."[2]

Legitimate differences of opinion will of course exist as to whether this or that country should be counted as belonging to the American economic empire. Baran and Sweezy offer the following list as being on the conservative side: The United States itself and a few Colonial possessions (notably Puerto Rico and the Pacific Islands); all Latin American countries except Cuba; Canada; four countries in the Near and Middle East; two counries in Africa and East Asia each; four countries in South and Southeast Asia; and one country in Europe. However, Canada as a capitalist dependency has profited most from the American connection in terms of its own economic development.

To begin with, Canada was a colony of France but England displaced her in 1763 as the ruling power in Canada. Till 1800 it was a sparsely populated area. People mere engaged in agriculture, forestry, fishing and fur trade. England supplied their consumer needs. British capital was gradually invested in mines, railways, transport and hydro-electric power. American capital came later entering all sectors of Canadian economy and superseded Britain as the dominant power in promoting the industrial development of Canada. Yet politically Canada remained attached to England in numerous ways. The North America Act of 1867 granted legislative and administrative autonomy to the people of Canada but its foreign policy was continuosly dictated by Great Britain. In the two world wars, Canada joined the war on the side of Great Britain against Germany almost spontaneously. After the second world war, both Britain and Canada act as if they are virtual satellites of the United States.

Taking advantage of England's engagement in the Nepoleonic Wars in Europe, the United states first persuaded Napoleon to sell off the large mid-Western colony of Louisiana and then President Madison declared war on England by attacking Canada. However, with the defeat of France in Europe, England decided to teach the arrogant Americans a lesson. Her naval troops attacked the Eastern coastal cities and even occupied Washington. A peace treaty was signed and the American dream of conquering Canada by force vanished. In 1824, President Monroe proclaimed what has since then become associated with his name the Monroe doctrine. This guaranteed joint Anglo-American domination of Canada, the Caribbean and Latin American countries and non-intervention by other European powers in North and South America. Canada thus emerged as a joint capitalist dependency of both Great Britain and the United States. Gradually, Canadian capital has displaced both British and U.S. capital as the major factor in the country's economy. Canada has, therefore, been accepted as the founder member of the Group-7 consisting of the seven most highly industrialized capitalist countries of the world. Other members of the G-7 are the United States, Germany, Japan, France, Italy and Great Britain.

**The Elitist Democracy**

With the growth of capitalism in Canada, indigenous as well as foreign-financed, a liberal-democratic polity has also grown on the home turf of the country. In such a system, votes are the nominal source of state power but monetary strength is the real source. This was recognised by Cheffins who pointed out how money played a big role in Canadian elections in view of large constituencies in which the Canadian electorate is divided in terms of the vast area that various candidates have to cover at the time of election campaigns. In election to the House of Commons as well as provisional legislatures, big corporations, including the multinationals, overtly and covertly provide funds to both the major parties viz the Liberal Party and the Progressive Conservative Party and, to a lesser degree, to other parties.

There is an element of contradiction in this system. The votes constituting a larg majority of the population may not own much property and yet they can form trade unions, political parties like the New Democratic Patry or the *Parti Quebecois*, and other mass organisations exercise political influence through them. If they win political power and then jeopardize the vested interests of the economic elites and the wealthy oligarchy, the system will face a crisis unless the dominant class abdicates without a fight. But we may discount this possibility as no privileged group has ever done this in histroy. In the case of Canada, the British-American bourgeoisie would have never allowed this to happen either.

In general, the ruling elite in Canada prefers democratic govenment to any kind of authoritarian rule. Popular endorsement of capitalist, oligarclic rule through a multi-party system gives it a kind of seeming pluralistic legitimacy. This enables Canada's policy to avoid certain real dangers of military or civilian

2. *Ibid* p. 194

dictatorship which destabilises many functional democratic regimes in Latin America or even Europe.

The capitalists in Canada do not resort to authoritarian methods in dealing with opposition movements. They even permit a separatist *Parti Quebecois* to hold a referendum to decide whether Quebec should stay in Canada or become independent. Similarly, the corporations give concessions to the working class to soften its political radicalism and weaken trade union militancy. Capitalists buy off labour leaders with money and by other means. They, therefore, never challenge the real bastions of oligarchic power in the economy. Labour capital relationship in Canada follows the US pattern rather than the British or European one which is much more conflictual than the North American trend.

For example, the Liberal-Conservative divide in Canada is more akin to the Democratic-Republican cleavage in the United States and much less akin to the Labour-Conservative rupture in the United Kingdom or the Left Right conflict in other European countries. The ruling elite in Canada has created such a machinery of government which checks deadlocks and stalemates that may result in the breakdown of democratic procedures. The number of political parties has been kept limited to prevent the government by unstable coalitions.

Canada has a second chamber, which has no elective element and yet it has a prestigious position in the constitutional system. Corporate funding of political parties makes the House of Commons as well as its government dependent upon and subservient to the moneyed class. Canada's bureaucratic, military and judicial elites, which exercise administrative, coercive and punitive functions, are drawn from the upper and middle strata of Canadian society and are the products of the privileged and elitist schools, colleges and universities not only of Canada but also of the United States, Great Britain and France.

In constitutional theory, the people exercise sovereign power. In actual practice, a relatively small wealthy elite rules supreme in Canada too, like any other capitalist democracy. Even then, democratic institutions are not merely a smoke-screen behind which sit a handful of power-hungry industrialists and financiers making decisions and issuing commands. Reality is much more complex than this. Bissonnette, Dawson, Stanley and Lamontagne have argued that Canada like all other Western democracies should be characterised as a pluralist democracy because all organised groups in Canadian society are capable of exercising influence and pressure on the government's decision-making. But the power of capital and labour as competing social groups to influence the course of administration and legislation is not equal and so Canada's political processes reflect imperfect competition, especially where the role of the elites and the masses is being considered. It is in this sense that we describe the political systems of all advanced capitalist countries, including that of Canada, as embodying the principles of an elitist democray.

There are many writers like Martin and Dawson who dispute the above formulation about the nature of Canadian democracy. According to them, the political system of Canada is highly pluralistic where several thousand freely formed associations coexist and compete for influence. In fact, Canada contains a large number of sub-cultures based on region, religion and ethnic origin. While the government is responsible to the organised public opinion, social structure is much more fragmented and incoherent Canadian society may not be open-ended, but unlike Britain, it has no traditional aristocracy. Yet it has a dominant social class, that forms the ruling elite and, thereby, invalidates the pluralistic thesis.

## SUGGESTED READINGS

Bissonnette, B. *Essai sur Constitution du Canada.*

Cheffins, R.I. *The Constitutional Process in Canada.*

Clokie, A. McD.,*Canadian Government and Politics.*

Dawson, R.M., *Democratic Government in Canada.*

Dawson, R.M.(ed) *The Government of Canada.*

Eggleston, W., Road to Nation-A Chronicle of *Dominion-Provincial Relations, Canada at Work;*

Lamontague,M., *Le Federalisme Canadien.*

Laskin, B., *Canadian Constitution Laws.*

Martin,C.B. *Foundations of Canadian Nationhood.*

Ricker, J.C., *How are we Governed?*

Stanley, F.G., *A Short History of the Canadian Constitution.*

Trudeau, P.E., *Federalism and the French Canadians.*

Willms,A.,(ed.) *Public Administration in Canada.*

Wade, M., *The French Canadians-1770-1967.*

# THE GOVERNMENT OF SWITZERLAND

## CHAPTER I

# The Swiss Political Tradition

### Special Case of Swiss Democracy

Switzerland is the ethnological as well as the geographical centre of Europe. It is a land-locked country situated in the heart of Western Europe covering an area of 15,976 square miles with a population numbering a little more than six and a half million and borders for a thousand miles upon three large neighbours—Italy, Germany and France—as well as on smaller Austria and tiny Liechtenstein. No natural boundary marks it off from the Germans to the north and east, from the French to the west and from the Italians to the south. Its central Alpine position has made it the source of several international rivers: the Rhine, flowing northward into the North Sea, the Danube and the Po flowing south-eastward into the Black Sea and into the Adriatic, and the Rhone flowing south-westward into the Mediterranean. All these rivers spring or receive affluents springing from the Swiss Alps and pass through or touch upon the territory of ten foreign countries.

The Swiss people are not a homogeneous whole. They sharply differ in race, language, religion, and even to a certain extent in civilisation. Yet in this diversity is to be found the unity of the Swiss nation, and Switzerland presents to the world the most striking example of not only a united people, "but one of the most united, and certainly the most patriotic, among the people of Europe." Secondly, as a result of her geographical position and her small size, Swizerland has succeeded in remaining aloof from the wars of Europe and in becoming centre of world activity by virtue of an internationally guaranteed neutrality. The neutrality of Swizerland was guaranteed by the Congress of Vienna in 1815 and reaffirmed by the League of Nations in 1920 and it formed the anchor of the nation's foreign policy during both World Wars.

Switzerland was the first in the world to experiment with republican institutions, and the only one State in Europe which has always been a republic. When the United States was born as an independent nation, Switzerland had behind it a republican tradition of some five hundred years. The impact of these republican institutions has been profound on the United States and other countries adopting the democratic way of political life. It is a government, moreover, under which the principles of direct democracy have been extensively applied. These devices of direct democracy were first adopted by the State of South Dakota in the United States in 1898, and set the ball rolling to vindicate the doctrine of popular sovereignty. Finally, Swizerland has worked out a system of government unique in character, but which in certain respects combines the stability of the American Presidential system with the responsibility of the Parliamentary system.

### Physical Characteristics

Switzerland is the "country of a thousand valleys" and the Swiss people dwell on both sides of a gigantic mass separated from one another by craggy heights and widespreading snow fields. Vast mountainous areas render about a quarter of the territory unproductive. The major portion of the remaining area is suitable only for pastures or for woodland, and only about 35 per cent is actually devoted to agricultural production. Agriculture on the whole supports 22.2 per cent of the entire population.

Nor has nature been bountiful in the mineral resources. Oil and coal do not exist and raw materials are almost entirely lacking. There is almost nothing of value which is exportable. The broken terrain of the country makes transportation and communications difficult. The only natural advantages are important sources of hydro-electric power.

The hostility of nature in Swizerland, however, has been "mastered by man, civilised by him and stamped everywhere by his presence, his labour and activities." Nature only permitted Switzerland to exist, but man has made it a fairly prosperous country with a reasonably stable economy. Agriculture has been maintained at a very high level and the Wahlen Plan carried out in the Second World War, represented the country's determined food policy to diminish her dependence on imported foodstuffs. She has admirably succeeded in it and today Switzerland produces no less than 80 per cent of her own needs and imports only 20 per cent. The Constitution empowers the Central Government to take measures to promote the general welfare and economic security of the citizens.[1] While promoting the general interest of the Swiss economy, the Central Government may enact regulations on the exercise of trade and industry and take measures in favour of specific economic sectors or professions. Where this is justified by general interest the Central Government is entitled to enact regulations departing, if necessary, from the principle of freedom of trade and industry in order to preserve important economic sectors or professions whose existence is threatened and to improve the skills of persons exercising an independent activity in those sectors or professions and to maintain a sound peasant population, ensure agricultural productivity and consolidate rural landownership.

Paradoxical as it may seem, Switzerland is primarily an industrial country and 45 per cent of her population is dependent upon manufacturing industries. She balances her otherwise deficit economy by the excess of exports of manufactured goods and in normal times Switzerland is among the nations of the world whose foreign trade per head of the population is the greatest. By virtue of her water power and skilled workmanship, she has developed highly especialised manufactures such as machinery, electro-technical supplies, watches and textiles. The natural beauty of her landscape lures hundreds and thousands of foreign tourists, summer and winter, and the Swiss hostel industry remains one of the best equipped and most intelligently directed in the world. The tourist trade, in fact, is one of the essential credit items in the Swiss balance of payments. All told, the Swiss are now a prosperous population and the striking feature of their prosperity is a significant degree of equality. There "is no proletariat, no misery and no hovels"[2] in Switzerland. Material anxiety exists nowhere and prosperity extends to everyone and everywhere. The standard of living of the people in general is comparatively higher than in many of her neighbouring countries. This astonishing success, the Swiss people owe primarily to their own labour "reinforced by a practical intelligence of quite an exceptional quality."

**Linguistic Divisions**

Linguistically Switzerland is heterogeneous and the Swiss nation defies all nationalistic canons of demographic and cultural unity. Almost three-fourths of her people speak German, one-fifth French, the remainder Italian, except for a few who speak Romanche, an ancient language of Latin origin. It must, however, be remembered that the linguistic groups are geographically sharply separated from each other by the Cantonal boundaries. Thus, the Ticino is almost exclusively (90.3 per cent). an Italian-speaking Canton, Geneva (80.6 per cent), Vaud (86.1 per cent), and Neuchatel (86.9 per cent) are solidly French-speaking; and all the remaining Cantons, except Berne and Fribourg, are almost exclusively German. Even in Berne the German population predominates over the French in the ratio of five to one; and in Fribourg the French population predominates over the German in the ratio of two to one. Romanche is the prevailing language in the Grisons.

The Swiss Constitution provides that four languages—German, French, Italian and Romanche—are the "national" languages of Switzerland but that only German, French and Italian are "official" languages. The various Cantons choose their own official language or languages. A noticeable feature of the present-day Swiss life is the "linguistic interpenetration" among the various Cantons. Almost all educated people in Switzerland use two or even three languages. Nevertheless it is a trilinguistic country and nothing whatever is done, officially or privately, to lessen the linguistic differences among the Swiss.[3] Nor is there the slightest suggestion of any linguistic propaganda. In fact, linguistic peace reigns in this happy land of the Swiss and differences of languages are regarded as a stabilising factor to their national unity.

1. Article 31. Also refer to Article 23.
2. Switzerland is, by per capita income, one of the richest countries in the world.
3. Article 107 of the Constitution provides that all three language groups must be represented on the Federal Court.

**Religious Identities**

Switzerland's religious diversity presented some grave problems in the past and it led to civil war and foreign strife. But fortunately for the national unity of the country, the religious and linguistic areas do not coincide, but overlap. The Protestants outnumber the Catholics in twelve Cantons of which nine are German and three French-speaking. The Catholics, on the other hand, outnumber the Protestants in ten Cantons, of which seven are German, two are French and one is Italian-speaking, Moreover, in most of the Protestant Cantons there are strong Catholic minorities whereas in eight out of the ten Catholic Cantons the Catholics cover 80 per cent of the total population. "This geographical and statistical distribution." observes Rappard, "of the two rival faiths even if it has not always prevented oppression obviously makes for mutual toleration."[4] The population as a whole is 57 per cent Protestant and 42.1 per cent Catholic.

The attitude of the Swiss to their religious differences is exactly the same as their attitude to their language differences. Religious minorties are highly respected and they do not coincide with linguistic minorities. One of the main purposes of the Federal Constitution set up in 1848 and amended in 1874 was to break the barriers created between Protestants and Catholics due to religious differences and, thus, to create a spirit of truly Swiss citizenship and guarantee certain fundamental rights to all Swiss people, no matter to which confession they had faith and to which part of the country they belonged. When the Constitution placed absolute reliance on matters of economic prosperity of the people and inculcated in them the spirit of national consciousness, it promoted and facilitated the growth of national loyalties. Today, there is complete religious toleration and the Swiss recognise the right of every one to profess the religion he prefers. The idea of oppressing religious minorities is foreign to the Swiss mentality and there is not a single Swiss who imagines that national unity can be furthered by confession in any particular religion. "Quite the contrary; here too," emphasises Andre Siegfried, "diversity is accepted as a condition of federal harmony for Swiss patriotism consolidates itself on a very different ground.".

**National Unity**

Switzerland is, thus, a land of paradoxes. It affords a striking example of a federal experiment which tends to overcome conflicting Cantonal interests without annihilating their identity. It also mocks at the principle of political "self-determination" for racial and linguistic groups and offers a splendid example for how statehood and national patriotism can be fostered in utter defiance of such a principle. Woodrow Wilson wrote in 1896: "The Cantons....having allied themselves....went on to show the world how Germans, Frenchmen, and Italians, if they only respect each other's liberties as they would have their own respected, may by mutual helpfulness and forbearance build up a union at once stable and free."[5] Woodrow Wilson himself was the father of the principle of self- determination.

But Swiss diversity is not confined only to language and religion. There are differences in the occupations of inhabitants, in the external conditions of their life, in their ideas and habits of thought. Then, there is the local pride which clings to time-honoured ways and customs and resists the tendencies, strong as they have become, that make for uniformity. Despite these differences, Swiss legal and moral unity has grown firmer with each passing generation.

They are an exceptionally united and an exceptionally patriotic nation. Bryce, while analysing the salient features of the Swiss nation, says: "A strenuous patriotism bracing up the sense of national unity, an abounding variety in the details of social, of economic and of political life, coupled with an attachment of local self-governments which having been the life-breath of the original Cantons, passed into the minds and hearts of others also, making them wish to share in the ancient traditions, and contributing to the overthrow of the oligarchy in the cities even where, as in Berne, it had been strongest." Thus, members of three races, even four "national" languages, and two religions have become one people.

## THE STRUGGLE FOR UNITY

**Early History**

Switzerland, as Andre Siegfried says, was not formed by unification but by aggregation. Originally, Switzerland consisted of a number of sovereign States without any co-ordinating central authority. These States comprised residents of different populations dwelling around the Alps. The inhabitants of these mountain valleys

4. Rappard, W. E., *The Government of Switzerland*, p. 11.
5. Wilson, W., *The State*, p. 301.

did not possess a common race or a common history or speak a common language, though they shared a common mode of life.

Towards the end of thirteenth century, however, three small Teutonic communities entered into a league of mutual defence to protect their common rights and privileges against the existing encroachments of their fedual lords; the most important being the Hapsburg rulers of Austria, themselves of Swiss origin, and then also Emperors of the Holy Roman Empire. The Hapsburg rulers made an attempt to reassert their fedual authority, but were met with successful resistance of the three confederated Cantons at the battle of Morgarten in 1315. During the next forty years, five more Cantons joined the confederacy of the original three. The confederation won its second victory over Austria in 1386 and thereby vindicated its *de facto* independence. For two and a half centuries thereafter the confederation maintained its existence, though the alliance was very often threatened by secessionist movement prompted by intercantonal strife.

The religious dissensions of the reformation period, once again, brought into prominence the secessionist tendencies. Half the Cantons embraced Protestantism and the other half adhered to the old faith. The confederation, however, survived, for the supreme interest of common defence held its members together. In 1648, the Treaty of Westphalia finally released the confederation from the suzerainty of the Holy Roman Empire and recognised its independent existence. By this time the number of the confederating Cantons had gone up to thirteen.

**Nature of the Ancient Confederation**

The authority of the confederation, thus, gradually extended over the greater part of the present Swiss territory. Although the Cantons proved unified enough to throw off outside control, they soon began to quarrel among themselves. In the management of their domestic affairs, the Cantons acted as completely sovereign entities. Their political institutions, too, varied greatly; the rural Cantons were pure democracies and governed themselves by meetings of the people; some, like Berne, were close oligarchies of nobles; and in others oligarchy was more or less tampered by a popular element.

Swizerland remained all through this period an alliance bound together only for offensive and defensive purposes. The Confederation, accordingly, had jurisdiction only over foreign relations. matters relating to peace and war, and inter- Cantonal disputes. These affairs were managed by a Diet which met at irregular intervals in one of the Cantons. The delegates who sat in the Diet were the agents of their Cantons and they acted according to their specific instructions. In the Diet a certain formal precedence was given to the larger Cantons, such as Berne and Zurich, but it was a constant source of irritation for others who insisted on the substance of their equality "and behaved in a manner not unlike that of a sovereign State participating in an international conference." The decisions of this assembly were not regarded legally binding unless they were unanimous. In fact, the Cantons looked at the Diet with suspicion and as a consequence of their strong local affinities had come to be firmly established.

It is interesting to note that some of the Cantons had by conquests acquired new territories and they regarded their acquisitions like subject areas denying to their inhabitants all rights and privileges which the Cantons claimed for themselves and their citizens.

**French Revolution and Restoration**

Then, came the French Revolution sweeping away all the local institutions. The armies of the French Revolution foisted the Helvetic Republic in 1798, upon the weak and disunited confederacy. But the Swiss reacted so strongly against the French-imposed Constitution that Napoleon was forced to restore the Constitution of the Cantons by the Act of Mediation of 1803. Under this Act six new Cantons were formed chiefly out of allied and subject territories speaking French and Italian. After the fall of Napoleon, the Congress of Vienna gave to Swizerland the old Confederate and Cantonal institutions of the eighteenth century and added three more Cantons to it. The total number of the Cantons thus forming the confederacy came to be 22.

Although the New Constitution did not establish any central authority as such but it did establish a Diet containing a representative of each Canton, voting on instructions. The Diet was competent to declare war, conclude peace, name ambassadors, and to levy troops in accordance with a system of Cantonal contingents. It could also send troops into any part of Switzerland threatened by disorder. The Cantons, however, maintained their complete internal autonomy which many of them now used to restore aristocratic regimes. They could, moreover, conclude treaties provided they were not prejudicial to the Confederation or to the right of other Cantons.

**Birth of Modern Switzerland**

The French suzerainty proved a blessing in disguise for it was between 1798 and 1815 that the basis of modern Switzerland had been firmly laid. The Act of Mediation added 6 more Cantons to the already 13. Three more, all French-Speaking were added in 1815, thus giving to Switzerland its present configuration. It was during this period that the trilingual status of the country, as it is today, was officially recognised. Finally, the French, liberal democratic and centralising influences began to manifest themselves into the Swiss political institutions. The Federal Agreement of 1815, therefore achieved, unity in diversity.

Partly as a result of the liberal revolution of 1830 in France, a movement arose to revise the Cantonal Constitutions in Swizerland in conformity with the democratic principles. In 1832, the Diet appointed a Commission to prepare a new or revise the federal pact. But it made no progress due to the serious religious differences. In 1845, the seven Catholic Cantons formed a separate league called the Sonderbund. The formation of this league led to a Civil War which was suppressed within a month.

The defeat of the seven Catholic Cantons was, in fact, the triumph for the movement of national unity. Influenced by the internal dissensions and motivated by the European liberal movement of 1848, the Swiss Diet now approved a new constitution which aimed to bring about a stronger and more highly organised government. Inspired to a certain extent by the example of the United States, the Constitution of September 1848 transformed Switzerland into a Federal Government.

**The Constitution of 1848**

The Constitution of 1848 was the child of compromise and it reflected the growth of new ideas with an attempt to retain ancient practices. The federating Cantons insisted on their retaining a sovereign character. A compromise was, accordingly, reached and the twenty- two Cantons remained sovereign "so far as their sovereignty is not limited by the Federal Constitution." The powers of the Federal Government extended to diplomatic and military affairs as well as to certain economic matters, such as posts, customs, weights and measures and such other matters in which concerted action was deemed necessary with a view to achieving national unity. The executive power was vested in a Federal Council consisting of seven members elected by the Federal Assembly.

The legislative power was vested in a Federal Assembly, divided into two Chambers; the Council of States equally representing the Cantons, and the National Council representing the population. The judicial power was vested in the Federal Tribunal, but it had no jurisdiction to declare laws unconstitutional. The Constitution guaranteed the sovereignty of the territories of the Cantons and authorised the Federal Government to intervene in Cantonal affairs without awaiting a request from the Cantonal authority in case of internal disturbance or threatened conflict between several Cantons.

**The Constitution of 1874**

The Constitution of 1848 remained in force for twenty-six years. In the meantime, the tendency towards greater centralisation became powerful, although the Federalists still advocated certain social and municipal privileges of the Cantons. The Radicalists, on the other hand, persisted in their demands for the abolition of such rights and privileges. They pleaded for certain inalienable rights and liberties for all the Swiss people alike under the protection of a unified and centralised law. They also desired for the nationalisation of railways under federal ownership, and that legislation should be referred to the referendum of the entire Swiss population, not as inhabitants of Cantons but as a single and unified nation.

The Radical movement carried with it a considerable majority of the public opinion necessitating thereby the revision of the Constitution of 1848. The Federal Assembly drew up a new Constitution and referred it to the people for their approval. It was adopted in April by a vote of 340,000 and 14½ Cantons against 198,000 and 7½ Cantons.

The new Constitution, which became operative on May 29, 1874, is now the working Constitution of Switzerland. It gave to the Federal Government centralized control over military matters and the initiative in unifying certain matters of commercial law. Since 1874, the Constitution has been amended a number of times. These amendments have still further centralised the powers of the Federal Government, have imposed upon the new government new tasks in the realm of economic regulation and social insurannce, and have increased the direct participation of the people in the process of legislation. In 1935, complete revision of the Constitution by popular initiative was requested by those groups who advocated strengthening the powers of the Cantons, and those who believed in the principle of occupational representation and its evolution into the coöperative state. But it was rejected by the people.

## SUGGESTED READINGS

Bonjour, Officer and Potter, *A Short History of Switzerland*

Kahn, Hans, *Nationalism and Liberty: the Swiss Example*

Seigfried, Andre, *Switzerland, A Democratic Way of Life.*

Solaveytchick, *George Switzerland in Perspective.*

# CHAPTER II

# Basic Features of the Swiss Confederation

The Republic of Switzerland, known by the formal title of Swiss Confederation, is composed of twenty-three "Sovereign Cantons", namely, Zurich, Berne, Uri, Schwys, Unterwalden (Upper and Lower), Glarus, Zug, Fribourg, Soleure, Basle (City and Rural), Schaffhauserrv, Appenzell (both Rhodes), St. Gall, Grisons, Aargau, Thurgau, Ticino, Vaud, Valais, Neuchatel, Geneva and Jura.[1] Three Cantons, Unterwalden, Basle[2] and Appenzell are further split up into half Cantons. Each half Canton is entirely independent of its twin and differs from a whole Canton only in two respects. A half Canton sends only one member to the Council of States, the Chamber representing the constituent units, instead of two as the full Cantons are entitled to. Secondly, a half Canton is entitled to cast a half vote on all questions relating to constitutional amendment,[3] whether full revision or partial revision. The subdivision into half Cantons was necessitated because of religious, historical or other local causes.

### Federalism

Switzerland's polity is federal, although Article I of the Constitution describes it as the Swiss Confederation. But it is a misnomer to call it a Confederation, in spite of the constitutional use of the term. A confederation implies a loose league of sovereign and independent States without a strong central authority and it has chances of dissolution. The Swiss Confederation, on the other hand, came into being as the Preamble to the Constitution asserts, "with the intent of strengthening the alliance of the Confederates and of maintaining and furthering the unity, strength and honour of the Swiss nation...." The Preamble further adds that in order to achieve the solidarity of the Swiss nation a "federal Constitution" has been adopted. Even if it be conceded that the Preamble to the Constitution has no juristic meaning and value, still it clarifies the intention of the Father-framers, the kind of polity they established and the express will of the people of Switzerland and the Cantons who adopted it at a referendum. The Cantons of Switzerland agreed to modify, like the original thirteen States of the United States, their erstwhile sovereignty in such a way as to grant adequate authority for national purposes to the Central Government of the 'Confederation''. The powers of the Central Government and the aim of the 'Confederation' find their expression in Article 2 of the Constitution. The aim of the 'Confederation', it says "is to preserve the outward independence of the fatherland, to maintain internal peace and order, to protect the freedom and the rights of the confederates and to promote their common prosperity." For the fulfilment of the aims of the 'Confederation' the subject matters to which the authority of the Central Government extends are: foreign affairs, questions of peace and war, conclusion of alliances and treaties, management and control of currency, communications, commerce, weights and measures, naturalisation and expatriation, higher education and research, conservation of natural resources, and all other fiscal matters concerning the prosperity of Switzerland.

Federation as a principle, is the combination of unity and diversity and it is the only answer in countries with deep-seated racial, cultural, religious or linguistic differences. It harmonises local autonomy with national unity and, thus, provides an equilibrium between the centripetal and centrifugal forces. The Central Government is assigned functions which are of national importance and general concern whereas matters of local interest that differ in different parts and sections of the country are left to the people of those areas for solution. In this way, a federal government presents a happy blending of cen-

1. Some of the French-speaking citizens of the Bernese Jura wished to be separated from the German-speaking Bernese of the rest of the Canton. A Cantonal initiative of Berne was rejected in 1959, but the demand for separation remained unabated and Jura was created a separate full Canton.
2. There had been a demand for the unity of Basle. It was refused in 1948 but it succeeded in 1960. A Constitutional Commission consisting of representatives of two Cantons was appointed to draft a new uhified Constitution.
3. The constitutional position of half a canton in found in Article 123.

tralization and decentralization.

The parallelism between the Constitution of Switzerland and that of the United States is close. Both have a federal polity envisaging dual governments of divided powers conferred by their respective Constitutions and which cannot be changed by either acting independently. The Swiss Constitution expressly declares that the Cantons "are sovereign insofar as their sovereignty is not limited by the Federal Constitution and, as such, exercise all rights which are not entrusted to the federal power."[4] The Constitution of the United States ordains that the powers "not delegated to the United States by the Constitution, nor prohibited to it by the states are reserved to the states respectively or to the people."[5] In each case, the constituent units of the federation have transferred specific powers to the federal government and reserved all residual powers for themselves. In both instances, in any case of conflict, over which authority has been transferred to the Central Government, the federal authority is supreme and its will prevails. That is the spirit of federalism which aims to give prestige and strength to the national government. If the constituent units toy with it, federalism in its essence disappears.

There are, however, two major differences between the Swiss and the American systems. In the first place, the Constitution, both in Switzerland and in the United States, is supreme, but the means of protecting that supremacy in Switzerland are juridically imperfect. Switzerland does not have judicial review of the constitutionality of federal legislation. Her legislative branch is supreme; its own interpretation of its constitutional powers is binding and final. Secondly, in the United States the federal administration is usually in a position to administer its laws. In Switzerland the obligation to carry out federal legislation frequently devolves upon the Cantonal Government. It has no organization of its own and possesses scanty means to have its laws enforced. All depends upon the goodwill and co-operation of the Cantonal Governments. Of Course, it goes to their credit that they have never left the National Government to hold the baby.

In the course of time, however, the growth of federal power became more and more pronounced. As the need for national unity increased and as problems calling for governmental regulation or assistance emerged, they overstepped Cantonal boundaries and assumed nationwide importance. Among these were military training, banking, patents, transportation, traffic in arms and alcoholic beverages, production and marketing of grains and railroads and radios both of which were nationalised. Agriculture, manufacturing and the tourist traffic were subsidised, industry was protected, import quotas were fixed, unemployment relief and compulsory insurance were initiated. When the Federal Government took to direct taxes and excise duties, it offered Cantons share in the new revenues which hitherto were the exclusive monopoly of the Cantons.

Four important factors have contributed to the process of centralisation; war, economic depression, the demand for ever increasing social services, and the mechanical and technological revolution in transport and industry. These factors are not peculiar to Switzerland. They are as much in the Swiss as in other federations. But the fact that Switzerland remains surrounded by three powerful neighbours, *viz.,* France, Italy and Germany, accelerated the pace of centralisation. In 1914 and especially in 1939 the Federal Assembly granted the Government exceptional and unlimited powers to protect the security, integrity and neutrality of the country, and to safeguard its credit, economic interests and food supply. These plenary powers involved restriction on the liberties and the rights of the Swiss to a staggering extent, but the people readily accepted them as necessary for preserving their independence and sovereignty. Both pro-Nazi and Communist organisations were suppressed. In August 1935, Professor Prozig of the Berne University was dismissed, because he had taken, as a leader of the Swiss National Socialist Party, oath of allegiance to Hitler. In October 1936, the Federal Council suppressed by law an irredentistic movement in Ticino, the Italian-speaking Canton. Likewise, the activities of the Communist Party were banned in the country and in 1935, Communist propaganda was prohibited by law. The extent of Swiss nationalism can be examined from the fact that in April 1937, the Canton of Neuchatel decided by a plebiscite, and for the first time in Switzerland's history, to suppress Communist organisations "for their super, and anti-

4. Article 3.
5. Tenth Amendment.

national activities."[6] After the army had been transferred to the Central Government, civil and criminal law became federal instead of Cantonal.[7] The motto: "one law and one army" was an endeavour to strengthen the cohesion of Switzerland.

These developments in the extension of the powers of the Federal Government have been viewed by many writers as alarming. When the War emergency was over or the country had been freed from the economic depression, it was expected that the range of federal action would decrease. But it has not happened so. Swiss economic life continues to be strictly controlled in its various aspects[8] and with it there is a corresponding growth of the federal bureaucracy and consequently a grumbling about its expense. "The danger of this tendency," says Andre Siegfried, "is that of the extent they suffer the encroachments of the central power the Cantons will gradually cease to be sovereign States at all and become simple district administrations carrying the behests of the Central authority." This is, however, an exaggerated view. The spirit of the Swiss Confederation, since its inception and particularly since 1848 when it became a really federal State, has always been to ensure and protect the autonomy of the Cantons, and to preserve their individual and separate entity. The Cantons remain the more genuine and more living democracies and the federative structure of the State, as Hans Huber says, "comes to complete both the idea of freedom and the idea of democracy." The Cantons are the constituent and pre-existing members of the Federal State. In fact, the Federal State was formed to unite and protect the freedom and rights of its constituent members.[9] The powers of the Cantons are original and they exercise all rights which are not delegated to the Federal Government. The Constitution guarantees to the Cantons their territory, their sovereignty, their constitutions, the liberty and rights of their people and the constitutional rights of citizens, and the rights and powers conferred by the people on the authorities. Article 16 of the Constitution authorises the Federal Executive to take any necessary measures, within the limits of its powers, to enforce these guarantees.

Although the sovereignty of the Cantons has steadily diminished in favour of the Confederation, nonetheless it is from the Cantons that the Confederation draws its authority and derives its constitutional usages. The Cantons are the original parts of the federal system of government and they retain their essential prerogatives. Maintenance of internal peace and security is their concern. Construction of public works[10] and highways,[11] provision for a system of public education, care of the social dependants, control of elections and local government are all their responsibility. It is only by being a citizen of a Canton that one acquires the citizenship of Switzerland[12] and Cantonal laws still determine many of the citizen's civil rights. Many affairs of the Central Government are managed by Cantonal Governments. Civil and criminal laws, federal subjects, are administered by the courts which are exclusively Cantonal. The Federal Government simply makes military regulations and appoints superior officers, but enforcement of those regulations, raising of certain contingents for the national army and provision of the personal equipment of each soldier, are the concern of the Cantons.[13] The Federal Tribunal has no officers of its own. It depends upon Cantonal Governments for the execution of its judgments.

To sum up, the Swiss Constitution expressly recognises the juridical personality of the Cantons in the composition of all federal organs. The Council of States represents the Cantons on the basis of equality and corresponds to the American Senate. The National Council represents the people in proportion to the number of electors in each Canton with the proviso that each Canton, no matter how small, shall have at least one deputy. The personality of the Cantons is also

---

6. As quoted in Ramesh Chandra Ghosh, the Government of the Swiss Republic (1953), p. 53 Geneva banned the Communist Party on 13th June, 1937. Vaud did the same by plebiscite on January 30, 1938, by 34,603 votes against 12,700 votes, *Ibid.*, fn.
7. Article 64 (1) and Article 64 bis (1)
8. Article 32 bis.
9. Article 2 .
10. Article 23, however, provides that the Central Government "is entitled in the interest of Switzerland, or a considerable part of it, to order public works at its own expense or to encourage such works by granting subsidies."
11. Article 36 bis (6). While recognising "the sovereignty" of the Cantons over national highways Article 36 bis (1 to 5) empowers the Confederation to build and maintain national highways.
12. Article 43.
13. Article 20 and Article 21 (2).

recognised in the process of amending the Federal Constitution. No change in the Constitutions can be considered legally adopted unless it is approved by a majority of votes of the citizens and also by a majority of the Cantons.

**A Comparatively Longer Document**

The Swiss Constitution is rather a lengthy document, much longer than the Constitution of the United States on which it is generally modelled. It goes into a good many details dealing with matters as fishing and hunting, qualifications of the members of the liberal professions, sickness and burial of the indigent, cattle diseases, gambling houses, and lotteries. All these matters in reality bleong to the sphere of ordinary rather than to that of constitutional legislation. Behind this plethora of details was perhaps the desire for sharp division of authority between the Cantons and the Federal Government.

**Spirit of Republicanism**

All through the Swiss Constitution there is in evidence a strong spirit of republicanism. This is, in fact, the very breath of the Swiss way of life. Article 6 of the Constitution requires the Confederation to guarantee the Cantonal Constitutions, provided that the latter ensure the exercise of political rights according to republican (representative or democratic) forms. The meaning of this provision becomes more clear when it is read along with Article 4. It says: "All Swiss citizens are equal before the law. In Switzerland, there shall be neither subjects, nor privileges of place, birth, person or family." This provision, according to Christopher Hughes, "is now a rule of law and incontestably the most active rule of law of the whole Constitution."[14] The founders of modern Switzerland were animated "by the desire to emancipate the individual from the shackles of the aristocratic, mercantilistic and clerical traditions which had for centuries limited"[15] the individual's freedom. They, accordingly, abolished all aristocratic and oligarchic privileges and guaranteed to the Swiss people equality before law. Every Swiss, man or woman, who has reached the age of twenty years and who is not excluded from the rights of active citizenship, has the right to determine his government, and the acceptance of the Constitution by the majority of the people, and its amendment at any time on popular demand.

There are, thus, in Switzerland no subjects, nor any privileges of rank, birth, person or family. All political institutions of the country—Federal, Cantonal and Communal—are elective in character, and the direct participation of the people in the affairs of government, and for making changes in the Constitution are the basic principles of the nation's political practices. The principle of republicanism and direct sovereignty of the nation is, indeed, the bulwark of Swiss democracy and the people have accepted it in a religious spirit.

**Civil Rights**

Inasmuch as the Swiss Federal State owed its creation largely to the liberal movement in the 1830's and 1840's the framers of the Federal Constitution were careful to include a number of provisions designed to protect the Swiss citizen against future arbitrary action on the part of the Cantons. Although the Constitution does not contain a formal Bill of Rights, nevertheless some two dozen Articles scattered throughout the document deal with the rights of individuals. These rights are elaborated in great detail. Not only are they defined as well as asserted, but in many cases the corresponding duties of the individual are also set forth.

The rights of the Swiss citizens, both guaranteed by the Federal Constitution and others guaranteed by his Cantonal Constitution, are protected by courts against infringement by any Cantonal authority. This protection can include an appeal to the Federal Tribunal[16] which is the highest Court in the land. In practice, such appeals are numerous, especially those concerned with a violation of the general right of equality before the law.

Citizenship in Switzerland has a three-fold basis: Communal, Cantonal and Federal. A person cannot be a Swiss citizen without being a citizen of a Canton and a person cannot be a Cantonal citizen without being a citizen of a Commune. The Constitution does not define citizenship. It simply provides that every citizen of a Canton is a Swiss citizen. Cantonal Constitutions pass responsibility to the lower level by providing that every citizen must also be a citizen of a Commune.

In practice, communal citizenship, and thus Swiss citizership, follows a modified rule of *Jus*

14. Hughes, C., *The Federal Constitution of Switzerland,* pp. 6-7.
15. Rappard, D.E., *The Government of Switerland*, pp. 108-09.
16.. Article 113 (1) (3).

*Sanguinis.* A child born of Swiss parents is, *ipso facto,* a citizen of his father's Commune of origin. A Swiss woman marrying a Swiss from another Commune loses the citizenship of her original Commune and becomes a citizen of her husband's Commune of origin. A child born of alien parents shall be a Swiss citizen by birth if its mother was born a Swiss citizen and if both its parents were resident in Switzerland at the time of its birth. The child shall acquire the citizenship of its mother's Commune of origin. Switzerland does not recognise the principle of *jus soli* when a child born of alien parents automatically becomes the citizen of a State on the soil of which it is born.

Swiss citizenship can also be acquired by naturalisation. Originally, the procedure to be followed and the fee to be paid varied from Canton to Canton and from Commune to Commune within the same Canton. This led to a scandalous abuse, especially during World War I, when anyone could purchase citizenship and this brought federal intervention. Article 44 now provides that Federal legislation "shall specify the conditions for the acquisition or loss of Swiss citizenship". The Federal law of 1920 standardized the classification of persons barred from acquiring citizenship and prescribed the minimum period of twelve years of residence before an alien could submit a petition for communal citizenship. Federal authorities were also given the power to disapprove any individual grant of citizenship.

In principle Swiss citizenship is inalienable. Article 44 (1) prescribes that no Swiss citizen "may be expelled from the territory of the Confederation or of his Canton of origin." It was only during World War II that an emergency law empowered the Government the right to deprive of their citizenship Swiss citizens having two or three nationalities if that fact could be construed to be a danger to the neutrality of Switzerland. A Law of 1952 also provides that second generation Swiss born abroad do not automatically become citizens of Switzerland. A Swiss woman who marries a foreigner may lose her citizenship unless she makes a declaration before marriage that she wishes to retain it. But these instances are just exceptions to the rule.

In general every Swiss citizen can settle in any place in the country. But the freedom of movement is hedged by various limitations and makes the scope of this right much less complete as compared with many other countries, for instance, in the United States. The Canton in which an individual may wish to settle can demand that he should produce a "certificate of origin" or some other document authenticating his identity from his Commune of origin. The Commune may refuse to issue such a certificate or some similar identifying document, or another Commune may decline to release it, under certain conditions such as the non-payment of particular taxes.

Even an individual in possession of a certificate of origin may be refused permission to settle in cases where the person in question had been deprived of his civil rights as a consequence of criminal judgment of a Court. Some other Canton may withdraw the right to reside in cases where an individual may have been "repeatedly sentenced for grave misdemeanour" or has "become a permanent burden upon public charity" and to whom the Canton or Commune of origin refused adequate assistance after having been officially requested to render it. In no case, however, is the Canton of origin permitted to refuse a Swiss the right to return.

In view of the right of Cantons to withdraw the privilege to reside from those who permanently depend upon public charity, the responsibility for the case of indigent Swiss citizens rests ultimately on the Cantons of their origin. Since quite a number of Swiss reside outside the Cantons of their origin, it is provided that the cost of relief shall be shared between the place of origin and the place of domicile according to a proportion based upon the length of time the pauper has resided outside the Canton of origin.

According to Article 4, "All Swiss are equal before the law." This is further amplified in the same Article by the statement that "In Switzerland there are neither subjects nor privileges of rank, birth, person or family." Article 60 adds, "All Cantons are bound to afford all Swiss citizens the same treatment as their own citizens in the fields of legislation and of judicial proceedings." Article 58 guarantees that no person may be deprived of his "constitutional judge; therefore no extraordinary courts of law may be set up." The same Article abolished ecclesiastical jurisdiction. In the eyes of the framers of the Constitution, these provisions were necessary to eliminate the creation of *ad hoc* courts such as those used for the persecution of the Liberals during the Sonderbund War and to keep ecclesiastical courts out of civil affairs. The provision regarding the constitutional judge" is now "only used against arbitrariness in sending people to one tribunal rather than to another or in refusing jurisdiction.''[17] Personal claims against a ''solvent debtor'' must be brought before the tribunal of the debtor's place of domicile and, as such, his property may not be seized or attached for personal claims outside the Canton in which he has his domicile. Imprisonment for civil debts is not permitted. The Constitution prohibits corporal punishment and the death penalty for political crime. A provision of the 1874 Constitution abolished the death penalty for other crimes, but it was reintroduced in 1878 as a result of constitutional amendment. The Federal Criminal Code 1942, reestablishes the prohibition on capital punishment except for serious crimes committed in times of war and during active military service.

Freedom of the press is guaranteed by Article 55. The original Article provided that Cantonal legislatures may enact measures ''for the repression of abuses'' and the Federal legislature ''has the right to prescribe penalties in order to suppress abuses directed against itself or its authorities.'' These provisions have been abrogated as a result of the operation of the Swiss Criminal Code.

The citizens are also guaranteed the freedom of association and petition. The freedom of association has been interpreted to include the formation of organised groups for religious, political, social, and economic purposes and it includes the right to assembly as well. This right is subject, however, to the provision that neither the purpose of the association nor the means it employs are in any way ''illegal or dangerous for the State.'' The Constitution provides that Cantonal laws shall lay down the measures required to repress the misuse of this right. As regards the right to petition, it should be noted that the competent Swiss officials make an effort to take most petitions seriously and redress grievances. But the right itself has lost a great deal of importance as a result of the adoption of the Constitutional initiative.

To safeguard against all possibilities of religious conflicts which for long had distracted Switzerland, the Constitution suggests various provisions. Freedom of belief and conscience are inviolable. No one can be forced to participate in a religious association, to attend religious teaching or to perform a religious act, nor he be subjected to penalties of any sort because of his religious education of children until they have completed their sixteenth year. Nor can his civil or political rights be abridged by any ecclesiastical or religious prescriptions. At the same time, no person can refuse to fulfil, on the ground of religious beliefs, any obligation which citizenship may demand. Moreover, no person can be compelled to pay taxes the proceeds of which go to finance a religious body to which he does not belong.

Article 50 guarantees the free exercise of the act of worship within the limits set by public order or morality. The Cantons and the Confederation may take appropriate measures for the preservation of public order and peace among the members of the different religious communities, as well as against encroachment by religious authorities on the rights of citizens and the State. Disputes of public or private law which may arise out of the creation of new religious communities or out of the splitting of existing communities may be brought before the competent authorities by lodging a complaint. Ecclesiastical jurisdiction has been abolished.

The Constitution also guarantees the right to marriage and it is placed under the protection of the Federal Government. This right cannot be limited for religious or economic reasons, nor on account of previous conduct or of other police considerations. A marriage which has been celebrated in a Canton or abroad according to the local legislation is recognised as valid within the whole territory of Switzerland. Through her marriage, the woman acquires the citizenship of her husband. Children born before marriage ''shall be legitimized by the subsequent marriage of their parents''. No bride-admission fee or nay other similar tax can be levied.

All Cantons are ''bound to afford'' all citizens the same treatment as their own citizens in the fields of legislation and of judicial proceedings. All transfer taxes on the moving of property inside Switzerland and all pre-emption rights of citizens of one Canton against citizens of other Cantons have been abolished. Federal legislation fixes the limits within which a Swiss citizen can be deprived of his political rights. Federal legislation lays down the necessary provisions concerning the extradition of the accused from one Canton to another. Extradition may not be made compulsory for political and press offences.

The Constitution guarantees the right of ownership. The Confederation and the Cantons,

17. Hughes. C., *The Federal Constitution of Switzerland*, p. 7.

to the extent allowed by their constitutional powers, can, however, by legislation and for reasons of public interest make provision for expropriation and restriction on ownership. In cases of expropriation and restriction of ownership fair compensation, equivalent to expropriation, shall be paid.[18]

**Democracy and Switzerland**

"Among modern democracies", writes James Bryce in the opening Chapter on the government of Switzerland, "which are true democracies, Switzerland has the highest claim to be studied. It is the oldest, for it contains communities in which popular government dates further back than it does anywhere else in the world; and it has pushed democratic doctrines further and worked them out more consistently than any other European States."[19] The principle of Swiss democracy is to be communal before being Cantonal, and to be cantonal before being federal. The basis of political authority is that of local autonomy and the popular will is formed from the bottom upward. Switzerland is a land of small communities, rural and urban, and Commune had been from the earliest time a potent factor in accustoming the people to control their own affairs. It is still the political unit of the nation and the focus of its public life. It is a means of educating citizens in public affairs and instilling in them the sense of civil duty. Both the Commune and the Canton appear to them the living realities of a direct or quasi-direct consultation of the people in all matters which concern their immediate administrative problems.

This democratic sense runs all through the federal Constitution and it may be safely said that Switzerland and democracy have now become almost synonymous. In spite of the tendency towards centralization, the introduction of the constitutional initiative in 1891, proportional representation for the election of the National Council in 1919, and of the optional referendunm on international treaties in 1921, sufficiently prove that the democratic purpose of the people which had created the present Swiss Republic in 1848 still remains intact. Rappard is of the opinion that the forms of democracy "have undoubtedly undergone a change under the impact of irresistible economic influences, but the spirit has remained the same."[20]

The Swiss faith in democracy as a political principle is most characteristically revealed in the people's extensive use of the instruments of direct popular government. The most ancient of these is *Landsgemeinde* or open town meeting in which every male adult can speak, make his own laws and elect officers. This over five hundred years old tradition of government still obtains in the five *Landsgemeinde* Cantons: Glarus, Appenzell Outer Rhodes, Appenzell Inner Rhodes, Obwalden and Nidwalden. In all other Cantons a representative republican form of government exists where a frequent use is made of the modern instruments of direct democracy, namely, the popular referendum and the popular initiative. The use of these instruments is also made for matters affecting the Confederation and international treaties.

**A Dynamic Constitution**

The Swiss Constitution is a living document and it presents a singular example of adaptability within the extent of a written Constitution. The Constitution has been so amended from time to time as to represent the popular aspirations consistent with the exigencies of time. The policy of nationalisation and the advancement of various state projects are clear indications of the country's drift towards the Welfare State. In fact, the emphasis in Switzerland, immediately after the Constitution of 1874 came into operation, had been on the protection of the individual rather than on the will to emancipate him. He has been protected against industrial exploitation by labour legislation in 1877, 1908 and 1920, against epidemics and other dangers to his health by various sanitary measures in 1897, 1905 and 1913 as well as against himself by the sundry forms of temperance and anti-alcoholic legislation in 1885, 1908 and 1930 and by anti-gambling measures in 1920. Article 35 prohibits the running of gambling houses and the Federal Government may also take appropriate measures concerning lotteries. Uniform laws on the employment of children in the factories and on the working hours of adult persons have been enacted and regulations are strictly enforced to protect the workers against the operation of unhealthy and dangerous industries. The protection of employees is legally ensured and adequate steps have been taken on the binding effect of collective labour and other

18. Article 22 ter.
19. Bryce, J., *Modern Democracies*, Vol. I, p. 367
20. Rappard, D.E., *The Government of Switzerland*, p. 111.

arrangements, which the Federal Government may deem necessary and expedient, between association of employers and employees with a view to furthering peaceful labour relations. Measures have been taken to encourage construction of houses and providing the opportunity for owning a dwelling or house. In order to prevent abuses in the field of rents and housing necessary legislation has been enacted. Laws have been made to regulate unemployment insurance which is obligatory and exceptions thereof have been laid down. Measures have also been adopted to promote an adequate old age, survivors' and disability insurance scheme. The Constitution empowers the Federal Government, within the limits of its constitutional powers, to have due regard to the needs of the family and legislate in the field of family compensation funds and institute maternity insurance.

But the great change was necessitated by the economic depression of 1930 when the workers, the farmers, and the middle-class all demanded State intervention to extricate them from the baneful results of their economic frustration, and to introduce schemes for their economic security. In order to protect her political independence and to save the country from the subversive elements either from the Right or the Left, and to safeguard her traditional neutrality during the two World Wars some restrictions were imposed on the liberty of speech and association of the citizens. The Swiss people have, however, always shown their love of personal liberty and whenever the Government has unduly interfered with it, they have consistently rejected at the polls even the most reasonable protective measures. In 1884, 1896, 1903, 1922, 1923, 1920. 1935, 1937, 1939 referenda on Bills intended to protect the community at the expense of the freedom of the individual gave expression to the liberal attitude of the people and the way in which they protected their most cherished liberties.

**Switzerland's Neutrality**

Switzerland has been a neutral country for more than four centuries. At the Paris Peace Conference in 1815, Swiss neutrality was recognised by Europe's great powers. After the First World War recognition of the neutrality of 1815 was renewed under Article 435 of the Treaty of Versailles of 1919. It found a basis in international law by the declaration of the Council of the League of Nations of May 14, 1938. With explicit reference to its neutrality Switzerland was granted the right not to take part in sanctions of the League of Nations.

The right of neutrality is the outcome of a process which has taken centuries to develop. It developed out of common law and is partly based upon common law even today. Despite Switzerland's affirmation to permanent neutrality, it does not find mention in any Article of the Constitution, except in Article 85 which deals with the competence of the Federal Assembly. But this Article, too, simply enumerates neutrality by providing that the two Chambers of the Federal Assembly may take measures "for the external security as well neutrality of Switzerland, declaration of war and peace." But it does constitutionalise neutrality of Switzerland and its recognition by international law enhances the stature of Switzerland as a peace-loving country which performs this humanitarian duty as an integral part of its policy of neutrality.

The Swiss population comprises groups from German, French and Italian spheres of cultures. Neutrality has played a decisive part in reconciling different mentalities and international interests. It became a uniting element, strengthening national unity. Neutrality protected Switzerland from disaster in two World Wars. Majority of the Swiss regard neutrality as an important factor in their national survival. They even rejected at a referendum, by a huge majority of the votes polled, the proposal for Switzerland joining the United Nations and in this process not even one of the cantons voted in favour of the proposal which had been passed earlier in 1981 by both the Houses of the Federal Assembly and had the full support of all major political parties.

**Amendment of the Constitution**

The Swiss Constitution is rigid and the procedure adopted to amend it is complicated. But it is by no means so difficult to put it in practice as in the United States. The method of revision is precisely stated in Chapter III of the Constitution of 1874. The revision of the Constitution may mean either a total revision or a partial revision. The former refers to the substitution of a new Constitution for the old one and the latter is only in relation to a specific provision of the Constitution.

The Swiss Constitution introduces the instruments of Constitutional Referendum and the Constitutional Initiative in the process of amending the Constitution. The Constitutional Referendum implies submission to popular vote all constitutional amendments for their final approval or disapproval. There are two aspects of popular vote. One is that all constitutional amendments must be ratified by a majority of the Swiss citizens, and by a majority of the Cantons. If the necessary majority cannot be obtained at both the levels, then, the amendment cannot become operative. Secondly, the constitutional initiative empowers the people themselves to propose either a total or partial revision of the Constitution.

The procedure prescribed for amending the Constitution is as follows:

(1) As said above, constitutional amendments may be total or partial. The Federal Legislature may initiate either type by the ordinary process of legislative action. The Federal Council may also draw up a proposal which is then submitted to the two Houses, the Council of States and the National Council, for independent deliberation or one of the two Houses may start the process. If both the Houses agree, it is submitted to the people, known as the compulsory constitutional referendum, for their verdict on the next convenient date. If a majority of the citizens voting at a referendum and majority of the Cantons approve it, then, the revised Federal Constitution or the revised part of it, as the case may be, is deemed to have been adopted. In determining the will of the Cantons, each Canton possesses one vote and each half Canton half a vote. The result of the popular vote in each Canton is considered to be the vote of that Canton.

If, however, only one House of the Federal Assembly agrees to the proposed total revision of the Constitution and the other House does not consent or if 100,000 Swiss citizens entitled to vote demand the total revision of the Constitution, the question whether such a revision should take place or not must be submitted in both cases to the vote of the Swiss people at a referendum. If the people at a referendum approve the total revision of the Constitution by a majority vote, new elections to both the Council of States and the National Council are held. Approval of the Cantons is not required at this juncture. After the elections had been held, the newly elected Council of States and the National Council proceed to consider the proposed revision. If both the Councils approve it, the revision of the Constitution is submitted to the vote of the people at a referendum. If it has been approved by the majority of the Swiss citizens voting and the majority of the Cantons, the revision comes into force.

Partial revision of the Constitution may be carried out either by means of a popular initiative, known as constitutional initiative, or in accordance with the forms laid down for federal legislation as analysed above. The popular initiative consists of a request, presented by 100,000 Swiss citizens entitled to vote, aiming at the introduction, setting aside or modification of specified Articles of the Constitution. If by means of a popular initiative several different provisions are to be modified or introduced into the Constitution, each one must be of a separate initiative request.

A constitutional initiative request may consist of a general proposal or take the form of a complete draft. A request in general terms for revision is just an indication of a desire by at least 100,000 Swiss citizens entitled to vote urging the need for a particular amendment which they deem necessary and expedient. A specific request, on the other hand, is a complete draft of the proposed amendment. If the request for amendment consists of a general proposal, both the Councils of the Federal Assembly should agree to it and if they approve, they shall prepare a partial revision in accordance with and in conformity to the lines of the proposal and submit their draft amendment to the people for adoption or rejection. If the Council of States and the National Council do not approve the revision, the question is submitted to the decision of the people. If the majority of the Swiss citizens entitled to vote decide in the affirmative (the Cantons are not counted in this procedure) the Federal Assembly shall undertake the revision in conformity with the decision of the people and submit it to a popular and Cantonal referendum.

If the proposal for a partial revision is in the form of a complete draft and if it meets with the approval of both the Councils of the Federal Assembly, it is submitted to the people and the Cantons for adoption or rejection. If the Councils disagree and do not approve the draft, they may prepare their own draft or recommend the rejection together with the draft proposed by the initiative to the decision of the people and the Cantons.

The procedure for partial revision on the initiative of the people may be summarised as follows:

1. If the demand for partial revision is unformulated, *i.e.,* it is couched in general terms, the Federal Assembly, if it approves it, frames

the amendment and, then, submits it for the ratification of the people and the Cantons;

2. If the Federal Assembly does not approve the amendment, then,

(i) the question whether there shall be a partial revision or not is submitted to the people for their decision. No reference need be made to the Cantons.

(ii) If majority of the citizens vote in favour of the revision, the exising Federal Assembly, although it had already expressed its disapproval of the proposed revision, is required to draft the amendment in conformity to the popularly initiated proposal and submit it to a referendum of the people and the Cantons;

3. If it is a formulated proposal, the Federal Assembly is first required to approve it and, then, it is referred to a referendum of the people and the Cantons. If the Federal Assembly does not approve of the revision, it may recommend to a referendum:

(i) that the proposed revision, may be rejected or

(ii) may frame its own counter-proposals and submit them along with the original popularly initiated proposal for the decision of the people and the Cantons.

The constitutional popular initiative was introduced at the federal level in 1891, subject to a petition by 50,000 eligible voters.[21] It has actually been employed for 67 times from the date of its introduction to 1976 and accepted for 18 times only. The compulsory constitutional referendum for the same period had been used for 102 times out of which the eligible voters accepted it on 82 occasions. The number of amendments to the Constitution are quite numerous and a few partial revisions have significantly altered the constituent parts of the Constitution. The vast majority of them have extended the competence of the Federal Government in various dimensions, particularly in restricting the freedom of trade and industry. Other amendments impose upon Swiss citizens the exacting standards of morality in matters of drink, gambling, etc.

The notable feature of the Swiss Constitution is its development through formal constitutional amendments alone. There is no growth through judicial decisions and precedents, because of the absence of the system of judicial review. The Federal Tribunal cannot declare *ultra vires* a law of the Federal Assembly. The Swiss theory is that the sovereign power should remain in the hands of the people or their representatives in the legislature. An initiative proposal to invest the Federal Tribunal with power to review legislation was rejected at a referendum in 1939. Hans Huber, who himself was a judge of the Federal Tribunal, remarked that the Swiss people "saw in the judicial examination of constitutional law an in-fringement of democratic principles."[22]

Another fact to be noted is that it is "easier for the Swiss people to amend their fundamental law than their ordinary statutes against the will of a hostile Parliament."[23] This is due to the reason that the Swiss people have no power of initiative in the matter of ordinary legislation. They can, on a petition of 50,000 citizens, demand a referendum on any federal law or decree, but they can never "directly provoke the adoption, repeal or amendment of a law by the Federal authorities." The proposals for constitutional amendments in Switzerland have been made by the people frequently.

## Swiss and American Constitutions Compared

A.B. Keith[24] has pointed out the following differences between the Swiss and the American Constitutions:

(1) The executive is vested in President in the United States and a Federal Council in Switzerland. It is a single executive in the former whereas it is collegial in the latter.

(2) In the United States the President is chosen by the Electoral College composed of elected representatives from each State, whilst in Switzerland the members of the Federal Council are elected by the Federal Assembly. In both countries the election has been intended to be indirect but it has become in reality a direct election in the United States.

(3) The Upper House or the Council of States in Switzerland has not the same weight in the constitution as the Senate in the United States since the consent of the latter is necessary before the President can make treaties or appoint public officers. Senate in the United States is the strongest Upper Chamber in the world. The House of Representatives has, therefore, been eclipsed by

21. In 1977 the number was increased from 50,000 to 100,000.
22. Huber, H., *How Switzerland is Governed*, p. 10
23. Rappard, W.E., *The Government of Switzerland*, p. 60.
24. Keith, A.B., *Constitutional Law*, pp. 28. 28-29.

the Senate. This is a unique feature of the American legislative system and, indeed, of a representative system of government. In Switzerland no distinction is made between the Upper and the Lower Chambers; both possess identical powers. This is again a peculiar feature of bicameralism in Switzerland. Bicameralism assigns to the Upper Chamber a role different from the Lower Chamber because one must not be the replica of the other. But Swiss bicameralism defies this basic principle of Second Chambers.

(4) Party government, and consequuent wirepulling exist in an exaggerated form in the United States, whilst in Switzerland it is almost entirely absent. This result, it would seem, follows from the manner in which the executives are appointed in the two countries, as well as from the fact that in the one case the executive is vested in a President, who appoints the various public officers, and in the other case in a Council. Switzerland, unlike other democracies, has not in any true sense a party government. There is the absence of party machinery and party-lines are rarely drawn. There are no party leaders as well and merit alone is the criterion for election to the Federal Council. Nor is there any opportunity for any one to extend patronage and distribute spoils.

(5) the States in the United States are forbidden absolutely to enter into treaties; the Cantons have a limited power. Cantons in Switzerland have a constitutional sanction to conclude treaties with each other or with foreign States concerning matters of public economy, neighbourly relations and police provided such treaties contain nothing contrary to the Confederation or to the rights of the other Cantons. All such treaties are subject to the approval of the Federal Council. If the Federal Council does not approve or another Canton raises an objection to them an appeal is lodged with the Federal Assembly for annulling the same.

(6) In Switzerland acceptance or rejection of a constitutional amendment must compulsorily be referred to the people. The Swiss voters also possess the right of constitutional initiative. In the United States neither of the two exists. In Switzerland, therefore, it is much easier to alter the Constitution than it is to change the Constitution in the United States.

(7) Laws of the Federal authority in Switzerland may be submitted on demand to a referendum, but not so in the United States. The national legislative referendum is applicable to federal laws, except budget and decrees, and since 1921 to international treaties. Within ninety days of the publication of a measure in the Federal Assembly either 50,000 citizens or eight Cantons may demand its submission to a referendum and the verdict of the people decides the fate of a measure.

(8) The Swiss federal judiciary cannot rule invalid a federal law, while, the United States Supreme Court often decides against federal legislation. In the United States supremacy of the judiciary is an accomplished fact whereas in Switzerland the Federal Assembly is supreme and the Constitution makes it so.

Today the Swiss political system has lost much of its originality. Direct democracy in the Cantons has become mostly unoperational. Referendum and intiative have become both irrelevant and ineffective. The Federal Concil has been reduced to the status and position of a parliamentary cabinet where the Socialists and other radicals often work as opposition.

## SUGGESTED READINGS

Bonjour, E., *The Real Democracy in Europe: the Example of Switzerland.*

Huber, Hans, *How Switzerland is governed?*

# CHAPTER III

# The Cantonal and Local Government

## The Communes and the Cantons

The principle of Swiss democracy, as said before, is "to be communal before being cantonal and to be cantonal before being federal." Switzerland is a union of highly developed autonomous communities within the federal State, and in the political life of the Swiss citizen the Canton looms larger than the federal State. The Commune is essentially the initial cell of Swiss democracy. It is the first basis of the administrative fabric, and a place which educates citizens in public affairs and instils in them a sense of civic duty. Then, come the Cantons, constituents of the Confederation.

"In the eyes of the citizen," writes Andre Siegfried, "the Canton is the living reality much more than the Confederation which may well appear to him as little more than a cold administrative mechanism. Each citizen feels himself a Swiss as a matter of course, but before being Swiss he is a native of Zurich or Glarus or Valais." He is the citizen of a Canton before being a Swiss citizen. Although, the present trend toward the nationalisation of political power and political loyalty have reduced their historic individuality and Cantonal feeling is slowly diminishing, yet the Constitution still recognises their sovereignty in so far as it "is not limited by the Federal Constitution, and as such, they exercise all rights which are not transferred to the federal power."[1] Cantons are still in fact the real centres of the political life of the nation. "It is to his Canton and to his city or village," writes Rappard, that a Swiss citizen "pays most of his direct taxes. It is to vote for and against cantonal and communal measures, for or against candidates to cantonal or communal office, that he is most frequently called to the polls. It was, until a generation ago, exclusively, and it still is mainly, on cantonal issues that political parties were and are formed and that many of the most important political battles are won and lost. Most constitutional changes were....wrought in the Cantons before they become ripe for consideration by the federal legislature."[2] We, accordingly, give precedence to Cantonal and Communal political institutions before we actually consider those of the Federal Government. Really Swiss politics are only half understood without a knowledge of local institutions.

## Constitutional Position of the Cantons

The Cantons twenty-three in number with three divided into half Cantons with their own separate governments—are very unequal in size and population. Their rights and powers correspond generally to those of the States in the American Union and the Australian Federal Commonwealth. Article 3 of the Swiss Constitution definitely specifies that residuary powers belong to the Cantons and that they are 'sovereign' within their sphere of jurisdiction. To the Federal Government are assigned specified powers. Each Canton possesses its own constitution and its own machinery of government—executive, legislative and judicial organs, a fiscal system and a civil service. And the Cantons control all forms of local self-government.

The Constitutions of the Cantons and half Cantons must comply with the provisions of the Federal Constitution. The Confederation guarantees the Cantonal Constitutions, provided that they: (a) do not contain anything contrary to the provisions of the Federal Constitution; (b) provide for the exercise of political rights in conformity with Republican representative or democratic forms of government; and (c) have been accepted by the people and can be amended on the demand of the absolute majority of the citizens. Within these limitations the Cantons are free to construct their constitutions and alter them as they please. In the beginning, the Cantonal Constitutions had been amended quite frequently and in some cases entailed a total revision. The net result of these amendments was that all the Constitutions, more or less, prescribe identical political institutions, except the four half Cantons

1. Article 3.
2. Rappard, W. E., *The Government of Switzerland*, *op cit.*, p. 31.

and one full Canton, five in all, where there is pure democracy.

**Two Types of Cantons**

Cantons are of two types—those ruled by primary, and those ruled by representative assemblies. To the first category belong the five pure democracies of Obwalden, Nidwalden, Appenzell Interior, Appenzell Exterior and Glarus. The first two are half-Cantons and they collectively make the Canton of Unterwalden. The third and the fourth, too, are half-Cantons making together the Cannton of Appenzell. Glarus is a full Canton. The origin of this curious institution of a half-Canton usually goes back to the simple fact that internal dissensions could not be settled except by territorial division. Obwalden and Nidwalden dissolved their common Landsgemeinde as early as 1432. Appennzell fell apart in 1592 as an outcome of the Reformation, which resulted in a half-catholic half-protestant Canton. The remaining twenty Cantons are representative democracies.

**The Landsgemeinde**

The Canton of Glarus and the four half-Cantons into which Appenzell and Unterwalden are divided still centre political authority in their over five hundred years old *Landsgemeinde* or annual assembly of all citizens which makes laws and elects officers, executive and administrative. In other words, the people directly exercise their superior power in an annual open air meeting, instead of through elected representatives.

The open-air meeting, called a *Landsgemeinde*, is held annually on a Sunday morning in April or May in the public square of the capital city or in a nearby meadow. Attendance is compulsory for all adult male citizens, but in practice all do not attend. The meeting is presided over by the head of the Cantonal Government in an atmosphere marked by solemnity, prayers, hymns and sometimes collective oaths. No turbulence and unusual activity or practice is ever in evidence. The proceedings are orderly and dignified and are usually witnessed by childern from other parts of Switzerland.

The *Landsgemeinde* elects by show of hands the Head of the Government, members of the Executive Council, the Cantonal representatives in the Council of States, judges and officials. The tradition is to re-elect the incumbents so long as they wish. The meeting further approves the accounts, votes the budget, and other legislative bills submitted to it. The *Landsgemeinde* has also the power to change the Cantonal Constitution.

The constitutional structure of a Canton consists of a Parliament, Landrat or the Cantonal Council, and an executive body, Regierungsrat or Council of State. The Landrat or the Cantonal Council is elected for a period of four years not by the *Landsgemeinde* but by separate electoral districts. This Cantonal Council is, in fact, a subsidiary legislature and attends to all the details that cannot be brought before the people in the open meeting, passes ordinances, votes the smaller appropriations, examines the accounts, and elects the minor officials. It also prepares the legislative work to be presented to the *Landsgemeinde.* This procedure is adopted obviously to prevent hasty and ill-considered action by the large public meeting. At one time the Cantonal Council tried to draw the whole control of legislative affairs into their own hands and no question could be brought in the *Landsgemeinde* without their approval. But after a good deal of struggle the people reasserted their right of private initiative. It is now the rule that one or more citizens can in some form propose any measure, provided notice had been given to the Cantonal authorities beforehand.

The Regierungsrat, or the Administrative Council, is usually composed of seven members elected by the *Landsgemeinde.* This is the Cantonal Executive Council and is presided over by the *Landammann* or the Head of the Government. The *Landamman* also presides over the *Landsgemeinde.*

## REPRESENTATIVE CANTONS

In all other Cantons representative Republican form of government prevails.

**The Great Council**

The legislative power and the supervision of administration is vested in a unicameral representative assembly of the Canton, variously named Great Council or Cantonal Council. All Cantonal legislatures are unicameral as a matter of tradition. As the instruments of initiative and referendum provide for popular control over legislation consequently no need is felt for the check provided by a second Chamber.

The membership of the Cantonal legislatures tends to be large in comparison with the size of the population it represents. In some Cantons the number is fixed by the Constitution. For example, the Constitution of Zurich calls for as many as 180 representatives. Generally speaking, the proportion between inhabitants and representative varies ranging from 1 to 250 to 1 to 4,000. The term of office of the legislators also varies. In most Cantons, it is four years; in the remainder it is from one to six years. The general tendency, however, is towards longer terms, because they are reluctant to go in for election so frequently. There must be at least one annual session to pass the budget. In some Cantons the legislature may be dissolved by popular vote. But with the general introduction of referendum the necessity of dissolving the legislature does no longer exist. Legislators in the Cantons receive no fixed salaries, but only a nominal sum per diem.

The powers of the Cantonal legislature include control and supervision of administration; control over the annual budget, loans, and taxations; power to declare a state of emergency and to call up Cantonal troops if necessary; to grant amnesty and pardon; ratification of inter-Cantonal treaties; election of superior judges in most of the Cantons and of the members of Cantonal authoritics dealing with education, church affairs and banking.

**Referendum and Initiative**

Every representative Canton provides for Constitutional Initiative and Compulsory Constitutional Referendum. That is to say, every Canton is required by the Federal Constitution to submit all changes in its Constitution for the acceptance or rejection by the people.[3] The Constitution can also be amended whenever the absolute majority of citizens demand it.[4] All Cantons go further and have the legislative referendum also and an assortment of other devices, varying from Canton to Canton, such as budget referendum, or a compulsory legislative referendum for laws entailing expenditure beyond a certain limit. Initiative on ordinary legislation is permitted. The effect of the operation of the popular instruments is that the citizens are called to the polls from four to eight, or even more times a year, and each time they are required to vote several issues.

**Cantonal Executive Power**

Each Canton is governed by a collegial executive body known as the Government Council in German-speaking Switzerland, and Council of State in the French part. The collegial system of executive is in harmony with the Swiss tradition and is a universal institution throughout Switzerland, both in the Cantons and the Federal Government. It is usually composed of five or seven members, but Berne and Appenzell and Interior Rhodes have nine and Nidwalden has eleven. The executive is a representative body of the political parties in the Canton. Sometimes deliberate effort is made to give the parties proportional representation. Broadly speaking, the executive council is a ''business board'' with little political colour. The councillors are elected for a term from one to five years; in most Cantons the term is four years.

The Chairman of the Council *Landammann,* is rarely elected for more than one year at a time, and is not immediately eligible for re-election. In some Cantons the Chairmen are elected by the Canton legislatures, in others by their colleagues and in the rest by the people. They do not enjoy any special power or authority. They are just like others in the Council.

The Councillors are usually re-elected and the Swiss tradition is that good men ought to continue in office so long as their health and ambitions permit. Consequently, although their terms are short, it is often looked upon as a life job. Their work is just like that of the Federal Councillors, divided into various departments and a councillor is usually the head of one department. They must appear and report to the State legislature on the Cantonal administration, take part in its debates, propose measures and draft when required by the legislature to do so. They also follow the federal example of not resigning even if the legislature does not support their plans.

In spite of the obvious subordination of the executive to the Cantonal legislature, it must be admitted that the position and the knowledge which the Councillors possess secure for them great influence with the Great or Cantonal Council. It has the strength which experience acquires by permanence in office and, as such the Executive Council supplies the chief impulse to the legislature.

## COMMUNES AND DISTRICTS

**The Communes**

There are now 3,118 Communes in Switzerland and they vary in size and population. They have the right of self-government within the limits prescribed by the Cantonal Constitu-

3. Article 6.
4. *Ibid.*

tions and the statutory laws of the Cantons concerned. In matters assigned to them, for example, education, public health, poor relief, water supply, police, etc., they have complete autonomy and in their administration they possess the same structure as the Cantons. The general direction of local affairs, the decision of all matters connected thereto and the appointment of the principal officers of the Communes are vested in the assembly of all adult citizens of the Commune. For the conduct of current business and for the execution of the communal law, the assembly of all the people elects a Council. In most of the French parts of Switzerland and particularly in the large Communes, the assembly of the people does not transact business directly. On the other hand, they elect a Communal Council which transacts business on behalf of the assembly of the people. The French Communes, therefore have two Councils: a large one which deals with questions of general policy and all matters of importance; second, a smaller executive body with the Mayor at its head and entrusted with the duty of the execution of communal laws. The decisions of the bigger Council, which may be called a municipal Parliament, are sometimes subject to referendum.

**The Districts**

The District is an intermediate division between the Canton and the Commune. But it does not constitute, except in a few places, a political community like the Commune. The District is merely an administrative unit. The chief district official is elected by the people and at some places he is assisted by a council with advisory functions. The district official represents the Cantonal Government in the district and, with the assistance of his subordinates, carries out its orders, executes the laws and acts as a link between the Canton and the Commune.

Swiss local government presents some significant features unknown elsewhere. Every Swiss citizen must be a citizen of some Commune before he can acquire the citizenship of a Canton and Switzerland. No foreigner can be naturalized in Switzerland who has not previously been declared acceptable as a member by a Commune. Secondly, the home Commune, as it is called, is ultimately responsible for him and his family. "The Federal Constitution assumes that, in case of their absolute indigence, this Commune must support them, wherever they happen to be living although it may of course oblige them to return to their political home."[5] Then, every Commune has an estate distinct from the one to which all residents contribute by taxation. The management of such an estate is reserved to the members of the Commune and not residents of the Commune. The law distinguishes between the local Commune, in which every citizen has an equal right to vote and is liable to equal taxation after three months of residence, and the Commune of origin or home Commune.[6] Then, the more important municipalities undertake and perform many economic activities which may be characterised as a socialistic tendency. The growth of this kind of municipal socialism in Switzerland has now become an important characteristic of Swiss political life in general though no socialist party has marked a conspicuous place for itself in the country.

While summing up the nature and importance of local self- government in Switzerland, James Bryce maintained that the Commune is not only the basis of the administrative fabric "but also the training which the people have received from practice in it has been a chief cause of their success in working republican institutions. Nowhere in Europe has it been so fully left to the hands of the people. The Swiss themselves lay stress upon it, as a means of educating the citizens in public work, as instilling the sense of civic duty, and as enabling governmental action to be used for the benefit of the community without either sacrificing local initiative or working the action of the central authority too strong and too pervasive."[7]

## SUGGESTED READINGS

Brooks, R.G. *The Government and Politics of Switzerland*

Sanser Hall Georges, *Political Institutions of Switzerland*

Rappord W.E., *The Government of Switzerland*

5. Rappard, W. E., *The Government of Switzerland,* p. 53.
6. *Ibid.*
7. Bryce, J., *Modern Democracies,* Vol. I, p. 375.

CHAPTER IV

# The Frame of National Government— The Federal Executive

**Organisation of the Executive**

The supreme directing and executive authority of the Confederation is exercised by a Commission of seven men[1] known as Bundesrat or Federal Council located at Berne. This Commission of seven men or Federal Council is chosen by the Federal Assembly for a term of four years (until 1931, for 3 years) from among all the Swiss citizens who are eligible to be elected to the National Council of the Federal Assembly. One of the members of the Federal Council is annually elected by the Assembly to serve as its Chairman and is designated President of the Confederation, while another is chosen as Vice-President.[2]

The term of office of the Federal Council coincides with the tenure of the National Council.[3] It is elected at the beginning of each National Council and is completely renewed after every General Election. Vacancies arising within the normal period of four years are filled at the next meeting of the Assembly for the unexpired term of office.[4] Although it is not required by the Constitution, the Federal Councillors are almost always chosen from among the members of the Assembly. When so chosen, they must resign their seats in the Legislature. The Constitution, however, prescribes that "no more than one person from each Canton may be chosen for the Federal Council."[5] Custom, on the other hand, insists one Councillor shall always come from Berne, another from Zurich and one from Vaud. This was, however, broken in the years from 1875 to 1881 and again from 1944 to 1947. The normal arrangement being that the Federal Council is composed of four German-speaking members, two from French-speaking part, and one member from Ticino, the Italian-speaking Canton. The wisdom of this distribution has been proved by long experience, because all the three language groups and both confessions are more or less fairly represented.

There have several times been proposals for direct election of the Federal Council by the people and there has twice been a referendum on the subject in 1900 and 1942. But it had been unsuccessful both times. Lowell thought that popular election of the Federal Councillors would intensify party rivalry extending its "influence over the whole range of policies, and produce a radical change in the character of public life." The national conventions which would come into existence for the nomination of the candidates, "would put an end to the low development of party which renders the permanent, business-like, non-partisan character of the Federal Council possible, which makes it their places permanently even when their policy does not prevail. The Councillors would become the standard-bearers of the different groups, and could hardly maintain the mediating attitude that has made their position unique among the governments of the world."[6] The proposal for direct election has each time been made to secure representation on the Council for an excluded party or section of the country. It may, therefore, be said, as Hughes remarks, "that the threat of proposing a constitutional initiative for direct election is the section behind the custom of having all main parties represented on the Federal Council."[7] This may be illustrated from the party representation in the Federal Council. In 1943 there were 3 Liberals, 2 Catholics, 1 Farmer and 1 Socialist. In 1951, 3

1. Article 95.
2. Article 98.
3. Article 96 (2).
4. Article 96 (3).
5. Article 9617.
6. Lowell, A. L., *Government and Parties in Continental Europe,* Vol. II, p. 320.
7. Hughes, C., *The Federal Government of Switzerland,* p. 108.

Radical Liberals, 2 Catholic Conservatives, 1 Social Democrat and 1 Peasant and Middle Class were chosen. The nature of representation remains more or less similar since then.

**Federal Council not a Partisan Body**

The Federal Council, says Bryce, "stands outside party, is not chosen to do party work, does not determine party policy, yet is not wholly without some party colour."[8] The Councillors are chosen neither from the parliamentary majority as in Britain, nor are they political leaders of different parties or groups, as it was in France, who coalesced to form a government. They are a heterogeneous group of politicians belonging to four different parties who are chosen for their capacity as administrators. Speakers or tacticians are not needed in the Swiss Executive. No matter how well-qualified on other counts, no one can expect to be elected to the Federal Council unless which, above all others, the Swiss demand of those who hold public office—modesty. In his previous Cantonal and national service, he must have left an image of a person dedicated to his work without thought of personal recognition. The office must seek the candidates, not the candidate the office. It is administrative skill, mental grasp, good sense, tact and temper, the sum total of the virtuous qualities that recommend a candidate for selection. According to Dicey two ideas underlie the institutions of Switzerland. The first is, the universal acceptance of the sovereignty of the people, and the second is, that politics is a matter of business with the Swiss people.[9] It is this second idea which guides the nation in the selection of their administrators and get their affairs managed by men of capacity.

Moreover, the Federal Council is not an independent or co-ordinate branch of government. It is essentially a business body subordinate to the Federal Assembly. It is not expected to frame and control the policy of the government. Its duty consists in conducting the administration and giving advice on legislation. Policy making is the function of the Federal Assembly and the Federal Councillors are there to carry out its behest. They are, indeed, the servants of the policy-making and policy-initiating body—the Federal Assembly—and, accordingly, they cannot be partisans. All differences among themselves, though they are chosen from different parties, are ironed out by a spirit of compromise as public opinion in Switzerland expects every one to subordinate his own feelings to the public good. Lowell rightly remarked that the influence of the Federal Council "depends to a great extent on the confidence in its impartiality, and hence its position is fortified by anything that tends, to strengthen and perpetuate its non-partisan character."[10]

**Long Tenure of the Councillors**

The obvious result is that the Federal Council is unique in its stability. It is virtually a permanent body, though chosen afresh every four years.

The old members are always re-elected as long as they care to serve. If the National Council is dissolved earlier than the end of its normal four-year term, the first business of the new Assembly is to elect the Federal Council and in practice it means re-electing the old members without any consideration of the change in the complexion of the National Council. The non-partisan character of the Council and the fact that the Councillors are irremovable from office further contribute to their lengthy tenure. The average period of service is more than ten years, but persons like Signor Guiseppe, Motta, a Federal Councillor from Ticino, have held office from 1911 to 1940. Dr. Phillippe Etter served for 23 years, Dr. Karl Koblet for 14 years, Dr. Max Petipierre for 10 years and Dr. Rodolphe Rubattal for 8 years.[11]

Two important reasons may be assigned for this lengthy tenure. One, of course, is that to the Swiss it seems as irrational for the State to lose a valuable administrator on account of a difference of opinion. Dicey likens the Swiss Federal Council to a Board of Directors of a joint stock company, and adds that there is no more reason for altering its composition if it is doing its work efficiently in the general interests than there is to alter the membership of such a board under similar circumstances. Second, when a Councillor dies or resigns, the range of candidates for the place is quite limited, for, in practice, Councillors are almost invariably selected from the members

8. Bryce, J., *Modern Democracies,* Vol. I, p. 394.
9. Dicey, A. V., *Law of the Constitution,* pp. 608-09.
10. Lowell, A. L., *Government and Parties in Continental Europe,* pp. 202-03.
11. Dr. Josef Escher succeeded Dr. Errico Celio in 1950 on his appointment as Swiss Minister in Rome. Herr von Steiger and Herr Nobles retired because of their age and were succeeded by Dr. H. Feldmann and Prof. M. Weber on December 3, 1951. From 1848 to 1978 there had been 86 Councillors and the average length of tenure had been 11 years.

of the Federal Assembly which is by no means a numerous body. Moreover, the Constitution ordains that no more than one member from a single Canton may be chosen, and by usage the Cantons of Berne, Zurich and Vaud must be represented. This limitation narrows the choice. Finally, the office itself does not carry a fabulous salary and other amenities are also meagre. The Federal Councillor now draws a salary of 110,000 Swiss francs per annum. It is certainly an improvement over what it was in 1848 and even 1959, but a large number of Federal Councillors remain men of the people. It is told of a Federal Councillor that when he was asked why he travelled third class, he replied, "Because there isn't a fourth." The Swiss people are frugal and simple in habits and they do not want public offices to become glamorous. Their call to a public office is duty and patriotic devotion. They let those continue in office who are dedicated.

**Organisation of Federal Administration**

The work of federal administration is divided into seven Departments, equivalent to the number of the Federal Councillors. The Departments are designated as: Political; Finance and Customs; Interior; Justice and Police; Public Economy; Posts and Railways; and Military Affairs. The allocation of Departments is made among the Councillors themselves by mutual arrangement. Each Councillar presides over a Department and as his tenure of office is pretty lengthy, he retains for practical reasons of convenience and economy, the same Department continuously. The assignment is, however, nominally made afresh every year. At one time there was a complaint that actual changes in the allotment were too frequent. It is no longer the case now and the complaint is that changes are not made often enough.

Although the business of the Federal Council is divided into different Departments and one of the members is at the head of each Department, yet the Constitution ordains that "decisions are taken by the Federal Council as a body."[12] This provision gives to the Federal Council a corporate personality and makes it corporately responsible. It acts as a collegiate body and its decisions always come from that body as a whole. The Constitution further prescribes that "in order to make deliberation valid, at least four members of the Federal Council must be present."[13] The Law of 1914 on the organization of Federal Administration also provides that the deliberations of the Federal Council shall be in private, that decisions shall normally be by count of hands, that there must be at least three votes, and a majority of the Councillors present, on the majority side, and that the President has a casting vote.[14] All this means that the Federal Council must meet at least once a week and its deliberations are secret. Four members of the Council constitute a quorum and decisions are taken on a majority basis, but all decisions must be supported by at least three members.

There has been some criticism on the corporate responsibility of the Federal Council, and it has long been said that "there are seven Federal Councillors, but no Federal Council." It is true that members of four different parties can hardly hammer out a common policy. Then, the Councillors are not obliged to stand by each other, or even to pretend to hold out the same opinions and there have been occasions when members of the Council have argued against each other in the Federal Assembly, when sharply divided on policy. Decision, moreover, is by a majority vote. But since the deliberations of the Federal Council are secret, and former Councillors are reluctant to recount their experiences, it is difficult to state definitely how much diversity of opinion ordinarily exists. It seems quite evident, however, that members of the Council do not carry their party principles too far. This is partly due to the Swiss habit of compromise and submission to the majority. But, as Hughes remarks, "the loneliness of the very high office and the greatness of responsibility can hardly fail to engender a corporate spirit; the essential element for obtaining genuine agreements—secrecy of discussion—is after all present."[15] The Councillors also know it that the final decision of all the most important questions rests with the Federal Assembly; the sovereign body whose servants they all are. The most routine decisions in the ordinary transaction of business are made by the Councillor competent in the matter and then placed before the Council for usual ratification. Thus, as a member of a collegiate body, since the Federal Council governs collectively, he shares responsibility to the

12. Article 103.
13. Article 100.
14. Articles 4, 6 and 7 of the Law of 1914.
15. Hughes, C., *The Federal Constitution of Switzerland*, p. 116.

public for the Council's actions. "The subordination of the individual member to the will of the government", remarks Erich Gruner, "may go so far that he is forced to advocate publicly solutions to controversial problems which he rejects personally."[16]

**The President**

The officer, whose constitutional title is the "President of the Confederation", is one of the seven Councillors and is chosen, as also the Vice-President, by the Federal Assembly from among the members of the Federal Council for a term of one year. Swiss democracy insists upon the principle of rotation and the Constitution expressly provides that the retiring President cannot be elected either as President or as Vice-President for the following year, and the same member cannot be Vice-President for two consecutive years. Usage, however, requires that the Vice-President succeeds the President and the two offices rotate among the members of the Federal Council according to seniority. New Federal Councillors serve beneath all their seniors before filling the Presidency and those who have filled the office go to the bottom of the list. It means that a Councillor can become a President for more than one term though not consecutively. M. Guiseppe Motta was five times President, Herr Muller was president in 1899, 1907 and 1913, and Dr. Phillipe Etter in 1939, 1942, 1947 and 1953. Dr. Max Petipierre had three terms.

Although the President of the Confederation holds an office of some dignity and enjoys some precedence over his colleagues, yet his precedence over the rest is merely a formal precedence. He is in no sense the chief executive. He is not even *primus inter pares*, as he becomes one like others after the expiry of a year. Nor is he the chief administrator as he has no more power than his colleagues and is no more responsible than other Councillors are for the governance of the country. All decisions emanate from the Federal Council as a single authority. The President is simply a Chairman of the Federal Council and presides over its meetings. As Chairman only, he exercises a casting vote and that, too, in case of a tie. Such official authority as he may exercise comes to him as a member of the Council and as head of one of the seven administrative departments. He gets a salary equal to each of his other colleagues,[17] except an additional allowance of 5,000 francs for meeting entertainment costs for the year of his office. Switzerland has no palatial Government House for its President and he is not even provided with an official car. There is no grandeur and as the Presidency confers a more or less nominal honour, Swiss citizens are apt to foreget who their President is "just now" although they are likely to know by name the majority of the members of the Federal Council.

If such are the powers and authority of the Swiss President, then, it is generally asked where is the need for such an office? The answer is simple. There are certain durties, such as receiving potentates and ministers of other countries, which are impossible for seven men to perform simultaneously. Besides, there are some ceremonial national duties which must necessarily be performed by some one. The functions of the President are laid down in the Law on the Organization of Federal Administration of 1914 and it gives him certain very limited emergency powers, general supervisory powers, and the responsibility for the Federal Chancellery. It, also, states that "the President represents the Confederation at home and abroad." Formerly, by virtue of the system known as the 'Presidential Department' the President of the Confederation was also head of the Foreign Office. But as the President changed annually the Foreign Department also circulated among the members of the Federal Council. The result was that there was no continuity of direction in the management of a branch of public business, which perhaps, more than any other, requires permanence. Under the influence of Councillor Numar Droz the experiment of disassociating the Presidency from the Foreign Department was tried during the years 1887-94. It was again tried in 1915-17, and was permanently adopted in 1920. At present, a Federal Councillor may well remain in the Department to which he was first appointed until he retires, may it be a Foreign Department or any other Department.

**Functions of the Federal Council**

Article 95 of the Constitution designates the Federal Council as "the supreme executive and governing authority of the confederation." As the supreme Executive of Switzerland, the Federal Council is entrusted with most of the

16. Gruner, Erich, *Modern Switzerland,* p. 342.
17. Those who are above 55 years of age are entitled to, after 10 years in office, a pension which varies between forty and sixty per cent of salary, according to their tenure of office.

duties that its counterparts have in other countries. In Switzerland, however, much of the responsibility is shared with other organs of Government. Article 102 contains a long list of the principal functions and duties of the Federal Council:

1. It conducts the affairs of the Confederation in accordance with federal laws and decrees.

2. The Federal Council must ensure due observance of the Constitution, the laws and decrees of the Confederation, and Federal Treaties. For the observance of international treaties, the Federal Government does not appoint its own officers. They are, as a rule, executed by the Cantonal authorities. The Federal Council is empowered to intervene and take necessary action, either on its own initiative or in response to an appeal against a grievance, if Cantonal Governments do not co-operate in the proper execution of federal laws, decrees and international treaties, unless the appeal is of the type which should go to the Federal Tribunal as provided in Article 113. In the classes of cases reserved for the Federal Tribunal, the Federal Council is entitled to take measures on its own initiative to secure the observance of the Constitution, "both to prevent the unlawful action and perhaps to remedy it, but without prejudice to an eventual appeal to the Tribunal."[18]

The Federal Council has exercised this authority with great tact and discretion by permitting elasticity in interpretation. Even where there is a sufficient cause of trouble with a Canton, its methods of compulsion and use of force are more consistent with the Gandhian technique. The subsidies given to the Canton are withheld and troops are sent "who accomplish their mission without bloodshed; for they do not pillage, burn or kill, but peaceably quartered there at the expense of the Canton, and literally eat it into submission. This is certainly a novel way of enforcing obedience to the law, but with the frugal Swiss it is very effective."[19]

3. According to a constitutional provision the Cantons must have their Constitutions and alterations sanctioned ('guaranteed') by the Federal Assembly. That is to say, the Federal Assembly has to pass an arrete granting or refusing the guarantee. It is the duty of the Federal Council to supervise the 'guarantee' of Cantonal Constitutions. The guarantee is granted provided that the Cantonal Constitution contains nothing contrary to the provisions of the Federal Constitution; that the Cantonal institutions are representative or democratic, and that such political institutions have the consent of the people.

4. The Constitution empowers both the Houses of the Federal Assembly, to each member of either House, to each Canton and half-Canton and the Federal Council to initiate legislation. In practice, however, it is the Federal Council which really initiates major portion of the legislation to be enacted. Whenever the Federal Council feels that some new legislative measure is expedient to be enacted or the prevailing laws need some amendment for the proper and efficient conduct of government's business or when it feels that the popular demand for a new law widely exists, it drafts the desired measure, with the help of its expert staff, and submits it to the Federal Assembly. When a proposal originates at the instance of a member, the Federal Assembly passes a resolution requesting the Federal Council "to address itself to the subject and prepare a bill." It also frequently advises either House of the Assembly or a Canton whenever asked to give advice on the form or substance of a measure. The Federal Assembly receives the recommendations of the Federal Council accompanying the draft bill with respect and hesitates to enact it when the report of the Federal Council is unfavourable. The Federal Council, thus, really initiates legislation and the Federal Assembly only amends it and that, too, when deemed necessary.

The legislative responsibilities of the Federal Council do not end here. As a general rule, a Councillor is assigned to guide the bill all the way through the legislative process. The bill is examined in the Committee in his presence and he gives his advice and comments. When it goes to either House of the Federal Assembly, the Councillor is there to introduce the bill, to explain its objects and purposes, and to defend it if necessary and in general acts "as its shepherd before the legislative wolves."[20] The result is, in the words of Professor Rappard, "one is forced to admit that the most responsible and influential work is that not of the so-called legislature, but of the executive."[21]

5. Deputies of both the Houses of the Fed-

18. Hughes, C., The *Federal Government of Switzerland,* p. 112.
19. Lowell, A. L. , *Government and Parties in Continental Europe,* Vol. II, p. 197.
20. Codding, G. A., *The Federal Government of Switzerland,* p. 93.
21. Rappard, W. E., *The Government of Switzerland,* p.84.

eral Assembly are given the right of interpellation. It is the duty of a member of the Federal Council to reply either immediately or at a later session. After the reply has been made, the Deputy, who initiated the interpellation, is given the opportunity to declare whether he was satisfied or not with the reply. If he is not satisfied, he can have recourse to motion or postulate. If the motion passes, the Council need not resign. Since 1946, the National Council has also made use of the "question hour". A deputy may question members of the Federal Council on any subject concerning the Federal administration.

6. As a result of the growing legislation and increasingly complex nature of governmental activities the Federal Assembly delegates to the Federal Council a great deal of discretion in the administration of Federal laws. The Federal Council issues rules and regulations thereunder which have the force of laws. Such rules and regulations are subject to the legislative referendum. There has been a steady increase in the power of issuing ordinances even in normal times. In times of emergency, the ordinance legislative power practically replaces normal legislation. It has become a custom at such times for the Federal Assembly to grant the Federal Council "full powers" to issue any ordinance it sees fit for the protection of Switzerland's neutrality and economic stability. In 1914 and 1939 the Federal Assembly conferred powers on the Federal Council which even permitted it to deviate from the Constitution.

7. The Federal Council examines the laws and ordinances of the Cantons that are required to be submitted for its approval. It also supervises the branches of Cantonal administration where such supervision is incumbent upon it.

8. It looks into the execution of judgments of the Federal Tribunal and of agreements and arbitration awards upon disputes between Cantons. The execution of the decisions of the courts and of many provisions of the Constitution, and of much federal legislation is left to the Cantons. If the Cantons fail to carry out these obligations, then, in the last resort the appeal is made to the Federal Council.

9. All federal appointments, except those entrusted to the Federal Assembly, the Federal Tribunal or any other authority, are made by the Federal Council. The Federal Council in practice delegates its right of appointment in very many cases to the various branches of administration and other independent authorities.

10. The Constitution debars Cantons from concluding among themselves separate alliances and all treaties of a political nature.[22] The Cantons may, however, conclude agreements among themselves concerning matters of legislation, justice and administration, provided such agreements are brought to the notice of the federal authority, which is entitled to prevent the execution of the agreements if they contain anything contrary to the Confederation or to the rights of other Cantons.[23] The Cantons also retain the right to conclude treaties with foreign States concerning matters of public economy, neighbourly relations and police provided such treaties contain nothing contrary to the Confederation or to the rights of other Cantons.[24]

The Constitution empowers the Federal Council to examine the agreements of the Cantons among themselves and with foreign States and sanction them if they are in accordance with the Constitution and the law otherwise the Federal Council can appeal to the Federal Assembly for annulling the same. All official intercourse between the foreign governments or their representatives takes place through the agency of the Federal Council.[25]

11. The Federal Council conducts the foreign relations of Switzerland, safeguards the extenal interests of the Confederation, ensures the external safety of the country, and maintenance of her independence and her neutrality. The Federal Council also negotiates treaties and ratifies them after approval of the Federal Assembly. It is incharge of external affairs generally.

12. It looks after the internal security of the Confederation, and the maintenance of peace and order. Actually, the maintenance of internal peace and order is the concern of the Cantonal governments. If internal order breaks down, then only federal intervention takes place. The Federal Assembly determines the measures to be taken[26] and the Federal Council looks after their implementation. What is presumably meant is that the Federal Council asks for an arrete, which the

22. Article 7(1).
23. Article 7(2).
24. Article 9.
25. Article 10(1).
26. Article 13(2).

Federal Assembly passes and the Federal Council carries out.

13. In the case of emergency, when the Federal Assembly is not in session, the Federal Council is empowered to call out troops and employ them as it may think fit. But it must convene a session of the Federal Assembly immediately, if the number of troops called out exceeds two thousand men or if they remain mobilised for more than three weeks.

14. The Federal Council is entrusted with the charge of the military affairs of the Confederation and of all branches of the federal administration. Article 13 of the Constitution provides that the Confederation may not maintain standing army. But Cantons can maintain a standing armed force, with the consent of the federal authorities, of not more than 300 men, not including police forces.[27] But the Confederation has the right to dispose of the army (consisting of troops of the Cantons and all Swiss who are subject to military service) as well as of the war materials provided for it and in time of danger, the Confederation has also the right to dispose directly and exclusively of all men not incorporated into the federal army as well as of all other military resources of the Cantons.''[28]

15. It examines the laws and decrees of the Cantons which require its approval and supervises such branches of Cantonal administration as are placed under its control. For instance, the organisation, management and supervision of primary education is a Cantonal concern, but such education must be compulsory and, in public schools, free of charge. Adherents of all religions and beliefs can attend public schools without being affected in any way in their freedom of creed. Article 27 of the Constitution authorises federal authorities to take appropriate measures against Cantons which fail to meet these requirements. Article 31 guarantees the freedom of trade and industry through the territory of the Confederation. But Cantonal regulations concerning the exercise of trade and industry and the taxes on such activities remain unaffected. However, such regulations shall not depart from the principle of freedom of trade and industry where the Federal Constitution provides otherwise.

16. It administers the Federal finances and prepares the budget and submits accounts of federal receipts and expenditure.

17. The Federal Council supervises the official conduct of all officers and employees of the Federal administration.

18. The Federal Council gives an account of its work to the Federal Assembly in each ordinary session, presents to it a report on the internal conditions in the country and foreign relations of the Confederation, and recommends for its consideration such measures which it thinks useful for promoting the general welfare. It also submits special reports when the Federal Assembly or either of its House demands.

19. Finally, the Federal Council has some powers of a judicial nature. It hears appeals of private individuals against decisions of the various Departments and against decision of the Federal Railway Administration. It has also appellate jurisdiction over decisions of the Cantonal governments in cases relating to discrimination in elementary schools, differences arising out of treaties relating to trade, patents, military taxation, question about occupation and settlement, consumption taxes, customs, Cantonal elections, gratuitous equipment of the militia.

**Executive Subordination to the Legislature**

The powers of the Federal Council are enormous. But in terms of law it is the servant of the Federal Assembly. This is essentially due to the theory of the Swiss Constitution that the executive is not an independent or co-ordinate branch of government. The Federal Assembly elects the Federal Councillors and their term of office coincides with that of the National Council. When the National Council is dissolved for total revision of the Constitution under Article 120, the Federal Council must also be re-elected for the remainder of the legislative period. The President and the Vice-President are also the nominees of the Assembly.

The functions of the Federal Council are only supervisory. The policy emanates originally and finally from the Federal Assembly. Article 71 of the Constitution contains the statement that the Assembly exercises the ''supreme power of the Confederation.'' And it is really so. The Federal Council has no initiative of its own, and when it exercises the prerogatives relating to foreign affairs, to the armed forces, or to the ordinary conduct of public administration there must be either previous authority of the Federal Assembly for all those acts or subsequent ratification. The Federal Assembly's practice of grant-

27. Article 19.
28. Article 20.

ing full powers in an emergency to the Federal Council definitely suggests that the Assembly can claim back the powers it effectively delegates. The Assembly, moreover, frequently issues directions in the form of resolutions or motions indicating the manner in which the Council's functions shall be discharged. The Council is also required to submit annual report to the Assembly. The report is debated, department by department, and finally sanctioned. The Council may also be required to make special report when the Federal Assembly or one section thereof demands it. The Councillors are not members of the Federal Assembly and yet they attend all plenary legislative sessions, answer questions, give explanations and join in debates. If the Federal Assembly disagrees with them or reverses their decisions in legislative or executive matters, the Councillors do not accept it a political affront and resign. On the contrary, they submit to the will of the Federal Assembly as the final authority and try loyally to carry out its directions. The Council, as Prof Dicey puts it, "is expected to carry out and does carry out, the policy of the Assembly, and ultimately the policy of the nation, just as a good man of business, is expected to carry out the order of his employer."[29] Lowell expresses the same idea a little more cogently. It is, he says, "a general maxim of public life in Switzerland that an official gives his advice, but like a lawyer or an architect, he does not feel obliged to throw up his position because his advice is not followed." He may not resign even when the personal policy of a Councillor has been rejected by the people. The resignation of Herr Welti, who resigned in 1891, when his railway nationalisation policy having been accepted by the Assembly was afterwards rejected by the people at the referendum, was declared as "unconstitutional."[30]

### Not a Parliamentary Type of Government

It follows, then, that the Swiss Federal Council is not a parliamentary cabinet. In reality it is highly misleading to name the Council a Cabinet, as some do. The term Cabinet implies a degree of party solidarity which the Swiss body does not possess. Party solidarity necessitates political homogeneity as team work demands oneness of purpose and aim. The ministers, who make the Cabinet, are the real functionaries, they belong to the parliamentary majority party, and are chosen to carry out party pledges. They are responsible to the legislature, individually and collectively, for all their official acts and remain in office so long as they retain its confidence which, for all intents and purposes, means the confidence of the people who elected them in majority. The Swiss Council, no doubt, is elected by the Federal Assembly, but the Councillors are not required by the Constitution to be members of the Assembly, and if they are, as they generally are, before their nomination as Federal Councillors, they must resign their seats therefrom. They become Councillors not because they belong to the parliamentary majority party or are the leaders of the political parties, but in their capacity as administrators and in conformity with Swiss democratic sense that they represent all interests, people and territories. It is true that they appear in both the Houses of the Federal Assembly, take an active part in debates, answer to questions put to them by members and have the right to voice proposals concerning the subject-matter under discussion,[31] yet they do not profess or advocate a policy. They simply participate in the debates of both sections of the Federal Assembly in a consultative capacity and have the simple right to express opinion and voice proposals concerning the subject-matter under discussion. It is for the Assembly to pay any heed to such proposals or not, or even to reject them summarily. Nor do the Federal Councillors vote on matters for decision before the Assembly because they have no *locus standi* in the organisation and membership of either House of the Assembly.

The law, no doubt, demands that the Federal Council should hold regular meetings once a week, its deliberations should be in private and decisions reached by majority vote,[32] and the Constitution insists that decisions shall be under the name and by the authority of the Federal Council.[33] Nonetheless the Federal Council is not a homogeneous whole and differences of opinion among the Councillors are permitted and allowed to become known. They occasionally speak on opposite sides in the legislature, although it goes to the credit of Swiss democracy that such differ-

---

29. Dicey, A. V., *The Law of the Constitution,* p. 611. Also refer to Bryce, *Modern Democracies,* Vol. I, p.446.
30. Encyclopaedia Britannica, 11th ed., p. 211. After the First World War, the number of such resignations has increased. Ghose, R. C., *The Government of the Swiss Republic,* p. 92.
31. Article 101.
32. Article 4, 6, 7. Organisation of Federal Administration and Law, 1914.
33. Article 100.

ences rarely cause trouble. But this is not the way of Cabinet government. Differences of any kind are not permitted in the ministerial ranks.

The Constitution also permits the Federal Council to recommend to the Federal Assembly for its consideration such legislative measures and decrees as it may think useful for promoting general welfare.[34] It is also very common for the Assembly to pass a resolution and request the Federal Council to prepare a Bill on some subject, and in fact all measures not introduced by the Federal Council are, as a rule, referred to it before they are sent to a Committee or taken up for debate. In this way, the Council exerts a great influence in shaping the actual legislation. Still, it does not give to the Federal Council a legal legislative leadership. Its role remains only advisory and here lies the fundamental difference.

But the real difference between a cabinet and Swiss Federal Council hinges upon their relationship with the legislature. A cabinet is created by the legislature and it exists on its confidence. In Switzerland the relations between the two are based upon an entirely different principle. While the connection between the Federal Council and the Federal Assembly is quite close and in many aspects akin to what it is between the cabinet and the legislature under a parliamentary system of government, yet the Federal Council neither leads nor controls the Assembly. The Assembly is the master and it possesses the supreme power in the Confederation; the Federal Council is just its subordinate authority. The Constitution does not make the executive an independent or co-ordinate department of Government. The Federal Council is not responsible to the Assembly in the same way as a cabinet is to the legislature. Moreover, resignation of a Councillor is not likely to bring a crisis. The Federal Councillors must not resign collectively or individually when their measures are rejected or their policies reversed by the Assembly. They continue in office no matter what the Assembly does to their Bills or executive orders. This is so, because the Federal Councillors do not initiate or control the policy and they are not collectively pledged to pursue it. They have no policy of their own. Nor can the Federal Council possess the power to dissolve the Federal Assembly or one of its Houses. Herein lies the real secret of the Federal Council's position.

**Not even a Presidential System**

If the Swiss Federal Council is not akin to a parliamentary Cabinet, it is not even the presidential type of executive. There is, indeed, no semblance between the two. The Federal Council is not like the executive in the United States, a separate branch of government. The American Presidency is a single executive and the Constitution assigns to the President independent and exclusive powers with a policy of his own. The President is, in brief, both an executive and the executive. Congress cannot encroach upon his constitutional rights, nor can it limit his actions. The only contact between the executive and the legislature is through the Presidential messages, otherwise neither he nor the members of his 'Cabinet' have any access to either House of Congress. The Secretaries, who are the administrative heads of the different Departments of Government and are said to make the President's Cabinet, are appointed by him and they remain in office so long as he wishes them to continue. It is for the President to decide when and how to consult them. It is, again, for the President to determine whether to accept their advice or not. They are the advisers of the President and they really make his 'family'. The office of the President does not depend upon Congress. He is popularly elected for a term of four years and his office goes by calendar. In fact, the Swiss Confederation has no President as the Cantons have no Governors in the real sense of the terms. The collegial system is the traditional form of Government and the only one in use in Switzerland.

The Swiss Federal Council is not a separate branch of government with an independent policy of its own. It has been given no veto upon laws to prevent encroachment upon its rights. Nor is it completely divorced from the legislature. The connection between the Federal Council and the Assembly is close and intimate. In fact, the Federal Council is very often described as the "Executive Committee of the Swiss Parliament." Whatever it be, it remains a fact that the Federal Council is not an independent authority at all, for its administrative acts are supervised, controlled or reversed by the Federal Assembly, the supreme authority of the Confederation.

**Plural Executive**

To sum up, the Swiss Federal executive is neither Parliamentary nor Presidential. It is unique by itself inasmuch as that it is collegial body of seven members who serve as the coun-

34. Article 102, Section 4.

try's supreme executive and governing authority. The framers of the Constitution rejected the American precedent of a single elected exponent of the country's executive power. They were not unconscious of the advantages of unity and continuity of action inherent in an elected President, But, as they said: "The Committee entrusted with the task of framing the Constitution could not think of proposing the creation of an office so contrary to the ideas and habits of the Swiss people who might see therein evidence of a monarchical or dictatorial tendency. In Switzerland one attached to councils....Our democratic feeling revolts against any exclusive personal preeminence."[35]

The Constitution in 1848, accordingly, entrusted the supreme directing and executive power in the Confederation to a Federal Council consisting of seven members, and the relevant provisions are still in force today. Having created a collegial executive, it was made to include the important features of both the parliamentary and presidential systems of government. The Swiss executive is the mixture of the two and the architects of the Constitution were original in giving to their country an absolutely new mechanism of government which combined the merits and excluded the defects of both the parliamentary and presidential systems. James Bryce correctly remarked that the Federal Council is not Cabinet like that of Britain and the countries which have initiated her Cabinet system, "for it does not lead the legislature, and is not displaceable thereby. Neither is it independent of the legislature, like the executive of the United States and of other republics which have borrowed therefrom the so-called 'Presidential system,' and though it has some of the features of both these schemes, it differs from both in having no distinctly partisan character."

This is surely the unique feature of the Swiss Constitution. In no other modern republic is executive power entrusted to a council instead of to an individual, and in no other free country has the working executive so little to do with politics. The Swiss Federal Council, to quote Bryce again, "stands outside party, is not chosen to do party work, does not determine party policy, yet is not wholly without some party colour." The practice now accepted and followed, since the election of 1959, is that the composition of the Federal Council should reflect as far as possible the strength of all the major political parties in order to ensure executive leadership and highly efficient government.

### Advantages of the Collegial Executive

The constitutional position and the work of the collegiate executive are really admirable, for it has some of the chief merits of the Cabinet system without the disadvantages. In Switzerland there is the same mutual confidence and co-operation between the legislature and the executive as it is obtainable under the Parliamentary system of government. But a Cabinet should advantageously belong to one single majority party in the legislature or to a combination of two or more parties who agree to work out a common political programme. The Swiss Federal Council, on the other hand, is representative of all the opinions and areas in the country, and still it is pledged to no political programme. Such a representative executive does not leave an opportunity for the opposition to grow and exist. When all the interests and opinions are given their due share of influence in the conduct of public affairs, it really means a democracy; a government of all by all and for all—a real government by consent. Then, the Federal Council is a reputed non-partisan body and its role is not only to advise and influence the Federal Assembly, but also to mediate, "should need arise, between contending parties, adjusting difficulties and arranging compromises in a spirit of conciliation."[36] This is not difficult in Switzerland because public opinion expects of every Swiss to subordinate his own feelings to the public good and, as such personal ambition in Switzerland has played smaller part than in any other free country. Lowell, accordingly, says that the Federal Council "may almost be regarded as a mainspring and is certainly the balance-wheel of the national government."[37]

Another advantage of the Swiss collegiate executive is its permanence and stability. As it is not dependent on the vote of the legislature for its life, the executive is stable, more or less permanent and certain to follow a coherent and consistent administrative policy. Moreover, the Swiss system enables proved administrative talent to be kept in the service of the nation, no matter what personal opinion they may hold on particular issues. Such a homogeneity in diversity, stability and continuity are inconceivable under a Parliamentary system of government.

35. As quoted in R. C. Brooks, *The Government of Switzerland,* p. 76.
36. Bryce, J., *Modern Democracies,* Vol. I, p. 398.
37. Lowell, A. L., *Government and Parties in Continental Europe,* Vol. I, p. 398.

Bryce has cogently said, "It (the Federal Council) provides a body which is able not only to influence and advise the ruling Assembly without lessening its responsibility to the citizens, but which, because it is non-partisan, can mediate, should need arise, between contending parties, adjusting difficulties and arranging compromises in a spirit of conciliation. It enables proved administrative talent to be kept in the service of the nation, irrespective of the personal opinions of the councillors upon the particular issues which may for the moment divide parties....It secures continuity in policy and permits traditions to be formed."

Finally, the Swiss system secures continuity in policy and permits traditions to be formed. When the members are appointed singly and at considerable intervals, it lifts the body above the transient impulses that stir in the people. There are no partisan commotions and flaring up of emotions. Both of these are really invaluable traditions in the life of a democratic nation and such traditions cement continuity in policy. It is often contended that continuity and traditions have the tendency to make administration "groovy", but this is hardly a danger in Switzerland where every citizen is imbued with a public spirit and where Councillors are always accessible, and in constant touch with the Assembly.

**Growth in Its Powers**

According to law the Federal Council is the Servant of the Federal Assembly, but in reality it is exactly not so. The Federal Council, observes James Bryce, "exerts in practice almost as much authority as do English, and more than do some French Cabinets so that it may be said to lead as well as follow."[38] A lengthy tenure of office adds to the Councillor's official prestige, administrative skill and political judgment. The mere fact that the Federal Assembly transfers to the Council most of the legislative initiative and very often seeks its advice on all measures offer to the Councillors vast opportunities to determine the tenor and direction of public policy.[39] The nature of modern legislation, which requires considerable technical knowledge, has further helped to transfer the legislative initiative into the hands of an expert body like the Federal Council.

With the help of its expert staff the Federal Council drafts bills and presents to the Federal Assembly, along with a well- reasoned report presenting the purpose of the proposed legislation and giving the reasons why it should not be enacted. Even in the case where the Federal Council drafts bills on the direction of the Assembly, it usually does not enact the draft law when the Council's report is unfavourable. Moreover, the Council enjoys the delegation of legislative powers and the rules and regulations framed thereunder are as valid as the law itself. Emergency powers of the Council are as significant as its ordinance making power. One of the most sweeping grant of power to any democratic executive whose country was not actually engaged in war was given in 1939 to the Federal Council.[40] It was passed in the form of an urgent federal arrete, not subject to the legislative referendum, only one day after the Federal Council made the request. The powers given to the Council by the Assembly went very far to suspending the Constitution altogether, made the government almost the sole legislature and did much to check the interplay of democratic institutions, specially of the referendum.

A steady growth in the powers of the Federal Council had been the course of Swiss constitutional history. Since the introduction of proportional representation, the Federal Assembly has ceased to be dominated by one or two political parties. It is increasingly turning out to be an arena of political higgling and haggling between a large number of parties with the consequent result that the Assembly does not today enjoy its past prestige and power. The Assembly's loss is the Federal Council's gain. Moreover, in the process of centralisation in Switzerland the authority of all the central institutions has considerably extended, but by comparison with the Federal Assembly the Federal Council has become more powerful and independent.

The contemporary tendency all the world over for strengthening the executive power has also helped to disturb the Swiss balance of power. Practically irremovable, and difficult to control by reason of the great technical complexity of its tasks, the Federal Council has, according to Andre Seigfried "gradually come to wield a quasi-absolute power". The two World Wars and the economic depression of 1930, were the most important of all the causes which have contrib-

38. Bryce, J., *Modern Democracies,* Vol. I, p. 397.
39. Refer to W. E. Rappard, *The Federal Government of Switzerland,,* pp. 82-85.
40. Codding, G.A. *The Federal Government of Switzerland,* p. 95.

uted to the growth of the powers of the Federal Council. In their efforts to maintain Switzerland's traditional neutrality and to protect the country's economy during and after the Wars, the Federal Assembly delegated "blanket" authority over matters, hitherto regulated directly by statute, to the Federal Council. In pursuance of these powers, the Council issued ordinances vitally affecting personal liberties and properties of the people. It also issued decrees relating to private law in the name of public security or necessity. The power of issuing ordinances, though it is a normal feature in the Continental countries, was hitherto unknown in Switzerland. Adopted as a measure of national expediency or exigency, it came to stay in Switzerland and has now assumed a normal character of the Federal Council's executive authority. Is this new development nct antagonistic to the traditional Swiss principle of legislative supremacy? The system of direct democracy, has probably given the most fatal blow to the supreme power of the Assembly. On many occasions legislative measures passed by the Assembly by a heavy majority have been rejected by the people. Even with regard to ordinary legislation the Federal Council in the words of Bryce, "is a guide as well as an instrument, and often suggests as well as drafts measures." When the supreme authority receives suggestions and accepts them, and allows the same suggesting authority to draft the legislative measure, it really does not remain supreme, though legally it may continue to be so.

## THE FEDERAL ADMINISTRATION

### Administrative Departments

The Federal administration is divided into seven Departments each headed by a Federal Councillor. By virtue of the law on the organization of Federal Administration of 1914, the Departments are: (1) The Political Department; (2) Department of the Interior; (3) Department of Justice and Police; (4) Military Department; (5) Department of Finance and Customs; (6) Public Economy; and (7) Traffic and Power. The Departments are allocated by the Federal Council itself among its members. Every Federal Councillor is also Deputy for another Department.

The functions assigned to Departments are constantly changing and the Law of 1914 is not a convenient document for determining the jurisdiction of each Department. Moreover, Article 23 of the 1914 Law gives the Federal Council power to determine what subject matters are to be delegated to the Departments "to deal with on their own, and provides for appeals to the Federal Council itself against such departmental decisions in certain circumstances."[41]

The Political Department embraces some political responsibilities, but it is essentially a foreign office and deals with foreign relations of the Confederation. Before 1914, this Department was known as the Presidential Department and it always went to the President of the Confederation. But this required an annual change, with the change of President and, accordingly, there was no continuity or direction which is so essential in the conduct of foreign affairs. Now the Political Department goes to one of the Councillors and it continues under him so long as he remains a member of the Federal Council, no matter whether he happens at the same time to be the President of the Confederation or not. Ernst Noles, the President for 1949, held charge of the Department of Finance and Customs while Dr. Max Petitpierre was in charge of the Political Department from 1945 to 1951 and continued to hold the same for another four-year term after his re-election. Since neutrality is an essential condition of Switzerland's domestic peace, the task of the Political Department is really arduous. The choice of the people in selecting a person who should shoulder this responsibility has been remarkable and it has fallen on such men as Ador (1917). Mota (1920-40), and Petitpierre.

"Neutrality has no value," writes Andre Seigfried, "unless the independence it represents is defended by force of arms." Neutrality, thus, includes the defence of Switzerland's own independence by force of arms, if necessary, and the Swiss guard themselves with vigilance and suspicion against any possible aggression from her neighbours. Military Department is, accordingly, the next most important. The Confederation is not authorised to maintain a standing army,[42] and standing army here means a mercenary army.[43] The Swiss army consists of conscripts, very small cadre of regular officers, and some maintenance troops. All Swiss youngmen of an adequate physical standard must do military service, except certain officials while in office and the clergy

41. Hughes, C., *The Federal Constitution of Switzerland,* p. 117.
42. Article 13.
43. Hughes, C., *The Federal Constitution of Switzerland,* p. 147.

of recognised denominations. Cantons are also permitted to maintain military contingents. The Federal Government exercises control over federal army, war material, organisation of the army and military education.

The functions of the Interior Department are miscellaneous and more or less similar to its counterpart in the United States. It is assigned the function of carrying out the Federal Government's policies with regard to education, public works, conservation, and public health. Of the remaining Departments, the Departments of Posts and Railways and Public Economy require a little consideration. The Confederation owns and manages the postal, telephonic, telegraphic, wireless and railway system. The Railways Administration is a separate entity though it functions under the control of the Department of Posts and Railways. It enjoys a considerable degree of autonomy and, *inter alia,* has a separate budget. The Department of Public Economy is concerned with industry, agriculture, and social insurance. It helps in the exploitation of natural resources and devises measures for accelerating Switzerland's productivity.

### The Civil Service

The personnel of the Swiss Civil Service is not numerous as in other countries in spite of the increase in the Federal Government's activities and a general tendency towards centralization. This is primarily due to the fact that the Federal authorities do not maintain their officers in the Cantons. All federal measures are put into execution by the local authorities. Apart from the employees of the post office, the railways and certain exceptional branches of administration there are no federal officials.

The two World Wars, however, have considerably added to the number of the civil servants. The magnitude of the increase can be examined from these figures. In 1939, the total number of the civil servants was 10,842 and in 1945 it increased to 29,630. After the War some reduction was brought about and the next year the number fell to 26,131. A further reduction by 8,000 was effected in the following years. In 1959 the central administration employed only about 17,554. Nonetheless, extension in the powers of the Federal Government is generally deemed in Switzerland as an encroachment on the autonomy of the Cantons. The growth of bureaucracy and the creation of bureaucratic mentality in administration "must tend in the long run," remarks Andre Seigfried, "to compromise the spirit of a regime which is founded on cantonal autonomy and popular delegation, that is to say, a regime which is founded on confidence in men rather than on administrative mechanism from which the human element tends to be more and more excluded."

The Federal civil servants, except a very few of the most important which lie in the gift of the National Assembly, and others appointed by the Federal Tribunal or other Federal authorities as the Federal Railway Administration, are appointed by the Federal Council and are dismissed by it for any dereliction of duty. Appointments to the higher posts are made usually for a term of four years subject to reappointment, which is just a mere formality. These appointments may, therefore, be described as permanent. There is nothing resembling the American Spoils System in Switzerland. Very rarely is any one dismissed for political reasons; nor do such reasons play great part in appointments. Moreover, meagreness of salaries does not make jobs worth struggling for in Switzerland, and public opinion, too, would reprehend any attempt to appoint incompetent men for party reasons. The retirement age is sixty-five years.

### The Federal Chancellory

The Federal Chancellory at the head of which is the Chancellor of the Confederation, is responsible for the secretarial business of the Federal Assembly and of the Federal Council.[44] The Chancellory is under the superintendence of the President of the Confederation, and the ultimate superintendence of the Federal Assembly. The Chancellor is elected by the Assembly in a joint session[45] for four years, but in practice he continues in office until he retires. The election has fairly political flavour, and regard is paid to the alterations of languages and confessions. The Vice-Chancellors are appointed by the Federal Council, and "one of them usually acquires a sort of moral claim to the office of Chancellor before the place falls vacant."[46]

The personality of the Chancellor is not important, for his duties are chiefly formal and mechanical. The office, however, is of consider-

44. Article 105.
45. Articles 92 and 85, Section 4.
46. Hughes. C., *The Federal Constitution of Switzerland,* p. 109.

able dignity and confers upon its holder a sort of honorary headship of the Federal Civil Services. "There is no British equivalent—but the functions have a faint similarity with those of the clerk of the County Council, while the prestige is not entirely unlike that of the Speaker of the House of Commons. His duties include:

(i) The clerkship of the Federal Council; and

(ii) The office of clerk-at-the-table of the two Houses and of the Federal Assembly in a joint session; his Deputy acts for him in the other House. His functions, as such, include the supervision of the shorthand, and the translation, and what we should call the office of the Sergeant-At-Arms;

(iii) The supervision of the publication of the legal acts of the Federal Assembly and the Federal Council;

(iv) The counter-signing of Federal Acts, and the organization of federal elections and initiative and referendum votes;

(v) Certain duties regarding organisation and methods of federal administration.

**Merits of the Swiss Administration**

Bryce points out two prominent merits of Swiss Government and administration in general. One is the cheapness of administration. Finances are carefully managed and current normal administrative expenses are kept appreciably down. It is true that the two World Wars meant a mounting expenditure beyond the financial capacity of Switzerland, but the people being thrifty and inquisitive, who apply to "public expenditure a vigorous standard such as that regulates a peasant household," their economy is relatively stable and the country has not to face serious financial embarrassments.

Purity, according to Bryce, is the second prominent feature of the Swiss administration. The Federal and Cantonal Governments are practically free from corruption and public scandals are rare, but when they occur "the guilty person however strong his position had been, must quit public life forthwith."

To this may be added the third, an efficient government. Professor G.J. Friedrich, an eminent student of Public Administration, goes so far as to say of Switzerland: "Except to the extent to which she was helped by the example of France and Germany, she is full proof of the contention that democracy is able to do a better job, in fact, than of other system. For there can be little question that upon close scrutiny by unbiased investigator the Swiss appear to have a more effective responsive officialdom than any other country except Sweden (and Sweden also is very democratically governed)."

# CHAPTER V

# The Frame of National Government—The Federal Assembly

## A Bicameral Legislature

The Federal Legislature, known as the Federal Assembly, is bicameral. Its two chambers are: Counsil des Etates, the Council of States, and Counsil National, or the National Council. The Swiss Parliament is supreme and the Constitution expressly states: "subject to the rights of the people and of the Cantons....The supreme power of the Confederation shall be exercised by the Federal Assembly."[1] The Assembly passes the law which may neither be vetoed by the President of the Confederation nor declared unconstitutional by any Swiss court. The supremacy of the Federal Assembly further means that other organs of Government are not coordinate and independent, but are subordinate to it, subject to the provisions of the Constitution. It not only legislates in legislative as well as constitutional matters, but it also chooses the members of the Executive—the Federal Council and elects the Judiciary as well as the Chancellor, who is the permanent head of the civil service. The directions of the Assembly are final and not subject to appeal. To put all this in the words of Rappard, the Federal Assembly is supreme "as long as it retains the confidence and performs the will of the electorate."[2] The electorate has the right to veto all the unpopular Bills by defeating them at a referendum and it has been done so often. "The Swiss voter," remarks Bryce, "always independent, is most independent when he had to review the action of his legislature."[3] There is, thus, no possibility in Switzerland of legislative tyranny, or tyranny of a parliamentary majority and this was fully demonstrated in 1884 in connection with the four laws, called at that time, "the four-humped camel" and characterised as "the high handed behaviour of the ruling majority of the Assembly." All these laws were rejected at a referendum.

## THE COUNCIL OF STATES

### Composition and Organisation

The Council of States represents the component units of the Confederation on the basis of equality and corresponds to the American Senate. Every Canton, no matter what its size or population, is entitled to two representatives, and every half-Canton one representative.[4] The total membership of the Council of States is, thus, 46—representing 23 Cantons, three divided into half Cantons.

Each Canton determines by its own laws the mode of election of the Deputies, the length of their terms of office, and the allowances paid to them. In certain Cantons Deputies are elected indirectly by their legislatures while in some others they are elected directly. In the Landsgemeinde Cantons they are elected by the Landsgemeinde. There is, accordingly, no uniform method of election, or a similar tenure of office or an equal fixed salary. The terms of office vary all the way from one to four years; three years being the most common. In St. Gallen it is one year. In two Cantons the Deputies may be recalled by the Cantonal legislatures before the expiration of their term.

The only restrictions on elections to the Council of States are contained in Articles 6, 81, and 108 of the Constitution. According to Article 6 all Cantonal elections must be democratic. Article 81 provides that members of the National Council and the Federal Council must not be at the same time members of the Council of States. Article 108 makes membership in the Council of States incompatible with membership on the Federal Tribunal.

The membership of the Council of States is usually quite stable as most Deputies are

1. Article 71.
2. Rappard, W. E., *The Government of Switzerland*, p. 56.
3. Bryce, J., *Modern Democracies*, Vol. I, p. 436.
4. Article 80.

reelected for as long as they wish to serve. The calibre of the Deputies is pretty high and they command sufficient experience in national and Cantonal public affairs. Only those who have proved their worth in Cantonal affairs are likely to be selected and quite often they are drawn from the Cantonal Executive Councils or their legislatures.

The Council of States must meet once a year in ordinary session on a day fixed by standing orders. Provision is made in the Constitution for the calling of special session either by the Federal Council, or on the request of one-quarter of the members of the National Council or of five Cantons.[5] The Council of States elects its own Chairman and Vice-Chairman for each ordinary and extra-ordinary session. But the Constitution provides that the Chairman or Vice-Chairman may not be chosen from the Deputies of the same Canton whose representative was Chairman during the ordinary session immediately preceding.[6] The effect of this constitutional provision is that the office circulates among Cantons.[7] The Chairman presides over the meetings of the House and is largely responsible for the determination of the daily order of business to be transacted. He votes in case of a tie, but in the elections of the members of the Federal Council, its President and Vice-President, Judges of the Federal Tribunal, the members of the Federal Insurance Court and the Commander-in-Chief the Chairman votes in the same manner as other members of the Council of States.

The attendance of an absolute majority of the total number of the Deputies (46) is necessary for the valid transaction of business,[8] that is, 24 members, and all questions are decided by an absolute majority of those voting.[9] The Deputies vote without instructions from their Cantons,[10] and this constitutional provision implies that the members of the Council of States do not represent separate Cantonal interests and they cannot be armed with definite instructions as to how they should vote on particular issues. "The programme which the Article implies," observes Christopher Hughes, "is that members should vote from their consciences and not from instructions"[11] of either the Cantonal legislatures or of their parties or other associations.

### The Council of States, A Weaker Chamber

The Council of States possesses equal rights and powers with the National Council. All legislative measures may be introduced in either of the two Houses and must be approved by both the Houses to become laws. In case of disagreement and when second deliberation too has yielded no results, the differences are submitted to a Joint Conference Committee. If the Joint Conference Committee fails in its efforts to reach an agreement, the bill in question is dropped. Neither of the two Houses enjoys priority even in regard to financial matters. The framers of the Constitution had really attempted to make the Council of States a close second to the American Senate, and occupy the same position of precedence in the framework of the national government. But the Council has failed, for several reasons, to fulfil the expectations of its makers. Its history has, in fact, been almost the reverse of the American Senate. The latter was in the beginning inferior, both in influence and public esteem to the House of Representatives. It was only in the second generation of statesmen that the Senate assumed its present dominating role. The Swiss Council of States, on the other hand, began its career with high hopes and great reputation, but gradually it receded into the background and men of energy and ambition began preferring to sit in the National Council. The Swiss Council of States, unlike the Senate, is given no special functions and the tenure of office of the Deputies being not uniform and in some cases even subject to recall, it provided little attraction for promising youngmen who looked on it as only a stepping stone to the National Council. Nor does it provide an element of continuity from which traditions might flow. When both the Councils possess equal powers and identical functions, the one which represents the people and is elected for a fixed period is sure to attract statesmen of reputation and add to its prestige and stature. It becomes the pivot of political authority and the

5. Article 86.
6. Article 82.
7. The position of the half-Cantons is not clear.
8. Article 87. It means that 24 out of 46 Deputies must be present. It is the duty of the Chairman of the Council to ensure this if necessary by roll-call.
9. Article 88. An absolute majority in Switzerland means 'more than half', *i.e.,* of those voting, of those present, of the whole Council. Hughes, C., *The Federal Constitution of Switzerland,* p. 99.
10. Article 91.
11. Hughes, C., *The Federal Constitution of Switzerland,* p. 104.

centre of weighted power. It is not surprising, therefore, if the Council of States enjoys less authority and influence than the National Council.

But it does not mean that the Council of States commands a distinctly subordinate position like other Upper Chambers in countries having Parliamentary type of government. It enjoys equal powers, constitutional, legislative and financial, with the other Chamber. Laws may originate in either of the two and must pass through both the Councils and therefore the Councils must agree between themselves which shall have 'priority' in any particular business. Annual business, such as the budget, goes one year to one Council first, the next year to the other Council first. The Council of States is not a submissive body. It often disagrees with measures passed by the National Council and not only insists on the disagreement, of course a rare event in the Swiss political life, but it also persists which means dropping of the bill. The National Council has no veto over its powers, legislative and financial.

The Council of States has, thus, preserved its distinct entity. Its deliberations are, as might be expected from its smaller size, more dispassionate and more detailed than those of the National Council. In particular, the members of the official committees appointed by the Council of States take a pride in the thoroughness of their reports. Talent also flows in the Council of States. Most of them are highly educated. Almost half of the membership of the Council in 1960 had been recipients of doctorates. Moreover, of late years there has been a tendency to make the terms of office of the members of the Council of States uniform, four years as that in the case of the National Council. Yet, the National Council is ultimately the more powerful. The obvious reason, and an important one for the weakness of the Council of States is that the House gets through its business, because of its small membership—46 only—more rapidly than the National Council. The result is that "often having nothing to do, it has acquired an undeserved reputation for idleness."

## THE NATIONAL COUNCIL

### Composition and Organisation

The important and influential Chamber, then, is the National Council, a representative House of the Swiss people. The composition and organization of the National Council, unlike the Council of States, are regulated entirely by the Federal Constitution.[12] Since 1963, it has a fixed membership of 200. The Deputies are elected directly by secret ballot and since 1910 by proportional representation.[13] Every Swiss citizen, man or woman, who has completed his or her twentieth year and who has not been deprived of his or her political rights by the legislation of the Confederation or of the Canton where he or she is the resident has the right to participate in federal elections and other federal polls,[14] as the referendum. But the right to be eligible for membership of the National Council extends to lay Swiss citizens only. The Constitution excludes clergies from becoming members of the National Council.[15] Each Canton or half-Canton, as the case may be, forms an electoral constituency.[16] Prior to the 1962 Amendment, the National Council was composed of Deputies "chosen in the ratio of one member for each 24,000 souls of the total population." An additional seat was allotted for any fraction over 12,000. As a result of the 1962 Amendment this procedure is no longer necessary. Article 72 (2) now provides that the seats shall be distributed among the Cantons and the half-Cantons in proportion to their resident population, each Canton and half-Canton being entitled to one seat at least. Detailed provisions in this respect have been laid down by a federal law.

The National Council is elected for four years. It is not subject to dissolution, except for total revision of the Constitution when one House differs from the other.[17] Qualifications for membership are the same as required for voting. But all clergy, executive and principal administrative servants of the Confederation, members of the Council of States, and the Federal Councillors are especially excluded and are not eligible for election.

The House elects its own Chairman and Vice-Chairman for each ordinary or extraordinary session, neither being eligible for the same office in the next consecutive regular session. The word "session" is interpreted as meaning the annual session provided in Article 86. The Chairman of the National Council is, thus, elected for

12. Article 73.
13. Before 1919 elections were by a single member constituencies with a second election if an absolute majority was not obtained at the first.
14. Article 74. Manhood suffrage was introduced in Switzerland as early as 1848.
15. Article 75.
16. Article 73.
17. Article 120(2)

one year. And the system of compulsory rotation of office, consistent with the Swiss tradition, is designed to guard against concentration of power in one man. It is also intended that the office should not be concentrated in any one party or Canton or linguistic group. The Chairman does not have extensive powers. He has a casting vote which he exercises in case of a tie according to the established usages of the House. But when the House assembles for purposes of election of the Federal Council, the Federal Court, the Chancellor and the General of the Federal army the Chairman votes in the same way as other members.

**Sessions and Debates**

The National Council meets in regular sessions at the beginning of December and has generally four sittings.[18] The sessions are very short lasting only about three weeks apiece. The Federal Council may summon an extraordinary session should an emergency arise.[19] The House meets at 8 a.m. in summer and at 9 a.m., in winter, every day except Saturday and Sunday. Attendance is regular and punctural and a member absenting himself without strong reasons is deemed neglectful of his duty. The House devotes itself strictly to the dispatch of business and the normal Swiss Deputy shows just the qualities that are associated with the Swiss character. A Swiss Deputy is 'solid, shrewd, unemotional or at any rate indisposed to reveal his emotions. He takes a practical commonsense and what may be called middle-class view of questions.'' The Swiss Federal Assembly is, therefore, the most business-like body in the world doing its work quietly. The debates are orderly and there are few set speeches. Rhetoric is almost unknown and the usual cheers and cries of approval or dissent are rarely heard. Obstruction is unknown and divisions are much less frequent. ''The sessions of the National Council,'' writes Andre Siegfried, ''are more like meettings of an administrative body affecting only indirectly those who are not immediately concerned—but what an efficient administration!'' Deputies may speak in any of the four national languages and every public document is published in German, French and Italian, three official languages. There are no official stenographers and the debates are scantily reported even in the leading newspapers. Occasionally, the Council may order the verbatim reporting and publication of important discussions.

The Constitution provides that both the Councils conduct business only when an absolute majority of their respective members is present, that is, 101 in the case of the National Council. All decisions are made by a majority of those voting with the exception of the approval of ''urgent'' arretes (decrees) which require the approval of a majority of all the members. But if 50,000 Swiss citizens entitled to vote or eight Cantons request a popular vote, the decrees put immediately into effect shall lose their validity one year after their adoption by the Federal Assembly if they have not been approved by the people during that period; in that case they may not be renewed.[20]

**No Official Opposition**

The role of political parties in the Swiss legislature is far inferior to that prevailing in Britain and other democratic countries. This is due to two reasons. Firstly, the National Council cannot displace the Federal Councillors. Secondly, even in the legislative sphere, the supremacy of the Federal Assembly is qualified by the ultimate sovereign power of the people and they can at a referendum negative the decisions of the Federal Assembly. There is neither any Treasury Bench nor one for Opposition, since neither exists. The Federal Councillors are not members of the legislature, though they can appear in any House of the Federal Assembly. But it does not entitle them to vote. When business relating to a particular Department is considered by either of the Councils, the Federal Councillor who heads the Department concerned attends, answers questions, gives explanations and joins in its debates. All this, however, does not give to the Federal Councillor the position and influence of a minister as under the parliamentary government. The

18. Article 86 provides that both Councils meet at least once a year for an ordinary session on a day to be determined by their rules of procedure. ''The practice is to count all the sittings of the Assembly in one year as a single session adjourned.'' The date of assembling for the ordinary session is fixed by law. The law on the Relations between the Councils of 9th October, 1908 fixes the 1st Monday in December as the start of the first part of the ordinary session and the first Monday in June as the start of the second part. The Councils also regularly hold ordinary sittings in March and September.

19. Article 86 provides that both the Councils shall be convened for an extraordinary session by decision of the Federal Council or on request from one-quarter of the members of the National Council or from five Cantons. Once only in 1891 both the Councils were convened on demand of a quarter of the members of the National Council.

20. Article 80 bis (2).

Federal Councillors are assigned seats on a dias right and left of the Chairman of the House. And as they are not members of the House, they cannot be leaders of a parliamentary majority party, no matter what personal influence they otherwise may wield. When there is no ministerial party there can be no Opposition. The Swiss people do not exhibit hostility. Nor do they make regular campaigns of it. They view legislation by its practical utility, no matter whether their own party or others sponsor it. The proof of such an attitude can best be illustrated from the fact that Deputies belonging to the same party do not necessarily sit together. They usually sit by Cantons irrespective of their party labels.

### Joint Sittings

Both the Councils sit separately to transact their ordinary business, but they meet in a joint session for three definite purposes:—

(1) to elect the Federal Council, the Federal court, the Federal Insurance Tribunal, the President of the Federal Council as also the Vice President who are both President and Vice President of the Confederation, the President and Vice-President of the Federal Court and of the Federal Insurance Tribunal, the Chancellor of the Confederation and the Commander-in-Chief of the Army;

(2) to exercise the federal power of pardon,[21] and

(3) to resolve conflicts of jurisdiction between the major federal organs.

When the two Councils sit together, the Chairman of the National Council presides and decisions are reached by a majority of all the Deputies voting together.[22]

## LEGISLATIVE PROCEDURE

The Constitution gives the right to introduce legislation to both the Houses of the Federal Assembly—the Council of States and the National Council—to each member of both the Houses, to each Canton and half-Canton, and the Federal Council. In practice, it is the Federal Council which initiates as well as introduces major portion of the legislation. When the Federal Council feels that some new legislation is necessary or the prevailing laws need amendments, for the efficient and proper functioning of the government, or when it feels that there is a popular demand for a new law, it proceeds on its own initiative to draft a Bill with the help of its expert staff. The draft-laws, together with the Federal Council's report suggesting its own views on the proposed legislation, are submitted to the two Houses o f Assembly for their consideration.

It the Federal Assembly itself or members of either House decide upon the need of some legislation, it requests the Federal Council to act through procedures known as the "motion" and the "postulate". A motion is a command of the Assembly to the Federal Council to act and such a command must be the result of the agreement of both the Houses. The postulate is of lesser gravity, but leads towards the same objective. Instead of "commanding" the Federal Council to submit a draft law, a postulate merely "invites" the Federal Council to act. It may originate in any of the two Houses and does not require the agreement of both. Immediately on receipt of the "motion" or "postulate" the Federal Council proceeds to draft the Bill on the lines proposed and presents the same with its report to the Federal Assembly. The Federal Council may also recommend in its report rejection of the proposed legislation. The Federal Council usually gives utmost consideration to motions and postulates, but it does not mean that it must necessarily comply with them as directed. "Motions are deemed to lapse when the signatories cease to be members of the Council, or if the motion is not discussed at all within two years, or is not answered by the Federal Council within four years.[23] Postulates have even shorter life span if not taken up by the Federal Council.[24]

Since both Houses of the Assembly have coequal powers and neither is superior to the other the Federal Council submits its Bills and messages to the Chairmen of the Council of States and the National Council at their first session. The Chairmen decide among themselves which House will be the first to deal with each piece of business. Unless the Federal Council has designated a bill as "urgent" the division of business must be sanctioned by each House. In case of

21. The difference between pardon and amnesty is that : (1) the former is an individual one whereas amnesty is a mass measure, and (2) the amnesty is in advance of sentence whereas pardon is subsequent to punishment. Hughes, C., *The Federal Government of Switzerland,* p. 95.
22. Article 92.
23. Hughes, C., *The Federal Government of Switzerland,* p.156.
24. *Ibid.*

"urgent" bills, the decision of the two Chairmen is binding. The bills are ordinarily sent to the appropriate committees immediately after the allotment of the business. The committees may hold their meetings in any part of the country and generally they carry their work in the interval between the sessions of the Assembly. The committees receive the secretarial assistance of the Federal Chancellory and may summon any official of the Federal Government for evidence, explanation and clarification. The committees seldom change the sense of the draft laws, but they often do make suggestions for amending the proposed laws. Minority reports frequently accompany the majority reports.

There are three stages in the discussion of a bill in each House. After receiving the report of the Committee, the House to which it is allotted first debates "entering upon the matter". If it is agreed upon, then, the House proceeds to discuss the bill clause by clause. After it has been fully discussed the bill is voted upon as a whole. If it is approved the bill is then sent to the other House wherein the same procedure is followed. "In exceptional cases, and in the event the draft bill is capable of being broken up logically each Houses simultaneously may take different Sections of the same bill for debate. As soon as each Section is approved by one House it is sent immediately to the other for consideration."[25]

When the bill has been passed by both the Houses, the Federal Chancery prepares the official text which is signed by the Chairmen and Secretaries of both the Houses. The text is then submitted to the Federal Council for publication and execution. It comes into effect, unless challenged by referendum, on the date fixed in the original bill, or if no date is mentioned within five days after publication.

### Deadlock between the Councils

The possibilities of a serious deadlock between the Council of States and the National Council are rare indeed. But it does happen, the Law on the Relations between Councils, 1902, as amended in 1939, sets forth the procedure to be followed. If the second House disagrees with the decision of the first, the bill is sent to the former for another deliberation. Only the points of difference are discussed, unless the changes are of such a nature as to necessitate a debate on the bill as a whole. This procedure continues until agreement is reached, or "until the two bodies agree to disagree." In that event, the points of difference are submitted to a Joint Conference Committee presided over by a member of the House which had originally rejected the bill or expressed disagreement thereon. If the Joint Conference Committee fails to reach an acceptable alternative, or if their proposals are refused, the bill in question is dropped.

## POWERS OF THE FEDERAL ASSEMBLY

### Competence of the Assembly

There are few constitutional limitations on the powers of the Federal Assembly within its own sphere of jurisdiction. Article 84 distinctly specifies that the National Council and the Council of States "shall deal with all matters which the present Constitution places within the competence of the Confederation and have not been attributed to another Federal authority." The framers of the Constitution did not deem it necessary to impose specific limitations on the powers of the Federal Assembly, as the power of the people can be invoked at a referendum to overrule the Assembly. Moreover, in a small country, like Switzerland, where the strength of the legislative bodies is small and the politicians are judged by the traditionally strict standard of honesty, the need for constitutional limitation does not arise as "public opinion would at once check any attempt by the Councils to extend their powers beyond the limits the Constitution prescribes."

Another peculiarity of the Swiss legislature is that both the Chambers are coordinate in all respects of their powers and functions. Legislative measures can be initiated in either Chamber and neither possesses the power to veto the other. The Federal Councillors, though members of neither Chamber, are required to appear and answer questions put to them equally in both. For certain purposes, like the selection of the Federal Councillors, its President and Vice-President, for decisions on conflict of jurisdiction between the Federal authorities, and for the granting of pardon, etc., the two Chambers sit together and vote as one Chamber. Besides, the Constitution can be amended, subject to certain other provisions, by the equal participation and agreement of the National Council and the Council of States. Finally, the makers of the Swiss Constitution did not pay much attention to the orthodox doctrine of the

25. Codding, G. A., *The Federal Government of Switzerland*, p. 83.

Separation of Powers. They vested the Federal Assembly with all kinds of authority, legislative, executive and judicial. In Switzerland there is a government by Assembly.

**Legislative Powers**

Federal Assembly is competent to enact all laws and decrees dealing with matters which the Constitution assigns to federal authorities, and make laws dealing with the organization and mode of the election of the federal authorities. It determines and enacts necessary measures to ensure the due observance of the Federal Constitution; the guarantees of Cantonal Constitutions and the territory of the Cantons, the fulfilment of Federal obligations; adopts measures ensuring the external safety of the country, her independence and neutrality; the internal safety of Switzerland, and the maintenance of peace and good order; enacts the annual budget of the Confederation, approves State accounts and decrees authorising loans. Finally, the Federal Assembly can demand all kind of information, which it deems necessary, on the administration of the Confederation and directs questions to the Federal Councillors. The Federal Council presents an annual report to the Assembly upon the internal conditions and foreign relations of the Confederation. It may also be required to make special report whenever either House of the Federal Assembly demands.

The Swiss Constitution provides that all laws passed and resolutions adopted by the Federal Assembly must be submitted to the people for their acceptance or rejection, if a demand to that effect is made within 90 days by 50,000 Swiss citizens or eight Cantons, provided it has not been declared urgent by the Federal Assembly. If a referendum is held and a majority of the people vote against the law, it becomes void. Before 1930, Federal decrees which were not general in character and which were declared urgent could not be submitted to referendum. The amendment of January 22, 1939 restricted the application of the urgency clause to only such decrees as were passed by a majority of all members of each of the two Chambers and had their duration definitely fixed.[26] Article 89 was amended again in 1949 and the present position is that 50,000 voters or 8 Cantons may demand referendum on a federal decree declared urgent. Such a decree will become inoperative one year after its adoption by the Federal Assembly, if it is not approved by the people within this period. Such a decree cannot be re-enacted.

The Federal Assembly is the judge and determines what laws or resolutions are urgent. Dr. Zellweger accuses the Federal Assembly of not using this discretion impartially in order to prevent popular action upon its measures. Two points may, however, be noted in this connection. First, the referendum for ordinary laws in the Confederation is optional or facultative. Second, there does not exist popular initiative on legislative measures in the Confederation.

**Executive Powers**

The Council of States and the National Council, at their joint sitting, elect the seven members of the Federal Council, its President and Vice-President, appoint judges of the Federal Court, the members of the Federal Insurance Court and the Commander-in-Chief. The right of election or confirmation in respect of other officers may be vested in the Assembly by federal legislation. The Federal Assembly supervises the activities of the civil service, and even decides administrative disputes and conflicts of jurisdiction between federal officials. It determines salaries and allowances of members of Federal Department and of the Federal Chancery, as also the establishment of permanent federal offices and the salaries in connection therewith.

The control of the federal army, too, is vested in the Assembly. It declares war and concludes peace, ratifies alliances and treaties. All treaties concluded by the Cantons between themselves or with foreign States must be confirmed by the Federal Assembly, provided that such Cantonal treaties are submitted to it only on appeal either by the Federal Council or another Canton. If the Cantons fail to execute federal laws or obligations, the Federal Assembly decides on the nature of intervention against the offending Canton or Cantons.

The amended Article 89 provides that international treaties which are of unspecified nature and cannot be denounced; provide for adherence to an international organisation; entail a multilateral unification of the Law must be submitted to the people for approval or rejection if 50,000 Swiss citizens entitled to vote or eight Cantons demand. This provision can also be extended to other treaties by a decision of both Houses of the Federal Assembly. Adherence to collective security or to supranational bodies

26. Article 89 bis (1).

must necessarily be submitted to the vote of the people and the Cantons. It is a compulsory referendum and not on demand.

**Judicial Functions**

The Federal Assembly grants pardon in joint session whereas amnesty is granted by two Chambers separately. It also hears appeals against the decisions of the Federal Council relating to administrative disputes.

**Constitutional Amendment**

The method and procedure of amending the Constitution has already been discussed.[27] When both the Chambers agree to revise the Constitution either wholly or partly, the proposed revision is submitted to the people for their acceptance or rejection. In case one of the Chambers does not agree to the proposed revision, the matter is then referred to the people for their decision whether they need such a revision or not. If the majority of people vote for revision new elections of the Federal Assembly are held to effect the revision. After having passed through the Federal Assembly, it is submitted at the referendum of the people and the Cantons.

The Swiss Constitution also provides for. constitutional initiative and here, too, the Assembly plays its due part, though the final arbiters are the people.

## THE DECLINE OF LEGISLATIVE SUPREMACY

The Constitution vests the supreme authority of the Confederation in the Federal Assembly subject to the rights of the people and of the Cantons. It is both a legislative and a Constituent Assembly and its laws can neither be vetoed by the President of the Confederation nor can these be declared unconstitutional by any Swiss court. Its supremacy is further established by the fact that other organs of the Federal Government are subordinate to its authority. The performance of the Federal Assembly is also impressive and the Swiss people, throughout its career, have not shown any real discontent over its working. It provides a national forum for the expression of differing points of views, it works quietly and without undue haste, and its cost is not excessive. Much contrary to the expectations of the constitution- makers, the history of bicameralism is eminently admirable. The two Houses have shown more harmony and the friction has been rare. In fact, seldom does one House seriously attempt to overthrow the decisions of the other on matters of national importance. And both have attracted highly talented statesmen and election to either of the two Houses is deemed a great honour.

It cannot, however, be denied that there has been a steady decline in the prestige of the Federal Assembly as a body. This is due to important reasons. In the first place, the process of direct legislation has considerably contributed towards the decline of its legislative supremacy. When Deputies know that ultimately authority vests in the people to accept or reject the laws they make, they take very little interest in the performance of their legislative duties. There is neither initiative nor the ambition to venture it. If the measure passed by the Federal Assembly succeeds at a referendum, the credit for it goes to the people and not to the legislature. If it does not succeed, the blame goes to the legislature. Such a feeling of frustration reduces the sense of responsibility and the legislature, as Bryce says, may be disposed to pass "measures its judgment disapproves, counting on the people to reject them, or may fear to pass laws it thinks needed lest it should receive a buffet from the popular vote." The history of popular voting discloses a marked tendency to reject measures that are in any way radical. The Swiss have also rejected all those laws that are too comprehensive, or complicated, or mean to effect too much at once. They know that they have the right of constitutional initiative and if need be they have the means to see the Constitution amended. This tendency also creates, amongst the legislators a condition of doubt or indecision, if not a feeling of helplessness.

Another reason for the weakness of the Assembly lies in the fact that down to the present day it has remained an assembly of notables, a non-professional parliament. Erich Gruner says, "In initiation of the expression 'militia army' the Federal Assembly is usually called a 'militia parliament.' Switzerland still cherishes the illusion that parliamentary work is not so demanding as to exclude the exercise of an ordinary occupation, and that the individual parliamentarian can continue to make living from his usual occupation despite the loss of time involved". During recent years there has been a shift towards a full-time parliamentary job, but this has not been accompanied by an adequate parliamentary salary. Swiss parliamentarians do not have offices, as-

27. Chapter II.

sistants, or secretaries to assist them in the performance of their duties. "Thus the work style of members of parliament," Gruner explains, "is characterised by chronic lack of time and by conflict between occupational and parliamentary demands."

The result is that the Assembly has tried to shift its responsibility and the lead is taken by the Federal Council. The Federal Council has now become the director of legislative process. It not only introduces legislation but initiates it too. The Council derives its authority from Article 102, Sec. 4, of the Constitution which reads: "It (Federal Council) shall submit to the Federal Assembly drafts of laws and decrees and shall give its opinion on proposals submitted to it by the Councils or the Cantons." The bulk of the legislation, therefore, originates from the Federal Council. Wherever the Federal Assembly makes a request to the Federal Council to initiate legislation on the special subject, it drafts the bill with the help of the expert staff at its disposal and forwards it on to the Assembly along with a well-reasoned report presenting the purport of the proposed legislation and giving the reasons why it should or should not be enacted. Even in the cases where the Assembly has requested the Federal Council to draft a piece of legislation, it usually does not enact the draft law when the Council's report is unfavourable.[28]

The members of the Federal Council also pilot bills in the Federal Assembly through all the stages of the legislative process. The Federal Councillor, who is assigned the bill, gives his advice and comments in the Committee and his role is significant there. "It is not necessary," remarks Prof. Rappard, "to have attended many such meetings to understand why the principlal actors are rarely the legislative members."[29] On the floor of the House of the Assembly which gets the priority to discuss it, the Federal Councillor again explains, elaborates, elucidates and defends or opposes, if necessary, the bill. The Federal Assembly has, thus, as Codding remarks, "been reduced, to a certain extent, to the position of an advisory body with the electorate exercising the real decision-making power." If a system of legislative initiative should also be adopted, as is being suggested, he further remarks, "there is little doubt that the prestige of the legislature would be even further lowered.[30]

In the opinion of Erich Gruner the Federal Assembly is wedged between the Federal Council, for which it can create difficulties but which it cannot overthrow, and a sovereign (the voters) who by means of the ballot (optional referendum and constitutional initiative) can question the policies of the elected authorities, or, on the contrary, can accelerate them." Answering to the question "Is the Swiss parliament weak?" Hughes says, "In the continuous process of legislation and administration its influence (of the Federal Assembly) is rather that of a source of light which makes a plant grow in a particular direction than that of a gardener who lops off a branch."[31] Hughes had in mind the classical parliamentary function—elections, control of administration, budget making and legislation. But the Federal Assembly makes up some of the deficiencies by the vigorous use of motions, postulates and interpellations. Since 1946 question hour has been introduced in the National Council and a Deputy can question a member of the Federal Council on any subject concerning the federal administration. It keeps the Councillors on their toes. Erich Gruner, accordingly, concludes: "If one may characterise the British parliament as a debating parliament and the American parliament as a cooperating one, the Swiss parliament merits the adjective threatening."[32] But the threats do not and cannot take a concrete shape to have the desired impact. The authority of the Federal Assembly is *de jure* "the supreme authority of the Confederation", when it was created and today even, but it is in fact the weakest link of the Swiss Government.

## SUGGESTED READINGS

Coddling G.A., *Federal Government in Switzerland.*

Hugges, C., *The Parliament of Switzerland.*

Lowell, A.L., *Government and Parties in Continental Europe.*

Wheare, K.C. *Federal Government.*

---

28. Codding, G. A., *The Federal Government of Switzerland,* p. 92.
29. Rappard, W. E., *The Government of Switzerland,* p. 85.
30. Codding, G. A., *The Federal Government of Switzerland,* p. 92.
31. Hughes, C., *The Parliament of Switzerland,* p. 165.
32. Gruner, Erich, *Modern Switzerland,* p. 352.

# CHAPTER VI

# The Frame of National Government— The Federal Court

## The Federal Court

The creation of a Federal Court was the chief institutional innovation of the 1874 constitutional revision. The Constitution of 1848 provided for the administration of justice in the Federal sphere, but it had no jurisdiction over conflicts of law between the Confederation and the Cantons or between the Cantons themselves. Such cases were heard and decided by the Federal Assembly. Even cases relating to the rights of the citizens could not be heard by the Federal Court unless they were referred to it by the Federal Council or the Federal Assembly. The Federal Court had no fixed location for the transaction of business and it lacked qualified professional personnel. A more serious weakness was its lack of authority. All this was changed by the Constitution of 1874. Article 106 says, "There shall be Federal Court for the administration of justice in so far as this is within the Federal competence." The Court, as at present constituted, first assembled in 1875 and "since then its jurisdiction has been enlarged several times chiefly at the expense of the Federal Council"[1]

The members of the Federal Court and their substitutes are elected by the Federal Assembly "which shall ensure that the three official languages of the Confederation be represented."[2] The organisation of the Federal Court and of its divisions, the number of its members and its substitutes, the duration of their term of office and their salary are determined by law of the Federal Assembly.[3] The Constitution does not prescribe any qualifications for the members of the Federal Court and their substitutes. It only says that any Swiss citizen who is eligible to the National Council may be appointed to the Federal Court.[4] The Constitution, however, imposes two restrictions.[5] (1) the members of the Federal Assembly and of the Federal Council and the officials appointed by these authorities may not at the same time be members of the Federal Court; and (2) members of the Federal Court may not hold another office, be it in the service of the Confederation or in the Cantons, nor any other profession or industry.[6]

Despite the absence of prescribed qualifications for the members of the Federal Court and their substitutes, due care is taken to select men of legal learning and ability. While predilection may sometimes be present in the appointments made by the Assembly, "it is not alleged that they not injured the quality of the bench, any more than the occasional action of like influences tells on the general confidence felt in England and (as respect the Federal Courts) in the United States in the highest courts of those countries."

The Law on Judicial Organisation of 1948, determines the organization of the Federal Court. It fixes the number of judges between 26 and 28; which is actually 26. There are also 11 to 13 substitutes. The actual number is 12. The term for which the judges of the court are elected is six years. But, as in the case of Federal Councillors, the judges may be, and often they are, re-elected. This practice of re-election has resulted practically into a life-tenure, thus, removing the danger to the independence of the judiciary which "might otherwise inhere in the brevity of the judges' legal term and in the influences which affect their original election."[7] In practice, judges resign in the year in which they become seventy. The Court has its own President and

1. Hughes, C., *The Federal Constitution of Switzerland,* p. 119.
2. Article 107 (1).
3. *Ibid.,* Section 2.
4. Article 108.
5. *Ibid.*
6. Before 1874 membership of the Federal Court was not incompatible with that of the Federal Assembly nor with following any other employment, and in fact was normally combined with one or both of these.
7. Shortwell, J. T., (Ed.), *Government of Continental Europe,* p. 354.

Vice-President elected for two years. They are not, however, immediately re-eligible.

The Federal Court is the only national Court. There are no inferior Federal Courts, except the assizes in which the country is divided for criminal cases. The reason is that the bulk of judicial work continues to be discharged by the Cantonal Courts. Nor has the Federal Court, as in the United States, a staff of its own all over the country for the execution of its decisions. Execution of judgments in Switzerland is the function of the Federal Council with an authority to act through Cantonal officials. Such a distinct organization gives to the Swiss Federal court a peculiar position among the federal judicial systems.

**Jurisdiction**

The jurisdiction of the Federal Court extends over civil and criminal cases and questions of public law. The Court has no power of interpreting the Constitution and declaring a federal law invalid. In other words, the Federal Court cannot question the validity of laws passed by the Federal Assembly. It can, however, inquire into the constitutionality of Cantonal laws and actions of Cantonal executives and sometimes Federal executives. But Prof. Hans Huber, at one time a Judge of the Federal Court, is of the opinion that the court will make an effort to interpret federal laws whose meaning is not clear in such a manner as to honour the intent of the Constitution.[8]

**(i) Civil Jurisdiction**

The Federal Court adjudicates civil disputes between the Confederation and the Cantons and between the Confederation and Corporations or private persons if the object of the dispute is of such importance "as shall be determined by federal legislation and if those corporations or persons are plaintiffs." Similarly, the Court decides between the Cantons themselves, and between the Cantons and Corporations or private persons if the object of the dispute is of such importance "as shall be determined by the federal legislation and if one of the parties so requires." The Court, further, decides disputes concerning loss of nationality (Statelessness) and disputes between Communes of different Cantons concerning questions of citizenship.[9] The Federal Court is also bound to adjudicate other cases if both parties agree to refer them to it and if the subject of the dispute is of such importance as shall be determined by federal legislation.[10]

The Civil jurisdiction of the Court expressly conferred by the Constitution has further been extended by virtue of the provision of Article 114 which authorises the Confederation to place "other matters" within the competence of the Court. The same Article confers on the Court powers to ensure the uniform application of laws relating to commerce and the transactions affecting movable property (law of contract and torts including commercial law of bills of exchange), suits for debts and bankruptcy, protection of copyrights and industrial inventions, including designs and models. Article 64 confers a general power on the Confederation to legislate in any fields of civil law. This all-embracing power conferred on the Confederation, *ipso facto,* enlarges the civil jurisdiction of the Federal Court.

**(ii) Criminal Jurisdiction**

On the criminal side, the court has original and exclusive jurisdiction in:

(a) Cases of high treason against the Confederation, revolt and violence against the federal authorities;

(b) Crimes and offences against the Law of Nations;

(c) Political crimes and offences which are either the cause or consequence of disorders and disturbances necessitating armed federal intervention;

(d) Offences committed by officials appointed by a Federal authority when brought before the Court by that authority.

The Constitution provides that the Federal Court shall pass judgment on the aforesaid criminal cases with the assistance of a jury to give a verdict on facts.

The Court also has original jurisdiction over other serious crimes such as counterfeiting and voting frauds. Cases of original jurisdiction, however, make up a very small proportion of the work load of the Federal Court.

Article 64 bis. empowers the Confederation to legislate in the field of criminal law. In criminal cases, as stated before, the Court holds assizes from time to time at fixed centers in which the country is divided for this purpose. In these assizes a section of court consisting of three judges, sits with a jury chosen by lot from the

8. See W.C. Rice's *Law Among States in Federacy,* p. 117.
9. Article 110.
10. Article 111.

neighbouring villages. Concurrence of five-sixths of the jury is necessary to convict an accused person.

The court sits in four chambers for exercising its criminal jurisdiction: The Federal Criminal Court; the Court of Accusation—this prepares business for the Federal Criminal Court and decides if there is *prima facie* case, and decides as to the place of criminal jurisdiction, *i.e.,* in which Canton. Then there is the Court of Cessation, and, finally, is the extraordinary Court of cessation of seven judges.

**(iii) Constitutional Jurisdiction**

The Federal Court has a limited constitutional jurisdiction. It adjudicates:

(1) conflicts of competence between the federal authorities on one side and authorities of the Cantons on the other side;
(2) disputes between Cantons in the field of the constitutional rights of citizens as well as individual complaints concerning the violation of inter-Cantonal agreements and international treaties.

In all the aforesaid disputes, the Federal Court applies the laws and generally binding decrees adopted by the Federal Assembly as well as the international treaties approved by the Federal Assembly.

The provision relating to the constitutional rights of citizens has been constructed by statute to include rights guaranteed by Cantonal as well as by Federal Constitutions. In all such cases of conflict of competence it is the duty of the Federal Court to uphold the Federal Constitution against the Cantonal, and the Cantonal Constitution against ordinary laws and decrees of the Cantons. The Federal Court can invalidate Cantonal laws and it can enquire into the constitutionality of actions of Canton executive officials. In practice, there are a great number of such appeals brought before the Federal Court each year, and the great majority of such appeals concern the guarantees of equality before the law as provided in Article 4 of the Constitution.

**Comparison with the United States**

The nature of the Swiss Federal Judiciary was discussed in Chapter II, and it was pointed out that it differs materially from the Federal Judiciary in the United States. The Swiss Federal Court though a national court, stands alone. It has not, like the American Supreme Court, subordinate courts spread over the whole country. Nor has it its separate officials to execute its judgments. The Court relies upon the Federal Council, acting through the Cantonal governments, for the enforcement of its decisions. But the real difference is between the powers of the two. The Federal Court is bound by an express provision of the Constitution to apply every law passed by the Federal Assembly. Article 113 provides that in cases of conflicts of competence between the federal authorities and Cantons, disputes between Cantons in the field of public law and complaints concerning the violations of the constitutional rights of citizens as well as individual complaints concerning the violations of concordants and international treaties, the Federal Court shall apply the laws and generally binding decrees adopted by the Federal Assembly. The Swiss Federal Court has, accordingly, no power to ascertain the constitutionality of Federal Statutes and such decrees of the Federal Assembly as are of general application. The Constitution has reserved for the Federal Assembly the right to interpret the Constitution and all laws passed thereunder. The Federal Assembly can put its own construction on every law which it has passed without the interference of any judicial authority to correct it. This is unpalatable to American lawyers who hold that the powers of legislature cannot go beyond those which the Constitution has conferred upon it. There cannot be security, the voice of America further contends, for the due observance of the Constitution, if its interpretation is left to be determined by the legislature which might have infringed its provisions. It would be tantamount to make the violating body the judge in its own case.

The Continental theory, on the other hand, subordinates the judiciary to the executive and the legislature. Some of the eminent Swiss Jurists regard the American system as more rational, still Switzerland has clung to the Continental tradition and there is no apparent likelihood of a change. Even if it may be conceded that the power of judicial review inheres in the Federal Court, it would hardly serve as an effective instrument since the sovereign people in Switzerland have the direct means of expressing their will at a referendum. A judicial decision declaring a law unconstitutional would interfere with their cherished constitutional right of accepting or defeating legislation passed by the Supreme Court of the United States. Many important matters are beyond the competence of the Court. Moreover, whereas cases of conflict of jurisdiction between the Federal authorities and Cantonal authorities are decided by the Federal Court, conflicts of jurisdiction between the Federal Court and the Federal Council are decided by the Assembly. The Federal Court has, therefore, no power, like the Supreme Court, to decide upon the question of its own competence. The Federal Court, in brief, since its establishment at Lausanne in 1875, has never enjoyed the prestige and independence of the American Supreme Court. "To endow it with the right of disavowing federal statutes would therefore be to impose on a much weaker Court a much heavier burden than that under the American judiciary sometimes seems to be staggering today."[11]

## THE FEDERAL ADMINISTRATIVE COURT

The Constitution established a Federal Administrative Court[12] to adjudicate administrative disputes falling within the scope of the Confederation and referred to it by federal legislation. The Administrative Court also adjudicates disciplinary cases of the Federal administration referred to it by federal legislation in so far as such cases shall not be referred to a special jurisdiction. The Court applies the federal legislation and the treaties approved by the Federal Assembly. The Cantons are entitled, subject to the approval of the Federal Assembly, to refer to the Federal Administrative Court for adjudication administrative disputes falling within the scope of their competence.

The organisation of federal administrative and disciplinary jurisdiction and its procedure has been determined by federal law. In 1925, the Federal Assembly by a resolution decided that the duties of the Administrative Court were to be exercised by the Federal Court. The Administrative Court is, therefore, not a separate court like the Swiss Insurance Tribunal or like the Administrative Courts in France and other Continental countries. It is a section of the Federal Court and, accordingly, a part of the ordinary courts, except that the Administrative courts use a different type of procedure from that used in the Federal Court.

## SUGGESTED READINGS

Bryce, J., *Modern Democracies, Vol. 1. Chaps. XXVII and XXXII*

Hughes, C, *The Federal Constitution of Switzerland*

Rappard, W.F., *The Government of Switzerland*

Tripp, M.L., *The Swiss and United States Federal Constitutional Systems.*

11. Rappard, W. E., *The Government of Switzerland,* p. 91.
12. Article 114 bis.

# CHAPTER VII

# The Referendum and the Initiative

### Direct Legislation

The institution of direct legislation is a distinctive feature of Swiss democracy. The method of popular legislation, *i.e.*, law-making by the citizens themselves and not by their representatives, is as old as Swiss history and it finds its fullest expression in the *Landsgemeinde,* the mass meetings of all citizens. The Landsgemeinde is still kept alive with its ancient traditions and practices in the four half-Cantons of Appenzell, Unterwalden, and in the Canton of Glarus. In the remaining Cantons the referendum and the initiative represent an effort to extend the idea of direct democracy in order to uphold the cherished conviction of the Swiss people that they are sovereign and they can assert their right by taking a direct part in the determination of the affairs of the State. Such an attitude of mind of the people has profoundly modified Swiss mechanism of government and influenced the world opinion in favour of these institutions.

"Nothing in Swiss arrangements," writes Bryce, "is more instructive to the student of democracy for it opens a window into the soul of the multitude. Their thoughts and feelings are seen directly, not refracted through the medium of elected bodies."[1] Switzerland is really speaking a type of "mixed democracy,"[2] wherein "the legislative will of the people is expressed both through legislatures and through direct popular votes in the form of the referendum and the initiative."[3] The plebiscitary rights, according to Erich Gruner, are "quasi-substitutes for parliamentary votes of no confidence, for which no provision is made in the Swiss system". Unlike the Swiss system, the American governmental system is not based on the idea of counterweights but on an equilibrium of three separate powers, the President, the Congress and the Supreme Court.

### The Referendum

Literally the word referendum means "must be referred." As a concept of Political Science, it means the process by which the verdict of the citizens eligible to vote is sought on a proposed law, fundamental or ordinary, and on which the legislature has already expressed its opinion. If it is approved by the majority of the voters voting, the law stands adopted. If it is rejected, it is given up. Referendum is really a consultation of the people on a law passed by the legislature before its final enactment. In short, voters approve or reject the legislation passed by the representative assemblies.

The referendum may be of two kinds: optional or facultative, and compulsory or obligatory. When a law, after it has passed through the legislature, is submitted to the people for their acceptance or rejection on a petition from the specified number of citizens, it is known as the optional or facultative referendum. In the case of compulsory or obligatory referendum all measures of a specified type must necessarily be referred to the people for their acceptance or rejection before they can become laws. The obligatory form is obviously more democratic, for it requires expression of popular opinion on every law. The Swiss, too, consider it preferable on practical grounds, because it "avoids the agitation necessarily involved in the effort to collect signatures to the petition for a referendum." And laws so approved by the people have a great stabilising effect as they have the impress of popular will.

### Forms of the Referendum

All amendments to the Federal and Cantonal Constitutions are subject to obligatory referendum and without such a process no constitutional change becomes final. The obligatory referedum for all changes in the Federal Constitution was introduced in 1848, and this provision has been continued in the Constitution of 1874. The prevailing Constitution also included the provision that Cantonal Constitutions must be similarly adopted in order to be guaranteed by the

1. Bryce, J., *Modern Democracies,* Vol. I, p. 415.
2. Marx, M., *Foreign Governments,* p. 390.
3. *Ibid.*

Federal government.[4]

The procedure applied in the Confederation for constitutional referendum has already been discussed.[5] To recapitulate it, proposed amendments for partial or total revision of the Constitution are usually passed first by the Federal Assembly in the same way as ordinary laws. Then, they are submitted at a referendum of the citizens entitled to vote and become valid only after having been approved by a majority of the popular votes cast at a referendum, and by a majority of the Cantons. The vote of each Canton or half-Canton is determined by its popular vote.

If one of the Houses of the Federal Assembly does not agree to the proposed amendment or revision, the matter whether such an amendment is necessary or not, is referred to the people at a referendum. If the majority vote is in the affirmative, then, fresh elections of the Federal Assembly are held. The newly elected Assembly undertakes the proposed revision and after duly passing it is submitted to the referendum of the people and Cantons for their acceptance or rejection.

If one of the Houses of the Federal Assembly does not agree to the proposed amendment or revision, the matter whether such an amendment is necessary or not, is referred to the people at a referendum. If the majority vote is in the affirmative, then, fresh elections of the Federal Assembly are held. The newly elected Assembly undertakes the proposed revision and after duly passing it, is submitted to the referendum of the people and Cantons for their acceptance or rejection.

The national legislative referendum is applicable to federal laws and general binding federal decrees, and since 1921 to international treaties concluded for an indeterminate duration and cannot be denounced; treaties that provide for adherence to an international organisation and those that entail a multilateral unification of the law. By a decision of both Houses of the Federal Assembly it may be made applicable to other treaties as well. Every Federal law after having been passed by the two Councils and a federal decree are published in the Federal Official Journal and sent to the Cantons to be circulated through the Communes. Within ninety days of circulation, 50,000 citizens entitled to vote or eight Cantons may demand their submission to a referendum. Similarly, 50,000 citizens or eight Cantons may demand submission of international treaties, as specified above, to a referendum for approval or rejection. All these are examples of optional referendum. Compulsory referendum is provided in Article 89 (5) and it is applicable in case of collective security organisations or to supranational bodies. It reads: "Adherence to collective security organisations or to supranational bodies shall be submitted to the vote of the people and the Cantons." This Section of Article 89 is essentially distinct from Section 3 of the same Article which reads: "Paragraph 2 (relating to submission of federal laws and binding decress to the people for approval or rejection if 50,000 citizens entitled to vote or eight Cantons) so demand."

The Cantons have never demanded referendum. The citizens do usually demand it. The opponents of the measures excite popular interest and secure the requisite number of signatures. The signatures are now often collected by sending reply-paid cards through the post to voters, who merely need to sign and drop the card into a letter box.[6] When the number of signatures sent in has been recognised by the Federal Council to be sufficient, it publishes the law to be circulated among the people all over the country, and fixes a day for voting, not before four weeks after the publication and distribution of the law.

Meetings are held at which members of the Federal Assembly and others advocate or oppose it. Articles on the main provisions of the law appear in the press. The arrangements for voting are made by the Cantonal authorities, but ballot papers are supplied by the Federal Government. The voting is held on a Sunday and takes place on the same day over the whole country. The polling is usually quiet and orderly and complaints of bribery and impersonation are seldom heard.

All Cantons, except those ruled by ***Landsgemeinde,*** provide for legislative referendum. In some it is obligatory, in others it is optional; where it is optional it depends upon a petition by a specified number of citizens, the number varying from Canton to Canton, to invoke it. In still other Cantons the referendum is obligatory for important financial laws only and optional for others.

**Forms of the Initiative**

The referendum has purely negative effect as it merely enables the people to reject measures

4. Article 6
5. Chapter II, *ante.*
6. Hughes, C., *The Federal Constitution of Switzerland,* p. 101.

passed by their representatives. The advocates of direct legislation, and more particularly the Swiss, plead that the legislature ought not to have the exclusive right to originate legislation. It ought to be, it is asserted, an inherent right of the citizens to propose legislation and when ratified by the popular vote, it must become law no matter even if it has been disapproved by the legislature. Such a device of popular legislation is called initiative. By means of initiative the voter can make his influence felt in those cases where the legislature may not want to adopt a constitutional amendment or a law.

The initiative is very often erroneously likened to a petition. But both essentially differ from one another. A petition is a mere popular submission made to the legislature suggesting the need for making a particular legislation. The legislature may or may not act upon it. But the initiative is the vindication of the sovereign power of the people as it takes effect without regard to the opinion of the legislature, and even against its wishes. It involves the actual proposal, by a portion of the electorate, of a law or a similar measure which may or may not be approved subsequently by the legislature but which, in any case, is usually submitted to a referendum decision of the voters. In brief, the voters initiate legislation they desire to have no matter whether it is approved or rejected ultimately.

The initiative may also take two forms: formulative, and in general terms. When the demand is couched in general terms it is the obligation of the legislature to draft, consider and pass the laws as desired by the required number of citizens, subject to the ratification of the people. If the proposal is formulated, in the form of a bill complete in all respects, it is the duty of the legislature to consider the measure as it is and the vote has to the taken on that text.

The right of constitutional initiative exists both in the Confederation and in the Cantons. Under it a minimum of 100,000 voters may petition for an amendment to the Federal Constitution either in the form of a request in general terms or formulated in the complete and final form of a bill. If the Federal Assembly approves a proposal submitted in general terms, it, then, proceeds immediately to draw up the amendment and submit it to the popular and Cantonal vote. If, however, the Assembly votes against it, the question is referred to the people whether or not the initiative proposal will be proceeded with. If it wins the majority of the popular vote, it becomes the duty of the Assembly, although it has already expressed its disapproval of the proposal, to put the amendment in form and submit it to the verdict of the people and Cantons. An unfavourable popular vote kills it.

If the initiative is formulated in specific terms, and if the Federal Assembly accepts it, the proposal is at once submitted for popular and Cantonal action in the usual manner. If the Assembly does not agree to the formulated proposal, they may either advise to reject the initiative or submit a counter-proposal along with the original one.

If the initiative contains a proposal for a complete revision of the Constitution, then the procedure is identical to the one explained previously,[7] when one Chamber of the Federal Assembly proposes the revision and the other opposes it.

Since there is no federal legislative initiative, the constitutional initiative has been used to place all kinds of matters in the Federal Constitution, for instance, the prohibition against Kosher slaughtering. The Constitutional initiative, on the other hand, has also been used for such politically significant purposes as the introduction of proportional representation and of the referendum on certain international treaties. Herman Finer says, that the "constitutional initiative (in Switzerland) is wide enough to include ordinary legislation when proposed as a constitutional amendment, and, this, which is found in some states of United States also, is a defect rather than a merit—to put ordinary laws into the Constitution."[8] There is indeed, no recognised criterion for determining whether a proposed measure is a constitutional amendment or ordinary law.

In the Cantons, however, there is legislative initiative. In all Cantons, except where laws are made in the *Landsgemeinde,* a prescribed number of citizens may either propose a new law or submit to the Cantonal legislature the principle on which they desire a new law to be based. In the latter case, the Council refers the question to the vote of the people. If the people approve it, then, the Cantonal Council prepares the law and it is submitted to the people for their acceptance or rejection. If the proposal is formulated, it goes straight to the people. But the Cantonal Council may suggest counter-proposals and refer them to

7. Chapter II, *ante*.
8. Finer, H., *The Theory and Practice of Modern Government,* p. 561.

people for their decision along with the original popularly initiated proposal.

**Working of Referendum and Initiative**

The Swiss citizens are constantly being called upon, either at the Federal or Cantonal level to express their opinion either by referendum or initiative. While legislative initiatives have remained limited to the individual Cantons, the constitutional popular initiative was introduced at the federal level in 1891, subject to petition by at least 50,000 (raised to 100,000 in 1977) eligible voters. The following two tables show how often these three instruments have been employed from the date of their introduction to 1976. The tables indicate the proportion of laws and binding decrees which have been subjected to the optional referendum and those for which the referendum was compulsory. The second table also shows how many constitutional initiatives have been submitted and the distribution of acceptances and rejection by the people.

TABLE I

**On Legal Level**

(Optional referendum)

| | *Absolute number of federal laws* | Submitted to referenda | Accepted | *Rejected* |
|---|---|---|---|---|
| | 1141 | 78 | 30 | 4.8 |
| Per cent | 100 | 6.8 | 2.6 | 4.2 |

TABLE II

**Constitutional Level**

| | Compulsory referendum | | | *Popular initiative* | | |
|---|---|---|---|---|---|---|
| | *Total* | *Accepted* | *Rejected* | *Total* | *Accepted* | *Rejected* |
| | 102 | 82 | 20 | 67 | 18 | 49 |
| % | 100 | 80 | 20 | 100 | 27 | 78 |

In the Cantons the consultation of the people is more frequent. The quorum of signatures required for submission of an initiative is particularly low ranging from 1000 to 5000 signatures. But its frequency is more in the German-speaking Cantons. In the German- speaking Cantons there is more jealousy and distrust of government and more confidence in the action of the people. Hence the referendum and the initiative are peculiar German institutions. The French, on the other hand, are less democratic in the Swiss sense of the term. They are by nature more inclined to follow the lead of the Government and although they have adopted the referendum, it is most exclusively optional and for that too, they have made little use of it.

**Character of the Laws Rejected**

From the above survey of the working of direct legislation in Switzerland it will be clear that the Swiss are asked to pronounce their judgment on a variety of problems including the highly technical. From the list of the measures rejected, a few inferences may be made. First, the history of popular voting reveals a marked tendency to reject measures that are in any way radical. It implies that the Swiss people by themselves are really more conservative than their representatives. But the conservatism of the people does not manifest itself so much in the Confederation as in some of the Cantons. The people also reject those laws that are too comprehensive, or complicated, or mean to effect too much at once. This tendency has one good result, for it shows that the Swiss want to understand the laws they are required to enact. Finally, the Swiss have rejected measures which involve spending of money. This tendency, which seems to be universal, applies especially to proposals, "for increasing the salaries of public officers, and in fact, the largest number of negative votes ever cast in a federal law were thrown against the Bill for pensioning officials." But whenever the government has appealed to the spirit of patriotic sacrifice, when the interest of national security seemed to justify such appeals, as it happened during the two World Wars, and in the period of economic depression, the people had readily responded to the needs of the nation and readily enhanced their personal and financial burdens.

The fact that a mere four per cent of the federal laws have been rejected by the voters at a referendum (see Table I) makes it evident that the main effect of the referendum consists in the prevention of undesirable laws. Because of the possibility that decisions of the Assembly may afterwards be submitted to a popular vote, attempts during recent times are made to obtain the consensus of interest groups concerned with a particular bill at the early stages of its initiation. It is really the interest groups, with mass support and vast financial resources, that they endanger any legislation that is a potential instigator of a referendum. But despite this preliminary processing the referendum may block the legislative impulse. "Thus, it may paralyse or sabotage vital

9. Hughes, C., *The Federal Constitution of Switzerland*, p. 101.

measures, and thereby exercise a latent breaking power against innovations''. The inevitable reforms, such as the introduction of woman suffrage and of social insurance, were delayed for decades and that federal unification, *e.g.* of the educational system, ''have been choked off. Absolutely essential adjustments in the federal system of taxation have been accomplished only painfully through 60 years of provisional measures.''[10]

Direct legislation, it was remarked in the beginning of the present Chapter, is almost peculiar to Switzerland and it has profoundly modified the character of the Swiss Government. Its institutions were planted in some other countries after World War I as a result of the people's reaction against representative democracy. Whatever be the degree of success there, it cannot be denied that the mechanism of direct democracy is a difficult operative ideal. It demands certain inherent qualities in the people where it is desired to be made operative. The success which popular legislation has achieved in Switzerland is due to the historical antecedents of the Swiss people, to their long practice of self- government in small communities, to social equality, and to the pervading spirit of patriotism and sense of public duty in them. Similar success cannot be expected in countries where similar conditions are not obtainable. In Switzerland direct legislation has a natural growth, or as Bryce says, it is ''racy of the soil. There are institutions which like plants, flourish only on their hill side and under their own sunshine.'[11]

Independence is the first quality which a Swiss citizen exhibits. Democracy without political parties is unthinkable and voting of any kind closely follows party lines. But in Switzerland party sentiments seldom dominate the minds of the Swiss citizens particularly when they are required to give their final judgment on legislation. The Swiss Constitution does not provide for the dramatic clashes of political parties and forces common in other countries. There have been instances when a displeasure at the conduct of a party created a prejudice against the measures it had put through the legislature, as it happened in 1884 when the people rejected all the four Bills due to the irritation caused among the minority parties in the Assembly. But this is a rare phenomenon in Swiss politics. The ''Swiss voter, always independent, is most independent when he has to review the action of his Legislature.'' Each proposal is generally dealt with on its merits. Party affiliations do not count when the Swiss dislike changing their members even when they championed the measures which they have rejected. ''As a general rule the Swiss tend to re-elect representatives whom they have disavowed, unless they have reason to suspect their patriotism.''[12]

Another quality in the Swiss is parsimony. Like the Scotch, they are thrifty, and ''in public matters positively penurious.'' A Swiss is averse to anything which can increase taxation and he cannot understand ''why officials should be paid on a scale exceeding what he earns by his own toil.'' With this attitude the Swiss examine all their political problems and institutions. As a corollary, it follows that they like their administrative machinery to be simple. And through all these ages the Swiss have jealously guarded their local sovereignty and have always resented the interference of the Central Government, although there has been a marked evolution in the popular mind towards centralization.

But the quality most important ''in a legislating nation as in a legislating assembly,'' says Bryce, ''is compounded of two things: judgment and cool-headedness, the absennce of passion and presence of intelligence.''[13] The Swiss are the embodiment of this quality which we may call a ''good sense.'' They are neither an emotional nor a passionate people. They are an educated nation and ''their best minds are more sagacious than imaginative.'' Having a long experience with the methods of direct democracy and its successful operation, the Swiss have formed the habit of voting in calm spirit. They are cautious in their judgment and the great majority of the nation have always shown resolute hostility to demagogic spirit. In 1981, for example, the Federal Assembly had voted in favour of Switzerland joining the United Nations. The motion had the full support of all the major Swiss political parties. Keeping to its policy of armed neutrality, the subject was discussed threadbare over the year and in March 1986, the proposal was finally rejected at a referendum by a high majority of 75.7 per cent of the votes polled, and not even

10. Gruner, Erich, *The Political System of Switzerland,* p. 349.
11. Bryce, J., *Modern Democracies,* Vol. I, pp. 453-54.
12. Rappard, W. E., *The Government of Switzerland,* p. 72.
13. Bryce, J., *Modern Democracies,* Vol. I, p. 435.

one of the Cantons voted in favour of it. It was a relatively very high turnout of voters at the referendum and shall, perhaps, remain unprecedented.

While comparing the working of direct legislation in other countries where it is practised in one form or the other, Dubbs says, "Survey the countries of the world, you may find elsewhere greater political achievements, but assuredly in no country you will meet as many good citizens of independent national and sound practical judgment; nowhere so great a number of public men who succeed in fulfilling their function in minor spheres with dignity and skill; nowhere so much a proportion of persons who, outside their daily round, interest themselves so keenly in the welfare and in the difficulties of their fellow citizens."

Compromise and tolerance are the most essential elements in the Swiss system of government. "A people more given to absolute or inclined to engage in extreme debates over abstratct principles would find the Swiss system unworkable."[14]

**Arguments in Favour of Referendum**

The principle of popular sovereignty finds its real expression in direct legislation rather than in a representative system. In a representative system genuine public opinion is unobtainable, for it is moulded and shaped by the partisan influences of the press, the platform and the propaganda. The referendum upholds the sovereignty of the people and is the surest method of discovering the real wishes of the people. It is an excellent barometer of public opinion. Moreover, a citizen knows better than his representatives what can serve him the best and enhance his interests. A law which comes direct and straight from the people carries with it fuller moral authority and commands more unquestioning obedience than a law made for them by the representatives.

The referendum minimises the importance of political parties and discourages partisan spirit. Then, it is a popular check on the vagaries of the legislature and the political machine. The frequent rejection by the people of measures passed by the legislature shows that the latter does not always know or give effect to the real will of the people. The referendum also ensures that laws opposed to the popular will have no chance of being enacted. It puts a veto in the hands of the people.

The referendum reduces the political high-handedness of the majority party. Under the representative system a law is usually what the parliamentary majority wishes it to be. It does not represent the will of the minorities. If, however, it is referred to the people before it can be finally enacted, the minorities do get an opportunity to adequately express their opinion and to muster strong their opposition, and if possible, to negative it. This is real democracy. Then, there is no time lag. Direct legislation, remarks Bryce, helps the legislature to keep in touch with the people at other times than at general election and in some respects a better touch, for it gives the voters an opportunity of declaring their views on serious issues, apart from the destructive or distorting influence of party spirit."

When the people feel and realize that they are the real legislators, their patriotism and their sense of responsibility are fully stimulated. Realisation of this fact is also the real political education of the citizens. This is the true price of democracy. Moreover, the process of direct legislation is conservative in character. The people will seldom introduce radical changes when they know that they are the arbiters on legislation. They realise, that if need be, they themselves can easily adjust laws to fulfil their needs. They do not, accordingly, press for sweeping changes.

The Referendum is the best means of resolying deadlocks between the two Chambers of the legislature. It is, again, a check on the powers of the legislature. In Switzerland the executive does not exercise veto on legislation. Nor does one Chamber override the other. They are coequal in powers. The only check available, therefore, is the popular vote. Finally, as Bryce says, "There must somewhere in every government be a power which can say the last word, can deliver a decision from which there is no appeal. In a democracy it is only the people who can thus put an end to controversy".

**Arguments Against Referendum**

One of the chief objections against the referendum is that it has undermined the prestige of the legislative assemblies and has adversely reacted on the quality of membership. When the representatives know that ultimately their efforts may be reversed, they will take little interest

14. Buell, L., *Democratic Governments in Europe,* p. 583.

in the discharge of their legislative duties. Moreover, it erodes responsibility by making the people, "an anonymous shifting abstraction," responsible. If the measure succeeds at the popular vote, the credit for it goes to the people and not to the legislature. If it does not succeed, the blame goes to the legislature. The status and authority of the legislature must, accordingly, suffer and the result is that the people become less deferential towards it. "Its sense of responsibility," says Bryce, "is reduced" and it may be disposed to pass "measures its judgment disapproves, counting on the people to reject them or may fear to pass laws it thinks needed lest it should receive a buffet from the popular vote."

The man in the street is not adequately qualified to form and deliver any opinion upon many subjects of legislation particularly when legislation has become so highly technical and complicated. A simple 'Yes' or 'No' does not indicate the real will of the people and their comprehension of the legislation which they accept or reject. The making of laws or their ratification demands from the people a great moral standard and it is this moral value which is first and last for the referendum's main justification. The people may be ever so shrewd and ever so willing to do their duty in accordance with the strict code of morality, but they have not, and cannot have, the knowledge needed to enable them to judge the implications of the proposed legislation. Nor can the pamphlets distributed and speeches made by the supporters and opponents of the measure convey to them the requisite knowledge. The interests of the people are really safer in the hands of representatives chosen for their talent and mature judgment than when submitted to the hazards of the popular vote. Then, the people must accept or reject the bill, no amendments are possible. The vote must be given for the whole bill. In fact, no amendments can be possible when the legislative assembly consists of the whole public.

Another criticism and, indeed, a really cogent one, relates to the small size of the votes cast at a referendum. It is asserted that the result of the ballot does not fairly represent popular opinion, because in most cases the opponents of the measure go to the polls in larger proportion than its supporters. The number of large abstentions at referendum also proves that many a voter either cares little for his civil duties, or knows his unfitness to perform them. Moreover, when people are frequently asked to cast their votes, they develop what may be called an "electoral fatigue." The net result is that the decision arrived at is invariably that of a minority of the citizens and it becomes difficult, under the circumstances, to know whether there is any public opinion at all on the question. Furthermore, the referendum sometimes involves unnecessary and harmful delay in passing many laws of vital national importance. All this takes away the educative value of the referendum. When citizens do not interest themselves in public affairs, direct legislation becomes a farce, pure and simple.

When a law is accepted at the referendum by a small majority, as it happened on the question of the Swiss Federal Penal Code, and on the Federal Economic Articles in 1938 and 1947 respectively with a majority of only 53 per cent in both the cases, its moral authority would suffer more than it would be the case had opinion been nearly equally divided in the representative legislature. In countries where direct legislation does not exist, a law passed by representative legislatures is accepted and no one cares to enquire what was the majority that passed it. It comes in the regular way from the usual organ of the people's will and it is accepted by the people in the usual way. But when it goes to the people for their acceptance every one is keen to know the majority that passed it. Those who opposed it carry on their opposition ceaselessly and openly, because they feel aggrieved to have been overridden by a negligible majority.

There is also no justification to hold that direct legislation lessens the evils of party system. As a matter of fact, political parties become more active when frequent votes are to be taken. The referendum accentuates political rivalry and partisan spirit, though this tendency has not been so prominent in Switzerland because of the habits of the people. The high cost per signature of securing the petition of 50,000 citizens for a challenge confines its use to corporate bodies—political parties, trade unions, pressure groups, etc., and increases their already strong influence on policies. "The vitality and influence of these non-public-law bodies," observes Christopher Hughes, "appears to a foreigner the most helpful sign in Swiss democracy, but the Swiss themselves are unanimous in deploring it; perhaps that is because they have deprived themselves of the counter-weight of strong political parties divided on issues of policy''[15]

One obvious result of the referendum is the movement of the centre of gravity from the legislature to the executive. In the first place, the Assembly prefers to delegate legislative powers to the Federal Council than to legislate itself, ''for less surface is thereby exposed to criticism: laws are drafted to avoid referendums. And secondly, the *Arretes* of the Federal Council not being exposed to challenge like those of the Assembly, in time of emergency the Federal Council has to do all the legislating.''[16] The will of the people finds no adequate channels of expression and effectiveness. Direct democracy and its often acclaimed advantages disappear. An executive which is neither responsible nor responsive and is, in fact, the servant becomes the master.

Finally, ''the most comprehensive but also the vaguest argument,'' says Bryce, ''adduced against the referendum is that it retards political, social and economic progress.'' Sir Herny Maine developed this point in his book, *The Popular Government,* in 1885, and it particularly impressed Englishmen who had associated masses with conservatism. But this argument is not supported by Swiss experience. It is true that prejudice or undue caution has in some cases delayed the progress of economic or social reforms which the Assembly proposed, but no general harm has followed in Switzerland from that conservatism.

**Arguments in Favour of the Initiative**

Arguments in favour of the referendum and the initiative are more or less identical. But as the conditions of the latter's application are different, it needs, therefore, to be considered separately.

The initiative is claimed to be the necessary development of the concept of popular sovereignty. The people, it is argued, cannot really be sovereign, if they act through representatives. Howsoever politically virtuous and best intentioned the representatives may be, they must act according to the party programme and the party whip which may even lead to misrepresentation of the people's will. It is, accordingly, claimed that there is no better means of adequately and genuinely expressing their will, except by their own voice and vote. The referendum gives to the people only negative right of either accepting or rejecting the legislation on which they are required to express their opinion. But the initiative gives them the positive right of framing laws which they feel they actually need. If the referendum ''protects the people against the legislature's sins of commission so the initiative is a remedy for their omissions.''

Next, if the legislatures are apathetic to the needs of the people, lag behind public opinion and primarily concern themselves to push through party programmes, then ''why should a body of persons chosen by the people close the door against the people themselves allowing only such proposals as take their fancy to pass through so that the people deal with them?'' A law initiated by the people, it is argued, is the expression of their experiences and the manifestation of their own will. There is spontaneity in obeying such laws and obedience to authority is *ipso facto.* Such political behaviour on the part of the citizens adds to the stature and stability of the government and all round reverence for the institutions of the country. Finally, the initiative minimises the possibility of political upheavals as there is no indefinite postponement of legislation which the people deem essential for their welfare. They act immediately and on their own initiative rather than to depend upon their representatives to feel their pulse and wait for the legislature to pass it.

**Arguments Against the Initiative**

But the initiative, like the referendum, reduces the authority and responsibility of the legislature. Making of laws, especially drafting of bills, is not the job of a man in the street. It is an arduous task which requires specialized knowledge and mature judgment which only experts connected with the work and members of the legislature acquire by long experience. An average man cannot and does not know the technicalities required in drafting bills. The result is that popularly initiated bills are often ''crude in conception, unskilled in form marred by obscurities and omissions.'' The language used in such bills is usually seriously defective and liable to many interpretations. In the Cantons where the legislative initiative has been much freely used, it has not been the parent of any reforms which might not have been obtained through the legislature. The people, on the other hand, have sometimes placed unwise laws in the Statute books. ''Sometimes the prudence of the Cantonal Councils,'' maintains Bryce, ''dissuading the people from the particular plan proposed and substitut-

15. Hughes, C., *The Federal Constitution of Swizerland,* p. 102.
16. *Ibid.,* p. 101.

ing a better one, averted unfortunate results, while in the case of an ill-considered banking law the Federal authorities annulled the law as inconsistent with the Constitution. Several times the people have shown their good sense in rejecting mischievous schemes proposed by this method.'' The much acclaimed advantages of initiative, therefore, are actually negatived by the practical results.

**Final Analysis**

In Switzerland, the opinions, both of scholars and statesmen, on the value of direct legislation are most divergent. Some extol it as the most perfect institution, in theory and practice, so far devised. There are others who decry it on the ground that people are consulted on matters which they do not understand and assert that the actual working of the system has been bad. Some reformers resent the delays and checks inherent in the referendum and some voters complain of the excessive demands made on their spare time. All the same, no one in Switzerland would now be seriously in favour of giving it up. If one were to ask, writes Rappard, the man in the street in Switzerland ''whether his country was on the whole satisfied with the results of her experiments with direct democracy, the answer would undoubtedly be in the affirmative, Indeed he might take exception to the term of experiments in this connection. The experimental stage is over and with it have gone as well the misgivings of the early enemies of the initiative and referendum as the blind enthusiasm of its first friends.''[17]

The people as a whole value the privilege. ''The people of modern democracies,'' writes Bonjour, ''is no longer the irresponsible demos which Aristophanes pilloried with his mordent pen in the Knights—a brutal, elderly and iracible epicure, a willing prey to the basest flattery. Today it is usually clear-sighted and obedient to its best impulse when its leaders know how to enlighten it by appealing to them....''[18]. The political party which holds the majority in the Federal Assembly or Cantonal legislatures, though sometimes annoyed at the results, has never tried to withdraw it. The Radicals deem it to be a necessary feature of democracy. The Conservatives and the Clericals consider it a necessary drag on hasty legislation. The institution has, thus, become permanent, ''not only because the people as a whole are not disposed to resign any function they have assumed, but also because it is entirely comfortable to their ideas and has worked in practice at least as well as a purely representative system worked before or would be likely to work now''. The institutions of initiative and referendum are the pivot upon which hinges the entire Swiss system of government. If they are abolished, the present relations among the executive, the legislature and the judiciary will have to be altered and either the American or the British system of government adopted. But the ordinary Swiss looks upon representative democracy, whether Presidential or Parliamentary, as a poor substitute for the exercise of real sovereignty by the people.

The Radical Party has constantly advocated the introduction of the legislative initiative for federal laws and recently it has been joined by the Socialists. Various arguments are used and repeated for the institution of the legislative initiative and one of a more practical nature is that it would eliminate the practice of using constitutional initiative to insert into the Constitution provisions that should ordinarily be drafted as laws. Various arguments against this institution are also advanced and the most familiar argument is that ''it would further reduce the importance of the Cantons and their protection against the encroachment of the Federal Government.''[19] There may be practical reasons to block the introduction of legislative initiative, but as an institution of direct democracy it is highly valued. The majority of the Cantons have the institution of the legislative initiative. Some of the American States introduced non-constitutional initiative simultaneously with the referendum on the Swiss model. Twenty States of the Middle and Far West already have the right of initiative. Whatever be the verdict on the initiative, the Swiss people, as Hans Huber has said, ''as a whole and in the Cantons have, by and large, given proof of great political maturity in referendum voting.''

## SUGGESTED READINGS


Gruner, Erich, *The Political System of Switzerland.*

Marx, M., *Foreign Governments.*

Munro, W.B. and Ayearst, M., *The Governments of Europe, pp. 725-750.*

Shotwill, J.T. and Others, *Governments of Continental Europe, pp. 351-356.*

Siegfried, Andre : *Switzerland : A Democratic Way of Life.*


17. Rappard, W. E., *The Government of Switzerland,* pp. 74-75.
18. Bonjour, E., *Real Democracy in Operation,* pp. 115-16.
19. Raphael also points out that if a majority of the voters and Cantons should be required for approval of a legislative initiative, ''the only distinction still existing between constitutional and ordinary legislative measures would disappear'' *The Government of Switzerland,* p. 770.

# CHAPTER VIII

# Political Parties and Interest Groups

## Nature of Political Parties

Switzerland is a democracy, but even in democracy, the individual alone is inevitably impotent unless he joins others with similarly minded fellow-individuals to exercise his political authority. When he does so it is the emergence of a political party, which is a necessary tool of democratic government.

In spite of the inevitability of political parties in the Swiss system of government, the Swiss Constitution, like that of the United States, contains no express mention of this instrument of democracy. Political parties in Switzerland have extra-constitutional growth. There is, however, an indirect reference to political parties in the Swiss Constitution since the introduction of proportional representation for the election of the National Council. Article 73, as amended on October 13, 1918, provides: "Elections for the National Council shall be direct. They shall take place according to a system of proportional representation, each Canton or half-Canton forming an electoral district." The principle of proportionality would be meaningless if it did not refer to the parties between whose elected representatives a proportion, similar to that prevailing between their electors, was to be established.

Switzerland too, like other Continental democratic States, relies upon a variety of political parties to organize and promote national opinion. In fact, nowhere else in Europe there are more chances of having political parties than in Switzerland. The suffrage is wide and the people have to vote upon public affairs very often. Then, there are so many diversities of racial character, of religion, of speech, of forms of industry, and of conflicting economic interests. All these diversities are a breeding ground for multiplicity of parties and their frequent regrouping. But it is fortunate for Switzerland that the lines of party do not coincide with those of race and language and nowhere else "has the ship of the State been so little tossed by party oscillations." There are four major political parties and there do not exist extreme differences in their political philosophy and social composition. As the Swiss love for "order and compromise is as strong in politics as it is elsewhere" the multiple-party system has not led to the instability that is found among two of Switzerland's close neighbours.

## History of Political Parties

The political history of the present Confederation begins with the overthrow of the Sonderbund to which a reference has been made earlier[1] and the adoption of the Constitution of 1848. The Constitution sealed the re-union of all the Cantons and created closer ties between them. At that time, federal affairs were dominated by two groups of politicians whose principal support came from the Protestant German Cantons and from Protestant French Cantons. These groups subsequently became known respectively as the Liberals and the Radicals. The former group, the Liberals, consisted of older men who advocated a liberal political philosophy of the traditional *laissez-faire* type, moral and cultural freedom for all, and republican political institutions. The Radicals were younger and progressive people and they were inclined towards a liberalism of more advanced type. They sought to extend political democracy through the institutions of the initiative and the referendum, and advocated a policy of economic liberty with a certain degree of State intervention. Despite their differences, the Liberals and the Radicals actively collaborated in bringing into being the Federal Constitution of 1874, and this document incorporates the philosophies of these parties and resents "centralistic, liberal, secular and democratic features."

Opposed to them was the Catholic Conservative People's Party. It consisted mainly of those elements which had formed the Sonderbund in 1846, and brought in the War of Secession in 1848. The Clericals were ultramontane in their views and were the champions of the Cantonal rights. The party paid, according to Zurcher, "only grudging allegiance to the constitutional

1. See *ante*, Chap. I.

settlement of 1848, into the acceptance of which it had been virtually coerced.'' This party now draws its members mainly from the Cantons where the Catholic majority is overwhelming. It is the most ardent, the most compact and the best organised of the Swiss political parties. The party still opposes certain provisions of the Federal Constitution that they regard as anti-Catholic or as anti-Clericals. It rejects all powerful State and espouses rights of the individuals in regard to family, school, and church. In general, it is hostile to centralisation.

Thus, at the advent of 1874, there were three political parties. The Liberals and the Radicals governed the country from 1848 to 1890 while the Catholic Conservatives remained in the Opposition. The Liberals commanded a large majority in the Federal Assembly and all the seven seats in the Federal Council belonged to them. An important feature of this period is that the Liberal Party's electoral strength decreased considerably whereas that of the Radicals increased enormoulsy. In time, the Radicals commanded a decided majority both in the Council of States and the National Council, but not in the Federal Council, because of the Swiss habit of re-electing the Councillors as long as they wished to serve. With their retirement, however, they were replaced by the Radicals and by 1899, the Federal Council's membership came to include a single Liberal Member.

When the only Liberal member of the Federal Council retired in 1891, the Assembly which was then manned by the Radicals, elected in his place a representative of the Catholic Conservative Party. The Liberal Party became the Opposition. The Radical Conservative Coalition begun in 1891, continued till 1948, when a Socialist found his way. With the resignation ofDr. Weber, the Socialist member of the Council, the Socialist Party decided not to put forward another candidate, The vacated seat was given to Catholic Party. In 1954, the Federal Council was made up of three Radicals, three Catholics, and one Farmer. But the withdrawal by the Socialist Party was temporary. In 1959, it put up two candidates and secured both the seats. The Federal Council then reflected for the first time the true party strength.

After 1880, Switzerland witnessed the rise of the Swiss Social Democratic Party. The Socialists, as their name suggests, were the followers of Karl Marx. The development of industrialization, and the growth of such industrial centres as Zurich, Winterthur, and Basel together with the large immigration of German working men, offered the best opportunity for propagating the socialist doctrines, and the party grew apace. At the end of the First World War, it claimed 41 seats, and in the elections of 1935 it secured 50 seats in the National Council and, thus, became in the next four years the dominant party; the Radical Liberals and Catholic Conservatives having 48 and 42 seats respectively. In 1939 its number fell to 45 as a group of Left-Wing Radicals broke away from the party. In 1943, it again went up to 56, but fell down to 48 in 1947 and in the elections of 1951 its strength stood at 49, and in 1959 at 51.

An important feature of the party system in Switzerland is that a certain conservatism governs the development of parties and none of them is extremist. The socialist of the Swiss Socialist Democratic Party is essentially practical and not revolutionary, although in the early days of its career it believed in the collective ownership of all the means of production, in an inevitable class struggle and, consequently, in violent and unconstitutional methods. But as Switzerland is a mountainous country of small holdings and the peasantry wedded to the soil with strong patriotic sentiments, the revolutionary aspect of socialism did not have much appeal for the people. Moreover, the Communal and Cantonal public enterprise, the nationalisation of rails and roads, forests, water power, etc., made the programme of the socialists less attractive. They were, accordingly, compelled to make their programmes less militant as compared with those of the socialist parties in certain other countries. The Swiss Socialist Democratic Party, therefore, reconciled itself to the democratic and constitutional principles. The Party has now openly declared its faith in an evolutionary form of socialism.

The Socialist Democratic Party is the most highly organised political party in Switzerland and it has its branches in all the Cantons. It stands for nationalization of industries and all private monopolies, higher wages, social security, compulsory liquidation of agricultural debts, unemployment relief, recognition of the right to work, and suffrage for women.

**Other Parties**

With the introduction of proportional representation in national elections in 1918, many more parties emerged in. The Farmers, Workers and Middle Class Party was organised in 1918 as a result of split from the Radicals because of dissatisfaction with the latter's agrarian policy. In 1929, the Radical conservative coalition was broadened to include a representative of the Farmers Party which claimed 31 seats in the National Council. In 1935, the Party could command only 21 seats and this number continues since then with a seat fluctuating this or that way. This fall-off was primarily due to the coming into existence of another agrarian party called the Young Farmers who secured four seats in 1935, 6 in 1943, 5 in 1947, 4 in 1951 in the National Council. The Farmers Party is intensely patriotic and vigorously favours measures for adequate national defence. Its programme is decidedly for the protection of agricultural interests and advocates a policy of advancement of agricultural interests by means of federal subventions.

Other minor parties, at present, represented in the National Council include the Independence Party formed in 1935, the Independent Social Democrats, the Nicole group which seceded from the socialists in 1939, and the Communists. The Communists, who now call themselves the Labour Party, have increased their following, but their success in the stable political conditions of Switzerland can never be phenomenal.

**Features of the Swiss Party System**

The Swiss party system is now more akin to the French rather than the Anglo-American system. The reasons for multiplicity of parties in Switzerland are obvious. It is a country of diversities, more Communal and Cantonal rather than federal in its political outlook and, consequently, the political parties, too, are not nationally organized. Switzerland, unlike other democracies has not in any true sense a party government. There are no nationwide elections for a national office such as that of a President. Elections to the Federal Assembly have a strong local colour. National party organizations are maintained now but really their practice is to constitute mere alliances for common nationwide purposes with otherwise independent Cantonal parties; the only exception being the Social Democratic Party.

Switzerland also disproves the contention that democratic government cannot work unless there is a definite majority party or a coalition of parties. Minority parties find representation in the Federal Council and in the Executive Councils of almost all the Cantons. This enables them to exert a direct influence on the conduct of public affairs. Thoroughly partisan administration is, therefore, out of question in Switzerland. There is also absence of strict party control in the Federal Assembly. Party lines are rarely drawn, except on measures that have an immediate bearing on party interests or on religion. The result is that there is the absence of party machinery. There are no national committees, no elaborate system of party caucuses and general conventions. The Radicals and the Clericals, and so the Socialists, do occasionally hold their Congresses, but they can have no resemblance with party meetings in the United Kingdom, India, and other countries.

Another feature of the Swiss party system is that there are no party leaders. The absence of party leaders is partly due to the non-party executive at the Centre as well as in the Cantons, and partly because the parties are divided on local rather than on national issues. Lowell says that it would be "more accurate to say that federal representatives are chosen by the Cantonal parties." The influence of the leaders consequently finds expression in their own Cantons and their power is local rather than national. Another reason is that there is no opportunity for anyone in Switzerland to extend patronage and distribute spoils. Finally, there is neither professionalism in politics nor party funds. Administration has attained in Switzerland a stage of business-like efficiency. Demagogues do not find favour with the Swiss people. Nor do the representatives find time, during the short sittings of Swiss Parliament of ten to twelve weeks, in a year, to permit "talkers and fighters." The Federal Assembly is the most business-like body in the world and it does its work quietly. Obstruction in the conduct of business is unknown and divisions are much less frequent.

Politics is run is Switzerland more cheaply than anywhere else in the world. Money for party purposes is needed only when the party requires scientific organization, meetings to be held for nursing the constituencies and diffusing literature. All parties, including the socialists, agree on three fundamentals: Swiss independence, Swiss neutrality, and Swiss trade. They may disagree on details and on the best method of achieving the objectives, but on the importance of the threefold goal there can be no difference of opinion. Then, there is no bid to capture the government. The defeat of a party leader in the elections is neither desired nor it is manipulated. In fact, pains are taken "to provide against such contingency." Politics, therefore, in Switzerland is unadulterated and a game of the veterans who play it in a sportsman spirit. There is complete absence of the motive of personal profit. "It is not worth anybody's while," writes Bryce, "to spend money on party work except for some definite public purpose. Nobody in Switzerland has anything to gain for his own pocket by the victory of a party, for places are poorly paid. Federal places do not change hands after an election. Cantonal places are not important enough to deserve a costly fight, nor could the expenditure of money at an election escape notice in these small communities."

The spirit of political parties is, thus, weaker in Switzerland than in most other democracies of the world. The political organizations are less tightly knit and less actively worked. In the mountainous and agricultural regions, there are only local questions that occupy the people. In the industrial parts of the country, political parties are more active, but their issues are so diverse and their problems so numerous, because of natural diversities, that it is impossible to give a general description of Cantonal politics. The result is that the parties in the Cantons are not necessarily the same as in the Confederation. They do not always even bear the same names. The Cantonal elections are usually fought on Cantonal and not on national issues. The Swiss while electing their representatives, respect ability and trust those whom they have long known as honest and courageous. Party enthusiasm and hero worship seem foreign to their nature.

Such a party system, as is obtainable in Switzerland, has tranquillizing, stabilizing and ennobling influence. There is no incentive to party organization and chances of a party warfare are reduced to a minimum. The extreme stability of the parties is the most remarkable peculiarity of the Swiss political life. The majority parties are not obliged to make any great effort to retain their positions. The minority parties become passive by the consciousness that they have no chance of getting control of the government. Moreover, politics in Switzerland is conducted almost without regard to party leanings. When one party has the stable support of a large part of the nation and its supremacy is firmly established, its members are not rigidly compelled to stand together for all intents and purposes.

**Interest Groups**

Interest groups activity in Switzerland, writes Codding, "is integrated, to a great extent, into the normal political process." This is essentially due to the presence of the multiple party system. Although there is no fundamental difference in the philosophy of the various Swiss political parties, but the political platform and activities of these parties do reflect the divergence of attitude and approach towards many of the major economic, social and political problems confronting the country. Interest groups, accordingly, find a party whose attitude reflects their approach to the problems and its solution and they join hands to make a common cause. If such a party does not exist, a new party, helped by the Swiss system of proportional representation, comes into existence. This is true both on the national as well as Cantonal levels.

The organisation of the Federal Assembly, brief sessions of both the Houses, and meagre salàries for the Deputies make it difficult for a professional politician to exist. Even the self-employed, such as, lawyers with private practice, hesitate to render parliamentary service. The result is that their places are taken by the Trade and Industrial union officials, and won by industrial executives all of whose salaries are assured during their parliamentary tenures. "There is also the traditional abhorrence of the Swiss voter for the professional politician. When men are drafted for political office, their backgrounds of success in private life, business, farming or labor (labour) union activity is usually the deciding issue". The nature of the system is consequently favourable to group activity.

Section 3 of Article 32 of the Constitution provides that "Interested economic organisations shall be consulted prior to the enactment of the executory legislation and may be called upon to cooperate in the application of executory legislations." The Federal Council has made it a practice to call upon interest groups that might be affected by new legislation to state their views and even help draft the new law. Testimony from the interest groups is also called for by the legislative committees which give new legislation its first close scrutiny. Interest group activity is, therefore inevitable at different stages of legislative process.

The interest groups are always active at the legislative referendum. If the law passed by the legislature conflicts with the views and interests of a particular group, it attempts to force a legislative referendum. The tendency of the Swiss voters "to reject a goodly portion of legislation when brought before them for the first time can be a powerful weapon." The constitutional initiative is also valuable. Although a constitutional initiative has a very little chance of being accepted by the voters, but the reference of an issue to the people for their verdict can have tremendous publicity value for the cause of the interest group.

Four of the most powerful interest groups are the Swiss Union of Commerce and Industry, commonly called the VORORT; the Swiss Peasants Union; the Swiss Federation of Trade Unions; and the Swiss Association of Arts and Crafts. All these four major interest groups are usually represented in the Federal Assembly. There are many other interest groups, which whether or not represented in the Federal Assembly can always bring their weight in favour of or against legislation affecting their interests. Some criticism of the existing interest groups has been voiced, but their supporters are in a great majority. Some contend that all interest groups must have their say in order to make it possible to determine what is the national interest. Others have faith that the manner of selecting legislators and the manner of selection and composition of the Federal Council, which is a collegiate body and plays an important role in the legislative mechanics, ensures that the Swiss public servant "will remain true to his political, legal and moral responsibilities". If worst comes to worst, the Swiss voter has confidence in his own ability to choose right from wrong. After all the majority has its ultimate weapons, the referendum, backed by the constitutional initiative.

## SUGGESTED READINGS


Bonjour, E.: *Real Democracy in Operation, The Example of Switzerland.*

Bonjour, E., Officer, H.S., and Potter, G.R.: *A Short History of Switzerland.*

Brooks, R.C.: *Government and Politics of Switzerland.*

Bryce, J.: *Modern Democracies,* Vol. I, Chaps. XXVII—XXXII.

Buell, R.L.: *Democratic Governments in Europe,* pp. 557-84.

Codding, G.R.: *The Federal Government of Switzerland.*

Ghosh, R. C.: *The Government of the Swiss Republic.*

Hans Huber: *How Switzerland is Governed.*

Hughes, C.: *The Federal Constitution of Switzerland.*

Kahn, Hans: *Nationalism and Liberty: The Swiss Example.*

Lowell, A.L.: *Government and Parties in Continental Europe,* Vol. II, Chaps. XI, XII.

Marx, M.: *Foreign Governments.*

Munro, W.B. and Ayearst, M.: *The Governments of Europe,* pp. 725-50.

Neumann, R.G.: *European and Comparative Governments.*

Ogg, F.A., and Zink, H.: *Modern Foreign Governments.*

Rappard, W.E.: *The Government of Switzerland.*

Sauser-Hall, Georges: *The Political Institutions of Switzerland.*

Shotwell, J.T., and Others: *Governments of Conntinental Europe,* pp. 351-6.

Siegfried, Andre: *Switzerland: A Democratic Way of Life.*

Solaveytchik, George: *Switzerland in Perspective.*

Spiro, Herbert, J. : *Government by Constitution,*

Tripp, M.L.: *The Swiss and United States Federal Constitutional Systems.*

Wheare, K.C.: *Federal Government.*

# CHAPTER IX

# The Swiss Political System

## Republican Legacy

The political system of Switzerland and its constituent Cantons is the product of gradual aggregation and evolution from its original communes, both rural and urban, that came into existence during the Middle Ages. The Alpine communities, living in practical isolation from each other, developed republican institutions from a very early phase in their political history. Their social and political structures represented a transition from their traditional, tribal, egalitarian and democratic features to medieval, feudalistic, patriarchal and oligarchical, characteristics. Pastoral communities preferred tribal, popular assemblies where their menfolk gathered to transact their political business periodically. Larger communes with a mix of agricultural and some industrial activities developed a class of landowning nobles and rich burghers. These communities graduated to elective Republics where the ruling aristocrats legitimized their power to govern on the basis of a semblance of popular consent obtained through pressure and even intimidation. The fact that the Swiss communes and Cantons were Republican did not mean that they were democratic in terms of their social and political system as well. In their actual working, they were entrenched oligarchies.

Rousseau was the first to idealize the city-state of Geneva in his *Social Contract* as a policy based on direct, participatory democracy forgetting its oligarchical base in the urban bourgeoisie and the absentee landowners. Since then, the Republican tradition and features of the Swiss political system have been magnified to celebrate Switzerland as a land of unprecedented 'democratic' virtues. Republicanism of the Swiss people was more a product of historical accident than a result of any popular initiative or national planning. Yet the Republican legacy is important for understanding the present character of Swiss political institutions.

The Republican legacy of Switzerland enabled the country to maintain a highly decentralized and autonomous structure for its Cantons and communes, which have experimented with their own mini-Republican institutions without any homogenising influence from any monarchical centre. We know that the Hapsburg dynasty, which ruled over the Austro-Hungarian Empire, was itself of the Swiss ethnic origin but it did not succeed in extending its overlordship over the Swiss Cantons as they jointly defended themselves from any encroachments by forming a League. The then 13 cantons united into a loose alliance and became formally independent of the Holy Roman Empire in 1648.

No addition was made to the number of Cantons till 1798. In that year, under the influence of France, the unified Helvetic Republic was formed. The ideas of the French Revolution were gradually penetrating the Swiss mountains, hills and valleys but they failed to satisfy the Swiss people, who loved their local liberties too much and could not think of sacrificing them at the altar of a centralised, national Republic. Had the Helvetic Republic survived, the Swiss people might have become a unified nation with a centralised administration on the French constitutional model. This did not happen because unlike France, the Swiss people did not constitute a homogenous linguistic nationality, nor even a compact religious community and no monarch had ever consolidated the separate, autonomous Cantons and communes into a well-ordered kingdom. Their fragmented, pluralistic and exclusivist Republican legacy precluded the emergence and stabilisation of any nation-based Republic. The Helvetic Republic formed on the French nationalistic model, therefore, could not last even for a decade.

Just five years after its creation, Napoleon Bonaparte gave a new constitution to the people of Switzerland through the Act of Mediation in 1803. Out of the lands, allied or conquered earlier, new Cantons were formed to increase their member to 19. After the defeat of Napoleon, Switzerland regained her complete sovereignty. In 1815, the Holy Alliance powers, Austria, Prussia, Russia, Great Britain and other European states, which assembled in the Congress of Vienna, guaranteed the perpetual neutrality of Switzerland along with the inviolability of her territoy. Through a Federal Pact, 3 new Cantons were added to complete the territorial boundaries of the country. In 1848, after a short Civil War between the Catholic and Protestant Cantons, in which the latter were victorious, a new Constitution was adopted without external interference. The 22 Cantons set up a Federal Government, consisting of a Federal Council, a Federal Parliament and a Federal Tribunal. This Constitution, in turn, was superseded on 29 May, 1874 by the present Constitution. Switzerland was thus transformed from a League of Republican Cantons into a multinational Federal Republic, though technically it was still designated as a Confederation, which was a misnomer.

### A Product of Historical Compromise

This functioning democracy of the Swiss Confederation disproves the thesis that the modern state should be founded on the principle of single nationality. About 19 Cantons are German-speaking, which could have become easily a part of the German nation. A section of the German speaking population was drawn towards Germany during the Nazi era but the Government suppressed this movement without much opposition. The German-speakinmg Swiss constitute 74% of the nation and are satisfied with 4 seats in a Federal Council of 7 members. The French-speaking Swiss form about 19% of the total population and have been allotted 2 seats on the federal Council. The Italian-speaking Swiss can claim a majority in only one Canton, Ticino, and constitute just 5% of the country's population and yet they permanently occupy one seat in the Federal Council.

The 'Federal Executive' thus represents a coalitional principle, in which 74% Germans are accorded only 57% share, 19% French get a weightage of 29% and 5% Italians receive a quota of 14%, thus respecting the terms of a historic compromise which is now about 150 years old. Within the same formula, the Protestants are given 4 seats (57%) and the Catholics are entitled to 3 seats (43%) in the Federal Cabinet. Further, two large Cantons, Berne and Zurich are always represented, no other Canton can claim more than one seat, and political parties should also be given proportional representation in the Federal Executive. Major parties such as Catholic Conservatives and Social Democrats usually get two seats each while three minor parties are accorded one seat each. Except for a short duration in 1950s when the Social Democrats refused to participate in the ruling coalition, there has been no formal opposition in the Swiss Parliament. Only a small group of Communists keeps away from this coalitional arrangement.

The Swiss Federal Council is thus a visible symbol of the harmony that now exists between major linguistic, religious and political groupings in the country. The German-speaking group in Federal Parliament usually nominates two Protestant and two Catholic representatives who may belong to the Conservative, the Social Democratic and the Peasant and Middle class parties. The French-speaking group nominates two Protestant representatives who may usually belong to the Social Democratic or Radical parties. The Italian-speaking group nominates one Catholic representative who may usually belong to the Radical or some other minor party. When a vacancy occurs, only one or two candidates can be identified in accordance with the criteria fixed on the basis of language, religion and party allegiance. But the historic compromise never fails to deliver results and disequilibrium is almost always avoided.

Unlike Belgium, whose neutrality was violated by Germany in both the World Wars, the strategic situation of Switzerland was such that no invading army felt the need to enter Switzerland in order to attack a third country. Moreover, the belligerents have used the neutral status of the country to maintain some minimum contact between them through the mediation of the Swiss Government. This gave the Swiss people full opportunity to maintain their federalized political institutions and system of participatory democracy in the stable condition undisturbed by warfare around their borders. While a large nation like France suffered Nazi occupation and the ignominy of a puppet Vichy regime, resulting in the disgrace of the Third Republic and the enfeeblement of the Fourth Republic after the war, there was no such catastrophic turmoil on the Swiss territory where its liberal political institutions kept on advancing on a leisurely pace both at 'Confederal' and Cantonal levels despite linguistic and religious schisms and political party cleavages. Otherwise, a Swiss General de Gaulle could have subverted the 1874 constitutional arrangement and imposed a Ceasarist constitution *a la* the Fifth Republic on Switzerland too. One may argue that England's insular separation from European convulsions and Switzerland's Alpine exclusion from the surrounding centres of catastrophic events have protected their democratic political evolution from being vitiated by any external intervention.

**Class Structure and Elites**

The Swiss society is quite different from other capitalist societies such as the United Kingdom, the United States, France and Canada discussed earlier in a multitude of ways. It has a different history, traditions, languages, cultures and institutions which distinguish Switzerland from all of them. But it shares two features with them: the first is that it is like them a highly industrialised society; and the second is that the largest part of the means of economic activity is there too under private control and ownership. As an advanced capitalist society, it may resemble even Japan in some respects, but it should be differentiated from under-industrialized countries such as India or Egypt, even though there too the means of production etc., are mainly under private ownership and control.

It is true, as Joseph Schumpeter pointed out, that "social structures, types and attitudes are coins that do not readily melt; once they are formed they persist, possibly for centuries; and since different structures and types display different degrees of ability to survive, we almost always find that actual group or national behaviour more or less departs from what we should expect it to be if we tried to infer from the dominant forms of the productive process."[1]

Yet the class structure and the nature of elite formation in Switzerland, despite its national peculiarities, is not very different from that of other countries of advanced capitalism. As Schonfield suggests, "there is a certain uniformity in the texture of their societies....and even more markedly in terms of their behaviour over a period of years, the similarities are striking."[2] Like other advanced capitalist countries Switzerland also has a notable 'public sector', which is mainly 'infra-structural and like them, the state there also plays a substantial role by way of regulation, control, co-ordination etc. Similarly, the state is by far the largest customer of the 'private sector', which depends upon the credits, subsidies and benefits that it dispenses.

In Switzerland, we find a vast scatter of individually or corporately owned small and medium-scale businesses, forming thousands of economic units. They constitute a distinct and important segment of the Swiss economy and profoundly influence the working of its polity as well. There is no doubt that economic trends adversely affect small and medium-sized enterprises. Consequently, many of them try to survive by becoming dependent on and subsidiary to giant corporations including the multinationals. Switzerland, being a tax haven, welcomes foreign capital. British, German and French capital is invested in mining, steel industry, tourism and other businesses including hydro-electric power. The Swiss banks retain enormous deposits from all over the world which are a great resource for the development of the national economy.

There is every reason to believe that the Swiss economy is now dominated by giant enterprises, both indigenous and foreign, in terms of management as well as the share of invested capital. Switzerland may keep out of the United Nations politically or the NATO militarily to protect its status of a neutralised state, but is has become fully integrated within the formidable capitalist complexes that have come into existence in Western Europe. The transnational character of this giant enterprise "has very large implications" for a small, multi-ethnic nation like Switzerland "not only in economic terms but in political terms as well."[3] The European Economic Community, with which this Alpine nation is informally allied in numerous ways, "is one institutional expression of this phenomenon and represents an attempt to overcome, within the context of capitalism, one of its major 'contradictions', namely the constantly more marked obsolescence of the nation-state as the basic unit of international life."[4]

There is to be found in Switzerland a relatively small class of the Swiss people with a sprinkling of aliens from other parts of Western Europe, particularly German and British, who own a markedly disproportionate share of the nation's wealth, and whose incomes are largely derived from that ownership. Taken together,

1. Quoted in R. Bendix, *Nation-Building and Citizenship*, p.8
2. A Schorfield, *Modern Capitalism*, p.65.3
3. See on this theme E-Mandel, "International Capitalism and 'Supra-Nationality'" in the *Socialist Register*, 1967.
4. R. Miliband, *The State in Capital Society* p.15.

here is the class which Marxists have often designated as 'the ruling class' of a capitalist country. This point may be debatable. But it is possible to note the existence of economic elites which as proprietors and managers command many of the most vital sectors of the Swiss economy. Again, in Switzerland too, the opposite end of social scale is occupied by a working class which is mostly composed of factory, hotel and mine workers with agricultural earners forming a steadily diminishing part of the labour force.[5]

The work process in the Swiss society, as anywhere under capitalism, remains one of domination and subjection. As Professor Dahrendorf points out, privileged birth accompained by education in elitist schools and universities ensures position of power in industry, banking and state bureaucracy. In a 'meritocratic' society like that of Switzerland, "the race is still rigged-against the working-class competitors."[6] A university degree only offers a start in the post university race. But here too the race remains rigged because several other factors materially affect career patterns. One of these is the net-work of 'connections' which links members of the elite groups. In contrast, the working-class families do not have good connections. An occasional success of a working-class youth does not disrupt the class hierarchy of a capitalist system. It rather strengthens it by creating a myth of 'equal opportunity' under liberal capitalism. Aristocratic elites have been assimilated to the world of industrial, financial and commercial enterprises through a process of 'bourgeoisification.' Today, bourgeois elites exercise a much greater degree of political power and influence than any other social class or group in the working of the Swiss political system.

Switzerland has not been involved in any war since its neutralization in 1815 and yet it maintains a large army and airforce. It has a well-entrenched military elite which promotes sentiments of patriarchy, male chauvinism and conservatism in the Swiss society. Though Federal Parliament favoured franchise for the Swiss women in 1959, the male electorate rejected it in a referendum and one of the arguments advanced against giving vote to women was that they are not full citizens of the Republic as they are incapable of bearing arms in its defence. Thus they could get voting rights only 12 years later in July,1971. The judges and bureaucrats are as status quoist in Switzerland as their colonels and brigadiers on most social and political issues. But the most significant aspect of the Swiss political system is the partial paralysis of its political parties which have almost completely surrendered their ideology and independent judgment to the requirements of a permanent, all-party coalition that governs the country as an instrument of the dominant classs. Almost continuous inclusion of two Social Democratic minters in the Government guarantees that class conflict will be effectively controlled in the interest of capitalist stabilization and liberal-democratic political equilibrium.

There is one last aspect of the process of legitimation to which reference must be made in the case of Switzerland. The most celebrated element of the Swiss Constitution is its provision for the institutions of direct democracy such as referendum and intiative and the phenomenon of an all-citizen people's assembly in one Canton and four Half-Contons. Actually, this limited experiment in the working of direct, participatory democracy has proved to be an anti-climax because the sovereign people have been even more conservative on social, economic and political issues than the political elites in Parliament. This shows the cultural hegemony of the dominant classes over the subordinate ones through the generation of a false consciousness among the masses by the elites. This legitimation cannot be attributed to the ameliorative capacities of capitalism only. Marx wrote in *Capital* that "The advance of capitalist production develops a working class, which by education, tradition, habit, looks, upon the conditions of that mode of production as self evident laws of nature.... the dull compulsion of economic relations completes the subjection of the labourer to the capitalist,"[7]

Ralph Miliband says, "Here, indeed, is 'socialisation', produced by the operation of system itself and only enhanced by the legitimation process."[8] In addition, the manipulative powers of the dominant cultural apparatus also shape the political behaviour of the masses. Moreover, classes, including the working classes tend to instil in their children the mental habits and ex-

5. For some relevant figures, see Russtt et al, *World Handbook*, pp. 177-179.
6. Ralph Militand, *The State in Capitalist Society*, pp. 40-41.
7. Karl Marx, *Capital,* Vol 1, p. 737.
8. R. Militand, *The State in Capitalist Society*, pp. 234-235.

pectations associated with their own class. They tell their children that the path to success lies not in rebellion but in conformity to the values, prejudices and ideas of the dominant class. In short, the subordinate condition of the working class is itself a major factor in its 'political socialisation.' This explains the genesis of popular conservatism in the Swiss political system of participatory democracy.

## SUGGESTED READINGS

Bonjour, E., *Real Democracy in Operation, The Example of Switzerland*
Huber, Hans, *How Switzerland is Governed*?
Kahn, Hans, *Nationalism and Liberty-The Swiss Example.*
Miliband, Ralph, *The State in Capitalist Society.*
Rappard, W.E., *The Government of Switzerland.*
Sauser-Hall, Georges, *The Political Institutions of Switzerland.*
Siegfried, Andre, Switzerland: *A Democratic Way of Life.*
Tripp, M.L., *The Swiss and United States Constitutional Systems.*
Woddis, Jack, *New Theories of Revolution.*

# THE GOVERNMENT OF JAPAN

## CHAPTER I

# The Constitution of Japan (1946)

### Japan's Political Tradition

The Japanese archipelago, situated off the east of the Asian Continent consists of the four principal islands of Honshu, Hokkaido, Shikoku, and Kyushu plus thousands of small islands. In area Japan is 369,622 square kilometers or 147,727 square miles (only for the area under actual administration of Japan) and it stretches 2,000 kilometers or 1,500 square miles in a north, south-west direction, between 27 and 45 degree north. Japan is roughly one-twentieth the size of the United States of America, one-eighth of the size of India, but is slightly larger than that of the United Kingdom or Italy.

Japan is an island empire characterised by complex features and this fact has profoundly affected the political character of the country during the past two thousand years and more. In the first place, the island and the mountains made land communications pretty difficult and, consequently, have produced regional outlook and psychology of the people. Each region has its own distinct history and traditions and possessed in the past some sort of political identity too. This sort of localism and fragmentation disappeared after the Restoration in 1868, when Japan was unified for the first time in her history. Yet this outlook did not disappear altogether from the minds of the people. Their political behaviour and, as such, the practical politics of the country are still prominently influenced by the historical legacy of the political decentralization and localism.

Secondly, Japan's insularity provided for her a well defined frontier which created amongst her people a sense of group identity and strong nationalist feelings. Japan's nationalism is proverbial. Then, unlike Korea, which is physically contiguous to China, the Japanese have developed their own culture by selecting only those elements of civilisation which suited their genius and served their needs. In due course such elements were assimilated into Japanese culture completely and "in such a manner as to lose their original identity, frequently giving rise to products far different from and even superior to original." The cultural homogeneity of the Japanese has produced such a sense of social solidarity amongst them that at no stage of Japan's history there has been development of any kind of racial antagonism. Racism, therefore, has been unknown throughout her history and racial problems have never arisen in Japanese politics for racial groups have never existed to form a minority. Japan had a population of 121,050,000 as of October 1, 1985 of which only 0.7 per cent belonged to registered minority group.[1] There is no other major nation with so small an admixture of identifiable minority elements. This also helps to explain the strong nationalism frequently displayed by the Japanese in modern times.

Their geographical isolation, common language and long history combined with racial identity to facilitate the development of very strong 'in-group' feeling against foreigners. The result is a nation which although subject to a number of domestic cleavages, has in the past usually presented a strong and united front to the rest of the world. Nature has also endowed Japan with a degree of national security. Prior to 1945 no one had ever successfully invaded Japan since the pre-historic times. Her national development was, therefore, achieved without the disruptive effects of foreign invasions and in accordance with the expression of the native genius. "This fact", according to Robert Ward "has had two

1. Only one million *burakumanis (untouchables)* and 600,000 Korean residents remain unassimilated.

prime consequences for the Japanese. First, it has enabled them to turn on and off almost at will the stream of intercourse with the Asian countries or the rest of the world. It made possible, for example, the effective adoption of deliberate policy of national seclusion for almost 250 years prior to 1854. Second, it has enabled the Japanese to concentrate exclusively and almost fiercely on domestic political issues, domestic power struggles and internecine strife with little or no concern for the effect that might have on the external safety of the nation. National security carried to this extent is unparalleled among the other great states of modern history.''[2]

There are three stages which cover the development of the Japan's constitutional history—from the dawn of history to 1185 A.D., from 1185 to 1868; and the third from 1868 onwards. Chitoshi Yanaga describes the three stages as pre-feudal period, the feudal period, and the post-feudal period. For our purposes we are primarily concerned with the post-feudal period.

The end of the eighteenth century witnessed vital changes in the social and political life of Japan. The country was being put to an increasing pressure for opening her ports to foreign ships and there appeared to be no alternative left to the Government but to revise the previous decision. There were also quite visible signs everywhere indicating decay of the feudalistic social and political structure. Historic clan enmities against the Tokugawa became significantly prominent. All these factors coupled with the dissatisfaction of the Samurai on their deteriorating economic and social status gave birth to a movement for the restoration of the power to the Emperor. The movement was strengthened when in 1854, Japan abandoned the policy of isolation and concluded a treaty of amity with the United States to be soon followed by similar treaties with other European countries. The enemies of the Shogun found a favourable climate to impress upon the Japanese people that such treaties posed a serious threat to the integrity of Japan and would lead to Western imperialistic exploitation. The movement gained momentum and its leaders rallied round the Emperor by proclaiming: ''Revere the Emperor, expel the barbarians.'' The Tokugawa regime ultimately collapsed. In 1867, Shogun Tokugawa declared the end of the military government *bakufu* and in 1868, the sixteen- year-old Emperor Mutshito ascended the throne.

The period intervening the Restoration and promulgation of the Meiji Constitution (1868-89) is described as pre-parliamentary. This period, according to Chitoshi Yanaga, ''was an interlude, a transition stage, between feudalism and constitutionalism which was dominated by a small oligarchy under an interim system of absolute monarchy.''[3] Every effort was made to stabilize monarchy and to make the Emperor's writ run throughout the length and breadth of the country. To mark the transfer of political authority, Edo was renamed Tokyo, and the Shogun's palace was taken over by the Emperor.

But it was not a smoother switchover at least in the first decade after the Restoration. Opposition was intense on all sides. The sweeping changes from feudalism to oligarchically-run absolute monarchy headed by a minor Emperor, were subjects of bitter dispute. In 1877, discontented Samurai rebelled. Conditions, however, settled down when the Satsuma Rebellion was put down. The time was, accordingly, opportune to determine finally the form of government which should mould and shape the destinies of the nation.

There was, however, a fundamental difference on this issue. The opposition was pretty vocal on demanding an early establishment of a representative parliament and organised political parties. The government was reluctant to accede to this demand in the beginning but ultimately yielded to the irresistible pressure and ceaseless agitation of the opposition. In 1881, the government declared that constitution providing for elective parliament would be promulgated in 1890. Immediately after this announcement political parties came into existence.

Prince Ito Hirobumi was entrusted with the task of formulating the Constitution. The Drafting Committee consisting of three members, including Ito Hirobumi completed their labour in 1888, and the Draft Constitution was submitted to the Privy Council for its approval. After receiving its approval the Constitution was bestowed on the Japanese nation as a gracious gift from the Emperor on 11 February, 1989. The Meiji Constitution, as it was officially known, remained in force until Japan's surrender to the Allied Powers on 2 September, 1945.

The Constitution remained in existence for

2. Ward, Robert E. and Macridis, Roy C. (Eds.), *Modern Political Systems : Asia,* pp. 39-40.
3. Japanese People and Politics, p. 18.

58 years, but it was never amended. The achievements of the Restoration and Meiji Constitution can best be summed up in the words of a publication, issued by the Bureau of Statistics, Office of the Prime Minister. It stated: "The Meiji Restoration was like the bursting of a dam behind which had accumulated the energies and forces of centuries. Japan set out to achieve in only a few decades what had taken centuries to develop in the West—the creation of a modern nation, with modern industries, modern political institutions and a modern pattern of society. The surge and ferment caused by the sudden release of energies made themselves felt overseas. Japan emerged victorious from the Sino-Japanese War of 1894-95 and the Russo-Japanese War of 1904-05. By the end of World War I, which she entered under the provision of the Anglo-Japanese Alliance of 1902, Japan was recognised as one of the world's greatest powers."[4]

While Japan's progress as a modern industrial nation and of the world's greatest powers was spectacular and speedy, there were problems which confronted the nation's social, economic and political life in the mid-twenties. The World Economic Depression of 1929 intensified all these problems. Elements, particularly in the army, who advocated that overseas expansion was the only solution of difficulties facing Japan, eventually dominated and controlled the national policy. The militarists and ultranationalists predicted the destiny of Japan to become an empire that would ultimately dominate all Eastern Asia. They, accordingly preached the doctrines of racist mythology, national superiority and divinely sanctioned imperialism. They engineered the establishment of Japan's domination over Manchuria and attempted other military ventures in China, and finally drove the nation into the Pacific War and disastrous defeat. After the War, Japan was placed under Allied Occupation, and a new Constitution, based on the ideals of democracy and peace, as conceived by the Occupation Authorities, was promulgated in 1947. Japan regained her independence in 1952, and a few years later was admitted into the United Nations.

### The Potsdam Declaration and Occupation

On July 26, 1945 in Potsdam, Germany, President Truman and Prime Minister Clement Attlee (who had just succeeded Winston Churchill), with the concurrence of Chiang Kai-shek, issued a declaration incorporating the terms for the surrender of Japan. It was essentially the handiwork of America, for it was drafted by the United States and was based on a paper originally prepared by two officials of the State Department. Russia was not a signatory to the Potsdam Declaration as she was then not at war with Japan. Two weeks later when Russia entered the War, she signified her approval to the principles contained in the Potsdam Declaration. Since the Potsdam terms of surrender have important bearing on the Constitution of 1946, these are quoted here in full :

"There must be eliminated for all time the authority and influence of those who have deceived and misled the people of Japan into embarking on world conquest, for we insist that a new order of peace, security and justice will be impossible until, irresponsible militarism is driven from the world.

Until such a new order is established and until there is convincing proof that Japan's war-making power is destroyed, points in Japanese territory to be designated by the Allies shall be occupied to secure the achievement of basic objective we are here setting forth.

The terms of the Cairo Declaration[5] shall be carried out and Japanese territory shall be limited to the island of Honshu, Hokkaido, Kyoshu, Shikoku, and such minor islands as we determine.

The Japanese military forces, after being completely disarmed, shall be permitted to return to their homes with the opportunity to lead peaceful and productive lives.

We do not intend that the Japanese shall be enslaved as a race or destroyed as a nation, but stern justice shall be meted out to all war criminals, including those who have visited cruelties upon our prisoners. The Japanese Government shall remove all obstacles to the survival and strengtening of democratic tendencies among the Japanese people. Freedom of speech, of religion and of thought, as well as respect for the fundamental human rights, shall be established.

4. p. 4.
5. The Cairo Declaration of Roosevelt, Chiang Kai-shek and Churchill of December 1, 1943, had provided that Japan would be deprived of all the islands in the Pacific which she had seized and occupied since the beginning of World War I and all that Japan had stolen from the Chinese, such as Manchuria, Formosa, and the Pescadores would be restored to the Republic of China. Japan would be expelled from " all other territories which she had taken by violence and greed." Korea "in due course" would become free and independent.

Japan shall be permitted to maintain such industries as will sustain her economy and permit the execution of just reparations in kind, but not those which would enable her to rearm for war. To this end, access to, as distinguished from control of, raw materials shall be permitted. Eventual Japanese participation in world trade relations shall be permitted.

The occupying forces of the Allies shall be withdrawn from Japan as soon as those objectives have been accomplished and there has been established in accordance with the freely expressed will of the Japanese people a peacefully inclined and responsible government.

The first offer of the Japanese Government to accept the terms of the Potsdam Declaration was delivered through the Swiss Government on August 10, 1945, "with the understanding that the said declaration does not comprise any demand which prejudices the prerogative of His Majesty as a Sovereign Ruler." The Allies in their reply referred to the position of the Emperor somewhat indirectly in the following terms : "From the moment of surrender the Authority of the Emperor and the Japanese Government to rule the State shall be subject to the Supreme Commander of the Allied Powers who will take such steps as he deems proper to effectuate the surrender terms. The ultimate form of government of Japan shall, in accordance with the Potsdam Declaration, be established by the freely expressed will of the Japanese people." This clearly implied that the Allied Powers would like to continue with the monarchy in Japan after Occupation subject to two conditions. Firstly, the Emperor would be subject to the authority of the Supreme Commander of the Allied Powers, and secondly, the future form of government, as also the role the Emperor would play therein, would be determined by the Japanese people themselves.

The assurances that the Emperor would continue to reign, and that the Japanese Government would continue in existence after the surrender were accepted by Japan. On September 2, 1945, Allied and Japanese representatives signed the Instrument of Surrender aboard the U.S.S. Missouri in Tokyo Bay. General Douglas MacArthur was appointed Supreme Commander for the Allied Powers to direct the Occupation and to effectuate the surrender terms which for brevity could be reduced to demilitarization, disarmament and democratization.

Although the Occupation was complete and the authority of the Supreme Commander for the Allied Powers was absolute, the Japanese Government continued as before with the Emperor at the head of the nation. The Allied Powers and for that matter the Supreme Commander never ruled Japan directly. This was unlike Germany. The relationship between the Supreme Commander and the Japanese Government was clearly stated in "United States' Initial Postsurrender Policy for Japan."[6] It was determined that:

"The authority of the Emperor and the Japanese Government will be subject to the Supreme Commander, who will possess all powers to effectuate the surrender terms and to carry out the policies established for the conduct of the occupation and the control of Japan."

"In view of the present character of the Japanese society and the desire of the United States to attain its objects with a minimum commitment of its forces and resources, the Supreme Commander will exercise his authority through Japanese Government machinery and agencies, including the Emperor, to the extent that this satisfactorily furthers United States' objectives. The Japanese Government will be permitted, under his instructions to exercise the normal powers of government in matters of domestic administration. The policy, however, will be subject to the right and duty of the Supreme Commander to require changes in government machinery or personnel or to act directly if the Emperor or other Japanese authority does not satisfactorily meet the requirements of the Supreme Commander in effectuating the surrender terms. This policy, moreover, does not commit the Supreme Commander to support the Emperor or any other Japanese Governmental authority in opposition to evolutionary change looking toward the attainment of the United States' objectives. The policy is to use the existing form of Government in Japan, not to support it. Changes in the form of Government initiated by the Japanese people or government in the direction of modifying its feudal and authoritarian tendencies are to be permitted and favoured. In the event that the effectuation of such changes involves the use of force by the Japanese people or government against

6. While the Potsdam conference was still going on, a highly important development in the area of policy formulation for a defeated Japan was taking place inside the U.S. Government. The State, War and Navy Co-ordinating Committee (SWNCO) produced a policy paper entitled "United States' Initial Post-surrender Policy for Japan." It was approved by the President and became the basis of policy that General MacArthur was to execute.

persons thereto, the Supreme Commander should intervene only where necessary to ensure the security of his forces and the attainment of all other objectives of the occupation.''

The Japanese Government was, therefore, an instrument by which the United States' objectives were to be realized. The authority of the Supreme Commander was complete in all respects and it was his ''right and duty'' to see that the changes which he deemed necessary and consistent with and in pursuance of those objectives were properly and expeditiously implemented. If the Emperor or any other Japanese authority did not meet the requirements of the Supreme Commander in effectuating the surrender terms, he could order changes in the governmental machinery or personnel as he deemed necessary or to act directly. The procedure actually adopted was that directions were issued under the authority of the Supreme Commander and the Japanese Government was required to act thereupon. The Occupation Authorities kept a close watch on the actions of the Japanese Government to ensure that the directions issued were faithfully observed. ''Of almost equal significance were the informal aspects of the relationship between the government and the occupation, ranging from 'suggestions' from General MacArthur to Japan's Prime Minister, through conferences between occupation authorities and Japanese bureaucrats, to private after-hour conversation between Japanese and Americans who found a common interest in solving the problems created by the peaceful evolution.''[7]

Demilitarization was relatively a simple problem and it was speedily and efficiently accomplished by the Occupation Authorities. By the end of 1948, Japan had been completely demilitarized. Democratization, however, was rather a complicated problem and it raised enormous difficulties. Any programme of democratization was deemed impracticable and futile unless a sizable Japanese population, especially its critical elements, were convinced of its value and supported its implementation. To enable the people to adequately appreciate the implications of a democratic set-up, the first attempt was made on October 4, 1945 by issuing a series of fundamental directives titled the ''Removal of Restrictions on Political, Civil and Religious Liberties.'' It was also enjoined upon the Japanese Government to forthwith release all political prisoners, to abolish all governmental agencies responsible for maintaining restrictions and discriminations, to remove all such officers from office and to bar their future appointments in any important capacity. The object was to abolish all privileges and vested interests and to create a climate of liberty in which the Japanese should be in a position to demand and safeguard the basic human rights hitherto denied to the people of Japan, and to provide them with an opportunity to determine their political fortune.

Closely in its wake, General MacArthur informed the Prime Minister of Japan on October 11, 1945 that ''in the achievement of the Potsdam Declaration the traditional social order under which the Japanese people for centuries have been subjugated will be corrected.'' Accordingly, the Supreme Commander required the Government to institute the following reforms : the emancipation of women by their enfranchisement, the encouragement of the labour unions, the opening of the schools to more liberal education, the abolition of ''systems which through secret inquisition and abuse have held the people in constant fear,'' and the democratization of economic institutions by curbing monopolies in order to widen the distribution and trade. The Shidehara Government in consultation with the Occupation Authorities immediately took measures to enact necessary laws relating to the social and political reforms in implementation of the policy of the Allied Powers.

Another directive from the Supreme Commander issued on December 15, 1945 demanded the abolition of Shinto, the State religion. The aim was to convert the Emperor from an absolute ruler with allegedly divine attributes to a mere mortal who serves as the symbol of the nation and of the people's unity. Two weeks after this directive which demanded abolition of Shinto, the Emperor declared in his 1946 New Year Message that the ties between the Throne and the people : ''do not depend upon mere legends and myths. They are not predicated on the false conception that the Emperor is divine and that the Japanese people are superior to other races and fated to rule the world.''[8] Thus, the ideological basis of ultranationalisam and militarism which had for centuries been the cult of the Throne was effaced from Japan. This was followed by a great purge.

7. Maki, John, M, *Government and Politics in Japan*, p. 50.
8. As cited in Theodore McNelly's *Contemporary Government of Japan*, p. 31.

On January 4, 1946, the Supreme Commander directed the Japanese Government to plan for the removal and exclusion from office of those persons arrested as suspected war criminals, commissioned officers in the Imperial Japanese Armed Forces and others who had served in the military police and secret intelligence and high ranking civilians in the Ministry of War and Navy, influential members of ultranationalistic, terroristic or secret patriotic organisations, persons influential in the activities of the Imperial Rule Assistance Association and other allied organisations, officials of financial and development organisations involved in Japanese expansion, Governors of occupied territories, and additional militarists and ultranationalists.

### First Effort to Revise the Japanese Constitution

The declared object of the Potsdam Declaration was to establish in Japan a peacefully inclined and respon-sible government in accordance with the freely expressed will of the Japanese people and it was made a condition precedent for the withdrawal of the Occupation Forces of the Allies. On October 4, 1945, General MacArthur urged upon Prince Konoye Fumimaro, Vice-Premier in the Higashi Kumi Cabinet, to take the initiative in revising the Meiji Constitution. Prince Konoye was not taken in the succeeding Shidehara Cabinet, but he managed to obtain a commission from the Emperor to investigate whether the Constitution required any revision and if so to what extent. Konoye held a number of private conferences with George C. Atcheson Jr., SCAP's[9] Political Adviser, and three U.S. State Department Officials who happened to be in Tokyo then. Various parts of the Meiji Constitution, which these officials felt required revision, were pointed out to Konoye, but no reference was made for the abolition of the institution of the Emperor.[10] There was, however, widespread feeling among the Allies that Konoye should have nothing to do with any scheme of constitutional reforms because of his alleged war guilt. It had been stated that the conference held between U.S. State Department officials and Konoye angered the Supreme Commander and he directed the former to have no more parleys with Konoye.

On November 1, SCAP Headquarters announced that MacArthur "had not chosen Konoye to reform the Japanese Constitution."

But Konoye continued on his job and late in November submitted his report on constitutional reforms to the Emperor. He recommended that the Meiji Constitution required revision with a view to strengthening the Diet, but such revisions should not destroy the basic principle of the Constitution that sovereignty resided in the Emperor. In December Konoye was indicted as a war criminal, but before he could be arrested, he committed suicide.

In October, just when Prince Konoye had obtained his commission from the Emperor authorizing him to investigate whether the Constitution needed revision, General MacArthur summoned Prime Minister Shidehara and pointedly advised him that the Government of Japan must immediately be reformed and, accordingly, the Constitution required to be liberalised. The Prime Minister pleaded that the legislation enacted by the Diet to enlarge the franchise and other reforms connected thereto adequately served the purpose and, consequently, there was no need to revise the Constitution. But MacArthur did not agree. He rather pulled up the Prime Minister and forced him to set up a committee to recommend proposals for reforms and revision of the Constitution.

The Committee on the Constitution, headed by Matsumoto Togi, was not in the beginning inclined to propose substantial alterations in the Constitution. But toward the end of December, when pressed hard, it was made to suggest some concrete proposals for revision. By that time the political parties, too, had presented their proposals for reforms. The Liberal and Progressive Parties proposed that the power of the Diet should be increased, but without impairing the principle that sovereignty resided in the Emperor. The Social Democratic Party recommended that while sovereignty resided in the State the political authority should vest in the Diet and the Emperor, the Diet sharing the most important part of it. The Communists, on the other hand, pleaded for the establishment of a Republic, and the trial of Emperor as a war criminal.

### MacArthur Constitution

The Matsumoto Committee submitted its draft of the revised Constitution on February 1, 1946, which was rejected by the Supreme Commander. He characterised it as reactionary. Mac-

9. Supreme Commander Allied Powers.
10. Theodore McNelly, *Contemporary Government of Japan,* pp. 37-38.

Arthur thereupon directed the SCAP Government Section to prepare the draft which should serve as a "guide" for the Japanese Government. In his directive to the SCAP Government Section, MacArthur's instruction was that "guide should provide for the institution of the Emperor, but the powers of the Emperor should be exercised according to the will of the people." The Government Section worked with utmost speed to prepare the draft Constitution and within a week's time it completed the job. The draft Constitution was presented to the Japanese Government on February 13. It is reported that General Courtney Whitely, Chief of Government Section, while presenting the draft Constitution which was intended to serve as a "guide" to the Cabinet, made its members clearly understand that if they did not accept the general principles contained therein, General MacArthur would present the Constitution straightway to the people of Japan and in that case "The person of the Emperor" could not be guaranteed.

The Shidehara Government was left with no option but to accept the draft. When it was shown to the Emperor he also observed that there was no other alternative. The Prime Minister, then, reported to his Cabinet that "we are making an extremely grave commitment in accepting such a Constitution as this. Perhaps this commitment will also bind our posterity. When this draft is made public, some will applaud and others will keep silence. The latter will undoubtedly be highly indignant at bottom towards us. However, I believe that we are following the only possible course in view of the situation confronting us." There was a deep sense of shock and it was known to all that almost all Ministers wiped tears from their eyes.

The adoption of the draft constitution was, thus, an accomplished fact. Still to observe the formality the draft was sent to the Matsumoto Committee to serve as a "guide." The Committee made some minor revisions in it in close consultation with the Government Section, SCAP. It was then sent back to the Cabinet. The draft was made public on March 6, as if it was actually Shidehara Government's own revision of the Constitution. To make it still reassuring an Imperial Rescript announced the adoption of the draft and explained the democratic principles on which it was based. General MacArthur, too, kept with the track and issued his approval of the draft constitution to authenticate that it was the handiwork of the Japanese themselves and not an American made constitution.

The Draft Constitution was, then, finally submitted to the Diet for its approval in accordance with the provisions of the Meiji Constitution. But the Houses of the Diet took pains to fully debate it "always honouring the fiction that it was of Japanese origin." The Diet made some minor alterations too. But all this was done with the final approval of the Occupation Authorities. The Diet gave its approval on October 7, 1946, and the Constitution was promulgated on November 3, 1946 to synchronize with the birthday of Emperor Meiji. The new Constitution became operative six months later on May 3, 1947. "It was the occupation," succinctly remarks Maki, "that originated, directed, and obviously controlled the drafting, the content, and the process of approval of the new Constitution."[11] It may aptly be called the MacArthur Constitution.

## BASIC FEATURES OF THE CONSTITUTION, 1946

### The Constitution as a Document

Although the Constitution was adopted as an amendment of the Meiji Constitution, 1889, but actually it was a total revision which drastically transformed the nature and structure of the Government in Japan. It consisted of 103 Articles grouped in XI Chapters (Chapter XI contains Supplementary Provisions, Articles 100 to 103) written in a simple style and easily comprehensible language. Both in broad principle and in specific details the Constitution of 1946 differs completely from the Constitution of 1889, which it replaced. Its three basic principles are : sovereignty of the people, the guarantee of the Fundamental Rights, and the renunciation of war, the last being a most peculiar feature of the Constitution and an object of the country's greatest Constitutional controversy. Japan's Constitution is the only instance which constitutionally renounces war.

The structure of the government which the Constitution sets up completely supplants the institutions Japan had proudly inherited since the "ages eternal." It was the avowed policy of the Allied Powers to obliterate the image of divinity which the Japanese people believed surrounded the Throne and to eliminate completely from their minds the concept of national policy. Shidehara

11. Maki, John M., *Government and Politics in Japan,* p. 80.

Cabinet had hoped that the process of democratization, which the Supreme Commander had urged as the most important element of the Potsdam declaration, would not entail demolishing the past entirely. They had, in fact, expected that the proposals of the Matsumoto Committee would form the basis of discussion and compromise in order that a part of the old system might be retained. The Supreme Commander, however, had left no alternative for the Shidehara Government but to accept the draft Constitution as prepared, under his instructions, by the SCAP Government Section. Although the draft constitution was claimed to serve as a "guide" for the Japanese Government, but in reality it was the Constitution they were required to accept and a few minor changes which the Matsumoto Committee and the Diet made therein had the full approval of the SCAP. This "American-inspired Constitution" is replete with the fundamentals of American political philosophy. "The Preamble to the Constitution," says Chitoshi Yanaga, "reminds the reader of the ideas and language of such historic documents as the Declaration of Independence, the Federalist Papers, the Preamble to the Constitution (of U.S.A.), the Gettysburg Address and even the Atlantic Charter."[12]

**Sovereignty of the People**

Sovereignty of the people which runs through the entire Constitution is its basic feature. It is a revolutionary change as it destroys the old principle of Imperial Sovereignty. The Meiji Constitution was a gift of the Emperor to the nation and its Preamble declared that "the right of sovereignty of State, We (the Emperor) have inherited from our Ancestors, and we shall bequeath to our descendants." It further provided, "the Empire of Japan shall be reigned over and governed by a line of Emperors unbroken for ages eternal." Article IV provided that "The Emperor is the head of the Empire, combining in himself the rights of sovereignty and exercises them according to the provisions of the Constitution."

Under the Constitution of 1946 sovereignty belonged to the people and that the Emperor was only the symbol of the State and unity of the people," and he derived his position from the will of the people with whom "resides sovereign power."[13] The transfer of sovereignty from the Emperor to the people finds full expression in the Preamble to the Constitution which states : "we the Japanese people, acting through our duly elected representatives in the National Diet....do proclaim that sovereign power resides with the people and do firmly establish this Constitution." It affirms that "Government is a sacred trust of the people, the authority for which is derived from the people, the powers of which are exercised by the representatives of the people, and the benefits of which are enjoyed by the people." Sovereignty of the people, the Preamble asserts, "is a universal principle of mankind" upon which the new Constitution of Japan is founded and the people of Japan through this Constitution "reject and revoke all Constitutions, laws, ordinances and rescripts" which are in conflict with this principle. Accordingly the Constitution established a representative and responsible government manifesting the will of the people at the national as well as the local levels. The institutions of referendum, initiative and recall also prevail in one way or the other. The appointment of the Judges of the Supreme Court is subject to review at a national referendum, first at the time of the General Election following their appointment and then at the first General Election after a lapse of ten years. The Supreme Court is the guardian of the rights of the citizens. Article 97 declares that Fundamental Rights as enshrined in the Constitution are for all time inviolate.

In his first address from the Throne Emperor Akihito pledged "anew that I shall observe the Constitution of Japan and discharge my duties as the symbol of the State and of the unity of the people." This made the position of the Emperor clear on the controversy that the Government decided Shintoistic enthronement ceremony might create "an atmosphere conducive to any revival of militarism." Prime Minister Kaifu conveyed people's thanks for the Emperor's pledge. He observed, "We, the people of Japan, revere Your Majesty as symbol of the State and of the unity of the people and pledge, with new resolve, to devote our utmost efforts to building a Japan open to the world, vigorously culturally rich, and practising world peace and the well-being of mankind." The Emperor's address was drafted by the Government.

**Fundamental Rights and Duties**

The Constitution bestows on the people a truly imposing list of Rights which itself is an expression of the sovereignty of the people.

---

12. Japanese People and Politics, p. 125.
13. Article 1.

Chapter III of the Constitution is exclusively devoted to the enumeration of these Rights. Out of a total of 103 Articles which comprise the Constitution, 31 are contained in Chapter III and embrace civil and political Rights as also Duties, though the latter are not many. The Rights are fully guaranteed and the Constitution declares them ''eternal and inviolate'' and include political, social and economic equality as well as suffrage, welfare and liberty for the people. All told, the emphasis throughout is on respect for the dignity of the individual. A section of the Japanese people feels that the constitutional emphasis on the role of the individual is rather excessive and suggests some modification thereto. But this suggestion has not been favourably accepted and the majority of the people believe that it is not desirable to effect any change.

**Renunciation of War**

A peculiar, rather unprecedented, feature of the Constitution is that it unequivocally renounces war for ever. Article 9, which constitutes a single Article in Chapter II and is titled ''Renunciation of War,'' reads : ''Aspiring sincerely an international peace based on justice and order, the Japanese people forever renounce war as a sovereign right of the nation and the threat or use of force as means of settling international disputes.'' It is provided that ''in order to accomplish the aim of the preceding paragraph, land, sea, and air forces, as well as other war potential, will never be maintained. The right of belligerency of the State will not be recognised.'' The Preamble enshrines the ideals of liberty and ''desire for peace for all time'' and the Japanese people pledged by their ''national honour to accomplish these high ideals and purposes'' by resolving that never again ''shall we be visited with the horrors of war through the action of government'' and expressed their determination to ''secure for ourselves and our posterity the fruits of peaceful co-operation with all nations and the blessings of liberty throughout the land.''

The constitutional provision of renunciation of war should, indeed, be the most cherished goal of State policy if all other States provided for the same in their Constitutions and their governments pursued the path of international amity by renouncing war and settling their disputes by and through peaceful means. But none has done it so far, not even the United States of America which was at pains to specifically enshrine it in the Constitution of Japan. The Occupation Authorities in their bid to militarily cripple Japan made this provision in the Constitution and also ordained that Japan would never maintain land, sea and air forces, as well as other war potential. The right of belligerency of the State is also not recognised by the Constitution. The provisions of Article 9 are, however, now interpreted by the Government to mean that defensive armament is permissible and the Constitution outlaws only war and threat or use of force as means of settling international disputes. ''It has been very plausibly argued,'' remarks Theodore McNelly, ''that war and threat or use of force as means of self-defence are permissible.''[14]

Prime Minister Kaifu's Government reinterpreted, early in November 1990, Article 9 of the Constitution relating to the renunciation of war in Chapter II. It was maintained that the Constitution does not debar the Government to send Japanese forces—regular military or specially raised corps—to help enforce peace in the world. Elaborating the point the Prime Minister asserted that since Japan was now an economic super power it must accept certain responsibility in the matter of a new world order and in pursuance of that role Japan would be justified in sending her defence forces to join a United Nations approved multinational force to enforce peace. Such an interpretation was unthinkable even a year before and it made some Japanese weary.

**Supremacy of the Constitution**

Article 98 specifically provides that ''this Constitution shall be the supreme law of the nation and no law, ordinance, imperial rescript or other act of government, or part thereof, contrary to the provisions thereof, shall have legal force or validity.'' It means that all laws, ordinances, imperial rescripts and Cabinet orders prevailing at the time when the Constitution became operative in 1947, and were inconsistent with the provisions of this Constitution became *ipso facto* invalid and consequently, inoperative. And after the Constitution became operative nothing shall be enacted by the Diet which is not consistent to and in accordance with the fundamental law of the country. Similarly, no act of government will be valid which is contrary to the provisions of the Constitution. Article 99 explicitly holds responsible all those engaged in public acts, the Emperor or the Regent as well as Ministers of State, mem-

14. Contemporary Government in Japan, p. 202.

bers of the Diet, judges and all other public officials, to uphold and respect the Constitution. It is their constitutional duty and any deviation therefrom makes them liable to punishment as prescribed by the Constitution or the laws made thereunder. Nothing in Japan, therefore, can be enacted or done by any agency of the Government which is not permitted by the Constitution. To safeguard against invasion on the liberties and freedoms of the people, Article 97 reiterates that the Fundamental Human Rights guaranteed by the Constitution "are fruits of the age-old struggle of man to be free; they have survived the many enacting tests for durability and are conferred upon this and future generations in trust, to be held for all times inviolate."

**Rigid Constitution**

The supremacy of the Constitution is ensured if it is not alterable under the ordinary law-making procedure. The Constitution of Japan prescribes the procedure for amending the Constitution and it is distinct from that of an ordinary law. It means that the Constitutional law is not at par with the statutory law and the former has precedence in status over the latter, that is, the constitutional law is fundamental and supreme. Article 96 provides that proposals for amending the Constitution may be initiated either in the House of Councillors or in the House of Representatives. Such a proposal must separately pass in each House by a majority of two-thirds or more of its membership. After the amendment has been passed by the Diet, it is submitted to the people at a referendum for their ratification. If majority of the people voting at the referendum approves it, it becomes an amendment of the Constitution and is immediately promulgated by the Emperor "in the name of the people."

The Constitution has not so far been amended even once. In spite of the strong pressure of the Conservatives for its revision and the setting up of a Commission on the Constitution under the law of the Diet,[15] the Constitution reads today as it did in 1947. The Commission on the Constitution has not yet finalised its deliberations.[16] Moreover, it is difficult to obtain a concurring vote of two-thirds or more of all the members of each House plus an affirmative vote of a majority of the votes cast at a referendum. Because of the relative difficulty of the amending process, the Constitution of Japan can reasonably be characterised as an example of a rigid Constitution.

If the Constitution has seen no amendment, it does not mean that the Constitution has not expanded. The laws enacted by the Diet, interpretation of the Constitution and elaboration of its provision by the courts have considerably helped the Constitution to grow, though the latter make a minor contribution. But a number of basic laws passed by the Diet have sufficiently supplemented the provisions of the Constitution as, for example, the Imperial House Law, the National Diet Law, the Finance Law, the Cabinet Law, the Public Autonomy Law. Since changes in the basic law can be made under the ordinary process of legislation, it renders the Constitution to some extent flexible.

**Judicial Review**

The Constitution explicitly vests in the Supreme Court the power of judicial review, though it establishes a unitary system of government. Article 81 provides that the Supreme Court is the court of last resort with power to determine the constitutionality of any law, order, regulation, or official Act, Here Japan introduces an American element of institutions. But whereas in the United States the Supreme Court does not derive its power of judicial review from the Constitution, the Japanese Supreme Court has the constitutional power to interpret the Constitution and to maintain its sanctity and supremacy.

The Supreme Court in Japan has not so far held, with the exception of certain laws passed to implement Occupation Directives, any law, order, regulation or official Act void and unconstitutional, but has upheld a few as constitutional. In the Sunakawa case (1959) the Supreme Court declared that the stationing of American forces in Japan did not violate Article 9 of the Constitution. It also set the principle that unless a treaty is "obviously unconstitutional and void, it falls outside the purview of the power of judicial review granted to the Court."

**Emperor the Symbol of the State**

The Constitution preserves the institution of the Emperor, but deprives His Majesty of all powers, privileges and prerogatives he formerly enjoyed and exercised. The Constitution now declares him to be the symbol of the State and of

15. The legally stipulated duties of the Commission are : "to study the Constitution, to investigate and deliberate on problems relating to it, and to report the results to the cabinet and through the cabinet to the Diet."
16. It was not until almost fifteen months after the law was passed that the Commission held its first meeting.

the unity of the people.[17] He has no powers and authority related to the Government. He performs only those "acts" which are enumerated in the Constitution[18] subject to the provision that the "advice and approval of the Cabinet shall be required for all acts of the Emperor in matters of State and the Cabinet shall be responsible thereof."[19] As the Emperor derives "his position from the will of the people,"[20] and he performs acts in matters of State as specified in the Constitution, he must do so on the advice and approval of the Cabinet.[21] The Constitution also prescribes that no property can be given to, or received by, the imperial Houses, nor can any gifts be made therefrom without the authorization of the Diet.[22]

**Parliamentary system of government**

The Government of the United States had decided to establish in Japan a Parliamentary system of government in preference to the Presidential system and the Secretary of State, Byrnes, had accordingly advised George Atcheson, Jr., SCAP's Political Adviser. But a peculiar feature of Parliamentary government, which the Constitution established in Japan, is that the Emperor does not perform even those acts and functions which are associated with the constitutional Head of the State, for example, appointment of the Prime Minister and dissolution of the legislature. The Emperor is the symbol of the State and of the unity of the people who derives his position from the will of the people. The Executive power is vested in the Cabinet and it is made collectively responsible to the Diet. The Prime Minister heads the Cabinet and a majority of the number of Ministers, including the Prime Minister, must be members of the Diet. The Diet designates the Prime Minister and on his resignation the Cabinet resigns *en masse*.[23] If the House of Representatives passes a no-confidence resolution or rejects a confidence resolution, the Cabinet resigns *en masse*.[24] All these are the attributes of a Parliamentary system of government and ensure the smooth working of the Cabinet. In the United Kingdom these well-recognised principles of the Cabinet government are the result of deep-rooted conventions. In Japan, they have been specifically incorporated in the Constitution and, thus, constitutionalised.

**A Unitary Constitution**

The 1946 Constitution of Japan is unitary and all authority flows from the Government at Tokyo, though there is much of devolution. The Provinces derive their authority in exercise of their jurisdiction and powers from the Acts of the Diet. The Diet may expand or diminish that authority and jurisdiction as and when it may deem necessary and proper. The provinces are, thus, subordinate units of Government and they do not possess plenary powers as in a federal polity.

**Diet is Bicameral**

The Diet is bicameral in structure and consists of two chambers : the House of Councillors and the House of Representatives. The House of Councillors consists of 250 members, out of which 150 are elected on a geographical basis whereas the remaining 100 are elected by the nation at large; a voter, thus, exercises two votes, one for the candidate in a local constituency and the other for the candidate in the national constituency. The term of office is six years with one-half of the Councillors retiring after every three years. The Chamber is not subject to dissolution. The House of Representatives consists of 511 members elected for a term of four years and the House is subject to dissolution. Both the Houses of the Diet possess identical legislative powers, but in case the House of Councillors makes a decision different from the House of Representatives and such a difference cannot be resolved in the Joint Committee of the two Houses, it becomes a law of the Diet when the House of Representatives passes the Bill for the second time by a majority of two-thirds of members present. The Constitution unequivocally establishes the supremacy of the House of Representatives over the House of Councillors in financial matters.

**Adult Suffrage**

Under the Meiji Constitution the House of

17. Article 1.
18. Article 7.
19. Article 4.
20. Article 1.
21. Article 7.
22. Article 8.
23. Article 70.
24. Article 13.

Peers—the Upper House—consisted of representative Peers, representatives of the highest taxpayers, and Imperial appointees whereas originally the House of Representatives was elected by a small electorate which met a high payment of tax. Women had no votes. With the enactment of universal suffrage in 1925, all males over 25 years of age were given the right to vote. The Constitution of 1946 made both the Houses representative in character and abolished the discrimination between sexes. Now all citizens of Japan, who are otherwise not disqualified by law, and have reached the age of 20 years, are given the right to elect their representatives for both the Houses of the Diet.

**Local Autonomy**

Finally, the Constitution prominently introduces the principle of local autonomy. Local Governments, prefectures and city, town and village municipalities have been granted by the Constitution extensive rights of self-government. Article 93 provides that the "local public entities shall establish assemblies as their deliberative organs" and that "the Chief executive officers of all local public entities, the members of their assemblies, and such other local officials as may be determined by law shall be elected by direct popular vote within their several communities." The Local Autonomy Law, 1947, which supplements Article 92 of the Constitution, provides for the exercise of initiative and recall by the voters of local entities. Such a democratic potential was hitherto unknown in Japan.

## RIGHTS AND DUTIES OF THE PEOPLE

**Fundamental Rights**

The Constitution bestows on the citizen of Japan an imposing list of civil and political rights and thirty-one Articles out of a total of 103 are contained in Chapter III under the caption "Rights and Duties of the people." It is probably one of the world's most detailed and ambitious constitutional statements which guarantees that these human rights "conferred upon the people of this and future generations of the people" are "eternal and inviolate."[25] The Constitution further provides that the freedoms and rights guaranteed to the people shall be maintained by the constant endeavor of the people, and enjoins upon them that they "shall refrain from any abuse of these freedoms and rights and shall be responsible for utilising them for the public welfare."[26] It means that the Constitution explicitly impresses upon citizens that vigilance is the price of democracy and since they have the inalienable right of determining their political destiny, they must not abuse any of these freedoms and rights and utilize them for their own good and the public welfare. Accordingly, the Constitution emphasises respect for the individual, without any kind of discrimination,[27] and guarantees to him the right to life, liberty and the pursuit of happiness, provided it does not interfere with the public welfare which would "be the supreme consideration in legislation and other government affairs."[28]

The provision in Article 11 that "the people shall not be prevented from enjoying any of the fundamental human rights....conferred....as eternal and inviolate rights" is an unconditional guarantee of rights and the Government is debarred from imposing any restriction or curtailment on their rights. But Articles 12 and 13 impose restrictions. Article 12 prescribes certain responsibilities for the people. The first is that they should maintain their rights through their constant endeavour and refrain from any abuse of them. Secondly, the people should be responsible for utilising their rights for the public welfare. Article 13 while declaring that all the people shall be respected as individuals, conditions their right of life, liberty, and the pursuit of happiness to the extent that none of them does interfere with the public welfare. Some fears have been expressed in Japan that incorporation of public welfare provision and making enjoyment of rights subject to public welfare is likely to be misinterpreted and the liberties of the people might be infringed or curtailed in the name of public welfare. It is argued that public welfare has ever remained a misleading concept. There is no activity of the State and no action of Government, down to the most ruthless and tyrannical, which has not been defended on the ground of public welfare. And Japan has a legacy of the long authoritarian tradition.

But this issue, as Maki observes, "'is an important one in every democracy, because it involves the balance between the enjoyment of

25. Article 69.
26. Article 11.
27. Article 2.
28. Article 13.

freedom by the individual and the good of the entire community.''[29] Rights cannot be divorced from obligations and human rights cannot subsist without limitations. While imposing responsibilities on the people of Japan, the Constitution also makes the Government responsible for serving the people's right to life, liberty and pursuit of happiness.[30] No representatives and responsible Government, which is accountable to the people, can afford to infringe, abrogate or abuse Fundamental Rights on the plea of public welfare which it cannot adequately defend. The Government is ever under scrutiny and it cannot forget that tomorrow is the day of election and it shall have to account for its public activities which it cannot adequately defend. The Supreme Court of Japan has upheld that public welfare is a valid justification to restrict freedom. But it has also equally insisted that the doctrine of public welfare ''cannot be used by any governing authority as an abstract justification for the limitation of freedom, it can be applied only under duly enacted legislation and under clearly defined circumstance.''[31] It is creditable that during the past four decades, since constitution became operative , there has been ''no erosion of any constitutionally guaranteed freedom through legislative, executive or judicial action.[32]

**Specific Rights**

Here is a summary of rights the Constitution guarantees to citizens : freedoms of thought, conscience, religion, assembly, association, speech, press and all other forms of expression, choice of residence and occupation, choice to move to a foreign country and to give up nationality, academic freedom,[33] freedom from discrimination in political, economic or social relations because of race, creed, sex, social status, or family origin,[34] equality before law and under the law, the inalienable right to choose public officials and to dismiss them, the right of petition for the redress of grievances, for the removal of public officials, for the enactment, repeal or amendment of laws, ordinances or regulations, or for other matters, the right to sue the State or public entity for damage resulting from an illegal act of any public official,[35] freedom to marriage based on mutual consent, equal rights of husband and wife, the right to maintain the minimum standards of wholesome and cultured living, the right to receive equal education correspondent to their ability, the right to work, the right of the workers to organise and bargain and act collectively, the right to own or hold property, and the right to due process of law.

From the rights and freedoms enumerated above, it should be noted that the concept of equality has received a prominent and practical place in the Constitution. Social equality is guaranteed by abolishing special privileges by not recognising peer and peerage and excluding any privilege from any award of honour or any distinction which is not limited to the lifetime of the recipient. No person can be held in bondage and involuntary servitude, except as punishment for crime. Equality of the sexes, the right to equal education and equality of rights of husband and wife enhance the dignity of the individual and his social stature. The equality before the law finds even more emphasis. Ten Articles out of a total of thirty-one in the Chapter on Rights and Duties are devoted to what may be characterised as the due process of law. It includes : freedom from deprivation of life or liberty or the imposition of other criminal penalty except according to procedure established by law, freedom of access to courts, no arrest or detention without immediate notification of the nature of the charges, privilege of counsel, security of home, papers and effects except under warrant, security against torture or cruel punishments, the right of speedy and public trial by an impartial tribunal, right of examination of witnesses and of compulsory process for obtaining witnesses in his behalf at a public expense, freedom from compulsion to testify against himself, freedom from being criminally liable for an act which was lawful at the time it was committed, or of which he has been acquitted, and from double jeopardy, and the right to sue the State for redress after acquittal following arrest or detention.

Political equality finds expression in guaranteeing universal adult suffrage with regard to the election of public officials, giving the people the inalienable right to choose public officials and

29. Maki, John H., *Government and Politics of Japan*, p.87.
30. Article 13.
31. Maki, John M., *Government and Politics of Japan*, pp. 37-38
32. *Ibid.*
33. Article 19 to 23.
34. Article 14.
35. Article 26.

to dismiss them, declaring all public officials as servants of the whole community, ensuring secrecy of ballot in all elections and not making a voter answerable, publicly or privately, for the choice he has made, and granting to every person the right of petition of the redress of damage, for the removal of public officials, for the enactment, repeal or amendment of laws, ordinances or regulations and for other matters. The Constitution guarantees that no person shall be in any way discriminated against for sponsoring such a petition.

The Constitution significantly guarantees the right to work and the right to decent living. The right to work is also an obligation and, thus, a duty of every citizen. Article 25 gives the right to decent living and guarantees that in all spheres, the State shall do its best to promote social welfare and security and public health. Article 29 concedes the right to property and it has been made inviolable, but private property may be acquired by the Government on payment of just compensation. The Constitution prescribes (Article 27) that standards for wages, hours of work, rest and other working conditions shall be fixed by law. But the right of the workers to organise and form union, bargain for their service prospects and to act collectively is guaranteed by Article 28. The Constitution, thus, gives to the workers the right to strike. The Constitution also ordains that children shall not be exploited.

**Duties**

The Constitution also places emphasis on the duties of the individual, though they are not many. Chitoshi Yanaga says that the "traditional attitude has for centuries been to emphasize duties practically to the exclusion of rights, this was especially the case under feudalism. For the purpose of encouraging democratic development it was imperative that individual rights be stressed to effectively counteract the altogether too powerful influence of the authoritarian tradition and its legacies in Japanese society. The result has been the inclusion of only a few basic obligations of citizenship......"[36] The duties and responsibilities of the citizen include : refraining from the abuse of any freedom or right, the responsibility for preserving and maintaining by constant endeavour the freedom and rights guaranteed by the Constitution,[37] the obligation to work which is also a right,[38] liability to taxation,[39] and the obligation of all people to have all boys and girls under their protection receive ordinary education as provided by law.[40]

Japan is the sole political example where a constitution imposed on the defeated nation by a Victorious Country has successfully worked for almost six decades. It has embraced the spirit of western liberalism and tried to reshape its conceptual assumptions in accordance with its own national ethos. A conservative political party has remained in power in Japan for long without interruption. Nationalism is still a strong political tendency.

36. *Japanese People and Politics*, p. 353.
37. Article 12.
38. Article 27.
39. Article 30.
40. Article 26.

# CHAPTER II

# The Executive

## The Emperor in History

Chitoshi Yanaga gives a matter of fact description of the Emperor. He says, "The Emperor has been and still is the living symbol of the nation's history, heritage, and achievements, of all that is glorious in the nation's past and present, of its continuity and durability. He is the incarnation of history and religion. In his person are epitomised the nation's hopes, aspirations and promise. He is the spiritual anchor, the moral rudder, and the political gyroscope that insure the safety and steadiness of the course of the ship of state. As a symbol he is enshrined in the hearts of the people who attribute everything good to his virtue."[1] He was and still is the nation's rallying point descending in direct and unbroken line from Amaterasu-Omikami, the Goddess of the Sun. The Emperor, pictured as a *Kami* or heaven-descended divine, sacred, virtuous and all-wise, became the accepted ideology of the State and these attributes of the monarch were taught in the schools. Near the entrance to every schoolyard there was a small shrine in which were installed the pictures of the Emperor and the Empress. Every schoolchild had to uncover and bow before this shrine each time he entered or left the school. "On national holidays, usually at 10 A.M. all Japanese inside or outside the country were supposed to bow respectfully in the direction of the Imperial Palace in Tokyo. It was a custom, not rigidly enforced, for Japanese to bow each time they passed the main entrance to the Palace ground."[2] It was sacrilege to discuss any aspect concerning the person of the Emperor.

The Emperor was, thus, for the Japanese State, the repository of sovereignty which was eternal and unalterable, that is. "co-extensive with the Heavens and with the Earth." His authority was supreme and inalienable to which all religiously bowed. In interpreting the Peace Preservation Law of 1925, which forbade *inter alia* advocating the alteration *Kokutai* or national polity, the Supreme Court declared that the Emperor, of a line unbroken for ages eternal, reigned and exercised sovereignty in Japan.

Despite this fact of political loyalty and unbounding reverence and devotion of the people, the Emperor actually possessed very little political power and His Majesty usually had never made any important political decision. At least during the past near about 800 years, he had always followed the advice of the effective government of the time that was in the saddle and was in no way responsible for the formulation and execution of public policy. The Emperor was the ceremonial head of the State and performed only the ceremonial functions. The Constitution of 1889 gave him absolute power. Article IV stated: "The Emperor is the head of the empire combining in Himself the rights of sovereignty, and exercises them, according to the provisions of this constitution." But even then, he had always acted on the advice of his Ministers. He did no wrong and performed no public act on his own initiative and responsibility. He could, thus, be described as the constitutional monarch even under the Meiji Constitution, the most powerful symbol of the unity and solidarity of the Japanese nation. The Japanese adored their nation by adoring the Throne and the Royal Family provided a useful focus for patriotism and patriotic devotion. Here the Emperor of Japan resembled the British monarch. "The reverence of the Emperor." writes Chitoshi Yanaga, "is almost unbelievable especially to those who have not witnessed its manifestation. Perhaps the British alone of the Western people today can come closest to understanding attitude toward the sovereign."

1. Chitoshi Yanaga, *Japanese People and Politics*, p. 129.
2. Maki, John M., *Government and Politics in Japan*, p. 113.

**The Emperor as He is Today**

In their bid to effect the doctrine *Kokutai* or national polity, which vested the power to rule ultimately in the Emperor, the Occupation Authorities strove to "humanize" the Emperor. They contrived a Constitution which reduced the Emperor to a mere symbol of the State and of the unity of the people. The Emperor derived his "position from the will of the people with whom sovereignty resides." With a view to vindicate the sovereignty of the people the ultimate authority of amending the Constitution is vested in the people themselves and the Constitution so amended, the Emperor proclaims it in the name of the people. It means that if the majority of the people acting through their representatives and ratified at a referendum so desire, the institution of the Emperor can be abolished. This is a revolutionary change and perhaps the Japanese will never venture to abolish it, yet it is a legal truth that they can do it if they so desire. It is an irony that the Emperor, who had advised his Cabinet on August 14, 1945, to accept the allied Surrender Terms in order to save national polity from destruction and the nation from annihilation, was left with no option but to accept the Constitution which ordained his own political demise. The mind of the Occupation Authorities and the shape of the things to come was fully reflected in the Emperor's New Year Day Rescript of January 7, 1946. He declared that the ties between him and his people "have always stood upon mutual trust and affection" and not "upon legends and myths," not are they "predicated on the false conception that the Emperor is divine and that the Japanes people are superior to other races and destined to rule the world."[3] It is reported that the day the new Constitution was made operative, Shimizu Cho, the Constitutional Adivser to the Emperor and Chairman of the Privy Council which approved the Constitution, drowned himself at Atami. The note, which Shimizu Cho left, read: "I have decided to die so that I from the spiritual world may help to protect our national polity and with the safe-being of His Majesty."[4]

There was almost the entire nation which thought likewise. In a survey conducted by the United Nations Educational and Cultural Organization, it was found out that "74 per cent of the Youth of postwar Japan strongly believe the Emperor remains as the very best, the symbol of the nation, not only on paper, but in the hearts and minds of the people."[5] This was really a shock for the Western nations especially Americans who had deliberately engineered the Constitution of 1946. Since the time Japan regained her independence determined efforts are afoot, restoring the universal reverence for monarchy as it prevailed before the defeat of Japan in 1945. The Conservatives are the most active and their advocacy is more enthusiastic. They hold that the Emperor's position as a mere symbol of the State and of the unity of the people "does violence to the historical tradition and sentiment of the people." Some of the critics of the Constitution maintain that Japan is not a constitutional monarchy, as it is claimed, but a Republic. They assert that the symbolic role of Emperor, derivation of his position from the people and their possessing the ultimate power of abolishing monarchy, and denial of even nominal powers to the Emperor are the characteristics of a republic although the Imperial Throne is dynastic. This is, however, a wrong interpretation of a republican form of government so long as the Imperial Throne remains dynastic. But the Conservatives cannot be induced to reconcile themselves to the position which the Constitution assigns to the Emperor. Accordingly, the Liberal and Progressive parties set up in 1954 their separate committees for a thorough study of the problem of constitutional revision with special reference to the powers and position of the Emperor. Both the committees came to the conclusion that the Constitution need be immediately revised and the position of the Emperor elevated to the constitutional head of the State as the British King is. The Government also appointed a Commission on the Constitution. Nothing tangible has yet come about, but there is a strong feeling among the Japanese people that the Emperor be restored to his former position. In some parts of Japan a movement called Kigensetsu (National Foundation Day) is strengthening its activities. Kigensetsu, February 11, is the traditional anniversary of the founding of the Japanese State by the first Emperor Jimmu Tennno in 600 B.C. It reveals the reverence and affection of the people of Japan towards the Imperial family

3. As cited in Chitoshi Yanaga's *Japanese People and Politics,* pp.137-38.
4. As cited in Theodore McNeley's *Contemporary Government of Japan,* p. 56.
5. UNESCO, Courier, August-Sept., 1954, pp. 12-35. Also refer to "Japanese Popular Attitude Towards the Emperor," *Pacific Affairs,* Dec., 1952, pp. 235-44.

of which the present ruler, Emperor Akihito, son of Emperor Hirohito, is the 125th in the line of succession. There has been only one dynasty which has ruled Japan in lineal succession unbroken for ages eternal.

**Succession to the Throne**

Article 2 of the Constitution provides that the Imperial Throne is dynastic and shall be succeeded to in accordance with the Imperial House Law enacted by the Diet. According to the Meiji Constitution the Imperial Diet could not amend or repeal the Imperial House Law which determined succession to the Throne. The Emperor alone, with the advice of the Imperial Family Council and the Privy Council, could amend it. But under the 1946 Constitution, it is the Diet alone which makes, amends or repeals the existing Imperial House Law enacted in1947, and which came into effect simultaneously with the inauguration of the Constitution on 3 May, 1947.

The Imperial House Law of 1947 provides that the "Imperial Throne shall be succeeded by a male offspring in the main line belonging to the Imperial lineage." Primogeniture is the rule with succession running through the main line and the law rigidly defines the composition of the Imperial Family. No adoption is permitted. If there is no member of the Imperial Family in the main line of succession, the Throne is passed to members of the Imperial Family next nearest in lineage precedence being given to the senior member of the senior line. The Imperial House Council, which consists of ten members[6] at a meeting presided over by the Prime Minister, may change the order of succession in the case the heir to the Throne suffers from an incurable and serious disease. A regency is established in case the Emperor has not come of age (18 years) or when the Emperor suffers from a serious disease, or there is a serious hindrance in the performance of his public acts. The regent performs his acts in the name of the Emperor. The Japanese Crown Prince Akihito on 22 September 1988, assumed all Imperial State duties as his father, 87 years old, Emperor Hirohito lay critically ill but stable. The Emperor had requested that all affairs of State be transferred to Akihito, his eldest son. Prince Akihito, however, was not named regent. The Cabinet meeting presided by Prime Minister Noboru Takeshita approved the Emperor's decision.

**Imperial Household Finances**

The Imperial Household affairs are now complete-ly under the jurisdiction and authority of the Diet. Before 1945, the Imperial Family was extremely wealthy and possessed extensive property holdings both in the land and big industries. The Emperor was "the greatest of the Zaibatsu (cartels) and exercised a powerful influence on the economy of the country." But now the greater part of that extensive property has been transferred to the State and the needs of the Imperial Household are provided by appropriations subject to the approval of the Diet. Article 8 of the Constitution specifically provides that "No property can be given to, or received by the Imperial House, nor can any gifts be made therefrom, without the authorization of the Diet."

The Imperial Family was reduced in size in 1947, when eleven princely families, consisting of fifty-one Princes and Princesses, renounced their status and privileges and became commoners. The Imperial Family now includes the families of the present Emperor Akihito and his brothers. The Constitution of 1946 has abolished the titles and, accordingly, the former eleven princely families are not even titled.

**The Emperor and His Functions**

Articles 1, 3 and 4 determine the position of the Emperor under the Constitution and Articles 6 and 7 list his functions. Article 1 makes the Emperor "the symbol of the State and the unity of the people, deriving his position from the will of the people with whom resides sovereign power." The effect of this Article is adequately expressed in Articles 3 and 4. Article 3 ordains that "The advice and approval of the Cabinet shall be required for all acts of the Emperor in matters of State, and the Cabinet shall be responsible therefor." Article 4 prescribes that the "Emperor shall perform only such acts in matters of state as are provided for in the Constitution and he shall not have powers related to government." The combined effect of all these provisions may, thus, be summed up:—

(1) that the emperor no longer exercises any power or authority relating to government;

(2) that he only performs certain acts in

6. The composition is : two members of the Imperial family, the Presidents and Vice-Presidents of both Houses of the Diet, the Prime Minister, the Head of the Imperial House Agency, the Chief Judge and one other Judge of the Supreme Court. Two members of the Imperial Family are chosen by election within the Imperial Family, and a Judge by other Judges of the Supreme Court.

matters of State and such acts are as specified in the Constitution. There is no prerogative which he enjoys and no privilege or authority he can exercise;

(3) that the advice and approval of the Cabinet is required for all acts of the Emperor and there is ministerial responsibility for all such acts;

(4) that the Emperor is only the symbol of the State and the unity of the people; and

(5) that the Emperor derives his position from the will of the people in whom resides sovereign power. If the people so will they can abolish monarchy and the Emperor deprived of his position.

Articles 6 and 7 specify the following acts in matters of State which the Emperor performs:—

(1) the appointment of the Prime Minister as designated by the Diet;

(2) the appointment of the Chief Judge of the Supreme Court as designated by the Cabinet;

The Emperor, with the advice and approval of the Cabinet, performs the following acts in matters of State on behalf of the people:—

(3) promulgation of amendments of the Constitution, laws, Cabinet orders and treaties;

(4) proclamation of General Election of members of the Diet;

(5) convocation of the Diet;

(6) dissolution of the House of Representatives;

(7) receiving of foreign ambassadors and ministers;

(8) attestation of instruments of ratification and other diplomatic documents as provided for by law;

(9) attestation of the appointment and dismissal of Ministers of State and other officials as provided for by law, and of full powers and credentials of Ambassadors and ministers;

(10) awarding of honours;

(11) attestation of general and social amnestry, commutation of general punishment, reprieve, restoration of rights; and

(12) performance of ceremonial founctions.

**Role of the Emperor**

The functions enumerated above are a part of the overall functions which generally belong to the head of the State. But all such functions the Emperor performs on behalf of the people and on ministerial advice and approval. Neither of them involves any initiative, discretion or influence on his part. The Constitution does not only debar him from performing any personal act relating to Government, but also so incapacitates him politically that the Emperor cannot even claim to be the chief of the State or the representative of the nation. "It appears," writes Theodore McNelly, "that the term symbol of the State" may have been suggested by the British Statute of Westminster (1931) which provides that British monarch is the symbol of the British Commonwealth."[7] But such a use of the term is not happy in the case of the head of a sovereign State as Japan is.

The Emperor is, thus, relegated to the position of mere cypher and he stands no comparison with the constitutional monarch of England who plays a definite role in the governmental process. The Emperor of Japan performs only ceremonial functions and nothing beyond. He has absolutely no discretion in the appointment of the Prime Minister as he must appoint one designated by the Diet. In keeping with the constitutional provision that the Emperor is merely the "Symbol of State" but not the head of State Japanese cabinets are never sworn in by the Emperor. They merely attend a formal ceremony at the Imperial Palace attesting to their appointment. Nor can he influence the dissolution of the Diet. It is the constitutional right of the Cabinet alone; the Emperor must accept the advice tendered and promulgate dissolution. Treaties are not negotiated and concluded in the name of the Emperor. He simply promulgates them on behalf of the people and as concluded by the Government and approved by the Diet. The assent of the Emperor is not needed to validate laws passed by the Diet. In England a Bill becomes a law after it is passed by Parliament and on receiving the royal assent. The King has the power to veto a Bill duly passed by Parliament, although it has never been done since 1707. The Emperor of Japan has no power to withhold assent. A Bill, *ipso facto* becomes law when passed by the Diet. The Emperor simply promulgates it. Finally, he does not enjoy the preregrative of mercy. The Emperor only attests general and special amnesty, commutation of punishment, reprieve, and restoration of rights.

The Emperor is, no doubt, provided with

7. Theodore McNelly, *Contemporary Government of Japan*, p. 59.

requisite information about the affairs of the State and political policies of the Cabinet, but he possesses none of those rights—the right to be consulted, the right to encourage, and the right to warn, which Bagehot assigned to the British King. And a King of great sense and sagacity, he further said, "would want no other."[8] The Emperor of Japan is never consulted and his opinion is not solicited on any matter related to Government by the Ministers. He performs only those functions which are specifically enumerated in the Constitution and that, too, on behalf of the people from whom he derives his position. The Ministers are responsible to the Diet for all such acts of the Emperor. He has neither a legal nor a theoretical right to intervene and influence important decisions. Asquith, in a Memorandum on the rights and obligations of the British King, wrote, "He (King) is entitled and bound to give his ministers all relevant information which comes to him, to point out objections which seem to him valid against the course which they advise, to suggest (if he thinks fit) an alternative policy. Such intimations are always received by ministers with the utmost respect and considered with more respect and defence than if they proceeded from any other quarter."[9] The moral influence of the Emperor of Japan is still considerable and he may exert it in exceptional circumstances, but it will be a purely personal function carrying with it the weight of his institutional prestige. Constitutionally, he has no *locus standi* to do so. Nor can the Emperor act as a mediator and use his prestige to settle conflicts as the British monarch has done on many occasions. The Constitution insists that he should not take interest in politics and express only shading of public opinion. In sum, Emperor Hirohito, and the present Emperor Akihito too, essentially symbolised continuity, but as far as can be seen, did not exert even limited political influence wielded by modern monarchs. When on 22 December 1985, Japan celebrated one hundred years of Cabinet government, the celebration was accompanied by the first ever visit by a Japanese Emperor to the residence and the main office of the Japanese Prime Minister to attend a gathering of past and present cabinet ministers. With the Emperor in attendance, nothing controversial was said. When Emperor Hirohito spoke briefly, all those attending stood, many with their heads bowed. The Emperor said that he expected the Japense people, from top to bottom, to contribute to the peace of the world and the welfare of mankind as well as the development of the nation.

It cannot, however, be denied that in spite of the political incapacitation of the Emperor, the popular attitude towards the throne remains unabated. The Emperor of Japan was and is still the most powerful symbol of the unity and solidarity of the Japanese nation. The Japanese adore nation by giving ardent adoration to the Throne. The Emperor symbolizes more than two thousand years of "Japaneseness" of the unity and stability of the nation and, thus, provides a strong focus for patriotism and patriotic devotion. "The reverence of the Emperor," observes Chitoshi Yanaga, "is almost unbelievable especially to those who have not witnessed its manifestation at first hand. Furthermore, it is unfathomable since it is an emotional and practically a religious manifestation. Perhaps the British alone of the Western people can come closest to understand the Japanese attitude toward the sovereignty,"[10].The role of the Emperor, therefore, cannot be discounted. He is the rallying point of the nation and majority of the Japanese people wish and strive to elevate him to the position and status of a constitutional head of the State. Parliamentary democracy requires the presence of some dignified and detached person who should play a definite role in the governmental process as the British Monarch does.

## THE CABINET

### The Cabinet System in Retrospect

The beginning of the Cabinet system in Japan goes back to the Imperial Ordinance of 1885, which set up the Cabinet. But it did not establish the Cabinet system of government as obtainable in Britain. In fact, it was unlike the evolution of Cabinet Government in Britain where the Cabinet was the last element to evolve. In Japan "the cabinet antedated the promulgation of the Constitution by four years and the opening of Parliament that is the Diet, by full half decade."[11]

But the beginning had been made, though in the Constitution of 1889, itself the terms "Cabinet" and the "Prime Minister" occurred

8. Bagehot, W., *The British Constitution* (The world classics ed.), p. 67.
9. Spender, J. A., *Life of Lord Oxford and Asquith,* Vol. II, pp. 29-30.
10. Chitoshi Yanaga, *Japanese People and Politics,* p.130.
11. *Ibid.,* p. 144.

nowhere. Article 55 simply stated that there would be "ministers of state" who were "to give advice to the Emperor and be responsible to it." From this provision it could be implied that the Meiji Constitution established a sort of Cabinet to advise the Emperor and be responsible to him for that advice.

Since the "ministers of state"[12] did not constitute a Council of Ministers and they were individually responsible to the Emperor alone, it was not necessary that they should have been members of the Diet and belonged to its majority party or a combination of parliamentary groups agreeing to form a Coalition Government. In the beginning, the Emperor selected his own Prime Minister on the recommendation of his advisers who included the Elder statesmen, the Lord Keeper of the Privy Seal and the Minister of the Imperial Household. The Prime Minister would, then, select the ministers in consultation with the Emperor. By the second decade of the present century, the Emperor began summoning, but not invariably, the leader of the majority party in the Diet and would command him to recommend other ministers. But the Prime Minister did not make a team by selecting ministers from his own political party. Besides the multiplicity of political parties, there were other considerations which weighed heavily with the Prime Minister in making his choice. He had always to give premium to the wishes of the oligarchy and the views of the armed forces. The obvious result was a weak Cabinet which had to work under various pressures and influences. Nobutaka Ike correctly remarks that "the power of the prewar Cabinet, therefore, was greatly circumscribed both in theory and practice. Nevertheless, of all the organs of government the Cabinet was perhaps most consistently in the public eye, and almost all political figures came to consider appointment as Prime Minister, or even as a Cabinet Minister, the crowning achievements of their careers."

**Cabinet System under the 1946 Constitution**

The terms "Cabinet" and the "Prime Minister" are now constitutionalized and the Constitution of 1946 incorporates all the basic principles which govern the system of cabinet government. The executive power vests in the Cabinet[13] and the Emperor is only the symbol of the State and of the unity of the people.[14] The Cabinet consists of the Prime Minister as its head and other Ministers of State who are appointed by the Prime Minister.[15] The Prime Minister is designated from among the members of the Diet[16] by a resolution of the Diet, and the post goes invariably to the leader of the majority party or majority coalition in the House of Representatives, as in 1983 when the New Liberal Club threw its 8 seats in coalition with the Liberal Democratic Party with 250 seats in a 512 House. The Prime Minister and other members of the Cabinet must be civilians[17] and a majority of them should be chosen from among the members of the Diet.[18] The Cabinet in the exercise of its executive powers is collectively responsible to the Diet[19] and the Prime Minister may remove the Ministers of the State as he chooses.[20] The Cabinet must resign when the House of Representatives either passes a no-confidence resolution or rejects a confidence resolution.[21] The Cabinet, thus, remains in office as long as it can retain the confidence of the House of Representatives. While the collective responsibility of the Cabinet is to the House of Representatives, individual Ministers are responsible to the Prime Minister and they can be removed from office at his will. A hand which had made them can also unmake them.

**Composition and Organization of the Cabinet**

The size of the Cabinet varies from time to time, but usually 16 Ministers of State are appointed. All Ministers are technically of equal rank and status. In practice, however, only twelve hold Portfolios and head the various Ministries. Ministers without Portfolios do not hold charge of Ministries and are as a matter of distinction designated State Ministers.

Cabinet meetings are held twice a week, on

12. Kahin, George McT. (Ed.), *Major Governments of Asia*, p. 193.
13. Article 65.
14. Article 1.
15. Article 66.
16. Article 67.
17. Article 66.
18. Article 68.
19. Article 66.
20. Article 68.
21. Article 69.

Tuesday and Friday, at the Prime Minister's official residence. The Prime Minister presides over meetings of the Cabinet and in his absence the Vice-Premier presides. It is an established practice now that Cabinet decisions must be unanimous. If a Minister does not agree to the decision or policy of the Cabinet, he should resign from office. The Cabinet proceedings are strictly secret and no minutes are maintained. The Ministers have explicit instructions not to divulge what transpires in the Cabinet meetings. The Cabinet Secretariat, headed by a Director and two Deputy Directors, assists in the work of the Cabinet, arranges the agenda, prepares documents and handles other matters. It is customary that the Director of the Cabinet Secretariat, and the Director and Deputy Directors of the Bureau of Legislation attend the meetings of the Cabinet, participate in its deliberations but they cannot vote.

Eighteen Ministries or Departments have been established in addition to the Prime Minister's Office. The Prime Minister himself heads his office and it is the nerve centre and operational matrix of the Government. The Cabinet Secretariat and the Legislative Bureau are the auxiliary organs of the Cabinet. The former is charged with the function of preparing the agenda of Cabinet meetings and other miscellaneous affairs of the Cabinet. The Legislative Bureau examines and drafts Government Bills and Cabinet orders as well as drafts of treaties and other matters of equal importance. There are three extra-ministerial agencies : the National Personnel Agency; the Commission on Constitution, and the Economic Planning Agency. The Board of Audit is independent of the Cabinet and it is constitutionally charged with the duty of finally auditing every year the accounts of the expenditure and revenues of the State.

The two principal committees of the Cabinet are the Ministerial Defence Council and the National Defence Council. The Ministerial Defence Council consists of the Prime Minister, Foreign Minister, Finance Minister, Agriculture and Forest Minister, International Trade and Industry Minister, the Transport Minister, and the State Minister who serves as Director of the Economic Planning Agency.The National Defence Council consists of the Prime Minister, Foreign Minister, Finance Minister and the State Minister serving as Director of the Defence Agency and Director of the Economic Planning Agency. The Prime Minister is the Chairman of both these Committees.

The average life of the Cabinet is a little more than ten months. Paradoxical as it may seem, Prime Ministers have been more durable than Cabinets. The average life of the Prime Minister is twenty-five months. Intra-party and intra-factional differences on policy or personnel of the Cabinet are the two main reasons for short Cabinet tenures. ''And there is constant factional and intra-party pressure on all Cabinets to step aside in favour of other deserving colleagues. The pressure is so strong on any Prime Minister that frequent Cabinet changes are almost the necessary political price for his own continuance in power.''[22] The factional feuds within the Liberal Democratic Party led to the desertion of seventy members and, consequently, defeat of the Government headed by Masayoshi Ohira on a no-confidence motion tabled by the Opposition in March 1980.

**Functions of the Cabinet**

According to the Meiji Constitution of 1889, the Executive power was vested in the Emperor. The Ministers of the State advised His Majesty. It was for the Emperor to make decisions and the Ministers exercised only those functions which the Emperor was pleased to delegate to them, though in practice the Emperor acted as a constitutional monarch. The Constitution of 1946 vested the Executive power in the Cabinet[23] and the Emperor possesses no powers related to the Government[24]. In regard to acts specified in the Constitution which the Emperor performs the advice and approval of the Cabinet is necessary.[25] There is no act which the Emperor can perform in his discretion. The Cabinet, thus, formulates and decides policy and co-ordinates and controls the Ministers and other agencies of administration.

But for the implementation of policy necessary legislation must be available. If the existing framework of law does not provide for it, old laws may be amended, or new laws enacted. Administration and legislation go together. It is

22. Robert E. Ward and Roy Macridis (Editors), *Modern Political Systems : Asia*, p. 97.
23. Article 65.
24. Article 4.
25. Article 7.

for the Cabinet to decide what laws need be amended and the new laws which are required and their priority. The Cabinet is, thus, the magnet of policy and it integrates and guides the work of the Legislature. It is the instrument through which the Executive branch of Government is linked with the Legislature. To express it in the words of Bagehot, in the context of the British Constitution, Cabinet is a "hyphen that joins, the buckle that binds the executive and legislative departments together".

But administration cannot be divided rigidly into eighteen or so Ministries. The action of one Ministry affects another and, indeed, every important problem cuts across departmental boundaries. It is the function of the Cabinet to coordinate the functions of several Ministries or Departments of Government. Finally, the Cabinet is responsible for the whole expenditure of the State and to raise necessary revenues to meet such expenditure.[26]

The functions stated above are the general functions inherent in a cabinet government and are of universal application. The Constitution of Japan, as a measure of abundant caution, specifies various functions with which Cabinet is charged. The most important of such functions are enumerated in Chapter V. Article 72 states: the Prime Minister representing the Cabinet :

(1) submits Bills to the Diet;
(2) reports on the general national and foreign affairs to the Diet; and
(3) exercises control and supervision over various administrative branches.

Article 73 prescribes that the Cabinet in addition to other general administrative functions, shall perform the following functions:—

(i) administer the law faithfully and conduct affairs of the State;
(ii) manage foreign affairs and conclude treaties, subject to the prior or subsequent, depending upon circumstances, approval of the Diet;
(iii) administer the civil service in accordance with standards established by law;
(iv) prepare the Budget, and present it to the Diet;
(v) enact Cabinet orders in order to execute the provisions of the Constitution and of law. However, it cannot contain penal provisions in such Cabinet orders unless authorized by law;
(vi) decide on general amnesty, special amnesty, commutation of punishment, reprieve and restoration of rights;
(vii) all laws and Cabinet orders are to be signed by the competent Minister of the State and countersigned by the Prime Minister.[27]

The Cabinet also performs functions connected with other organs of Government:

(a) advises the Emperor on acts in matters of State;[28]
(b) designates the Chief Judge of the Supreme Court;[29]
(c) appoints Judges of the Supreme Court, excepting the Chief Judge[30] and Judges of the inferior courts from the list of persons nominated by the Supreme Court.[31] The Chief Justice of the Supreme Court is designated by the Cabinet and appointed by the Emperor;
(d) determines the convocation of extraordinary session of the Diet;[32]
(e) convenes, in time of national emergency, the House of Councillors in emergency session when the House of Representatives has been dissolved;[33]
(f) advises the dissolution of the House of Representatives to the Emperor,[34]
(g) advises promulgation of general election of the members of the Diet;[35]
(h) advises the convocation of the Diet,[36]
(i) expends monies from the Reserve Fund to meet unforeseen deficiencies in the Budget and get subsequent approval of Diet,[37]

26. Article 86 also states : "The Cabinet shall prepare and submit to the Diet for its consideration and decision a budget for each fiscal year."
27. Article 74.
28. Article 3.
29. Article 6.
30. Article 79.
31. Article 80.
32. Article 53.
33. Article 54.
34. Article 7.
35. *Ibid.*
36. *Ibid.*
37. Article 87.

(j) submits final accounts of expenditures and revenues of the State and the statement of audited report prepared by the Board of Audit of the Diet every year,[38] and

(k) submits reports at regular intervals and at least annually to the Diet and the people on the State of national finances.[39]

On December 22, 1985, Japan celebrated one hundred years of Cabinet Government. On that date in 1885 the Emperor Meiji inducted the Cabinet. Japan's fast-paced effort to catch up with the West was already under way. The Japanese wanted to modernise politically as well as economically and they saw that the two processes were inextricably linked. But the record of Cabinet development over the last more than one hundred years is ambiguous. It has been continuous but not continually meaningful. The fact that a Cabinet has been always in place has not meant that it was always in command. The institution became decreasingly relevant in the nineteen twenties and thirties as the military increasingly dominated the political process. The Cabinet was not able to clearly assert itself again when the crucial decision to surrender at the end of World War II was required.

The Japanese Cabinet has not even been in the ascendancy since democracy was restored after War. Often the politicians have spent so much time and energy competing for cabinet office that the net result has been domination of the decision-making process by the bureaueracy. Factionalism within the ruling Liberal Democratic Party over the last 35 years has made frequent cabinet reshuffles mandatory. The bureaucracy has supplied the continuity, which the decision-making process required, and which ministers had not always been able to supply.

## THE PRIME MINISTER

### Designation and Appointment

There is no Act of British Parliament which establishes the office of the Prime Minister in the United Kingdom.[40] But the Constitution of Japan specially provides for it, and determines his status. Article 6 of the Constitution provides that the Emperor shall appoint the Prime Minister as designated by the Diet. This is repeated in Article 67 with a further addition that the Prime Minister shall be designated from among the members of the Diet by a resolution of the Diet. At the same time, the Constitution requires that the Prime Minister and other Ministers must be civilians.[41] It, however, does not provide that the Prime Minister must always belong to the Lower House (House of Representatives) of the Diet. Legally, therefore, if the Prime Minister belonged to the Upper House (House of Councillors) there is no constitutional bar to it. But it has never happened since the Constitution became operative in 1947, and it is now a well established practice that the Prime Minister must come from the House of Representatives. That the Prime Minister should belong to the House of Representatives is implied in proviso to Article 67. It provides that if the House of Representatives and the House of Councillors disagree, and if no agreement is reached in a Joint Committee of both Houses, or if the House of Councillors fails to make designation within ten days after the House of Representatives has made designation, the decision of the House of Representatives is the decision of the Diet. Added to it is the constitutionally ordained responsibility of the Cabinet to the House of Representatives. Since the Prime Minister leads the Cabinet, it is logical to infer that he belongs to that House to which the Cabinet is constitutionally responsible.

The procedure actually followed in designating the Prime Minister is the same in both the Houses of the Diet. For clarity it may be divided into two stages. The first stage consists in nominating the candidates. If one single Party commands a majority, its leader will be automatically designated as a majority of the members present and voting is required to designate the Prime Minister. If one single Party does not command a majority and a few of the political parties combine to form the majority coalition, its leader is again an obvious choice. If this is not possible, parties nominate their candidates for the office of the Prime Minister. Since voting is on strict party lines, none can command a majority vote. In that case the first two candidates securing maximum votes run the final nomination and one securing the majority of votes stands designated. In the

38. Article 90.
39. Article 91.
40. The Ministers of the Crown Act, 1937, recognized for the first time the office of the Prime Minister and First Lord of the Treasury.
41. Article 66.

event of a tie, decision is made by lot. This completes the first stage or step in the designation of the Prime Minister. Then, a resolution of formal designation is presented and voted upon in both the Houses of the Diet. In the event of disagreement between the two Houses, a Joint Committee is appointed to resolve the difference. If the Joint Committee does not come to a decision and the disagreement continues, the decision of the House of Representatives finally prevails and that decision is deemed as the decision of the Diet. This actually occurred in 1948, when Prime Minister Ashida won over his rival, Yoshida. Toshiki Kaifu, who was elected President of the ruling Liberal Democratic Party was designated Prime Minister on August 1989 over-riding the House of Councillors' choice of the Socialist Leader, Miss Takako Doi, a former Professor of constitutional affairs. The person so designated by the Diet becomes the Prime Minister on appointment by the Emperor. The appointment by the Emperor is a sheer ceremonial function as he is not legally competent to refuse such an appointment.

An unprecedented display of factional infighting within the Liberal Democratic Party created a piquant situation. The Party had secured 259 seats in the 511 member House of Representatives in October 1979 General Election. It should have been a routine procedural formality for the Lower House, voting automatically the leader of the largest Party to the office of the Prime Minister. The normal practice in the Liberal Democratic Party has been that its Parliamentary leadership goes to its Party President. As such, Masayoshi Ohira should have been the sole choice. But Takeo Fukuda, of the same party and the former Prime Minister, staked his claim in an open defiant manner and contested the election. Ohira was designated Prime Minister by 138 votes against 121 for his rival in the second ballot with 250 abstentions. All Opposition parties refused to participate in the election and cast blank votes. It was for the first time in Japan's parliamentary history that two men from the same party were pitted against each other for the Premiership and it was only the third time that a parliamentary election for government head went to the second round.

**Powers of the Prime Minister**

The extent of the powers of the Prime Minister can well be appreciated from his constitutional position as the chief executive, and the head of the administration. Article 66 of the Constitution declares the Prime Minister as the head of the Cabinet. He appoints Ministers and possesses the undisputed right to keeping them in office at his pleasure.[42] He represents the Cabinet in submitting Bills, reporting on general national affairs and foreign relations to the Diet, and exercising control and supervision over various administrative branches.[43] All laws and Cabinet orders are signed by the competent Ministers and countersigned by the Prime Minister.[44] The Prime Minister presides at the Cabinet meetings[45] and decides disputes of jurisdiction among Ministers of Cabinet.[46] The Prime Minister may suspend the official act or order of any administrative office pending action by the Cabinet.[47] The identity of Ministers is unknown to law without the Prime Minister. Article 70 of the Constitution declares that the entire Cabinet must resign in case there is a vacancy in the post of the Prime Minister. It falls within the special competence of the Prime Minister to fix the date of the Diet elections, to convene the Diet, and to conclude and ratify international agreements.[48] With a constitutionalised office as the head of the Cabinet and the enormous powers which the Constitution conferred on the Prime Minister, his position is not a whit less than his prototype in Britain. Under the Meiji Constitution, the Prime Minister was not more than *primus inter pares,* first among equals. His appointment was a matter of imperial prerogative and all officers of the State, civil and military including the Ministers of States, were appointed and dismissed by the Emperor.[49] Now the Prime Minister is a member of the Diet and a leader of the Party in majority. He is vested with the power to appoint his Ministers and they retain office at his pleasure, though the Cabinet as a whole is collectively responsible to the Diet. In

42. Article 68.
43. Article 72.
44. Article 74.
45. Cabinet Law, Article 4.
46. Cabinet Law, Article 7.
47. Cabinet Law, Article 8.
48. *Statistical Handbook of Japan,* 196, *op. cit,* p. 104.
49. Article 10, *Constitution of Japan,* p. 1889.

the appointment of Ministers, he has the right to select his own team which in his opinion would be able to ensure the solidarity and stability of the Government. There may be certain political exigencies which may influence his choice, but the last word rests with him. It is his decision, choice and preference which the Emperor must accept. The Emperor simply performs a ceremonial function and attests the appointment and dismissal of ministers.

It is, thus, the constitutional authority of the Prime Minister to ask a colleague to resign and if the does not, to dismiss him from office as Prime Minister Katayama and Yoshida did. The Prime Minister can also reshuffle his Cabinet as and when he likes and this happens frequently in Japan. Prime Minister Yoshida is famous for the number of Ministers he had appointed. "Twice Mr. Kishi and twice Mr. Ikeda made wholesale changes in the personnel of their cabinets in such a way that the 'reconstructed' cabinet (Kaizo naikaku) were virtually new ones."[50] There is another important power which the Constitution vests in the Prime Minister. No legal action can be taken against Ministers, during their tenure of office, without the consent of the Prime Minister.[51] As head of the Cabinet, the Prime Minister calls the meetings of the Cabinet and presides over its proceedings, thereby holding a tight rein over the members.

There are no rules, customs and precedents governing the transaction of business in the Cabinet meetings. Nor is there a quorum fixed for the meeting and votes are never taken. Decisions must always be unanimous. The members express their views on the issues before the Cabinet, discuss pros and cons and strive to arrive at an agreement. The Prime Minister sums up the results of discussion and determines the consensus of opinion. Being head of the Cabinet and leader of the party in office, the Prime Minister enjoys a position of pre-eminence which enables him to impose his decision. He enjoys great power especially in emergency. The Prime Minister is empowered to proclaim national or local emergencies. He is also competent to issue direct orders to the public authorities in the areas involved in emergency proclamations.

The Prime Minister is the voice of the Cabinet in the Diet. He alone is authorized by the Constitution to submit Bills and reports on general national affairs and foreign relations to the Diet. He also exercises control and supervision over various administrative branches. The Prime Minister is, thus, the Manager-in-Chief of the Government's business. The Cabinet law empowers him to decide disputes of jurisdiction between one Minister and the other,[52] and may even suspend the official act or order of any administrative office pending action by the Cabinet.[53] These powers of the Prime Minister together with the constitutional provision that all laws and Cabinet orders require counter-signatures of the Prime Minister eclipse the position of the Ministers.[54] The Prime Minister is really the master of the Government, for he makes and unmakes the government and determines the policies at the meeting of the Cabinet of which he is the head. And for the members of the Cabinet, he appoints them and can dismiss them. An apt description of the position of the Prime Minister of Japan is, therefore, in essence similar to the one Jennings gives to the British Prime Minister, "He is, rather, a sun, around which planets revolve."

**Position of the Prime Minister**

In spite of that much of similarity between the position and role of the Prime Minister of Japan and that of the Prime Minister of Britain, the former enjoys more powers and he has stronger hold over his colleagues in the Cabinet as well as on the Diet. There are two important provisions in the Constitution which make his position unrivalled and his authority supreme. He appoints his Ministers of State and removes them from office "as he chooses."[55] In terms of law, Ministers in Britain are responsible to the sovereign whereas in Japan they are legally responsible to the Prime Minister. Secondly, the Prime Minister, "representing the cabinet, submits bills, reports on general national affairs and foreign relations to the Diet and exercises control and supervision over various administrative

50. Theodore McNelly, *Contemporary Government of Japan*, p. 85.
51. Article 75.
52. Article 4, Cabinet Law.
53. Article 7, Cabinet Law.
54. Article 72, *Constitution of Japan*, 1947.
55. Article 68, *Constitution of Japan*, 1947.

branches."[56] This provision in Article 72 has the impact of American Constitution which establishes the Presidential system of government and is akin to the annual and other periodical messages of the President to Congress.

In Britain a Minister introduces and pilots a public Bill. In Japan a legislative measure is submitted in the name of the Prime Minister to the Presiding Officer of the House in which the Bill is desired to be introduced. This simple provision, though in practice innocuous, gives to the Prime Minister a position of legal precedence and official prestige and status over his colleagues in the Cabinet. Moreover, the Constitution further sanctifies the position of the Prime Minister when it prescribes (Article 70) that when there is a vacancy in "in the post of the Prime Minister.... the Cabinet shall resign *en masse*." It means that the identity of the Ministers is not known in law without the Prime Minister. In Britain, too, the position is precisely the same, though it is the result of a well-recognised convention. But to give it a constitutional sanction is to establish legally that the Prime Minister is the kingpin of the Executive power of the State.

There is yet another provision in the Constitution which significantly enhances both the authority and influence of the Prime Minister in the context of the government machinery. Article 75, which has generally remained obscure, provides that the Ministers of the State "during their tenure of office shall not be subject to legal action without the consent of the Prime Minister. However, the right to take action is not impaired thereby." It means that no legal proceedings of any kind or nature can be instituted against a Minister without the prior consent of the Prime Minister, and that in the eyes of law the Prime Minister has the constitutional right to prevent the legal action intended to be taken. When the consent of the Prime Minister is the *sine qua non* of a legal action to be taken against a Minister, his authority becomes peerless in relation to other Ministers. It also implies that so long as a Minister continues his unflinching loyalty and allegiance to the Prime Minister, he remains immune from any legal proceedings against him for his official acts. The pith of this provision is that so long as the Prime Minister commands a comfortable majority in the Diet there is no possibility of manoeuvring with the legislative majority with a view of ousting the Ministry from office. But factional infighting in the Party and revolt of members within the Party may cause the defeat of the ruling party as it happened in March 1980 when 70 members of the Liberal Democratic Party deserted and Ohira's Government fell on a motion of no-confidence tabled by the Opposition.

There is nothing like the individual responsibility of a Minister in Japan as it is in Britain. The Constitution empowers the Prime Minister to remove a Minister from office as and when he chooses to do so. A breath which has made Ministers can also unmake them, though the position is not exactly the same as it is with the President's cabinet in the United States. The Prime Minister in a Cabinet system of government must ensure his majority in the legislature and should be able to lead and control the body to which the Cabinet is responsible as a whole. But the constitutional authority of the Japanese Prime Minister makes his position pre-eminent.

So vast is the extent and effect of the authority of the Prime Minister over his colleagues and, consequently, on the Cabinet that very often a question is posed "Whether the Diet was not responsible to the cabinet rather than the cabinet to it." The Constitution makes the Diet the sole law-making organ of the State and it controls the Executive through various devices of a Parliamentary system of government which have been constitutionalised. But in actual practice, the Prime Minister leads and controls the Diet. He has the constitutional power to dissolve the House of Representatives and with the dissolution of that House, the House of the Councillors "is closed at the same time." This means the demise of the Diet as a whole save that the Cabinet may in time of national emergency convoke the House of Councillors in an emergency session. The threat of dissolution, therefore, is like a big stick that keeps the House of Representatives together. It really makes the members of the House amenable to the wishes of the Prime Minister. Two examples will illustrate the point at issue. In 1948, Ashida Hitoshi resigned. Yoshida, one of the candidates for the Premiership, persuaded Yanazaki Takeshi not only to resign his seat in the House of Representatives in order to facilitate his election, but also managed to be designated by the Diet as a Prime Minister. Yanazaki Takeshi, it may be noted, was the likely choice of the Diet. In 1953, Prime Minister Yoshida insulted

56. *Ibid.*

the Diet by calling a member of the House of Representatives a stupid fool during the course of a debate. The House took umbrage over his indignity and a motion of no-confidence was initiated against the Government. The Prime Minister immediately obtained an imperial Rescript dissolving the House of Representatives. In the following General election Yoshida's Party again came into power, though with a reduced majority, and he was designated Prime Minister by the Diet.

These Constitutional provisions, notwithstanding the position of the Japanese Prime Minister is not on the same pedestal as those of the Prime Minister of Britain and India. Parliamentary system envisages alteration in government which is not possible in Japan. The Liberal Democratic Party has been in command of the government during the past more than thirty years and there seems no possibility of the parties in Opposition to oust it. General elections in Japan do not determine the leadership of the government and the nation, to the same extent, as they usually do elsewhere. No Prime Minister can be certain that the inevitable Liberal Democratic Party's electoral victory will assure his continued prime ministership. As things stand, Prime Minister Yasuhiro Nakasone ended his second and final term as Liberal Democratic Party President and, as such, Prime Minister in October 1987. He managed an extension in his term for another year as a result of the Party's electoral victory in the 1986 elections and his other national and international achievements in the political sphere. But before the proposal for his extension could mature, other leaders in the Party, such as Foreign Minister Shintaro Abe, Finance Minister Noburo Takeshita and Party's Executive Council chairman Kiichi Miyazawa sought to succeed Nakasone. In Japan, there is nothing as party allegiance and personal loyalty which are the hallmark of the British Parliamentary system.

The rule is that Japanese Prime Ministers are much more chairmen of the Board, rather than pilots at the helm, or, as Takeshita himself put it to a reporter: "I am not a leader who says follow me." Takeshita was a very much traditional style Japanese politician, who preferred to pursue consensus before taking action, in contrast to Nakasone who gave the Prime Ministership a much higher profile, especially abroad, often by promising action before consensus had been agreed. Takeshita returned the Japanese premiership to the self-effacing low-posture image which it has enjoyed for most of the 32 years of the Liberal Democratic Party rule.

Another important fact that has undermined the position and prestige of the Prime Minister is the fact that choosing a Prime Minister has become a difficult task in these days. It is not as though candidates are scarce, only that many are reluctant to take over the responsibility under the circumstances that had discredited the ruling Party, which alone is the Liberal Democratic Party. Prime Minister Noboru Takeshita acknowledged on April 12, 1989 of collecting 200 million Yen in political funds and donations. In announcing his decision to resign on April 25, he apologised. "The Recruit question has caused a grave crisis for nation's parliamentary democracy," he said in the statement. To make matters worse, there came up the issue of Sousuke Uno's involvement with a geisha. The Liberal Democratic Party desperately looked for a person who would be able to stem the rot and put the Party back where it was a year or so ago. It was with this hope that the Liberal Democratic parliamentarians had gone along with Toshiki Kaifu the present incumbent Prime Minister. One of the campaign issues of the February 1990 General Election was the call for clean policies in the wake of the Recruit scandal.[57]

### The Civil Service

The Civil Service in a modern State is the core of government. The Cabinet formulates policies, but the real work of administration is done by thousands of civil servants who staff the various Ministries or Departments of Government. It is not the business of a Minister, who heads the Department, to work the Department. His business is to see that the Department pursues a determined policy and it functions efficiently in that particular direction. Those who actually run the Department and implement the policies of the Government constitute the civil service of the country. They have a permanent status and tenure and are selected for their administrative capacity alone and are graded accordingly. They have no

57. Recruit Conglomerate, one of the fastest growing firms in Tokyo, sold in 1986, unlisted stocks in a subsidiary at a basement price and also surreptitiously financed " sells" to about 160 politicians and influential people, mostly LDP and its allies. The share known in over the counter market, OTC as "political stocks" apparently because of the insides information, soared soon after 1986. The fortunate owners unloaded them as the stock issue skyrocketed, yielding them huge profits.

interest in party politics and remain rigidly neutral and rigorously impartial in economic and political issues. Permanency of tenure gives them security of service and furnish to Ministers, who are amateurs in administration, and the legislature all necessary information for shaping and enacting policies on a multitude of subjects. Laski has aptly said that "every State is enormously dependent upon the quality of its public officials." The welfare of the people, therefore, normally depends upon the honest performance of the duties assigned to the civil servants, high and low. Their duties have become tremendously complex and onerous with expansion in the scope of governmental activities. The responsibilities devolving on the civil servants demand greater expertise knowledge, promptness in the performance of their duties, efficient diagnosis of the social ills and suggestion of appropriate remedies, and consequently tendering service with equal fidelity whatever government may come and go.

### The Civil Service Before 1946

Japan had nothing like the civil service until the seventh century. The patriarchal clan system had seriously undermined the authority of the Emperor and in their bid to strengthen the political structure, the Japanese looked to China for inspiration, which was then at the height of her glory. They found that the most important factor that contributed to China's greatness and power was her highly developed administrative system. Japan, accordingly, imported from China a highly centralised administrative system with the Confucian tradition that conferred high prestige upon the government officials. But there was one major difference. Whereas in "China the civil service had been instituted to destroy the old power structure based on the aristocracy," in Japan, "it was used to strengthen the political structure dominated by the aristocracy." For a little over five centuries the administration of national affairs was concentrated in the hands of civilian aristocracy which operated out of the Imperial court at the national capital.

Feudalism lasted for nearly seven centuries. The administrative system that developed during this period was dominated by the military and hierarchical organization and it was based upon the strong bond of fidelity between the lord and the vassal. It was precisely not a civil service system "but a feudal bureaucracy based on status, and official posts were hereditary." In the early years of the Meiji era, the officials of the State were largely drawn from the old Samurai-class, but soon there spread a strong feeling of discontentment against the government personnel and the method of entry into the service. It was complained that appointments went generally to friends of those already in the service and the able and talented youngmen were eliminated from entering public service. The agitation had the desired effect and in 1885 the foundation of a modern civil service was laid by adopting the principle that appointments to government posts should be based on competitive examination. The first examination for recruitment to second and third rank services was held in 1887. There was no competitive examination for recruitment to first rank service and it embraced Cabinet Ministers, ambassadors and highest judicial officers, accounting for less than five per cent of the total number of civil servants.

### Civil Service under 1946 Constitution

Under the Meiji Constitution all government officials were appointed by the Emperor and they remained in service at the pleasure of His Majesty. Imperial Ordinances rather than laws enacted by the Imperial Diet determined the conditions of the Imperial Civil Service. Since it was an Imperial Civil Service, in "its dealings with the public the Japanese bureaucracy acquired the reputation of being arrogant and over-bearing. Officials were, in theory responsible to the Emperor, and, therefore, each official was vested with a segment of imperial authority."[58] At functions of the Imperial Court the officers of the first rank were placed in precedence with the President of the House of Peers and the Speaker of the House of Representatives. And as the officials were responsible to the Emperor "and not to the public, officialdom was never very much concerned with the matter of public relations."[59]

The Constitution of 1946 changed the entire concept of public service. Article 15 provides : (1) the people have the inalienable right to choose their officials and to dismiss them, (2) all public officials are servants of the whole community and not of any group thereof. If any public official does any wrong to a person and the person concerned suffers damage through an illegal act of such officials, he can sue for redress as provided by law. The National Service Law enacted

58. Kahin George McT. (ed.) *Major Governments of Asia*, p. 197.
59. *Ibid.*

in 1947, provides "for servicewise standards of personnel administration." The National Personnel Authority, which was set up in 1949 and administers the National Public Service Law, is "charged with the responsibility of introducing democratic methods, providing scientific personnel management, and creating a job classification system."[60]

All public officials are now divided into two categories, Special Government Service, and the Regular Government Service. In the Special Government Service are included members of the Cabinet, all such positions the appointment of which requires approval of the Diet, high officials in the Imperial Court, Judges, Ambassadors and Ministers, Diet employees, common labourers, and employees of State Corporations. The Regular Government Service includes the personnel of the National Government, administrative and clerical, except those classified belonging to the Special Government Service.

The National Public Service Law is essentially concerned with the Regular Government Service. The National Personnel Authority, modelled after the Civil Service Commission of the United States of America, administers the National Public Service Law. It functions independently of the Diet and the Cabinet and consists of three Commissioners, one of whom is the Chairman. The Chairman is appointed by the Cabinet with the approval of the Diet. The functions of the National Personnel Authority, *inter alia,* are : to conduct the civil service examinations, classify position, promote employee training and welfare, deal with employee grievances, fix hours of work, leave of absence, temporary retirement. discipline compensation for illness and injury while on duty, issue directives within the law, which are binding on all Departments, and to recommend administrative and salary reforms to the Cabinet and Ministries.

Consistent with the demands of expanding governmental activities there has been an enormous increase in the size of the national government employees. Just before the War in 1940, the National Government had, excluding the military and certain temporary employees, a total of 231, 898 persons on its pay roll. In 1960, the figure was 1, 428,049, a more than five-fold increase. In 1963, it touched a total of 1,851,777 and this figure has since substantially increased. Out of this huge total of national employees a little more than five thousand belonged to the higher civil service comprising the first, second and third grades in the administrative service. Access to these positions is usually restricted to persons who pass the Higher Civil Service Examination, and the training and preparation of this Service are rigorous.

Despite the institutional changes referred to above, "the Japanese bureaucracy continues to be officious and given to feeling of self-importance."[61] Summing up the nature of the Japanese civil service, Robert E. Ward says,[62] "Displays of individual initiative on the part of junior employees are not highly valued. Loyalty and obedience to superiors, tact, anonymity, patience, and a capacity for the endless details and rituals of administration are the normal virtues. Personal and job security is complete, accountability to the public is practically nil." Confucianism had normally exalted the role of the government officials and this idea continues to prevail during the present time too. The public at large also stresses the superiority of the officials and obedience to their authority. And then the civil service is a step up the social ladder. Thus, it "hardly needs to be emphasised," remarks, Chitoshi Yanaga, "that, while under the new Constitution it has "been made very clear, that Government officials are public servants, it will be some time before the new legal status is accepted socially and psychologically by the officials themselves as well as the general public."[63]

Another feature of higher bureaucracy in Japan is that it is deeply involved in politics. Ever since the War such an involvement has become notable. It is now believed that one of the best ways to begin a political career is to enter the civil service. After retirement, which is comparatively at an early age and the pension is inadequate, an aspiring civil servant is apt seriously to consider a political career as the crowning of his ambitions. He has "already proved his administrative competence, and he enjoys a measure of prestige in his home community where people regard him as a home-town boy who made good, and they take a personal interest in his political career."[64] Ac-

60. *Statistical Hand-Book of Japan,* 1964, p. 107.
61. Kahin George McT (Ed.), *Major Governments of Asia,* p. 198.
62. Ward and Macridis (Eds.), *Modern Political Systems : Asia,* p. 101.
63. Chitoshi Yanaga, *Japanese People and Politics,* p. 311.
64. Theodore McNell, *Government of Japan,* p. 93.

cording to the analysis given by Robert E. Ward, in 1959, 84 members of the Lower House (18 per cent of the total membership) and 81 members of the Upper House (32 per cent) were former career civil servants. Some 35 per cent of the Cabinet members holding office between 1954 and 1961 were civil servants[65] and most of the post-War Prime Ministers have had long careers in the civil service—Shidehara, Yoshida, Kishi, Ikeda, Fakuda and Ohira. ''Bureaucrats naturally regard their own opinion,'' concludes Theodore McNelly, ''as more informed than that of the laymen, and Cabinet Ministers, with bureaucratic origins often take a scornful attitude towards legislators, the press and the general public. Ikeda Hayato was notorious for his lack of tact before he became Prime Minister.[66]

## SUGGESTED READINGS

Chitoshi Yanaga, *Japanese People and Politics*

Kahin, George McT, *Major Governments of Asia*

Maki, John M., *Government and Politics of Japan*

McNelly, Theodorie, *Contemporary Governments of Japan.*

Ward and Macridis, *Modern Political Systems: Asia*

Word, Robert E., *Japan's Political System*

Wint, Guy (ed.) *Asia Handbook.*

65. Ward and Macridis (Eds.), *Modern Political Systems : Asia,* p. 102.
66. Theodore McNelly, *Contemporary Government of Japan,* pp. 49-95.

# CHAPTER III

# The Diet

### The Diet

The Constitution describes the Diet or Parliament of Japan as the highest organ of State power and the sole law-making organ of the State.[1] It further states that the Diet consists of two Houses, the House of Representatives and the House of Councillors.[2] These two provisions are sharply distinguishable from the corresponding provisions of the Meiji Constitution. The Emperor, according to that Constitution, had alone the right of sovereignty and the sole ultimate repository of State power and he exercised "the legislative power with the consent of the Imperial Diet." Moreover, the Emperor and the Cabinet both had the power to issue decrees which had the force of law. The Constitution of 1946, which became operative in 1947, vests sovereignty in the people and the Diet, which is the expression of the will of the people and is the sole law-making organ of the State. "The Government has thus been transformed from an Emperor-centred to a Parliament-centred mechanism,"[3] and the elected representatives of the people are charged with the task of deliberating on national policies, formulated by the Cabinet, which body is collectively responsible to the Diet,[4] approving them finally, and enacting them into laws to make them valid for implementation and obedience.

Although the Diet reflects the opinion of the people, it also guides and leads public opinion. It is here that the representatives of the people ventilate grievances and seek redress. The Opposition opposes and criticises the policies and actions of the Government while the Party in office explains and clarifies in order to make issues intelligible to the people. It is a government by publicity and is subject to daily and periodic assessment. In other words, Diet is the national forum where all kinds of matters are debated and discussed and it equips the people with sufficient political knowledge to determine what policies and politics they will like to own. Since the powers of the Diet extend to all aspects of government activity, its authority is all-embracing. It deliberates and legislates, sanctions and controls the finances of the State, designates the Prime Minister who forms the Government and controls it hrough many processes. The government is ever under scrutiny of the Diet and the Constitution now vests it with investigative power,[5] which the Imperial Diet did not possess under the Meiji Constitution.

### A Bicameral Legislature

Japan has a bicameral legislature since 1890. Under the Meiji Constitution the Upper House was named as the House of Peers and it consisted of 416 members made of Peers, representative Peers, representatives of the highest taxpayers, and Imperial appointees. "It was natural, given its make up, that House of Peers was highly conservative, and since its powers were equal to that of the House of Representatives, it served for decades as a bulwark against popular control of the government."[6] The Lower House, the House of Representatives, was elected by a small electorate which met a high payment of tax. Originally, it consisted of 300 members. Women had no votes. In 1902 tax qualification was reduced and the membership increased. With the enactment of universal suffrage in 1925, which entitled all males over 25 years of age to vote, the

1. Article 41.
2. Article 42.
3. Ward and Macridis (Editors), *Modern Political Systems : Asia,* p. 92.
4. Article 65.
5. Article 62.
6. Kahin, George McT. (Ed.), *Major Governments of Asia,* p. 189.

number was set at 466. The term of office of the members was four years. But there were serious limitations on the powers of the House of Representatives, particularly relating to finances.

The Occupation Authorities, especially General MacArthur, favoured a unicameral legislature by doing away with the House of Peers as nothing resembling with it was desired to be put in its place. There was also a strong objection to an Upper House constituted on the basis of vocations or economic groups. But the Japanese did not favour tampering with bicameralism. They felt that an Upper Chamber in any democratice set-up was necessary as a check against hasty and ill-considered legislation. It was, accordingly proposed that a House of Councillors be established consisting of "members elected for the various districts or professions and members appointed by the cabinet upon resolution of a committee consisting of members of both Houses."[7] The Occupation Authorities eventually agreed to retain bicameralism, but the Upper House consisting of only elected members, representing all the people and not of groups or any section of society.

## THE HOUSE OF COUNCILLORS

### Composition

The House of Councillors, which replaced the House of Peers, consists of 252 members. The Constitution does not fix the number of the Councillors. It simply says: "The number of the members of each House shall be fixed by law."[8] The Law has now fixed the number at 252 out of which 152 are elected on a geographical basis, that is, from forty-six electoral districts in which the country is divided and correspond with the prefectures, and the remaining 100 are elected by the nation at large. The former are known as local constituencies and the latter national constituency. The number of seats going to a prefecture is roughly in proportion to its population and they vary from two to eight seats. For example, Tokyo and Hokkaido return eight Councillors each, while Osaka returns six. As the elections from the prefectures and the nation at large are held simultaneously, a voter exercises two votes, one for the candidate in the prefectural or local constituency, and the other for a candidate in the national constituency.

The members of the House of Councillors are elected for six-year term with one-half elected every three years.[9] There is no dissolution of the House. Since the terms are staggered, after the expiry of every three years, 76 members are chosen from the prefectural or local constituencies and 50 from the national constituencies. The idea of introducing two categories of constituency was to have a dissimilar composition as compared with the House of Representatives, and to attract eminent candidates of national stature who do not get themselves involved in the rough-and -tumble of partisan policies.

Qualifications for membership of the Diet (House of Councillors and the House of Representatives) are fixed by law. But the Constitution itself emphasises that there shall be no discrimination because of race, creed, sex, social status, family origin, education, property or income. The idea is to stress that privileges of any kind, as were found in the composition of the House of Peers under the Meiji Constitution, have been abolished altogether, and that women enjoyed the same rights as men.[10] The minimum age fixed for a Councillor is 30 years and he must fulfil all other qualifications which are prescribed for a voter. But the Constitution prohibits anyone to remain a member of both Houses simultaneously."[11] The House itself decides disputes relating to qualifications of members and there is no appeal in this respect to any other authority.[12] In order to deny a seat to any member, it is necessary to pass a resolution by a majority of two-thirds of the members present in the House.[13]

Members enjoy complete freedom of speech and they are not liable outside the House for speeches, debates or votes cast inside the House.[14] Moreover, except for cases provided by law, they are exempt from apprehension while the House is in session. Any member apprehended before the opening of the session shall be freed during the terms of the session upon demand

7. As cited in Theodore McNelly's *Contemporary Government of Japan*, p. 102.
8. Article 43.
9. Article 46.
10. Article 43, *The Constitution of Japan*, 1946.
11. Article 48.
12. Article 55.
13. *Ibid.*
14. Article 51.

of the House.[15] The members receive annual payment as determined by law in addition to the daily allowance when the House is in session and free railway passes. They are also entitled to a special allowance to defray the expenses of mailing documents and carrying on correspondence when the House is in session. There is provision for retirement pension too. The Chairmen of the Standing Committees are provided with official automobiles.

**The Session**

The House must meet once a year in a regular session.[16] It is usually opened in December by the Emperor who delivers a brief message to a joint session of both the Houses. Extraordinary Sessions are called by the Cabinet whenever deemed necessary. If one-fourth or more of the total members of the House demand for convening an Extraordinary Session, it becomes the duty of the Cabinet to do so.[17] When the House of Representatives is dissolved, the House of Councillors "is closed at the same time." The Cabinet may, however, convoke the House of Councillors in emergency session if the conditions of national emergency prevail in the country.[18]

The quorum for the transaction of business is fixed at one-third of the total membership of the House.[19] Deliberations of the House are open to public[20] unless it is a secret meeting on the demand of two-thirds of the members present.[21] The House is required to keep a record of its proceedings which must be published and made available to the general public, except such parts of the proceedings of the closed session as require secrecy. Upon demand of one-fifth of the members present, votes of the members on any matter be recorded in Minutes.[22] All decisions are taken by a majority vote of the members present, except otherwise provided by the Constitution. In case of a tie, the Presiding officer exercises a casting vote.[23]

**The Presiding Officer**

The House of Councillors elects its own President and Vice-President. The President presides over the sittings of the House and controls its proceedings. In the absence of the President, the Vice-President presides. The House establishes its rules for the conduct of meetings, proceedings and internal discipline and may punish members for disorderly conduct. In order to expel a member from the House, a majority of two-thirds of members present must pass a resolution to that effect.[24] In case of a tie, the Presiding Officer is entitled to a casting vote.[25]

**Committees of the House**

The House has two types of Committees—standing and special—to deal with different matters. Previously, the House had twenty-two Standing Committees. Now their number stands at sixteen: Cabinet, Local Administration, Judicial, Foreign Affairs, Finance, Education, Social and Labour, Agriculture and Forestry, Commerce and Industry, Transportation, Postal Services, Construction, Budget, Audit, House Management and Discipline. A Councillor must be a member of at least one Standing Committee, but he must not serve on more than three committees.

**Functions of the House of Councillors**

Functions of the House of Councillors are:

**Legislative Functions**

The Constitution confers identical legislative functions on the House of Councillors and the House of Representatives. Article 41 says that the Diet is the highest legislative organ of State power and the sole law-making organ of the State. Article 59 further says that a Bill becomes a law on passage by both the Houses. It means that a legislative measure may be introduced in either of the Houses and when passed by them separately, it becomes a law and must be promulgated accordingly. But after having conceded that much to the House of Councillors, the Constitution establishes the supremacy of the House of Representatives. It is provided that in case the House of Councillors makes a decision different

15. Article 50.
16. Article 52.
17. Article 53.
18. Article 54.
19. Article 56.
20. Article 57.
21. *Ibid.*
22. Article 57.
23. Article 56.
24. Article 58.
25. Article 56.

from the House of Representatives, it becomes law of the Diet when the House of Representatives passes the Bill for the second time by a majority of two-thirds of members present and voting. But this provision does not preclude the House of Representatives from calling for the meeting of a joint committee of both Houses, provided for by law. If such a difference cannot be resolved in the joint meeting, it becomes a law of the Diet when the House of Representatives repasses the Bill by a majority of two-thirds or more of the members present and voting. The Constitution also provides that if the House of Councillors fails to take final action within 60 days excluding the recess period after receipt of the Bill from the House of Representatives, it may be taken by the House of Representatives to constitute a rejection of the Bill by the House of Councillors.[26] The final word, therefore, rests with the House of Representtives.

**Financial Functions**

Consistent with the democratic theory and the practice of Parliamentary system of government, Money Bills do not originate in the House of Councillors. The Constitution specifies that the Budget must be submitted first to the House of Representatives and when it passes therefrom it goes to the House of Councillors. If the House of Councillors makes a decision different from that of the House of Representatives and when no agreement can be reached even in a joint committee of both the Houses, provided for by law, or when it fails to take final action within 30 days after receipt of the Budget approved by the Lower House, the decision of the House of Representatives becomes the approval of the Diet.[27] In matters of budget, therefore, the function of the House of Councillors is significant.

Articles 83 to 91 contained in Chapter VII of the Constitution enumerate the powers of the House of Councillors which it exercises together with the House of Representatives. It is provided in clear terms that the power to administer national finances shall be exercised by the Diet. Both the Houses modify the existing taxes or impose new ones, authorise the expenditure of money and assume obligations by the State, approve the Budget for each fiscal year as prepared and submitted by the Cabinet, authorise and approve expenditure from a reserve fund to provide for unforeseen deficiencies in the Budget and approve the appropriation of expenses for the Imperial Household. Final accounts of the expenditure or revenues of the State are required to be audited annually by a Board of Audit and submitted by the Cabinet to each House of the Diet for its acceptance. The House of Councillors, like the House of Representatives, is also responsible for approving the Government's settled accounts. At regular intervals and at least annually the Cabinet is required to report to both the Houses of the Diet and the people on the state of national finances.[28]

**Administrative Functions**

The Cabinet is the creation of the Diet and is headed by the Prime Minister. The Constitution requires that all members of the Cabinet be civilians and that a majority of their number, including the Prime Minister, be members of the Diet. Custom has, however, established that the Prime Minister invariably belongs to the House of Representatives and an overwhelming majority of the Ministers are chosen from the same House. Not more than three or four Ministers are taken from the House of Councillors. The Prime Minister is designated by a resolution of the House of Representatives and the House of Councillors. If, however, the House of Representatives and the House of Councillors disagree and if no agreement can be reached in the joint committee of both the Houses, or if the House of Councillors fails to make designation within 10 days after the House of Representatives has made its designation, the decision of the House of Representatives is the decision of the Diet.[29] The final determination in the designation of the Prime Minister is, therefore, that of the House of Representatives and to its choice the House of Councillors must submit.

The House of Councillors does not control the Government and can bring no crisis by passing an adverse vote. According to Article 66 the "Cabinet is collectively responsible to the Diet," which in terms of law means both the House of Councillors and the House of Representatives. But when read with Article 69 responsibility really means to the House of Representatives. It specifies, that when the House of Representatives passes a resolution of no confidence in

26. Article 59.
27. Article 60.
28. Article 90.
29. Article 67.

the Cabinet, or rejects a confidence resolution, "the Cabinet, shall resign *en masse,* unless the House of Representatives is dissolved within 10 days." Thus, when the House of Representatives passes a no confidence motion against the Government or rejects a vote of confidence in the Government, it must either resign or advise dissolution of the House of Representatives within ten days of the passing of resolution to seek the verdict of the electorate. The House of Councillors is not dissolved. The new election of the House of Representatives will, then, determine the party to form the Government.

It does not, however, mean that the Councillors have no hand in influencing administration. The members of the House of Councillors can seek information from the Government on any aspect of administration through the medium of questions. "Question hour" in the life of the Parliamentary government plays a significant role and it tends to keep the Government within bounds. The members may also seek redress of grievances or bring to the notice of the Government a matter of public importance of which the Government has not taken any cognisance by passing a resolution to that effect. The Constitution enjoins on the Cabinet to report at regular intervals and at least annually to both the Houses of the Diet on the state of national finances, and the Prime Minister, representing the Cabinet, on general national affairs and foreign relations.[30] Finally, the House of Councillors together with the House of Representatives has been given investigative functions. According to Article 62, each House of the Diet "may conduct investigations in relation to government, and may demand the presence and testimony of witnesses, and the production of records." The House of Councillors in this way exercises a continuous supervision over the administration, particularly relating to efficiency and honesty of Government.

**Judicial Functions**

The House of Councillors, together with the House of Representatives, constitutes the court of impeachment for the trial of Judges of the Supreme Court. Article 64 of the Constitution provides that "the Diet shall set up an impeachment court from among the members of both Houses for the purpose of trying Judges against whom removal proceedings have been instituted." Matters relating to impeachment are provided by law. The Court of Impeachment, as now constituted, consists of 14 members equally drawn from the House of Councillors and the House of Representatives. The members of the Court elect one from among themselves to be a presiding officer. The law also sets up an Indictment Committee, consisting of an equal number of members of both the Houses of the Diet, which prefers charges for removal against a judge or judges to be impeached. A member of the Indictment Committee cannot simultaneously be a member of the Court of Impeachment.

**Constituent Functions**

The House of Councillors and the House of Representatives both exercise equal powers of amending the Constitution. Amendment to the Constitution can be initiated by either House of the Diet and it must pass separately by a majority of two-thirds of the total membership of the House of Councillors and the House of Representatives, and then it is submitted to the people for their approval at a referendum.

**Electoral Functions**

The House of Councillors together with the House of Representatives performs many electoral functions. The procedure adopted for the selection of the Prime Minister has already been described. The Constitution definitely prescribes the participation of both the Houses in the designation of the Prime Minister.[31] The qualifications of the members of both the Houses and their electors are fixed by law of the Diet. The only limitation that the Constitution places is that there shall be no discrimination because of race, creed, sex, social status, family origin, education, property or income.[32] The Diet is also competent to enact laws regarding the formation of electoral districts, method of voting, and other matters pertaining to the method of election of members of both the Houses.[33] Each House is competent to judge disputes relating to qualifications of its members. However, in order to deny a seat to any member, it is necessary to pass a resolution by a majority of two-thirds or more of the members present.[34] The House of Councillors elects its

30. Article 72.
31. Article 67.
32. Article 44.
33. Article 47.
34. Article 57.

own President and Vice-President, and other officials of the House.[35]

**House of Councillors at Work**

As said earlier, General MacArthur had desired a unicameral legislature and the first draft of the Constitution was accordingly formulated. But the Japanese leadership was strongly opposed to this proposal and the Constitution of 1946 established a bicameral legislature. Since the Constitution had set up a Parliamentary system of government, it was, natural that the popular chamber should remain the focus of authority and the Upper Chamber was to exercise only a restraining, moderating and dignifying influence, and to provide continuity and stability to the Diet. The members of the House of Councillors are elected for a term of six years, one-half retiring after every three years. As the House is not subject to dissolution, there is continuity in its life and the members usually serve for their full term of six years. The law of the Diet prescribes that members of the House of Councillors must at least be thirty years of age and they should be chosen from two different kinds of constituencies: 100 from the national constituency and 152 from the local or prefectural constituencies. The intention was to combine the advantages of informed local representation with those of a panel of nationally eminent candidates. But after more than four decades of the working of the Constitution, the House of Councillors is not greatly different from the House of Representatives either in terms of age or politics.[36] It has become practically a partisan body as the House of Representatives is. There are, however, some eminent statesmen who are chosen from the national constituency, the bulk of those so chosen probably represent organizations having branches or influence in several heavily populated areas of Japan *e.g.*, labour unions, big business and nationally organized interest groups.[37] There are just a few independent candidates and the rest are the nominees of the political parties and subject to their rigid control The party composition of the House of Councillors closely resembles to that of the House of Representatives.

The House of the Councillors has in practice not fulfilled the purpose of exercising a restraining influence against hasty and ill-considered legislation. When the same Party controls both the Houses and the Party composition therein remains more or less the same at every election, there is no possibility of any disagreement between the two Houses and the Bills pass through *ipso facto*. Rigidity of party discipline does not permit opposition of any kind to the Government's policy with the result that the House of Councillors has become a recording Chamber. There is a growing feeling among the Japanese that the House of Councillors as constituted at present makes little contribution to the role it is expected to play and, accordingly, some kind of reform is urgently needed in its composition. It has been suggested that the House should be made a Chamber representing professions and other elements of the electorate; the original point of view expressed by the Japanese in 1946, but not accepted by the Occupation Authorities.

## THE HOUSE OF REPRESENTATIVES

**Composition and Tenure**

The House of Representatives is the Lower Chamber of the Diet and consists of 512 members elected for a four-year term. Originally, the total membership of the House was fixed at 466. On restoration of Amami Island to Japan by the United States of America in 1953, its strength was raised to 467. Since the House is subject to dissolution, it does not run a full term. General Elections have taken place at intervals ranging from six and half months to three years and eight months. Candidates are returned from a total of 118 so-called "medium sized" constitutencies, each constituency returning from three to six members, on population basis, except the constituency of Amami Islands which is represented by one member. Despite that each constituency returns several members, each elector casts only one vote. The Japanese system is a form of "limited voting," that is, the voter is permitted to vote for fewer candidates than the number of seats to be filled from a constituency.

The Public Offices Election Law of April 1950, guarantees the right of vote to practically all Japanese citizens, male or female, who have reached the age of twenty years. A candidate for membership to the House of Representatives should be twenty-five years of age and he must have been resident of the locality from which he seeks election continuously for a period of three months. But locality rule in Japan does not mean

35. Article 58.
36. Theodore McNelly, *Contemporary Government of Japan*, p. 103.
37. Ward and Macridis (Eds.), *Modern Political System : Asia*, 92.

actual residence in the constituency as the rigid practice in the United States is. It simply means having a legal domicile and being registered there. A candidate for the House of Representatives must meet all other qualifications as those prescribed for voters. No one can be a member of both the Houses at the same time. Nor can he hold any other office under the Government. Disputes relating to qualifications of the members are judged by the House of Representatives itself. However, in order to deny a seat to any member, it is necessary to pass a resolution by a majority of two-thirds or more of the members present.

Members of both Houses enjoy complete freedom of speech and they are not held liable outside the House for speeches made or votes cast inside the House. Members of both the Houses are exempt from apprehension, except in criminal cases, while the Diet is in session. Any member apprehended before the opening of the session is freed during the term of the session upon demand of the House. The Constitution provides that members of both Houses shall receive appropriate annual payment from the national treasury in accordance with the law. The law provides for a handsome annual salary in addition to the daily allowance when the House is in session, free railway passes between Tokyo and homes of the members and some special allowances and other facilities. There is also a provision for retirement pension for members.

**Sessions**

The Constitution specifically mentions two types of sessions of the Diet: the regular or ordinary session, and an extraordinary session. An ordinary session of the Diet is convoked once a year,[38] but Cabinet may convoke an extraordinary session, whenever necessary, to take up emergency matters which cannot wait until the next regular session. If one-fourth of the total numbere of members of either House make a demand that the Diet should be convoked in an extraordinary session, the Cabinet must summon it.[39] There is also a provision for a special session. According to Article 54, when the House of Representatives is dissolved there must be a General Election of members of the House of Representatives within 40 days from the date of dissolution, and the Diet must be convoked within 30 days from the date of the Election. The purpose of such a special session of the Diet is to elect a Prime Minister who should form the government, and to dispose of the unfinished business left over because of dissolution. When the House of Representatives is dissolved, the House of Councillors must immediately go into adjournment. But in times of national emergency, the Cabinet may convoke it in emergency session to take action on urgent measures. Measures adopted by the House of Councillors in emergency session are provisional and they become null and void unless assented to by the House of Representatives within a period of 10 days after the opening of the next session,[40] which is usually a special session.

Business cannot be transacted in the House unless one-third or more of total number of members of the House are present,[41] that is, 171 members out of a total membership of 512 must at least be present for the valid transaction of business. All matters are decided by a majority vote of those present, except as provided for in the Constitution.[42] In case of a tie, the Presiding Officer, the Speaker, and in his absence the Deputy Speaker, exercises a casting vote and decides the issue.[43]

There is a constitutional sanction that deliberations in each House of the Diet should be public.[44] It means that the sessions of each House of the Diet are open to public unless a majority of two-thirds of the members present in a House pass a resolution that a secret meeting of the House be held.[45] Under the Meiji Constitution the Cabinet could alone demand a secret meeting of the House. But under the Constitution of 1946, it is the House itself which decides by a two-thirds majority that there should be a secret meeting. The Cabinet has absolutely no say in the matter. Each House of the Diet is required to keep a record of its proceedings. Such a record is required to be published and made available to

38. Article 52.
39. Article 53, *Constitution of Japan,* 1946.
40. Article 54.
41. Article 56.
42. *Ibid.*
43. *Ibid.*
44. Article 57.
45. *Ibid.*

public, except such parts of the proceedings of a secret session as may be deemed to require secrecy.[46]

**Organisation of the House**

The organisation of the House of Representatives is quite simple. The first business of the House when it assembles immediately after the General Election is to elect a Speaker and a Deputy Speaker or Vice-Speaker. The Speaker presides over the meetings of the House and in his absence the Vice-Speaker presides. It is, therefore, the first step in the organization of the House that the Presiding Officer may be elected, for it is only after his election that the business of the House can be transacted. The House makes its own rules pertaining to meetings, proceedings and internal discipline.[47] For deliberative purposes the House functions either in plenary session or in committees. There are 16 Standing Committees of the House and most of these Committees correspond to Ministries or Departments of the Government. The House may also appoint special Committees for the study of particular problems or proposals. Each party is represented in the Committees on the basis of party strength in the House. Each member must serve on at least one Standing Committee and on not more than three Committees.

**The Speaker**

Under the Meiji Constitution the members of the House of Representatives did not elect their Speaker. The House would nominate three members and the Emperor selected one out of them to act as the Speaker. The Constitution of 1946 specifically provides that each House shall select its own presiding officer, and empowers him in case of a tie to decide the issue by his casting vote. So important is the office of the Speaker that no business of the House can be transacted without him. Even the designation of the Prime Minister, urgent as it is, has to wait until after the Speaker and his Deputy are chosen.

Normally, the Speaker is the nominee of the Party in majority in the House of Representatives and he is elected for the life of the House, that is, for 4 years, provided it is not dissolved earlier. If the Party in office does not command an absolute majority, but only a working majority with the support of some other party or parties, the Speakership can go to a party other than the Government Party as it happened in the Fifth Yoshida Government. The Speaker of the House of Representatives is, accordingly, a party man and he does not renounce his party affiliations after his election to that office. Nor does it apply to him, as it does to the Speaker of the British House of Commons, once a Speaker always a Speaker, so long one wishes to be. A Speaker of the last House may not be elected to the House after the fresh elections by the new House even if the same Party is returned in majority and forms the government. He may not be elected to the House at the General Election. To ensure his re-election to the House, the Speaker must remain a partisan to further the interests of his Party and aid the government Party, of which he is the nominee, in pushing through its legislative programme. The Speaker in Japan, therefore, is not the impartial umpire in the House and custodian of the rights of its members whether they belong to the Treasury Benches or the Opposition. His role is very much akin to that of his counterpart in the United States of America.

The Speaker presides over the meetings of the House of Representatives. It is his foremost function to maintain order and decorum in the House so that the proceedings are conducted smoothly and efficiently, and there is expeditious disposal of the business before the House. In case of disobedience to his orders or disorderly conduct or use of unparliamentary language, the Speaker may deny to such a member the right to speak. If the unruly behaviour still continues, the may adjourn the House. But in order to expel a member from the House for his disorderly conduct, the Constitution demands that the House should pass a resolution to that effect supported by a majority of two-thirds or more of the members present. If the visitors to the House exhibit disorderly conduct, the Speaker is empowered to order expulsion of such visitors or order that the visitors' gallery be cleared in entirety.

The Speaker determines the order of business, fixes the time limit on debates and interpellations, gives floor to the members who wish to participate in debates, applies closure, and, thus, brings the debate to an end. He puts the motion to vote and announces the results. In case of a tie, he exercises his casting vote and decides the issue. Immediately after the Bill is introduced in the House, the Speaker, as a rule, refers it to the

46. *Ibid.*
47. Article 58.

appropriate Standing Committee or a Special Committee of the House. He formally appoints the members and chairmen of the Standing Committees. The Speaker functions as the official representative of the House with all other agencies outside it. He proposes executive sessions and approves the appointment of government members for the purpose of assisting Cabinet Ministers in the Diet. He may appear before any Committee of the House, including the Joint Conference Committee, and tender his views and opinion on the matter before the Committee for investigation. The Speaker is empowered to accept the resignation of a member of the House when it is not in session.

The Speaker receives a salary equivalent to that of the Prime Minister and the Chief Justice. He also ranks high in precedence.

**Supremacy of the House of Representatives**

The Constitution definitely establishes the supremacy of the House of Representatives and it is in accordance with the theory and practice of the Parliamentary system of government. In the creation of the Cabinet and in its retention in office the House of Representatives is the dominant Chamber. In the process of law-making it has the final say. The House of Representatives can override the House of Councillors in the event of irreconcilable disagreement between the two Houses or delay or inaction on the part of the House of Councillors in legislative or financial matters. The exact role of the House of Councillors is to delay the enactment for a specified period of time (60 days in the case of legislative measures and 30 days in respect of the Budget) and not to be a rival Chamber.

**Legislative Functions**

As said earlier, a legislative measure must pass through both the Houses in order to become a law. But if one House disagrees with the other and if the disagreement cannot be resolved even in a Joint Committee of both the Houses the Constitution vests the House of Representatives with an overriding power over the House of Councillors. Article 59 specifies that a legisative bill which is passed by the House of Representatives and upon which the House of Councillors makes a decision different from the House of Representatives and the diference persists in spite of the efforts of the Joint Committee of both the Houses to resolve it, it becomes a law on its being passed a second time by the House of Representatives by a two-thirds majority of the members present. The Constitution empowers only the House of Representatives to call a meeting of the Joint Committee.[48]

The Constitution also provides that if the House of Councillors fails to take final action on a bill passed by the House of Representatives within a period of sixty days (excluding the recess period) after its receipt from the House, the House of Representatives may take such an inaction on the part of the House of Councillors as a rejection of the measure by it. If the House of Representatives again passes the bill by a majority of two-thirds or more members present, it becomes a law of the Diet and is promulgated accordingly.[49] But a legislative measure which the House of Representatives rejects cannot be recognised or revived by the House of Councillors. The final authority of law-making, therefore, rests with the House of Representatives.

**Financial Functions**

The House of Representatives has control over the purse along with the House of Councillors. But, here too, the Constitution unequivocally establishes the supremacy of the House of Representatives over the House of Councillors. This is, indeed, the prerequisite of the system of responsible government. According to Article 60 the budget must first be submitted to the House of Representatives. It is further provided that the approval of the budget by the House of Represenatives becomes the approval of both the House of the Diet, if the House of Councillors makes a decision different from that of the House of Representatives and when no agreement can be reached through a Joint Committee of both Houses, or when, it fails to take action within 30 days after the receipt of the budget approved by the House of Representatives. The same provision applies to ratification of treaties.[50]

Chapter VII of the Constitution, covering Articles 83 to 91, contains powers which the House of Representatives together with the House of Councillors exercise with respect to national finances: the Diet determines the manner in which the finances are to be administered, modifies the existing taxes or imposes new ones,

48. Article 589.
49. *Ibid.*
50. Article 61.

authorizes the expenditure of money and assumes obligations by the State, considers and approves the budget for each fiscal year prepared and submitted by the Cabinet, authorises and approves expenditure from a reserve fund tc provide for unforeseen deficiencies in the budget, approves the appropriation of expenses for the Imperial Household, receives from the Board of Audit, through the Cabinet, the audited accounts of the expenditure and revenues of the State, and receives reports at regular intervals, but at least once a year, from the Cabinet on the state of the national finances.

**Executive Functions**

A third great function of the House of Representatives is controlling the executive. It creates the Cabinet and the Cabinet is collectively responsible to the House of Representatives. This is the basic feature of the Cabinet system of government as established in Japan. The Prime Minister heads the Cabinet. Legally, he is designated by the Diet, but in actual practice he is the choice of the House of Representatives. The Constitution provides that if the House of Representatives and the House of Councillors disagree and no agreement is reached even in the meeting of the Joint Committee of both the Houses, or, if the House of Councillors fails to make designation within ten days after the House of Representatives has made its choice, the decision of the House of Representatives is final and is deemed the decision of the Diet.[51] The Emperor "appoints" the Prime Minister as designated by the Diet.[52]

With the appointment of the Prime Minister formation of the Cabinet begins. The Constitution simply says that a majority of the number of Ministers must be chosen from among the members of the Diet,[53] and all of them must be civilians.[54] In practice, however, except for three or four Ministers who belong to the House of Councillors, the remaining twelve or thirteen invariably have been chosen from the House of Representatives. And with the stability of the party system in Japan, they are taken from the majority party in the House of Representatives of which the Prime Minister is the head. The Cabinet advises and approves all acts of the Emperor in matters of State and is responsible thereof.[55] Whereas the individual Ministers can be removed from office by the Prime Minister,[56] the Cabinet as a whole can only be dismissed by the House of Representatives. Article 69 provides that if the House of Representatives passes a no-confidence resolution, or rejects a confidence resolution, the Cabinet resigns *en masse* unless the House of Representatives is dissolved within ten days.

It means that the Cabinet remains in office as long as it can retain the confidence of the House of Representatives. As soon as its confidence is lost, it must resign as a whole thereby providing an opportunity to the Opposition to form the government. If the Government does not resign, it advises dissolution of the House of Representatives. The House of Councillors is never dissolved. There must be a General Election of members of the House of Representatives within forty days from the date of dissolution.[57] The principle of collective responsibility of the Cabinet can best be ensured if a Cabinet has the power to dissolve the Chamber to which it is responsible. Collective responsibility of the Cabinet is further emphasised by Article 70. It says that when there is a vacancy in the post of the Prime Minister, the Cabinet shall resign *en masse.* The identity of the Cabinet, of which the Prime Minister is the head, is unknown to law without the Prime Minister and in his absence it does not exist. And the Prime Minister is the leader of the majority party or parties in the House of Representatives.

Responsibility and control go together. There are two important methods by which the House of Representatives maintains its control over the Executive. The first is through the medium of questions and interpellations . It provides an opportunity to the members of the House to seek information on various matters of administration and seek redress in case of abuse of authority. The late Professor Laski succinctly said that parliamentary government "lives and dies by publicity it can secure not only on government operations, but on all the knowledge it can obtain on the working of social processes."

51. Article 67.
52. Article 6.
53. Article 68.
54. Article 66.
55. Article 3.
56. Article 68.
57. Article 54.

The Constitution of Japan requires the Prime Minister to report on general national affairs and foreign relations to the Diet.[58] The Cabinet also reports at regular intervals, and at least annually, to the Diet and the people on the state of national finances.[59] Report on natinal finances embraces all the aspects and problems of administration. All kinds of treaties must also be ratified by the Diet[60] though concluded by the Cabinet.

The second instrument of controlling the Executive is the criticism which is constantly aimed at the Government in the House of Representatives. The House of Representatives is also a debating society and this is done when Bills before the House are being discussed and debated. In fact, the entire policy of the Government is under review on all such occasions. Since the defeat of a Bill means the defeat of the Government, the Opposition makes a bid to expose the Government and if possible to depose it. The Government on its part makes all-out efforts to defend its policies and actions. Another opportunity for criticism is provided when the national finances are discussed by the House, more especially the proposals for expenditure.

In addition to these, the most extreme form of Opposition attack on the policy of the Government is the vote of no-confidence in the Ministry. The Constitution accords to the vote of no-confidence a constitutional sanctity. Article69 provides: ''If the House of Representatives passes a no-confidence resolution, or rejects a confidence resolution, the Cabinet shall resign *en masse,* unless the House of Representatives is dissolved within ten (10) days,'' This provision is vindication of the principle of collective inisterial responsibility (Article 66) and is the *sine qua non* of a responsible government. A resolution of no-confidence is of crucial importance, because it decides the fate of the Ministry. So long as the Ministry commands a comfortable majority in the House of Representatives such a motion is of no consequence. But still it creates a stir in the Ministry and shakes its prestige. All the same, it ensures accountability of the Goernment to the Diet and keeps the Government vigilant not to attract such an eventuality.

The House of Representatives spearheaded by the Opposition, accordingly, provides ample opportunities for controlling the Cabinet which is vested with the Executive power. The Constitution also provides for setting up committees of investigation by each House of the Diet. These committees may conduct investigation in any matter relating to Government and demand the presence and testimony of witnesses, and the production of records.[61] Investigation by committees is an effective method of supervising and controlling administration, though it seems incongruous in a system of government in which ministerial responsibility is its basic element and is constitutionally provided. However, investigation by committees, as in the United States, has not much to commend.

**Judicial Functions**

Article 64 provides that the Diet ''shall set up an Impeachment Court from among the members of both Houses for the purpose of trying those judges against whom removal proceedings have been instituted.'' Article 78 further provides that ''Judges shall not be removed except by public impeachment....'' The Court of Impeachment so set up consists of fourteen members, seven from each House of the Diet, and tries those judges against whom removal proceedings have been instituted by an Indictment Committee. The Indictment Committee, too, consists of an equal number of members from each House of the Diet. No one can be a member of the Court of Impeachment and the Indictment Committee simultaneously.

**Constituent Functions**

Amendments to the Constitution can be initiated in either House of the Diet and when the motion passes by a two-thirds majority of all the members of each House separately, it is submitted to the people for their approval at a referendum where it is required to have an affirmative vote of a majority of all votes cast. The House of Representatives and the House of Councillors can, thus, initiate constitutional amendments by a concurring vote of two-thirds or more members of each House.

**Electoral Functions**

The House of Representatives together with the House of Councillors designates the Prime Minister. If both the Houses disagree and

58. Article 72.
59. Article 91.
60. Article 73.
61. Article 62.

no agreement can be reached even through a Joint Committee, or the House of Councillors fails to make designation within ten days after the Lower Chamber has made designation, the decision of the House of Representatives is accepted the decision of the Diet. Both the Houses determine by law the qualifications of the members and their electors with the proviso that there shall be no discrimination because of race, creed, sex, social status, family origin, education, property or income. Each House is the judge of disputes relating to qualifications of its members. But in order to deny a seat to any member, it is necessary to pass a resolution by a majority of two-thirds or more of the members present. Electoral districts, method of voting and other matters pertaining to the method of election of members of both Houses are determined by law of the Diet.

## LEGISLATIVE PROCEDURE

### Peculiarities of the Legislative Procedure

The legislative procedure in Japan is sharply distinguishable from the one prevailing in other countries with a Parliamentary system. It is simple and matter of fact. There are just three stages which cover the career of a Bill : Introduction; Committee stage; and consideration in the plenary session of the House. The same procedure is followed in both the Houses. When both the Houses pass a Bill, it becomes an enactment of the Diet. The Emperor simply promulgates it. He has no power to veto it.

Normally, the aims and objects of the bill are not explained in the plenary session of the House on introduction. However, if the Committee on Ways and Means deems such an explanation necessary in respect of a particular Bill, the explanation is made before it is referred to a Committee. Another important feature of the legislative procedure is the Opposition's resort to obstructionist tactics, which take various forms and some of them are unprecedented in the legislative history. The neverdecreasing majority commanded by the Liberal Democratic Party since 1955, has relegated the Socialists and their allies in a permanent minority. Since voting in the House of Representatives runs strictly on party lines, the Opposition puts determined obstruction to at least delay the enactment of Government Bills. They not only resort to filibustering, but even climax the obstruction by riots and use of violence on the floor of the House and the streets. There is another device of obstruction. The frustrated Opposition would block the corridors of the Diet in order to prevent the Speaker of the House of Representatives in calling the House to order. On various occasions the Speaker had been compelled to call in the police to physically remove the members preventing him from convening the House. There is still another tactic of boycotting the planary sessions of both the Houses and the Committee meetings.

### Kinds of Bill

Bills are of two kinds: Government Bill and Members Bills. A Government Bill and a Member's Bill may not differ in their content and both may relate to public matters. But a Government Bill is introduced in either House of the Diet by the Prime Minister himself or by one of the Ministers on his behalf. A Member's Bill originates from a Member of the Diet. If a Government Bill is defeated, it brings crisis in the Government which may result into either resignation of the cabinet or dissolution of the House of Representatives. But it is not so in the case of a Member's Bill.

### Introduction of the Bill

A Government Bill is always in pursuance of the policy determined by the Cabinet and it may aim at either amending the existing law or bringing on the statute a new law. The proposal for either of it originates from one of the Ministries, where it undergoes through various stages and thorough grooming in the departmental channels. When finally approved by the Minister concerned, the draft Bill goes to the Bureau of Legislation where it is subjected to expert examination. From here it goes to the Cabinet Secretariat. Finally, it is submitted to the Cabinet for its approval.

If the Cabinet approves the draft Bill, it is ready for introduction in either House of the Diet. It is submitted in the name of the Prime Minister to the Presiding Officer of the House in which the Bill is desired to be introduced, except for Money Bills which must be introduced in the House of Representatives. When a legislative Bill is introduced in the House of Councillors, its copy is required to be submitted to the House of Representatives within five days of its introduction. The same procedure is followed if it is introduced in the House of Representatives.

The Speaker of the House of Representatives or the President of the House of Councillors, as the case may be, refers the Bill to the proper Committee of the House on the recommendation of the Way and Means Committee. If a Bill is considered urgent, its examination by the Committee may be omitted by the decision of the Steering Committee. "This procedure is employed especially in the case of a Member's Bill on which the understanding of the Committee that would have deliberated on it has been obtained in advance." Normally, a Bill is not considered in the plenary session of the House. If, however, the Ways and Means Committee considers it necessary the explanation is made in the plenary session before it is referred to a Committee of the House.

**Committee Stage**

Committee stage is the most important stage in the career of a Bill. The Bill may be referred to either a Standing Committee or a Special Committee of the House and it has the power to pigeonhole it, if the Bill is deemed, "not worthy necessary or desirable." It is, thus, tantamount to killing the Bill. The Committee holds public meetings and may require the attendance of the Prime Minister, Ministers, and Government officials. They are required to answer to questions directed to them and make explanation on the Bill. The Committee may also summon publicmen to express their opinions on the Bill. It may make "investigating trips including travels abroad," if considered necessary. The Committee has always at its disposal the services of the Diet staff, including experts and researchers, for advice and guidance. It may also use the services of the National Diet Library for a thorough study and scrutiny of the Bill and may demand, as often as necessary, opinion of the Bureau of Legislation on matters legal, constitutional and administrative. If the Bill involves consideration by more than one Committee, it is jointly considered.

**Consideration by the House**

After the Bill has been thoroughly examined, scrutinized and approved by the Committee, it is reported to the House for deliberation and a vote. The Chairman of the Committee presents the report together with the minority report, if any. The House then discusses and deliberates upon the report. Amendments can also be moved by the members. After all the clauses have been read and voted, the Bill as a whole is voted upon. In the event of a tie, the Presiding Officer casts a deciding vote.

**A Bill Becomes a Law**

After the bill has passed through one House it is immediately sent to the other where it undergoes the same procedure. If the second House approves it, it becomes an enactment of the Diet and is transmitted to the Emperor for 'promulgation'. It becomes a law. If the House of Councillors rejects the Bill passed the House of Representatives and no agreement could be reached in a Joint Committee of both the Houses, or the House of Councillors fails to take action within 60 days of its receipt, it becomes an enactment of the Diet when passed for the second time by the House of Representatives by a majority of two-thirds or more of the members present.

**The Budget**

A different procedure is followed in the enactment of the budget. According to Article 60, the budget must be submitted to the House of Representatives. It cannot originate in the House of Councillors. When the budget passes through the House of Representatives, it is transmitted to the House of Councillors. If the House of Councillors makes a decision different from the House of Representatives and when the Joint Committee of both the Houses fails to reach an agreement, or when the House of Councillors fails to take action on it within 30 days of its receipt, the decision of the House of Representatives is the decision of the Diet, that is, as if both the Houses of the Diet have approved the budget.

It is the constitutional duty of the Cabinet to prepare and submit to the Diet for its consideration and decision a budget for each fiscal year. The process of formation of budget starts sometimes in September when the Finance Ministry examines the estimates submitted by the various Ministries. This is an arduous task as it requires close examination of all such estimates which are very often exaggerated and consequently require drastic trimming. The draft budget is ready by January for the consideration of the Cabinet and its discussion may extend to quite a number of meetings. When full agreement has been reached in the Cabinet, the budget proposals are referred back to the Ministries for overhauling their estimates. The Finance Ministry then receives the final estimates from each Ministry. The Finance Minister in the light of such estimates prepares the budget which incorporates the statement of revenues and expenditure for the ensuing financial year commencing from April. The draft budget is again submitted to the Cabinet for its final approval.

The Budget Bill is introduced in the House

of Representatives in the later part of January. Its introduction is followed by the speeches of the Prime Minister, the Foreign Minister, the Finance Minister and the Director of Economic Policy Board. The House of Councillors usually receives the Budget Bill the next day after its introduction in the House of Representatives. However, according to rules its submission may not be delayed beyond five days. The Prime Minister, the Foreign Minister, the Finance Minister and the Director of the Economic Policy Board also address the House of Councillors and they explain the various aspects of the policy involved and implications of the Budget.

After the explanation of the Prime Minister and other Ministers, the Speaker refers the Budget Bill to the Standing Committee on the Budget which consists of 51 members. The Committee thoroughly examines all proposals relating to revenue and expenditure and probes into each item. The Prime Minister, Ministers and officials of the Finance Ministry appear before the Committee to answer to questions, make explanations, elaborate and remove ambiguities and doubts. The Committee meets as a whole, except for a day or two when it divides into sub-committees. The sittings of the Committee are open to public.

After the completion of its deliberations, the Chairman of the Budget Committee submits the report to the House of Representatives. The House discusses the Budget Bill for a period of three to four weeks. It may accept the recommendations of the Budget Committee in toto or accept them with amendments. The decision of the plenary session may or may not be the same as that of the Budget Committee. But rejection of the Budget Bill by the House of Representatives brings the downfall of the Government or the Cabinet may decide the dissolution of the House.

The Budget Bill as passed by the House of Representatives is transmitted to the House of Councillors for its consideration. As pointed out earlier, if the House of Councillors does not agree with the decision of the House of Representatives and if the disagreement is not resolved even in the Joint Committee of both the Houses, or the House of Councillors fails to consider the Budget Bill within 30 days of its receipt, the decision of the House of Representatives is final and in terms of the Constitution, it is the decision of the Diet. The Budget becomes operative on April 1. If, for certain reasons, the Budget Bill is not passed before April 1, then, it is necessary for the Diet to pass provisional Budget on a monthly basis until such time as it is finally passed.

**Committees of the Diet**

The Committees of the Diet are the core of the legislative process in Japan. Their origin goes back to the Meiji Constitution when five Standing Committees were set up in each House of the Imperial Diet. But these Committees did not play a vital role then as they do now since most of the legislative business was transacted in the plenary session of the two Houses. Under the Constitution of 1946, originally, the House of Councillors and the House of Representatives each had 22 Standing Committees. Their number was subsequently reduced to 16 and it stands now. There are in each House Standing Committees on : Cabinet, Local Administration, Judicial Affairs, Foreign affairs, Finance, Education, Welfare and Labour, Agriculture, Forestry and Fisheries, Commerce and Industry, Transport, Communications, Construction, Budget, Accounts, Steering and Discipline. Most of these Committees correspond to the Ministries of the Government.

A Standing Committee may consist of thirty, forty or fifty members except for Discipline, and Steering and Accounts Committees, which have a membership of 20 and 25 each respectively. Soon after both the Houses of the Diet have elected their Presiding Officers, the next step is the selection of the Committees. Members of each Committee are appointed by the Presiding officer of the House concerned on the basis of the party strength in the House. According to the law of the Diet, each member must serve on at least one Standing Committee but not on more than three Committees. Chairmanships of the Committees are allocated to the parties roughly in proportion to the number of seats each party commands in the House. Since the Liberal Democratice Party commands nearly two-thirds of total membership in each House, the Government Party monopolises the Chairmanships of almost all the Standing Committees. Committee Chairmansip is the most coveted since it carries with it great prestige. "Not only is a chairman able to influence the legislative programme of the government but is able to enjoy the prerequisites and compliments of his office which are considerable. As presiding officer, the Chairman not only opens and closes the meetings of the Committee but works out the agenda, determines the order of business and regulates the speed of deliberations. He is in control of the various stages of the Committee's work, questioning, debate, and decision. In his capacity as the spokesman and representative of the Committee in all its external relations and negotiations, he becomes a key figure.''[62]

The Standing Committees are highly important organs of law-making and they have the power to kill legislative proposals or to enable them to succeed. Upon them devolves the primary responsibility of selecting those legislative proposals submitted by the Government and recommending them for approval and enactment. All proposals for legislation undergo an onerous process of examination and scrutiny and in order to hammer them through the Committees hold public meetings, in which witnesses representing different shades of opinion and interests are summoned to tender evidence and to make available all kinds of material, exhibits and documents to authenticate their point of view. Refusal to appear before a Committee is subject to a contempt charge.

The Standing Committees have been subjected to a severe criticism, particularly with regard to their numbers and the manner in which they function. The Committees are, it is said, too numerous in each House and, consequently, the affairs of the nation are divided into rigid watertight compartments. The government is a single whole and it requires an integrated action to solve the national problems. As the real work of examination, investigation and determination is done in the Committees, many of the details of facts and other relevant information remain unknown to the legislators who are not Committee members. Even the aims and objects of a Bill, according to the rules of legislative procedure, are not explained in the plenary session of the House. There is, accordingly, lack of interest among the members of the Diet. ''This makes it difficult if not impossible to effectively dramatize the general debates on the floor of the House. In fact, it can often lead to the minimizing of the usefulness as well as the effectiveness of the general floor debate. It has also contributed to extremely poor attendance at plenary session except for very special occasions.''[63] Moreover, the Standing Committees more or less correspond to the Ministries and there is a close link between both. Many Japanese believe that this system of close linkage between the Legislative and Executive branches has tended to strengthen the role of the Executive. ''Typical of the system has been the appointment to the appropriate Committee of Diet members with backgrounds, if not careers, in the matching ministry or executive agency. This creates a situation in which the bureaucratic loyalties of the committee members may outweigh their legislative responsibilities and their constitutional position as members of the highest organ of state power.''[64]

According to Chitoshi Yanaga the Japanese Committee system is a great obstacle to development of integrated and broad view of national problems. Seikai Orai calls it the ''cancer of the Diet'' which seriously hampers its activities and functions nullifying the constitutional provision that the Diet is the highest organ of State power. Prof. Ardath Burks would say that the Japanese Committee system is much suited to the Presidential system of government rather than to a Parliamentary democracy. Analysinng the demerits flowing therefrom, he *inter alia*, remarks that special interests dominate and influence the discussions and decisions of the committees and the Diet, as such, becomes ''a notorious tool for promotion of narrow committee interests.''

Each House may establish Special Committees, too, by a special resolution of the House. They are *ad hoc* Committees set up to study particular problems or proposals and as soon as they complete their work, they become non-existent. The Standing Committees, on the other hand, are appointed for the duration of the session and a Bill appropriate to the subject-matter of the Committee is referred to it. The life of a Special Committee may extend beyond the session of the House in which it was created. The Chairman of a Special Committee is appointed by the members of the Committee itself and all matters before it are decided by a majority vote. The Chairman exercises a casting vote in case of a tie. Like the Standing Committees, the Special Committees, too, hold public hearings and can summon witnesses and demand production of any record or material. After the investigation is over the Committee reports to the House. If the report is not unanimous, both the majority and minority reports are submitted. Commenting upon the im-

62. Chitoshi Yanaga, *Japanese People and Politics*, p. 197.
63. *Ibid.*
64. Maki, John M., *Government and Politics in Japan*, p. 96.

portance of the Special Committees, Chitoshi Yanaga writes: "Actually, so far as the general public is concerned, it is the work of the Special Committees which attracts widespread attention and interest because of the emergency or sensational nature of most of the subject-matter handled."[65]

The Constitution establishes two other kinds of Committees, the Joint Committee of both the Houses, and the Committees of Investigation. Article 59 provides that in case the House of Councillors and the House of Representatives make different decisions on a legislative Bill the House of Representatives may call a meeting of a Joint Committee of both Houses for resolving the disagreement. Similarly, a Joint Committee may be set up for resolving differences between the House of Councillors and the House of Representatives with regard to the budget, treaties, designation of the Prime Minister and constitutional questions. A Joint Committee consists of 20 members, equally drawn from the Houses, and elected by the members of each House from amongst themselves. The members elected from each House select their own Chairman and each Chairman alternatively presides over the meeting of a Joint Committee.

Article 62 of the Constitution provides for setting up the Committees of Investigation by each House of the Diet. These Committees are empowered to conduct investigations of affairs relating to Government and may demand the presence and testimony of witnesses, and the production of records. Since the Constitution became operative a few such Committees, such as a Committee on Illegal Disposal of Government Property, and a Committee to examine the revision proposals of Japan-United States Security Treaty, had been set up. In most cases the Committees investigating Government operation assemble facts and submit reports on their findings and are content to stop there. However, in some cases they go a step further and pass judgment or make recommendations.

The Legislative Committee is yet another Committee. It is a Joint Committee of both the Houses and consists of 18 members, 10 from the House of Representatives and 8 from the House of Councillors, elected by each House from amongst its own members. This Committee has nothing to do with legislation. Its function is to ensure effective operation of the Diet and to maintain a smooth working relationship between the House of the Councillors and the House of Representatives. The Committee submits its reports to the Speaker of the House of Representatives and the President of the House of Councillors at every session of the Diet.

## SUGGESTED READINGS

Kahin, George McT, *Major Governments of Asia.*

Halliday & McCormarck, *Japanese Imperialism Today.*

Kahn, Herman, *The Emerging Japanese Superstate.*

Maki, John M, *Government and Politics of Japan.*

Thayer, Nathaniel B., *How the Conservative Rule Japan?*

Ward, Robert E., *Japan's Political System.*

65. *Japanese People and Politics*, p. 184.

## CHAPTER IV

# The Judiciary

### Judiciary under The Meiji Constitution

There was a complete transformation of the Judicial system in Japan during the Meiji period. The old antiquated concepts of legal system developed during feudalism were abandoned and new codes patterned on the Continental jurisprudence were enacted with the advice of German and French Jurists. Anglo-Saxon jurisprudence had no place therein. Judiciary was, accordingly, not an independent branch of the Government, but an arm of the Executive administered by the Ministry of Justice. Although judges were required to administer law impartially, but their dependence on the Ministry hardly guaranteed independence for them. There did not exist the rule of law and *salus populi suprema lex,* the welfare of the people is the supreme law, constituted the basis of the legal system. It was not within the competence of the courts to hold any law or executive order invalid. Nor could the courts safeguard the liberties and rights of the people. In case of disputes between the government and citizens the ordinary courts had no jurisdiction. Administrative adjudication was the concern of the Court of Administrative Litigation.

There were three kinds of courts: Ordinary Civil and Criminal Courts; Courts of Administrative Litigation; and Military Court. At the apex of the ordinary civil and criminal courts was the Supreme Court consisting of 45 Judges divided into 9 divisions of 5 Judges each. The Supreme Court exercised original and appellate jurisdiction. In case of treason and serious offences against the Imperial Family, its jurisdiction was original. On the appellate side, it heard appeals both in civil and criminal cases from the lower courts.

Next to the Supreme Court were seven High Courts, one for each Province. The High Courts heard appeals from the lower courts. Then, there were 50 District Courts, at least one in each Prefecture. The District Courts tried more serious criminal and civil cases. At the bottom were Local Courts, a little more than 300 in number, which had the jurisdiction in minor cases.

The Court of Administrative Litigation was patterned after its French counterpart and was based on the Prince Ito's belief that "if administrative activities were placed under the scrutiny and control of judicature, and if courts of law were given the power to review and invalidate administrative acts, the Executive would be subordinated to the Judiciary. thereby impairing the integrity and effectiveness of the executive branch."[1]

### Judicial System under the 1946 Constitution

Like various other institutions in Japan, the judicial system too was greatly changed under the impact of the Occupation Authorities. The changes effected related to the structure of the courts and judicial procedure and were in conformity with the democratic philosophy of law and jurisprudence as cherished by the Americans. "It is perhaps not surprising," wrote Nobutaka Ike, "given the nature of the occupation, that many ideas and practices of Anglo-Saxon origin were incorporated into the judicial system thereby changing its orientation which was fomally predominantly Continental."[2] Even the oath of office "has been introduced in both form and language very much like that which obtains in the United States"[3]. Here is a summary of the changes which constitute the features of the Japanese Judicial system now.

The Constitution separates the Judiciary

1. Chitoshi Yanaga, *Japanese People and Politics,* p. 355 f.n.
2. Kahin, George McT. (Ed.), *Major Governments of Asia,* p. 199.
3. Chitoshi Yanaga, *Japanese People and Politics* p. 348.

from the Executive and makes it an independent branch of Government. Article 76 vests "the whole judicial power" in a Supreme Court and in such inferior courts as may be established by law. It further provides that no extraordinary tribunal shall be established "nor shall any organ or agency of the Executive be given final judicial power." In order to emphasise the independent status of the Judiciary the Supreme Court actually controls all judicial affairs of the country. According to Article 77 the Supreme Court is vested with the rule-making power under which it determines the Rules of Procedure and of Pratice, and of matters relating to attorneys, the internal discipline of the courts and the administration of Judicial affairs.

The Constitution guarantees the independence of Judges and ensures the dignity of the Judiciary. It ordains that all Judges shall be independent in the exercise of their conscience and bound only by the Constitution and the laws.[4] The Chief Justice of the Supreme Court is designated by the Cabinet and appointed by the Emperor.[5] This procedure is designed to place the Chief Justice on the same level of rank and dignity as the Prime Minister. Judges of the Supreme Court are appointed by the Cabinet[6] whereas judges of the inferior courts are appointed by the Cabinet from a list of persons nominated by the Supreme Court.[7] Judges are liable to removal only by impeachment unless judicially declared mentally or physically incompetent to perform official duties. No disciplinary action against Judges can be taken by any Executive organ or agency.[8] Judges of the Supreme Court and inferior courts receive, at regular stated intervals, adequate compensation which cannot be decreased during their terms of office.

The Constitution applies the principle of popular sovereignty on the Judges of the Supreme Court too. Their appointment is reviewed by the people at the first general election of the members of the House of Representatives following their appointment and every ten years thereafter. If the majority of the voters disapprove the appointment, the Judge is dismissed.[9] Judges of the inferior courts are appointed for a term of ten years subject to reappointment. No judge of the Supreme Court has so far been voted out of office and the judges of the inferior courts are invariably re-appointed. Yet it is a constitutional fact that their tenure at both levels is subject to review.

There is a complete separation of judicial administration from criminal investigation by placing the Procurator's (Prosecutor's) office under the control of the Ministry of Justice. The Judges and the procurators consequently work independently of each other; both are separate and distinct functionaries. The procurators are civil servants working under the supervision and control of the Minister of Justice whereas the Judiciary is a separate and independent branch of the Government.

The principle of the Rule of Law has for the first time been introduced in Japan. There is now only one system of courts throughout the country and only one system of law to which all people are amenable. The whole judicial power is vested in the Supreme Court and other inferior courts and no extraordinary tribunal exists to administer justice. Nor is any organ or agency of the Executive given final judicial authority. Accordingly, the Court of Administrative Litigation was abolished and administrative litigation is now placed within the jurisdiction of regular courts. Trials are conducted in open court and judgment is declared publicly. If the court unanimously determines that publicity of the trial proceedings is dangerous to public order or morals, the trial may be conducted privately. But trials relating to political offences, offences involving the press or cases wherein the rights of people as guaranteed by the Constitution are in question must always be held publicly.[10]

The Code of Criminal Procedure and the Code of Civil Procedure assign to the courts a far greater role to play than was the case previously. Warrants for arrest and detention can now be issued only by the judges, the courts are to start with the presumption of innocence of the accused in criminal cases, and the legal validity of confession has been greatly limited. Judicial decisions are now rendered in a simple colloquial language and, above all, the Constitution itself is couched in a simple and matter of fact language intelligible to the average Japanese.

4. Article 76.
5. Article 6.
6. Article 79.
7. Article 80.
8. Article 78.
9. Article 79.
10. Article 82.

The Supreme court is the court of last resort with the power to determine the constitutionality of any law, order, regulation, or official act.[11] The Constitution is, therefore, supreme and the supreme Court has been explicitly given the right of judicial review.

The Constitution guarantees to citizens fundamental Rights and the courts are the custodian of all such rights. Article 11 unequivocally declares: "These fundamental human rights guaranteed to the people by this Constitution shall be conferred upon the people of this and future generation as eternal and inviolate rights." Article 97 repeats this assurance by emphasising that the Fundamental human rights "by this Constitution guaranteed to the people of Japan are fruits of the age-old struggle of man to be free; they have survived the many exacting tests for durability and are conferred upon this and future generations in trust, to be held for all time inviolate." Article 98 establishes the supremacy of the Constitution by asserting: "This Constitution shall be the supreme law of the nation and no law, ordinance, imperial rescript or other act of government, or part thereof, contrary to the provisions hereof, shall have legal force or validity." It is for the Supreme Court to determine the constitutionality or otherwise of any law, order, regulation or official act.

Another feature of the judicial system in Japan is the system of courts of Domestic Relations. These courts are half arbitral and half judicial tribunals composed of judges and laymen and they decide cases involving domestic relations and juvenile delinquency.

Finally, the Supreme Court, as Maki remarked, "has adhered strictly to the principle of the separation of powers but has honoured equally the doctrine of legislative supremacy."[12] The Court has insistently safeguarded its sole right to exercise the whole judicial power and resolutely resisted any interference on the independence of the courts. On the other hand, the Supreme Court has also consistently refused to declare legislative and executive acts unconstitutional. The Court has argued that to declare such acts as unconstitutional would be the violation of the principle of separation of powers as well as the doctrine of legislative supremacy. The proper "remedy for legislation not clearly constitutional is a political one, that is, the sovereign people can pass judgment on the Diet and on the Cabinet by means of the ballot."[13]

### Organization and Functions of the Courts

The Judiciary consists of the Supreme Court, 8 High Courts, 6 High Court Benches, 49 District Courts (with 235 branches) and 570 Summary Courts. There are also 49 Courts of Domestic Relations or Family Courts (with 235 branches).

### The Supreme Court

At the apex of the judicial structure is the Supreme Court located at Tokyo. It consists of a Chief Judge and fourteen other Judges; fifteen in all. The Chief Judge is appointed by the Emperor upon designation by the Cabinet, while all other Judges are appointed by the Cabinet and "attested" by the Emperor. The law provides that ten Judges, out of a total of 15 including the Chief Judge, must be legal experts of not less than 20 years' professional standing and the remaining five Judges may be learned persons of experience but necessarily in the field of law. This is designed to permit a more democratic and varied representation of expertise on the highest tribunal of the nation. The appointment of Judges, of the Supreme Court is subject to review at a national referendum, first at the time of the General Election following their appointment and then at the first General Election after a lapse of ten years. There has been no case of dismissal as such so far. But the system of popular review "could conceivably result in drawing the court into the rough and tumble of partisan politics."

Judges of the Supreme Court are required to retire at an age fixed by law, which is 70 years. The minimum age of a Suprme Court Judge is fixed at 40 years. Judges cannot be removed from office except by public impeachment unless judicially declared mentally or physically incompetent to perform official duties. No disciplinary action against Judges can be administered by any Executive organ or agency. The Constitution demands that all Judges shall be independent in the exercise of their conscience and in order to ensure their independence adequate compensations are guaranteed, which cannot be decreased during their terms of office.[14]

The Supreme Court is the Court of the last

11. Article 81.
12. Maki John M., *Government and Politics in Japan,* p. 107.
13. *Ibid.*
14. Article 79.

resort with powers to determine the constitutionality of any law, order, regulation or official act. The power of judicial review is, thus, explicitly vested in the Supreme Court. In all cases involving questions of constitutionality the Grand Bench of the court of all 15 Judges, 9 constituting a quorum, hears the appeals. In other cases in which issues of law are involved appeals are heard by a petty Bench consisting of five Judges, three constituting a quorum. The Supreme Court is the highest court of the land and its decisions are subject to no further review. Its jurisdiction is exclusively appellate. The Court limits itself to the points of law while hearing appeals and its decision are rendered by the majority opinion of the court. Except on special occasion, the decisions are always written.

The Supreme Court is vested with the rule-making power under which it determines the Rules of Procedure and of Practice, and of matters relating to attorneys, the internal discipline of the courts and the administration of judicial affairs. Public Procurators are subject to the rule-making power of the Supreme Court. This is, indeed, a sweeping power. The Supreme Court may delegate some of its rule-making authority to lower courts. This is how the Supreme Court exercises supervision and control on the entire judicial system in the country. A key organization through which the court exercises its broad powers of judicial control is the Legal Research and Training Institute, established by law under the jurisdiction of the Supreme Court. Among other things, the Institute is responsible for the training of every person interested in a legal career. No one can, thus, become a judge, a lawyer, or a public prosecutor unless he graduates from the Institute or has undergone a course of in-service training there. The Suprme Court also operates similar institutes for training of the clerks of the court and family court probationers. Judges of the inferior courts are appointed by the Cabinet out of the list of nomination made by the Supreme Court, and it supervises the inferior courts in matters of administration.

**Position and Role of the Supreme Court**

The Occupation Authorities had intended that the Japanese Supreme Court should play the same role and acquire the same position in the body politic of the country as the United States Supreme Court, though Japan does not make a federation. The Constitution vests the Supreme Court with the whole judicial power and it is explicitly stated that no "extraordinary tribunal shall be established, nor can any organ or agency of the Executive be given final judicial power."[15] It is the final court of appeal and its jurisdiction is appellate alone. It exercises powers of supervision and rule-making and, these powers are, indeed sweeping. The Constitution ensures the independence of the Judges and ordains that they would dispense justice according to their conscience and "shall be bound only by this Constitution and the laws."[16] The method of appointment of the Chief Justice places him at par with the Prime Minister in dignity and prestige. The Judges are subject to impeachment, but no Judge has been impeached so far. They are themselves extremely conscious of maintaining high standard of impartiality, efficiency and morality. Though, their appointment is subject to the review of the people, but their appointment is invariably approved by securing 90 per cent and more approved votes. In the General Election of 1949 all the fourteen Judges were "enthusiastically" approved.

The Supreme Court is the court of last resort with power to determine the constitutionality of any law, order, regulation or official act.[17] The power of judicial review, which the Constitution vests in the Supreme Court, makes it the guardian of the Constitution. It has admirably protected the rights of the citizens and has withstood all inroads made by any authority on the Constitution and independence of the Judiciary. The Judicial Committee of the House of Councillors passed a Resolution in 1949 that under Article 62[18] of the Constitution the Diet be empowered to investigate Court decisions and thereby determine on the nature of the decisions rendered by the Court and discuss the attitude of the Judges. The Supreme Court held the resolution unconstitutional and declared that the Diet had no such authority and it was in contravention of the provisions of the Constitution guaranteeing the independence of the Judiciary. In another case the Court decided that capital punishment did not

15. Article 76.
16. *Ibid.*
17. Article 81.
18. Article 62 says : "Each House may conduct investigations in relation to government, and may demand the presence and testimony of witnesses, and the production of records."

infringe the provisions of Article 36[19] so long as the due process clause embodied in Article 32[20] was duly observed. In 1952, Suzuki Mosaburo, Chairman of the Left Socialist Party, challenged in the Supreme Court the organisation of the National Police Reserve as it violated Article 9 of the Constitution which renounces war and the threat to or use of force. The Supreme Court refused to comment on the abstract problem of the constitutionality. In 1959, the court reversed the decision of the Tokyo District Court in the Sunakawa case and held that the Court should not involve itself in political and inter-State conflicts and controversies. The Court held that the stationing of American forces in Japan did not violate Article 9 of the Constitution. It also set the principle that unless a treaty is "obviously unconstitutional and void, it falls outside the purview of the power of judicial review granted to the Court."

The Sunakawa case decision provoked the former Socialist Prime Minister, Katayama Tetsu, who characterised it as a "betrayal of the people's trust in the Supreme Court as a watchdog of the Constitution." The Court relying upon the doctrine of Separation of Powers recognised supremacy of the Diet and held that the proper remedy for legislation not clearly constitutional is a political one, that is, the sovereign people can pass judgment on the Diet and on the Cabinet by means of the ballot. In a landmark decision the Supreme Court ruled that the 1983 election for the House of Representatives was a clear violation of the constitutional promise of equality before the law, given the enormous discrepancy in the value of one vote in many constituencies. The Court did not declare the 1983 election to be invalid, but it hinted strongly that it might so rule if another election was held based upon the current maldistribution of parliamentary seates. Since then, there has been a great deal of talk about electoral reform but no action has been taken so far and the Japanese gerrymander continues.

### High Court

In the second rank below the Supreme Court, are the 8 High Courts. The jurisdiction of a High Court extends to the region to which it is assigned and, accordingly, it has a regional jurisdiction. The number of Judges differs from one High Court to the other. Tokyo has 64 Judges whereas Saporro has only 7. The Court operates through a Bench of three Judges, but in case of trial for crimes to overthrow the Government the Bench consists of five Judges. Judges are appointed for ten years, although there is no restriction on their being re-appointed, provided that they shall be retired at the age of 65. They are nominated by the Supreme Court. Judges must have at least ten years' experience in a judicial capacity, or as a Procurator or as a practising lawyer.

### District Courts

Beneath the High Courts are 49 District Courts (with attached courts of Domestic Relations), one in each of Prefectures, except for Hokkaido which has four. The Judges of the District Courts are similarly appointed as Judges of the High Courts and they must possess similar qualifications. District Courts are the principal trial courts and exercise a general jurisdiction over all civil actions not specially given to other courts. A single judge presides over the courts, except for more serious cases when a panel of three judges conducts the trial.

The District Courts have attached courts of Domestic Relations, 49 in number with 235 branches. These courts are peculiar to Japan and are designed to promote harmonious relationship within the family and among relations. A Court of Domestic Relations or a Family Court, as it is now popularly designated, is composed of one judge and two intelligent and experienced laymen. These courts provide facilities for the out-of-door settlement of disputes relating to probate and domestic disputes, such as, divorce, alimony, breach of promise, inheritance, property division, adoption, guardianship, and other similar matters. Normally, judicial procedure is not followed in every case as there are chances of settlement outside the court. To the best, Family Courts may be characterised half arbitral, half judicial.

### Summary Courts

The last are 570 Summary courts which are at the base of the judicial pyramid in Japan. These courts handle minor civil and criminal cases. In civil cases the amount involved should be less then 5,000 Yens and in criminal cases the sentence awarded to an accused should be less than a month. The presiding officer has a broad

19. Article 36 provides : "The infliction of torture by any public officer and cruel punishments are absolutely forbidden."
20. Article 32 reads : "No person shall be denied the right of access to the courts," Also refer to Article 31.

latitude in the conduct of trials. Judges of the inferior courts, like High Court and District Judges, are appointed by the Cabinet from a list of persons nominated by the Supreme Court, and their appointment is for ten years, although there is no restriction on their being reappointed. They retire at the age of 65.

## SUGGESTED READINGS

Chotoshi Yonagar, *Japanese People and Politics.*

Maki, John M., *Government and Politics of Japan.*

Norman, E.Herbert, *Japan's Emergence as a Modern State.*

Ward, Robert E., *Japan's Political System.*

# CHAPTER V

# Political Parties

### Historical Background

Political parties did not emerge in Japan as a result of the establishment of Parliamentary system of government in 1947. Their origin goes back to 1874, though there were no political parties then in the real sense of the term. They were political clubs and societies. Early in January 1874, Itagaki organized a political association called the Patriotic Public Party to carry on a movement for the realization of liberty and attainment of popular rights. Immediately afterwards a "Memorial for the establishment of popular Representative Assembly was presented to the Emperor. It caused a stir in the country and had a magnetic effect on the people. But the Emperor's Government undertook measures to suppress the movement and the Patriotic Public Party went out of existence after only two months of its establishment. In 1878, the party was revived with the avowed object of pressing forward its original demand for the establishment of a representative assembly. It had somewhat an inflammatory effect. The Government first used suppressive measures to crush the agitation, but soon realized the futility of the oppressive policy and ultimately bowed to the popular demand. An Imperial Rescript issued on October 18, 1881 declared that the national assembly would be established in 1890.

Six days after the issuance of the Imperial Rescript the Liberal Party was established and it became the vanguard of the movement for popular government. Closely in its wake came the Progressive Party, popularly known as the Reform Party, which advocated liberalism of the British type and freely preached the philosophy of Bentham and John Stuart Mill. The Government was alarmed by the activities and programmes of both the Liberal and Progressive Parties and in order to counteract their influence on the people, it backed the founding of the Imperial Party. The Imperial Party was for all intents and purposes a Government supported party. Its membership comprised Government officials, Buddhist and Shinto priests, and nationalist scholars who were the product of government schools.

All the three parties disbanded in 1885, partly as a result of Government's repressive policy directed against the Liberal and Progressive Parties and partly as a consequence of their internal dissensions. Ito, who had by then come back from Germany, was strongly opposed to political parties and the caused the liquidation of the Imperial Party. Ito became Prime Minister in 1885. He pushed ahead, with the support of Inoue, the Foreign Minister, his programme of Westernization, which stongly aroused the champions of civil rights, "as well as the nationalists and the chauvinists." Inoue's attempt in 1887 to make concessions in the negotiations for treaty revisions was denounced by Agriculture and Commerce Minister Tani and it was followed by a scathing criticism of the Government by the various segments of the Japanese society. Goto strongly appealed to the sentiments of the people and exhorted them to join the forces against the Government. Members of the disbanded Liberal Party, the nationalists and the conservatives all joined togethher and formed a "Greater Coalition of Parties."

The Government accepted the challenge and issued on December 19, 1887, a Peace Preservation Ordinance which authorized the expulsion of all those engaged in anti-government activities from an area within a radius of seven and a half miles from the capital. Near about 600 people were expelled as a result of this ordinance. The movement then spread to the outlying areas. In the meanwhile Ito was successful in bringing Okuma, his old colleague with whom he had parted political company in 1881, in Government as Foreign Minister. " In the succeeding government headed by Kurado, Okuma became the mainstay of the Cabinet and actually came to lead if not dominate it."

Immediately after the Meiji Constitution became operative in 1889, Prime Minister Kurado declared his faith in the supra-party government and he was supported by Ito, who was the President of the Privy Council. The Prime Minister succeeded in winning over Inoue, Goto and Itagoki and they were taken in the Cabinet. "All these political leaders," observed Chitoshi Yanaga, "fought against the ruling oligarchy espousing the cause of liberalism and popular rights. Yet, when lured with government posts of sufficient prestige, they gave up their fight and gladly joined the ranks of those in power. Their devotion to the ideals of responsible government or even to political parties was not only weak and expediential but easily purchasable.[1] That was the nature of political parties in Japan till 1890.

When Sino-Japanese War came in 1894, opposition against the Government ceased altogether. But soon after the cessation of hostilities the two leading Opposition parties realised "that for years they had been duped, bought and exploited by the government and it was imperative they abandon their useless and harmful struggle with each other and join forces in the fight against their common political enemy, the Satsuma-Choshu clique that was in control of the government.[2] They founded a party in 1898, a merger of the defunct Liberals and Progressives.

Roundabout the century another dramatic development took place in the growth of political parties. Prince Ito, who had all through these years, bitterly opposed political parties, became their supporter. He declared that for good and efficient government political parties were essentially necessary and, accordingly, in 1900, he founded a party known as the Association of Political Parties. Till 1913, those who had been affiliated with the Progressive Party did not regroup to form another party. They were content to form coalitions. It was only between 1913 and 1925 that Constitutional Association, which had the support of elder statesmen and business leaders and advocated the establishment of constitutional government, was organised World War too had created an impact on the Japanese people in favour of democratic institutions and it appeared by 1920 that a full-fledged parliamentary government would soon be established. Beginning from Kato Takakira, the President of the Constitutional Association, till the assassination of Inuki Tsuyoshi in 1932, party leaders, except once for General Tanaka Giichi, headed the Government.

One important feature of this period was that the political parties depended heavily on the big industrial combines, *Zaibatsu,* which supplied them with funds to fight elections. Some of the business magnates supported the opposing parties at the same time in order to win the support of the government, no matter which party came into power. This "alliance between the parties and the *Zaibatsu* naturally caused the public to be suspicious that the government was partial to the interests of the big business, and these suspicions seemed to be confirmed by the frequent charges of bribery and corruption that were aired in the Diet, principally by the party which happened to be in Opposition at the moment."

There were some other reasons, like the growth of big cities and localisation of industries, formation of labour unions, spread of education, the growth of white-collar class, etc., which created a political awakening amongst the Japanese people and they demanded enlargement of the suffrage and consequently the right to vote. But paradoxical as it was, most of the Japanese leaders were reluctant to enlarge the electorate. The bureaucrats, too, considered it ominous. They thought that enlargement of the electorate would bring social instability which would prove highly injurious to the growth and development of the country and its people. But the popular demand could no longer be resisted and in 1923, all male Japanese people of 25 years of age and more were given the right to vote.

But with the extension of suffrage, the Diet passed the Peace Preservation Law which provided punishment extending to ten years for persons guilty of joining societies and organizations advocating a change in the Constitution, the Emperor institution and in the ownership of private property. This punitive legislation, however, did not deter the growth of radical parties. The Farmer-Labour Party was established in 1925 to achieve equality and the greatest good of the masses as its goal. Back in 1892, Socialism had found its way in Japan when the radical faction in the Liberal Party separated and established the Oriental Liberal Party. After quite an upheaval in the career of the socialist parties with different

1. *Japanese People and Politics,* p. 221.
2. *Ibid.*

labels, in 1922 the Japan Communist Party found its way. It was banned in 1923, but was again revived in 1927 followed by severe suppression in 1928, and by 1932 its central leadership was completely destroyed.

In spite of the fact that various socialist parties including the Anarchist and Syndicalist groups had come and gone during this period, they had created an indelible impression on the working class. They, however, failed to carry the voters along with them primarily due to their internal strife and government's repression. In the 1928 elections, the first on the basis of universal manhood suffrage, the four socialist parties ran 88 candidates but could capture only 8 seats in the House of Representatives. After that they failed to enlist even this meagre support of the electorate and by 1930 suffered a great setback.

The conservative parties, too, suffered from deep factionalism. Accordingly, they commanded neither reasonable respect nor a continuous support from the electorate. None of them had a clear and definite programme. Lack of responsibility to the Diet made the government irresponsible and the members had no effective means to control it. The militarists seized the opportunity. They attributed the distress caused by the economic crisis, political, distress prevailing in the country, and diplomatic failures in the international field to the scandalous behaviour of the political parties and the politicians. People, too, had lost faith in the ability and integrity of the political parties to solve the national and international problems which confronted the country. The party government came to an end in 1932. The militarists who had come into power exercised such a pressure that ultimately in 1940, the political parties found their complete exit. From 1940 to 1945, there existed only one body in the country, the Imperial Rule Assistance Association, "a mild version of a totalitarian party."

## POST-WAR POLITICAL PARTIES

### Re-appearance of Political Parties

After the exit of political parties from the national scene for about a decade and a half they re-appeared in 1945, when as a prelude to the setting up a democratic setup of government the Occupation Authorities issued a directive to the Japanese Government on October 4, 1945 for removal of restrictions on political, civil and religious liberties. The Japanese Government was directed to immediately abrogate the operation of all provisions of laws, decrees, orders, ordinances and regulations which restricted freedom of thought, of religion, of assembly, of speech and press. The Directive also ordered the Japanese Government to release all political prisoners. A week later, General MacArthur desired that the Government should adopt, as rapidly as possible, the emancipation of women by granting them the right to vote, to encourage formation of labour unions, and endeavour to democratize economic institutions.

The Directive proved a green light for the resumption of political activities and consequently reappearance of political parties. In the first General Election held in April 1946, there were as many as 260 "parties" excluding scores of organizations which could not be counted as political parties. After the first mushroom growth, four political parties—the Liberal Party, the Progressive Party, both conservatives in spite of their attractive labels, the Social Democratic Party, and the Japan Communist Party—finally stabilized themselves. In 1955, the Liberal and Progressive Parties merged into one and the new Party was named the Liberal Democratic Party. The reunification of the Socialists, who had hitherto been engaged in stormy conflict among themselves, alerted the conservatives to take stock of their future. Thus, in 1955 there emerged what could be described as a formal two-party system. But the unification among the Socialists was only a temporary phase. There were again factional splits and in 1959, the Socialist Democratic Party was divided into two separate parties, the Socialist Party (the old left-wing) and the Democratic Socialist Party.

### Characteristics of the Party System

Here are some of the important characteristics of the Japanese party system:—

The Meiji Constitution established a bicameral legislature. Though the House of Representatives was directly elected and was subject to dissolution, yet it did not establish a cabinet system of government. It only envisaged it. In 1900, when Prince Ito felt the political expediency of forming a party government and declared that the Constitution nowhere prohibited a party government that political parties took a firm root in the administration of the country. From 1924 to 1932, party leaders headed the government.

The Constitution of 1946 clearly established the Parliamentary system of government. The Emperor is the symbol of the State and the Cabinet is vested with the Executive power. The Constitution requires that the Prime Minister, who heads the Cabinet, should be designated from among the members of the Diet and a majority of the Ministers constituting the Cabinet must be chosen from among the members of the Diet. The Constitution also provides for the collective responsibility of the Cabinet to the Diet, and the Diet is subject to dissolution. All these are the characteristics of a party government which should come into office as a unit and go out of office as a unit. The Cabinet makes a team, the members of which play the game of politics under the captaincy of the Prime Minister. In order to put a united front they swim and sink together. Homogeneity is, therefore, the essence of their existence and solidarity ensures their stability in office. Party system is, as such, the basis of the cabinet government. Yet, the Constitution does nowhere mention the party system. It is an extra-constitutional growth in Japan as it is in other democratic countries having parliamentary system of government.

For the smooth working of such a system of government, it is desirable that there should be a two-party system, one in office and the other in Opposition. But the bane of Japanese politics is the multiplicity of political parties. In the pre-war era there were as many as 260 parties at one time and when the Constitution of 1946 became operative the number was more than 260. They could not really be characterised as political parties. They were just various groups and associations and the result of various traits of Japanese character. Habits of nations, like that of individuals, seldom die and the multiple party system continues as before causing considerable complexity in the political life of the country.

Splits and merger of the parties is a regular feature in Japan. Fondness of variety and newness have an admirable appeal to the Japanese and both these factors constantly account for the growth of splits and the multiplicity in the number of the parties. Most, if not all, these mergers have been effected by incompatible groups for expediency and have been marriages of convenience. Even members who bolted the party, as well as splinter parties, have been re-admitted without much ado into the parties. Political parties change their labels with the greatest of ease and without changing their policies. More often than not names are changed merely to accommodate the newly won members or simply to give the psychological effect and illusion that the party is making a fresh start.[3]

The process of merger was highlighted in 1955, when the Conservatives and the Socialists both closed their ranks and formed two distinct political parties. Some optimists fervently predicted that the two party system had finally been established in Japan. But factionalism soon plagued the unity of the Socialists and after a truce of only four years they again divided and formed two separate parties. The Liberal Democratic Party remained united since then and it had been the ruling party since 1955. But internal strife had ever remained rampant among the conservatives as ever before. The socialists and the conservatives are "congeries of factions" and if the latter had remained united it was political expediency. If they had separated, their ruling position disappeared and it is precisely this condition that prevails now. Remember that there have been years of unexampled prosperity and freedom from national crisis in Japan."

None of the parties in Japan are mass organization. They are largely associations of professional politicians who centre their activities in Tokyo. They operate among a coterie of professional politicians and administrators and their prime focus of attention is the House of Representatives which actually designates the Prime Minister and provides a majority of ministers. Seldom do they go in their constituencies to nurse them and lead the people. There may be scattered prefectural and local party offices, but their contribution in the basic party offices is negligible. All important work is done at the party headquarters. The Diet-centred nature of the political parties makes them essentially parliamentary parties. Here Japan is akin to France.

Another important feature of the party system in Japan is the steady influx of the officials, serving and retired, into the parties and the Diet. A well recognised political axiom in Japan is to enter the civil service with a view to begin a political career. A civil servant who has ambition of becoming a minister must at some point run for a seat in the Diet. "Since about 1949, the number of ex-bureaucrats in the conservative parties have increased appreciably until in recent

3. Chitoshi Yanaga, *Japanese People and Politics*, p. 239.

years they represent about one fourth of the members of the House of Representatives belonging to the Liberal Democratic Party.''[4] In four Cabinets between 1957 and 1960 the ex-officials had held about one-half of the Cabinet posts. Most of the post-war Prime Ministers have had long careers in civil service as Shidehara, Yoshida, Ashida, Kishi, Ikeda, Fakuda and Ohira. The result is that the ''Japanese politics has undergone a kind of bureaucratization,'' and as such, there has come into being concentration of party activities in the Diet oblivious of the importance and role of the extra- parliamentary segment of the party.

Localities are still a strong factor in the Japanese politics. The electors generally prefer to vote for a candidate who belongs to them rather than to a party and the programme it stands for. The theory of ''friends and neighbours'' determines the choice and it is an important aspect of the electoral behaviour in Japan. It is believed that the candidate who lives in the immediate vicinity is most likely to best represent the local interests.

Till recently, religion had not provided a basis of organization of political parties. There were no religious blocs and no religious dominated parties. It was complete secularization of politics and politicians did not use religion for political purposes. But in the sixties there emerged a neo-religious political party, the Komeito Party, which is the political arm of the Sooka Gakkai, a militant Buddhist organization. The Komeito Party set up its candidates in the 1967 mid-term elections and secured 25 seats. In the elections of 1969 the strength of the Party went up to 47. In 1972, it secured 30 seats, and since then it constitutes a vital political force in Japan.

## PARTIES AND POLICIES

### Liberal Democratic Party

The Liberal Democratic Party, which is now in power, was established in 1955 as a result of the merger of conservative groups. The Liberal Party and the Democratic Party (previously the Progressive Party) unified to counteract the unity of the Socialists. The Liberal Democratic Party stands for the preservation of the principle of popular sovereignty, respect for and protection of the worth and dignity of the individual, his rights and freedoms, clean government, revision of the Constitution with a view to elevate the position and status of the Emperor as Head of the State in place of the symbol of the State, restoration of the right to defence of the country, limited rearmament for self-defence, educational and technological development, expansion in foreign trade and planned industrial growth, industrial peace and workers' welfare and application of social security on a broader national base, a diplomacy closely associated with the United Nations which will bring Asia closer to the rest of the world, co-operation with the free world and especially with the United States, a cautious approach to the normalization of relations with the People's Republic of China and Soviet Russia.

The Liberal Democratic Party considers itself a national party and seeks support from all strata of the population. But the Party is backed most heavily by rural communities, owners of commercial and industrial establishments in the towns and cities, and high level administrative personnel in Government agencies and of corporation executives. The Party is headed by the president, who is chosen by a party conference consisting of Party members of the two Houses of the Diet, and delegates chosen by the prefectural branches of the Party. The Party President is elected for a period of two years at a time and Party rules prescribe his election for two consecutive terms. By virtue of his position as President of the Party, he is the presumptive Prime Minister when the Party forms the Government. Other important officials are the Secretary-General, the Chairman of the Executive Council, Chairman of the Political Research Committee and the Party Discipline Committee. The Headquarters of the Party are at Tokyo and it is there that vast majority of the Party's work is transacted. In fact, for purposes of most policy decisions and day-to-day business, the Party is almost exclusively controlled by its higher membership normally resident in Tokyo, although ultimate authority rests with the Party Conference or Congress. The Party claims a total registered membership[5] of more than 2,500,000, and American commentators hold that it is in the neighbourhood of 400,000.[6]

The Liberal Democratic Party came into

4. Kahin, George McT, *Major Governments of Asia,* p. 232.
5. Ward and Macridis (Editors), *Modern Political Systems : Asia,* p. 72.
6. Also refer to Robert A. Scalapino and Junosuke Masumi, *Parties and Politics in Contemporary Japan,* pp. 83-85.

power in 1955 together with the Socialists. Since Socialists were sharply divided amongst themselves there was possibility to oust them from office. But the Liberal Democratic Party itself is torn into factions and it is estimated there are now 13 factions,[7] each having its own following in the House of Representatives. It is, therefore, difficult, as Ward and Macridis observe, "to describe accurately, the leadership of the Liberal Democratic Party. Superficially, the party is led by its President who, since this is normally the majority party, is also apt to be the Prime Minister of Japan. But when we look more closely, we soon see that the Liberal Democratic Party really has no single leader. In fact, it is in some ways more accurate to view it as a loose coalition of factions united for purposes of campaign and legislative strategy rather than as a unified national party."[8] This came true in December 1966, when as a result of a revolt within the Party, headed by Fujiyama the Diet was dissolved and General Election held in January 1967. The ruling Liberal Democratic Party again came into majority, with Eisaku Sato as the Prime Minister, but the dissidents posed a threat to the leadership of Sato.

In March 1980 seventy dissidents deserted the ruling party and together with the Opposition ousted Ohira's Government from office on a vote of no-confidence. The House of Representatives was dissolved and the Party surged back to power with a comfortable majority. The only answer to the Liberal Democratic Party's victory is that the Japanese voter does not see a practical alternative to the ruling Liberal Democratic Party and conforming to the conservative habit of voting he "votes for the devil he knows." The second factor that helped the Liberal Democratic Party to bag a comfortable majority is, what the Japanese political scientists describe, "the sympathy vote." The death of the incumbent Prime Minister, Masayoshi Ohira, ten days before the poll helped the Party. As the Chairman of the Buddhist-oriented Komeito Party said, "We really had a difficult battle because we lost a clear target of attack" in Ohira's death. Ohira was vehemently criticised both within the Party and outside it because of his close connection with the former Prime Minister Kakeui Tanka (1972-74) who was on trial for his alleged involvement in a Lockheed bribery scandal. Ohira was also accused within his own Party of having won its presidency in the 1978 biennial election through massive enrolment of bogus members with the funds coming from Tanka.

In the 1983 elections to the House of Representatives, the Liberal Democratic Party won 250 seats whereas its strength was 131 in the House of Councillors. The Prime Minister, Yasuhiro Naxasone, who was also the President of the Liberal Democratic Party, gambled in calling an election to the House of Representatives well 18 months ahead of schedule and it paid off more than handsomely. The Party tightened up its grip on both the Houses by winning in July 1986, 300 seats, giving it an absolute majority and increased its tally from 131 to 142 seats in the House of Councillors. Japan's Prime Minister Toshiki Kaifu led the party to a victory in one of the most crucial elections for the House of Representatives in February 1990 General Election. The Party won 275 seats in the election for 512 seats.

**Japan Socialist Party**

In October 1955, the Japan Socialist Party was established under the Chairmanship of Mosaburo Suzukoi. The Party emerged as a result of the reunification of left and right-wing Socialists who had been split for years. But they again separated in 1959, and the Democratic Socialist Party was established on January 24, 1960 by dissident right-wing members of the Socialist Party. The Japan Socialist Party is now the second largest Party in the Diet. It commanded 118 seats in the House of Representatives in 1972, and it held at its peak in 1976 with 123 seats. It came down to 107 in October 1979. Its hold in terms of the percentage of votes gained has steadily declined from 29 per cent in 1969 to 19.7 per cent in 1979. The chances for the Socialist Party to come to power are remote. In July 1986 elections the Japan Socialist party conceded to the Liberal Democratic Party 27 seats in the House of Representatives. It was for the first time that the Socialists got a less than three-digit total. It came down to 85 as compared with 112 in 1983. In the February 1990 General Election the Party won 136 seats increasing its strength by 51 seats. The Party had a majority in the House of the Councillors. The Socialist Party, under the leadership of Miss Takako Doi, could not succeed in its bid to dislodge Japan's long one-Party rule, apparently because of Opposition disunity.

7. Theodore McNelly, *Contemporary Government of Japan*, p. 122.
8. Ward and Macridis (Editors), *Modern Political Systems : Asia*, p. 73.

The platform of the Japan Socialist Party may be described as follows: re-adjustment of Japan's foreign relations with emphasis being put on the establishment of a collective non-aggression and mutual security system including Japan, United States and the Soviet Union (now defunct) demobilization of the present defence forces and creation of a democratic national policy; establishment of democracy and the socialization of major industrial and financial institutions to create a welfare and cultural State; attainment of a self-sustaining economy and the development of land to absorb the unemployed. The Party aims to achieve its objective through peaceful revolution, that is, by obtaining an absolute majority in the Diet in accordance with democratic forms. A socialist administration would first be established and stabilised and the capitalist society would then steadily be converted into a socialist society.

The Party claims to be class-mass party, with its nucleus the working class, and a union of toiling classes made up of farmers, fishermen, small and medium commercial and industrial enterprises, intellectuals and others constituting the great majority of the people. Japan Socialist Party too is highly centralised in Tokyo, where an elaborate Party Headquarters is maintained. At the top is the national convention, which meets every year, and is made up of delegates of local Party units and affiliated organizations. The convention elects a Central Executive Committee, its Chairman and Secretary-General. The convention is the ultimate source of policy and adopts the party platform.

**The Democratic Socialist Party**

The reunification of the Socialists in 1955 did not eliminate the ideological and the personal feuds which had ever plagued the Socialist movement in Japan. They remained together for four years and the eventual split came in October 1959, when a group within the Japan Socialist Party led by Nishio Suehiro, issed a statement that "there is an urgent desire in Japan for a democratic socialist party which, while abiding by parliamentarianism, will fight for extreme leftists and rightists and promote the general welfare of all sections of the working people, without special favour or partiality to labour union." The members of the "Socialist Reconstruction League" led by Nishio formally selected from the Socialist Party to organise a "genuine" Socialist Party. It actually came into being on January 24, 1960 and was named the Democratic Socialist Party.

At the time of their separation the dissidents had the support of some 35 Socialist members in the House of Representatives and their number increased to 40 before the General Election in December 1960. They fared poorly in this election securing only 17 seats. In the General Election in December 1963, the Party captured 23 seats and in December 1969, it won 31 seats. In December 1972 elections the strength of the Party was reduced to 20. In 1979 the Party increased its strength to 41. But in 1986, it could win 26 seats only whereas in 1983 the Party had won 38 seats. The organisation of the Democratic Socialist Party resembles that of the Japan Socialist Party. At the head of the Party is the Chairman of the Executive Committee with the Secretary-General who is incharge of administration. The ultimate authority is vested in the Party Congress.

The policy of the Democratic Socialist Party may be summarised as follows:

(1) opposition to capitalism and totalitarianism of both the right and the left;
(2) respect for the dignity of the individual;
(3) pursuit of an independent foreign policy; and
(4) establishment of a Welfare State through planned economy and socialist means.

**The Communist Party**

The Communist Party was formally organised in 1922, but it remained outlawed until after World War II. The Party has run candidates in all the General Elections since 1946, but its electoral and parliamentary successes have been modest. The Party reached the peak of its strength in the 1949 General Election, when it polled 5.6 per cent of the total votes and won 35 seats in the House of Representatives. In 1960 election it had 3 seats each into the House of Representatives and the House of Councillors. In the election of 1963, the Communist Party won 5 seats in the House of Representatives. In 1969 election it secured 14 seats but in the 1972 elections the Party could capture 40 seats and in 1979, 42 seats. In the 1986 elections the Party barely managed to hold its own; remaining static at 26 seats. In 1990 too there was not much appreciable improvement.

According to recent survey, membership of the Communist Party is about 370,000.[9] All Japan Congress constitutes the supreme authority

9. *Facts about Japan,* Public Information and Cultural Affairs Bureau, Ministry of Foreign Affairs, Japan.

within the Japan Communist Party. The Congress is now convened after every two years. Delegates to the Congress are elected by Party members through their local organizations. The Congress formulates the Party platform, discusses governing regulations, lays down the principles of political action. Since the Congress does not meet regularly, it does not actually initiate policy. The principle of democratic centralism rigidly operates. The Party Congress elects the members and candidates of the Central Committee. There is a Central Committee Directorate of eight members. The Central Committee meets at least once every three months. The Secretariat of the Central Committee consists of ten members and is headed by the Secretary-General. The Party Congress also elects a Central Control and Supervision Committee.

**Communists only Principled Lot in Japan**

The Japanese political system with its six major parties launched on October 8, 1996, a 12 day period of campaigning for the October 20 elections. Every party has either imported or exported defectors except the Japanese Communist Party. In the eyes of every commentator, it is like Ceaser's wife, beyond suspicion.

The head of the Japanese Communist Party, Tetsuo Puwa (66) still retaining the title Presidium chairperson, can draw crowds on a rainy. Tokyo day that are larger than what the Japanese Communist Party did in the cold war days. In August, 1996 Yutaka Vano was elected as Mayor of Konae, a suburb of Tokyo. This surprise was followed by a victory for the Communist-backed independent candidate in the Adachi ward mayoral election. Adachi became the only Communist supported mayor in Tokyo's 23 wards. What this suggests, together with the large crowds is that even in the post-cold war era, despite relations with Russia not yet normalised, people are unwilling to reject a candidate merely because he is backed by the JCP.

Until the 1978 mobilisation campaign of the Liberal Democratic Party, the Japanese Communist Party had the largest membership of any party in post war Japan at 370,000 with a third of them women. Rather than go after votes by changing its principles, the JCP is a rarity in that it is saying its principles have stood the test of time, therefore the people should come after them.

**The Komeito Party**

The political aims of the Komeito Party include creating a Welfare State based upon respect for humanity and human socialism and establishing a clean parliamentary and democratic system of government. It calls for an independent foreign policy and advocates for a step-by-step dissolution of the U.S.-Japan Security Treaty in line with a strengthening of the United Nations' security functions. The Komeito Party is a Buddhist-oriented party and is steadily making its impact on the Japanese politics. In 1974, it had 30 members in the House of Representatives and eleven in the House of Councillors and in 1979 it further improved its strength in both the Houses. But in the July 1986 elections, the Komeito, which is a centrist Party won 57 seats and lost only one seat, as compared with its total of 58 in 1983.

**New Liberal Club**

Since 1976, some Liberal Democratic Party supporters have switched to a splinter, the New Liberal Club. The Club was set up in that year by dissidents claiming to be disgusted with corruption among top Liberal Democratic Party leaders. But the Club dropped from 17 seats in the House of Representatives in 1976 at the height of the storm touched off by a Lockheed bribery scandal, involving former Prime Minister Kakeui Tanka, to only 4 in the October 1979 round.

**SUGGESTED READINGS**

Chitoshi Yanaga – *Japanese People and Politics*

Scalapino and Masumi, *Parties and Politics in Contemporary* Japan.

Thayear, Nathaniel B, *How the Conservatives Rule Japan* ?

# CHAPTER VI

# The Japanese Political System

### Strategy of Modernisation

Western Europe's large leap forward in the direction of modernity and industrial growth need not necessarily have prevented modernisation and economic development in other countries but for the decisive intervention by imperialist powers. This can be clearly seen in the history of the only Asian nation that succeeded in escaping imperialist domination and in attaining a relatively high degree of economic advancement. Had India been permitted the Japanese option by escaping British rule, she "might have found in the course of time a shorter and surely less tortuous road towards a better and richer society. That, on that road she would have had to pass through the purgatory of a bourgeois revolution, that a long phase of capitalist development would have been the inevitable price that she would have had to pay for progress, can hardly be doubted. It would have been, however, an entirely different India (and an entirely different world), had she been allowed as some more fortunate countries were—to realize her destiny in her own way, to employ her resources for her energies and abilities for the advancement of her own people."[1]

Japan's modernisation and industrialisation at a rapid rate after the Meiji Restoration of 1868 shows that the above scenario for India and other underdeveloped countries is by no means purely hypothetical. Japan's unprecedented development as a free nation took place when Western capitalism was destroying India, conquering Africa, partitioning China into spheres of influence, and subjugating Latin America. Social conditions in Japan were as favourable, or as unfavourable, to economic development as anywhere else in Asia. In fact, Japan, with its purely feudal organisation of landed property and its developed small peasant economy, was torn by all the internal tensions and conflicts of a feudal society and consequently, it "was perhaps even more tightly locked in the strait jacket of feudal constraints and restrictions than any other pre-capitalist country."[2]

For two centuries, before the bourgeois revolution from above, efforts were made by feudal rulers of Japan to suppress growth and change. "Society was frozen into a legally immutable class mould... Maintenance of the warrior class continued to take the surplus of society, learning little for investment... the closed class system smothered creative energies and tended to freeze labour and talent in traditional occupations."[3] Yet under this rigid crust of feudal rule, there also took place a rapid accumulation of capital in the hands of the mercantile class. A measure of the wealth amassed by this class is the amount of 1,781,000 ryo which the members of the trading guilds paid to the government, technically as a loan but actually as a gift, a sum equivalent to one year's expenditure of the the state of that time.

There is no doubt that the pressures coming from the rising bourgeoisie brought about the Meiji Restoration because the rapidly growing capitalist relations were rupturing the fetters of the feudal order, though political significance of the mounting opposition of the lower *samurai* class and of peasant uprisings too should be recognised. Paul Baran says: "As in all revolutions, it was a combination of heterogeneous social groups that accomplished the overturn of the *ancien regime*. But while the most active and most conspicuous among them were the *declasse* warriors and the frustrated intellectuals, the embittered feudal lords and the disgruntled courtiers.... yet it was the rising bourgeoisie that determined both the direction and the outcome of the movement, and it was the capitalist class that reaped the political and economic fruits of the Revolution,"[4]

---

1. Paul Baram, Political Economy of Growth, pp. 284-285
2. Ibid., p.286
3. Thomas C. Smith, *Political Change and Industrial Development in Japan.,* Chapter II.
4. Paul Baran, *The Political Economy of Growth,* pp.287-288

The Meiji Revolution succeeded in creating the political and economic framework necessary for capitalist development. The new regime drastically shifted the nation's gears and provided a great impetus to primary accumulation of capital as well as to its transfer from purely commercial to industrial pursuits. The economy being predominantly agrarian with about three-fourth of the population engaged in agriculture, the bulk of the economic surplus was extracted from the peasants. The strategy of Japans development was the curious blending of continued feudal relations in agriculture with a strong, centralised, capitalist-dominated state promoting energetically the growth of capitalist enterprise.

For Japanese capitalism, the rural districts and villages played the role of an internal colony. The policy of ruthless direct extraction from peasants was supplemented by keeping the wages of non-agricultural workers down to rock-bottom in order to maximise the aggregate economic surplus. The feudal lord ceased to be a territorial magnate investing his freshly capitalised wealth in banks, stocks, industries or landed estates, and so joined the small financial oligarchy."[5] Although the utmost was being done to fill the coffers of the bourgeois class, it failed to induce a spurt of investment in industrial development. Some merchants like the Mitsui did shift their capital to industry but others stuck to trade, moneylending and commodity speculation. Japan was still going through the mercantile phase of capitalism. It was the modernised, capitalist state created by the Meiji Revolution that launched Japan on the road of industrial capitalism.

The Meiji state went much further. It invested heavily in construction of railways, in shipbuilding, in basic industries, in a communications system, in production of machinery etc. The state enterprises, when they became profitable, were sold to private buyers for 15 to 30 per cent of the amounts which they cost the government. The profits earned by the Mitsui, Mitsubishi, Sumitomo, Okura and other future 'Zaibatsu', through government contracts earlier and from 're-privatized' enterprises later, were truly fabulous. The so-called daring and innovating entrepreneur of the bourgeois mythology was nowhere present in this scenario of Japan's industrial progress. In fact, from its inception, "a bourgeois-dominated regime" served "as a vigorous and relentless engine of capitalism."

This became possible because "Japan had very little to offer either as a market for foreign manufacturers or as a granary of raw materials for foreign industry." [6]

By this time, Western penetration of Asia had reached a point of exhaustion and no European power was interested in the conquest of Japan. The growing rivalry among the imperialist powers also prevented them from invading Japan. However, the threat of Western intervention acted as a great stimulant to Japan's economic development. "The exceptional Japanese receptiveness to Western knowledge... was largely due the fortunate circumstance that Western civilization was not brought to Japan at the point of a gun, that Western thought and Western technology were in Japan not directly associated with plunder, arson, and murder as they were in India, China and other now underdeveloped countries."[7]

**From Militarism to Fascism**

The advent of capitalism neither revolutionized nor disintegrated Japanese agriculture. The evidence shows that an initial shock of some severity caused by the Meiji Revolution was followed by a lasting equilibrium. "The landlord", as Barrington Moore puts it,"was the key to the new system."[8] Morris has estimated "that the landlord took from three-fifths to two-thirds of the physical product of the land between 1873 and 1885..... under the system prevailing between the World Wars, the tenant turned over half his crop to the landlord."[9]

The Japanese landlords were able to block all attempt aimed at serious land reforms. As was expected, they would appeal to nationalist traditions in order to deny the realities of conflicting economic interest. This is one of the main features of fascism. The example of fascist demagoguery can be found in the following statement issued by the Japanese Landowners'

5. Norman, E. Herbert, *Japan's Emergence as a Modern State., op. at., p.94*
6. *Ibid.*, op. cit. p.46
7. Panl Baram, *The Political Economy of Growth.* p.296
8. Moore, Barrington, Jr., *Social Origins of Dictatorship and Democracy,* p. 282
9. *Ibid., p. 285*

Association in 1926: "Remembering the splendid tradition of our nation, with sovereign and subjects forming one whole, and reflecting on the glorious history of our national development in the past, let us emphasize the harmonious relations between capital and labour, and especially cultivate peace between landowners and tenant farmers and thus contribute to the development of our agricultural villages. What sort of devils are they who furiously strike fire bells when there are no fires and incite to a class struggle, provoking animosity against landowners by exciting tenant farmers? If these malicious designs go unrestricted, what will become of our national existence?... we are determined, therefore, to cooperate with those who hold the same ideas, to arouse public opinion, and to establish a more suitable policy."[10]

The peasants were ruthlessly exploited by this landowning class, which offered to Japanese society neither artistic culture nor the security of earlier rulers in the countryside. It contributed "scarcely more than pious protofascist sentiments. A class that talks a great deal about its contributions to society is often well along the road to becoming a menace to civilization." A landlord class of this type relies on a substantial dose of repression to maintain its dominant social position and temperamentally likes the ascendancy of militarists and fascists in the state system. In practice, this also means that "capitalist elements are not strong enough to introduce new forms of repression on their own."[11]

Thus from the beginning of the modern period, commercial and agrarian elites had combined in order to keep the populace in its place at home and enable Japan to seek military glory abroad. Brown in *Nationalism in Japan* points out that conquest of colonies was in the minds of Japanese rulers from the beginning. "Rich Country-Strong Army" was their favourite slogan. In 1871, Yamagata Aritomo said,"Our army is in the midst of reorganisation ... in a year or so, foundations of the military system will be established and there probably will not be any obstacles to prevent the sending of an army to the continent."[12] Repression at home and aggression abroad were the main features of the Japanese variant of developing totalitarianism.

The correspondence of the vital interests of Japanese capitalism with the military requirements for national survival, even national glory, was of tremendous significance in determining the rapid speed of Japan's economic and political development during the late nineteenth and early twentieth centuries. Huge investments were made in basic industries, shipbuilding and armament production. The bourgeois rulers harnessed the patriotic and martial ferver of the *declasse* military castes for building a strong, modern economy. Within fifty years "the concentrated monopolistically controlled industry provided a firm basis for an impressive military potential which, combined with the purposefully nurtured chauvinism of the *samurai* and their descendants, turned Japan from an object of imperialist intrigues into one of Western imperialism's most successful junior partners."[13] As Lenin put it, "by their colonial looting of Asian countries the Europeans managed to harden one of them — Japan for great military exploits that assured it of an independent national development."[14]

**The Nature of Japanese Fascism**

According to Barrington Moore, the rise of Japanese militarism and fascism may be divided into three phases. The first one, characterised by the failure of agrarian liberalism, ended with the adoption of a formal constitution and superficial elements of a parliamentary regime in 1889. The second phase closed with the failure of democratic forces to break through the barriers imposed by this system, clearly visible with the onset of the great depression in 1929. The failure of the 1930s leads to the third phase of a war economy and the Japanese version of a militarist-fascist dictatorship.

By the early thirties, the weak parliamentary democracy was perishing under the final blow of the Great Depression. However, it did not happen in a dramatic fashion *a la* Hitler's usurpation of the Weimar Republic. In the case

10. Quoted by Ladijinsky, W., in "Farm Tenancy and Japanese Agriculture", *Foreign Agriculture*, Vol.1, No 9, (Sept, 1937), pp. 441-449
11. Moore, Barrington Jr., *Social Origins of Dictatorship and Democracy,* p. 287
12. Ike, Neboutaka, *The Beginning of Political Democracy in Japan*,. p.51
13. Paul Baram, *The Political Economy of Growth, p. 298*
14. V.I.Lenin, *Sochinenya* (Works), 4th Edition, Vol.15, p.161.

of Japan it is more difficult to draw a sharp distinction between a democratic and a fascist phase than in the German instance. In foreign affairs, it began with the conquest of Manchuria in 1931. In domestic affairs, the assassination of Prime Minister Inukai and an attempted *coup d' etat* on 15 May, 1932 marked the end of the hegemony of the politicians, leading to the ascendancy of the militarists and crypto-fascists.

In 1932 a small group of peasants led by a Buddhist monk planned to assassinate the 'ruling clique' responsible for the misery of the peasantry. They killed a former Finance Minister, Inoue, and the Chief Director of Mitsui, Baron Dan, before the plot was uncovered. A band of young naval and army cadets then attacked the *Zaibatsu*, political leaders, and men around the Emperor "to save Japan from collapse," as they claimed. One unit shot the Prime Minister, others killed police chiefs, court officials and capitalists. This violence initiated a period of semi-militarist dictatorship which ultimately led to outright fascist totalitarianism a few years later.

Four years later in 1936, Japan had a relatively free election. The Conservative *Minseito* party fought it on a slogan–'What shall it be, parliamentary government or Fascism?' got 205 seats and defeated the fascists who got only 6 seats while a labour party, *Shakai Taishuto,* received 18 seats. To this defeat, a section of the army reacted with another attempted *coup* known as 26 February (1936) Incident. Several high officials were killed and a fascist 'new order' was proclaimed by the rebels. High army authorities refused the use of force to crush them. Since the Satsuma Rebellion, this was the biggest crisis of State in Japan. However, this 'fascism from below' was defeated through diplomacy. It was essentially the anticapitalist, left-wing of Japanese fascism, which was sacrificed to 'fascism from above' i.e. right-wing pro-capitalist fascism.

Barrington Moore says "Respectable fascism now made rapid strides. National mobilization was decreed, radicals were arrested, political parties were dissolved and replaced by the Imperial Rule Assistance Association, a rather unsuccessful copy of a Western totalitarian party. Shortly afterward Japan joined the anti-Comintern. Triple Alliance dissolved all trade unions, replacing them with an association for 'service to the nation through industry'. Thus by the end of 1940 Japan displayed the principal external traits of European fascism."[15] Unlike Nazi Germany, no blood purge was necessary to exclude the right-wing radicals from power. Japanese big business successfully resisted attempts to subordinate profits to patriotism. The whole period of military hegemony and fascism was very profitable to capitalists.

Industrial output increased from 6 billion yen in 1930 to 30 billion in 1941. The share of heavy industry in the total industrial output rose from 38 per cent to 73 per cent in the same period. "By nominally yielding to government control the *Zaibatsu* were able to obtain fairly complete domination of all industry. The four great *zaibatsu* firms, Mitsui, Mitsubishi, Sumitomo, and Yasuda, came out of the Second World War with total assets of more than 3 billion yen, compared with only 875 millions in 1930," [16] In the Asian version of fascism, The army played a different political and social role from that of the German army under Hitler. Japan was backward relative to Germany and its agrarian sector was far more important. The Japanese military leadership, therefore, could not so easily dismiss agrarian demands.

For the same reason, sections of the Japanese army intervened in the political arena by attempting *coups d'etat* in a distinct contrast to the behaviour of the German army. Japanese fascism differed from its European counterpart in other respects as well. "There was no sudden seizure of power, no outright break with previous constitutional democracy, no equivalent of a March on Rome, partly because there was no democratic era comparable to the Weimar Republic. Fascism emerged much more 'naturally' in Japan; that is, it found congenial elements in Japanese institutions even more than it did in Germany. Japan had no plebeian *Fuhrer* or *Duce*. Instead the Emperor served as a national symbol in much the same way." [17]

Unlike Fascist Italy and Nazi Germany, Japan did not have a really effective single mass party. The Imperial Rule Assistance Association was an artificial structure created from the above with no popular base. Lastly, the Japanese fascists did not have a racial enemy like the Nazis had found in the Jews. In spite of the above difference, there were basic similarities between

15. Barrington Moore Jr., *Social Origins of Dictatorship and Democracy,* p. 301
16. *Ibid,* p. 302
17. *Ibid,*. p. 304

the Asian and European versions of fascism. Germany, Italy and Japan entered the industrial world at a later stage. In these countries, dictatorial regimes were established whose main features were aggression abroad and repression at home. In all fascist countries, the social basis of their rule was an alliance between the capitalist class in cities and a land-owning class in villages. Finally in Europe as well as Japan, a form of rightist radicalism emerged as a consequence of petty-bourgeois and peasant discontent under developing capitalism. The radical slogans were used earlier by these repressive regimes but soon this spurious radicalism was suppressed in order to consolidate the alliance with monopoly capital.

During the totalitarian phase of Japan's modern history, the peasantry was integrated into the national structure in a way that is broadly similar to Tokugawa methods for penetrating and controlling rural population. These arrangements show compatibility between significant aspects of Japanese feudalism with its twentieth-century totalitarian institutions. The oligarchical structure, internal solidarity and strong vertical bonds with higher authorities continued in Japan's villages with little change during and after the transition to modern production for the market. The landlords maintained most of the old village structure because they could extract in this way and sell enough of a surplus to stay on top of the hierarchy.

Here is a lesson for all societies which attempt a non-revolutionary transition to modernity, democracy and development, including India. Barrington Moore says, "The adaptability of Japanese political and social institutions to capitalist principles enabled Japan to avoid the costs of a revolutionary entrance onto the stage of modern history. Partly because she escaped these early horrors, Japan succumbed in time to fascism and defeat. So did Germany for very broadly the same reason. The price for avoiding a revolutionary entrance has been a very high one. It has been high in India as well. There the play has not yet reached the culminating act, the plot and the characters are different. Still, lessons learned from all the cases studied so far may prove helpful in understanding what the play means.".[18]

**Post-War Capitalist Democracy**

The state intervention in every aspect of economic life, a characteristic of post-war capitalist democracy, is nothing new in the history of capitalism. Even in the countries most dedicated to *laissez faire* capitalism, state intervention has been of crucial intervention, especially in any period of crisis. While advanced capitalism provides a broadly similar socio-economic environment for political life, politics itself can often be exceedingly dissimilar. For example the twentieth century capitalism provided the context for Baldwin's Conservative rule in Britain, for Nazi totalitarianism in Germany, Roosevelt's New Deal in the United States and the Asian brand of fascism in Japan. "The notion that capitalism is incompatible with.... authoritarianism may be good propaganda but it is poor political Sociology." [19]

In post-war society of capitalist Japan "aristocracy still carries a good deal of *cachet,* but the business classes are no longer conscious of being *parvenu* and socially inferior to any other group or class." [20] A Japanese writer says that in Japan "today those who engage in commerce and industry are considered the pillars of the community and find easy entry into the most respected levels of society. Seekers of wealth no longer need to be apologetic.... The change in the ethos is but one measure of this rise of business to a position of dominance in the political life." [21] A.B. Cole points out that "the top bracket of business executives has already superseded the older *Zaibatsu* families, and has become the principal elite in post war Japan. "[22] As suggested by Abegglen and Mannari, "For Japan, the largest proportion by far the business leaders is drawn from fathers who were themselves executives or owners of large enterprises, with the sons of landlords and small businessmen second and sons of labourers nowhere."[23] R.P. Dore also notes "The total absence in the Japanese sample of the sons of manual labourers and tenant farmers in the recruitment of comtemporary Japanese business

18. Barrington Moore, Jr., *Social Origins of Dictatorship and Democracy*., p. 313
19. R.Miliband, *The State in Capitalist Society,* p. 82
20. *Ibid.,* p. 42
21. *N. Ike, Japanese* Politics, p.82
22. A.B. Cole, *Japanese Society and Politics- The Impact of Social Stratification and Mobility on Politics,* p.86
23. Abegglen and Mannari "Leaders of Modern Japan: Social Origins and Mobility" in *Economic Development and Cultural Change,* Vol 9, no 1, part 2, p. 112

leaders."[24]

Japan's privileged classes, having lost their fascist masters and protectors, now found a new set of protectors, and rulers in the shape of their American conquerers and occupiers. Defeat in war and the collapse of the fascist dictatorship raised the spectre of social revolution but the U.S. occupation authorities had no desire of allowing any radical change in Japan. In fact, an occupation by the American army was an absolute guarantee to Japan's dominant classes that any threat to them will be opposed, if necessary with the full force of military power. Indeed defeat at the hands of the United States provided an additional bonus to the Japanese capitalist class as this rid its members of indigenous rulers whose failure in war had turned them into encumbrances which they could not have been able to remove on their own.

At the end of war, it appeared that General MacArthur's programme of purging 'pro-fascist' elites in Japan might push 'democratisation' too far as to make the pre-war business elites lose hope of coming back to power. Japanese capitalists also distrusted the policies of 'decartelisation' proclaimed by the victorious allies. But all such fears proved to be highly exaggerated. The 'artificial revolution' forced upon Japan and Germany at the end of the war "brought no permanent stigma to those who had led their country to ruin; neither country emerged into sovereignty with any important reservation against the employment of nationalist fanatics of the thirties and forties, even in the most responsible positions."[25] Thus in both Germany and Japan, the former fascists and businessmen were running the post-war 'democratic' regimes.

It was a form of 'palace revolution' involving the return of older elites in place of the 'fascist' upstarts. Shift in the power structure accurred mainly within a middle-and upper-class context and did not change their hegemony. As for 'decartelisation,' the programme proved to be abortive. Halliday points out that "a list of 1200 firms to be broken up was compiled; this was progressively reduced until there were only 19 firms on the list—and when nine of these had been dealt with the board set up by SCAP (composed of five prominent US businessmen) decided enough had been done" [26] A few years later after the war, big business in defeated Japan was bigger than ever and launched on a spectacular course of expansion. Thus capitalists in post-war Japan achieved a position in society which was more eminent than at anytime in the past.

As Ralph Miliband puts it, "the postwar triumphs of capitalism in Germany, Japan and Italy were hardly a case of the Phoenix rising from the ashes. The Phoenix had been alive and prospering throughout the years of dictatorship and terror. Defeat at the hands of the Western powers merely gave it the chance to do even better. For the business and other elites of these countries, those years were not a dark hiatus between overthrow and restoration. There was no overthrow and there was therefore no need for restoration."[27]

The most visible innovation of the MacArthur Constitution was the renunciation of war as an instrument of national policy by Japan. Japan's defence became the responsibility of the United States under a Security Treaty signed by both the countries. Japan's armed forces demobilized and armament factories ceased production of arms and ammunition. Yet Japan has been allowed to build and augment its Self-Defence Forces equipped with modern weapons. These so-called Self-Defence Forces, in fact, constitute a fully equipped, modernized armed force. The ratio of officers in the army and air force is five times larger than what it should be, which ensures a rapid increase of recruits whenever required. This shows that Japan's disarmament is unreal. Militarism and national fanaticism remain part of the ruling class ideology. The military elite has an honoured place in post-war Japanese society, economy and polity despite its invisibility. The 'industrial-military' complex is not a figure of speech but a solid fact, cemented by a genuine community of interests. Despite its relative enfeeblement in numbers, the role of the military elite in the post-war management of capitalist democracy is not insignificant.

Prime Minister Kishi spoke in favour of acquiring nuclear weapons by Japan as early as possible: "Not all nuclear weapons can be considered as falling within the purview of this prohibition (Article 9 of the Constitution). If there is nuclear weapon that can be considered as solely a defensive weapon, then it is not

24. Ward and Rustow (eds) *Political Modernisation in Japan and Turkey*, p.203
25. J.D.Montgomery, *Forced to be free- The Artificial Revolution in Germany and Japan*, p.35
26. J Halliday, "Japan—Asian Capitalism" in *New Left Review*, no.44, July-August, 1967, p.11
27. Ralph Miliband, *The State in Capitalist Society*, pp. 87-88

outside the realm of possibility for Japan to possess it." [28] By 1962 Japan's armed forces had 243,923 men, the navy 469 ships totalling 128,000 tons and the airforce 1100 planes. In the decade 1954-1963 defence expenditure rose form 135 billion yen to 247 billion yen.

Japan still looks at East and South-east Asia as its Zone of action and expansion. By 1969 it was making 97 per cent of its own ammunition and 84 per cent of its aircraft, tanks, guns, naval craft and other military equipment. It was the fourth country to launch a space satellite and it is technologically prepared to produce nuclear weapons. As three branches of its forces are heavily over-officered, which means they could be expanded at a short notice. Japan's forces are already the seventh strongest in the world. They are just "short of a leap to a full-scale offensive nuclear strategy."[29] In absolute terms, Japan's military expenditures are very high and have been rising from year to year." Japan's seizure of the Tiaoyu islands in the winter of 1970-71 went almost unnoticed."[30] Japan has worked as a junior partner of the United States in all its wars against the Asian nations by supplying arms, ammunition and other material for waging power.

As Halliday and McCormack have pointed out, "Weapons for use in the Korean and Vietnam wars played a crucial part in Japan's postwar economic recovery and growth. U.S. military procurements in Japan between 1951 and 1960 amounted to 6 billion dollars.... The Japanese economy was largely moulded by the demand for war materials."[31] Military- industrial solidarity, which began during the pro-fascist period, has now been institutionalised under post-war capitalist democracy. "The practice of 'descent from heaven', by which youthful admirals, generals and other military officials retire from their posts to join companies engaged in defence-related works is a long-established one. During the 'Defence Secrets scandal of 1967-8 it was learned that there were 265 Defence Agency officials, who had retired between 1962 and 1967, who were so engaged."[32]

In post-war Japan, the Liberal Democratic party has emerged as the permanent ruling group except for a very short stint by an opposition coalition. The party came into existence as a result of the merger of two conservative parties in 1955 and since then it has been in power almost without any interruption. Both in terms of its any social composition and actual politics, it represents the corporate rich of the Japanese society. It is heavily financed by big business and pursues policies dictated by this class. The administrative and judicial elites, like business and political elites, are educated in Tokyo University and a few other elitist institutions and work through a network of common friends and relatives. Nepotism and corruption have become part of Japanese party politics and administrative institutions. Despite these negative points, 'Japan Incorporated' has made tremendons economic progress making Japan the second largest economy in the world. Capitalist democracy in Japan is so far a success story. Pre-war fascism has assumed the form of an entrenched, reactionary conservatism under American hegemony.

## SUGGESTED READINGS

Baran, Paul A., *The Political Economy of Growth.*

Chitoshi Yanaga, *Japanese People and Politics.*

Halliday, J., and McCormack G., *Japanese Imperialism Today.*

Kahin, George McT, *Major Governments of Asia.*

Kahin, Herman, *The Emerging Japanese Superstate.*

Maki, John M., *Government and Politics of Japan.*

McNelly, Theodore, *Contemporary Government of Japan.*

Miliband, Ralph, *The State in Capitalist Society.*

Moore, Barrington Jr, *Social Origins of Dictatorship and Democracy.*

Norbeck, Edward, *Changing Japan.*

Passin, Herbers, *The United States and Japan*

Storry, Richard, *A Short History of Modern Japan*

Takahashi, Kamekichi, *The Rise and Development of Japan's Modern Economy.*

Thayer, Nathaniel B., *How the Conservatives Rule Japan.*

Ward and Macridis, *Modern Political Systems: Asia.*

Ward, Robert E., *Japan's Political System.*

Thayear, Nathamiel B, How the Conservatives Rule Japan?

28. Quoted by Wolf Mendl, "Japan's Defense Problems," *Yearbook of World Affairs,* 1968, p.135
29. J.Halliday and G.McCormack, *Japanese Imperialism Today,* p.83
30. *Ibid.,* p.97
31. *Ibid.,* pp. 108-109
32. *Ibid.,* p. 109

# THE GOVERNMENT OF THE PEOPLE'S REPUBLIC OF CHINA (CONSTITUTION OF 1982)

## CHAPTER I

## The Chinese Political Tradition

### People's Republic

There is a saying in the People's Republic of China: ''Tsou, tsou; ts'ou, ta'ou, kai kai'' (Act, act you will make mistakes; correct them, correct them). Forty centuries of slow change lay behind China when the Communists took over the country in 1949 and brought to an end, as the Preamble to the 1954 Constitution of the People's Republic of China declared: ''a long history of oppression and enslavement.'' The new Republic set before it the fundamental task of bringing about, step by step, the socialist industrialisation of the country and, step by step, to accomplish the socialist transformation of agriculture, handicrafts and the capitalist industry and commerce. By 1954, it was claimed that the necessary condition had been created for planned economic construction and gradual transition to Socialism. On September 20, 1954, the First National People's Congress solemnly adopted at its first session, held in Peking, the Constitution of the People's Republic of China. The Constitution ''consolidates the gains of the Chinese People's Revolution and the political and economic victories won since the founding of the People's Republic of China; and, however, it reflects the basic needs of the State in the period of transition, as well as the general desire of the people as a whole to build a socialist society.''[1]

In a few years of the establishment of a People's Democratic Dictatorship, Chinese Communists surprised the world by their success in boosting industrial production, by extending strong and effective government throughout the country, by building massive army, in fact, wholesale militarization, and by improving the living conditions of industrial workers. In the international affairs the Constitution pledged the People's Republic to a firm and consistent policy ''for the noble cause of world peace and the progress of humanity.'' But within just three years of its career, China began itself indulging in expansionism. It pounced upon Tibet and subjugated it. After consolidating its conquest there, it penetrated in the Indian territory, repudiated the International frontier, the McMahon Line, and launched an undeclared war. The Constitution had unequivocally declared that China had already built an indestructible friendship ''with the great Union of the Soviet Socialist Republics.'' But soon China's relations with Soviet Russia deteriorated verging on open hostility and ideological denunciation.

### The People and the Country

China is the world's most populous country. The 1982 census counted 1,000 million people as compared with the 1972 census which counted a population of 723.07 million people. China has succeeded in its reducing birth rate by an impressive 34 per cent between 1965-70 and 1970-80. The Government has now introduced a system of incentives and disincentives to induce people to observe one-child family norm in order to achieve zero population growth rate by the turn of the century.

China's territorial boundary is spread over 3,800,000 square miles. On the north are Himalayan ranges and on the south and east is the

1. Preamble to the *Constitution of the People's Republic of China,* 1954.

erstwhile Soviet Union. The People's Republic of China consists of provinces, autonomous regions and municipalities directly under the Central Government. The capital is Beijing.

Only a few million Chinese work in industry. Nearabout 70.3 per cent of the population is rural and essentially depend upon agriculture. There is too little good arable land in China to meet the needs of the population. Much of the country consists of desolate plains, barren mountains and winding paths, with paddy fields filling every inch of arable land. A bad season leaves millions hungry. No Government of China has yet been able to control the gods of weather. Malcolm MacDonald, who arrived in Hongkong on November 3, 1962, after a four-week tour of China, said, "The people and Government of China are confident but not complacent. They know and admit they are still inexperienced in modern affairs and the task of turning their colossal teeming country into a modern industrial and agricultural State is gigantic." MacDonald predicted it would take "a considerable number of years" for China to be "independent agriculturally" and "many more years than that before it achieved industrially." The position is not radically bright even today. Under the Sino-American agreement, China was committed to buy six million tons of foodgrains annually from 1981 to 1984. Such massive imports of foodgrains greatly worried the Chinese leadership, as the country was committed to attaining self-sufficiency in food under the four-point modernisation programme on which Deng-Xiaoping and his associates, including the Premier, had staked their reputation and future. But this was too optimistic a hope due to the woeful shortage of arable land in China, coupled with vagaries of nature.

There is a good deal of empirical evidence to suggest that the average growth rate of Chinese economy during 1950-78 was nearly 6 per cent and in per capita terms 4 per cent. More significantly industrial production had grown at the rate of 9.5 per cent. With the help of the population and growth rate strategy, China was able, in a brief period of little more than two decades, to eradicate the worst form of poverty. There is no affluence but there is no destitution. It achieved a high literacy percentage and managed to provide adequate health facilities for the entire population. The economy of the country during recent years has been restructured with clear incentive for private enterprise and invitation to foreign capital investment. Such a reorientation of economic policy is logical in the perspective of the four modernisation goals—modernisation of agriculture, industry, science and technology, set before the nation at the National People's Congress Session held in September 1980. The earlier Plan (1976-85) was consequently abandoned and the new formulated in the light of new economic policy and experience of the past few years.

China is inhabited by various races, but the Hans, that is the Chinese, constitute the vast majority, only six per cent of the total population is non-Chinese and there are 12 racial groups with over 100,000 persons each. Some of the important of such groups are the Chuang, Hui, Uighur, Tibetan, Korean, Thai, Mongolian and Manchu. Despite racial and other diversities, linguistic and cultural homogeneity makes Chinese a strong and united nation. Their literature, customs, traditions, beliefs and faiths have all been greatly influenced by Confucianism. Their language and common acceptance of ideas, customs, philosophies, as Winfield remarked, "created a basic unity and homogeneity which has been binding in spite of differences in topography, climate, even in spite of variations in spoken language brought about by the absorption of new racial groups,"[2]

The official language is Chinese, although there are more than 150 Chinese dialects and other languages. Before 1949, religion-wise break up of the people was : Taoist, Confucianist 75 per cent, Buddhist 16 per cent, Muslims 8 per cent and Christians 1 per cent. Although the Constitution guarantees freedom of conscience and religion, but it also provides that the people shall enjoy "freedom not to believe in religion and to propagate atheism." Like other Communist countries, China, too, promotes atheism and discredits all kinds of religion.

## HISTORY OF THE CONSTITUTION

### From the Ancient to Manchu Dynasty

The history of the development of the Chinese people covers different periods, the ancient period is older than the Greek and Roman civilisations. Till the emergence of the Tang dynasty (618-907) A.D.) several dynasties had ruled over the different parts of the country. The Tang dynasty was followed by several others till the rise

2. Winfield, G. F., *China—The Land and the People*, p. 7.

of Manchu dynasty towards the close of the sixteenth century. Twelve emperors of the Manchu dynasty ruled and during this period the empire was consolidated and it prospered and progressed.

The East India Company carried on its trade with China in 1664, and it destroyed the monopoly of the Portuguese that they had hitherto enjoyed. The British merchants were only concerned with the accumulation of huge profits to themselves and consequently they freely encouraged the trade in opium oblivious of its effect on the health and earning capacity of the Chinese. The trade in opium resulted into the First (1841) and Second (1858) opium wars. One of the important causes of the opium wars was the Government's opposition to the British carrying on trade with Chinese people in opium, which had been declared as a contraband. But the real fact leading to both the wars was the anxiety of the British to get special rights and privileges, including equality of status, in dealing with the Chinese Government in China. The War of 1841 ended with the treaty of Nanking which provided, *inter alia,* cession of the Island of Hongkong to Britain, payment of 15 million dollars to British merchants as compensation, opening of ports of Canton, Aninoy, Foochow, Ningpo and Shanghai to British trade and residence. The treaty also guaranteed equality of status to the British. These terms were deemed essentially humiliating and there spread a wave of resentment throughout the country. The Chinese Government later on granted similar concessions to the Americans too.

The second opium war started on the British taking side of the Americans and French in their conflict with the Chinese over the abuses of extra-territoriality and also for the reason that the British merchants smuggled into Chinese territory contraband and other goods. The end of the Second War gave significant rights to foreigners in China, particularly to British and French. Later, similar rights were conceded to Americans also. All told, the total effects of both these wars were the political humiliation and economic bankruptcy of the Chinese. All this was attributed to the weakness of Manchu Government. The enlightened class of Chinese succeeded in making the people to rise against the Government at various places. The uprising was, no doubt, crushed with the help of foreigners, but it created an upsurge in the country which set the ball rolling for supplanting the Manchu dynasty. In the meanwhile a war was fought between China and Japan over the Korean question. Japan insisted on the recognition of Korea as an independent State whereas China claimed Korea as its tributary. China was defeated and Korea was declared an independent State.

China had to pay an indemnity to Japan also. But the most important sequel of China-Japanese war was a threat to the integrity of China. The Western Powers took advantage of the miseries of China and offered to lend her money freely to enable to pay the indemnity to Japan for concessions of trade. Russia, France and Germany made their own demands to obtain spheres of influence and each one succeeded in getting its own price. But in these concessions Britain saw a threat to her dominant position in China. As a result of the Spanish American War, 1898, the United States had annexed Philippines and she naturally became interested in the Western Pacific and in China itself. John Hay, the Secretary of State, then enunciated the "Open Door" policy, which should provide equal opportunity to all nations to trade with China. All these happenings aroused China's deep indignation and it gave birth to a new revolutionary nationalist movement pledged to free the country from foreign domination and to establish a republican government in the country after overthrowing the Manchu regime.

**New Chinese Nationalism**

Sun Yat-Sen was the moving force of this movement. So zealously did he plunge himself in it that in 1895, he had to flee from China with a price on his head. Boxer uprising is the most important phase of the revolutionary movement. A secret society of the Boxers, outwardly started with the object of training youngmen in gymnastics and boxing, had its avowed object of overthrowing the Manchu dynasty, which they held responsible for the surrender of China to foreign powers. The Boxers, accordingly, directed their activities on attacking the foreign legations and Chinese Christians and glorified their existence by killing a few of foreign diplomats. The foreign powers combined together and raised forces to combat the Boxers, but they did not succeed beyond protecting their legations. It was at this stage that the United States came forward with its policy of "seeking a solution which may bring about permanent safety and peace to China, preserve Chinese territorial and administrative entity, protect all rights guaranteed to friendly powers by treaty or international law, and safeguard for the world the principle of equal and impartial trade with all parts of the Chinese empire." Russia did not accept the policy enunciated by the United States and occupied Manchuria. The Allied armies reached Peking for the relief of the foreign legations placing China entirely at their mercy. The outcome was the Boxer Protocol signed on September 7, 1901.

The Boxer protocol was not a treaty as it did not require ratification. In fact, its terms had been fulfilled by the Chinese Government even before it could be signed. The terms provided for repatriations for the assassinated, punishment for the authors of the crime, payment of indemnity of four hundred and fifty taels with interest at four per cent to be paid in thirty-nine years, occupation by allied troops of twelve specified places for keeping open communications between Peking and the Sen, improvement of commercial relations by amending the commercial treaties, etc. The Boxer movement though apparently suppressed, but the revolutionary spirit of the Chinese remained unabated and soon there emerged the Reformist Movement. The Reformist Movement, like its predecessor Boxer Movement, was anti-foreign and it aimed at overthrowing the Manchu dynasty. It also aimed to reform the entire life of the Chinese people by improving their social, economic and political lot. The young Chinese trained in western methods of education and institutions spearheaded the movement which soon spread even in the remotest parts of the country. Province after province revolted and the six-year-old Manchu Emperor abdicated paving the way for the establishment of a republic in 1911.

Sun Yat-Sen after his flight from China had directed the revolutionary movement from abroad. When the Manchu Emperor abdicated and the peace conference convened by various participants in the Reformist Movement was in session, he came back home and was elected the provisional President of the Republic of China. But the revolutionaries were divided amongst themselves in different parts of the country. In the South, Yuan Shih-Kai was declared President of another republic. Sun Yat-Sen was anxious to maintain the unity of the country and, accordingly, he resigned from the provisional Presidentship in favour of Yuan. Trouble again brewed up when the most powerful group under Sun Yat-Sen organised itself as Kuomintang, the National People's Party in 1912. Yuan obtained huge debts from England, France, Germany, Russia and Japan and declared himself Emperor in 1915. The Kuomintang revolted against Yuan who was obliged to postpone his coronation and eventually to restore the republic. But he soon died early in June 1916 and the former Vice President Li Yuan Hung became the President of the Republic, thus, establishing once again the unity of the country under the leadership of the Kuomintang.

The First World War dragged the Chinese Republic in new difficulties. China sought help from the United States to preserve neutrality. But when Japan entered the war on the side of the Allies she presented China with twenty-one demands. The Japanese demands were heavily tilted against China, but there was no way out and she was forced to concede fifteen out of twenty- one demands. Japan's position was, thus, inconceivably strengthened in the Far East. The Treaty of 1921, signed by nine powers[3] bound the signatory powers : (1) to respect the sovereignty, the independence and the territorial and administrative integrity of China; (2) to provide the fullest and most unembarrassed opportunity to China to develop and maintain for herself an effective and stable government; (3) to use their influence for the purpose of effectually establishing and maintaining the principle of equal opportunity for the commerce and industry of all nations throughout the territory of China; (4) to refrain from taking advantages of conditions in China in order to seek special rights or privileges which would abridge the rights of subjects or citizens of friendly States, and from counteracting action inimical to the security of the State. By another treaty, China's right to enjoy tariff autonomy was also recognised.

The October Revolution in Russia and the establishment of the Soviet State in 1917, affected the politics of China too. A number of prominent Chinese nationalists thought that only a Socialist State of the Soviet pattern could remove the economic and political ills of China. The advocates of the Marxian thesis became the left-wing of the revolutionaries. The Kuomintang opposed the Communists, who were under the guidance of Joffe, the Russian Representative. But in 1923, Sun Yat-Sen entered into an alliance with the Communists. They were allowed to enter the Kuomintang while retaining their own party or-

3. Great Britain, France, Italy, Belgium, the Netherlands, Portugal, Japan, the United States and China.

ganisation. The Russians, keen to help them in establishing their national independence, sent Borodin to Canton to organise a new revolutionary republic in China and General Blucher to train the revolutionary army. Chiang Kai-shek, who had been in Russia as Sun's emissary, was placed at the head of the Whampa Military Academy, which produced the new leaders of the Chinese army. The intensive propaganda of the Communists and devoted indoctrinating of the youth created bright chances of China's becoming red. Sun Yat-Sen died in 1925, and the Kuomintang acknowledged Chiang Kai-shek as their chief leader. But Sun's death had removed the unifying factor and soon open conflict arose between the Communists and the Kuomintang.

Chiang Kai-shek was an able military general and his military successes resulted in the new unification of China. The old Republic came to an end as also the Nanking Constitution under which it had worked. After establishing his leadership and influence of the Kuomintang, Chiang Kai-shek resigned his military post and under the law of October 25, 1928, established a new national government at Canton and put himself at its head. A National People's Convention adopted on May 12, 1931, a provisional Constitution which aimed to put into action Sun's three principles of People's Government, People's Livelihood, and People's Nationalism, that is, freedom from foreign control.

The events, then, followed are swift to some extent. In 1931, Japan occupied Manchuria and set up there a puppet government with a new name "Manchukus." The League of Nations failed to prevent Japan from violating its covenant and the terms of the Nine Power Treaty of Washington in 1921, to which Japan herself was a signatory. Chiang Kai-shek was left smarting under humiliation. During the Second World War Japan threw her lot with the Axis powers and China seized the opportunity and joined the Allies. Japan had occupied some part of the territory of China during the War. With the active aid of the Allies, China succeeded in getting it back and strengthened its position to the extent that it was included amongst the five great powers to get a permanent seat in the Security Council. The American forces and money also helped Chiang to combat the Communists who had started a virulent propaganda against his government. But the Communists with Russia's unprecedented help were able to drive Chiang's Government in the Island of Formosa in 1947. It was triumph for Communism and China became red. A People's Republic of China was established.

**The Provisional Constitution**

When the Communists came to power they did not base their government on a formal constitution analysing the machinery of government. Nor did they attempt one for the first five years of their career. There existed alone the Chinese People's Political Consultative Conference, a numerous body of 662 delegates representing the various political parties including the Communist Party, the various regions, mass organisations, the People's Liberation Army and the overseas Chinese. It was a motley of delegates, but with a common programme set forth by Mao Tse-Tung, which hinged upon his thesis of People's Democratic Dictatorship. It really served the provisional constitution for half a decade. The Organic Law consisting of 31 Articles was promulgated and it outlined the machinery of government which was to bring forth the fulfillment of the Common Programme and the basis for drafting of the constitution.

**Drafting of the Constitution**

A Committee to draft the constitution for the People's Republic of China was appointed in January 1953, under the Chairmanship of Mao Tse-Tung. The draft of the constitution was made available to the Conference, which accepted it in March 1954. Like the Stalin Constitution, and in order to give it the complexion of the constitution ordained by the people themselves, it was submitted for discussion to the selected people representing different democratic parties and groups, and people's organizations of all sections of society. The discussions lasted for two months and certain amendments were also suggested thereto. The draft of the constitution thus amended was published and circulated amongst the people for general discussion. It was estimated that about 150,000 million persons participated in the public discussions for over two months. Here, too, the procedure was identical to the one adopted in Russia in 1936. The draft of the constitution was further amended in the light of suggestions emerging from these public discussions, which were formally adopted by the Central People's Government Council on September 9, 1954. The final draft was, then, reported to the First National People's Congress at its first session on September 20, 1954. In pursuance of this Constitution new governmental organisation was set up on November 4, 1954.

**The 1954 Constitution**

The 1954 Constitution of the People's Republic of China summed up the struggle of the Chinese people to overthrow colonialism, feudalism and capitalism and proclaimed that the newly formed State was a single-multi-national State wherein all nationalities in China were united in one family of free and equal nations. The Constitution, accordingly, guaranteed equal status to all nationalities, prohibited discrimination or oppression against any nationality and acts which undermined the unity of the nation. All nationalities enjoyed freedom to use and foster the use of their spoken and written languages, and to preserve and reform their own customs or ways of life. The Constitution also guaranteed regional autonomy to all those national minorities whose people lived in compact communities. National autonomous areas were the inalienable parts of the People's Republic of China.

The Constitution established a democratic State led by the working class and based on the alliance of workers and peasants. It established a people's democratic dictatorship in order to build a prosperous and happy socialist society. But the establishment of the People's Republic of China would not usher in all at once a socialist society. Till the socialist society was built, the fundamental task of the State, during the transition period, was step by step, to bring about the socialist industrialisation of the country, and, step by step, to accomplish the socialist transformation of agriculture, handicrafts and capitalist industry and commerce.

The Constitution contained a separate Chapter on Fundamental Rights and Duties of citizens. It recognised seven basic freedoms, inviolability of home and privacy of correspondence. Women enjoyed and exercised equal rights with men in all spheres of political, economic, cultural and domestic life and the State protected marriage, the family, the mother and child. The right to elect and stand for election was extended to all citizens who had reached the age of eighteen years. The duties of the citizens were more or less the same as prescribed in the Soviet Constitution of 1936. The Constitution granted the right to asylum to any foreign national for supporting a just cause, for taking part in the peace movement or for engaging in scientific activity.

The 1954 Constitution was a brief document. It was really a transitional instrument. The National People's Congress was the highest organ of State authority and the sole legislative instrument in the Republic. It was a unicameral legislature elected for a term of four years. If for some exceptional circumstances new elections could not be held, the term of the sitting members was prolonged until the first session of the succeeding Congress. The Constitution required that the Congress should be convened once a year by its Standing Committee. Elections to the Second and Third Congress were held in accordance with the provisions of the Constitution and their sessions were annually convened. But no elections to the Congress were held from 1964 to 1974 and not a single session of the Congress was convened during this span of a decade.

The Standing Committee was the highest functioning organ of State authority which acted on behalf of the Congress between its sessions. Even this body did not meet after 1966 without amending the Constitution. The work of the Government was carried on by the extra-constitutional authority of the Chinese Communist Party hierarchy. The Constitution did not contain any provision relating to the role of the Communist Party, except for a perfunctory reference to "democratic Centralism" in Article 2. Both the Preamble to the Constitution and Article 19 simply acclaimed the Party that led the people of China to finally achieve their great victory in the people's revolution against imperialism, feudalism and bureaucratic capitalism. But the Party itself was paralyzed as its highest organs were replaced by the "proletarian headquarters" of Mao Tse-tung, which consisted of a small group of functionaries loyal personally to Mao. The "proletarian headquarters" was proclaimed the "sole leading organ of the entire Party, the entire Army and the entire Country.

**Constitution of 1975**

On 18 January 1975, the official communique announced that the session of the Fourth People's Congress was held from 13 to 17 January and passed a resolution expressing the conviction that China could be built into a powerful modern socialist country in another twenty years or so. Nothing was said about the revision of the Constitution in the official communique, but in the news trickling out through diplomatic sources and the Soviet Press it was revealed that the New Constitution had been passed. The first authoritative comment on the new Constitution appeared in *Pravda* on February 5, 1975 and it was reproduced in the *Soviet Review*.

The 1975 Constitution, it was pointed out, enhanced the role of the people and legalised the structure of the State set-up that functioned during the last decade. The Chairman of the Chinese Communist Party was to be the Commander-in-Chief of the Armed Forces, in- cluding the Militia, and that many State, Party and military posts could be simultaneously held by the same persons. The ''revolutionary committees'' were put on a constitutional basis and were invested with the functions of the common organs of the local people's assemblies. They were also given power to appoint the chairmen of courts and relieve them of their posts.

The Preamble to the Constitution of 1975 embodied the philosophy of the Constitution. It explicitly affirmed the principle of direct Party rule which had been paralysed during the Cultural Revolution and the following years. It clearly defined the existing social order and made explicit its ideological principles. In the end, it appealed to the people of all nationalities ''to unite to win still greater victories.''

The 1975 Constitution itself recognised the leading role of the Communist Party and stated with unmistakable clarity that the Communist Party of China was the ''core of the leadership of the whole Chinese people''. The Constitution also declared that the working class ''exercised leadership over the State through its vanguard, the Communist Party of China''; the National People's Congress was ''the highest organ of State power under the leadership of the Communist Party, the National People's Congress appointed and removed the Premier of the State Council and the members of the State Council on the proposal of the Central Committee of the Communist Party of China. Thus, the 1975 Constitution explicity affirmed the principle of centralised and direct Party rule over the Government and the Armed Forces which included Militia as well. The Constitution abolished the office of the Chairman of the Republic.

The striking feature of the Fundamental Rights incorporated in Chapter IV was that the Constitution conceded to the people the freedom of procession and the freedom of strike. The Constitution also omitted certain duties earlier prescribed by the 1954 Constitution, for example, to uphold the discipline at work, to keep public order and to respect social ethics.

**The Constitution of 1978**

Within three years of the existence of 1975 Constitution the National People's Congress was presented on March 1, 1978 with the draft of the revised Constitution which made provision of China's ambitious modernization plans. The draft Constitution also called for ''consolidating the socialist economic base'',, and ''developing the production forces at high speed''. This process, it was claimed, necessitated changes in the Articles of the 1975 Constitution covering State organs and personnel, and in order to give full play to socialist democracy to arouse the ''socialist enthusiasms of the people of all the nationalities to strive for the fulfilment of the central task for the new period.''

The fifth National People's Congress adopted on 3 March, 1978, the new Constitution. The Preamble to the Constitution was a thesis in Mao Tse-tung's leadership and his achievements. The 1978 Constitution for the first time highlighted the role of the Army by providing (Article 19) that the Chinese Liberation Army ''is the workers' and peasants' own armed force led by the Communist Party of China''. It was ''the pillar of the dictateorship of the proletariat'' commanded by the Chairman of the Central Committee of the Communist Party. The State devoted major efforts to the revolutionization and modernization of the Chinese Liberation Army, and strengthening the building of militia. Article 58 imposed ''The lofty duty'' of every citizen to defend the Motherland and resist aggression. The fundamental task of the armed forces was to safeguard the socialist revolution and socialist construction, to defend the sovereignty, territorial integrity and security of the State and to guard against subversion and aggression ''by social imperialism, imperialists and their lackeys.''

The Bill of Rights embodied in the Constitution was impressive as it embraced the political, social, cultural and economic life of the citizens. The Constitution expressed these Rights in absolute and unqualified terms. But the real position was different. All the Chinese people did not enjoy all the freedoms enshrined in the Constitution. There were categories of people who were ''non- people. This point was elaborated by MaoTse-tung himself. He declared that there were certain categories of people, such as ''the henchmen of imperialism, the landlord class, the bureaucratic capitalists as well as the reactionary clique of the Kuomingtang" who were 'non-people'. The law clearly prohibited the imperialists, the feudalists and the bureaucrats to exercise the right to vote and stand for election.

Another striking feature of the Constitution was that citizens enjoyed freedom of procession, demonstration and the freedom to strike, and had the right to "speak out freely, air their views fully, hold great debates and write high-character posters." But neither of these freedoms could he exercised against the constitutionally established ideology of the socialist State based upon Marxism-Leninism-Maoism thought.

The Constitution precisely defined the ideological basis by upholding the leading position of the Marxism-Leninism-Mao Tse-tung thought in all spheres of ideology and cultures. Art and culture, the Constitution prescribed, must be socialist culture- oriented based upon Marxism-Leninism-Mao Tse-tung thought.

All organs of State were required to maintain close contact with the masses of the people, rely upon them, heed their opinions, be concerned with their weal and woe, streamline administration, practise economy, raise efficiency and combat bureaucracy. Article 16 of the Constitution set the norms, and prescribed that the personnel of organs of State should earnestly study Marxism-Leninism-Mao Tse-tung thought wholeheartedly; serve the people; endeavour to perfect their professional competence, take an active part in collective productive labour; accept supervision by the masses; be models in observing the Constitution and law; correctly implement the policies of the State; seek the truth from facts and must not have recourse to seek personal gain.

The National People's Congress was the highest organ of State power and all authority emanated from it. It was both a legislative and Constituent Assembly; supervised the enforcement of the Constitution and Laws; decided on the choice of the Premier on the recommendation of the Central Committee of the Communist Party and on the choice of members of the State Council on the recommendation of the Premier; elected the President of the Supreme Court and Chief Procurator; examined and approved the economic plans, the State budget and the final state accounts; decided the question of war and peace and exercised such other functions as the National People's Congress deemed necessary.

Since the Congress met in session only once in a year, the Constitution provided for a Standing Committee to act and function on its behalf. It was the permanent acting body of the Congress. The Chairman of the Standing Committee performed all those functions which prior to 1975 belonged to the Chairman of the Republic; the office since abolished. The State Council composed of the Premier, the Vice-Premiers, the Ministers and the Ministers heading the Commissions, was the organ of state power. It was the highest organ of State administration entrusted with the duty to see the proper implementation of the policy decisions it determined through the administrative departments and agencies into which the central administration was divided.

The role of the judiciary was given minor significance and it took only three Articles to describe it including the People's procuratorates. For the whole Republic there was the Supreme People's Procuratorate entrusted with the duty of exercising procuratorial authority to ensure observance of the Constitution and law by all departments under the State Council, the local organs of the State at various levels, the personnel of the organs of the State and the citizens.

## SUGGESTED READINGS

Endicott, John E. and Heaton, W.R., *The Politics of East Asia : China, Japan, Korea.*

Misra, Kalpana, *From Post-Maoism to Post-Marxism.*

Moore, Barrington, Jr., *Social Origins of Dictatorship and Dictatorship.*

Skocpol, Theda, *States and Social Revolutions.*

Waller, Derek J., *The Government and Politics of the People's Republic of China.*

# CHAPTER II

# The Constitution of 1982

## Change of Policy

The Third Session of the Fifth National People's Congress that concluded its deliberations in the first week of December 1980 was momentous as a process to streamline and strengthen the institutional framework that had begun after Mao's death. It strongly reflected the deep-felt concern of the present leadership to ensure that China would not in future be rocked by political eruptions of the kind that occurred under Mao, with disastrous consequences to the country's development and the Party's morals. Retreat from the Cultural Revolution of the sixties was presented to the outside world in soft and undazzling language, although by then mopping up of the movement was common knowledge and shifts in policies emerging from the deliberations of the Fifth National Congress were the culmination of that process.

The Central Committee of the Communist Party headed by Hua Guofeng, who was also the Prime Minister, determined "new political norms and principles," four in number : to separate Government and Party posts and thereby to end the concentration of too much power to individual leaders; to consolidate the concept of collective leadership; to induct relatively younger men into responsible positions to pave the way for orderly transition in future; and to end the practice of life-long political vocation for ageing leaders. In conformity with these norms and principles Hua announced in the National People's Congress his own resignation from the post of the Prime Minister along with seven Vice-Premiers. He retained his Party post as its Chairman and the Chief of the Party's Military Commission. The seven Vice-Premiers, who too had resigned also retained their Party posts.

The emphasis on decentralisation and liberalisation of the economy was also evident in the deliberations of the National People's Congress. This was again an unmistakable departure from the past line. The pragmatic acceptance of the realities of commodity economy and "responding to the needs of the market" in Hua's speech would have been unthinkable in Mao's time. Two changes in this respect were significant. The first was the introduction of a systematic taxation scheme which covered not only joint ventures started with Chinese and foreign investment in the process of modernization, but also the individual citizens. The second was the new citizenship law which banned dual nationality, except in cases where (as in Vietnam) a person was forced to adopt foreign nationality. This change ran counter to the basic Chinese understanding of the status of those born to Chinese parents irrespective of the place of birth. Every overseas Chinese was entitled so far to keep Chinese nationality in addition to his local status.

China's new socialist economy was to have a big place for the private sector. This was indicated by Xue Muqiao, adviser to the State Planning Commission and Director of the Economic Research Institute. He said at a seminar attended by businessmen and diplomats from several countries that China needed "a multi-faceted economy which includes a private sector" and "joint- socialist-private enterprise in which public stock would be owned by workers." The private sector's role had so far been confined largely to small individual enterprises mostly ethnic overseas Chinese. Xue Muqiao explained that private capital should "cover the holes" in the socialist systems. He did not spell out the "holes," but it was made amply clear that large and small private sector and joint enterprises would help to spur China's modernisation.

In this process of modernization the problem of population figured prominently and in order to restrict its growth, the National People's Congress in 1980, passed a new marriage law raising the age of marriage to 22 for males and

20 for females from 20 and 18 respectively, and also made it a duty for the married to practise family planning. The law, however, was not binding on the minorities, and much younger marriages.

**Draft of the 1982 Constitution**

The National Constitutional Revision Committee adopted a new draft of the Constitution of the People's Republic of China on April 21, 1982. The Revision Committee, presided over by Peng Zhen, Vice-Chairman of the Committee, reviewed, for ten days, article by article a revised draft of the Constitution submitted by the Committee's Secretariat, held discussion and made changes therein. The session of the Committee adopted a proposal that the draft be submitted to the Standing Committee of the National People's Congress for deliberations and approval before it was made public for nationwide discussion.

The Standing Committee at its 23rd Session that opened on April 22, 1982 considered the revised draft of the Constitution consisting of a preamble and four chapters containing 140 articles. The greatest change in the draft constitution was the reinstatement of a Chairman of the People's Republic and the establishment of a Central Military Council of the People's Republic to lead the armed forces of the country. The draft constitution as approved by the Standing Committee was made public for nationwide discussion, a usual practice both in China and U.S.S.R. One cannot possibly say with certainty the extent of amendments to the draft constitution emerging out of the nationwide discussion and the number and nature of the suggested amendments that were finally accepted by the National People's Congress.

**The New Constitution**

The draft constitution was adopted on December 4, 1982 by the Fifth National People's Congress at its Fifth session. It is fourth in the series; three in 1954, 1975 and 1978 preceding it. With the lone exception of Thailand, China has had more Constitutions than any other Asian country. The 1954 Constitution wore a transitional outlook and was to be basically amended once China had fully moved from the period of people's democracy to socialism. China had not moved to socialism both in 1975 and 1978 when it had new Constitutions. Nor has the fourth adopted in 1982. It acknowledges its achievement. It firmly pronounces that in some respects China has to continue within the framework of people's democracy and cannot hastily advance on the socialist path. The Preamble made this important aspect amply clear. It stated that under the leadership of the Communist Party and the guidance of Marxism-Leninism and Mao Zedong thought, the people of all nationalities will adhere to the people's democratic dictatorship and follow the socialist road, "steadily improve socialist institutions, develop socialist democracy, and improve, socialist legal system and work hard and self-reliantly to modernize industry, agriculture, national defence and science and technology step by step to turn China into a socialist country with a high level of culture and democracy."

This is a sharp break with the Constitution of 1975 which had spelled out a radical framework for the socialist development. In fact, it is denunciation of Maoism as is evident from the speech of Peng Zhen, Vice-Chairman of the Constitutional Revision Committee that he made at the 23rd Session of the Standing Committee of the National People's Congress. While explaining the principal points of the revised drafts he said, "since the founding of the People's Republic, China has had three Constitutions: the 1954 document was comprehensive in content, while 1975 and 1978 documents, restricted by the historical conditions at that time, were undesirable."[1]

**Constitution as a Document**

The 1982 Constitution, unlike its predecessor constitutions, is quite comprehensive and contains 138 Articles. The Constitution of 1954 contained 106 Articles though it was a transitional constitution. The Constitution of 1975 was the briefest in the series with 30 Articles in all. The 1978 Constitution contained 60 Articles, besides a lengthy Preamble. The pattern of the 1982 document differs from its predecessors in another respect and it is important to mark a break with the past. The Chapter on Fundamental Rights and Duties of Citizens constituted the penultimate chapter in the Constitutions of 1954, 1975 and 1978 whereas in the 1982 Constitution it gets a place of precedence as Chapter Two, before Chapter Three, describing the structure of the State and it is in consonance with the practice in the Western democratic countries.

The 1982 Constitution aimed at righting the

1. Preamble to the Constitution of the People's Republic of China, 1954, p. 134.

wrongs of the Cultural Revolution (1966-1976), setting the country on the path of stability and modernization, and granting the Chinese citizens extensive freedoms and rights which are positive in essence and favourably compare with the Bill of Rights in Western democracies. The Constitution legitimises the guidelines and principles formulated since 1978 to develop a socialist democracy and legal system and reverses the effect of the Cultural Revolution which was characterised by social turbulence, economic decline and violation of people's "democratic rights." The provisions of the Constitution promote an active, stable and unified political system. Peng Zhen, Vice Chairman of the Constitutional Revision Committee, in a report to the National People's Congress, which adopted the document on December 4, 1982, said that the new Constitution "sums up the historical experience of China's socialist development, reflects the common will and fundamental interests of all nationalities in the country, conforms to the situation in China and meets the needs of socialist modernization."

The needs of social modernization are stated in the Preamble to the Constitution: "The basic task of the nation in the years to come is to concentrate its efforts on socialist modernization." The Chinese People, the Preamble adds, are determined to work hard and self-reliantly to modernize industry, agriculture, national defence, and science and technology "step by step to turn China into a socialist country with a high level of culture and democracy."

The Preamble also stresses that China follows an independent foreign policy based on mutual respect and territorial integrity, mutual non-aggression, non-interference in each other's internal affairs, equality and mutual benefit, and peaceful co-existence through developing diplomatic relations and economic and cultural exchanges. "China consistently opposes imperialism, hegemonism and colonialism, works to strengthen unity with the people of other countries, supports the oppressed nations and the developing countries in their just struggle to win and preserve national independence and develop their national economies, and strives to safeguard world peace and promote the cause of human progress."

**General Principles**

Following the introductory section, constituting the Preamble, is the first chapter—"General Principles"—whose Articles cover the stipulations on the nature of the State.

The first Article in the Constitution states: "The People's Republic of China is a socialist State under the people's democratic dictatorship led by the working class and based on the alliance of workers and peasants." A people's democratic dictatorship, Peng Zhen explained, "means that the State practises democracy among the greatest number of people while narrowing the target of dictatorship to just a handful of people (forces and elements which are hostile to, and try to undermine the socialist system). Article 1, therefore, contains the provision that the socialist system is the basic system of the People's Republic of China and "sabotage of the socialist system by any organization or individual is prohibited."

Here is a break between the earlier Constitutions and the Constitution of 1982. The precise definition of the Chinese State had varied in each Constitution. All had included the phrase that the system was "led by the working class and based on the alliance of the peasants and workers," but in the 1954 Constitution the State was a "people's democratic State" and in the 1975 and 1978 Constitutions it was "the dictatorship of the proletariat." Another significant departure from the 1978 Constitution is on the role of the Communist Party of China. Article 2 of the 1978 Constitution stated: "The Communist Party is the core of leadership of the whole Chinese people. The working class exercises leadership over the State through its vanguard, the Communist Party." The 1982 Constitution omitted this provision altogether and there is no mention of the Party in the Constitution except in the Preamble.

Article 3 of the 1982 Constitution introduces a new element that did not exist in the earlier Constitutions. It provides that the National People's Congress and the local congresses at different levels are instituted through democratic election. They are responsible to people and subject to their supervision. All administrative, judicial and procuratorial organs are created by the people's Congresses to which they are responsible and under whose supervision they operate. The division of functions and powers between the central and local organs is guided by the principle of giving full play to the initiative and enthusiasm of the local authorities under the unified leadership of the Central authorities.

The People's Republic of China is a single multinational State. There are 56 nationalities and Article 4 declares that all nationalities are equal.

Discrimination against and oppression of any nationality are prohibited. Any acts that undermine the unity of the nationalities or instigate their secession are legally banned. The people of all nationalities have the freedom to use and develop their own spoken and written languages, and to reform their "own ways and customs."

On the reunification of China, the Chapter on General Principles contains an Article (31), stating: "The State may establish special administrative regions when necessary. The systems to be instituted in special administrative regions shall be prescribed by law enacted by the National People's Congress in the light of the specific conditions." The Preamble to the Constitution enjoins a "lofty duty of the entire Chinese people including our compatriots in Taiwan, to accomplish the great task of of reunifying the motherland." After reunification with the mainland, according to Peng Zhen, Taiwan can enjoy a high degree of self-government as a special administrative region. "This power of self-government means, among other things, that the present social and economic system in Taiwan, its way of life and its economic and cultural relations with foreign countries will remain unchanged."

The General Principles also codify the new economic policies formulated and practised since 1978 to promote socialist modernization. The Constitution re-affirms public ownership of the means of production as the basis of China's socialist economic system, and calls for the development of diverse economic forms—state, collective and individual—while upholding the authority of the state sector. Though the socialist ownership is stressed, the Constitution also allows for the coordinated growth of the national economy through a comprehensive balancing of a planned economy with the supplementary role played by market supply and demand. In views of the past excessive and rigid control over planning and administration, the Constitution sets forth varying decision-making powers to state and collective owned enterprises in operation and management.

In order to accelerate the process of modernization and consistent with the new socialist economy as stated by Xue Muqiao, Adviser to the State Planning Commission, private sector is to have a big place now. "We need," he declared "a multi-faceted economy which includes a private sector," and "joint- socialist-private enterprise in which public stock would be owned by workers." Article 18 of the General Principles provides that China permits foreign enterprises, other foreign economic organisations and individual foreigners to invest in China and to enter into various forms of economic co-operation with Chinese enterprises and other economic organisations in accordance with the law of China. All such foreign economic enterprises as well as joint ventures with Chinese and foreign investment located in China, shall abide the law of China and, at the same time, their lawful rights and interests shall be duly protected.

On the philosophical side, a salient feature of the 1982 Constitution, is the increase in Articles on "socialist spiritual civilization," which according, to Peng Zhen, is manifested in higher education, scientific and cultural level, and in higher ideological, political and moral standards. Article 24 specifies: "The State strengthens the building of socialist civilization through spreading education in higher ideals and morality, general education and education in discipline and the legal system, and through promoting the formulation and observance of rules of conduct and common pledges by different sections of the people in urban and rural areas."

This Article stipulates that the State advocates the civic virtues of love of the motherland and it educates the people in patriotism, collectivism, internationalism and communism and in dialectical and historical materialism. The Article also stipulates opposition to "capitalism, feudalist and other decadent ideas."

Included, as well, in the Chapter on General Principles, is a section in Article 2 which stipulates that all power in China belongs to the people, and that the people will administer State affairs and manage economic, cultural and social affairs in accordance with the law. In the aftermath of the Cultural Revolution and in the light of experience, China has restored to the Constitution not only what was relevant on the fundamental rights of citizens in the 1954 Constitution (rights omitted in the next two constitutions of 1975 and 1978) but made these provisions more specific and comprehensive.

During the Cultural Revolution people were arrested at will, placed on secret trial and given arbitrary sentences. Since 1976 after Mao's death, and especially since 1978, China has formulated new criminal and procedural laws and regulations to develop democratic processes and improve the legal system. All such measures are now enshrined in the Constitution and dignity of the Constitution and law is required to be preserved at all levels. No organisation or individual does enjoy the privilege of being above the Constitution and law. Article 5 states: "All State organs, the armed forces, all political parties and public organizations and all enterprises and undertakings must abide by the Constitution and the law. "All acts in violation of the Constitution and the law must be looked into."

Article 9 of the 1978 Constitution provided that the State protected the right of citizens to own lawfully earned income, savings, houses and other means of livelihood. The 1982 Constitution inserts a new provision in the right to property. Article 13 guarantees "by law the right of citizens to inherit private property." Inheritance of property does not fit into the Marxian concept of socialism, but the People's Republic of China also permits existence of capitalist enterprises, and invites investment of foreign capital and protects both by law.

The Chinese constitution of 1982 established the supremacy of Dengist concept of governance. It retains the primacy of the Communist Party at the state level but sheds the ideological assumption of a command economy. Mao as a person is still revered but his ideological legacy has been largel repudiated. China today has constructed an edifice of Capitalism within the frame work of a communist party-led state structure, still dominated by the Chinese Communist Party.

# CHAPTER III

# Fundamental Rights and Duties of Citizens

The 1982 Constitution incorporates in Chapter Two an impressive list of Fundamental Rights and quite a few of them do not exist even in the Constitutions of some democratic countries of the West. The Chapter on Fundamental Rights also presents a discernible difference from the previous Constitutions. Fundamental Rights, in the earlier Constitutions, were relegated to a secondary position and were incorporated in the penultimate Chapter. They were also scanty in their content. The number of Articles in the Chapter on Fundamental Rights and Duties in the 1982 Constitution is 24 as compared to 16 in the 1978 Constitution. The newly-added contents which stress citizens' fundamental rights include: all citizens are equal before the law; personal dignity of citizens is inviolable. Insult or slander against any form is prohibited; extra-legal detention of citizens, or extra-legal deprivation or restrictions of citizens' freedom of persons by other means, is prohibited; and the freedom and privacy of correspondence of citizens are protected by law.

For the first time, rights of citizens are constitutionally rendered inseparable from their duties. Every citizen enjoys the rights guaranteed by the Constitution and law and simultaneously it is his duty to abide by the Constitution and law and respect the rights of his fellow citizen. Another innovation included in the fundamental rights is the duty of the State and society to ensure the livelihood of the retired personnel. The State and society also help to make arrangements for the work, livelihood and education of the blind, deaf-mutes, and other handicapped persons. Marriage, the family and child are protected by the State. Both husband and wife have the duty to practise family planning. Whereas it is the duty of parents to rear and educate their children likewise it is the duty of children to support and assist their parents. Violation of the freedom of marriage is prohibited. Maltreatment of old people, women and children is also prohibited.

**Right to Equality**

Article 33 defines citizenship. All persons holding the nationality of the People's Republic of China are citizens of China and they are equal before the law without any discrimination of nationality, race, sex, occupation, family background, religious belief, education, property status, or length of residence. Equally, all citizens who enjoy rights must perform the duties prescribed by the Constitution and the law. Rights and duties are, therefore, inseparable and they go together for all citizens of the People's Republic of China.

**Political Rights**

All citizens who have reached the age of 18 have the right to vote and seek election to any office of a State organ, regardless of nationality, race, sex, occupation, family background, religious belief, education, property status or length of residence except persons deprived of political rights according to law. Article 18 of the 1978 Constitution specifically deprived of political rights, as prescribed by law, those landlords, rich peasants and reactionary capitalists who had not yet been reformed. Article 35 of the 1982 Constitution does not specify ineligibility of a particular category of persons. It is to be determined by law. A similar provision existed in Article 85 of the 1954 Constitution.

In addition to the basic freedoms deemed as the pillars of democracy, the 1978 Constitution conferred on the citizens the freedom "to strike" and "have the right to speak out freely, air their views fully, hold great debates and write big-character-posters". The Constitution of 1982 went a little ahead conferred on the citizens the freedom of speech, of the press, of assembly of the association and also the right to procession and demonstration.[1]

1. Article 87 of the 1954 Constitution also conferred the right to freedom of procession and freedom of demonstration.

But all these freedoms are not absolute, although there is no specific provision in Article 35 itself that may restrict the enjoyment of the basic freedoms. Article 51 of the Constitution, itself a fundamental right, however, imposes broad limitations on the enjoyment of all kinds of rights irrespective of their contents. It stipulates: "The exercise by citizens of the People's Republic of China of their freedoms and rights may not infringe upon the interests of the state, of society and of the collective, or upon the lawful freedoms and rights of other citizens." If the provisions of Article 51 are coupled with Article 28 of Chapter one—the General Principles—the precise position with respect to enjoyment of basic rights and freedom becomes self-evident. It states: "The state maintains public order and suppresses treasonable and other counter-revolutionary activities; it penalizes actions that endanger public security and disrupt the socialist economy and other criminal activities, and punishes and reforms criminals." The phrase "criminal activities" is all-embracing and may take cognisance of any activity which may be deemed criminal in the context of expediency of circumstances. And when the State undertakes to reform criminals, they are essentially the persons who are deemed criminals according to the prevailing political climate in the country.

Nothing can, therefore, be said, spoken or demonstrated against the socialist state under the people's democratic dictatorship. The Preamble enjoins on the Chinese people of all nationalities that under the leadership of the Communist Party and the guidance of Marxism-Leninism and Mao Zedong Thought to continue to adhere to the people's democratic dictatorship and follow the socialist road. The Preamble ends by exhorting "The people of all nationalities, all state organs, the armed forces, all political parties and public organizations and all enterprises and undertakings in the country" to "take the Constitution as the basic norm of conduct, and they have the duty to uphold the dignity of the Constitution and ensure its implementation."

There was a democratic ferment in China when widespread students' demonstrations swept the country in the first week of December 1986. The students demanded more democratisation and more reforms. Deng Xiaoping regime was certainly more democratic than its predecessor and there was an awareness on the part of Chinese leadership of the need for democratisation. But the Chinese leadership was in no mood to accept and launch another revolutionary movement at that juncture when Deng's economic reforms had met with severe criticism from the conservative elements in the Communist Party of China. The Government, therefore, promulgated stringent regulations, banning '*inter alia*' unannounced demonstrations and the putting up of unsigned posters in public places. The penalty for violation of the ban was a stiff five-year imprisonment. But the students not only succeeded in defying the ban, they also secured the release of demonstrators who were arrested. What made the movement significant was the fact that the students agitating for democracy and freedom, had succeeded in securing support from a section of the Chinese bureaucracy.

**Freedom of Religious Belief**

Citizens of China enjoy freedom of religious belief. No state organ, public organisation or individual may compel citizens to believe in, or not to believe in, any religion. Nor may they discriminate against citizens who believe in, or do not believe in, any religion. The State protects normal religious activities of all denominations. But no one may make use of religion to engage in activities that disrupt public order, impair the health of citizens or interfere with the educational system of the State. Religious bodies and religious affairs are not subject to any foreign domination.

There is enough available evidence now that freedom of religious belief in China was sufficiently curtailed till recently. The wholesale persecution of Chinese Muslims evoked widespread resentment among Muslims of the world. Christians and Buddhists (or Lamaists), too had been subjected to more or less the same treatment. The campaign against counter-revolutionaries was linked in 1951 with an intensive programme to subordinate religion to the State. In March 1951 a ruthless drive against Taoist societies and Christian missionaries was launched. Since 1979, however, various religions have gained a measure of toleration for their religious practices. Temples and mosques have been re-opened after being closed since the start of the Cultural Revolution. The ethnic upheaval and simultaneous rise of fundamentalism culminating into the disintegration of the Soviet Socialist Republics has made a sea-change in the policy and attitude of the Chinese Communist rulers towards ethnic minorities, their religion and culture.

**Inviolability of Person and Home**

Articles 37 and 39 deal with the inviolability of the person and home of a citizen, Article 37 guarantees the freedom "of person of citizens." No citizen may be arrested except with the approval or by decision of a people's procuratorate, which is reponsible for legal supervision, or by decision of a people's court, and arrests must be made by a public security organ. Unlawful deprivation of citizens' freedom of person by detention or other means is prohibited as also the unlawful search of the person of citizens. This extra-legal detention of citizens, or extra legal deprivation or restriction of citizens' freedom of person by other means is an improvement on Article 47 of the 1978 Constitution. It did not also provide for prohibition of unlawful search of the person of citizen.

Article 39 guarantees the inviolability of the home of citizens. Unlawful search of, or intrusion into, a citizen's home is prohibited.

**Personal Dignity of Citizens**

Another newly added Article in the Chapter on Fundamental Rights is the personal dignity of citizens. Article 38 makes the personal dignity of citizens inviolable and prohibits insult, libel, false charge or "frame-up" directed against citizens by any means or form.

**Privacy of Correspondence**

The freedom and privacy of correspondence of citizens are protected and it is another newly added provision that did not exist in the earlier Constitutions. Article 40 provides that the freedom and privacy of correspondence of citizens are protected by law. No organisation or individual may, on any ground, infringe upon the freedom and privacy of citizens' correspondence. But this right is not absolute. It is provided that public security or procuratorial organs are permitted to censor correspondence, in accordance with procedures prescribed by law, in order to meet the needs of State security or of investigation into criminal offences.

**Right to Criticise**

Citizens have the right to criticise and make suggestions to any State organs or functionary. They have also the right to make to relevant State organs complaints and charges against, or exposures of, any State organ or functionary for violation of the law or dereliction of duty. But fabrication or distortion of facts for the purpose of libel or frame-up is prohibited.

The State organ concerned must deal with complaints, charges or exposures made by citizens "in a responsible manner after ascertaining the facts." No one may suppress such complaints, charges and exposures or retaliate against the citizens making them. Citizens who have suffered losses through infringement of their civic rights by any State organ or functionary have the right to compensation in accordance with the law.

**Right to Work**

Article 48 of the 1978 Constitution provided that citizens had the right to work and to ensure that they enjoyed this right. The State would provide employment in accordance with the principle of overall consideration, and, on the basis of increased production, the State would gradually increase payment for labour, improve working conditions, strengthen labour protection and expand collective welfare. The 1982 Constitution renders work both the right as well as the duty. It places more emphasis on duty and holds work as "the glorious duty of every able bodied citizen." All working people in State enterprises and in urban and rural economic collectives are enjoined to perform their tasks with an attitude consonant with their status "as masters of the country." The State promotes socialist labour emulation, and commends and rewards model and advanced workers. The State also encourages citizens to take part in voluntary labour in order to inculcate in them the spirit of patriotism and dedication to the motherland.

In order to ensure the enjoyment of the right to work, the State provides necessary vocational training to citizens before they are employed and using various channels creates conditions for employment, strengthens labour protection, improves working conditions and, on the basis of expanded production, increases remuneration for work and social benefits.

The concept of socialist emulation was borrowed from the erstwhile USSR Constitution and it means the mass movement of working people for higher productivity. A socialist society, it is explained, cannot achieve the desired results unless labour is imbued with socialist ideas and a socialist mind. The workers must exhibit a sense of duty in their work and, therefore, it contradicts the right to procession and demonstration as provided in Article 35.

**Right to Rest**

Closely allied to the right and duty to work is the right to rest which is concomitant to socialist labour discipline and achievement of high productivity. The State, accordingly, provides and expands facilities for rest and recuperation of working people, and prescribes working hours and vacations for workers and staff.

**Right to Retirement**

The State prescribes by law the system of retirement for workers and staff in enterprises and undertakings and for functionaries of organs of State. The livelihood of retired personnel is ensured by the State and society. Earlier Constitutions did not provide for retirement and a guaranteed livelihood for retired personnel.

**Right to Material Assistance**

Citizens have the right to material assistance from the State and society when they are old, ill or disabled. The State develops the social insurance, social relief and medical and health services that are required to enable citizens to enjoy the right to material assistance. The State and society ensure the livelihood of disabled members of the armed forces, provide pensions to the families of martyrs and give preferential treatment to the families of military personnel. Article 50 of the 1978 Constitution did not provide for the preferential treatment to families of military personnel. Similarly, it only ensured the livelihood for the families of martyrs. Article 45 of the 1982 Constitution provides for pensions to such families.

This Article also provides that the State and society help in making arrangements for the work, livelihood and education of the blind, deaf-mutes and other handicapped citizens. There was no similar provision in the earlier Constitutions.

**Right to Education and Research**

Citizens have the duty as well as the right to receive education and the State promotes the all-round moral, intellectual and physical development of children and young people. Article 51 of the 1978 Constitution simply provided that the citizen had the right to education and did not prescribe it a duty as well. Duty to receive education implies that parents must compulsorily send their children to schools to receive education.

Citizens also enjoy the freedom to engage themselves in scientific research, literary and artistic creation and other cultural pursuits. The State encourages and assists creative endeavour conducive to the interests of the people that are made by citizens engaged in education, science, technology, literature, art and other cultural work.

**Equality of Women**

Women in the People's Republic of China enjoy equal rights with men in all spheres of life, political, economic, cultural and social, including family life. The State protects the rights and interests of women, applies the principle of equal pay for equal work for men and women alike and trains and selects cadres from among women.

**Protection of Marriage and Family**

Marriage, the family and mother and child are protected by the State. Both husband and wife have the duty to practise family planning. Article 53 of the Constitution of 1978, provided that the State advocates and encourages family planning. The 1982 Constitution makes it a constitutional duty both for husband and wife to practise family planning.

Parents have the duty to rear and educate their minor children, and children who have come of age have the duty to support and assist their parents. This guaranteed duty of parents and children is more or less identical to the provisions of the 1977 Constitution of the USSR. Citizens in Soviet Russia are obliged to concern themselves with the upbringing of children, to train them for socially useful work, and to raise them as worthy members of a socialist society. Likewise, it is the duty of children to care for their parents and help them.

Another innovation provided by Article 49 of the 1982 Constitution of the People's Republic of China is that it prohibits violation of freedom of marriage and maltreatment of old people, women and children. Even the 1977 Constitution of the USSR did not provide for prohibiting the maltreatment of old people, women and children.

**Rights of Chinese Nationals**

Article 50 protects the legitimate rights and interests of Chinese nationals living abroad and lawful rights and interests of returned overseas Chinese and of the family members of Chinese nationals residing abroad. The protection of the lawful rights and interests of returned overseas Chinese is in pursuance of the new citizenship law (1980) which bans dual nationality, except in cases where (as in Vietnam) a person is forced to adopt foreign nationality.

**Interests of the State**

The exercise by citizens of their freedoms and rights may not infringe upon the interests of the State, of society and of collective, or upon the lawful freedoms and rights of other citizens. Such categorical prohibition did not exist in the earlier Constitutions.

## FUNDAMENTAL DUTIES

Every right has a corresponding obligation or duty. Without duties there can be no rights. A valid claim is both a right and duty. Harold Laski aptly said, ''He that will not perform functions cannot enjoy rights any more than he who will not work ought to enjoy work.'' Without corresponding obligations the whole concept of rights becomes meaningless. As the State, acting through the government, maintains and coordinates rights, it is the duty of every citizen to help the government in realizing the purpose of the State for which it exists. This means that a citizen owes a duty to the State as organised in government. That is the theory of rights.

The 1982 Constitution of the People's Republic of China constitutionalised the basic principle of rights by providing in Article 33 that every ''citizen enjoys the rights and at the same time must perform the duties....'' The earlier Constitutions simply carried a list of duties incorporated in the Chapter on the Fundamental Rights and Duties of Citizens but neither of them categorically spelt out that rights and duties are inseparable and that a citizen enjoys the rights and at the same time performs the duties.

Apart from the Articles relating to fundamental rights where duties are specifically stated along with a particular right—Article 42 (the right as well as the duty to work), Article 46 (duty as well as the right to receive education), Article 49 (the duty to practise family planning), and Article 51 (in the exercise of rights a citizen may not infringe upon the interests of the State, of society and of the collective, or upon the lawful freedoms and rights of other citizens)—the Constitution prescribes the following duties for citizens.

### Unity of the Country

The foremost duty of every Chinese citizen is to safeguard the unity of the country and the unity of all its nationalities. The People's Republic of China is a multi-national State comprising fifty-six nationalities with their own distinct customs, beliefs, languages and mode of life. The people of all nationalities in China, says the Preamble to the Constitution, have jointly created ''a splendid culture and have a glorious revolutionary tradition.'' Both the victory of China's new-democratic revolution and the success of its socialist cause have been achieved by the Chinese people of all nationalities. In the struggle to safeguard the unity of the nationalities and as such of the country, ''it is necessary,'' the Preamble adds, ''to combat big-nation chauvinism, mainly Han chauvinism, and also necessary to combat local-national chauvinism.'' Discrimination against and oppression of any nationality and acts that undermine the unity of the nationalities or instigate their secession are prohibited[2]. The State, accordingly, suppresses treasonable and other counter-revolutionary activities, penalises actions that endanger public security and disrupt the socialist system.[3]

### To Abide by the Constitution

Article 53 enjoins on all citizens to abide by the Constitution and the law, keep State secrets, protect public property and observe labour discipline and public order and respect social ethics. China is a socialist State under the people's democratic dictatorship and it is the basic system of the country as manifested in the Constitution. Sabotage of the socialist system by any organisation or individual is prohibited.[4] All State organs, the armed forces, all political parties and public organisations and all enterprises and undertakings must abide by the Constitution. No organisation or individual is above the Constitution and the law.[5] The Constitution is the fundamental law of the State and it commands supreme legal authority. The citizens have, therefore, as the Preamble says, ''the duty to uphold the dignity of the Constitution and ensure its implementation.''

### To Safeguard the Honour of China

It is the duty of citizens of China to safeguard the security, honour and interests of the motherland. They must not commit acts detrimental to the security, honour and interests of the Motherland. The Preamble exhorts the Chinese people to fight against all forces and elements, both at home and abroad, that are hostile to China's socialist system and try to undermine it.

2. Article 4.
3. Article 28.
4. Article 1.
5. Article 5.

**Defence of the Motherland**

It is the sacred duty of every citizen of the People's Republic of China to defend the Motherland and resist aggression. It is the honourable duty of all citizens to perform military service and join the militia in accordance with the law. All able-bodied persons who are young and within the range of specified age limit, as prescribed by law, have the constitutional duty to perform military service both during peace and war time in order to keep the country prepared to meet aggression of any kind.

**To Pay Taxes**

It is the duty of citizens of the People's Republic of China to pay taxes in accordance with the law. Tax is a compulsory contribution by citizens to meet the expenditure of the State and there is no *quid pro quo* in it. It is the duty of every citizen to pay taxes, national and local, punctually and regularly to enable the government to perform its functions adequately, efficiently and effectively.

## SUGGESTED READINGS

Bannerji, Shibnath- *The Chinese Government and Politics*

Waller, Derek J. *The Government and Policies of the People's Republic of China.*

# CHAPTER IV

# The National People's Congress

### Highest Organ of State power

The National People's Congress is the highest organ of State power[1] and all authority of the People's Republic of China flows from it. Till 1982, it was the sole legislative authority of the country and now, according to the Constitution of 1982, it is exercised both by the National People's Congress and its Standing Committee[2] which is a permanently acting body. It amends the Constitution and supervises its implementation, elects the President and Vice-President of the Republic and recalls or removes them from office; decides on the choice of the Premier, Vice-Premiers, State Councillors, Ministers and the Auditor-General and Secretary-General of the State Council and recalls or removes them from office; elects the Chairman of the Military Commission and decides on the choice of other members of the Military Commission, elects the President of the Supreme Court, Procurator-General and recalls or removes from office all these incumbents; examines and approves national plans; examines and approves the State budget; alters or annuls improper decisions of the Standing Committee: approves the establishment of provinces, autonomous regions and municipalities directly under the Central Government; decides on the questions of war and peace, and exercises such other functions and powers as the highest organ of State power should exercise.[3] The Constitution, thus, confers on the National People's Congress unlimited powers and authority.

### A Unicameral Legislature

The National People's Congress is a unicameral legislature in a unitary multinational State. It is composed of deputies elected by provinces, autonomous regions and municipalities directly under the Central Government, and by the armed forces. All citizens of China who have reached the age of 18 years have the right to vote and stand for election, regardless of nationality, race, sex, occupation, family background, religious belief, education, property status, or length of residence except persons deprived of political rights according to law. The number of deputies and the manner of their election are prescribed by law.[4] All the minority nationalities are entitled to appropriate representation.[5] The total number of Deputies to the Fifth National People's Congress in 1983 approximated 3,300. In 1988 the membership approximated 2,700.[6]

Election of deputies is conducted by the Standing Committee of the National People's Congress for a term of five years. Two months before the expiration of the term of the Congress, the Standing Committee is required by the Constitution to ensure that the election of deputies to the succeeding National People's Congress is completed. Should exceptional circumstances prevent elections to the succeeding Congerss, it may be postponed by a decision of more than two-thirds majority vote of the number of members of the Standing Committee of the current People's Congress and its term extended. But elections to the succeeding National People's Congress must be completed within one year after the termination of such exceptional circumstances. The Constitution is silent on the nature of those exceptional circumstances.[7]

The National People's Congress meets

1. Article 57.
2. Article 58.
3. Articles 62 and 63.
4. Article 34.
5. Article 59.
6. The Fourth Congress had a total membership of 2,835 deputies.
7. Article 60.

once in a year and is convened by its Standing Committee. A session may be convened at any time the Standing Committee deems this necessary, or when more than one-fifth of the deputies so propose.[8] There is no provision in the 1982 Constitution, as it was in the earlier Constitutions, for advancement or postponement of a session.[9] It means that session of the Congress must now be convened once every year. When the Congress meets, it elects a Presidium. The organisation and working procedure of the Congress and its Standing Committee are prescribed by law.

**Privileges and Duties of Deputies**

No deputy may be arrested or placed on criminal trial without the consent of the Presidium of the current session of the National People's Congress or, when the Congress is not in session, with out the consent of its Standing Committee. Deputies may not be called to legal account for their speeches or votes at meeting of the People's National Congress.[10]

Article 76 provides that Deputies must play an exemplary role in abiding by the Constitution and the law and keeping State secrets and, in production and other work and their public activities, assist in the enforcement of the Constitution and the law. Deputies should maintain close contact with the units which selected them and with the people, listen to and convey to the appropriate organs the opinions and demands of the people and work hard to serve them. They are subject to the supervision of the units which elected them. The electoral units have the powers, through procedures prescribed by law, to recall deputies.

**Functions and Powers**

The National People's Congress exercises the following functions and powers:

(1) The Constitution amending power rests with the National People's Congress. Amendments to the Constitution may be proposed either by the Standing Committee of the National People's Congress or by more than one-fifth of the Deputies to the Congress. If the proposed amendment or amendments are adopted by two-thirds majority of all the Deputies, the Constitution stands amended.

The process of amendment has varied with each Constitution in the series. The Constitution of 1954 provided that a majority of two-thirds vote of all the Deputies was necessary for adopting a constitutional amendment. The 1975 Constitution substituted the two-thirds majority vote to a simple majority of the Deputies and the Constitution of 1978 even dropped this. It only provided that the Constitution would be amended by the National People's Congress. The 1982 Constitution restored the original majority of two-thirds as it existed in the 1954 Constitution.

The National People's Congress supervises the enforcement of the Constitution. The duty of upholding the dignity of the Constitution is so vital that the Constitution makes every organ of State authority to ensure its implementation. All acts in violation of the Constitution "must be looked into." The Constitution defines the "basic system and basic tasks of the state in legal form", it is, accordingly, the fundamental law of the State and has supreme legal authority.

(2) The National People's Congress enacts and amends basic statutes relating to criminal offences, civil affairs, the State organs and other matters on which the Congress may deem necessary and expedient to legislate. The power to legislate on subjects other than those mentioned above is exercised by the Standing Committee of the Congress. In the earlier Constitutions the National People's Congress possessed the sole authority to enact statutes. The law-making process consequently suffered enormously, particularly since 1965. The National People's Congress, because of its huge number of members and a brief session once in the year, and that, too, often postponed, gave just formal approval to the bills already formulated and as a result the Standing Committee had been performing the real act of legislation. This process has been legitimised under the 1982 Constitution. Enactment of statutes, with the exception of those which should be enacted by the National People's Congress, has been transferred to the Standing Committee of the Congress.

(3) The National People's Congress elects the President and the Vice-President of the Republic for a term of five years each. The offices of the President and the Vice-President were abolished by the 1975 Constitution. The 1982 Constitution restored both these offices which had existed under the 1954 Constitution.

8. The earlier Constitutions had no such provision.
9. Under the 1954 Constitution no session of the Congress was convened from 1964 to 1974.
10. Article 74.

(4) The Congress decides on the choice of the President of the Republic, and also decides on the choice of the Vice-Premiers, State Councillors, Ministers incharge of ministries or commissions. It has also the power to recall or remove from office all the aforesaid incumbents. The Standing Committee, however, decides, when the National People's Congress is not in session, on the choice of Ministers in charge of Ministries or Commissions upon nomination by the Premier.

(5) It elects the Chairman of the Central Military Commission and, upon the nomination by the Chairman, other members of the Commission. The Congress also recalls or removes from office all such incumbents. It also elects the President of the Supreme People's Court and the Procurator-General of the Supreme People's Procuratorate and may recall or remove them from office.

(6) The Congress examines and approves the plan for the national and social development, and the State Budget, and the reports on their respective implementation. It alters or annuls inappropriate decisions of the Standing Committee of the Congress. The Congress also approves the establishment of provinces, autonomous regions, and municipalities directly under the Central Government, and decides on the establishment of special administrative regions and the systems to be instituted there.

(7) Decisions on questions of war and peace are taken by the National People's Congress. But when the Congress is not in session the Standing Committee decides on the proclamation of state of war into the event of an armed attack on the country or in fulfillment of international treaty obligations concerning defence against aggression.

(8) Finally, there is a general provision vesting the National People's Congress with authority "to exercise such other functions and powers as the highest organ of state power should exercise." This power of the Congress is not bound by any limitation and may embrace any subject or matter.

Deputies to the National People's Congress have the right, in accordance with procedure prescibed by law, to submit bills and proposals within the scope of its functions and powers. The Deputies have also the right to address questions, in accordance with procedure prescribed by law, during the sessions of the Congress to the State Council or the ministries and commissions, "which must answer the questions in a responsible manner."[11]

The Congress establishes a Nationalities Committee, a Law Committee, a Financial and Economic Committee, an Education, Science, Culture and Public Health Committee, a Foreign Affairs Committee, an Overseas Chinese Committee and such other special Committees as are necessary. These special committees work under the direction of the Standing Committee when the Congress is not in session. The Special Committees examine, discuss and draw up relevant bills and draft resolutions under the direction of the Congress and its Standing Committee. The National People's Congress and its Standing Committee may, when they deem it necessary, appoint committees of inquiry into specific questions and adopt relevant resolutions in the light of their reports. All organs of State, public organisations and citizens concerned are under a constitutional obligation to supply the necessary information to those Committees of inquiry when they conduct investigation.[12]

## THE STANDING COMMITTEE

The Standing Committee of the National People's Congress is the permanent working organ of the Congress. As the Congress meets only once in a year and that too for a brief session, it appoints a committee to act on its behalf, during the interval preceding the next session of the Congress, in carrying out the powers and functions that the Constitution confers on it as the highest organ of State power. The Standing Committee, being the creature of the Congress that acts on its behalf, is constitutionally bound to submit a report to the Congress of all its actions and activities and is responsible to the Congress to all intents and purposes.[13] The Congress also alters or annuls inappropriate decisions of the Standing Committee. Hitherto the Standing Committee did not exercise legislative functions. The 1982 Constitution empowers it to enact or amend statutes with the exception of those which should be enacted by the National People's Congress.[14] This has been done to streamline administration and it was one of the significant innova-

11. Article 73.
12. Article 71.
13. Article 69.
14. Article 67(2).

tions that the framers of the 1982 Constitution had introduced. The other in this process is the provision that the National People's Congress must meet in session once in a year. No session of the Congress was convened between 1964 to 1974. Till the Constitution of 1982 became operative the session of the Congress could be "advanced or postponed."

**Composition and Organisation**

The Standing Committee is composed of the Chairman, the Vice-Chairmen, the Secretary-General and the members,[15] all told about 200 in number, and are elected by the Congress. Minority nationalities are entitled to appropriate representation on the Standing Committee. The term of the Standing Committee is five years, but the National People's Congress has the power to recall them from office. No one on the Standing Committee can hold any post in any of administrative, judicial or procuratorial organs of the State.

A significant feature of the 1982 Constitution is limiting the tenure of important State functionaries to two consecutive terms, thus, eliminating the *de facto* system of life-long tenures that had hitherto existed. Accordingly, the Chairman and the Vice-Chairmen of the Standing Committee can not serve for more than two consecutive terms.[16]

The Chairman of the Standing Committee convenes its meetings and presides over them. The Vice-Chairmen and the Secretary-General assist the Chairman in the performance of his functions.[17] Executive meetings of the Committee with the participation of the Chairman, the Vice-Chairmen and Secretary-General "handle the important day-to-day work" of the Committee.[18] The Standing Committee exercises its functions and powers until a new Standing Committee is elected by the succeeding National People's Congress.[19] The organisation and working procedure of the Committee are prescribed by law.

The office of the President of the Republic was abolished by the 1975 Constitution and the dignified functions of that office were vested in the Chairman of the Standing Committee. He performed the functions of receiving foreign diplomatic envoys, promulgated law and decrees, ratified treaties concluded with the foreign States and other ceremonial functions. With the restoration of the office of the President of the Republic by the 1982 Constitution, those powers have been taken back from the Chairman of the Standing Committee.

**Powers and Functions**

In Western democracies the function of interpreting the constitution which is written rests with the judiciary and the process is known as the judicial review. In the United States there is no direct authority in the Constitution which empowers the Supreme Court to declare the constitutionality of any act, federal or State, and interpret the Constitution. But Chief Justice Marshall declared in *Marbury* v. *Madison* (1803) that judicial review is a part of the constitutional law of the country and it is inherent in a written constitution. In India, the Constitution specifically provides for judicial review.

But in Communist countries, though the Constitutions are written, the judiciary is specifically debarred from interpreting the Constitution. In the People's Republic of Chian the power to interpret the Constitution is vested in the Standing Committee of the National People's Congress. The theory of separation of powers has no relevance in a Communist polity.

The Standing Committee shares with the National People's Congress the power to legislate. The National People's Congress enacts and amends the basic statutes and the nature of these basic statutes is explained in Article 62 (3) of the Constitution. With the exception of those Statutes "which should be enacted by the National People's Congress," the Standing Committee is competent to enact or amend on residuary matters. All those persons who are members of the Standing Committee, together with Deputies to the National People's Congress, have the right, in accordance with the procedures prescribed by law, to submit bills and proposals within the scope of the respective functions and powers of the National People's Congress and its Standing Committee. The Standing Committee can also propose amendments to the Constitution.

The Standing Committee enacts, when the National People's Congress is not in session,

15. Article 65.
16. Article 66.
17. Article 68.
18. *Ibid.*
19. Article 66.

partial supplements, and amendments to statutes enacted by the Congress provided that such partial supplements and amendments do not contravene the basic principles of these statutes. The Committee also interprets these statutes. The Constitution is silent on the nature of the statutes that the Committee interprets. But the blanket provision that the Standing committee exercises the power "to interpret statutes" embraces the basic statutes that the National People's Congress had enacted as well as the statutes enacted by the Standing Committee itself.

The Committee also examines and approves, when the National People's Congress is not in session, partial adjustments to the plan for national economic and social development and to the State budget that prove necessary in the course of their implementation.

Supervision of the work of the State Council, the Central Military Commission, the Supreme People's Court and the Supreme People's Procuratorate is another important function of the Standing Committee. It annuls those administrative rules and regulations, decisions or orders of the State Council that in its judgment contravene the Constitution and the statutes. The Committee also annuls those local regulations or decisions of organs of State power of provinces, autonomous regions and municipalities directly under the Central Government that contravene the Constitution, the statutes or the administrative rules and regulations of the State Council.

When the National People's Congress is not in session, the Standing Committee decides upon nominations made by the Premier, on the choice of Ministers in charge of ministries or Commissions, the Auditor-General or the Secretary-General of the State Council; decides upon nomination by the Chairman of the Central Military Commission, choice of other members of the Commission; appoints and removes Vice-Presidents and Judges of the Supreme Court, members of the Judicial Committee and the President of the Military Court at the suggestion of the President of the Supreme Court; appoints and removes Deputy Procurator-General and procurators of the Supreme Procuratorate, members of the Procuratorial Committees and Chief Procurator of the Military Procuratorate at the suggestion of the Procurator-General of the Supreme Procuratorate, and approves the appointment and removal of the chief procurators of the people's procuratorate of provinces, autonomous regions and municipalities directly under the Central Government.

The Standing Committee decides on the appointment and recall of plenipotentiary representatives abroad. It decides on the ratification and abrogation of treaties and important agreements concluded with foreign States. This power of appointment and recall of ambassadors accredited to the foreign States, decision on the ratification and abrogation of treaties and important agreements concluded with foreign States is the exclusive power of the Standing Committee whether the National People's Congress is in session or not.

When the National People's Congress is not in session, the Standing Committee decides on the proclamation of a state of war in the event of an armed attack on the country or in fulfilment of international treaty obligations concerning common defence against aggression. The Committee decides on general mobilization or partial mobilization and decides on the enforcement of martial law throughout the country or in particular provinces, autonomous regions or municipalities directly under the Central Government.

The Standing Committee institutes systems of titles and ranks for military and diplomatic personnel and other specific titles and ranks, and institutes State medals and titles of honour and decides on their conferment. The Committee also decides on the granting of special pardons.

Finally, the Standing Committee is empowered, to exercise such other functions and powers as the National People's Congress may assign to it.

**Role of the Standing Committee**

The Constitution holds the National People's Congress as the highest organ of State power and its jurisdiction extends to all subjects and matters and the Constitution empowers it "to exercise such other functions and powers as the highest organ of state power should exercise." It elects the members of the Standing Committee and has the power "to recall, all those on the Standing Committee." It can alter or annul inappropriate decisions of the Standing Committee. Though a creature of the National People's Congress to which body it is responsible and reports on its work, the Standing Committee eclipses the authority of the National People's Congress in practice. The actual functionary for the exercise of the powers and functions of the Congress is its

Standing Committee; the permanent and continuing working organ of State power in fact and law.

The National People's Congress meets once in a year for a short period and with its colossal membership of approximately 2,700 and that, too, assembled in a unicameral legislative chamber, it has neither the time nor the means to deliberate and discuss on all those issues that come before the Congress for approval and adoption. It only puts formal approval over already formulated bills by the Standing Committee and endorses the decisions taken by the Committee during the period that intervened between one session of the Congress and the other. Even if the Congress can find time to examine any matter and action taken, it is only *ex post facto* attempt which has practically no utility. Before 1982 the National People's Congress was the sole Legislative Assembly and the Standing Committee formulated the legislative measures and resolutions and they were approved the the Congress as a matter of routine. The *de facto* system of legislation has been legitimised by the 1982 Constitution and the Standing Committee has been empowered to enact and amend statutes with the exception of basic statutes that the Congress can only enact or amend. But even basic statutes can be supplemented and enacted by the Standing Committee, when the Congress is not in session, provided that they do not contravene the basic principles of these statutes.

As an interpreter of the Constitution and the statutes, whether basic or enacted by itself, the authority of the Standing Committee is final and unquestionable. To give a phrase a new interpretation is to give it a new meaning, and to give it a new meaning is to change it. Though it is absolutely not possible that the interpretation given by the Standing Committee may even smack of a deviation from the Party line, yet in terms of Constitution the exclusive power of the Standing Committee to interpret the Constitution and the statutes makes its authority unique from all other organs of State power including the National People's Congress.

The Standing Committee is alone responsible for completing elections of the deputies to National People's Congress two months before the expiration of its five-year term. If, however, exceptional circumstances prevent such an election, it may be postponed by decision of a majority vote of at least two-thirds of the members of the Standing Committee. The election of deputies to the succeeding National People's Congress is required to be completed within one year after the termination of such exceptional circumstances. But who determines the existence of exceptional circumstances and their termination? All such decisions are taken by the inner circle of the Party and, then, there is inter- locking of government and the Party at all levels of the organs of State particularly at the top level and both the Party and the political system in China, as it was in the USSR, are based on the principle of democratic centralism, which has been sanctified by the Constitution in Article 3 of Chapter One—General Principles. All the same, the importance of the Standing Committee in the matter cannot be denied. Then, the Standing Committee convenes the annual session of the National People's Congress and it may be convened "at any time the Standing Committee deems this necessary." There was no such provision in the earlier Constitutions.

The Standing Committee supervises the work of the State Council, the Central Military Commission, the Supreme People's Court and the Supreme People's Procuratorate. It is claimed that the supervision system provided by the 1982 Constitution has the same functions as "Constitutional Committees or courts of other countries. Our system conforms to the conditions of legal system of our country."[20]

The Standing Committee can also annul those administrative rules and regulations, decisions or orders of the State Council that contravene the Constitution and the statutes. It can also annul those local regulations or decisions of the provinces, autonomous regions and municipalities directly under the Central Government that contravene the Constitution, the statutes or the administrative rules and regulations.

The Standing Committee exercises extensive power of appointment, in some instances when the National People's Congress is not in session, and in others under the jurisdiction assigned to the Standing Committee itself. Coupled with it is the Committee's power of removal of a category of functionaries from office on its own determination.

In the domain of foreign affairs the powers exercised by the Standing Committee are impressive and vital too. It alone decides the appointment and recall of envoys accredited to foreign States and decides on the ratification and abroga-

20. "Nobody is above Constitution and Law," excerpts from Renmin Ribao (People's Daily) circulated by the Embassy of People's Republic of China, New Delhi.

tion of treaties and important agreements concluded with foreign States. When the National People's Congress is not in session, the Standing Committee decides on the proclamation of a state of war and in the event of an armed attack on the country or in fulfilment of international treaty obligations concerning common defence against aggression. The Committee also decides on general mobilization or partial mobilization and on the enforcement of martial law throughout the country or in particular provinces, autonomous regions or municipalities under the Central Government.

The Constitution also empowers Standing Committee, when the Congress is not in session, to enact partial supplements and amendments to statutes that have been enacted by the Congress and examines and approves partial adjustment of the plan for national economic and social development and the State budget that prove necessary in the course of their implementation.

Such is the extent of the authority of the Standing Committee that no other organ of State power can rival it. It, however, goes to the credit of the Standing Committee that it has exercised its powers judiciously, effectively and efficiently, though the centre of direction remains the inner circle of the Communist Party of China. Those who direct the Party find their due positions in the Standing Committee, the State Council and the National People's Congress. This fact of synchronisation of determination of policies and decisions at all higher levels of powers is the leading reason for the Standing Committee to become the real and actual centre of the exercise of State power. Peter S. Tang aptly said, "...like the Presidium (USSR), the Standing Committee serves as a small and manageable group for giving the necessary legal form and authority to acts of State which are essentially decided upon in higher councils of the Party."

## SUGGESTED READINGS

Bannerjee Shibnath , *The Chinese Government and Politics.*

Kahin, George McT, *Major Governments of Asia.*

Walen, Derek J., *The Government and Politics of the People's Republic of China.*

# CHAPTER V

# The President of the Republic

The Constitution of 1982 restored the offices of the President and the Vice-President of the Republic[1] that had existed under the Constitution of 1954, but ceased to exist with the enforcement of the 1975 Constitution. Liu Shaochi had succeeded Mao in this post of the President till the outbreak of the Cultural Revolution when he was removed from the office and disgraced. According to the 1975 and 1978 Constitutions the duties and functions of the President of the Republic, which were essentially dignified or ceremonial, were conferred on the Chairman of the Standing Committee. The Chairman of the Standing Committee presided over the work of the Standing Committee, received foreign diplomatic envoys and in accordance with the decisions of the National People's Congress or its Standing Committee promulgated laws and decrees, dispatched and recalled plenipotentiary representatives abroad, ratified treaties concluded with foreign States and conferred State titles. The Vice-Chairman of the Standing Committee assisted the Chairman of the Standing Committee in his work and could exercise part of the Chairman's functions and power on his behalf.

**Election and Term of Office**

The President of the Republic of China is elected by the National People's Congress for a term of five years, for the same term as that of the National People's Congress. Any citizen of the People's Republic of China who has the right to vote and to stand for election and has reached the age of 45 years[2] is eligible for election as President of the Republic. The Constitution also provides for the office of the Vice-President of the Republic, who assists the President in his work. The Vice-President fulfils all the conditions of the President for his eligibility to the office and is elected in the same way and for the same term as the President. Both the incumbents of these two offices can not serve for more than two consecutive terms.

If the office of the President falls vacant, the Vice-President succeeds to the office of the President. In case the office of the Vice-President falls vacant, the National People's Congress elects a new Vice-President to fill the vacancy. In the event that the offices of both the President and the Vice-President fall vacant, the National People's Congress elects a new President and a new Vice-President. Prior to such elections, the Chairman of the Standing Committee temporarily acts as the President.

The Vice-President assists the President in his work. The Vice-President ''may exercise such parts of the functions and powers of the President as may be deputed by the President.[3] He is, thus, the agent or deputy of the President with no plenary powers. He exercises the power of the President only when he succeedes to the Presidency.

**Functions of the President**

The President, in pursuance of decisions of the National People's Congress and its Standing Committee, promulgates statutes; appoints and removes the Premier, Vice-Premiers, State Councillors, Ministers in charge of ministries and commissions and the Auditor-General and Secretary-General of the State Council. He confers State medals and titles of honour and issues orders of special pardons. The President proclaims martial law and a state of war and issues mobilization orders. Under the 1954 Constitution the Chairman of the Republic commanded the armed forces and was also the Chairman of the National

1. The incumbents of both these offices were designated as Chairman and Vice-Chairman of Republic by the 1954 Constitution.
2. Under the 1954 Constitution the age fixed for eligibility was 35 years.
3. Article 82.

Defence Council.[4] Whenever he deemed necessary, the Chairman convened a Supreme State Conference and acted as its chairman. He submitted the views of the State Supreme Conference to the National People's Congress, the Standing Committee, the State Council or other bodies concerned for their consideration. The 1982 Constitution did not revive these powers of the President.

## THE STATE COUNCIL

The State Council is the Central Government of the People's Republic of China and it is the executive body of the highest organ of State power; it is the highest organ of State administration. Being the highest executive body of the highest organ of State power, it is but natural that the top Party political leaders are associated with this decision-making organ of the Government in order to ensure the proper implementation of such decisions through the administrative departments and agencies into which the central administration is divided.

### Composition of the State Council

The State Council is composed of the Premier, the Vice-Premiers, the State Councillors, the Ministers in charge of ministries, the Ministers in charge of Commissions, the Auditor-General, and the Secretary-General. The organisation of the State Council is prescribed by law. The Premier has overall responsibility for the effective and efficient functioning of the State Council where- as the Ministers have overall responsibility for the ministries or commissions under their charge.

The choice of the Premier is decided by the National People's Congress upon nomination by the President of the Republic whereas the choice of the Vice-Premiers, State Councillors, Ministers in charge of ministries or Commissions and the Auditor-General and the Secretary-General of the State Council is decided upon the recommendation of the Premier.[5] The term of office of the State Council is five years. The Premier, Vice-Premier and the State Councillors can serve only for two consecutive terms.[6] The National People's Congress has the power to recall or remove from office the Premier, Vice-Premiers, State Councillors, Ministers in charge of ministries or commissions and the Auditor-General and the Secretary-General of the Council.[7] The Standing Committee decides, when the National People's Congress is not in session, on the choice of Ministers in charge of ministries or commissions or the Auditor-General and the Secretary-General of the State Council upon the nomination by the Premier.[8]

### Working of the State Council

The Premier directs the work of the State Council. The Vice-Premiers and State Councillors assist in the work of the Premier.[9] The Premier has overall responsibility for the State Council and the State Council is responsible, and reports on its work, to the National People's Congress or, when the Congress is not in session, to its Standing Committee.[10]

The Ministers in charge of Ministries or Commissions are responsible for the work of their respective departments and convene and preside over ministerial meetings or commission meetings that discuss and decide on major issues in the work of their respective departments. The ministries and commissions issue orders, directives and regulations within the jurisdiction of their respective departments and in accordance with the statutes and the administrative rules and regulations, decisions and orders issued by the State Council.

The State Council establishes an auditing body to supervise through auditing the revenue and expenditure of all departments under the State Council and of the local governments at different levels, and those of State financial and monetary organisations and enterprises and undertakings. Under the direction of the Premier, the auditing body independently exercises its power to supervise through auditing in accordance with the law, subject to no interference by any other administrative organ or public organisation or individual. The State Council has a Secretariat under the direction of the Secretary-General of the Council. Steps are being taken to reduce the number of staff in the State Council

4. Article 85.
5. Article 62.
6. Article 87.
7. Article 63.
8. Article 67 (9).
9. Article 88.
10. Article 92.

and rationalise the portfolios of various ministries. About one-third of the State Council membership was axed in 1982.

In order to streamline the functioning of the State Council, the Constitution now stipulates that the executive meetings of the State Council are composed of the Premier, the Vice-Premiers, the State Councillors and the Secretary-General of the State Council. The Premier convenes and presides over the executive meetings as well as plenary meetings of the State Council. It means that numerous Ministers, Vice-Ministers and chiefs of commissions and Bureaus will now be normally excluded from the executive meetings of the Council and, thus shall be manageable meetings facilitating speedy transaction of work which was hithero retarded by unmanageable composition of the State Council. The Constitution definitely distinguishes between the executive meetings and plenary meetings of the council,[11] both convened and presided over by the Premier. The 1954 Constitution also made this distinction.

**Functions and Powers**

The State Council adopts administrative measures, enacts administrative rules and regulations and issues decisions and orders in accordance with the Constitution and the Statutes. It submits its proposals to the National People's Congress or its Standing Committee, when the Congress is not in session, for necessary approval and implementation. The Council lays down the tasks and responsibilities of the ministries and the commissions to exercise unified leadership over the work of the ministries, and commissions and to direct all other administrative work of a national character that does not fall within the jurisdiction of the ministries and commissions. It exercises unified leadership over the work of local organs of State administration at different levels throughout the country and also lays down the detailed division of functions and powers between the Central Government and organs of State administration of provinces, autonomous regions and municipalities directly under the Central Government.

The Council draws up and implements the plan for national economic development and social development and the State budget. It directs and administers economic affairs and urban and rural development, affairs of education, science, culture, public health, physical culture and family planning. It also directs and administers civil affairs, public security, judicial administration, supervision and other related matters. Conduct of foreign affairs and conclusion of treaties and agreements with foreign States, direction and administration of the national defences, affairs concerning the nationalities and safeguarding the rights of minority nationalities and the right of autonomy of the national autonomous areas constitute another important bunch of the functions and powers of the State Council.

The Council protects the legitimate rights and interests of Chinese nationals residing abroad and protects the lawful rights and interests of returned oversea Chinese and of the family members of Chinese nationals residing abroad.

It alters or annuls inappropriate orders, directives and regulations issued by the ministries and commissions and of local organs of State administration at different levels. The Council approves the geographic division of provinces, autonomous regions and municipalities directly under the Central Government, and approves the prefectures, counties, autonomous counties, and cities.

The Council of State shares with the Standing Committee the power to decide on the enforcement of martial law in parts of provinces, autonomous regions and municipalities directly under the Central Government. But it has no power to decide on enforcement of martial law throughout the country. It is within the exclusive jurisdiction of the Standing Committee.

The Council examines and decides on the size of administrative organs and, in accordance with the law, appoints, removes and trains administrative officers, appraises their work and rewards and punishes them. The National People's Congress or its Standing Committee may assign to the Council of State with such other functions or powers as may be deemed necessary and expedient. A similar provision has been made in Article 67 (21) relating to the powers and functions of the Standing Committee. But it is in sharp contrast to the general and all embracing power that Article 62 (5) confers on the National People's Congress. The Congress can exercise such other functions and powers as the highest organ of State power may decide. The Standing Committee and the State Council can exercise only such functions and powers as the National Peo-

11. Article

ple's Congress may "assign" to them.

## THE CENTRAL MILITARY COMMISSION

The Central Military Commission, directly under the National People's Congress, is an innovation of the 1982 Constitution and it sharply departs from the earlier Constitutions. It does not quite compare with the National Council of Defence presided over by the Chairman of the Republic as it existed under the 1954 Constitution. The Constitution of 1975 abolished the National Council of Defence and the 1982 Constitution gives the 1954 Defence Council absolutely a new orientation. The National Military Commission is a numerous body composed of a Chairman and other members. The Chairman is elected by the National People's Congress and the choice of other members of the Commission is decided, upon nomination by the Chairman, by the Congress.[12] The National People's Congress may also recall or remove them from office.[13] The Commission is responsible to the Congress and its Standing Committee.[14] The Standing Committee also supervises the work of the Commission.[15] The Central Military Commission is, therefore, not a part of the State Council though it forms a part of Chapter Two of the Constitution which, *inter alia,* deals with the State Council.

The Constitution of 1978 vested the command of the armed forces of China in the Chairman of the Central Committee of the Communist Party. It also stipulated that the Chinese People's Liberation Army "is the workers' and peasants' own armed force led by the Communist Party of China; it is also the pillar of the dictatorship of the proletariat."[16] In order to avoid concentration of power of commanding the armed forces into the hands of a single person, the 1982 Constitution places its command under a collective organisation—the Central Military Commission—whose work is under the constant supervision of the Standing Committee. The Chairman of the Commission has overall responsibility for the Commission and he is responsible to the National People's Congress and its Standing Committee. The term of office of the Central Military Commission is five years. It is a single five-year tenure for the Chairman of the Commission as well as for its other members. The Constitution specifically fixes two-tenure consecutive election of the President of the Republic, Vice-President of the Republic, the Chairman of the Standing Committee, the Premier, Vice-Premiers and State Councillors, the President of the Supreme Court and the Procurator-General, but it is only one-term tenure in the case of the Chairman as well as other members of the Central Military Commission. Xu Bing, a researcher with the Law Institute of the Chinese Academy of Social Sciences, says: "Most countries place their heads of States in command of their armed forces. But our armed forces are under an organization so as to guarantee that the command of the armed forces does not fall in the hands of one person, but remains in the hands of the people."[17] Article 29 of the Constitution declares that the armed forces of the People's Republic of China belong to the people."

### Appraisal of the State Council

The powers and functions of the State Council are very wide and impressive. There is no sphere of administration which it does not direct and control. The Constitution ordains the State Council as "the highest executive body of the highest organ of State power." It is the creature of the National People's Congress and reports and is responsible to it for the exercise of its functions and powers or when the Congress is not in session to its Standing Committee. The Standing Committee enforces the responsibility of the State Council by its supervisory power over its work. It may also annul those administrative rules and regulations, decisions, or orders of the State Council that contravene the Constitution or the statutes. The responsibility of the State Council, or the Ministers in charge of ministries and commissions is further invoked through the medium of questions, which the deputies have the right to address during the sessions of the National People's Congress and by members at meetings of the Standing Committee. The Constitution categorically stipulates that the State Council or the ministries and commissions "must answer the questions in a responsible

12. Article 62 (6).
13. Article 63 (3).
14. Article 94.
15. Article 67 (6).
16. The Constitution of the Republic of China, 1978, Article 19.
17. "New Constitution is uniquely Chinese," Special to China Daily and circulated by the embassy of the People's Republic of China, New Delhi.

way''.

The 1982 Constitution also strengthens the position of the Premier which had been eroded during the Cultural Revolution. The 1978 Constitution did not assign any function or position of eminence to the Premier *vis-a-vis* other members of the State Council except that the National People's Congress decided on the choice of other members of the State Council upon recommendation of the Premier. The choice of the Premier rested with the Central Committee of the Communist Party[18] and this choice the National People's Congress accepted invariably.

The 1982 Constitution retrieves the position of the Premier. The nomination of the Premier now rests with the President of the Republic and the National People's Congress makes the choice. The Congress decides on the choice of the Vice-Premiers, State Councillors, Ministers in charge of ministries and commissions, the Auditor-General and the Secretary-General of the State Council upon recommendations by the Premier. The position of the Premier is further strengthened by the Constitution by stipulating that the Premier has overall responsibility for the State Council, that the Premier directs the work of the Council and that the Vice-Premiers, and State Councillors ''assist'' the Premier in the work of the Council. The Constitution also provides that the Premier convenes the executive as well as plenary meetings of the State Council and presides over both. The executive meetings of the Council are composed of the Premier, the Vice-Premiers, the State Councillors and the Secretary-General of the State Council and it means exclusion from executive meetings of the Council of other categories of ministers. It is a sort of ''inner council'' and was created in order to rationalise administration which was almost in shambles.

Despite all these efforts to restore the pre-eminence of the Premier, his position cannot be compared with his counterpart under a cabinet system of government. In a country where democratic centralism is the key-note of the administrative and political set-up, the position of the Premier and, in fact, all other functionaries of the State is dwarfed by the top-level Party men who determine the Party line, no matter whether they are young or old. The basic system of the State may be ''democratic'', in reality it is minus democratic principles and practices. In a socialist State democratic centralism cannot and does not permit otherwise.

Even the Constitution itself does not allow freewheeling to the State Council within the sphere of functions assigned to it. The Standing Committee of the National People's Congress supervises its work and annuls those rules, and regulations, decisions or orders of the Council that may, in the judgment of the Committee, contravene the Constitution and the statutes. The Standing Committee interprets the Constitution and the statutes also and the meaning it gives is final and unchallengeable. It has been aptly said that the supervision system that the 1982 Constitution provides ''has the same functions as Constitutional Committees or Courts of other countries'' and the Chinese system ''conforms to the conditions and legal system'' of that country.

## SUGGESTED READINGS

Bannerjee Shibrath, *The Chinese Government and Politics.*

Endicoft, John E.rd Heaton, W.R., *The Politics of East Asia : China, Japan, Korea*

Kahin, George McT, *Major Governments of Asia.*

Waller, Derck J. *The Government and Politics of the People's Republic of China*

Ward and Macridis, *Modern Political Systems : Asia.*

18. *The Constitution of the People's Republic of China,* 1978, Article 22 (4).

# CHAPTER VI

# The Judicial System

**Role of the Judiciary**

The judiciary plays an insignificant role in a socialist system and is even scantily described in the Constitutions of their respective countries. Under the 1954 Constitution of China twelve brief Articles in all including the system of people's procuratorate, dealt with the judiciary. The 1975 Constitution devoted only six printed lines and the 1978 Constitution took three Articles to describe it, one exclusively dealing with the people's procuratorate. The 1982 Constitution is no exception to this pattern, though it has thirteen Articles in all, five are devoted to the procuratorate system.

Socialist countries reject the Anglo-Saxon jurisprudence and the theory of the Separation of Powers has no place in this system. The socialist jurisprudence regards Judiciary as an arm of administration and its role is to provide a machinery for easy and speedy decision of cases and, more importantly, to educate the citizens to uphold and strengthen the socialist system in a spirit of dedication to the socialist ideology. The Preamble to the 1954 Constitution and the Organic Law of the People's Courts stated that the People's Courts in all their activities would educate citizens in their loyalty to the country and voluntary observance of laws. The law of the country was and is construction of socialism guided by Marxism—Leninism and Mao Zedong Thought. The 1982 Constitution defines the basic system and basic task of the State in legal form. Since it is the fundamental law of the land and supreme legal authority, "the country", as the Preamble says, "must take the Constitution, basic system and basic tasks of the State in legal form. Since it is the fundamental law of the land and supreme legal authority, "the country must take the Constitution, as the basic norm of conduct," and they have the duty to uphold the dignity of the Constitution and ensure its implementation, that is, maintain, preserve and strengthen the socialist State under the people's democratic dictatorship. It is, accordingly, the duty of the courts to inculcate in citizens the spirit of devotion to the cause of socialism, to observe the basic norm of socialist conduct; to safeguard the unity of the country, to abide by the Constitution and law and to help the State in suppressing treasonable and other counter-revolutionary activities and penalise actions that endanger the public security and disrupt the socialist economy and other criminal activities and reform the criminals.

**Organisation of Courts**

The judicial authority of the People's Republic of China is exercised by the Supreme People's Courts, and the local people's courts at all levels. The Constitution also establishes military courts and special people's courts. But the people's courts are the only judicial organs of the State. The organisation of the people's courts is prescribed by law. All cases handled by the people's courts except for those involving special circumstances as specified by law, are heard in public and the accused has the right to defence. Citizens of all nationalities have the right to use the spoken and written languages of their own nationalities in court proceedings. The people's courts and procuratorate are required to provide translation for any party to the court proceedings who is not familiar with the spoken or written languages in common use in the locality. The people's courts, in accordance with the law, exercise judicial power independently and are not subject to interference by administrative organs, public organisations or individuals.

The people's courts constitute the collegiate system in the administration of justice. The Constitution of 1978 provided that, in accordance with the law, the people's courts "apply the system whereby representatives of the masses participate as assessor in administering justice"

(Article 41). It further provided: "with regard to major counter-revolutionary or criminal cases, the masses should be drawn in for discussion and suggestions." There is no identical provision in the 1982 Constitution, as in Article 41 of the 1978 Constitution. It simply says that the organisation of courts is prescribed by law. The prevailing law provides for the collegiate system in the administration of justice. In cases of first instance justice is administered by a collegiate bench consisting of a judge and people's assessors, with the exception of simple civil cases, minor criminal cases and other cases provided by law. In cases of appeal or protest, justice is administered by a collegiate bench of judges. People's courts at all levels set up judicial committees and justice is administered by a collegiate bench consisting of a judge and people's assessors, with the exception of simple civil cases, minor criminal cases and cases otherwise provided by law. In cases of appeal or protest, justice is administered by a collegiate bench of judges. Members of judicial committees of local court are appointed and removed by the people's congresses at the corresponding levels upon the recommendation of the presidents of the local people's courts. Members of the judicial committee of the Supreme People's Court are appointed and removed by the Standing Committee of the National People's Congress at the suggestion of the President of the Supreme People's Court. Meetings of the judicial committees of different sets of courts are presided over by the presidents of the concerned courts. The Procurator-General of the Supreme People's Procuratorate and local people's procuratorate at the corresponding levels have the right to attend such meetings and participate in the discussion. The task of the judicial committees at all levels is to sum up judicial experience and to discuss cases of great importance or difficult cases as well as other questions relating to judicial work.

An appeal may be brought by a party from a judgment or order by a local court as a court of first instance to the court of the higher level in accordance with the procedure prescribed by law. The people's procuratorate may lodge a protest against such a judgment or order before the court at the next higher level in accordance with the procedure prescribed by law.

If a person sentenced to capital punishment considers as erroneous the judgment or order of an intermediate court as a court of last instance, he may apply to the court at the next higher level for re-examination. A judgment of a basic court and a judgment or order of an intermediate court in case of capital punishment, is required to be submitted to the higher court for approval before execution. If the president of a court finds, in a legally effective judgment or order of his court, some definite error in the determination of facts or application of law, he must submit his judgment or order to the relevant judicial committee for disposal. If the Supreme Court finds some definite error in a legally effective judgment or order of any lower court, or if an upper court finds such error in such judgment or order of a lower court, they have the authority to review such cases themselves or to direct a lower court to conduct a retrial. If the Supreme People's Procuratorate finds some definite error in legally effective judgment or order of a court at any level, or if it finds such error in such a judgment or order of a lower court, they have the authority to lodge a protest against the judgment or order in accordance with the prescribed procedure of judicial supervision.

The Supreme People's Court is responsible to the National People's Congress and its Standing Committee. The Standing Committee supervises the work of the Supreme People's Court. Local courts are responsible to the local people's congresses at corresponding levels and are subject to their supervision. The judicial work of the lower courts is subject to their supervision by the upper courts. The judicial administration at all levels is directed by the judicial administrative organs.

The term of the President of the Supreme People's Court is five years and he does not serve for more than two consecutive terms. The Standing Committee appoints and removes Vice-Presidents and judges of the Supreme People's Court and members of the Judicial Committee. Presidents of local courts are elected by the people's congresses at the corresponding levels and other judges are appointed and removed by the Standing Committees of the local people's congresses. The Standing Committee also supervises at its corresponding level the work of people's court.

Citizens who have the right to vote and stand for election on attaining the age of 18 years are eligible to be elected as people's assessors. Their term of office and the method of their selection is decided by the Ministry of Justice. The assessors exercise their functions in the courts, are members of the division of the courts in which they participate, and have equal rights with the judges.

**Basic People's Courts**

Basic People's Courts are County People's Courts and Municipal People's Courts; People's Courts of autonomous counties and People's Courts of municipal districts. A basic court is composed of a president, one or two Vice-Presidents and judges. The court may set up a criminal division and a civil division, each with a chief judge and when necessary, associate other judges. A basic court may, according to the condition of the locality, population and number of cases, set up people's tribunals. A tribunal is a component part of the court and its judgments and orders are judgments and orders of the basic court.

Basic courts take cognisance of civil and criminal cases of first instance, except such cases as are otherwise provided by laws. Besides trying cases the courts settle civil disputes and minor criminal cases which do not need a trial, direct the work of conciliation committees and direct the judicial administrative work within their competence.

**Intermediate People's Courts**

Intermediate People's Courts are established in various areas of a province, autonomous regions, and municipalities directly under the Central Government, large municipalities and administrative counties. An intermediate court is composed of a President, one or two Vice-Presidents, chief judges of divisions and judges. It has a criminal division and a civil division, and such other divisions as may be deemed necessary.

Intermediate courts take cognisance of cases of first instance assigned to them by law to their jurisdiction; cases of first instance transferred from the Basic Courts, appeals and protests against judgments and orders of the Basic Courts, and protests lodged by the People's Procuratorate in accordance with the procedure of judicial revision.

**Higher People's Courts**

Higher courts are those of provinces, autonomous regions and municipalities directly under the Central Government. A higher court is composed of a President, Vice-Presidents, chief judges of divisions, and judges. The court has criminal division and a civil division and such other divisions as may be deemed necessary.

Higher People's Courts take cognisance of cases of first instance assigned to their jurisdiction, cases of first instance transferred from lower courts, appeals and protests against judgments and orders of lower courts, and protests lodged by the Procuratorate in accordance with procedure of judicial supervision.

**The Supreme People's Court**

The Supreme People's Court is at the apex and is the highest judicial organ. It supervises the administration of justice by the local people's courts at different levels and, by the special people's courts. It is composed of a President, Vice-Presidents, Chief Judges of divisions, associate chief judges of divisions, and judges. It has a criminal division and a civil division, and such other divisions as may be deemed necessary.

The Supreme People's Court takes cognisance of cases of first instance assigned by law and statutes to its jurisdiction or that case which the court considers that it should try; appeals and protests against judgments and orders of High Courts and special courts; protests lodged by the Supreme People's Procuratorate in accordance with the procedure of judicial revision.

## PEOPLE'S PROCURATORATE

**People's Procuratorate**

The people's procuratorates are State organs of supervision. For the whole Republic of China there is the Supreme People's Procuratorate headed by the Procurator-General who is elected for a term of five years by the National People's Congress and is subject to recall or removal by the Congress. The Procurator-General cannot serve for more than two consecutive terms.

The Supreme People's Procuratorate directs the work of the local people's procuratorates at different levels and of the special people's procuratorates. People's procuratorates at higher levels direct the work at lower levels. People's procuratorates, in accordance with the law, exercise procuratorial power independently and are not subject to interference by administrative organs, public organisations or individuals. The Supreme People's Procuratorate is responsible to the National People's Congress and its Standing Committee. The Standing Committee supervises the work of the Supreme People's Procuratorate. The Standing Committee also appoints and removes Deputy Procurator-General and procurators of the Supreme People's Procuratorate, members of the Procuratorial Committee and the Chief Procurator of the Military Procuratorate at the suggestion of the Procurator-General of the Supreme People's Procuratorate. The Standing Committee approves the appointment and removal of the chief procurators of the people's procuratorates of provinces, autonomcus regions and municipalities directly under the Central Government. Local people's procuratorates at different levels are responsible to the organs of State power at the corresponding level which created them and to the people's procuratorates at higher levels.

Local organs of the people's procuratorate and special people's and military procuratorates exercise procuratorial authority within the limits prescribed by law. The people's procuratorates are State organs of legal supervision and it is their duty to see that resolutions, orders and measures of the local organs of state power conform to the Constitution and law, and that the Constitution and law are observed by persons working in these organs and by all citizens. The procuratorates investigate, prosecute and sustain the prosecution of criminal cases. They also see that the investigation departments, in performing their duties, conform to the Constitution and law, to see that the judicial activities of the people's courts, the execution of sentences in criminal cases, and the activities of departments in charge of reform conform to the law, and to institute or intervene in legal actions with regard to important civil cases which affect the interests of the State and citizens.

The work of the Procuratorate is closely associated with the judicial courts. Being the official guardian of the Constitution and law and, consequently, that of the judicial and social legality, it is the duty of the Procuratorate to investigate all cases of sabotage of the socialist system, to investigate all cases of treasonable and revolutionary activities and actions that endanger public security and disrupt the socialist economy and see that the criminals are adequately punished. The Procuratorates being organs of legal supervision also protect the fundamental personal rights of citizens and safeguard the inviolability of their persons. No one may be arrested except with the approval and decision of a people's procuratorate or by decision of people's court.

The institution of the people's procuratorate is unique in the judicial system of China, as it was in the USSR. The powers of the Procurator-General are so extensive and his authority is so pervasive that it embraces all organs of administration, the army, public organisations, and all enterprises or organisations and citizens. In the discharge of supervisory functions, the Procurator-General has to ensure that there is the correct application and strict execution of the Constitution and laws by all ministries, commissions and other organs of State power at all levels as well as by officials and citizens of China. The Constitution invests the procuratorates with authority to exercise procuratorial power independently and none of them at any level are subject to interference by administrative organs, public organisations or individuals.

## SUGGESTED READINGS

Bannerjee Stribnath, *The Chinese Government and Politics.*

Kahin, George McT, *Major Governments of Asia*

Waller, Derek J., *The Government of the People's Republic of China..*

# CHAPTER VII

# The Communist Party of China

## Party the Leader and Core of the Country

The general programme of the Chinese Communist Party declares that as the "highest form of class organisation, the party must strive to play a correct role as the leader and core in every aspect of the country's life." Liu Shao-chi, in his report on the Draft Constitution of the People's Republic of China (1954) presented to the First National People's Congress, said that the leadership of the Communist Party of China was essential not only to the Chinese people's democratic revolution, but also to the realization of socialism. "It must also combat any tendency to departmentalism, which reduces the party's role and weakens its unity." Though there was no mention of the Party in the Constitution of 1954 and the Party existed outside the administrative machinery of the State, yet as a teacher and leader of the people, it functioned as the prime force inside the structure of the State. In the politics of China there was only one party which operated and as it was the revolutionary party which had ousted the previous regime and established the People's Republic of China, it was certainly the decision-making centre and implementing orgainstation to the realisation of socialism. The members, therefore staffed all the key positions in the government. Explicit injunctions welded them into a disciplined body under central direction from Party organisation and officials at parallel or higher levels. Its leaders decided government policy regardless of their titles or constitutionally vested responsibilities. The Party's ideology was the only officially propagated doctrine mandatory for members and non-members alike. Party members were not to limit their loyalties just to Government and, thus, become the tools of 'departmentalism.' They were enjoined to respectfully and rigidly accept the higher directions of the Party. The Party constitution prescribed that: "Party decisions must be carried out unconditionally. Individual Party members will obey the Party organisation, the minority should obey the majority, the lower Party organs, and all constituent Party organs throughout the country shall obey the National Party Congress and the Central Committee."

This is democratic centralism. Article 2 of the 1954 Constitution also emphasised the practice of centralism within the structure of the State. It read: "The National People's Congress, the local people's congresses and other organs of the State practise democratic centralism." In his Report on the Draft Constitution, Liu Shao-chi explained this provision in the Constitution and said: "Our system of democratic centralism is explained by the fact that the exercise of state power is unified and concentrated in the system of people's congress....we Marxist-Leninists have long since publicly declared that we stand for centralism...In the Draft Constitution, we have combined a high degree of centralism with a high degree of democracy. Our political system has a high degree of centralism but it is based on a high degree of democracy." Mao Zedong, in his book, *On Coalition Government*, stated that the political system of China was "at once democratic and centralised, that is, centralised on the basis of democracy and democratic under centralized guidance." Democratic centralism is, therefore, a keynote of Communist doctrine and it is applied meticulously at all levels, governmental and social.

The democratic aspects of "democratic centralism" are manifested in free discussions before decisions are taken and in election of higher, bodies by lower groups. Elections are unanimous otherwise it creates factionalism and decisions once arrived at must be obeyed rigorously and regularly. Deviation therefore is indiscipline which is a heinous crime in Communist ideology. The General Programme of the Communist Party of China repeats at every step that "the party is a united militant organization, welded together by a discipline which is obligatory on all its members."

**Party under the 1975 Constitution**

The 1975 Constitution not only constitutionalised the Communist Party of China, but in unmistakable terms established the rule of Party, which had been virtually displaced by the revolutionary committees set up during the Cultural Revolution in the body politic of the country. It declared that the Communist Party of China "is the core of the leadership of the whole Chinese People" and "the working class exercises leadership over the State through the vanguard of the Communist Party of China." The National People's Congress was the highest organ of State "under the leadership of the Communist Party of China." The National People's Congress appointed and removed the Premier and the members of the State Council "on the proposal of the Central Committee of the Communist Party of China." The Chairman of the Central Committee of China commanded the armed forces and the Chinese People's Liberation Army and the People's militia were led by the Communist Party.

The Constitution, thus, explicitly affirmed the principle of centralised and direct Party rule over the Government and the Armed forces. The Preamble summed up the achievements of the Party during the last 20 years and recounted that the people of all nationalities continuing their triumphant advances under the leadership of the Communist Party achieved great victories in socialist revolution and socialist construction and the great Proletarian Cultural Revolution and consolidated and strengthened the dictatorship of the. proletariat. The Premble also committed China to "continued revolution" under the guidance of the Party and emphasised that the country must adhere to its basic line and policies for the entire historical period of socialism and persist in continued revolution. Continued revolution, it was asserted aimed to resolve the contradictions which the danger of capitalist restoration and the threat of subversion and aggression by imperialism and social imperialism had created. The Constitution expressed the confidence of the Chinese people that led by the Communist party "they will vanquish enemies at home and abroad and surmount all difficulties to build China into powerful socialist State of the dictatorship of the proletariat so as to make a great contribution to humanity."

**Party under the 1978 Constitution**

The 1978 constitution of the People's Republic of China was the replica of its predecessor Constitution so far as the role of the Communist Party was concerned. The Preamble to the Constitution recounted the heroic struggle of the Chinese people, led by the Communist Party of China and "headed by our great leader and teacher Chairman Mao Zedong" finally overthrew the reactionary rule of imperialism, feudalism and bureaucratic capitalism, winning complete victory in 1949 and founded the People's Republic of China. The Constitution also set forth the general task for all the Chinese people under the leadership of the Communist party to usher in an era of prosperity and socialist enthusiasm. It was the fundamental duty of citizens that they should support the leadership of the Communist Party and support the socialist system, the Preamble added.

Article 1 of the 1978 Constitution declared that the People's Republic of China was a Socialist State of the dictatorship of the proletariat led by the working class and based on the alliance of the workers and peasants. This was followed by Article 2 stipulating that the Communist Party of China was the core of the leadership of the whole Chinese people and the working class exercised leadership over the State through its vanguard, the Communist Party of China. The Chairman of the Central Committee of the Communist Party commanded the armed forces of China and Article 19 further stated that the Chinese Liberation Army was the workers, and peasants' own armed force led by the Communist Party of China and it was the pillar of the dictatorship of the proletariat. The Constitution assigned to the armed forces the task of safeguarding the socialist revolution and socialist reconstruction. The National People's Congress decided on the choice of the Premier of the State Council upon the recommendation of the Central Committee of the Party.

**Party under the 1982 Constitution**

The Cultural Revoluation had marked a stage in the implementation of the policies of Mao Zedong. The higher organs of the Party and the State were replaced by the proletarian headquarters of Mao Tse-tung, which consisted of a small group of functionaries loyal personally to Mao. This "headquarter" was proclaimed "the sole leading organ of the entire party, the entire army and the entire country." A mechanism of power was built in which a definite place was given to the Communist Party on a new basis and the central link of the system consisted of revolutionary Committees, which replaced the former Party and State organs. The Constitution of the Party was accordingly, changed and the central and local commissions were, *inter alia,* abolished. The Eleventh Party Congress, the first without Mao Zedong and Chou Enlai, which met in September 1977, changed for the fourth time the Party Constitution in order to overhaul the Party set-up to prevent future usurpation of power by a small coterie. An attempt was made to return to the positive traditions of the Party which included strengthening of discipline, democratic relations, free expression of opinions and greater respect for the interests of the masses. The Party organisation was overhauled from top to bottom and one of the safeguards introduced was the revival of central and local Commissions.

Despite denunciation of Mao's policies and the disaster he wrought on the Party and the State, his shadow still loomed large in the Party. This factonalism in the Party was evident from the fact that he still remained "our great leader and teacher" and "all our victories in revolution and construction" as the Preamble to the 1978 Constitution declared, "have been won under the guidance of Marxism-Leninism-Mao Zedong Thought. The fundamental guarantee that the people of all our nationalities will struggle in unity and carry the proletarian revolution through to the end is always to hold high and staunchly to defend the great banner of Chairman Mao." In all there were five such references to Mao in the Preamble to the 1978 Constitution, two years after his death, and was even described as the founder of the People's Republic of China. In the Preamble to the Constitution of 1982 there are two references to Mao-Zedong Thought "which integrates the concrete practice in China." The 1982 Constitution, thus, follows the treand of downgrading the stress on Mao, but of not pushing de-Maoification too far.

The Chinese Constitutions do show in their Preambles an increasing tendency to mention the leadership of the Communist Party in making and sustaining the revolution. There were two such references in the 1954 Constitution, three in the 1978 Constitution and no less than four in the 1982 Constitution. The Preamble to the 1982 Constitution declares that both the victory "of China's new democratic revolution and the successes of its socialist cause have been achieved by the Chinese people of all nationalities under the leadership of the Communist Party of China and the guidance of Marxism-Leninism and Mao Zedong Thought, and by upholding truth, correcting errors and overcoming numerous difficulties and hardships." The Preamble exhorts the people that the basic task of the nation in the years to come "is to concentrate its efforts on socialist modernization. Under the leadership of the Communist Party of China and the guidance of Marxism-Leninism and Mao Zedong Thought, the Chinese People of all nationalities will continue to adhere to the people's democratic dictatorship and follow the socialist road, steadily improve socialist institutions, develop socialist democracy, improve the socialist legal system and work hard and self- reliantly to modernize industry, agriculture, national defence and science and technology, step by step to turn China into a socialist country with a high level of culture and democracy."

There is no provision in any Article of the Constitution which may describe the role of the Communist Party. The People's Republic of China is now a socialist State under the people's democratic dictatorship led by the working class and based on the alliance of workers and peasants (Article 1). Article 2 of the 1978 Constitution was dropped altogether. The command of the army no longer vests in the Chairman of the Central Committee of the Party. The Central Military Commission directs the armed forces of the country (Article 93). The armed forces of China belong to the people. Their tasks are to strengthen national defence, resist aggression, defend the motherland, safeguard the people's peaceful labour, participate in national reconstruction and work hard to serve the people (Article 29). The Premier is no longer the choice of the Central Committee. He is now chosen by the National People's Congress on nomination by the President of the Republic (Article 62 (S)).

The Communist Party of China having, led the people in formulating the 1982 Constitution, is determined to lead the people in upholding the dignity of the Constitution and enforcing it firmly. The new Party Constitution adopted by the 12th National Conference of the Communist Party of China held in September 1982 stated, "All the activities of the Party should be in accordance with the Constitution and the law" and the Constitution defines the basic system and the basic tasks of the State in legal form. The

Communist Party is still the vanguard of the people but the role it plays is subject to the Constitution which is the fundamental law of the land.

**Membership and Organisation**

In 1921, thirteen anarchists, radicals and Marxists met in Shanghai and established the first Congress of the Chinese Communist Party. In 1951, the membership of the Party had gone to 5.8 million and in another decade it went up to 17 million. In August 1977 the membership exceeded 35 million, in 1980 it was over 50 million and in 1986, it exceeded 62 million. The membership is strictly limited. Anyone who has attained the age of eighteen and who does work and does not exploit the labour of others is eligible to become a member. But a candidate must be recommended by two full members of the Party. If the Party branch as well as the next Party committee approve, he is given a probationary status. After a satisfactory completion of one year of "elementary education", during which "political qualities" are carefully observed, he is admitted as a full member of that group which approved him first for the probationary status.

At the bottom of the organisation is the local cell and the local branch chooses delegates to county or municipal Party Congress, which in turn elects the Provincial Party Congress. The Provincial Congress sends delegates to the National Party Congress which then chooses a 201-man Central Committee. The Central Committee is the highest leading body of the Party when the National Party Congress is not in session. The elections at all levels of the Party are to be periodically held, but in practice they have proved to be less than periodic and at the higher levels the Party positions were held beyond their constitutional tenure. This life-long tenure trend has now been ended. The Provincial Party Congresses are to elect the National Party Congress every five years, but actually only two such Congresses were elected during eighteen years, the seventh in 1945 and the eighth in 1956. Again, after thirteen years the ninth Congress was called in 1969 to legitimise the results of the Cultural Revolution and the tenth was convened in 1974 which was necessitated to "consolidate and multiply the achievements of the great proletarian cultural revolution." The eleventh Congress was held from August 12 to 18, 1977. Now it is held regularly.

The National Party Congress, consisting of more than one thousand and five hundred members, is elected for five years and it must meet every year unless the Central Committee decided that "extraordinary conditions" do not permit such a meeting. There has been only one meeting till 1956 and subsequently at irregular intervals. It means that the Central Committee has exercised its extraordinary power of not convening annual meetings of the National Party Congress at regular intervals. Since the Congress elects the Central Committee "and therefore is legally superior to it, failure to convene the parent body removes the problems of co-responsibility to the membership at large. In this manner, reality mirrors theory, reversing the image in the process." In fact, the Congress does not elect the Central Committee. It is the outgoing Politburo and to be more precise its Standing Committee of seven men, which actually selects the Central Committee. The Standing Committee of the Politburo includes the top-ranking leaders, and the choice actually rests with them.

The Central Committee does not even formulate policy. It is a numerous body which meets once or twice yearly and that, too, for only a brief period. It is on record that at times of particular or prolonged crisis, the Central Committee does not meet at all. No Central Committee plenum was held in 1960, despite the marked deterioration of Sino-Soviet relations and the decline of agricultural productivity that had begun in 1958, when the tenth plenum of the Central Committee met in 1962, only four days were allotted for discussion of Party as well as national affairs. Taking into account the infrequency and short duration of its meetings, the Central Committee functions mainly as a sounding board for previously determined policy.

The Politburo with membership of twenty-three is the core of the important deision-makers and "probably acts as a controlling nucleus for the larger body." The Central Committee is important to the Politburo because it transmits and implements Politburo decisions. Central Committee's endorsement of Politburo actions gives the policies a legitimacy "far beyond that which is possible through Press announcement." Consistent with the principle of democratic centralism it is obligatory on all to accept and implement all such decisions without demur. Here is a matter of fact summing up of the position and functions of the Central Committee.....The Central Comnitee is too large and meets too infrequently and too briefly to be the real decision-making centre of the CCP (Chinese Communist Party). Yet it is much more than a rubber stamp for Politburo. It gives legitimacy to Politburo decisions in accordance with the party constitution. It transmits decisions to lower levels linking the peak of the political pyramid with its mass base (more than other million basic level organisations). It provides status to worthy party members and, finally, offers a proving ground for potential leaders."

The Politburo, like other Party organs, is a numerous body and has, accordingly, its Standing Committee which constitutes the brain trust of the Politburo. It has always included top party leaders, as it once had Mao Zedong, Chou En-lai, Chow Ch'en Yun and Teng-Hsais-ping. With the Party Chairman, the Premier and other galaxy of Party leaders it is but natural that the Standing Committee should constitute the apex of the policy formulation.

Among other organs of the Central committee the most important are the Secretariat and Departments, such as, the Rural work, Industrial work, Social Affairs, and the Control Commission. The Secretariat monitors the execution of policy on a daily basis through the Party Central organs, bureaus and Committees. The Control Commission, according to Party rules, examines and deals with cases of violation of the Party Constitution, Party discipline, Communist ethics, and state laws and decrees on the part of Party members and deals with appeals and complaints from party members. It originally consisted of seventeen regular and four alternative members. In September 1962, the tenth plenary session of the Eighth Central Committee decided to enlarge the membership in order "to strengthen the work of the Party Control Commission." Enlargement of the membership of the Control Commission emphasised the importance of this organ which was entrusted with the duty to combat "improper" attitudes and "sectarian" tendencies of the Party members. The Party rules explained that every member "has the duty to report to the party Control Committees whatever he knows about infractions against party rules, party discipline, communist morality, national laws and decrees on the part of other party members. Moreover, it is his duty to help the Party Control committee struggle against such phenomena."

## SUGGESTED READINGS

China's Constitution of 1982

Bannerjee, Shibnath, *The Chinese Government and Politics.*

Endicott, John E., and Heaton, W.A., *The Politics of East Asia : China, Japan, Korea.*

Johnson, Chalmers (ed) Ideology and Politics of *Communist China*

Lenis, John, (ed) *Party Leadership and Revolutionary Power in China.*

Miera, Kalpama, *From Post Maoism to Post Marxism*

Schurmann Franz, *Ideology and Organisation in Communist China.*

Townsend, James, *Political Participation in Communist China.*

Waller, Derek J., *The Government and Politics of The People's Republic of China.*

# CHAPTER VIII

# Democratic Ferment

## Demand for More Reforms

Student agitation is not a new phenomenon in China. Since 1919 students have been a vocal political force fighting authoritarianism and corruption. This political role of the students was sanctified by the 1982 Constitution when Article 35 conferred on citizens the right to freedom of speech, of press, of assembly, of asscciation, of procession and demonstration. This troublesome right, which even Sun-Yat-Sen, the father of New Chinese Nationalism, would never have conceded, ignited the spurt of student unrest first in 1986 and again in April-May 1989 eventually culminating on June 3-4, 1989 at Tiananmen square in Beijing, in the massacre of hundreds of unarmed youngmen and women at the hands of the People's Liberation Army (PLA). How- ever, it has since become known that many in the People's Liberation Army feel shame at having fired at the young students spearheading the demand for more democratic reforms.

In December 1986 student unrest, which swept through nearly a dozen cities, was in favour of democracy and freedom. Deng Xiaoping's regime was certainly more democratic than its predecessor and there was an awareness on the part of the Chinese leadership of the need for democratization. But the leadership was in no mood to accept and launch another revolutionary movement at that juncture when Deng's economic reforms had met with severe criticism from the Conservative elements in the Communist Party of China. The pace of change that the students wanted alerted Deng Xiaoping and Hyaobang, the General Secretary of the Chinese Communist Party, and even had initially sympathised with the students' demand in their quest for a more "open" China. The Government in a bid to arrest the movement promul gated stringent regulations banning unannounced demonstrations and the putting up of unsigned posters in public places. The penalty for violating the ban was five years hard labour in prison.

In mid-January 1987, a meeting of the Party's Politburo was held and the Secretary-General Hu Yobang was forced to resign, and some of China's intellectuals were attacked, demoted, and expelled from the Party. The Chinese citizens were, thus, once again, forcefully reminded of the sanctity of the four principles of China's policy. These principles were: to uphold he socialist road; to uphold the democratic dictatorship; to uphold the primacy of the Communist Party of China; and, to support the primacy of Marxist-Leninist-Mao-Zedong Thought. Both the Government and the Communist Party made it unequivocally clear that nobody would be permitted to challenge these four cardinal principles which embodied the rules of prolonged struggle for the integration of Marxist-Leninist theory with the practice of Chinese Revolution.

The democratic turmoil subsided, but not the democratic fervour that culminated into the June 3-4, 1989 nightmare of the Tiananmen Square. In his June 9, 1989 speech, so far the ultimate official pronouncement of what had happened in China, Deng Xiaoping said, "It started as student unrest, then it developed into a turmoil. And finally, it turned out to be a counter-revolutionary rebellion." That was the official version. But how is one to describe the military operation in Beijing on the night of June 3-4, against unarmed mass of students mostly in their teens? "The brutal suppression" of a "peaceful student movement" was the invariable description given by countries adhering to the Western type of democratic government. The leaders of China's Republic and the Communist Party on the other hand, called it the liquidation of a "gang of counter-revolutionaries" who were determined to overthrow the socialist system. No matter how you describe it, it needs no great perspicacity to see that what happened first in December 1986 and, then, in April-May ending on June 3-4, 1989, had its seeds in the changes Deng Xiaoping himself had ushered in. If it was a "counter- revolution," Deng was its architect. That he did not want his policies to have the effects they had is of no consequence.

**Analysis of the Factors Responsible**

At the beginning of 1989, a leading Chinese economist noted three phases in a "sweet and sour decade" from the end of 1978. The first and sweet period, period of six years saw the "heady" result of agriculture reforms in rapid and phenomenal increase in food output and labour productivity. In the second period from late 1984 to late 1987, rural growth lost its momentum, and reforms in the industrial sector, despite an astounding rise in investment and production, began to show the distorting effects of unrestricted industrial growth. With mounting inflation close to 30 per cent in 1989, inceasing income disparities and alarming spread of corruption, the decade was turning sour. A thriving black market had become important area of corruption which was also rampant at almost every level of State and party administration.

Corruption is, undoubtedly, related to the price system, but a mere general explanation for the widespread prevalence of this vice is a new culture attached to easy and rapid money-making without any qualm of conscience. And when the market is flooded with consumer goods, it becomes a direct incentive for larger income disregardful of its source.

Regional income disparities were inherent in Deng's plan of liberalisation-action which created the eastern "gold coast." But personal and sectional disparities were the most important. A private person in construction, for example, earned twenty times more as much as the average urban income. Rural prosperity under the new dispensation was not evenly distributed. According to the estimate there were 100 million unemployed or under-employed peasants. Then, there was a floating estimated population of 50 million peasants who moved to urban areas from time to time causing a big strain on urban economy. The imbalance so created generated crime. There were also some 20 million migrant workers who added to the woes of the urban population. These bare facts evidently well establish how defective Deng's reforms scheme was.

The general economic improvement was unquestionably impressive, but in the wild pursuit of prosperity, there had hardly been any pretence of egalitarian and moral concern and the people at large paid scant respect to China's "fine tradition" of plain living and hard struggle. It really became anachronistic in the context of the prevailing philosophy when the paramount leader declared: "to get rich is glorious." Money became an end and not a means. It did not matter how it was to be amassed as the measuring rod of glory was the amount of wealth the individual possessed. It meant that even corrupt practices were permissible in the pursuit of achieving glory.

Among those denied this glory were people engaged in what an American economist described as "knowledge-extensive" work, more "elegantly but loosely" described as intellectuals. Deng Xiaoping did make efforts to rehabilitate the intellectuals after the Cultural Revolution, but their economic condition only worsened in relative terms. In 1978, "brain workers in State employment earned just 2 percent more than manual workers; in 1986, on the eve of the first democratic upsurge, the latter earned 10 percent more than the brain workers."

This was an immediate cause of discontent in the academic community. Only a fourth of some Chinese students who went to the United States of America in the past 10 years were said to have returned home. Many more who had gone to various European countries and Japan did likewise. This process had two implications. Those who had lived in the foreign countries savoured the blessings of economic prosperity and political freedom. They could visibly see and feel that these people with whom they were living in the pursuit of acquisition of knowledge were enjoying a much higher standard of living without sacrificing individual liberty. China cut a poor figure by comparison. Those who could not go abroad for obvious reasons felt frustrated and deeply hurt as their cynicism had grown because of the way Party links at home influenced the prospects of employment.

The frustration of rural unemployed youth tended to be most socially disruptive. The prosperity of the rural new-rich did not assure them that opportunities were unlimited, and there was no longer Party compulsion or ideological motivation for collective work. Often drawn to the cities, they remained a source of potential trouble, as some of them did show during the student unrest in Beijing both in 1986 and 1989. Neither the rural nor the urban youth found much inspiration for a better life in the ways of self-seeking Party cadres.

The Cultural Revolution was the great disservice that Mao did to the Party and the people. In it, most loyal Party members had been hounded out and many done to death. All intellectuals were cruelly punished. All this had virtually destroyed their faith in the goodness of Mao and the greatness of the Party, thus, choking all channels of ideological faith and pursuit of the desired goal.

In 1986-87 the Communist Party of China felt concerned about the attitude of Chinese students and launched a fact-finding exercise. The Party had always attached great importance to ideological orientation, and each army unit, every school and university had a Party cell which monitored and guided mental attitudes. In 1987, a long questionnaire was circulated to students at all levels to elicit information: (1) why they (students) take to the streets and demonstrate, (2) why the Chinese youth, who is brought up entirely on the Marxist thought since his childhood, evinces such a keen interest in western philosophy; and (3) why students show such suicidal tendencies at the slightest setback.

The survey found that the students had become blase and entered the Party not through conviction and ideological urge but for self-advancement. The Vice-Chairman of National Education Council, Liu Chung-teh, concluded in 1987 that the two main factors responsible for this were the "negative" effect of the Cultural Revolution, and the growing outside contact as a result of the Party's economic liberalisation programme.

Not only was ideological education, as the Party leadership admitted, neglected during the past decade, visitors to China in recent years also spoke of moral vacuum, evident in sharp increase in crime, prostitution and general permissiveness. Apart from the high living by the new-rich, there had grown a consumerist and imitative culture, inevitably inspired by ideas and models imported from the West. From time to time Chinese leadership had bemoaned the existence of this "spiritual pollution", but it could hardly be checked so long as the door remained open for modernization and thousands of foreigners daily intermingled with the Chinese in China. Alien political ideas were bound to find their way into an ideological vacuum. Added to these was the dawn of Gorbachev era in the Soviet Union. If the USSR could woo democracy and liberalise its institutional framework within the socialist society, why not China? They loudly questioned.

Party leaders, like Deng Xiaoping had themselves suffered harsh and humiliating treatment from Mao for their "dissent" which was nothing more than a plea for liberalisation, the same plea which the students and intellectuals had made in 1986 and in Tiananmen Square in Beijing beginning in April 1989 and culminating into the tragic events of June 3-4. In early May Party leaders like Chao Tse- Yang and Li Ping had shown an understanding attitude. The Party itself realised that in dealing with students, one has to think not only of logic (what is right and what is wrong) but of human emotions. Chao and Li Ping visited the fasting students in the hospital, and Li even gave a good chit to them by saying that they were "patriotic" and "enthusiastic." There was nothing then to suggest the "savage crackdown" which was to come only a fortnight later.

Almost two months after the "crackdown" of students, senior Chinese leaders and media officials claimed that the situation was "back to normal." In an informal talk with a visiting Indian Press delegation on August 2, 1989 Li Tie Ying, Politburo member and Education Minister, indicated that with the return to normalcy China would pursue "with greater vigour" the earlier policies of socialist reforms and the opening up of the economy. "We have achieved positive results by following these policies in the last decade. We will make a few adjustments when we make an assessment later," he said.

The Party's Politburo announced, sometime later "seven tasks of great concern to the people." All these tasks, interestingly related to one of the basic demands of the student demonstrators—the elimination of corruption amongst the Chinese Communist Party and Government officials. Other demands relating to this important aspect included the closing down of commercial firms by the children of high Party officials, including Deng Xiaoping's son, cancelling the special supply of food- stuffs of leading officials and banning the use and import of foreign cars by high party and government officials.

Li Tie Ying said that the student demonstrations were "manipulated" by "a handful of conspirators" who wanted to overthrow China's socialist system and the Communist Party. Under the garb of slogans about "democracy, human rights and freedom," they actually "wanted to restore capitalism." He accused "hostile international forces," especially the United States' Congress of interfering in China's internal affairs. He asserted that China would continue to strive to bring about socialism under the leadership of the Chinese Communist Party, and any action in opposition to the party would end up in turmoil. The message Li conveyed to the West was that Beijing was ready to deal with it on the terms of a China under the Communist Party.

According to Shao Huaze, the Editor-in-chief of the *People's Daily*, those journalists who took part in the pro-democracy demonstrations would not be punished. "None of them have been removed from the posts, but they would have to undergo political re-education." Only those who committed criminal acts were to be dealt with severely.

The Government launched a massive campaign to educate the public on the "real facts" of the student movement and in order to show the People's Liberation Army (PLA) in a different light, television serials on their heroic war exploits were shown daily.

The events of June 3-4, 1989 showed up some of the major deficiencies of the Chinese political system. The foremost among them was the weakness, even irrelevance, of institutions. The Communist Party of China was hardly called to action in dealing with the "counter-revolutionary rebellion." The Central Committee of the Party did not meet during the two months of the crisis, from mid-April to mid-June. Nor was a session of the Standing Committee of the National People's Congress convened. The arteries of command and control were seized by an exceedingly small number of leaders, the majority of whom did not even sit in the Politburo, but had been retired from active political roles.

Deng Xiaoping's failure to build institutional scaffoldings of a regime of liberalisation and modernization allowed a "turmoil" to swell into a "rebellion" in a matter of six weeks. The system did not know how to deal with it. In the great institutional vacuum, restoration of order-the old order—had to be left first to the People's Liberation Army (PLA) and then largely to the internal security apparatus. Socialist legalism another laudable objective of Deng's programme of reforms, took a back seat as leaders of the unofficial students' and workers' unions were hauled out of their homes or hiding places and thrown into prison.

Those who helped Deng to suppress the "rebellion" asserted their opposition to his strategy of economic reforms. They had long held the view that the often hasty and impatient search for financial business, trade and technological linkage with the capitalist countries had not only gravely distorted China's socialist economy by allowing the creation of large and strate- gically important capitalist conclaves, but nearly devastated its socialist ideology and values. They blamed the liberal openings to the capitalist world for the high incidence of "official profiteering;" the Chinese name for corruption in high places.

The capitalist countries had invested $11.5 million in modernizing China's industrial base. All this suffered major setback, because all those countries withheld any further aid to China. Even the World Bank stalled a $ 60 million agriculture loan, and suspended indefinitely S 700 million in other credits. The Asian Development Bank shelved a loan of $ 25 million to China's Siponese Petro- chemical Company. The Japanese Government echoed American concerns about developments in China and withheld certain major transfer of money and technologies.

The real loss for China was the confidence of the vast segment of democratic opinion all over the world. Throughout the upheavals even in the dark days of the Cultural Revolution, a solid body of democratic opinion all over the world stood by China. It was the steadfast good will of this segment that the Chinese leadership had forfeited by the barbarities committed on the Tiananmen Square on June 3-4, 1989, and the wave of suppression that continued for a pretty long time afterwards. It was estimated that more than 4,000 protesters languished in jail and scores had mounted the gallows. Two months after one member of the Chinese Communist Party had fled abroad, China announced the dismissal and expulsion of two prominent dissidents from the Party. The *People's Daily* said on August 10, 1989 that Yan Jiaqi former adiser to ousted Party chief Zhao Ziyang and head of a key Political Science Institute, and historian Bau Zunx had "clung to a bourgeois liberal stand and undertaken evil activities to overthrow the leadership of the Communist Party."

Yan fled to France after the Beijing bloodshed and from there called for a non-violent overthrow of the Beijing Government. After the

1986 student demonstration, the Provincial Governments showed little enthusiasm in arresting the young leaders of the democracy movement. In 1989, too, many of the leaders of the movement spread out to the Provinces in the hope that the Party's provincial leaders did not share the hardliners' perception of the "rebellion." Consequently, they would be in a position to make another bid for the massive demand for democracy. If the events in Western European Countries and the USSR itself, where Communism is a stale talk now and the Communist Party has been liquidated, is any guide it may happen any time or at the latest on the demise of Deng Xiaoping who is in his declining years at the age of 87. Deng is now off the stage of active politics of power.

China's Prime Minister, Li Ping, however, is not repentant on the use of military force in June 1989 to crush anti-government protests and he publicly refused to rule out doing it again. Addressing the customary Press Conference after the fortnight-long plenary session of the People's Congress, he said, on 10 April 1991, that history was vindicating his Government's action. "Had we not been forced to take resolute measures, China would be bogged down in economic crisis and political instability, at least as serious as in countries that used to be socialist." His obvious reference was to the East European countries. There was a hint of mellowing of Li's tone in talking about the 1989 protests. He said it was "entirely understandable that people should have different perceptions of unrest because of their different values and ideologies."

**Impact of Political Developments in Soviet Russia**

Notwithstanding proclamations by top Chinese leaders that the political developments in the Soviet Union will have no effect on the pursuit of socialism in China, indications are to the contrary. The Premier, Li Peng, has assertively said that conditions in China differ widely from those in the erstwhile Soviet Union and hence Beijing's steadfastness in sticking to hardline Marxist-Leninist policy would not be influenced by the developments in the homeland of Marxism-Leninism. However, reports leaking out of China have spoken of fears expressed by hard line leaders about the effects of the Soviet situation being felt in the country.

The latest such indications come in a report published by Hong King's *South China Morning Post* which quoted a Chinese Communist leader, Chen Yun, as having called on the Party to do its best to prevent the emergence of a "Yeltsin-like figure" in China. Quoting unnamed sources, the newspaper reported that the "conservative patriot," in a briefing to "intimates" soon after the failure of the *coup* in Moscow, said that the Party must draw the "right lesson" from the crumbling of Communism in the Soviet Union and the ascending of bourgeois liberal politicans.

The Chinese fears about their Communism facing a fate similar to the Soviet Communist Party is not hard to understand. As the Soviet Union disintegrates, with thirteen Republics having declared their independence, the Beijing's leaders are deeply concerned that ethnic nationalism in the vast Central Asian steppe will spill over into China's sensitive border regions. To China's west lie the three Republics of Kazakhstan, Kirghizia and Tajikistan. The mostly Muslim Kazakhs, Kirghis and Tajik who live in these Republics speak a Turkie language similar to that spoken by their predominently Muslim brethren in China; the Uighurs, Kazakhs, Kirghis and Tajiks of Xijiang Province.

To China's North is Mongolia, the former Soviet satellite that abandoned Communism in 1990. The two million Mongolians there share a common heritage with China's estimated 4 million Mongolians most of whom live in Inner Mongolia.

China's 55 different minorities make up about 7 per cent of the total population. It will not be, therefore, wide of the mark to say that ethnic nationalism, already a source of serious tension in some regions, could fuel nascent separatist sentiment in China.

**SUGGESTED READINGS**

Goldman, Merle; *Sowing the Seeds of Democracy in China : Political Reform in the Deng Xiaoping Era.*

Harding, Harry, *China's Second Revolution : Reform After Mao.*

Misra, Kalpana, *From Post-Maoism to Post-Marxism. The Erosion of Official Ideology in Devy's China.*

# CHAPTER IX

# The Chinese Political System

### Imperial System and Feudalism

The character of traditional Chinese political system has become subject to a terminological debate. Terms such as 'gentry', 'feudalism' and 'bureaucracy' have been used to describe that system. The issue here is to determine how the upper classes were connected with landed property who also enjoyed near monopoly of bureaucratic posts in the state. Some Western scholars emphasize that the Imperial state in China was a form of Oriental despotism governed by a bureaucratic *literati* which was a group of Confucian scholars. The Marxists criticise this view arguing that the ruling class gentry in China was essentially feudal in character which exploited the peasantry, extracting an economic surplus from the tillers of the soil by virtue of their ownership of land.

The Chinese Communists treat the Imperial era and even the Kuomintang period as a form of Feudalism. But there was no system of vassalage in Imperial China and only very limited grants of land in return for military services. "Nevertheless," the Marxist stress on landlordism is thoroughly justified."[1]. He adds, "Even the Emperor was a super-landlord who collected grain from his subjects. If the Imperial system relied to such a great extent on collection in kind, we may be sure that it prevailed quite widely elsewhere."[2].

As already indicated, the landlord relied on the Imperial bureaucracy to safeguard his property rights. As Owen Lattimore has remarked, behind each Imperial project was a powerful minister, and behind each minister a powerful body of landlords. These facts bring the Oriental agrarian bureaucracy and the idea of water control into proper perspective. Thus the bureaucracy constituted an alternative way of squeezing economic surplus from the peasants. For the landlord, Confucian doctrines and the system of examinations gave legitimacy to his superior social status.

Imperial Chinese society never created an urban trading and manufacturing class comparable to that which grew out of the later stages of Feudalism in Western Europe. With the decay of the Imperial apparatus, visible during the eighteenth century, its capacity to control commercial elements declined. By the second half of the nineteenth century, the traditional rule of the feudal, scholar-official had disintegrated in the coastal cities. After the conclusion of the Opium War in 1842, the *comprodores* spread through all the treaty ports of China. When Chinese industry began on its own in a modest way in 1860s, it did so under the shadow of provincial gentry, who hoped to use modern technology for their separatist ends. Military aims were in the forefront and so production of arms was stressed. As this early push toward industrialisation came from provincial foci of power, with very little support from the Imperial government, it was more of a disruptive than a unifying factor.

Thus China, like Russia, entered the modern era with a numerically small and politically dependent middle class. This class did not develop an independent ideology of its own as it did in Western Europe. Even then it played a significant role in undermining the Manchu state. The growth of this class in coastal China led to the break up of the Empire and creation of "regional satrapies in a way that foreshadowed the combination of 'bourgeois' and militarist roles in the hey-day of the warlords (roughly 1911 to 1927) and on into the Kuomintang era."[3]. A substantial amalgamation gradually took place between sections of the landlord class and leaders in trade, finance and industry.

This amalgamation provided "the chief

1. Barrington Moore Jr, *Social Origins of Dictatorship and Democracy,* p.163
2. *Ibid.,* p. 168
3. *Ibid.,* p. 177

social underpinning of the Kuomintang, and attempt to revive the essence of the Imperial system, that is, political support of the landlordism with a combination of gangsterism indigenous to China and veneer of pseudo-Confucianism that displays interesting resemblances to Western fascism."[4] This combination arose in a large measure out of the failure of the landowning gentry to achieve the transition from preindustrial to commercial forms of farming. Under conditions of an abundant labour and simple technology, there was no need for a Chinese landowner to rationalise production for the limited, urban market. When and where the market did grow, it turned the gentry into *rentiers* with bureaucratic connections rather than into agrarian entrepreneurs.

Hence, the Chinese landed upper classes failed to develop any significant principled opposition to the Imperial system. Western notion of parliamentary democracy did not appeal to the Chinese scholar-gentry. In Europe under feudalism aristocrats obtained immunities, privileges and a corporate identity that created a demand for representative institutions culminating in parliamentary democracy. Landed property in Chinese society could not serve as a basis for political power separate from the political mechanism of the Imperial state. The fact that circumstances precluded the emergence of a liberal aristocratic opposition decreased the capacity of the Chinese polity to respond successfully to a totally new historical challenge that came from Western imperialism.

A serious dilemma faced the Manchu regime during the final five decades of its rule. "On the one hand, it needed greater revenue to put down the internal rebellion and face foreign enemies. On the other hand, it could not obtain this revenue without destroying the whole system of gentry privileges. To raise adequate revenue would have required the encouragement of commerce and industry. The fact that foreigners managed the customs made such a policy even more difficult. "[5].

Theda Skocpol points out, "Yet the Chinese Empire did decline, opening the way to the revolutionary destruction of the gentry... Essentially, China came under extra-ordinary pressures from imperialist industrial nations abroad. This happened even as long-gestating internal developments were unbalancing the system from within precisely in ways that made it unlikely that Imperial authorities would, or could, respond effectively to the foreign threat. "[6].

Barrington Moore points out, "a regime, many of whose key features had lasted for centuries, simply fell apart in less than a hundred years under the impact of western blows.... In China... the final period of anarchy lasted much longer. As a minimum, one might date it from the proclamation of the Republic in 1911 to the formal victory of the Koumintang in 1927. the latter initiated a weak reactionary phase".

There was a symbiotic relationship between the landlord and the Chinese warlord. The system of requisitions, taxes in labour and kind, compelled the peasants to support the cities in the rural areas. Merchants too joined hands with the landlords foreshadowing the class coalition of the Kuomintang. In the new situation, the successors to the old ruling class sought without success an alliance with the new forces. These "successors were to be landlords pure and simple, gangsters, or a combination of the two, a tendency that lay just below the surface in Imperial times."[7].

**The Kuomintang Interlude**

With significant Communist and Soviet assistance, the Kuomintang had won control of a large part of China in 1927 working out from its base in the south. This success was mainly due to the support which its armies had so far received from the peasants and the workers. The Kuomintang's social program gave it an advantage over the warlords. It was hoped that its 'revolutionary' ideology might enable it to unify China by defeating the warlords.

When the nationalist forces reached Shanghai, the Kuomintang leader betrayed the revolutionary cause. "On April 12, 1927, his agents, together with others on the spot, including French, British, and Japanese police and military forces, carried out a mass slaughter of workers, intellectuals, and others accused of sympathizing with the Communists. "[8]. Chiang's victory in-

4. *Ibid.*, p. 178
5. *Ibid.*, p. 182
6. Theda Skocpol, *States and Social Revolutions.*, p.73
7. *Ibid.*, p.186
8. Harold Isaacs, *Tragedy of the Chinese Revolution.*, pp. 180-181

itiated a new phase in Chinese politics. He unified China with imperialist support and promised suppression of Communism and agrarian discontent by using military force.

Commercial elements were weakening the peasantry and concentrating wealth in the hands of a new social formation—a fusion between sections of the old ruling class and new social strata rising in the towns. This fusion formed the social basis of the Kuomintang. Its agrarian policy was aimed at maintaining or restoring the *status quo*. The presence of the Communist rival polarised the situation making Kuomintang policy even more oppressive. "The Communists act as the inheritors to temporarily fanatical peasant rebellions; the National Government and the Kuomintang to ascendant mandarinates."[9].

Industry failed to register significant advance under the Kuomintang. It cannot be attributed to Japanese blockade and occupation alone. An important factor was the continuing opposition from the landlords to China's transformation into an industrial power. China preferred to import military equipment instead of building up its own industrial base. China remained industrially backward because the landowning class retained through the Kuomintang the substance of political control and leadership.

The two decades of Kuomintang rule show some features of the reactionary phase of the European response to industrialisation, including some totalitarian, characteristics. The social basis of the Kuomintang was an opportunistic but contradictory coalition between the rural landlords and the urban capitalists. "The Kuomintang, through its control of the means of violence, served as the link that held the coalition together. At the same time its control of violence enabled it to blackmail the urban capitalist sector and to operate the machinery of government both directly and indirectly. In both these respects the Kuomintang resembled Hitler's NSDAP."[10]

However, there are important differences between the social bases and historical circumstances of the Kuomintang fascism and Germany's National Socialism. These differences account for the relatively weak character of the Chinese reactionary phase. One of the causes was the lack of a strong base in industry in the case of China. Japan's invasion of China further weakened the native capitalist element and prevented the Kuomintang fascism from assuming an expansionist character. For these reasons. "The Chinese reactionary and protofascist phase resembles that of Franco's Spain, where an agrarian elite also managed to stay on top but could not execute an aggressive foreign policy, more than it does corresponding phases in Germany and Italy."[11].

During its revolutionary phase, prior to attaining power, the Kuomintang had identified itself with the Taiping Rebellion of China's peasantry. After the conquest of state power, the Party under Chiang Kai-shek's leadership did an about-turn, identifying itself with the Imperial system and its superficial Restoration of 1862-1874. [12]. It was a "a switch that recalls the early behaviour of Italian fascism. After victory, the doctrine became a curious amalgam of Confucian elements and scraps taken from western liberal thinking. The latter...had entered through the influence of Sun Yat-sen... The analogies to European fascism arise mainly from the pattern and shadings of emphasis that Chiang Kai-shek...placed upon these disparate elements."[13].

In Chiang Kai-shek's *China's Destiny,* there is practically no discussion of the social and economic factors that had brought China to her current state of degradation. Any serious analysis of these issues could have alienated upper class support to the Kuomintang. In this lack of a realistic analysis of socio-economic issues, its ideology reminds us of European fascism. In the Confucian theory of a benevolent elite that also assumes a heroic and martial character, the Kuomintang doctrine resembled western fascism. Chiang says, "Excessive personal liberty... cannot be allowed to exist either during wartime or in the postwar period." He quoted Sun Yat-sen to justify this, "In order to resist foreign oppression, we must free ourselves

9. Paul M. Linebarger, *The China of Chiang Kai-shek.*, p. 233
10. Barrington Moore, Social Origins of Dictatorship and Democracy. pp. 196-197
11. *Ibid.*, p.197
12. Mary C.Wright, *The Last Stand of Chinese Conservatism.*, p. 300. For an analysis of the Kuomintang ideology, see pp. 301-312
13. Barrington Moore Jr., *Social Origins of Dictatorship and Democracy.*, pp. 197-198

from the idea of 'individual liberty' and unite ourselves into strong cohesive body."[14].

Chiang's talk about 'political tutelage' and preparation for democracy was mainly rhetoric. Actual policy was not to disturb the *status quo* and even to distort facts in order to idealize the past. Mary C.Wright has argued this point cogently in her book, *The Last Stand of Chinese Conservatism,* reminding that this distorted patriotic idealization of the past is one of main stigmata of European fascism. Another feature is the Kuomintang's effort to suppress native Communism by the use of force, which is again a major characteristic of Western fascism. This shows that fascism as an ideology dominated Japan and Kuomintang China in Asia as well as Germany and Italy in Europe, at the same time, as a single complex unit, affecting their social, political, and intellectual climate and movements, though in different ways.

**Failure of the Bourgeois Republic**

Like most revolutions, the bourgeois revolution of 1911 gave rise to great hope and euphoria in China and the people looked to it as a panacea for the country's ills and miseries. But the demise of the old dynasty did not lead to the creation of a bourgeois-democratic state. As soon as Sun Yat-sen was proclaimed Provisional President of the Republic, Yuan Shih-Kai, a reactionary General, forced the abdication of the nationalist leader and assumed the position himself. The Republican ideals were soon given up as the new dictator Yuan was proclaiming his ambition to found a new dynasty.

It was recognised that the transformation of China into a modern democratic nation could not be achieved by one simple revolution. From 1911 to 1925 China faced one of the most chaotic, confusing and disunited periods of her history. As C.P. Fitzgerald traces the collapse of the revolution through the tragi-comedy of General Yuan's rule to the dissolution of all central government into regional warlordism, he points out that the bourgeois revolution discredited not only the old monarchical system but also the credentials and ideals of the new republican regime.

According to Fitzgerald, the Chinese became "completely disillusioned with the false gods of the west. They turned restlessly to some other solution." Soon the news of the Russian Revolution reached China., "Here was a new model, and what is more important, a model bearing none of the stigma of western colonialism. To young Chinese intellectuals trapped in the dark ages of modern Chinese history between warring factions of venal warlords and encroaching foreign powers eager to 'cut up the Chinese melon'; this new doctrine had a strong appeal."[15]

As the events proved, the bourgeois Republic was destined to end neither in democracy nor in a new dynasty, but in chaos. The foreign powers, including Japan, were hostile to the Republican cause. Strong republican China would banish Japan's dream of her continental empire and put an end to semi-colonial domination of China by other imperialist powers. But the emerging Republic did not exactly cover itself with glory by its mal-functioning. "The Parliament, elected in 1912, was a travesty of democracy. Votes were openly sold and openly quoted on the market. The members, when they met, devoted all their time to appropriate large salaries to themselves. Without roots in Chinese history, without tradition and without honesty, the organs of democracy presented a shameful picture of irresponsibility and corruption. Truly 'a monkey had dressed up in the roles of Duke Chou'."[16].

To the President, Yuan Shih-Kai, the spectacle of the Republic's degeneration was quite welcome as it gave him an opportunity to intrigue to found his own personal dynasty. He secured a large loan from the European powers, without the Consent of China's Parliament, and thus flouting the constitution he made himself independent of it. Then began the process of assassinating or exiling prominent Republican leaders. "The dynasty was proclaimed, the President, Emperor-elect, performed, for the last time in history, the rite of ploughing and sacrifice at the Temple of Agriculture and the Altar of Heaven, and the date of his enthronement was announced."[17].

By a historic irony, the Republic was saved by Japan's presentation of the notorious Twenty-

14. Chiang Kai-shek, *China's Destiny.*, p. 208
15. Franz Schurmann and Ordville Schell (eds) *Republican China*, p.22
16. C. P. Fitzgerald, *The Birth of Communist China,* p. 47
17. *Ibid.*, p. 48

one Demands, which if accepted would have made China a virtual Japanese protectorate extinguishing her independence. Yuan accepted these demands in part but this destroyed his prestige. A military revolt in Yunnan and a wide-spread threat of a civil war forced Yuan to abandon his dynastic plans. The Republic was technically saved. But the Republican party had played no role in crushing the monarchical movement. Only the jealous generals had any hand in Yuan's overthrow. In Peking a succession of weak cabinets occupied office but the Republic failed to recover its former position. In the South, Sun Yat-sen established a rival regime of the Republican party, which was itself dependent on the good will of the local military satraps. [18].

With the disintegration of the bourgeois Republic, the generals, nicknamed the warlords, became the real rulers of China in different regions. "They supported or betrayed the government for money; they warred upon each other to secure richer revenues, they organised the opium trade, sold the official posts, taxed the people for years in advance, squeezed the merchants, and finally, immensely rich, allowed for a last payment, their troops to be defeated, and retired to the safety and ease of the foreign concessions in Shanghai or the British colony of Hong-Kong."[19].

The Chinese Revolution had become an incomprehensible chaos. The military rulers had alienated both the *literati* and the peasantry. No contest was visible between democracy and tyranny on the basis of principles. Throughout the period of warlord rule, from 1916 to 1925, conditions steadily deteriorated in the cities as well as the villages. In this period of disastrous floods and famines, democracy and the West's image had been discredited and cast aside. It is true that democracy was never given a fair trial in the early period of Republican China. Bourgeois democracy "had never taken root in this alien soil, and... the pitiful travesty of the early Republic was neither an example of democracy nor a proof of its failure."[20].

Yet this was the image that the Chinese people witnessed of democracy in their country. "In the name of Parliament they had seen gross and shameless corruption; in the name of democracy they had seen nothing but weak and bad government, military usurpation, violation of law, every kind of oppression and national decline....the Chinese people were completely disillusioned with the false gods imported from the West."[21] Another effect of this tragicomedy was to discredit still further the fallen Empire. "The Chinese are not romantic, particularly in politics. No lost cause appeals to the Chinese, no fallen house receives sympathy or support. What has fallen is down and can never be raised up. There have been no restorations in China, no Jacobites, no ghosts from the political past....No one really thought that new dynasty, encumbered by the memories of the past, would prove able to steer China on to a new course. By 1920 it was clear that western democracy was not the solution and tacitly it was abandoned even by the revolutionary element."[22]

**Towards People's Democracy**

Nationalists and Communists alike consider the May Fourth Movement of 1919 as the culmination of China's cultural revolution. It also marks the beginning of modern nationalist struggle against foreign domination. The student-led demonstrations and the great general strike in Shanghai and other cities convinced many Chinese intellectuals that alliance with the masses was the only road to revolution and regeneration. The Russian Revolution of 1917 inspired many Chinese to study Marxism and Li-Ta-chao, the future Communist leader, "wrote prophetically of Russia and China's common revolutionary destiny.... Within a decade Marxism had become the dominant mode of thinking in both Communist and non-Communist intellectual circles."[23].

The Chinese Communist Party was formed in Shanghai in July 1921. Soon it entered into an alliance with the Kuomintang under Sun Yat-sen's leadership. But Sun died in 1925 and Chiang broke the United Front by resorting to White Terror against the Communists. When Chiang's brutality forced the Communists un-

18. *Ibid.*, pp. 50-51
19. Quoted in Schurmann and Schell (eds), *Republican China.*, p. 31
20. Quoted in *Ibid.*, p. 33
21. C.P. Fitzgerald, *the Birth of Communist China*,. p.53
22. *Ibid.*, p. 54
23. F. Schurmann and O. Schell(eds), *Republican China*, p. 87

derground, he cut them off from the workers of the city, but he could not break their contact with the agitated peasantry. The Communists started forming soviets in the areas liberated by them. Thus an 'armed revolution' came into existence confronting an 'armed counter-revolution' in China. After the famous Long March, the Communists established their own government in the Northwest. The Japanese invasion of China persuaded the Kuomintang and the Communists to form the Second United Front.

In 1945 the Japanese surrendered. China was now free from foreign invaders. But as soon as the Japanese laid down their arms, the old rivalry began between the Kuomintang and the Communists. The United Front, which was always vulnerable, collapsed. America helped Chiang to occupy Northern Chinese and Manchurian cities. The Communists moved into the countryside surrounding the urban centres. Despite American support, Chiang's army was routed in the Civil War. People's Republic of China came into existence in 1949. The Nationalists were driven out of the mainland and took refuge in the island of Taiwan where they are still ruling under American protection.

Mao has explained the nature of the people's democratic revolution in China in the following words, "The first imperialist world war and the first victorious social revolution, the October Revolution, have changed the whole course of world history and ushered in a new era....In this era, any revolution in a colony or semi-colony that is directed against imperialism *i.e.* against the international bourgeoisie or international capitalism, no longer comes within the old category of the bourgeois democratic world revolution, but within the new category. It is no longer part of the old bourgeois, or capitalist, world revolution, but is part of the new world revolution, the proletarian-socialist world revolution."[24].

The social basis of the People's Democratic State was a four class coalition of the workers, the peasants, the petty-bourgeoisie and the national bourgeoisie under the leadership of the Chinese Communist Party. It was directed against the feudal landowners, the bureaucratic capitalists and the imperialists. According to Mao, the proclamation of the Chinese People's Republic in 1949 was the consummation of the new-democratic revolution which would create conditions for a continued revolution in the direction of socialism. The socialist transformation of China's economy was completed under Mao's leadership within a decade. Yet Mao was convinced that antagonistic contradictions still vitiated the Chinese society.

Mao Zedong pointed out, "In China although the main socialist transformation has been completed with respect to the system of ownership, and although the large-scale and turbulent class struggles of the masses characteristic of the previous military periods have in the main come to an end, there are still remnants of the overthrown landlord and comprador classes, there is still a bourgeoisie and the remoulding of petty bourgeoisie has only just started. The class struggle is by no means over. The class struggle between the proletariat and the bourgeoisie, the class struggle between the different political forces, and the class struggle in the ideological field between the proletariat and the bourgeoisie will continue to be long and tortuous and at times will become very acute. The proletariat seeks to transform the world according to its own world outlook, and so does the bourgeoisie In this respect, the question of which will win out, socialism or capitalism, is still not really settled."[25]

In the cultural revolution, the radical wing of the Communist Party led by Chairman Mao fought against the 'capitalist-roaders' through a nation-wide campaign in which the workers and the youth were encouraged to participate in large number. Mao declared that representatives of the bourgeoisie have sneaked into the Party, the government and the army, occupying the highest posts in certain cases. They have also infiltrated into literary, educational and cultural institutions. All these bourgeois elements, he said, are counter-revolutionary revisionists who are conspiring to seize state power and establish a dictatorship of the bourgeoisie. Mao, therefore, asked the people to smash their plots for restoring capitalism in China.

After Mao Zedong's demise, the same revisionists and 'capitalist-roaders', led by Deng Xiaoping, who were denounced and persecuted during the cultural revolution, seized state power. The new ruling elite condemned the

24. Mao Zedong, "On New Democracy" in *Selected Works.*, Vol. 2., pp. 343-344
25. Mao Zedong, *Four Essays on Philosophy., p. 115*

so-called 'cultural revolution' as a naked power struggle waged by a clique of the so-called 'radicals'. It disrupted production and inhibited economic development and demoralized the honest and hard-working Party and State cadres and leaders. Deng Xiaoping accused the 'gang of four', which also included Mao's wife, that it was trying to establish a 'fascist-type' dictatorship on the pretext of implementing the 'great proletarian cultural revolution'. The moderate ruling group gradually reversed the 'socialist' policies initiated by Maoist radicals in the sphere of agriculture and re-intorduced privatization in industry, commerce and banking. Even foreign capital has been invited to contribute to China's industrialization in selected zones set up in the coastal provinces.

**The Cultural Revolution**

The Great Proletarian Cultural Revolution, as Mao called it, was in the direct tradition of Mao's conception of revolution as a continuing process. "Central to this conception is the idea that the existing situation must be constantly reviewed and called into question to prevent the re-emergence of the former exploiting classes in positions of influence, in the form of repeated 'class struggle' movements, and a whole series of policies of 'thought reform' and 'rectification' movements."[26]. The basic concept behind these campaigns has been that the human values and cultural norms are the crucial factor in the functioning of society; and that even a political revolution and seizure of state power leading to collective ownership of the major means of production cannot guarantee the success of a socialist revolution unless there is also a revolution in men's mode of thought.

The old morality was derived from the old bourgeois society of capitalism, private property and self-interest. The new morality must be related to socialism, collective property and public interest. Mao believes that bourgeois culture and ideas will not disappear on their own, they will have to be driven out and then replaced by socialist values and culture. The Cultural Revolution aimed at changing men's minds and, in addition, replacing the personnel wielding power that still retained older modes of thinking, burgeois or feudal. One distinguishing feature of the Cultural Revolution was the role played by a new extra-Party organisation of the youth, the Red Guards, that came into existence to spearhead it.

According to Mao's theory, classes continue to exist under soialism; these are not classes in the traditional Marxist sense which are related to the ownership of property like landlords, peasants, capitalists and workers. They are rather functional classes such as managers, party leaders, state officials intellectuals, peasants and workers. Contradictions still exist between them which may develop into sharp hostilities. Unless they are properly resolved, they can lead to a fundamental conflict between rulers and ruled. This happened in Russia after the death of Stalin. Through the Cultural Revolution, Mao wanted to escape from Russia's fate of backsliding into ideological revisionism.

*Liberation Army Daily* in its editorial on the 3rd November 1966 explained the nature and purpose of the Cultural Revolution in the following words, "Conducted mainly in the ideological field, fundamentally it is a great revolution to destroy the thousands-of -years old concept of private ownership and establish the socialist concept of public ownership.... Ideas, culture, customs, habits, political views, legal concepts, views on art and so on are all ideological forms in society, which generally go under the name of culture. Why must we carry out a cultural revolution in the period of socialism ? The reason is that the economic base of society has undergone fundamental change.... Since the economic base has changed. the ideological super-structure must change accordingly to keep step with it. Otherwise it will obstruct the forces from developing, lead to the loss of the already-won fruits of the revolution, and give rise to revisionist rule and the restoration of capitalism."[27].

In 1964, Mao claimed that literary and artistic circles had behaved for the last fifteen years as arrogant bureaucrats, had not identified with the workers and peasants and had not reflected socialist revolution and socialist construction. In 1965 he criticized the reactionary bourgeois authorities in the universities. In 1966 certain party leaders of Peking and their journals were attacked for their pro-capitalist views. *Peking Review* declared, "The overthrown bourgeoisie, in their plots for restoration and sub-

26. Stuart Schram, *Mao Tse-tung,*quoted in *The Chinese Road to Socialism,*. p. 99
27. Quoted in E.L. Wheelwright and Bruce McFarlane, *The Chinese Road To Socialism*., pp. 106-107

version, give first place to ideology, take hold of ideology and the superstructure. The representatives of the bourgeoisie...did all they could to spread bourgeois and revisionist poison through the media of literature, the theatre, films, music, the arts, the press, periodicals, the radio, publications and academic research and in schools etc., in an attempt to corrupt people's minds... as ideological preparation... for capitalist restoration. "[28].

After some time, the Eleventh Plenary Session of the Eighth Central Committee of the Chinese Communist Party adopted the sixteen points on August 8, 1966, as guidelines for the Cultural Revolution. The decision specified that "at present our objective is to struggle against and over-throw those persons in authority who are taking the capitalist road...so as to facilitate the consolidation and development of the socialist system."[29].

Mao and his allies were using the Red Guards as the spearhead of the new revolution. They were offered free rail transport anywhere in China, free food, and free lodging in schools and colleges. Millions of these young men and women came to Peking to be addressed by their leader, who exhorted them to fan out to other cities and the countryside. There was some violence. The 'capitalist-roaders' were beaten up, the temples were desecrated and houses of the 'bourgeoisie' were ransacked and their goods confiscated. Mao emphasized the people's right to rebel as the great truth of Marxism. He talked of "bombarding the Party headquarter". It is easy to see why. The Maoists were at that time the minority group in the Party Central Committee. Of seven members of the former Standing Committee, Liu Shaoqi, Deng Xiaoping, Zhu Deh and Chen Yun were "rightists", only three stood with the "proletarian line", Mao Zedong, Lin Biao, and Zhou Enlai. The task was to overthrow those in authority, smash the Party and State apparatus and assert the supremacy of "revolutionary committees" set up by the "proletarian headquarters" of the cultural revolution.

By April 1968, the Cultural Revolution in China had entered a new stage. The proletarian headquarters around Mao had seized power in twenty-three out of twentyseven provinces; Mao's ally, Zhou Enlai had also established full control over the Central Government; and an attempt was being made to run a modern economy on "moral incentives" and "mobilization of the masses" with profound effects on production and efficiency. The latest phase was featured by the overthrow of an elite group of party bureaucrats, managers, technocrats and state functionaries. "Maoists did *not* see the Cultural Revolution as a zigzag stage in the policy and tactics between Left and Right, or as an opportunity for the Left to push ahead to a new advance, The issue between them and the Liu Shaoqi group was seen as being *Over the whole nature and raison d.'etre of the socialist revolution.*"[30]. The cultural revolution signified that the struggle between "two lines" in the Communist Party had been transformed into the struggle between "two roads" — capitalism and socialism-in the national arena.

## Socialism with Chinese Characteristics

The last phase of Mao Zedong's life saw a high degree of polarisation between the ultra-leftist radicals of Shanghai led by Jiang Qing and the supporters of Zhou Enlai and Deng Xiaoping. A basic conflict between them centred on their experiences during the Cultural Revolution and their responses towards its legacy. Jiang's group believed that the class struggle between the proletariat and the bourgeoisie was an important feature of an early socialist society and during that phase the danger as well as the possibility of capitalist restoration was very real. They emphasized high levels of collectivisation, normative incentives, indigenous technological development and an open education system. The moderates stressed pragmatic policies in agriculture, industry and education which were more result-oriented and less ideological. As Kalpana Misra put it, 'Evaluating socio-economic policies in terms of developmental imperatives and efficiency they perceived ultra-leftist pre-occupation with class and class conflict as antithetical to their goals.[31].

Mao's approach at this time was dualistic. He tacitly supported the leadership of the moderates in the economic sphere but at the same time encouraged the ultraleftist criticism of their

28. *Peking Review.*, June 10,1966
29. *Eastern Horizon.*, January 1967
30. E.L.Wheel Wright and Bruee McFarlance, *The Chinese Road to Socialism.*, p. 122
31. Kalpana Misra, *From Post-Maoism to Post-Marxism.*, p. 117

economic policies. "The twin campaigns to Restrict Bourgeois Right and Strengthen the Dictatorship of the Proletariat that dominated the Chinese media in 1975-76 aimed specifically at undermining the legitimacy of moderate economic initiatives and labelling them ideologically suspect tactical expedients."[32].

In 1981-82, the moderate reformers were in a stronger position. The controversy over stages was finally settled in their favour. The definition of socialism as public ownership of the means of production and distribution according to work was now recognized as the correct description of socialist society. An economic reform was expedited during the 1980s. However, the reality of economic liberalisation became inconsistent with such a statist conception of the socialist economy. Deng's intervention on behalf of the reformers propelled the Chinese economy further in the direction of liberalisation. Zhao Ziangs followers used the inherent contradictions of the half-way reform to press for further acceleration and deepening of the reform process.

Zhao Ziang pointed out that China's "per capita GNP still ranks among the lowest in the world... the backwardness of the productive forces determines the following aspects of the relations of production: socialisation of production.... is still at a very low level; the commodity economy and domestic market are only beginning to develop; the natural economy and semi-natural economy still constitute a considerable proportion of the whole; and the socialist economic system is not yet mature and well-developed."[33]. Given this under-development of its produtive forces, China's primary stage of socialist development "was destined to span almost a century and a half. During this stage China would accomplish industrializing and modernization of production, which many other countries had achieved under capitalist conditions."[34].

The thesis that China was then in the primary stage of socialism aimed at clarifying the nature of both 'right' and 'left' mistakes. On the one hand it criticised the view that China could not take the socialist road without going through the stage of fully developed capitalism. On the other hand, it argued against skipping over stages and attempting policies appropriate to a much higher level of development as this was sheer utopianism. On the basis of a proper understanding of the current stage of growth, it was possible for Dengist leadership to devise suitable policies for the building of "Socialism with Chinese Characteristics."

In fact, this thesis about the primary stage of development could not provide a proper ideological justification sought by the Dengist leadership. The developments related to structural reform as well the inconsistencies inherent in the theory of the 'primary stage of socialism' rendered the definition of socialism in the early 1990s quite ambiguous. They undermined the credibility of their claim that China was still engaged in building 'socialism' of any stage, primary or otherwise. "A premature declaration of socialism simply highlighted the fact that China's socialist transformation' was in essence an administrative decree and not in any way a reflection of objective reality."[35]

In late 1980s and early 1990s, when economic crisis and rampart bureaucratic corruption prevailed, some radical reformists advocated elimination of price controls, establishment of full-fledged market economy, even the abolition of public ownership and the institution of private property rights. "As a fulfilment of Maoist prophecy that such a state of affairs would eventually lead to 'capitalist restoration' some of the most vocal of Chinese reformers now insistently pressed for the substitution of public ownership with private-property relations."[36].

The theory of the primary stage of socialism failed to counter Zhao Ziang's critics both on the left and the right. From the moderate perspective it could not provide legitimation either to the system or generate support for the goals of the leadership. The rightists felt that Zhao's approach did not go far enough because they had by then completed the transition from revision to renunciation of the socialist protect. For Mao, 'payment according to work' was 'the

32. *Ibid.*, p. 118
33. Zhao Ziang, :"Advance Along the Road of Socialism with Chinese Characteristics," report delivered at the 13th Conference of the Communist Party of China on 5 October, 1987
34. Kalpana Misra,"*From Post-Maoism to Post-Marxism.*, p. 111
35. *Ibid.*, p. 113
36. *Ibid.*, p. 114

exchange of equal values' that prevailed in capitalist economy. The dangers of extolling this principle as a positive socialist method of distribution, as Deng Xiaoping and his supporters were doing, were correctly pointed out by Yao Wenyuan.

This Chinese critic of Dengist policies predicted that "a small number of people will in the course of distribution acquire increasing amounts of commodities and money through certain legal channels and numerous illegal ones; capitalist ideas of amassing fortunes and craving for personal fame and gain, stimulated by such 'material incentives' will spread unchecked; phenomena such as the turning of public property into private property, speculation, graft and corruption, the theft , and bribery will increase; the capitalist principle of the exchange of commodities will make its way into political and even into Party life, undermining the socialist planned economy ; acts of capitalist exploitation such as the conversion of commodities and money into capital, and labour power will occur.... as a result, a small number of new bourgeois elements and upstarts.... will emerge from among Party members, workers, well-to-do peasants, and personnel in state organs. When the economic strength of the bourgeoisie has grown to a certain extent, its agents will demand political rule, demand the overthrow of the dictatorship of the proletariat and the socialist system, demand a complete changeover from socialist ownership, and openly restore and develop the capitalist system."[37].

The early post-Mao debate on 'the bourgeois right' developed out of the need to invalidate the leftist 'egalitarianism' and argue that China's socialist development was not be sabotaged by the new Dengist socio-economic policies. The controversy over whether class should be defined primarily on economic basis or in terms of ideological and political criteria also was likewise concerned with the denial of the hostile emergence of new exploitative social classes in 'socialist' China. For the moderate leaders and intellectuals, who were criticised as the 'capitalist roaders' in the past, the emphasis on economic criteria was quite necessary at this stage but this assertion brought them into conflict with the growing reformist trend towards privatization. The radical reformers found political criteria more useful for understanding the new role of capital in the increasingly market-oriented economy. "For very different reasons, Mao's most vociferous critics found themselves in agreement with his position on class status."[38].

In addition to superstructural elements inherited from the old social order, a second source of class polarization and capitalist restoration, according to Mao, was bureaucratic degeneration and an alliance between party-state bureaucracy and the liberal and technocratic intelligentsia. The revolts of intellectuals, students and other strata in Eastern Europe, the 'cult of the expert' advocated by Liu Shaoqi, Deng Xiaoping and others and their opposition to the Socialist Education Movement had convinced Mao that a 'bureaucratic-political' nexus was emerging in China also which would obstruct further advance towards socialism. The post-Mao Dengist leadership reversed Mao's preference for continuous revolution in favour of an elite-guided process of steady economic development based on pragmatic planning and professional expertise.

After his rehabilitation, Deng restored the legitimacy of the 'revisionist' cadres and denounced the 'falsehoods' which were 'peddled by the Gang of Four (his term for the overthrown radical leaders). Deng's argument for dismissing the existence of a bureaucratic class was that the Communist cadres did not own the means of production and, therefore, it was not possible for them to exploit the workers or the peasants. Dengist educational reforms focused primarily on the tasks of economic modernization. The significance of differential access to education in systems in which the power and privileges enjoyed by the elite cannot be inherited has been highlighted by many writers. Paul Sweezy singled out privileged access to education as "probably the most important way in which the bureaucracy reproduces itself as a class."[39]. The emergence of a powerful and wealthy group of industrial and commercial entrepreneurs reinforced the 'bureaucratic bourgeoisie within the Party' because it could assist them through bureaucratic manipulation of the partially pri-

37. Yao Wenyuan, "On the Social Basis of the Lin Biao Clique", *Hongi.*, no. 4(1975) pp. 20-29
38. Kalpana Misra, *From Post-Maoism to Post-Marxism.*, p. 149
39. Paul Sweezy, "Towards a Programme of Studies on the Transition to Socialism," in Paul Sweezy and Charles Bettelheim, *On the Transition to Socialism.*, New York: Monthly Review Press, 1972, pp. 123-135

vatized economy.

As a shrewd observer explains it, "Party-state functionaries' privileged and monopolist access to and control over material resources, capital base, licensing etc., along with connections and networks put them in a unique position to exploit the opportunities offered them from economic liberalization. The beneficiaries of half-way economic reform were the bureaucrat capitalists whose new-found channels for amassing wealth would be undermined by a return to the structures, norms, and values of the planned socialist economy, whereas a transition to a complete market, i.e., a full-fledged capitalist restoration would deny them their special inside tracks."[40].

According to Charles Bettelheim, all Soviet-type societies eventually degenerated into bureaucratic or state capitalism and after the collapse of Communist Party rule in these countries, they are trying to create market-oriented economies, although the remnants of state capitalism still co-exist with the new features of market capitalism in all these societies. In China, the Dengist leadership introduced strong elements of market capitalism and capitalist social relations without completely demolishing the earlier structures of state capitalism and the command economy. Here we had a curious spectacle of the Communist Party itself presiding over the liquidation of its own revolutionary legacy.

## SUGGESTED READINGS

Andors, Stephen, *China's Industrial Revolutions, Politics, Planning and Management.*

Balazs, Etienne, *Chinese Civilization and Bureaucracy.*

Bettelheim, Charles, *Cultural Revolution and Industrial Organisation in China.*

Ch'en Jerome, *Mao and the Chinese Revolution.*

Chiang Kai-shek, *China's Destiny.*

Fitzgerald, C.P. *Revolution in China.*

Isaacs, Harold R. *Tragedy of the Chinese Revolution.*

Miliband, Ralph, *Marxism and Politics.*

Misra, Kalpana, *From Post-Maoism to Post-Marxism.*

Moore, Barrington Jr., *Social Origins of Dictatorship and Democracy.*

Pye, Lucien W., *The Spirit of Chinese Politics* Schram, Stuart R., *The Political Thought of Mao Tse-tung*

Schurmann, F., and Schell, O.,(eds), *Republican China; Communist China.*

Skocpol, Theda, *States and Social Revolutions.*

Wheelwright, E.L., and McFarlane, Bruce, *The Chinese Road to Sócialism.*

Wright, Mary C., *The Last Stand of Chinese Conservatism.*

40. Kalpana Misra, *From Post-Maoism to Post-Marxism.*, p. 173

# PART II

# THE GOVERNMENT OF THE INDIAN REPUBLIC

# CHAPTER I

# The Nationalist Movement

## Rise of Nationalism

Nationalism is a feeling of territorial patriotism or a sense of identification of the individual with the entire people of the land. This consciousness is fostered by the development of a common language, expansion of education and means of communication and transport, growth of political parties, democratic institutions and a free press, and by the active participation of the people in government and other public affairs. The sentiment of national unity is forged among the people through struggle for independence. The exploitation and repressive policies of the rulers whip up anti-government feelings which find expression in some form of political action, constitutional or revolutionary. The pace and growth of a national movement, however, depend upon various factors, like the quality of leadership, the spirit of discipline and sacrifice among the people and the national and international situation.

In India, whose political history extends over centuries, the political and national unity, though formulated as a concept even in earlier times, was never consciously realised at any time before the nineteenth century. The country had a cultural and social unity which sustained her people through several political vicissitudes. Politically, too, a very large part of India had, for certain periods, been consolidated, especially under the Mauryas, Kushans, Guptas and Mughals, and in time of common danger people in various parts of the country had demonstrated a unique solidarity. The country had also known both the monarchical and republican forms of government and representative institutions, described as "little republics", had functioned in villages for centuries. Whatever the form of government, the Indian polity, broadly speaking, was characterised by its ethical basis, the prevalence of popular will and a concern for the general well-being. But, unfortunately, India as a country never exhibited political stability for a long period. Nor did it become a nation in the modern sense of the term, as was perhaps nowhere else during that period. Apart from the feeling of territorial affinity as a consequence of living together, there was never an organised and deliberate effort made to promote the sentiments of national unity. Tara Chand states the bare truth that "The hard moulds into which groups and communities were enveloped did not permit them to be fused together" into a politically conscious society.[1]

No doubt the rulers and people of India had offered successful resistance to some foreign aggressors and India's military history is replete with individual and collective valorous deeds and acts of chivalry, patriotism, self-sacrifice and undaunted courage, but generally personal rivalries and political intrigues, casteism and regionalism had always marred political unity that had attained great fame for her cultural and spiritual heritage. It was primarily for dissensions among the warring rulers of post-Aurangzeb India that just a handful of the British who came to trade and lived on the sufferance of the Mughal and other Indian authorities, gradually extended their political domain. It was because of their superior military organisation and better army and their successful political strategy of exploiting internal strifes that the East India Company vanquished the Mughals, the Marathas, and the Sikhs and by

1. Tara Chand, *History of the Freedom Movement in India,* Vol. I, p. 4.

the middle of the nineteenth century practically the whole of India was held under their sway.

The British in India restored peace where life and limb was in danger. The theoretical basis of political unity was provided by the British Crown holding together the British and Princely India. The period from 1858 to the end of First World War presented a picture of the administrative unification of India. The country was knitted together by a uniform post and telegraph system and its distant and far-flung parts were linked up with a network of roads and railway communications. A single currency prevailed from Kashmir to Cape Comorin and a customs union was built around the country within which the economic life was integrated. In a mult-lingual country, English, though a foreign language, enabled people from the various areas to converse with one another and to associate socially and politically. A uniform system of education also contributed to the political unity of the country.

These were some of the blessings of the British regime which made India a political unit and a geographical entity, but by themselves these could not have galvanised the country into a dynamic nation. What actually led to the emergence of a single independent union at the end of the British rule in 1947 was the prolonged and bitter political struggle of the Indian people which "gave to the sense of Indian nationhood a significance which a mere unified administration or a common education could not have given." India's freedom struggle which passed through many upheavals, unfolds a poignant and inspiring drama of the emancipation of 400 million odd Indians from the political bondage of the mightiest empire of the world.

## FACTORS STIMULATING THE GROWTH OF NATIONALISM

### Pre-'Mutiny' Developments

Most of the earlier invasions of India were short-lived like those of Alexander, the Huns, the Sakas, Mahmud Ghaznavi, Shahab-ud-din Ghori, Timur, Nadir shah and Ahmed Shah. The conquests of Turks and Mughals, however, were of a different nature. These invaders settled permanently in India and were absorbed in the Indian society. But the 'conquest' of India by the East India company was a new experience for the Indian people. Unlike the previous conquerors, who either withdew or made India home, the British turned the country into a political dependency of Great Britain. They did not rest at that. They shattered the economy, killed industry, transformed the land system, perpetuated economic exploitation in the interest of their own country and the people groaned under the heels of a foreign imperialist power.

The reckless policy of political expansion pursued from the time of Clive to that of Dalhousie, annexation of the Princely States through the policy of escheats, annexation and the doctrine of lapse, the arrogance of the company's officials, ill-conceived agrarian changes and the expropriation of some landlords alienated a large number of Indian Princes and the landed aristocracy and left behind a blazing trail of discontent and disaffection throughout the country. The Muslim and Hindu families, tribes and castes, which were nurseries for the supply of soldiers, administrators and leaders were ostracized from the offices of the Company's government and were condemned to serve as helots. The learned classes, who had enjoyed a great patronage under the ruling Princes and the feudal lords were gradually squeezed out of their profession. The masses, too, who had generally remained indifferent to political vicissitudes in the past, felt deeply aggrieved for having been hit hard by land policy of the Company. Heavy assessment, the unceasing growth of population and its ever-increasing pressure on land further depressed their already miserable standard of living. They virtually lived on the verge of starvation.

Haughty and arrogant attitude of Europeans towards Indians, both high and low, the inaccessibility of the British officials, the exclusion of Indians from all high offices of the Company and denial of all kinds of rights to Indians all combined together made the Company's regime highly unpopular.

The alarm caused by the rapid spread of Western civilisation in India and the proselytising activities of Christian Missionaries also significantly contributed to inflame anti-British feelings. Sir Syed Ahmed Khan, a great admirer of the British, drew attention thus to these apprehensions of Indians, Hindus and Muslims alike : "There is no doubt that all persons whether intelligent or ignorant, respectable or otherwise, believed that the Government was really and seriously desirous of interfering with the religion and customs of the people, converting them all, whether Hindus or Mohammedans, to Christianity, and forcing them to adopt European manners and habits."

The political awakening among certain

sections of the people, therefore, arose out of resentment against the Company's unjust and exploitative policies. A bitter feeling grew that the evils from which the people suffered were the outcome of Farangi's (foreigner's) rule and the periodical famines in the first half of the nineteenth century were linked with the sacrilegious way of life of the Kristan (Christians).[2] The misery that followed in the wake of famines kept alive the feeling of anger and hostility against the Company's regime.

The socio-religious movements among the Muslims and the Hindus in the first half of the nineteenth century also helped, for different reasons, in fostering national consciousness among the two communities. They awakened pride in the ancient religions and engendered dissatisfaction against foreign rule which was considered to be threatening the indigenous culture.

The Wahabi movement,[3] which was initiated in Arabia, preached a return to primitive Islam and extolled its glory, made a great impact on the minds of Indian Muslims, who were in the slough of despondency. As ex-rulers of the country, the Muslims nursed a great resentment against the British and their rule which had deprived them of all the advantages and blessings which had belonged to them as ruling community. The Company's Government, on its own part, was suspicious of the Muslims lest they should make a bid to regain their lost power. They looked upon the Muslims as their enemies and resorted to a policy of isolating them from the Hindus. A clear enunciation of this policy was given by Lord Ellenborough. He wrote to the Duke of Wellington, after the fall of Kabul and Ghazni, that whereas Muslims, as a class, had wished for the defeat of the British forces, the Hindus were delighted on their victory. He, then observed, "It seems to me most unwise, when we are sure of the hostility of one-tenth, why not to secure the enthusiastic support of the nine-tenths which are faithful." He, again, wrote to the Duke of Wellington, "I cannot close my eyes to the belief that what race (Muslims) is fundamentally hostile to us, and, therefore, our true policy is to conciliate the Hindus."[4]

Thus, began the systematic policy of 'Divide and Rule' , which gave not only a severe blow to the pride and respectability of the Muslims, but also emasculated them politically and economically. The upper class Muslims, who previously thronged the military profession, were kept out of the Company's army as, it was believed, their exclusion, was necessary for the safety of the British Empire in India. The substitution of English as the official language minimised the chances of the Muslims for recruitment to the civil services, for they clung to the old orthodox traditions of religious education and turned their back on the new learning of the *franks* (Englishmen).

On the other hand, the Hindus promptly and eagerly seized the opportunity and made the best of Western education for advancing their professional interests. Consequently, the Muslims were excluded from the lower administrative posts as well as from other soft-handed professions. The Hindu collectors of revenue were elevated to the position of landlords with the result, as Sir William Hunter pointed out, "that most of the Muslim Houses of Bengal either disappeared or were submerged beneath the new strata of society which had developed........."[5] In the Punjab, where the Muslims were in a dominant majority, their condition was not a bit better. The revenue system introduced there produced a class of money lenders who were more often than not Hindus, since usury is banned by the Quran. The Hindu money lenders throve upon the misery of the Muslims and did not hesitate even to deprive them of their land. Such expropriation, according to Thornborn, had proceeded to a dangerous extent.[6] Apart from these setbacks the deliberate policy followed by the Company's Government to liquidate indigenous industries and handicrafts ruined the professions of weavers and other Muslim artisans.

The cumulative effect of this loss of political power by and the economic degradation and social humiliation of the Muslims produced in them a deep sense of frustration and resentment

---

2. Christians who had no scrupples either for the cow or the pig.
3. The Wahabi Movement aimed at establishing in India Dar-ul- Islam and declared *Jihad* first against the Sikhs and later against the British after the conquest of Punjab. The Muslims were repeatedly told that no True Believer could live loyal to an infidel Government without perdition of his soul. Patna was the centre of the Wahabi movement and activities in British India.
4. Refer to Lajpat Rai's *Unhappy India,* p. 400.
5. Hunter, W. W., *The Indian Musalmans,* p. 163.
6. Refer to Thornborn's *Musalmans and Moneylenders.*

against the British. The Wahabi movement made a great appeal to them in that mood. Syed Ahmed Shah, the Wahabi leader, "stirred the Muslim population to its depths, and a wave of enthusiasm swept over the country. So elemental was its force that William Hunter had called it one of the greatest religious revivals known to Indian History."[7] The Wahabis organised the impoverished peasants in Bengal and fomented agrarian revolts. In the 1857 'revolt' they took a leading part and continued their ceaseless efforts to penalise the British administration and even after that.

The Hindus, on their part, were also influenced by certain reform movements which vitalised their social and religious life. Hinduism, which had, for five hundred years, been the religion of a subject race, was in a moribund condition. The Hindu society was sullied by superstitions, decaying customs and strange cults and its philosophy was embroiled in the superstructure of priest- ridden practices. Such a state of affairs afforded an opportunity to Christian missionaries to embark on a policy of extensive proselytisation. Although their activities met with some success in the beginning, soon they produced a strong reaction, especially in Bengal which had the deepest impact. Raja Ram Mohan Roy, the founder of Brahmo Samaj, in the first half of the nineteenth century, attempted to reform Hinduism by rationalising it on the basis of the old Hindu scriptures. He struck a new note of social reform by upholding the cause of women, preaching the abolition of Suttee and urging upon the Hindus to undo the evils of caste system and idolatry. Although his reform movement met initially a small success, it was the precursor of other and more significant movements "which in the course of a century transformed Hindu religious thought and reorganised Hindu Society." It was the reformed Hinduism which became the basis of India's national unity and the spring-board of the national movement.[8]

On the political side, too, Raja Ram Mohan Roy blazed the path of constitutional agitation in the country by advocating that the people of India had the same capability for improving as any civilised people in the world. He belonged to that class of politically conscious Indians who had learnt to apply the lessons of English literature, political thought and history to his own country and to ask the rulers for an enlightened system of government. He championed the liberty of the press and the rule of law. Thus, with Raja Ram Mohan Roy started renaissance which steadily gathered strength, and from reform the spirit of revolt emerged.

To sum up, the first half of the nineteenth century witnessed a simmering of national consciousness in the country, but there was no organised platform as yet. There was a seething discontentment against the Company's regime, but for different reasons among different sections of the people. Some progressive British administrators had forewarned the Company of the consequences of their retrogressive policies and prophesied that either those policies would foment a spirit of discontent or, if this did not happen, the people would sink in character. Their foreboding proved true. Despite the skilful policy of 'Divide and Rule' the Company could not stem the tide of political uprisings which broke out from time to time and as far back as the early part of the nineteenth century.[9] The last and the most severe uprising was the "Revolt" of 1857 that shook the East India Company's administration to its very foundations.

### The "Revolt" of 1857

Starting as a military uprising at Meerut on May 10, the 1857 "Revolt" rapidly turned into a sort of "War of Independence"[10] The sepoys gave a political touch to the struggle by placing themselves under the leadership of Bahadur Shah, the last Mughal King at Delhi, and proclaimed him Emperor of Hindustan. Although initially they had taken up arms against the East India Company for the protection of their religion, they eventually fought for India's political independence in a bid to establish a political system indigenous to the soil. In many places, especially in the North-Western Provinces, Oudh and Bihar, the civil population rose independently of the 'mutineers.' No doubt, several heterogeneous elements that joined the revolt had diverse motives. Their activities were not wholly inspired by patriotic impulses and were not well co-ordinated and planned, but they were well

7. Mehta and Patwardhan, *The Communal Triangle in India,* p. 95.

8. Panikkar, K. M., *Common Sense about India*, p. 21.

9. Important among them were the Bareilly rising of 1816, the Cole outbreak of 1831-32, the Ferazee disturbances at Barisal in 1831 and later at Faridpur in 1837, the Moplah outbreaks of 1819 and 1851, 1852 and 1855, and the Santhal insurrection of 1855- 56.

10. *1857–A Pictorial Representation,* p. XV.

united in their hatred of the British masters. The struggle cemented different elements, commanding a wide popular support. For the first time Hindus and Muslims in certain places fought together against the alien ruler. Though the concept of an Indian nationality was in embryo yet, and, largely feudal loyalty served for partriotism,[11] a large number of the people of India felt happy that they had something in common as against the British, in spite of their racial, religious and linguistic differences.

The revolt was quelled by the mighty hand of the British, but not the urge for freedom. The revolt had the seeds of nationalism and the spark of revolution. Like Julius Caesar who was more powerful dead than alive, the Mutiny of 1857 became a symbol of challenge to the mighty British power in India. It remained a shining example for the nationalists, revolutionaries and anarchists alike. The unknown heroes of 1857 as well as those well-known, like Nana Sahib, Rani Lakshmibai of Jhansi, Tatya Tope, Bahadur Shah and Kunwar Singh, became national heroes and champions of national freedom. The stories of their heroic struggle and bravery inspired the Indian people in the twentieth century. Popular songs and ballads kept their memory alive and animated the fighters for freedom to keep the torch of liberty burning.

**Growth of Nationalism after 1857**

After the restoration of British authority, the Government took immediate measures of precaution to avoid all risks of insurrection. The Mughal line was virtually extinguished; Bahadur Shah was captured and his two sons were shot dead after capture. All the lands of the mutineers in Oudh were confiscated. The army, which took the initiative in the outbreak, was thoroughly reorganised and the scheme of division and counterpoise dominated the defence policy of British India. Tribal and communal loyalties were encouraged to prevent the growth of the sentiment of national unity among the army. People's contact with the army was sealed and even Indian newspapers were not allowed to reach the military personnel. An impregnable force of British troops was stationed in India and the artillery was placed exclusiely in the hands of Europeans. The British troops, which alone were equipped with more effective weapons of warfare, were always stationed with the Indian regiments in all important centers of the country to serve as 'internal security' troops. To preclude the chance of any future rebellion breaking out in the country, the right of using firearms by the Indian civil population was drastically restricted.

In regard to Indian States, a dual policy was pursued. On the one hand, all possible steps were taken to make them militarily weak and harmless. The Princes were reduced in rank and status, legally and theoretically by the Royal Titles Act, 1876,[12] and in practice by the assumption of rights and privileges under the cloak of 'paramountcy.' On the other hand, an effort was made to conciliate the ruling families by assuring them their future stability. The policy of 'Divide and Rule' was followed ruthlessly and the split between the Hindus and Muslims was deliberately and systematically encouraged.

It was, however, realised that the police power alone would not provide a firm footing to British Imperialism and a semblance of benevolent government was deemed necessary. The Company's rule was, thus, brought to an end and the Government was transferred to the British Crown. The new regime was heralded by Queen's Proclamation, which struck a new note of moral basis for British rule in India. The Indian Councils Act, 1861, was enacted, by which the number of Additional members was increased and for the first time Indians were associated to elicit popular reaction to legislative and administrative measures as a much-wanted safety valve.

These measures gave some satisfaction to the people and raised the hope that they would open a new chapter of good and responsible government in the country. But the solemn assurances made in the Queen's Proclamation were followed more in the breach than in the observance. In fact, the era of British administration by the British Crown was a period of broken pledges. The disillusionment and frustration caused by the violation of assurances was the most potent factor in converting the goodwill of Indians into a spirit of hatred and animosity against British rule, and sharpened the edge of the nascent spirit of nationalism, the growth of which wa the characteristic feature of this period.

Very soon the post-Mutiny era was vitiated by a spirit of racialism and arrogance on the part of the ruling class. The reasons were not far to seek. The 'Revolt' of 1857 had left behind a

11. Sen, S. N., *Eighteen Fifty-seven,* pp. 411-413.
12. Lord Lytton proclaimed to the Indian people at a *durbar* the new title of Queen Victoria, the "Queen Empress of India."

tradition of suspicion and deep hostility on both sides. Sir Edward Thompson observed, "Right at the back of the mind of many an Indian the Mutiny flits as he talks with an Englishman—an unavenged and unappeased ghost."[13] The Indians could not forget the sacrifices they had made in their bid to free the country from the alien rulers and the woeful memories of the wholesale massacre and other brutalities committed by the British soldiers not only in the course of military campaigns but in a spirit of sheer revenge even after the Mutiny had been suppressed. Garrat remarked that "The English had never attempted to remove the irritation caused by their behaviour after the Mutiny, and from that time we must date the long and bitter estrangement between the two races. Born of hatred and fear, it was nourished on a series of unfortunate incidents, most of which were the direct result of the new spirit which the Mutiny encouraged amongst Europeans."[14]

The feelings of the British towards Indians both at Home and in India were those of active hatred and they looked upon them "as the creature half gorilla, half negro."[15] The most rabid anti-Indian amongst them openly preached and practised racial exclusiveness. They regarded an Indian as a black heathen worshipping stocks and sones and swinging himself on bamboos like beasts.[16] To accept him as the equal of a Britisher, as declared in the Queen's Proclamation, appeared to them nothing short of heresy.[17] The conception of race superiority among the British could be fathomed from certain maxims which guided their conduct towards Indians. The first was that the only thing that an Indian would understand was fear; second, the life of a European was worth those of many Indians; third, that England had been forced to lose many lives and spend millions of pounds to hold India and, therefore, deserved some more substantial recompense than merely the privilege of governing the country in a spirit of wisdom and unselfishness.[18]

Intoxicated with power and flushed with the consciousness of their inherent superiority as a race, the British civil servants ignominiously treated even distinguished Indians of high merit.[19] They looked on Indians as a race to whom rules of decent conduct need not apply. The facilities of communication and speedy means of transport had brought about a great change in their attitude. They could now live along with their families in India and visit their homes frequently. Thus, they ceased to look upon India as their "adopted home" and gradually caste-barriers arose between Indians and Englishmen, increasing thereby "bitterness, hostility and fear." Blunt wrote in 1909, "The English woman in India during the last thirty years has been the cause of half the bitter feelings there between race and race........It is her constantly increasing influence now that widens the gulf of ill-feeling and makes amalgamation daily more impossible."[20] A saying went round that where two English families lived, there were three gardens, one, of course, being the club. But their clubs were closed to Indians. They could not tolerate Indians even travelling with them in the upper class railway compartments. Assaults on innocent and helpless Indians, and striking of Indian servants on the slightest provocation were accidents of common occurrence. The planters especially surpassed others in their brutalities on Indian coolies (labourers), and still they went unpunished. The administration of criminal justice had become a judicial scandal. "The long succession of murders and brutalities perpetrated by Englishmen on Indians which either went unpunished or for which, at the demand of the whole European community, only a small penalty was exacted.

13. Thompson, Sir Edward, *The Other Side of the Medal,* p. 29.
14. Garrat, G. T., *An Indian Commentary,* p. 116.
15. *Idem.,* p. 114.
16. Henry Cotton, *New India,* pp. 46-47.
17. Sir Henry Cotton wrote : "Ten years have elapsed since the Mutiny, but the Mutiny was in the early days of my service a living memory in the minds of all. When I first arrived in the country, it was duly enjoined upon me as a matter of vital importance that I should insist on all the outward and visible signs of deference and respect which Orientals with a leaning to sycophancy, resulting from generations of subjection and foreign rule, are only too willing to accord. Although I was a very *chota* (small) *sahib* (officer), and posted only to the humble office of Assistant to the Magistrate and Collector of a district, I was early taught that, though I might be but a fly on the wheel of the official hierarchy, I was, in the eyes of the people among whom I lived, a representative of the Government and entitled as such to rights and privileges on no account to be a foregone. Such was the atmosphere in which we lived; we are directly encouraged to assume an attitude of a patronising and superior character...........The old Haileybury stone still pervaded the civil service......."Henry Cotton, *Indian and Home Memories,* pp. 65-66.
18. Garrat, G. T., *An Indian Commentary,* p. 118.
19. Blunt, W. S., *India Under Ripon, A Private Diary,* p. 74. Also refer to Blunt's *Ideas About India,* p. 46.
20. Blunt, W. S., *India Under Ripon, A Private Diary,* p. 261. Also Spear, T. J. P., *The Nabobs,* p. 141.

The scandal of which there were many flagrant instances in the sixties"[21] continued for long. On the other hand, Indians were more severely punished even for the slightest offence or discourtesy to the Britishers.[22] The obvious result was increased racial bitterness between the rulers and the ruled and it was, in the opinion of Garrat, a direct cause of the growth of nationalism. It had been correctly said that the racial arrogance of the Britishers made the British rule more unpopular and hated in India than probably any other single factor. Lord Lytton wrote to the Secretary of State for India, Lord Salisbury, on September 28, 1876 : "The prevalent brutality towards natives of the lower orders, the crystallised official formality towards natives of highest class, and it is really a wonder that our rule is not more unpopular than it is......I am convinced that the greatest danger we have to deal with in India is from the Whites."

Government services have always carried social distinction besides providing opportunities of employment to the people. Any Government which discriminates among the services is bound to provoke discontentment. After 1857, the bureaucracy in India provided this gun-powder in abundance and as Raghuvanshi pointed out, "the cry of Indianisation of the services was the starting point of political agitation."[23] With the spread of Western education the number of educated Indians increased considerably, but the Government had neatly excluded them from all positions of trust and responsibility. It was the monopoly of the Britishers, and Indians, as Surendranath Banerjea said, "were the helots of the land, the hewers of wood and the drawers of water."[24] The Royal pledge to the people for free admission to services on the basis of merit alone still sanctified the professions of the Government, but as Lord Lytton confessed, these pledges were not intended to be carried out. In a confidential Minute he wrote : "We all know that these claims and expectations never can or will be fulfilled. We have had to choose between prohibiting them (Indians) and cheating them, and we have chosen the least straightforward course......Since I am writing confidentially, I do not hesitate to say that both the Governments of England and India appear to me up to the present moment unable to answer satisfactorily the charge of having taken every means in their power of breaking to the heart the words of promise they had uttered to the ear."[25]

The admission of Indians to the Indian Civil Service, which provided the steel framework of the British administration, was intentionally made difficult. The competitive examination was held in London and the age of entrance was fixed at twenty-one years. But these conditions made it extremely difficult for Indians to compete in the examination. Despite these difficulties some Indians succeeded in qualifying for it. But for one reason or the other obstacles were placed in the way of successful candidates in joining the service. In 1869, Surendranath Banerjea moved the Queen's Bench for a writ of *Mandamus* and the court upheld Banerjea's contention and ordered that he should be admitted to the service.[26] The Civil Service Commissioners had to suffer Banerjea in the Indian Civil Service, but two years afterwards he was dismissed from service on a "wicked proceeding" instituted against him.[27] The other victim of the bureaucratic fury was Aurobindo Ghosh, who came out successful in the main examination, but was disqualified in the riding test.

These cases created a furore in the country and formed the basis of political agitation. Surendranath Banerjea and Aurobindo Ghosh became national heroes and pioneers of the national

---

21. Garrat, G. T., *An Indian Commentary* pp. 116-17. Also refer to Theodore Morrison, *Imperial Rule in India,* pp. 27-28.
22. Lord Lytton wrote to the Secretary of State for India, August 27, 1876 : "Since the Fuller case has led me to look more carefully over the recent verdicts of the Courts in cases affecting natives, I have been quite *horrified* by their apparent injustice. Fuller, with the approval of High Court, was fined Rs. 30 for unintentionally killing his syce (groom). The other day a native was *transported for life* for stealing 4 annas." *Lytton Papers*.. Quoted in Tara Chand, *History of the Freedom Movement in India,* Vol. II, p. 487.
23. Raghuvanshi, V.P.S., *Indian Nationalist Movement and Thought,* p. 22.
24. As quoted in Annie Besant, *How India Wrought for Freedom,* p. 174.
25. Refer to the Presidential Address of Gopal Krishna Gokhale delivered at the Benares session of the Indian National Congress (Twenty-first Session, 1905). *Idem.,* p. 420. Lord Hamilton, the Secretary of State for India, wrote to Lord Elgin on May 7, 1897 : "I do not think we should put very prominently forward the Queen's Proclamation of 1858. As a piece of English it is fine, but 40 years' practice has shown the extreme difficulty of giving effect to the academic utterances as to equality of race...." As quoted in the *History and Culture and Indian People, British Paramountcy and Indian Renaissance, op. citd.,* Vol. X, Part II, p. 400.
26. Surendranath Banerjea, *A Nation in Making,* pp. 15-16.
27. The proceedings were instituted under Act XXXIX of 1850. "Many years afterwards", wrote Surendranath Banerjea, "a Lieutenant-Governor told me that it was a wicked proceeding". *Idem.,* p. 29.

movement in the country. Banerjea founded the Indian Association in 1876, which was intended to represent the views of the educated middle-class community and was to serve as "the centre of All-India movement" on the conception of a united India. He had four objectives in view : (1) the creation of a strong body of public opinion in the country; (2) the unification of the Indian races and peoples upon the basis of common political interests and aspirations; (3) the promotion of friendly feelings between Hindus and Mohammedans; and (4) the inclusion of the masses in the great public movements of the day. The Indian Association, wrote Banerjea, "materially helped to promote these ideals. They were the natural and normal development of the efforts of great men of the past, under the new conditions created by the closer touch of our best minds with the political thought and activities of the West.[28]

In 1877, the Secretary of State for India, the Marquis of Salisbury, reduced the maximum limit of age for the open competitive examination for the Indian Civil Service from twenty-one to nineteen years. Indians regarded it as a deliberate attempt to blast the prospects of Indian candidates for entry into the Indian Civil Service. The Indian Association immediately resolved to organise a national movement with a view to agitating for raising the maximum age limit and holding of simultaneous examinations both in Britain and India. As a result of the vigorous campaign initiated by Surendranath Banerjea public opinion was whipped up in the country, and, consequently, it was decided to send an All India Memorial to the House of Commons, followed by a deputation to place these grievances before the British Government and to enlist the sympathies of the British people. Thus, a common platform emerged in India through the Indian Association which united the people through a sense of common grievance and the inspiration of a common resolve. Reactionary policies are often the creators of great public movements and the Civil Service Movement found its culminating expression in the Congress movement.

The soil for the growth of nationalism in Victorian India was also prepared by various socio-political factors. Among these were the establishment of political stability and a strong centralised system of administration which provided an umbrella for the attainment of a representative government. The establishment of peace set the people free to turn their minds to economic and political affairs.

The unification of the country and the spread of Western education widened opportunities for employment in the administrative services, the legal profession, business, insurance, banking, industry and allied vocations and enterprises, which having been set up on a national basis, contributed to the development of a national sentiment. The rapid disintegration of indigenous institutions and the growth of modern economic groups, diversification of occupations and mobility of labour with sharp class consciousness, created in the minds of all an awareness that they were the people of India and that their weal and woe were common.

With this orientation of the social set up emerged a politically conscious middle-class intelligentsia, which became the spearhead of the national movement in the country. The rise of this class in the post-Mutiny period was a social development of great significance, for these people "pulled society out of the medieval rut and ensured her development on modern lines."[29] With the growth of the vernacular press and the emergence of political organisations the influence of this class spread among the masses, who were still politically ignorant and inert.

The malcontents of today are the revolutionaries of tomorrow, and of all the malcontents the unemployed and the starving are the worst. In 1880, Sir William Hunter wrote : "there remain millions of Indians who go through life on insufficient food." Even Lord Salisbury, as Secretary of State for India, confessed in 1875 that British rule was bleeding India white. The economic structure of the country had become subservient to the British exploitative system. Agriculture, the mainstay of India's economy, was allowed to deteriorate miserably while the pressure of population on land increased as the population expanded and indigenous industries decayed. At the Second Session of the Indian National Congress, D.E. Wacha drew attention to the poverty of the Indian population and pointed out that the condition of the ryot had steadily deteriorated since 1848 and that 40 millions of people had only one meal a day, and not always that. He attributed this pitiable condition to an unparalleled drain of wealth from India to Great

28. *Idem.*, pp.42-43.
29. Raghuvanshi, V.P.S., *Indian Nationalist Movement and Thought*, p. 25.

Britain.[30] Dadabhai Naoroji in India[31] and William Digby in Britain[32] exposed, by an array of statistics and facts, how British policy was directly responsible for the deteriorating economic condition of India. Educated Indians were deeply moved by the grim picture of India's poverty drawn by these intellectual giants. They realised the menace of the foreign rule and it helped in rousing their political conscience.

Recurring famines in the country emasculated rural India. As compared to seven famines in the first half of the nineteenth century, the second half had to undergo the misery of twenty-four famines with a total of over 28 million deaths. The famine of 1877 was, according to R.C. Dutt, "a calamity unprecedented in its intensity within the memory of living men."[33] Five million people perished. But Nero was fiddling while Rome was burning. Lord Lytton, the then Governor-General, in utter disregard of the economic distress in the country, held an Imperial *durbar,* to declare the assumption of Imperial Titles by the Queen and his own accession to the office of Viceroy. Immediately after the assumption of office, Lytton despatched a Mission to Kabul, which eventually involved the Government of India in the Second Afghan War.[34] This Imperialist war put India to a staggering loss of twenty million sterling and a damning slight to the British prestige and authority into the bargain.[35] Had this amount been expended on important irrigation projects, as recommended by Sir Henry Cotton to the Select Committee of the House of Commons and in the same year in which the Afghan War had begun, it would have saved millions of Indian cultivators from distress and famines for all time. This callous manifestation of British Imperialism in India evoked deep resentment among the people and their reaction was canalised in the form of agrarian anti-tax riots in the Deccan. The state of things by the end of Lord Lytton's regime was, as Sir William Wedderburn summed up, "bordering upon a revolution."[36]

The evolution of political progress in every country has generally begun during the reign of malevolent rulers. In Britain it began with King John and in India it was ensured during the Viceroyalty of Lord Lytton. Throughout his tenure of office Lytton pursued a policy of repression and enacted measures that helped to stir the educated community into life, which, according to Surendranath Banerjea, "years of agitation would perhaps have failed to achieve."[37] Lord Lytton, in the opinion of the Duke of Devonshire, was the very reverse of what an Indian Viceroy ought to have been, lacking in imagination and unsympathetic even to the legitimate aspirations of the Indians.[38] His abolition of import duty on British cotton goods in the face of stout opposition of the majority of the Members of his Executive Council, who were themselves Europeans,[39] the enactment of the Arms Act, which made an invidious distinction between the Indians and the Europeans,[40] and the Vernacular Press Act,[41] were the most oppressive and discriminatory measures which were vociferously condemned by the educated Indian community. "These ill-started measures of reaction", remarked Sir William Wedderburn, "combined with Russian methods of police repression brought India un-

30. Refer to Pattabhi Sitaramayya, *History of the Indian National Congress,* Vol. I, pp. 86-87.
31. Dadabhai Naoroji, *Poverty and Un-British Rule in India.*
32. William Digby, *'Prosperous' British India.*
33. Dutt, R.C., *India in the Victorian Age,* p. 427.
34. Lord Lytton was armed, before his departure from England, with secret instructions embodied in the Secretary of State's Dispatch, February 28, 1876.
35. Gladstone in his Midlothian speech, denounced the policy of the Conservative Government and characterised it as "untrue, arrogant and dangerous." Morley, *The Life of William Ewart Gladstone,* Vol. II, p. 595.
36. Pattabhi Sitaramayya, *History of Indian National Congress,* Vol. I, p. 8.
37. Banerjea, Surendranath, *A Nation in Making,* p. 63.
38. Mazumdar, A. C., *Indian National Evolution,* p. 31.
39. The Import duty which stood at 10 per cent in 1860 was reduced to 5 per cent in 1875. In 1877, the House of Commons adopted a resolution calling upon the Government of India to repeal without delay the cotton duties. When the question came before the Viceroy's Executive Council, a majority of the Members were opposed to this repeal. Lord Lytton exercised his veto. The duty on coarse cotton goods was repealed in 1879.
40. While the Act permitted foreigners belonging to any nationality and coming to India, to keep arms freely, it required every Indian to obtain a licence.
41. Vernacular Press Act IX of 1878. The Act empowered a Magistrate or a Collector to order any Editor of a Vernacular newspaper to enter into a bond not to publish anything likely to excite feelings of disaffection against the Government or antipathy between persons of different races, castes and religions. In case of contravention of this regulation the newspaper was first warned of the offence and if it reoccurred, its equipment was liable to be seized. For those who did not enter into a bond, they were required to submit proofs before publication for scrutiny to the officers appointed by the Government.

der Lord Lytton within measurable distance of a Revolutionary outbreak."[42]

The successor of Lord Lytton was a true Liberal of the Gladstonian era. Lord Ripon believed, as a good Christian, that "righteousness exalteth a nation". He sympathised with the aspirations of the Indians and attempted to undo what his Tory predecessor had done. He concluded a treaty with the Amir of Afghanistan and repealed the Vernacular Press Act. He also took immediate steps to abolish the judicial disqualification of Indians based on race distinctions. According to the old Criminal Procedure Code (1873) no Magistrate or Sessions Judge could try a European British subject, unless he were himself of European birth. By 1883, some of the Indian members of the Covenanted Service had risen by seniority to the stage when they could become Magistrates and Judges in the Courts of Sessions. Lord Ripon felt that it would be highly invidious, if they were not given the same rights and privileges as their European colleagues in service. A Bill was, accordingly, introduced in the Supreme Council by the Law Member, Sir Courtney Ilbert, seeking to remove the existing anomaly by giving Indian Magistrates jurisdiction over European offenders.

But this was too much for the British community to swallow. They were already nursing a strong grievance against the liberal policies of Lord Ripon. To regard an Indian as an equal of his British colleagues appeared to them nothing short of heresy. Ripon was vilified and openly insulted. A social boycott was declared against the Governorr-General and even some Members of his Executive Council refrained from attending social functions at the Government House. It was reported that 'a confederacy of blusters' was formed to overpower the sentries at the Government House, to put the Viceroy on board a steamer at Chanderpal Ghat and to deport him to England.

The press in England also became violent against the Viceroy. This wild agitation alarmed the Home Government. The Secretary of State devised a compromise which practically defeated the purpose of the Ilbert Bill.[43] Lord Ripon's efforts to remove race distinctions were, thus, foiled. But the Anglo-Indian agitation taught the "Indian leaders of political thought, hitherto steadfast in their faith in British justice, that without vigorous and countrywide agitation they could not hope to combat successfully the reactionary forces at work. Thus, did the people of India learn to distinguish between the liberty-loving British nation in whose sense of justice they had placed implicit faith and the British bureaucracy and community in India from whom they despaired of getting fair play."[44]

The periods of the Viceroyalty of Lord Lytton and Lord Ripon were, therefore, the seed time of Indian nationalism. It was during their period that Indians began to feel that the time had come when they should unite in an organised effort to obtain for themselves the freedom enjoyed by the British in their own country and the same representative and effective voice in their country's administration. The Indian Association organised the first National Conference in December 1883 at the Albert Hall. About a hundred people attended the Congress and the first meeting commenced with the recitation of a national hymn. In his opening speech Anand Mohan Bose declared that the Conference was the first stage towards a national parliament. The agitation of the Anglo-Indians over the Ilbert Bill taught Indians the great value of political agitation carried on the basis of a united front. The imprisonment of Surendranath Banerjea strengthened the growing bonds of fellowship and good feeling between the different Provinces. The conference could not be organised next year, but the great International Exhibition held at Calcutta in 1884, "further convinced the Indian leaders of the possibility of carrying on an all-India agitation on sound lines."[45] Thus, ensued the era of political agitation.

Racial discrimination, repression and cruel

---

42. Wedderburn, W., *Biographical Sketch of Allan Octavian Hume*, p. 101.

43. Lord Ripon had to yield. His government then proposed, with the approval of the Secretary of State for India, that "the extended powers should only be granted to Sessions Judges and District Magistrates and that the High Court should have power to transfer the hearing of the case from one court to another." But even this did not satisfy the Europeans and Ripon "had to stop further." A new Act was passed in 1884 which allowed the Indian District Magistrates and Sessions Judges power to try Europeans on the condition that a European accused could demand a trial by Jury half of which were to consist of Europeans or Americans.

44. Surendranath Banerjea was convicted for contempt of court for publishing a leaderette in the *Bengalee* on April 2, 1883 and sent to prison for two months. Surendranath Banerjea claimed the hounour of being the first Indian of his "generation who suffered imprisonment in the discharge of a public duty." *A Nation in Making*, p. 74.

45. Raghuvanshi, V.P.S., *Indian Nationalist Movement and Thought*, p. 42.

economic exploitation had made the Indian people aware of the curse of political subjugation and had disturbed political waters. But more than these were other catalysts which forged stable bonds of national unity and fostered political awakening. Among them was the imposition of an alien, though rich language, for the purpose of administration and its inevitable emergence as a common medium of communication and self-expression. In introducing the English language Lord Macaulay had a limited purpose, namely, to build a new educated class of English-speaking Indians meant initially to provide a link between the rulers and the ruled and to interpret British ideas and institutions to their countrymen. But it proved a blessing in disguise for Indians. English became a common all-India language of the educated Indians living in various parts of the country, thus, forging a new bond of political unity in multi-lingual society. Till the close of the nineteenth century the acquisition of knowledge in English was confined to a microscopic minority of the population of a small upper class and some sections of the lower-middle classes. But its influence was sufficient to create ferment in the domain of ideas and to mould Indian political thought.

Through the channels of the English language came the liberal ideas of the West; which stirred the imagination of the Indian people and roused them from their slumber. It unfolded to them the dynamic concepts of liberty, democracy, rule of law, and the modern forms of government. The inspiring ideals of the French and American revolutions and philosophies of Milton, Burke, Mill, Macaulay, Spencer, Garibaldi, and Karl Marx came within their ken. Through this medium dawned the marvels of modern science and technology and the knowledge of international developments. As a result of this impact mental stirrings were produced, reason and judgment replaced blind faith and belief and superstition yielded to a rational outlook. The average Indian had never before thought in terms of freedom and individual initiative. He had mostly been swayed by the ideals of submission and renunciation. With the development of English education politically conscious Indians imbibed the ideas of political freedom and the principles of democratic and constitutional government, and began to apply them to their own country. Ramsay MacDonald observed, "Herbert Spencer's individualism and Lord Morley's liberalism are, as it were, the only battery of guns which India has captured from us, and condescends to use against us."

The press in India also played a very important part in disseminating news and views and helping to create an enlightened public opinion. After the abolition of censorship on the press by the Government of Sir Charles Metcalfe in 1835, the Vernacular Press made rapid progress. By the turn of the century Indians owned and managed about 476 newspapers and most of them were conducted in the vernacular. The Indian owned press focussed attention on the failings and unpopular measures of the Government and became a vehicle for ventilating popular grievances. The Anglo-Indian Press, on the other hand, was pro-Government and anti-national and openly preached the race superiority of Europeans. The Indian Press advocated racial equality and strove to forge national unity in order to combat racial inequality. The Anglo-Indians, therefore, *en bloc,* held that the Indian press preached sedition. Lord Lytton's attempt to gag it by enacting the Vernacular Press Act, 1878, created a great political commotion. The Act was later withdrawn, but it brought home to Indians the fact that the main obstacle in the way of their progress was their slavery and that some kind of political organization was necessary to mobilise the people for freedom. The establishment of the Indian National Congress changed immediately the tone of both Indian and Anglo-Indian Press, "and brought politics in the forefront of discussion in both cases. The more important of Indian papers now sought to educate the public in the ideals of the Congress, and some even overstepped the limit of moderation set by their institution as its standard. The Anglo-Indian Press, with a few exceptions, criticised the political ideals of the Congress as chimerical and was definitely hostile to it. In this way they reflected the British attitude which was opposed to all political aspirations of India."[46]

The writings of Indian patriots also played a notable part in creating a sense of national consciousness and patriotism. This literature revolutionised Indian thinking and contributed to the birth of extremism in India. A number of distinguished writers in Bengal, who had permanently

46. *The History and Culture of the Indian People, British Paramountcy and Indian Renaissance, op. cit.,* Vol. X, Part II, p. 251.

enriched her language, preached the national sentiments through the medium of novels, poems, songs and essays. This literature proved to be the most valuable aid in the struggle for freedom.[47] The same holds more or less true of other parts of the country. Literature in Bengali, however, outnumbered the rest. Bankim Chandra Chatterjee's *Anand Math* had been called by some "The Bible of modern Bengali patriotism", and it was in that book that the song *Bande Mataram* first appeared. *Ananda Math* had also served as a text of revolutionary nationalism in Bengal.

The recovery of Indian History, a process which began with the decipherment of Asokan inscriptions, greatly spurred the growth of the national movement. It led to the inculcation of a national image in the minds of the people. Before this "such national pride as India had was local pride : the Marathas, the Rajputs, the Andhras and all other peoples had racial memories of their greatness, but none of them had pride in India. When the History of India was gradually unfolded through archaeology, epigraph and other fields of scholarship, an image of united Indian nation emerged which pictured them as one of the great historic peoples of the world who had contributed to the growth of civilisation. That History which not only bore witness to a continuing civilisation in India, with its achievements in many fields, religion, literature, philosophy, art, architecture, etc., to which every part of India had an equal right, but to a glorious tradition of cultural expansion overseas and across deserts which founded cities, States and Empires had actively carried on an international life in the not too remote past, created in the minds of the people of India pride of Indianness. Without this new self-image, the political unity of India would have been artificial."[48]

European scholars, like Max Mueller, Monier Williams, Roth, Sassoon, Burnouf, Jacobi and Colebrooke, helped the educated Indians to rediscover their own culture and civilisation and the world to know the secrets of India's great cultural heritage. They held Indian civilisation and culture superior and thereby kindled in the bosom of Indians the fire of patriotism which was put aflame by Indian scholars, like Ranade, Raja Rajindra Lal Mitra, Har Prasad Shastri and Dr. Pandu Sen.

Even this national image created by the historic researches might have remained an empty dream like the concept of Arab unity, but for the active national movement which began in the latter half of the nineteenth century. "That provided a focus for the dispersed feelings of patriotism, which, under a uniform system of education, a growing sense of Indianness and the common suffering under foreign rule, had developed."[49]

---

47. In 1859, Ranglal Banerjee came out with a play "Padmini" wherein the hero made the following inspiring speech :

    "Who wants to live in disgraceful dependence,
    Who likes to wear shackles of slavery,
    It is hell to remain in slavery for ages,
    A day's freedom is but a crown of joy,
    He is worthy of life and strength,
    Who liberates his country by sacrificing himself."

    As quoted in Hemendra Nath Gupta, *The Indian National Congress,* p. 16. Reference may also be made to a drama, *Bharat Mata,* wherein the following song occurred :-

    "O India, gloomy is thy face,
    Beautiful that was as the moon,
    Tears flow from thine eyes,
    Throughout the day and night."

    As quoted in Bipin Chandra Pal's *Memoirs of My Life and Times,* Vol. I, p. 227.
48. Talk by Sardar K. M., Panikkar on "Political Oneness", broadcast from A.I.R. Delhi, May 15, 1962.
49. *Ibid.*

# CHAPTER II

# The Indian National Congress and the Demand for Parliamentary Institutions

## An Era of New Political Life

The post-1857 period in India assumed a new dimension under the impact of Western education and other social and political developments. The people having been completely disarmed, the freedom struggle in India could have only a civil rather than a military basis. Though the spirit of violence was not altogether dead and occasionally violent uprisings broke out in the country during the second half of the nineteenth century,[1] an intellectual movement of a non-violent nature now dominated the Indian mind. The spread of English education increased the strength of that class of Indians who were influenced by Western political thought and the technique of political agitation that prevailed in Britain. The more politically conscious people in the country, accordingly, took to agitating public opinion against the evil effects of the British administration in India rather then practising violence. Dadabhai Naoroji and men of his way of thinking, although they had no intention of questioning the British overlordship, desired nonetheless that the Indian government should be guided more in the economic interest of India. They felt that to accelerate the economic and political progress of the country, it was essential to educate British public opinion in respect of India's true condition and Britain's duty towards Indians.

Dadabhai Naoroji collected a band of workers and, together with W.C. Bonerjee, established the London Indian Society, which carried on useful propaganda. On December 1, 1866, the East India Association came into being.[2] The object of this body was to bring together Englishmen and Indians "on a common platform not only for the ventilation of Indian grievances but also for the removal of the erroneous impression" that India was unfit for any form of representative institutions. Gradually the influence of the Association began to be felt in Parliament. Whenever Indian questions were discussed, several members of Parliament, either on the promptings of the members of the East India Association or inspired by their discussions, spoke with knowledge about the needs and aspirations of the people of India and brought informed criticism to bear on the solution of Indian problems.

Within two years of its establishment, the East India Association had demonstrated what a wide field of work lay ahead and Dadabhai Naoroji was deputed to India to establish branches of the Association and collect funds. Three branches of the Association were established in Bombay, Calcutta and Madras in 1869.[3] In 1870 was started the Sarvajanik Sabha[4] with the main object of serving as a bridge between the government on one hand and the people on the other. Mahadev Govind Ranade was the strong man behind the activities of the Sabha and it was at his feet that Joshi, Gokhale and Tilak received their first lesson in public service. In 1867, Surendranath Banerjea established the Indian Association at Calcutta.[5] In 1884, the Mahajan Sabha was founded in Madras. The Sabha

---

1. Like the Wahabi, the Kuka and the Income-tax and Indigo riots.
2. For a list of the first members of the East India Association see its Journal, Vol. I, No. 2, pp. 117-20. Though there were a number of Indian names, Europeans preponderated.
3. The East India Association, however, gradually sank in importance after 1884 due to a change in the attitude of Englishmen towards India.
4. It originally started as Poona Association in 1867 on the lines of the Bombay Association.
5. *A Nation in Making,* p. 42. Surendranath Banerjea thus explained the need for such an association : "After my return from England in June 1875, and along with the work of organising the students and infusing in them a new life and spirit, I began seriously to consider the advisability of forming an Association to represent the views of the educated middle-class community and inspire in them a living interest in public affairs. There was indeed the British Indian Association........; but it was essentially and by its creed an Association of landholders. Nor did any active political agitation, or the creation of public opinion by direct appeals to the people, form a part of its recognised programme. There was, thus, the clear need for another political Association on a more democratic basis........" *Idem.,* Vol. I, pp. 166-68.

summoned a conference in December of the same year and during its four-day session discussed a paper recommending the expansion of the Legislative Council to the maximum number of its membership as provided in the Act of 1861, and the appointment of non-official members on a representative basis. It also recommended the separation of the judicial from the revenue functions. It was decided to send a memorial on these lines to the government.

The Bombay Association established in 1852, was replaced by the Bombay Presidency Association in 1885. It commanded an eminent position as a public body under the able direction of Ferozeshah Mehta, Kashinath Trimbak Telang and Badruddin Tayabjee. It "showed considerable activity in the early days of its existence. By resolutions, memorials and public meetings it focussed the general feelings of the community on all matters of common interest."[6] But after the founding of the Indian National Congress in December, 1885, "the main activities of India flowed through that great channel, leaving the other fields high and dry."[7]

**Birth of the Indian National Congress**

The birth of the Indian National Congress was the culminating point of India's political awakening in the nineteenth century. It was the first all-India association of a permanent nature, and with it began a new era in the political life of India. For more than twenty years after it came into being "it completely dominated the political life of India and gave a shape and form to the ideas of administrative and constitutional reforms which formed the chief planks in the political programme of India. Even though the Congress ceased to play the dominant role in Indian politics after the split at Surat in 1907, it served the very useful purpose of keeping alive an all-India political platform which enabled Gandhi to revitalise this great organisation and make it a fit instrument for leading India, stage by stage, to its goal of independence."[8]

Allan Octavian Hume, a retired member of the Indian Civil Service, took the initiative.[9] In March 1885, a notice was issued convening the meet of the first Indian National Union at Poona in the following December. The circular notice conveying the dates for holding the conference at Poona, *inter alia,* stated that the "direct object of the conference will be : (1) to enable all the most earnest labourers in the cause of national progress to become personally known to each other; (2) to discuss and decide upon the political operations to be undertaken during the ensuing year." Indirectly, the circular added, this conference will form the germ of a Native Parliament, and, if properly conducted, will constitute in a few years an unanswerable reply to the assertion that India is still wholly unfit for any form of representative institutions."[10]

The conference could not be held at Poona due to some sporadic cases of cholera having occurred there. The venue was, accordingly, shifted to Bombay and thenceforward it came to be called "the Congress." Seventy-two Indians drawn from various parts of the country, representing different classes and communities and speaking one common language (English) met as scheduled. Never before had so important and comprehensive an assemblage occurred within historical time on the soil of India. W. C. Bonerjee was elected the first President of the Congress. He laid down its objects under four heads :

"(a) The promotion, by personal intimacy and friendship amongst all the more earnest workers in our country's cause in the various parts of the Empire;

(b) The eradication, by direct personal intercourse, of all possible race, creed, or provincial prejudices amongst all lovers of our country, and the fuller development and consolidation of those sentiments of national unity that had their origin in our beloved Lord Ripon's ever memorable reign;

(c) The authoritative record, after this, has been carefully elicited by the fullest discussion, of the matured opinions of the educated classes in India on some of the more important and pressing of the social questions of the day;

(d) The determination of the lines upon and methods by which during next twelve months it

6. Mody, H., *Pherozeshah Mehta,* Vol. I, pp. 166-68.
7. *The History and Culture of the Indian People, British Paramountcy and Indian Renaissance, op. citd.,* Vol. X, Part II, p. 516.
8. *Idem.,* p. 524.
9. Allan Octavian Hume (1829-1912) had served the Government of India since 1846, but was removed from the post of Secretary to the Government of India by Lord Lytton in 1879 for holding independent views and expressing them frankly and fearlessly. Hume retired from service in 1882.
10. Annie Beasant, *How India Wrought for Freedom,* pp. 3-4.

is desirable for Native politicians to labour in the public interests."

The birth of the Indian National Congress was epoch-making as it "crystallised for the first time the new political forces in India, which till then had been localised and scattered.[11] According to Pattabhai Sitaramayya, "that what had been a vague idea floating generally in the air and influencing simultaneously the thought of thoughtful Indians in the north and the south, the east and the west, assumed a definite shape and became a practical programme of action."[12] The special correspondent of *The Times,* reporting on the inaugural session of the Congress, wrote : "For the first time, perhaps, since the world began India as a nation met together."[13] It marked a spectacle of national unity, a demonstration of people's sense of solidarity based on common aims and grievances.

Indian leaders, Dadabhai Naoroji, W. C. Bonerjee, Ferozeshah Mehta and others, who gave their unflinching help and unceasing co-operation to Hume in establishing the Indian National Congress, though not tools in his hands "were not interested in leading a popular movement of liberation either." Dadabhai Naoroji had cherished, throughout his political career, the fervent hope that if the British people remained true to themselves and to their traditions, they could certainly help Indians to attain parliamentary institutions. His faith in the sense of fairness of the British people was reflected in his censure of the bureaucratic government in India as "Un-British". W. C. Bonerjee, the first President of the Indian National Congress, spoke the mind of the delegates assembled in its 1885 session at Bombay when he declared that the demand for political progress was not incompatible with their thorough loyalty to the British Crown, and in "meeting to discuss, in an orderly and peaceful manner, questions of vital importance affecting their well-being." He further asserted that in organising themselves "they were following the only course by which the Constitution of England enabled them to represent their views to the ruling authority."[14] Revolutionary politics, as such, did not suit the temper of the Indian upperclass intelligentsia of those days. Even Surendranath Banerjea ruled it out as unsuited to the circumstances of India and as fatal to its normal development, along the line of peaceful and orderly progress."[15]

If Hume was the father of the Indian National Congress, Lord Dufferin, the Viceroy, was the god-father. Hume's original idea, according to Wedderburn, was that the provincial organisations, like the Indian Association, the Bombay Presidency Association, and the Mahajan Sabha of Madras, were to take up political questions whereas an All-India organisation, which he contemplated to establish, should concentrate on social questions. But "it was apparently by Lord Dufferin's advice that he took up the work of political organisation, as the matter first to be dealt with."[16] This is supported by W. C. Bonerjee. When Hume went to Simla early in 1885, he met Lord Dufferin and consulted him on his scheme of things. "Lord Dufferin took great interest," wrote Bonnerjee, "in the matter, and, after considering it for some time he sent for Mr. Hume and told him that, in his opinion, Mr. Hume's project would not be of much use. He said that there was no body of persons in this country who performed the functions which Her Majesty's Opposition did in England. The newspapers, even if they really represented the views of the people were not reliable and as the English were necessarily ignorant of what was thought of them and their policy in native circles, it would be very desirable in their interests as well as the interests of the ruled that Indian politicians should meet yearly and point out to the Government in what respect the administration was defective and how it could be improved and he added that an assembly such as he proposed, should not be presided over by the Local Governor, for in his presence the people might not like to speak out their mind."[17]

Hume was convinced by Lord Dufferin's reasoning, according to Bonerjee, and when he

11. Rafiq Zakaria, *Rise of Muslims in Indian Politics—An Analysis of Developments from 1885 to 1906,* p. 47.
12. Pattabhi Sitaramayya, *The History of the Indian National Congress,* p. 11.
13. *The Times,* London, February 1, 1886.
14. Presidential Address, Bombay Session, 1885, Banerjee, A. C., *Indian Constitutional Documents,* Vol. II, p. 84.
15. *A Nation in Making,* p. 43. R. C. Mazumdar advances evidence to show that Surendranath Banerjea was deliberately excluded at the inception of the Indian National Congress. *The History and Culture of the Indian People, British Paramountcy and Indian Renaissance, op. citd.,* Vol. X, Part II, pp. 532-34.
16. Wedderburn, W., *Biographical Sketch of A. O. Hume,* pp. 59-60.
17. Bonerjee, W. C. *Introduction to Politics (1898),* and as cited in Pattabhi Sitaramayya, *History of the Indian National Congress,* Vol. I, p. 15.

placed his two schemes, his own and Lord Dufferin's before leading politicians in Calcutta, Bombay, Madras, and other parts of the country, they unanimously accepted Lord Dufferin's scheme and proceeded to give effect to it. Thus, was established the Indian Union, afterwards rechristened the Indian National Congress. Bonerjee also in clear terms stated that Dufferin had made it a condition with Hume that his "'name in connection with the scheme of the Congress should not be divulged so long as he remained in the country, and his condition was faithfully maintained and none but men consulted by Mr. Hume knew anything about the matter."[18]

Professor Sunder Raman, who also attended the first session of the Congress, gave a somewhat different version. He said that Hume's original idea was to rouse the conscience of the English people through persistent agitation in Britain. But when he revealed his scheme to Dufferin, the Viceroy told him that agitation in Britain would be a futile attempt and the best course would be to confine it to India alone by Indians themselves through some organised all-India body under his leadership.[19]

But Lord Dufferin himself categorically contradicted both these views and unequivocally stated that he had thought that the Congress would devote and direct its attention only to social questions. This point he made clear in his speech at the Saint Andrew's Day Dinner on November 30, 1888. Lord Dufferin said in his speech : "When the Congress was first started, I watched its operations with interest and curiosity and I hoped that in certain fields of useful activity it might render valuable assistance to the Government. I was aware that there were many social topics connected with the habits and customs of the people which were of unquestionable utility, but with which it was either undesirable for the Government to interfere, or control.......When Congress was first started, it seemed to me that such a body, if they directed their attention with patriotic zeal to those (social questions) and cognate subjects, as similar Congresses do in England, might prove of assistance to the government and of great use to their fellow citizens; and I cannot help expressing my regret that they should seem to consider such momentous topics, concerning as they do the welfare of millions of their fellow-subjects, as beneath their notice, and that they should have concerned themselves instead with matters in regard to which their assistance is likely to be less profitable to us."[20] R. C. Majumdar is of the opinion that the view that Hume's original plan was to set up merely a non-political organization "cannot be easily reconciled with his 'appeal' (addressed to the graduates of the Calcutta University on March 1, 1883), and possibly Dufferin's share in this project has been misunderstood or exaggerated."[21] But Majumdar has "no doubt whatsoever that the Congress was really designed to arrest the progress of the revolutionary outbreak,"[22] and that in setting up this organisation Hume had the advice and blessings of Lord Dufferin.

**Rift in the Lute**

The first session of the Indian National Congress held in Bombay ended with three cheers for Hume, and Hume returning the greetings with three cheers for Her Majesty the Queen Empress. The second session was held at Calcutta, Dadabhai Naoroji presiding. Lord Dufferin received some of the delegates as "distinguished visitors to the capital" and also invited them to a garden party at the Government House. The third Congress met at Madras in Dec. 1887, and Badruddin Tyabji was elected President for that session. Lord Connemara, the Governor of Madras, entertained the delegates as Lord Dufferin had done the previous year. But soon after the Madras session, there was a rift in the lute and the bureaucracy fell foul of the Congress." Conservative opinion in Britain and India had received the birth of the Congress with considerable misgivings and hostility. *The Times* felt so much perturbed that it plainly told the "Hindu agitators" that it was by force that India was won and "it was by force that India must be governed."[23] Sir Henry Maine, the former Law Member of the

18. *Ibid.*
19. Andrews, C. F., and Mukherjee, G., *Rise and Growth of Congress in India,* pp. 122-4.
20. Bannerjee, A. C., *Indian Constitutional Documents,* Vol. II, p. 96.
21. Majumdar, R. C., *History and Culture of the Indian People, British Paramountcy and Indian Renaissance,* Vol. X, Part II, p. 531.
22. *Ibid.* Hume himself said, "A safety-valve for the escape of great and growing forces, generated by our own action, was urgently needed, and no more efficacious safety-valve than our Congress movement could possibly be devised." Wedderburn, W., *Biographical Sketch of A. O. Hume,* p. 77.
23. *The Times,* London, February 1, 1886.

Governor-General's Executive Council, wrote to Lord Dufferin on June 2, 1886, "There is the rather melancholy consideration that the ideal at which the educated natives of India are aiming, is absolutely unattainable. How can 180 millions of souls govern themselves ?"[24] In his *Essays on Indian Topics,* Theodore Beck, Principal of the Muhammadan Anglo-Oriental College, Aligarh, maintained that the Congress would inevitably develop into a "deadly engine of sedition" and warned the Government that if it allowed the Congress to spread its propaganda of the reform of Councils and constitutional agitation, the result would be "the massacre of Englishmen, their wives and children."[25] He argued that the talk of constitutional agitation was a perversion of language which would ultimately lead to bloodshed and mutiny.[26] Sir John Strachey, like Theodore Beck, accused the Congress of being a seditious organisation which was veiled under the expression of loyalty, and contended that since the ignorant masses could not follow the intricate limitations of constitutional agitation, they would only be excited by the Congress to bring about a revolution.[27] Lord Dufferin himself reacted sharply to the Congress demands. He wrote to Sir Henry Maine, May 9, 1886, "There is a mischievous busy-body of the name of Hume, whom Lord Ripon had rather feted and who seems to be one of the chief stimulators of the Indian Home Rule Movement. He is a cleverish, a little cracked, vain, unscrupulous man.....very careless truth."[28]

In spite of the moderate demands of the Congress for reforms, repeated from year to year, there was no sympathetic response. Hume was shocked and pained by the stolid indifference displayed by the Government and "no less by the misguided hostility shown towards the Congress by the official circles and by the minority communities in India, who represented the Congress movement as an attempt to subvert the government and establish a *Hindu Raj.*" Hume, therefore, decided to start a public agitation against the reactionary measures and menacing policy of the Government by means of public meetings, pamphlets and leaflets on the model of the Corn Law agitation in Britain. He appealed for funds and went round the country along with other leaders of the Congress holding a thousand meetings. Arrangements were also made for the distribution of half a million pamphlets translated into twelve Indian languages. Two of them *A Congress Catechism* and *A Conversation between Maulvi Fariduddin and Rambaksh of Kambakhtpur* showing by a parable the evils of absentee State-landlordism, however benevolent the intention might be, were widely circulated. In a speech delivered at a public meeting at Allahabad on April 30, 1888 and subsequently published in the form of a pamphlet, *A Speech on the Indian National Congress, Its Origin, Aims and Objects,* Hume stoutly defended his action of mass organisation. A similar campaign was organised in Britain by Dadabhai Naoroji with the sympathy and support of Englishmen like Sir William Hunter, Sir Henry Cotton, David Yule and many others.

The activities of Hume and his colleagues alarmed the authorities in India. The reactionaries amongst them desired to suppress the Congress and even recommended that Hume should be deported. The hostility of the Anglo-Indians was not a whit less. *The Calcutta Review,* in its issue of January 1889, observed, "The Congress then is something more than a Political Club. It is a Revolutionary League.........It is obvious that agitation is on foot which may in certain events lead to the most serious consequences to the government and the country." Lord Dufferin lashed at the Congress in his Saint Andrew's Day Dinner speech. He said that the Congress represented "a microscopic minority" and it did not represent India. He then asked : how could any reasonable man imagine that "the British Government would be content to allow this microscopic minority to control their administration of that majestic and multiform empire for whose safety and welfare they are responsible in the eyes of God and before the face of civilisation." The Viceroy even charged the Congress with exciting hatred "of the people against the public servants of the Crown in India."[29]

The increasing number of Muslim delegates attending the sessions of the Congress was really more unnerving than anything else that the

24. *Dufferin Papers*
25. Theodore Beck, *Essay on Indian Topics,* Pioneer Press, Allahabad, 1888, "In What Will it End ?" p. 105.
26. *Idem.,* pp. 117-119.
27. Strachey, Sir John, *India, op. citd.,* p. 22.
28. *Dufferin Papers.*
29. Banerjee, A. C., *Indian Constitutional Documents,* Vol. II, pp. 94-97.

British bureaucracy could put up with. Official and non-official influence was set to work to misguide the Muslims and other loyalists that the Congress was seeking to establish a *Hindu Raj* in the garb of a demand for representative government. In order to kill the Congress countrywide demonstrations were engineered, and several anti-Congress Muslim and other organisations, like the United Indian Patriotic Association, and the British Indian Association of Oudh, were set up. Counter-propaganda was started by issuing anti-Congress literature for dissemination among the Members of the British Parliament and the public in general.

**Technique of "Political Mendicancy"**

Despite the hostility of the bureaucracy in India and the adverse criticism of the Muslim and loyalist elements, the Congress forged ahead. Its propaganda in Britain and its emphasis on constitutional agitation won for it an increasing number of British supporters and sympathisers.[30] The Congress maintained great moderation and dignity even in criticising the Government and its policies. The criticism that its leaders made was not against Englishmen or the British nation. It was directed against the defective system of Government in India, which was an autocratic despotism. Having faith in the British sense of justice, its leaders did not pitch their demands very high. They believed in winning India's freedom by gradual stages and sincerely thought that the British form of parliamentary government was a far off ideal.

Imbued with the spirit of Victorian liberalism, the Congress leaders sought to achieve their objectives by constitutional means and cautious agitation. The Congress was concerned with reforms and not freedom, educating public opinion and agitating through meetings, pamphlets and leaflets. According to Dadabhai Naoroji what India had to learn from Great Britain was to agitate most loyally through petitions, demonstrations and meetings all quiet, peaceful and decorously but enthusiastically conducted. It was for this reason that their technique of attaining their objectives was nicknamed "Political Mendicancy" by the extremists, who sought to make the nationalist movement more broad-based and revolutionary in character.

**Modest Demands**

In the first few sessions the Congress drew attention of the Government to the appalling poverty of the country and asked for suitable enquiry and redress. It criticised the Government measures and policies from the national point of view and championed the rights and liberties of Indians at home and abroad. Among the important demands were : abolition of the Council of India, reform and expansion of the Supreme and Provincial Legislative Councils, holding of Indian Civil Service Examinations simultaneously in India and Britain, appointment of Indians to higher posts, reduction in military expenditure and training of Indians for commissioned posts in the army, separation of the judiciary from the executive, repeal of various repressive laws and removal of restrictions on the Indian press, reduction in salt duty and land revenue, change in tenancy laws to protect the peasants against landlords. repeal of cotton excise duty, protective tariffs for Indian industries, opening of agricultural banks to provide easy credit to the tillers, revival of old industries and starting of new ones.

The popular agitation for the association of Indians with administration bore some fruit. Lord Ripon introduced reforms in the field of local government. This opened a new chapter of Local Self-government in India, although the measures were half-hearted and a poor substitute for the full-blooded local autonomy which functioned in ancient India. The British authorities thought that only by learning to manage their local affairs could Indians acquire the experience of representative government.

But the bureaucracy did not take very kindly even to these paltry reforms. Although it was anxious to enlist the co-operation of the people in the task of government, the adoption of the parliamentary system of government, reached in Great Britain by degrees and trials, was considered out of the question for the politically immature India. The British Government was, therefore, reluctant to concede the modest demands for the expansion of Legislative Councils by the addition of elected Members. The Congress leaders, on the other hand, argued that good government was not possible without its being representative. As regards the argument that Indian masses were steeped in illiteracy and were not fully alive to their political responsibilities, their answer was that such a state of affairs existed even in Britain when the Reforms Act of 1832 was passed. It was pointed out that half of Brit-

30. For instance, David Yule, W. S. Caine, Charles Bradlaugh, Samuel Smith and Dr. Clarke. The visit of Members of Parliament to India and their presence at the Congress sessions became an annual event.

ain's male population and three-fourths of the females were then even unable to sign their names on their marriage certificates.

The Congress, finding itself absolutely ignored by the Government of India, turned to Britain and the constant pressure brought on the British government and public made a dent in its intransigence. The British Government grudgingly introduced a Bill in Parliament in 1890 to counteract the Bill sponsored by Charles Bradlaugh. The chief features of Bradlaugh's Bill were : a system of election through electoral colleges and restriction of official elements to not more than one- fourth. The 1892 reforms were, thus, an attempt at compromise "between the official view of the councils of pocket legislatures and the educated Indian view of them as embryo Parliaments."

**Widening of the Gulf**

Some of the other demands of the Congress were also partially accepted by the British Government in due course. For instance, a number of posts hitherto reserved for the Indian Civil Service were transferred to Provincial Civil Services, enabling Indians to hold those posts. A Resolution in favour of holding simultaneous examinations for the Indian Civil Service in India and Britian was passed in the House of Commons in 1893, though it was brought into actual effect long afterwards. The views of the Congress on problems affecting India, such as the North-West Frontier Policy, the Plague Regulations, the famine grant, and the financial relations of Britain and India, had also prevailed. The Royal Commission on Public Finance held that the charges placed on India were unfair to the extent of a quarter of a million sterling per year. In accepting the finding of the Commission, the British Government conceded to India a small measure of financial justice.

This was the credit side of the constitutional agitation, but there were several other modest and minimum demands, fervently made by the Congress old-guards, that were not conceded because of the pressure of the bureaucrats in India and the vested interests of British capital.

The drama of Indian nationalism, sustained by the ideas of the National Conference, and the Indian National Congress, moved through its second act during the second half of nineteenth century. The old divided and casteridden India began to recede, yielding place to a new India animated by a new spirit of nationalism. This phase constituted a landmark in the history of India, as no clear trace of it was available in earlier periods. With the Moderates still holding the ground, the technique of constitutional agitation was by that time fully evolved. Political mass meetings all over the country, political associations at centres with branches in the *mofussil* areas, memorials and petitions both to Indian and Home Governments, and organisations and individual efforts to educate public opinion in England and interest it in the Indian affairs all these became the standard forms of political activity in India. In the context of World history, this was a period when several other European countries, like France, Spain, Germany and Italy, attained their political unity and their examples inspired people of the countries held in political bondage to break their chains.

The turn of the century witnessed fresh developments of far reaching consequence which gave a new direction to Indian politics. The sand started slipping from under the feet of the Moderates and a wave of extreme nationalism began to sweep over the placid waters. The bureaucracy, on the other hand, switched on to the policy of centralisation and officialisation, contrary to the spirit of the time. But "with each advancing year nationalism, which became the dominant factor in India's freedom movement and the stabilisation of parliamentary institutions, cast its lengthening shadow over the fortunes of the British rule in India."

The hallmark of Lord Curzon's administration was distrust of Indians and belittling of their ability and honesty. Not a representative government, but an inexorable quest for efficiency became the objective of that regime. That policy fanned extremism in Indian politics and widened the gulf between the Government and the restive political India. Educated young men "highly sensitive and touchy, holding extremist views and impatient of delay in achieving freedom" mustered within the Indian National Congress and pressed for a radical change in the policy of constitutional agitation, which had not succeeded either in securing representative government or changing the long suffered arrogance, hostility and high-handedness of the bureaucracy in India.

The new generation, therefore, pulsating with a new vision, became impatient with the imbecile technique of "political mendicancy" and felt that reforms could be secured only by political action and not by appealing merely to the good sense of the English people. The study of Western thought instilled in them the feeling that self-government was the inalienable right of the people. *Swaraj* became the political sheet-anchor of the extremists. But the British Government, under the influence of the vested interests in Britain as well as in India, contended that Indians were not fit for it yet. Repression and reform became the keynote of their policy. Arguments against the fitness of Indians for self-government were refuted by Indian leaders, historians and archaeologists and a wave of deep resentment spread over the whole country against the policy of wanton repression. This reaction found manifestation in extreme nationalism of various brands.

## EXTREMISM, CAUSES OF ITS GROWTH

### Misrule of the Tory Government

The growth of the extreme type of nationalism in India was the product of the misrule of the Tory Government. From 1885 to 1902, Lord Salisbury headed the British Government, except during the brief intervals when the Liberals were in power.''[31] Although not an Imperialist himself, Salisbury had ''the capacity to yield, and to drift with the tide when he could not oppose it.''[32] Lord Hamilton, who presided at the India Office from 1895-1903, had no sympathy with the people of India. He wrote to Curzon on September 20, 1899, ''I think the real danger to our rule in India, not now but 50 years hence, is the gradual adoption and extension of Western ideas of agitation and organisation; and if we could break the educated Hindu party into two sections holding widely different views, we should, by such a division, strengthen our position against the subtle and continuous attack which the spread of education must make upon our present system of Government.'' Hamilton was indifferent even to the economic distress of the people and stood by unconcerned during the period of unparalleled calamities of war, famine and pestilences, which characterised eight years of his stewardship of the India Office.

Lord Elgin, who came to India as Governor-General with traditions of peace and goodwill towards Indians, felt helpless, confronted as he was, with an unsympathetic Secretary of State and the hardened bureaucrats who surrounded him in his Council. The lingering suspicion in the minds of Indians that India was exploited for the benefit of Britain, initially aroused by the policy of free trade, was intensified by fiscal and financial measures adopted in the last decade of the century.In 1896, the import duty on foreign cotton was lowered to 3 ½ per cent on the representation of Lancashire manufacturers and exporters. A countervailing excise duty was also imposed on Indian manufactures. It caused a stir in the country. The mercantile community which was hardhit, fretted and fumed but to no avail.[33]

Lord Bacon correctly said that ''much poverty and much discontentment prepare the ground in which revolutions germinate.'' Beginning from the last decade of the nineteenth century, India passed through unexampled economic distress. There was all round economic depression and the lower middle-class people were the worst sufferers. Besides, the country suffered from natural calamities. Floods, famines, plague and earthquake had devastated the country and the people died like mosquitoes.''[34] But the Government stood by unconcerned and did nothing to improve the economic lot of the people. Unemployment amongst the educated classes, especially in Bengal, produced a ferment of anti-British feelings. The Sedition Committee expressed the opinion that the economic discontent of the *Bhadrolok,* for centuries peaceful and unwarlike, was responsible for the intensity of nationalist feelings in Bengal.

It was in this period charged with commotion that the classic works, Dadabhai Naoroji's *Poverty and Un-British Rule in India,* and William Digby's *'Prosperous' British India*, appeared. They carried a factual account of India's poverty and misery and drove home to the people the curse of British Imperialism. According to Jawahar Lal Nehru these books ''played a revolutionary role in the development of our nationalist thoughts. In spite of the moderate outlook of the authors of these books they gave ''a political

31. February to July 1886, and from 1892 to 1895.
32. Dutt, R. C., *India in the Victorian Age*, p. 442.
33. R. C. Dutt, thus, writes, : ''The result of this iniquitous legislation combined with the famines and currency legislation, has been disastrous..........New Mills are struggling into existence in spite of every check, but the output in yarn and piece goods shows a lamentable decline.'' Dutt, R. C., *India in the Victorian Age,* p. 544.
34. Two severe famines in quick succession broke out in 1896-97. By the spring of 1897, over four million people were receiving relief and mortality was extremely heavy. Lovat Fraser, *India Under Curzon and After,* p. 444.

and economic foundation to our nationalism."[35]

It was at this grave moment, as the Famine Commission observed, that Elgin's Government embarked upon the costly and extensive trans-frontier military operations at the bidding of the Secretary of State for India. In 1895, Surendranath Banerjea warned the Government against this "wrong and ruinous" policy. "Let me tell the Government of India", he said, "in your name (delegates of the Congress at the Poona session) that the true scientific frontier against Russian invasion does not lie in some remote inaccessible mountain, which has yet to be discovered, nor is it to be found in the House of Commons as someone said; but it lies deep in the heart of loyal and contented people."[36] That was the true voice from the heart of India, but there was no change in the Government's policy. In 1900, a fresh famine broke out over a large area and it lasted three years during which millions of men perished, Tens of thousands were still in relief camps when the gorgeous Delhi *darbar* was held in January, 1903.[37] "As a pageant", wrote Lovat Fraser, "the Durbar was without precedent in the history of Asia, and probably its magnificence will never again be equalled."[38] But unprecedented, too, was the misery of the Indians; which had no equal before or after.

These events produced a seething discontentment in the country and fed political extremism. During the 1896-97 famine, Bal Gangadhar Tilak, the most outstanding of the new group of extremists, started a no-tax campaign amongst the peasantry of the Deccan. He organised a corps of volunteers to tour through the villages and to explain to peasants their rights to relief and remission of land revenue under the Famine Relief Code. He told the people, "If you have money to pay Government dues, pay them by all means. But if you have not, will you sell your things away only to avoid the supposed wrath of subordinate government officers ? Can you not be bold, even when in the grip of death ? We can stand any number of famines, but shall we do with sheepish people ?"

Tilak voiced his feelings in the columns of his Weeklies, the *Mahratta,* English, and the *Kesari,* in Marathi. Both these papers became powerful organs to spread the principles and policies of the new wave of nationalism. In the *Kesari*, January 12, 1897, he reviewed the work of twelve years of the Indian National Congress and suggested what its future course of action should be. Tilak wrote, "For the last twelve years we have been shouting hoarse, desiring that the Government should hear us. But our shouting has no more affected the Government than the sound of a gnat. Our rulers disbelieve our statements or profess to do so. Let us now try to force our grievances into their ears by strong constitutional means. We must give the best political education possible to the ignorant villagers. We must meet them on terms of equality, teach them their rights and show them how to fight constitutionally. Then only will the Government realise that to despise the Congress is to despise the Indian nation. Then only will the efforts of the Congress leaders be crowned with success. Such a work will require a large body of able and single-minded workers, to whom politics would not mean some holiday recreation, but an every-day duty to be performed with strictest regularity."

Bubonic plague, following in the wake of the famine in Deccan, provided a further edge to bitterness. By the end of 1898, the recorded number of deaths reached an under-estimated total of 1,73,000. To prevent the spread of the disease the Government adopted some measures which evoked resentment. The military were called to help the civil authorities in that process. Without observing any customary formality, soldiers entered residential quarters, examined indiscriminately men, women and children, segregated those suspected of disease and had them sent to isolation camps. All this produced a deep sense of estrangement amongst the people. More than two thousand people of Poona, Hindus and Muslims, submitted a memorial to the Government, protesting against the conduct of British soldiers engaged in enforcing the plague rules. It had no effect on the government. Tilak took up the issue in the *Kesari* and severely criticised the official measures. Desperate but helpless people resorted to rioting and on the night of the celebrations of Queen Victoria's Diamond Jubilee, two English officers, W.C. Rand, Assistant Commissioner of Poona, and his companion, Lieutenant C. E. Ayerst, were killed in the streets of Poona. Similar riots took place in Bombay.

The disturbance was quelled with a heavy

35. Jawaharlal Nehru, *Autobiography*, p. 426.
36. As cited in Annie Beasant, *How India Wrought for Freedom,* p. 209.
37. The great Coronation Assemblage to celebrate the Coronation of Edward VII.
38. Lovat Fraser, *India Under Curzon and After,* p. 232.

hand and Chapekar brothers, suspected of murder at Poona, were arrested and tried. Damodar Chapekar was sentenced to death and executed. Coercion was intensified, for the authorities suspected in these riots a regular conspiracy to overthrow the Government. In that mood the official wrath fell on Tilak and on July 27, 1897, he was arrested for "exciting and attempting to excite feelings of disaffection to the Government", through certain articles entitled "Utterances of Shivaji", and was sentenced to eighteen months rigorous imprisonment. With the "martyrdom of Tilak extremist agitation struck root in the soil." A "nation is in tears," said Surendranath Banerjea.[39]

**Repressive and Reactionary Policy**

The Government, in its determination to suppress the so-called terrorist activities, followed a policy of rigorous persecution. It passed laws to restrict the liberty of the press, empowered magistrates to bind down editors of newspapers, and to send them to prison in default of security without trial for any specific offence. N. Subba Rao Pantulu, Chairman of the Reception Committee of the fourteenth Congress, expressed his deep and painful concern at the provocative attitude of Indian officials "who saw conspiracy where there was none, who narrowed personal liberty in times of peace, brought in laws against sedition, and made distinction between the British-born and the Indian subjects of the Queen Empress."[40] In 1896, the doors of the Roorkee Engineering College were closed to Asiatics of pure descent domiciled in India. Thus, the Government of India, as Anand Mohan Bose expressed it, gave "privilege to illegitimacy" by not excluding admission to the College to Asiatics of impure descent.[41] Romesh Chandra Dutt cogently remarked that he could hardly remember any time "when the confidence of the people of India in the justice and fair play of English rulers was so shaken as it has been within the last two years."[42]

In this way, in the words of C. Jambulingam Mudaliar, an Empire which had been consolidated "by confidence and goodwill has been converted into a Government of suspicion and distrust.....A permanent bitterness of feeling has taken root over the land, over its whole length and breadth."[43] The new Sedition Law placed speakers and editors of Indian origin on a level with robbers and vagabonds. It was the worst affront to the self-respect of Indians and it created a woeful sense of estrangement between the people and the Government. Lord Elgin's silly declaration that India had been conquered by the sword and by the sword it should be held, fanned popular discontent and indignation into flame. Gokhale had issued a warning to the Government as far back as 1892, that its reactionary policies were an invitation to the danger ahead. The Government paid no heed to his sane advice, and to the changing mood of the people.

But the Moderates in the Congress were fully seized of the real situation in the country. In October, 1900, Hume, Wedderburn and Dadabhai Naoroji addressed a manifesto to the Congress President, wherein they represented that "a very critical stage in the history of the organisation, possibly a parting of ways, has now been reached." Whether the constitutional technique of agitation, they observed, could succeed any more depended upon the attitude and action of the people. But "We, who were among its originators, have now well-nigh completed our work as pioneers, we have given the lead to young men and must look to them to take up in large measure the burden of the work." The younger men had already pronounced on the futility of the ideology and methods of the pioneers and decided upon a more revolutionary method which would yield quicker and better results.

**Lord Curzon's Affront to Indians**

When Lord Curzon landed in Bombay on December 30, 1898 the people gave him a cordial welcome in the hope that he would govern India in accordance with the best traditions of British rule. In December 1898 the President of the Madras Congress, Anand Mohan Bose, warmly welcomed the appointment of Lord Curzon as Viceroy and said, "Let a nation which is Christian endeavour truly to show the ideal of Christ, to carry out the divine command of doing to others what they would have wished done to themselves in the exercise of its power in its attitude towards Indian aspirations." Yet, in No-

39. As cited in Annie Besant, *How India Wrought for Freedom*, p. 259.
40. *Idem.*, p. 271.
41. *Idem.*, p. 272.
42. *Idem.*, p. 273.
43. *Idem.*, p. 275.

vember 1900 Lord Curzon wrote, "The Congress is tottering to its fall and one of my greatest ambitions while in India is to assist it to a peaceful demise."[44] The new Viceroy excelled his predecessors in exhibiting Imperialist arrogance and insolence and soon showed by his acts that he considered Indians definitely inferior. Bitter feelings were roused against him by his fetish of efficiency, by his unbridled egoism and racial arrogance, and by his attempt to disrupt the unity of the Bengal Province, under the cover of administrative convenience. The end of his regime, which had shown British rule at its worst, was a welcome break. Virtually, the country heaved a sigh of relief. Even a Moderate like Gopal Krishna Gokhale offered his thanks to the Almighty on this occasion. He compared Curzon with Aurangzeb and said, "There we find the same attempt at a rule excessively centralised and intensely personal, the same strenuous purpose, the same over-powering consciousness of duty, the same marvellous capacity for work, the same sense of loneliness, the same persistence in a policy of distrust and repression, resulting in bitter exasperation all round. I think even the most devoted admirer of Lord Curzon cannot claim that he has strengthened the foundations of the British rule in India."[45]

Lord Curzon, immediately after his arrival, trumpeted that his authority over the sub-continent of India was absolute and without his authority "a sparrow can scarcely twitter its tail at Peshawar." At the Delhi *Durbar*[46] in celebration of the coronation of Edward VII, Curzon acted as if he was the King himself and not His Majesty's Viceroy. He insulted the Princes who could trace their lineage to the Sun and the Moon. His curtailment of the powers of the Calcutta Corporation, his Official Secrets Act, his officialisation of the Universities, and his Tibetan expedition were some of the execrable instances of Curzon's administration. The Official Secrets Act authorised the arrest of anyone on mere suspicion and it was made the responsibility of the accused person to prove his innocence. The Act was not only odious and iniquitous but monstrous. Gokhale said it was "impossible to speak with patience or moderation on the subject." The Universities Act jammed educational progress, bureaucratised education, reduced the independence of the Universities, and throttled private education. Surendranath Banerjea, moving a resolution in the nineteenth Congress, said that the new fangled Imperialism was darkening the prospects of human freedom and that Lord Curzon's "name would go down to posterity indissolubly linked with a reactionary and retrograde measure which has been condemned by the unanimous opinion of the educated India."[47]

Such was the tense atmosphere in the country when Lord Curzon added insult to the injury by making adverse reflections on the character and ability of the Indian people. He declared in his Budget speech, March 1904, that the highest ranks of civil employment must as a general rule be held by Englishmen, as only the members of a ruling race possessed the qualities essential for the performance of the task. But even more galling to the sense of self-respect of the Indians were his utterances at the Calcutta University Convocation. He made the imputation that Indians were by their environment, their heritage and their upbringing unequal to the responsibilities of high offices under the British rule. While emphasising the importance and function of a University in moulding the character of the youth, he said, "We have hardly learned how to light the lamp of the soul.....We have to save the rising generation from walking in false paths and to guide them into right ones." Having said so, he warned the Bengalis against flattery, vituperation and eloquence. "All I say to you", Curzon said, "do not presume upon this talent." Curzon, thus, nakedly abused the Bengalis and concluded his address by saying that India was not a nation.

"Nations are swayed", succinctly remarks Masani, "by sentiments as are individuals."[48] The sentiments of the Indian people were outraged by these vituperative outpourings of Curzon. Mammoth meetings were held in all the important cities of India, condemning the representative of the King Emperor for casting aspersions on the character of the people. Lord Curzon's behavior turned many a Bengali into an

---

44. Curzon to Hamilton, November 1900, as quoted by Daniel Argove in his *Moderates and Extremists in the Indian Nationalist Movement,* p. 95.
45. As quoted in Annie Besant, *How India Wrought for Freedom,* p. 417.
46. The Durbar cost India £ 360,666. Morley, J., *Recollections,* Vol. II, p. 166. Lal Mohan Ghosh, President of the 1906 Congress Session, denounced the Delhi Durbar as "a pompous pageant to starving people."
47. As quoted in Annie Besant, *How India Wrought for Freedom,* p. 383.
48. Masani, R.P., *Britain in India,* p. 79.

extremist. Even the sober leaders of the Congress felt extremely disgusted. In that temper moderation was naturally discounted and extremism gained ground. For this change in the political climate Curzon must be held personally responsible to a large extent.

**The Partition of Bengal**

On top of all this came the decision to partition the historical Province of Bengal, which acted like match-stick that applied fire to the political gun-powder. Not only was the Partition a sinister move with the real aim to drive a wedge between the Hindus and the Muslims[49] and to hold India by dividing the people on the basis of communal animosity,[50] but the way in which the scheme was enforced under threat of British bayonets pushed the political unrest to the danger point and let loose a wave of terrorism in the country. Besides, suppressing the national forces with an iron hand, government officials fomented communalism. Encouraged and pampered, the anti-social elements among the Muslims indulged in open violence, looted Hindu shops, burnt their homes, desecrated their temples and carried away Hindu widows. Sir Bampfylde Fuller, the Lieutenant-Governor of Bengal, said in a jest that he had two wives, one a Hindu and the other a Muslim, and the latter was a favourite. Whether it was a jest or not, the joke was taken in earnest by the Muslims who generally believed that the British authorities would not take notice of their excesses and that they could have a free hand in the affair.

The Partition of Bengal led directly to the growth of extremism. "This is how extremists are created", declared Gokhale in anguish. Surendranath Banerjea and Bipin Chandra Pal took the lead and the Bengalis carried on a virulent agitation for the annulment of the Partition. The people in Bengal initiated the Swadeshi and boycott movements, which spread like wild fire throughout the country. Protest meetings, huge processions and bonfires of foreign goods became a daily feature with the Bengalis. The indiscriminate prosecution of the school lads and the circular banning the recital of Bande Mataram in public places intensified the agitation. People observed the Partition Day[51] as a day of national mourning and humiliation. Efforts to ease the situation through a high-powered deputation failed. Gokhale and Lajpat Rai were sent to London to appeal to the British Government to undo the wrong, but they came back empty-handed. In disgust Lajpat Rai gave the message to his countrymen that if they really cared for their country, they would themselves have to strike the blow for freedom.[52] Frustration was deepened even among the Moderates, who could not keep a hold on the political situation. This was reflected when Gokhale said that young men were "beginning to ask what was the good of constitutional methods, if it was only to end in the partition of Bengal."

**Race-conscious Arrogant Behaviour of the Anglo-Indians**

Among other important factors which fomented anti-British feelings and egged on extremism was the race-conscious arrogant behaviour of the Anglo-Indians and the anti-Indian policy of the Anglo-Indian press. Fed on anti-Indian propaganda, British soldiers and other British residents in India assaulted Indians, causing the death of many of the victims. In almost all such cases the white culprits escaped without any, or with proportionately very light, punishment. The brutish murderous assault by three drunken British soldiers on Dr. Suresh Chandra Sircar, a medical practitioner at Barrackpur in 1898

49. Lord Curzon went on tour in February 1904, in Eastern Bengal "to feel the pulse" of the people. Lovat Fraser reported that swarms of small boys greeted Lord Curzon in the streets, carrying placards on which was inscribed the legend : "Do not turn us into Assamese." Curzon told the people at a public meeting at Dacca that he had never cherished the intention ascribed to him by the placards and that the people of Eastern Bengal "must be the head and heart of any.....new organism, instead of the new extremities." Lovat Fraser, *India Under Curzon and After*, p. 381.
50. The final division was that a new Province of Assam and Eastern Bengal was created. It included Assam, the three Divisions of Chittagong, Rajshahi and Dacca and a few minor pieces of territory. The total area of the new Province was 106,540 square miles with a population of 31 millions; 18 million Muslims and 12 million Hindus.
51. October 16, 1905, the day on which the Partition of Bengal was effected.
52. At the Benares session of the Congress in 1905, Lajpat Rai congratulated Bengal on its splendid opportunity of heralding a new political era for the country and said that the English expected them to show more manliness in their struggle for liberty. They must show that they were "no longer beggars, and that we are subjects of an Empire where people are struggling to achieve that position which is their right." If other Provinces followed the example of Bengal, said Lajpat Rai, "the day was not far distant when they would win." As quoted in Annie Besant, *How India Wrought for Freedom*, pp. 427-28.

shocked the whole country. But the special jury, most of whom were European lawyers of the Calcutta High Court, acquitted the accused persons of the charge of murder and found them guilty of only causing grievous hurt. There were several other soul-stirring cases of blatant racialism in the country.[53] These cases even touched the chord of Lord Curzon's heart, who, thus, conveyed his resentment to the Secretary of State : "I do not know what you think of these cases. They eat into my very soul."[54]

The Anglo-Indian press helped in spreading the venom of racial arrogance and very often lent support to the white criminals and even abetted them to crime. When the attempt to shoot Kingsford miscarried, but resulted in the death of two English ladies, the *Asian* of Calcutta wrote, "Mr. Kingsford has a geat opportunity, and we hope he is a fairly decent shot at a short single range. Mr. Kingsford will manage to secure a big 'bag' and we envy him for his opportunity."[55] *The Civil and Military Gazette of Lahore,* and some other important Anglo-Indian papers openly abused educated Indians and used ignominious names for them. Nevinson writes that educated Indians "were spoken of as 'babbling B.A.s', 'baseborn B.A.s', 'a class that carries a stigma', and so on."[56] And yet there was no penalty for such writings which incited racial hatred.[57] The young Indians pulsating with fresh ideas of freedom could not tolerate such an outrageous treatment and the popular unrest keyed on to a high pitch.

**Fresh Wave of Revivalism**

The desire for freedom was also inspired by a fresh wave of religious revivalism, which was a curious blending of politics with religion, the urge to orient towards the past which conjured up a golden age of peace and plenty. The physical unity, which British rule had brought about through a Central Government as well as by the expansion of the means of communication and transport, was reinforced by the knowledge of a common rich heritage and the cultural unity of the country. Researches about the ancient polity and representative institutions gave tongue to the extremists who regarded foreign rule as the cause of all ills in India. Several eminent scholars of Indology counteracted the theories of Western scholars by pointing out that a representative form of government and enlightened public opinion were not foreign to India. These theories fed the Indian politicians to retort that if India had a self-government in the remote past there was no reason why it could not have it in the twentieth century. The concept of a new India, free from the aliens, wherein a democratic society was to be established according to the genius of the people, was mirrored in the image of Mother India, garbed in queenly attire. The idealization of India in the *Bande Mataram* song, the preachings of lessons from the Gita as well as from the life histories of heroes like Rana Pratap and Shivaji, created a new fervour in the political life of the country.

The renaissance created a revulsion against things Western and gave rise to love of things Indian. It promoted a new sense of patriotism and nationalism in the country. It also became the mainspring of the activities of Lokmanya Tilak, Aurobindo Ghosh, Bipin Chandra Pal and Lajpat Rai –leaders of the extremist wing in the Indian National Congress. Tilak, who was the foremost among them, was described by Valentine Chirol as "one of the most dangerous of pioneers of the disaffection" and "truly the father of Indian unrest."[58] Tilak was probably the most erudite of the Sanskrit scholars of the day and was proud of India's ancient glory. He devoted himself to educational activities in order to inculcate the spirit of true nationalism among the young men and through them to raise the status of India to heights reminiscent of the past. He hated and denounced the British and he hated them not because they had overthrown the Peshwas but because the impact of Western education had

53. In one such case several British soldiers outraged an Indian woman to death. Not only was punishment not meted out, but the military authorities on the spot showed a culpable disposition to hush up the whole matter, and were abetted in their attempt by the local civil officials. In 1902, the troopers of a cavalry regiment beat an Indian cook to death for having refused to procure an Indian woman for them.
54. Ronaldshay, *Life of Curzon,* Vol. II, p. 246.
55. Nevinson, H. W., *The New Spirit in India,* pp. 29.
56. *Idem.,* pp. 17-18.
57. Sir Henry Cotton wrote in 1904, "It is a grave symptom that the official body in India has now succumbed as completely as the non-official to anti-native prejudices." He further added, 'We now see a state of things in which the Indian community exists alone on the one side, while both classes of Englishmen, official as well as non-official, are united on the other." Cotton Sir Henry, *New India,* pp. 50-51.
58. Chirol, Valentine, Sir, *Indian Unrest,* pp. 40-41.

destroyed Hindu culture and polluted Hindu society.[59] Bent on the eradication of the despicable influences of Western education, Tilak thought of demolishing British rule itself. He, therefore, started a movement called the Maharashtra School of Nationalism, based on a revival of the memory of Shivaji. He drew his sanction from the Gita which teaches action and declares that kshatriya commits no sin if he kill his foe.[60]

Tilak resuscitated the Ganpati celebrations, revived the Shivaji festival, organised the Hindu youth into anti-cow killing societies and established *Akharas* and *Lathi* Clubs throughout Maharashtra. He exhorted his followers to emulate the example of Shivaji to kindle in them a heroic determination to achieve freedom from the British, and to defend the interests of the Hindu religion, of which Ganpati was the protector. "Lectures, processions, singing parties", Tilak declared, "are the invariable accompaniment of the festival and they not only afford an outlet to the religious zeal of the people but help in fostering the national sentiment also and creating interest in the outstanding questions of the day."

The Province of Bengal, exasperated by the regime of Lord Curzon, with Partition forced down its throat against the united will of the Bengalis, was the first disciple to accept Tilak's teachings. The Bengal School of Nationalism led by Bipin Chandra Pal and Aurobindo Ghosh was influenced by the neo-Vedantic movement of Swami Vivekanand which sought to realise the old spiritual ideas of the Aryan race by the idealization and spiritualization of the contents and actual relations of the life.[61] Sometimes old gods and goddesses were interpreted in a way suitable for rousing national sentiments and hopes among the people. The ancient idealism of the *Shakti* cult was revived and all the forms and symbols of Hindu worship were given a new meaning. "This wonderful transfiguration of the old gods and goddesses", observed Bipin Chandra Pal, "is carrying the message of nationalism to the masses of the country." The goddess *Kali* or *Durga,* he said, had no message for the weakling. *Durga Puja* was originally a ceremony associated with war and that the animal sacrifices were intended to quicken the martial spirit of the Indian race.

Aurobindo recalled the glory of the Indian heritage and propounded that "independence is the goal of life and Hinduism alone will fulfil this aspiration of ours." Lajpat Rai, in the Punjab, pooh-poohed westernised Indians who were blindly imitating Western customs and ways of life and were forgetting their own sublime culture.

### Humiliation of Indians in British Colonies

Certain external factors, too, helped the growth of nationalism in India. While the country was internally in ferment, the people of India witnessed their brethren in South Africa and other British Colonies subjected to odious racial discrimination and humiliation. Valentine Chirol, special correspondent of the *London Times,* who visited India during the Viceroyalty of Lord Minto, admitted that "much bad blood had undoubtedly been created by the treatment of British Indians in South Africa and the attitude in British Colonies towards Asiatic immigrants."[62] Lajpat Rai gave a pathetic account of the status of Indians and the humiliating treatment which they received abroad. "The Indian", he wrote, "carried the badge of political subjection with him. The British Colonies, more than any other country, bang their doors on him. He is a pariah all over the world."[63]

The miserable plight of Indians abroad roused great indignation in Indian National Congress. Since 1894, the Indian National Congress had been protesting against the disabilities from which Indians suffered in the British Colonies, and had prayed to Her Majesty's Government

59. Tilak came from a family which had been in the service of the Peshwas and, accordingly, his mind was moulded in an atmosphere where the memories of Maharashtra's glorious past were fresh. His love for Hindu religion and pride in its ideals and institutions made him the champion of India's superiority. In order to rally the Hindu masses under one political flag, he introduced the public festival of Ganesh and Shivaji's anniversary celebration.

60. Tilak declared, "Great men are above the common principles of morality.......The Divine Krishna's teachings in the Gita, tell us we may kill even our teachers and kinsmen and no blame attaches if we are not actuated by selfish motives .....If thieves enter our house and we have not sufficient strength to drive them out, should we not, without hesitation, shut them and burn them alive..........." As quoted in M.A. Buch, *Rise and Growth of Indian Militant Nationalism,* p. 28.

61. Vivekananda declared in a speech, "O, ye brave men, take courage, be proud that you are an Indian, and proudly proclaim I am Indian—every Indian is my brother.....The soil of India is my highest heaven. India's good is my good.." *The Life of Swami Vivekananda,* Vol. IV, p. 185.

62. Chirol, Valentine, Sir, *Indian Unrest,* p. 34.

63. Lajpat Rai, *Young India,* p. 80.

and the Government of India to safeguard their interest and endeavour to remove their grievances. But it had no effect.[64] At the session of the twenty-first Congress, B. N. Sarma spoke out boldly, warning Britain that in the Empire there could not be permanently a racial supremacy, one race dominating the other. "If we are true to ourselves", he said, "then the race which has produced greatest philosophers, the greatest statesmen and greatest warriors shall not crouch for this or that favour at the hands of other people. It is then and then alone that the South African problem, as well as other Indian problems will find their solution."[65]

### Foreign Influences

The socio-religious awakening, the political and economic exploitation, racial arrogance and repressive measures had produced sharp anti-Imperialist feelings by the end of the nineteenth century and in that atmosphere any single blow on the citadel of Imperialism was a matter for rejoicing and a source of inspiration to nationalist India. The defeat of Italy by Abyssinia in 1896, was hailed in India and, as Garrat said, "added fire to Tilak's agitation."[66] The nationalist movement in Egypt, Persia and elsewhere thrilled the people of India and stimulated their national fervour. The victory of Japan in the Russo-Japanese War in 1905, exploded the myth of European invincibility and the prestige of Great Britain received a setback in the Boer War.[67] These events put fresh heart into Indian politics and sharpened the edge of militant nationals. The phenomenal rise of Japan to power stimulated many Indians and they began studying her history and the causes of her growing ascendancy. Her success was attributed, besides other factors, to the unique patriotism and spirit of nationhood and self-sacrifice of the people. These virtues, it was thought, could infuse a new life even into a subjugated and dismayed country like India to free herself from the British bondage. These feelings were strengthened by the study of the lives and works of Mazzini, Garibaldi and Cavour.

The beginning of the twentieth century was a period of new awakening in the East. A sense of Asian solidarity was growing. This new consciousness came as a result of the feeling that there existed fundamental unity between India, China and Japan and that if that unity was to be maintained, they must fight unitedly against the menace of European Imperialism. But the Indian people were conscious that their country could play her part only after attaining an independent and free government of their own and they firmly determined to get it.

## PARTING OF THE WAYS

### Two Wings in the Congress

As described earlier, the rumblings of extremism had been in evidence since 1894, but there was no formal division of the Congress into the Moderates and the Extremists. Up to 1905, both worked in alliance. But since then the cleavage between these tow wings had marked the beginning of a new ferment in the national history of India. The dragon-teeth sown by Lord Curzon ripened into a sinister harvest. Gokhale, who presided over the Benares session of the Congress, remarked that he had been called to take charge of the vessel of the Congress with rocks ahead and angry waves beating around, and invoked the divine guidance.

The 1905 session of the Congress at Benares was held at the time when the wounds caused by the Partition of Bengal were quite fresh and there was unprecedented commotion in the country.[68] The official report of the 1905 session observed : "Never since the dark days of Lytton's Viceroyalty had India been so distracted, discontented, despondent; the victim of so many misfortunes, political and other; the target of so much scorn and calumny emanating from the highest quarters— its most moderate demand ridiculed and scouted, its most reasonable prayers greeted with a stiff negative; its noblest aspirations spurned and denounced as pure mischief or solemn nonsense; its most cherished ideals hurled down from their pedestal and trodden under foot."[69] Yet, the Moderates stuck to their guns

64. In 1903 the Indian National Congress passed a resolution strongly protesting against the hardships and disabilities of the Indians living in the British Colonies and prayed to the British Government to devise adequate measures to ensure the position of equality to Indian emigrants with the European subjects in all the British Colonies.
65. As cited in Annie Besant, *How India Wrought for Freedom,* p. 425.
66. *An Indian Commentary, op. citd.,*p. 134.
67. The British Government had waged war against Transvaal and one of the declared causes of the Boer War was the treatment meted out to the Indians. But the irony was that the British Government not only connived at, but sometimes even encouraged anti-Indian legislation aiming to seriously curtail the rights and status of the Indians.
68. The Partition came into effect on October 16, 1905.
69. As quoted in Ramna Rao, *A Short History of the Indian National Congress,* p. 52.

and advocated and insisted on constitutional means for gradually achieving self-government in India. Gokhale, in his Presidential Address, thus defined the goal of the Congress ".......that India should be governed first and foremost in the interest of Indians themselves, and that in course of time a form of government should attained in this country similar to what exists in the self-governing Colonies of the British Empire. For better, for worse, our destinies are now linked with those of England and the Congress freely recognises that whatever advance we seek must be within the Empire itself."[70] He declared that the advance towards self-government could "only be gradual, as at each stage of the progress it may be necessary for us to pass through a brief course of apprenticeship before we are enabled to go to the next one; for it is a reasonable proposition that the sense of responsibility, required for the proper exercise of the political institutions of the West, can be acquired by an Eastern people through practical training and experiment only."[71]

Although the Moderates were in majority in the Congress, they were losing ground, for even their modest demands did not evoke any response in the official quarters. At the 1904 Congress session it was resolved that a deputation, under the leadership of Sir Henry Cotton and the President for the year, should wait upon Lord Curzon and present to him resolutions passed at that session, which, *inter alia,* included the Indianisation of the services, elimination of the causes of poverty, an enquiry into the conditions of the peasants and the enlargement of the Councils. Lord Curzon refused to receive the deputation and characterised the activities of the Congress as the mere letting of "gas". It was, then, decided to send a deputation, consisting of Gokhale and Lajpat Rai, to London and to present Indian grievances before the British public.

Meanwhile, the Liberals came into power in 1905, and John Morley became the Secretary of State for India. Indians, particularly the Moderates, felt happy over the change of Government in England as the Liberals, while in Opposition, had given a promise of a fair deal and of great reforms. Morley's espousal of India's cause had always been vigorous, and naturally high expectations were placed in him. But Gokhale and Lajpat Rai, during their stay in London, realised that "the speeches of a Party in Opposition are more dictated by expediency than by the principles for which the Party stands, that an imperceptible but nonetheless noticeable change occurs in the persons as soon as they shift from the Opposition to the Treasury benches; that where Indian affairs were concerned the party labels of Liberals and Conservatives have no meaning and above all that Morley's liberalism which had excited great hopes, had deserted him, and what remained of it was geographical in its scope, confined to England alone.[72] At the Benares session of the Congress, Lajpat Rai informed the delegates that the British public was too busy with their own affairs and that Indians would have to carve out their own political destiny.[73]

At the 1905 session of the Congress a difficult situation arose, which caused a serious crack in Congress unity. In January, 1906, the Prince and Princess of Wales were scheduled to visit India. The extremists in the Congress had threatened to boycott the Royal visit and the Viceroy felt uneasy about it. Minto had met Gokhale and had taken an assurance from him that the Congress would make its earnest and best efforts to make the Royal visit a success. Accordingly, the Moderates desired to move a resolution in the open session of the Congress, pledging a welcome to the Royal visitors. It proved a spark in the arsenal of sullenness and caused an explosion. The contingent of Bengali delegates became boisterous and vehemently denounced this move of the Moderates. The Maharashtra and Punjab leaders were prevailed upon to pacify the indignant Bengalis and it was with great difficulty that they agreed to let the resolution be passed in their absence. But the Moderates had to make a show of compromise with the extremists. Gokhale, in his Presidential Address, condemned the Partition of Bengal as a "cruel wrong" and denounced Lord Curzon's assertion that the agitation was "manufactured". He praised the heroic stand of the Bengalis against the oppression of a harsh and uncontrolled bureaucracy. Gokhale declared that nothing more intense, widespread and spontaneous had been seen in Indian political agitation and justified the *Swadeshi* and *boycott* movements as a political weapon.

Thus, although an open rift was avoided at

70. Banerjee, A.. C., *Indian Constitutional Documents,* Vol. II, p. 203.
71. *Ibid.*
72. Ishwari Prasad and K. S. Subedar, *A History of Modern India,* pp. 344-45.
73. Lajpat Rai, *Young India,* pp. 169-70.

the 1905 session, it left behind a trail of sharp dissension among the Congress members. Relations between the two groups were further estranged during the course of the year. The Secretary of State for India had categorically declared in Parliament that the Partition of Bengal was a settled fact and that it could not be undone. The extremists, therefore, wanted to intensify their struggle against the Partition by capturing the Congress and putting Tilak in the chair for the 1906 session, which was to meet in Calcutta.

This was too much for the old guards, and they outwitted the extremists by putting Dadabhai Naoroji in the chair. Their move was successful, but the extremists scored a few points in the game. Resolutions were passed at the Calcutta session on all the four important issues which they had professed for, that is, *Swaraj, Swadeshi, boycott* and national education. The keynote of Dadabhai's Presidential Address was *Swaraj* or self-government and the Congress switched on to a new objective. Self-government like that of the United Kingdom or the Dominions was declared to be the goal of India.

A rift between the two sections of the Congress was again averted, but not for long. Sharp differences between the two sections persisted with regard to the method of winning *Swaraj*. The boycott resolution was another bone of contention. The Moderates never desired it to be used as a political weapon to bring British rule to an end. They intended to confine its application only to Bengal as a gesture of protest against the Partition of Bengal. The extremists, on the other hand, aimed at using it as a political weapon embracing within its fold the boycott of foreign goods as well as the boycott of offices. They wanted the people to refuse to associate with the Government in any form and to extend the boycott movement to the whole country. Tilak explained the objective in his speech before a Calcutta audience. He said, "If you have not the power of active resistance, have you not the power of self-denial and self-abstinence in such a way as not to assist this foreign government to rule over you ? This is boycott, we shall not have their goods, we shall not give them assistance to collect revenue and to keep the peace. We shall not assist them in fighting beyond the frontiers or outside India with Indian blood and money. We shall not assist them in carrying on the administration of justice. We shall have our own courts and when the time comes we shall not pay taxes. Can you do that by your united efforts ? If you can, you are free from tomorrow."[74] Lajpat Rai upheld *Swadeshi* and boycott as the religion of new India; the manifestation of self-sacrificing patriotism; the means of moulding a self-reliant Indian nation and the spearhead of India's national struggle against British rule.[75] He discarded the Moderates' plea of co-operation with the Government on attaining self-government steadily and gradually, and asserted that it was folly to interpret India's status of political subservience as a beneficial school for political apprenticeship.[76]

### The Surat Split

During 1907, relations between the Moderates and extremists reached the breaking point. Lord Minto, who had succeeded in introducing communalism into Indian politics, was hobnobbing with the Moderates for seeking their co-operation in the reforms which were on the anvil. This annoyed the extremists, for they had no faith in the capacity of the Moderates to negotiate with the Government. The object with which the Muslim League was founded further exasperated the extremists. They thought of the one and the only course left for them and it was to make a bold bid to capture the Congress at its ensuing annual session in 1907. For this purpose, they wanted to propose the name of Lajpat Rai as President for the Surat Session. The Moderates, who were still in majority in the Congress, opposed the move and, instead, proposed the name of Rash Behari Ghosh. Although Lajpat Rai refused to contest the presidency,[77] the extremists persisted in opposing the nomination of Rash Behari Ghosh.

Towards the approach of the Surat session, Aurobindo Ghosh called upon the extremists to counter the Moderates and set up a separate "Nationalists' Conference." The first Nationalists' Conference was held in Haripur in the outskirts of Surat on December 23, 1907. It was presided over by Aurobindo Ghosh and addressed by Tilak. Entrance to the conference was restricted to persons who openly declared that they were

74. Bal Gangadhar Tilak, *His Writings and Speeches* (192), p. 77.
75. "The Swadeshi Movement", *Indian Review,* May 1906, pp. 353-56.
76. "The National Outlook", *Modern Review,* March 1907, p. 205.
77. Lajpat Rai declared, "I will be the last person to allow myself to be made the reason or occasion for any split in the national camp."*Indian Review,* December 1907, p. 960.

Nationalists. The Conference passed resolutions on total boycott and complete independence.[78]

There were two groups in the Nationalists' Conference too. One led by Tilak had no intention to cause a split in the Congress[79] and the other led by Aurobindo Ghosh sought to capture the Congress or wreck it. The Moderates, on the other hand, had anticipated the secession of the extremists from the Congress and this was evident from the undelivered presidential address of Rash Behari Ghosh. He declared, "The National Congress is definitely committed only to constitutional methods of agitation to which it fast moved. If the new party does not approve of such methods and cannot work harmoniously with the old, it has no place within the pale of the Congress. Secession, therefore, is the only course open to it."[80]

The Congress met on December 26, 1907. As soon as Surendranath Banerjea formally introduced the president-elect, Rash Behari Ghosh, tumultuous hisses and shouts deafened Banerjea's speech. The meeting ended in a fiasco. Next day, the Congress met again, when invective was used and grave disorder was apprehended. The meeting was dispersed by the Police. The extremists left the Congress in disgust, leaving the Moderates in possession of the field. A committee, consisting of Ferozeshah Mehta, Dinshaw Wacha and Rash Behari Ghosh, met in April 1908, at Allahabad and drew up a constitution of the Congress. It clearly specified that the object of the Indian National Congress was the attainment of *Swaraj* within the British Empire, to be achieved strictly by constitutional means and by gradual reform of the existing system of administration. Every delegate to the Congress had to express in writing his acceptance of this article of the constitution. The constitution also laid down the disciplinary rules which ensured the exclusion of rebellious members from the Congress.

Under the new constitution of the Congress passive resistance and boycott, which had been adopted only the previous year as means for achieving the objectives of *Swaraj,* were ruled out. "What happened at Surat," wrote Annie Besant, "was the saddest episode in the story of the Congress." It caused an unfortunate split in the nationalist ranks and discredited the organisation. The Moderates closed the doors of the Congress to those who did not pledge themselves to its way of self-government and the methods of constitutional agitation.[81] By offering a mild dose of 1909 Reforms, the Government secured the co-operation of the Moderates. The Government was happy at the split, but still had an apprehension lest the Congress should ultimately become an extremist organisation.[82]

With the object of the Congress clearly defined under the amended constitution, it met in 1908 at Madras, when Rash Behari Ghosh was re-elected President. A resolution was passed, welcoming the Reform proposals of Morley and Minto and the hope was expressed that the Reforms would be worked in a liberal spirit. Surendranath Banerjea, who moved the resolution, enjoined upon the delegates that the reforms should be considered "as a message of conciliation." A resolution expressing detestation of the acts of violence in some parts of the country was also moved from the chair. By another resolution ill-treatment of Indians in South Africa was condemned, the annulment of the Partition of Bengal was demanded, and the *Swadeshi* movement was given unrestricted support.

## SUGGESTED READINGS

Desai, A.R., *Social Background of Indian Nationalism.*

Dutt, R.P., *India Today.*

Gandhi, M.K., *My Experiments with Truth.*

Lajpat Rai, *Unhappy India.*

Nehru, J. L. *Autobiography Whither India.*

Raghuvandir, V.P.S. *Indian Nationalist Movement and Thought.*

Sitarammaiya, P., *History of the Indian National Congress.*

Tara Chand, *History of Freedom Mavement.*

Tilak, B.H., *Writings and Speeches.*

78. Tilak emphasised at the Nationalists' Conference, "we have not come to cause a split in the Congress, we do not want to hold a separate Congress, our policy is not destruction but progressive."
79. *The Surat Congress,* Natesan, Madras 1908, Presidential Address, p. 29.
80. *Ibid.*
81. Annie Besant, *How India Wrought for Freedom,* p. 465.
82. Morley, J., *Recollecions,* Vol. II, p. 201.

# CHAPTER III

# The Rise of Muslim Communalism

## The Policy of "Divide and Rule"

*Divise et impera* is an old maxim of statecraft which has invariably been followed by all conquerors in all lands and in all ages. Once the validity of the foreign rule is admitted, no special blame can be attached to the rulers for having recourse to the policy of 'Divide and Rule'. The British in India would have been no exception, if, like other conquerors, they too had followed that policy. But the servants of the East India Company had resorted to such a policy much earlier when the validity of their rule in India could not be admitted. They knew too well the weaknesses of India's political fabric. Internal disunity caused by narrow jealousies, dissensions, greed, and communal and local loyalties had ever plagued India at every stage of her history and the same tendencies and influences had paved the way for British Rule in India. Malcolm was stating a bare truth when he said that Hindustan could never have been subdued but with the help of her own children. The British played successfully one dynasty or power against another and, thus, subdued the country. This policy of 'Divide and Rule' or 'counterpoise' of native against native equally stood them in good stead in holding the people in bondage.

## Anti-Muslim Policy

After the annihilation of the Mughal Empire the Muslims as a community were segregated and the Britishers pursued a systematic policy of enfeebling them economically and politically, lest they might venture to regain what they had lost. Even as late as 1824-25, Bishop Heber observed that "the Mohammedans are hostile to the English as those who have supplanted them" and believed that "if a fair opportunity offered, the Musalmans, more particularly, would gladly avail themselves (of it) to rise against us."[1] And, as said earlier, Lord Ellenborough wrote in 1843, "It seems to be most unwise when we are sure of the hostility of one-tenth, not to secure the support of the nine-tenths who are faithful. I cannot close my eyes to the belief that this race (Muslims) is fundamentally hostile to us and therefore our true policy is to conciliate the Hindus."[2] He believed that the best way of restoring "equilibrium between the two religions," Hindus and Muslims, was to bring "the Mohammedans to their senses."[3] Lord Dalhousie's attitude towards the Muslims was not a whit less inimical. He really revealed his mind in a private letter to one of his friends on August 18, 1853. "The King of Oudh", he wrote, "seems disposed to be bumptious. I wish he would be. To swallow him before I go would give me satisfaction. The old king of Delhi is dying. If it had not been for the effete folly of the Court (of Directors) I would have ended with him the dynasty of Timur."[4]

In the "revolt' of 1857, Hindus and Muslims joined together to overthrow the British and both suffered heavily, but the common belief among Englishmen was that Muslims had been mainly responsible for the Mutiny. For the Muslims "the rebellion of 1857", according to Rafiq Zakaria, "was not just a revolt against the British; it was their last desperate bid for the recovery of their privileges.....They detested the Cross because it had replaced the crescent."[5] To put it in the words of Sir S. H. Cunningham, "The Musalman had a personal grievance. He was feeling the dual pain of humiliated authority and tarnished prestige."[6] The result was that during and after the Mutiny "the Mohammedans" as the biographer of Sir Syed Ahmed Khan says, "were under a cloud. To them were attributed all the horrors

1. Bishop Heber, *Narrative of a Journey,* Vol. I, p. 198.
2. Rafiq Zakaria says that Lord Ellenborough not only had a soft corner for the Hindus : "'he made no secret of his contempt for the Muslims." *Rise of Muslims in Indian Politics,* p. 4.
3. Law, Sir Alganon(Ed.), *India Under Lord Ellenborough,* p. 65.
4. *Private Letters of the Marquis of Dalhousie,* p. 262.
5. Rafiq Zakaria, *Rise of Muslims in Indian Politics,* pp. 5-6.
6. Cunningham, Sir S. H., *Earl Canning,* p. 65.

and calamities of the terrible time."[7] The European community residing in India openly preached and urged upon the Government an anti-Muslim policy. The European inhabitants of Calcutta submitted a petition to the 'Home' authorities demanding the recall of Lord Canning, as the Governor-General did not support the anti-Muslim cry raised by the European community in India.

Lord Canning was not recalled, but the British Government, as William Hunter pointed out, "turned upon the Musalmans as their enemies."[8] The post-Mutiny period was perhaps the darkest period in the history of Indian Muslims. The heavy hand of reprisal ruined many families which had enjoyed both prestige and power. It was a great blow to their pride and respectability. It was difficult for them to forget that they were once the conquering and ruling people and had enjoyed all the privileges which belonged to a ruling class. "The sense of frustration, the memories of glories departed and consciousness of the fact that the Hindus had stolen a march over them in every sphere,"[9] fostered communal loyalties in them.

**Socio-Economic Decline of the Muslims**

The reaction of the British conquest on the minds of the Muslims and Hindus was bound to be different.[10] Whereas the Hindus welcomed British rule in India and regarded it as a benign Act of Providence which brought them deliverance from the tyranny of Muslim rule,[11] the hostility of the Muslims towards the English was unbounded. They regarded them as their bitterest foes, since they had usurped their political authority. As the past rulers of the country, the Muslims resented their new position and sulked in their tents. The British, on their part, adopted a continuous policy of suppression towards them. In Bengal the object of the land settlement was to bring the old Muslim nobility and official class to a position of social degradation. The Hindu collectors of land revenue were elevated to the exalted position of landlords.[12] In the Punjab, where the Muslims were in a dominant majority, their condition was not a whit better. The revenue system introduced there produced a class of moneylenders who were Hindus since usury is banned by the Quran. The Hindu moneylenders throve upon the misery of the Muslim peasantry. They did not hesitate even to deprive them of their lands. Such expropriation, according to Thornborn, had proceeded to a dangerous extent.[13]

The exclusion of the Muslims from Government services was calculated and wholesale. The upper class Muslims, who had taken to the military profession as their *beau ideal,* were mostly kept out of the army as the Government believed that their exclusion was necessary to their safety. William Hunter stated that "no Mohammedan gentleman of birth can enter our regiments" and as an illustration explained that "how a ridiculous small numbers" of Muslims held commissions from the Governor-General and "as far as I can learn, not one from the Queen."[14] In the civil services their position was worse. None of them could find their way in the Covenanted Civil Service or up to the Bench of the High Court.[15] In some cases vacancies advertised clearly stated that the appointments would

7. Graham, P. F. I., *Life and Work of Sir Syed Ahmed Khan,* p. 40.
8. Hunter, W. W., *Indian Mussalmans,* p. 147.
9. Raghuvanshi, V.P.S., *Nationalist Movement and Thought in India,* p. 95. Rafiq Zakaria says that though deprived of position and authority, the Muslims looked down upon the Hindus as if the latter "were still under some Muslim Monarch. This attitude of self-deception brought upon them disastrous consequences. The alien government went ahead with its plans, contemptuous of their opposition; while the Hindus made the most of every opportunity, in a way glad that the Muslims had left them with an open field." *Rise of Muslims in Indian Politics,* p. 9.
10. *The History and Culture of Indian People, op. cit.,* Vol. X, Part II, p. 295.
11. This is evident from the statement of Raja Ram Mohan Roy who in his "Appeal to the King in Council" against the Press Regulations referred to the "despotic power of the Moghul Princes" and offered thanks "to the supreme Disposer of the events of this universe, for having unexpectedly delivered this country from the long-continued tyranny of its former rulers, and placed it under the Government of the English,—a nation who not only are blessed with the enjoyment of civil and political liberty, but also interest themselves in promoting liberty and social happiness, as well as free inquiry into literary and religious subjects, among those nations to which their influence extends." *Ram Mohan Roy—Works,* pp. 439, 445-46, 462, 465.
12. According to James O' Kinesly, the Permanent Settlement in Bengal "elevated the Hindu collectors, who, up to that time, had held but unimportant posts, to the position of landholders, gave them a proprietary right in the soil and allowed them to accumulate wealth which would have gone to the Musalmans under their own rule." As quoted in W.W. Hunter, *The Indian Mussalmans,* p. 160.
13. Refer to Thornborn's *Mussalmans and Moneylenders.*
14. Hunter, W.W., *The Indian Mussalmans,* p. 159.
15. *Ibid.*

be given to none but Hindus.[16] If no bar was placed on their entry, the Muslims soon found themselves edged out by the Hindus. The substitution of English as the official language had given the Muslims a grievous setback. Their religious beliefs and racial pride made them cling to the old orthodox traditions of religious education and they turned their back on the impious new learning of the *farangis* (Europeans).[17] The Hindus on the other hand, welcomed the new change and "rushed to adjust themselves to the new situation. They took full advantage of the official encouragement, and in commerce, education and professions found new avenues to carve out a bright future for themselves."[18]

The British policy aimed at destroying indigenous industries and handicrafts had a crushing effect on the Muslims, as millions of weavers and other artisans belonged to their community. Thrown out of employment, "Where were they to go ? Their old profession was no longer open to them; the way to a new one was barred. They could die, of course.....They did die in tens of millions."[19] Lord Bentinck, the Governor-General, reported in 1834, that the misery hardly finds a parallel in the history of commerce. Those who survived took to the land which hardly had the capacity to receive them. Consequently, appalling misery and privation haunted the Muslims.

The Muslims were, thus, gradually ousted from their lands and their offices; "in fact everything was lost save their honour." The Hindus, from a subservient state, came into the lands, offices and other worldly advantages of their former masters. "Their exultation knew no bounds, and they trod upon their heels." The result was that "The Musalmans would have nothing to do with anything in which they might have to come into contact with the Hindus."[20]

The social degradation and utter poverty of the Muslims also prevented the growth of a Muslim middle class, while among the Hindus it gradually developed and gained shape. This uneven and unbalanced development of the two major communities had a great impact on the future politics of India, and "certainly herein lies," says Zia-ul-Hasan Faruqi, "the complex socio-economic ground where the seeds of communalism were sprinkled and watered by the religious and cultural bickerings to develop into a thorny bush which subsequently inflicted bleeding wounds on the unity of India and finally divided into two parts."[21]

**The Aligarh Movement**

The Aligarh Movement[22] started by Syed Ahmed Khan[23] played a vital role in the evolution of Muslim political consciousness. His objective was to draw the Muslims from the sloth of backwardness and conservatism, to instil into them a desire for Western education and culture, to improve their status and to dispel from the minds of

16. According to the analysis made by the *Aligarh Institute Gazette*, February 25, 1882 (p. 219), in 1871, the proportion of Mohammedans to Hindus in the uncovenanted civil service was 1 : 10 and in the judicial and revenue departments only 19 out of 185 high officials were Muslims.
17. This view is contradicted by Ziya-ul-Hasan Faruqi. He says, "During the period under review (1800-1857) they (Muslims) were deliberately being isolated from all places of position and prestige and constantly kept out of Government services. The excuse was that the Muslims themselves were responsible for this state of affairs, for they kept on clinging to the old type of education and refrained from joining the new schools. But this is an allegation without any foundation; and if it be accepted, what treatment was meted out to them when they started learning English ? They also desired to enter the services of the Company, but they received only discrimination, sometimes mild, often ruthless, and the door was closed against them." *The Deoband School and the Demand for Pakistan,* pp. 13-14.
18. Ziya-ul-Hasan Faruqi, *The Deoband School and the Demand for Pakistan,* p. 13.
19. Jawaharlal Nehru, *The Discovery of India,* p. 277.
20. Sayani, R. M., Presidential Address, Twelfth Indian National Congress, Calcutta Session, 1896. Banerjee, A.C., *Indian Constitutional Documents,* Vol. II, p. 165.
21. Ziya-ul-Hasan Faruqi, *The Deoband School and the Demand for Pakistan,* p.16.
22. Syed Ahmed Khan's efforts to regenerate the Muslim community and to lay the foundation of modern educational avenues for his coreligionists came to be known as the Aligarh movement. He selected Aligarh as the centre of his activities for various reasons. One of them was that Aligarh and its neighbouring districts had a predominantly Muhammedan population and a Muhammedan feudal aristocracy from whom he hoped to receive substantial financial support for the growth of the college he had decided to start.
23. Syed Ahmed Khan (1817-1898) traced his descent from Hazrat Husain and would often speak of the prophet as "my grand- father". At the age of 20 he took service with East India Company as *sarishtadar*. His mother, who had been Syed Ahmed's only parent, guardian and guide since he was 19, had inculcated in him great respect for authority. Thus, during the Mutiny his loyalty to the British remained unshaken and the Government granted him pension of Rs. 200 a month for life and the life of his eldest son. In 1869, he was awarded Third Class of the Star of India and in the same year was granted a sum of £250 per annum, for two years. He retired from service in 1876 and in 1888 the title of knighthood of the Order of the Indian Empire was conferred upon him.

the English people the illusion that the Muslims were primarily responsible for the Mutiny.[24] Under the Aligarh Movement an educational scheme was formulated which sought to combine the Western system of education with the basic teachings of Islam rationalistically interpreted for the Indian Muslims.

Syed Ahmed Khan formed, in 1870, a Committee for the better diffusion and advancement of knowledge and learning among the Mohammedans of India. The Committee began collecting funds for establishing a college and enlisting the support of influential Muslims. But it met with stout opposition from the Muslim public in general, especially the *ulema* (religious divines). They were offended by the so-called rationalistic interpretation of Islam, which constituted one of the objectives of Syed Ahmed's educational schemes. The *ulema* held it anti-Islamic.

Syed Ahmed Khan put before himself the target of rupees two lakhs for starting the college. But the response from the Muslims was poor and there were slim hopes of reaching the target in view of the vehement opposition of the *ulema* and the orthodox Muslim press. Maulvi Sameeullah Khan, Syed Ahmed's close associate, advised him to start the college immediately even though the required amount of money was not available. The beginning was made by opening an English medium school in 1873, with L.G.I. Siddons as its Headmaster. Siddons later became the first Principal of the Muhammedan Anglo-Oriental (M.A.O.) College.[25]

The foundation stone of the college building was laid by Lord Lytton on January 8, 1877.[26] In an address of welcome presented to the Viceroy the College Committee described British rule in India as "the most wonderful phenomenon the world has ever seen", and added, that the College aimed at educating the Muslims so that they should be able to appreciate the blessings of British rule; "to dispel those illusory traditions of the past which have hindered our progress; to remove those prejudices which have hitherto exercised a baneful influence on our race; to reconcile oriental learning with Western literature; to inspire in the dreary minds of the people of the East the practical energy, which belongs to those of the West; to make the Musalmans of India worthy and useful subjects of the British Crown; to inspire in them the loyalty that springs not from servile submission to a foreign rule, but from genuine appreciation of the blessings of the good government." These are the objects, the address concluded, "which the founders of the college have prominently in view."[27]

Lord Lytton, in his reply to the address of welcome, described the ceremony as constituting "an epoch in the social progress of the Muhammadans in India under the British rule." He also welcomed the establishment of the M.A.O. college for "one special reason." There was no object, he said, "which the Government of India has more closely at heart than that the plain principles of its rule should be thoroughly intelligible to all its subjects, from the highest to the humblest." This, the Viceroy believed, could be achieved by "a body of cultivated natives...than twice the number of English officials or twenty times the number of European scholars."[28]

The establishment of the College was hailed by the Anglo-Indian press and the British officials alike.[29] Mr. Keene, the Director of Public Instruction, North-Western Provinces, observed that the establishment of the M.A.O. College marked an epoch and "was likely...to form the germ of a very wide and important movement that would live in History......"[30] Exactly the same views had been expressed by the College

24. Immediately after the Mutiny, Syed Ahmed wrote a pamphlet entitled *Asbab-i-Baghawat-i-Hind* (The Causes of the Indian Revolt) wherein he rebutted the charges against the Muslims and pleaded that the British authorities should not punish the poor Muslims for the follies and faults of Bahadur Shah, the Mughal Emperor. In 1860-61, he wrote a series of pamphlets entitled: *The Loyal Muhammedans of India* wherein he deprecated the wholesale denunciation of Muslims as a race and tried to establish that Islam and Christianity were so akin to each other that the Muslims were not permitted by their religion to wage a war against the British who were Christians by faith.

25. Originally, the M.A.O. College Committee wanted that the college should be confined to Muslims alone. But eventually it was decided to keep its portals open for the Hindus too, because of the "goodwill, sympathy and generosity" displayed by "the Hindu nobility and gentry." The Maharajas of Patiala, Benares and Vizianagram gave handsome donations.

26. The College Committee had first requested Sir John Strachey and then Lord Northbrook to lay the foundation stone, but they could not do so due to their official pre-occupations.

27. Supplement to the *Aligarh Institute Gazette,* January 12, 1877.

28. Nawab Mohsin-ul-Mulk (Editor), *Addresses and Speeches relating to the Muhammedan Anglo-Oriental College,* pp. 22-23.

29. Lord Lytton promised a monthly donation of Rs. 500 from his own purse. Prominent among other British donors were Lord Northbrook, Sir William Muir, Sir John Strachey, and Sir William Hunter.

30. *The Aligarh Institute Gazette,* January 19, 1877, p. 41.

Committee in their welcome address presented to Lord Lytton. The address said, "from the seed we sow today, there may spring up a mighty tree whose branches like those of the banyan of the soil, shall in their turn strike firm roots into the earth and themselves send forth new and vigorous samplings."[31] As Rafiq Zakaria remarks, "......its (M.A.O. College) foundation proved a landmark in the annals of Muslim education. Moreover, its leaders and students soon began to shape even the political future of their co-religionists. In fact, within less than a decade, its luminaries collectively described as the 'Aligarh School' assumed an almost monopolistic control of Muslim affairs. From them went the word to the newly educated Muslimss and in nine cases out of ten they respected the word; in consequence, for more than two decades, Aligarh turned out to be the focal point of Muslim activities, educational, social and political."[32]

Many causes could be assigned for the turn in Muslim politics and that too in favour of the Aligarh School. One of them, according to Theodore Morrison,[33] was "certainly political."[34] Syed Ahmed Khan's open and unceasing opposition to the Indian National Congress not only brought him the support of many British bureaucrats; they also helped to bring round within his fold the Muslim Zamindars, who were anxious to have some medium to express their loyalty to the British. Another important cause was the anti-cow-killing agitation started by the Hindus in many important cities and towns. It created a sense of uneasiness among the Muslims and "it led them to look for religious affinities with the British." And hence, "the whole tendency of the time", comments Morrison, "was to bring the Muhammedans and the English together."[35] Syed Ahmed Khan worked very hard to achieve it and he admirably succeeded in his efforts.

Syed Ahmed Khan was vehemently opposed to the Indian National Congress and he openly confessed that he had "undertaken a heavy task against the so called Indian National Congress."[36] He dissuaded the Muslims from joining it as he apprehended that their participation in any kind of nationalist movement would be suicidal to the interest of the Muslim community.[37] If the Muslims were involved in any agitation at that stage of their political existence and their sentiments roused there might be, he feared, a repetition of the happenings of 1857. With the avowed object of combating the nationalist forces in the country,[38] he not only exhorted the Muslims to remain aloof from the Congress, but also instilled into them the idea that the British Government would most certainly give beneficial positions to them, provided they did not give rise to suspicions of disloyalty. He, therefore, advised his co-religionists that the best and only course for them was to remain in faithful alliance with the British Government.

The Indian National Congress in its first session in 1885 had demanded the reform and expansion of the Supreme and local Legislative Councils by the admission of a considerable proportion of elected members and the creation of similar councils for the North-Western Provinces and for the Punjab. It also urged that all budgets should be referred to these councils for consideration and their members be empowered to ask questions. Moreover, a Standing Committee of the House of Commons should be constituted to receive and consider any formal protest that might be recorded by majorities of such Legislative Councils against the exercise by the Executive of power, which would be vested in it, of overruling the decisions of such majorities. It also asked for the appointment of a Royal Commission to inquire into the working of the Indian administration, and prayed for holding simultaneously examinations for the Indian Civil Service

31. These sentences were *verbatim* repeated in the address presented to Sir Charles Crosthwaite, Lieutenant-Governor of North-Western Provinces in 1894, *Aligarh Institute Gazette*, November 13, 1894, p. 119.
32. Rafiq Zakaria, *Rise of Muslims in Indian Politics*, p. 181.
33. Morrison (1863-1936) succeeded Theodore Beck as Principal of the M.A.O. College in 1899 and held the post till 1905.
34. Morrison, Theodore, *History of the M.A.O. College from its foundation to the year* 1903, p. 10.
35. *Ibid.*
36. Graham, G.F.I., *Life and Work of Sir Syed Ahmed Khan*, p. 273.
37. W. S. Caine, a Member of the British Parliament, who visited India in 1888, wrote, "Sir Syed tells me that he and his friends took no notice whatever of the first Congress at Bombay; but the second one, meeting at Calcutta, attracted more attention and a number of leading Muhammedans met privately to consider what their attitude should be and decided that no official notice should be taken." *India as Seen by W. S. Caine*, p. 28.
38. In 1888, Sir Syed Ahmed Khan founded the United Indian Patriotic Association and its membership consisted of both the Hindus and the Muslims, but it soon developed into a purely Muslim organisation. Some of the Muhammedan Associations affiliated to the United Patriotic Association formulated rules to expel those Muslims from their ranks who either belonged to the Congress or were in any way sympathetic to it.

both in England and India, and for raising the examination age to twenty-three years. These demands were repeated, with certain modifications on the elective principle and grant of franchise, at the 1886 Congress session held at Calcutta. All these resolutions not only led to a bitter controversy between officials and non-officials, but also between Hindu and Muslim leaders, particularly on proposals relating to the reform of the Councils and reconstruction of the public services.

Just a month before the scheduled meeting of the Calcutta session of the Congress, Syed Ahmed Khan wrote a lengthy leading article in *Aligarh Institute Gazette* wherein he strongly condemned the Congress and characterised its programme as ''seditious.'' He raised the question, ''Is the State of the country adapted to popular Government ?'' and himself gave the reply, ''certainly not.''[39] The Reception Committee of the Calcutta Session of the Congress took some concrete steps to ensure adequate representation of the Muslims in its deliberations and, accordingly, wrote letters to two Muslim organisations—the Central National Muhammedan Association and the Muhammedan Literary Society—requesting them to send delegates. But their response was not favourable and both these organisations disapproved of the items on the agenda.

Twenty-seven Muslims attended the second Congress, Dadabhai Naoroji presiding. In his presidential address he defined the scope of the Congress and pointed out that it was a purely political body and it should deal only with the political matters, on which Indians were united. The Third Congress was held at Madras in December 1887. Badruddin Tyabji, a prominent Muslim leader of Bombay, was selected as its president. The efforts of the Congress to attract more Muslims to attend the session infuriated Syed Ahmed Khan and he delivered on December 28, 1887, the same day the Congress was meeting at Madras, a speech at Lucknow scathingly condemning the Congress. He disparagingly declared that the Congress movement would not do good to anybody, except a few Bengalis, ''who at the sight of the table-knife crawl under a chair.'' He held that the Congress demand of establishing parliamentary institutions in India was a ''useless uproar'' and warned the Muslims that if they joined the Congress ''nothing but national disaster lay in store for them.'' He advised his co-religionists to remain steadfastly loyal to the British Government, if they did not want their community to grow under the yoke of the future Hindu rule.[40]

Syed Ahmed Khan developed his thesis on three main points :

(1) That the Hindus and the Muslims constituted ''two different nations ''irrespective of the fact that they ''drink from the same well, breathe the air from the same city and depend each on the other for his life.'' To illustrate his point Syed Ahmed Khan posed a question, ''Now suppose that all the English were to leave India, then who would rule the Country ?'' Is it possible ''that under these circumstances the two nations—the Mohammedans and Hindus—could sit on the same throne and remain equal in power ?'' He himself replied, ''Most certainly not. It is necessary that one of them should conquer the other and thrust it down.'' To hope that both could remain equal in power was to wish for ''the impossible and the inconceivable.''

(2) That representative institutions were ''unsuited to the conditions of India.'' Syed Ahmed explained, let us suppose that the right to universal franchise had been given to Indians and the highest and the lowest all enjoyed the right to vote. What would happen then ? In such an eventuality, he said, the Hindus would cast their votes in favour of the Hindu candidates and the Muslims for Muslim candidates. The result would be that the Hindu candidates would have ''four times as many votes'' as the Muslim candidates because their population is four times as numerous.'' Could the Muslims in such a situation safeguard their interest?, he posed the question. He himself replied, ''It would be like a game of dice, in which one man had four dice and the other one.''

(3) That it would be discreet and beneficial for the Muslims to rely entirely on the British Government for safeguarding their interests and for their effective representation in administration. He enjoined upon the Muslims to unite and co-operate with the British, because, according

39. *The Aligarh Institute Gazette,* November 23, 1886.

40. The Lucknow meeting was attended by the taluqdars of Oudh, members of the government services, the Army, the professionals of Law, the press and the priesthood, Syeds, Shaikhs, Mughals and Pathans belonging to some of the noblest families in India, and representatives of every Muslim school of thought, from the orthodox Sunni and Shia Maulvis to the youngmen trained in Indian Colleges or in England. *The Pioneer,* Allahabad, January 11 and 12, 1888.

to the teachings of the Quran, "our nation cannot expect friendship and affection from any other people."

*The Times* described Syed Ahmed Khan'sLucknow speech as "one of the most remarkable political discourses ever delivered by a native of India."[41] The Muslim press, too, generally hailed the speech. The *Muslim Herald* wrote in its leading article, "The Syed does not mince matters but hits out straight from the shoulder like the giant he is. In a mawkish time, enslaved by senseless conventions, it is a relief to find one man at least who, avoiding periphrasis, honestly calls a spade a spade.......We proudly accept the Syed as our leader and exponent—the summit and the crown of Islam, a faith that binds together with the withes of iron 50,000,000 Indian Musalmans. Sir Syed leads the way. His speech sounds the keynote of our policy."[42] but the speech created a stir in the Congress, especially amongst the Bengalees who felt bitterly hurt. Lajpat Rai published towards the end of 1888, four "open letters to Sir Syed Ahmed Khan,"[43] wherein he challenged Sir Syed's attack on the Congress and his "two-nation" theory. He charged Syed with going back on his earlier advocacy of Hindu-Muslim co-operation as both constituted a single nation.

The Aligarh movement, thus, grew anti-Congress and anti-Hindu. It, no doubt, brought about the political and social regneration of the Muslims but at the same time widened the political cleavage between the Hindus and the Muslims and created a distinct Muslim unit in Indian politics. Pakistan today claims Sir Syed Ahmed Khan as one of the founder fathers of the country."[44] It is true. The father of the Muslim "nationhood" was not Jinnah but Sir Syed. The arguments that Jinnah advanced in support of the two-nation theory were precisely the same that Sir Syed used in opposing the Congress. Even the words used by Jinnah were the same used by Sir Syed in his speeches and writings. It is often stated that Sir Syed had previously advocated Hindu-Muslim unity and co-operation and references are made to his various speeches delivered at Gurdaspur and Lahore in the Punjab. But this is not supported by facts. Sir syed was first and last a Muslim and a Muslim's point of view was essentially different from an Indian's point of view.[45] Nationalism, as Coupland has said, "feeds on memories, but the memories of the Moslems were concerned with Islam than India; they did not share with their Hindu fellow-countrymen's pride in a record of civilisation stretching far into the past...."[46] Therefore, Sir Syed's "supposed advocacy of Hindu-Muslim unity", remarks M. S. Jain, "is a myth created by interested persons. The concept of a united Indian nationality never crossed his mind" and all those statements which advocated Hindu-Muslim unity were a mask to secure financial assistance for the M.A.O. College from the Hindus.[47]*The Aligarh Institute Gazette* makes a revelation. Its issue of June 23, 1871 contains a statement that "by the pretext of this (Hindu-Muslim) unity we get our work done."[48] Sir Syed was so keen to get subscriptions, from any quarter for the Aligarh College that in one of his private letters he wrote, "We would accept donations for the College on whatever condition one would offer."[49]

**Role of European Principals of Aligarh College**

The British Principals of Aligarh College played a key role in enticing educated Muslims away from the nationalist forces. Theodore Beck, who took over the Principalship of the Muhammadan Anglo-Oriental College in 1883, was described as an Empire-builder in far off lands.[50] Rafiq Zakaria describes him in many ways "the counterpart of Hume" as what the latter did for the Congress, Beck "did for the Aligarh Movement."[51] Mohsin-ul-Mulk publicly confessed that after the death of Sir Syed it was to Beck that the Muslims turned "for no man except Sir Syed

41. *The Times,* London, January 16, 1888.
42. Quoted in Rafiq Zakaria, *Rise of the Muslims in Indian Politics,* p. 56.
43. These letters were first published in *The Tribune,* Lahore (October 27, November 17, December 5 and 19, 1888) and later published by him in a book entitled : *The Man in his word.*
44. Refer to Symonds, R., *Makers of Pakistan*
45. Abdul Aziz, *Pakistan* (Urdu), p. 30.
46. Coupland, R., *The Constitutional Problem in India,* p. 33.
47. Jain, M. S., *The Aligarh Movement,* p. 137.
48. P. 338.
49. *Khatoot-i-Sir Sayyid,* pp. 219-20 and as quoted in . M. S. Jain *The Aligarh Movement,* p. 141.
50. On Beck's death in 1899, Sir John Strachey paid him the handsome tribute : "An Englishman who was engaged in the empire building activities in a far off land, had passed away. He died like a soldier at the post of his duty."
51. Rafiq Zakaria, *Rise of Muslims in Indian Politics,* p. 317.

had worked with such zeal and unselfish devotion for their cause."[52] Immediately before his departure from London, Beck made a speech which was clearly indicative of his mission in India. He said that parliamentary system in India was most unsuited and it would be a futile attempt if representative institutions were introduced in the country. "The Muslims", he declared, "will be under the majority opinion of the Hindus, a thing which will be highly resented by Muslims and which, I am sure, they will not accept silently."[53]

Incidentally, Beck's arrival in India synchronised with the year when Syed Ahmed Khan had delivered a speech in the Supreme Legislative Council, deprecating the elective principle of representation, as "the larger community would totally override the interest of the small community." He underlined the elements that divided Hindus and Muslims and stressed the wide chasm that prevented the two communities from constituting a single nation. "India a continent in itself", Syed Ahmed said, "is inhabited by vast population of different races and different creeds; the rigour of religious institutions has kept even neighbours apart—the system of caste is still dominant and powerful...One section may be numerically larger than the other, and the standard of enlightenment which one section of the community has reached may be far higher than that attained by the rest of the population. One community may be fully alive to the importance of securing representation on the local boards and the district councils, whilst the other may be wholly indifferent to such matters.....The system of representation by election means the representation of the views and interests of the majority of the population."[54]

Theodore Beck, a Tory by political faith who took pride in the imperialist greatness of Britain, found in Syed Ahmed Khan the fulfilment of his mission. *Pax Britannica* was the guiding principle of Beck's life and he was convinced that an alliance between the Muslims and the British would preserve the *British Raj* for ever whereas Hindu-Muslim understanding and cooperation would ultimately ruin the British imperial majority in India. He succeeded in winning the confidence of Syed Ahmed Khan, the noblest and the most gifted with whom he had "ever enjoyed intimate personal intercourse."[55] Beck cemented Syed Ahmed's belief that while an Anglo-Muslim alliance would ameliorate the conditions of Muslims as a community, the nationalist alliance would lead them once again to a state of sweat, toil and tears. As Principal of the college, he, together with other English Professors, strove to instil into the young Muslim students the benefits of loyalty to the *Raj* and trust in the sincerity of the British. Even anti-Hindu sentiments were often encouraged.

Syed Ahmed's Lucknow speech can, without hesitation, be attributed to Beck's inspiration. Just a month before the Lucknow speech, Beck had published in *The Pioneer,* Allahabad, two articles expressing identical views.[56] Beck repeated the same ideas in London in 1895. Addressing the London Muslim Association, he emphasised the impossibility of Hindu-Muslim unity and deprecated the idea of establishing a democratic government in India, as such a system would make the Muslims slaves of the Hindus for all times to come. He warned them not to repeat the mistakes of 1857 and, therefore, not to join the seditious Indian National Congress.

Thus, the Muslims were isolated from the main stream of national politics and were used as pawns in the communal politics of the country in a bid to perpetuate the British Raj. When Charles Bradlaugh introduced a Bill in the British Parliament in 1889, embodying the elective principle in the organisation of the Legislative Councils, Beck sponsored a memorial on behalf of the Muslims, representing that democratic institutions were not suitable to India, inhabited as it was by divergent communities and interests. Again, early in 1890, on Beck's suggestion, Sir Syed decided to present a petition signed by nearly 40,000 Muslims, through Sir Richard Temple, to the House of Commons praying that Parliament would not introduce the principle of election in any scheme of reforms of the Councils. Such a step, the petitioners prayed, would "destroy that even-handed justice which has been hitherto the basis of British rule and place them (Muslims) and other minorities in an almost intolerable subjection to classes actively hostile

52. *The Pioneer,* Allahabad, November 29, 1899.
53. As quoted in Mohammed Noman, *Muslim India,* p. 52.
54. Speech delivered in the Supreme Legislative Council on the Central Provinces Local Self-Government Bill, 1883.
55. *The Pioneer,* Allahabad, November 28, 1887. Also refer to Beck's speech on Sir Syed's death as reported in the *M.A.O. College Magazine,* April 1898.
56. November 2 and 3, 1887.

to their welfare."

It was mainly due to the efforts of Beck that the United Indian Patriotic Association was established in 1889. But it did not serve the desired purpose. On December 30, 1894, Sir Syed convened a meeting and explained the implications of the elective principle embodied in the Rules made under the Indian Councils Act, 1892, and the resolution of the House of Commons in favour of simultaneous examinations for the Indian Civil Service. He pointed out that the Muslims were, as a result, "in a very awkward dilemma." They should, therefore, organise themselves and form an association for representing Muslim interests both before the Government of India and the British public. He pointed out two serious defects from which the United Indian Patriotic Association suffered—a joint organisation of Hindus and Muslims and its object was to create public opinion. The Muslims, he asserted, were in need of an *exclusive* organisation of their own which was not to indulge in any political agitation. Nor was it to hold public meetings nor to affiliate other associations to it.

The question of protecting the political rights of Muslims, Beck added, had become serious because of two agitations.......surging throughout the country......for some years." One, he said, was the Indian National Congress, which was entirely opposed to Englishmen. The second, movement against cow-slaughter, was against the Mussalmans. To prevent cow-slaughter, the Hindus boycott their opponents to starve them into submission. This has resulted into bloody riots in Bombay, Azamgarh, etc. Since the Englishmen and the Mussalmans had become the targets of these two movements, it was necessary, therefore, he added, that both should unite in opposing both. "We should carry on propaganda in favour of true loyalty and unity of action", he emphasised.

At the end of Beck's address and on Sir Syed's suggestion the Muhammadan Anglo-Oriental Defence Association of upper India was established.[57] Beck went home in 1895. There he addressed the members of the London branch of the Association and publicly declared that Anglo-Muslim unity was possible, but Hindu-Muslim unity was not possible under any circumstances.

Theodore Morrison succeeded Beck after his death in 1899. Morrison had had his training from Beck and he faithfully "continued to follow" in the footsteps of his predecessor in the Empire-building mission. He, too, denounced the establishment of democratic institutions in India and declared that if established, they "would reduce minorities to the position of hewers of wood and drawers of water." On the death of Morrison in 1936, *The Times* wrote, "'But he will best be remembered as an accomplished interpreter of Indian Muslim life and sentiment; he was indeed, one of the makers of the Muslim renaissance in India."[58] W.A.J. Archbold, who succeeded Morrison in 1905, accomplished the rest. He was an ambitious Englishman fired with the late Theodore Beck's zeal to serve the Muslim community. In collusion with Colonel Dunlop Smith, Private Secretary to the Viceroy, Lord Minto, Archbold manoeuvred the scheme of communal representation.

The role of the three Principals of the M.A.O. College was, therefore, quite significant in Muslim politics. Every one of them took an active interest in the Indian political controversies and on not a few occasions were able to guide the Muslim leadership in Aligarh "in the particular channels they wanted."[59] There are some critics who blame the British Principals of the M.A.O. College for Sir Syed's anti-Congress and anti-Hindu views, particularly Principal Beck whom a few described as his "political father."[60] This is historically incorrect, yet it cannot be denied that Beck played "the greatest role, in Britishing the whole gambit of Muslim politics during this period. He prepared the material with which Sir Syed fought the Congress". It would, therefore, be no exaggeration to say, as Zakaria suggests, that, "but for Beck's initiative and help, many of Sir Syed's political and educational schemes would not have flourished."[61]

57. The main objects of this Association were : (1) to place the opinions and views of the Musalmans before the British people in general and the Government in particular and to protect their political rights; (2) to prevent political agitation from spreading among the Musalmans; (3) to support measures designed to strengthen British rule in India; (4) to help the Government in maintaining peace and foster a spirit of loyalty.

58. *The Times*, London, February 15, 1936.

59. Rafiq Zakaria, *Rise of Muslims in Indian Politics*, pp. 184-85.

60. See Asoka Mehta and Achyut Patwardhan, *Communal Triangle in India*, pp. 58-59, and Gurmukh Nihal Singh's Presidential Address to the Indian Political Science Conference, Agra session, published in the *Indian Journal of Political Science*, Vol. IV, p. 382.

61. Rafiq Zakaria, *Rise of Muslims in Indian Politics*, p. 318.

**Reversal of Government Policy**

The activities of Theodore Beck coincided with a deliberate change in the policy of the Government towards Muslims. The policy of splitting the two major communities and playing Muslims against Hindus had really begun with the re-organisation of the army. The Indian army before the 'Mutiny' consisted of Hindus, Mussalmans, Sikhs and Poorbias, all mixed up. In 1858, Syed Ahmed Khan had deplored the fact that the two antagonistic races, Hindus and Muslims, should have been placed in the same regiment thereby providing them with an opportunity for development of feelings of brotherhood and comradeship in making common effort for liberation. He maintained, "If separate regiments of Hindus and separate regiments of Muhammedads had been raised , this feeling of brotherhood could not have arisen."[62] Sir John Lawrence was also of the same opinion. He maintained, "Among the defects of the pre-Mutiny army, unquestionably the worst, and the one that operated most fatally against us was the brotherhood and homogeneity of the Bengal army, and for this purpose the remedy is counterpoise, firstly, the great counterpoise of Europeans, and, secondly, of the native races."[63] To provide a safeguard against Mutiny, the Peel Commission, in its report on military reorganisation submitted in 1889, recommended that the army should be composed of different nationalities and castes, and as a general rule, mixed promiscuously through each regiment."[64] The object of the whole reorganisation scheme, *inter alia,* was to set caste against caste, religion against religion, and company against compnay. Sir Charles Wood, the Secretary of State for India , had earlier written to Sir Hugh Rose, "I wish to have a different and rival spirit in different regiments, so that Sikh might fire into Hindoo, Goorkha into either, without any scruple, in case of need."[65] The Army Commission of 1879 had strongly emphasised this principle of *'Devise et Impera.'*[66] The reorganisation of the army, after the Mutiny, thus, destroyed the sentiment of unity, and regiments, battalions and companies based on sectarian, class and caste distinctions created parochial loyalties.

In 1871, Sir William Hunter[67] in his book, *Indian Mussalmans : Are they bound in conscience to rise against the Queen ?*, drew the attention of the British Government to the grievances of the Muslims and to their complaints of British : "Want of sympathy, want of magnanimity mean malversation of funds, and great public wrongs spread over a century."[68] Hunter pleaded for justice for Muslims and urged upon the government for the removal of the causes of their discontent.British officers in India had by then realised that any more enfeebling of the Muslim community was neither politic nor warranted by the exigencies of time.[69] It was, therefore, considered expedient to take the Muslims into alliance rather to continue with the policy of distrust and suspicion about them, especially when the Government was confronted with a new threat of nationalism of the growing westernised middle-class who were predominantly Hindus.[70] Some of the British officials publicly declared that the political interests of the Muslims were identical with theirs. Sir John Strachey attacked the whole concept of the Indian National Congress by asserting that there was no country as India and that there were no Indians in the sense of a united people who were bound by racial, cultural, or linguistic ties. He, accordingly, claimed that there could be no Indian nation or any representation of Indian nationality.[71] Lord Lytton wrote to the Secretary of State for India, Lord Salisbury, that it entirely depended upon the

---

62. Syed Ahmed Khan, *Causes of Indian Revolt,* pp. 54-55.
63. As quoted in Mehta and Patwardhan, *The Communal Triangle in India*, p. 54.
64. *Report of the Peel Commission,* XIV.
65. Letter dated February 26, 1862. In his Minute of December 8, 1888, Lord Dufferin emphasised that the British "should always remember the lessons which were learnt with such terrible experience thirty years ago......."
66. *Report,* para 50. The Army Commission of 1879 was presided over by Sir Asley Eden.
67. A Civil Servant.
68. Hunter, W.W., *Indian Mussalmans,* p. 159.
69. Lord Mayo realised the seriousness of the situation and directed that more encouragement should be given to the Muslims in the matter of education so that they should not lose the advantages, both material and social, which the other subjects of the Empire enjoyed. Refer to Resolution Nos. 300-310. (Home Department), dated August 7, 1871, Also refer to Resolution (Home Department), dated June 13, 1873. In one of his Notes the Governor-General wrote, "We have not only failed to attract the sympathies and confidence of a large and important section of the community but we have reason to fear that we have caused positive disaffection."
70. Smith, W.C., *Modern Islam in India,* p. 196.
71. Strachey, J., *India : Its Administration and Progress,* pp. 2, 308.

policy of Her Majesty's Government "whether the sentiment of our Muhammedan subjects is to be an immense security or an immense danger to us."[72] The change in the British policy was gradual, but it was definitely evident that it marked, as Coupland said, "the end of the decline" of the Muslims "and the beginning of the recovery."[73]

The policy of alienating the Muslims from and using them as a counterpoise against the Hindus took a definite shape in 1888, when Hume started his mass movement and the official attitude towards the Congress became specifically antagonistic. When on January 4, 1887, Lord Dufferin reported to the Secretary of State for India about the abstention of the Muslims from the annual sessions of the Congress, Lord Cross wrote to the Viceroy, "This division of religious feeling is to our advantage." The views of Lord Dufferin, too, had changed by then. In his Saint Andrew's Day speech he rebuffed the Congress leaders, described the Congress as representing a "microscopic minority" and declared that "in the present condition of India there can be no real or effective representation of the people with their enormous number, their multifarious interests and their tessellated minorities." Lord Dufferin was also responsible for initiating the theory of special importance of Muslims in Indian politics, and reminded them that "fifty millions of men are themselves a nation—and a very powerful nation."[74] Lord Salisbury declared in a public speech in London that it was impossible for Britain to hand over the Indian Muslims to the tender mercies of a hostile numerical majority.[75]

Dufferin and Salisbury roused the feelings of the Muslims against the Hindus and it was not strange, in the circumstances, that the principle of separate representation was smuggled into the Indian Councils Act of 1892, although the Act itself had nothing to do with it. Nor had any organised association of the Muslims put forth such a demand. It was introduced silently; it was in the "directions issued to those charged with the duty of framing regulations as to the classes and the interests to whom representation was to be given that the Muslims were named as a class to be provided for."[76]

Both the Aligarh Movement and the definite policy of 'Divide and Rule' increased the friction between Hindus and Muslims and communal disturbances grew in frequency.[77] The British Government made a virtue of the hostility between the two communities as a safeguard of the Empire in spite of the administrative difficulties involved therein. Lord George Hamilton, the Secretary of State for India, wrote to the Viceroy, Lord Elgin (October 3, 1895), "Sandhurst (Governor of Bombay) sent me details about the riot at Dhullia. The Mahomedans were clearly in the wrong. These outbreaks are, from administrative point of view, regrettable, but they do seem to me to strengthen our position generally as reminders of what was the condition of India before our authority was established and what it would be if abolished."[78] Two years later (May 7, 1897) Hamilton, again wrote to Elgin, "I am sorry to hear of the increasing friction between Hindus and Mahomedans in the N. W. (North-West) and the Punjab. One hardly knows what to wish for—unity of ideas and actions would be very dangerous politically, divergence of ideas and collision are administratively troublesome. Of the two latter is the least risky, though it throws anxiety and responsibility on those on the spot where the friction exists."[79]

Here is a weighty rebuttal of the argument put forward by quite a few that there was not any "hard and fast policy of 'divide and rule', pursued by either the British Cabinet or the various Viceroys."[80] Rafiq Zakaria's estimate "'that the British policy was not 'divide and rule'—division was already there; it was to use Curzon's classic phrase 'to hold the scales even' between the Hindus and Muslims",[81] is neither convinc-

72. Lytton, *Personal and Literary Letters of Lord Lytton,* Vol. II, p. 65.
73. Coupland, R., *The Indian Constitutional Problem,* p. 32.
74. *Indian Speeches of Lord Dufferin* (Modern Review, 1911), Vol. I, p. 303.
75. As quoted in M. Noman, *Rise and Growth of the All-India Muslim League,* p. 55.
76. Ambedkar, B. R., *Pakistan,* pp. 240-41.
77. Serious Communal riots broke out at Lahore and Karnal (1885), Delhi (1886), Hoshiarpur, Ludhiana, Ambala, Dera Ghazi Khan (1889), and Palakad in the Salem district of Madras (1891). The year 1893 was one of the worst.
78. For details refer to *History and Culture of Indian People, British Paramountcy and Indian Renaissance, op.cit.,* Vol. X, Part II, p. 325.
79. *Ibid.*
80. Refer to Rafiq Zakaria, *Rise of Muslims in Indian Politics,* p. 354; and Jain, M.S., *The Aligarh Movement,* pp. 119-21.
81. Rafiq Zakaria, *Rise of Muslims in Indian Politics,* p. 354.

ing nor borne by public testimony. Did Curzon not create a Muhammedan Province by partitioning Bengal, comprising a region where the followers of Islam were to be in ascendancy? Did not Sir Bampfylde Fuller pursue a deliberate policy to establish a religious feud between the two communities ? Bampfylde Fuller merely gave formal and official expression to a bare truth when he represented the Hindus and Muslims as his two wives, the latter being the favourite one. "Those who are familiar with the stories of *Suorani* and *Duo-rani* (favoured and discarded queens) in Indian folk-tales will easily understand the full implications of this. The 'Divide and Rule jack boot' was still there—only it was on the other leg."[82] Lord Minto's Viceroyalty entrenched Muslim communalism by introducing the undemocratic and anti-national communal representation and separate electorates. Lord Minto, as his biographer stated, "had liking for the Muhammedans."[83] Rafiq Zakaria also admits this fact when he says that Lord Minto "was not only sympathetic to them but also realised that the Muslims could provide a good brake against any hasty Hindu demands for constitutional advancement."[84]

**Impact of Religious Revivalism**

Communal politics was also accentuated by movements of religious revivalism. The Wahabi movement left behind a trail of communal consciousness in the Muslims, which militated against the growth of secular nationalism among them. It was purely a Muslim movement and was directed against non-Muslims, the infidels, although in its later phase it became violently anti-British. An aggressive form of Hindu Revivalism, particularly under the Arya Samaj movement,[85] further sharpened the edge of communal disharmony between Hindus and Muslims.[86] The communal passions so aroused were fanned by the Anglo-Indian officials and the press.[87] Revivalism be it Hindu or Muslim, aptly remarks Raghuvanshi, "was certainly not a happy development for the growth of a sturdy nationalism in which Hindus and Muslims could sink their differences."

The leaders of the nationalist movement, who were predominantly drawn from the Hindu community, based nationalism on the glory of the Hindu religion and the traditions of the Hindu history. Tilak, Pal and Ghosh brothers, spearheads of the nationalist movement during the close of the nineteenth century, drew inspiration from India's past, cited episodes from the history of Hindu India, and tried to infuse national pride and self-respect into the masses by utilising the Hindu gods and heroes. In a multi-religious society, Hindu nationalism was bound to weaken its secular character. Nationalism, thus, expressed in religious terms and clothed in religious mystical forms, had no appeal for the politically conscious middle-class Muslims. It rather alarmed them and the Aligarh Movement contrived all possible means to counteract nationalism and identified it with Hindu communalism out to establish *Hindu Raj*. The name of Shivaji was an inspiration to the Hindus who held Aurangzeb in open contempt. The reverse was the case with the Muslims. The Rajput heroes like Rana Pratap, were the idols of the Hindus and enemies of the Muslims. The Third Battle of Panipat was the occasion of national mourning for the Hindus but of great deliverance for the Muslims.[88]

One of the many reasons why the nationalist movement did not draw within its orbit wide sections of the Muslim community even when the Indian National Congress had become a vital and acknowledged political force in the country, was that the nationalist movement continued to have a Hindu religious tinge. *Ram Rajya,* whatever be its significance, was unpalatable to the Muslims, if not for anything else, at least for its name.

**The Partition of Bengal**

The Partition of Bengal, as seen earlier, was used as a major device by Lord Curzon to drive a wedge between the Hindus and the Muslims.

82. *History and Culture of the Indian People, British Paramountcy and Indian Renaissance, op. cit.*, Vol. X, Part II, p. 324.
83. Buchan, John, *Lord Minto,* p. 243.
84. Rafiq Zakaria, *Rise of Muslims in Indian Politics,* p. 146.
85. Swami Dayananda Saraswati founded the Arya Samaj in 1875. The most important characteristic feature of the Arya Samaj was its emphasis on *Shuddhi* or reconversion of millions of Hindus who had been either willingly or forcibly converted into other religions. *Shuddhi* was strongly resented by the Muslims and it had ever been a source of chronic feud between the two communities.
86. Valentine Chirol observed that Hindu revivalism was as "consistently anti-Muhammedan as anti-British, and even more so." *Indian Unrest,* p. 120. Also refer to Jawaharlal Nehru, *The Discovery of India,* pp. 313-14.
87. Refer to Rafiq Zakaria, *Rise of Muslims in Indian Politics,* pp. 354-55.
88. *The History and Culture of the Indian People, op. cit.* Part II, p. 330.

In the name of Islam and its ascendancy, he inflamed the sentiments of the Muslims, who were initially against any kind of division. The Viceroy toured the area that was to comprise Eastern Bengal, held consultations with the Muslims, dwelling upon the advantages that would accrue to them as a result of partition, and canvassed their support for the success of his scheme. In one of his speeches, Lord Curzon promised that partition "'"would invest the Mohammedans of Eastern Bengal with a unity which they had not enjoyed since the days of the old Mussalman Viceroys and Kings."[89] Official influence was exercised to win over those who opposed partition.[90]

The division of Bengal on communal lines, and the anti-Hindu policy pursued by Sir Bampfylde Fuller, roused the Muslims to acts of violence. According to Nevinson, "priestly Mullahs went through the country, preaching the revival of Islam, and proclaiming to the villagers that the British Government was on the Mohammedan side, that the law courts had been specially suspended for three months, and no penalty would be exacted for violence done to Hindus or for the loot of Hindu shops or for the abduction of Hindu widows. A red pamphlet was everywhere circulated maintaining the same wild doctrines."[91] Riots broke out at many places, including Dacca, and for three days and nights "the Muslim mob ruled and looted to their heart's content the rich Marwari jewellers."[92] Nevinson toured the riot affected areas immediately after and thus described the situation : "A few lives were lost, temples were desecrated, images broken, shops plundered, and many Hindu widows were carried off. Some of the towns were deserted, the Hindu population took refuge in any 'pacca' house...women spent nights hidden in the tanks, the crime known as 'group rape' increased, and throughout the country districts there reigned a general terror which still prevailed at the time of my visit."[93]

Through such heinous deeds, directly abetted by Lord Curzon's regime, the Government sought to sharpen the edge of communal politics as a counterpoise to the growing strength of the extremists. To keep away Muslims from the *Swadeshi* and *boycott* movements, which the Bengalis had started as weapons for the annulment of partition, a propaganda was carried on by the agencies of the Government that the benefit of this movement would accrue only to the industrialists, who were predominantly Hindus. After having kindled the flames of communalism, partition was annulled. This gave "a rude shock to the Muslims, they felt once again betrayed." They believed that the Hindus had forced the government to abolish partition. This led the Muslims to think that without organization, sufferings and sacrifices nothing could be achieved from the government. Blind loyalty was nothing but weakness."[94]

**Strategy of Separate Electorates**

The strategy of Lord Curzon and his successors was to set one religion against the other and class against class in order to shatter the image of national unity and to disintegrate the feelings of solidarity. For this purpose he had partitioned Bengal, and had thought of establishing a Council of Princes. But in the latter attempt he did not succeed. When Lord Minto became Viceroy in 1905, he was confronted with a very tense situation in the country. In order to enfeeble the growing popularity of the Indian National Congress, he revived the attempt at the establishment of the Council of Princes and enthusiastically pushed through his plan. The Viceroy even corresponded with the Princes on the subject with a view to obtaining "mutual co-operation against a common danger." He wrote to the Secretary of State, "I have been thinking a good deal lately of a counterpoise to Congress aims. I think we may find a solution in the Council of Princes; or on the elaboration of that idea, a Privy Council not only of native rulers, but of a few other big men to meet, say, once a year for a week or a fortnight at Delhi, for instance."[95]

The response of the Princes to the Viceroy's communication was encouraging and they even recommended certain specific measures, which the government should take to combat the "common danger" of the Indian National Con-

89. As quoted by Ram Gopal in his *Indian Muslims,* p. 91.
90. Nawab Salimullah, who had condemned partition as a "beastly arrangement", was won over by advancing him a loan of £100,000 on a nominal rate of interest.
91. Nevinson, *The New Spirit in India,* p. 192.
92. *Idem.*, p. 193.
93. *Idem.*, p. 195.
94. Ziya-ul-Hasan Faruqi, *The Deoband School and the Demand for Pakistan,* p. 48.
95. Marry, Countess, Minto, *India : Minto and Morley,* pp. 28-29.

gress. But the Secretary of State did not agree with the proposal of the Viceroy, as he had complete faith in the loyalty of the Princes and was convinced of their full support against any kind of upsurge. What really worried Lord Morley was the growing sense of national consciousness among the Muslim younger generation. In spite of the efforts of Sir Syed Ahmed Khan and his followers and the policy of the Government of India for alienating the Muslims from the Hindus, Western education had created the same awakening in them as it had done among the educated Hindus during the last quarter of the nineteenth century. Thus, Morley wrote to Minto, "everybody warns us that a new spirit is growing and spreading over India.......Be sure that before long the Muslims will throw in their lot with the Congress against you."[96] Minto agreed with Morley and wrote him, "The younger generation (of Muslims) were wavering, inclined to throw in their lot with the advanced agitators of the Congress, and a howl went up that the loyal Mohammedans were not to be supported, and that the agitators were to obtain their demands through agitation."[97]

Lord Minto, at the behest of the Secretary of State, soon began to elaborate the scheme of reforms which should at least satisfy the moderate element in the Congress. But Minto's real concern was to devise means for weaning the Muslims from the politics of the country and obliterating from their minds the sense of nationalism. So, before the intended reforms could take shape, a scheme for winning the Muslims had taken a tangible form. A deputation of the Muslims was arranged to meet the Viceroy to present their demands to His Excellency. The main actors in the drama were Principal Archbold of the Aligarh College and Colonel Dunlop Smith, Private Secretary to the Viceroy.

A deputation, consisting of thirty-five prominent Muslims drawn from different Provinces and led by His Highness the Aga Khan, met the Viceroy on October 1, 1906, and presented to him an address in which they made two important demands on behalf of the Muslim community. The first was that the position accorded to the Muslim community in any kind of representation should be commensurate with their numerical strength and also with their political importance and the value of the contribution "they make to the defence of the Empire," and consistent with "the position they occupied in India a little more than a hundred years ago." Secondly, that the methods of nomination and election had failed to give the Mulsims a proper type or adequate number of representatives and if the principle of election was to be accepted by the Government in the forthcoming reforms, they should be given the right of sending their own representatives by themselves through separate electorates comprising the Muslims alone, beginning from the local bodies and going up to the Imperial Legislative Council including the Senates and Syndicates of the Indian Universities. In addition to these two important demands the deputation also asked for greater representation of the Muslims in the services of the Government, and protection of their interests if an Indian was to be appointed a member of the Governor-General's Executive Council. The address concluded that "in furthering Muslim interest, Government will be only strengthening the bond of loyalty and laying the foundation of their political advancement and prosperity."

Lord Minto expressed his entire agreement with the demands of the deputation and promised that in any system of "representation whether it affects a municipality or a district board or a legislative council in which it is proposed to introduce or increase an electoral organisation the Muslim community should be represented as a community." The Viceroy also sympathised with the extra claims of the Muslim community and said, "You justly claim that your position should be estimated not only on your numerical strength, but in respect of the political importance of your community and the services it has rendered to the Empire." He further observed, "I am entirely in accord with you. Please do not misunderstand me; I make no attempt to indicate" by what means representation of "the communities can be obtained, but I am as firmly convinced as I believe you to be, that any electoral representation in India would be doomed to mischievous failure which aimed at granting a personal enfranchisement regardless of the beliefs and traditions of the communities composing the population of this continent." Finally, the Governor-General gave an assurance that the

96. January 6, 1960. *Idem.*, p. 330.

97. *Ibid.* Some of the younger Muslims had even suggested that the best course for the Muslims was to join the Congress in large numbers, play their part in its activities and to ensure the protection of their rights and interests. Refer to Rafiq Zakaria, *Rise of Muslims in Indian Politics*, p. 96.

political rights and interests of the Muslims "will be safeguarded in any administrative reorganisation with which I am concerned, and that you and the people of India may rely on the British *Raj* to respect, as it has been its pride to do, the religious beliefs and the national traditions of the myriads composing the population of His Majesty's Indian empire."

The Anglo-Indian officers and the European population in India were jubilant at the success of this "command performance."[98] The Viceroy himself wrote that October 1, 1906, was "a very eventful day : as some one said to me, "An epoch in Indian history."[99] An official of the Government of India wrote to the Viceroy, "I must send Your Excellency a line to say that a very big thing has happened today. A work of statesmanship that will affect India and Indian history for many a long year. It is nothing less than the pulling back of twenty-six millions of people from joining the ranks of the seditious opposition."[100] The biographer of Lord Minto described the Viceroy's speech to the deputation as "a charter of Islamic rights."[101]

Coupland rejects the argument, so often advanced, that the Simla Deputation "was engineered" to meet the Governor-General and the main actors in the drama were Principal Archbold of the Aligarh College, and Colonel Dunlop Smith, the Private Secretary to the Viceroy. He says, "there is no evidence to suggest that the deputation was in any sense engineered. It was actually organised by the well-known Moslem leader, Nawab Mohsin-ul- Mulk."[102] M. S. Jain[103] and Rafiq Zakaria[104] who have made special study of the Aligarh Movement, support Coupland's conclusions.

The Aga Khan deputation received a good press in Britain. The same day when the deputation waited on Lord Minto, *The Times* published an article extolling the wisdom of the Muslims and observed that "they had never been enamoured of representative institutions on the European model and that there was no nation in India as there was in Britain. " Other British papers, too, wrote in the same tone. "It appears from these articles, wrote Tufail Ahmed, "how the English press looked upon Indians being one nation with a sense of shock and heart- burning and how pleased they were to see it broken into pieces and how proud they felt in setting the Indians against one another on the basis of religion and of creating lasting hostility between them."[105] The Government of India searched for a pawn on the chess-board of Indian politics and they found it in the willing Muslims who desired to have their special claims recognined in the impending constitutional reforms and to establish their separate political existence. Buchan gave true expression to the British policy when he said that Lord Minto's "speech undoubtedly prevented the ranks of sedition being swollen by Moslem recruits, an inestimable advantage on the day of trouble which is dawning."[106]

Lord Morley did not initially approve of separate electorates. His objection was two-fold. Firstly, that it would create an invidious distinction between the Muslims and the Hindus, and secondly, that it would give the Muslims in several cases two votes instead of one. On the contrary, he suggested a scheme of joint Electoral College, but ultimately succumbed to the pressure of Minto. The system of separate electorate was, thus, introduced in the teeth of the opposition of nationalist India. The system was mischievous, as it threatened to break India's political unity and was sure to have adverse effects on the growth of a nationalist spirit. A Muslim remarked, "The attempt on the part of my co-religionists to create an irreconcilable Ulster in India is not very laudable". He most prophetically added that "this will veritably be the open-

98. An expression used by Maulana Mohammed Ali in his Presidential Address at Coconada session of the Indian National Congress.
99. Mary, Countess, Minto, *India : Minto and Morley,* pp. 46-47.
100. *Ibid.*
101. Buchan, John, *Life of Lord Minto,* p. 244
102. Coupland, R., *The Constitutional Problem in India,* p. 336. f.n.
103. Jain says, "Thus,........it can be stated that the whole responsibility for the deputation must rest on the Muslim community which planned and worked for it. The Indian nationalists, in their pious wish to ignore the fact of Muslim communalism, straightway branded the deputation of 1906 as a "command performance' without looking to the role Muslims played at the time." *The Aligarh Movement,* pp. 153-56.
104. Rafiq Zakaria writes, "Hence, far from being a 'command performance', the deputation was the last desperate effort of Mohsin-ul-Mulk and his friends to retrieve the position in their own community and to win over the British to their side." *Rise of Muslims in Indian Politics,* pp. 359-61.
105. M. Syed Tufail Ahmed, *Musalmanon Ka Roshan Mustaqbil* (Urdu), p. 3693
106. Buchan, John, *Life of Lord Minto,* p. 244.

ing of Pandora's box and India will then be confronted with a grave situation of the first magnitude."[107]

Several members of the Muslim community later felt that in asking for communal electorates they had committed a serious mistake. Ramsay MacDonald wrote in 1911, that "several people spoke to me with bitterness about the way that certain of their leaders had consented to play a game planned for them by the Anglo-Indian officials." Whatever might have been the difference among the Muslims as to the wisdom or folly of the step, there was a general agreement among progressive Indians that the scheme of communal representation was a clever move on the part of Lord Minto and his Government to prevent the Indian people from uniting and from depriving the Reforms of 1909 of much of their utility. In this game a large number of Muslims agreed to play to the tune of their political masters.

After the introduction of communal representation the cleavage between the two communities widened and there existed constant tension between the Hindus and the Muslims. According to the Indian Statutory Commission the communal tension was "'a manifestation of the anxieties and ambitions aroused in both communities by the prospect of India's political future. So long as the authority was firmly established in British hands and self-government was not thought of, Hindu-Moslem rivarly was confined within a narrow field....there was little for members of one community to fear from the predominance of the other. The comparative absence of communal strife in the Indian States today may be similarly explained. Many who are well acquainted with the conditions of British India a generation ago would testify that at that epoch so much good feeling had been engendered between the two sides that communal tension as a threat to civil peace was at a minimum. But the coming of the Reforms and the anticipation of what may follow these have given new point to Hindu-Moslem competition."[108] But the Commissioners did not say nor would have they said, who created the feelings of communal strife between the Hindus and the Muslims.

### The All India Muslim League

Five days after the Aga Khan deputation had met Lord Minto at Simla, the Indian correspondent of *The Times* reported, "The Muhammedan delegates assembled here discussed informally the question of forming an association with a view to safeguarding the interest of the community throughout India. It was decided in the first place to organise political associations which should send representatives to a central body."[109] This was corroborated by the Aga Khan himself. He wrote in his *Memoirs,* "Mohsin-ul- Mulk and I, in common with other Muslim leaders, had come to the conclusion that our only hope lay along the lines of independent organisation and action, and that we must secure independent political recognition from the British Government as a nation within a nation."[110]

But Nawab Salimullah Bahadur of Dacca took the initiative.[111] He circulated a letter containing a plan for "the Muslim All-India Confederacy." The *raison d' etre* of the plan was to establish a political party with the sole aim of protecting and propagating the Muslim cause. Though Salimullah's scheme had definitely a little scope and was defective, but it was the embryo from which the Muslim League emerged.[112] Salimullah's plan became the basis of discussion at Dacca on December 30, 1906.[113] A provisional Committee was formed with Viqar-ul-Mulk and Mohsin-ul-Mulk as Joint Secretaries. The committee was entrusted with the task of framing a constitution of the Muslim League within four months. The committee was also authorised to convene a representative meet-

107 *The Awakening of India,* p. 129.

108. Report of the Indian Statutory (Simon) Commission, Vol. I, p. 29.

109. *The Times,* London, October 6, 1906.

110. Aga Khan, *Memoirs,* p. 76. In a letter dated October 29, 1906, the Aga Khan informed Colonel Dunlop Smith about the formation of the proposed organisation and also told him that during his absence from India Nawab Mohsin-ul-Mulk would not do anything "before first finding out if the steps to be taken has the full approval of Government privately,........"*Minto Papers,* Vol. No. 126.

111. Syed Ameer Ali, founder of the Central National Muhammedan Association in 1877, had since then urged the Muslims to organise themselves into a distinct political group, but Sir Syed had always opposed the idea. Refer to his "Memoirs" in *Islamic Culture,* Vol. V, No. 4, p. 540, and "India and the New Parliament", *Nineteenth Century,* August, 1906, pp. 257- 58.

112. Syed Razi Wasti, *Lord Minto and the Indian Nationalist Movement,* p.77.

113. After the conclusion of the All India Muhammedan Educational Conference, a special meeting of the delegates to the Conference was convened, under the presidentship of Nawab Viqar- ul-Mulk, to discuss the issue of forming a political association of the Muslims.

ing of the Indian Muslims at a suitable time and place and put the proposed constitution before that body for its final approval and adoption.

The Muslim League, thus, came into being on December 30, 1906. Its aims and objects remained undefined till its Karachi session in 1907, when they were given definite shape :

(1) "To promote among the Musalmans of India feelings of loyalty towards the British Government, and to remove any misconception that may arise as to the intentions of the Government with regard to any of its measures;

(2) To protect and advance the political rights and interests of the Musalmans of India and to place their needs and aspirations before the government in temperate language;

(3) So far as possible and without prejudice to the objects mentioned above, to promote friendly feelings between Muslims and other communities of India."

The formation of the Muslim League was a great landmark in the history of Indian politics, for it was under the aegis of this body that a large number of Muslims, mostly Nawabs, Landlords and title holders, kept communalism alive and prevented the bulk of Muslims from falling in line with the national forces in the country. The League realised the hopes of the Britishers by consistently fighting the growth of secular nationalism and thereby providing a convenient argument to British Government for denying independence to India. "Minto's policy saw its culmination when the Moslem League fought for recognition as the sole representative body of the Indian Musalmans"[114] and finally it was to split India into two parts.

**Hindi-Urdu Controversy**

But nothing alienated the two communities from each other as did the Hindi-Urdu controversy. Though primarily a language controversy, it roused such passions on both sides that its repercussions on inter-communal relations were grave and far-reaching. It originally started at Benares in 1867, when Hindus organised a movement to replace Urdu by Hindi and the Persian script by the Devanagari script. Immediately, after the anti-Urdu campaign, Syed Ahmed Khan, it is reported, "told his superior officer, Mr. Shakespeare, that he was convinced after the anti- Urdu agitation of the pro-Hindi Hindus that there was no hope of any kind of joint action by Hindus and Muslims. Muslims, he said, had to organise themeselves on their own to safeguard their heritage."[115]

Hindi-Urdu controversy was confined essentially to North where the British administrators, when Persian remained no longer the Court language, were faced with the question : which was the language of North India, Urdu as written in the Persian script or Hindi with its Devanagari script.[116] Obviously, the Hindus insisted on the replacement of Urdu by Hindi in Devanagari script whereas the Muslims were vehemently opposed to it. Sir George Campbell, the Lieutenant-Governor of Bengal, was the first to initiate the introduction of Hindi in Bihar, which then formed part of Bengal. In 1872, he issued instructions that in future Hindi in Devanagari script should replace Urdu for the transaction of all official business in the Patna and Bhagalpur Divisions. This was sharply resented by the Muslims and they strove for the withdrawal of this order, but George Campbell remained adamant.

The order, however, remained more or less a dead letter under George Campbell's successor, Sir Richard Temple. The Hindus, in their turn, resented the lukewarm attitude of Sir Richard Temple towards Hindi. Under Sir Ashley Eden Hindi, again, became a live subject and the Government of Bengal issued clear directions that from January 1, 1881, Hindi in Devanagari script would be exclusively used in all official documents and that the issuing of any document in the Persian script by the courts, except as exhibits, "was absolutely forbidden." Police officers and subordinate services were warned that those who did not possess a working knowledge of the Devanagari script would be replaced by those who were competent for the transaction of official business in that script.

These orders and the firm determination of Sir Ashley Eden to enforce them rigidly deeply antagonised the Muslims against the Hindus. They thought that it was at their instance that Urdu had been replaced in Bihar. Angry representations were made to the Government and whenever there was an opportunity, forceful demonstration of their anger was made. The aggressively communal attitude of many newspapers aggravated the already strained relations between the two communities. Syed Ahmed

114. Das, M. N., *India Under Morley and Minto*, p. 182.
115. Rafiq Zakara, *Rise of Muslims in Indian Politics*, pp. 293-94.
116. As quoted in above, p. 301.

Khan particularly became more bitter and declared that "the adoption of the Nagari character and the Hindi language will greatly injure educated Musalmans in both official and private life. It will in fact be the greatest injury save deprivation of their religion."[117]

Early in 1882, a fierce controversy was raged in the Punjab over the use of Urdu or Hindi. The Arya Samaj enthusiastically advocated the use of Hindi as the most suitable language "for the rejuvenation of Hindu nationality." In a speech in April, 1882, at Ambala, Lajpat Rai opposed the use of Urdu and expressed his conviction that the political solidarity of the Hindus demanded the development of Hindi into the national language of India. In the North-Western Provinces also the relations between the two communities were embitterred on the language issue. In 1883 a suggestion emanated that the character of the court language should be changed from Persian to Devanagari script. It proved a spark. The entire Muslim official class in the Province arrayed itself against the suggestion and violent protests were raised both in the public and in the press. Syed Ahmed Khan advised the Muslims to form the *Ajuman-i-Himayat-i-Urdu* in all the Provinces in order to safeguard the interests of the Urdu-speaking people. A central committee was also formed with Syed Ahmed Khan himself as its Secretary.

With the formation of the Indian National Congress in 1885, there was lull in the language controversy. The emphasis of the Congress leaders was on Hindu-Muslim unity and they would not side with any movement which would alienate the Muslims from the Hindus. However, another spurt came in 1898, when the leading Hindus of N.W. Provinces and Oudh waited in deputation upon Sir Antony MacDonnell, the Governor of the Province, and impressed upon him the desirability of introducing Hindi in Devnagri script as the Court language. Sir Antony, while conceding to the demand, deprecated any hasty change in the existing practices of the courts and Government offices. However, two years later by a Government resolution Devanagari character was given the same status as the Persian character and the use of both the languages was permitted in courts and offices. It was also decreed that no person "shall be appointed, except in purely English office, to any ministerial appointment henceforward unless he can read and write both the Nagari and Persian characters fluently."[118]

This infuriated the Muslims as the "new order not only hit them economically, but culturally." They could swallow the abolition of Urdu in Bihar "but to strike against it in its very home"— the United Provinces—was too severe a blow. Besides, they felt the blow rather intensely because "it came so soon after the death of Sir Syed; somehow they believed that if he had been alive such a disaster would never have befallen them."[119] Sir Antony MacDonnell was described as "an enemy of Islam" and a "'pro-Hindu satrap." An Urdu Defence Association was formed which carried on virulent propaganda against Hindi. All this annoyed the Governor. He asked Nawab Mohsin-ul-Mulk to desist from fomenting agitation and sever all his connections with the Urdu movement; otherwise he would not be allowed to continue as the Secretary of the Muhammedan Anglo-Oriental College, Aligarh. Mohsin-ul-Mulk had to retreat. "This role of a partisan on behalf of the Government towards which they were taught to have an attitude of unconditional loyalty was terribly shocking to the Muslims as a whole; particularly the younger generation at Aligarh was completely disillusioned and became suspicious of the British professions of friendship with them."[120]

But the hostility of the Muslims was concretely directed against the Hindus, as the Government, it was firmly believed, was favouring them. The glee of the Hindu press on this issue was too exuberant not to be noted by the Muslims.[121] The Hindus, on their part, nourished a grievance that the Government had abdicated in favour of the Muslims in not firmly implementing its own decisions. All this foreboded a deep rift which sought to cleave society and culture into two irreconcilable groups.

## SUGGESTED READINGS

Humayan Kabir, *Muslim Politics.*

M.A. Jinnah, *Some Recent Speeches and Writings.*

Moin Shakir, *Khilaft to Partition.*

W.C. Smith, *Modern Islam in India.*

117. Sir Antony MacDonnell was the Commissioner of Patna Division under Sir George Campbell and was actively associated with the introduction of Devnagri characters in Bihar.
118. *Government Gazette*, North-Western Province and Oudh, Part VI, April 21, 1900.
119. Rafiq Zakaria, *Rise of Muslims in Indian Politics,* p. 304.
120. Ziya-ul-Hasan Faruqi, *The Deoband School and the Demand for Pakistan,* p. 47.
121. Rafiq Zakaria, *Rise of Muslims in Indian Politics,* pp. 308-9.

# CHAPTER IV

# The British Legacies

On 15 August 1947 the British rule in India came to an end and the power was transferred to two independent Dominions, India and Pakistan. On 26 January 1950, India adopted a new Constitution and became a sovereign democratic republic. But this is too simple a way to explain the two momentous events, one, the end of the rule in a country considered to be a jewel of the British Crown, and, the other, devising the constitution which was to foster the achievements of many goals and fulfilment of aims and aspirations of the millions who had hitherto been groaning under the heels of alien rulers. Morris-Jones says, "We have to ask : how new was the new republic and what was handed over along with 'power'?"[1] The answer to both these questions is rooted in the constitutional history of India. Modern India is the product of centuries of evolution and the impact of Western ideas and institutions had a prolonged effect on what India is today.

## 'COMPANY BAHADUR'

### Traders Become Rulers

The British came to India early in the seventeenth century, but the traders soon became rulers, Sir Thomas Roe, who represented the British merchants at the Mughal court, had a word of advice for his countrymen. He told them, "Let this be received as a rule that if you will profit, seek it at sea and in quiet trade; for without controversy it is error to effect garrisons and land wars in India." This advice was not, long heeded to. As early as 1687, during the reign of Aurangzeb, the Directors of the Company instructed their chief representative in Madras "to establish such a polity of civil and military power, and create and secure such a large revenue to secure both....as may be the foundation of a large, well grounded, secure English dominion in India for all time to come"[2].

The position in India changed significantly after the death of Aurangzeb. On the passing away of a strong ruler, the process of disintegration started and the principal and ancillary organs of administration began to work at cross purposes. Internal dissensions and weakening of the hold of the Central Mughal Government provided favourable opportunities to the British. In 1705 the Company sent an embassy to the Mughal court and wrested from the weak ruler extensive privileges throughout the Empire, including the right to trade in Bengal free of all duties, to rent additional territory around Calcutta, and the right to coin money in Bombay and to circulate it throughout India. "The *firman* of 1716-1717 became known as the 'Magna Carta' of the Company, the major step in the establishment of this new type of politico-commercial power on Indian soil."[3] When in 1757 at the battle of Plassey Clive defeated the Nawab of Bengal, it was inevitable that the Company should become the leading political power in India. The Battle of Buxar (1764) completed what Plassey had begun and, as Ramsay Muir remarked, "It finally rivetted the shackles of the Company's rule upon Bengal". The work of Clive was continued by Warren Hastings (1774-84) and Lord Wellesley (1798-1805). After the two Sikh wars the Sikhs were defeated and Punjab was added to the territories of the Company. In 1856, Lord Dalhousie annexed vast kingdom of Oudh.

Thus, by the middle of the nineteenth century most of India was controlled by the British, either directly by the East India Company or indirectly through the system of treaties and alliances with the Princely States. Some of the former Indian States were annexed by the Company under the doctrine of lapse and principle of escheat, especially during the Governor-Generalship of Lord Dalhousie. Dalhousie completed the process of consolidation of British control in India.

### Company and the British Government

But soon the criticism against the Com-

1. Morris-Jones, W. H., *The Government and Politics of India,* p. 2.
2. Quoted in R.C. Majumdar, H. C. Raychaudhri, and K. Datta, *An Advanced History of India,* p. 639.
3. De Riencourt, *The Soul of India,* p. 199.

pany's rule mounted high on the score that the opulence and arrogance of the servants of the Company returning home had corrupted the British way of life and demoralised its politics. Although the servants of the Company amassed wealth, the Company itself was faced with a serious financial crisis. The reckless policy of the Company's servants and its expanding political commitments in India soon made the Company bankrupt. The British Government could not remain quiet and appointed two Parliamentary Committees in November 1772'' to enquire into the affairs of the East India Company. The Select Committee and the Secret Committee submitted twelve and six reports respectively, all highly condemnatory and described the woeful tale of the affairs of the Company indicting Clive for his unpardonable sins in India. The British Government decided to ''regulate the Government of the East Indies'' and on May 13, 1773, Lord North introduced a Bill in Parliament.

The East India Company Act, 1773, commonly known the Regulating Act, altered the form of Government in the Company's territories in India, thereby firmly establishing the right of British Parliament to regulate the affairs of the Company and shape its political destiny. The Act recognised the authority of the Company to carry on hostilities and to make treaties with the native powers in India. This provision changed the position of the Company from a trading corporation to a political body.

But the Regulating Act proved a crude attempt at providing a satisfactory governmental machinery. The one established violated ''the first principles of administrative mechanics.''[4] It soon broke down under the stress of Indian circumstances and its own inherent defects. The Pitt's India Act, 1784, and a series of supplementary measures that followed removed the defects and laid down the principles on which Indian affairs for the next three-quarters of a century were conducted. The Act differentiated between the political and commercial activities of the East India Company and for all political transactions placed it in direct and permanent subordination to the British Government. The Act also brought the Governor-General of India into close relationship with the British Government by creating an ''Indian Ministry within the framework of the British Government without appearing to do so.'' The Charter Acts of 1793 and 1833 progressively whittled down the other powers of the Company. The most important of these was the Act of 1833.

The Act of 1833 made the Company's position more anomalous by declaring it as a trustee of His Majesty the King of the United Kingdom. It put an end to the commercial activities of the Company and centralized the administration, especially legislation. It brought into existence for the first time a properly styled Central Government whose foundation had been laid by the Charter Act of 1773. At the time of the expiration of the Act of 1833, a class of politically conscious Indians stirred and made efforts to bring to an end the reactionary regime of the East India Company. But the Charter was renewed. The Act of 1853 retained the Company until Parliament should otherwise direct. The system of centralized administration and legislation continued.

The Charter Act of 1853 paved the way for the assumption by the Crown of the governance of India. It gave no definite renewal of the Charter for a specified term of years as former Charters had done. The ''Mutiny'' in 1857, brought about the extinction of the Company and the assumption of the administration of India by the British Crown. The Act for the Better Government of India, 1858, finally, relieved the Company of its political responsibilities and provided for the direct assumption of the Government of India by the Crown acting through a Secretary of State. The transfer of power, however, was no more than a formal change. It was the culmination of the process that had begun in 1784, if not 1773.

## BALANCE SHEET OF THE COMPANY'S ADMINISTRATION

### Credit Side

''The East India Company,'' wrote Marshman, ''was created two hundred and fifty years before for the purpose of extending British commerce to the East; and it transferred to the Crown on relinquishing its function an Empire more magnificent than that of Rome''[5]. This magnificent Empire was not built without blunders and even heinous political crimes. ''To disguise them and to maintain that the British administrators were always swayed by impeccable motives and unerring statesmanship is to produce an unrealistic and impossible picture, for we are

4. *Report on Indian Constitutional Reforms,* para 30, p. 17.
5. Marshman, J.C., *The History of India,* Vol. II, p. 457.

dealing after all with the human agency. But when all necessary qualifications are made the annals of the company form one of the most fascinating pages in History."[6] This statement does not come from an impartial historian, nonetheless it cannot be denied that there were statesmen in the service of the company who evolved a high standard of humanitarian administration. They "were filled with a deep sense of mission. To them goes the credit of raising the administration of the East India Company from the counter to the pedestal of trusteeship. Even when they were engaged in building it, they were contemplating its end. The instability of empires, even the mightiest, was ever before their eyes and their ideas about government and its obligation to the governed were cast in the loftiest mould."[7] Wellesley, Hastings, Munro, Malcolm, Elphinstone and Bentinck belonged to the succession of enlightened statesmen whose nation-building activities and reforms deserve just appreciation.

During the period of the Company's regime serious attempts were made to provide an effective government capable of maintaining law and order. The Company succeeded therein, though not without initial blunders. By slow degrees an efficient covenanted civil service of character, ability and experience was evolved out of the older system of pure jobbery and corruption. Hastings, Munro and Elphinstone even tried to pave the way for the Indianisation of the services. While introducing the Charter Bill of 1833, which expressly provided that no subject of the Crown should be, by reason only of his religion, decent or colour, be disqualified for any place in the Company's service,"[8] Macaulay declared in the House of Commons[9] that he would to the last day of his life feel "proud of having been one of those who assisted in the framing of the Bill which contains that 'noble clause'."

A working settlement of land revenue and the organisation of civil and criminal justice were effected in order to ensure the provision of a just government. The extirpation of human sacrifice, the extinction of slavery, the abolition of *sati* and infanticide and the suppression of *thuggee* laid the foundations of a humane social system. In fact, a constant war was waged against some barbarous customs then prevalent in India. John Lawrence adopted as his motto "the new trilogue of the British Government : thou shalt not burn thy widows; thou shalt not kill thy daughter and thou shalt not bury thy lepers alive."

Measures of famine relief were taken to relieve suffering. Efforts were made to develop means of communication and transport as well as irrigation to arrest the recurring threat of famines. The extension of the Grand Trunk Road, the great arterial highway across India, was vigorously pushed and completed in 1853, and before Lord Dalhousie relinquished his office, a network of hundreds of miles of railways was under construction. Telegraphic communication was established between Calcutta, Madras, Agra and Peshawar, and the postal system was brought within easy reach of the poor, and from one end of the country to the other. Lord Dalhousie had fervently supported the policy of digging canals and the Bari Doab Canal venture was completed in 1859. The Godavari works and Krishna River canal too fructified.

The adoption of the Western system of education and the recognition of the right of Indians to places in the Company's service, though "imperfectly conceded and treacherously delayed"[10] were valuable incentives to national consciousness and political advance in India.

### Other Side of the Medal

Whatever may be the degree of excellence of the Company's administration on abstract principles or for its specific achievements, the real merit of an administrative system is evidenced by the views and reactions of those who bore the brunt of it and were directly affected by it. From Raja Rammohan Roy, father of political liberalism in India, to organised political opinion as expressed in the petitions of the British Indian Association,[11] the Madras Native Association,[12] and the Bombay Association,[13] the Company's regime was regarded as outmoded and they boldly demanded a better and nobler administration based on the model of the British Government. Their persistent demand for various re-

6. Roberts, P. E., *History of British India,* p. 24.
7. Masani, R. P., *British in India,* p. 24.
8. Cl. 87.
9. July 10, 1833.
10. Phillips, C.H., *East India Company,* p. 297.
11. Parl. Papers H. L., No. III of 1952-53, pp. 249-51.
12. Parl. Papers, H.C., No. 768 of 1952-53, p. 120; and H.C. No. 426 of 1852-53, p. 438.
13. Parl. Papers, H.C. No. 426 of 1852-53, p. 476.

forms must be taken as a fair measure of their condemnation of the Company's administration in India. Liberal- minded Englishmen, like Sir John Shore, Sir Thomas Munro, Sir John Malcolm, and George Thompson, also joined the Indians in condemning various aspects of the administrative system of British India.

The foremost of all that compels attention about the first century of British rule in India was the appalling poverty and grinding distress to which the people were reduced by the ruin of indigenous industry, oppressive land-tax and perpetual drain of wealth.[14] Indians were reduced to passive onlookers; they had no place or power in the administration of their own country. They were excluded from the dignity of offices which even the lowest Englishmen could not be prevailed upon to accept. The curse of political subjugation with all the attendant evils, so pathetically described by Munro, exercised a degenerating influence upon the life and character of the people at large. The early dreams and enthusiastic hopes of the small band of English-educated Indians were giving place to disillusion and despair, while the common people, full of discontent and disaffection, bided their time in sullen resentment, marked by occasional outbursts of violence. By the time the British completed the first hundred years of their rule, they gained the whole of India, but lost their hold on the hearts of the Indians

## THE BRITISH CENTURY

### Unification of India

Approximately a century elapsed between the zenith of the power of the East India Company during the Governor-Generalship of Lord Dalhousie (1848-57) and the end of the British rule in 1947. This century began with the "Mutiny" and the assumption of the Government of India by the Crown and the century ended with the withdrawal of the British and the creation of two sovereign and independent States : India and Pakistan. During this period the British restored peace where life and limb was in danger. The political unity was provided by the Crown holding together the British and Princely India. The period from 1858 to the end of the First World War presented a picture of the administrative unification of India. The country was knitted together by a uniform post and telegraph system and its distant and far-flung parts were linked with a network of roads and railway transport. A single currency prevailed from Kashmir to Cape Comorin and a customs union was built around the country within which the economic life of the country was integrated. In a multi-lingual country, English, though a foreign language, enabled people from the various areas to converse with one another and to associate socially and politically. A uniform system of education also contributed to the political unity of the country. Various steps in the direction of self-government, beginning from the Councils Act of 1861 to the Government of India Act, 1935 were taken and they together trained the people in the art of limited and responsible government and finally helped to galvanise the country into a dynamic nation.

### The Pattern of British Rule

The British developed an effective system of administration, patterned after the system evolved during the earlier century. Independent India adopted in large measure the same system and continues with it since then. This is a legacy of fundamental importance.

Political India consisted of two parts, British India and the Indian States, some 562 in number, governed by the Rulers of these States, who were assured by Queen Victoria in her Royal Proclamation that there would be no encroachment on their territory, personal rights and privileges, all treaties made with them by the East India Company would be maintained and their rights and dignity honoured. Some of these States were as large as the major States of Western Europe, and since they existed in all parts of the country and "covered nearly two-fifths of the total area, a political map of India prior to partition looked like a piece of crazy quiltwork."[15] The Princes governed these States subject to the authority and supervision of the Political Department of the Government of India which was under the direct charge of the Governor-General. A Resident was appointed in each State and he was usually the effective source of power. The interference of the Political Department in the internal affairs of the States was proverbial.

British India was divided into eleven Provinces at the time of partition with a Governor at the head. Before the Reforms of 1918, Provinces were limbs of a highly centralised administration, though various measures had introduced an ele-

14. Refer to R. C. Dutt's *India under Early British Rule*, and *India in the Victorian Age*.
15. Palmer, Norman D., *The Indian Political System*, p. 59.

ment of decentralisation. The Acts of 1919 and 1935 demarcated the jurisdiction between the Central and Provincial Governments. The Provinces enjoyed certain amount of autonomy in their affairs first under the system of dyarchy, and thereafter as a result of Provincial autonomy. But responsible government in the provinces was introduced under heavy restrictions and safeguards and the mighty hand of the Governor-General entered all the spheres of the Provincial administration. The Governor-General and the Viceroy, the twofold title which the head of the Government of India bore till 1947, was assisted by an Executive Council which consisted before 1908 of all European members. The Governor-General had the power to override the majority opinion of the Council, if, in his opinion, any measure affected essentially the safety, tranquillity, or interests of the British possessions in India. The Governor-General, on his part was responsible to the Secretary of State for India and through him to the British Cabinet and Parliament. The Secretary of State was provided with a Council known as the Council of India. The intention was to provide him with expert advice on affairs relating to India. With the establishment of telegraph communication between England and India in 1870, and the policy of substitution of private letters and telegrams for official correspondence, both the Secretary of State and the Governor-General ignored their Councils on all important matters. From here onwards the administration of affairs in India was subjected to more direct and effective control from London.

The Provinces were divided for purposes of administration into divisions, districts and tehsils or taluks. At the head of the division, which comprised a number of districts, was the Commissioner. The district was the hub of the administration and the district officer, designated as the Deputy Commissioner or Collector, combined multifarious and diverse functions, and was charged with the duty of administering the affairs of the district, with the maintenance of law and of revenue. Alongside the District Officer would be the specialist officers, such as the Superintendent of Police, Civil Surgeon, Executive Engineer and others. These specialist officers would be responsible so far as specialist service itself was concerned to appropriate departments of the Provincial government but in general district administration they would all come under the District Officer to whom they would look for leadership. Thus generalist administrator was the Provincial Government's maid of-all-work and being the Government's representative on the spot he symbolised its authority and prestige; the physical embodiment and symbol of British *Raj.*

A district was divided into a number of Tehsils or Taluks. A Tehsil or a Taluk consisted of a number of villages. In every village there would be the headman and the patwari (accountant for land revenue purposes). Both these incumbents in the village represented the Government. This was the framework which was inherited by the new regime of Independent India.

The Indian Civil Service was, without doubt, the most valuable of the British bequests to Independent India. It consisted of small administrative aristocracy (fewer than 2,000), largely Indianized by 1947, 'generalist' and non-technical in nature, "highly educated and carefully selected by a difficult competitive examination, remarkably adaptable, almost entirely free from corruption, exceptionally devoted to duty imbued with intense *esprit de corps,* and perhaps most important of all, *pan Indian* rather than regional or provincial in its loyalties."[16] The members of this service maintained the highest standards of efficiency and integrity and manned most of the key administrative posts. They were often criticised for developing a spirit of elitism and an exaggerated sense of their own importance. But ""in a country", as Morris-Jones has said, "where any kind of government employment carried appropriate prestige, membership of the highest service of all lifted a man into a social stratosphere."[17] To belong to the Indian Civil Service was not simply a guarantee of good, interesting and lucrative job, it was practically the sole repository of power. From its ranks were drawn not only the district officers, commissioners, senior officials of the Provincial and Central Governments but also Governors of most of the provinces, the members (until 1921, and in part until 1937) of the Provincial Executive Councils and most of the members of the Governor-General's Executive Council and even some of the memberships of the Secretary of State's Councils.

With the transfer of power, the British as

16. Hansen, A.H., and Janet Douglas, *India's Democracy,* p. 23.
17. Morris Jones, W.H., *The Government and Politics of India,* p. 23.

rulers withdrew, but the great machine of government continued intact. "Its build and shape, its manner of working, the relations of its parts—all these were firmly present, constituting an enormous fact."[18] Many Indian politicians, who acquired office after 1947, regarded the members of the Indian Civil Service, initially, as imperialism's Trojan Horse and the most extreme of them demanded its abolition. But Nehru and Patel, who had learned to appreciate their adaptability, efficiency and integrity warned caution. They emphasised that, administratively continuity was the best policy. Patel, in an impassioned defence of the all-India services, said in the Constituent Assembly in 1949, "I have worked with them during this difficult period......Remove them and I see nothing but a picture of chaos all over the country." Without the Indian Civil Service orderly administration might have collapsed and regional separatism triumphed. With it and its successor, the Indian Administrative Service, India had a "steel frame", but far from being the virtual master of India the civil servants had to become its servants.

At the time of transfer of power in 1947, five hundred non-British Indian Civil Service officers were available. Today, their cadre is extinct, either by death, resignation or retirement. A handful of them who were till recently available held key positions in the Union and the State administration. Some retired members of the Indian Civil Service till recently were posted in various trouble-shooting roles.

## STEPS TOWARDS SELF-GOVERNMENT

### Major Landmarks

Equally important, although of more controversial significance, was the experience of self-governing institutions which Indians acquired under various schemes of reforms, especially those that the British conceded in their later days. India's political leaders inherited the machinery of Government which carried the accumulated wisdom of the six major landmarks that had determined the course of the British rule and helped to prepare Indians for the assumption of political responsibility in 1947. A federal polity and the parliamentary system of government find their manifestation in these landmarks and both these legacies constitute, *inter alia,* the basic structure or framework, the concept used by the Supreme Court, of the 1950 Constitution.

The Government of India Act, 1935 was the penultimate chapter of rather a long story in the development of self-governing institution with a rudimentary beginning in 1861. The Indian Councils Act, 1892 was definite advance over its predecessor, the Councils Act, 1861. The changes it introduced however slight to give satisfaction to the growing politically conscious Indians, made a beginning in the direction of giving to the Councils the form of parliamentary institutions, despite the disclaimer of the Government both in India and Britain. By conceding the elective principle, though limited and indirect, and by granting the right to interpellation, and discussion on the budget, the Act of 1892 paved the way of further reforms. The non-official members were in the minority in the Councils and their functions were rigidly fettered, but they had the opportunity to express their opinions, criticize the administration and seek redress for the grievances. In spite of their defects and shortcomings, the Morley-Minto reforms (1909) constituted an important stage in the evolution of the representative institutions in India. The changes may not have been wholly parliamentary, but the Legislative Councils served a forum for the expression of public opinion and the non-official members assumed the role of the Opposition. They also used the Councils as platforms for educating the people in the affairs of the country. The Councils had become deliberative bodies, if not controlling the executive.

Controlling the executive is the essence of parliamentary system and the Government of India Act, 1919, introduced it partially under the system of dyarchy in the Provinces. The Government of India Act, 1935, abolished dyarchy in the Provinces and introduced instead provincial autonomy with ministerial responsibility, though under heavy restrictions and safeguards. The Congress Party formed ministries in seven out of eleven Provinces and in coalition with parties other than the Muslim League . When the "interim" Government was formed at the Centre, both members of the Congress Party as well as other parties had acquired considerable knowledge of, and what was important respect for parliamentary procedures and conventions. According to Morris-Jones, the Act of 1935 made three contributions to the Indian political development. "It established a full regime of responsible government in the provinces operated on an exceptionally elaborate division of powers *vis-a-*

18. *Ibid.*, p. 25.

*vis* the Centre,'' is the first among those three. Doubts about the appropriateness of the legacy of parliamentary system of government were expressed then and even now have not been laid to rest. All one can say is that neither in 1947 nor subsequently was there any coherent and generally acceptable alternative.

**The Policy of ''Divide and Rule''**

Of all the legacies of the British rule in India the legacy of communalism is the most cruel and it finds its echo from the days of the East India Company. It however, took a concrete shap during Lord Curzon's Viceroyalty. The strategy of Lord Curzon and his successors was to set one religion against the other and class against class in order to shatter the image of national unity and to disintegrate the feelings of solidarity that the Indian National Congress had created right from its inception in 1885. Curzon partitioned Bengal in order to drive a wedge between the Hindus and Muslims, under the cover of administrative convenience, but it was entirely on communal line. Minto abetted the Muslims to form a separate organisation of their own and, thus, helped the establishment of the Muslim League. He also prevailed upon Lord Morley, the Secretary of State for India, to concede to the demand of the Muslims for separate electorates comprising the Muslims alone and weightage in services.

Curzon had kindled the baneful communal consciousness by partitioning Bengal and carving out Eastern Bengal and Assam as a separate province with a Muslim majority. Morley-Minto reforms gave it a more concrete shape and by spreading communalism, through separate electorates, achieved the greatest victory for the British Empire in the Twentieth century. The system of communal representation was opposed to history and all codes of political morality. It had nowhere existed before and perhaps nowhere else it had been planned even by the worst followers of Imperialism to divide the people of a country in this manner. ''A political barrier'', wrote Nehru, ''was created round them (Muslims), isolating them from the rest of India and reversing the unifying and amalgamating process which had been going on for centuries........'' The ultimate result was the partition of India in 1947. Communalism still plagues Indian politics and it is the most cruel legacy of the British rule.

**Division and Independence**

Lord Louis Mountbatten was appointed the Governor-General of India to prepare the ground for the transfer of power. His instructions were to strive for obtaining a unitary government for British India and the Indian States on the basis of the Cabinet Mission Plan. Only if by October 17, 1947, he found that there was no prospect of reaching a settlement between the two major parties, he should think of other means. Mountbatten set about most expeditiously and zealously on his mission immediately after assuming office on March 24, 1947. Within a few days he could know that his instructions were out of date and there was no alternative to division of India. The Muslim League had become desperate and the new Viceroy was a close witness to communal rioting and fires of frenzy happening all over the country, urban and rural.

Lord Mountbatten prepared a plan for partition and referred it to the leaders of the Congress and the Muslim League to know their reactions. On May 18, the Governor-General left for London to discuss his Plan with the Prime Minister and the Secretary of State. The Cabinet approved the Plan. Having obtained the green signal, the Viceroy returned to India to make the announcement incorporating the Plan itself, on behalf of His Majesty's Government.

The Congress accepted the Plan and so did the Sikhs. Jinnah did not give anything in writing, although he assured the Viceroy that he would do all in his power to get the Plan accepted by the Muslim League. The Mountbatten Plan was simple. India was to be divided into two Dominions—India and Pakistan. The North-West Frontier Province, the Muslim-majority parts of Punjab and Bengal, Sind and Baluchistan and Sylhet amalgamated with Eastern Bengal were to become parts of Pakistan.

**The Indian Independence Act, 1947**

The stage was, thus, set for transfer of power. On July 2, 1947 the Draft of the Independence Bill implementing the political settlement in accordance with and in conformity to the announcement of June 3, 1947 was circulated to the leaders of the Congress and the Muslim League for their consideration. The Bill was introduced in Parliament on July 5 and after having passed through both the Houses it received the Royal assent on July 18, to become operative on August 15, 1947. As a result of the setting up of the new Dominions on August 115, His Majesty's Government ceased to have responsibility as respects the Government of any territories which, immediately before August 15, were included in

British India. The suzerainty of His Majesty over the Indian States lapsed and they became independent in their political relations with the Government of the Austin Dominions.

The British legacies are clearly visible in various articles of the Indian Constitution which literally valodated the theory and practice of British democracy within the framework of the Republic state structure. The British conventions of parliamentary government apply to the Indian system of parliamentary governance both at the levels of the Centre and the component states, though these conventions have not been stated in the body of the constitution. They are just assumed and have become operational in the actual working of our Constitution.

## SUGGESTED READINGS

Bettelheim, Charles, *India Independent*

Barrington, Moore, *Social Origins of Dictatorship and Democracy.*

Desai, A.R. *Social Background of Indian Nationalism.*

Dutt, R.P., *India Today.*

Granville Amtiu, *Indian Constitution — A Cornerstone of a Nation.*

Marnis Jones, W.H., *The Government and Politics of India.*

Rudolph and Rudolf, *In Pursuit of Lakshmi*

## CHAPTER V

# Making of the Constitution : Basic Decisions and Objectives

### Making of the Constitution

The right of the people to determine the form of government under which they would live and to frame their own constitution, despite repeated disavowal by the British Government, was finally conceded in March, 1942 when Sir Stafford Cripps brought to India reform proposals of the War Cabinet. The Cripps Proposals were rejected, but the right of Indians to frame their own constitution through a Constituent Assembly was established. It was reiterated in the March 15, 1946 statement of the Prime Minister, Clement Attlee. While recognising India's right to independence, he said, "......What form of government is to replace the present regime is for India to decide, but our desire is to set up forthwith the machinery for making the decision."

In pursuance of the Prime Minister's statement elections to the Constituent Assembly were held in July, 1946. The Muslim League won all but seven of the seats reserved for Muslims and the Congress secured 203 of the General seats. The Congress had also succeeded in capturing one Sikh and four Muslim seats, thus, making a tally of 208 seats out of a total of 296 seats allotted to the Provinces. The Indian States were to have 93 seats. The representatives of the States of Baroda, Bikaner, Jaipur, Jodhpur, Rewa, Udaipur and Patiala entered the Assembly in April, 1947. Representatives of States, other than Jammu and Kashmir, and Hyderabad, Junagadh and two more States, entered the Assembly subsequently. Jammu and Kashmir and Hyderabad came in after the accession of these States in October, 1947 and November, 1948 respectively.

The Constituent Assembly was a galaxy of top-ranking leaders of the Congress and the Muslim League, veteran statesmen, seasoned administrators, eminent jurists, in fact, people drawn from all walks of life and all parts of the country. In the selection of its candidates for election to the Constituent Assembly, the Congress adopted two basic norms : (*i*) that the Congress candidates should represent the country as a whole and various viewpoints within the Party itself must find due representation; and (*ii*) due care should be taken to bring on its list candidates capable of representing country's dynamism irrespective of party affiliations. It was, accordingly, ensured that persons of exceptional ability outside the Congress Party found places in the Constituent Assembly, and that minority communities were justly represented. The Cabinet Mission Plan had guaranteed seats for Muslims and Sikhs only and no provision was made for the representation of other minorities, such as, Parsis, Anglo-Indians, Indian Christians, members of the Scheduled Castes and even women. In some cases, instructions were issued by the Congress Working Committee to the Presidents of the Provincial Congress Committees to recommend the names of specified persons for nomination.[1] All minority communities were represented usually by the members of their choice. The Indian Christians had seven members, the Anglo-Indians three and Parsis three. After the partition the total number of representatives of the minorities, including Muslims, was 88 out of 233 seats allotted to the Provinces; 37 per cent of the total population of the Provinces. There was hardly any shade of opinion not represented in the Constituent Assembly.

After partition the Congress majority in the Assembly jumped to 82 per cent. There was no conceivable opposition. The twenty-eight Muslim League members from the non-Pakistan Provinces, who took their seats in the Assembly, were separately divided among themselves. The Muslim League was "suspect" in India and Pakistan having been created there was no motivating force which could bind them together in a cohe-

1. Among them were Alladi Krishnaswami Ayyar, N. Gopalaswami Ayyangar, B. R. Ambedkar, Hriday Nath Kunzru, K. Santhanam, M. R. Jayakar, Sachchidananda Sinha and K.M. Munshi, Tej Bahadur Sapru declined to accept the nomination due to illness.

sive body. Nor was there any dynamic leader to whom they would have looked for guidance. Their only aim was to safeguard the interests of the Muslims who had not opted for Pakistan. They still feared Hindu domination and, therefore, turned to Nehru and the Congress leadership for the protection of the interests of their community. The Constituent Assembly was the Congress. At the Centre and in the Provinces there were Congress Governments too. As Granville Austin has said, "The Assembly, the Congress, and the government were, like the points of a triangle, separate entities, but, linked by overlapping membership, they assumed a form infinitely meaningful for India."[2]

The Constituent Assembly met as scheduled on December 9, 1946. The Muslim League boycotted its deliberations, although the December 6 statement of the British Government had accepted the Muslim League's interpretation of the grouping clause. Jawaharlal Nehru moved the Objectives Resolution on December 13, 1946 and described it as a "solemn pledge to the people" which they would redeem in the constitution that they would frame. On the motion of M. R. Jayakar's amendment the discussion on the Objectives Resolution was postponed so as to enable representatives not only of the Muslim League, but of the Indian States, too, to participate in the deliberations of the Assembly.

The Assembly was adjourned till January 20, 1947, but the Muslim League continued with its boycott when it met after the adjournent. After the acceptance of partition the position was entirely changed. Jinnah and the league leadership agreed that the League members of the Assembly from the non-Pakistan Provinces should participate in its deliberations, and play their part in the framing of the future constitution of India, with a view to securing the interests of the Mussalmans, who were to remain in India, by providing effective safeguards. When the Assembly met for the fourth session on July 14, 1947 the Muslim League members from the non-Pakistan Provinces took their seats and declared themselves as "loyal and law-abiding citizens of India." Now, the Constituent Assembly was not bound by the provisions of the Cabinet Mission Plan. It was, competent to chalk out its own course and to establish a federation of its own choice, with as strong a Centre as desired.

**Task of the Constitution-Makers**

But partition had made the task of the Constitution-makers tremendously arduous. The problems they had to tackle were many and difficult to resolve. They had to devise a scheme of government for 400 million people in no way homogenous and alike. There were scores of communities speaking different languages, professing different faiths, practising different customs, following different traditions and emphasising different cultures. The demand of the Muslim League for the division of India on religious basis, culminating ultimately in slicing territories in the Wast and the East, had completely changed the pattern of the political set-up originally contemplated. The first task of the Constitution-makers, therefore, was to adequately provide for the unity and integrity of the country in the presence of a foreign State within the very compound of India.

The creation of Pakistan did not mean the total exit of the Muslims from India. More than ten per cent of the total population of the country was left on the Indian side of the border and that, too, in the same Provinces from where the cry that Islam was in danger was raised first. Having been left leaderless and forsaken by their own coreligionists whose battle they had fought, these political orphans were to be rehabilitated with adequate guarantees for the protection of their religion and culture. The object was to instil in them the sense of belongingness to India and the faith of a unified nation. Together with the problem of the Muslims, and equally important, was the problem of nearabout forty-million untouchables, numerous other minority groups, backward people and areas, like tribes and tribal areas, who were to be protected from the the centuries-old oppression and suppression.

Then, there was the baffling problem of the Indian States, 562 in number. The declaration of lapse of Paramountcy on transfer of power had created an intriguing situation. The States were left free "to enter into a federal relationship with the successor Government or Governments or failing this, enter into political arrangements with it or them."[3] Interpreted in terms of law, the Memorandum prepared by the Cabinet Mission on "States, Treaties and Paramountcy" and endorsed by the Mountbatten Plan left any Prince or a combination of Princes free to declare his or

2. Granville Austin, *The Indian Constitution : Cornerstone of a Nation*, p. 9.
3. *Memorandum of the Cabinet Mission on "States, Treaties and Paramountcy,"* May 12, 1946.

their independence and even to enter into negotiations with any foreign power and thus become islands of independent territory within the country. In fact, some States, such as Hyderabad and Junagadh, had begun to flirt with foreign States. Junagadh, a small State in Kathiawar, acceded to Pakistan, and Pakistan accepted the accession, even though the population of the State was predominantly Hindu. Apparently, the Nizam of Hyderabad desired to maintain an independent status. Envoys from the Nizam's court, together with intermediaries, like Sir Walter Monckton, went silently to and from Delhi "carrying terms and proposals, feelers and conditions." By November, 1947, no more than a Standstill Agreement could be secured from him, prolonged negotiations failed to persuade His Exalted Highness to accede to India.

The position of the Indian National Congress was clear enough on the issue of Indian States. On July 15, 1947 the All-India Congress Committee categorically rejected the claim of some of the States and the theory of Paramountcy. Speaking at this meeting Nehru said that the States have only two alternatives : they could join the Union of India either individually or in groups. "There is no third way out of the situation—third way meaning Independence or special relation to a foreign power." Coupland had aptly said, "India could live if its Muslim limbs in the north-west and north-east were amputated but could it live without its heart ?" The heart of India was its Princely States. The foremost concern of the Government of Independent India was to conserve the heart of India.

Immediately after the plan to partition and grant of Independence on August 15, 1947 was announced, the Interim Government decided to set up a State Ministry to deal with the problem of Indian States. This Ministry was placed under the charge of Sardar Vallabhbhai Patel. By August, 1947, all the 562 States, with the exception of Hyderabad, Jammu and Kashmir and Junagadh, had been persuaded by a combination of cajolery and firmness, to sign Instruments of Accession and Standstill Agreements which had the effect of surrendering their powers in the three fields of foreign relations, defence and communication, and maintaining unchanged all arrangements in other matters.

The unity of what had been left as India after the partition was so vital that the Government of India "could not view with equanimity and trifling with it"[4] The people of Junagadh forced the Nawab to flee to Karachi and in November 1947 the Muslim Dewan of the State was compelled to invite the Government of India. Junagadh became a part of the Union of India as a result of plebiscite in February, 1948. In Hyderabad the situation became explosive as a result of disorder that broke out inside the State, fanned by the Communist-led peasants of Telengana and the ugly acts of a violent fanatical group of Muslim militants, Razakars. Even raiders from Hyderabad made incursions into Indian territory. Indian troops were, consequently, ordered to enter Hyderabad and after four days of 'police action' the Nizam capitulated. He agreed to accede to the Indian Union in November, 1948 and became the nominal head of the State.

Along with Hyderabad, Kashmir was another problem. The Maharaja of Jammu and Kashmir refused to accede either to Pakistan or India prior to August 15, 1947. In October, 1947 the Pathan tribesmen from Pakistan raided Kashmir and threatened its capital, Srinagar. The Maharaja in desperation sought military aid from India which was given only on his agreeing that the State of Jammu and Kashmir should accede to India. For the Government of India it was announced by Lord Mountbatten as Governor-General that "as soon as law and order have been restored in Kashmir and her soil cleared of the invader, the question of the accession should be settled by reference to the people." Although a cease-fire was agreed upon on January 1, 1949, through the good offices of the United Nations, the Kashmir question has been the major issue in dispute between India and Pakistan ever since. The cease-fire line has became a *de facto* frontier.

The work accomplished by Sardar Vallabhbhai Patel in the States Ministry rationalised the political map of India by the merger or the consolidation and integration of the Indian States. It was a silent revolution and India was unified as never before in her history. No fewer than 216 smaller States were abolished as separate units and merged into the Provinces. States numbering 275 in all were integrated to form five new Unions with a Rajpramukh as the head of a Union of States. The Rajpramush was chosen by the States integrated into a Union. Sixty-one States were brought under direct Central administration either as separate units or in consolidated

4. *White Paper on Indian States,* July 1948, p. 18.

blocks. The States of Hyderabad, Mysore and Jammu and Kashmir were left unaffected by these changes.

The White Paper on Indian States had said that Indian independence would have no meaning if the people of the States did not have the same political, social and economic freedom, as those enjoyed by the people of the Provinces. All the Princely States, save for a few enlightened States, such as Mysore, were notoriously backward and even feudal. The makers of the Constitution had therefore, to devise means to make them as viable and sizable units with democratic institutions. The process of integration and democratization began after their accession to India.

## BASIC AIMS AND OBJECTIVES

### Basic Objectives

To forge unity out of numerous diversities, both natural and artificial, was therefore, the foremost task of the Constitution-makers. But their real and stupendous task was, as Jawaharlal Nehru explained in the Constituent Assembly, "'to free India through a new constitution, to feed the starving people and to clothe the naked masses, and to give every Indian the fullest opportunity to develop himself according to his need."[5] On the mid-night of August 14, 1947 Nehru in a moving speech called upon the members of the Constituent Assembly to take a pledge of dedication of service to India and humanity. "Long ago," he said, "we made a tryst with destiny, and now the time comes when we shall redeem our pledge not wholly or in full measure, but very substantially........." To the people of India, Nehru made a fervent appeal "for co-operation in the great adventure of building the noble mansion of free India where all her children may dwell." The task of the Assembly was to devise a constitution that would serve the ultimate goal of social revolution, "of national renaissance." Simple drafting of the fundamental rights and moral precepts of a preamble were only a parchment of paper unless the political machinery established by the constitution did not foster or at least permit a social revolution to reach the destination.

The basic aims and objectives of the new State of India find their expression in the Objectives Resolution approved by the Constituent Assembly on January 22, 1947 and the most significant statement of such aims and objectives is found in the Preamble to the Constitution of 1950. Thus, the foundation of the constitutional structure was laid by the Objectives Resolution which prescribed :

"(1) This Constituent Assembly declares its firm and solemn resolve to proclaim India as an Independent Sovereign Republic and to draw up for her future government a Constitution;

..............

(4) Wherein all power and authority of the Sovereign Independent India, its constituent parts and organs of government, are derived from the people; and

(5) Wherein shall be guaranteed and secured to all the people of India justice, social, economic and political; equality of status, of opportunity, and before the law; freedom of thought, expression, belief, faith, worship, vocation, association and action, subject to law and public morality; and

(6) Wherein adequate safeguards shall be provided for minorities, backward and tribal areas, and depressed and other backward classes; and

(7) Whereby shall be maintained the integrity of territory of the Republic and its sovereign rights on land, sea, and air according to justice and the law of civilised nations; and

(8) This ancient land attains its rightful and honoured place in the world, makes its full and willing contribution to the promotion of world peace and the welfare of mankind."

These fundamental Objectives, which were to guide the deliberations of the Constituent Assembly, may, thus, be stated :

(1) that India is to be an independent sovereign Republic;

(2) that it is to be a democratic Union with equal level of self-government in all the constituent parts. "There cannot be," as Nehru emphasised, "different standards of freedom as between the peoples of the states and the people outside the states;"

(3) that all power and authority of the Union Government and Governments of the constituent parts is derived from the people;

(4) that the constitution must strive to obtain and guarantee to the people justice based upon social, economic and political equality, equality of opportunity and equality before the law;

(5) that there should be freedom of thought,

5. *Constituent Assembly Debates*, Vol. II, p. 316.

expression, belief, faith, worship, vocation, association and action, subject to law and public morality;

(6) that the constitution should provide just rights for minorities, backward and tribal areas, and depressed and other backward classes so that they may be equal participants in and recipients of social, economic and political justice; and

(7) to frame a constitution which should secure for India a due place in the comity of Nations and to contribute to the promotion of world peace and the welfare of mankind.

With well-defined objectives before them the Constituent Assembly established eight major Committees[6] to provide bricks and mortar for the constitutional structure. Either Patel, Nehru or Prasad chaired each of these committees and in many cases the other two or Azad, were present. With seven other Assembly members,[7] these leaders constituted an inner circle in the Committees of the Assembly. The inner circle demonstrated the inter-locking of the three organisations—the Party, the Assembly and the Congress Governments at the Centre and the Provinces—for with one exception all were also members of the Congress or of the Central Government.[8] After partition, the Constituent Assembly was a one- party body in an essentially one-party country. In other words, the Assembly was the Congress and the Congress was India.

The Drafting Committee[9] appointed by the resolution of the Constituent Assembly on August 29, 1947 submitted its report on February 21, 1948. The Draft Constitution was presented to the Constituent Assembly on November 4, 1948, for consideration, thereby providing a sufficiently long opportunity to the public, the press and the Provincial Legislatures to discuss it and focus public opinion. Its first reading comprised general discussion which commenced on November 4 and continued till November 9. Then began the second reading or consideration of the clauses of the Draft and it continued from November 15, 1948 to October 17, 1949. As many as 7,635 amendments were tabled out of which 2,473 were actually moved and discussed. The Assembly again sat on November 14, 1949, for the third reading of the Draft and it concluded on November 26. On this date the Constitution received the signatures of the President of the Constituent Assembly and it was declared passed.

The final session of the Constituent Assembly was held on January 24, 1950. It unanimously elected Rajendra Prasad the first President of the Republic of India under the new constitution which came into force on January 26, 1950. This date was specifically chosen for the inauguration of the Indian Republic, as it was on January 26, the Indian National Congress had passed the historic resolution at its Lahore session to win independence. Since then this resolution was repeated every year at public meetings all over the country till India became independent in 1947.

It was the Congress Expert Committee,[10] presided over by Nehru, that set India to her present Constitution. This Committee was appointed by the Congress Working Comittee to prepare materials for the Constituent Assembly and six of its eight members had been elected to that body. Vallabhbhai Patel was not a member of the Committee, but he attended many committee meetings. Other invitees were V. K. Krishna Menon, A. Appadorai, Mridula Sarabhai, and Raja Hathee Singh. The Committee drew widely upon the mature experience of advanced democratic countries. The Union Constitution Committee ransacked all the known constitutions of the world. They borrowed freely from the Government of India Act, 1935, although they deviated from it wherever they believed it was necessary.

## BASIC DECISIONS

Seven of the decisions regarding the nature of the new State which were made with due

---

6. Rules, Steering Advisory, Drafting, Union Subjects, Union Constitution, Provincial Constitution, and States. The Assembly had a total of more than fifteen committees. The Advisory Committee had two Sub-Committees, Fundamental Rights and Minorities.
7. G. B. Pant, P. Sitaramayya, A. K. Ayyar, N. G. Ayyangar, K. M. Munshi, B. R.Ambedkar, S. Sinha.
8. Nehru, Patel, Azad, Ayyangar and Sinha were the members of the Central Government, Pant was the Chief Minister of Uttar Pradesh ; Prasad was President of the Assembly, Munshi and Sinha were members of the Congress Working Committee, Ayyangar was neither a Minister nor a member of the Congress.
9. It consisted of seven members with B. R. Ambedkar as Chairman. The other members were : N. Gopalaswami Ayyangar, Alladi Krishnaswami Ayyar, K. M. Munshi, Saiyad Mohd. Saadulla, N. Madhava Rau, and D. P. Khaitan. Sir B. L. Mitter, though originally appointed a member, was unable to attend the Committee meetings after the first meeting as he ceased to be a member of the Constituent Assembly.
10. The Committee was formed on July 8, 1946 and consisted of Asaf Ali, K.M. Munshi, N. G. Ayyangar, K. T. Shah, K. Santhanam (all members of the Constituent Assembly), Humayun Kabir and D. R. Gadgil.

consideration, but without significant opposition were : India should have a written constitution, it should be a federal State; it should be a republic; it should have a parliamentary democracy; it should be a member of the Commonwealth of Nations; it should be a secular State; and, it should be a Welfare State.

**A Written Constitution**

For a federal State the constitution must almost necessarily be a written constitution which defines the relations between the Central Government and the regional Governments, demarcates the sphere of each, and is paramount to the constitutions of regional Governments, if each component part of the union has its own separate constitution. To base the arrangements which are inherent in a federal polity "upon understandings and conventions," as Dicey said, "would be certain to generate misunderstandings and disagreements."[11] Moreover, the demand for Constituent Assembly and the making of constitution by that body postulates that it must be a written constitution.

There were other compelling reasons for India to opt for a written constitution and that, too, for an elaborate and detailed document. India inherited a written constitution in the Government of India Act, 1935, one of the longest pieces of legislation ever enacted by the British Parliament. This Act, supplemented by the Indian Independence Act, 1947, another elaborate measure of the British Parliament with certain amending statutes passed by the Constituent Assembly of India, gave the Indian Union a working constitution till 1950 when the new Constitution became operative. The Constitution-makers thoroughly familiar with the provisions and implications of the 1935 Act, and with the practical experience of the machinery of Government then available instinctively borrowed profusely from it and in many cases entire Sections from the Act were transferred to the new Constitution. The members of the Assembly believed that to effect a smooth transfer of authority from the British Indian Government to the Government of India a variety of details should be included in the constitution in order to preserve administrative continuity and efficiency. At the time of Independence, India inherited a well-established system of constitutional law. "To have recreated this body of law in the form of legislation to be passed after drafting a constitution of broad principles seemed to Assembly members a difficult if not a dangerous proposition."[12]

Then, the task of the Constitution-makers was pre-conditioned by inescapable factors of previous regime and the politico-economic set-up of the vast sub-continent. Highly divergent elements had to be welded together and units widely differing from one another were to be brought together in an organic unification. These differences created difficulties in the legislative and administrative set-up and the Constitution originally provided for four distinct types of units–Part A, Part B, Part C, and Part D of the First Schedule–on a different constitutional level. Moreover, the unity of what was left as India was so vital a necessity for the political strength, full economic development, and the cultural expression of the people that the Constitution-makers followed the precedent of Canada and prescribed, in the federal polity they established a full-dressed constitution for the States comprising the Indian Union. The Constitution also elaborately dealt with the complicated problem of relations between the Union and the States as well as inter-State co-ordination and adjudication of disputes relating to water of inter-State rivers or river valleys. Not oblivious of the centrifugal forces that worked in India from the dawn of her history and in order to checkmate any recurrence of fissiparous tendencies arising out of various divergent elements in the Indian social life, the Constitution-makers armed the Union with adequate powers to meet any contingency whenever any grave threat, internal or external, appeared or was likely to appear threatening the unity and security of India. Rajendra Prasad gave a matter of fact analysis in his observations to the Constituent Assembly on November 26, 1949. He said, "India today needs nothing more than a set of honest men who will have the interest of the country before them. There is a fissiparous tendency arising out of various elements in our life. We have communal differences, caste differences, language differences and so forth."[13]

Referring to the detailed nature of the constitution, Prasad observed, " The Constitution has gone into great details regarding the distribution of powers and functions between the Union and the States in all aspects of their administrative

11. Dicey, A.V., *Law of the Constitution*, p. 142.
12. Granville Austin, *The Indian Constitution : Cornerstone of a Nation*, p. 327.
13. *Constituent Assembly Debates*, Vol. X, p. 891.

and other activities. I do not wish to pass any judgment on this criticism and can only say that we cannot be too cautious about our future, particularly when we remember the history of the country extending over many centuries."

The problem relating to public services, special classes, like Anglo-Indians, Scheduled Castes and Scheduled Tribes required in the opinion of the Assembly members, special constitutional provisions and they were duly provided. Similarly, the question relating to official language and regional languages has been specifically dealt with in the Constitution. Provisions relating to higher judiciary were also included so as to put its independence beyond the reach of Parliament. The Constitution embodies an elaborate List of Fundamental Rights as also the Directives Principles of State Policy. Some of these rights are unknown to other constitutions and their inclusion was necessitated by the peculiar conditions and circumstances prevailing in India. The theme of social revolution runs throughout the proceedings of the Constituent Assembly and in their efforts to achieve that end an elaborate Bill of Rights was engrafted on the parliamentary system of government and a federal system was supplemented by provisions for centralization of power whenever national interests demanded the strength of the unitary system.

The Constitution of a country cannot be divorced from the facts of history. It is, therefore, not surprising that the Constitution-makers would have produced quite a comprehensive document which at places entered into comparatively detailed provisions. The predominance of the lawyer element in the making of the Constitution might have been another contributory factor. But as K. C. Wheare explained, "in the long process by which the Government of India Act, 1935 was framed, the people in Britain learned much of the difficulties of making a Constitution of India, and any one who followed the discussions of these years, in which Indians and British alike strove to devise a good government for India will be slow to criticise the work with which the Indian Constituent Assembly has done. It has been a tremendous task and to have produced a constitution at all which can command so wide a measure of agreement is a great achievement."[14]

The constitution as finally emerged out of the Constituent Assembly consisted of 395 Articles and Eight Schedules. The Ninth Schedule was added by the Constitution (First Amendment) Act, 1951, and the Tenth by the Constitution (Fifty-second Amendment) Act, 1985. The total number of amendments so far made is 74 and many more are on the anvil. No other constitution in the world is so long. President Neelam Sanjiva Reddy in his broadcast to the nation on the eve of 32nd anniversary (1979) of the Independence Day bemoaned the "steady and cumulative deterioration of standards in public life and public morality" and the contempt with which principles of life had been compromised and the basic values of life treated. He considered that the time was ripe now for enlightened public opinion in the mainstream of national public life "to review the provisions of the Constitution in the light of working it over for the last three decades."

No other Constitution in the world is so long and detailed, even ponderous, as the 1950 Constitution of India in its present shape. M. V. Kamath humorously remarked in the Constituent Assembly, "The emblem and the crest that we have selected for our Assembly is an elephant. It is perhaps in consonance with that, that our Constitution is the bulkiest that the world has produced."[15]

### Constitution-Amending Process

Jennings has said that the Indian Constitution is too long and detailed and too rigid. What makes the Constitution so rigid, he explains, "is that in addition to somewhat complicated process of amendment, it is so detailed and covers so vast a field of law that the problem of constitutional validity must always arise."[16] Long and detailed it certainly is on sound grounds in the eyes of the Assembly members, but rigid it has not proved to be. Nor was it the intention of the Constitution-makers to make it rigid. The method of amendment is not complicated as Jennings holds it to be. It is simple, though not far from easy. It has sought to avoid the difficult processes laid down by the American and Australian Constitutions. K. C. Wheare says that the Indian Constitution strikes a good balance between extreme rigidity and too much flexibility. Nehru explained the reasons for it. He told the Constituent Assembly, "while we want this constitution to be as solid and as permanent as we can make it,

14. Gupta, Madan Gopal (Ed.), *Aspects of the Indian Constitution*, p.79.
15. *Constituent Assembly Debates*, Vol. VII, p. 1042.
16. Jennings, W. I., *Some Characteristics of Indian Constitution*, pp. 9-10.

there is no permanence in constitutions. There should be certain flexibility. If you make anything rigid and permanent, you stop the nation's growth, the growth of a living vital, organic people........In any event, we could not make this Constitution so rigid that it cannot be adapted to changing conditions. When the world is in turmoil and we are passing through swift period of transition, what we may do today may not be wholly applicable tomorrow."

It is important to note that the rigidity or flexibility of the amending process essentially depends upon in practice, on the complex of political parties at the Centre and in the States, and the attitude the Supreme Court may take in the final analysis. In the absence of a single party commanding a dominant majority in both Houses of Parliament, as in the case of Congress (I) minority Government headed by P. V. Narasimha Rao, no amendment can succeed as it would be impossible to secure the requisite majority–absolute as well as two-thirds in each House–as required under Article 368 of the Constitution. The Janata Party that assumed office in April 1977, was committed to repealing the Constitution (Forty-second Amendment) Act, 1976, in toto. Though the Janata commanded a comfortable majority in the House of the People (Lok Sabha), it was in minority in the Council of States (Rajya Sabha). The Constitution (Forty-third Amendment) Bill, 1977, was introduced in the House of the People and it passed therefrom. But the Amendment Bill was allowed to languish in the Council of States on fear to be outvoted there. It was after prolonged discussions with the leaders of the Opposition and with a good deal of give and take with the leader of the Congress Parliamentary Party that the Forty-third and Forty-fourth Amendments could pass in both the Houses of Parliament and in this process the Janata had to depart from its electoral commitment and that, too, on some crucial provisions of the Forty-second Amendment.

In case different political parties and groups constituting United Fronts were to form coalition governments, both at the Centre and in the States, the probabilities of such a contingency not being remote, the amending process in regard to the entrenched provisions can hardly operate as they require for their amendment not only a majority of total membership in each House of Parliament and a majority of not less than two-thirds of members present and voting but also ratification by at least one-half of the number of State Legislatures. Such a situation had arisen after the 1967 General Elections when the Constitution remained static till 1971 mid-term elections to the House of the People. One of the reasons which can convincingly be assigned for dissolving the Assemblies of the nine Northern States by the Janata Party Government in April, 1977 was the obvious apprehension that the process of ratification by the States of the various provisions inserted in the Constitution by the Forty-second Amendment, and to which the Janata Party was committed to repeal would not be forthcoming if the Congress Party remained in majority in all those States. It was exactly the same apprehension when Mrs. Gandhi's Government dissolved the Assemblies of those States once again in February 1980; political vengeance besides.

Judiciary also plays a key role in determining the rigidity of the Constitution. The majority decision in *Golak Nath* case nearly paralysed the amending process. Five to six Judges majority held that in future Parliament would not abridge or abrogate Fundamental Rights through the normal procedure prescribed in Article 368 for amending the Constitution. The Constitution (Twenty-fourth Amendment) Act, 1971 restored to Parliament the power to amend the Constitution including the Chapter on Fundamental Rights. In *Keshavanadna Bharati,* popularly known as the Fundamental Rights case, the Supreme Court reversed the stand taken by the Court in the *Golak Nath* case, but it put a rider on the power of Parliament by ruling that it had no power to change basic structure or framework of the Constitution.

The Constitution provides for three different methods of amending it :

The first mechanism of the amending process relates to Articles which are amendable under the substantive part of Article 368, that is, when an amending Bill is introduced in either House of Parliament and passed in each House (i) by a majority of the total membership in each House and (ii) by a majority of not less than two-thirds of the members present and voting in each House.

The second mechanism embraces Articles specifically mentioned under the proviso to Article 368 items (a) to (e). Amendment to any of these Articles requires not only a majority of total membership in each House and majority of not less than two-thirds of the members present and voting in each House but also ratification by at least one-half of the State Legislatures. The reasons for entrenching these Articles were given by Ambedkar in the Constituent Assembly. He explained, "If the members of the House who are interested in this are to examine the articles that have been put under the proviso, they will find that they refer not merely to the Centre but to the relations between the Centre and the Provinces (States). We cannot forget the fact that we have in a large number of cases invaded provincial autonomy, we still intend and have as a matter of fact seen to it that the federal structure of the Constitution remains fundamentally unaltered."[17] To amend the provisions laying down the distribution of powers and of revenue without permitting the provinces or the States "have any voice is in my judgment altogether nullifying the fundamentals of the Constitution,"[18] he added.

The entrenched provisions are :

(1) The method of election of the President of India (Art. 54 and Art. 55);
(2) Distribution of Legislative powers between the Union and the States (Articles 245 to 255, Chap. I of Part XI; Seventh Schedule);
(3) Extent of the Executive power of the Union and the States (Articles 73 and 162);
(4) Representation of the States in Parliament;
(5) Provisions relating to the Supreme Court and High Courts (Articles 134-147, Chapter V of Part VI, and Article 241);
(6) Amendment of the Constitution (Article 368).

The third category includes provisions in the Constitution which permit easy changes to be made with or without constitutional amendment. Generally, such provisions are alterable by a simple majority vote in each House of Parliament, followed by Presidential assent. Nearly two dozen Articles of the Constitution thus provide for their own alteration, and the pattern is a standard one. Whatever the Article establishes—for example, the qualifications for citizenship, the salaries and allowances of the Supreme Court and High Court Judges, the States that have to be bicameral legislatures—is to remain in force "until Parliament otherwise provides." Formal amendments in all such cases are not effected but otherwise they have the effect of making changes in the constitutional law.

But the most striking example of provisions alterable by simple majority vote in Parliament and assented to by the President are Articles 1, 2 and 3. Article 1 lays down that India shall be a Union of States and these States are named in the First Schedule and the Fourth Schedule of of the Constitution. Articles 2 and 3 empower Parliament to form new States and to alter the areas, boundaries or names of the existing States or to cause a State to disappear entirely by merging it with another State or States. A Bill effecting such changes may be introduced in either House of Parliament on the recommendation of the President. The President is required to refer such Bill to the Legislature of the State or States so effected for expressing its or their views thereon within the specified period of time or within such periods as the President may allow. After the expiry of the said period the Bill is introduced in Parliament. Article 4 (2) expressly states that such a law shall not be deemed as an amendment of the Constitution for the purposes of Article 368, but the fundamental importance of these Articles can in no way be minimised. They can change the political map of India and yet they are not governed by the provisions of Article 368.

The three mechanisms of the amending process were a compromise worked out by the Drafting Committee and were designed, as Ambedkar told the Constituent Assembly, to achieve a flexible Constitution. The compromise was between a small group of Assembly members who recommended the adoption of an amending process like that of the United States and a somewhat larger group that advocated amendment of all the clauses of the Constitution at least during the initial period by a simple majority of each House of Parliament. But Ambedkar asserted that the Constitution was a fundamental Document and utter chaos would result if it could be amended by a simple majority of Parliament.[19] Such a unique process of amendment of the different provisions of the Constitution did not hitherto exist in any other written Constitution. Commenting upon it, K.G. wheare remarked, "this variety in the amending process is wise but it is rarely found."[20]

17. *Constituent Assembly Debates,* Vol. IX, pp. 1661-63.
18. *Ibid.*
19. *Constituent Assembly Debates,* Vol. IX, pp. 1662-63.
20. Wheare, K. C., *Modern Constitutions*, p. 143.

A few observations may be noted with regard to the procedure for amending the Constitution. The right of initiating an amendment is vested exclusively in the Union Parliament. The Constituent States have no jurisdiction to propose a constitutional amendment except under article 169 (1) when the Legislative Assembly of a State may propose for the creation or abolition of a Legislative Council (Vidhan Parishad). Nor is the right to initiate a constitutional amendment conceded to the people. The exclusion of the constituent States from the amendment process is a negation of the well-accepted federal principle and contrary to the practice followed in other federal countries. The Drafting Committee claimed to have largely followed the model set by the Canadian federation, but even in Canada the Provincial Legislatures had the unfettered power of amending the Provincial Constitutions by the ordinary process of legislation, excepting on one point only, *viz.,* the office of the Lieutenant-Governor.[21]

The Rules of Procedure and Conduct of Business of the House of the People (Lok Sabha) as framed under Article 118 of the Constitution provided that the rules of procedure applicable to any ordinary Bill shall also apply to a Constitution Amendment Bill.[22] It means that Article 368 of the Constitution is not a code in itself and the procedure prescribed therein for amending the Constitution is to be supplemented by Rules made by each House of Parliament regulating its procedure and conduct of business. The Supreme Court held in *Shankari Prasad Singh Deo* v. *Union of India* that "having provided for the constitution of Parliament and prescribed certain procedure for the conduct of its legislative business to be supplemented by each House, the makers of the Constitution must be taken to have intended to follow that procedure so far as it may be applicable consistently with the express provisions of Article 368."[23]

The procedure followed in adopting the first twenty-three amendment Bills was to obtain special majority-at least half the membership of the House and not less than two-thirds of the members present and voting—at all stages of the consideration of a Bill. The two amendment Bills, to abolish the Privy Purses (twenty-sixth amendment) and to do away with the privileges of the members of the Indian Civil Service (twenty-eighth amendment) fell through at the consideration stage as both the Bills could not secure the requisite two-thirds majority of the members present and voting. The Rules Committee of the House of the People thereupon brought about a fundamental change which now prescribes that the special majority will be required only at the final stage of voting on the Bill. In the earlier stages a simple majority shall be sufficient.

The Rules Committee also took note of the fact that in the case of "omnibus" Bills involving the amendment of various Articles of the Constitution on different aspects and subjects, members of the House might be divided in their views on different provisions. To obviate such contingencies, the Rules Committee recommended that a Constitution Amendment Bill should deal with a single subject only. Accordingly, two separate amending Bills—the first inserting "amount" in place of "compensation" in Article 31, and the second seeking to abolish the Privy Purses and Privileges of Princes, Articles 291 and 362—were introduced and enacted separately. But this norm was not observed in the case of the Forty-second, Forty-third and Forty-fourth amendments. The Forty-second and Forty-fourth amendments covered the whole gamut of the constitutional framework, the former containing 59 Sections and the latter 45 Sections. The Forty-third amendment had 11 Sections.

The Indian Constitution, like that of the United States, does not prescribe any time limit within which State Legislatures may ratify or reject the amendments referred to them. Nor has Parliament done so on its own initiative, however urgent and time-bound the amendment may be, as the Forty-fifth Amendment was. The Constitution is also silent whether it is necessary that the amending Bill required to ascertain the will of the States must be transmitted to all the States or it is enough if it is submitted to some of them to ensure the requisite majority of the States. The situation did arise in the case of the Twenty-third Amendment Bill. The Constitution was notified to have been amended before some of the States had signified their approval. The Mysore (now Karnataka) Legislative Assembly strongly protested against this procedure. The amendment seeking to include Sikkim as an associate State of the Union became operative immediately after the requisite half the number of the States had

21. Section 82(1), The North America Act 1867 (now the Canadian Constitution Act).
22. Rule No. 159.
23. *All India Reporter,* Supreme Court, 428.

given their assent thereto. Similarly, the Thirty-sixth Amendment including Sikkam as the twenty-second State of the Union of India, and the Thirty-eighth Amendment making emergency not justiciable by courts, received the assent of the President immediately after half the States had ratified and became operative. This procedure has now become the norm and has been invariably followed in all the subsequent amendments.

When the procedure to amend the Constitution is the same as in the case of ordinary legislation, can the President withhold his assent thereto after the amending Bill has been duly passed by both the Houses of Parliament ? Article 368 originally did not make any reference to the President's power to withhold his assent and, accordingly, the Presidential assent was taken as a matter of sheer formality. The question of withholding assent could only arise when the procedure prescribed in Article 368 had not been followed. Since the controversy whether the President could exercise his veto power had lingered on all those years and even eminent jurists expressed the opinion that the President had and could exercise his discretionary power if he was satisfied that the situation so demanded, the Twenty-fourth Amendment (1971) inserted, as a measure of abundant caution, in renumbered Clause (2) of Article 368 that an amending Bill duly passed by two Houses of Parliament '''shall be presented to the President who shall give his assent to the Bill and thereupon the Constitution shall stand amended in accordance with the terms of the Bill.''

### A Federal Polity

The Constitution-makers of Independent India were in no doubt that a large new State, faced with the problem of establishing a central authority strong enough to govern a vast area inhabited by millions of people with different historical and linguistic backgrounds and interests, must inevitably be some form of federal structure. With the integration of Princely States, the formation of federation had become a *fait accompli.* The Butler Committee in 1929 had said that ''politically there were two Indias.......The problem of statesmanship is to hold them together.''[24] But holding them together was simply not sufficient. They were integrated in the Indian Union and Sardar Patel could rightly claim that it was not ''an alliance between democracies and dynasties, but a realUnion of the Indian people built up on the basic concept of the sovereign people.'' He also maintained that the Constitution ''removes all barriers between the people of the States and the people of the Provinces and achieves for the first time the objective of a strong democratic India built on the true foundation of a cooperative enterprise on the part of the people of the Provinces and States alike.''[25] For Ambedkar the Constitution of India ''is a single frame from which neither (Provinces or States) can get out and within which they must work.''[26]

The Assembly members were not wedded to the narrow ideas of federalism and they were not at all committed to follow the path carved out by the framers of the American Constitution. They firmly believed that India had unique problems to solve the like of which had not confronted other federations in history. Some of these required immediate effective solution, others demanded concerted policy and united efforts. There was, accordingly, near unanimity among all sections of the Assembly to have a strong centre possessing an overriding authority. The proceedings of the Constituent Assembly significantly reveal that whereas there were strong protests over the distribution of powers and revenues between the Union and the units and on the effects of emergency provisions on the federal structure there was none of the deep seated conflict of interests as between the Northern and Southern States in the Philadelphia Convention in 1787, or between Ontario and Quebec in Canada. The relative absence of conflict between the *Centralists* and the *Provincialists* smoothened the task of the Constitution-makers. ''They were the members of a family'' as Granville Austin put it, ''who, for the first time in possession of their own house, must find a way to live together in it. If their life was not to grind to an acrimonious halt, the members' relationships must by compromise be made mutually satisfactory.''[27] Drawing upon the experiences of the older federations, the Father-framers adopted the policy of ''pick and choose'' to see what would suit the genius of the nation best.[28] This policy of ''pick and choose'' with a firm determination to have a strong central

24. As cited in the White Paper on Indian States (198), p. 123.
25. *Constituent Assembly Debates,* Vol. V, p. 161.
26. *Ibid.*, Vol. VII, p. 34.
27. Granville Austin, *The Indian Constitution : Cornerstone of a Nation,* p. 192.
28. *Constituent Assembly Debates,* Vol. XI, p. 654.

authority produced an unusual political structure that defied the traditional basic principles of a federal polity and set up a new pattern of relationship between the Union and the States. Nowhere in the Constitution the word federation has been used. Article I simply described India as a Union of States.

The use of the expression Union of States was deliberate and Ambedkar explained in the Constituent Assembly the significance of the use of this expression instead of the expression "federation". He said, "It is true that South Africa which is a unitary State is described as a Union. But Canada which is a Federation is also called a Union. Thus, the description of India as a Union, though its Constitution is Federal, does no violence to usage. But what is important is that the use of the word 'Union' is deliberate. I do not know why the word "union' was used in the Canadian Constitution. But I can tell you why the Drafting Committee used it. The Drafting Committee wanted to make it clear that though India was to be a Federation, the Federation was not the result of an agreement by the States to join in a Federation, and that, the Federation not being the result of an agreement, no State has the right to secede from it. The Federation is a Union because it is indestructible. Though the country and the people may be divided into different States for convenience of administration, the country is one integral whole, its people a single people living under a single *imperium* derived from a single source. The Americans had to wage a civil war to establish that the States have no right of secession and that their federation was indestrucible. The Drafting Committee thought it was better to make it clear at the outset rather than to leave it to speculation or to dispute.[29]

**Nature of the federal polity**

The antecedents of India's peculiar needs, that necessitated such a nature of the federal polity, are to be found in the Indian history of the British period, especially of thirty years before Independence, in the anxieties and turmoils accompanying partition, in the religious fanaticism, and in the brutal murder of innocent people that the Constitution-makers themselves saw in the streets of Delhi and even outside the precincts of the Constituent Assembly building. They also witnessed the ghastly murder of the Father of the Nation on January 30, 1948. "The light," as Nehru said, in broken tones, over the All India Radio, "has gone out of our lives and there is darkness everywhere."

The problems confronting India and the legacy of the generation had not changed with the Independence of the country. At the time of the constitution-making the disruptive forces were already revealing symptoms of revival. It was a time when the great blood bath that accompanied partition was followed by invasion on Kashmir by Pakistan tribals. Not all the States had agreed to integrate in India and, as said earlier, some were flirting with foreign countries and had declared their independence. The whole country was, side by side, overwhelmed with economic crisis and famine conditions prevailed in many areas. There was the Communist insurrection in the Telengana region and Razakar[30] trouble in Hyderabad. It was, therefore, not surprising that in the midst of these disturbing conditions, the Union Government would have been given power, under the constitution, to meet the menace of disruptive forces, to curb the bane of communalism, regionalism and linguism, to vigorously save the economy of the country from disaster, to effectively meet administrative challenges created by partition and transfer of power and instil confidence in the minds of the people by settling some five and half million Hindus and Sikhs who had crossed from West Pakistan to India. "We have to deal," declared Nehru, "with a situation in which, if I may say so, if we do not try to our utmost the whole of India will be a cauldron within six months......And I don't know whether it will not be a cauldron in next six months due to the economic situation."[31]

It the exigencies of the present as well as the pattern of the past impelled the Constitution-makers to create a strong central authority, anxieties of the future were no less compelling. The immediate goal of social revolution, improving the standard of living and increasing industrial and agricultural productivity provided yet other reasons for a strong central authority which should show effective and impressive results. Although some Assembly members, K. Santhanam was one of them, argued that welfare of the people should be the responsibility of the Provincial (State) governments, most of them believed

29. *Ibid.*, Vol. VIII, pp. 42-43.
30. An extremist Islamic para-military movement.
31. Speech at a meeting of the Negotiating Committee of the Chamber of Princes and the States Committee of the Constituent Assembly.

that regional governments would be frail reeds to such a heavy and new responsibility. This duty, they asserted, should rest with the Union in order to make a national effort to achieve the objectives in view. The attributes of a strong Union authority, explained Balkrishna Sharma, "are that it should be in a position to think and plan for the well-being of the country as a whole, which means.......having the authority to co-ordinate (and)....the power of initiative. It should be in a position to supply the wherewithal to the provision for their better administration wherever the need arises. It should have the right in times of stress and strain to issue directions to the Provinces (States) regulating their economic and industrial life in the interest of the nation as a whole."[32] G. L. Mehta observed, "We must not also forget that economic forces and strategic considerations today tend to invest the Centre with large powers. If we organise economic development and social welfare as people organise for war, then the State of the future will have to be a positive State, it will have to be a social service State. It will require large finances, and more or less homogenous economic conditions will have to be maintained in order to achieve these purposes."

It may, thus, be summed up that the history of the past, the contemporary situation and the needs and hopes of the future were the three important factors which created a demand for a strong Centre. There were some prominent members of the Assembly who pointed out that centralization was justified not merely by the peculiar conditions which were characteristic of India, but it was a trend in all the federal States to counteract the disadvantages resulting from a constitutional distribution of powers. Alladi Krishanaswami Ayyar stressed this point and said, "In view of the complexity of industrial trade and financial conditions in the modern world, and the need for large-scale defence programmes, there is an inevitable tendency in every federation in the direction of strenghtening the federal government." The Draft Constitution in several of its provisions had, he added, "taken note of these tendencies instead of leaving it to the Supreme Court to strengthen the Centre by a process of judicial interpretation."

It does not, however, mean that the concept of tight federation remained unchallenged. Some of the members expressed the view that the constitution actually provided for a formidable unitary constitution and reduced the States to the position of "glorified district boards." Mehbub Ali Beg and N. G. Ranga apprehended that the emphasis on centralization and the easy means with which the Union Government could convert the federal system into a unitary one might lead to "totalitarianism and absolute negation of democracy."[33] Hirday Nath Kunzru said that the provisions of the Constitution opened the possibilities of the States being treated "as though they were children and the President a village schoolmaster."[34] K. Santhanam was of the view that a Centre with fewer powers would really be stronger than one with too many powers.[35] But the task of the Constitution-makers was made easier by the existence of a powerful single-party with nation-wide authority and by the absence of strong regional parties.

The controversy on the nature of the Indian federation did not come to an end even after the Constitution became operative in 1950. After the Fourth General Elections in 1967, with some nine non-Congress Governments in the States and a depleted Congress majority in Parliament until mid-term Parliamentary poll in 1971, the controversy assumed added importance. Even those in office did not lag behind. Ministers of the Union Government, from time to time, gave expression to their feelings, decrying the tendency towards the increasing concentration of authority and urged the need for decentralization of power to make the democratic process and concept of federalism more concrete and tangible to the common man. Prominent among them were: H. M. Shah, Union Minister of Industries, T. T. Krishanamachari, one of the architects of the Constitution, H. V. Pataskar, Governor of Madhya Pradesh and a former Union Minister.

The growth of regional parties gave a fillip to the controversy and its advocates became more articulate. The Dravida Munnetra Kazgham Party of Tamil Nadu demanded in 1967 greater autonomy for the States and even threatened to secede. Its successor, the Anna Dravida Munnetra Kazgham, a splinter group of DMK, which came into power in 1977 and again in 1991 is as vocal on this issue as its parent body. The Marxist

32. *Constituent Assembly Debates,* Vol. V, p. 77.
33. *Ibid.,*Vol. VII, pp. 296 and 350.
34. *Ibid.,* Vol. X, p. 369.
35. *Ibid.,* p. 364.

Chief Minister of West Bengal, Jyoti Basu, wrote letters on Decembers 1, 1977, enclosing a memorandum approved by the West Bengal Council of Ministers, to all Central Ministers, State Chief Ministers and Ministers, Legislators at the Centre and in the States and others seeking their support for a national debate on his Government's demand for greater State autonomy. He went to Srinagar to elicit the support of the National Conference President and Chief Minister of Jammu and Kashmir, Sheikh Mohammed Abdullah, which was readily available. The Sheikh advocated that the Centre should possess a few enumerated powers and the residuary powers be vested in the States. Prakash Singh Badal, who headed the Akali-Janata coalition Government in Punjab was the ardent advocate of Jyoti Basu's demand for greater autonomy, although the Akali Dal had been giving dubious meanings to the concept of greater autonomy. The main thesis of the Akalis is to be found in the Anandpur Sahib resolution which unequivocally declared the Sikhs to be a nation. The Akali Dal launched "Dharam Yudh" (holy war) in August 1982 for the fulfilment of their religious and political demands rivetting on an autonomous Sikh state wherein Sikhs should dominate and their religion governed the administration. The Anandpur Sahib resolution conceded to the Central Government four enumerated subjects foreign affairs, defence, currency and communication, : and the residuary powers rested with the units. The extremists among the Akalis unfurled the banner of "Khalistan" in the Golden Temple, their holiest Shrine, Amritsar, and declared Punjab to be an independent and sovereign Sikh state.

The Janata Party in its election manifesto for the Sixth House of the People election 1977, listed decentralisation as one of the party's objectives to be achieved. But the Janata repudiated its electoral objectives after coming into office. Prime Minister Morarji Desai rejected the demand for State autonomy and asserted that there were enough powers with the States. Minister of State for Home Affairs, Dhaniklal Mandal, pointed out in the House of the People (February 22, 1978) that the existing constitutional provisions were adequate and called for no amendment. The issue was once again raised at a meeting of the Parliamentary Consultative Committee for the Home Ministry on December 22, 1980 and it was likewise turned down. It was pointed out from the Government side that granting more powers to the States would create more problems, rather than solve existing ones.

In March 1983, the Chief Ministers of three Southern States (Tamil Nadu, Andhra and Karnataka) and the Union Territory of Pondicherry established the Coun- cil of Chief Ministers of Southern States in order to form a common forum for the redressal of their grievances and demand greater autonomy for the States, especially financial. Pressurised by circumstances, particularly emerging in Punjab and Jammu and Kashmir, and alarmed on the developments in the Southern States, Prime Minister Indira Gandhi announced the appointment of a Commission, headed by the former Judge of the Supreme Court Ranjit Singh Sarkaria, to review the Centre-State relations in their entirety keeping in view the unity of the country. The Prime Minister's concept of centre-state relations was that a strong centre was necessary for strong component units of the Indian Union as both go together to cement the unity of the country. The Chief Ministers of the Southern States as well as other Opposition parties firmly believed that strong states was the *sine qua non* of a strong centre and it was the basic requirement of a federal polity. Their ranks have since swelled.

No federal polity has worked strictly in accordance with the constitution on which it is based. Various forces emerge as a consequence of which the working constitution becomes different from the original instrument. The form of constitution remains the same, but the spirit and substance of it undergoes a change. The American federation began its career with the theory of State rights. Today, the National Government is unrecognisable. It has become more powerful and the process of centralization is at its peak, that is, the National Government has assumed influence or control over functions which formerly were considered under State jurisdiction. Canada began its federal career with the scales heavily tilted in favour of the Central authority. Today, the Canadian Provinces enjoy powers almost greater than those the States do in the American federation.

The existence of a strong centre is not inconsistent with the theory and practice of federalism. Each country evolves its own pattern of Union-State relations in the light of its historical background and its political, economic and social conditions. But a strong centre must not be a dominant centre which should render regional governments hapless and helpless or in the words of Riker to "overawe the constitutional governments.''[36] During the last forty-two years the Government of India has unquestionably established its dominant role and extended its influence and control over the subjects within the exclusive jurisdiction of States. Even the Constitution was amended to effect transfer of subjects, such as, education and forests, on the State List to the Concurrent List.[37] The Constitution (Forty-second Amendment) Act, 1976, inserted a new Article 257A empowering the Union Government to deploy any armed forces of the Union or any other force to the control of the Union for dealing with any grave situation of law and order in any State. Many regarded this provision as a silent transfer of federalism into virtual unitarianism. K. Santhanam described it as paramountcy of the centre in place of a strong centre as visualised by the Founding-fathers. The Constitution (Forty-fourth Amendment) Act, 1978, omitted Article 257 A, but Entry 2A in the Union List, relating to deployment of armed forces inserted by the Forty-second Amendment, was retained. However, an assurance was given in Parliament that the Central forces would be deployed with the consent of the State concerned. Gyani Zail Singh, the then Home Minister in Mrs. Gandhi's Government, all the same, asserted in the House of the People that the Centre would not wait for a request from a State for the deployment of Central forces in case of communal riots and atrocities on Harijans and would itself take the initiative if the circumstances so demanded.

### Factors Responsible for Growth of Central Control

Many factors have helped in growth of central influence and control over the States during all these years. The first is the legacy of the British rule. Independent India inherited the tradition of a strong centre from the British. Before the Government of India Act, 1935, became operative on April 1, 1937 India had a unitary system of Government and the Provincial Governments were virtually the agents of the Government at Delhi. The 1935 Act set up a federal system (which did not become operative), but the Provinces became autonomous within the sphere assigned to them. There was really no autonomy for them as the Central Government continued to exercise its control and direction through devices like the Governor's special responsibilities and his obligations to act in his individual judgment. When the Governor acted in his discretion in the exercise of any of such powers, he was responsible to the Governor-General and through him to the Secretary of State for India. It had been the maxim of British policy that whenever some reforms accompanied by devolution of authority were conceded the tight control under the mechanism of superintendence and direction of the Government of India would remain the basic feature of all such reforms.

When India became Independent, the Government of India Act, 1935, provided a working machine in the Provinces. It was, therefore, not possible to start afresh. According to Ivor Jennings, the Government of India Act, 1935, was a bad precedent for the Constitution of an independent country,[38] for the scheme of federation as embodied in the 1950 Constitution is fundamentally the same as under the 1935 Act. Having no experience of participating in the federal system other than the one working in the country, the Constitution-makers could not think otherwise than to apply their knowledge which they had acquired all through those years, 1937 onwards. Nehru had probably foreseen it. He could not at that stage of the constitutional developments in India anticipate the shape of the things to come and the compelling exigencies which free India would have to face and resolve, but the importance of a strong centre was significantly apparent in Nehru's thinking. Nehru spoke for the Congress and the Congress spoke for the country after Independence. And the four leaders of the Constituent Assembly—Nehru, Patel, Prasad and Azad—were the four heroes of the independence movement.

There is another important point. The actual experience with the working of provincial autonomy, even within the restricted scope provided by the 1935 Act, was too short a period for the politically conscious sections of the people to become firmly attached to the concept of provincial autonomy. A few of them who could know what it precisely meant had to swallow the unitary provisions, especially relating to emergency, on the assurance of their leaders in the Constituent Assembly that those would not be required in practice. The emergency provisions in the 1950 Constitution resembled closely to those of the pre-Independence period against which they had

36. Riker William, H., *Federalism : Origin, Operation, Significance,* p. 86.
37. Six subjects in all were brought on the Concurrent List by the Forty-Second Amendment.
38. Jennings, W. I., *Some Characteristics of the Indian Constitution,* p. 56.

campaigned ardently. But the same persons who were governing the country were responsible for drafting the constitution and their awareness of the issues involved made the Assembly members to agree finally. Despite the assurances given and hopes expressed in the Constituent Assembly, resort to emergency provisions, particularly, under Article 356, forms a very important feature of Indian politics. The suspension of the Constitution of a State has been more often abused rather than used as a measure of last resort.

"Looking at the Centre for leadership and guidance may be regarded as part of India's culture."[39] It rather runs in the blood of Indians and they have always found solace in the authority and might of the Central Government. It has not a whit diminished with the setting up of a federal polity with limited and divided powers. Every person high or low, educated or otherwise, a politician or a layman begins from above for the solution of his problems or the redress of a grievance unmindful of the barriers which a federal polity creates. Worst of all are the demands to the President for suspending the constitution of a State or revoking it. Such demands have been made even by persons tall in political maturity and those who had been publicly condemning the presence of Articles 356 and 357 in the Constitution. Jayaprakash Narayan demanded it for the State of Bihar by dismissing the Ghafoor Ministry. Morarji demanded it for Gujarat by dismissing Chamanbhai Patel Ministry[40] on a threat of interminable fast. Once it had been conceded, Morarji asked for the revocation of the President's Rule. Whatever be the merits or justification for the demand by these political dignitaries, it is the political habit of the people that illustrates the point of finding ultimate refuge in the Central authority.

The uni-party rule and the charismatic leadership are the most important factors to strengthen the centralizing process. With Nehru as the unquestioned leader in the formative period of new India and the Congress Party in a virtually unchallengeable position at the Centre and more or less in an identical position in all the States for seventeen years, the power, control and prestige of the Union Government was tremendously augmented. When one single party rules the nation, without any electoral shock for such a long time, and more so when the same party had struggled for more than half a century to win freedom for India and achieved it, it regards itself as the custodian of that nation. With the traditions of a national movement reflected in its centralized structure, the central leadership of the Congress Party issued command policies and treated the State Governments as subordinates. When the State units of the Party organisation are ignored at every step and they have no voice, even a feeble one, in determining the party policy, the growth of predominance of the central authority is the natural consequence thereof. K. Santhanam aptly remarked that it was "the democratic centralism of the Congress during all these years that was responsible for the strength of the Central Government and the relative subordination of State Government."[41]

It had another aspect also. The State units of the Congress Party organisation prepared the list of candidates to contest elections to the State Legislatures, but the final selection had always been made by the Central Parliamentary Board of the Party. The persons who had the luck to be nominated as Party candidates and succeeded in the elections would always look to their benefactors at New Delhi and act on the cue emanating therefrom. Even nominations for the leadership of the State Legislature Party were and are made by the central Leadership. Quite often the person so nominated would be imported into the States to lead the Government. The Chief Ministers and the legislators, thus, became the mouthpiece of the Central Government. A breath that had made them could also unmake them. Punjab Chief Minister Ram Krishan would describe himself as the "driver of the High Command."

After the General Elections of 1967 Congress lost its majority in some nine States and the non-Congress governments of the United Front came into office. The sense of consciousness and self-assertiveness of these States increased and they became quite vocal about the Centre-State relations. The Leftist Governments in Kerala and West Bengal adopted an open policy of confrontation and defied the authority of the Union Government on a number of issues. The Union Government itself in minority in Parliament, after the 1969 Congress split, and dependent upon its existence on the support of the Communist Party, Dravida Munnetra Kazhagam (DMK) and the Akalis had to swallow the bitter pill. The DMK

39. Venkatrangaiya, M., and Shiviah, M., *Indian Federalism,* p. 96.
40. Jayaprakash Narayan supported Desai's demand.
41. Santhanam, K., *Union-State Relations in India,* pp. 61-62.

Government in Tamil Nadu became vocal in its demand for autonomy to the States. But the 1971 mid-term Parliamentary poll and the General Elections to the State Assemblies, except Tamil Nadu, in March 1972, brought the Congress back to the same position that existed before 1967. The charismatic leadership of Mrs. Indira Gandhi gave a new direction to the Indian politics. The manner in which she dealt with the Bangladesh issue and the victory in war with Pakistan evoked widespread respect to the extent of worship for her. The Congress Party and its central bodies drew inspiration from Mrs. Gandhi notwithstanding her rebuttal to the contrary. The Central leadership of the uni-party in office assumed the role of the patriarch in controlling and running the administration of the States. The Janata Party followed close in the heels of the Congress when it came into power in March 1977 and soon dissolved the Assemblies in nine States in an earnest bid to establish a uni-party government at the Centre as well as in those States. The Party organisation was also similarly centralised and the Central leadership nominated Chief Ministers to be formally elected by the State Legislative Party and quite often replaced them at will. Old habits seldom die and Mrs. Gandhi again did the same in the States in 1980 what she had been doing earlier to 1977. This time criterion of personal loyalty weighed with her more heavily in selecting candidates for the State Assemblies and nominating Chief Ministers. Rajiv Gandhi did precisely the same as his mother did and there was absolutely no deviation in his style of functioning and the element of personal loyalty weighed as heavily and extensively as before.

Financial authority, like political authority, under a federal scheme should be decentralised as financial independence is a large part of general independence. According to the 1950 Constitution the taxes on the Legislative List remain much the same as under the Government of India Act, 1935. While the proceeds on the taxes within the State List are entirely retained by the States, the proceeds of some of the taxes in the Union List are to be assigned or may be assigned wholly or partly to the States. The residuary taxing authority rests with the Union. Besides these, the Constitution provides for payment of grants. Under Article 275 Parliament is empowered to make such grants as it may deem necessary to give financial aid to any State which is in need of assistance. It is for Parliament to determine the extent of the grant and it may vary from State to State according to the needs of each. Under Article 282 the Union and the State Governments are given the general power to make grants for any public purpose even if it is not within their respective legislative competence.

In both income tax and excise duties there has been continuous rise in the share of State Governments. While in 1952 the States used to receive 50 per cent of the net proceeds of the income tax and no share in the excise revenue, their share in these, as consequent upon the recommendations of the Sixth Finance Commission, had gone up to 80 per cent of income tax and 20 per cent of the Union excise duties. However, the States are now entitled to receive revenue from auxiliary taxes which hitherto were non-shareable. The biggest transfer of resources is of grants-in-aid which are generally given to comparatively backward States and these have been stepped up by three and a half times over the recommendations of the Fifth Finance Commission from Rs. 711 crores to 2,510 crores. Financial assistance and grants-in-aid are a prolific source of central control and direction. They are made subject to conditions and are fallowed by regulatory authority of the Union Government.

Also, the transfer of resources from the Centre to the States occurs for meeting the deficits of States on plan expenditure. While the States have to share 50 per cent of the aggregate public sector plan expenditure, the resources normally accruing to them from this purpose are not more than 20 per cent and 80 per cent of these resources accrue to the Union Government. As a result of continuously mounting expenditure of States on Plan and non-Plan expenditure and their inflexible resources, the gap between resources and expenditure between the States has been considerably widening. Despite liberal transfers from the Centre, the State Governments resorted to the technique of overdrafts which the Union Government converted into loans. This created an embarrassing situation for the States. "The predominance of discretionary grants," as G. Ramachandran pointed out, "has given to the Central Government a powerful leverage in influencing the policies and programmes of State Governments even in spheres such as education, medical and public health, which are constitutionally within the competence of States." Among the various factors which have been a constant source of irritation between the Centre and the States, he adds, the preponderance of discretionary grants and loans should be assigned an important place."[42]

The Study Team of the Administrative Reforms Commission observed, "To some extent financial dependence of the States is desirable as representing a centripetal force. But the magnitude of such dependence makes a qualitative difference when the extent of dependence goes too far, wrong attitudes begin to make an appearance among those responsible for financial management in the States as well as the Centre."[43] In the States excessive dependence on the Centre tends to produce irresponsibility and operational inefficiency. At the Centre dominant financial power in relation to States gives central authorities exaggerated notions of their importance and knowledge and does not allow sufficient place to the point of view of the States. It is important, therefore, the Study Team of the Administrative Reforms Commission suggested, that "the degree of financial dependence of the States on the Centre should be reduced to the minimum because that minimum would be adequate from the point of view of giving the Centre controlling powers in the context of national integration."[44]

But the main focus of study in the causes of the ascendancy of powers of the Union *vis-a-vis* the States is the Planning Commission. Though not a creation of the Constitution, not even endowed with a statutory sanction, this extra constitutional authority has assumed the role of the architect of India's destiny. The Five-Year Plans have reduced the federal structure to almost a unitary system and the authority of the States has been brought to a marginal phenomenon. Planning for purposes of economic development, remarks Santhanam, "practically superseded the federal constitution so far as States were concerned but this supersession was not legal or constitutional but was by agreement or consent."[45] Planning has been comprehensive and it has covered all the sphere of activities of both the Union and the States. In fact, it has even covered the sphere of literature and sports. Under educational planning, grants have been given for establishing gymnasia, or cricket coaching, etc. "So the planning may in some sense be called totalitarian, but for the evil association of the world totalitarianism."[46]

Planning and federalism make uneasy partners and the emphasis on the former has profound effects on Union-State financial relations. The Planning Commission is a centrally created, centrally financed and a centrally controlled body. Till recently, half the number of its members were the nominees of the government. The Prime Minister has been its Chairman and the Union Minister of Planning, its Vice-Chairman, except during certain years. The Janata Party Government reconstituted the Planning Commission with a new Vice-Chairman and two new full time members. The three Cabinet Ministers—the Finance Minister, the Defence Minister and the Minister for Home Affairs— were all included, thus, supplementing economic expertise with political backing. Mrs. Indira Gandhi reversed the process initiated by Morarji Desai and appointed in 1980 the Planning Minister as the Commission's Vice-Chairman. The position was again reversed when National Front Government came into power in 1989 and continues to be so till now. But at no stage now or before, the States have been represented on the Commission and it accounts for the Commission's centralised approach.

The Constitution-makers had visualized planning as a joint venture and consequently included "Economic and Social Planning" in the Concurrent List. The importance of subjects included in the State List in developmental planning is brought about by the fact that more than 60 per cent of the expenditure of the total expenditure of planning in all the Five-Year Plans is on all such subjects. But during all these years the role of the Centre in the formulation and execution of plans "became paramount and that of the States quite subsidiary."[47] It is true that partnership between the Centre and States has become more real in successive exercises and the Planning Commission has taken due notice of this important fact. In shaping the Plan at different stages and giving it a final form the National Development Council—a representative body of the States Chief Ministers—is consulted and its approval is sought. But the role of the National

42. G. Ramachandran, "Centre-State Relations," (*Paper contributed to the National Convention of Union-State Relations,* 1976), pp. 231-32.
43. Report of the Study Team on "Centre-State Relations," *Administrative Reforms Commission,* Vol. 1, 1968, p. 23.
44. *Ibid.*
45. Santhanam, K., *Union-State Relations in India,* p. 42.
46. *Ibid.*
47. Venkatrangaiya, M., and Shiviah, M., *Indian Federation* p. 107.

Development Council is only formal. It has neither the time nor the expert knowledge so essentially required to scrutinise the Plan as formulated by the Planning Commission.[48]

In addition to the schemes included in the State Plan there are some outside them known as "Centrally sponsored schemes." These schemes are sponsored by the Centre and executed by the State Governments under the technical guidance and supervision of the appropriate Ministries of the Union Government. In the beginning the Centrally sponsored schemes were just a few but now their number has sufficiently multiplied. They deal with subjects enumerated in the State List with the result that the supervision and control of the Union Ministries has penetrated into the State Ministries. "To this extent the result, for all practical purposes, is to make such subjects concurrent or central by the central donor."[49] The Forty-second Amendment transferred education, forests, population control and family planning and a few more subjects to the Concurrent List.

Article 365 of the Constitution gives a general power to the Union Government that if a State Government failed to give effect to, or comply with any directions given in the exercise of its executive power, the President may declare that a situation had arisen in which the Government of the State cannot be carried on in accordance with the Constitution. This provision is a paradise for the Union Government to assert its authority and bring the defaulting State Governments under its unitary control. The satisfaction of the President that a situation has arisen in which the Government of the State cannot be carried on in accordance with the provisions of the Constitution is final and conclusive.

Article 355 confers a duty on the Union Government to protect the States from external aggression and internal disturbance and to ensure that the government of every State is carried on in accordance with the provisions of the Constitution. If the President either on a report from the Governor of a State or on his own satisfaction believes that the State cannot be governed in accordance with the provisions of the Constitution, he may by proclamation assume the functions of the State executive and declare that the powers of the State Legislature shall be exercised by or under the authority of Parliament. But Governors in quite a number of instances abused this power vested in them under Article 356 and recommended the imposition of the President's rule under suspect circumstances. A provision included in the Constitution (Article 355) charging the Union to maintain integrity of a constituent unit of the federation has very often been used to coerce a State Ministry when it did not belong to the same party or when central leadership desired to improve its party's image in the State or even to remove dissensions and replace it by another leader to become the Chief Minister. Since 1950 the President's rule, excluding its imposition in one single stroke on nine States in April 1977 and once again, in February 1980, has been imposed on different States for more than eighty-four times. Save a few occasions, the action taken on the defaulting States can be described as political and having no constitutional justification.

The Governor, therefore, is not an inert cypher. He occupies a pivotal position in the State Government as an instrument of Central vigilance and control. He is appointed by the President but in terms of constitutional practice he is actually appointed by the Prime Minister and retains office at his pleasure. It is, under the circumstances, not difficult to appreciate that a Governor may become suspect of acting under the pressure of the Union Government in relation to his functions in the State of which he is the Head. When the Party in power in a State is different from the party in power at the Centre, the Governor and his Council of Ministers are likely to pull in different directions if the interests of the Union and the State differ. The Union Government may even use the Government for influencing or controlling the policy of the State Government and if the Governor fails to impress the State Ministry with his directions from the Union Government, the President may on his report take over administration of the State notwithstanding the majority it commands in the State Legislature. It happened in 1970-71 in the States with non-Congress Governments and in 1976 in Tamil Nadu with DMK Party in office. Early in 1991, the DMK Government was again dismissed by the President. Normally, the President is moved to action under Article 356 on the report of the Governor. But in this case the President dismissed the Ministry without having re-

48. Report of the Study Team on Centre-State Relations, *Administrative Reforms Commission*, Vol. 1, pp. 102-04.
49. *Ibid.*

ceived any report from the Governor for such an action. Though within the bounds of law, the action of the President was widely criticised and was deemed even suspect. It damaged the dignity and office of the President.

Then, the Governor can withhold assent to a Bill passed by the State Legislature or to reserve it for the considertion of the President. "On what ground then except that of the Union Government's discretion," asked Kogekar, "can the Governor stultify the Legislature's Power ?"[50] Acting on the advice of the Prime Minster, the President may return the Bill for reconsideration by the State Legislature for reasons stated or even veto it without assigning any r easons.To be safe, it may be pigeonholed as the Constitution does not prescribe time limit for Presidential consideration.

The constituent units have no independent power of amending the constitution and the process involved therein, except for a few specified matters in Article 368 when ratification by Legislatures of at least half the number of States is necessary to render the amendment valid. The law of Parliament may even change the political map of India. Whenever a change in the name, areas or boundaries of a State is proposed to be altered, the President simply ascertains the views of the Legislature of a State or States concerned which must be expressed within the period specified by the President. The views of the States or State Legislatures concerned are not binding on the President. Even a decision abolishing the Legislative Council in a State, if it has one, or for its creation in a State without one, depends on the law of Parliament.

The scheme of distribution of subjects between the Union and the States follows essentially the pattern of the Government of India Act, 1935, and it is heavily tilted in favour of the Union. If both the Union and a State legislate on a matter contained in the Concurrent List and if the law made by the State Legislature is repugnant to any provision of the law made by Parliament on the same subject, the Union law supersedes the State law. Parliament is also empowered, under Article 249, to legislate on any matter in the State List, if the Council of States (Rajya Sabha) passes a resolution by a two-thirds majority declaring a particular subject or subjects to be of national interest. When the Legislature of one or more States determine by a resolution that Parliament should legislate on a particular matter in the State List, Parliament can make laws with respect to that particular matter or matters.[51] Finally, Article 253 empowers Parliament to pass legislation implementing any treaty, agreement or convention with another country or any decision made at any international conference, association or other body.

Then, there is the Election Commission established under Article 324. It is a centralised election machinery which is required to surperintend, direct and control elections not only to Parliament but also to the State Legislatures. There is also the Comptroller and Auditor-General, appointed by the President, who keeps careful vigilance not only on the finances of the Union but also of the States. As Comptroller, he controls the issue of public money, his duty being to satisfy himself that no money is paid out of the exchequer without proper legal authority. As auditor, he audits the accounts and reports annually to the President or Governors of States, as the case may be.

**Proposals to Remove the Imbalances**

The working of the Constitution, therefore, establishes that since 1950 many events that had occurred have a direct or indirect bearing on the Centre-State relations. Presenting the 1961 budget to the Tamil Nadu State Assembly, C. N. Annadurai said, "There has been a considerable change in the matrix of Centre-State financial relations since the provisions of the Constitution in this regard were settled. There have been a number of new trends and developments which could not have been visualised when the Indian Constitution was framed.....Through a new institution (Planning Commission) which was beyond the ken of the architects of the Constitution, the Centre has acquired still more large powers, causing concern about the position of the States." He emphasised the need for setting up a high-powered Committee to examine the working of the Constitution and for re-allocating powers, if necessary, between the Union and the States. Annadurai had earlier expressed the view that the powers which strictly came under the State sphere were being slowly taken over by the these Centre, "We must correct this," he urged, "and leave thee powers to the States."

It was in this context that the Tamil Nadu Government set up a committee, under the chair-

50. "Some Characteristics of the Indian Constitution," *The Indian Journal of Political Science,* April-June, 1950, p. 62.
51. Article 252 (2).

manship of Dr. P. V. Rajamannar.[52] The terms of reference of the committee, which reflected the DMK Government's policy, were to consider the entire question regarding the relationship that should subsist between the Centre and the States in a federal set-up and to examine the existing provisions of the Constitution and to suggest measures necessary for augumenting the resources of the States without prejudice to the sovereignty and integrity of the country as a whole. The Committee submitted its report in May 1971. The recommendations of the Committee amounted to a demand for rewriting many of the basic provisions of the Constitution, though it disclaimed any intention to disturb the essential framework of the Constitution. The Committee, accordingly suggested a series of changes that would divest the Centre of a range of fiscal, legislative, regulatory and emergency powers. In federalism, the Committee observed, the national and State Governments exist on the basis of equality and neither has the power to make inroads on the definite authority and functions of the other unilaterally. Their model was the United States Constitution.

The Centre-State relations became the subject of investigation by the Administrative Reforms Commission in the mid-sixties. In order to probe thoroughly the various issues involved in this relationship the Commission appointed a Study Team headed by M.C. Setalvad, the former Attorney-General of India. On the basis of the report of the Study Team, the Commission submitted its own report on June 19, 1969. Referring to the controversies that had arisen between the Centre and the States, the Commission observed, "but these controversies pertain mostly to matters administrative and financial and not to constitutional issues." Eminent political leaders of various political parties that appeared before the Commission emphasised their faith in the Indian unity, though they argued for more autonomy and initiative for the States. The Commission, accordingly, did not think it necessary to suggest any amendment to the Constitution. They, however, made recommendations to the delegation of more financial and administrative functions and powers to the States with the twin objectives of making the relations between the Centre and the States more smoother and introducing efficiency and economy in the administration of the Union and State Governments. The Commission believed that the amendment of the Constitution was not a solution of the problems of Centre-State relationship. It should be sought "in the working of the provisions of the Constitution by all concerned in the balanced spirit in which founding-fathers intended them to be worked."

The Union Government completely ignored the Rajamannar Committee Report, but accepted the view of the Administrative Reforms Commission. The Government felt that the existing provisionsof the Constitutionwere adequate to meet any situation or resolve any problem that might arise between the Centre and the States. It was the firm conviction of the Government that the basic scheme of the Indian Constitution was a federation with a strong Centre, and the doctrine of a nebulous and weak Centre, as envisaged in the Rajamannar Committee Report, ran counter to the concept of the powers of the Union Government accepted by the Constituent Assembly. However, the Government thought that there was room for strengthening of the financial powers of the States and steps were taken in that direction. Decentralization was one of the two items on the March 1977 poll manifesto of the Janata Party. The Union Commerce Minister, Mohan Dharia, declared on June 6, 1977 at Madras that the Janata Party Government which stood for decentralization of powers to "ensure real power lay with the people" would give more powers to the States to make them strong. Once this was achieved there would be no need for any regional party to raise the State autonomy demand. But nothing happened during three years of Janata Lok Dal rule. Mrs. Gandhi's Government adhered to the old stand, although decentralization remained an unceasing dogma of every Government. Compelling reasons, however, influenced the decision of the Government of India when Prime Minister Indira Gandhi announced in March 1983 the appointment of Sarkaria Commission to review the Centre-State relations.

### Sarkaria Commission Report

The three-member Commission, consisting of Justice Ranjit Sigh Sarkaria, a retired Judge of the Supreme Court (Chairman), B. Sivaraman and S.R. Sen (Member) on Centre-State relations, submitted its Report, covering 5,000 pages, to the Prime Minister on October 20, 1987. The Commission was appointed on June 9, 1983 at the height of the Akali agitation in Punjab. It was initially given one year to complete its work,

52. Dr. A Lakshmana Swami Mudaliar and P. Chandra Reddy were its two other members.

but its term was extended four times until October 31, 1987 to report on the entire gamut of the Centre-State relations. The summary of the Report was officially released on January 30, 1988.

The Sarkaria Commission has refrained, in the main, from making any radical recommendations on institutional structures. It outright rejected the demand for curtailing the powers of the Centre and maintained that a strong Centre is necessary to preserve national unity and integrity of the country. In its view the fundamental provisions of the Constitution have done reasonably well and withstood the stresses and strains of the heterogeneous society in throes of change and, consequently, it does not find any need for drastic changes.

In the financial sphere also the Commission did not see any justification for major modification in the basic scheme of the Constitution dividing the fields of taxation between the Centre and the States. It has, however, favoured amendments to the Constitution to provide for sharing of corporation tax and levy of consignment tax and tax on advertisements in broadcasting.

The Commission has, in fact, dealt with financial relations between the Centre and the States in detail. It has rejected almost all the suggestions to shift the taxation powers of the Centre to the States. Some of the subjects suggested for such shifting are terminal taxes on goods and passengers by railways, estate duty, banking, etc. The suggestion to provide for levy of additional sales tax in lieu of excise has also been rejected. Regarding agricultural income tax, the Commission has concluded that the opinions are divided and, accordingly, the matter should be examined in depth. The Commission is also not in favour of suggestion that devolution of funds to the States would be made automatic. It has recommended that an expert committee should be set up to examine taxation reforms and resource mobilization.

The Commission has observed that the present division of functions between the Finance Commission and the Planning Commission is reasonable and should continue. The terms of reference of Finance Commission, however, be drawn up in consultation with the State Governments. Similar expert bodies should be set up at the State levels also, the Commission proposed. Observing that the need for national planning is undisputed, the Commission observed that planning and implementation should be a cooperative process between the Centre and the States. The Commission is not in favour of granting of an exalted autonomous status to the Planning Commission. The Commission also recommended that the loan grant pattern of Central assistance should be reviewed and the number of centrally sponsored grants for projects should be kept to the minimum.

The Commission felt that the supremacy of Parliament envisaged in Articles 246 and 254 is essential and needs no modification. The only suggestion given in this respect is that residual matters other than taxation could be in the Concurrent List. Without directly referring to the Anandpur Sahib resolution the Commission expressed the view that there should be no limiting of the powers of the Union. Various suggestions asking for the transfer of subjects to the State or Concurrent List have been rejected. Transfer of subjects like preventive detention, education, labour, and electricity, the Commission says, could disturb the basic scheme of the Constitution and, therefore, is uncalled for. The Commission has, however, recommended a process of consultation by the Centre on all the Concurrent subjects, which is not being done at present.

The Commission has made a strong case for inter-State Council, which it names inter-Governmental Council, under Article 263. The Council could, however, be used only for the purposes mentioned in the aforesaid Article. The National Development Council, the Commission recommends, should be retained and the Zonal Councils activated.

On the deployment of Central forces, it has been recommended that the Union Government should have full powers to decide on such deployment and the State concerned should cooperate. The deployment could be made regardless of the wishes of the State Government, if necessary. However, there should be no change in the relationship between the Union armed forces and the State civil authorities. The Centre should consult and seek co-operation of the State Government before declaring a particular area within the State as a "disturbed" one.

The Commission has rejected all suggestions to modify the role of the Council of States (Rajya Sabha) and the Centre's power to the reorganisation of the States. The Commission has emphatically suggested the retention of the existing provisions in the Constitution. No change is also necessary to amend the procedure laid down in Article 368 in relation to the State of Jammu and Kashmir. While reiterating that the supremacy of the Union in the executive field should remain intact, it has recommended that more extensive and generous use of Article 258 should be made to decentralize Central powers.

The Commission has categorically rejected the demand for autonomy for radio and television. The Commission has upheld the Union Government's contention that broadcasting should remain with the Centre and that the present moment was not appropriate for granting autonomy to the two mass media. It should, however, he ensured, the Commission observed, that there should be decentralisation to a reasonable extent in the day-to- day operations of the radio and the television, and use of simple Hindustani for broadcasts is encouraged. It suggested that Hindi used in broadcasts should be enriched by assimilating common words from Hindustani and other languages referred in Article 351 (directive for development of Hindi language) Eighth Schedule.

The Commission said effective steps should be taken to uniformly implement the "three language formula" in its true spirit in the interest of the unity and integrity of the country. The Commission noted that in the process of developing Hindi, it is neither desirable nor necessary to replace commonly understood terms by difficult Sanskritised words. The Commission said that Government service is an important avenue for the educated in India. Proficiency in a particular language need not be insisted upon at the time of recruitment to ensure that language is not used as a factor to create difficulties in recruitment or subsequent career in the service.

The Commission, however, gives to state language primacy in the transaction of governmental work. The work of the Union and State Governments, which directly affects the local people, must be carried out in the local language. The Commission has observed that this is even more important in a welfare state.

It is, therefore, necessary that all forms, applications, letters, Bills, notices etc. are available in the local language as well as the official language. This is of equal relevance to State Governments which have sizeable linguistic minorities concentrated in certain areas. The Commissioner of Linguistic Minorities should be activated.

On civil services, the Commission said that there should be no move to disband the all-India services as it would undermine national integrity. The Union Government should persuade the States to agree to the constitution of all-India services for education, engineers, medical and health as recommended by the Estimates Committee. It also suggested that after creating a pool of officers from the Centre and States in agriculture, cooperation and industry, all-India services in these sectors could be set up.

Emphasising the need for further strengthening of th services through periodical dialogue between the Union and the States, there should be an element of compulsion in the matter of deputation of officers of all-India services to the Union. Every all-India service officer, whether a direct recruit or promotee, should be required to put in a minimum period under the Union Government and for this purpose, the minimum number of spells of deputation to Union should be laid down for direct recruits and promoted officers separately.

The Commission recommended that all-India services should be further strengthened. This could be achieved through well-planned improvement in selection, training, deployment, development and promotion policies and methods. The present accent on generalism should yield place to greater specialisation in one or more areas of public administration.

The Commission urged the Union Government to dissuade State Governments from using the powers of transfer, promotion, posting and suspension of all-India services in order to "discipline" them. The Commission is of the view that no change is necessary in the present disciplinary procedures and rules relating to all- India service officers, except in the matter of suspension.

The Commission suggested the setting up of an advisory council for personnel administration of the all-India services with the Union Cabinet Secretary as chairman. The advisory council would advise the Union and State Governments. It should meet periodically and regularly and suggest solutions to the problems offered to it by the Union and State Governments.

The Sarkaria Commission recommended that the institution of Governor must stay, but has given in its report comprehensive guidelines for appointment of Governor. It says that a politician from the ruling party at the Union should not be appointed as Governor of a State which is being ruled by some other party or combination of other parties. It has been suggested that Article 155 of the Constitution should be suitably amended to prescribe consultations with the State Chief Minister on the appointment of the Governor. The Commission has stipulated that a person to be appointed as a Governor should satisfy the following criteria :—

He should be eminent in some walk of life; he should be a person from outside the State; he should not be too intimately connected with the local politics of the State; and he should be a person who has not taken too great a part in politics generally, and particularly in the recent past. The Commission has recommended that the Vice-President of India and the Speaker of the House of the People may be consulted by the Prime Minister in selecting a Governor. The consultation should be confidential and not a matter of constitutional obligation.

The Governor's tenure of office of five years in a State should not be disturbed, except very rarely and that, too, for extremely compelling reasons. The Commission has recommended that as a matter of convention, the Governor should not on demitting his office be eligible for any other appointment of office of profit under the Union or a State Government, except for second term as Governor or election as Vice-President of India. Such a convention should require that after quitting or laying down his office, the Governor shall not return to active partisan politics. The Commission has also recommended that a Governor should, at the end of his tenure, irrespective of its duration, be given reasonable post-retirement provisions for himself and for his surviving spouse. The aim of the Commission is to make apolitical person as Governor.

Article 356 of the Constitution, the Commission recommends, should be invoked for Central intervention in States very sparingly and only as a measure of "last resort." The Centre should step in only when all available alternatives fail to prevent or rectify a breakdown of constitutional machinery of the State. Before taking action under Article 356, any explanation received from the State Government should be taken into account. However, this may not be possible in a situation when not taking immediate action would lead to disastrous consequences. The Commission has suggested that when an "external aggression" or "internal disturbance" paralyses the State administration creating a situation drifting towards a potential breakdown of the constitutional machinery of the State, all alternative courses as available to the Union under Article 356 should be exhausted to contain the situation.

In a situation of political breakdown, the Governor should explore the possibilities of having a government enjoying majority support in the State Assembly. If it is not possible for such a government to be installed and if fresh elections can be held without avoidable delay, he should ask the outgoing Ministry, if there is one, to continue as a care-taker government provided the Ministry was defeated solely on a policy issue. The Governor should then dissolve the Assembly, leaving the resolution of the constitutional crisis to the electorate. During the intervening period, the care-taker government should be allowed to carry on the day-to-day government but prevented from taking any policy decision.

The Commission has pointed out that if these important ingredients were absent, it would not be proper for the Governor to dissolve the Assembly and install a care-taker government. The Governor should then recommend proclamation of President's rule, but without dissolving the Assembly.

The Commission has recommended that every proclamation be placed before each House of Parliament at the earliest, in any case before the expiry of the two-month period contemplated in Clause 3 of Article 356. The State Assembly should not be dissolved either by the Governor or President before Parliament considers the proclamation. Article 356 should be suitably amended to ensure this. The Commission has also recommended that all material facts and grounds on which Article 356 (I) is invoked should be made an integral part of the proclamation issued under the Article.

The Commission is of the view that normally, the President is moved to action under Article 356 on the report of the Governor. The report of the Governor is placed before each House of Parliament. This report of the Governor which is crucial in the political life of the State concerned should be a "speaking document," containing a precise and clear statement of all material facts and grounds on the basis of which the President may satisfy himself as to the existence or otherwise of the situation contemplated in Article 356.

The Commission is of the view that when a resolution passed by the Legislative Assembly of a State for the abolition or creation of a Legislative Council in the State is received, the President shall cause the resolution to be placed, within a reasonable time, before Parliament together with the comments of the Union Government. Parliament may accept or reject the request contained in the resolution. If the resolution is adopted by Parliament, the Union government shall introduce necessary legislation for implementation by amending the Constitution, if necessary.

A major recommendation of the Commission relates to time-bound completion of the consultative process for appointment of High Court Judges. The Commission says that Article 217 relating to appointment and conditions of office of a Judge of a High Court should be amended and another clause be inserted. The clause suggested by the Commission says that : "The President may, after consultation with the Chief Justice of India, make rules for giving effect to the provisions of clause 1 of the Article, and in order to ensure that vacancies in the posts of Judges in the High Courts are promptly filled in, these rules may prescribe a time schedule within which the various functionaries having consultative role in the appointment of Judges under the Article shall complete their part of the process."

The Commission has come out against the transfer of Judges of High Courts without their consent. It has been recommended that the convention that High Court Judges were not transferred without their consent should continue to be observed. The Commission also felt that the advice given by the Chief Justice of India regarding a proposal to transfer a Judge from one High Court to another, after taking into account the latter's reaction and the difficulties, if any, should as a rule of prudence be invariably accepted by the President and seldom departed from. It also felt that as a matter of healthy practice the Chief Justice of India should before formulating an opinion in his individual judgment as to the proposed transfer of a Judge from one High Court to another, take into confidence two senior Judges of the Supreme Court and obtain their views.

The Commission has also found a case for providing safeguards against misuse of powers relating to appointments of Commissions of Inquiry. It does not, however, find it necessary to amend the Constitution for the purpose. In its opinion the fact that power is capable of being misused, is no ground for amending the Constitution.

The Commission has suggested that the safeguards can be :

That no Commission of Inquiry against an incumbent or former Minister of a State Government on charges of abuse of power or mis-conduct shall be appointed by Union Government unless both the Houses of Parliament, by resolution of majority of members present and voting, require the Union Government to appoint such a Commission.

No Commission of Inquiry shall be appointed to inquire into the conduct of a Minister (incumbent or former) of a State Government with respect to a matter of public importance touching his conduct while in office unless the proposal is first placed before the Inter-State Council (which the Commission designates as inter-governmental Council) and has been cleared by it.

Appropriate safeguards on these lines be provided in the Commissions of Inquiry Act, 1952 itself against the misuse of this power, while appointing a Commission to inquire into the conduct of a Minister or Ministers of a State Government.

The Commission suggested the formation of a Standing Committee for the Union Territories. All matters which need to be sorted out between the Central Government and the Union Territory with a Legislature may be dicussed by the Standing Committee. The Committee may have the Union Home Minister as Chairman and the Lieutenant-Governor and Chief Minister of the Union Territory as members. When a matter concerning a Union Ministry other than Home Affairs comes up before the Committee, the Central Minister concerned may be associated. But the Standing Committee may not deal with matters which can appropriately be discussed in the Zonal Council or in the National Economic and Development Council.

The Sarkaria Commission, to sum up, does not favour structural changes, regards the existing constitutional scheme and provisions relating to the institutions basically sound, not only to preserve and protect the unity and integrity of the country, but also to coordinate a uniform, integrated policy on issues that concern the nation as a whole. The distribution of powers, between the Union and the States, made by the Constitution reconciles the imperatives of a strong Centre in a plural society with the need of State autonomy, the Commission noted. At the same time, the Sarkaria Commission makes out strong case in the interest of harmony for changes in the functional or operational aspects, be it with regard to the appointment of Governors, use of Article 356, the High Court Judges especially relating to their appointment and transfer from one High Court to another, the setting up of the Inter-Governmental Council (Inter-State Council provided in Article 263) for resolving Centre-State problems, the National Development Council to get constitutional status, enlarging financial resources of the State, restraints on Central law making on Concurrent List subjects and the role of the Planning Commission.

All this means rejection of not only the Akali Dal's demands as enshrined in the Anandpur Sahib resolution, CPI(M)'s demand for greater autonomy, but also the philosophy behind the Telugu Desam's position that the Centre is a myth. The Commission has also rejected the suggestions of the West Bengal Government, CPI(M), the DMK and the AIADMK for abolishing the post of Governor or doing away with the all-India Services. Whereas in the appointment of Governor, it has recommended that the Constitution should formally stipulate that the Centre must consult the Chief Minister of a State before appointment, the Commission has made concrete suggestions regarding the exapansion of All-India Services and strengthening of the personnel management.

The rationale of the Sarkaria Commission is clear. It wants an element of trust, mutual accommodation and understanding to impregnate in the dealings of the Centre and the States the lack of which, it has impliedly conceded, had led to distortions in the last forty years of the life of Independent India. The Commission Report on the whole vindicates the stand taken by the Congress (I) in its memorandum, though it suggests flexibility (in the Centre-State dealings) of an order that had not been evident in the past under the Congress rule.

All the political parties, however, have not taken kindly the recommendations of the Sarkaria Commission, well argued and balanced as they are. The United Akali Dal Leader and former Pubjab Chief Minister Prakash Singh Badal described the report as dishonest. Ramkrishna Hegde, former Chief Minister of Karnataka State, accused the Commission of adopting "one-sided approach" and regretted that it should have marred its work by pronounced centrist bias. CPI(M) General Secretary, E.M.S. Namboodiripad, said that the Sarkaria Commission had been guided by the politics of Congress (I) and the Bharatiya Janata Party which advocated a strong Centre in the name of national unity, thus, negating State autonomy leading to tensions between the Centre and the constituent States.

The Home Minister told the Parliamentary Consultative Committee attached to his Ministry on July 16, 1988, that the Centre was keen on eliciting the opinion on the recommendations of the Sarkaria Commission from the State Governments, Members of Parliament and others before taking any decision on the serious issues of Centre-State relations. But no action was taken by the Congress(I) Government on any matter. Nor did the succeeding National Front and Samajwadi Janata Governments make any serious attempt. The only creditable achievement had been the setting up of the Inter-State Council under Article 263 of the Constitution for which a strong case was made by the Sarkaria Commission.

The Inter-State Council met in October 1990 and appointed a Sub- Committee to consider the recommedations of the Sarkaria Commission. The first meeting of the Sub-Committee was held on September 24, 1991 and some concrete suggestions were produced in the sphere of legislative relations between the Centre and the States. The most important of them was the acceptance of the Sarkaria Commission's recommendation providing for extensive consultations with States before the Centre legislates on any subject included in the Concurrent List. The Prime Minister P.V. Narasimha Rao, addressing the concluding session of the two-day conference of Governors, December 27-28, 1991, declared that the future Centre-State relations would be based on a spirit of co- operation with States advising the Centre on matters concerning them. He also explained that the National Development Council (NDC) had constitued a Standing Committee to go into the question of Centre-State relations in its entirety.

The role of the Inter-State Council and its Sub-Committee assumes a crucial importance in view of the stengthening of secessionist tendencies in the three border States of Assam, Punjab and Jammu and Kashmir and the growth of centrifugal forces elsewhere in the country. Much of the restiveness of the States could be traced to the fact that the resources of the States have not grown commensurate with their added responsibilities as constituent units of the Welfare State, which has increased their reliance on the Centre even in the sphere earmarked for them. This has been compounded by the blatant misuse of office of the Governor to dismiss State Governments found inconvenient by the Party in office at the

Centre and the denial of any role to the States in deciding the criteria for devolution of funds.

Besides the alarming happenings in Kashmir and Punjab, the inter-caste communal tensions building up elsewhere, the deepening economic and social disparities and the regional imbalances emerging from time to time, there is a cause of real concern. Certain foreign developments deepen the fears about the future of the Indian federation. If the once mighty Soviet Union can be reduced to a mere Commonwealth of twelve Sovereign and Independent Republics, how can it be taken for granted that the foundation of the Indian federation will remain unshaken. In a significant statement Prakash Singh Badal, President of the moderate faction of the Akali Dal and a former Chief Minister of Punjab, sounded a note of warning lest India goes the Soviet way and demanded that India should be decalred a Commonwealth of autonomous States and all the autonomous States be given full constitutional rights to pursue their regional, ethnic and religious identities.[53]

The very thought whether India as a federation will survive may appear blasphemous, but considering the unseemly happenings all over the country the need to correct the distortions in the Indian federal set up has become imperative. It is, indeed, unfortunate that no government and no political party has taken a decisive step in that direction. There have been only half-hearted attempts to tackle this problem of restructuring the Centre-State relations. In this context the observation of Rasheeduddin Khan, a political scientist, that "There is a historic warning focus in India, to put our house in order, before accumulated problems erode and dismantle our unique federal identity" is significant.

In his study of Indian federalism,[54] Rasheeduddin Khan, not only places the problem in the right perspective but spells out a design for change which will correct the imbalances in the Indian Federal set-up. His plan has four major aspects each of which calls for close study. They are : territorial re-organisation of the existing States; recasting Centre-State relations on a rational and co-operative basis; activisation of the Panchayati Raj and Nagarpalika system at the grassroot level; and, building a consensus among the people and the political parties on the four "critical value" of the Indian Republic—democracy, secular polity, social justice and federal-nation building.

The stress laid by the Prime Minister P.V Narasimha Rao at the Governors' Conference, December 27-28, 1991 on need to foster the cooperative spirit in working the federal principle is a welcome step in the right direction. He made a sound appeal for the revitalisation of the co-operative spirit. The maintenance of a free and pluralised society and the formulation and implementation of public policy on a consensual basis can be assured through a genuine devolution of powers and responsibilities to the lowest levels of governmental organisation and through the establishment of a system based on a true co-operative federal spirit.

**The Republic of India**

The Preamle to the Constitution declares that India is a sovereign democratic Republic. The Indian Independence Act, 1947, contained the constitutional relationship of the Crown of Britain and the Dominion of India by providing, that the Governor-General of India would be appointed by the King and he represented His Majesty for the purpose of the Government of the Dominion. Free India had two Governor-Generals—Lord Mountbatten and C. Rajagopalachari. The 1950 Constitution brought to an end this constitutional relationship and with its inauguration India became completely independent and sovereign. The Objectives Resolution of the Constituent Assembly contained the words "Independent and Sovereign." Later on the word "Independent" was dropped to avoid tautology.

It has been argued that the word "Democratic" used before the word "Republic" is redundant. But really it is not so, for democracry does not involve the existence of a republican form of government. It may be obtainable under hereditary monarchy as well, as in Britain. A republican government, according to Madison, "derives its power directly or indirectly from the great body of the people, and is administered by persons holding their offices during pleasure for a limited period or during good behaviour. It is essential in such a goverrnment that it be derived from the great body of the society, not from an inconsiderable proportion, or a favoured class....." The President of India is indirectly elected by the representatives of the people for a

53. Speech delivered at a public meeting at the historic Jor Mela at Fatehgarh Sahib in Patiala district on (now itself a district) December 27, 1991.
54. Rasheeduddin Khan, *Federal India: A Design for Change.*

period of five years. The Council of Ministers, which aids and advises the President, is constituted from the party or parties commanding majority in Parliament. Though appointed for a period of five years, Ministry remains in office so long as it can retain the confidence of the representative Chamber of Parliament, House of the People, elected by adult franchise. The expression 'democratic republic', therefore, does not only emphasise the elective principle governing the head of the State, but it also provides the means for the realisation, for all citizens of India of justice, liberty, equality and fraternity, the four pillars of democracy. In other words, the Preamble establishes in form as well as in substance a government of the people, for the people and by the people.

**Parliamentary Democracy**

The Constitution establishes a parliamentary system of government both at the Centre and in the States. It was rather a foregone conclusion that the new Indian State would be a parliamentary democracy. From the British, educated Indians learned the principles of parliamentary democracy and demanded for their own country the same political institutions as they had in Britain. The Congress leaders, in fact, had always couched their demands before Independence in terms of parliamentary democracy. The Commonwealth of India Bill and the Nehru Committee Report both proposed a parliamentary system of government for free India as did the Sapru Report in 1945. The Draft Constitution of Free India published by the groups of the Left, the Centre and Rights—those of the Marxist, M. N. Roy, of the Socialist Party, and the Hindu Mahasabha, a communal party—all envisaged a parliamentary system of government for the constitution of India.

The British Government had persistently rejected the Idian demand for establishing parliamentary institutions on the British model on the ground that they were neither suited to nor were desirable for India. The reforms introduced from time to time for the governance of the country were always halting, yet rudiments of responsible government were always there and the legislatures had attracted among their members many statesmen unrivalled for their deep learning and debating skill. In the early years of the twentieth century, the Central Legislature had the distinction of having leaders of the stature of Gopal Krishna Gokhale, Surendranath Banerjea and V. S. Srinivasa Sastri. Under the Montagu-Chelmsfofd reforms, it included eminent men like Vithalbhai Patel, Motilal Nehru, Madan Mohan Malaviya, M. A. Jinnah and S. Srinivasa Iyengar. At a later stage veterans like Bhulabhai Desai and S. Satyamurthi. By 1947 the British constitutional practices had taken roots in India and after Independence the Governor-General's Executive Council functioned as a cabinet.

It was, therefore, not surprising that at the time of framing the constitution if the Assembly took inspiration from Britain. Jawaharlal Nehru,Sardar Vallabhbhai Patel, B. R. Ambedkar, K.M. Munshi, Alladi Krishanswami Ayyar and N. Gopalaswami Ayyangar, who dominated the Constituent Assembly and were the architects of the constitution, were admirers of the British system of government. Why, said Munshi, in the Constituent Assemby, should India turn its back on a hundred-year-old tradition of Parliamentary government.[55] Speaking in the House of the People (Lok Sabha) on March 28, 1957 Jawaharlal Nehru said, "We chose this system of parliamentary democracy deliberately; we chose it not only because to some extent we had always thought on those lines previously, but because we thought it in keeping with our own old traditions, not the old traditions as they were, but adjusted to the new conditions and new surroundings. We chose it—let us give credit where credit is due because we approved of its functioning in other countries, more especially in the United Kingdom."

Parliamentary system is both responsible and responsive. There is both a daily and periodic assessment of the responbsibility of government. It can meet the crisis in the social and political life of the nation swiftly, adequately and effectively as there is no working at cross purposes between the executive and legislative wings of the government. The system, therefore, secures swiftness in decision and vigour in action and enables the Government to press through such legislation as it thinks it is needed, and can conduct both domestic and foreign policy with the confidence that its majority will suppport it against the attacks of the Opposition. The Ministers being in constant touch with the Opposition as well as in still closer contacts with the members of their own party can feel the pulse of the

55. *Constituent Assembly Debates,* Vol. VII, pp. 284-5.

legislature and through it the ebb and flow of the public opinion. The Government under such a system cannot act arbitrarily as everyday is a day of reckoning in the life of parliamentary government.

**India in the Commonwealth**

Though India had decided to be Republic and it ended all constitutional relationship with the British Monarch, yet in 1949 the Constituent Assembly decided that India would continue her membership of the Commonwealth, whose head the British Monarch was. India was, therefore, the first nation to reconcile the incompatibles of the repulicanism and Monarchy. This she did at a time when Ireland was breaking away from the Commonwealth and was proclaiming itself as a republic in reaction, primarily, to the unpleasant symbol of Monarchy.

India's membership of the Commonwealth was agreed to at a special meeting of the Commonwealth Prime Ministers, held in London in late April, 1949. This decision was embodied in a declaration of the conference and was ratified by the Constituent Assembly of India in a resolution moved by the Prime Minister. Nehru explained that in this resolution "nothing very much is said about the position of the King except that he will be a symbol." The King, he explained, had no function at all. He had a certain status. The Commonwealh as such "is not a body, if I may so; it has no organisation through which to function and the King also can have no functions," added the Prime Minster.

There was a spate of criticism on India's membership of the Commonwealth. It was argued that acceptance of the King as Head of the Commonwealth was incompatible with the Republic status and the sovereign character of India. Some regarded this membership as a great betrayal and the greatest mistake committed by the Congress Party after the partition of India. This accusation has since been repeated so often. The Communist Party of India had been severe in attack. A resolution was moved in the Council of States (Rajya Sabha), on December 7, 1956 urging India's withdrawal from the Commonwealth. The Election Manifesto of the Hindu Mahasabha declared in 1957 that there was "no other alternative for a self-respecting nation but to sever its incogruous connection with the Commonwealth."

The Commonwealth agreement of April, 1949 was really an instrument of compromises. It was a kind of improvised political device intended to reconcile two apparently inconsistent factors, namely, India's decision to adopt a republican form to and continue membership of the Commonwealth. But the agreement has no legal significance. It is extra-constitutional. "It is an agreement by free will," as Nehru said, "to be terminated by free will." It has not even the formality which normally accompanies treaties, he added. "By remianing within the Commonwealth, India has the right to be represented at the Commonwealth Conferences, and the right to be consulted and kept informed on Commonwealth matters. Decisions at Commonwealth Conferences are not binding on her against her will. No treaty with a foreign power, and no declaration of war by a member of the Commonwealth is binding on India without her express consent." In the course of a broadcast from the All India Radio, New Delhi, on May 10, 1949, the Prime Minister asserted that the Commonwealth "is not a super-State in any sense of the term. We have agreed to consider the King as the symbolic head of this free association. But the King has no function attached to that status in the Commonwealth. So far as the Constitution of India is concerned, the King has no place and we shall have no allegiance to him.." Vallabhbhai Patel also expressed exactly the same opinion at a Press Conference on April 28, 1949. But whatever be the legal position of the Commonwealth Agreement and the advantages flowing from such membership, it cannot be denied that India's membership of the Commonwealth and accepting the King or Queen as a symbol of free association, is a constitutional anomaly in a Republic. Robert G. Menzies, leader of the Opposition in Australia, correctly remarked on April 28, 1949, "how a nation can become Republic by abolishing allegiance to the Crown and at the same time retain membership of a united Commonwealth which is and must be basically a Crown Commonwealth is a complete mystery."

The Commonwealth is not a relationship between India and Britain. It is a relationship between India and fifty other countries of the world of which Britain is only one. Britain is no longer the leader of the Commonwealth, though she remains important because of her historical role. Nehru saw the great possibilities of a multiracial Commonwealth, the value of a meeting place for nations. Intervening in the debate on the resolution of the Communist Members of the Council of States (Rajya Sabha) urging upon the

Government to withdraw from the Commonwealth, Nehru analysed the reasons and advantages which accrued to India from her membership. He asserted that it has been the privilege and policy of India "to be a bridge between countries and not to break bridges that already exist." India, he added, "does not want to break her links, nor does she desire now, with the outside world. In fact, she wanted and still wants to strengthen and develop them."

Nehru was, as President Fakhruddin Ali Ahmed said, "the builder of the Commonwealth." He paved the way for new republican countries to join the Commonwealth on a footing of equality and reap the benefits of a mutual consultation and co-operation, avoiding all causes of tensions. As in Nehru's days, India continues to value the Commonwealth link not merely because of past associations, "but because it has the capacity to advance the larger world causes to which India is committed—world-peace, internal understanding and developmental co-operation among the peoples of the world and the elimination of the causes of tensions among nations." The Commonwealth, in sum, is an essay on international understanding and co-operation and remarkable experiment in international living and free and voluntary association among fifty nations "based on mutual respect, a sincere desire to understanding each other's viewpoints and problems and co-operation in common interests of their people."[56] Addressing the opening session of the Commonwealth Prime Ministers' Conference on June 8, 1977, Morarji Desai said, "In participating in this great momentous meeting, I have only one desire and one ambition, and that is to ensure that we bring to bear on our problems a common urge to come together rather than to drift apart." The Prime Minister of India added that as he looked around the table he could not help feeling that "We are a United Nations in miniature" and expressed the view that in course of time, "this institution will set a pattern for the formation of Commonwealth of nations, reflecting a veritable mirror of the world. It is that hope and that aspiration to which I cling with all sinceritty of conviction and it is that ideal which gives me strength in sustaining my attachment of this great institution."[57]

### A Secular State

A secular State is primarily devoted to political order and freedom and pursues policies in promoting economic stability and welfare of the people. It is a system of government which is conducted in conformity with the needs of the world on the basis of fundamentals and methods provided for modern civilisation by science or technique. A secular State is not to be guided in the performance of its functions and discharge of duties by the teachings of any religious faith or creed practised within its territories, no matter what the numerical strength of its followers may be. A secular State does not allow its resources and prestige to be utilised for the propagation of any particular religion. It allows freedom of religion to all, provided such freeedom is exercised subject to law and morality. According to P.B. Gajendragadkar, secularism is the pragmatic approach to the problem of society. It is not anti-God or anti-religion. "So long as religions keep themselves within their bounds," the State "does not seek to interfere with them."[58] Nehru objected strongly to any efforts to perpetuate "a complete structure of society......by giving it religious sanction and authority." He desired that State which "protects all religions, but does not favour one at the expense of others and does not itself adopt any religion as the State religion." He described the decision of the Pakistan Constituent Assembly in November 1953, to make Pakistan an Islamic Republic as "a medieval conception......totally opposed to any democratic conception."

The secular basis of India is a revolutionary departure from the traditional approach to the problems of political obligation. Nehru was a leading champion of the concept of the secular State and, to use the words of Chester Bowles, creation of India as a secular State may in time to come would "be accepted as one of his greatest achievements,"[59] Nehru had a deep aversion to the intrusion of religion in the politics of a country and it had been his constant concern to transform

56. Inaugural address at the Twenty-first Commonwealth Parliamentary Conference held at New Delhi on October 28, 1975. *The Times of India,* New Delhi, October 29, 1975.
57. *The Times of India,* New Delhi, June 9, 1977.
58. Address on "Secularism and the Indian Constitution." *The Times of India,* New Delhi, November 23, 1965. Also refer to the proceedings of the seminar on "Secularism" organised by Indian Law Institute in collaboration with the Education Commission appointed by the Government of India.
59. Chester Bowles, *Ambassador's Report*, p. 104.

India from a caste-ridden society in which communalism constitued a major threat to "a national State which includes people of all religions and shades of opinion and is essentially secular as a State."[60] He declared in the House of the People that "Religion is all right when applied to ethics and morals, but it is not good if mixed up with politics."[61]

The facts of history, the events leading to the partition of India on the basis of religion and aspirations of the people to make India strong and united all combined together to make a secular approach to the problems of the new State as an indispensable condition. In a country inhabited with diverse religious beliefs and creeds, particularly when such differences coincided with differences of social organisation and customs the only answer to the question of the role of religion in the new republic was a secular State, in which every citizen would have the right to practise his own faith and possess the same social and political rights as every other citizen. The State must be neutral in all matters of religion and is not organised along religious lines.

There was originally no specific provision in the Constitution which declared that India was a Secular State. The Forty-second (Constitution Amendment) Act, 1976, inserted in the Preamble the word 'secular' and it now reads : "We, the People of India, having solemnly resolved to constitute India into a Sovereign Socialist Secular Democratic Republic and to secure to all its citizens......"The three pillars of the Constitution are sovereignty, socialism and secularism and on them stands the constitutional structure which secures for all citizens justice, liberty and equality. The basis of secularism is ethics and dedication to its promotion is the striving to bring about a society of equality and justice where liberty prevails all round.

Principles of secularism are, however, embodied in the various provisions of the Constitution, especially in many Articles in Part III dealing with Fundamental Rights and in Article 325 which provides for one general electoral roll for every territorial constituency for election to either House of Parliament or either House of the State Legislature. It is expressly provided that "no person shall be ineligible for inclusion in any such roll or claim to be included in any special electoral roll for any such constituency on grounds only of religion, race, caste, sex, or any of them." The Constitution thereby abolished separate communal rolls which had plagued Indian politics since the Morley-Minto Reforms of 1909.

The part played by the national movement for freedom in promoting the idea of secularism and a secular State is shown unmistakably in the resolution passed by the Congress at its Karachi session in 1931. Having affirmed the idea of religious liberty and adequate protection to minorities the resolution emphatically asserted that "the State shall observe religious neutrality to all religions." This resolution is a key to understanding the attitude adopted by the Constitution-makers nearly twenty years later; embodying in the Constitution the guarantees of State's neutrality in the matter of religion and faith. The debates in the Constituent Assembly leave little doubt that the intention of the members was not the secularisation of the State in the sense of its complete dissociation from religion. They intended the State to observe religious neutrality by according equal treatment to all religions and religious minorities.

The Constitution of India really lacks what is regarded as the basic requirements of a secular State notwithstanding insertion in the Preamble in 1976 of the term secular. A secular State is one where there is a complete separation between the church and the State, as in the United States of America. India has no established church as in Great Britain and in some other countries, particularly Islamic. In India, all religions are placed on a footing of equality and this principle of religius equality does not make her a secular State. No doubt Nehru and many leading men of the country have described India as a secular State, but Nehru himself stated as early as 1954, that the use of the term "secular" to describe the nature of Indian State was "perhaps.....not a very happy one," and the term was being used "for want of a better word". Dr. S. Radhakrishnan observed that "the religious impartiality of the Indian State is not to be confused with secularism or atheism. Secularism as here defined is in accordance with the ancient religious traditions of

60. Speech at Aligarh in 1948, quoted in Donald E. Smith, *Nehru and Democracy*, p. 147. Contrast it with Gandhi's ideals. He wrote in his *Autobiography*, "I can say without the slightest hesitation, and yet in all humility that those who say that religion has nothing to do with politics do not know what religion means". This was Gandhi's approach to purify politics and make love and truth as its basis. *Story of My Experiments with Truth*, p. 615.

61. Speech in the House of People, September 17, 1963.

India.''[62] It is significant to note that the proceedings of the Constituent Assembly show that two attempts made to introduce the word ''secular'' in the Constitution had failed.

Nevertheless, it cannot be said that the Indian State does not possess some characteristics of a secular State. Instead of creating a wall of separation between the State and religion ''it looks on religion with benevolent neutrality and treats all of them equally. The State confers a wide freedom of religion on the individual and the religious denomination, making it subject to regulation only in the interest of social welfare and reform.''[63] In regard to relations betwen the State and the individual all citizens are to be treated alike, and none is to be discriminated against by reason of his religion and faith.

The question whether India is a secular State is thus answered by Eugene Smith : ''My answer is a qualified 'yes'. It is meaningful to speak of India as a secular state.....India is a secular state in the same sense in which one can say that India is a democracy. Despite various undemocratic features of Indian politics and Government, parliamentary democracy is functioning, and with considerable vigour. Similarly the secular state; the ideal is clearly embodied in the Constitution, and it is being implemented in substantial measure. The question must be answered in terms of a dynamic state which has inherited some difficult problems and is struggling to overcome them along general sound lines.''[64] Of all the legacies of the British rule in India, the legacy of communalism is the most cruel. It divided India and even partition did not succeed in eliminating its ravaging effects. Of India's social diversities, that which stems from religion ''has been,'' as Morris-Jones says, 'the best known for its profound influence in politics.''[65]

There is no specific provision in the Constitution that provides against communalism or prohibits political activities by religious groups as such. Presumably the Constitution-makers did not envisage the emergence of these ugly forces in view of the marked strength of the national feeling after the achievement of Independence and the bitter experience of partition. Professor Dalme points out that in the Indian context the content of secularism stemmed from the country's concern to bury the two-nation theory that had caused immeasurable communal strife in the sub-continent.[66] But communalsim and seperatism are again the grim realities and both offer a serious challenge to the integrity of the State. The now abandoned secessionist movement of the Dravida Munnetra Kazgham (DMK), the unceasing demand of Sikh ''homeland'' verging on ''Khalistan'' as the extremists among them proclaim as the ultimate goal of the survival and glory of the Sikh Panth, and the communal poison emitted by the Jamiat-i-Islami, Vishwa Hindu Parishad and some other parties of their ilk in the North and particularly by the anti-seculars and fundamentalists, shake the indissolubility of the Union and secularism, which constitute two of the four fundamentals of the Indian Constitution. If the Constitution-makers had envisaged the emergence of these politically ugly forces, they would probably have had made specific and explicit provision to deal with them vigorously and effectively. It cannot, however, be denied that any challenge to the integrity of the Union and importation of religion into politics are against the spirit of the Constitution.

**A Welfare State**

The objective of the Constitution-makers was to draft a constitution of socio-economic revolution and they incorporated many provisions in the Constitution to make India a Welfare State. The basic aims of a Welfare State were clearly foreshadowed in the Preamble to the Constitution and in virtually all of Part IV containing the Directive Principles of State Policy. The Preamble was patterned along the lines of the Objectives Resolution and it is a ''key to open the minds of the Constitution-makers.''[67] Justice Hidayatullah said that ''the Preamble resembles the Declaration of Independence of the United States, but is really more than a declaration. It is the soul of the Constitution as it lays down the pattern of the society which it states is sovereign, socialist, secular, democratic republic and secures to all its citizens justice, social, economic and political and promotes among them all fraternity assuming the dignity of the individual and

62. As cited in Ved Prakash Luthera, *The Concept of the Secular State and India,* p. 155.
63. Setalvad, M. C., ''Secularism in India,'' Talk broadcast over the All India Radio, New Delhi, January 31 and February 1, 1963.
64. Donald Eugene Smith, *India as a Secular State,* pp. 449-500.
65. Morris-Jones, W. H., *Parliament in India,* p. 26.
67. Refer to S.C. (1960) 3S.C.R. 250, 281.

the unity of the nation.''[68]

Democracy not only requires equality but also justice. The essence of justice is the attainment of happiness and good of all as distinguished from the happiness and good of individuals or even the majority of them. Justice in this sense cannot be secured unless there is a society of equals in status and opportunity. Equality of status and opportunity are not available unless all sections of the people are equally in a position and circumstances to benefit from the social order that prevails. The Indian Constitution not only prohibits discrimination on grounds of birth, sex, religion , caste and creed, but also adequately provides for the promotion of the interests of the Backward Classes and areas. It seeks to remove all inequalities created by inequalities in the possession of wealth and opportunity, race, caste and religion by providing just and human conditions of work, maternity relief, leisure and cultural opportunity to every individual, prevention of exploitation in labour and industry, free education for all and the like. The ideal of economic justice the Constitution promises to secure by directing the State policy towards equality of reward for equal work, by the distribution of ownership and control of material resources of the community so as to subserve the common good and operation of economic system in such a way that it does not result in the concentration of wealth and the means of production to the common detriment.

Jawaharlal Nehru emphasised in a speech in the Constituent Assembly on the imperative needs for India to move into the modern world of science and technology for bringing into existence a social order in which there would be rapid rise in the standards of living with equitable distribution of wealth and equality of opportunity for all to carve out a career for themselves so that all of them may live with dignity and happiness. Since Independence India has been following the path of democratic planning to estabilsh a Welfare State ''by compressing the history of centuries into a few decades.''[69] The Five-Year Plans placed economic development in the framework of social justice. Removal of poverty and attainment of self- reliance were the two major objectives of the Fifth Plan and so is that of the Sixth, the Seventh, the Eighth and the Ninth. Special and concerted effort has been paid to the removal of social and legal disabilities imposed under traditional caste and feudal institutions, such social evils like untouchability, bonded labour and dowry, and economic evils like the feudal zamindari system. In order to make equal opportunities to the poor and Backward Classes and areas, laws dealing with Community Service, such as, health, education, etc., have been enacted and various projects have been pursued by providing much investment. Particular attention is paid to social security for industrial workers under the Schemes of Employees State Insurance and Employees Provident Fund. The Welfare Services for the handicapped and the maladjusted have been provided either directly by the State or grants are given to voluntary welfare institutions providing such services. Concerted efforts are being made to end poverty and unemployment and it is the basic commitment of the Government. The Desai Government declared to end unemployment and poverty within a span of ten years. Mrs. Gandhi's Government was also committed to the eradication of these two social evils, but it is a slow process and cannot be solved within a specified period of time. Rajiv Gandhi's Government was wedded to the programme of carrying the country to the twenty-first century so that India may stand as a peer with other developed countries. But within limited resources, hefty deficit financing, mounting loans, unfavourable balance of trade, and other visible constraints especially all-round corruption at all levels of authority, it seems to be an urealistic aspiration and it proved to be so.

**Universal Suffrage**

The decisions analysed above were made by the Constituent Assembly with a little debate and discussion that Norman Palmer regards them ''assumptions rather than decisions.''[70] But two other decisions that the Assembly made entailed prolonged debates which often generated heat and even today many people, for various reasons, entertain doubts about their wisdom. The first decision related to the reorganisation of States along with linguistic lines. The decision about the linguistic States was taken against the consistent opposition of Nehru and Patel. Linguistic States have revealed the strength of regional against national loyalties and regional loyalties have shown their ugly head in various forms resulting into the fragmentation of the national

68. Hidayatullah, M., *Democracy in India and the Judicial Process*, p. 51.
69. Jagannadhan, V., ''Welfare State in India,''Aiyar, S.P. (Ed.), *Perspectives on the Welfare State*, p. 250.
70. Palmer, Norman, D., *The Indian Political System*, p. 105.

life. The demand for regional states has no end and remains unabated.

The introduction of adult suffrage without qualifications of any kind was the boldest step taken by the Constitution-makers and it was an act of faith they had placed in the common man. Since 1920 the Indian National Congress had demanded adult suffrage for the people of India, but the British did not concede even a fragment of it. Under the Government of India Act, 1935, only 14 per cent of the total population of the country secured franchise, women constituting a negligible portion of the total electorate. Prior to that time the electorate had been only about one-fifth as large. In the first General Elections in 1952 the number of eligible voters increased to 173 million and in the 1977 election to the Sixth House of the People (Lok Sabha) the electorate numbered 322 million. It increased to 349 million in January 1980 election to the Seventh House of the People, and 520 million to the Tenth Lok Sabha in 1991.

Nehru and others in the Constituent Assembly believed that the system of adult suffrage with direct election was the pillar of social revolution. Way back in 1935, he wrote : "an assembly selected (would) represent the people as a whole and (would) be far more interested in the economic and social problems of the masses than in the petty communal issues which affect the small groups."[71] Nehru wrote these words about Constituent Assembly, but their applicability to Legislatures is evident. A few believers of the "Gandhian constitution" pleaded in the Constituent Assembly for indirect election to the Legislature by making a village and its panchayat as the base. The Assembly members did not find it feasible. Many believed that to confine adult participation in elections to the creation of panchayats would be politically dangerous. Alladi Krishanswami Ayyar said, "The Assembly has adopted the principle of adult franchise with an abundant faith in the common man and the ultimate success of democratic rule, and in the full belief that the introduction of democractic government on the basis of adult suffrage will bring enlightenment and promote the well-being, the standard of life, the comfort, and the decent living of the common man." He clearly said that the only alternative to adult suffrage " was some kind of indirect election based upon village community or local bodies and by constituting them into electoral colleges .......That was not found feasible."[72]

Article 326 of the Constitution provides that elections to the House of the People and to the Legislative Assembly of every State shall be on the basis of adult suffrage. That is to say, every person who is a citizen of India and who is not otherwise disqualified is entitled to be registered as a voter at any such election. Adult suffrage is the acceptance of the fullest implication of democracy and it is the most strikingg feature of India's Constitution. "In fact," K. M. Panikkar said, "it may well be claimed that the Constitution is a solemn promise to the people of India that the legislature would do everything possible to renovate and rebuild society on new principles"[73] based upon economic and material progress of the masses with a view to take them out from centuries of mental and psychological stagnation and passivity.

Adult suffrage gave a voice, indeed, power to millions of people who hithertofore had depended on the whims of others for even vague representation of their interests and redress of grievances. Now they themselves have the power to elect their representatives in whom they repose confidence and who depend upon their existence on the mandate of the people which is sought periodically. Moreover, direct elections have brought national awareness to individuals living in villages. Rural India is deeply soaked in local politics and local loyalties and both these factors have impeded the growth of national unity and progress. Direct elections based on adult suffrage were designed to supplant local loyalties and parochial considerations of caste and religion by national awareness as the electorate demonstrated to some extent in the 1977 and 1980 Parliamentary polls as well as in December 1990 and May-June 1991. Highlighting the implications of adult franchise, Panikkar said, "adult suffrage has social implications far beyond its political significance. Many social groups previously unaware of their strength and barely touched by political changes that had taken place, suddenly realised that they were in a position to wield power."[74]

The voting figures of the General Elections

71. Jawaharlal Nehru, *Unity of India*, p. 23.
72. *Constituent Assembly Debates*, Vol. XI, p. 835.
73. Panikkar, K. M., *Hindu Society at Crossroads*, pp. 63- 64.
74. *Ibid.*

so far held reflect a high degree of political awareness and popular participation. But adult franchise has not achieved what the Constitution-makers had designed to defeat. Direct elections have helped the mushroom growth of political parties and groups with local and regional roots. The local parties have promoted not only narrow loyalties and factionalism, but have abetted caste and class consciousness in the form that had not existed before. The selection of candidates and election results have usually followed religion and caste lines and all parties, irrespective of their labels and professions, blatantly indulge in these vote catching devices. The venom of cummunalism is not spared to be injected and no party can claim exception to it, even those who swear by secularism. The voting pattern, both in urban and rural areas, is the same. In constituencies where candidates belong to two different religious communities, voters are urged to cast their votes in favour of their co-religionists and appeal in the name of religion is as forceful today as it was in the pre-Independence period. Muslims and Sikhs claim that religion and politics for them are inseparable. Care is also taken that candidates belonging to that community, sect or caste are put up for election which constitutes the majority of the electorate in a particular constituency. Thus, the elements that help the growth of political culture have no occasion to germinate.

# CHAPTER VI

# Fundamental Rights

## Demand for Declaration of Rights

Before the enactment of the 1950 Constitution there was no charter of fundamental rights of a justiciable nature, although the demand for such rights and their constitutional guarantees had its deep roots in the nineteenth century. It was implicit in the formation of the Indian National Congress in 1885, which wanted the same rights and privileges for Indians that the British enjoyed in their own country. The promoters of the Indian National Congress emphatically demanded an end to discrimination inherent in a colonial regime. Perhaps, the first implicit demand for fundamental rights appeared in the Constitution of India Bill, 1895. This bill, described by Mrs. Annie Besant as the Home Rule Bill, envisaged to guarantee to all citizens freedom of speech and expression, right to personal liberty, inviolability of one's house, right to property, equality before the law, equality to admission to public offices and right to petition for redress of grievances. Immediately after the publication of the Montagu-Chelmsford Report, the Indian National Congress, at its Bombay session in August 1918, demanded that the new constitution of India should contain a "declaration of the rights of the people of India as British citizens," guaranteeing equality before the law, freedom of speech and press, and protection in respect of liberty, life and property.

By the mid-twenties, Congress and Indian leaders had acquired a forceful consciousness of their rights which was influenced by various factors, especially by the experience of World War I, the deep disappointment which the Montagu-Chelmsford Reforms had caused, President Woodrow Wilson's support for self-determination and M.K. Gandhi's arrival in India and his active participation in the politics of the country. The Constitution of the Irish Free State in 1921, which contained a Bill of Rights, had also a profound effect on political thought in India. The Commonwealth of India Bill, drafted by the National Convention under the inspiration of Mrs. Annie Besant in 1925, embodied a declaration of rights more or less similar to the provisions of the Irish Constitution.

Within two years of the publication of the Commonwealth of India Bill came the announcement of the appointment of the Indian Statutory (Simon) Commission. To set a model for the Simon Commission, the Forty-third Annual Session of the Congress at Madras in 1927 resolved that the Working Committee be empowered to set up a Committee "to draft a Swaraj Constitution for India on the basis of a declaration of rights." The Nehru Committee was, accordingly, appointed in 1928, which included in its membership representatives of all the political parties. The Nehru Committee in its report included a comprehensive bill of rights and in recommending their declaration the Committee urged that "Ireland is the only country where conditions obtaining before the Treaty are nearest approach to those we have in India. The first concern of the people of Ireland was, as it is indeed with the people of India today, to secure fundamental rights that had been denied to them". Another reason why India attached importance to the declaration of the fundamental rights, in the opinion of the Committee, was the unfortunate existence of communal differences in India. "Certain safeguards and guarantees," the Committee urged, "are necessary to create and establish a sense of security among those who look upon each other with distrust and suspicion. We could not better secure the full enjoyment of religious and communal rights to all communities than by including them among the basic principles of the constitution." The Committee added, "It is obvious that our first care should be to have our fundamental rights guaranteed in a manner which will not permit their withdrawal under any circumstances."

In 1931, the Indian National Congress passed a Resolution on Fundamental Rights. In order to end the exploitation of the masses, the Resolution emphasised, political freedom must include real economic freedom of the starving millions. It was further declared that any constitution which might be agreed to on behalf of the

Indian National Congress should provide, or enable the Swaraj Government to provide, for certain fundamental rights and duties. But the British Government was in no mood to reconcile itself to this primary demand of the Indians. In fact, such a demand was unsuited to the British genius. The Simon Commission had ridiculed the idea of fundamental rights. "Abstract declarations", the Commission observed, "are useless unless there exists the will and the means to make them effective."[1]

All the same, the matter came up for consideration during the Round Table Conferences. At the Second Round Table Conference, M. K. Gandhi, the sole representative of the Indian National Congress, circulated a memorandum, *inter alia,* demanding that the new Constitution should "include a guarantee to the communities concerned for the protection of their cultures, languages, scripts, education, profession and practice of religion and religious endowments." Another memorandum on the subject was put forward jointly by the representatives of the minorities. Ramsay MacDonald, the then Labour Prime Minister, announced that he felt the need of incorporating fundamental rights in the proposed constitution of India for safeguarding the interests of the minorities. Immediately after came the National Government into power with Ramsay MacDonald as Prime Minister, but with a clear majority of the Conservatives in the Government. This made a sharp swing in the official policy. Lord Reading and Sir John Simon were vehement in opposing the inclusion of fundamental rights in the new constitution for India. The Indian representatives at the Conference could not agree amongst themselves on the basic problems of constitutional reforms and, accordingly, the issue of fundamental rights also lapsed.

The Joint Parliamentary Committee on the Government of India Bill, 1934, endorsed the observations of the Simon Commission on the demand for a constitutional guarantee of fundamental rights to subjects of British India. The Committee, however, conceded that there were some legally recognised principles which could be included in the new constitution and, accordingly, the Government of India Act, 1935, conferred certain rights and forms of protection on British subjects in India.[2]

The subject of fundamental rights came up for active consideration in the deliberations of the Conciliation Committee, also known as the Sapru Committee, appointed by the All-Parties Conference (1944-45). The Committee was of the opinion that fundamental rights were not only "assurances and guarantees to the minorities but also prescribing a standard of conduct for the legislatures, governments and the courts."[3] The Committee further said that it was for the Constitution-making body to settle the list of fundamental rights and, then, to decide about their division into justiciable and non-justiciable rights and to provide in the case of the former, suitable machinery for their enforcement. A few months more than a year later the Constituent Assembly of India began framing the Fundamental Rights and the Directive Principles of State Policy, the former justiciable and the latter non-justiciable. The most striking feature about the treatment of rights in the Sapru Report was the distinction between justiciable and non-justiciable rights.

### Constituent Assembly and Fundamental Rights

The Cabinet Mission Plan conceded the demand for the Constituent Assembly as well as the need for a written guarantee of fundamental rights in the Constitution of India. It recommended the appointment of an Advisory Committee on the Rights of Citizens, Minorities and Tribal and Excluded Areas, containing the interests affected, which would prepare a list of fundamental rights and also to recommend their inclusion in the State or the Union List. By the Objectives Resolution introduced by Jawaharlal Nehru and adopted on January 22, 1947, the Constituent Assembly solemnly pledged itself to draw up for India's future governance a constitution wherein "shall be guaranteed and secured to all the people of India, justice, social. economic and political, equality of status, of opportunity and before the law; freedom of thought, expression, belief, faith, worship, vocation, association and action, subject to law and public morality."

Two days after adopting Objectives Resolution, the Constituent Assembly elected an Advisory Committee for reporting on minorities, fundamental rights and on the tribal and excluded areas. The Advisory Committee consisted of 54 members with Sardar Vallabhbhai Patel as its Chairman. The Committee was constituted on

1. *Report of the Indian Statutory (Simon) Commission* , Vol. II, Para 36.
2. Refer to Sections 275 and 297 to 300 of the Government of India Act, 1935.
3. *Constitutional Proposals of the Sapru Committee* (1945), pp. 256-57.

February 12, 1947, with five Sub-Committees one of which was to deal with fundamental rights.[4] The draft report of the Sub-Committee was circulated to its members with the explanatory notes on various clauses prepared by B.N. Rau, Constitutional Adviser to the Constituent Assembly. These were thereafter discussed in the Sub-Committee in the light of the comments offered by the members and the final report was submitted to the Chairman of the Advisory Committee on April 16, 1947. The Advisory Committee accepted the recommendations of the Sub-Committee : (1) for division of rights into justiciable and non-justiciable rights; that is, rights enforceable by appropriate legal process and rights consisting of directive principles of state policy, which though not enforceable in courts, were nevertheless to be regarded as fundamental in the governance of the country; (2) certain rights being guaranteed to all persons and certain others to citizens only; and (3) all such rights being made uniformly applicable to the Union and the units. The Constituent Assembly adopted all these recommendations and the Constitution of 1950 contains two Chapters—Chapter III enumerating the Fundamental Rights and Chapter IV dealing with the Directive Principles of State Policy. The Constitution (Forty-second Amendment) Act, 1976, inserted a new Chapter Part IV A containing fundamental duties which are covered by Article 51A.

**Some Features of the Fundamental Rights**

The Constitution sets out a most elaborate declaration of human rights as compared with the Bill of Rights contained in any other existing constitution of importance. The provisions of Chapter III are detailed covering a variety of topics and some are purely the outcome of the peculiar social conditions, prevailing in India,[5] but aiming to build a new social structure on the ruins of old time-worn social order based on inequality, untouchability, status–caste and religious considerations and economic exploitation. The new social order envisaged in the Fundamental Rights is intended to help the growth of new sociological processes forging thereby an integrated homogeneous community free from exploitation of any kind and social disability of any nature.

Whereas some of the rights conferred by the Constitution are limited to citizens such as freedom of speech, assembly and cultural and educational rights, in the case of others, as equality before the law, religious freedom, etc., such a limitation does not exist; these are applicable to citizens and aliens alike. The relevant Articles of the Constitution make use of the two terms 'citizens' and 'persons' and they are indicative of the distinction between citizens and aliens. Even in the absence of such a distinction all the rights could not have been available to citizens and aliens alike, but the matter would have remained undecided until the Supreme Court had determined so.

Some of the provisions of Chapter III of the Constitution are of the nature of prohibitions and place constitutional limitations on the authority of the State, for instance, no authority of the State can deny to any person equality before the law or the equal protection of the laws; discrimination against any citizen; and no titles other than a military or academic distinction can be conferred. From the point of view of an individual, such rights may be termed as negative rights. The remaining provisions of the Chapter on Fundamental Rights, as such, can be said to contain positive rights of the individuals. In spite of this distinction no clear-cut line of division can be drawn between the two. There is, however, one important distinction between them. The provisions which impose constitutional limitation on the authority of the State are binding for all intents and purposes and any action, legislative or executive, which contravenes any of these provisions, would be void altogether. The provisions relating to individual rights, on the other hand, are subject to the regulation of the State within certain prescribed limits and restrictions so imposed cannot be held to be void unless they travel beyond those limits.

The Fundamental Rights place limitations on all kinds of authority that has either the power to make laws or have discretion vested in it. The Fundamental Rights are, accordingly, binding on the Union Government, the State Governments and the local bodies including village Panchayats, and other authorities within the territory of India. Article 12 of the Constitution defines the State, inclusively, to mean the Government and Parliament of India and the Govern-

4. The Sub-Committee on Fundamental Rights consisted of J. B. Kripalani, M. R. Masani, K. T. Shah, Rajkumari Amrit Kaur, Alladi Krishnaswami Ayyar, Harnam Singh, Maulana Abul Kalam Azad, B. R. Ambedkar, Jairamdass Daulatram and K.M. Munshi. The President of the Committee was authorised to nominate additional members.
5. Articles 15(2), 15(4), and 17.

ment and Legislature of each of the States and all local or other authorities within the territory of India or under the control of the Government of India. Ambedkar made this point clear in the Constituent Assembly. He explained that the object of the Fundamental Rights was two-fold. "First, that every citizen must be in a position to claim those rights. Secondly, they must be binding upon every authority.....upon every authority which has got either the power to make laws or the power to have discretion vested in it. Therefore, it is quite clear that if the Fundamental Rights are to be real, then they must be binding not only upon the Central Government, they must not only be binding upon the Provincial Government.......they must also be binding upon District Local Boards, Municipalities, even authority which has been created by law and which has got certain power to make laws, to make rules, or make by-laws."

Absolute or unrestricted rights are not possible. This is the position in Britain, although there are no constitutional guarantees of fundamental rights in that country.[6] In the United States there are no direct restrictions imposed by the First Ten Amendments which determine the American Bill of Rights. But under the doctrine of Police Power the Supreme Court has recognised the inherent power of the State to impose such restrictions on Fundamental Rights as may be deemed reasonable to protect the common good. The Constitution of India, on the other hand, imposes direct limitations on Fundamental Rights. Ambedkar, while introducing the Draft Constitution and supporting the restriction clauses, maintained, "what the Draft Constitution had done is that instead of formulating fundamental rights in absolute terms and depending upon our Supreme Court to come to the rescue of Parliament by inventing doctrine of police power, it permits the State directly to impose limitations upon the fundamental rights."[7] Courts in India cannot, therefore, question the propriety of legislation once it has been established that it is within the competence of the legislature to make such a law or in any way to modify its effect on the ground that it seeks to "unduly restrict personal liberty."[8]

The Constitution of India, thus, did not recognise the supremacy of the judiciary against the Legislature, although the Constitution gave to the judiciary the power to review legislation repugnant to the Fundamental Rights. The position before February 1967 was that Parliament would abrogate or abridge Fundamental Rights by amending the Constitution under the provisions of Article 368 and thereby override the unwholesome decision of the Judiciary simply by securing the requisite special majority, which the Congress Party had commanded in Parliament all those years. In 1961 and 1963, the Supreme Court declared that the Kerala and Madras Land Reform Acts, which provided for a ceiling on land holdings, were bad. In the wake of these declarations the Seventeenth Amendment was enacted in 1964 whereunder 44 laws passed by both the States were included in the Ninth Schedule in order to maintain them valid. A good number of writ petitions challenging the competence of Parliament to enact the Seventeenth Amendment were moved in the Supreme Court. The Supreme Court by a 6-5[9] ruling on February 27, 1967 reversed its earlier decisions[10] and declared that Parliament has no power to abridge or take away Fundamental Rights by amending the Constitution under Article 368. Chief Justice Subba Rao, speaking for the majority, declared, "The Constitution has given by its scheme a place of permanence to the fundamental freedoms. In giving to themselves the Constitution, the people have reserved the fundamental freedoms to themselves. Article 13 merely incorporates that reservation. The importance attached to the fundamental freedoms is so transcendental that a bill enacted by a unanimous vote of all the members of both Houses (of Parliament) is ineffective to derogate from its guaranteed exercise....." The Court rejected the Government's argument that if the power to amend the Constitution was not all-comprehensive, no way would be left to change the structure of the Constitution or to abridge the Fundamental Rights even if the whole

---

6. *Liversidge* v. *Anderson* (1942).
7. *Constituent Assembly Debates,* Vol. VIII, p. 41.
8. *Lakhinarayan* v. *Prov. of Bihar* (1949). Also refer to *Gopalan* v. *The State of Madras.*
9. *Golak Nath and Others* v. *State of Punjab, All India Reporter,* 1967, Supreme Court 1943. The majority opinion was expressed by two separate judgments; one by the Chief Justice Subba Rao for himself and Justices J. C. Shah, S. M. Sikri, J. N. Shelat, and C. A. Vaidialingam, and the other by Justice M. Hidaytullah. The dissenting Justices were Wanchoo, Bhargava, Bachawat, Ramaswami and Mitter.
10. *Shankar Prasad Singh Deo and others* v. *Union of India and Others, All India Reporter,* 1951, Supreme Court 458; and *Sajjan Singh* v. *The State of Rajasthan, All India Reporter,* 1965, Supreme Court 845.

county demanded such a change. It was declared that "this visualizes an extremely unnforceeable and extravagant demand; but even if such a contingency arises, the residuary power of the Parliament may be relied upon to call for a Constituent Assembly for making a new Constitution or radically changing it."

The resultant position was that the amendment of the Fundamental Rights was not forbidden, but the Supreme Court reserved to itself the power of determining in each specific case whether the amendment in question took away or abridged those rights contained in Part III of the Constitution. Thus, the precariously balanced six to five decision established the supremacy of the Judiciary so far as Fundamental Rights were involved. The Supreme Court of India, like its counterpart in the United States, assumed the role of a super legislature because what is taken away by the Justices from Parliament is taken away from the people.

The Constitution (Twenty-fourth Amendment) Act, 1971, was enacted to get over the difficulty created by the *Golak Nath* case. The amendment empowered Parliament to abrogate any of Fundamental Rights including the right, under Article 32, to move the Supreme Court for the enforcement of Fundamental Rights. The validity of this amendment was questioned in the Supreme Court through a series of writ petitions. In *Kesavananda Bharati* v. *The State of Kerala* the Court reversed the *Golak Nath* case judgment by upholding the validity of the Twenty-fourth Amendment and thereby restored the supremacy of Parliament in regard to legislation on Fundamental Rights, a position that existed prior to 1967. But the Court also ruled that Parliament cannot alter the basic structure or framework of the Constitution. What exactly did the basic structure mean, the Court said nothing about it. The Thirty-fourth Amendment enacted in 1974 put out of the pale of judicial review a bunch of laws designed to alter the structure of the ownership of agricultural land and tenurial relations. The Thirty-ninth Amendment (1975) sought to amend the Ninth Schedule of the Constitution so as to bring within its scope 38 Central and certain State enactments and thereby protecting them from challenge in any court of law on the ground of violation of any of the Fundamental Rights.

Soon in the wake of the Thirty-ninth Amendment came the Fortieth in May, 1976, which provided for addition of 64 Central and State laws in the Ninth Schedule with a view to protecting them from challenge in the courts on constitutional grounds. By including these nine Central Acts and fifty-five State laws in the Ninth Schedule, the new doctrine of the Congress Government that the Directive Principles of State Policy should prevail over Fundamental Rights was reaffirmed in no uncertain terms.

The President of the Indian National Congress appointed the Swaran Singh Committee on Constitutional Reforms early in 1976. The Committee suggested that primacy of the Directive Principles of State Policy must be proclaimed once for all and no law giving effect to Directive Principles should be called in question on the ground of infringement of any of the Fundamental Rights. The Constitution (Forty-second Amendment) Act, 1976, was mainly based on the recommendations of the Swaran Singh Committee Report.

The Janata Party, formed just before the Parliamentary elections held in March 1977, pledged in its manifesto "to rescind the 42nd Amendment." The electorate reposed their confidence in the Janata and the Party assumed office on the 25th March. In the April session of Parliament the Government introduced the Constitution (Forty-third Amendment) Bill seeking to repeal, *inter alia*, Article 31-D. The Bill was passed in the House of the People but before the Council of States could consider it, the Bill was virtually withdrawn. The Janata Government apprehended that the Bill might be overthrown by the Council of States where the Congress Party still commanded a massive majority. However, as a result of consensus between the Prime Minister and leaders of the Opposition parties the Constitution (Forty-third Amendment) Act, 1977, *inter alia,* omitted Article 31-D, saving the laws in respect of anti-nationl activities, and anti-national associations, and Article 32A, constitutional validity of State laws not to be considered in proceedings under Article 32. Thereafter, consensus was also reached on the provisions of the Forty-fourth Amendment Bill and it became an Act of Parliament in 1978. Though a comprehensive Act, the Forty-fourth Amendment did not rescind the provisions of Article 368 Sections 4 and 5; the former debarring the courts to question on any ground the validity of any amendment (including the provisions of Part III) and the latter declaring that there shall be no limitation whatever on the constituent power of Parliament to amend by way of addition, variation or repeal the provisions of "this Constitution under this article."

The supremacy of Parliament, thus, remained unchallenged, though the decision in the *Kesavananda Bharati* case and reaffirmed in *Indira Gandhi* v. *Raj Narain* still prevailed. The validity of the Forty-second Amendment was questioned through various writs and the Supreme Court in the *Minerva Mills* case struck down in May 1980 Sections 4 and 55 of the Amendment incorporated in Articles 31-C and 368 (4) (5) of the Constitution. The Court held that giving boundless and unchallengeable power to Parliament is violative of the basic structure or essential features of the Constitution and, accordingly, void in terms of the *Kesavananda Bharati* judgment of April 24, 1973.

Another important feature of the Fundamental Rights is that there is a special constitutional provision (Article 32) for their enforcement. The right to move the Supreme Court for the enforcement of Fundamental Rights is itself a guaranteed right under Article 32. A citizen whose rights have been infringed by any public authority in India can move the Supreme Court by appropriate proceedings for the enforcement of his rights and the Court is empowered to issue directions or orders including writs in the nature of *Habeas Corpus, mandamus,* prohibition, *quo warranto* and *certiorari,* whichever may be appropriate. The State High Courts have also the power of issuing writs under Article 226 and enforce rights in the same manner within the limits of their respective jurisdictions. Thus, the constitutional remedies after the enforcement of Fundamental Rights are made available to every citizen and within his easy reach. But during the operation of emergency, under Article 352, the President may by order suspend the right to move any court for the enforcement of any rights mentioned in the Presidential order except the rights conferred by Articles 20 and 21—protection in respect of conviction for offences, and protection of life and personal liberty.

Fundamental Rights can also be restricted or suspended. Article 33 provides that Parliament may by law determine to what extent any of the rights conferred by Part III shall, in their application to members of the Armed Forces or the Forces charged with the maintenance of public order, be restricted or abrogated so as to ensure the proper discharge of their duties and maintenance of discipline among them. The special feature of the Indian Constitution is that the provisions of Article 33 apply not only to the Armed Forces but also to the ordinary police and the civil employees in the defence establishment as also the office bearers of their Unions.

Rights relating to freedoms as contained in Article 19 may be suspended during the period when the Proclamation of Emergency is in operation. Article 358 (1) provides that while a Proclamation of Emergency is in operation, "nothing in Article 19 shall restrict the power of the State as defined in Part III to make any law or to take any executive action which the State would but for the provision contained in that Part (Part III—Fundamental Rights) be competent to make or to take." But any law so made, shall to the extent of incompetence, cease to have effect as soon as the Proclamation of Emergency ceases to operate. If the Proclamation of Emergency is in operation only in any part of the territory of India, any such law may be made, or any such action may be taken, under Article 358 (1) in relation to any State or Union Territory in which the Proclamation of Emergency is not in operation, if the security of India or any part thereof is deemed to be threatened by activities in that part of the territory of India in which the Proclamation of Emergency is in operation.

The Janata Party's 1977 election manifesto stated that the right to property would be removed from the Chapter on Fundamental Rights and made "a legal right enforceable in a court of law." In fulfilment of its election commitment, the Constitution (Forty-fourth Amendment) Act, 1978, abolished the right to property as a Fundamental Right[11] and, accordingly, omitted the sub-heading "Right of Property" occurring after Article 30 and Article 31 which guaranteed to every person the right not to be deprived of his property except by authority of law. Omission of right to property from Part III of the Constitution does not affect the right of a citizen to acquire, hold or dispose of property.[12] Nor can it be acquired except by the authority of law. The only difference that its omission from the Chapter on Fundamental Rights makes is that while under the omitted constitutional provision the right to property could be adversely affected by a constitutional amendment in accordance with the prescribed procedure whereas now the right to prop-

11. Section 6.
12. Article 300A inserted by the Constitution (Forty-fourth Amendment) Act, 1978, S. 34.

erty can be modified by a law passed by Parliament in accordance with the procedure adopted for ordinary laws. The sanctity hitherto attached to the right to property as an inalienable right, therefore, disappears by its omission from the Chapter on Fundamental Rights.

There are no natural or unenumerated rights under the Indian Constitution. The Supreme Court has definitely held that unless there is an express provision in the Constitution with which the Act of a Legislature conflicts, it cannot be held to be void merely on the ground of its being inconsistent with what the court considers to be the spirit of the Constitution.[13] In other words, a right which has not been enumerated and expressly declared to be a Fundamental Right in Part III of the Constitution is not a Fundamental Right.[14] It does not, however, mean that there are no rights apart from those included in the Fundamental Rights. But all such rights are ordinary rights and not Fundamental Rights and they cannot be enforced in the Supreme Court under Article 32 or in the State High Courts under Article 226. The legal remedies provided under Article 32 are only applicable to Fundamental Rights.

During the past few years the Supreme Court has widened the scope of basic human rights by adopting a pro-active approach and entertaining public interest litigation coming before it from any source, even an item published in a newspaper or submission made through a mere letter. In spelling out the Directive Principles of State Policy, the framers of the Constitution had laid down the broad contours of just social order, but it was left to the political process and the judicial system to fill in the gaps. The political process had been slow, tardy and haphazard, although it had been instrumental in introducing a certain amount of change. The judicial system had tended to reserve its attention and energies for those who could pay to seek redress for the damage done to them for infringement or violation of their rights. The poor had no access to the courts. The legal system has become so costly that the poor people are priced out of the legal system. By entertaining public interest litigation the Supreme Court has opened the portals of justice for the poor enforcing their fundamental right to live with human dignity.

Finally, there are the Directive Principles of State Policy as contained in Chapter IV. In considering the question of fixing the Fundamental Rights and incorporating them into the Constitution, the Advisory Committee appointed by the Constituent Assembly, came to the conclusion that the Fundamental Rights should be divided into two parts—the first justiciable and the other nonjusticiable. The non-justiciable rights are put under the heading Directive Principles of State Policy and according to Article 37 they are not enforceable by any court, "but the principles laid down are nevertheless fundamental in the governance of the country and it shall be the duty of the State to apply these principles in making laws." To put it in a more matter of fact language, whereas the Fundamental Rights are in effect, injunctions prohibiting Government from doing certain things, the Directive Principles are affirmative instructions to Government to do certain things.

Whatever be the legal nicety between the Fundamental Rights and the Directive Principles of State Policy, the Constitution of India, as Granville Austin says, is "a social document, the majority of its provisions are either directly aimed at furthering the goals of the social revolution or attempt to foster this revolution by establishing the conditions necessary for its achievement."[15] The core of the commitment to the social revolution lies in Parts III and IV, in Fundamental Rights and in the Directive Principles of State Policy. Both together constitute the conscience of the Constitution. They had their roots in the struggle for independence and were included in the Constitution in the expectation that one day the tree of true liberty and justice would bloom in India. The Fundamental Rights and the Directive Principles connect India's future, present and past "adding greatly to their significance of inclusion in the Constitution, and giving strength to the pursuit of the social revolution in India."[16]

## SOME SPECIFIC FUNDAMENTAL RIGHTS

### The Right to Equality

The right to equality guaranteed in Part III of the Constitution has no socialist implication. It is essentially negative in character and is intended to remove the social and civic disabilities

13. *A. K. Gopalan* v. *State of Madras.*
14. For example Chapter IV incorporating Article 300A carries the Heading "Right to Property."
15. Granville Austin, *The Indian Constitution : The Cornerstone of a Nation,* p. 50.
16. *Ibid.*

from which the masses of India had suffered all through these ages. Democracy can only exist and flourish amongst a society of equals and the Indian Constitution makes social and civic equality as the bedrock of Indian polity. It guarantees equality of all persons before the law, prohibits discrimination on grounds of religion, race, caste, sex or place of birth as between citizens, grants to all equality of opportunity in the matter of public employment, and abolishes untouchability on the one side and titles on the other.[17] Citizens may not be denied admission to educational institutions maintained by the State or receiving aid out of State funds on the grounds only of religion, race, caste, or language. Minorities may establish their own schools and government may not discriminate against them in making grants on the grounds of religion, race or language.

The Supreme Court bench consisting of Justice O. Chinnappa Reddy, Baharul Islam and A. P. Sen held in *Randhir Singh's* case that the "right to equal pay for equal work" is a fundamental right and enforceable as such. The Court ruled that construing Articles 14 (right to equality before the law) and 16 (right to equality of opportunity in matter of job opportunity and public appointment) in the light of Article 39 (d)—that there is equal pay for equal work for both men and women—the principle of equal opportunity for equal pay is deducible from those Articles and may properly be applied to cases of unequal scales of pay based on no classification or irrational classification though those drawing the different scales of pay do identical work under the same employer."

Some exceptions are, however, inevitable and the Constitution sets out these exceptions. A legislature may make laws with special provisions for women and children. The Constitution (First Amendment) Act, 1951, further provided that "Nothing in this Article (15) or in clause (2) of Article 29 shall prevent the State from making any special provision for the advancement of any socially and educationally backward classes of citizens or for the Scheduled Castes and the Scheduled Tribes." Another exception made is with regard to the equality of opportunity in public employment. Parliament may confine employment under State or local authority to residents. A State may also provide for the reservation of appointments or posts for members of backward classes, which, in the opinion of the State, are not adequately represented in the services under the State. Offices connected with religious or denominational institutions may be reserved for the adherents of a particular religion or belonging to a particular denomination.

The right to equality, therefore, aims at protecting citizens against discriminatory treatment by the State in the fields of administration and legislation, to advance the uplift of the socially backward classes even to the exception of granting them special privileges for removing other and cruder forms of social inequality. Such social customs and disabilities as enforced segregation of the so-called untouchables at wells, in streets, schools and places of worship are declared illegal. In fact, the Constitution bans all kinds of untouchability specified and unspecified and uplifts more than 50 million untouchables from their age-old degraded social status. The right to equality, in sum, fosters the social revolution by creating a society egalitarian to the extent that all citizens are to be equally free from coercion or restriction by the State, or by the society privately. Liberty is no longer the privilege of the few, but a social content and right of all, high and low, men and women irrespective of religion, caste and creed.

### The Right to Freedom

The right to freedom is covered by Articles 19 to 22 and embraces the classical liberties of the individual. Of these, Article 19 is the most important as it originally guaranteed six fundamental rights, which may be described as six freedoms, *viz.,* (a) freedom of speech and expression; (b) freedom of assembly; (c) freedom of association; (d) freedom of movement; (e) freedom of residence and settlement; and (f) freedom of property,[18] and (g) freedom of profession, occupation, trade or business. All these freedoms are the most important ingredients of human happiness and progress, as without them no individual can rise to the full stature of his personality. The Preamble of almost every Constitution epitomises these freedoms and declares them as its objectives. For instance, the Preamble to the Constitution of the United States, *inter alia,* declares "to secure the blessings of liberty to ourselves and to our posterity." The Preamble to the Indian Constitution declares that one of its objectives is

17. Articles 17 and 18.
18. Freedom of Property as contained originally in sub-clause (f) has been omitted by the Constitution (Forty-fourth Amendment) Act, 1978, S. 2.

to secure to all citizens "Liberty of thought, expression, belief, faith and worship."

Article 19 may be divided into two parts. The first is the declaration of rights. The second part contains limitations [clauses (2) to (6)] each governing one or more clauses of the first part. Consistent with the theory that rights can never be absolute, the Constitution imposes specific limitations on their exercise and enjoyment. This is an improvement on the American Constitution which leaves the determination of restrictions and adjustment of conflicting interests of the individual and society to the courts. The Constitution of India defines the scope of limitations and authorises the State to restrict the exercise of freedoms guaranteed by Article 19 within the restricting clauses of the Article. It has been maintained that these limitations are, in fact, a partial justification of the American doctrine of Police Power.

The limitations imposed on the freedom of speech and the right to property were substantially modified by the Constitution (First Amendment) Act, 1951. The scope of the freedom of speech under the original provision was exceptionally wide. There were only four reservations restricting this right, *viz.*, laws relating to libel, slander and defamation; contempt of court; decency or morality; and security of the State. Thus, "public order" was not one of the purposes for which the freedom of speech could be restricted. Similarly, incitement to an offence was not made one of the objects to restrict the freedom of speech. The Supreme Court held in a series of cases that a law restricting the freedom of speech and not relating to defamation or contempt of court and not involving offences against decency or morality would be *ulta vires* unless it related to any matter which undermined the security of, or tended to overthrow the State. The 1951 Amendment added three more reservations to existing list contained in Article 19(2). The new reservations were : (1) friendly relations with foreign states; (2) public order; and (3) incitement to an offence. With the inclusion of these three additional reservations the right to freedom of speech was considerably curtailed and the scope of interference appreciably widened, provided the courts could be satisfied about the reasonableness of restrictions. By reasonable restrictions, the Supreme Court meant restrictions which are not excessive in nature and beyond what is required in the interests of the public. The Supreme Court also held that "the determination by the Legislature of what constitutes a reasonable restriction is not final or conclusive; it is subject to supervision by this Court. In the matter of Fundamental Rights the Supreme Court watches and guards the rights guaranteed by the Constitution and in exercising its functions it has the power to set aside the Act of the Legislature if it is in violation of the freedoms guaranteed by the Constitution."[19]

The Constitution (Sixteenth Amendment) Act, 1963, added the "Sovereignty and integrity of India" as one of the grounds in the interests of which Legislatures could impose reasonable restrictions on freedom of speech and expression, assembly, and forming of associations, or unions. Asoke K. Sen, the Law Minister, while moving a motion to refer the Constitution (Sixteenth) Amendment Bill to a Joint Committee of Parliament, said in the House of the People on January 22, 1963 that powers were also being taken to impose restrictions on those individuals or organisations who wanted to make secession from India as political issues for the purposes of fighting elections. This, he maintained, had become necessary as some decisions of the Supreme Court made it clear that Article 19 of the Constitution in its present form was not enough to ban secessionist activity. He further said that it was also being provided that any persons who wanted to stand as a candidate for a seat in the Assembly in a State or in the House of People or a State Council or the Council of States should take an oath, pledging himself to uphold the sovereignty and integrity of India. This would ensure that no candidate would make secession a political issue in the elections. Furthermore after elections, every member would have to take another oath, pledging himself to the same thing, namely, upholding the sovereignty and integrity of India.

Similarly, sub-clauses (b) and (c) of Article 19 (1) confer the freedom to assemble peaceably and to form associations or unions. The freedom to speech is complimentary to the freedom to assemble and the freedom to form associations or unions. The Sixteenth Amendment, however, restricted their scope. Clauses 3 and 4 of Article 19 empower the State to make any law imposing, in the interests of sovereignty and integrity of India or public order or morality reasonable restrictions on the exercise of these freedoms.

Other rights guaranteed by Article 19 may

19. *Chintaman Rao* v. *The State of Madhya Pradesh,* A.I.R. 1954 S.C., 118.

be briefly stated. The right to move freely is the right of movement unchecked and unrestricted anywhere within the territory of the Indian Union, subject to such restrictions as are imposed by any existing law or such as the State may in future impose in the public interest or to safeguard the interests of any Scheduled Tribes. In times of emergency, such as war, every citizen cannot claim as a matter of right access to places considered of military or strategic importance. Similarly, when an epidemic spreads in one part of the country, people may be prohibited by law from entering or leaving the affected area in the interest of public health. The freedom of movement also does not take away the right which law gave to the Government to extern any person from any part of the country for a particular period in the interests of maintenance of law and order,[20] as also to detain any person for sufficient grounds if the public interest demanded it.[21]

Allied to the right of free movement is the right to reside and settle in any part of the territory of India. This right is limited by reasonable restrictions in the interests of general public or for the protection of the interests of Scheduled Tribes.

Finally, the right to practise any trade or profession is subject to the right of the State to prescribe professional or technical qualifications to enable a citizen to become a lawyer or an engineer. This restriction is natural and necessary. The Constitution (First Amendment) Act, 1951, further empowered the State to reserve to itself the right to carry on any trade, business, industry or service either directly or through State controlled corporations to the complete or partial exclusion of private citizens. The purpose of the amendment was explained by the Law Minister during the course of debate on the Amendment Bill. He said that the State Governments would gradually take to nationalization; hence it was necessary that the Constitution should be amended to provide authority for the same. Article 19(6) was, therefore, amended to avoid the adverse implications of this decision as far as State trading was concerned. The reasonableness of any law permitting nationalization of any trade or business cannot be a subject of judicial review.[22]

It will, therefore, be obvious that under the amended Clause (6) of Article 19 the restrictions on the right of carrying on any trade or profession, etc., fall into three classes : (a) reasonable restrictions imposed under the general power in the interest of the general public; (b) restrictions in the form of professional or technical qualifications; and (c) any law relating to carrying on trade or business or industry or service by the State or corporation owned or controlled by the State. Restrictions imposed in the interests of general public give a very wide scope for interference and can include all matters affecting public welfare, such as, public safety, public health, public morals, etc. Reasonable restrictions include "prohibition", having regard to the exceptional circumstances which involve patent and widespread danger to the community. It may, accordingly, prohibit a citizen from carrying on a particular trade, business or profession.[23] The State may also create a monopoly in relation to any trade which is liable to cause injury to the public,[24] or any trade in commodities essential to the life of the community.[25]

## Life and Liberty as Rights

The rights guaranteed in Articles 20, 21 and 22 relate to the individual's personal liberty and collectively come under the sub- heading "Right to Freedom." These rights strengthen the liberties conferred on citizens under Article 19. Article 20 deals with certain Fundamental Rights of a person accused of a crime and embodies certain important principles of criminal jurisprudence, Clause (1) of the Article embodies the principle that no one should be made to suffer any punishment for an offence under any law not in force at the time of the commission of an offence. Similarly, no person shall be subject to a penalty greater than that which might have been inflicted under the law in force at the time of the commission of the offence. Clause (2) of the same Article embodies the fundamental principle that no one should be placed in jeopardy twice for the same offence. The principle underlying this clause is the same as underlies the "double jeopardy" clause of the American Constitution,though the words used are different. Clause (3) gives effect

20. *N.B. Khare* v. *State of Delhi,* 1950.
21. *A.K.Gopalan* v. *State of Madras,* 1952.
22. *Saghir Ahmed* v. *State of U.P.,* A.I.R., 1954 S.C 224; *Ramchandra Palai* v. *State of Orissa,* A.I.R. 1956 S.C. 298.
23. *Commr. Narendra* v. *Union of India,* A.I.R. 1960 2 S.C. 375.
24. *Cooverji* v. *Excise Commissioner,* A.I.R., 1954 S.C. 220.
25. *P.T. Society v. R.T.A.* 1960 S.C. 801.

to the principle that no one should be compelled to give evidence against himself in a criminal case. This clause follows the language of the Fifth Amendment of the Constitution of the United States, though the rule laid down in the Indian Constitution is "narrower than the American rule as expanded by interpretation."[26]

The Constitution (Forty-fourth Amendment) Act, 1978, prohibited the suspension, by Presidential Order, during the operation of the Proclamation of Emergency, the right to move the Supreme Court by appropriate proceedings, including the writ of *habeas corpus*, for the enforcement of rights conferred by Article 20—protection in respect of conviction for offences.[27] Nor has the State the power to make any law or take executive action restricting, abridging or abrogating the rights guaranteed under Article 20.[28]

Article 21 guarantees to every person the most essential of all rights, the right to life and personal liberty, which the Article says cannot be taken away except according to procedure established by law. The Constitution permits the continuance of preventive detention, but only in accordance with the laws providing for it. This Article is not intended to be a constitutional limitation upon the powers of the legislatures. The object is simply to serve as a restraint upon the Executive so that it may not proceed against the life or personal liberty of the individual save under the authority of some law and in conformity with the procedure laid therein. The procedure so laid down must be in conformity with Article 22 of the Constitution.

The phrase "established by law" means enacted by law and the word "law" means State-made law. No person can, accordingly, claim that the procedure prescribed by law does not conform to the principles of natural justice. Explaining the implications of the phrase "established by law", Justice Das observed that Article 21 defines the ambit of the right to life and personal liberty.[29] It is not an absolute right but is a qualified right "a right circumscribed by the possibility or risk of being lost according to the procedure established by law. It is for Parliament to enact a law changing the procedure and once it is changed that procedure becomes the procedure established by law. When a person is deprived of liberty otherwise than procedure established according to law, it is only then the courts will interfere. It is not for the courts to determine whether the law is reasonable or not.[30]

From 1950 to 1977, the Supreme Court took the view that Article 21 is a protection only against executive action which does not have the warrant of law behind and, therefore, if there was a law, it is good enough. It may prescribe any procedure. So long as it prescribes some procedure, it would meet the requirements of Article 21, But in *Maneka Gandhi's* case, the Supreme Court decided for the first time that the procedure to meet the test of Article 21 must be reasonable, fair and just. Just any procedure will not do. It must satisfy the test of reasonableness. The Court held that the concept of reasonableness runs like a golden thread through the entire fabric of the Constitution. Article 14, which guarantees equality before the law, also postulates reasonableness and non-arbitrariness; Article 19 contemplates reasonableness and so also does Article 21.

During the operation of the Proclamation of Emergency the right to move the Supreme Court by appropriate proceedings for the enforcement of the right to the protection of life and liberty conferred by Article 21 cannot be suspended. By inserting this provision the Constitution (Forty-fourth Amendment) Act, 1978, nullified the effects of the Supreme Court decision during the Emergency in what came to be known as the *Habbeas Corpus* case (*A. D. M. Jabalpur* v. *S. S. Shukla* 1976 (supp.) SCR, 172). In this case the court ruled that in view of the Presidential Order under Article 359 of the Constitution suspending the enforcement of Fundamental Rights no person had any *locus standi* to move any writ petition for *habeas corpus* or any other writ, or order or direction to challenge the legality of an order of detention on the ground that the Order was not under or in compliance with the statute or was illegal or was vitiated by *mala fides*, factual or legal, or was based on extraneous considerations. Justice H. R. Khanna dissented from the majority opinion of the Court.

Article 22 of the Constitution gives certain constitutional rights to arrested persons and also lays down certain fundamental rules with regard

26. Basu, Durga Das, *Commentary on the Constitution of India, op. cit.*, p. 149.
27. Article 359 (1).
28. Article 359 (1A).
29. AI.R. 1950 S.C. p. 114.
30. *Ram Singh* v. *State of Delhi*, (1951) S.C.R., 451.

to preventive detention. It may, however, be noted that provisions relating to preventive detention are peculiar inasmuch as the Constitution of India permits resort to preventive detention even in peace time. In other democratic countries preventive detention is usually a method resorted to in emergencies like war. Preventive detention in India for reasons connected with the security of the State, or the maintenance of public order, or maintenance of supplies and services essential for the community, is on the Concurrent List[31] but preventive detention for reasons connected with defence, foreign affairs, or the security of India is within the exclusive competence of Parliament.[32]

The first two clauses of Article 22 deal with detention under the ordinary law and prescribe the procedure when a person is arrested. It ensures : (i) right to be informed of the grounds of arrest; (ii) right to consult and to be defended by a legal practitioner of his choice; (iii) right to be produced before a magistrate within twenty-four hours; and (iv) freedom from detention beyond the specified period of twenty-four hours except by order of the magistrate.

The remaining clauses of this Article relate to preventive detention. Detention can be of two types : punitive and preventive. A preventive detention is intended to detain a person, without trial and without any charge of commission of an offence. It is a measure to intercept a person as a matter of precaution before he actually commits an offence. No offence is proved nor any charge is formulated, but there is a strong suspicion or reasonable probability that the individual commits or is likely to commit acts prejudicial to the welfare of the society, the security of the State and the stability of the Government established by law. It is not a criminal conviction which can only be warranted by legal evidence. The person under detention (detenu) is not given immediately on his arrest reasons for such arrest and detention. Neither he has any right to consult a lawyer, nor is he to be produced before a magistrate within twenty-four hours. Provisions of clauses (1) and (2) of Article 22 do not apply to a person arrested or detained under any law providing for preventive detention as also to any person who for the time being is an enemy alien.

Preventive detention legislation contemplates executive action for holding a person in custody for indefinite period without trial. The specific heads of prejudicial activities for which preventive detention can be effected are contained in List I, Entry 9 and List III, Entry 3, of the Seventh Schedule to the Constitution. The sole justification for arrest is the satisfaction of the competent administrative authority or suspicion of reasonable probability of the detenu committing or likely to commit an act which may either cause harm to society or endanger the security of the State. Such detention is outside the reach of Article 19(1) (d) which guarantees the right to all citizens to move freely throughout the territory of India.

Article 22 clauses (4) to (7), however, provide safeguard against the rigours of preventive detention :

(1) detention canot last for more than three months, except on the report of the Advisory Board consisting of persons who are, or have been, or are qualified to be appointed as, Judge of the High Court, has reported before the expiration of three months that there is in its opinion sufficient cause for such detention;[33]

(2) the period of detention can in no case exceed beyond the maximum period prescribed by law made by Parliament;

(3) the detaining authority shall, as soon as may be, communicate to the detenu the grounds on which the detention has been made and shall afford him the earliest opportunity of making a representation against the order of his detention.

(4) the communication conveying the grounds of detention shall contain facts, except those that cannot be disclosed for reasons of public interest;

(5) Parliament may by law prescribe the circumstances under which, and the class or classes of cases in which, a person may be detained for a period longer than three months under any law providing for detention without obtaining the opinion of the Advisory Board;

(6) the maximum period for which any person in any class or classes of cases may be detained under any law providing for detention;

(7) the procedure to be followed by an Advisory Board in an inquiry.

**Right against Exploitation**

Articles 23 and 24 come under the subheading right against exploitation. Article 23 categorically prohibits all traffic in human beings

31. Article 246, Seventh Schedule, List III, entry 3.
32. *Ibid.*, List I, entry 9.
33. Article 22(4) substituted by The Constitution (Forty-Fourth Amendment) Act, 1979, S. 3.

and *begar* and other similar forms of forced labour. Traffic in human beings is evidently a very wide expression and would embrace not only the prohibition of slavery and bonded labour but also traffic in women for immoral or other purposes. Contravention of this prohibition has been made an offence punishable in accordance with law. The Constitution-makers had in mind the widespread evil custom of forced labour without remuneration or just a nominal remuneration verging on pittance prevalent in the country since ages. The National Survey Organisation, commissioned by the Planning Commission, had estimated the bonded labour in the country at 3.45 lakh. Of this number 2.14 lakh had been identified and 1.75 lakh of them had been rehabilitated. The responsibility of rehabilitating the bonded labour lay with the State Governments, but the Labour Minister told the House of the People (Lok Sabha), on March 23, 1987 that the State Governments were not responsive and, therefore, an exact estimate of the existence of bonded labour and their rehabilitation was not possible to give.

Clause 2 of Article 23, however, provides for the power of the State to impose compulsory service for public purposes. The expression public purposes has nowhere been defined, but it must include an object or aim in which the general interest of the community, as opposed to particular interst of individuals, is directly and vitally concerned.[34] The expression "public purpose", as Ambedkar explained to the Constituent Assembly, "includes any object or aim in which the general interest of individuals is directly or vitally involved.[35] Compulsory service for public purposes necessarily includes military service as it is a service for a public purpose to maintain the sovereignty and integrity of the country. In *Dulal Samanta* v. *District Magistrate, Howrah,* the Calcutta High Court held that the "conscription for police or military service is neither *begar* nor traffic in human beings and is, therefore, not hit by Article 23."[36] In *Atma Ram* v. *State of Bihar* it was held that the provision in the Bihar Finance Act, 1950, making it obligatory on owners of motor vehicles to collect rent and taxes imposed on freights was within the exception of Article 23 (2) which allowed the State to impose compulsory service for public purposes.[37]

Article 24 provides that no child below the age of fourteen years shall be employed to work in any factory or mine or engaged in any other hazardous employment. Here the Indian Constitution goes ahead of the American Constitution wherein there is no express prohibition against the employment of children in any factory or mine or in other hazardous occupations.

**Right to Freedom of Religion**

The Preamble to the Constitution expresses a resolve of the people to constitute India into a Sovereign Socialist Secular Democratic Republic[38] in order to ensure, among other things, "Liberty of thought, expression, belief, faith and worship." The secular principle thus accepted by the people of India was made fundamental and enshrined in Part III of the Constitution as contained in Articles 25 to 28. These rights have a wide scope and include both the personal and social aspects of religion and are equally enjoyed by all persons living in India, citizens and aliens. The Constitution guarantees to all personss freedom of conscience, and to profess,[39] practise and propagate any religion subject to the prescribed limitations of public order, morality and health and other provisions of Part III. The Constitution, as such, does not only guarantee the freedom of religious faith and belief but it protects also acts done in pursuance of religion and this is made clear by the use of expression "practice of religion." All rituals, ceremonies, observances and modes of worship which are considered as integral part of a religion are permitted to be practised unhindered provided they do not offend any of the prescribed limitations.

But religious freedom and freedom of conscience do not diminish in any manner the regulatory power of the State given to it by the provisions of the Constitution. Religious freedom stands harmoniously with other Fundamental Rights. Religious institutions[40] being on the Con-

34. *State of Bihar* v. *Kameshwar Singh,* A.I.R. 1952 S.C. 252.
35. Refer to *Constituent Assembly Debates,* Vol. VIII, pp. 809-10; as also to *State of Bihar* v. *Kameshwar Singh,* A.I.R. 1952 S.C. 252.
36. A.I.R. 1958 Cal. 265.
37. A.I.R. 1954 Pat. 359.
38. Substituted by the Constitution (Forty-second Amendment) Act, 1976, for the words "Sovereign Democratic Republic."
39. The wearing and carrying of *Kirpans* (Swords) is deemed to be included in the profession of the Sikh religion. Article 25 Explanation I.
40. Seventh Schedule, List III, Entry 28.

current List, the right of freedom to religion does not, accordingly, prevent the State Legislatures to enact any law regulating or restricting any economic, financial, political or other secular activity of a religious body, nor render invalid laws throwing open public religious institutions formerly reserved for a section of the adherents of any one of the Hindu, Sikh, Jain, or Buddhist religions, to all adherents of that religion. Similarly, religious freedom is no bar to social welfare and reformatory legislation, though the Muslim Women (Protection of Rights on Divorce) Act, 1986, is a retrograde and discriminatory measure.[41]

Since the provision of Article 25 is analogous to the first amendment to the United States Constitution and certain articles in other Commonwealth Constitutions, the Supreme Court of India has largely based its reasonings on judgments delivered by apex courts in those countries. In the National Anthem case the Supreme Court decided in August 1986 (*Bijoe Emmanuel* v. *State of Kerala)* that the expulsion of three school students[42] for not singing the National Anthem was violative of Article 25 of the Constitution. It was held by the Supreme Court in 1958 that Article 25 embodied the principle of tolerance which has throughout been the characteristic feature of the Constitution and emphasised the secular motive of the Republic.

Underlining the same sentiments, the Supreme Court judgement in the instant case stated,'' Article 25 is an Article of faith in the Constitution, incorporated in recognition of the principle that the real test of a true democracy is the ability of even an insignificant minority to find its identity[43] under the country's constitution. This has to be borne in mind in interpreting Article 25.'' The judgment also held that the Court cannot go into the reasonablemess of a particular religious belief or practice. The question is whether the belief is held genuinely and conscientiously. If it is genuinely held, practices which do not violate public order, morality and health cannot be banned.

The judgement makes a third crucial point to be considered when Fundamental Right to freedom of conscience and religion is invoked. It says that the act complained of as offending the right must be examined to discover whether such act is to protect public order, morality or health and whether it is authorised by law made to regulate or restrict any economic, political or secular activity which may be associated with religious practice or to provide for social welfare and reform.

A large volume of cases decided by the Supreme and High Courts on Article 25 raise the question whether a particular practice is a part of religion or not. A government employee in the State of Uttar Pradesh, for instance, claimed that taking a second wife is part of his religion and a service rule banning it violated Article 25. The Allahabad High Court rejected the plea. The same High Court had held in the case of a Muslim that taking four wives is not part of Islam, though the personal law allows a Muslim male to do so. The Bombay High Court has held that polygamy is not a part of Hindu religion. The Kerala High Court has held that a student cannot claim freedom of conscience to come in improper dress in the college against the college rules. A Hindu lady who refused to produce her photograph for identification purpose claimed the right to freedom of religion, but the Calcutta High Court rejected the defence.

The Supreme Court has held that the Tandava dance in processions or public places by Anand Margis carrying lethal weapons and human skulls was not an essential rite. In a recent case relating to the shifting of Muslim graves in Varanansi, the Court held that there was nothing in Islam which prohibits the shifting of graves.

Even the right to practice religion is not absolute and is subject to public order, morality and health empowering the State to make laws restricting, economic, political or secular activity, though such activity may be associated with religious practise, the Supreme Court has held. The State has the power to legislate for social

---

41. The Act denied to divorced Muslim women the right to seek maintenance from their husbands under Section 125 of the Criminal Procedure Code.
42. The students belonged to Jehvoh Witnesses; a religious group founded in the United States in 1872, by Charles Taze Russel. The Jehvoh Witnesses believe that the world power and political parties are unwitting allies of Satan. They refuse to vote, run for public office, serve in the armed forces, salute the flag, stand for the national anthem or recite pledge of allegiance. They interpret the Bible literally and had at one time come to the conclusion that Jesus Christ would return in 1874 and millions of people living in the 1940's would never die.
43. Jehvoh Witnesses in the United States had taken 45 cases to the Supreme Court and have won significant victories for the freedom of religion and speech. Canada, Australia and Great Britain have also to cope with tricky legal questions raised by them.

welfare and reform and any such legislation may extend even to some interference with the practice and propagation of religion. For instance, on the vexing question of religious processions, which often end in bloody riots, the Supreme Court has repeatedly granted powers to the authorities to control or even ban such activities. In the Varanasi graves case, it reiterated in 1984 that "the exercise of fundamental rights is not absolute and must yield to maintenance of public order."

All religious denominations are guaranteed autonomy, the right to establish institutions, and the right to acquire and deal with property, but only subject to public order, health and morality. No one can be compelled to pay taxes for the propagation or maintenance of any religion and religious instruction is not to be given in schools and colleges wholly maintained out of government revenues. But religious instruction may be imparted in private institutions receiving a grant from public funds or recognised by the State provided no pupil is given religious instruction or made to attend religious worship in a building attached to the institution without his consent, or, if he is a minor, his guardian's consent.

**Cultural and Educational Rights**

Apart from individual's rights and freedoms, the Constitution recognises and guarantees certain non-political rights of the religious, cultural and linguistic minorities, groups or sections of the people. Article 29 guarantees to every minority or section of the people to preserve its language, script and culture notwithstanding the provisions of Article 343 under which the official language of the Union shall be Hindi in Devanagari script. Clause (2) of the same Article provides that no citizen may be denied admission to State and State-aided educational institutions on the grounds only of religion, race, caste or language. Article 30 guarantees to all minorities whether based on religion or language the right to establish and administer their educational institutions and the State shall not discriminate against them in making grants on grounds of religion, race or language.

There is implicit in the right conferred by Article 30(1) the right to impart instruction in their own institutions to the children of their own community in their own language. To deny it is tantamount to depriving it of the right conferred by Artcle 29(1) which guarantees to conserve language or script of a minority community and the right to establish and administer educational institutions of their choice under Aricle 30(1). Article 30 came for discussion in Kerala Education Bill, 1957. Since this Bill, which was reserved for the consideration of the President, imposed serious limitations on the right of the minorities in the administration of their institutions aided and recognised by the Kerala Government, the President referred some of the provisions of the Bill to the Supreme Court for its advisory opinion. The Court expressed the opinion that the minority community "can effectively conserve its language, script or culture by and through educational institutions and, therefore, the right to establish and maintain educational institutions of its own choice is a necessary concomitant to the right to conserve its distinctive language, script or culture and that is what is conferred on all minorities by Article 30(1)........." There is no constitutional right, the Court remarked, to receive State aid. "If the State does grant aid, it cannot impose such conditions (*e.g.,* that the State will acquire the institution or will take over the management if certain things are not done) as will deprive it of its right under Article 30 (1). The State cannot take over the management of schools established by minority communities on the plea that it (State) seeks to do so or introduce free and compulsory education as required by Directive Principles." The object can be fulfilled through the State-owned or State-aided institutions, the Court said :[44]

A special Constitution Bench of the Supreme Court declared on April 26, 1974 that the provisions of the Gujarat University Act, 1949, as amended in 1972, governing the affiliation of minority colleges, transforming them into constituent colleges of the University, regulating the appointment and service conditions of the staff and providing for arbitration of disputes, violated the fundamental right of the minorities to administer educational institutions of their choice.[45] The Supreme Court, thus, reaffirmed the rights enshrined in Articles 29 and 30. "There can be no surrender of constitutional protection of the right of minorities to popular will masquerading as the common pattern of education," Justice Mathew remarked. This ruling by the Court followed two writ petitions filed by the Ahmedabad

44. A.I.R. 1958 S.C. 856.
45. A.I.R. 1974 S.C. 1389.

St. Xavier's College Society and others.

But in its judgment on November 17, 1986, the Supreme Court declared as ''discriminatory and void'' Section 12 of the Delhi School Education Act which exempts unaided minority institutions from the provisions of the Act (Sections 8 to 11) dealing with the terms and conditions of employees of recognised private schools''. The Bench held that ''regulatory measures which are designed towards the achievement of the goal of making the minority educational institutions effective instruments for imparting education cannot be considered to impinge upon the right guaranateed by Article 30(1) of the Constitution.'' The Court ruled that the requirement (prescribed by Section 10) is a permissible regulation aimed at attracting competent staff and consequently at the ''excellence of the institution.'' The provisions of the Act made applicable to unaided minority educational institutions by this judgment related to payment of scales of pay and allowances, medical facilities, pension, gratuity, provident fund and other prescribed benefits, etc. to the employees of recognised private schools at rates not being less than those allowed to the employees of the corresponding schools run by the Government authority.

The Constitution (Forty-fourth Amendment) Act, 1978, inserted a new Clause 30 (1A) after Article 30 which ordained that in making any law providing for the compulsory acquisition of any property of an educational institution established and administered by a minority, the State shall ensure that the amount fixed by or determined by such law for the acquisition of such property ''is such as would not restrict or abrogate the right guaranteed in Article 30'' —Right of minorities to establish and administer educational institutions. Whereas the amendment conceded to the State the power to acqurie property of an educational institution established and administered by a minority, it is obligatory for the State to ensure that the amount fixed for compensation of that property is adequate enough so that it may enable that minority to establish and administer a similar institution at an other location.

**Right to Property**

The consensus reached between the Government and the Opposition parties on April 20, 1978 on deleting the right to property from Chapter III on Fundamental Rights and giving it a statutory status was reflected in the Constitution (Forty-fourth Amendment) Act, 1978, by inserting a new Chapter IV with the heading Right to Property and incorporating Article 300-A which ordains that ''No person shall be deprived of his property save by authority of law.'' Section 5 of the Amendment omitted the sub-heading ''Right to Property'' occurring after Article 30. Article 31A and Article 31C have been suitably amended as to omit all references to the right to property. Similarly, Section 2 omitted Sub-cl-(f) in Article 19(1) that read ''to aqcuire, hold and dispose of property.'' This change does not in any way affect the right of a citizen to hold, acquire or dispose of property except that under the omitted provisions the right to property could be adversely affected only by a constitutional amendment and in accordance with the procedure prescribed under Article 368, whereas under Article 300–A the right to property can be modified by a law passed by Parliament in accordance with the procedure adopted for enactment of an ordinary law. But it does affect the sanctity of property as an inalienable basic right.

The Constitution, however, retains Articles 31A and 31B–saving of laws providing for acquisition of estates, etc., and validation of certain Acts and Regulations. The effects of both these Articles are very wide and were intended to validate the acquistion of zamindaries on the abolition of Permanent Settlement without interference from Courts.

Article 31A provides that no law, past or future, affecting rights of any proprietor or intermediate holder of any estate or taking over the management of property by the State for a limited period either in the public interest or in order to secure the proper management of the property, or the extinction or modification of any rights of managing agents, secretaries or treasurers, managing directors or managers of corporations or any voting rights of shareholders, or extinction or modification of rights under mining leases and other similar agreements regarding any mineral or mineral oil or the permanent termination or cancellation of any such agreement, lease or licence shall be deemed void on the ground that it is inconsistent with, or takes away or abridges any of the rights by Article 14 or Article 19. If any law is made by the legislature of a State, the provisions of Article 31A shall not apply unless it had been reserved for the consideration of the President and received his assent.

The Constitution (Seventeenth Amendment) Act, 1964, added another provision to Article 31A. It provided that where any law makes any provision for the acquisition by the State of any estate and where any land comprised therein is held by a person under his personal cultivation, it shall not be lawful for the State to acquire any portion of such land as is within ceiling limit applicable to him for the time being or any building or structure standing thereon unless the law relating to the acquisition of such land or structure, provides for payment of compensation at a rate which shall not be less than the market value of such a property.

Article 31B was inserted to save the Acts, and Regulations specified in the Ninth Schedule of the Constitution notwithstanding any decision of a court or tribunal that any of these Acts, Regulations or provisions is void on the ground that it takes away or abridges or is inconsistent with any of the Fundamental Rights as contained in Part III of the Constitution. This Article, however, reserves the power of the competent Legislature to repeal or amend any of the Acts or Regulations included in the Ninth Schedule.

Article 31C inserted by the Twenty-fifth Amendment Act, provided that no law passed to give effect to the Directive Principles of State Policy in Article 39 Clauses (b) and (c) would be deemed to be void on the ground that it was inconsistent with, took away or abridged any of the Rights conferred by Articles 14, and 19, and no law containing a declaration that it was for giving effect to such policy would be called in question in any court that it does not give effect to such policy. When such a law was made by the State Legislature, the provisions of Article 31C would not apply unless such law having been reserved for the consideration of the President has received his assent.

In *Keshavananda Bharati* case the Supreme Court allowed the Directive Principles of State Policy as contained in Article 39 Clauses (b) and (c) to override the Fundamental Rights. But the Court also held that any law declared by Parliament to give effect to these two Directive Principles would be subject to judicial review in order to determine whether the law did in fact achieve that objective. To nullify this effect of the Supreme Court's ruling, the Constitution (Forty-Second Amendment) Act, 1976, amended Article 31C and established the primacy of the Directive Principles. The Supreme Court struck down in the *Minerva Mills* case Article 31C as it changed the basic structure of the Constitution in terms of the *Kesavananda Bharati* case.

**Right to Constitutional Remedies**

Article 32 guarantees to every citizen the right to move the Supreme Court by appropriate proceedings for the enforcement of Fundamental Rights. And for that purpose the Supreme Court is given general powers to safeguard the Fundamental Rights as well as the power to issue directions or orders or writs in the nature of *habeas corpus, mandamus,* prohibition, *quo warranto* and *certiorari,* whichever may be appropriate, for the enforcement of any of the Fundamental Rights. A right without a remedy is a meaningless formality. Ambedkar described in the Constituent Assembly that remedies provided in Article 32 are '''the heart and soul of the Constitution.'' Before 1978, enforcement of rights, as mentioned in the Presidential Order, could be suspended, under Article 359, when a Proclamation of Emergency was in operation. The Presidentail Order could also suspend the enforcement of Articles 20 and 21. The Forty-fourth Amendment Act amended Article 359 to the extent that enforcement of rights guaranteed under Articles 20 and 21 cannot be suspended even during the operation of Emergency.

Hitherto resort to the suspension of the enforcement of Fundamental Rights had been made in the event of actual aggression. But lately it has been used for economic offences too on the ground that such offences constitued as serious a threat to the security of the country as an external aggression or internal disturbance and deserved to be dealt with on the same basis. Enforcement of Fundamental Rights for economic purpose was suspended by the Presidentail Order on November 16, 1974 in the case of persons detained under the Maintenance of the Internal Security Act, 1971 as amended by the Ordinance of September18,1974, and subsequently on December 23, 1974 under the Conservation of Foreign Exchange and Prevention of Smuggling Activities Act, 1974.

The Constitution (Forty-second Amendment) Act, 1976, debarred the Supreme Court, under the newly inserted Article 32A, from considering the constitutional validity of any State law in any proceedings under Article 32 unless the constitutional validity of any Central law was also an issue in such proceedings. Article 32A was, however, omitted by the Constitution (Forty-fourth) Act, 1978.

### Application of Rights to Armed Forces

One of the points that came at an early stage for consideration was the extent to which Fundamental Rights would apply to the members of the armed forces. By virtue of their nature of service and position, they had necessarily to be subject to a conduct and discipline not entirely consistent with the exercise of fundamenal rights as they would apply to an ordinary citizen. This fact was realised at the preliminary stages in the discussions of the Sub-Committee on Fundamental Rights. K. M. Munshi had provided in his draft that Union legislature by law be entitled to determine to what extent any of the fundamental rights should be restricted or abrogated for the members of the armed forces or forces charged with the maintenance of the public order to ensure the fulfilment of their duties and the maintenance of discipline. Munshi's reservation was accepted and adopted by the Advisory Committee and finally adopted by the Constituent Assembly with a minor verbal change suggested by Ambedkar.

Article 33 of the Constitution provides that Parliament may by law determine to what extent any of the rights conferred by Chapter III on Fundamental Rights shall, in their application to the members of the Armed Forces; or the members of the Forces charged with the maintenance of the public order; or persons employed in any bureau or other organisations established by the State for purposes of intelligence or counter-intelligence; or persons employed in, or in connection with the telecommunication systems set up for the purpose of any Force, bureau or organisation of the members of the Armed Forces or for purposes of intelligence or counter-intelligence be restricted or abrogated so as to ensure the proper discharge of their duties and the maintenance of discipline among them.

### Indemnity to Public Servants

At the revision stage, the Drafting Committee introduced a new Article 34 providing for indemnity to poublic servants and others for any action taken by them for maintenance or restoration of order in any area where martial law was in force. Justifying the need for such a provision, the Drafting Committee observed that the fundamental rights as contained in Part III might prevent validation by the legislature for acts done during the period when martial law was in force and also prevent the indemnifying of persons in the service of a Union or a State or other persons in respect of actions taken by them during such period.

In the Constituent Assembly when Article 34 came for consideration a number of amendments were proposed and of these one moved by Shibban Lal Saxena sought deletion of the Article on the ground that it might lead to excesses by officers working in the martial law area in the hope of indemnification by an Act of Parliament. Ambedkar replying to the debate maintained that if Article 34 was not included, the administration of martial law would not be possible.

The Assembly rejected the amendments and adopted Article 34. It provides that Parliament may by law, notwithstanding the provisions in Part III relating to the Fundamental Rights, indemnify any person in the service of the Union or of a State or any other person in respect of any act done by him in connection with the maintenance or restoration of order in any area within the territory of India where martial law was in force or validate any sentence passed, punishment inflicted, forfeiture ordered or other act done under martial law in that area.

### Legislation to Give Effect to Rights

Article 35 empowers Parliament to make laws with respect to any matter under Clause 3 of Article 16 (requirements as to residence to classes or class of employment or appointment); Clause 3 of Article 32 (empowering any court to exercise jurisdiction with respect to enforcement of Rights); Article 33 (modification of Rights in their application to Armed Forces); and Article 34 (restrictions on Rights while martial law is in force in any areea). Parliament has also the power to prescribe by law punishment for those acts which are declared to be offences under Part III in case of their violation. Clause (b) of Article 35 provides that in case ofActs already in existence which provide punishment for breach of fundamental rights, unless and until Parliament makes another provision, such laws would continue in operation.

## NATURE OF FUNDAMENTAL RIGHTS

### Rights not Sacrosanct

The Fundamental Rights were intended to serve three important purposes, namely, (i) to prevent the Executive from acting arbitrarily; (ii) to ensure some amount of security and protection to various types of minorities; and (iii) to promote and foster social revolution by establishing the conditions necessary for achieving justice, social, economic and political. But the Supreme Court, some eminent jurists and teachers in Political Science as well as quite a few prominent public men considered the rights contained in the Chapter on Fundamental Rights (Part III) as immutable and transcendental. In a series of judgements the Supreme Court described them as "paramount", "sacrosanct,"[46] "rights reserved by the people",[47] "inalienable and inviolable"[48] and "transcendental."[49] The immutability and permanence of the Fundamental Rights were sought to be established first on the reasoning that these rights are rooted in the doctrine of natural law and were, therefore, 'natural rights' as expressed in the traditional parlance and, secondly, on the ground that they have been given a place of permanence by the Constitution within its scheme.[50]

But the Fundamental Rights as contained in Part III of the Constitution, are neither rooted in the doctrine of natural law nor are they based on the theory of 'reserved rights'. They are conferred rights and embody the social values of the present generation. As the social values are not static, the Fundamental Rights are subject to changes and modifications in order to fulfil the aspirations of man in the context of his changed conditions and the environment in which he lives. Even the Supreme Court admitted in the *Gopalan* case that the provisions of Part III of the Constitution strike a balance between a written guarantee of individual rights and the collective interests of the community.[51] Justice J. M. Shelat of the Surpeme Court observed in a lecture delivered on December 18, 1966, that a study of the provisions of Part III "will at once show that while laying down the various fundamental rights of citizen, they also effectuate a reconciliation between them and the general needs and welfare of the society and the nation. By so doing, Part III leaves the door ajar for the functional working of the Constitution in future." The provisions of Part III themselves provide," Justice Shelat explained, "that these Fundamental Rights must yield to reasonable restrictions, the imposition of which may become necessary to satisfy the changing necessities and situations which might arise from time to time."[52]

It was, therefore, not the intention of the Father-framers to render the rights sacrosanct otherwise they would not have ventured to strike a balance or effectuate a reconciliation between them and the needs and welfare of society. Rights are dynamic realities and they have never been intended to be impediment to progress, development and advancement. They are conferred in fulfilment of the aims of the new social and economic order envisaged in the Directive Principles of State Policy set out in Part IV of the Constitution. But not in the manner in which the Constitution Forty-second Amendment had done by not even leaving a hazy line of demarcation between the Fundamental Rights and the Directive Principles and, thus, riding roughshod over the intentions of the Constitution-makers. The Amendment was, in fact, designed to personify the absolute authority of the Executive by removing all limitations on the amending power of Parliament and depriving the Courts of their jurisdiction to call in question any amendment of the Constitution. Speaking for himself and Justices Gupta, Untwalia and Kailasam in *Minerva Mills* case, Chief Justice Chandrachud observed, "Our Constitution is founded on a nice balance of power among the three wings of the State, namely, the Executive, the Legislative and the Judiciary. It is the function of the Judges, nay their duty, to pronounce on the validity of laws. If Courts are totally deprived of that power, the fundamental rights conferred upon the people will become mere adornments because rights without remedies are as writs in water."

46. *A.N. Gopalan* v. *State of Madras* (1950). S.C. J. (1950) S.C.R. 88, p. 198.
47. *State of Madras* v. *Champakam Dorairajan* (1951) *S.C.J.* 313 (1951) *S.C.R.* 825.
48. *M.S.M. Sharma* v. *Shri Krishan Sinha* (1959) *S.C.J. 925,* (1959) *I.S.C.R.* (Supp.) 806.
49. *Ujjam Bai* v. *State of U.P.* (1963) *I.S.C.R.* 778; A.I.R. 1963 S.C. 1621.
(1967) 2 S.C.J. 486 pp. 498-99.
50. *Golak Nath and others* v. *State of Punjab.*
51. Refer to Shetty. K. P. Krishna, *Fundamental Rights and Socio-Economic Justice in India,* p. 19.
52. Rajendra Prasad Endowment Lectures, *The Spirit of the Constitution* (Bharatiya Vidya Mandir 1967), p. 31.

# CHAPTER VII

# Directive Principles of State Policy and Fundamental Duties

### Beau Ideal in the Constitution

If the Preamble is the key to the understanding of the Constitution or to open the mind of its makers, the Directive Principles of State Policy, as enshrined in Part IV, are its beau ideal. It is here that the Constitution-makers poured their mind by setting forth the humanitarian socialist principles which epitomised the hopes and aspirations of the people and declared them as fundamental in the governance of the country. They are affirmative instructions from the ultimate sovereign to the State authorities, which are the creature of the Constitution established by them, to secure to all citizens justice – social, economic and political; liberty of thought, expression, belief, faith and worship; equality of status and opportunity; and to promote among them all fraternity assuring the dignity of the individual and the unity and integrity of the nation.[1]

It is the duty of all the authorities of the state to direct their activities in such a manner so as to secure the high ideals set forth in the Preamble and copiously analysed and enshrined in Part IV of the Constitution. The Directive Principles of State Policy are an amalgam of diverse subjects embracing the life of the nation and include principles which are general statements of social policy, principles of administrative policy, socio-economic rights, and a statement of the international policy of the country. B.R. Ambedkar told the Constituent Assembly that every Government, Central, State and local "shall be on the anvil, both in the daily affairs and at the end of a certain period when the voters and the electorate will be given an opportunity to assess the work done by the Government...... While we have established political democracy it is also the desire that we should lay down as our ideal economic democracy....... There are various ways in which people believe that economic democracy can be brought about, we have deliberately not introduced in the language that we have used in the Directive Principles something which is fixed or rigid. We have left enough room for the people of different ways of thinking, with regard to the reaching of the ideal of economic democracy. Our object in framing the Constitution is two-fold : (i) to lay down the form of political democracy, and (ii) lay down that our ideal is economic democracy, and also to prescribe that every Government, whatever is in power, shall strive to bring about economic democracy ......."[2]

The idea of making a constitutional declaration of social and economic policy is the recognition of the ideal of a service State in place of a regularoty State which found expression in the 1931 Karachi resolution of the Indian National Congress. The Karachi resolution held that in order to end the exploitation of the masses, political freedom should include economic freedom. Most of the members of the Constituent Assembly, and especially the select group in the Fundamental Rights Committee, were quite familiar with the political thinking at that time, the practice that the United States of America had of late adopted and the manner in which the Federal and State Governments had begun playing an every increasing role in the nation's social and economic life. They had also closely watched the fact that most of the new Constitutions that came into being after World War I, particularly of Germany and East European countries, had recognised that one of the chief

1. The Constitution (forty-second Amendment) Act, 1976, adds in the Preamble to the Constitution "integrity" after "unity" and it now reads "unity and integrity of the Nation."
2. *Constituent Assembly Debates*, Vol. VII, pp. 494-95.

functions of the State must be to foster and secure the social well-being of citizens and the economic prosperity of the nation.[3] The Irish Constitution, too, had greatly impressed the wide range of members of the Constituent Assembly. The long-standing affinity of the Indian National Congress with the Irish Nationalist Movement made the example of constitutional declaration expressed in the Irish Directive Principles of State Policy especially attractive to the Congress Assembly members, particularly the socialist-wing within its fold. But the most weighty support came from B.N. Rau, the Constitutional Adviser to the Constituent Assembly, Alladi Krishnaswami Ayyar, B.R. Ambedkar and K.T. Shah. Of the four, B.N. Rau was the most influential. He emulated in his *Constitutional Precedents* the Irish example of distinguishing between justiciable and non-justiciable rights. His *Precedents*, during the actual drafting of the Directive Principles, supplied the members of the Sub-Committee on Fundamental Rights with at least five of the original twelve provisions and the preamble of the Principles.[4]

**Directive Principles and Fundamental Rights**

With the precepts set out in the Directive Principles, which were the offspring of the Objectives Resolution, few if any members of the Constituent Assembly disagreed. Almost the only critical voices were those of members who believed that the provisions of the Directive should be justiciable if they were to be adequate to their task, and those of a few members who had, "a quarrel" with a particular provision within the Principles. T.T. Krishnamachari, who described the Directive Principles as "a veritable dustbin of sentiment........sufficiently resilient as to permit any individual of this house to ride his hobby horse into it, " could find few supporters. But Krishnamachari himself became less critical some two months after giving his speech on his appointment as a member of the Drafting Committee.

The initial approach of the Sub-Committee on the Fundamental Rights was to make no distinction between positive obligations and negative liberties as it was deemed to reflect the national demand. But immediately after the Sub-committee had drafted the negative rights, its members began talking of a section of non-justiciable rights. At the meeting held on March 31, 1947 it was decided to include the "Directive Principles of the Social Policy", as they were then called, with a preamble explaining that they were for the general guidance of all the authorities of the government and were not enforceable in any court. Thus, the break with the Fundamental Rights weas made.

But B.N. Rau suggested that it was to be occasionally necessary for the State to invade private rights in the discharge of one of its fundamental duties, as for example, to raise the nation's standard of health, of living, etc., and the Fundamental Rights being justiciable and the Directive Principles being without any legal force, the private right might override the public weal. He, accordingly, recommended for the careful consideration of the Sub-Committee whether "the Constitution might not expressly provide that no law made and no action taken by the State in discharge of its duties under Chapter III of Part III (Directive Principles in his Draft of the Constitution he submitted to the Drafting Committee) shall be invalid by reason of its contravening the provisions of Chapter II (Fundamental Rights)." [5] Rau's suggestion did not receive a favourable response and the Directives as finally incorporated in the Constitution are distinctly demarcated from the Fundamental Rights so far as their enforcement is concerned.

The Fundamental Rights are justiciable and Article 32 of the Constitution guarantees to all citizens the right to move the Supreme Court for their enforcement in case of violation or their abridgement by any authority of the State. It means that the Fundamental Rights are mandatory whereas the Directive Principles are declaratory as they have expressly been excluded from the purview of the courts. If any authority of the State does not take any positive action in promoting the objects set forth in the Chapter on the Directive Principles no action can be taken

3. Agnes Headlam Morley, *The New Democratic Constitutions of Europe*, p. 264.
4. Compare with the text of the Directive Principles as they were first presented to the Constituent Assembly in August 1947.
5. Rau, B.N., Notes on Certain Clauses of his Draft Constitution dated October 7, 1947, Shiva Rao, B., *The Framing of India's Constitution*, Vol. II. Also refer to Rau, B.M., *India's Constitution in the Making*, p. 333.

against that authority in a court of law. But the courts are bound to declare as void any law or executive action if it violated or infringed any of the provisions of the Chapter on Fundamental Rights. In case of conflict between the two, the Fundamental Rights shall prevail.

Conflicts between the Directive Principles and Fundamental Rights may arise due to several reasons and one of the important reasons is the presence of Clause 2 of Article 13 which stipulates that "The State shall not make any law which takes away or abridges the rights conferred by this Part (Part III Fundamental Rights) and any law made in contravention of this clause shall, to the extent of contravention, be void." It meant, till the enactment of the Twenty-fourth Amendment, and, finally, the Forty-second Amendment, that the State could not, while implementing Directive Principles, make laws in contravention of the Fundamental Rights. Nor could a citizen invoke the sanction of the Directive Principles in support of his claims under the Fundamental Rights. Jawaharlal Nehru was not oblivious of conflicts to arise between the Directive Principles and the Fundamental Rights. Speaking on the Constitution (First Amendment) Bill, he pointed out how such a conflict could arise. He observed, "The Directive Principles of State Policy present a dynamic move towards a certain objective. The Fundamental Rights represents something static, to preserve certain rights which exist. Both again are rights. But somehow and sometime it might so happen that, that dynamic movement and that standstill do not quite fit into each other."[6]

The Judiciary resolves such conflicts. The Supreme Court till recently took a firm stand that the Directive Principles could not override the Fundamental Rights and they must conform to and run subsidiary to the latter. *The State of Madras v. Champakam Dorairajan* was the first case decided by the Supreme Court in this respect. The Supreme Court upholding the decision of the High Court of Madras in the instant case ruled that the Chapter on Fundamental Rights is sacrosanct and not liable to be abridged by any legislative or executive act or order except to the extent provided in the appropriate Articles in Part III. In an analogous case the *State of Madras v. C.R. Srinivasan* the Supreme Court held that the Directive Principles of State Policy being non-justiciable could not override a Fundamental Right. As a result of these judgments and as also the one in *B. Venkataraman* v. *The State of Madras*, the Constitution (First Amendment) Act, 1951, was enacted and a new Clause 4 was inserted in Article15. It provided, "Nothing in this Article or in Clause (2) of Article 29 shall prevent the State from making any special provision for the advancement of any socially and educationally backward classes of citizens or for the Scheduled Castes and the Scheduled Tribes." Despite this amendment the courts continued to emphasise the subordinate character of the Directive Principles.

But a change in the attitude of the Supreme court was discerned in the *State of Bihar v. Kameshwar Singh* and *Bijoy Cotton Mills Ltd.* v *The State of Ajmer*. In the first case the validity of the Zamindari Abolition Act was questioned on the ground that it violated the guaranteed Fundamental Right to property. Justice M.C. Mahajan speaking for the Court upheld the validity of the Zamindari Abolition Act on the reasoning that the implementation of the Directive Principles set out in Article 39 was such a public purpose. It was held that the Zamindari Abolition Law, which intended to do away with the concentration of large tracts of land in the hands of a few individuals and benefits large number of tenants must be deemed to be for the public purpose. In *Bijoy Cotton Mills Ltd.* v. *The State of Ajmer* the Court did not subscribe to the view that the Minimum Wages Act unreasonably restricted the right of the employers. In a unanimous judgment delivered by Justice Mukherjee, the Court ruled that "securing of living wages to labourers, which ensure not only bare physical subsistence but also maintenance of health and decency, is conducive to the general interest of the public. This was one of the Directive Principles of State Policy embodied in Art. 43 of our Constitution" and, therefore, a reasonable restriction on the employers'right to carry on business could be imposed by the State.

In *M.H. Quereshi v. The State of Bihar,* the Supreme Court was called upon to give its decision on the validity of Bihar, Uttar Pradesh and Madhya Pradesh laws which banned the slaughter of certain animals including cows. Chief Justice S.R. Das, who delivered the opinion of the Court, held that the State cannot make any law which takes away or abridges the rights con-

6. *Lok Sàbha Debates* (1951). II. Cols. 8822-3.

ferred by Chapter III of the Constitution which enshrines the Fundamental Rights. "The Directive Principles cannot override this categorical restriction imposed on the legislative power of the State. A harmonious interpretation has to be placed upon the Constitution and so interpreted it means that the State should certainly implement the directive principles but it must not do so in such a way that its laws take away or abridge the Fundamental Rights for otherwise the protective provisions of chapter III will be a mere rope of sand." This decision is almost reminiscent of *Champakam Dorairajan* case, although the Court introduced the doctrine of harmonious interpretation or construction as a technique of interpretation.

'*In re on the Kerala Education Bill*, 1957,' the Supreme Court was called upon to give its opinion, *inter alia*, on the relationship between the Fundamental Rights and the Directive Principles. Chief Justice S.R. Das, speaking for the Court held that "although this legislation may have been undertaken by the State of Kerala in the discharge of the obligation imposed on it by the Directive Principles it must nevertheless subserve and not override the Fundamental Rights. The Directive Principles have to conform to and run subsidiary to the Chapter on Fundamental Rights." This opinion reiterated the views expressed in the Cow Slaughter case without reintroducing any new innovation in the application of the doctrine of harmonious construction.

But there was a change in judicial thinking and the first indication of it was noticed in the statement of Justice Mudholkar in *Sajjan Singh v. State of Rajasthan*. In this case, the argument before the Supreme Court was that if the Fundamental Rights were not made subject to the amending process of the Constitution there was a danger that the much needed dynamic change or development in the Indian society would be hampered. Though he did not dismiss the argument advanced as of no consequence, he expressed the opinion that even if the Fundamental Rights were taken as unchangeable, the much needed dynamism could be achieved by properly interpreting the Fundamental Rights in the light of the Directive Principles. He-observed that the Directive Principles "are also fundamental in the governance of the country and the provisions of Part III of the Constitution must be interpreted harmoniously with these principles." Two important points may be noted in the opinion expressed by Justice Mudholkar, although he also envisaged the application of the doctrine of harmonious construction. He takes cognisance of the fundamental nature of the Directive Principles and in case of conflict between the Fundamental Rights and the Directive Principles suggests to resolve it by interpreting the former in the light of the latter. His approach in resolving the conflict is to ensure dynamism in the socio-economic structure in the Indian society. To interpret the Fundamental Rights in the light of the Directive Principles is "definitely to give new meaning, new content and new dimension to the former so that not only the latter could be implemented fully and effectively but the former could find themselves in tune with the changed conditions and the new social order brought about by implementation of the Directive Principles."[7]

The majority opinion in the *Golak Nath* Case rejected the government argument that if Parliament was not given the power to amend the Constitution it would be difficult to implement the Directive Principles and there would be a revolution in the country. The Court declined to take a decision on this hypothetical situation and held : "if it is the duty of Parliament to enforce the Directive Principles it is equally its duty to do so without infringing the Fundamental Rights. The Constitution-makers thought it could be done and we also think that the Directive Principles could reasonably be enforced with the self-regulatory machinery provided by Part III of the Constitution." Proceeding further, Chief Justice K. Subba Rao said, "Nor can we appreciate the argument that all the agrarian reforms which Parliament in power wants to effectuate cannot be brought about without amending the Fundamental Rights". It was in this context that the Chief Justice observed, "The Fundamental Rights and the Directive Principles of State Policy enshrined in the Constitution formed an 'integrated scheme' and was elastic enough to respond to the changing needs of the society."[8]

The doctrine of "integrated scheme" enun-

7. Shetty, R.P. Krishna, *Fundamental Rights and Socio-Economic Justice in the Indian Constitution*, p. 103.
8. *Golak Nath v. State of Punjab* (1967) 2 S.C.J. 436

ciated by Chief Justice Subba Rao admits two important results. In the first place, since Part III and Part IV of the Constitution form an integrated scheme they, undoubtedly, stand on a footing of equality and, therefore, the theory of subordination enunciated by the Supreme Court in *Champakam Dorairajan* case and reiterated in the *Cow Slaughter* case and the *Kerala Education Bill* stands completely repudiated. Secondly, the doctrine of "integrated scheme" established the elasticity of the Fundamental Rights and Fundamental Rights, as such, must respond to the changing needs of the society reflecting the aspirations of the people. The Directive Principles of State Policy are the conscience of the Constitution and the reservoir of the people's aspirations. Fundamental rights can, therefore, never be static. They change in their content with the changing needs of the society and justify their dynamism. It is, accordingly, clear that the doctrine of "integrated scheme" and the theory of "elasticity" of Fundamental Rights establish that Fundamental Rights must be interpreted in the light of the Directive Principles so that the State may be able to carry out its socio-economic obligations imposed on it by the Preamble and Part IV of the Constitution. The Constitutional duty of the State is spelt out in Article 38 which is the keystone of the Directive Principles. It is the star by which the Government is required to chart its course.

If the provisions contained in Part III cause hindrance in the discharge of a constitutional duty, as cast upon it by article 37, the government must strive to remove those hindrances and both the Twenty-fourth and Twenty-fifth Amendments of the Constitution sought to do it. The Constitution (Twenty-fourth Amendment) Act, 1971, set up a mechanism for amending the Constitution and thereby removed the hindrance that the *Golak Nath* case had created. It also amended Article 13 by inserting a new Clause (4) which provided that nothing in this Article shall apply to any amendment of this Constitution. The Constitution (Twenty-fifth Amendment) Act, 1971, deleted the word "compensation" occurring in Article 31(2) and substituted it by the word "amount." It also inserted Clause (2B) in the same Article thereby nullifying the effect of the judgment in *Bank Nationalisation case*. Another new Article 31-C was inserted providing that no law seeking to enforce the Directive Principles of State Policy in clauses (b)[9] and (c))[10] of Article 39 would be held invalid on the ground that it involved any of the Fundamental Rights conferred by Articles 14, 19 or 31. Moreover, declaration in the clauses (b) and (c) of Article 39 would render such law immune from challenge in any court. The amendment also provided that no law containing such a declaration could be called in question on the ground that it did not in point of fact promote the Directive Principles of State Policy. The State Legislatures were empowered to enact such laws as ordained by Article 31C with the proviso that such laws after passing from the State Legislature should be reserved for the consideration of the President.

Explaining the import of the contents of the Twenty-fifth Amendment, V.R. Krishna Iyer (afterwards a Judge of the Supreme Court) remarked that it introduced the new Article 31C whereby a marriage between the most vital Directive Principles and the most potent Fundamental Rights has been effected. A harmony has been established by this provision that no law made to give effect to the Directive Principles specified in Clauses (b) and (c) of Article 39 shall be deemed to be void on the ground that it takes away any of the Fundamental Rights guaranteed by Articles 14, 19 and 31."[11] The Supreme Court in the *Kesavananda Bharati* case upheld Article 31C recognising the competence of the Legislature of enacting laws to give effect to the Directive Principles in Clauses (b) and (c) of Article 39, but struck down the provision that "no law containing a declaration that it is for giving effect to such policy shall be called in question in any court that it does not give effect to such policy." The Court also ruled that though by Article 368 Parliament is given powers to amend the Constitution, that power cannot be exercised so as to alter the basic structure of the Constitution.

To nullify the effect of the *Kesavananda*

---

9. Clause(b) Provides, "that the ownership control of the material resources of the community are so distributed as best to subserve the common good."
10. Clause (c) provides, "that the operation of the economic system does not result in the concentration of wealth and means of production to the common detriment."
11. Aiyar, S.P. and Raju, S.V. (Eds) *Fundamental Rights and the Citizen*, p. 110.

*Bharti* case the Constitution (Forty-second Amendment) Act, 1976, amended Article 31C by providing that no law giving effect to the policy of the State towards securing all or any of the Directive Principles laid down in Part IV shall be deemed to be void on the ground that it is inconsistent with, or takes away or abridges any of the rights conferred by Articles 14, 19 or 31.[12] As a measure of abundant caution Article 368 was also amended by inserting Clauses (4) and (5) debarring the courts from questioning the validity of amendments made and bestowing upon Parliament powers without any limitation to amend any provisions of the Constitution.

The validity of the Forty-second Amendment was questioned in the *Minerva Mills* case. On May 9, 1980 the Supreme Court applied the ruling in the *Kesavananda Bharati* case and held unanimously that Section 55 of the Forty-second Amendment was void. It also held by a majority of 4 to 1[13] that section 4 of the Act amending Article 31C which exempts from challenge any law which enforces any of the Directive Principles on the ground that it violates Article 14 or Article 19 is also void because it "damages thc basic essential features of the Constitution and destroys its basic structure." Justice Bhagwati in his dissenting judgment held that the amended Article 31C, "far from being damaging the basic structure of the Constitution strengthens and reinforces it by giving fundamental importance to the rights of the members of the community as against the rights of a few individuals and furthering the objective of the Constitution to build an egalitarian social order where there will be social and economic justice for all......"

The *Minerva Mills* case established the supremacy of the Fundamental Rights and every legislation or constitutional amendment made in furtherance of the Directive Principles is subject to the scrutiny of the courts to determine whether it is violative of the Fundamental Rights, particularly, Articles 14 and 19.

No less a person than Justice Frankfurter of the United States, whom Rau had consulted, was of the view that the Directive Principles should prevail in case of a conflict with the Fundamental Rights and this should be secured by an express provision in the Constitution. Rau's suggestion did not receive a favourable response then and "wisely", as A.G. Noorani remarks, the constitution-framers made Fundamental Rights "justiciable in explicit terms and directive principles non-justiciable as explicity. A chastened B.N. Rau himself came to regard the directives rather like the Instrument of Instructions issued to Governors."[14]

But perusal of debates on the Directive Principles in the Constituent Assembly reveals a few important facts. Firstly, the Directive Principles had been made unenforceable not to render them ineffective or that they should remain like a cheque on a bank payable at the convenience of the bank, as Prof. K.T. Shah believed them to be if not made justiciable within a specified time limit. The intention was, as Ambedkar explained to the Constituent Assembly, that " in future both the legislature and the executive" should not merely pay lip-service to these principles but they should be made "the basis of all legislative and executive function that they may be taking hereafter in the matter of governance of the country." It was not an attempt, he added, to incorporate in Chapter IV, the positive mandates to the State and prescribe the manner in which those mandates were to be realised. The Directive Principles were intended to impart continuity to the national policies and their flexibility made it possible for the parties of the Right and the Left to strive in their own way to reach the ideals of social and economic democracy whenever they would get an opportunity to form the Government after having received the verdict of the people at the polls, he emphasised.[15]

Secondly, positive emphasis has been laid on the fundamental nature of the Directives so that an express duty may rest on the State to adequately discharge its constitutional obligations. The aim of the Constitution-makers was to establish a state which should be a democracy not

---

12. The Constitution (Forty-fourth Amendment) Act, 1978, has dropped Right to Property from Chapter III-Fundamental Rights.
13. Cheif Justice Y.V. Chandrachud, Justices A.C. Gupta, N.L. Untwalia, and P.S. Kailasam. Justice P.N. Bhagwati dissented.
14. Noorani, A.G., "Reviewing Fundamental Rights", *Indian Express.*, New Delhi, September 4, 1980.
15. *Constituent Assembly Debates,* Vol. VIII, p. 382.

only in the political area where legislative authority is based on adult franchise and the executive is parliamentary, but also to promote a Welfare State, where social and economic democracy must also prevail. The Directive Principles establish the conditions necessary for its achievement. Article 36 lays down that the State "shall strive to promote the welfare of the people." Ambedkar explained that the word "strive" had been purposely used 'because their intention was that however adverse the circumstances that stand in the way of government in giving effect to these principles and however impropositious the time might be they should always strive for the fulfilment of the Principles. Otherwise it would be open to the government to say that circumstances were not good and the finances were so bad that they could not implement them."[16]

The Constitution-makers, therefore, vested in the people of India the power and the means to compel the Government of the day to implement the Directive Principles or even at a time when it is not financially and administratively possible for it to do. The Constitution established a parliamentary system of government. The mechanism of such a system enables the citizens to watch, and scrutinise the acts of the Government and assess the impact of its performance on the body politic of the country and on the well-being of the common man. At the time of the General Election people measure Government's success or failure in the light of the achievements and fulfilment of the goals prescribed by the Constitution. To ignore the Directive Principles is to ignore the substance provided in the Constitution, hopes held out to the nation and the very ideals on which the constitution is built. If the government, irrespective of its party label, pursues a policy which is in accordance with the Principles enunciated in the Constitution and caters to their sense of justice, the electorate will endorse its policy and allow it to continue in office. otherwise, they will repose their confidence in another party. Parliamentary system accepts alteration in government and the vigilant public opinion is the sanction behind it. It is for this reason that the Constitution-makers deliberately introduced in the language they have used in the Directive Principles something which is not fixed or rigid . They have left enough room for the the people of the different ways of thinking to go to the electorate and persuade them that their policy and programme are the best way of reaching economic democracy; the fullest opportunity for all people to act in the way they want to act.

Finally, the Directive Principles of State Policy, according to the framers of the Constitution, are like the instrument of instructions flowing the from the sovereign people to the state directing them to do certain things. These directions are as much binding on the Legislature and on the Executive as they are on the Judiciary. All these wings of the Government are its component parts and they collectively express the will of the State. It is, therefore, the duty of the Judiciary to safeguard the Directive Principles from the vicissitudes of the fortune of the political parties that come and go out of office from time to time. As the Directive Principles are intended to impart continuity to the national policies, as they represent the deliberate wisdom of the nation through the Constituent Assembly, it is for the courts to see that this continuity does not become the plaything of party politics and, consequently, retard the progress of their fulfilment. Moreover, many of the Fundamental Rights are subject to reasonable restrictions in the interests of public. In interpreting these rights, which are justiciable, the Constitution-makers had imposed on the courts a duty to lay down the canons for determining what is "reasonable" and a "public interest" and while doing so due emphasis must be placed on the Directive Principles as the Constitution holds them fundamental in the governance of the country. This path was set in *Kameshwar Singh* and *Bijoy Cotton Mills* cases. In both these cases the Supreme Court laid down two rules of construction : (*i*) that in case of conflict between the right of the individual and laws aiming to implement socio-economic policies in pursuance of the Directive Principles greater weight should be given to the latter; and (*ii*) that every socio-economic legislation enacted in pursuance of the Directive Principles should be construed as one purporting to "public interest" or as a "reasonable restriction" on the Fundamental Rights. Justice Mudholkar applied the same approach in *Sajjan Singh* case when he enunciated the doctrine of "dynamism," and the theory of "elas-

16. Ibid, Vol. VIII, pp. 594-95.

tic" Fundamental Rights, as enunciated by Chief Justice K. Subba Rao in the *Golak Nath* case, implies the same principle or rule of construction. All of them are not only in consonance with the provisions of the Article 37 of the Chapter on the Directive Principles of State Policy but in complete conformity with the intentions of the Constitution-makers as well as which find their echo in the Preamble to the Constitution.

**What Directives Have Wrought**

The significance of the Directive Principles, as said earlier, was appreciably realised by almost all the members of the Constituent Assembly. They firmly believed that certain social values especially those related to economic rights, embodied in Part III of the Constitution, were meaningless to large sections of the people if poverty, with all its attendant evils of economic and social distress was to haunt them at every step and account for their inexplicable sufferings. Their primary concern was to usher in a new social order in which justice, social, economic and political shall inform all institutions of the national life. For the fulfilment of this objective the State has been charged to make effective provisions for securing the right to work, to education and to public assistance in case of unemployment, old age, sickness and disablement, and in other cases of undeserved want.[17] These are the minimum requirements of civilised existence and it is the foremost duty of every State, whatever be its label, to ensure that all these basic necessities of life are available to all individuals. The pith of the Directive Principles has a deep impact on a democtraic set-up. If democracy is to survive, it must establish and nurture a society resting on social justice. This is the only peaceful and evolutionary method otherwise the answer is revolution. The Constitution-makers adopted the former by playing the role of a constitutional reformer and "attired the aspirations of the people with a constitutional role." The result was the establishment of the socio-economic justice in the Preamble of the constitution, which is to be implemented by the State to achieve the goal.[18]

The Supreme Court in its judgement related to conditions of workers in Asian Games (1982) projects heralded a silent legal revolution. It clothed million of workers in the factories, fields, mines and project sites with basic human dignity. They got fundamental rights to minimum wages, drinking water, shelter, creches, medical aid and safety in their respective professions. Justice P.N. Bhagwati and Baharul Islam, who delivered the judgement, strongly defended the public interest litigation and criticised lawyers, journalists and "self-styled human rights activists" who thoughts that by entertaining such cases the highest court in the land was simply wasting its time. The judgment said that the public interest litigation was a co-operative effort on the part of the petitioner, the authorities and the Court. The State, which is usually the respondent must welcome it as it would give it an opportunity to right the wrong.

But the Directive Principles have been sceptically received by some eminent authorities. K.C. Wheare has doubted "whether there is any gain, on balance, from introducing these paragraphs of generalities into a constitution."[19] He is of the view that a Constitution should include only those provisions which can be capable of enforcement and are obligatory on the State. Ivor Jennings has been unduly severer in his criticism. He said,"the ghosts of Sidney and Beatrice Webb Stalk through the pages of the text. Part IV of the Constitution expresses Fabian Socialism without the Socialism, for only the nationalisation of the means of production, distribution and exchange is missing; but nationalisation for the Fabians was a means to an end and not an end itself; the end is quite adequately expressed in the Constitution." Jennings also questioned the reasonableness of inserting in a constitution a collection of political principles which "obviously derive from English experience in the nineteenth century and are deemed to be suitable for India in the middle of the twentieth century." He added that the ideas expressed in Part IV would survive for a generation and some of them may even survive for longer period. "The question whether they are suitable for the twentieth century, when the Constitution may still be in operation, cannot be answered, but it is quite probable that they will be entirely outmoded."[20]

The Communists in India have also been

---

17. Article 41.
18. Shetty, K.P. Krishna, *Fundamental Rights and Socio-Economic Justice in the Indian Constitution*, p.108.
19. Wheare, K.C., *Modern Constitutions*, p. 69.
20. Jennings, W.I., *Some Characteristics of the Indian Constitution*, p. 31.

harsh in assessing the utility of the Directive Principles. Tushar Chatterji, a Communist Member of Parliament, moved a resolution in the House of the People, urging for the appointment of a 15-member Parliamentary Committee to inquire into the implementation of the Directive Principles embodied in the Constitution. While moving his resolution, Tushar Chatterji catalogued the failures of the government and maintained that the common people did not feel any difference from the State of affairs that existed today. "Several problems", he maintained, "like food, education and health still remained unsolved while the life of the common people had become more burdensome and difficult. They could not but feel that these solemn declarations in the Constitution were not directives but only 'decoratives' in the Constitution."[21]

Many of the points raised by Tushar Chatterji, way back in 1958, are correct and the gap between the poor and the rich has become more wide. But it cannot also be denied that the problems of eradication of poverty, achieving full employment, appreciably raising the living standard and equitable distribution of national wealth are colossal indeed, and no government, whatever be its complexion can achieve miracles. It will take several decades to achieve the goal set in the Directives and establish a Welfare State wherein social and economic democracy would prevail.

It cannot, however, be overlooked that the policy of the government from the beginning of India's republican career has been shaped according to the Directive Principles and every decision of the Planning Commission has been guided or coloured by these Principles. This is more than evident in the social, labour and economic legislation undertaken by the government and its industrial, agricultural and taxation policies. The Taxation Enquiry Commission, 1953-54 was asked to examine the tax structure and to suggest measures to reduce the inequalities of income and wealth, analyse their effects on development of the productivbe enterprises and on the inflationary process. The Industrial (Development and Regulation Act) 1954, and the establishment of the Monopolies Inquiry Commission in 1965 were aimed to achieve the objective outlined by the Taxation Inquiry Commisssion in terms of its reference. The Monopolies Commission made probing inquiries into the causes and extent of concentration of economic power in private hands, the factors responsible for monopolistic tendencies in the national economy and their social consequences. It recommended the constitution of a permanent body "with the duty and responsibility of exercising vigilance, and for taking action to protect the country against dangers of concentrated economic power, consumers' co-operatives, etc." and recommended that appropriate legislation should be enacted accordingly. The Government acted promptly in accepting and implementing the suggestions of the Monopolies Inquiry Commision. This is not a complete picture, but it is suggestive of the various steps taken at the Union level in realizing the content of the Directive Principles.

At the State level, legislation to abolish intermediaries and Zamindari systems and land reforms was enacted in the early years of 1950 and, today, land, both urban and rural, is subject to ceilings and the surplus land as a result thereof has gone to the weaker sections of the community , though its pace is inexplicably slow in some States. In pursuance of the Directive Principles to organise village panchayats and to promote cottage industries in order to ensure decentralised and composite democracy in the form of self-governing village communities requisite legilsation was passed and adequate funds provided. While initiating the debate in Parliament on the economic policy in India, C.D. Deshmukh, the then Finance Minister, declared that whereas the development of major industries must continue in national interest, it was necessary to develop small-scale and village industries "with great opportunities for employment and more and more chance of improving the resources of the population." Prime Minister Nehru, intervening in the debate, reaffirmed the policy of his Government of bringing about a casteless and stateless society through the peaceful and cooperative method. He asserted that the biggest private sector in the country was "the private sector of the peasant with his small holdings."

The Janata Government was wedded to the Gandhian way of life and a decentralized and composite democracy was the first item on its agenda. The national development plan for 1977-78 was, accordingly, recast with an allocation of as much as 30.4 per cent of the funds for agriculture and allied services and provision of schemes to create 2.5 million jobs. Announcing the new thrust of the Government on farming and rural infrastructure, the Finance Minister,

H.M. Patel, explained to the House of the People during his Budget speech that the entire plan strategy was oriented towards according primacy to agriculture, priority to rural development and eradication of the unemployment within a time limit. "The Sixth Five Year Plan of Rs. 97,500 crores expected the economy to grow at 5.2 per cent per year and at the higher rate of 5.5 per cent in the 10 years thereafter and bring down the percentage of people below the poverty line from the existing 48 to 30 by the end of the sixth Plan period. Employment will increase at a rate faster than the growth in the labour force."

The principle of international peace and security enshrined in Article 51 finds its full expression in the external policy of India. Jawaharlal Nehru's doctrine of dynamic neutrality, India's deep faith in co-existence, her advocacy of *Panch Sheel* and acceptance of those lofty ideals of peace and mutual tolerance by the major countries of the world is the greatest contribution which Independent India can claim. India has, indeed, saved the world from disaster. Michael Foot wrote, in 1955, "power corrupts and the world owes Independent India an immense debt for helping to save us from the corruption of power on an international scale which might so easily have led us to disaster."[22] The five principles : (1) mutual respect of each other's territorial integrity and sovereignty; (2) non-aggression; (3) non-interference in each other's internal affairs for any reasons, either of an economic, political or ideological character;[23] (4) equality and mutual benefit; and (5) peaceful co-existence—contained in the *Panch Sheel*—helped to outlaw from the minds of the Heads of the great States the possibility of war, little, of course, knowing that one of the signatories to the *Panch Sheel* would, become an aggressor. Addressing the Constituent Assembly at mid-night on August 14, 1947, Rajendra Prasad said, "we have only one ambition and that is to make our contribution to the building of peace and freedom for all.' India has striven to hold steadfast to this spirit which inspires the last of the Directives, though herself victim of four wars. Her recent normalisation of diplomatic and trade relations with these neighbouring countries reiterates India's dedication to international peace and security.

**Classification of the Directive Principles**

The first two Articles (36 and 37) of the Chapter on Directive Principles of the State Policy are general in character and deal with definitions, legal effects and objectives. The remaining Articles may, for purposes of clarity, be grouped into three distinct categories : (i) those that aim to shape India into a Welfare State; (ii) those that aim to shape India into a Gandhian State; and (iii) those that aim to promote international peace.

(i) Article 38 (1) provides that the State shall promote the welfare of the people by securing and protecting as effectively as it may a social order in which justice, social, economic and political shall inform all the institutions of the national life. Clause (2, inserted by the Forty-fourth Amendment, provides that the State shall, in particular, strive to minimise the inequalities in income, and endeavour to eliminate inequalities in status, facilities and opportunities, not only amongst individuals but also amongst groups of people residing in different areas or engaged in different vocations. Thus, promotion of the welfare of people, both residing in urban and rural areas and engaged in different vocations is the objective which the Constitution sets forth by striving to secure a social order where justice, social, economic and political, shall prevail. Welfare and justice are, accordingly, the twin object of the Constitution. Article 39 then, proceeds to particularise some of the methods by which the object of general welfare, through justice, can be obtained and the basis of the new social order established. This Article finds adequate support from the provisions about a casteless and classless society. With this end in view the State shall direct its policy in securing :—

I (a) adequate means of livelihood for all citi zens, men and women equally;
(b) distribution of wealth so as to subserve the common good;
(c) the operation of the economic system which does not result in the concentration of wealth and means of production to the common detriment;
(d) equal pay for equal work for both men

22. *The Tribune*, Ambala Cantt, August 15, 1955.
23. An Amendment to Clause 3 was made to the *Panch Sheel* in the joint declaration signed in the Moscow by the Prime Ministers of India and the Soviet Union. The original Clause 3 read : "Non-interference in each other's affairs". The amendment added the following words : "for any reasons, either of an economic, political or ideological character.

and women;[24]

(e) protection of adult and child labour;

(f) the Forty-second amendment altered the original clause, which read : "protection of child and youth against exploitation and against moral and material abandonment,"to emphasise the constructive role of the State with regard to children. It now provides that the "children are given opportunities and facilities to develop in a healthy manner and in conditions of freedom and dignity and that childhood and youth are protected against exploitation and against moral and material abandonment.

(g) provision of work and education for all people, relief in case of unemployment, old age, sickness and disablement and in other cases of undeserved want;

(h) just and humane conditions of work and maternity relief;

(i) a living wage and decent conditions of work for all workers, agricultural, industrial or otherwise as to ensure to them sufficient leisure and enjoyment of social and cultural opportunities;

(j) to secure the participation of workers in the management of undertakings or other organisations engaged in any industry. (This provision was inserted by the Forty-second Amendment as Article 43A);

(k) free and compulsory education for all children until they reach the age of fourteen years;

(l) raising the level of nutrition and the standard of living and the improvement of public health;

(m) to secure that the operation of the legal system promotes justice, on a basis of equal opportunity and in particular, to provide free legal aid to ensure that opportunities for securing justice are not denied to any citizen by reason of economic or other diabilities. (This provision was inserted by the forty-second Amendment as a new Article 39A); and

(n) to endeavour to secure for the citizens a uniform civil code throughout the country.

II. Some of the Directive Principles are in accordance with and conform to the Gandhian way of life and fulfil the requirements of Gandhi's conception of the State. These Directive Principles enjoin that :

(a) the State shall take steps to organise village panchayats and endow them with such power and authority as may be necessary to enable them to function as units of self-government;

(b) the State shall endeavour to promote cottage industries on an individual or cooperative basis in rural areas;

Both these provisions aim at *Sarvodaya* or pure socialism as Prof. S.N. Aggarwal called it.[25] *Sarvodaya* is the Gandhian technique of decentralised economy and composite democracy in the form of self-dependent and self-governing village communities or panchayats.

(c) to promote with special care the educational and economic interests of the weaker sections of the people, and, in particular of the Scheduled Castes and the Scheduled Tribes in order to protect them from social injustice and all forms of exploitation;

(d) to bring about prohibition of consumption, except for medicinal purposes, of intoxicating drinks and of drugs which are injurious to health;

(e) to take steps to organise agricultural and animal husbandry on modern and scientific lines and,, in particular take steps for preserving and improving the breeds, and prohibiting the slaughter of cows and calves and other milch and drought cattle;

(f) to protect and improve the environment and safeguard the forests and wild life of the country, (This provision has been inserted by the Forty-second amendment as Article 48A);

(g) to protect, preserve and maintain places of national and historical importance; and

(h) to take steps to separate the judiciary from the executive; and to secure for citizens a

---

24. Refer to the Supreme Court judgement in the writ petition of constable Randhir Singh. Justices O. Chinnapppa Reddy amd Baharul Islam allowed the writ petition and ruled that the right to the "equal pay for equal work" is a fundamental right and enforceable as such.

25. "Socialism and Sarvodaya", *The Hindustan Times*, New Delhi, January 1, 1955.

uniform civil code throughout the country.

III. In the international field India shall strive:
   (a) to promote international peace and security;
   (b) to maintain just and honourable relations between nations;
   (c) to foster respect for international law and treaty obligations; and
   (d) to encourage settlement of international disputes by arbitration.

## FUNDAMENTAL DUTIES

### Need for Inclusion in the Constitution

Incorporation of a charter of Fundamental Duties in the Constitution is one of the important features of the Constitution (Forty-second Amendment) Act, 1976. The Swaran Singh Committee on constitutional reforms, appointed by the Congress President, was asked in a resolution of the All-India Congress Committee, passed at its meeting in New Delhi on May 29, 1976 to formulate proposals to fill what was widely considered a historical lacuna to India's charter rights. Within the Congress the sentiment was fairly strong that the Constitution-makers went, in the first flush of Independence, to great lengths to articulate the citizen's fundamental rights in the Constitution but overlooked the need to prescribe the corresponding fundamental duties and obligations. The political crisis that strained the Indian democratic system in the last sixties and again in 1974 and 1975 was one of the compelling reasons to necessitate the inclusion of what the Constitution-makers had in their wisdom omitted, although there was some suggestion at the time when the Constitution was drafted that his important aspect should not be ignored.

Nor is the issue of enumerating the citizen's fundamental duties to society and State in a Constitution totally without a precedent. Nearly fifty countries, as Vinod Sethi enumerated, have incorporated duties in their constitutions,[26] and Japan is one of them whose basic document was consulted by the makers of the Indian Constitution. The Japanese Constitution spells out explicitly some of the citizen's countervailing duties in the same breath as his Fundamental Rights. "Rights and Duties of the People" are enshrined in Chapter III of the Constitution.

The Swaran Singh committee proposed an 8-Point code of "fundamental duties" which, after due process of public consultation, were proposed to be enshrined in the Constitution. The proposed duties were :

(1) To respect and abide by the Constitution and the laws.
(2) To uphold the sovereignty of the Nation and to function in such a way as to sustain and strengthen its unity and integrity.
(3) To respect the democratic institutions enshrined in the Constitution, and not to do anything which may impair their dignity or authority.
(4) To defend the country and to render national service including military service when called upon to do so.
(5) To abjure communalism in any form.
(6) To render assistance and co-operation to the state in the implementation of the Directive Principles of State Policy, and to promote the common good of the people so as to subserve the interest of the social and economic justice.
(7) To abjure violence; to protect and safeguard public property and not to do anything which may cause damage and destruction to such property.
(8) to pay taxes according to law.

### Duties Analysed

The Constitution (Forty-second Amendment) Act, 1976, inserted a new Chapter Part IV-A and listed in Article 51A the following ten duties—

" (a) to abide by the Constitution and respect its ideals and institutions, the National Flag and the National Anthem.
(b) to cherish and follow the noble ideals which inspired our national struggle for freedom;
(c) to uphold and protect the sovereignty, unity and integrity of India;
(d) to defend the country and render national service when called upon to do so;
(e) to promote harmony and the spirit of commonbrotherhood amongst all the

---

26. "The Fundamental Duties", *Indian Express*, New Delhi, September 30, 1976.

people of India transcending religious, linguistic and regional or sectional diversities; to renounce practices derogatory to the dignity of women,

(f) to value and preserve the rich heritage of our composite culture;

(g) to protect and improve the natural environment including forests, lakes, rivers and wild life, and to have compassion for living creatures;

(h) to develop the scientific temper, humanism and the spirit of inquiry and reform;

(i) to safeguard public property and abjure violence,

(j) to strive towards excellence in all spheres of individual and collective activity so that the nation constantly rises to higher levels of endeavour and achievement."

The Fundamental Duties inscribed in the Constitution are a mixed bag of expectations and exhortations. Quite a good number of these items are those which are enforceable today even without their being specifically incorporated in the Constitution. In this category fall the items to abide by the constitution, respect the National Flag and the National Anthem, to defend the country and render national service when called upon to do so and safeguard public property. To uphold and protect the sovereignty, unity and integrity of India draws sustenance from the same moral source from which the Constitution's Sixteenth or anti-sessionist amendment itself stems.

The three most important items in the list of Fundamental Duties are those requiring the citizens to respect the ideals of the Constitution and the institutions it establishes, to promote harmony and the spirit of common brotherhood amongst all the people of India professing different religions, speaking different languages, practising different customs and inhabiting different parts of the country, and to safeguard the public property and to abjure violence. These are clearly intended to meet certain specific political threats that democracy in India has to contend with.

The Indian Charter of Fundamental Duties is unique to include the duty to develop the scientific temper, humanism and the spirit of inquiry and reform. It has been incorporated to eradicate superstitions in which India is deeply soaked and to remove the bane of religious fanaticism, regional chauvinism and linguistic frenzy which have ever plagued India and retarded her unification into a cohesive society. The duty to renounce practices derogatory to the dignity of women and to preserve the rich heritage of India's composite culture are two other moral codes to ennoble the society. These are, in fact, homilies to be taught in schools and colleges rather than to be incorporated in the Constitution as Fundamental Duties.

# CHAPTER VIII

# The President

## The Nature of the Union Executive

One of the important questions to engage the attention of the Constitution-makers related to the nature of the Executive. Ambedker observed in introducing the constitution in the Constituent Assembly : "A student of constitutional law, if a copy of a constitution is placed in his hands, is sure to ask two questions. Firstly, what is the form of Government that is envisaged in the Constitution; and secondly, what is the form of the Constitution ? For these are the two crucial matters which every constitution has to deal with."[1] From the earlier stages of the discussion on the principles of the new constitution there was an overwhelming opinion in favour of the parliamentary system of government.[2] In the Memorandum on the Principles of the Union Constitution,[3] submitted by Alladi Krishnaswami Ayyar and N. Gopalaswami Ayyangar, for the consideration of the Union Constitution Committee, it was specifically suggested that the Executive "power of the federation will, subject to the provisions of the constitution, be exercised by, or on the authority of a Council of Ministers, to be called the Cabinet, which will be collectively responsible to the House of Representatives."[4] It may, however, be noted that at this stage it was contemplated to confer certain special powers on the President. In his Memorandum on the Union Constitution and Draft Clauses prepared by the Constitutional Adviser (May 30, 1947) for the use of the Union Constitution Committee, it was provided that "there shall be a Council of Ministers, with the Prime Minister at the head, to aid and advise the President in the exercise of the functions, except in so far as he is required by this constitution to act in his discretion." The President was also to be vested with specified special responsibilities in the exercise of his functions and where any special responsibility of the President was involved, he exercised his discretion as to the action to be taken. But to safeguard against the arbitrary use of discretionary authority by the President, the Constitutional Adviser had provided for the creation of a Council of State, a kind of Privy Council. This was a system of checks and balances designed to prevent both the President and the Ministry from resorting to an arbitrary use of untrammelled authority.

This matter was considered by the Union Constitution Committee on June 8 and 9, 1947. The Committee generally agreed that the Union Executive should be of the parliamentary type and that the President should have no special responsibilities as suggested by the Constitutional Adviser in his Memorandum and that he should exercise his powers, including the power to dissolve Parliament, only on the advice of his Ministers. This recommendation of the Committee also made the Constitutional Adviser's proposal for the setting up of the Council of State infructuous.

When the Report of the Union Constitution Committee came up for consideration before the Constituent Assembly, there was general agreement for establishing a parliamentary executive. The critics of such a system of government, Kazi Syed Karimuddin and Hussain Imam, however, moved an amendment proposing a non- parliamentary executive. Hussain Imam thought that the system of government obtaining in the United States of America, was "more democratic and based on better and sounder principles" than the parliamentary system of the British type. The Constituent Assembly finally accepted the principle of a parliamentary executive collectively responsible to the representative chamber of Parliament and the Drafting Committee based the Draft Constitution on this concept.[5]

1. *Constituent Assembly Debates,* Vol. VII, pp. 31-32.
2. Refer to the questionnaire issued by the Constitutional Adviser, B. N. Rau, to the Members of the Central and Provincial Legislatures, March 17, 1947. *The Framing of India's Constitution, Select Documents, op. cit.* Vol. II, pp. 434-51.
3. Circulated to the Members of the Committee on June 4, 1947.
4. *The Framing of India's Constitution, Select Documents, op. cit.,* Vol. II, p. 546.
5. *Constituent Assembly Debates,* Vol. IV, p. 921.

In the Draft Constitution of February, 1948, there was a provision made for an Instrument of Instructions, as embodied in the Government of India Act, 1935, for Governors alone. The Drafting Committee decided, on further consideration, to remedy the omission and provide one for the President too. Accordingly in October 1948, the Committee gave notice of an amendment to Article 62 of the Draft Constitution, proposing to add a new clause : "In the choice of the Ministers and the exercise of his other functions under this Constitution the President shall be generally guided by the instructions set out in Schedule III-A...."

Ambedkar's amendment adding a clause in the Constitution for an Instrument of Instructions to guide the President in the exercise of his functions was accepted by the Constituent Assembly. On October 11, 1949, however, when the new Schedule III-A containing the Instrument of Instructions was due to be considered by the Assembly, T. T. Krishnamachari expressed the desire of the Drafting Committee that the proposal for the inclusion of the Instrument of Instructions to the President should be dropped. He also moved that a similar Instrument already included in the Draft Constitution for Governors as the Fourth Schedule, should be omitted and also the consequential clause.

The Drafting Committee appeared to have been persuaded by Jawaharlal Nehru to accept the view that the Council of Ministers should be collectively responsible to the representative chamber of Parliament and, under the circumstances, it would be impolitic to confer on the President, through the Instrument of Instructions, powers that might give him an effective voice in the formation of the Council of Ministers or in moulding the policies of the government. Alladi Krishnaswami Ayyar forcefully put this point in the Constituent Assembly. This view was accepted and the proposal to omit the Instrument of Instructions and the related clause was approved.

## The President of India

The Constitution provides for a President of India and the executive power of the Union including the Supreme Command of Defence Forces is vested in him. But the executive power of the Union vested in the President must be exercised in accordance with the Constitution and the Constitution prescribes that there shall be a Council of Ministers with the Prime Minister at the head to aid and advise the President in the exercise of his functions and the advice so tendered is binding on the President.

It is significant to note that the Constitution simply creates the office of the "President of India." Nowhere does it say that the President is either the head of the State or the head of the Executive. The omission is deliberate. The Union Constitution Committee proposed to call the President the "Head of the Federation,"[6] but the Drafting Committee omitted both the words 'Head' as well as 'Federation' and created the President of India. When this article of the Draft Constitution was being discussed in the Constituent Assembly Prof. K. T. Shah moved an amendment that "the Chief Executive and Head of the State in the Union shall be called the President."[7] Ambedkar opposed it and said, "His (Shah's ) amendment, if I understood him correctly, is fundamentally different from the whole scheme as has been adopted in the Draft Constitution. Prof. Shah uses the words 'Chief Executive and the Head of the State.' I have no doubt about it that what he means by the introduction of these words is to introduce the American presidential form of executive but not parliamentary form of executive which is contained in the Draft Constitution."[8]

The Constitution, therefore, establishes a parliamentary form of government and the head of the State is a necessary adjunct of such a system no matter whether he is a King or a President. The real functionaries are the responsible Ministers who make and run the government. Jawaharal Nehru told the Constituent Assembly, "We want to emphasise the ministerial character of the Government, that power really resided in the ministry and in the legislature and not in the President as such."[9]

## Demand for Presidential System

Although the Constitution established a parliamentary system and it had been working at the Centre and the States, eminent opinion in the country veered round the Presidential system, especially after the 1967 General Election and its advocates were many. Even K. M. Munshi, who

6. Report of the Union Constitution Committee, July 4, 1947. *The Framing of India's Constitution, Select Documents, op. cit.*, Vol. II, p. 578.
7. *Constituent Assembly Debates*, Vol. VII, p. 969.
8. *Ibid.*, p. 974.
9. *Constituent Assembly Debates*, Vol. VII, p. 734.

was one of the 7-man Committee which drafted the Constitution and most eloquently championed the cause of parliamentary democracy in the Constituent Assembly, expressed the opinion in 1967, that if he were to frame a constitution for the country again he would favour the Presidential system as in the United States. He said, "Those of us who supported the British Cabinet system, to which we were accustomed, thought that it would work effectively in India, but I must confess that we have failed to evolve the two-party democratic tradition necessary to support the Cabinet system..........The Cabinet system of Government has not been a success......We are heading towards a situation in which either the presidential system or military rule would become inevitable."[10] K. S. Hegde, Chief Justice of the Delhi High Court and afterwards a Judge of the Supreme Court, said on April 15, 1967, that the Constitution should be reshaped to provide, among other things, for the Presidential form of Government for the multiplicity of political parties might soon lead India to conditions similar in pre-de-Gaulle France."[11] Madhu Limaye, then a Member of Parliament, speaking on "Future of Parliamentary Democracy in India," observed that many people in India were doubting whether democracy was successful in India. Some were thinking whether the Presidential form of Government, "would not be better than the present Parliamentary form of Government." Limaye was of the opinion that adoption of Presidential form of Government "involving separation of executive and legislative functions might foster national feeling during the election of the President and may also help the emergence of two strong contending parties or a coalition of parties."[12]

There is, however, no denying the fact that the democratic instinct of Indians had proved immature. The bane of defections that followed in the wake of 1967 General Election and the most reprehensible manner in which the non-Congress Opposition parties indulged, both inside and outside the Union and State Legislatures, vulgarised politics and seriously undermined the future of parliamentary democracy in India. Elections to the Sixth House of the People in March 1977, the polarisation of the political parties and the emergence of responsible Opposition,and its leader having been given an official recognition and status seemed to augur well and set a bright future for the smooth functioning of parliamentary democracy. But the old game of defections was again allowed to pollute politics and the Janata ruling party played the major role. The Executive Committee of the Janata Party at a meeting held on April 24, 1977, decided that members of the Council of States (Rajya Sabha) and the State Assemblies desiring of joining the Party would be admitted "without any condition or reservation."[13] Indians are proverbial worshippers of the rising sun and when the power hungry politicians got the cue from the ruling party, they *en masse* deserted the parties on whose tickets they had been elected and the nefarious game of defections had then a full swing.

Vayalar Ravi, a former Congress Working Committee member, told newsmen at Trivandrum on May 10, 1977 that a move to convene a Constituent Assembly was initiated during the period of Emergency and a bill to introduce the Presidential system of government got ready by Mrs. Gandhi's Government. Sanjay Gandhi, the Prime Minister's son, was the prime force behind these, he disclosed, which were, however, scotched by the opposition within the Congress Party.[14] The Prime Minister, Mrs. Gandhi, stoutly contradicted the information, that had trickled out to the press, when the matter was raised in Parliament. It is on record now that in October 1975 a demi-official paper, "A Fresh Look at Our Constitution : Some Suggestions", advocating a Presidential system was circulated and sent to the Judges as well.[15] In 1976, several Pradesh Congress Committees advocated the setting up of a Constitutent Assembly. The move was abandoned and, instead, the Forty-second amendment was adopted in December 1976.

---

10. As reported in *The Hindustan Times*, New Delhi, January 28, 1967.
11. Seminar organised by the Bar Association of India. *The Indian Express*, New Delhi, April 17, 1967.
12. Meeting organised by the Progressive Group, Bombay, September 2, 1967. *The Hindustan Times*, New Delhi, September 4, 1967.
13. *The Times of India*, New Delhi, April 25, 1977.
14. *Indian Express*, New Delhi, May 11, 1977.
15. Justice V. R. Krishna Iyer of the Supreme Court and Justice T. U. Mehta, publicly admitted about the circulation of such a paper. On January 2, 1980, shortly after his retirement as Chief Justice of Himachal High Court, Justice Mehta recalled how in 1975 a "mysterious paper" was circulated to all judges. It suggested both a Presidential form of government and a Superior Council of Judiciary to interpret the Constitution and to suparvise the performance of Judges. He expressed his belief that the cyclostyled paper was distributed by the Law Minister.

The issue remained more or less dormant during nearly three years of the Janata-Lok Dal rule. But it triggered again soon after Mrs. Gandhi returned to power in January 1980 and more particularly after the Supreme Court decision in the *Minerva Mills* case on May 9, 1980. On May 11, 1980 laying the foundation stone of a telephone exchange building at Sangareddy, the headquarters of the Medak district in Andhra Pradesh, Communication Minister C. M. Stephen said that the Supreme Court judgment (in Minerva Mills case) holding that Parliament does not have unrestricted power of amending the Constitution and that Fundamental Rights are more important than Directive Principles laid down in the Constitution "posed a new challenge to the ruling party, and we will face it."[16] Dr. Chenna Reddy, the Andhra Pradesh Chief Minister, renewed in most unequivocal terms the demand for a Presidential system on June 22, 1980 at Hyderabad in a speech delivered in the presence of the Union Law Minister Shiv Shankar. Chenna Reddy repeated its plea for the second time at New Delhi on June 7, 1980. He even spelt out the details of his scheme clearly enough. His suggestions created a furore in the Council of States (Rajya Sabha) on June 9, 1980 and anxious queries were made by the Opposition members. The Union Minister of Law and Justice, Shiv Shankar, assured the House that there was no thinking on the part of the Government to introduce a Presidential form of government in the country and "it is not necessary at this stage to do so." The Law Minister described Dr. Chenna Reddy's views as '"individual opinion" and it was a case of individual's freedom of expression.[17]

But it did not end the matter there. All the Opposition parties combined together to forestall the designs, if any, of the ruling party. Even a memorandum was submitted to the President for his intervention in checkmating the proposed changes and substituting Presidential for a Parliamentary system. Kuldip Nayar reported in the *Indian Express,* December 15, 1980, that President Neelam Sanjiva Reddy was opposed to the Presidential System of government and he reportedly told some Indian leaders, the other day that there was no possibility of the system being introduced at least for twenty months "as long as I am there" (President Reddy completed his term of office in July 1982). But the President snubbed a reporter at Hyderabad when he was asked about his views on the Presidential system and angrily replied that : "the President does not make statements." The Bharatiya Janata Party President, A. B. Vajpayee, alleged, on December 13, 1980 at Gwalior, that there was a "two-year plan" to install Mrs. Indira Gandhi as the country's President by changing the Constitution.[18] The Bharatiya Janata Party at its Bombay Session in a resolution on the political situation warned the country against the "sinister designs" of the ruling party to replace the Parliamentary system by the Presidential form of government and push India under an "authoritarian rule."[19]

When Dr. Chenna Reddy's suggestion of the Presidential system was being discussed in the Council of States,[20] the Chairman, M. Hidayatullah, characterised the suggestion of the Andhra Pradesh Chief Minister as "straws in the wind" and appealed to the members that they should not get unnecessarily agitated. The remark evoked loud protest from the Opposition, but what happened subsequently cannot be lightly brushed aside. When the Maharashtra Chief Minister A.R. Antulay, had spoken so trenchantly against the existing parliamentary system and pleaded for the need to change the system whether before a gathering of lawyers or at the session of the All India Congress (I) Committee and suggested that the Congress (I) should start a dialogue on this question and a special session of the AICC (I) should be convened to consider the issue, one cannot consider his utterances as that of a lone soldier. He even suggested holding of a referendum on the Presidential system.[21] There was certainly a powerful lobby within the Congress(I) to bring about the change and Antulay was one of the selected instruments for the propagation of an idea. Even the Law and Justice Minister, Shiv Shankar, told the House of the People that he personally felt that the Presidential form was a highly democratic form of government. Mrs. Indira Gandhi did not say anything categorical on the subject, but her observations

16. *The Tribune,* Chandigarh, May 13, 1980.
17. *The Times of India,* New Delhi, June 10, 1980.
18. *The Sunday Standard,* New Delhi, December 14, 1980.
19. *Indian Express,* New Delhi, December 14, 1980.
20. June 9, 1980.
21. *India Express, New Delhi, January 28, 1981.*

at the All India Conference of Lawyers that she inaugurated in October 1980 that why "many who swear by democracy should shy away from discussion of a matter of public importance" and her remarks at a news conference at New Delhi that the Presidential system was "democratic" in content, were significant. When many speakers in the All India Congress Committee session in December 1980 commendingly referred to the Presidential system and sought a switchover, there was not a word of disapproval by her. She smiled when a group of 25 American students from New York asked her, on January 27, 1981, about the controversy regarding the Presidential form of government. Specifically they asked whether it was ruled out forever. The Prime Minister said, she did not think there would be a Presidential form of government in the near future and added that it was, however, "everybody's case that the Presidential system was less democratic. The question was of finding out what effectively worked in Indian conditions and of obtaining peoples' participation."[22]

More recently, it had been vigorously advocated by Vasant Sathe, when Minister of Communication in Rajiv Gandhi's Government and again when the Congress was out of office in 1991. Rama Krishna Hegde, who was the critic of the Presidential system became its ardent supporter. However, the most unambiguous endorsement has come from the Bharatiya Janata Party, which adopted the Presidential form of government as part of its programme at the Vijayawada conference. Vasant Sathe later clarified that he had not advocated a switch to the Presidential system. "All I had been pleading for is that within the existing system, we should have a directly-elected chief executive who, although chosen by the people, would be responsible to Parliament. This slight change is necessary because the existing structure has proved to be weak."

In the last week of January 1987, a debate was opened by 20 eminent citizens who questioned the relevance of the Indian Constitution as an instrument of social change. The Twenty believed that the distorted functioning of parliamentary democracy was responsible for all that ailed India today and that drastic constitutional reforms were the solution. The reforms suggested ranged from direct election of the Prime Minister by the people entitled to vote (which certainly is tantamount to the Presidential system though they shied away from saying so) to proportional representation in Parliament and the State Legislatures.

The ranks of the no-changers are equally numerous and articulate. They include eminent jurists like N. A. Palkhivala, H. M. Seervai and L. M. Singhvi. The Supreme Court Bar Association is as vocal as the pro-changer lawyers. In a resolution passed at an emergency meeting on November 17, 1980 the Supreme Court Bar Association condemned the "sinister attacks" on parliamentary democracy and independence of judiciary and assailed the argument that the Prime Minister must have all the powers of the President of the United States to maintain the unity and integrity of the country.[23] Palkhivala, way back in 1979, pleaded for changes in the Constitution and argued the case for a change to the Presidential System[24], but soon there was a wavering shift in his stand. He says that he was wrong and the people who support the Presidential form are wrongly motivated and authoritarian. "When your house is on fire, you do not decide whether your bed room should be converted into a study", he says.[25] H. M. Seervai believes that the advocacy for adopting Presidential System "is mistaken and is based on general and emotional grounds."[26] Justice V. R. Krishna Iyer, talking to newsmen at Chandigarh on May 11, 1980 said that the Presidential form had a great potential for subversion of democracy in a large and diverse country like India with indigent and illiterate people. He remarked that any change from the present form of government would have to undergo the test that "it does not violate the basic structure of the Constitution."[27]

To substitute a Presidential system to a

22. *The Hindustan Times,* New Delhi, January 28, 1981.
23. As reported in *Indian Express,* New Delhi, November 18, 1980.
24. Palkhivala in his Convocation Address to the Madras University, 1979, expressed the view that a Presidential System "tailored" to meet our requirements could be introduced in our Constitution by a valid constitutional amendment without altering the basic structure. Also refer to his article "Has the Constitution Failed ?" *The Illustrated Weekly of India,* Bombay, September 16-22, 1979, and address to a seminar on "Challenge Ahead" at Calcutta on April 20, 1980. *The Times of India,* New Delhi, April 21, 1980.
25. "Case against Presidential System", *Indian Express,* New Delhi, November 20, 1980.
26. *The Times of India,* January 28, 1980.
27. *Indian Express,* New Delhi, January 28, 1981.

Cabinet system is not to amend the Constitution, as Antulay maintained, or to have a directly elected chief executive responsible to Parliament within the existing system as Vasant Sathe suggested, but to rewrite large parts of it. It is an impossible task to re-write large parts of the Constitution and to tailor them to meet the requirements of the country. The Constitution is an organic whole and it cannot be changed piecemeal. In determining the nature of the Executive, the Constituent Assembly decided that it should be of parliamentary type and in consonance with the basic principles of that system of government it had to enact other provisions which would harmonise with the parliamentary system and make it function smoothly. If the Presidential system is to be adopted and the powers and functions vested in and exercised by the Council of Ministers are to be conferred on the President as the Chief Executive, who shall be both the head of the Government and the State, corresponding changes shall have to be made in the States. One cannot think of a constitution having two diametrically opposed systems of government, one for the Union and the other for the States and that too in a federal polity. If the Presidential system is conceded at both levels, it would immediately involve the question of mode of electing the President and the Governors. Then the existing powers of the President and the Governors would have to be considered *de novo* and various other constitutional provisions, including administrative relations between the President and Parliament and the Governors and State Legislatures. They shall have to be redefined in conformity to the basic principles of the Presidential system hinging upon separation of powers. And if the principle of free and limited government is to be the *sine qua non* of such a system as it was with the Founding Fathers of the Constitution of the United States, the system of checks and balances is its *raison d' etre* and it shall have to be devised and incorporated in the various provisions of the Constitution.

The Presidential system, therefore, cannot be introduced without re-writing the Constitution. The Supreme Court ruled in the *Keshavananda Bharati* case that the basic structure of the Constitution cannot be changed. This principle was followed in *Mrs. Indira Gandhi* vs. *Raj Narain* election case and re-affirmed in the *Minerva Mills* case. The Parliamentary system of government is the foundation on which the entire machinery of Government, both at the Centre and the States, is erected. "To pick up the foundations of the Executive and Legislatures and build a new structure on new foundations is to make a new Constitution and not to amend the old one. Such purported amendment would be void under Article 368 as altering more than the basic structure of our Constitution.[28]

It is not the Constitution which has failed the people, says Palkhivala, "but it is our chosen representatives who have failed the Constitution." The structure has been "erected by architects of consummate skill and fidelity; its foundations are solid, its compartments are beautiful; its arrangements are full of wisdom and order; and its defences are impregnable from without. It has reared for immortality, if the work of man may justly aspire to such a title. It may nevertheless perish in an hour by the folly, or corruption, or negligence of its keepers THE PEOPLE", he added. But the foundations of the Constitution "have been shaken by the folly of the people, the corruption of our politicians and the negligence of the elite. In just thirty years, we have reduced the noble processes of our Constitution to the level of a carnival of claptrap, cowardice and chicanery."[29] Ambedkar poignantly remarked in the Constituent Assembly, that if the Constitution "which was given by the people unto themselves in November 1949 did not work satisfactorily at any future time, we would have to say not that the Constitution has failed but the man is vile". These words of the architect of the Constitution have proved to be prophetic. The life style of Indians during the past four decades has brought utter disillusionment. India's problem is in the crisis of character and the decline of integrity "which should be loadstar. We are in danger of fast becoming a philistine nation, a society without inspiration."[30] It is, therefore, a crisis of substance and not form, a crisis of functioning and not in structure.

### Qualifications for Election as President

The Constitution requires that the President should be a citizen of India, must have completed the age of thirty-five years and be qualified for election as a member of the House

28. Seervai, H. M., "Presidential System—II Studies in Comparison", *Indian Express,* New Delhi, November 21, 1980.
29. Palkhivala, N.A. "Has the Constitution Failed ?", *The Illustrated Weekly of India,* Bombay, September 16-22, 1979.
30. Singhvi, L. M., Bhagwati Singh Mehta Memorial Lecture, Jaipur, *The Hindustan Times,* November 2, 1980.

of the People. But he must not at the time of his election hold any office of profit under any Government, Union or State or local. A person, however, is not to be deemed to hold any office of profit by reason only that he is the President or Vice-President of the Union or the Governor of any State or is a Minister for the Union or for any State. The President must not be a member of either House of Parliament or a State Legislature, and if he is, he must vacate his seat in that House before he enters upon his office as President. In order to prevent abuse of authority by such candidates, the Constitution vests the superintendence, direction and control for the election of President in the Election Commission which, in its turn, is subject to the control of Parliament.

Prior to the Thirty-ninth Amendment all doubts and disputes arising out of or in connection with the election of a President or Vice-President were inquired into and decided by the Supreme Court, whose decision used to be final.[31] The Constitution (Thirty-ninth Amendment) Act, 1975, deprived the Supreme Court of this jurisdiction and empowered Parliament to regulate by law, all matters relating to and connected with the election of a President or Vice-President, including the grounds on which such election could be questioned. The amendment contemplated to set up an authority or body to inquire into and decide all such disputes. The validity of the law regulating such disputes, the setting up authority or body to inquire into and the decision of that authority or body was not to be called in question in any court. The Constitution (Forty-fourth Amendment) Act, 1978, restored to the Supreme Court, its original power of inquiring into and deciding all doubts and disputes relating to the election of a President or Vice-President. The newly inserted Article 71 further provided that if the election of a person as President or Vice-President is declared void, acts done by him in the exercise of the performance of the powers and duties of President or Vice-President, as the case may be, on or before the date of the decision of the Supreme Court shall not be invalid by reason of such a decision.

The Constitution (Eleventh Amendment) Act, 1961, inserted clause 4 in Article 71 providing that the election of a President or Vice-President shall not be called in question on the ground of existence of any vacancy for whatever reason among the members of the electoral college electing him. In other words, it is not a valid ground to contend that the existence of a vacancy in the electoral college renders the election of a President or Vice-President void or Presidential or Vice-Presidential election may not be held till the electoral college is complete for all intents and purposes.

**Term of Office**

The President holds office for a term of five years and is eligible for re-election. He may resign before the expiry of his term and in such an eventuality the resignation is required to be addressed to the Vice-President who shall forthwith communicate it to the Speaker of the House of the People. But the Constitution makes no provision for meeting a situation arising from the resignation of the acting President. V. V. Giri, who acted as President after the death of Zakir Hussain, expressed his desire on July 16, 1969 to resign in order to contest the Presidential election scheduled for August 16, 1969. Since the Constitution did not provide for a clear cut direction in regard to a situation where the Vice-President was acting as President, V. V. Giri resigned from the office of the Vice-President, in accordance with the advice of the Attorney-General, and addressed his letter of resignation to the President of India. Copies of the letter sent to the President's Secretariat were forwarded to the Prime Minister and the Chief Justice of India.

**Mode of Election**

The mode of election of the Indian President is completely different from that under the American Constitution. It is a unique election in that the representatives of the people choose the President. As Dr. Rajendra Prasad put it, "The President is elected by representatives who represent the entire population twice over, once as representatives of the States and again as their representatives in Parliament." Jawaharlal Nehru commended this as the right method to choose a good man who can efficiently and with dignity play the role as a constitutional head. If the President was to be directly elected, Nehru told the Constituent Assembly, "and yet (we) did not give him any real powers, it might become slightly anomalous" especially since "we wanted to emphasize the ministerial character of

31. Article 71 (original) provided : "All doubts and disputes arising out or in connection with the election of a President or Vice-President shall be inquired into and decided by the Supreme Court whose decision shall be final." The Supreme Court decided under this provision the election petitions against President V. V. Giri (1970) and President Fakhruddin Ali Ahmed (1974).

the Government that power really resided in the Ministry."[32]

The qualifications prescribed are simple. Any citizen of India who has completed 35 years of age and is qualified for election as a member of the House of the People (Lok Sabha) is eligible to contest provided his nomination is backed by not less than 10 electors as proposers and at least 10 electors as supporters.

The President is elected by the members of an electoral college consisting of the elected members of both the Houses of Parliament and the elected members of the Legislative Assemblies of the 25 States. Nominated members of these Houses and the elected members of the Assemblies of the Union Territories are excluded. The Constitution lays emphasis on uniformity in the scale of representation of the different States and the parity between the States as a whole and the Union through the determination of the value of the votes based on the population of the States.

In simple language, the complicated formula would mean that the value of the vote of every elected member of the Legislative Assembly of a State is determined by dividing the population of the State by the total number of elected members of the Assembly and by 1,000, and if there is any remainder of not less than 500 after such division, then the vote of each member is further increased by one. To illustrate it :

$$\left.\frac{\text{Total population of the State}}{\text{Total number of elected members in the Legislative Assembly of a State.}}\right\} \text{Divided by } 1{,}000$$

The value of the vote of an elected member of either House of Parliament is worked out by dividing the total number of votes assigned to the members of the Legislative Assemblies of all the 25 States by the total number of the elected members of both the Houses of Parliament, fractions exceeding one-half being counted as one. The Constitution also lays down that till we reach the year 2000 and a census is taken thereafter, the population for the determination of the value should continue to be the 1971 census figures.

In the election, the system of proportional representation by means of a single transferable vote is followed as provided in Article 55. The ballot is secret. The candidate who secures votes more than or equal to the quota of votes is declared elected. If at the first count no candidate is able to secure the required quota of votes, the candidate securing the least number of votes is eliminated and his votes are transferred among other candidates according to the second preference on the ballot papers of voters who gave him first preference. The process of elimination and transfer of votes continues, till such a candidate is found who has obtained the required quota of votes. Disputes, if any, about the election of the President are heard and decided by the Supreme Court.

The Presidential and Vice-Presidential Act, 1952, in its operation through the first five elections was found inadequate in many respects to cope with complex situations. The elections to the highest office became a free-for-all with non-serious candidates who did not have the capacity to put up even a symbolic fight jumping into the fray. The legislative measures taken in 1974 to curb this undesirable development and inject seriousness into the election came not a day too soon. The law now lays down that : (1) a candidate's nomination papers should be proposed by at least 10 electors and seconded by an equal number; (2) a sum of Rs. 2,500 should be deposited along with the nomination; and (3) a petition challenging an election can be filed in only by a contesting candidate or 20 or more electors jointly.

**Eligibility for re-election**

On the question of re-eligibility the Constitution does not impose any express restriction as to the number of terms, consecutive or otherwise, for which a person can be elected President. It simply provides that "A person who holds or who has held, office as President shall, subject to the other provisions of this Constitution, be eligible for re-election to that office." The Union Constitution Committee had recommended that a retiring President would not seek election beyond the second term and the Constituent Assembly accepted this suggestion. But when the Draft Constitution came under discussion, the point was made that, if there was a capable and efficient man, there was no reason why he should not be allowed to serve the country beyond two terms and, accordingly, K. C. Sharma moved an amendment for removing the restriction that the President would be eligible to hold office for two terms

32. *Constituent Assembly Debates,* Vol. IV, pp. 713-4.

only.''[33] Ambedkar accepted the amendment and restriction on the eligibility for re-election was withdrawn.

Rajendra Prasad was elected the first President of India by the Constituent Assembly on January 24, 1950. He was elected for the second time under the normal working of the Constitution in 1952. In 1957, when time came for Presidential election, Nehru hoped and expected that Prasad would step down in favour of the Vice-President, S. Radhakrishnan. But Rajendra Prasad declined to do so and there was a minor crisis within Congress Party. Rajendra Prasad continued in office till 1960, the aggregate period of two terms, and in 1960, he himself announced that he would not run for the third term. A Convention was, thus, set for a two term tenure.

**Impeachment**

The President is liable to impeachment for violating the Constitution. The expression ''Violation of the Constitution'' has nowhere been defined. The manner in which impeachment proceedings take place is covered by Article 61. It provides that either House of Parliament may prefer the charge for impeaching the President by moving a resolution, provided fourteen days' notice has been given to that effect by not less than one-fourth of the total membership of the House initiating the charge of impeachment. When the House initiating the charge passes a resolution to impeach the President, the other House as a consequence thereof investigates the charge so made. But instead of making the investigation itself, the House may delegate the work of investigation to any court or tribunal appointed by the House for that purpose. The President has the right to appear in person or be represented at such investigation. If the House investigating the charge passes a resolution by a two-thirds majority of the total membership of the House that the charge has been sustained, the President is removed from his office the day on which such a resolution is passed.

No President has been impeached so far, though efforts were made twice in 1970 and 1979 for initiation of impeachment proceedings against V. V. Giri and Neelam Sanjiva Reddy respectively, but in both the cases the proposals were ultimately dropped.

**Succession of Presidency**

The Constitution provides for succession to Presidency after the expiration of the term of office of the President, by reasons of his death, resignation or removal. Article 62(1) states that election to fill a vacancy shall be completed before the expiration of the term of office of the President. If the office of the President becomes vacant owing to the death, resignation or removal or to any other cause before the expiry of his term, the election of a new President must be held as soon as possible, but in no case later than six months from the date of the occurrence of the vacancy.[34] In the meantime, the Vice-President acts as President till the date on which a new President enters upon his office.[35]

But the Constitution does not provide for a situation in which the offices of both the President and the Vice-President become vacant. To remedy the omission Parliament passed in May 1969, the President (Discharge of Functions) Act, providing for the discharge of President's duties in certain contingencies and putting the Chief Justice of India, or in his absence, the seniormost Judge of the Supreme Court in the line of succession. On the resignation of the Acting President, V. V. Giri, the Chief Justice of India M. Hidayatullah, succeeded Giri till the Presidential elections were held and the newly elected President assumed office. The Home Minister made it clear in Parliament that the Act in no way intended to determine succession to the Presidency. It was just to fill a vacuum if the Vice-President who can act as or discharge the functions of the President, is for any reason incapacitated or is not available.

**Oath or Affirmation by the President**

Every President and every person acting as President or discharging the functions of the President is required, under Article 60, before entering upon his office to make and subscribe in the presence of the Chief Justice of India or, in his absence, the seniormost Judge of the Supreme Court available, an oath or affirmation in the prescribed form. The oath or affirmation demands from him :

(1) to faithfully execute the office of the President or discharge the functions of the President;

(ii) to preserve, protect and defend to

33. *Ibid.*, Vol. VII, pp. 1023-24.
34. Article 62(2).
35. Article 65.

the best of his ability the Constitution and the law; and

(iii) to devote himself to the service and well- being of the people of India.

## THE VICE-PRESIDENT

### The Vice-Presidency

The Constitution provides for the Vice-President and the office is modelled partly on the similar institution in the United States. Like the American Vice-President, the Indian Vice-President is the ex-officio Chairman of the Council of States (Rajya Sabha), the Upper Chamber of the Union of India. The similarity between the two offices ends here. In the United States, the Vice-President must possess all the qualifications of a President and he is elected by the same popularly elected electoral college which elects the President. The reason is obvious. The American Vice-President succeeds to the Presidency in the event of the President's death, resignation, incapacity or removal and continues in the office for the unexpired portion of his predecessor's term. The Vice-President of India, on the other hand, only acts as President in any casual vacancy in the office of the President until a new President is elected and enters upon his office, as did V. V. Giri on the death of Zakir Hussain, and B. D. Jatti on the death of Fakhruddin Ali Ahmed. The terms of office of the American President and Vice-President are identical and both are liable to removal by impeachment. The Vice-President of India is elected for a term of five years by an electoral college consisting of members of both Houses of Parliament and is liable to removal from office by a resolution of the Council of States passed by a majority of all the then members of the Council and agreed to by the House of the People.

But the most important dissimilarity between the two offices relates to their duties and functions. The Vice-President of India is the *ex-officio* Chairman of the Council of States and he draws his salary as an incumbent of that office. In between the sessions of the Council of States he may even go abroad on a goodwill mission or on an invitation from foreign Governments, as did Radhakrishnan, Zakir Hussain, G. S. Pathak, B. D. Jatti, R. Venkataraman and Shankar Dayal sharma on many occasions. But neither he speaks for the Government nor has he any participation, either directly or indirectly, in the affairs of the Government. The Vice-President of India does need no training in administration, like his counterpart in the United States, as he fills only a casual vacancy and takes over the Rashtrapati Bhavan until the President resumes his duties or a new President is elected, in no case later than six months from the date of the occurrence of the vacancy, and enters upon his office.

A neat distinction need be made when the Vice-President acts as the President and when he is discharging the functions of the President. The Vice-President acts for the President in the event of his death, resignation or removal until a new President is elected and he enters upon his office. But when the President is unable to discharge the functions relating to his office owing to absence, illness, or any other cause, the Vice-President discharges his functions until the date on which the President resumes his duties. Radhakrishnant wice discharged the functions of the President and once Zakir Hussain when President S. Radhakrishnan fell ill and Jatti for N. Sanjiva Reddy when he went to the United States for treatment. The Vice-President, whenever, he acts as President, exercises all the powers of the President and is entitled to such emoluments, allowances and privileges as may be determined by Parliament and until provision to that effect is made, such emoluments, allowances and privileges as are specified in the Second Schedule. But when the Chief Justice of India discharges the functions of the President, as envisaged in the Presidential (Discharge of Functions) Act, 1969, his emoluments, allowances and privileges remain the same as those of the President and Parliament cannot alter them.

### Election of the Vice-President

The Vice-President is elected by the members of an electoral college consisting of the members of both Houses of Parliament in accordance with the system of proportional representation by means of the single transferable vote. The voting is by secret ballot. The Vice-President must not be a member of either House of Parliament or a House of the State Legislature and if he is of either of them, he shall be deemed to have vacated his seat in that House on the date on which he enters upon his office as Vice-President. No person shall be eligible for election for Vice-President unless he is a citizen of India, has completed the age of thirty-five years, and is qualified for election as a member of the Council of States and he must not hold any office of profit under the Government of India or the Government of any State or any local or other authority subject to the control of any of the said Governments. But a person shall not be deemed to hold any office of profit by reason only that he is the President or Vice-President of the Union or the Governor of any State or is a Minister either for the Union or for any State.

The term of office of the Vice-President is five years. But he may resign from his office before the expiry of the normal term. The letter of resignation is to be addressed to the President of India. When V. V. Giri resigned on July 20, 1969, he addressed his letter of resignation to the President of India, although he himself was the Acting President. This procedure he followed on the advice of the Attorney-General. The Vice-President may also be removed from office by a resolution passed by a majority of all the then members of the Council of States and agreed to by the House of the People. The Vice-President continues to hold office, notwithstanding the expiration of his term, until his successor enters upon his office.

**Duties of the Vice-President**

The duties of the Vice-President, as said earlier, are two-fold. He is the *ex-officio* Chairman of the Council of States, presides over its meetings, and draws his salary in that capacity. Though the office of the Vice-President is created by the Constitution, but he draws no salary in that capacity. When the Vice-President acts as President of the Republic or discharges the functions of the President, he ceases to perform the duties of the Chairman of the Council of States and is, accordingly, neither entitled to any salary nor allowances payable to that office. When the Vice-President acts for or discharges the functions of the President he exercises all the powers of the President and enjoys all the privileges of that office.

## POWERS AND DUTIES OF THE PRESIDENT

**Executive Powers**

The President, unlike his counterpart in the United States, has no power of control and supervision over the Ministries of the Union Government. They are presided over by Ministers whose advice is binding on him in the exercise of his functions. The President is only a necessary adjunct of the Governmental machinery. His authority is formal, though all executive actions of the Union Government must be expressed to be taken in the name of the President. For that matter all contracts and assurances of property made on behalf of the Government of India are expressed to be made by the President and executed in such manner as the President may direct. Moreover, all officers of the Union are his officers and, consequently, his subordinates, and he has the right to be informed of all the affairs of the Union. The President also makes rules for the convenient transaction of the business of the Government of India and for the allocation among Ministers of the said business. He has the right to be kept informed by the Prime Minister of all decisions taken by the Council of Ministers and seek such other information regarding the affairs of the Government of India as he may consider necessary and expedient. The President may also ask the Prime Minister to submit for the consideration of the Council of Ministers any matter on which a decision had been taken by a Minister but which has not been considered by the Council. He may also require the Council of Ministers to reconsider the advice tendered to him, either generally or otherwise.[36]

All important appointments are made by him and they include the Prime Minister of India, other Ministers of the Union, the Attorney-General of the Union, the Comptroller and Auditor-General, Judges of the Supreme Court and the High Courts and the State Governors. Before appointing Judges, the President is bound to consult servicing Judges, and he will be bound to make these appointments on the advice of the Ministry. With regard to the appointment of the Prime Minister, the choice of the President is obvious when the Constitution enjoins that the Council of Ministers shall be collectively responsible to the House of the People. Collective responsibility can only be enforced when the Council of Ministers is a team which plays the game of politics under the captaincy of the leader of the party in majority in the House of the People. The President may have some discretion in the selection of the Prime Minister, if no single party has a majority. But even in that case it is the duty of the President to turn to a person who must be able to secure colleagues and with his colleagues he must be able to secure the collaboration of the House of the People. Following the death of Nehru, Dr. Radhakrishnan swore in G. L. Nanda, the seniormost member of Nehru's cabinet, as interim Prime Minister pending selection of a

36. Substituted by the Constitution (Forty-fourth Amendment) Act, 1978, S. 11.

new leader by the Congress Legislature Party in Parliament. He repeated it in 1966 on the death of Lal Bahadur Shastri and his decision was appreciated. Gyani Zail Singh straightway administered the oath of office to Rajiv Gandhi, when he was only a member of Parliament and had not been elected leader of the Congress Legislature Party in Parliament, after the assassination of Indira Gandhi. It was a bold decision based on the shrewd assessment of the prevailing situation, though a complete departure from the established convention. Rajiv Gandhi's landslide victory at the polls shortly thereafter fully vindicated Zail Singh's decision. In contrast, Neelam Sanjiva Reddy landed himself in a serious controversy in 1979 by calling upon Charan Singh to form the government after the fall of the Janata Government headed by Morarji Desai. Charan Singh could not face Parliament and bowed out within a few months.

Besides the appointment of high dignitaries of the State referred to above, the President has also the power to appoint the following administrative commissions : An Inter-State Council, the Union Public Service Commission and a Joint Commission for a group of States, the Finance Commission, the Election Commission, a Commission to report on the administration of Scheduled Areas, Special Officer for Scheduled Castes and Scheduled Tribes, a Commission to investigate into the condition of backward classes, and a Commission on Languages. But all this he does on ministerial advice.

The President has the power to remove his Ministers, the Attorney-General of India, and the Governors of the States. But ministerial dismissal by the head of the State is not the essence of a parliamentary system of government. No Government in Britain has been dismissed by the Sovereign since 1783 and no Monarch may today venture it, whatever be the legal opinion, unless he or she is determined to gamble in the most dangerous manner. The role of the Indian President with relation to his Ministers is identical to that of the British Monarch. Ambedkar emphasised this point in the Constituent Assembly. He asserted, "Beyond the identity of names of the Heads of Governments of the Indian Union and the U. S. A., there is nothing in common between the form of government prevalent in America and that proposed in the Indian Constitution." He further added that the place of the President of India "in the administration is that of a ceremonial device on the seal by which nation's decisions are made known. He will be generally bound by the advice of the Ministers. He can do nothing contrary to their advice; nor can he do anything without their advice. The President of the United States can dismiss any Secretary at any time. The President of the Indian Union has no power to do so, so long as his Ministers command a majority in Parliament." It is the Parliament's privilege to vote down the Ministry.

**Military and Foreign Affairs**

The Constitution vests in the President the Supreme Command of the Defence Forces, but he is expressly required to exercise this power in conformity with law. Parliament has exclusive legislative power relating to the defence forces, war and peace. Declaration of war and peace, as under the British Constitution, is an executive function, but the Indian President will not declare war or deploy the force without or in anticipation of Parliamentary sanction.

All matters affecting relations with foreign countries are within the exclusive legislative competence of Parliament[37] and, as such, executive power relating to foreign affairs is exercised by the Union and the diplomatic business is conducted in the name of the President. Diplomatic envoys and consular agents are accredited in his name. All treaties and international agreements are negotiated and concluded in the name of the President, provided they do not involve the secession of the territory, payment of money or a change in the law made by Parliament. But this power of treaty-making can be restricted by Parliament under article 53(3) (b), which provides that "nothing in this Article shall...........prevent Parliament from conferring by law functions on authorities other than the President."

**Legislative Powers**

The President is a component part of the Union Parliament. Article 79 provides that there "shall be a Parliament for the Union which shall consist of the President and two Houses to be known respectively as the Council of States and the House of the People." The powers vested in the President in relation to legislation are :

The President has the power to summon and prorogue Parliament and dissolve the House of the People (Lok Sabha). The power to summon Parliament is, however, subject to the condition

37. Seventh Schedule, List I, entry 14.

imposed by Clause (1) of Article 85, that is, the President must summon Parliament within six months from the last sitting of a session. If he fails to summon it within the prescribed time, there will be a breach of the Constitution. The President has also the power to summon a joint sitting of both Houses of Parliament in case of a deadlock between them over a non-Money Bill.

Power of dissolution is one of the most important features of a parliamentary government. Dissolution means the end of the life of the representative House of the Legislature and calls for a fresh election. During the last more than a hundred years in Britain there is no instance of refusal of a dissolution when advised by the Prime Minister. Nevertheless, the opinion has always prevailed in that country that the Monarch is free to disregard such an advice if he feels that the Prime Minister's right to ask for dissolution is being put to serious abuse. There had been two definite occasions during the last seventy years or so when dissolution took place at the express desire of the King.

The issue of dissolution came up for active consideration before the Constituent Assembly of India when Prof. K. T. Shah moved an amendment to Article 69 of the Draft Constitution, which corresponds to Article 85 of the 1950 Constitution, making it obligatory for the Prime Minister to give in writing the reasons for the dissolution of the House of the People. Ambedker in reply (May 18, 1949) said that if the object of Prof. K. T. Shah was that the Prime Minister should not arbitrarily ask for dissolution, the object would be served if the convention regarding dissolution was properly observed. His exposition was that before granting the Prime Minister's proposal for dissolution, the President should ascertain the feelings of the House by exploring the chances of another Ministry. If he found that "the feeling was there that there was no other alternative except dissolution, he would as a constitutional President undoubtedly accept the advice of the Prime Minister to dissolve the House." This exactly is the practice followed in Canada. Ambedkar admitted in the Constituent Assembly that in a parliamentary government there are only two prerogatives which the Head of the State may exercise. One is the appointment of the Prime Minister and the other is the dissolution of Parliament.

On December 7, 1970 the President dissolved the House of the People on the advice of the Prime Minister. In her special broadcast to the nation justifying a Parliamentary poll a good one year ahead of schedule, Mrs. Indira Gandhi declared that she needed a fresh mandate from the people in order to remove the obstacles to her socialistic and secular policies. But what was expedient for Mrs. Gandhi was not acceptable to others. Several Opposition parties protested against dissolution and even a seasoned statesman Acharya Kripalani characterised it as a major danger to democracy. In his article : *Dissolution of Lok Sabha*, he pointed out that power "is useful for serving a legitimate national cause. Power for its own sake or that of an individual is dangerous. Let the nation beware betimes."[38]

Some of the political parties which challenged the Prime Minister's right to govern as head of the minority Government challenged her right to advise dissolution and since it was the first and, consequently, unprecedented act of dissolution some odd suggestions were made. The then Jana Sangh Chief, Atal Behari Vajpayee, asked the President not to accept the Prime Minister's advice and suggested that he should tell the Prime Minister that the House "should pass a resolution recommending dissolution of it." Another suggestion made was that the President should seek an advisory opinion of the Supreme Court. Some others suggested that the President should act "independently and a national caretaker Government be formed." It was even urged that Parliamentary election should not be held before the scheduled time because of the costs and the administrative inconvenience involved therein.

All these arguments were not only irrelevant but the obvious expression of political immaturity. While it may not be mandatory for the President to accept the Prime Minister's advice for dissolution, there is no reason why the President should refuse to accept such advice, when the Prime Minister intends to receive a new mandate from the electorate which may not be available from their representatives. It is an appeal to the people, the ultimate sovereign and quite clearly the lesser sovereign (their representatives) cannot veto the larger sovereign. Mrs. Gandhi's Government had lost its moral right to stay in office when the Supreme Court struck down the Presidential Order on the de-recognition of the Princes. It was, accordingly, right and

---

38. *Indian Express*, New Delhi, December 31, 1970.

proper that the electorate would have been given earliest possible opportunity to give its verdict on the conduct of the Government. The constitutionality of Presidential action in dissolving Parliament was, therefore, beyond challenge. If he would have refused to the Prime Minister's advice to dissolve Parliament the President would have involved himself in active politics; the role which the Constitution never intended for him.

But dissolution of the House of the People in August 1979 dragged President Sanjiva Reddy in an ugly political controversy. The decision of the President to dissolve the House of the People on the advice of the Prime Minister, who had failed to face Parliament as commanded by the President himself, and ask Charan Singh to continue as Prime Minister, rejecting the claim of the Leader of the Opposition to form the Government on the specific understanding that he would establish his claim to majority on the floor of the House within a period of time the President might prescribe, certainly violated not only the principle he had himself once enunciated so categorically but the very conventions on which hinge the functioning of parliamentary democracy and in utter disregard of the intentions of the framers of the Constitution. The criticism was so bitter among the critics that one group, Janata Party headed by Chandra Shekhar, threatened to initiate proceedings for impeachment of the President. N. A. Palkhivala observed that the President's decision to dissolve the House of the People "is, to use the language of studied moderation, unjustified to the point of constitutional impropriety."

It is certainly the President's prerogative that he may refuse dissolution if he felt that circumstances justified such a refusal. This is evident from the provision of Article 85 (2) (b) which says that the President "may from time to time dissolve the House of the People ". The contrast is significant in the use of the word "may" here. Most of the Articles relating to the powers of the President use the mandatory expression "shall". Article 85(1) itself ordains that the President "shall from time to time summon each House of Parliament .........but six months shall not intervene between its last sitting......and the first sitting in the next session."

But dissolution is always an exceptional remedy and President Reddy could well reject the advice tendered by Charan Singh Cabinet without proper assessment on the floor of the House whether Jagjivan Ram's claim could be sustained or not. If Charan Singh could be put in office of the Prime Minister as leader of the minority group that had defected from the Janata Party and his was not even a recognised party of the House, on the commitment that he would seek a mandate from the House "the earliest opportunity, say by the third week of August" the same principle could be applied to Jagjivan Ram when he was the recognised leader of the Opposition and the single largest recognised party of the House.

The President is empowered by Article 86 to address either House of Parliament or both Houses assembled together, and for that purpose require the attendance of Members. But it is not mandatory. Article 87(1), however, makes it obligatory on the President that he "shall" address both Houses of Parliament assembled together at the commencement of the first session after each General Election and at the commencement of the first session of each year and inform Parliament of the causes of its summons. The President's address corresponds to the Speech from the Throne in Britain and as in that country it is used for political purposes in making pronouncements of policy of the Government, both on the domestic and foreign affairs. The address of the President as the Speech from the Throne in Britain, is the handiwork of the Prime Minister, though formally endorsed by the Cabinet in India. The President has to read it as it is. He cannot skip over any portion of the address, as was done by the West Bengal Governor Dharam Vira. The President, unlike a Governor, has no discretion to exercise and if there is presumed to be any, the Constitution Forty-second Amendment as also the Forty-fourth Amendment expressly provide that there is none.

Clause (2) of Article 86 empowers the President to send message to either House of Parliament with respect to a Bill then pending in Parliament or otherwise, and a House to which any message is so sent shall with all the convenient dispatch consider any matter required by the message to be taken into consideration. This power given to the President is, indeed, very wide as the message may relate to any pending Bill or to any other matter before Parliament. But such a power is incongruous in the context of a parliamentary system as established in India. It corresponds to the American President's power of sending message to Congress covering a vast range of problems indicating the needs of the government and the necessity of either amending the existing law or enacting new legislation. But the American Presidency is not a part of the legislature and the Presidential message is a gesture to friendly legislators by the President to support his policy and initiate the required measures. The President of India stands in no such need. His advisers are a part of Parliament, chosen from it and responsible to it. They are always in Parliament to initiate new legislation or to offer amendments to the old, explain policy and defend administration, and to participate in debates. If the President sends a message on a Bill which has ministerial support, it has no use and the President unnecessarily drags himself into politics. The real power of the President, like the British Monarch, depends upon "his willingness to keep off politics." If the President sends a message contrary to and without the ministerial advice, then he ventures to interfere with the constitutional responsibility of the Council of Ministers to Parliament and obviously defies the advice tendered to him by the Council of Ministers in the exercise of his functions thereby violating the Constitution and, consequently, making himself liable to impeachment. This is not likely to happen, but no one can predict the folly of human nature.

The President is required to lay before Parliament the Budget, and Supplementary Budget, if any; the report of the Comptroller and Auditor-General of India relating to the accounts of the Government of India; the recommendations of the Finance Commission and the explanatory memorandum of action taken thereon; reports of the Union Public Service Commission; and various other reports like the report of the special officer for Scheduled Castes and the Tribes; and the report of the Commission to investigate into the conditions of the Backward Classes. He recommends measures to Parliament involving the expenditure of Union moneys. These functions the President clearly exercises on ministerial advice.

The recommendations of the President are necessary before legislation can be introduced for the reorganization of States or alteration of State boundaries. The views of the State Legislature or Legislatures must be ascertained before such a recommendation is made and the views so expressed are not binding on the President. As the President shall act on the advice of his Ministry it rests upon the decision of the latter whether the Bill should be introduced in opposition to the views of the State Legislatures or not.

Similarly, sanction of the President is necessary before legislation can be introduced relating to Money Bills, Bills involving expenditure, Bills affecting taxation in which States are interested. No Bill imposing restrictions on freedom of trade can be introduced in the State Legislatures without the previous sanction of the President.

When a Bill passed by both the Houses of Parliament is presented to the President, he may take any of the following three steps as provided by the Constitution :

(1) he may give his assent to the Bill;

(2) he may withhold his assent;

(3) he may return it, if it is not a Money Bill for the reconsideration of both the Houses of Parliament with a message for : (a) a total reconsideration of the Bill, or (b) a partial reconsideration of the Bill, or (c) he may propose amendments to the Bill.

Withholding assent to a Bill passed by Parliament, is inconsistent with the principle of ministerial responsibility and the President is not likely to venture it. The President has been given the power of veto over legislation with the intent that like the Sovereign in Britian he, too, should never use it. So long as the Council of Ministers commands a majority in Parliament and as long as Parliament remains representative of the people, it carries with it the mandate of the political sovereign. If the President withholds his assent he tampers with the will of the political sovereign expressed through their representatives.

If the President sends back a Bill for reconsideration and if such a Bill passed again by both Houses of Parliament with or without amendments as contained in the Presidential message, the President must give his assent thereto. This is of the nature of a 'suspensive veto' and is more or less identical to the suspensive veto power of the American President. The Constitution does not prescribe any time limit within which the Bill must be returned by the President for reconsideration. It simply says, "The President may as soon as possible return the Bill after it is presented to him." Can the President indefinitely keep the Bill pending ? The principle of ministerial responsibility again intervenes with political consequences if the President tries to put it in cold storage.

In fact, the provision of returning Bills after they are passed by Parliament, is opposed to the basic principles of a parliamentary government. It is tantamount to directing the Ministry to revise its policy. If the President objects to some provisions of the Bill or had to offer some suggestions thereon, the best opportunity for him was to communicate his views to the Cabinet before the introduction of the proposed legislation in Parliament. The Constitution imposes a duty on the Prime Minister to communicate to the President all decisions of the Cabinet relating to the affairs of the Union and proposals for legislation and to furnish such information regarding administration of the affairs of the Union and proposals for legislation as the President may call for.

The Constitution-makers perhaps did not foresee that by borrowing the instrument of 'suspensive veto' from the American Constitution they were not only creating legal complications but political confusion too. Rajendra Prasad, in spite of his unequivocal declaration on the nature of the Constitution in the Constituent Assembly, as its President, attributed to the office of President of India enormously greater powers than those given by the Constitution. On September 15, 1951 he sent a note to the Prime Minister in which he expressed the desire to act solely in his own judgement, independently of the Council of Ministers, when giving assent to Bills, when sending messages to Parliament and when returning Bills to Parliament for reconsideration. This desire was inspired by the Hindu Code Bill which had just been introduced in the provisional Parliament. Prime Minister Jawaharlal Nehru immediately wrote back to the President and reminded him that "These were serious matters of great constitutional importance. They might involve a conflict between the President on one side and the Government and Parliament on the other. They would inevitably raise the question of the President's authority and powers to challenge the decision of Government and of Parliament. The consequences would obviously be serious." He further added that "in our view, the President has no power or authority to go against the will of Parliament in regard to a Bill that has been well considered by it and passed. The whole conception of constitutional government is against any exercise by the President of any such authority."[39]

The President replied to the Prime Minister on September 18, 1951 wherein he maintained that the Constitution "confers in unequivocal words on the President the right to address and send messages to Parliament........Similarly, it also confers on him in unequivocal terms the right to declare either that he assents to a Bill or he withholds assent therefrom when it has been passed by Parliament and presented to him........The meaning of the words which are clear and unequivocal in our Constitution is, I take it, sought to be curtailed by importing and reading into our Constitution certain practices and conventions of the British Constitution. While it is to be hoped that ordinarily and in most cases no difference between the Government and Parliament on the one hand and the President on the other will arise, and the President will act in accordance with the convention of the British Constitution that the King acts on the advice of his Ministers occasions requiring the President to take an independent line of his own cannot be altogether and entirely ruled out." After assigning his reasons for not always acting on the advice of his Ministers, the President wrote that in his view the Constitution "does not admit of a wholesale importation of all practices and conventions of the British Constitution." The President added that he would be the last person to create any conflict and would be prepared to go to the farthest extent to avoid it, if he could do it consistently with his conscience and his views about the Constitution. But "the time for taking any decision by me," he concluded, "has not yet come, and still, hope that it may not come. When it comes, I will, of course, write to you and the Cabinet giving my reasons for any decision that I may take. I can only give you the assurance that I shall not take any decision without giving my fullest consideration to all aspects of the question, particularly the question of constitutional correctness and propriety.[40]

The Prime Minister referred the contents of the President's letters to Alladi Krishnaswami Ayyar and the Attorney-General, M. C. Setalvad, for their opinions. The Attorney-General communicated his opinion on September 24, 1951 and informed the Prime Minister that the functions of the President "cannot be exercised by him without the concurrence of his Ministers and that in exercising them he is bound to act in accordance with the advice tendered by his Ministers.[41]

Alladi Krishnaswami Ayyar wrote two letters to the Prime Minister, the first on September

39. Letter from Jawaharlal Nehru to Dr. Rajendra Prasad, September 15, 1951. Munshi, K. M., *Indian Constitutional Documents,* Vol. I, p. 583.
40. *Ibid.,* pp. 585-86.
41. *Ibid.,* pp. 592-93.

20, 1951, wherein he expressed the opinion that it was perfectly clear that the President "is in every respect in the position of a constitutional monarch in England or his representative in the Dominions, namely, the Governor-General and that there is no sphere of his functions in respect of which he can act without reference to the advice of his ministers. This holds good in respect of his duty to assent to bills as to other matters. Though the Constitution does not go into details in this regard, Article 74 of the Constitution is sufficiently clear on this point." In his second letter, October 8, 1951, he wrote that the President's argument, if conceded, "will upset the whole constitutional structure envisaged at the time when the constitution was passed, make the President a sort of dictator answerable to no one and will reduce the Indian Constitution to a hybrid type which has its counterpart neither in what is known as the Presidential type of Government as obtained in America nor the cabinet type of government known to Britain and the Dominions nor to the system of government obtaining in France which in several respects approximates to the system of government obtaining in Britain and the Dominions." He added that Prasad "seems to read every article of the Constitution in which the expression 'President' occurs as conferring powers upon the President in his individual capacity without reference to the Cabinet or the Council of Ministers." But Article 74 "is all pervasive in its character and does not make any distinction between one kind of functions and another. It applies to every function and power vested in the President whether it relates to addressing the House or returning a Bill for reconsideration or assenting or withholding assent to the Bill. It will be constitutionally improper for the President not to seek to be guided by the advice of his Ministers in exercising any of the functions legally or technically vested in the President. The expression aid and advice in Article 74, cannot be construed so as to enable the President to act independently or against the advice of the Cabinet."[42] A. G. Noorani succinctly says that "Dr. Prasad's demarche thus helped clarify the position once for all, though with results he could have hardly liked."[43] The amended Article 74 now places the matter beyond the reach of any controversy. The advice tendered by the Council of Ministers is binding on the President. What he can do is that he may require the Council of Ministers to reconsider such advice and he is statutorily bound to act in accordance with the advice tendered after such consideration.

President Zail Singh's non-assent to the Postal Interception Bill (the Indian Post Office (Amendment) Bill, 1986) revived an issue which remained unsettled from the early days of the Constitution—the relative powers of the constitutional Head of the State and the elected government, commanding majority in Parliament, under Parliamentary system, the specific provisions of the Constitution and the well-recognised conventions governing such a system notwithstanding. A Bill amending the Indian Postal Act, 1898, and empowering officials of the Union and State Governments to intercept mail of citizens, passed by Parliament in its winter session 1986, was sent to the President in the normal routine for his assent. But while some other measures sent by the Government were received back with the Presidential approval, the amending Postal Bill was not. Instead of according assent, the President sent the Bill to the Law Ministry with several suggestions for its review. The clarifications submitted to the President did not satisfy him, in particular on Clause 26 which gave the Government power to intercept a citizen's mail as it ran counter to the 1968 recommendations of the Law Commission, and was violative of the provisions enshrining fundamental rights to freedom of speech and expression.

The President under Article 111 has the power to withhold assent to a measure and send it back to Parliament with a message that it be reconsidered or indicate the desirability of a particular amendment. Since President Zail Singh did not return it to Parliament and kept it pending, ultimately leaving to his successor to take action as he deemed necessary a political motive would certainly be seen in the entire process, rationale of the review of the Bill aside.

Even under the formal provisions of the Constitution, the President's power of vetoing a Bill is limited, for if the Parliament passed the Bill again in the original form, it is constitutionally obligatory on him to assent to it. So far there has been only one instance of the exercise of President's veto power. It was in regard to the PEPSU Appropriation Bill in 1959 when this State was under the President's rule. But it was sent to the President for assent a day after when

42. *Ibid.*, pp. 593-94.
43. "The President—II", *Indian Express*, New Delhi, March 21, 1967.

the President's rule had ended. President Rajendra Prasad took the position that it was *ultra vires* of Parliament to exercise the legislative power of the PEPSU State and withheld assent. It did not lead to any constitutional crisis perhaps because only a technicality was involved.

The President also gives assent or may withhold his assent to Bills passed by the State Legislatures, but reserved for his consideration by a Governor. Where the Bill is not a Money Bill, the President may direct the Governor to return the Bill to the House, or as the case may be, the Houses of the Legislature of the State together with such a message. When a Bill is so returned, the House or Houses shall reconsider it accordingly within a period of six months from the date of receipt of such message and, if it is again passed by the House or Houses with or without amendment, it shall be presented to the President for his consideration.

On August 8, 1948 Rajendra Prasad wrote to B. N. Rau seeking clarification whether a Governor could in his discretion withhold assent from a Bill passed by the State Legislature; and if the Governor referred the Bill to the President, could the President then assent or withhold assent in his discretion ? His argument was that if the Ministry at the Centre was the same as in the Province (State), presumably meaning that both could easily be Congress Ministries, the provision would be meaningless. The answers to Rajendra Prasad's questions lie in the Draft Constitution itself and the relevant Articles thereto are 175, 176, 143 (1). The Governor was given only those discretionary powers which were explicitly provided in the Draft Constitution (Article 143) and this power was not given in the case of assenting to or withholding assent from Bills or of referring them to the President, except that in certain situations the Governor could in his discretion refer a Bill back to the Legislature together with his recommendations. If the Legislature again passed that Bill, with or without recommendations of the Governor, the Governor was bound to give his assent thereto (Article 175). When the Bill was referred to the President by the Governor, he could assent to it, withhold assent or refer it back to Provincial (State) Legislature. No mention of discretionary power of the President was made in Article 176. It was, accordingly, clear that the President was in this case, too, bound to act on the advice of his Ministers.

The issue of reservation of Bills for the consideration of the President has become a matter of practical importance since 1967 when parties in power in some States are different from one at the Centre. It is possible that some of them may undertake legislation within their legal competence to give shape to their own economic and social ideologies and quite conceivably they may conflict with the policies and ideology of the party in power at the Centre. Should a Governor reserve such legislation for the consideration of the President and if he does, should the Union Government advise the President how he should deal with the reference; whether he should return it to the State Legislature with a message for reconsideration, withhold his assent or keep the Bill pending indefinitely as no time limit is prescribed for the President to signify his assent ? Surely, it was not the intention of the Constitution-makers to vest the Union Government in a Federal polity with such a sweeping power as to reduce the States to the subordinate position of mere administrative units as was the case before 1920. There is also a similar provision in the Constitution of Australia empowering the Governor of a State to reserve a Bill for the consideration of the Crown and not of the Governor-General. Secondly, the Crown is advised by the State Cabinet and not by the Commonwealth of Australia Cabinet. It, thus, clearly establishes that the Australian Constitution does not tamper with the autonomy of the States. This is precisely what a federal polity demands. It is, accordingly, hoped that the President of India would exercise his judgement, when confronted with such a situation, after seeking the views of the State cabinet and if need be, the advice of the Supreme Court as was done in the case of the Kerala Education Bill passed by the Communist Government when it was earlier in power : "This alone would place the President," says Asoka Chandra, "in correct relationship with States and conforming to the democratic principles of federal State."[44]

The President has been given far-reaching power in the sphere of legislation when Parliament is not in session. In no country with a written Constitution and the parliamentary type of government is the chief of the State the repository of such prodigious legislative power. Clause (1) of Article 123 provides : "If at any time, except

44. "Scope for President to use his Judgement," *The Statesman*, New Delhi, March 31, 1967.

when both Houses of Parliament are in session, the President is satisfied that circumstances exist which render it necessary for him to take immediate action, he may promulgate such Ordinances as the circumstances appear to him require." Clause (2) of the same Article provides that the Ordinance has the same force and effect as an Act passed by Parliament. The Ordinance so promulgated must be laid before both Houses of Parliament immediately after it reassembles. If Parliament disapproved the Ordinance it lapses. If it is not disapproved, it will automatically cease to operate at the end of six weeks from the reassembly of Parliament. Since the maximum period which can elapse between two sessions of Parliament is six months, the minimum duration of Ordinance, unless previously terminated by Parliament, can be six months and six weeks. The President may withdraw the Ordinance at any time.

The Ordinance issuing power of the President is a relic of the Government of India Act, 1935. In Britain the Executive does not possess such an independent power of legislation. There is no precedence of such a power to exist in the Dominions. In the United States all legislative power is vested in Congress and it cannot delegate its authority of law-making to any other authority. But the President of India is empowered to issue Ordinances when Parliament is not in session and these Ordinances have the force and effect of law as passed by Parliament. The courts cannot question the *bona fides* of the President's action in issuing an Ordinance or whether there existed reasonable necessity for such an action. The President is the sole judge of the necessity of issuing an Ordinance and he is not to give reasons for promulgating it. To dispel any kind o doubt in that respect the Thirty-eighth Amendment inserted a new Clause (4) in Article 123. It provided : "Notwithstanding anything in this Constitution, the satisfaction of the President mentioned in Clause (1) shall be final and exclusive and shall not be questioned in any court on any ground." The courts could not even examine the Ordinance promulgated and see whether it had been issued within the scope of powers conferred by the Constitution. The satisfaction of the President was final and conclusive and not subject to judicial review. This provision was deleted by the Forty-fourth Amendment.

The Ordinance issuing power vested in the President is of the nature of an emergency power to meet the extraordinary situation in which it is not possible for the Executive to get the necessary legislation enacted immediately by Parliament. Ambedkar explained to the Constituent Assembly that "it is not difficult to imagine cases where the powers conferred by the ordinary law may be deficient to deal with a situation which may suddenly and immediately arise. The emergency must be dealt with and it seems to me that the only solution is to confer on the President the power to promulgate a law which will enable the executive to deal with that particular situation."[45] Both the wording of Article 123 (1) and Ambedkar's defence of it make it clear that an Ordinance must be resorted to only in the event of emergency when immediate Executive action is called for.

But there had been a tendency on the part of the Government to resort to the Ordinance-making power oftener than seems desirable. Mrs. Gandhi's Government had seen appropriate to promulgate in ten weeks between Parliament's last session and the Winter Session in November 1980 spate of Ordinances and nearly half of the 20-odd Bills that came before Parliament during the Winter Session were measures to replace some of the 19 Ordinances that had been promulgated. One of these Ordinances was promulgated one week before Parliament was to reassemble. The Opposition from all sides of the House gave vigorous expression over this misuse of the Executive power which the Chairman of the Council of States and the Speaker of the House of the People endorsed.

Ananthasayanam Ayyanger, who was Speaker in 1959, presiding over a symposium on : "Law and Democracy in India,"[46] deplored the arbitrary manner in which the Executive was prone to use the Ordinance-making power of the President. "At time one felt," he said, "that the promulgation of an Ordinance was delayed until a Parliament session was prorogued." Such a procedure was highly objectionable, and "a negation of parliamentary democracy." When the framers of the Constitution provided that any Ordinance issued must receive legislative sanction within the specified period, they were anxious that, as far as possible, democratic procedures and processes should be enforced by the

45. *Constituent Assembly Debates*, Vol. VIII, p. 214.
46. *The Tribune*, Ambala Cantt., February 9, 1059.

party in power in making laws. And, thus, emergency powers were to-be exercised sparingly and only in case of real emergency. The Executive has paid scant attention to the intention of the Constitution-makers during the last more than two decades and conventions about the Executive's self-restraint as were built up under Jawaharlal Nehru's stewardship have been nullified. The Government cannot technically be faulted for arguing that what it has done is absolutely constitutional. But common sense and conventions suggest that promulgation of indiscriminate Ordinances does not strengthen the free institutions to which India is constitutionally committed.

Finally, the President nominates twelve members to the Council of States from among persons having special knowledge or practical experience of Literature, Science, Art and Social Service. He may also nominate two Anglo-Indians to the House of the People if no Anglo-Indians otherwise get themselves elected to the House.

### Judicial Powers

The President may grant pardons and reprieves, and suspend, remit or commute sentences to persons convicted by Court Martial, and in all cases in which sentences to death have been passed. But the President's power of pardon does not affect the similar power of the Governors of the States and military officers with respect to Court Martial. The President's power of pardon covers offences under acts relating to matters on the Union List. It does not relate to offences committed against matters on the Concurrent List unless Parliament has expressly excluded the executive power of the State of such matters.

The President's power of pardon is exercised on the advice of Ministers.[47] In Britain pardoning is a Royal prerogative. But it is primarily a matter for the Home Secretary and the Royal share is mainly formal.

### Miscellaneous Powers

There are many miscellaneous powers of the President : making of rules as to the manner in which orders and instruments made by the Government of India, in the name of the President, shall be authenticated; rules for the convenient transaction of the business of Government of India and for allocation among ministers of the said business; rules, in consultation with the Chairman of the Council of States (Rajya Sabha) and the Speaker of the House of the People (Lok Sabha), as to the procedure with regard to joint sittings of, and communications between, the Houses. The President's approval is also necessary for rules made by the Supreme Court for regulating the practice and procedure of the Court. The President makes regulations determining the number of members of the Union Public Service Commission, their tenure and conditions of the service, etc. He also makes regulations specifying the matters in which it shall not be necessary to consult the Union Public Service Commission in respect of the services of the Union.

The Constitution also confers on the President the power of taking the opinion of the Supreme Court on questions of public importance involving a question of law as well as a question of fact. It means that the President can refer to the Supreme Court the question whether a proposed Bill will be *ultra vires* of the powers of the legislatures. The advisory opinion given by the Supreme Court is not binding on the President.

## EMERGENCY POWERS

One of the major issues to engage the attention of the Constituent Assembly members was the inclusion of adequate provisions in the Constitution which would enable unified, speedy and effective action in situations of emergent nature. The familiarity with and experience of the exercise of emergency powers during the British rule formed the background to shape the decisions of the Constitution-makers on this vital and most pressing issue of the day.

The Drafting Committee provided for two separate situations envisaged in the Draft of the

47. Rajendra Prasad "did not act as a signing machine when dealing with appeals for clemency." He examined each case thoroughly and satisfied himself that the accused had been provided with proper defence and frequently called the Home Minister or his Deputy for information about appeals. Datta, C. L. *With Two Presidents, The Inside Story,* p. 45. G. B. Pant, the Home Minister, was reported to have said that Prasad "himself looked into each case so very carefully that the Home Ministry simply forwarded these cases to him and abided by his decision whatever it might be, without question or delay" *The Tribune,* Ambala Cantt., April 7, 1963. Early in November 1981, Billa and Ranga, sentenced to death in the Chopra children murder case, questioned the validity of the President's rejection of their mercy petitions. The Chief Justice of India constituted an emergency bench, which sat at his residence on a non-working day, to hear the petition. While admitting the petition the Chief Justice asked if there was a proper policy which determined the President's decision in mercy petitions. The court thus became a party to challenge what has so far been regarded as the President's absolute discretion to grant or deny reprieve to persons under death sentence. The Supreme Court had itself confirmed their death sentence on an appeal. The petition was finally dismissed but the interference of the Supreme Court is significantly important.

Constitutional Adviser—a national emergency affecting the security of the Union or any part thereof, and an emergency confined to a Province (State). Draft Article 275 empowered the President, when he was satisfied that there was a grave emergency whereby the security of India was threatened, whether by war or domestic violence, to issue a proclamation of emergency making a declaration to that effect. It was also made clear that a proclamation of emergency could also be issued before the actual occurrence of war or domestic violence if the President was satisfied that there was imminent danger thereof. The proclamation would cease to operate after six months unless approved by resolutions of both Houses of Parliament. Draft Article 276 gave the Union Government full power during the period the proclamation of emergency remained in force to issue directions to State Governments as to the manner in which their executive authority was to be exercised. Articles 277, 278 and 279 supplemented the powers so conferred either by legislation or otherwise.

Two important amendments were subsequently made to the emergency provisions by the Drafting Committee. The first was a new article which placed on the Union Government a duty of protecting every State, and the second was the responsibility of an intervention in a State when it was faced with the threat of a breakdown of the constitutional machinery. The President was competent to act on the basis of a report of the Governor or otherwise.

The proposal relating to financial emergency was introduced by Ambedkar on October 16, 1949. The financial emergency provisions enabled the Union Government to direct a State to reduce the salaries and allowances of all or any class of its staff as well as those of the Judges of the Supreme Court and High Courts. An express provision was also added that failure on the part of any State to comply with any directions would be deemed to be a failure to carry on the government in accordance with the provisions of the Constitution.

At the revision stage the Drafting Committee decided to introduce a new article of general application in the Constitution that non-compliance with the directions issued to a State Government, as in the case of financial emergency, would be deemed to be a failure on the part of the State Government to carry on the government of the State in accordance with the provisions of the Constitution. The intention was to make its application uniform and, accordingly, a new Article 365 was inserted in the Constitution.

**Kinds of Emergency**

Part XVIII of the Constitution incorporating Articles 352 to 369 deals with the emergency provisions which are divided under three distinct heads :

(1) *An emergency arising out of a threat to the security of India or any part of it by war or external aggression or armed rebellion.* A Proclamation of Emergency may be made by the President at any time if he is satisfied that the security of India or any part thereof is in danger or is likely to be in danger either due to war or external aggression or armed rebellion.

(2) *Failure of constitutional machinery in a State.* The President is empowered to make a Proclamation when he is satisfied that the government of a State cannot be carried on in accordance with the provisions of the Constitution, either on the report of the Governor of the State or otherwise.

(3) *Financial Emergency.* The President is empowered to make a declaration of financial emergency whenever he is satisfied that the financial stability or credit of India or any part thereof is threatened.

The two kinds of Proclamation—Proclamation of Emergency (Articles 352 and 360) and Proclamation of failure of constitutional machinery in a State (Article 356)—differ on the grounds leading to the Proclamation as well as to the effects. The Proclamation of Emergency may be necessitated whenever the security of India or any part of it is threatened or is deemed to be threatened either due to war or external aggression or armed rebellion, or whenever the financial stability or credit of India is threatened. The Proclamation of failure of constitutional machinery, on the other hand, is necessitated whenever the Government of a State cannot be carried on in accordance with the provisions of the Constitution. A threat to the security of India or a threat to her financial stability may not lead to the Proclamation of failure of the constitutional machinery in a State. The obvious grounds in the latter case is either failure of the constitutional machinery in a State, or the refusal of a State to discharge its constitutional obligations.

When a Proclamation of Emergency declaring that the security of India or any part of the territory thereof is threatened by war or external aggression or armed rebellion, is in operation provisions of Article 19, basic freedoms, may be suspended by a law or an executive action. The President may also suspend by an Order the right to move courts for the enforcement of such Fundamental Rights, except fundamental rights enshrining Articles 20 and 21, as are specified in the Presidential Order. Nothing of this kind shall happen when a Proclamation of failure of the constitutional machinery in a State is made. Neither any of the Fundamental Rights are suspended nor the right to move courts for the enforcement of Fundamental Rights is liable to be suspended.

Secondly, the object of a Proclamation of Emergency is to confer wider powers, executive and legislative, upon the Union Government in order to meet the threat to the security of India or its financial stability. The State authorities do not cease to function. The organs of the State Governments continue to function as before under normal conditions, except that (i) the Union Government can give directions to the States as to the manner in which the executive power thereof is to be exercised; (ii) the legislative competence of the Union Parliament is widened and it acquires the power to legislate on subjects included in the State List; and (iii) the President is empowered to modify, by his own Orders, the provisions of the Constitution with regard to financial matters. But in case of a Proclamation of failure of the constitutional machinery the Government of the State concerned is superseded by the Union, except the High Court. The State Legislature is suspended or dissolved and the State executive in whole in part.

### Emergency due to External Aggression or Armed Rebellion

A Proclamation of Emergency may be issued by the President, under Article 352 (1), if he is satisfied that a grave emergency exists whereby the security of India or of any part of the territory of India is threatened, whether by war or external aggression or armed rebellion.[48] Originally, a Proclamation of Emergency could not be made in respect of part of the country. It applied to the country as a whole. The Constitution (Forty-second Amendment) Act, 1976, enables the President to make a Proclamation of Emergency either in respect of whole of India or of such part of its territory as may be specified in the Proclamation.[49]

The reasons leading to the declaration of emergency may be actual occurrence of war or external aggression or armed rebellion or a threat thereto. It means that a Proclamation declaring Emergency can be made even before the actual occurrence of war or external aggression or armed rebellion, if the President is satisfied that there is an imminent danger thereof. The satisfaction of the President, which means the satisfaction of his Council of Ministers,[50] is the only determining factor whether any cause for declaration of emergency exists or not. A Proclamation of Emergency may be varied or revoked by a subsequent Proclamation.

As a measure of abundant caution and to safeguard the abuse of emergency powers vested in the President under Article 352, the Constitution (Forty-fourth Amendment) Act, 1978, provides that the President shall not issue a Proclamation declaring Emergency or a Proclamation varying such Proclamation unless the decision of the Union Cabinet (that is to say, the Council consisting of the Prime Minister and other Ministers of Cabinet rank appointed under Article 75) that such a Proclamation may be issued has been communicated to him in writing.[51]

A Proclamation of Emergency is required to be laid before each House of Parliament and it ceases to operate at the expiry of one month[52] unless before the expiry of that period it has been approved by resolutions of both Houses of Parliament by a majority of total membership of each House and by a majority of at least two-thirds of the members of the House present and voting.[53] If a Proclamation is issued at a time when the House of the People (Lok Sabha) has been dissolved or its dissolution takes place during the

48. Subs. by Constitution (Forty-fourth Amendment) Act, 1978, S. 37 for "internal disturbance."
49. Section 48, (w.e.f. 3.11.1977).
50. Whenever the Constitution requires the satisfaction of the President or Governor for the exercise by the President or Governor of any power or function, the satisfaction required by the Constitution is not the personal satisfaction of the President or Governor but the satisfaction of the President or Governor in the constitutional sense in the Cabinet System of Government, that is, satisfaction of his Council of Ministers on whose aid and advice the President or Governor generally exercises all his powers and functions (1974) 2SCC 832.
51. Article 352(3).
52. Subs. by the Constitution (Forty-Fourth Amendment) Act,1978, S. 37 for "two months."
53. Article 352(6), *Ibid.*

period of one month, in that case the Proclamation must be approved by the Council of States (Rajya Sabha) by a majority of its then, total membership and by a majority of not less than two-thirds of its members present and voting. It must also be approved by the newly elected House of the People by a majority of its then total membership and two-thirds of the members present and voting. If the House of the People (Lok Sabha) does not pass such resolution within thirty days of its first sitting the Proclamation ceases to operate after the expiry of thirty days from the date on which the House sits after its reconstitution.

If the House of the People approves the Proclamation, it continues in operation for a period of six months and it shall cease to operate, unless previously revoked, after the expiry of six months from the date of passing of the second resolution by the House of the People. The Proclamation can be renewed for a further period of six months at a time and for "so often"[54] as deemed necessary if the resolution to that effect is each time passed by each House of Parliament by a majority of the total membership of that House and by a majority of not less than two-thirds of the members of the House present and voting. It means that the duration of the Emergency, after the expiry of one month from the time of its Proclamation, cannot exceed for more than six months at a time, but there is no limit on the total length of time during which the Proclamation of Emergency can continue to remain in force provided each time before the expiry of six months it is approved by each House of Parliament by the prescribed majority of the then total membership and two-thirds majority of the members present and voting.

If the dissolution of the House of the People (Lok Sabha) takes place during any period of six months and a resolution approving the continuance in force of the Proclamation of Emergency has been passed, by the prescribed majority, by the Council of States (Rajya Sabha) but no resolution to that effect had been passed by the House of the People (Lok Sabha) before the expiry of six months, the Proclamation shall cease to operate after the expiry of thirty days from the date on which the newly elected House first sits, unless its continuance in force is duly approved by the requisite majority of the total membership of the reconstituted House and by a majority of not less than two-thirds of its members present and voting before the expiry of the specified period of thirty days.[55]

In order to remove all doubts about the declaration of a Proclamation of Emergency and to remove ambiguities, if any, in Article 352, the Constitution (Thirty-eighth Amendment) Act, 1975, inserted two Clauses (4) and (5) therein. The Constitution (Forty-fourth Amendment) Act, 1978, omitted Clause (5) and renumbered Clause (4) as Clause (9) which reads : "The power conferred on the President by this Article shall include the power to issue different Proclamations on different grounds, being war or external aggression, armed rebellion[56] or imminent danger of war or external aggression or armed rebellion, whether or not there is a Proclamation already issued by the President under Clause (1) and such Proclamation is in operation." This provision removes all doubts whether the President can issue another Proclamation of Emergency on any other ground when one Proclamation is already in operation. There can be a series of permissible Proclamations provided the grounds in each case are different. For example, a Proclamation on the ground of armed rebellion can go together with a Proclamation of threatened external aggression or even a third may be added if the ground is different.

Clauses (7) and (8) deal with the procedure for revoking a Proclamation declaring Emergency or a Proclamation varying such Proclamation issued subsequently if the House of the People passes a resolution disapproving, or, as the case may be, disapproving the continuance in force of such a Proclamation. If the House of the People is in session a notice in writing signed by not less than one-tenth of the total number of members of the House of the People may be addressed to the Speaker signifying their intention to move a resolution for disapproving, or, as the case may be, for disapproving the continuance in force of a Proclamation declaring Emergency, under Clause (1) of Article 352 or a Proclamation varying such Proclamation under Clause (2) of the same Article. If the House of the People is not in session the notice signifying the intention to move such a resolution is to be addressed to the President of India. On receipt of such a notice by the Speaker if the House of the

54. Proviso to Article 352(5), inserted by *Ibid.*
55. Proviso to Article 352(5), *Ibid.*
56. Subs. by *Ibid.*, for "internal disturbance."

People is in session, or the President, if the House is not in session, a special sitting of the House shall be held within fourteen days from the date on which the notice is received. If the House of the People passes the resolution disapproving the Proclamation declaring Emergency or disapproving the continuance in force of such a Proclamation, the President shall revoke Proclamation declaring Emergency or disapproving of its continuance in force. Revocation of the Proclamation is the exclusive privilege of the House of the People. The members of the Council of States have neither the right to initiate a resolution revoking Emergency nor a resolution passed by the House of the People to that effect is subject to their approval. The Constitution is also silent about the majority required in the House of the People supporting the resolution revoking the Proclamation.

Prior to the enactment of the Forty-fourth Amendment Act, 1978, there did not exist any provision in the Constitution authorising the members of the House of the People to move a resolution for disapproving a Proclamation of Emergency or its continuance. The decision of revoking it rested with the President alone. The House of the People could only disapprove the resolution of the Government seeking the approval of the House for continuing in force for the prescribed period of time a Proclamation of Emergency.

**Effects of Proclamation of Emergency**

While a Pro lamation of Emergency is in operation the following constitutional consequences come into effect:

Notwithstanding anything in the Constitution, the Executive power of the Union extends to the giving of directions to any State as to the manner in which its Executive power thereof is to be exercised. If a Proclamation of Emergency is in operation in any State or part of its territory, as specified in the Proclamation, the Executive power of the Union shall extend by giving directions to any other State or part of its territory, in which Proclamation is not in operation, if the security of India is threatened by activities in that State or in any part of its territory.

The power of Parliament to make laws with respect to any matter shall include power to make laws conferring powers and imposing duties upon the Union or officers and authorities of the Union relating to that matter or matters notwithstanding that it is not included in the Union List of the Seventh Schedule. If the operation of Emergency is confined to a specified State or part of its territory, the power of Parliament to make laws conferring power and imposing duties upon Union or officers and authorities of the Union shall extend to any other State or part of its territory, in which the Proclamation of Emergency is not in operation, if the security of India is threatened by activities in that State or in any part of its territory.

Parliament shall have the unrestricted power to make laws, while a Proclamation of Emergency is in operation, for the whole or any part of India with respect to any of the matters enumerated in the State List of the Seventh Schedule. Laws so made by Parliament shall become inoperative six months after the Proclamation has ceased to operate, except as things done or omitted to be done before the expiration of the said period.

Any law made by the Legislature of a State, which is inconsistent with such laws made by Parliament will be void to the extent of inconsistency.

During the period of the operation of a Proclamation of Emergency the President may, when Parliament is not in session, promulgate Ordinances in respect of matters enumerated in the State List. The President's legislative power under Article 123 is enlarged accordingly.

Parliament has the power to extend its own life beyond five years, by law, while a Proclamation of Emergency is in operation for a period not exceeding one year at a time. Such an extension in its term cannot last beyond six months after the Proclamation has ceased to operate.

The President may, while a Proclamation of Emergency is in operation, by his Order modify the provisions of Articles 268 to 279 relating to the distribution of revenues with a view to securing revenues for the Union to meet the situation created by Emergency. But every such Order made by the President shall be laid before each House of Parliament immediately after it is made. In no case shall such Orders be valid beyond the financial year in which the Proclamation of Emergency ceases to operate.

While a Proclamation of Emergency is in operation in India or any part of the territory thereof nothing in Article 19 shall restrict the power of the State to make any law or take any executive action impairing or abrogating Fundamental Rights. But any law so made or executive action taken otherwise than a law must contain a recital to the effect that such law or executive action taken is in relation to the Proclamation of Emergency. Any law so made or executive action taken shall, to the extent of incompetency, ceases to operate.

Where a Proclamation of Emergency is in operation the President may by Order declare that the right to move any court for the enforcement of Fundamental Rights, except under Articles 20 and 21, as may be specified in the Presidential Order and all proceedings pending in the courts for the enforcement of such rights shall remain suspended for the period during which the Proclamation remains in force or for such shorter period as may be specified in the Presidential Order. Every Order made by the President shall be laid before each House of Parliament "as soon as after it is made." The Constitution does not fix any time limit for the Order to be placed before Parliament. It is for the President to determine when the Order shall be laid before Parliament.

While the Presidential Order suspending the right to move courts for the enforcement of specified rights in the Presidential Order, except under Articles 20 and 21, is in operation nothing shall restrict the power of the State to make any law or to take executive action which the State, but for the provisions contained in Part III is competent to make or take. Any law made or executive action taken must contain a recital to the effect that such law or executive action is in relation to the Proclamation of Emergency in operation. But any law so made shall, to the extent of incompetency, cease to have effect as soon as the Presidential Order ceases to operate. If a Proclamation of Emergency is confined to a particular territory such a law or executive action may be extended to any other State or Union Territory in which the Proclamation of Emergency is not in operation, if the security of India or any part thereof is threatened by activities in or in relation to the part of the territory of India in which the Proclamation of Emergency is in operation.

The Presidential Order suspending the enforcement of rights, except Articles 20 and 21, may extend to the whole or any part of the territory of India. but where a Proclamation of Emergency is in operation only in a part of the territory of India, any such Order shall not extend to any other part of the territory of India unless the President is satisfied that the security of India or any part of its territory is threatened by activities in or in relation to the part of the territory of India in which the Proclamation of Emergency is in operation and considers that such extension is necessary.

**Failure of the Constitutional Machinery**

Article 355 imposes on the Union Government the duty to protect every State against external aggression or internal disturbance and to ensure that the government of every State is carried on in accordance with the provisions of the Constitution. Article 356 further provides that if the President, on receipt of a report from the Governor of a State or otherwise, is satisfied that a situation has arisen in which the government of a State cannot be carried on in accordance with the provisions of the Constitution, the President may by Proclamation :

(a) assume to himself all or any of the functions of the government of the State including all or any of the powers vested in or exercisable by the Governor or any body or authority in the State other than the Legislature of the State;

(b) declare that the powers of the State Legislature shall be exercisable by or under the authority of Parliament;

(c) make such incidental and consequential provisions as may appear to the President to be necessary or desirable for giving effect to the objects of the Proclamation, including provisions for suspending, in whole or in part, the operation of any provisions of the Constitution relating to any body or authority in the State.

If the Proclamation has declared that the powers of the State Legislature shall be exercised by or under the authority of Parliament, it shall be competent :—

(a) for Parliament to confer on the President the power of the Legislature of the State to make laws, and to authorise the President to delegate subject to such conditions as he may think fit to impose, such power to any other authority to be specified by him in that behalf;

(b) for Parliament, or for the President or other authority in whom such power to make laws is vested, to make laws conferring powers and imposing duties, or authorising the conferring of powers and the imposition of the duties upon the Union or officers and authorities thereof;

(c) for the President to authorise when the House of the People is not in session expenditure from the Consolidated Fund of the State pending the sanction of such expenditure by Parliament.

Clause (2) of Article 357 substituted by Constitution (Forty- second Amendment) Act, 1976, provides that any law made in exercise of the power of the Legislature of the State by Parliament or by the President or other authority so appointed, shall after a Proclamation made in case of failure of the constitutional machinery, continue to remain in force after the Proclamation has ceased to operate until altered or repealed or amended by the State Legislature concerned or other competent authority.

The President, however, cannot assume to himself any of the powers vested in or exercisable by the High Court. Nor can he suspend, either in whole or in part, the operation of any provision of the Constitution relating to High Courts.

The Proclamation may be revoked or varied by a subsequent Proclamation. Every Proclamation issued in connecution with the failure of constitutional machinery in a State requires to be laid before each House of Parliament and it ceases to operate, except where it is a Proclamation revoking a previous Proclamation, after the expiry of two months unless before the expiration of that period it has been approved by resolutions of both Houses of Parliament. If a Proclamation is issued at a time when the House of the People (Lok Sabha) is dissolved or the dissolution takes place within the specified period of two months and the House had not passed a resolution approving the Proclamation, it should be approved by the Council of States (Rajya Sabha) before the expiration of two months subject to the approval of the newly elected House of the People (Lok Sabha) within thirty days of its first sitting. If the reconstitued House of the People does not pass such a resolution approving continuance in force of the Proclamation before the expiry of thirty days, it ceases to operate after the expiry of that period.

A Proclamation approved by both the Houses, unless revoked, ceases to operate on the expiry of six months[57] from the date of issue of the Proclamation unless again approved "so often" before the expiry of six months at a time, but no such Proclamation shall in any case remain in force for more than three years. It means the maximum period for which the Proclamation can remain operative is three years, but it is to be renewed each time after expiry of every six months.

In order to safeguard against the abuse of power under Article 356 the Constitution (Forty-fourth Amendment) Act, 1978, substituted a new clause for clause (5). It provides that a resolution with respect to the continuance in force of a Proclamation for any period beyond one year from the date of issue of the Proclamation shall not be passed by either House of Parliament unless :

(a) a Proclamation of Emergency is in operation, in the whole of India, or in the whole or any part of the State, at the time of passing of such resolution, and

(b) the Election Commission certifies that the continuance in force of the Proclamation is necessary on account of difficulties in holding general elections to the Legislative Assembly of the State concerned.

The Proclamation of failure of constitutional machinery in the State of Assam was, accordingly, revoked early in December 1980, before the expiry of a year ending on December 12 and again in February 1983.

The expression used in Article 356 that "the government of the State cannot be carried on in accordance with the provisions of the Constitution" has a very wide scope. There is no necessary connection between the conditions of Emergency due to war, external aggression or armed rebellion or a threat thereto and failure of the State government to work according to the Constitution. But a Proclamation of failure of the constitutional machinery in a State or States can be made, if the President is satisfied that the measures taken to meet the Emergency created due to war or external aggression or armed rebellion or a threat thereto, under Articles 352 and 353, are not adequate or are not likely to be adequate. The President can also make a Proclamation of failure of the constitutional machinery, if he is satisfied that there is a political breakdown and there is no stable majority in the State Legislature to form the Ministry or the party

57. Subs. by the Constitution (Forty-Fourth Amendment) Act, 1978, S. 38 for "one year." The Forty-Second Amendment had substituted "one year" for "six months" as it originally existed.

wrangles within the majority party itself do not satisfy the conditions of a stable government, as it happened in four States Punjab, Travancore-Cochin, Patiala and East Punjab States Union and Andhra of the pre-States reorganisation period. But it became a common feature of the United Front Governments after the 1967 General Elections. The constituent parties and groups of these Fronts could not form effective alliances and there was no common goal and no common approach to the problems they had to face. The only concern of the component units of the United Fronts was to get into power, to oust the partners and to create a constitutional crisis wherever and whenever possible.

The Janata Government adopted an unprecedented procedure in declaring the dissolution of the Assemblies in the nine Congress ruled States in the North, putting them under the President's Rule under Article 356 and holding fresh elections. Home Minister Charan Singh asked the Chief Ministers of these nine States, immediately after the elections to the Sixth House of the People in March, 1977, to advise their Governors to recommend to the President dissolution of the State Assemblies as the Congress had lost confidence of the people of those States by totally rejecting the candidates put up by the ruling party in the elections to the House of the people. But State Governments did not accept the Home Minister's suggestions and, consequently, President's Rule was imposed under Article 356 in all these States.

However impressive the political consideration, the precedent set by the Janata Government seems to have become the norm of practical politics. Immediately after assuming office in January 1980, the Congress (I) Government, with a massive majority in the House of the People, began to talk in the language of the Janata Government and in February 1980, decided to dissolve nine State Legislatures where parties other than the Congress (I) were in office. But the logic of the then Home Minister Zail Singh's proposal for an "automatic dissolution of Opposition-led State Assemblies after the Lok Sabha elections" is neither consistent with the existing provisions of the Constitution nor is it in consonance with the nature of a federal polity, which the Constitution establishes. Nor was it ever the intention of the Constitution-makers to choke the channels of responsible government through dubious means and intentions.

Finally, failure to comply with the directions of the Union Government may also lead to the Proclamation of failure of the constitutional machinery. It is important to note that in order to issue a Proclamation of failure of the constitutional machinery in a State the President need not wait for the report of the Governor as it had been done so often but more particularly in 1977 and 1980 when nine State Assemblies were dissolved each time at one stroke and, once again, in 1991 in Tamil Nadu. The President is empowered to take action on his own initiative and it is all a matter of his satisfaction.

The powers of the President to supersede the Government of a State are very wide and even drastic and they received stiff opposition from some of the top-ranking members of the Constituent Assembly when the relevant provisions were under discussion on its floor. Some of them condemned the provisions as "far too sweeping thus reducing provincial autonomy to a farce." H. V. Kamath informed the Assembly that he foresaw the possible end of democracy in India in the form of a Hitler-like takeover of the Union Government. He particularly referred to the use of the word "otherwise" in Article 278 of the Draft Constitution (corresponding to Article 356 of the Constitution) and said that it was "a diabolical word in this context" and prayed for its dele- gation.[58] Hriday Nath Kunzru's criticism went much deeper into the problems of government and in the responsibilities, in a free society, of the governed. He argued that if real responsible government was to be established in the Provinces (States), "the electors must be made to feel that the power to apply proper remedy, if any mismanagement occurred, rested with them. It depended upon them to choose their representatives who would be capable of working in accordance with their best interest." If the Union Government or Parliament were given a power to interfere and manage their affairs, there was a danger that whenever there was a dissatisfaction in the State, appeals could be made to the Union Government to come to their rescue.

It proved to be true. Even statesmen of the status of Jayaprakash Narayan and Morarji Desai demanded the promulgation of President's rule in the States of Bihar and Gujarat respectively. Desai threatened to go on hunger-strike if his demand was not conceded. And when his object

58. *Constituent Assembly Debates*, Vol. I, p. 140.

was fulfilled, he demanded its revocation.

Ambedkar's defence of emergency provisions in the Constituent Assembly showed that he was alive to Kunzru's apprehensions. He asserted that there was a possibility of "these Articles being abused and being employed for political purposes." He expressed the view that it would be proper and just that these provisions would never be brought into operation and they would remain a dead letter. But what Ambedkar had thought did not actually happen. The provisions of Article 356 have been used all these years for purely political purposes and dubious methods have been used to supersede the State governments and impose the President's rule. It began with Nehru in the State of Kerala in 1959 and since then it has been used for 83 times and, probably, no State escaped from the grips of Article 356.

### Application of the Emergency Provisions to the State of Punjab

To meet the growing menace of secessionism and extremism that had plagued Punjab since early 80's, the Constitution (Fifty-ninth Amendment) Act, 1988, inserted Article 359 A providing for the modifications in Article 352, 358 and 359—Emergency provisions in their application to the State of Punjab.

In Article 352 in Clause (1) the following was substituted after the opening portion :

"If the President is satisfied that a grave emergency exists whereby—

(a) The security of India or any part of the territory thereof is threatened, whether by war or external aggression or armed rebellion; or

(b) the integrity of India is threatened by internal disturbance in the whole or any part of the territory of Punjab he may by Proclamation, make a declaration to that effect in respect of the whole of Punjab or of such part of the territory thereof as may be specified in the Proclamation."

As a consequence of this provision relevant modifications to this effect were to be substituted at the appropriate places in the remaining part of Article 352 as well as in Article 358–dealing with suspension of provisions of Article 19 during Emergency. In Article 359 dealing with suspension of the enforcement of rights during Emergency only Article 20—protection in respect of conviction for offence—was to be excluded from suspension and not both the Articles 20 and 21—protection in respect of life and personal liberty—as ordained by the Constitution (Forty-fourth Amendment) Act, 1978.

### Financial Emergency

If the President is satisfied that a situation has arisen whereby the financial stability or credit of India or any part of the territory thereof is threatened he may, under Article 360, by a Proclamation make declaration of Financial Emergency. A Proclamation of Financial Emergency, like a Proclamation of Emergency due to war or external aggression or armed rebellion or a threat thereto, is to be laid before each House of Parliament and remains in force for a period of two months. It ceases to operate at the expiration of that period unless it has been approved by resolutions of both Houses of Parliament. If a Proclamation is issued at a time when the House of the People (Lok Sabha) is dissolved or its dissolution takes place within two months of issuing of the Proclamation and the House has not passed a resolution of its continuance in force, it must be approved by the Council of States (Rajya Sabha) within the specified period of two months and by the newly elected House of the People within thirty days of its first sitting. If no resolution approving the resolution is passed by the House within that period of thirty days the Proclamation ceases to operate after the expiration of thirty days from the date when the House meets for its first sitting. A Proclamation of Financial Emergency may be revoked or varied by a subsequent Proclamation. Unlike the Emergency under Article 352, due to war, external aggression or armed rebellion, the Constitution does not provide for either the majority necessary for approving the resolution by both Houses of Parliament for continuance of Financial Emergency after the expiry of two months or its revocation on a resolution by the House of the People.

During the period a Proclamation relating to Financial Emergency is in operation, the executive authority of the Union extends to the giving of directions to any State to obsreve such canons of financial propriety as may be specified in the directions, and the giving of such other directions as may be deemed necessary and adequate by the President for maintaining the financial stability and credit of India. Notwithstanding anything contained in the Constitution, such directions may :

1. (a) ask a State to reduce salaries and

allowances of all or any class of public servants connected with the affairs of the State;

(b) reserve all Money Bills or other Bills to which the provisions of Article 297 (Financial Bills ) apply for the consideration of the President after they have been passed by the State Legislature, and while a Proclamation of Financial Emergency is in operation, the President is competent to issue directions for the reduction of salaries of all or any class of public servants connected with the affairs of the Union including the Judges of the Supreme Court and the High Courts.

**Emergency Powers Examined**

Emergencies must arise in the life of every nation and there must be adequate provisions to meet them. Self-preservation is the first law of every nation and there must necessarily exist the competence to meet exigencies when they arise. The capacity for protection and self-defence is a necessary concomitant of sovereignty and nationhood. The Central Government, therefore, in every State is constitutionally made responsible for protecting the country from external aggression and securing it from internal disturbances and violence. During periods of emergencies fundamental rights and othe constitutional guarantees are so modified as not to impede the Executive in taking such action as it may deem expedient and necessary. In Britain, the maxim is *inter arma silent leges,* when there is an armed conflict the laws remain silent and the courts have tolerated it in the interests of the country. But almost in every country the Executive assumes emergency powers under Legislative authority. In Britain Parliament itself endows the Executive with authority to arrest without trial suspected persons by passing such Acts as the Defence of the Realm Act, 1914, and Emergency Powers (Defence) Act, 1939. And a distinction is always made between an emergency due to war and an emergency due to internal disorder. Whatever be the nature and extent of emergency, the Rule of Law is always kept unimpaired.

The Constitution of theUnited States does not specifically provide for any kind of emergency. The Supreme Court, too, has held that "emergency does not create power"; nor does it increase the power already given in the Constitution. The Constitution simply provides that the United States shall guarantee to every state in the Union a Republican form of government, and shall protect each of them against invasion, and on application of the Legislature or of theExecutive (when the Legislature cannot be convened) against domestic violence. In pursuance of this provision, the National Government has exercised tremendous powers. But the Constitution ordains that "The privilege of the writ of *habeas corpus* shall not be suspended unless when in cases of rebellion or invasion the public safety may require it." Thus, only actual invasion or rebellion justifies the suspension of the writ of *habeas corpus*. Internal disturbance, such as a strike or any other similar cause, does not justify it. It has been, further, held that the power to suspend the writ is the exclusive right of Congress, and it is for the courts to determine whether the Constitution justifies or not the exercise of this right by Congress.[59] There is no provision in the Constitution which empowers either the Executive or the Legislature to suspend any of the Fundamental rights either during war or any other emergency. In *Home Building Association* v. *Blaisdell,* the Supreme Court ruled that "Even war does not remove Constitutional limitations safeguarding essential liberties." Every restriction on the rights and liberties of the people as a result of "police power" of the State "must be weighed by balance of justice." India followed the Weimar Constitution and vested the President with vast emergency powers, although unlike the German President, he acts on the advice of his Council of Ministers and on assuming emergency powers he is guided by the advice of his Ministers who derive their authority from and are responsible to Parliament. A Proclamation of Emergency s constitutionally required to be laid before each House of Parliament and it ceases to operate after the expiry of the specified time unless it is approved by both Houses of Parliament. But till 1978, the Constitution did not provide adequate safeguards to prevent an ambitious Prime Minister from indiscriminately invoking the emergency powers to perpetuate himself or herself in power, as Mrs. Indira Gandhi did in 1975. A Proclamation of Emergency on the ground of internal disturbance, as originally provided in Article 352, was issued on the night of June 25, 1975 before the Cabinet approved it. It was just

59. *Ex parte Miligan.*

an *ex post facto* approval of the subservient Cabinet when it came before it on the morning of June 26. The Thirty- ninth Amendment had inserted clause (5) in Article 352 which provided that the satisfaction of the President with regard to the declaration of emergency was final and conclusive and it could not be questioned in any Court of Law on any ground. The President could also suspend by Order the right to move courts for the enforcement of any of the Fundamental Rights including the protection of life and liberty, and, consequently, a writ of *habeas corpus* could not be moved by a person arrested or detained.

The Constitution (Forty-fourth Amendment) Act, 1978, remedied the damage done by Mrs. Gandhi in declaring emergency without consulting her Cabinet and provided other safeguards to prevent its abuse. In Article 352 (1) "internal disturbance" was omitted and substituted by "armed rebellion", which is specific and is in the nature of "internal insurrection", to borrow a phrase from the American Constitution. The President shall not issue a Proclamation of Emergency for any reason unless it is a decision of the Union Cabinet (that is to say, the Council consisting of the Prime Minister and other Ministers of Cabinet rank) and communicated to the President in writing that such a Proclamation may be issued. The President, if he so desired, may require the Cabinet to reconsider its decision. Clause (5) inserted by the Thirty-ninth Amendment providing that the satisfaction of the President was final and conclusive and it could not be questioned in any court of law has been omitted and any person can now challenge the validity of a Proclamation of Emergency.

A Proclamation of Emergency ceases to operate after the expiry of one month unless it has been approved before the expiry of that period by resolutions passed by both Houses of Parliament supported by a majority of the total membership of that House and by a two-thirds majority of the members of that House present and voting. The President shall also revoke a Proclamation if the House of the People passed by an absolute majority a resolution disapproving or, as the case may be, disapproving the continuance in force of such a Proclamation. The power of the President to suspend the right to move courts for the enforcement of Fundamental Rights under Article 359 has also been amended. Rights guaranteed under Article 20—protection in respect of conviction of offences—and Article 21—protection of life and liberty—have been protected and remedies for their enforcement can be secured by appropriate proceedings in the Supreme Court or a High Court.

Even this is not enough. The issuance of a Proclamation of Emergency is an executive action and it is a two-pronged weapon which can be used if the President is satisfied that a grave emergency exists whereby the security of India or any part of the territory thereof is threatened, whether by war or external aggression or armed rebellion. It remains in force for a period of one month without reference to Parliament, except that it is to be laid before each House of Parliament. Parliament can intervene only if its continuance in force is deemed necessary and expedient on the expiration of one month. The right of the Executive, therefore, to issue a Proclamation of Emergency remains unfettered for a period of one month. In almost every other country the Executive assumes emergency powers under Legislative authority. And emergency in India does not cease when the conditions necessitating it cease to exist. It continues in force till it is revoked by a subsequent Proclamation initiated by the Executive or its continuance in force is disapproved by resolutions of both Houses of Parliament supported by the requisite majority in each House, or the House of the People itself passes a resolution that it should be revoked. But a Government commanding a comfortable majority in both the Houses of Parliament and determined that it should continue in force can checkmate Parliament to have its way. There is no time limit for which a Proclamation is to continue in force. The only safeguard is that it is renewable after every six months. Moreover, Proclamation of one kind of Emergency is no inhibition for the President to issue another Proclamation for a different reason. There can be series of Proclamations in operation at the same time provided that the grounds are different. When a series of Proclamations are in operation at the same time and the specified time of their expiration of six months in each case is different the country is likely to suffer from continuous conditions of Emergency on different grounds.

The power of the President to suspend the right to move courts for the enforcement of any of the Fundamental Rights, except under Articles 20 and 21, is only *ad interim* power, for every Order issued by the President, as soon as may be after it is made, is to be laid before Parliament. But it is for the Executive to determine the time when it should be laid before Parliament. The

Constitution does not fix any time-limit.

Though there is no necessary connection between a Proclamation of Emergency issued under Article 352 (1) and failure of the constitutional machinery under Article 356 (1), but the President if he is satisfied that the measures taken by a State Government or a number of State Governments, under Articles 352 and 353, are not adequate or likely to be adequate to meet the requirements of Emergency by war or external aggression or armed rebellion or a threat thereto he may issue a Proclamation declaring the breakdown of constitutional machinery in a State or a number of States and assume to himself all or any of the functions of the Government of the State or a number of States. It is rather unprecedented that in a federal polity the Central Government may go to the extent of superseding the government of a constituent unit and abrogate its constitution except for provisions relating to the High Court so long as a Proclamation of Emergency remains in force. Whereas the Constitution does not fix any time limit for the continuance in force of a Proclamation of Emergency, the maximum period for which the President's rule in a State can remain in force is fixed at three years. But this limit was exceeded in the case of Punjab by amending the Constitution on the ground of disturbed conditions in the State. Whatever be the compelling reasons supersession of the Constitution of a constituent unit and imposition of the Central rule therein is in no way a redeeming feature of which a federal polity should feel proud.

## ROLE OF THE PRESIDENT

### Constitutional Position of the President

The role which the President can play in the body politic of the country had remained the subject of wide controversy till 1976, when the Constitution (Forty-second Amendment) Act, decided the controversy by providing in Article 74(1) that the President in the exercise of his functions shall act in accordance with the advice of his Council of Ministers. This was reinforced by the proviso to Article 74(1) by the Constitution (Forty-fourth Amendment) Act, 1978, which made the position of the President unambiguously clear and definite beyond any doubt. What he can do now is that he may require the Council of Ministers to reconsider the advice tendered to him, and the President "shall act in accordance with the advice tendered after such reconsideration." Coupled with it is clause (3) of Article 352 substituted by the Constitution (Forty-fourth Amendment) Act, 1978, which provides that the President shall not issue a Proclamation of Emergency or a Proclamation varying such Proclamation "unless the decision of the Union Cabinet (that is to say, the Council consisting of the Prime Minister and other Ministers of Cabinet rank appointed under Artcle 75) that such a Proclamation may be issued has been communicated to him in writing." Therefore, the satisfaction of the President to issue a Proclamation of Emergency under Article 352(1) is to all intents and purposes the satisfaction of the Cabinet which is collectively responsible to the House of the People and not to the President.

It does not, however, mean that the President is mere figurehead or "a magnificent cipher." This, according to K. Subba Rao, the former Chief Justice of India, "is a cynical view."[60] His office is of great dignity and he exercises a great influence over the policies and administration of the government. The President represents the majesty of the State, is at the apex though only symbolically, and has rapport with the people and the parties, being above politics. Acting on ministerial advice does not necessarily mean immediate acceptance of the Ministry's first thoughts. The President can state all his objections to any proposed course of action and ask his Ministers-in-Council, if necessary, to consider the matter. It is only in the last resort that he must accept their advice. This is *raison d'etre* of proviso to Article 74(1) inserted by the Forty-fourth Amendment.[61] The President's vigilant presence makes for good government, if only he uses the right to be consulted, the right to encourage and the right to warn, to borrow Bagehot's words. A President of great sense and sagacity would want no others.

If the Constitution divests the President of power, it does not mean that he exercises no influence. There is a good deal of difference between power and influence. Jennings, while dealing with the powers and position of the Brit-

60. As reported in *Indian Express,* New Delhi, May 30, 1969.

61. N. K. Palkhivala is of the opinion that when Charan Singh's Cabinet resigned in August 1979, his advice to the President to dissolve the House of the People was not binding on the President. "To say that the advice of that cabinet in favour of dissolution was binding on the President is to say that a Cabinet which has never lived with Parliament has a right to demand its death. Surely there are less dangerous ways of mocking the Constitution." The President's Decision : Consequences of Dissolution., *The Times of India,* New Delhi, August 24, 1979.

ish King says, "A function to be exercised on advice is not formal or automatic."[62] A King must be persuaded on many occasions and on occasions the King may do the persuading. Jagjivan Ram, who had been a Union Minister almost all the time since Independence till August 1979, said that the President of India "exercises his moderating influence and inspires or moulds policies and actions so silently and unobtrusively that many are prone to think that, unlike any other Head of a State, he neither reigns nor rules.[63]

Although the President does not attend the meetings of the Cabinet yet he must keep himself abreast of what the Cabinet does and what the public feels. Article 78 imposes a constitutional duty on the Prime Minister to keep the President informed of all decisions of the Council of Ministers relating to the affairs of the administration of the Union and proposals for legislation; to furnish such information relating to the administration of the affairs of the Union and proposals for legislation as the President may call for; and if the President so requires, to submit for the consideration of the Council of Ministers any matter in which a decision has been taken by a Minister but which has not been considered by the Council of Ministers. This he may do to enable the decisions of the individual Minister to become articulate through the channel of collective responsibility and, as such, the solidarity of the Council of Ministers.

When Draft Article 65, corresponding to Article 78 of the Constitution, was being discussed, Law Minister B. R. Ambedkar explained to the Constituent Assembly members that the practice (as it existed on the eve of the commencement of the Constitution) was to send "weekly summaries prepared by each Ministry containing decisions taken by it to the Cabinet and the Governor- General. If on perusal of these summaries the Governor-General thought that a particular decision taken by a Minister was not good, he would place that matter for reconsideration of the Cabinet." He recalled that the provisions of Draft Article 65 (Article 78 of the Constitution) were intended to clarify the relationship between the Council of Ministers and the President. The Union Constitution Committee had omitted all references to the authority of the President and his relations with the Council of Ministers, excepting that their function was to aid and advise the President. The Drafting Committee thought it imperative to fill in the gap. Justices V. R. Krishna Iyer and P. N. Bhagwati referring to Article 78, in *Shamsher Singh and Ishwar Chander Aggarwal* v. *The State of Punjab*, observed, that this Article "wisely used, keeps the President in close touch with the Prime Minister on matters of national importance and policy significance, and there is no doubt that the imprint of his personality may chasten and correct the political government, although the actual exercise of the functions entrusted to him by law is in effect and in law carried on by his duly appointed mentors, *i.e.* The Prime Minister and his colleagues."

Emphasising the importance of relations between the President and the Prime Minister, as envisaged in Article 78, V. V. Giri said that the President can play a useful role by exchanging views "frankly and freely concerning Government constantly—as I and the Prime Minister have done." Narrating the experiences of his term of office to the Reporter of the *Press Trust of India,* President Giri remarked, "Taking an overall view of my tenure, though I cannot say that I am satisfied with the results achieved it is for the Government to implement policies and programmes. I have in my humble way put forward from time to time concrete proposals designed to find solution to some of the most urgent problems facing the country."[64] But the relationship between President Neelam Sanjiva Ready and Morarji Desai was less than cordial and there was practically no consultation between the two. Speaking at a reception accorded to Sanjiva Reddy by the citizens' committee Hyderabad, immediately after entering Rashtrapati Bhavan, he said, "I am not a President to play the second fiddle. This they know at Delhi."[65] This was an aggressive way of saying what Giri had said and it was perhaps Reddy's reaction against the label of "rubber-stamp" the Janata Party used for his predecessor Fakhruddin Ali Ahmed, and was accused of his "timid performance" during the 1975 Emergency. But Reddy had not been steady in his pronouncement during his tenure of office. The consultations between Reddy and Mrs. Indira Gandhi were regular, but sans cordiality. Mrs. Gandhi's consultations with President Gy-

62. Jennings, W. I., *Law and the Constitution,* p.98.
63. Refer to *Ajatshatro,* edited by Valmiki Chowdhury.
64. *Indian Express,* New Delhi, August 19, 1974.
65. *The Statesman,* New Delhi, October 10, 1977.

ani Zail Singh were regular and deeply cordial, though vital differences between the two had emerged on the Punjab crisis.

But the relationship between President Gyani Zail Singh and Prime Minister Rajiv Gandhi created a crisis of "confidence and morality" as Madhu Dandavate, Janata Member of the House of the People (Lok Sabha) described it. Rajiv Gandhi had not honoured in its letter and spirit his obligations under the Constitution to the Head of the State and deviated form the well-established convention of regular consultation between the two. He called on the President at Rashtrapati Bhavan only on two occasions during his tenure of first two years in office. Jawaharlal Nehru created the convention of visiting the President every week on Monday at 10 A. M. After the 1962 war with China, the then President Radhakrishnan, requested Nehru, who was not keeping good health, instead of reporting to him every week to do so every month. This was the convention followed by successive Prime Ministers, except Morarji Desai, but still he observed the possible outward constitutional formalities.

The uneasy relationship between the Prime Minister and the President, which had been Delhi's most open secrets for close two years and written about in the print media frequently, was highlighted by the Opposition on the discussion on the motion of thanks to the President in both the Houses of Parliament. Intervening in the debate in the House of the People on March 2, 1987, the Prime Minister observed that he and his Ministers had kept the President informed about important developments and on matters of national interest. Also there was no question of choking the constitutional authority of the President as regards reconsideration of any advice given by the Cabinet, he said. He pleaded with the Opposition not to politicise the office of the President and keep it above politics.

The Prime Minister would not have made this claim in Parliament as he knew as well as any one else that it was not true that he and his Ministers had kept the President fully informed on important matters. The President repudiated the statement of the Prime Minister in his letter dated March 9, 1987 and it somehow leaked and was reproduced in *Indian Express,* New Delhi. Among other things, the President said in his letter that "as you are aware the factual position is somewhat at variance with what has been stated by you" in Parliament on March 2 and that "I am constrained to say that certain well-established conventions have not been followed", that "I have not been briefed on matters relating to accords finalised in respect of Assam, Punjab and Mizoram," that "when I had specifically requested you to meet me after my visit to Jammu and Kashmir last year, there was no response from you," that "I have brought to your notice that reports of some commissions of inquiry had not been sent to me long after the receipt by the Government", and "that politicisation of the office of the President was started not by the Opposition as alleged by the Prime Minister in Parliament, but by an honourable member of the ruling party in April 1985, who was subsequently elevated to the Council of Ministers."[66] The letter ended thus : "You may share these with Parliament so that full facts are known to the people's representatives."

The Prime Minister sent a detailed reply to the President's letter followed by two meetings, which continued to be more or less regular, indicating that the process of consultation between the Head of the State and Head of the Government had well retrieved. The Prime Minister and the Ministers briefed the President on various issues, but differences still persisted between the two on the interpretation of Article 78. The President claimed his unfettered constitutional right to ask for any kind of information relating to the affairs and transactions of the Government whereas the Prime Ministers, supported by a resolution of the Cabinet, invoked the provisions of Article 74(1) and would not concede to the President that much of free-wheeling. It was, therefore, for the Prime Minister and the Council of Ministers to determine and decide the extent of information that could be furnished to the President and on matters deemed appropriate which might be constitutional. It meant that the powers of the President to seek information were limited and that he was guided in that respect on the advice of his Council of Ministers.

The result of this unfortunate controversy over the relationship between the Prime Minister and the President had done considerable damage to the individuals and the institutions involved in it. The President in his letter of March 9, 1987 to

66. Reference was to K.K. Tewari, Member of the House of the People, who accused the President on the floor of the House for harbouring extremists in the Rashtrapati Bhavan.

the Prime Minister had succinctly said, "........but I do feel that if relations between the Prime Minister and the President are maintained in line with the letter and spirit of the Constitution, keeping national interest paramount there will be no room for comment or speculation from any quarter. This delicate relationship has to be nurtured by mutual trust, concern for conventions and empathic and free exchange of views."

It, once again, revived the issue of the powers of President *vis-a-vis* the Prime Minister which had been a subject of controversy since the time of the first President, Dr. Rajendra Prasad. But never before the controversy acquired the dangerous overtones it had acquired then. Somnath Chatterjee, lawyer and Member of Parliament. while delivering A. K. Gopalan lecture in New Delhi on April 19, 1987, on the "Role of the President and the Prime Minister in the Constitution," argued that the President has the authority to dismiss the Prime Minister, dissolve the House of the People (Lok Sabha) and call for fresh elections if a situation warranted such action. Referring to the controversy relating to Article 78, he maintained that unfortunately some people in the ruling party were arguing that the Prime Minister could supply only such information as he thought proper or necessary. This amounted to placing the Prime Minister above the Constitution and it was fraught with dangerous consequences, including the President exercising his authority to dismiss the Prime Minister.[67]

There was widespread speculation that the President was planning what would amount to a *coup* against a duly elected Prime Minister commanding two-thirds majority in the House of the People (Lok Sabha). First, rumours that the Gyani was contemplating such a move began to float from individuals claiming to be close to the President, in the summer of 1986. These rumours acquired a new urgency in the wake of the Gyani's letter of March 9, 1987 to Rajiv Gandhi which happened to be followed by sensational but unsubstantiated charges of corruption. These rumours gained sufficient credence that the Gyani had been consulting lawyers on the issue of the powers of the President under the Constitution. Zail Singh confirmed that he had studied the pleas of the prosecution of Prime Minister "most carefully" and sought legal opinion from different people because "I can only sanction what is legally sustainable. I cannot act of pique." He told Pritish Nandy, editor of the *Illustrated Weekly,* Bombay, in an exclusive interview : "I have already taken too many controversial steps. I must leave something for my successor too." He added, "Just because Rajiv Gandhi has humiliated me in so many ways does not mean that I can dismiss him or sanction prosecution proceedings. I must act with dignity and propriety. I must act as President of India."[68] Rajiv Gandhi and his Government was so much afraid of unpredictable Gyani Zail Singh that in an unprecedented move the Prime Minister did not advise the President, when the winter session of the 1987 Parliament came to an end, to prorogue the House of the People (Lok Sabha); though the Council of States (Rajya Sabha) was. The way in which the mind of the President worked is revealed in an Urdu couplet which he recited entirely out of context at a farewell meeting with reporters in Bangalore on July 14, 1987 :

> "Main jin haathon men phool ke guldaste de kar aya tha,
> Ab wohi haath pathar le kar meri talash men hain."
> (The hands in which I had placed a bouquet of flowers are today after me with a stone).

The President often writes to the Prime Minster and expresses his views on various important matters. There were many occasions in the past when the President and his Prime Minister exchanged strongly worded correspondence over many issues. Differences arose between Rajendra Prasad and Jawaharlal Nehru in 1950 on the Hindu Code Bill and the Government had to postpone the consideration of the Bill for some time.

Another important issue on which the President and the Prime Minister differed was the introduction of Hindi for official purposes. The President advised the Prime Minister to speedily and vigorously encourage the use of Hindi so that it might become the sole official language as early as possible. Nehru, on the other hand, argued that the pace of Hindi in Government offices should not be forced because of practical difficulties in using it at all levels, and, secondly, it would meet stiff opposition from non-Hindi-speaking areas, especially from the South. Rajendra Prasad, therefore, did not act as mere figurehead during his tenure of office. He tried to

67. *The Hindu,* New Delhi, April 23, 1987.
68. *Illustrated Weekly of India,* Bombay, July 19-25, 1987.

influence the decisions of the Cabinet. When Rajendra Prasad retired from his office as President, the Prime Minister and Parliament paid warm tributes to the ability and tact with which he had conducted himself as the constitutional Head of the State. The address presented to him on May 8, 1962, *inter alia,* said, "By your qualities of unostentatious grace, your utter simplicity, clarity of outlook, deep humility and broad humanity, you invested a special meaning and significance in your choice as President. As the first President of India, you have enriched and embellished the office and are leaving behind inspiring traditions."

Radhakrishnan during his tenure of office had been exceptionally frank in publicly giving expression to his views. In his Republic Day broadcast on January 25, 1963, he said : "Our credulity and negligence are responsible for our reverses" in NEFA. In a speech in Bomaby, the President declared India's reverses as "a matter of sorrow, shame and humiliation." In November, 1963, in his Convocation address delivered at the Uttar Pradesh Agricultural University, the President attributed stagation of agriculture to "lack of true, wise leadership and administrative inefficiency." In a broadcast to the nation on January 25, 1964, Radhakrishnan cautioned against complacency towards corruption and said, "It would be well to recognise that the tolerance of our society for weak, inefficient and unclean administration is not unlimited." But his broadcast to the nation on January 25, 1967, came from an anguished heart. He warned the nation that the "prospect of a revolution" was "inescapable," if unruly behaviour, fasts and violence in the country did not end. Describing 1966 as the worst year since Independence, full of natural calamities and human failures, the President said that even after making allowance for all difficulties of the situation, "We cannot forgive widespread incompetence and the gross mismanagement of our resources."

In spite of this open criticism of the Government's policy, Nehru, Shastri and Mrs. Gandhi got on well with Radhakrishnan. Unlike Rajendra Prasad, Radhakrishnan did not claim larger powers than commonly allowed to the President. He was the Philosopher President and as an upholder of the Constitution, he was a wise Head of the State who advised, warned and encouraged as the occasion demanded. On the death of Prime Minster Nehru, the President in broadcast to the nation said : "Nehru held the office of the Prime Minster of our country since the dawn of independence; and in the long years of his Premiership tried to put our country on a progressive, scientific, dynamic and non-communal basis. His steadfast loyalty to certain fundamental principles of liberalism gave direction to our thought and life..........He used the existing social and political institutions and breathed in them a new spirit, a new vitality." Radhakrishnan congratulated the Prime Minster and the Government and the Chiefs of Staff "on the hard and excellent work which they and those working under their leadership" did during the Indo-Pakistan conflict in 1965.

The President, in brief, like the King of Britain, has not merely been constitutionally romanticised but actually vested with a pervasive and persuasive role. While he plays such a dynamic role, he is not a rival centre of power in any sense and must abide by and act on the advice duly tendered to him by his duly constituted Ministers, except in a narrow territory (appointment of the Prime Minster and dissolution of Parliament) which is sometimes slippery, as in the case of Charan Singh's appointment as Prime Minster by the President in July 1979 and dissolution of Parliament in August 1979 and both these acts of President Sanjiva Reddy attracted widespread criticism, though not without substance. Prof. N. V. Pylee considers that President Reddy "was clearly guilty of violating the Constitution" by permitting Charan Singh as Prime Minster, after the dissolution of Parliament, without satisfying even the basic constitutional requirements as the Constitution "does not have any specific provision for a caretaker government.."

It has been rightly said that the voice of reason is more readily heard when it can persuade but no longer coerce. With extensive political knowledge and wide experience at his command, the President may influence the decisions of his Ministers and help even in moulding the policy of the government. As a friend of the Ministers, he may resist the advice tendered to him, but he must not carry his point so far as to threaten the stability of the Government. Even "When the President", said V. V. Giri, "expressed his view" publicly on matters of common concern—sometimes vital to the functioning of our democracy— he does not do so to embarrass the government but to strengthen their hands in dealing with them.[69]

In the final analysis the Presidency is what its occupant makes of it. The President must have a dynamic personality, political wisdom and independence of mind and intellect. His influence will be strictly in proportion to the quality of his personality and character. It depends also on the President's relations with his Council of Ministers. The history of Presidency under Rajendra Prasad and Sarvapalli Radhakrishnan, in spite of the former's controversial statement of November 28, 1960, and the latter's public criticism of the Government, is resplendent with what a sagacious occupant of that august office can do in dispelling all doubts, real or imaginary, regarding the possible abuse or misuse of the President's powers. Both have set precedents which help to fulfil the objectives of the Father-framers of the Constitution. Neelam Sanjiva Reddy was a controversial President and despite his unpredictable prouncements, he fulfilled his duties to the best of his wisdom and upheld the prestige of the august office that he occupied. Of all the Presidents he alone worked with three Prime Ministers, each differing from others not only in views, style of functioning and temperament but in party loyalties. By holding to the sound principle that the Head of the State and head of the Government should work harmoniously he adjusted himself to a Janata Prime Minster, a Lok Dal Prime Minister and the Congress (I) Prime Minister despite his relations with Morarji Desai were far from cordial and the same was true of his relations with Mrs. Indira Gandhi. This could have led to serious difficulties, but Reddy never tried to impose his views on the Government of the day and precipitate a constitutional crisis. He had to tackle difficult issues the like of which his predecessors were never called upon to deal with and succeeded to tide them over to the best of his wisdom and political experience he had gained in various capacities of his political career, although his decision to ignore Jagjivan Ram's claim as the new leader of the Janata Parliamentary Party and to ask Charan Singh, a defector from the Janata Party, to form the Governmet shall ever remain controversial as no sagacious President would have attempted it.

The Seventh President Gyani Zail Singh categorically stated after his election that he would function strictly in accordance with the Constitution. A nominee of Prime Minister Indira Gandhi, whose loyalty had been his only asset and had paid him rich dividends. He is humble and soft by temperament but he is one of the shrewdest and most experienced politicians in the country today. It is a matter of common knowledge that the President had differences with Prime Minister Indira Gandhi on the Government's handling of the Punjab crisis. The President confessed to Khushwant Singh that he was kept in dark about 'Operation Bluestar' and only learnt of it over the radio. He added that the President had also told him that if he had been informed of the operation in advance he would have dissuaded the Prime Minister from taking such an adventure.[70]

Virtually all Presidents of India thus far have come from a political background—certainly Gyani Zail Singh, who as Union Home Minister and also earlier as Chief Minister of Punjab and President of the Congress (I) was involved in matters of political controversy. It is quite understandable that there might have been variances, even sharp, between Prime Minster Rajiv Gandhi's perception of political problems and issues and President Gyani Zail Singh, but he had the constitutional right to know the inner thinking and decisions of the political government on a range of domestic and international matters and seek necessary information on all matters of State. No matter who leaked the President's letter of March 9, 1987, challenging the veracity of the Prime Minister's statement in Parliament on March 2 and 4 it sought to prove that Rajiv Gandhi did not speak the truth, or the whole truth, when he said that he had been keeping the President fully briefed on all important issues. Did not the Prime Minister reveal in 1985 that he departed from the various past conventions and one of them, of course, was the fulfilment of his constitutional duty under Article 78? It goes to the credit of Gyani Zail Singh that he subdued the humiliation or to put it rather mildly mistreatment by those who claimed to be the people's representative till he was forced to clarify the points involved in March 2 and 4 statements of the Prime Minister made in Parliament.

69. But President Sanjiva Reddy's plea for greater autonomy to the States, made in the course of his Patel Memorial Lecture on October 31, 1981, triggered a storm of controversy and was certainly embarrassing to the Government in the explosive situation created by the demand for the greater autonomy and prolonged unrest in the North-East. It was hailed by the CPM and the Akali Dal.

70. *The Times of India,* New Delhi, April 21, 1987.

Nor did he fall in the trap that was laid for him by the Opposition parties to precipitate a constitutional crisis which would have put into jeopardy the future of democracy itself in India, though he kept the atmosphere so heavily charged with suspicion by his pronouncements that no one was quite prepared to discount the possibility that President Gyani Zail Singh would not spring an unpleasant surprise on the nation[71] before he formally laid down office on July 25, 1987.

R. Venkataraman assumed office of the President of the Republic of India on July 25, 1987 and reminded the nation, in a brief speech delivered at the Central Hall of Parliament, the need for consolidation and confidence. He cautioned that "too many institutions and relationship have suffered an erosion of confidence. This cannot but have disastrous consequences." He said, "As I enter office today in all humility, I wish to assure the nation that I shall endeavour to deserve the trust and confidence reposed in me. In the discharge of my responsibilities, namely, to preserve, protect and defend the Constitution, I shall strive to follow the illustrious tradition set by eminent Presidents like Dr. Rajendra Prasad, Dr. Radhakrishnan and Dr. Zakir Hussain. I will neither fail to exercise the duties and functions attached to this high office, nor stray beyond the powers enshrined in the Constitution by the founding fathers."

In an exclusive interview with Promila Kalhan Venkataraman who was then Vice-President of India and a Congress (I) nominee for Presidency, expressed the view that the President of India was not meant to be a second seat of power by the Founding Fathers of the Constitution of India. He can guide, advise and warn the Government and should the Constitution seem to be leaking down, he can take necessary action to protect it. Otherwise his role is limited". When asked, suppose the Prime Minister does not listen to the advice of the President, what can the President do about it ? "Nothing ," he replied. The interviewer intervened and said, I suppose much depends on the personality of the President. His answer was "that is for you to say."[72]

No President of India has in the last forty years been faced with turmoils, moral and political, which challenged his objectivity as President R. Venkataraman had. But he faced all sorts of situations with courage and discreetfully and proved worthy of the office he held. A false step would have created difficulties for him and inflict a serious damage to the Presidency.

## SUGGESTED READINGS

*Constituent Assembly Debates.*

Granville Austin, *The Indian Constitution - A Cornerstone of a Nation.*

Jennings W-1, *Some Characteristics of the Indian Constitution.*

Morris- Jones, W.H. *The Government and Politics of India.*

71. Addressing a crowded "Meet the Press" programme at Chandigarh on July 19, 1987, asked by a persistent journalist about the likelihood of his decision to grant permission to sue the Prime Minister President Gyani Zail Singh said the matter was under consideration. As another reporter persisted that there was hardly a week before he relinquished office, he retorted back: "yes I have about a week to take decision." He also said that "the Constitution gives vast powers to the President which have to be used with discretion."
72. *The Hindustan Times Sunday Magazines,* July 5, 1987.

# CHAPTER IX

# The Council of Ministers

## The Real Executive

If the President is the constitutional Head of the State the real executive is the Council of Ministers established by Article 74 (1) with the Prime Minister at the head to aid and advise the President in the exercise of his functions and he is constitutionally required to always act in accordance with such advice. The question whether any, and if so what, advice was tendered by Ministers to the President cannot be inquired into by any court. Article 361 (1) also provides that the President shall not be answerable to any court for the exercise and performance of the powers and duties of his office. The question of ministerial advice cannot be brought before courts and personal immunity from legal action, whether during office or thereafter, is given to the President for any act done or purporting to be done by him in the exercise and performance of those powers and duties. It also establishes that the relations between the President and his Ministers are confidential. The principle involved in these provisions is similar to the doctrine of the British Constitution that the "king can do no wrong." It means that the President of India, like the British Monarch, may not perform any public act involving the exercise of discretionary powers except on the advice of his duly constituted Ministers. And for every act performed in the name of the President the Ministers are responsible to the House of the People. To put it in a matter of fact language, the President can do nothing right or wrong, of a discretionary nature and having a legal effect. His name cannot be referred to in connection with any public act anywhere in courts or within and outside Parliament. Nor can any Minister plead the orders of the President in defence of a wrongful act or for any error of omission and commission and thereby shield himself behind the legal immunities of the occupant of the Presidential office.

Before 1978 the Constitution simply provided for the Council of Ministers and the use of the term Cabinet in the context of the machinery of government was nowhere mentioned. Immediately after the transfer of power in August 1947, no distinction was made between the Council of Ministers and the Cabinet. Both the terms were used interchangeably. All Ministers, except the Prime Minister, enjoyed the same position, status and powers. But the Prime Minister and other Ministers were not oblivious of the confusion thus caused. In order to make the position of the Ministers precise and define their powers, Gopalaswamy Ayyangar, a senior member of the Council of Ministers, was entrusted with the task of studying the problem of Cabinet organisation and to make recommendations. The Ayyangar Report, submitted in November, 1949, recommended the categorization of Ministers on the British pattern and defining the powers and responsibilities of each category of Ministers.

The Constitution of India did not take cognisance of the three-tier Ministers as recommended by the Ayyanger report. But the Council of Ministers formed by Jawaharlal Nehru under the new Constitution took due care to adopt this categorization of the Ministers and since then it has become entrenched in the political system of India. The Council of Ministers consists of : Ministers, who are members of the Cabinet; Ministers of State, who are not members of the Cabinet but are of the Cabinet rank; and Deputy Ministers. Cabinet Ministers usually less than twenty, are the most influential and outstanding leaders of the party included in the Council of Ministers. They meet collectively in Cabinet meetings, held normally once a week, decide upon policy, and in general head the important Ministries of the Union Government. Ministers of State, though formally of Cabinet status and are paid the same salaries as the Cabinet Ministers, do not attend and participate in the deliberations of the Cabinet meetings unless specially invited when something relating to their Ministries, if they hold independent charge of such Ministries or when the Cabinet Ministers with whom they are attached cannot attend the meeting has to be decided by the Cabinet. Next in rank are the Deputy Ministers. They are junior Ministers and their task is to assist the Ministers with whom they are associated in their administrative and parliamentary duties.

But the Constitution (Forty-fourth Amendment) Act, 1978, has institutionalized the term Cabinet by recognizing it and distinguishing it from other Ministers who are members of the Council of Ministers. The newly inserted Clause (3) in Article 352 provides that the President shall not issue a Proclamation of Emergency or a Proclamation varying it "unless the decision of the Union Cabinet (that is to say, the Council consisting of the Prime Minister and other Ministers of Cabinet rank appointed under Article 75)" is communicated to him in writing.

**Size of the Council of Ministers**

The Constitution does not fix the size of the Council of Ministers. It is for the Prime Minister to determine its size according to the exigencies of the time and requirements of the situation. But the choice of the Prime Minister is limited to the extent that he must consider the claims and views of the leading members of the Parliamentary party in both Houses.[1] The need to give representation to important regions and communities are two other important factors which no Prime Minister can afford to ignore. Important States, Like Uttar Pradesh, Bihar, West Bengal, Maharashtra, Gujrat, Punjab[2] and Tamil Nadu have never remained unrepresented. Like- wise, important communities, such as Muslims and Sikhs, must always be properly represented.

One result of this part of regional and communal representation is that the size of Council of Ministers has remained big and often unwieldy. Nehru was often criticised for keeping large Council of Ministers. In November, 1962 a resolution was moved in the House of the People (Lok Sabha) recommending reduction in the size of the Council of Ministers and emphasised the need for exercising rigorous austerity in ministerial circles. Nehru opposed the resolution and pointed out that Emergency created by war with China had actually increased the work-load of the Government. The Council of Ministers formed by Lal Bahadur Shastri in 1964 consisted of 51 members, sixteen of them were Cabinet Ministers. Soon after his election as leader of the Congress Parliamentary Party, Shastri declared that a large Cabinet would be fully justified in view of the vastness of the country and the nature and complexity of the problems confronting it. Mrs. Indira Gandhi, during the eleven years of her tenure, kept the number around sixty and the number of Cabinet Ministers varying from fifteen to eighteen. Morarji Desai kept his Council of Ministers at as low a number as nineteen for four months but all Cabinet Ministers. Addition was, however, made by including Ministers of State, but kept the total below forty.

The Administrative Reforms Commission in its Report, on the *Machinery of the Government of India and its Procedure of Work*, recommended that the strength of the Council of Ministers should normally be 40 and only under special circumstances it might go up to 45. It was suggested that the three-tier system in the ministerial set-up should be continued. The Commission recommended a compact cabinet consisting of not more than 16 Cabinet Ministers "to ensure homogeneity, speed and purposeful functions should constitute the norm." The collective responsibility of the Council of Ministers to the House of the People necessitates that all its members must belong to the same party and believe in the same policy in order to provide a stable government under a unified command of the homogeneous and disciplined leaders. But when emergencies upset the normal conditions and the nation faces some crisis, the national government may be established to solve all such problems through the common and concerted efforts of the representatives of all parties. Nehru included in his Council of Ministers, formed in January, 1950, five non-Congressmen—B.R. Ambedkar, Syama Prasad Mukherjee, Baldev Singh, Gopalswami Ayyangar and Shanmukham Chetty. But gradually the number of non-Congressmen was reduced and by 1958 all the senior posts in the Council of Ministers were held by Congressmen. Nehru did not consider feasible the suggestion made in 1962, when China had attacked India, for a broadbased Council of Ministers. Mrs. Indira Gandhi rejected the insistent demand of the Opposition to form a national government after the 1969 Congress split and when she headed the minority government. The Government formed by Charan Singh in July 1979 was a minority Government with Congress (S)[3] as its partner

1. Mrs. Indira Gandhi in the composition of her Council of Ministers in January 1980 considered personal loyalty to her in the days of her political distress a superior claim.
2. Except when no elections were held in the State both for Parliament and the State Assembly.
3. A faction led by Swaran Singh.

with the support of Congress (I)[4] which was withdrawn subsequently followed by the resignation of the Prime Minister and his Council of Ministers. The Chandra Shekhar Government was also a minority government with the assured support of Congress (I) and so is one headed by P. V. Narasimha Rao. Narasimha Rao called it a consensus Government as he chose to adopt a conciliatory approach right from the beginning. "My style of functioning is to be one of consensus. I will not, the Congress (I) will not ride rough-shod", he declared in the House of the People (Lok Sabha) while replying to the debate on the motion of the confidence in July 1991.

Morarji Desai committed a constitutional breach by being sworn in as the Prime Minister on March 24, 1977 without a Council of Ministers. Article 74(1) provides that there shall be a Council of Ministers with the Prime Minister at the head to aid and advise the President in the exercise of his functions. For two days there was no Council for Desai to lead and to aid and advise the President. Any advice tendered to the President by the Prime Minister for two days, when the first instalment of Ministers with Moraraji Desai as its head was sworn, was not in terms of Article 74(1) and actions of the President during this period were bad in the eyes of law and violative of the principle of collective responsibility. This unhappy breach of constitutionalism set a precedent for Chief Ministers in quite a number of States when in June 1977, they assumed their offices alone without the Council of Ministers again to be repeated by Congress (I) Chief Ministers in 1980, 1982 and 1983. In the States it has become a norm of practical practice.

## BASIC PRINCIPLES OF PARLIAMENTARY GOVERNMENT

### Cabinet is the Driving and Steering Force

The cabinet is a wheel within a wheel. Its outside ring consists of a Party that has a majority in the House of the People (Lok Sabha), the next ring being the Council of Ministers of different ranks, and the smallest of all being the cabinet containing the Party leaders who really matter. By this means is secured that unity of Party action which depends upon placing the directing power in the hands of a body small enough to agree and influential enough to control. The cabinet is, thus, the driving and steering force in the Parliamentary machine of government.

Such a system of government hinges upon well-established and universally recognised principles some of which have been constitutionalised and find expression in the various provisions of the Constitution. Cabinet itself, which had prior to 1978 an extra-constitutional growth, is now a part of Article 352(3) together with the office of the Prime Minister. This provision also makes cabinet distinguishable from the Council of Ministers and renders it a policy-formulating and decision-making body.[5] Articles 74 and 75 of the Constitution incorporate the principles that govern the functions of the Parliamentary government and they are basic in its life. Article 74 (1) enjoins that there shall be a Council of Ministers with the Prime Minister at the head to aid and advise the President who shall act in accordance with the advice so tendered. The President is vested with the power to refer the advice so tendered for there consideration of the Council of Ministers. But he is bound to act in accordance with the advice thus tendered after such reconsideration.

Article 75 provides that the Prime Minister shall be appointed by the President whereas other Ministers shall be appointed by him on the advice of the Prime Minister. The Council of Ministers is collectively responsible to the House of the People (Lok Sabha) while individual Ministers hold office during the pleasure of the President which for all intents and purposes means the Prime Minister. A Minister including the Prime Minister, who for six consecutive months is not a member of either House of Parliament ceases to be a Minister after the expiry of that period unless he had been elected to be a member of either the House of the People or the Council of States.

But all these provisions, though vital, are neither full nor positive and many important points involved therein for the smooth functioning of Parliamentary democracy have been left to be determined by conventions and usages. There is some supreme virtue in leaving them subject to conventions and usages. The conventional element makes the working of Parliamentary democracy flexible and, consequently, easily adjustable to meet the emergencies or any other special circumstances that may confront the nation. A discreet use of the convention lubricates the machinery of government which otherwise could crack under the rigidity of law.

4. Led by Mrs. Indira Gandhi.
5. Article 352(3).

### Constitutional Head of the State

The Head of the State in a Parliamentary system of government must not be the directing and deciding factor responsible before the nation for the measures taken. The whole executive power is exercised in his name by the political men who belong to the majority party in the representative legislative chamber and are responsible to it for all public acts individually as well as collectively. If the representative chamber does not approve their policies or endorse their actions, they must quit office and make room for others who can retain its confidence. As the Head of the State takes no part in the politics of the country, he does not participate in the confidential discussions (deliberations of the Cabinet) in which his Ministers formulate policy and decide the advice they would tender him.

The object of the Constitution framers was to make the President, like the British Monarch and that he should act on the advice tendered to him by his Ministers. The Constitution, no doubt, uses the traditional language of the Canadian and South African Constitutions that the Council of Ministers will "aid and advise" the President in the exercise of his functions and powers, but it does not do any damage to the basic requirements of Parliamentary democracy. The expression "aid and advise" is a stereotyped phrase of constitutional law and practice. It has no relevance to its use in the ordinary dictionary sense. It is a term of art which has historically acquired a special meaning well understood by constitutional lawyers. In explaining the form of government and the role of President, Ambedkar explained to the Constituent Assembly that the "President of the Indian Union would be generally bound on the advice of his Ministers. He can do nothing contrary to their advice."[6]

Originally, the Constitution made no specific provision that the President must act as advised by the Council of Ministers. The Constitution-framers thought that the binding nature of ministerial advice was the *sine quo non* of the Parliamentary system and it was a universally recognised practice from which and about which there could be no doubt. It would, thus, be futile to make any specific provision of this vital truth in the Constitution itself. Moreover, the Constitution nowhere vested the President with any discretionary and individual judgment powers. They, accordingly, thought that lack of such a provision is an adequate safeguard to any kind of doubt about the exercise of Presidential authority.

Bit it did not happen that way. The first President of India Dr. Rajendra Prasad believed that in certain exceptional circumstances the President may not act on the advice tendered to him by his Council of Ministers. The thesis assumed added importance and became rather sharp when K. M. Munshi, then one of the living architects of the Constitution who had forcefully advocated in the Constituent Assembly the importance of adopting the Parliamentary system wrote in January 1963, that judged by the well-accepted canons of interpretation a person on whom a duty is cast or in whom a trust is invested is bound to exercise his own discretion in relation to the duty or trust and cannot be deemed to have been deprived of it by implication.[7]

To dispel all doubts and as a measure of abundant precaution the Constitution (Forty-second Amendment) Act, 1976, amended Article 74(1) which read "....The President who shall, in the exercise of his functions, act in accordance with such advice." The Constitution (Forty-fourth Amendment) Act, 1978, substituted a provision to Article 74(1) providing for a little free-wheeling for the President by giving him the choice, if he so required, to refer the advice so tendered "either generally or otherwise" to the Council of Ministers for reconsideration, but such advice, after reconsideration, was made binding on the President. The function of the Council of Ministers is, thus, to decide and for the President to advise if he feels that their decision stands in need of some advice.

### Ministers Chosen from Parliamentary Majority

The essence of the Parliamentary government is that Ministers should be members of the Legislature and belong to the majority in its representative chamber. The membership of the Legislature gives to Ministers a representative character and invokes their responsibility for all acts of omission and commission to those who gave them the mandate to govern through the chamber which is the repository of their will. It also binds the Executive and Legislative authorities together and there can be no working at cross purposes between the two wings of the Government. It is in this context that Bagehot made his

6. *Constituent Assembly Debates,* Vol. VIII, p. 53.
7. *The Times of India,* New Delhi, Republic Day Supplement, January 26, 1963, p. VII.

classic statement that Cabinet is a hyphen that joins, the buckle that fastens the Executive and Legislative Departments. Moreover, membership of the Legislature provides Ministers an effective opportunity to present, advocate and to defend their views and proposals and get them endorsed by the representatives of the people.

There is no constitutional bar in India to a person, who is not a member of either House of Parliament to become a Minister and there are scores of instances, the most recent being of Prime Minister P. V. Narasimha Rao and the Finance Minister Manmohan Singh. Both were without having seats in either House of Parliament when appointed Ministers. But a Minister so appointed ceases to hold office if for a period of six consecutive months he is not a member of either House of Parliament. It means that every Minister who has no seat in Parliament must become a member of either House of Parliament or quit his office.

**Leadership of the Prime Minister**

The Council of Ministers is a team that plays the game of politics under the captaincy of the Prime Minister. The Prime Minister is the leader of the Parliamentary majority Party and Ministers work and function under his leadership. In terms of the Constitution, Ministers are appointed by the President on the advice of the Prime Minister, but in actual practice they are his nominees and his advice to the President in proposing their names for appointment is binding. The Prime Minister's choice in selecting the Ministers is limited no doubt but once the choice has been made and submitted for the Presidential appointment, there can be no deviation therefrom. It is also the constitutional right of the Prime Minister to retain a Minister, to shift him from one Ministry to another or sound him to resign or to dismiss him if the Minister becomes defiant. The identity of the Ministers is unknown to law without the Prime Minister. They remain in office as long as he is there. If he resigns their resignation is *ipso facto.* A Party, in brief, lives on Party spirit and as an instrument of government it preserves its continuous corporate identity on the leadership of the Prime Minister. All this secures unity and close association between Ministers on one side, and the Cabinet and the Parliamentary majority on the other.

**Ministerial Responsibility**

Ministerial responsibility is the essence of the Parliamentary system of government and collective responsibility is Britain's principal contribution to modern political practice. Ministerial responsibility means, in the first place, that Cabinet Ministers preside over the administrative Departments of the Government and for the effective and efficient working of their respective charge, they are individually responsible to and answerable to the legislature. In the second place each Minister largely shares a collective responsibility with other Ministers for anything of high importance that is done in every branch of public business besides his own. The Ministry is a unit, it comes into office as a unit and goes out of office as a unit. The Ministers belong to the same Party or a combination of parties if there is not one single party in majority under the recognised leadership of the Prime Minister and they swim and sink together. Solidarity is the prerequisite condition of the Cabinet system. It is binding, accordingly, on every member of the Cabinet and every political officer outside the Cabinet, no matter what his rank is, to present a common front and pursue an agreed policy for which all accept responsibility and on which they stand or fall together. A Minister who is not prepared to defend a Cabinet decision must resign and if he does not, then, he is liable to be dismissed from his office.

The Constitution expressly provides for the collective responsibility of the Council of Ministers to the House of the People (Lok Sabha). This provision gives a constitutional sanctity to Britain's principal contribution of collective responsibility. It means that the Council of Ministers remains in office as long as it can retain the confidence of the representative chamber of the Legislative. There is, however, no provision in the Constitution for the individual responsibility of the Ministers. It simply provides that Ministers hold office during the pleasure of the President which in practice means the pleasure of the Prime Minister. It is rather rare for the Prime Minister to venture a dismissal of a colleague. Morarji Desai instead of exercising his prerogative of asking Charan Singh and Raj Narain to resign convened an emergency meeting of the Cabinet and 14 Ministers backed the decision of the Prime Minister in asking them to withdraw from the Cabinet. It was virtually their dismissal.

**Secrecy**

If collective responsibility is to be really effective; it is imperative that the Cabinet should deliberate in secret and its proceedings remain highly confidential. "There must be", as Lord Salisbury said, "irresponsible licence in discussions."[8] If mature, rational and independent contribution to the process of policy-making is desired from men who are engaged in a common cause and who come together for the purpose of reaching an agreement, secrecy of the proceedings and the views expressed by the participating members in the discussion must be ensured. Publicity reduces the independence of mind of ministers in relation to each other and harmony of views becomes impossible. Moreover, a knowledge of differences among Ministers makes difficult the unflinching support of the whole Party to the policy adopted. It also offers vulnerable points to the attacks of the opposition which is ever vigilant to plague the Government at every step.

The Cabinet in India is a secret body collectively responsible for its decisions. The Oath of Secrecy which every Minister is required to take before entering upon his office imposes a constitutional obligation not to disclose any Cabinet secret. Moreover, Cabinet decision is an advice to the President and the President's sanction is necessary before any sort of publicity may be given to that advice. When a Minister resigns as a result of differences of opinion or is asked to resign, Rules of Procedure and Conduct of Business in Parliament permit him to make a personal explanation to the House without raising a debate.[9]

There are other means by which more or less reliable information regarding the views expressed and decisions taken often get out. In every country either the Prime Minister, or some other Minister on his behalf, gives to the press a guarded statement on the Cabinet decisions in order to promote opinion about the policy which the Government has decided to pursue. Then, the press has its own methods of sneaking in and Ministers are quite vulnerable. Prime Minister Lal Bahadur Shastri established the system of public relations and Cabinet decisions, which were not of a confidential nature, were released to the Press by the Cabinet Secretariat at the end of every meeting. The advisability of such public relations was proposed to Jawaharlal Nehru on several occasions, but he did not favour it. Mrs. Indira Gandhi continued with the change introduced by Lal Bahadur Shastri and the practice continues since then.

8. Cecil Gwendolen, *Life of Lord Salisbury*, Vol. II, p. 233.
9. Rule 218.

**How the Cabinet Works**

The Cabinet generally meets once a week, but when Parliament is in session or when urgent matters requiring immediate decisions, arise, it may hold more than one meeting. The meetings are usually held at Rashtrapati Bhavan, where the office of the Cabinet Secretariat is located. Sometimes Cabinet meetings were held at the Houses of the Ministers both under Nehru and Shastri. Morarji Desai revived this practice which was abandoned by Mrs. Gandhi. Chief Ministers may be asked to attend the meetings when matters relating to their States are discussed in order to arrive at a positive decision. P. C. Sen, West Bengal Chief Minister, and Orissa Chief Minister, Biju Patnaik, attended the Cabinet meetings on June 6, 1963 when the food problem in the eastern region was causing concern. Patnaik was also consulted on defence problems immediately after the Chinese attack in October, 1962, and given a room in the Ministry of External Affairs. Experts on matters of technical nature, such as military, scientific or economic may be invited to explain personally the issues involved in such matters. The Deputy Chairman and members of the Planning Commission attend when problems relating to their respective charge are brought on the agenda.

The agenda is prepared by the Cabinet Secretariat in consultation with the Prime Minister. There are no definite rules determining the subjects for discussion in the Cabinet. Matters of a routine nature are decided by the Minister in consultation with the Prime Minister or these may be referred to the Appropriate Cabinet Committee and subsequently confirmed by the Prime Minister. The Prime Minister himself may take the decision and later inform the Cabinet. H. M. Patel, who had been the Cabinet Secretary, says that Prime Minister Jawaharlal Nehru himself had repeatedly taken decision on his own in respect of matters relating to the External Affairs Ministry without the Committee of the Cabinet for Foreign Affairs being aware of them. He further says that the Cabinet itself had been ignored by the Prime Minister even more frequently and that "several senior ministers have also tended to take a leaf out of the Prime Minister's book and to by-pass the Cabinet. They do not do so on thier own. They obtain the Prime Ministers concurrence to a line of policy which they advocate and then without waiting for the approval of the Cabinet go forward treating the Prime Minister's approval as the approval of the Cabinet."[10] This is supported by N. V. Gadgil, who had been Cabinet Minister from 1947-52.[11] Mrs. Indira Gandhi "simply informed" the Cabinet about the declaration of internal emergency in June 1975 and dissolution of the House of the People in January, 1977.

Every matter that comes for the Cabinet discussion is accompanied by an explanatory memorandum. If the matter concerns more than one Ministry, all the concerned Ministries submit their explanatory memoranda, which are circulated among all Cabinet Ministers well in advance of the scheduled meeting. An item not on the agenda can be raised at the meeting with the permission of the Prime Minister, provided it is of great urgency. The Prime Minister presides at the meetings and in his absence the Deputy Prime Minister, if there is one. In the absence of both, the seniormost Minister used to preside. During the tenure of Mrs. Gandhi's Prime Ministership, the seniority list was abandoned and the names of Ministers appeared alphabetically. The Prime Minister named the person who would act in her absence and this practice was continued during her second tenure in office in 1980 and still continues to be the practice.

The Administrative Reforms Commission suggested that the office of the Deputy Prime Minister should be regularised and the Prime Minister needs institutional support for ensuring efficient and effective functioning of the governmental machinery. Originally, Morarji Desai had no Deputy Prime Minister, but exigencies of tottering Janata Party and in his anxiety to save the Government from exit from office, compelled him to appoint two Deputy Ministers—Charan Singh Deputy Prime Minister No. 1 and Jagjivan Ram Deputy Prime Minister No. 2. A unique precedent in the annals of any country with Parliamentary system of government.

There is no quorum for a Cabinet meeting. Its duration depends upon the nature of the items on the agenda. Discussion ensues on each item and it is frank and often blunt. Differences are resolved by mutual discussion, and discussion continues until an agreement is reached. Votes are never taken.[12] The decisions taken are forwarded to the Ministers for necessary administrative action.

**Cabinet Committees**

The burden of the Cabinet is titanic. It cannot meet its stupendous task when it generally meets once a week and that too far a short duration.[13] Then, it has too many members for effective discussion and all of them, except the Minister Without Portfolio, if there is one, are heads of the Ministries and they are too occupied in their departmental and parliamentary duties. Moreover, the Cabinet has neither the time nor is it able to tackle all the numerous details relating to administration. The result is emergence of Cabinet Committees. The Committees help the Cabinet to discharge its responsibilities efficiently and expeditiously. Some of these Committees are continuous and, thus, permanent, others are *ad hoc,* that is created for single time-limited matter. An *ad hoc* Committee is set up to deal with a special problem or a critical situation and is composed of Ministers primarily concerned with the problems at issue. It deliberates, reports and disbands. A special committee of the Cabinet was constituted in November, 1964 to examine the charges of corruption against the Orissa Chief Minister and some of his other colleagues. In 1962, the Emergency Committee was set up soon after the Chinese invasion. Such Emergency Committees were twice again set up in 1965 and 1971 after Pakistan had attacked India. A Cabinet Committee was also appointed on the reorganisation of Assam. In July 1987 a special Cabinet Committee was set up under the Chairmanship of the Prime Minister, Rajiv Gandhi, to tackle the problem created by the worst drought of the country. In October 1991, a Cabinet Committee, under the chairmanship of the Prime Minster (Narasimha Rao) was appointed to monitor prices.

Before 1970, there were four Standing Committees : Foreign Affairs, Economic Affairs, Internal Affairs, and the Parliamentary Affairs. In 1970 the Internal affairs Committee and the Foreign Affairs Committee were replaced by the Political Affairs Committee under the chairmanship of Prime Minister. Other Committees, new or reconstitued were : Economic Co-ordination Committee, Family Planning Committee, Food

10. Aiyar, S.P., and Srinivasan, R. (Edts.), *Studies in Indian Democracy,* pp. 205-206.
11. Gadgil. N. V., *Government from Inside,* Chap.VI.
12. According to Krishna Menon, "The Cabinet never votes." *The Times of India,* New Delhi, October 23, 1968. Also refer to Gadgil, N. V., *Government from Inside,* Chap. VI.
13. The longest session was for four hours at a stretch on October 14, 1964 to consider the outlines of the Fourth Five-Year Plan.

and Agriculture and Rural Development Committee, Committee on Accommodation, Appointment Committee, and the Parliamentary Affairs Committee. The Prime Minster again reconstitued the Committees in 1974. The functions of these Committees were also revised.

The Janata Government decided to undertake a systematic programme of dismantling the superfluous administrative apparatus built up by the Congress Government during all those years. Among the steps taken were to reduce the number of Cabinet Committees. Only four Committees were set up instead of over a dozen in the Congress administration. Previously, the same group of Ministers sat on at least half a dozen Committees, excepting that there was only one additional Minister on each Committee. The system often led to delay and sometimes even confusion.

The number and composition of the Cabinet Committees are largely determined by the Prime Minister. They combine two functions : co-ordinating the various Ministries and decentralising the policies. The Committees can also be employed to keep critical problem under continuous review. By including non-Cabinet Ministers, whenever deemed appropriate, in their deliberations, the committee system can extend the Cabinet's co-ordinating activity to wider areas of governmental affairs. It is also possible for the senior members of the permanent services to attend Cabinet Committee meetings as adviser to their Ministers.

The Cabinet Committees report to the whole Cabinet and seek to submit agreed reports and recommendations. A Minister, who is not satisfied with such recommendations, can appeal to the Cabinet where differences are tried to be resolved. If the Minister is not reconciled to the decision taken by the Cabinet, he may resign.

**Cabinet Secretariat**

As said earlier, India has adopted the British model of setting up a Cabinet Secretariat. The Department of Cabinet Affairs, under the Cabinet Secretariat, had an important and co-ordinating role in the process of decision-making at the highest level and operated under the direction of the Prime Minister. Its functions included the submission of cases to the Cabinet and its Committees, preparation of the records of the decisions taken and follow-up action on their implementation. It also serviced the Committees of Secretaries which met periodically, under the chairmanship of the Cabinet Secretary to consider and advise on problems requiring inter-ministerial consultation and co-ordination. The Cabinet Secretariat formulated the Rules of Business and allocated the business of the Union Government to the Ministries and Departments under the direction of the Prime Minister and with the approval of the President. The Department of Cabinet Affairs obtained and circulated to the President, the Vice-President, the Council of Ministers and other important functionaries periodical summaries and notes on important developments in each Ministry.

Prime Minster Moraraji Desai, who was the Chairman of the Administrative Reforms Commission, in an effort to give implementation to the recommendations of the Administrative Reforms Commission, decentralised the work of administration in order to make it result-oriented and also responsive to the people. Decision-making which was hitherto concentrated at the level of the Prime Minister's Secretariat and the Cabinet Secretariat, rested with each Ministry; it looked after its own work without having to look up to some higher body for routine approvals. The Cabinet Secretariat, thus, resumed its original role as a co-ordinating body and to process proposals sent by the various Ministries for the consideration of the Cabinet. Since the departure in the process of decentralization was a complete departure from the past practice, it necessarily cautioned gradualism. As a preliminary step the Department of Personnel and Administrative Reforms went back to the Home Ministry and Revenue Intelligence to the Finance Ministry. The underlying idea of decentralization was to make the administration more responsive to the people and the points of contact between it and the people should be increased. There should be a quick method of redressal of grievances and routine decisions concerning the people should be taken with utmost speed.

After the return to power in 1980, Indira Gandhi restored the Secretariat to its earlier size and even expanded the establishment to some extent. But after Rajiv Gandhi became Prime Minister, it got further expanded to the size of a full-fledged Ministry wielding enormous power in the higher direction of Government. Apart from a Secretary, a special Secretary, four Additional Secretaries, four Joint Secretaries, three Directors and several Deputy Secretaries, there were several senior officers of the rank of Secretaries like the Information Adviser and Security Adviser in the Prime Minister's Secretariat. It inevitably led to a lot of criticism from other sections of the Government about the style of functioning and the kind of supervisory role it sought to establish over the working of the Whole Government. It compelled the Prime Minster to take a fresh look and see how best his Secretariat could improve its role without treading on the toes of the senior Ministers or interfering unduly with the performance of their Ministries and Departments. The Cabinet Secretariat with its reformed role still functions but the appointment of the Cabinet Secretary has become a political appointment now and it does not augur well.

**Prime Minister's Secretariat**

In this process of decentralization and in order to cut necessary administrative frills, the Prime Minister's Secretariat was renamed as Prime Minister's Office. The origin of the Prime Minister's Secretariat goes back to August, 1947, when it was devised to serve the purpose of a centre of information and a channel of communication between the Prime Minster and the Union Ministers. It had nothing to do with decision formulation. But Lal Bahadur Shastri's failing health in 1964 made him to lean heavily on his Secretariat and it reassumed the role of a regular department functioning under a Secretary. Instead of remaining an information pipeline the Secretariat became a top decision-influencing body. Mrs. Indira Gandhi reorganised the Secretariat so that it would function as a reservoir of knowledge and an effective centre of liaison between the Union Ministries and the State Governments in dealing with the problems of national importance. The Research and Analysis Wing (RAW) was expanded and activised so that the Prime Minister should be kept posted with matters and men in the country. During the past few years of Mrs. Gandhi's first tenure of Prime Ministership the RAW played a significant role even in politics within the Union Government and between the Union and the States.

The Prime Minister's Secretariat had to a large degree brought about co-ordination among Civil Servants, Ministers and the Prime Minster *inter se.* But it had also been instrumental in concentrating powers at the top level. The three advisers of the Prime Minister—L. K. Jha, P. N. Haksar and Yashpal Kapur—at one time exercised influence and authority in no way inferior to that of a Union Minster. L. K. Jha played an important role in negotiating the Kutch Agreement in 1965. P. N. Haksar was sent to Dacca to discuss matters of urgent and vital importance with Sheikh Mujib-ur-Rahman. He also took an active part in negotiating an important agreement with Pakistan foreign Minister Aziz Ahmed in the Delhi Conference of 1973. The Prime Minister's Secretariat issued a circular to all the Union Ministers on October 8, 1974 asking them to send to the Prime Minister's Secretariat copies of the Statements to be made to Parliament and notes on supplementary questions on such statements.

The role of the Prime Minister's Secretariat had been the subject of frequent criticism in Parliament. A demand was made by the Janata Party to Prime Minster Morarji Desai for a thorough probe into the activities of the Research and Analysis Wing of the Secretariat. As a result of the process of decentralization some 600 officers working in the RAW were posted in their Home States and the Secretariat was shorn of its name as well as powers. The Prime Minister's office consisted of the Principal Secretary, the Private Secretary and a few personal assistants. The rest of the staff was scattered. In Desai's view one of the main reasons for the alienation of the people from the Congress Government was centralisation of decision-making apparatus under the Prime Minster. The system had led to concentration of power in the hands of Mrs. Gandhi and a small group of officials in the Cabinet Secretariat and the Prime Minister's Secretariat and resulted in the taking up decisions in an undemocratic manner.

## FUNCTIONS OF THE CABINET

**Extent of Functions**

Cabinet is the supreme directing authority, the magnet of policy, which co-ordinates and controls the whole of the executive government of the Union and integrates and guides the work of the Parliament. The most authoritative statement about the functions of the Cabinet in Britain was made in Report of the Machinery of Government Committee (1918) and these functions legitimately go with the Cabinet wherever such a system of government exists. The Committee listed three functions :

(a) "the final determination of policy to be submitted to Parliament;
(b) the supreme control of the national executive in accordance with the policy prescribed by Parliament; and
(c) the continuous co-ordination and limitations of the interests of several Departments."

A Parliamentary system of government on the British model is operative in India, but the Cabinet in India performs certain functions which the British Cabinet dare not assume. For instance, article 123 of the Constitution empowers the President to promulgate Ordinances which shall have the same force and effect as an Act of Parliament. Such Ordinances are issued and promulgated on the advice of the Cabinet under the authority of the President. Fundamental Rights as contained in Article 19 may be suspended when a Proclamation of Emergency is in force and the decision to declare Emergency and suspension of Fundamental Rights, as contained in the Presidential Order, including the enforcement of such rights, is that of the Cabinet and not of the Prime Minister alone.[14] Decisions relating to the reorganisation of the States and alteration in their boundaries are taken by the Cabinet. All such decisions are in the final analysis subject to the approval of Parliament, but so long as the Government commands a comfortable majority Parliament simply gives its approval.

**Policy-Determining Functions**

Cabinet is deliberative and policy formulating body. It discusses and decides all sorts of national and international problems confronting the country. The Cabinet always attempts to reach unanimous agreements embodying Government's policy so that it presents to Parliament and to the world at large a united policy of action. This is the essence of collective responsibility. If an individual Minister finds it impossible to agree with policy determined by the Cabinet, the only course left for him is to resign rather than to plague the Cabinet. As a policy-determining body, the Cabinet meets regularly once a week and takes decisions on all vital issues and other matters emerging from various Ministries and earmarked for Cabinet discussion. The Cabinet, thus, supplies leadership, initiative and resourcefulness.

While the Cabinet has determined on a policy the appropriate Ministry carries it out either by administrative action within the framework of the existing law or by submitting a new proposal for legislation to Parliament. Legislation is the handmaid of administration and Cabinet is the instrument which links the Executive wing of Government to the Legislative—"the hyphen that joins, the buckle that fastens the executive and the legislative departments together," in the classical expression of Bagehot. In this way the Cabinet directs Parliament for action and it gets the approval of its policy with a majority in Parliament. Cabinet, as such, leads Parliament.

These are essentially legislative functions of the Cabinet. But in a modern State, as Jennings has said, "most legislation is directed towards the creation or modification of administrative powers." No vivid distinction, as a matter of reality, can be made between legislation and administration. The Cabinet plans the legislative programme at the beginning of each session of Parliament and determines priorities. Legislative measures are introduced either by a Cabinet Minister or by some other Minister acting on the Cabinet's approval. No Minister can introduce a legislative measure on his own initiative. It is for the Cabinet to decide what Bills shall be promoted in a session of Parliament. In matters of legislation, therefore, the control of the Cabinet over the Council of Ministers is unchallengeable. It will be more correct to say that the Cabinet Ministers formulate policies, make decisions and draft Bills on all significant matters which in their judgement require legislative attention, asking of Parliament, only that it gives sanction to such decisions and policies by considering them and taking the necessary vote. The Cabinet really legislates with the advice and consent of Parliament. The time of summoning and prorogation of Parliament is decided by the Cabinet. Dissolution of Parliament, which decides the fate of various parties, is the decision of the Cabinet, though the Prime Minster of India like his British counterpart, exercises it is as a matter of right.

**Supreme Control of the Executive**

The Cabinet is not an Executive instrument in the sense that it possesses any legal powers. The Constitution vests the Executive authority in President, exercisable by him either directly or through officers subordinate to him. The real functionaries are the Ministers. Ministers preside over the Ministries of Government, and carry out the policy determined by the cabinet and approved by Parliament. In carrying out the work of their Ministries, Ministers, whether in the Cabinet or not, must faithfully follow the directions of the Cabinet in enforcing its decisions and

14. Article 235 as amended by the Constitution (Forty-fourth Amendment) Act, 1978, as also Article 358.

policies. Any deviation therefrom is against the rigid discipline of party government and, consequently, may lead to the removal of a Minister who defies the principle of party unity. The Cabinet is, thus, the supreme national Executive. It superintends, supervises and directs the work the Civil servants do all over the Union. All questions and problems which are likely to focus the attention of Parliament are considered in the Cabinet and decisions taken thereon to prevent a multiplicity of votes in important debates.

The power of delegated legislation has still more enhanced the Executive authority of the Cabinet and the Ministers. Legislation during recent times has become more voluminous and more technical and Parliament very often passes laws in skeleton form leaving it to the Council of Ministers or Ministers in charge of the appropriate Ministries to fill in the details and make Rules and Regulations in order to give effect to such laws.

**The Cabinet as a Co-ordinator**

The essential function of the cabinet is to co-ordinate and guide the functions of the several Ministries and Departments of Government. Administration cannot be rigidly divided into twenty or more Ministries. The actions of one Ministry may affect the work of another Ministry. In fact, every important problem cuts across departmental boundaries, and the Cabinet performs the vital task of co-ordinating policy. On purely inter-departmental matters endeavour is made by the Ministries to resolve their differences and reach agreement. If no agreement can be reached, then, the Prime Minister acts as an arbitrator and co-ordinator. In the last resort, the appeal is to the Cabinet. The Minister who does not agree to the Cabinet decision must resign. This means not only the linking of specific administrative decisions by reference to a general policy, but the expression of the same general policy in legislation.

The emergence of the Cabinet and the increased problem of co-ordination in the context of the Welfare State and implementation of Five-Year Plans have brought about a significant expansion in the work of the Cabinet Secretariat. The Cabinet Secretariat takes down and circulates the decision of the Cabinet, its Committees and Sub-committees. It circulates the agenda and the background papers to Cabinet Ministers. The Prime Minister and the Chairmen of the Cabinet Committees now primarily rely upon the corps of their expert assistants in the Cabinet Secretariat to supply them with the requisite information and advice in integrating the work of the different Ministries. There are also the Committees of the Secretaries of the Ministries which meet periodically under the chairmanship of the Cabinet Secretary, to advise the Cabinet on problems of interministerial consultation and co-ordination.

**Control over Finance**

Two more functions may be added to those enumerated above. The first is that the Cabinet is responsible for the whole expenditure of the State and for raising necessary revenues to meet it. In Britian, the annual Budget statement is excluded from the scope of the Cabinet decisions. But being a matter of political importance, it is always brought before the Cabinet and the Chancellor of the Exchequer makes an oral statement about it a few days before his Budget speech. On the estimates the control of the Cabinet is complete. If there are new proposals to taxation policy they must be considered at length by the Cabinet before the Budget is produced. In India, too, the Cabinet does not discuss the Budget. But the Finance Minister generally keeps his colleagues in the picture so far as a proposal may affect matters which come within their purview. The final decision is that of the Finance Minister. The detailed taxation proposals are shown to the Prime Minister. The Prime Minister may take one or more of his senior colleagues in his confidence and direct the Finance Minister to do so. But the proposals are divulged to the Cabinet only on the day when the Finance Minister is to make his budget speech in Parliament. The Cabinet can, however, examine the Budget proposals after it has been presented to Parliament and insist on modifications. It can even overthrow it altogether, but this may be done only at the risk of the resignation of the Finance Minister and damage to the prestige of the Government. If the secrecy of the Budget is to be ensured, then, the Finance Minister, as British Prime Minister Anthony Eden, said, "is wise if he shares his burdens to some extent with the Prime Minister," but "clearly he cannot share them with the whole Cabinet."

C. Rajagopalachari severely criticised the Budget procedure followed in India. Commenting upon the Budget proposals for 1963- 64 which imposed an additional taxation burden of Rs. 275 crores in a single year, he said, "The way in which budgets are made and got ready for presentation leaves no room for the whole or material section of the Cabinet to examine and advise upon it, or even to go through it. In order to safeguard secrecy all consultation is avoided. The Budget is hatached by the officials working under the nominal guidance of the Finance Minister.'' If both the Prime Minster and the Finance Minster, he added, happened to be persons ''blissfully ignorant of the business of the budget-making, when all the economy of the county comes under the direct or indirect influence of the budget; the consequences are, what we see now, disastrous.''

**Control over Appointments**

Appointments do not normally come before the Cabinet for discussion. But all major appointments, such as those of Governors and other appointments to the key positions, must be mentioned in the Cabinet before they are made public. This is tantamount to seeking the approval of the Cabinet though as a matter of reality it may be a sheer formality. But the control of the Cabinet is obviously there.

## THE PRIME MINISTER

**Office of the Prime Minister**

The powers and functions of the Prime Ministers of India and Britain are to a great extent similar as both these offices are the product of a Parliamentary system of government. Both are central to the formation of the governments of their countries, central to their lives and central to their death. Lord Morley's description that the Prime Minister is the ''keystone of the Cabinet arch'' is a classical exposition, but he also added that the Prime Minister could assume powers not inferior to that of a dictator so long as he enjoyed the confidence of the House of Commons. The Indian Prime Minister, Mrs. Indira Gandhi, assumed this role after declaring internal Emergency. But whatever be the magnitude of the authority of the British Prime Minister, he can never be a ''grand vazier'' as Gladstone declared. Harold Wilson, former Labour Prime Minister, described the role of the Premier as ''conducting an orchestra and not playing instrument himself.'' Mrs. Gandhi played the instrument herself and the rest danced to the tune she produced.

In some other important aspects, too, both these offices differ from one another. The office of the Prime Minister of India is created by the Constitution and his role, though not precisely defined, is statutorily made manifest. The office of the British Prime Minister is the result of sheer chance and accident and the role he plays in the body politic of the country is the consequence of slow and steady growth beginning from Walpole. It is, again, the result of a convention that the British Prime Minister belongs to the House of Commons to which Chamber the Ministry is answerable.[15] It is also a convention that the Ministers of one Chamber have no access to the other Chamber and take part in the discussions of the other House. The Indian Constitution does not say whether the Prime Minister should belong to the House of the People or to either House or be a Member of Parliament at all. But conventions and the basic requirements of a responsible government do demand that he should be a member of the representative House at the time of his appointment.

Though the first Lord of the Treasury, the British Prime Minister does not hold charge of any particular department, he confines himself to general supervision and overall control of the Government. But in India, Prime Ministers have invariably held charge of some Ministry or Ministries. Nehru headed the External Affairs Ministry and the Atomic Energy Department. Shastri took over the portfolio formerly held by Nehru, but within six weeks of his assumption of office he gave up the External Affairs for reasons of health. Mrs. Indira Gandhi retained for herself only the Department of Atomic Energy in 1966 and afterwards had with her Planning, Electronics and Space in addition to Atomic Energy. Morarji Desai retained Planning and other Departments held by Mrs. Gandhi. Mrs. Gandhi during her second innings in 1980, held charge, *inter alia* of Defence, Mines and Planning but afterwards gave up Defence retaining Atomic Energy, Space, Science and Technology. In addition to the portfolios inherited by Rajiv Gandhi from his mother he was also a Minster for Defence for sometime, and then, took over finance when V. P. Singh was switched over to the Defence in February 1987. In the Cabinet reshuffle on July 25, 1987, the Foreign Minister was assigned Finance and the Prime Minister took over foreign Affairs from him. The practice is now so firmly entrenched that all Prime Ministers have held charge of quite a number of Departments.

15. Since 1903 no Peer has been appointed as the Prime Minister, except Lord Home in 1963. But within ten days after his appointment he renounced peerage.

Chandra Shekhar had at one stage charge of as many as twenty-three Departments. A more or less similar pattern remained with Narasimha Rao.

**Appointment of the Prime Minister**

The Constitution is silent how the President shall choose the Prime Minister. It does not also say whether he should necessarily belong to the House of the People or may be a member of either House of Parliament. If the letter of the law is to be followed strictly, a Prime Minister may be appointed without his being a member of either House of Parliament, as P.V. Narasimha Rao was, for a period of six months and after the expiry of that period he must seek election to either House. But this shall be against the theory and practice of the Parliamentary system of government as it vitiates the principle of ministerial responsibility. The convention is that the Head of the State summons the leader of the Party or group commanding a majority in the House of the People to form a Ministry. It would be immaterial whether the Party is a single Party or a coalition and if a coalition whether formed before or after the election. If no Party has a majority, the President should ordinarily exercise discretion and summon the leader of a party or group most likely to be able to form a Ministry. Where the former governing Party had lost its majority, the President should call upon the leader of the Opposition Party to form a Ministry even if it is smaller in number than the former governing Party. This rule is based on the principle which requires the mandate of the electorate is to be respected. but this rule can apply only if there is a reasonable possibility of the minority Opposition Party being able to form the Ministry and to carry on the Government by commanding a majority in the House.

However, appointment of Charan Singh as Prime Minister was bad by any canon of constitutional propriety and it evoked widespread criticism bringing the institution of Presidency into the arena of party politics.[16] On July 15, 1979, Prime Minister Desai submitted "his own resignation" and that of his "Council of Ministers" to the President, because the Janata Party had lost the absolute majority in the House of the People and, at the same time, informed him that his Party continued "to be the largest singly Party" in the House. Desai had expected that the President would invite him as leader of the single largest Party in the House to form the new government. But the President asked Y.B. Chavan, the Leader of the Opposition in the House of the People, to explore the possibilities of forming a government. Chavan reported to the President his failure to form an alternative government. The President, then, wrote identical letters to Morarji Desai and Charan Singh to prove their claims to form a Ministry. Desai subsequently resigned from the leadership of the Janata Party when he found that the list of his supporters submitted to the President included the names of some Congressmen and also retired form active politics. The Janata Party, then, elected Jagjivan Ram as its new leader.

Desai's complaint against the President that he was not fair to him and that he was bound to call him first, instead of Y.B. Chavan, to form a new government since he headed the largest single party in the House of the People was not tenable. Morarji Desai had no right to be an aspirant for the office by virtue of having resigned, when the Janata Party had been reduced in strength as a result of internal dissensions in the Party, in the face of the no-confidence motion moved by the leader of the Opposition which had acquired certainty of success. Sir Ivor Jennings in his classic *Cabinet Government* clarified the point. After making an unaswerable case for asking the Leader of the Opposition to form a new government no sooner the Government was defeated whether at the polls or in the House, Jennings made the proviso that "Where a Government resigns owing to internal dissensions it does not necessarily follow that the Opposition must take office." The Queen "must ascertain the views of all interested parties" and she is entitled "to consult whom she pleases, and the precedents give her full liberty."

The Janata Party was reduced in its strength as a result of its internal dissensions and its leader could not be invited to form a government even if it was the largest single Party in the House so long as its leader remained Morarji Desai and against whose stewardship the Party broke up in protest resulting into a certain defeat on a motion of no confidence. Desai would have resigned from the leadership of the Party simultaneously with his own and that of his Council of Ministers' resignation. But Desai defied the well-established and recognised conventions of the Parliamentary system of government and retained the

16. Refer to Chapter VIII. *ante*.

leadership till circumstances compelled him to quit and retire from active politics. There would have been a greater merit in the Janata case if Desai would have relinquished the leadership to give a new leader a chance to try his luck.

Equally serious was Charan Singh's disqualification who sabotaged his own Government and then himself defected when Parliament was not in session. Consistent with standard of political morality Charan Singh would not have been in the running for Prime Ministership. At the time of the adjournment of Parliament he was part of Desai's Government (Deputy Prime Minister No. 1) and he defected, when Parliament was not in session, to a party which had not been recognised by Parliament and engineered to become its leader. But it was Charan Singh's ambition of life to become the Prime Minister of India and he seized the opportunity by claiming a majority only on the strength of support from the Congress headed by Indira Gandhi. By ignoring the claim of Jagjivan Ram that he could establish his majority at the floor of the House and appointing Charan Singh as Prime Minister, the President elevated opportunism "to the status of national policy." It was also betrayal of the electorate for the Janata conglomeration won the 1977 Parliamentary election as well as Assembly elections in the nine North States on the platform of ending authoritarianism whose undisputed symbol, they held, was Mrs. Gandhi. By consorting with her merely to achieve power and to fulfil the ambition of his life, Charan Singh showed utter contempt for the electorate on whose mandate he and others of the erstwhile Lok Dal Members had been elected.

The best course for the President was if neither of the two contenders, Desai and Charan Singh, would have been asked to establish their claims to form an alternative government. If not for any other reason, it would have been just punishment for unscrupulous politicians for their petty manoeuvres. And when Desai had resigned from the leadership of the Janata Parliamentary Party, there was no other choice for the President but to give chance to the new leader of the Janata Party when Jagjivan Ram had offered himself to substantiate his majority on the floor of the House. His failure to prove his credentials would have saved the Presidency from disrespect and no *mala fide* would have been hurled on Neelam Sanjiva Reddy.

The appointment of Rajiv Gandhi on October 31, 1984, after the assassination of Mrs. Indira Gandhi, even before he was elected leader of the Congress Parliamentary Party was clearly an exercise of President's discretion. Some eyebrows were raised as it violated the established convention governing the appointment of a Prime Minister in such a contingency, that is, the sudden death of the Prime Minister and when there is no Deputy Prime Minister or the party had not elected its leader. The Opposition parties and the commentators remarked that Rajiv Gandhi regarded it as his "natural right" to succeed his mother and Gyani Zail Singh has his own explanation to offer in electing Rajiv Gandhi. He told Pritish Nandy, editor of the *Illustrated Weekly of India*, "Look, everyone knows how much I loved Jawaharlal Nehru and Indira Gandhi. I would do anything for them. Yet, the nation was more important to me. So I spent a lot of effort trying to genuinely assess Rajiv before I swore him in. I didn't let my love for Nehru family overwhelm my love for the nation. Rajiv's sweetness and simplicity appealed to me. He seemed a man capable of leading the nation and appealing to the masses. He was gentle, soft spoken, decent."[17]

### Role of the Prime Minister

The Prime Minister is the keystone of the Cabinet arch. In his hand is the key of the government. His functions and duties are wide and his authority enormous. K.T. Shah expressed apprehension in the Constituent Assembly about the concentration of power in the Prime Minister and said that such a concentration of power "may very likely militate against the working of the real responsible and democratic government."[18] Not in identical terms, Ambedkar too admitted that the Prime Minister is by far the most powerful man in the country. He maintained, "if any functionary under our constitution is to be compared with the United States President, he is the Prime Minister and not the President of the Union."[19] The comparison between the Prime Minister and the American President is not apt as both these offices belong to two distinct and opposite systems. Yet it cannot be denied that the Prime Minister commands a pivotal position and the entire Cabinet system revolves around his office.

17. *The Illustrated Weekly of India*, Bombay, July 19-25, 1987, pp. 12-13.
18. *Constituent Assembly Debates*, Vol. VIII, pp. 114-46.
19. *Ibid*., p. 998.

There is positive provision in the Constitution conferring so vast powers on the Prime Minister, but the spirit of the Constitution and the principles on which it is based are as cogent sources of authority as specific provision in the Constitution.

The Prime Minister forms the Council of Ministers, determines its sizes, decides the persons to be included in the Council of Ministers, names the Ministers to constitute the Cabinet and allocates offices. He may even select his colleagues from outside the ranks of his Party, as Nehru did in 1950.There is nothing in the Constitution which may bind the Prime Minister in the selection of his team to make the Council of Ministers. But there are certain political considerations, party obligations, geographical considerations and representation of various minorities, which no Prime Minister can venture to ignore. Mrs. Gandhi put at the top considerations of personal loyalty during her difficult days in forming her 1980 Council of Ministers. There are some leaders in every Party whose ranking is so high, their influence and following so dominating and personality so towering that their inclusion in the Council of Ministers is taken for granted even though the Prime Minister may be keen to exclude them. Similarly, in the allocation of portfolios they may demand what they wish to have and the Prime Minister has no choice but to yield. They may safely decline what is given, if the assignment is deemed not consistent with their standing in the Party or even liking. Vallabhbhai Patel would have accepted nothing short of Home Affairs, State and Broadcasting. T. T. Krishnamachari declined to rejoin the Cabinet after the 1962 elections unless he was given the Finance Ministry, though he joined later as Minister of Economic Production, very soon to step into the Finance Ministry.

It is the undisputed right of the Prime Minister to shuffle and reshuffle his pack as and when he likes. He is free in the exercise of his judgment to make such appointments as may seem appropriate to him for the stability, effectiveness and efficiency of the Government. He has the unfettered right to review, from time to time, the allocation of offices among the various Ministers and to decide whether that allocation still remained the best that could be effected. In July 1965, S.K. Patil resisted Nehru to shift him from Ministry of Food to Railways. But once he resigned under the Kamraj Plan, which really was a device to get rid of inconvenient Ministers whom otherwise Nehru was hesitant to remove, it was his final exit from the Council of Ministers. In July, 1969, Mrs. Indira Gandhi deprived Morarji Desai of the Finance Ministry and left him to continue as Deputy Prime Minister alone, the position he did not accept and resigned. In accepting Desai's resignation the Prime Minister asserted her unfettered right to allocate offices as she deemed best. In 1970, she shifted Y.B. Chavan from Home to Finance and Dinesh Sigh from External Affairs to the Minister of Industrial Development to be finally dropped in 1971. Mrs. Gandhi reshuffled her Council of Ministers six times between 1971 and 1974, minor changes apart. On the sixth reshuffle, October 19, 1974, she changed the portfolios of her senior colleagues and dropped five. Morarji Desai made minimal changes during his tenure of twenty-seven months whereas Mrs. Gandhi did it twice during the first eleven months of her office in 1980 and many more followed with a major reshuffle in February 1983. Rajiv Gandhi holds record. During the first two-and-a-half years of his tenure in office, he shuffled and reshuffled his Council of Ministers nine times.

Both as a captain of the team and head of the administration, it is the prerogative of the Prime Minister to ask anyone of his colleagues, whose presence in the Ministry is deemed prejudicial to the stability, efficiency, integrity or policy of the Government, to resign. If he defaults, he may be dismissed. Mohan Dharia was virtually dismissed on March 2, 1975 for his public utterances supporting Jayaprakash Narayan's movement in Bihar. The Prime Minister wrote to Dharia that his retention in the Council of Ministers was no longer possible and that the President was being advised accordingly. Dharia, immediately after receiving the Prime Minister's letter resigned. Divesting Morarji Desai of his Financial portfolio without even informing him earlier had a ring of dismissal, though the Prime Minister did not tell it specifically. Morarji Desai wrote separate letters to Charan Singh and Raj Narain on June 29, 1979 to withdraw from the Cabinet. Mrs. Gandhi silently dropped her trusted lieutenants V. C. Shukla, Kamalpati Tripathi and Kedar Pandey. Vishawnath Pratap Singh, Defence Minister in Rajiv Gandhi's Government resigned in April 1987. It was a well-calculated move on the part of V.P. Singh the implications of which were not understood then. V. P. Singh dropped his own creator and the Deputy Prime

Minister Devilal as he had established himself a scheming rival.

The Prime Minister possesses the power of dissolution. Dissolution of the House of the People means that the members hold their seats in the House at the mercy of the Prime Minister's use of this "terrifying power", for it entails new elections with all the uncertainties and vicissitudes involved in election. The threat of dissolution, thus, always hangs like a sword of Damocles. On December 7, 1970 the President dissolved the House of the People on the advice of the Prime Minister. 1971 Parliamentary elections returned the Congress with a massive majority. Mrs. Gandhi again advised the President to dissolve the House of the People in January 1977. The following elections in March 1977 swung the pendulum against the Congress uprooting it in North India. Mrs. Gandhi also lost the election. In August 1979 Charan Singh advised the President to dissolve the House of the People and order new elections. The advice tendered by the Prime Minister was variously criticised as it came from a person who could not face the House of the People to receive its mandate. Even the action of the President was criticised in dissolving the House. New elections were held in January 1980 and Mrs. Gandhi's Congress was returned with massive majority.

As Chairman of the Cabinet, the Prime Minister attracts "special kind of loyalty, engendered by the vague feeling that business is expedited and improved by order and that one must be prepared to suffer the chairman's ruling for the sake of the collective enterprise."[20] Ministers may differ behind closed doors, but they must finally agree if party solidarity is to be maintained and collective responsibility ensured. The possibilities of disagreement are, indeed, rare. A difference between two Ministers or Ministries can be settled by private consultation or by arbitration by the Prime Minister. If differences emerge out of the Cabinet discussions the chairman of the Cabinet occupies a position of pre-eminence which enables him to impose the decision. Moreover, the Prime Minister is the leader of the Parliamentary Party and his fifteen or more colleagues in the Cabinet owe him a personal allegiance and party loyalty. He also controls the agenda for the Cabinet meetings. It is for the Prime Minister to accept or reject proposals for Cabinet discussion, but no Prime Minister will like to embarrass himself by a complaining colleague that an important matter was not placed on the agenda, especially when the Party in power, as the Janata was, a combination of heterogeneous constituent units with no common ideology to bind them and guide their actions, or minority Government, as at present headed by P.V. Narasimha Rao, wherein every single member constitutes the strength of Government and ensures its stability.

The Prime Minister is the Manager-in-Chief of the Government's business. He supervises and co-ordinates policies of the several Ministers and Ministries. He must see the Government as a whole and bring the variety of governmental activities into reasonable relationship with one another. It is, however, not possible for a Prime Minister in any part of the democratic world to exercise his control and supervision over all the Ministries and Departments of the Government. The province of the state, too, has vastly expanded. The responsibilities of the Prime Minister have, therefore, tremendously increased and are being shared by his colleagues, who constitute the inner Cabinet and the work of co-ordination is done by various Committees of the Cabinet. Still, the Prime Minister is supposed to exercise a general supervision over all Ministries and Departments and he has the right to be consulted on all matters important or minor, controversial or otherwise. B.K. Kaul, Principal Private Secretary to the Prime Minister in his examination before the Public Accounts Committee, on a question about the supervisory functions of the Prime Minister, said, "The Minister-in-charge of each Ministry is responsible for the affairs of the Ministry. Under the Cabinet system of government, the minister is the highest person-in-charge of a Ministry. He is directly responsible to the Prime Minister." When asked, cannot the Prime Minister sit in judgment over other Ministers, he replied, "He can. Ultimately the Prime Minister is responsible."[21]

Apart from the overall supervision of the administration of the Union Government, the Prime Minister exercises special responsibility towards foreign, defence, finance, home and economic affairs. He may not hold charge of the Foreign Affairs Ministry, but his control over the foreign policy and in the appointment of diplo-

20. Finer, Herman, *The Theory and Practice of Government*, p. 592.
21. Public Accounts Committee 1952-53, Seventh Report on Appropriation Accounts (Civil), 1949-50, Vol. II, Evidence, pp. 21-22.

matic missions is unchallengeable. He is the spokesman of the Government on all international matters and every statement he makes and every word he utters is searched for meaning in foreign offices throughout the world. The Prime Minister's figure looms large in world. Nehru was his own Foreign Minister. Shastri and Mrs. Gandhi retained this Ministry for a brief period and so was Rajiv Gandhi. But the Tashkent Agreement was on Shastri's own initiative supported by a few Ministers and Civil Servants present on the occasion. Mrs. Gandhi was primarily responsible for taking decisions on such grave issues as the Indo-Soviet Treaty and Bangladesh. Rajiv Gandhi himself was responsible for Indo-Sri Lanka accord.

Similarly, the relation of the Prime Minister with the Defence Ministry is close and active. During war the responsibility for defence and foreign affairs essentially devolve upon the Prime Minister assisted by the Defence Minister, Foreign Affairs Minister and the Chiefs of Staff. Nehru himself made the decision on ceasefire with Pakistan in 1947 and to take the Kashmir issue to the United Nations. The conduct of the two more wars with Pakistan in 1965 and 1971 was guided by Shastri and Mrs. Gandhi and the credit for victory on both the occasions went to the two Prime Ministers.

No less is the Prime Minister's hold on the economic affairs. He must always have a full grasp of important policies and programmes, like land reforms, industrial advancement and production, food, irrigation, prices and other problems of identical importance. The Prime Minister is the chairman of the Planning Commission and the National Development Council. Mrs. Indira Gandhi was the author of the Twenty-point Economic Programme which formed the hub of economic policy of her Government. Rajiv Gandhi gave a new orientation to the programme and its progress was regularly monitored at the highest level. The policy of industrial liberlisation and other economic reforms initiated by the Congress (I) Government in June 1991 were the child of Narasimha Rao himself, though formally endorsed by the Cabinet.

By the same token internal peace and security of India is the basic responsibility of the Union Government and in pursuance of it Mrs. Indira Gandhi declared internal Emergency in June 1975 on her own initiative and informed the Cabinet of it the next day. The Punjab, Assam and Mizoran accords were the result of Rajiv Gandhi's own determination. There might have been private consultations with his close confidants but none of them was the result of a Cabinet decision. It is generally the decision of the Prime Minister to determine whether the Government of a State be carried on in accordance with the provisions of the Constitution and action under Article 356 should be taken or not. The appointments of the State Governors and judges of the Supreme Court and High Courts, subject to the constitutional requirements, are made by the Prime Minister.

The Prime Minister is the leader of the House of the People. All principal announcements of policy and business of the Government are made by him and all questions of non-departmental affairs and critical issues relating to national and international matters are addressed to the Prime Minister. The Prime Minister initiates and intervenes in debates of general importance and also possesses an immediate authority to correct what he may regard as the errors of omission and commission of his colleagues in the Council of Ministers. Nehru appeased an angry House of the People by promising an immediate inquiry when the Food Minister vainly tried to assure the House that it need not feel concerned over the fertilizers. When the Law Minister introduced the Representation of the People's Bill at the fag-end of the session of Parliament and hinted at further legislation by the President during the recess it angered the House. The Prime Minister intervened and promised that it would only be done by Parliament and, if necessary, the session of Parliament might be lengthened. With Nehru the Opposition parties, though ineffective, enjoyed influence and the Prime Minister's strength rested not only on the majority that the Congress Party commanded, but from both sides of Paliament. There was, however, a serious breach between Mrs. Gandhi and the Opposition after 1971. Between November, 1969 and February, 1971 the minority Government headed by Mrs. Gandhi yielded on many occasions to the Opposition pressures. After the 1971 electoral majority the rift between the Government and Opposition became more sharp. It is true that the Opposition, too, behaved irresponsibly and harassed the Government sometimes ruthlessly. But Mrs. Gandhi and her colleagues completely ignored the Opposition parties, except the Communist Party, and even questioned the relevance of Opposition in India. Morarji Desai, on the other hand, consulted the Opposition on all important matters and an attempt was made to reach a consensus on national issues, such as the election of the President and the anti-defection legislation. The Leader of the Opposition enjoyed the status of a Minister. But the cleavage between the ruling Congress (I) Party, after it came into office in January 1980, and the Opposition parties had become alarming. The frustrated Opposition parties mauled by the electorate with no possibility of return to power in the very near future together adopted the attitude of confrontation at every step with the Government. They were so vertically and horizontally divided that they could not agree on a common programme to present a united Opposition, but they readily joined hands together to agitate against the Government without the slightest consideration to national interests. Their meeting point was to hunt out Mrs. Gandhi from office.

Rajiv Gandhi took the Opposition parties into confidence and tried to ascertain their views and reactions on important national and international issues. He consulted the various Opposition parties if a consensus candidate could be agreed to for the eighth Presidential election. But the Opposition was in complete disarray. A regional partly. Telugu Desam, was the main Opposition group in the House of the People. Quite a number of conferences and conclaves were convened to form an alternative party to the Congress and even a confederation of the parties was suggested, but unity could not be forged. Confrontation with the Government remained their point of agreement on the floor of the House or the threats to take the issues to the streets as the Bharatiya Janata Party frequently resorted to. Non-Congress Chief Ministers in their meeting on April 25, 1987 decided to conduct mass movements in their respective States on issues directly affecting the people and to press for greater reform of Centre-State relations though all the issues involved therein were pending with the Sarkaria Commission which had submitted its Report but the Government was to consider it before taking any final decision. A minority Government can ill-afford to ignore the opposition and consensus is the keynote of Narasimha Rao's Government. The Opposition too refrains from taking any bold decision and oust the Government from office so soon after the two General Elections within a short span of eleven months.

The Prime Minister is the channel of communication with the President on matters of public importance and the Constitution itself establishes this channel when Article 78 prescribes it a duty of the Prime Minister that he should communicate to the President the decisions of the Cabinet and provide information that he needs. It also enjoins on the Prime Minister to provide to the President such information relating to the administration of the affairs of the Union and the proposals for legislation that the President may call for. It is inconceivable that in the discharge of what are laid down as the *duties* of the Prime Minister to the President, the Council of Ministers—in effect the Prime Minister—should be the determining authority and that it should be vested with unfettered discretion on the nature and timing of the information to be submitted to the President. Article 74(1), which provides that the President in the exercise of his functions shall act in accordance with the advice of the Council of Ministers, cannot be read so as to reduce other provisions of the Constitution to a nullity.

But the nature and extent of information required and sought by the President, under Article 78, is obviously subject to the test of relevance and reasonableness and must not be interpreted in a fundamentalist or overweening way. This right to information is indeed a necessary adjunct to the President's playing his constitutional role effectively. The President is envisaged to represent the nation, ensuring that the rules of the Constitutional game and 'fair play' are observed. He is also entitled to advise and caution the Government, though obviously what impact the advice will have depends on the holder of the office and how much the Council of Ministers and Parliament respect his wisdom, sagacity and integrity.

The Prime Minister is the chief adviser of the President and in emergencies, he or she will consult him, though there was a breach when Mrs. Indira Gandhi presented the Proclamation declaring internal Emergency in June 1975 without prior consultation with the President. Nor did she brief the President on the "Blue Star Operation." He learnt it from the news bulletin broadcast by the All-India Radio. Rajiv Gandhi did not consult him on the various accords he concluded.

The patronage exercised by the Prime Minster is enormous. All major appointments are really made by him. In the course of making such appointments, he, no doubt, receives the advice of his colleagues, but the ultimate choice belongs to him.

The general election is in reality the election of the Prime Minister. The slogan in the

1952, 1957 and 1962 General Election was "to vote for the Congress and strengthen the hands of Nehru." The Congress and Nehru had become synonymous. He had no visible grip on the Party machine, but his sway over the people was greater and more absolute than that of any other democratic statesman elsewhere. Writing about Prime Minister Nehru, Hiren Mukherjee, the Communist M.P., said, "If to a public figure nothing is more rewarding than the love of his people, Jawahar Lal Nehru has been one of the most fortunate persons in creation. Apart from Gandhiji, no one, in India has been recipient in recent decades, of such abounding love—and, while the Mahatma commanded a sort of reverence, Nehru has evoked the people's affection. Even Subhash Chandra Bose, in some ways a more dynamic person, lacked the secret of Jawaharlal's personal fascination for all varieties of people."[22] K.R. Srinivsa Iyengar, writing under the caption : *The Prime Minster,* observed "when he (Nehru) enters an assembly, be it a Select Committee or a mass rally, the effect is invariably the same. All eyes converge towards him, all hands clasp in eager affectionate welcome as if to a preordained tune, and a hushed expectancy watches his intrepid movements and strains to catch his words and whispers. The men are a little out of breath, the women are almost overwhelmed."[23] Prime Minster Nehru was, thus, the virtual leader of his Party and he towered above all in national stature. In fact, he had acquired world stature and even his bitter political adversaries acclaimed him as such. "May this gentle colossus," prayed Hiren Mukherjee, "stride the Indian scene for as long as we care to foresee in the future."[24]

The Prime Minister moulds and guides public opinion by receiving deputations and discusses issues, by public speeches at party conferences, and on other important occasions which demand proper attention. The role which a Prime Minster played in assuming leadership of the party depends upon his personality, his prestige and even his strategy. Jennings says, "since his personality and prestige play a considerable part in moulding public opinion he ought to have something of the popular appeal of a film actor and he must take some care over his make up—like Mr. Gladstone with his collars, Mr. Lloyd George with his hair, Mr. Baldwin with his pipes and Mr. Churchill with his cigar." Nehru and the nation were personified. In the beginning of her career as Prime Minister, Mrs. Indira Gandhi's assets were her youth, her strong sense of duty and her unquestioned dedication to the country's interests and good. She had a hold on the people's imagination. After the nationalisation of 14 major Banks in July, 1969, Mrs. Gandhi's popularity ran at a peak according to a Gallup Poll reported by E.P.W. Da Costa.[25] The survey conducted by him disclosed that in August 1969, her peak popularity rose to 71 as compared to 45 in October 1966 and 41 in August-September 1967. "This is high," said da Costa, "but short of the Indian peak of 97 which Lal Bahadur Shastri reached after 22-day hostilities in 1965. Nevertheless, the ascent from 41 to her peak figure of 71 is a clear indication that the Prime Minister has emerged in the arena of India's most popular leaders which includes her father and Lal Bahadur Shastri." It proved true in the mid-term 1971 elections to the House of the People, when she secured a massive mandate from the electorate for her policies and programmes. The manner in which she dealt with the Bangladesh issue and the successful end of war with Pakistan within a brief period of two weeks evoked widespread respect for her and raised Mrs. Gandhi's stature as Prime Minister to unprecedented heights. There was "Indira Wave", as described in terms of politics.

But her popularity waned after 1973. This swing can be attributed to diverse factors, but importantly to the uncertain and instable economic conditions in the country and the never-ending price rise which completely disillusioned the people. All this was coupled with Jayaprakash Narayan's movement in Bihar and his tirade against the Prime Minister herself. The Opposition parties, more especially the Congress (O), seized the opportunity under Jayaprakash's umbrella with the avowed object of defaming Mrs. Gandhi and dislodging her from office. Even Jayaprakash Narayan gave a call for her removal from office and branded her as an unabashed dictator and the leader of corruption and other malpractices who had amassed wealth from questionable quarters. Finally, came the Allahabad High Court judgment on June 12, 1975, which

22. "Symposium on Nehru," *The Illustrated Weekly of India,* Bombay, August 16, 1959.
23. *The Hindustan Times,* Sunday Magazine, November 13, 1953, p. 1.
24. "Symposium on Nehru", *The Illustrated Weekly of India,* Bombay, August 16, 1989.
25. *The Hindustan Times,* New Delhi, August 28, 1969.

disqualified her to hold an elective post for a period of six years.

Just thirteen days after the Allahabad High Court judgment, the country was brought under a state of internal Emergency. No other office under the Constitution suffered so much damage as did that of the Prime Minister of India. On January 18, 1977, Mrs. Indira Gandhi advised the President to dissolve the House of the People (Lok Sabha) and order fresh elections. The Opposition Parties formed a common Janata Front and contested the elections. The people, who had lost faith in Indira Gandhi's leadership and the Party she headed, withdrew their mandate. The Congress (I) was routed in North India and Mrs. Gandhi was defeated in her own Constituency which she had nursed so fondly all those years.

The nation looks to the Prime Minister for leadership. But it is the democratic leadership that the Prime Minister under a Cabinet system is called upon to provide; a leader of a team, ensuring that it functions as a team. It is the Prime Minister who tenders the advice of the Council of Ministers to the President. If the Prime Minister simply informs the Cabinet of such a vital matter as the declaration of Emergency and the subservient Cabinet endorses it without demur, there is neither team nor its captain. Ambedkar uttered the warning in the Constituent Assembly on November 25, 1949 as it concluded its labours. He told the Assembly members "to observe the caution which John Stuart Mill has given to all who are interested in the maintenance of democracy, namely, not to lay their liberties at the feet of even a great man, or trust him with powers which enable him to subvert their institutions." This caution, he added, was far more necessary in the case of India than in the case of any other country. "For in India *bhakti* or what may be called the path of devotion or hero-worship, plays a part in politics unequalled in magnitude by the part it plays in the politics of any other country in the world. *Bhakti* in religion may be a road to the salvation of the soul. But in politics, *bhakti* or hero-warship is a sure road to degradation and to eventual dictatorship.

Rajiv Gandhi succeeded his mother and in the January 1985 Parliamentary elections he swept to power on the kind of vote not even Jawaharlal Nehru and Mrs. Indira Gandhi received in their days. It was a rather indulgent electorate, caught in anxiety after Mrs. Gandhi's assassination, that placed Rajiv Gandhi on the high pedestal with over 400 seats in the House of the People. The young Prime Minster, at the age of 40, was idealized both by the people and the media. He was contemptuous of the run-of-the-mill Congressmen so much so that he called them power brokers at the Party's centenary celebrations in December 1985. He had sought to project himself "Mr. Clean" determined to carry the country to the twenty-first century by his innovative schemes and projects and dynamic government that would work "fast." He adopted a series of policies which were very different from Mrs. Gandhi's as in the case of accords in respect of Punjab, Assam and Mizoram. Much of the intelligentsia saw Rajiv Gandhi as a successor to Nehru and not to Mrs. Gandhi.

But within a short span of twenty-eight months of his assumption of office, his popularity began to subside. What is significant is the speed at which his popularity graph began dipping, particularly with the leakage of President Gyani Zail Singh's letter of March 9, 1987 to the Prime Minister closely followed by the Fairfax controversy, the result of the Assembly elections in the States of West Bengal and Kerala and then the controversial Bofors deal. The Opposition got hold of some issues on which it could embarrass the Government and it did well. Failure of the Punjab policy, the rout of the Congress (I) in the Haryana Assembly elections followed by expulsion of Vishawnath Pratap Singh from the Party to join Arun Nehru and Mohammed Arif Khan, his former Ministers, who had earlier been expelled for their anti-party activities, further worsened the image of Rajiv Gandhi and there was total loss of his credibility among the masses in general. Similarly, the United States' determination to step up military-cum-economic assistance to Pakistan and to ignore Islamabad's bid to acquire nuclear weapons capability was testimony to the collapse of Rajiv Gandhi's America policy. Questions about the durability of the Prime Minister's leadership and even the country's stability began to be asked. Former President Sanjiva Reddy was invited for consultation on the national problems by the Prime Minister in end May 1987. He told press persons that during his talks with the "Young Prime Minister" for over an hour they discussed many issues, but Rajiv Gandhi was not clear about the dimensions of the problems facing the country. He was "in a state of confused mind with regard to their solution." He further said, "I had been there to give a bit of my mind to Mr. Rajiv Gandhi in resolving the problems.......It is now for the Prime

Minister to consider them in the interest of the nation.''[26]

**Position of the Prime Minister**

This makes the position of the Prime Minister clear. An appraisal of the Indian Prime Minister's position under the Constitution was made by the Administrative Reforms Commission headed by Morarji Desai. Its report said : ''The Constitution accords the Prime Minister a special position in the executive machinery of Government. He is not only the head of the Council of Ministers—*pimus inter pares*—but also the President's principal adviser. The high position invests him with the special responsibility to see that the institution functions as a team, that the rule of collective responsibility is effectively enforced, that policies are made objectively and realistically after due study and deliberation and are motivated by the national interests, that they are implemented properly and effectively, that administration is responsive to the people's needs.''

But in actual practice the Prime Minister is not *primus inter pares;* not even in Britain. Discussing the position of the British Prime Minister, Herbert Morrison says, ''As the head of the Government he is *primus inter pares.* But it is today far too modest an appreciation of the Prime Minister's position.''[27] Jennings says that Prime Minister is not merely *primus inter pares*. He is not even *inter stellas luna minores* (a moon among lesser stars). ''He is rather, a sun around which planets revolve.''[28] The earlier conception of the Prime Minister as first among equals, *primus inter pares,* does not reflect the real difference in status and responsibility between the person who holds the first position, and is the Prime Minster, and even his senior colleagues. While refuting the charge of C.D. Deshmukh that the two crucial decisions on Bombay, which caused his resignation from the Council of Ministers, Nehru declared in the House of the People on July 30, 1956, ''After all, I am the Prime Minister of India and the Prime Minister is the Prime Minister. He can lay the policy of the Government........I know something of democratic procedure......I know something of what the Prime Minister's duties are and that in the Constitution the Prime Minister is the linchpin of the Government. To say that the Prime Minister cannot make a statement is a monstrous statement itself......I am something more than the Prime Minister of this country, and we are all something more. We are the children of Indian revolution.''[29]

The authority of the Prime Minister is great if he is keen to assert himself to the full position he occupies. The office of the Prime Minister in India is created by the Constitution and his authority carries with it constitutional sanction. In a judgment on the right of the Prime Minister to continue in office after Parliament had been dissolved, the Supreme Court held that to accept the plea that the Council of Ministers ceases to hold office ''would be to change the whole concept of the Executive. It would mean that the President need not have a Prime Minister to aid and advise him in the exercise of his functions.'' If Article 52 which provides that there shall be a President 'is mandatory,'' the Court ruled, ''so is Article 74 (1) which says that there shall be a Council of Ministers with the Prime Minister at the head to aid and advise the President in the exercise of his functions.'' While expressing no firm opinion on the plea of N.A. Palkhivala, Mrs. Indira Gandhi's counsel, that an absolute stay on the Allahabad High Court judgment disqualifying her to hold any elective post should be granted as the theory of balance of convenience was in her favour, Justice Krishna Iyer observed, ''The Prime Minister is the central figure who decides crucial internal and external policy........Although collective Cabinet responsibility was the essence of the democratic process, the personality of Prime Minister has a telling effect on democratic government. (Therefore) the balance of convenience would be in favour of continuance of the same team (Council of Ministers) which was animated by the presence of the key personality within the Council of Ministers.''

The Prime Minister is the king-pin in the system of Cabinet Government. On him rests the entire machinery of administration : its stability and policy continuity. To defy his authority and challenge his position is suicidal to the political ambition of a Minister unless the Prime Minister has handled his job so badly that there is a widespread feeling of his unfitness for it. Nehru even thought of dismissing Sardar Patel. It was reported that the Prime Minister told his Deputy

26. *The Hindu,* New Delhi, June 2, 1987.
27. Morrison, H., *Government and Parliament,* p. 97.
28. Jennings, W.I., *Cabinet Government,* p. 183.
29. Brecher, Michael, *Nehru, A Political Biography,* p. 485.

that he had the right to select his colleagues and he could dismiss him if his views differed from the policy of the Cabinet.[30] Ambedkar resigned from the Government and complained in the statement of his resignation that many Ministers had been given three or four portfolios so that "they had been overburdened. Others like me have been wanting more work. I have not been considered even for holding a portfolio temporarily when a minister-in-charge has gone abroad for a few days." Nehru accepted the resignations of Morarji Desai, S.K. Patil, Lal Bahadur Shastri, Jagjivan Ram, K.K. Shrimali and Gopala Reddy under the Kamraj Plan because it provided him an opportunity to get rid of some or the incompetent inconvenient colleagues whom he was hesitant to remove in the normal way. Lal Bahadur Shastri and Jagjivan Ram were dropped in order to keep up an appearance of impartiality in accepting these resignations. Morarji Desai had to quit unceremoniously from Mrs. Gandhi's Cabinet as Charan Singh and Raj Narain had to do from Morarji Desai's Cabinet. Similar was the fate of V.C. Shukla and Kamalapati Tripathi in 1981, Kedar Pandey in 1983 and Ghani Khan Chowdhry in May 1987. V.P. singh dismissed his Deputy Prime Minister Devi lal.

After Lal Bahadur Shastri's election as leader of the Congress Parliamentary Party an impression went round that he would be just an equal in the Cabinet and would always consult on all matters of importance not only his ministerial colleagues, but also the President of the Congress Party and its other leaders who had helped him in his election. Shastri immediately scotched all such conjectures. In a statement made at Nagpur on June 16, 1964 he said, "I cannot effectively function as Prime Minister of India if I yield to any pressure from any quarter." Kamraj had openly stressed the necessity of building a "collective leadership" to fill the gap created by the demise of Nehru, a charismatic figure. But as events proved Shastri was, in the words of Frank Moraes, "nobody's puppet". He did not live long enough "to put the issue of his overriding authority as Prime Minister to test but before his death, he had indicated the drift of his mind. He was not willing to fit snugly into the framework of a cosy collective leadership, or to adapt himself to rule by consensus.[31]

Mrs. Indira Gandhi inherited all those disabilities when she succeeded Shastri. She had the added disadvantage of age too. The top leadership of the Congress Party, responsible for her election as leader of the Parliamentary Party, deemed her succession as an interim arrangement. She, too, was rather shaky in the beginning, but with greater political stability, after the 1971 poll, Mrs. Gandhi showed signs of greater maturity and a new confident personality emerged. She succeeded in eclipsing her powerful colleagues in the Cabinet. The stature she attained after India's victory over Pakistan and the manner in which Bangladesh issue was resolved, Mrs. Gandhi would "brook no rival, and before her authority ministers cower. Among some, including Chavan and Jagjivan Ram, subservience is possibly explained by the fact that at one time or the other the Prime Minister has caught these veteran war horses prancing on the wrong foot in the wrong pastures."[32] Mrs. Gandhi revived the inner or "kitchen" cabinet, the practice which Shastri had abandoned, in the very first year of her assumption of office. Dinesh Singh, C. Subramaniam and Ashoka Mehta were her close confidants. But there was a significant difference in the style of Nehru and Mrs. Gandhi's inner Cabinet. Nehru included in his inner Cabinet senior Ministers and the inner body was something like a "policy" or "partial" Cabinet.[33] But Mrs. Gandhi would trust her junior colleagues. She also received counsel from other trusted colleagues, Uma Shankar Dikshit and Durga Prasad Dhar, and from outside the Council of Ministers. D. P. Mishra, Nandini Satpathy, S.S. Ray, D. K. Barooah and Rajin Patel were her close confidants. She heavily leaned on her younger son Sanjay Gandhi and after his demise her elder son Rajiv Gandhi was her constant

30. Gadgil writes, "......the schism between the viewpoint of Vallabhbhai (Patel) and Nehru began to come to surface gradually. Nehru was displeased with a speech made by Vallabhbhai in Varanasi......The differences between them became sharper as time went on. It was rumoured then that Nehru had given a hint to Vallabhbhai through one of his confidants that he might have to go if he did not behave. I do not believe there could have been any such hint. But I know for certain that Nehru's favourites and sycophants were quite capable of creating such mischief." Gadgil, N.V., *Government from Inside*, p. 150.
31. Frank Moraes, *Witness to an Era*, p. 263.
32. *Ibid.*, p. 253.
33. Patel, Azad, Ayyangar, Kidwai, Desai, Menon and Shastri were its members at one time or the other. Nanda, Krishnamachari and Shastri formally assisted him in the last months of his office.

political aide and even assumed extra-constitutional authority.

Morarji Desai had no inner circle to consult. Nor could he afford to attempt one in a strife-ridden Council of Ministers and warring constituent units of the party that he headed. He told Pritish Nandy, Editor of the *Illustrated Weekly of India,* "I always listened to my colleagues.....and did what was right for the nation."[34] In Rajiv Gandhi's case power fell into his lap at a young age of 40 and without any experience of the intricacies of politics, he was in a hurry to reach the 21st century without realising that the present had to be a bridge between the past and future. He selected a coterie of persons young in age who had no roots in a democratic movement. If Rajiv Gandhi had not appointed his friends as his counsels officially, he lent his ears to Amitabh Bachchan, Romi Chopra, Rajiv Sethi and ex-Captain of the Indian Airlines Satish Sharma. The result was complete failure on all fronts, domestic and international and utter loss in prestige and credibility.

The actual power of the Prime Minister, however, varies according to his personality and the extent to which he is supported by his Party. His prestige, no doubt, is one of the elements that makes for the success of the Party as he goes to the electorate not as an individual, but as a leader of the Party. So long as he retains the hold on his Party, he is, able within limits, to dictate to his Party. The mighty power of Nehru was of his dynamic personality and he reigned supreme over his Party and the Government that he headed. "Many of his colleagues and, or Party high-ups," wrote Radhakrishnan, "received the shock of their lives when Nehru asked them to explain obscure reports published in the papers, with the relevant cutting pasted faithfully on the note paper."[35] Nehru combined the two posts of the Congress Party President and the Prime Minister from 1951 to 1954. Thereafter, he received unequivocal respect, affection and regards from the Presidents who followed him. The Congress Party had, in fact, always looked to the Prime Minister for political guidance and his leadership was never questioned. Nehru too treated the Party President and the Working Committee with the utmost consideration nd never denigrated publicly the organisation. He consulted the Working Committee frequently on matters of national importance and valued the suggestions proposed by them. In case of difference of opinion, he had the capacity to bring round the Working Committee to his Cabinet's point of view. He had also the capacity to yield to the opinion of his Cabinet colleagues and the Parliamentary Party in the wider national interests. The Congress Parliamentary Party demanded Krishna Menon's resignation in 1962, when China attacked India and the Indian army suffered a series of reverses. Nehru defended Menon in the Parliamentay Party and vaguely threatened to resign. It was reported that one of the leaders in the Party said, "If you continue to follow Menon's policies, we are prepared to contemplate that possibility." Nehru yielded and Menon had to resign. This is the specimen of Nehru's respect for democratic and human values.

Shastri in the beginning showed deference to the wishes of the Congress President, but soon he assumed the role of equality and a little later he clearly established his dominant position. He also played prominent part in the re-election of Kamraj as the Congress President. But the relations between Mrs. Gandhi and the Congress President became strained from the very start, although Kamraj had played the key role in her selection as leader of the Parliamentary Party. She did not consult the Congress President on such important matters as the devaluation of the rupee as well as on the decision of the Indo- US Foundation and the election of her some men to the Central Election Committee of the Party. The Prime Minister, as Rajni Kothari remarked, "appeared to be no longer a prisoner of Kamraj and looked forward to an equal partnership with the Congress President."[36]

But soon she began to assert herself. After having consolidated her position in the Government Mrs. Gandhi strove to make mark on the Party and even challenged Kamraj insisting on the nomination of Dr. Zakir Hussain for the Presidency. Relations between the Party and Mrs. Gandhi's Government deteriorated after the 1967 General Election when the top Party leaders, like Kamraj, S. K. Patil and Atulya Ghosh, lost the poll. The rift between the Congress President, S. Nijalingappa, and Mrs. Gandhi became sharp and the 1969 Presidential election brought the breaking point. Mrs. Gandhi wanted that the choice of the Presidential candidate should be the exclusive

34. *The Illustrated Weekly of India,* Bombay, February 2, 1986.
35. *The Tribune,* Ambala Cantt., November 13, 1955.
36. Rajni Kothari, "*India : The Congress System of Trial*", Asian Survey, February 1968, p. 89.

concern of the Prime Minister whereas the Congress President asserted that it was the right of the Central Parliamentary Board. When the Central Parliamentary Board selected Neelam Sanjiva Reddy as the Congress candidate for the presidential poll, Mrs. Gandhi complained that by imposing the decision on her the office of the Prime Minister had been denigrated. "All over the world", she said in anguish, "the impression had gone round that the Prime Minister is demoted in her own organisation. No democracy can function if the head of the Government is insulted in the Party."[37]

Mrs. Gandhi had "the reputation of never forgetting and more ominously, she never forgives."[38] The "insult" of imposing the Presidential candidate was to be avenged and thus began conflict, confrontation and split. Mrs. Gandhi clarified the position of the Prime Minister *vis-a-vis* the Congress President and the Working Committee. Addressing the general body of the Congress Parliamentary Party on August 29, 1969 she explained that the sphere of the Congress President was the Party which laid down broad policies. But the implementation of policies and programmes rested with Parliament and the State Legislatures. The leader of the Parliamentary Party, as the Prime Minister, had responsibility not only to the Congress Parliamentary Party, but to the State Governments and the nations of the world. Therefore, it would not be proper to fetter the discretion of the Prime Minister.[39] But the Congress President warned his partymen against the evil of "personality cult" which was reflected in the speeches of the Prime Minister and her desire of freedom of vote in the ensuing Presidential election; one was the nominee of the Congress and the second an independent having the tacit support of Mrs. Gandhi.

The Indian National Congress was split and Mrs. Indira Gandhi became the undisputed leader of the Party then known as the Indian National Congress (Ruling). In the initial stages after the split she even toyed with the idea of becoming the Congress President,[40] but hesitated lest the accusation of "personality cult" might be confirmed. The nationalisation of the top fourteen Banks, her utterances promising economic and social justice, the massive 1971 poll majority, the successful end of Bangladesh crisis and the victorious end of the war with Pakistan inspired confidence in the mind of the people in a manner unparalleled in the history of the Indian National Congress. The Congress and its competent bodies at all levels of the organisation completely surrendered to Mrs. Gandhi the authority to take decision on the issues involved, to nominate Chief Ministers of the States and even the members of the *ad hoc* committees where the Pradesh Congress Committees had been superseded. The Congress President Jagjivan Ram (1969-71), D. Sanjivayya (1971-72), Shankar Dayal Sharma (1972-74) and D. K. Barooah all echoed her tune of thought. Except Jagjivan Ram, the remaining three were her nominees. But Barooah surpassed them all when he publicly declared that 'India is Indira, and Indira is India."

The Party abdicated in favour of the Prime Minister and, thus, began an era of constitutional despotism and sycophancy. Both the Prime Minister and the Party had to pay a very heavy price for the concentration of authority and the role played by the "caucus". Fifty Congress members of both Houses of Parliament gave to the Congress President a letter, immediately after March 1977 elections, demanding his (Barooah's) resignation. Mrs. Gandhi also came under severe criticism for allowing the emergence of "caucus" which wielded undemocratic power during the nineteen months of Emergency. Demand was also made to purge the Congress, if its politics was to be purified and even Mrs. Gandhi's removal from the Party would not have been a surprise. But Mrs. Gandhi found her survival in splitting the Congress for the second time and became the President of the group : Congress Conventionists, to be finally known as Congress (Indira) or Congress (I).

It is the paradox of Mrs. Gandhi's popularity that even in the dark days of her political career there was no revulsion against her popular rating as assessed by E.P.W. da Costa in August 1977. In January 1980 Parliamentary elections the electorate reposed their confidence in the indispensability of Mrs. Gandhi at the critical juncture of India's political career after Independence and returned her Congress with a massive majority. They re-affirmed their confidence in her again in the Assembly elections in nine Northern States and in the following by-elec-

37. *The Statesman,* Calcutta, August 17, 1969.
38. Frank Moraes, *Witness to an Era,* pp. 263-64.
39. *The Sunday Standard,* New Delhi, August 31, 1969.
40. Krishnan, T.K. Kunhi, *Chavan and the Troubled Decade,* p. 289.

tions. But the political upheaval of 1977 had made no change in Mrs. Gandhi's style of functioning. She rode the crest and combined the office of the Prime Minister and the Presidentship of the Party designated as Congress (Indira). An important criterion, she adopted in the second spell of her office in selecting her team of Ministers was the unflinching loyalty of a person in her days of distress. This criterion was rigidly applied in the selection of Party candidates for contesting elections to the House of the People and the State Assemblies. Subservience to the Party leader at all levels was as vigorous as before. Zail Singh, the then Home Minister, described "Indiraji" as his *rahnuma* (patron)[41] and she was patron of all whether they had given public expression to their feelings or not. She still believed in *ad hocism* and no Party elections were held, either in the Central organisation or in the Provincial Committees. The State Chief Ministers were her nominees and they held office at her pleasure. The State Party bosses were her creation and they changed at her will.

Way back in 1957, N.V. Gadgil, former Union Minister (1947-52) wrote that the position of the Prime Minister "is a peculiar one. In the Cabinet, he naturally claims that it is his responsibility that the decisions of the Government are in conformity with the broad principles and policies laid down by the Congress. In the Working Committee, where he cannot escape dominating, he represents the Government and is in a stronger position to necessarily press his views, backed up as they are by administrative experience." Many merits, he added, are claimed for such a position of the Prime Minster as he constitutes an effective connecting link between the Government and the Party organisation as represented by the Working Committee. "But the disadvantage which is inherent in a situation of this kind," Gadgil remarked, "is equally overwhelming, *viz.*, that the Prime Minister is invested with formidable power and influence and unless he be a genuine democrat by nature he is very likely to become a dictator."[42] Nehru was a sensitive democrat, a great humanist, averse to power politics. Mrs. Gandhi had a past. She always told her countrymen that Nehru was her teacher, her Guru, and pledged to uphold all the human and democratic values which her father had painstakingly nourished. But history's verdict is that she failed to maintain the Nehru legacy.

Morarji, on the other hand, was a democrat who had a firm belief in the rule of law and dignity of the individual. His had been a remarkable political life moulded by Gandhi and his own strong often rigid views how he should conduct himself, the Party and the govern- ment. Many disagreed with some of his views and found the ring of self-righteousness often through his preaching. In politics man proposes and circumstances dispose and this is precisely what happened during Desai's tenure of Prime Ministership. His misfortune was that he had the Government of a squabbling and undisciplined Party which even effected the style of his Ministers. They contradicted each other and one another. Cohesion at any stage had not been their concern both in the Party and the Government. At one stage, with few exceptions, there was a race among them for self-promotion. Without any official restraint or political decorum, they talked to the Press, to the public and against each other including the Prime Minister. A Prime Minister commands from his colleagues party loyalty and personal allegiance and it is the strength of the office he holds and ensures team spirit. Morarji Desai could not get either. Charan Singh and Jagjivan Ram did not forget that their claims had been ignored and Prime Ministership was gifted to Desai by Jayaprakash Narayan. The split and inner-party fights posed an insurmountable problem and Desai was not strong enough to hold the Government and Party together. He cogently summed up this deplorable aspect of the affairs of the Janata Party. During the 'meet-the-Press' programme he pointed out that the Janata Party was formed by six different parties which had been criticising each other for thirty years. The parties had come together as all wanted to be together but habits which were thirty years old could not vanish overnight. When asked was it proper for any Minister to publicly state his views till the Government took a decision ? The Prime Minster said that "it would be much better if everyone in this country understood what was proper and what was not." "But how many do so ?", he asked. He added that he had been drawing their (Ministers) attention and this was having its impact. Patience was needed to educate

41. As reported in *The Tribune,* Chandigarh, March 21, 1980.
42. Gadgil, N. V., "The Government and the Party," *The Indian Journal of Public Administration,* New Delhi, October-December 1957, p. 354.

a person, he remarked.[43] Nothing more could be expected in reply from a hapless and helpless Prime Minister.

Rajiv Gandhi became complacent after the enormous success that he achieved in the first two years of his assumption of office as Prime Minister and President of the Congress (I) both rolled into the one. He felt that he had massive support both inside and outside Parliament and became a little more aggressive in moving the country faster to his cherished goal of the 21st century. He was oblivious of the constraints of democracy, the inertia of administration,[44] the vastness and complexity of the land and the pressure of population, particularly of the people struggling to find a place in the sun.

Most importantly Rajiv Gandhi was oblivious of what has come to be known in the vocabularly of American politics as the "Nixon effect." Whenever a leader is returned to power with a massive majority and also combines unto himself the command of the organisational wing of the Party, he begins to operate carelessly. Without due regard to scruples, with a touch of arrogance, he grievously offends his supporters in the Party. Rajiv Gandhi made himself inaccessible to his Party colleagues and treated them as ordinary members of the public; he would reshuffle his Council of Ministers as if it was a pack of cards; and that he would not listen to the advice of his senior Cabinet Colleagues. Even more important that the Congress leaders of standing would be as afraid of him as they were of Mrs. Indira Gandhi after she had split the Congress in 1969, driven out of the organisation those who had dared oppose her and established her supremacy in it. Whatever resistance had survived in the Congress and surfaced in the wake of electoral debacle in 1977 got eliminated when Mrs. Gandhi again split it in 1978. It was this organisation which Rajiv Gandhi had first lorded over as General Secretary and then inherited on October 31, 1984. Its leading lights could not legitimately have been expected to be guided by anything otherwise than the survival instinct. Here we can do no better than paraphrase Oliver Goldsmith and say :

Ill fares the system to hastening ills a prey,
Where power accumulates and men decay.

## SUGGESTED READINGS

*Constituent Assembly Debates.*

Granville Austin, *The Indian Constitution —A corner-stone a Nation.*

Hanson, A.H. and Janet Douglas, *India's Democracy.*

Jennings, W.I. *Some Characteristics of the Indian Constitution.*

Palmer, Norman, D., *The Indian Political System.*

43. As reported in *The Times of India,* New Delhi, February 29, 1980.
44. In a public speech the Prime Minister stated that "Our administrative mechanism is cumbersome, archaic and alien to the needs and aspirations of the people."

# CHAPTER X

# Parliament

### Unity through Popular Government

The predominant aim of the Constituent Assembly members when framing the legislative provisions of the constitution, was to create a basis for the social and political unity of the country. They chose to do this by welding the diversified Indian elements and interests into one mass electorate having universal, adult suffrage and by providing for the direct representation of the voters in the popular assemblies. This bold step completely overturned the constitutional pattern left by the British rule. The Executive and Judicial provisions of the Government of India Act, 1935, were adapted to India's needs by the Assembly with some major changes of substance, but with few of form. It was not so with the legislative provisions. These had to be entirely remade to incorporate the aims and objectives the nation had set before it.

Under the Act of 1935, not only did the Provinces lack even a semblance of popular government, but the small electorate that existed was thoroughly fragmented. The franchise was restricted by property, educational and other qualifications to near about 15 per cent of the entire population and this narrow electorate was split into not less than thirteen communal and functional sectors for whose representation seats were reserved, and that too with weightage in many cases, in the various legislative bodies. Election to the Lower Chamber of the Central Assembly was indirect on the basis of communal and functional electorates consisting of the members of the Provincial Assemblies. Evidently, the members of the Constituent Assembly could not hope to succeed in their mission to achieve national unity and stability "by perpetuating a system of government that accentuated existing cleavages in Indian society and tended to create new ones."[1]

In their efforts to remove all such cankers from the body politic of the country the Assembly members decided to provide universal adult franchise and joint electorates, by replacing communal electorate. There was to be neither weightage of representation for minorities nor reservation of seats, except for Scheduled Castes and Backward Tribes and that, too, for a short period.[2] The Lower Chambers, both at the Centre and in the States, were to be directly elected by adult suffrage. Only the Upper Chambers, at both levels, were to be, in part, indirectly elected. The members of the Council of States ( Rajya Sabha) were to be elected by the members of the State Assemblies whereas the Legislative Councils, except for those nominated,[3] were to be elected from territorial constituencies by special electorates of the members of municipal, district and other forms of local government, of the university graduates and of teachers in Higher Secondary Schools. The restrictions on the powers of the Legislatures, as under the 1935 Act, were removed and all powers exercised by parliamentary bodies in federal representative democracies were given.

### Parliament not a Sovereign Body

Parliament is the name given by the Constitution to the Union Legislature and it consists of the President and two Houses known respectively as the Council of States (Rajya Sabha) and the House of the People (Lok Sabha). The President is a constituent part of Parliament just as the Monarch is in Britain. But the American President is not a constituent part of Congress. The Constitution of the United States provides, "All legislative powers herein granted shall be vested

---

1. Granville Austin, *The Indian Constitution : Cornerstone of a Nation*, p. 145.
2. Seats were reserved for Scheduled Castes and Tribes for ten years from the commencement of the Constitution in the Lower Houses of the State Assemblies and in the House of the People (Lok Sabha). The President was empowered (likewise State Governors) to nominate not more than two Anglo-Indians to the Lower House if he believed that the community was not sufficiently represented. This provision has five times been extended and appears to have become retrenched in the system. It is reservation *par excellence*.
3. In Upper Houses there were also to be (12) members nominated by the President, and a Governor (one-sixth of the total membership of the Upper House) with special qualifications in the fields of literature, science, art, co-operative movement and social service.

in the Congress of the United States, which shall consist of a Senate and a House of Representatives.''

Though the Constitution of India adopts the language of Britain in describing its Legislature at the Centre, and makes the President, like the Monarch of that country, a constituent part of Parliament, yet the Indian Parliament is not sovereign Legislature like the British Parliament. It functions within the bounds of a written Constitution setting up a federal polity and a Supreme Court invested with the power of judicial review. The legislative competence of Parliament is limited, during normal times, to the subjects enumerated in the Union List and the Concurrent List in the Seventh Schedule of the Constitution. Besides, its supremacy within its own sphere of jurisdiction is limited by the Fundamental Rights guaranteed to the citizens in Part III of the Constitution. Article 13 Clause (2) prohibits, subject to specified restriction, the State from making any law which would take away or abridge any of the Fundamental Rights. Where the State makes a law in contravention of the Fundamental Rights, that law shall, to the extent of contravention, be void.

In Britain no formal distinction is made between constitutional and other laws and the same body, Parliament, can change or abrogate any law whatsoever and by the same procedure. The Constitution of India, on the other hand, makes a distinction between statutory law and constitutional law and prescribes a special procedure for amending the latter as incorporated in Article 368. The Supreme Court held in *Keshavananda Bharati* v. *The State of Kerala* that Article 368 does not enable Parliament to alter the basic structure or framework of the Constitution. The term basic structure is a vague and general term and the Judges themselves did not offer a common agreed meaning. Some included Fundamental Rights and federation in the concept of basic structure while others saw no limit to the amending power of Parliament. The Constitution (Forty-second Amendment) Act 1976, provided that Parliament had full power to amend the Constitution and no Amendment made under article 368 could be questioned in any Court on any ground. The validity of the Forty-second Amendment was questioned and in May 1980 the Supreme Court struck down in the *Minerva Mills* case Section 55 of the Amendment incorporated in Clauses (4) and (5) of Article 368 as it altered or destroyed the basic structure or framework of the Constitution. It was affirmation of the *Keshavananda Bharati* case (1973) judgment. Unless this Judgment is reversed by the Court on the review application of the Union Government or a new amendment of the Cnstitution is enacted and the Supreme Court upholds that amendment, the power of Parliament cannot extend beyond the limitations placed by the Constitution and the Supreme Court.

Despite these limitations on the authority of Parliament, it is the pivot on which revolves the whole machinery of the Government. Its legislative competence embraces a large field and its financial powers are vast. Its sanction is also necessary for declaring war and making peace. Parliament and the State Legislatures have equal rights to make laws in respect of subjects in the Concurrent List, but if a law enacted by a State Assembly is not in conformity to the law passed by Parliament, the law made by Parliament prevails. Parliament can also legislate on any subject in the State List if the Council of States declares by a resolution that it is necessary in the national interest to do so. During Emergency all restrictions on the legislative and financial jurisdiction of Parliament disappear.

**Parliament is Bicameral**

One of the most vexing questions of Political Science, wrote B. N. Rao in his *Constitutional Precedents* was the problem of second chambers. The first bicameral legislature was established in New Delhi under the Government of India Act, 1919, but the Upper House was never intended to have a federal role in the sense of providing for equal representation to the various Provinces. In 1919, the federal issue did not arise and the Government of India was constructed on the basis of devolution of authority from the Centre. In the federal structure as envisaged by the Nehru Report, the Upper House would have existed primarily to provide an opportunity for reconsideration of legislation in a ''somewhat cooler atmosphere''[4] than that obtaining in the Lower House. Such a precaution was considered especially necessary owing to the existence of sharp communal differences that had been marked in the working of the Lower House at the Centre as well as in the Provinces.[5] The Nehru Committee rejected the argument that in a federal polity the constitu-

4. *Nehru Report*, p. 94.
5. *Ibid.*, pp. 94-95.

ent units should be equally represented in the Upper House, as in the United States' Senate, "in view of great differences in size and population of our Provinces." Yet it did recommend the number of representatives assigned to small Provinces could be increased so that their relationship to the great Provinces should not be "wholly disproportionate." The Committee felt that as the members of the Upper House were to be elected by the Provincial Legislatures, it would give the Provinces a feeling of being represented at the Centre.

The same reasons for not having equal representation of the constituent units in the Upper House were cited by the Federal Structure Sub-Committee at the Round Table Conference. The Sub-Committee added that it doubted if equal representation "would commend itself to general public opinion."[6] The Government of India Act, 1935, gave expression to this view point. The Sapru Committee made no recommendations on the subject, and, thus, the issue came to the Constituent Assembly.

The Union and Provincial Constitution Committees considered the question of second chambers in the meetings separately held in June 1947. The Union Constitution Committee was in favour of an Upper House of the State legislatures. Provincial representation was to be one member for each million of population upto five millions and one for each two millions of population thereafter. The maximum representation of a Province was to be twenty.[7] The Report of the Union Constitution Committee is silent for its rejection of equal representation of the constituent units. It may, however, be surmised the members of the Committee agreed with the views expressed in the Nehru Committee Report and at the Round Table Conference. They might also have feared, as B. N. Rau did, that if they allowed equal representation to all units of the Federation, the Provinces "would be swamped" by the Princely States when they acceded to the federation.[8]

The Constituent Assembly considered the report of the Union Constitution Committee during July and August 1947. The debate centred on the role of the second chambers in modern democracies and the necessity of any Upper House in a federal Legislature was discussed only once and that too cursorily. N. Gopalas-wami Ayyangar told the Assembly that "the need for a second chamber has been felt practically all over the world wherever there are federations of any importance." Dealing with the role of the second chambers, he said, "After all, the question for us to consider is whether it performs any useful function. The most that we expect the Second Chamber to do is perhaps to hold dignified debates on important issues and to delay legislation which might be the outcome of passions of the moment until passions have subsided and calm consideration could be bestowed on the measures which will be before the Legislature; and we shall take care to provide in the Constitution that whenever on any important matter, particularly matters relating to finance, there is a conflict between the House of the People and the Council of States, it is the view of the House of the People that shall prevail. Therefore, what we really achieve by the existence of this Second Chamber is only an instrument by which we delay action which might be hastily conceived, and we also give an opportunity, perhaps to seasoned people who may not be in the thickness of the political fray, but who might be willing to participate in the debate with an amount of learning and importance which we do not ordinarily associate with House of the People. That is all that is proposed in regard to this Second Chamber. I think, on the whole, this balance of consideration is in favour of having such a Chamber and taking care to see that it does not prove clog either to legislation or administration."[9] It is significant to note that Ayyangar made no attempt to justify the existence of the Council of States on any of the grounds which are generally responsible for establishing a second chamber in a federation, especially giving equal representation to the federating units. The new Constitution also did not reflect it. Nor do the powers and functions of the Council of States demonstrate its federal character as a custodian of the interests of the constituent units.

## COUNCIL OF STATES (RAJYA SABHA)

### Composition and Organisation

The Constitution fixes the maximum strength of the Council of States (Rajya Sabha) at 250 including 12 nominated by the President to represent literature, science, art and social service. The maximum number of seats is 34 in the case of Uttar Pradesh and the minimum is 1(one) each for Sikkim, Nagaland, Manipur,

6. *Report of the Federal Structure Sub-Committee to the RTC;* Cmd. 3778, p. 218.
7. UCC report, para 14; *Reports, First Series,* p. 54.
8. Rau, B. N., in a note to his Memorandum on the Union Constitution of May 30, 1945.
9. *Constituent Assembly Debates*, Vol. IV, p. 644.

Tripura, Meghalaya and Mizoram. The representatives of States are elected by the elected members of their Legislative Assemblies in accordance with the system of proportional representation by means of the single transferable vote. In the case of the Union Territories, members are chosen in such a manner as Parliament may by law determine.

The principle of nomination was the subject of a good deal of criticism in the Constituent Assembly. Some members characterised it as an undemocratic and reactionary element of membership in a democratic republic. Representation of the States on the basis of population and inclusion of nominated members, it was contended, violated the federal principle too. During the early Constitution-making debate an amendment to establish a single chamber was moved, although it was defeated. When in the later debate on the Draft Constitution an attempt was again made for a single Chamber Legislature, Ananthasayanam Ayyangar defended the Upper House as a way to utilise the services of persons of intellectual capacity and experience of affairs without imperilling the administration. But all such arguments were in favour of bicameralism, and not in defence of the composition of an Upper House in a federation. Nor could it be claimed that the Council of States so constituted would serve as a defence for smaller States. The Council is a continuous body and is not subject to dissolution. Its life is for six years, one-third of the number of members retiring after every two years.

**Qualifications for Members**

To be qualified, a candidate for election to the Council of States should be :

(a) a citizen of India, and makes and subscribes before a person authorised by the Election Commission an oath and affirmation that he will bear true faith and allegiance to the Constitution of India as by law established and that he will uphold the sovereignty and integrity of India;

(b) not less than thirty years of age; and

(c) possessing such other qualifications as may be prescribed by Parliament. Under the Representation of the People Act, 1951, a candidate for election to the Council must be a parliamentary elector in the State from which he seeks election.

The qualifications required for eligibility to the Council of States are the same as those required for the House of the People except that the age in the case of the latter must not be less than twenty-five years. The framers of the Constitution thought that higher qualifications would tend to give greater dignity to the House and, at the same time, higher average ability. The functions, observed Ambedkar, that a member "is required to discharge in the House require experience, certain amount of knowledge and practical experience in the affairs of the world, and I think if these additional qualifications are accepted, we shall be able to secure the proper sort of candidates who would be able to serve the House better than a mere ordinary voter might do."

**The Presiding Officer**

The Vice-President of India is the *ex officio* Chairman of the Council of States and finds a close parallel in the Vice-President of the United States who is the President of the Senate. The Vice-President of India like his American counterpart, is not a member of the House and both have no right to vote except in the event of a tie. But the President of the Senate is just a moderator. He cannot control debate through the power of recognition; he must recognise the members in the order in which they rise. The Chairman of the Council of States in India enjoys an exalted position. He recognises members to the floor, allots time,[10] decides point of order, maintains order and relevancy in debates, puts questions and announces results. The American Vice-President permanently relinquishes the office of the President of the Senate on his succession to Presidency, but the Vice-President of India fills only a casual vacancy and reverts to his original office of Chairman as soon as the contingency of his acting President is over.

The Council of States elects a Deputy Chairman from amongst its own members and he presides at the sittings of the House in the absence of the Chairman or during any period when the Vice-President is acting, or discharging the functions of the President. In the absence of both the Chairman and the Deputy Chairman from any sitting of the House such person, as may be determined by the Rules of Procedure of the Council of States, acts as Chairman. If no such

10. Chairman M. Hidayatullah fixed a duration of eight minutes per question.

person is present, some other member as the Council may determine acts as Chairman.

The Chairman may be removed from office by a resolution of the Council of States, provided at least fourteen days' notice for the intention to move such a resolution has been given, by a majority of all the then members of the Council, and agreed to by the House of the People. While such a resolution of removal is under consideration of the Council, the Chairman neither presides at any sitting of the Council nor can he exercise a casting vote in case of equality of votes, but he has the right to vote on such a resolution on the first instance. He has the right to speak in, and otherwise to take part in the proceedings in the Council. The Deputy Chairman is also subject to removal in the like manner, except that the resolution of his or her removal does not require the agreement of the House of the People as it is necessary in the case of the Chairman. The salaries and allowances of the Chairman and the Deputy Chairman are determined by Parliament and are charged on the Consolidated Fund of India. The office of the Vice-President carries no salary by itself.

## FUNCTIONS OF THE COUNCIL OF STATES

### Legislative Functions

The process of making laws is the business of the Parliament as a whole, that is, the President, the Council of States (Rajya Sabha) and the House of the People. The House of the People by itself can do nothing, although the actual powers exercised by the President and conferred on the Council of States (Rajya Sabha) are subject to specific limitations. All Bills, other than Money Bills, may originate in either House and no Bill can become a law unless agreed to by both the Houses and assented to by the President. It means that the power of initiating legislation on any non-Money Bill belongs to the Council of States and the House of the People, and such a Bill in order to become law must be agreed to by both the Houses. When a Bill is amended in either House, such amendment must be agreed to by both the Houses. In case of disagreement made in the Bill, the President may summon both the Houses in a joint sitting for the purpose of deliberating and voting on the Bill. At the joint sitting questions are decided by a majority of the members of both Houses present and voting. A Bill thus agreed to and passed is deemed to have been passed by both Houses. The method of joint sitting also applies when a Bill is passed by one House and sent to the other but is not passed within six months after its reception by the other House, excluding any period of prorogation or adjournment over four days.

The Council of States (Rajya Sabha), thus, possesses co-ordinate legislative powers with the House of the People. Unlike the Parliament Act of 1911 as amended in 1949, in Britain, there is nothing in the Indian Constitution which may limit the legislative powers of the Council of States. On the other hand, the Council of States may press an issue to the extent of summoning joint sitting of the two Houses for the resolution of any disagreement. The Banking Service Commission (Repeal) Bill was passed by the House of the People (Lok Sabha) on December 5, 1977, but rejected by the Council of States (Rajya Sabha) three days later. The President summoned a joint session of the two Houses to meet on May 16, 1978 to consider the Banking Service Commission (Repeal) Bill. It was the first joint session of Parliament since May 1961 when the two Houses met to resolve differences over the Dowry Prohibition Bill. But in a joint sitting the position of the Council of States becomes weaker as its membership is in a minority of 1 to 2 (250 to 544) with membership of the House of the People. The Council can, at most, delay legislation passed by the House of the People for a period not exceeding six months. It cannot permanently kill it.

### Financial Functions

The position of the Council of States (Rajya Sabha) in respect of Money Bills is definitely inferior to that of the House of the People (Lok Sabha). The Constitution defines a Money Bill and it is expressly provided that the decision of the Speaker of the House of the People (Lok Sabha) whether a Bill is a Money Bill or not shall be final. The Constitution prescribes that a Money Bill shall not be introduced in the Council of States and it is barred from rejecting or amending a Money Bill. After a Money Bill has been passed by the House of the People (Lok Sabha), it is transmitted to the Council of States (Rajya Sabha) for its "recommendations" within a period of fourteen days. It is for the House of the People to accept or reject such "recommendations." In case it rejects the "recommendations," the Bill is deemed to have been passed by both Houses in the form in which it was passed by the House of the People. If the Council of

States does not return to the House of the People within fourteen days a Money Bill with or without its recommendations,'' it is deemed to have been passed by both Houses in the form in which it was passed by the House of the People.

The right to vote supplies is perhaps the greatest privilege of a legislative body and under the Constitution this right is the exclusive privilege of the House of the People. The Council of States simply discusses the budget. Demands for grants are not submitted to the Council.

**Administrative Functions**

The Council of States does not control the Executive as the Constitution makes the Council of Ministers responsible to the House of the People. In fact, control and responsibility go together. But the Council of States can influence the Executive in two ways. First, by eliciting information about the actions of Government and secondly, by criticism aimed at the Government. The most effective instrument by which the Council of States seeks information from the Government is through the instrument of oral or written questions together with supplementaries. The normal occasion for criticism of the Executive is debate on a motion of adjournment and the Council shares this privilege with the House. The policy of the Government is really under review when laws are made and the motion of thanks on the address of the President is being discussed. In order to defend the policy of the Government, Ministers are there and some of them are appointed from among its members. The Constitution permits a Minister, who is not a member of the Council, to speak in, and otherwise to take part in its proceedings, though he has no right to vote in that House. The Council, however, cannot bring about the downfall of the Government as the Constitution makes it responsible to the House of the People alone. But the Council amended the President's address to Parliament in January 1980 by the combined strength of the Opposition which commanded a majority. This was the first time since the promulgation of the Constitution in 1950 that the President's address had been so amended and it set an unusual precedent.

**Constituent Functions**

The Council of States exercises constituent functions along with the House of the People. A Bill to amend the Constitution may originate in either House. But all Constitution-amending Bills, except the Constitution (Fortieth Amendment) Bill, 1975, have been initiated in the House of the People. A Bill amending the Constitution under article 368 must pass in each House by a majority of not less than two-thirds of the members of that House present and voting. But if such amendment seeks to make any change in Article 54 (election of the President), Article 75 (manner of election of President), Article 73 (extent of executive power of the Union), Article 162 (extent of executive power of the State), Article 241( High Courts for Union territories), or Chapter IV of Part V (the Union Judiciary), Chapter V of Part VI (High Courts), or Chapter I of Part XI (Legislative relations between the Union and the States), or any of the Lists in the Seventh Schedule, or any representation of States in Parliament, or the provisions of Article 368 (amendment of the Constitution ) the amendment also requires to be ratified by the Legislatures of not less than one-half of the States by resolution to that effect passed by those Legislatures before the amendment Bill is presented to the President for assent.

The Constitution does not prescribe any procedure for settling differences between the two Houses in case of disagreement on an amendment Bill. The procedure prescribed in Article 108 in case of disagreement on ordinary legislation does not apply to Bills amending the Constitution. Hari Chand is of the opinion that the House of the People represents the will of the people and, consequently, the will of the people must prevail and the Council of States must not become an obstacle in the way of the popular Chamber. "Moreover, in case the amendment relates to any of the entrenched provisions, the interests of the States are not in danger, because the amendment would require ratification by at least half the States Legislatures and the States can take care of their interests better than the Upper House. "[11] But this is not a correct appraisal. The Council of States defeated the Constitution (Twenty-fourth Amendment) Bill, 1970, though by only a fraction of vote, and, again, in 1977 discussion on the Forty-third Amendment Bill was postponed till the next session of Parliament apprehending stout opposition by the Congress (I) which then commanded a majority in the Council. The Opposition also successfully thwarted the Constitution (Forty-fourth Amend-

---

11. Hari Chand, *The Amending Process in Indian Constitution*, p. 25.

ment) Bill which was intended to amend the distortions wrought by the Constitution (Forty-second Amendment) Act, 1978, as viewed by the Janata Government and had been passed by an overwhelming majority in the House of the People.

**Miscellaneous Functions**

The miscellaneous functions of the Council of States are :—

(1) The elected members of the Council of States participate in the election of the President of India. The President is elected by an Electoral College consisting of the elected members of both Houses of Parliament and the elected members of the Legislative Assemblies of the States.

(2) The President is liable to be impeached and a resolution to impeach the President may be moved in any House of Parliament and such a resolution must be passed by two-thirds majority of the total membership of that House. When this has been done, the charge is investigated by the other House or by a Court or Tribunal to which that House may refer the Impeachment charge to be investigated. A vote by two-thirds of the total membership of the House which investigates it is necessary for the impeachment to succeed. It means that if the Council of States initiates proceedings of impeachment the House of the People investigates the charge, and if it is initiated by the House the Council investigates and the impeachment, succeeds if the investigating House passes a resolution by a two-thirds majority of its membership. The Council of States, thus, enjoys co-equal powers with the House of the People in the process of impeachment of the President.

(3) The Vice-President of India is elected by an electoral college consisting of the members of both Houses of Parliament and may be removed from his office by a resolution of the Council of States and agreed to by the House of the People.

(4) A Judge of the Supreme Court or a High Court may be removed for misbehavior or incapacity on the address passed by both Houses of Parliament, supported by a majority of the total membership of, and a two-thirds majority of the members present and voting in each House. Here, too, the powers of the Council of States are identical to those of the House of the People. Agreement of the Council is also necessary if action is to be taken against the Chief Election Commissioner, Comptroller and Auditor-General of India and the members of the Union Public Service Commission.

(5) The report of the Union Public Service Commission, the Comptroller-General, the Scheduled Castes and Tribes Commission and the Finance Commission and are considered both by the Council and the House.

(6) If the Government makes a proposal to take an appointment from he purview of the Union Public Service Commission, both the Houses must agree to its exclusion.

(7) The Council may declare by a resolution, passed by two-thirds majority of its members present and voting, that it is necessary or expedient in the national interests that Parliament should make laws with respect to any matter enumerated in the State List. Such a resolution remains in force for a period not exceeding one year.

(8) The Council is also empowered under Article 312 to create one or more All India Services, if the House of the People declares by a resolution supported by not less than two-thirds of the members present and voting that it is necessary or expedient in the national interest to do so.

(9) The approval of the Council of States is necessary for the continuance of a Proclamation of Emergency (Article 352), failure of constitutional machinery in a State (Article 356), and financial emergency (Article 360) , beyond the specified period of time. If the House of the People stands dissolved when a Proclamation is issued or it is dissolved before the expiry of the specified period of time the Council of States alone is to judge the necessity of the continuance of a Proclamation issued under either of the aforesaid Ar-

ticles. If it does not approve, the Proclamation ceases to operate.

(10) Every Order made by the President suspending the enforcement of Fundamental Rights is required to be laid before each House of Parliament.

(11) The delegated legislation made and rule framed thereunder by various Ministries must be approved by both Houses.

**Role of the Council of States**

The Council of States was intended to be less powerful and influential than the House of the People and this is in accordance with basic principles which govern the functioning of the Parliamentary system. The Constitution does not give to the Council specific powers to control the Executive. A motion for lack of confidence in the Government cannot be moved therein. It has, no doubt, the right to seek information from the Government through the instrument of questions and supplementaries, to discuss and criticise its policy through debates, and to draw attention to matters of urgent public importance, through the "calling attention" motions but the Council can not plague the Ministry and oust it from office. The Constitution recognises and ordains the collective responsibility of the Council of Ministers to the House of the People alone.

The Council has co-ordinate powers with the House of the People in ordinary and amending legislation only in theory. It cannot veto legislation passed by the House of the People, but can only delay it. If the differences between the two Houses cannot be settled in the ordinary process of the legislation the President may summon a joint sitting of the two Houses where the will of the House of the People prevails because of its numerical superiority. In matters financial, the Council is absolutely powerless, even not at par with the British House of Lords. Money Bills originate in the House of the People and if a question arises whether a particular Bill is a Money Bill or not, the decision of the Speaker is final. The House of the People simply transmits a Money Bill to the Council for " recommendations" and it is required to return it within fourteen days of its receipt. If it is not returned within the specified time or returns it with "recommendations" which are not acceptable to the House of the People, the Money Bill is deemed to have been passed by both Houses, in the form in which it was originally passed by the House of the People. Demands for grants are not submitted to the Council; sanctioning of public expenditure is the exclusive right of the House of the People.

The Council does not even serve the purpose of a federal second chamber. Neither the critics of a Second Chamber in the Constituent Assembly nor its supporters did advance a single federal argument. The well-accepted practice of a federal polity is to make the Upper Chamber a representative House of the constituent units and its constitution is based upon equality by representation irrespective of the size and population of the federating units. The Council of States does not accord equal representation to the States of the Union of India. It is not, at the same time, the voice of the States and has no power to safeguard their interests. The justification of the Council of States, remarks Morris-Jones, "has always been in terms of 'second thought' rather than 'State rights.'" [12] On no occasion the federal conscience of the members of the Council of States revolted whenever the State Assemblies were dissolved; even nine Assemblies twice at one stroke in 1977 and 1980, without any valid reason or cause and contrary to the expectations of the framers of the Constitution.

It does not, however, mean that the Council of States occupies the same pitiable position as French Council of Republic under the Constitution of the Fourth Republic. Nor is it so ineffective as the Canadian Senate. "There is a misconception," wrote B.D. Jatti, Vice-President of India, "about the powers of the Rajya Sabha in financial matters." [13] It is true, he says, that Money Bills cannot be introduced in the Council and it is deemed to have been passed by both Houses if the Council does not make any "recommendation" within fourteen days and if "recommendations" are made it is up to the House of the People to a accept or reject such "recommendations." But the Constitution also provides that the Union Budget is to be laid before both the Houses of Parliament and it is discussed in the Council also, although the demands for grants are to be made only in the House of the People. A practice has, however, come into vogue that the Council of States discusses the working of

12. Morris-Jones, W.H., *The Government and Politics of India,* p. 193. Also refer to N. Gopalaswami Ayyangar's observations in the Constituent Assembly, *Constituent Assembly Debates,* Vol. IV, p. 644. and cited *ante.*
13. "Role of Elders", *The Tribune*, Chandigarh, January 26, 1975.

three or four important Ministries as it chooses during the Budget session. The reports of the Comptroller-General relating to the accounts of the Union are also laid before both Houses. The Council of States is also represented on two of the financial committees of Parliament—the Committee on Public Accounts, and the Committee on Public Undertakings.

The Council of States has, thus, a fairly adequate opportunity in influencing and even shaping the financial affairs of the country. It has not hesitated to recommend quite a number of amendments in the Income-Tax Bill, 1961 and the House of the People accepted all the proposed amendments.

The Council of States significantly performs the function of influencing the Government and weightage is given to the views expressed on the floor of the House by elder statesmen and eminent parliamentarians. Since the Council is smaller in membership and less worried by the pressure of work, the debates in the Council are less frequently subject to time control through time limits. The Council provides a calmer atmosphere where members can debate controversial questions in well-informed and objective manner. The debates are often outspoken marked by dignity and a remarkable responsiveness of public opinion. The tradition of dignified debates, observed, B.N. Banerjee, "which was built up by the House is the result of a happy combination of circumstances not the least of which is the fact that the five Chairmen of the Rajya Sabha [14] so far are among the most eminent person experts in their own lines." All these persons "have given an aura of dignity to the atmosphere of the House by conducting the proceedings with judicious combination of firmness and flexibility."[15]

The co-equal powers of the Council of States on constitutional amendments are of great importance. The House of the People cannot by itself amend the Constitution unless the Council agrees to such a change. The provisions of Article 108 governing the joint sittings of the two Houses in case of disagreement do not apply to Bills amending the Constitution. The Constitution (Twenty-fourth Amendment) Bill, 1970, which was passed by an overwhelming majority in the House of the People, was defeated in the Council of States by only a fraction of vote and, consequently, the amending Bill fell through. Apprehending stout opposition to the Constitution (Forty-third Amendment) Bill, 1977, its decussion was postponed till the next session of Parliament. The Council refused to adopt the Constitution (Forty-fourth Amendment) Bill 1978 except with five amendments. The Congress Opposition stalled on April 11, 1977 the final passage of the two official Bills, one to extend the term of Goa, Daman and Diu and Mizoram Assemblies, and the other to extend the term of the Delhi Metropolitan Council. Intervening in the discussion on a non-official Bill moved by the Communist Member Bhupesh Gupta seeking to amend Article 368 to provide that in the event of a disagreement between the two Houses over an amendment Bill of the Constitution there should be a joint session for resolving the differences, the Law Minister said that such suggestions were considered in 1971 and found unnecessary.[16]

Even with regard to ordinary legislation referred by the President to a joint sitting of the two Houses under article 108, B.N. Banerjee, the Secretary-General of the Council of States, rebutted the argument that the views of the House of the People will invariably prevail because of its numerical superiority. He explains that the critics of the Council of States "ignore the fact that a disagreement which may arise on important issues may not be the House *qua the House* but may arise on the basis of policies and approaches of the different political parties in the two Houses on the various issues. It is possible to contemplate a situation in which the decision of the Lok Sabha may be outvoted in joint sitting of two Houses.[17] There have been only two joint sittings of both Houses so far in order to resolve a deadlock on the Dowry Prohibition Bill in May 1961, and on the Banking Service Commission (Repeal) Bill in May 1978. In the Dowry Prohibition Bill one of the most important amendments, which the Council of States had been insisting from the beginning and the House of the People had been refusing to accept, was adopted at a joint sitting in May 1961.

The Constitution confers on the Council two special powers exclusively exercised by it

---

14. S. Radhakrishnan, Zakir Hussain, V. V. Giri, G. S. Pathak, B.D. Jatti, (M. Hidayatullah, and R. Venkatraman). The eighth Chairman, Dr. Shankar Dayal Sharma was another illustrious Vice-President.
15. "Rajya Sabha at work", Shakdhar, S. L. (Ed), *The Constitution and Parliament of India,* p. 314.
16. As reported in *The Times of India*, New Delhi, March 20, 1976.
17. "Rajya Sabha at work," Shakdhar, S.L. (Ed.), *The Constitution and Parliament of India,* p. 311.

and not shared with the House of the People. As stated earlier, Parliament is empowered to legislate with respect to any matters on the State List of the Seventh Schedule if the Council of States declared by a resolution that it is necessary or expedient in the national interest that Parliament should make laws thereon. Again, under Article 312 if the Council passes a resolution declaring that it is necessary or expedient in the national interest to create one or more All-India services common to the Union and States, Parliament will have the power to create by law such services. The Council of States twice passed such resolutions in 1961 and 1965. The resolution passed on December 6, 1961 recommended the creation of Indian Service of Engineers, the Indian Forest Service and Indian Medical and Health Services. On March 30, 1965 the Council passed a resolution for the creation of the Indian Education Service, though both these resolutions have not been implemented so far.

As a body which is not subject to dissolution but which perpetually renews itself every two years, the Council of States symbolises the permanence and continuity of Parliamentary institutions of the country. This continuity acquires a special significance when the House of the People stands dissolved and the Council of States is to discharge the Constitutional obligation under Articles 352, 356 and 360 relating to declaration of Emergency either due to war or external aggression or armed rebellion or threat thereto; breakdown of the constitutional machinery in a State; or financial Emergency.

These specific constitutional provisions make the Council of States an integral part of the machinery of Government. It is true, that the Council of States was not designed to vie with the House of the People, but it was not also the intention of the Constitution-makers to render the Council to play the "humble role of an unimportant adviser" or an occasional check on hasty legislation. In practice, the Council has, from the beginning of its career, played its role effectively in the affairs of the State and has vigorously focussed the attention of the Government on many matters of special importance in the life of the nation. In 1969, the Council passed the resolution that "this House is of the opinion that Government should take legal and other steps for the abolition of privy purses and privileges of ex-rulers before presentation of the general Budget in the coming February session of Parliament." The Council also acclaimed the nationalisation of the fourteen banks. The vigilant members of the Council made persistent demands during discussions for inquiring into the charges against the Punjab Chief Minister Partap Singh Kairon, grant of industrial licences to the Birlas and the affairs of Dharam Teja and Jayanti Shipping Company. Likewise, public attention on alleged irregularity in respect of import licences to some firms of Pondicherry was focussed for the first time through a starred question on August 27, 1974. Again, on August 10, 1978 the Council of States adopted a resolution demanding a probe into allegations of corruption against members of the families of Prime Minister Morarji Desai and Home Minister Charan Singh. The Chairman, B.D. Jatti, pointed out that the motion was necessarily a "recommendation" and it was for the Government to accept or not. When the Government decided not to accept the "recommendation", the Council asserted itself in a way thwarting the proceedings of the House compelling the Prime Minister to announce the Government's decision to refer the charges as contained in the resolution of the Council to the Chief Justice eventually leading to Vaidialingam probe which indicted the close relations of Desai and Charan Singh. The important committees, like the Committee on subordinate Legislation and Committee on Government Assurance have always played an effective role in influencing and supervising the administrative actions of the Government. The Committee on Petitions has proved to be a useful forum for ventilating the grievances of the public and getting redressed. B.D. Jatti, the former Vice-President of India and the Chairman of the Council, asserted that the Council of States "by its record of work has proved to be an effective force and I can say with confidence that in the years to come the critics of the second chamber are bound to find themselves in negligible minority."[18]

The Council of States has certainly belied the apprehensions of the critics of bicameralism in the Constituent Assembly that the Council will be "a clog in the wheel of progress of India", or that it could serve to keep the capitalistic outlook safe in India and that it would be a "unnecessary drain on our poor economy." The world has come a long way from Abbe Sieyes who disfavoured bicameralism with the epigram : "If a

18. "Role of the Elders," *The Tribune*, Chandigarh, January 26, 1975.

second chamber dissents from the first, it is mischievous; if it agrees it is superfluous'' Democracy proved that neither it is mischievous nor superfluous. The role and relevance of bicameralism has now veered round to John Stuart Mill who wrote, ''A majority in a single Assembly .........easily becomes despotic and overweening, if released from the necessity of considering whether its acts will be concurred by another constituted authority.'' India has a long tradition of its assemblies going down to the post-Vedic period and that heritage finds expression in a verse from Mahabharata inscribed on the opening page of ''Twenty-five years of Rajya Sabha'' brought out by the Rajya Sabha Secretariat in 1977 :

> That's not an Assembly where there are no eldermen,
> Those are not elders, who do not speak with righteousness.

But there is one aspect against which the Council of States must guard itself. While welcoming the sixty-four new members of the Council of States on April 6, 1960, Vice-President Radhakrishnan called upon them to fight ''inertia, obscurantism, reaction and superstition.'' These are the evils from which second chambers suffer in general and invite a widespread demand for their abolition. The Council of States should not be allowed to become a political prisoners' home. Law-making is a specilised job; and a modicum of technical knowledge and a certain intellectual ability are essential even to understand the problems that confront Legislatures in our times. The criterion laid down in the Constitution for nominations is a partial indication of what is expected of a second chamber. But it is evident from the nominations so far made that to a great exent the intentions of the framers of the Constitution have not been realised. The Congress did not always consciously try to fill the nominations with a corpus of special knowledge such as cannot be ensured in the House of the People.[19] Nor have the indirect elections of the remaining members introduced a body of seasoned parliamentarians, who might import into the debates ''an amount of learning and importance'', as Gopalswami Ayyangar argued in the Constituent Assembly. According to Morris-Jones the Council of States has three outstanding merits : ''It supplies additional political positions for which there is a demand, it provides some additional debating opportunities for which there is occasionally need, and it assists in the resolution of the legislative time table problems.'' It is, accordingly, incumbent on all political parties to help the Council of States to play its requisite role by sending to it members whose party grading may be low but I.Q. is high.

''But the House of the Elders is no longer elderly, feels the Chief Reporter, S. P. Agarwal, of the Council who retired recently after covering the Upper House for over thirty years. His observations are relevant to the atmosphere that now prevails in this House as compared to 1952, when it began its career. The first ten years of the Council of States were the House's finest hours. During this period there was hardly an occasion to call the House to order. Even if a member spoke for an hour he was heard with respect and without interruption. Points of order were rare. According to Agarwal there were less than a dozen expuctions during this period. Members themselves withdrew any word they felt was unparliamentary.

But the change began in the early seventies and ''the Rajya Sabha today has become more youthful. It is now vibrating with the situation prevailing outside in the country. The quality of the debate as also the composition is not as merited today as it was in the past. A major time of the House is lost in personal and party squabbles. Scant attention is paid to the rules of procedure and the rulings of the Chairman are invariably defied. Use of unparliamentary language and unruly behaviour rule the day. There are ''half a dozen expunctions in every session'' and not a day passes without an order that a Member's speech should not be recorded. The practice of ordering the House reporters not to take notes as the Member refuses to listen to the Chairman's entreaties to be seated has become ''in vogue'' since seventies.[20] Walk-ups is a normal feature.

---

19. C.C. Desai (Swatantra) moved in the House of the People a non-official Constitution Amendment Bill seeking to abolish nominations to the Council of States. His contention was that provisions of Article 80 had been misused. P. Govinda Menon, Law Minister, who intervened in the debate, said that it would be prudent to leave this provision alone so long as it did not prove injurious to the country's interests. He maintained that any human institution was prone to lapses. It could even be said, he added, that an element of patronage was inherent in any system of nominations. But it was undeniable that many of the nominated members had made significant contribution to the debates through their specialized knowledge.
20. *Indian Express*, New Delhi, August 4, 1982.

But the most disturbing development is the defiance of the Chairman's rulings and often use of in decorous language on his observations and comments on minor points at issue or when the Chairman performs his duty to protect the right of a Private Member in seeking more information on a question raised. Such an attitude of the parliamentarians and more so of seasoned Members of the House and Ministers, too, not only undermines the authority and dignity of the Chair, but the prestige of the House itself. A sharp clash between the Chairman, M. Hidayatullah, and the leader of the Janata Party of the House marked the start of the proceedings on September 15, 1981. Seconds after the Chairman occupied his seat and called for the first question, Piloo Mody stood up to ask him when he and some of his colleagues could raise certain issues in his (M. Hidayatullah's ) presence in the House. The Chairman told him that he did not have to guarantee his presence in the House, but "You can certainly come to my chamber and raise anything you want." When Mody sharply insisted that the members of the House were entitled to raise matters in the House in his presence and not in his chamber, the Chairman reminded him, "Nobody seems to have told you that you are sometimes inclined to be rude." Mody retorted, "I am inclined to be rude as I am recipient of rudeness also. I hope you will take it in the same spirit."[21]

But Pranab Mukherjee's behaviour, who was the Finance Minister and the Leader of the House, reveals more than it can be described. On November 2, 1982, the Chairman intervened on behalf of a Member who was not satisfied with the Finance Minister's replies to a question on World Bank loans to developing countries. The Minister replied that he had already given the requisite information. But the Chairman did not agree with him. The Minister thereupon became sharp in his reply. The Chairman told him, "There is such a thing as politeness." Mukherjee retorted, "Yes, that is why I do not want, that you should come between me and the Member." The Chairman reminded him, "I will, that is why I am sitting in the Chair." Mukherjee curtly replied, "I will accept your ruling without any question.....But don't have a running commentary. Let me answer the question in my own way."[22]

Relevant proceedings of the Constituent Assembly suggest that rewarding talent was not the sole aim of the Constitution-makers in providing for nominated members. They visualised the Council of States as a mechanism for moderating, rather than rivalling or thwarting the House of the People (Lok sabha).[23] One member likened the Upper Chamber to the saucer that might cool the beverage in a cup but which could never threaten the cup. If the Council of States was to mellow the Lower House's emotions with fresh reflection, the nominated members were to be of a special value as they were expected to add a component wisdom that was not only specialised but also detached and non-partisan. But this precious expectation has not been fulfilled as nominations have now degenerated into party spoils.

Even biennial elections to the Council of States are being fought strictly on party lines and selection of candidates is made purely on party considerations. Those who, per chance, were non-party nominees they did not remain aloof from active politics and many formally joined the ruling party as it was rewarding to do so. The Anti-defection law is now a great deterrent, but such nominations are not likely to disappear altogether. The voting pattern of most others shows that they have generally sided with the Government whatever be the merit of the measure under consideration. Independence and talent are guarantees against the principle of nomination in vogue.

**Relations between the Houses**

Jawaharlal Nehru gave a succinct exposition about the relations of the Council of States and the House of the People. "Under our Constitution," he explained, "Parliament consists of two Houses, each functioning in the allotted sphere laid down in the Constitution...........sometimes we refer back to practice and conventions prevailing in the Houses of Parliament of the United Kingdom and even refer erroneously to an Upper House and Lower House. I do not think that is correct...........To consider either of these Houses an Upper House or a Lower House is not correct Each House has full authority to regulate its procedure within the limits of the Constitution. Neither House by itself constitutes Parliament. It is the two Houses together that are the Parliament in India. The successful working of our constitu-

21. As reported in *Indian Express,* New Delhi, September 16, 1981.
22. As reported in *The Times of India., New Delhi, November 3, 1982.*
23. *Constituent Assembly Debates,* Vol. IV, pp. 928 ff.

tion, as of our democratic structure, demands the closest cooperation between the two Houses." The Council has powers similar to those of the House of the People, except in matters financial and responsibility of the Council of Ministers. The party composition of both Houses remained similar till March, 1977 when Congress lost its majority in the House of People but regained its previous position after January 1980, though it did not command a two-third majority. Even the social composition of the Council and the House resembles each other. The Council had its members the galaxy of some eminent personalities who served the Council since it came into existence; Pattabhi Sitaramayya, Sardar K. M. Panikkar, Dr. Tara Chand, Dr. Radha Kumud Mukherjee, Prof. S. N. Bose, B.R. Ambedkar, Alladi Krishnaswami Ayyar, P. N. Sapru, G. S. Pathak, M. C. Setalved, M. C. Chagla, C. K. Daphtary, K. Santhanam, Rama Krishna Rao, Dr. Ramaswami Mudliar, R.R. Diwakar and Bhupesh Gupta are a few of the many more. The procedure for the conduct of business in both Houses is also not appreciably distinguishable. The Council has a regular question hour [24] and the same half-an-hour discussion procedure as in the House of the People. From 1964 the revised Rules of Procedure provide for discussion on matters of urgent public importance. Petitions for redress of grievances can be made to the Council. A new Committee, namely, the Committee on Subordinate Legislation has since been extended by including within the ambit of its functions various rules, regulations and orders framed in pursuance of the Constitution also. [25] The Committee on Government Assurances has also been set up.

The Government, too, had made an effort to introduce first in the Council of States an increasing number of public Bills. Since 1952 up to the end of December 1974, 312 Government Bills were introduced in the Council. From the analysis of the subject-matter of those Bills it can definitely be said that quite a good number of them were of immense social, educational and legal importance. Apart from the Hindu Marriage and Divorce Bill, 1952, the Hindu Minority and Guardianship Bill, 1953, the Hindu Succession Bill, 1954 and the Hindu Adoptions and Maintenance Bill, 1956, some of the more important legislative measures introduced in the Council were the Working Journalists (Industrial Disputes) Bill, 1955, the Children Bill, 1959, the Foreign Marriage Bill 1963, the Press Council Bill, 1963, the Banaras Hindu University (Amendment) Bill 1964, the Jawaharlal Nehru University bill 1964, the Monopolies and Restrictive Trade Practices Bill, 1967, the Medical Termination of Pregnancy Bill, 1969, the Code of Criminal Procedure Bill, 1970, the Foreign Contribution (Regulation) Bill, 1974. The Constitution (Fortieth Amendment) Bill, 1975 was also initiated in the Council of States.

The Council of States, thus, started its career on the same lines as the House of the People. But being a chamber primarily intended for reflection, its members had the psychological realisation of its inferiority and, consequently, they felt frustrated. There had been also vehement critics of bicameralism who strongly pleaded for its abolition. But, "it is the habit of institutions," as Morris-Jones had remarked, "to give birth to loyalties."[26] The Council, therefore, tried to assert itself in order to remove the impression of its inferiority. A bitter rivalry between the two Houses soon developed despite the dominating position of one party in both Houses.

The first clash between the two Houses occurred during the Budget session of 1953 when the Council of States refused to accept the position of subordination by disallowing the Law Minister, a member-Minister of the Council, to appear before the House of the People, on its call, to clear some misunderstanding that had arisen on the Income-Tax (Amendment) Bill, 1952. The Council of States thereupon passed a resolution that "this Council is of the opinion that the Leader of the Council (Law Minister Biswas) be directed not to present himself in any capacity whatsoever in the House of the People." It angered the members of the other House and they asserted that Ministers were responsible to the House of the People and doubted the propriety of the Council's resolution." There would have been an open rupture if the tactful intervention of the Prime Minister had not saved the situation.

Soon there was another occasion for conflict. In January 1953 the Rules Committee of the Council of States sent its proposals with regard to the Public Accounts Committee to the House

24. When the Council met for the first time in May 1952 the question hour was restricted to only twice a week.
25. Previously the Committee examined and scrutinised rules, regulations and orders in pursuance of legislative functions only.
26. Morris-Jones, W.H., *Parliament in India,* p. 255.

of the People. It had suggested that the Council should have either a Public Accounts Committee of its own, or seven of its members should be added to make it a joint committee of both Houses. The Public Accounts Committee passed a resolution that a joint committee of the two Houses or a separate committee of the Council "would be against principles underlying the Constitution." The Rules Committee of the House of the People, which considered the proposal of the Rules Committee of the Council, agreed with the opinion expressed by the Public Accounts Committee in its resolution. The matter would have ended there, but the motion of the Prime Minister in the House "to recommend to the Council of States that they nominate seven members to associate with the Public Accounts Committee of this House" brought the issue in the open. The motion of the Prime Minister did not envisage a Joint Public Accounts Committee of two Houses, yet it caused a good deal of criticism and resentment in the House of the People. It was on the assurance of the Prime Minister that the Committee would be a Committee of the House of the People under the control of the Speaker and that the financial powers of the House were in no way threatened that the motion was finally passed in December 1953 and the seven members of the Council of States joined the Public Accounts Committee in May 1954. Similar difficulties arose with regard to the composition of Joint Committees of both Houses and somewhat sullenly the House of the People agreed to the proposals of the Council of States.

The Chatterjee incident engendered still more excitement and resentment. N.C. Chatterjee, a Member of the House of the People, was reported to have said that the Upper House, "which is supposed to be a body of elders, seems to be behaving irresponsibly like a pack of urchins." The question of privileges was raised in the Council of States and the Chairman directed the Secretary of the Council to ascertain the facts. The House members objected to the letter of the Council Secretary inquiring from N. C. Chatterjee whether the report was correct. The Speaker held that the Secretary's letter was more "in the nature of a writ" and suggested that the reference to this particular issue, and the general problem of procedure in such cases be made to a joint meeting of the Privileges Committees of both Houses. The Council agreed to the Speaker's suggestion and the two Privileges Committees worked out an acceptable procedure for cases where a member of the House commits a breach of the privileges of the other.

The Chairman of the Legislative Council (Rajya Sabha) M. Hidayatullah, while interpreting Rule 187 relating to the rights and privileges of the members of the Upper House on the Parliamentary Committee on Public Undertakings gave his ruling, July 1982, that members of the Council on this Committee were "associate members." As a consequence of this ruling the Opposition members of the Council in Public Undertakings Committee and the Public Accounts Committee resigned *en bloc*. The opposition members unanimously demanded that Rule 187 be so amended as to remove the anomaly at the earliest. The Speaker of the House of the People in his ruling on the issue recalled what Jawaharlal Nehru had said on May 13, 1953 in support of the motion for association of members of the Council of States with the Public Accounts Committee and observed, "It has been ceaseless endeavour" to live up to Nehru's sagacious counsel "in letter and spirit". Intervening in the discussion, Finance Minister Pranab Mukherjee assured the Council, on August 2, 1982, that it would not be difficult to sort out the matter on the basis of the usages, practices and conventions and the Speaker's ruling of July 28, 1982 that members of both Houses of Parliament were equal in every respect.

These disputes brought into prominence the question of the utility of the Council of States. A Private Member moved a resolution in the House of the People in April, 1954 demanding the abolition of the Upper House. Some Members of the House belonging to the Congress Party and the Leftists advanced the same old familiar argument that the Council of States was a stronghold of reactionary elements and a device to flout the voice of th people. One Member spoke about "the mad drive towards equalisation of powers and functions." Some argued for the retention of the Council of States but urged that its members should be chosen differently. The Government view was that the Council of States had not been given a fair trial and that it was too early to pronounce a judgment on its utility. Once again, after two decades, Niren Ghosh, Marxist member of the Council, while welcoming B.D. Jatti, on assuming the office of the Vice-President of India and, as such, Chairman of the Council on August 31, 1974, on behalf of his Party, said that the Council of States represented the States of the Union and the nationalities of the Union and accordingly, deserved to be "upgraded" in its parliamentary powers. He suggested that the Constitution be so amended as to give equal powers, to the Council of States and the House of the People.[27]

Unless it is acceptably proved that democracy does not need a second chamber, and more so a federation, it is not democratic to urge for its abolition. Institutions are always reluctant to vanish and it does not seem likely that public opinion could be made to agree to the liquidation of the Council of States. But enjoyment of identical powers and functions by both of Houses means a sheer duplication and the advantages of such a system of legislature are questionable. Democracy has decidely made the representative Chamber a predominant partner, and the second Chamber is created to exercise a moderating influence, a couterposise to democratic fervour, a safety which lies to sober second thought and, consequently, a check on hasty and ill-considered legislation. It serves as a brake, but not too tight a brake which may lead to an open rupture between the two Chambers. The intention of the framers of India's Constitution was significantly clear on this point and the Constitution itself is quite specific about it. Once this point is appreciated by both the Houses the cause or causes of conflict, if any, are sure to disappear and each House will shine within its allotted sphere of functions. Incredible as it may seem, even a former Prime Minister is known to have told some senior Members of the Council of States on more than one occasion that the "Lok Sabha is the real Parliament. We are directly elected by the people not indirectly. Whom does your House represent? It should be abolished." He altogether forgot that India is a federation for which second Chamber is the prerequisite condition as it represents the States, its constituent units.

Such like utterances create confusion and friction without realising the repercussion on the body politic. Morris-Jones has succinctly said, "What is certain is that peaceful co-existence is difficult if the two Houses continue to desire to perform the same functions." If their roles are not soon distinguished, "the tradition of rivalry will soon become established and the Council will continue to attract a large number of persons who would have been more readily found themselves in the House of the People." The practice of rivalry is most wasteful exercise of political energies "and it can only serve to lower Parliament as a whole in public esteem,"[28] he added.

B. D. Jatti foresees an important role that the Council of States may play in the body politic of the Country. He maintains, "In view of the present political set-up in the country a situation may arise when the governments in a number of States may be run by political parties other than the party at the Centre and this will have its impact on the Rajya Sabha. Then the Rajya Sabha will have an important role to play in handling the problem of federal adjustment."[29]

## THE HOUSE OF THE PEOPLE (LOK SABHA)

### Composition and Organisation

The House of the People (Lok Sabha) is the representative Chamber of Parliament of India. It had a maximum membership of 525; not more than 500 members chosen by direct election from territorial constituencies in the States and not more than 25 members from the Union Territories chosen in such a manner as Parliament by law provided. The Constitution (Thirty-first Amendment) Act, 1973, increased the upper limit for representation of the States to 525 and set the limit for representation of the Union Territories at 20. The Goa, Daman and Diu Reorganisation Act, 1987, necessitated further change in the composition of the House of the People. Article 81 now provides that subject to the provisions of Article 331, relating to nomination of not more than two members of the Anglo-Indian Community the House of the People shall consist of :

(a) not more than five hundred and thirty members chosen by direct election from territorial constituencies in the States, and

(b) not more than twenty members to represent the Union Territories, chosen in such manner as Parliament may by law provide.

A person is qualified to be chosen to fill a seat in the House of the People if he :-

(a) is a citizen of India, and makes and subscribes before some person author-

27. As reported in *The Hindustan Times*, New Delhi, September 1, 1974.
28. Morris-Jones, *Parliament in India*, p. 262.
29. *The Tribune*, Chandigarh, January 26, 1975.

ised in that behalf by the Election Commission an oath or affirmation according to the form set out for the purpose in the Third Schedule to the Constitution;[30]

(b) is not less than twenty-five years of age; and

(c) possesses such other qualifications as may be prescribed in that behalf by or under any law made by Parliament.

In the case of a seat reserved for the Scheduled Castes in any State, a candidate for election to the House of the People should be a member of any of the Scheduled Castes, whether of that State or of any other State and should be a elector for a parliamentary constituency. In the case of a seat reserved for Scheduled Tribes in any State, he should be a member of any of the scheduled Tribes, whether of that State or of any other State and should be an elector for any parliamentary constituency.

A person is disqualified for being chosen as, and for being a member of either House of Parliament :—

(i) if he holds any such office of profit under the Government of India or the Government of any States as is declared by Parliament by law to disqualify its holders;

(ii) if he is of unsound mind and stands so declared by a competent court;

(iii) if he is an undischarged insolvent;

(iv) if he is not a citizen of India, or has voluntarily acquired the citizenship of a foreign State, or is under any acknowledgment of allegiance or adherence to a foreign State; and

(v) if he is so disqualified by or under any law made by Parliament.

Article 103 deals with the decision on questions as to disqualification of members. Originally, it provided that all questions about the disqualification of a person would be decided by the President in accordance with the opinion rendered by the Election Commission. The Constitution (Forty-second Amendment) Act, 1976, substituted a new Article providing that the question whether a member had become subject to any of the disqualifications mentioned in Article 102 (1) or as to whether a person, found guilty of a corrupt practice at an election to a House of Parliament under any law made by Parliament was disqualified, including the question as to the period of disqualification, would be decided by the President after consulting the Election Commission. The Election Commission might hold any inquiry for this purpose as it deemed fit. The decision of the President in this respect was final.

The Constitution (Forty-fourth Amendment) Act, 1978, omitted Article 103 as inserted by the one restoring the original position. It now provides that the question whether a member has become subject to any of the disqualifications mentioned in Article 102 (1) shall be referred to the decision of the President and his decision shall be final. But before giving any such decision, the President shall obtain the opinion of the Election Commission and act according to such opinion.

The Union Constitution Committee had recommended a term of four years for the House. The Drafting Committee accepted the opinion of de Valera, and changed it into five years. The Draft Constitution in a footnote explained the justification for this change. It said, "The Committee has inserted 'five years' instead of 'four years' as the life of the House of the People as it considers that under parliamentary system of government the first year of a Minister's term of office would generally be taken up in gaining knowledge of the work of administration and the last year would be taken up in preparing for the next general election, and there would thus be only two years for effective work which should be too short a period for planned administration."

## THE SPEAKER

### Office of the Speaker

The House elects its own Speaker from among its members to preside over its sittings and conduct its proceedings. The Speaker vacates his office if he ceases to be a member of the House. He may at any time resign from his office or may be removed on a resolution passed by a majority of all the then members of the House. Fourteen days' notice for moving such a resolution is required to be given. The Speaker does not vacate his office on the dissolution of the House; he continues in office until immediately before the first sitting of the reconstitued House after the dissolution.

30. Inserted by the Constitution (Sixteenth Amendment), Act, 1963. The form of an oath or affirmation is :
"I, A. B., having been nominated as a candidate to fill a seat in the Council of States (or the House of the People) do swear in the name of God/solemnly affirm that I will bear true faith and allegiance to the Constitution of India as by law establilshed and that I will uphold the sovereignty and integrity of India.

The Constitution also provides for the office of the Deputy Speaker and he performs the duties of the Speaker when the latter is absent or while the office of the Speaker is vacant. In Britain the Speaker is indispensable and without him the House can not meet. In India, on the other hand, the Constitution definitely provides, that while the office of the Speaker is vacant the duties of the office shall be performed by the Deputy Speaker. And if the office of the Deputy Speaker, too, happens to be vacant, then, the duties of the office of the Speaker shall be performed by such member of the House, as the President may appoint for the purpose. When both the Speaker and the Deputy Speaker are absent from any sitting of the House one of such members as may be determined by the Rules of Procedure of the House acts as Speaker. The Rules of Procedure and Conduct of Business in Parliament, 1950, provide that at the commencement of the Parliament or from time to time as the case may be, the Speaker nominates from amongst the members of Parliament a panel of not more than six chairmen any one of whom may preside in the absence of the Speaker and the Deputy Speaker when so required by the Speaker or in his absence by the Deputy Speaker. If none of the chairmen of the panel be available, the House may choose one of its members to act as Speaker. Neither the Speaker nor the Deputy Speaker is to preside while a resolution for his own removal is under consideration, although he is entitled to be present, speak in and otherwise to take part in the proceedings of the House. He shall also have the right to vote but only in the first instance on such resolution or on any other matter during such proceedings. But he does not exercise a casting vote in the case of an equality of votes.[31]

The Constitution gives to the Speaker only a casting vote to be exercised in the case of equality of votes. This provision incorporates the British convention that the Speaker of the House of the Commons does not vote except in case of a tie. But the British Speaker usually endeavours to give the casting vote in such a way that it does not make the decision final, thereby extending to the House another opportunity to consider the question.

The Constitution provides that the Speaker and the Deputy Speaker shall receive such salaries and allowances as may be determined by Parliament and they are charged on the Consolidated Fund of India.

31. Article 96 (2).

**Position of the Speaker**

The office of the Speaker is of much dignity, honour and authority. Like the Speaker of the British House of Commons, the Speaker of the House of the People (Lok Sabha) interprets the will of the House and speaks for it as well as to it. He is the custodian of the dignity of the House and an impartial arbiter in its proceedings. Speaking in the Constituent Assembly of India (Legislative), on March 8, 1948, on the occasion of the unveiling of the portrait of the late V.J. Patel, the Prime Minister observed : "Now, Sir, specially on behalf of the government, may I say that we would like the distinguished occupant of this Chair now and always to guard the freedom and liberties of the House from every possible danger, even from the danger of executive intrusion. There is always that danger—even from a National Government that it may choose to ride roughshod over the opinions of a minority, and it is there that the Speaker comes to protect each single member, or each single group........ Vithalbhai Patel....laid the foundations of those traditions which have already grown up round the Chair.......I hope that those traditions will continue, because the position of the Speaker is not an individual's position or an honour done to an individual. The Speaker represents the House. He represents the dignity of the House and because the House represents the nation, in a particular way, the Speaker becomes the symbol of the nation's liberty and freedom. Therefore, it is right that that should be an honoured position, a free position and should be occupied always by men of outstanding ability and impartiality.'

Vithalbhai Patel may be regarded as the first Speaker in India, though his official designation was the President of the Legislative Assembly, who laid the foundations of the office by following the British traditions. Immediately after his election to the Chair in 1925, he declared himself a no party man and rigidly abstained from any kind of political activity. He had established such a firm reputation as a Speaker and his position was so unchallenged that in spite of the many remarkable rulings he gave which were not to the liking of the Government of the day he was unanimously elected to the Chair both by the official and non-official members of the Assembly of that day. And when the urge to participate in the Civil Disobedience Movement of 1930 came Patel resigned from his office. But the

Congress was the first to violate the conventions associated with the office of the Speaker in Britain and so scrupulously observed by Vithalbhai Patel. Mohammed Yakub succeeded Patel, but he was there only for a session. Ibrahim Rahimtoola, who succeeded Yakub soon after his election to Chair, resigned for reasons of health. Then, came Shanmukham Chetty. But at the next General Election, Shanmukham Chetty was opposed and defeated by the Congress candidate. Since then, the retiring Speakers have always been opposed in the General Election and the Speakers themselves, till the election of N. Sanjiva Reddy, retained their active party affiliations. On May 17, 1967 when Reddy was elected Speaker of the Fourth House of the People, he observed, "My office requires of me to be impartial and judicious in the conduct of my work. I can assure you with all the force at my command that I will try to live up to this requirement and maintain the high traditions set by my predecessors. As a necessary corollary to this resolve, I resign my membership of the party (Congress) to which I had the honour to belong for 34 years. So long as I occupy this Chair it shall be my endeavour to see that all sections of this House get an honest impression that I do not belong to any party at all." When Gurdial Singh Dhillon was elected Speaker in August 1969, he resigned from the Congress Party in Parliament but continued to be a member of the Congress Party.

N. Sanjiva Reddy resigned from the Speakership in 1969 and was nominated the Congress candidate for the Fourth Presidential election. Reddy was again elected the Speaker of the Sixth House of the People as a Janata Party candidate. But this time he did not resign from his party. He took, on the other hand, active part in the party politics. Reddy disclosed the mind of his Party when he told the newsmen at Hyderabad on April 9, 1977 that the Forty-third Constitutional Amendment Bill, which sought to reduce the term of the House of the People and the State Assemblies to five years, was introduced in Parliament with the Presidential election in mind. He also said that the Bill was introduced to "respect the feeling of Mr. Jayaprakash Narayan who wanted the States also to go to polls.[32] Addressing a public meeting at Tirupati on April 12, 1977, Reddy asked the Janata Party workers to find out what was wrong with their campaigning in the South. He asked the rural youth, especially the educated, to tour the villages and explain to the people why the Janata Party was voted to power in the North and how the unity of the country should be preserved. "There is no question of North versus South in elections," he added.[33]

The Congress Working Committee in a resolution determined that the Speakers, both in the States as well at the Centre, should keep back from Congress election. But this decision of the Working Commute did not imply that they could remain members of the Congress Party. This point was further made clear by G.V. Mavalankar, Speaker of the First Lok Sabha. Speaker maintained, the speaker in India is not today absolutely out of the political arena as the speaker of the House of Commons though with very extensive limitations on his activities. He may continue to be a member of his Party, but he should not take part in the affairs of the party, particularly in regard to matters which are likely to come before the House for discussion and decision. We have also considered it proper that he should not take sides in public controversies in respect of matters likely to come before the House. In short, he should not identify himself with any propaganda or express any opinions which are likely to embarrass his position as the presiding authority or is likely to create an impression that the Speaker is a partisan."

Mavalankar admitted that the logical corollary of the Speaker's position in Britain is that his seat is not contested in the General Election and he is elected Speaker so long as he wishes to be so elected irrespective of his party affiliation. But "with the present state of political consciousness of public life in India," Mavalankar added, "it is too much to expect that people with different ideologies will all respect the convention of not contesting the election of the Speaker and it is this aspect which very seriously affects the adoption in toto of all British conventions in respect of the office of the Speaker."[34]

32. *The Sunday Standard*, New Delhi, April 10, 1977.
33. *The Statesman*, New Delhi, April 15, 1977.
34. More, S.S., *Practice and Procedure of Indian Parliament*, p. 79.

Mavalankar considered the British precedent an ideal to be reached in course of time. [35]

Mavalankar followed the middle course between the two schools of thought in India; the new school which urged the impartiality of the Chair does not depend on the nature of the Speaker's outside activities and accordingly, did not accept the British model of absolute severance from politics, and the older orthodox school which insisted on the adherence to the British model and emphasised that impartiality demanded sincere attempts to break previous political connections. According to Mavalankar's middle course, the Speaker may not be a partisan yet he still remains a party man and is the choice of his party. But every party man has his own prejudices and the prejudices of a promoted politician are, indeed, very strong. The Chair, under such circumstances, cannot command that much reverence as it does in Britain for its impartiality. The result was the first motion of no-confidence moved against the Speaker on December 18, 1954. It was condemned by the Prime Minister as "vicious" and he described the Opposition responsible for it as "incompetent and frivolous." The motion was lost on a voice vote, but it had a lesson. It gave a setback to the dignity of the Chair and, as such, to the dignity of Parliament.

The Socialist Member of Parliament, Madhu Limaye, gave a notice, on March 3, 1975, of a no-confidence motion against Speaker Gurdial Singh Dhillon "for having lowered the prestige of the office." It was also signed by Piloo Mody (BLD) and S.N. Mishra (Congress O). Listing thirteen charges against the Speaker, Madu Limaye, *inter alia*, accused Dhillon for having wilfully abolished the right of the members to raise points of order and having "continually and arbitrarily" disallowed, in total violation of the rules, questions highly embarrassing to the Government. It was also alleged that the Speaker constantly interrupted even those members who were speaking with his permission and not letting them complete their submissions.

The notice was subsequently withdrawn for reasons best known to Madu Limaye and his associates. But the result of such motions of no confidence against the Speaker and especially charging him for having lowered the prestige of office by partiality towards the Government is disastrous. Such ugly scenes, as disorderly defiance of Speaker's rulings, interruptions by raising irrelevant points of order and staging a walk-out had become a common feature of the proceedings of Parliament prior to the Sixth House of the People elections. Speaker Hukam Singh, addressing a conference of Presiding Officers on October 29, 1966, stressed the need for finding a "permanent and lasting" solution of the problem of "repeated disorders" in Parliament and State Legislatures. [36] Satyanarayan Singh, Union Minister for Parliamentary Affairs, called for a "Pathological diagnosis" of the causes of disorderly scenes in India's Legislatures[37] President Giri, in his inaugural address to the Speakers' Conference in New Delhi, in December 1970, raised the question whether any useful purpose was served by framing codes of conduct for legislators. "No member of Parliament or of a legislative body", he said "can hope to impress his constituents by some act of his or some sensation" which makes headline news. But the majority of the Legislators, the President observed, do not share this view. "In any event", he further added, "there is no evidence that any member has in the slightest degree impaired his career by being the storm centre of disorderly scenes in Parliament or a State Legislature. Otherwise it is difficult to see why noisy interruption of parliamentary proceedings is becoming more and more frequent after e ach successive election.[38] The Speaker's continued association with his party is an undeniable and a potential cause

35. The Conference of the Presiding Officers of Legislative bodies held at Trivandrum in July-August, 1951, passed the resolution: "The conference is of the opinion that it is desirable in the interests of the development of free democratic institutions in this country that following the practice of the British House of Commons a convention should be established to the effect that the seat from which the Speaker or the Chairman stands for election should not be contested......The necessary corollary of the full establishment of this convention would be that the Speaker or Chairman would not take part in any party politics. The conference feels that such convention is a healthy one and its growth should be encouraged." *Journal of Parliamentary Information,* Vol. I, p. 141. The National Committee of the Samyukta Socialist Party decided on October 17, 1968 that the Party would not oppose, in any election, a Speaker who had immediately on assumption of office renounced his Party affiliation. It called on other political parties to follow suit. *The Tribune*, Ambala Cantt. October 19, 1968.
36. *The Hindustan Times,* New Delhi, October 29,1966.
37. Presidentail Address delivered at the Fifth All India Whips' Conference, Bangalore, January 3, 1966. *The Hindustan Times,* New Delhi, January 5, 1966.
38. *The Times of India*, New Delhi, December 30, 1970.

of such a vicious circle. When sitting Speakers, as Gurudial Singh Dhillon can be switched over to ministerial posts, there is ample justification for lack of confidence in the impartiality of the Speaker and distrust thus caused breeds disorderly scenes and unruly members.

But Balram Jakhar, Speaker of the Seventh House of the People, excelled his mentor Gurdial Singh Dhillon. *The Tribune* reported[39] that the Speaker joined five Congress (I) leaders from Punjab[40] on April 30, 1980 in Delhi "to screen the list of seekers of the party tickets" and in doing so had "violated" one of the "most sacrosanct conventions of the democratic form of government." It caused not a few eyebrows to be raised among veteran parliamentarians and sparked a controversy in the whole country. Despite the rebuttal of Darbara Singh, the Punjab Chief Minister, Gurdial Singh Dhillon and Satpal Mittal, two other participants in the meeting, confirmed the Speaker's presence and sought to make it a non-issue by adding that Jakhar was there "merely" for consultation in regard to the party candidates for the Assembly segments forming his parliamentary constituency. Once the Speaker was elected on party ticket, Dhillon argued among other things, "the party's claim to utilize his services was natural."[41] Whatever be the justification, Jakhar's presence in a party meeting for the selection of party candidates for the Assembly poll is a matter of serious concern for the future of the parliamentary system in which the Speaker occupies a key position. The image of his independence and impartiality is shattered and what happens everyday on the floor of the House is its clear testimony.

The House of the People (Lok Sabha), on April 15, 1987, rejected by a voice vote the no-confidence motion against Speaker Balram Jakhar. The motion specifically brought out the charge that the Speaker had barred Parliament from discussing vital constitutional and procedural issues and the burning problems of the day; the obvious reference was to his ruling of March 19, 1987 as a result of which members were not permitted to raise a discussion on the relationship between the President and the Council of Ministers under Article 78 of the Constitution. The Speaker had also ruled that even during the discussion on a motion of censure or no-confidence directed against the Council of Ministers "the relationship between the President and the Prime Minister or the Council of Ministers, including the advice tendered or exercised or correspondence exchanged between them cannot be allowed to be brought in to influence the debate." Madhu Dandavate, Janata member, described during the acrimonious discussion of the motion of no confidence the ruling of the Speaker as a piece of "misrepresentation of the Constitution, rules of the House and precedents." Such an accusation, whether legally correct or not, certainly reflects on the dignity and impartiality of the Speaker and erodes his authority.

In the Eighth Lok Sabha no Party commanded a majority. But the Janata Dal and its National Front Allies could count on the avowed support of the Left Parties and the BJP and were thus assured a working majority in the House. Rabi Ray was elected the Speaker, though much against the wishes of V. P. Singh. It goes to the credit of Rabi Ray that he did act with exemplary impartiality during his all too brief term as Speaker. He was even called upon to give a ruling on the question of disqualification of certain members who violated the anti- defection law by crossing the floor which he did with objectivity.

The election of Shiv Raj Patil as Speaker of the Tenth Lok Sabha without a contest was rather dramatic as his success was assured the moment the Bhartiya Janata Party, the main Opposition Party in the Lok Sabha with a strength of 117, expressed itself in favour of support to his candidature. From the beginning the Congress (I) was keen that its nominee should occupy the key post notwith- standing its minority status. Yet it did not make any serious effort to reach consensus on this matter, particularly with the Janata Dal and the Left who had all along persisted with the candidature of Rabi Ray. Having come to realise that Ray did not stand a chance of making the grade the National Front finally decided not to press its claim describing the understanding between the Congress and the BJP as a clandestine arrangement and an opportunistic idea. It was the contention of the Prime Minister P .V. Narasimha Rao, that it was imperative for the Congress (I) to bag the Speakership "if the Gov-

39. *The Tribune*, Chandigarh, May 3, 1980.
40. The five leaders were : Giani Zail Singh, Darbara Singh, Gurdial Singh Dhillon, Buta Singh and Sat Pal Mittal. Mrs. Gandhi was "present at the meeting throughout."
41. Gurdial Singh Dhillon's statement issued on May 4, 1980 from Amritsar, The Tribune, Chandigarh, May 5, 1980.

ernment is to run'' implying thereby that a smooth functioning was next to impossible if the post went to a candidate belonging to some other party.

In fact, there has been no precedent of an Opposition candidate occupying the office of Speaker so far and the ruling Party must have felt that it should not give up its right if it even meant making certain compromises in achieving the desired goal. This indeed was the refrain of the Prime Minister when he categorically asserted that they had to brush aside all inhibitions and do everything that was needed to ensure that the ruling Party candidate was elected Speaker whatever the cost might be. Two important results emerge from this. The first is that unlike Britain, Speakership in India is a post not an institution and, secondly, the post of a Speaker is partisan institution as its incumbent must be a partyman.

**Powers and Functions of the Speaker**

The functions and authority of the Speaker in India resemble more or less to those of the Speaker of the British House of Commons. He speaks for the House and to the House and, as such, is the principal spokesman of the House. Messages on behalf of the House and to the House are sent or received with the authority of the Speaker. All Bills passed by the House are authenticated by his signatures before they are sent to the Council of States for its consideration or the President for his assent. He receives all petitions, appeals, messages and documents addressed to the House and all orders of the House are executed through him.

Communications from the President to the House are made through the Speaker. When a message from the President, whether with respect to a Bill pending in Parliament or otherwise, is received by the Speaker, he reads it to the House and gives necessary directions in regard to the procedure to be followed for the consideration of matters referred to in the message, and in giving those directions he may suspend or vary those to such extent as he may deem necessary. Similarly, all communications from House to the President are made through the Speaker in the form of a formal address after a motion has been made and carried by the House.[42]

The Speaker presides over the sittings of th House and conducts its proceedings. He decides who shall have the floor and all speeches and remarks are addressed to the Chair. He proposes and puts the necessary questions and announces the results. In consultation with the Leader of the House, the Speaker determines the order of business, the time to be allotted for different kinds of business, and sees that it is taken up and finished according to the Time Allocation Orders. He is the final judge to decide on the admissibility of questions, resolutions and motions. He must also certify, under Article 110 of the Constitution, whether a Bill is a Money Bill or not. Every Money Bill, when it is transmitted to the Council of States is so certified by him, as also when it is presented to the President for his assent. The Speaker does not vote except in the case of a tie.

The Speaker does not take part in the deliberations of the House except in the discharge of his duties as the presiding officer of the House. He may, however, either on a point of order, or on a request made by a member, address the House at any time on a matter under consideration with a view to help and aid members in their deliberations.[43] Such instances are rare,[44] but whenever he addresses the House those expressions are not to be taken in the nature of a ruling.

The Speaker exercises his powers and functions partly under the Constitution and partly under the Rules of Procedure of the House. He has also the power to deal with all matters which are not adequately provided for in the Rules of Procedure. He has, in fact, done so quite frequently and now all such precedents have been embodied in book form as Directions of the Speaker and are made available to the members of the House. The Speaker maintains perfect order and decorum in the House and has wide powers to check disorder, irrelevance and unparliamentary language or behaviour. A member who shows disrespect to the Chair by not obeying his order may be punished by suspension from the service of the House, and any reflection on the action or character of the Speaker for his ruling is a grave breach of order which will receive immediate and serious reproof. If the Speaker is of the opinion that a word or words used in the debate are defamatory or indecent, or

42. Rule 47. A common example is the Motion of Thanks adopted in the House on the President's address to the two Houses of Parliament assembled together. Such a motion is conveyed by the Speaker to the President.
43. Rule 360.
44. For instance, Speaker, Mavalankar elucidated a procedure which he desired the House to follow in regard to the debate on the report of the States Reorganisation Commission. Lok Sabha Debates (II), 9-12-1955 and 14-12-1955.

unparliamentary or undignified, he may, in his discretion, order that such word or words be expunged from the proceedings of the House.[45] He may direct any member guilty of disorderly conduct to withdraw from the House, or adjourn[46] or suspend the business of the House in case of grave disorder. However, when strong feelings exist or are aroused in the House, there are times when the Chair can appropriately be deaf or indeed blind.''[47]

The Speaker announces the closure of debates, is the guardian of the privileges of the House and protects the interests of the minorities. He also protects the encroachments by the Government. When Ministers tend to encroach upon the rights of the members or refuse to answer questions, or circumvent the answers, or do not give sufficient information, it is, then, to Mr. Speaker that the members appeal to safeguard and enforce their rights against the Executive.[48] Various powers are conferred on the Speaker in relation to questions to Ministers. Though the guiding principles regarding admissibility of questions are laid down in the Rules of Procedure, their interpretation is vested in the Speaker. He may also vary the Question Hour, waive the rules relating to notice of questions, and permit a question to be asked at short notice if it relates to a matter of public importance and is, in his opinion, of an urgent character. Provision has been made in the Rules for half-an-hour discussion on matters arising from the answers to questions provided they are of sufficient public importance, but the decision as to whether a matter conforms to the requirements of the relevant Rules rests with the Speaker.

The Speaker also decides about the admissibility of resolutions and motions. He decides whether a motion expressing want of confidence in the Council of Ministers is in order, and whether a ''cut'' motion is or is not admissible under the Rules. His consent is required to a motion to adjourn the House for the purpose of discussing a definite matter of public importance, to a motion for discussing a matter of general public interest, and to any motion for adjourning the debate on a Bill. His consultation is also necessary for the presentation of petitions to the House, for calling the attention of a Minister to any matter of urgent public importance and for any member to point out a mistake of accuracy in a statement made by a Minister or any other member of the House. Further, the consent of the Speaker is required by a Minister desiring to make a personal statement explaining the reasons of his resignation from his office. The Speaker's permission is likewise necessary if a member of the House wants to make a personal explanation. He can refer any matter to the Privileges Committee.

But the chief function, and an arduous too, of the Speaker relates to the judicious conduct of debates. He fixes a time limit for speeches, selects amendments to a Bill or resolution to be discussed by the House. The Speaker is, in fact, ''lord of the debate.'' He must see that the debate centres on the main issue before the House and members do not wander accidentally or deliberately, in the realm of irrelevance. Then, there are constant appeals to him for his ruling on point of procedure and his ruling is final which must be accepted without demur. They constitute precedents which are collected for future guidance and cannot be questioned on a substantive motion. It is said of the Speaker of the British House of Commons that the Prime Minister ''can do nothing right, but Speaker can do nothing wrong.'' This is, however, not true in India. Defiance of the rulings of the Speaker is rule now rather than an exception. When, Speakers do not eschew party connections and are active participants in the affairs of the party, the respect and obedience which the

45. Rules 353, 356 and 380.
46. The Speaker adjourned the House on February 17, 1981 when some Congress (I) and Lok Dal members pushed and pummelled each other, were engaged in scuffles and exchanged a few blows.
47. Kaul, M. N., and Shakdhar, S.L., *Practice and Procedure of Parliament* (1972), p. 101. Also refer to the observations of the Speaker in the British House of Commons, *House of Commons Debates*, 1-2-1972, c. 239.
48. The Speaker expressed his unhappiness in the House on November 16, 1971 at the spate of Ordinances issued by the Government during the brief inter-session period of two months. He observed that he would invite the attention of the Government to the need for justifying the ''emergency and urgency'' to promulgate these Ordinances. *Indian Express*, New Delhi, November 17, 1971. Speaker Balram Jakhar also expressed his concern on the Seventeen Ordinances issued in between the period of the close of the Budget Session and the Winter Session in November 1980.

Chair should command disappears with loss of faith in the independence and impartiality of the Speaker.

The Speaker appoints Chairmen of all committees of the House. "The Speaker", writes S. L. Shakdhar, "is the supreme head of all Parliamentary Committees set up by him or by the House. He issues directions to the Chairmen in all matters relating to their working and the procedure to be followed. He guides them holding periodical consultations with the Chairmen and the members. The Speaker reads all reports of the Committees and keeps in touch with their activities. All difficulties and matters of importance are referred to him for guidance and advice."[49] He sees that any notice issued by a Committee or a minute of dissent of a member does not contain any words, phrases or expressions which are argumentative, unparliamentary, irrelevant, verbose or otherwise inappropriate. He may, accordingly, amend it, if deemed necessary, before circulation. The Speaker himself is the *ex-officio* Chairman of some of the Committees of the House such as the Business Advisory Committee, Rules Committee and the General Purposes Committee.

The Speaker presides over the joint sitting of both Houses of Parliament, whenever the President calls it in the event of the disagreement between the House of the People and the Council of States and all the rules of Procedure operate in regard to the joint sitting under his directions and orders. However, if at any sitting of the House of the People a resolution for the removal of the Speaker from his office is under consideration, he is not to preside at that sitting. The Constitution also prescribes certain of his duties : he is empowered to adjourn the House or to suspend its sitting in the event of the absence of a quorum; and he is authorised, in his discretion, to permit any member of the House who is unable to express himself in Hindi or in English to address the House in his mother tongue . He has also the power to recognise parties and groups in the House of the People.

The Speaker is the *ex-officio* President of the Indian Parliamentary Group, which in India functions as the National Group of the Inter-Parliamentary Union and the Main branch of the Commonwealth Parliamentary Association. He nominates, in consultation with the Chairman of the Council of States, personnel for various parliamentary delegations to foreign countries. He may lead these delegations himself. The Speaker is also the Chairman of the Conference of Presiding Officers of Legislative Bodies in India.

The House of the People has its own Secretariat and the conditions of service of persons appointed to the secretarial staff of either House of Parliament are regulated by law of Parliament. The secretariat staff of the House functions directly under the control of the Speaker and is responsible to no other authority. The Speaker also controls the premises of the House and his authority within and without the House is undisputed. He regulates admission of "strangers" and Press correspondents to the galleries and other precincts of the House. Visitors and Press correspondents, after their admission to the galleries, are subject to the discipline and orders of the Speaker. In the event of breach of his orders he may punish them by stopping their admission either for a definite or an indefinite period or, in serious circumstances, involving contempt of the House or its members or the committees, censure them or, in extreme cases, commit them to prison. Summons to offenders are issued under his authority and it is sufficient for the courts if his orders merely state that the person is required to appear before the House on the charge of contempt of the House or a breach of privilege.

The Speaker is, thus, the impartial custodian of the rights of the members of the House. For him the humblest back-bencher is not less than a member, nor is the greatest Minister more than a member. He seldom speaks, but when he does, 'he speaks for the House not to it." The essence of his impartiality lies in the way he maintains an atmosphere of fair play by ensuring that the Opposition have an opportunity to express their views and criticism, yet at the same time, seeing that there is no parliamentary obstruction to hinder the Government in the task of governing the country. The powers vested in the Speaker are intended to enable him that the House functions smoothly and it transacts its business effectively, efficiently and expeditiously. The Speaker would not, therefore, exercise his powers arbitrarily or in such manner as to prevent the House from functioning as the Speakers of the West Bengal and Punjab Legislative Assemblies did in 1967-68. The Page Committee, while commenting upon the duties and responsibilities of the Speaker and his relations with the House,

49. Lal, A.B. (Ed.), *The Indian Parliament*, p. 34.

observed, "The fundamental principle is that the House, subject to the provisions of the Constitution, is sovereign in the matter of its own rules of procedure and conduct of business.......Hence whatever powers have been conferred by the rules on the Speaker are intended to serve one purpose, *i.e.,* the House should be enabled to function at all times in the interest of the country and the powers conferred on the Speaker, should be used by him in the interest of the House."[50] The Speaker must, therefore, possess high and varied qualities of character and intellect. He should be able, vigilant, thoroughly conversant with he Rules of Procedure and precedents, imperturbable, tactful and should possess a sense of humour to relieve not only tensions in the House but also at times to relieve its monotony. This is a gift which may be either natural or cultivated, but it is certainly a weapon of great potency with a wise and capable Speaker. Addressing the 52nd Annual Con- ference of the Speakers of legislative bodies of India in October 1986, Balram Jakhar, Speaker of the Lok Sabha, likened the Speakers to wild horses whose rider was the State Legislature. "They would want to tame you, but never get tamed. For if you do so, you would be dragged all along." The Speaker should be "firm with a smile."

The Thirty-ninth Constitution Amendment Act, which has since been rescinded, intended to protect the Speaker, because of the dignity of the office that he occupied, from the jurisdiction of the courts in respect of all disputes arising out or in connection with his election to the House of the People.

## FUNCTIONS OF THE HOUSE

India is a Union of States and, accordingly, all legislative power is divided between the Union and the States. Parliament has exclusive power to make laws with respect to matters enumerated in the Union List—List I in the Seventh Schedule to the Constitution. With respect to the Concurrent List—List III— both Parliament and State Legislatures have concurrent powers. Subject to the provisions of the Constitution, Parliament has the power to make laws for the whole or any part of India whereas the jurisdiction of State extends to the whole or any part of the State. No law made by Parliament shall be deemed to be invalid on the ground that it will have extraterritorial operation. When a Proclamation of Emergency is in operation, Parliament has the power to make laws for the whole or any part of the territory of India with respect to any matter enumerated in the State List— List II— though on the expiry of six months after the Proclamation has ceased to operate such laws cease to have effect. Parliament has also the power to legislate for two or more States by their consent and it is open to other States also to consent to or adopt such legislation. In case of repugnancy between the law of the Union and the law of a State, the former shall prevail. Residuary powers rest with the Union.

The entries in the Union, Concurrent and State Lists are only legislative heads or fields of legislation and, as such, they demarcate the area over which the appropriate legislature can operate. From the classification of matters into the three Lists, competence of the House of the People has been questioned from time to time on particular matters before the House. It is the accepted practice in the House of the People that the Speaker does not give any ruling on a point of order raised whether a Bill is constitutionally within the competence of the House. The House also does not take a decision on the specific question of *vires* of a Bill.[51] The members express their views in the matter and advance arguments for and against the *vires* for the consideration of the House and the issue is decided accordingly. There have, however, been occasions when the Speaker leaving the ultimate decision on the matter to the House has expressed his own views on the *vires* of Bills. In order to help the House and the Speaker to decide disputed or complicated legislative proposals before the House, the Attorney-General may address the House on the suggestion of the Speaker or the House itself and give his opinion on the legal and constitutional aspects involved therein.

### Legislative Functions

The process of making laws is the business of Parliament as a whole; President, the Council of States and the House of the People.

The House can by itself do nothing, although the actual powers of the President and the Council of States are subject to limitations. A non-Money Bill may originate in any of the two Houses and it must be passed by both Houses if it has to become law. The House of the People, unlike the British House of Commons, has no

50. As cited by Kaul, M.N., and Shakdhar, S.L., *Practice and Procedre of Parliament,* p. 103.
51. Kaul, M. N., and Shakdhar S. L., *Practice and Procedure of Parliament,* p. 473.

means to over-rule the Council of States. In case of disagreement between the two Houses or if more than six months elapse from the date of the receipt of the Bill by the other House without the Bill being passed by it, the President may sommon a joint sitting of both the Houses. If at the joint sitting the Bill is passed by a majority of the total number of members of both Houses present and voting, it shall be deemed to have been passed by both Houses of Parliament. Here lies the supreme position of the House of the People. The will of the House is bound to prevail at the joint sitting on account of its numerical strength.

**Financial Functions**

"Who holds the purse, holds the power," wrote Madison in the *Federalist*. It is through the control of the nation's purse that the House enjoys real supremacy over the Council of States. The Constitution provides that a Money Bill shall not be introduced in the Council of States. It should originate in the House of the People and when it passes therefrom, it is transmitted to the Council of States for its recommendations. The Constitution further requires that the Council of States should return the Bill to the House with or without its "recommendations" within fourteen days from the date of the receipt of the Bill by the Council. If the House accepts any of the "recommendations" made by the Council, the Bill is deemed to have been passed by both Houses of Parliament with those amendments. If the House does not accept the "recommendations" of the Council, the Bill is deemed to have been passed by both Houses of Parliament in the original form as passed by the House of the People. If a Bill passed by the House and transmitted to the Council is not returned within fourteen days of its receipt, it is deemed to have been passed by both Houses of Parliament, after the expiry of fourteen days, in the form in which it was passed by the House of the People. The Council of States can only delay the enactment of a Money Bill for a period of fourteen days. Demands for grants are not submitted to the Council of States. The sanctioning of expenditure is the exclusive privilege of the House of the People.

**Electoral Functions**

The elected members of the Both Houses of Parliament form a part the Electoral College for the election of the President of India; the other part of the Electoral College being the Elected members of the Legislative Assemblies of the States. The Vice-President is elected by the members of an Electoral College consisting of the members of both Houses of Parliament. In the process of election of both the President and the Vice-President the House of the People enjoys co-equal powers with the Council of States.

**Controlling the Executive**

But the most important function of the House is that of controlling the executive. The Constitution makes the Council of Ministers collectively responsible to the House of the People and the responsibility of the Council of Ministers to the House involves a constant control of the House over the Government; control and responsibility go together. Responsibility of Government means its resignation from office whenever the policy of the Government proves fundamentally unacceptable to the House. An obligation, therefore, rests on the House to exercise a day-to-day scrutiny over the activities of the Government in such a way that fundamental disagreement between the Executive and the representatives of the people will be clear and manifest. If the actual and possible mistakes of the Government were not apparent, the Government might become irresponsible. Control by the House prevents irresponsibility since Ministers are constantly conscious of the fact that they will be called to account.

The House maintains its control in two ways. The first is the constant demand in the House for information about the actions of Government. The second is the criticism that is constantly aimed at the Government in the House. These two methods are closely related to each other and take various forms. The most effective instrument by which the House seeks information from the Executive is the oral or written questions. Any member of the House may, by following prescribed Rules, direct questions at Ministers and the Ministers at the beginning of each sitting of the House devote almost an hour to answering questions that have been put to them. The institution of asking questions is as highly developed in India as it is in Britain and is prominently distinguished from some of the Dominion countries, like Austaliia.[52] It is generally the most

52. Sir Anthony Eden, in his tour of the Commonwealth, is said to have felt more at home in the Indian Parliamment's Question Hour than he had been in the Australian Parliament. Morris-Jones says, "While the form of the initial question is firmly disciplined, the freedom given to the putting of supplementaries is fairly large and ministers cannot use escape routes on too many occasions." *The Government and Politics of India*, p. 197.

interesting part of the proceedings of the House and it provides the time when a member can make his mark and when Ministers, too, can make or mar their reputations. A member may also move for obtaining returns or supplying information on matters of public importance.[53] Information may,again, be obtained by the House regarding the administration by appointing Parliamentary Committees.

The House is also a debating assembly. "A society," writes Laski, "that is able to discuss does not need to fight, and the greater the capacity to maintain interest in discussion, the less degree there is of an inability to effect the compromises that maintain social peace."[54] The most important function of the Opposition is to discuss and criticize matters of administration and policy making and to make the Government to defend its intentions and practices. The best opportunity for the Opposition to criticize governmental policy as a whole is when it debates the reply on the Address of the President to Parliament. Another opportunity is when public finance, more especially proposals for expenditure, are under discussion. At this stage, the action of every individual Minister and his Ministry is under review. Demands for supplementary estimates similarly offer an opportunity for criticism. It must, however, be said that till March, 1977 there was no well-organised strong Opposition to create an effective stir in Government by its criticism. The Janata Government recognised the worth of responsible Opposition within the framework of a parliamentary system and accorded to the Leader of the Opposition the status of a Minister of the Cabinet rank with all the privileges attached to the office. But after January 1980 the Opposition was in complete disarray and there was no cohesion among the various Opposition parties and groups to present a united front and arrest the vagaries of the Government effectively and in a responsible spirit. Proper restraint on the actions and policies of the Government is not possible under the circumstances, except the pre-planned obstructionist strategy followed by walk-outs.

In addition to these regularly scheduled debates, any member of the House may, after the notice and subject to the rules governing it, move a resolution expressing lack of confidence in the Council of Ministers. Motion for a vote of no confidence is really a crucial occasion in the life of the Government as it decides its fate. So long as a Government can command a comfortable majority,[55] it is not possible for such a motion to get through, still it creates embarrassment the ranks of the Ministry and agitates public opinion.[56] The most normal occasion for the criticism of the Executive is debate on a motion of adjournment. A member may, during a sitting, move the adjournment of the House for discussing a definite matter of urgent public importance. If the Speaker admits the motion, then, a full debate on the issue is held. The policies and actions of the Government are exposed by the Opposition and its lapses highlighted. The Government stoutly defends with reasoned arguments substantiated by authentic official material. If the Government fails to convince the House it must face the consequences.

There is another kind of adjournment motion and it may be called the emergency adjournment motion. It is intended to raise discussion on matters of urgent public importance for a short duration and for calling attention of the Government. No formal motion is allowed. What the Rules require is that a member wishing to raise a debate should give a notice to the Secretary of the House clearly and precisely specifying the matter to be discussed. The notice must be supported by at least two other members. If the Speaker admits the notice, he will fix a day, in consultation with the Leader of the House, for discussion. The duration of the debate does not exceed two and a half hours. What is important to note here is that even a Government which commands an overwhelming majority in the House cannot prevent the ventilation of an important grievance and the Constitution gives to every member freedom of speech in Parliament. The Half-an-Hour Discussion on matters arising out of questions, also, affords opportunities for ventilating grievances. Other opportunites for raising debates include the moving of resolutions and No-Day-Yet-Named motion.

53. As in the case of Sirajuddin and Co., Fairfox and Bofors gun deal cases in March-April 1987.
54. Laski, H., *Parliamentary Government in England,* p. 149.
55. Morarji Desai's Government resigned in July, 1979 on reduced strength of the Party when the vote of confidence moved by Y. B. Chavan was under discussion.
56. Not infrequently the Opposition behaves irresponsibly as it happened on the motion of no-confidence against the Government in November 1968. The liberty to oppose the Government was fully exercised by Opposition parties, but when the turn came for the leader of the Government (Prime Minister) to reply, Mrs. Indira Gandhi was ruthlessly shouted down. This is tantamount to destroying the values of parliamentary government.

Another device for raising important matters and ventilating whatever has happened and agitating the Members is the 'Zero Hour' practice. It is entirely an Indian innovation and is unknown to the Rules of Procedure and Conduct of Business in the House. Nobody can say how did it originate and acquire the name. But the practice goes back to early 1950 during the tenure of Speaker Hukam Singh. Immediately after the Question Hour and before other business was taken up the Speaker would permit ordinary Members of the House, who otherwise were overshadowed by the presence of a host of veteran parliamentarians, to bring to the notice of the Government important matters and seek redress. The Members, thus, found that their voice counted and began to use the opportunity freely and since it was an interregnum between the Question Hour and the other business to be taken up it came to be known as the Zero Hour.

Originally, it was useful device conducted in an atmosphere of orderly and fruitful proceedings, but soon it declined into a line of disorder, uproar and pandemonium, often unbecoming of Parliament and almost invariably unproductive. On February 17, 1981 the House was adjourned in a state of shock when Congress (I) and Lok Dal Members freely exchanged blows. On August 22, 1978 a Lok Sabha bulletin informed Members that there was no Zero Hour in the Rules of Procedure and Conduct of Business in the House. Anybody desiring to raise a matter of wide public importance had to give appropriate notice under the relevant Rule. "Members are requested not to raise matters without the specific approval and consent of the Speaker." On a Member's plea that it had been the practice of the House and the decision be reconsidered, the Speaker commented, "May I tell you that there is nothing like Zero Hour." Speaker Hegde after consulting leaders of various political parties, offered to substitute five statements each day under Rule 377 after giving due notice to the Speaker and obtaining his consent. That system has worked well. It was, for instance, under Rule 377 in the Monsoon Session in 1979 that the Congress (I) managed to raise the matter of the Desai-Charan Singh correspondence and the related corruption charges, after having tried unsuccessfully to raise it in other forms under other Rules. Consent is given to almost every matter sought to be raised. Despite this outlet for Members' grievances, Zero Hour lives on and thrives amidst uproarious scenes verging on even vilification.

**Constituent Functions**

The House together with the Council of States has the power to amend the Constitution. A Bill to amend the Constitution may originate in either House and it must be passed by each House of Parliament by a majority of its total membership as well as by a two-thirds majority of the members present and voting. The Constitution, as said before, does not prescribe the method of resolving differences between the two Houses over a proposed amendment of the Constitution. Article 108 relates to the procedure prescribed for resolving the differences over a legislative measure and does not apply to a constitutional amendment.

**Miscellaneous Functions**

Parliament has the power for the removal of Judges of the Supreme and High Courts on the grounds of proved misbehaviour or incapacity and address for such a removal is required to be passed by each House of Parliament supported by a majority of the total membership of that House and by a two-thirds majority of the Members of that House present and voting. The removal of the Chief Election Commissioner and Comptroller and Auditor-General of India is subject to the same procedure as in the case of Judges. Either of the two Houses may prefer a charge for impeachment of the President. If the charge is preferred by the House, the Council of States investigates to or causes it to be investigated. The impeachment succeeds when the Chamber investigating the charge passes a resolution supported by a two-thirds majority of members present and voting that the charge is sustained. The removal of the Vice-President is only subject to the approval of the House of the People after a resolution to that effect has been passed by a majority of all the members of the Council of States. Approval of both the Houses is necessary at all stages and every time for the continuance in force of a Proclamation of Emergency, under Article 352, Proclamation declaring the failure of the constitutional machinery in a State, under article 356, and proclamation relating to financial emergency, under Article 360, beyond the specified period of time and when its operation is intended to be extended after the expiry of that period. Rules and Regulations made by the various Ministries and Departments under the authority of delegated legislation are approved by both the

Houses. The reports of the Union Public Service Commission, the Comptroller and Auditor-General of India, the Scheduled Castes and Tribes Commission and the Finance Commission are presented to both Houses for their consideration. If the Government makes a proposal to take an appointment out of the purview of the Union Public Service Commission, both the Houses should agree to such an exclusion.

## LEGISLATIVE PROCEDURE

The Constitution does not prescribe a detailed legislative procedure. It merely says that a Bill, other than a Money or Financial Bill, may originate in either House of Parliament, and a Bill shall not be deemed to have been passed by Houses of Parliament unless it has been agreed to by both Houses, either without amendment or with such amendments only as are agreed to by both Houses. A Bill pending in either House does not lapse if Parliament is prorogued. The dissolution of the House of the People causes the lapse of any Bill which is pending in it or which has been passed by the House but is pending in the Council of States. But a Bill which originated in the Council and is still pending there does not lapse on account of dissolution. When the President has notified his intention to summon a joint sitting of both Houses of Parliament, a subsequent dissolution of the House of the People does not cause the Bill to lapse.

The rest is covered by the Rules made by Parliament. These Rules prescribe an identical procedure in both Houses. A legislative Bill is required to be read three times in each House before it can be deemed to have been passed by both Houses of Parliament. An ordinary legislative measure may be introduced either by a Minister or by a Private member. In the former case, it is known as a Government Bill and in the latter case it is classified as a Private Member's Bill. A Government Bill and a Private Member's Bill both undergo an identical procedure. The three readings of a Bill involve four stages. The first reading relates to the motion to introduce a Bill and on its adoption the Bill is deemed to have been introduced. The Billl is also deemed to have been introduced if it is already published in the *Gazette of India*. The second reading consists of two stages. The first stage constitutes discussion of the principles of the Bill and its provisions generally on any of the following motions :— that it be taken into consideration; that it be referred to a Joint Committee of both the Houses with the concurrence of the Council of States; that it be circulated for the purpose of eliciting public opinion. Second stage in the Second Reading constitutes clause-by-clause consideration of the Bill as introduced or as reported by a Select or Joint Committee, as the case may be. The third reading refers to the discussion on the motion that the Bill (or the Bill as amended) be passed.

The Bill is, then, transmitted to the other House for its concurrence. A message from the originating House signed either by the Presiding Officer or the Secretary is sent to the other House. The message is read in the House and copies of the Bill are laid on the table. Thereafter any Minister may give notice that the Bill be taken into consideration. The subsequent procedure of discussion and amendment is the same as in the originating House. After the Bill is passed by the receiving House, it is sent back to the originating House with amendments if any. If the receiving House passes the Bill in the same form in which it came from the House of its origin, it is presented to the President for his assent. The President may give his assent thereto, or withheld it, or return it for reconsideration of the Houses, with or without a message suggesting amendments. When the Bill so returned by the President has been reconsidered by both the Houses and is again passed by the two Houses with or without amendments and presented to the President for his assent, the President can no longer withhold it, and must give his assent thereto. A Bill, thus becomes law.

If a Bill passed by one House and transmitted to the other is amended by that House, it goes back to the House where it originated. If the House originating the Bill does not agree to the amendment or amendments or makes further amendments to which the other House does not agree, the President may summon a joint sitting of the two Houses. The Speaker presides and the Rules of the House of the People are made applicable at a joint sitting. Amendments can be moved at a joint sitting, but only such amendments are admissible as have been made necessary by the delay in the passage of the Bill, or may arise out of amendments, if any, proposed by one House and rejected by the other. The decision of the Presiding Officer with regard to the admissibility of amendments is final. The Bill is deemed to have been passed by both the Houses if a majority of the members present and voting at joint sitting agree to it.

A Joint session may also be summoned if a Bill passed by one House is rejected by the other, or if more than six months elapse from the date of the reception of the Bill by the other House without the Bill being passed by it.

### Private Members' Bill

Since 1965 the last two and a half hours of the Friday sittings are normally allotted for the transaction of Private Members' Business. Private Members' Business consists of Resolutions and Bills. The Speaker decides which of the two are to be dealt with on a particular Friday. In practice, it means that every alternate Friday is made available for Private Members' Bills, the other Friday being devoted to Private Members' Resolutions.

The Procedure in the case of Private Members' Bill is the same as for Government Bills, except for some special features. The notice for leave to introduce a Bill must be accompanied by a statement of objects and reasons, the recommendation and sanction of the President required for the introduction or consideration of the Bill, memoranda showing the financial effect of the Bill, etc. A notice may be disallowed, if it is not complete in any respect or the Bill is otherwise defective. The Speaker has the inherent power to disallow notice of a Bill, if he thinks that it is not proper to include it in the List of Business. There is a Committee on Private Members' Bills and Resolutions consisting of not more than 15 members nominated by the Speaker for one year. The Chairman is appointed by the Speaker from among the members of the Committee. If the Deputy Speaker happens to be a member of the Committee, he is appointed Chairman automatically. The functions of the Committee are :

(1) To examines every Bill seeking to amend the Constitution before a motion for leave to introduce the Bill is included in the List of business. The Committee since its inception has taken this matter very seriously and laid down certain principles. One of these states that "the Constitution should be considered as a sacred document—a document which should not be lightly interfered with and should be amended only when it is found absolutely necessary to do so.....Such amendments should normally be brought by government."

(2) To examine all Private Members' Bills after they have been introduced and before they are taken up for consideration in the House and to classify them according to their nature, urgency and importance into two categories : Category A and Category B. Bills in Category A have precedence over those in Category B.

(3) To recommend the time that should be allocated for the discussion of the stage or stages of a Private Member's Bill and also to indicate the different hours at which the various stages of the Bill in a day shall be completed.

(4) To examine every Private Member's Bill which is opposed in the House on the ground that the Bill initiates legislation not within the legislative competence of the House. The Speaker considers such objection *prima facie* tenable.

(5) To recommend time limit for the discussion of Private Members' Resolutions and the ancillary matters.

### Financial Legislation

The principles involved in the financial procedure are essentially the same as followed in the British House of Commons. Financial initiative in both the countries is the exclusive right of the Government. Secondly, the House of the People in India, as the House of Commons, has the exclusive right to vote supplies and to sanction the levy of taxes and imposts. Finally, in both countries, taxation, and appropriation and expenditure from public funds need legislative authorization.

The Constitution provides for a special procedure in regard to Money Bills. A Money Bill may not be introduced in the Council of States and it cannot be introduced without the recommendation of the President. When it is passed in the House of the People, it is transmitted to the Council of States, with the Speaker's certificate that it is a Money Bill and the decision of the Speaker on this point is final. The Council of States cannot reject a Money Bill, but it may, within fourteen days of its receipt, return it to the House of the People with its "recommendations". The House may either accept or reject all or any of the "recommendations" of the Council of States. If the House of the People accepts any of them, the Money Bill shall be deemed to have been passed by both Houses with those amendments. If the House does not accept any of the "recommendations" of Council of States, the Money Bill shall be deemed to have been passed by both Houses in the form in which it was passed by the House of the People. If the Bill is not returned to the House within fourteen days, it shall be deemed to have been passed by both Houses at the expiration of the stipulated period in the form in which it was passed by the House of the People. When it is presented to the President for assent the provision by which the President may return the Bill to the Houses for reconsideration (Article 111) does not apply.

A Money Bill cannot be introduced or moved except on the recommendation of the President. According to Article 110 a Bill is deemed to be a Money Bill if it contains only provisions dealing with all or any of the following matters :

(a) the imposition, abolition, remission, alteration or regulation of any tax;
(b) the regulation of the borrowing of money or the giving of any guarantee by the Government of India, or the amendment of the Laws with respect to any financial obligation undertaken by the Government of India;
(c) the custody of the Consolidated Fund[57] or the Contingency Fund of India,[58] the payment of money into or the withdrawal of money from any such fund;
(d) the appropriation of moneys out of the Consolidated Fund of India;
(e) the declaring of any expenditure to be expenditure charged on the Consolidated Fund of India or the increasing of the amount of any such expenditure;
(f) the receipt of money on account of the Consolidated Fund of India or the Public Accounts of India or the custody or the issue of such money or the audit of the amounts of the Union or of a State; or
(g) any matter incidental to any matter referred to above from (a) to (f)."

The use of the word "only" at the beginning of the definition of a Money Bill is significant. The Constitution prescribes two conditions for a Bill to be regarded as a Money Bill. Firstly, it must deal with all or any matters contained in Article 110 (i). Secondly, the provisions of the Bill must deal only with such matters and not with any other matter. It is, therefore, not possible to enact as a Money Bill anything which changes the law in other respects. It must be a Money Bill, pure and simple. A Bill which imposes fines, penalties, or licence fees, or deals with taxes imposed by the local authorities is neither a Money Bill nor a Financial Bill. A Money Bill when it is presented to the President of India for his assent must be accompanied by a certificate of the Speaker that it is a Money Bill. The President shall not withhold his assent from a Money Bill passed by Parliament. This is in pursuance of the supremacy of Parliament in the matter of finance.

It is necessary to distinguish Money Bill from Financial Bills. Money Bills are those which are defined in Article 110 as referred to above. Financial Bills are other Bills containing financial provisions but to which the provisions of Article 110 are not applicable. Financial Bills also cannot be introduced without the recommendation of the President, and must not be introduced in the Council of States. Whereas a Money Bill is transmitted to the Council of States for its consideration and "recommendations" alone and it has no right to amend it, a Financial Bill can be amended by the Council. It rests with the Speaker of the House of the People to determine whether a Bill is a Money Bill or not. The Council of States has no right to question the certificate subscribed by the Speaker that the Bill is a Money Bill.

### The Budget

The Constitution has adopted the fundamental principles governing the British financial system, that is, parliamentary control over the receipt and expenditure of public Money. These principles are :

(1) no tax can be imposed except with the authority of Parliament;
(2) no expenditure can be incurred except with the sanction of Parliament;
(3) no tax can be imposed or expenditure incurred unless asked for by the Executive. It means that financial initiative rests with the Executive alone; and
(4) all expenditure except that specifically charged by any enactment of Parliament requires to be sanctioned on an annual basis. This is called the principle of annuality.

The expenditure for any financial year, the period between April 1 and March 31, must therefore, be sanctioned either totally or in part by Parliament before the expiry of the previous

57. All funds received by the Government of India form the "Consolidated Fund of India' from which alone the Government withdraws money for its expenditure and repayment of debts.
58. A reserve fund called the 'Contingency Fund of India' is placed at the disposal of the Government to meet the unforeseen requirements exceeding the authorised expenditure. The fund facilitates advances subject to subsequent regularization. It is, in brief, grant in advance pending completion of the regular procedure.

financial year. That is to say, the Annual Financial Statement or the Budget must be passed whether totally or in part before March 31 of each year. The Budget is ordinarily presented to Parliament in the month of February each year in two parts—the Railway Budget and the General Budget. The Railway Budget exclusively deals with the receipts and expenditure relating to Railways and it is separately presented by the Minister for Railways. The General Budget deals with estimates of all the Departments of the Government of India excluding Railways and is presented by the Finance Minister. The procedure in case of the Railway Budget and the General Budget is the same.

The Budget or the Annual Financial Statement, as the Constitution names it, must show separately the expenditure charged on the Consolidated Fund of India and the sums required to meet other expenditure proposed to be made from the Consolidated Fund of India. It must also distinguish expenditure on revenue account from other expenditure. The expenditure charged on the Consolidated Fund of India comprises :

(a) the emoluments and allowances of the President and other expenditure relating to his office;
(b) the salaries and allowances of the Chairman and the Deputy chairman of the Council of States and the Speaker and the Deputy Speaker of the House of the People;
(c) debt charges for which the Government of India is liable including interest, sinking fund charges and redemption charges and the expenditure relating to the raising of loans and the service and redemption of debt;
(d) (i) the salaries, allowances and pensions payable to or in respect of judges of the Supreme Court,
(ii) the pensions payable to or in respect of the Federal court,
(iii) the pensions payable to or in respect of judges of any High Court which exercises jurisdiction in relation to any area included in the territory of India or which at any time before the commencement of the present Constitution exercised jurisdiction in relation to any area included in a Province corresponding to a State specified in Part A of the first Schedule;
(e) the salary, allowances and pension payable to or in respect of the Comptroller and Auditor-General of India;
(f) any sums required to satisfy any judgment, decree or award of any Court or arbitration tribunal;
(g) any other expenditure declared by the Constitution or by Parliament by law to be so charged.

The expenditure charged on the Consolidated Fund of India is not submitted to the vote of Parliament, but either House of Parliament can discuss it. It is non-votable. The other expenditure is submitted in the form of demands for grants to the House of the People. The House may assent, or refuse assent to any demand, or assent to any demand subject to a reduction of the amount specified therein. It is, votable, but no demand for grant can be made except on the recommendation of the President.

The Annual Financial Statement or the Budget has to pass through five stages : (1) Introduction or presentation; (2) General discussion; (3) Voting of demands; (4) Consideration and passing of the Appropriation Bill, and (5) Consideration and passing of the taxation proposals; the Finance Bill.

(1) *Introduction or Presentation.* The Budget session of Parliament commences in mid-February when the Railway Minister introduces the Railway Budget and subsequently the Finance Minister introduces the Financial Statement in the House of the People. It is accompanied by the Budget Speech made by the Finance Minister. It is an important event as it unfolds the fiscal and economic policy of the Government for the ensuing year. The copies of the Budget together with the Explanatory Memorandum are printed and circulated among members for their reference. The Budget contains the estimates of receipts and expenditure. The Explanatory Memorandum contains a comparative statement of such receipts and expenditure for the current year and the next year and reasons for any increase or decrease in the amounts. The memorandum also furnishes the information relating to estimates.

(2) *General discussion.* After the Budget has been presented, money has to be

asked for as Demands for Grants. Here the Budget is dealt with in two stages—a general discussion, and the demands for specific grants. A general discussion of the Budget as a whole is spread over 3 or 4 days. It is customary for the leader of the Opposition to initiate the discussion. No discussion of details and no cut motions are in order at this stage. It is a general discussion which covers all items of expenditure including those that are 'charged' and are excluded from vote. The discussion relates to the policy of the Government involving a review and criticism of the administration of the various Departments, the general problems connected with nation's finances and the principles involved in the Budget proposals. Following the British practice, the major part of the time for the Budget discussion is allowed to the Opposition to review the work of the Government for the year and ventilate grievances of the people. The discussion is political rather than financial. No vote is taken during the general discussion. But the Finance Minister has the right to reply at the end of the discussion.

(3) *Discussion and Voting.* With the general discussion the work of the Council of States is complete so far as the Annual Financial Statement is concerned. But the House of the People, after general discussion is over, proceeds to the voting of demands not charged on the Consolidated Fund of India. The voting of demands is the exclusive privilege of the House and the Council has no share in it. The House of the People has the following powers in respect of each demand : (i) to assent to the demand; or (ii) to refuse it; or (iii) to reduce it. The House has no power to increase a demand, or to alter the destination of a grant, or to put any condition as to the appropriation of the grant.

The time for debates on the estimates is determined by the Speaker in consultation with the Leader of the House. Reports of the activities of different Ministries during the preceding year are circulated among the members for their references. When the demand for grant of a Ministry is moved it comes under scrutiny and the debate, which usually extends to not more than two days, rivets on the working of the Ministry and its administrative policy. But the real debate takes place when amendments are proposed either for the reduction of the amount demanded or for the omission or reduction of any item in any grant.The voting on the demands must conclude on the fixed day when closure is applied and all outstanding demands are put to vote and disposed of, no matter whether they have been discussed or not..

(4) *Appropriation Bill.* The next stage is the Annual Appropriation Bill which must be passed into a statute. All the demands voted by the House of the People and the expenditure charged on the Consolidated Fund are put together and incorporated in a Bill called the Annual Appropriation Bill. The allotment of time for the different stages of the Bill is determined by the Speaker and debate on the second reading of the Bill is general. When the Bill is moved for consideration, debate is restricted to those points only which have not been discussed during the debate on estimates. Amendments may be moved for reduction in the expenditure alone. No amendments to the grant as voted by the House previously or altering its destination or varying the amount charged on the Consolidated Fund are admissible.

The Appropriation Bill having passed through all the stages is finally voted upon. If passed by the House of the People, it is certified by the Speaker as a Money Bill and transmitted to the Council of States. The Council must return it to the House with its "recommendations" within fourteen days. It is for the House to accept or reject these "recommendations," if any. The assent of the President to the Appropriation Bill is just a matter of formality. He cannot return a Money Bill for reconsideration.

An Appropriation Act embodies the authority given by the House, with the assent of the President, to Government to spend money as authorized in the Act. Without such an authority the Government cannot incur any expenditure. The Comptroller and Auditor-General of India would hold a payment illegal and unauthorized if it were made without authorization in the Appropriation Act. If the Government subsequently finds that the money granted under any head is insufficient for its need, it again comes to the House for a supplementary grant. The supplementary grants are embodied in one or more Appropriation Bills which must be passed by the House before the end of the financial year.

(5) *The Finance Bill.* The Finance Bill incorporates the financial proposals of the Government for the ensuing year and is presented to Parliament at the same time as the Budget. The procedure followed is that of a Money Bill. The Discussion of the Finance Bill in the second reading is confined to general principles. It is only in the Select Committee that the Bill is considered in detail and amendments are moved. Clause by Clause consideration of the Bill follows after the presentation of the Committee Report. The scope of amendments is limited to proposals for the reduction or abolition of a tax. The financial proposals become operative immediately after presentation of the Budget under the Provincial Collection of Taxes Act, 1931. The Finance Bill must be passed before the end of April.

Since the expenditure sanctioned in the preceding Budget expires on March 31, and the discussion on the Budget for the current year can go on till the end of April or beyond, it becomes necessary to keep the Government functioning pending the final supply. The Constitution, accordingly, provides for grants in advance to be made by Parliament, that is, Vote on Account. The House of the People votes provisionally early in March about a 12th of the estimated expenditure under various grants. The necessary Appropriation Bill for this amount as also a similar amount in respect of the "charged" expenditure is passed. There is no discussion on a Vote on Account as it is an unavoidable formality and a sheer necessity.

## PARLIAMENTARY COMMITTEES

### The Committee System

The principle of appointing committees is not a modern development. It is as old as Parliamentary system itself. The British Parliament soon after its organisation realised that, as a deliberative body, it could not do its work effectively and efficiently, although the business it transacted at that stage of its career was very light and simple. It, accordingly, started the practice of appointing its committees and delegating to them the more detailed consideration of work. With the growth of the parliamentary work and with a view to ensure its smooth, efficient and expeditious disposal the utility and the number of committees increased tremendously, and the House of Commons today relies more on Committees for expertise scrutiny and consideration of legislation and other matters which Parliament is to decide and determine.

The history of the committee system in India goes back to 1854 when the first legislature was established. The Legislative Council appointed its own committee to consider what should be its standing orders. Since then it became a practice of the Council to appoint from time to time committees to deal with varied matters. The existing Committees, may be divided into : (i) Ad-hoc Committees, and (ii) Non-Ad-hoc Committees. In the former category come Select Committees and Joint Committees. Committees in the latter category may be classified according to their functions. The following classification borrowed from S. S. More's *Practice and Procedure of Indian Parliament*[59] presents a matter of fact analysis ;

(a) Committees to inquire :
   (1) Committee of Petitions.
   (2) Committee of Privileges.
(b) Committee to scrutinise :
   (1) Committee on Government Assurances.
   (2) Committee on Subordinate Legislation.
(c) Committees of an administrative character relating to the business of the House :
   (1) Committee on Absence of Members from the sittings of the House.
   (2) Business Advisory Committee.
   (3) Committee on Private Members' Bills and Resolutions.

59. pp. 516-17.

(4) Rules Committee.

(d) Committees dealing with provision of facilities to Members :

(1) General Purpose Committee.

(2) House Committee.

(3) Library Committee.

(4) Joint Committee on Salaries and Allowances of Members of Parliament.

(e) Financial Committees :

(1) Estimates Committees.

(2) Public Accounts Committee.

(3) Committee on Public Undertakings.

The Ad Hoc Committee may be broadly classified under two heads :

(1) An Ad-hoc Committee constituted from time to time, either by the House of the People on a motion adopted in that behalf, or by the Speaker, to inquire into and report on specific subject.[60]

(2) Committees set up to advise the House. Under this classification come Select or Joint Committees on Bills which are appointed on a motion made in the House to consider and report on a specific Bill.

A Committee on Public Undertakings has recently been constituted to investigate into the working of public undertakings.

**Select Committees**

Select Committees are appointed on individual Bills and for making some investigation, inquiry or compilation. The first Select Committee was appointed in 1954 and since then the succeeding Legislatures have invariably appointed numerous such committees. Select Committees, whether for a Bill or for making other investigation, have proved themselves a convenient instrument for detailed examination of Bills and other problems under inquiry. The Speaker remarked in 1955: "when we meet in the committee we do not represent parties, we function as a whole House and we do what, we think, the best in the interest of the House." The Parliamentary Committees help to save time for the House to discuss important matters and prevent Parliament from getting lost in details and thereby losing its hold on matters of policies and broad principles. Apart from this, the very complexity and technical nature of the modern business makes it necessary, that it should be closely scrutinised in a business-like manner, availing of outside technical or expert advice, whenever necessary. The Speaker, accordingly, aptly suggested that the House should rather appoint large Select Committees and leave the "matter to be thrashed out there than in a bigger House."

Members of a Select Committee are appointed or elected by the House itself or nominated by the Speaker. The willingness of the members desired to serve on the committee is ascertained before a proposal for appointment or nomination is made. The chairman is appointed by the Speaker from among its members, but if the Deputy Speaker happens to be a member of the committee, he shall be appointed chairman. One-third of the total membership constitutes the quorum and majority vote determines the decision of a committee. The chairman is entitled to a casting vote in case of a tie. A committee can appoint its own sub-committee. The meetings of a committee are private and are normally held in the precincts of Parliament House. It may send for persons to give evidence and produce papers and records. The report is presented by the chairman of the committee or a member authorised by the committee. Members dissenting from the majority report may submit minutes of dissent. The Speaker has the power to give directions to the committee with a view to regulating its procedure and the organisation of its work. The committee becomes *functus officio* as soon as it has presented its final report.

**Joint Committees**

In order to avoid duplication of proceedings a Bill may be referred to a Joint Committee composed of members of both Houses. A Joint Committee also saves time and helps to bring about and develop good understanding, an appreciative spirit and co-operation between the representatives of both the Houses. A motion for the appointment of a joint committee and reference of a Bill to such a committee after being carried out in the originating House, is transmitted to the other House for its concurrence. The member-in-charge of a Bill indicates the number and names of the members constituting the committee from the House to which he belongs as also the number of the members from the other House. The proportion of members from the House of the People and the Council of States is two to one.

## INDIVIDUAL COMMITTEES

**Business Advisory Committee**

The Business Advisory Committee of the Lok Sabha consists of the Speaker and not more

60. For instance, the Committee on the Conduct of a Member Mudgal case 1951; the Committee on the Conduct of certain Members during the President's Address; Railway Convention Committee; and the Committee on Bofors guns deal.

than fourteen members nominated by him. The Speaker is its *ex-officio* chairman. As the membership of Committee is limited and there are quite a large number of Opposition groups, it is not possible for the Speaker to nominate members from each and every group. However, in order to make the Committee as broad-based as possible certain prominent unattached members and members of some of the Opposition groups, who do not find representation in the Committee, are invited by the Speaker to attend its sittings. The invited members have neither the right to vote nor are they counted for the purpose of a quorum.

The function of the Business Advisory Committee is to recommend the time that should be allocated for discussion of the stage or stages of such Government Bills or the business which the Speaker in consultation with the Leader of the House may direct to be referred to the Committee. The Committee can indicate in the proposed time table the different hours at which the various stages of the Bill or the business should be completed.

**Committee on Private Members' Bills**

This Committee consists of not more than fifteen members nominated by the Speaker. The Deputy Speaker is invariably its member and as far as possible every section of opinion of the House is represented thereon. The functions of the Committee are : to examine and classify all Private Members' Bills according to their nature, urgency and importance; to allot time to Private Members' Bill and resolutions; to examine Private Members' Bills seeking to amend the Constitution before their introduction in the House; to examine a Private Members' Bill which is opposed in the House on the ground that the Bill initiates legislation outside the legislative competence of the House and to perform such other functions as may be assigned to it by the Speaker from time to time.

**Committee on Petitions**

Article 350 entitles a citizen to submit representation for the redress of grievance to any officer or authority in the Union or a State. It is also considered an inherent right of a citizen to present a petition to Parliament ventilating public grievances and offering suggestions on matters of public importance. Rules of the Lok Sabha (160-67) provide for such petition to be presented.

A petition must be submitted to the House with the consent of the Speaker and it should concern some matter engaging the attention of the House, or some matter which falls within the cognisance of a court of law. A petition cannot be presented if it involved expenditure from the Consolidated Fund of India, or pertains to financial matters. A petition is usually presented by a Member who has to give advance notice of his intention to summit it to the House. On the day fixed for its presentation, the Speaker calls out the member's name and he presents the petition indicating briefly its subject-matter. The House thereupon is seized of it and the petition is remitted for consideration of the Committee of Petitions.

The Committee on Petitions is nominated by the Speaker and consists of not less than fifteen members in proportion to the strength of the parties or groups so as to make it representative of all shades of opinion in the House. It examines the merits of the petitions and makes recommendations to the House after taking such evidence as it may deem necessary. No minutes of dissent can be appended to the Report of the committee.

Balram Jakhar, former Speaker of the Lok Sabha, exhorted the Chairmen of the Committees on Petitions of various legislatures, to gear themselves up by reviewing the existing working procedures and devising new ones, if necessary, to handle increasing cases in the future. Legislatures are not "elitist bodies," he affirmed. They are primarily representative institutions of the people and must protect their interests, freedom and public weal. The Committees on Petitions because of the nature of their functions are placed in a unique position to bring the people closer to the legislatures. Therefore, the procedures, "style of working and attitude of the committees should be such as would encourage more and more citizens to approach them for help". Begum Abida Ahmed, who headed the Lok Sabha's Committee on Petitions said, "Our effort should be to strengthen the Committees to an extent, that the common man may look to them with great expectations for redressal of grievances and fulfilment of aspirations."

**Committee on Government Assurances**

While replying to questions and supplementaries in the House or in the course of discussion on Bills, Resolutions and other Motions, Ministers sometimes give assurances or undertakings either to consider a matter or to take action thereon or to provide to the House full information later. The Speaker appoints for one year a Committee of the House consisting of fifteen members on Government Assurances with a view to scrutinising assurances thus made and to report to the House whether such assurances, undertakings and promises have been fulfilled or not. If implemented, the extent of their implementation and whether such implementation was within the time necessary for this purpose. Statements showing action taken by Government in implementation of the assurances are laid periodically on the Table of the House by the Minister of Parliamentary Affairs. No Minister is nominated to this Committee. The Council of States has no such Committee.

**Committee on Privileges**

Members of Parliament enjoy certain amenities, exemptions and privileges to protect their functional freedom individually and the dignity and authority of Parliament collectively. Where there is any question of an alleged breach of a privilege, the matter may be examined by the House but generally it is referred by the House to its Committee of Privileges for examination, investigation and report.

Some of the immunities, exemptions and privileges so enjoyed by members of Parliament are specified in the Constitution, some are contained in statutes, some in the Rules of Procedure and Conduct of Business of the two Houses, and some till recently were based on precedents and conventions of the House of Commons. The Constitution itself provided that until Parliament by law defined these privileges from time to time, if necessary, they would be those of the House of Commons, and of its Members and Committees, at the commencement of the Constitution. The Constitution (Forty-second Amendment) Act, 1976, amended Article 105 (3) and omitted the reference to the British House of Commons and laid down that the powers. privileges and immunities of each House of Parliament would be those of each House that existed at the commencement of the Forty-Second Amendment and as might be evolved by each House from time to time. This provision had not been brought into force till 1978 when the Constitution (Forty-fourth Amendment) Act, 1978, restored the original Clause 3 of Article 105 providing that the powers, privileges and immunities of each House of Parliament, and of the members and committees shall be such as determined by law and till such law is made, they shall be the same as obtaining immediately before the coming into force of Section 15 of Forty-fourth Amendment.

It is now more thanfour decades that the Constitution came into force, but the parliamentary privileges have not so far been codified. The citizen has, therefore, to consult what the law of British Parliamentary privileges was as on January 26, 1950, what the privileges of the Indian Legislatures and, correspondingly, his rights *vis-a-vis* the Legislatures are. This situation operates to the detriment of citizen's Fundamental Rights. "But it would seem", A.G. Noorani remarks, "that the legislators are more concerned about their privileges than the rights of citizens" and there appears to be a consensus "about retaining parliamentary privileges in their existing nebulous state."[61]

The Committee of Privileges was first appointed by the Speaker in April 1950. Initially ten Members were appointed to the Committee and now it consists of fifteen Members nominated by the Speaker at the commencement of the House. It examines every issue referred to it, determines whether the facts reveal a breach of privileges and makes its recommendations to the House. On a motion made to that effect, the report is taken into consideration. The House may agree or disagree with the recommendations of the Committee or may agree with amendments and action may be taken accordingly.

**Committee on Subordinate Legislation**

The Indian Legislatures have been delegating the rule-making power for more than a century now, but parliamentary control over subordinate legislation is a recent innovation. Since 1953, a Committee on Subordinate Legislation has been constituted by the Speaker for one year. In making selection from panel of names submitted by the Leader of the House and and by the leaders of other parties and groups, the Speaker gives preference to those who have legal background and experience. The main functions of the Committee are to examine and determine :

(1) whether the Rules, Regulations and Orders are in accordance with the general objects of the Constitution or the Act under the authority of which they are made;
(2) whether they contain matters which should be properly dealt with in an Act;

61. Noorani, A.G., "Need to Codify Parliamentary Privileges," *The Sunday Standard*, New Delhi, February 12, 1978.

(3) whether they contain the imposition of any tax;
(4) whether they directly or indirectly bar the jurisdiction of the courts;
(5) whether they give retrospective effect to any of the provisions where the Act or Constitution does not confer such authority;
(6) whether they involve expenditure from the Consolidated Fund or the public accounts;
(7) whether they appear to make any unexpected or unusual use of the powers conferred;
(8) whether there have been justifiable delays in the publication of the Rules or in laying them before Parliament;
(9) whether for any reason they call for any elucidation.

If the Committee is of the opinion that any Order should be annulled wholly or partially, or should be amended in any respect, it reports that opinion, together with the grounds thereof to the House. If the Committee opines that any other matter relating to any Order should be brought to notice, it may report that opinion and matter to the House. Usually, the Committee makes one report to the House during a session. Reports of the Committee are not discussed in the House, but it keeps a constant watch on the implementation of its recommendations. The Ministers concerned are asked to furnish from time to time a statement of action taken or proposed to be taken by them on the recommendations made by the Committee and on the assurances given by them through correspondence with the Committee. The progress of implementation of the various recommendations is reported to the House by the Committee from time to time.

**Committee on Absence of Members**

Article 101 (4) of the Constitution provides that if for a period of sixty days a Member of either House of Parliament is, without permission of the House, absent from all meetings thereof, the House may declare his seat vacant. Till the Budget session of 1954, the Speaker would read to the House applications for leave and then ascertain the wishes of the House thereon. But thereafter a Standing Committee was set up comprising fifteen Members nominated by the Speaker for one year. This committee considers applications of Members for leave for absence from the sitting of the House. It examines the cases of Members who had been absent for a period of sixty days or more without permission. The Committee recommends to the House whether absence without permission should be condoned or not. In one case it has so far recommended that absence without permission of a Member should not be condoned. The Council of States has no such committee.

**Rules Committee**

Article 118(1) of the Constitution empowers each House of Parliament to make rules for regulating the procedure and conduct of its business. The Rules Committee has been constituted in pursuance of this provision. It is nominated by the Speaker–the Chairman, and consists of fifteen members. The Speaker–the Chairman, is its ex-officio Chairman. The committee so nominated holds office until a new committee is nominated.

The function of the Committee is to consider matters of procedure and conduct of business in the House and to recommend any amendments or additions to the Rules of Procedure and Conduct of Business that may be necessary. Apart from the members of the Committee some other Members of the House may also be invited to attend particular sittings of the Committee. Till 1954 amendments to the Rules of Procedure were made by the Speaker–the Chairman, but now the recommendations of the Rules Committee are placed before the House and adopted.

**Committees Dealing with Facilities**

Besides these, there are three committees dealing with provision of facilities to Members : the General Purposes Committee; the House Committee; and the Library Committee. The function of the General Purposes Committee is to consider and advise on such matters concerning the affairs of the House as may be referred to it by the Speaker. The House Committee deals with matters of accommodation, food and medical aid for members. The functions of the Library Committee are : to consider and advise on such matters concerning the Library as may be referred to it by the Speaker, to consider suggestions for the improvement of the Library, and to assist members in fully utilising the services provided by the Committee.

**Committee on Estimates**

To ensure parliamentary control over grants made to the Government and to supervise and control the actual appropriation, Parliament exercises close scrutiny of public accounts through two of its Committees—the Public Accounts Committee on Estimates was constituted for the first time in 1950, replacing the then Standing Finance Committee of Parliament. Speaker Mavalankar observed in the Lok Sabha : "Consequent upon the provisions of Articles 113 to 116, as also independently thereof, it was felt to constitute a Committee on Estimates for better financial control of the House over expenditure by the Executive. The chief function of this Committee will be to examine such of the estimates as may seem fit to it and to suggest economies consistent with the policy underlying the estimates. There will be, in addition, usual Committee on Public Accounts. The functions of these Committees will be complementary and, it is expected, they will not only give a picture of the entire financial position but the Committees will be mutually helpful in examining the finances for the future in the light of expenditure in the past.."

The Committee on Estimates consists of not more than thirty Members who are elected by the House from among its Members every year according to the system of proportional representation by means of the single transferable vote. The motion for election of members of the Committee is moved by the Leader of the House at the commencement of each House of the People and in subsequent years by the Chairman of the Committee before the term of that Committee is due to expire. In order to maintain continuity in membership of the Committee a convention has been established since 1955-57 that while nominating Members for election parties and groups in the House should keep in view that as far as possible nearly one-third of the Members retire every year and two-thirds of the outgoing Members are returned. A Minister is not elected to the Committee, and if any Member after his election to the Committee is appointed a Minister, he ceases to be a member of the Committee from the date of his appointment. The Chairman of the Committee is appointed by the Speaker from among the members of the Committee. It is a Committee of the House of the People exclusively and unlike the Public Accounts Committee no member of the Council of States is associated with it.

The function of the Committee is to scrutinize the Budget estimates for the year, to suggest economies in the expenditure, improvement in organisation and other steps for increasing efficiency, to find out whether the money is well laid out and also to suggest the form in which the estimates should be presented to Parliament. Usually the Committee functions through the Sub-Committees, one corresponding to one or more Departments, and their reports are submitted both to the House and to the Government. The Committee does not complete its work with the final passage of the Budget. It continues with its labours throughout the year and exercises scrutiny over one Department or the other as it chooses and deems necessary.

As a convention, the Reports of the Committee on Estimates, like those of the Public Accounts Committee, are not discussed in the House. It is again a convention that the recommendations of a Parliamentary Committee are regarded as directions, and accordingly, the recommendations of the Committee on Estimates are generally accepted by the Government and acted upon. After the Committee's report has been presented to the House, copies thereof are forwarded to the Ministry or Department concerned with a request that replies to recommendations be sent not later than six months from the date of its presentation to the House. On receipt of the statement showing the action taken by the Government, it is examined by the Study Group appointed for this purpose and is placed before the Chairman together with the findings of the Study Group. If there is any point, which in the opinion of the Study Group or the Chairman, requires consideration by the Committee, it is specially referred to it. On the basis of the comments made by the Committee, or the Study Group, a draft "Action Taken Report" is prepared which is again considered by the Study Group. After the Chairman's approval it is circulated to the members of the committee. The report is finalized by the Chairman on the basis of the comments received from the members and presented to the House.

Commenting on the utility of the Committee on Estimates, Asok Chanda says, "In recent years, however, the Committee's contribution has been more impressive.......While the Committee refrains even now from openly criticizing the policy implicit in the estimates, its examination does often indirectly reflect on the manner in which a particular policy has been evolved or is being implemented. There has also been considerable improvement in the organisation of the Committee and in its technique, which has better equipped it to fulfil its responsibilities. Even though it works within the limitations inherent in a democratic form of government, its contributions are tending to become more and more effective in economizing national expenditure.''[62] Morrison Jones is rather critical of the role of the Estimates Committee. Its Members, he says, ''are supposed to look for possible economies but they have in fact been happy to rule out the faint line between economy and efficiency. Further, they have not hesitated to recommend in the name of efficiency large administrative reforms and even reorientation of policy. Their audacity occasioned strong comment and it may be that they have in the last few years been more modest in the scope of their reports.'' But ''of their growing competence and effectiveness as a control over ministries,'' he adds, ''there can be no doubt. If they find less to be indignant about it, it is in part because their influence is now automatically reckoned with.''[63]

**The Public Accounts Committee**

The Public Accounts Committee considers the Appropriation Accounts in details and it is the twin brother of the Estimates Committee. Public Accounts Committee were for the first time constituted at the Centre and in the Provinces as early as 1923. But they met under the chairmanship of the Finance Member of the Governor-General's or Governor's Executive Council. Their secretariat consisted of the Finance Department and their role was technicalities. Moreover, the position of the Auditor-General was more governmental than independent and he was in no sense a servant of the Legislature.

In 1950, the Public Accounts Committee was made a real parliamentary committee. The Comptroller and Auditor-General is an important adjunct of the Committee. His audit reports stand automatically referred to the Committee. When the official witnesses are being examined by the Committee, the Comptroller and Auditor-General sits to the right of the Chairman and assists him as the evidence is being taken. With the permission of the Chairman, he may ask a witness to clarify a point and he may further make a statement on the facts of the case. The Committee consists of not more than fifteen members who are elected by the House every year from among its Members according to the principle of proportional representation by means of the single transferable vote. A Minister is not elected a member of this Committee, and if a member, after his election to the Committee, is appointed a Minister, he ceases to be a member of the Committee from the date of his appointment. Since 1954, seven members of the Council of States have been associated with the Committee.[64] The Chairman of the Committee is appointed by the Speaker from among the members of the Committee.

The main function of the Public Accounts Committee is to scrutinize the Appropriation Accounts of the Government of India and other accounts laid before the House and the report of the Comptroller and Auditor-General of India and to satisfy itself that moneys shown in the accounts have been legally disbursed, that expenditure conforms to the authority that governs it and that re-appropriation has been according to rules. The Committee has also to examine the statement of accounts showing the income and expenditure of State Corporations, trading and manufacturing schemes and concerns and projects of autonomous and semi-autonomous bodies whose audit is conducted by the Comptroller and Auditor-General.

The Report of the Comptroller and Auditor-General of India furnishes the Public Accounts Committee with most of the material on which it functions. The Committee has, however, the power to scrutinize and report on almost any matter relating to the management of public finance. The report of the Comptroller and Auditor-General is taken up Ministrywise, and the Departmental Secretaries are required to appear as witnesses to elucidate and explain the observations of audit, in order to enable the Committee to reach final conclusions and formulate its recommendations. The examination of the Committee extends ''beyond the formality of the expenditure to its wisdom, faithfulness and economy.'' Specifically, the examination covers the manner in which approved policy is being implemented, the degree of efficiency and economy with which plans and programmes are being executed and the manner in which discretionary powers are being exercised. The Committee is not concerned with the policy of the method of expenditure. The question whether there is any extravagance or waste in carrying out that policy is within the competence of the Committee. Whenever the

62. Asok Chanda, *Indian Administration*, p. 186.
63. Morris-Jones, W.H., *The Government and Politics of India*, p. 196.
64. A motion in connectioin with the nomination by the Council of States of the seven members is moved in the House of the People every year by the Chairman of the outgoing Committee or the Leader of the House, as the case may be.

Committee decides to examine a matter involving serious financial irregularities, it may appoint a Sub-Committee to go into the matter. A Sub-Committee so appointed, has the powers of the undivided Committee and its report after the Committee's approval, is deemed to be the report of the whole committee.

The utility of the Public Accounts Committee is immense. It is a representative Committee of all shades of opinion and Members of Parliament, who constitute the Committee, recognise the question of public accounts as a national question and, accordingly, its deliberations and findings are devoid of party feelings and partisan approach. It directly contacts the executive officers, the administrators and all those who spend money and, thus, direct elucidation of the disputed matters can be sought from these officials. It may even summon further evidence, oral and documentary. If necessary, evidence may be taken on oath, but in practice that is not done by any Select Committee except in very special cases.

This is a post-mortem examination, all the same, very effective. The Committee has no power to complete any administrative action to be taken on its observations, but that has not detracted from the effectiveness of its recommendations. Recommendations of the Committee are treated with respect by the Government and most of them are accepted and implemented. In case of disagreement between the Government and the Committee with respect to any recommendation the Government must apprise the Committee of the reasons that might have weighed in not accepting or implementing a recommendation. The views of the government are considered by the Committee and it may, if deemed necessary, present a further report to the House. In the event of difference of opinion between the Government and the Committee remaining unresolved, the matters are referred to the Speaker for his guidance. The House seldom discusses reports of the Committee, but Members may use observations of the Committee in their speeches during the discussion on the Budget, demands for grants, etc. However, if there is a specific issue, over which there is difference of opinion between the Committee or the Government or a Minister, that issue can be brought before the House for discussion on a motion.

The utility of the Public Accounts Committee has been variously interpreted. Asok Chanda says that its power is indirect "and lies nominally in the potential results of its reports and the publicity which it is able to give to the question it investigates and in the moral effect of its criticism."[65] Morris-Jones puts it in another way. He says, "The fact that their scrutiny is *ex-post facto* is less important than that the government has continuously to act in the knowledge that scrutiny of any item may take place and that waste and impropriety may be widely exposed in the House and the Press. The fact that the Government replies to the Public Accounts Committee are often vague and cool is less important than that behind the reply there has often been embarrassment and some resolve not to let it happen again."[66]

Five important points were made by the Finance Minister in his address to the Chairmen of the Public Accounts Committees of the Lok Sabha and the State Assemblies in September 1986. First, that the Public Accounts Committees should while relying on the Comptroller and Auditor-General's report, also take into confidence the Finance Ministry or the Finance Departments of State Governments. Second, that the Public Accounts Committees would discharge their functions more effectively if they gave up their pre-occupation with nit-picking issues of non-compliance with rules and regulations, etc., and instead took a broader view, from time to time. Third, that in view of the resources constraint, which involves having to choose between different projects, the Public Accounts Committees should seek the assistance of the Comptroller and Auditor-General in drawing up a list of projects and programmes that have lost their relevance so that these can be scrapped and the money thus saved diverted to more useful programmes or projects. Fourth, that the Public Accounts Committees should insist on accounts of the previous year being presented in the winter session at the latest, instead of having to wait for almost two years. Lastly, that the accounting practice of State Governments, specially at the district treasury level, should be strengthened along the lines suggested by the Finance Ministry in 1976.

These suggestions deserve to be taken seriously. The Public Accounts Committees should

65. Asok Chanda, *Indian Administration,* p. 183.
66. Morris-Jones, W.H., *The Government and Politics of India,* pp. 195-96.66.

take up the really serious issues and give up their excessive preoccupation with trivial. The crux of the issue is watch-dog function that the Public Accounts Committees are supposed to perform. While by and large they have discharged this function reasonably well, they have mostly succeeded in highlighting relatively minor financial irregularities. The bigger sins of omission and commission, such as time and cost over-runs, poor choice of technologies, bad project planning and implementation, etc., have escaped their notice. N.C. Ranga, who was Chairman of the Central Public Accounts Committee in 1958-59, said, "It is a notorious fact that politics comes in as one of the elements to bloat demands and expenditures; inefficiency and indifferent management of funds, whether from the Centre or the States, have become endemic feature, that result in heavy wastage of public funds."

**Committee on Public Undertakings**

The demand for a separate committee on Public Undertakings goes back to 1953. Speaker Mavalankar, in a letter dated December 19, 1953, wrote to the Prime Minister that there was a general feeling in favour of setting up a Standing Committee to examine the working of autonomous Corporations. He pointed out that the Estimates Committee and the Public Accounts Committee were already overburdened with work and would not, therefore, be able to find time to go into the working of the Corporations. But the Prime Minister did not accept the suggestion and the matter lingered on till 1964 when a Committee on Public Undertakings was constituted.

The Committee on Public Undertakings consists of not more than ten members elected by the House of the People from among its members according to the principle of proportional representation by means of the single transferable vote. Five members from the Council of States elected in the same manner, are associated with the Committee. The members of the Council are invited to associate with the Committee on a motion adopted by the House and concurred by the Council. A Minister is not elected a member of the Committee. If a member elected to the Committee is subsequently appointed Minister, he ceases to be a member of the Committee from the date of his appointment. The chairman is appointed by the Speaker from among the members of the Committee.

The functions of the Committee are :

(1) to examine the report and accounts of the such public undertakings as have been specifically allotted to the Committee for this purpose;

(2) to examine the reports, if any, of the Comptroller and Auditor-General on the Public undertakings;

(3) to examine, in the context of autonomy and efficiency of public under takings, whether the affairs of the public undertaking are being managed in accordance with the sound business principles and prudent commercial practices; and

(4) to exercise such other functions vested in the Public Accounts Committee and the Estimates Committee in relation to the public undertakings specified for the Committee as are not covered by (1), (2), and (3) above and as may be allotted to the Committee by the Speaker from time to time.

The Committee shall, however, not examine and investigate any of the following matters:-

(a) matters of major Government policy as distinct from business or commercial functions of the Public undertakings;

(b) matters of day-to-day administration; and

(c) matters for the consideration of which machinery has been established by any special statute under which a particular undertaking is established.

The total Government investments in public undertakings in different States amounted to Rs. 25,000 crores on March 31, 1983. The Committee has investigated into and examined all aspects of the working of these undertakings. One innovation introduced by the committee is the "horizontal study," where some aspect of the working of all public undertakings is studied and norms of performance, cost, practices, etc., are set down.

The Committee in its 32nd report voiced concern at the gradual erosion of the decision-making powers of the public sector enterprises. It noted that to ensure an efficient running of the public sector companies the Industrial Policy Resolution, 1956, had clearly stated that the managers should have the largest possible measure of freedom. It is precisely for this reason that the then prevailing practice of having departmental undertakings was jettisoned and public sector firms were set up as corporate entities. Over the years, however, the autonomy that these corporate entities should have enjoyed and exercised, was gradually encroached upon and they came to be run as mere extensions of the ministries. According to the Committee, although on paper the public sector managers enjoy large autonomy, ministries and government departments have virtually usurped their decision- making powers. The Committee has recommended that "necessary ground rules should be laid down to restrict the Government directions only to matters of policy without transgressing into the spheres of detailed administration."

**Consultative Committee**

Apart form the Committee of the Legislative Assembly, prior to 1950, members of both Houses of the Central Legislature also served on the Standing Advisory Committees attached to various Departments of the Government of India. All these Committees were purely advisory bodies and functioned under the control of the Government and the Minister incharge of the department acted as the Chairman of the Standing Advisory Committee. After the 1950 Constitution became operative, the position of the Central Legislature changed, significantly and these Committees were consequently abolished. But the Government had been seriously thinking all that time how to associate the members of the Parliament with the working of various Ministries and Departments of the Government and thereby provide them with opportunities for discussion of broad policies of the Government in an informal manner. In 1954 the Government decided to establish Informal Consultative Committees for the various Ministries. But the Opposition parties and groups did not take kindly to the Consultative Committee. As a result of discussion between the Government and the Opposition at different levels in 1969, it was decided to delete the word "Informal" from their nomenclature. Mutually agreed "Guidelines" were also formulated to regulate their functioning. The Government, however, did not accept the suggestion of the Opposition for the formation of the Parliamentary Committees in place of Consultative Committees.

Members of both Houses of Parliament are nominated on the Consultative Committees for various Ministries by the Minister of Parliamentary Affairs, on the basis of preference indicated by the members themselves or by the party leaders. Members of the Opposition parties are nominated in proportion to their numerical strength in Parliament. Every Opposition party or group has, thus, its fixed quota for representation on the Consultative Committees and these parties and groups are free to nominate their members on more than one Committee within the quota allotted to them. The unattached members, and members belonging to the ruling party are nominated on the basis of the preferences indicated by them and sent individually to the Department of Parliamentary Affairs. The Committees are reconstituted every year and a member once assigned a Committee for a Ministry, according to the preference indicated by him, continues to be a member of that Committee unless he himself opts for another Committee. The Minister concerned presides over the meetings of the Consultative Committee attached to his Ministry. The Committees provide a forum of informal discussions between the members, Ministers and senior officials of the Government on the problems and policies of the Government relating to administration in a manner which is not practicable on the floor of the House. The deliberations of these Committees are informal and no reference to the discussions held in the meetings is made on the floor of the House and it is binding on the Government as well as the members of the Committees.

Members of these Committees are free to discuss any matter which can appropriately be discussed in Parliament. The practice is to invite suggestions and items for discussion from members and thereupon agenda with notes is prepared and circulated among members. The Committees cannot summon witnesses, to send for or demand the production of any files, or to examine any official records. The Chairman of the Committee may, however, furnish any additional information required by members. A brief record of the discussion in the meeting of a Committee is prepared and circulated among members, except in the case of Ministries of Defence, External Affairs and Department of Atomic Energy :

In matters where there is unanimity, the Government normally accepts the view of the committee subject to the following exceptions :

(i) any view having financial implications;
(ii) any view concerning security, defence, external affairs and atomic energy; and
(iii) any matters falling within the purview of an autonomous corporation.

If the Government finds it difficult to accept the view of the committee, the reasons thereof are explained to the members of the Committee.

But the Consultative Committees, it is widely felt, do not function as committees and still less discharge the functions of consultation except in a purely formal sense. The committee, attached to a Ministry, does not meet by itself without the Minister to discuss or deliberate. It is convened by the Minister. Polemics and partisanship are as present in the committees' deliberations as they are in Parliament itself. The duration of the meeting is decided by the Minister concerned who presides as chairman. The frequency of the meeting varies from two to six per year. Each meeting lasts about a couple of hours unless it is extended to the following day as it happened on January 25, 1978 in the case of the committee attached to the Ministry of External Affairs.

The need for effective Parliamentary Committees is being widely recognised and there was a demand of a cross-section of the Members in the House of the People for increased powers and functions to Parliamentary Consultative Committees. Members generally wanted their status as Standing Committees to be restored so that they might share some of the burdens of Parliament. The Parliamentary Affairs Minister, Ravindra Verma, ruled out the demand and asserted that the Consultative Committees were functioning satisfactorily and the present Government (Janata) had no proposal to increase their powers.

A proposal to do away with the Consultative Committees and replace them with Subjects Committees, as the Public Accounts Committee and the Public Understanding Committee of Parliament, had come up during the late half of 1989. It was considered with some trepidation by the Congress Government of the day headed by Rajiv Gandhi. Even though the move had the backing of the then Speaker of the Lok Sabha Balram Jakhar, it remained a non-starter as the Ministry of Parliamentary Affairs was opposed to it as also various other Ministries and Departments who had expressed strong reservations about such Committees. The Subjects Committees pertaining to agriculture, environments, and science and technology were, however, subsequently set up, though they have so far remained only on paper.

It was reported in September 1991 that the Lok Sabha and Rajya Sabha Secretariats were making a fresh attempt to resurrect the proposal to do away with the Consultative Committees.[67] But it again created a mild flutter in the Ministry of Parliamentary Affairs. The lobby in the Government was for continuing the system of consultative committees. In their opinion the idea of having subjects committees was sought to be pushed by the Secretariats of the Lok Sabha and Rajya Sabha allegedly to enlarge their sphere of influence. This is, however, neither a valid nor a logical argument to rebut the cogency of proposal. Several veteran Members of Parliament during the recently concluded 1991 Budget session of Parliament underlined the need for setting up subjects committees ensuring thereby a proper scrutiny of the functioning of various Ministries and Departments and accountability fixed in case of any lapse or dereliction. But the Minister of Parliamentary Affairs had obliquely ruled out the setting up of subjects committees on the ground that the country had given itself a "Parliamentary system of functioning".

## THE DECLINE OF PARLIAMENT

Speaker Balram Jakhar, delivering the Presidential address at the conference of presiding officers at Hyderabad on December 28, 1981, described the tendency to "decry and berate" legislatures as "dangerous." He said in his view all the talk one heard of declining image of the legislatures stemmed from insufficient appreciation of the role that belonged to the legislature in a democratic polity. The representative institutions, he added, performed a crucial role as the central arena where all the competing forces in the polity, ideas, ideologies and interests, were brought face to face for organised interaction. "If the corporate conscience of the community is to find voice and assert itself it can be done only in a legislature—a people's forum, by the people's representatives. Who else can espouse and uphold the cause of the poor, downtrodden and the defenceless."[68]

The Parliamentary system of Government that India deliberately adopted ensures harmonious co-operation between the executive and legislative branches of government and there is no working at cross purposes between these two wings of government. Ministers are the heads of the various administrative departments, and, at the same time, they are members of the majority party in the legislature. Being in constant touch with the Opposition as well as in still closer contact with the members of their own party the

67. As reported in *The Times of India*, New Delhi, September 27, 1991.
68. As reported in *The Times of India*, New Delhi, December 29, 1981.

ministers can feel the pulse of the legislature and through it the pulse of the public opinion and can thereby obtain useful criticism, in a friendly way of their measures. The members of the legislature can also call to the attention of the Government any grievance felt by their constituents and secure redress. The system, according to James Bryce, secures "swiftness in decision and vigour in action, and enables the Cabinet to press through for such legislation as it thinks with the confidence that its majority will support it against the attacks of Opposition."[69]

The essential feature of Parliamentary democracy is a certain degree of moderation among the political parties, or what may be described political forbearance. The minority agrees that the majority should govern and the majority agrees that minority must criticise and even depose the Government if it can carry with it the majority in the legislature. The Opposition is the prospective Government and it understands and observes the rules of the game, as the majority does. The Government so arranges the parliamentary programme as to give the due opportunity to the Opposition to discuss and criticise its actions. The Government even becomes wiser by that criticism and arrives at a compromise. This is the essence of discussion and parliamentary government succeeds *par excellence* in this respect. The situation of ruthless opposition prevails only when extremist and anti-democratic forces gain a substantial membership in the legislature which they proceed to terrorise and ridicule. Parliamentary system recognises and welcomes differences and it provides the machinery for their expression. But these differences must not go so far as to make the work of Government impossible. If such things are allowed to happen, as they do in India, it is the end of parliamentary democracy.

In the 1950's and early 1960's India had the moral strength of a nation on the move. Jawaharlal Nehru, the first Prime Minister, nurtured the parliamentary institutions and even his stout critics never disputed that he made a unique contribution towards strengthening the foundations of parliamentary democracy in India "The universal admiration Nehru commands on this score" explains Atal Behari Vajpayee, "was not because of any exceptional parliamentary skills that he possessed; it was because of his sincere respect for Parliament and his regard for parliamentary propriety and procedures."[70] Even when his dominance in Parliament was complete and the House of the People was often referred to as his "sounding board," Nehru sought to carry it with him on all important matters instead of imposing his will on it. He would neglect any of other responsibility but not attendance in Parliament when it was in session. Hiren Mukherjee, in his reminiscences, *Portrait of Parliament,* recalled : "Till a few months before his death, Jawaharlal Nehru dominated Parliament....This was not on account of any oratory.........This was not on account of any mastery over the intricacies of procedure, which he never claimed. Rather it was on account of innate and unfailing respect which he had for Parliament as the symbol of the people's power and as good a repository as could be devised of their collective wisdom in our kind of society.........Respect for the House is the foundation of good Parliamentarianism—never to hedge or dodge, being ready to admit errors with grace and always come out clean." When allegations of corruption were levelled in Parliament against Pratap Singh Kairon or K. D. Malviya or T. T Krishnamachari, Nehru's initial response used to be of annoyance and anger. He felt that the Opposition "was unjustifiably pillorying colleagues of his for political gain." But when the facts marshalled by Opposition members "seeped home to make it evident that here was in fact a *prima facie* case, Mr. Nehru did initiate inquiries against these three. Ultimately all three had to go."[71] He respected the Opposition point of view on many occasions and yielded to the criticism with grace.

Undoubtedly, Parliament's functioning left much to be desired even during Nehru's time. Nevertheless, Nehru was greatly missed within a few years of his death. The decline of Parliament became so pronounced by the early seventies that the years under Nehru appeared in contrast as Parliament's "Golden period." The split in the Congress and proclamation of Internal Emergency in June 1975 inflicted a grievous blow to the parliamentary institution provoking a veteran to remark : "Our problem is no longer one of how to strengthen Parliament. We have now to save Parliament."

In their earnest effort to make Parliament a model of dynamism the Founding Fathers en-

69. Bryce, James, *Modern Democracies*, Vol. II, pp. 510-11.
70. "The Decline of Parliament," Express Magazine, *Indian Express* (Sunday Edition) December 6, 1981, p. 1.
71. *Ibid.*

grafted an innovation in the Constitution empowering Parliament to lay down additional qualifications for becoming a member of either House apart from being qualified to be an elector.[72] This provision according to Ambedkar, was intended to ensure that men of better calibre than an ordinary elector adorned both the Houses of Parliament. But no additional qualifications to achieve that end have as yet been framed. Provision was also made in Article 80 (a) for the nomination by the President of twelve members of the Council of States consisting of persons "having special knowledge or practical experience" in respect of such matters as literature, science, arts and social service. This provision was intended to enable the Government to make available to Parliament the services of distinguished persons who were election shy and would not like to be involved in the rough and tumble of politics. Several eminent men in their respective fields adorned, generally in the first two decades the Council of States. But since 1971, this provision has been observed more by breach and without any respect to the intention of the Constitution-makers. Nominations are now regarded as the choicest plums in the basket of the ruling party to be distributed among the faithfuls and discredited loyal partymen at the polls.

By all standards it has been acknowledged that the quality of debates in the House of the People (Lok Sabha) as well as interventions have gone down. One has only to recall how in the early days of the House the debates were not only scintillating but well-informed. This was not just because there were giants in the House in those days, but both on the Treasury and Opposition benches, individual members did a lot of homework, prepared thoroughly before they spoke and acquainted themselves convincingly. In fact, many a member made his tenure in Parliament a period of self-education, a stint for enlightenment. Both among the ruling and Opposition members of Parliament one would find self-made specialists who took their job seriously and with a clear sense of devotion to the national interest as members of the highest legislature of the country.

But the quality of the membership has deteriorated over the years. For this the leadership of every political party is responsible. Party tickets for parliamentary elections are no longer given on considerations of merit, on the potentiality of a person to develop as a serious and dedicated member of the highest legislature of the country, but on consideration other than merit. The process of selecting candidates now is the usual routine recommendation of the State units to be chosen finally by the central parliamentary board of the party. Invariably all parties selected their candidates on the basis of their pull with the communal, caste and bloc votes. The Janata Party, till its disintegration, had a fixed quota of candidates for each of its constituent units. In all elections since 1971, the personality of Mrs. Indira Gandhi became the only focal point of party propaganda. After the second split of the Congress in 1978, the faction headed by Mrs. Indira Gandhi became Congress (Indira) and in the 1980 Parliamentary elections loyalty to Mrs. Gandhi during days of her political distress was the major criterion for selecting party candidates. Unflinching loyalty to a person is a unique norm for selecting party candidates and it has no parallel in the annals of any country with a democratic system of government. Such a criterion produces a breed of the sycophants and not parliamentarians. They do not represent the people in the national forum but a single person whose behests they unhesitatingly obey and follow. They, thus, sacrifice their independence of judgment and narrow their horizon of approach to the solution of the national problems. Parliament is a deliberative assembly of one nation, with one interest, that of the whole nation. Sachchidananda Sinha, Provisional Chairman of the Constituent Assembly, quoted in his inaugural address the words of Joseph Story :........ "Republics are created —theses are the words that I commend to you for your consideration—by the virtue, public spirit and intelligence of citizens. They fall when the wise are banished from the public councils because they dare to be honest, and the profligate are rewarded because they flatter the people in order to betray them." Sachchidananda Sinha's words have proved prophetic. A decade or so back Nani A. Palkhivala wrote that after thirty years of independence, "Indian democracy has reached the nadir because in our average politician we have the pathetic amalgam of lack of true intellect with lack of character and lack of knowledge."[73]

Sir Ivor Jennings has succinctly analysed the role of the Opposition in a parliamentary system of government. The Government governs

72. Article 84 (c).
73. "Has the Constitution Failed ?" Nani A. Palkhivala, the *Illustrated Weekly of India*, Bombay, September 16, 1979.

and the Opposition criticises. "Failure to understand this principle," he lamented "is one of the causes of the failure of so many of the progeny of the Mother of Parliaments and of the suppression of Parliamentary government by dictatorship." Attacks upon the Government and the individual ministers are the functions of the Opposition. It adopts Sir Toby's advice "so soon as ever thou seest him, draw; and, as thou drawest, swear horrible." That duty is the major check which the Constitution provides upon corruption and defective administration. It is also the means through which individual injustices are prevented. The House of Commons, Jennings points out, 'is at its best when it debates those individual acts of oppression or bad faith which can never be completely overcome in a system of government which places responsibility on such minor officials as police officers. It is the public duty of the Opposition to raise such questions. It is a duty hardly less important than that of Government."

The role of the Opposition which Sir Ivor Jennings emphasises relates to a country with two-party system as it had till recently in Britain. However, there are still two major parties, Conservative and Labour, and among them the Government alternates one in power and the other in Opposition. India has a multiple-party system with only four recognised national parties and a score of others including the regional parties. Opposition is, therefore, a motley of groups with no unity of purpose or ideology to hold them together for a concerted action. Disraeli believed that "no government can long be secure without a formidable Opposition." The Opposition parties and groups in India are so sharply divided among themselves that they do not see, as they had not seen before until 1977, any chance of their being able to come to power in the foreseeable future. The Janata miracle of 1977 is not likely to repeat itself. This psychological factor affects the thinking and strategy of the Opposition.

When the Congress was at its crest after 1971 parliamentary elections, the Party President Dev Kanta Barooah said : "Our country can do without Opposition. They are irrelevant to the history of India." The second part of this observation is all too sadly true in practice. In Britain, according to the ancient theory, service in the House of Commons is like a jury service, not a right but duty. In India, the politicians are driven always by the quest of obvious authority. In a status conscious society, as India is, politicians are incapable to grasping that a subtle form of power can also be exercised by those who do not hold ministerial office. Self-seeking men of limited vision view the Opposition "as the refuge for failure and the nursery of frustration. They fail utterly to realise that those who oppose also serve a valid purpose in a parliamentary democracy."

The first part of Barooah's comment is irrelevant in the context of the parliamentary system of government that the Constitution establishes and shall remain so as long as such a system endures. Opposition is the life blood of the parliamentary government. The Janata Government in 1977 recognised the indispensability of the Opposition by recognising the leader of the Opposition, Y.B. Chavan, who led the Congress Parliamentary Party. He was paid a salary from the exchequer and was given the status of a Cabinet Minister. The Congress(I) ruling party did not abandon this practice and it is well-trenched now. But the effectiveness of the Opposition does not exist in the midst of multitude of Opposition parties and groups and, particularly, when a regional party, Telugu Desam, constituted the largest Opposition group in the Eighth House of the People (Lok Sabha). They were strange bed fellows to combine them together. In a vain bid to form an alternative to Congress (I) various conclaves and conferences were convened during the many years suggesting even a confederation of the non-Congress (I) Opposition parties, but insurmountable hurdles plagued their efforts at every stage. An "Activist,"[74] writing under the caption "What must Opposition Do ? Other than Heckle the Government,"[75] suggested, *inter alia*, "What we in that loosely called collectivity, the 'national opposition' need to do urgently is above all to regain our identity. Only then can our purpose and role follow, and only then credibility be restored, not otherwise....Our public image is even worse....People are not ready yet to put destinies into our hands again."

An important feature of a successful parliamentary system is a certain degree of moderation among the political parties and accordingly,

74. An important leader of he Opposition "Activist" wrote under a pseudonym so that the propositions, he suggested, may be considered independently of who he was and which group he belonged to.

75. *The Times of India*, New Delhi, July 30, 1986.

both the party in power and Opposition should understand and observe the rules of the game. A simple practice of British politics, is, "If you wish to govern, you must show yourself to be governed." This rule acts as a powerful and valuable stimulus both to the majority and the minority. Just as the party in power must reconcile differences with the Opposition in order to ensure a stable government representing public opinion and to win approbation of the electorate who gave them the mandate to govern, similarly, the Opposition must remain moderate and sensible, if they are to win approval as an alternative government. When political parties become intolerant of one another and virulent in opposition and attacks, orderly government cannot exist. For the success of the Parliamentary system of government rational and responsible Opposition is as necessary as the rational and tolerant majority imbued with the sense of give and take.

That precisely does not exist in India. The ruling party is intolerant and irrational in its approach and the Opposition, no matter what its label is, resorts to every trick, every method of obstruction and filibuster. And if everything else fails even force may be applied. It also claims its rights to go to the streets and organise agitations against the Government in order to achieve its objective. What began in the sixties in the aftermath of the Sino-Indian border conflict, as outbursts of anger and frustration of an Opposition then venting the national mood in Parliament, has over the years become a recognised parliamentary practice. Pran Chopra gives a graphic picture of the functioning of the House of the People. He writes, "It should make a true democrat weep to see what happens daily on the floor of Parliament, especially the Lok Sabha. Pandemonium has become a daily event, with members outshouting everyone instead of trying to outargue anyone. Defiance of the Speaker has become a habit with some, disregard of the rules a habit with many. Interrupting one another is more the rule than the exception, and the resulting din overpowers everyone's ability to think."[76]

But what happened in the House of the People in a brief first session of the Seventh House of the People shall perhaps remain unprecedented. A group of young ruling party members resorted to obstreperous heckling of some of the more important Opposition members on practically everyday, sometimes even when the Leader of the House was present. Not a single senior member of the ruling party made an effort to control their partymen. Indeed, they seemed to offer encouragement by their own comments about the Opposition. Frank Anthony (Nominated) had, earlier, mentioned that the House had sometime tended to become what he called a bear garden. "It has been a matter of sadness to some of the senior members that certain members almost specialised in an attitude of defiance of the chair." He also stated again that "there might be a tendency, because of its overwhelming strength." In the Eighth House of the People the discussion on the "Bofors Kickbacks" issue, the Opposition charges were sometimes explicitly stated but were more often insinuated with a viciousness rarely seen before. Ajoy Biswas, the CPM member from Tripura, went down in history as one who had been suspended for the entire session. When the Speaker asked Defence Minister K.C. Pant to read the motion on the Bofors panel, he rushed to the well of the House and snatched the papers from him. The Eighth House of the People truly touched its nadir in July-August 1987.

The Council of States was seen by the Constitution-makers as a foil to the tyranny of the majority entrenched in the House of the People. The elders in the Council were expected to bring to bear on the legislative business a measure of detachment and freedom from partisan passion. But these expectations were soon belied. The working of the Council of States has not been substantially different from the Lower House. The proceedings of the Upper House are as boisterous as in the Lower House. The sharp clashes between the Chairman, who also was the Vice-President of India, and Piloo Mody, Leader of the Janata Party and the Leader of the House Pranab Mukherjee, who also was the Finance Minister, and the indecorous language used by them towards the Chair, has, perhaps, not a parallel even in the House of the People."[77]

Two results flow from the above analysis : the apathy of the members in the transaction of the business of Parliament and its shrivelling sessions. Both are interconnected and importantly contribute to the decline of Parliament. Parliament in India has its own clearly set-out Rules of Conduct and Procedure as the Mother

76. "The Twilight of Parliament," *The Tribune*, Chandigarh, September 8, 1978.
77. See *ante*.

of Parliaments has May's Parliamentary Practices. The only difference between the two is that while working in the British Parliaments their observance is the rule, their breach the exception. In India, it is just the other way round. No other Parliament has a so-called Zero-hour [78] which begins at the end of the Question-hour. While the Presiding-Officer is calling upon Ministers to lay papers on the table, there may be many as two dozen members on their feet clamouring for his attention to make statements on matters of public importance, special mentions, call attention motions or points of order. It is free play for all and the rules are cast to the winds. The pleadings of the Speaker that they should speak one by one are of no avail. Speaker Balram Jakhar's admission that the image of Parliament must be protected led to the thinking that Zero-hour might be abolished. But members are not prepared to surrender their this cherished right of redressal of grievances. The then Bharatiya Janata Party President, Atal Behari Vajpayee, said at Vijayawada on September 13, 1982, that any attempt to do away with the Zero-hour in Parliament would be stoutly resisted by the Opposition. He maintained that it was an Indian innovation which "would help accelerate the pace of socio-economic transformation."[79] But no one realises that every minute of Parliamentary Session is estimated to cost the exchequer about Rs. 800.[80]

Question-hour is the most effective instrument in a parliamentary democracy for seeking information from the executive. Questions asked, oral or written, bring to light the activities of government and subject the Government to public scrutiny, and this is, according to Herman Finner, "The fundamentally characteristic way of keeping the Cabinet painfully sensitive to publics opinion."[81] The proceedings of each House of Parliament in India begin with the Question-Hour. Twenty questions are listed for each day and it is rare that more than four are taken up in the hour scheduled. While the questioner is putting his or her supplementaries, a dozen or more hands are raised to catch the eye of the Presiding Officer. There are cries from the different corners of the House addressed to the Speaker, "Look this side, Sir ! And this side too ! Why do you always look right or left and never in the front ?" Supplementaries usually take the form of speeches with lots of interruptions. The requests from the Speaker not to make speeches but ask questions remain unheeded and his admonitions go unheard. Tempers are frayed, unparliamentary expressions are used and ordered to be expunged. They are expunged from the record and banned to the Press, but hundreds of visitors in the galleries of the House everyday hear them and spread vastly exaggerated accounts of what transpired in the House. It lowers in the public eye the dignity and prestige of Parliament and, *ipso facto,* of the representatives whom they had elected.

Equally disquieting are the twin tendencies of absenteeism and thin attendance. "Sometimes just five members conduct the business", H. V. Kamath observed in March 1979 while a Business Advisory Committee Report was beeing discussed. "Heaven help us for democracy cannot go on at this rate," he commented with feeling. Professor P. G. Mavalankar had in that same discussion explained "quite a large number of our friends" come only when they had to speak in a discussion. "They then attend, speak and go away." He added "I suppose all of us ought to take things seriously.......It is only a microscopic minority who take Parliament seriously and who sit in the House from say, 10.30 a.m. to 6.30 p.m." The Minister of Parliamentary Affairs agreed with this. He said, "I agree there are Hon'ble members who sit through in the House and there are others who come, sit for some time, and then go away." This was, he added, " a question which should be posed to the conscience of all members." A House of People (Lok Sabha) bulletin had in March 1979 suggested, citing previous ruling of the Speakers, that it was a breach of Parliamentary etiquette and a discourtesy to the House for members to come in only to make a speech and go away, and it had no effect at all on the Honourable Members.

This casual attitude of members towards the proceedings of Parliament is embarrassing to the Government and so often Ordinary Bills and even Constitution Bills had collapsed. The 46th Amendment Bill collapsed because a large number of members belonging to the ruling party had been in Parliament at the time of the division, but

78. See *ante.*
79. As reported in *The Hindustan Times,* New Delhi, September 14, 1982.
80. This was revealed by Shyam Lal Yadav, Deputy Chairman of the Council of States (Rajya Sabha) in his Key-note address on "Question hour : how to make it more effective." As reported in *The Times of India*, New Delhi, January 23, 1983.
81. Finer, Herman, *Government of Greater European Powers,* p. 162.

not in the House. The 47th Amendment Bill faced the same fate as befell the 46th. The First, Seventh, the Seventeenth and Nineteenth Constitution Amendment Bills had earlier fallen through for want of the prescribed majority.

Even during the discussion on the Punjab crisis, a crucial issue agitating the nation and on the resolution of which depended the unity of the country, there was perceptibly high rate of absence when the Home Minister spoke. If the House was not adjourned it was not because more than the requisite number of 55 members was present[82] but the Speaker who alone has to decide on the quorum thought it discreet not to press for it.[83] The Postal Amendment Bill, which sought to reduce one of the vital fundamental rights conferred on a citizen by Article 19 of the Constitution, was passed when only 20 members were present in the House. In case the President had assented to this bill, it would not have been a legally enacted measure and its validity was liable to be challenged in a court of law on that ground. During the debate on the President's address (1987)—the major debate which is generally taken up first during the budget session—one could see a lack of quorum, though this embarrassment was ignored.

This is not a recent development. This irresponsible absenteeism has been increasing over the years and there are absolutely no extenuating circumstances in defence of this conduct of the members of Parliament. They are paid fairly well and their perks are considerable. They are extremely touchy about their privileges, perquisites and other trappings that go with their high status and they can be pugnacious in defence of these. But their attitude towards the rightful role that the great institution of Parliament must play has become despairingly cynical. They do not seem to bother even if the august House does not meet. This, unfortunately, is true as most of the Treasury benches, enjoying even a virtual four-fifths majority, as of disparate Opposition groups. Otherwise, a vigilant Opposition could have easily embarrassed the complacent, indolent and disorganised ruling party by mustering quorum of its own and the most controversial Postal Amendment Bill would have foundered on the floor of the House of the People.[84]

When the guillotine was applied in the House of the People (Lok Sabha) debate on budgetary demands for Ministries and Departments, the executive was allowed to get away with the authority to spend during 1987-88 more than Rs. 21,000 crores without Parliamentary scrutiny. It was then a record, for the demands of as many as 20 Ministries and four Departments, including Industry, Commerce, Planning and Programme Implementation, Textiles, Food and Civil Supplies, Steel and Mines, Surface Transport, Tourism and Health and the entire range of science subjects consisting of Atomic Energy, Space, Ocean Development and electronics, could not get a chance to be considered. The number of Ministries whose demands the House was able to discuss in some detail were just 10 and it might have been even less, had not the time for putting an end to all discussions on demands been extended by two sittings. During the Budget session in 1986, the House discussed at length the demands for 11 Ministries and five Departments. The previous year (1985), the figure was 15 Ministries and five Department. In 1991 the guillotine cut short the debate on the demands for grants of various Ministries except five Ministries. This was claimed as an improvement on the Lok Sabha's performance in 1990 when it had a detailed examination on the functioning of only four Ministries. In 1992 demands of seven Ministers could be discussed and 35 guillotined involving demands totalling Rs. 233, 398 crores. This sorry state of affairs continues unabated year after year.

It is hardly a happy development that the number of Ministries and Departments whose budgetary demands the House of the People is able to discuss in details keeps dwindling. Speaker Balram Jakhar was himself exercised over this development not long ago and spoke more than once of the need to ensure genuine

82. Article 100 (3) of the Constitution provides that the quorum to constitute a meeting of either House shall be one-tenth of the total number of the members of the House.
83. Article 100(4) states that if there is no quorum, it shall be the duty of the Chairman or Speaker or person acting as such to adjourn the House or to suspend the meeting until there is a quorum.
84. The Congress (I) Parliamentary managers took a serious view of the large-scale absence of party members. In what is described as a strong plea for taking Parliament seriously, the Minister of Parliamentary Affairs (H.K.L. Bhagat) wrote to all party members (March 1987) to guard against absenteeism. The letter was supplemented by verbal exhortations. It had been suggested that the members should not leave Delhi during the session without informing party whips and that too if they had pressing reasons. While in Delhi, they should make it a point to be present in the House. If that was not possible, they should be in Parliament House to be able to respond to the quorum bell. The conveners of the State Committees were urged not only to ensure that the members from their respective States attend, but also in monitoring the response to his exhortations.

parliamentary scrutiny of the Budget through Standing Committees.

S. N. Mishra, a senior Janata Member of Parliament, complained in the 1979 Budget Session of the House of the People that duration of Parliament's sessions has of late been shrinking. He also complained that of the available time too little is being devoted to budgetary control and policy debates and too much to other less consequential matters. The Leader of the Opposition, C. M. Stephen (Congress I) supported Mishra, Atal Behari Vajpayee also complained of shrivelling sessions of Parliament.[85] A resolution passed at the instance of the General Purposes Committee of Parliament in 1955, laid down criteria for the duration of sessions. By and large these recommendations were followed until 1980. As against an average of 25 weeks per year in earlier days, it only met for 19 weeks in 1980 and 21 weeks in 1981. "By itself, this curtailment in the duration of Parliament's sessions," says Atal Behari Vajpayee, "would seem a minor matter. But in actual fact, it is symptomatic of the present Government's allergy to parliamentary accountability, bordering on contempt for the institution and a desire to limit its role." [86] But will extension in the duration of Parliament serve any useful purpose in the presence of absenteeism and thinness in attendance except a toll on the exchequer ?

It is time that Parlilament itself decided on how to improve its own functioning. As Speaker Balram Jakhar suggested and some Members of Parliament are also seriously concerned over this, for going in for the Committee system; that each Member is attached to one or more Committees dealing with a specific subject and they would specialise in the subject concerned with the help and cooperation of the Ministry concerned. This would perhaps facilitate more serious functioning by the Member while the duration of the plenary session could be gainfully reduced.

Whatever be the remedy, the present malaise of conspicuous absenteeism of Members of Parliament must be sternly checked and here the Opposition must accept its due share for this sordid state of affairs. When Athens was a democracy then a Greek dramatist, Aristophanes, said about its people :

> "It's your fault, people of Athens who live
> On public money, but all you think about
> Is private gain, every man for himself."

Obviously Aristophanes meant the politicians of Athens who were losing the essence of democracy while they were still working a democratic constitution. It is equally applicable to parliamentarians in India because their functions and performance is betrayal of the trust reposed in them by the vast concourse of humanity that voted them to be their representatives.

## SUGESTED READINGS


Alexandrovicz, C.H., *Costitutional Developments in India.*

Bettelheim, Charles, *India Independent.*

Blacklerburn, *Explosion in a Subcontinent Constituent Assembly Debates*

Granville Austin — *The Indian Constitution —A Cornerstone of a Nation.*

Jennings, Ivor, *Some Characteristics of the Indian Constitution.*

Rudolph, L.I. and Rudolph S.H., *In pursuit of Lakshmi. the Political Economy of the Indian State*

Selbowne, D. *An Eye to India.*

Shukla, V.N. *Constitution of India.*


85. "The Decline of Parliament," Express Magazine, *Indian Express* (Sunday Edition), December 6, 1981.
86. *Ibid.*

# CHAPTER XI

# The Supreme Court

## Constitution of the Supreme Court

The Constitution provided for the establishment of a Supreme Court of India consisting of a Chief Justice and until Parliament by law provided a larger number, not less than seven Judges. The Supreme Court (Number of Judges) Act, 1956, raised the maximum number of Judges to ten and this number was again raised in 1960 to fourteen including the Chief Justice. The Supreme Court (Number of Judges) Amendment Act, 1977, provided that the maximum number of Judges, excluding the Chief Justice, shall be 17. It has since been increased to 26.

There is no minimum number of Judges fixed by the Constitution, except for the provision in Article 145 relating to Rules of Court. Clause (3) of this Article provides that the minimum number of Judges who are to sit for the purpose of deciding any case involving a substantial question of law and to the interpretation of the Constitution or for the purpose of hearing any reference under Article 143, advisory jurisdiction of the Court, shall be five. The Constitution (Forty-second Amendment) Act, 1976, inserted a new Article 144A which provided that the minimum number of Judges constituting the Bench for disposal of questions relating to the constitutional validity of laws would be seven. But the Constitution (Forty-third Amendment) Act, 1977, omitted Article 144A thereby restoring the original position. Article 145 (2) empowers the Supreme Court, with the approval of the President, to make rules, subject to the number of five Judges constituting a Constitutional Bench, the minimum number of Judges who are to sit for any purpose, and may provide for the powers of single Judges and Division Courts. Rules of the Supreme Court provide that subject to other provisions of these rules, every cause, appeal or matter shall be heard by a Bench consisting of not less than three Judges nominated by the Chief Justice.

If at any time there is no quorum of Judges available to continue or hold any session of the Supreme Court, the Chief Justice of India, may, with the previous consent of the President and after consultation with the Chief Justice of the High Court concerned, request a Judge of the High Court, qualified to be a Judge of the Supreme Court, to attend the sittings of the Court as an *ad hoc* judge for such period as may be necessary. He shall remain a High Court Judge and his duties at the Supreme Court are additional, but during his attendance at the Supreme Court he has all the jurisdiction, powers and privileges of a Supreme Court Judge.

The Constitution also provides that the Chief Justice of India may at any time, with the previous consent of the President, request any person who has held the office of a judge of the Supreme Court or of the Federal Court or who has held the office of a Judge of a High Court and is duly qualified for appointment as a Judge of the Supreme Court[1] to sit and act as a Judge of the Supreme Court. While so sitting and acting he is entitled to such allowances as the President may by order determine and has all the jurisdiction, power and privileges of a Judge of the Supreme Court, ''but shall not otherwise be deemed to be, a Judge of that Court.'' It is important to note that while absence of a quorum of the permanent Judges of the Supreme Court is a condition for the appointment of an *ad hoc* Judge, there is such condition when a retired Judge of the Supreme or Federal Court or a person who held the office of a Judge of a High Court is requested to sit and act as a Judge of the Supreme Court. He may be asked to sit and act at any time by the Chief Justice with the previous consent of the President.

A person to be appointed a Judge of the Supreme Court must be a citizen of India and has been a Judge of one or more High Courts for five successive years or an advocate of one or more High Courts for ten successive years or is, in the opinion of the President, an eminent jurist. Every Judge of the Supreme Court is appointed by the President by warrant under his hand and seal after consultation with such of the Judges of the Su-

1. Inserted by the Constitution (Fifteenth Amendment) Act, 1963.

preme Court and of the High Courts as the President may deem necessary for such a purpose, but the Chief Justice of India must always be consulted.[2] A Judge holds office until he attains the age of sixty-five years.[3] He may, by writing under his hand addressed to the President, resign his office.[4] He is also liable to be removed from his office by an order of the President after an address by each House of Parliament supported by a majority of the total membership of that House and by a majority of not less than two-thirds of the members of that House present and voting has been presented to the President in the same session for such removal on the ground of proved misbehavior or incapacity.[5] Parliament may regulate by law the procedure for the presentation of the address and for the investigation or proof of the misbehavior or incapacity of a Judge. No person who has held office of a Judge of the Supreme Court shall plead or act in any court or before any authority within the territory of India after retirement or resignation or removal from office. Before entering upon his office a Judge makes and subscribes before the President or some other person appointed in that behalf by him an oath or affirmation that he shall to the best of his ability, knowledge and judgment perform the duties of his office without fear or favour, affection or ill will and that he will uphold the Constitution and the laws.

**Appointment of Chief Justice**

The appointment of A.N. Ray, a sitting Judge of the Supreme Court, as Chief Justice of India, on the retirement of S.M. Sikri in April 1973, in supersession of three others,[6] who were senior to him on the Bench, precipitated an unprecedented situation in the history of the Judiciary in India. The three Judges whose claims to the office of the Chief Justice were overlooked resigned. In Parliament and elsewhere, there was a sharp reaction to the appointment of Justice Ray with accusations of political motivation behind it. The Supreme Court Bar Association as also the Bar Associations of High Courts in all the States, barring a sprinkling of individual members, passed resolutions protesting against the action of the Union Government. The resentment was more bitter when Justice M.H. Beg superseded Justice H.R. Khanna early in 1977.

Article 124(2) provides for the appointment of Judges of the Supreme Court by the President after consultation with the Chief Justice of India and such of the Judges of the Supreme Court and High Courts in the States as he may deem necessary. But no such provision exists in the matter of appointment of a Chief Justice. Hitherto the practice was to appoint the seniormost Judge of the Supreme Court as Chief Justice in consultation with the retiring Chief Justice. In the appointment of Justice Ray this practice was not followed and the retiring Chief Justice, S. M. Sikri, was never consulted at any stage. Chief Justice Sikri came to know of the appointment, as he said in a statement, only through the news broadcast by the All India Radio, Delhi station.[7] A point of law was raised in the Delhi High Court in respect of Ray's appointment. The petitioner prayed for a writ of *quo warranto* against the Chief Justice of India on the ground that the appointment of Justice Ray was in violation of Article 124 (2) as the mandatory consultation was not made and as the rule of seniority, which inheres in that Article, was not followed and that the appointment made was *mala fide*. By the time the writ petition was filed the Judges who had been superseded resigned and the petition was rejected.

The Law Commission, chaired by M. C. Setalvad and containing such distinguished

2. The Chief Justice of India, Y.V. Chandrachud, expressed the opinion that the prevailing system of appointment of Judges deserved a "decent burial." He suggested that the responsibility of recommending names for appointments that at present rested exclusively on the discretion of the Chief Justice, be entrusted to a body which may include three Judges, two members of the bar, two representatives of the Government, and two nominees of the Opposition. The idea was to make merit a critical criterion by making the selection process an open one. Justice P.N. Bhagwat, too, felt that the existing constitutional provisions were not adequate. Instead, there should be a collegium to make recommendations. He did not spell out its composition. But a committee on the reforms of the Indian legal system, at the conference organised by the Indian Law Institute under the chairmanship of Soli Sorabjee, suggested setting up a collegium comprising the Chief Justice of India and three seniormost Judges should decide upon the appointment of Judges and the decision of the collegium should be submitted to the President and it must be binding on the Government of India.
3. The Constitution (Fifteenth Amendment) Act, 1963, inserted clause (2A) in Article 124 providing that the age of a Judge of the Supreme Court shall be determined by such authority and in such manner as Parliament may by law provide.
4. Justice Baharul Islam resigned in January 1983 in order to contest a House of the People seat in Assam due to be held in mid-February 1983.
5. Article 124(4).
6. Justices J.M. Shelat, K.S. Hegde and A.N. Grover.
7. *The Tribune*, Chandigarh, April 29, 1973.

members as G. S. Pathak, S. M. Sikri, M. C. Chagla, N. A. Palkhivala, had urged in 1958 that succession of an office of this character (Chief Justice) should not be "regulated by mere seniority." The Commission emphasized the point that a successful Chief Justice needed qualities of leadership and administrative ability not expected of his associates, however erudite and senior in their tenure in the Court. They even made a special plea for youth "carrying a freshness and vigour of mind which have their advantages as maturity and experience flowing from age." They suggested the possibility of taking a person from "outside;" preferably from the Chief Justices of the various High Courts or outstanding Judges of such Courts. The Commission observed, "It is therefore necessary to set a healthy convention that appointment to the office of the Chief Justice rests on special consideration, and does not as a matter of course go to the seniormost puisne Judge." The Study Team of the Administrative Reforms Commission, whose Chairman C.D. Deshmukh was, recognised this point and recommended that "seniority-based elevations resulting in markedly short tenures," as in the case of the Chief Justice, should be altered.

At 61, Justice Ray had a term close to four years in contrast to weeks and months which Justice Shelat and Hegde could look forward to if they had been appointed in succession according to the convention of seniority while the third of the superseded Judges, A. N. Grover, would had enjoyed a longer tenure than Justice Ray if he had been selected. The Government, once it decided to break the sequence of seniority, probably decided to go in for what it considered to be the most suitable choice.

The seniority convention has not been followed in the appointment of Chief Justices of High Courts or to elevation from High Courts to the Supreme Court.[8] The seniority rule in the appointment of the Chief Justice of India has, therefore, no legal basis. But it is fair enough to question the timing of the Government's decision to break with the convention and practice of all these years. Although the Government had accepted the Law Commission's recommendations in 1960, it had not felt it necessary to put the same in effect until April 1973, except in the appointment of P. B. Gajendragadkar as Chief Justice under more extenuating circumstances. Nowhere is a convention so suddenly thrown to the winds, remarked Justice M. Hidayatullah, "immediately after the delivery of the judgment." Shelat, Hegde and Grover were members of the thirteen-member Constitution Bench which heard the *Kesavananda Bharati* case and delivered the judgment on April 24, 1973. The intentions of the Government became suspect and a wild cry went around the country that the Government was penalising the Judges for their independence and impartiality.

A public controversy on the appointment of the Chief Justice again started much earlier to the retirement of M. H. Beg on February 22, 1978. The two seniormost Judges were Y.N. Chandrachud and P. N. Bhagawati. Fifty-two public men and advocates in Bombay[9] issued on January 6, 1978 a memorandum questioning the desirability of the Union Government appointing either Justice Y. V. Chandrachud or Justice P. N. Bhagwati as the Chief Justice of India on the ground that in their view they did not qualify for this office of the highest importance, because both had decided against the citizen and in favour of the State in the *Habeas Corpus* case during the Emergency."[10]

In a separate Press statement, M.C. Chagla too argued against the appointment of Justice Chandrachud because of his "misdeed" during the emergency which "is a very grave one" because he held in the *Habeas Corpus* case along with his three other colleagues and against the emphatic opinion of his senior colleague, Mr. Justice H. R. Khanna and nine High Courts, that, by reason of the Presidential decree suspending Article 21, no one had the right to move Courts for a writ of *habeas corpus* against his order of detention, however illegal, unjustified or *mala fide* the order might have been. He appealed even to Jayaprakash Narayan "to raise his voice

8. A.N. Grover was appointed to the Supreme Court in 1968 when two other Judges, including the Chief Justice, were senior to him in the Punjab and Haryana High Court. Ranjit Singh Sarkaria of the same Court was elevated to the Supreme Court Bench leaving behind many Judges, including the Chief Justice, senior to him. J.R. Madholkar, a Bombay High Court Judge, was appointed Supreme Court Judge in 1960 superseding all the Chief Justices of High Courts in India, as his position amongst permanent judges of the various High Courts was at No. 7. A.N. Ray came to the Supreme Court superseding many judges of the West Bengal High Court.
9. Among the signatories were S.M. Joshi, A.D. Gorwala, Mrs. Durga Bhagwat, Marathi Writer, A.I. Samson, a retired Judge, Ram Jethmalani, Iqbal Chagla. A.G. Noorani, Anil Diwan, S.K. Mukherji and R. Mathalone.
10. As reproduced in *The Times of India,* New Delhi, January 7, 1978.

against what might be considered as a national disgrace and I also appeal to our Prime Minister (Morarji Desai) to intervene and not to permit this appointment to be made which is contrary to the highest standards of judicial office.''[11] But the Government appointed Justice Y.V. Chandrachud to succeed Justice M. H. Beg as Chief Justice of India and upheld the principle of seniority. In pursuance of this principle P. N. Bhagwati succeeded Chandrachud and R. S. Pathak succeeded Bhagwati on his retirement on December 31, 1986. Ranganath Mishra succeeded Chief Justice Pathak and K.N. Singh succeeded Mishra. K. N. Singh had a tenure of just two weeks. He was succeeded by Chief Justice M. H. Kania.

The Law Commission's 80th Report on ''the appointment of Judges'' was presented to the Council of States on January 28, 1980. The Report was prepared by its former Chairman, Justice H. R. Khanna.[12] It recommended that the principle of seniority should be strictly followed by the Government in the appointment of the Chief Justice of the Supreme Court. The Commission said that departure from this principle in the past had aroused controversy and affected the image of the office of the Chief Justice. It was observed that ''The vesting of unbridled power in the executive to depart from this principle may be absurd.'' The Commission suggested that, if at all, the Government proposes to depart from this principle of seniority, the matter should be referred to a panel consisting of all the siting Judges of the Supreme Court. In case of difference of opinion, the decision of the majority view would prevail.

As for the other Judges of the Supreme Court, the report suggested that the Chief Justice of India should consult two of his seniormost colleagues before recommending a name. His recommendation to the President should reproduce the views of each of them. Any recommendation of the Chief Justice which carried the concurrence of his two seniormost colleagues should normally be accepted. The Commission also suggested that ''no one should be appointed to the Supreme Court as Judge unless for a period of not less than seven years he has snapped all affiliations with political parties and unless during the preceding period of seven years he has distinguished himself for his independence, dispassionate approach and freedom from political prejudices, bias or leaning.'' Merit alone should be the consideration for the appointment of Judges and no consideration should be shown to the fact that certain minorities are not too well represented on the Bench. Even where regard is to be had for representation of different regions, the best person from the region should be appointed.

**Independence of the Judiciary**

The members of the Constituent Assembly envisaged the judiciary as a bastion of rights and justice and in their efforts to achieve this ideal they were careful to keep it out of politics. How was politics to be kept out of the Courts ? ''The Assembly's answer", as Granville Austin says, ''was to strengthen the walls of the fortress with constitutional provisions.''[13] The suggestions of the Sapru Committee were their guide in this respect. The Committee had recommended that Judges of the Supreme Court should be appointed by the Head of the State in consultation with the Chief Justice of India and they should be removed from office on grounds of misbehavior or infirmity of the mind by the Head of the State with the concurrence of a special tribunal.[14] The salaries of the judges and their strength was to be fixed by the constitution and would be neither varied to a Judge's advantage or disadvantage without the sanction of the Head of the State and the recommendation of the Supreme Court and the Government. The Committee, however, rejected the idea of an address by Parliament, which was used in England for the removal of judges because it did not consider it right and proper that judge's conduct should form the subject of discussion in the heated atmosphere of a political Assembly.''[15]

The members of the *Ad Hoc* Committee on the Supreme Court appointed by the Constituent Assembly, took a somewhat different view of these matters, but the Assembly ultimately framed provisions closer to those of the Sapru Committee. In the matter of the Appointment of the judges the *Ad Hoc* Committee sought greater safeguards and declared that it would not be ''expedient'' to leave their appointments ''to the unfettered discretion of the President of the Un-

11. *Ibid.*
12. Besides Justice Khanna, the other signatories to the Report were S.M. Shankar, T.S. Krishnamurthy Iyer and P.M. Bakshi.
13. Granville Austin, *The Indian Constitution : Cornerstone of a Nation,* pp. 175-76.
14. *Sapru Report,* clause 13, pp. xi-xii.
15. *Ibid,* para 226,198.

ion." The Committee suggested that the President should nominate puisne Judges with the concurrence of the Chief Justice, and this nomination would then be subject to confirmation by a panel composed of Chief Justices of High Courts, some members of both Houses of Parliament, and the law officers of the Union. In the alternative, the panel of Chief Justices of the High Courts should submit three names to the President who would choose one of them with the concurrence of the Chief Justice of India.[16]

The Union Constitution Committee agreed with the suggestion of the Ad Hoc Committee that the salaries, allowances, etc., of the Judges should not be included in the Constitution, but did not accept the suggestions for the selection of Judges. Instead, returning to the method of the Sapru Report, it recommended that Judges be appointed by the President in consultation with the Chief Justice and such other Judges of the Supreme or High Courts as might be necessary.[17] The Constituent Assembly accepted this recommendation with little debate and this provision ultimately became part of the constitution.[18] But there was a sharp divergence of opinion on the removal of the Judges. Alladi Krishnaswami Ayyar proposed that Judges should be removed by the President for incapacity or proved misbehaviour on an address by both Houses of Parliament. It was opposed by M. A. Ayyangar. He proposed that they should be removed by a special tribunal consisting of sitting and former Supreme and High Court Judges.[19] The Constituent Assembly adopted Ayyar's amendment and finally it became Article 124 (4) of the Constitution. Ayyar also defended the exclusion from the Constitution laying down the salaries of Judges. He believed that "from the very nature of things" all such provisions could not be included in the Constitution, which should embody only the "main heads". It should be left, he maintained, for a "Judicature Act to be passed by the Assembly to implement the powers that are conferred under the Constitution."[20] The Drafting Committee did not agree with Ayyar on this point.

The Drafting Committee framed nearly all the judicial provisions in its meetings from December 10 to 17, 1947. The Committee set the number of Judges at seven, subject to change by Parliament, and they retired on attaining the age of sixty years. Their qualifications were also laid down and the procedure for removal from office was stiffened by requiring the address of Parliament passed in each House by a majority of total membership of that House and two-thirds majority of the members of that House present and voting. The judges were debarred from practising at the Bar after retirement. Their salaries, allowances, leave and pensions were to be determined by Parliament and until it did so they were to be as laid down in a Schedule to the Draft Constitution. But none of the rights and privileges of a Judge could be varied to a Judge's disadvantage during his tenure of office.

The Constituent Assembly undertook detailed consideration of the judicial provisions of the Draft Constitution on May 24, 1949. The appointment of the Judges still remained a matter of concern and one of the Assembly members, S. L. Saxena, suggested that their appointments should be confirmed by two-thirds of the members of both the Houses of Parliament so that their independence may not be "compromised."[21] But Ambedkar did not agree. He defended the draft proviso which was finally adopted.[22] The matter of salaries, allowances, etc., of the Judges was another point of keen discussion. The ultimate decision in this respect was taken by the Cabinet and approved by the Assembly. Patel circulated a secret note on May 31, 1949 in the Cabinet. It recapitulated the previous discussions on this point and noted that in the light of these discussions and the views of Chief Justice and the Prime Minister, he had agreed that in order to have "a first rate Judiciary in India" the salaries of the Judges should be fixed in the Constitution in order to attract "first rate men to accept these appointments." The note also listed the salaries and allowances considered to be necessary to achieve the goal of "a first rate judiciary in India."[23]

Ambedkar, accordingly, moved on July 30, 1948 a new Article 104 in the Draft Constitution that Judges should be paid the salaries specified

16. *Ad Hoc Committee Report,* para 15-16; *Reports. First Series,* p. 66.
17. Minutes of the meeting of the Union Constitution Committee, June 11, 1947. *Reports, First Series,* p. 57.
18. Article 124 (2).
19. Minutes of the meeting of the Union Constitution Committee. *Reports, First Series.* p. 895. Removal by a tribunal had B.N. Rau's support also.
20. *Ibid,* p. 890.
21. *Constituent Assembly Debates,* Vol. VII, p. 231.
22. *Ibid.,* p. 258.
23. Refer to Granville Austin, *The Indian Constitution : Cornerstone of a Nation,* pp. 182-83.

in the Second Schedule, but their privileges and allowances should be determined by Parliament and until Parliament decided on them, they should be specified in the Schedule. The Assembly adopted the new provision after a inconsequential debate.[24] Thus, the Constitution guarantees to the Judges of the Supreme Court both security of service and emoluments. These provisions are intended to make the Judiciary independent, impartial, incorruptible, and having the courage and conviction to do the right as defined by law.

There is, however, a lacuna in the system which impairs the guarantee of judicial independence of the Supreme Court Judges. Judges are permitted after their retirement or resignation chamber practice, which involved advisory work. The Law Commission deplored this concession and pointed out its repercussions. "The possibility of their being able to advise rich clients," the Report of the Commission said, "after their retirement may tend to affect their independence on the Bench. In any event, if judges are to be permitted to practise by giving advice after retirement, the public would be apt to think that in dealing with the cases of such litigants whom they may hope after retirement to be asked to advise, the judges do not act impartially."

Strictly speaking, M. Hidaytullah, a former Chief Justice of India, should not have accepted the post of the Vice-President. Nor P. N. Bhagawti would have agreed to his name to be proposed by the Opposition as one of consensus candidates for the post of the eighth Vice-President. Not long ago a report circulated that another former Chief Justice of India might be appointed ambassador to the United States. The number of retired Judges of the Supreme Court heading Commissions appointed by the Government of India and State Governments are innumerable to count and it looks as if Judges increasingly feel no compulsion in accepting assignments from the Government. Such appointments always give a feeling that some of the Judges want to stay on the right side of the Executive to have "something good" waiting for them in their days of retirement. People's confidence in the Judiciary is, consequently shaken.

Independence of judiciary militates against any commitment of Judges except to the Constitution and laws. It entails keeping the scales even in any dispute between the rich and the poor, the mighty and the weak, the State and the citizen. It calls for administration of justice without fear or favour. Such independence, postulates freedom from bias and refusal to get aligned to any party. A court room, says H. R. Khanna, a former Supreme Court Judge, "is not a pulpit nor a place for crusades in the robe of judges to propagate their favourite ideologies. Persons aligned with any political party or committed to some particular economic ideology cannot bring to bear a dispassionate approach to their task of deciding cases." He further adds a judge under "the scheme of our Constitution must be independent and impartial. He cannot, in order to be true to his office, worship simultaneously at two shrines–the shrine of justice and the shrine of his favourite political and economic ideology."

## JURISDICTION OF THE COURT

### General Provisions

The powers and functions of the Supreme Court are reflected in its jurisdiction. The Constitution vests the Supreme Court with original and appellate jurisdiction. The original jurisdiction mainly extends to matters regarding the interpretation of the provisions of the Constitution which arise between the Union and the States and the States *inter se.* The original jurisdiction also extends to issuing orders in the nature of writs for the enforcement of Fundamental Rights. The Constitution (Forty-second Amendment) Act, 1976, inserted a new Article 131A vesting in the Supreme Court the exclusive jurisdiction in regard to questions as to the constitutional validity of the central laws. The Constitution (Forty-fourth Amendment) Act, 1978, however, repealed Article 131 A.

The appellate jurisdiction of the Supreme Court extends to all matters from the High Courts in the States as well as from other specified tribunals. The Supreme Court may also grant special leave to appeal from any judgment, decree or final order of a High Court if it is satisfied that the case involves a substantial question of law as to the interpretation of the Constitution.

There are some general provisions in the Constitution which sufficiently widen the scope of the Supreme Court's jurisdiction. The Supreme Court is declared to be a Court of record and has all the powers of such a Court including the power to punish for contempt of itself. A Court of record is a court whose acts and proceedings are enrolled for perpetual memory and

24. *Constituent Assembly Debates,* Vol. IX, pp. 10-13.

testimony. These records are of such high and super-eminent authority that their truth is not to be called in question in any court, though the Court of Record itself may amend clerical slips and errors. A Court of Record has the power to fine and imprison for contempt of its authority and the Constitution expressly provides for it.[25] The President may consult the Supreme Court if at any time it appears to him that a question of law, or fact, has arisen or is likely to arise, which is of such a nature and of such importance that it is expedient to obtain an opinion upon it.

The Constitution provides for the enlargement of the jurisdiction of the Supreme Court by the law of Parliament with respect to any matters in the Union List.[26] The Government of India and the Government of a State may confer by special agreement and if Parliament makes law to that effect, on the Supreme Court jurisdiction and power with respect to any matter within their common competence.[27] Such an enlargement of jurisdiction may be in respect of the original or appellate jurisdiction of the Supreme Court.

Parliament may by law confer on the Supreme Court power to issue directions, orders or writs, including writs in the nature of *habeas corpus, mandamus,* prohibition, *quo warranto* and *certiorari,* or any of them, for any purpose other than enforcement of Fundamental Rights.[28] While the power of the Supreme Court to issue directions, orders or writs for the enforcement of Fundamental Rights is conferred by the Constitution itself and is guaranteed by it, the power of the Supreme Court to issue directions, orders or writs for any other purpose depends on the Act of Parliament.

The Constitution (Forty-second Amendment) Act, 1976, inserted a new Article 139A providing that the Supreme Court may on an application made by the Attorney-General transfer to itself cases involving the same or substantially the same questions of law pending before the Supreme Court or a High Court or before two or more High Courts and dispose of all such cases. The Constitution (Forty-fourth Amendment) Act 1978, enlarged the scope of such transfer of cases by substituting a new clause (1) to article 139A and also adding a Proviso thereto. Article 139A(1) now provides that the Supreme Court may, if it is satisfied, on its own motion or on application made by the Attorney-General of India or by a party to any such case that cases involving the same or substantially the same questions of law are pending before it and one or more High Courts or before two or more High Courts and that such questions are substantial questions of general importance, withdraw the case or cases pending before the High Court or High Courts and dispose of all these cases itself; provided that the Supreme Court may after determining the said question of law return any case so withdrawn to the concerned High Court together with copy of its judgment and the High Court shall proceed to dispose of the case in conformity with such judgment.

The Constitution (Forty-fourth Amendment) Act, 1978 retained Clause 2 of Article 139A as provided in the Forty-second Amendment. It provides that the Supreme Court may, if it deems expedient so to do for the ends of justice, transfer any case, appeal or other proceedings pending before any High Court to any other High Court.

Parliament may by law make provision for conferring on the Supreme Court such ancillary powers, not in- consistent with any of the provisions of the Constitution, as may appear to be necessary or desirable for the purpose of enabling the Court more effectively to exercise the jurisdiction conferred upon it by the Constitution.[29] Accordingly, Parliament has by the Code of Criminal Procedure (Amendment) Act, 1952, empowered the Supreme Court to transfer a criminal case or appeal from one High Court to another.

In recent times, the Supreme Court has assumed an important role in the field of public interest litigation and in the words of Chief Justice Y.V. Chandrachud the Court has become "a bulwark against all assumption and exercise of excessive powers" in cases like the Bhagalpur blindings, the flesh trade, detention of children and eviction of pavement dwellers.

Finally, the Supreme Court, subject to the provisions of any law made by Parliament and with the approval of the President, may make rules for regulating generally the practice and procedure of the Court.[30] In pursuance of this

25. Article 129.
26. Article 138(1).
27. Article 138 (2).
28. Article 139.
29. Article 140.
30. Article 145 (1).

provision, the Supreme Court has made the Supreme Court Rules, 1950.

**Original Jurisdiction**

In a federal polity the powers between the Union and the State Governments are delimited and demarcated and, accordingly, it necessitates the presence of an independent judicial authority empowered to interpret the Constitution and secure the rights of the federation and the federating units. The Constitution of India vests the Supreme Court with original and exclusive jurisdiction in any dispute :

(a) between the Union Government and one or more States; or

(b) between the Union Government and any States on one side and one or more States on the other; or

(c) between two or more States, if the dispute involves any question of law or fact on which the existence or extent of a legal right depends. That is to say, the despute between the Union and the States or between the States *inter se* must relate to some justiciable right. Where the claim made by one of the parties is not dependent on law or fact but on extra legal considerations and hypothetical assumptions, the Supreme Court has no original jurisdiction. Thus in order to involve the original jurisdiction of the Supreme Court two conditions must be present : (1) as to the parties, and (2) as to the nature of the dispute. If these two conditions are not satisfied, a suit cannot be brought before the Supreme Court.

The Supreme Court does not entertain disputes, on its original side, to which citizens are a party. Suits by individuals against the Union or a State can be brought in ordinary courts and would come up to the Supreme Court only in appeal, if the requirements relating thereof are satisfied. The Constitution also excludes from the original jurisdiction disputes relating to water of inter-State rivers or river valleys referred to a special statutory tribunal, matters referred to the Finance Commission, adjustment of certain expenses between the Union and the States, and bar to interference by courts in disputes arising out of certain treaties, agreements, etc.

Where cases involving the same or substantially the same question of law of general importance are pending before the Supreme Court and one or more High Court or before two or more High Courts, the Supreme Court, if satisfied, on its own motion or on an application made by the Attorney-General of India or by a party to any such case withdraw the case before the High Court or High Courts to itself and dispose of all such cases; provided that the Supreme Court may after determining such questions of law return any case so withdrawn with a copy of its judgment to the High Court from which the case has been withdrawn, and the High Court shall on receipt of it proceed to dispose of the case in conformity with that judgment.

The Supreme Court has been invested with special jurisdiction and responsibility in the matter of the enforcement of Fundamental Rights and in exercise of this jurisdiction the Court has the power to issue directions, orders or writs in the nature of *habeas corpus, mandamus,* prohibition, *quo warranto* and *certiori,* whichever may be appropriate. The Constitution also provides that Parliament may by law confer on the Supreme Court power to issue directions, orders or writs in the nature of *habeas corpus, mandamus*, prohibition, *quo warranto* and *certiorari* for any purpose other than the enforcement of fundamental Rights. In the exercise of its original jurisdiction the Supreme Court may, thus, issue, directions or orders in the nature of these writs for the enforcement of Fundamental Rights and others purposes. Whereas the jurisdiction of the Supreme Court for issuing writs in the case of Fundamental Rights is concurrent with the High Courts under Article 226, the right to move the Supreme Court by appropriate proceedings for the enforcement of Fundamental Rights is guaranteed under Article 32. No such responsibility is laid on the High Courts. The Supreme Court held in *Romesh Thapar* v. *State of Madras* that Article 32 provides a guaranteed remedy for the enforcement of Fundamental Rights, and this remedial right is itself made a Fundamental Right. The Supreme Court is the protector and guarantor of fundamental rights and it cannot consistently with the responsibility so laid upon it refuse to entertain applications seeking protection against infringement of such rights. A citizen can resort directly for such relief to the Supreme Court without first resorting to the High Court under Article 226 of the Constitution.'' But the remedy under Article 32 is available only in the case of an infringement of a Fundamental Right and cannot be extended to cover cases of infraction of any other constitutional right. The Supreme Court has also laid down that a petition under Article 32 must establish not only that impugned law is an infringement of a Fundamental Right but that it also affects or invades the Fundamental right of the petitioner guaranteed by the Constitution.

The Constitution (Thirty-ninth Amendment) Act, 1975, ousting the Supreme Court from exercising jurisdiction on matters relating to or connected with the election of a President or Vice-President has been rescinded and the old position under Article 71 (1) is restored.[31] All doubts and disputes arising out or in connection with the election of a President or Vice-President are inquired into and decided by the Supreme Court and its decision is final.

**Appellate Jurisdiction**

The appellate jurisdiction of the Supreme Court covers cases in constitutional matters (Article 132), civil and criminal cases (Articles 133, 134) and in cases by special leave of the Supreme Court against judgment, order, etc., of any court or tribunal in India (Article 136). The Supreme Court as the highest court of appeal stands at the apex of the Indian judicature. Its appellate jurisdiction is much wider than that of the Supreme Court of the United States which concerns itself only with cases arising out of federal jurisdiction, or the validity of laws. M.C. Setalvad said, in his speech at the inauguration ceremony of the Supreme court, that the writ of the Court "will run over territory extending to over two million square miles inhabited by a population of about 300 millions..........It can truly be said that the jurisdiction and powers of this court in their nature and extent are wider than those exercised by the High Courts of any country in the Commonwealth or by the Supreme Court of the USA........"In fact, the Supreme Court has shown willingness to entertain appeals not only from ordinary courts but also from industrial courts, election tribunals and other quasi-judicial bodies.

(i) *Constitutional cases.* An appeal lies to the Supreme Court from any judgment, decree or final order of a High Court in India, whether in a civil, criminal or other proceedings, if the High Court certifies that the case involves a substantial question of law as to the interpretation of the Constitution. The Constitution (Forty-fourth Amendment) Act, 1978, inserted Article 134(A) which provides that every High Court, passing or making a judgment, decree, final order, or sentence; under Article 132(1) or 133 (1) or 134 (1) may, if deems fit, on its own motion, and if an oral application is made, by or on behalf of the party aggrieved, immediately after passing or making of such judgment, final order or sentence shall determine whether a certificate that the case involves a substantial question of law as to the interpretation of the Constitution may be given or not. Where such a certificate is given any party in the case may appeal to the Supreme Court on the ground that the question of law, which is substantial, has been wrongly decided. Where the High Court has refused the issuing of such a certificate, the Supreme Court may, if it is satisfied, that the case involved a substantial question of law as to the interpretation of the Constitution, grant special leave, under Article 136, from such judgment, decree, final order or sentence. Prior to the Forty- fourth Amendment, the appellant, if the High Court had granted a certificate to appeal to the Supreme Court, could take other grounds, with the leave of the Supreme Court, also in support of his appeal and the new grounds taken might not be constitutional. This provision of Article 132 (3) has been omitted by the Forty-fourth Amendment.

It follows that the final authority for interpreting the Constitution rests with the Supreme Court whatever be the nature of the suit of proceedings. It may, however, be noted that the case appealed in the Supreme Court, either when the High Court grants a certificate or where the Supreme Court grants special leave, must involve a question of law and it must be a "substantial" question of law as to the interpretation of the Constitution. "Substantial" here means a question regarding which there is a difference of opinion and which has not been finally settled by a judicial decision. It must not be a question of fact and it must not be a question of interpretation of any other law which does not involve interpretation of the Constitution.

(ii) *Appeals in Civil matters.* Article 133 originally conferred a right to appeal to the Supreme Court in civil proceedings against a judgment, decree or final order of a High Court if it certified that the amount involved in disputes was not less than Rs. 20,000 or that it involved directly or indirectly some claim or question respecting property of that value, and that the case was fit one for appeal. But if the High Court's judgment

31. The Constitution (Forty-fourth Amendment) Act, 1978, S. 10.

confirmed a judgment of an inferior court a further certificate that the appeal involved some substantial question of law was required.

The right to appeal in civil cases involving Rs. 20,000 confronted the Supreme Court with the load of work which it could not cope with. The Law Commission recommended that valuation should not form the basis of an appeal case and it should be immediately dispensed with. Accordingly, the Thirtieth Amendment was passed in 1972 which provides that civil appeal shall lie with the Supreme Court if the High Court certified that the case involves a substantial question of law of general importance and that in the opinion of the High Court the said question needs to be decided by the Supreme Court. This the High Court may do, if it deems fit, on its own motion or on an oral application of the aggrieved party immediately after the passing or making of the judgment, decree or final order.[32] It means that civil appeals involving only important questions of law of general importance or a substantial question of law on the interpretation of the Constitution will go to the Supreme Court and valuation can not be the only reasonable and logical yardstick for a right to appeal. Moreover, no appeal shall, unless Parliament by Law otherwise provides, lie to the Supreme Court from the judgment, decree or final order of one Judge of a High Court.

(iii) *Appeals in Criminal Cases.* In criminal cases the appeal lies to the Supreme Court as of right in cases : (a) where a lower court passes an order of acquittal of an accused person but the High Court reverses the order of acquittal on appeal and sentences the accused person to death; (b) where the High Court withdraws for trial before itself any case from a subordinate court and, after trial, convicts the accused person to death; or (c) where the High Court certifies, under Article 134A, that the case is a fit one for appeal to the Supreme Court either on its own motion or on an oral application made by the aggrieved party immediately after passing the judgment. Parliament may by law confer on the Court any further powers to entertain and hear appeals from any judgment and final order or sentence in a criminal proceeding of a High Court in the territory of India subject to such conditions and limitations as may be specified in such law.

But so long as Parliament does not legislate as such the Constitution intends, that, except in cases referred to above, the State High Courts shall normally be the final courts of appeal in criminal matters. Hence where the High Court grants a certificate that the case is a fit one for appeal to the Supreme Court it should do it in exceptional cases where it is manifest that by disregard of legal process or by violation of the principles of natural justice or otherwise substantial and grave injustice has been done.[33]

(iv) *Appeal by special leave.* Article 136 confers very wide and discretionary powers on the Supreme Court in the matter of granting special leave to appeal from any judgment, decree, determination, sentence or order in any cause or matter passed or made by any court or tribunal in India, other than Military Tribunal and Court Martial. Whereas Articles 132 to 135 deal with ordinary appeals to the Supreme Court, Article 136 vests in the Supreme Court a plenary jurisdiction in the matter of entertaining and hearing appeals by granting of special leave against any kind of judgment or order made by a court or tribunal in any cause or matter. It means that leave to appeal may be granted notwithstanding the limitations contained in Articles 132 to 135 and notwithstanding the fact that the High Court has refused leave to appeal. The power of the Supreme Court to grant special leave to appeal is, thus, not subject to any constitutional limitation. It is entirely left to the discretion of the Supreme Court. Broadly speaking, the Suprme Court would exercise this power to give relief to the aggrieved party in cases where the principles of natural justifice have been violated or a tribunal fails to exercise jurisdiction or acts in excess of jurisdiction or acts illegally, even though the party may have no footing on appeal as of right.

Moreover, the special leave to appeal cannot be only from a High Court. It may be from any court or tribunal, other than Military Tribunal and Court Martial, in the territory of India. The Supreme Court has, accordingly, power to grant special leave to appeal from the judgment or an interlocutory order of a court subordinate to the High Court or a tribunal, the duties and functions of which are similar in the nature of those of a court.[34] The Supreme Court has also held in *Raja*

32. Article 134A inst. by the Constitution (Forty-fourth Amendment) Act, 1978, S. 19.
33. *Mohinder Singh* v. *The State,* A.I.R. 1952 S.C. 415.
34. *Durga Shankar* v. *Raghuraj Singh,* A.I.R. 1954 S.C 520; *Bharat Bank Ltd.* v. *Employees of Bharat Bank,* A.I.R. 1950, S.C. 188.

*Krishna Bose* v. *Binod Kanungo* that even when the Legislature states the the orders of a tribunal under an Act like the Representation of the People Act shall be conclusive and final, the Court can interfere under Article 136 as the jurisdiction conferred by this Article cannot be taken away or whittled down by the Legislature. The discretion of the Court, so long as the provision of Article 136 remains, is unfettered.

As regards the precise extent of the jurisdiction under Article 136, the Supreme Court has held that "It is not possible to define with any precision the limitations on the exercise of the discretionary jurisdiction vested in the Supreme Court by the constitutional provision made in Article 136. The limitations, whatever may be, are implicit in the nature and character of the power itself. It being an exceptional and overriding power, naturally it has to be exercised sparingly and with caution and only in special and exceptional situations. Beyond that it is not possible to fetter the exercise of this power by a set formula or Rule.[35] The Court, as said earlier, does not grant special leave to appeal unless it it specifically shown that exceptional and special circumstances exist, that substantial and grave injustice has been done and the case in question presents feature of sufficient gravity to warrant a review of the decision appealed against.

Justice S. Murtaza Ali and O. Chinappa Reddy gave a new dimension to the interpretation of Article 136. Soundarapandian, brother of the deceased, had come to the Supreme Court against the acquittal of P.S.R. Sadhamantham by the High Court. The Court observed that the fact that the Criminal Procedure Code does not provide for private parties to move against acquittals, had not relevance to the question of the power of the Supreme Court under Article 136. The Supreme Court's appellate power under article 136, the Court ruled, not circumscribed by any limitation as to who may invoke it is "exercisable outside the purview of ordinary law" to meet the pressing demands of justice. It was the practice of Supreme Court to permit invocation of its plenary or appellate power under Article 136 in exceptional circumstances, as whether a question of law of general public importance arises or a decision shocks the conscience of the Court. But the Supreme Court can also interfere even with findings of fact, making no distinction between judgments of acquittal and conviction if the High Court had acted "perversely or othrwise improperly." The Court will not not abjure its duty to prevent violent miscarriage of justice by hesitating to interfere when interference is imperative, the Court observed.

In April 1979, the Supreme Court approached the Union Government with a suggestion that it should amend Article 136 to limit its powers to hear and admit only those special leave petitions which concerned constitutional matters. The Government expressed its inability to accept the suggestion, but advised the Supreme Court that it could itself restrict its powers to grant special leave to appeal. The rule about special leave petition till July 1978 was that it could be filed in the Supreme Court if the High Court against whose judgment an appeal was sought to be made had rejected permission. The rule was relaxed by the Supreme Court in July enabling an aggrieved party to come to it straight without waiting for the permission of the High Court concerned. Though the relaxation was aimed to helping the litigants, it caused a spurt in the number of special leave petitions compelling the Supreme Court to approach the Government for amending Article 136.

**Advisory Jurisdiction**

The President may under Article 143(1) make a reference to the Supreme Court for its consideration and opinion any question of law or fact which is of such a nature and of such public importance that it is expedient to obtain the Court's opinion on it. The President may refer such a question not only where it has actually arisen but also where it appears to the President that it is likely to arise. The President can, accordingly, refer to the Supreme Court the question whether a proposed Bill will be *intra vires* of the Constitution. Such references are heard by a Bench consisting of at least five Judges and the Court follows the procedure of a regular dispute that comes before it. The opinion of the Court is pronounced in open Court. It may not be a unanimous opinion and the dissenting Judges can give their separate opinion. But the opinion of the Supreme Court is not binding on the President as it is not of the nature of a judicial pronouncement. It is also not obligatory on the Supreme Court to give its opinion; it may or may not.

Under Clause (2) of Article 143 the President may refer to the Supreme Court for its opinion disputes arising out of any treaty, agree-

35. *Dhakeswari Cotton Mills Ltd.* v. *Commissioner of Income Tax,* A.I.R. 1955, S.C. 65.

ment, etc., which had been entered into or executed before the commencement of the Constitution. In the case of such references, it is obligatory for the Supreme Court to give its opinion to the President.

Technically, no court in India is bound by the advisory opinion of the Supreme Court but such opinions are always respected by the courts. The opinions given by the Supreme Court in the Delhi Laws Act, 1912, and the Kerala Education Bill, 1957, have often been referred to and cited in Courts. In the conflict between the Uttar Pradesh Legislative Assembly and the Allahabad High Court, it was argued before the Supreme Court that it was only in respect of matters falling within the powers, functions and duties of the President that he was competent to frame questions for the advisory opinion of the Supreme Court. The Court held that words in Article 143 (1) were wide enough to empower the President to forward to the Supreme Court for its advisory opinion any question of law or fact which had arisen or was likely to arise, provided it appeared to the President that such a question was of such a nature or such public importance that it was expedient to obtain the opinion of the Court on it.

A reference was made in connection with the Indo-Pakistan Agreement relating to the exchange of enclaves (Berubari Union, 1958) in 1960. The opinion of the Supreme Court in this case was against the views of the Government of India which had held that Parliament was competent to implement the agreement by an ordinary law and that amendment of the Constitution was not necessary. In 1974, a reference made to the Supreme Court related to the Presidential election due to be held in August, 1974. The Opposition parties in Parliament had contended that the electoral college constituted for the election of the President, under Article 54 of the Constitution, would be incomplete as the Gujarat Assembly stood dissolved with the imposition of the President's rule in that State. After prolonged hearings the Supreme Court rendered the opinion that the Presidential election must be held before the expiration of the term of the office of the present incumbent irrespective of the dissolution of one or more Legislative Assemblies and their members not participating in the Presidential election. Another reference made by the President to the Supreme Court related to the Jammu and Kashmir Resettlement Bill, 1982, which has since become an Act of the State Legislature. The latest reference made by the President related to the Cauvery water dispute between the State of Karnataka and Tamil Nadu.

The advisory function of the Supreme Court is analogous to that performed by the Privy Council in Britain. Section 4 of the Judicial Committee Act, 1883, provides that His Majesty may refer to the Judicial Committee of the Privy Council "such matters whatsoever as His Majesty shall think fit." The Committee shall, where a reference is made to it, hear and consider the same and advise the Queen. But the dissenting opinions are not delivered in the Privy Council. Similarly, Section 60 of the Canadian Supreme Court Act, 1906, authorises the Governor-General to refer important questions of law and fact and obtain the opinion of the Supreme Court thereon. The Supreme Court is bound to entertain and answer the references and the answers are advisory. But the Constitution of the United States does not contain any corresponding provision and the Supreme Court has constantly refused to pronounce advisory opinion upon abstract question of law. To do so, the Supreme court held, would be incompatible with the position the Court occupies in the Constitution of the United States.[36]

There had been a good deal of difference of opinion among the jurists and political thinkers in India on the advisability of placing a constitutional obligation on the Court to give an opinion to the Executive on questions of law.[37] The framers of the Constitution, however, thought it expedient to confer advisory functions on the Supreme Court.[38]

### Power to Review its own Decisions

Like the highest court in other countries the Supreme Court of India, too, is not bound by its own decisions. It can reconsider its own decisions provided that such review is in the interest of the community and justice. An application for review may be filed with the Registrar of the Court within thirty days after its judgment is delivered in appeal and it should briefly and distinctly state the grounds for review. The application for re-

36. *Muskrat* v. *United States.*
37. Also refer to opinion of Professor Flex Frankfurter ( a Judge of the U.S. Supreme Court). This is quoted in Shukla, V.N., *Constitution of India,* p. 142.
38. Section 213 of the Government of India Act, 1935, conferred advisory jurisdiction on the Federal Court.

view must also be accompanied by a certificate by the Counsel that it is supported by proper grounds. Any such review is undertaken by a larger Bench than the one which passed the original judgment. The Supreme Court's power to review its earlier decisions helps it to correct any decision which may be deemed erroneous.

## JUDICIAL REVIEW

### Supreme Court, Guardian of the Constitution

The power of the courts to interpret the Constitution and to secure its supremacy is inherent in any Constitution which provides Government by defined and limited powers. Madison explained, ''a limited constitution......one which contains specified exceptions to the legislative authority.....can be preserved in no other way but through the medium of the courts of justice, whose duty it must be to declare all acts contrary to the manifest tenor of the Constitution void. Without this, all the reservations of particular rights or privileges amount to nothing.'' This point was succinctly explained by Chief Justice Marshall of the United States in *Marbury* v. *Madison.* He declared that the Supreme Court determined the constitutionality or otherwise of laws, Federal and State, and this power with the Supreme Court was a necessary consequence of the Constitution, otherwise declaration of the supremacy of the Constitution had no meaning.

Like the Constitution of the United States, there is no express provision in the Constitution of India declaring the Constitution to be the supreme law of the land. Perhaps, the Constitution makers deemed such a declaration superfluous as they would have believed it to be clearly enough implied when all organs of the Government, Union and State, owe their origin to the Constitution and derive powers therefrom and the Constitution itself cannot be altered except in the manner specifically laid down in Article 368. The status of the Constitution as fundamental law, Justice K.K. Mathew, a former judge of the Supreme Court of India, said, was determined by two factors : its efficient cause, and its formal cause. The efficient cause was none other than the ''supposed original will of the People of India.'' The Constitution was ''the covenant of the people of India and embodiment of their conception of the higher law governing current legislation and other activities of the Government. Else, there was no significance in a written Constitution framed by the People.'' The original will was prior and superior to the will of any representative assembly of the people and as the expression of the original will the Constitution is binding on all subsequent legislative, executive and judicial bodies. Under the aspect of formal cause, he said, the Constitution was fundamental law in that it prescribed ''certain decisive principles of lasting value of political rule to ensure the just exercise of powers by the State.''[39]

The philosophy of judicial review is, thus, rooted in the principle that Constitution is the fundamental law. As the Constitution is primarily an instrument to distribute political power, it is hard to escape the necessity of some body with authority to declare when the prescribed distribution has been disturbed. The Supreme Court is expressly given the power to interpret the Constitution (Articles 132/147), declare the law (Article 141), and enforce the limitations of the rule of distribution of legislative powers between Parliament and State Legislatures, and other constitutional limitations, for instance, prohibition against enactment of laws in derogation to the Fundamental Rights (Article 12 (2)). It is the duty of the Judges to uphold the Constitution and owe ''true faith and allegiance to the Constitution of India.''[40] When a contradiction between the Constitution and enacted law is alleged to exist and is proved in the course of judicial proceedings, it is the duty of the Judges to resolve the contradiction. If it cannot be harmonised and violates the Constitution, the enactment should be declared void and consequently unconstitutional thereby rendering it inoperative. Justice Das, in *A. K. Gopalan* v. *The State of Madras*, observed,''.....in so far as there is any limitation on the legislative power the Court must, on a complaint whether such limitation has been transgressed, and if there has been any transgression the Court is bound by its oath to uphold the Constitution.''

The power of judicial review exercised by the Supreme Court does in no way make it a rival to Parliament. Nor does it assume such extensive powers of judicial review as its counterpart in the United States exercises. There is difference in the very nature of the federation in the two countries. The exhaustive enumeration of powers of the

39. First Sir Tej Bahadur Sapru Memorial Lecture on ''Democracy and Judicial Review'', *The Statesman*, New Delhi, March 27, 1976.

40. Form of Oath or affirmation made by a Judge before entering upon his office, Article 124(6), Third Schedule IV.

Union and the States, the vesting of residuary power and the power of issuing directions in the Union, and overriding powers in emergencies minimise the possibilities of disputes to arise between the Union and the States. The power of invalidating laws vested in the Supreme Court on the ground of contravention of the Fundamental Rights differs from that of the United States' Supreme Court. There is, under the Constitution of India, no 'due process' clause and no doctrine of 'judicial supremacy.' The 'due process' clause and the doctrine of 'judicial supremacy' have made the United States Supreme Court the arbiter of social policy; a kind of super-legislature. In India, on the other hand, there had prevailed, till 1967, the doctrine of legislative supremacy, subject to the constitutional limitations. The Supreme Court exercised the judicial review power not out of any desire "to tilt at legislative authority in crusader's spirit, but in the discharge of the duty plainly laid upon" the Court by the Constitution.[41] It declared an Act void where it was in clear contravention of the Constitutional limitations, but it did not question the policy involved in the legislation. While the Court was always vigilant to prevent any encroachment by the Legislature upon the Fundamental Rights, it was yet not a third chamber sitting in judgment on the policy laid down by the Legislature and embodied in the legislation which the Supreme Court was considering. The Supreme Court itself defined its role in *A. K. Gopalan* v. *The State of Madras.* It was observed that in India the position of the judiciary "is somewhere between the Courts in England and the United States....no scope in India to play the role of the Supreme Court in the United States." The authority of the Court was to be exercised in such a manner that neither Parliament nor the Executive should exceed the limits set on them by the Constitution and if they ever did, the Court had the power to halt it.

But the majority judgment in the *Golak Nath* case disturbed the balance hitherto maintained. In 1951, the Supreme Court rejected the argument that the amending power of Parliament under Article 368 did not extend to Fundamental Rights. The decision was unanimous. The same argument was again rejected in 1964 but by a majority of three Judges against two. It was raised again in 1967 and this time the Court accepted the argument by a majority of six to five. Chief Justice Subbo Rao defined Fundamental Rights as primordial, transcendental and immutable and were, therefore, beyond the reach of Parliament and the amending power under Article 368. Two important results flowed from the majority judgment in the *Golak Nath* case. Firstly, it placed a permanent restraint on power of Parliament to pass any amendment of the Constitution which had the effect of taking away or abridging Fundamental Rights. Secondly, the Directive Principles of State Policy should be enforced without amending the Fundamental Rights. Thus, the delicate and difficult problem of adjusting Fundamental Rights and restrictions thereon to the ever-changing and unforeseen social demands became the sole responsibility of the judiciary and, consequently, ultimate supremacy under the Constitution came to be vested neither in the people nor in their representatives in Paliament but what at any given moment was the majority opinion of the Supreme Court.

This assertion of judicial power led to furious controversy and the parliamentarians repudiated it through the Twenty-fourth Amendment of the Constitution, which restored to Parliament the power to amend the Constitution including the Fundamental Rights. The Twenty-fifth Amendment inserted a new immunity clause 31-C which provided that no law seeking to enforce the Directive Principles under clauses (b) and (c) of Article 39[42] shall be invalid on the ground that it violated some Fundamental Rights in Articles 14, 19 or 31. Both these Constitutional Amendments were challenged in the Supreme Court. In the *Kesavananda Bharati* case the Supreme Court reversed its earlier decision on the *Golak Nath* case and upheld the power of Parliament to amend by way of addition, variation or repeal any provision of the Constitution provided it did not alter the basic structure of the Constitution.

But there was a considerable difference of opinion among the Judges delivering the majority judgment in the *Kesavananda Bharati* case on the concept of basic structure or framework of

41. *The State of Madras* v. *V.G. Rao,* A.I.R. 1952 S.C. 196.
42. Clauses (b) and (c) of Article 39 provide that the State shall, in particular, direct its policy towards securing:
"(b) that the ownership and control of the material resources of the community are so distributed as best to subserve the common good;
(c) that the operation of the economic system does not result in the concentration of wealth and means of production to the common detriment."

the Constitution. As the concept remained undefined, the last word with respect to what exactly did it mean and consequently Parliament's power to amend the Constitution still rested with the Supreme Court. The validity of the Thirty-ninth Amendment ousting the jurisdiction of the Supreme Court to decide disputes relating to the election of the President, the Vice-President, the Prime Minister and the Speaker of the House of the People was questioned in Mrs. Indira Gandhi's election appeal against the judgment of the Allahabad High Court disqualifying her for a period of six years, on the ground that it evaded the authority of the Supreme Court, which was at the apex of the judiciary, and, therefore, altered the basic structure of the Constitution. The majority of the Judges answered in the affirmative.

The Constitution (Forty-second Amendment) Act, 1976, denied the Supreme Court the jurisdiction to go into the validity of any amendment passed by Parliament in accordance with the procedure laid down in Article 368, and the power of Parliament to amend any provision of the Constitution was without any limitation whatsoever. The role of the Supreme Court as protector of Fundamental Rights was reduced first by making the Directive Principles supersede the Fundamental Rights and then circumventing the jurisdiction of the Courts under Article 368 (4) to question the validity of any amendment. Then, the Supreme Court alone could examine the validity of any Central Law, but it could not be declared invalid unless two-thirds of the Judges of a mandatory seven-member Bench declared it so. The Forty-third Amendment (1977) omitted Article 144-A and restored the *status quo ante,* that is, a Constitution Bench consisting of five[43] or more Judges would decide all cases of constitutional validity.

The Janata Party was committed to undo the distortions of the Forty-second Amendment, but the Constitution (Forty-fourth Amendment) Act, 1978, did not touch Clauses (4) and (5) of Article 368 and the position with regard to the amending power of Parliament *vis-a-vis* the Supreme Court remained as it was before the commencement of the Forty-fourth Amendment. The validity of the Forty-second Amendment was questioned in the *Minerva Mills* case and the Supreme Court struck down these two Clauses (4) and (5) of Article 368. Likewise, Article 31C, which provided that all laws which have nexus with any Directive Principles of State Policy "shall be deemed to be void" on the ground that they are "inconsistent with, or take away or abridge any of the rights conferred by any provision" of the Chapter on Fundamental Rights was also struck down. The Court held that to abrogate the Fundamental Rights while supporting to give effect to the Directive Principles is to disarray the essential feature of the Constitution.

The Constitution (Forty-second Amendment) Act, 1976, was intended to assert the sovereignty, and supremacy of Parliament, especially with regard to its power to amend the Constitution. The need for such an amendment had arisen because the Supreme Court's decision in the *Keshavananda Bharati* case laying down by a majority that Parliament has no power to alter the basic features of the Constitution and without defining what those basic features were."

The theory about the sovereignty of Parliament in a federal polity is not even a legal fiction. This point was convincingly explained by Motilal Setalvad in the Hamlyn lectures which he delivered at the Inns of Court in London in 1960. He pointed out, "The very purpose of a written constitution is the demarcation of the powers of the different departments of Governments so that the exercise of these powers may be limited to their particular fields. In countries governed by a written constitution, as India is, the supreme authority is not Parliament but the Constitution." Setalvad then explained why the founding fathers had in this regard departed from the British practice which they had so closely followed in other respects. "The Indian legislatures," he said, "had not the age- old ancestry and traditions of the British Parliament. India is a country of vast distances inhabited by People....in varying stages of development. A democracy means a Government by the majority. In such a Government it becomes necessary to safeguard the essential freedoms of the citizens, and particularly of the citizens constituting the minorities." The distinctions made by Setalvad have been much forcefully emphasised by an eminent scholar D. W. Brogan. Speaking about the United States of America he said, "American law and constitu-

43. Article 145(3) provides : "The minimum number of Judges who are to sit for the purpose of deciding any case involving a substantial question of law as to the interpretation of this Constitution or for the purpose of hearing any reference under Article 143 (Advisory opinion) shall be five."

tional practice are designed to minimise inequalities between States, between sections, between minorities and majorities and between individuals, while English practice is designed to give full effect to majority opinion—although there is no greater inequality than that of members."

What Brogn says about the United States equally applies to India. In a highly pluralist society as one in India united in a federal polity no single constitutional organ of Government can be invested with sovereign power and, accordingly, there can be no escape from a system of checks and balances so that there can be no concentration of power in any particular organ of the State. A federation postulates dual polity and it establishes a government of limited and divided powers with a view to safeguarding the encroachment of such powers by any other authority at any level. The arrangement of Government as established by the Indian Constitution was designed to promote co-operation among the three branches as well as checking and balancing them.

The Preamble to the Constitution declared the broad and enduring purposes which it was expected to serve. In seeking these purposes the Constitution may be amended from time to time. But these purposes embodied the aspirations of the entire people, who gave the Constitution to themselves, and not to the transient and changing objects of a particular party. It is, therefore, the supremacy of the Constitution and it cannot be made the object of the vagaries of the fluctuating majorities.

**Role of the Supreme Court**

On January 28, 1950, the Supreme Court of India held its inaugural sitting. Since then, it has been functioning as one of the foremost institutions of India's republican democracy and as an instrument of rule of law. Placed as it is at the apex of a single unified judiciary, it is not only the final court of appeal in all matters, but has also been made the ultimate interpreter of the laws and the Constitution, the arbiter of federal disputes and the constitutional interpreter of the Fundamental Rights of individuals and of minority groups. In addition to ordinary channels of appeal the Constitution confers on the Supreme Court extraordinary powers where justice might require the interference of the Court. Its power to grant special leave to appeal from the decision of any court or tribunal, except military tribunals, is not subject to constitutional limitations. It is entirely the discretion of the Supreme Court and it may give relief to any aggrieved party even to a private party, in cases where the principles of natural justice have been violated or if the court at any level had acted perversely or otherwise improperly.

The Supreme Court in recent times has assumed the role of a "bulwark against the assumptions and exercise of excessive powers" as Chief Justice Y.V. Chandrachud said at the Law Day function held on November 26, 1981. He pointed out that a liberal democracy like one in India did not mean that the will of the people was law. The people's will become a law only "when it conformed to recognised normative procedures and did not violated the fundamentals of the Constitution." That is why, the Chief Justice asserted, the courts were the hand-maids of liberal democracy without which there could be no independent authority to examine "whether the limits of popular will were exceeded in any manner." Consequently, the court is today engaged in "public interest" cases and more and more lawyers, journalists and law leaders are coming to the Court with grievances of the poor and the illiterate, the silent majority. The view taken by the Court in liberalising the rules of *locus standi* has widened the scope of citizen to move the Court even when his fundamental rights are not violated. Any members of the public, can move the Court even by writing a letter and the Court entertains the letter as a writ petition "casting aside all procedural and technical rules."[44] The Chief Justice in December 1982, gave a call for what he termed "judicial activism" by which courts "interpreted and created laws" for the welfare for whom they were intended.

The Supreme Court is a Court of record and the acts and proceedings of such a Court are of such high and super-eminent authority that their truth is not to be called in question in any court. Its decisions are binding on all courts in India and the supreme and overriding status of its judgments is placed beyond the reach of ordinary legislative enactments. The consultative functions of the Supreme Court are important inasmuch as it can pronounce advisory opinion even upon abstract questions of law. The opinion so expressed is not of the nature of judgment and,

44. Justice P.N. Bhagwati, "How the Supreme Court Enforces Citizen's rights," Express Magazine, *Indian Express*, New Delhi, January 31, 1982.

accordingly, not binding on the courts, although such opinions carry great weight and authority with all courts and tribunals.

The writ of the Supreme Court runs over more than eight hundred million people. In sheer amplitude of judicial powers and the variety and range of jurisdictions, the Supreme Court of India is without a rival in any other system in the world. Alladi Krishnaswami Ayyar rightly observed that the Supreme Court has more powers than any other Supreme Court of the world. The United States Supreme Court does not have the kind of wide appellate jurisdiction as the Supreme Court of India exercises.

But the primary duty of the Supreme Court is to interpret the Constitution and determine laws. Sir Maurice Gwyer, at the inaugural sitting of the Federal Court on December 6, 1937, said that while declaring and interpreting the law, "it will always be our endeavour to look at the Constitution of India, whether in its present form or in any other form which it may assume hereafter, not with the cold eye of the anatomist, but as a living and breathing organism which contains within itself, as all life must, the seeds of future growth and development.... The Federal Court will declare and interpret the law and that I am convinced, in no spirit of formal or barren legalism. But I do not want to be misunderstood. This Court can, and I hope will, secure that those political forces and currents, which alone can give vitality to Constitution, have free play within the limits of the law; but it cannot under the cover of interpretation alter or amend the law; that must be left to other authorities. Nevertheless, within the limits I have indicated, I do not doubt that the Federal Court can make and perhaps decisive contribution towards the evolution of India into a great and ordered nation, a link between the East and the West, but with a policy and civilization of its own." Chief Justice Kania said on the day of the inaugural sitting of the Supreme Court on January 28, 1950 : "The Supreme Court, an all-india Court, will stand firm and aloof from party politics and political theories. It is unconcerned with the changes in the government. The Court stands to administer the law for the time being in force, has goodwill and sympathy for all, but is allied to none. Occupying that position we hope and trust the Court will maintain the high traditions of the nation and in stabilising the roots of civilisation which have twice been threatened and shaken by two world wars, and maintain the fundamental principles of justice which are the emblem of God." The first Attorney-General of India, M.C. Setalvad, in his speech at the inaugural sitting, *inter alia,* said : "The detailed enumeration of fundamental rights in the Constitution and the provisions which enable them to be reasonably restricted will need wise and discriminating decisions. On the Court will fall the dedicated and difficult task of ensuring the citizen the enjoyment of his guaranteed rights consistently with the rights of the society and the safety of the State."

The lengthy statements on the inaugural functions on two momentous occasions succinctly explain the role of the highest court of the country in shaping her destiny. The Supreme Court cannot afford to remain oblivious of the "new atmosphere," as Nehru put it, in the country and should not interpret the Constitution and law, to use Maurice Gwyer's words, in "a spirit of formal or barren legalism." Justice Frankfurter of the United States Supreme Court said that statesmanship was needed on all hands to avoid a tragic and dangerous confrontation between the legislative and judicial wings of the government and this could be avoided by judicial restraints. Justice Holmes, of the same court, had also remarked that the Supreme Court was not the only guardian of the peoples' freedom and that Legislatures were equally their guardians.

The Legislatures are, indeed, equal guardians of the people's freedom, provided the majority party should not go amuck. No doubt, the Supreme Court performs judicial functions, but it has to deal with many issues and controversies which bristle with partisan origins and political consequences. A constitutional court, interpreting the Constitution and determining law, however, moderate and self-restrained, cannot evade or avoid pronouncement on matters political irrespective of its own views on judicial activitism. It cannot reamin unconcerned about complaints of arbitrariness and turn a blind eye to unreasonable invasions of fundamental rights. It cannot countenance, except at the cost of sacrificing its noble mission and mandate under the Constitution, any excessive claims of unlimited power.

The first two decades of the Supreme Court's career were fruitful years. As the custodian of the constitutional system and the legal process it strove to stabilise the aspirations of the new nation, strove to relieve the tensions confronting a developing country, resolved the conflicts of a diverse and open society and accommodated and adjudicated antagonistic demands for justice. In the performance of this arduous and stupendous task the Supreme Court acted with utmost erudition, understanding and wisdom and commanded the confidence and respect of the people in a larger measure than any other institution in the country. But of late, there has been an erosion in the dignity and prestige of the Supreme Court and it began with the decision in the *Golak Nath* case. The judgment in the Bank Nationalisation case and the Presidential Order derecognising the Princes met with the cry that the Court was reactionary. It was around this time that Mohan Kumaramangalam made his plea that India's Judiciary should be committed on certain socio-economic matters and his views were put into action by appointing A. N. Ray Chief Justice of India (April 1973) in preference to presumably three not "committed" colleagues, except to the Constitution. This policy of judicial appointments was universally denounced in India as subversive to the independence of the judiciary.

The appointments to the higher judiciary have ever been the subject of criticism and the sentiments expressed by eminent jurists are too numerous to quote. As far back as 1958, the Law Commission in its Fourteenth Report referred to the unsatisfactory selection of judicial personnel and remarked : "........The almost universal chorus of comment is that the selections are unsatisfactory and that they have been induced by executive influence. It has been said that these selections appear to have been made out of considerations of political expediency or regional or communal sentiments. Some of the members of the Bar appointed to the Bench did not occupy the front rank in the profession, either in the matter of the legal equipment or of the volume of their practice at the Bar. A number of more capable and deserving persons appear to have been ignored for reasons that can stem only from political or communal or similar grounds......" Justice M.H. Beg again superseded Justice H. R. Khanna on the retirement of Chief Justice Ray and when Beg was to retire in February 1978, the appointment of the Chief Justice took an ugly shape. Y.V. Chandrachud, the seniormost Judge, was vehemently criticised and it became a matter of widespread public controversy. The memorandum by fifty-two public men of Bombay addressed to the Minister of Law and Justice to the Government of India, on January 1978, said, in part that the doctrine of "Committed Judges", as it came to be called, was implemented by the Government of India not only in the matter of appointment to the Supreme Court Bench but also in regard to appointment to the High Court Benches. How far it proceeded became evident when Judges of the Supreme Court and of the High Courts began going around delivering political speeches, a practice which was criticised by the Supreme Court itself. The result of this policy became all too clear during the dark months of the Emergency when Mr. Justice A.N. Ray, the then Chief Justice of India, and some of his colleagues showed themselves to be, in the words of Lord Atkin apropos his colleagues in the famous case of *Liversidge* vs. *Anderson* "more executive minded than the executive." M.C. Chagla considered the appointment of Chandrachud "would be making ourselves the laughing stock of the whole judicial world. Mr. Chandrachud would have been ostracised–but instead of doing that, we are going to give him the accolade of judicial approval."

In the *Habeas Corpus* case [45] Chief Justice Ray, Justice Beg, Chandrachud and Bhagwati concurred in holding that "In view of the Presidential Order dated 17th June 1975 no person has any *locus standi* to move any writ petition under Article 226 before a High Court for *habeas corpus* or any other writ or order or direction to challenge the legality of an order of detention on the ground that the order is not under or in compliance with the Act or is illegal or is vitiated by malafides factual or legal or is based on extraneous considerations." Justice H. R. Khanna alone dissented and he had to pay a price for his dissent. He was superseded in January 1977, and Justice M.H. Beg was appointed the Chief Justice of India. On July 14, 1976, Jayaprakash Narayan in a statement had said, "As far as the judiciary, I must say that the High Courts have come out with flying colours in the present crisis. But the record of the Supreme Court is unfortunately very disappointing mainly because Mrs. Gandhi has packed it with pliant and submissive judges except for a few"

Even if it is conceded that the future norm for appointment to the Bench shall be on political basis, even then it is expected that judges would maintain postures of strict neutrality. Once elevated to the Bench their biases would be constitutional and judicial not political or ideological. "The primary duty of the judges", says H. R.

45. *A.D.M. Jabalpur* vs. *S. Shukla.*

Khanna, former Judge of the Supreme Court, "is to uphold the constitution and the law without fear or favour and in doing so they cannot allow any political ideology which might have caught their fancy to colour decision. The sobering reflection has always to be there for judges, as said by a great master, that the Constitution is meant not merely for their way of thinking but for people of fundamentally differing views."[46]

The same standard applies to a judge's post retirement demeanour, Judges of the Supreme Court are supposed to retire quietly into oblivion. It is universally recognized that a Judge's conduct should be free from temptation or fear even after he leaves the Bench. That, at least, was the intent of the framers of the Constitution in inserting Article 123 (7), that prescribes that no person who has held office as a Judge of the Supreme Court shall plead or act in any Court or before any authority within the territory of India. But if sitting Judges near retirement start hankering after entering or returning to politics, it is likely to affect their judicial decisions. The unhealthy trend of sitting Judges entering active politics started in 1967. The then Chief Justice Subba Rao, committed judicial impropriety when he accepted the Opposition's invitation to become its candidate for the 1969 Presidential poll and resigned from his office. Subba Rao's willingness to become the Opposition's nominee soon after his crucial judgment in the *I.G. Golak Nath* vs. *The State of Punjab* was widely criticised and propelled the highest Court of the country into political controversy. The image of the Supreme Court–as being above politics and political leanings–never recovered from the jolt given to it by Subba Rao. The former Judge of the Supreme Court H. R. Khanna was caught in the political web by accepting to enter Charan Singh's Ministry, though he immediately afterwards resigned. But the political lure was there when he contested the 1982 Presidential election as combined Opposition's candidate knowing it full well that the chance of his success was really remote. The image of the Supreme Court received another grievous blow when a sitting Supreme Court Judge Baharul Islam, who was due for retirement by the end of February in 1983, resigned in January to be able to contest the Barpeta House of the People seat on the Congress (I) ticket.[47] Baharural Islam's resignation came barely a month after his (and Justice R.B. Mishra's) controversial judgment in the Patna Urban Cooperative case in favour of the Bihar Chief Minister Dr. Jagannath Mishra, who stood accused of forgery and corruption. The third Judge hearing the case, Justice V.D. Tulzapurkar, dissented. Perhaps, there might be no link between Baharual Islam's resignation and his judgment in the Patna Urban Cooperative case, but his subsequent actions compounded the widespread misgivings which that judgment had aroused.[48] A review application was filed in the Supreme Court pleading that Justice Baharul Islam's judgment was politically motivated as he became Congress (I) nominee for the Barpeta House of the People seat. The Court unanimously decided to hear the appeal challenging the judgment of the Patna High Court upholding withdrawal of the criminal case against Dr. Jagannath Mishra.

There is evidence to suggest that a few of the Judges of the Supreme Court adjusted their antenna to "know what would suit the Government in power." Judgments in one era compared to those of another show how things changed under two different regimes. A note was circulated among High Courts after the triumph of the Janata Party in the Parliamentary poll in March 1977. The note on behalf of a Committee of Judges of the Supreme Court proposed a code of ethics for the Judges to check "the deterioration of standards and fall in values." The main point emphasized was "a solemn undertaking" not to drink either in public or private. This was obviously to please Prime Minister Morarji Desai. But the most objectionable part of the code was to be enforced through law. Chief Justice Beg, in his covering letter dated October 10, 1977, to the Chief Justices of High Courts, said, "I am glad to be able to inform you that the present Government is very willing to strengthen our hands and to help us move in the right direction by any legislation which may be necessary for this purpose." S.N. Mishra raised the issue in the House of the People on December 9, 1977, and observed that the code of conduct was a clear insult to the Judges of the High Courts and it would be a sad

46. "Judges As Knight Errants," H.R. Khanna, *The Times of India,* New Delhi, February 5, 1983.
47. Retired Judges have entered politics, like K.S. Hegde, H.R. Khanna and H.R. Gokhale, but they did not resign as Judges, like Subba Rao and Baharul Islam.
48. Baharul Islam was a member of the undivided Congress and represented it in the Council of States for two terms before being inducted as a Judge of the Assam High Court. He retired in 1980 and soon thereafter was elevated to the Supreme Court.

day when the Judges would have to obtain character certificates periodically even if they be from their fellow-Judges. Chief Justice Beg actually issued and was later forced to withdraw, a contempt notice to newspapers who transmitted to the people the code of ethics, in the formulation of which the Chief Justice of India had taken the initiative, and had questioned its propriety. Chief Justice Beg had dismissed, it is important to recall, the Allahabad High Court judgment setting aside Mrs. Indira Gandhi's election as erroneous though Mrs. Gandhi's appeal before the Supreme Court was heard in terms of an amended electoral law which precluded the examination of the merits of the case. In laying down his office of Chief Justice of India in February 1978, Justice M.H. Beg gave expression to the noble sentiments of a Judge when he said that if the Judges of the Supreme Court had become pliant to the dictates or directions of the Executive, the sooner the Court was wound up the better for the country.

After his elevation in February 1978, Chief Justice Y.V. Chandrachud made an unprecedented public statement that he had spent sleepless nights, but he did not have the courage to give a contrary decision in the *Habeas Corpus* case in 1975. Justice Chandrachud did not act according to the dictates of his conscience and clearly violated the oath of his office that he "will duly and faithfully and to the best of his ability, knowledge and judgment perform the duties of his office without fear or favour, affection or ill will." Justice H.R. Khanna, who gave the dissenting judgment, and Judges of the nine High Courts who had ruled likewise, were also living under the same grave circumstances and conditions of 1975. Justice Khanna's dissenting judgment was acclaimed by the foreign press and jurists. *The New York Times* commented that it deserved to be engraved in letters of gold.

Chief Justice Chandrachud did another disservice to his august office. The issue relating to charges of corruption against some family members of the Prime Minister Morarji Desai and Home Minister Charan Singh were highly contentious and for months continued to arouse considerable passion. Later in 1978 when the Council of States was paralysed for weeks because the Government was not willing to abide by its resolution calling for probe either by a commission of inquiry or the Committee of the House, then, the Information Minister Lal Krishna Advani, who was also the leader of the Council of States (Rajya Sabha), had felt constrained to resign from the Union Government. The Prime Minister, Morarji Desai, thereupon agreed to refer the matter to the Chief Justice of India to look into it and the Chief Justice agreed. But he finally refused to look into the charges of corruption. Many eyebrows were raised that the Government should have resorted to the expedient of referring the matter to the Chief Justice of India and that he would have agreed to look into it. The Chief Justice's final conclusion to refuse it was neither flattering to his prestige nor to the dignity of the office he occupied. If he would have agreed, as he did it initially, and whatever his findings would have been, the office of the Chief Justice of India would have been dragged into public controversy damaging the image of the highest judiciary in the country. Charan Singh said in the House of the People on December 2, 1978 that the Chief Justice would have no authority to compel attendance of any person for being examined as a witness or production of documents.

The image of Justice P. N. Bhagwati is more controversial. In their memorandum, addressed to the Law Minister, fifty-two public men and advocates in Bombay, wrote, "though public memory is short, one can recall Justice Bhagwati sharing public platforms with the then leaders of the emergency. He made no secret of his identification with the then current 'ism' and with the leaders of emergency." Justice Bhagwati wrote a letter to Mrs. Indira Gandhi in eulogistic terms lauding her electoral victory in January 1980. In the opening paragraph of his letter he wrote : "It is a most remarkable achievement of which you, your friends and well-wishers can be justly proud." He reminded her of the heavy responsibility that rested on her shoulders and people's expectations from her. He had gone on to add, "you have become the symbol of the hope and aspirations of the poor hungry millions of India who had so far nothing to hope for and nothing to live for and who are now looking up to you lifting them from dirt and squalor and freeing them from poverty and ignorance...." The concluding paragraph said, "today, the reddish glow of the rising sun is holding out the promise of a bright sunshine. May, that sunshine fill our hearts with joy and bring comfort and cheer to the poor, half naked, hungry millions of our countrymen. That is my only prayer to God on this occasion."

Justice Bhagwati's letter attracted severe criticism among the public, the Bar and among some Judges of the Supreme Court too. The

Supreme Court Bar Association even decided, to censure the conduct of the Judge which was "contrary to the principle of judicial independence." Addressing the Indian Law Institute, New Delhi, on March 22, 1980, Justice T.D. Tulzapurkar voiced his concern over some Judges hovering round the seats of political power. He said that they hobnobbed with Ministers and law officers and sought favours. Referring indirectly to the letter of Justice Bhagwati, he said, "The recent news items which you all must have read have caused great anguish and pain to me and many of my colleagues who have expressed their resentment. It is a very disturbing trend damaging the image of judiciary from within and must be deprecated." He reiterated that if Judges started sending "buquets of congratulatory letters to a political leader on is political victory, eulogizing him on the assumption of a high office in adulatory terms, the people's faith in the judiciary will be shaken; and if this can happen now, the day will not be far off when Judges may, even seek appointments and wait on him and other persons who count and that will be the saddest day for the country and the judiciary."[49]

There was another aspect of Justice Bhagwati's letter to Mrs. Indira Gandhi. He had mentioned that mounting arrears had been clogging the judicial machinery and stressed that the position was almost desperate and "yet there did not seem to be any sense of urgency in the court." This raised a pertinent question whether it was decorus for a sitting Judge to criticise brother Judges on the Bench and that too in a letter written to the Prime Minister.

These are trying times in the history of the Supreme Court and the lustre that it shed is fast fading. A judge, especially of the highest court of the country, like Ceasar's wife, must be above suspicion. Threats to judicial independence and integrity emanate from within and without. Vigilant guardians of an independent judiciary are always alert and ready to protest encroachments from the domain of the Supreme Court. But not much thought has been given to the harm that judges' public postures might inflict on the judiciary. A former Judge of the Supreme Court, H. R. Khanna, said, "Institutions are normally strong enough to withstand external threats but they give way and start crumbling when some of those manning them, attack them from within and indulge in what is akin to an act of sabotage.[50] Earlier, C.K. Daphtry speaking at the Law Day function organised by the Supreme Court Bar Association, expressed his unhappiness at the lack of unity among judges. Referring to the Judges case, he pointed out that today when a judge referred to another judge "as my brother, "it would be doubtful if he meant it all.[51] When Kuldip Nayyar gave to his article, appearing in *Indian Express,* March 1980, the caption, "Judge, Judge Thyself," he epitomised the whole truth.

The Chief Justice of India was seriously mauled when his colleagues constituting the seven-member Bench, which heard the Judges case, decided to make public his affidavit containing his confidential discussions with the Law Ministry. The four to three majority judgment held that the Chief Justice of India's opinion did not have primacy over that of the Delhi High Court's Chief Justice. Justice P. N. Bhagwati even described the Chief Justice of India as a "litigant" in the case. N.A. Palkhivala commented that Justice Bhagwati was in error in describing the Chief Justice of India a "'litigant" into "contest" with Chief Justice K.B. N. Singh of the Patna High Court. He added, "No doubt every Judge has the jurisdiction to decide rightly or wrongly. But what is regrettable is that the judgment of Bhagwati J. dealing with the transfer of Chief Justice Singh was couched in language which occasionally lapses into questionable taste when dealing with the conduct and affidavit of the Chief Justice of India."[52] Justice Bhagwati found Chief Justice Chandrachud's affidavit as "vague and indefinite, delightfully vague" a "little intriguing" and "the Constitution incantation." No less damage was done to the position of the Chief Justice of India and the importance of upholding the prestige of that office by the statement of President Neelam Sanjiva Reddy made on his behalf by the Solicitor-General in the Supreme Court, to the effect that the Chief Justice of India did not have any personal discussion with him regarding the transfer of Chief Justice K.B. N. Singh of the Patna High Court to Madras High Court, despite the erroneous interpretation of Sanjiva Reddy on the ex-

49. *The Statesman,* New Delhi, March 23, 1980.
50. "Judges as Knight Errants : A case of self-inflicted injury," *The Times of India,* New Delhi, February 5, 1983.
51. As reported in *The Hindustan Times,* New Delhi, November 27, 1981.
52. Nani A. Palkhivala, "Aspects of the Judge's Case–1." *Indian Express,* New Delhi, February 3, 1982.

pression "President of India." Reddy had interpreted the expression to mean the person of the President as distinct from the office of the President.

During recent years another unhealthy practice has developed. Some Judges of the Supreme Court expound their own views and question the soundness of judgments of other Judges outside the Chambers. While delivering the lecture on : "Judiciary–Attacks and Survival" at Pune on October 28, 1992, Justice V. D. Tulzapurkar criticised the interim order in the Bihar Blinding cases passed by a Bench consisting of Justices, P. N. Bhagwati and R. S. Pathak and charged these two Judges for violating the spirit of Article 21 of the Constitution which ensures fair trial in conformity to procedure prescribed by law.

Close on the heels of Justice Tulzapurkar's Pune lecture came a speech by Justice O. Chinnappa Reddy at a seminar on "Socialism, Constitution and the country Today" in New Delhi. Justice Reddy called for the transfer of the Right to work, living wage and decent conditions of work from the Chapter on the Directive Principles of State Policy to the Chapter on Fundamental Rights. He advocated abolition of private ownership of means of production, denounced the "bourgeoisie feeling class" and ended up by declaring that "it is not the judiciary but Parliament and the Government that have failed the people." Justice Reddy ctricised the Indian Constitution for not being a true socialist Constitution. To add to it, the speeches delivered by Justice P. N. Bhagwati, D. A. Desai, and O. Chinnappa Reddy at the Indo-German Seminar reeked of politics and were, undoubtedly highly controversial in glaring contrast to the Paper submitted at the seminar by Justice E.E. Venkataramiah. The greatest asset of the Judiciary is public perception and acceptance of it as an impartial body. Decisions of Judiciary suspected of partisanship, philosophical slants and ideological tilts cannot be acceptable to all sections in an open society as one in India

"What is more perturbing," says Soli J. Sorabjee, "is the phenomenon, which, if unchecked, is now threatening to become a trend, of delivering judgments of utmost importance without any real judicial consultation and deliberation among all members of the bench who heard the case."[53] The requirement that the judgment of a court should be the result of collective deliberation composing the Court is founded upon the fundamental principles essential to the due administration of justice. Every judicial act which is done by several ought to be concluded after discussion and after deliberately weighing the arguments of each other. That was stated way back in 1884 by Sir Henry Barnes, Chief Justice of the Allahabad High Court and was reiterated about a century later in 1980 by Justice P.N. Bhagwati as a judge of the Supreme Court.

The first departure from this sound principle was made by Chief Justice Subba Rao in April 1967 in a case involving the important issue of a fundamental right. The case was heard by a five-member bench and the judgment was reserved. On April 9, 1967 Subba Rao announced that he would resign his office of Chief Justice on April 11 and contest the Presidential election. He had prepared the majority judgment for himself and Justices Shelat and Vaidyalingam, but "apparently" the draft judgment was not circulated earlier to other judges, Hidaytullah and Bachawat, and delivered the Judgment on April 10. Justice Hidaytullah and Bachawat expressed their dissent the same day but gave reasons subsequently on April 24, 1967. Since it was not in keeping with the temperament and spirit of those times to publicly criticise in judgments their judicial brethren who participated in the case, Justice Hidaytullah in his dissenting judgment made a significant comment "For reasons, into which it is not necessary to go here, our judgment could not be delivered with the judgment of the Chief Justice."

In one of the most far-reaching judgments in the *Keshavananda Bharati* case there was no exchange of draft judgments amongst the judges who constituted the Bench, although in this case the unique doctrine of basic structure was evolved.[54] The same disturbing phenomenon recurred in 1980, and again in a case of great constitutional importance–*Minerva Mills*–involving the constitutionality of certain provisions of the Constitution (Forty-second Amendment) Act, 1976. This time Justice P.N. Bhagwati com-

53. "The Supreme Court of India–I : Erosion of Judicial Collectivism," *The Times of India,* New Delhi, January 5, 1987.
54. According to Justice Chandrachud, who sided with the majority, there was not sufficient time, after the conclusion of arguments, for an exchange of draft judgments amongst all the judges : "We sat in full strength of 13 to hear the case and I hoped that after a free and frank exchange of thoughts, I will be able to share the views of someone or the other of my esteemed brothers. But we were overtaken by adventitious circumstances......."

plained that as a dissenting member that no judicial conference or discussion among the judges was held nor any draft judgment circulated with the result that he did not have the benefit of knowing the reasons for the judgment of the Chief Justice Chandrachud and three other judges who spoke for the majority. After deploring this practice Justice Bhagwati warned that, "this would introduce a chaotic situation in the judicial process and it would be an unhealthy precedent.......For good measure he confronted the majority with Chandrachud's dicta in *Keshavananda Bharati* about the necessity of a free and frank exchange of views."

In the celebrated Judges case (*S.D. Gupta* vs. *Union of India*) it was just a day before the due date of retirement of Justice A.C. Gupta, a member of the Bench hearing the case, that full draft of the judgments was circulated amongst the judges constituting the Bench. Impending retirement of Chief Justice Chandrachud on July 11, 1985 was "another casualty" in the case of *Tulsiram Patil*. In the dissenting judgment Justice Thakkar "bitterly protested" about the receipt of the full draft of the judgment running into 237 pages prepared by Justice Madon for the majority, only in the morning of July 11, less than 3 hours before the deadline for pronouncement of the judgment in the Court.[55] With anguish he said, "If only there had been a meeting in order to have a dialogue, there might have been a meeting of minds.

The retirement syndrome struck again. The Constitution Bench presided over by Chief Justice P. N. Bhagwati heard the case concerning the withdrawal of prosecution against Jagannath Mishra, former Chief Minister of Bihar. Judgment was reserved in September 1986. Chief Justice Bhagwati was due to retire on December 21, 1986. The judgment was pronounced on December 20, 1986, which happened to be Saturday, a day before Bhagwati's retirement and, once again, without discussion amongst the judges. Justice Khalid, who was a party to the majority judgment, had gone on record as saying, "It is unfortunate that a discussion could not be held about this case by the judges who heard this case." Justice Khalid was even unhappy at the admission of the review petition in the *Jagannath Mishra* case. He was particularly dismayed at the review Bench deciding to admit the petition and rehear the case but choosing not to give any reason for its views.

In the final analysis, the deep fissure running through the Supreme Court is in the full glare of public eye. The Supreme Court dismayed its admirers by its extraordinary action in holding a sitting at the residence of the Chief Justice on a Saturday morning to stay the execution of Billa and Ranga in order to examine whether or not the President acted correctly in rejecting their mercy petition. The Court later vacated this stay as summarily as it had ordered it. This was followed by the *West Bengal Electoral Rolls* case by the unhappy twist and turns before its final hearing by a five-member Bench. Five senior counsels through a signed statement charged the three-member Bench with bias and urged that the *West Bengal Electoral Rolls* case be shifted to some other Bench. Equally regrettable was the tussle that developed between the three-member Bench headed by Justice D. A. Desai and Justice Sabyasachi Mukherjee of the Calcutta High Court, who had given a stay order in the *West Bengal Electoral Rolls* case. Justice Mukherjee took exception to the "unprecedented" directive conveying to him vacating the stay order by the Supreme Court through a "lightening " telephone call.

The pattern of four to three or three to two divisions on all substantive issues, the diametric divergence of views expressed by the judges, the whispers of political affiliations of individual judges, the clash of personal ambitions and mutual conflicts and clashes have created an irreparable damage to the highest Court of the country. H. R. Khanna has correctly said, "It takes years to build the institutions.....But institutions can be destroyed overnight by the ambition, waywardness, caprice, pettiness or weakness of adventurists or self-seekers. They can be damaged also by those who cave in under fear and even by the well-intentioned who might be carried away by the exuberance of their ideas."[56]

In the end , it must be emphasised that an honest and independent judiciary is the most valuable possession a democracy can claim to have. Nothing must be done to malign or denigrate it. Let not the judges give cause for complaint or murmur. Not only their judicial dealings but their conduct out of court must inspire public

55. Justice A.C. Gupta was due to retire on December 31, 1981 and the full draft of the judgments was circulated on December 30.
56. "Judges As Knight Errants : A case of self-inflicted injury," The *Times of India*, New Delhi, February 5, 1983.

confidence. A.N. Grover, a former Judge of the Supreme Court, with a nostalgic pride recalls the esteem with which the judiciary was held a little over fifty years ago. The social intermixing, he recounts, between he Bench and the Bar was more of a "public nature like participation in big parties and functions and individual members of the Bar and the Bench did not socialise except in a few cases." After attaining independence, over the years, a good deal of change has come about and appropriately Justice Grover gives to his article the caption : "Judiciary–fall in values." There has been, he writes, erosion of solidarity, the code of professional ethics is not being properly followed in certain cases, the social intermixing between lawyers and judges had increased "to an extent where there is lot of loose talk of favouritism." It was essentially the Bar that was responsible for initiation of inquiring into the corruption charges against the Supreme Court Judge, Mr. Justice V. Ramaswami.

# CHAPTER XII

# The Union and the States

### Original Units of the Union

Before 1947 there were politically two Indias—British India governed by the British Crown according to the laws passed, from time to time, by the British Parliament and enactments of the Indian Legislature, and the Indian States, 562 in number and popularly known as Princely States, under the suzerainty of the British Crown but for the most part under the personal rule of the Princes. In 1950 when the new Constitution of the Republic of India came into being, the Indian States had been liquidated and the country welded into a single political entity. Three different patterns were discernible in the process of the integration into the Union of India.

(1) 216 State having a population of over 19 million were merged in the neighboring Provinces which were designated in the Constitution as Part A States;

(2) 61 States having a population of about 7 million were constituted into newly formed Centrally administered units known as Part C States;

(3) 275 States with a population of about 35 million were integrated to create new administrative units, namely, Part B States of Rajasthan, Madhya Bharat, Travncore-Cochin, Saurashtra and Patiala and East Punjab States Union (PEPSU);and

(4) 3 States, Hyderabad, Jammu and Kashmir and Mysore, became Part B states.

The constituent units of the Union of India were, therefore, divided into three categories. Part A States included Assam, Bihar, Bombay, Madhya Pradesh, Madras, Orissa, Uttar Pradesh, West Bengal and Punjab. The Andhra State was created in 1953 out of Telgu-speaking areas of Madras, making a total of 10. Part B States were 8–Hyderabad, Jammu and Kashimir, Madhya Bharat, Mysore, Patiala and Punjab States Union, Rajasthan, Saurashtra, and Tranvancore-Cochin. The State of Jammu and Kashmir though specified in Part B of the First Schedule, was placed on a special footing and there was special Article (370) in the Constitution dealing with it. Other Part B States were covered by Article 238 in Part VII of the Constitution.

Part C States consisted of Ajmer, Bhopal, Coorg, Delhi, Himachal Pradesh, Kutch, Manipur, Tripura, and Vindhya Pradesh. Cooch-Behar, which was originally a Part C State, was subsequently merged with West Bengal. Bilaspur too, was originally a separate unit in Part C but was afterwards merged in Himachal Pradesh.

### Disparate status of the units

A peculiar feature of the Indian Constitution was the disparate status of the constituent units. The Drafting Committee explained the reasons for this disparity. The Committee said, "In article I of the Draft, India has been described a Union of States. For uniformity the Committee has thought it desirable to describe the units of the Union in the new Constitution as States, whether they are known at present as Governors' Provinces, or Chief Commissioners' Provinces or Indian States. Some differences between the units there will undoubtedly remain in the new Constitution and in order to mark this difference, the Committee has divided the States into three classes; those enumerated in Part I of the First Schedule, those enumerated in Part II, and those enumerated in Part III."[1] The Constitution maintained this difference and established three categories of States giving each category a pattern and status of its own.

The status of Part A and Part B States was based on the concept of federalism, but there were a few significant differences in the governance of the two. The head of a Part A State was a Governor appointed by the President for a period of five years. The head of a Part B State was a Rajpramukh and the office was hereditary in the case of Hyderabad and Mysore. The head of the Jammu and Kashmir State was designated Sadar-i-Riyasat and he was elected by the Legislature for a period of five years. A Rajpramukh of a Union of States was the ruler of one of the principal constituent States and was elected by

1. *Draft Constitution of India,* p. iv.

the Council of Rulers of the States forming that Union. The Rajpramukh was to be recognised by the President. The President also recognised the Sadar-i-Riyasat of Jammu and Kashmir, although it was just a formality. But the main feature that distinguished Part B States from Part A States was provision contained in Article 371 which vested in the Union Government the authority of exercising general control over the Governments of those States for a period of ten years from the commencement of the Constitution, or for such longer or shorter period as determined by Parliament. It was further provided that Part B States must comply with such particular directions as would be given to them from time to time by the President. And the directions were in practice so ubiquitous and frequent that the control exercised by the Union Government was characterised by many as "the new paramountcy." The State of Mysore was, however, exempted from such a control.[2]

Part C States which ranked lowest in the hierarchy were administered by the Union Government on a unitary basis. The Constitution clearly specified that the President would administer these States and in administering them he might act through a Lieutenant-Governor or a Chief Commissioner to be appointed by him, or through the Government of a neighboUring State.[3] The Constitution further provided that Parliament might create by law or continue by law local legislatures for these States and specify their functions.[4] Parliament was also authorised to create for each of such States a Council of Advisers or Ministers.[5] Parliament, accordingly, passed the Government of Part C States Act, 1951, providing for the setting up of the Legislatures and Ministries in Part C States. But this devolution of powers to Legislatures and Governments of Part C States did not detract the legislative authority of Parliament over those States or from the responsibility of the Union Government to Parliament for their administration. It was really unfederal to deem Part C States as the units of a federation.

Apart from the States of the Union, the Constitution also provided for the administration of the Territories in Part D and other Territories including the acquired territories but not specified therein. The only Territory specified in Part D was the Andaman and Nicobar Islands. A Territory, unlike a State, did not form a unit of the Union of India and as such it essentially differed from the States of the Union in matters of representation in the Union Parliament. Representation in the Council of States was only limited to the States[6] and a Territory being not a unit of the Union did not have representation there. The people of the State and the Union had representation in the House of the People by virtue of the Constitution, whereas representation of the people of a Territory depended upon legislation by Parliament.[7]

The Territory was administered by the President through a Chief Commissioner or other authority appointed by him, and by regulations which had the force of an Act of Parliament.[8] The legislative powers of Parliament also included matters in the State List.[9] The authority of the Union Government, administrative and legislative, including the regulation-making power, was, thus, complete in all respects.

But public opinion, both within and without the Part B and Part C States, had been constantly critical of this constitutional anomaly which, it was argued, offended the principle of equality of status between the constituent units of a federation. It also contradicted the principle of equal rights and opportunities for the People of India. The States Reorganisation Commission was "impressed by the weight of the public sentiment on this matter" and recommended that the existing constitutional disparity between the different units of the Union should disappear as a necessary consequence of reorganisation. "The only rational approach to the problem, in our opinion," observed the Commission, "will be that the Indian Union should have primary constituent units having equal status and a uniform relationship with the Centre, except where, for any strategic security or other compelling reasons, it is not practicable to integrate any small area with the territories of a full-fledged unit."[10] The Commission held that the classifi-

2. Proviso to original Article 371.
3. Original Article 239 (1)
4. Original Article 240 (1) (a).
5. Original Article 240 (1) (b).
6. Fourth Schedule, Article 80 (1) (b).
7. Article 81 (1) (b).
8. Article 243 (2), repealed by the Seventh Amendment Act, 1956.
9. Article 246 (4).
10. *Report of the States Reorganisation Commission,* para 237.

cation of States into three categories had been adopted essentially as a transitional expedient and was not intended to be a permanent feature of the constitutional structure of India. Part B States, the Commission recommended, should be equated with Part A States by omitting Article 371 of the Constitution and by abolishing the institution of the Rajpramukh. The institution of the Rajpramukh, observed the Commission, "has a political aspect" and large section of public opinion views its continuance with disfavour on the ground that it "ill accords with the essentially democratic framework of the country."[11]

With regard to Part C States, the Commission recommended that with the exception of Delhi, Manipur and Andaman and Nicobar Islands, which should be centrally administered, the remaining States in this category should to the extent practicable, be merged in the adjoining States.[12] Such of the States as could not be merged in the adjoining areas for security and other imperative considerations should be administered by the Centre as Territories.[13]

According to the States Reorganisation Commission the component units of the Indian Union were to consist of two categories :

(a) "States" forming primary federating units of the Union; and

(b) "Territories" centrally administered.

The Government of India announced on January 16, 1956 its acceptance of the recommendations of the State Reorganisation Commission for the abolition of the constitutional disparity of the different States such as Part A, B and C States, and the abolition of the institution of the Rajpramukh.

**The New Political Map of India**

As a result of reorganisation, the Union of India was to consist of 14 States and 6 Territories. States were : Andhra Pradesh, Assam, Bihar, Bombay, Kerala, Madhya Pradesh, Madras (Tamil Nadu), Mysore (Karnataka), Orissa, Punjab, Rajasthan, Uttar Pradesh, West Bengal and Jammu and Kashmir. The six Territories were : Delhi, Himachal Pradesh, Manipur, Tripura, the Andman and Nicobar Islands, the Laccadive Miniocy and Amindivi Islands (Lakshadweep). No territorial change was made in the case of Assam, Uttar Pradesh and Jammu and Kashmir. Kerala was a new name, although it represented substantially the old States of Tranvancore-Cochin. The Kannada-speaking areas, which had been brought together, retained the name of Mysore. Andhra Pradesh was the combination of the States of Hyderabad and Andhra. The case for an enlarged Andhra State was forcefully stated by the Reorganisation Commission, though they favoured the formation of such States five years thence. The formation of the new Bombay State was based on a formula suggested by the Commission, though its territorial complex had to be altered to some extent by Parliament so as to consolidate in one State all the Marathi and Gujarati-speaking people, The exclusion of Himachal Pradesh and Tripura from the States of the Punjab and Assam respectively was decided after taking into consideration the wishes of the people and the immediate needs of those areas regarding their economic development.

The political map of India redrawn in 1956 had to be changed on May 1, 1960, when the State of Bombay was bifurcated into Maharashtra and Gujarat. The Union of India, then, consisted of 15 States and 6 Territories. It was again changed on August 1, 1960 when the Prime Minister announced in Parliament the decision of the Government for the creation of Nagaland as a new State—the 16th in the Republic. The Constitution (Thirteenth Amendment) Act, created the State of Nagaland, comprising the territory known as the Naga Hills, Tuensang Area and covering an area of about 6,000 square miles inhabited by 400,000 Nagas. Once again, the political map was changed by creating the seventeenth State of Haryana on November 1, 1966. Punjab was divided into Punjab and Haryana with portions of territory going to Himachal Pradesh, a Union Territory. Himachal Pradesh attained statehood in January 1971 and became the eighteenth State.

The Government of India announced on September 11, 1968 its decision to constitute an autonomous State–Meghalaya–within the State of Assam, consisting of the hill districts of Garo and Khasi and Jowai (Jaintia) in the first instance.[14] The autonomous districts of Mikir Hills

11. *Ibid.*, para 242.
12. *Ibid.*, para 268.
13. *Ibid.*, para 267.
14. Garo and Khasi Hills and the Jowai forming parts of the autonomous State of Meghalaya covered a population of 7,90,000.

and North Cachar Hills were given the option to join the autonomous State of Meghalaya through a two-third majority vote in their respective District Councils. Meghalaya, comprising the Garo and Khasi and Jowai (Jaintia) came into existence on April 2, 1970. As a result of the scheme to reorganize the north-eastern region of the country, Manipur and Tripura became States and Meghalaya was also elevated to the status of a full fledged State in December 1971.[15] Two new Union Territories of Mizoram and Arunachal Pradesh emerged out of the existing Mizo district and NEFA respectively. This made a total of twenty-one States comprising the Union of India. The thirty-Sixth Amendment created the Twenty-second State of Sikkim. Early in 1987, Arunachal, Mizoram and Goa were elevated and the total number of States constituting the Union of India came to twenty-five.

## ZONAL COUNCILS

Two new features of the 1956 scheme of reorganisation, not relatable to the States Reorganisation Commission's Report were the formation of Zonal Councils and the setting up of Regional Committees of the Legislature in the Punjab and Andhra Pradesh. The Zonal Councils were intended to provide a forum for inter- State co-operation and an effort, in association with the Union Government, for the settlement of inter-State disputes and the formulation of inter-State development plans. The Regional Committees of the Legislature in Punjab and Andhra Pradesh were intendent to be set up with the object of catering to the special needs of the regions concerned within the framework of a unified State structure.

### Zones and Zonal Councils

The States Reorganisation Act, 1956, divided the States and the Territories as reorgainsed (excluding the Andman and Nicobar Islands and the Laccadive, Miniocy and Amindivi Islands) into five Zones and established a permanent Zonal Council for each of them. The five Zones were:

(1) the Northern Zone comprising the States of Punjab, Rajasthan, Jammu and Kashmir; and the Union Territories of Delhi and Himachal Pradesh;
(2) the Central Zone, comprising the States of Uttar Pradesh and Madhya Pradesh;
(3) the Eastern Zone, comprising the States of Bihar, West Bengal, Orissa and Assam; and the Union Territories of Manipur and Tripura;
(4) the Western Zone, comprising States of Bombay and Mysore; and
(5) the Southern Zone, comprising the States of Andhra Pradesh, Madras; and Kerala with Mysore as a permanent invitee.

As a result of quite a number of reorganisations which have since then taken place the grouping of the States and Union Territories in different Zones at present is :

(1) The Northern zone consists of States of Haryana, Himachal Pradesh, Jammu and Kashmir, Punjab, Rajasthan; and the Union Territory of Chandigarh and Delhi;
(2) The Central zone comprises the States of Madhya Pradesh and Uttar Pradesh;
(3) The Eastern Zone comprises the States of Bihar, Orissa and West Bengal;
(4) The Western Zone consists of the States of Gujarat, Maharashtra , Goa and the Union Territory of Dadra and Nagar Haveli; and
(5) The Southern Zone comprises the States of Andhra Pradesh, Karnataka, Kerala, Tamil Nadu and the Union Territory of Pondicherry.

For the North-Eastern region there is a body similar to the Zonal Council to deal with matters of common interest to the States of Assam, Arunachal Pradesh and Mizoram. The North-Eastern Council which came into being on August 8, 1972, has certain additional functions. It has to formulate a unified and co-ordinated regional plan (which is in addition to the State Plans) covering matters of common importance. In respect of projects or schemes intended to benefit two or more States, the Council has to recommend the manner in which they may be executed, managed or maintained, their benefit shared and the expenditure incurred. The progress of implementation of the Plan and the expenditure thereon are supervised by the Council. The Council has to review from time to time the measures taken by the States for maintenance of security and public order and, as and when necessary, recommend further measures in this be-

15. On November 10, 1970, the Prime Minister made a statement in Parliament announcing the Government's acceptance of Meghalaya's demand for full statehood. The decision to grant statehood to Manipur and Tripura, the Prime Miniter said; ''necessitated a fresh look at the State of Meghalaya.''

half.

**Birth of the idea of Zonal Councils**

The idea of Zonal Councils arose from the just and wholesome revulsions against the ugly passions disclosed by the reactions of linguistic communities in connection with the proposals of the States Reorginsation Commission. Before concluding his speech on the Commission's Report in the House of the People (Lok Sabha) on December 21, 1955, the Prime Minister commended to the House the idea of dividing India, after Reorganisation of States, into four or five areas and setting up an Advisory Zonal Council in each of them to ''develop the habit of co-operative thinking.'' The Prime Minister made no secret of what he would do if left to himself. He said, ''The more I have thought about it, the more I have been attracted to something which I used to reject previously and which I suppose, is not at all practicable now. That is, the division of India into four, five or six major groups regardless of language, but always I will repeat, giving the greatest importance to the languages in those areas. I do not want this to be a step to suppress language, but rather to give it encouragement. That, I fear, is a little difficult. We have gone too far in the contrary direction.But I would suggest for the consideration of this House a rather feeble imitation of that. That is, whatever final decisions Parliament arrives at in regard to these States, we may still have what I would call Zonal Councils, for four or five States, as the case may be, having a common council.......'' The Prime Minister indicated that the Zonal Councils would be advisory bodies. ''Let us see how it develops,'' said Nehru.''Let the Centre be associated with it for dealing with economic problems as well as the multitude of border problems and other problems that might arise.''

The feeler thrown by the Prime Minister was received by the House with enthusiastic cheers, and approving nods from some prominent members of the Opposition were also witnessed. The result was that idea of the Zonal Council had quick maturity and found expression in the resolution of the Government of India published on January 16, 1956, containing decisions on most of the States Reorganisation Commission's proposals. It stated that ''the Government of India propose, simultaneously with the creation of the new States, to establish Zonal Councils, which may deal with matters of common concern to the States in different Zones, including economic planning and questions arising out of reorganisation.'' Part III of the States Reorganisation Act provided for five Zones and the composition and functions of the Zonal Councils.

A Zonal Council was established for each of the Zones. While forming the division of these zones several factors, such as the natural divisions of the country, requirements of economic development, cultural and linguistic affinities, means of communication and requirements of security and law and order, were taken into account. The Northern Zone with its headquarters at New Delhi was inaugurated on April 24, 1957, the Central zone with its headquarters at Allahabad in May, 1957, the Eastern Zone with its headquarters at Calcutta on April 30, 1957, the Western Zone with its headquarters at Bombay on September 20, 1957, and the Southern Zone with its headquarters at Madras on July 11, 1957.

**Composition of the Councils**

The Zonal Council for each Zone consists of the following members :

(i) a Union Minister appointed by the President;

(ii) the Chief Minister of each such State to be nominated by the Governor;

(iii)where any Union Territory is included in the Zone, one member for each Territory to be nominated by the President.

The Zonal Council for each Zone has also a body of Advisers consisting of :

(a) one person nominated by the Planning Commission;

(b) Chief Secretaries in the States included in the Zone; and

(c) Development Commissioners in the States included in the zone.

The Advisers assist the Zonal Council in the performance of its duties. They also have the right to take part in the discussion of the Council or of any committee of the Council of which the adviser may be named a member. But no adviser has a right to vote at a meeting of the Council or of any such committee.

A Zonal Council may from time to time by resolution passed at a meeting appoint committees of its members and advisers for performing such functions as may be specified in the resolution. The Council may nominate and associate with any such committee such Union Ministers or Ministers in the States included in the Zone and officers of the Union Government or State Government as it may think appropriate. A person associated with a committee of a Zonal Council has the right to take part in the discussions of the Committee, but without the right to vote. The Advisers of the Council, too, who are members of the committees, have no right to vote. A Committee so appointed shall observe such rules of procedure in regard to the transaction of business at its meetings as the Zonal Council may, with the approval of the Government of India lay down from time to time.

The Union Minister nominated by the President to a Zonal Council is its Chairman. The Chief Ministers of the States included in the Zone act as Vice-Chairmen of the Council for that Zone by rotation, each holding office for a period of one year at a time. Each Zonal Council has its own Secretariat consisting of a Secretary, a Joint Secretary and such other officers as the Chairman of the Council may consider necessary to appoint. The Chief Secretaries of the State represented in Zonal Council shall each be the Secretary of the Council by rotation and hold office for a period of one year at a time. The Joint Secretary is chosen from amongst officers not in the service of the States represented in the Council and is appointed by the Chairman of the Council. The Secretariat of each Council is located at such place within the Zone as the Council may determine.

Each Zonal Council meets when summoned by the Chairman. Unless otherwise determined by the Council itself, the Zonal Council for each Zone shall meet in the States included in that Zone by rotation. The Chairman presides at the meeting of the Council and in its absence the Vice-chairman. If both the Chairman and Vice-Chairman remain absent, any other members chosen by the members present, from among themselves shall preside at a meeting of the Council. The Chairman shall observe such rules of procedure in regard to the transition of business at its meeting as the Council may, with the approval of the Union Government, lay down from time to time.

All questions at a meeting of Zonal Council are decided by a majority of votes of the members present. In the case of equality of votes, the Chairman or, in his absence, any other person presiding has a casting vote. The proceedings of every meeting of a Council are forwarded to the Union Government and also to each State Government concerned.

**Objectives of the Councils**

The Councils are deliberative and advisory bodies competent to discuss matters of interest to some or all of the parties represented in them, namely, the Union, the States or the Union Territories. They may advise the Central Government and the Government of each State concerned as to the action taken or to be taken an any such matter. It has been provided that the Zonal Councils may in particular discuss and make recommendations regarding :

(a) any matter of common interest in the field of economic and social planning;
(b) any matter concerning border disputes, linguistic minorities, and inter-State transport; and
(c) any matter connected with or arising out of the Reorganisation of States.

Provision has also been made for the holding of joint meetings of two or more Zonal Councils.

When the Constitution of India was being framed, some statesmen expressed the view that India should adopt a unitary rather than a federal system of Government. They pointed out that federalism would encourage fissiparous tendencies, make economic planning difficult and prevent administrative uniformity. The framers of the Constitution preferred the federal to the unitary system as they thought that federalism alone could forge unity out of the wide cultural and social diversity in the country and prevent heavy concentration of power which was incompatible with democratic practice. They were, however, not oblivious of the cogency of the arguments of the opponents of federalism and provided for a federal polity with an exceptionally strong unitary bias.

Two factors during recent years led to the revival of the demand for a unitary form of Government–the bitter controversy and ugly incidents which followed the publication of the States Reorganisation commission Report[16] and

16. The fear of separatist forces anticipated in the linguistic provinces was reflected in the motion submitted by P.S. Deshmukh to the Steering Committee of the Constituent Assembly. Deshmukh recommended that for a variety of reasons, including the "bitter passions" aroused by the linguistic provinces controversy, the Draft Constitution should be forgotten and instead the Constituent Assembly should draw up a constitution providing India with a unitary government. Similarly, Maulana Abul Kalam Azad in a note on "Education in the Union and Concurrent List", dated May 19, 1948, pointed out that "'the demand for linguistic provinces and other particularistic tendencies" were gathering strength in the country, and the only way of maintaining Indian solidarity was "to give a commanding position to the Centre in the new constitutional set-up."

the realization that the presence of small States as constituent units of a federation stands in the way of the effective implementation of development plans. Switching on to the unitary system of government is really not the panacea for India's ills at this stage. But to bring about the "emotional integration of India," as Prime Minister Nehru fervently appealed in Parliament, is no doubt the desideratum and the scheme of Zonal Councils was an inspired idea. The Zonal Counsils are purely deliberative and advisory bodies intended to foster habits and institutions of economic cooperation and administrative coordination among the States within each Zone. The co-operation and coordination thus brought about is sure to contribute to the proper integration of the development programmes of the Zones by easing the rigidities and artificial barriers occasioned by the interference of State boundaries and they may in time prove to be valuable correctives, on the psychological and emotional plane, to the rivalries and separatist tendencies promoted by the more extreme types of linguistic claims. Referring to the Zonal Councils, Pandit Govind Ballabh Pant rightly remarked in Parliament "while the States have to be carved in accordance with their natural affinities, the supreme objective of strengthening the unity, the cohesion of the nation and the country, has to be given the first and foremost consideration....So far as the economic and developmental requirements of the country are concerned, these linguistic affinities do not mark the bounds of the various territories. Rivers do not determine their course in accordance with the language of the people who make them their homes. The mines that lie deep down in the bosom of the earth do not follow any regional pattern much less any linguistic pattern. So for the purpose of economic development at least, if not for anything else, it would be desirable to have councils of this type. Besides, they should serve to heal the wounds that separation may cause in some places." The scheme of Zonal Councils is the test in the art of living together. They are the flexible instruments to develop inter-State cooperation and the best example of co-operative federalism.

The main objectives of the Zonal Scheme can best be described in the words of Pandit Pant, which he outlined at the inaugural meeting of Northern Zonal Council:

"(1) to achieve an emotional integration of the country;

(2) to hope in arresting the growth of acute State conscience, regionalism, linguist and particularist trends;

(3) to help in removing the after-effects of separation in some cases so that the processes of reorganisation, integration and economic advancement may coalesce and synchronise;

(4) to enable the Centre and the states, which are dealing increasingly with matters economic and social, to cooperate and exchange ideas and experience in order that uniform policies for the common good of the community are evolved and the ideal of a socialist society is achieved;

(5) to co-operate with each other in the successful and speedy execution of major development projects; and

(6) to secure some kind of political equilibrium between different regions of the country."

While the scheme of the Zonal Councils was received generally with enthusiasm, apprehensions had also been expressed that it was too idealistic a venture and that it might result in a Zonal Council either absorbing the participating States, or Councils developing into powerful bodies which would weaken the Centre. But this is not a correct appraisal of the Zonal Councils. The Zonal Councils are deliberative bodies whose task is to advise the Union Government and the participating State Governments for action to be taken in matters of common interest. Their advisory functions are confined to securing better co-ordination within the different Zones, promotion of collective approach and effort to solve problems common to all the units within a Zone. They are intended to foster inter-state concord and thereby strengthen and invigorate the Union as well as the states. Pandit Pant clarified this point at the inaugural meeting of the Northern Zonal Council. He said, "The Councils, as I have already observed, are advisory bodies. But if they are to serve the purpose for which they have been constituted, their recommendation will need to be treated with consideration and respect. The success of the experiment will depend to a large extent on the outlook which the state Governments bring to bear on their deliberations, their ability to appreciate each other's point of view and their readiness to reconcile the state aspect of different problems with their inter-state aspect." The creation of the Zonal Councils does not, therefore, in any way detract from the content of the legislative and executive powers of the states.

The idea of providing a meeting ground for inter-state co-operation in matters of common interest to states is by no means peculiar to India. In the United States of America, beginning with the inter-state Parole and Probation Compact of 1934, collective State action by means of compacts had been utilised to promote inter-state cooperation. Some agencies created to secure inter-state co-operation include a Legislative Reference Bureau, Inter-state Commissions, Conferences on current governmental problems, Conferences of state executives, administrators, and judges and regional associations. In Australia, in the same way, inter-state co-operation had taken various forms.

In India the Zonal Council idea dates back to the Coupland Plan, though it was a device suggested to give economic complexion to certain political plans. After independence, a Joint Advisory Council for Punjab, PEPSU, and Himachal Pradesh was set up and it continued to be in existence till the Northern Zonal Council came into being. In fact, it was the pioneer in initiating the Zonal idea. Another such example of regional co-operation was the Bhakra Control Board on which Punjab, PEPSU, Rajasthan and Himachal Pradesh were represented. The Zonal Councils are an inter-state forum where the states are associated with each other to promote and facilitate co-operrative efforts towards the economic and social development of each Zone and, as a consequence of that, towards the unity and welfare of the nation. The unity and welfare of the whole country is the essence of the emotional integration of India. Pandit Pant epitomised the whole truth when he said that "no region could prosper unless the security and unity of India were completely ensured and generated for today, for tomorrow and for ever."

Generally, social and economic interests cut cross state lines and are of either regional or national concern. Greater co-ordination of social and economic policies and planned and orderly development of the resources of the country can be ensured if major policy decisions are not compartmentalised in the state-moulds. They must be fully studied and discussed with their impact on territories contiguous and the people inhabiting those areas who are to share the weal and woe resulting from such policy decisions. The then Madras Finance Minister C. Subramaniam, while inaugurating the quarterly meeting of the southern Indian Chamber of Commerce on November 12, 1958, pleaded for a Zonal approach while formulating the Third Five-Year Plan for the country. He suggested that instead of assessing the resources of each state separately and planning state-wise a combined and co-ordinated Zonal approach should be made to planning. This, he maintained, besides eliminating regional disparities would avoid lopsided development of a particular state.[17] Pandit Pant appealed to the Southern Zonal Council meeting to set the overall economy of the South, rather than of the individual states, as the guiding principle. Pandit Pant's appeal had an effect and the states of Andhra and Madras were knit into economic agreements, which hitherto had taken regional-political colour. Wider economic cooperation was envisaged in the proposal to set up a regional grid linking the power systems of Madras, Andhra, Mysore (now Karnataka) and Kerala. There are some who entertain serious doubts about the utility of the Zonal Councils in dealing with questions connected with, or arising out of the re-organisation of the states, such as, border disputes, linguistic minorities and inter-state transport. It is further contended that in such matters it is impossible for neighbours to come to an agreement by mutual discussion. The Governments of Andhra and Madras failed to settle even minor border disputes. Maharashtra and Mysore (Karnataka) waged their endless controversy. A proposal that Nehru should convene a conference of the Chief Ministers of Andhra, Maharashtra and Mysore (Karnataka) for a discussion of Krishna-Godavari waters dispute and then suggest his own solution was mooted, but without any tangible result.[18] In fact, even minor disputes about persons and places arouse more passion and create a deep sense of regional loyalties which had ever been the bane of Indian politics. On one occasion Nehru went so far as to suggest that if there was a choice between national unity and the Third Plan he would abandon the Plan rather than risk disunity.

The Congress President, Sanjiva Reddy, in his address to the Congress Session at Bhavnagar, suggested that the separatist tendencies could best be countered by arming the five Zonal Councils, which had so far served as advisory bodies, with the authority to "back up their solution and

17. *The Tribune*, Ambala Cantt., November 14, 1958.
18. *The Times of India*, New Delhi, March 21, 1963.

implement them." He maintained that "Decisions taken at Delhi may not take fully in account all the local needs......Decisions at the State level may not reflect fully the needs of national importance. It is obvious therefore that a *via media* establishment is needed to decide the problem at an intermediary level."

The first and somewhat critical reaction to the Congress President's suggestion of giving statutory powers to the Zonal Councils came from the then Praja Socialist Party Chairman, Asoka Mehta. He expressed the view that though seemingly attractive, Sanjiva Reddy's proposal for stronger Zonal Council was not without dangers. The alternative solution that Mehta offered was to build a strong Centre with special powers to protect the rights of linguistic minorities. "The proper approach, in our opinion," he maintained, "is to strengthen the Centre. The Union Government should have wider concurrent powers and be given direct responsibility in certain matters, such as protecting the legitimate rights of linguistic minorities in the states. The Union Government should have the powers and the will to arbitrate in inter-state disputes quickly and firmly......"[19]

The Punjab delegates to the Bhavnagar Congress session supported the idea of a non-official resolution recommending the division of India into five Zones superseding the existing constituent states. Recently, a few more have spoken up and asked for a reversal of the policy of linguistic states. Virendra Patil, then Chief Minister of Mysore (Karnataka), suggested the formation of Zonal States; earlier, S. Nijalingapa, the Congress President, had spoken of the disintegrating impact of linguism on India's unity. V.V. Giri, as Vice-President of India, expressed the opinion that linguistic states must go. The Working Committee of the Jana Sangh, on April 4, 1969, demanded the constitution of a States Reorganisation Commission to examine in its entirety the question of redemarcation of state boundaries to reconcile the regional aspirations with the paramount need of national unity and security.

This is, no doubt, a gigantic task and it is doubtful now if the states will agree to the redistribution of their boundaries on basis other than language or abdicate any of their powers to the Zonal Councils, as was suggested by Sanjiva Reddy. In any case, the arming of the five Zonal Councils with wider powers is not likely to avert the main danger which India faces today. The threat of the disruptive forces at work, and which is much wider than ever before, can be countered only by creating a national consciousness that cuts across communal, casteist and linguistic divisions.

Whatever be the merits of Zonal Councils in creating them and the initial high hopes placed on them in bringing abut emotional integration of India, they are almost dormant now. President Giri, delivering the inaugural Govind Vallabh Pant memorial lecture, on April 10, 1972, regretted that Zonal Councils, instead of becoming "instruments of unity and great cohesion among states" have become "partially dormant."[20] He maintained that Govind Vallabh Pant had visualised the Councils as a means of bringing about greater understanding among the states and a common approach to problems and warned against letting discussion on Union-State relations and inter-state problems degenerate into conflicts between rival parties and competing ideologies. But the results had not been achieved and his labours seemed to be frustated. The President passionately pleaded that the progress of the people was not a divisible commodity. "A sense of partnership" he pointed out, "in the welfare of the people as a whole, and not a sense of partisanship, is the only constructive way of solving these differences and problems arising between the component units of the Union of India."

## CENTRE-STATE RELATIONS

### Legislative Relations

The essence of federalism is the division of the powers between the national Government and the state Governments. Within the spheres allotted to them, the National and state Governments are supreme and their authority is coordinate. Conflict of jurisdiction arising between the two sets of Government is decided by an independent judiciary, Federal or Supreme Court.

The scheme of distribution of powers is determined by the peculiar political conditions under which it comes into existence. In the United States when thirteen sovereign States agreed to federate, they were anxious not to permit their complete subordination to the Na-

19. *The Statesman*, New Delhi, January 9, 1963.
20. *The Times of India*, New Delhi, April 12, 1972.

tional Government. They would only agree to vest it with certain specified powers of common concern and national importance, retaining the rest for themselves. The Constitution of the United States, accordingly, contains only one list of subjects to be administered by the Central Government and the residuary powers remain with the States.[21] Through interpretation of the Constitution, under the leadership of Chief Justice John Marshall, not only a trend toward increased powers of the Central Government emerged, but also a field of concurrent legislation developed. On some matters such as bankruptcy, weights and measures, harbour regulations, both Congress and the state Legislatures may legislate, but state legislation shall take effect only in the absence of federal legislation.

But Canadian Constitution is just the other way. The Canadians had before them the experience of the working of the American Federal system extending to nearly about a century. They had also witnessed the American Civil War in 1861, and carefully watched the long and bitter controversy over rights of the states, which culminated in the tragic Civil War. It was natural, therefore, that they would have agreed to make the Centre strong and vest it with more powers. The North America (now Canada) Act, 1867, contained two Sections or Lists in which the powers of the Centre and the Units (Provinces) were enumerated, leaving the residuary powers to the Dominion Parliament. Besides, the Dominion Government was authorised by the opening para of Section 91 "to make laws for the peace, order and good government of Canada, in relation to all matters not coming within the class of subjects by the Act assigned exclusively to the Legislatures of Provinces......." Section 93 of the Act gave the Provinces control over education subject to the intervention of the Dominion Government in some specific cases. Section 92 specified the exclusive powers of the Provinces. There was also a small Concurrent List comprising agriculture, and immigration and in case of conflict between the Dominion and Provincial laws, the Dominion Law prevailed. Old age pension was added to the Concurrent List in 1951, but the Dominion Law did not affect in any form the existing or any future Provincial Law. Australia broadly followed the American system, because the problem of federation there was different from that in Canada and much more like that of the United States. Political conditions prevailing there permitted its adoption. The Australian Constitution contains only one List enumerating the powers of the Federal Government and the powers of the States are residual.

The Government of India Act, 1935, contained three Lists—Federal, Provincial and Concurrent—and the residuary powers were given to the Governor-General in his discretion. The method of distribution of powers adopted was neither American nor Canadian. It was necessitated by the political conditions then prevailing in India. In the three Round Table Conferences preceding the enactment of the Act of 1935, there was a substantial difference of opinion between the Hindus and the Muslims with regard to the allocation of residuary powers. The Hindus, favouring a strong Centre, insisted that residuary powers should be given to it, whereas the Muslims favoured strong Provinces and demanded that residuary powers should go to them. To solve the conflicting claims, the device adopted was to enumerate exhaustively the exclusive powers of the Centre and the Provinces so as to reduce "the residue to proportions so negligible that the apprehensions which have been felt on one side or the other are without foundation."[22] The Joint Parliamentary Committee explained the need for having a Concurrent List. It said, "Experience has shown both in India and elsewhere, that there are certain matters which cannot be allocated exclusively either to a Centre or to a Provincial Legislature, and for which, though it is often desirable that Provincial Legislature should make provision, it is equally necessary that the Central Legislature should also have a legislative jurisdiction, to enable it in some cases to secure uniformity in the main principles of law throughout the country, in others to guide and encourage provincial efforts, and in others, again to provide remedies for mischiefs arising in the provincial sphere but extending or liable to extend beyond the boundaries of a single province."

The scheme and principle of distribution of powers in the Constitution of India substantially remain the same as it was under the Government

21. The Tenth Amendment reads : the powers not delegated to the United States by the Constitution, nor prohibited to it by the States, are reserved to the States respectively." The prohibitions imposed on the National Government are stated in Article 1, Section 9, and first ten Amendments, and the restrictions imposed on the State Governments are enumerated in Article 1, Section 10.

22. *Joint Parliamentary Committee*, Reports para 49.

of India Act, 1935. There are three Lists : the Union List, the State List and the Concurrent List. Parliament has the exclusive power of making laws with respect to matters which are enumerated in the Union List which contains 97 subjects. The State Legislatures have the exclusive powers of making laws with respect to matters enumerated in the State List containing 66 subjects. As regards matters which are enumerated in the Concurrent List, 47 in number, both Parliament and state Legislatures have concurrent powers with the proviso that in case of a conflict, the Central Law must to the extent of repugnancy, prevail over the state Law. If, however, the state Law has been reserved for, and received the President's assent, it will prevail over the Central Law unless and until Parliament passes a new law overruling the provisions of the state Law.

The Constitution (Forty-second Amendment) Act, 1976, inserted four new Entries—17-A, 17-B, 20-A, and 33-A and substituted Entry 25 with new matters in the Concurrent List. Entries 17-A and 17-B include Forests and protection of wild animals and birds. Entry 20-A relates to population control and family planning and Entry 33-A deals with weights and measures except establishment of standards. Administration of justice, constitution and organisation of all courts, except the Supreme Court and the High Courts have been inserted in entry 11-A. Entry 25 substitutes education including technical education, medical education and Universities, subject to the provision of entries 63, 64, 65 and 66 of List I; vocational training and technical training of labour. Most of these entries were originally on List II–State List.'

The residuary power, the Constitution gives to Parliament. This is unlike the Government of India Act, 1935, which vested residuary power in the Governor-General who could in his discretion assign to the Centre or the Provinces legislative powers regarding subjects not mentioned in any of the three Lists.

The enumeration of subjects in the three Lists is extremely detailed and an attempt has been made to exhaust all the activities of ordinary government.

While the Constitution confers exclusive jurisdiction upon the State Legislatures to make laws with respect to matters enumerated in the State List Articles 249-253 provide for certain cases in which Parliament is empowered to legislate with respect to any matter in the State List whenever the Council of States passes a resolution supported by a two-thirds majority of the members present and voting that such legislation by Parliament is necessary or expedient in the national interest. Laws so made by Parliament remain in force for a period not exceeding one year unless continued under a fresh resolution for a further period of one year. It shall, to the extent of incompetence, cease to have effect on the expiration of a period of six months after the resolution has ceased to be in force.

The Government resolution invoking Article 249 of the Constitution, the first of its kind, empowering Parliament to legislate on certain matters to deal with terrorism along the border areas was passed on August 13, 1986. The resolution was passed with an official amendment to incorporate a preamble setting the government's intention to limit Parliamentary legislation to the country's north-western border. The preamble read: Whereas the situation in Punjab and other areas in the north-west borders of India has become extremely grave due to infiltration from across the north-western borders and unabated terrorist activities in the border areas."

The Punjab Cabinet endorsed Punjab Chief Minister Surjit Singh Barnala's criticism of the government's resolution under Article 249 passed by the Rajya Sabha empowering Parliament to legislate for certain matters included in the State List. The Punjab Chief Minister had the grievance that at no stage was he consulted about the invocation of Article 249. But the resolution never became operative and was allowed to lapse on August 12, 1987. The Statutory resolution empowered Parliament to make laws with respect to specified matter for a period of one year "from 12th August, 1986."

The division of powers in the American Constitution is rigid and no change can be made therein without amending the Constitution. In Australia, too, amendment of the Constitution is required for transferring to the Commonwealth Parliament any of the powers substantially given to the state by the Constitution. In Canada the Dominion Parliament is competent to make laws on matters provincial or local when they assume national importance. But it has no power to legislate on a matter which comes directly within the exclusive Provincial List. Whenever any matter assumes national importance, the Union Parliament can legislate for "the peace, order and good Government of Canada" and it is for the courts, and not Parliament, to determine whether necessity for such assumption of powers by Parliament exists or not. In India, on the other hand, when the Council of States determines that a subject has assumed national importance and passes a resolution to that effect with the requisite majority, Parliament becomes competent to invade the State List to the extent that the resolution goes. The House of the People has no say in the matter and it is the exclusive concern of the Council of States. The power of Parliament in this respect is, no doubt, temporary, yet it is indicative of the tendency of the Constitution towards unitariness. No other federal constitution makes a similar provision as it is not in conformity with the federal principle.

The Indian Constitution reserves for the Union the power to invest itself with overriding authority in emergencies. Article 250 empowers Parliament to legislate with respect to any matter in the State List during the operation of Proclamation of Emergency. A Proclamation of Emergency may be issued if the President is satisfied that the security of India or any part thereof is threatened either by war or external aggression or armed rebellion or even if the threat of either of these exists. It is for Parliament, and not for courts, to determine the expediency of a Proclamation of Emergency and once Proclamation of Emergency comes into operation, the Constitution, for the period of Emergency becomes in effect unitary and Parliament can legislate on any matter in all the three Lists. The Executive authority of the Union being coordinate with its legislative authority, during the operation of Emergency, the Union Government has the power to give directions to the State Governments how they should exercise their Executive authority.

The Constitution also provides for emergency powers to deal with a breakdown of the Constitution in a State. If the President is satisfied, on the report of a Governor or otherwise, that the Government of a State cannot be carried on in accordance with the Constitution, or where any State had failed to comply with the directions of the Union Government, the President may hold that a situation has arisen in which the Government of the State cannot carried on in accordance with the provisions of the Constitution and issue a Proclamation transferring the legislative powers of the State to Parliament.

The exclusiveness of the State List is further modified by Article 252 which empowers Parliament to legislate on any subject in the State List, if the Legislatures of two or more States resolve to make a request to Parliament to that effect. The laws so made by Parliament can also apply to other States which may adopt them after making their request in the same manner. Once Parliament is empowered to legislate at the request of the State Legislatures, the jurisdiction of the latter is excluded from those matters.

Entry number 14 of the Union List confers on Parliament exclusive power to make laws with respect to "entering into treaties and agreements with foreign countries and implementing of treaties, agreements and conventions with foreign countries." Article 253 empowers Paliament to make any law for the whole or any part of the territory of India for implementing any treaty, agreement or convention with any other country or countries or any decision made at any international conference, association or other body. Thus, in order to implement any treaty or agreement with a foreign country, Parliament's power of legislation is not confined to matters on the Union List and the Concurrent List. It can pass an Act dealing with a matter on the State List if the implementation of any kind of international treaty or agreement so necessitates it. And the law so passed by Parliament shall not be invalidated on the ground that it contains some provisions relating to matters on the State List. This is really sweeping power and it has no parallel even in Canada. In *Attorney-General of Canada* vs. *Attorney-General of Ontario* the Privy Council held that "in a federal State where legislative authority is limited by a constitutional document or is divided up between different legislatures in accordance with the classes of subject-matter submitted for legislation......the obligation imposed by treaty may have to be performed, if at all, by several legislatures; and the executive have the task of obtaining the legislative assent not of the Parliament to whom they may be responsible but possibly of several parliaments to whom they stand in no direct relation. The question is not how the obligation is formed, that is the function of the executive but how is the obligation to be performed and that depends upon the authority of the competent legislature or legislatures."

## ADMINISTRATIVE RELATIONS

### Union and States and States *inter se*

Co-operation and goodwill are the two essential prerequisites which minimise friction inherent in a dual system of government and ensure smooth and proper functioning of the administrative machinery. But there are always in every federal scheme of government certain forces, seen or unseen, at work which if unchecked by law encourage disruptive tendencies and jeopardise the solidarity of the State. Provision has also to be made for meeting emergencies which either may emerge from the actual working of the federal scheme or to meet the new conditions and circumstances which may result from differences arising between the independent functioning of authority in the two sets of Government. Finally, the National Government is responsible for the peace, order, good government and security of the country as a whole. All these factors necessitate cooperation in the administrative sphere of the Centre and the States. In fact the success and strength of the federal polity depend upon the maximum of co-operation and co-ordination between each set of authorities and between States *inter se.*

Administrative relations between the Union and the States of a federation may be examined under two headings : (1) techniques of Union control over States; and (2) inter-State comity.

**Union Control over the States**

During Emergency the control of the Union Government over the States in India is complete in all respects, and the Constitution will work as if it were a unitary government. During normal times the Union government exercises control over the States through different methods and agencies. This may be examined under the following heads : (i) directions to the State Governments, (ii) delegation of functions, and (iii) All-India services.

(i) *Directions to the State governments*

The idea of the Union Government giving directions to the State Governments is foreign and repugnant to the Constitution of the United States. The Framers of the Indian Constitution borrowed it from the Government of India Act, 1935. The Constitution, accordingly, gives the Union Government the power to give directions to the State Governments.

(a) A constitutional obligation is placed on the State Governments : (1) to ensure compliance with the laws made by Parliament, and (2) not to impede or prejudice the exercise of the executive power of the Union within their respective territories. In either case the Union Government may give for the purpose such directions to a State as may appear to it to be necessary and expedient. When both these provisions are put together they unprecedentedly widen the authority of the Union Government, for they restrict, both positively and negatively, the executive authority of State and give ample scope to the Union Government for exercising its executive functions unrestricted in any way. The sanction behind the directions of the Government of India is the provision of Article 365 which says : "Where any State has failed to comply with, or to give effect to, any directions given in the exercise of the executive power of the Union under any of the provisions of this Constitution, it shall be lawful for President to hold that a situation has arisen in which the government of the state can not be carried on in accordance with the provisions of this Constitution." It means that if a State has failed to comply with the directions of the Union, the President may declare under Article 356, that there has taken place a breakdown of the Constitution in the state and he may assume to himself all or any of the functions of the Government of the State.

But Kerala Government refused to comply with the provisions of the Essential Services Maintenance Ordinance 1968, and regretted its inability to issue instructions to district authorities to take suitable action, including arrest of and institution of cases, against persons instigating employees who were willing to work. The attention of the Kerala Government was invited to Article 256 of the Constitution which provided that the "executive power of every State shall be so exercised as to ensure compliance with the laws made by Parliament and any existing laws which apply in that State, and the executive power of the Union shall extend to the giving of such directions to a State as may appear to the Government of India to be necessaary for that purpose." The State Government informed the Government of India that all actions necessary and found suitable were being taken, keeping in view the provisions of Article 256. Clarifying the position taken by the Kerala Government, the Chief Minister, E.M.S. Namboodiripad, said that his Government had only used its discretion in the application of the Ordinance in regard to arrest and prosecution of those inciting or taking part in the September 19, 1968 token strike. The attitude of the State government left no option for the Government of India but to post Central Reserve Police without previously intimating the State Government.

The Kerala Government protested to the

Union Government against posting of Central Government Police without their consent and characterized it as an invasion on the autonomy of the State. The United Front Government of West Bengal also challenged the right of the Union Government to deploy Central Reserve Police in the State, especially after the Cossipur Gun and Shell factory firing incident. The Constitution (Forty-second Amendment) Act, 1976, inserted Article 257-A empowering the Government of India to deploy any armed force of the Union or any other force subject to the Union for dealing with any grave situation of law and order in any State. The armed force so deployed was to act in accordance with the directions as the Government of India might issue and it was to be in no way subject to the superintendence and control of the State Government unless otherwise provided in such directions. As a measure of abundant caution Entry 2-A was inserted in List I—Union List—which dealt with the deployment of any armed force of the Union or any other force subject to the control of the Union in any State in aid of the civil power. The Constitution (Forty-fourth Amendment) Act, 1978, omitted Article 257-A, [23] but Entry 2-A in List I of the Seventh Schedule was retained. When the Forty-fourth Amendment Bill was being discussed in Parliament, the Prime Minister and the Home Minister gave a categorical assurance that deployment of any armed force of the Union would be subject to the request made by the State Government. But Giani Zail Singh, then Home Minister in the Congress (I) Government, made a public statement that in the event of communal riots and atrocities on Harijans the Union Government would be competent to deploy armed forces of the Union without waiting for the request coming from the State Government.

(b) The Union Government may give directions to a State as to the (1) construction and maintenance of means of communication declared to be of the national and military importance, and (2) measures to be taken for the protection of railways within the States, provided that in either case compensation shall be paid to the States in respect of the extra cost incurred for the purpose.

Communications generally, are a State subject, vide Entry 13, List II—State List. Article 257 (2) empowers the Union Government to give directions to a State to construct and maintain means of communication which the former may declare to be of national or military importance. It means, that while the Government of India may itself construct and maintain means of communication necessary for the exercise of its powers over naval, military and air force works [Entry 4, List I–Union List—and proviso to Article 257 (2)], it may also direct the States to construct and maintain such means of communication which may be important from the national or military stand point.

Similarly, railways are a Union subject and Police, including Railway Police, is a State subject. The executive power of the Union to give directions to a State for the protection of the railways includes the power of the Government of India to give directions to a State Government to employ its police force for the proper protection of the railways and their property and, if necessary, to employ additional police subject to contribution by the Union as provided in Article 247 (4).

(ii) *Delegation of Functions*

Article 258 provides that the President may with the consent of the Government of a State entrust either conditionally or unconditionally to that Government or its officers functions in realtion to any matter to which the executive power of the Union extends. Parliament may also by law entrust functions to a State Government or its officers in relation to any matter over which the State Legislature has no jurisdiction. In such a case there shall be paid to the State compensation for the extra cost of administration incurred by the State in connection with the exercise of those powers and duties.

According to Article 258–A, inserted by the Constitution (Seventh amendment) Act, 1956, the Governor of a State may with the consent of the Government of India entrust, either conditionally or unconditionally, to that Government or its officers functions in relation to any matter to which the executive power of the State extends. The Constitution, thus, provides for inter-level delegation of functions.

Mention may also be made that Article 355 imposes a duty on the Union to protect every State against external aggression and internal disturbance and to ensure that the government of every State is carried on in accordance with the provisions of the Constitution.

(iii) *All-India Services*

23. The Constitution (Forty-fourth Amendment) Act, 1978, S. 33.

defence and general welfare of the United States and to borrow money on the credit of the United States. In Canada, the Union Parliament has the power to raise money by any mode or system of taxation and to borrow money on public credit. In Australia, the Centre and the States have concurrent powers of taxation except that the imposition of custom and excise belong exclusively to the Commonwealth.

In India the Drafting Committee had recommended that in view of the unstable conditions prevailing in 1948, the existing distribution of the sources of revenue under the Government of India Act, 1935, should continue for at least five years after which a Finance Commission be appointed to review the position. The Constitution made a provision for the appointment within two years of the inauguration of the Republic, or thereafter at the expiration of every fifth year or earlier, a Finance commission consisting of a Chairman and four other members.[34] The duties of the Commission are to recommend to the President the distribution of the taxes which are distributable between the Centre and the States and the principles on which grants-in-aid should be made out of the Union revenues to the States, and make recommendations or any other matter referred to in the interest of sound finance.[35] The Constitution thus provides for a new solution to the problem of distributing the public revenues. It is a flexible method and the whole division comes under review after every fifth year and even earlier.

**Allocation of Revenues**

The taxes on the Legislative Lists remain much the same as under the 1935 Act. The States are absolutely entitled to the proceeds of taxes on the State List and the Union takes the proceeds of taxes on the Union List and of any tax not mentioned in any List. There are no taxes on the Concurrent List. While the proceeds on the taxes within the State List are entirely retained by the States, the proceeds of some of the taxes in the Union List are to be assigned, or may be assigned wholly or partly to the States. The residuary taxing authority rests with the Union. The Constitution distinguishes four categories of Union taxes which are available, wholly or in part, to the States.

(i) Duties levied by the Union but collected and wholly appropriated by the States : Stamps duties in respect of bills of exchange, cheques, promissory notes, bills of lading, letters of credit, insurance, transfer of shares, debentures, proxies and receipts, and excise duties on medicines and toilet preparations containing alcohol.

(ii) Taxes levied and collected by the Union but whose net proceeds are wholly assigned to the States include :

(a) duties in respect of succession to property to other than agricultural land;
(b) state duty in respect of property other than agricultural land;
(c) terminal taxes on goods and passengers carried by railway, sea or air;
(d) taxes on railway fares and freights;
(e) taxes other than stamp duties on transactions in stock-exchanges and future markets;
(f) taxes on the sale or purchase of newspapers and on advertisement published therein; and
(g) taxes on the sale and purchase of goods in the course of inter-State commerce and trade.

(iii) Taxes levied and collected by the Union but whose net proceeds are shared between the Union and the States. The only tax which comes under this category is the Income Tax. The Corporation Tax is not shared, but belongs exclusively to the Union. Agricultural Income Tax is a State subject and, therefore, does not come under this category. After deduction of sums attributable to the Union Territories and to Union emoluments, the net proceeds of Income Tax are divided between the Union and the States and among different States as prescribed by the orders of the President after considering the Report of the Finance Commission.

Parliament may, for Union purpose, impose surcharges on those duties or taxes which are available for distribution, but it may not alter the rates of taxes in which States are interested except on the recommendation of the President..

(iv) Taxes which are levied and collected by the Union but whose net proceeds are shared between the Union and the States. Under this category come Union excise duties other than those on medicinal and toilet preparations. The excise duties on medicinal and toilet preparations are wholly, as said in item (i) assigned to the

34. Article 280 (1).
35. Article 280 (3).

States.

**Grants-in-Aid**

The Constitution provides for three kinds of grants to the States from the Union resources. Under Article 273 the States of Assam, Bihar, Orissa and West Bengal are given grants in lieu of export duty on jute and jute products. The sums of such grants-in-aid may be such as prescribed by the President. These sums are to be paid to the States so long as the export duty on jute and jute products continues to be levied by the Government of India or until the expiration of ten years since the inauguration of the Republic, whichever is earlier.

There is general provision of grants to the States in Article 275. Parliament is empowered to make such grants as it may deem necessary to give financial assistance to any State which is in need of Assistance. It is for Parliament to determine the extent of the grant and it may vary according to the needs of the different States. Apart from this, it is the constitutional duty of the Union to finance schemes it has approved for the welfare of the Scheduled Tribes and for raising the level of administration of the Scheduled Areas. There is special provision for a grant to Assam and to any other autonomous State formed within the State of Assam under Article 244A, in respect of their tribal areas.

Under Article 282 the Union and the State Governments are given power to make grants for any public purpose even if it is not within their respective legislative competence. Financial assistance or the grants-in-aid are prolific source of Central control and direction. They are made subject to conditions and are followed by regulatory authority of the Union Government. It is a matter of common experience that one who pays the piper has a loud voice in calling the tune.

**Exemption from Taxation**

The Constitution also follows the general provisions of the Government of India Act, 1935, and exempts the property of one Government from taxation by another. Article 285 provides that unless Parliament declares otherwise, Union property is not subject to State taxation, but shall continue to pay existing dues to local authorities until Parliament stops it. A State may not tax electricity supplied to the Government of India or a railway unless permitted to do so by Parliament. Without the consent of the President, a State may not tax water or electricity supplied or controlled by any authority established for regulating or developing any inter-State-river or river-valley.

The property and income of a State are exempt from Union taxation, but this exemption does not extend to a trade or business carried on by the Government of a State, unless Parliament declares by law such trade or business incidental to the ordinary functions of Government.

**Power of Borrowing**

Generally the power of borrowing is only incidental to the power of the Government and no specific provision is made in a Constitution as regards the limits and modes of borrowing, but the Constitution of India makes a specific provision in this respect. The Union Government is empowered to borrow upon the security of the Consolidated Fund of India, subject to the limits and conditions as Parliament may impose.[36] Thus, the power of borrowing of the Union is subject to the limits as prescribed by an Act of Parliament. But the Constitution itself imposes limitations on the borrowing powers of the States in addition to conditions which the State Legislature may impose. A State can borrow only within India and cannot raise a new loan without the consent of the Union Government if there is outstanding any part of a previous loan guaranteed by the Union or owed to it, The Union Government may make loans to States subject to the conditions imposed by Parliament, or may guarantee loans to States, provided that the limits set by Parliament to Union loans are not exceeded.

**Financial Emergency Powers**

The Financial Emergency powers, as provided in Article 360 have as far reaching effects as those relating to legislative and administrative spheres. A Proclamation of Financial Emergency may leave the States with no other resources than those available from taxes on the State List, for the President may, while the Proclamation is in operation, suspend any of the provisions of the Constitution relating to grants and to the sharing of Union Taxes. If the President is satisfied that the financial stability of India or any part thereof is threatened, he may issue a Proclamation empowering the Union to give directions controlling a State's financial activities and require State Money Bills to be reserved for consideration by the President.

36. Article 292.

### Comptroller and Auditor-General

The Comptroller and Auditor-General of India is appointed by the President and he performs such duties and exercises such powers in relation to the accounts of the Union and the States and of any other authority or body as Parliament may prescribe by law. The accounts of the Union and of the States are to be kept in such form as the President may, on the advice of the Comptroller and Auditor-General of India prescribe.

## CENTRE AND STATES

### Centre-State Relations

The relationship between the Centre and the States covers a wide range and embraces a very large part of the functions and activities in the administrative, social and economic spheres. Since 1950, many events have occurred which have a direct or indirect bearing on the Centre-State relations. For instance, the Planning Commission was set up by a resolution of the Government of India in March 1950 with the object of accelerating the economic growth of the country and to meet the social urge for the extension of social services. Though not a creation of the Constitution not even endowed with a statutory sanction, the Planning Commission assumed the role of the architect of India's destiny. There were widespread complaints and it was contended that Five-Year Plans had reduced the federal structure to almost a unitary system. Presenting the Budget to the Tamil Nadu Legislature, on June 17, 1967, C. N. Annadurai observed, "There has been a considerable change in the matrix of Centre-State financial relations since the provisions of the Constitution in this regard were settled. There have been a number of new trends and developments which could not have been visualised when the Indian Constitution was framed....... Through a new institution which was beyond the ken of the architects of the Constitution, the Centre has acquired still larger powers, causing concern about the position of the States." The reorganization of the States in 1956 and thereafter, especially with the emergence of non-Congress Governments in some States after the 1967 General Election and split in the Congress in 1969 gave to the issue of Centre-State relations a new dimension and importance.

### Investigation by Administrative Reforms Commission

The Centre-State relations became the subject of investigation by the Administrative Reforms Commission in the mid-sixties. In order to probe thoroughly the various aspects of the issues involved in this relationship, the Commission first appointed a study team headed by M.C. Setalvad. On the basis of the report of this study team, the Administrative Reforms Commission submitted its own report on June 19, 1969 to the Government. Referring to the controversies which had arisen between the Centre and the States, the Commission observed : "but these controversies pertained mostly to matters administrative and financial and not to constitutional issues. Eminent leaders of various political parties who appeared before the Commission emphasised their faith in the Indian unity though they argued for more autonomy and initiative for the States." The Commission, therefore, did not think it necessary to suggest any amendments to the Constitution. They, however, recommended for delegation of more financial and administrative functions and powers to the States "with the twin objective of making the relations between the Centre and the States more smoother and introducing efficiency and economy in the administration of the Union and State Governments." It is not in the amendment of the Constitution, the Commission asserted, "that the solution of the problems of the Centre-State relationship is to be sought, but in the working of the provisions of the Constitution by all concerned in the balanced spirit in which the founding-fathers intended them to be worked."

### Rajamannar Committee

On September 22, 1969 the Tamil Nadu Government constituted a committee consisting of Dr. P.V. Rajamannar, Dr. Lakshmanswami Mudaliar and P.C. Chandra Reddy to examine the entire question regarding the relationship that should subsist between the Centre and the States in a federal set-up and to suggest suitable amendments to the Constitution so as to secure utmost autonomy to the States. The Committee presented its report to the Tamil Nadu Government in May 1971. The pith of the report is to alter the theme of subordination of the State "running right through the Constitution." The Committee felt that the prevailing unitary trends are mainly due to the certain provisions in the Constitution which confer special powers on the Centre; one-party rule, both, at the Centre and in the States; inadequacy of States' open fiscal resources and consequent dependence on the Centre for financial assistance; the institution of Central planning and the role of the Planning Commission. "In a federation", the Committee observed "The national and State Governments exist on a basis of equality and neither has the power to make inroads on the definite authority and functions of the other unilaterally. In India, however, the national Government is vested with powers on certain occasions to invade the legislative and executive domain of the States."

The Rajamannar Committee recommended among other things quite a number of constitutional amendments. Its recommendations, the Committee asserted, enlarge the autonomy of the State consistent with the integrity of the country. The Committee disclaimed any intention to disturb the essential framework of the Constitution. "Our aim was not to destroy the present Constitution and frame another in its stead, our intention was not to 'grasp this sorry scheme of things' and to 'shatter it to bits' and then remould it nearer to the heart's desire."

The Committee came down strongly on Article 365 which entitled the Centre to supersede a State Government, by assuming to itself under Article 356, the powers of the State Government concerned and recommended the repeal of this Article along with others tending to usurp or constrict powers of the States. At the same time, the Committee recommended that the Governor should be appointed always in consultation with the State Cabinet, or alternatively in consultation with a high power body specially constituted for the purpose. The Governor should be ineligible for a second term in office and he should be liable to removal only for proved misbehavior or incapacity after inquiry by the Supreme Court. It also recommended that there should be a constitutional provision enabling the President to issue instrument of instructions to the Governor laying down guidelines in respect of matters on which the Governor should consult the Centre or those on which the Centre could issue directions to him. The instrument should also lay down principles for the Governor to act as Head of the State, including the occasions for the exercise of discretionary powers. The provisions in the Constitution that the Ministry holds office during the Governor's pleasure should be omitted.

Regarding emergency provisions in the Constitution, especially emergency confined to a State (Articles 356 and 357) the Committee recommended the provisions to be totally omitted. Alternatively, sufficient safeguards should be provided in the Constitution to secure the interests of a State against the arbitrary and unilateral action of the party in the power at the Centre. If the provisions, as now obtaining in the Constitution, were to remain, the only contingency which might justify the imposition of President's rule was the complete breakdown of law and order in a State, when the State Government itself was unable or unwilling to maintain the safety and security of the people and property in the State. Also, the President, before issuing a Proclamation of superseding the State Government, should refer the report of the Governor to the State Legislative Assembly for its views.

The Committee suggested the setting up of an Inter-State Council consisting of the Prime Minister and the Chief Ministers to decide on matters of interest to more than one State and all matters of national importance, except defence and foreign affairs. The Committee insisted that the decisions of the Council should ordinarily be binding on the Centre and the States. If the Central Government were to disagree, the reasons for such disagreement with the decisions of the Council should be explained to Parliament and the Legislatures of the States. The Committee also recommended regional representation on the Union Cabinet and equal representation of all States in the Council of States (Rajya Sabha). In the House of the People (Lok Sabha) the number of seats fixed for each State in 1951 should remain unaltered, except where there was increase in population.

The Committee also made several recommendations about the distribution of powers between the Centre and the States. It suggested the appointment of a "High Power Commission, for the redistribution of specific powers from the Union and Concurrent Lists to the State List. Pending the decisions by such a Commission, the Committee made its own recommendations regarding transfer of subjects to the State List. The Committee recommended that the residuary power of legislation and taxation conferred by Article 248 and Entry 97 of the Union List should be vested in the State Legislatures. The Committee argued that with the detailed listing of matters in the three Lists there was no need to provide for the residuary powers. But if it was deemed necessary to continue with it, such power should belong to the States as in the United States. It also recommended that the State Legislature should possess the power to amend or repeal an Act passed by Parliament under Article 252 (Power of Parliament to legislate for two or more States by consent and adoption of such Legislation by any other State). The ratification of Amending Bill of the Constitution should be by three-fourths of the State Legislature or at least two-thirds of the total population of the country.

The emphasis on autonomy became particularly sharp in the Committee's recommendation on financial relations. It recommended that major part of Union Government's power of taxation should be transferred to the States and to vest the States with powers of individual licensing, except for industries of national importance or of all-India character or which have a capital of Rs. 100 crores. The Committee would make the Government of India responsible for providing the foreign exchange needed by any industrial undertaking licensed or started by a State through block grants on the recommendations of a Permanent Finance Commission or in consultation with the Planning Commission. The Committee recommended that the Finance Commission should be a permanent body with its own secretariat, and to reduce the Central control over the planning programme in the States. It recommended that the existing Planning Commission be set up with only an advisory role. The Committee also recommended establishment of Planning boards in the States.

All decisions relating to inter-State rivers should be taken by the Supreme Court and satisfactory provisions in the Constitution should be made for implementing its decision. At the same time, the Committee recommended that no appeal from a High Court should lie in the Supreme Court in ordinary, civil, criminal or other matters whatever the pecuniary interests involved and whatever the sentence imposed, except in a case involving constitutional issues or the interpretation of a Central Act. It also suggested that the State Legislatures should have a voice in the removal of High Court Judges.

The Committee's quest for an "ideal federal system" led it to suggest restrictions not only on the power of Parliament and the Government of India, but also on the jurisdiction of the Supreme Court "to a degree which will reduce the Court's authority enormously and deprive the country of the immense good which the Court had done and is capable of doing."[37] In reply to a question from V.S. Maniam that the committee's recommendations to curb the appellate authority of the Supreme Court had been described by some critics as "Most reprehensible," Dr. Rajamannar sharply reacted to it. "What we have suggested", he said, 'is what obtains in other countries with a federal system of government. The classic instance is the Supreme Court of U.S.A."[38] Without considering whether the changes recommended were necessary or beneficial, the Committee, simply took the Constitution of the United States as its beau-ideal and sought to refashion the Supreme Court of India accordingly. No less startling is the Committee's proposal that the State Legislature should have a voice in the removal of High Court Judges.

It is important to note that the Committee was asked by its terms of reference to suggest constitutional changes not to secure the extent of autonomy necessary for proper governance, but the "utmost autonomy" possible in a federal set-up. One can understand autonomy if it is construed as synonymous with decentralization, but the concept of "utmost autonomy" is incongruous with a federal set-up as it can lead only to anarchy. The Rajamannar Committee suggested deletion of Articles 256 and 257 of the Constitution in their entirety. These Articles empower the Union Government to issue directions to the State Governments to ensure that the latter comply with and do not impede or prejudice, the laws of the Union or the Union Executive in the exercise of its authority. Together with it, the Committee suggested the repeal of emergency provisions, especially Articles 356, 357 and 365. This would reduce the Centre to complete impotence in dealing with any State which chooses to defy it or even where there is danger of the administration breaking down because of ministerial instability.

The Rajamannar Committee report is wholly unsatisfactory. But it does not mean that the Report lacks a constructive character altogether. Its comments on the financial aspects, on the Planning Commission and on the Governors are important and need serious consideration. There is a very strong case reforming the present system, but not its replacement. The Rajamannar Committee's grievance is not the abuse of the Constitution but the Constitution itself.

The Central Government completely ignored the Rajamannar Committee Report. Its

37. A.G. Noorani, "Centre-State Ties–a wrong approach." *Indian Express,* New Delhi, July 18, 1971.
38. *The Sunday Statesman,* New Delhi, July 4, 1991.

contention throughout had been that since the Committee was set up by the Government of a State, it had nothing to do with its report. Reacting to the demand for the appointment of a high-power commission on the questions of giving more powers to the States, the Prime Minister expressed the view that the Constitution itself was capable enough to deal with any problem emerging form the Centre-State relations and consequently there was no necessity to review the Constitution as recommended by the Rajamannar Committee. The Prime Minister also pointed out that the real problem in the Indian federal system was in respect of sharing the scarce resources and as long as resources remained scarce, changes in the Constitution would be of little help.

The Central Government accepted on March 13, 1975, the Administrative Reforms Commission view that no changes in the Constitution were called for to ensure proper and harmonious Centre-State relations. The Union Cabinet felt that the existing provisions of the Constitution were adequate to meet any situation or resolve any problem that might arise between the Centre and the States. In coming to this decision, the Cabinet also took note of the recommendations of the Rajamannar Committee as well as the White Paper presented by DMK Government to the State Assembly in April 1974.The Cabinet's considered view was that the White Paper of the Tamil Nadu Government had proposed even drastic changes than those proposed by the Rajamannar Committee. It felt that the proposals made by Tamil Nadu Government would alter the basic structure of the Constitution and such a major change was "neither necessary nor feasible."

The Union Cabinet felt that the basic scheme of the Indian Constitution was a federation with a strong Centre and that the doctrine of a nebulous and weak Centre ran contrary to the concept of powers of the Union Government accepted by the Constituent Assembly. It recalled the observation of Jawaharlal Nehru, as Chairman of the Union Power Committee of the Constituent Assembly in July 1947 that "the soundest framework of our Constitution is a federation with a strong Centre." However, the Cabinet thought that there was room for strengthening the financial powers of the States. The Government processed the issues involved and some headway was made.

**The Demand for Greater Autonomy**

There is not a single democratic federation in which argument about the division of power and authority between the Union and its constituent units is over. It is a continuous process and it is the scope and quality of the debate that matters to solve the problems emerging in such a polity. But the demand for greater autonomy for the States became much louder and unrealistic after the Janata Party's victory at the polls in 1977. The Janata Party, coming into power as it did on the tidal wave of popular revulsion against Emergency, was committed to restoring public faith in open, democratic governance and part of that commitment included political and Economic decentralisation, which, in simple words, meant more powers of the States. Some of the "proposals for a comprehensive Bill to amend the Constitution", which the executive of the Janata Parliamentary party debated, included provisions restoring to the States the autonomy taken away from them during the Emergency, such as the reinclusion of forestry and education in the State List and abolition of Article 257-A, inserted by the Forty-second Amendment Act, enabling the Central Government to deploy Union armed forces in any State on its own discretion and initiative.

This gave a fillip to the demand for greater autonomy for the States and it started in West Bengal immediately after the June 1977 Assembly poll, and the CPM-led Left Front Government assumed office. The CPM Party was Janata's ally in the March 1977 Parliamentary poll. In October 1977, the West Bengal Chief Minister, Jyoti Basu, held discussions in Srinagar with his counterpart in Jammu and Kashmir, Sheikh Mohammed Abdullah. Initially, the discussion for greater autonomy between the two began as a quiet dialogue, but soon it assumed the "character of a pioneer movement," when Punjab also became their ally.

The Jyoti Basu-Sheikh Abdullah talks were followed by a meeting of the CPI(M) in West Bengal and a subsequent resolution on the subject by the West Bengal Government. Dr. Ashok Mitra, the State Finance Minister, kept the issue alive by his proposal to hold a conference of the States to consider the financial relation between the Centre and the states and the Akali Party invited the conference to be held in the Punjab. Next followed a Press Conference held by Sheikh Abdullah in New Delhi, on January

29, 1978, in which he suggested the extension of Article 370 (which governs the relation of Jammu and Kashmir with the Union) to the other states. Endorsing the stand taken by West Bengal Chief Minister, for review of the Centre-State relationship, he asserted that only strong states could lead to a strong Centre.[39]

The West Bengal Chief Minister wanted the Preamble of the Constitution to be amended to include the word "federal" in the rest of the Constitution. According to him, only foreign relations, defence, communications, currency, economic co-ordination and related matters should fall within the exclusive jurisdiction of the Union. Article 248 (relating to residuary powers of legislation) should be amended and Article 249 be deleted in order to deprive Parliament of the right to legislate on matters not enumerated in the Union or Concurrent lists, Articles 356 and 357 (provisions in case of failure of constitutional machinery in states and exercise of legislative powers under Proclamation issued under Article 356) and Article 360 (provisions as to financial emergency) should be deleted, and 75 per cent of all revenues collected by the Centre under whatever head should go to the state. Thus, among the proposals that Jyoti Basu had made, the key ones are not those which relate to the share of the states in the Central Government's revenues and planning, though these are vitally important for which the states have always clamoured irrespective of the labels of their Governments.

**Anandpur Sahib Resolution**

The Working Committee of the Akali Dal, at its meeting on 11 December 1972, appointed a Sub-Committee, with Surjit Singh Barnala,[40] as Chairman, to "drawing up" the draft of a 'policy programme.' The Surjit Singh Sub-Committee presented its report at the meeting of the Working Committee held in Anandpur Sahib on 16-17 October 1973. The Working Committee approved the report after a "close discussion" for being placed before the General House of the Akali Dal..

The purposes of the Akali Dal set forth in the Anandpur Sahib resolution, *inter alia* were : "to preserve and keep alive the concept of distinct and independent identity of the Panth (described as Sikh nation) and to create an environment in which national sentiments and aspirations of the Sikh Panth will find full expression, satisfaction and growth." The operative part of the Anandpur Sahib resolution related to the political goal of the Akali Dal; the ultimate objective of which was the "pre-eminence of the Khalsa (pure Sikhs)." The new Punjab, which would be achieved by merging all those Punjabi-speaking areas "deliberately kept out of Punjab," would constitute a single administrative unit "Where the interests of the Sikhs and Sikhism are specifically protected."

In this new Punjab and other States the "Centre's interference" would be restricted to: foreign relations, defence, currency and general communications. All other subjects would be in the jurisdiction of Punjab and other states which would be fully entitled to frame their own constitutions on these subjects for administration. For the administration of the aforesaid four subjects assigned to the Centre "Punjab and other states would contribute in proportion to representation in Parliament." In pursuance of this political goal, the Akali Dal would endeavour "to have the Indian Constitution recast on real federal principles, with equal representation at the Centre for all States."

It is unlikely that the country will accept a revival of the Cabinet Mission's Scheme in respect of the Union's powers as suggested by Jyoti Basu, Sheikh Abdullah and the Akalis in the Punjab, whose extremists even claim that India is a multinational State. But Prime Minister Morarji Desai's refusal either to reopen the whole gamut of Centre-State relations or even to consider of convening a conference to discuss the issue, was perhaps too brusque. Dialogue is the essence of any relations between the Centre and constituent units of a federation as both are the integral parts of a polity and a federal polity is yet to be devised which satisfactorily answers all problems for all times. This is, however, not to suggest that the Constitution should be rewritten in order to remove the imbalances and distortions.

It does not, however, mean that the Constitution is perfect in matters of financial relations. There are shortcomings which need be removed. For instance, the constitutional allocation of finances between the Centre and the states is

39. *The Times of India,* New Delhi, January 30, 1978.
40. Other members of the Committee were : Gurcharan Singh Tohra, Jiwan Singh Umranangal, Gurmit Singh, Dr. Bhagat Singh,Balwant Singh, Gian Singh Rarewala, Prem Singh Lalpura, Jaswinder Singh Brar, Bhag Singh, Major-General (Retd.) Gurbux Singh Badni and Amar Singh Ambalavi.

hardly fair to the latter. Then, the Centre has leverage in the distribution of taxes collected on behalf of the states as also in the matter of discretionary grants. The distribution of pool taxes is determined by the periodic Finance Commission and the grants-in-aid by the Planning Commission, the extra-constitutional body. The Report of the Administrative Reforms Commission noted that "the main grievances lie in the financial field" and conceded that "there was weight in the argument that as the Planning Commission is a body established by the Central Government by an executive order, it would be desirable for another body created by law, to be entrusted with the responsibility of formulating the principles governing the allocation of plan grants. Accordingly, we have recommended that the Finance Commission should be entrusted with the responsibility." The Report was submitted in June 1969 and since then much has happened to call for a review of the kind which the Administrative Reforms Commission undertook at the Centre's instance, without protest from any state, but with no tangible result. Clearly, the states need less inelastic and less inadequate resources to meet their own requirements and need to be less dependent on the Centre for grants. The study team of the Administrative Reforms Commission remarked that the excessive dependence of the states on Centre has tended to produce irresponsibility and operational inefficiency. At the Centre dominant financial powers in relation to the states have given Central authorities exaggerated notions of their importance and knowledge with the result that little allowance is made for the points of view of the states. It is important, therefore, in the study team's view that the degree of financial dependence of the states on the Centre should be reduced to the minimum, because that minimum would be adequate for the Centre having controlling powers in ensuring national integration.

**Sarkaria Commission**

Prime Minister Indira Gandhi announced in Parliament, on March 24, 1983, the appointment of a Commission, under the Chairmanship of Justice Ranjit Singh Sarkaria, to review the existing arrangements between the Centre and the states. The Commission submitted its Report to the Prime Minister on October 20, 1987. The recommendation of the Commission are still in the process of discussion in the Inter-State Council, which was recently established under Article 263, as recommended by the Sarkaria Commission.

**Demand for Greater Devolution of Power**

Delivering the Maulana Azad Memorial Lecture on "Maulana Azad and United India", in New Delhi on May 7, 1992, President R. Venkataraman said that dividing forces in India would never succeed in achieving their goal even though regional imbalances still continue to plague the economy. But he cautioned that it was prudent to take note of the changing moods of the people in India and elsewhere. Man's urge for freedom reflects itself in several facets such as political institutions, economic regimen and social status. The urge for greater say manifests itself increasing by these days, be it in Panchayat institutions, or the State's affairs or economic, social and other activities, he said, adding that the growing demand for greater devolution of power and authority by the states has to be taken note of and "accommodated, if we were to hold in check the divisive forces in society." The Constitution of a country "has to grow with the changing needs of society and absorb progressive trends so as to reflect the will of the people," the President emphasized."[41]

Earlier, the political resolution of the Bharatiya Janata Party, moved by L.K. Advani, at Antyodayanagar, Gandhi Nagar, on May 3, 1992, castigated the Narasimha Rao Government for making a mess in Kashmir, Punjab, Assam and North-Eastern States and demanded the appointment of a national commission to suggest decentralization of political and economic powers. Simultaneously Chief Ministers of non-Congress governed states are grouping together to exercise pressure on the Centre for giving the states more financial as well as legislative powers. The initiative was taken by the Chief Ministers of Uttar Pradesh and Rajasthan, though no less vocal the Chief Minister of Orissa had throughout been. The Uttar Pradesh Chief Minister had warned the Centre of the dire consequences if the President's rule, under Article 356, was imposed on the States.

The demand for more greater autonomy, especially with regard to the finances has become more vocal after the U.F. combine consisting of 13 political parties, horizontally and vertically

41. As reported in *The Hindu*, New Delhi, May 8, 1992.

ideologically different to one another, the demand has become more loud and stringent. Southern States stand in the front line. Farooq Abdulla contested the 1996 elections in clear terms: "Back to the original autonomy which was the basis of Sheikh Abdullah to join the Indian Union."

## SUGGESTED READINGS


Alexandrovicz, C.H., *Constitutional Developments in India.*

*Constituent Assembly Debates.*

Granvill Austin - *The Indian Constitution - A Cornerstone of a Nation.*

Morris -Jone, W.H., *The Government and Politics of India.*

Rudolph & Rudolph, *In Pursuit of Lakshmi, The Political Economy of the Indian State*

K. Mathew Kurden & P.N. Vargese (eds.) *Union State Relations.*

Shukla, V.N., *Constitution of India.*

# CHAPTER XIII

# The State Executive

### Office of the Governor

The Governor of a State is appointed by the President by warrant under his hand and seal. The term of the office is five years, but he holds it at the pleasure of the President. In the early stages of the drafting process of the constitution it was thought that the Governor should be directly elected by the people. The Drafting Committee feared friction between the elected Governor and popular ministry[1] and suggested an alternative mode of appointing a Governor. The proposal was that the State Legislature should suggest a panel of four persons (who need not be the residents of the State) and the President would appoint one of the four as Governor. Although the principle of election had until the last some supporters, but some of the Assembly members who had originally held this view came to favour nominated Governors.[2] Jawaharlal Nehru explained that he had come to favour nominated Governor partly because it would keep the Centre in touch with the States and would remove a source of possible "separatist tendencies."[3] The Constituent Assembly rejected both the proposals, of direct election and the selection out of a panel of four elected by the State Legislature, in favour of nomination by the President. It was unequivocally made clear that the Governor would not be an instrument of the Union Government. The Drafting Committee too expected the same role the Governors to play. T. T. Krishnamachari said in the Assembly that he would at once "disclaim all ideas, as far as I am concerned, that we in this House want the future Governor who is to be nominated by the President, to be in any sense the agent of the Central Government. I would like that point to be made very clear, because such an idea finds no place in the scheme of the Government we envisage for the future"[4] Krishnamachari's views on the role of the Governor were confirmed by the Committee of Governors appointed by President V.V. Giri in November 1971.

But the future could not sustain Krishnamachari's claim nor the views of the Governors Committee could have any impact on the course of events. As the coarse love of never runs smooth so does the course of politics. For example, the unusual procedure adopted in Commander Nanavati's case in suspending the sentence passed by the Bombay High Court pending the disposal of his application for leave to appeal to the Supreme Court proved that the Governor, a promoted politician, and the State Ministry when they belonged to the same ruling party, could be made to succumb to the command of the Central Government, whatever be the merits of such a behest. When the representatives of Commander Nanavati appealed to the Government of Bombay to suspend his sentence, it felt that it was an unusual procedure and decided to seek the Centre's advice. The opinion given by the Centre might not be interpreted as a direction, and it might not have even violated any legal or constitutional provision but it did show how the Centre could dictate its mind. When the Bombay Government was hesitant to adopt the unusual procedure, the Centre should have given its thought, whatever considerations might have weighed with it, to that aspect of the matter before tendering the necessary advice. The Full Bench of the Bombay High Court held that the order of the Bombay Government suspending the life sentence of Commander Nanavati had not been shown to be "unconstitutional or contrary to law." All the same, the Court expressed its profound regret at the use of extraordinary powers in the Nanavati case.

The essential idea of having a nominated Governor was to have a person as the Head of the State who should maintain himself on a higher plane and would hold the scales even without any

1. *Draft Constitution of India,* p. 7.
2. Among them were T.T. Krishnamachari, Mrs. Durgabai, B.G. Kher and Pandit Govind Ballabh Pant.
3. *Constituent Assembly Debates,* Vol. VIII, pp. 454-6.
4. *Constituent Assembly Debates,* Vol. VIII, p. 4.

political considerations, and, if necessary, to stand up on his own against the State Government as well as against the Union Government. The Governor "is the representative not of a party," observed the Chairman of the Drafting Committee, "he is the representative of the people as a whole of the State. It is in the name of the people that he carries on the administration. He must see that the administration is carried on a level which may be regarded as good, efficient, honest administration."[5] The Governor was, therefore, neither expected to be a puppet in the hands of the State Ministry nor should he become a mere instrument in the hands of the Union Ministry." But how far partymen specially if they happen to be candidates defeated at parliamentary elections," pertinently puts N. R. Deshpande, "can stand squarely against Cabinets whether in the States or at the Centre, particularly against the latter, is highly problematical." Hitherto, barring a few appointments, Governors have been appointed purely on party considerations. And, then, Governorship is interchangeable with the State Chief Ministership or Ministership at the Centre at any time when deemed politically expedient.[6]

## Qualifications and Conditions of Office

A Governor must be a citizen of India and at least thirty-five years of age. He must not be a member of either House of Parliament or of a House of the Legislature in any State. If he is a member of any Legislature, he vacates his seat on assuming office. Nor shall the Governor hold any office of profit.[7] He is entitled, without payment of rent, to the use of his official residences and is also entitled to such emoluments and allowances and privileges as may be determined by Parliament by law. Until provision was to be made by Parliament the salary of the Governor was fixed by the constitution at Rs. 5,500 per mensem plus allowances and privileges as the Governor of the Corresponding Province, was entitled to immediately before the commencement of the Constitution. The Governors (Emoluments, Allowances and Privileges) Amendment Act, 1986, doubled the monthly emoluments of Governors to Rs.11,000 with retrospective effect from April 1,1986. Their emoluments and allowances are not to be diminished during their terms of office.

Two conventions are now well established with regard to the appointment of a Governor. In the first place, the Governor must be acceptable to the State to which he is likely to be appointed. The Administrative Reforms Commission shared the view that the convention is a healthy one and should continue. The practice is that the Union Government consults the Chief Minister of the State concerned prior to the appointment of a Governor. The Union Government has also conceded that if a Chief Minister bases objections on grounds that are valid, or at least agreeable,the Union may drop his name. But the Union is not prepared to concede to any Chief Minister the right of veto on the ground that the proposed nominee is a member of a particular political party, or that he is drawn from the ranks of the civil or defence forces. The Administrative Reforms Commission had recommended that Judges on retirement should not be appointed Governors. However,a Judge who entered public life on retirement and became a legislator or held an elective office might not be considered ineligible for appointment as Governor. But the Government does not share this view. It feels that barring retired Judges for being appointed as Governors is going beyond the scope of Article 157 and there may be no particular advantage in rigidly excluding Judges without reference to the merit of individual cases.

The second convention is that person selected must normally be an outsider,that is, resident of another State. While expressing his fears in the Constituent Assembly on an elective Governor, Jawaharlal Nehru said that it would be infinitely better if a Governor was not intimately connected with the local politics and factions in a State and should be a more detached figure,acceptable to the State no doubt,but not known to

5. *Ibid,* pp. 546.
6. For instance, K.M. Munshi, Sri Prakasa, N.V. Gadgil, V.V. Giri, K.N. Katju.
7. Raghukul Tilak was appointed Governor of Rajasthan in early May, 1977 and the date of his arrival at Jaipur had also been announced. When he did not arrive on the appointed day, it was being said that a constitutional hitch had arisen over his appointment. Tilak was a member of the Rajasthan Public Service Commission in the fifties and Article 319 (a) debars a former member of the Public Service Commission from taking up a Government job. Later it was pointed out that the Governor of a State is not a Government employee since he was appointed by the President and drew his salary from the Consolidated Fund. This point was clarified by the Supreme Court on May 4, 1979 in Dr. Raghukul Tilak's case. The court said, "It is no doubt that the Governor is appointed by the President which means in effect and substance the Government of India, but that is only a mode of appointment and it does not make the Governor an employee or servant of the Government of India...."

be a part of its party machine.[8] So far there had been only two exceptions to this practice, the first Governor of West Bengal, H.P. Mukherjee, and the Governor of Mysore (now Karnataka), who was formerly the ruler of the Mysore State and later its Rajpramukh.

A Governor holds office for a period of five years and it is subject to extension. The Administrative Reforms Commission suggested that a Governor should not be eligible for further appointment after the completion of his term. The Rajamannar Committee also took an identical view. But the view of the Union Government was that a Governor should not ordinarily be eligible for further appointment after the completion of his term, but no express restriction should be placed thereon.

A Governor may resign sooner or may be removed earlier, as Tamil Nadu Governor Prabhudas Patwari was removed in 1980 and Raghukul Tilak, Rajasthan Governor,in 1981,as he holds office during the pleasure of the President which for all intents and purposes means the pleasure of the Union Ministry. But he cannot be recalled on the demand of the State Ministry. The United Front Government of West Bengal demanded the immediate recall of Governor Dharam Vira. The Union Government categorically rejected the demand. The Opposition in the Karnataka Assembly demanded first that Governor Uma Shankar Dikshit should resign; because he was a partisan and, subsequently, the demand for this recall was also made. To yield to demand for recall amounts to the exercise of a right to a dismissal of a Governor by the State Ministry.

The Provincial Constitution Committee had proposed for the appointment of a Deputy Governor in each State, but the Drafting Committee did not accept the proposal. The Committee was of the view that it would be sufficient to include a provision in the Constitution enabling the State Legislature or the President, if the Governor was to be appointed by him,to make necessary arrangements to discharge the functions of the Governor in an unforeseen contingency. The Committee made a specific suggestion that it could be laid down in advance that the Chief Justice of the State would fill the casual vacancy.[9] It is now a well recognized convention to appoint the Chief Justice of the High Court of the State where the vacancy suddenly occurs. But Sri Prakasa, who had been a Governor himself, regarded it a bad convention.[10]

The Constitution (Seventh Amendment) Act, 1956, makes a provision in Article 153 for the appointment of the same person as Governor for two or more States. The States with common Governor retain their own separate Legislatures and Councils of Ministers; and they function separately of each other. The common Head is the only link between them as far as their individuality is concerned. Where the same person is appointed as Governor of two or more States, the emoluments and allowances payble to the Governor are allocated among the States in such proportion as the President may by Order determine. The States of Punjab and Haryana,immediately after the organisation of Punjab in 1956, had a common Governor for some time and so had Assam and Nagaland.Till recently, the States of Assam, Manipur, Meghalaya and Nagaland had a common Governor. Now it is one for Assam and Meghalaya.

The President may also appoint the Governor of a State as the Administrator of an adjoining Union Territory, as in the case of Chandigarh, and in that case he acts as Administrator independently of his Council of Ministers.

The Governor is not answerable to any court for the exercise and performance of the powers and duties of his office or for any act done by him in the exercise and performance of those powers and duties. No criminal proceedings can be instituted or continued against the Governor in any court in respect of any act done in his personal capacity during his term of office whether before or after he entered upon office as Governor. But such proceedings can be instituted or continued after the Governor demits his office and the period for which civil proceedings could not be instituted or continued shall be excluded for the purpose of the law of limitation.

## ROLE OF THE GOVERNOR

### Dual Role

Until the passing of the new Constitution in1950,the Governor-General of India had a dual function to perform. He was both a representative of the Crown and the link between the Crown and the Government of India through which the Crown and the British Government exercised its

8. *Constituent Assembly Debates,*Vol. VIII, pp. 454-56.
9. *Draft Constitution of India,* pp. 7-8 and footnote to Article 138.
10. Sri Prakasa, *State Governors in India,* p. 41.

control and authority. With the introduction of Provincial autonomy, under the Government of India Act,1935, the Provincial Governors also came to assume a dual position. In relation to the Provincial Government, the Governor, except for the functions in the field of special responsibilities and discretion, became the constitutional head and he acted on the advice of his Council of Ministers responsible to the Provincial Legislature. But whenever the Governor acted in the discharge of his special responsibilities or in the exercise of his discretion, he acted independently of his Council of Ministers and was subject to the authority, superintendence and control of the Governor-General and through him to the British Government. This historic role of the Governor of having to assume a dual character continued under the 1950 Constitution. He bears certain responsibilities to the President as executive head of the State and is,thus, a link with the Union. In order to assume this vital role and function effectively in the discharge of his responsibilities that the Constituent Assembly abandoned the original proposal of an elective Governor.

The dual function of the Governor may be divided into two separate fields : (1) the State field and (2) non-State field.

## THE STATE FIELD

### Discretionary Powers

The form of Government in States, as at the Centre, is parliamentary and this is the basic feature of the Constitution. The Constitution provides that there shall be a Council of Ministers with the Chief Minister at the head to aid and advise the Governor in the exercise of his functions,except in so far as he is by or under the Constitution required to exercise his functions or any of them in his discretion. The Constitution nowhere confers on the President discretionary powers, though the issue had remained controversial. In order to remove doubt about it the Forty-second Amendment specifically made the advice tendered to him by the Ministers binding. The Forty-fourth Amendment added proviso to Article 74 (1) and introduced a little element of flexibility by allowing the President the option to refer back the advice for reconsideration of the Council of Ministers, but the President must act on the advice tendered to him after reconsideration.

The Constitution makes no attempt to define the discretionary powers of the Governor, except those expressly stated in the Constitution relating to certain matters concerning the administration of tribal areas in Assam and Meghalaya, the Tuensang area of Nagaland and the Hill areas of Manipur, and the Telengana region of Andhra Pradesh and the maintenance of law and order in Nagaland. The Constitution (Thirty-sixth Amendment) Act, 1975, confers on the Governor of Sikkim special responsibility "for peace and for an equitable agreement for ensuring the social and economic advancement of different sections of the population of Sikkim" and in the discharge of his special responsibility; the Governor, subject to such directions as the President may, from time to time, deem fit to issue, act in his discretion. The President may by order made with respect to the State of Maharashtra or Gujarat provide for any special responsibility for the establishment of separate development boards for Vidarbha, Marathwada and rest of Maharashtra or as the case may be Saurashtra, Kutch and the rest of Gujarat, for equitable allocation of funds for development expenditure on the above areas, and an equitable arrangement providing adequate facilities for technical education and vocational training, and adequate opportunities for employment in service under the State Government in respect of all the said areas.

Article 163(2) gives to the Governor more or less a *carte-blanche* by providing that if any question arises whether any matter is or is not a matter with respect to which the Governor is by or under the Constitution required to act in his discretion, the decision of the Governor in his discretion shall be final and the validity of anything done by the Governor shall not be called in question on the ground that he ought or ought not to have acted in his discretion. Read with it are the provisions of Article 160. This Article, which is seldom noted, highlights the potentialities of the office of the Governor. It provides that the President may make such provision as he thinks fit for the discharge of the functions of the Governor of a State in any contingency not provided for in Chapter II of Part VI relating to the Governor. In the hands of an astute Governor all these powers can assume great significance.

### Appointment of the Chief Minister

Besides these express and defined discretionary powers, the discretion of the Governor extends to certain undefined and unregulated fields. The foremost among them is the discretion to choose the Chief Minister on whose advice the Ministers are to be appointed. As the Constitution enjoins collective responsibility of the Council of Ministers to the State Assembly, it is obvious that the Chief Minister should be a person who commands a majority in the State Assembly and he selects his team from that majority of the legislators so that all together may play the game of politics and ensure a stable government. If there is a clear majority of one party the task of the Governor is not difficult and there is no dispute about it. The Governor summons the leader of the majority party and commissions him to form the Government. If no party commands a real majority, especially in a multiple party system, the Governor exercises a definite discretion in the choice of a Chief Minister. It is here that acute controversy may arise and even resort to courts is likely to be made, as in U.P. in November 1996. Under compelling reasons the aggrieved party took the matter to the Allahabad High Court which gave its verdict against the decision of the governor.

The ministerial imbroglio in the states of Madras and Travancore Cochin after the first General Elections produced unsavoury repercussions on the political life of the country and the evolution of democratic institutions. The Congress failed to secure a clear majority in the Madras State Assembly and the party was in disarray. The outgoing Congress Ministry recommended to the Governor the nomination of C. Rajagopalachari to the Legislative Council and the Governor accepted the recommendations. Immediately after his nomination the Governor summoned Rajagopalachari as the "prospective leader" of the Congress Legislature Party and commissioned him to form the Government. This enraged public opinion and the validity of Rajagopalachari's nomination to the State Legislative Council was challenged in the Madras High Court. Still worse was the nomination of Morarji Desai, who had been earlier defeated at the poll for Assembly seat, to the Bombay Legislative Council, and his appointment as the Chief Minister. The Governors' Committee (1971) severely opposed the practice of appointing non-legislators or nominated members of the State Legislative Council as Chief Ministers. But this practice though unhealthy is well entrenched.

In Travancore Cochin (now Kerala)with the breakdown of the Congress Government in 1953, the Assembly was dissolved although the Leader of the Opposition asked the Rajpramukh to allow him to form a coalition Government of the United Front of the Leftists, excluding the Praja Socialist Party. In the elections that followed no party could secure a majority, but the Rajpramukh summoned the Leader of the Praja Socialist Party,with only 19 members out of a total membership of 118 in the State Assembly. This was bad enough. But the worst was the Kerala Governor's action in commissioning Achyuta Menon, a Member of Parliament, to form the Ministry after the resignation of Namboodiripad Ministry in 1969.

After the General Elections in 1967 a piquant situation arose in some of the States where no single party could claim a clear majority to form the Government, although the Congress had emerged in all those states as the largest party. The non-Congress parties expressed the view that in such a situation the Governor must invite the Opposition to form the Government and if the Opposition failed it was only then that the Governor should carry out his "soundings" to ascertain who could command the requisite majority. This issue was closely examined by the Governors'Committee. The Committee expressed the opinion that the leader of the largest single party, when no party commands an absolute majority, has for that reason alone no absolute right to claim that its leader should be summoned to form the government to the exclusion of others. The relevant test was "not the size of the party but its ability to command the support of the majority in the Legislature," the Committee maintained. The Committee suggested that if prior to the General Election some parties combine on an agreed programme or an electoral understanding and if such a combination gets a majority, the Governor may invite the commonly chosen leader of the combination; to form the Government. If the combination comes into existence after the General Election with a view to forming the Government, the leader of such a combination should also be elected by all the members of the parties or groups. The task of the Governor, the Committee explained, becomes easy under the circumstances as it avoids the necessity of the Governor checking up with different leaders or individuals as to their allegiance. Conflicting claims have quite frequently been made and undemocratic devices are often resorted to establish the facade of majority.

**Dismissal of a Chief Minister**

Dismissal of a Chief Minister, which implies *ipso facto,* dismissal of the Ministry, has generated the most acute controversies and passions in the recent years, When the West Bengal Chief Minister, Ajoy Mukherjee, was dismissed by Governor Dharam Vira, it was argued that the Governor should have acted like the British Crown and , accordingly, he could not dismiss the Chief Minister unless he himself resigned or there was an adverse vote against him in the State Assembly. This is the correct position, provided the Chief Minister continues to receive the same support of the same coalition or party, on the basis of which he was appointed. Ajoy Mukherjee headed the United Front Government and the group of legislators led by P.C. Ghosh was one of its constituent groups. P .C . Ghosh and his follower legislators defected from the United Front and the Governor asked the Chief Minister to forthwith summon the Assembly, in order to ascertain whether his coalition still enjoyed the majority. The Chief Minister did not agree with the Governor. The Governor thereupon made his own assessment of the strength of the United Front Government in the Assembly and as he thought that the Front no longer enjoyed the majority support, Ajoy Mukherjee was dismissed from the office of Chief Minister. The action taken by the Governor was challenged in the West Bengal High Court through a writ petition. Justice B.C. Mitra upheld the action taken by the Governor and ruled that the Governor "had absolute, exclusive, unrestricted and unquestionable discretionary power" to dismiss Chief Minister and appoint some other person as the Chief Minister and to appoint a Council of Ministers on his advice.[11]

But the action taken by Uttar Pradesh Governor, Gopala Reddy, in dismissing Chief Minister Charan Singh was not in conformity with the well-accepted canon of constitutional propriety, though in the eyes of law his action was unquestionable. The Congress (R), a participant in the Government headed by Charan Singh, withdrew its support and the Congress Ministers demanded in a meeting of the Cabinet that the Chief Minister should immediately summon a meeting of the State Assembly in order to measure the strength of his BLD (Bharatiya Lok Dal) Party on the floor of the House. Chief Minister did not originally accept the suggestion,but subsequently agreed that the Assembly should meet on October 6,1970. But before the Assembly could meet on the scheduled date, the Governor dismissed the Chief Minister from office as he was satisfied on his own assessment that the Chief Minister had lost the majority support in the State Assembly. This was done on October 2,1970. Both the State Government and the Union Government became political suspects and the non-Congress elements, inside as well as outside the State,characterized the Governor's action as the rape of democracy.

The legal position with regard to the dismissal of a Chief Minister is clear. Ambedkar explained to the Constituent Assembly that as the Ministry held office during the pleasure of the Governor, "he has to see whether and when he should exercise his pleasure against the Ministry." In *M.P.Sharma* v. *P.C. Ghosh* the West Bengal High Court ruled that collective responsibility of the Council of Ministers to the State Assembly does not in any manner fetter or restrict the pleasure of the Governor during which Ministers hold office. But this is precisely not the essence of a parliamentary system of government and more so when the polity is federal. Unrestricted power vested in the Governor to dismiss a Chief Minister commanding a majority in the State Assembly is sure to strain Centre-State relations, particularly when the Party in power in a State is different from the Party in Office at the Centre. The action of the Governor is sure to be construed as suspect. In the absence of well-recognized conventions in the exercise of discretionary power by the Governor to dismiss a Chief Minister, it will be safe to state that a Chief Minister must not be dismissed except on an adverse vote by the State Assembly or unless there are special exceptional circumstances compelling the dismissal. What those exceptional circumstances can possibly be, it is difficult to define. But if the Governor is convinced that the Ministry has lost its majority and he does not or hesitates[12] to immediately summon the State Assembly for its verdict,or the Chief Minister does not resign on an adverse vote on the floor of the House,[13] or the Ministry indulges in political

---

11. *M.P. Sharma* v. *P.C. Ghosh,* West Bengal C.W. N. 328.
12. Gurnam Singh, Chief Minister of Punjab, hesitated to resign when his own Akali Party revolted and the Appropriation Bill was defeated. The Governor, D.C. Pavate, sent an oral message, through his secretary, to Gurnam Singh, that he would be dismissed if he did not resign by next morning. Pavate, D.C., *My Days as Governor,* p. 31.
13. DMK Ministry headed by M. Karunanidhi was dismissed, in January, 1976, on serious charges of corruption. Sarkaria Commission was appointed to inquire into the charges. Chandra Shekhar told the Press in January 1992 that he had advised the President to dismiss the DMK Government in Tamil Nadu and impose President's rule because of his "national duty" when he was Prime Minister." He told reporters that he tried to pursuade then Chief Minister M. Karunanidhi to change his ways at least twice, when he did not agree, it was his "national duty" to dismiss the DMK Ministry. As reported in *The Pioneer*, New Delhi, January 16, 1992.

manoeuvring to keep itself in office,or that it is engaged in political activities which are likely to endanger national security, or carries out maladministration and corruption to secure political advantages,the Governor shall be within his right to exercise his discretion in dismissing such a Ministry. If a Chief Minister is found guilty of corruption or nepotism by an independent tribunal and declines to resign, the Governor would be entitled to dismiss him.[14]

B. R. Ambedkar was clear on the point that a Minister,Central or State, could be dismissed on the ground of corruption. He explained to the Constituent Assembly that it would be perfectly open to the "President to call for the removal of a particular Minister on the ground that he is guilty of corruption or bribery or maladministration, although the particular Minister probably is a person who enjoyed the confidence of the House. I think honourable members will realise that the tenure of a Minister must be subject not merely to one condition but to two conditions and the two conditions are purity of administration and confidence of the House." The Governor can exercise this power as much as the President. But if he is to wield such power, he must act with manifest impartiality. The dismissal of Dev Raj Urs Ministry in Karnataka early in January 1978, ignoring the demand that it be allowed to demonstrate its majority in the State Assembly,was an action which had little to commend it. For many months Dev Raj Urs had been engaged in a bitter political war with K.H. Patil,the President of the Pradesh Congress Committee,and as a consequence the administration was paralysed. As members of the party abandoned Dev Raj Urs in numbers, and as allegations of corruption against him were being made before the Grover Commission, he was losing control of the situation, no doubt, but the Governor ought to have given him the opportunity of a test to measure his strength in the State Assembly, especially as that test was only three days away from the day of his dismissal. The Governor could wait for another three days as he had held so far and the Grover Commission Report was not expected to submit its interim report at an early date.

When there was a vertical split in the ruling Telugu Desam Party 109 members of the Andhra Pradesh Legislative Assembly with N.T. Rama Rao and 91 with the splinter group headed by the Telugu Desam leader, Nadendla Bhaskara Rao, neither had overall majority in the House. Here steps in the discretion of the Governor. When the Congress (I) with 58 members expressed support to N. Bhaskara Rao, Ram Lal, the State Governor,called upon him to form the Ministry, and following the example of President Sanjiva Reddy in asking Charan Singh to form the Government although Morarji Desai, the outgoing Prime Minister, had the largest single group in the House of the people (Lok Sabha), he asked the new Chief Minister to prove his strength on the floor of the House within one month. The Jammu and Kashmir Governor,Jagmohan, followed the same example when the Kashmir National Conference split into two and he dismissed Dr. Farooq Abdullah's Ministry.

The action of Governor Ram Lal was vehemently criticized throughout the country on his refusal to give N.T.Rama Rao time to test his strength on the floor of the Assembly and his permission to Bhaskara Rao to prove his majority "within a month."Mrs. Indira Gandhi intervened and Ram Lal resigned which was for all intents and purposes his recall as N.T. Rama Rao was given an opportunity to prove his strength and was, once again, inducted as Chief Minister. Governor Jagmohan's dismissal of Dr.Farooq Abdullah was well-orchestrated and here again the henchman was the Congress (I).

**Power of Dissolution**

The Constitution gives to the Governor the power of dissolution and the convention is that it is always done on ministerial advice. The Constitution does not bind the Governor as Article 74(1)binds the President to always act on the advice of his Council of Ministers. A question, therefore, arises whether the Governor is bound to dissolve the State Assembly when advised by the Chief Minister who has lost his majority in the Legislature?In Britain the convention is that the Prime Minister who has been defeated in the House of Commons has the right to advise the King to dissolve the House and order fresh elections and this advise is invariably accepted by the Monarch. It has been argued that the British precedent should be a model for India, especially in the States which are cluttered with regional parties divided both horizontally and vertically and loyalties always shifting. The pattern is a coalition ministry, if no single party succeeds in

14. Pratap Singh Kairon, Punjab Chief Minister, Biren Mitra, Orissa Chief Minister and Bakshi Ghulam Mohammed, Chief Minister, Jammu and Kashmir, were indicted for corruption, but they resigned when adverse verdicts were given against them.

securing a majority. If the coalition breaks up or the Chief Minister ceases to command a majority and is defeated on an adverse vote, there can be no legitimacy in asking for dissolution. If such demand is conceded there shall be a series of mid-term elections in the State as the life of a coalition ministry is always precarious. In such circumstances, the Governor is within his right to decline to accept the advice of the Chief Minister to dissolve the State Assembly. The Governor has again the right to dissolve the Assembly if the Chief Minister ventures to take shelter under Article 174(1),which allows a gap of six months between two sessions, when he had lost the majority support either because of defections or because some of the constituent parties in the coalition government withdrew from it and in spite of the advice of the Governor to establish his majority on the floor of the Assembly. In such an eventuality before ordering dissolution of the Assembly, the Governor may assess the possibilities of forming an alternative Government. But it involves the risk of horse- trading, not a rare phenomenon in State politics.

**Discretion is neither Arbitrary nor Capricious**

But acting in discretion does not mean acting arbitrarily or capriciously. Discretion in its ordinary meaning signifies unrestricted exercise of choice or will; freedom to act according to one's own judgment."But when applied to public administration, it means a power or right conferred upon them by law, of acting officially in certain circumstances according to the dictates of their own judgment or conscience uncontrolled by the conscience or judgment of others. Discretion is to discern between right and wrong, and therefore whoever hath power to act at discretion is bound by the rule of reason and law.''[15] Discretion must, therefore, be exercised honestly on judicial grounds and substantial reasons. The Constitution meant the Governor to act generally on ministerial advice but reserving to himself certain discretionary powers to be exercised by him untrammeled by ministerial control. At the Governors conference in November, 1970 Mrs. Indira Gandhi told the Governors, ''You can be the guide, philosopher and friend to your respective governments, while also discharging your constitutional responsibilities.''[16] Some of these responsibilities are in express terms whereas others flow ineluctably from the Governor's position as a constitutional head of the State functioning under a parliamentary system.

The Constitution vests in the Governor the following discretionary powers and these are spread over in different parts :

(1) The appointment of the Chief Minister [Article 164(1)];
(2) Dismissal of Ministers [Article 164(1)];
(3) Dissolution of the Assembly [Article 174 (2) (b)];
(4) Requiring the Chief Minister to submit information relating to legislative and admistrative matters [Article 167(b)];
(5) Requiring the Chief Minister to submit for the consideration of the Council of Ministers any matter on which a decision has been taken by a Minister but which has not been considered by the Council of Ministers [Article 167(c)];
(6) Withholding assent to the Bill passed by the Legislature and sending it back for reconsideration [Article 200];
(7) Reserving a Bill duly passed by the State Legislature for the assent of the President [Article 200];
(8) Seeking instructions from the President before promulgating an Ordinance dealing with certain matters [Article 213(1)];
(9) Submission of a Report to the President advising breakdown of the constitutional machinery in the State [Article 356];
(10) In the case of the Governor of Assam certain administrative matters connected with the Tribal Areas and settlement of disputes between the Government of Assam and the District Councils of an autonomous district with respect to mining royalties [Schedule Sixth Paras 9(2)and 18 (3)]; and
(11) Special responsibility of the Governor of Sikkim for peace and for equitable agreement for ensuring the social and economic advancement of different sections of the population of Sikkim.

Alexanderowicz expressed the opinion that in the exercise of his functions in the undefined field the Governor will be under the complete control of the President. He advanced the argu-

15. Tomlin's Law Dictionary.
16. *Indian Express,* New Delhi, November 31, 1970.

ment that if a Governor chooses to exercise his discretion independently of the President and for that matter the Union Government, the President will be entitled to withdraw his pleasure of continuing the Governor under Article 156(1).[17] But this is not a correct appraisal. It is a well-recognized principle of constitutional law that an authority vested with constitutional and statutory powers must exercise powers on his own judgment, as the Maharashtra Governor did in the matter of A.R.Antulay's prosecution,even where they are discretionary. If he does not exercise his judgment and act on the dictation of some other authority, the exercise of such power would be bad and the action of the Governor is justiciable in courts. In the exercise of his discretion, therefore, in appointing the Chief Minister or in removing him from office or in dissolving the State Assembly or even in recommending to the President the taking over of the State Government under Article 356, the Governor must act on his own judgment. It will be unconstitutional and unlawful for the President, that is, the Union Government, to try to interfere or influence the exercise of discretion by the Governor.

## THE NON-STATE FIELD

### Governor as Representative of the Union

The functions of the Governor in the non-State field are embodied in Part XI of the Constitution. Article 256 enjoins that the executive authority of a State shall be so exercised as to ensure compliance with the laws made by Parliament. Article 257 provides that the executive power of a State shall be so exercised as not to impede or prejudice the exercise of the executive power of the Union and the executive power of the Union extends to the giving of directions to a State as may appear to the Union Government to be necessary for that purpose. The executive power of the Union also extends to giving directions to a State for the construction and maintenance of means of communications declared to be of national or military importance, and also for giving directions to take measures for the protection of the railways within the State. Under Article 258 the Union Government may entrust the State Government or its officers functions in relation to any matter to which the executive power of the Union extends.

All these provisions unprecedentedly widen the authority of the Union Government and restrict both positively and negatively the executive authority of the State Governments. The sanction behind the directions of the Union Government is the provisions of Article 365. It provides that if a State Government fails to comply with or to give effect to any directions given by the Union Government the President may declare the failure of the constitutional machinery in that State and may assume to himself all or any of the functions of the State Government. It means that the authority of the Union Government runs parallel to the authority of the State Government. This is a clear departure from the doctrine of a constitutional government in a State according to which the Governor acts on the advice of his Council of Ministers. In regard to these matters the Governor cannot act on the advice of his Council of Ministers if it runs counter to the directions of the Union Government. For the proper carrying out of these directions, he may so distribute the business of the Government that the directions are fully carried out. In last resort, he may recommend to the President to declare breakdown of the constitutional machinery of the State.

The role of the Governor is significantly marked when he performs the constitutional duty to report to the President whether a situation has arisen under which the Government of his State cannot be carried on in accordance with the provisions of the Constitution and, accordingly, the State should come under the President's rule. This constitutional power of the Governor has become extremely controversial. Although the Constitution empowers the President to take over the Government of a State without the Governor's report if he is satisfied that such a course should be taken under Article 356,all the thirty-six cases, prior to the dismissal of the Ministries and dissolution of the nine State Assemblies in April 1977 and once again in February 1980, by the President himself,[18] are cases on which action had been taken on the report of the Governors. It is pointed out that it is here that the Union Government can pressurize the Governor to report in such a manner that the State Government could be dismissed and the dismissal of Charan Singh Ministry in 1970 in Uttar Pradesh is familiarly cited. But Charan Singh himself in his capacity as the Union Home Minister, attempted to pressurize some of the Governors of nine Northern

17. Alexanderowicz, N.H., *Constitutional Development in India*, p. 145.
18. The States were: Punjab, Himachal Pradesh, Haryana, Uttar Pradesh, Bihar, West Bengal, Orissa and Rajasthan.

States in which Assemblies were desired to be dissolved in April, 1977 and the Bihar Governor, Jagan Nath Kaushal, did not submit to such pressure. Another important instance of such a pressure was the dismissal of the Karunanidhi Ministry in Tamil Nadu in January 1976 on the inspired report of the Governor. Home Minister Zail Singh did not pressurize the Governors for the dissolution of the nine Assemblies. It was done on the satisfaction of the President himself, but the Home Minister did pressurize the Governors themselves to resign. In a press interview he said, "It is proper for all political appointees including Governors to resign immediately after a change of government at the Centre. At least democratic traditions demand it"; a bad logic and ill-conceived argument in a federal polity.

The intention of the Constitution-makers was that while sending his report to the President the Governor would act on his own judgment. It is certainly an improper use of his constitutional power, if the Governor acts under pressure of any kind or dictation from any quarter. The President, that is, the Union Ministry, too must act *bona fide* and reasonably. He must have authentic material and convincing data with him to sustain his judgment that the Government of a State cannot be carried on in accordance with the provisions of the Constitution. If the judgment of the Governor in making his recommendation seems to be coloured, insufficient or lacks authority, the President should not accept the Governor's recommendation and exercise his own independent judgment. If the Governor and the President both do not act *bona fide* and reasonably and on material which can constitutionally sustain their action redress can be sought in a court of law. Dismissing suits by the State Governments on the dissolution issue in 1977, Chief Justice M.H. Beg stressed that the Supreme Court had never abandoned its constitutional functions as the final judge of constitutionality of all acts purported to be done under the authority of the Constitution and it had not refused to determine question of either of fact or law so long as it had found itself possessed of power to do it and the cause of justice capable of being vindicated by its actions.

The imposition of the President's rule in the States of Rajasthan, Haryana and Uttar Pradesh after the elections of 1967 presents a revealing study. An impression went round that Governor Sampurnanand acted as a partisan and the Congress Government at the Centre had designed to come to the aid of the Rajasthan Congress Legislature Party, which was plagued by defections and faced with hostile Opposition, by imposing the President's rule within a few hours of its assumption of office. The Haryana non-Congress Government headed by Rao Birendra Singh fell on March 21, 1967 a prey to the latest sickness in Indian politics–opportunistic politicians who oscillate across the floor of the Legislature uninhibited by any principle. Although Rao's Ministry commanded forty members in an effective Assembly of seventy-eight, the Governor dismissed the Ministry and the President's rule was imposed. In his report to the President the Governor wrote, "majority of today can be a minority of tomorrow and cannot be relied upon." But a sordid drama was enacted in Uttar Pradesh, when on September 29,1970 the Governor sent his report recommending imposition of the President's rule. President Giri was on a visit to the Soviet Union and he signed at Kiev (Ukraine) on October 1 a Proclamation taking over the administrationa of Uttar Pradesh. The document along with the Governor's report was brought from Kiev by a special courier and the President's rule was imposed on October 2.The Samyukta Socialist Party's move to impeach the President was based on the ground that he had not asserted himself enough, and had without objectively applying his mind to the Uttar Pradesh situation "rubber-stamped the illegal Union Cabinet decision based on an incompetent report by the Governor." But not a little finger was raised when the Tamil Nadu Chief Minister was dismissed in January 1976, perhaps it was due to Emergency.

The Governor not being a representative of a party, but the representative of the people of the State as a whole, should keep himself off politics. As an impartial umpire his work is to see that the game of politics is played according to the rules, leaving the politicians to fight out the disputes amongst themselves. He should not conduct himself in a manner which suggests that he is inclined to support one party at the expense of the other. The rigours of Article 356 can be mitigated once the public is convinced that the Governor is in a position to exercise his own judgment unfettered by pressures form the Centre.

This problem involves two inter-connected issues. The first is the appointment of a Governor and the second relates to his removal from office. In order to give true meaning to the office of the Governor, it is imperative to choose a proper person for filling the office. It should not be treated as a last refuge of politicians who were either rejected at the polls or pushed out of leadership by more dynamic rivals in the Party. Nor should the Governorship be treated as a sort of cold storage of politicians who could be brought back to active politics when deemed expedient.[19] If a Governor becomes an active politician and even partisan, like Ajit Prasad Jain,[20] Sampurnanand, and Gopala Reddy, Governorship forfeits popular confidence and dignity of the office disappears. They really surrender themselves to their benefactors at New Delhi. It is, therefore, highly desirable that outstanding persons in the political, social and educational life of the country, with an unimpeachable reputation of honesty of purpose and conviction,and who are not controversial figures should be appointed to this august office. The Sakaria Commission, too, made more or less indentical recomendations regarding the appointment of a Governor.

Girja Shankar Bajpai, H.P. Modi, K.M. Munhi, Mrs. Sarojini Naidu, Sri Prakasa and Kailash Nath Katju, who adorned the Raj Bhavans in the early period after Independence, are some of the shining examples who exercised a healthy influence in an unseen manner over the administration and affairs of their States. They functioned as elder statesmen outside the clash of party or parochial interests, though they were political appointees. Even during the near recent times Nawab Ali Yavar Jung. C.P.N. Singh and D.C. Pavate are still remembered with respect and affection. Nawab Ali Yavar Jung, Governor of Maharashtra, had a bearing and mind that evoked the affection of all and his advice was always valued. after years in retirement, had the reputation, despite his known failings, of a man with a mind of his own and who exuded authority. Pavate minced no matters and was straight and frank. He commanded unequivocal respect and admiration from the Akali-Jan Sangh Coalition Government in Punjab. But there is a qualitative change in the calibre of the present-day Governors,not because most of them are political appointees,but because some of them are ''utterly and incorrigibly unfit for anything except to use their Raj Bhavans opportunity as a rest cure.'' Political appointees in the past were neither physically nor mentally decrepits. Morarji Desai's Government, however, seemed to have a weakness for Heads of State ''who had long ceased to function on ally cylinders'', but carried their own fads to become the norms of their official residence and style of life. The Tamil Nadu Governor, Prabhudas Patwari brought the office of the Governor into contempt with antidiluvian ways. He disregarded the rules and norms that go with the name of the place and position and rigidly introduced his own philosophy of life in the Raj Bhavan.

The tenure of the office of the Governor is equally important. A Governor holds office for a period of five years or he may be removed earlier as he holds office during the pleasure of the President. It has been rightly suggested that independence of the Governors in the performance of their duties and functions can be secured if the term of office is not extended beyond the prescribed period of five years and they are not eligible for any future assignment after their retirement either under the Union or a State Government. Holding the office at the pleasure of the President, which really means the pleasure of the Union Ministry, the lure to get extension and the attraction of an equally lucrative and prestigious assignment after retirement induce a Governor to become subservient to the Union Government. Accordingly, a provision in the Constitution should be made for a term of five years only and he must not be removed from office unless it be for proved misbehavior.

The removal from office of the Tamil Nadu Governor Prabhudas Patwari in October 1980, followed by the Rajasthan Governor in August 1981,and the resignation of Tarloki Nath Singh, West Bengal Governor, ''on the advice of the Union Home Minister, Mr. Zail Singh''[21] in September 1981 have set bad and dangerous precedent as it vitally involves the dignity of the office of the Governor and more so when the removal is arbitrary and capracious exercise of powers. Appointed by the President, the Governor holds office under the Constitution during ''the pleasure of the President.'' But the expression ''Pleasure''does not give *carte-blanche* for arbitrary action. The Constitution also uses the same expression in Article 75(2) for the tenure of

19. Jogendra Singh, Governor of Rajasthan and R.D. Bhandare, Bihar Governor, were drafted by the Congress to contest the 1977 elections to the House of the People.
20. Ajit Prasad Jain, Governor of Kerala, took active part while in office in canvassing support for Mrs. Indira Gandhi's election as the leader of the Congress Parliamentary Party to become the Prime Minister.
21. Statements by T.N. Singh at Varanasi on September 15, 1981, and as reported in the *Times of India,* New Delhi, September 16, 1981.

the Ministers *vis-a-vis* the President and a similar expression in Article 164(1) regarding the Ministers in the States *vis-a-vis* Governors. The Supreme Court aptly remarked that there is no worse way to read a Constitution literally. The President can in no way dismiss a Governor without a cause than he can the Prime Minister or a Union Minister. The nature of the cause would vary with the office but in each case there must be an assigned cause appropriate to the office and acceptable to the law. But the removal fom office of the Nagal and Governor, M. M. Thomas, did not violate the constitution in dissolving the State Legislative Assembly on the advice of the Chief Minister Vamuzo, on March 27, 1992 an asking him to continue as the caretaker Government. The Central Government has indeed, no role to play in the action taken by the Governer and he was not ound to consult the President before dissolution of the State Assembly under Article 174 (b) of the Constitution.

The issue of removal of the Governor was debated in the Constituent Assembly on May 31,1949. Ambedkar rejected the suggestion that "certain grounds should be stated in the Constitution itself for the removal of the Governor". But he did not reject the necessity for the existence of "legitimate ground" for removal. He maintained that the President will enjoy certain discretion but the courts have always held that discretion is the antithesis of caprice."It seems, therefore," he argued, "quite unnecessary to burden the Constitution with all these limitations stated in express terms when it is perfectly possible for the President to act upon the very same ground under the formula that the Governor shall hold office during his pleasure." Earlier, T.T.Krishnamachari,another member of the Drafting Committee, had, *inter alia*, told the Assembly Members that if it was considered necessary that "the Centre must have some powers reserved for itself in order to ensure good government in the provinces" (states), those powers can be provided for. But, he immediately added, "There is no need for us to adopt an outworn system,a system which has grown, because of historic traditions, because of that figment of imagination which was actually translated into practice by British Ministers, namely, the preservation of the prerogative of the Crown in the Dominions."

The framers of the India's republican Constitution, as A.G.Noorani says, "declined to give the expression 'During pleasure'(from the Latin "*dorante bene placito*") the significance it has in English law in regard to the Crown's powers since the feudal era." The Supreme Court made an authoritative exposition on May 4,1979, in *Dr. Raghukul Tilak's* case when his appointment as Governor of Rajasthan was challenged. The Court said, "It is no doubt true that the Governor is appointed by the President which means in effect and substance the Government of India, but that is only a mode of appointment and it does not make the Governor an employee or servant of the Government of India. So also it is not material that the Governor holds office during the pleasure of the President. It is a constitutional provision of the determination of the term of office of the Governor and it does not make the Government of India an employer of the Governor....This office is no subordinate or subservient to the Government of India. He is not amenable to the direction of the Government of India. His is an independent constitutional office which is not subject to the control of the Government of India. He is constitutionally the Head of the State..." A Head of the State cannot be removed from office arbitrarily and it was not the intention of the Constitution framers to leave him unprotected against arbitrary dismissal as in the case of Patwari, Tilak, T.N. Singh and a few others.

It is also of fundamental importance that healthy conventions may be evolved to guide the Governor in the exercise of his discretion in the undefined field. It is equally important that a healthy code of conduct should be prescribed to enable the Governor to independently discharge his responsibilities to the President under Articles 356 and 357 and other emergency provisions. Ashoka Sen suggested that a body of constitutional experts should be set up representing Parliament, the State Legislatures and also the Union Government and the State Governments which should be charged with the duty of drawing up a code of conduct guiding the President and the Governors in the exercise of their respective functions under the emergency provisions of the Constitution.[22] During the last forty-two years, excluding dissolution of nine State Assemblies in April 1977 and,once again of the same number in February 1980,the President had taken over the State Governments more than fifty-seven times. The longest spell of about five years in one go was in the State of Punjab and the Constitution had to be amended each time to meet the statutory

22. Sen, Ashoka, K., *Role of Governors in the emerging Pattern of Center-State Relations in India,* p. 71.

requirements.

Punjab was the first State to be brought under Central rule after the Constitution came into force. It was on June 20,1951, that the then Congress Chief Minister Dr. Gopi Chand Bhargava, got on the wrong side of the Congress High Command and was directed to resign. Dr. Rajendra Prasad did not like the way party considerations had weighed in decisions at the government level. The Constitution had been in vogue for a little over a year and President Prasad was keen to establish sound precedents in regard to Centre-State relations, particularly in the matter of taking over the State administration.

Bad precedents seldom die as bad habits and the first bad precedent became a trend-setter. The prophetic words of Dr. Rajendra Prasad are a commentary on "unedifying" manner in which the constitutional processes have been interrupted for nearly four score times and no State has escaped from its onslaught. There is an endless clamour now for deleting Article 356 if State autonomy in a federal polity is to be safeguarded.

The Draft Constitution contained an Instrument of Instructions for the Governors and the Constituent Assembly had adopted it as well as the provision dealing with it. But both were omitted subsequently. It was felt that the matter should be left to conventions rather than to put it in the body of the Constitution as a Schedule. Dharam Vira, who had been the Governor of Punjab, West Bangal and Mysore (Karnataka), expressed the opinion that in the present context when political loyalties were shifting fast and when multi-party Governments and Governments different politically from that operating at the Centre were functioning in the States, it would be desirable to define the powers of the Governor. This would obviate, he explained, to a great extent conflicting reaction by different Governors on identical circumstances. "There can, however, be no guideliness," he said, "which can cover all situations and in these circumstances a Governor will have in any case to exercise his own discretion and judgment."[23] Dharam Vira's proposal was that if a number of constitutional experts and jurists sit together and think over the problem, they might be able to work out in various circumstances under which it would be necessary to have greater clarity in regard to the functions and duties of a Governor.

President V.V.Giri appointed a committee of five Governors[24] on November 30,1970 to consider and formulate norms under the Constitution and also to look into the question of providing guidelines for the Governors to ensure uniformity of action in identical situations. The Committee submitted its report on November 26, 1971. The report,in the words of President Giri, represented the "pooled wisdom of all the Governors" and some of its conclusions "will become the subject-matter of public discussion and may be even controversy.[25]

## Governors' Committee

According to the official announcement the Governors'Committee was asked to study and report on the three issues mentioned by the President in his address to the conference of the Governors on November 20,1970, *viz.,* the appointment of the Council of Ministers, the summoning, prorogation and dissolution of the State Legislature, and the failure of the constitutional machinery in a State.

The Committee came to the conclusion that no guidelines could be provided and that, in each situation, the Governor concerned would have to take his own decision. But it suggested a system of pooling of information by a special wing in the President's Secretariat. Such an arrangement,the Committee said, aimed at putting the Governors in possession of authentic information regarding political and constitutional developments in the States from time to time. The proposed wing in the President's Secretariat, the Committee explained, would ascertain all the facts and circumstances relating to each situation which might arise from time to time requiring action by a Governor in the exercise of his powers and the reasons for the action taken by him in a particular situation. The facts as ascertained could then be confidentially communicated to all the other Governors with the permission of the President.

At the very outset the Committee categorically rejected the doctrine of the Governor being the President's agent. It emphatically held that the Governor, as Head of the State, "Has his functions as laid down in the Constitution itself

23. "Interview with Dharam Vira", *The Hindustan Times,* New Delhi,October 11, 1969.
24. Bhagwan Sahay (Jammu and Kashmir); B. Gopala Reddy (Uttar Pradesh); V. Vishwanathan (Kerala); Ali Yavar Jung (Maharashtra); and S.S. Dhawan (West Bengal).
25. Before submitting the report to the President, the Committee decided to circulate the draft report to all the Governors for eliciting their comments so that the final report should be prepared in the light of their views.

and is in no sense an agent of the President'', not even when the Government of a State had been taken over by the President under Article 356. ''The Governor does not'', the Committee observed, ''by virtue of anything contained in the Constitution, become an agent of the President.''

The Committee was opposed to Legislative action to cheek defections[26] and floor crossings for that ''would interfere with the right of dissent and would not permit genuine changes of conviction or dissatisfaction with the party and its leadership, for example, where promises or programmes remain unfulfilled.'' But the Committee would like the legislator who changed his party to seek re-election. ''This is different,'' the Committee said, ''from curbing the right of dissent or change and is in essence an extension of the exercise of responsibility which is at the root of our Constitution. ''Morally, too, in the opinion of the Committee,'' this would be the right course to adopt and may certainly restrict defections prompted only by reasons of self-interest or pursuit of power.''

With regard to the discretionary powers of a Governor, the Committee felt that these were not exhaustive. ''Even though'', the Committee observed, ''in normal conditions the exercise of the Governor's powers should be on the advice of the Council of Ministers occasions may arise when the Governor may find that, in order to be faithful to the Constitution and the law and his oath of office, he has to take a particular decision independently. It is however, realised that, in the scheme of our Constitution, such occasions will be extremely rare.'' Even in the sphere where the Governor is bound to act on the advice of his Council of Ministers, it does not mean, in the opinion of the Committee, immediate and automatic acceptance by him of such advice. In any relationship between the Governor and his Council of Ministers, it added, the process of mutual discussion was implicit, and the Governor "will not be committing any impropriety if he states all his objections to any proposed course of action and asks the Ministry to reconsider the matter. ''In the last resort, the Committee said,"he is bound to accept its final advice but the Governor has the duty to advise the Ministry as to what he considers to be the right course of action, to warn the Ministry whenever he thinks that it is taking wrong step, and to suggest to it to reconsider the proposed course of action.'' For the proper discharge of this duty, the Committee suggested, the Governor must have authentic information from his own Government and from the Union Government. The rules of transaction of business of the State should provide for such information to be supplied to the Governor and for the Union Government itself to keep the Governor duly informed.

As regards the appointment of the Chief Minister, the Committee thought, the leader of the largest single party in the Assembly (when no party had an absolute majority)has for that reason alone no absolute right to claim that he should be summoned to form the Government to the exclusion of others. The relevant test for a Governor ''is not the size of the party but its ability to command the support of the majority in the Legislature, It may be that a party, even though leading in relative strength in a Legislature, may not be able to obtain the support of other members.'' In contrast, the Committee explained, a numerically smaller party may command majority support with the help of other parties or groups. The Governor has, thus, first and essentially to satisfy himself that the person whom he invites to form the Government commands or is likely to command a majority support in the Legislature. It may even be that the leader of the party which is in a minority in the Legislature ''may also be invited to form a Government without that party necessarily entering into a combination with other parties provided that the Governor is satisfied that such a minority party leader will be able to command the support of other parties in the Assembly for its policies.''

If prior to a General Election,some parties combine on an agreed programme or an electoral understanding that if such a combination gets a majority they will form the Government and if such combination does secure the majority,the Governor may invite the commonly chosen leader of the combination to from the Government, be cause the electorate in returning such a combination in majority had already prior knowledge that it would be called upon to form the Government. The Governor in inviting such a leader,would be acting in accordance with the wishes of the electorate. Where no such arrangement existed among the parties prior to a General Election and a combination or a coalition comes

---

26. In pursuance of the Fifty-second Constitution Amendment Act, 1985, the Anti-defection Law was enacted and its validity was upheld by the Punjab and Haryana High Court in May, 1987. It has also been endorsed by the Supreme Court.

into existence after the elections with a view to forming the Government, various difficulties arise. In such a case, the Committee suggested, the leader of such a combination should also be elected by all the members of the parties or groups. This will avoid the necessity of the Governor checking up with different leaders or individuals as to their allegiance to the leader. Today,Governors often find themselves in the unenviable position of getting conflicting lists with names overlapping and having to send for individual members to ascertain their loyalty or allegiance to a particular group. This had been,the Committee remarked,one of the most distressing features of our political life in some of the States. If a convention was adopted, it was suggested, by which the leader of a coalition, like the leader of any political party, is chosen by election at a meeting of all the members of the different parties forming the coalition, the task of the Governor will be rendered easier.

The Committee is opposed to non-legislator or nominated members of the Legislature being chosen leaders and becoming Chief Ministers. It suggested, that if, in very exceptional circumstances, "a person who is not already elected is chosen as leader and is invited to be the Chief Minister,he must stand for election within the shortest possible time and, if not elected, should quit office forthwith." Inviting a non-member, the Committee strongly felt, is wrong,worse still is to nominate a person to the Legislature in order to make him a Chief Minister. Such a course, in the opinion of the Committee, "is contrary to the basic concept of parliamentary government."

Other Ministers are appointed on the advice of the Chief Minister, but there should be no "undue delay between the Chief Minister's acceptance of office and his tendering of advice to the Governor in regard to the appointment of the other Ministers," the Committee observed. There had been instances in which, on the formation of a new Government, the Chief Minister was sworn in and the appointment of other Ministers was kept pending. "This practice is clearly unconstitutional because Article 163 (1) speaks of the Council of Ministers, and the Chief Minister by himself without even a single other Minister, cannot be said to constitute a Council of Ministers."

As far as the Governor's pleasure is concerned the Committee was of the opinion that the test of confidence in the Ministry should normally be left to a vote in the Legislative Assembly. A Chief Minister's refusal to test his strength, when the Assembly is not in session, on the floor of the Assembly can well be interpreted as *prima facie* proof of his no longer enjoying the confidence of the Legislature. In such circumstances, the Governor" would be in duty bound to initiate steps to form an alternative Ministry." If that is not possible, he ought to report to the President,under Article 356, and recommend the dissolution of the Legislative Assembly.

But what happens if a coalition breaks up, and the Chief Minister demands the resignation of his colleagues with whom he is no longer in accord without submitting his own resignation? The Committee's answer was, "when the Chief Minister heads a single party Government, his pre-eminence is unquestioned, but in a coalition or a multi-party government, his pre-eminence is derived solely from agreement among the partners". Thus, the Chief Minister in a coalition cannot claim the right of advising the Governor in the appointment or dismissal of Ministers in such a manner as to break the arch and yet claim the right to continue as Chief Minister .Therefore,in the opinion of the Committee, the Chief Minister cannot break up the coalition by seeking to dismiss the Ministers representing the partnership, and yet claim to remain in office himself. On the other hand,the Committee held that if some Minister in a coalition "belonging to a particular party or group themselves resign due to disagreement with the Chief Minister or any other reason, the Chief Minister may not necessarily resign." If, however, his majority in the Assembly is threatened by such resignations, it would be expected of him to demonstrate his continuing strength in the Assembly by advising the Governor that the Assembly be summoned within the shortest possible time and obtaining its verdict in his favour.

The Committee made a fair discussion on the Governor's power of dissolution and his power, under Article 356, to report to the President a breakdown in the constitutional machinery of the State. On the point of dissolution the Committee was of the view that if a Chief Minister clearly lost his majority in the Assembly and faced a noconfidence motion or had yet to get the Budget adopted by the Assembly, the Governor should explore the possibility of forming an alternative Government and, failing that, act under Article 356. The Committee observed that "recourse to Article 356 should be the last resort for a Governor to seek.''

Briefly stated, the Governors' Committee has defined the role of the Governor in several ticklish situations. It clearly states that the Governor will be well within his right to dismiss a Chief Minister, if he is satisfied, that the Chief Minister has lost a majority in the Legislature and either refuses or is reluctant to test his strength on the floor of the House. The Committee also notes that the choice of the Chief Minister and imposition of the President's Rule under Article 356 are not the only two situations when the Governor has to act without consulting his Council of Ministers. Other occasions may arise where the Governor may find that to be faithful to the Constitution and the laws and his oath of office, he has to take his decision independently. The Bombay High Court and the Supreme Court upheld the decisions of the Maharashtra Governor, in ordering prosecution of A.R. Antulay, former Maharashtra Chief Minister, and ruled that the Governor was empowered to act independently and was not bound to seek the advice of the Council of Ministers.

The Committee has not wisely sought to lay down any rigid guidelines. Quite apart from the fact that it is hardly possible to provide for every contingency, such guidelines may be counter-productive in the sense that they may place the Governor in a strait jacket from which he may not be able to free himself even when circumstances so demanded. The Committee rightly remarks that ''the working of the Constitution during the past twenty-one years has exposed not so much weakness in the Constitution or its alleged misuse by Governors as weaknesses in the country's political life.'' Therefore, in the purposeful evolution of conventions in a Parliamentary system of Government the political parties, as much as the Govenors, have a primary responsibility. It is the existence of the multiple parties and the development of the ''SVD politics''-amorphous coalitions brought together by the lure of office rather than any clear political principles or programmes–that has thrown a labyrinth of problems.

The Committee's report, in the opinion of A.G.Noorani,''is a curate's egg. It is good in parts, inadequate in some and totally wrong in one major aspect. Still it is a notable contribution and one can hope that before long an all party committee will draw on it and provide a fairly definitive set of norms and conventions.''[27] The Prime Minister, Mrs. Indira Gandhi, had proposed at the Governors' Conference to consult the various political parties to help evolve a code for Governors to act under the Constitution. The proposal did not take a concrete shape.

To aid the Governors, the Committee suggested the setting up of a special wing in the President's Secretariat to collate and make available authentic information regarding political and constitutional developments in all the States from time to time. This is a valuable innovation of great practical utility to Governors for taking appropriate decisions and ensuring a certain uniformity of approach in establishing.sound conventions and precedents.

**Final Analysis**

The exact position and role of the Governor in the body politic of the country figured prominently in the deliberations of the Constituent Assembly. While none advocated that he should be an autocrat, it was widely felt that he should be invested with adequate powers to insure the maintenance of high standards of government. This view was upheld by Jawaharlal Nehru and Sardar Vallabhbhai Patel. In his Memorandum on the Principles of a Model Provincial Constitution prepared by the Constitutional Adviser, it was provided that there shall be a Council of Ministers to aid and advise the Governor in the exercise of his functions ''except in so far as he is by or under this constitution required to exercise his functions or any of them in his discretion.'' In a note appended thereto, the Constitutional Adviser observed that while for the most part the Governor would act on the advice of his Ministers, there were certain functions which even a responsible Head had to exercise in his discretion, namely, the choice of the Prime (Chief) Minister, the dissolution of the Legislature (in certain events), and so on.[28]

The Memorandum prepared by the Constitutional Adviser was discussed by the Provincial Constitution Committee, headed by Sardar Vallabhbhai Patel,and divergent views were expressed about the functions of the Government. The final proposals of the Committee were incorporated in its report:Memorandum on the Principles of a Model Provincial Constitution. The report envisages the conferment of ''special re-

27. ''Governor's Role in People's Raj'' *Indian Express*, New Delhi, January 16, 1972.
28. *The Framing of India's Constitution, Select Documents*, op. cit., Vol. II, pp. 657-63.

sponsibility"[29] on the Governor besides discretionary powers. Sardar Patel,who presented the report to the Constituent Assembly on July 15,1947, assured the members that vesting the Governor with discretionary powers would in fact be no invasion on the ministerial responsibility as it was not the intention of the Committee to confer on the Governor any special powers in a situation involving a grave menace to the peace and tranquillity of a Province."The Committee in settling this question", he explained, "intended to convey that the Governor shall have only the authority to report to the Union President about the grave situation arising in the Province (State) which would involve a great menace to the peace of the Province." As regards other discretionary powers, he asserted, that the power of summoning and dissolving the State Legislature "is normal which is given in every constitution to a Governor, and therefore there is nothing special about it."

As it emerged out of the Constituent Assembly the discretionary powers became exercisable not for certain purposes but in relation to certain specific functions. Adopting this plan, the Draft Constitution specified in various Articles spread over in different parts of the Draft certain matters in which the Governor would be required to act in his discretion.[30] This issue was considered by a Special Committee appointed for the purpose at its meeting held on April 11, 1948.It decided that in view of the change that the Governor should be nominated, instead of being elected, all references to exercise of functions by the Governor in his discretion should be omitted from the Draft Constitution. The proposal of the Special Committee was,however, not adopted and no amendment was suggested by the Drafting Committee to Article 143.

When Article 143 of the Draft Constitution was under consideration in the Constituent Assembly, H .V. Kamath moved an amendment seeking to delete all references to the exercise of discretionary powers by the Governor. But Ambedkar, contrary to his previous statement wherein he had categorically maintained that the Governor would always be required to act on ministerial advice, took a different stand this time. He maintained, "The retention in, or vesting the Governor with, certain discretionary powers is in no sense contrary to, or in no sense a negation of responsible government."[31] He externsively cited the examples of Canada and Australia and opposed Kamath's amendent. The Constituent Assembly supported Ambedkar and negatived the amendment.

The Constitution meant the Governor to act generally on ministerial advice but reserving to himself certain discretionary powers to be exercised by him untrammelled by ministerial advice. Ambedkar pointed out two types of duties a Governor was to perform. In the first type, he assigned him the duty to see "whether and when he should exercise his pleasure against the Ministry" that is, the Governor has to see that the Ministry continues to run the administration smoothly, efficiently and effectively. Secondly, it is the duty of a Governor to advise his Ministers,to warn them, to suggest an alternative and to ask the Government to reconsider the whole issue."[32]But the ultimate decision should be that of the Council of Ministers. He should resist the advice tendered to him,but he must not persist. The decisions are taken by the Council of Ministers and it is the duty of the Chief Minister to communicate to the Governor all such decisions and proposals for legislation (Article 167). As a channel of contact and communication, he retains to himself the old dual role of the Governor and must act independently of his Council of Ministers on all such matters on which he is constitutionally entitled to receive instructions from the President."The Governor" explained K.M. Munshi, " is the watchdog of constitutional propriety and the link which binds the State to the Centre thus securing the constitutional unity of India."[33]

The office of the Governor was never meant to be an ornamental sinecure. He is not required to be an inert cypher and his "character, calibre and experience must be of an order that enables him to discharge with skill and detach-

29. Namely, the prevention of any grave menace to the peace and tranquillity of the Province (State).
30. Appointment and dismissal of Ministers; summoning and dissolving of State Legislature; power to return to the Legislature for reconsideration of a Bill submitted to the Governor for his assent; issuing a proclamation of emergency suspending Ministers and assuming to himself executive functions of the State; appointment of the Chairman and members of the State Public by the Supreme Court.
31. *Constituent Assembly Debates,* Vol. VIII, pp. 489-502.
32. *Ibid.,* p. 546.
33. *Kulpati Letter No. 103 to Bharatiya Vidya Bhavan,* Bombay.

ment his dual responsibilities towards the Centre and towards the State executive of which he is the constitutional head.''[34] There is no substance in the assertion of Mrs. Vijaya Lakshmi Pandit,who resigned from the Governorship of Maharashtra,that the office of the Governor should be abolished. She felt that the only thing that could influence a person to accept Governorship was the salary that the office carried. She also expressed her dissatisfaction with everything that the Governor and the *Raj Bhavan* stand for. Sometimes the criticism has been even indecorus. A Chief Minister once described the Governors as ''nothing but expensive irritations.'' Commenting upon the observations of Mrs. Pandit, Sri Prakasa replied, ''It would indeed by a pity if any office is maintained in a democracy that serves no useful purpose and it will be a greater pity if the only thing that can induce any person to accept the office is its salary.''[35] Sri Prakasa held that "the only official emblem today of the unity of the country is the Governor."He had a feeling that "even the President is not so.''[36]

The question of the abolition of the office of the Governor does not arise.[37] Even if it is abolished the day-to-day duties pertaining to the office of the head of State, that is, the dignified functions,will have to be performed by some one. In the beginning things went smoothly and relations between Governors and Chief Ministers were happy and cordial. The relations between the Governors and the Union authorities too extended to the Governors the regard and consideration consistent with the dignity of their office. The people at large gave them the same respect and courtesy as in the past. But soon they were relegated to a position derogatory to their power and position. When the ''defeated Generals of a victorious army'' were raised to the position of authority and dignity as a consolation of their electoral and other discomfiture, it was small wonder that such men were least concerned with their duties and obligations and readily surrendered themselves to their benefactors in New Delhi, Sri Prakasa wrote that Jawaharlal Nehru "not only dealt with the Chief Ministers over the heads of the Governors,but in some cases, to my personal knowledge, he gave authority to non-officials particularly ladies to do things in the Raj Bhavans, which were the Governor's residence and over which he was supposed to have full authority–without as much as consulting or even informing the Governor.'' [38]Sri Prakasa takes another instance. He says, ''In the beginning the Central Ministers took the place of the old Executive Councillors of the Viceroy whose place in the warrant of precedence was below that of the Governors, The Prime Minister,however,decreed that the Governors,except in their own States,were lower than Central Cabinet Ministers.[39]

It is on record that many of the Chief Ministers even ignored the constitutional obligations under Article 167 to keep their Governors fully informed about the affairs of the State. Under the colour of "aid and advise",Chief Ministers arrogated to themselves the power to nominate Judges and Vice-Chancellors.[40] Complaints to Jawaharlal Nehru, on the occasion of the annual conference of the Governors and otherwise too,''about the high-handedness'' of the Chief Ministers yielded no results. Every time,wrote K.M. Munshi, ''the matter was mentioned at the Governors' conference, Jawaharlal Nehru laughed it out.''Thus, in anguish, perhaps, Munshi described his job as Governor ''to run a hotel and entertain guests.''[41] The obvious result was that the Chief Ministers were, if not encouraged

34. *Report of the Study Team of the Administrative Reforms Commission on Centre-State Relationship,* Chap. XVIII, p. 272.
35. Sri Prakasa, *State Governors in India,* pp. 63-64.
36. ''Governor's Lot Worsening : Reappraisal Overdue''. *The Tribune,* Chandigarh, April 7, 1960.
37. At a symposium on the ''Role and Position'' of the Governors, organised by the Indian Paliamentary Association, Ramamurty, Satish Chandra Aggarwal and Bal Krishan Menon, all Members of Parliament, urged the abolition of the office. Memoranda were also submitted to the Sarkaria Commission, reviewing the Centre-State Relations, suggesting that the office of the Governor should be abolished. The most articulate was the Telugu Desam Party headed by Andhra Chief Minister N.T. Rama Rao.
38. ''Governor's Lot Worsening : Reappraisal Overdue'', *The Tribune,* Chandigarh, April 17, 1969.
39. *Ibid.*
40. Girja Shankar Bajpai, when Governor of Bombay, insisted that in his capacity as the Chancellor of Poona University he was not bound to accept the advice of his Ministry in nominating the members of the Senate. His contention was upheld by the Attorney- General. In the newly established Universities, as in the Punjabi University, Patiala, and Guru Nanak Dev University, Amritsar, the Vice Chancellors are appointed by the Chancellors on the express advice of the State Government. Similarly, Fellows are nominated by the Chancellor on the advice of the Government. Despite the clear provisions of the Punjabi University, Patiala, Act, Dr. Chenna Reddy, as a Chancellor of the University, did not accept the State Government's recommendation for the appointment of the Vice-Chancellor.
41. As cited by Pavate, D.C., *My Days as Governor,* p. 9.

over, they were certainly allowed to keep in direct touch with the Central authorities on the heads of the Governors.

The whole purpose of the Governorship was, thus, nullified and the intention of the Constitution-makers that the Governor was to be a link between the Union Government and the States was defeated and the main actors in this drama were Nehru and the Chief Ministers themselves who were active participants in the various committees of the Constituent Assembly where provisions of the Constitution were actually hammered. But with the coming into power of non-Congress coalitions consisting of eight or nine units even fourteen, professing different ideologies and pursuing different objectives, after the General Election in 1967 in a good many States, and more especially what happened in Bengal, it dawned upon the Union Government and others to properly assess and appreciate the role of the Governor in a federal polity as in India, and the peculiar and diverse conditions obtaining in every State essentially influenced by the people and their behaviour as electors and their representatives. One of the former Union Ministers who had then become Governor of a State exhorted other Governors "to recover their constitutional status as the Centre and the States were no longer controlled by the same party. Dharam Vira, the Mysore (Karnataka) Governor, also said that it was the responsibility of the Governor to see that the Government of the State ''is run in accordance with the letter as well as with the spirit of the constitution. When political parties change on account of shifting loyalties it becomes very necessary that the Governor should be very vigilant in order to ensure that the government is run by a party or collection of parties which have the majority in their favour. He has to ensure that by taking shelter behind certain constitutional lacuna a minority government does not continue to function indefinitely. He has also to exercise considerable discretion at the time of the formation of a government. If there are multi-party groups coming together this discretion has to be exercised very carefully to ensure that the group or the party which wants to form the Government is really in a majority and can form a stable Government,''[42]

President V.V. Giri, in his concluding speech at the Governors' conference on November 21,1970, observed,"A Governor in spite of the difficult position in which he functions today and in spite of the fact that he may be liable to criticism, has to assert himself in upholding his constitutional duty.''[43] He added,''While it is always open to Governor to seek the views of others whenever important issues come before him, it must definitely be understood that the ultimate decision is always entirely of the Governor".The recommendations of the Governors' Committee assigned a specific and powerful role to the Governor. The Committee noted that the choice of the Chief Minister and imposition of President's rule are not the only two situations where the Governor has to act independently of his Council of Ministers. Other occasions arise where the Governor"may find that to be faithful to the Constitution and the law and his oath of office, he has to take a particular decision independently.''

For the functioning of the constitutional government in a State, the Governor provides the kingpin on which the entire machinery of the State must revolve. He summons the Legislature, prorogues and dissolves it. He chooses the Chief Minister and commissions him to form the Council of Ministers. Having installed the Government in office, he must continue to perform his legal,constitutional and conventional functions in order to enable the Government to be conducted properly and efficiently. It is his duty to see that the State Government functions in accordance with the Constitution and in conformity to the directions issued by the Union Government in pursuance of the provisions in Part XI, Part XVIII and other parts of the Constitution. In his capacity as a representative of the President,the Governor must diligently perform his dual role of sending a report to the President and if any serious emergency including the breakdown of the Constitution appeared and keep that report secret from his Council of Ministers. The Governor,thus,forms a stable link between the Union Government and the State Government and embodies in his office the machinery through which Government in a State may function in accordance with the Constitution.

In normal conditions, the Governor exercises his functions on the advice of his Council of Ministers. But consistent with the theory and practice of a responsible system of government,

42. ''Interview with Dharam Vira'', *The Hindustan Times*, October 11, 1969.
43. *The Sunday Tribune*, Chandigarh, November 22, 1970.

it does not mean immediate and automatic acceptance by him of such advice. In any relationship between the Governor and his Council of Ministers the process of mutual discussion is implicit and the Governor does not commit any impropriety if he states all his objections to any proposed course of action and asks the Council of Ministers to consider and even reconsider the matter, after obtaining any clarification he intends to seek. But in the last resort, he is bound to accept the Council of Ministers' final advice. In Bagehot's classical exposition of the role of the head of a State with a parliamentary system of government; the Governor has the duty to advise the Ministry as to what he considers the right course of action, to warn the Ministry whenever he thinks that it is taking a wrong step and to suggest to it to reconsider the proposed action in the light of his advice and warning.

Apart from being the symbol of the State, the Governor is the representative of the people. There should at least be one functionary in the State to whom all parties and interests can look up for disinterested advice, guidance and support. And no one can perform this function better than the Governor whose office, in some of its responsibilities, has been conceived and created for this purpose. Generally speaking, a Governor is an elderly person who has had experience of life in various spheres and departments of national activity; and ordinarily he is capable of giving advice. In India reverence to age is a part of her culture and, as such, the Governor can prove to be the best instrument of reconciling the differences between the Government and the Opposition on a good number of measures and thereby ensure political stability in the State. Kailash Nath Katju,who had been Governor of Bihar and Orissa States, succinctly said, ''Non-possession by you (Governors) of any political powers makes no difference at all. I think the Governor of a State under the Constitution can easily gain that respect and affection from the people under his care, if he himself leads a dedicated life.''[44] But it need be re-emphasised that if the Governor is to judiciously exercise his functions and duties, the President should appoint only those persons who are truly worthy of the office. Dharam Vira appropriately said that the ''time is past when the post of Governor was considered to be a sinecure for political pensioners,inconvenient politicians or aging civil servants. ''It is now obvious,'' he added, that a Governor "should be chosen with great care and should be people who in times of emergency, can deliver the goods.''[45]

But whatever care may be taken promoted politicians seldom forget their past prejudices,they often make political statements which are highly damaging to the office they hold. In the General Election of 1957 no party could secure majority in the Orissa State Assembly. The Jharkhand Party promised continuous support to the Congress Party and the Governor, Bhim Sain Sachar, called upon H.K. Mahatab to form the government. During the swearing in ceremony, the Governor was reported to have made a political speech. According to Surendranath Dwivedi, Chairman,Utkal Praja Socialist Party, the Governor had said that he would watch with ''personal interest'' the endeavours of the Chief Minister for securing a maximum of co-operation of others besides the present supporters.[46] The Governor of Orissa, Y.N. Sukhthenkar, in 1958, in his anxiety to keep the Congress Party in office kept the resignation of the Mahatab Ministry under consideration and subsequently allowed Dr. H.K. Mahatab to withdraw the resignation of his Ministry. The Governor had asked the leader of the Opposition to produce a list of members of the State Assembly who would support him. He, then,went to New Delhi to meet the President, the Prime Minister and the Home Minister to apprise them fully of and give them his views on the situation and, finally, on return from New Delhi rejected the claim of the leader of the Opposition that he commanded a majority on the ground that no names of his supporters had been supplied.[47] The ruling Legislative United Front Party in its meeting on May 21,1972 levelled serious charges against the Orissa Governor Joginder Singh. It was alleged that, among other things, the Governor had allowed Raj Bhavan to be used as a "centre of intrigue"against the coalition Government.[48] B.N.Joshi, General Secretary of the Rajasthan Congress Committee, criticised what he described as ''partisan statement'' made by the Governor, Raghukul Tilak, soon after he assumed office on May 12,1977. At a Press Con-

44. *The Tribune,* Chandigarh, October 22, 1971.
45. *The Illustrated Weekly of India,* Bombay, June 4, 1972.
46. *The Hindustan Times,* New Delhi, April 16, 1957.
47. *The Hindustan Times of India, New Delhi,* May 25, 1958.
48. *The Times of India,* Bombay, May 27, 1972.

ference he is reported to have said that he hoped the Janata Party would be able to overcome its problems of adjustment and that it would be a misfortune if the party broke up.[49] Referring to his appointment, Tilak said,he was to assume office on April 6, 1977, but he wanted time to consider whether he could serve the people by working for the (Janata) Party or as Governor.[50] The Governor also blamed civil servants for the "art of sycophancy"that some of them had developed in the past thirty years, of course his reference was to the Congress regime. When active politicians are elevated to this high office they make a mess of their position. The Uttar Pradesh Governor, C.P.N. Singh, who had been recalled after years of retirement,declared at a Press conference on May 18,1980 that he would not allow any"irresponsible combination of political groups" to form a Ministry in Uttar Pradesh in case no single party secured absolute majority in the ensuing Assembly elections. At the same time, he made it clear that he would try to ensure a stable Ministry through a "permutation of political parties which could form such a government.''[51] There was a sharp reaction to the Governor's statement which the Opposition leaders described as "threat to the Opposition parties and indirect support to the Congress (I).[52]

To sum up, in theory, politics and office of the Governor of a State ought to be far apart. And yet the country has seen Governors playing politics with impunity. Ram Lal while in the Hyderabad Raj Bhavan being a classic example as also Jagmohan in Srinagar during his first tenure.[53] In their case,however,it was a game of politics at the behest of others. That saw a major indignant ground swell against the Congress (I) in both the States, Andhra Pradesh and Jammu and Kashmir. There are others who have been occupying Raj Bhavans and playing politics locally or back in their own perishes. Of late, one who made and played politics with least concern for propriety was the Rajasthan Governor Vasantrao Patil. He came down from Jaipur, and camping in his son's house in Bombay, demanded that the Maharashtra Chief Minister S.B.Chavan be dismissed. Patil had proclaimed to newsmen in Bombay that he did not see any incompatability between the position of a Governor and his recent role in Maharashtra.''I am a Congress (I) man first,and Governor next,'' was his rationale.

Two results emerge from this analysis and both are closely interconnected. The integrity of State politics is vital for the political health of the country and a major corrective effort is necessary to remove the distortions that have overcome an office of great constitutional importance–the office of the Governor. During the past more than thirty years the office of the Governor has been misused and generally the Governors had been made handmaids not only of the Union Government,but also of the ruling party at the Centre as well. Not only the prestige of the office suffered a serious decline but politics in the States became yet more unstable and unprincipled. The conventions of the parliamentary system of government are much the same for the President as they are for the Governor and so, substantially, are constitutional provisions in so far as they deal with their position as head of a State in parliamentary democracy. Importantly, there is another aspect of the Governor's position and it is the federal aspect. His position is a dual one. He is appointed by the President on the advice of the Union Government and holds office at his pleasure. At the same time, he is the constitutional Head of a member-State of the federal Union–the eyes and ears or confidant of the Union Government and the conscience keeper of the State's Chief Minister at one and the same time.

It was abundantly made clear in the Constituent Assembly, particularly by T.T.Krishnamachari, that the Governor ''who is to be nominated by the President,to be in any sense an agent of the Central Government.'' He emphasised this point and made it unambiguously clear ''because such an idea finds no place in the scheme of Government we envisage for the future. ''This has since been confirmed by the Report of the Committee of Governors (1971). The Committee emphatically held that the Governor as Head of the State has his functions as laid down in the Constitution itself and is in no sense an agent of the President, not even when the Government of a State has been taken over by the President under Article 356. But numerous instances are there that prove that most of the Governors have all these years, especially since

49. *The Times of India*, New Delhi, May 15, 1977.
50. *The Statesman*, New Delhi, May 14, 1977.
51. *The Times of India*, New Delhi, May 19, 1980.
52. *The Statesman*, New Delhi, May 20, 1980.
53. Jagmohan dismissed Dr. Farooq Abdullah and appointed G.M. Shah, who publicly declared in October 1987, that he was a ''Pakistani,'' Chief Minister with a bunch of defectors from Farooq Abdullah's National Conference Party.

1969,been used as agents of the Centre and they had very often been used against non-Congress Governments in the States. Even Charan Singh tried to use this device in dismissing the non-Congress Ministries in the nine Northern States in 1977.

It is also hard to believe that the Constitution framers had even in mind to place the constitutional Head of the State in so delicate a position and leave him unprotected against arbitrary dismissal by the Centre as was done in the case of Prabhudas Patwari, Ragukul Tilak and T.N. Singh, who was "advised" to resign. Arbitrary dismissal really makes a mockery of federalism as the Governor is the Head of a member-State. Federalism is based on equality of status and co-ordinate powers bet- ween the two sets of government.

It is,therefore, necessary to correct the present imbalance in regard to the Governor's office by giving him greater independence *vis-a-vis* the Centre. And the crux of the problem is that there is something fundamentally wrong with the procedure of appointment of Governors. In view of the statement made by Giani Zail Singh, the then Home Minister, in March 1980, that it is "proper for all political appointees including Governors to resign immediately after a change of government at the Centre; at least democratic traditions demand it, it is significantly necessary that the Governor's appointment should not be left to the caprice of the Union Home Ministry. Nor should it be left to the predilections of the State Chief Minister. In the Lal Bahadur Shastri Memorial Lectures at Poona University on "Conflict between the Centre and States", K. Subba Rao, former Chief Justice of India, suggested that the Governors "should be appointed by the President in consultation with Ministers but on the advice of a high-powered body...and he should be removable only on basis of a verdict of misconduct pronounced by the Supreme Court. A Governor so removed should not be eligible for any Central, State Government position." It is a bit cumbrous and seems radical reform. Nath Pai, a member of Parliament, suggested that the appointment of a Governor should be subject to the ratification by Parliament. The proposal merited serious consideration, but the Government was in no mood to accept it. An innocuous proposal is to give the Governor a fixed term in office and make him removable only for proven misconduct. This simple reform alone will make the Governor far more independent than he is today. It will also enable him to be more candid in his dealings with the Chief Minister and pointing out the lapses in the State administration.

## THE COUNCIL OF MINISTERS

### The Council of Ministers

The Constitution provides that there shall be a Council of Ministers with the Chief Minister at the head to aid and advise the Governor in the exercise of his functions except in so far as he is by or under the Constitution required to act in his discretion. The Governor appoints the Chief Minister and other Ministers are appointed by the Governor on the advice of the Chief Minister.[54] While the Council of Ministers is collectively responsible to the Legislative Assembly of the State, Ministers hold office during the pleasure of the Governor. There is no provision in the Constitution for individual responsibility of the Ministers to the Legislative Assembly. Individual responsibility is covered by the provision that Ministers hold office during the pleasure of the Governor and the pleasure of the Governor really means the pleasure of the Chief Minister. When a Minister does not agree with the policy of the Council of Ministers, or he does anything else which compromises the solidarity and stability of the Government, constitutional propriety as well as a duty demand that he should immediately resign when a hint is given by the Chief Minister. If he does not resign, then, it is the right of the Chief Minister to advise the Governor for his dismissal. Ambedkar emphasised this point in the Constituent Assembly.

Joint responsibility is the first necessity of a responsible government and the most essential fact for a successful democratic administration. The Ministry is one and indivisible and its solidarity demands a "common front" both within and outside the Legislature. A Minister differing from the policy determined by the Cabinet must resign from the Government. If he does not resign, then, the decision of the Cabinet is as much his decision as that of his colleagues even if he

54. Governor Pavate wrote, "The usual procedure is that a Chief Minister considers certain persons for appointment as Ministers and advises the Governor to appoint them. The Governor considers the names carefully before doing so." Without disclosing the name, Prakash Singh Badal expressed a desire to the Governor to expand his Council of Ministers by including a Jana Sangh member of the Assembly who was reported to have agreed to defect if he was sworn in as a Minister immediately. The Governor refused to make the appointment under the circumstances. Pavate, D.C., *My Days As Governor*, p. 162.

protested against it in the Cabinet. It means that the Minister cannot rebut the criticism of his opponents on the plea that he did not agree to the decision when the matter was being discussed in the Cabinet. And for that matter, all Cabinet secrets must be most scrupulously guarded. This strict discipline in the responsible system of government rigidly insists if mature, rational and independent contribution to the policy-making is desired from men who are engaged in a common cause and who come together for the purpose of reaching an agreement. "It is, however, not unusual in our country," said K.M. Munshi, "to find a differing Minister's views appearing in the daily papers on the morning after a Cabinet meeting."[55]In the states differences among the Ministers and among some Ministers and the Chief Minister are more frequent and pronounced than at the Centre. Factions among state parliamentary parties have been a rule rather than an exception. Intrigues against other colleagues and the Chief Minister have followed factious struggle. In almost all the states these have been furthered by the rift between the head of the political party in the state and the Chief Minister. When Ministers contradict each other, cracks appear in the government fabric which are injurious and possibly fatal to good government. When intrigues and factious struggle amongst the Ministers enter the body politic that is the end of responsible government and this is the hard lesson Indians have learnt by years of experience.[56]

The number of the Ministers is not fixed. It is for the Chief Minister to determine the size of the Council of Ministers and he does so as the requirements of the occasion may demand. The only constitutional requirement is that in the states of Bihar, Madhya Pradesh, and Orissa the Council of Ministers must have a Minister in charge of Tribal Welfare and the same Minister may also be entrusted with the welfare of the Scheduled Castes and Backward Classes in the state.

It has often been complained that the Councils of Ministers in the states are unduly large and it heavily burdens their exchequers. Prior to 1962, this criticism was untenable. Their number was nowhere larger than the actual needs of a good and efficient administration. The necessities of a Welfare State incredibly expand the functions of Government and correspondingly the number of the Departments of the government. Responsible government demands that all Departments must be presided over by a political chief to see the proper implementation of policy and be answerable to the Legislature for its work. But not in the manner which Coalition Governments, after1967 General Election, had done in a good number of the states. In a new and small state like Haryana, for instance, more or less every legislator was an aspirant for ministership and he defected from his parent party to be sworn on the same day. In fact, ministership was a bait to defect and crossing of floor had become a normal feature of the political life of the state raising the total number of the Council of Ministers to a staggering figure of 34 of a total State Assembly membership of 81. Lachhaman Singh Gill's minority Government in Punjab consisted of seven Cabinet Ministers,three Ministers of State and three Deputy Ministes. Three more Ministers were added after about a week of its existence, making a total of sixteen Ministers out of a total 19 MLAs forming the Janata Front. The Janata Party had issued a directive that the strength of the Ministry should not exceed ten per cent of the total membership of the State Assembly. But in almost all the states where the Janata Party formed Governments in North India the norm was violated and with the connivance of the Central Parliamentary Party Sheikh Mohammed Abdullah began with seven-member Ministry on July 9,1977 and within four days increased the number to twenty-three, the largest in the state history. The total number of members of the National Conference in the Assembly was 47. But Andhra Pradesh established a record when Anjiah constituted a 61-member Council of Ministers. There were loud protests and on the intervention of Congress (I) President the number was reduced to 45 early in February

55. *Kulpati's Letter* No. 103 to *Bharatiya Vidya Bhavan*, Bombay, *op. citd.*
56. One of the Ministers of State, Tarlochan Singh Ryasti, in the Badal Ministry in Punjab, while analysing the reasons for reverses of the Akali Dal in the 1972 mid-term Parliamentary poll, in a pamphlet issued by him, openly demanded an inquiry into the allegations of corruption against his colleagues in the Council of Ministers and also demanded a reduction in the size of the Ministry which was too big for a small State like Punjab. D. C. Pavate, who was then Governor, said that the Badal Ministry consisted of 27 members out of a total strength of 58 Akali legislators and sharp differences arose among them on the distribution of portfolios. Discontentment among a few more Akali legislators spread who were not included in the Ministry. "An impression had been created that a number of Akali MLAs would leave the Akali Dal and form a coalition government with the Congress (R) or form a government with the support of Congress." Pavate D.C., *My Days As Governor*, p.189.

1981. Bihar at present takes the lead and Haryana is a close second. Prime Minister P.V. Narsimha Rao expressed himself against "oversized" Cabinets both at the Centre and in states and multiplicity of Corporations to accommodate a large number of persons.[57] But Kerala Chief Minister, K. Karunakaran, ruled out cuts in his Ministry. He felt that it was unworkable in Kerala which has multiparty government.[58] A similar view was expressed by the Bihar Chief Minister.

The Constitution nowhere mentiones the word Cabinet. It provides for a Council of Ministers both at the Centre and in states. The Cabinet was an extra-constitutional growth at both the levels. The Councils of Ministers formed at the Centre since 1950, made a definite distinction between "Ministers of Cabinet" and "Ministers of State". No such distinction was made in the states until after the 1962 General Election. Now this categorisation of Ministers of different status is complete in all states. Even Deputy Chief Ministers have been appointed in some of the states. Uttar Pradesh had two in 1979 just as there were two in the Union Government. But it is the Cabinet Ministers alone who meet in a body, deliberate and formulate policy and constitute a Cabinet. The Cabinet Ministers preside over the different Departments of Government and see that the policy collectively determined by the Cabinet is properly implemented. If a Minister of State holds an independent charge of a Department, he attends the meetings of the Cabinet and participates in its deliberations when problems relating to his Department are under discussion. Deputy Ministers and Parliamentary Secretaries have no berth in the Cabinet. Their task is to assist the Ministers, to whom they are attached, in their administrative and Parliamentary duties. The Parliamentary Secretaries are neither Ministers nor do they exercise any powers. They are assigned duties as the Minister in charge of the Department to which they are attached may consider necessary. But all of them, who make the Council of Ministers are members of the State Legislature, and if they were not at the time of their appointment they must get themselves elected within a period of six months,belong to the majority party or a combination of parties commanding a majority or support of the majority of members, and are collectively responsible to it.

57. *The Hindustan Times*, New Delhi, January 19, 1972.
58. *The Times of India*, New Delhi, January 20, 1972.

**Dismissal of Ministry**

Dismissal of Ministry by the Head of the state is not an accepted axiom of parliamentary system of government under normal conditions. But if the Governor is convinced that the Ministry was indulging in political manoeuvring to keep itself in office, and, consequently, jeopardising the interests of the state, or that it was engaged in activities which were likely to endanger national security or unity, he can in his discretion dismiss such a Ministry. B.R. Ambedkar's clarification on this issue to the Constituent Assembly left no room for controversy. Speaking on June 2,1949, he told the Assembly Members, "My submission is that although the Governor has no function still, even the constitutional Governor, that he is, has certain duties to perform. His duties, according to me, may be classified in two parts. One is, that he has to retain the Ministry in office. Because the Ministry is to hold office during his pleasure, he has to see whether and when he should exercise his pleasure against the Ministry..."

After careful consideration of the constitutional position, the Kerala Enquiry Committee of the Indian Commission of Jurists, consisting of N.H. Bhagwati, M.P.Amin, former Advocate-General of Bombay, and N.K. Nambiar, a constitutional lawyer, opined, "Where, therefore, the Governor is satisfied that the Ministerial orders are in violation of the law, it is not only his right, but his duty as guardian of the Constitution, which he has sworn to preserve, protect and defend, to correct and rectify, and, in the last resort, to dismiss the Ministry, if recalcitrant. A Governor who fails in his duty, must be deemed to be privy to the violation of the law; and his position will become wholly untenable. It may be that on the dismissal of Ministry, the Governor might be unable to find an alternative Ministry commanding a majority in the Legislature. But, in that event, he has the right to order a dissolution of the Legislative Assembly and direct fresh elections."

The opinion expressed on November 11,1967 by a spokesman on behalf of the Union Government was that when in his judgment, the Governor is duly satisfied that the Chief Minister no longer commands support of the majority of Assembly members, he would be justified in the exercise of his discretionary functions to dismiss the Council of Ministers. In such a case, there can be no question of his acting on the advice of his Council of Ministers. This action, he elaborated, can be taken on the basis of any material or information available to him, even, if such material or information might be extraneous to the proceedings of the Legislative Assembly. The Home Minister asserted in the Council of States (Rajya Sabha) that the discretion of a Governor was not justiciable.[59] The Union Law Minister endorsed in the House of the People (Lok Sabha) the opinion expressed on behalf of the Home Ministry and opined that in dismissing the Ajoy Kumar Mukherjee Ministry in West Bengal, the Governor had acted "in the interest of the country and the Constitution."[60]

The Presiding Officers of the Legislative bodies of India, assembled in a conference on April 6-7, 1968 at New Delhi, adopted a resolution recommending to the Government of India to take urgent and suitable steps to evolve conventions in regard to the powers of the Governors to summon or prorogue the Legislatures and dismiss Ministers. By implication the resolution had disapproved of the action of West Bengal Governor in assuming to himself the power to judge the support of the Ministry. The resolution stated that the question whether a Chief Minister has lost the confidence of the Assembly shall at all time be decided into the Assembly.[61] The resolution of the Conference of the Presiding Officers runs contrary to the stand taken by the Home Ministry and the Law Minister himself that a Chief Minister holds office at the pleasure of the Governor. The Punjab Governor D.C. Pavate wrote to Chief Minister Gurnam Singh, who had earlier been defeated on the floor of the Assembly, asking him to resign at once otherwise "I would be required to dismiss him."[62]

But the constitutional competence of a Governor's action in dismissing an elected government is not open to question today. Both the West Bengal High Court and, later, the Supreme Court-which dealt with similar questions arising from the Governor-Speaker controversy in Punjab-clearly upheld the Governor's action in two situations as constitutionally competent. In *The State of Punjab* vs. *Baldev Prakash and Satpal Dang* the Supreme Court held that the Governor's powers being untrammelled by the Constitution and an emergency having arisen the action (of the Governor) was 'perfectly understandable" and consequently. the resummoning of the Legislature by the Governor was a step in the right direction. The Court upheld the constitutional validity of the two Appropriation Acts of the Punjab which the Punjab and Haryana High Court had earlier struck down. In another case of the Probationers in the Punjab Judicial Service, Justice Bhagwati and Iyer held. "In all his (Governor's) constitutional functions, it is the Ministers who act. Only in the narrow area specifically marked out for discretionary exercise by the Constitution, he (Governor) is untrammelled by the State Minister's acts and advice. Of course, a limited free-wheeling is available regarding choice of the Chief Minister and the dismissal of the ministry as in the English practice adapted to Indian constitution."

**Chief Minister**

The practices of the parliamentary system of Government and those that govern the office of the Prime Minister in Britain have been followed to a considerable extent in the working of the Union Government in India and the position of the Indian Prime Minister,like his counterpart in the 10 Downing Street,is unchallengeable which no other colleague of his can rival. But the Chief Ministesr in majority of the States do not enjoy that unique position of exceptional and peculiar authority. Members of the majority parties in the State Legislatures and Ministers themselves have not exhibited sufficient discipline of solidarity and team work. Personal differences, intra-party conflicts, clamour for offices, favouritism and even casteism, regionalism and communalism are so prominently in operation that the career of a Ministry is always in jeopardy. So long as one single party reigned supreme in nearly all the States major splits between the groups within the party were avoided by the stern hand of the Congress Parliamentary Board. But after the 1967 General Election,when the stronghold of the Congress loosened,the splits hitherto curbed violently reappeared. In fact,there was an open revolt. Even ambitious veterans either left the Congress or joined hands with other groups with whom they had nothing in common except the desire to oust the Congress from power. The situation did not appreciably improve when the

59. As reported in *Indian Express,* New Delhi, November 21, 1967.
60. Speech in the House of the People, December 4, 1967, *The Times of India,* New Delhi December 5, 1967.
61. As reported in the *Statesman,* New Delhi, April 8, 1968.
62. Pavate, D.C. *My Days As Governor,* p. 131.

Janata Party came into power in 1977. In the States of Bihar,Madhya Pradesh and Uttar Pradesh, and Haryana there was an open revolt on the selection of party leaders in the State Assemblies and even the Central leadership was accused of partisanship and favouritism and in most of the cases it was true.

One of the main factors responsible for the disintegration of the Congress was the mighty hand of the Central Parliamentary Board which always dictated and imposed its decisions on the State Legislature Party. The Board seldom allowed the Party to elect its leader to become a Chief Minister and select his colleagues in the Council of Ministers. The Chief Ministers were very often directed in the replacement of Ministers and even the Chief Ministers themselves. For instance, Bhim Sain Sachar in the Punjab was replaced by Pratap Singh Kairon. Ram Kishen was not the State Legislature Party's choice and he himself proclaimed *ad nauseam* that he was the "driver" of the High Command. The practices established by the Congress neither helped to uphold the authority of the Chief Minister nor sustained collective responsibility. In reality it helped to aggravate group manipulation and created conditions of schism in the Council of Ministers thereby utterly damaging the authority and prestige of the office of the Chief Minister. A party must freely elect its own leader and the leader should be free in shaping his Government according to his own views of what is likely to work best. A leader imposed from above cannot command the spontaneous esteem and unequivocal loyalty of his colleagues,and his colleagues in the Council of Ministers should be only those persons who owe to their chief personal loyalty as well as party allegiance; the *sine qua non* of team work. An imposed leader from above meets the fate of Kedar Pandey and Abdul Ghafoor in Bihar, Ghanshyam Oza and Chimanbhai Patel in Gujarat. H.N. Bahuguna in Uttar Pradesh, S.B.Chavan in Maharashtra and scores of others like them.

It has now become almost a principle that the Chief Minister will be a nominee of the High Command which in terms of Congress (I) meant its President, Mrs. Gandhi and Rajiv Gandhi.The State legislators are never allowed to make their choice by a free and secret ballot. Either one is selected or some sort of nebulous consensus is sought to be brought about at New Delhi. After 1980 elections to the State Assemblies it was found that none of the members of the majority party in most of the States could command sufficient support to hold the office of the Chief Minister and, consequently, persons elected to Parliament were sent to the States to pilot their Governments. This happened in Rajasthan, Uttar Pradesh,Orissa, Maharashtra and subsequently in Andhra Pradesh. And the test of selection was personal loyalty to Mrs. Gandhi, which was really unfortunate as it seriously undermined the dignity of the office of the Chief Minister. But the Congress(I) Party had to pay price for this indiscreet policy in the January 1983 Assembly elections in the States of Andhra Pradesh and Karnataka. The Congress(I) Party since then has retreated from this practice and the State Legislature Party elects its own leader. But the factionridden Congress (I) has not a consensus candidate with-the result that the Central Parliamentary Board appoints its observers, who carry the mind of the Congress President who is also the Prime Minister, to sort out the differences and reach consensus. This is, in fact, a veiled imposition of a leader as one will not like to go on the wrong side of the Party President and lose the grace of the Prime Minister.

There is another tendency that has prominently emerged as a result of Centre's tightened control. In spite of the talk of decentralization of power,there has been an increasing tendency to concentrate power and decision-making. After Independence the States were headed by stalwarts like B.G.Kher, B.C.Roy, K.Kamaraj, G.B.Pant who were held in high esteem by the Prime Minister. Instead of their having to run to New Delhi for seeking advice and approval,they only came when invited for consultation on any key national and international issues. Jawaharlal Nehru respected the federal principle and he allowed the States freewheeling within their own area of jurisdiction. Latterly,this quality of the Constitution has been diluted in various overt and covert ways. The Chief Ministers retain their camp offices at the State Capitals and they rush to New Delhi for advice and consultation on trivial matters. All Congress (I) Chief Ministers have done well to note, that regional satraps who try to survive without the Party President cum Prime Minister's blessings will speedily be cut down to size.

**Duties of the Chief Minister**

The Constitution prescribes that it shall be the duty of the Chief Minister:

(a) to communicate to the Governor all decisions of the Council of Ministers relating to the administration of the affairs of the State and proposals for legislation;

(b) to furnish such information relating to the administration of the affairs of the State and proposals for legislation as the Governor may call for; and

(c) if the Governor so requires to submit for the consideration of the Council of Ministers any matters on which decision has been taken by a Minister but which has not been considered by the Council.

But once the matter so referred is approved by the Council of Ministers it becomes binding on the Governor. The Constitution nowhere empowers the Governor to re-open any decision already taken by the Council of Ministers. It is only the decision of an individual Minister that can be referred to the Consideration of the Council of Ministers. It has been asserted that the provision empowering the Governor to direct the Chief Minister to submit for the consideration of the Council of Ministers any matter on which decision has been taken by a Minister is not in accord with the principle of collective responsibility. But it is not exactly so. So long as one single Party commands a clear majority in the State Legislature and the Council of Ministers is a homogeneous team, the possibility of a Minister taking a decision on any matter of policy independently of the Council of Minister or taking an important matter upon which there is no Cabinet decision or his acting contrary to the decision already taken by the Cabinet, is very rare. But when it is a coalition government, in which many groups combine without having any common basis of policy, such an eventuality may arise, as it did happen in Uttar Pradesh,Madhya Pradesh and West Bangal, when Ministers took action on matters upon which there were no Cabinet decisions and even made declaration of policies which happened to be contrary to the decisions of the Cabinet itself. It is only here that the intervention of the Governor is needed to safeguard the principle of collective responsibility enshrined in the Constitution,that is,to direct the Chief Minister to submit for the consideration of the Council of Ministers any matter on which decision has been taken by a Minister. Dealing with this aspect, K.M. Munshi said in the Constituent Assembly, "there is no harm,but there is great advantage if the Governor exercises his influence over his Cabinet. As I have said we have single parties in the provinces now but a time might come when there will be many parties, when the Premier (Chief Minister) might fail to bring about compromise between the parties and harmonious policies during a crisis. At that time the value of the Governor would be immense and from this point of view I submit, that the powers that are given here are legitimate powers given to a constitutional Head and they are essential for working out a smooth democracy and they will be most beneficial to the Ministers themselves because then they will be able to get confidential information and advice from a person who has completely identified himself with them and get accessible to other parties."[63]

## SUGGESTED READINGS

Bettelheim, Charles, *India Independent.*

*Constituent Assembly Debates.*

Alexandrivicz, C.H. *Constitutional Developments in India.*

Granville Austin, *The Indian Constitution – A Conrnerstone of a Nation.*

Ivor Jennings, *Some Characteristics of the Indian Constitution.*

Mornis Jones –*Indian Constitution, Government and Politics of India.*

Shukla, V.N., Constitution of India.

63. *Constituent Assembly Debates*, Vol. VII, p. 130.

# CHAPTER XIV

# The State Legislature

### The State Legislature

The Legislature of a State consists of the Governor and one House or, as the case may be,two Houses. Bihar, Jammu and Kashmir, Karnataka, Maharashtra and Uttar Pradesh have two Houses whereas the remaining twenty States are unicameral.''[1] Parliament can, by law, provide for the abolition of an existing Legislative Council or for the initial creation of Council if the proposal is supported by a resolution of the Legislative Assembly (Vidhan Sabha) passed by a majority of the total membership and by two-thirds majority of those present and voting. The procedure regarding the creation or abolition of a Legislative Council (Vidhan Parishad) is similar to the one provided in the Government of India Act,1935. Ambedkar,while explaining the reasons for adopting this procedure, said in the Constituent Assembly ''The provision of this Article follows very closely the provision contained in the Government of India Act,1935, Section 60 for the creation of the Legislative Council and Section 308 which provides for the abolition. The procedure adopted here for the creation and abolition is that the matter is really left with the Lower Chamber, which by a resolution may recommend either of the two courses that it may decide upon. In order to facilitate any change made either in the abolition of the Second Chamber or in the creation of a Second Chamber provision is made that such a law shall not be deemed to be an amendment of the Constitution, in order to obviate the difficult procedure which has been provided in the Draft Constitution for the amendment of the Constitution.''[2]

### Bicameral Legislature

The Memorandum on the Principles of a Model Provincial Constitution circulated on May 30,1947,by the Constitutional Adviser provided for a single chamber, called the Legislative Assembly. The Note added to the Memorandum pointed out that under the Government of India Act, 1935,the Provinces of Assam, West Bengal, Bihar, Bombay, Madras and the United Provinces had bicameral legislatures and whether any State was to have a bicameral legislature or not would probably have to be left to decision of the representatives of that State in the Constituent Assembly. In case any State decided to have two chambers,the second chamber would be called the Legislative Council.

The Provincial Constitution Committee decided that as a general rule,there should be only a single chamber legislature in all the States. But the Committee agreed that two chamber legislatures might be constituted in States where special circumstances existed. In a Note added to the Report, the Committee proposed that the members representing the different States in the Constituent Assembly should meet separately and come to a final decision whether to have a second chamber for their State or not. A Sub-Committee consisting of B.G. Kher, Pattabhi Sitaramayya, P. Subbarayan and Kailash Nath Katju was constituted to determine the composition and mode of representation of members of the Legislative Council in case a State decided to have a second chamber. The Sub-Committee recommended that the membership of the second chamber, if decided to have one, should not be more than a quarter of the total membership of the Legislative Assembly, and that there should be,within certain limits,functional representation on the lines of the Constitution of Ireland. It was, accordingly, recommended that the composition of the Legislative Council should be one-half to be elected on functional representation on the Irish pattern; one-third to be elected by the Legislative Assembly of the State through the method of proportional representation, and one-sixth to be nomi-

1. Although the Constitution (Seventh Amendment) Act, 1956, provides for the creation of a Legislative Council in Madhya Pradesh, it had not yet been constituted. But it is included in Article 168 which states that the Legislature in Madhya Pradesh shall consist of the Governor and two Houses.
2. *Constituent Assembly Debates,* Vol. IV, p. 14.

nated by the Governor on the advice of his Ministers.

These proposals of the Sub-Committee were accepted by the Provincial Constitution Committee. The Constituent Assembly discussed the recommendations on July 18 and 21, 1947 and were adopted with some amendments. The Constitution, thus, provides a divergent practice of bicameral legislatures in the States. It also provides for the abolition of the Council in a State which has one, or for its creation in the State without one. But it does not involve amendment of the Constitution. The procedure, provided in Article 169, prescribes: on a resolution passed by a majority of the total membership of the Legislative Assembly and by two-thirds majority of the members present and voting either for the creation or abolition of a Legislative Council, Parliament enacts a law in deference to such a resolution.

Legislative Council had a chequered career in the States where they were established. Originally, Bihar, Bombay, Madras, Punjab, Uttar Pradesh and West Bengal in Part A States and Mysore among Part B States had bicameral Legislatures. Of the fourteen reorganised States in 1956 ten werc to have bicameral Legislatures : Andhra Pradesh, Bihar, Bombay, Madhya Pradesh, Madras, Mysore, Punjab, Uttar Pradesh, West Bengal and Jammu and Kasmir. With the creation of Maharashtra and Gujarat States in 1960, Gujarat opted for a single chamber and so did Haryana on the division of Punjab in 1966. In Punjab and West Bengal the Legislative Councils were abolished in 1969. The Uttar Pradesh Assembly also voted for the abolition of the Council on April 29,1970. But on May 4, just after three days, Speaker A.G. Kher confirmed in the State Assembly that a formal resolution urging revocation of the abolition of the Council had been received by him and Uttar Pradesh bicameral legislature continued. In Bihar the Assembly passed in its 1970 Budget Session a resolution recommending the abolition of the Council. But in December the Assembly adopted by 186 to 55 votes, a non-official resolution seeking postponement of the abolition Bill till May 1974. No action has since been taken and Bihar too continues with a second chamber. Andhra Pradesh Legislative Assembly, immediately after Telugu Desam assumed office in January 1983, passed with overwhelming majority a resolution to abolish the Legislative Council. The Union Government declined to take action on the resolution on the ground that since Telugu Desam had only 6 members in the 90-member Legislative Council, it had no right to demand its abolition; not a valid argument as it contravened the provision of Article 169 of the Constitution. The Union Government ultimately succumbed when the Andhra Pradesh Assembly passed the resolution for the second time and the Legislative Council was thus abolished in that State. Tamil Nadu soon followed Andhra Pradesh and now only five States of the Union of India have bicameral legislatures.

## LEGISLATIVE COUNCILS

### Composition and Organisation

The Legislative Council of a State comprises not more than one- third of the total number of members in the Legislative Assembly of the State and in no case less than 40 members.[3] About one-third of the members of the Council are elected by members of the Legislative Assembly from amongst persons who are not its members; one-third by electorates consisting of members of municipalities, district boards and other local authorities in the State which Parliament may by law specify; one-twelfth by registered graduates of more than three years' standing; and one-twelfth by registered teachers in educational institutions not lower in standard than secondary schools. The remaining members are nominated by the Governor from among persons who have distinguished themeselves in the field of literature, science, art, co-operative movement and social service. The system of election prescribed for all such categories is that of proportional representation by means of the single transferable vote. The Councils are not subject to dissolution but one-third of their members retire every second year. A member who remains absent for a period of sixty days from all its meetings without permission vacates his seat.

The Council along with the Assembly must be summoned at least twice a year and not more than six months would intervene between the last sitting and the first sitting in the next session. The Governor prorogues the Council. He may address the Council separately or both the Houses together. The Governor may send messages to the Council in respect of a Bill pending before it, suggesting any changes of modifications which he deems necessary and such messages must be

3. The Legislative Council of Jammu and Kashmir has only 36 members vide Section 50 of the Constitution of Jammu and Kashmir.

considered at the earliest possible opportunity. Every Minister and the Advocate General of a State has the right to speak in, and otherwise to take part in the proceedings of both Houses and any Committee of the Legislature of which he may be named a member. But a Minister is entitled to vote only in that Houses of which he is a member.

The Council chooses from amongst its members a Chairman and a Deputy Chairman. Both vacate their offices if they cease to be members of the Council or resign form its membership. They can also be removed by a resolution of the members of the Council, provided fourteen days' notice to move such resolution of removal had been given. When the resolution for removal is under discussion against the Chairman or the Deputy Chairman, the concerned person shall not preside at the sitting of the Council, although he may be present at such a sitting and has the right to speak in, and otherwise to take part in the proceedings of the Council. He shall be entitled to vote only in the first instance on such resolution or on any other matter during such proceedings. In case of equality of votes he does not exercise a casting vote to which he is otherwise entitled under Article 189.

The Chairman presides at all sittings of the Council and in his absence the Deputy Chairman. During the absence of both the Chairman and the Deputy Chairman, such other person as may be determined by the rules of procedure of the Council shall preside; or if no such person is present, such other person as may be determined by the Council shall act as Chairman. While the office of the Chairman is vacant, the duties of his office are performed by the Deputy Chairman. If the office of the Deputy Chairman is also vacant, such member of the Council as the Governor may appoint shall perform all such duties connected with the office of the Chairman.

**Functions of the Council**

A Bill other than a Money Bill or Finance Bill may originate in either House of the legislature, if it is bicameral. A Bill is not deemed to have been passed by the State Legislature unless it has been agreed to by both the Houses. If the Council does not pass a Bill, or it is passed by the Council with amendments to which the Assembly does not agree or three months elapse from the date on which the Bill is laid before the Council, it again goes to the Assembly. The Assembly may pass the Bill with or without amendments suggested by the Council and then transmit it to the Council for its consideration. If the Council again rejects the Bill, or it is not passed within one month from the date on which the Bill is laid before the Council or is passed with amendments to which the Assembly does not agree, the Bill is deemed to have been passed by the two Houses in the form in which it was passed by the Assembly for the second time. The Legislative Council cannot kill the Bill. It can only delay it for a period of four months.

The functions of a Legislative Council in respect of Money Bills are similar to those of the Council of States (Rajya Sabha). No Money Bill can be introduced in a Legislative Council. After a Money Bill has been passed by the Legislative Assembly, it is transmitted to the Council for its recommendations. The Council is required to return the Bill with its recommendation within fourteen days. The Assembly may either accept or reject such recommendations. If it rejects them, the Bill is deemed to have been passed by both the Houses in the form in which it was passed by the Legislative Assembly. If the Bill is not returned within fourteen days, it is deemed to have been passed by both the Houses at the expiration of the said period in the form in which it was passed by the Assembly.

The Legislative Council has, thus, neither the initiative nor any effective voice in respect of money or financial matters. It can only make recommendations within the specified period of fourteen days and it is for the Legislative Assembly either to accept or reject such recommendations. If the Council fails to make any recommendation within fourteen days after receiving the Bill, it is deemed to have been passed by both the Houses of the Legislature in the form in which it was passed by the Legislative Assembly. The real power in financial and money matters belongs to the Assembly.

The Council does not control the Ministry. The Constitution specifically provides that the Council of Ministers is collectively responsible to the Legislative Assembly. No adverse vote of the Council can bring the Ministry to crisis. The members can, however, put questions and ask supplementaries on matters connected with public administration, move, discuss and pass resolutions on any matter of public importance and relating to the administration of the State. Rules of Procedure of the Legislative Council also provide for Calling Attention Notice.

### Utility of the Councils

Whatever reasons might have weighed with the Provincial Constitution Committee that the members of the Constituent Assembly representing different Provinces (States)should meet separately and decide whether to have a second chamber or not, it is, undoubtedly, clear that the Constitution-makers were themselves uncertain of the utility of the Legislative Councils. By providing for their abolition by an ordinary legislative process the Councils were given only a very subordinate and tentative place in scheme of the State Government. The Legislative Councils are not only second chambers, wherever they exist, but also secondary chambers. They have practically no control over Money Bills. A Money Bill must originate in the Legislative Assembly and having passed thereform, it is simply transmitted to the Council for its recommendations. The Council must return the Bill to the Assembly within fourteen days of its receipt either with or without its recommendations. But the recommendations are not binding on the Assembly. If the Assembly rejects these recommendations or the Council does not make any recommendation within the specified period of fourteen days, the Bill becomes law on receiving the assent of the Governor. All that the Council can do is to delay a Money Bill for fourteen days. Nor are its powers effective in respect of non-Money Bills. The Council can only delay the passage of a non-Money Bill for a period of four months. The Constitution does not even make a provision for joint sittings in case of disagreement between the two Houses. The will of the Assembly must ultimately prevail.

Despite all this,there are many staunch advocates of bicameral Legislatures in the States.[4] They do not regard second chamber a futile institution and argue for it as a democratic necessity; a check on hasty and ill-considered legislation. Legislative Councils,they assert, adequately serve this purpose and from their performance in the States in which they exist their role as revisory chambers is fully established. The amendments proposed to the Bills by the Council have generally been accepted by the Assemblies and the speeches of elder statesmen and veteran politicians, who compose the membership of the Councils, are heard with keen attention and respect. In India respect to age, experience and maturer judgment is a heritage and their impact on public opinion is immense. Presiding officers of the Legislative Councils,who met at Patna in August, 1970, demanded the retention or restoration of Legislative Councils and described the popular campaign to abolish them as "a part of conspiracy to murder democracy in India." They even sought amendment of the Constitution to provide for Councils in the States where they did not exist. The Punjab Legislative Assembly passed a resolution on March 29, 1976, recommending to Parliament that it should provide for the creation of a Legislative Council, which was earlier abolished in 1969, in the State.[5] Moving the resolution the Minister for Parliamentary Affairs, Umrao Singh, said that in all democratic countries there were two Chambers, one which was chosen on the basis of adult franchise through direct election while the other had members representing special interests and minorities, such as, graduates, intellectuals and teachers. The Upper House, he maintained, was not for persons or parties but for giving representation to wider interests.

The atmosphere in the Councils, it is argued, is serene and is particularly suited for initiating non-controversial legislation. Passions do not run high there and political antagonism does not assume so much bitterness as in the Assembly, because the Council cannot bring about a crisis in the Government. The result is a high order of debates and full consideration of the pros and cons of the legislation under discussion or matter under review. In financial matters, too, Legislative Councils have their own contribution to make which is by no means negligible. The Constitution provides that the Annual Budget is to be laid before both the Houses of the Legislature and discussed. The report of the Comptroller and Auditor-General is also required to be laid before both Houses. The Council is also represented in the Public Accounts Committee.

But the critics of the second chambers in the States are no less vehement. They assert that the Legislative Councils are composed of diverse elements, differently elected and include nominated members too. A chamber so heterogeneously constituted can neither properly serve the purpose of a revising chamber nor can it act as an effective brake against hasty and ill considered

4. Sir Prakasa, "Abolition of Upper Houses : The Other Side of Issue", *The Tribune,* Chandigarh, June 6, 1969.
5. The resolution was passed by 64 to 26 votes. Members belonging to Akali Dal, CPI and CPI (M) voted against. The Council has not been restored so far. The proposal has, once again, been revived by the Beant Singh Government.

legislation. It is also maintained that there is a dearth of representatives for both the Houses in every State and the Legislative Councils being what they are have not been able to attract whatever talent and experience is available. Moreover, the party in power has always used the Council as a spring-board for its own power and patronage rather than to establish it as a forum of talent and eminence. Sometimes nominations are made to enable certain persons to become Ministers or even Chief Ministers,as C. Rajgopalachari in Madras, Morarji Desai in the erstwhile Bombay State and Gyani Gurmukh Singh Musafir in the pre-organised Punjab State in 1966. The installation of Mandal as Chief Minister of Bihar after the defeat of M.M.Sinha's Ministry was rather dramatic. In a majority of cases nominations have seldom fulfilled the requirements of the Constitution that the members nominated shall be persons having special knowledge or practical experience in respect of such matters as literature, science, art, cooperative movement and social service.

If the Legislative Councils do not fulfil the democratic demands of a double chamber, it is a sheer hoax of democracy to continue with them. D.C. Pavate, who had been Governor of Punjab, says, "For some mysterious circumstances the founding fathers of the Constitution have provided bicameral legislatures in most of the States" and characterised their existence as "just an exercise in delaying legislation."[6] The leader of the BKD Party in the Uttar Pradesh Assembly, Udit Narayan Sharma, stated on April 29, 1970, when the resolution recommending the abolition of the Legislative Council was being discussed, that the Council served no useful purpose and often it made mockery of democracy. To support his argument he maintained that the Assembly had passed the Motion of Thanks to the Governor, but the Council had rejected it, simply because non-Congress Government was in office whereas Congress commanded a majority in the Council. The SSP legislator, Anant Ram, participating in the debate made a point that the Council served no useful purpose as out of 400 Bills referred to it, only four were amended by the Council. He even levelled charges of corruption against members seeking election to the Council and indignantly said that it was a matter of shame that an industrialist "has got himself elected to the Vidhan Parishad (Legislative Council) by buying votes of M.L.A.s." In indirect elections, he added, "voters could be corrupted. Capitalists' attempt to get into the Lower House rarely succeeded, but many of them had managed to become members of the Upper House."[7]

As far back as 1953 the Bombay State Assembly voted for abolition of its Legislative Council by 182 votes to 31. Conformably to the United Front's 32-point programme, West Bengal Government announced its intention in March 1969 to seek the abolition of the Legislative Council. No one, including the Opposition in West Bengal Legislative Assembly, had a good word for the Council and the resolution for its abolition was passed unanimously. It was also abolished in the Punjab[8] followed by Andhra Pradesh and Tamil Nadu. Many other States in which Legislative Councils existed began to appreciate that the scheme of bicameralism was completely out of accord with any sense of constitutional proportion or propriety. It was an expensive experiment and an unnecessary drain on the meagre resources of the States. The Governments in West Bengal, Punjab, Andhra Pradesh and Tamil Nadu,while pleading for the abolition of their Legislative Councils, laid particular stress on the cost of maintaining them. In West Bengal and Punjab it cost each State exchequer Rs.17.72 lakhs a year.

The plain fact is that Legislative Councils in the States have been found to be an expensive luxury and no tears are shed over them, except by the members deprived of cushy seats or the party bosses who shall be handicapped by their abolition in the task of providing some profitable occupation or a sinecure to party rebels or election financiers. Far from functioning as indispensable revisionary bodies, Councils have gradually become political sanctuaries and like the fifth wheel of the coach have turned out to be superfluous, if not positive hindrance. Hardly any of the Legislative Councils can claim to have acted as an effective brake on legislative despotism.

---

6. Pavate, D.C., *My Days as Governor,* pp. 102-3.
7. *The Times of India,* New Delhi, April 30, 1970.
8. Abolition of the Legislative Council makes a revealing study. Whereas Chief Minister Gurnam Singh wanted its immediate abolition, Sant Fateh Singh, President of the Shiromani Akali Dal, was in favour of its retention. D.C. Pavate, who was then the Governor of the Punjab, noted that the Chief Minister prevailed on the Prime Minister, "to push the abolition of the Council through Parliament speedily." Pavate, D.C., *My Days as Governor,* p. 104.

Legislative procedures are cumbersome enough without them. Nor are they sensitive barometers of public opinion. Their utility, if any, is vitiated by their composition.

## THE LEGISLATIVE ASSEMBLY

### Composition and Organisation

The Legislative Assembly is the popularly elected chamber and is the real centre of power in a State. The maximum strength of an Assembly must not exceed 500 or its minimum strength fall below 60,except the Legislative Assemblies of Arunachal, Goa, Mizoram and Sikkim. The demarcation of territorial constituencies is to be done in such a manner that the ratio between the population of each constituency and the number of seats allotted to it, as far as practicable, is the same throughout the State. Apart from these general provisions regarding the representation of Scheduled Castes and Scheduled Tribes (except the Scheduled Tribes in the autonomous districts of Assam)in the Legislative Assembly of every State.[9] Seats are also reserved for the autonomous districts of the State of Assam.[10] Provision has also been made to nominate one member of the Anglo-Indian Community, if the Governor is of the opinion that the community is not adequately represented in the Assembly.[11]

The duration of the Assembly, unless sooner dissolved was originally fixed at five years. The Forty-second Amendment Act increased it to six years, but the Forty-fourth Amendmend Act again reverted to five-year term. When a Proclamation of Emergency is in operation, Parliament may by law extend the term beyond five years for a period not exceeding one year at a time. But such an extension must not continue beyond six months after a Proclamation of Emergency has ceased to operate.[12]

The qualifications for membership of the Legislative Assembly are the same as for members of the House of the People. A candidate for election to the Assembly must be a citizen of India,not less than twenty-five years of age, makes and subscribes before some person authorised in that behalf by the Election Commission an oath or affirmation that he will bear true faith and al- legiance to the Constitution of India as by law established and that he will uphold the sovereignty and integrity of India,and possesses such other qualifications as may be prescribed by Parliament. No person can be a member of both Houses of the State Legislature at a time if there is a Legislative Council in that State. No person can also be a member of the Legislatures of two or more States. The Assembly may declare vacant the seat of any member who absents himself from all its meetings for sixty days without the permission of the Assembly.

A person is disqualified for being chosen as a member of the Assembly : if he holds any office of profit under the Government of India or the Government of any State,other than an office declared by the State Legislature by law not to disqualify its holder; if he is of unsound mind and stands so declared by a competent court; if he is an undischarged insolvent; if he is not a citizen of India, or has voluntarily acquired the citizenship of a foreign State,or is in acknowledgment of allegiance or adherence to a foreign State; if he is so disqualified by or under any law made by Parliament. A person shall not be deemed to hold an office of profit under the Government of India or the Government of any State by reason only that he is a Minister either for the Government of India or any State Government. If any question arises as to whether a member of the State Legislature is subject to any of the aforesaid disqualifications, the question shall be referred for the decision of the Governor and his decision shall be final. But before giving decision on any such question, the Governor must obtain the opinion of the Election Commission and he is required to act according to such opinion.[13] The decision of the Governor is the opinion of the Election Commission.

The Governor may from time to time summon the House or each House of the State Legislature to meet at such time and place as he thinks fit,but not more than six months shall intervene between its last sitting in one Session and its first sitting in the next Session. The Governor may from time to time prorogue the House or either House and dissolve the Legislative Assembly.

The Governor may address the Legislative Assembly or in case of a State having a Legislative Council either House or both Houses assembled together. He may send messages to either

---

9. Article 332 (1).
10. Article 332 (2).
11. Article 333 .
12. Article 172, proviso.
13. Article 192 as amended by the Constitution (Forty-fourth Amendment) Act, 1978, S.25.

House on a Bill pending before the Legislature, suggesting any changes or modifications which he may deem necessary . It is the duty of the House to which such a message is sent to consider it with all possible dispatch. The Constitution imposes a duty on the Governor to address the new legislature after every General Election and at the commencement of its first Session every year and inform the Legislature of the causes of its summons. The Legislature is required to provide in its rules for the allotment of time for the discussion of the Governor's address. The debate and voting on the address, in fact, constitutes an annual vote of confidence in the Council of Ministers.

Every Minister and the Advocate-General for a State have the right to speak in both Houses, if it is a bicameral legislature, and to take part in their proceedings as well as in their Committees. But a Minister is entitled to vote only in that House of which he is a member.

The quorum to constitute a meeting of a House of the State Legislature is ten members or one-tenth of the total number of members of the House,whichever is greater, if until the State Legislature by law otherwise provides.[14] All questions at any sitting of the House are determined by a majority of votes of the members present and voting, other than the Speaker or Chairman, or person acting as such. The Speaker or the Chairman shall not vote in the first instance but he shall have and exercise a casting vote in the case of equality of votes.

**The Speaker**

The Assembly chooses two of its members as the Speaker and the Deputy Speaker. A Speaker vacates his office if he ceases to be a member of the Assembly. He may also resign his office at any time. A Speaker may be removed from office by a resolution of the Assembly passed by a majority of all the then members of the Assembly after fourteen days' notice of the intention to move such a resolution. But he does not vacate his office on the dissolution of the Assembly. He continues to be the Speaker until immediately before the first sitting of the Assembly after the dissolution. While the office of the Speaker is vacant, the Deputy Speaker performs his duties.

The duties and powers of the Speaker are, broadly speaking, the same as those of the Speaker of the House of the People (Lok Sabha). The Speaker is an independent and impartial presiding officer and has been invested with all the powers consistent with the dignity of the Chair and necessary to ensure the orderly conduct of the business of the Assembly. He is empowered to admit questions, resolutions and motions and allots time to the different kinds of business before the Assembly. He determines, in consultation with the Leader of the House, the order of business and fixes the time-limits to speeches. He maintains proper order and decorum in the House and has the power to ask a member to withdraw from the House for any violation of the rules of the House or to suspend him for a whole session if his conduct is grossly disorderly or, is in flagrant disregard of the authority and rulings of the Chair. The Speaker nominates the panel of Chairmen and the Chairmen of the Select Committees on Bills as well as of other Committees of the House. He interprets the Rules of the Assembly and decides all points of order and questions of procedure. His ruling cannot be contested; it is final.

The Speaker, in brief, is the impartial custodian of the rights of the members of the House. But the high traditions of the office and the great reverence in which the Speaker should be held are altogether absent in the States of India, Exchanges of hot words between the Speaker and some members are not infrequent. There have been limitless number of cases in which a member who is 'named'had refused to apologise or quit the Chamber on being called upon by the Speaker to do so. Frequently, services of the Marshal are requisitioned to make a recalcitrant member to leave the House in obedience to the instructions of the Speaker. The Uttar Pradesh Assembly provided an unprecedented instance on September 8,1958 in which the Marshal was compelled to requisition the help of the armed constabulary to turn out the leader and members of the Socialist group who defied the Speaker's order to quit the House. But what happened in West Bengal on September 21,1959 was disgracefully reckless. Not only did members of the Congress Party and the Opposition, notably the Communists,indulged in shouting down one another, but also hurled shoes at one another. As if this was not enough three mikes were pulled from their sockets and thrown at the Treasury Benches. Two members challenged each other on the floor

14. Clauses 3 and 4 of Article 189 restored by the Constitution (Forty-fourth Amendment) Act, 1978, S. 45 by repealing S. 31 of the Constitution (Forty-second Amendment) Act, 1976, which had omitted them.

of the House and later exchanged blows in the lobbies until they were separated by the sober colleagues. In the Madhya Pradesh Assembly one member, disregarded the authority of the Chair, obstructed the proceedings of the House, and rushed to the dais and caused criminal assault on the Deputy Speaker who was on the Chair on March 16, 1966. Another member used insulting language against the Chair and threw chappal (footwear) towards the Chair. The House expelled them by adopting motions and declared their seats in the Assembly vacant. They challenged the decision of the House in the High Court in writ petitions,but the Court upheld the decision of the House. These are just few of scores of such examples and some are even disgraceful.

The Speakers, too,have very often not acted with due discretion. The Speaker of the erstwhile Patiala and East Punjab States Union was saved from removal from office by the prorogation of the House by the Rajpramush. Another Speaker apologised to the House when his conduct was sought to be discussed by a privilege motion. Yet another tried to explain away the offending remarks and even offered to expunge them from the proceedings. In Andhra Pradesh the leave to move the resolution against the Speaker was refused because the requisite support of the members was not forthcoming. The West Bengal Speaker adjourned the Assembly *sine die*, soon after it met on November 29,1967,as he thought that the dismissal of the United Front Ministry and appointment of Dr.P.C.Ghosh as Chief Minister by the Governor were unconstitutional and invalid "since it has been effected behind the back of this House." He also said that he might again adjourn the Assembly, *sine die,* if it was reconvened by the Governor "unless I change my view that the appointment of Dr. P.C. Ghosh as Chief Minister and the summoning of the House on his advice unconstitutional and invalid." The Speaker did it for the second time when the House met for the Budget session. In Punjab, Speaker Joginder Singh Mann adjourned the Assembly for two months when the Financial Statement had been laid before the House and the financial business was about to be gone through. The Speaker had to face two motions expressing no confidence in himself and the Assembly was adjourned most probably to escape or evade the consequences of these motions.

Such actions on the part of the Speaker neither add to the dignity of the Chair nor do they help the growth of traditions associated with the office of the Speaker. India has not in the last four decades evolved any concept of non-partisan Speakership. There have been numerous instances of Speakers becoming Chief Ministers or Ministers at the Centre. One was appointed a member of the Union Public Service Commission. The result is, what is happening in the Chambers of the State Legislatures. In August 1969, the Speaker of Assam Legislative Assembly was *gheraoed* and microphones were uprooted by some of the members. There, at least, no violence was attempted on the person of the Speaker. But just a fortnight later, in the Uttar Pradesh Assembly shoes,seat-cushions and booklets were thrown at the Speaker. The Speaker called the Marshal and the police to eject Opposition members,while the Deputy Speaker,who belonged to the Opposition, shouted at the police to get out of the Chamber. Much worst is happening today than that happened yesterday.

**Functions of the Assembly**

The State Legislature has exclusive power over subjects enumerated in List II (State List) and Concurrent powers over those enumerated in list III (Concurrent List). But if Parliament passes a law on a matter contained in the Concurrent List, the State Legislature is not competent to pass law on the same subject. If the State Legislature, on the other hand, has passed a law on a subject given in the Concurrent List, Parliament, too, can pass a law on the subject and the State law becomes inoperative to the extent it is repugnant to the Union law. The State law, however, prevails notwithstanding such repugnancy, if it was reserved for the President and had received his assent.

The Constitution also imposes the following restrictions on the powers of the State Legislatures even within their exclusive jurisdiction:

(1) Some State laws will be invalid unless they are reserved for consideration of the President and are assented to by him, for example, laws passed by the State Legislatures for the acquisition of property; laws in respect of concurrent matters which are repugnant to earlier legislations of Parliament; laws providing for the imposition of taxes on the sale or purchase of commodities declared by Parliament to be essential for the life of the community.

(2) Some Bills require the previous sanction of the President before they can be intro-

duced in the State Legislatures, for instance, Bills seeking to impose restrictions in the public interest on the freedom of trade,commerce or intercourse within or without that State.

(3) Parliament is also empowered to legislate with respect to a matter in the State List if the Council of States (Rajya Sabha) declares by a two-thirds majority that it is expedient in the national interest for Parliament to do so. Such a resolution remains in force for a period of one year at a time, but not exceeding a total of two years.

(4) While a Proclamation of Emergency is in operation Parliament has the power to legislate with respect to any matter in the State List.

(5) In case of failure of the constitutional machinery in a State, the President may suspend the State Legislature and vest its powers in Parliament.

A Bill, other than a Money Bill, may originate in either House of the State Legislature, if there is a Legislative Council. A Bill is deemed to have been passed by the Houses of the Legislature when it is agreed to by both the Houses, which for all intents and purposes means the Legislative Assembly. The Council cannot force its decision on the Assembly. It can simply delay the passage of a Bill for four months. In brief, all legislative power of the State, subject to the power of issuing Ordinances by the Governor when the Legislature is not in session, is concentrated in the Assembly.

The control of the Legislative Assembly is complete over the finances of the State. All Money Bills must originate in the Assembly and its verdict must prevail in all respects. In case there is a Legislative Council, it must return a Money Bill to the Assembly within fourteen days of its receipt with or without recommendations. If it is not returned within that period, or the recommendations are not acceptable to the Assembly, the Bill is deemed to have been passed by both Houses in the form in which it was passed by the Legislative Assembly. The Annual Financial Statement or the Budget is required to be laid before the House or the Houses of the State Legislature. All proposals for expenditure, except the expenditure charged on the revenues of the State which can be discussed but not voted upon by the State Legislature,are submitted to the Legislative Assembly in the form of demands for grants. The voting of grants is the exclusive privilege of the Assembly and it has the power to pass or reject a demand or to reduce its amount, though it has not the power to increase the amount. It is, further, provided that no tax will be levied in a State without the sanction of the Legislative Assembly.

The control of the Assembly over the administration of the State is a logical conclusion of the parliamentary system of Government. The Council of Ministers is formed out of the majority party in the Assembly,and it is collectively responsible to it. No one can continue to remain a Minister for more than six consecutive months without a seat in the one or the other House of the Legislature. The salaries and allowances of the Ministers are voted by the Assembly.

The Assembly can seek information from the Government on any matter of public administration by means of questions and supplementaries. It can also move and pass resolutions recommending to the Government steps which should be taken on matters of public importance. The Assembly may censure the Government if it does not approve its policy and pass a vote of no-confidence, entailing the resignation of the Ministry.

The Legislative Assembly forms part of the Electoral College for electing the President.

## LEGISLATIVE PROCEDURE

### Legislative Procedure

The Constitution prescribes the most important rules of procedure of the State Legislatures and they are covered by Articles 196-221. Detailed rules have been left for determination by the State Legislatures themselves. The rules prescribed by the Constitution are similar to those prescribed for Parliament. Articles 107-111, and the rules formed by the State Legislatures follow the model of Parliament as incorporated in its Rules of Procedure and Conduct of Business.

### Legislative Bills

Accordidng to the Legislative procedure a Bill other than a Money or Finance Bill, may originate in either House of the State Legislature which has a Legislative Council. A Bill shall not be deemed to have been passed by the Houses of the Legislature of a State having a Legislative Council unless it has been agreed to by both Houses,either without amendment or with such amendments only as are agreed to by both Houses. The prorogation of a House or Houses does not involve the lapse of a Bill pending in the State Legislature. Bills pending in the Council but which have not been passed by the Assembly do not lapse on a dissolution of the Assembly.

The dissolution of the Assembly causes the lapse on any Bill which is pending in it, or which has been passed by it but is pending in the Legislative Council.

In case of disagreement between the Legislative Assembly and the Legislative Council over a Bill, the Constitution does not provide for a joint sitting of both Houses, as it is in the case of the Union Parliament, for the resolution of such disagreements. Disagreements between the two Houses of the State Legislature are resolved by the simple expedient of the Assembly passing the disputed Bill for the second time. The Constitution says,if a Bill has been passed by the Legislative Assembly and transmitted to the Legislative Council and (a) is rejected by the Legislative Council, or (b) more than three months elapse from the date of its receipt by the Legislative Council without the Bill being passed by it, or (c) a Bill is passed by the Council with amendments to which the Legislative Assembly does not agree, then the Assembly may pass the Bill again either in its original form or with such amendments as have been suggested by the Council and agreed to by the Assembly. When the Assembly passes the Bill for the second time it is transmitted to the Legislative Council and if (a) the Bill is, again rejected by the Council, or (b) more than one month elapses from the date of its receipt by the Council without the Bill being passed by it, or (c) the Bill passed by the Council with amendments to which the Assembly does not agree, the Bill is deemed to have been passed by both the Houses of the State Legislature in the form in which it was passed by the Legislative Assembly for the second time.

When a Bill has been passed by the State Legislature it is presented to the Governor for his assent. The Governor may either give his assent to the Bill or withhold his assent thereform or may reserve it for the consideration of the President or he may return it with a message for reconsideration in whole or in part or may suggest amendments, thereto. In the last case, if the Bill is again passed with or without amendments, the Governor must give his assent thereto.

**Different Stages in the Passage of a Bill**

A Bill other than a Money Bill, in order to become a law, has to pass through three readings in each House, if the State has a bicameral Legislature. The first reading covers the introduction of the Bill. The motion for leave to introduce a Bill is a formal business. The member asking for leave makes a short speech. By convention no debate takes place at this stage and the Speaker immediately puts the question. If the House grants the leave,the mover of the Bill rises to say, "Sir, I introduce the Bill." No speech is made on the contents of the Bill nor does any other member speak on the motion or the BIll. If a motion for leave is opposed, the Speaker permits the member moving the Bill to make a brief explanatory statement and so does the member opposing it. Then, the question is put to the House. But if the Opposition attacks the Bill on the ground of incompetency of the Legislature to consider it, the Speaker permits a full discussion thereon.

After the Bill has been introduced, it is immediately published in the State Government Gazette. The Speaker may permit the publication of the Bill in the Government Gazette before the motion for leave to introduce the Bill has been made. In that case, it is not necessary to move for leave to introduce the Bill and if the Bill is afterwards introduced it is not necessary to publish it again. The first reading of the Bill is now complete.

The second reading of the Bill is divided into two stages. The first stage consists of a general discussion on the Bill and the second stage relates to the discussion of clauses, schedules and amendments. The first stage in the second reading begins when the member in whose name the Bill stands moves one of these motions: (a) that it may be taken into consideration either at once or at some future date to be mentioned; or (b) it be referred to the Select Committee of the Houses; or (c) to Joint Committee of the two Houses, if there is a Legislative Council in the State; or (d) it be circulated for the purpose of eliciting public opinion. It is here that the member-in-charge of the Bill explains the purpose and objects of the Bill, gives the background of bill, explains the circumstances in which the Bill is necessary, and gives such other material information as may be necessary in respect of the Bill. The Opposition opposes the Bill, but the discussion must be confined around the principles of the Bill and its general provisions. No amendment to the Bill can be introduced at this stage,except for amendments to the motion that the Bill be taken into consideration or it be referred to a Select Committee or it be circulated for eliciting public opinion.

When the motion that a Bill be referred to a Select Committee is made, the member-in-charge of the Bill indicates the names of members who would constitute the Select Committee as also the date by which the Select Committee should submit its report to the House. The Select

Committee usually consists of ten to fifteen members and only such members are appointed as are willing to serve on it. The mover ascertains in advance from such members their willingness to serve on the committee. The Speaker nominates one of the members of the committee to be its chairman. The Committee thoroughly examines the Bill and all its provisions, discusses it clause by clause, may ask for relevant papers and records,may hear expert evidence and representatives of special interests affected by the measure and suggest its own changes and modifications. The Chairman of the Committee, then, presents the Report to the House. He may make any remarks, but he has to confine himself to a brief statement of facts and there can be no debate on it. The Report and the Bill, as amended by the Select Committee, are published in the State Government Gazette.

After the Report has been presented,the member-in-charge of the Bill may move: (1) that the Bill as reported by the Select Committee be taken into consideration;or (2) that the Bill be recommitted either (a) without limitation or (b) with respect to particular clauses or amendments only, or (c) with instructions to the Select Committee to make some particular additional provision in the Bill. If the member-in-charge of the Bill moved that the Bill be taken into consideration, any member may move an amendment that the Bill be recommitted. Then, follows the final stage and the third reading of the Bill when a motion is made that the Bill be passed. After such a motion has been made no amendment,except that which is formal,verbal or consequential to an amendment to the Bill, can be made. The discussion on a motion that the Bill be passed is confined to either support or rejection of the Bill as a whole.

After the House has passed the Bill, it is transmitted to the other House, if there is one, where it undergoes the same process. When the Bill has been passed by the House or Houses it is submitted to the Governor for his assent and if it is assented to by him or by the President, when reserved for his consideration, it is published in the State Government Gazette as an Act of the State Legislature.

**Money Bill**

A Money Bill or Financial Bill must originate in the Legislative Assembly. It cannot be introduced in the Legislative Council if the State has one. If any question arises whether a Bill is a Money Bill or not the decision of the Speaker of the Assembly thereon is final and the Speaker shall endorse a certificate on such a Bill that it is a Money Bill when it is transmitted to the Legislative Council or to the Governor for assent. A Money Bill cannot be introduced or moved except on the recommendation of the Governor. After a Money Bill has been passed by the Assembly, it is transmitted to the Legislative Council, if the State Legislature is bicameral, for its recommendations. The Council is required, within fourteen days of its receipt, to return the Bill to the Legislative Assembly with its recommendations. The Assembly may accept or reject the recommendations so made. If the Assembly does not accept any of the recommendations, the Money Bill is deemed to have been passed by both Houses in the form in which it was originally passed by the Legislative Assembly. If the Legislative Council does not return the Bill with its recommendations within the prescribed period of fourteen days, it is deemed to have been passed, on the expiration of the said period, in the form in which it was passed by the Legislative Assembly.

## FINANCIAL PROCEDURE

The principles underlying the financial procedure in the State Legislatures are the same as in the Union Parliament and they are in complete accord with the system of representative government and a sound system of public finance. The Government has, in the first place,the exclusive right to initiate financial legislation. Secondly, the Legislative Assembly alone has the power to make grants and to appropriate funds for different items of expenditure and to impose taxes and authorise borrowing by the Government. Finally, statutory authorization is necessary for all expenditure out of the Consolidated Fund and for all taxes imposed.

**Annual Financial Statement**

In every financial year the Governor shall cause to be laid before the State Legislature an Annual Financial Statement or Budget. The Annual Financial Statement must clearly show separately the expenditure charged on the Consolidated Fund, and must also distinguish expenditure on revenue account from other expenditure. The following expenditure is charged on the Consolidated Fund:—

(1) the emoluments and allowances of the Governor and other expenditure relating to his office.

(2) the salaries and allowances of the Speaker and the Deputy Speaker of the

Legislative Assembly, and of the Chairman and the Deputy Chairman of the Legislative Council in the case of States with bicameral Legislatures;

(3) the interest, sinking fund charges and other debt charges of the States;

(4) the salaries and allowances of the Judges of the High Court;

(5) sums required to meet any judgment, decree or award of any Court or arbitral tribunal; and

(6) any other expenditure declared by the Constitution or by the State Legislature by law to be so charged.

It may be noted that the Constitution declares the following sums also to be expenditure charged on the Consolidated Fund of the State;

(a) the administrative expenses of a High Court including all salaries, allowances and pensions payable to the officers and servants of the Court [Article 229 (3)]; and

(b) sums necessary to meet the expenses of the State Public Service Commission, inclouding any salaries, allowances and pensions payable to the members or staff of the Commission (Article 322).

The expenditure charged on the Consolidated Fund of the State is not subject to the vote of the State Legislature. But the Legislature can discuss the estimates of the expenditure. The other expenditure is submitted in the form of demands for grants to the Legislative Assembly. The Assembly has the power to discuss, assent or refuse to assent to any demand, or to reduce the amount of the demand. It cannot, however, either propose new grants or increase the amount of the demand. No demand for a grant can be made except on the recommendation of the Governor, that is, on the responsibility of the Ministry.

**Stages in Financial Legislation**

There are five stages in the passage of the Annual Financial Statement or the Budget. The first stage covers the presentation of the Annual Financial Statement by the Finance Minister to the State Legislature. The presentation of the Annual Financial Statement is accompanied by an explanatory speech. After a few days, there is a general discussion on the proposals and members of the Legislature express their opinion on the policy of the Government. A fixed number of days, usually three or four, are allotted for this purpose, and it finishes the second stage. In the third stage voting of grants takes place. A separate demand is made for each department by the Minister-in-charge and it is here that the department comes under full scrutiny. A vote to reject or reduce the demand may be made by any member,but it is not within the competence of members to propose either new grants or an increase in the amount demanded. About twenty days are usually allotted for the voting of grants. On the last date and one hour before the adjournment of the sitting of the Assembly all demands which have not been disposed of till then are put to vote. No amendment or discussion is allowed on such demands. They must be accepted or rejected by the Assembly.

The next stage is the Annual Appropriation Bill which must be passed into a statute. After the grants have been made by the Assembly,a Bill is introduced to provide for the appropriation out of the Consolidated Fund of the State of all moneys required to meet (a) the grants so made by the Assembly, and (b) the expenditure charged on the Consolidated Fund of the State. No amendment, which will have the effect of varying the amount or altering the destination of any grant so made can be proposed in the Bill. The decision of the presiding officer whether an amendment is admissible or not is final. The Appropriation Bill having passed through all stages is finally voted upon and if passed by the Assembly, it is certified by the Speaker as Money Bill and transmitted to the Legislative Council, if there is one in the State.

Another step in the completion of the Annual Financial Statement is the passage of the Finance Bill. A Bill which sets out the ways and means by which revenues necessary for meeting the expenditure of the State for the ensuing year are to be raised is called the Finance Bill. The Finance Bill is presented to the State Legislature at the same time as the Budget and the procedure followed is that of a Money Bill. The Bill must be passed before the end of April, but the financial proposals become operative immediately after the presentation of the Budget under the Provisional Collection of Taxes Act,1931.

**SUGGESTED READINGS**

Alexandrovicz, C.H., *Constitutional Developments in India.*

*Constituent Assembly Debates.*

Kothari, Rajni, *State Against Democracy.*

Morris-Jones, *The Government and Politics of India.*

Shukla, V.N. *Constitution of India.*

# CHAPTER XV

# The State Judiciary

## The High Courts

The High Courts had been functioning in India for nearly ninety years when India became Independent and these High Courts had an eminent record of independence and impartiality. But all the Provinces of pre-Independent India did not have High Courts. The Calcutta High Court exercised jurisdiction over Assam and the Patna High Courts over Orissa. The United Provinces had two High Courts,the Allahabad High Court and the Chief Court with its headquarters at Lucknow. Both these courts exercised appellate jurisdiction. By July 1948, however every Province had a High Court of its own. Originally, the 1950 Constitution provided for a High Court in each Part A and Part B States. Parliament was also empowered to create a High Court, or extend the jurisdiction of a neighbouring Part A or Part B State to a Part C State. There were, as such, 18 High Courts and 7 Judicial Commissioners' Courts, one for each Part C State other than Coorg and Delhi.

The reorganization of the States reduced the number of the High Courts, but with Sikkim becoming the twenty-second State of India and having its own separate High Court, the number was again eighteen including three having jurisdiction over more than one State. The Punjab and Haryana High Court has jurisdiction over the States of Punjab and Haryana. Gauhati High Court's jurisdiction extends over Assam, Manipur, Meghalaya, Nagaland, Mizoram and Arunachal. The Bombay High Court's jurisdiction now extends to Goa. Among the Union Territories, Delhi alone has a High Court of its own.[1]

The position of the High Courts in India materially differs from that of the State courts in most other federations, notably that of the United States of America. In America the State Courts are constituted under the State Constitutions and, consequently, they have no connection with the federal judicial system. The method of appointment of judges, their service conditions and the jurisdiction of the State Courts differ from State to State. In India all High Courts are constituted under one constitution with uniform jurisdiction and conditions of service of the Judges and they are subject to transfer from one State to another. The State Governments have no control over the High Courts. Nor can they alter the constitution or organisation of the High Courts. It can be done only either by amending the Constitution or the law of Parliament.

A High Court consists of the Chief Justice and such other Judges as the President may from time to time deem it necessary to appoint. Originally, proviso to Article 216 empowered the President to appoint as many Judges as he might deem necessary from time to time, and also fixing from time to time the maximum strength of each High Court. The Constitution (Seventh Amendment) Act, 1956 omitted the proviso as it was considered to be of little significance from the practical point of view since the Presidential Order could be changed from time to time.

## Appointment of Judges

The Constitutional Adviser suggested, in his Memorandum of May 30, 1947 on the Provincial Constitution that the High Court Judges might be appointed by the Governors with the approval of two-thirds of the members of the State Council.[2] The proposal to set up a State Council was abandoned and the Provincial Constitution Committee, accordingly, recommended that Judges should be appointed by the President in consultation with the Chief Justice of the Supreme Court, the Governor of the Province and the Chief Justice of the High Court of the Provinces (States), except when the Chief Justice himself was to be appointed. Explaining the proposal in the Constituent Assembly, Sardar Vallabhbhai Patel said that the proposal was designed to ensure fair appointments to the High

1. Bombay has territorial jurisdiction over Dadra and Nagar Haveli; Calcutta over Andaman and Nicobar Islands; Kerala over Lakshadweep; Madras over Pondicherry; Punjab and Haryana over Chandigarh.
2. A body in the nature of the Privy Council to be set up at the Centre to advise on several matters. See *ante*.

Courts so that the Judiciary should be above the suspicion of party influence.[3] The Constituent Assembly accepted the proposal.

The President appoints the Chief Justice of a High Court by warrant under his hand and seal after consultation with the Chief Justice of India and the Governor of the State. But in making the appointments of Puisne Judges, the President consults in addition the Chief Justice, of the High Court to which they are being appointed.[4] A Judge of a High Court must be a citizen of India and (a) must have held for, at least, ten years a judicial office in the territory of India, or (b) must have been for, at least, ten years an advocate of High Court. The Constitution does not provide for the appointment of non-practising lawyers as Judges of High Court. But a person is qualified for appointment as a Judge of the Supreme Court if he is, in the opinion of the President, a distinguished jurist.

The Law Commission in its 80th Report on "the method of appointment of Judges" which was presented to the Council of States (Rajya Sabha) on January 28, 1980, opined that the present scheme was basically sound but some marginal improvements were necessary. The Chief Justice of a State High Court should consult two of his seniormost colleagues before recommending a name and this should be normally accepted by the Government. The Chief Justice's recommendation should be accepted by the Chief Minister within a month and outside limit of seven months should be fixed for acceptance. The Commission did not rule out a direct meeting between the Chief Justice and the Chief Minister to resolve any dispute over choice. The Chief Minister should only have a right to comment on the name or names proposed by the Chief Justice. The Commission rejected the proposal that the Chief Justice should propose a panel of names since it would dilute its majority. The minimum age of a Judge should be 45 years. For persons recruited from the Bar directly, the age should be 54.

As for the Chief Justice, only the seniormost person should be chosen. As the proposal to the office of the Chief Justice emanated from the Chief Minister himself, he should confine himself to taking the initiative for the appointment of the Chief Justice based on the principle of seniority. If for any reason this was not considered feasible, the proper course would be to select some Judge from outside the State. It should, however, be ensured that the Judge so appointed as Chief Justice should have been on the High Court Bench for a sufficiently long time and should be senior enough as a Judge as not to cause resentment among the senior Judges of the High Court that some one junior in service had been appointed in supersession of their claim. In no case should a junior Judge of the High Court be appointed as Chief Justice in supersession of a senior.

The Commission coupled its suggestion with another salutary suggestion. It recommended that persons to be appointed to the High Courts or Supreme Court should not have "any affiliation with a political party continuously for seven years preceding their appointment."

Considerable controversy revolved on the unanimous recommendation of the Consultative Committee of Parliament attached to the Ministry of Law and Justice that the Chief Justice and at least one-third of the number of Judges of a High Court should be from outside the State under its jurisdiction. The Law Minister took note of the consensus at the meeting. On July 24,1980, the Law Minister assured the House of the People (Lok Sabha) that the Government would seek the guidance of the Supreme Court while evolving a mechanism on the appointment of Chief Justices of the High Courts. He explained that the Bar Council had passed the resolution expressing its disapproval on the presumption that the Government had already taken a decision on the issue. Reiterating the Government's commitment to the independence of the judiciary, the Law Minister said he was even prepared to entrust the Supreme Court with the job of evolving the mechanism for the appointment of Chief Justices. The Chief Justice of India was initially not favourably inclined to the proposal as, in his opinion, it would effect the efficiency of the judiciary. His main argument was that Judges have to deal with the local sentiments, traditions, customs and language. The consensus of the Council of Chief Ministers of the four Southern States was review of Centre-State relations and, *inter alia,* to safeguard the independence and competence of the judiciary by ensuring that High Court Judges were familiar with the language and customs of the concerned State.

3. *Constituent Assembly Debates,* Vol. IV, p. 710.
4. Article 217.

The original Article 224 made provision for the attendance of retired Judges at sittings of the High Court, similar to the one in the case of the Supreme Court. But the Constitution (Seventh Amendment)Act, 1956, conferred on the President the power of making appointments of temporary additional and acting Judges. Additional Judges may be appointed for a period not exceeding two years when it appears to the President that by reason of increase in the business of a High Court or arrears of work such appointments are necessary.[5] A duly qualified person may be appointed by the President as an acting Judge when a permanent Judge is absent from the duties of his office or is acting as Chief Justice. He shall continue to act until the permanent Judge has resumed his duties.

Article 224-A makes provision for the appointment of retired Judges at sittings of High Courts. The Chief Justice of a High Court may at any time, with the previous consent of the President, request any person who has held the office of a Judge of any High Court in India to sit and act as a Judge of the High Court of that State. While so sitting and acting he is entitled to such allowances as the President may by order determine and has all the jurisdiction, powers and privileges of a Judge, but is not otherwise deemed to be a Judge of that High Court.

Originally, Judges held office until they attained the age of sixty years. The Constitution (Fifteenth Amendment) Act, 1963, raised the age of retirement from 60 to 62 years. But a Judge may resign office or may be removed from his office by the President in the same manner as a Judge of the Supreme Court may be removed. Judges of the High Courts, accordingly, enjoy a security of tenure similar to that of the Judges of the Supreme Court. They can be removed only on the ground of proved misbehaviour or incapacity by the President on an address of Parliament adopted separately by each House by a majority of its total membership as well as by a two-thirds majority of those present and voting.

It is easier to amend the Constitution than to remove a judge from his office. Whilst expecting high rectitude from the dispensers of justice the Constitution guarantees them virtual irremovability in order to ensure independence of the judiciary. On June 24,1948, Jawaharlal Nehru stated in the Constituent Assembly that our judges should be "first-rate" men of the "highest integrity" who "should stand up against the executive government and whoever may come in their way."

The Constitution originally provided that a person who had retired as a Judge of a High Court could not plead or act in any Court or before any authority within the territory of India. The Constitution (Seventh Amendment) Act, 1956, partially modified the bar on retired High Court Judges. The amended article 220 now permits a retired High Court Judge to practise before the Supreme Court and any High Court other than the one in which he was a permanent Judge. But the Law Commission has criticized this provision and recommends for its abolition.

The salaries of the High Court judges cannot be varied and neither Parliament nor State Legislatures have any power in this matter. The President, however, is empowered to reduce the salaries of the Judges during the operation of the Proclamation of Financial Emergency. Allowances and rights in respect of leave of absence and pension of the Judges are determined by an Act of Parliament. Neither the allowances of a Judge nor his rights in respect of leave of absence or pension shall be varied to his disadvantage after his appointment. Salaries and allowances of the Judges have been charged on the Consolidated Fund of the State and hence are not votable. Their pensions are charged on the Consolidated Fund of India.

**Transfer of Judges**

Article 222 provides for transfer of a Judge from one High Court to another. The President may, after consultation with the Chief Justice of India, transfer a Judge from one High Court to another. According to the original provision a Judge transferred from one High Court to another was entitled to a compensatory allowance. This

5. The Government of India had been giving "piecemeal" extensions to additional Judges of several High Courts. Among the Judges favoured with short-term extensions were Justices O. N. Vohra, S. N. Kumar and B.S. Wad of the Delhi High Court. Fearing that they might not be given a further extension by the Government for reasons other than judicial, V.M. Tarkunde moved the Supreme Court with a request that the Government be asked to decide about their future most expeditiously. The Constitution Bench directed the Government on May 8, 1981 to take a decision at least ten days before the short-term extension of the three Judges expired. The Government granted only one year's extension to Justice Wad and refused to grant any extension to the other two Judges, though they were senior to Justice Wad. Justice Kumar went to the Supreme Court for redressal. For months the Supreme Court heard the arguments and in some aspects the case took an ugly shape. The majority opinion upheld the action of the Government.

was considered to have no justification and the Constitution (Seventh Amendment) Act, 1956, amended Article 222 to that extent. But the Constitution (Fifteenth Amendment) Act,1963, restored the original position and clause (2) which was omitted by the Seventh Amendment Act now provides that when a Judge has been transferred from one High Court to another,he shall be entitled to receive in addition to his salary such compensatory allowance as may be determined by Parliament and, until so determined, such compensatory allowance as the President may by order fix.

Between 1950 and 1975 judges of various High Courts were transferred; in each case with the consent of the judges transferred. Even when the States were reorganised and when the States of Maharashtra and Gujarat were carved out of the State of Bombay, only those judges of the existing Bombay High Court were transferred to the new High Court of Gujarat who consented to such transfer. During the Emergency in 1975, sixteen judges from various High Courts were transferred after consultation with the Chief Justice of India, A.N. Ray, to promote "national integration". One of these sixteen judges filed a writ petition in the Gujarat High Court against the orders of his transfer to Andhra Pradesh High Court and it succeeded. The Union Government filed an appeal in the Supreme Court. The Supreme Court decided by a majority of 3:2 that the President in consultation with the Chief Justice of India could transfer a Judge of the High Court under Article 222 in the "public interest "and the consent of the concerned judge was not a prerequisite.

The Consultative Committee of members of Parliament attached to the Ministry of Law and Justice unanimously recommended on June 7,1980 that the Chief Justice and at least one-third of the Judges of a High Court should be from outside the State under its jurisdiction. It also urged the Government to strictly implement in letter and spirit the provision of Article 222 of the Constitution relating to the transfer of Judges from one High Court to another. The Law Minister, P. Shiva Shankar,took note of the consensus at the meeting about the higher judiciary and said the mechanics of such appointments would have to be worked out in detail so that these could be implemented without discrimination.

Normally,the appointment of Chief Justices of High Courts and transfer of Judges should be above controversy and totally free of political motivation. But following the unhappy experience of Emergency period and the irresponsible talk by politicians of a "committed judiciary" fears were expressed in certain quarters, including the vast majority of lawyers in the country,that the new system being considered for senior judicial appointments and their transfers might be prompted by extraneous considerations. The recommendation of the Consultative Committee was designed to eliminate the chances of local prejudices and pressures determining the outcome of cases so as to ensure full justice to everyone. Such postings might in fact prove all to the good. The Law Commission's 80th Report presented to the Council of States (Rajya Sabha) on January 28, 1980, favoured the evolution of a convention according to which one-third of the judges in each High Court should be from another State. "This would have to be done through the process of initial appointments,and not by transfer ." However, the Commission approved the transfer of a Judge to preserve "the image and good name of the judiciary". But the Commission added the proviso that "no judge should be transferred without his consent from one to the other unless a panel consisting of the Chief Justice of India and his four seniormost colleagues finds sufficient cause for such a course. In case of differences between the members of the panel, the view of the majority should be taken to be the view of the panel." The Chief Justice of India was originally opposed to the transfer of Judges, as a matter of policy, as distinct from individual cases, but ultimately he veered round the Government's point of view.

**Jurisdiction of the High Courts**

The Constitution does not attempt detailed definitions or classification of the different types of jurisdiction of the High Courts. It was presumed that the High Courts which were functioning with well-defined jurisdiction at the time of the framing of the Constitution would continue with it and maintain their position as the highest courts in the Statue. The Constitution,accordingly, provided that the High Courts would retain their existing jurisdiction subject to the provisions of the Constitution and any future law that was to be made by the Legislature. This was affirmed by the Supreme Court in *National Sewing Thread Co. Ltd.* v. *James Chadwick and Bros. Ltd.(1953)*

Besides the normal original and appellate jurisdiction, the Constitution vested in the High

Courts four additional powers: (1) the power to issue writs or orders for the enforcement of Fundamental Rights or for any other purpose; (2) the power of superintendence over subordinate Courts; (3) the power to transfer cases to themselves pending in the subordinate Courts involving interpretation of the Constitution; and (4) the power to appoint officers.

The Constitution (Forty-second Amendment) Act,1976, denuded the High Courts of substantial powers and jurisdiction. Section 38 of the Amendment Act substituted a new Article for the original Article 226. While the High Courts still exercised the power tc issue writs or orders in the nature of *habeas corpus, mandamus, prohibition, qua waranto* and *certiorari,* or any of them for the enforcement of Fundamental Rights, but they could no longer exercise jurisdiction in any case where there was an invasion of a legal right. The words "for any other purpose" originally inclouded in Art:cle 226 were omitted and in their place quite a restricted jurisdiction was provided, that is in (a) cases where there was a contravention of a statutory provision causing substantial injury, and (b) cases where there was an illegality resulting in substantial failure of justice. In either case the court had to be satisfied before issuing directions, orders or writs that there was no other remedy available in any law to seek redress. Provision was also made that the High Courts would not issue interim order ordinarily except on notice to the other side and after giving the other side the opportunity to be heard. An exception could be made in cases where the loss or damage could not be compensated in terms of money. But an interim order would not be granted if the effect of such an order was to delay any inquiry into a matter of public importance or any investigation or inquiry into an offence punishable with imprisonment or action for the execution of any work cr project of public utility.

The newly inserted Article 226A debarred the High Courts from considering the constitutional validity of any Central law in any proceeding under Article 226. Hitherto the courts could consider the constitutional validity of both the Central and State laws in writ proceedings or otherwise. Article 131 A, also inserted by the Forty-second Amendment Act,1976, (S. 23) conferred upon the Supreme Court alone the exclusive jurisdiction in regard to questions involving the constitutional validity of central Laws. Article 228 was amended to provide that where a High Court was satisfied that a case pending before it involved any question as to the constitutional validity of any Central law or of both Central and State laws, the High Court was required to refer it for the decision of the Supreme Court.

The newly inserted Article 228A provided for the minimum number of Judges of a High Court who would sit for determining any questions to the constitutionality of any State law. The minimum number of Judges comprising the Constitution Bench was fixed at five. But where the number was less than five in a High Court all the Judges of that High Court would constitute the Bench. If the number of the Judges were five or more the decision as to the constitutional validity of law in question was to be determined by a two-thirds majority of the Judges sitting on the Bench. If the number was less than five, the law in question could not be declared invalid unless all the Judges held it to be so.

The Constitution (Forty-third Amendment) Act, 1977, made drastic amendments to the provisions of the Forty-second Amendment Act. It, *inter allia*, omitted Article 131A (exclusive jurisdiction of the Supreme Court in regard to questions as to the validity of Central laws), Article 226A (constitutional validity of Central laws not to be considered in proceedings under Article 226) and Article 228 A (special provisions as to the disposal of questions relating to constitutional validity of State laws). The rest was achieved by the Constitution (Forty-fourth Amendment) Act, 1978, by substantially amending Article 226 (power of High Courts to issue certain writs).

The High Courts are primarily Courts of appeal. Only in matters of admiralty, probate, matrimonials, contempt of Court, enforcement of Fundamental Rights and cases ordered to be transferred from a Lower Court involving the interpretation of the Constitution to their own file, they have original jurisdiction. The High Courts of Bombay, Calcutta and Madras exercise original civil jurisdiction when the amount involved exceeds specified limit. In criminal cases it extends to cases committed to them. On the appeal side they entertain appeals in civil and criminal cases from their subordinate courts as well as from their original side. For historical reasons and as a result of the specific provisions in the Government of India Act,1950, no High Court had any original jurisdiction in any matter concerning revenue. The 1950 Constitution removed this restriction. The Forty-second Amendment Act again took it away by omitting proviso to Article 225. But it has been restored by the Constitution (Forty-fourth Amendment) Act, 1978; the jurisdiction as it existed at the commencement of the Constitution in 1950.

The jurisdiction as well as laws administered by a High Court can be effected both by Parliament and State Legislature. Parliament exercises exclusive power to make laws touching the jurisdiction, power, and authority of all courts with respect to subjects on which it is competent to legislate. It can also legislate on subjects in the Concurrent List. Similarly, a State Legislature has power to make laws touching the jurisdiction, powers and authority of all courts within the State with respect to all subjects enumerated in the State List and in the Concurrent List. But with respect to matters in the Concurrent List the Union Law normally prevails in case of conflict.

**Power to Issue Writs**

Before the commencement of the Constitution in 1950 only the High Courts of Calcutta, Madras and Bombay had the power to issue certain prerogative writs within their original jurisdiction. Article 226 of the Constitution now empowers every High Court, throughout the territories in relation to which it exercises jurisdiction, to issue to any person or authority, including in appropriate cases, any Government, within those territories, directions, orders or writs, including writs in the nature of *habeas corpus, mandamus, prohibition, quo warranto* and *certiorari,* or any of them, for the enforcement of any of the Fundamental Rights and for any other purpose. The Constitution Forty-second Amendment Act, 1976, omitted the provision "for any other purpose" but the Forty-fourth Amendment Act, 1978 restored it.

The Forty-fourth Amendment Act inserted new clause (3) in Article 226 providing that where any party against whom an interim order, whether by way of injunction or stay or in any other manner is made on a writ petition without furnishing to such party copies of such petition and all documents in support of the plea for such interim order, and giving such party any opportunity of being heard makes an application for the vacation of such order and furnishes a copy of such application to the party in whose favour such order has been made or the counsel of such party, the High Court shall dispose of the application within a period of two weeks. If the application is not disposed of within the prescribed period of two weeks, the interim order shall on the expiry of that period, stand vacated.

Although the Supreme Court and the High Courts have concurrent jurisdiction in the enforcement of Fundamental Rights, the Constitution does not confer on the High Courts the special responsibility of protecting Fundamental Rights as the Supreme Court is vested with such a power. Under Article 32 the Supreme Court is made the guarantor and protector of Fundamental Rights whereas in the case of High Courts the power to enforce Fundamental Rights is part of their general jurisdiction. This special and unique position of the Supreme Court was emphasised by Justice Patanjali Sastri in *Romesh Thapar* vs. *The State of Madras.* It was observed, ".....Article 32 provides a 'guaranteed' remedy for the enforcement of those (fundamental) rights, and this remedial right is itself made a Fundamental Right by being included in Part III. This Court is thus constituted the protector and guarantor of Fundamental Rights and it cannot, consistently with the responsibility so laid upon it, refuse to entertain applications seeking protection against infringement of such rights."

**Power of Superintendence**

Every High Court has power of superintendence over all courts and tribunals throughout the territories in relation to which it exercises jurisdiction. In the exercise of the power of superintendence the High Court may call for returns from such courts, make and issue general rules and prescribe forms for regulating their practices and proceedings and prescribe forms in which books, entries and accounts shall be kept by the officers of these courts. The Constitution, accordingly, vests in each High Court, as the highest Court within its territorial jurisdiction, a special power and responsibility over all courts so that the judicial institutions in the State function properly and discharge their duties according to law. The power of superintendence over subordinate courts and tribunals is both judicial and administrative and the Constitution does not place any restriction on the exercise of this power, This point was made clear by Justice Nasir Ullah Beg of the the Allahabad High Court in *Jodhey* v. *State.* The Court observed, "On a proper interpretation of this clause it is difficult to my mind to hold that the powers of superintendence are conferred only on administrative matters. There are no limits, fetters or restrictions placed on the power of superintendence in this clause and the purpose of this clause seems to be to make the High Court the custodian of its jurisdiction and to arm it with a weapon that could be wielded for the purpose of seeing that justice is met out fairly and properly by the bodies mentioned therein."

**Transfer of Certain Cases**

If the High Court is satisfied that a case pending in a court subordinate to it involves a substantial question of law as to the interpretation of the Constitution, it may transfer the case to itself. After the case has come to the file of the High Court, it may dispose of the whole case itself, or may determine the constitutional question so involved and return the case to the court from which it had been withdrawn together with a copy of its judgment on such question and direct it to dispose of the case in conformity with such judgment. The Constitution, thus, denies to subordinate courts the right to interpret the Constitution so that there may be the maximum possible uniformity as regards constitutional decisions. It is, accordingly, the duty of the subordinate courts to refer to the High Court a case which involves a substantial question of law as to the interpretation of the Constitution and the case cannot be disposed of without the determination of such question. The High Court may also transfer the case to itself upon the application of a party in the case.

**Court of Record**

The High Court is a court of record and has all the powers of such a court including the power to punish for contempt of itself. The two characteristics of a court of record are that the records of such a Court are admitted to be of evidentiary value and that they cannot be questioned when produced before any court, and that it has the power to punish for contempt of itself. Neither the Supreme Court nor the Legislature can deprive a High court of its power of punishing a contempt of itself.

**Officers and Servants of the High Court**

Article 229 empowers the Chief Justice of a High Court to appoint officers and servants of the Court for the efficient performance of its functions. The Governor may in this respect require the Court to consult the State Public Service Commission. The Chief Justice is also authorised to control the conditions of service of the High Court staff subject to any law made by the State Legislature in this respect. The administrative expenses of the High Court are charged on the Consolidated Fund of the State. In *Pradyot Kumar* vs. *The Chief Justice of the Calcutta High Court* (1956), it was held that "a power of appointment includes the power to suspend or dismiss." The Chief Justice has, thus, the power to suspend or dismiss any officer or servant from the service of the High Court.

## SUBORDINATE COURTS

**Subordinate Judiciary**

Before the transfer of power the subordinate judiciary, particularly on the criminal side, did not command the unflinching confidence of the people for its independence and impartiality. Both the Indian Statutory Commission and the Joint Select Committee on Indian Constitutional Reform dwelt on this aspect and emphasised the paramount importance of an independent and fair-minded judiciary enjoying the confidence of the people. The Joint Select Committee laid special stress on the need for a competent subordinate judiciary in India "who are brought most closely into contact with the people, and it is no less important perhaps indeed even more important, that their independence should be placed beyond question than in the case of the superior judges."[6]

The Government of India Act, 1935, partially removed the existing defects on the civil side, but nothing tangible was done in the case of the magistracy on the criminal side. The District and Sessions Judges were appointed by the Governor, after consultation with a High Court, in his individual judgment.[7] Subordinate Civil Judges were recruited as a result of competitive examination and the government made rules, in consultation with the Public Service Commission and the High Court, defining the qualifications required. Their postings and promotions rested with the High Court. But in the case of District and subordinate Magistrates appointments were made by the Provincial Government under the provisions of the Code of Criminal Procedure and there was no obligation to consult the High Court. Nor was there any obligation to consult the High Court for their postings, transfers, promotions or for investing any of them with special criminal powers. The District Magistrate was also the principal District Officer, and the Collector. Am-

6. Joint Select Committee on Indian Constitutional Reform, Report (1934), para 337.
7. Government of India Act, 1935, Section 254.

bedkar correctly pointed out in the Constituent Assembly that the magistracy was sentimentally connected with the general system of administration.[8]

Originally, neither the Draft Constitution prepared by the Constitutional Adviser in 1947, nor the one prepared by the Drafting Committee in 1948, contained any specific provision on the subordinate judiciary. The intention at that time was that services of all types should not be included in the Constitution but were to be regulated by Acts of the appropriate Legislatures. The Conference of the Federal Court and the Chief Justices of High Courts held in March 1948, prominently discussed the omission to provide specifically for the subordinate judiciary in the constitution. The conference regarded it as most essential that the members of the subordinate judiciary should not be exposed to the extraneous influence of the party in power. In a Memorandum incorporating comments and suggestions on the Draft Constitution, Judges observed, "So long as the subordinate judiciary, including the District Judges, have to depend upon the provincial (state) executive for their appointment, posting, promotion and leave, they cannot remain entirely free from the influence of members of the party in power and cannot be expected to act impartially and independently in the discharge of their duties. It is, therefore, recommended that provisions be made placing exclusively in the hands of the High Courts the power of appointment and dismissal, posting, promotion and grant of leave in respect of the entire subordinate judiciary including District Judges."[9]

The Drafting Committee accepted these suggestions. The Committee came to the conclusion that the time was appropriate for assimilating the civil and criminal justice and placing them equally under the control of the High Courts. The Drafting Committee, accordingly, drafted new provisions and inserted a new Chapter VIII in Part VI of the Draft Constitution containing Articles 209-A, 209-B and 209-C. These provisions regarding the Subordinate Judiciary came for discussion in the Constituent Assembly on September 16, 1949. In moving the new Article, Ambedkar made some changes. The promotion and posting of the District and Sessions Judges, which under the Draft Constitution, were the functions of the High Courts, were now made the responsibility of the Governors in consultation with the High Courts. Whereas in the Draft Articles, as first proposed, the High Courts were vested with full powers in regard to the posting and promotion of all members of the subordinate judiciary, the amended Articles confined this power of the High Courts to the subordinate civil judiciary alone. A new Article was added to provide that the procedure laid down for the civil judiciary would apply to the magistracy exercising criminal jurisdiction if the Governor by public notification so directed and that too subject to such exceptions and modifications as he might specify. In defending these changes Ambedkar observed. "The Drafting Committee would have been very happy if it was in a position to recommend to the House that immediately on the commencement of the Constitution, provisions with regard to the appointment and the control of the civil judiciary by the High Court were also made applicable to the magistracy. But it has been realized that the magistracy is intimately connected with the general system of administration. We hope that the proposals which are now being entertained by some of the Provinces to separate the judiciary from the executive will be accepted by the other Provinces so that the provisions of Article 209-E would be made applicable to the Magistrates in the same way as we propose to make them applicable to the civil judiciary. But some time must be permitted to elapse for the effectuation of the proposals for the separation of the judiciary and the executive. It has been felt that the best thing is to leave this matter to the Governor to do by public notification as soon as the appropriate changes for the separation of the judiciary and the executive are carried through in any of the Provinces."[10]

The Constituent Assembly finally adopted the Articles proposed by Ambedkar and they became Articles 233 to 237 of the Constitution.

### Appointment of District and other Judges

The Constitution divides judicial posts into two categories. The higher categories include District and Sessions Judges, Judges of the City Civil Courts, Additional District and Sessions Judges, Joint District and Sessions Judges, Assistant District and Sessions Judges, Chief Judges of Small Cause Courts, Chief Presidency Magistrates and Additional Chief Presidency Magis-

8. *Constituent Assembly Debates,* Vol. IX, p. 1571.
9. *The Framing of India's Constitution, Select Documents,* Vol. IV, p. 186.
10. *Constituent Assembly Debates,* Vol. IX, p. 1571.

trates. The second or lower category includes other civil judicial posts inferior to the post of a District Judge. Appointments to posts in the higher category are made by the Governor of the State in consultation with High Court exercising jurisdiction in relation to such State. No person, other than one already in the service of the Union or to the State, is eligible for appointment in this category except an advocate or a pleader of seven years' standing and is duly recommended by the High Court for appointment.

All appointments in the lower category, *i.e.,* other judicial posts inferior to the posts of a District and Sessions Judges, are made by the Governor of a State in consultation with the Public Service Commission and the High Court exercising jurisdiction in relation to such State. The practice that exists in most States is that the Public Service Commission conducts a competitive examination for recruitment to the judicial service of the State. The Commission prescribes certain minimum educational and professional qualifications for candidates competing for this examination. The required vacancies are filled up from amongst the list of successful candidates in order of merit. The selected candidates are given special training for a certain period before regular appointment to the service. Thereafter, they come under the superintendence of the High Court in the discharge of their responsibilities.

The control over District Courts and courts subordinate thereto has been vested in the High Court. Article 235 provides that '"the control over District Courts and courts subordinate thereto including the posting and promotion of and the grant of leave to, persons belonging to the judicial service of a State and holding any post inferior to the post of the District Judge shall be vested in the High Court............'' The control by the High Court, accordingly, includes control over the posting, promotion and grant of leave to persons belonging to the judicial service and holding posts inferior to that of a District Judge. All subordinate courts, in brief, are placed under the administrative control of the High Court. Postings and promotions of District judges are made by the Governor in consultation with the High Court.

**Criminal Courts**

Every district in a State has both civil and criminal courts. On the criminal side there is a great measure of uniformity throughout India as the Code of Criminal Procedure applies to all courts. At the head of a district is the Sessions Courts presided over by a Sessions Judge. A Judge of a Sessions Court may pass any legal sentence, but a death sentence is subject to confirmation by the High Court. Sometimes he is assisted by Additional Sessions Judges. Subordinate to a Sessions Judge, who is also a District Judge, is a hierarchy of different grades of Civil and Criminal Courts. Besides hearing suits, the civil courts exercise jurisdiction over several matters such as arbitration, guardianship, marriage, divorce and probate. Quasi-judicial tribunals distinct from the ordinary courts have also been set up under certain special Acts for determining some types of civil rights. In some cases, appeals lie from their orders to the ordinary civil courts. But when no such right is given, they are subject to the constitutional right of superintendence of High Courts.

The constitution and organisation of criminal courts and their procedure are regulated by the Code of Criminal Procedure, 1973 which became operative on April 1, 1974, repealing the Code of Criminal Procedure, 1898. The Code of 1973 provides separate sets of magistrates for performing the executive and judicial functions. The Executive Magistrates are under the control of the State Government whereas Judicial Magistrates are under the control of the High Court. On the executive side, for each District there is a District Magistrate and under him work a number of Executive Magistrates. These Magistrates continue to deal with problems relating to the maintenance of law and order and the prevention of crime. On the judicial side, the judicial hierarchy of magistrates consists of the Chief Judicial Magistrates at the district level and the Judicial Magistrates of the first and second class. Broadly speaking, Magisterial functions, which are essentially judicial in nature, are the concern of the Judicial Magistrates. In metropolitan areas, with population of more than 10 lakhs, there are Metropolitan Magistrates who exercise larger powers for quicker disposal of cases.

The Code of Criminal Procedure 1973, has ushered in radical changes. The new Code provides for the separation of Judiciary from the Executive on an All-India basis. There is now complete separation from April, 1974 in all the States and Union Territories, except Jammu and Kashmir, Nagaland and tribal areas. Several other important changes designed to expedite the disposal of cases, to improve efficiency, to prevent abuses and to afford relief to the poor sections of the community have been brought about.

The system of appointing honorary magistrates or justices of the peace has been abandoned. Instead, a provision has been made for the appointment of retired or serving officers of Government as special magistrates with summary powers to try special categories of petty cases. The jury system has also been abolished.

Under the Code, every person arrested with or without warrant is required to be informed of the grounds of his arrest and in bailable cases has right to be released on bail. No person can be kept in police custody during investigation for a period exceeding fifteen days, even by an order of the court. No person can be kept on remand by order of the court for more than sixty days in any case. After the expiry of that period if the challan is not put up in a court, he is entitled to be released on bail. Provisions relating to bail have been liberalised and anticipatory bail can be granted in certain cases.

Another major change is the doing away with preliminary inquiry in sessions cases. The powers of revision conferred on superior courts cannot be exercised in respect of interlocutory orders. In order to ensure speedy disposal of cases the provision relating to compulsory stay of proceedings on the mere intention of the party to move for a transfer of the case has been omitted. But stay of proceedings can be obtained from superior courts in proper cases. Provision has also been made to afford an opportunity to the accused to make his representation, if any, on the punishment proposed to be given after conviction. The provision for demanding security from habitual offenders has been extended to anti-social offenders, such as, smugglers, blackmarketeers and persons, who default in provident fund contribution or commit offense under the Untouchability (offences) Act etc.

It has been compulsory to give a copy of the first information report to the informant. If a police officer refuses to record the information, the aggrieved party can send it by post to the Superintendent of Police, who will pursue the matter. Limits have been prescribed for the duration of security proceedings. Such proceedings shall ordinarily terminate, if they are not concluded within a period of six months. In cases where the offence is punishable with imprisonment for a period of two years or less, the investigation, if not completed within six months, can be stopped by a magistrate. Periods of limitation on a graded scale for launching criminal prosecutions have been provided in cases not punishable with imprisonment for more than three years.

**Civil Courts**

Throughout India, excepting the ''Presidency'' Towns–Bombay, Calcutta and Madras–the District Civil Court is presided over by a District Judge who is also the Sessions Judge. The Court of the District Judge is the principal civil court in the district and exercises both judicial and administrative powers. It exercises both original and appellate jurisdiction in civil cases and has wide powers under Special Acts, such as, Succession Act, the Guardians and Wards Act, the Provincial Insolvency Act, and the Divorce Act. The District Judge has the power of superintendence over subordinate courts exercising civil jurisdiction in a district.

Next to the District Judge's court is the court of a Civil or a Senior Subordinate Judge. This court has jurisdiction over cases of any amount. In the States where there are courts of Civil Judges they have no appellate jurisdiction whereas the courts of Senior Subordinate Judges excerise appellate power in minor cases. Below them are the courts of Subordinate Judges or Munsiffs as they are named in Bihar, Orissa, Uttar Pradesh and Assam. Subordinate Judges exercise appellate power in minor cases. Below them are the courts of Subordinate Judges or Munsiffs may be of the First or Second Class with varying jurisdiction. Appeals from the Subordinate Civil Courts lie, in the first instance, to the District Court if the amount involved does not exceed five thousand rupees. If it exceeds five thousand rupees, appeals lie to the HIgh Court. Rights of second appeal differ in different States, but there is a right of second appeal on a point of law, or on account of a substantial defect in procedure, or when the Court of first appeal differs on a question of fact from the court of first instance.

Small Causes Courts have been established in big towns for the expeditious disposal of cases not involving difficult questions of law and where the amount involved does not exceed two thousand rupees, or one thousand rupees, or five hundred rupees as the State Government may determine. Small Causes Courts follow summary procedure and the judgments are not ordinarily appealable though error in law may be rectified in revision.

In some States, Village Panchayats have been invested with power to try minor civil cases involving movable property. The decisions of the Panchayats are not appealable.

## SUGGESTED READINGS


Bettelheim, Cherles, *Indian Independence.*

Desai, A.R., *Social Background of Indian Nationalism.*

Granville Austin, *The Indian Constitution, A Cornerstone of a Nation.*

Hanson O.H. and, Janet Douglas *India's Democracy.*

Jennings, *W.I., Some Characteristics of the Indian Constitution.*

Karunakaran, K.P., *Democracy in India.*

Kothari, Rajni, *Stage Against Democracy.*

Morris-Jone, W.A., *The Government and Politics of India.*

Palmer, N.D., *The Indian Political System.*

Rudolph & Rudolph, *In Pursuit of Lakshmi*

Shukla, V.N., *Constitution of India.*

# CHAPTER XVI

# Services Under the Union and the States

### How the Government Operates

Government, whether Union or State, operates through its Secretariat. The Secretariat,both at the Centre and in a State, is divided into Ministries and Departments among whom various subjects of governmental activity are distributed according to administrative convenience. Each Ministry is presided over by a Minister. In most of the Ministries of the Union Government there is at least one Deputy Minister, who is also a member of the Council of Ministers. But a Deputy Minister does not hold separate charge of a Ministry. His task is to assist the Minister, with whom he is associated, in his administrative and parliamentary duties and he may be compared to a Parliamentary Secretary in Britain; a "Junior Minister."

Besides the political heads of various Ministries of Government there are a number of permanent officials and clerical staff. At the head of each Ministry is the permanent Secretary, till recently a member of the Indian Civil Service, which is extinct now with the retirement of the last incumbent in March 1980, or Indian Administrative Service, who occupies a position of the very highest responsibility and importance. In fact, the Secretary is the key man in the Ministry who helps his political chief to see that the Ministry works efficiently and in particular direction. The Secretaries have in most cases been so long attached to their respective ministries that they acquire complete grasp of affairs within their own spheres and provide "a permanent brains trust" to the Ministers who are amateurs in the art of administration. Then, there are in the Ministry, possibly an Additional Secretary, a Joint Secretary, a Deputy Secretary, an Under Secretary, Assistant Secretaries, Superintendents and many others who do merely secretariat work of a purely routine character. Highest and lowest, these non-political agents of administration make up, in general, the Civil Service. Their tenure of office is permanent and they continue to function regardless of political changes. They are outside the domain of politics and this is the most important feature of the Civil Service. Lord Balfour has given a true picture of the position which Civil Servants occupy in Britain and it is applicable similarly to the Civil Service in India. The Civil Servants, wrote Lord Balfour, "do not control policy; they are for that very reason an invaluable element in Party Government. It is through them, especially through their higher branches, that the transference of responsibility from one party or one minister to another involves no destructive shock to the administrative machine. There may be change of directions, but the curve is smooth."[1] The Civil Servants, in brief, keep the wheels of governmental machine going and act as agents for the fulfilment of the policy of the party in office; the policy formulated during the election and formally endorsed by Parliament. They are a link between successive ministries, and repository of principles and practices which endure while governments come and go. Their rigid neutrality in the party political issues is the first code of their official conduct and they serve with equal fidelity whatever be the complexion of Government. All Civil Servants owe a temporary allegiance to the party in power and its programme, no matter what their bias or personal conviction. "The first thing," observed Viscount Attlee, "a Minister finds on entering office is that he can depend absolutely on the loyalty of his staff and, on leaving office, he will seldom be able to say what the private political views are even of those with whom he has worked most closely."[2]

### Functions of a Ministry

The functions of a Ministry may broadly be said to be four. First, a Ministry must answer for its administration to the public. Administration does not operate in the vacuum. Since it translates policy into practice, the policy, which has received the approval of the people and endorsement of the Legislature, must be capable of

1. *Introduction to Bagehot's English Constitution,* p. XXIV.
2. "Civil Servants, Ministers, Parliament and the Public," *The Indian Journal of Public Administration,* April-June 1955, p. 96.

explaining itself. It means the accountability of administration to both the Legislature and the public. As this accountability is to be effected through those who are responsible for administration, the Ministry must provide to their political chief all relevant information so that he may be able to defend the actions of his Ministry in the Legislature and in the public forums. The work of the Ministry must, therefore, be conducted in such a way and its policy so framed that it should be capable of "articulate rational defence."

The second function of the Ministry is the drawing up of its policy. Policy, really, is formulated by the Cabinet. But all details of the working out of the policy so formulated and all routine business connected thereto are left to various Ministries of the Government. Very often the Ministry may itself suggest proposals within the framework of the policy of the government. Such proposals may either be the outcome of the Ministry's own administrative experience or may be the result of the directions given to it by its political chief. Whatever be its origin, the Ministry prepares the draft of the scheme, works out its details in accordance with the general policy determined by the Cabinet and consults the interests likely to be affected by it. If the scheme of the policy cannot be carried out within the framework of the existing law, then, it passes into the stage of proposals for a Bill. After its approval by the Cabinet it is drafted as a Bill to be laid before the Legislature at the Centre or in the States, as the case may be. The Bill is sponsored and piloted by the Minister-in-charge of the Ministry to which it relates and it is his responsibility to see it through. But the members of the Civil Service have to remain in attendance in the Legislature to assist the Minister with information and advice, whenever he is under fire in the House. It will, thus, be clear that even if the inspiration of the Bill may have come from the Minister, the preparatory work is the task of the Ministry and in great part the result of the influence exerted by the permanent Secretary. "The second thing a Minister will discover on entering office,'" wrote Attlee, "is that the Civil Servant is prepared to put up every possible objection to his policy, not from desire to thwart him, but because it is his duty to see that the Minister understands all the difficulties and dangers of the course which he wishes to adopt."[3]

Most modern statutes are "skeleton legislation." Legislatures legislate in general terms only, empowering the Ministries to give effect to the statutes. The rules and regulations so made have the force of law. The Ministry will, probably, concurrently with its preparation of the Bill work out regulations and subordinate acts of legislation and shortly after the Bill becomes law will issue them in the form drafted by the Law Department. In the application of the rules and regulations to specific cases, the Executive often assumes a quasi-judicial role. Innumerable kinds of judicial or quasi-judicial functions arise in the course of administration of public services, particularly those which affect the individual welfare of large sections of the community. In fact, the switching over of the functions of the State from negative to positive has necessitated it for Legislatures to act along two lines especially. In the first place, Legislature delegates a certain broad rule-making authority to the administration and, secondly, authority is conferred upon administration, in certain cases to adjudicate controversies. Decisions of these kinds are not truly judicial as they do not determine legal rights. They are, however, an extremely important means by which administration makes policy and shapes the nation's future within the framework of powers agreed to by Parliament.

Finally, the function of the Ministry is to implement policy. When the policy has been determined, presented and sanctioned, it becomes the duty of the permanent officials of the Ministry to see that it is faithfully carried out, even if the policy is not what they might have urged. Sir Warren Fisher cogently explained the principles on which Civil Servants in Britain act. It will be instructive to quote them here. Fisher says, "Determination of policy is the function of Ministers, and once a policy is determined it is the unquestioned and unquestionable business of the civil servant to strive to carry out that policy with precisely the same goodwill whether he agrees with it or not. That is axiomatic and will never be in dispute. At the same time, it is the traditional duty of the civil servants, while decisions are being formulated, to make available to their political chiefs all the information and experience at their disposal, and to do this without fear or favour, irrespective of whether the advice thus tendered may accord or not with the Minister's initial view. The presentation to the Minister

3. *Ibid*, p. 96.

of the relevant facts, the ascertainment and marshaling of which may often call into play the whole orgainsation of the Department, demands of the civil servant greatest care. The presentation of inferences from the facts equally demands from him all wisdom and detachment he can command."[4] There is little evidence in England of Civil Servants sabotaging the policy of the responsible political head of their Department.

R.K. Ramadhyani, writing on the Role of Civil Servants, says, "The civil Servant has thus the dual role of being the executive for the policy of a party and of being its interpreter; he is also in a good measure a maker of policy on its behalf. It is mainly in executing the policy of the party that conflict may arise; it can only be secondary in making new or subsidiary policy. A Civil Servant, exercising his democratic right of vote may have even cast his vote against the party which has come into power. He is now called upon to implement the policy of the party and very clearly he is in duty bound to do so, as he is not a ruler by himself but a public servant. It is his duty, therefore, to try to understand the policy of the party which has the mandate of the people and to implement it in the most faithful way. If he did not do so he would not be true to the democratic form of government which requires that for the time being the rule of the majority has to be accepted by the minority."[5]

## Organisation of the Civil Service

The guiding principles of Civil Service orgainsation are very simple and obvious. They are three : a unified service, recruitment by open competition, and classification of posts into intellectual for policy, and clerical for mechanical work to be filled separately by separate examination. The division of Civil Servants into these two categories is essential for the proper performance and co-ordination of functions and for making policy responsive and responsible. In the clerical category may be placed all such work as is either of a simple mechanical kind or consists in the application of well-defined regulations, decisions and practices to particular cases. In the other category—intellectual for policy—may be placed all such work as is concerned with the formulation of policy, the revision of existing practice of current regulations and directions, and the orgainsation and directions of the business of government.

The administrative class is pivotal and directing class of the whole Civil Service. "They are responsible," as Herman Finer says with reference to the British administrative class, "for transmitting the impulse from their political chief, from the statutes and declaration of policy, through the rest of the service and out to the public."[6] On this class rest, in India as in Britain, the responsibilities for formulating departmental policy and for controlling and directing the various Ministries. They are a body of advisers who find solutions that arise outside the normal routine of departmental work, supply suggestions which may form the ingredients of supreme policy and interpret regulations applying to difficult cases. The Directive Principles of State Policy enshrined in the Constitution, the realization of the objective of a Welfare State on a socialistic pattern and the prodigious effort involved in the proper execution of Five-Year Plans have created new responsibilities and onerous tasks for the whole administration and particularly for the administrative class. Their duties have become all-comprehensive and embrace planning, control and guidance of the entire economic as well as social life of the nation.[7] "When it becomes the central purpose and justification of government," wrote Sukhthankar, the then Cabinet Secretary, "while adhering to democratic values and methods to find a rich social and economic content for freedom to bring about equality of opportunity for all and to secure the maximum development of the human and material resources of a vast country, the administration faces new and immensely vital tasks." These new and immensely vital tasks "require the proper development of new arts of what may be called social and economic engineering."[8]

For the efficient performance of these heavy and arduous duties the administrative officers must necessarily possess a trained mental equipment of a higher order, capable of ready mastery of complex and intricate problems. They must also possess virtue of human sympathy. Prime Minister Jawaharlal Nehru reminded his

4. As quoted in Jennings' *Cabinet Government,* pp. 114-15
5. *Hindustan Times,* New Delhi, May 10, 1957.
6. *The Theory and Practice of Modern Government,* p. 767.
7. Introduction to Public Administration in India, Report of a Survey by Paul H. Appleby.
8. Govind Ballabh Pant, "Public Servant in a Democracy," published in the *Indian Journal of Public Administration,* July-September 1955, p. 181.

audience consisting of civil servants at Kurnool, on December 9, 1955 of the exact purpose of the Services. "The Services", he explained, "as their name implies are supposed to serve, obviously. Serve who ?—society, the people, the country. Why I say this, because the test, always, has to be how far the Services, whether as a whole or any individual member of them are serving the larger causes that society has, that the nation has."[9] The qualities exactly wanted in public servants must, therefore, be : initiative and enterprise, planning and organizing capacity, efficiency, honesty, loyalty, political neutrality, width of social outlook and the spirit of social service.

The British Civil Service is world famous for its political neutrality, impartiality and integrity. "The characteristic which has long been recognised in the British administrator," observed the Report of the Committee on the Political Activities of the Civil Servants, "and extolled as a special virtue is his impartiality and, in his public capacity, a mind untinged by political prepossession." But this traditional concept of political neutrality is undergoing, as S. Lall observed, "radical change under the impact of many factors some of which are common to all nations and others special to under-developed countries like India. The concept is being rapidly transformed, without a conscious realization and neutrality to a positive, non-partisan participation in the management of country's affairs."[10] The process of decision is no longer exclusively confined to the Ministers. It is diffused over the entire system of Government. The Ministers may ultimately mould and shape policies, but all such policies are being constantly readjusted "in a seamless web of a multiplicity of agencies." This complexity and dispersal of the decision-making process in the scale and scope of governmental activities (particularly in matters of welfare and State enterprise), the pressure thrown up by the democratic processes involved in the establishment of an egalitarian society and the increasing complexity of modern society. "The higher echelons of the Civil Services today not only advise and assist the Ministers in the formulation of policy; they indirectly influence decision." The dichotomy of the governmental process into politics and administration, *i.e,* 'decision' and 'execution' no longer exists.

**Committed Bureaucracy**

In his presidential address to the All-India Congress Committee's Calcutta session in December 1972, Shankar Dayal Sharma (currently Vice-President of India) described the present administrative machinery as being ill-suited to be an effective instrument of social change. He dwelt at length on the need for a complete overhaul of the administrative machinery which, he said, "does not have the necessary commitment and perspective" for putting through a plan for "the socialist transformation of our people's lives."[11] While commending the statement on the economic policy to the Subjects Committee of the Congress on December 27, 1972, the Planning Minister, D.P. Dhar, enunciated its "fundamental objective" as increased production in agriculture and industry. This process, he said, should go hand in hand with social justice. "We make a commitment that production in both the sectors has got to be achieved in a stipulated period. And for this we must not depend upon bureaucracy." Many results in the past, Dhar explained, "got bogged down in the quagmire of bureaucratic corruption and inefficiency, in spite of clear enunciation of objectives."[12] On the penultimate day of the Congress plenary session, December 28, 1972, the Prime Minister, Mrs. Indira Gandhi, stressed the need for administrative reforms, emphasizing that a system inherited from colonial rule could not keep pace with the changed mood of the nation.[13]

Clearly, an administrative structure that served British colonial needs is no longer relevant, but it makes no plea for a committed bureaucracy. A committed bureaucracy is possible only in a totalitarian regime, for a committed administration and democratic procedures are directly incompatible. Commitment in this context means a dedicated endorsement of whatever is prescribed by the party in power. But the most significant aspect of a democratic system is that it allows for an alternative government. A committed bureaucracy will then mean that the entire bureaucratic set-up would have to go with every change in the party complexion of the government. A politically neutral administration, re-

9. Published in the *Indian Journal of Public Administration*, October-December 1955, p. 289.
10. "Civil Service Neutrality," *Indian Journal of Public Administration*, January-March 1958, p. 1.
11. *Indian Express*, New Delhi, December 27, 1972.
12. *The Times of India*, New Delhi, December 29, 1972.
13. *The Statesman*, New Delhi, December 30, 1972.

sponsive to the policies prescribed by the party in power is quite a different thing from the kind of commitment which has been fashionable with the Congress leaders to demand from all sections of the government including the Judiciary. The Congress Parliamentary Party executive set up a nine-member committee "to consider problems of administration and suggest remedial measures. The Committee could not complete its labours before the Congress went out of office in April, 1977. Obviously, the emphasis of the Committee would have been on "commitment." But in democracy, no party remains in power perpetually and the concept of a committed bureaucracy presupposes that the administration is not at the disposal of any party other than one in power.

**Classification of Services**

In countries with a federal polity, it is usual for the Central Government and the Governments of the constituent units to have separately organsied services for the administration of subjects falling within their respective spheres of jurisdiction. In India, too, there are two sets of services, Central Services and State Services. The Central Services are concerned with the administration of Union subjects, such as, Foreign Affairs, Defence, Income Tax, Customs, Posts and Telegraphs etc., and the officers of these services are exclusively in the employ of the Union Government. The subjects within the jurisdiction of the States, such as public order, local Government, education, public health, agriculture, land revenue, veterinary, etc., are administered by the State Services and the officers of thse services are exclusively in the employ of their State Governments. In addition to these two classes of Services, the Constitution also provides for the All-India Services, a form of personnel organisation which has no parallel in any other federal country, except Pakistan. The All-India Services are common to the Union and the States and are composed of officers "who are in the exclusive employ of neither and may at any time be at the disposal of either." The Constitution at its commencement named two such Services, the Indian Administrative Service and the Indian Police Service.[14] It is further provided that other All-India Services, including an All-India Judicial Service,[15] may also be created by Parliament, if the Council of States (Rajya Sabha) declares by a resolution supported by not less than two-thirds of the members present and voting that it is necessary or expedient in the national interest to do so. A resolution was adopted by the Council on December 6, 1961, to the effect that it was necessary and expedient to the national interest that Parliament should by law provide for the creation of Indian Forest Service and it was constituted with effect from July 1, 1966. In 1965 the Council approved the setting up an Indian Agricultural Service and the Indian Educational Service. Although both these Services have not so far come into existence, but it does indicate the trend of administrative thinking in the sixties. "It is curious", says S.P. Aiyar, that "services which had been abolished because they were considered to be the creations of an imperial power and running counter to the genuine spirit of provincial autonomy were again sought to be resurrected.'[16]

Ambedkar explained in the Constituent Assembly the reasons for making this extraordinary provision for the creation of All-India services particularly the Indian Administrative Service. He said, "The dual polity which is inherent in a federal system is followed in all Federations by a dual service. In all Federations there is a Federal Civil Service and a State Civil Service. The Indian Federation, though a dual polity, will have a dual service, but with one exception. It is recognised that in every country there are certain posts in its administrative set-up which might be called strategic from the point of view of maintaining the standard of administration....... There can be no doubt that the standard of administration depends upon the calibre of the Civil Servants who are appointed to these strategic posts........ The Constitution provides that without depriving the States of their right to form their own civil service there shall be an all-India Service recruited on All-India basis with common qualifications with uniform scale of pay and members of which alone could be appointed to these strategic posts throughout the Union." The members of the Indian Administrative Service, therefore, man administration both at the Centre as well as in the States. Referring to three All-India Services—Engineering, Medical and Forests—the Home Minister, Lal Bahadur Shastri, said at Tirupati on September 25, 1962, that these three proposed services were being constituted to bring about homogeneity and unity in the

14. Article 312 (2).
15. Article 312 (1) as amended by the Constitution. (Forty-second Amendment) Act, 1976.
16. Maheswari, B.L. (Ed.), *Centre-State Relations*, p. 200.

administration. This was one of the recommendations, Shastri added, of the States Reorganization Commission.[17] The States Reorganisation Commission having bowed in 1956 before the demand for linguistic States, it sought to counter any tendency therein for disintegration by recommending new All-India Services. The Government of India zealously pursued it and made the State Chief Ministers to agree at a special 'integration' conference in August 1961, to the creation of three All-India Services—Engineering, Medical and Health and Forest—but they resisted the proposals for a fourth, for Education. The All-India Services, thus, came increasingly to be seen as a great force in national integration.

But after the 1967 General Election, the spirit for more State rights took a concrete shape when the Tamil Nadu Government appointed the Rajamannar Committee to examine the entire relationship that should subsist between the Centre and the States in a federal set-up with reference to the provisions of the Constitution of India. The Rajamannar Committee Report (1971) devoted one full Chapter to the Civil Services in India. It regarded with apprehension the nature of Article 312 which does not provide for consultation with the States prior to the passing of a resolution by the Council of States (Rajya Sabha) for the creation of an All-India Service, or at any other stage before constituting such a service. The Committee's main grievance was that Article 312 gives complete and final authority to the Union Government which can, if it so chooses, brush aside any suggestion made in that respect by a State Government. The Committee quoted with approval the views of the Study Team of the Administrative Reforms Commission that in a federal set-up "to have an All-India Service that serves the needs of the States but is controlled by the Union is an unusual feature." The Committee also recalled the statement made by the Joint Parliamentary Committee (1934) that the existence of All-India Services was incompatible with provincial autonomy.

### The Indian Administrative Service

The Civil Service in India may be divided into three categories : the All-India Services, the Union Services, and the State Public Services. All-India Services are those specified in Article 312 (a) of the Constitution, namely, the Indian Administrative Service and the Indian Police Service. A few more have since been created. Union or Central Services include services in the various administrative departments of the Government of India such as the Indian Foreign Service, the Indian Revenue Service, the Indian Audits and Accounts Service, the Indian Railways Service, and the Indian Posts and Telegraphs Services. There are several engineering and other ministerial services.

The successor to the Indian Civil Service, the "steel frame" of the British Indian administration, is the Indian Administrative Service. The control and management of the Indian Administrative Service (IAS) as S.B. Bapat explained "is necessarily a joint co-operative affair."[18] The Service is organsied in the form of a number of I.A.S. cadres for each State. Recruitment to the Service is made by the Union Government on the result of a competitive examination conducted by the Union Public Service Commission. The officers recruited are allotted to different State cadres. The strength of each cadre is so fixed as to include a reserve of officers who can be deputed for service under the Union Government for one or more "tenures" of three, four or five years before they return to their State cadre. This arrangement is claimed to have the advantage of having at the disposal of the Union Government the services of officers with first-hand knowledge and experience of conditions in the States. And the States have officers, after their return to the State cadre, who are fully familiar with the policies and programmes of the Union Government.

There is yet another distinctive feature of the Indian Administrative Service. It is a multi-purpose Service composed of "generalist administrators" who are expected, from time to time, to hold posts involving a wide variety of duties and functions. At one time they may be responsible for the maintenance of law and order, at another time for the collection of revenue, regulation of trade, commerce or industry, and still at another they may be engaged in welfare activities like education, health, labour and development and extension work in agriculture and reconstruction. Thus, the administrators get a general training in more or less every branch of administration. There are two definite advantages of such a system of service. According to the arguments

17. *The Tribune,* Ambala Cantt, September 27, 1962.
18. "The Training of the Indian Administrative Service". *The Indian Journal of Public Administration,* April-June 1955, p. 119.

of Macaulay and Jowett, it is a better qualification for intellectual work than a special training, and that success in such a kind of training is likely to indicate desirable qualities of character. Secondly, it accounts for the liberal outlook of the administrators.

The method of recruitment to the Indian Administrative Service, the Indian Foreign Service and the Indian Police Service combines a written examination of high standard. Till recently the written test included compulsory papers and a number of optional papers, the precise mix being different for Indian Administrative Service and the Indian Foreign Service on the one hand, and the Indian Police Service on the other, selected from a group so made as to compel the candidates to go outside the range of subjects which they might have studied at the university level. The written examination was followed by a searching personality test. Candidates had to secure a certain minimum percentage of marks in the aggregate of compulsory and lower optional papers before they could be called for interview. For a period, it was the rule, that a candidate could be failed on personality test alone. A change was subsequently brought about and the interview marks were simply added to those of written papers. This method of recruitment, according to S.P. Bapat, ensured that the youngmen recruited to service "possess not only a high level of intelligence and academic learning, but an adequate measure of the qualities of personality and character, such as, discernment, clarity of thought and expression, intellectual integrity, self-confidence, self-possession, breadth of outlook and sense of moral and social values–qualities which must be looked for in persons holding responsible, administrative positions in any democratic welfare state."[19]

The scheme of examination hitherto followed has undergone a substantial change since 1979, primarily as a result of administrative compulsions. In 1976, 30,739 candidates applied for 679 vacancies in the Indian Administrative and Indian Police Service and the non-technical higher Central Services. Out of this number 17,645 candidates appeared at the examination out of which 1,157 were declared qualified for the interview and as a result of that 679 were finally declared recruited to these Services in accordance with the vacancies in each.

In order to get out of the difficulty of growing number of candidates when the vacancies were limited to around 700, the Kothari Commission was appointed on Recruitment Policy and Selection Methods in 1974. The Commission submitted its report in 1976 and recommended, which was accepted by the Government, a new scheme of examination consisting of two parts : a preliminary examination (objective type) and the Civil Service main examination which includes a written examination and interview. The preliminary examination, consisting of one compulsory and one optional papers, serves the purpose of a screening test. For example, in 1979 out of a total of 67,500 candidates at the preliminary test well over 60,000 were weeded out and in 1980 out of a total of 65,000 candidates 9,000 were declared eligible for the main examination. In 1981, roughly 8,600 wrote the Civil Service (Main) Examination. According to the UPSC Report 2.29 Lakhs applied for the Preliminary Examination and only 1.10 Lakhs (about a tenth of the number) appeared for the examination, and of it 11, 250 qualified for the Main Examination. As regards the academic background of the aspirants to the I.A.S. in the recent years they have ranged from the professionally qualified like Chartered Accountants, Engineers from ITTs and even M.B.B.S. from prestigious institutions to doctorates in different disciplines. The first ranker in the I.A.S. for 1990 was on Engineering graduate from the ITT, Madras. This shows when there are a multiplicity of career options available in today's context, unlike the early Fifties and Sixties, the I.A.S. is still considered a coveted Service. The successful candidates at the Preliminary test sit for the Main Examination consisting of eight Papers and an interview. Of these eight papers, English, one language and General Studies (consisting of two papers) are compulsory and a candidate has an option to select two other subjects out of a long list of subjects taught at the Universities.

What the administration really needs today is leadership. "Leadership in administration," writes K.N. Butani, "translated into practical realities, implies that leaders must have 'spring' and vitality in them to be able to top the immense potentialities of human endeavour for creative activity. By dash, enthusiasm, and zest for work, they should be able to infect the entire team they command with a pioneering spirit of endeavour and towards feats of administrative achieve-

19. *Ibid.*

ment.''[20] It, therefore, makes it imperative that men of the special merit who exhibit attributes of leadership by their decisiveness and dash at interview should be recruited in the administrative service. Mere possession of academic qualifications and passing the written examination is not enough. Interview unfolds the depth of a candidate and his potentialities in meeting situations and resolving matters which his diverse duties entail. There is, consequently, no merit in the argument about the futility of interview test.

But the Administrative Service has neither been able to maintain the high standard of quality for which it was reputed nor is it able to attract young shoots possessing the qualities an administrative officer must essentially possess–judgment, *savoir faire,* insight and fair-mindedness. The Service does not attract the youngmen who attain front rank eminence at the Universities. There is a ''flight of quality personnel'', as S. P. Aiyar puts it to the private sector, where salaries are handsomely lucrative, perquisites attractive, amenitives many, and there is freedom from all kinds of political pressure.[21]

This apart, the Administrative Service has not been able to strengthen the foundation of the Service. Political environment of the country has never allowed conventions and norms of administrative behaviour to evolve. The plague spot is the endless efforts of all State Governments to increase the quota of promotees from their own service and, consequently, diminishing the percentage of direct recruits to enter the service through the competitive examination. Another inroad was made by the special recruitment in 1956 and the short service commission personnel of the Armed Forces in 1962 to be followed in 1971, on the basis of a simplified three-paper test. The Study Team of the Administrative Commission observed in its Report that as a result ''of this heavy dilution, the IAS has lost, or was never allowed to develop its character.''

But the worst aspect of the policy-making in personnel administration is the decision of the Government to accept the introduction of all regional languages, included in the Eighth Schedule to the Constitution, as the media of examination. Until 1969, the only language allowed was English. After that the Union Public Service Commmission accepted regional languages as media of examination in two subjects, essay and general knowledge. Not more than one out of 10 candidates was found to use an Indian language instead of English in these two papers. The Union Public Service Commission had been insisting on a gradualist approach to the switching over to Indian languages, even if only as an option to begin with.

This gradualism was not intended to obstruct the fulfilment of the official commitment made in 1969 to promote the use of Indian languages in the Union Public Service examinations nor of the recommendations to the same effect made by the Kothari Commission, appointed in 1974 at the instance of the Union Public Service Commission and in consultation with the Union Government. The Union Public Service Commission's policy of gradualism aimed at doing enough spade work without endangering the standards not only of the examinations and of the services whose key personnel the examinations supplied and on which riveted the general administration of the whole country.

When the Janata Government, with strong pro-Hindi and anti-English elements, came into power, it decided to rush things during its term of office and accepted the Kothari Commission proposals and offered candidates the choice of writing all their papers in an Indian language, if they wished to. The Union Public Service Commission conducted its first Central Service examination (a collective name for all types of administrative examinations) in 1979. According to the Chairman of the Union Public Service commission, Dr. M.B. Sahre, out of 7,500 candidates who took the main examination, after weeding out 60,000 at the preliminary examination, only 14 per cent chose to write their papers in an Indian language; 86 per cent opted for English.[22] In 1981 roughly 8,600 candidates wrote the Civil Service (Main) Examination and as the Union Public Service Commission Report for 1981-82 presented to Parliament in March 1983, revealed that there was poor response to the option to answer papers in the regional languages. Tamil Nadu and the Hindi region both scored poorly, though their record was a shade better than that of most other languages. Overall, the number of candidates writing their public service examination in the regional languages is

20. ''Leadership in Administration'', *The Indian Journal of Public Administration,* October-December, 1956.
21. Maheshwari, B.L. (Ed.), *Centre-State Relations,* p. 208.
22. 12 per cent comprised Hindi-users and 2 per cent the remaining languages—34 candidates used Telugu, 26 Bangla, 13 Tamil and 8 Malayalam.

negligible.

These figures establish that the demand for "indigenisation" has no effective support from the candidates, who prefer, in the main, to go on using English. The demand for "indigenisation" really comes from the State Governments, all of which nurse a grievance about their States being "under-represented" in the Central Services and which see the use of Indian languages in the Union Public Service examinations as the short-cut to rectifying that "imbalance". In the absence of some kind of standardization or equivalence in multi-lingual marking that is acceptable to all the language groups, the use of Indian languages will lead to all the chauvinistic malpractices and each State Government will seek to pack the Service with entrants speaking the language of the State. This will mean, according to a former member of the Union Public Service Commission, "the funeral of the All-India Services."

Some members of the Council of States (Rajya Sabha) demanded, in a discussion on the 1977-78 Union Public Service Commission Report, change in the existing examination and recruitment methods used by the Commission. The Members who made this demand believed that the present system of choosing entrants favoured those who belonged to the "urban elite." Their contention was that the mode of examination and recruitment should be so designed that large number of intelligent youngmen and women from the rural areas might be able to join the main administrative services. One of the reasons that weighed with the Janata Government in permitting the option to use Indian languages for all the papers in the Central Services examinations was precisely to reduce the dominance of the "urban elite" in the Union Public Service Commission examinations. In 1977, the two-day Conference of Chairmen of State Public Service Commissions made an identical recommendation.

There can be no objection in principle to the recommendation that the recruitment to the superior Central and State Services should be on the basis of "intrinsic merit and potentiality" rather than articulation and sophisticated manners. But the ideal aimed at lowering standards to encourage rural entrants bristles with too many fallacies to create a strong and independent corps of civil servants capable of handling difficult situations, often taking unpopular decisions, resisting populist pressures and wisely advising politicians on the most effective course. It was, indeed, a welcome step when interviews were placed at par with the written examination, thereby depriving candidates from upper-class homes and English medium schools of their initial advantage. There is likely to be more depletion of the urban groups with the full penetration of regional languages as a medium of interviews.

Hitherto the age limits for recruitment were 21-24 years. The Janata Government raised it to 21-28 years ostensibly to benefit boys and girls for rural areas, who start education later than urban boys and girls. Since then the tinkering with the age limit had taken place arbitrarily, and in a surprising move the Narasimha Rao Government decided to raise the upper age limit for the Civil Service Examination to be held in 1992 to 33. The Kothari Committee which went into the question of age limit said that the entire process of examination should ensure identification of the really capable among the competing candidates and that the interest of these candidates would be adequately protected by having the upper age limit at 26 years with the usual relaxation for the Scheduled Caste and the Schedule Tribe candidates. Even in respect of number of attempts the Kothari Commission strongly urged that it must be restricted to two. The Public Services (Qualifications for recruitment) Committee appointed by the Government as early as in 1955 had said that the mental qualities as also the personality can be tested in one or at the most two examinations. Expert opinion also supports the view that the innate mental and analytical qualities may at best be tested in the first two or three examinations. Why exactly the number of permissible attempts should have been raised from three to four is again unclear. Ad hocism in a matter of such vital importance must be given up.

The rise in age defeated the basic idea of "catch them young" as a process of recruitment in the civil services. The study made at the Lal Bahadur Shastri National Academy of Administration made in 1982, revealed that most candidates selected for the Indian Administrative Service in recent years had a "national outlook," the average age of the probationer being 27, some of them tended "fixed opinions" and it occasionally became difficult to "mould them into the ethos of the service. A large number of candidates clearing the examination, taking the age of relaxation, were already married with two or three children. They no longer had the vigour and enthusiasm one finds in those belonging to the age group of 20-25. They also lacked stamina and strength to undergo tough training and initial hardwork; they become risk conscious.'' This apart, they were more vocal, articulate, assertive, prone to defy authority and discipline and sometimes leading to gross misbehaviour which caused incalculable damage to the administrative system.[23]

**Paralysis of Bureaucracy**

An honest and efficient bureaucracy is an important and indispensable limb of a sound administration. Lord Macaulay tersely state this bare truth when he declared in British Parliament that ''the character of the Governor-General (of India) is less important than the character of the Administrator by whom the administration is carried.'' Under a parliamentary system of government the character of the Minister is less important than the character of his civil servants. The civil services provide the framework of the administration of the country. The Ministers make policy decisions. In arriving at these decisions and looking to the consequences, they may, if they choose, seek the advice of civil servants, but the ultimate decision has necessarily to be that of Ministers. It is, however, in the area of implementation of these decisions that the role of administrators and other civil servants is of great significance. A feeling of confidence in civil servants is one of the essentials for drawing the best out of them. It had, to be ensured that this confidence is not impaired for the civil services keep the government as a going concern. It corrects the risks involved in decisions taken under pressure with its expertise and ascertainable knowledge. It oils the machinery of politics by relating the popular will to what a detached and disinterested experience indicates to be practicable. Its authority is that of influence, not that of power. It indicates consequences but it does not impose commands. Patel realised it and Nehru eventually veered round to the point of retaining the Indian Civil Service. They strove to enshrine the structure of an independent, impartial and irremovable civil service, a British legacy, in various provisions of Part XIV of the Constitution.

In the Nehru era all the proprieties and norms of minister-administrator relationship were maintained, though at occasions they too played favourites. They all operated on a limited canvas and the bureaucracy's capacity to fight back, to repair the damage, to restore the sanctity of the confidential reports and to uphold the norms of seniority remained, in the main, intact. In the States, however, the conditions were not ideal and a few of the officers, for example, N. Banerjee in Bihar and Dr. Nabogopal Das in West Begal, were compelled to resign in sheer disgust. But such occurrences were then exceptions rather than the rule, not *vice-versa,* as seems to be the case at present.

Now there is paralysis of bureaucracy and erosion in the morale of civil servants. A survey of administration reveals a painful study. Barrenness of ideas pervades civil service, the old dedication and efficiency have vanished, initiative is totally lacking, integrity and probity remain merely shadows of their past reality and general overall flabbiness and sycophancy prevails. To cover up their errors and misdeeds the political bosses make civil servants a target of attack for any shortfalls or mishaps in the administration. When they use harsh and unrestrained language to denigrate civil servants in the open it is not realised that such behaviour not only sullies the image of civil service but also seriously affects the capacity of officers, especially at the district level, to deal with piquant situation and difficult issues involved in matters of administration. Vallabhbhai Patel gave a note of warning in the Constituent Assembly when he said, ''........as a man of experience I tell you, do not quarrel with the instruments with which you want to work. It is a bad workman who quarrels with his instruments. Take work from them. Every man wants some sort of encouragement. Nobody wants to put in work when everyday he is criticised and ridiculed in public. Nobody will give you work like that.''[24]

This parlous State of administration is a two-fold problem. First, the quality of bureacracy has been diluted over the years due to the decline

23. On October 4, 1981, during a trek to Badrinath as part of training, V.K. Singh, a probationer, was allowed to have got drunk, misbehaved with a woman colleague and even brandished with the fire arm. His male colleagues, who were eye witnesses, overpowered Singh before he could do more harm. Singh had earlier ''withdrawn'' from the National Defence Academy, Khadkwasla. The Director of the Mussoorie Administrative Academy, P.S. Appu, reported the matter to the Home Ministry, and insisted that the least ought to be done was to terminate his probation. The Home Ministry, under political pressure tried to shield Singh, thus impelling the Director to seek premature retirement in protest.

24. *Constituent Assembly Debates,* Vol. X, pp. 42 ff.

in the standards of education, inroad on administrative services made by special recruitment in 1956, 1962 and 1971, job reservation mania, raising the state service quota from 25 to 33 per cent with a still more clamour of rise, as particularly in Uttar Pradesh and all this leading to class exclusiveness, overstaffing, unionisation and proliferation of inservice rivalries. There is yet another factor and it has proved to be very harmful. during the British regime the supremacy of the Indian Civil Services was an undisputed fact. It was accepted by other "Imperial Services as a matter of course. But in Indpendent India the Indian Police Service did not accept the supremacy of the Indian Adnubstratuve Service. It was rather made the target of attack and abuse. Apart from the struggle between the two All-India Services for sharing in the plumb jobs, the class and caste antagonism has seriously embittered their relation and created bad blood through the entire bureaucratic labyrinth. No less important is the sharp controversy between the generalist and the specialists.

The second problem is the anxiety of the politicians to bend the civil service to their will and there has been no dearth of high-ranking civil servants enthusiastically willing to do the politician's behest for unworthy motives of their own. This phenomenon is not of recent origin, though it reached its apogee during the last few years. It first appeared in the States and its pacesetters were Pratap Singh Kairon in Punjab and Bakshi Ghulam Mohammed in Jammu and Kashmir. Both Kairon and Bakshi had no respect for independent, honest and efficient administrators. They loathed rules and regulations and disdained the cardinal principle of administration in a democratic set-up that the civil servant "acts as the hands and feet of the minister and and the two must work in unison." They regarded them as tools and expected secretarial notings which should conform to their aims. Those who succumbed had their rewards; coveted assignments, important postings, out-of-turn promotions and sharing the spoils. Those who hesitated to fall in line had to pay heavy price—transfer to inconvenient positions and out of way places tantamount to demotion, or transfer without any assignment or were asked to proceed on leave, withholding of promotions and even suspension.

The Kairon-Bakshi culture soon spread to other States. The forces unleashed by them were strengthened further by the political instability ushered by the Fourth General Election in 1967 and the growing infighting within the Congress Party in States where it had managed to remain in power. Attempts were made to politicise the service and to identify some officials with one or the other of the political parties. The downfall drift thereafter was swift and was also dangerous in consequences. The well- entrenched practice that prevails now is that on the eve of election there are mass transfers of administrative heads of districts as also of police officers. These transfers are made on the assumption that some of them are regarded as more pliable and amenable to the wishes of the party bosses. In simple words, it means distrust of some public servants and expression of great confidence in others. This confidence or lack of it has nothing to do with merit, impartiality or efficiency of the officer concerned. It is a question of the equation he is likely to establish with his new masters and this in turn is influenced by how far he had involved himself with the previous Government and how far he is prepared to fall in line with the new one. With the change in the complexion of Government the Secretaries to the Government are also changed; sometimes wholesale. In common parlance it is described as "shake up". The fluctuating fortunes of parties effect the fortunes of individual officers and play a vital role in their careers. They would, therefore, instead of concentrating on the discharge of their official duties, get engrossed in playing their part to help one or the other political groups. The civil servant becomes a political activist.

This phenomenon hitherto confined to the States showed its ugly face at the Centre after the Congress split in 1969. Those who imported it into New Delhi were the champions of "committed bureaucracy" which had no use for rebels. The first systematic effort to put pliant persons in key positions in the Secretariat, intelligence services and public sectors was made during the Emergency. Hundreds of officials were shuffled around at the Centre and in the State ostensibly to give a dynamic push to Mrs. Gandhi's 20-point programme and the family planning drive. But the results were disastrous as the rulers of the day themselves admitted.

After March 1977 General Election it was hoped that the Janata Government would restore the balance as it enjoyed initially among a large section of the bureaucracy sympathy and respect since it was committed to dismantle the coercive apparatus of the Emergency. But the way it sought to browbeat the top bureaucrats into convenient decisions put even the so-called excesses of the Emergency into shade. Scores of officers were arraigned before the Shah and other Commissions and, in a vast majority of cases, the whole operation had the trappings of witch-hunt. "The scandalous manner in which so upright and outstanding a civil servant as Mr. B.B. Vohra has been treated" writes Inder Malhotra, "will always remain an indictment of both the Janata and Lok Dal Governments."[25]

Despite the assurance given by Mrs. Gandhi immediately after the change of Government in January 1980, to the Secretaries of various economic Ministries that she would turn the new leaf nothing was done to restore the self-confidence and self-esteem of civil servants at the top who were afraid of taking even routine decisions during the three years of Janata-Lok Dal rule. On the other hand, politicalisation of the bureaucracy was carried a stage further. The new Government acted with alacrity in making widespread changes in key posts in various Union Ministries, the public sector, the Delhi Administration and such sensitive organisations as the Intelligence Bureau,, the CBI and the Central Reserve Police. The Civil Servants put under "cloud" were those who were associated with the processing of cases against Mrs. Gandhi, Sanjay Gandhi, and her colleagues or were working in the Commissions of inquiry set up against her or her colleagues. The then Union Home Minister, Gyani Zail Singh, designed a "loyalty" test to screen some senior officials. Some thirty top men were forced to proceed on leave or were not given any alternative assignment. They drew their salaries from the public exchequer but had no job for months together. Civil Servants who were conspicuously associated with Emergency and who later stood firm in their loyalty to Mrs. Gandhi were rehabilitated. While some had been given the post held prior to 1977, others were promoted or given coveted assignments.

According to B.K. Nehru at the root of maladministration from which India is suffering is the "Varna Sankar" that has been caused "by increasing practice of ministers not to concern themselves so much with polity as with individual cases." He assigns various reasons why Ministers are mostly engaged in and prefer to decide individual cases. One of the important reasons, he emphasizes, is "the financial corruption prevalent among many of the several hundred ministers who are normally in office in this country has reached scandalous proportions. A minister who refrains from deciding individual cases is likely to remain poorman."[26] It is a matter of common knowledge and belief and the young entrepreneurs trumpet it openly and without any reservation that there is no transaction involving a Government department, no issue of a licence for setting up a new factory, starting a new industry or expanding an old one, no permit for export, no dealing with any commercial undertaking needing sanction of the Government in which the politician concerned does not insist on a substantial gift for his party and his own pocket. Bureaucrats, of course, claim their due share. The Ministers expect secretarial notings which conform to their aims and civil servants demand price for this piece of dishonesty. There is *quid pro quo*. Those who do not fall in line earn the displeasure of their superiors and have to pay for it; the familiar transfers, withholding promotions or even suspension. Dr.N.B. Prasad, former Chairman of the Natural Gas Commission, the man who put India on the international oil map, was transferred when he dared to disagree with the Janata Petroleum Minister H.N. Bahuguna on the purchase of a drilling rig from Holland. When Congress returned to power in 1980, Prasad as Power Secretary was again in trouble. This time he objected to the import of two old power plants from France annoying a powerful ruling party leader. Prasad was quickly transferred and he eventually resigned from Government service in disgust.

There are two other important factors that essentially contribute to this dismal state of affairs. Here bureaucracy plays the positive role. The reason for creating All-India Services, particularly the Indian Administrative Service, Ambedkar explained to the Constituent Assembly, was that certain posts in the administrative set up of the country "are strategic from the point of view of maintaining the standard of administration...and members of which (All-India Services) alone could be appointed to these strategic posts throughout the Union." The Service has been organised in the form of a number of I.A.S cadres for each State. The strength of each cadre is so fixed as to include a reserve of officers who can be deputed for service under the Union Govern-

25. Malhotra, Inder, "Ministers vs. Civil Servants," *Sunday Review, The Times of India*, New Delhi, June 1, 1980.
26. Nehru, B.K., "Decline of the Civil Service," *The Tribune*, Chandigarh, April 28, 1980.

ment for one or more tenures of three, four or five years before they return to their State cadre. The advantage claimed for such an arrangement is that the Union Government has at its disposal the services of officers with first-hand knowledge and experience of conditions in the States and when they return to their State cadre, the States have officers who are fully familiar with the policies and programmes of the Union Government.

But the Civil Servants themselves have striven to wreck this noble ideal of the Constitution makers. There is a craze to stay at New Delhi and once an officer comes on a tenure he seldom likes to go back to his State. Inder Malhotra writes,"The late Sir Girja Shankar Bajpai, the archetypal civil servant if ever there was one was nearly driven to tears in the early fifties when the found that most of his colleagues would do almost anything to stay on in Delhi rather than to go back to the State."[27] They manipulate and manoeuvre with politicians to ensure their stay at New Delhi and the Ministers oblige them because they are always willing to bend over backwards to do the politicians' behest for unworthy motives of their own. B.B. Vohra extensively quoted in support of his contention that he was let down as badly by his peers as by Mr. Morarji Desai and Mr.Charan Singh. The process was reversed by Rajiv Gandhi. The Prime Minister directed all the Ministries that officers for more than five years' stay in New Delhi should be reverted to their State Cadres and banned re-employment of superannuated persons and if they were already in employment no further extension should be given and where possible their services terminated. But it did not work well in the desired direction and the Prime Minister himself reversed his own scheme in the back gear and once an exception was made it snowballed into full action. The position was not exactly so bad as before, but there was no well-defined norm to be adhered to. Rajiv Gandhi created history when he sacked in pubic the permanent head of the Indian Foreign Office, A.P. Venkateswaran.

Then, it is passion with almost all top-ranking civil servants approaching the age of superannuation, to explore all possibilities for an extension and if it was not possible, then, either to get a diplomatic assignment or a place in some State Raj Bhavan. When there is a scramble for extensions or diplomatic or gubernatorial assignments,the senior civil servants are easy tools in the hands of Ministers to dance to their tune They become abject sycophants and without any qualm of conscience say yes to every suggestion without any regard to consequence.

During the seventh Gobind Ballabh Pant memorial lecture which B.K. Nehru delivered at India International Centre, New Delhi, he described civil servants in India a plaything of politics who "instead of administering the law are being compelled to carry out the wishes of ever changing Ministers." He tore apart any myth that might be existing that civil servants in India were being allowed to perform their roles. He analysed the causes of increased ministerial interference in the work of civil servants and suggested, as remedial measures,a procedure laid down through legislation for appointments, posting and transfers of civil servants; increasing their salaries substantially to make them impervious to corruption and "reprofessionalising" the service, "The canker of careerism, sycophancy, indiscipline, factionalism,lack of integrity and pursuit of self-interest which is attacking the system will automatically largely disappear when the political interference from which it emanates has been eliminated," he explained.

In his letter addressed to the Bihar Chief Minister Jagannath Mishra, refusing his promotion to the Commissioner's grade in the Indian Administrative Service, A.K. Chatterjee wrote on September 23,1981,"An honest and upright public servant finds himself absolutely irrelevant in the present set-up. He becomes a meaningless label in a system based on favouritism and geared to serve the interests of political functionaries and their dear and near ones alone." Chatterjee's protest acted as a catalyst to the growing resentment among the civil servants against political interference, and the Bihar I.A.S. Association passed a resolution expressing solidarity with him and asking other services to also protest "against the dominance of political bosses which tended to incapacitate the public servants from giving free and fearless advice." A.V.R. Reddy in September 1982 came out with a blistering indictment of the Andhra Pradesh politicians. Parakh, another Indian Administrative Service Officer, who succeeded Reddy and was replaced by the Telugu Desam Government in 1983, followed in his predecessor's footsteps. His statement was less provocative,but he made the point

27. Malhotra, Inder, "Ministers Vs. Civil Servants" *Sunday Review, The Times of India,* New Delhi, June 1, 1980, p. 1.

about the wisdom of frequent and abrupt transfers of officials in key positions and its impact on the morale of the civil service as a whole.

These isolated cases permanently bring into focus the disturbing indications of the decay of India's political system. It also makes clear that there are capable civil servants who believe firmly in the concept of trusteeship which the British Government inculcated in Indian Civil Servants.[28] Young I.A.S. officers, full of idealism, hopes and new ideas,soon encounter the pernicious power and influence of the deceitful political operative and his ubiquitous businessman-contractors friends; it is an encounter the bureaucrats invariably lose. Under the circumstances the civil servants who retain the courage to resist deserve full support. If it is more of them,it should act as a curb on politicians who run riot.

**Recruitment and Conditions of Service**

"The method of responsible Government to be successful in political working," observed the Joint Select Committee on Indian Constitutional Reform, 1933-34,"requires the existence of a competent and independent Civil Service staffed by persons capable of giving to successive Ministers advice based on long administrative experience,secure in the positions, during good behaviour, but required to carry out the policy upon which the Government and Legislatures eventually decide."[29] So long as politicians can influence in any vulgar sense appointments and promotions, there is, as Ivor Jennings says, "a risk of toadying flattery and self-seeking" and the mind of the Minister will always be devoted to the need of rewarding his followers. The whole administration must,under the circumstances, deteriorate both in tone and efficiency and the services may be depleted of able, efficient, honest and experienced persons. The method of selection for the various posts in the public services and their conditions of service are, therefore, matters of supreme importance in order to secure a continuous inflow of competent men of the right type.

The Drafting Committee thought it advisable that detailed provisions relating to the services should be regulated by Acts of the appropriate Legislatures rather than by constitutional provisions.[30] The Constituent Assembly accepted this recommendation of the Drafting Committee and the Constitution lays down certain general provisions, leaving the detailed rules of recruitment and conditions of service of persons serving the Union and the States to be determined by the appropriate Legislatures.[31]

The Constitution provides that except where a different provision is made, as in the case of the Judges of the Supreme Court and of the High Courts,the tenure of office of all persons holding Government posts under the Union, including posts connected with defence services, is during the pleasure of the President, and any person who is a member of the Civil Service of a State or holds any post under a State holds office during the pleasure of the Governor. Dismissal or removal of a Civil Servant cannot be effected by an authority subordinate to that by which he was appointed. And no dismissal, removal, or reduction in rank of a Civil Servant can take place until he has been given a reasonable opportunity of showing cause against the action proposed to be taken against him. But this requirement is not necessary:

(i) where dismissal or removal or reduction in rank takes place as a result of the conviction of a public servant on a criminal charge; or

(ii) where the authority empowered to dismiss or remove a person or reduce him in rank is satisfied that for some reason,to be recorded by that authority in writing, it is not reasonably practicable to give that person an opportunity of stating his case; or

(iii) where the President or the Governor, as the case may be, is satisfied that in the interest of the security of the State it is not expedient to give such an opportunity to that person."

28. Every warrant of appointment issued by the British Crown carried the preamble, "Our Trusty and Wellbeloved....." Every public servant in Britain is beloved of the Crown and enjoys its trust. In return, he carries the burden of trusteeship of the task assigned to him and is, therefore, expected to discharge his duties bearing faith in his trust. The officers of the British empire in India were appointed by Royal warrant and, consequently, carried with them the trust reposed in them. The officers of the East India Company bore no such trust and the notoriety they gained for their rapaciousness and preference for private profit over public gain bears the testimony of history and needs no recounting.

29. Vol. I, para 274.

30. *The Draft Constitution of India,* xi, para 16.

31. Article 309. Also refer to Entry 70 of the Union List and Entry 41 of the State List, Schedule VII.

If any question arises whether it is reasonably practicable to give to any person an opportunity of showing such cause, the decision thereon of the authority empowered to dismiss or remove such person or to reduce him in rank, as the case may be,shall be final.

The Constitution (Forty-second Amendment) Act,1976, denies to Government servants the opportunity to make a representation at the second stage of inquiry against the penalty proposed to be imposed. Article 323-A empowers Parliament to make a law for adjudication of service disputes by administrative tribunals. Service matters have,therefore,been taken outside the jurisdiction of the courts. But the power of the Supreme Court under Article 136 to grant special leave to appeal will remain.

**Public Service Commissions**

"Wherever democratic institutions exist, experience has shown that to secure an efficient civil service it is essential to protect it so far as possible from political or personal influences and to give it that position of stability and security which is vital to its successful working as the impartial and efficient instrument by which governments, of whatever political complexion, may give effect to their policies."[32] Public Service Commissions are fundamental to the very conception of a democratic government, for they perform a very important and vital function in a democracy. Their primary objective is to establish a Civil Service free from personal and political influence and to secure to civil servants protection from victimization and injustice. They provide effective instruments by which governments professing different political faiths and pursuing different ideologies can give effect, through an efficient and impartial Civil Service, to their programmes and policies. Independence, impartiality and integrity constitute the essential characteristic features of a true and efficient Public Service Commission.

The Government of India Act,1919,provided for the establishment of a Public Service Commission in India. But no action was taken thereon. The Royal Commission on Superior Civil Services (Lee Commission),1924,gave particular attention to the matter and recommended that the statutory Public Service Commission envisaged in the Government of India Act,1919,"Should be established without delay."[33] It was only in October 1926, that a Public Service Commission was established at the Centre. In 1929, Madras established its own Public Service Commission. The Punjab Legislative Council enacted legislation for the establishment of a Commission, but it could not come into existence due to scarcity of finances.

The Indian Statutory (Simon) Commission recommended the establishment of Public Service Commission in all the Provinces."We have no doubt", the Commission observed, "of the necessity for the establishment of Provincial Public Service Commissions if an efficient and loyal public service is to be maintained.[34] They thought that the protection of the services from political influence was an essential condition of the constitutional advances they recommended. It was, accordingly, suggested that provision should be made in the Government of India Act that, if any Provincial Legislative Council did not pass within a prescribed period an Act for the establishment of a Public Service Commission,with a constitution and functions approved by the Secretary of State in Council,the Provincial Government "shall be required (1) to conduct its recruitment through the agency of the Central Public Service Commission;(2) to submit appeals from members of the provincial and subordinate services to the same body; and (3) to accept and apply the same convention in regard to the Commission's recommendations as are accepted by the Government of India."[35] The Government of India Act, 1935, accordingly, provided that "there shall be a Public Service Commission for the Federation and a Public Service Commission for each Province." Provision was also made whereby the same Public Service Commission could serve the needs of two or more Provinces jointly.

The Commission was purely an advisory body. Appointments to the Commission were made by the Governor-General or Governor, as the case might be, acting in his discretion. At least half of the number of members of a Commission were to be from the services who had held office under the Crown for ten years or more. The tenure of office of the members and conditions of their

32. *Report of the Royal Commission on the Superior Services in India (Lee Commission),* para 24.
33. *Ibid.*
34. *Report of the Indian Statutory Commission,* Vol. II, para 339.
35. *Ibid.* Bombay and Sind had a Joint Commission as also Punjab and North-West Frontier Province, and one Commission served Bihar, Orissa and the Central Provinces.

service were determined by regulations made by the Governor-General and Governors. The functions of the Commissions were enumerated in the Act itself but the Governor-General and Governor acting in their discretion could exclude any matter from the purview of the Commission concerned. It may, however, be noted that in practice all services functioning in the sphere in which the Governor-General or a Governor acted in his discretion were excluded from the purview of the respective Commissions.

The Constituent Assembly had,thus, before it the Government of India Act,1935, outlining the composition and functions of the Public Service Commissions together with fairly well-established traditions relating to their working. The Union Constitution Committee and the Provincial Constitution Committee did not find it necessary to go into their details and recommended that provisions regarding the Public Service Commissions should be on the lines of those in the Government of India Act,1935. But there was one important difference in the recommendations of these Committees. Whereas the Union Constitution Committee had recommended that the appointment of the Chairman and members of the Federal (Union Public Service) Commission should be made by the President on the advice of his Ministry, the Provincial Constitution Committee had suggested that Provincial (State) Commission Members, including the Chairman, should be appointed by the Governors acting in their discretion, However, in presenting the Report of the Committee to the Constituent Assembly on July 15,1947, Sardar Vallbhbhai Patel said that the appointment of the Chairman and members of the Provincial (State) Public Service Commissions would generally be made by the Governor on the advice of his Cabinet or Ministry.[36]

In pursuance of the Reports of the Union Constitution Committee and the Provincial Constitution Committee the Constitutional Adviser in his Draft of October 1947, included provisions for Public Service Commissions which closely followed the Government of India Act, 1935. The Drafting Committee in its Draft of February, 1948,adopted the Constitutional Adviser's Draft. In May 1948,a conference of the Chairmen of all the Provincial Public Service Commissions and the Chairman and members of the Federal Public Service Commission was held and some suggestions were made for incorporation in the Constitution.[37] The more important of these suggestions were:

(1) Provision should be made in the Constitution that the procedure prescribed for the removal from office of Judges of the Supreme Court and High Courts and the Comptroller and Auditor General would be followed also in the case of the members of the Public Service Commissions.

(2) Following the Government of India Act,1935, the Draft had provided that less than one-half of the number of members of a Public Service Commission should be persons who had held public office for at least ten. years. The conference suggested that in order to provide for the representation of all the interests involved,this percentage should be reduced to one-third.

(3) Provision should be made that the conditions of service of member of a Public Service Commission should not be varied to his disadvantage during his tenure of office.

(4) The Chairmen of Public Service Commissions like the members, be eligible to hold office after retirement with the permission of the President or Governor as the case might be. The conference thought that while all restrictions on the future employment of Chairman and members of the Commission should not be abrogated,the services of such experienced men should, if necessary, be available to the Government.

(5) Before the President or the Governors made regulations excluding any matter from the purview of the Public Service Commission,the appropriate Commission itself should be consulted.

(6) While it could not be made obligatory on the Government to accept the advice of a Commission in all cases, provision should be made for reports of the Public Service Commissions to be compiled annually and laid before the appropriate Legislature, and in particular for a list of cases to be placed before the Legislature where the advice of the Commission had not been accepted.

These suggestions were cast in the form of draft amendments and the Drafting Committee considered them together with the views of the

36. *Constituent Assembly Debates,* Vol. IV, p. 581.
37. *The Framing of India's Constitution, Select Documents,* Vol. IV, p. 411.

Ministry of Home Affairs and the Law Ministry. The amendments proposed by the Drafting Committee were considered by the Constituent Assembly on August 22 and 23, 1949. In the course of revision Articles relating to the Public Service Commissions were renumbered 315 to 323.

**Appointment and Terms of Office**

The Constitution provides for a Public Service Commission for the Union and a Public Service Commission for each State. But if the Legislatures of two or more States authorize it by resolution, Parliament may establish a Joint Commission for those States. The Union Public service Commission may perform the functions of a State Public Service Commission at the request of the Governor of a State, and with consent of the President.[38] The Union Territories are served either by the Union Public Service Commission or by the Public Service Commission of an adjoining State.

The Chairman and other members of the Union Public Service Commission or a Joint Commission are appointed by the President and in the case of a State Public Service Commission by the Governor of the State. One-half of the members of a Commission, Union or State, must have held office for at least ten years either under the Government of India or under the Government of a State. A member holds office for six years or until he attains, in the case of the Union Commission the age of sixty-five years and in the case of a State Commission or a Joint Commission the age of sixty-two years whichever is earlier. A member of a Public Service Commission is, on the expiration of his term of office, not eligible for reappointment to that office.[39] The Chairman of the Union Commission is ineligible for further appointment either under the Government of India or under the Government of a State. But a member of the Union Commission is eligible for appointment as Chairman of the Union Commission or Chairman of a State Commission. The Chairman of a State Commission is eligible for appointment as Chairman or a member of the Union Commission or Chairman of any other State Commission. A member of a State Commission is eligible for appointment as Chairman or a member of the Union Commotion or as Chairman of that or any other State Commission. None of them, however, is eligible for any other employment either under the Union Government or under the Government of a State.[40]

Employment under Government has been interpreted to mean employment which is paid by the Government. The Universities and public corporations are independent legal entities with their own independent financial resources and, accordingly, employment under such bodies is not employment under Government. Some States have appointed retired persons or who had resigned from the Public Service Commissions to statutory bodies. In the case of universities interchange between the Vice-Chancellorship and membership of a Public Service Commission has almost become a regular feature. A new precedent was set in April, 1977, when the President appointed Raghukul Tilak, a retired Chairman of the Rajasthan Public Service Commission, as Governor of Rajasthan. The explanation offered was that a Governorship was not employment under Government as the salary of the Governor was paid out of the Consolidated Fund. The Supreme Court upheld the contention of the Union Government and ruled that the appointment of Raghukul Tilak was in order and, therefore, valid. A.K. Kidwai, former Chairman of the Union Public Service Commission, was appointed Governor of Bihar in1978,after the resignation of Jagan Nath Kaushal.

The number of members constituting the Union Public Service Commission and the conditions of their service, or of a Joint Commission, are determined by the President and in the case of State Commissions by the Governor by regulations.[41] It has since been decided that there shall be six to eight members of the Union Commission and usually three for the State Commissions. The conditions of service of a member of a Public Service Commission cannot be varied to his disadvantage after his appointment.[42] The entire expenses of the Commission, including the salaries and allowances of its members, are charged on the Consolidated Fund of India and in the case of a State Public Service Commission on the Consolidated Fund of the State.

The Chairman or any other member of Public Service Commission may be removed from his office by order of the President on the

---

38. Article 315.
39. Article 316.
40. Article 319.
41. Article 318.
42. Proviso to Article 318.

ground of misbevariour and the Constitution prescribes the procedure to prove misbehaviour.[43] The ground or grounds of misbehaviour are referred to the Supreme Court by the President. The Supreme Court then conducts the inquiry in accordance with the procedure prescribed under Article 145 of the Constitution and submits a report to the President . Pending inquiry in the Supreme Court, the President in the case of the Union Commission or a Joint Commission and the Governor in the case of a State Commission may suspend from office the Chairman or any other member of the Commission against whom a reference has been made to the Supreme Court.

The President may by order remove from office the Chairman or any other member of a Public Service Commission on any of the following grounds:

(a) if he is adjudged an insolvent; or
(b) if he engages during his term of office,in any paid employment outside the duties of his office; or
(c) if he is, in the opinion of the President, unfit to continue in office by reason of infirmity of mind or body.

If the Chairman or any other member of a Public Service Commission becomes in any way concerned or interested in any contract of agreement made by or on behalf of the Government of India or a State Government or in any way participates in profits accruing thereof or in any benefit or emolument arising therefrom except as an ordinary member of an incorporated company,he shall be deemed to be guilty of misbehaviour under Article 317 (1).

There was no provision in the Government of India Act,1935, for the removal and suspension of members of the Public Service Commissions. All such matters were governed by rules framed by the Governor-General and the Governors acting in their discretion. Article 317 of the Constitution now empowers the President alone to remove members of a Public Service Commission. He does so by his Order, without any formality, when a member is adjudged an insolvent, or he engages himself in any other employment or he is deemed unfit to continue in office owing to infirmity of mind. But removal on grounds of misbehaviour involves the observance of certain procedure as provided in the Constitution. The Constitution also provides an instance of misbehaviour.

### Functions of Public Service Commissions

The Constitution prescribes the following functions of the Public Service Commissions, both Union and States.[44]

(1) to conduct examination for appointments to the Union and State Services respectively;
(2) to assist the States in framing and operating schemes of joint recruitment for any service for which candidates possessing special qualifications are required, if two or more States make such a request to the Union Public Service Commission;
(3) to give advice:
   (a) on any matter referred to them relating to methods of recruitment to civil services and for civil posts;
   (b) on the principles to be followed in making appointments, and in making promotions and transfers from one service to another and on the suitability of candidates for such appointments, promotions or transfers;
   (c) on all disciplinary matters including memorials or petitions on such matters;
   (d) on a claim made by any person who is serving or has served under the Government of India or a State Government that the costs of defending legal proceedings against him in respect of acts done or purporting to be done in the execution of his duty should be borne by the Government; and
   (e) on any claim for the award of a pension in respect of injuries sustained by a person while serving under the Government in a civil capacity and any question as to the amount of any such award.
(4) any other matter referred to a Public Service Commission which the President or, as the case may be, the Governor of a State may refer to them.

Normally, a Public Service Commission must be consulted in all matters relating to methods of recruitment,on the methods to be followed in making appointments, promotions and transfers from one service to another, on the suitability

43. Article 317 (1).
44. Article 320.

of applicants, on disciplinary matters affecting any person in a civil capacity, on claims submitted by civil servants for payment of costs incurred in defending legal proceeding and compensation for injuries sustained in the execution of their duties and for the award of pensions. But the Constitution also empowers the President and the Governors to make regulations specifying the matters in which, either generally or in particular circumstances, the Commission may not be consulted.[45] No reference need be made to the Public Service Commission on matters relating to the reservation of appointments of posts in favour of backward classes, Scheduled Castes and Scheduled Tribes.[46]

In 1961 an amendment was made which provided, "It shall not be necessary for the President to consult the Commission in any case where he proposes to make an order of dismissal, removal or reduction in rank after being satisfied that such action is necessary in the interest of the security of the State." In 1962, following the Proclamation of Emergency similar amendments were made curtailing the advisory functions of the Commission. All regulations made by the President or the Governor specifying the matters in which it is not necessary to consult the Commission are to be laid before the appropriate Legislature and are subject to legislative control and modification.[47]

Under Article 321 of the Constitution, the functions of the Union or a State Public Service Commission may be extended by an Act of Parliament or, as the case may be,by a State Legislature. Such an Act may bring within the scope of the functions of the Commission matters connected with the services of public institutions, such as, Public corporations and local bodies, under the Union or a State Government. The need for bringing such institutions within the purview of the Public Service Commissions is undeniable in view of the greater emphasis on the utility of public corporations and such other institutions in the context of the increasing activities of a Welfare State. These institutions employ an ever-increasing number of officials.

**Independence of the Commissions**

The Constitution contains the following guarantees to secure independence of the Commissions in the discharge of their duties:

(1) The Public Service Commissions are constitutionally created and are in no way subordinate either to the Executive or the Legislature. Parliament can neither abolish them nor alter their powers and functions, except by following the process of constitutional amendment which is a difficult and cumbersome procedure.

(2) The term of office of a member is fixed by the Constitution and no one is eligible for reappointment to that office on the expiration of his term.

(3) Removal or suspension of a member can only take place in accordance with the procedure and for reasons prescribed in the Constitution.

(4) The conditions of service of a member can not be varied to his disadvantage after his appointment. The salaries and allowances of the members and staffs of the Commission as well as expenditure incurred on their upkeep are charged on the Consolidated Fund. The Commissions are, accordingly, not subject to the vote of Parliament or a State Legislature, and, consequently, not subject to the vagaries of fluctuating majorities.

(5) In order to avoid the suspicion that promise or prospects of further employment under the Government might operate or be used to influence the Judgment of the members of the Commissions, the Chairman and members, on ceasing to hold office, become ineligible for further employment under Government except:

(i) that the Chairman of a State Commission is eligible for appointment as Chairman or a member of the Union Commission or as Chairman of any other State Commission;

(ii) that a member of a State Commission is eligible for appointment as Chairman or a member of the Union Commission, or as Chairman of that or any other State Commission; and

(iii) that a member of the Union Commission is eligible for appointment as Chairman of the Union Commission or Chairman of a State Commission.

(6) In order to ensure their reasoned judgment, their independence and impartiality, the makers of the Constitution had intended that only men of mature age and long experience should be elevated to the Public Service Commissions. The age of retirement has been, accordingly,

45. Proviso to Article 320.
46. Article 320 (4). Also refer to Article 16 (4) and 335.
47. Article 320 (5).

fixed at sixty-two years for the members of the State Commissions and sixty-five for members of the Union Public Service Commission.

All these constitutional provisions have not fulfilled the expectations of the makers of the Constitution. In actual practice appointments to the Commissions, particularly in the States, have often been made on political considerations thereby lowering their prestige in the eyes of the public. In fact, due advantage has been taken of the absence of qualifications and mode of selection of the members of the Commissions by certain State Governments, with the result that appointment to the Public Service Commissions is deemed by many aspirants as reward for their party service. At the Union level, except for Shivashunmugam Pillai,who was a former Speaker of the Madras Legislative Assembly,[48] no politician has been appointed on the Commission. In the States, it is just the reverse. The Law Commission made a pointed reference to the shocking state of affairs prevailing in the States. The Commission said: "Having regard to the important part played by the Public Service Commission in the selection of the subordinate judiciary, we took care to examine as far as possible the Chairman and some of the members of the Public Service Commissions in the various States. We are constrained to state that the personnel of these Public Service Commissions in some of the States was not such as could inspire confidence from the points of view of either efficiency or impartiality. There appears to be little doubt that in some of the States appointments to these Commissions are made not on considerations of merit but on grounds of party and political affiliations. The evidence given by members of the Public Service Commissions in some of the States does create the feeling that they do not deserve to be in the responsible posts they occupy. In some of the Southern States the impartiality of the Commissions in making selections to the judicial service was seriously questioned."[49] An ex-Chairman of the Madhya Pradesh Public Service Commission said, "The constitutional independence given to the Commission is largely vitiated by vesting the appointment of Members in the hands of the Governor, i.e., the Chief Minister in actual practice. The Chief Minister often appoints persons on political, communal, regional and other grounds, and not solely on merit, such persons usually find it difficult to resist ministerial pressure and influence in carrying out their duties in an independent and impartial manner..."[50]

But what happened in Bombay (now Maharastra) will perhaps remain unprecedented in the history of Public Service Commissions in India. A Deputy Minister in the Bombay Government was appointed a member of the Commission from the quota reserved for civil servants. "Although the appointment," says B.A. V. Sharma, "seems to fulfil the legal niceties it was clearly against the spirit of the Constitution. There cannot be a worse example of a party government ruthlessly seeking to promote its interests and that of a party member in total disregard of constitutional propriety."[51]

**Commission an Advisory Body**

Although the Constitution provides that the Union and State Public Service Commissions shall conduct examinations for appointments to the Civil Services of the Union and that of the States and normally they shall be consulted in all matters relating to methods of recruitment, yet the status of the Public Service Commissions is advisory. The use of the words "shall be consulted" in Article 320 (3) is significant of the meaning. The Public Service Commission merely gives its opinion with regard to the suitability of a candidate for the post under consideration to the President or, as the case may be, the Governor, and it is not obligatory on the latter to accept that opinion or recommendations. Sometimes the Government directs the Public Service Commission to recommend more names than the available posts and makes selection of its own out of the panel of names so recommended without adhering to the priority recommended by the Commission. The Constitution,however, provides that it is the duty of the Union Commission and the State Commission to present annually to the President or, as the case may be, the Governor, a report as to the work

48. He was a member of the Union Public Service Commission from 1955 to 1961.
49. Law Commission of India, *Fourth Report, Report of Judicial Administration,* Vol. I, Ministry of Law, Government of India, New Delhi, 1958, p. 171.
50. Rege, D.V., "The Public Service Commission. Its Powers and Functions—A Critical Assessment" in *Studies in State Administration,* Edited by G.S. Halappa, p. 134.
51. Sharma, B.A.V., "Public Service Commissions in India", *Studies in Indian Democracy,* Edited by Aiyer, S.P., and Srinivasan, R, p. 227.

done by the Commission. Immediately after the receipt of such a report the President or the Governor is required to lay it before each House of Parliament or the State Legislature together with a memorandum of the cases where the advice of the Commission was not accepted and the reasons for such non-acceptance.[52]

It would, thus, appear that the framers of the Constitution have made a specific provision that the Legislatures of the Union and the States are the ultimate judges of Governments' actions. This provision simultaneously ensures that consultation with the Commission is not overlooked, that the advice of the Commission is as a rule accepted, and that the Governments are free in cases where they consider the matter of sufficient importance to follow their own judgment provided they are prepared to justify their action before the Legislature.[53] The Union Government have had to consult the Union Commission every year on more than seventy-five thousand cases and the number of cases in which the Commission's advice was not accepted was just 57 times between 1950 to 1985. But it increased to 92 times between 1985 to 1990 (the figures beyond 1990 are not available). The annual average, thus, shot up to 18.4 cases as against 1.6 cases in the first 35 years. The UPSC noted that what was "particularly disturbing" was that in several cases the Government did not give the reasons for the rejection of the Comission's advice. Citing the instance of 10 cases of non-acceptance in 1990, it was revealed that the Government failed to provide reasons for rejection in three cases. Out of these three, two cases pertained to appointment by promotion and one to transfer on deputation.

The States present a yet more gloomy picture. The State Public Service Commissions provide sufficient material to support that inadequate respect is shown by the State Governments to the recommendations of the Commissions. Even more grave are certain unpublished allegations of interference, direct and indirect, by authority and pressures to influence decisions. The most painful is the widespread public belief that money factor is one of the major criteria in selecting candidates. The removal of the Chairman of the Haryana Public Service Commission and the indictment of the Punjab and Haryana High Court hardens into reality.

52. Article 323.
53. Bapat, S.B., 'Public Service Commissions—An Indian Approach,' *The Indian Journal of Public Administration,* January-March 1956, p. 589.

## CHAPTER XVII

# Administrative Tribunals

### Role of Administrative Tribunals

The Swaran Singh Committee on Constitutional Reforms, appointed by the Congress President early in 1976, recommended the setting up of administrative tribunals by a law of Parliament for determining disputes relating to the recruitment and conditions of service of the employees of the Union and the State Governments including the employees of any local or other authority within the territory of India or of a Corporation owned and controlled by the Government, industrial and labour disputes, and disputes relating to revenues, land reforms, ceiling on urban property, and the procurement and distribution of foodgrains and other essential commodities.

One justification of administrative tribunals is that in their absence the law courts are extremely overworked and consequently there is inordinate delay in the disposal of cases which need expeditious decisions. The Swaran Singh Committee expressly stated that the objective should be that "the matters going before these tribunals are decided fairly and expeditiously." But it may be added that the tribunals have advantages over the courts for citizens and the State alike. Tribunals are cheap, speedy, less legal formalities to be observed, easily accessible to the public and are composed of experts in the matter to be dealt with. Tribunals have, as the Law Commission put it, "certain inherent advantages like cheapness, procedural simplicity and availability of special knowledge." If procedural safeguards are ensured the administrative tribunals have the qualities mentioned in the Franks Committee Report.[1]

The Report of the Franks Committee is a document of great importance. The conclusion of the Committee is that the administrative tribunals are not part and parcel of the machinery of Government. They are independent organisation of adjudication for the impartial assessment of individual's claim. "We regard both tribunals and administrative procedures," the Committee said "as essential powers to society. But the administration should not use these methods of adjudication as convenient alternatives to the courts of law." The emphasis of the Report is that whosoever be the arbiter of the rights of the individual, he must be an independent arbiter and the scope for decision must be confined to points of law; neither to policy, nor to administrative expediency. The procedure that has been recommended by the Committee is : openness in inquiry or hearings, fairness and impartiality.

The three points on which the Franks Committee based its Report were : (1) all decisions of administrative tribunals should be subject to review by ordinary courts on points of law; (2) the decision should be entrusted to a court rather than to a tribunal in the absence of special considerations that make a tribunal more suitable and if possible to a tribunal rather than to a Minister; and (3) the determination that the citizen should not suffer in the protection of his legal rights from the substitution of a tribunal or ministerial inquiry or hearing for a court of law. The tribunals, as the Law Commission said, "will be useful as a supplementary system" to the hierarchy of courts. To the courts must, therefore, belong the final responsibility for pronouncing what the law is in regard to the subjects assigned to the tribunal.

But the Constitution (Forty-second Amendment) Act, 1976, expressly excluded the courts from exercising jurisdiction over the tribunals from clause (1) of Article 227 and inserted clause (5) providing that nothing in Clause (1) shall be construed as giving to a High Court any jurisdiction to question any judgement of any inferior court which was not othewise subject to appeal or revision. Articles 323-A and 323-B that authorised Parliament and the State Legislatures to establish administrative tribunals also expressely stated that appropriate legislature may exclude, in the law that it makes, the juridisdiction of all courts, except the juridisdiction of the

1. A Committee appointed by the British Government in 1955 under the Chairmanship of Sir Oliver Franks. The Report was submitted in August 1957.

Supreme Court under Article 136, with respect to the disputes and complaints falling within the jurisdiction of the tribunals, and provide for the establishment of a hierarchy of tribunals.

The Constitution (Forty-fourth Amendment) Act, 1978, amended Article 227, relating to power of superintendence over all courts by the High Court, by substituting for clause (1), as amended by the Forty-second Amendment, which now reads : "Every High Court shall have superintendence over all courts and tribunals throughout the territories in relation to which it exercises jurisdiction." It also omitted clause (5) inserted by the Constitution (Forty-second Amendment) Act, 1976, but retained the provisions of Article 323-A (2) (d) and Article 323-B(3)(d) permitting exclusion of jurisdiction of all Courts except the jurisdiction of the Supreme Court under Article 136 (special leave), with respect to disputes and complaints of service of persons appointed to public services or of any local or any other authority or of any corporation owned or controlled by the Government.

But the remedy of appeal to the Supreme Court by grant of special leave is not adequate. Apart from the fact that it is expensive, inconvenient and shall greatly increase the work-load of the Suprme Court, there shall be confusion in the administration of law. The jurisdiction of superintendence vested in the High Courts ensures that the Courts or tribunals should conform to the law laid down by the courts. If the High Courts cease to exercise this jurisdiction as the Supreme Court remarked in a case where an administrative tribunal declined to follow a High Court ruling, "there would be confusion in the administration of law and respect of law would ir- retrievably suffer." Some of the disputes before the tribunals involve complex questions which can best be resolved by the courts. The jurisdiction of superintendence vested in the High Courts "is to be excersied," as the Supreme Court put it, "most sparingly in appropriate cases" to keep courts and tribunals "within the bounds of their authority and not for correcting mere errors."

**Tribunals Relating to Service Matters**

Administrative tribunals in respect of service matters have been treated separately under Article 323-A, and it is only the law of Parliament which establishes such tribunals, one for the Union and a separate one for each State or for two or more States. These administrative tribunals shall adjudicate on matters of disputes and complaints with respect to recruitment and conditions of service of persons appointed to public services and posts in connection with the affairs of the Union or of any State or of any local or other authority within the territory of India or under the control of the Government of India or of any Corporation owned and controlled by the Government.

The law of Parliament establishing such administrative tribunals should clearly specify the jurisdiction, powers (including the power to punish for contempt) and authority which may be exercised by each of such tribunals, provide for the procedure (including provisions as to the limitation and rules of evidence) to be followed, exclude the jurisdiction of all courts, except the jurisdiction of the Supreme Court under Article 136, with respect to the disputes and complaints in respect of service matters, and provide for the transfer to each such administrative tribunal of any case pending before any court or authority immediately before the establishment of such tribunals.

Article 371- D empowers the President to make by Order with respect to the State of Andhra Pradesh special provisions for equitable opportnunities and facilities for the people belonging to the different parts of the State in the matter of public employment and in the matter of education. The law of Parliament setting up administrative tribunals and defining their jurisdiction should expressly state the repeal or amendment of any such Presidential Order.In order to ensure the effective functioning, speedy disposal of cases and enforcement of the orders of the tribunals, the law should also contain such supplemental, incidental and consequential provisions as Parliament may deem necessary.

**Tribunals for other Matters**

Article 323-B empowers appropriate Legislature, Parliament or State Legislature, competent to make laws with respect to such matters, to provide for the adjudication or trial by tribunals of any disputes, complaints or offences with respect to all or any of the following matters :

(a) levy, assessment, collection and enforcement of any tax;
(b) foreign exchange, import and export across customs frontiers;
(c) industrial and labour disputes;
(d) land reforms by way of acquisition by the State of any estate as defined in Article 31-A in Chapter III dealing with Fundamental Rights, or any of the rights

or the extinguishment or modification of any such rights or by way of ceilings on agricultural land or in any other way;

(e) ceiling on urban property;

(f) elections to either House of Parliament or either House if it is unicameral.

(g) production, procurement, supply and distribution of foodstuffs ( including edible oilseeds and oils) and such other goods as the President may, by public notification, declare to be essential goods and control of prices of such goods;

(h) offences against laws with respect to any of the aforesaid matters [(a) to (g)] and fees in respect of any those matters; and

(i) any matter incidental to any of the aforesaid matters specified in (a) to (h).

A law made by the competent Legislature with respect to the matters enumerated above should provide for the establishment of a hierarchy of tribunals, define the jurisdiction, powers (including the power to punish for contempt) and authority which may be exercised by each tribunal, specify the procedure (including provisions as to the limitations and rules of evidence) to be followed, and exclude the jurisdiction of the Supreme Court under Article 136, with respect to all or any of the matters falling within the jurisdiction of such tribunals. Provision must also be made for the transfer to the relevant tribunal of any cases pending before any court or any other authority immediately before the establishmet of these tribunals. With a view to ensuring effective functioning of the tribunals, speedy disposal of cases and enforcement of the orders of the tribunals, the law should contain such supplemental, incidental and consequential provisions as the appropriate legislature may deem necessary.

# CHAPTER XVIII

# Elections and Parties

## India's "Act of Faith"

The decision of the Constituent Assembly to give every adult Indian, male or female, the right to vote under a system of universal and direct suffrage, was, as Alladi Krishnaswami Ayyar described it, an act of "abundant faith in the common man and the ultimate success of democratic rule."[1] It was the culmination of the Congress demand which had become a *sine qua non* of independence. Under the Government of India Act. 1935, the electorate was honeycombed with fifteen different kinds of voters with reserved seats.[2] Separate communal electorates had plagued the Indian politics since their introduction in 1909. The framers of the Indian Constitution would have none of them. Article 325 states that no person shall be eligible for inclusion......in any special electoral roll....on grounds only of religion, race, caste, sex or any of them." Articles 330 and 332, however, provide for reservation of seats for Scheduled Castes and Scheduled Tribes for the House of the People (Lok Sabha) and every State Assembly[3] (Vidhan Sabha). Provision has also been made for the nomination of not more than two members to the House of the People (Lok Sabha), and one member to the State Legislative Assembly (Vidhan Sabha) if the Anglo-Indian community is not adequately represented therein.

Part IV (Articles 324-329) of the Constitution of India deals with Elections. Every citizen of India who is not less than eighteen years of age except those who are mentally unsound or who had been found guilty of criminal or corrupt practices, have the right to vote for elections to the House of the People and to the Legislative Assembly of every State. The Constitution creates an Election Commission charged with the superintendence, direction and control of all elections to Parliament, to the State Legislatures and to the offices of the President and the Vice-President of India. The Election Commission consists of the Chief Election Commissioner and such other Election Commissioners as the President may determine their number from time to time. The Chief Commissioner acts as the Chairman of the Commission in case there are other Election Commissioners as well. Before each General Election the President may, after consultation with the Chief Election Commissioner, appoint Regional Commissioners to assist the Election Commission in the performance of its functions. The Chief Election Commissioner is liable to removal from office in like manner and on the like grounds as a Judge of the Supreme Court. The conditions of his service cannot be varied to his disadvantage after his appointment. But Election Commissioners and Regional Commissioners, if any, can be removed only on the recommendation of the Chief Election Commissioner.

In 1951-52 when Independent India held her first General Elections for 489 seats to the House of the People (Lok Sabha) and for approximately 3,300 seats to the State Assemblies with over 176,000,000 voters, their organisation presented a mammoth task. The Election Commission had to tide over many difficult situations and solve the riddles of many complex problems. The registration of voters created special problems arising from the linguistic complications, the difficulty of diverse traditions about surnames, the religious inhibitions of the Hindu women to communicate the names of their husbands and the ambiguous status of hundreds of thousands of refugees who had migrated from Pakistan. Above all was the problem of illiteracy. No fewer than 80 percent of the voters were illiterate and to obviate some of the problems thus created, the use of symbols and the multiple ballot box scheme were employed. At least 80 parties contested the elections and if individually oriented groups be

1. *Constituent Assembly Debates,* Vol. XI, p. 825. The Election Commission later characterised it, "an act of faith–faith in the common man of India and in his practical commonsense." *Report of the First General Election in India,* 1951-52, Vol. 1, p. 10.
2. Article 331.
3. Article 333.

included the figure would be 190. Nearly 17,500 candidates contested the elections. More than one-third of these ran as independents; only 240 were women. Fourteen of the larger parties were recognised as the national parties and each one of them was assigned a symbol for its exclusive use throughout the country. Each of the other parties was assigned a symbol either by the National Election Commission or by a State Election Commission. Each polling booth had to contain as many ballot boxes as there were candidates contesting election from that constituency. Almost in all parts of the country, particularly in rural areas, separate facilities had to be provided for women voters.

The Election Commission set up 200.000 polling booths and stations to cater to 176,000,000 eligible voters and manned some two and a half million ballot boxes. Some one million Government officials were drafted to supervise the actual voting. But the sheer size of election operation was not the only hurdle to be crossed. In the remoter areas physical communications presented the most exacting difficulties. In some of these areas elephants had to be commandeered for transport and "at least one election official had to cope with the experience of guarding polling booths against a marauding tiger."

It was the world's largest exercise in democracy and for the Western observers it was a unique occasion. They wondered how in an under-developed country, whose people were mostly illiterate, tradition-bound, unaccustomed to the idea as well as practice of direct adult franchise and unfamiliar with the ways and tenets of democracy, this gigantic experiment would succeed. Many of them predicted that the whole thing would degenerate into a shamble. But it succeeded admirably and the Indian electorate redeemed the "act of faith" the Founding-fathers had reposed in them. The polling continued for four months, from October 25,1951 to February 21,1952 and despite the difficulties of geography and climate the voters braved the weather and distance. They came to the polling stations, attired in gala dresses, men and women, on foot, on bullock carts, camels and elephants, on bicycles, by public conveyance, and by almost every conceivable means of transportation. Most of them took their responsibilities seriously. The turnout of the voters was impressive, except in a few parts of the country, as in most of Rajasthan. Of the 176,000,000 eligible voters, 88,600,000 or slightly more than 50 per cent actually voted and nearly 106,000,000 valid votes were cast. Bearing in mind that the rate of illiteracy was nearly about 80 per cent the turnout must be regarded as a remarkably high proportion, particularly when we remember that just one-fifth of the eligible number of voters had any previous experience of voting. As many as 1,635,000 votes were invalidated. Inevitably there was some misunderstanding and confusion. The voters had to cast votes simultaneously for the State Assembly and the House of the People. In a double-member constituency two votes had to be cast in each instance instead of one. Many voters, for lack of experience and literacy, left their ballots on top of the ballot boxes, or on the floor of the booth instead of dropping them in ballot boxes.

**Elections**

The technique of election campaigns and the tools employed in the First General Election remained the same in the subsequent elections too. They have some familiar features with other countries of the West and some are native to the soil. The usual common techniques are public meetings, speeches by the top-ranking party leaders on hurricane tours throughout the length and breadth of the country, canvassing by the candidates together with the influential men of the area from house-to-house, exchange of salutations, handshaking, and hugging, with a pat to the children to create an emotional impact, partisan appeals and profuse promises. Temples, mosques and gurdwaras are the usual platforms for communal parties where even religious passions are aroused. The unity of the community constitutes the focal point of appeal. Certain techniques extensively used in the Western countries were not available until the June 1977 Assembly elections in the nine Northern States and Tamil Nadu. The All-India Radio was not a significant factor in the previous election campaigns. The Radio was used by the Government agency to explain the voting procedures and urging the voters to exercise their cherished right of franchise. Excerpts from the election manifestoes of the parties were read from time to time; the ruling party always commanding the advantage. Television did not exist till recently and it does not cover the whole country even now. The Janata Government initiated for the first time in May 1977, broadcasts on the Radio and Doordarshan (television) by the leaders of the national parties, but only once or twice and for a limited duration.

The tools used in election campaigns are varied and often fascinating but jarring too. Some of the parties and candidates are really ingenious in devising novel election tools in reaching the remote areas. Real ingenuity is reflected in many of the placards and posters littering every available space on the walls of the houses and commercial premises. Slogans are painted on the roads too.

In towns, cities and villages loud speakers mounted on motor cars, jeeps, tongas (hackney carriages) and bicycles blare the names of candidates and their election symbols in almost unceasing babel of sounds right from early in the morning till late at night, much to the agony of the student community and discomfiture of the public. The slogan for the Congress candidates was vote for the Congress and strengthen the hands of Nehru or Indira Gandhi. The slogan of the Janata Party in 1977 was Jayprakash Narayan's message: ''Democracy V. Dictatorship.''

Taking out processious is another familiar tool of election campaigning. Truck loads of shouting young people, most of whom are generally in their teens and quite a few of them are hired, cruise through the streets and along the highways. Sometimes, processions are preceded by bands or *bhangra* (dancing) parties. Torchlight processions are also taken out and street-corner meetings are held. The candidates are keen that their supporters should fly atop their houses and commercial premises the party flags to exhibit their electoral solidarity in that area, though it is not an exact barometer of actual assessment. Money power is another secret tool and the poor very often succumb to such a temptation

Since 1967 disruption of political meetings has taken the main form of violence. There were stray cases even before, but such incidents are of usual occurrences now. In 1967,there were as many as 474 reported disturbances during the sixty days preceding the poll and in 8 per cent of these cases deaths or serious injuries occurred. In West Bengal, when political murders reached a figure of 1,200 in 1970 doubts were seriously sexpressed whether an election could be held at all. Troops were, however, called to help the civil authorities in holding peaceful elections. The troops fanned in the entire State and despite extensive patrolling 120 deaths occurred during the seven weeks of intensive campaigning. In other States violence was less extreme,although Bihar saw some bloody affrays,—a product of caste rivalries,—and both Uttar Pradesh and Gujarat had serious Hindu-Muslim riots and the police had to resort to firings and the imposition of curfews. The March 1977 elections to the House of the People passed off without any serious incidence of violence, but in June 1977, Bihar, West Bengal and Uttar Pradesh again fell prey to violence and the police had to resort to firing. Later, political murders took place in Jammu and Kashmir. Home Minister Charan Singh told the House of the People that cases of violence were less in number in 1977 as compared with 1971. Comparisons are always odious and there is no denying the fact that violence is a serious blot on the electoral record of India. In Uttar Pradesh, Bihar and Madhya Pradesh electoral violence is near-endemic. In May 1981 in the nine Assembly polls 21 people died and for the first time six candidates were among the dead, three in Uttar Pradesh, two in Bihar, one in Gujarat. While most of the 21 slayings were in Uttar Pradesh and Bihar, corpses were strewn around seven (out of nine) States, including hitherto trouble-free Punjab. Capturing of polling booth has now become a routine process by organised and armed gangs of hoodlums. especially in Bihar. During the 1971 General Election, for instance, of 66 cases of booth capturing throughout the country as many as 52 took place in Bihar. In the 1977 General Election Bihar and West Bengal shared the honour of booth capturing equally. Against the 32 booths forcibly seized in Bihar, 31 were similarly taken over in West Bengal. There is ample evidence on record that even dacoits are wooed by politicians for support at the polls in the Chambal region of Madhya Pradesh and Uttar Pradesh. A top official was reported to have said in Gwalior that the dacoits ''are like any other vote banks for political parties.''[4] An elected member of the Uttar Pradesh Assembly sent to a notorious dacoit of Muzaffarnagar (U.P.) a letter of thanks and gratitude for his support in May 1980 election.

Until the Fourth General Election in 1967, Congress, while polling less than half of the votes cast for members of the House of the People,won 70 per cent or more of the seats. The next largest was the Communist Party of India whose strength fluctuated between sixteen and twenty-nine seats. No other Party could get enough members to be

4. The *Hindustan Times*, New Delhi, December 24, 1979.

of any real significance in 1952 and veered round this number until 1962. The Jana Sangh which began its career with three seats in 1952 increased its position to six in 1957 and fourteen in 1962.

But the Congress could not dominate the State Assemblies. In 1952 it failed to win an overall majority in the Patiala and East Punjab States Union (PEPSU),[5] Travancore Cochin,[6] Orissa and Madras. In the newly created Andhra Pradesh, the Congress could secure only forty seats against forty-one gained by the Communists. In Kerala the Communists formed the Government in 1957 by routing the Congress. In Orissa the Congress Government had to depend for its existence on the active support of the Jharkhand Party. Andhra Pradesh and Orissa soon came under the President's rule. Kerala, too, had a spell of the President's rule. In the mid-term elections the Congress gained a stable majority as a result of electoral agreements with the Socialists and the Muslim League. In Orissa the Congress, again, could not muster an absolute majority and it formed coalition Government with locally-based Ganatantra Parishad. Madhya Pradesh Congress Government fell victim to internal factionalism with the consequence that the President's rule had to be imposed. In the third General Election the share of the Congress seats in the State Assemblies fell from 68.4 per cent in 1952 to 61.3 per cent followed by the same difficulties as before, although rather less severe. The Congress Government in Kerala was shortlived and,once again,the President's rule had to be imposed. In Madhya Pradesh the Congress Government had to depend upon the support of the Independent members.

Two results emerge from this study of the election results between 1952 and 1962. In the first place,Indian politics were more "competitive" at the State level than at the Central level, and secondly, there were certain areas where the weakness of the Congress was particularly marked. At the national level there were no real issues to be isolated, except those arising from different personalities. Broadly speaking, the people voted either for the Congress or against the Congress. The Congress had to its credit the achievements of the national movement. It won for India freedom and the memories of Gandhi were still fresh in the minds of the masses. Nehru, with his charismatic personality led the party and his name had a magic effect on the electorate. But the Congress was also vulnerable because over the years it had alienated many people and regions for one reason or another. Almost everyone who was frustrated and unhappy with his lot in life accused the party in power and that was Congress. The reorganisation of the States in 1956 created a big dent in the solidarity of the Party and its cohesiveness was severely disturbed in the regions which were deemed to have been adversely affected by the scheme of reorganisation. In the elections for the members of the State Assemblies local issues and grievances, therefore, predominated. These varied from State to State, and, indeed, from constituency to constituency. The agitation, for instance, started by the Samyukta Maharashtra Samiti and the Maha Gujarat Janata Parishad, two opposition organisations, the former for the creation of a united Maharashtra State and the latter for the separation of the Gujarati-speaking from the Marathi-speaking areas, became so violent and effective that in 1957 elections the Bombay Congress Party found its former massive majority reduced to a highly precarious one. Both these front organisations secured support from almost all sections of the people without any party compulsions. It must also be noted that though the Congress was a dominant party, both at the Centre and in the States, it was not the first choice of the majority of the people, for less than half of the voters had always cast their votes for the Congress candidates.

The leaders of the Congress Party were alarmed at these disturbing trends. The vulnerability of the Congress was revealed in the 1967 elections. In the House of the People its majority was reduced from 361 to 284; a precarious majority, for factionalism in the party had reached a stage where majority could not be safely relied upon. With the split in the Congress in 1969, the Congress lost majority in the House of the People. Sixty-five members of the House broke from it and sat with the Opposition. The minority Government of Mrs. Indira Gandhi was 52 votes short of an absolute majority and it could remain in power with the support of the Communists, the Akalis and Dravida Munnetra Kazagham.

But the situation for the Congress was far worse in the States. Bihar, Punjab, West Bengal, Orissa, Madras and Kerala were all lost. In Rajasthan it secured 89 seats out of a total of 184 and in Uttar Pradesh 199 out of a total membership of 425. In Kerala the tally was 9, in Madras

5. PEPSU disappeared after its merger with Punjab in 1956 as a result of reorganisation.
6. Travancore Cochin became Kerala after reorganisation.

50, in Orissa 31 and in West Bengal 127. The Opposition parties had become wiser by then. Hitherto the simple majority voting system had operated in favour of the Congress. The fragmentation of the Opposition enabled it to win seats on minority votes. Electoral pacts,if any,were few and perfunctory. In the 1962 elections some of the Opposition parties used the strategy of electoral agreements effectively and on a large scale and it yielded good dividends.

These electoral alliances, which had eaten into Congress majority in the States, do not fully explain the bad shape the Party had assumed. For instance, despite the electoral alliances in Gujarat and Madhya Pradesh most of the Congressmen succeeded in retaining their seats. Here the State Congress parties remained comparatively united and the alliances could not create a big dent on their solidarity. But in those States where the Congress parties were prey to intense factionalism and the Opposition alliances were powerful the damage was marked. And once the Opposition gained the day, ambitious politicians found adequate opportunities to prance into new pastaures. Formerly, to be outside the Congress was to be in political wilderness. In 1967, there were several alternative homes for the politically ambitious and frustrated adventurers. Thus started the game of defections and floor crossing. Another factor worth mentioning was the growth of factionalism in the Congress Central Election Committee, a body responsible for the final selection of candidates. This factionalised body discounted merit and partisan candidates were selected. These candidates had less vote-getting capabilities and their loyalty to the party itself was sure to be weak. Way back in 1954, Dunichand Ambalavi, wrote, "I know enough of the working of the Congress machinery and that of the Punjab Election Board of which I was a member in 1951-52. Pre-planned designs, duplicity and what not played greater role in the selection of candidates than any consideration of honesty, fair-play and recognition of the claims of deserving candidates."[7] If such things become a repeat performance at the highest level where final selections are made, the result is sure to be runious for the party, he added.

The major political effect of the 1967 elections was the proliferation of the unstable governments in North India and some other States. These coalition Governments had nothing in common to bind them together. Their instability was essentially due to the diversity of their political components or to what an Indian journalist described as "ideological promiscuity."[8] In most cases it was only the desire to power which brought them together and consequently the creation of political majorities to support them in the Legislatures proved extremely difficult. The habit of floorcrossing was another plague spot that left the Governments uncertain and, therefore, impotent. The outcome was the imposition of President's rule in one State after another. The midterm elections in February 1969 in Uttar Pradesh, West Bengal,Bihar and Punjab in no way improved the situation. This mini-general election involving some two-thirds of the electorate followed the trends of 1967. The public disenchantment with the United Front Governments in no way proved advantageous for the Congress either. A divided house was finally split among two rivals, never to combine again.[9]

In December 1970, Mrs. Indira Gandhi thought it expedient to seek a fresh mandate. She advised the President to dissolve the House of the People and order fresh elections. It is important to note that elections to the House of the People were delinked form elections to the States of Orissa,Tamil Nadu and West Bengal. Mrs. Gandhi's decision to hold fresh elections was not received enthusiastically by her own partymen. Many of the observers regarded it as a desperate gamble. She made a direct appeal to the nation to help her to carry out an effective implementation of social and economic programme through democratic processes. "Poverty" the Congress manifesto ended,"must go. Disparity must diminish. Injustice must end." To carry out the entire programme, Mrs.Gandhi explained to the electorate, a strong and stable Government committed to radical policies and backed by a decisive majority in Parliament was necessary.

The nation responded to Mrs. Gandhi's call and Congress in securing a massive majority of 352 seats in a House of 518–122 more than it held at the time of dissolution. It polled 43.64 per cent of the votes cast. For the Opposition parties,both right and left, it was a complete disaster. The strength of the Congress (O)was reduced from 66

7. *The Tribune,* Ambala Cantt. June 2, 1959.
8. As cited in Hanson, A.H., and Janet Douglas, *India's Democracy,* p. 59.
9. There was another split in January 1978, and Mrs. Gandhi was the main actor in this drama too.

to 16 seats and it polled 10.56 per cent of the votes cast. The Swatantra,which had 44 seats in 1967, could retain only 8 seats with 3.08 per cent of the total electorate. The Samyukta Socialists lost 20 of their 23 seats and Jana Sangh sank from 35 to 21 and the Communists from 29 to 24. The only major party to improve its position was the Marxist Communist Party. It secured 25 seats. Regional Parties, with the exception of DMK and the Telengana Praja Samiti, which demanded a separate State for Telengana,were erased from the national political scene. DMK won 18 seats.

In two of the three States in which elections were held simultaneously the Congress led by Mrs. Gandhi—(Congress) (R), Ruling Congress as it was then known—made spectacular gains. In Orissa, previously ruled by Swatantra-led coalition, it secured 51 seats and emerged as the largest party. In West Bengal it secured 105 seats as against 111 of the CPI (M), showing a gain of 50 on its performance of the undivided Congress. Congress (R) formed Government in coalition with the Communist Party of India, the Bangla Congress and the Forward Bloc,both regionally based parties. The DMK was given a free run for the Assembly seats on the undertaking that it would not contest the Congress (R) candidates in the ten House of the People seats.

The Congress (R) swept the polls in other States too when elections were held subsequently. Parliamentary elections to the Sixth House of the People were normally due to be held in March 1976. But internal Emergency was declared on the mid-night of June 25, 1975 and subsequently the term of Parliament and the State Assemblies was extended for a period of one year. In January 1977 the Prime Minister advised the President to dissolve the House of the People and order fresh elections. The elections were held in March 1977. Immediately after the Presidential Order dissolving the House of the People, Emergency was relaxed and all the political leaders detained were released. Four Opposition parties—the Congress (Organisation), Jana Sangh, Bharatiya Lok Dal, and Socialist Party—combined together in a single party to contest elections on a common symbol. Jayaprakash Narayana, God-father of the Janata Party, gave a call to the people not to miss the opportunity election had offered to choose between freedom and slavery—for the country, for themselves and for their children. He declared that Janata Party was committed to restoration of Fundamental Rights and the Rule of law.[10] Jagjivan Ram, the Agriculture Minister, resigned from the Union Cabinet and the Congress on February 2, 1977 and formed a new party, the Congress for Democracy. Jagjivan Ram declared at a Press conference that his party would have electoral adjustments with the Janata Party. The Janata and the Congress for Democracy had a common symbol on the ballot papers.

Of the 188,438,910 valid votes, the votes polled by the national parties were:

| | | |
|---|---|---|
| Janata-CFD | 81,355,333 | (43.17 per cent) |
| Congress | 65,088,520 | (34.54 per cent) |
| CPI | 5,310,775 | (2.82 per cent) |
| CPI (M) | 8,103,723 | (4.30 per cent) |
| Others | 17,247,100 | (9.15 per cent) |
| Independents | 1,333,452 | (6.02 per cent) |

The Janata-CFD tally did not include the Votes polled by the combination in Tamil Nadu,where it contested on the symbol of the Congress(O).

The combine polled more than 50 per cent of the votes in the seven States and two Union Territories. They were: Bihar 65.01, Haryana 70.35, Himanchal Pradesh 58.37, Madhya Pradesh 57.95, Orissa 51.77, Rajasthan 65.21, Uttar Pradesh 68.03, Chandigarh 66.13 and Delhi 68.15.

The Congress polled majority votes in three States and three Union Territories. They were : Andhra Pradesh 57.36, Karanataka 56.74, Assam 50.56, Lakshadweep 58.59, Andaman and Nicobar Islands 58.54 and Arunachal Pradesh 56.34. The Party did not win a single seat in Himachal Pradesh, Haryana, Punjab, Uttar Pradesh, Delhi and Bihar. In Rajasthan and Madhya Pradesh the Congress won one seat each. In other words, out of 237 seats in seven States and two Union Territories in Northern and Central India, the Congress won just two seats. The Janata Party's performance was equally bad in the South. In Andhra Pradesh, Karnataka,Tamil Nadu, Kerala, Pondicherry, Lakshadweep, and the Andaman and Nicobar Islands, only six seats went to the Janata Party and there was only one recognisable national personality, Neelam Sanjiva Reddy,subsequently to become President of India, figuring in the ruling Party as a representative of the South.

The CPI, which secured seven seats against 23 in 1971, polled only 2.82 per cent of the votes compared with 4.73 per cent last time. It, however, obtained more than 4 per cent of the votes

10. *The Indian Express*, New Delhi, January 30, 1970.

in five States—Manipur 11.50, Kerala 10.38,West Bengal 6.49, Bihar 5.63 and Tamil Nadu 4.60—to be recognised as a national party. The CPI(M) received 4.30 per cent of the votes this time against 5.12 per cent in 1971. This party fought the Parliamentary election in alliance with the Janata Party and won 22 seats as compared with 25 in 1971.

The regional parties and Independents generated 15.17 per cent of the votes and annexed 60 seats against 22.13 per cent and 65 seats in 1971. Among the regional parties which gave an impressive performance were: the National Conference (2) which contested in Jammu and Kashmir in alliance with the Congress, the Kerala Congress (2) and other parties (Muslim League 2 and RSP I), all CPI-led ruling front Kerala,the Peasants and Workers Party (5), an ally of the Janata Party in Maharashtra, Akali Dal (9) an ally of the Janata Party in Punjab, the United Democratic Front (1) in Nagaland, All-India Anna Dravida Munnetra Kazagham (18) in Tamil Nadu and Pondicherry (1), and Maharashtrawadi Gomantak Party(1) in Goa, Daman and Diu. The percentage of votes polled by these parties together with other smaller parties in the respective States were : Jammu and Kashmir 34.99, Kerala 24.31, Maharashtra 10.24, Punjab 40.57, Nagaland 51.68,Tamil Nadu [including DMK, AIADMK, and Congress (O)] 48.05,Goa 40.52 and Pondicherry 53.32.

In mid-April 1977, The Union Home Minister "appealed" to the Chief Ministers of the nine States—Punjab, Himachal Pradesh, Haryana, Rajasthan, Uttar Pradesh, Bihar, Madhya Pradesh and Orissa where the Congress suffered a rout in the March elections to the House of the People—to advise the Governors to dissolve their Assemblies and immediately seek a fresh mandate from the people. The "appeal" was not accepted and the President issued proclamations declaring breakdown of the Constitution in these States and dissolved the State Assemblies. Tamil Nadu was already under the President's rule since January 1976. The elections to the State Assemblies of these States were held in early June. Elections to the Jammu and Kashmir State Assembly,which had been dissolved earlier by the Governor on the advice of the Chief Minister were held in the end of June.

The Janata Party again swept the polls in the States of Himachal, Haryana, Rajasthan, Uttar Pradesh, Bihar, Madhya Pradesh and Orissa. The public support for the Party,though somewhat dissipated, was still solid enough and in no State did it receive less votes than Congress in its heyday. In the Punjab there was Akali-Janata and CPI(M) alliance. In West Bengal CPI(M) went alone and for the first time came into power in its own right, without being dependent on the support of partners in a coaliation. In Tamil Nadu All-India Anna Dravida Munnetra Kazhgam won as many as 129 seats in 234 member House. The DMK secured 49 seats. In Jammu and Kashmir for the first time since independence, the voters had an option between two national parties (Congress and Janata) and one local party (National Conference) and they exercised their vote in favour of the National Conference with a predominant majority.

In July 1979 the Janata Party disintegrated and apprehending certain defeat on a vote of no-confidence moved by the Leader of the Opposition,Y.B.Chavan, in the House of the People, against the Janata Government, Prime Minister Morarji Desai submitted to the President his own resignation as well as that of his Council of Ministers. After prolonged consultations and discussions, the President appointed Charan Singh, heading the Lok Dal-Congress (U) coalition with outside support of the Congress (I). The President, while appointing Charan Singh as Prime Minister, had fettered him with the condition that he would seek confidence of the House of the People within a month's time. But Congress (I) subsequently withdrew its support from the Government and the Lok Dal-Congress (U) coalition could not command sufficient support in the House to steer through the condition of seeking a vote of confidence and, consequently,resigned. Prime Minister Charan Singh advised the President, on the basis of the decision of his Cabinet, to dissolve the House of the People and command fresh elections. The President thereupon dissolved the House of the People and the Lok Dal-Congress (U) coalition remained in office as a care-taker Government till fresh elections were held in January 1980. Congress (I) headed by Mrs. Indira Gandhi received massive mandate from the electorate virtually routing all other parties contesting the mid-term Parliamentary election.

Following the precedent set by the Janata Government in February 1977, the Congress (I) Government also dissolved the State Assemblies where non-Congress (I) Governments were in power. Switching over loyalties, a proverbial feature of Indian politics, had started much earlier, even before the Parliamentary elections in January 1980. Bhajan Lal, the Haryana Chief Minister, took the lead and along with 37 members of the State Janata Legislative Party, joined Mrs. Gandhi's Congress and others joined them afterwards. In Himachal defections from the Janata ruling party reduced Shanta Kumar's Government into minority and the Congress (I) leader, Ram Lal, took over the Government. In the States of Punjab, Uttar Pradesh, Madhya Pradesh, Bihar, Orissa, Rajasthan and Maharashtra Congress (I) secured respectable majorities and formed Governments in those States. The position as it existed in May1981 was that Congress (I) Governments ruled in the sixteen States and in the remaining six, CPI(M) was in power in Kerala, Tripura and West Bengal, All-India Anna Dravida Munnetra Kazhagam in Tamil Nadu, the National Conference in Jammu and Kashmir and Sikkim Congress in Sikkim. The same old pattern of uni-party Goverment both at the Centre and in the States, was once again, repeated. Both in the January 1983 Assembly elections Congress (I) lost its ruling position both in Andhra Pradesh and Karnataka. Tripura went to the CPI (M) for the Second time.

**Parties: (1) Congress**

The Indian National Congress was the ruling party at the Centre from 1947 to March 1977 when the Janata Party stepped in its place. It reigned supreme in all the States, except for a short spell in Kerala, till the 1967 General Election when its fortune began fluctuating. Till 1980 it was totally eclipsed in the Northern States. Although it was the ruling party in the States of Maharashtra,. Andhra Pradesh, Karnataka and Assam, but was in disarray as a result of defections and internal dissensions eventually resulting into the Party's second split in January 1978. In Kerala it was in coalition Government with the Communist Party and the Muslim League.

In conversation with Michael Brecher, Krishna Menon described the one great advantage that Congress had over its competitors. "The great strength of the Congress Party," he said, "is that they have a place in the hearts of the people. There is nothing to take its place. I mean you cannot compare it to a Western political party; it is not strictly a party, it has got a mystique; it is a movement still." But after Independence the Congress had to play a very different role. It had become the successor to the British authority in India. There was at that time much heart-searching and stock-taking in the Congress ranks as to whether the Congress should continue to function when its mission of winning freedom for India had been fulfilled. Gandhi himself felt that the Congress should dissolve and turn itself in a Lok Sewak Sangh (Society for the service of the people),because he did not want the child of his toils and symbol of national unity to become the plaything of politics and be reduced to the position of a mere party manoeuvring for power. The majority in the Congress, however, as Prof. Avasthi says, "declined to commit political 'harakari' and decided to stand forth as a political party in the usual sense of the terms." The Congress thus, ceased to be an omnibus organisation which could contain almost any Indian who wanted his country to be free. It became instead a political party, which was at the same time the Government of Independent India. It meant that Congress could not command the support and respect of all those comrades who had fought together the battle of freedom. Gandhi's assassination so soon after Independence also removed from the scene the most unifying influence of all and, then followed the process of disintegration in the Party. The Socialists, who formed the left-wing of the Congress, separated and established a new party under the leadership of Jayaprakash Narayan. Sarat Chandra Bose formed another party, the Socialist Republican. A few more members of the Congress Party in the Central Legislature formed the Socialist Democratic Party under the leadership of Prof. K.T.Shah. Some were expelled, or were forced out by the change in Congress Policy.

But the Congress retained some of its former mystique and influence. It was Gandhi's party which had led India to freedom and the Government was headed by Nehru whose role in the freedom movement was revered by all. He was the beau ideal of the old and young alike and the Congress still tried to be all things to all men. "I have begun with Congress", said an old man in a rural constituency, "have stayed with Congress and will end with Congress, because Congress is the first party. The flowers that bloom in the field, the crops that grow in the field, they are there because of Congress." Such sentiments generally expressed the feeling of millions of Indians in whose hearts respect for Congress remained unshaken.

The younger generation did not have any such memories to recall. Their parents might have recited to them the anecdotes of the national movement. The Congress leadership, too, continued to remind them of the glorious achievements the Party had to its credit. But past is past with distant and fading memories. The Congress old guard had practically disappeared and even among the middle-aged Congress leaders very few had "graduated from British jails." Here lies part of the explanation of both Congress's former dominance and its decadence.

A second and equally important explanation is to be found in political organisation of the Congress. It is the only political group in the nation with a truly all-India organisation. Its lowest organisational unit is the committee in a village or town or city ward. The line of organisation extends from the local committee to other committees in larger sub-divisions of the State,to Pradesh(State) Committees,and from the Pradesh Committee to the Central party apparatus, headed by the all-India Congress Committee and the Working Committee. Theoretically, the annual session of the Congress is the supreme policy-making body, but in practice it is of the nature of party rally which brings together the leaders of the party and thousands of delegates. The delegates and others who attend the annual session listen to the reports from party committees, and they endorse, usually without much debate, large number of resolutions, formulated or at least approved by the party's High Command.

There are three successive stages whereby the Congress built itself into a genuine national party. Originating amongst a "microscopic minority," to use Lord Dufferin's language, of Westernised professional men, at the beginning of the present century, the Congress began to recruit support from the indigenous business community. When Gandhi entered upon the political scene, it stretched towards the masses. Although it rarely reached the lower strata of society, the Congress became popular among the middle strata such as peasant proprietors, tradesmen and skilled artisans. With Independence and Congress having succeeded to authority, its appeal extended to even more socio-economic groups and the response was astounding as the people regarded it the only political vehicle for the realisation of their aspirations. Those who chose to remain outside the party itself would at least cast their votes for the Congress, though they might have disagreed with many specific items of Congress policy, as they respected it as an effective organisation capable of delivering whatever "goods" there were to deliver. The organisational effectiveness, therefore, goes a long way to explain the former Congress dominance.

The recruitment of members from a wide spectrum of caste and interest groups was undoubtedly a source of strength for the Congress, as it increased immensely its vote catching capacity and Nehru could raise the slogan in 1953 that "the Congress is the country and the country is Congress." But it gradually became transformed into a source of weakness. This process of aggregation and accommodation was much more difficult for local leadership. The locals were faced with the choice of preserving their own leadership by discouraging recruitment, or winning additional votes by bringing into organisation new elements which might subsequently displace them. True, that with Independence rapid avenues became available for local leaders to realise their political aspirations, but it also tended to reinforce factionalism which is characteristic of all Indian organisations and associations. The factions are like miniature parties within the broad party. Their numbers and strength varied from area to area but on the whole one may agree with Paul Brass, who studied the Uttar Pradesh area, that "organisationally, Congress is a collection of district factions and state factions forming alliances and developing hostilities in a constant struggle for positions of power and status in Congress-controlled institutions."

In the beginning actual factions were not entirely "chaotic or anemic" in their mode of operation. They were tolerated by the central leadership on the ground that factionalism within the party served some useful purpose. It was considered a democratic process as factions were the agents of political recruitment which widened the base for grassroot political participation and kept the party responsive to the constantly changing political environments. But there was another side of it too. Factionalism made the process of decision-making difficult and lengthy. It made the central leadership paralysed as the leadership increasingly preoccupied itself with the maintenance of internal unity of the party to the exclusion of any other objective. Moreover, as Baldev Raj Nayar Remarked, "the spectacle of constant bickering amongst Congressmen, the public display of inner party controversies and the open defiance of party discipline make not only for the denigration of the Congress Party, but also lead to a contempt for the political system and party itself.''

The organisation of the party in power is expected to work in close harmony with, and always be willing to be guided by and support the ministerial wing. The head of the organisation, the party President, and the Leader of the Parliamentary wing, who is the Prime Minister, should, in theory at any rate, always work hand in hand in order that the party policies and programmes are duly implemented. But Nehru and the other top leaders firmly believed that having accepted the parliamentary system and the constitutional doctrine of ministerial responsibility of Parliament and through it to the people, the role of the organisational wing was only to take broad decisions on party programme and organising its members for electoral and ''constructive'' work. The practical difficulties of such a separation of powers are obvious and there were quite a few influential members in the party who bitterly complained that intra-party democracy was being thrown overboard.

At the Centre, ''the Prime Minister and the Congress President tended to regard each other at best with suspicion and at worst with outright hostility.''[11] J.B. Kripalani, who succeeded Nehru as President of the Party, when the latter became Prime Minister, tried to insist that political decisions should be made in consultation with the Working Committee. Kripalani had already taken measures to insulate the Working Committee from the governmental influence by limiting the number of ministers among its members to one-third of the total membership. Both Nehru and Patel ''fought him vigorously'' with the result, that, within two months of Independence, Kripalani tired of the struggle, resigned from the Congress presidency and, soon after, from the party to become its veteran foe. He formed a new Party,the Kisan Mazdoor Praja Party (KMPP). Purshottam Das Tandon, who became the President in 1950, also challenged Nehru and he, too, was forced to resign. Thereafter Nehru himself became the President and combined the two posts, Prime Ministership and the presidency of the party, for some years. According to Frank Moraes, this victory for the parliamentary wing created ''a Congress habit of mind...which led the overwhelming bulk of the party to look to the Prime Minister and not to the President of the Congress for the political guidance.''

Nehru's successor to the presidency, U.N. Dhebar, was hand-picked and he was not at all prominent in the higher circles of the party or of the Government. In 1969, Dhebar was succeeded by Mrs. Indira Gandhi. Mrs. Gandhi's successor was D. Sanjivayya, a comparatively young Chief Minister of Andhra Pradesh. Thus,whether he held the position of Congress President or not, Nehru had been the unquestioned leader of the party as well as the nation, till his death in 1964.

Nadar K. Kamraj was the President when Nehru died and he managed the succession of Lal Bahadur Shastri to Prime Ministership. Kamraj and his 'Syndicate'—a small group of the Working Committee—contrived to establish the principle of collective responsibility and it was claimed by influential Congressmen that there existed one. Shastri lived for a short time and apparently there was no conflict between him and the Congress President. Kamraj, again, succeeded in installing Mrs. Indira Gandhi as the Prime Minister. Kamraj did not favour the selection of Morarji Desai, another candidate, as strong-willed and obstinate he was, he might not get on smoothly with the party. Indira Gandhi, on the other hand, would depend upon the Congress President for advice and guidance, being a woman and inexperienced. But she soon asserted her independence. Kamraj himself lost control over the party after his defeat in the 1967 elections and many of the other ''tallest poppies,''such as, Atulya Ghosh and S.K. Patil. The relations between the ministerial and organisational wings became so sour that party unity could no longer be maintained. The split over the Fourth Presidential election in 1969 left the Congress a divided camp and a party of hostiles in search of an opportunity to run down one another. The public clash between the Congress President, Nijalingappa, and Mrs. Gandhi took away the simple grace which party solidarity demanded.

The Working Committee comprising the Nijalingappa group expelled Mrs. Gandhi from the party for her ''constant denigration of the organisation...acts of indiscipline'' and '' a basic and overriding desire to concentrate all power in her own hands,'' and called upon members of the Congress Parliamentary Party to elect a new leader. The other half of the Working Committee (10 out of 21) led by Mrs.Gandhi countercharged Nijalingappa and his syndicate for reducing to mockery democracy and discipline within the

11. Hanson, A.H., and Janet Dougals, *India's Democracy,* p. 70.

Congress "by small coterie equating itself with the entire organisation" and "ousted" Nijalingappa from Congress Presidentship. The Congress split, into Congress (Ruling) under Mrs. Gandhi and Congress (Organisation) under Nijalingappa, was complete.

In the States the conflict between the Chief Ministers and the Presidents of the Pradesh Congress Committees was even sharper, but its pattern varied from State to State. Y.B. Chavan, for instance, kept the Maharashtra organisational wing under his tight control whereas in West Bengal it was just the reverse. Here, Atulya Ghosh, the organisational leader, maintained dominance over the ministerial wing. In other States, "the fortunes of battle rocked to and fro with varying results". In Uttar Pradesh the battle had always been too severe and many a time ministries had fallen as a result. In many States the Legislature parties and the Pradesh Congress Committees functioned as virtually two independent parties and the supporters of the organisational wing acted in the manner of an Opposition and on occasions embarrassed the government by tabling motions critical of the Government. Whenever the Central leadership tried to intervene,it met with partial success and that, too, temporarily to flare up again. After the declaration of Emergency these rifts did not abate,but they took a new form. The Pradesh Congress Committees and the Legislature parties became beggars at the gate of not the Central leadership but the Prime Minister. They would invariably seek the good offices of Mrs. Gandhi to intervene. Many Pradesh Committees were superseded on her behest and replaced by the *ad hoc* committees manned by the personnel of her own choice. The Chief Ministers were made and unmade by her with rivalries to recur again but leaving behind a corps of disgruntled Chief Ministers removed by Mrs. Gandhi. They formed the core of the Congress for Democracy and the Janata Party and helped the disintegration of the Congress and its humiliation at the March and June 1977 elections.

The Congress after the 1967 elections stood discredited at the bar of public opinion. Factions were rampant in the Party and the average Congressman was collecting dividends on his past investment. Sidhartha Ray,former Judicial Minister of West Bengal,said in the State Assembly in 1958 that the Congress Party and administration were"helping in building up a morally corrupt and physically weak nation."[12] Dunichand Ambalavi,wrote in 1959. "If I were to narrate all that has happened inside and in the name of the Congress since the advent of freedom it would be a harrowing and distressing story. In the General Elections of 1951-52, many Congress notables in the Punjab, acted upon the adage 'make hay while the sun shines.' Some of them who could not and did not go to the Punjab Legislative Assembly made piles of money."[13] Pyarelal, a former Private Secretary to Gandhi, wrote, "It has to be admitted that India today is far from realising the picture of what Gandhiji called 'India of my dreams.' Bribery and corruption are rampant all round, and on all accounts it is at worse than it was under British rule. Favouritism and nepotism and failure of the judiciary to give unadulterated justice to the people in innumerable cases is a distressing fact."[14] C.D. Deshmukh maintained that it was now recognised that the administrative machinery at all levels was "erratic and inadequate. The Public heard of nepotism, high-handedness, gerrymandering,feathering of the nest through progeny and many other sins of commission and omission."[15]

There was a close association between factionalism and patronage which assumed different forms and toadying of the worst kind. The distribution of favours was, of course, the most important of the weapons that a dominant faction could wield. If used judiciously it could bring together the whole State organisation in a unity,but this was a precarious unity and was achieved at a perilous cost. It debased the nation and deprived it of credibility. It was experimented on a large scale and one of its most successful practitioners was Pratap Singh Kairon, the Punjab Chief Minister (1956 to 63). He managed his unruly followers and opponents by what he described as "the American technique"—everyone had his price. So was Atulya Ghosh of West Bengal. He once admitted that under his leadership the Pradesh Congress Committee had become "a place for spoils and favours"—a situation he justified on the grounds that the alternative was mobocracy, which indeed it seemed to have been. The leadership in the States corrupted the people in order to strengthen their base of authority and status

12. *The Tribune,* Ambala Cantt., March 26, 1958.
13. *The Tribune,* Ambala Cantt., June 2, 1959.
14. *The Tribune,* Ambala Cantt., October, 2, 1954.
15. V.S. Srinivasa Sastri Endowment Lecture, Madras University, July 11, 1959, *The Hindustan Times,* New Delhi, July 12, 1969.

and the vicious circle grew like a snowball. The corrupted themselves would become corrupters to strengthen their own party position. There could be no more damaging indictment of Congress rule than the observations made by the Election Commission in its report on the Fifth General Election, 1971-72. It asked, "How can we expect that the election would be corruption-free when the whole country in every sphere and department of life and activity is plunged in the sea of corruption?" The Congress rule had become synonymous with the "licence, permit and quota raj." The Tarkunde Committee on election reform, appointed by Jaya Prakash Narayan, expressed the view in its report in February 1975, that among the political parties the Congress had the greatest access to business finance "by reason of its power of patronage."

In all elections since 1971 the personality of Mrs. Gandhi became the only focal point of party propaganda. Both the party's election manifesto and its publicity literature exalted her as an incomparable leader with the power to solve all problems of the country. "She is", declared in one of the advertisements in newspapers, "the only national leader whose image is enshrined in the hearts of the people." Nehru had raised the slogan in 1953 "the Congress is the country and the country is Congress." The tradition of heroworship was carried to such extreme lengths that no less a person than the Congress President equated India with Indira. But the March 1977 elections proved otherwise. Emergency took its toll and the Prime Minister herself was defeated in a constituency that she had nursed so fondly. For the Congress, the election was the end of the road until the Party purified itself or to put it in the words of Brahmanada Reddy, it goes "back to its pre-independence modes of service and sacrifice."[16] Immediately after relinquishing her office as Prime Minister, Mrs.Gandhi went in political seclusion. There were speculations that she intended to stage a comeback. In reply to a question at a Press Conference whether Mrs. Gandhi was returning to active politics, the Congress President said, "I do not know. She seems to have said that she is not returning to active politics."[17] Asked if this was good for the party,he said that she must have taken the decision for the good of the party. All sane elements in the Congress believed that Mrs. Indira Gandhi should leave the party alone if it was to survive. But she found her survival in splitting the Congress for the second time and engineering for herself the Presidentship of the split group, Congress conventionists and finally known as Congress (Indira).

Within two months after the second split in January 1978, Mrs. Gandhi had amply demonstrated her mettle. February 1978 State Assembly elections in Karnataka, Andhra Pradesh and Vidarbha in Maharashtra established beyond doubt that she was the principal architect of Congress (I) success. In Andhra Pradesh, for instance, hit by the worst-ever cyclone in its history in November 1977, the ruling Congress was humbled and the breakaway Congress (I) firmly established its credentials as a legitimate heir to the legacy of the undivided Congress. The Janata,which had made a strenuous effort to capture power, could barely retain its status as the main Opposition Party in the new Assembly. The Congress was reduced to party of 30 members in the 294-member Assembly. The performance of Congress (I) was equally stunning in Karnataka and it became partner in the coalition government in Maharashtra on terms of equality.

In the official Congress there were two strong groups, one favouring unity with Indira's Congress and the other strongly opposing it. Mrs. Gandhi responded to the call for unity and prolonged parleys were held. But all proved futile because those who did not want to return to her fold and whom she did not want to return to her by themselves made not much difference to the country's political scene, except Y.B. Chavan and he, too, exercised some influence in Maharashtra alone. Mrs. Gandhi, accordingly, dictated her own terms for merger of the two wings. Swaran Singh, who headed the other Congress, ultimately reported to his Working Committee on March 12, 1979 that Congress(I)was uncompromising on every issue and it had refused to agree to modalities which would have meant that the two parties were coming together on terms of equality. An impression was rather sought to be created that it was the Congress that had to merge in Congress (I). The Working Committee, then, decided to break off unity talks.

The January 1980 Parliamentary elections

16. *The Times of India,* New Delhi, August 1977.
17. *Ibid.*

once again proved that Mrs,Indira Gandhi was by far the most charismatic and astute political leader that India had produced since Jawahalal Nehru. The massive majority she secured in the Hrouse of the People (Lok Sabha) was a rare personal triumph for her more especially when she and her Party had lost the people's confidence almost completely in 1977. Mrs. Gandhi showed her indomitable will in the way she overcame the trauma of her personal tragedy and politically rehabilitated herself and her Party. Her ceaseless political tours which took her to almost every part of the country all the way from Udhampur (Jammu) to Kanya Kumari, backed by a well-organised election and publicity machine, put her way ahead of her rivals. But she could not ignore the important part of this election that the votes cast in favour of the Congress were barely 43 per cent of the total votes cast. It meant that 57 per cent of the voters voted against her and her party, the Congress.

Despite the lessons of Emergency, Mrs. Gandhi's style of functioning remained the same. She combined, without regular election, Presidentship of Congress (I) with the office of the Prime Minister which she held, thus, obliterating the neat line drawn between the organisational and parliamentary wings of the party. No election was held for any of the Congress committees in any of the State and the same old style of *ad hocism* was the rule. This led to groupism and dissensions in the ranks of the Party. In the absence of recognised leadership at the State level, most State governments were riven by differences and disaffection erupting in ministerial crises from time to time and urgent problems which required immediate solution were put in cold storage. The condition was really chaotic. She warned and even reprimanded her warring partymen and legislators, but it had no effect. She really failed to display the same mettle,which marked her in the 1980 elections in disciplining her own Party. The centralisation of the Party had, no doubt, smothered inner- party democracy, but it had made the party no more cohesive. It progressively diminished the central leadership's effectiveness since it was so deeply involved in sorting out parochial quarrels that would once have been settled locally.

With the Party's bastions in the South stormed, it faced an uncertain prospect in the 1985 Parliamentary election. Since the fear of incurring Mrs. Indira Gandhi's displeasure and the awe of her charisma had become less effective the result was that as the next Parliamentary election approached, more and more members of Parliament started seriously thinking whether they would not be better off by throwing in their lot with some other party. That had been the lesson in the history of political parties in India and Andhra Pradesh and Karnataka opened the way. But Mrs. Gandhi was not oblivious of these likely developments. Closely on the heels of the Andhra Pradesh and Karnataka debacle and with an eye on the 1985 Parliamentary election, she initiated measures to revamp the Party and the Government. She made changes in the Cabinet and let the Maharashtra and Himachal Pradesh Congress (I) Legislative parties choose successors to Balasaheb Bhosle and Ram Lal as an earnest effort of her intention to let Party unit run their own show. She appointed Kamalapati Tripathi as the working President and responsible for party affairs. She appointed C.M. Stephen and Rajiv Gandhi as General Secretaries of the party and later convened a meeting of Pradesh Party Presidents and Secretaries to rejuvenate the organisation with an announcement that party elections at all levels would be complete by July,1983.

She also made changes in the Union Cabinet and sought to tone up the functioning of the bureaucracy and to come down on corruption and waste. She wanted to lick her Party into shape and deliver the government that worked that she promised in the 1980 election campaign so that by the time the 1985 Parliamentary election came round, she and her Party should be strong to meet any challenge. But the real problem of the Party was the neglect of grassroot sentiments all these years which had encouraged contention among local factions. A government cannot run affairs of a nation effectively unless it is backed by a dynamic organisational infrastructure of the ruling party.

Rajiv Gandhi succeeded Mrs. Indira Gandhi after her assassination on 31 October 1984,as Prime Minister and President of the Congress (I). In his capacity as President of the party he expressed his firm resolve to depart from the old practice and to take early steps to conduct the party poll and, thus, to put an end to what the commentators had described all these years as the "President's rule" in the Congress (I). In December 1985,at the Congress centenary session in Bombay, he vowed to eliminate the "power brokers" who stepped up their activities and the "moneybags" to help them to recruit non-existent persons as part of organised jockeying for elective positions. He also showed his keenness to entrust the affairs of the party to younger people. The generational change was sought to be accelerated and this produced a sharp reaction, even stiff resistance. It was the clash between the old guard and the younger lot that added a new dimension to the tussle of positions of vantage in the party. The reluctance of the old timers to give up the levers of power was matched by the grabbing proclivities of the freshers. The latter had the advantage of support and encouragement from the top whereas the former feared edging out with humiliation, and the end of their long political career.

This clash was in the making for the past two years (1987) if one were not to take into account the period when Rajiv Gandhi influenced party decisions in his capacity as the General Secretary of the All-India Congress Committee (I) during the life time of Mrs.Gandhi or the impact of Sanjay Gandhi's emergence on the party's functioning. When Rajiv Gandhi became the Prime Minister and the President of the Congress (I) the clash surfaced on the eve of the 1985 House of the People (Lok Sabha) poll–at the time of the selection of candidates. He wanted a total break with the past and opposed the renomination of a large number of old foggies in the House of the People (Lok Sabha). Kamlapati Tripathi,otherwise not very effective as working President of the party cautioned against wholesale changes,and was able to exert some restraining influence. The compulsions of the elections led to a give-and-take though the compromise clearly weighed in favour of Rajiv Gandhi. But the induction of younger members in the Union Council of Ministers from January 1985 onwards and the changes in the organisational set-up in the States alarmed the old timers. The subsequent signals perturbed them further. Their anger found expression in derisive references to "computer boys" or "childish" ways of running the affairs of government and the party.

The response to the challenge posed by tussles and clash was different—postponement of the party poll. At a press conference in February 1987 in response to some pithy queries Rajiv Gandhi mentioned difficulties posed by the scrutiny of the party electoral rolls to screen out bogus members. As regards "concentration of power", he said he did delegate authority to the Vice-President and the working President and if they had gone now it was not his fault. It was clear from the remarks of Rajiv Gandhi at the press conference that his ideas of reorganising the party set-up were limited to the removal of the working President Kamlapati Tripathi and the Vice-President Arjun Singh. These two extra constitutional authorities were created in totally different circumstances but got embroiled in equally sharp controversies. Kamlapati Tripathi was inducted as working President around the time when Rajiv Gandhi became General Secretary after the death of his younger brother Sanjay Gandhi in 1980. Indira Gandhi obviously had in mind a blend of experience and dynamism. In the peculiar situation after her assassination, however, Tripathi lost whatever little relevance he had till then. The veteran could not be removed but the gap was filled early in 1986 with Arjun Singh's appointment as Vice-President. They were provided with a large team of General Secretaries, including some who had been dropped from the Council of Ministers. The experiment did not work. Though Arjun Singh was to work under the guidance of, and at the directions of the working President, the two could not establish even a semblance of working relationship. Kamlapati Tripathi was gradually sidelined as Arjun Singh took important decisions either on his own or under the advice of Rajiv Gandhi or his aides. The task of removing Kamlapati Tripathi, if not Arjun Singh, from his controversial position turned out to be tough as he refused to catch hints and defied the cajoling by M.L. Fotedar, who acted as Secretary to Rajiv Gandhi in his capacity as party President. To get over the irksome situation, a new device was thought of—all the office-bearers were required to quit and later, while the General Secretaries were allowed to continue, the resignations of the working President and Vice-President were accepted.

The phenomenon of bogus members was not new, but had been evident from the time the Congress assumed power at the Centre and in the States after Independence and its membership became the vehicle of high positions. Even before 1947, when the Congress was in no position to distribute rewards and patronage,the scramble for party office used to be acute. But neither the intensity of feeling aroused by the contests nor the gigantic nature of the scrutiny task deterred those controlling the party on various occasions from conducting the elections. The norms changed from 1973 onwards when Indira Gandhi acquired total control of the party machine with her supremacy and its ready acceptance by the party members at all levels with senior leaders taking pride in "democratic centralism" that replaced the electoral process. The Emergency period strengthened these trends, leading to the emergence of extra-constitutional authorities both in the working of the Congress (I) and the Government. Surprisingly, appropriate lessons were not learnt as the rout of the Congress in 1977 could have been averted had the party scrupulously adhered to democratic principles in its working, though it might be an over-simplification, but the denial of inner party democracy certainly did contribute to Mrs. Indira Gandhi's fall. After her return to power in 1980 no attempt was made to do away with the new culture which had struck deep roots.

That legacy Rajiv Gandhi inherited. The Congress (I) Party remained very much Rajiv Gandhi's Party, as it was her mother's during her life time. The Party continued to have nominated leadership from the apex down to the lowest level and as a important corollary to this practice, the Chief Ministers in the Congress (I) governed States were picked up by the decision-makers at the Centre if and when the occasion arose. Most of these Chief Ministers who occupied these posts were not chosen by their respective Legislative parties. A breath that made them could also unmake them.

Rajiv Gandhi combining unto himself the Prime Ministership and the post of the President of the Congress (I) became power-intoxicated. He was arrogant in his postures and entirely cut off from the masses. The 1989 election to the Lok Sabha threw the Congress (I) out of office. It secured just 197 seats of a total 510 contested with 39.5 per cent of the total number of votes cast. With- in less than a year another election to the Lok Sabha was necessitated. The Congress vote declined from 39.5 per cent in 1989 to 37.3 per cent in May-June 1991 elections. Despite this drop the Party won 225 Seats, 28 more than 1989. The reason for this increase in the number of seats was a more divided opposition vote than in 1989. As a result of February 19, 1992 elections to the Lok Sabha in the Punjab State and by-elections in other States the strength of the Congress has gone up to 243 seats.

After Rajiv Gandhi's assassination on May 21, 1991, P.V. Narasimha Rao occupied for the interim period, the office of the Congress (I) President as also that of the Prime Minister of India by virtue of being a leader of the largest single Party in the House of the People, though he himself was not a member of either House of Parliament. It was for the first time in the history of Independent India that a non-member of Parliament was summoned by the President to form the government.

Narasinha Rao firmly committed himself and the Congress (I) Party to restore internal democracy in the Party and as a consequence to hold elections at all levels of the Party organisation and saddle the duly elected members in office. He also promised to rigidly adhere to the democratic norm of 'one man one post '. The process of elections is more or less complete now. Narasinha Rao has been unanimously elected President of the All India Congress Committee and together with the office of the Prime Minister the norm of 'one man one post' has not been adhered to.

**(2) Janata Party**

Janata Party was the successor to Congress as a ruling party at the Centre. In the June 1977 elections it succeeded in ousting the Congress Governments in the States of Himanchal Pradesh, Haryana, Rajasthan, Uttar Pradesh, Madhya Pradesh, Bihar and Orissa. In Punjab the Akali Party was in alliance with Janata and CPI(M). In Jammu and Kashmir, West Bengal, Tamil Nadu and Kerala the Janata fared miserably. No elections were held in Assam, Maharashtra, Andhra Pradesh and Karnataka and Congress Governments remained there in office, although consistent with India's political culture there had been spate of defections and floor crossings, especially when the Janata Party kept its "doors open" to members of the Council of States (Rajya Sabha) and the States Assemblies."[18]

The formation of the Janata Party was the result of tentative steps taken inside Tihar Jail, Delhi, as described by Atma Singh, former Punjab, Development Minister. He said that twenty prominent leaders of the Bharatiya Lok Dal, Congress (Organisation), Jana Sangh and the Socialist Party—all detained under the Maintenance of Internal Security Act—met on February 6,1976 in a closed door meeting under the chairmanship of Charan Singh, the Bharatiya Lok Dal leader. They were allowed to go out of the room only after they had endorsed the decision, initiated by

18. Announcement made by Janata Party General Secretary Surendra Mohan on April 26, 1977, *The Hindustan Times*, New Delhi.

Prakash Singh Badal (Akali Dal), to constitute a United Party to fight the Congress. After a month Charan Singh was released on parole and he was authorised to meet Jayaprakash Narayan to announce the formation of the Janata Party.[19] The Emergency was relaxed in January 1977, and all Opposition leaders were released from detention to enable the political parties to contest elections to the Sixth House of the People scheduled to be held in March.

On January 20, 1977, Morarji Desai announced that the four Opposition parties—Bharatiya Lok Dal, Jana Sangh, Congress (O) and Socialist Party—had combined into an alliance to contest the elections as a single Janata Party. The newly created combination received the blessings of Jayaprakash Narayan who announced its main aims at a Press conference. He said that the main aim of the Janata Party would be to decentralise power, so that people even in the remotest villages could participate in the making of decisions and plans that concern them. And of course the party will revive the strength of independent institutions like the judiciary and the Press that act as a check against authoritarian rule.'' The Janata Party, he added, ''is committed to follow Gandhian principles in evolving its socio-economic programme for in spite of much talk about 20 and more points, the conditions of the poor have deteriorated.''

In accordance with the aims outlined by Jayaprakash Narayan the main thrust of the Janata Party's manifesto, released on February 10, 1977, was the use of Gandhian principles and policies to restructure the economy. By doing so, it hoped to focus attention on agriculture and unemployment and ''ensure decentralisation of economic and political power.'' If returned to power, the Janata Party promised to lift the Emergency, restore Fundamental Rights, repeal Maintenance of Internal Security Act, seek to rescind the Constitution (Forty-second Amendment) Act, 1976,and other such measures that ''will free the people from the bondage of fear and restore to the citizen his fundamental freedoms, and to the Judiciary its rightful role.'' The Party would work for devolution and decentralisation of power and seek a national consensus in favour of smaller districts and smaller development blocks ''so as to encourage democratic participation and sound economic management and micro-planning.''

The manifesto in its section on a ''new economic charter'' affirmed the right to work. It was felt that ''this could be realiasable ideal only if we move towards the establishment of an economy in which agriculture and cottage and small industries have primacy and are not sacrificed to the big machine and big city.'' The large-scale industry would be confined to production of goods not otherwise possible or for defence needs. The property right was proposed to be deleted from the Fundamental Rights leaving this as an ordinary statutory right, the object being to ensure economic reforms, such as land reforms, were not held up. The Party believed that ''it is possible to eliminate destitution within a decade'' by raising every family above the poverty line, and would attempt to achieve the objective ''through appropriate economic policies that promote self-employment and provide employment, education and social services to every citizen.'' Priority was to be given to agriculture and rural reconstruction ''which must constitute the base of our development planning.'' Landlordism was to be abolished and holdings below 2.5 hectares were to be exempted from payment of land revenue.

The Janata Party's foreign policy would reflect the nation's enlightened interest and its aspirations and priorities at home. It would oppose all forms of colonialism, new-colonialism and racialism. It stood ''for friendship for all.'' The manifesto affirmed the party's commitment to genuine non-alignment free from attachment to any power bloc. It would strive for the peaceful settlement of all international disputes and work with other Third World nations to establish a new and just international economic order. With India's neighbours, the Party would strive to resolve such outstanding issues as remained pending or unsettled and would consciously promote a ''good neighbour policy.'' It stood for regional cooperation for the common good and for global detente free of new blocs or spheres of influence and based on universal and general disarmament.

The four combining parties for purposes of elections to the House of the People (Lok Sabha) formally merged into the Janata Party on May 1, 1977, the Congress for Democracy, led by Jagjivan Ram, joining on May 6. It was polarisation of the political forces the need for which had originally become articulate after the Uttar Pradesh elections in 1974. The Bharatiya Kranti

19. *The Tribune,* Chandigarh, August 2, 1977.

Dal (BKD) President Charan Singh summoned a convention of non-Communist Opposition parties to consider the possibilities of merging the various parties and groups into a single cohesive political party which should provide an alternative to Congress. The merger decision, first announced on April 1, 1974, led to a rift in the Bharatiya Kranti Dal and the Swatantra Party, the remnants repeatedly questioning the groups' voluntary dissolution. Minoo Masani and the Tamil Nadu Swatantra unit also revolted. Congress (O), Jana Sangh, Muslim League, DMK and the Akai Dal had their own reservations and, finally, they could not be persuaded to merge and form a new party. But as a result of the ceaseless efforts of Charan Singh and Biju Patnaik, the Bharatiya Lok Dal was formed in August 1974 by the merger of seven non-left parties. Welcoming the formation of the Bharatiya Lok Dal, Acharya J.B. Kripalani said that the Dal should put all ideologies and programmes on the shelf.

The main problem that confronted the Janata Party after a little more than two years of the final merger of five parties was the inability of its leaders and the constituent parties to forget their pre-merger political identities. The words 'constituent' and 'erstwhile' to identify former units of the Party recurred with increasing frequency and not even an attempt at the fiction was made that the Janata Party was undivided. Jayaprakash Narayan frankly stated that the groups and parties that had joined the Janata Party "have yet to forget their past allegiances and the party has yet to function as a well-knit body." He, however,expressed the hope that the party would be able to overcome their "internal feuds as they had no alternative and would be finished if they broke up." C.B. Gupta and Jagjivan Ram also spoke out and Gupta even threatened to quit the Janata Party unless something was done to correct a situation wherein "profession and practice differ so blatantly—even in the beginning..."[20] Jagjivan Ram was forthright when he observed that the Janata Party was still a conglomeration of different groups which had failed to merge their identities with the new Party. He added, "It seems these groups will think of their narrow interests even after five years when, in the event of elections, they will demand their shares of representation."[21]

There was an apologetic reference to teething troubles and, rather more sophistically, to the contention that differences were the normal features of a healthy democracy; the same old argument that the Congress had advanced when factionalism plagued it at every level. But the Congress was a more homogeneous organisation and its aggregative capacity was more. It consisted of diverse groups, interests and factions between which compromise, although difficult, proved possible until very recently. But ideologically there was nothing common among the merging units of the Janata and despite the earnest wooing of Charan Singh they could not earlier be brought together in Bharatiya Lok Dal. Not even an effort was made to extinguish former identities. Indeed on the contrary there was an assertion of their rights and grievances. The scramble for assembly tickets in June 1977 elections, for ministerial posts and for Party offices and endless exchange of accusations within the party were alarming. A recital of the Janata infighting in Uttar Pradesh and Madhya Pradesh and elsewhere was superfluous when considered in the context of fisticuffs that occurred in West Bengal, Rajasthan and Punjab and severe tension which developed between secular and communal elements.

This sort of thing seemed endemic to the Indian political scene, but in odd juxtaposition to the Janata's assurances of a "total revolution." The Janata spirit evaporated soon after the poll victory in March 1977, and the central leadership was to be held responsible for it. "The first sin, " as Inder Jit wrote, "was committed when the time came to choose the leader of the Janata Parliamentary Party. Some of the groups met in quiet conclaves to determine informally who should or should not be backed for the Prime Minister's office. A dismayed J.P. tried to remedy the situation following his arrival in New Delhi, but succeeded partially."[22] Jagjivan Ram and his men of the Congress for Democracy not participating. Once this hurdle was crossed the constituent units of the Janata, as they then were, started functioning aggressively and soon each was demanding an equal (or reasonable) share in the Union Cabinet. The top leadership decided on a quota system for the first Cabinet list, two each for the constituent units and for the independent Chandra Shekhar- Dharia group and one for the Akalis with whom the Janata was in alliance in

20. *Indian Express*, New Delhi, July 24, 1977.
21. *The Statesman*, New Delhi, July 20, 1977.
22. *The Tribune*, Chandigarh, August 2, 1977.

Punjab.

This was the beginning of the "rot of group functioning" and it spread with all the unfortunate consequences and many even hazarded speculation about the future of the Janata Party. The National Executive of the Janata Party was named on quota and so was the Executive of the Parliamentary Party. Even the General Secretaries for both the organisational and ministerial wings were appointed on the quota basis. That was not all. "Fuel is now proposed to be added," wrote Inder Jit, "to the fire through a provision of the constitution framed for the Janata Parliamentary Party." This provided for elections to the party executive on the basis of proportional electoral device designed to give representation to various parties and groups which otherwise would have remained unrepresented. It has no place in the context of an integrated party for the purpose of its internal elections, except to breed groups and, if some exist already, to perpetuate groupism and, thus, create a body riddled with vested interests.

Another ticklish issue that immediately confronted the Prime Minister was the expansion of the Union Ministry. For months when the Janata Party assumed office, the Council of Ministers consisted of the nineteen Cabinet Ministers sworn in March 1977. On the calculation that there would be an expansion shortly after the budget session the various groups in the Parliamentary Party were working on their strength and their claims accordingly. In terms of the parties which comprised the ruling formation, the Congress (O) was regarded as over-represented compared to the BLD-Jana Sangh combine which was believed to be the largest single group. Representation of Muslims was another problem.

The dictionary meaning of the word "merger" is synonymous with absorption. But at no stage the seed of absorption was allowed to germinate and make Janata a well-integrated party. It is true, emotional integration does take some time, for merging units have to overcome their sense of insecurity. A Janata leader explained, "the Ganga and Jamuna meet at a sangam in Allahabad. But the waters of the two rivers retain their colour and identity for quite some distance." But not in the manner in which Janata Party functioned. Selfishness, sectarianism and narrow-mindedness had no place whatever in the organisation whose leaders swore by Gandhian Principles.

The Janata Party did not function even as SVD (Samyukta Vidhayak Dal), an innovation of 1967, but a loose SVD. In the SVD each constituent at least knew where it stood *vis-a-vis* the others. But in the Janata Party no constituent unit knew what precisely its position was. Power can combine even desperate elements together for some time but not for ever and this element essentially accounts for the withering away of the Party of Jayaprakash Narayan's dream who had expressed even from his death-bed his sorrow and deep anguish on the functioning of the Party. He predicted its demise if the Janata did not mend itself by halting groupism and if the drift was allowed to go beyond a point of no return. It proved true and the Janata Party disintegrated by three successive splits. Raj Narain formed the Janata (S) after he was asked to quit the cabinet. Charan Singh's defection was stabbing at the back. He was the Deputy Prime Minister No. 1 in the Desai Government and wrecked the Janata Party to become Prime Minister. It was the fulfilment of his life's ambition. Charan Singh formed his own Lok Dal and Raj Narain's Janata (S) merged with it.

No less was Morarji's contribution to the disintegration and decline of the Janata Party. Within the first year of Janata's tenure in office, it was more than evident that Desai's leadership was inadequate. The public disenchantment was openly shared by important Ministers who began to speak of Janata's non-performance. Through all this Desai remained unmoved and unmoving until he was face to face with defeat on a vote of no confidence. Even after the resignation of his Government, he did not resign from the leadership of his Parliamentary Party until compelling circumstances (inclusion in his list of supporters submitted to the President were found to contain 21 number of Congress members of Parliament) forced him to quit politics. But it was too late then for the new leader of the Janata Party to restore its image. Desai spent all the store of political goodwill with which Janata Party had begun in his bid to attain Prime Ministership. No one can dispute that throughout his political career Morarji Desai was mad for power. But there was no method in his madness. What else could one think of Desai's statement that he saw nothing wrong in making government with Mrs. Gandhi's support if it came unsought.

In the 1980 Parliamentary elections the battered Janata could secure just 31 seats (Bihar 8, Gujarat 1, Haryana 1, Karnataka 1, Madhya Pradesh 4, Maharashtra 8, Rajasthan 4, Uttar

Pradesh 3, Delhi 1). In March 1980, Jagjivan Ram quit Janata to form the 'real Janata' and then suddenly realised that it was a grave mistake that he committed by joining the Janata Party. Next month (April 1980) its Jana Sangh constituent and some others formed a new party, Bharatiya Janata Party. With this fifth split, the Janata Party, did not dissolve. But its existence could no longer be of much consequence. The fifth split was the most serious blow to what was created in 1977. The Party was undoubtedly much weakened when the Bharatiya Lok Dal group broke away, but it survived as a just credible political force. When Jagjivan Ram and his followers left, what was damaged was more than party's reputation than its organisational strength, which derived largely from that of its Jana Sangh component. But Jana Sangh's withdrawal and forming a separate party left Janata, with a few prominent and several not so prominent politicians, with little effective following.

The Janata Party is at present in total wilderness, though still hugging the fond hope that by intensive nursing of the people, it can become an alternative to Congress (I). It is, however, doubtful if the spirit of 1977 can be recaptured. It remains the amalgam of a few nationally recognised names but it has not been able to identify its ideological base in terms of the economic policies and political appeal.

The 1996 elections of the House of the People (Lok Sabha) elected a hung Parliament. The Bharatiya Janata Party was the largest Party in the House but it could not muster support from any other Party and the President had no other alternative but to call the leader of the Bharatiya Janata Party to form the Government. But this minority Government remained in office just for13 days when it resigned as it could not face the vote of confidence as all other parties had combined to defeat the non-secular government. It consequently offered an opportunity to a combine of 13 parties, Janata Dal taking the lead to form the Government with the avowed support of the Congress from the outside. But the life of the UF Government seems to be precarious with the election of Sita Ram Kesari as the President of the Congress and the leader of the Congress Parliamentary Party. Sita Ram Kesari has declared that the support of the Congress to the UF Government ought not to be taken for granted. It will depend upon the issues and their merit being consistent with the policy of the Congress.

**(3) The Communist Party**

The Communist Party rose in the course of India's struggle for freedom as a result of the Indian revolutionaries who drew their inspiration from the Great October Revolution. "The Communist Party of India," reads the Party's Constitution "is the political party of the Indian working class, its vanguard, its highest form of class organisation. It is a voluntary organisation of workers, peasants and of toiling people in general devoted to the cause of socialism and communism." The aim of the Communist Party is the achievement of power by the working people; the establishment of a people's democracy led by the working class, based on the alliance of the working class, and peasantry, and the realisation of socialism and communism. Its programme includes defence of the vital interests of the masses, steady improvement in their living conditions and abolition of social and economic inequalities. It fights against all obstructionist conceptions and practices such as communalism, caste, untouchability and the denial of equal rights for women. "The Communist Party upholds freedom of conscience and the rights of all minorities. It fights for rights and welfare of the people of tribal areas.....Fighting against all separationist and disruptionist trends and movements the Communist Party struggles for balanced development of all regions, for equality and equal treatment for the people of all linguistic regions as a sure foundation of Indian unity."

The 1967 Election Manifesto outlined the programme for immediate measures. With the implementation of this programme the Communist Party intended to save the country from "the present crisis, stimulate production in industry and agriculture, ensure at least minimum needs of living life, strengthen and extend democracy and avert the danger of India falling a helpless victim to American neo-colonialism." The broad features of the programme were total elimination of foreign monopolies, annulment of all collaboration agreements, taking over by the State of all foreign trade, effective measures to curb the monopolists and to break up in particular the 75 monopoly houses exposed in the Monopolies Commission Report, replacement of the Fourth Plan by a People's Plan, nationalisation of banks, mopping up the accumulated wealth of the monopolists and former princes, overhauling the entire present tax structure, abolition of land revenue to be replaced by a steeply graded tax on agricultural incomes, with exemption for all uneconomic holdings, democratisation and reorganisation of the public sector, assurance of minimum need-based wage, enforcement of effective and far-reaching land reforms, wider power and authority, particularly in economic and financial matters, to be given to the State.

The party believed that in order to ensure rapid and faithful implementation of urgently needed democratic reforms the first step was to clean up and overhaul the State administration. With this end in view the parliamentary system should be strengthened by abolishing the Emergency powers of the President and his power to dismiss a State Government so long as the latter enjoyed the confidence of the Legislature. The institution of the Governor should be abolished and the costly and superfluous Upper Houses be substituted by Standing Committees with representatives of all parties. Proportional representation should be introduced.

In the 1971 elections the Party raised a battle cry for the rout of "right reaction" and an appeal was made to the electorate to bring about a new House of the People (Lok Sabha) which should have a firm left and democratic reorientation and was committed to effecting basic changes in the Constitution. The Constitution must be amended to place Parliament's supremacy and the will of the people, expressed through Parliament, beyond all challenge by the Judiciary, including the Supreme Court. This implied, the manifesto explained, that Parliament must resume its power to amend the Chapter on Fundamental Rights. The Constitution should also be amended to make it obligatory on the part of the Judiciary "to interpret legislations for social and economic changes, not for restricting their scope or for protecting the vested interests, affected by them, but for the promotion of social justice and progress." The Judiciary must be guided by the Preamble and the Directive Principles of State Policy in dealing with such measures. The Party emphatically reiterated its earlier stand for the abolition of the posts of Governors and Upper Houses of the Legislatures both at the Centre and in the States, drastic revision of the Emergency powers, particularly those that affect the democratic rights and weaken democracy. Ironically, the Communist Party of India gave an all-out support when in June 1975, internal Emergency was proclaimed.

The Party re-affirmed its well-known position on major economic and political issues. In subsequent years it advocated the takeover of the wholesale trade in foodgrains and other essential commodities and nationalisation of textile, sugar and jute industries and all banking business. The Party's hostility towards the United States of America in the field of foreign policy had been its stand all along. The Party called upon the voters to give a clear mandate in favour of "progressive and democratic forces", and to defeat the "reactionaries," without defining precisely what did it want.

The methods of the CPI to achieve its objective had all through been the familiar agitation, direct strike and sabotage. But consistent with the changes in the Soviet Communist Party thesis, it was admitted that in India, too, a peaceful social change was possible and where a parliamentary system existed the transformation of the capitalist community could be achieved without violent revolution. Accordingly, the CPI amended its constitution by providing, "the Party strives to achieve full democracy and socialism by peaceful mass movement, by winning a majority in Parliament and by backing it with mass sections, the working class and its allies can overcome the resistance of the forces of reaction and ensure that Parliament becomes an instrument of the people's will for effecting fundamental changes in the economic, social and state structure."

The Party's electoral prestige has steadily declined. In the 1980 election to the House of the People it won only 10 seats. Dange's relinquishing the Presidentship of the Party and formation of a separate faction (Dange group) had weakened the party base and its credibility. The CPI and the CPM, each for its own reasons, are coming closer to each other. The CPI Central Executive, at its session in January 1981, made the formation of a nation-wide "left and democratic front" its major plan. The Party did not show signs of softening its hostility to Mrs. Gandhi's Government. Ever since the Emergency experiment, the CPI no longer believed that the Congress (I) represented the "progressive bourgeoisie." While Moscow remained favourably disposed to Mrs. Gandhi, as was reflected in Brezhnev's visits to India, it did not seem to have influenced the CPI's attitude. All the same, CPI has been dwarfed by the CPM and it feels safer in a "left and democracatic front" than in a purely "left front" where the CPM's greater strength and electoral prestige would inevitably make itself felt to its disadvantage.

**(4) Communist Party (Marxist)**

There was split in the Communist Party of

India after the Vijayawada Congress of 1961. The split in the Communist movement, according to the Communist Party's Election Manifesto (1967), had seriously affected the mass movement as well as the struggle for forging broad unity of the Left and democratic forces. The Communist Party of India, the Communist Marxists claimed was a group of Dange revisionists out to pursue their opportunity line of class-collaboration. Taking advantage of the bourgeois chauvinism raised in connection with the India-China conflict, the revolutionists "joined hands with the bourgeois landlord government (Congress) to open the country to American penetration, the dire effects of which they are seeing today." The revisionists (Communist Party of India) had neither ideologically nor organisationally, they asserted, any right to call themselves by the old name. The Communist Party of India (Marxist) is the only party that stood firmly and constantly for socialism. It rejected the Communist Party's commitment to the "parliamentary road to socialism" and most important was the replacement of the work-cell as the basic unit by the residence-based branch.

The Communist Party (Marxist) aims at socialisation of the means of production and this can be achieved under a proletarian State alone. It is in the proletarian State that the exploitation of man by man can be abolished and, thus, help to solve the problems of poverty and impoverishment. The Party firmly believes that the road to socialism can be opened only through the establishment of a State of People's Democracy led by the working people and replacing the present bourgeois-landlord State, led by the big bourgeoisie. This can be achieved by developing determined mass struggles on the basis of growing unity and consciousness of the people. The party works determinedly for organising people's struggle for livelihood, democracy and power. It believes and advocates in *bandhs, gheraos* and student struggles. The 1967 Election Manifesto of the Party said, "The mighty Bengal Bandhs, the Kerala, Bihar and U.P. bandhs have set the pace for the new movement. Millions have participated in these struggles and braved the firing squads of the police to defend their livelihood and liberties. These have been followed by the mighty wave of student struggle of the working class, salaried employees and finally the employees of the government ........ Never before since independence India witnessed such mighty struggles." The Party, the Manifesto further said, "with its militant and revolutionary tradition calls upon the people to rout the Congress and endorse the Party's electoral programme which alone shows a way out of the present critical situation."

The Party stands for the sovereignty of the people, annulment of the Emergency powers of the President, proportional representation, regional autonomy for tribal areas, an equal right for all citizens, equality of all languages, widest autonomy of the States comprising the Union of India, and abolition of the institution of Governors. The role played by Governors showed, the 1971 Election Manifesto of the Party said, that they invariably act as the instrument of the Centre against the people of the States and powers of the President enable him to take over the administration of a State for months and run it without the consent of the people. In order to make the powers and functions for the State real, it demands transfer of the subjects in the Concurrent List of the Seventh Schedule to the States, a larger allocation of resources to the State including a share of 75 per cent of all Central taxes, and complete control of a State Government over all its officials belonging to All-India Services.

The Party directed sharp criticism on the Judiciary and maintained that the courts must function as the instruments of the peoples' will and not as instrument opposing popular progress. The people should have complete freedom to dispense with the services of the judges who hold up the march of progress. On the economic side the Party stands for taking over the landlord's land and its distribution among agricultural labour and poor peasants gratis, cancellation of debts owed by peasants, agricultural workers and small artisans, equitable distribution of food to the people of urban and rural areas, State trading in foodgrains and entire surplus of the produce of landlords and rich peasants to be compulsorily procured. Effective price control is sought through nationalisation of banks, State trading in foodgrants etc. Drastic reduction in taxation is proposed and taxation on all necessities of life is to be abolished. The Party proposes reduction in defence expenditure, abolition of land tax, irrigation cess and other cesses and surcharges on uneconomic holdings. The Party will stop all further American aid, impose moratorium on all foreign payments, nationalize all foreign trade, and all foreign capital in plantations, mining, oil refineries, shipping and trade.

With relation to internal trade and commerce the Party champions nationalisation of banks, monopoly concerns and other big industry wherever necessary. It advocates a people's economic plan of development and urges that, if returned to power, development of public sector with the utmost rapidity will be undertaken, and the private sector and profits therefrom will be strictly controlled.

In international relations, the Party stands for independent foreign policy based on opposition to imperialism, especially American imperialism, colonialism and neo-colonialism and support to all freedom struggles. It believes in and supports the policy of co-existence and friendship with the peace-loving countries and a firm solidarity with Afro-Asian people. Break with British Commonwealth is its avowed object. It firmly believes and will strive for a peaceful settlement of dispute with Socialist China and creation of friendly relations with China in the interest of Asian freedom, of all disputes with Pakistan and promises "revision of all cultural agreements with foreign countries with a view to eliminating all those provisions that enable foreign powers to penetrate into the social and cultural life of the nation." The Party is also pledged to take new initiatives to organise common struggle of all the anti-imperialist countries, particularly those of Asian and African against the increasing penetration of the American, the West German, Japanese, and the imperialist powers in the economy, political life, cultural activities and in the military affairs of the newly independent countries.

The 1977 manifesto was essentially an indictment of the Congress Government for proclaiming Emergency, enactment of the Forty-second Amendment and the untold sufferings of the people during the nineteen months of Emergency. It called upon the electorate to unmask the efforts of the Congress Government to make the world believe that the Indian people are not willing to accept the dictatorship of the Congress Party by voting everywhere against the Congress policies on all fronts. "It is the task of the left and democratic forces to put before the people a comprehensive programme to defend the people and their liberties."

The CPI (M) put forward the following programme and called upon all Left and democratic parties and forces to rally round it and vote against Congress policies :

(1) Release of all political prisoners and withdrawal of warrants, repeal of the 42nd Constitution Amendment and other repressive laws like MISA and the Press Objectionable Matters Act; (2) Takeover of foreign capital, ban on entry of multinationals and investment of private foreign capital; (3) Moratorium on foreign debt payment; (4) Nationalisation of monopoly houses, nationlization of sugar, textile, jute, cement and drug industries; adequate financial and other assistance to small and medium industries; (5) Takeover of foreign trade; (6) Ending of corruption and bureacratism in the public sector undertakings; (7) Restoration of democratic and trade union rights and collective bargaining through trade unions whose representative character must be decided by secret ballot of the workers; need-based minimum wage and full neutralization of the rise in the cost of living; withdrawal of the Bonus Act; measures against victimization; (8) Abolition of landlordism by taking over the entire land of the landlords and labourers and poor peasants; Cancellation of debts of peasants, landless labourers and rural poor and provision of adequate and cheap credit to them; supply of inputs and essential articles at cheap rates to them; remunerative prices for their produce to be ensured through government purchase; lowering of taxes and other levies on the peasants, firm measures against social oppression of Harijans; (9) bringing down of prices by drastically reducing taxes and levies on essential articles; State takeover of wholesale trade in foodgrains and the essential articles and their distribution under supervision of People's Committees; compulsory procurement of all the marketable surplus of foodgrains of all landlords; (10) Right to work to be made a fundamental constitutional right, and (11) Compulsory free education up to the age of 14 and eradication of iliteracy; and (12) A foreign policy of consistent anti-imperialism and close co-operation with Socialist countries.

The CPI (M) established itself as a major party in West Bengal and Kerala, where it became the dominant party in the United Front Governments which emerged from the 1967 elections. Subsequently, it received setbacks in both States. In West Bengal it was challenged by the Congress and outflanked by a third and even more revolutionary Communist Party, the Communist Party (Marxist-Leninist). In Kerala, it was forced to yield office to a CPI-led Government, enjoying Congress (R) support. In 1971, CPI (M) secured only two out of nineteen House of the People seats whereas in 1977 it won none. In West Bengal the

CPI (M) had a setback in 1971 elections and its tally was 24 against 29. In 1977 the party went in for alliance with the Janata Party and secured 17 seats. But in the Assembly elections it went alone and for the first time came into power in its own right and continues in the saddle since then. It routed both the Janata and the Congress in January 1978 elections in Tripura and formed the Government and continues to be in office.

Most of the Communist success, electorally and otherwise, has been achieved in areas with high literacy rates and high voting turnouts. The educated unemployed provide them with a high proportion of consistent support. Like other parties, the Communists, too, have marked caste affiliations in certain areas. Oddly enough, their supporters are by no means invariably at the bottom of the social scale. in Andhra, for instance, they formerly had the support of the Kammas, a caste which included many substantial landlords.

The CPI (M) has also given priority to the question of forming a "left and democratic front," thus, shedding some of its hesitation on this issue. Substantial sections within the important West Bengal unit were hostile to Congress (U) and the Janata, the two partners in the proposed alliance. But the organisational wing of the Party was pressed to fall in line with the national policy. It, however, has nothing in common with the Bharatiya Janata Party which is regarded fundamentally communal party. The CPI (M) by more or less repudiating Chinese foreign policy had also moved closer to the CPI in its assessment of the international scene. But the Question of unity between the two wings of the Communist Party is a misplaced speculation. It came into power in its own right and coutinuous to remain in the saddle since then. West Bengal does not change colours easily. After 14 years of CPI (M)–led Left Front the red bastion emerged victorious again in 1991. CPI (M) secured 188 seats, CPI 16 and others 57. The Congress (I) came a poor second with 43 seats out of total of 294 Assembly seats. The CPI (M)-led Left Democrtic Front (LDF) lost to the Congress (I)-led United Democratic Front (UDF) in the State of Kerala. The CPI (M) won 29 seats only out of a total of 140 seats in the State Assembly.

The disintegration of the Soviet Union and collapse of communism there and the East European countries had no impact on the policy and strategy of CPI (M). The Party still steadfastly adheres to Marxism-Leninism and holds Mikhail Gorbachev responsible for the whole debacle. That is the crux of the Party's policy resolution at its Madras session in January 1992.

## THE ELECTION COMMISSION

### The Electoral Machine

Elections are central to the functioning of modern democracies as they constitute the principal mechanism for exercising the control of the people on their representatives and give legitimacy to govern in a democratic system. Free and fair elections are the *sine qua non* of the democratic system and as a consequence thereof the machinery of conducting elections and the personnel manning it assume key importance in a country's political life.

India incorporates such a system in the Constitution and in the various legislative measures enacted pursuant to the constitutional provisions. There are certain basic elements in the electoral system, namely, universal adult suffrage which entitles every citizen who is not less than eighteen years of age, provided he is not otherwise disqualified, the right to be registered as a voter. Then, there is the principle of 'one man one vote' and the method of direct election to the House of the People (Lok Sabha) and the Legislative Assemblies of the States. There are adequate provisions to ensure participation of the deprived sections of society (Scheduled Castes and Scheduled Tribes) by reserving constituencies for them. The management and conduct of elections on such a large scale, as in India with 520 million eligible voters in 1992, is entrusted to an independent Election Commission and it has been accorded Constitutional status. Efficiency, impartiality and adequacy of the Electoral machinery, thus, provide for free and fair elections, without them elections lose their savour and it becomes a futile exercise in the realm of a democratic system. Recent elections held in November 1989 and May-June 1991 have, however, cast apprehension on the office of the Election Commission, as a weak, ineffective and a partisan institution. The large-scale violence, both capturing and unbecoming malpractices together with muscle and money power are a black spot on the electoral machinery in India.

## ELECTION COMMISSION

### Apex Body

The superintendence, direction and control of preparation of the electoral rolls and the conduct of all elections to Parliament, State Legislatures, and of elections to the offices of the President and Vice-President under the Constitution are vested in the Election Commission consisting of the Chief Election Commissioner and such number of the Election Commissioners as the President may from time to time fix.[23] The appointment of the Chief Election Commissioner and the Commissioners is made on behalf of Parliament. When any other Election Commissioner is so appointed, the Chief Election Commissioner acts as Chairman of the Commission. Before each General Election to the House of the People and to the Legislative Assembly of each State and biennial election to the Legislative Council (Vidhan Parishad) of each State having such Council, the President may also appoint after consultation with the Election Commission such Regional Commissioners as he may consider necessary to assist the Election Commission in the performance of its functions.

The conditions of service and tenure of office of the Election Commissioners and the Regional Commissioners are determined by the President by Rule. The Chief Election Commissioner is liable to be removed from office in like manner and on the like grounds as a Judge of the Supreme Court and the conditions of his service cannot be varied to his disadvantage after his appointment. Any other Election Commissioner or Regional Commissioner shall be removed from office on the recommendation of the Chief Election Commissioner.[24]

Two Regional Commissioners were appointed for a period of six months during the General Election held in 1951-52 and since then no such appointment has been made. Except on two brief occasions, there were Deputy Election Commissioners in the Commission. The Commission has one Deputy Election Commissioner at present. The Commission has its own nucleus of staff.

**Subordinate Officers**

Among the subordinate election officials are the Chief Electoral Officers for each State to aid in the preparation of the electoral rolls. Others include Electoral Registration Officers, revising authorities for deciding claims and objections to the draft electoral rolls, and Returning Officers (and Assistant Returning Officers) for conducting elections in each constituency. They all are drawn from the higher cadres of Government employees in each State. In addition to these, there are thousands of presiding officers, polling officers and others for conducting the polls. For the election of 13 members to the House of the People (Lok Sabha) and 117 Members of the Legislative Assembly in the State of Punjab in February 1992, more than 94,000 personnel of different categories were drafted.

In the process of amending the election laws and statutory rules, the role of Chief Electoral Officer in a State has been expanded and as a result the Election Commission has acquired the major responsibility for his election. In the initial stages, the Chief Electoral Officers were appointed by the State Governments. Subsequently the changes in the Rule redefined this officer "appointed by the State Government with the concurrence of the Election Commission." Provisions in the two amending Acts of 1956 clearly specified that the selection of the Chief Electoral Officer in a State would be made by the Election Commission. At the same time, authority has been delegated to the Chief Electoral Officer in each State to supervise election procedures from the early stages of preparing and revising electoral rolls. The initial responsibility for supervising the conduct of elections now rests with the Chief Electoral Officers, subject to the "Superintendence, direction and control of the Election Commission."

## ELECTORAL REFORMS

The necessity of reforming the electoral system is as old as the first 1951-52 General Election. But it did not take a tangible shape. Nor had any voice been raised from the non-ruling parties against this basic exercise of democracy and the problem as it has aggravated over the years. When the National Front Government, headed by Vishwanth Pratap Singh, the Janata Dal Parliamentary party leader, assumed office in 1990, it appreciated the urgency of the problem and appointed a Committee chaired by the then Law Minister Dinesh Goswami to study in details the problem of electoral reforms and make necessary recommendations. In pursuance of the Goswami Committee recommendations three separate Bills were introduced in the Council of States (Rajya Sabha). The Bills could not make any headway and are still pending there and are

---

23. In 1989 the one-member Election Commission became a multi-member body with the appointment of two other Election Commissioners, S.S,. Dhanoa and V. Seigell, both former civil servants, the first from I.A.S. and the second form IPS. The multi-member Election Commission however, remained in existence just for 79 days, and once again it became a one-member Commission.
24. Article 324.

likely to be allowed to lapse. Law Minister Vijaya Bhaskar Reddy in the Narasimha Rao Congress (I) Government had repeatedly assured the Parliament that the Government was serious about electoral reforms and would soon introduce a comprehensive Bill.

**Piecemeal Electoral Reforms**

For the present, the Government resorted to issuing Ordinances and that, too, in a piecemeal manner incorporating some reforms which the political expediency demanded. The first in the series of these Ordinances was the one issued on January 4, 1992. The Government had first decided to move for consideration one of the three pending Bills in the Council of States (Rajya Sabha) and informal consultations were held with the Opposition leaders. But for some inexplicable reason the Bill did not find a place in the Official Legislative Business and the Ordinance was issued in an attempt to bypass Parliament and was occasioned by the proposal initiated by the Government to hold elections in the State of Punjab after a gap of 57 months President's rule in that State.

The Ordinance provided that Parliamentary and State Assembly elections would not be countermanded if an Independent candidate died before the poll. The Law Minister said in a Press interview that the Punjab Government had been keen on the amendment of Representation of the People's Act so that the elections in the State slated for mid-February 1992, were not affected owing to terrorist violence against Independent candidates. Militants shot dead 23 candidates during the campaign period in May-June 1991 propsed elections. This led to the countermanding of the involved Parliamentary and Assembly seats.

The second Ordinance to amend the Representation of the People Act curtailed the time for election campaigning from 20 days to 14 days. While it may be welcomed by various political parties so far as it helps in the present Punjab situation, the political parties may subsequently find it impractical to cover the vast Parliamentary constitutencies in a short span of 14 days. It may not be possible for a candidate to contact personally the electorate in his House of the People (Lok Sabha) constituency, which often has one million votes. And in India, personal contact during electioneering has its personal appeal and the technique is well entrenched.

But that is not the end of electoral reforms. The focus in fact should be on the larger question of regulating the proliferation of non-serious candidates who have severely burdened and trivialized the electoral process. There were over 5,000 Independents in the 1991 House of the People (Lok Sabha) polls, a majority of whom were in a fray only for cheap self-publicity. Previous Election Reforms Committees have proposed numerous amendments to tackle the problem of multiplicity of candidates including a substantial increase in the security deposit; not allowing a candidate to contest more than one constituency; and the most radical though innovative alternative, to disqualify a candidate from standing in an election for some time; if he failed to secure one-fourth of the total number of votes cast. Law Minister Vijaya Bhaskar told the PTI correspondent in an interview on December 29, 1991, that the Government was considering ways and means of preventing ''frivolous'' candidates from entering the election arena. One of the proposals, he added, was to make a provision that every candidate is sponsored by at least ten elected members of either of Panchayats or cooperative societies; not a difficult requirement in the final analysis under the prevailing political climate in India.

He also said that a legislation for fresh delimitation of the House of the People (Lok Sabha) and State Assembly constituencies was ready and would be introduced in the Budget session of Parliament commencing on February 24, 1992.[25] While there will be no increase in the total number of seats at both the levels of the Legislature, there would be changes in the reserved seats, he added. Those seats would be rotated from a constituency where the Scheduled Caste and the Scheduled Tribe votes are the highest to the second highest.

One of the Bills on electoral reforms pending before Parliament was about the composition of the Election Commissions whether it should remain one-man body, as it is, or more than one-member, to ensure greater impartiality. This is now one of the pressing demands of the Opposition parties. The National Front and the Left Front are its vocal advocate. This combine submitted on March 4, 1992 a notice, signed by 122 Members of Parliament, to the Speaker to move a motion of impeachment against the Chief Election Commissioner, T.N. Sheshan, for his ''mis-

25. Constitution (Seventy-first Amendment) Act, 1992, provides for fresh delimitation on the basis of 1991 census. Thus, the embargo that was placed by the Forty-second Amendment Act, 1976, has been removed.

behaviour, and illegal, partisan and arbitrary actions'', during the conduct of the various elections held during his tenure.[25a]

Moreover, a single individual at the helm of affairs is not a very satisfactory arrangement for controlliing the expanding work of the Election Commission, especially with the addition of some 50 million voters consequent on the lowering of voting age to 18 years. Also there seems to be a possibility that the Election Commission may be entrusted with the onerous job of conducting Panchayat Raj polls. A measure of reform should be to keep the Election Commission a three-member body manned by persons of exceptional integrity and proven calibre.

But neither of the three Bills pending in Parliament nor the latest Ordinances that had been promulgated in pursuance of electoral reforms deal directly with the basic distortions of the electoral process. They represent no counter to the money and muscle power so widely rampant at all levels of elections of the legislative and local bodies and continue to manipulate the popular mandate, or to the often grossly misused might of official machinery.

When democracy becomes corrupt, the best gravitate to the bottom, the worst float to the top, and the vile is replaced by the more vile. Henry George's words seem prophetic if one looks at the composition of the 1991 elected members of the Bihar Legislative Assembly to illustrate the magnitude of the problem. At least 40 of 323 legislators have proven criminal record and 10 out of this number are hardened criminals. They belong to various political parties and were elected by margins that many of the State's top respected and veteran leaders cannot boast of. Other States, as Utter Pradesh and Madhya Pradesh do not sufficiently lag behind, though in numbers they stand no comparison to the State of Bihar. One of the former Ministers, belonging to the Janata Dal (Samajwadi) party in Uttar Pradesh, was arrested on the basis of heinous criminal offences and he contested for the State Assembly seat in the 1991 elections while lodged in the jail and won by a thumping majority.

The criminal politician nexus, which flowered in 1977 when both the Congress (I) and the Janata Party gave tickets to criminals in their eagerness to capture the maximum number of seats both in the House of the People (Lok Sabha) and the State Assemblies that went to the polls, has in the last decade and half become an accepted fact of political life in India, importantly in the States of Hindi-belt.

## ANTI-DEFECTION LAW

### In Retrospect

The defectors had plagued the Indian politics since the Fourth General Election in 1967. Not that it was a new phenomenon peculiar to India, but the dimensions it assumed and the ugly form it took for ministerial rewards in return was unprecedented and it has now become an integral part of the country's political life. In one single year 438 legislators defected with 210 being rewarded ministerial berths. Over the period March 1967 to August 1970, the Governors' Committee (1971) headed by Bhagwan Sahay reported 1,240 defections, with a sample showing rewards of ministership in one-fifth of the cases. Ministries tumbled with ease, supported by unscrupulous Governors with avowed leanings towards a particular political party, which at that point of time was the Congress. The concern for such a state of affairs was voiced in the House of the People (Lok Sabha) and was reflected in the debates of the House on August 11, November 24, and December 8, 1967 and it led to the appointment of a high-level committee[26], with Y.B. Chavan as Chairman, to consider the problem of legislators changing the allegiance from one party to another and their frequent crossings of the floor. The Committee was required to examine this problem in ''all its aspects and make recommendations in this regard.''

Analysing the motives behind the change in allegiance the Committee stated in its Report : ''Following the Fourth General Elections, in the short period between March 1967 and February 1968 the Indian political scene was characterised by numerous instances of changing of party allegiance by Legislators of several states. Compared to roughly 542 cases in the entire period between the first and Fourth General Election at least 438 defections occurred in these 12 months alone. That the lure of office played a dominant part in decisions of legislators of the

25A It is doubtful if the notice will fructify because the Bharatiya Janata Party has decided not to go along with the National Front-Left Front Combine. L.K. Advani, the Leader of the Opposition in the House of the People told the Press that ''we are charry of resorting to extreme measures like impeachment.'' *The Statesmen*, New Delhi, March 5, 1992.

26. It was a distinguished committee that included Jayaprakash Narayan, Madhu Limaye, S.N. Dwivedi, P. Govinda Menon (Law Miniter) two former Attorneys-General, M. Setalvad, and C.K Dephtary, and S. Mohan Kumarmangalam

States of Bihar, Haryana and M.P. (Madhya Pradesh) Punjab, Rajasthan, U.P. (Uttar Pradesh) and West Bengal 1165 were included in the Council of Ministers which helped to bring into being by defections........"

The Committee also took upon itself the onerous task of defining "defection." This definition, which was drafted by Jayaprakash Narayan himself, was accorded general approval of the Committee, was as follows : "An elected member of a legislature who has been allotted the reserved symbol of any political party can be said to have defected, if after being elected as member of either House of Parliament or of the Legislative Council or the Legislative Assembly of a State or Union Territory, he voluntarily renounces allegiance to, or association with, sush political party, provided his action is not in consequence of decision of the party concerned."

The Report of the Committee came for discussion in the Council of States (Rajya Sabha) on August 12, 1969. Once again divergent views on remedies of defection were expressed, though everybody showed deep concern at the menace of the defections. On July 24, 1970, Union Cabinet approved a draft of the legislation on defection, which was later discussed on December 10, 1970, in a conference of Opposition leaders, convened by Prime Minister Indira Gandhi. Again, the same old line of differences of opinion was voiced and, accordingly, no agreement or consensus could be arrived at. Keeping in view the sentiments of the Opposition leaders, the Prime Minister declared that no Bill on defections would be moved in the Fourth Lok Sabha.

On May 16, 1973, Uma Sankar Dixit, the then Home Minister, sought leave of the House of the People (Lok Sabha) to move Constitution (Thirty-second Amendment ) Bill, 1973, which aimed to meet the menace of defections. The Bill provided (a) disqualification of those legislators who leave a party voluntarily, and (b) disqualification of those legislators who voted in the House of which they were members in defiance of the Party Whip. The provision was considered sinister and destructive of the principle of accountability to the House of the People (Lok Sabha) and Legislative Assembly (Vidhan Sabha) of a State as also of freedom of speech and vote of legislators. N.A. Palkhivala spoke very emphatically against the Bill and considered it "truly savage", on "absurd proposition, which no Constitution of any mature nation had ever contained." He said, "No greater insult can be imagined to Members of Parliament and State legislators than to tell them that once they become members of a political party, apart from any question of party constitution and any disciplinary action the Party may choose to take, the Constitution of India itself expects them to have no right to form judgment and no liberty to think for themselves, but they must become soulless and conscienceless entities who would be driven by their political party in whichever direction the party chooses to push them. If we pass this proposed provision into law and Constitutional disqualification for a member who honestly votes or abstains from voting we shall make ourselves the laughing stock of the world."

In the wake of such a stout opposition to the Bill, both within and outside Parliament, the Government did not push it forward and instead made a motion for reference of the Bill to a Joint Committee of both the Houses of Parliament. The Bill, however, lapsed in the Committee itself, when the House of the People (Lok Sabha) was dissolved in 1977. A fresh attempt was made by the Janata Government in August 1978 to introduce the Constitution (Forty-Eighth Amendment) Bill which contained, more or less, identical provision for disqualification of a member as the 1973 Constitution Amendment Bill, that is, if he voted or abstained from voting contrary to the Party Whip. Thus, both the Bills of 1973 and 1978 sought to punish honest dissent. It was vehemently opposed by the General Secretary of the ruling Janata Party, Madhu Limaye, on the floor of the House itself. Citing the Keshavanand Bharati case, he said that the proposed Constitution Amendment Bill was against "the basic features of the Constitution. It militates against the funda- mental principles..... It is beyond the competence of this Parliament.....this is a battle between dictatorship and democracy. This is a battle between bossism and freedom of Members of Parliament......This is the most sinister bill, that has come before the Lok Sabha (House of the People)." Madhu Limaye was not only supported by the Opposition Members but several other Members of the ruling party as well. The Bill, thus, ran into rough waters and rather than force defeat in the House, it was deemed politically prudent by the Government to withdraw it unconditionally.

**The Anti-defection Act, 1985**

After the 1985 elections to the House of the People (Lok Sabha) in which Congress (I) led by

Rajiv Gandhi won a three-fourth majority, the entire atmosphere was changed into euphoria. The Opposition had not been able to recover from its humiliating defeat at the polls and was nothing but a babble of tongues. The Rajiv Gandhi Government introduced Constitution (Fifty-second Amendment ) Bill, 1985, on January 23 to fulfil electoral commitment of the Congress (I) to ban defections. The Bill roadrollered through the Parliament without any opposition. There were two notable objectors to the Bill, Soli Sorabjee and Madhu Limaye, both out of Parliament. The Bill was not referred to the State Legislatures for their ratification under article 368 (2). It received the assent of the President on February 15, 1985 and became operative on March 1, 1985. The Amendment Act added a new Tenth Schedule to the Constitution incorporating the provisions of what it came to be known the Anti-Defection Act, 1985. Thus, what could not be done in past more than two decades was achieved in Janurary 1985. This amendment put a seal on the "fate of a possible genuine dissent in Indian Parliamentary democracy."

The Act provides that the seat of the elected Member of Parliament or the Legislative Assembly of a State Legislature shall fall vacant on the following contingencies :—

(a) if he voluntarily gives up the membership of a political party on whose symbol he had been elected; or

(b) if he votes or abstains from voting in the House of which he is a member contrary to any direction issued by the party to which he belongs without obtaining prior permission of the competent authority of his party and such act of voting against the directive issued or abstention therefrom has not been condoned within fifteen days from the date of such voting; or

(c) if an independent member after his election joins any political party; or

(d) if a nominated member joins from the date he took oath as a member of the House to which he had been nominated. A nominated member of a House where he is a member of any political party on the date of his nomination as such member, shall be deemed to belong to such political party.

But the aforesaid provisions relating to disqualification of a member or members shall not apply in the following cases :

(i) *Party split*. Where there is a split in the political party and the member or members concerned belong to a faction arising out of such split and the group thus splitting consists of not less than one-third of the total membership of the original party in the House;

(ii) *Party merger*. Where two or more political parties have decided to merge by a two-thirds majority of the total membership of the party in the Legislature concerned.

*Exemptions*. The aforesaid provisions relating to disqualification shall not apply to a person who has been elected to the office of the Speaker or Deputy Speaker of the House of the People (Lok Sabha) or the Deputy Chairman of the Council of States (Rajya Sabha) or the Chairman or Deputy Chairman of the Legislative Council (Vidhan Parishad) of a State :

(a) if he, by reason of his election to such office, voluntarily gives up the membership of the political party to which he belonged immediately before his election and does not so long he continues to hold such office thereafter, rejoin that political party or become a member of another political party; or

(b) if he, having given up by reason of his election to such office, his membership of the political party to which he belonged immediately before such election, rejoins such political party after he ceases to hold such office.

**Decision On Questions of Disqualification**

(1) Para 6 of the Anti-defection Schedule 1985, lays down that if any question arises as to whether a member of a House has become subject to disqualification, the question shall be referred for the decision of the Chairman or, as the case may be, the Speaker of such House and his decision shall be final : Provided that where the question which has arisen is as to whether the Chairman or the Speaker of a House has become subject to such disqualification, the question shall be referred for the decision of such member of the House as the House may elect and his decision shall be final.

(2) All proceedings as stated above in relation to any disqualification of a member of a House shall be deemed to be proceedings in Parliament within the meaning of Article 122 (Courts not to inquire into proceedings of Parliament) or, as the case may be proceedings in the Legislature of a State within the meaning of Article 212 (Courts not to inquire into proceedings of the Legislature).

Para 7 of the Tenth Schedule is by far important. It bars the jurisdiction of courts in such cases of disqualification on grounds of defection.

It provides that "notwithstanding anything in this Constitution, no Court shall have any jurisdiction in respect of any matter connected with the disqualification of a member of a House under the Schedule."

Para 8 of the Tenth Schedule authorises the Chairman or the Speaker of a House to make rules for giving effect to the provisions of the Schedule and the rules so framed were approved by the House of the People (Lok Sabha) on December 16, 1985. The Lok Sabha (Disqualification on Ground of Defection) Rules, 1985 stipulated that every such petition alleging disqualification should be addressed to the Secretary-General of the Lok Sabha, containing a concise statement of the material facts against the alleged Member or Members of the Parliament. It is provided that the Speaker would seek the reply from the affected party within seven days after receiving the petition from the leader of the party concerned. The decision of the Speaker in this regard shall be notified in the Official Gazette and forwarded to the Election Commission and the Government of India. Likewise, the State Legislatures framed their own Rules and Regulations, for the application of disqualification of their respective members in cases of defections.

**Evaluation of the Act**

The Anti-defection Act, 1985 was widely acclaimed by the Congress (I) and some other political parties. But it suffered from serious flaws and misgivings, Neither a public debate on its specific provisions had been initiated nor any attempt was made by the Congress (I) Government to seek a consensus of other political parties in its favour. It was simply rushed through in Parliament and, as such, was widely believed that the legislation was designed to benefit the ruling party alone.

The definition of the term "defector," as contained in the Act, does not cover the honest dissenter who defies the Party Whip on a Bill to which he is conscientiously opposed and the defeat of such a Bill in the House would not effect the survival of the Government. The Constitution (Thirty-second Amendment) Bill, 1973, which aimed to meet the menace of defection, provided disqualification on two counts : (a) of those members who left a party voluntarily and (b) those who voted in the House in defiance of the Party Whip; precisely the same provisions as are contained in the Anti-defection Act, 1985. The Thirty-Second Amendment Bill which also contained similar provisions was abandoned in face of wide averse public opinion.

The Governors' Committee (1971) was opposed to legislative action to check defections and floor crossings for that would not permit genuine changes of conviction or dissatisfaction with the party and its leadership, for example, where promises or programmes remained unfulfilled. But the Committee would like the legislator or legislators who changed their party to seek reelection. "This is different," the Committee noted, "from curbing the right of dissent or change and is in essence an extension of the exercise of responsibility which is at the root of the Constitution." Morally too, in the opinion of the Committee, "This would be the right course to adopt and may certainly restrict defections prompted only by reasons of self-interest or pursuit of power."

But the Anti-defection Act, 1985, legitimises defections through the device of "party split" and "party merger." The process of both the devices is easy and for all intents and purposes is an *alibi* for defection. In case of "party split" one-third of the total membership of the party in the House if they form a distinct and separate group arising out of such split do not attract the penalty of disqualification under the law. In case of "party merger" the prescribed majority is two-thirds of the total strength of the original party in the House . As a result, there was a Government of defectors at the Centre following the defection of thirty-seven members of the Janata Dal headed by V.P. Singh. Chandhra Shekher submitted to the Speaker of the House of the People (Lok Sabha) the list of these thirty-seven members on November 6, 1991, and informed him about the split in the Janata Dal, a constituent of the National Front, and the formation of a new political party. Chandra Shekher staked his claim with the breakaway group of the Janata Dal, as "unattached," a new addition in the vocabulary of the Anti- defection Act, 1985, and the creation of the Speakar, with the outside support of the Congress (I) Party. Intrinsically speaking the Janata Dal Party and the Government formed by Vishawanth Partap Singh as its leader was also a government of defectors as almost all the members of the newly formed Janata Dal were either expelled form the Congress (I) Party or had defected therefrom. Some of the more clever out of them continued to remain members of the Congress (I) Party and either voted with the Party or abstained from voting, though they criticised the policy of the Party both inside and outside Parliament. The Congress (I) did not venture to take action against them for tactical political reasons.

The three suggestions made by President R. Venkataraman in his speech on December 27, 1991 to the Conference of Governors, had most probably the feelings of a provenly defective, Anti-defection law which could enable just a handful of defectors, as in the case of Chandra Shekher, to assume the reins of office at the Centre. The first suggestion was that the size of the Ministry should "be limited to one-tenth of the size of the popularly elected legislators." Secondly, the defector should "be debarred from any political office, elective or otherwise, for the duration of the legislature to which he had been returned by the electorate". Lastly, he said, "In matters pertaining to the anti-defection law, judicial directives are sometimes issued to the Governor, placing that office in a situation of delicacy." The President suggested that the office of the Governor be insulated "from such piquant situations."

The problem facing the country is to devise a set of rules which will curb corruption and the corrupt practices go with it. Probity, says A. G. Noorani, "cannot be legislated, but corruption can be punished and deterred to a certain extent." The size of the Ministry is one of the patent factors of corruption. The Committee on Defection recorded in 1969 "unanimous agreement" on the recommendation to limit the size of the Council of Ministers. There was also agreement that the size of the Council should have some relation to the size of the Legislature. But the curb can be evaded by providing what President R. Venkataraman described as "a ministerial type of *sine- cure*." It is, therefore, no less essential to put these plums of office jobs beyond the grasp of defectors. Dev Raj Urs had as many as 47 Members of the Legislative Assembly of Karnataka members of land tribunals and another 47 as members of State Boards and Corporations. Bhajan Lal in Haryana and Laloo Prasad Yadav in Bihar, during recent times are close rivals of Urs in their patronage and vitiating the country's polity.

Para 6 of the Anti-defection Act, 1985, provides that any question regarding disqualification arising out of the defection is to be decided by the Chairman or the Speaker of the House, as the case may be, and his decision shall be final. It also provides that all proceedings of Parliament and the Legislature of a State as, the case may be shall be deemed to be proceedings of the Legislature concerned and, accordingly, the validity of such proceedings cannot be called in question in a court of law on the ground of any alleged irregularity of procedure. Para 7 of the Tenth Schedule bars in clear terms the jurisdiction of the courts in respect of any matter connected with the disqualification of a member of a House under the Schedule.

The Report of the All-Party Committee on the Electoral Reforms submitted in May 1990, recorded that all political parties, except the Congress (I), felt that the power of deciding legal issue of disqualification should not be left to the Speaker. Upholding the validity of Anti-defection Act, 1985, by a 3-2 majority, the Constitution Bench of the Supreme Court ruled that the Speaker's or the Chairman's order, as the case may be, under the Act were open to judicial review. Since the Speaker or the Chairman, as the case may be, acts as a "tribunal" in giving his decision on a case of defection, Para 7 of the Tenth Schedule of the Constitution which bars the jurisdiction of the courts is, therefore, unconstitutional. It went against the stated objective of providing "a remedy for the evil of unprincipled and unethical political defections" by giving immunity to presiding officers of the Legislatures from "allegations of mala-fide and non- compliance with rules of natural justice", the Court held.

The Supreme Court also observed that "the disqualification imposed by Para 2 (1) (b) must be so construed as not to unduly impinge on the said freedom of speech of a Member." This would be possible, the Court noted, if Para (1) (b) is confined in its scope by keeping in view the object underlying the amendments contained in the Tenth Schedule, namely, to curb the evil or mischief of political defections motivated by the lure of office or similar considerations."

The Court said that the stated objective could be achieved if the disqualification incurred on the ground of voting or abstaining from voting by a member was confined to cases where a change of government was likely to be brought about or was prevented by such action. In the alternative, the same could be said when such voting or abstinence was on a matter which was a major policy and programme on which the political party to which the member belonged went to the polls.

At present under Para 2(1)(b) a member incurs disqualification if he votes or abstains from voting in the House contrary to any direction issued by the political party to which he belongs without obtaining prior permission. The Court held that the words "any direction" required to be construed harmoniously with the other provisions of the anti-defection law which define and limit the contours of its meaning. There was, therefore, no justification to give words wider meaning. The Court said voting or abstinence from voting by a member against the direction by the political party by such a motion would amount to disapproval of the programme on the basis of which he went before the electorate and got elected and, such voting or abstinence would lead to a breach of the trust reposed in him by the electorate. "Keeping in view the consequences of the disqualification it would be appropriate that the Whip should be so worded as to clearly indicate that voting or abstaining would result in incurring disqualification," the Court observed.

The majority judgment was delivered by Justice M.P. Venkatchallaiah, Justice K. Jayachandra Reddy and Justice S.C. Agarwal.

In a separate dissenting judgment Justice L.M. Sharma and Justice J.S. Verma held the entire anti-defection law unconstiutional. The Judges held that the law violated the basic structure of the Constitution. They said constitutional scheme for decision on questions of disqualification contemplated adjudication by an independent authority outside the House. Namely, the President or the Governor in accordance with the opinion of the Election Commission all of whom were high constitutional authorities with security of tenure independent of the will of the House.

**Suggestions of the Speakers**

The Speakers Conference held in New Delhi on February 11, 1992, specially convened to consider the possible changes in the Anti-defection Act, 1985, unanimously agreed that the decision of the Speaker or Chairman, as the case may be, in all matters of disqualification of a member or members of a House on the ground of defection should be outside the jurisdiction of the Courts as provided in Para 7 of the Tenth Schedule of the Constitution. The Presiding Officers felt that Para 7 which was recently struck down by the Supreme Court should be restored and the law should be ratified by the required number of State Legislatures under Article 368 (2) of the Constitution.

The Speakers also generally agreed that the Supreme Court verdict on the legal validity of the Anti-defection Act, 1985, should be respected. But at the same time, they felt that the proceedings in the matter relating to determination of disqualification of a Member of Parliament or a Member of the State Legislature should be treated as proceedings of the Legislature concerned, as provided in Para 6 of the Tenth Schedule, and should, therefore, bar the Jurisdiction of the Courts within the meanings of Articles 122 and 214 of the Constitution respectively. They felt that it was a matter of "mutual respect" for the Legislature and the Judiciary and each one organ of the State should refrain from intervening in the matters of the other.

There was also unanimity among the Speakers on the need for curbing the defections as such. Some of the participants suggested that "wholesale defections" should be outlawed and, for that matter, they felt, that the condition of one-third split in the party should be modified. For genuine split in a party at least half of its members, it was suggested, should part company with the parent party. It was also suggested that the defectors should not be eligible to hold any office, including the ministership, for some time so that a Member was not lured to another party on some consideration.

There was also unanimity amongst the Speakers on the need for providing a permanent machinery for review of the orders of the Speaker disqualifying a Member from the House, to meet the ends of natural justice. There was, however, difference of opinion on the form of such a machinery. It was also felt that the determination of the issue whether a Member had incurred disqualification should not be done by a Speaker alone, but it should be referred to a committee of the House.

It was proposed that the recommendations of the Conference would first be discussed with the leaders of the various political parties in Parliament and State Legislatures, and then be forwarded to the Government for amendments in the Anti-defection Act, 1985. It is a lengthy process and how long does it take to effect the desired amendments swings in politics which is highly unpredictable in the present context.

**Parties Favour Amendment**

A meeting of major political Parliamentary parties, convened by the Speaker of the House of the People (Lok Sabha) on February 5, 1992 recommended amendment of the Anti-Defection Act to avert any confrontation between the Legislature and the Judiciary on its implementation. The Lok Sabha Secretariat Press note said, "The consensus at the meeting was, that with a view to maintaining healthy and harmonious relations between the legislature and the judiciary, it was necessary that the decision of the Supreme Court should be respected by the presiding officers of all the legislative bodies in the country". The Government may prepare a draft of amendment to the existing law, the Press note said, and added that it could be referred to the Joint Select Committee of Parliament for discussion.

The meeting also felt the matter could be discussed in other form, like the Presiding Officers' Conference and various Political Parties.

**Presiding Officers' Conference**

Presiding Officers of Legislatures, on February 11, 1992, called for the creation of an authority, to review their decisions under the Anti-Defection Law. This was one of the major amendments to the Anti-Defection Law recommended by the Presiding Officers of "almost all the State Legislatures" at a conference chaired by the Speaker of the House of the People (Lok Sabha), Shivraj Patil.

According to the Press release issued by the Lok Sabha Secretariat, the Presiding Officers suggested the creation of the authority on the grounds that they should not be "answerable in the court of law for what they do while conducting the business of the House". It was proposed that such an authority could be the Governor or the President or a body of Speakers or a body of other persons.

They also pointed out that some of the terms used in the Anti-Defection Law such as "split", "merger", and "political parties" were ambiguous and needed to be clearly defined. Another amendment suggested was that the law should be "very clear on the activities of the political parties inside and outside the House, on expulsion and on the term 'unattached' used in the decisions of the presiding officers."

The Presiding Officers also suggested that members changing their parties "may not be given political positions." Besides, there was a debate on the provision of one-third of the members of a Party being allowed to defect without attracting disqualification under the Tenth Schedule.

Though extraneous to the Presiding Officers' Conference, it shall be worthwhile to refer to the opinion of the veteran BJP leader Atal Behari Vajpayee. On March 12, 1992, addressing a Press Conference at Lucknow, he demanded to review the Anti-Defection Act. He argued that the provision in the Act on split in political parties needs to be waived off completely as it was being misused. He suggested that any member of State Legislature or Parliament quitting the Party on whose ticket he had won the election would be forced to resign from his seat in the Legislative concerned and seek a fresh mandate.

## SUGGESTED READINGS

Kothari, R, *Politics in India.*

Kochanak, S.A., *The Congress Party.*

Weiner Myron, *Party-building in a Nation.*

# CHAPTER IXX

# The Indian Political Tradition

India's relatively stable democracy and slow but steady economic development during the last five decades of independence appear exceptional to many observers. The existence and survival of the Indian democratic state and its capacity to oversee a reasonably sustained economic growth can be explained partly in terms of "the legacies of statelessness and state formation that distinguish India from most Third World countries. Their proximate determinant was the viceregal state of the British Raj. Their more distant determinants included the Mughal empire from whose ideas and practice the British benefited and which the British assimilated, and the imperial states and regional kingdoms of ancient and medieval India."[1]

The troubled political history of many Asian and African countries, during the last several decades, has shown that the task of state building must precede parallel nation building and economic development. "Contrary to prevailing assumptions of scho-larship and policy in the generation since decolonization, states create nations and economies more than nations and economies create states."[2]

**The Sub-continental Empire**

India's political tradition of stateness is rooted in its ancient and medieval history. Unlike some emergent states in Africa, it was not imported from Europe. In ideological and constitutional terms, it was not a foreign transplant though British rule in some ways did influence state formation and the level and quality of stateness in India. But British rule in turn was built on Mughal rule and incorporated many of its characteristics. The historical legacies of the sub-continental empires more than two millennia ago had established conceptions and institutions of the state that provided models for the contemporary multinational state of the Indian Republic. Regional kingdoms, however, constituted the principal state from the seventh to the sixteenth century. But the sub-continental state conception had already been realized in the Mauryan empire, particularly under Asoka (312-185 B.C.), and under the imperial rule of the Guptas (A.D. 319-540).

India's ancient empires had established their hegemony in the entire sub-continent over diverse regional kingdoms, thus, creating the structures and conceptions of a pan-Indian state. The concept of a *Chakravarti* ruler remained a part of India's political history sometimes as a reality and sometimes as an ideal to be pursued by powerful conquerers. Indian political tradition reflects a dialectical tension bet- ween these ever present regional political identities and the perennial quest for an imperial state. "The history of Indian state formation is more comparable to that of Russia and China, where empires became multinational states, than to that of Western Europe, where regional kingdoms were transformed into absolute monarchies and then nation-states."[3] Had the Holy Roman Empire embodied itself in a modern European polity, it could have resembled the modern Indian Republic. In fact, the regional kingdoms have remained in dialectical relation with the sub-continental empire thoughout Indian history. Today the dialectical relationship manifests itself through a federal form of government in the Indian Republic.

On the Indian sub-continent, the regional kingdom and the 'national' polity became the 'recessive' but the 'multinational' empire the 'dominant' form of the state. The Mughal, British and Indian states of the modern age incorporate the dialectical tension between these two alternating state forms in India's political tradition. India's sub-continental empires created means of penetration and domination which can be compared to those developed by European

1. Rudolph & Rudolph, *In Pursuit of Lakshmi* : *The Political Economy of the Indian State,* p. 60.
2. *Ibid.*, p.60.
3. *Ibid.*, p.64.

absolutism in the seventeenth and eighteenth centuries. these were: centralized fiscal instruments in the possession of the king; patrimonial agrarian bureaucracies barred from control of the means of adminis-tration and also from inheriting their office and estates; and armies financed and controlled by the king and not by feudal chiefs or independent military adventurers. Such arrangements were already in force in the fourth-century B.C. Mauryan imperial state and discussed in Kautilya's Arthashastra [4]

However, their realization has differed over time. Reinforced in later imperial states, they have weakened under enfeebled emperors or under regional satraps, whose officials seize control over estates, office, army and treasury through manipulation or use of force. The Mughals succeeded in constructing a centralized military-revenue arrangement, the *mansabdari,* which enabled it to extract the resources and maintain the army to conquer and govern an extensive empire. "Comparable in size to the domains of Charler V, the Mughal empire probably controlled its area more severely. The emperor's dominion was exercised through a centrally appointed court nobility, the *mansabdars,* not through decentralized prebendiaries as in European feudalism,"[5] Noble estates were not hereditary. The Mughals were influenced by Ottoman models of administration and revenue collection, though the Ottoman were more ruthless in eliminating intermediary classes than the Mughals. The local rulers and chiefs survived in India, forming intermediary layers of political, economic, and cultural autonomy. This contrasts with the model of 'oriental despotism' expressed in the Ottoman empire as well as with Russian Trarist absolutism.

The administrative-revenue system of the Mughal rulers provided the network, units and methods of revenue collection and the conceptions of maintaining social peace. the division of the country into *subahs, sarkars,* and *parganas* was perpetuated in British administrative divisions. The *zebt* method of measuring land for fixing revenue travelled from the administrations of Sher Shah and Akbar to Cornwallis and the British rule. In the latter period of Aurangzeb's rule and under the last Mughal rulers, the authority and capacity of the state appreciably declined. It was restored under British viceroys, who revived and reformulated the notions and practices of the imprial state bequeathed from the Mauryan times.

Imperial states created the myths, rhetoric and symbols of the king's eminence and the state's glory. Both the Mughals and the British benefited from the age-old and pervasive Hindu concept of a universal emperor, the *Chakravarti rajadhiraja,* who performed the *Ashwamedha* sacrifice. Akbar became a *shahanshah* (king of kings) and Queen Victoria assumed the gran title of Empress to legitimize their authority ever the Indian elites and masses. Such iconography, rituals and sanctification elevated the ruler to a god-like status, who became an object of awe, wonder and celebration. "Here too there was continuity between British and Mughal empires. The British used Mughal ceremonies and language to revitalize the universalism and mystique of the imperial state. Through ceremonial enactments that closely emulated Mughal patterns, they revived in Queen Victoria's time imperial grandeur and patrimonial ties in *durbars,* jubilees, and coronation ceremonies and rituals of loyalty between the Queen-Empress and her subjects."[6]

The realization of the sub-continental state has waxed and waned in history. The Mughals and the British in their own different ways revived and restored the structures of the sub-continental imperial state after defeating their regional challengers. The creation of India and Pakistan in 1947 and Bangladesh in 1971 left the sub-continent with one sub-continental imperial state and two latter-day representatives of the regional kingdom in a dialectical tension between them. In contrast with modern European states, which destroyed or absorbed regional identities, the Indian state has tried to accommodate regional cultures and identities through federal arrangements.

The strategy propounded in the fourth century Arthashastra—that subordinate rulers shall he preserved and respected in their customs and territorial jurisdiction, via tribute and respect, the superior authority of a king of kings—

4. See A.L. Basham, The Wonder that was India, Chap. 4, and Romila Thapar, Asoka and the Decline of the Mauryas.
5. Rudolph & Rudolph, *In Pursuit of Lakshmi : The Political Economy of the Indian State,* p. 65.
6. *Ibid.,* p. 66.

governed the statecraft of the sub-continental empires in Mauryan, Mughal and British times. After independence, India's federal system became its modern embodiment within the twentieth-century model of the sub-continental state.

**Society, State and Individual**

The state-society relationship, as Rudolphs put it, can be measured on a continuum ranging from complete state domination of society to complete societal dominance over the state. They identify four potential positions on the continuum; (1) totalitarian, in which the state totally dominates society, creating and controlling social institutions, maintaining a closed social order, and using force and terror to secure compliance; (2) autonomous, in which the state can be independent because of its insulation from social forces, the only limits on its actions being consent and legitimacy; (3) constrained, in which the state's freedom to act is limited by the representation of organised social interests; and (4) reflexive in which the state lacks self-determination because organised social classes have seized state authority and its resources. A particular state's location on the continuum would depend "on historical circumstances, including ideology, leadership, conjunctural effects, and the balance of public and private power.[7]

The Indian state is the residual legatee of a long tradition of high stateness that goes back to ancient imperial states and medieval regional polities. More recently, this high stateness, expressed in terms like *sarkar* (government) and *raj* (rule) is derived from more recent Mughal and British empires. After independence, the Indian Republic can be located in the middle positions of the continuum, autonomous or constrained, rather than at its extremes, totalitarian or reflexive. The state as a third actor began its career in independent India as a creature of Nehruvian 'socialism', which was independent of the class politics of both private capital and organised labour. "For Nehru, socialism meant using the planned development of an industrial society to eliminate poverty, provide social justice, create a self-reliant economy, and assure national independence and security in world politics. In a mixed economy, the state would occupy the commanding heights."[8]

Apart from Nehruvian consensus on the mixed economy, traditional Hindu and imported liberal state theory have also made termendons impact on state formation and the level and quality of stateness. Hindu theory emphasizes family, caste, clan, and tribe. Liberal theory regards the individual as the basic unit of society. Liberal theory also stresses the contractual basis of obedience and authority. Hindu theory is related to *danda niti* (science of punishment) and *Arthashastra's* real politik. It differs sharply with liberal conception of right reason and natural law as the source of order and morality. Yet the two theoretical traditions converge with respect to the priority of social values over state goals. The *Dharmashastras* constitute fundamental prescriptive canons of Hindu culture in a society where the ruler and the ruled are equally bound by them. The doctrine implied restraints on the king's power inherent in the *danda niti* as liberal doctrines of consent and natural rights did in relation to the western state. The good Hindu king was required to protect the laws of the self-regulating orders of society.

At the extreme, both liberal and Hindu state theory reach the point of anarchism. This is suggested by the convergence of Thoreau and Gandhi on the philosophy, legitimacy and importance of civil disobedience to resist the state that violates social values and ethical norms of good and just governance. The founders of the Republican constitution benefited from the legacy of high stateness bequeathed to them by the political tradition of the Mauryan, Mughal and British sub-continental state. But they were obliged to combine the principles of centralization with a parallel system of regional autonomy, derived from the political tradition of self-administering regional kingdoms.

Rudolphs conclude this dialectical interpretation of the Indian state by saying: "The ideas and practice of the sub-continental imperial state from Mauryan to British times and the Hindu conception that social order requires the state's force, left a legacy of high stateness. On the other hand, the sovereignty-limiting ideas and practice of the regional kingdom and of the Hindu and liberal conceptions that society is prior to and autonomous of the state created a legacy of low stateness. These paradigms and

7. *Ibid.*, p. 61.
8. Rudolph & Rudolph, *In Pursuit of Lakshmi : The Political Economy of the Indian State*, p.62.

parameters structured the possibilities and choices of those who created independent India's state.''[9] The nature of the state cannot be determined *a priori* from theory. State-society relationships vary with historical circumstances and the process of state formation produces polymorphous entities. Peter Nettl, therefore, argued that high and low stateness varied with historical experience, political, cultural and structural legacies.[10]

**Obstacles to Democracy**

By the time of Queen Elizabeth I in England, the Mughal conquerers of India had established in India what Karl Wittfogel called an oriental despotism. Barrington Moore prefers to call it ''an agrarian bureaucracy or an Asian version of royal absolutism, rather more primitive than that of China, a political system unfavourable to political democracy and the growth of a trading class. Neither aristocratic nor bourgeois privileges and liberties were able to threaten Moghul rule. Nor were there among the peasants any forces at work that would have been likely to produce either an economic or a political break with the prevailing society.''[11] Village community and caste system prevented peasant discontent from taking the form of massive rebellion as in the case of China.

When the Mughal system simply broke down due to lack of qualitative change and the dynamics of increasing exploitation produced by its system of tax-farming, the collapse gave the European bourgeoisie the chance to establish its colonial foothold in the eighteenth century. There were then powerful obstacles to modernization and democracy in India's social structure prior to the British conquest. The British rule damaged the artisan castes and promoted the rise of a parasitic landlord class. The colonial regime, the foreign bourgeoisie and the native landlords extracted a substantial economic surplus from the impoverished peasantry. The British presence, the failure of 1857 rebellion, and the character of Indian society ruled out the Japanese path to moder-nity and industrial development. Hence, economic stagnation continued thoughout the British era and indeed into the present day.

However, the British rule prevented the formation of the reactionary coalition of landowning elites with a weak bourgeois class and thereby, along with British cultural influence, made a small contribution to political democracy and bourgeois parliamentarism. The Indian manufacturers felt cramped by imperialist policies and allied with the nationalist movement. ''As the nationalist movement grew .... Gandhi provided a link between powerful sections of the bourgeoisie and the peasantry through the doctrines of non-violence, trusteeship and glorification of the Indian village community. For this and other reasons, the nationalist movement did not take a revolutionary form ... The outcome of these forces was indeed political democracy, but a democracy that has not done a great deal toward modernizing India's social structure. Hence, farming still lurks in the background.''[12]

According to Moreland, the fundamental features of the traditional Indian polity were a sovereign who ruled, an army that supported the throne, and a peasantry that paid for both. To this trio one should add the institution of caste for a better understanding of Indian society. The weakness of a national aristocracy was an important obstacle in the growth of parliamentary democracy from native soil. Land was held in theory and to a great extent in practice at the pleasure of the ruler. Again there was no such thing as the inheritance of office and so each generation had to make a fresh start.

By skimming off most of the economic surplus generated by the peasants, the Mughal rulers avoided the dangers of an aristocratic attack on their power. At the same time, wasteful use of surplus seriously limited the possibilities of the kind of development that could have broken through the agrarian order and established a new kind of society. ''The point deserves stressing since Marxists and Indian nationalists generally argue that Indian society was on the point of bursting through the fetters of an agrarian system when the advent of British imperialism crushed and distorted potential developments in this direction. This conclusion seems quite unwarranted on the basis of the evidence, which gives strong support to the opposite thesis : that neither capitalism nor

---

9. *Ibid.* p. 68.,
10. J.P. Nettl, ''The State as Conceptual Variable, *World Politics* 20 (July 1968), p. 566.).
11. Barrington Moore Jr., *Social Origin of Dictatorship and Democracy.* p. 315.
12. Barrington Moore Jr., *Social Origin of Dictatorship and Democracy*, p. 316.

parliamentary democracy could have emerged unaided from seventeenth century Indian society."[13]

Cities like Agra, Lahore, Delhi and Vijayanagar rivalled the splendour of Rome, Paris and Constantinople but they were not centres of trade and commerce. Despite the Protestant ethic of the Baniyas, there was no vibrant middle class in Indian cities. The French traveller Bernier says, "There is no middle estate. A man must be either of the hihest rank or live miserably."[14] The Mughal legal system was behind that of Europe and no merchant could seek the protection of his rights from the court with the help of a lawyer as this profession was non-existent. The Mughal system was too predatory in relation to merchants as well as other property- owners. Yet chieftains and *zamindars* were left alone as long as they paid their taxes.

These local despots were too parochial and disunited to challenge and substitute for royal absolutism as the English aristocracy did from the days of Magna Carta. But they played a political role when the imperial system decayed and became more oppressive by becoming the rallying point for peasant rebellions. "Native elites together with the peasants could not wield India into a viable political unit on their own. But they could punish the errors of foreigners and make their position untenable. This the peasants did under the Moghuls, and with new allies, under the British; similar tendencies remain apparent even in the third quarter of the twentieth century."[15]

By the middle of the eighteenth century the Mughal bureaucratic hegemony had decayed into a system of petty kingdoms frequent at war with one another. This opened way for imperialist intervention and subsequent conquest of India. "As one looks back over the record, it is easy to conclude ... that the dynamics of the Moghul system were unfavourable to the development of political democracy or economic growth in anything resembling the Western pattern. There was no landed aristocracy that had succeeded in achieving independence and privilege against the monarch while retaining political unity. Instead their independence, if it can be called that, had brought anarchy in its train. What there was of a bourgeoisie likewise lacked an independent base. Both features are connected with a predatory bureaucracy, driven to become ever more grasping as its power weakened, and which by crushing the peasants and driving them into rebellion returned the subcontinent to what it had often been before, a series of fragmented units fighting with one another, ready prey for another foreign conquerer."[16]

The character of upper classes and political institutions prevented India's progress towards capitalism and political democracy. Besides, a closer look at the place of the peasants in India's social structure will account for their poor productivity and apparent political docility. The structural contrast with China is quite striking. In India, the higher castes had the best land and could command the labour of the lower castes. As an organization of labour, caste in the countryside was a cause of poor cultivation. As the organization of authority in the local community, caste inhibited political unity. The system emphasized the individual's duty to the caste, not individual rights against society. "In the willing acceptance of personal degradation, by its victims and the absence of a specific target for hostility, a specific locus of responsibility for misery, the Indian caste system strikes a modern Westerner as a curiously intensified caricature of the world as Kafka saw it."[17]

### Imperialism and India's Underdevelopment

India's political tradition was abruptly unsettled and ruptured by imperialist intervention in the eighteenth century which started the process of India's underdevelopment. When this intervention began, India was predominantly a feudalistic society. Of course, there are far-reaching differences between the European serfdom and pre-capitalist social structures of Japan, China and India but they had this similarity that the ruling class extracted an economic surplus from the peasants, though by different methods. So one should bear in mind that histories of feudalism, despite divergences, contain substantial similarities. Though many historians still object to the general applicability of the term

13. *Ibid.*, p. 321.
14. Quoted in W.H. Moreland, *India at Death of Akbar*., p.26.
15. Barrington Moore Jr., *Social Origin of Dictatorship and Democracy,* p. 326.
16. Barrington Moore *Jr., Social Origin of Dictatorship and Democracy* pp. 329-30.
17. *Ibid.*, pp. 340-41.

'feudalism', there is a wide consensus on the proposition: "that the pre-capitalist order, be it in Europe or be it in Asia, had entered at a certain state of its development a period of disintegration and decay. In different countries this decomposition was more or less violent, the period of decline was shorter or longer — the general *direction* of the movement was everywhere the same."[18]

There were three interrelated processes in this change. First, there was a notable increase in agricultural output accompanied by growing feudal pressure on the peasants, leading to their discontent and revolt and the creation of a potential industrial labour-force. Secondly, there was increased division of labour, evolution of the class of merchants and artisans and the growth of towns. Thirdly, there was visible accumulation of capital in the hands of the expanding class of traders and rich farmers. In the words of Marx, "what enables money wealth to become capital is on one hand its meeting with free workers; is secondly its meeting with equally free and available for sale means of subsistence, materials, etc. that were otherwise... the property of the now dispossessed masses."[19] However, it is the primary accumulation of capital to which strategic significance should be given. To quote Marx again, "Capital formation does not stem ... from landed property ... nor from the guild ... but from merchant and usurer wealth."[20]

The state, as it came under the influence of capitalist interests, became increasingly active in aiding and advancing the emerging entrepreneurs. Marx said, "they all employ the power of the state, the concentrated and organisd force of society, to hasten, hothouse fashion, the transformation of the feudal mode of production into the capitalist mode, and to shorten the transition."[21] Western Europe's large leap forward need not necessarily have prevented economic growth in other countries like India. As Andre Gunder Frank testifies, development in Western countries was accompanied by simultaneous process of underdevelopment in colonies and semi-colonies. At the time of Western interaction, "the primary accumulation of capital was making rapid progress, crafts and manufacturing expanded, and mounting revolts of the peasantry combined with increasing pressure from the rising bourgeoisic shook the foundations of the pre-capitalist order. This can be seen whether we consider the early history of capitalism in Russia ... or whether we retrace the beginning of capitalism in India..."[22] Marx said, "The country that is more developed industrially only shows to the less developed the image of its own future."[23]

In colonies like India, the colonizers "rapidly determined to extract the largest possible gains from the host countries, and to take their loot home ... they engaged in outright plunder or in plunder thinly veiled as trade, seizing and removing tremendous wealth from the places of their penetrations,"[24] In the words of Maurice Dobb: "In the cruel capacity of its exploitation colonial policy in the seventeenth and eighteenth centuries differed little from the methods by which in earlier censuries crusaders and the armed merchants of Italian cities had robbed the Byzantine territories of the Levant,"[25] Marx points out, "the treasures captured outside Europe by undisguised looting, enslavement and murder flowed back to the mother country and transformed themselves into capital."[26] These 'unilateral transfers' of wealth multiplied economic surpluses available to Western capitalism for its growth and damaged the capacity of colonies like India to develop by robbing them of these aggregates of wealth and capital.

The record of India's exploitation from the days of the East India Company has been summarized by a British economic historian, an authority not suspect of anti-British, prejudice as follows; "Up to the eighteenth century, the economic condition of India was relatively advanced, and Indian methods of production and

18. Paul Baran, *The Political Economy of Growth*, p. 268.
19. Quoted in *Ibid.*, p. 269.
20. Quoted in *Ibid.*, p. 270.
21. Karl Marx, *Capital* (ed. Kerr), Vol.1. p. 823.
22. Paul Baran, *Political Economy of Growth* , p. 272.
23. Karl Marx, *Capital* (ed. Kerr), Vol. 1., p. 13.
24. Maurice Dobb, *Studies in the Development of Capitalism*, p 208.
25. *Ibid.*, p. 209.
26. Karl Marx, *Capital*, (ed-Kerr), Vol. 1 p. 826.

of industrial and commercial organisation could stand comparison with those in vogue in any other part of the world ... A country which has manufactured and exported the finest muslins and other luxurious fabrics and articles when the ancestors of the British were living an extremely primitive life, has failed to take part in the economic resolution initiated by the descendant of those same wild barbarians."[27]

This failure was not due to some peculiar inaptitude of the Indian race because "the great mass of the Indian people possess a great industrial energy, is well-filled to accumulate capital, and remarkable for a mathematical clearness of head, and talent for figures and exact sciences. Their intellects are excellent."[28]

Brooks Adams compares India's plunder by the British with the worst examples of such loot in history : The Roman proconsuls who squeezed out of a province the means of building marble palaces and obtain other luxuries just in a year and the Spanish Viceroys of Peru or Mexico who after plundering and killing the natives of Latin America, entered Madrid with a long train of gilded coaches and of sumpter-horses trapped and shod with silver. The British had outdone all of them.[29] "Very soon after Plassey the Bengal plunder began to arrive in London, and the effect appears to have been instantaneous, for all authorities agree that the industrial revolution," the event which has divided the nineteenth century from all antecedent time began with the year 1760."[30]

Romesh Dutt concludes by saying : "In India, the state virtually interferes with the accumulation of wealth from the soil, intercepts the incomes and gains of the tillers ... leaving the cultivators permanently poor ... In India, the state has fostered no new industries and revived no old industries for the people ... In one shape or another all that could be raised in India by an excessive taxation flowed to Europe, after paying for a starved administration ... Verily the moisture of India blesses and fertilizes other lands."[31]

The calamity that the invasion of British capitalism brought upon India assumed staggering proportions. It is true that the process of transition from feudalism to capitalism has caused a vast amount of misery, suffering and starvation everywhere. Yet accumulation of capital ultimately served to lay the foundations for the eventual expansion of industrial output and productivity. Paul Baran points out: "Indeed, there can be no doubt that had the amount of economic surplus that Britain has torn from India been *invested in India,* India's economic development to date would have borne little similarity to the actual sombre record. It is idle to speculate whether India by now would have reached a level of economic advancement commensurate with its fabulous natural resources and with the potentialities of its people. In any case, the fate of the successive Indian generations would not have resembled even remotely the chronic catastrophe of the last two centuries."[32]

But the harm done to India's economic capacity was exceeded by the lasting damage inflicted upon the people as Marx put it: "All the civil wars, invasions, revolutions, conquests, famines strangely complex, rapid and destructive as the successive action in Hindustan may appear, did not go deeper than its surface. England has broken down the entire framework of Indian society, without any symptoms of reconsolidation yet appearing. This loss of the old world, with no gain of a new one, imparts a particular kind of melancholy to the present misery of the Hindu and separates Hindustan, ruled by Britain, from all its ancient traditions, and from the whole of its past history."[33]

The British administration of India systematically destroyed all the fibres and foundations of Indian society. Its land and taxation policy ruined the rural economy and created a class of parasitic landlord and moneylender. Its commercial policy destroyed the artisan class and created the filthy slums of Indian cities filled with millions of hungry and sick paupers. Its economic policy prevented indigenous industrialisation and promoted the proliferation of speculators, petty businessmen, agents and

27. Vera Anstey, *The Economic Development of India* (4th edition), p.5.
28. Quoted in Marx, "*The Future Results of British Rule in India* in Marx and Engels, *On Britain*, p. 398.
29. See T.B, Macaulay's *Lord Clive.*
30. *The Law of Civilisation and Decay, An Essay on History*, pp. 294 ff.
31. R.C. Dutt, *Economic History of India,* (7th edition), pp. viii-xi
32. Paul Baran, *The Political Economy of Growth*, pp. 281-282.
33. Karl Marx, "British Rule in India," in Marx and Engels, *Selected Works,* Vol 1, p.313.

sharks of all types preying upon the miserable people of a decaying society. To quote from Kaye's *Life of Metcalfe,* "It was our policy in those days to keep the natives of India in the profoundest state of barbarism and darkness, and every attempt to diffuse the light of knowledge among the people, either of our own or of the independent states, was vehemently opposed and resented,"[34]

Jawaharlal Nehru says: "British rule thus consolidated itself by creating new classes and vested interests who were tied up with that rule and whose privileges depended on its continuance. There were the landowners and the princes, and there were a large number of subordinate members of the services in various departments of the government ... To all these methods must be added the deliberate policy, pursued throughout the period of British rule, of creating divisions among Indians, of encouraging one group at the cost of the other,"[35] It is thus a fair assessment of the impact on India of two centuries of exploitation by Western imperialism and a correct analysis of the causes of India's continued underdevelopment, when Nehru further says: "Nearly all our major problems today have grown up during British rule and as a direct result of British Policy; the princes; the minority problem; various vested interests, foreign and Indian; the lack of industry and the neglect of agriculture; the extreme backwardness in the social services; and above all the tragic poverty of the people."[36]

**Independence and Partition**

Despite serious obstacles, an independent Indian bourgeoisie, as distinguished from a compradore mercantile class, did not come into existence during the period of British rule. A few industrial houses like the Tatas and the Birlas even played a monopolistic role in India's industrial development. They extended moral and material help to the nationalist leaders in organising an anticolonial movement against the British rulers. Indian National Congress during the Gandhian era-1919-47 was financially supported by the Indian bourgeoisie. The Muslim League, from the beginning, was a movement supported by the Muslim landowners in the United Provinces but acquired some strength when the Muslim bourgeoisie from the Bombay Presidency extended its support to it. Similarly, the financial backing of the Marwari-Gujarati capital was crucial for the National Congress.

The Non-Co-operation Movement of 1920-21 was one of the landmarks in the Gandhian era. Others were the civil disobedience movement of 1930-31, the Individual *Satyagraha* of 1940 and Quit India Movement of 1942-45. Almost all of them combined legal and extra-legal methods of struggle. Gandhi and his followers questioned the moral right of the imperialists to rule over India and courted imprisonment by violating their unjust laws. But he also tried to negotiate with the British rulers and to reach agreement with them in a spirit of conciliation. This strategy of struggle followed by compromises suited the Indian bourgeoisie perfectly which was itself vacillating in its attitude towards imperialism.

A fundamental characteristic of the movements led by Gandhi was its emphasis on non-violence. Even those disciples of Gandhi, who did not accept non-violence as a creed, accepted it as a practical and expedient policy. "Gandhi was a unique leader in many respects. He tried to fulfil many different functions. He was a social reformer, a nationalist leader and a world prophet. This created a lot of confusion among those who could only think within established framework. Some of them accused him of revivalism and others of reckless revolutionary activities. And many contended that he was strengthe-ning anarchy in the country."[37] An Indian Marxist noted about Gandhi: "The fact that India chose to remain a secular republic is in large measure to him. The Hindu communalist felt at an enormous disadvantage in combating him since it was impossible to contest the Indianness or the 'Hinduness' of the man of the man or to dispute that. What he was telling the people sprang from the very depths of the traditions of India."[38]

While the form of Gandhi's thought and expression was based on Hindu and religious idioms and terminology to some extent, the content of his message was secular, national

34. Quoted in Paul Baran, *The Political Economy of Growth,* p. 283.
35. Jawaharlal Nehru, *The Discovery of India,* pp. 304-05.
36. *Ibid* pp. 306-07.
37. K.P. Karunakaran, *Democracy in India,* p.12.
38. Mohit Sen, The *Indian Revolution,* p.20.

and universal. Within India, he was the greatest force in favour of democracy and modernisation. He fought for the people's right to civil liberties in the Non-co-operation and Khilafat movements. Later, he struggled for the economic rights of the poorest of the-poor the right to make salt. In 1940, he protested against the British decision to make India a belligerent without her consent in an imperialist war. By 1942, he demanded that the British should quit India. In 1947, he stood for the country's unity and independence but without partition as this, he thought and feared, could lead to a communal holocaust and ethnic cleansing in both the countries. When the partition became inevitable he fought the battle against communal killings and fanaticism almost single-handed. Ultimately, a Hindu zealot shot him because of his convictions. Gandhi's incompromising nationalism, humanism and secularism became inseparable ideological components of Indian political tradition.

In a way, Gandhi and his philosophy of 'non-violence' can be interpreted as representing the ideology of the Indian bourgeoisie. This class did not want a violent anti-imperialist revolution with the support of the peasants and workers as this could lead to their own overthrow eventually. When the Congress leadership led by Patel and Nehru accepted the Mountbatten plan of India's partition into two independent dominions in 1947, it was fulfilment of the aspirations of the Indian bourgeoisie as well as the ambitions of M.A. Jinnah and the Muslim bourgeoisie represented in the Muslim League.

D.G. Tendulkar, the authoritative biographer of Gandhi, records the events of 15 August, 1947 as follows: "There were festivities all over the land. But the man who, more than any one else had been responsible for freeing India from the alien rule did not participate in the rejoicings. When an officer of the Information and Broadcasting Department of the Government of India came for a message, Gandhi replied that he had 'run dry.' When told again that if he did not give any message it would nor be good, Gandhi replied : "There is no message at all; if it is bad, let it be so." (Vol. VIII, pp. 95-96).

It may also be noted that on 26 January, 1948, the first time Independence Day was being celebrated in free India and just four days before his martyrdom — Gandhi said: "This day, 26th January, is Independence Day. This observance was quite appropriate when we were fighting for independence we had not seen, nor handled. Now? We have handled it and we seem to be disillusioned. At least I am, even if you are not." (Vol. VIII, p. 338). Disillusioned by the moral degradation of the ruling Congress Party, he even recommended its dissolution, withdrawal from politics and conversion into a Lok Sevak Sangh, *i.e.,* a non-governmental organisation for social service. He said that the Congress as a propaganda vehicle and parliamentary machine had outlived its utility.

Commenting upon the gulf between Gandhi on the one hand and Nehru and Patel on the other which was evident between 1945 and 1948: E.M.S. Namboodiripad pointed out: "It was this change in the position of the bourgeoisie as a class and its individual representatives that brought it into conflict with Gandhi, the man who still clung to the ideals which he had been preaching in the days of anti-imperialist struggle. The moral values which he had preached in the days of anti imperialist struggle now became a hindrance to the politicians who came to power. Gandhi, on the other hand, remained true to them and could not reconcile himself to the sudden change which occurred to his former colleagues and lieutenants .... We may conclude by saying that Gandhi became the Father-of-the-Nation, precisely because his idealism to which he adhered to in the years of anti-imperialist struggle became practically useful political weapon in the hands of the bourgeoisie in the latter days of his life, because his idealism did in the post-independence years become a hindrance to the self interest of the bourgeoisie."[39]

Nehru was another important leader and thinker who contributed to the growth of India's political tradition both before and after independence. Gandhi had nominated him as his political heir despite differences in their political outlook and philosophy on some issues. Nehru was firm believer in the ideals and institutions of bourgeois democracy and liberalism. The non-communal approach to politics was interpreted by Nehru in Western secular terms. In his *Autobiography* and *Whither India,* he expressed some intellectual appreciation of the

39. E.M.S. Nambordiripad, *The Mahatma and the Ism*, p. 117.

Marxist tradition, 'socialism' and Soviet Russia but kept away from the politics of both the Congress Socialist Party and the Communist Party of India as well as the working-class movement. This made him an acceptable leader of the Indian bourgeoisie both during the anti-colonial struggle and after the formation of the Indian Republic. He also kept away from Subhash Bose's radicalism and pragmatism.

During the World War II, he remained sympathetic to the cause of the Democracies against the Fascist aggressors and supported the Soviet Union against Nazi Germany and the Republic of China against Japan. He opposed Bose's plan for seeking India's liberation with the Japanese support. "Nehru's greatest contribution lay in giving a definite international outlook to the Indian nationalist movement— He conceived the Indian nationalist movement as a part of the world-wide movement against imperialism. In fascism, he perceived the dangers to individual freedom and he was of the view that, under no circumstances, should Indian nationalism ally with fascism even if the fascist governments were fighting the Western imperial powers like Great Britain and France."[40] Thus, the political tradition of India's National Movement was not only liberal and democratic in a general sense, it was also at the same time anti-fascist in a specific sense which in a way was the extension of its deep-rooted anti-imperialism.

Modern India, however, also saw a strong Muslim separatist movement, which culminated in the creation of a separate Muslim state , under the leadership of Mohammed Ali Jinnah. But the ideology of Muslim separatism began with Sir Syed Ahmed. Unfortunately, the Muslim political tradition in India was characterized by the almost total failure of the Muslim intelligentsia to separate religion and politics and to achieve a secular outlook as well as their unwillingness to adapt themselves to the demands of reason, liberalism, modernisation and secularism. Khilafat Movement, which was supported by Gandhi, was a means to achieve the goal of Pan-Islamism, an ideal rejected by nationalist Turkey. The movement had no intrest in democracy and no commitment to India's composite nationalism. It is a sad reality that those who followed the technique and strategy of this Pan-Islamic movement fought the battle of Pakistan and won it.

Iqbal, the celebrated poet who wrote *Sare Jahan se achcha Hindostan hamara* (our India is the best in the world), also become the prophet of Muslim separatist ideology. Moin Shakir says, "Iqbal did not have sufficient courage to break with traditional Islam completely and accept the spirit of modern science. His thought is replete with paradoxes and antiquarianism. He failed to assimilate liberal forces and could not completely free himself from the moorings of tradition. His inconsistences and contradictions make it difficult to regard him as a systematic thinker or a consistent philosopher.[41]

W.C.Smith says, "Iqbal was himself a bourgeois and in some respects a contented one, he never really deserted his class."[42]

Abul Kalam Azad and Abdul Ghaffar Khan were two Muslim leaders of stature who understood the true nature of composite Indian nationalism, democracy, freedom, parliamentarism and secularism. While Azad was also a great thinker, Gaffar Khan was a great leader of the Pathans who converted them to the Congress ideology of auti-imperialism and non-violent struggle. Professor Mohammad Habib says this about Maulana Azad , "His thought was correct; and his faith in God, in his country and in himself was so firm that he would neither bend nor break owning to the onslaught of the mad-dogs of Muslim communalism. In those days the Muslim Unveresity had become 'the armoury of the Muslim League" and I have good personal experience of that mad-dog Muslim communalism, which has fortunately be taken itself to Pakistan, where it is controlled by military regiments. "In the whole history of Muslim India," no one thinker and scholar has been more intensely hated by his coreligionists than Maulana Azad during the ten years preceding the Partition. Jinnah took every opportunity of insulting him; the Muslim press kept on cursing him, he was abused from every communal platform"[43].

The real ideologue of the separatist Muslim

40. P. Karunakaran, *Democracy in India,* p.16.
41. Moin Shakir, *Khilafat to Partition,* p. 123.
42. W.C. Smith, *Modern Islam in India,* p.112.
43. M. Habib's "Introduction" To Moin Shakir's *Khilafat to Partition,* p. xx.

political tradition in India was none other than Mohammed Ali Jinnah. Though in the beginning, he started as a nationalist leader of the moderate Gokhale school. At that time he was the most secular of all Muslim leaders. He was least interested in Islam and had no knowledge of its scriptures. He accepted the principles of nationalism, democracy, secularism and unity of the country. As a liberal, he stood for the ideals of individual liberty, absence of fanaticism, and constitutionalism. He said that the people should learn to separate religion from politics. He was a great lawyer who defended Tilak in the court when the British were determined to persecute him for his militant nationalism. He was metamorphosed completely after a few decades into a Muslim communal bigot and an advocate of the two- nation theory which became the ideological basis of the Pakistani state.

The portrait of Jinnah would remain incomplete if we do not state the fact that as a politician he was remarkably callous. "When a group of Aligarh Muslim students ventured to ask him what would be the fate of Indian Muslims he said he would give his answer when the time came. But when the time came, he declared: 'I have written off the Mussalmans of India.'"[44] Jinnah personally and his Muslim Leage were never actively involved in any anticolonial struggle directed against the British rulers. The only stuggle he led just before partition was the socalled 'Direct Action ' directed against the Hindus in Bengal and Punjab. This resulted in large-scale ethnic cleansing of both Hindus and Muslims in North India but Jinnah did not shed a tear and had no plan or patience for peaceful transfer of the two communities across the newly created borders of India and Pakistan.

Jinnah argued that the Congress was a Hindu body, Swaraj meant Hindu Raj and National Government, by implication, would be Hindu Government. He gave an ideological and religious interpretation to the Two-Nation Theory. He argued that the Muslims in India are a nation who must preserve their culture and identity in a separate state of Pakistan. Democracy in united India would be the 'fascist' rule of the Congress-led Hindu majority. Jinnah described the Congress organization led by Gandhi as a "Fascist Grand Council under a dictator who was not even a four-anna member of the body."[45]

Democratic rule will lead, he said, to the complete destruction of what is most precious in Islam; it will culminate in the creation of private armies of both the communities and to civil war.

Thus the conception of Indian nationalism and a central, sub-continental government was a mental luxury of the Hindu leaders. Another ingredient of the Two- Nation Theory was the emphasis on the 'Historical' and 'Spiritual' differences existing between the Muslims and the Hindus. The history of one thousand years, said Jannah, failed to unite them into one nation. Therefore, "the artificial and unnatural methods of a democratic constitution will not create a sense of nationality." Jinnah held that Hinduism and Islam are "two entirely distinct and separate civilizations," the Hindus and Muslims, therefore, belonged to two antagonistic religions with different social customs, rival philosophies and two distinct bodies of literature, they did not inter-marry and did not inter-dine, and they belonged to two dissimilar societies, which were governed by two different social and legal codes. "They govern not only his law and culture but every aspect of the social life and such religions, essentially exclusive, completely preclude that merging of identity and unity of thought on which Western democracy is based and inevitably bring about vertical rather than the horizontal division democracy envisages."[46]

There is another aspect of the Muslims separatist political tradition. The leadership of the Muslim League was in the hands of the North Indian landowners and the Gujarati Bohra bourgeoisie. The Muslim landlords were apprehensive of losing their lauded property as the Congress was committed to a policy of radical land reform at that time. The Muslim bourgeois class was not happy about the competition which it had to face from a richer Hindu bourgeoisie. A separate homeland could provide a refuge and better opportunity for trade, industry and profits. Penderal Moon rightly says, "The truth

44. *Ilid,* p.xxi.
45. *Recent Speeches and Writings of Mr. Jannah,* p. 233, Quoted in *Khilafat and Partition*, p.190.
46. Quoted in Moin Shakir, *Khilafat to Partition* , p. 191.

is that for the Muslim bourgeoisie the idea of a state, however poor, in which they and not the Hindus would be rich-men and hold all the best posts in government service, industry and commerce had a powerful attraction."[47]

According to Moin Shakir, "The Two-Nation Theory and the demand for Pakistan indicates the peculiar non-national trait of the Muslim mind. It was a self-defeating project and an escape from hard realities."[48] Dr. S. Ansari argues that a careful study of Indian Islam reveals that "Islam in India is an Arabic version of *Sanatana Dharma* just as Sikhism and Arya Samaj are more or less Gurmukhi or Hindu Editions of Islam.[49] Ansari also stated that the two-nation theory was a myth, a camouflage to cover up humiliation in the social sphere, and inequality in the economic field. "The story of the growth of the Muslim League is the story of the rise of the Muslim middle class. Moreover, the young bourgeoisie—both Muslims and Hindus — felt the need of having the state in its own hands. Therefore, Jinnah was more interested in the political liberation of the Muslims than in the social and economic emancipation of the exploited masses.[50] Pakistan was thus a new state of the Muslim Indian bourgeoisie.

In 1971, there was another partition of the Indian subntcontinent when Bangladesh came into existence, demolishing M.A. Jinnah's theory of separate nationalism on purely religious basis. It invalidated his theory of 'two nations' creating a Bengali state out of Pakistan, demonstrating the significance of Bengali sub-nationalism. In secular India, linguistic sub-nationalism was contained within a secular, federal and democratic political structure.

## SUGGESTED READINGS

Baran Paul, *Political Economy of Growth.*
Bettleheim, Charles, *India Independent.*
Blackburn, R. *Explosion in a Sub-continent*
Desai, A.R., *Social Background of Indian Nationalism*
Dutt, R. Plame, *India Today.*
Gough and Sharma (eds) *Imperialism and Revolution in South Asia.*
Karunakaran, K.P. *Democracy in India.*
Moore, Barrington Jr., *Social Origins of Dictatorship and Democracy.*
Namboodiripad, E.M. S., *Conflicts and Crisis*
Nehru, Jawaharlal, *Discovery of India*
Rudolph, L.I. and Rudolph S.H., *In Pursuit of Lakshmi, the Political Economy of the Indian State.*
Selbourne, David, *An Eye to India.*
Shakir, Moin, *Khilafat to rtition*
Shukla, V.N. *Constitution of India.*
Smith, W.C., *Modern Islam in India.*
Woodruff, Philip, *The Men Who Ruled India.*

47. Penderal Moon, *the Future of India*, p. 27
48. Moin Shakir, *Khilafat to Partition*, pp. 204-05
49. S. Ansari, *Pakistan*, p. 25.
50. *Ibid.*, p. 27.

# CHAPTER XX

# The Indian Political System

### Early Years of the Republic

The Indian Republic, according to Paul Baran, during its early years, when it was being governed under the undisputed leadership of Jawaharlal Nehru, could be described as a nation-state with a 'New Deal' orientation. A New Deal type regime like that of independent India was brought to power by a broad popular movement. Its primary and unifying objective was to overthrow the colonial rule and replace it by a government of national independence. "Struggling against imperialism and its domestic ally, the feudal comprador coalition," the national movement assumed the charecter of a united front of "the progressive bourgeoisie striving to find a road towards industrial capitalism, of intellectuals seeking a better future for their country, and of active elements of the urban and rural proletariat rising against the misery and oppression of imperialist comprador domination." However, an essentially reactionary segment of the feudal aristocracy also "joined the nationalist camp, interested primarily in deflecting popular energies from the struggle for social change into a fight against foreign subjugation"[1].

Immediately after independence, the unity of the nationalist movement was subjected to severe strains and stresses. Earlier also, its right-wing was afraid that the national struggle might create conditions favourable to a social revolution by mobilising and organizing the peasants and workers. Therefore, it sought to exclude or minimize the role of the popular masses in the anti-imperialist front and adopted a policy of negotiations and compromises with the imperialist authorities. Its left-wing was anxious to combine the goals of social justice with those of national freedom and insisted on greater mass participation in anti-imperialist struggle. Yet so long as the primary goal of national freedom was not attained, "the fight for national independence over-shadowed and absorbed the struggle for social progress."[2]

Earlier the centripetal forces of the national united front were stronger than the centrifugal elements. This scenario began to change after the formation of the Indian Republic. Weakened by World War II, Great Britain was compelled to grant political independence to South Asian countries like Burma, India, Pakistan and Sri Lanka. As John Foster Dulles put it,"When the fighting in World War II drew to a close, the greatest single political issue was the colonial issue. If the West had attempted to perpetuate the *status quo* of colonialism it would have made violent revolution and consequent defeat inevitable. The only policy that might succeed was that of bringing independence peacefully"[3]

With the problem of national independence resolved, the basic class conflict of an antagonistic society became intensified in India. While some significant, central issues of social and economic development were actually linked with the questions of national freedom, there were some other issues actually which were being obscured and confused by it. For example, the oppression and exploitation of the peasantry by the landowning aristocracy or the strangulation of industrial development by monopolistic capital was merely a *national* question, it was more a *social* problem, to be faced and to be resolved in that way. Thus, the nationalist movement, after acquiring power in the Indian Republic, entered a process of disintegration. The socially antagonistic elements, tenuously integrated during the era of anti-imperialist struggle, became more or less quickly polarized into opposing class parties or fractions within the frame work of a new political order. The break-up between the Indian National Congress on

1. "Paul Baran, *Political Economy of Growth*, p. 366.
2. *Ibid.*, p. 36.
3. John Foster Dulles, *War and Peace*, p. 76.

parties on the other signified this schism in the early years of the Indian Republic.

The speed of this breakdown of national unity depended upon the accentuation of the internal class straggle in the context of the specific historical circumstances of a country. In China the advanced urban proletariat had played a decisive role in the anti-imperialist straggle and was strong enough to organise and assume the hegemony of the peasantry's armed struggle for an agrarian revolution. In this service, the split in the national front proceeded very rapidly. Its bourgeois, capitalist, component, frightened by the spectre of a social revolution. Turned swiftly against its former ally, and its mortal enemy of the future. In fact, it did not hesitate to make common cause with feudal elements representing the main hindrance to its own development, with the impesialist overlords just overthwon by the national liberation, and with the comprador groups threatened by the political retreat of their foreign protectors. They proved the correctness of Lord Acton's aphorism, that "the bonds of class are stronger than those of nationality."[4]

Under such conditions "the political independence barely won turns into a sham, the new ruling group merges with the old ruling group, and the amalgam of property—owning classes supported by imperialist interests uses its intire power to suppress the popular movement for genuine national and social liberation and reestablishes the *ancien regime* not *de jure but de facto.* China under the Kuomintang, Pakistan, South Korea, South Vietnam typify this process."[5] India under the Congress rule during the early years of the Republic did not succumb to this degeneration. This is because the popular pressure for social liberation was less pronounced in India at the time of the attainment of national freedom.

The working class during the first decade after independence was politically and numerically weak and the peasantry except in certain pockets, was politically passive due to its age-old servitude and deeply rooted religions superstitions. In these circumstance, the Indian bourgeoisie felt more secure and tried to prevent the potential upsurge of social-revolutionary forces " by making an all-out effort to lay the foundations for the evolution of an indigenous industrial capitalism, to create a modern capitalist state." The success of such an undertaking depended "on the quality of its leadership, on its determination to dislodge the feudal and comprador elements from their position of dominance, on the intensity of the resistance on their part, and on the extent to which the inter-national constellation permits the elimination or considerable weakening of the support given to these strata by the world's imperialist powers."[6]

In India, the united front of anti-imperialist forces was still, though precariously, intact, and provided the broad political basic for the government of the national bourgeoisie. But this breadth of the national coalition which accounted for the great electoral strength of the Congress Party in sweeping general elections at this time was also responsible for paralysing the administrative machinery of the state. Though the Congress leadership still enjoyed the overwhelming media and popular support, it encountered some unsurmountable obstacles in formulating and implementing a programme of social and economic change. While intending to promote the growth of capitalist industrialization, it lacked courage to offend the interests of the landlords. While trying to reduce the most outragious inequalities, it failed to interfere with the vested interests of the traders and usurers. It wished to improve the miserable condition of the workers but was also fearful of antogonising capitalists. Though anti-imperialist by tradition, the Congress was now courting favours from foreign capital.

The contradictions of Nehru's policy were limitless. On the one hand, Nehru assured the Indian capitalists that he was determined to promote and protect their private property. On the other, he promised the nation and the working class a 'socialist pattern of society.' Nehru was presiding over a Bonapartist regime which stood above the struggle of opposing classes though this merely reflected the stage which the class struggle had reached in Indian society at that time. Nehru was anxious to reconcile irreconcilable needs, to compose radical differences and to find compromises where

4. John Edward Dalberg Acton, *Essays on Freedom and Power,* p. 224.
5. Paul Baran, *Political Economy of Growth,* p. 368.
6. *Ibid,* p. 369.

cal differences and to find compromises where decisions could not be avoided. Losing much precious time in bridging recurring conflicts, the *Congress system,* as Rajni Kothari puts it, substituted minor reforms for radical changes and revolutionary phrases for revolutionary actions. The Congress Party thereby endangered not only the very possibility of implementing its proclaimed programmes but even its very tenure in office.

Paul Baran's judgment on the achievement of the so-called Nehruivian Congress is harsh but, nevertheless, true. He says, "Handicapped by the heterogeneity and brittleness of its social foundations and by the ideological limitations resulting therefrom, the essentially petty bourgeonis regime is incapable of providing genuine leadership in the battle for industrialization, is powerless to mobilize what is most important: the enthusiasm and the creative energies of the broad popular masses for a decisive assault on the country's backwardness, poverty, and lethargy."[7] In India, it is only the state that can mobilize the surplus present potentially in the economic system. It alone has the capacity to employ it for the expansion of the nation's productive forces. In India the amount of resources seized by the state is much *smaller* than the potential economic surplus. Even more important is the fact that the use made of it, despite good intentions, does not provide for rapid and balanced economic growth. As the *Economist* commented, "like the Red Queen, India has to run fast even to stand still."[8]

**Persistent Centrism of Indian Politics**

According to Lloyd and Susanne Rudolph, the outstanding characteristic of Indian politics has been its persistence of centrism. During three decades and five successive Lok Sabha Elections (1952, 1957, 1962, 1967, and 1971), the Indian National Congress was the dominant party among India's several parties. The ruling Congress Party benefited from three factors: (1) It had an apex body with a leadership and national goals which provided democratic legitimacy and bargaining power for a sub-continental state that included different regional political parties, (2) a centrist ideology of secularism, liberal democracy, socialist pattern and mixed economy; and (3) a pluralist basis of support that encompassed several interests, strata, communities and regions. These features also applied to the Janata Party, which won the sixth Lok Sabha election in 1977; the Congress led by Indira that won the seventh Lok Sabha election in 1980 and the Congress led by Rajiv in the eighth Lok Sabha election of 1984; and the several parties that split from Congress from time to time.

The reasons for this continued feature of dominant centrist trend in Indian politics have been listed by Rudolph and Rudolph as follows: "(1) The marginality of class politics, (2) The fragmentation of the confessional majority: (3) The electoral strength of disadvantaged confessional and social minorities, (4) The increasing political consciousness and effectiveness of "bullock capilatists' and 'backward classes;' (5) The imperatives of capturing power in Delhi; (6) The constraints imposed on India's federal system by cultural diversity and social pluralism; and (7) The advantages that accrue to a centrist national party or coalition when parliamentary seats are won by pluralities in single-member constituencies."[9]

An important condition for centrism is the marginality of class politics at national level. To some, class politics may seem inevitable in India with so much poverty, injustice and inequality. But the weakness of class organization and lack of class consciousness in the subordinate classes are the principal factors which have made class polarization difficult to achieve at an all-India level. Groups representing language, caste, community, and region and those speaking for scheduled castes, tribes and Muslims have been more successful than class-oriented organizations in creating a sense of identity and in influencing political decision-making.

Unlike Europe, Labour, Socialist and Communist Parties have not yet become national role-players and all-India phenomena and so there in no direct and visible confrontation between labour and capital. There is no national Conservative party either. The Swatantra Party was the closest approximation to an Indian Conservative party but its existence proved ephemeral. The Bharatiya Jan Sangh and its

7. *Ibid,* p. 370.
8. "India—Progress and Plan" (22 January 1955).
9. Lloyd Rudolph and Susanne Rudolph, *In Pursuit of Lakshmi,* p. 19.

progeny the Bharatiya Janata Party constitute an amalgam of *hindutva* and conservatism but its has yet to overcome its Hindi heartland identity. At present, corporate capital in India finances two major political parties, the Indian National Congress and the Bhartiya Janata Party. But they have yet to establish their authenticity as class-oriented right parties of the conservative type, though they are in the process of doing so as their common support to policies of economic liberalistion, privatization and globalization has shown during the previous two decades.

But it is difficult to agree with the thesis of the Rudolph couple that the two historic adversaries are playing a marginal role in Indian politics just because it is not adequately reflected in the nomenclature of political parties or the ideological masks that they wear. Nor can it be explained by the so called centrality of a third factor, the state. The state in India has built a public sector only to promote the growth of a private sector and bureaucratic capitalism and corporate capitalism have been intimate allies under the benevolent guardianship of a ruling elite under the Congress or Non-Congress system of governance.

The fragmentation of organized labour into severnal national federations has not prevented it from waging local and nation-wide struggles both against the state bureaucracy and private capital. Organized capital has also been quite influential in promoting its class interests through financing political parties and through pressuring state administration. Even the Rudolph couple has to conclude by saying: "Business' interests in India, while not publicly represented in comparative party politics (this statement is doubtful), are better represented than those of organized labour in bureaucratic, parliamentary, and (informal) party processes... business interests in India focus their attention on executive agencies... Business contributions to political parties are an invisible but important channel of influence... Private-sector capitalists can also influence how the government applies and implements controls and regulations that affect very major area of decision: investment, expansion, new products, foreign exchange and collaboration, location, and pricing."[10]

India's 'permit-licence raj' gave private-sector capitalism protected markets and monopoly profits. Even the Birla-owned *Hindustan Times* admitted in its editorial, "Over the last thirty years of Indian socialism and mixed-economy, the private sector has flourished and prospered many times over; much of the prosperity can be traced to the private sector's capacity and ability to influence governmental policies and laws,"[11] Rudolphs point out, "This interpretation of the relationship between private-sector capitalism and the state has led the neo-Marxist left to argue that the tail wags the dog, that despite the state's socialist claims and its command of the economy's industrial and financial heights, it serves capitalists and capitalism."[12]

But this view, according to Rudolphs, ingnores the "dependent nature of private capitalism in India. He quotes with approval Kochanek's opinion in this context," Business has never succeeded in blocking or even in modifying a major distributive policy in India... (it) could not delay or modify the decisions to nationalize life insurance... (or) stop the nationalization of private sector banks... what business *can* do however, is to try to convert a redistributive issue into a regulatory issue in which its interest seems self-evident rather than self-serving."[13] By 1984, state capitalism was perceived by its critics as the problem rather than the solution. This shift in the public perception of the state affected its legitimacy in directing the planned and private-sector economies and enhanced private capital's public standing and prestige in relation to state capitalism. "Despite this altered ideological climate, the state as third sector continued to dwarf both of the historic adversaries of class politics, capital as well as labour. Neither was in a position to challenge the centrist feature of Indian politics."[14]

### Confessional and Minority Politics

The term 'confessional' may sound unfamiliar to Indian ears. It has been used by Lloyd Rudolph and Susanne Rudolph to denote non-secular, communal or religion-oriented politics in the Indian context. Centrist ideology in India

10. Rudolph and Rudolph, *In Pursuit of Lakshmi* pp. 31-32.
11. *The Hindustan Times,* February 6, 1984.
12. Rudolph and Rudolph, *In Pursuit of Lakshmi,* pp. 32-33.
13. Kochanek, *Business and Politics in India,* p. 329.
14. Lloyd Rudolph and Susanne Rudolph, *In Pursuit of Lakshmi,* p. 35.

includes secularism as a part of its liberal ethos Despite temptations to adopt a Hindu identify and programme, the Congress and other centrist parties have retained their commitment to secularism. In Western Europe the roots of confessional politics go back to the Reformation in the sixteenth century. It unleashed a civil war in several Europan countries. But it also gave birth to a secularizing process that contributed to the separation of church and state and to religious tolerance. In modern Europe, we have Christian Democrats and Christian Socialists who pursue policy aims which are consistent with their religious beliefs.

It is the European sense of confessional politics that the Rudolph couple has in mind when he intends to find out whether confessional politics in India could again give rise to a 'destructive' cleavage in Indian politics. The obvious aspirant for national confessional politics is the 'Hindu majority.' But this majority, according to them, is an 'artifact of categorization' that encompasses a diversity of gods, goddesses, holy texts, social customs, ontologies and epistomologies. "Without an organized Church, it is innocent of orthodoxy, heterodoxy, and heresy. Thus, until the transforming historical events and experiences that surfaced during the Janata government (1997-79) and crested in the early 1980s, the 'Hindu majority' remained an illusory support base for a national confessional party. At the same time, minority religious communities—Muslims, Sikhs, and Christians were able to play a role in state politics."[15] More important, the Hindu majority was more fragmented along sect, caste, class and regional lines of cleavage than were India's minority religious communities.

Before the emergency regime of Indira Gandhi, its was the Jan Sangh and Rashtriya Swayamsevak Sangh that articulated and propagated the ideology of Hindu nationalism. Hindu confessional politics was India's counterpart to the ideology of Islamic Pakistan. However, the ideological and military threat of Pakistan could not sustain and give much political support to Hindu confessional politics before 1980. Jan Sangh could capture only 9 per cent votes in 1967 and 7.4 per cent in 1971 Lok Sabha elections which were its best performances. The break-up of Pakistan in 1971 as a result of India's military victory reduced the potential influence of Hindu confessional politics for a decade.

The Indian Republic began its career with a powerful commitment not only to a secular state but also to secularism as an ideology. It was challenged after 1980 when growing conflict among Hindus, Sikhs and Muslims made the latent contradictions manifest. The contradiction in the Indian concept of secularism was its simultaneous commitment to equal citizenship and to autonomous committees. Group identities were equally recognized by the British and nationalist rulers and this obstructed the growth of the concept of equal citizenship based on the rights of the individual. For Gandhi, confessional politics was a vehicle of community refom — Khilafat agitation, campaign for Gurdwara reform and the ongoing massive campaign, against untouchability politicized Muslim, Sikh and Hindu communities.

By contrast, Nehru could not take religion seriously or recognize groups as valid components of the Indian nation. For him, the Muslim League before partition was just a group of Muslim landlords and nothing else. He did not visualize that this landlord clique could lay the foundation of an independent Muslim nation. He dismissed Hindu Mahasabha, Jan Sangh and the Akalis as political groups, which have no future in a secularist, Indian Republic. He thought that confessional politics was irrelevant in the context of more important issues of economic development, democratic rights of individuals and social and cultural modernization.

In the 1980s, the Hinduism that had been an 'artifact of categorization' began to transform itself into a *Hindutva*, a condition of national consciousness. This development created an environment for the growth of a national Hindu confessional politics. Religious celebrations, demonstrations and performances began to acquire all-India dimensions. Hindu festivals became the occasions for displaying Hindu solidarity and militant nationalism. The Vishwa Hindu Parishad organized the Hindu holy men and their lay devotes into a noisy, strident and militant forum trying to play the role of a vanguard for Hindu nationalism. The Bajrang Dal emerged as the lumpen stormtroopers of

15. *Ibid.* p. 37.

the Sangh *parivar* embracing the BJP, RSS, and the VHP. Romesh Thapar observed in 1986, "Imagine sects of Hindu priests... moving from mandatory caste signs to other symbols of the faith—dhoti-clad, bare to the waist, trident equipped, and with the *bodi* tuft of hair.... soon the cult could take over in our offices as an exercise of the fundemental rights embodied in our Constitution... the Muslims could overnight don the red fez.. to this could be added the trimmed beard of the *mullahs* and *maulvis*.. we are on the edge of encouraging a multitude of what are called 'psyches' one for each community, each caste, each tribe. "[16]

Hindu confessional politics became a form of cultural nationalism for the Hindu heartland states. It was also exported to states where Hindus are a minority like Kashmir's Jammu region, the Punjab and Christianized North-East. Besides, it spread to Maharashtra and Gujarat which are closest to Hindi Heartland culture. The Janata Party's victory in 1977 put the advocates of Hindu confessional politics in the Central Government for the first time. The issue of conversion and the content of textbooks was used to articulate the Hindu grievances and to argue that Hinduism was threatened by India's minority religions. "The supporters of the Hindu backlash alleged that the minorities were privileged and pampered... Congress governments... were charged with appeasing the minorities out of political expediency."[17]

The cohesiveness and scale of India's minority groups contributes to the illusory nature of the Hindu majority. It also constitutes a hindrance to the practice of Hindu communal politics and obstructs the functioning of a Hindu confessional party. India's minorities like the American blacks, appear to share a 'group consciousness '. This helps them to achieve relatively higher levels of political participation than their social and economic status would lead one to expect. Group consciousness persuaded Muslims and scheduled castes to vote in larger proportions for the secularist Congress than did other voters in the first-three general elections. However, since the fourth general election, Muslims and scheduled castes have voted less cohesively as compared to the scheduled tribes. Electoral support of Muslims and *dalits* is vital for success especially in the five Hindu Heartland states of northern India. In these states vote swings have been widest since 1967. Minorities are very significant in number in just those states where elections since 1967 have been most volatile. These states elect 39 per cent of parliament's 545 members. The three minorities together constitute 37 per cent of the electorate in Biher, Uttar Pradesh and Madhya Pradesh, 34 per cent in Rajasthan, and 23 per cent in Haryana. Congress victories in 1971, 1980, and 1984 were due in part to strong support among minorities. Defeats in 1977, 1989, 1996, 1998 and 1999 low voter support in 1980 and 1991 were associated with defection by the miniorities.

The electoral successes of the Congress Party under Jawaharlal Nehru, Indira Gandhi and Rajiv Gandhi were largely enabled by support from India's largest minorities, Muslims and the Scheduled Castes. Janata's' success in 1977 election reflected a new minority alienation from Congress. Since 1980 in both centre and state elections, the minority constituencies have consistently voted for the winning party, if it was at the same time a centrist party as well. The distribution of minority electoral support in the last seven parliamentary elections from 1977 to 1998 indicates that the minorities, rather than engaging in bloc voting for Congress, have responded to the centrist appeals of winning parties. Lloyd and Susanne Rudolph point out correctly, "Parties whose ideology, policies, and electoral strategy do not attend to representing minority interests and identities cannot compete for power at the national level. Centrist parties, in the coded language of Indian politics, espouse secularism and socialism to signal their regard and concern for the 38 per cent of the electorate who are poor and oppressed minority voters".[18]

## Bharatiya Janata Party—Origins

In order to understand the genesis of the Bharatiya Janata Party, it is necessary to go back to Hindu Mahasabha, which was the Hindu confessional party before independence, the Rashtriya Swayamsevak Sangh, which was founded by Dr. Hedgevar in 1925 and the Jan Sangh, which was founded by Dr. Shyama

16. *Economic and Political Weekly,* January 7, 1986.
17. Rudolph and Rudolph, *In Pursuit of Lakshmi*, pp. 41-42.
18. *Ibid,* p. 49.

Sangh, which was founded by Dr. Shyama Prasad Mukherji just before the first general election in 1952. Its ideological inspiration also came from Hindu-minded Congressmen like B. G. Tilak, Lajpat Rai, Madan Mohan Malaviya, Vallabhbhai Patel and P. D. Tandan. Besides, both the present BJP and its predecessor Jan Sangh have been closely associated with non-confessional right wing parties like the Swatantra Parlay founded by C. Rajgopalachari, which later merged with the Bharatiya Lok Dal, led by Charan Singh. In 1950s it was also allied to Ram Rajya Parishad and Hindu Mahasabha, which were both Hindu confessional groups, at the parliamentary level.

Righwting political parties could be divided into two categories:(1) feudalistic, communal and confessional groups., and (2) conserative, bourgeois- oriented groups. In the first general election the rightwing parties, including the confessional groups, secured 3,30,00,000 (three crore and thirty lakh) votes, which was 70 per cent of the votes secured by the Congress Party. The Communists and Socialists together got 2,80,00,000 (two crore and eighty lakh) votes. Even then, Congress secured 375 seats, the rightwning parties got only 75 seats, and the Left had to be satisfied with just 49 seats. Among feudal, Communal and confessional groups the Jan Sangh has a prominent place. In the first Lok Sabha election it got 3.5 per cent votes and stood fifth in its ranking.

Jan Sangh, Hindu Mahasabha, and Ram Rajya Parishad together secured one crore (1,00,00,000) votes. These three parties believed in the ideology of Hindu nalionalism and the ideals of Hindu culture and were hostile to Islamic Pakistan, western culture, Christianity, socialism, communism, Soviet Russia and Communist China. These parties denigrated Prime Minister Nehru as the 'Nationalist Muslims', a' Russian- Chinese agent' or an ' ape who imitates the west ' all the time. The RSS and the Anand Marg participated in politics in a clandestine manner. These elements were responsible for the assassination of Mahatma Gandhi. Some critics have considered them the Indian versions of fascism. During the pre-emergency period, the Hindu Confessional forces and their reactionary allies had openly ganged up against the Congress regime.

Among the conservative bourgeois-oriented groups main allies of Jan Sangh were the Swatantra Party and the BKD. C. Rajgopalachari founded the Swatantra Party in 1959 as classic rightwing and prol business party. Like Jan Sangh, both Swatantra and BKD opposed Congress-sponsored and Left-supported policies of land reforms, the setting up of co-operative institutions, growth of the public sector, planning and socialism. All of them supported development through capitalism and private enterprise, demanded subsidies for rich farmers, reduction of income tax, facilities for foreign investments and an end to the 'licence permit raj'.

The principal supporters of the Swatautra Party set up institutions like the 'Forum for Free Enterprise,' and the 'Federation of Indian Agriculturists'. In the 1962 Lok Sabha elections, the Tata industrial house provided enormous financial support to the Swatantra Party. This was because the Swatantra Party's programme had incorporated the demand of India's monopoly capital that the state should abandon its strategy of promoting 'state socialism' and adopt the policy of encouraging private capital including foreign capital. However, Charles Betthheim said," Even then big capitalists, despite their great fondness for the Swafatra Party, have not severed their relationships with the Congress Party. It seems that they have perhaps helped the Swatantara Party so that they can create an alternative to Congress in future and if the Congress Party were to desert them in order to support some other vested interests, then the other party could be used to put pressure on Congress."[19]

In addition to monopoly capitalists, the princes and landowners also joined the Swatantra Party and the Ganatantra Parishad in Orissa, which represented the feudal forces there, merged with this party. Maharani Gayatri Devi led this party in Rajasthan. In Andhra Pradesh, rich farmers joined this party. In 1967 Lok Sabha elections, Jan Sangh secured 35 seats but the Swatantra Party got 44 seats and became the main opposition group. The righist parties together could win, more than 100 seats. Except West Bengal and Kerala, rightwing parties were the chief components of the several non-Congress governments which were set up at state level in different states between 1967 and 1972.

19. Charles Bettleheim, India Independent, p. 350

came an important political constituent of the right wing governments that were set up in Uttar Pradesh, Madhya Predesh and Bihar. In Punjab, the Jan Sangh and the Akali Dal formed an alliance.

In 1971 Lok Sabha election, Jan Sangh, Congress-O (a splinter group led by Morarji Desai), Swatantra Party, BKD and Lohia Socialists formed a 'Grand Alliance "to fight Indira-led Congress-R. This grand coalition had 160 seats in Lok Sabha be fore the general election but could get only 50 seats in the new Lok Sabha. Indira Gandhi swept the mid-term polls and established a stable government obtaining a two-third majority in the fifth Lok Sabha. India's victory in the Bangladesh war further strengthened Indira Gandhi's position as a national leader and Congress Party supremo. However, she made certain mistakes in running the government and could not find answers for resolving the growing economic crisis. She toppled opposition-led governments in the states without discretion and changed even Congress chief ministers just to assert her imperial authority. Her authoritarian tactics displeased all right-wing parties, antagonized left-wing political formations except CPI and even some Congress factions.

Jaya Prakash Narayan emerged from his political hibernation to lead an anti-Congress youth movement which had its major base in Gujarat. It later spread to Bihar. Narayan raised the slogan of 'Total Revolution' and overthrow of the corrupt Congress regime led by Indira Gandhi. When JP movement, supported by student and opposition groups including Jan Sangh, started gathering momentum, Indira Gandhi imposed a national emergency putting a large number of agitating leaders and their followers in prison. The rigours and excesses of the emergency regime united all struggling opposition parties into an all-inclusive political formation, once Mrs. Gandhi decided to lift the emergency after a period of 'dictatorial' repression extending to eighteen months.

Jan Sangh also merged its identity in the new political formation designated as the Janata Party. Other political parties, which joined the Janata band-wagon, included Congress-O led by Morarji Desai, BKD led by Charan Singh, the Socialists led by Madhu Limaye etc. and Congress for Democracy led by Jagjivan Ram. The victorious Janata Party got 300 seats in the Lok Sabha out of 542 with 43 per cent votes. The defeated Congress Party was reduced to 153 seats with 34 per cent votes. Janata Party dissolved nine state governments by proclaiming President's rule holding new elections and winning most of them. CPI (Marxist) came to power in West Bangal in 1977 and since then it has been winning all state and parliamentary elections which have been held there.

In the sixth Lok Sabha, Jan Sangh led by A. B. Vajpayee, external affairs minister had ninety seats (31 per cent),

Bharatiya Lok Dal led by Charan Singh, some ministers, had fifty-five (19 per cent), the socialists led by George Fernandes, industries minister, had fifty-one (17 per cent,) and Congress for Democracy, led by Jagjivan Ram, defence minister, had twenty-eight (10 per cent). When the Janata Party broke up into its constituent fractions, the Jan Sangh component, after the seventh Lok Sabha elections, reconstituted itself as the Bharatiya Janata Party. In 1980, the BJP had only 16 seats. In the next Lok Sabha election in 1984 it was almost wiped out by Rajiv Gandhi hurricane and left with just two seats there.

**Minority and Coalition Governments**

Bharatiya Janata Party's electoral success in the ninth Lok Sabha elections in 1989 was a morale- booster for the party. From the incredibly low figure of two seats in the eighth general election, its score now jumped to 85 seats. It was able to improve its tally to 120 seats in the tenth Lok Sabha in 1991. During this interregnum, the party's ideologue and leader, A.B. Vajpayee had endeavoured to give a new centrist image to the BJP distancing it from the right-wing, communal programme of the Jan Sangh. He also appreciated Gandhi's economic ideas and JP's philosophy of *Sarvodaya* and decentratised democracy. But L.K. Advani continued to emphasize BJP's commitment to the saffron programme of *hindutra* and cultural nationalism. But Vajpayee was quite determined to give a more liberal, secular and democratic image to Hindu nationalism, in spite of its latent contradictions.

This was done by interchanging and absorbing the values and experiences of the JP movement (1973 – 75), the emergency resistance struggle (1975-77), and the Janata experiment (1977-80), The RSS- BJS legacy was sought to be diluted by the social vision of the Janata-JP movement. However, this was more a mask than a real transformation. Yet it worked for some time. The emergence of V.P.Singh's Jan Morcha in 1987 represented a crucial development in Indian politics. After some time, he succeeded in forging a united opposition party—the Janata Dal. V.P. Singh followed a clever policy of equidistance from both the BJP and the Left. Despite differences on some major issues like Art. 370 etc. the BJP and Janata Dal entered into a mutually beneficial seats arrangements without entering into an electoral alliance.

In a protest against Rajiv Gandhi's refusal to resign on the Bofors issue, the entire opposition, including two BJP members, resigned from Lok Sabha. The Bofors corruption issue proved decisive in the defeat of Congress in 1989 elections. As a result, the Janata Dal, led by V.P. Singh, which secured 142 seats formed a minority government with the outside support of both the BJP and the Left. V.P. Singh minority government survived for a year but L.K. Advani's Rath Yatra, his arrest by Laloo Prashad's government in Bihar, the contentious issue of Ram Janmabhuni Temple, the sudden implementation of the Mandal Report giving 27 per cent representation to the OBC's created fissure in the JD-BJP coalition. V.P.Singh government fell when Congress and BJP ganged up to overthrow it. The outcome was another minority government led by the rump Janata Dal under Chandra Shekhar's leadership, which was supported by Rajiv Gandhi's Congress from outside. It was a case of a tail wagging the dog. This government also fell after a few months when Congress withdrew its support on a non-isssue.

This led to the holding of midterm elections in 1991, the tragic assassination of Rajiv Gandhi by alleged LTT extremists and the return to power by a minority Congress regime led by Narasimha Rao. Rao engineered defections from Jharkhand and some other parties and succeeded in gaining absolute majority in Parliament and governed for a full term of five years. The general election for the eleventh Lok Sahba again resulted in a fractured verdict but the BJP for the first time emerged as the largest single party in Indian Parliament. Dr S.D. Sharma, the President of India, then created history of some sort by inviting the BJP leader, A.B.Vajpayee, to form a government. The BJP remained in power uncomfortably for just thirteen days, could not find a single additional supporter to its otherwise impressive tally of 160 seats, and tendered its resignation when it lost the confidence vote in the Parliament. Consequently, two minority third front governments were successively installed led by Deve Gowda and I.K.Gujral respectively which were at the mercy of Sita Ram Kesri-led Congress Party. Both the governments were toppled when the cynical Congress leadership decided to withdraw its external support, thus, forcing mid-term elections in March 1998.

The outcome of the 12th Lok Sabha elections in March 1998 was far from being conclusive. This fragmented verdict was not entirely unexpected. Neither the BJP nor the Congress, even with their socalled alliance partners, could manage to secure a clear majority in Parliament, although the BJP did emerge as both the largest single party and as the leader of the largest alliance of parties. "The performance of the BJP", as the *Economic and Political Weekly* admitted, "marks, once again, an advance for the party in terms of the number of seats won, the proportion of votes polled and the evidence of expansion of support for it to new parts of the country."[20] Despite Sonia Gandhi's high profile campaign, the party failed to increase its tally of seats in the new house and its share of votes was actually smaller this time than in 1996.

It was the United Front, the aspiring third force in Indian politics, which came out the worst off in these elections, with the Janata Dal, the socalled leader of this third force, was almost decimated. Along with the decline of the JD, the regional components of the erstwhile United Front, such as the DMK, the TMC, the TDP and the AGP also suffered severe losses. They should now worry about threats to their position in their own states while their role at the national level has been consideradely diminished. The vote for the Left parties, confined as they are to Kerala and West Bengal, has further declined from 9.1 per cent to 7.7 per cent though by default they have remained the principal actors in the diminished third front.

The seats and votes lost by the JD and constituents of the United Front have gone to other single-state splinter parties such as the

20. *Economic and Political Weekly*—Editorial, 7 March, 1998

AIDMK, BJD, RJD, making for the fractured and inconclusive electoral outcome. The CPI(M) and the CPI, in a typical Pavlovian reaction, declared that their parties and the United Front would support a Congress government to prevent the BJP form coming to power. However, the support of the TDP, once convener of the United Front, now extended to the BJP led government proved crucial in the formation of A.B. Vajpayee's Ministry. The new BJP led government naturally lacked any ideological and programmatic coherence, as was the case with the two United Front governments, which had ruled for the last twenty-one months. With the aid of a lack-lustre, chauvinistic national agenda, which ostensibly excluded some controversial issues like Ayodhya, Art. 370 and the Uniform Civil Code, the main concern of this opportunistic and unprincipled alliance government was mere physical survival at any cost.

The Editorial concluded by saying : "It will equally naturally have to get busy actively covering up well established cases of corruption and abuse of governmental authority, whether it be Bofors or the venalities of that current object of adoration of BJP leaders, J Jayalalitha, to mention just two out of an indeed rich pantheon. It may even be pushed into tampering with the Constitution to dismiss this or that duly elected state government. Such in sum is the quality of governance that is in store for the citizen, though the political fixers and wheeler-dealers, the self styled king makers and 'Chanakyas' will be undoubtedly in their elements once again"[21] Most of this prognosis about the BJP-led coalition government has proved correct. This government was essentially a regime of the Hindu Right, diluted and shaped to an extent, by the narrow interests of some of its coalition partners. It was finally brought down by the defection of the largest and most volatile ally, the AIDMK.

The BJP regime was communal and divisive in its outlook and approach. It colluded with the RSS's longstanding project of minority-baiting. It permitted the most fascistic members of the saffron outfit to unleash the politics of hatred and terror especially against the Christian minority, ostensibly on the issue of 'conversion.' Although the national agenda of governance excluded the BJP demands on the Ram temple, Article 370 and Uniform Civil Code, the regime endangered the nation's commitment to secularism and the scarcity of the rule of law Murli Manohar Joshi's plan even attempted to saffronise education, though it proved abortive A.B.Vajpayee "hijacked India's independent and peace-oriented, nuclear policy, twisted it out of shape, and imposed on the people of India and Pakistan a dangerous costly new nuclear arms race. It has only undermined bilateral relations with China and Pakistan, before attempting unsuccessfully and unconvincingly to repair some of the damage. Its economic policy, following the Pokhran nuclear explosions and the imposition of sanctions by the United States and some of its allies, was...a policy of 'placating foreign governments and international capital by offering economic concessions, through greater liberalisation, greater incentives for foreign investors and offerring the opportunity to enter captive Indian markets and buy up domestic assets cheaply;"[22]

In addition, the BJP regime put destabilising pressure on federalism and co-operative Center-State relations by using Article 356 to dismiss the elected RJD government in Bihar, thus cynically threatening the existence of other legitimate governments at the state level. "Through its determination to hang on to power after clearly forfeiting parliamentary legitimacy, it forced the polity to register a new low in sordid opportunism and horse-trading. In sum, the BJP led regime set an unmatched - and difficult to match- record of divisive, reactionary and chauvinist misgovernnance."[23] Yet the people of India showed a better judgment of this government of the Hindu Right, when they booted out these saffron governments in Rajasthan and Delhi and disallowed the BJP to win power in Madhya Pradesh.

The state elections showed that the masses of the people were alienated by sharp rises in the prices of essential commodities and by the communal, divisive and inept governance. The constant tensions and vacillations within the coalition government were reflective of this truth of alienation from the electorate. It appeared that the saffron cause was in headlong retreat

---

21. *Economic and Political Weekly* — Editorial, 7 March, 1998, p. 491.
22. *Frontline*, Editorial, May 7,1999, p. 7.
23. *Ibid*, p. 7.

retreat in the national political arena. The pendulum had swung in favour of the BJP's main antagonist, the Congress-I led by Sonia Gandhi. The only viable interim government that can be formed, before the elections for the 13th Lok Sabha, would conceivably be a minority Congress-I government supported from outside by all anti-BJP partices. This interim regime can serve two constructive purposes, First, it must recommit the Indian state to a course of secular democracy. Secondly, it must enable the nation to get off the nuclear tiger.

The fall of the BJP led coalition government clearly demonstrated how the Indian political system, which was based on one party dominance in the past, has been transformed into a chaotic multi-party system. The following is the detailed pattern of voting on the crucial confidence motion on 17 April, 1999, in the 12th Lok Sabha, having an effective strength of 542 members:[24]

| **Those voting Against-270** | | **Those voting For - 269** | |
|---|---|---|---|
| Congres-I | 139 | BJP | 182 |
| CPI(M) | 32 | Samata | 12 |
| AIDMK | 17 | Telugu Desam | 11 |
| SP | 20 | BJD | 9 |
| RJD | 16 | Akali Dal | 8 |
| CPI | 8 | Trinamul | 7 |
| Janata Dal | 6 | DMK | 6 |
| RSP | 5 | Shiv Sena | 6 |
| BSP | 5 | PMK | 4 |
| RPI | 4 | INLD | 4 |
| TMC | 3 | MDMK | 3 |
| F.B. | 2 | Lok Shakti | 3 |
| IUMI, | 2 | National Conference | 2 |
| Majlis (Owaisi) | 1 | Maneka Gandhi | 1 |
| Janata Party | 1 | TRC | 1 |
| ASDI | 1 | RJP (Anand) | 1 |
| Arunachal Cong.(M) | 2 | 1Arunachal Cong. | 1 |
| AIIC(Ola) | 1 | HVP | 1 |
| SJP | 1 | SDF | 1 |
| NC (Soz) | 1 | Independents | 3 |
| Kerala Congress | 1 | (Satanam Singh, | |
| Buta Singh | 1 | Lallungmauna and | |
| PWP | 1 | S.Biswamuithiary) | 1 |
| | | MSCP | 1 |
| | | Nominated | 2 |

R. Muthiah (AIDMK) did not vote; Kim Gangte (CPI) and Malti Devi (RJD) were absent; Speaker-1, Vacancies–2.

**Another Mid-term Election**

After the defeat of the BJP-led government on 17 April, 1999, the Congress led by Sonia Gandhi decided, with the concurrence of her chosen party leaders, particularly Arjun Singh, to explore the possibility of setting up a Congress-led minority government with the outside support of all other parties and individuals that had voted to overthrow the Vajpayee government. The CPI(M) leader, Harkishan Singh Surjeet tried to secure the support of the left and other secular parties for the proposed Congress-led minority government. The leader of the Samajvadi Party, Mulayam Singh, and the leaders of the Revolutionery Socialist Party and the Forward Bloc with 27 votes refused to support any prospective Congress government. The leader of the Bahujan Samaj Party with 5 members said that she could not pledge her support to any government in advance. Mrs Gandhi, therefore, could gather support only from 239 MPs which was not enough to form a new government. The proposal to set up Jyoti Basu as the new Prime Minister remained a non-starter as the Congress declared that it could not lend its support to 'any third or fourth front government' at that late stage. Earlier the CPI(M) itself had scuttled the candidature of Jyoti Basu for the post.

On 26 April, 1999, President K.R.Narayanan dissolved the 12th Lok Sabha after getting recommendation from the caretaker Vajpayee government for doing the same. A Rashtrapati Bhawan communique said that the President has, by his order under sub- clause (b) of clause two of Article 85 of the Constitution, dissolved the 12th Lok Sabha. The four page communique observed tersely that "the ruling alliance lost its majority because of lack of cohesion within its ranks and those who voted out the alliance showed the same disunity while trying to form an alternative government. In this situation, the President reached the conclusion that time had arrived for the democratic will of the people to be ascertained once again, so that a government can be formed, which can confidently address

24. *The Hindu,* 18 April,1999; (Note— Total strength of Lok Sabha is 545).

the urgent needs of the people."[25]

The communique referred to the ruling alliance's plea that since the opposition had failed, the BJP should be given another chance to form its government. The President turned down the request finding no merit in its proposal. The President told Congress Chief Sonia Gandhi that inviting the Congress when its support base in the Lok Sabha remained well short of the ruling coalition's proven strength of 269, was out of the question. The President added, "The recourse to dissolution on the defeat of a minority/coalition government arises when it appears to the President that a stable government connot be formed without a general election"[26]

Thus, the 12 the Lok Sabha has had the shortest term so far— a little over 13 months or 412 days in all. Constituted on 10th March, 1998, it had to be dissolved on 26th April, 1999 after the BJP- led coalition government, headed by Atal Behari Vajpayee, lost the confidence vote by a wafer thin margin of one vote. With the opposition attempts to form an alternative government ending in a stalemate, the dissolution was the only option left before President Narayanan.

The ninth Lok Sabha which saw two Prime Ministers — V.P.Singh and Chandrashekhar — was the second shortest completing only 15 months. Constituted on 2nd December 1989, the House was dissolved on 13th March, 1991, after a series of crises destabilized the V.P. Singh and Chandrashekhar governments, both of them minority regimes, supported from outside by the BJP, (CPI(M) and the Congress-I respectively. The life of the 11th Lok Sabha, which saw the arrival and departure of three successive Prime Ministers, was also cut short by the inherent dangers of all minority regimes which depend on the external support of a single party.

While A.B.Vajpayee resigned after being unable to cobble together a majority in the 11th Lok Sabha, H.D. Deve Gowda had to quit when Sita Ram Kesri suddenly withdrew the Congress -I support to his government. I.K. Gujral presided over a similar United Front government, minus Deve Gorda, but he also had to quit unceremoniously when Kesri employed the same trick to unseat him from his post. The 11th Lok Sabha had a life of 18 months- and-a-half only from 15 May 1996 to 4 December, 1997.

In the last one decade, the only exception to this rule was the 10th Lok Sabha which continued for its full five years term. It was a minority government too but its leadder P.V. Narasimha Rao was able to establish his majority in the Lok Sabha by successfully engineering defections from some smaller opposition parties. The 10th Lok Sabha was formed on 20th June, 1991 and was dissolved on 5th May, 1996.

**The Twelve Lok Sabhas**[27]

| Date of Constitution | Date | Dissolution |
|---|---|---|
| First Lok Sabha | 17.4.1952 | 24.4.1957 |
| Second Lok Sabha | 5.4.1957 | 31.3.1962 |
| Third Lok Sabha | 2.4.1962 | 3.3.1967 |
| Fourth Lok Sabha | 4.3.1967 | 27.12.1970 |
| Fifth Lok Sabha | 15.3.1971 | 18.1.1977 |
| Sixth Lok Sabha | 23.3.1977 | 22.8.1979 |
| Seventh Lok Sabha | 10.1.1980 | 31.12.1984 |
| Eighth Lok Sabha | 31.12.1984 | 27.11.1989 |
| Ninth Lok Sabha | 2.12.1989 | 13.3.1991 |
| Tenth Lok Sabha | 20.6.1991 | 10.5.1996 |
| Eleventh Lok Sabha | 15.5.1996 | 4.12.1997 |
| Twelfth Lok Sabha | 10.3.1998 | 26.4.1999 |

There has been a quantitative shift in the Indian political system from one-party dominance of the Nehru-Gandhi era to multi-party fragmentation of the last decade which has led to instability of Indian cabinets and the consequential shortening of the life span of the Lok Sabha. Bourgeois Parliamentarism is at its best when it succeeds in developing a stable two-party system. By its failure to do so, capitalist democracy in India is facing a crisis, plunging its political economy in turmoil. The next Lok Sabha election returned BJP-led alliance to power with A.B. Vajpayee as the Prime Minister. This government is likely to survive for a full term of five years.

## SUGGESTED READINGS

Alexandrovicz, C.H. *Constitutional Developments in India.*

Baran, Paul, *Political Economy of Growth.*

Bettleheim Charles, *India Independent.*

Desai, A.R., *Soial Background of Indian Nationalism.*

Dutt. R. Palme, *India Today.*

Gough and Sharma (ed), *Imperialism and Revolution in*

25. *The Times of India*, 27 April, 1999.
26. *Ibid*, p. 1.
27. *The Hindu*, 27 April, 1999, p. 8.

*South Asia.*
Karunakaran, K.P. *Democracy in India.*
Kothari Rajni, *Politics in India.*
Kochanak, Stanley A., *Business and Politics in India.*
Moore, Barrington Jr, *Social Origins of Dictatorship and Democracy.*
Morris-Jones, W. H, *the Government and Politics of India.*
Namboodiripad E.M.S, *Conflicts and Crisis.*
Nehru, Jawaharlal, *Discovery of India.*
Palmer, Norman D. *The Indian Political System.*
Rudolph and Rudolph, *In Pursuit of Lakshmi—The Political Economy of the Indian State.*
Selbourn, David, *An Eye to India.*
Shukla, V.N. *Constitution of India.*
Weiner, Myron, *Party-building in a Nation.*

**Journals**

1. *Economic and Political Weekly*
2. *India Today*
3. *Frontline*
4. *Outlook*
5. *Seminar*
6. *The Indian Journal of Political Science.*

# CHAPTER XXI
# Politics, Ideology and Governance

## Politics and Ideology

During the last two decades, Indian politics has become more directly oriented towards important issues of governance than to competing and conflicting motivations of ideology. The Congress party has now rejected the Nehruvian ideology of socialist pattern of society and planned economy and the United Progressive Alliance (UPA) led by the Congress leadership has whole heartedly accepted the liberal capitalist model of economic development for the country.

The preceding government of the National Democratic Alliance (NDA) led by the Bharatiya Janata Party also rejected its ideology based on Swadeshi and Hindutva in order to pursue the goal of India's economic development based on the western models of liberalisation and preference for private enterprise including a larger role for foreign capital. The Socialist groups gave up their 'socialistic' programmes and splintered into tiny fragments aligning either with the NDA or the UPA. The disappearance and disintegration of the Communist States including the Soviet Union has sobered the Indian Left resulting in a tactical alliance between the Congress-led UPA government and the Communist parties in Indian Parliament. The West Bengal Chief Minister, who leads a CPM-led government openly invites outside Indian and foreign capital for the development of his state.

Lal Krishna Advani told the Bharatiya Janata Party's national executive on 18 September, 2005, "In a democratic, multiparty polity, an ideologically driven party like the BJP has to function in a manner that enables it ... to reach the large sections of the people outside the layers of all ideology."

Prime Minister Manmohan Singh told the 40th Indian Labour Conference that appropriate and relevant labour laws are in the interests of labour and in the interests of the nation as a whole. Trade unions should, therefore, give up their old ideological approach based on class antagonism. The Communist Chief Minister of West Bengal spoke at a seminar in Kerala, "Why should we oppose foreign companies if they bring in jobs? Why should we oppose shopping malls from MNCs if they provide employment to our jobless youth." He thus pleaded for a non-ideological approach to the role of foreign capital in contributing to India's economic development. Referring to the views of these leaders, Vidya Subramaniam rightly concludes:

> "Three leaders from three different political formations. Yet, a common thread runs through the thoughts of Manmohan Singh, Lal Krishna Advani and Buddhadeb Bhattacharjee. It cannot be ideology that bonds Centrist Singh, Hindutva Advani and Communist Bhattacharjee. What is evident here is quite the opposite—a certain impatience with ideology, an urge to break free of dogma and rigid party politics and move with the times. Singh and Bhattacharjee run governments whereas Advani was in government until May 2004."[1]

This shared outlook emphasises the derive for economic reforms, integration with the world and dilution of ideology. It also signals the rightward shift of governance. It moves towards a consensus for market-centred pragmatism.

As cabinet minister in NDA government, Advani advocated the separation of governance from ideology. He said that large areas of governance have no connection with any

1. (Seminar, January 2006, p. 52)

ideology. Good governance is possible only when administrative issues are depoliticised and de-ideologised. Yet he contradicted himself when he exulted in Narendra Modi's electoral victory in Gujarat saying that it signified that "the ideology of cultural nationalism propagated by the BJP will find wide-scale applicability all over India."

The BJP returned to the good governance theme for the assembly elections in November 2003. However, after BJP's defeat of the 'India Shining' campaign in the Lok Sabha elections of 2004, Advani himself conceded the futility of separating governance and ideology. He told the BJP's National Council meeting on 6 April 2005:

> "No single reason was responsible for our electoral setback. However, ... one of the important reasons ... is this — We must continually nurse our own ideological and organisational constituency. Just as every MP or MLA has to nurse his constituency well in order to be able to get re-elected, every political party has to nurse its core constituency of ideological supporters and organisational workers in order to be able to win a renewed mandate. During the NDA government's six years in office, we focused so much on issues of development and governance that we somehow neglected ... those who support us and work for us because of our ideology."[2]

**Ideology and Governance**

When the UPA came to power, Prime Minister Manmohan Singh also became a convert to the principle of separation between governance and ideology. Sonia Gandhi as head of the Congress party would focus on ideology and political issues while he would deal with the reformist and pragmatic agenda of governance and economic development. This division of labour implied that Central Government would concentrate on administration, the party executive would be separately concerned with electoral mobilization.

Meanwhile, Advani underwent another change in his perspective when he praised Mohammad Ali Jinnah as a secular leader. The RSS leadership demonised Advani but he advised the BJP to reach out to those outside "The layers of all ideology." Though Advani had been the intolerant face of Hindutva, he now turned towards a more inclusive concept of nationalism. Vidya Subrahmaniam emphasizes an important point:

> "Overnight, the BJP chief transformed from respected party leader to villain and betrayer. However, the reaction of party and parivar appeared to have only further convinced Advani that the way forward lay in moving away from ideology. That the BJP's allies swung to his support bears out this reasoning Advani would be acceptable as prime minister for the precise reason that he would be unacceptable to the parivar. A similar mismatch was Atal Behari Vajpayee's winning card".[3]

Advani's new assessment of Jinnah as a 'secularist' resulted in his isolation from the R.S.S. and V.H.P. (Vishwa Hindu Parishad) ideologues of Hindutva. However, it made Advani as the epitome of moderation and an advocate of inclusion. He criticized the role of the R.S.S. functionaries in trying to control the BJP policies. In doing this, he was moved by the needs of governance arguing for the subordination of its ideology. For this, he was obliged to give up the highest elected office of his party in December, 2005.

But the new pragmatism was not confined to the congress and BJP leadership alone. When the Narsimha Rao–Manmohan Singh team initiated the economic reforms in 1990s, they were fully backed by the BJP as well. However, the Indian Left continually opposed these policies at that time. This situation has considerably changed now. Today we find

2. Quoted in Seminar, January 2006, p. 53
3. (Seminar, January 2006, p. 54)

Bhattacharjee, the Communist Chief Minister of West Bengal, speaking the language of market-friendly economic reform. After his visit to Singapore, he exhorted Bengal to 'reform or perish' and accept the policies of liberalization and globalization. He promised strike-free environment to the Information technology, welcomed private capital initiative for the modernisation of the Kolkata airport and even invited foreign investments for speeding up the process of industrialization in West Bengal.

Despite this exuberant display of pragmatism, "the divide between government and ideology/politics remains a problematic one". This makes easy theorising a problematic one. Vidya Subramaniam points out:

> "Whatever the compulsions of governance government and party are not mutually exclusive. ... Those in government draw their mandates from and have to discharge their duty to the party. Government policy is shaped by party manifesto and is expected to factor in political feedback; and it is in populist mode that prime ministers and chief ministers seek votes. ... To argue for separation of governance and politics is to liberate the former from accountability and to undermine the independent nature of government and party."[4]

Thus, Manmohan Singh's policy of governance must be in tune with the ideology and politics of the Congress party led by Sonia Gandhi. Advani's conversion to moderation does not imply the rejection of the BJP's Hindutva vision. Bhattacharjee is subject to the authority of the CPM's politibureau and must practise his new-found love for economic reforms under its directions. When Jyoti Basu was invited by the National Front to become India's Prime Minister, the CPM's politibureau did not permit him to accept the post. The UPA government based on external support of the Left cannot separate the issues of governance from the impact of ideology and party polities.

4. Seminar, January, 2006, pp. 54-55.

**TABLE 1**

**Lok Sabha Elections of 1999 and 2004**

**Total Seat = 537**

**Vote by Party and Alliance in 1999**

| | Seats Contested | Seats Won | % of Vote |
|---|---|---|---|
| 1. **BJP and Allies** | 597 | 299 | 40.8 |
| 2. BJP | 340 | 182 | 23.7 |
| 3. Telugu Desam | 34 | 29 | |
| 4. Janata Dal (U) | 61 | 20 | |
| 5. Shiv Sena | 63 | 15 | |
| 6. DMK | 19 | 12 | |
| 7. Others | 80 | 41 | |
| 8. **Congress and Allies** | 584 | 134 | 34.1 |
| 9. Congress | 453 | 112 | 28.4 |
| 10. AIDMK | 29 | 10 | |
| 11. RJD | 60 | 7 | |
| 12. Others | 42 | 5 | |
| 13. CPM | 72 | 32 | |
| 14. CPI | 54 | 4 | |
| 15. BSP | 224 | 14 | |
| 16. S.P. | 151 | 26 | |
| 17. NCP | 30 | 6 | |
| 18. Others | | 22 | |

**TABLE 2**

**National Election Result – May 2004**

**Total Seat = 543**

| Party | Seats Contested | Seats Won | No. of Votes | % of Votes |
|---|---|---|---|---|
| Congress | 417 | 145 | 103408949 | 26.53% |
| BJP | 364 | 138 | 86371561 | 22.16% |
| CPM | 69 | 43 | 22070614 | 5.66% |
| BSP | 435 | 19 | 20765229 | 5.33% |
| SP | 237 | 36 | 16824072 | 4.32% |
| Telugu Desam | 33 | 5 | 11844811 | 3.04% |
| Rashtriya Janata Dal | 42 | 24 | 9384147 | 2.41% |
| Janata Dal (U) | 73 | 8 | 9144963 | 2.35% |
| AIDMK | 33 | 0 | 8547014 | 2.19% |
| Trinamool Congress | 33 | 2 | 8071867 | 2.07% |
| DMK | 16 | 16 | 7064393 | 1.81% |
| Shiv Sena | 56 | 12 | 7056255 | 1.81% |
| NCP | 32 | 9 | 7023175 | 1.80% |
| Janata Dal (S) | 43 | 3 | 5732296 | 1.47% |
| CPI | 34 | 10 | 5484111 | 1.41% |
| Biju Janata Dal | 12 | 11 | 5082849 | 1.30% |
| Akali Dal | 10 | 8 | 3506681 | 0.90% |
| Lok Jan Shakti | 40 | 4 | 2771427 | 0.71% |

| Party | Seats Contested | Seats Won | No. of Votes | % of Votes |
|---|---|---|---|---|
| R.L.D. | 32 | 3 | 2463607 | 0.63% |
| Telangana R.S. | 22 | 5 | 2441405 | 0.63% |
| PMK | 6 | 6 | 2169020 | 0.56% |
| AGP | 12 | 2 | 2069600 | 0.53% |
| Jharkhand Mukti Morcha | 9 | 5 | 1846843 | 0.47% |
| R.S.P. | 6 | 3 | 1689794 | 0.43% |
| Other Parties | — | 21 | — | — |
| Independents | — | 18 | — | — |

TABLE 3

**Votes and Seats of Major Parties in 2004 elections As Compared with those won in 1999 elections**

| Party | Votes | Change | Seats | Change |
|---|---|---|---|---|
| Congress | 103,405,272 | –1.6 | 145 | +32 |
| BJP | 85,866,593 | –1.5 | 138 | –44 |
| CPM | 22,061,677 | +0.3 | 43 | +11 |
| CPI | 5,434,738 | –0.1 | 10 | +6 |
| DMK | 7,064,393 | +0.1 | 16 | +4 |
| JD (U) | 9,924,209 | –0.5 | 8 | –11 |
| NCP | 6,915,740 | –0.5 | 9 | +1 |
| RJD | 9.613,302 | –0.5 | 21 | +12 |
| BSP | 20,713,468 | +1.1 | 19 | +5 |
| BJD | 5,084,428 | +0.1 | 11 | +1 |
| Trinamool Congress | 8,647,771 | –0.5 | 2 | –8 |
| S.P | 16,645,356 | +0.5 | 36 | +10 |
| Akali Dal | 3,506,681 | +0.2 | 8 | +6 |
| Shiv Sena | 7,056,075 | +0.2 | 12 | –8 |
| Telugu Desam | 11,844,811 | –0.6 | 5 | –24 |

The three tables will help us in analysing the transition which is taking place in the evolution of the Indian political system. It shows the eclipse of the dominant mono-party system which characterized the functioning of the post-colonial India from 1947 to 1977. The next three decades represent a chaotic development of a plethora of regional and caste-based political parties which now align either with the Bharatya Janata Party or the Indian National Congress to form a coalition government at the centre. The BJP-led coalition of about 20 political groups ruled India from 1998 to 2004. Since then a Congress-led UPA government in ruling the country, assisted by a similar number of small regional parties plus outside support of the Left Front.

**Victory of a Congress-led Coalition**

The victory of the United Progressive Alliance led by the Congress in the 2004 general elections was quite astonishing. It appears that Sonia Gandhi's leadership has re-established the primacy of the Nehru-Gandhi family in running the political affairs of the country. Like Indira Gandhi in 1971-77 and Rajiv Gandhi in 1984-89, she too holds the key to power in the Indian polity. Rahul Gandhi has become a member of the Lok Sabha and is being groomed for potential leadership of the nation. Indira Gandhi had similarly tried to groom, first Sanjay and then Rajiv to succeed her. Like Indira, Sonia too says that the Congress stands for the 'common man' — (*Aam Admi*).

In 1991, Sonia had been the first choice of the congress working committee for the top job in the government and the party but she declined the offer. She agreed to lead the Congress seven years later when the party was in decline. In 1999, after the fall of the BJP government, she faced a serious challeng to her leadership on account of her Italian origin. Sharad Pawar, the former leader of the Congress in Lok Sabha, led the attack. The BJP questioned her foreign origin as well as her Roman Catholic religious affiliation.

In 1999, Sonia led her party to second place in Parliament. But in 2004, she led the Congress-led coalition to victory. Her foreign origin was no longer a serious issue. When she declined the Prime Minister's post, her gesture was even more appreciated. She proposed Man Mohan Singh's name for the Prime Minister's job. Sonia is the head of her party as well as the chairperson of the UPA in Parliament. She is viewed by critics as the wielder of real state power in the Indian Republic.

Yet this is not the whole truth. The Congress has only 145 members in the Lok Sabha with a total membership of 543. The BJP has 138 members which is just seven seats less. Yogendra Yadav points out that the allies of the Congress scored much more impressive gains and helped the senior partner to win 54 seats in their dominant regions.[4] The long period of

4. *Economic and Political Weekly*, December 18, 2004, pp. 5583–98.

Congress dominance is now a thing of the past. Its share of popular votes in 2004 elections has declined to just 26.53 per cent. Its proportion of seats in the Lok Sabha in just 26.7 per cent. This is quite in contrast with Indira Gandhi's achievement in 1971 when the Congress won 350 seats in a house of 520. Rajiv got even a larger majority in 1984.

The weak position of Sonia-led Congress in quite evident, if we consider large regions across the country. Both Congress and BJP have at present only marginal support in the states of Uttar Pradesh, Bihar and West Bengal. Except Narsimbha Rao (1991–96) and Atal Bahari Vajpayee (1999–2004), no other Prime Minister has ruled India without his party controlling Uttar Pradesh.

The Congress lost Tamil Nadu in 1962 and has failed to win power therefor more than four decades. The Congress has been unable to win any election in West Bengal since 1977. It has been out of power in UP and Bihar since 1989. It lost Gujarat in 1985 and has been unable to regain power there. In Maharashtra, the Congress shares power with NCP. It has lost power to BJP in Rajasthan, Madhya Pradesh, Chhattisgarh and Jharkhand recently. Except Andhra Pradesh, the Congress is weaker in other southern states at present.

The allies who share power in the Congress-led coalition have joined the UPA for a simple reason If they remain divided, they cannot wield any power. Unity enables them to exercise the power of governance. Mahesh Rangarajan says:

> "Congress has had to stoop to conquer. In the process, it has paid a price: many regional satraps have got a share of power. The new era of coalition government under Congress leadership is a product of strategic weakness and tactical flexibility. ... Nevertheless, the victory is impressive. Congress has worked out agreements with some of the very forces that were once implacably opposed to it lenuous set of alliances underpins the present UPA government. Most prominently, the 61 member Left Front led by the Communist Party of India (Marixst), the world's most successful Marxist party in any democracy, has extended support even though virtually all its PMs fought and defeated Congress candidates at the hustings."[5]

The present case is different from the situation in 1969–71, when the CPI was the key ally of Indira-led Congress but did not have substantial mass following. Indira Gandhi jailed several leftist and regionalist leaders during the Emergency (1975–77). But now many former anti-Congress socialists like Ram Vilas Paswan are backing Sonia-led UPA. In 1969–71 and 1991–93 Congress Prime Ministers ruled without having a majority in Parliament but they never thought of sharing power with other parties. As recently as 1999, even Sonia Gandhi had dismissed all talk of the Congress forming a Third or Fourth front with like-minded parties and possible allies in governance. Sita Ram Kesari had brought about the downfall of the United Front governments led H.D. Deve Gowda and Inder Kumar Gujral.

### Changes in Electoral Strategy

After a long period of sitting in opposition, the Congress decided to rework its electoral strategy. The Congress and Nationalist Congress Party were adversaries in the 1999 state election in Maharashtra. Yet both formed a stable government which lasted for five years. In 2000 the Congress entered into a coalition with RJD in Bihar and both the parties gained substantially in the subsequent Lok Sabha election of 2004 as a result of this alliance.

In 1984 Indira Gandhi toppled a legally elected government in Jammu and Kashmir. Sonia Gandhi adopted a different strategy in 2002 by sharing power with the regional People's Democratic Party and both these parties could have their chief minister by rotation. The Congress defeat in three states of Rajasthan, Madhya Pradesh and Chhattisgarh in December 2003, persuaded the congress leadership to revise its future strategy in the

5. *Economic and Political Weekly*, August 6-12, 2005, Vol. XI, No. 32, p. 3599.

light of the Shimla resolution of July 2003 that permitted sharing of power with allies.

Further, a series of state level alliances helped the Congress party to emerge out of its political isolation. Six years of the BJP-led government in New Delhi created a need for tactical cooperation between Congress and the Leftist parties. In this scenario, the Left bloc opted for extending support to the UPA government without joining it. Congress also accepted DMK as its ally, though this party had earlier joined the NDA government also.

Sonia Gandhi has tried to secure the kind of social support which Indira Gandhi enjoyed in 1980. Like India, she has portrayed herself as the protector of *subaltern* groups such as dalits, adivasis and Muslims. In 2004 election too, Congress and its allies received the support of a majority of these underprivileged groups. Two major dalit-led groups entered into pre-poll pacts with Congress in Maharashtra and Bihar.

The Bahujan Samaj Party who not an electoral ally but its leader Mayavati was among the first to extend her support once the results were declared. Religious minorities, like dalits and adivasis, are now returning to their traditional political loyalty towards the Congress though gradually. BJP's strident campaign against Sonia's foreign origin has helped her in gaining the support of the religious minorities as well as subordinate groups like lower castes and underprivileged women.

The Gujarat massacres of Muslims in 2002 resulted in coming together of all anti-Hindutva forces around the secularist banner. It also helped in the consolidation of dalits and other backward classes around the Congress and its other political allies in north Indian states. The new allies of Congress now compensated for its own halting and lukewarm policy in championing the cause of the downtrodden classes. The Congress also benefited from the widespread hostility to the NDA government, which was viewed as an upper-caste oriented and city-central political formation by a large section of the electorate. The disgruntled elements did not necessarily vote for the Congress but they brought down the BJP-led regime from power by alienating a section of the middle class which had supported it earlier.

However, the Congress party has been unable to restore the traditional 'coalition of extremes' under which Brahmins and some other upper castes had united with dalits, adivasis and Muslims to vote this party into power in several general elections after independence. In 2004, the lower classes did not support congress to that extent. The BJP-led NDA retained a lead of 20 per cent among high-caste voters. However, caste and class are not exactly identical. It is still a fact that higher social status is often a factor in achieving higher education, access to wealth and political power.

As Yogendra Yadav points out, the support of those peasant castes and social classes whose political assertion has played such an important role in Indian politics since 1989, has not necessarily benefited the Congress party.[6] The voters turned away from the N.D.A. but they preferred parties like the Samajvadi party to the Congress. The success, structure and functioning of the UPA government would depend on how far it is able to fulfil its mandate.

**India's Coalition Experience**

The first true coalition government at the centre took office only in 1998. Earlier, the Janata Party government formed in 1977 was also a art of coalition disguised as 'merger' which could not obliterate the separate identity of the constituent groups. Morarji Desai also accepted Akali Dal and Congress for Democracy, led by Jag Jeevan Ram, as his allies. However the Janata Party had a majority of its own.

In 1989, V.P. Singh's National Front evolved a new concept of forming a minority government with outside support from the BJP and the Leftist parties which were ideologically opposed to each other. This experiment was only short-lived. In 1998, A.B. Vajpayee was more successful in forming a coalition

6. *Economic and Political Weekly*, August 21, 1999, pp. 2393–99; *Seminar* No. 526, pp. 64-70.

government based on a common minimum programme. At that time, his alliance had only 253 seats in Lok Sabha falling short of majority by 20 seats. But he could get external support from Telugu Desam Party of Andhra Pradesh to establish his majority in Parliament.

The present UPA regime will have to learn and unlearn from the experiences of the outgoing NDA regime. The older Congress-dominated polity that emerged from the first general elections of 1952 came to an end in 1989. Yogendra Yadav has argued that the new system crystallised only in 1991. He is right as there was a vestige of an anti-Congress front that displaced Rajiv's party from power in 1989. Yet the same election also marked a new low for Congress from which it has failed to recover despite befriending its former ideological opponents, that was inconceivable in the past.

Since then, no political party has secured an absolute majority in the Lok Sabha to form a government on its own. But from around 1999, as Wallace and Roy rightly suggest, "a bimodal mode of power began to take shape with the BJP and the Congress heading rival fronts," About a quarter of a voters is still outside the fold of the two alliances. Some parties, like DMK, may shift allegiance between one poll and another. Yet the two fronts are now almost permanent entities.

According to Yogendra Yadav, the general election of 2004 marked a 'moment of closure' for the broadening of democratic opportunities that had become apparent at the base of the polity during the preceding fifteen years. The assertion by dalits and adivasis, higher voting in elections in north India, tactical voting by religious minorities, a larger presence of women in polities, the assertion of regional and sub-regional groups were the features of the change.

Society was polarised in north India between the supporters of Hindutva and the similarists, though this had limits in view of the social and regional heterogeneity of the country. The movements ran into their limits though after leaving strong marks on the body politic. No subsequent government was able to discard V.P. Singh's implementation of the Mandal Commission Report regarding reservation of 27% posts to the backward classes in the central government. Despite counter-mobilization that set clear limits to the BJP-sponsored Hindutva agenda, these are visible signs of a permanent consolidation of a Hindu vote bank as a significant social force in Indian politics.[7]

**Engagement with Marginalized Social Groups**

It has been argued that the opportunities for empowerment that opened up in the Indian political system in the late 1980s have now been foreclosed. A process of containment has set in. Caste and region based mobilization is now disconnected with the wider politics of socio-economic justice. What 2004 election marks is less 'a moment of closure' than a revival of closer engagement with marginal social groups.

Let us look at the nature of Congress history in this connection. Mahatma Gandhi negotiated with B.R. Ambedkar to create a system of joint electorates where only members of the 'depressed classes' could contest elections. In a similar view, Nehru implemented the formation of linguistic states despite his earlier antipathy to the scheme. Similarly, Indira Gandhi adopted parts of the Communist Party's economic programme and also inducted key members of the religious minorities and lower castes into powerful positions.[8] Congress policy towards popular movements has been that of containment coupled by an assertion of its leadership role. This was true of debit struggles in north India as well as tribal struggles in central India.

However, in contrast to the past, the Congress capacity to assimilate smaller political entities is limited. Smaller groups now defy easy co-optation. Congress absorbed anti-caste rebels in Maharashtra making the Ambedkarite Republican Party dysfunctional

7. Subas Palshikar 'Majoritarian Middle Ground', *Economic and Political Weekly,* December 18, pp. 5426-30.
8. Inder Malhotra: *Indira Gandhi–A personal and Political Biography,* London, 1989, pp. 123-29.

there. But it has failed to contain the Bahujan Samajvadi Party's increasing popular support in Uttar Pradesh at present. Congress also succeeded in coopting tribal leaders like Jaipal Singh and Sibhu Soren in Jharkhand. However, it has now limited capacity to absorb tribal political leaders, least in the north-eartern states. Ravinder Kumar says that even before independence, the Congress had a tenuous social base among the underprivileged but tilled towards propertied groups. However, the working of the dynamics of democracy has changed the Congress perspective during the last fifteen years. Even then, there is no question of Congress absorbing the regional lower caste-led outfits with which it has forged electoral alliances in Uttar Pradesh, Bihar or Jharkhand.

**Congress Record of Destabilizing State Governments**

The UPA government now must break with the Congress party's long record of destabilizing state governments. This dates back to the dismissal of the first elected Communist government of E.M.S. Namboodiripad in 1959, after which Congress forged an alliance with the Muslim League. Both Indira Gandhi and Rajiv Gandhi dismissed several state governments on the ground that the general elections had deprived them of their mandate. In view of the viability of other of the two major national parties to aspire to power in several key states, it is also difficult for them now to dislodge popularly elected state governments on grounds of constitutional breakdown or an emergency.

The NPA government repeatedly tried to dismiss the Bihar government but failed to do so. Indira Gandhi had made maximum use of the Article 356 to distabilize several state governments. But this is now an impossible task for Manmohan Singh. Paul Brass had highlighted this in *The Politics of India since Independence* and was centrally concerned with dynamic of Congress-Controlled Union government and opposition-ruled states. Now it is not only the Congress but the time have also changed. States possess greater freedom to exist and work in a system which is more federal in substance now.

**More Critical Attitude to Hindutva**

Congress has now adopted a more critical attitude towards the Sangh parivar ideology of Hindutva. This will create more spaces for new types of engagement across the communal divide. Sonia Gandhi's leadership has also seen the party to return to a hardline approach against communal mobilization. The opportunity to cooperate also comes because public opinion was polarised during the NDA rule.

Sonia Gandhi since 1998 has ended the Congress policy of what was known as 'soft' Hindutva. In the past, Congress has been a loosely defined middle-of-the-road political party rather than a cadre-based and ideologically strong organisation. The 'soft Hindutva' stance emerged during the last period of Indira Gandhi's rule. There was an element of anti-minority sentiment in Indira Gandhi's handling of politics in the states of Jammu and Kashmir and Punjab. As Jaffrelot says, "this erosion of secularism was not new but was without precedent in its scale."[9]

This appeasement of Hindutva continued till the 1990s though this co-existed with appeasement of Muslim communalism. The example was the Shah Bano case in 1986 when Rajiv Gandhi enacted a highly gender-biased law to appease conservative Muslims. There no doubt that this policy was not approved by all sections of Congress.

Congress went on ignoring the implementation of the Mandal Commission Report which was submitted in 1980. The reason was that the Congress did not want to politicise caste cleavages among Hindus and followed an opportunist policy of playing on majority fears of Khalistani and Pakistani-Kashmiri terrorism. This phase ended only in the late 1990s.

The consolidation of the BJP as nucleus of a ruling coalition forced Congress to change its strategy and tactics. Its support to the united Front government was the prelude to a realignment of forces. In her first campaign speech in 1999 as Congress president, Sonia

9. Christophe Jaffrelot: *The Hindu Nationalist Movement and Indian Politics*, Penguin, Delhi, 1996, pp. 330-37.

Gandhi rejected the old accusation that the RSS provided the ideological background for Mahatma Gandhi's murder.

It should be noted that when the results of the 1999 election were being announced, Harkishen Singh Surjeet, the general secretary of the Communist Party (Marxist) mentioned the possibility of external, issue-based support for a Congress-led government. Laloo Prasad Yadav, possibly the biggest political beneficiary of Mandal-based mobilisation also extended his support to Congress. This indicated that there was an important shift in the Congress policy towards Hindutva. It appeared that it was now determined to give battle to the rising pro-Hindutva forces.

However, this confrontationist attitude towards the pro-Hindutva forces was not followed with consistency. In the state assembly elections in Gujarat in 2002, held in the shadow of some of the worst communal massacres of Muslims in the history of 'secular' India, the Congress went out of its way to minimise the significance of those issues which affected the minority community. As Mani Shankar Aiyar recently admitted with rare honesty, this strategy was not only highly unprincipled but proved evenbrally quite unsuccessful.[10]

## The Issue of Socio-Economic Justice

The issues of soft Hindutva and lower caste and adivasi assertion are interlinked as two rival notions in Congress strategy. In the past, when Bharatiya Jan Songh was marginal force, MP Chief Minister Ravi Shankar Shukla took action against missionaries in the adivasi areas. In UP, Chief Minister C.B. Gupta marginalised Urdu, which was welcomed by all pro-Hindu organisations.

At that time, the Congress just made informal and tactical arrangements with peasant and lower caste rebels against the old order. Socio-cultural charges in north and central India now have made it difficult for the Congress to ignore newly assertive social groups. Mean while, RSS and BJP have also infiltrated peasant and adivasi groups and tried to indoctrinate them. This indicates that the wider issue of social and economic justice will figure more prominently in political debate in the coming years.

There are distinct reasons why socio-economic changes did not occur in the late 1980s and 1990s despite noisy movements clamouring for them. One was the relative fuzziness of several newly empowered groups that led them to issues beyond specific symbolic ones. Many dalit and back-word class based parties demanded more reservations in the government sector. Once this was achieved and private sector reservation did not make much head way, they are agitating for more jobs.

However, these OBCs, dalits and adivasis are opposing another kind of reservation, which is based on gender. They are opposing one-third reservation the women in legislatures, in education and in employment. Pratap Bhanu Mehta has argued that lower-caste uprisings are not directed against the caste system as such but only against what they visualize as the special privilages of the upper caste gentry.[11]

P. Sainath in his articles in the *Hindu* has drawn attention to widespread distress of the peasantry in Andhra Pradesh and other states. The UPA government must take into account the critiques of the developmental models that obstructed all-round growth. Much of the green revolution belt in Andhra Pradesh, Punjab and Maharashtra has now seen distress and indebteness even among the rich peasants. The UPA government must implement a new model of rural financing and better safety nets for those who earn their living by working on land. It must pass a radical land reform law as well.

## Development-Related Issues

Congress is relatively better placed to engage with several of the development-related problems than its opponent, the BJP. There is no previous example of industrializing a large country like India by democratic methods. Yet the progress so far is in the right direction.

10. Mani Shankar Aiyar: *Confessions of a Sealar Fundamentalist,* Penguin, Delhi, 2004, p. 15.
11. Bhanu Pratap Mehta: *The Burden of Democracy,* Penguin, Delhi, 2003, pp. 75-77.
12. Sudha Pai: *Dalits and the Unfinished Social Revolution,* Sage, Delhi, 2002.

Some serious achievements of the newly assertive movements are sometimes overlooked. As Sudha Pai says, the Bahujan Samaj Party has taken initiatives to widen land reboms in UP and also given sanitation facilities to underprivileged sections.[12] West Bengal has shown how local bodies can improve the governance of forest resources to enable poor people to share forest products.[13]

It is important to emphasize that Congress as the centrist social force has sometimes tried unsuccessfully to tame the newly assertive groups. As part of the UPA, the centrist and the leftist forces can accelerate the process of pro-people economic development. The logic of forming the UPA was to lock the BJP out of power. The UPA emphasises the human dimension of liberalisation so that the benefits of economic development may reach the sections who did not gain from the reforms introduced by Manmohan Singh as finance minister from 1991 to 1996.

The internal rifts within the UPA are evident in the debates over the Employment Guarantee Act. Neo-monetarists suggest the possible outlay of over 3,00,000 million rupees a year but the leftists look to its benefits to the poor. The expansion of rural credit is demanded by those with a base among agriculturists but is opposed as a populist diversion by those who are committed to fiscal reform.

In a society which is still predominantly agrarian with its two-third labour force engaged in cultivation, agriculture cannot be ignored. The last decade saw greater disparity between urban and rural incomes and a slow-down in job creation in both farm and factory. In 155 out of 600 districts, left-wing extremist violence cannot be delinked from the phenmenon of rural unemployment and under-employment. India may have a fourth of the world's software engineers but it also has one of three desperately poor people in the world.

The UPA government has to fulfil its promise to the people. But this has been made difficult by the mood of fiscal rectitude which is also shared by many key economic decision-makers in the Congress party. On the other hand, there is great pressure from its Leftist and regional allies to increase expenditure on people's welfare. The solution is possible by balancing these requirements and by providing more incentives for growth in agriculture and ensuring an end to growing unemployment by creating more jobs. Mahesh Rangarajan remarks:

> "The need for balance has become more pronounced in the post-reform era when the level of disparity in a society already typified by hierarchy and privilege has to all evidence, increased very markedly. This is clear in regional terms, with the south and the west making the most significant gains in investment and much of north India lagging far behind. This is even sharper in social indicators."[14]

The success of the UPA government will depend on its capacity to carry out its program of rapid economic development which should also lead to social and economic justice by uplifting the condition of the masses.

**Managing the UPA Coalition**

The United Progressive Alliance government has completed one year and eight months and like the preceding N.A.D. government, may last for five years completing its full term. The relatively smooth induction of the 14-party UPA cabinet with many experienced ministers, generated political confidence. The National Common Minimum Programme pledged to strengthen secularism and work for economic growth with a human face. Although a minority coalition government, the Congress got a disproportionately large share in the UPA ministry. This has provided greater stability to the new regime as compared to the outgoing BJP-led government.

The Left Front's promise to extend outside support to the UPA coalition over a full parliamentary term has further stabilised the Congress-led government. Yet this coalition

13. K. Sivaramakrishnan: "Co-managed Forests in West Bengal" *Journal of Sustainable Forestry,* 7 (1998), pp. 23-51.
14. Mahesh Pangarajan: *Economic and Political Review,* "Polity in Transition" August 6, 2005, p. 3604.

regime faces grave political challenges. The first is the complexity of the NCMP's agenda such as expanding the gains of liberalisation to underprivileged groups. Secondly, conflicts of interest within the coalition threaten to derail its plans. The capacity of the UPA to preserve political unity and act on its agenda depends on the ability of its leaders to manage the coalition and achieve proper balance between conflicting interests.

How well is the Congress, the fulcrum of the UPA, qualified to manage the problems that a coalition regime at the centre necessarily has to resolve? Has the Congress leadership, which resisted the necessity of federal coalition politics till recently, changed its outlook? Both Sonia and Manmohan Singh talked about the party's ambition to reclaim its majority status in Parliament in a near future during its Hyderabad Session held in January 2006. An analytical review of the UPA's electoral strategies and economic politics of past 18 months reveals the risks that we ahead if the Congress and its allies are unable to cooperate in managing their coalition.

Has the Congress developed further trust among its allies? Has it viewed the UPA as a durable coalition strategy to challenge the BJP-led alliance in future? Or, is it a make-shift arrangement based on expediency? The Congress manoeuvres over the last 18 months indicate the latter and show its desire of regaining its political ascendancy.

These manoeuvres began in June 2004 when it refused to accept Samajvadi party as a part of its coalition though it announced its support to the UPA immediately after the elections. Congress also excluded the SP from the drafting of NCMP. Since then, Congress is following a hostile policy towards Mulayam Singh's government in Uttar Pradesh. Though Mayawati's BSP also extended its support to the UPA after elections, she is also being treated as a political ontorchable by the Congress party. This hostility towards both SP and BSP is due to the Congress party's ambition to regain majority support in Uttar Pradesh, where it has been reduced to a marginalised group of 9 MPs. But this is not the proper way to treat its allies.

However, Sonia Gandhi's decision to refuse the P.M.'s post made it earlier for the NCP to overlook its earlier opposition to her prime ministerial candidacy. Sharad Pawar has got the agricultural portfolio and there is almost complete harmony between Congress and NCP at present. The DMK, despite its conflicts with the Congress leadership in the past, is a satiated group in the UPA in terms of the cabinet posts and a promise to repeal the POTA and to grant Tamil, the status of a classical language.

Congress rewarded Laloo Prasad with the coveted Railway ministry but its alliance with Ram Vilas Paswan's Lok Jan Shakti in the first Bihar election antagonised the RJD, though it rectified its error in the next Bihar election by aligning with Laloo's RJD. However, the role of Buta Singh as Bihar's Governor has created loss of face to the UPA government. The fact that Lok Jan Shakti and Rashtriya Janata Dal fight against each other in Bihar creates a difficult situation for the Congress leadership at the centre.

In Jharkhand, the Congress party unilaterally decided to enter into an alliance with the Jharkhand Mukti Morcha without consulting either the Left Front or the RJD. This proved to be a blunder. The ensuring 'friendly contests' between UPA's partners allowed an unpopular BJP to win this election. Sanjay Ruperelia concludes:

> "The Congress apposite for reclaiming a foohold in involant northern states where it is weak is understandable. Yet it is one thing for the Congress to secure greater representation in various states and another to assume its right to dominate. Moreover, seeking to recover its position by playing off its formal allies has proven disastrous. State based parties increasingly wish to exercise power at the centre as well as the regions. The old formula of 'you can run the centre, let us control the state' is no longer possible in an era of ascendant regional power. Yet a new principle is yet to be found. Hence, the imperative

that faces the UPA — to devise a durable coalition strategy based on genuine power-sharing between the Congress and its state-based partners, and amongst them in turn. Without such a plan, relations between the main constituent parties will remain precarious, with self-destructive consequences."[15]

**Mechanisms of Coalition Decision-Making**

A coalition requires that party leaders make binding decisions by adjudicating competing demands. In theory, the cabinet is the place where these functions have to be performed. Effective cabinet functioning also requires the full participation of its constituents, the building of consensus over policy issues and self-imposed discipline to implement collective decisions. Disciplined single-party governments can enforce unity through whips. Forging unity in multi-party coalition cabinets is more difficult. The loyalties of ministers are diverse. This makes enforcement of even agreed policies difficult.

The saving grace is that the larger party distributes cabinet posts among its allies and formulates official consensus to retain their confidence in Parliament. However, the existence of external power centres that wield authority in a party or parties that provide critical outside support to the government, without joining the cabinet, complicates the Indian experience in coalition's functioning.

Let us consider the functioning of the UPA coalition in detail. First is the question of Manmohan's authority as Prime Minister and the degree of influence that Sonia Gandhi exercises on him as the party chairperson. The concern about the PMs authority is misplaced. As a top economist with technocratic ability and honesty, the PM enjoys growing respect in his party and also among the allies. His relationship with Sonia Gandhi reflects a division of labour which allows both to function effectively in their respective spheres.

In contrast, the far more difficult problem for the functioning of the UPA as a collective decision-making body concerns Congress-Left Front relations. The CPM was afraid that it would not be able to exercise sufficient control over economic policy by joining the cabinet. Its central committee therefore decided to extend outside support only to the UPA government. Other left parties followed CPM's example. In the beginning their commitment to the UPA seemed solid. The CPM had supported Congress through indirect electoral alliances in Andhra Pradesh and Tamil Nadu. The party permitted Som Nath Chatterjee to occupy the Speaker's post on the request of the UPA.

In return for the support, the Congress agreed to protect the existing pro-labour laws, to review the 2003 Electricity Act and to desist from privatising profit-making public sector enterprises, by including these commitments in the National Common Minimum Programme. Yet the possibility of conflict could not be ruled out. The first basic principle of the NCMP was to promote "social harmony and peace" by pledging rapid pro-poor development, higher public investment in education, health and infrastructure, and employment for the rural and urban poor.

Yet this agreement on the policy aims could not eliminate disagreement on the means—hard choices over fiscal policy and details of policy implementation NCMP's silence on these questions foreshadowed a potential opposition by the Left Front to the strategy and tactics pursued by the Congress-controlled economic ministries of the UPA government. Purnima Tripathi points out that the government's introduction of various economic measures created great dissatisfaction in the Left. The Planning Commission Chairman's decision to invite World Bank representatives to participate in consultative review committees of the Tenth Plan earned the anger of several Left economists forcing their dissolution. The interest rate out to the Employees Provident Fund also led to Left protest. The decision to raise the foreign direct investment (FDI) cap in

15. Sanjay Ruperalia: "Managing the United Progressive Alliance", Economic and Political Weekly, June 11-17, 2005, p. 2410.

the insurance, civil aviation and telecommunication sectors also displeased the left leaders.

Finance minister, Chidambaram, increased expenditure on social development items in the 2005 union budget. But he relied on over confident fiscal estimates which proved unrealistic. There is lack of consultation between the UPA ministries and the Left leaders on many schemes of social development which has led to frequent controversies between them According to a senior Left Front leader, the Congress "believes that this is not a coalition government but a government run by the Congress Party alone. They will have to come out of this mindset and internalise the coalition dharma, otherwise they will invite trouble for themselves."

Whatever the differences, the Left cannot afford to topple the UPA. The first imperative is to keep the BJP out of power. The LF's own pursuit of liberalisation in West Bengal also makes its radical declarations at the centre more problematic. Its current predicament forces a re-examination of the policy of outside support and whether participation in the UPA government would not have served the interests of the Left better. The Congress has effectively pursued its preferred economic reforms. This has changed the terms of power vis-a-vis the Left and have shown the importance of formal ministerial participation.

**Challenges of a Multi-Party Government**

Governing a diverse multi-party government involves numerous challenges. The inexperience of the Congress. has been a liability in this respect. Its on going conflict with the Left Front should not blind the Congress to larger political realities. The May 2004 verdict represented a protest against rising social inequalities. Failure to address these concerns will enable the Left to protest and undermine the credibility of the UPA government. Electoral fortunes of the Congress will depend on redressing the inequities of liberalisation, which was promised by the Congress manifesto before elections.

For these reasons, the constitution, status and functioning of the Coordination Committee is important. Does it meet regularly? Who can convene its meetings? How much can it influence policy-making of the level of government? It cannot dissolve policy differences. Yet it can soften hostile positions and lead to mutual accommodation. This would reduce making public appears to the NCMP. The UPA should avoid a replay of the United Front when "damaging public debate over the locus of authority slowed down policy decisions, depleted political trust and sapped the energies of government."[17]

As Manmohan said, "life is never free of contradictions ... we will have to find a practical way." (*The Hindu*, May 28, 2004). Politics requires skilled political judgement. The question is whether the Congress can fashion a larger political bargain to manage or transform the array of interests within the UPA. This requires greater willingness to share power better and govern more collectively. It should have a better planning for its future.

A crucial requirement for the Congress is to rebuild its organisational strength on the ground. Yet party-building in the states will necessitate its conflict with its political allies. Developing a powerful coonter-bloc against the BJP requires that the Congress must develop with its allies common political strategies that can mobilise the poor and distribute the gains of development more widely over the long term.

Failure to deliver on its promises, the appearance of drift and dissention from within, all of these constitute real political threats to the UPA. The dangers of complacency are real. The fortunes of the BJP appear diminished for the moment after its defeat in May 2004 elections. A return to militant Hindu nationalism may hasten its decline at the national level. However, it would be a mistake to underestimate the party's capacity to

16. Purnima S. Tripathi: "A Performance Deficit", *Frontline*, September 25, 2004.
17. Sanjay Ruparelia: "Managing the United Progressive Alliance", *Economic and Political Weekly*, August 11-17, 2005, p. 2411.

regroup. The popularity of Hindutva in certain sections of the electorate cannot be ignored, Moreover, as the NDA showed) the agendas for economic reform and Hindutva-oriented policies's can be pursued simultaneously. At state level, Modi has pursued a similar polity in Gujarat.

The national vote share for the BJP in 2004 was, at approximately 22% which was just 4% less than that of the Congress. This provides the BJP a basis for recovery. History shows the party's capability to oscillate between militant ethno-religious mobilisation for power and creating moderate political coalitions to implement economic reforms along the liberal capitalist model.

The unexpected electoral verdict of May 14, 2004 has provided a great opportunity to the United Progressive Alliance to restore the fabric of secularism, to extend benefits of economic growth to masses and secure a just peace in Kashmir. The achievement of these objectives will not be easy. The Congress must learn to manage the UPA coalition in such a way as to ensure maximum economic development and expansion of its benefits to underprivileged sections of the Indian society. That alone can guarantee the UPA a full term and possibly return to power in the next general election.

**Supreme Court on Assembly Dissolution**

The decision of the UPA government on dissolution of the Bihar state Assembly on the recommendation of the then Governor, Buta Singh, was declared unconstitutional by the Supreme court. The diametrically opposite views expressed by the supreme court judges in their reasoning were based on the land mark Supreme Court decisions in the Bommai case and the Rajasthan case.

The majority view, castigating governor Buta Singh and quashing the decision to dissolve the assembly, was by Chief Justice Y.K. Sabharwal, and supported by Justice B.N. Agarwal and Justice Ashok Bhan. The minority views, upholding the dissolution of the House, were tendered through separate judgements by Justice K.G. Balakrishnan and Justice Arijit Pasayat.

**Majority Judgement**

1. The May 21 report recommending dissolution was based on a "mere suspicion whims and fancies of the governor;"

2. This whimsical report was accepted as gospel truth by the Union council of ministers without any verification of the facts;

3. Clearly, the governor had misled the council of ministers which led it to advise the President to dissolve the assembly;

4. Buta Singh's action, based on his fanciful assumptions, preventing staking of claim by a political party, if allowed to stand would be destructive of the democrative fabric;

5. No governor can recommend dissolution of House to prevent a majority, even if cobbled together, from *staking* claim to form government;

6. Buta Singh's action was a mere pretence; the real objective was to do prevent Nitish Kumar from *staking* claim to form government;

7. Governor is not an avlomatic political ombudsman;

8. Adjudication of defection is not within the domain of governor.

**Minority Judgement**

1. Between March and May 2004, JD(U) had never approached the governor to state claim to form government;

2. There is no material to show that breakaway faction of LJA joined JD(U) alliance;

3. Therefore, governor did not act hastily to dissolve the assembly to prevent JD(U) alliance from forming the government;

4. Position would have been different had the governor rejected their claim;

5. No possibility of formation of government even after assembly kept in suspended animation for three months; the only solution in such a scenario is fresh elections;

6. In such a fluid political situation, allegations of allurement and horse-trading can certainly be taken into consideration by the governor;

7. Governor's recommendation for dissolution on the ground that the majority is being cobbled together by unethical means, is

not unconstitutional; it may be a wrong perception but certainly not irrational, irrelevant and extraneous.

Reeling under the scathing criticism of his "coloured" exercise of power in the dissolution of the Bihar assembly, the only action of governor Buta Singh found to be acceptable was that he was within his rights to dissolve the assembly even before it had met. The governor was blamed for almost all his actions by the 3 : 2 majority.

Justice Sakhar wal declared, "There is no restriction under Article 174 (2) (B) of the constitution stipulating that the power to dissolve the legislative assembly can be exercised by the governor only after its first meeting."

Shivraj Patil, the UPA home minister, said: "The fact that it was a split verdict that out of the five judges two approved of the governor's action suggests it was not entirely mala fide."[18]

## SUGGESTED READINGS

1. Almond, Grabriel A., *Comparative Politics Today*.
2. Riker William H., *Theory of Political Coalitions*.
3. Journals: *Economic and Political Weekly, Frontline*, Indian Journal of Political Science *India Today, Outlook* and *Seminar*.

18. *The Times of India*, January 26, 2006, p. 12.

# Index

# POLITICAL SCIENCE

## INDIA'S CONSTITUTION

**M.V. Pylee**

**CONTENTS :** Introduction ● Preamble, Territory and Citizenship ● Fundamental Rights and the Directive Principles ● The Machinery of the Union Government ● Government Machinery in the States ● The Federal System ● Miscellaneous Provisions ● Appendix ● Selected Bibliography ● Index

**Code : 17 161** **11th Rev. Edn. 2005** **ISBN:81-219-0403-X**

## POLITICAL THEORY

**V.D. Mahajan**

**CONTENTS:** Political Theory ● Approaches to Political Analysis ● Methodology of Political Science ● Political Science and its Relation to Allied Sciences ● The Nature and Scope of Political Science ● Politics and Society ● The State ● The Political System ● Political Culture and Political Socialisation ● Power, Authority and Legitimacy ● Political Modernisation and Political Development ● Origin of the State ● Evolution of the State ● Sovereignty ● Citizenship ● Rights and Duties Liberty ● Equality ● Property - Justice ● Law Forms of Government ● The Constitution of the State ●Theory of Separation of Powers ● The Legislature ● Problems Relating to Voting and Representation ● The Executive ● The Judiciary Political Parties and Pressure Groups Public Opinion ● Local Government ●The End and Functions of the State Liberal ●Theory of the Nature and Functions of thestate ● Marxian Theory of the Nature and Functions of the State ● The Welfare State Utilitarianism ● Individualism Idealist Political Theory ● Socialism Marxism and Bolshevism ● Fascism and Nazism ● Democracy Nationalism and internationalism Imperialism ● Political Thought of Harold J. Laski ● Political ● Thought of Mahatma Gandhi ● Index

**Code : 17 021** **4th Edn. 2003** **ISBN:81-219-0369-6**

## PRINCIPLES OF POLITICAL SCIENCE

**A.C. Kapur**

**CONTENTS: Part I :** Nature and Scope of Political Science ● Modern Politics ● The Nature of the State ● Origin of the State ● The Evolution of the State Nationalism ● Sovereignty ● Relation between the Individual and the State Rights and Duties ● Liberty and Equality ● Relations between States ● **Part II:** Forms of Government ● Parliamentary, Presidential and Totalitarian Patterns ● Separation of Powers ● The Framework of Government ● Constitution ● The Electorate and Representation ● The Legis,lature ● The Executive Consultative and Advisory Bodies ●The Judiciary ● The Party System Public Opinion ● Local Government ●The Finances of the State ● **Part III:** The Limits of Political Control ● Theories of the Sphere of State Activity ● Gandhian Way of Life ● Index

**Code : 17 001** **20th Edn. 2004** **ISBN:81-219-0276-2**

## INDIAN ADMINISTRATION

**Vishnoo Bhagwan & Vidya Bhushan**

**CONTENTS :** ● Evolution of Indian Administration ● Envionmental Setting ● Cental Political Executive ● Structure of Administation ● State Adiministration ● Cente-State Relations ● Public Sevices ● Machiney for Planning ● Public Undertaking ● Control of Public Expenditure ● Administration of Law and Order ● District Administration ● Panchayati Raj ● Urban Local Government ● Administration for Welfare ● Issue Areas in Indian Administration ● Annexure-I : Office Administration ● Annexure-II : Salient Features of the Indian Constitution ● Annexure-II : Tenth Five Year Plan ● Annexure-IV : Prime Minister's Secretariat ● Annexure-V : Cabinet Secretariat ● Annexure-VI : 12th Finance Commission ● Annexure-VII : Income Tax Department ● Annexure-VIII : All India Service Exam nation- Revamping ● Annexure-IX : Padmanabhaiah Committee ● Annexure-X : Takyo Anti-Corruption Conference ● Appendix : Concerning New Government at the Centre

**Code : 17 163** **4th Rev. Edn. 2005** **ISBN:81-219-0402-1**

## INDIAN POLITICAL SYSTEM

**(Indian Government & Politics)**

**R.C. Aggarwal**

**CONTENTS : Part I:** Imperialism and Nationalism ● Toughest Armed resistance to British Imperialism (How Indians lost their cherished possession of independence? Background) ● Disastrous Effects of British Imperial Rule in India (Gravest discontent and disaffection unleashes armed struggle against it) ● Nationalism Triumphs over Imperialism: India -Gains Independence ● Landmarks in Indian Constitution (Acts of 1909, 1919 and 1935) ● Legacies of the Old System and Decisions of the Constituent Assembly, Indian Political System, **Part II:** Modern Indian Constitution (legal Instrumentof Indian Political System), Framing of the Constitution: Its basic Objective and

Philosophy • Sources of the Constitution • Salient Features of the New Constitution of India •Nature of Federal System Fundamental Rights and Duties • Directive Principles of State Policy • The Union Executive • Union Parliament, Reorganisation of States, State Executive and Legislature • Relations Between the Union and the States Zonal Councils •Judiciary and Judicial Review • Administration of Delhi and other Union • Territories • The Comptroller and Auditor • General and Attorney General of India • Amendment of the Indian Constitution • Social Justice and Weaker Sections • Official Language and Decisions of Supreme, Court • Public Services and Public Service Commission • Planned Development • District Administration in India • Panchayati Raj or Local Self • Government • **Part III:** Indian Political System at Work or Nature of Indian Politics • Political Dynamics or Indian Political Parties • Pressure Groups, Politics of Defections (Political Turn-Coatism) • Linguism in Indian Politics • Caste in Indian Politics • Communalism in Indian Politics (Secularism and Its Problems) • Regionalism and Secessionism in Indian Politics • Efforts Towards National Integration •Coalition Politics in India or Opposition in Indian Politics • Prospects of Parliamentary Democracy in India • Election and Voting Behaviour (is to 10th General Elections) • Appendices • Index

**Code : 17 124** **5th Edn. 2003** **ISBN:81-219-283-5**

## SELECT CONSTITUTIONS

**A.C. Kapur & Revised by K.K. Misra**

**CONTENTS** : **Part I:** The Government of United Kingdom • The Government of United States • The Governmentof France • The Government of Canada • The Government of Switzerland • The Government of Japan • The Government of The People's Republics of China, **Part II:** Government of the Indian Republic •The Nationalist Movement •The Indian National Congress and the Demand for Parliamentary Institutions • The Rise of Muslim Communalism • The British Legacies • Making of the Constitution: Basic Decision and objectives Fundamental Rights • Directive Principles of State Policy and Fundamental Duties • The President •The Council of Ministers Parliament •The Supreme Court •The Union and the States • The State Executive• The State Legislature • The State judiciary • Services under the Union and the States • Administrative Tribunals • Elections and Parties •The Indian Political System • Index

**Code : 17 003** **15th Edn. 2002** **ISBN:81-219-0713-6**

## PUBLIC ADMINISTRATION

**Vishnoo Bhagwan & Vidya Bhushan**

**CONTENTS : Part I:** Introduction •Meaning, Nature and Scope of Public Administration • Importance of Public Administration •Public Administration and other Social Sciences • New Dimensions of Public Administration • **Part II:** Organisation in General • General Aspects of Administration • Principles and Tools of Administration • Legislature as a Board of Directors • The Chief Executive as General Manager • **Part III:** Organisation • Principles and Structure Organisation and its Principles Staff • Line and Auxiliary Agencies • Organization of Department • The Bureau and Board of Commission • Field Establishments • Public Enterprises • Independent Regulatory Commissions • **Part IV:** Management • Management • A Conceptual analysis Leadership • Policy Formation Decision-Making • Planning • Coordination • Delegation and Communication • Supervision • Public Relations • **Part V:** Personal Administration • Civil Servants and their Role Problems of Personnel Organisation Recruitment of Personnel • Training • Promotion, Advancement • Transfer • Public Employees Organization • Economic Civil Services in India •Need and Evolution • Corruption in Public Services • Generalist vs. Specialist • **Part VI:** Administrative Improvement • Administrative Procedure • Organisation and Methods • **Part VII:** Administrative Law and Adjudication • **Part VIII** : Financial Administration • Administrative Legislation • Delegated Legislation • Administrative Adjudication • Administration and Finance • The Budget • The Finance Ministry • Budgetary Process in India • Parliamentary Control over Finances • Accounting and Audit • Parliamentary Control Over Finance • Financial Committees • **Part IX:** Control over Administration • **Part X:** Local Administration • State-Local Relations • Panchayati Raj • Community Project Administration • District Administration • Municipal Government in India • Appendices • Index

**Code : 17 009** **8th Rev. Edn. 2005** **ISBN-.81-219-0340-8**

## POLITICAL THEORY

**Eddy Asirvatham**

**Revised by K.K. Misra**

**CONTENTS** : The Nature, Scope and Methods of Political Science • Politics as a Social process • History, Political Theory and Ideology • The Nature of the State • The Origin of State • The Historical Development of the State •The Social Contract •Theory of Hobbes, Locke and Rousseau • The Justification and End of the State • The Proper Sphere of State Action • The Welfare State • Theory of State: Its Comparative Dimensions •Nature of State in Capitalist Society • Nature of State in Socialist Systems • Comparing the Nature and Role of the State in Developed and Developing Societies •Theories of Rights Particular Rights • Liberty and Equality • The Concept of Equality Sovereignty • Political Pluralism Law • The Concept of Justice • Classification of States and Constitutions •

Organisation of Government • Democracy • Theories of Democracy • Liberalism and Utilitarianism in Politics• Idealism and Pragmatism in Politics • Nationalism • Imperialism and internationalism • The Evolution of Communistic • Thought • Marxist •Theories of Alienation • Freedom • State and Revolution • Socialism after Marx • Fascism and Nazism • The United Nations • Political thought of Mahatma Gandhi • Political Philosophy of Laski Comparative Study of Ideologies • Bibliography • Index

**Code : 17 149** **13th Edn. 2004** **ISBN:BL -219-0346-7**

## POLITICAL THEORY

**(Principles of Political Science)**

**R.C. Aggarwal**

**CONTENTS : Part 1:** Nature, Scope and Methods of Political Science • Behavioural Revolution in Political Science • Post-Behaviouralism Relation of Political Science to Other Social Sciences State, State, Nation and Nationality • The Nature of the State, Idealistic or Metaphysical Theory, Theories Regarding the Origin of the State (Divine, Force and Patriarchal Theories) • Origin and Evolution of State (The Contract Theory, Evolutionary Theory and Evolution of the State) • Sovereignty and Pluralism • Concept of Welfare and Secular • State • Relation Between the Individual and State (Citizenship, Rights and Duties) • Liberty and Equality, State • Law and Punishment . international Law (Relations between States and Theories of Coexistence, Panch Sheel Internationalism and United Nations • Forms of Government (Monarchy Aristocracy, Democracy and Dictatorships) Forms of Government (Unitary and Federal Governments •Forms of Government (Parliamentary and Presidential) • Constitution of the State, Organs of Government (Legislature) • Franchise, Elections and Minority Representation Organs of Government (Executive) Organs of the Government Judiciary) •Theory of Separation of Powers • Political Parties • Local Self • Government Public Opinion • **Part II:** Political System, Political System (General System Theory and System Theory of Morton) • Political Culture • Political Socialisation • Power Influence, Authority and Legitimacy-Political Elites • Modernisation and Political Development • Nationalism and Imperialism **Part III** Individualism • Utilitarianis Socialism, Communism and Collectivism, Anarchism Syndicalis Guild Socialism, Fascism and Nazis • Gandhism and Sarvodaya • **Part IV** Marxist Theory about the Origin the State • Marxist •Theory of Rights Marxist Concepts of Liberty • Equality Property • Justice • Pressure Group • Miscellaneous Topics

**Code : 17 022** **8th Edn. 2004** **ISBN:81-219-0664-4**

## CONSTITUTIONAL GOVERNMENT IN INDIA

**M.V. Pylee**

**CONTENTS :** • Introductory •The Growth of Constitutionalism in India • Preamble, Territory and Citizenship • Fundamental Rights and Directive Principles • The Government of the Union •The Machinery of Government in the States •The Federal System •The Comptroller and Auditor General of India • Bibliography • Index of case • General Index

**Code : 17 130** **5th Rev. Edn. 2003** **ISBN:81-219-2203-8**

## CONSTITUTIONAL DEVELOPMENT AND NATIONAL MOVEMENT OF INDIA

**(Freedom Movement, Acts and Indian Constitution)**

**R.C. Aggarwal**

**CONTENTS : Part I:** Constitutional Development of India - Regulating Actl Pitts India Act and the Charter Act of 1813 • Constitutional Development upto 1853 A.D. • **Part II** National Movement (Struggle for Freedom Against Foreign Rule) • 6 March of British Imperialism (Toughest resistance offered by the Indians) •Disastrous Effects of British Imperialism (Armed uprisings against it before 1857) • First Armed Struggle for Freedom, 1857 and Act of 1858 Act of 1861 A.D. • Rise of Nationalism and Birth of Congress • Act of 1892 Moderate and Extremist Programme of Congress, Revo-lutionary movement in India and abroad • Rise and Growth of Communalism •Morley • Minto Reforms (Act of 1909) • The Impact of the First Great War and The Home Rule Movement •Government of India Act, 1919 •Nature and Working of Dyarchy in the Provinces • Non-Co-operation Movement and Swaraj Party • Civil Disobedience Movement • Socialist and Communist Trends in National Movement • Central Government ( Act of 1935) • Provincial Governments (Act of 1935) • Working of the Provincial Autonomy • Quit India Movement and Dawn of Independence (Triumph of Nationalism over Imperialism; Imperialists Quit, Pakistan Established) • Some Prominent Leaders of Freedom Struggle • Heroic Struggle for Freedom in Assam • **Part III:** Modern Indian Constitution (Greatest Instrument of Legal Political System) • Framing of the Constitution: Its basic objectives and philosophy •Sources of the Constitution •Salient Features of India's New Constitution • Nature of the Federal System • Fundamental Rights and Duties • Directive Principles of State Policy (Positive Directions for State) • The Union Executive • Union Parliament •Reorganisation of States, State Executive and Legislature • Relations between the Union and the States •Zonal Councils • The Judiciary and judicial Review (Landmark Judgements of the Supreme • Administration of Delhi and other Union Territories •Social Justice and Weaker Sections •Amendments of Indian Constitution • The Comptroller and Auditor-General and Attorney- General of India •Indian Administration and Some

Miscellaneous Topics • Public Services (Bureaucracy) and Public Service Commission • Planning Commission and Five Year Plans • District Administration in India • Panchayati Raj or Local Self Government • Political Dynamics (Indian Political Parties) • Pressure Groups (Anonymous Empire) • Appendices • Index

**Code : 17 031** **14th Rev. Edn. In Press** **ISBN:81-219-0565-6**

## लोक प्रष्ठासन के सिद्धान्त

### विज़्णु भगवान एवं विद्या भूज़्ण

**विज़्रय-सूची: भाग-१** परिचय- लोक प्रष्ठासन का अर्थ, प्रकृति और क्षेत्र • लोक प्रष्ठासन का महत्त्व • लोक प्रष्ठासन तथा अन्य सामाजिक विज्ञान • **भाग-२** सामान्य प्रष्ठासन • प्रष्ठासन के सामान्य पक्ष • प्रष्ठासन के सिद्धांत तथा उपकरण • मुख्य निज़्पादक • **भाग-३** संगठन- संगठन तथा इसकी मूलभूत समस्याएं • स्टाफ, लाइन तथा सहायक एजेंसियां • विभाग का संगठन • ब्यूरो तथा बोर्ड अथवा आयोग • क्षेत्रीय प्रतिज़्ठान • सार्वजनिक उद्यम • स्वतन्त्र विनियामक आयोग **भाग-४** प्रबन्ध-प्रबन्ध • नेतष्टत्व • नीति-निर्माण • निर्णय-निर्धारण • नियोजन • समायोजन • प्रत्यायोजन तथा संचार • पर्यवेक्षण • लोक • सम्पर्क **भाग-५** प्रष्ठासनिक सुधार-संगठन तथा प्रणाली **भाग-६** • कार्मिक प्रष्ठासन-सिविल सेवक तथा उनकी भूमिका कार्मिक • संगठन की समस्याएं • भर्ती • प्रष्ठिक्षण • पदोन्नति • सरकारी कर्मचारी संगठन • लोक सेवाओं में भ्रज़्टाचार • सामान्यवादी बनाम विष्ठोज़्ज्ञ वाद विवाद • **भाग-७** प्रष्ठासकीय कानून और न्यायिक निर्णय-प्रष्ठासकीय कानून • प्रतिनिहित विधान • प्रष्ठासकीय न्याय निर्णय • **भाग-८** वित्तीय प्रष्ठासन • प्रष्ठासन एवं वित्त • बजट • वित्त मंत्रालय • भारत में बजट निर्माण प्रक्रिया • वित्त पर संसदीय नियंत्रण-लेख एवं लेखा परीक्षण • वित्त पर संसदीय नियंत्रण-वित्तीय समितियां • **भाग-९** प्रष्ठासन पर नियंत्रण • प्रष्ठासन पर नियंत्रण • **भाग-१०** स्थानीय प्रष्ठासन-पंचायती राज • जिला प्रष्ठासन

**Code : 17 028** **6th Rev. Edn. 2001** **ISBN:81-219-0438-2**

## राजनीति विज्ञान के सिद्धान्त

**(Theory of Political Science)**

### अनूप चंद कपूर एव

### संष्ठोधित कृज़्णकान्त मिश्र

**विज़्रय-सूची: भाग-१** राजनीति विज्ञान की प्रकृति और उत्पत्ति • राजनीति विज्ञान की प्रकृति और क्षेत्र • आधुनिक राजनीति • राज्य की प्रकृति • राज्य की उत्पत्ति-1 • राज्य की उत्पत्ति-2 • राज्य का विकास • राज़्ट्रवाद • राज्य की संप्रभुता • व्यक्ति और राज्य के बीच संबंध-1 • स्वाधीनता और समानता • व्यक्ति और राज्य के बीच सम्बन्ध कानून-II • राज्यों के बीच सम्बन्ध **भाग-२: राज्य का संगठन** • सरकार के रूप • सरकार के रूप-एकात्मक और संघात्मक • संसदीय अध्यक्षात्मक तथा अधिनायकवादी प्रणालियां • ष्ठाक्तियों का पृथक्करण • राज्य का संविधान • निर्वाचक और प्रतिनिधित्व • विधानमण्डल • कार्यपालिका • परामर्ष्ठा समितियाँ और मन्त्रणा निकाय • न्यायपालिका • दल-प्रणाली • लोकमत • स्थानीय सरकार • राज्य का वित्त-प्रबन्ध • **भाग-३** राज्य के कार्य • राजनीतिक नियन्त्रण की सीमाएँ • राज्य-कार्य क्षेत्र के सिद्धान्त • राज्य-कार्य क्षेत्र के सिद्धान्त-समाजवाद • राज्य के कार्य क्षेत्र-साम्यवाद • गाँधीजी का जीवन-दर्ष्ठान • पारिभाज़िक ष्ठाब्दावली

## राजनीति विज्ञान

### संष्ठोधित एवं परिवद्धित संस्करण

### एं'डी॰ आष्ठीर्वादम् एवं कृज़्णकान्त मिश्र

**विज़्रय-सूची:** राजनीति-विज्ञान का स्वरूप • राजनीति और सामाजिक और सामाजिक प्रक्रिया • राजनीति के उपागम और दष्टिज़्टकोण • राज्य का स्वरूप • राज्य की उत्पत्ति • समाज, राज्य और नागरिकतां • राज्य का विकास • स्वतन्त्रता, समानता, सम्पत्ति और न्याय • हॉब्स, लॉक और रूसो का सामाजिक संविदा सिद्धान्त • राज्य का औचित्य और उद्देष्ठय • राज्य का उचित कार्य-क्षेत्र • लोक कल्याणकारी राज्य • अधिकार सम्बन्धी सिद्धान्त • विष्टिज़्ट अधिकार • राजनीतिक बहुलवाद • सम्प्रभुता के सिद्धांत •

कानून और राज्य • राज्य के उदारवादी तथा मार्क्सवादी सिद्धांत • राजनीतिक व्यवस्थाओं के रूप • राज्यों तथा संविधानों का वर्गीकरण • सरकार का संगठन • लोकतन्त्र के सिद्धांत • स्थानीय स्वशासन • राजनीति में उपयोगितावाद • राजनीति में आदर्शवाद • राष्ट्रवाद, साम्राज्यवाद और अन्तर्राष्ट्रवाद • साम्यवाद विचारधारा का विकास • मार्क्स के बाद समाजवाद • फासिस्टवाद और नाजीवाद • संयुक्त राष्ट्र संघ • महात्मा गांधी की राजनीतिक विचारधारा • विचारधाराओं की तुलनात्मक समीक्षा • लास्की का राजनीतिक चिंतन • क्रियावाद तथा बहुलवाद • उदारवादी विचारधारा • मार्क्सवाद का मूल्यांकन • फासीवाद की आलोचना • राज्य का वर्ग चरित्र • अधिकार और स्वतंत्रता • लोकतांत्रिक समाजवाद • अंतर्राष्ट्रीयता का आदर्श • आधुनिक राजनीति और व्यवहारवाद तथा व्यवहारवादी क्रान्ति

**Code : 17 152** **12th Edn. 2004** **ISBN:81-219-0896-5**

## RESEARCH METHODOLOGY

**R. Cauvery, U.K. Sudha Nayak, M. Girija & R. Meenakshi**

**CONTENTS : Part -I :** Nature, Scope And Methodology of Business Economics • Concepts of Social Science Research • Stages in Reseach Process • Hypothesis • Theory and Facts of Social Science • The Design of Research • Methods of Data Collection-I • Methods of Data Collection-II • Sampling • The case Study Methods • Survey Methods • Technique of Interviewing • Questionnaire • Schedule • Data Processing • Analysis and Interpretation of Data • The Research Report • Value Judgements

**08 215** **4th Edn. 2004** **ISBN : 81-219-2220-8**

## भारतीय संविधान का विकास तथा राष्ट्रीय आन्दोलन

**आर.सी अग्रवाल**

**विषय-सूची: • पहला खण्ड : भारतीय स्वतंत्रता आन्दोलन तथा संवैधानिक विकास** • भारत में ब्रिटिश साम्राज्यवाद का कठोरतम मुकाबला • ब्रिटिश साम्राज्यवाद के घातक परिणाम तथा (1857 से पूर्व) विद्रोह • भारत का प्रथम स्वतन्त्रता संग्राम, 1857 • 1861 का अधिनियम, तथा अन्य • **दूसरा खण्ड : भारत का आधुनिक संविधान** • भारत के नए संविधान की विशेषताएं तथा संघवाद • मौलिक अधिकार और राज्य-नीति के सिद्धान्त (उच्चतम न्यायालय के निर्णयों के सम्बन्ध में) • संघीय कार्यपालिका (राष्ट्रपति, प्रधानमंत्री तथा मंत्रिमण्डल) • संघीय संसद • राज्यों का पुनर्गठन तथा कार्यपालिका (राज्यपाल तथा मंत्रिपरिषद) • संघ तथा राज्यों में संबंध • न्यायपालिका का संघटन और उच्चतम न्यायालय के महत्वपूर्ण निर्णय तथा न्यायिक पुनरीक्षण एवं अन्य

**Code : 17 059** **20th Edn. Rev. 2001** **ISBN:81-219-2040-X**

## स्वतंत्रता आन्दोलन का इतिहास

**पुखराज जैन**

**विषय-सूची:** • ऐतिहासिक पृष्ठभूमि : हमारा देश परतन्त्र क्यों हो गया, कैसे हो गया? • ब्रिटिश साम्राज्य का उद्देश्य और प्रकृति • 1857 का स्वतंत्रता संग्राम • स्वतंत्रता आन्दोलन (1858-80) • भारतीय राष्ट्रीय कांग्रेस की स्थापना • उदारवादी और उग्रवादी राष्ट्रीय आन्दोलन • क्रांतिकारी विचारधारा और आन्दोलन • राष्ट्रीय आन्दोलन का गाँधी युग • देशी रियासतों में राजनीतिक चेतना और जन-आन्दोलन • राष्ट्रीय आन्दोलन की लक्ष्य सिद्धि : स्वतंत्रता की प्राप्ति • राष्ट्रीय आन्दोलन की बाधाएं : साम्प्रदायिकता, अस्पृश्यता तथा अन्य

**Code : 13 169** **1st Edition : 1988**

## भारतीय स्वतंत्रता संग्राम तथा संवैधानिक विकास

**बी.एल. ग्रोवर एवं यशपाल**

**विषय-सूची: • भाग-I** औपनिवेशिक काल में संवैधानिक विकास (मध्य 18वीं शताब्दी से 1947 तक) • **भाग - II** स्वतंत्रता संग्राम • **भाग - III** भारतीय गणतंत्र का संविधान (1950 से आजतक) • **भाग - IV** विषय परक सारांश • परिशिष्ट (क-झ) • अनुक्रमणिका

**Code : 13 051** **1st Edition : 1985** **ISBN:81-219-0910-4**

# IMPORTANT ENCYCLOPAEDIAS ON SOCIAL SCIENCES

## INTERNATIONAL ENCYCLOPEDIA OF GOVERNMENT & POLITICS

**2 VOLUMES (H.B.)**

**Frank N. Magill, editor**

Code : 23 195 — Rs. 6,500.00 (Set)

## WORLD ENCYCLOPEDIA OF PARLIAMENTS AND LEGISLATURES

**2 VOLUMES (H.B.)**

**George Thomas Kurian, editor**

**Code : 23 179** — **$ 275.00**

**Exclusive reprints from S. Chand**

## INTERNATIONAL ENCYCLOPEDIA OF TERRORISM

**Martha Crenshaw and John Pimlott, editors**

**Code : 23 184** — **Rs. 4,500.00**

## ENCYCLOPEDIAS OF SOCIOLOGY I, II

**Frank N. Magill, editor**